About SIGCHI and ACM

CHI 2011 is sponsored by ACM's Special Interest Group on Computer-Human Interaction (ACM SIGCHI). The scope of SIGCHI consists of the study of the human-computer interaction processes and includes research, design, development, and evaluation efforts for interactive computer systems. The focus of SIGCHI is on how people communicate and interact with a broadly-defined range of computer systems. SIGCHI serves as a forum for the exchange of ideas among computer scientists, human factors scientists, psychologists, social scientists, designers, educators, and practitioners involved in the design, implementation, and evaluation of interactive computing systems. Nearly 5,000 professional members of the SIGCHI community work together toward common goals and objectives. Visit SIGCHI at http://www.sigchi.org.

ACM, the Association for Computing Machinery http://www.acm.org/, is an educational and scientific society uniting the world's computing educators, researchers and professionals to inspire dialogue, share resources and address the field's challenges. ACM strengthens the profession's collective voice through strong leadership, promotion of the highest standards, and recognition of technical excellence.ACM supports the professional growth of its members by providing opportunities for life-long learning, career development, and professional networking. ACM offers its 87,000 global members cutting-edge technical information through world class journals and magazines, dynamic specia linterest groups and globally recognized conferences.

Welcome from Chairs

Over the last year or so, we have been blessed with the challenge, the opportunity, and the distinct pleasure of organizing the CHI 2011 Conference on Human Factors in Computing Systems, the premier international conference for the field of human-computer interaction.

CHI 2011 takes place in gorgeous, energetic, sophisticated Vancouver BC, a city renowned for its innovation in entertainment, sustainability, accessibility, and inclusivity. The New York Times calls it, "a liquid city, a tomorrow city, equal parts India, China, England, France and the Pacific Northwest." Vancouver lays a beautiful backdrop for our conference, which boasts nearly 30 years of wonderful work.

Behind the success of the conference is our diverse community of faculty and students, of researchers and practitioners, of young and, well, also of experienced. It is a community of designers, technologists, psychologists, social scientists, biologists, artists, engineers, anthropologists, musicians; the list goes on. Wherever we are, we are always a community of near and far. Most impressively, ours is a community that cares deeply about innovating, learning, sharing, and interacting; all with the common goal of using technology to shape the way people around the world live and play.

Returning attendees will recognize the general conference format - 2 days of small intimate workshops, followed by 4 days of technical content, all surrounded by social and intellectual exchanges. In addition to the familiar venues that form the core of the conference, we have also arranged various special events, such an keynotes by Howard Rheingold and Ethan Zuckerman; invited talks by ACM SIGCHI award winners Terry Winograd, Larry Tesler, Alan Newell, and Clayton Lewis; an HCI museum exhibit hosted by Bill Buxton; and a panel celebrating Stu Card's achievements and contributions to the field of HCI.

With the record number of submissions and accepted content this year, we hope that you will utilize the print and electronic programs, but also the daily CHI Madness presentations that provide a glimpse of the day ahead. In the interest of continuing to evolve the conference to best serve our needs, we will experiment with shorter talks this year (20 minute slots for long pieces of content and 10 for shorter ones) to infuse even more energy into the program. We will also have a pretty full slate of social media applications to help you connect with other attendees and to provide you with the fullest experience possible.

It has been quite the ride, and we'd like to thank everyone involved and welcome you all to the conference. We hope that CHI 2011 inspires you reflect on the past, the present, and perhaps most importantly, the future of the people and body of work that is ACM SIGCHI. We hope you enjoy CHI 2011 in Vancouver and that you have a great time "Connecting..."

Desney Tan
CHI 2011 General Conference Chair
Microsoft Research

Bo Begole
CHI 2011 Technical Program Chairs
PARC

Wendy Kellogg
CHI 2011 Technical Program Chairs
IBM Research

From ACM SIGCHI's President and Vice President for Conferences

SIGCHI is proud to sponsor the premier annual conference in the field of human-computer interaction. Past CHI conferences have been known for being the stage of new developments and advances in HCI, and for memorable events. CHI 2011 is no exception. We are extremely grateful to the CHI 2011 Conference Chair Desney Tan, to Technical Program Chairs Bo Begole and Wendy Kellogg, and to their wonderful crew, who succeeded to build an impressive program and experience.

CHI, the conference that is organized on behalf of ACM's Special Interest Group on Computer-Human Interaction (SIGCHI) is an ideal forum for people to meet formally as well as informally, to exchange knowledge and views, to share experiences, and to learn. The CHI conference brings together professionals from research and practice; people from industry, academia, and from government; long-term veterans of HCI, young professionals and students; all in an environment designed to encourage interaction. We invite you to actively participate in that interaction: introduce yourself to people, interact with presenters and speakers, renew old friendships and make new ones.

SIGCHI is an international community of professionals who share an interest in the many diverse facets of HCI. SIGCHI is committed both to advancing the field of HCI, to facilitate exchange of information within the SIGCHI community, and to support students to enter the domain.

The CHI conference is arguably the single most visible activity of SIGCHI, but we also sponsor and support a wide range of specialized conferences in areas ranging from interactive systems design to user interface technology to computer-supported cooperative work to "intelligent" user interfaces. Visit the SIGCHI website at http://www.sigchi.org to find our conference schedule, listing upcoming as well as past conferences.

SIGCHI and ACM produce some of the most respected publications in the field. All members receive interactions, a highly-acclaimed magazine covering the broad field of HCI and user interface design. ACM Transactions on Computer-Human Interactions (ToCHI), now in its 17th year, is our flagship journal - a quarterly publication with the top-quality archival research aimed at researchers and those translating research into practice.

SIGCHI is truly an international organization, with 32 local chapters and 3 student chapters in 19 countries on 5 continents. We encourage all SIGCHI members to join their local chapter - or if there isn't one in your area, we would love to help you create one. And don't forget virtual communities! SIGCHI hosts dozens of electronic mailing lists on topics ranging from HCI and the Web, to HCI educations, to public policy and beyond. Those lists range from dozens of subscribers to thousands, and are an excellent way to keep up with the field and with friends and colleagues.

Finally, on behalf of ACM SGICHI, we again want to thank the conference committee and all of the hundreds of volunteers who make this conference possible. Their work makes this a rewarding experience for all of us.

Gerrit C. van der Veer
SIGCHI President

John "Scooter" Morris
SIGCHI Vice-President for Conferences

CHI 2011 Table of Contents

CHI 2011 Table of Contents

CHI 2011 Table of Contents

CHI 2011 Table of Contents

Driving

Session Chair: Dario Salvucci, *Drexel University*

Meetings & Interaction Spaces

Session Chair: Wendy Ju, *Stanford University*

Art, Music & Movement

Session Chair: Amy Voida, *University of California, Irvine*

Facebook

Session Chair: Daniela Busse, *SAP*

Health 3: Online Communities & Social Interaction

Session Chair: Julie Kientz, *University of Washington*

CHI 2011 Table of Contents

CHI 2011 Table of Contents

Volume 2

Ambient & Peripheral Computing

CHI 2011 Table of Contents

CHI 2011 Table of Contents

CHI 2011 Table of Contents

CHI 2011 Table of Contents

CHI 2011 Table of Contents

Multi-touch

Session Chair: Tomer Moscovich, *INRIA*

Pointing 2: Fitts Law

Session Chair: Shumin Zhai, *IBM Research*

Evaluation and/or Design Based on Many Users

Session Chair: Manfred Tscheligi, *University of Salzburg*

Homeless Users

Session Chair: Phoebe Sengers, *Cornell University*

Visual Analytics

Session Chair: Jeffrey Heer, *Stanford University*

CHI 2011 Table of Contents

CHI 2011 Table of Contents

CHI 2011 Table of Contents

CHI 2011 Table of Contents

CHI 2011 Table of Contents

CHI 2011 Table of Contents

CHI 2011 Table of Contents

CHI 2011 Table of Contents

CHI 2011 Table of Contents

CHI 2011 Table of Contents

CHI 2011 Table of Contents

CHI 2011 Table of Contents

CHI 2010 Organizing Committee

Conference Chair
Desney Tan, *Microsoft Research*

Conference Chair Assistant
Saleema Amershi, *University of Washington*

Technical Program

Chairs
Bo Begole, *PARC*
Wendy A. Kellogg, *IBM Research*

Technical Program Chairs Assistant
Manas Tungare

Papers
Geraldine Fitzpatrick, *Vienna University of Technology*
Carl Gutwin, *University of Saskatchewan*

alt.chi chairs
Daniel Wigdor, *Microsoft*
Patrick Baudisch, *Hasso Plattner Institute*

Case Studies Chair
Manfred Tscheligi, *University of Salzberg*

Courses Chairs
Nancy Frishberg, *MSB Associates*
Regina Bernhaupt, *IRIT -- University of Toulouse*

Doctoral Consortium Chairs
Mary Beth Rosson, *Penn State University*
Saul Greenberg, *University of Calgary*

Interactivity Chairs
Jan Borchers, *RWTH Aachen University*
Lyn Bartram, *Simon Fraser University*
Sid Fels, *University of British Columbia*

Panels Chairs
John C. Thomas, *IBM Research*
Simone Barbosa, *PUC-Rio*

Poster Chair
Anthony Tang, *Georgia Tech*

Special Interest Groups (SIGS) Chairs
Ido Guy, *IBM Research*
Daphne Raban, *University of Haifa*

Student Design Competition Chairs
Stephen Brewster, *University of Glasgow*
Youn-kyung Lim, *KAIST*

Video Chairs
Michael Bernstein, *Massachusetts Institute of Technology*
Shahram Izadi, *Microsoft*

Work-in-Progress (WIPs) Chairs
Brian Bailey, *University of Illinois, Urbana-Champaign*
Mark Newman, *University of Michigan*

Workshops Chairs
Daniela Busse, *SAP Labs (Palo Alto)*
Catalina Danis, *IBM Research*

Core Communities

Communities Chair
Arnie Lund, *Microsoft*

Design Community Chairs
Scott Pobiner, *Parsons The New School for Design*
Carla Diana, *Smart Design*

User Experience Community Chairs
Elizabeth Buie, *Luminanze Consulting*
Jhilmil Jain, *Microsoft*

Engineering Community Chairs
Ruven Brooks, *Independent Consultant*
Keith Butler, *University of Washington*

Management Community Chairs
Jim Nieters, *Yahoo!*
Carola Fellenz Thompson, *Mindjet*

FEATURED COMMUNITIES

Child Computer Interaction Community Chairs
Janet C Read, *University of Central Lancashire*
Panos Markopoulos, Eindhoven University of Technology
Allison Druin, *University of Maryland*

Games and Entertainment Community Chairs
Regina Bernhaupt, *IRIT - University of Toulouse*
Katherine Isbister, *NYU-Poly*

Health Community Chairs
Gillian R. Hayes, *University of California, Irvine*
Madhu Reddy, *The Pennsylvania State University*

Sustainability Community Chairs
Azam Khan, *Autodesk Research*
Eli Blevis, *Indiana University-Bloomington*

PARTICIPATION & VOLUNTEERING

Student Volunteer Coordinators
Aaron Houssian, *Philips Research, TU/Delft*
Vicky McArthur, *York University*

Madness Chairs
Paul André, *University of Southampton*
Max L. Wilson, *Swansea University*

Social Media Chair
Cliff Lampe, *Michigan State University*

Publicity Chair
Kirstie Hawkey, *University of British Columbia*

SPONSORS, EXHIBITS, & TECHNOLOGY

Sponsors and Exhibits
Carol Klyver

Registration Coordinator
Yvonne Lopez

Design Directors
Oscar Murillo, *Microsoft*
Cole Benson, *University of Washington*

Webmaster
Lydia Chilton, *University of Washington*

Proceedings & Program Chairs
Aurélien Tabard, *IT University of Copenhagen*
Max Van Kleek, *Massachusetts Institute of Technology*
Nirmal Patel, *Georgia Tech*

Technology Liaisons
Scooter Morris, *University of California, San Francisco*
Sara Drenner, *Inuvo*

LOGISTICS

ACM Staff Liaisons
Ashley Cozzi, *Association for Computing Machinery*

CMC Staff Liaisons
Scooter Morris, *University of California, San Francisco*

Conference Logistics
Janeé Pelletier, *Conference & Logistics Consultants*

CHI 2011 Sponsors, Supporters, Champions, Contributors, & Friends

CHI 2011 Champions

Bloomberg

Microsoft

ebay | PayPal

NSF

Google

SAP

CHI 2011 Contributors

Autodesk

IBM Research

Graphisme, animation et nouveaux médias
gran
Graphics, Animation and New Media

NOKIA

event/burn

Friends of CHI

Adobe Systems, Inc.

Disney Research

FX Palo Alto Laboratory, Inc.

University of Maryland

Yahoo!

University of Michigan

Enhancing Interactional Synchrony with an Ambient Display

Madeline Balaam
Culture Lab,
Newcastle University,
Newcastle, UK,
madeline.balaam@ncl.ac.uk

Geraldine Fitzpatrick
Vienna University of Technology
Vienna, Austria,
geraldine.fitzpatrick@tuwien.ac.at

Judith Good
HCT Group,
University of Sussex
Brighton, UK,
J.Good@sussex.ac.uk

Eric Harris
HCT Group,
University of Sussex
Brighton, UK,
erich@sussex.ac.uk

ABSTRACT
Nonverbal communication is an essential part of face-to-face social interaction, conveying information about emotion and interpersonal relationships. The rigorous sensing capabilities of pervasive technologies and the subtle nature of ambient technologies make them ideal to support the production of nonverbal communication in social interactions. In this paper we present a study using an ambient technology that supports nonverbal communication, and specifically nonverbal behaviours associated with rapport. We show that an ambient display can influence a participant's nonverbal behaviour, and that participants are not aware of this change in their behaviour. We discuss these findings in terms of the design and ethical issues that it raises, and define an agenda for future work.

Author Keywords
Ambient display, biofeedback monitor for social interaction, social interaction, face-to-face interaction, rapport, interactional synchrony.

ACM Classification Keywords
H5.3. Group and Organization Interfaces: Synchronous.

General Terms
Design, Experimentation

INTRODUCTION
In recent years technologies have been deployed within social situations, for example, to initiate social interaction [24, 27], support group work [18], show interactional patterns, and share ideas [10]. Further to this, technologies [29], are being used to measure interactions in order to understand the impact of social dynamics and nonverbal behaviours on processes like decision making or software development [31]. This is an important advancement for HCI since nonverbal communication is central to social interaction [2, 31], and to date, the majority of technologies that support face-to-face social interaction have tended to focus on supporting the informational, or verbal aspects of interactions.

Research suggests that being adept at encoding (sending) and decoding (receiving) nonverbal communication has a positive effect on social interaction. For example, these skills are positively correlated with social competence, high quality interpersonal relationships and smooth social interactions [15, 26]. The significance of these skills is widely recognised by the lay-person, with many books and courses available to help individuals learn to better encode and decode nonverbal communication. It is however interesting to note that nonverbal communication is thought to be performed subconsciously [23, 30, 34], and as a consequence, the intentional, or conscious encoding of nonverbal communication can lead to poorer results [23, 34]. This has led others to suggest that teaching, or training nonverbal communication skills will require extremely rigorous and multiple sessions of practice in order to be successful [30].

The intriguing subconscious elements of nonverbal communication suggest that pervasive and ambient technologies have the potential to support nonverbal communication. For example, due to the sensing capabilities of these technologies, they can be applied within authentic interactional contexts to provide continual subtle support for the encoding and decoding of nonverbal communication, in real time, and in a rigorous manner. Additionally, these technologies may be able to provide such support in a subconscious manner [33], reflecting the mode through which nonverbal communication is thought to be produced. Nevertheless, although some research is beginning to explore how pervasive technologies might *measure* nonverbal communication [31], research has yet to explore how these technologies might be used to support the encoding, or decoding of nonverbal communication in real time throughout face-to-face social interactions.

In this paper, we bring together research from social psychology with advances in HCI to explore a new role for pervasive and ambient technologies in supporting face-to-face social interaction. Focussing initially on the ambient aspects, we present an exploratory study which investigates how an ambient display that responds to specific nonverbal behaviours within face-to-face social interactions impacts on the perceptions and the mechanics of an interaction. After reviewing current approaches for pervasive technologies that support face-to-face interactions, and the role of nonverbal behaviours in communication, we describe a study, undertaken to evaluate the impact of an ambient display on participants' self reports and observers' perceptions of a social interaction, as well as to better understand the issues of designing and deploying such technologies. In the final section of this paper we discuss the results of this study along with the design and ethical implications of this work.

The main contribution of this work is to identify the potential value of ambient displays in supporting the subconscious elements of face-to-face social interaction and to articulate future research directions to be explored from an HCI perspective. The results of this work will be of interest to those seeking to support face-to-face communication, collaboration, and group work, as well as those seeking to improve or teach social skills.

RELATED WORK

There are a number of technologies which seek to support face-to-face interaction [9, 16, 24]. One application area helps strangers make contact with one another, with a substantial portion focussed on conferences and networking experiences. Three examples are Ticket2Talk [24], which uses RFID nametags to display information about a conference attendee's interests whenever they stand near a display, iBand [16], a wearable technology that exchanges personal information, similar to that found on a business card, through a handshake, and GroupWear [9], also nametags that share ideas and exchange information.

All of these systems attempt to ease the burden and embarrassment experienced in beginning conversations with a stranger, serving as a catalyst to "break the ice" in initial meetings [16]. They are designed to help people network, and find people with similar interests. Studies indicate that some participants appreciate help in putting a face to someone's name, or initiating conversation [24]. Some of these prototypes are also moving to commercial products (http://www.ntag.com). However, these systems demand somewhat extrovert behaviour, as noted in [25] where some attendees reported feeling uncomfortable with the "loud announcement" of their presence in an area, and where participants still needed to feel comfortable talking to a stranger about one of their interests.

The informational element is only one aspect of human communication. Both paralinguistic (i.e. intonation, speed, tempo and voice quality) and nonverbal communication (i.e. gestures, facial expressions, posture) play a significant role in the success of an interaction [15, 17, 31, 37]. HCI research has explored how paralinguistic aspects can be sensed and augmented to support social interaction. For example, both DiMicco [12] and Ara [1] have used microphones as sensors to display data back to participants with regard to turn taking behaviours within group conversation, with the aim of supporting reflection on behaviour. DiMicco's visualisations of turn taking during a group interaction allow viewers to understand who is extroverted in a group, who is dominant, who is quiet, and who sided with whom during a debate [12]. Meeting Mediator [18] utilises the Sociometer sensing device [29] to collect paralinguistic data about a social interaction, and provide a real-time personal peripheral display on a mobile phone depicting the amount each participant has spoken, and the overall interactivity of the meeting. The results of a deployment suggest that Meeting Mediator reduces the amount of overlapping speech, as well as shortening individuals' speaking time.

Whilst moving on from supporting the purely linguistic aspect of human communication, these systems still place the emphasis of what makes for a successful interaction on the amount and evenness of vocalisation from each individual member. The importance of nonverbal communication in social interaction is widely recognised [9, 17, 31, 37], yet, apart from research on issues such as gaze and video framing in video-conferencing e.g., [28] it remains relatively unexplored in terms of how new forms of technology might support the nonverbal aspects of face-to-face communication (see [27] for an exception).

Nonverbal communication consists of signals encoded through facial expressions, gestures, postures, spatial behaviour and non-verbal vocalisations [2]. Nonverbal communication is said to have taken place when one person influences another (whether consciously, or unconsciously) through any (and more) of the signal channels listed earlier [2, 11]. Research suggests that it communicates information about emotion, interpersonal relationships, and is an essential aspect of social competence [2, 7, 20, 22, 37].

Rapport is one element of social interaction that is strongly encoded through nonverbal communication [37], and additionally theorised as key to the development of interpersonal relationships, and the success of an interaction [5]. Rapport is believed to be crucial to develop trust, to create closeness, and be included in a group [22], as well as to help interactions feel smooth [36]. In industry, managers and sales people are often taught specific nonverbal techniques to promote rapport with colleagues and clients [19]. Tickle-Degnen et al [37] conceive of rapport as being the experience of three components: mutual attentiveness, positivity, and coordination, each of which is encoded and decoded through nonverbal communication. For example, coordination (sometimes termed "interactional synchrony") has been defined as a combination of postural synchrony and movement synchrony [7].

Bernieri et al. have conducted a number of studies to explore how rapport is encoded in nonverbal signals, along with how observers understand rapport in others [for example 5, 7]. Their results suggest, dependent of course on the context surrounding the interaction, that feelings of rapport are strongly correlated with interactional synchrony (or, coordination) and interactant proximity. However, Bernieri et al's research also suggests that there is a disconnect between how rapport is encoded, and how observers decode rapport from nonverbal signals, with observers judging the amount of rapport present in a social interaction based on the expressivity of individuals, i.e. the amount an individual talks, smiles, and uses expressive facial expressions and gestures. They conclude that this expressivity of individuals drives social judgments, even though rapport is actually encoded through much richer and diverse nonverbal signals.

Bernieri et al's work identifies an area within social interaction where some key nonverbal channels are often not attended to when making important social judgements. Our research explores the extent to which an ambient display can be utilised to amplify (or make more salient) the wide range of rich, and sometimes overlooked, nonverbal signals through which rapport is encoded. In this sense rapport acts as a test bed within which we can explore the potential for technologies to support nonverbal communication in face-to-face interactions. The study described here explores the following research questions: 1) Can nonverbal signals associated with rapport be amplified with an ambient technology to make them more salient and available for social judgement? 2) Is it possible to influence feelings of rapport by amplifying the nonverbal signals associated with rapport? 3) Can such amplification impact on the nonverbal communication within an interaction? 4) How is a such a technology perceived by potential users?

THE AMBIENT DISPLAY

There are few available guidelines to inform the design of ambient displays that amplify nonverbal signals. We therefore based the design of our display (see Figure 1) on a set of self-generated criteria: the display should not be distracting; the display should appear neutral; the display should show potential to make available the patterning of cues for subconscious processing; the display should not jar with the study environment. Given these criteria, water seemed a promising design metaphor. The visual for the display was adapted from 'Water' by Rui Gil[1]. The passive version of the display is a dark blue textured visual akin to waves. The ambient version of the display is subtly animated, giving the appearance of small ripples on the surface, in response to the sensing of the nonverbal manifestations of rapport (see Figure 1). For this study, the sensing of the nonverbal correlates of rapport was carried out by Wizard of Oz (WoZ). By utilising WoZ, we replicate an envisaged future scenario where participants in a social interaction might wear pervasive devices, e.g., as part of clothing, or something akin to Sociometer [29], or alternatively, interact in a room embedded with sensors or image recognition systems that capture the gestures, postural changes, eye gaze, and back-channel responses (e.g. "uh ha", head nods, etc.) that correlate with feelings of rapport [7] to control an ambient display.

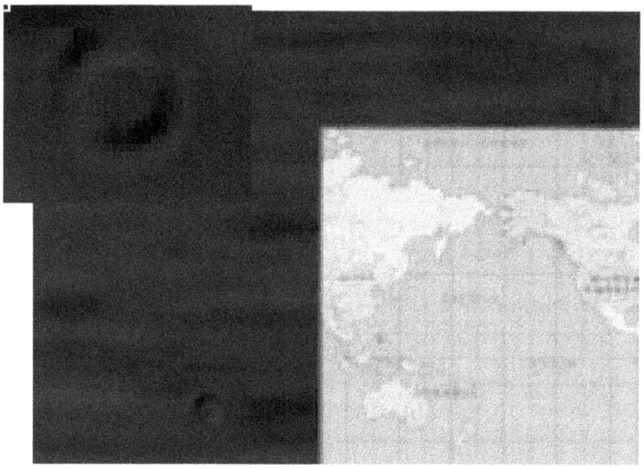

Figure 1. A Section of the Ambient Display which Surrounds a Map Used to Aid a Holiday-Planning Task. Small Ripples Appear in Response to Nonverbal Correlates of Rapport. (See Top Left Corner for an Enlarged Ripple).

STUDY DESIGN

The primary aim of this study was to investigate whether an ambient display, responding to the nonverbal manifestations of rapport, has the potential to impact on participants' self reports of rapport, and observers' judgements of interactional synchrony. To explore this question we adapted a study design first utilised by Bernieri et al [7] which explored the relationship between self reports of rapport, observer reports of rapport, and the body language of participants in a holiday planning activity.

Holiday Planning Interaction

16 adults (8 women and 8 men) took part in the initial holiday planning part of this study. Participants were recruited via general university mailing lists. Each participant was compensated £10 for their time. The 16 adults were organised into 8 unacquainted pairs of same-sex participants (this differs from [7] where mixed-sex pairs were used). Using a repeated measures study design, each pair completed a holiday planning task twice. To support the holiday planning task, each pair worked with a wall-projected display of a world map (this differs from [7] where a physical map of the world and $20,000.00 of play money were used). In both interactions, the map was surrounded by the ambient display (Figure 2 shows the relative size of the map and ambient display to two male participants of average height): in the experimental condition, the display responded to nonverbal communicative acts associated with rapport, while in the control condition, the display remained static. Half of the participant pairs experienced the responsive ambient display during their first holiday planning interaction, and the second half experienced it during their second holiday planning interaction. In a further variation from [7], to provide two conditions with which to assess the impact of the ambient display, the planning activity was also varied to

[1] licensed under Creative Commons Attribution-Share Alike 3.0 license. http://openprocessing.org/visuals/?visualID=66. License: http://creativecommons.org/licenses/by-sa/3.0/.

maintain interest in the task. In one condition participants planned a holiday for themselves (as in [7]), while in the second condition, they planned a holiday for an older person of their choice. Again, the conditions were counterbalanced.

To avoid influencing the results of the study, the participants were told at the outset that the study was concerned with the experience of stress in planning activities and how stress impacts decision making and collaboration.

Responding to the Nonverbal Manifestations of Rapport

In the future we envisage that pervasive and wearable technologies, building on advances made by devices such as Sociometer [29], will be capable of automatically capturing participants' body language and therefore nonverbal behaviours associated with rapport. At this stage of the overall research project we wanted to decouple the questions around how rapport could be detected by technology from the question of whether ambient displays can amplify nonverbal behaviours linked to rapport, and the impact of such a display. For this reason, we adopted a WoZ approach to control the ambient display. Different individuals have different levels of interpersonal sensitivity leading to different perceptions of interpersonal body language and cues. To counter this, the same researcher manually triggered a median of six ripples to appear on the responsive ambient display whenever she observed participants manifesting nonverbal behaviours associated with rapport. Each ripple dissipated over nine seconds, growing from a diameter of 25mm to 100mm. The placement of each ripple on the ambient display was determined at random by a computer program. The schedule for detecting rapport was adapted from Bernieri et al [6]. Back channel responses and eye contact were also included in the response schedule to take into account work which suggests these behaviours, depending upon the context, are also associated with feelings of rapport [7, 17]. Hence ripples were triggered in response to:

- simultaneous movement (e.g. when the participants show change in movement that start, stop, change speed, or change directions at the same instant).
- tempo similarity (e.g. when the participants share the same rhythm in their gestures and movements).
- coordination (e.g. when the participants' behaviours mesh or combine evenly and smoothly).
- posture matching (e.g. when the participants share the same postures.) (See Figure 2 for an example).
- back channel responses (e.g. head nods, utterances showing agreement / listening such as "uh ha").
- eye contact (e.g. when participants engaged direct eye gaze).

Holiday Planning Procedure and Data Collection

At the start of the session each pair was asked to spend several minutes introducing themselves to the other participant. The participants were then asked to complete a first holiday planning task together whilst being video recorded, as described in the previous section. At the end of this task the participants individually completed a questionnaire which collected self reports of rapport (the rapport criterion measure). The rapport criterion measure (labelled post-task questionnaire during the study) contains 29 items, initially derived by Bernieri et al [7] from Tickle-Degnen and Rosenthal's theoretical and empirical exploration of rapport [37]. The rapport criterion measure asked participants to "rate yourself in the previous interaction on the following characteristics: smooth, bored cooperative, satisfied, comfortable, awkward, engrossed, involved, friendly, active and positive." The second half of the measure asked participants to "rate the interaction between you and your partner on the following characteristics: well coordinated, boring, cooperative, harmonious, unsatisfying, uncomfortably paced, cold, awkward, engrossing, unfocussed, involving, intense, unfriendly, active, positive, dull, worthwhile, and slow." Each item was rated on a Likert scale from 1 = not at all, to 9 = very. In addition, and to support the story told to participants regarding the purpose of the study, participants were asked to complete a simple self report measure of stress. This scale was included to add weight to our initial explanation of the study, it is not relevant to the current investigation, and will not be discussed further.

After a short break, the pair completed the holiday planning task for a second time, changing conditions as described earlier. At the end of the interaction the participants completed the rapport criterion measure, and a simple self report measure of stress for a second time. Following this, a semi-structured interview was conducted with each participant, covering questions such as their satisfaction with completing the holiday planning task, and their thoughts on the responsive ambient display. The participants were then debriefed. Each interview was transcribed and a theme-based analysis was conducted.

All of the interactions were recorded on three video cameras, with two cameras positioned to capture the participants' facial expressions, and a third capturing the broader interaction from the back of the room (see Figure 2). Video recording started directly after a researcher introduced the holiday planning task to participants.

Figure 2: Depicting View of Broader Interaction. Also Showing an Instance of Posture Matching.

Observer Judgements of Nonverbal Behaviours

In addition to exploring the impact of our visualisation on self reports of rapport, we were also interested in the impact of our ambient display on observers' judgements of the nonverbal behaviours within the interaction.

Here, we utilised Bernieri et al's methodology for collecting observer judgements of interactional synchrony [6], as a means of understanding how the ambient display may have influenced one aspect of how rapport is manifested through nonverbal communication [6, 7, 37]. As detailed by, and replicating, their study [6], we extracted the second minute of each holiday planning interaction from the video data collected from the video camera at the back of the room. This video data was then treated to remove sound, as well as remove any movement from the ambient display. Finally a mosaic effect was applied to the video to focus attention on the timings and patterns of movements, rather than other salient features of social interaction, such as facial expression. These one minute video segments were then used as stimuli for judgements of interactional synchrony. According to Bernieri et al [6] this technique has the advantages of enabling a observer to focus on the overall behaviour of interactants, rather than fine-grained analysis of a few distinct behaviours. The method does not attempt to define what it means to be coordinated; it simply assumes that when behaviours are harmonised, simultaneously occurring, and similar that observers will perceive these behaviours as synchronous. Additionally, such a technique is scalable enabling studies to show statistical power.

Twelve untrained observers served as judges of interactional synchrony. These observers were recruited from within the University, but were neither participants, nor involved in the project. Observers received no compensation for their participation. Our untrained observers were asked to access a web-based form, to view and rate each anonymously named video in turn. Before the observers completed the judging task, they were introduced to the concept of interactional synchrony (amalgamated from [6]) as follows:

"We consider interactional synchrony to be a dynamic aspect of interpersonal coordination where the movements of interacting individuals become organised in time and space. Things appear coordinated, harmonised and synchronous to the degree that they constitute a perceptual unit, when they appear to fit together".

Each observer was then asked to rate each video segment along three Likert scales described as follows: coordination (to what extent do the pairs' behaviours mesh or combine evenly and smoothly), simultaneous movement (e.g. if one person kicks their foot at the precise instant another swings their arm it is considered a simultaneous movement), and posture similarity (e.g. are they both sitting upright? Do they both have one hand on a hip?). The observers scored each measure on a scale from 1 = "no X" to 8 = "a lot of X".

RESULTS

This section provides an analysis of the relationship between the ambient display, self reports of rapport, and observer judgements of rapport. We also provide a themed analysis of the interview data.

The Relationship between Self Reports of Rapport and the Ambient Display

All 29 items of the rapport criterion measure were highly intercorrelated. The Cronbach alpha reliability coefficient for the entire scale was 0.90.

A rapport score was calculated for each individual in each interaction as the mean score reported across all items of the rapport criterion measure. A pair rapport score in each interaction was calculated as the mean of the two rapport scores calculated for each individual belonging to the pair. There was very little difference between the mean individual rapport score for interactions where an ambient display amplified nonverbal behaviours associated with rapport ($M = 181.81$, $SD = 21.88$), and where the ambient display remained static ($M = 181.62$, $SD = 22.35$). Similarly, there was very little difference between the mean pair rapport score for an interaction when supported by a responsive ambient display ($M = 181.81$, $SD = 12.93$), and when no support was offered via the ambient display ($M = 181.62$, $SD = 15.60$). Two Wilcoxon signed-rank tests confirmed no significant differences between these pairs of scores.

The Relationship between Observers' Judgements of Nonverbal Behaviours and the Ambient Display

The level of reliability for each of the three measures of interactional synchrony (coordination, simultaneous movement, and posture similarity) was high, with the calculated Cronbach's alpha for coordination = 0.84, for simultaneous movement = 0.91, and for posture similarity = 0.77.

An observer judgement of coordination was calculated for each video as the mean value of observers' ratings of coordination associated with that video. The same procedure was followed for simultaneous movement, and posture similarity. For each video, interactional synchrony was calculated as the mean value of the associated observer judgements of coordination, simultaneous movement, and posture similarity.

Figure 3 presents the mean of each observer judgement for the two conditions. The bar chart illustrates a general positive trend where the responsive ambient display resulted in higher observer judgements of coordination, posture similarity, simultaneous movement, and interactional synchrony. A Wilcoxon signed-rank test indicates that the participants showed significantly more interactional synchrony when their encoding of nonverbal manifestations of rapport were supported by an ambient display (M = 4.88, SD = 0.88), than when not (M = 4.31, SD = 0.98), T = 1.00, p = 0.01. In addition, the participants were significantly more coordinated when supported by an ambient responsive display (M = 4.90, SD = 1.01), than when not (M = 4.40, SD = 1.14), T = 4.00, p = 0.05. Finally, the pairs were also found to show significantly more posture similarity when supported by a responsive ambient display (M = 5.37, SD = 0.56) than when not (M = 4.66, SD = 0.99), T = 1.50, p = 0.03.

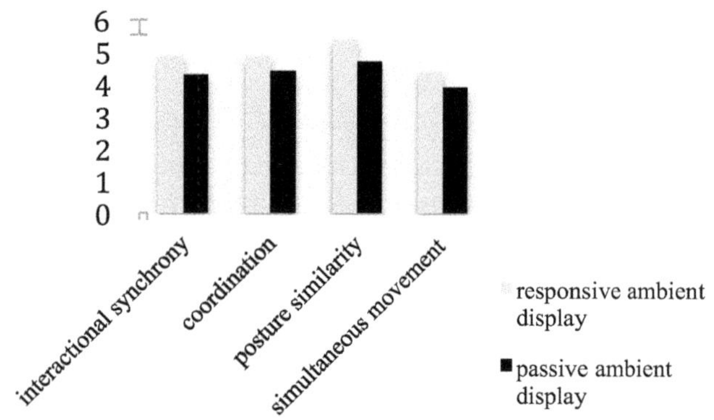

Figure 3: Mean Interactional Synchrony Ratings as a Function of the Amplification of Rapport through an Ambient Display

Participants' Thoughts on an Ambient Display that Supports Nonverbal Communication

A semi-structured interview was conducted with each participant after they completed both holiday planning tasks to understand their experience of taking part in the study, their thoughts on our representation of rapport, as well as to provide inspiration to further the design of technologies to support face-to-face interaction. The interviews were conducted in the same room as the study, with the length of interview variable, lasting between 20 and 40 minutes. A qualitative inductive analysis was applied to the data with themes identified by the authors based on both a deep reading of the data and the study's research questions. Here we provide an overview of the interview data around two main themes: representing social interaction; appropriateness of technology in face-to-face interaction.

Representing Social Interaction

At the outset of the interview all participants were asked whether they had noticed any movement on the display during either of the holiday planning tasks. Half (8) of the participants reported that they did not notice any change in the ambient display. The remaining participants reported to have noticed movements on the display whilst they had completed the task, but had thought the movements were completely unrelated to their interaction, or the task. In fact, the majority of these participants reported that they had thought the ambient display was a screen saver.

For the half who reported having noticed movement on the display, only two participants reported that the ambient display was a distraction from the social interaction, with one participant reporting that she found herself watching the ambient display whilst completing the planning task with her partner.

Participant 10: *"Yes, I thought it was a screensaver, because I... I don't know. I guess I didn't think about it, because it's got programme bars, so it's not a screensaver, but that's what I thought it was and I found myself watching it..."*

After this line of questioning the participants were debriefed, and told the real purpose of the study. The interview then moved on to focus on the future design of ambient displays for social interaction. There was agreement amongst participants that a representation of social interaction should not distract from the interaction itself. Additionally, several participants felt that the function of the technology would need to be obscured - otherwise participants worried that the ambient display may cause unnecessary anxiety. For example, two participants were concerned that an ambient display such as this might highlight less positive interactions, and instigate a negative feedback loop.

Participant 17: *"So, if you had a very disharmonious interaction, you might have the chance of instigating a negative feedback loop where you kind of start to go downhill and then the environment changes, and that makes you more angry and then..."*

Both Participant 9 and 12 felt that the function of the technology would need to be hidden in order to be effective.

Participant 9: *"That was... I felt manipulated at that point, so I think there's a point at which... if one's aware of it, then you're... you have to start changing it, I'd have thought..."*

Participant 12: *"Yes, if you knew too much about the workings of it, then it would become less effective then."*

Additionally, some participants thought that if the technology was understood by users, then it might become a stigma, indicating to others that a particular person had difficulty in social interactions.

Participant 3: *"...so just bringing something like that to anything and people knowing about it immediately puts... you know, think that you're trying to hone your skills or you're not confident, so I don't think that... I wouldn't want that, I suppose."*

The Appropriateness of a Technology that Supports Nonverbal Communication

A section of the interview probed whether there was a use for technologies that support nonverbal communication within face-to-face interactions. Five participants felt that technology had no place providing this sort of support. For example Participant 7 told the interviewer:

Participant 7: *"...if I think about communication technology for example, that wouldn't have a purpose in face-to-face communication, because I don't need any technology to make my communicating easier with someone, because he's next to me."*

Participant 9 thought that the technology was superfluous since, as humans, we are already very well aware of social signalling.

Participant 9: *"I prefer to respond to the person and have eye contact or not have eye contact. I mean, I'm either engaged or not engaged with them. I'm not so sure how much external things like that... I think it's a bit too much for people to have to know that that's going to be a signal that... in a way, we all know our signals."*

Some participants were enthusiastic for a technology that would support face-to-face communications, and particularly if it would be beneficial for some people who might otherwise have difficulties in social interactions.

Participant 18: *"With the subtler points, like with people who are shy people and people might interpret that shyness wrongly when they are actually trying to get across these other feelings, than it could be really useful for some people."*

DISCUSSION

The data presented in the Results section indicates that our amplification of rapport through an ambient display increased the amount of interactional synchrony, and more specifically, the amount of coordination and posture similarity seen within an interaction by untrained observers. At the same time, interactants themselves were seemingly unaware of these increased behavioural manifestations of rapport, with no significant differences in their self reports of rapport between conditions. Although this study is based on a small sample size, these significant results are intriguing. Our main contribution here then is an initial exploration of the potential value ambient displays might show in supporting the subconscious non-verbal elements of face-to-face social interaction as well as to articulate avenues for further exploration.

Whilst we based out study on a social science study [7] to explore rapport, we made several changes to the method in order to address our research questions regarding ambient displays. For example, our participants did not use physical money, or a physical map in planning their holidays. Although these changes are relatively small, they are important. Bernieri et al hypothesised that the physical elements of the task (money and map) were influential on the amount of interactional synchrony experienced by participants [6]. This renders a direct comparison between our results and Bernieri et al's dataset difficult. As such, the discussion presented here focuses on the research questions driving this work, and the ethical questions surrounding ambient displays such as the one presented here.

Pervasive Technology Can Influence Interactional Synchrony in Interactants

As described above, interactional synchrony appears to increase, as measured by untrained observers, when an ambient display is used to amplify the nonverbal signals associated rapport. This is an important finding when taking into account the available empirical evidence that links synchronous movement to feelings of trust, smoothness in an interaction, and relationship building [22, 37]. What is of further interest is the finding that although participants' nonverbal communication was perceived to have changed when the ambient display responded to behavioural manifestations of rapport, participants were unaware of this change. The statistically significant change in nonverbal communication did not impact upon the participants' self reports of rapport. In other words, although the participants manifested increased rapport in a bodily sense, this did not feed into a greater sense of rapport in a conscious, or cognitive sense.

There are a number of reasons why this could be the case. For example, it is possible that the modality chosen to represent interactional synchrony was incorrect. Half of the participants were aware of movement on the ambient display, and some reported that this movement had been distracting. From this we might infer that the display reduced eye contact as the representation drew the eyes from an interactional partner, even if only for a short period. Literature suggests that eye contact is a crucial element of social interaction, impacting upon turn taking behaviours [17]. It is also linked to two components of rapport: mutual attentiveness, and positivity [37]. So, by reducing the amount of eye contact, we may have inadvertently negatively affected judgements of positivity and mutual attention, and thereby feelings of rapport.

Further to this, Tickle-Degnen et al have theorised about the relative importance of three nonverbal components of rapport (positivity, mutual attentiveness, and coordination) throughout the lifetime of a relationship [37]. In this model, positivity is considered to be particularly important to feelings of rapport in initial encounters among strangers, whilst coordination becomes more important to the evaluation of rapport in later interactions, where there is an increased familiarity amongst participants. As such, it is possible that although increased coordination was experienced by participants, these experiences of greater coordination did not feed into participants' models of what rapport feels like in initial interactions between unacquainted people, or in addition that this increased coordination was countered by a decrease in mutual attentiveness, and positivity. Further work collecting observer judgements of mutual attentiveness and positivity would allow us to assess this hypothesis.

Finally, the statistically significant differences in observers' perceptions of nonverbal communication were small. As such, perhaps these changes in behaviour were not sufficiently perceivable by those individuals taking part in the interaction to feed into their interpersonal judgements.

Influencing Social Interaction Subconsciously

The interview data suggests that the display was subtle enough that half the participants seemingly did not notice changes in its appearance over the course of the 10 minute interaction. Even when participants reported being aware of the movement on the display, they dismissed this movement as a screen saver which had no relation to themselves, or the interaction. Yet, the ambient display which amplified nonverbal manifestations of rapport did indeed appear to influence the overall level of interactional synchrony, and more specifically the level of coordination, and posture similarity within the interaction as judged by untrained observers. The visible availability of additional information via the ambient display, reflecting the nonverbal communication, seemingly reinforced and enhanced participants' behaviour and interactional body language without the participants being aware of this influence. This suggests that the ambient display may have contributed to the subconscious processing of nonverbal communication, as described by [23]. This finding complements [33], where ambient displays seemed to subconsciously encourage healthy lifestyle choices.

The ambient display discussed in this paper could be described as a ambient persuasive technology [14]. The ambient display, and the results of its application so far raise ethical questions, particularly when one considers the empirical link between interactional synchrony and trust [22]. In effect future iterations of such a technology may have the potential to subconsciously change people's attitudes about a given person (or product), which in turn may influence conscious decision making processes.

However, it is important to emphasise that people already make these subconscious social judgements [23, 30] and that the technology described here is only *responding* to the nonverbal manifestations of rapport as displayed by the participants. In this sense it is very much like the technologies described by Berichevsky et al [4], it is a technology that amplifies human behaviour to possibly persuasive ends, but without the human behaviour, this technology has no persuasive power. This argument is entangled with the current workings of our technology: at present, the display and its response to synchronous movements are under the control of a "wizard". If further work with future iterations of the technology show that amplifying synchronous movement leads not only to greater coordination within an interaction, but that this coordination can be converted into a greater sense of rapport, then an individual outside of the interaction continuing to control the visual representation, and amplifications could arguably be less ethical. At present, we believe that the amplification of nonverbal social signals has to be directly coupled with those social signals occurring within the interaction to influence feelings of rapport. That said, this is an important avenue for further research, the results of which will guide the ethical application of technologies that support nonverbal communication in face-to-face interaction.

Additionally, as the technology moves out of the control of the "wizard", and into the control of sensors and what will effectively be an automated decision making technology, there will be new ethical implications. It will be important to understand the potential impact of the technology making errors when identifying and amplifying behaviours that appear to be related to rapport. For example, how would such a technology differentiate between an interactant mocking, rather than mirroring another, and what would the impact of mistaken amplifications be?

Applications for Ambient Displays in Social Interaction

Supporting the Production of Nonverbal Communication

This study points to the potential for technology to provide real time support to interactants in the production, or encoding, of nonverbal communication during face-to-face interactions. However, whilst our data analysis suggests that the ambient display may have engendered more encoding of "useful" nonverbal behaviours, the increased availability of these behaviours did not translate into feeling that the interaction was more successful. It will require further work to unpack why this is the case, but we are particularly interested in how a modality might better amplify moments of interactional synchrony, and are currently investigating whether other modalities might be better suited to amplifying such moments.

The results from this study suggest that ambient and pervasive technologies could support nonverbal communication for a range of different users and contexts. For example, some research suggests that those who feel excluded from a social group (and therefore perhaps shy people) encode more of the nonverbal communicative acts that lead to smoother interactions than the non-excluded [21]. In corroboration, there is evidence that shy people believe that the nonverbal signals they produce are often ignored in favour of the talkativeness, and the self expression of others [35]. This position is supported by research [7] which indicates that social judgements are often made based on more extroverted behaviours such as smiling, and talkativeness. As such, shy people may be contributing to a social interaction in a nonverbal manner, but these contributions may be overlooked in favour of more explicit social signals. It also suggests that shy people may feel happy contributing to an interaction through nonverbal channels, where they may feel uncomfortable maintaining an interaction by verbal means. Future work within this area could seek to develop ambient displays, and pervasive technologies that can amplify, or draw attention to, a shy participant's contributions to a social interaction, and as a result make this nonverbal contribution to a social interaction more available to the non-shy.

Better Supporting Collaboration within Groups

There are a number of pervasive technologies currently available that support face-to-face group work [for example 12, 18]. These technologies tend to emphasise the role that turn taking, and evenness in contribution play in good collaboration. Yet, research conducted with children solving a maths problem in small groups suggests that it is not necessarily evenness in turn taking that leads to successful collaborations [3]. Instead the critical difference was the way in which a group responds to suggestions and possible solutions from individuals. In tandem with this, the researchers found successful collaborations featured greater amounts of *connected* turn taking – where the conversations of participants were well aligned to a particular topic, or problem. To aid this mutual attention, groups coordinated themselves and their work through the use of physical artefacts in the environment, conversational devices, and *coordinated* physical movements. Barron [3] therefore argues that groups must not only focus on the content space of a task, or problem, but also on the relational space. Given the positive influence our technology had on coordination, future iterations of our technology may be well placed to support this relational aspect of group work.

Challenges in Applying an Ambient Display to Support Social Interaction

There are some continuing design challenges around creating technologies that can support nonverbal aspects of face-to-face communication. For example, we found that there was a mixed desire amongst our participants for this type of support. In particular, our participants worried about the negative connotations of such a technology, for example, people being able to see the success (or not) of their interactions and conversations, and the stigma that could be attached to using such a technology. To counter this, some of the participants felt that the function of the technology would need to be obscured from users in order for it to remain effective (a need supported by [23]). These comments lend support to our choice to create an ambient display, rather than a display that used numbers or words to denote nonverbal communication within the social interaction. It also suggests a delicate balance regarding the visibility (or perceptibility) of the ambient display and its purpose. For example, how should design balance the need to provide socially anxious people with a more salient means of participating, whilst not distracting interactants from their conversation, or producing negative judgements about an interaction, or indeed a person?

CONCLUSIONS AND FUTURE WORK

The work described here has sketched the possible opportunities for research around ambient and pervasive technologies which support nonverbal communication. Further research is needed, for example, to understand whether other modalities may be more appropriate for amplifying nonverbal communicative acts, and, whether the fine-tuning of modality can translate the enhanced encoding of nonverbal communication seen in this study to an improvement in the decoding of nonverbal communication. Considerable technical effort will also be required to design pervasive sensing technologies that are able to detect the nonverbal behaviours relevant to social interaction and respond in real time. Our investigations have shown that an ambient display has the potential to influence the nonverbal communication within pairs completing a collaborative task. In addition, the data collected suggests that the ambient display was operating on a subconscious level, scaffolding individuals' use of nonverbal communication without his or her conscious awareness. This work takes a small step towards defining a role for ambient and pervasive technologies that moves beyond supporting solely the information and verbal aspects of face-to-face interactions and collaboration, to technologies that support the interpersonal and relational aspects of social interaction.

ACKNOWLEDGEMENTS

This work has been funded by the EPSRC, grant number EP/F064330/1. Many thanks to all the participants and observers who contributed to our study and Dr. Amanda Carr who kindly guided our statistical analysis.

REFERENCES

1. Ara, K., et al., Sensible Organisations: Changing out Businesses and Work Styles through Sensor Data. *J. of Information Processing 16*, (2008), 1-12.
2. Argyle, M., *Bodily Communication*. Methuen, London, (1975).
3. Barron, B., When Smart Groups Fail. *J. of Learning Sciences 12*, 3 (2003), 307-359.
4. Berdichevsky, D. and Neuenschwander, E., Towards an Ethics of Persuasive Technology. *Comms. of the ACM 42*, 5 (1999), 51-58.
5. Bernieri, F., Coordinated Movement and Rapport in Teacher-Student Interactions. *J. of Nonverbal Behaviour 12*, 2 (1988), 120-138.
6. Bernieri, F., Davis, J., Rosenthal, R., Knee, R., Interactional Synchrony and Rapport: Measuring Synchrony in Displays Devoid of Sound and Facial Expression. *Personality and Social Psych. Bulletin 20*, (1994), 303-311.
7. Bernieri, F., Gillis, J., Davis, J., GRahe, J., Dyad Rapport and the Accuracy of Its Judgement across

Situations: A Lens Model Analysis. *J. of Personality and Social Psych. 71*, 1 (1996), 110-129.

8. Berzowska, J. Memory Rich Clothing: Second Skins That Communicate Phsyical Memory. In Proc. *Creativity and Cognition*, ACM (2005), 32-40.
9. Borovoy, R., Martin, F., Resnick, M., Silverman, B., *Groupwear: Nametags That Tell About Relationships*, In Proc. *CHI* ACM (1998), 329-330.
10. Borovoy, R., Martin, F., Vermuri, S., Resnick, M., Silverman, B., Hancock, C., Meme Tags and Community Mirrors: Moving from Conferences to Collaboration. In Proc. *CSCW* (1998), 159-168.
11. Bull, P., *Posture and Gesture*. Pergamon press, (1987).
12. DiMicco, J.M., Pandolfo, A., and Bender, W. Influencing Group Participation with a Shared Display. In Proc. *CSCW*, ACM (2004), 614-623.
13. Falk, J., Björk, S., *The Bubblebadge: A Wearable Public Display*, In Proc. *CHI 1999* ACM (1999), 318-319.
14. Ham, J., Midden, C., and Beute, F. Can Ambient Persuasive Technology Persuade Unconsciously? Using Sublimial Feedback to Influence Energy Consumption Ratings of Household Appliances. In Proc. *Persuasive Technology*, ACM (2009)
15. Hodgins, H. and Zuckerman, M., The Effect of Nonverbal Sensitivity on Social Interaction. *J. of Nonverbal Behaviour 14*, 3 (1990), 155-170.
16. Kanis, M., Winters, N., Agamanolis, S., Gavin, A., Cullinan, C., Toward Wearable Social Networking with Iband. In Proc. *CHI*, ACM (2005), 1521-1524.
17. Kendon, A., *Conducting Interaction: Patterns of Behaviour in Focused Encounters*. Cambridge University Press, Cambridge, (1990).
18. Kim, T., Chang, A., Holland, L., Pentland., Meeting Mediator: Enhancing Group Collaboration Using Sociometric Feedback. In Proc. *CSCW*, ACM (2008), 457-466.
19. Laborde, G., *Influencing with Integrity: Management Skills for Communication and Negotiation*. Crown House Publishing, (1998).
20. LaFrance, M., Nonverbal Synchrony and Rapport: Analysis by the Cross-Lag Panel Technique. *Social Psych. Quarterly 42*, 1 (1979), 66-70.
21. Lakin, J., Chartland, T., and Arkin, R., Nonconscious Mimicry as an Automatic Behavioural Response to Social Exclusion. *Psych. Science 19*, 8 (2008), 816-822.
22. Lakin, J. and Chartrand, T., Using Non-Conscious Behavioural Mimicry to Creat Affiliation and Rapport. *Psych. Science 14*, 4 (2003), 334-339.
23. Lieberman, M., Intuition: A Social Cognitive Neuroscience Approach. *Pysch. Bulletin 126*, 1 (2000), 109-137.
24. Mccarthy, J., McDonald, D., Soroczak, S., Ngyuyen, D., Rashid, A., *Augmenting the Social Space of an Academic Conference*, In Proc. *CSCW*, ACM (2004) 39-48.
25. McDonald, D.W., McCarthy, J., Soroczak, S., Nguyen, D., Rashid, D., Proactive Displays: Supporting Awareness in Fluid Social Environments. *ACM Trans. Comp.-Hum. Interaction 14*, 4 (2008), 1-31.
26. Monfries, M. and Kafer, N., Neglected and Rejected Children: A Social-Skills Model. *The J. of Psych. 121*, 4 (1987), 401-407.
27. Narumi, T., Akagawa, T., Ah Seong, Y., Hirose, M., An Entertainment System Using Thermal Feedback for Increasing Communication and Social Skills. *Lecture Notes in Com. Sci. 5690*, (2009), 184-195.
28. Ngyuyen, D., T., and Canny, J. More Than Face-to-Face: Empathy Effects of Video Framing. In Proc. *CHI* ACM (2009), 423-432.
29. Olguín Olguín, D. and Pentland, A. Sensible Organizations: A Sensor Based System for Organizational Design and Engineering. In Proc. *Workshop on Organizational Design and Engineering* (2009)
30. Palmer, M. and Simmons, K., Communicating Intentions through Nonverbal Behaviours: Conscious and Nonconscious Encoding of Liking. *Human Comm. Research 22*, 1 (1995), 128-160.
31. Pentland, A., *Honest Signals - How They Shape Our World.* MIT Press, Cambridge, MA, (2008).
32. Reeves, B. and Nass, C., *The Media Equation: How People Treat Computers, Television, and New Media Like Real People and Places*. CSLI Publications, California, (1996).
33. Rogers, Y., Hazelwood, W., Marshall, P., Dalton, N, S., Hertich, S., Ambient Influence: Can Twinkly Lights Lure and Abstract Representations Trigger Behavioral Change. In Proc. *Ubicomp 2010*, ACM (2010) 261-270.
34. Schlenker, B. and Weigold, M., Interpersonal Processes Involving Impression Regulation and Management. *Annual Review of Psych. 43*, (1992), 133-168.
35. Scott, S., *Shyness and Society: The Illusion of Competence*. Palgrave Macmillan, (2007).
36. Stel, M. and Roos, V., Mimicry in Social Interaction: Benefits for Mimickers, Mimickees, and Their Interaction. *Brit. J. of Psych. 101*, (2010), 311-323.
37. Tickle-Degnen, L. and Rosenthal, R., The Nature of Rapport and Its Nonverbal Correlates. *Psych. Inquiry 1*, 4 (1990), 285-293.

Issues in Evaluating Ambient Displays in the Wild: Two Case Studies

William R. Hazlewood, Erik Stolterman, Kay Connelly
Indiana University School of Informatics and Computing
Bloomington, IN 47405, USA
{whazlewo, estolter, connelly}@indiana.edu

ABSTRACT
In this paper we discus the complex task of evaluating ambient displays, concentrating on issues within in-situ deployments. We start by describing how these technologies have been evaluated in lab settings, where the focus has been primarily on issues of usability, and argue strongly for the necessity of in-situ evaluation. We then present two case studies involving in-situ evaluations, and from these derive issues that hindered the researchers from being able to delve more deeply into the overall impact of their implementations. We conclude with our own suggestions on possible alternatives to explore for evaluating ambient displays, which are based on the issues derived from our case studies.

Author Keywords
Ambient Displays, Feedback, Evaluation Studies, Case Studies, Methods.

ACM Classification Keywords
H5.m. Information interfaces and presentation (e.g., HCI): Miscellaneous.

General Terms
Design, Human Factors, Measurement, Performance

INTRODUCTION
Over the last decade the advent of ubiquitous computing research has piqued an interest in alternative displays that can provide useful information while blending smoothly into the surrounding environment. These devices are distinguished from more typical informational displays in that they are designed to be minimally attended and perceivable from outside of a person's direct focus of attention, providing a level of pre-attentive processing without being unnecessarily distracting. Such technologies are intended to be embedded in existing environments, often appropriating unused physical and visual aspects of everyday objects to provide an information channel that can be *easily ignored* when there are more important matters requiring attention [19]. Because they can be easily "tuned out," informational displays such as these may offer a solution to the possible threats of information overload some have predicted as a side effect of ubiquitous computing environments becoming more common [26]. The challenge we face is how to provide in-depth evaluations on something that is defined as blending with the surrounding world, and meant to be (in some respects) ignored.

While many interesting ambient display technologies have been explored over the last decade, there is a lack of research discussing the difficulty involved in *evaluating the general impact and effectiveness of such technologies*. The lack of research on the evaluation of ambient displays is due in part to the sheer difficulty involved in developing prototypes and implementing user studies for this class of technologies [5]. Since ambient displays are designed to be highly subtle and used indirectly, traditional user interface evaluation methodologies targeting task-oriented users do not provide enough methodological support for the study of how these technologies are experienced in actual contexts of use, or how people's relationship with the technology changes over long periods of time.

By definition, these technologies do not function as intended until they have properly blended into the everyday environment [14], which is difficult to accurately simulate inside a controlled laboratory. Studying these technologies is further complicated in that a sort of paradox arises where intrusively observing the use of an ambient display hinders it from functioning as intended. Direct observation and probing from researchers is a constant reminder that something out-of-the-ordinary is present, and directs the subject's attention unfairly. It is likely that the more aggressively or intrusively one tries to observe people's interactions, the less these results will be an accurate reflection of actual use. Hence, special care must be taken when designing evaluative studies on ambient displays. Since few long-term or in-situ studies have been conducted, it is not clear how to accurately gauge the effectiveness or impact of systems with such atypical styles of use.

In this paper we argue that ambient displays, in all their many forms, constitute a new form of user experience that is radically different from the traditional focused task-oriented user situation. As a consequence we argue for methodological development when it comes to evaluation of these technologies. This paper is based on two case studies, both examples of ambient technology evaluated in real-world settings. We conclude the paper with a discussion of the insights on evaluation derived from the two cases. We also present some possible directions for further methodological development when it comes to evaluation of ambient technology.

RELATED RESEARCH

The concept of an ambient display has its genesis in Mark Weiser's seminal paper, *Designing Calm Technology*. In this paper Weiser describes a project he called "The Dangling String," which consists of a simple cable hanging in the corner of a room that twitches whenever a packet of information is sent over the local network. If there is little network traffic, the string hangs motionless, but as traffic increases the string wiggles and twitches chaotically. While there are a number of ways to inform people of the local level of network traffic, the advantage of this particular display is that it conveys information in a simple and subtle manner, allowing people in the office to *just know* when the network is under heavy usage without having to think about it. Weiser proposed that this form of representation would allow information to move easily from the periphery of our attention, to the center, and back. So, despite being ubiquitous, such displays could also be easily ignored or disregarded when more pressing concerns required one's attention [24].

Hiroshi Ishii's group at the MIT Media Laboratory further explored the concept of ambient displays by producing several unique implementations, such as ambientROOM [14], the Water Lamp, and Pinwheels [8]. Examples like these allude to several potential advantages from designing technologies that are subtle and make use of our peripheral awareness. However, since the majority of such implementations have not been evaluated [16], and no agreed upon evaluation metrics exists, it is difficult to articulate their overall value.

Evaluations on Ambient Information Devices

While there have been several innovative ambient displays with little or no formal evaluation [e.g., 4, 12, 15, 20, 24], there are some early implementations which have provided important initial evaluations in an attempt to expose how people react to ambient displays, for example LumiTouch [6] and AudioAura [18]. These examples, however, report few details, and focus mainly on informal user feedback. The LumiTouch was given to users who were not emotionally involved with one another, and after using it for a short time comments were collected regarding each individual's experience. In AudioAura nine participants were given a brief introduction, and then asked to complete a set of self-paced tasks, followed by a questionnaire where comments and suggestions were encouraged.

Whereas AudioAura and LumiTouch were intended for designated users, many ambient displays have been designed for public spaces where the information presented can be absorbed by anyone who happens to walk by [e.g., 12, 15, 25]. As with the previous examples, evaluations for these installations typically involve informal interviews focused heavily on the initial levels of *enjoyment* when interacting with the display but little in the way of long-term effects or general impact.

Laboratory Evaluation Styles

In more elaborate evaluations of ambient displays, methods have focused mainly on the *functionality* and *usability* of the implementation itself. For example [2] describes a device called the "WaterBot" which was developed to encourage water conservation by providing subtle visual and audio cues to those using a water faucet. It was evaluated in a controlled study where ten participants were asked to wash their hands thoroughly in a sink with the WaterBot installed. To gauge the intuitive aspects of the device, participants were not told any details about the device, or its intended function. As they washed their hands repeatedly, the WaterBot cycled through its modes as the researchers observed and recorded the subject's comments. This evaluation provided important insights into how the users made sense of the WaterBot's cues, which could be generalized to show how people might interact with devices they have never before encountered. However, since the study was conducted in a controlled laboratory where participants were requested to complete a task under observation, it is unlikely that the WaterBot ever became embedded into the participant's environment as Weiser suggested. Because of this, we have no real knowledge of the long-term impact this display could have on behavior. It could very well be that during regular use, those using WaterBot would simply become unaware of its presence, or just ignore it intentionally once they were not being observed.

In [7], a system called "eye-q" was developed in which two small LEDs were embedded into a pair of eyeglasses. These LEDs were intended to deliver simple visual cues in the wearer's peripheral visual field without disrupting their vision, or diverting their existing focus of attention. To evaluate this display, a thorough set of experiments were conducted to test the subject's ability to perceive the cues given by the glasses while the subject was focusing on separate primary tasks, which required varying levels of concentration. The study showed that the display was less noticeable when users were under higher workload conditions. This result implies that the information from the display *can* inherently shift to the background when the user needs to focus on something else, but just as with the WaterBot, the eye-q studies were conducted in a controlled laboratory setting, where it is likely that the participants were more sensitive to the display than they might be in a natural setting. It is still unclear whether this display would function as it did in the lab or if it would become one of the many notifications people simply tune out permanently.

An evaluative framework was developed specifically for ambient displays in [16], where the authors successfully modified a version of Neilson's heuristics for evaluating usability, to specifically address the design of ambient displays. However, while this method is good for locating problems of usability due to design flaws, such analyses tell us only about the *potential* success of an ambient display, not how such displays function once no one is prompting their consideration.

We have come to realize that there are limits on what can be learned about ambient displays in a laboratory setting, particularly implementations that do not address specific tasks or goals. To advance research in ambient displays *new evaluation methods must be explored* that can account for the special requirements necessary for these technologies to function as intended, particularly the blending of these displays into the environment.

Our conjecture is that new methods will require studies focused specifically on *in-situ* deployments conducted over *long periods of time*. This arrangement seems to be the only way to allow a display to become truly *ambient* within a given environment. However, studies like this are difficult and time consuming since they often involve observing low intensity usage styles (e.g., only brief glances at a display) [13]. Also, the ambiguous nature of *use* of these displays demands a rethinking of evaluation. As Hallnäs and Redström state, technologies like these are neither works of art, nor tools with explicit uses, even though they share properties with both [10]. Our goal is to explore more broadly how such studies could be conducted, derive exactly what factors can be measured, and determine what these factors can tell us about the impact ambient displays have in actual contexts of use.

In the following sections, we present two case studies where an ambient display was developed and evaluated in-situ. These case studies are presented in brief, but full accounts can be found in [11] and [21]. These studies were initially not designed as studies of evaluation methodology, but both present evaluation challenges that initiated this paper and our examination of evaluation methodology. The two studies each offer a set of evaluation issues and have provided us with the material necessary for a deeper discussion on evaluation.

CASE STUDY 1: STUDENT FEEDBACK ORB

In the first study, a simple ambient display was developed and deployed in an exploratory long-term, in-situ, study. Considering the research motivations, an initial set of four rubrics was derived for this study's development.

(i) Make use of a simple mechanism

The authors did not want to complicate their study with dense or highly abstract mappings of symbols to meanings, or use anything that would require significant training in order to be understood.

(ii) Provide an information source that was of high interest to the participants

The information channels commonly used for ambient displays typically include sources that can be constructed from publicly available data streams. To create a system that provides information that is potentially more engaging, the authors chose to create a custom information channel specifically tailored to the participants' interests.

(iii) Be conducted outside of a laboratory setting

The authors wanted to observe a display embedded at a level where participants interact with it naturally, and figured that this would not be accomplishable unless the display was placed in the participants natural setting (i.e., a real home or office).

(iv) Run for an extended time

This rubric was to ensure that the display became embedded into the participant's surroundings, and fully integrated with daily routines. Also, this time frame allowed the display to overcome any initial novelty effects.

To satisfy (i), the authors made use of an existing commercial device known as the "Ambient Stock Orb" from AmbientDevices.com [1]. For (ii), the authors focused on university instructors as the participants in the study, and created an information channel that allowed students to provide feedback regarding their learning experiences. For (iii), the authors simply give an Ambient Orb to each of the participating instructors, and told them to situate the orb wherever they felt it was most appropriate. Finally, for (iv) the system was structured so that it could run automatically, logging information for as long as the study conditions would allow.

The Ambient Display

The final system consisted of an Ambient Orb set to reflect the overall daily confidence levels of students within a particular course, and convey this information to the instructor using a predefined color scale. Additionally, a way for the instructors to view more detailed feedback information was provided in case they were curious as to why their orb had changed one way or the other. Below is a detailed description of the different components of this display.

The Ambient Orb

The Ambient Orb consists of a small sphere made of frosted glass containing an array of multicolored LEDs (see Figure 1, bottom right). These LEDs allow the orb to shift smoothly between thousands of different colors, which are configured by way of an embedded cellular chip communicating with a national pager network in the United States. The result is an information appliance that does not require an existing network connection to function.

The Custom Information Channel

To provide a custom information channel, the system sent automated emails to each participating student, asking them to give a general confidence rating over their understanding of the materials covered in class. This email was sent after each class, and consisted of an HTML formatted message containing a single Likert scale which the students could click (see Figure 1, top). To supplement the data represented on the orb, a separate information page was developed which the instructor could reference through the web. This page contained a histogram showing the actual scores received in real time, and a small bit of extra statistical information (see Figure 1, bottom left).

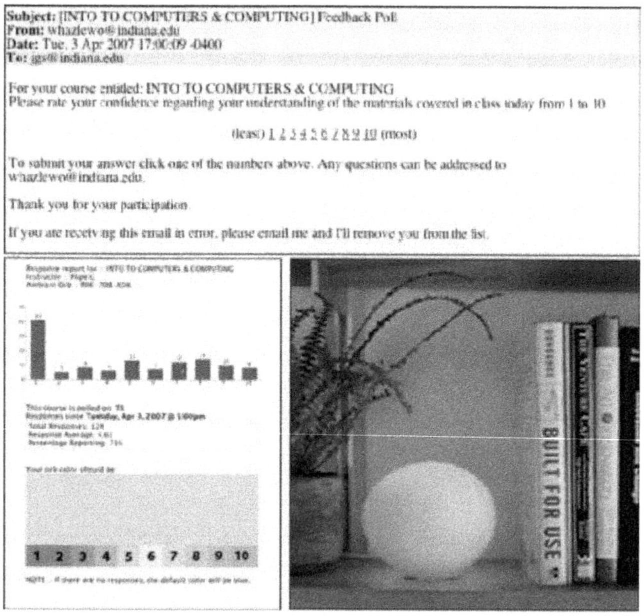

Figure 1: The automated email (top), Informational website (bottom, left), and the Ambient Orb (bottom, right)

Evaluation

Six instructors were gathered from four different departments at the authors' university to participate in this study. Each of the instructors were met with individually, given an orb, and instructed on how it functioned. The instructors were told how to tell if the orb is working correctly and that they should be able to place it anywhere they desired.

Once the orbs were working, and the instructors understood how to use them, the authors began recruiting students from each instructor's class. During this recruitment, students were informed that participants would be receiving an automated email after each class asking them to answer the following question:

"Please rate your confidence regarding your understanding of the materials covered in class today from 1 to 10."

It was explained that to respond they simply had to click on one of the hyperlinks embedded inside the email, that their participation was voluntary, and that the instructor would have no knowledge of who was participating. This was important so that the students were comfortable in giving negative responses.

The instructors were informed that the orb was set to show the average score given by the students on a scale of 1 to 10, with 10 being the best, that the scores were mapped to a color scale ranging from red to yellow to green, and provided the URL for accessing their own supplemental information page. Finally, it was explained that the instructors were not expected to use the system one way or another and that they should feel free to check the information page anytime they wished.

Abridged Study Results

Except for two instructors (*Instructor 2* and *Instructor 3*) who joined after the initial study had begun, the system ran for 68 days. Since this was an exploratory study, there was no specific phenomenon being measured. The authors were mostly interested in any interesting outcomes that could be used to inform future in-situ studies of ambient displays.

The observation process was made difficult by the fact that the authors constrained themselves from directly observing the participants. The reason for this is that they believed that continually probing the instructors would constantly force the display in the foreground of the participant's attention, keeping it from blending into the surrounding environment and becoming *truly ambient*. The authors chose instead to monitor whatever information was possible *without* disturbing the instructors during the study. However, the pool of non-intrusive monitoring sources was very sparse. The authors had access to the web server hosting the information web page for each instructor's orb, so the frequency which the instructors accessed this resource could be monitored, and they could observe how the students were reporting responses to the biweekly polls. Lastly, they knew structured interviews could be conducted without contaminating the use of the display after the study had concluded. Described below are the observations made along with the interpretations of the authors.

Information Web Page Access

It was surprising how infrequently some of the instructors accessed the informational web page for their orbs. The authors had predicted that the majority of instructors would access the informational site somewhat frequently at the beginning of the study until they became more accustomed to reading the Ambient Orb, but as shown in Table 1, several of the instructors only accessed the informational web page a few times over the entire course of the study. Towards the midpoint of the study an email was sent out reminding the instructors of the informational web page's existence, which may account for the *only* accesses by some of the instructors. Instructors 1, 5, and 6, were the most infrequent visitors to the information web page. During the post-study interviews, the instructors were asked to give their opinion on the value of having the Ambient Orb paired with the informational web page.

Instructor 5 responded:

Instructor 5: "I preferred to look at the website, quite frankly, because it gave more information. The average is kind of a limited score, I preferred the website because of its additional information, and I know how many responses are contributing to the score. Some may not care, but for me, from a research background, teaching, I obviously want to know more information."

However, later in the same response this instructor states:

Instructor 5: "I wouldn't say the orb was a waste, I used that as a barometer on how frequently to go check the web site. I didn't check the website necessarily a whole lot. I checked the orb a lot, and if I'd seen changes I would have gone to the website."

Instructors 1 and 6 both agreed that while they liked the information in the web page more than the orb, they did not feel that they had to check the web page unless prompted to by the orb.

From one point of view, such statements support the value of this display. It was clear that the information was valuable to the instructor, but the Ambient Orb acted more as a filter that informed the instructor that they did not *need* to bother checking the detailed information on the web page. However, during the study a concern was that the lack of access to the informational web page meant that the instructors had simply forgotten about its existence. Despite the initial desire to avoid polling the instructors, the authors decided to send out an email reminding them about the informational web page. The email had a URL embedded in it which they most of them clicked, but even after this reminder there were few accesses to the page. This event is an indication of the difficulty with non-invasive studies. The authors found the lack of access to the web a problem with the study, while it could as well have been an indication of the opposite. That is, that the instructors felt satisfied with the Orb and the ambient information.

To better understand the instructor's own perception of their reliance on the system, they were asked to report how often they made use of the web page. Their responses support what is shown in the logs:

Instructor 1: "I didn't check it often, [the orb] was pretty much always the same color."

Instructor 5: "I'd guess I've checked it about 5 or 6 times. I would have checked it more often had I had more change in the color. That would have prompted me to check again. I had such consistency in color that I didn't go look at the web much. When I did it was just because I was curious about the distribution."

These responses indicate that the instructors were indeed *aware* of the web page's existence, but never felt a compulsion to access it.

Observations on Evaluation Issues

Several issues in regard to the challenges of setting up in-situ long-term evaluations of ambient technologies were observed in this study. Some of the most important findings are:

Limited forms of observation. The non-intrusive observation methods that the authors restricted themselves to made it extremely difficult to collect useful information that would expose anything meaningful about the display. However, it is the nature of in-situ studies that one has little control over the environment in which a technology is situated. Since we cannot reliably predict what variables will be beneficial in such evaluations, it becomes more important to look for ways to record *anything* that can be logged so that this data is available when researchers realize they need it *post hoc*.

No control of context. While the authors' ambient display functioned exactly as it was designed, the custom information channel did not record any radical events to observe. It would have been beneficial to their analysis to have an occasion where the students reported an extreme lack of confidence over a topic so that the instructor's orb would have dipped into the red. Such an event would have provided something to focus on to during the concluding interviews. Unfortunately, as stated above, when studying displays in-situ, one has little influence over the occurrence of interesting events.

Non-task oriented. The information device discussed here was not intended to address any specific task (e.g. alter the pacing of course topics, or increase the average grades of the students), it only provided information the authors believed could be somehow beneficial to the instructors; information that is just *good to know*. Since the authors were not trying to alter any specific opinion or behavior, it was difficult to know in advance what would potentially be of interest to measure as an effect of the use of the device.

Difficulty measuring awareness without contamination. The study was aimed at examining how the device would influence the instructors' general awareness of their students' confidence. The concluding interviews provided some indications, but while the system was deployed it was difficult to examine the thoughts of the subjects without influencing their actions and personal reflections.

Accounting for overly subtle presentation. While the display functioned technically, for the purposes of this evaluation the method of presentation was far too subtle. Of course the rate of change in an ambient display will influence how near or far it is to the observer's direct focus of attention, but if it is too static, then the display may become nonexistent to the observer. To increase the noticeability of this display the authors could have set it to display rate-of-change rather than the averages, and still have something that contains the specific qualities of an ambient display.

CASE STUDY 2: CLOUDS AND LIGHTS

The second study explores the evaluation issues that arise when developing an ambient display for a shared public space rather than one designed to convey information towards a specific user. To account for a more general audience, displays such as these have to present information content that is *less* personal, and somewhat generalized, such as weather or stock values [9]. For example, [17] describes a public display that conveys the relative economic strength of the Euro, the Dollar, and the Yen, using the heights of water jets within a stylized fountain. Another display within this theme is "The Source," which is an ambient display developed for the London Stock Exchange. This display consists of a grid of 162 steel cables running from floor to ceiling within the 32-meter high atrium in the center of the building. This system of cables supports a 9x9x9 matrix of 729 translucent spheres, which can travel up and down the cables, and illuminate in a manner similar to the Ambient Orb. Throughout the day the form and motion of the installation are determined by real-time stock information. At the end of the day the spheres return to their cubed arrangement, and the spheres illuminate to show the stock market's closing price.

With each of these displays, the information presented is not directed at any particular individual. Instead, the information is simply put in the open, with no specific intention as to how this information is to be appropriated by those walking by. Again, it is simply information that is potentially *good to know*. How then, does one go about evaluating the impact of an informational display such as this? One way would be to place such a display in a location where the information would have an effect on some observable behavior, and watch to see how that behavior changes after deployment.

In the study discussed here, a series of three large-scale ambient displays was deployed in a shared space, with the intent of altering a simple behavior. Similarly to "The Source," these displays were situated within the atrium of a newly constructed building. Atriums such as these are ideal for ambient displays, as they often act as a channel through which many people have to travel from one location in the building to another. The behavior selected for augmentation was whether people decided to take the stairs or the elevator when moving through the building. This was done by constructing a system to log the usage of these resources, along with a series of three separate displays conveying stair vs. elevator usage in different ways. The construction of this system was no trivial task, requiring over nine months of research and development, and consultation from a wide range of experts.

The Ambient Display(s)

Rather than a single display, three different displays were implemented. These displays were intended to work together as a single system in order to subtly alter the behavior of those within the building. Each of these displays is briefly described below.

The Clouds

This display consists of two separate clusters of spheres, colored orange and gray, which move up and down independently. The orange spheres represent the usage of the elevators while the grey spheres represent the stairs. The relative heights of the clouds change depending on the number of people who use the stairs versus the elevator, repositioning themselves every quarter hour. The higher up the orange cloud the more people are using the stairs and the higher up the grey cloud the more people are using the elevator (Figure 2, left).

Follow the Lights

This display is designed as an abstract representation intended to be playful and interactive, with the aim of luring and encouraging people to take the stairs. It was implemented using a series of interconnected LEDs embedded into the existing carpet tiles (Figure 2, right). As someone enters the building and walks toward the elevator, the lights begin to twinkle in a pattern that flows toward the stairwell. If the same person continues on to the elevator, the lights begin to slowly pulsate red, as if to imply that the display is becoming annoyed at the person ignoring its suggested path.

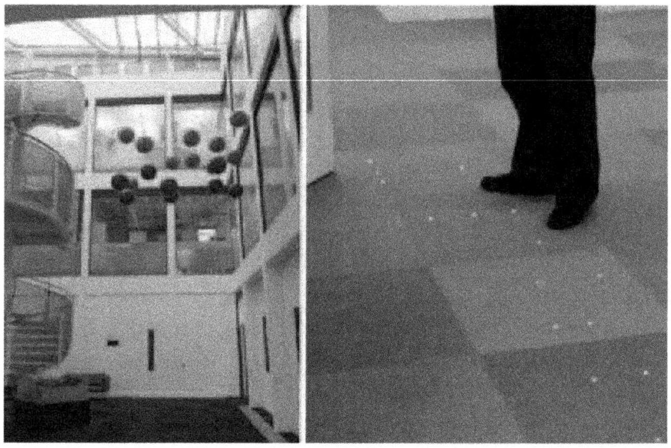

Figure 2: The Clouds (left) and Follow-the-Lights (right)

The History

This display consisted of a simple set of dynamic pie charts displayed on a large existing plasma display situated near the entrance of the atrium (Figure 3). The design was deliberately more literal than the other two, and gave those within the building a historical perspective of the stair vs. elevator usage throughout the week.

Logging the amount of stair and elevator usage was done by placing pressure sensitive mats beneath the carpet at the thresholds of each stairwell and elevator within the building. The data from these mats was forwarded to a central machine and aggregated.

Evaluation

In order to see if behavior had changed the authors developed a baseline data set by running the pressure mat sensors for six months prior to the deployment of the ambient displays. Once the baseline data had been collected, the system of displays was installed over a weekend when no one was in the building. The authors wanted to record people's initial reactions, and observe how they went about making sense of the displays naturally. The authors decided to propagate information about these displays only by word of mouth. All project members were told to explain the displays and the general project goals to anyone who asked directly, but avoid making any sort of broadcast announcement.

Figure 3: The History

With the system deployed, an 8-week evaluative study was initiated. This study was conducted using a mix of different data collection methods, including: observations and interviews *in situ*; an online survey sent to all building occupants after four weeks; and the data logged by the sensor network. The first two weeks after deployment consisted exclusively of remote observation. This involved project members inconspicuously positioning themselves within the atrium, and taking copious semi-structured notes using a template generated prior to the study. This template noted group size, trajectories of people moving through the space, whether they stopped and discussed the displays, and what they discussed. In weeks 2-4 interviews were conducted where project members approached 25 people randomly as they entered the atrium. These people were asked whether they had noticed the displays, and what exactly they thought the displays meant. This included note taking as before, along with some audio recording. At the midpoint of the study, and email was sent out to the entire population of the building (approx. 200 people), asking them to participate in an online survey. The four-week mark was selected because it was predicted that this was adequate time for most people to have noticed the display, and for the initial novelty factor to wear off. The survey consisted of 13 questions regarding their use of the building, where they were located in the building, and what their impressions/interpretations were of the various displays. Finally, to analyze the actual behavior versus perceived behavior, the responses to this online survey and face-to-face interviews were compared with the log data recorded by the physical sensors.

Abridged Study Results

In terms of people's ability to understand the meaning of these displays, *Follow-the-Lights* was found to be the most intuitive according to the survey and interviews. By week 4 of the study most had figured out that Clouds were supposed to represent some relationship between the stairs and the elevators although few knew the exact mapping between the display and the information it was providing. During interviews people reported a wide variety of interpretations as to exactly how this mapping worked. Additionally, many reported that they would just prefer to have a simple numerical representation rather than the abstract displays.

In terms of behavioral change, when people were asked whether the displays had caused them to alter their behavior, the vast majority stated that the displays had no effect on them personally. However, when the baseline data was compared with what was being captured by the floor sensors after the displays had been deployed, a statically significant change in the ratio of elevators versus stairs was detected. This implies that the displays were having some sort of effect on people of which they were not even aware.

Observations on Evaluation Issues

As with the previous case, this study provided several insights into the issues that arise when conducting such evaluations. Some of our findings are:

Notions of 'user' and 'use' are ambiguous. When observing/evaluating a public ambient display like this one, it's not clear exactly who the users are. Technically, it is *anyone* who could potentially occupy the space. This could include the people who work in the building, the cleaning crews, the caterers, and any visitors. In addition, it is not clear how to evaluate *use* since we have not established what it means to be *using* the display (e.g., are we using it just by being in the same space, or does it require direct observation and consideration? When exactly are we *not* using it?). This issue makes it difficult to establish any precise expected outcome of the system, and further complicates the decision as to what should be measured. How exactly does one conduct a user study when they do not have a specific user, or a defined task?

To what extent is it acceptable to directly interfere with people in the study? In this study, people in the building were observed and interviewed frequently, which of course influenced the overall public awareness of the system. At the same time, direct input from the public provided rich insights into how people value, and think about, the display. This hints at a possible tradeoff between preserving the natural environment in which a display is employed, and the quality of data collected via the study.

Discrepancies in self-reflection. The opinions and behaviors reported in the interviews did not match what was captured with the sensors logging actual use. While it has become agreed upon that people are not generally good at self-report, this can be seen as a potential opening for evaluations that compare and contrast data from several sources. How to accomplish this (i.e., what sources and how to gather data) is not obvious.

DISCUSSION

The goal of an in-situ study is to observe a technology or practice in a natural context of use. Of course any time we observe or probe for insights, we are having some sort of effect on the *authenticity* of this natural context. With many technologies this lack of authenticity does not hinder researchers from collecting valuable insights, but in the case of ambient displays, which are intended to blend into the surroundings, it would seem that *any* amount of probing would contaminate the potential findings.

In the case of many public ambient displays, there is no specifically targeted user, no uniquely specified task, and it is not always the case that the designer has any real intent as to how the information being presented is to be used. In some cases, studying the use of a real ambient display in-situ may be impossible. For instance, one of the pre-defined information channels for the Ambient Orb is the U.S. National Threat Level, which has only gone red once since it's creation in 2002. It is not necessarily the case that this is a bad display, or that people would not be aware of it. There would just not be many ways in which researchers could establish the overall usefulness of such a display until some national catastrophe was to occur. While there are available ways to incorporate some form of gaze/glance detection into the design of a display, there does not seem to be a way to measure how frequently someone inadvertently siphons information from something that enters our field of view.

Implications for research

Based on our findings we are convinced that evaluation "in the wild" of ambient displays poses severe problems. We have discussed some of them above with the purpose of making them as visible as possible. Our assumption is that there will be a continued increase in use of ambient technology in all forms. So, the question then becomes, how can HCI research approach this evaluation challenge? Here we discuss some potential strategies.

The methodological approach

The most obvious and natural direction would be for the HCI research community to engage in a continuous methodological development based on the rich knowledge already existing in the field in regard to evaluation and testing. There exist already a large number of evaluation methods and techniques that might be possible to adapt and redesign. Of course, this development has to be carefully crafted to engage with the unique issues related to ambient technology.

For example, to address the lack of anomalous events observed in both our cases, one could incorporate artificial events into the structure of a study. This would allow researchers to impose a small level of influence over the in-situ environment, potentially without corrupting this environment's natural state. This practice could have ethical concerns however, dependent on the sensitivity of the information being conveyed by the ambient display. For instance, we would want to consider very carefully the ramifications of implying to an instructor that his or her students are giving negative feedback, when they are not. Such a method would have to be considered on a case-by-case basis.

This is only one example of what might be done, however, it shows that there are potentially great opportunities to creatively develop new methods for specific ambient devices and contexts of use.

The design approach

An approach that is somewhat different would be to augment the way ambient technologies are designed so that the technology and devices themselves include functions and features that make evaluation a *built-in* property. To some extent this is what the simple logging of visits to the informational web site provided in our first case, and the tracking of behavior changes in the second case.

Another possible example of this approach is presented in [22], where the authors incorporated gaze detection into their evaluation of an ambient display. This allowed the authors to—at the very least—know if their display ever actually entered the field of view of those within the space. Such information could be correlated with other measurements to provide a better picture of how the display is functioning. Other things that would aid in these evaluations would include: absolute location tracking (to know how long a person was in the presence of the display), and galvanic skin response (to correlate any physiological responses to changes in the display).

As we learned from our case studies, neither the *user* nor the *use* of such displays is always clear. Hence, it is hard to predict what data will be useful once the analysis begins, or which data could be beneficial to gain deeper insight into other forms of observation (e.g., surveys). With the second case study for example, contrasting the results of an online questionnaire with the automated data logging provided by the pressure mats led to the primary finding (i.e. that the display seems to be having an unconscious effect on behavior). We anticipate that as new technologies for monitoring human behavior and physiological responses become more refined, these *built-in* possibilities will become more available and less intrusive to the user and hence provide more opportunities for automatic capturing of data, leading to richer analysis and interpretation opportunities.

A major advantage of this approach is, of course, that the researchers do not need to directly interact with the subjects in order to gain the extra information. A possible disadvantage is in the possible issues of privacy that could be introduced by this form of monitoring. Such issues may, to some degree, also be handled with careful design of the technology since the purpose of these studies is not necessarily based on the actions of one individual user, allowing us to disregard information on individuals.

The "Darwin" approach

This approach is based on the assumption that generally good technologies prevail over time in a manner analogous to Darwinian Natural selection. Here, the method would involve building a large number of different ambient displays, situating them in real environments, and letting them function until time reveals which implementations have a propensity for sustained use, and which eventually become discarded.

When using this method however, the concept of *best* must be carefully operationalized when dissecting the features or attributes that make up a particular ambient display. This is because it is not always a specific attribute that determines the success or failure of an implementation. Rather, it is the total collection of attributes that dictate whether or not it will succeed. For instance, many point out that the Betamax video standard provided superior video quality to the more successful VHS format, implying that video quality was not the only attribute that mattered. Initially, the VHS format offered a much lager storage space (3 hours vs. 1 hour for Betamax), and VHS players were much cheaper to produce. Continuing the Darwin analogy, the combination of these factors provided the VHS format a stronger reproductive advantage over Betamax, and hence it was able to survive longer.

Evaluating ambient displays in this fashion would focus more on rigorous *post mortem* analysis rather than monitoring activities, and development of in-depth user studies. It is plausible that analyzing failed or successful designs, perhaps using theoretical frameworks such as Actor-Network Theory, or Distributed Cognition, could expose general characteristics or qualities. These could, in turn, be used to produce new design principles specific to the development of ambient displays.

The Interaction Criticism approach

Due to growing interest in topics such as affective computing, experience design, and intimate and embodied interaction, some are calling for an increased awareness of "the symbolic level of mood and meaning" within the field of Interaction Design [23]. To address this, some suggest that an expressive language of interaction design be explored and developed. A possible solution offered by Bardzell et. al. [3] is to incorporate an *interaction criticism* phase into existing interaction design processes. This phase would resemble the style of critical analysis employed among music, film and literary critics, as well as academic criticism in art and architecture. In these cases, a critic is able to apply interpretive reasoning to some of the more subjective aspects of a given artifact. This ability comes from developing a level of expertise on a given subject (e.g. ambient displays) through lengthy encounters, theories, and in the examination of other works of criticism from peers and colleagues. Such a method would involve the creation of a community of practitioners who routinely evaluate each other's designs via criticism, and use this criticism to help interpret observations made of these displays in contexts of use.

A justification for this approach is that many of those who are developing ambient displays are either artists themselves, or are borrowing heavily from the fine arts and architecture. For example, the "DataFountain" and "The Source," were both produced by artists. Hence, it is reasonable that we would also adopt some of the forms of evaluation used within these disciplines.

CONCLUSION

We have argued for the necessity of conducting long-term in-situ studies to better understand how people make use of ambient displays. From the two case studies presented here, we have identified several issues that should be considered when developing similar studies on this kind of technology, and a series of alternative approaches for evaluation that warrant investigation. We believe that the classification of these issues will require further iteration in order to become more specific, and more theoretical work has to be done to refine the approaches. For instance, there is a need to define or redefine already established concepts such as *use*, *user*, *interaction*, *awareness*, *attention*, *presence*, and others in the context of in-situ ambient displays.

We have proposed four potential directions (approaches) that HCI research could develop in order to better handle evaluation of ambient displays. However, we do not foresee any of these approaches to be the only way forward, and we anticipate that all of these approaches will likely be developed in relation to additional theoretical work. Additionally, we believe that the methods proposed in this article warrant further investigation as a possible means of adding richness and depth to existing evaluations, and we would expect future evaluations to incorporate some form of hybridization of these approaches. This work represents only the early steps of a vein of research that will eventually lead to the development of frameworks and methodologies appropriate for understanding how people will live and interact with this particular technology.

ACKNOWLEDGMENTS

We would like to thank all those who aided in the construction of the instillations presented within our case studies, as well as the conference reviewers for their insightful comments.

REFERENCES

1. Ambient Devices, "The Ambient Stock Orb." http://www.ambientdevices.com/cat/orb/orborder.html (accessed September 20, 2010).
2. Arroyo, E., Bonanni, L., and Selker, T. 2005. Waterbot: exploring feedback and persuasive techniques at the sink. In *Proceedings of* CHI '05. ACM, New York, NY, 631-639.
3. Bardzell, J. and Bardzell, S. 2008. Interaction criticism: a proposal and framework for a new discipline of hci. In *Proceedings of CHI'08*. ACM, New York, NY, 2463-2472.

4. Brewer, J., Williams, A., and Dourish, P. 2005. Nimio: An Ambient Awareness Device, Demonstration at the European Conference on Computer-Supported Cooperative Work (ECSCW). 18--22 September 2005, Paris, France.
5. Carter, S., Mankoff, J. 2004. Challenges for UbiComp evaluation, technical report UCB/CSD-04-1331, computer science division. University of California, Berkeley.
6. Chang, A., Resner, B., Koerner, B., Wang, X., and Ishii, H. 2001. LumiTouch: an emotional communication device. In *Proceedings of CHI '01*. ACM, New York, NY, 313-314
7. Costanza, E., Inverso, S. A., Pavlov, E., Allen, R., and Maes, P. 2006. eye-q: eyeglass peripheral display for subtle intimate notifications. In *Proceedings of* MobileHCI '06, vol. 159. ACM, New York, NY, 211-218
8. Dahley, A., Wisneski, C., and Ishii, H. 1998. Water lamp and pinwheels: ambient projection of digital information into architectural space. In *Proceedings of CHI 98*. ACM, New York, NY, 269-270
9. Greyworld, "The Source (2004)." June 20, 2004.http://greyworld.org/archives/31 (accessed September 20, 2010).
10. Hallnäs, L. and Redström, J. 2001. Slow Technology – Designing for Reflection. *Personal Ubiquitous Comput.* 5, 3, 201-212.
11. Hazlewood, W. R., Dalton, N., Marshall, P., Rogers, Y., and Hertrich, S. 2010. Bricolage and consultation: addressing new design challenges when building large-scale installations. In *Proceedings of DIS '10*. ACM, New York, NY, 380-389.
12. Heiner, J. M., Hudson, S. E., and Tanaka, K. 1999. The information percolator: ambient information display in a decorative object. In *Proceedings of UIST '99*. ACM, New York, NY, 141-148.
13. Holmquist, L.E.. 2004. Evaluating the comprehension of ambient displays. In *CHI '04 extended abstracts on Human factors in computing systems* (CHI '04). ACM, New York, NY, USA, 1545-1545.
14. Ishii, H., Wisneski, C., Brave, S., Dahley, A., Gorbet, M., Ullmer, B., and Yarin, P. 1998. ambientROOM: integrating ambient media with architectural space. In *Proceedings of CHI 98*. ACM, New York, NY, 173-174
15. Ishii, H., Ren, S., and Frei. P. 2001. "Pinwheels: visualizing information flow in an architectural space," In *Proceedings of CHI '01 extended abstracts on Human factors in computing systems*, pp. 111-112, 2001.
16. Mankoff, J., Dey, A. K., Hsieh, G., Kientz, J., Lederer, S., and Ames, M. 2003. Heuristic evaluation of ambient displays. In *Proceedings of CHI '03*. ACM, New York, NY, 169-176.
17. Mensvoort, K. "DATAFOUNTAIN - Money currency rates displayed with an internet enabled water fountain." http://www.koert.com/work/datafountain/ (accessed Sep 20, 2010).
18. Mynatt, E. D., Back, M., Want, R., Baer, M., and Ellis, J. B. 1998. Designing audio aura. In *Proceedings CHI'98*. ACM Press/Addison-Wesley Publishing Co., New York, NY, 566-573.
19. Olivier, P., Cao, H., Gilroy, S. W. and Jackson, D. G. 2006. Crossmodal Ambient Displays. In *Proceedings of British HCI* 2006, Springer, London, 3-16
20. Redström, J., Skog, T., and Hallnäs, L. 2000. Informative art: using amplified artworks as information displays. In *Proceedings of DARE'00*. ACM, New York, NY, 103-114
21. Rogers, Y., Hazlewood, W. R., Dalton, N., Marshall, P., Pantidi, N. and Hertrich, S. 2010. Ambient Influence: Can Twinkly Lights Lure and Abstract Representations Trigger Behavioral Change? In *Proceedings of Ubicomp '10*, 2010 (in press).
22. Shen, X., Eades, P., Seok-Hee, H., Vand Moere, A. 2007. Intrusive and Non-intrusive Evaluation of Ambient Displays. In *Proc. of 1st Workshop on Ambient Information Systems*. Colocated with Pervasive 2007, Toronto, Canada. vol. 254, May 2007.
23. Smith, G. What is interaction design? In Moggridge, B. *Designing Interactions*. The MIT Press, 2007.
24. Weiser M, Seely Brown J. Designing calm technology. PowerGrid Journal 1.1.1996. Available at: http:// www.powergrid.com/1.01/calmtech.html
25. White, T. and Small, D. 1998. An interactive poetic garden. In *Proceedings of CHI'98*. ACM, New York, NY, 335-336.
26. Wurman, R. S. 2001. Information Anxiety. Doubleday, New York.

Does MoodyBoard Make Internet Use more Secure? Evaluating an Ambient Security Visualization Tool

Alexander De Luca[1], Bernhard Frauendienst[1], Max-Emanuel Maurer[1], Doris Hausen[1], Julian Seifert[2], Niels Kammerer[1], Heinrich Hussmann[1]

[1]Media Informatics Group, University of Munich [2]MHCI, University of Duisburg-Essen

{alexander.de.luca, max.maurer, doris.hausen, hussmann}@ifi.lmu.de

{frauendi, kammerer}@cip.ifi.lmu.de, julian.seifert@uni-due.de

ABSTRACT

Internet users are targets for ever-advancing phishing- and other attacks. The risks are, for example, to disclose credit card information or passwords to unauthorized instances. One approach to help users with insecure situations is provided by MoodyBoard, which uses ambient information to highlight potential risks. In this paper, we present findings from an evaluation of this system. Two user studies were conducted in order to find out whether an ambient security tool can protect users during sensitive tasks. We designed a pilot study to find out whether users understand the warnings and a security study to see if it helps to protect users from phishing attacks. Results show that MoodyBoard users behaved significantly more secure.

Author Keywords

Security, Awareness, Ambient visualization, MoodyBoard.

ACM Classification Keywords

H5.2. [Information interfaces and presentation (e.g., HCI)]: User Interfaces – Evaluation/methodology.

General Terms

Experimentation, Human Factors, Measurement.

INTRODUCTION

Frauds on Internet services like phishing are widely covering the media these days. Scams are improving every day but simple attacks already do the trick. From habituation effects [2] to overlooking important warnings [10] there are different reasons why people fall for phishing. Lack of interest in security [9], wrong mental models [4] or lack of knowledge [7] can open security holes. We cannot expect users to solve these problems. We have to work with them together to do so [1].

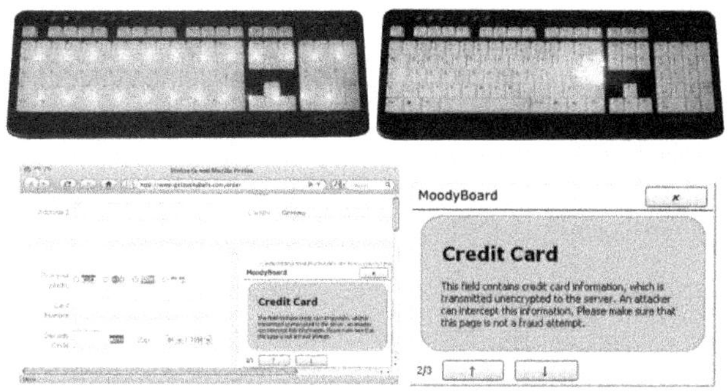

Figure 1: Top: The MoodyBoard prototype can glow in arbitrary colors. The return key can be lit seperately. Bottom: Message window after pressing the help button.

Current work on supporting users to make secure decisions when using Internet services often focuses on improving warnings. They are either blocking – forcing the user to decide upon an action [5] – or non-blocking, leaving it to the users to heed the warning or not [5,10]. While blocking warnings can become quickly annoying and fail due to habituation effects, non-blocking warnings are often simply overlooked or not understood. Another approach is teaching users to behave more securely and identify threats [6].

In this work, we introduce a fourth approach. Instead of relying on teaching, blocking or non-blocking warnings, ambient security notifications are used. Ambient notifications could be categorized as non-blocking warnings. However, there is one major property that sets them apart: a non-blocking warning can usually only occupy limited space of the user's screen. This limitation does not exist for ambient information. Thus we can use a very intense warning while not actively blocking the user's current task.

As the tool of choice, we decided to use MoodyBoard, which has been developed in several recursive steps to support users in security sensitive tasks [3]. In short: MoodyBoard is a keyboard that can glow in arbitrary colors (see figure 1, top). The concept is promising but has not been evaluated yet. In this work, we therefore provide an evaluation of the concept based on two consecutive user studies. The results of the studies show that this kind of ambient warning can significantly improve secure behavior.

MOODYBOARD

The prototype is a stripped down version of a Revoltec Lightboard XL standard layout keyboard, extended with strips of RGB-SMD-LEDs, which illuminate the whole key area (figure 1, upper left). The Return key is separately lit (figure 1, upper right). The wrist rest holds a small vibration motor. The original backlight switch was remodeled into a help button. Pressing the help button displays a message containing information on why the specific notification was triggered (figure 1, bottom). The LEDs allow us to change the luminosity and colors in arbitrary ways, which is necessary since only hard changes of those values are likely to get the user's attention [8].

A Firefox extension connects the hardware with the browser interface. It allows for MoodyBoard notifications to be "attached" to DOM-events on arbitrary HTML elements using XPath expressions. The improved version for the security study additionally displays messages for each notification when the help button is pressed. For more information on MoodyBoard, please refer to [3].

PILOT STUDY

It is essential for security notifications that the user understands them in order to work. Therefore, a first user study was conducted to gather information about the participants' interpretations of MoodyBoard notifications and whether they match their actual meaning.

Study Design and Procedure

The physical setup resembled a standard desktop environment and consisted of an LCD screen, mouse and MoodyBoard (without help button) connected to a laptop.

The study involved four tasks whose order was perfectly counterbalanced. For each, the participant had to complete a task on a web page, three of them included payment and entering credit card information, the fourth was to enter a comment. One of the payment sites was SSL encrypted and resulted in green light upon focusing the credit card field. The other pages were unencrypted and showed red illuminations when sensitive data was entered or submitted, with exception of the "comment" task, which also showed green light due to the non-sensitive nature of the data.

The study was set up in an empty room. Each participant was handled separately. After entering the room, they were provided a small introduction to the scenario and a list of tasks already in the appropriate order. During each task, after the MoodyBoard feedback was triggered, users were asked to share their opinion as to why this particular feedback was provided in this situation. They also had to rate its appropriateness on a five-point Likert scale (1="not appropriate at all", 5= "very appropriate"). Their answers were written down and matched against two central points – encryption status and sensitivity of data – in order to calculate to which extent they coincided with the actual implementation. Finally, after completing the tasks, participants were asked to fill out a questionnaire.

Participants

24 participants (eight female) were recruited. Their average age was 25 years (21 - 31). About two thirds were students with a background in computing science, the rest had a diverse background.

Results

The results showed that users often had problems interpreting the feedback MoodyBoard gave. We calculated an overall match ratio of 35%. Match ratio refers to the intersection of the users' interpretation and the actual technical reasons for a notification. Even more, only five participants had a perfect match, each on exactly one task. On the other hand, all users recognized the red messages to be warnings, and over half associated them with the security of private data.

In the post-study questionnaire, users voted average on a five-point Likert scale that the information given from MoodyBoard was sufficient (Median=4). However, the need for more information was rated only slightly less important (Median=3).

Essentially, our main findings from this study are that MoodyBoard is capable of attracting the user's attention, but more – preferably context-sensitive – information needs to be provided to produce a sensible reaction. That is, a help button as envisioned in the concept seems highly necessary. Additionally, (red) warnings were not only more efficient, they were also interpreted more accurate. That is, we decided to abstain from positive notifications since they caused more confusion than adding benefit.

SECURITY STUDY

The security study took place at our premises and had a similar physical setup as the pilot study. The main goal was to find out whether MoodyBoard can provide appropriate feedback to make Internet use more secure.

Study Design and Procedure

At the beginning of the experiment, the participants got an introduction to the study which was disguised as an Internet surfing behavior experiment. Before starting with the practical part, the users were asked to fill out a pre-questionnaire, which contained questions regarding their Internet expertise. Based on these, the participants were either marked as experts or not and were assigned to the two groups respectively. This allowed for an equal amount of experts in both groups.

The investigator asked the participants to perform some urgent tasks for a "good friend" who had to go to his grandmother's funeral. The tasks were done "at the friend's home" whose computer was equipped with MoodyBoard (not in the control group). Four different tasks, together with the required input data, were handed out to the participants in written form. Two tasks required passwords (for an auctioning site and a payment service), the other two the use of credit card information (payment for a travel and a gift order). For each participant and each data type, one website was randomly assigned as being a phishing site. These used slightly modified URLs and were unencrypted. All sites, phishing or not, were hosted on our own servers (spoofing the URLs) to avoid connectivity problems.

To the experimental group, MoodyBoard was introduced as being able to notify about different situations (security was never mentioned) and that the reasons for the notifications could be looked up by pressing the help button. In this group, the use of unencrypted websites in combination with sensitive data triggered warnings: red glowing keyboard for password and credit card fields and a red blinking return key plus vibration for submit buttons. Alarms were triggered whenever an input field got the focus (e.g. was clicked) or the submit button was hovered by the mouse pointer. Pressing the help button displayed a warning that data would be submitted over an unencrypted channel and that the page should be checked for integrity. As opposed to the pilot study, "secure" situations did not trigger notifications. The interaction was filmed with a camera for later analysis (mainly verifying if phishing websites were identified or not). In the end, the investigator briefed all participants in both groups about the experiment and asked them to fill out a final questionnaire containing questions related to phishing.

We applied a mixed-model design with two groups. The between-group variable was *MoodyBoard* (yes or no). Within the groups, a repeated-measures design was used. The independent variables were *data type* (password and credit card number) and *phishing* (yes or no). The dependent variable measured was *security* (number of identified phishing websites). To minimize learning effects, a 2x(4x4) Latin square was used. The "2x" refers to the fact that firstly the phishing sites were evenly assigned to a 4x4 block, which was then duplicated, inverted, and its last two rows and columns swapped. This required a minimum of eight users per group. For each possible setup, a bookmark set was provided (and loaded) that had to be used by the participants.

The goal was to measure whether MoodyBoard helped to identify more phishing websites. The only condition under which a phishing website was counted as recognized was when the participant aborted the task. This was possible since in the introduction, it was emphasized that the personal data should be treated with care as if it was a real situation. The only means for the control group to identify a phishing website were standard browser methods: certificates were displayed or not and the URLs could be checked. Thus, the main hypothesis was that MoodyBoard users would identify significantly more phishing websites than users in the control group.

Participants

We recruited 32 participants, 16 per group. Group 1 (control) had an average age of 23 years (21 – 27, eight female), group 2 (MoodyBoard) of 24 years (22 – 27, seven female). Having 16 users per group allowed for perfectly applying the Latin square design as described in the previous section. Expert users were mostly computer science students, while the other participants were diverse. Not only did both groups include the same number of experts, additionally there were equally as many as non-experts (eight in each group).

Results

Phishing

Overall, 24 (38%) out of the 64 phishing sites were identified. 18 (56%) out of 32 in the MoodyBoard group were found, compared to only six (19%) in the control group. In nine instances, participants aborted the task after using the help button and reading the explanations. There was no difference between experts and non-experts (twelve phishing sites each). Most identified phishing websites were in the credit card conditions (16 in total; eleven of them with MoodyBoard) while only eight (seven with MoodyBoard) password phishing sites were identified. Taking a closer look at the data reveals that only users that found the credit card phishing site were able to identify the password phishing site. Additionally, only one user in the control group found the password phishing site. MoodyBoard performs better than what we know from current non-blocking warnings [5] and similar to advanced blocking warnings [7] while not interrupting the current workflow of the user.

A mixed-model ANOVA confirmed these results. It revealed a significant main effect for the between-group variable *MoodyBoard* ($F_{1,30}=9.956$; $p=.004$). This means that participants in the MoodyBoard group were significantly more likely to identify a phishing website which supports the main hypothesis. The main effect of *data type* was highly significant as well ($F_{1,30}=16.351$; $p<.001$; Greenhouse-Geisser corrected). Therefore, the results that more credit card phishing sites were identified did not come up randomly. This is very interesting since the password-protected sites in the study were both highly sensitive too (e.g. online payment). It seems that users still considered credit card information as more sensitive. This might explain, why, in contrast to password sites, five people found the credit card phishing sites without MoodyBoard support. Finally, no significant interaction effects were found (all $p>.05$).

The questionnaire (experimental group) gives further insights. Even though usefulness of MoodyBoard notifications was rated averagely (Median=3), the participants that correctly identified phishing websites rated it very high (most 4 or 5). Furthermore, all four participants that did not use the help button rated usefulness very low (1,1,1,2). This supports the finding of the pilot study, that this button is essential. It is thus not surprising that some participants mentioned that the help messages should always be displayed at least for the first visit of a website.

False positives

Another interesting finding was on falsely identified phishing websites. Despites happening only three times, all cases occurred in the MoodyBoard group and all for credit card. As mentioned before, genuine websites did not trigger any notifications. So why did these false positives occur? In one case, a user stopped the task (which we defined as "phishing identified") since she was "*not sure whether this is really the trip my friend wanted to book*". The other two were users that also found the real phishing sites. Finding them might have made them suspicious with respect to phishing attacks in the experiment.

Why MoodyBoard users fell for phishing attacks

Finally, we wanted to know what reasons made users fall for phishing attacks, especially in the MoodyBoard group. One user stated that she recognized the wrong URLs but thought they were necessary for the experiment (see limitations section). More interesting are reasons based on wrong interpretation of the notifications. As stated in the study description, participants were only briefed that MoodyBoard would give them feedback during surfing the Internet. Security was not mentioned at all. Thus, three users interpreted the warnings with respect to the current task. For instance, two participants thought that the red light indicated a mistake during input (e.g. a spelling mistake). Another user was sure that the glowing enter button told him not to forget to submit the form. None of them used the help button, which avoids such misinterpretations. We argue that these situations would not happen in a real situation, in which a user knows what MoodyBoard is designed for. Still, evaluating a "worst case" scenario reveals the most interesting findings.

Limitations of the Results

Testing the security of a system in a lab study is rather hard. Users tend to behave more carelessly and do not feel in real danger, which is supported by the artificial setup. It is likely that the results for both groups are affected by this fact. It is also hard to hide the real meaning of a study and we cannot say for sure that none of the users knew what it was really about. Nevertheless, the experiment is a good indication on how MoodyBoard or a similar ambient notification system can unobtrusively support users in security relevant tasks.

The lack of a condition using only software notifications in the experiment only allows for theoretically comparing the system to such approaches. Thus, we can only state that the current MoodyBoard concept is a valuable tool to protect users but we cannot say how much more beneficial it is compared to a software only solution.

Even though neither in the pilot nor the security study did participants overlook the ambient notifications, we did not explicitly test required intensity, or compare different setups for notifications. Thus, we cannot state which parameters make an ambient security notification visible and "important enough" for users to interrupt their tasks.

CONCLUSION AND FUTURE WORK

In this work, we presented an evaluation of MoodyBoard based on two consecutive user studies. The results show that MoodyBoard positively influenced secure behavior even though misinterpretations of notifications occurred. In an informed user group however, such interpretations as seen in the security study, are less likely.

The main advantage of MoodyBoard is that it does not block any screen real estate but at the same time can deliver very intense, noticeable non-blocking warnings without interrupting the user's current task. The notifications are also visible to anyone nearby which might raise privacy issues in shared working environments (like offices). For instance, repeated red glowing keyboards might raise suspicion about colleagues.

For future work, it would be interesting to see how MoodyBoard performs in a real world setting. However, it is extremely hard or impossible to measure its efficiency in such a setting. Nevertheless, qualitative results of a real world long-term study could be very insightful.

REFERENCES

1. Adams, A. and Sasse, M. A.. Users are not the enemy. Commun. ACM 42, 12 (Dec. 1999).
2. Amer, T.S., Maris, J.B. Signal words and signal icons in application control and information technology exception messages – hazard matching and habituation effects. Tech. Rep. Work. Paper. Series 06-05, Northern Arizona University, Flagstaff, AZ, October 2006.
3. De Luca, A., Frauendienst, B., Maurer, M., and Hausen, D. 2010. On the design of a "moody" keyboard. *In Proc. DIS '10*. Aarhus, Denmark, August 16 - 20, 2010.
4. Dhamija, R., Tygar, J.D., Hearst, M. Why phishing works. *In Proc. CHI '06*. Montréal, Québec, Canada, 2006.
5. Egelman, S., Cranor, L. F., and Hong, J. You've been warned: an empirical study of the effectiveness of web browser phishing warnings. *In Proc. CHI '08*, Florence, Italy, 2008.
6. Kumaraguru, P., Sheng, S., Acquisti, A., Cranor, L. F., and Hong, J. Teaching Johnny not to fall for phish. *ACM Trans*. Internet Technol. 10, 2, Article 7, June 2010.
7. Sunshine, J., Egelman, S., Almuhimedi, H., Atri, N., Cranor, L.F. Crying Wolf: An empirical study of SSL warning effectiveness. *In Proc. USENIX '09*.
8. Ware, C. Information Visualization, Second Edition: Perception for Design. Morgan Kaufmann, 2004.
9. Whitten A., Tygar J.D. Why Johnny can't encrypt: A usability evaluation of PGP 5.0. *In Proc. USENIX '99*.
10. Wu M., Miller R.C., Garfinkel S.L. Do security toolbars actually prevent phishing attacks? *In Proc. CHI '06*. Montréal, Québec, Canada, 2006.

Peripheral Computing During Presentations: Perspectives on Costs and Preferences

Shamsi T. Iqbal, Jonathan Grudin and Eric Horvitz
Microsoft Research
One Microsoft Way, Redmond, WA 98052
{shamsi, jgrudin, horvitz}@microsoft.com

ABSTRACT

Despite the common use of mobile computing devices to communicate and access information, the effects of peripheral computing tasks on people's attention is not well understood. Studies that have identified consequences of multitasking in diverse domains have largely focused on influences on productivity. We have yet to understand perceptions and preferences regarding the use of computing devices for potentially extraneous tasks in settings such as presentations at seminars and colloquia. We explore costs and attitudes about the use of computing devices by people attending presentations. We find that audience members who use devices believe that they are missing content being presented and are concerned about social costs. Other attendees report being less offended by multitasking around them than the device users may realize.

Author Keywords

Attention, multitasking, presentation, laptops

ACM Classification Keywords

H.5.m. Information Interfaces and Presentation (e.g., HCI): Miscellaneous.

General Terms

Experimentation, Measurement.

INTRODUCTION

The pervasive use of mobile computing devices such as laptops, tablets, and smartphones is a feature of the modern-day landscape. These devices enable users to tap into a tremendous amount of information and to communicate virtually anywhere and anytime. With the benefits come costs. Such costs are revealed in a stream of media reports about accidents or operational aberrations linked to the extraneous use of mobile devices in situations such as driving cars and trains, piloting commercial airplanes, and even during real-time newscasts [8].

Whether the costs of peripheral computing outweigh the benefits will depend on the individual and the situation. Much research has focused on identifying costs of multitasking in domains such as desktop computing and driving, where division of attention may be common or even unavoidable [1, 6]. Our work examines the extent to which people are aware of such costs when they multitask in a context typically associated with a single focus of attention. The multitaskers we studied believe that they are paying a price, yet engage in peripheral activities. We also find that concerns that they report about how their behavior is perceived may not be well founded.

Our study focuses on multitasking during colloquium-style presentations. For those attending, computing devices can enhance a presentation when used as an auxiliary source of information or for note-taking, but they are often used for unrelated tasks such as checking and sending email or text messages. In meetings and classroom lectures where attention is mandatory, device use is viewed with caution for these reasons [5]. However, for the type of presentations considered in this paper, attendance and attention is voluntary. In these settings, access to peripheral computing may raise the likelihood that people will attend, and thus get some exposure to content they would otherwise miss entirely. Beyond understanding the effects of device use, we are interested in whether speakers or other listeners consider device use impolite in these settings.

We studied perceptions of audience attitudes and behavior in colloquium-style presentations at Microsoft Research. These widely-publicized talks are open to all employees. Motives for attending vary. In contrast to course lectures, speakers are not responsible for ensuring that material is learned. In finding more awareness of the costs of peripheral computing and more acceptance of device usage than expected, we identify challenges in managing attention where technology is ubiquitous.

PILOT STUDY OF SELF AWARENESS OF INATTENTION

As five colloquium-style presentations in Microsoft Research lecture rooms were concluding, we distributed a brief paper questionnaire to audience members in the room (averaging 35; others watch live video feeds). To avoid influencing the responses, we did not describe the specific purpose of the survey. An early question was "Which of these best describes your experience today?" followed by the choices "I picked up all of the lecture information that would be useful to me," "I picked up most of the lecture information that would be useful to me," and "I missed significant information." Several unrelated questions

	Reported getting all useful information	Reported missing useful information
Had laptop	19 (41%)	27 (59%)
No laptop	72 (57%)	54 (43%)

Table 1. Breakdown of useful information reported as learned across attendees with and without device

followed. The final question was the only one to mention technology: "Which of these items did you have with you in the lecture?" followed by the choices Tablet, Laptop, Phone, Pen, and Paper. We did not ask whether a device was used for extraneous computing, to avoid any hint of the study purpose that could bias responses.

172 audience members completed the questionnaire. 46 had brought laptops with them. We observed the audiences, noting that most laptop carriers used them during the lectures. Only a few people used phones during the lectures.

Laptop possessors were more likely to report that they missed useful information (Table 1). The difference is significant, with one-tailed LOR of 0.64, $z=1.83$, $p=.034$. Not all laptop possessors used them; the effect is probably stronger among people who do use them.

It is likely that a significant portion of laptop users who reported that they missed useful information linked their peripheral device use to the presumed loss of content. That such participants multitask is evidence that they perceive tangible benefits in device use that outweigh the cost of possibly losing useful information. However, in a setting where the expected norm is paying attention to the speaker, device usage could be influenced by perceptions of social costs, such as incurring the disapproval of speakers or other attendees. Our next study examined this issue through direct data collection.

STUDY OF PERCEIVED COSTS AND BENEFITS OF MULTITASKING DURING LECTURES

Understanding why audience members choose to use devices despite potential costs could lead to better policies regarding multitasking or to changes in presentation styles. Also, mismatches in speaker and audience perceptions could presage changes that will align perceptions. Towards this goal, we investigated in detail how speakers and audience members (device users and non-users) reacted to multitasking, posing these questions:

1. What are speakers' assessments of costs and benefits of the use of devices by members of the audience?
2. What do audience members believe about the influence of multitasking on speakers and others in the audience?

Methodology

Surveys were administered to speakers and their audiences. Survey questions covered the prevalence and patterns of device usage during lectures, perceived social impact, benefits and distraction costs, and strategies to manage attention. All participants received a small gratuity.

Participants

The speaker survey was administered to external speakers, including university professors and industry researchers, and to members of our research organization who frequently deliver lectures to academic and industry audiences. External speakers were contacted through their hosts and handed a survey before or after their talk. The same survey was made available online to employees with lecturing experience. The audience survey was sent to employees via a lecture announcement mailing list.

Survey Results

The speaker survey received 62 responses out of 250 survey recipients (11 external, 51 internal). The audience survey drew 112 responses from a distribution list of about 1000.

Perceived prevalence of device usage

Only 16% of the speakers reported that they never or rarely noticed audience members using a device. About 75% estimated that over 10% of audience members used devices. Some speakers estimated device usage to be over 50%.

40% of audience members reported using laptops and 33% reported using smartphones during at least one in four of the lectures that they attend. The 60% who do not frequently use devices reported being somewhat distracted by people who do (67% for laptops, 42% for smartphones). 56% reported being distracted by laptop use only when it was conspicuous; 35% reported not being affected at all. For smartphones, 42% reported being affected only when conspicuous and 51% not at all.

Patterns of device usage by audience members

Only 24% of laptop users and 8% of smartphone users reported using devices solely for lecture-related tasks such as taking notes, looking up references, or communicating about the lecture. The rest reported unrelated content generation (writing or editing text, code, diagrams, etc.), communication, web access, awareness (checking status or incoming information), and the reading of content unrelated to a lecture. Over 80% reported using devices for awareness and communication 'occasionally,' 'often,' or 'always.' Half reported browsing the web for content unrelated to the presentation.

When do people turn to a device for tasks unrelated to the lecture? About 75% report often using a device when a lecture does not meet expectations. 5% reported always switching in this situation. Need, desire, and choice to multitask also arose when they were "interested only in parts of the lecture" (10% always, 65% often).

Benefits, Costs and Social Implications

Table 2 summarizes responses to questions on perceived costs and benefits on a Likert scale of 1 (strongly disagree) to 7 (strongly agree). We contrast responses of speakers to audience members for both laptops and smartphones.

There was wide agreement that laptop use can enhance presentations, although audience members were more positive about this than speakers. Speakers did not feel that smartphones could enhance the experience; audience members showed high variance on this issue. Both groups

		Speaker	Audience	P
Device use supplements lecture	Laptop	**4.65***	**5.48****	0.023
	Smartphone	**3.21****	3.34	0.755
	P	0.00	0.038	
Device use enables multitasking	Laptop	**4.5**	**5.00***	0.187
	Smartphone	3.97	**5.00***	0.006
	P	0.02	0.17	
Device use distracts from lecture	Laptop	**5.76****	3.76	0.001
	Smartphone	**5.62****	3.84	0.001
	P	0.27	0.025	
Multitasking is impolite		3.84	**5.48****	0.001
It is a part of today's world		**5.13 ****	**4.9****	0.39
Multitasking should be minimized at lectures		**4.44**	**4.19**	0.437

Table 2. Mean ratings of benefits, costs and social perception of device use (1=strongly disagree, 4=neutral, 7=strongly agree). p values across rows indicate difference between laptops and smartphones, and down columns indicate difference between speaker and audience. Bold values significantly different from the neutral rating of 4; * indicates $p < 0.01$ and ** indicates $p < 0.001$.

agreed that laptops can help listeners multitask, but only audience members felt that smartphones can.

Speakers felt that laptops and smartphones distract their users. Audiences were more neutral. Close to 50% of device users asserted that despite missing some information while interacting with devices, the benefits of peripheral computing make such usage worthwhile (see Figure 1).

Audience members reported feeling that device usage could be disrespectful, but the speakers themselves tended to disagree (M = 3.84, where 4 is neutral). Device users who know that they are not fully attentive may feel somewhat disrespectful (or may feel that they should report that they feel this way): 62% of respondents who rated disrespect high (6 or 7 on the 7-point scale) also reported high laptop usage, and 71% reported heavy smartphone use in lectures.

Speakers cannot be sure what a device is used for, which may deter them from attributing disrespect. One wrote:

> "It's hard to tell whether the device is used in a positive way (e.g., taking notes) or a negative way (e.g., distracted by IM)... I find that in general such use is for email/IM and not for enhancing the lecture experience, therefore high use equates to low interest and attention. A note taking participant is looking up at you frequently or while typing - an inattentive user is looking down and reading."

Speakers also realize that the ability to use a laptop could induce busy people to attend:

> "There are many reasons to use a laptop that might be tied to the talk (taking notes or looking up a paper the talk reminded you about). Additionally, there are many demands on everyone's time. Presumably if they are at my talk, they found it important enough to want to hear what I have to say while trying to balance that with other demands on their time."

This sentiment was echoed by audience members, who widely opined that banning devices would be detrimental: "I don't think things should be changed because I think the benefits of the work (and non-work which can be beneficial too) people do during lectures outweigh the loss of information resulting from less attention." Most reacted negatively to the idea of turning off wireless access during presentations.

However, some dissented, maintaining that paying attention should be the top priority of people in the room:

> "I think people should be discouraged from coming to lectures if folks can't pay attention to what the speaker has to say. There is nothing worse than having someone doing other work and not paying attention to what is happening in the room. However, I wouldn't want to ban laptops as taking notes via laptop is important."

Others noted that device users could position themselves to minimize distracting the speaker or other audience members. Most accept that multitasking is a feature of our world and accept it when it is discrete.

We asked people whether they would feel more comfortable using devices if more people around them did. Most said that the behaviors of others did not influence them, but some felt that additional usage would increase social acceptability:

> "...as that would be an indication of the cultural norms for that setting' and 'the more using their laptop, the more the perceived acceptance of using a laptop during a lecture.'

Some expressed concern about their image and felt that seeing others use devices reduces guilt about marginal behavior: "just because I won't be as obvious" and "because there is a safety in numbers and for myself, I feel device usage is slightly bad behavior." The overall tone reflected the survey finding that audiences feel that device use could create a poor perception of the audience by the speaker (M = 5.1), even though most speakers did not report such feelings.

Strategies for managing attention

74% of laptop users and 71% of smartphone users reported

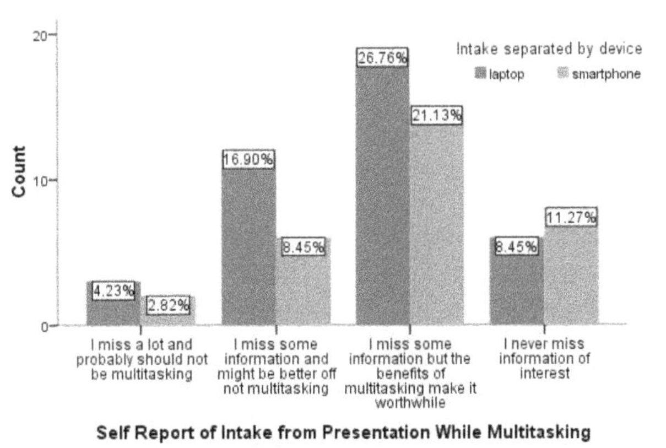

Figure 1. Audience perceptions of balance between intake of information from presentation and multitasking on device. The *y* axis shows count of respondents agreeing with the statement on the *x* axis (% of total respondents are on each bar).

mostly focusing on the talk and occasionally switching to a device when other tasks demand attention. As one user said:

> "While my use of devices at lecture tends to be limited, I occasionally need to: - look at the slides directly on my laptop (maybe i am a slide ahead or behind or it is hard to see the screen from my seat) - keep an eye for high priority email that may come my way. - take a couple of notes (as opposed to typing every word the speaker says) - look up some related information online There may be rare occasion where someone may show up at a talk and find out it is quite different then what they expected. While in general it would be best to leave at that point, there may be occasion where it would create too much disruption and using your device discretely is a better way to go."

Device users also reported a desire to demonstrate to speakers that they are paying attention. Frequent eye contact, asking questions, and putting away a device were commonly cited ways to show interest and respect.

67% of speakers considered device use an indicator of loss of interest in their lecture, but only 23% reported acting on it in real time. 12% reported tailoring lectures in advance to take audience multitasking into account. One commented:

> "When I seem to be losing the audience for any reason, I modify my delivery. Lots of heads down over laptops with users appearing to be reading rather than mostly looking up while writing means that they have drifted off into email or web pages and I need to pull them back in."

Reservations about modifying lectures to incorporate or inhibit device usage include the ambiguity of use, which could be for taking notes, looking up related material and references, or tweeting about the talk. In the colloquium setting we studied, most speakers felt that it was up to audience members to decide how to focus their attention.

DISCUSSION

Related studies report on costs [2, 5] and benefits [3, 4] of using laptops in classroom settings, where students are expected to devote full attention. Campbell and Pargas [3] note that laptop use in classroom settings can be "beneficial and integral" to learning and identify opportunities for educators to adapt lesson plans to exploit devices. Hembrooke and Gay [5] highlight disruptive effects of laptop use on learning, and attribute reduced performance to distractions from applications that divert attention from lectures. Barkhuus [2] found polarized uses of laptops in classrooms: both as a supplement to a lecture and for multitasking on unrelated tasks such as surfing the web, email, and working on other assignments. For business meetings, another setting where a single focus of attention is often expected, Newman [7] studied sources of disruption and found that laptop users often drift to less relevant activities, have difficulty reengaging in the conversation, and when they do may raise topics that are no longer relevant.

In the setting we studied, speakers do not have formal accountability for teaching. Listeners have discretion about attending and paying attention. Less obligated to attend to the lecture, our participants may assume greater flexibility to focus on peripheral tasks as long as their behavior is not socially disruptive. The fact that attendees used computers during lectures for which they felt they missed potentially useful information and where they expressed concern about speaker attitudes suggests that behavioral changes in this setting may be difficult to enforce through persuasion or policy. Instead, speakers could engage a dual-tasking audience by such means as walking through the audience while speaking, mentioning people who are present by name, and creating tasks for them during the lecture. This is an even more salient consideration in settings where speakers have greater responsibility for audience learning.

We focused on perceptions of distraction and social costs of device usage. Future research complementing these studies could explore device usage for parallel social interactions related to the lecture. Also, detailed in-situ studies of attention-switching and its effects on information intake, coupled with assessed participant interest in the lecture, could provide insight into behaviors and outcomes.

CONCLUSION

We identified attitudes and behaviors related to the use of computing devices during presentations. Our findings suggest that multitasking is likely to continue and become more acceptable in practice. To succeed in the colloquium lecture context we studied, speakers should consider adjusting presentations to a world in which audiences are poised and ready to divide attention with other tasks and interests, made available through connected computing devices.

ACKNOWLEDGMENTS

We thank all the survey respondents and presentation attendees who kindly responded to our surveys.

REFERENCES

1. Bailey, B.P. and Konstan, J.A. On the Need for Attention Aware Systems: Measuring Effects of Interruption on Task Performance, Error Rate, and Affective State. *J. Computers in Human Behavior*, *22* (4). 709-732.
2. Barkhuus, L. "Bring your own laptop unless you want to follow the lecture": alternative communication in the classroom. In *Proc. GROUP '05*, 2005, 140-143.
3. Campbell, A.B. and Pargas, R.P. Laptops in the classroom. In *Proc. SIGCSE '03, 2003*, 98-102.
4. Golub, E. On audience activities during presentations. *J. Comput. Small Coll.*, *20* (3). 38-46.
5. Hembrooke, H. and Gay, G. The Laptop and the Lecture: The Effects of Multitasking in Learning Environments. *J. Computing in Higher Education, 15* (1). 46-64.
6. Horrey, W.J. and Wickens, C.D. Examining the Impact of Cell Phone Conversations on Driving Using Meta-Analytic Techniques. *Human Factors*, *48* (1). 196-205.
7. Newman, W. and Smith, E.L. Disruption of meetings by laptop use: is there a 10-second solution? In *CHI '06 extended abstracts*, 2006, 1145-1150.
8. Ophir, E., Nass, C. and Wagner, A.D., Cognitive Control in media multitaskers. In *Proc NAS*, (2009), 15583-15587.

An Exploratory Study of Input Modalities for Mobile Devices Used with Museum Exhibits

Priscilla Jimenez
Department of Computer Science - UIC
Chicago, IL, United States
pjimen5@uic.edu

Leilah Lyons
Department of Computer Science - UIC
Chicago, IL, United States
llyons@uic.edu

ABSTRACT
New of mobile device features and the growing proportion of visitors carrying mobiles allow the range of museum exhibit design possibilities to be expanded. In particular, we see opportunities for using mobiles to help exhibits scale up to support variable-sized groups of visitors, and to support collaborative visitor-visitor interactions. Because exhibit use is generally one-time-only, any interfaces created for these purposes must be easily learnable, or visitors may not use the exhibit at all. To guide the design of learnable mobile interfaces, we chose to employ the *Consistency* design principle. *Consistency* was originally applied to desktop UIs, so we extended the definition to cover three new categories of consistency relevant to ubiquitous computing: *Within-Device Consistency*, *Across-Device Consistency* and *Within-Context Consistency*. We experimentally contrasted designs created from these categories. The results show small differences in learnability, but illustrate that even for one-off situations learnability may not be as important as usability.

Author Keywords
Ubiquitous Computing, Mobile Devices, Opportunistic User Interface, Museums, Collaboration.

ACM Classification Keywords
H.5.2 Information Interfaces and Presentation User Interfaces (Evaluation/Methodology, Interaction styles and Input devices and strategies).

General Terms
Experimentation

INTRODUCTION
Science museums receive hundreds of thousands of visitors every year [e.g. 1]. A growing percentage of museum visitors will be carrying smart devices along on their visits. While museums are interested in providing mobile visitor experiences, the ever-evolving nature of mobile devices poses challenges for learnable interface design. At the beginning of 2010, when this study was performed, the developments for mobile devices included multi-touch screens, accelerometers, GPS and Wi-Fi, which we anticipated could be used to provide wholly new ways for users to interact with both the devices and with each other. We were interested in the possibility of allowing visitors to use their personal devices as opportunistic user interfaces (O-UIs) to highly-interactive software-based museum exhibits [17], but little is known about how to design such interfaces. There are ample practitioner examples[1] and accounts of mobile device use in museum literature [e.g., 26], and a few examples in the academic HCI literature [e.g., 25], but most uses of mobiles in museums have been in the form of electronic guidebooks for individual use [10, 26], not as tools for collaboratively interacting with exhibits directly, which in our opinion is more in keeping with the highly-interactive, highly social nature of many museum exhibits. As consequence, we have turned to the more theoretical Human Computer Interaction (HCI) literature for guidance on how to design these UIs.

In looking for design principles that might apply in this context, the notion of interface *Consistency* seems to be an important one to consider, since it is a design strategy for decreasing learnability time of UIs. Learnability is important because the average amount of time visitors interact with a museum exhibit is about four minutes [4].

We built a prototype of a computer-based museum exhibit which uses mobile devices as input interfaces. In addition to providing museum visitors an easily learnable input interface to interact with museum exhibits, our goal is to provide an input interface that promotes collaboration within a group, because most visitors attend in groups [15]. We selected three different metaphors to guide the design of three different UIs. In selecting these metaphors, we used the notion of *Consistency* to guide the designs. However, as this work will show, *Consistency* must be redefined for use in a multi-device interface context. It is also an imperfect guide, because one must consider the competing demands of learnability vs. usability, and because *Consistency* does not speak to the goal of providing an interface that is expected to promote sociability.

In this paper we show the full results of a work in progress presented in [13]. First, we are going to detail principles

[1] For example, The Metropolitan Museum of Art, the Tate Gallery, the Museum of Modern Art, among many.

involved in the selection of the UIs implemented in the mobile device, followed by the related work focused in design of museum exhibits and UIs. Then, we are going to provide a brief description of our application and user study. Finally, the paper will present the results of our March 2010 research study followed by the conclusions.

BACKGROUND AND PRIOR WORK

Smart devices have new interaction capabilities, like multi-touch screens and accelerometers, but the biggest determinant in selecting an input method is how learnable the interface is, since visitors first concern when approaching an interactive exhibit is how to interact with it [7], and this learning process should be considerate within the 4-minute span visitors usually spend at a museum exhibit [4].

One canonical approach to maximizing interface learnability is to rely on *Consistency*, a design principle of interfaces, which recommends adopting an existing "look and feel" that users are likely to be familiar with [19]. The definition of consistency has usually been related to software interface design, and it usually has been strongly tied to output (i.e., the graphical arrangement and appearance of the user interface), but not input (with the layout of keys on keyboards the lone exception). The Consistency design principle, put broadly, recommends that interfaces which have similar operations should use similar elements for similar tasks. In [9], consistency was described in three different senses: *Internal Consistency* refers to designing operations to behave the same *within* an application; *External Consistency* refers to designing operations and interfaces to be the same *across* applications; and *External Analogic* or *Metaphoric Consistency* refers to designs that may use metaphors or analogies to objects, attributes or relations in the world outside of computer interfaces.

These three types of consistency might not be totally applicable, since they were originally developed for single-user desktop graphical UIs and we are designing for a multi-device multi-user interface. Thus, we redefine the different senses of *Consistency* for a multi-device, multi-user context. In this context *Internal Consistency* refers to when a UI design is consistent with the design of previous applications developed for the mobile device (*within-device* consistency). We redefine *External Consistency* to refer to when a UI design will be consistent with other common handheld input devices (*across-device* consistency). Because these devices are "objects in the world outside of [a given device's] interface," *across-device* consistency also incorporates the notion of External Analogic/Metaphoric Consistency. Even with these redefinitions, however, we are still left with a range of options. Would *internal, within-device consistency* (remaining true to the dominant input styles for the device) be more effective than *external, across-device consistency* (adopting other familiar device input styles) when using the device in a wholly new way?

Moreover, which external metaphors should be selected (i.e., which other devices should we look to) to attain *across-device consistency*? In this latter question, we are guided by the context of museums themselves – the social shared nature of exhibit use. A (perhaps counterintuitive) risk we most balance is making the mobile interfaces *too* engaging. A known problem with the use of mobiles in museums is that intensive interactions with devices can work at cross-purposes to the museum context and actually inhibit interaction with exhibits and result in isolation from other visitors [10]. In museums, visitors need to be free to interact with one another, and to interact bodily with the space of the museum itself. So the across-device metaphors selected should be those known to encourage engagement with a larger, social and embodied space (not just a display screen). This illustrates the fact that when applying consistency principles to ubiquitous computing, one must look beyond just the realm of devices: an interface must be consistent within the context of the device's use (*within-context consistency*); in this case, a social, informal, highly-interactive learning environment.

In this work, we experimentally contrast several possible approaches: across-device consistency, within-device consistency, and a combination of across-device and within-context consistency (see Table 1 for an overview).

Applying External, Across-Device Consistency

Relying on External Consistency might suggest that adopting an interface that emulates a gamepad controller input style would be effective, since the vast majority of users have employed directional keypads as inputs to single or multi player home game systems. This type of control is held in the hand, where the digits (especially thumbs) are used to provide input via action buttons and a four-way directional controller (sometimes referred to as a "D-pad"). Very few contemporary smart devices have physical D-pads, but they can be emulated with on-screen buttons. A favorable result in terms of learnability and ease-of-use is expected with the implementation of gamepad metaphor.

Applying Internal, Within-Device Consistency

Users do not often use software-emulated gamepad controllers on their smart devices, so that approach might not actually increase learnability. Instead, it might be wiser to remain internally consistent with the usual "look and feel" of these devices themselves, and use the multi-touch input style employed by most smart phone applications. In [11] it was stressing the importance of the task domain and making a mechanism that matches the user thoughts and goals known as direct manipulation. In a multi-touch input interface style, the concept of direct manipulation interfaces implemented with the usage of finger movements allows the user to directly manipulate objects and immediately receive feedback. Thus, the implementation of this interface also promises to be highly learnable and usable.

Combining External, Across-Device Consistency with Within-Context Consistency

Across-Device consistency alone might suggest that we consider taking advantage of device accelerometers to emulate the "look and feel" of Nintendo's "Wiimote," but there are other consistency principles at play in this scenario as well. The rapid adoption of Nintendo's accelerometer-based "Wiimote" shows that even a wholly new user interface design can be easily learned if it relies on an embodied input method. Moreover, embodied input methods take to user attention (especially visual attention) away from the device itself, encouraging users to engage with both the physical and social spaces that surround them, as evidenced by the success of the Wii^{TM} at engaging a broad demographic range of users [29] in joint physical activities. For this reason, we view the use of a Wiimote-like metaphor as having within-context consistency, since interaction with the social and physical realms are important to museum activities. Also, since museums have a diverse demographic of visitors, especially in terms of age, the success of the Wii at the elderly [18, 27] is yet another argument for the within-context consistency of the Wiimote as design metaphor. The implementation of this interface may not be as effective as the previous ones in terms of learnability or ease-of-use, since the ergonomics of mobile devices differ from Wiimotes, but it might better promote collaboration and avoid the concerns about the heads-down effect or visitor isolation.

Consistency Principles	DK	MT	DT
Internal, Within-Device Consistency	No	Yes	No
External, Across-Device Consistency	Yes	No	Yes
Within-Context Consistency	No	No	Yes

DK = Emulation of gamepad controller, MT = Use of multi-touch mobile feature, DT = Emulation of a Wiimote

Table 1. An outline of the consistency principles applied in the three tested user interface conditions.

Consistency and its Discontents

Many writers have presented cases in support of user interface consistency as a reliable principle that designers should consider. Rubinstein and Hersh provide guidelines for better design in [21], and outright recommend that designers "Build consistent human interfaces." The rationale is the "consistent myth": users perceive systems as clear and effective, because consistency helps them to know how the system will behave in all circumstances. Polson [20], states that consistency reduces training when new interfaces are introduced to user. Smith and Mosier [24] present a guideline for designing user interfaces in which consistency is the design principle most recommended.

On the other hand, there are some others that argue that consistency is an unreliable guide. Grudin [9] states when user interface consistency becomes our primary concern, our attention is directed away from its proper focus: users and their work. He presented three cases and examples in which consistency is not reliable guide to follow. In his paper, he presents conclusions. (1) Most of the design choices can be better understood through the analysis of the users work. (2) Although it seems reasonable to think that a consistent interface will be easy to learn, there are situations in which ease of learning can conflict with the ease of use. If learnability impedes a good performance, consistency is working *against* a good design, and then in these cases priority must be established in the interface design. (3) Interface design is an engineering problem that forces tradeoffs among many factors, and then in which case a fully consistent system is not practical.

As can be seen, *Learnability* and *Usability* are important aspects to satisfy when designing UIs, and succeeding in fulfilling one does not imply the other. Thus, *Learnability* vs. *Usability* is important to attend to, thus we will assess it in our experiments.

Group Usability of Mobile Devices in Museums

The majority of museum visitors attend in social groups [15], but prior studies of mobile device use in museums reveal that a major complaint associated with the use of mobiles is a feeling of isolation [e.g. 3, 10], so if we make use of the devices we must also take care to preserve social interactions within groups. Several other HCI researchers have come to the same conclusion, and have specifically designed proofs-of-concepts for how mobile applications can support social activities in museums. In this section we situate our work in relation to these prior projects.

Prior work that attempted to encourage collaborative interactions in museums [19, 20, 21, 22, 23] with mobile devices has one common element: in all cases, the activity involved visiting different exhibits, a *cross*-exhibit interaction. This differs from our approach in that the proposed application in this research study is not intended to be a kind of mobile museum guide or to augment museum exhibits with further information. Instead, we want to use O-UIs to support deep engagement with a *single* exhibit, and with the social context surrounding that exhibit. An interesting thing to note about the pro-collaboration designs in the prior work is that they encourage *non*-co-located collaboration: the activities tend towards "treasure hunts" that encourage visitors to split up to gather information [5, 8, 14, 31, 32]. While collaboration certainly can happen while visitors are separated, we are more interested in. Collaboration that can occur in a collocated space, as conversations are known to play a major role in the informal learning processes in museums [2, 6].

EXPERIMENTAL DESIGN

This research study asks participants to use mobile devices to join a collaborative software activity shown on a large shared display. Shared displays have been used in previous works supporting public, informal interactive experiences [e.g. 16, 17, 28]. Large shared displays allow the participants to observe the current state of the shared activity, and in theory each participant has an equal opportunity to contribute to the task. We wish to explore impact of different modalities of providing input via mobile devices, on three areas: 1) the learnability and ease-of-use of the UIs, 2) the impact of input method on sociability and joint efforts to achieve a common goal and 3) the feasibility of the input method for use in museums exhibits.

In this research study we tested three input conditions that attempt to replicate the three design approaches described above: a Directional Keypad (DK) that employs the external, across-device consistency principle, a Multi-Touch (MT) interface that employs the internal, within-device consistency principle, and a "Device Tilt" Wiimote-style input (DT) that employs a combination of the external, across-device consistency principle and the internal, within-context design principle for ubiquitous computing settings. We do not expect that the outcome of this experiment will completely favor one input style for all three criteria (learnability & ease-of-use, sociability & collaboration, and museum feasibility). In fact, we suspect that both the DK and the MT conditions will be easier to learn and use, and consequently may also be more feasible for museum use. However, we suspect that better sociability will be observed in the DT condition, based on its similarity to Wiimotes. Our anecdotal experience indicates that Wiimote users seem more likely to critique, comment, laugh, and share tips with one another, especially during the initial learning phase, possibly because the embodied nature of the control allows users a greater visual access to the actions of their partners than traditional gamepads.

Application Overview

Many applications could be created for our configuration (shared display as a common screen and mobile devices as controllers), allowing one physical installation to present many exhibits. For our experiment, though, we chose the *Tangram*, an old Chinese geometry puzzle, in which the player is challenged to put together seven geometric pieces 'tans' to fit an outline without overlapping them. The idea for the task came from prior experimental work studying the collaboration of visitors while using computer-based exhibits, which also made use of tangrams as the activity [22]. Tangrams are useful for experimental purposes because while they provide a genuine intellectual challenge in keeping with what may be found in hands-on museums, at the same time they do not require prior content knowledge, obviating the need for ancillary exhibit materials that might distract from the task and skew measures. For the purpose of studying interaction design, Tangrams are also useful because they provide opportunities for rich 2-dimensional input: the tans can be translated in two dimensions, rotated, and may need to be flipped when forming certain shapes.

When implemented in a museum, the application created for this study, *WeTangram*, would be hosted on a computer hidden in an exhibit and presented on shared display (see Figure 1). Museum visitors would download a free "satellite" application to their mobile device, which communicates wirelessly with the main *WeTangram* application. Once all of the participants are connected via Wi-Fi with the exhibit (shared display) and identified using a nickname, they attempt to work together to complete a tangram outline in the least possible time to attain a high score. Each participant uses his or her device to manipulate – move, rotate or flip - only one tan at a time from the set of seven pieces. He/she has the option of dropping the piece and choosing another if available. The "holder" of a piece is recognized by a different border color that matches with the color of the participant's name on the shared display.

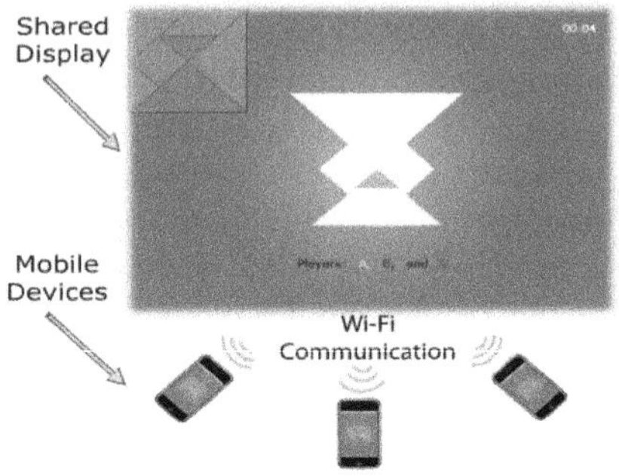

Figure 1. WeTangram application.

METHODOLOGY

Participants

For this study, we recruited a convenience sample of thirty under 30-year-old university students as ten groups of three. We chose groups of three because prior research [30] has found that a triad is the optimal size to solve collaborative math problems that involve a reasoning task. In addition, because we used within-device consistency as a design principle, we required participants to be active users of mobile devices with touch screen features because our use case presupposes visitors will use their own phones, but we did not place restrictions on prior Wii or D-pad experience because such visitors may have varying prior experience. (93% were regular users of D-pad controllers and 53% were regular users of Wiimote)

Experimental Conditions

This experiment evaluated three different input styles for an *iPod Touch/iPhone* interface to a shared museum exhibit. *Directional_Keypad* (see Figure 2, left) implements the external, across-device consistency principle by emulating a D-pad. It displays directional keys on the mobile device screen, and by pressing the buttons the users are able to move (up, down, left, right) a fixed small amount, rotate (left, right) by 45°, or flip a tangram on the y-axis. *Multi_Touch* (see Figure 2, middle) implement the internal, within-device consistency principle. It allows users to freely move a piece using one finger gestures, freely rotate left/right using two finger gestures, or flip tangram pieces using a finger tap. This input style is included because it is the dominant input approach used for smart devices like the *iPhone/iPod touch*. *Device_Tilt* (see Figure 2, right) implements a combination of the external, across-device and within-context consistency principles. It allows users to freely move by slowly tilting (vertically via pitch and horizontally via roll) and rotate (left, right) pieces by 45° by sharply rolling the device. This input style is included because of its similarity to the Wii controller, although the specific control actions were developed formatively to account for hardware differences.

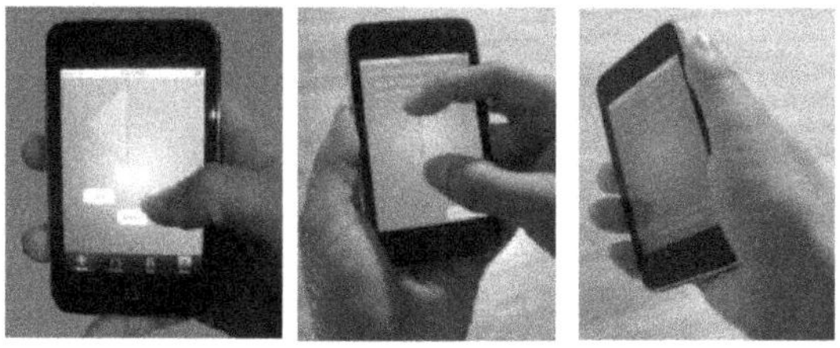

Figure 2. From left to right: the Directional_Keypad (DK), Multi_Touch (MT) and Device_Tilt (DT) interfaces.

Evidence

Here we describe the measures used to assess the three interfaces.

Learnability and Ease of Use

Subjective reflections about learnability and ease of use were gathered using Likert scale questions in a post-questionnaire.

Sociability and Collaboration

The level of co-player integration was studied through interaction logs and videotapes of behavior. The logs were used to measure each participant's *Effort Distribution*, i.e., the degree of contribution to the final solution in terms of placed tans. Because we wish to produce interfaces that encourage socialization and collaboration, the number of speaking turns were counted as the *Amount of Verbal Communication*. This information also used to compute the *Distribution of Conversation* to determine if the talk was equally distributed or dominated by one or two participants.

Museum Feasibility

The *Total Solution Time* recorded by the log data helped us find out if the application is viable to use within the 4-minute or less span visitors usually spend at a museum exhibit [4]. Moreover, museums, especially science museums, are meant to be institutions that provide their visitor enjoyable learning experiences [12]. Thus we gathered subjective enjoyment ratings using a Likert scale in a post-questionnaire and used video to code the times when users showed expressions consistent with enjoyment (e.g., laughs or smiling).

Task Description

The participants were asked to work together to solve a tangram puzzle. Because the experiment used a repeated-measures experiment design, we used paradoxical tangram problems [23]. These consist of seemingly identical tangram figures, so they are of roughly similar difficulty levels, but solving one puzzle will not help one know how to solve the others (see Figure 3).

Procedure

Groups were given instructions and asked to answer individually a pre-study questionnaire. Following this, each group tested the application using the three different input styles and three different paradoxical tangram shapes (see Figure 3). No exploration time was given, as learnability was what we wanted to study. To balance the practice effect, an incomplete repeated measures design was used, rotating the orderings for the input interface styles and the tangram silhouettes using the Latin Square technique. This technique ensures that all possible combinations of input interface and tangram problem being tested, and occur exactly once in each row and column as shown in Table 2. In each group, after the three trials were completed, every participant individually filled out a post-questionnaire.

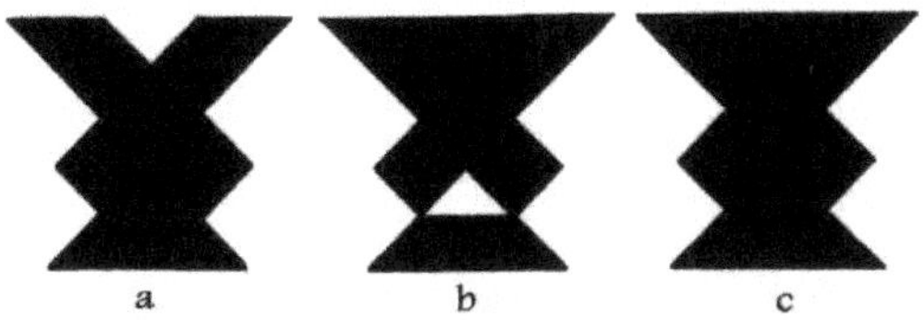

Figure 3. Paradoxical Tangram problems used in this study.

Group	Trial 1	Trial 2	Trial 3
1	DKa	MTb	DTc
2	DTa	DKb	MTc
3	MTa	DTb	DKc
4	DKc	MTa	DTb
5	DTc	DKa	MTb
6	MTc	DTa	DKb
7	DKb	MTc	DTa
8	DTb	DKc	MTa
9	MTb	DTc	DKa
10	DKa	MTb	DTc

Table 2. List of conditions that were tested: (DK) Directional_Keypad, (MT) Multi_Touch, and (DT) Device_Tilt. a, b, and c represent the paradoxical tangram problems depicted in Figure 3

RESULTS

Learnability

Participants were asked to rank the three interfaces according to how easy they thought each was to learn (see Figure 4). We can see that 67% of the participants ranked the *DK* interface as the easiest to learn to use, while 33% of the participants were most in favor of the *MT* interface, and no participants ranked the *DT* interface as the easiest to learn. The 90% Confidence Intervals (CIs) for the easiest rank values are shown in Figure 5. A chi-square test of goodness of fit was performed to determine whether the interfaces were equally ranked as the easiest to learn. $X^2(2, n = 27) = 18, p < 0.001$. Then we can conclude that *DK* is the interface easier to use for this experiment.

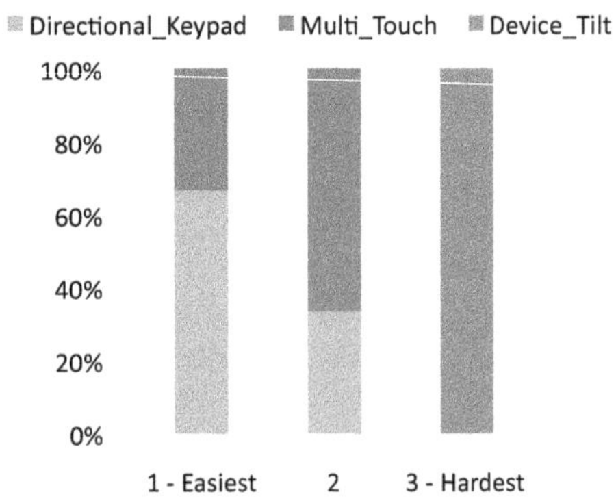

Figure 4. Responses to forced ranking question: "Ranking in terms of Ease of Learning."

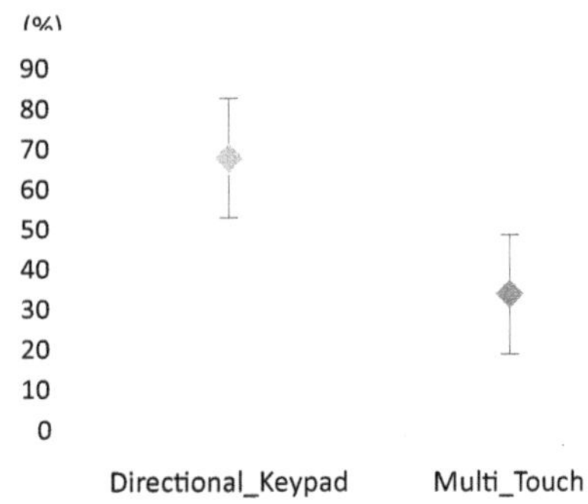

Figure 5. 90% CIs for the interfaces raked as easiest to learn.

This result was expected, because *DK* has the longest history of use as an input strategy, and is still in use today in most video game controllers. From the observation of the sessions and videotapes, we also realized that *DT* was the hardest interface because of the lack of affordances for holding the device as a controller which is intended to be held in a single orientation. Unlike a Wiimote, which has an ergonomic design for a particular holding orientation, it was observed that the participants hold the mobile device in different ways in order to provide input to the exhibit.

Ease of Use

The results concerning ease-of-use were broken into two categories: ease-of-moving and ease-of-rotating. The Likert responses to ease-of-moving are: *DK* (M = 4.0, Mdn = 4, SD = 0.89), *MT* (M = 4.5, Mdn = 5, SD = 0.73) and *DT* (M = 2.3, Mdn = 2, SD = 0.89), where 5 represents "very good" and 1 represents "very bad". A Friedman ANOVA by ranks $F(2, 30) = 47.82$, $p < 0.0001$ indicates that the measures were significantly different from each other. The results concerning ease-of-rotating are: *DK* (M = 4.2, Mdn = 4, SD = 0.89), *MT* (M = 4.2, Mdn = 5, SD = 0.86) and *DT* (M = 2.0, Mdn = 2, SD = 1.07), where 5 represents "very good" and 1 represents "very bad." The result of the Friedman ANOVA by ranks $F(2, 30) = 44.22$, $p < 0.0001$ indicates a significant difference in responses. These results indicate that *MT* is the interface that users consider easiest to use, and implies that internal, within-device consistency is superior for usability.

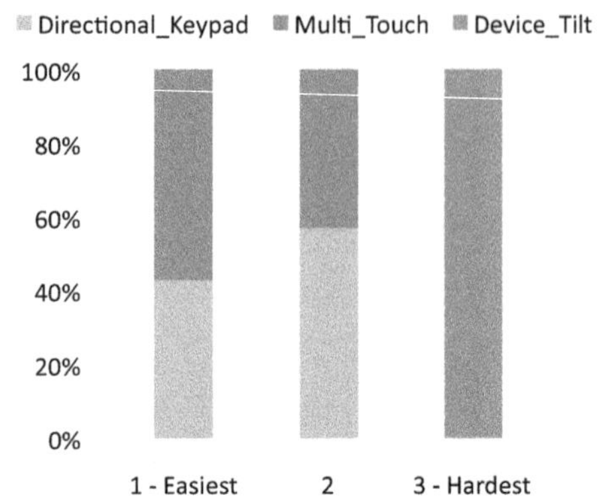

Figure 6. Responses to forced ranking question: "Ranking in terms of Ease of use."

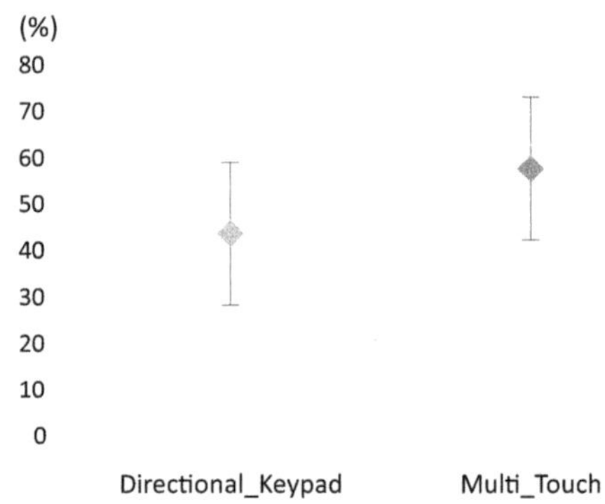

Figure 7. 90% CIs for the interfaces raked as the easiest of use.

Participant's opinions about the tested UIs showed that 57% of the participants ranked the *MT* interface as the easiest of use, while the 43% of the participants were in favor of *DK*, and no participants ranked the *DT* interface (see Figure 6). The 90% CIs (± 15.39%, see Figure 7) indicate that there is a fair amount of overlap between *MT* and *DK*, although a Chi-square test of goodness of fit $X^2(2, n = 28) = 14.86$, $p < 0.001$, determines that the ease of use ranking for the three input interfaces was not equally distributed.

Sociability and Collaboration

To know the distribution of individual contribution to the final solution, the *Effort Distribution,* we first computed the standard deviations (SD) across the number of correctly placed tans per participant in each trial, and then we calculated the averages of these SDs for each UI condition. As in this activity, we have seven tans and three participants per trial; the ideal value for the SD is 0.58, resulting of any combination of (2, 2, and 3) that represents the number of tans placed for each participant. We do not expect to get the ideal value of the SD. However, to identify the input interface that tends to better support the degree of contribution per participant to the final solution we looked for the input interface closest to the ideal value.

The averages are summarized as *DK* (M = 1.25, SD = 0.56), MT (M = 1.09, SD = 0.70) and *DT* (M = 1.61, SD = 0.85).

Although the *DK* and *DT* samples are normally distributed, the *MT* sample did not meet the criteria in order to perform a one sample *t*-test. In the three cases, we can see that those average values diverge from the desired value, but the results of the *MT* interface are the closest to the desired value and in which its SD encompasses the desired value of 0.58. This might suggests *MT* is the interface that tend to support an equally contribution to the final solution.

These values agree with the anecdotal observation that in some *DT* interface tests the participants did not know how to rotate or move the tans. When these participants realized that one of his/her partners mastered these actions, they decided to stop trying and leave the device to the side for a while (without diminishing their apparent interest in their partners' interaction with the activity). Unfortunately, we did not observe any similar behavior associated to the *DK* interface to explain its uneven *Effort Distribution*.

To measure collaboration among the participants based on the *Amount of Verbal Communication*, we analyzed the videotapes of each session and coded the dialogue data and participants' interaction. Each participant's remark in the session script was classified as an ON-COLLABORATIVE or OFF-COLLABORATIVE remark. For example, "Ok, we need to take out those triangles" would be an ON-COLLABORATIVE remark and if the remark was a personal opinion like "I think once you get used to it, it is fun" it would be classified as an OFF-COLLABORATIVE remark because it does not assist the group in the joint task. Additionally, if an ON-COLLABORATIVE remark was related to help with the puzzle solution it was tagged as ON-COLLABORATIVE/SOLVING PROBLEM, but if the ON-COLLABORATIVE remark was related to help with the interface interaction it was tagged as ON-COLLABORATIVE/INTERFACE.

The average within-group utterances per minute, regardless of classification (ON-COLLABORATIVE + OFF-COLLABORATIVE), are: *DK* (M = 4.90, SD = 1.86), *MT* (M = 4.58, SD = 1.59) and *DT* (M = 4.45, SD = 2.25). Since the samples in *DK* were not normally distributed, we could not perform one-way ANOVA to determine which one promotes more overall conversation among the participants.

The ON-COLLABORATIVE utterances per minute *DK* (M = 4.20, SD = 1.56), *MT* (M = 4.13, SD = 1.81) and *DT* (M = 3.65, SD = 1.97) indicate roughly similar rates of collaborative conversation across all conditions, confirmed by a repeated measure one-way ANOVA F (2, 27) = 0.46, p = 0.6394. This result indicates that the values obtained about collaboration are not significantly different among the three interfaces, so we cannot draw a strong conclusion based on the raw amount of verbal communication.

To measure the *Distribution of Conversation*, we computed percentages of ON-COLLABORATIVE remarks per participant. One of our goals was to design interactive exhibits that support equal collaboration among the players. What this means in terms of measurement is, that when we coded the number of pro-collaborative remarks, no one participant is seen as the main "driver" of the collaborative activity – since this activity was tested with three players, it was hoped that each player would have a percentage of collaborative participation around 33%.

To obtain the percentage of collaborative participation per user, we counted the number of a user's ON-COLLABORATIVE remarks and divided by the total number of ON-COLLABORATIVE remarks of the whole group. These percentages of collaborative participation are shown in a frequency distribution table (see Figure 8). The reported results in the graph suggest that this kind of group activity and the usage of mobile devices support our goal; the majority of participants, in the three tested interfaces, fall into the range of 21% to 40% which is near the 33% ideal distribution of collaborative actions across partners.

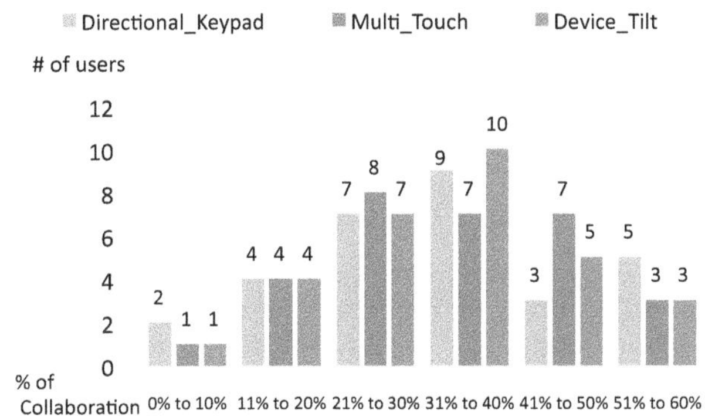

Figure 8. Frequency distribution of the proportion of users' remarks coded as collaborative.

Some differences emerge, however, when we computed standard deviations (SDs) – a measure of dispersion – of the collaborative conversation within each group. Then we calculated the averages of these SDs. As we expect an equal collaboration among participants, the ideal value of the computed averages should be the closer to zero. Thus, a lower value implies a more equitable conversation pattern. The average values of the collaboration proportion are *DK* (M = 15.6, SD = 9.19), *MT* (M = 15.3, SD = 7.87) and *DT* (M = 12.3, SD = 8.29). These reported values suggest that the *DK* and the *MT* interfaces are farther from the desired value comparing to the *DT* interface, consequently the *DT* interface has more of a tendency to promote equal collaborative conversation among the participants. We also counted the number of times in which a participant volunteered to manipulate a tangram piece, because we wanted to know if a tested UI influenced this behavior. The values obtained are: *DK* (M = 2.7, SD = 2.79), *MT* (M = 2.0, SD = 3.0) and *DT* (M = 4.0, SD = 3.0). These two trends are in keeping with the within-context consistency principle used in designing the *DT* interface, which should promote sociability. Unfortunately, it could not be verified statistically since not all the UIs reported values which were normally distributed.

Museum Feasibility

The success of a museum exhibit rests on whether or not visitors enjoy interacting with it, and whether or not it can be used within a short timeframe. Thus, we need to evaluate if the use of these UIs affect the spent time by visitors in an exhibit. Figure 9 shows that *MT* supports the activity in order to solve the problem in the least possible time, which is consistent with its superior usability, as reported above. Half of the groups using the *MT* interface finished the activity within the 4-minute timeframe we expected.

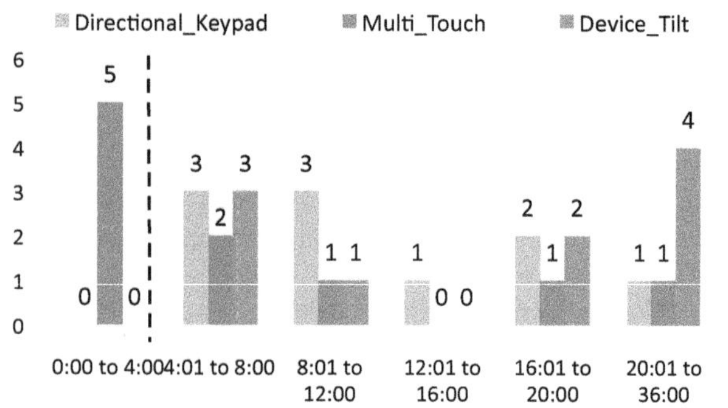

Figure 9. Number of groups whose total solution time falls within a given 4-minute range.

To measure enjoyment ratings, we analyzed the videos to quantify the times in which participants laugh or smile while using the device. The results of this analysis are: *DK* ($M = 1.6$, $SD = 3.4$), *MT* ($M = 3.1$, $SD = 3.3$) and *DT* ($M = 27$, $SD = 23$). Since the samples in *DK* were not normally distributed we could not statistically verify the differences of these values, but looking at them it is apparent that the participants using *DT* exhibited more behaviors associated with enjoyment, which we expected from our use of the within-context consistency design principle.

The results concerning enjoyment are shown in Figure 10. We can observe that 71% of answers indicated that *MT* was the most enjoyable interface, 25% of the answers were in favor of *DT* and 4% of the users reported *DK* as the most enjoyable UI. The 90% CIs which are shown in Figure 11 indicate a clear distinction across interfaces in terms of enjoyment, confirmed by a Chi-square test of goodness of fit X^2 (2, $n = 28$) = 20.22, $p < 0.001$. While these results confirm that the most usable interface, *MT*, was the most enjoyable, it is surprising that 25% of respondents ranked the *DT* as the most enjoyable to use, despite its poor ranking for both learnability and usability (although it is consistent with *DT*'s high rates of coded laughter and smiles). This indicates that usability and learnability measures might not be sufficient to predict the ultimate user's preferences for O-UIs in a museum exhibit context.

The responses concerning the UI preference for controlling a museum exhibit are depicted in Figure 12. The graph shows that 79% of responses point to *MT*, leaving 14% in favor of *DK* and 7% for *DT*. The 90% CIs (see Figure 13) once again indicate a clear distinction between the different interfaces, confirmed by a Chi-square test X^2 (2, $n = 29$) = 27.78, $p < 0.001$. These results indicate, perhaps unsurprisingly, that usability is associated with a preference for an interface in a museum context. What is striking, however, is that the interface associated with highest learnability, *DK*, does not rank high on our museum feasibility measures.

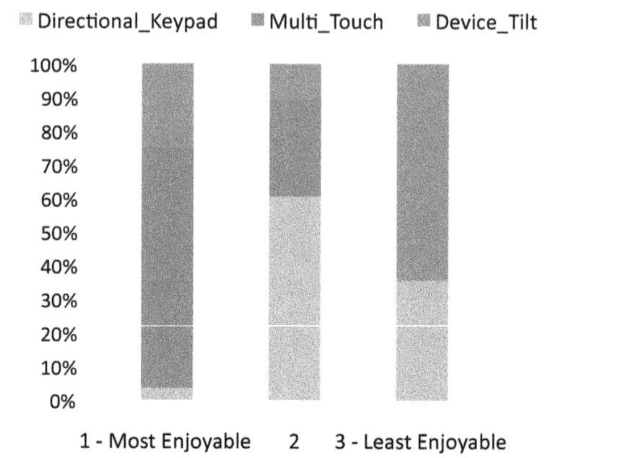

Figure 10. Responses to forced ranking question: "Ranking in terms of Enjoyment."

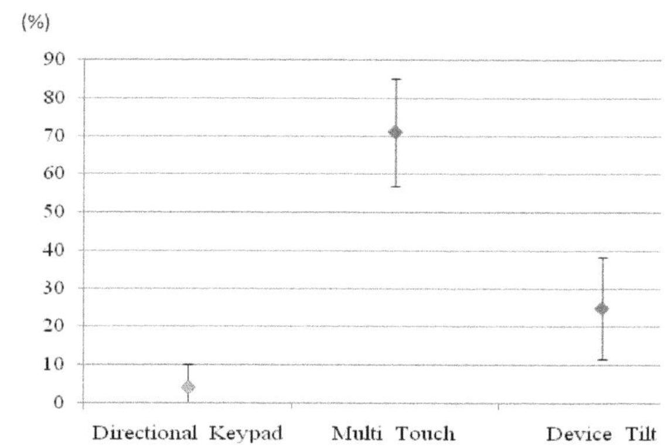

Figure 11. 90% CIs for the interfaces raked as the most enjoyable interface.

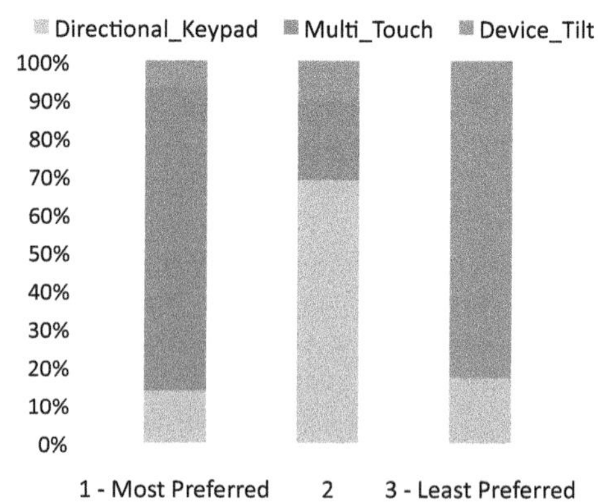

Figure 12. Responses to forced ranking question: "Ranking in terms of preference to use to control a museum exhibit."

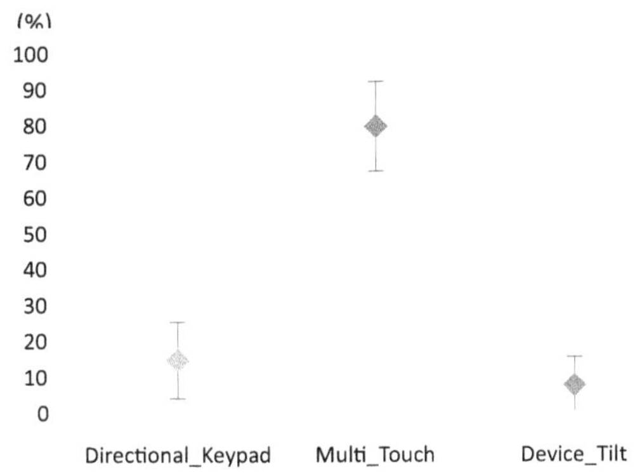

Figure 13. 90% CIs for the interfaces raked as the preferred to use to control a museum exhibit.

CONCLUSIONS

In terms of *usefulness*, the reported results place the *Multi_Touch* interface above the *Directional_Keypad* interface, even though the participants ranked *Directional_Keypad* as the easiest to learn. This shows that our prior assumptions about the critical role of learnability in the design of O-UIs for exhibits may have been wrong, or at least, the learnability differences were slight enough to be outweighed by usability issues. We also could see that *Multi_Touch* is the interface that enables the participants to have better performance, to solve the problem in a shortest time compared to the other two UIs, perhaps because it affords more direct manipulation. This result confirms that easy-to-learn and easy-to-use do not always come together, and further, suggests that neither learnability nor usability alone are enough to predict the ultimate users' preferences for O-UIs. It also suggests that using Internal, Within-Device Consistency as design guideline may be appropriate for O-UIs like multi-device interfaces to museum exhibits.

In terms of *Enjoyment* ratings, the participants ranked the *Multi_Touch* interface as the most enjoyable, but we also notice that even thought the *Device_Tilt* interface was more difficult to learn and use than the other two UIs, some of the participants reported this interface as the most enjoyable, an oddity that was reflected in their observed affective responses (smiling and laughing), indicating that designers might want to consider Within-Context consistency in their designs for O-UIs. This work did not test the combination of Within-Context consistency and Internal, Within-Device consistency, but these results suggest that this may be a target for future work. Indeed, several participants suggested, unprompted, that we should consider implementing a mixed UI using the *Multi_Touch* and *Device_Tilt* interface, so this should be further examined.

In terms of *Sociability & Collaboration,* we could not find significant differences among the UIs to help us to drawn strong conclusions about whether one UI promotes more participation or collaboration among the interfaces. The results related to *Effort Percentage* suggest the *Multi_Touch* interface might promote more equal participant effort during the activity, suggesting that good usability is needed to promote even participation, and in turn, collaboration. The summarized data related to the *Amount of Verbal Communication* did not report a considerable difference among the UIs. Finally, the data related to *Distribution of Collaboration* did not show outstanding differences among the UIs either, although the *Device_Tilt* interface tended to promote a more equal collaborative conversational participation among the users, as its Within-Context consistency might suggest. O-UI designers may wish to employ this design guideline, but it does not seem to be necessary for ensuring collaboration. It is more likely that the structure of the shared activity itself has more bearing on collaboration than the UI, if one may judge by the way other researchers developing collaborative mobile activities in museums have independently converged on the use of games with independent roles to induce collaboration.

The principle of External, Across-Device consistency implemented in the *Directional_Keypad interface* showed good results in terms of learnability, but increased learnability did not help participants attain good performance, nor did it contribute to enjoyment or participant judgments about the appropriateness of the UI for a museum context. When External, Across-Device consistency was combined with within-context consistency in the *Device_Tilt* interface, the learnability benefits disappeared, likely due to the differences in ergonomics between Wiimotes and mobile devices. This suggests that merely using a *metaphor* of interaction is not sufficient when applying the External, Across-Device consistency principle to ubiquitous computing interfaces. By removing consistency from the realm of displays, we must begin to incorporate notions of physical space (embodiment, and in turn, ergonomics) into consistency.

Although the end product of this work was intended for science museums, these findings are likely to hold in any situation with a one-off use case (e.g. other museums, bars, airports). The experimental approach used here revealed some tradeoffs that will help designers make decisions when employing smart devices as opportunistic user interfaces in informal collaborative contexts. Generally speaking, using Internal, Within-Device Consistency to design an interface produced the best results.

ACKNOWLEDGMENTS

We thank the LTG Lab members for their opinions and suggestions while designing the WeTangram application. As well as, all the UIC students that participated in the experimental phase of this research.

REFERENCES

1. Annual Report 2008. http://www.exploratorium.edu/about/annualreport.pdf
2. Ash, D. Dialogic inquiry in life science conversations of family groups in a museum. *Journal of Research in Science Teaching*, 40(2), 138-162. 2003.

3. Bellotti, F., Berta, R., Gloria, A., and Margarone, M. User testing a hypermedia tour guide. Pervasive Computing, 1(2), 33-41, 2002
4. Borun, M., Chambers M., and Cleghom, A. Families are learning in science museums. *Curator: The Museum Journal*, 39(2), 123-138, 1996.
5. Cabrera, J. S., Frutos, H. M., Stoica, A. G., Avouris, N., Dimitriadis, Y., Fiotakis, G., and Liveri, K. D. Mystery in the museum: collaborative learning activities using handheld devices. In *Proc. MobileHCI* 2005, ACM Press (2005), 315-318.
6. Callanan, M. A., & Jipson, J. L. Explanatory Conversations and Young Children's Developing Scientific Literacy. In K. Crowley, C. D. Schunn & O. Takeshi (Eds.), *Designing for Science: Implications from Everyday, Classroom, and Professional Settings.* Lawrence Erlbaum. 21-49, 2001.
7. Carlisle, R.W. What Do School Children Do at a Science Center?. *Curator: The Museum Journal*, 28 (1), 27-33, 1985.
8. Dini, R., Paterno, F., and Santoro, C. An environment to support multi-user interaction and cooperation for improving museum visits through games. In *Proc. MobileHCI 2007*, ACM Press (2007), 515-521.
9. Grudin, J. The case against user interface consistency. *Commun. ACM*, 32 (10), 1989, 1164-1173.
10. Hsi, S. The Electronic Guidebook: A Study of User Experiences Using Mobile Web Content in a Museum Setting. In *Proc. WMTE 2002*, IEEE CS Press (2002), 48-54.
11. Hutchins, E. L., Hollan, J. D., and Norman, D. A. Direct manipulation interfaces. *Human-Computer Interaction.* 1 (4), 1985, 311-338.
12. ICOM Code of Ethics for Museums. http://icom.museum/ethics.html.
13. Jimenez, P. and Lyons, L. Studying Different Methods of Providing Input to Collaborative Interactive Museum Exhibit Using Mobile Devices. In Proc. WMUTE 2010, IEEE CS Press (2010), 225-227.
14. Klopfer, E., Perry, J., Squire, K., Jan, M., and Steinkuehler, C. Mystery at the museum: a collaborative game for museum education. In *Proc. CSCL 2005.* International Society of the Learning Sciences, 316-320.
15. Korn, R. An analysis of differences between visitors at natural history museums and science centers. *The Curator: The Museum Journal*, 38 (3), 150-160, 1995.
16. Leikas, J., Stromberg, H., Ikonen, V., Suomela, R. and Heinila, J. Multi-user mobile applications and a public display: novel ways for social interaction. In *Proc. PerCom* 2006, IEEE CS Press (2006), 66-70.
17. Lyons, L. Designing Opportunistic User Interfaces to Support a Collaborative Museum Exhibit. In *Proc. CSCL 2009,* ISLS 2009, 375-384.
18. Neufeldt, C. Wii play with elderly people. *Enhancing Interaction Spaces by Social Media for the Elderly: A Workshop Report.* IISI 2009, 6 (3), 50-59.
19. Olson, D.R. *Building Interactive Systems: Principles for Human Computer Interaction (1st Ed.).* Florence, KY: Cengage Learning, 2010.
20. Polson, P. The consequences of consistent and inconsistent user interfaces. *Cognitive Science and Its Applications for Human-Computer Interaction*, 59-108, 1988.
21. Rubinstein, R. and Hersh, H. *The Human Factor: Designing computer systems for people.* Digital Press, Bedford, Mass., 1984.
22. Scarlatos, L. An application of tangible interfaces in collaborative learning environments. In *Proc. SIGGRAPH* 2002, ACM Press (2002), 125-126.
23. Slocum, J. *The Tangram book.* Sterling Publishing, 100, 2001.
24. Smith, S. and Mosier, J. *Guidelines For Designing User Interface Software.* ESD-TR-86-278. Bedford, Mass., 1986.
25. Stock, O., and Zancanaro, M. *PEACH: Intelligent Interfaces for Museum Visits.* Springer-Verlag. 2007.
26. Tallon, L., and Walker, K. *Digital Technologies and the Museum Experience: Handheld Guides and Other Media.* AltaMira Press, 2008.
27. Theng, Y., Dahlan, A. B., Akmal, M. L., and Myint, T. Z. An exploratory study on senior citizens' perceptions of the Nintendo Wii: the case of Singapore. In *Proc. i-CREATe 2009.* ACM Press (2009), Article 10.
28. Vajk, T., Coulton, P., Bamford, W. and Edwards, R. Using a mobile phone as a "Wii-like" controller for playing games on a large public display. *International Journal of Computer Games Technology*, Hindawi Publishing Corp, 2008, Article 4.
29. Voida, A. and Greenberg, S. Wii all play: the console game as a computational meeting place. In *Proc. CHI 2009,* ACM Press (2009), 1559-1568.
30. Wiley, J., and Jensen, M. When three heads are better than two. In *Proc. CogSci* 2006, 2375-2381.
31. Yatani, K., Sugimoto, M. and Kusunoki, F. Musex: A System for Supporting Children's Collaborative Learning in a Museum with PDAs. In *Proc. WMTE 2004*, IEEE CS Press (2004), 109-113.
32. Yiannoutsoua, N., Papadimitrioua, I., Komisa, V. and Avourisb N. "Playing with" Museum Exhibits: Designing Educational Games Mediated by Mobile Technology. In *Proc. IDC 2009.* ACM Press (2009), 230-233.

"I Lie to Myself that I Have Freedom in My Own Schedule": Productivity Tools and Experiences of Busyness

Gilly Leshed
Department of Communication
Cornell University, Ithaca, NY 14850, USA
gl87@cornell.edu

Phoebe Sengers
Information Science Department
Cornell University, Ithaca, NY 14850, USA
sengers@cs.cornell.edu

ABSTRACT
This paper examines the relationship between experiences of busyness in everyday life and the use of productivity tools, including planners, calendars and to-do lists. Field study findings demonstrate that American individuals across a demographic range have internalized a cultural emphasis of busyness as a moral value to construct positive identities as busy individuals. At the same time, they struggle with a sense of conflict around busyness, reflected in real-life experiences of clashing priorities, fantasies of downtime, and struggles with anxiety, guilt, and loss of control. Our findings also point to the ways digital and non-digital productivity tools are embedded in experiences and coping practices around busyness. Grounded in our observations we propose design principles for productivity tools that support users' identities as busy people but also address some of the perils of the American busyness ethic.

Author Keywords
Busyness, productivity tools, qualitative field study.

ACM Classification Keywords
H5.m. Information interfaces and presentation (e.g., HCI): Miscellaneous.

General Terms
Design, Human Factors.

INTRODUCTION
There is a heavy emphasis in contemporary American culture on busyness, i.e., being in a constant functional, action-oriented state [5]. The jury is still out on whether Americans' work time, paid and unpaid, across genders and occupations, objectively increased or decreased in the past few decades [27 vs. 26]. But busyness is not simply about factually having a lot to do; instead, it is the valuing of "doing more in less time," as well as concrete practices and habits in individuals' daily lives that instantiate this idea.

CHI 2011, May 7–12, 2011, Vancouver, BC, Canada.

In this paper we examine the relationships between everyday busyness experiences in the US[1] and the use of productivity tools, i.e. digital and non-digital tools and artifacts for managing one's time, tasks, and activities, including planners, calendars and to-do lists. We report on a field study of experiences of busy lives and how people from multiple perspectives and demographic backgrounds cope with these experiences. Our findings show that participants have internalized the cultural norm of busyness, seeing being busy an important part of their identities and establishing this in the ways they use their productivity tools. At the same time, our participants' accounts suggest a fundamental sense of conflict around busyness and its costs. Based on our findings, we suggest design guidelines for productivity tools to both support users' identities as busy individuals and provide alternative responses to the downsides of busyness.

Productivity Tools in a World of Busyness
In American culture, a busy lifestyle at work, home, and leisure may signify an ethic to lead action-oriented, productive lives. When asked how one is doing, people often respond, "Busy, busy." The value of busyness is so ingrained in work and leisure that for many it is hard to imagine a life that is not busy. This busyness ethic stands in contrast to alternative cultural norms, such as Latin-American expectation of being late, the Italian siesta, and eschewal of production on Saturdays by Orthodox Jews.

In the American cultural context, a common solution for managing a life perceived as busy is to adopt strategies for optimizing what to do at any given moment in order to be highly efficient [4] and get things done [2]. Productivity tools put such strategies into practice. For instance, Remember The Milk is a popular web application for managing one's to-do items (www.rememberthemilk.com), and RescueTime logs and analyzes time spent on computer applications and websites to boost one's productivity (www.rescuetime.com). These two examples are the tip of the iceberg of IT solutions designed to handle ever-more tasks, activities, commitments, contacts, opportunities, and information. These solutions include, for example, email clients that automatically categorize and prioritize incoming

[1] While our findings are limited to the US, research in other countries such as Canada and the Netherlands [10,36] suggests related ideas of busyness may extend to other nations.

messages to reduce cognitive load, awareness tools that help people find the most appropriate times to contact others, online calendars for efficient multi-party scheduling, and personal information management tools for organizing, storing, and retrieving increasing amounts of documents and information in computer desktops and on the web.

Why do Americans, equipped with a profusion of productivity solutions, feel ever more busy? In part, new information and communication technologies, such as cell phones, email, online calendars, and social media and networking sites, offer not only productivity and efficiency, but also affordances for new pursuits and temporal experiences [33]. These experiences include, for instance, fragmentation and micro-coordination of activities [15] and working in unanticipated times and locations between planned tasks and meetings [24]. These affordances may in turn be fostering high levels of busyness.

In this study, we look at how busyness is experienced, enacted, and responded to in everyday life, and show how individuals' mundane experiences materialize cultural-level norms. We specifically examine the role that productivity tools play in these micro-practices of busyness. What does real American busyness look like on the ground, and how are productivity tools deployed in it? Based on this analysis, we suggest how productivity tools can be better designed to respond to people's experiences of busyness.

FIELD STUDY

Previous ethnographic studies have documented everyday activities, coping strategies, and consequences of experiencing busyness in the workplace and the home [5,17]. These accounts mention the use of productivity tools as part of individuals' efforts to maintain order in their busy life pursuits. Another approach focuses on the use of productivity tools, such as calendars [7,22], email [35], and to-do lists [3], acknowledging the busyness norm in everyday work and home life. In this study, we integrate these two approaches to understand the role that productivity tools play in experiences of busyness, following Wajcman's call for empirical studies addressing the reciprocal relationship between technological innovation and changing time experiences [33]. Between November 2009 and April 2010 we interviewed individuals to understand their daily experiences of busyness and coping strategies, and the use of productivity tools for managing their time and activities.

Participants

In order to include diverse perspectives, we recruited participants from various ages, occupations, and backgrounds. We advertised in community centers, contacted people we thought might have interesting perspectives, and used snowball recruitment. 13 people from a US college town volunteered, each receiving a $20 gift card for participating. Five participants were males and 8 females, in ages from 24 to 75 years (median=38), and 7 were parents. They varied in economic status and occupation, as shown in Table 1.

Method

We met participants for an interview at the time and place of their preference: their home, workplace, a café, etc. We asked participants to have with them ready the tools they use to manage and organize their time and daily activities. Participants showed us physical artifacts such as planners, appointment books, wall calendars, and to-do lists, as well as digital tools like email applications and phone calendars (Table 1 and Figure 1). Interviews were loosely structured, covering three main areas:

1. Daily activities at work, home, and elsewhere; planned and spontaneous activities; deviations from routine; etc.
2. Tools used for managing time and schedule or record activities; what each tool is used for and how; usefulness of and problems with each tool; etc.
3. Feelings and values of busyness and time and task management; whether participants feel more or less busy than others; if they would like to change how they spend their time; etc.

Pseudonym	Gender	Age	Self identification	Productivity tools discussed in interview
Tammy	F	35	Afterschool childcare assistant director	To-do lists, weekly planner
Sarah	F	32	Mother of 3, part time fitness instructor	Wall calendars
Robin	F	30	Community center childcare staff, returning undergraduate student	Weekly planner, school syllabi, running logbook, to-do list in notepad, email, bills payment notebook
Ben	M	24	Musician and afterschool counselor	—
Gina	F	38	"Professional slipper through the cracks of society"	Weekly planner, journal notebook, home chores list
Diana	F	25	Nanny and community college student	Calendar and notes on phone
Keith	M	48	Delivery company truck driver (married to Margie)	Day timer book, company pad computer, to-do lists
Margie	F	48	Stay-at-home mom (married to Keith)	Weekly planner, wall calendar
Nick	M	49	Artist-activist and musician, single father	Weekly planner, to-do lists, email
Stephanie	F	32	Hairdresser and mother of 3 children	Salon appointment book, personal monthly planner, family wall calendar, email on phone
Kurt	M	75	Retiree, widower, formerly college staff member	Weekly planner
Ann	F	58	University professor and department chair	Calendar, task list, and email on phone
Manuel	M	42	Assistant professor, husband and father of 2	Weekly planner, to-do list on office board, family calendar

Table 1. Field study participants, how they identify themselves, and their productivity tools

Interviews lasted 45-100 minutes, and were audio recorded and transcribed. We used open coding to analyze the data, searching for common concepts and identifying themes that reoccur in the data. We next report on these themes and the uses of productivity tools related to each one, organized into three subsections: a pervasive busyness culture, everyday experiences, and strategies for coping with busyness.

FINDINGS

A Pervasive Culture of Busyness

First, our findings confirmed that participants are enacting a culture of busyness. They described long days full of activities at work, at home, in school, and elsewhere. Ann, for example, a university department chair, attends meetings, runs a research lab, writes grants, supervises students, and handles emails early in the morning, late at night, and in between everything else. Keith, a truck driver, spends 10-11 hours hustling through his daily delivery route. Sarah, mother of three young children, cares for the family and the house, teaches fitness classes, trains for triathlons, and volunteers at her children's schools. Even when engaged in fun or leisure activities, our participants seemed task-oriented. For example, Diana describes her packed weekends: "*Sometimes I'll schedule myself so that I'm doing things*

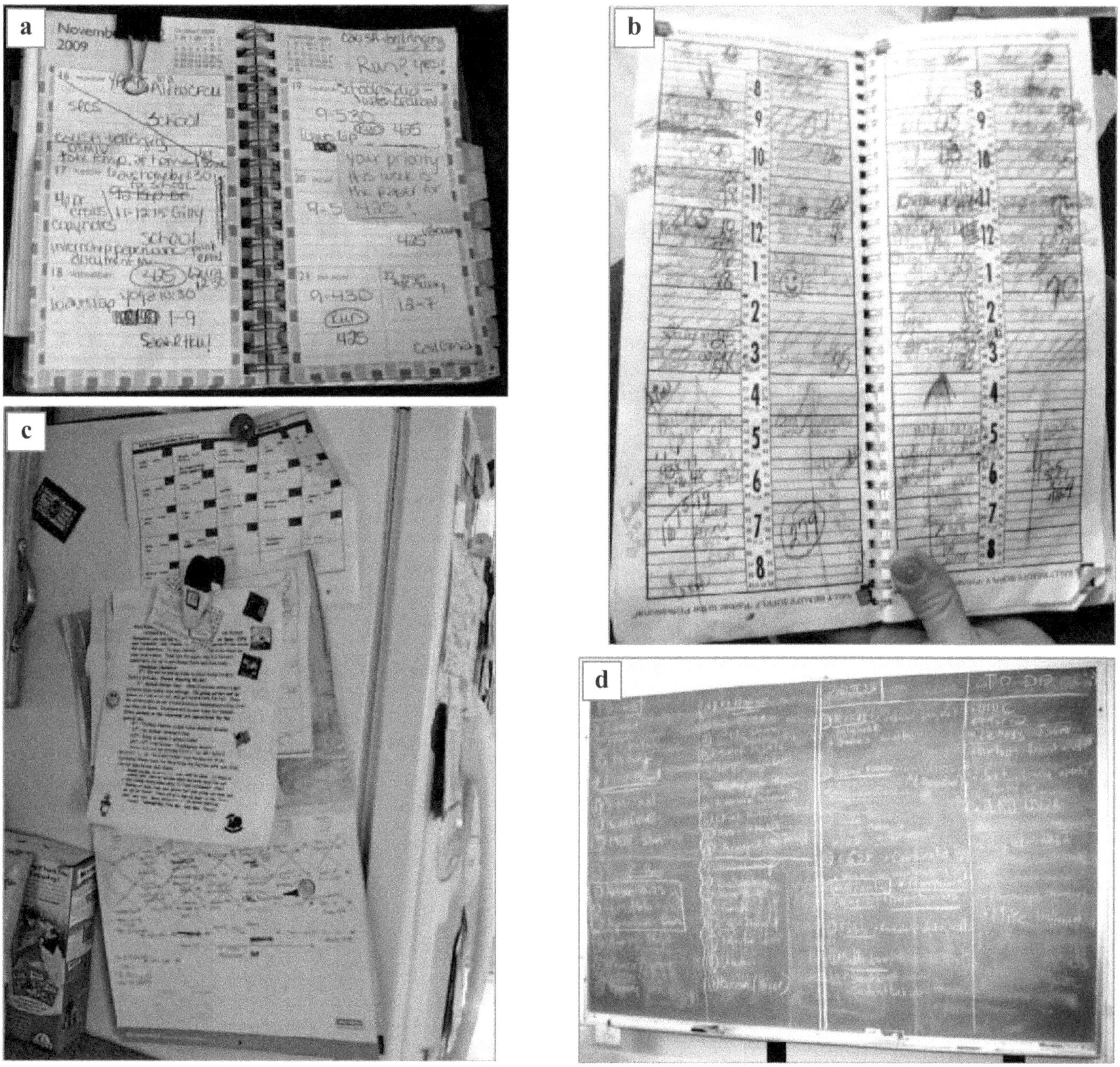

Figure 1. A sample of participants' productivity tools: (a) Robin's weekly planner; (b) Stephanie's salon appointment book; (c) Sarah's family calendars; (d) Manuel's to-do list on his office board

straight through the weekend and then if my sister calls me and wants to hang out, I can't 'cause I'm too busy." The one participant who admitted not being busy, Ben, a band drummer and an afterschool counselor, appeared uneasy sharing that he has a lot of free time to "just" hang out.

Being busy, it became clear, is ingrained in how participants view the world and establish their identities in a specific socio-cultural context. Across occupations and stages of life, they consider being busy an important **personal value**: rewarding, fulfilling, and meaningful; as Tammy says: *"I try to fill the day with accomplishments, meaning, getting things done. And at night, at my time off, as long as everything that needs to be done is done, then I can relax and feel good about it."* Busyness is also seen as a **social norm**, illustrated in the account by Margie, who is married to Keith and mom to Jessica, a disabled 14-year-old:

> *"My husband thinks I don't do anything all day, that I sit and somehow magically the food appears on the table before or shortly after he arrives home, and the house is clean [...], and the child is taken care of [...]. It was very difficult for me when he broke his back and he was home [...]. I felt like there was somebody over my shoulder and I couldn't get anything done [...]. I'm sure that he went back to work convinced that I did nothing all the time."*

Productivity tools seem to play an important role in formalizing one's busy selfhood. Participants often described their days by reading from their tools the details of their activities and tasks and the times in which they accomplished them. They see their productivity tools as essential to their ability to get things done, and as such, supporting their identities as busy people. Robin, juggling a full-time childcare job, studying for a bachelor's degree after a 10-year hiatus, and marathon training, explains the significance of her planner: *"I don't fall behind [...]. I know when I have to be some place, and I know what I need to focus on for that day. I can't just do whatever I feel like doing."*

But while productivity tools help relieve the anxiety associated with packed schedules and too many activities and tasks, this comes with a price. To keep up, participants describe how they perpetually fill up their planners, calendars, and task managers with appointments and tasks; Nick says about his to-do list, *"I'm moving forward but always behind [...] I'm always taking care of old ones but I'm always adding to it."* Further, many express fear of losing their tools. Tammy describes a time when she forgot the planner at home: *"without the planner I feel anxious because I'm supposed to be working off the list!"* These findings indicate a tension between wanting to abide by norms of busyness and the strain that may be associated with this desire.

Experiences of Busyness

Doing and Being

Some participants distinguished between tasks they want to get done with and activities they find rewarding and meaningful. For example, Sarah considers the time spent preparing to go for a workout as wasted, taking away from time of actually exercising. Kurt's morning includes an hour of open-ended reflection and retrospective writing, after which he runs errands and works on house projects. He values accomplishing house projects, but finds deeper meaning in non-task-oriented reflection. Stephanie consciously combines her weekly grocery shopping with spending time with a friend: *"we go get coffee, spend our time at Wegman's [supermarket], [...] and it's just like a girls' time. And then we get our groceries, we're getting the job done."*

Our participants generally aim the use of their productivity tools for practical tasks and activities. They use these artifacts to plan for, remind, document, and prepare for things to do: appointments, meetings, work tasks, homework, workouts, and more. In this sense, these artifacts are seen as supporting one's **doing** rather than what they define as the more in-depth significance of their **being**. Kurt says about his weekly planner: *"It gives me a general structure of what I will be doing, not what I will be thinking or emoting."*

However, the prosaic details of routine actions can also be thought of as defining a person's identity. For instance, Sarah knows that getting her children ready for school or waiting for them to finish their karate class substantiate her identity as a mother, even if she does not savor these mundane activities. This is in accordance with the concept of human agency in Giddens' Structuration theory, that humans simultaneously act and reflexively consider the meanings of their actions, thus coupling the concepts of 'human being' and 'human doing' [13].

Accordingly, we found evidence that productivity tools not only play a functional role, but also give a sense of fulfillment, meaning, and identity. Gina, for example, cuddles her planner as she talks about it, calling it *"my very best friend."* She intentionally chose an attractive-looking planner, and uses it not only for appointments and tasks, but also to record thoughts, feelings, recipes, and books she wants to read. Keith records in his day timer productivity-oriented details such as the time he started his route, number of stops and packages he delivered and picked up, and driving distances. Yet, he considers it a personal diary:

> *"By filling this out at lunch break and then at the end of the day, it's like markers, it's like chapters in a book. [...] I know if I'm having a good day, bad day, or so-so day. [...] I live and die by this thing. Could I survive without it? Yeah, but I wouldn't have the same sense of... accomplishment."*

These findings suggest that productivity tools have a deeper role beyond simply helping people functionally get things done. These tools also help people feel valuable, accomplished, and satisfied; they materialize people's identities and thereby help people both **do** and **be**.

Doing Nothing

When asked, each participant described moments of "doing

nothing" differently: Keith sleeps in and reads the newspaper on Sunday morning; Robin "goofs off" on social networking sites; Nick lingers after a meal instead of doing the dishes; Tammy relaxes on the patio chair. Others say they never really "do nothing", but sometimes get close: Sarah snuggles with her youngest daughter, thinking in her head what to do next; Kurt watches TV on Sunday nights when he doesn't feel like *"doing something intentional"*; And Manuel realizes, *"it will be nice just to have a little time in which you are really not using your mind or your body."*

The latter quote exemplifies a desire for moments of unwinding or relaxation. Stephanie enjoys her 40-minute commute, away from both work and family, listening to her favorite music and sipping coffee. Robin purposely takes Friday nights off: *"you just need to sit there and not do anything and vegetate, because you're just brain-overloaded."* Keith, constantly on the rush at work, is appreciative of unplanned downtime: *"If I'm under-dispatched [...], then I'll do something spontaneous. Go buy a newspaper or go chat with somebody, [...] once in a while the dispatcher screws up and under-dispatches you [...] I take it as a gift from the heavens."*

At the same time, some participants worry about having downtime. Used to a high pace job, Ann expresses uneasiness when work slows down: *"when there's a break or in the summer, there is a lot of I-should-be-doing-something guilt that drags along."* Sarah says: *"There is always something that can be done [...] I'm not really comfortable not doing anything"*. Other accounts indicate a tension between valuing downtime on its own right and justifying it as purposeful relaxation so that one can get back to being busy.

Time for relaxing, unwinding, lingering, or goofing off is similar to the concepts of dead times [24], plastic time [25], British pottering [32], and liming in Trinidad [20]. Whether planned or spontaneous, we found these times to be marginalized and seen as gaps between task-oriented times. They do not appear in participants' productivity tools, even when planned. Instead, productivity tools are reserved for **doing something**, and moments of **doing nothing** have to fit in the blank spots.

Publicly Busy

Experiences of busyness have a strong social component: one's daily schedules and activities are often affected by and affect others. First, participants express commitment to activities that involve others. For example, despite Ann's time-consuming administrative duties, she prioritizes helping colleagues: *"co-professors, postdocs, the people here [...], when they need something I try to make that happen."* Forgetting or being late to social commitments breaks codes of behavior; Ben admits that he is often late to work, which is *"not a good reputation to have."* Social commitments therefore reflect ways in which busy identities become real through being performed (or underperformed) for and with others [14].

Productivity tools reflect the importance of such performance through being particularly used to track participants' activities that pertain to others. For example, Margie marks her daughter's school schedule in her planner to make sure she is home when Jessica arrives from school. Kurt explains what kinds of activities he writes in his planner: *"If it involves other people, where I need to make contact, and not forget it, I'll put that. That's number one."*

Second, when others are involved, one has to coordinate mutual activities to ensure the flow of their own schedules, which is in itself a source of busyness. Sharing productivity tools is one way to support such mutual coordination, at work and at home. Stephanie's salon appointment book always stays at work for other hairdressers to add or update appointments if a client calls when she is out; and Sarah writes her weekend workouts on the family calendar and encourages her husband to put his fishing plans there too so that they are each aware of when the other will be out.

However, some participants are reluctant to share their productivity tools with others. Ann, for example, accessing her online calendar on her phone, stopped using the university system that made her schedule visible to others besides her assistant: *"Not that I have anything to hide, it's just that I don't want everyone else running my life. [...] When I was on this public one, they'd say, I noticed you have this time from 2 to 3 on Friday, and I would be, that's my writing day. So I've had to block things out a little bit more."* Similarly, Stephanie blocks personal times using scribbles in her salon appointment book (Figure 1b) so that other salon employees know when not to schedule clients, but don't know exactly what she will be doing at these times.

These findings suggest a tension between maintaining others' awareness and retaining privacy and control. Despite efforts to apply IT solutions for shared spaces, activities, and calendars that improve coordination among employees [23] and family members [7,21], there might not be a single solution that fits individuals' particular understanding of what should be shared, with whom, and when. We discuss some design principles for handling these tensions below.

Redundancies and Inconsistencies in Productivity Tools

Often, participants showed us a range of digital and analog productivity artifacts and tools (Table 1), raising questions about how they deal simultaneously with all these tools. We observed that each tool offers specific purpose, value, function and materiality, seamlessly integrating with the other tools. Robin's planner (Figure 1a) is a central organizer with pointers to details in her school syllabi, email, running plan, and bill payment notebook. Stephanie maintains a concrete distinction between work and home by keeping her appointment book at the salon (Figure 1b), a family wall calendar at home, and a personal monthly planner in her purse to synchronize between the two. Sarah keeps on the kitchen refrigerator the primary family calendar and "back-up" calendars sent from school with activities, snacks, and volunteering reminders (Figure 1c). Manuel maintains his schedule in a weekly planner he carries everywhere, and visualizes the "big picture" of his work with a list of tasks and projects on his office blackboard (Figure 1d).

At the same time, one instrument may be used for several, seemingly inconsistent purposes. Robin showed us a Post-It note in her planner that says "wash sleeping bag": *"I went camping this summer and I still have not washed my sleeping bag [...]. I keep moving the little Post-It note, because I know it's one thing I can push off."* Figure 1a shows another Post-It note with a message Robin wrote to herself: *"Your priority for this week is the paper for 425!"* Post-It notes offer Robin two distinct affordances: they stand out for highlighting important tasks, and can be moved around for low-priority tasks. This system makes sense for her, despite its inconsistency to the external observer.

Using tools inconsistently or redundantly may require extra work to maintain them simultaneously, synchronize them, and remember how they integrate, implying a difficulty in creating efficient systems that "work". At the same time, these "systems" are uniquely created and appropriated for each person's own purposes and specific needs and as such make sense for them and fit with who they are, and respondents showed little difficulty in managing their integration. We discuss later the extent to which the materiality of physical artifacts may extend to digital productivity tools.

Coping with Busyness

Setting Goals and Priorities

In a busy world where people feel there is a lot to do and not enough time, they must continually negotiate what to spend their time on. Our participants attempt to manage this by setting priorities based on their life perspectives, and, based on these priorities, determine what to do at any given moment. This leads to unique experiences of busyness, where individuals attempt to orient their everyday activities toward identity constructing goals.

For instance, for Nick, parental commitments such as driving his daughter to the mall take precedence over some personal activities as working on his website, but he makes sure nothing interferes with his daily yoga exercise. Diana, who recently moved out of her parents' home, explains how her goals influence her time-spending choices:

> *"Setting up goals where I want to be involves time management. If I want to become healthy then I'm going to set aside time to work out, and if I want to be healthy I'm going to have to set a time to go grocery shopping to buy the foods I need. And if I want to go to school, I'm going to have to set aside time to work on my homework. And I keep my schedule open to work a lot, like, I'll choose work over play now, because I want to save money."*

While the strategy of optimizing activities by setting and following priorities may appear obvious and is a mainstay of the time-management self-help literature, it is important to highlight that this way of thinking may not necessarily be a natural human condition, but rather a pervasive habit shaped by living in circumstances that call for never-ending activity. In a culture where productivity experts exhort people to prioritize, it is remarkable how widely ingrained this practice actually is, or at least is reported to be. It demonstrates the degree to which a busyness orientation has been incorporated into people's everyday lives.

We observed, similar to [3], that planning and recording activities and events in productivity tools are often used to highlight one's goals and priorities. For example, Robin wants to get into a PhD program in psychology and be financially secure after experiencing a divorce and layoff. She writes tasks that pertain to these priorities in her planner and syllabi, marking high-priority tasks using circles, colors, and Post-It notes (Figure 1a): *"I've highlighted this 425 because I know I have to sit down and do the research for that paper and that's really important."* Sarah writes her teaching schedule and her children's afterschool activities on the family calendar to highlight their importance, despite those being routine and mostly consistent (in contrast to [7]). And while Tammy writes home chores in her to-do list, Margie does not, explaining: *"things that are ingrained like grocery shopping, laundry, that sort of stuff doesn't go in there, because it's just what I do."*

These findings again suggest that these tools play a broader role beyond offering time and task management or as memory aids. The **use** and **non-use** of productivity tools, for example, recording a task or an event (or not), can be seen as a way one defines what specific details in their life experiences are important, thereby identifying their personal goals and priorities and constructing one's identity.

Dealing with Conflicts and Constraints

However, life sometimes gets in the way. Keith would rather spend more time with his family and as an athletic coach, and Margie would want to work outside of the house (*"I never really saw myself as necessarily being a stay-at-home mom forever"*). Yet, Keith has to work overtime to provide for Jessica's living and medical expenses, while Margie does the nursing care. Margie describes how her daily schedule is dictated by taking care of Jessica:

> *"Basically my day is driven by her. I have to do what she has to have done, because she isn't physically able to do much of anything for herself. So if she has homework that requires being written out, I have to sit with her and write it out, I'm her scribe. And she has breathing treatments at night, she has feeding that has to be hooked up. [....] So when she's home and her nurse shifts are done, then I'm her nurse, basically."*

The circumstances Keith and Margie face do not afford simply setting life goals and pursuing activities to achieve them. Instead, they had to readjust their priorities in order to make peace with real-life constraints. They compensates a little for their pushed-off passions and aspirations: Margie runs a card-making business from home, and Keith coaches adult swim groups on Monday evenings, justifying it as enough to maintain the spark of coaching (*"I go to my island two hours a week and it just realigns my world"*).

We observed that participants use their productivity tools in idiosyncratic ways in coping with conflicts. Manuel writes in his weekly planner with pencil to make it easy to update his schedule; Tammy rewrites unfinished tasks in the next day's to-do list; Stephanie blocks openings in her calendar knowing she might be running late with clients and will need to catch up; and Ann, so used to double-booking, marks in purple events she will not attend in her color-coded digital calendar. Although productivity tools are often designed within a mindset of "set your goals, decide on the activities that will let you achieve them, and carry out those activities," users uniquely appropriate their tools to renegotiate goals and revise activities on the fly in a world of changing schedules due to dynamic interactions, conflicts and constraints. Gina eloquently expresses the contradictions involved in these negotiations: *"I'm not as organized as I'd like to be, but I know that without something like this to even deviate from, I'd be completely sunk."*

Planning

One of the most significant strategies we observed in coping with busyness given changing constraints, conflicts, and responsibilities is planning. Plans, even those not eventually followed, help participants organize and prioritize their activities, coordinate with others, and anticipate what their schedules are going to look like. For example, Ben describes how he had planned to help at a music concert one night and drive his girlfriend to a medical appointment early next morning, setting two alarm clocks to wake up on time. Robin reorganizes her work hours to fit her marathon training plan. Keith follows his daily route with a plan of packages delivery and pickup, their order and addresses, on the company's pad computer. Although the nature of these plans and the level of control over them vary, participants appreciate having plans because they give a sense of systematicity for getting things done.

Seemingly, our data demonstrate existing stereotypes about the degree to which individuals control their plans, for example, that blue-collar workers are less in control whereas academics can decide on their schedules and tasks. So Ann, a university department chair, can decide if she will travel to Europe for a conference and what research projects to embark on. But facing a myriad of choices of how to carry out her job and struggling to keep up with all the commitments and changes in her daily schedule, she sometimes feels she is losing control (*"I lie to myself that I have freedom in my own schedule"*). In contrast, Keith does not control much of his daily plan (*"I can't control the number of stops, the number of pieces or how the truck's loaded, all I can do is go faster or slower"*), but being able to predict what his day will look like makes him feel in control. This suggests that at a deeper level, **having control** and **feeling in control** are not the same.

Ideally, once plans are made they are to be followed. In reality, they are continually interrupted by impromptu circumstances. Stephanie, for instance, tries to follow the daily plan of clients' appointments written in her salon appointment book, but occasionally a client is late, causing her to run behind schedule. Thus, despite being important for anticipating what will happen, plans are not deterministic, but open-ended, suggestive, and subject to change. Margie's plans change frequently because of unexpected school work demands for Jessica or, worse, because of sudden medical complications:

> *"I like being able to write things down, I like kidding myself that my life is predictable. I could plan to do anything I wanted, and I have accepted now [...] that it's gonna go up the smoke. If I spend too much time downstairs working and I'm late starting whatever I wanted to do upstairs that day, [Jessica] will inevitably come home with 4 hours worth of homework."*

> *"We have a family motto to make wishes not plans, because for a long time whenever we would make plans, we'd get tickets to go to something, inevitably she would get sick, and we'd have to give that up."*

Therefore, while productivity tools are designed to rationally make plans and follow them, real life is full of unexpected, changing interactions and situations. This is the core argument in Suchman's "Plans and Situated Actions" [29], which distinguishes between formal representations of courses of actions and situated real life experiences, and recognizes the dynamic negotiation between the two. Similarly, we do not argue that plans embedded in productivity tools do not matter. They serve an important role in creating feelings of control, order and predictability, negotiating priorities and goals, and as such, constructing identity. This is true even when participants do not create their own plans, when planning happens only mentally, or when plans continually change. The need for order might be a fundamental human trait; as Swan et al. put it, "in ordering things, materially, we unavoidably order ourselves" [30].

DISCUSSION

The results of our study point to two primary topics of discussion: the ways in which participants have incorporated broader cultural norms of busyness into their personal identities through daily experiences and use of productivity tools, and the gaps and glitches in their experiences that suggest underlying conflicted relationship with busyness. Below, we discuss each topic and its implications for the design of productivity tools. Note that our analysis is derived from US-based interview accounts; other cultural perspectives and additional data collection methods would likely lead to different design opportunities.

Enacting Busyness

Our analysis demonstrates how participants enact cultural norms of busyness through their daily practices. Whether or not they are objectively busy, participants certainly *feel* busy and incorporate that sense into their activities and habits. We do not argue that individuals are 'cultural dopes' [11], mindlessly following norms of busyness; rather, given the situations they find themselves in and the cultural alternatives available for them to think those situations through and weigh their opportunities, desires, and values, a focus on busyness becomes a natural choice. An important aspect of this is that busyness is not simply a rational means to an end but has become itself part of Americans' identity and source of fulfillment. So, for example, participants justify moments of downtime by a need to "charge the batteries," given the negative value associated with "doing nothing" in their cultural context.

Our findings further suggest that in experiencing and dealing with everyday busyness, productivity tools have a broader role beyond merely offering a way to organize and prioritize many to-do items or coordinate busy schedules. Participants use these tools to renegotiate their goals and priorities, feel socially committed, manage ever-changing real-life interactions, feel in control, and organize not only what they do, but also who they are. As such, these tools are what Foucault calls "technologies of the self" [9]—tools and techniques through which humans constitute themselves, by engaging in processes in which they define and produce the ethical self-understanding of the 'truth' of their own thoughts and practices. Further, through idiosyncratic use, personalization, and appropriation of an array of productivity tools, these tools play an important emotional role in their users' lives. Our finding are underscored by other studies showing that tools embedded in everyday practices extend beyond their original intent, toward constituting one's personal identity and social values through use and appropriation [e.g., 19,31,34].

Allow Personalization

Our findings show that the idiosyncratic uses and appropriations of productivity tools play important roles in how participants perceive themselves as busy individuals. For example, a calendar book is used by Kurt to plan his upcoming week and anticipate his schedule, by Keith to post-hoc log his work activities and feel satisfied by seeing the details accumulate, by Tammy to list her to-do items and feel accomplished in crossing them out, and by Gina to write down anything that bubbles up in her mind and needs to be recorded at the moment. The material qualities of the calendar book, with pages that can be flipped back and forward and without restrictions for what can be written in them enables a variety of emerging appropriations.

We suggest that designers of productivity tools should welcome unexpected uses as their design iteratively develops beyond mere scheduling or task management. One way to achieve personal appropriation is by keeping the system open for multiple interpretations of how it should be used and experienced [28], where the 'final design' is creatively constructed as the user interacts with the system over time [34]. For example, while email was originally designed as a communication medium, people also use it to manage their tasks and archive information [35]. Allowing users to send themselves email and to create email folders allowed for the emergence of these uses. Another example would be to provide easy access to archived calendared events in a digital calendar. This can offer opportunistic reflection on one's past activities beyond simply managing one's schedule, translating the idea of flipping pages in a calendar book.

Offer Heterogeneity

A quick review of commercial productivity software reveals "all-in-one" solutions for managing emails, schedules, contacts, and tasks (e.g., Microsoft Outlook, Lotus Notes, and Google Apps), protocols for synchronizing calendars, email, and other data between multiple platforms, and web applications accessed from any browser on any machine. Fusing together or synchronizing tools for various contexts and functionalities offers convenience and efficiency, for example, by automatically sending an email when a meeting has been updated. However, Ann's decision not to be on the university's online scheduling system and Robin's suite of calendars, syllabi, and other tools she constantly synchronizes, exemplify the value one may find in maintaining tools detached from a global system.

We suggest that designers of productivity tools consider the specific, heterogeneous functions they want to support before offering an all-encompassing solution. Allowing users to decide what tools to combine and what to leave unconnected offers an additional dimension of personalization and control, allowing users to choose what fits their own identities as busy individuals.

Gaps and Glitches

The overwhelming majority of our participants made clear that being busy is an important part of their identity, and, furthermore, that they enjoy being busy. Our first set of design implications aims to support these practices. At the same time, conflicts and struggles began to emerge through our conversations that suggest a dark side to the American busyness ethic. First, the pervasive desire to be busy stands in contrast to an anxiety associated with having to keep up with the norm, as well as to a longing for and appreciating relaxation and downtime. Second, whereas participants used productivity tools to maintain a sense of control over their schedules and lives, realizations that this sense of control is illusionary glimpsed through their accounts (see also [6]). Third, our findings point to a mismatch between supporting public awareness and retaining privacy and control over one's schedules and activities. Fourth, participants perpetually readjust plans and renegotiate priorities to settle conflicts and constraints between what they find meaningful and what needs to be done.

These findings suggest a significant design opportunity for productivity tools that take into account these forgotten or marginalized aspects of busyness experiences. We are inspired in this by Dunne and Raby's notion of designing for neglected, negative aspects of human experience as a design ethic [8], as well as by Agre's call to open up new spaces for design by inverting core design assumptions [1]. In the case of productivity tools, the design of tools for time, task, and activity management tends to centralize concepts of rational planning, "getting things done", and a fast pace of life. In contrast, neglected but valued aspects of people's experiences with busyness – spontaneity and dynamic interactions, downtime, and slowness – are marginalized, opening an opportunity for alternative design.

Design for Underload and Slowness

Current productivity tools are designed with the assumption that one can better cope with busyness by becoming more efficient and productive. For example, a task manager that keeps track of many to-do items and a scheduling system that helps juggle many appointments relieve the burden of having to keep everything in one's mind. However, these systems are designed within a mindset that one *should* have a lot of to-do items and appointments and that one *should* juggle and manage rather than cut them back.

Our observations suggest that the other side of busyness—slack, inefficient time use, downtime, and slowness—is predominantly ignored in productivity tools. Instead, designers could acknowledge a fundamental need for inefficient downtime, non-functionality, slowness, and gaps between busy times [25,32]. HCI researchers have successfully introduced purposeful slowness into the home and leisure domains [12,16]; this may also benefit businesses and organizations [18]. For example, purposefully delaying email delivery (e.g., realsnailmail.net), while it has drawbacks such as email arriving too late, might in turn evoke reflection on one's level of commitment and about opportunities versus losses in inefficiency and non-productivity.

Highlight Situated Interaction

Productivity tools are designed to help cope with busyness by helping create formal representations of one's daily actions, tasks, and schedules. Our findings, however, suggest that participants incessantly negotiate between what the formal plan pushes toward and dynamically changing daily interactions, experiences, conflicts, and constraints.

We suggest that designers should be wary about creating representations in productivity tools that immerse users in them too much. For example, calendar systems may assist in scheduling multi-party meetings, but everyone must represent all their engagements in the system, "blocking" personal times [23], not leaving room for spontaneity and unmediated engagements. Instead, acknowledging and emphasizing the opportunistic, plastic character of the openings in one's schedule [25] as well as the ephemeral, improvised nature of plans and other formal representations [29] may help downplay the authority of the system and prepare users to better handle unexpected situations.

CONCLUSIONS

Our empirical analysis demonstrates that our relationship with busyness is more complex than that suggested by a simple emphasis on efficient "getting things done" in the manner that drives much of the research and design of productivity tools. While American users of productivity tools have internalized cultural norms of busyness, engagement with productivity tools is not simply an attempt to optimally organize one's schedule and activities, but also includes significant social and emotional dimensions. Engagement with productivity tools is accompanied by a sense of pride in accomplishments, personal feelings of control over one's life, and constructing and reflecting on one's identity. Awareness of these dimensions affords new design opportunities for productivity tools to support not only busyness management but also the emotional and personal journeys through which users are traversing in their lived experiences and identity construction.

Our observations of gaps and glitches in everyday experiences of busyness further suggest a more intricate perspective on busyness than simple idealization. Our participants detailed significant challenges they experience when coping with their busy lives, including guilt or anxiety over how well one measures up to the cultural ideal of a busy citizen, moments of awareness of an actual lack of control over one's schedule despite a superficial sense of freedom, or inability to engage in downtime. The conflicts with what it means to be a busy person suggest an opportunity to intervene with design for alternative values. Our current endeavor in this direction is the GoSlow program that plugs serendipitous moments of pause and reflection into a calendar on one's mobile phone. This highlights the ideas of designing for underload, but can be taken up by users in many different ways and in various contextual situations.

Our work raises questions about the larger context within which productivity tools are embedded, a fast-paced culture with a strong busyness ethic seen as a personal value and a social norm. While redesigning productivity tools may not necessarily change cultural norms, our design suggestions highlight the ethical responsibility of designers to take an active role and make informed choices instead of succumbing to cultural norms allegedly beyond their control. Despite socio-cultural forces, technology may be designed to open a window for slowing down and self-expression as well as speeding up and uniformity.

ACKNOWLEDGEMENTS
We thank Eric Baumer, Carman Neustaedter, Alex Taylor, and especially Lucian Leahu for helpful feedback and advice. This work was supported by NSF grant ISS-0847293.

REFERENCES

1. Agre, P. 1997. *Computation and human experience.* Cambridge, UK: Cambridge University Press.
2. Allen, D. 2001. *Getting things done: the art of stress-free productivity.* New York: Penguin.
3. Bellotti, V., Dalal, B., Good, N., Flynn, P., Bobrow, D.G., & Ducheneaut, N. 2004. What a to-do: studies of task management towards the design of a personal task list manager. *Proc. CHI '04.* 735-742.
4. Covey, S.R. 1990. *The seven habits of highly effective people.* New York: Simon & Schuster.
5. Darrah, C.N., Freeman, J.M., & English-Lueck, J.A. 2007. *Busier than ever! why American families can't slow down.* Stanford, CA: Stanford University Press.
6. Davidoff, S., Lee, M.K., Zimmerman, J., & Dey, A.K 2006. Principle of smart home control. *Proc. UbiComp '06.* 19-34.
7. Davidoff, S., Zimmerman, J., & Dey, A.K. 2010. How routine learners can support family coordination. *Proc. CHI '10.* 2461-2470.
8. Dunne, A. & Raby, F. 2001. *Design Noir.* Basel: Birkhäuser.
9. Foucault, M. 1988. Technologies of the self. In L.H. Martin, H. Gutman & P.H. Hutton (Eds.), *Technologies of the self: A seminar with Michel Foucault* (pp. 16-49). Amherst, MA: University of Massachusetts Press.
10. Frissen, V.A.J. 2000. ICTs in the rush hour of life. *The Information Society*, 16, 65-75.
11. Garfinkel, H. 1967. *Studies in ethnomethodology.* Englewood Cliffs, NJ: Prentice Hall.
12. Gaver, W., Bowers, J., Boucher, A., Law, A., & Pennington, S. 2007. Electronic furniture for the curious home: assessing ludic designs in the field. *IJHCI*, 22(1-2): 119-152.
13. Giddens, A. 1984. *The constitution of society: outline of the theory of structuration.* Berkeley, CA: UC Press.
14. Goffman, E. 1959. *The presentation of self in everyday life.* New York: Doubleday.
15. González, V.M. & Mark, G. 2004. "Constant, constant, multi-tasking craziness": managing multiple working spheres. *Proc. CHI '04.* 113-120.
16. Hallnäs, L. & Redström, J. 2001. Slow technology: designing for reflection. *Pers. Ubiq. Comp.*, 5(3), 201-212.
17. Hochschild, A.R. 1997. *The time bind: when work becomes home and home becomes work.* NY: Metropolitan Books.
18. Honore, C. 2004. *In praise of slowness.* NY: Harper.
19. Kaye, J., Vertesi, J., Avery, S., Dafoe, A., David, S., Onaga, L., Rosero, I., & Pinch, T. 2006. To have and to hold: exploring the personal archive. *Proc. CHI '06.* 275-284.
20. Miller D. & Slater, D. 2000. *The Internet: an ethnographic approach.* New York: Berg.
21. Neustaedter, C. & Bernheim Brush, A.J. 2006. "LINC-ing" the family: the participatory design of an inkable family calendar. *Proc. CHI '06.* 141-150.
22. Neustaedter, C., Brush, A.J., & Greenberg, S. 2009. The calendar is crucial: coordination and awareness through the family calendar. *ToCHI*, 16(1), 1-48.
23. Palen, L. 1999. Social, individual and technological issues for groupware calendar systems. *Proc. CHI '99.* 17-24.
24. Perry, M., O'hara, K., Sellen, A., Brown, B., & Harper, R. 2001. Dealing with mobility: understanding access anytime, anywhere. *ToCHI,* 8(4), 323-347.
25. Rattenbury, T., Nafus, D., & Anderson, K. 2008. Plastic: a metaphor for integrated technologies. *Proc. UbiComp '08.* 232-241.
26. Robinson, J.P. & Godbey, G. 2005. Busyness as usual. *Social Research*, 72(2), 407-426.
27. Schor, J.B. 1991. *The overworked American: the unexpected decline of leisure.* NY: Basic Books.
28. Sengers, P. & Gaver, W. 2006. Staying open to interpretation: engaging multiple meanings in design and evaluation. *Proc. DIS '06.* 99-108.
29. Suchman, L. 1987. *Plans and situated actions.* New York: Cambridge University Press.
30. Swan, L., Taylor, A.S., & Harper, R. 2008. Making place for clutter and other ideas of home. *ToCHI*, 15(2), 1-24.
31. Taylor, A.S. & Swan, L. 2005. Artful systems in the home. *Proc. CHI '05.* 641-650.
32. Taylor, A.S., Wyche, S.P., & Kaye, J. 2008. Pottering by design. *Proc. NordiCHI '08.* 363-372.
33. Wajcman, J. 2008. Life in the fast lane? Toward a sociology of technology and time. *Brit. J. Soc.*, 59(1), 59-77.
34. Wakkary, R. & Tanenbaum, K. 2009. A sustainable identity: the creativity of an everyday designer. *Proc. CHI '09.* 365-374.
35. Whittaker, S. & Sidner, C. 1996. Email overload. *Proc. CHI '96.* 276-283.
36. Zuzanek, J., Beckers, T., & Peters, P. 1998. The 'harried leisure class' revisited: Dutch and Canadian trends in the use of time from the 1970s to the 1990s. *Leisure Studies*, 17, 1-19.

Homebrew Databases: Complexities of Everyday Information Management in Nonprofit Organizations

Amy Voida, Ellie Harmon & Ban Al-Ani
Donald Bren School of Information and Computer Sciences
University of California, Irvine
{amyvoida, ellie.harmon, balani}@uci.edu

ABSTRACT
Many people manage a complex assortment of digital information in their lives. Volunteer coordinators at nonprofit organizations are no exception; they collectively manage information about millions of volunteers every year. Yet current information management systems are insufficient for their needs. In this paper, we present results of a qualitative study of the information management practices of volunteer coordinators. We identify the resource constraints and the diverse and fluid information needs, stakeholders, and work contexts that motivate their information management strategies. We characterize the assemblages of information systems that volunteer coordinators have created to satisfice their needs as 'homebrew databases.' Finally, we identify additional information management challenges that result from the use of these 'homebrew databases,' highlighting deficiencies in the appropriateness and usability of databases and information management systems, more generally.

Author Keywords
Homebrew databases, information management, nonprofit, NPO, volunteer coordination, volunteer management.

ACM Classification Keywords
H.4.1 [Information Systems Applications]: Office Automation

General Terms
Design, Human Factors

INTRODUCTION
> This is where we get crazy. This is nuts. We actually—we don't have a database of our volunteers.... I shouldn't say that. We have probably seven databases for volunteers. All of them have different information. It took us three to four months to even figure out who had what databases (P1).

People manage a complex assortment of digital information in their lives. In the workplace, the volume and diversity of information to be managed poses a significant challenge for knowledge workers [4]. In the home, people manage ever-larger collections of digital information—media, in particular [20].

Some consumer applications provide databases tailored to support the management of specific types of data for individuals or small groups (e.g., iTunes). In contrast, enterprise applications (e.g., PeopleSoft) are designed to manage vast amounts of complex organizational data. Somewhere in between lie the information management needs of many people—people with information that is more complex than a music library but who are unable to confront the overhead involved in designing, learning and using enterprise database systems.

During our research with nonprofit organizations, we discovered one class of workers, volunteer coordinators, with compelling information management needs that fall in this middle ground. In the United States, where this research took place, approximately 63.4 million people (~27% of the population) volunteered for a nonprofit organization last year [6]. In order to manage this massive number of volunteers, 62% of charities and 37% of religious congregations have a paid staff member who coordinates volunteers [24]. Volunteer coordinators must manage a diversity of information associated with their volunteers, such as demographic, contact and scheduling information. Although volunteer coordinators work in an organizational context, there is typically little, if any, organizational information technology in place to support their information work. With little or no formal training in information systems, volunteer coordinators have created their own unique 'homebrew' information management systems, taking advantage of whatever media and technologies they have access to. However, the complexity of these homebrew solutions—for example, seven databases about volunteers with so many different owners that it took months to find them all (P1)—highlights deficiencies in the appropriateness and usability of databases and information management systems, in general.

In this paper, we present results of our qualitative, empirical study of the information management practices of volunteer coordinators. We describe their information needs and the context and constraints that motivate their choices about how to manage information. We characterize the resulting assemblage of resources, media, and technology they draw upon as 'homebrew databases.' A *homebrew database* denotes an assemblage of information management resources that people have pieced together to satisfice their information management needs. In our research, these assemblages sometimes included actual database software, but typically consisted of other resources such as spreadsheets, email clients, and paper records. Regardless of the systems used to manage this information, participants still referred to this assemblage as their "database" or "databases." We follow their lead, then, in calling these systems homebrew databases, although we emphasize that the media and technology they are composed of are not all technically databases, even though most of the types of data that our participants worked with would be well suited to being managed in a database system. To conclude, we unpack the challenges arising from the use of homebrew databases and discuss implications for the design of databases and information management tools.

RELATED WORK

Information Management in Knowledge Work

Studies of workplace information management have typically focused on how people manage particular types of information, such as files [1], email [2, 25], or schedules [19]. This application-centric research has highlighted the extent to which personal information management tools have been overloaded to accommodate other information management needs. For example, email was used for task management, calendaring, and reminding [2, 25]; calendars were used for task management, contact management, and accounting [19]. The use of multiple applications, each suited to a particular task or genre of information and each incurring its own information management overhead, has led to problems of fragmentation [3].

Other research has examined information management at the intersection of various tools and media. Boardman and Sasse studied the use of three information management tools—files, email, and bookmarks; their findings suggest that individuals' information management strategies vary dramatically across these tools [4]. Researchers have also explored the complementary affordances and use of paper and digital media in information management [15, 21].

We extend this body of research by exploring the synergies and conflicts that arise when multiple tools are overloaded and used simultaneously for information management. In addition, we provide a complementary perspective on work practices; instead of setting our unit of analysis on a particular application or type of information, as most research in this area has done (see [15] for a notable exception), we examine the more holistic work practices of a particular class of knowledge worker, enabling us to better understand the relationships and movement among multiple systems used within the context of work.

The Usability of Database Systems

As early as 1978, human factors researchers suggested that attention be paid to the usability of database systems [22]. In the intervening years, SIGMOD, the ACM Special Interest Group on Management of Data invited two keynote speakers to address database usability [9, 11]. Jagadish et al. noted that database research has followed two main paths towards increased usability—exploring query interfaces and personalization. However, their assessment of the overall usability of databases is a clear call to action:

> ...when we see how information is created, accessed, and shared today, database technology remains only a bit player: much of the data in the world today remains outside database systems. Even worse, in the places where database systems are used extensively, we find an army of database administrators, consultants, and other technical experts all busily helping users get data into and out of a database.... Unfortunately, databases today are hard to design, hard to modify, and hard to query [11].

Our study of volunteer coordinators' homebrew databases reinforces this call to action. We provide a concrete context for understanding specific usability challenges that individuals face when in a position to incorporate the use of databases into their information management strategies.

Information Technology in Nonprofit Organizations

Studies of information technology use in nonprofit organizations (NPOs) have focused on diverse application areas, from use in fundraising [10] to inter-organizational coordination [13, 23] to IT management, more broadly [17]. More generally, this related work foregrounds the underlying context and constraints of technology use within NPOs—the significant resource and expertise constraints influencing technology use, the ways that volunteers change the dynamic of the organization and influence technology use, and the underutilization of technology when NPOs do not see a connection between technology use and their underlying mission or values (see, in particular [7, 14, 17]). Researchers have also observed instances in which the databases used by an NPO were augmented for "day-to-day operations," either by paper-based records [13] or by additional, partially redundant databases [16].

We extend this work by unpacking reasons why volunteer coordinators augment databases and explore the additional challenges that arise as a result of the use of multiple tools.

METHOD

Participants

We recruited 23 participants (22 female) who were responsible for managing volunteers in an NPO. For some participants, the work of volunteer coordination comprised their full-time jobs. Other participants undertook this coordination work alongside other responsibilities within the organization (e.g., fundraising, communications, or administration). Other participants were volunteers, themselves, and took on the work in retirement or in addition to another full-time, paying job.

We recruited participants in three different metropolitan areas in the western United States, primarily via snowball sampling. We also advertised the research at a volunteer recruitment fair on a university campus. We continued recruiting participants until we had achieved data saturation and sampling breadth along two dimensions: the size of the volunteer program and the domain of the nonprofit. Participants represented volunteer programs along a continuum from those just starting to recruit volunteers to those managing established programs with ~2300 volunteers. Participants also represented seven of nine major classes of nonprofits, including arts, education, environment, health, human services, foreign affairs, and public benefit (e.g., community service clubs) [18].

Data Collection

We conducted semi-structured interviews using a protocol designed around the following areas of interest:

- The background of the organization, its mission, and the ways that the interviewee believed her work and the work of the volunteers contributed to this mission;
- The background of the interviewee, how she came to work in volunteer management, and whether she had received any formal training for her work;
- The nature of the work undertaken by the interviewee, with an emphasis on coordination work both within and outside of the organization; and
- The role of digital and analog technologies in her work.

During the interview, we also asked participants to sketch their social networks. We prompted participants to indicate specific information interdependencies with each colleague or group of colleagues as well as the technologies used to communicate or coordinate with each.

Interviews lasted 60 minutes, on average. We conducted all interviews singly or in teams of two, and all researchers used the same interview protocol. Researchers met weekly while collecting data to discuss the interview data and to revisit the protocol, where necessary, in light of each new interview. We interleaved data collection and data analysis.

Data Analysis

The research team collaboratively analyzed each interview transcript. The most prevalent topic discussed was the "databases" that were variously used, worked-around, and/or abandoned by the participants. In this analysis, then, we focused on the interview data that related in some way to what participants referred to as their "databases" and to information management, more broadly. Using inductive qualitative methods [8], we iteratively developed a coding scheme related to participants' information management practices. Our initial set of codes typically related either to specific kinds of information management challenges or to rationales for using particular systems. Subsequent iterations of the coding scheme helped to differentiate between challenges rooted in the work context and challenges created (or exacerbated) by the participants' choice of systems. In addition, we identified clusters of systems that shared similar motivations for adoption and resultant challenges for information work. Our final iteration of the coding scheme helped us focus on the cyclic nature of information management strategies.

VOLUNTEER COORDINATION: AN OVERVIEW

The volunteer coordinator manages an organization's volunteer program, which is "a vehicle for facilitating and coordinating the work efforts of volunteers and paid staff toward the attainment of organizational goals" [5]. Additionally, our results suggest that from a public-facing perspective, the volunteer coordinator is "the port of entry for volunteers to get engaged in [an] organization" (L2[1]). The volunteer coordinator recruits, trains, places, follows up with, and recognizes volunteers, while continually working to keep them engaged within the organization. However, the work of the volunteer coordinator is not wholly outward facing; much of the work involves coordination within the organization, as well. Volunteer coordinators work with other staff members to help identify volunteer opportunities throughout the organization. They maintain an acute awareness of all programs and activities carried out across the organization, "...stick[ing] your nose into everything that's going on in the rest of the organization because you have volunteers everywhere" (D2). Both for herself and for others, the volunteer coordinator generates numerous reports about volunteers and about the state of volunteerism within the organization.

HOMEBREW DATABASES: CASE STUDIES

Managing information about an organization's volunteer base—such as names, contact information, and schedules—is central to the work of volunteer coordination. Here, we describe two different case studies of homebrew databases in order to exemplify the most common information management strategies used by participants in this research.

A Youth Development Nonprofit's Homebrew Database

O1 is one of two volunteer coordinators at a local affiliate of a national youth development NPO. She works half-time and manages a new group of 60–120 volunteers per quarter.

O1 collects information about potential volunteers via email. Once a potential volunteer RSVPs for an orientation and training session, O1 transfers his or her name and contact information to an Excel spreadsheet associated with the given month's training session. O1 maintains separate spreadsheets for the RSVP lists to different events as well as separate spreadsheets for current and past volunteers:

> I have this very massive, detailed RSVP to the training list for every month that I update pretty much every day and there's – it's color coordinated, it's all fancy (O1).

O1 collects information from confirmed volunteers via several paper-based forms: a signed volunteer contract; questionnaires about their skills, interests, schedules and availability; and a background check provided by the local police department. O1 then copies selected information from these forms by hand onto index cards, one per

[1] We refer to each of our participants based on the domain of work undertaken by their NPO [18]. For example, NPOs working in the area of housing and shelter have a domain code that begins with the letter "L." Multiple participants within the same domain are differentiated numerically (e.g., L1 and L2).

volunteer, and staples the index card to the front of each volunteer's packet of information as a quick reference. She uses these cards to help in placement and scheduling:

> You should see me.... I collect their packet and I staple it all and I have their...index card with their name, I highlight their name, their availability and their email address. It's like I see it all there because it's on a couple different pieces of paper and I sit there...with my chart and I figure out, you know, where I'm going to put who.... (O1).

After O1 places and schedules volunteers, these packets of information are filed alphabetically in a three-ring binder for the current quarter. O1 is in the process of entering volunteer contact information into a database used by the rest of the organization but has not yet caught up with the data entry backlog. As a result, she noted that when the NPO's "emails go out, our volunteers don't get those...."

Instead, O1 sends her own e-newsletter to the volunteers. O1 was originally cutting and pasting email addresses from her Excel spreadsheets into Outlook, but because it took too long, she had an intern help her re-enter all the volunteer information into Outlook. Unfortunately, the distribution lists are too long to use within Outlook, so she has returned to cutting and pasting from her Excel spreadsheets.

O1 uses another quarterly set of three-ring binders to log volunteer hours. All volunteers have a separate page in the binders where they are responsible for signing in and out and logging their hours worked each time they volunteer.

A Human Services Nonprofit's Homebrew Database

P1 is the volunteer coordinator at a local affiliate of national human services NPO. The national organization has a suite of web-enabled databases for tracking volunteers, donors, and clients, but these tools do not fully meet the needs of the local NPO. Because of this, the local NPO maintains their own homebrew database for ~2300 volunteers.

P1 first collects information about potential volunteers from a website when they register for orientation and later via a set of paper applications filled out at that orientation. P1 tracks the application process on paper until the prospective volunteer passes a background check. Then, the documents are scanned onto a shared network drive, and some data are manually entered into the homebrew database.

The foundation of this homebrew database is a shared Microsoft Outlook address book. Information about each volunteer, including his or her name and contact information, is managed in an address book entry. Extra fields are repurposed to store additional information such as race, ethnicity and job title. When volunteers attend training sessions or receive certifications, this information is tracked in the free-form notes section of their address book entries. The volunteers, themselves, are also given paper certificates as a record of their training, which can be used as a backup for the NPO's data: "we ask everybody to hold onto them just in case, because of us and our crazy databases" (P1).

Although the Outlook address book is set up to be shared throughout the organization, many of P1's colleagues prefer to maintain their own copies of the information. In fact, most departments maintain separate, somewhat-duplicate rosters of volunteers:

> Yes. It's on our server. But, again, some people don't use it. They want to create their own. That's what had happened, there are probably about eight different Outlooks that were out there.... So when I got here I was, like, "You are kidding me." So when they would say, like, "Can you do an hourly report, how many hours our volunteers have done in the last..." I was, like, "What? Can I even get a roster of our volunteers?" (P1)

P1 and her colleagues also maintain a "massive Excel spreadsheet" for tracking the hours of ~1500 adult volunteers. (Hours of ~800 youth volunteers are kept in a separate spreadsheet.) The spreadsheet-based system has recently evolved from one-file-per-month-per-department to a single shared file used for an entire year. This file has been enhanced to include formulas for calculating things like volunteer hours across departments and months. To keep the formulas working, anyone doing data entry has to add new volunteers at the bottom of the first page of the spreadsheet, out of alphabetical order. Each department is responsible for collecting their volunteers' hours and entering them in this shared spreadsheet.

P1 maintains contact with volunteers via a bi-monthly e-newsletter. She sends newsletters in batches using Outlook, "four separate e-mails because it will drag our server down so quickly." Volunteers also receive NPO-wide e-newsletters from the marketing department. As such, P1 is also responsible for entering volunteer contact information into the separate system used by marketing.

P1 is currently in the process of trying to streamline her information management practices. She is working with a software engineer who has volunteered his services full-time to the organization (a short-term arrangement). The volunteer is building a Microsoft Access database that they hope will be used throughout the organization to manage volunteer data:

> Without [this volunteer], I don't know where we'd be right now, frankly. Because he spends all of his time building [the database] while we are running the department.... So I don't know how we would do [it], because it's a full-time job in and of itself (P1).

HOMEBREW DATABASES: THE CONTEXT OF INFORMATION MANAGEMENT

Our results suggest that volunteer coordinators' choices and configurations of homebrew databases are motivated by a number of salient features of their work contexts.

The Diversity and Fluidity of Information Needs

Volunteer coordinators manage a diversity of information:

- *Individual volunteers*: names, contact and demographic information, schedule and availability, photos, program areas, skills/certifications, experience, dates and times of volunteer service, valuation of the volunteer's time (for calculating in-kind donations), background check, and liability waivers or other signed contracts.

- *Groups of volunteers* (e.g., corporate employees or church youth groups): name of the organization sending the volunteers, group leader name and contact information, group size, skills or physical abilities of the group, number of staff needed to supervise the group, total people-hours volunteered, and photos of the group.
- *Volunteer opportunities*: description of the opportunity, number of volunteers needed, schedule (dates and times), location, experience or training required, program area or department, and name of the supervisor.
- *Volunteer events* (e.g., orientations, training sessions, feedback roundtables, and recognition ceremonies): names and contact information for individuals who have RSVPed and often what informational resources the individual has already been sent.

This diversity of information needs is due, in part, to the complexity of the volunteer coordinator's job. In many cases, one individual manages the equivalent of an entire human resources department. The diversity is also due to the different kinds of stakeholders that must be supported; volunteers, nonprofit staff members, and representatives of other organizations all have information needs that the volunteer coordinator has to fulfill.

Volunteer management is also characterized by a fluidity of information needs. Volunteer coordinators reported frequently changing information management strategies to respond to new information needs from internal and external stakeholders, for example, as a result of new funding opportunities. In addition, many of the volunteer coordinators we interviewed had been working at their job for less than a year and/or were part of a new volunteer coordination department. As such, information needs were still evolving as the individuals and departments came to better understand their job or role within the organization.

The diversity and fluidity of information needs manifests in system requirements for *supporting diverse types of data*, from photos to scheduling information to legal documentation. Further, *underlying schemas and reports need to change as information needs change*.

The Diversity and Fluidity of Stakeholders

Volunteer coordinators work with a diversity of stakeholders, both internal and external to the organization:

- *Volunteers* typically approach the volunteer coordinator via email with inquiries about opportunities to volunteer. They send information about themselves, their interests and schedules. They RSVP for orientation and training sessions. In some instances, particularly when working with children, they are responsible for obtaining a background check and ensuring that the resulting paperwork is on file with the nonprofit. Volunteers sign in at the nonprofit and log their hours when volunteering. Some volunteers request reports about how many hours they have worked so that they can add that information to their résumé or provide verification for a community service requirement (e.g., at school). Many volunteer coordinators also reported continually reaching out to new demographics of volunteers; their efforts helped ensure a continued diversity of volunteers.
- *Group leaders* represent volunteers from other organizations, such as religious institutions or corporations. Group coordinators sign up to volunteer on behalf of their groups and negotiate terms of service with the volunteer coordinator (e.g., what service activities would be done as well as who would provide supplies for the project). Most commonly, group coordinators maintain their own rosters of volunteers, reporting to the nonprofit volunteer coordinator information about the number of volunteers who should be expected.
- *Institutions* such as schools or the criminal justice system send volunteers to the NPO to fulfill a specific number of service hours. These institutions have additional information needs including volunteer contracts with expectations for both the volunteer and the nonprofit, timesheets to be signed, and evaluations to be written.
- *Other Staff Members within the Nonprofit* (e.g., program and event coordinators) work with the volunteer coordinator to identify volunteer opportunities, create job descriptions, identify required training or expertise, provide scheduling information, and estimate the number of volunteers needed. The volunteer coordinator matches volunteers with these opportunities.
- *Accounting and development departments* within the NPO also have specific information needs. Some accountants maintain records about volunteer service hours to track in-kind donations. Data about hours volunteered are also frequently used by colleagues working on grant writing and development.

Volunteer coordinators also manage a fluid group of stakeholders. Some are working to provide a greater number of episodic—short term or one-time—volunteer opportunities to bring in new volunteers; others are constantly reaching out to new demographics of volunteers.

The diversity and fluidity of stakeholders manifests in requirements that systems can *scale gracefully*, both in terms of the amount and kind of data within the system as well as the number of users of the system.

The Diversity and Fluidity of Work Contexts

Many volunteer opportunities happen in the community—at schools, building sites, urban shelters or food pantries, settings without consistent or predictable information systems infrastructures. Some NPOs offer volunteers the opportunity to respond in crisis situations, as well. In these situations, the timing of volunteer work, the location of the service opportunity, and the quality of the infrastructure (information technology or otherwise) cannot be predicted in advance. These contexts for volunteer work and, therefore, the contexts for the work of the volunteer coordinator are diverse and changing. This diversity and fluidity manifests in requirements that systems be *accessible from multiple locations*, whether that access is mobile, web-based or otherwise.

Constraints in Time, Funding, and Expertise

The work of volunteer coordinators is characterized by pragmatic constraints in time, funding, and expertise. Many volunteer coordinators work only part-time in that capacity. In addition, many volunteer coordinators reported that interactions with volunteers and clients were the "real" work; the related information management responsibilities, although important, were less of a priority to them.

The work of volunteer coordinators is also constrained by funding. In particular, organizational information system infrastructure seemed to be more commonly allocated to support engagement with donors than with volunteers.

Finally, the work of volunteer coordinators is constrained by a general lack of expertise in information systems. Many volunteer coordinators were trained in the domain of the nonprofit (e.g., biology or education) or otherwise had received little training in information systems designed for organizational contexts. Many of the volunteer coordinators were relatively new to the organization or their departments were new. Thus, there was also frequently a lack of expertise in the organization's information systems (if they existed at all). Finally, some volunteer coordinators rely on volunteers to help with their information management; because of the fluidity of volunteers, there can also be a general lack of expertise within the volunteer pool, as well.

These constraints mean that *learnability* is a key factor in the adoption (or abandonment) of information systems. In lieu of time and funding for extensive training, participants believed that they and their volunteers should ideally be able to 'walk-up-and-use' information systems.

HOMEBREW DATABASES: THE MULTIPLICITY OF SYSTEMS

The diversity and fluidity of information needs, stakeholders, and contexts as well as time, funding, and expertise constraints all factor into decisions about which information systems to use. As these factors change, so do the assemblages of systems that are used to manage that information.

The volunteer coordinator's homebrew database is often distributed across numerous different systems. As such, the vast majority of volunteer coordinators have to manually enter information about volunteers into multiple information systems, including calendar systems, spreadsheets, address books, and other databases. Each application enables the data to be used in different but equally important ways. When NPOs collaborate with other organizations or are local affiliates of a national NPO, they often have to enter and maintain information in databases owned and managed by these other groups, as well.

When a volunteer coordinator matches a volunteer with an opportunity, the management of information about that volunteer often transfers to another staff member within the organization—typically either a program or event manager. These individuals often have more specific information needs driven by the particularities of their programs or events. For example, the volunteer coordinator at an animal welfare NPO recruited volunteers to foster animals in their homes. The foster program manager maintained information about these volunteers in her database—the animal database; the volunteer coordinator had to manually move those data over to her own volunteer database to consolidate volunteer information in one place:

> They enter foster hours when a foster kiddo [animal] is returned. Then their database, which was our animal database, which is not our volunteer database, generates the number of hours that were put in, averaged at about two hours a day. And then we take those and put those into ours... (D2).

In some instances, volunteer coordinators reported that even when they had a shared infrastructure for maintaining volunteer information, other staff members frequently duplicated information to customize it for their own needs. Practices of syncing back to the shared "database" were tenuous at best: "[A co-worker] would take my information, copy it and drag it into hers. I didn't know, always, if she was making changes" (P1).

This multiplicity of systems and duplication of data leads to (1) overhead for entering data into multiple systems, (2) version control issues in which information falls out of sync among "databases" and, (3) the abandonment of certain "databases" and the relinquishing of the functionality afforded by that particular "database." Indeed, L2 reported that her biggest frustration was that...

> ...nothing syncs. You have to do multiple entries for everything. And at the point when you have to do multiple entries is when you don't do entries. You know, it just is so time-consuming and redundant that you have so many other things to do, that you just don't have the time to enter it (L2).

Volunteer coordinators typically create their homebrew databases by drawing from three classes of systems: *personal office applications*, *paper*, and *enterprise or custom databases*. In addition to the overall challenges resulting from the use of multiple systems, each class of systems creates its own challenges for information management. Each volunteer coordinator created her own unique assemblage of systems and typically experienced a subset of these challenges related to the particular classes of systems present in her homebrew database.

Personal Office Applications as "Databases"

Despite the quantity and complexity of the information managed, most volunteer coordinators use personal office applications such as Microsoft Excel and Outlook for managing volunteer data. These tools are not merely part of a larger information workflow. Rather, nearly all of the volunteer coordinators in our study use one of these tools as a primary repository for some form of information, even at organizations managing over 1,000 volunteers.

Most volunteer coordinators use multiple spreadsheets to track different but often overlapping kinds of information—for example, corporate, regular, and prospective volunteers; volunteers by department; and hours by department.

Volunteer coordinators also track volunteer information in email address books and in email messages, themselves. Some volunteer coordinators use email as the primary "database" for storing all volunteer information. Others use multiple address books, shared address books, user-customizable fields, and hierarchical distribution lists.

The problems that arise from the use of personal office applications as "databases" center on issues of scale and inaccessibility. Personal office applications fail to scale along three dimensions: number of users, number of records, and dimensions of data. First, although these applications allow for some collaboration, granting access to a large number of users means that shared files are often locked for editing. Second, the increase in the number of records stored in individual spreadsheet files, for example, leads to situations in which a file grows too large to open in a reasonable amount of time. Limitations of personal e-mail clients means that e-mails intended for wide distribution cannot be sent to hundreds (or thousands) of individuals:

> We were crashing the system for a year and a half and no one told us. {Laughter} Our network would go down every time we sent an email out to all the volunteers, but there was never the connection made. And one day I was pulled over to the data room and, "Do you recognize these email addresses?" I'm like, "Yes, those are our volunteers!" (D2)

Working around these issues requires the adoption of additional systems (e.g. email marketing services) or the additional effort of separating recipient lists into multiple smaller sets and manually sending out emails in batches. Third, personal office applications do not scale well for tracking information along multiple dimensions. For example, when tracking volunteer hours, some coordinators found it difficult to maintain data both from an individual perspective (e.g., for recognizing service) and from a departmental perspective (e.g., for documenting the total monetary value of volunteer work for a particular program).

Another problem with using personal office applications as "databases" is the inaccessibility of the data. Volunteer coordinators frequently create reports about volunteers' service. Although the Outlook address book, for example, is easily adapted to store additional information, it does not provide tools to generate these kinds of reports. Volunteer coordinators struggle to access and aggregate data siloed in multiple files, or worse, multiple programs:

> I guess what's tricky for me is I don't really have one database or one list of everyone. They're in these different spots. So if I wanted to, like, do a mass email to everyone, I don't have that capability (C2).

Additionally, information stored in personal office applications is difficult to access from off-site locations, where a significant amount of volunteering takes place.

Although these problems related to scale and inaccessibility are significant, it is also important to understand why something like Outlook may be a *good* choice for managing human resources information in the first place. Tools like Outlook and Excel satisfy many of the constraints within which volunteer coordinators work: they are already available on NPO computers and do not require additional expense or training. The fluidity of stakeholders—volunteers, in particular—means that technologies need to be familiar and accessible to many people. In addition, personal office applications can be appropriated flexibly and generally provide basic multi-user functionality.

Paper-Based "Databases"

Perhaps more surprising than the pervasive use of personal information management tools is the extent to which volunteer coordinators, even in large organizations, use paper as a substantive part of their information management workflow. This was the case for half of our participants, who often noted the seeming absurdity of the situation:

> We give anniversary pins, you know, for every year and then every subsequent five years. From what I understand somebody went through our paper files and figured [it] out, looked at the orientation date. And we have over 1,000 volunteers! (P1)

Many volunteer coordinators collect applications and contracts on paper-based forms. Volunteers frequently report hours on paper sign-in sheets. Liability waivers and emergency contact forms are almost always kept on paper; these records are typically maintained at a worksite and only later archived at the organization's primary office. Sometimes a subset of information from these forms is entered into a computer-based information management system. In one NPO, paper forms are scanned into the computer, although the data stored on them is not translated from handwriting to queryable digital text. In many cases, forms remain paper-based and destined for filing cabinets.

Paper "databases" suffer from similar issues of scalability and inaccessibility as personal office applications, only magnified. Searching, sorting, and aggregation require that information either be processed manually or duplicated in the computer, both of which are time consuming tasks.

Yet, paper fills many information management needs of volunteer coordinators. For many participants, paper plays a key role in supporting collaborations:

> We have it that way in a physical book because myself, [my supervisor, and a co-worker from another department] all look at the book from time to time and see what's open, so it's getting kind of toted everywhere (L1).

With multiple users, a single copy of a paper-based "database" does not lead to version control problems. In a number of instances, when computer-based "databases" were duplicated and drifted out of sync, a common strategy was to revert to the use of paper-based systems to have one, easily identifiable, master copy of the data. Paper-based "databases" also serve as a functional lowest-common denominator in organizations where not all employees have access to the same technological infrastructure or the skills to use it. A volunteer coordinator at one NPO schedules volunteers on a print out given to her by the project coordinator because she does not have access to the application that he uses to plan the work (L2). A volunteer coordinator at another NPO tracks volunteer hours on paper because the volunteers work in a kitchen without a computer (K1). The portability of paper, then, is also an asset, particularly for NPOs that work at off-site locations.

Finally, paper is also useful for maintaining a shared awareness of processes. For example, P1 uses checklists and a series of trays to track the state of volunteer applications, not only for herself, but also for the office volunteers who come in and out throughout the day. By having information sorted based on applicants' standings, someone can immediately see what task to start on next.

Enterprise and Custom Databases

Roughly one-third of participants use some form of enterprise-level or custom database software. These range from full-featured database systems designed specifically for NPOs, like The Raiser's Edge[2], to more general business-oriented tools, such as ConstantContact[3]. One volunteer coordinator at a youth services NPO, for example, has appropriated VolunteerMatch[4] for managing many of her volunteer information needs:

> All of our short-term opportunities are directly linked to VolunteerMatch. So, anyone who looks for that short-term opportunity will show up in that reporting system. So, we have a way of capturing all of their data and their information and pulling – downloading reports (O2).

This one service allows her to manage sign-ups and scheduling, access information about each volunteer, and run reports to target new opportunities to individuals who had volunteered for similar activities in the past.

However, none of the volunteer coordinators have been successful in transitioning entirely to a single database, even one designed specifically for NPOs. Those who use an enterprise-level database do so alongside other tools. Many volunteer coordinators who expressed interest in enterprise or custom databases also expressed concerns that using a new piece of software—especially database software—would require dedicating time and money to develop the system and train people to use it:

> I know everything that we've looked at, I think you feel like you still kind of have to build a lot and that it's not as easy to set up as you kinda hope it would be (P1).

In addition to setup time, volunteer coordinators who were currently using databases experienced them as introducing new data entry and data management overhead: "The problem is it's a full-time job. Literally, I could sit at a computer nine hours a day and enter in those volunteer applications" (O2). Thus, even organizations that had functional databases are not able to fully utilize them:

> So, I guess that's part of the daily [work], too, is the input of the night before's volunteer hours, which is a little backed up right now... My volunteer who does that has been sick for a while.... We try to keep up with it and it just gets away from you. We could use extra hands, but that means extra computers and extra spots to sit (K1).

Additionally, data in databases are often perceived as not being accessible or in a usable format. Because different stakeholders often have different information needs, even when a volunteer coordinator uses a database to manage the majority of her information, she often reported exporting data to an Excel spreadsheet for herself or other collaborators, recreating the challenges of data redundancy that the database is intended to mitigate: "Once they're all there [the information is in the database], I can make this beautiful Excel sheet of all their information..." (O1).

Furthermore, information management is not the real work of volunteer coordination; it is overhead. While a few participants had volunteers who were willing to help them manage data, many felt that data management is the most undesirable task that could be given to a volunteer:

> It's like [my volunteer here]. He could be playing golf right now. The weather is perfect. And yet he's here, you know, sitting doing the most boring task there is (P2).

Issues of scale were the primary motivators for volunteer coordinators to transition to enterprise-level software. Coupled with this, ongoing difficulties managing duplicate and inconsistent data drove the vast majority of volunteer coordinators to seek out more centralized options.

HOMEBREW DATABASES: A CONTINUAL CYCLE OF RECONFIGURATION

Volunteer coordinators create particular assemblages of information management systems to satisfice their needs. Each type of system—personal office applications, paper, and enterprise databases—has its own set of shortcomings, at best, and exacerbates the challenges of information management, at worst. Nearly all of the volunteer coordinators in this study are frustrated with their current assemblages of systems and most are looking for better solutions—ideally, finding one system that can do everything. The problem is that no such solution exists:

> The problem is that all needs to be in the same software. This is what we struggle with. We can't figure it out... having all that stuff together in one software would be great. We were looking at some stuff... but nothing—nothing does it all (L2).

In lieu of a system that can do everything, volunteer coordinators continually reconfigure their homebrew databases—swapping one system for another and hoping the new set of systems will help reduce overhead in managing information. We heard over and over again that volunteer coordinators were in the process of migrating their data from one application to another.

Yet each transition to a new system creates additional work. Existing data either has to be ported—frequently necessitating manual re-entry of the data or selective copying and pasting—or abandoned. New systems rarely, if ever, encompass the same set of features or afford the same degree of flexibility as previous systems. Changes in the information managed by one application influence information management in others.

[2] http://blackbaud.com/products/fundraising/raisersedge.aspx
[3] http://constantcontact.com
[4] http://volunteermatch.org

Our data suggest the prevalence of a recurrent cycle—with each reconfiguration of the homebrew database demanding additional data management overhead and new data management practices. The new homebrew database, never quite addressing all the volunteer coordinators' information management needs or creating new challenges of its own, causes the cycle of reconfiguration to continue.

Volunteer coordinators also reported one additional catalyst that helps to perpetuate the cycle of reconfiguration—the fluidity of stakeholders. Information systems, particularly enterprise or custom databases, often rely on the expertise of someone who may not have a long-term commitment to the organization. When a local expert ceases to be available, the homebrew database has to be reconfigured so that the remaining volunteers and staff can manage the data.

FUTURE RESEARCH AND DEVELOPMENT

The results of this study suggest two trajectories for future research in databases and information management. We believe the outcomes of this future work may be valued not only by volunteer coordinators but also by the many individuals who need to manage information too complex for paper or personal office applications, but who cannot confront the overhead of using enterprise "solutions."

Towards More Human-Centered Databases

One significant trajectory for future research involves the design of more human-centered database systems. Such systems need to be accessible to individuals with limited technical expertise. Although there are some products like FileMaker and Microsoft Access intended to fill this need, these systems still require too much technical expertise to be usable by volunteer coordinators and many others who comprise the volunteer workforce. Indeed, one participant noted that a FileMaker database had to be abandoned when the resident expert left the organization (A2).

The challenge of creating more human-centered databases is not simply a matter of creating more usable interfaces for creating databases—both FileMaker and Access provide numerous templates and visual programming tools. It is also a matter of revisiting the complex models that underlie contemporary database systems. Jagadish et al. have called for "database systems that reflect the user's model of the data, rather than forcing the data to fit a particular model" [11]. In this research, we have begun to gather empirical evidence about how individuals construct representations of their own data. When considering requirements for more human-centered database systems, researchers might consider the ways that participants in our study modeled and managed their data:

- Volunteer coordinators chunked conceptually similar data into multiple, distinct information repositories and genre-specific applications. This observation suggests that human-centered databases need to support the management and integration of multiple types of data.
- Volunteer coordinators continually updated the underlying structure of their homebrew databases to reflect new information needs. This observation suggests that human-centered databases need to support evolving models, allowing the underlying schemas to change gracefully as information needs change.
- Volunteer coordinators reported that scalability was one of the most significant catalysts for the reconfiguration of their homebrew databases. This observation suggests that databases need to scale more gracefully and be useable from the very beginning of a volunteer coordinator's information management process through the maturation of the volunteer program. Databases are currently optimized for supporting very large datasets, but researchers should also consider what it would mean to provide database design and management tools with minimal adoption barriers for individuals with small-scale datasets, to encourage adoption from the outset.

Towards Migration, Import, Export & Syncing Standards

Even with the development of more human-centered databases, it is conceivable that volunteer coordinators will still manage some redundant data across multiple information systems. The volunteer coordinators in this study identified the migration of data between applications as a source of significant overhead. Volunteer schedules that were maintained in a calendar, for example, could not be exported into a spreadsheet to track hours. And while Outlook provided features to exchange data between an address book and an Excel spreadsheet, neither application provided a synchronization capability for data stored partially in one location and partially in another.

These observations suggest that another fruitful trajectory for future research would be the continued development of standards and interaction mechanisms for migrating data between applications, including importing, exporting, and syncing datasets. Although a number of standards (e.g., HTTP) and file formats (e.g., XML and OPML) have been developed to facilitate data exchange among applications, the corresponding tools for managing the mappings among application-specific data fields within these files and automating synchronization across data repositories have neither reached the same level of maturity nor become accessible enough for people without technical expertise.

CONCLUSION

In this paper, we have made the following contributions:

- We characterized the diversity and fluidity of the context and constraints of the work of volunteer coordinators and identified the associated challenges related to information management;
- We described the information management strategies of volunteer coordinators, characterized the homebrew databases they created, unpacked the reasons why they created these systems, and identified the additional information management challenges that were generated by these homebrew solutions;
- We proposed two trajectories for research—more human-centered databases and migration standards—that

would better support the information management needs of volunteer coordinators.

More broadly, this research foregrounds the pervasive influence and implications of evolution in information management. The nature of volunteerism evolves; the role of volunteerism within an NPO evolves; the kinds of information needed to understand volunteerism evolves; the information management practices of volunteer coordinators evolve; and the configurations of homebrew databases evolve. Although this research focuses on the information management of volunteer coordinators, researchers who study broader classes of knowledge workers have noted the importance of evolution, as well—that the meaning of information to a knowledge worker evolves over time (e.g., [12]). As a research community, then, we ought to consider the ways that information systems can be designed to evolve, as well—alongside individuals, groups, and organizations.

ACKNOWLEDGEMENTS

We thank our participants for sharing their time and experiences with us. This research was supported by a grant from the Center for Organizational Research at the University of California, Irvine.

REFERENCES

1. Barreau, D. and Nardi, B.A. Finding and reminding: File organization from the desktop. *ACM SIGCHI Bulletin 27*, 3 (1995), 39–43.
2. Bellotti, V., Ducheneaut, N., Howard, M., Smith, I. and Grinter, R.E. Quality versus quantity: E-mail-centric task management and its relation with overload. *Human-Computer Interaction 20*, 1 (2005), 89–138.
3. Bergman, O., Beyth-Maron, R. and Nachmias, R. The project fragmentation problem in personal information management. *Proc. CHI 2006*, ACM Press (2006), 271–274.
4. Boardman, R. and Sasse, M.A. "Stuff goes into the computer and doesn't come out": A cross-tool study of personal information management. *Proc. CHI 2004*, ACM Press (2004), 583–590.
5. Brudney, J.L. Designing and managing volunteer programs. In R.D. Herman (Ed.), *The Jossey-Bass Handbook of Nonprofit Leadership and Management*. Jossey-Bass, San Francisco (1994), 279–302.
6. Bureau of Labor Statistics, US Department of Labor. Volunteering in the United States—2009. http://www.bls.gov/news.release/pdf/volun.pdf.
7. Burt, E. and Taylor, J.A. Information and communication technologies: Reshaping voluntary organizations? *Nonprofit Management & Leadership 11*, 2 (2000), 131–143.
8. Corbin, J. and Strauss, A. *Basics of qualitative research: Techniques and procedures for developing grounded theory* (3rd ed.) Sage Publications, Los Angeles, 2008.
9. Date, C.J. Database usability. *ACM SIGMOD Record 13*, 4 (1983), 1.
10. Goecks, J., Voida, A., Voida, S. and Mynatt, E.D. Charitable technologies: Opportunities for collaborative computing in nonprofit fundraising. *Proc. CSCW 2008*, ACM Press (2008), 689–698.
11. Jagadish, H.V., Chapman, A., Elkiss, A., Jayapandian, M., Li, Y., Nandi, A. and Yu, C. Making database systems usable. *Proc. SIGMOD 2007*, ACM Press (2007), 13–24.
12. Kidd, A. The marks are on the knowledge worker. *Proc. CHI 1994*, ACM Press (1994), 186–191.
13. Le Dantec, C.A. and Edwards, W.K. Across boundaries of influence and accountability: The multiple scales of public sector information systems. *Proc. CHI 2010,* ACM Press (2010), 113–122.
14. Le Dantec, C.A. and Edwards, W.K. The view from the trenches: Organization, power, and technology at two nonprofit homeless outreach centers. *Proc. CSCW 2008,* ACM Press (2008), 589–598.
15. Mackay, W.E. Is paper safer? The role of paper flight strips in air traffic control. *ACM Trans. Computer-Human Interaction 6*, 4 (1999), 311–340.
16. McPhail, B., Constantino, T., Bruckmann, D., Barclay, R. and Clement, A. CAVEAT exemplar: Participatory design in a non-profit volunteer organisation. *Computer Supported Cooperative Work 7*, 3–4 (1998), 223–241.
17. Merkel, C., Farooq, U., Xiao, L., Ganoe, C., Rosson, M.B. and Carroll, J.M. Managing technology use and learning in nonprofit community organizations: Methodological challenges and opportunities. *Proc. CHIMIT 2007*, ACM Press (2007), Article 8.
18. National Center for Charitable Statistics. *National taxonomy of exempt entities.* http://nccs.urban.org/classification/NTEE.cfm
19. Palen, L. Social, individual and technological issues for groupware calendar systems. *Proc. CHI 1999*, ACM Press (1999), 17–24.
20. Sease, R. and McDonald, D.W. Musical fingerprints: Collaboration around home media collections. *Proc. GROUP 2009*, ACM Press (2009), 331–340.
21. Sellen, A.J. and Harper, R.H.R. *The myth of the paperless office*. MIT Press, Cambridge, MA, 2002.
22. Shneiderman, B. Improving the human factors aspect of database interactions. *ACM Trans. Database Systems 3*, 4 (1978), 417–439.
23. Stoll, J., Edwards, W.K. and Mynatt, E.D. Interorganizational coordination and awareness in a nonprofit ecosystem. *Proc. CSCW 2010*, ACM Press (2010), 51–60.
24. Urban Institute. Volunteer management capacity in America's charities and congregations: A briefing report, 2004. http://www.urban.org/publications/410963.html.
25. Whittaker, S. and Sidner, C. Email overload: Exploring personal information management of email. *Proc. CHI 1996*, ACM Press (1996), 276–283.

How a Freeform Spatial Interface Supports Simple Problem Solving Tasks

Eser Kandogan, Juho Kim[+], Thomas P. Moran, Pablo Pedemonte*

IBM Research - Almaden
650 Harry Rd.
San Jose, CA 95120
{eser,tpmoran}@us.ibm.com

[+]MIT CSAIL
32 Vassar St.
Cambridge, MA 02139
juhokim@mit.edu

*IBM Argentina
Ing. Butty 275 – C1001 AFA
Buenos Aires, Argentina
ppedemon@ar.ibm.com

ABSTRACT
We developed DataBoard, a freeform spatial interface, to support users in simple problem solving tasks. To develop a deeper understanding of the role of space and the tradeoffs between freeform and structured interaction styles in problem solving tasks, we conducted a controlled user study comparing the DataBoard with a spreadsheet and analyzed video data in detail. Beyond improvements in task performance and memory recall, our observations reveal that freeform interfaces can support users in a variety of ways: representing problems flexibly, developing strategies, executing strategies incrementally, tracking problem state easily, reducing mental computation, and verifying solutions perceptually. The spreadsheet also had advantages, and we discuss the tradeoffs.

Author Keywords
Spatial Interfaces, Freeform Interaction, Problem Solving, Spreadsheets.

ACM Classification Keywords
H5.m. Information interfaces and presentation (e.g., HCI): Miscellaneous.

General Terms
Human Factors

INTRODUCTION
Everyday we need to solve simple problems and make practical decisions at home and at work, from making the wedding invitation list, to arranging schedule for a customer visit, and distributing work items in a group. Often such decisions involve a number of items to be organized or categorized to further the work and deal with constraints, for example, assigning software defects to developers in a balanced way considering the priority and difficulty of the defects, among other factors.

Spreadsheets are often used for such problems to enable people to lay out information in a table to help them make decisions (often collaboratively). Using a spatial representation, such as a table, engages people's natural spatial and perceptual skills to simplify choice, perception, and mental computation [12]. Spreadsheets allow users to arrange data in rows and columns, sort, and perform calculations. Pen and paper or sticky notes on whiteboards are also commonly used to solve small problems on the spot [4]. Freeform interfaces mimic paper or board in the sense that they aim to provide a fluid natural interaction space to arrange information flexibly without the constraint of a table, as in spreadsheets. Freeform graphical, multi-modal, and tangible interfaces have been introduced to support users in tasks that require flexibility such as note-taking, brain-storming, and collaborative design, with varying degrees of costs and benefits [1,3,7,8]. Both freeform and structured spatial interfaces have their upsides as well as downsides. The tradeoff between freeform and structure is the main theme throughout this paper.

We are developing DataBoard to occupy a potential sweet-spot in the spectrum of spatial interfaces, specifically geared towards simple problem solving tasks. Users can jot down information related to their tasks in a freeform manner anywhere in the space in a simple point-click-type style. Yet, they can also arrange information into lists, piles, and tables and flexibly move items between them. For example, when making a wedding invitation list, one might begin by jotting down names of people, quickly organize them into lists of the brides' and grooms' side, personal or work friends, and local or remote people, and reorganize them to satisfy desired constraints flexibly.

As we continued to consider different use cases and add new features to DataBoard, a fundamental question kept coming: How, if at all, does freeform interaction help users, especially in problem solving tasks? To directly investigate that question, we conducted a controlled study to compare a very basic version of DataBoard as a freeform interface (with the ability to snap objects into lists) with a spreadsheet interface as a structured interface.

Our aim was not just to compare two different interfaces in terms of task performance, but to develop a deeper understanding of the role of space, spatial interaction, and the features of freeform and structured interfaces in problem solving tasks. We carried out a detailed analysis of video data collected during the experiment. Our results show that a freeform spatial interface enables better task performance and memory recall than a tabular interface. From our detailed observations, we argue that freeform interaction enabled participants to (1) flexibly represent attributes of the problem in the freeform space in order to better develop strategies; (2) execute their strategies incrementally, easily tracking state as they proceeded; and (3) easily verify and tweak their solutions.

In this paper we briefly describe DataBoard, present our study method and findings, describe our observations in depth, and discuss how freeform interaction supports problem solving.

RELATED WORK

Spatial Interfaces

GUIs are inherently spatial interfaces, and they vary on the spectrum of freeform vs. structured interactions. Desktop systems, for example, offer some level of freeform interaction in that users can move objects anywhere on the desktop. On the other hand, modern spreadsheets such as Microsoft Excel™ provide a tabular layout and allow users to organize, transform, and visualize data only within a table.

Some tasks, particularly those creative in nature, are potentially better suited for freeform interactions, such as brainstorming [7], mind-mapping [17], planning, design [4], note taking [8], collaborating in the workplace [18], and organizing photos [11]. Freeform interactions could foster the creative process by allowing the users to rapidly externalize thoughts without the constraints imposed on the use of space and transform them informally into useful organizations [1,2, 22]. For example, Microsoft OneNote™, a planning and note taking application, allows users to create several types of information and place them anywhere on the page. In OneNote users can also create lists or tables, and place them anywhere on the page, if they need to provide some structure to content created. Unlike DataBoard, however, desired structure needs to be predetermined, in that users start by creating a list, and adding information to it. Whereas in DataBoard users can simply start creating pieces of information and combine them into lists and tables as they work, and flexibly move them between lists. Another way to structure information is using page-level templates (as in Microsoft PowerPoint™), while still giving the user flexibility to organize information.

Space and Cognition

The distributed cognition literature emphasizes the importance of space and external representations in problem solving [23,24], wherein space can be intelligently utilized to generate and arrange external representations to aid problem solving by simplifying choice, utilizing perception, and minimizing internal computation [12]. Because most problems are difficult to solve only with internal (mental) representations, people often externalize information to distribute the cognitive overhead. In doing so, the nature of the representation used in problem solving can dramatically affect how people think about the problems and how long they take to solve them [23]. There is also a variety of work on how people code, use, and manipulate spatial information [16]. Manipulation can be epistemic, in that it does not directly improve the current state to be closer to the goal state, in contrast to pragmatic steps taken to solve a problem directly [13].

Use of space in regards to recall is also well-studied [9,10,21]. Studies of office workers to locate items in their offices identified different strategies people use for filing and retrieving information [15]. Other studies suggest that relying on location information alone for recall may be insufficient [10], especially if organization was not based on some logical structure [14]. However, user involvement in organizing the space helps recall [19].

DATABOARD

We designed DataBoard, a web-based freeform spatial interface, to help users in everyday problem solving tasks. The motivating example was management of software defects in our group. We found that the web-based defect tracking system we have been using with its rigid tabular interface was severely limiting for reviewing, categorizing, prioritizing, and distributing defects to team members during our weekly meetings.

The central idea of DataBoard is to enable users to organize and augment semantically-meaningful "domain objects" (as in [18]) such as defects in software development. Domain data is imported from a specialized application and laid out on DataBoard, where the user can interact within a freeform space, creating organizing structures (such as lists) and modifying underlying data as a result of such spatial interactions; and finally exporting the updated objects back to the application. For example, in our group meeting, we can import defects into a list on the board and then use the freeform space to "play" with them to represent their importance and urgency and discuss how they relate to each other. Then, at the end of the meeting we prioritize and assign them to the members of the team.

Using DataBoard users can create simple text, images, links, person objects by simply pointing anywhere on the layout, clicking and typing text, URLs, email addresses, which could be used to automatically create objects of different types (Figure 1). For example, an email address would be automatically mapped to a person using company address

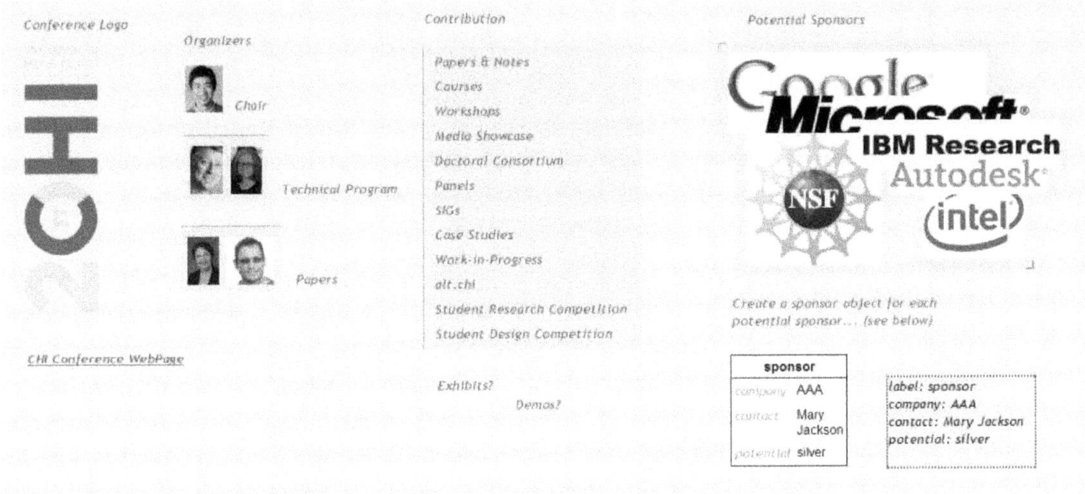

Figure 1. DataBoard supports users to create simple text, images, links, person, and user-defined objects on a two-dimensional layout flexibly through simple point-click and type. Users can move objects to snap to or overlap each other to organize them into lists and piles, respectively.

book and transformed into a Person object. Users can also create arbitrary user-defined objects with a simple syntax of name-value pairs. Finally, users can organize these objects into lists and piles, if they wish to. For the purposes of this paper, we will not go into much detail of DataBoard, but rather focus on the study and observations on the use of space and spatial interaction in problem solving.

STUDY

The promise of freeform spatial interfaces, like DataBoard's, was quite intriguing and seemed to apply to a lot of other everyday small-scale problem solving tasks. Thus, we wanted to develop a deeper understanding of how the use of space and freeform interaction contributed to our improved problem solving. To that end we designed a controlled study to see if there are performance improvements over tabular interfaces, and we especially wanted to pinpoint what aspects of the freeform spatial interaction contributed to that effect by carefully observing people behavior in problem solving tasks.

Hypotheses

In this experimental study we tested three hypotheses:

H1. Task Performance. Freeform spatial interaction will lead to shorter task performance times in problem-solving tasks over tabular spreadsheet based interfaces.

H2. Solution Quality. Freeform spatial interaction will lead to better solution quality in problem-solving tasks over tabular spreadsheet based interfaces.

H3. Memory Recall. Freeform spatial interaction will lead to better recall in problem-solving tasks over tabular spreadsheet based interfaces.

Design

A repeated measures within-subjects design was used in the experiment. The independent variables were Interface (Spreadsheet, DataBoard) and Task Type (Balancing, Scheduling). The dependent variables were Task Performance Time, Solution Quality, and Memory Recall Errors.

Each participant was brought in one at a time, and performed four tasks, two balancing and two scheduling tasks, one on DataBoard and one on Google Spreadsheet. The balancing task was to distribute a set of objects into three groups based on two attributes of the objects such that the number of objects in each group would be equal with attribute values balanced across groups. For example, given 18 software defects, the task was to assign these defects to three developers such that each would get an equal number of defects, where the distribution of defect priorities and the sum of difficulties would be balanced across developers. In the DataBoard case, participants started with an initial set of defects and they were tasked with moving these defects into three groups with a header of the developer's name (Figure 2). In the Spreadsheet, likewise participants started with an initial set of defects and they were tasked with assigning them to developers by filling in the developer column with A, B, or C (Figure 8).

The scheduling task was to order a set of objects in two lists based on dependencies between objects and another attribute of the objects. For example, given 8 defects, with different dependencies and priorities, the task was to assign these defects to two developers such that dependencies were observed and preference was given to higher priority defects. As such, unlike the balancing task, the order of the objects in the scheduling task was important. In the

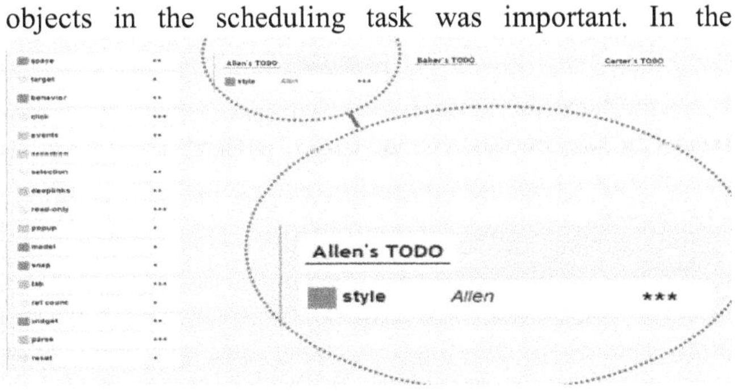

Figure 2. Balancing Task in DataBoard for Defect domain. Participants assigned defects to three developers by moving them from the original list on the left into one of the lists for a developer (enlarged in blue dotted lines)

DataBoard case, participants started with an initial set of defects and they were tasked with moving these defects into two lists with a header of the developers' name. In the Spreadsheet, likewise participants were tasked with assigning defects to developers by filling in the developer column with A or B and determining the order by typing 1, 2, 3, or 4.

To reduce an order effect in performance for the second interface, a parallel task domain was used on the second interface. For example, if the first domain was the software defects, the second interface used the class domain, where in the balancing tasks participants balanced the class load for three professors based on class difficulty and level (PhD, MS, and BS). The scheduling task in the class domain was about registering for classes based on prerequisites and class levels. Each task domain had the same number of objects (e.g. defect vs. class) and same number of groups/lists to distribute to (e.g. three professors, three developers) and tasks were isomorphic in terms of complexity.

The order of interfaces and tasks were counter-balanced. For example, participant S1 did balancing task first with Spreadsheet and then with DataBoard and scheduling task first with DataBoard and then with Spreadsheet. Participant S2 had the tasks the other way around. Participant S3 had the interfaces the other way around. The order of task domain was also counter-balanced.

Task Performance was measured with a stop-watch, started and stopped with the explicit command of the participant. The Solution Quality was assessed by experimenters and measured by the minimum number of steps to reach to a solution that satisfied all constraints of the task (e.g. balance of defect distribution based on priority and difficulty). Memory Recall tasks were given immediately after each session and inquired about the state of the participant's solution, such as the number of Ph.D. level classes for professor A. Different tasks were given at the end of each session to limit potential preparation. Memory Recall was measured by the absolute difference of the participants answer with the correct answer, ranged from 0 to 3, 0 being the perfect match. Participants who couldn't answer the memory recall task were given 3, which was the maximum possible distance from the correct answer. Memory Recall tasks were added later on as an afterthought thus only 12 participants were able to perform these tasks.

Procedure

Before starting the experiment, participants were briefed about the study and procedures to be used. They were assured that the experiment was measuring the effectiveness of the interface conditions not their own abilities to solve problems. With their permission, all experiment sessions were recorded on video in HD format to facilitate in-depth study of the strategies and actions. All sessions took place in a quiet study room.

Participants filled out a pre-questionnaire on their experience with spreadsheets, software development, and bug tracking systems. Afterwards, participants took a 3-minute spatial ability test, which contained Cards Rotation Tests [6]. Next, participants received a five-minute training on both interfaces, and reviewed features like sort and column/row move in Spreadsheet, and object selection, move, and list interaction in DataBoard. Participants then performed a training task on both interfaces to have hands-on experience using the interfaces in problem solving tasks.

Each experiment session consisted of four tasks, where participants performed two balancing and two scheduling tasks using the Spreadsheet and DataBoard interfaces. Before each session participants were reminded to think aloud, which they did to varying degrees. After reading the instructions for a particular session, participants were asked about their strategy in order to help them think in advance about the problem in order to minimize the effects of variances in strategy planning on task performance. It also helped to ensure that the problem was well-understood.

After each session participants were immediately asked to perform a quick memory recall task, followed by a subjective evaluation of the task difficulty and interface appropriateness for the current session. Upon completion of all the experiment sessions, participants filled an online post-questionnaire, where they answered questions to discuss features of Spreadsheet and DataBoard which supported or hindered their task performance, compare task difficulties in both interfaces, and whether and why they used external aids such as paper.

Participants

18 volunteers (7 female, 11 male) participated in the experiment. Participants ranged in ages from mid 20s to mid 40s, had an average skill level of 3.5 (1: novice, 5: expert) in spreadsheet use, 3.6 in software development, and 2.6 in bug tracking system use. Participants were a mix of college students and professionals with backgrounds on several fields of science, including computer science, physics, and social sciences. Participants received a lunch coupon in exchange for their help in the experiment.

Apparatus

Both conditions of the experiment were conducted on a web browser, displayed on a 20" LCD flat panel display in full-screen mode. Participants were given the option to use a mouse, a trackpoint, or a touchpad as the pointing device and pen and paper to use in their tasks.

RESULTS

Task Performance

The mean task performance times for the balancing task were 323.4 sec. (SD=206.6) with Spreadsheet and 231.5 sec (SD=143.6) with DataBoard, and for the scheduling task, 198.5 sec. (SD=81.8) with Spreadsheet and 142 sec. (SD=104.5) with DataBoard (Figure 3).

Repeated measures analysis of variance showed a main effect of Interface ($F_{Interface}(1,32) = 8.77$, $p < 0.01$) thus suggesting H1 is supported. No impact of interface order was observed on task performance ($F_{Interface*InterfaceOrder}(1,32) = 0.12$, $p > 0.5$). ANOVA on spatial ability incorporated as a covariant did not yield a significant difference ($F_{Interface*SpatialAbility}(1,31) = 0.17$, $p > 0.5$).

Solution Quality

Mean solution quality (as measured by minimum number of steps to satisfy all problem constraints from the participant's final solution) for the balancing task were 0.61 (SD=0.92) with Spreadsheet and 0.33 (SD=0.77) with DataBoard, and for the scheduling task, 0.94 (SD=1.06) with Spreadsheet and 0.72 (SD=1.07) with DataBoard. Repeated measures analysis of variance showed no main effect of Interface ($F_{Interface}(1,34) = 1.35$, $p > 0.2$) thus suggesting H2 is not supported.

Memory Recall

Mean memory recall errors for the balancing task were 0.83 (SD=0.83) with Spreadsheet and 0.42 (SD=0.9) with DataBoard, and for the scheduling task, 1.5 (SD=1.24) with Spreadsheet and 0.67 (SD=0.98) with DataBoard (Figure 3). Repeated measures analysis of variance showed a main effect of Interface ($F_{Interface}(1,22) = 4.84$, $p < 0.05$) thus suggesting H3 is supported. Note memory recall tasks were only conducted on 12 participants.

Subjective Evaluation Ratings

Subjects rated task difficulty for each interface after each session on a scale of 1 to 5 (1: very hard, 5: very easy). Mean ratings of the balancing task were 2.56 (SD=1.38) with Spreadsheet, and 3.44 (SD=0.98) with DataBoard, and of the scheduling task, 3.0 (SD=0.77) with Spreadsheet and 3.72 (SD=0.67) with DataBoard, with a main effect of the Interface (Kruskal-Wallis (KW), $p < 0.05$).

Subjects rated appropriateness of the interface, on a scale of 1 to 5, (1: not really, 5: very much). Mean ratings of the balancing task were 2.33 (SD=1.24) with Spreadsheet and 4.14 (SD=0.83) with DataBoard, and of the scheduling task, 2.28 (SD=0.82) with Spreadsheet and 3.83 (SD=0.98) with DataBoard, with a main effect of Interface (KW, $p < 0.01$).

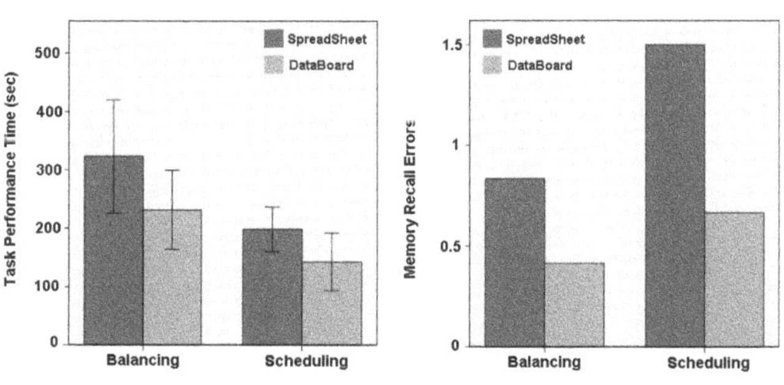

Figure 3. Task Performance Times and Memory Recall Error by Task and Interface. (Error Bars shown for +/- 2 SE)

Post Questionnaire

When asked about what helped or hindered their task performance on Spreadsheet, 10 out of 18 participants mentioned sort, particularly for categorizing information visually for easy verification. Despite availability of sorting, five participants mentioned that they had trouble mapping their tasks onto the tabular format, particularly for balancing tasks when all categories where in a single column (as opposed to three for example for balancing task, one for each developer). This was also an issue for scheduling tasks, as one participant said, not being able to map dependencies on the tabular format, "It was hard to keep in mind dependencies." One participant mentioned that even with sort he needed a way to more clearly separate rows. Four participants mentioned difficulty of keeping track of their state, and found it difficult to use expressions even as simple as sum and count, like one participant who put it as "Calculations might have helped, if I had known the right spreadsheet magic...."

Regarding DataBoard, 6 participants felt that lack of sorting hindered their task performance, while 3 mentioned ability to do calculations would have been nice for DataBoard. On the other hand, participants overwhelmingly (11) liked the visual nature of DataBoard in problem solving and suggested it helped them in their tasks by allowing them organize data in 2D, particularly to represent problem states, as one participant resembled it to a "parking lot" where you could solve parts of the problem in different places. Visual layout was also considered helpful for "visually balancing by just looking" thus reducing the need for calculation. Most participants felt that spatial interaction helped them "more effectively tune their solution". Three participants mentioned problems with spatial interaction particularly that the list interaction mechanisms could have been better designed and undo was difficult.

Participants were divided evenly regarding which task was more difficult, 8 suggested balancing task, 8 scheduling tasks, and 2 suggested about the same. On the other hand participants overwhelmingly said that Spreadsheet (12) was more difficult than DataBoard (3), while remaining said they were about equal.

Six participants used paper as an aid to help them solve problems such as calculating sums of difficulties, drawing dependency graphs, and remembering problem states at specific points, but 4 said they didn't but they should have used paper for similar reasons.

In concluding remarks, participants felt that DataBoard was really useful in their problem solving tasks, particularly for "manually solving simple problems." One participant found that "DataBoard was a lot more useful than I thought it would be," and another said "[It] opened my eyes to a new kind of dealing with data." Scalability was brought up as a specific concern with DataBoard, as one participant said: "I wonder if DataBoard would scale as much as the Spreadsheet when we get to many characteristics." The scalability of DataBoard remains to be tested, as our focus currently was simple everyday problems with a small number of objects (less than 50). Many subjects found tabular layout of spreadsheets to be limiting despite the availability of the column/row move feature in Google Spreadsheets – in fact that is why we chose Google Spreadsheet over other spreadsheet applications. This would make the interactions comparable to DataBoard both in terms of treating objects as a unit as well as in terms of interaction style. Even though participants were shown how to move rows and columns during training, many of the participants except one did not move rows and columns in the Spreadsheet condition. We believe that the visual affordances of the spreadsheet were so strong that a column/row move action was contrary to what users expected in a strict grid representation. One participant said "even though I knew I could move rows around, it never occurred to me to do so during the tasks."

VIDEO ANALYSIS

To develop a more in-depth understanding of the findings from the controlled experiment we analyzed video captured during the experiments. One of the researchers coded all the video from the experiment sessions, where events were identified and time-stamped. No additional coding by another researcher was conducted as coding was not subject to interpretation but rather focused on Next, itime-stamping events, such as typing in a number on a column in the spreadsheet or moving an object under a column in the DataBoard case.

Coding

Aside from obvious events such as, START, TALK, END, we coded action events as <OBJECT> <COLUMN> {<POSITION>}, when a participant moved (or entered text to that effect in Spreadsheet) an object to a column, optionally at a specific position, and SORT, when participant sorted (in the Spreadsheet), and NOTE to code external action such as using paper.

Additionally, we divided each session into three sequential phases: Prepare, Execute, and Verify & Recover. Prepare phase covered all actions such as sorting and moving objects in free space and lasted until the first actual assignment was made, followed by Execute which lasted until all objects were assigned, at which point we considered an initial complete solution was reached, and lastly a Verify and Recover phase in which participants tried to improve upon their initial solution. Note that this doesn't mean that participants did not perform, for example, verification in the Execute phase; it was merely our definition of gross phases of problem solving.

Observations

We identified three different strategies in our observations: 1) *Incremental* (with Trial & Error), 2) *Heuristic* (with Tweaking), and 3) *Decompose and Recompose*. Incremental strategies sought to solve the problem by reducing the scale of the problem linearly at each step. Heuristic approaches employed a general scheme to get to an initial solution very quickly and focused on fixing the initial solution thereafter. The Decompose and Recompose strategy divided the problem into smaller, more manageable parts and then merged them to achieve a solution. Below we describe our observations for both balancing and scheduling tasks and describe specific instances of each of these strategies in the experiment. The participants reported below were selected based on the differences in task performance times, in one way or another, and based on the commonality of the strategy and actions.

Balancing Task

We report our observations of S2 and S15, who performed faster with DataBoard (DB), and S4, who performed slightly faster with Spreadsheet (SS).

Decompose and Recompose + Incremental: S2. In the DB case, S2 spent considerable time planning and organizing defects into groups based on priority and difficulty (Figure 4). Then, she started distributing defects one row at a time with defects having the same difficulty and priority. She compensated differences in difficulty on subsequent rows when possible. Finally, she counted defects based on priority and difficulty across developers.

Figure 4. S2 spent considerable time decomposing the problem space by organizing defects into groups based on priority and difficulty levels.

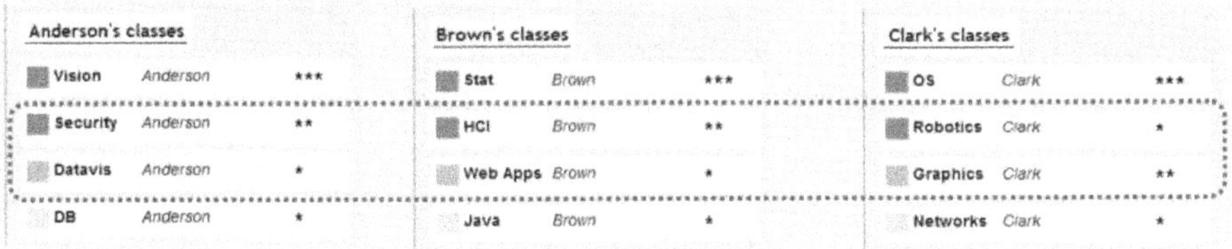

Figure 5. S15 trying to maintain balance on subsequent rows by compensating difficulties (indicated by *s) on the second row 2, 2, 1 with difficulty levels on third row 1, 1, 2.

Next, in the SS case, S2 started by sorting first by class-level and then by difficulty, which gave a good overview of the distribution of classes. She then started distributing classes of same level and difficulty but had trouble balancing once the obvious ones (equal level and difficulty) were assigned. To help in her task, she created tables to keep track of the distribution by level and difficulty, but spent a lot of time doing this as she had trouble maintaining the table. She gave up on the table and tried sort by class level, which gave a reasonable view of the solution state. After a few more assignments she was done.

Analysis. In both cases S2 employed a combination of Decompose and Recompose and Incremental strategies. In the DB case S2 decomposed the problem by arranging defects into groups based on priority level and difficulty and thereafter executed fairly optimally in an incremental fashion. S2 was able to proceed carefully on each row, and arrived to an initial solution which was the correct solution. Tackling the problem one row at a time helped S2 execute with awareness of the problem state on each row and verify easily at the end. In the SS case, she decomposed the problem easily by leveraging sort and began an incremental strategy. Once the obvious assignments were made, S2 started to have a hard time keeping tally of assignments. Creating summary table didn't help, and she lost quite a bit time. In the end another sort came to rescue.

Incremental: S15. In the DB case, S15 did not do any preparation but proceeded in a very orderly, incremental manner by picking and choosing the right mix of classes based on class level and difficulty from the original list, and making assignments for one row at a time. On each row he either completely balanced classes or, he tried to compensate for it on the next row (Figure 5).

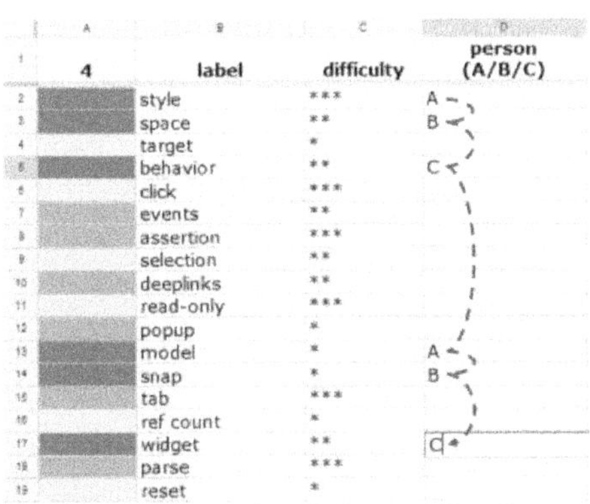

Figure 6. S15 trying to assign defects to developers in order (A, B, and C) by priority but also trying to balance of the difficulties on each set of assignments (A, B, C).

Next, in the SS case, S15 started again in a similar fashion assigning defects to A, B, and C in order (Figure 6). He tried to maintain balance but when only three defects remained he concluded that he can't as remaining defects had different difficulties. He cleared completely, sorted by difficulty, and then by priority. He prepared expressions to sum difficulty levels by priority. He calculated that he needed total difficulty to be 12 for each developer. Thus, he assigned 2 defects from each priority level, totaling 12 in terms of difficulty and assigned them one at a time to developers. He did not do any verification. Performance time, even only counting the time after cleanup, was still a lot longer compared to DB. (267 sec. in SS vs. 92 in DB)

Analysis. In the DB case S15 successfully completed a purely incremental strategy and found the solution easily with no verification necessary at the end. In the SS case he applied the same incremental strategy but failed as defects being dispersed in the layout made it difficult to balance. After clearing he utilized a Decompose and Recompose strategy by sorting and got a good sense of the distribution. After several calculations he transformed the problem into a computational problem and solved it as such.

Heuristic (with Tweaking): S4. In the SS case, S4 applied a heuristic approach and started by going from highest difficulty down, independent of priority levels, and assigning defects to developers in sequence, A, B, and C and got to an initial solution quickly. She tweaked her solution by first sorting on priority and counting difficulties for each person and tried to balance it by swapping defects. She did so in an optimal way.

Next, in the DB case, the participant proceeded in a similar fashion by distributing classes of the same difficulty to professors in order of A, B, and C, if possible at the same class level. Towards the end the participant performed a quick check of the distribution of class levels by professor and completed by swapping the differences. The participant did a very quick check at the end.

Analysis. In both DB and SS cases participant followed the same strategy with similar performance levels. When the strategy was well-thought to its finest detail in advance performances turned out to be similar.

Scheduling Task

We report our observations of participants S1, who performed faster with DataBoard, and S2, who performed faster with Spreadsheet.

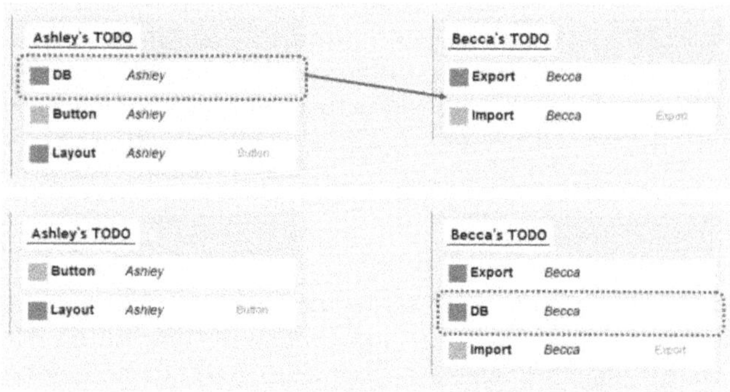

Figure 7. a) Upon seeing a priority violation across developers, i.e. Layout on Ashley vs. Import on Becca, S1 fixed it easily by moving DB to Becca, pushing Import down automatically.

Incremental (with Trial and Error): S1. In the DB case, the participant started first by assigning the high priority defects to developers by taking dependencies into account. As she was assigning the remaining defects, S1 recognized a priority violation across developers and fixed it easily by moving a high priority defect to the other list shifting down defects accordingly (Figure 7). She then assigned the remaining defects to developers in order of priority, and quickly verified the solution.

Next, in the SS case, S1 started by sorting classes on class level and set the schedule order first (without assigning class type yet). Immediately after a few assignments she began taking prerequisites into account. Once all schedule assignments were completed, she assigned class types. Despite spending considerable time on verification (30 sec.) she didn't reach to an optimal solution, and failed on several violations of class level (Figure 8).

Analysis. The participant started in both cases by following a similar strategy, i.e. starting with high priority defects or classes and then considering dependency as needed. In both cases the participant didn't follow an optimal path to the solution yet in the DB case he was able to quickly fix it as DataBoard allowed for quick changes to ordering, facilitating flexible problem solving. In the SS case it took longer to come to an initial solution. While S1 reached to an optimal solution in the DB case, in the SS case she failed to see several violations of class level constraint because of the way classes were organized, as they were sorted by class level not by schedule order.

Decompose and Recompose: S2. In the SS case, the participant quickly developed a strategy based on specific decomposition of the defects by dependencies and priorities and executed his plan by focusing solely on ordering of classes in the schedule. The participant then assigned them to developers randomly. He did a very quick check at the end and completed the solution optimally.

Next, in the DB case, participant spent considerable time planning his strategy by organizing classes in the free space based on the prerequisites and class levels (Figure 9). His solution was just to move this onto the solution space

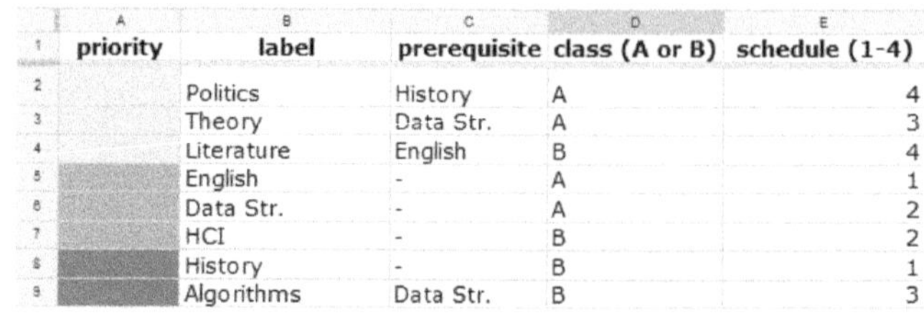

priority	label	prerequisite	class (A or B)	schedule (1-4)
	Politics	History	A	4
	Theory	Data Str.	A	3
	Literature	English	B	4
	English	-	A	1
	Data Str.	-	A	2
	HCI	-	B	2
	History	-	B	1
	Algorithms	Data Str.	B	3

Figure 8. When classes were sorted by class level, S1 failed to see several violations of class level constraint.

(under class types) where he would combine several of these dependency graphs into two lists of class types. He did so in an optimal number of steps.

Analysis. In the DB case planning in free space turned out to be useful in terms of thinking about and planning for the problem but didn't carry performance benefits in the solution of the problem, particularly as it wasn't easy to move objects from the planning space to the solution space. In the SS case having a very concrete and specific plan in advanced enabled easy execution.

DISCUSSION – FREEFORM SPATIAL INTERACTION

To discuss the tradeoffs between freeform and structured spatial interaction, as they relate to the phases and strategies of problem solving we identified, we use Kirsh's categories of the use of space to organize our comparison [12]. Kirsh proposed three main categories of use of space: spatial arrangements that simplify choice, spatial arrangements that simplify perception, and spatial dynamics that simplify internal computation [12].

Simplifying Choice

Arrangements that simplify choice use spatial affordances to encode actions, which help by reducing the search space or suggesting available actions. This plays an important role in the planning phase of problem solving tasks, and as such it is crucial for strategies with heavy planning phases, such as Decompose and Recompose. In freeform spatial interfaces, we argue that the ability to map problem space features more flexibly without the constraints of the

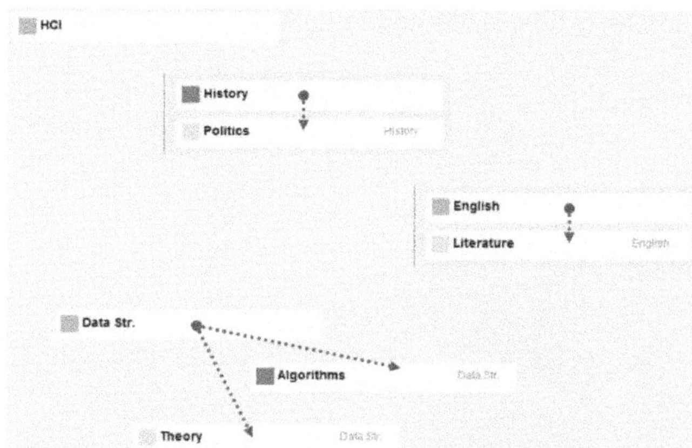

Figure 9. Participant S2 spent considerable time organizing classes in free form based on dependency and class level.

structure of tabular interface made it more applicable to a wider range of problems. In our post-interview, participants mentioned this issue particularly for scheduling task on the tabular layout, preferring the freeform nature of DataBoard. Even for the balancing task, the tabular layout's strong affordances limited participants; and they didn't consider arranging defects in flexible groups, as the DataBoard participants using the Decompose and Recompose strategies did in arranging defects by difficulty and priority. In the spreadsheet, the sorting operation was utilized heavily to compensate, but still the sorted arrangement was linear and didn't lend itself to the clear visual separations of objects that participants wanted. Also, for incremental strategies we saw that at each step of the process participants chose suitable objects from the unassigned set to make informed choices going onward.

Simplifying Perception

Spatial arrangements can also help simplify perception by making problem properties noticeable and thus making it easy to monitor the problem state. This was especially crucial for incremental approaches, where participants needed to track solution state at each step along the way. Many participants had problems in tracking state in the Spreadsheet interface, because objects were dispersed throughout the list, making it difficult to notice violations of problem constraints. This happened in situations as simple as ranking of red-orange-yellow priorities, as well as in situations with more complex dependency constraints. For heuristic approaches, which heavily rely on visual recognition of the solution state, it is critical to notice violations in the complete solution.

Simplifying Internal Computation

Problem solving is a complex cognitive task, involving representation, computation, and verification. Spatial interfaces allow users to represent the semantics of the problem spatially and visually. For example, consider the balancing task. On DataBoard assignments are represented by a list of objects under each assignee. When the user moves objects on the layout, from one list to another or onto free space, the user is intending to change assignments. On the spreadsheet, assignments are represented symbolically by names in the assignee column.

Easing internal (mental) computation involves creating visual cues to make certain properties explicit, thus bypassing the need for computing. This was particularly important for incremental approaches and to some degree in the recompose phase. Arranging defects with the same difficulty on the same row, or even compensating differences in the next row, was much easier given the horizontal arrangement of defects on DataBoard, essentially representing the summation of defect difficulties.

Spreadsheets have powerful operations, such as sorting and computation. Sorting groups assignments so that the distribution is clear and reduces internal computation. Spreadsheets also support defining computational formulas. For example, formulas to count assignments and sum up difficulties can help the user see the conformance of the problem state to the problem constraints. Yet, we saw little use of such formulas in our experiments, even though participants were fairly experienced spreadsheet users. The issue here wasn't that participants didn't know the sum and count functions; it was specifying what cells to apply these functions to. This was especially difficult, because all assignments were on a single column and it was difficult to specify cell ranges by assignee.

The DataBoard system used in the study did not provide such computational operations. However, it would be easy to add computations on spatial structures (e.g., formulas to count or add property values of items in lists) [5]. But note that spatial arrangements (e.g. horizontal alignment) reduced the need for such explicit computations.

There is an interesting tradeoff. While manually arranging items takes time, it cognitively involves the user; and thus the problem state is thoroughly understood and becomes memorable. While sorting in the spreadsheet is fast, it is perceptually jarring (as positions of objects change abruptly) and doesn't require cognitive involvement; and as such state may be less well understood and remembered.

Temporary Planning Spaces

Strategies had differing emphases in the planning, execution, and verification and recovery phases and thus made differing uses of space. In the DataBoard, a number of participants created separate planning spaces, where they represented problem space features, such as distribution of defects by priority and difficulty or dependency graph-like arrangements of defects. One of the participants called this a "parking lot," where one could temporarily park their partial solutions. In the Spreadsheet, participants had overlapping uses of space during planning and execution. A few participants created separate spaces where they did verification. They created tables to manually keep tally of assignments, but had problems updating the counts. In DataBoard, on the other hand, some participants had difficulty moving spatial arrangements off the planning spaces and merging them into the solution spaces. This was in part due to the fact that DataBoard didn't support list merge, as well as some specific list implementation issues.

CONCLUSION

Freeform satial interfaces help users to (1) flexibly map the problem onto a freeform arrangement and plan their strategies accordingly; (2) execute their strategies incrementally and easily check their actions at each step, leveraging reduced internal computation; and (3) verify and tweak their complete solutions easily, due to clear perceptual arrangements of objects in the space. These benefits, however, don't come for free, as they require involvement and effort from the users and thus may degrade overall performance.

There is a spectrum of spatial interfaces from completely freeform to completely structured. In this paper, we compared two specific instances of spatial interfaces near the ends of the spectrum. Our main goal was to further our understanding of spatial interfaces in support of problem solving tasks. We believe that there is benefit if we can provide a general way to transform structured domains onto freeform interfaces, augmented by some structuring and computational capabilities, to support more effective problem solving of common problems in these domains.

ACKNOWLEDGMENTS

We thank Steve Whittaker, Paul Maglio, and Chris Campbell for their input into the design and analysis of the study and Jeff Heer for suggesting important related work.

REFERENCES

1. Antle, A.N., Droumeva, M. and Ha, D. Thinking with hands: An embodied approach to the analysis of children's interaction with computational objects. In *Proc. CHI '09*, ACM, 2009, 3961-3966.
2. Arias, E., Eden, H., Fischer, G., Gorman, A., and Scharff, E. 2000. Transcending the individual human mind-creating shared understanding through collaborative design. *ACM Trans. Comput.-Hum. Interact.* 7, 1 (March 2000), 84-113.
3. Agarawala, A. and Balakrishnan, R. 2006. Keepin' it real: pushing the desktop metaphor with physics, piles and the pen. In *Proc.* CHI '06. ACM, 1283-1292.
4. Bailey, B.P. and J.A. Konstan. Are Informal Tools Better? Comparing DEMAIS, Pencil and Paper, and Authorware for Early Multimedia Design. In *Proc. CHI '03*, ACM, 2003, 313-320.
5. Burnett, M., Atwood, J., Djang, R., Gottfried, H., Reichwein, J., Yang., S. Forms/3: A First-Order Visual Language to Explore the Boundaries of the Spreadsheet Paradigm, *Journal of Functional Programming* 11(2), March 2001, 155-206.
6. Ekstrom, R. B., French, J.W., Harman, H.H., and Derman D. (1976). *Manual for Kit of Factor-Referenced Cognitive Tests*. Princeton, NJ: Educational Testing Service.
7. Hailpern, J., Hinterbichler, E., Leppert, C., Cook, D., and Bailey, B.P. 2007. TEAM STORM: Demonstrating an interaction model for working with multiple ideas during creative group work. In *Proc. Creativity & Cognition* (C&C '07). ACM, 2007, 193-202.
8. Hinckley, K., Zhao, S., Sarin, R., Baudisch, P., Cutrell, E., Shilman, M, Tan, D. InkSeine: *In Situ* search for active note taking, In *Proc. CHI '07*, ACM, 2007, 251-260.
9. Jacob, R. J., Ishii, H., Pangaro, G., and Patten, J. 2002. A tangible interface for organizing information using a grid. In *Proc. CHI '02*, ACM, 2002, 339-346.
10. Jones, W. P. and Dumais, S. T. 1986. The spatial metaphor for user interfaces: experimental tests of reference by location versus name. *ACM Trans. Inf. Syst.* 4, 1 (Jan. 1986), 42-63.
11. Kang, H., Bederson, B.,B., Suh, B. Capture, Annotate, Browse, Find, Share: Novel Interfaces for Personal Photo Management. *Int. J. Hum. Comput. Interaction 23*(3): 315-337 (2007).
12. Kirsh, D. The intelligent use of space, *Artificial Intelligence*, v.73 n.1-2, p.31-68, Feb. 1995
13. Kirsh, D. and Maglio, P. On Distinguishing Epistemic from Pragmatic Action. *Cognitive Science 18*, (1994), 513-549.
14. Lansdale, M. W. Remembering about documents: memory for appearance, format, and location. *Ergonomics*, 34, 8 (1991), 1161-1178.
15. Malone, T.W. How do People Organize their Desks? Implications for the Design of Office Information Systems. *ACM Transactions on Office Information Systems 1,* 1 (January 1983), 99-112.
16. Mandler, J. M., Seefmiller, D., Day, J. On the coding of spatial information. *Memory & Cognition* 5, 1 (1997), 10-16.
17. Millen, D. R., Schriefer, A., Lehder, D. Z., and Dray, S. M. 1997. Mind maps and causal models: using graphical representations of field research data. In *CHI '97 Extended Abstracts,* ACM, 265-266.
18. Moran, T. P., van Melle, W., and Chiu, P. 1998. Spatial interpretation of domain objects integrated into a freeform electronic whiteboard. In *Proc. UIST '98*. ACM, 1998, 175-184.
19. Naveh-Benjamin, M. Coding of Spatial Location Information: An Automatic Process? *Journal of Experimental Psychology: Learning, Memory, and Cognition 13,* 4 (1987), 595-605.
20. Norman, D., & Hutchins, E. Computation via direct manipulation. Final Report to Office of Naval Research, Contract No. NOOO14-85-C-0133. University of California, San Diego, 1988.
21. Robertson, G., Czerwinski, M., Larson, K., Robbins, D. C., Thiel, D., van Dantzich, M. Data Mountain: Using Spatial Memory for Document Management. In *Proc. UIST '98*, ACM. 1998, 153-162.
22. Warr, A. and O'Neill, E. Tool Support for Creativity using Externalisations. In *Proc. Creativity and Cognition* (C & C '07). ACM, 2007, 127-136.
23. Zhang, J. The Nature of External Representations in Problem Solving. *Cognitive Science 21*, 2 (1997), 179-217.
24. Zhang, J. and Norman, D. A. Representations in Distributed Cognitive Tasks. *Cognitive Science 18*, 1 (1994), 87-122.

Utilizing Multimedia Capabilities of Mobile Phones to Support Teaching in Schools in Rural Panama

Elba del Carmen Valderama Bahamondez[♦□], Christian Winkler[♦], Albrecht Schmidt[□]

[♦]Paluno, University of Duisburg-Essen
Gerlingstr. 16, 45127 Essen, Germany
{elba.valderrama-bahamondez, christian.winkler.pc}@uni-due.de

[□]VIS, University of Stuttgart
Universitätsstr. 38, 70569 Stuttgart, Germany
albrecht.schmidt@acm.org

ABSTRACT
Providing good education is one of the major challenges for humanity. In many developing regions in the world improving educational standards is seen as a central building block for improving socio-economic situation of society. Based on our research in Panama we report on how mobile phones can be used as educational tools. In contrast to personal computers mobile phones are widely available and in Panama over 80% of the children have access to phones. We report on four different studies building on one another. We conducted surveys, focus groups, and group interviews with several hundred teachers and pupils to assess opportunities, needs, and threads for using phones in teaching and learning. Based on the feedback received we created a set of use cases and finally evaluated these in a field study in a rural multigrade school in Panama. Our findings suggest that current phones with multimedia capabilities provide a valuable resource for teaching and learning across many subjects. In particular recording of audio and video, programs for drawing, and taking photos were used in very creative and constructive ways beyond the use cases envisioned by us and initial skepticism of parents turned into support.

Author Keywords
Developing countries, learning, children, mobile phone

ACM Classification Keywords
H5.m. Information interfaces and presentation (e.g., HCI): Miscellaneous; K3.1 Computers and Education: Computer Uses in Education

General Terms
Human Factors

INTRODUCTION
Improving education is a major concern in many countries around the world. From a governmental perspective, improving education is an investment in the country's future that can result in economic growth and increased global competitiveness. For individuals and families in these developing regions, the motivation to participate in education is typically very high, since education is seen as a way to improve personal living conditions and gain in the long term prosperity. Nevertheless, resources for education are limited both on a national level (e.g. budgets available for schools) and on a personal level (e.g. time available for learning).

The use of new technologies to improve education is tempting but very difficult at the same time. New technologies often seem to offer easier and wider access to educational materials and means for improving learning efficiency. At the same time, there is also a very strong cultural influence on how schools are organized and how teaching is conducted. The agreement within a society on what knowledge

Figure 1. Views of the School El Retiro

Figure 2. A student recording his voice in the English lesson using a multimedia phone

and skills are important is deeply rooted and not easily changed. Thus, the approach taken in teaching and the relationship between the teacher and pupil is very much dependent on the culture and must be respected when introducing new technologies. If these technologies impose certain teaching/learning paradigms, even if considered superior to the traditional way of teaching, they are likely to fail.

In contrast to personal computers (PC) mobile phones have become widely adopted around the world, including developing regions. In comparison to PCs mobile phones are easier to administrate and users have a great interest in keeping the devices functional at all times as they use them as communication devices. Additionally there is already an established local infrastructure for buying, maintaining, and repairing phones.

In our research we assess the potential of mobile phones as learning tools. The vision is that in the near future students and pupils would use mobile phones as educational device that offers them much of the functionality traditional PCs offer (as well as additional capabilities for multimedia documentation) and that phones can be used for learning at school. In contrast to previous research, we explore the design space of inherent capabilities of mobile phones, which are only enhanced by some generally useful applications (e.g., drawing application).

In this paper we report on our findings on emergent mobile phone usage and our experience with using mobile phones in the teaching context in schools in Panama. In order to understand how mobile phones are currently used and how widespread access to these devices is, we started our exploration by conducting a survey asking 300 pupils and 85 educators across Panama about current practice. Based on these findings we continued by conducting group interviews and design sessions in two iterations, first with 37 and the second time with 190 teachers in order to understand their needs for support in teaching. In these sessions we especially aimed at uncovering potential use cases, anticipated threats, and expected problems. Our approach was to look at ways in which mobile phones can be useful tools within the current educational system and the current ways of teaching. Based on the rich information that we received we finally designed a field experiment with 40 pupils and 3 teachers in a rural multigrade school (see Figure 1), which is the most common school type in Panama, to explore and evaluate different use cases for mobile phones as teaching aids (Figure 2 as an example use case).

The surveys, interviews, and field study were conducted in Panama and hence the findings apply in the first place there. However in the course of the research we discovered more and more that teachers appropriated the phone as a tool to their personal style of teaching. We see this as an indicator that the approach we describe in this paper could be exemplary for other developing regions and potentially also for developed countries.

The rest of the paper is structured as follows: In the next section we discuss related work in developing countries. We then give a short overview of the educational situation in Panama and describe in detail the proliferation of computer and mobile phones and their application in rural and urban areas. We then describe the initial concerns and opportunities seen by teachers collected in group interviews. In the main part of the paper we provide a comprehensive description and results of the two weeks field study conducted in a rural school. The paper then wraps up with discussion and conclusion.

RELATED WORK

In the literature we find several learning approaches for using computers and mobile phones for unprivileged.

One approach are low cost laptops specially designed for children, where the most outstanding project is the OLPC [8]. It is equipped with multimedia, collaborative UI (Sugar) and educational software. Authors of OLPC claim that children learn mainly by creating and sharing with their peers using only the laptops. Despite all the efforts, the OLPC have not been received by the developing countries as expected [10]. There have been concerns that this learning model would not fit educational curriculum, requirements and policies of some developing countries [10].

Mischief [13] is a project that investigates the use of multiple mice connected to a large display. This approach allows children to work simultaneously on the screen and supports cooperative work and learning. This approach is very economic but is difficult to use in common multigrade school environments, where children from different grades and learning backgrounds share the same classroom. In addition, in a large audience [14], it seems to be difficult to visualize all mice on screen.

Since mobile phones are popular in developing countries [9], this motivated several researchers to explore their usage for learning, with encouraging results. Kam et al. [1, 3, 6] implemented games on mobile phones for learning English as a second language based on traditional game practices in India. Kumar et al. [1] explored the unsupervised learning with mobile phones in the everyday life of rural children in India, while Kam et al. [6] do this in school settings. Results indicate introduced software and technology motivated children in learning [1] and that mobile games can be useful for learning in unprivileged areas only if the local game practices are well understood and considered [3,6]. In MobilED [2] Ford and Leinonen created an alternative approach to the Wikipedia where users can search and edit content through the use of audio and SMS.

M4Girls [11] and Mobi [12] looked at supporting Mathematics learning for students in South Africa. Both approaches considered the educational curriculum, the cultural-social context of the country, and the available technologies. Frohlich et al. [4] and Reitmaieer et al. [5] explored usage of the phone camera plus audio to support storytelling practices in underprivileged areas in India an Africa respectively. The study was focused on adults.

Besides, Hollow and Masperi [7] explored the use of a video-audio player customized handheld device in primary schools in Malawi. Here, children had access to different lessons installed on the mobile devices. The audio-visual lessons were explained by cartoons and were interactive by means of multiple-choice tests. Children could not pass to the next lesson until they answered the tests correctly.

In most of the learning approaches for developing countries presented here [1,6,7,8,11,12,13], researchers have implemented their own applications integrating multimedia features. At least in rural school environments there has not been any exploration in the use of multiple, default mobile phone features without installing any additional learning software. Different from [1] we found (1) an opportunity to use mobile phones to support other subjects besides language learning, (2) particular benefits of mobile phones for multigrade classroom environments, and (3) different, naturally evolved scenarios for mobile phone usage in class.

EDUCATIONAL SITUATION IN PANAMA

Panama has a very young population and a large portion of the population is at school age: 39% of Panamanians are between 0-19 years. Hence, maintaining schools, providing sufficient educational material and having enough qualified teachers is a great challenge. A large portion of multigrade schools (74%) – where pupils of different school-grades share the same classroom – is found in rural areas. This highlights the efforts to maximize the utilization of resources. All children are required to attend school from ages 5 to 17 (13 years of school). Panamanian laws also guarantee them free access to public education. The major subjects taught in schools are Spanish (the native language for most pupils), Mathematics, Science, Social Sciences (Geography and History) and English (as a foreign language). Topics are based on the National Educational Curriculum [15]. The vast majority of children attend public schools. Schools are classified in urban, rural and difficult access area schools according to where they are located.

Government and Teachers Perspective on Technological Challenges in Education

We met with the Secretary of State for Education, the Head of National Education, and Head of Primary Education of Panama. During these meetings, they explained to us the situation and their opinions on implementing new technologies in the schools, i.e. computers in Panamanian schools. With the high number of students and a lack of human resources and infrastructure, their limited budget is often used to fulfill other priorities. In difficult access area schools, the existence of computer labs is almost zero. Overpopulation of children in classrooms and the multigrade system both limit the children's access to computers. Another concern is the security of the equipment. In some areas, computers have been "lost". A further worry is allowing children access to the Internet. They do not want children to visit unsuitable sites. Another problem is computer maintenance.

RESEARCH METHODOLOGY

We realized four studies that can be grouped in three stages. In stage (1) we used surveys to analyze the access and use of technology by teachers and children and to get initial clues where and how mobile phones could support the learning-teaching process. In stage (2) we used focus groups, interviews, and paper prototyping, in two different studies to validate findings from stage 1, discuss about benefits and concerns of using mobile phones in class and extract teachers' ideas and opinions for using mobile phones as educational tools. Finally, we conducted a field study in stage (3), to explore how pupils and teachers make use of multimedia phones in a classroom setting and to validate the results from previous stages.

STAGE 1: ACCESS AND USE OF TECHNOLOGY BY TEACHERS AND CHILDREN

In Panama, as in Latin America in general and in other developing regions, there exists a digital division between urban and rural schools, which we wanted to capture in the survey. We realized the survey in May 2009.

The survey was conducted in three typical public schools in Panama, where two were urban schools located in Panama City and the other a rural school located in Panama East. The interviews were conducted during a 12-day period in May 2009. In total, 300 children were interviewed – 148 from urban schools and 152 from rural schools. The children were between 9 and 17 years of age. The average age was 12.4 years. 52.2% of the students were male. Additionally, 85 teachers were interviewed, of whom 65% were female. These initial findings have been reported in detail in [16], here we summarize the most important findings.

Access to Technology

Although we expected a higher penetration of mobile phones than access to computers, the actual numbers were still surprising: 97.6% of teachers and 80.3% of schoolchildren had access to a mobile phone. This is in accordance with the worldwide trend [9] of mobile phone penetration in developed as well as developing countries. Children have limited access to computers and Internet at home: in fact, in the case of children in urban areas 11.9% have computers without Internet and 49.3% with Internet access at home; from children in rural areas, 14,6% have computers with Internet and 11,4% without Internet. A considerable number of teachers and pupils have modern mobile phones. About 60% of the educators and 77% of children have access to mobile phones with Internet access and/or an integrated camera.

Potential Usage of Mobile Phones for Learning

In order to see where mobile phones could be best used as learning platforms, the children were asked about subjects where they have the most difficulties in learning and where they might want help with (e.g., through learning games). Additionally, we asked them how they get to and from school to get a better picture of possible user scenarios where children might be able to learn with mobile phones. Answers indicate many children (44.2%) would appreciate help in Mathematics, especially multiplication.

Some children felt that they "*cannot learn the multiplication table*" or do "*not [have] much time to practice*". Although most children saw their main problems in Mathematics, the overall responses differed greatly between rural and urban areas. Students in rural areas wanted support in a more diverse set of subjects, whereas students in urban areas were largely concerned with Mathematics.

We also asked teachers which subjects they thought children struggled with and could benefit from the use of technology (computer and/or mobile phones). The majority of teachers considered Mathematics (94.8%), English (35.1%), and Spanish (25.6%) as the most difficult subjects. Teachers stated that children in primary schools "*do not know the multiplication table*" and those in middle schools exhibit a "*lack of [basic mathematical principles]*" and "*do not know the four basic arithmetic operations*".

When we asked teachers about their opinions on educational applications on mobile phones, in particular for mathematical exercise (e.g basic Arithmetic) and English learning, 75% supported the idea of reinforced Mathematic learning and 54.1% supported the idea of English language learning.

STAGE 2: TEACHERS OPINION OF USING MOBILE PHONES IN CLASSROOM

Based on findings from our previous survey we wanted to explore some concrete ideas how teachers think mobile phones can be used in class. So we conducted focus groups and a large interview with a paper prototype.

Focus Group

In December 2009, we realized three focus groups with a total of 37 teachers in 3 different schools, two urban and one rural school. There were 28 male and 9 females with an average of 42,9 years old. We asked the participants regarding their expertise using PCs and mobile phones. The rating scale was from 1 to 5, where 1 meant no experience and 5 meant expert user. Participants have had an average expertise of 2.94 using a computer and an expertise of 3.6 in the use of mobile phones. This implies that 82% of participants were more experts using mobile phones than computers.

Most teachers liked very much the idea of using mobile phones for supporting teaching: "*they (children) really like this thing and are more expert than me*"; "*I think with mobile phones children will be very enthusiastic*". But two teachers were strongly against using mobile phones in classroom, "*I do not agree using mobile phones for learning in special Mathematics because (they) lead children to be more dump and dependent... computers do everything*".

According to the teachers, main concerns with the use of mobile phones are the security, distraction, and behavior problem among students, as one commented to us: "*Imagine large classes of 30 and even 40 students with mobile phone, how I control that (they) use it properly.*"

Two teachers had already used mobile phones in class with their pupils "*I was tired that my students filming me all the time and put me in the Internet... I am cabinetmaking teacher and because of the limited class time I have not enough time to review their works, ... so one day I tell them open your (mobile phone) camera and take a picture of your work ... they were so enthusiastic and concentrated taking the pictures... next day everyone wanted to show me and explain their works... since then I do not experience such bad behavior and I continue time to time using the phone in my class.*"

Many teachers agreed upon the key being the multimodal usage, especially combining audio, pictures and text. As well as to design applications as games to prevent children from becoming bored. All teachers considered the SMS exchange as strong problem for learning Spanish. The shortness and incorrect writing of the words are their main concerns. In general, they welcomed the help of mobile phones for Math, Spanish and English and perhaps also other subjects.

Paper Prototype

During three weeks of February we had the chance to interview around 190 teachers, which represented 1% of the teacher population in Panama. The teachers interviewed were representative of urban, rural and difficult access areas and we met them in groups of 30-40. We presented them a big paper prototype with an example of a mobile learning platform, where teachers would be able to create tasks and send to their pupils. The paper prototype was informed from our results of our previous focus groups. In total, we presented four (2x2) paper prototypes: one pair that would allow creation of mathematics tasks and another pair for science tasks, each pair consisting of one prototype representing a child's phone and the other a teacher's phone. The majority of the teachers (80%) liked the idea of using mobile phones easily in class. Teachers stated that students are very good with new technologies and are able to work with it. However, they think "*if we ever work with such phones... we have to receive good training on how to use it or otherwise children will know more than us*".

STAGE 3: FIELD STUDY IN THE CLASSROOM

Motivated by the findings from previous stages, including the high accessibility of mobile phones and teachers and children welcoming mobile phone usage, we decided to conduct a field study in a school. Our goal with the field study was to explore the design space of using mobile phones inside the classroom that fit with the local educational curriculum and teachers' needs. This goal splits into the following research questions: (1) how can multimedia capable mobile phones be used for learning in real classroom settings?; (2) how do teachers and pupils embrace the use of mobile phones to support common learning tasks in-situ?; (3) how will teachers integrate mobile phones in their daily teaching plan?

The findings from stage 1 stated that (1) pupils living in rural areas have much lower access to computers at home than their urban peers, (2) children in rural areas seem to welcome the support of the mobile phone in all the core subjects, including Maths and (3) teachers agree on expecting benefits of using mobile phones in multigrade schools. Thus we decided to start our field study with rural multigrade schools and then extend it to urban schools.

User Study Settings

The user study was realized with students and teachers from 4th, 5th and 6th grade of the school El Retiro (see Figure 1). The school is located in the province of Coclé, around 120 kilometers from Panama City. The school El Retiro is classified as rural multigrade school. The school-grades are organized as follows: 1st and 2nd grade are together in one classroom; likewise 4th and 5th grade are together. Kindergarten, third, and sixth grade have their own classroom. Most of the habitants of El Retiro live from the agricultural activities, and as workers of the two main luxury hotels located in Coclé. The families there have low income. Although it is located in the rural area, the school is one of the few schools privileged with a computer lab with (very slow) Internet access.

In order to avoid any bias a mobile phone was given to each participant. The model used was a Nokia 5530 XpressMusic, which was provided by Nokia for the duration of the study. This model was selected because it includes robust and rich multimedia and communication features. In addition it provides touch screen interaction (with fingers and stylus), thereby enables, e.g. drawing apps.

Since a modern mobile phone is in Panama, similarly to most places around the world, a status symbol and also the monetary value (retail price in the US in 2010 about 150U$) of these mid-range phones is in this region significant (a phone represents 60% of a typical monthly salary in this community) we decided that the phones were only used by the pupils in school and were not taken home in order to minimize the risk of theft or mugging. The teachers received the phones first, and they were encouraged to use the phone during the time of the field study also as their regular phone.

For the pupils we decided to start with the highest grade and introduce the mobile phone there first. The rational for this was that this reduces the potential for bullying and at the same time allowed a step-by-step introduction. We then continued to introduce the phones to the next lower grade and so on. We anticipated an effect (1) that the younger children would then be eager to try it out if the older children had it first and (2) that older children could help explaining how the phones work and provide additional support. Both expectations were well met and the introduction went without difficulties. Every child used the same unique phone during the whole field study. The mobile phones were delivered daily at the beginning and returned at end of each class that the teacher planned to involve cell phones. In order to introduce the use of mobile phone to pupils, to help when required and to observe the development of the field study, the first author of this paper stayed in the classroom.

On all children's mobile phones a logger application had been installed which ran transparently in background, autostarting on system boot, and cross-monitored with another watchdog application. The logger records every few seconds which applications are actively used by the participants. The data is logged with timestamp to a text file per day. Additionally, every 20 seconds the logger takes a screenshot of the active application of the pupil while the phone is in use (i.e. not in sleep mode). The application was written in Python (logging, picture taking) and Symbian C++ (access to system APIs). The data was logged to hidden folders on a 4GB SD card. The data could only be accessed by inserting the SD card directly into a computer. Hidden files and folders prohibited images from being erased by children as well as from appearing in the picture gallery.

The user study was realized from September 6th to 17th, 2010. The schedule in the school was from 8 a.m. to 1:30 p.m., thus five and a half hours. The school-hour in multigrade schools is 60 minutes. On average, children used the mobile phone around three to four hours daily, which represents between 54% and 72% of daily school time.

Besides the information we got from the logger file we realized two surveys (one before and one after the study), a final group interview, and a daily observation of pupils' interaction with the mobile phone. In the first survey, we asked children and teachers about their expectations on how to use a multimedia mobile phone for learning. At the end of the study, all participants filled in a post study questionnaire about their feedback and opinion of the study. Additionally we interviewed all the children to discuss about their learning experience during the study. We also met some parents to get their opinion about the use of mobile phones to support learning.

Participants

In total 40 children and 3 teachers participated in the user study. The mean age of the pupils was 10.5 years and 20 were girls. In the sixth grade and fifth grade there were 13 pupils each, and in fourth grade there were 14 pupils. The participating teachers were the teacher of sixth grade, fourth-fifth grade, and the English teacher. From the 40 children, only 4 children said they had a computer at home, but 39 children stated that someone in the family had a mobile phone at home. Even 10% of the children participants owned a personal mobile phone. There were 7 children that had never used a mobile phone before. Children have had no experience with touch screens before.

Description of the tasks

The first day we gave a general overview of the multimedia capabilities of the mobile phones to all teachers of the school. Then we asked teachers to design practicing tasks that utilize mobile phones and are according to the learning goals and content they had planned to teach in the near future. Additionally, based on previous findings, we asked teachers to focus on Mathematics, Spanish, English, and

Nature Science. However, teachers were free to add additional subjects in which to use the phones in the field study.

With respect to phone capabilities, we studied four main multimedia features, which are: 1) taking a picture and recording a video, 2) watching a video, 3) recording voice and listen to it and 4) painting and writing with the stylus.

For camera, video, and audio functions only those integrated with the mobile phone have been used. For evaluating the use of the stylus with the touch screen, third-party software was used, namely PaintPad (www.zensis.com) and Sticky Notes Touch (www.offscr.com). The former allows drawing and painting from blank as well as painting on saved images. StickyNotes simulates a post-it pinboard where users can pin hand-written messages.

The description of the activities realized during the field study including tasks, multimedia features used, and learning content is presented in table 1.

Watching Video

The activity of watching video was realized in Mathematics, Spanish and Nature Sciences, as described in table 1. All teachers used this feature to introduce a new topic, following the same pattern: pupils observed the video several times; after that teachers reinforced the concept with explanations and discussion with the pupils; then pupils saw the video one more time. In the end, the teacher realized other activities to extend and reinforce the topic either with or without mobile phone. The videos lasted between 1:10 and 9:38 minutes. Because of the considerable size of the videos (between 3 and 142 MB) they were installed on pupils' phones before the class.

The videos that children observed were either watched online (table 1: f), downloaded and saved on children phones (table 1: a), or own home-made videos. In the first case, the Internet connection was so slow that this form of watching video was tried only once and later replaced by the option of download, save and install on children's phones the day before the lesson. The third case is interesting to clarify: some videos were made by the grade teacher (see table 1: d) but also one teacher requested an external Math pedagogue to create the video to introduce the concept of measuring an area using the International System of Units (table 1: b). This topic seems to be complex in rural areas, both to teach and to learn. Multigrade teachers in Panama have no specialization in any specific subject, but have a general background. In the video the Math teacher recreates the size of the square meter and its submultiples with the real measure.

During the observation of videos pupils were fully concentrated and most of them played the videos longer and more often than required while waiting for peers to finish. In standard class situations, children are often distracted and miss part or all of teachers' explanations and the lesson. It carries out that children are often too shy to ask the teacher to clarify on open questions. When watching lessons from video, pupils can easily repeat parts of the video they missed or did not understand.

Children and teachers stated that watching videos helped pupils in understanding the class. One teacher said *"it (video) can help the student to learn easier through repeating"*, another said *"when students see the video three or four times, they have almost learned the lesson"*. Children also welcome the use of watching videos, as one pupil commented to us *"(videos) explained me better (the lesson)"*.

Educational Goal	Learning activities using the mobile phone
Mathematics: History of the longitude measures (6th)	(a) **Watching** a **video** about the history of the measure and the International System of Units as introduction of the topic; pupils in group of 2-3 **film** using part of their own body to measure e.g.: blackboard, books, walls, etc.
Measures of Area using the International Systems of units: square meters(6th)	(b) Children **watched a** customize **video** introducing the concept of square meter, its multiples and submultiples, then in the yard, children represent the size of a square decameter and **take a picture** of it
Addition of homogeneous fractions (4th) and multiplication - division of fractions (5th)	(c) Children **watched a video** introducing the concept of addition with homogeneous fractions. (d) **Watching video** about the concept of multiplication and division of fractions respectively.
Multiplication table (4th)	(e)Children **listen an audio** file and with the multiplication tables recorded by the teacher
Spanish: Graphemes of questionable writing in building homophones words in the context of a sentence (6th)	(f) Children opened Youtube, search and **watched a video online** (use of B-V). (g) Either **teachers take picture** of orthographical tasks (use of S-C-Z) from the Spanish book and **send via Bluetooth** to the children. Or **children take picture** directly from the Spanish books task. (use of B-V) (h) Children solve the tasks with **paint pad** (figure 3), then they **save and sent the filled task** to the teacher **via Bluetooth**
English Practicing future tense (6th); Practicing reading and pronunciation (6th)	(i) Teacher **recorded herself (audio)** reading an English letter using future tense in their phone; the file was installed on the children´s phones; pupils **listened to it** while reading the letter from the book (figure 2), then children **recorded themselves reading** aloud the letter; finally teacher and children listened to all recorded audio
Months of the year and days of the week(6th)	(j) Children individually prepared a speech about it, **filmed** in groups of two with children switching roles (speaker/cameraman).
Listening (5th and 4th)	(k) Teacher **recorded English nursery rhymes**, then pupil **listened** and extracted known words
Nature Sciences: Biology Human reproduction and sexuality(4th, 5th),	(l) Teacher **took a picture** of an exercise about the human reproductive system, sent it **via Bluetooth** to pupils, then children solved the exercise using **PaintPad**, saved it and sent it back to the teacher, who evaluated it using **PaintPad**. (figure 3)
Sexual reproduction of the plants (5th)	(m) Children were asked to go the garden and to **make a video** about the part of the flowers
Nature Sciences: Ecology Fossil fuel energy sources (6th)	(n) Teacher set pupils a questionnaire for pupils to **look up answers in Google**; then they **created a video** in groups of 3 where the pupils act as interviewee, interviewer and cameraman. (o) Building of a conceptual map about petrol using the **stylus** and the **StickyNotes Application**
Social Sciences: Privatization and globalization (6th)	(p) Children prepared for a debate where in groups of 3 pupils recreated a talk-show using the **video camera** of the phone.
Religion: Love and respect your father and mother (6th)	(q) Pupils painted (using **paintPad**) the history of the Bible; then **sent it via Bluetooth** to the teacher (figure 3).

Tabla 1. Learning activities realized during the field study

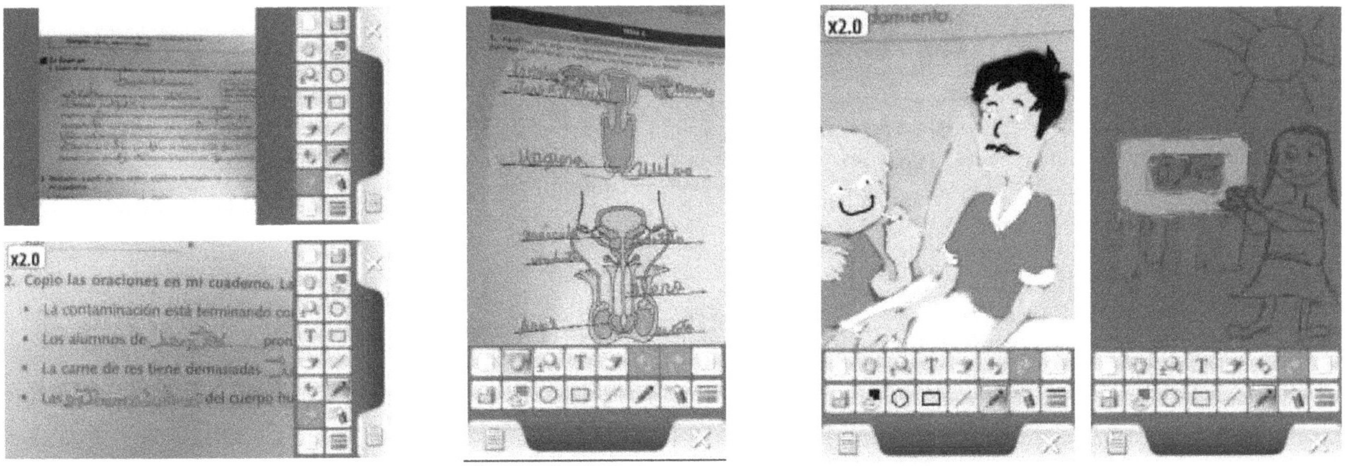

Figure 3. Different usage of photo annotation as used by students. Left: Filling a Spanish orthographic task 6th grade; middle: writing the parts of the human sexual reproductive organs 5th grade, right: painted pictures of a bible story

Recording Video by Pupils

In contrast to watching video, this feature was used by teachers to extend, review and reinforce a topic. Debate, dramatization, speech, and dialog were common activities which teacher used to help pupils learn the concept. Teachers stated that using the video camera enhances the motivation and involvement of pupils to do these tasks. Pupils showed their motivation with filming in that they did not stop before every group member was content with the result. Repeating the film-takes could as well help pupils indirectly in learning the lesson.

Pupils filmed individually as well as in small groups. Teachers later reviewed recorded footage. Filming videos was one of the most preferred activities and pupils found it simple to use "*for me it is very easy... only I press a button and I am filming*".

Recording and Playing Audio

Teachers used this activity especially in English (see table 1 and figure 2), but also in Mathematics (see table 1: e). Pupils found this feature to be very practical for improving the pronunciation in English and welcomed it more than we expected: "*I can hear me and correct pronunciation errors*". Teachers stated that when children record their own voice when reading, and later play it, it supports (1) the self- evaluation and self-critical spirit of the pupils, both important aspects for the teaching-learning process, (2) the improvement for pronunciation and listening to English.

In our pre-study questionnaire half of the 5th grade children answered they imagine mobile phones helpful for learning multiplication tables; not with pictures, games or text as we imagined, but with voice. They stated that with the cell phone they have the opportunity to record the multiplication table talking or singing, and listen repetitively. From our observation and talks with teachers, we think the reason of this preference can be: (1) the usual technique in this classroom for learning the multiplication table being iterative listening and repeating in choir (auditive memory) and (2) different from lower grades where pupils learn the concept of multiplication, on fifth grade pupils already knowing the concept of multiplication, with the requirement for visualizing the concept being lower.

Take a photo, Writing and Painting

One activity proposed from teachers was to take a picture of a task in the book, then let children fill it in, and finally send it back to the teacher. Books are only lent to the children, thus they are not allowed to write into them. So either children have to handwrite the exercise or pay to receive a copy of the practice. Teachers commented "*they manage that pencil (stylus) just as it (was) a real one*". For several examples see Figure 3, a) in Spanish, b) Biology, and c) in Religion. Painting and drawing still plays a role in upper levels of primary schools and not only in arts. In subjects like Nature Science and Religion, painting is among the main activities done in class. In sixth grade a teacher asked pupils to paint and illustrate a reading from the Bible, which can be seen in Figure 3. PaintPad was more successful than we expected, as one pupil said "*I love it... I can erase, change color and repaint again ... in the paper I cannot erase or change colors after I started*". *I feel phone*

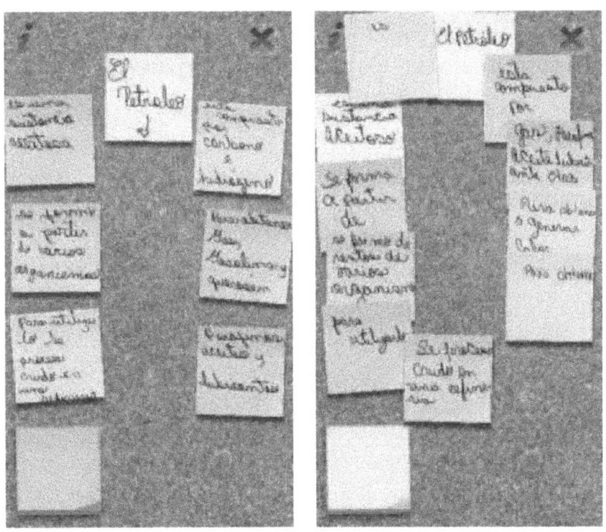

Figure 4 Conceptual map done by pupils of 6th grade using Sticky Notes Touch®.

was helpful for learning about female and male reproductive system and was very funny to write on the phone"

Finally in the class of Nature Science, children once used StickyNotes to create a conceptual map (see table 1: o and figure 4). From our observation and conversation with children they missed from this a mechanism to erase letters and not to "trash" the whole note away. It is important to note that the creation of conceptual maps is the most common practice in Panamanian schools to summarize what children have learned.

Interaction and behavior of the children in class

Although children had no experience with such phones, they learned very fast how to use them. After the second use of any multimedia function, most of the children had no more questions regarding the use of the mobile phone. Even more, sending a file via Bluetooth was explored only three times with sixth grade and two students were able to do it alone the second time. According to our observation children who had not used a mobile phone before, at the end of the study, were similarly skilled as others. The most difficult task was writing with the virtual keyboard, especially for those not familiar with mobile phones. During the 2nd week, there was no question how to use a function of a mobile phone in 6th grade. Fourth and fifth grade still had some questions because they started with the study two days later than 6th grade.

According to the teachers, pupils were much more involved and participative in the class, and more enthusiastic and concentrated in the realization of the tasks with the cell phones.

After the field study we asked children if they perceived a change in the interaction and behavior of the pupils in the classroom using a mobile phone. Most of the children, 84%, stated that they feel to learn more using a mobile phone, 54% stated that they participated more actively in the tasks, and around 65% of children stated that classes were more interesting and funny using a mobile phone. 63% of children stated that with mobile phones they were more collaborative with their peers. Only 3 students stated that class interaction was equal to that without cell phones.

Use of mobile phone by gender and age

At the beginning, boys seemed to be more comfortable and learn faster using the phone than their girl peers. During the first day of the user study in 6th grade, four of the first five children that finished the activity were boys. Consequently we got more questions from girls the first day.

Our recorded screenshots indicate that boys were more curious than girls and explored the phone more eagerly than girls – though this gap decreased a little by the second week. The most explored and used applications by boys were games, filming and taking pictures. Possible explanations for this are 1) that according to teachers the female pupils behaved and are better students than their male peers, and 2) boys at the beginning finished many of the tasks quicker than girls and therefore had more free time while waiting for girls to finish.

Another interesting aspect was the carefulness. Girls have been more careful in completing the tasks with the mobile phone, especially when painting with PaintPad. E.g., girls painted slowly and if the painting did not satisfy them, they repeatedly started over. In contrast most boys did not, which can also explain why girls took longer to finish.

Children learned by doing, they were not intensively trained in any of the features used. Further, age played a significant role as well. Comparing children of 6th, 5th, and 4th grade, higher grades learned faster to use the functions of the mobile phones. However we think with more training children of 4th grade could compete with their higher peers.

Teachers and children alone

Can children and teachers get along integrating the mobile phones in the learning activities without our supporting attendance? This was the question raised at the end of the study. So we decided to conduct a last day trial with 6th grade without us, where teacher and children worked completely alone. The teacher advised two activities: first children had to look up information about nature gas (Nature Sciences) in the mobile Internet (in teamwork) and then they should create a video with the information found. The second task was to take a photo of a learning task in the Spanish book, fill it out and send it to the teacher via Bluetooth.

According to the film we captured, screenshots and the teacher's opinion, the activity worked very well; she commented to us *"there were no questions on how to do they just knew how to do everything (on the phone)"* *"they were concentrated..."*. The only problem was that phone memory was full and she could not receive all works.

Multigrade classroom

In our study we also observed that integrating mobile phones in class helps to free some time for teachers, especially valuable in multigrade classrooms. One example of the field study: While pupils of fifth grade were making a video about the parts of flowers in the garden (table 1: m), the teacher gave a Math lecture to the pupils of 4th grade. When fifth grade pupils returned, the teacher reviewed their videos while children of 4th grade were solving a Mathematic practice related to the lecture before.

Feedback from the participants

Children and teachers reported positive feedback from the features used. We asked teachers to evaluate the usefulness of the multimedia functions used during the study on a 1-5 scale, where 5 meant strong agreement that it was useful. All the functions were considered between useful and highly useful: Play a video 4.5; Record a video 4.9; Take a picture plus Paintpad 5.0; Record voice and play audio 5.0. Table 2 shows a summary of pupils' opinions. We asked pupils from 6th grade about their opinion on using sticky notes: 85% of pupils considered it easy to use and liked it,

77% considered it interesting, 69% of them considered it was funny and 85% think it supported them in learning.

Item	Watch Video		Record Video		Voice		Paint Pad®	
	Y	N	Y	N	Y	N	Y	N
It was easy to use	89	11	89	11	89	8	92	8
I like it	95	5	97	3	92	8	97	3
It was funny to use	89	11	86	14	95	5	92	8
It was interesting	89	11	89	11	84	16	92	8
I feel it help me to learn better and more	86	14	89	11	86	14	89	11

Table 2. Opinion of the students about the use of some multimedia functions in percentage.

Parents feedback

At the end of the user study we met five mothers and three fathers of the participants from 6th grade in order to know their opinion about the study. From the 8 participants, only one male had never used a mobile phone before, the others owned a mobile phone. We presented some of the works done by the children with the mobile phones.

Parents were very astonished when seeing the works realized by the children with the mobile phone since they did not expect such outcomes. As one father commented "*at the beginning when my child told (me) about this (study) I was very skeptical of using (mobile) phones in the class...but now I am surprised and really see (it) would be very useful in class*". At last, one mother commented at the same respect "*I did not know all the things that are possible to do with a cellphone.*""

Similarly to teachers' concerns in our surveys, the main concern of parents was bad use of the cell phone, for example playing or accessing/recording inadequate material. Nevertheless, parents saw more benefits than risks using the mobile phone and were conscious of their role as supervisor of their children: "*it is important that (we) control that the children use them correctly*" and "*having the right supervision from us at home and teachers at school, I see no problem of using them (mobile phones) for learning*".

All the parents welcomed the idea of using a mobile phone for learning. They mainly think that children will be much more motivated and involved in class; as one mother said "*my son was extraordinary motivated (during) this two weeks to go to the school*"; another mother commented "*for children learning using a mobile phone is amusing*".

DISCUSSION

More than expected, in Panama access to mobile phones is much higher than to traditional computers. We were surprised how many of currently used phones had cameras and multimedia capabilities, suggesting that many people have mid-range phones. In our study we chose a phone model that is currently at the upper end of mid-range phones and has many features of a simple smart phone. We expect that these capabilities will be available also in the low-end phones over the next years. Many of the functions used rely on a touch screen with a stylus. However, our studies revealed that teachers are able and willing to create tasks that fit the phones available. Moreover, based on our good experience in the field study, we think that providing Internet access via the phones is manageable. Letting children know that using the device is not an uncontrolled space (as their interactions are logged) helps to ensure responsible behavior.

In the surveys and focus groups we asked children and teachers to speculate about potential uses of the mobile phone as educational device and got valuable responses on how to create successful learning environments in a developing country context. Though major parts of the field study were inspired by these comments, over the course of the study we got interesting findings that validated, but also contrasted, contradicted, and extended the suggestions made. Hence we argue that the use of surveys and focus groups only is not sufficient to understand requirements and to design deployments. In the surveys, using phones as educational devices was often seen as using the phone instead of a computer. In the field study we realized that standard video and audio capabilities, comparable limited on traditional PCs, were considered among the most useful functions for supporting learning because both allow children to create and to replay content.

Primed by having computer labs in schools, teachers were concerned about managing the phones and the infrastructure and teaching children how to use them. With traditional PCs this is in many schools the central issue. Here we see an interesting advantage of mobile phones. In the field study we could observe that children learned very fast using the new device after a short introduction. As the children used the phones as a personal device (each child had one phone) while in school they felt ownership and also had the opportunity to explore on their own pace. We observed that some children gained skill very fast and then were able and willing to help their peers. Though, we observed a gender difference in the approach of exploring devices. Further, our positive expectations on introducing phones top down (starting from highest grade) were met.

To our surprise we could witness how teachers embraced the new technology. Teachers learned within days to make use of the phone as a teaching resource and discovered new opportunities for using it in class. Several of the ideas, especially with taking photos and annotating them, were mainly developed and refined by the teachers. Having the simple usage model of a phone and in some cases the paint application enabled a versatile use without requiring a complex learning platform. For teachers it was a great value to tailor the content in an easy way to their current teaching plan. Here the multimedia recording turned out to be a very valuable resource. We learned that providing pre-fabricated digital content might be very difficult, as it would need to fit the teacher's plan and style of teaching. By providing tools where teachers can move their content easily into the digital domain we expect that many teachers can be won over as it eases their effort for preparation.

Before the field study, teachers and especially parents were worried that mobile phones might not be useful and distract the children from learning. Furthermore they did not see a link between a PC and a mobile phone and most of them could not imagine how a mobile phone could be used in a sensible way in school and for teaching. However, after the field study parents saw a clear benefit in using mobile phones in the school context, even though they were initially skeptical. They were surprised of the activities done with the phones and proud of the products their children created with these devices.

CONCLUSION

In this paper we presented our research on how multimedia rich phones can aid or support the school education in rural areas in developing countries. We conducted our research with children living in urban as well as rural areas, which had low access to computers but high access to mobile phones Besides, a considerable percentage of teachers and pupils reported to have access to modern mobile phones that include multimedia and networking features, i.e. integrated audio player, integrated camera and Internet access.

The findings we gained from surveys, interviews, and discussions with several hundred teachers and pupils show that pupils and teachers seemingly welcome edutainment applications on their handsets, in special for Mathematics and languages. Besides, standard multimedia phones showed to be a versatile and resourceful tool and our findings in the field study suggest that multimedia phones are ready to be used in class as they are, even without external learning applications installed. Phone manufacturers and service providers can take this as advice to equip their phones with some applications (drawing, multimedia annotation, easy import of traditional media) that are generally useful in the educational context when targeting developing markets.

The results of our final field study can be summed up to the following two key findings: (1) Rather than preparing mobile phones with pre-edited content, teachers were creative to fit features of the mobile phones into their teaching plan and (2) recording video and painting on the phone were the activities that children liked most to do.

Similar to earlier reports, we also observed a higher degree of concentration, involvement, motivation, and participation in the realization of the tasks given when pupils learned with mobile phones. However, this finding is not fully conclusive because of the limited duration of the field study and because pupils might have been influenced by the technology novelty effect. In the same direction we cannot conclude that pupils learn more effective using mobile phones. This would require a long-term study evaluating pupil progress over time. We are planning on conducting such a study in the near future.

Besides, we are going to evaluate in more detail the large amounts of application data we logged to see how the data supports our qualitative findings and provides us even deeper insights. Further we want to extend our field study to children in urban areas.

ACKNOWLEDGMENTS

This research has been conducted within the project “Embedded Interaction” and “Mobile Interaction with Pervasive User Interfaces” funded by the DFG. We thank Nokia for supporting us by providing phones for the field study. We are especially thankful to Jonna Häkkilä and Jarmo Kauko for their help and for sharing their insights.

REFERENCES

1. Kumar, A., Tewari, A., Shroff, G., et al. Exploratory Study of Unsupervised Mobile Learning in Rural India. In *Proc. CHI 2010*, ACM Press (2010), 743-752.
2. Ford, M., Leinonen, T. MobilED – Mobile tools and services platform for formal and informal learning. AU Press (2009), 195-214.
3. Kam, M. Mathur, A., Kumar, A., and Canny, J. Designing Digital Games for Rural Children: A Study of Traditional Village Games in India. *In Proc. CHI 2009*, ACM Press (2009), 31-40.
4. Frohlich, D. Rachovides, D. Riga, K., et al. StoryBank: mobile digital storytelling in a development context. *In Proc. CHI 2009*, ACM Press (2009), 1761-1770.
5. Reitmaier, T., Bidwell, J. and Marsden, G. Field testing mobile digital storytelling software in rural Kenya, I*n Proc. Mobile HCI 2010,* ACM Press (2010), 283-286.
6. Kam, M., Kumar, A., Jain, S., Mathur, A., and Canny, J. Improving literacy in rural India: Cellphone games in an afterschool program. *In Proc. ICTD 2009,* IEEE Press (2009), 139-149.
7. Masperi, P. and Hollow, D. An evaluation of the use of ICT within primary education in Malawi. *In Proc. ICTD 2009,* IEEE Press (2009), 27-34.
8. OLPC http://laptop.org/en/laptop/index.shtml
9. ITU. Measuring the Information Society. The ICT Development Index. Geneve, Switzerland: International Telecommunication Union ITU 2009
10. Kraemer, K., Dedrick, J., and Sharma, P. One Laptop Per Child: Vision vs. Reality. Communications of the ACM, 2009, 52(6). 66-74.
11. M4Girls.http://www.nokia.com/NOKIA_COM_1/Corporate_Responsibility/World_map/pdf/MEA/CI_OnePager_South_Africa_m4girls.pdf, retrieved Sept. 20, 10.
12. Mobi. http://www.mymobi.co.za/mobi_signin.php
13. Moraveji, N., Kim, T. Ge, J., et al., Mischief: Supporting Remote Teaching in Developing Regions. *In Proc. CHI 2008*, ACM Press (2008), 353-362.
14. Moraveji, N., Inkpen, K., Cutrell, E., and Balakrishnan, R. A Mischief of Mice: Examining Children’s Performance in Single Display groupware Systems with 1 to 32 Mice. *In Proc. CHI 2009,* ACM Press (2009), 2157-2166.
15. Meduca. Dirección Nacional de Currículo y Tecnología Educativa. Educación Básica General. Programa de Cuarto, Quinto y Sexto Grado (2002).
16. Valderrama Bahamondez, E., Schmidt, A. A Survey to Assess the Potential of Mobile Phones as a Learning Platform for Panama. Ext. Abstract CHI 2010, ACM Press (2010), 3667-3672

Infrastructures for Low-cost Laptop Use in Mexican Schools

Ruy Cervantes[1], Mark Warschauer[2], Bonnie Nardi[1] and Nithya Sambasivan[1]

Department of Informatics[1]
University of California, Irvine
{ruy,nardi, nsambasi}@ics.uci.edu

Department of Education[2]
University of California, Irvine
markw@uci.edu

ABSTRACT
In recent years, a number of low-cost laptops have been created for children's education, most notably the XO, developed by One Laptop per Child to embody principles of constructionist learning, and the ClassmatePC, designed by Intel to fit within and improve traditional education. We report on a series of field studies in Mexican elementary schools that deployed the XO or ClassmatePC. Although both devices are promoted as valuable for improving education in developing countries, our studies suggest that creating the social and technical infrastructures needed to sustain school laptop use is far more complex than what technology designers assume.

Author Keywords
Low-cost laptops, infrastructures, developing countries, OLPC, XO, ClassmatePC, education, Mexico, ICT4D

ACM Classification Keywords
K.3.1. Computer uses in education: collaborative learning, computer-assisted instruction. K.4.2. Computers and society: social issues. H.5.m. Information interfaces and presentation (e.g., HCI): Miscellaneous.

General Terms
Human factors.

INTRODUCTION
In the last five years, there has been a strong push to create low-cost laptops for children in developing countries. These efforts—from the computer industry, non-governmental organizations, and governments—were triggered by the One Laptop per Child (OLPC) project [15], which sought to create radical educational change by massively distributing its XO laptop to developing countries. Envisioned as a response to the problems of educational systems in the developing world, including shortage of teachers and lack of material resources, the XO laptop purportedly embodied the principles of constructionist pedagogy to empower students to learn on their own, without support from teachers [6,7]. Constructionism [25] departs from traditional education by emphasizing students' construction of their own artifacts and knowledge. The XO's most prominent competitor is the ClassmatePC, created by Intel. Unlike the XO approach, the ClassmatePC was designed to be compatible with and integrated into traditional educational systems [33]. Large sales deals recently secured by Intel in Brazil and Argentina [1] are signaling a growing market preference for the ClassmatePC.

To further understand the role of laptops in elementary education in developing regions, we conducted case study research on laptop programs in a select group of Mexican schools. From research conducted in developed countries (e.g., [35]), we know that successful school laptop programs need supporting socio-technical infrastructures, such as electricity, networks and tech-support infrastructures, as well as trained teachers, staff, and pedagogical materials. HCI research has started to look at educational ICTs in developing countries (e.g., [16]), but the laptop as an educational tool is yet to be investigated. A body of research is needed to design educational technologies that can be supported in resource-constrained environments.

The objective of our research was to understand which resources constituted the socio-technical infrastructures that supported the use of laptops in elementary education in a developing country, the specific functions of these infrastructures, and how these infrastructures were created in resource-constrained environments. We found an ecology of socio-technical infrastructures supporting the laptop programs in schools. These infrastructures included the laptops; physical infrastructures, such as the electrical system, buildings, and furniture; and social and organizational infrastructures, such as management, technical support, pedagogical support, and parental involvement. The educational impact of laptops did not solely depend on the economic resources of the school or on the type of laptops used. Although the socio-economic status (SES) of the schools affected their ability to build infrastructures, we found that the enthusiasm, commitment, and training of teachers, staff, parents, and students, along with the support of external organizations, helped create support infrastructures for laptops, despite limited resources. We found that what laptops can achieve depends heavily on school context, including factors such as teacher preferences, organizational values, and existing norms.

In this paper, we discuss how school communities achieved, or did not achieve, the support infrastructures for these laptops. Our study explains the mundane tasks by which people created complex socio-technical support infrastructures when resources were constrained. Finally, we articulate some of the opportunities for ICT designers in supporting technology-enabled educational change, such as leveraging the assets of school communities implementing laptop programs, empowering the community to create the support infrastructures for laptop usage, and considering implementation models other than one-to-one computing.

RELATED WORK AND THEORETICAL MOTIVATIONS

Several low-cost computers aimed for the developing world have failed to be adopted, as designers overlooked users' contexts [24]. Analyses of educational ICTs in developing countries have studied the different actors and entities necessary to create support infrastructures [8,24,27,34,35], and how the relationships are negotiated [20]. These analyses are useful for aiding policy-making but lack the detail required for technology design. Recent work in HCI has started to cover this gap; Kumar et al. [16] identified educational opportunities for out-of-school mobile learning in India, concluding that learning will increase according to the availability of appropriate sociotechnical infrastructures.

We need accounts of how laptop infrastructures are constituted in practice to better understand how relationships between material resources and communities create these infrastructures [32]. Infrastructures are broad underlying frameworks encompassing physical, social, and cultural resources that enable groups, organizations, or societies to function in certain ways [19]. Given the centrality of social resources in educational activities, we focus on the role of the social to study laptop infrastructures. The question for us is not only *what* resources make up laptop infrastructures, but also *when* those resources make an infrastructure [32], i.e., what kinds of interactions between things and people help develop an infrastructure. Star and Ruhleder found that infrastructures are built on an installed base of inherited strengths and limitations, reach beyond a single event or site, are embedded into other structures and social arrangements, are learned as part of membership with incoming members having to learn them, are linked with conventions of practice as they shape and are shaped by communities, are transparent until they break down, and take time and negotiation to adjust with other systems with which they are involved [32]. Star and Ruhleder's framework provides us with specific notions to discuss the complexities of creating laptop infrastructures, allowing us to relate our work to the growing body of HCI literature that has looked at the infrastructures sustaining ICTs in different contexts.

Scholars in sociotechnical analysis of computing infrastructures have studied multiple contexts [17,18,14,19,30,32,38], but we are not aware of infrastructure studies of education in the developing world. Social accounts of technological infrastructures used by professionals have documented how the material and social conditions of developing countries constrain interactions [14,38]. Interactions are shaped by a lack of organizational resources [17] and accountabilities across multiple organizational levels [18,30]. We argue that many previously identified constraints are present in laptop infrastructures of resource-constrained schools, such as material infrastructures that are less robust than in high-income countries; concerns of insecurity and theft; underdeveloped staff; and accountabilities at multiple levels including to school boards, districts, and state and federal ministries of education. Our study contributes to the sociotechnical analysis literature by showing how creating support infrastructures is a matter of dealing with multiple socio-technical constraints that interact in complex ways.

ICT4D and HCI4D literature have informed our views of how infrastructures are built in constrained environments. Studies examining large scale ICT projects for school children (e.g., [8,24]) have found them sustainable only if they address local communities' current practices [10] or if they create opportunities for new practices profiting from existing sociotechnical infrastructures [26]. We are informed by studies critiquing the personal-use private-ownership paradigm in developing countries, where, due to sociotechnical constraints, a shared use model is often more appropriate [24,31], including multiple mice per computer [31]. Ames has studied the country-wide XO deployment in Uruguayan elementary schools [6]. Our work differs from Ames' project by comparing deployments of two different technological platforms—Classmate and XO—and by looking at the Mexican educational system, which has many more social and organizational deficiencies than the Uruguayan educational system. Our study contributes to ICT4D and HCI4D by providing designers with a holistic view of the complexities of creating laptop infrastructures for educational change and by showing how communities can leverage the ecology of tools, policies, and programs to create their self-reliant and sustainable infrastructures. We contribute to HCI4D by studying technology use in Mexico, a high mid-income country facing the challenge of unequal distribution of socio-economic and pedagogical resources.

Our understanding of the human infrastructure in educational ICT has been influenced by the education literature, which has established teachers and pedagogical support as crucial resources for educational ICT projects. Mere access to technology does not automatically enable students to use computers to educate themselves, especially in low-SES environments, if students lack social support at home or school [8,12,22,34,35]. Teachers are a fundamental part of the infrastructure to support laptops, providing the instruction, mentoring, and modeling required for learning. Teachers are also users of the technical and pedagogical infrastructures in the classroom. Although ours is not an education-focused paper, the empirical data presented here serve the educational community in research and policy-making to better understand the challenges that teachers, staff and parents face when creating laptop support infrastructures in resource-constrained environments.

BACKGROUND

Mexico is a mid-income country with strong socio-economic disparities. Since many who can afford it seek education in private institutions [11], the majority of public schools serve less advantaged students. Programs to upgrade infrastructure and introduce ICTs in education have sought to overcome disparities with mixed results [21]. Curriculum reform aiming to prepare students for the 21st century has been difficult to implement due to deficiencies in teacher training [28]. The "Mochila Digital" (Digital Backpack), a large-scale project started in 2008 by the private Telmex Foundation, distributed 50,000 XO laptops in about 1,200 Mexican elementary public schools in cooperation with the Ministry of Education [2,3]. Participating schools received 40 XO laptops to be shared among all students. On a smaller scale, Intel's World Ahead program ran a series of pilot projects in Mexican elementary schools beginning in 2007 to test its ClassmatePCs [13], providing both laptops and substantial administrative and training support [33].

STUDY RATIONALE

Our case study was designed to understand the socio-technical infrastructures that support a laptop program. We selected five different schools in two Mexican cities, segmenting them by SES and by type of laptop deployed, namely Classmate and XO. We segmented the schools by SES into two high-SES and three low-SES schools (see Table 1), which allowed us to contrast how people created laptop support infrastructures in resource-constrained environments and in high-resource environments. Segmenting by type of laptop helped us determine if the support infrastructures were different in each case, and if differences in type of laptop brought changes in their educational function. The schools in our sample had different degrees of internal organizational maturity and of support from parents and external organizations. Contrasting these differences allowed us to understand how organization and support enable, or not, the creation of socio-technical infrastructures. Another dimension against which we compared how infrastructures were formed was the age of the laptop program at each school, varying from a few months to two school years. The final criterion for the design of our study was the use model of the laptop followed at each school. The largest XO implementation in the world, Plan Ceibal in Uruguay [4] follows a one-to-one use model. However the largest XO implementation in Mexico, Mochila Digital, and other smaller implementations, follow a shared use model. Peru's nationwide implementation [36], and a smaller program in Haiti [23], also have moved towards a shared use model. Given the prevalence of the shared use model in Mexico, we selected a majority of sites that followed this practice.

METHODS

We conducted 128 hours of observations (see Table 1) to examine the role of laptops in teaching and learning activities, the resources needed to conduct these activities, and how teachers and staff prepared for these activities. We documented our observations with extensive field notes, photographs of in-class interactions of teachers and students, and collection of samples of work of students and pedagogical materials. We observed classroom activities that did and did not involve laptops, teacher meetings, school assemblies, parent meetings, and social gatherings of teachers and staff. We also observed laptop support activities, such as how laptops were charged, stored, and transported to the classroom.

We conducted 41 semi-structured interviews of 20 to 60 minutes with staff, teachers, parents, and students. In these interviews we asked teachers, staff and parents about their perception of the laptop project, the history and development of the programs, and the process to implement the program, and the social, organizational, pedagogical and technical resources necessary for the program. We asked students, teachers, and staff about the educational uses and practices that involved laptops, and compared their responses against our observations, to be able to understand to what degree the perceived uses corresponded to observed use. We digitally recorded, coded, and transcribed all

	Conocerte	Del Valle	Miguel Hidalgo	Independencia	Octavio Paz
Location	Guadalajara	Guadalajara	Puebla	Guadalajara	Guadalajara
SES	High – Private	High – Private	Low – Public	Low – Public	Low – Public
Laptop Type	ClassmatePC-1	ClassmatePC-1	ClassmatePC-1	XO-1	XO-1
Program	Independent	Intel supported pilot	Intel/State govt. pilot	Mochila Digital	Mochila Digital
Active period	2007-2009	2007- date	2007- date	2009-date	2009-date
Laptop ratio	1-to-1	1st yr., 1-to-1. Then shared.	Shared	Shared	Shared
No. laptops	60	40	50	40	40
Observations	N/A.	Nov/09: 10 days. ~40hrs.	Dec/09: 10 days. ~40hrs.	Dec/09-Mar/10: 6 days. ~24hrs.	Dec/09-Mar/10: 6 days. ~24hrs.
Interviews	1 staff member, 2 teachers	7 students, 1 teacher, 2 staff, 2 parents.	8 students, 3 teachers, 1 staff, 4 parents.	5 teachers, 1 staff.	3 teachers, Principal.

Table 1: Characteristics of the observed urban elementary schools in Mexico.

interviews, and coded the field notes and pictures. Our coding was bottom-up, and the themes reported in our findings emerged from the data. The field researcher is Mexican and was educated there; all fieldwork was conducted in Spanish. Translations from Spanish are ours. Pseudonyms are used for schools and people.

THE SITES

Low-SES schools

We had three public, low-SES schools in our sample. The Miguel Hidalgo School ClassmatePC program was sponsored by Intel and the Puebla State Ministry of Education. Independencia and Octavio Paz schools were part of the Mochila Digital program and used XO laptops.

The Miguel Hidalgo School, a public elementary school in the city of Puebla, started its ClassmatePC program with 50 laptops in October 2007 [13]. The school had ample prior experience using ICTs. It has had a computer room since 1998. The principal was supportive of technology projects, and the school's technology coordinator was trained in both technology and ICT pedagogy. Both sponsors gave ample technical and pedagogical support to the school, and their pedagogical support personnel frequently visited the school.

The XO schools, Independencia and Octavio Paz, were located in low-SES neighborhoods of Guadalajara. Independencia was a stable older school with veteran teachers. Parents had a seemingly good relationship with the school authorities. Octavio Paz School was relatively new and growing fast. Lower grade classes had close to 50 students each, and classroom space was running out. School administrators indicated that parental participation was low, which they attributed to long working hours of low-income parents. The XO laptops were delivered to Independencia and Octavio Paz in spring 2009. Technical training was provided only to two staff or teachers per school, and not until October of that year. Those trained were expected to replicate the training to their peers. The XO schools faced numerous technical problems, as discussed below.

High-SES schools

The two high-SES schools were located in wealthy neighborhoods of Guadalajara. Both were running ClassmatePC laptop programs. These private schools had well-trained teachers and a good relationship with parents. Both schools have had well-equipped computer rooms for at least 10 years. Most classrooms in these schools had LCD projectors and a computer for the teacher. The Del Valle school program was also initiated as an Intel sponsored pilot project in 2007. During the first year, the school's 40 ClassmatePCs were allocated on a one laptop per student basis to all sixth grade students. After the first year, laptops were used on a shared basis among grade four-to-six students. The other private school, Conocerte, independently acquired ClassmatePCs in 2007, to implement a one-to-one laptop program in grades 5 and 6. The program lasted until spring 2009 (see discussion below). Students' parents covered the cost of purchase of laptops, and laptops were managed by the school's technology coordinator. After several months, students were allowed to take the laptops home. As Conocerte had the longest running one-to-one laptop program in Mexico that we were aware of, we decided to include the school in our sample, even though the program was no longer active at the time of our visit. We interviewed extensively the two teachers who had used the laptops with their classes and a technical support staff member.

FINDINGS

More than the laptop, it was the support infrastructures that made an educational difference. In low-SES schools, both using XOs and ClassmatePCs, much effort was expended to build infrastructures to enable students to access learning environments that they had no access to otherwise. Schools that solved the access issue—all high-SES schools and one low-SES—built infrastructures to capitalize on students' enthusiasm for technology to motivate them to be more independent learners. Schools changed their teaching and learning practices, only after their infrastructure was solid, and teachers had enough technical and pedagogical support to change their practices. How laptops were used to transform educational practices was determined by the skills and interests of the teachers, the motivation of students, and the values of the schools, rather than the affordances of the laptops alone.

Learning environments are laptops plus teachers

Most of the low-SES students' previous experience with technology was restricted by either limited physical access or limited social support. According to teachers, between a half and one-third of students in the observed schools had computers and Internet access at home. Though cybercafés were ubiquitous, few low-SES parents felt comfortable letting their elementary school children attend them or could afford the costs. Low-SES students who did find outside access to computers often lacked mentors. Only some students had parents, older siblings, or other relatives with extensive computer experience. Many had to learn computer skills on their own.

Laptop programs provided the opportunity to access educational resources because students could use laptops with the guidance of a teacher or technology coordinator in an environment conducive for learning. The use of XOs by two 3rd grade groups at Independencia illustrates how laptops plus teachers made the difference to create a productive learning environment. In "3-A", students used the XO without teacher supervision, as their teacher was not trained to use the XO. When the teacher handed out the laptops, she told students that they could "chat." Some students started communicating using the Chat program, but others were not able to figure it out, leaving them frustrated. Students of "3-B" conducted an educational activity which consisted of playing the popular song "Brother John" using TamTam, an XO music creation program. Their teacher printed the activity handout from the Mochila Digital's support site. Using the handout and their teacher's assistance, students could play the song on their own. The activity of 3-A had little educational value, as many students had chatted before at cybercafés and those who were not able to chat did not receive guidance to use the program. In contrast, the activity of 3-B allowed many students to create music on the computer for their first time.

It is pretty but not practical

Making the laptops "practical" to use, and easy to integrate into teaching and learning practices, was a function of the organizational capacity of the school, and not necessarily linked to its SES. Miguel Hidalgo had a solid internal organization, support from parents, and good relations with the Ministry of Education. With the advice of the Ministry of Education, the school built a "charging center" to charge and store all laptops. Its cost of nearly $700 US was paid for by parents. In contrast, the electrical infrastructure at Octavio Paz was unreliable. The principal bought some power-strips to charge the laptops at the single electrical outlet of each classroom, making laptop charging labor-intensive. This inconvenience made Octavio Paz's teachers characterize the XO laptops as "pretty" but not "practical". The lack of engagement between Octavio Paz staff and the parents made it impossible to raise funds for a reliable electrical infrastructure.

In high-SES schools, where providing laptops and physical infrastructures was not a problem, social organization was still crucial for using laptops reliably. When the technology coordinator at Conocerte, a high-SES school, resigned, the laptop program was officially ended. Still, many parents continued to buy netbooks for their children, and these students regularly brought their netbooks to school. However, teachers had reservations about using the netbooks in class, as some students had "inappropriate" material on their netbooks, such as violent videos, and teachers were also worried about computer viruses. Conocerte teachers told us they had felt much more confident in the laptops when the technology coordinator used to manage the program and help ensure that the machines were used for educational purposes.

Elsewhere, lack of local knowledge of its SugarOS made the XO difficult to maintain. Between a half and a third of XO machines of the Mochila Digital schools were received with a software-lock, as the security layer of SugarOS, called "BitFrost," had no activation key. Loading the keys on the computers was relatively complex for a non-technical user. Also, the laptops were not configured to access the Internet. Technical support was provided mainly over the phone, with no in-person support. Technical support of Mochila Digital was slow to respond, and schools could not use local technical expertise since SugarOS was virtually unknown.

Insecurity and robbery are a reality in Mexico, and it was a concern in all schools, directly impacting access to computing. At the high-SES Del Valle School, all of the laptops were stolen from a locked room a few weeks before our arrival. To carry on with their activities, and also to allow us to perform the study, the school borrowed laptops used at a sister campus for a few weeks. Staff explained to us that it would take months to replace the stolen laptops. The robbery made evident the vulnerability of computing infrastructures to the larger social context of a country where even low-cost laptops are valuable items.

One-to-one is aspired to, but sharing is more practical

One-to-one laptop programs were practically achievable in only one school. Even if a one-to-one laptop program was an aspiration for most teachers and staff, the laptops' cost and lack of requisite socio-technical support made this goal infeasible. Only Conocerte, the most privileged school, was able to sustain a one-to-one program for a prolonged period. For the technology coordinator of Del Valle, a high-SES school, a sustainable one-to-one program was achievable in two years, after lobbying with school authorities, building a school network, and working out financing with parents.

Low-SES schools shared laptops, given the lower capacity of their social and physical infrastructures, and the perceived benefit of giving access to all schools students as opposed to a single class with a one-to-one program. At the Miguel Hidalgo School, the principal chose to share their 50 ClassmatesPCs laptops among the twelve groups of the school, over having a single group in a one-to-one program. The principal considered that sharing was better, as all students would have a "chance to open [their] minds" to new ways of learning using the laptops under the guidance of their teachers. The value of using laptops was in increasing the access to technology for all students, beyond making teaching and learning more efficient.

Sharing laptops entailed practical problems, as neither laptop was designed for multiple users. First, transporting laptops between classrooms was an issue. Schools established weekly schedules to allocate a couple of hours per group. And moving laptops from classroom to classroom required coordination and time. For instance, at the Miguel Hidalgo school, each group picked up the laptops from the media room and took them to their classroom (see figure 1). This routine was time-consuming; it would have been more efficient to set up the laptops permanently at the media room. But taking "the technology inside the classroom", the technology coordinator explained, was something that students "liked and were excited about" as it made students feel closer to technology, especially to those with no computer at home. The second

Figure 1: Students transporting the laptops to their classroom.

issue was storing students' work. Miguel Hidalgo's laptops were labeled so each student would work on the same machine every time, storing their work in a folder with their name. In schools using XOs, students were not able to save their work on the laptop, as it had limited memory and the OS had no folders. At the Independencia School, some teachers asked students to buy USB flash drives, but only one third of parents were able to buy them. Students shared their drives with others who did not have one, but the practice was ineffective and many times the work was lost.

Improving the low-SES schools' infrastructures for implementing schoolwide one-to-one laptop programs requires a holistic approach. Nation-state support is required as few parents can pay for laptops or requisite infrastructure upgrades. Electrical installations for most classrooms were inferior. Storage arrangements would have to be made in many overpopulated classrooms, and schoolwide wireless networks would need to be established. Outside of a few schools, more attention to building the social infrastructure in support of laptop use is required. However, the technology coordinator of Miguel Hidalgo felt that at well-organized low-SES schools such as hers, with "good teachers and staff," a one-to-one laptop program would be implemented with positive educational results.

Building the community that builds the infrastructure

For low-SES schools, creating organizations that build reliable infrastructures in a context prone to breakdowns was crucial, and required great effort. Some community-building practices were mediated by the use of the laptops themselves. To increase the involvement of parents at Miguel Hidalgo school, they would be regularly invited to educational events to use the laptops with their children. We observed an event where parents worked with their children creating a Word document about the most important values of their family. These kinds of events allowed parents—with little experience with computers—to experience first-hand the power of laptops at school.

Involving and supporting teachers was fundamental for the continuity and success of the program. Technology coordinators and support staff were key to supporting teachers' involvement. Ms. Alejandra, a teacher at Miguel Hidalgo School explained that "the teacher" was the most important resource for a laptop program. Ms. Marian, the technology coordinator at Miguel Hidalgo, explained that her responsibility was "to guide the teacher so he or she can effectively see the laptop as something positive". For this, Marian had the support of personnel from Intel and the Ministry of Education. Marian invited teachers with poor computer literacy skills to follow the computer literacy lessons imparted to students. Sometimes students would help teachers in their learning process (see figure 2). This strategy helped to train teachers and integrate them to the laptop program by making teachers feel comfortable as technology learners, without losing face with their students. This way, Marian was able to "change the culture of the teachers," to become lifelong learners of technology.

Building a social network of teachers beyond the school was viewed as important. At Independencia, the laptop program coordinator explained that one of the challenges for program continuity was sustaining teacher motivation. She believed that enabling teachers to acquire continuous ICT training would be the key. As part of the solution, she pictured a network of teachers who could share their uses of technology in the classroom, creating a sense of belonging and support. But this network was difficult to bring about, as the Mochila Digital schools were spread out around the city. Online networks could be a solution, but those take time to build well and had not been developed.

Motivating students with their laptop enthusiasm

Schools with more stable laptop infrastructures, namely Del Valle, Conocerte, and Miguel Hidalgo, were able to use students' enthusiasm for laptops to motivate them to work independently. Teachers could capitalize on students' enthusiasm by continuously creating activities in which students experienced a new way of learning that was more enjoyable, more dynamic, and closer to their interests. Laptops became an auxiliary tool to capture students' attention, create supporting material for difficult subjects, and help students produce higher quality work.

Developing students' motivation was a blend of laptop affordances and social practices. Students enjoyed using laptops as they were perceived as aesthetically pleasing. Students of lower grades (1st through 4th) liked the small size of the laptops and keyboard, though the keyboard size started to bother some 5th and 6th graders. Beyond the affordances of laptops, their major value was in the social practices they allowed. Teachers were able to include multimedia resources that captured students' attention and supported their understanding of complicated material. Using laptops created opportunities to include students' technology interests, such as computer gaming, or using social networking sites. For instance, an English teacher encouraged students to use the Facebook game "Pet Society" to increase their vocabulary. Furthermore, teachers perceived that any activity done at the computer more easily caught students' attention. A Del Valle teacher suggested that students felt more compelled to work when using laptops, as technology was "part of them [...] they were born with it".

Since few schools had laptops, owning these devices became an occasion to interact with outsiders interested in

Figure 2: Student teaching her teacher how to use the laptop.

the programs. These interactions furthered the sense of teachers and students participating in something special. Miguel Hidalgo, for example, was featured in the local media, closely observed by another research team besides ours, presented in state government meetings as a model for ICT integration, and participated in contests and special activities. The laptop program there allowed some students to gain recognition, such as two 2nd grade students who received a public award in an inter-school writing contest for student using ClassmatePCs. Their laptop program also gave students the opportunity to interact with people from outside of the country; one project coordinated by Intel pedagogical support staff brought selected students into online discussion with students in Germany to discuss girls' rights in their respective countries.

At Independencia, and Octavio Paz, unstable infrastructures made it difficult to use laptops as a motivational device. At Octavio Paz, with little pedagogical support and difficulties in setting up the laptops, a teacher tried using the XOs as a recompense for her students' discipline, exchanging students' attention during class for letting them play with the XOs using any games such as Mazes for a few hours a week. The strategy only worked a few times, given the difficulties to charge the XOs and the lack students' interest to play with the machines without an objective.

The use of laptops depends on the infrastructure

The two high-SES schools were able to consistently integrate the laptops into their teaching and learning practices. How laptops were used was greatly influenced by teachers' preferences and skills. Both teachers who had used the laptops at Conocerte were highly competent and ready for change, but with different preferences. Adolfo, passionate about electronic music composition, implemented many multimedia production activities. Students in his class made electronic music to represent aspects of the city's geography. To help them, he learned how to use free sound editing software, installed it on each of the machines, and taught students how to use it. Alicia, who was more inclined towards mathematical and analytical aspects, took advantage of Excel and PowerPoint to teach students to create conceptual maps to visualize different perspectives on complex issues.

The school's values were another subtle but powerful influence on how laptop affordances transformed teaching and learning, as seen in differences between the two high-SES schools deploying ClassmatePCs. Conocerte School focused on cultivating students' creativity and autonomy through project work; this was reflected in how laptops were used as described above. Del Valle, which took a more traditional approach to academic achievement, emphasized more structured learning activities under careful teacher supervision. The efficiency of laptops helped students at Del Valle worry less about their work presentation and focus more on the quality of their answers, yet students adhered closely to teacher instructions per the overall values of the school.

We observed that the capacity to change teaching and learning practices increased when certain preconditions were met, including consistent access to technology, a prepared and committed teaching staff, and support from external organizations, district authorities, and parents. Creating the infrastructures for transformative uses was not only dependent on economic resources. While higher economic resources at high-SES schools helped to create physical infrastructures, a strong social organization was most important. At the wealthiest school in our study, Conocerte, the laptop program was completely halted once the technology coordinator resigned. And the low-SES Miguel Hidalgo school successfully leveraged its strong organizational capacity and external support to transform educational practices. Constant dialogue between teachers and technology coordinators at the school greatly facilitated educational change there. Concrete methods for using laptops were worked out during the teachers' weekly lesson planning time, as the technology coordinator worked together with the teachers to plan their their classroom activities. The dialogue also gave the technology coordinator an appropriate perspective of the laptops, as "one more tool", albeit a powerful one, for education.

DISCUSSION

In each of the five schools, socio-technical infrastructures shaped the use and educational value of laptops. These findings are in line with other reports [12,20,22,34,36,37] on how the "social envelope" surrounding ICTs influences the educational benefits of these technologies. To develop support infrastructures, the entire school community had to work in concert, making use of local and global resources. We can summarize several features related to infrastructures for learning with laptops, as follows.

Achieving educational change was not a product of the principles embodied by the laptops. OLPC believed that as the XO embodied the principles of constructionism it would function as a "Trojan Horse…a backdoor into overhauling the entire education system" of countries [9,6], making education more creative and student centered. In contrast, Intel described the ClassmatePC as a tool more centered in teachers and traditional learning, which could "easily integrate into their curriculum," that could be "locally appropriated, easily deployed" [5]. But, in spite of different intentions of the two laptops designs, in this small sample, the Classmate was being used for constructivist purposes more than the XO, showing that the way a device is used depends greatly on its adoption by a community in local context, according to its sociotechnical infrastructure, rather than just the intent of the designers.

Developing a strong human infrastructure allowed schools to use laptops to deliver educational value. Even with its material constraints, the low-SES Miguel Hidalgo school was able to use laptops to educate and motivate its students as it had well-trained staff and teachers. As ICTs only become useful when meaningful social practices are created around using these technologies [34], strong community support becomes crucial for effective use of laptops. Practices are learned from peers, parents, teachers and other role models. In low-SES schools, children often lack home access to knowledgeable computer users. But the organization and community support at Miguel Hidalgo allowed creating these social practices. The training and technical support programs were key for the success of the Intel sponsored pilots of our sample, showing the importance to develop social infrastructures. But the results of these ClassmatePC pilots, especially of the observed low-SES school cannot be immediately replicated. Miguel Hidalgo was a school out of the norm when compared with the other low-SES schools of our sample, as it had strong internal organization and efficient support from Intel and the government. The Mochila Digital schools we visited needed time and support to develop their social infrastructures: much stronger technical support, teacher training, and community support was need at these schools to get educational value out of the laptops. Scaling up programs to support the development of schools' social infrastructures remains a challenge. Comparing to another development effort, even India's Hole in the Wall project, which began by giving children unfettered access to kiosk computers without mediation by adults or organizations, has evolved to focus more on building ties with schools, teachers, and local communities as mediators of learning [8]. Walter Bender, former OLPC president of software and content, recently suggested that OLPC should also strive for building sociotechnical support infrastructures [34].

Building strong infrastructures supporting the laptops was dependent on the social conditions of each school. Creating an appropriate physical infrastructure was, especially in low-SES schools, dependent on the ability of the school to organize the community. Miguel Hidalgo, which had an efficient organization, was able to create a charging center, whereas the Octavio Paz School, which had problems with its parents' association, was not. Also, the ability to develop the human infrastructure through teacher training was affected by the wage structure. Many teachers had no free time to attend training sessions as they held multiple jobs to supplement their income. These dependencies between infrastructures ran across multiple organizational and social levels, further increasing their complexity. To take full advantage of the capabilities of the laptop infrastructure, educational plans and standardized tests created at federal and state levels have to be updated. Servicing laptops, in response for example to the Bitfrost locking of the XOs, depended both on the Mochila Digital tech support team and the school's technology coordinator.

Working out how laptops could fit into existing practices of school communities was fundamental to adoption. Miguel Hidalgo's teachers and technology coordinator could visualize new uses of laptops only when working together in the teachers' weekly planning sessions, an existing practice. When infrastructures have matured, they are learned as part of the membership of a community of practice. But the teachers' community had no precedent for how to use the laptop infrastructures. So the technology coordinator and teachers had to work out new uses of the laptop infrastructures. Technology coordinators were central in integrating laptop infrastructures into daily practices, and thus assumed the role of what Nardi and O'Day termed a "keystone species" [22].

But achieving the adoption of laptops needs dialogue at multiple levels, from curriculum reform at a national level, to the practicalities of each teacher's weekly lesson planning. Schools running laptop programs for a longer time had developed more stable infrastructures, as they had had greater opportunity to negotiate appropriate changes. The Miguel Hidalgo School had experience in both building relationships with its local community and in developing training and curriculum reforms with Intel pedagogical support staff and Puebla state Ministry of Education officials. This gave Miguel Hidalgo much more stable laptop infrastructures than those of the newly implemented Mochila Digital's schools, in which these dialogues and processes had not occurred.

Laptops had to be shared to work within the schools' existing infrastructural capacity. The initial designs of the XO (explicitly) and ClassmatePC (implicitly) assuming a one-to-one model of student use were out of synch with the infrastructures of the resource-constrained schools in our study. None of the laptop implementations at low-SES schools had a one-to-one program. Only Conocerte, the wealthiest school in our sample, was able to sustain a one-to-one laptop program for a prolonged period, and that later collapsed as well. The inability to move to a one-to-one program was not only due to the cost of laptops, but also due to the insufficient physical and social infrastructure to maintain, deploy, and effectively use a large number of laptops. In contrast, a shared use model at low-SES schools allowed all students a chance to meaningfully use computers, while not straining infrastructures. This observation is consistent with the case of the large XO implementation in Peru, first launched as a one-to-one program but then expanded as a shared use program to better match the country's infrastructural capacity [36].

Most of those we interviewed understood that schools had to upgrade their physical and organizational infrastructures before venturing into one-to-one programs. This belief was against OLPC's "saturation" principle of immediate one-to-one implementation. This principle downplays the need for a physical and social infrastructure to sustain a large-scale laptop deployment, whether to charge, maintain, and repair laptops or to ensure that they are used effectively. This downplaying of the critical role of community support—from technology coordinators, teachers, parents and others—has had negative consequences in OLPC deployments around the world [36]. For example in Uruguay, more than a quarter of the country's 400,000 XOs are non-functioning due to hardware of software problems [29]. In Alabama, after the Mayor and City Council launched a program despite opposition from teachers and the school district, laptops were seldom used in schools, large numbers become unusable due to hardware or software problems, and funding for the program was eventually discontinued [36].

Technology designers should understand that the nature and development of infrastructures depends on context. What was taken for granted in high-SES schools, such as adequate electrical systems or physical space, became a major obstacle for some low-SES schools. Simple schemes for distributing technology do not work if a suitable sociotechnical infrastructure is lacking. We saw how the laptop program in the highest SES school collapsed when the technology coordinator resigned, even as parents continued buying laptops for their children. Furthermore, the opportunities to change educational practices depended on the context: the skills and preferences of teachers and students, the values of the school, and the values of the larger educational systems in Mexico all determine what is practical to change. In the cases of the Del Valle and Conocerte schools, similar laptop affordances were used very differently, suggesting that laptop infrastructures are shaped by school values. It is not possible to introduce new educational models, as OLPC sought to do with constructionism, without a comprehensive approach to change the culture and practices of schools and teachers. The only way to transform education is to engage the whole community in a dialogue for creating change, as was being done at Miguel Hidalgo. The involvement of teachers is vital, as it is their role to facilitate learning practices in classroom. As teaching and learning practices with laptops were new in these schools, it was necessary to create an environment where teachers could be seen as learners of technology and experiment with new ways of working.

OPPORTUNITIES FOR LAPTOPS IN EDUCATION

We face the challenge of creating sociotechnical infrastructures that support large-scale educational change. The design of XO and Classmate assume a one-to-one use model. However, this model for personal use and private ownership makes assumptions based on the conditions of developed countries [31]. In most of our cases, laptops had to be shared to increase reach, lower costs, and be sustained within limited physical and social infrastructures. "One laptop per child" obscures the complexity of supporting laptop usage. The whole school community contributes to laptop infrastructures and use.

An ecology of technologies, community programs, and policies is needed to make effective use of laptops in education. Support technologies include hardware and software to share, maintain, and secure laptops, and to facilitate interactions among teachers, students, and parents. Programs to build technical and pedagogical capacities, motivate, and engage the school community can help ensure the sustainability the laptop infrastructures. To take advantage of laptops, educational systems in developing countries have to engage in comprehensive reforms to update their curricula, transform student testing, and promote the professional development of teachers. These ecologies must operate within educational systems with chronic organizational deficiencies and within the socio-economic problems of developing nations. Actors from all levels (policy makers, technology developers, educational authorities, school staff, teachers, and parents) have to participate in these ecologies. Monolithic approaches for change through injection of a new device will not work. Schools need building blocks that can be shaped according to their particular context, to cultivate the conditions in which educational change can emerge.

The designers of these ecologies can take advantage of a number of assets school communities have to create laptop infrastructures. Enthusiasm for technology can be capitalized on to build the motivation of both students and adults, as laptop activities with parents and pupils at Miguel Hidalgo School showed. A motivated community will have the creativity and perseverance needed to build a laptop infrastructure. Changing certain community rules can positively impact individuals' abilities to contribute towards the laptop infrastructures. For example, providing norms and structures for teachers to be learners of technology in their own groups can encourage teachers to update their skills and practices and strengthen the human component of infrastructures for laptop use. Dialogue is central to expand the construction and use of laptop infrastructures. Spaces for dialogue have to be created within existing practices. We saw how, if members of the community are questioned at the right moment, new uses for the infrastructures become clear, as shown when the technology coordinator talked to teachers during their weekly planning.

Each school should cultivate the "keystone species" [22] of teachers and technology coordinators. Mentor teachers will require support in the educational system, for example, through extra paid professional development time. While paid technology coordinators require extra resources, they can have an enormous impact on helping teachers integrate laptops with school practices. Socio-technical infrastructures supporting laptops cannot be immediately implemented, as communities take time to mature.

We agree with Pal et al. [24] on the appropriateness of the shared laptop use model for most of the schools in the developing world. In low-income countries, sharing a limited number of laptops puts much less stress on fragile school infrastructures, both physical and social, than providing one laptop to every child. In mid- and high-income countries, it is possible to transition to a one-to-one model, as the infrastructures of the whole educational system and each school strengthen, as demonstrated by the evolution of many laptop programs in US schools [35]. Software for laptop infrastructures should be suitable for a shared use model. Rollout strategies for large laptop programs should follow a staged implementation in certain grade levels or subject areas first, so that requisite physical and social infrastructures can be developed over time.

CONCLUSION

In the near future we will likely see more governments and institutions investing in laptops for basic education. The emphasis of these projects should be on building the basic sociotechnical infrastructures that will enable students to engage in meaningful learning with laptops. Given the complex environment of schools in developing countries, introducing new technologies is not easy. Support infrastructures for laptops are dependent on the context of each community, and it is only with full community participation that laptop infrastructures can be developed. As designers of technology, we should understand that laptops for education are not devices for individuals, but rather are part of a large sociotechnical infrastructure created by the whole school community. Designs should take a holistic approach, thinking about the ecology of tools, policies, and programs that each community will mix and match to create their own laptop infrastructure. Low-cost laptops can be used to promote educational change in developing countries, if the enthusiasm that these devices evoke is leveraged to promote the growth of organizational capacities, upgrade teachers' skills, and create a better overall educational environment for students.

ACKNOWLEDGMENTS

We thank teachers, staff, and the Ministries of Education in Jalisco and Puebla for facilitating our visit. A UC MEXUS grant made this work possible.

REFERENCES

1. Brazilian Ministry of Education plan large deployment with Mandriva Linux on Intel-powered classmate PCs. http://www2.mandriva.com/en/news/?p=145&s=0.
2. Mochila Digital. www.mochiladigitaltelmex.com.mx/.
3. OLPC Mexico. wiki.laptop.org/go/OLPC_Mexico.
4. Plan Ceibal. www.ceibal.edu.uy/.
5. Intel's Vision for Low Cost Netbook Laptops for Children and Schools Worldwide. www.classmatepc.com/vision/.
6. Ames, M. Hacker Learning? The Social Meanings of One Laptop Per Child. 2008.
7. Ananny, M. and Winters, N. Designing for Development: Understanding One Laptop Per Child in its Historical Context. *ICTD* (2007).
8. Arora, P. Hope-in-the-Wall? A digital promise for free learning. *British Journal of Educ. Technology 41*, 5 (2010).
9. Bender, W. Radio Open Source interview. 2007. olpctalks. com/walter_bender/bender_radio_open_source.html.
10. Best, M.L. and Kumar, R. Sustainability failures of rural telecenters: Challenges from the sustainable access in rural india (sari) project. *ITID 4*, 4 (2008).
11. Bracho, T. Desigualdad educativa. Un tema recurrente. *Revista Mexicana de investigación educativa 7*, (2002).
12. Giacquinta, J.B., Bauer, J.A., and Levin, J.E. *Beyond technology's promise: an examination of children's educational computing at home*. Cambridge Univ. Press, 1993.
13. Heredia Escorza, Y. and Lozano Rodríguez, A. El uso de computadoras ClassmatePC en una escuela primaria del estado de Puebla: un estudio descriptivo. 2008.
14. Irani, L., Dourish, P., and Mazmanian, M. Shopping for sharpies in Seattle: mundane infrastructures of transnational design. *ICIC* (2010).
15. Kraemer, K., Dedrick, J., and Sharma, P. One laptop per child: vision vs. reality. *Commun. ACM 52*, (2009).
16. Kumar, A., Tewari, A., Shroff, G., Chittamuru, D., Kam, M., and Canny, J. An exploratory study of unsupervised mobile learning in rural India. *CHI* (2010).
17. LeDantec, C. and Edwards, K. The view from the trenches: organization, power, and technology at two nonprofit homeless outreach centers. *CSCW* (2008).
18. LeDantec, C. and Edwards, K. Across boundaries of influence and accountability: the multiple scales of public sector information systems. *CHI* (2010).
19. Lee, C.P., Dourish, P., and Mark, G. The human infrastructure of cyberinfrastructure. *CSCW* (2006).
20. Luyt, B. The One Laptop Per Child Project and the negotiation of technological meaning. *First Monday 13*, (2008).
21. Muñoz-Izquierdo, C. and Magaña Rodriguez, R. Un acercamiento a la eficacia de los Programas del gobierno federal orientados a mejorar la calidad de la educación básica. *Revista Mexicana de Investigación Educativa 13*, (2008).
22. Nardi, B. and O'Day, V. *Information Ecologies: Using Technology with Heart*. MIT Press, 2000.
23. Näslund-Hadley, E., Kipp, S., Cruz, J., Ibarrarán, P., and Steiner-Khamsi, G. *OLPC Pre-Pilot Evaluation Report (Haiti)*. Inter-American Bank Education Division.
24. Pal, J., Patra, R., Nedevschi, S., Plauche, M., and Pawar, U.S. The Case of the Occasionally Cheap Computer. *ITID 5*, (2009).
25. Papert, S. *Mindstorms: Children, computers, and powerful ideas*. Basic Books, 1993.
26. Patel, N., Chittamuru, D., Jain, A., Dave, P., and Parikh, T.S. Avaaj Otalo: a field study of an interactive voice forum for small farmers in rural India. *CHI*, (2010).
27. Peña-Lopez, I. From Laptops to Competences: Bridging the Digital Divide in Education. *Revista de Universidad y Sociedad del Conocimiento 7*, (2010).
28. Pineda Pineda, I. Compentencias para el desarrollo del trabajo docente en la escuela primaria. *Congreso Nacional de Investigación Educativa*, (2010).
29. Plan Ceibal. Síntesis del informe de monitoreo del estado del parque de XO a abril de 2010. http://www.ceibal.org.uy/.
30. Ribes, D. and Finholt, T. Tensions across the scales: planning infrastructure for the long-term. *GROUP*, (2007).
31. Sambasivan, N., Cutrell, E., Toyama, K., and Nardi, B. Intermediated technology use in developing communities. *CHI* (2010), 2583-2592.
32. Star, S.L. and Ruhleder, K. Steps toward an ecology of infrastructure: Design and access for large information spaces. In J. Yates and J. Van Maanen, eds., *Information technology and organizational transformation: history, rhetoric, and practice*. SAGE, 2001.
33. Vota, W., Derndorfer, C., and Berry, B. One laptop per child overview. 2009. www.olpcnews.com/files/ One_Laptop_Per_Child_Overview_2009.pdf.
34. Warschauer, M. *Technology and social inclusion: rethinking the digital divide*. MIT Press, 2004.
35. Warschauer, M. *Laptops And Literacy: Learning in the Wireless Classroom*. Teachers College Press, 2006.
36. Warschauer, M. and Ames, M. Can One Laptop per Child Save the World's Poor? *Journal of Intl. Affairs*, (2010).
37. Warschauer, M., Cotten, S., and Morgan, A. One Laptop Per Child Birmingham: Case Study of a Radical Experiment. manuscript submitted for publication.
38. Wyche, S.P., Smyth, T.N., Chetty, M., Aoki, P.M., and Grinter, R.E. Deliberate interactions: characterizing technology use in Nairobi, Kenya. *CHI*, ACM (2010)

Utilizing DVD Players as Low-Cost Offline Internet Browsers

Gaurav Paruthi
Microsoft Research India
v-gaupa@microsoft.com

William Thies
Microsoft Research India
thies@microsoft.com

ABSTRACT
In the developing world, computers and Internet access remain rare. However, there are other devices that can be used to deliver information, including TVs and DVD players. In this paper, we work to bridge this gap by delivering offline Internet content on DVD, for interactive playback on ordinary DVD players. Using the remote control, users can accomplish all of the major functions available in a Web browser, including navigation, hyperlinks, and search.

As our driving application, we map the entirety of schools-wikipedia.org – encompassing 5,500 articles and 259,000 screens – to a double-layer DVD. We evaluate our system via a study of 20 low-income users in Bangalore, India. Using our DVD as reference, participants are able to answer factual questions with over 90% success. While most participants prefer to use a computer if one is available, for resource-poor environments the DVD platform could represent a viable and low-cost alternative.

ACM Classification Keywords
H.5.2 User Interfaces; K.3.1 Computers and Education

General Terms
Human Factors, Design

INTRODUCTION
While many of us in the industrialized world have come to rely on having continuous access to the Internet, we represent a small minority: as of 2009, nearly three quarters of the world's population are classified as Internet non-users [2]. In countries such as India, Internet penetration stands at 5.7% [4] while the penetration of broadband is less than 1% [5].

At the same time, developing regions have witnessed significant penetration of other information and communication technologies, including television and DVD players. In India, 58% of households have television and 9% have DVD players; DVD penetration is expected to rise to 21% by 2013 (exceeding the projected penetration of Internet-enabled PCs, which stands at 8.9%) [4]. Even in rural villages and urban slums, households often manage to acquire and sustain TVs and DVD players – as well as DVDs themselves, which are widely copied and distributed through informal markets.

In this paper, we aim to enable new and interesting interactions with an old piece of technology: the DVD player. While DVD players are typically used for watching movies, they also include a rich set of interactive features that are rarely utilized to their full potential. Just as one can use a DVD menu to select the chapter of a movie, it is possible to map hundreds of thousands of menus to a single disc and navigate between them using the remote control [1]. This opens the door to new applications, including the delivery of offline Internet content for browsing on TV and DVD.

As an initial exploration of this idea, we have mapped the entirety of Schools-Wikipedia [6] to a DVD. The DVD contains about 5,500 articles from Wikipedia, which translate to over 259,000 interactive screens on TV. Unlike prior efforts to map Wikipedia or other Internet content to DVD, our disc is playable in off-the-shelf DVD players without any dependence on a computer. Our DVD offers navigation functions that are comparable to a Web browser, including search, hyperlinks, scrolling, and a back button (see Figure 1).

This paper makes two contributions. First, we present an innovative and generalizable design for navigating and searching offline Internet content using the DVD platform. Second, we demonstrate that our design is usable via a study of 20 low-income users in Bangalore, India. Our conclusion is that while TV-DVD is not superior to a computer for delivering offline Internet content, it can nonetheless provide similar functionality at much lower cost.

RELATED WORK
We are unaware of any other tools or techniques for viewing offline Internet content on DVD players. While there are many efforts to build an offline version of Wikipedia on CD or DVD (e.g., [7]), none of the discs produced to date work on an ordinary DVD player. They utilize HTML or compressed formats that require a computer for playback.

The WikiReader [8] is a $99 portable device designed specifically for reading Wikipedia. It can hold 3 million articles, compared to the 5,500 articles that we fit on a double-layer DVD. However, WikiReader omits all images, limits the display to black and white, and has a 240 x 200 resolution (less than that of a TV). The primary advantage of our solution is to leverage existing household technologies to enable anyone to copy and distribute the disc at very low cost.

Step 1: Home Page. Numbered links can be followed by pressing the corresponding key on the remote control. The user advances to the search page by pressing "1".

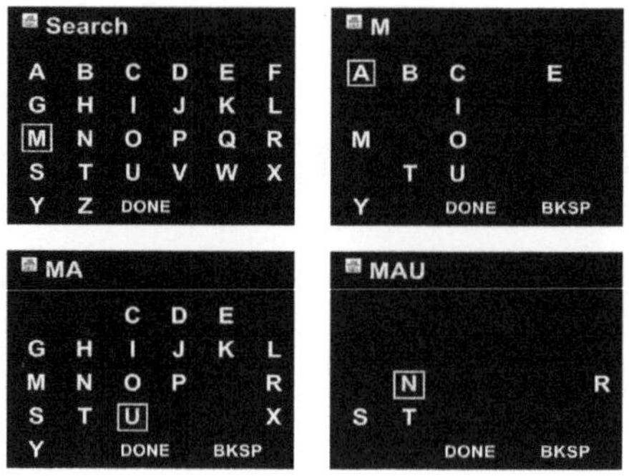

Steps 2-5: Search Pages. Using the arrow keys and select button, the user spells out the search term one letter at a time. In this case, after 4 letters the system jumps to the appropriate index page.

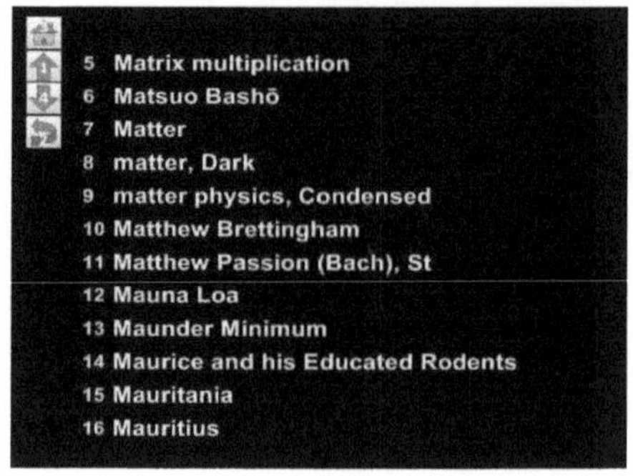

Step 6: Index Page. The user selects the desired article from the index using the number keys on the remote control. In this case she enters "12", for Mauna Loa.

Step 7: Content Page. The user arrives at the desired article. She can scroll up and down by using the "1" and "4" keys, respectively. In this cases she presses "4" in order to scroll down.

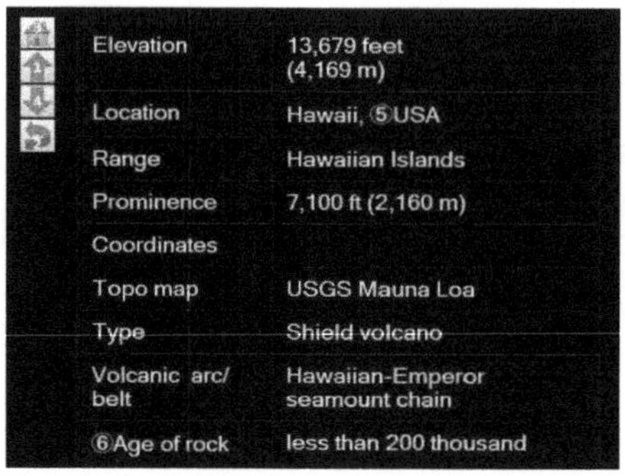

Step 8: Content Page. In addition to scrolling, the user can press "2" to go back, or "3" to return to the home screen. In this case the user presses "4" to scroll down further.

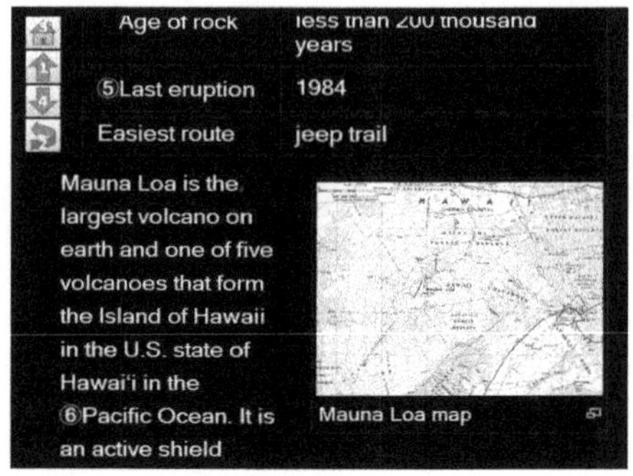

Step 9: Content Page. The user finds the information she was seeking: Mauna Loa last erupted in 1984. To learn more about eruptions, she can follow the hyperlink by pressing "5".

Figure 1. Example interaction with Schools-Wikipedia on TV-DVD. This example traces the steps needed for a user to answer one of our test questions: when was the last eruption of Mauna Loa?

In India, there are varied educational materials available on DVD, for example, from BookBox or Pebbles Infotainment; however, interactivity is almost completely absent. Conversely, in the United States, companies such as Screenlife have exploited many of the interactive capabilities of DVDs, but have focused on games rather than educational content.

Prior research has investigated the use of interactive DVDs in low-income schools in India [1], but focused on the domain of children's books and PowerPoint teaching aids. Researchers have also established guidelines for usable DVD menu design [3], though their focus is on movie DVDs and there is little overlap with our inquiries in this paper.

SCHOOLS-WIKIPEDIA ON DVD

We highlight the most interesting challenges and design decisions in mapping Schools-Wikipedia (a subset of Wikipedia intended for offline use) to DVD. Our discussion spans navigation, search, formatting, and our implementation.

Navigation

Navigating offline Internet content on DVD represents an interesting challenge. Instead of using a mouse and keyboard, the only input device available is the DVD remote control. (While it could also be possible to utilize the buttons on the DVD player itself, these generally represent a subset of what is available on the remote.) On DVDs, all navigation is done by selecting one of the options (or *links*) on an interactive menu. There are two ways to follow a link. The first is to highlight the link using the arrow keys and then to activate it using the select key on the remote control. The second is to press a number key directly; typing the number n on the remote will activate the nth link on the menu.

Our DVD uses a combination of these mechanisms for navigation. On the search pages (Figure 1, Steps 2-5), the user spells out the search term, one character at a time, using the arrow and select keys. We judged this to be simpler than typing a number, since there are 26 letters of the alphabet and most selections would require a tedious two-digit entry. However, for the home page, index page, and content pages (Steps 1, 6, and 7-9), we utilize the number keys for navigation. On all pages, links that are labeled with a yellow number can be followed by typing that number. In addition, on content and index pages, the numbers 1 through 4 are tied to specific functions: 1 scrolls up, 2 goes back, 3 goes to the home screen, and 4 scrolls down. The scrolling functions are assigned to keys 1 and 4 because of their intuitive vertical alignment on most DVD remote controls. The back key is limited in that it only stores a history of one page; pressing back twice will return to where the user started.

Search

Indexing and search is a critical component of Wikipedia and other Internet resources. However, search is especially challenging to provide on DVD players, as they have very primitive computational abilities. In particular, it is not possible to programmatically render text on the screen; one can only display frames of MPEG2 video that are stored on disc.

Our solution to this problem is to *simulate* the experience of search by pre-rendering all possible search screens and linking them together in a fixed configuration. For example, in Figure 1 (Steps 2-5), the user has the experience of selecting letters and appending them to the search term at the top of the screen (M, MA, MAU, etc.). However, in actuality, the DVD player is transitioning between separate menus, each of which has been pre-rendered to display a fixed string at the top. While it would require a large number of menus to represent all possible combinations of characters, we decrease the storage requirements drastically by prohibiting the user from spelling any word which does not correspond to an article on the disc. For example, in Figure 1, after the user has entered "M", the letter "Z" is removed from the options for the second character because no entries starting with "MZ" are available. Using this strategy, we require only 675 screens to cover all 4-letter prefixes that the user could search for; in comparison, an exhaustive enumeration of all 4-letter strings would require $26^4 = 456,976$ screens, which would likely exceed the capacity of the DVD.

Once the user has entered a requisite number of characters, the DVD automatically jumps to an index page, where all topics on the disc are sorted alphabetically. Our disc performs this jump when either: 1) the prefix entered by the user identifies a unique page of the index, or 2) the user has entered five characters. In the latter case (which is rare), the user may have to scroll through one or two pages of the index to find what she is looking for. Note that a given title is indexed multiple ways; for example, "St Matthew Passion (Bach)" is also indexed as "Matthew Passion (Bach), St" so that the user can find it when searching for "Matthew".

Formatting

Our design underwent many iterations to improve the readability of text on TV-DVD. We performed our testing on a second-hand analog TV (obtained for $50) that is representative of those found in the rural developing world. We found that using a white sans-serif font on a black background led to the best readability; serif fonts were particularly hard to read, as the thin lines caused an appearance of flickering on the screen. We also chose a relatively large font size, to enable viewing from a distance even on low-resolution screens.

Finally, to maximize the number of screens that could fit on the DVD, we simplified some of the Wikipedia content. We eliminated the bibliography from each page, as well as external links and the capability to zoom in on pictures.

Implementation

To generate the images for use on DVD, we render the HTML pages in a Web browser and take screenshots via .NET controls. We utilize a separate tool (details forthcoming) to author the DVD. One limitation of our tool is that the DVDs produced are compatible with many but not all DVD players, as different vendors appear to implement slightly different functionality. We are working to improve the compatibility of our disc in preparation for a broader deployment.

(a) Using computer (b) Using TV-DVD

Figure 2. User completes exercise on (a) computer and (b) TV-DVD.

We note that there is nothing fundamental in our implementation that restricts it to Wikipedia. The same infrastructure could be used to map general HTML content – complete with hyperlinks, indexing, and search – to interactive DVD.

USER STUDY

The goal of our user study is to assess whether low-income users in a developing-country context can utilize offline Internet content on DVD to accurately and efficiently retrieve needed information.

Participants

We conducted our user study with 20 participants (9 female) across two locations in Bangalore, India. 17 participants were enrolled in a non-profit IT training center that offers subsidized courses for people from low-income backgrounds, while 3 were support staff in an office facility. The average age of participants was 21 years (min 16, max 40). Participants had completed 12.6 years of schooling on average (min 11, max 15); also, 9 participants were currently enrolled as students. All participants were equipped with basic digital literacy skills and were comfortable reading English.

Only 25% of participants owned a computer at home, though 50% used a computer daily and 90% used a computer weekly (or more frequently). None of the participants had Internet access at home, though 10% used the Internet daily and 45% used the Internet weekly (or more frequently). In contrast, 100% of participants had a TV at home and 75% had a DVD player at home. Only one person had seen Wikipedia before.

Methodology

Our study represents a within-subjects design in which participants answer questions using both Wikipedia on computer and Wikipedia on TV-DVD. Both configurations utilized Schools-Wikipedia [6], a validated subset of 5,500 Wikipedia articles intended for offline use in schools. As Schools-Wikipedia does not include a search engine, the computer setup (Figure 2a) featured a custom Google search that indexed only pages hosted on schools-wikipedia.org; this search was set to the home page and default search engine of the Web browser. The TV-DVD setup (Figure 2b) utilized a 10-inch black-and-white TV (obtained new for $20 in India) and a generic DVD player, which was used to play our DVD.

	TV-DVD	Computer
Correctness	**91.0%** (± 5.3%)	**92.8%** (± 4.5%)
Time per Question	**1:41** (± 0:15)	**1:47** (± 0:27)

Figure 3. Main results of our user study. Time is given in minutes and seconds. Figures in parentheses represent 95% confidence intervals.

To evaluate the technologies, we asked participants to answer a set of 10 factual questions, including (for example) "what is the capital of Ukraine?" and "what year will Haley's Comet appear next?". We designed these questions to be 1) previously unknown to the participants, 2) answerable by viewing a (clearly-associated) Wikipedia article, and 3) answerable near the "beginning" of that article – within the first page of the computer screen, or the first 1-4 screens on TV-DVD. We divided the 10 questions into two equal groups; half of the participants completed Group A on computer and Group B on TV-DVD, while the other half did the opposite. All participants used the computer prior to TV-DVD, as we anticipate that many of our target users would explore Wikipedia on computer prior to utilizing our disc.

The specific experience of each participant was as follows. We started with informed consent and a demographic survey. Then, on the computer, we conducted a brief 1-on-1 training session in which the researcher demonstrated how to answer a practice question. The participant then answered two practice questions on their own, receiving help from the researcher and also asking the researcher as many questions as they liked. Subsequently, the participant completed five test questions on computer, with minimal assistance supplied by the researcher[1]. Following completion on computer, the training and testing process was repeated on TV-DVD. The session closed with an exit interview. We compensated participants Rs. 100 (about $2.20) for their time, which was usually between 60 and 90 minutes. We also gave all participants a complimentary copy of Schools-Wikipedia on DVD.

Results and Discussion

Our main results appear in Figure 3. In terms of success rate, participants correctly answered 91.0% of questions using TV-DVD and 92.8% of questions using computer. Both of these rates are very high, and while the average for computer is higher, the difference is not statistically significant.

Also evident in Figure 3 is the time required on each platform: participants spent an average of 1:41 per question on TV-DVD but 1:47 per question on computer. While the difference is not significant, it is interesting that TV-DVD was competitive with computer (and faster on average). We attribute this to two factors. First, as the computer screen has a higher resolution than the TV screen, it displays more content at a given time. This distracted participants in some cases, especially when the answer appears in Wikipedia's summary table (which appears in the corner on computer, but is shown first on TV-DVD). Second, some participants were slow typing on QWERTY keyboards, and benefited from the alphabetical layout of letters on TV-DVD.

[1]Across 210 questions, the researcher supplied a hint in 5 cases – 3 for DVD and 2 for computer – only when it became apparent that a participant was stuck.

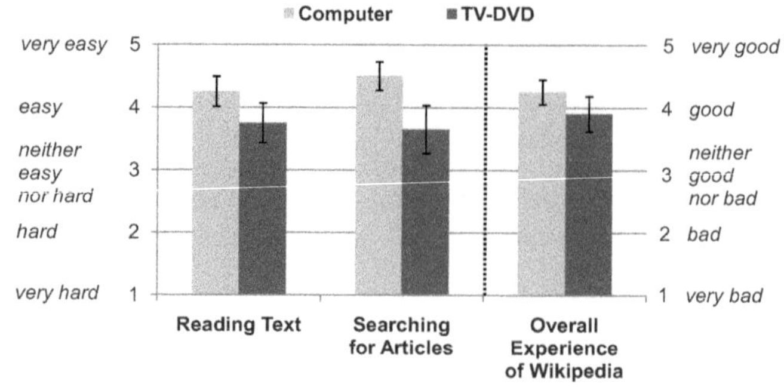

Figure 4. Users' opinions regarding the difficulty of reading text and searching for articles as well as their overall experience of Wikipedia. Error bars represent 95% confidence intervals.

Qualitative feedback was also gathered, and results appear in Figure 4. On computer, all but one participant judged it to be "easy" or "very easy" to read text and search for articles, while on TV-DVD participants indicated that it was significantly harder to read text ($p < 0.02$) or search for articles ($p < 0.01$). Regarding participants' overall experience, everyone indicated that the experience on computer was either "good" or "very good", while for TV-DVD three participants assigned neutral or negative labels. The overall experience on computer was rated significantly higher than that of TV-DVD ($p = 0.05$). Nonetheless, 25% of participants reported that they preferred TV-DVD to computer, and 90% said that they would use Wikipedia on TV-DVD if the computer was not available – as is the case in 75% of their homes.

CONCLUSIONS

Offline Internet content on interactive DVD has the potential to reach a large part of the developing world, due to the relatively high penetration of TVs and DVD players. In this paper, we show that the DVD platform is capable of supporting the core functionality of Web browsers – including navigation, hyperlinks, and search – by mapping the entirety of schools-wikipedia.org to a double-layer DVD. Our user study suggests that while the DVD platform is not superior to a computer, it nonetheless represents a usable and viable alternative for finding needed information at very low cost.

ACKNOWLEDGMENTS

We are very grateful to Augustine Thomas, Sunita, and Mini from the Hope Foundation, as well as all of the participants in our study, for their generous time and support.

REFERENCES

1. Gaikwad, K., Paruthi, G., and Thies, W. Interactive DVDs as a Platform for Education. In *ICTD* (2010).
2. ITU. World Telecommunication/ICT Indicators Database. http://www.itu.int/ITU-D/ict/statistics/, 2009.
3. Kappel, K., Tomitsch, M., Költringer, T., and Grechenig, T. Developing user interface guidelines for DVD menus. In *CHI Ext. Abstracts* (2006).
4. Screen Digest. Market Research Report, 2010.
5. Telecom Regulatory Authority of India. Press release no. 42, Sep 2010.
6. Schools Wikipedia. http://schools-wikipedia.org, 2010.
7. Wikipedia on DVD. http://www.wikipediaondvd.com/site.php/, 2010.
8. WikiReader. http://thewikireader.com/, 2010.

Importance-Driven Compositing Window Management

Manuela Waldner[1], Markus Steinberger[1], Raphael Grasset[2], and Dieter Schmalstieg[1]

[1]Institute for Computer Graphics and Vision
Graz University of Technology
Graz, Austria
{ waldner | steinberger | schmalstieg }@icg.tugraz.at

[2]HIT Lab NZ
University of Canterbury
Christchurch, New Zealand
raphael.grasset@canterbury.ac.nz

ABSTRACT
In this paper we present importance-driven compositing window management, which considers windows not only as basic rectangular shapes but also integrates the importance of the windows' content using a bottom-up visual attention model. Based on this information, importance-driven compositing optimizes the spatial window layout for maximum visibility and interactivity of occluded content in combination with see-through windows. We employ this technique for emerging window manager functions to minimize information overlap caused by popping up windows or floating toolbars and to improve the access to occluded window content. An initial user study indicates that our technique provides a more effective and satisfactory access to occluded information than the well-adopted Alt+Tab window switching technique and see-through windows without optimized spatial layout.

Author Keywords
compositing window management, visual saliency, space management, transparency

ACM Classification Keywords
H.5.2 Information Interfaces and Presentation: User Interfaces—*Windowing systems*

General Terms
Design, Human Factors.

INTRODUCTION
Although more than 25 years have passed since the emergence of the WIMP metaphor, the window concept still prevails as the unique interface to control multiple applications on the screen. Today, the need of information workers for multiple applications to successfully complete a single task and the common usage of floating menus or multiple windows per application, lead to a standard desktop being cluttered with a large number of open application windows. Even with increasing display space, users just tend to keep more application windows open [13].

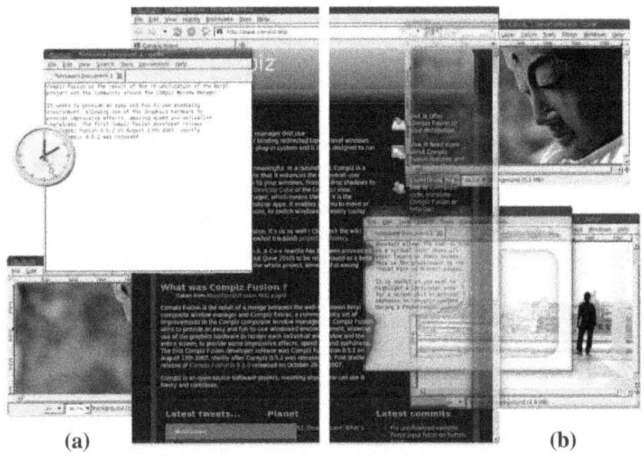

(a) (b)

Figure 1. (a) Conventional overlapping windows occlude important information in obscured windows. To reveal this information, the user has to change the window layout manually. (b) Importance-driven compositing spatially arranges occluded windows and applies see-through compositing to maximize content visibility and interactivity.

Most current window managers employ multiple overlapping windows and leave the spatial arrangement of the individual windows merely to the user. As a result, important information may be hidden in occluded windows (Figure 1a) and users spend a significant amount of time switching between windows to reveal obscured content [13].

Different window management techniques to increase the amount of simultaneously visible information have been explored. Automatic window layout techniques (*e.g.*, [18, 3]) reduce the amount of window overlaps and, as a result, the empty screen space. A limitation of these systems is the lack of knowledge about the application content. Therefore, windows are treated as "black boxes", which does not leave much room for *overlap-avoidance* [3] if the screen is cluttered with a large number of windows. On the other hand, transparency can be employed to reveal the content of occluded windows. However, transparency alone does not ensure that important hidden content is actually revealed. If highly salient window content overlaps, visual differentiation between window layers becomes difficult for the user. These situations can be resolved with an optimized spatial layout which minimizes information overlap.

In this paper, we therefore propose importance-driven compositing – a new window management approach for see-through user interfaces. We base our work on recently established compositing window managers, which have access to the window textures after the window content has been rendered into video memory. Importance-driven compositing window management analyzes these window textures to identify perceptually important window regions to optimize the spatial window layout for see-through compositing (Figure 1b). To identify the importance of a window and its content, we rely on a visual attention model describing how much a location in an image stands out from its surroundings [17]. In summary, our contributions are:

- Using visual saliency as an importance measure of application window content and the concept of *importance maps* as unified, image-based importance representation for compositing window managers,
- a window management approach combining spatial window layout optimization with see-through compositing for maximum information visibility and interactivity,
- a hardware-accelerated implementation for real-time usage in an established windowing system, and
- a validation of our approach through an initial user study indicating a benefit of our technique for accessing occluded content compared to traditional Alt+Tab window switching and *free-space transparency* [16].

We will present novel window management functions based on importance-driven compositing to improve the access to occluded information by a new window switching approach and a semi-automatic window layout technique. We also introduce functions to decrease occlusion of window content by pop-up windows or floating menus.

RELATED WORK

With the steadily increasing number of open, overlapping application windows, users are required to apply some sort of *occlusion management* technique [8] to discover and access occluded window content. To bring occluded windows to the front, window managers provide window lists, sequential window switching techniques (such as Alt+Tab or *stack leaving* [9]), or space-filling window layouts (such as Apple's Exposé[1]). However, explicit window switching has been described as tedious [10]. Subsequently, we discuss two window management approaches alleviating the need to switch windows explicitly by increasing the amount of simultaneously visible information on the screen: see-through windows and automatic spatial window layouts.

See-Through Windows

See-through user interfaces were first introduced by Bier *et al.* [5] as movable filters operating on the underlying graphics object. Today, advances in hardware-accelerated window management (such as *Metisse* [6]) have made enhanced window rendering techniques, such as transparencies, geometric deformations, or change visualizations [4], widely available. Most up-to-date window managers support half-transparent rendering of application windows to show information hidden underneath. However, experiments have shown that simple alpha blending either causes readability problems with foreground items or decreases the perception of the background image – depending on the chosen alpha level [12, 2]. Outlines of text and icons [12] and *multiblending* [2] have been shown to improve recognizability of blended content. *Dynamic transparencies* [11] help to increase background visibility and were demonstrated to reduce targeting performance only marginally. For see-through window management, Ishak and Feiner [16] apply *free-space transparency* only to "unimportant" (white) window regions. This guarantees that important content in top-level windows is preserved. However, it does not guarantee that important content in occluded windows is actually revealed. If important content in the occluded windows is located underneath the important regions of the overlay window, the user has to manually re-arrange windows to access hidden content. This limitation is the main motivation for our approach: we use window importance not only for see-through compositing, but also for an optimized spatial window layout which minimizes overlaps of important regions.

Spatial Window Layout

Window layout techniques like overlap-avoiding dragging [3] or constraint-enabled window management [1] spatially arrange windows to avoid window overlaps. For both techniques, a sufficiently large screen is required to accommodate for all the non-overlapping windows in their original size. Other techniques only temporarily change the window layout for certain situations, for instance if a physical occlusion of user interface elements has been detected [27] or if the user wants to copy-and-paste between overlapping windows [7]. All of these examples treat windows as simple rectangular shapes – irrespective of their content. For our window layout routine, we were inspired by the field of augmented reality, where a common task is to annotate real-world objects in video images with virtual labels. To find the optimal placement for the label, the video images are analyzed (*e.g.*, [19, 24]). We extended this approach for compositing window management where we treat windows as image templates with the objective of finding the window layout with the least information overlap.

To deal with limited screen space, window layout techniques often apply some sort of deformation to the windows. For instance, tiled window managers (*e.g.*, [18]) have to resize windows to keep all windows visible without an overlap. Automatic down-sizing introduces the risk of clipping important content at the window's boundary. Therefore, others crop windows to preserve only the most relevant regions of context windows (*e.g.*, [15, 20]). However, in these systems the user has to define the relevant regions manually, which can be a tedious task. In contrast, importance-driven compositing automatically identifies perceptually important window regions, by image-based analysis of window textures.

Task management systems (*e.g.*, [23, 22]) apply perspective transformations or down-scaling to context windows, while the focus windows remain in the center of the screen. How-

[1] `http://www.apple.com/macosx/what-is-macosx/expose.html`

ever, content can be too small or skewed to allow for details to be perceived. Furthermore, interaction with transformed windows is not possible in these examples. Thus, users have to perform explicit window switches to access and manipulate information in transformed windows. A main distinguishing aspect of our work is that we use unimportant screen space – potentially embedded within windows – to show important elements of occluded windows in original size. Content is neither distorted nor shrunk and fully interactive, if visible. This allows the user to look up and interact with the fine-grained content in occluded windows without explicitly bringing them to the front.

IMPORTANCE-DRIVEN COMPOSITING

Importance-driven compositing analyses the importance of window content to find an optimal spatial window layout – in terms of visibility and interactivity of occluded content – for see-through window interfaces. Our approach is composed of four steps:

1. The creation of desktop and window *importance maps* containing image-based descriptions of important regions,
2. a *window layout* routine, placing occluded windows to minimize the overlap between important regions,
3. importance-driven see-through *compositing*, applying per-pixel transparencies to reveal important content of occluded windows, and
4. *interaction* techniques allowing the user to access and manipulate content in occluded windows.

In the following, we will discuss these steps in more detail.

Importance Map

We introduce importance maps as unified image-based representation of importance in windowing systems: *window importance maps* are extracted from each window's content using a model of saliency-based visual attention. In our system, the window's content is given as an image – more specifically as a *texture*, as we are relying on a hardware-accelerated window rendering (similar as described in [6]).

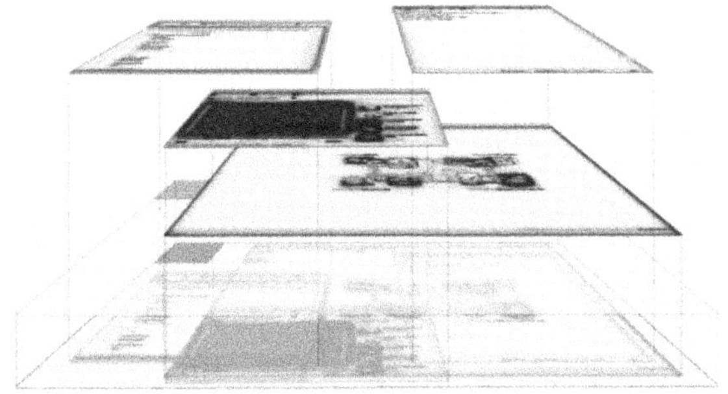

Figure 2. Window importance maps (2, blue) are created for each window individually and accumulated with high-level information (1, red) to a common desktop importance map (0, green). Dark areas represent high importance.

Window importance maps are accumulated into a common *desktop importance map*, which can be extended by high-level information provided by the user or derived from the physical screen setup. Windows are added to the desktop importance map from front to back – ensuring that recently used windows are prioritized for layout and compositing. Figure 2 shows individual window importance maps, high-level information, and the merged desktop importance map. The resulting desktop composition is depicted in Figure 3(8).

Visual Attention

Saliency is a measure of how much a location visually stands out from the surrounding image regions [17, 21]. Typically used bottom-up saliency features are regions of high changes in luminance, color opposition, orientation changes, and motion. For our window importance maps, we apply the conspicuity analysis proposed by Mendez *et al.* [21], which extracts pixel-wise saliency values based on an analysis of lightness, red-green and blue-yellow color opposition, to the (dynamic) textures of the windows. In addition, we measure visual changes in occluded windows and temporarily increase importance in regions where content has changed. Visual changes caused by user interaction, such as scrolling the window content, are ignored. The importance maps in Figure 2 show that user interface elements and information content, such as text or images, are assigned high importance values. In particular, the video in the center window of Figure 2 is highly salient due to additional motion. Homogeneous background regions have low importance – independent of their background color.

High-Level Importance

In addition to the accumulated window importance maps describing importance based on visual perception, the desktop importance map can also contain high-level information. For instance, a user might want to keep desktop regions uncovered from application windows to have access to frequently used desktop icons [14] or to avoid windows spanning across physical monitor bezels on multi-monitor settings [10]. This importance information can be accumulated into the desktop importance map – for instance by automatically adding a one-pixel line of high importance along monitor bezels. In the example map of Figure 2, the user manually selected the upper left corner of the screen as high-importance desktop region, where window placement should be avoided.

Window Layout

The aim of the window layout routine is to spatially arrange windows so that important regions of occluded windows are moved to desktop areas of little importance. Therefore we consider both, each window's individual importance map (Figure 3(2)) and the desktop importance map describing the current distribution of information over the desktop (Figure 3(3)), to find the optimal window placement. Figure 3 shows the layout step for a single window and the resulting desktop composition. The optimal window placement is determined by considering three influencing factors described in the following (*c.f.*, Figure 3(4-6)).

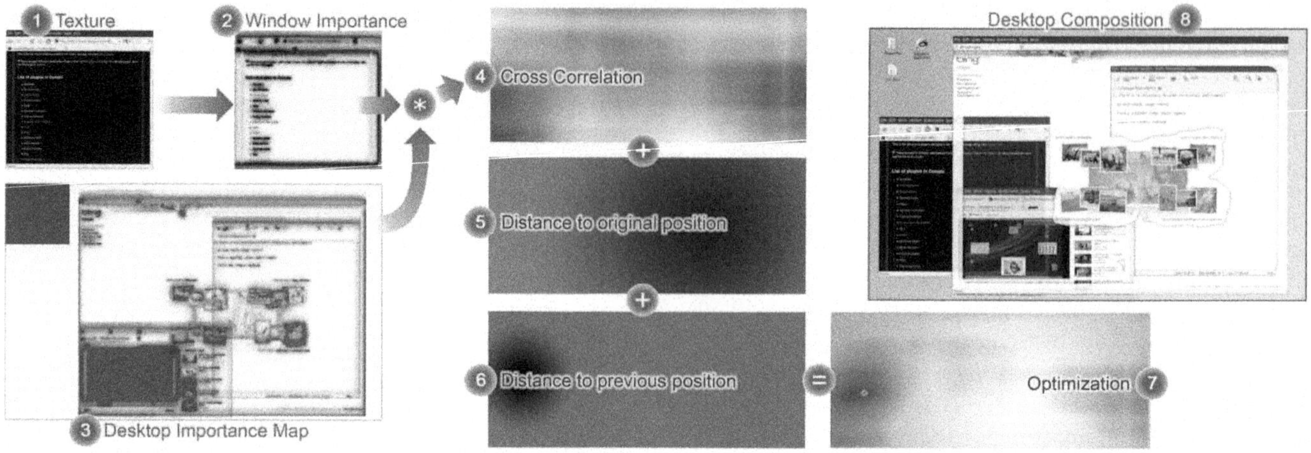

Figure 3. Overview of importance-based compositing for a single window: (1) from the window's texture, (2) the window importance map is created. (3) Given the desktop importance map, the window layout routine finds the optimal placement considering (4) the information overlap, (5) the distance to the original window location, and (6) the distance to the previous location. (7) The combination of these factors gives an optimization problem with the solution marked as a green dot (window center). (8) Finally, the window is rendered to the existing desktop content.

Firstly, the overlap of information in the window (I_w) and the already existing information on the desktop (I_d) shall be kept low. The information overlap can be formulated as a cross-correlation of the two importance maps I_w and I_d:

$$J_i(\vec{p}) = \sum_{(x,y)\in\Omega_w} I_w(x,y) \cdot I_d(\vec{p} + (x,y)),$$

where (x, y) visit all discrete positions in the window texture Ω_w, and $\vec{p}$ is the window location. Secondly, the location $\vec{p}$ should have little displacement from the original window location $\vec{p}_o$, which is defined by the location where the window has been mapped or manually positioned by the user. Thus, this term is responsible for maintaining a certain degree of spatial stability. Thirdly, the resulting window location $\vec{p}$ should vary minimally from the location in the previous frame $\vec{p}_p$. In other words, jitter should be minimized.

These requirements can be formulated as an optimization problem over all possible window locations $\vec{p}$ (Figure 3(7)):

$$J(\vec{p}) = \omega_i J_i(\vec{p}) + \omega_d D(\vec{p}_o, \vec{p}) + \omega_j D(\vec{p}_p, \vec{p}),$$

where J is the associated cost function to be minimized, composed by a weighted sum of the information overlap J_i, and the distance D to the original location (window displacement) and previous position (jitter). The individual weights (ω) vary for the presented window manager functions described further below in the paper.

To reduce the number of potential window locations ($\vec{p}$), the search space can be decreased by additional constraints. For instance, windows can be bound to certain screen regions or to "parent" windows. In addition, we limit the maximal window movement over time. This introduces smooth frame-to-frame animations and helps the user keep track of window movements. Window content is never placed outside the screen boundaries. This decreases the search space for large windows, while maximized windows will not be re-positioned at all.

Our algorithm treats multiple windows sequentially in a greedy manner. For each window, the best placement is determined by solving the optimization problem as stated above. Subsequently, the window's importance map is added to the desktop importance map at the determined location. The modified desktop importance map then serves as an input for the next window's placement. As the windows being traversed first have more freedom in finding a good placement, more recently used windows are implicitly prioritized.

Compositing

Importance-driven see-through compositing reveals occluded content by applying pixel-wise transparencies. We implemented two well-known compositing techniques from the field of technical illustrations and volume rendering [26]: *ghosting* and *cut-aways*.

Ghosting determines each window pixel's alpha value $\alpha_w(x, y)$ by evaluating the importance ratio of the window's importance map $I_w(x, y)$ and the desktop importance map $I_d(x, y)$ at the respective pixel:

$$\alpha_w(x,y) = \frac{I_w(x,y)}{I_w(x,y) + I_d(x,y)}.$$

Thereby, it ensures that the most important features of each window are visually preserved (Figure 4a). However, if the window layout routine cannot spatially separate important regions (for instance due to high information density), important features in overlapping windows compete for visual prominence.

Cut-aways put more emphasis on the windows' stacking order: they ensure that the most prominent features of the overlay windows are preserved. Only if the desktop's importance map value is below a certain threshold, the obscured window's content is revealed. Smooth blurring and desaturation of obscured window content provide subtle depth cues. This approach is similar to free-space transparency [16], where

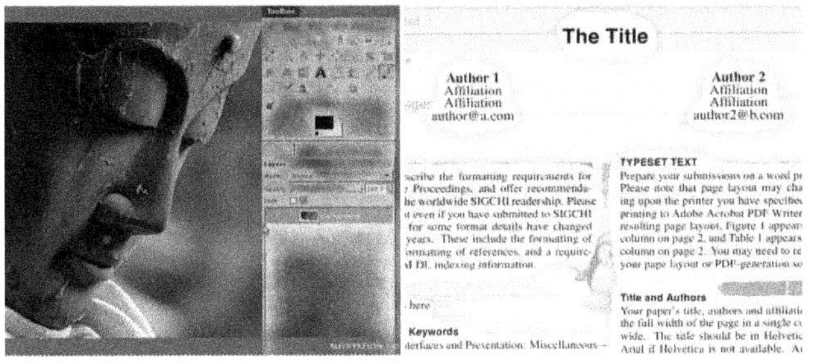

(a) (b)

Figure 4. See-through compositing: (a) Ghosting and (b) cut-aways.

transparency is only applied to white regions in overlay windows. Our cut-away technique differs from free-space transparency, as we apply hard boundaries between the foreground and the background and add shadows to visually indicate depth layers (Figure 4b).

Interaction

Importance-driven compositing window management allows users to interact with visible portions of occluded windows – even if located within the boundaries of an overlay window. We rely on the simple assumption that the user aims to interact with the visually most prominent window at the current mouse pointer location. We therefore set the input focus according to the compositing result: the window with the overall highest contribution to the pixel's color below the mouse pointer is activated.

WINDOW MANAGEMENT FUNCTIONS

Based on the concept of importance-driven compositing, we subsequently present novel window management functions for overlapping windows. Clearly, applying see-through window compositing to all application windows at all times interferes with focused attention [12] – the ability to focus entirely on a single item without visual interference from other items. Therefore, our suggested functions apply importance-driven compositing either temporarily or solely to a subset of windows.

Uncovering Windows

Hutchings *et al.* [13] found that window switching is a frequent activity and that most windows are activated for less than four seconds. This indicates that users often only need to skim the content of a secondary window to resume their primary task, such as reading a bit of documentation, checking if a new e-mail has arrived, or retrieving the result of a calculation. With sequential window switching techniques, the user has to perform multiple operations: initiate the window switch, identify and select the window of interest, perform the actual operation, and repeat the window switching step to return to the previous window. Not surprisingly, "the need to Alt-Tab" has been described as tedious [10].

To reduce the number of necessary activities to quickly access occluded content, we use importance-driven compositing to uncover information in occluded windows on demand. By pressing a keyboard combination, spatial window layout

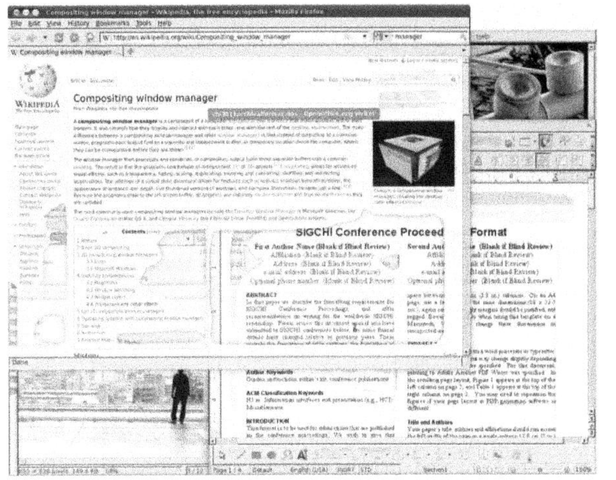

Figure 5. Unimportant window regions are temporarily cut away and occluded windows are spatially arranged to reveal obscured content. The user directly interacts with the otherwise invisible document content uncovered below the browser window.

and cut-away compositing is applied to all occluded (unminimized) desktop windows (*c.f.*, Figure 5). Top-level windows are not re-positioned. Penalties on window displacement for the layout algorithm are kept low to give more emphasis on minimizing the information overlap than a stabilized window layout. We discard the window title bars from occluded windows, as they have a high visual saliency but little benefit for user interaction in this situation. As input is redirected to the most salient window at the cursor location, simple operations in occluded windows – such as pressing a button – can be accomplished while exposing occluded content without actually bringing the window to the front. To signal which window currently holds the input focus, we increase the active window's overall alpha value and show its title at the left upper window corner (as for the document editor in Figure 5). When releasing the key combination, the active window under the pointer is brought to the front and the other occluded windows return to their original locations.

Semi-Automatic Window Layout

When working with large-scale monitors, users rarely maximize windows. Instead, they often "carefully coordinate" their windows and keep a small portion of occluded windows visible for direct access [14]. This window arrangement alleviates the need for explicit window switching. However, manually arranging the windows is rather time-consuming and keeping important elements visible for easy window identification requires frequent re-adjustment as other windows are moved.

We use importance-driven compositing as a semi-automatic window layout technique which is initiated when the user starts dragging a window. All windows – except for the window currently being dragged – become subject to semi-automatic window layout. As the user drags a window, underlying windows are re-positioned to avoid information overlap (Figure 6). In addition, ghosting allows the user to see the content underneath while keeping the title bar

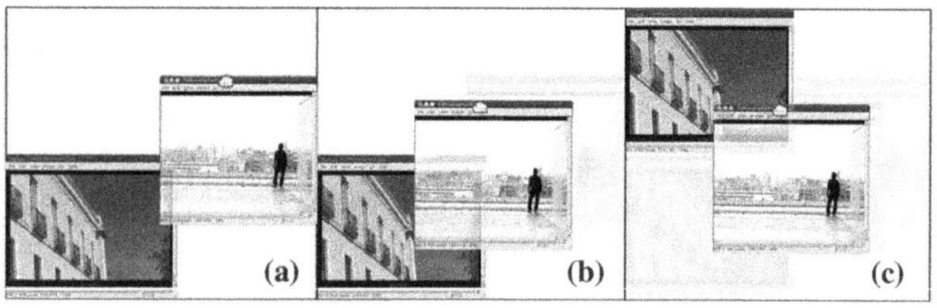

Figure 6. Semi-automatic window layout: (a-b) the user drags a window towards the left, which causes an overlap with another window. The window layout persists as long as the amount of covered information is low. (c) If more information is occluded, the obscured window is re-positioned to leave the most important window content uncovered. Window trails were added for illustration purposes.

pressed. As the user releases the mouse button, the applied layout persists and the windows become fully opaque again.

In contrast to the previously described window uncovering function, we treat the window being dragged as a black box (*i.e.*, the window importance map is uniformly high) as the aim is to optimize the layout for opaque windows. However, we do consider the importance of content in the windows underneath. In case the dragged window is moved on top of other windows, the layout function re-positions these occluded windows so that only unimportant regions are covered. Penalties for window displacement and jitter are high to keep the spatial window layout as persistent as possible.

Users can furthermore influence the resulting layout by providing high-level desktop importance information. They can define desktop regions where window placement should be avoided or prioritize certain regions.

Pop-Up Window Placement

Windows popping up without the user triggering it usually signals events which require the user's attention. Examples are dialogs indicating a new e-mail, instant messages, or a completed file operation. Immediate user activity is not always necessary. Yet, dialog windows popping up on top of the window stack – sometimes even obscuring the main interaction item – necessitate the user to interrupt the current task and undertake immediate action.

To minimize user interruption, we apply importance-driven compositing to pop-up dialogs. Newly created windows from the class "dialog" are automatically positioned to avoid an overlap with the content of other windows. Cut-aways are employed to ensure the readability of foreground information, as depicted in Figure 7. Users can directly interact with dialog windows wherever visibility is given. To bring the dialog window to the front as a conventional opaque window, the user employs a simple shortcut. If the user does not interact with the dialog within 10 seconds after creation, the window moves to the back of the window stack as a conventional occluded window.

Intelligent Floating Toolbars

Floating toolbars or tear-off menus are commonplace in many applications, such as word processors or image editing software. Instead of docking a menu to the window's boundary, the user can detach it and re-position it anywhere on the screen. Floating toolbars usually stay on top of the main application window to enable quick access to important user interface elements. Thereby, toolbars can lead to an occlusion of the main window content.

We allow the user to interactively pick floating toolbars for importance-driven compositing using a shortcut or a context menu entry. Once selected, the toolbar window is re-stacked behind the main application window and re-positioned to avoid an overlap with the main content. Ghosting maintains the most important content of both, toolbar and main window. We constrain the layout algorithm to apply only minimal displacement from the menu's previous and original location. As a result, the toolbar will minimally adjust its position as the user manipulates the main window's content, offering a trade-off between spatial stability and avoiding occlusion of important content. Consider, for instance, the floating menu shown in Figure 8: as the user scrolls the content, the menu is set to empty document spots but is never moved too far from its original location.

Users can bind a toolbar to a main window by using a context menu entry or by dragging it within the boundaries of the parent window and not moving it for a second. Automatic toolbar placement is then restricted to the interior and the immediate surroundings of the parent window. If the main window is moved, the toolbar is re-placed accordingly. To detach the toolbar from its parent, the user drags it outside the parent window's boundaries. Visual feedback of the binding/unbinding operation is provided by animated icons.

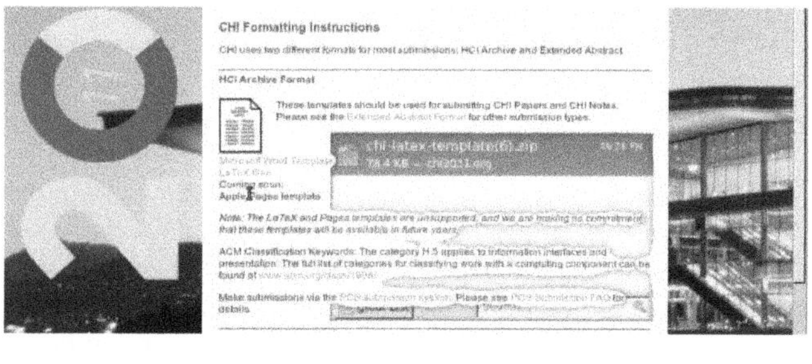

Figure 7. Importance-driven compositing takes care that the pop-up dialog does not occlude important website content while keeping the most important elements of the dialog visible.

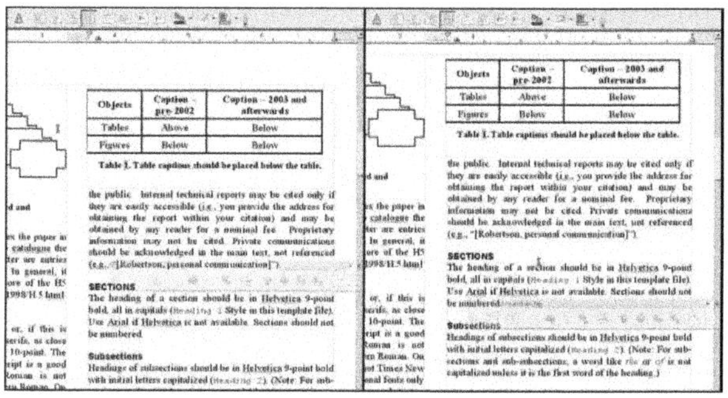

Figure 8. A floating menu is re-positioned automatically while scrolling the document to avoid overlap with textual content.

Our system supports independent application windows to reach similar functionality as floating application toolbars – similar to user interface "holes" to access auxiliary applications [25]. For instance, the user can attach a calculator to a programming environment or a sticky note to a document editor and access them like conventional user interface elements of the main application.

IMPLEMENTATION

Tremendous processing capabilities are nowadays available in form of graphics processing units (GPUs) in virtually every PC system. Yet, they remain mostly unused for common window operations. In our system, we formulate computationally expensive tasks (such as the saliency computation or the window layout routine) using advanced GPU languages - namely, the OpenGL Shading Language[2] (GLSL) and the Open Computing Language[3] (OpenCL) - to support real-time interaction. For our prototype, we extended the OpenGL-based compositing window manager Compiz[4] for the X Window System of Linux. On a Quad-Core 2.80 Ghz CPU and NVIDIA GeForce GTX 480, for a desktop resolution of 1280x1024, placing and rendering a window of approximately 500x300 pixels requires 6ms. For a conventional office scenario with five managed windows, we obtain an average frame rate of 20 fps.

Window importance maps are extracted from the individual windows' textures by using a GLSL implementation of Itti's visual attention model [17], as proposed by Mendez *et al.* [21]. Visual window changes are monitored through window *damage* events, *i.e.*, notifications of window region updates provided by the X Window System. These damage regions are merged into the window's importance map.

For the computationally expensive evaluation of the window layout cost function, we execute a two level parallel search in OpenCL. The best location found on a lower resolution is refined locally to give the new window location.

The final window compositing step is realized as a GLSL fragment shader, which is applied to the translated windows. The compositing shader determines per-pixel alpha values and evaluates each pixel's neighborhood for blurring and shadowing, according to the chosen compositing technique. The shader is also responsible for merging the window's importance map with the desktop importance map and to determine the most salient window at the respective pixel. This information is queried each time the mouse is moved, to find the active window at the current mouse pointer location. To redirect the mouse pointer input to an obscured window, we temporarily raise the window in the window manager's stacking order (refer to Stürzlinger *et al.* [25] for technical solutions and limitations for input redirection in the X Window System). Although this modifies the window manager's stacking order, we do not alter our traversal order for layout and compositing to keep the desktop visually consistent.

[2] `http://www.opengl.org/documentation/glsl/`
[3] `http://www.khronos.org/opencl/`
[4] `http://www.compiz.org`

EXPLORATORY USER STUDY

We conducted a preliminary user study to judge the usability of importance-driven compositing for accessing content in occluded windows. For that purpose, we compared it with two other window management techniques for three different tasks. The tasks were designed to simulate real information work situations, where users have to skim through information in occluded windows or quickly interact with obscured content before resuming the main task.

We hypothesized that importance-driven compositing will be advantageous compared to sequential window switching for quickly looking at information in occluded windows, as the number of necessary steps to reveal occluded content is reduced. Furthermore, we expected a performance benefit of importance-driven compositing for simple interaction tasks in occluded windows, as we provide the facility to directly interact with user interface elements in occluded windows.

We compared the following three window management techniques for revealing occluded window content:
Alt+tab (AT) in combination with conventional overlapping windows is a standard window switching technique provided by all major operating systems and served as a control condition. The employed Alt+Tab switcher by the Compiz window manager shows small previews of all windows when activated by the Alt+Tab sequence (Figure 9a), and allows for sequential window selection by pressing the tab key.
Free-space transparency (FST), proposed by Ishak and Feiner [16], applies transparency to unimportant window regions of overlay windows using a smooth gradient between transparent and opaque regions. We simulated FST using importance-driven compositing without the layout routine (Figure 9b). Instead of the original notion of unimportant window content (white pixels), we used our importance maps to define transparency values. FST does not allow users to directly interact with the occluded content. Therefore, we provided the "pie menu" proposed by the authors, which shows a circular menu of all the windows lying underneath the current pointer location, to bring occluded windows to the front. Participants had to press Start+tab to retrieve this menu and then click on a window preview to bring the desired window to the front.
Importance-driven compositing (IC) was employed to uncover occluded windows on demand, as described further above. To initiate IC, participants had to press the key combination Start+w. As long as the keys were pressed, occluded windows were spatially arranged, cut-aways were applied and interactivity for the most salient window underneath the pointer was ensured (Figure 9c).

Participants were asked to solve a visual search task. Questions were presented in a textual format and the users had to identify specific items in occluded windows. They were presented with a maximized main window and five small object windows behind the main window, which were arranged in a cascaded fashion. The object windows always contained an image of a 2D geometric primitive and – depending on the task type – a small textual label and a button. The main window contained the question the users had to answer and

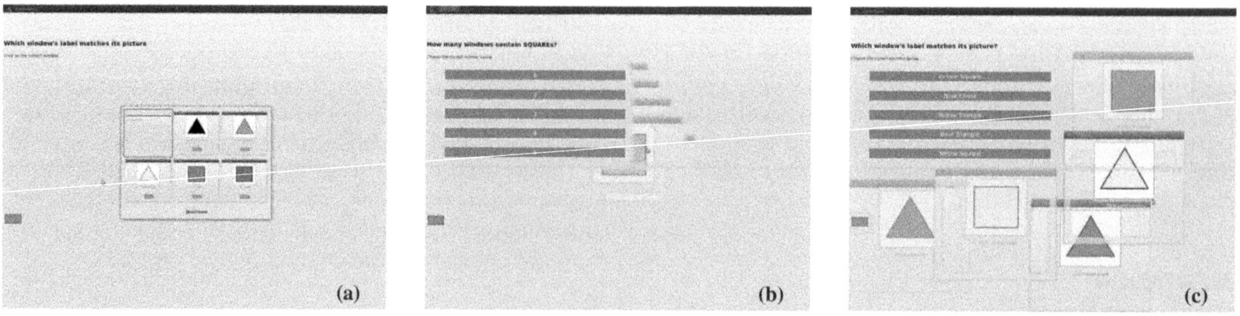

Figure 9. The three window management techniques and the three task types in our experiment: (a) overlapping windows with the Alt+Tab menu for the interact task, (b) free-space transparency with the count task, and (c) importance-driven compositing with the read task.

a list of solutions (in two task types). The following three task types had to be solved:

Count: Participants were asked to search for a certain 2D geometric primitive (*e.g.*, square) in the five object windows, count its occurrences, and select the number of occurrences from the list of solutions in the main window (*c.f.*, Figure 9b). This represents a scenario where users have to get an overview of all the windows and identify them based on a strong visual feature, which is also clearly visible in a scaled window representation.
Read: Participants had to find the only object window which contained a textual label (*e.g.*, *"This is a yellow triangle"*) that matched the associated picture of a geometric primitive (*c.f.*, Figure 9c). Subsequently, they had to select the same label from the list in the main window. This represents a scenario where the user has to switch to a window containing textual information required for the main task. Note that the text labels were too small to be readable in the FST pie menu and AT preview menu.
Interact: The task was similar to the read task, except that the validation of the matching label was selected by a push button directly in the object window (*c.f.*, Figure 9a). The task was designed to represent situations where the user has to shortly interact with an occluded window before resuming the main task.

We recruited 15 participants (4 female, aged 15 to 32) from a local high school and university. All participants were experienced computer users and tested for color-blindness. Nine participants are using Microsoft Windows as a primary operating system, three employ Linux and three use Mac OS X. Twelve of the participants use Alt+Tab "often" to "very often" to switch windows, followed by the window list in the task bar, which is employed frequently by eleven participants. None of the participants stated using one window switching technique exclusively.

The study was conducted on a PC running Linux Ubuntu 10.04 with a 1280x1024 17" monitor. We measured the completion times (time between appearance of a question and selecting an answer) and error rates for each task item. Participants were also handed out a preference questionnaire at the end of the experiment. A semi-structured interview was conducted to collect subjective feedback. For each technique, participants had a short practice session (6 questions). The order of the techniques and tasks was counter-balanced. Each user had to complete four repetitions for each task in every technique. For the interact task and read task, the stacking position of the window containing the correct label was balanced across the repetitions.

Results

We conducted a 3 (Technique: AT, FST, IC) x 3 (Task: Count, Read, Interact) repeated measures ANOVA ($\alpha = .05$) to evaluate completion times. Bonferroni adjustments were applied for post-hoc comparisons. We found a main effect for Technique ($F_{2,28} = 82.231, p < .001$) and Task ($F_{2,28} = 18.182, p < .001$), as well as a borderline significant interaction between the two factors ($F_{4,56} = 2.601, p = .046$). Post-hoc comparisons showed that IC (6.2s) was significantly faster than both, FST and AT (13.9s and 8.4s). AT was also faster than FST. However, IC was only faster than AT for the read and interact tasks. For the count task, there is no significant difference between IC and AT, but both techniques were performing better than FST. Figure 10 illustrates the completion time results.

Participants generally committed few errors with 97% of the questions being answered correctly. The highest error rates were collected for FST in the count and read tasks (10.0% and 6.7%, respectively).

Participants were asked to rank the three techniques on a seven-point Likert scale. A Friedman non-parametric test revealed a significant difference between user preferences ($\chi^2(2) = 23.414, p < .001$). Post-hoc comparisons using

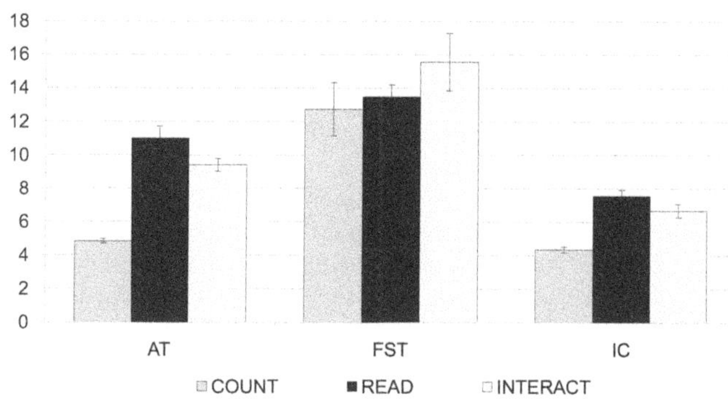

Figure 10. Completion times (seconds) for the three conditions (AT, FST, and IC).

Wilcoxon Signed Rank tests with Bonferroni adjustments showed that IC (6.33) was rated significantly higher than AT (4.73), and that both techniques were evaluated higher than FST (2.47). In the interview, participants mentioned the readability of small text and the ability to interact with obscured user interface elements as main reasons to rank IC higher than FST and AT. FST was primarily disliked for the pie menu to access occluded windows, which was described as hard to use, because only the windows located underneath the pointer were shown. Due to the initial cascaded window layout, only the top-most object window was fully visible (*c.f.*, Figure 9b). Therefore, several users commented that they did not know which windows were located beneath the mouse pointer and, as a consequence, which windows were included in the menu. One user summarized interaction with FST as: *"Transparency and not being able to interact [with occluded content] is very exhausting"*.

We also asked the participants which technique they preferred for the three tasks. For the interact task and read task, IC was chosen by the majority (15 and 12 participants out of 15, respectively). In the interview, most participants stated that IC was most appropriate for the read task as the text in obscured windows was readable, in contrast to the small menus of AT or FST. For the interact task, participants mentioned the ability to directly interact with occluded content without explicitly selecting the corresponding window as exceptionally useful. For the count task, AT was the most preferred technique (selected by 8). Participants commented that the menu of AT provided a good overview, so they could immediately see which images were available.

The results partially support our hypotheses: IC indeed provides an advantage for quickly looking at content in occluded windows. However, compared to AT, the performance advantage is only significant for accessing fine-grained information (as in the read task). The benefit of IC for simple interaction in occluded windows was confirmed by the results of the interact task.

DISCUSSION AND FUTURE WORK

The results of our experiment indicate that importance-driven compositing supports users in skimming through information in occluded application windows. Users described the access to occluded information as "more fluid" compared to sequential window switching menus, as only one activity was necessary to extract information from an occluded window. Another distinguishing aspect is the ability to directly interact with content of occluded windows without explicitly selecting the window in a separated user interface. Participants commented that this feature created a sense of "direct" interaction on the occluded content.

We consider the encouraging results of our exploratory user study as starting point for more empirical evaluations on importance-driven compositing. We will address potential limiting factors of our system which have not been captured by our experiment, such as the effect of automatic window re-arrangements on spatial memory or the effect of a dense information display on focused attention. To assess the suitability of visual saliency as primary measure of importance, we still need to thoroughly investigate whether traditional bottom-up saliency features are sufficient to describe the importance of window content – from user interface elements to various content like text, images, videos, or complex visualizations. Longitudinal studies will help to assess the benefits and limitations of our proposed window management functions in more realistic settings.

With importance-driven compositing, the desktop is not just a collection of (window) rectangles but rather a rich information map. We showed that we can leverage this importance measure for new interaction techniques on window manager level, which would otherwise require access to the application's content. It can also be employed as unified interface to implement previously suggested window management techniques, such as *free-space transparency* [16], *multiblending* [2], or *clipping lists* [20], as fully functional window manager extensions. Image-based representations of physical occlusions can serve as influence to the desktop's importance and thus generate *occlusion-aware* window layouts [27] automatically.

In the future, we will investigate how our importance model can be enriched by techniques for automatic extraction of individual user interface components [25], user-defined window constraints [1], or *fine-grained window management* [7], which takes into account the context of a user's action on a window. We also consider to add scaling as additional optimization factor to our layout routine. Shrinking and expanding regions of low importance can lead to a more flexible content arrangement, especially for large windows. Finally, our prototype has to be considered as proof-of-concept implementation. We demonstrated the feasibility of using state-of-the-art GPU languages in window managers. Yet, system performance can – and should – be further enhanced. Besides low-level optimizations for the GPU code, high-level observations of window changes could be used to trigger only partial importance map updates.

CONCLUSION

We presented importance-driven compositing window management which considers the importance of window content for an optimized spatial window layout in combination with see-through compositing. The aim of the technique is to optimize visibility and interactivity of important content contained in multiple overlapping application windows. Importance is defined by an image-based analysis of visually salient features within window textures. Based on importance-driven compositing, we presented new window management functions to minimize information overlap and to ease the access to occluded content. Results of a preliminary experiment indicate that users could extract fine-grained information and perform easy interaction tasks in occluded application windows faster and with greater subjective satisfaction compared to overlapping windows with sequential Alt+Tab switching. In comparison to free-space transparency [16], users appreciated the increased content visibility due to a more appropriate spatial window layout and the ability to directly interact with occluded content.

ACKNOWLEDGEMENTS

The authors would like to acknowledge Erick Mendez for providing the GLSL implementation for the saliency computation. This work was funded by the Austrian Research Promotion Agency (FFG) BRIDGE 822716.

REFERENCES

1. G. J. Badros, J. Nichols, and A. Borning. Scwm: An extensible constraint-enabled window manager. In *Proc. USENIX 2001*, pages 225–234. USENIX Association, 2001.
2. P. Baudisch and C. Gutwin. Multiblending: displaying overlapping windows simultaneously without the drawbacks of alpha blending. In *Proc. CHI 2004*, pages 367–374. ACM, 2004.
3. B. A. Bell and S. K. Feiner. Dynamic space management for user interfaces. In *Proc. UIST 2000*, pages 239–248. ACM, 2000.
4. A. Bezerianos, P. Dragicevic, and R. Balakrishnan. Mnemonic rendering: an image-based approach for exposing hidden changes in dynamic displays. In *Proc. UIST 2006*, pages 159–168. ACM, 2006.
5. E. A. Bier, M. C. Stone, K. Pier, W. Buxton, and T. D. DeRose. Toolglass and magic lenses: the see-through interface. In *Proc. SIGGRAPH 1993*, pages 73–80. ACM, 1993.
6. O. Chapuis and N. Roussel. Metisse is not a 3D Desktop! In *Proc. UIST 2005*, pages 13–22. ACM, 2005.
7. O. Chapuis and N. Roussel. Copy-and-paste between overlapping windows. In *Proc. CHI 2007*, pages 201–210. ACM, 2007.
8. N. Elmqvist and P. Tsigas. A taxonomy of 3d occlusion management for visualization. *IEEE TVCG*, 14:1095–1109, September 2008.
9. G. Faure, O. Chapuis, and N. Roussel. Power tools for copying and moving: useful stuff for your desktop. In *Proc. CHI 2009*, pages 1675–1678. ACM, 2009.
10. J. Grudin. Partitioning digital worlds: focal and peripheral awareness in multiple monitor use. In *Proc. CHI 2001*, pages 458–465. ACM, 2001.
11. C. Gutwin, J. Dyck, and C. Fedak. The effects of dynamic transparency on targeting performance. In *Proc. GI 2003*, pages 105–112, 2003.
12. B. L. Harrison, H. Ishii, K. J. Vicente, and W. Buxton. Transparent layered user interfaces: an evaluation of a display design to enhance focused and divided attention. In *Proc. CHI 1995*, pages 317–324, 1995.
13. D. R. Hutchings, G. Smith, B. Meyers, M. Czerwinski, and G. Robertson. Display space usage and window management operation comparisons between single monitor and multiple monitor users. In *Proc. AVI 2004*, pages 32–39. ACM, 2004.
14. D. R. Hutchings and J. Stasko. Revisiting display space management: understanding current practice to inform next-generation design. In *Proc. GI 2004*, pages 127–134, 2004.
15. D. R. Hutchings and J. Stasko. Shrinking window operations for expanding display space. In *Proc. AVI 2004*, pages 350–353. ACM, 2004.
16. E. W. Ishak and S. K. Feiner. Interacting with hidden content using content-aware free-space transparency. In *Proc. UIST 2004*, pages 189–192. ACM, 2004.
17. L. Itti, C. Koch, and E. Niebur. A model of saliency-based visual attention for rapid scene analysis. *PAMI*, 20(11):1254–1259, 1998.
18. E. Kandogan and B. Shneiderman. Elastic windows: evaluation of multi-window operations. In *Proc. CHI 1997*, pages 250–257. ACM, 1997.
19. A. Leykin and M. Tuceryan. Automatic determination of text readability over textured backgrounds for augmented reality systems. In *Proc. ISMAR 2004*, pages 224–230. IEEE Computer Society, 2004.
20. T. Matthews, M. Czerwinski, G. Robertson, and D. Tan. Clipping lists and change borders: improving multitasking efficiency with peripheral information design. In *Proc. CHI 2006*, pages 989–998. ACM, 2006.
21. E. Mendez, S. K. Feiner, and D. Schmalstieg. Focus and context in mixed reality by modulating first order salient features. In *Smart Graphics 2010*. Springer, 2010.
22. G. Robertson, E. Horvitz, M. Czerwinski, P. Baudisch, D. R. Hutchings, B. Meyers, D. Robbins, and G. Smith. Scalable fabric: flexible task management. In *Proc. AVI 2004*, pages 85–89. ACM, 2004.
23. G. Robertson, M. van Dantzich, D. Robbins, M. Czerwinski, K. Hinckley, K. Risden, D. Thiel, and V. Gorokhovsky. The Task Gallery: A 3D Window Manager. In *Proc. CHI 2000*, pages 494–501, 2000.
24. E. Rosten, G. Reitmayr, and T. Drummond. Real-time video annotations for augmented reality. In *Proc. ISVC 2005*, pages 294–302. Springer, 2005.
25. W. Stürzlinger, O. Chapuis, D. Phillips, and N. Roussel. User Interface Façades: Towards Fully Adaptable User Interfaces. In *Proc. UIST 2006*, pages 309–318. ACM, 2006.
26. I. Viola, A. Kanitsar, and M. E. Groller. Importance-driven volume rendering. In *Proc. VIS 2004*, pages 139–146. IEEE Computer Society, 2004.
27. D. Vogel and R. Balakrishnan. Occlusion-aware interfaces. In *Proc. CHI 2010*, pages 263–272. ACM, 2010.

Content and Hierarchy in Pixel-Based Methods for Reverse Engineering Interface Structure

Morgan Dixon, Daniel Leventhal, and James Fogarty
Computer Science & Engineering
DUB Group, University of Washington
{mdixon, dlev, jfogarty}@cs.washington.edu

ABSTRACT
The rigidity and fragmentation of GUI toolkits are fundamentally limiting the progress and impact of interaction research. Pixel-based methods offer unique potential for addressing these challenges independent of the implementation of any particular interface or toolkit. This work builds upon Prefab, which enables the modification of existing interfaces. We present new methods for hierarchical models of complex widgets, real-time interpretation of interface content, and real-time interpretation of content and hierarchy throughout an entire interface. We validate our new methods through implementations of four applications: stencil-based tutorials, ephemeral adaptation, interface translation, and end-user interface customization. We demonstrate these enhancements in complex existing applications created from different user interface toolkits running on different operating systems.

Author Keywords
Prefab, pixel-based reverse engineering, content, hierarchy.

ACM Classification Keywords
H5.2. Information interfaces and presentation: User Interfaces.

General Terms
Human Factors

INTRODUCTION AND MOTIVATION
Nearly every modern graphical user interface (GUI) is implemented using some form of GUI toolkit. Toolkits provide libraries of widgets and associated frameworks that reduce the time, effort, and amount of code needed to implement an interface. Although these toolkits have enabled many successes of the past forty years of human-computer interaction research and practice [19], the current state of toolkits has become stifling [8, 12, 21].

Specifically, researchers and practitioners are limited by the *rigidity* and *fragmentation* of existing toolkits. Rigidity makes it difficult or impossible for an application developer to modify a toolkit's core behaviors. Similarly, application rigidity generally precludes modification and customization of existing interfaces (except in limited ways envisioned and supported by an application's original developer).

Fragmentation results from the fact that people generally use many different applications built with a variety of toolkits. Each is implemented differently, so it is difficult to consistently add new functionality. Researchers are often limited to demonstrating new ideas in small testbeds, and practitioners often find it difficult to adopt and deploy ideas from the literature. These challenges limit the progress and impact of interaction research [8, 12, 21].

Because all GUIs ultimately consist of *pixels*, researchers have proposed methods for enhancing existing interfaces based only upon pixel-level interpretation. Pixel methods were initially proposed to support research in interface agents and programming by example [23, 25, 26, 32, 33]. More recent research examines broader opportunities for pixel-based methods: ScreenCrayons supports annotation of documents and visual information in any application [22], Sikuli applies computer vision to interface scripting and testing [3, 31], Hurst *et al.* use pixel-based methods to improve the accessibility API's target detection [15], and Prefab enables real-time modification of existing interfaces based on pixel-level interpretation [4].

The capabilities of these and other pixel-based systems are inherently defined and limited by a system's ability to meaningfully interpret raw interface pixels. This paper advances state-of-the-art systems by presenting the first pixel-based methods for real-time interpretation of interface content and hierarchy. Specifically, we build upon Prefab's pixel-based models of widget layout and appearance [4]. We first introduce the use of hierarchy to characterize complex widgets. We then introduce content regions and show how they enable efficient recovery of widget content. Finally, we show how these insights can be combined to recover a hierarchical interpretation of an entire interface. We validate our novel methods in a set of applications that demonstrate new capabilities enabled by interpretation of content and hierarchy, and we discuss future research opportunities suggested by this work.

Figure 1 illustrates several applications enabled by our new pixel-based methods. A pixel-based implementation of Kelleher and Pausch's *Stencils-based tutorials* [16] uses interface hierarchy to robustly reference specific widgets (i.e., differentiating among identical widgets by their position in the hierarchy). Our implementation of Findlater *et al.*'s *Ephemeral Adaptation* [5] is independent of interface implementation and leverages our models of content regions to create the necessary gradual onset animations. A

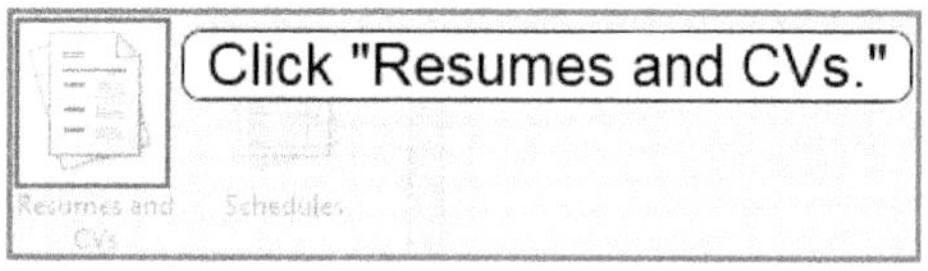

Kelleher and Pausch present the use of stencils to provide tutorials directly within the context of an interface [16]. This is a screenshot of our pixel-based implementation of a tutorial for downloading résumé templates in Microsoft Office 2010.

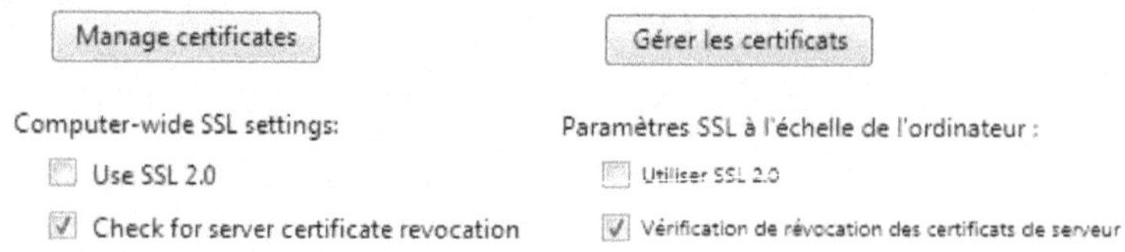

We present a GUI translator that works solely from an interface's pixels. Our translator identifies, interprets, and translates textual content while maintaining the same look and feel as the original application. Here is a portion of a Google Chrome Options dialog running in Microsoft Windows 7, translated from English into French.

Findlater *et al.*'s Ephemeral Adaptation improves targeting performance by reducing visual search while maintaining spatial consistency [5]. Likely targets appear as normal, but unlikely targets are initially missing and slowly fade in. This is a screenshot from our implementation of the technique in the context of a Skype settings dialog box running on Mac OS X.

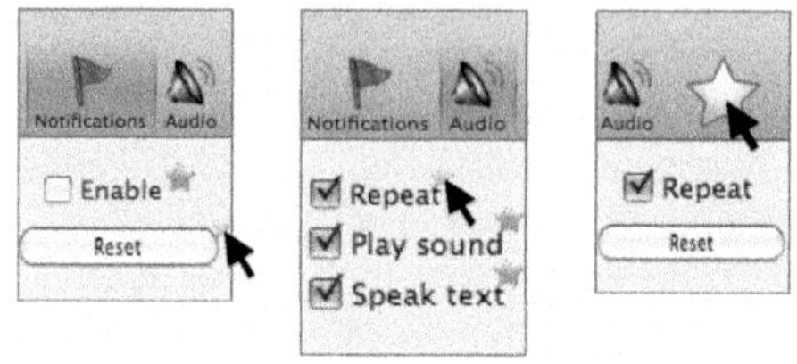

Our methods enable end-user customization of everyday interfaces. We implemented a technique that allows end-users to aggregate commonly used widgets of a tab control into a "favorites" tab. This is shown here in the context of the Skype settings dialog. Clicking on stars (left) adds the corresponding widgets to the "favorites" tab (right).

Figure 1: We introduce new pixel-based methods to reverse engineer interface content and hierarchy in real time. These methods enable a new range of advanced behaviors that are agnostic of an application's underlying implementation. All of these enhancements are implemented in the Prefab system and are discussed in greater detail later in this paper and in our associated video.

translantion enhancement highlights our real-time identification of interface content by extracting text, translating it, and re-painting it in the interface's original look and feel. Finally, adding *customization* to an existing interface illustrates support for managing occlusion and rendering new content using our pixel-based models.

The contributions of this work to pixel-based methods are:

- Methods for hierarchical models of complex widgets. These improve model implementation, example-based prototype creation, and runtime widget detection.
- Methods for modeling widget content regions. These enable efficient runtime recovery and interpretation of widget content.
- Methods for example-based parameterization of widget content regions. This is challenging because examples include content that should not be part of a prototype.
- Methods for recovering the content and hierarchy of an entire interface. This enables DOM-like interpretations of interfaces independent of their implementation.
- Validation of our methods in a set of novel pixel-based applications. These demonstrate our core methods and also illustrate opportunities to leverage our methods in addressing other challenges, such as robustly referencing widgets, re-rendering interfaces from pixel-based models, and managing interface occlusion.

RELATED WORK

This paper's pixel-based interpretation of interface content and hierarchy is implemented within the Prefab system [4]. To provide a context for our current contributions, we first discuss several relevant aspects of prior research and then review key components of the Prefab system.

Interpreting and Customizing Existing Interfaces

Our work is informed by GUI toolkit research [19]. For example, Hudson and Smith propose toolkit support for separating interface style from content, drawing an analogy to painting the same text with different fonts [13]. Hudson and Tanaka develop toolkit methods for painting stylized widgets, including an eight-part border defined by fixed corners and variable edges [14]. Our reverse engineering strategy turns such methods for painting interfaces on their heads: an eight-part model can be used to characterize many widget borders regardless of whether they were painted using Hudson and Tanaka's method. This paper is based on similar insights regarding tree-based interface layout and common approaches to painting variable content within widgets. We thus leverage knowledge of toolkit methods but remain independent of any particular toolkit.

Extensive research has examined interface customization. Most is limited to the web, where the Document Object Model (DOM) provides a structured representation of an interface. ChickenFoot [2] and CoScripter [18] are classic examples, and systems like Highlight extend these ideas to task-centric re-authoring for mobile devices [20]. Systems like Clip, Connect, Clone [6], d.mix [10], and Vegemite [17] demonstrate promising end-user mash-up methods.

For non-web interfaces, structure analogous to the DOM is provided the accessibility API. Stuerzlinger *et al.'s* research on User Interface Facades uses the accessibility API to enable runtime interface modification [27]. Compared to pixel-based methods, accessibility APIs are advantageous because they can access information that is not visible, such as items contained in a closed drop-down menu. Direct access to an interface's underlying data also removes the possibility for recognition errors. On the other hand, accessibility APIs require additional implementation effort to correctly expose hooks into an interface's underlying state. Toolkits generally attempt to provide default implementations, but many widgets are missing from the accessibility API because of application failures to implement necessary hooks. Hurst *et al.* found roughly 25% of widgets are completely missing from the accessibility API's view on many common applications [15]. The severity of this problem is magnified by the fact that it can be corrected only by an application's original developer (or somebody else with the application source). Pixel methods have the critical advantage that they do not require cooperation from the original application. The application exposes its pixels as normal, and anybody can then use those pixels as a basis for additional functionality. For example, Hurst *et al.* show a hybrid technique that uses pixel-based methods to augment the accessibility API to improve target boundary detection [15]. Our current work focuses on pixel-based methods, presenting advances toward a DOM-like representation obtained entirely from pixels without cooperation of an underlying application. Deeper exploration of additional hybrid techniques is an important opportunity for future work.

The most relevant prior work is therefore that examining pixel-based interface interpretation. Classic work by Zettlemoyer *et al.* examined widget identification in IBOTS and VisMap [32, 33] for interface agents and programming by example [23, 25]. Their methods require code-based descriptions of individual widgets, and Zettlemoyer *et al.* report 40% of VisMap code is specific to particular Microsoft Windows widgets. Our methods use examples to describe widget appearance, making it possible to scale to address the fragmentation of current interfaces. Perhaps more importantly, continued development of Zettlemoyer *et al.*'s methods in Segman found their performance insufficient for real-time demands of interactive applications [26]. In an interactive context, Olsen *et al.*'s ScreenCrayons leverages the universality of pixels to associate ink annotations with images of interfaces, but does not interpret those images [22]. Tan *et al.*'s WinCuts allows subdivision of windows with a copy-paste metaphor, but does not attempt to interpret or modify content [29]. Yeh *et al.*'s Sikuli uses template matching and voting based on invariant local features to identify occurrences of a target in an image of an interface (requiring 200msec to find all occurrences of a single target) [3, 31]. None of these existing pixel-based methods are capable of real-time interpretation of content and hierarchy, and so none are capable of the demonstrations presented in this paper.

Prefab

Prefab modifies the apparent behavior of existing interfaces using pixel-based interpretation with input and output redirection. Figure 2 illustrates a basic mechanism, where (1) a *source* window bitmap is captured, (2) the source image is interpreted, (3) the modified interface is presented

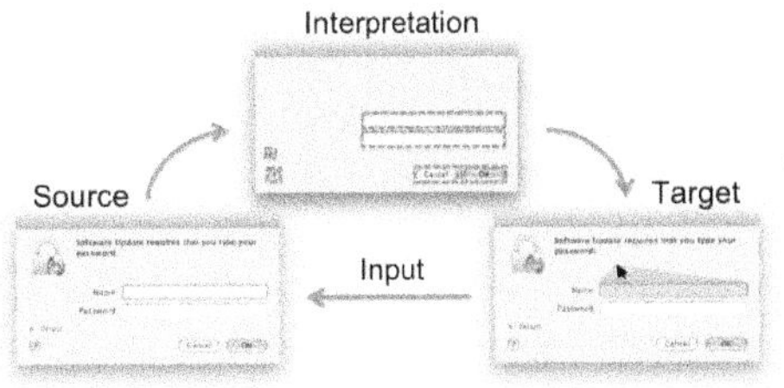

Figure 2: Prefab combines pixel-based interpretation with input and output redirection, allowing it to modify an interface independent of that interface's implementation. This requires real-time pixel-based interpretation.

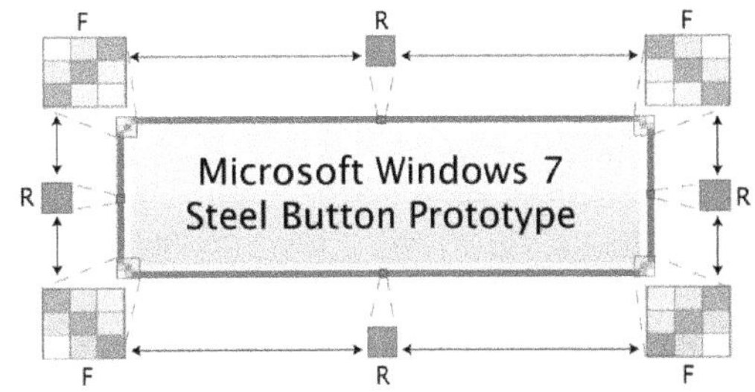

Figure 3: This Prefab prototype for Microsoft Windows 7 Steel buttons is an example of an eight-part model. Four features define the corners, each edge is defined by a region, and constraints require the parts form a rectangle. This prototype recognizes all Microsoft Windows 7 Steel buttons, independent of their interior content.

in a *target* window (with the source potentially hidden using virtual desktop methods), (4) input in the target is mapped back to the source, which then (5) generates new output that is captured and used to update the target. Prefab is the first system to combine pixel-based methods with input and output redirection, allowing it to modify an interface independent of that interface's implementation.

This requires interpreting images of an interface many times per second, which Prefab accomplishes using four major types of components: *models*, *prototypes*, *parts* (including *features* and *regions*), and *constraints*.

Models consist of abstract *parts* and concrete *constraints* on those *parts*. A typical *model* might include several *constraints* requiring that *parts* are adjacent. The *parts* are abstract, so a *model* does not describe any particular widget or set of widgets. Instead, a *model* describes a pattern for composing *parts* to create a widget.

Parts can be either *features* or *regions*. A *feature* stores an exact patch of pixels (exact colors in an exact arrangement). A *region* stores a procedural description of an area (e.g., painting a gradient or a repeating pattern). Because the same *parts* can be arranged in multiple ways, they alone do not describe any particular widget or set of widgets.

Prototypes parameterize a *model* with concrete *parts*, thus characterizing both the arrangement and the appearance of those *parts*. A *prototype* therefore describes a particular widget or set of widgets (e.g., the Mozilla Firefox Home toolbar button, all Microsoft Windows 7 Steel buttons).

Figure 3 presents an example eight-part *prototype* that parameterizes an abstract *model* of an eight-part border with *parts* corresponding to a Microsoft Windows 7 Steel button. It recognizes all Microsoft Windows 7 Steel buttons, independent of their interior content. Prototypes that assign different pixels to its parts can recognize different styles of buttons or different widgets that paint a border. Prefab is implemented as a library of *prototypes* with methods for applying those *prototypes* to identify widgets. Specifically, Prefab locates all *features* in a pass over an image and then tests the *regions* and *constraints* of potential *prototypes*.

Creating a *prototype* by manually specifying the *parts* of a *model* is possible, but tedious and error-prone. Prefab helps by fitting *prototypes* from examples. We have found that the most appropriate *prototype* for a widget is typically the one which requires the *fewest pixels* to explain its appearance. The intuition behind this approach is similar to the minimum description length principle, a formalization of Occam's Razor in machine learning [24]. Prefab uses a branch-and-bound search to determine what assignment of parts to a model best explains an example. For example, the prototype in Figure 3 is learned from a single example of a Microsoft Windows 7 Steel button. This ability to quickly create new prototypes is important to Prefab's potential for scaling to address GUI toolkit fragmentation.

INTERPRETING CONTENT AND HIERARCHY

This section addresses key challenges facing Prefab and other pixel-based systems. We first address the complexity of widgets with multiple components by introducing *hierarchical models.* We then address the difficulty of modeling unpredictable content by leveraging knowledge of containment in *content regions*. Finally, we combine and extend these ideas to enable efficient interpretation of the *content and hierarchy of an entire interface*.

Hierarchical Models

The eight-part model in Figure 3 was the most complex model explored in Prefab's initial development. Although Prefab's original methods can characterize many widgets, significant challenges arise when considering more complex models needed to represent widgets consisting of multiple components. Figure 4 illustrates this by comparing the modeling of a *slider* with that of a *scrollbar*.

Figure 4a shows a five-part model of a slider, consisting of a feature for the thumb, features for the trough endpoints, and regions for the variable-length trough. This model effectively characterizes many sliders. Although a scrollbar might seem to have a similar layout, Figure 4b shows that scrollbars vary the size of their thumb to illustrate what portion of the scrollable area is currently within view. A single feature is therefore insufficient for characterizing the scrollbar thumb, so we replace the feature with eight parts describing a thumb of varying size. If we want our model to represent the buttons at either end of the scrollbar, we also need to replace the end features with eight parts. Figure 4c shows the resulting model, which characterizes

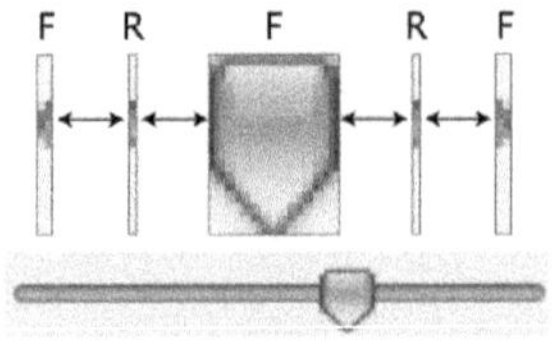

4a: Prefab's original methods support a five-part model of sliders.

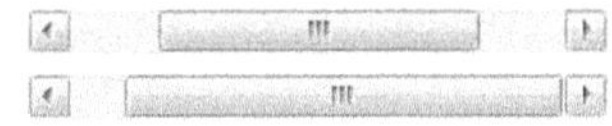

4b: Scrollbars vary their thumb size, so cannot be modeled with five parts.

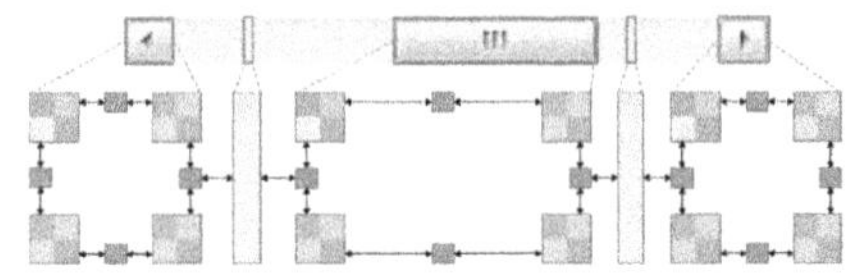

4c: This model accounts for the presence of scroll buttons and the varying size of the scroll thumb, but is too complex for practical use.

4d: Other types of scrollbars arrange buttons differently, which would require still greater complexity in the above model.

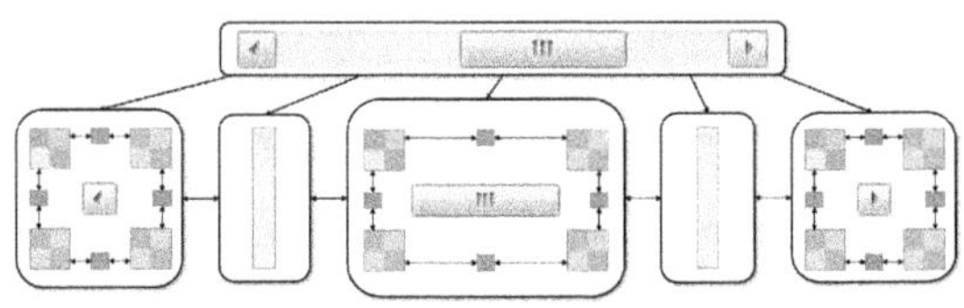

4e: Hierarchical models simplify the implementation, example-based parameterization, and recognition of complex widgets.

Figure 4: This paper introduces hierarchical models of widget layout, improving Prefab's support for complex widgets defined by hierarchies of simpler components.

the components of these scrollbars but has become too complex for practical use. It is difficult to correctly implement, and its many parameters create a high branching factor that makes it computationally expensive to fit prototypes from examples. The effort to implement and optimize complex models can be justified when they characterize a wide variety of widgets, but this model still does not characterize some common scrollbars. For example, Figure 4d shows a scrollbar from Mac OS X's Cocoa toolkit painted with both scroll buttons together.

The solution to these modeling challenges comes from the insight that complex widgets are typically defined by a hierarchy of simpler widgets. We introduce hierarchical models of widget layout, as illustrated with a scrollbar model in Figure 4e. This extends Prefab's original notion of delegating regions to procedural code (e.g., a gradient or a repeating pattern) by allowing delegation to another model. Portions of a hierarchy can be re-used in implementing multiple models. A model can account for portions of the hierarchy appearing in different arrangements or being optionally absent. The hierarchy can also be used when fitting prototypes from examples, with annotations of simpler components (e.g., the scrollbar thumb) constraining a search of the overall hierarchy. At runtime, hierarchical prototypes are identified by locating simpler components and then testing constraints and regions in the hierarchy.

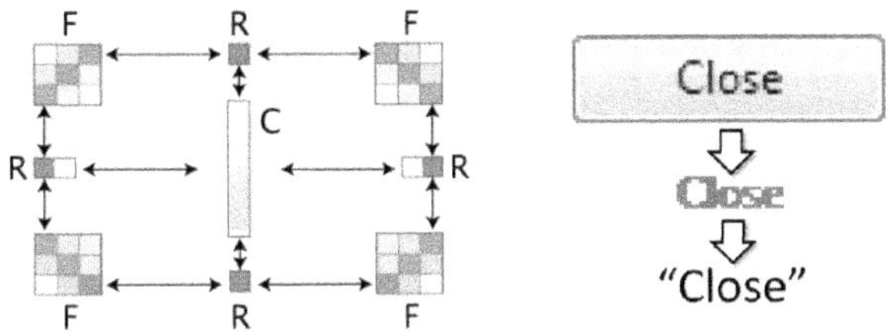

Figure 5: This prototype for Microsoft Windows 7 Steel buttons is an example of a nine-part model. Our nine-part model is identical to the eight-part model in Figure 3 except for the addition of an interior content region. This prototype's content region has been parameterized as a single repeating column. At runtime, content within a button is obtained by differencing the repeating column against the pixels inside the button's content area.

Content Regions

Prefab's pixel-based methods are built on the insight that the pixels of a widget are procedurally defined. This is critical to Prefab's real-time performance, as it allows exact feature matching as a basis for prototype detection. But some interface content varies dramatically and cannot easily be identified through exact matching. For example, modern toolkits often employ sub-pixel rendering and anti-aliasing techniques in text rendering. This improves readability, but also modifies text's pixel-level appearance in unpredictable ways. The same characters can be rendered as many different combinations of pixels. Prefab's original methods therefore could not address the recovery of widget content (e.g., Figure 3's prototype can identify Microsoft Windows 7 Steel buttons, but cannot recover their label).

We address this challenge by building upon several insights. First, toolkits construct interfaces as trees. Second, content appears at the leaves of a tree (i.e., labels and icons do not contain other widgets). Every piece of content is therefore contained within a parent. Third, the parents of these leaf nodes paint simple backgrounds (often a single color, sometimes a simple gradient). This is critical to interface usability, as a person must be able to easily see the content painted over that background. Instead of directly modeling unpredictable content, we introduce *content regions* that model the much simpler background of a parent and efficiently identify content using runtime differencing.

Figure 5 illustrates a nine-part model of a border with an interior content region (i.e., it is identical to the eight-part model from Figure 3 except for the addition of the interior content region). The model's constraints require that the content region describe every pixel not accounted for by the corner features or the edge regions. In this case, a prototype of the Microsoft Windows 7 Steel Button parameterizes the content region with a single repeating column. At runtime, content is obtained by differencing the repeating column against pixels inside the button's content area. Figure 5 illustrates this differencing with red pixels in an example button. A character recognition algorithm is then applied to recover the text "Close". Because such character

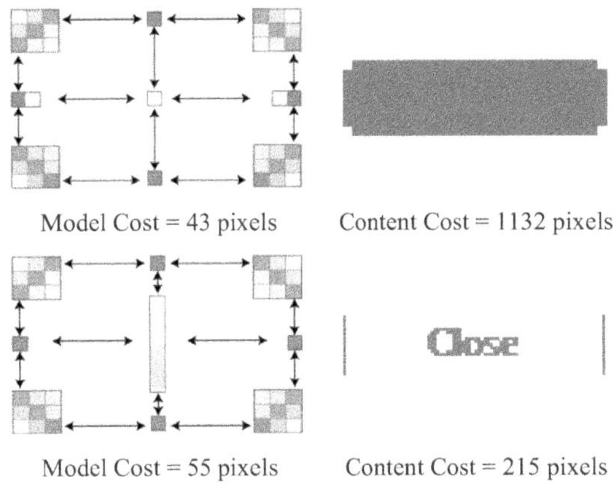

Figure 6: These are both valid nine-part prototypes for a single example of a Microsoft Windows Vista Steel button. They incur total costs of 1175 and 270 pixels. Prefab thus prefers the nine-part prototype shown in Figure 5, which costs only 246 pixels and is also more general. Note that Figure 5's prototype also identifies the correct content.

recognition is relatively expensive, it is important to note that our content region method identifies a small portion of an interface to which more expensive methods are applied. Its computation can also be cached, as there is no need to re-execute an interpretation of identical content pixels.

Parameterizing Content Regions by Example

Recall that Prefab supports the use of *examples* to create prototypes. Parts are assigned by a search minimizing the number of pixels needed to describe those examples in a manner consistent with the model. Like other regions, content regions are modeled as procedural methods for pixel generation (e.g., painting a single color, repeating a pattern, painting a gradient). Prefab's original methods cannot be applied to content regions because each example contains unpredictable content. A simple part cannot characterize this content, and so the search fails to fit a good prototype that generalizes from the example.

We address this problem by defining the cost of a potential prototype as the sum of two components: *model cost* and *content cost*. As before, the model cost is the number of pixels used to define the parts of a prototype. The content cost is the number of pixels in an example that do not match the prototype specified by a content region. The intuition behind this approach is that minimizing the sum requires the search to both *describe* the background and *identify* the foreground. Because we lack a meaningful method for generating that unpredictable foreground, we pay full cost for the pixels it occupies. Note that this is a generalization of Prefab's original method, as content cost is always zero in models without content regions.

As an example, Figure 5's prototype sets the width and height of each corner feature to three, top and bottom edge depths to one, and left and right edge depths to two. The content region is a repeating column of pixels. With these settings (selected by the branch-and-bound search), the prototype has a model cost of 57 (9 for each corner, 6 for the edges, and 15 for the content region). The text results in a content cost of 189 (the red pixels shown on the right side of Figure 5), yielding a total cost of 246 pixels.

In contrast, Figure 6 shows two other prototypes the search might consider for the same example. The first has the same corners and edges but attempts to fit a single color to the background of the content region. This improves its model cost to 43, but the poor match results in a content cost of 1142 and a total cost of 1175 pixels. The second example has the correct content region with the corner and edge configuration from Figure 3 (which was fit to an eight-part model that does not consider content). Specifically, notice its left and right edges are 1 pixel wide. This results in a model cost of 55 (9 for each corner, 4 for the edges, and 15 for the content region), but the content cost is increased to 215 by two 13-pixel columns at either end of the content region. Its total cost is 270 pixels. These and other prototypes are rejected, with the search ultimately selecting the configuration from Figure 5 as the best fit.

Note that the content region in Figure 5 has actually resulted in a better characterization of the prototype's other parts. Without a content region, there is no reason for Prefab to determine that the left and right edges of this example are two pixels wide (and so it finds the prototype form Figure 3). The inclusion of a content region has in this case lead Prefab to produce a prototype that describes *every pixel* in the example. Our validating applications present implications of this more complete interpretation.

Interpreting Content and Hierarchy in an Entire Interface

The intuition behind our methods for individual widgets can be extended to support pixel-based interpretation of content and hierarchy in an entire interface. Instead of considering content only in terms of text within a button, the necessary insight is that every widget is content relative to its parent. Our challenge is to recover the content and hierarchy of the entire interface while retaining Prefab's performance. We implement this in four steps, as illustrated in Figure 7.

We first apply Prefab's library of prototypes to locate widgets. This uses feature-based detection to identify a set of widget occurrences. We then organize the detected occurrences into a tree. The root is the image itself (typically a top-level window in Prefab's current input and output framework). The tree is constructed using constraints provided by each occurrence's model. These typically enforce spatial containment within a content region of the occurrence. The primary exception is for widgets that float above an interface (e.g., tooltips, popup menus, drop-down boxes). Tagging prototypes of these widgets allows our tree construction algorithm to link them directly to the root.

This organizes occurrences that were detected using our feature-based methods, but we still need to apply our differencing method to locate unpredictable content from content regions. It is important this differencing respect the

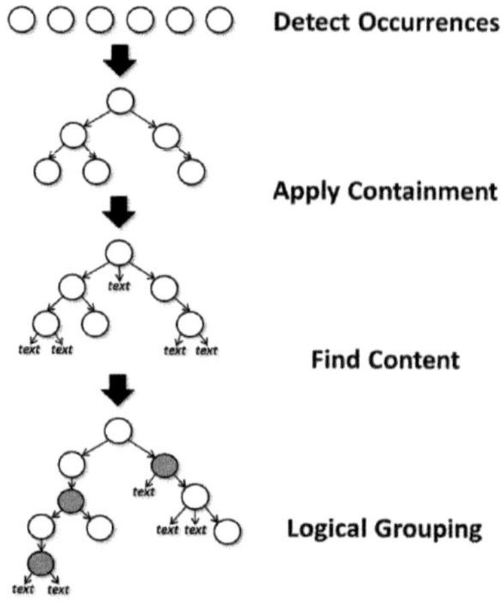

Figure 7: We interpret interface content and hierarchy by detecting widget occurrences, applying containment to construct a tree, finding content within widgets, and logically grouping nodes within the tree.

existing hierarchy (i.e., nested widgets must consider the proper background and must not generate spurious content in areas owned by children). Our current implementation uses a post-order traversal. We generate a composite background image when traversing down the tree, then test and mark pixels when traversing back up the tree. Widgets only test pixels within their content regions that were not marked by children. Identified content is interpreted and added as a child of the widget that detected it.

The resulting tree includes all detected widgets arranged by their containment. Additional organization can be added by considering that siblings in this *visual* tree may suggest an additional component in a *logical* tree. For example, several pieces of text might be grouped together and then related to an adjacent checkbox. Prior research has developed methods for semantic grouping of widgets [7]. Given our focus on pixel-based detection of the visual tree, we perform logical grouping using a set of heuristics.

VALIDATION THROUGH APPLICATIONS

This paper presents new methods for real-time pixel-based interpretation of widget content and hierarchy. Because this is a new capability, there is no reasonable comparison to other approaches for obtaining the same effect. We instead validate and provide insight into our work through a set of demonstrations. We select these with the goal of illustrating a range of complexity in applying our methods.

All of our applications are implemented in Microsoft's C# running on Microsoft Windows 7 and using redirection provided by Prefab. We use remote desktop software to demonstrate enhancements running on Mac OS X interfaces. Prefab thus continues to run on the Microsoft Windows 7 machine, adding its enhancements based entirely on the pixels delivered through the remote desktop connection. We apply enhancements to a variety of well-known applications to highlight that our methods are independent of the underlying implementation.

Stencils-Based Tutorials

Kelleher and Pausch's *Stencils-based tutorials* provide help directly within applications using translucent stencils with holes to direct a person's attention to the correct interface component [16]. Such an enhancement is difficult to broadly deploy because of the rigidity and fragmentation of existing applications and toolkits. It is beyond the capabilities of previous pixel-based systems because authoring such a tutorial requires support for referencing *specific* interface elements. For example, there may be several buttons of identical appearance within an interface, but only one of them is the appropriate next action.

Figure 1 and our associated video show our Prefab implementation of Stencils-based tutorials. The tutorial instructs a person on how to download résumé design templates in Microsoft Word 2010. Our video highlights the real-time responsiveness enabled by our new methods.

Stencils-based tutorials are a straightforward application of widget hierarchy. Knowledge of the full hierarchy allows us to reference widgets using simple path descriptors on the tree. We implemented this demonstration by building prototypes to identify the majority of widgets in Microsoft Office 2010. For example, we used nine-part models to characterize many of the containers and buttons. We also used one-part models to identify less structured content (e.g., the icons used to represent different types of templates). These one-part models are typically easy to construct (i.e., a model of the background of their parent makes it trivial to segment the one-part example). We converted Prefab's hierarchical interpretations into an XML format, allowing the use of XPath descriptors to reference widgets within the hierarchy. Tutorials are thus authored as a list of XPath descriptors paired with textual instructions for each step. Additional capabilities could be developed, and we have not yet explored the best approach to an authoring tool, but this demonstration highlights our use of the pixel-based hierarchy to reference specific widgets.

Ephemeral Adaptation

Findlater *et al.* developed Ephemeral Adaptation, an adaptive technique that improves performance by reducing visual search time and maintaining spatial consistency [5]. Ephemeral Adaptation helps draw visual attention to likely targets in an interface. Specifically, likely targets appear as normal within an interface, but unlikely targets are initially missing and then slowly fade in. Despite the promise of this technique, it has been difficult to evaluate in realistic use or to widely deploy in everyday software. A pixel-based implementation is beyond prior systems for two reasons. As before, it requires the ability to reference specific widgets (e.g., to monitor how frequently they are clicked in order to model which are likely targets). In addition, this application requires the ability to remove unlikely targets from the interface and then render their gradual onset.

Figure 8 and our associated video show our implementation of Ephemeral Adaptation using Prefab within a Skype settings dialog box running in Mac OS X. Upon moving between tabs, likely targets in each tab are initially visible. Unlikely targets then fade in over time. This enhancement uses a nine-part prototype of the tab pane and various prototypes for each of the interior widgets. We use our XPath descriptors to tally the frequency of interaction with each widget and use a simple model of likely targets (the most commonly-used widgets in each tab).

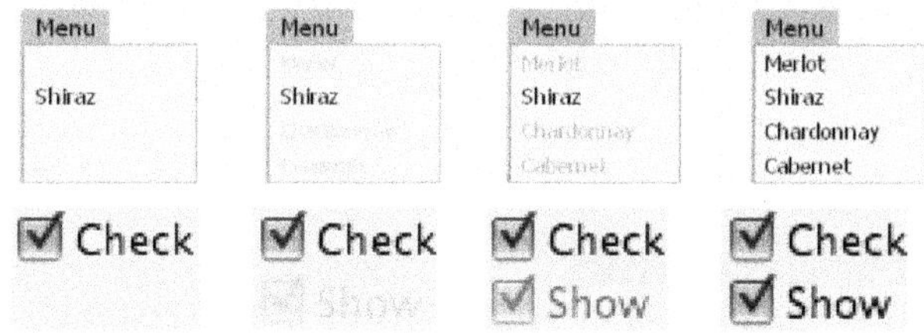

Figure 8: Findlater *et al.*'s Ephemeral Adaptation technique uses the gradual onset of unlikely targets to facilitate easier targetting of likely targets [5]. This image shows Findlater *et al.*'s original implementation of a menu testbed together with our pixel-based implementation within a Skype dialog running on Mac OS X.

We render the gradual onset animation using the content region from the tab's nine-part model. Specifically, we render tab background (i.e., the pixel-level appearance of its content region) as an overlay at the location of each unlikely widget. We then gradually fade this overlay from opaque to transparent. This creates the illusion that the widget is gradually fading into view. Note this technique requires identifying all of the content throughout the interface in order to appropriately animate its onset, a capability not supported by prior pixel-based methods.

Language Translation

In addition to pixel-based *identification* of interface content, our methods can help enable real-time *interpretation* of interface content. To demonstrate this, we implemented a pixel-based enhancement that automatically translates the language of an interface and then presents the translated content in the same look and feel as the original interface. Because of the rigidity and fragmentation of current tools, interfaces usually must be translated by their original developer (or somebody else with the application source). Our methods allow anybody to translate an interface and could thus form a basis for community-driven translation (similar to advances in social accessibility [28]). To the best of our knowledge, ours is the first method for real-time translation of interfaces independent of their underlying implementations. Although translation is not the same as complete localization, it is an important step.

Figure 1 and our associated video show our translation enhancement applied to a Google Chrome Options dialog running on Microsoft Windows 7. The left image illustrates a portion of the original dialog in English. The right image shows that same portion of the dialog with the text translated into French. Our associated video also includes a Spanish translation of the same dialog. We implemented

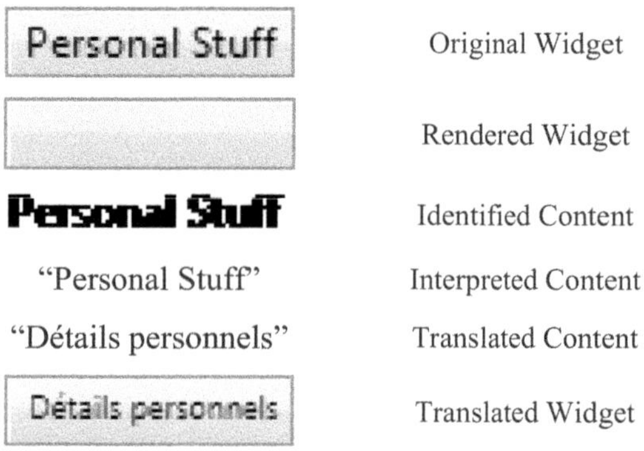

Figure 9: We use our knowledge of interface content and hierarchy to implement a translation enhancement that preserves the look and feel of the original application. A translated widget is rendered by compositing the translated text with its prototype's content region.

this by interpreting textual content identified by our methods, translating that text, and then rendering the new text in the original interface. Our associated video shows this enhancement running in real-time. This requires identification and interpretation of content occur quickly enough to handle the appearance and movement of content within a scroll pane.

There are several potential approaches to interpreting screen-rendered text [30]. Our current implementation uses an ad hoc template matching method, leaving integration of more advanced methods as an opportunity for future work. Importantly, our methods separate the identification of text from interpretation of that text. The interpretation of a region of pixels can thus be cached to eliminate potentially expensive re-interpretation of those same pixels (e.g., using a hash of the pixels). In our video, each piece of text is interpreted only the first time it appears. We then translate it using a machine translation service. As the text moves within the scroll pane, our content detection recovers the same pixels and retrieves the text from cache.

To maintain the application look and feel, we paint the translation into the original interface. This is implemented by using each widget's content region to render an overlay masking its content (i.e., its English text). The translated text is then rendered within the bounds of the original content region. For example, Figure 9 shows a button before its translated text is rendered. Because English text is typically shorter than translated text, we adjust the font size of the translated text to fit in the available region. Our next demonstration explores a more sophisticated modification of the interface to accommodate new content.

Interface Customization

Our pixel-based interpretation of interface hierarchy also provides a framework for modeling some common forms of *occlusion* in interfaces. Occlusion is at the very core of the desktop metaphor, as it allows interfaces to limit the complexity of presented interfaces via the illusion that additional portions of the interface continue to exist even

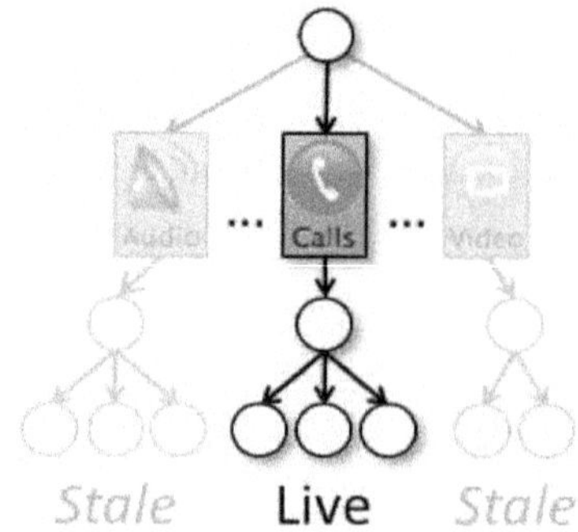

Figure 10: We use our knowledge of hierarchy to manage widget occlusion in a tab pane. We store the most recently observed image of each widget, annotating occluded widgets to indicate those images are currently stale.

when they are not visible. For example, tab controls use occlusion to limit attention to related subsets of complex interfaces. Existing pixel-based methods are strictly limited to interpreting visible portions of an interface. The need to observe an interface is inherent to pixel-based methods, but we can use our knowledge of interface hierarchy to help manage common forms of occlusion.

Figure 1 and our associated video present a demonstration of this in the context of interface customization. Instead of automatically adapting an interface according to widgets that are likely to be used, this example allows people to manually flag widgets as "favorites" for quick access. Figure 1 shows this applied to the same Skype dialog box from our Ephemeral Adaptation example. A small star is added to each widget in the interface. Clicking this star adds the widget to a "favorites" tab we added to the interface. Viewing that tab presents all starred widgets and allows interaction with each of them. As with all of our demonstrations, this is implemented using pixel-based interpretation with input and output redirection.

The management of occlusion is inherent to this example. We enhance the hierarchy to store the most recently observed version of each tab (using our XPath descriptors to reference each tab and its contents). We annotate these nodes in the hierarchy as *stale* to capture the fact they are occluded. Figure 10 depicts a simplified snapshot of the interpreted hierarchy with occluded nodes. If a "favorite" widget is currently occluded in the source window, it is painted using its stale version from the hierarchy. When a person moves to interact with a widget, synthetic input events are generated to bring that tab of the source window into view (i.e., to ensure that portion of the hierarchy is responsive to interaction via standard redirection mechanisms). Synthetic events could also be generated to regularly poll stale portions of the hierarchy, but this was not needed in our demonstration.

This example also demonstrates the use of our pixel-based methods to add new elements to the interface. Nine-part models of the window, the tab button container, and the tab pane are used to create a larger version of the window, insert the new "favorites" tab button, and to render the blank tab area into which "favorite" widgets are added. Figure 1 and our associated video show the added tab button and the extended window. We view this as an initial peek into opportunities to fundamentally transform the rigidity and fragmentation of existing interfaces.

DISCUSSION AND LIMITATIONS

This paper advances state-of-the-art pixel-based systems by presenting the first methods for real-time interpretation of interface content and hierarchy. We now briefly discuss some important aspects of our pixel-based interpretation and identify some opportunities for future work.

For the sake of clarity, this paper presents the simplest description of our pixel-based methods for interpreting interface content and hierarchy. A variety of optimizations could improve performance. For example, the entire interpretation process can be implemented using lightweight incremental evaluation to compute exactly the sub-tree of the hierarchy that could possibly have changed between successive frames [11]. Many stages in the process can allow a multi-core approach (e.g., siblings can detect content simultaneously). Given these and other potential optimizations, we generally do not expect performance to be problematic in most applications. Our implementation currently computes frame differences to efficiently detect features and uses parallelization when interpreting content. We currently re-compute the entire hierarchy whenever Prefab identifies new features. Our associated video shows multiple demonstrations that interpret content and hierarchy in real interfaces of existing applications with computations between frames typically under 100msec. We believe this is sufficient for the applications we explore.

The preparation of our demonstrations highlighted another advantage of our approach to interpreting interface content and hierarchy. If our methods are applied to an interface that contains widgets that are not already in Prefab's prototype library, the parents of those currently unknown widgets identify their pixels as content. We used this fact to quickly extract the examples used to create prototypes for our demonstrations, and we believe it could provide a basis for an improved prototype authoring tool.

Our translation demonstration currently uses an ad hoc approach to text interpretation (exact matching against a library of labeled character snippets). Off-the-shelf OCR technologies are generally ineffective because of the extreme low resolution of typical interface text. We previously noted the availability of recognition methods for screen-rendered text [30], but these are not optimized for Prefab's scenario. A deeper investigation of robust text interpretation methods is an opportunity for future work.

We have noted the existence of prior work examining logical grouping of interface elements [7]. It is unclear whether these methods are compatible with the real-time requirements of pixel-based interpretation. The tree-based organization of interfaces and our ability to interpret visual containment provides an important advantage: we can likely consider only logical groupings of siblings. Based on the hierarchies we have encountered in our work, there are typically a small number of siblings in any given node (i.e., most interface elements are intentionally designed to contain a small number of content items). Our current implementation uses simple heuristics to perform logical grouping. For example, checkboxes are matched to their corresponding content using a threshold on the proximity of the nearest text. Future work can explore more advanced approaches to creating logical groupings by matching elements of an interface. Errors in an automated process could be also corrected by storing annotations that record the need for a specialized grouping (e.g., using our XPath descriptors to override the default behavior).

This paper focuses on core methods for interpreting content and hierarchy together with demonstrations of their value in example applications. There is a significant opportunity for future work that more thoroughly characterizes these and other pixel-based methods. Such work might examine the variety of widgets encountered in applications in the field, how well pixel-based methods can characterize those widgets, how many types of models and parts are necessary, and which of those models and parts are most broadly effective. Our pixel-based methods are the first to rival the accessibility API in terms of completeness, so comparisons between our methods and the accessibility API may be appropriate. Such a comparison should preferably go beyond simple frequency of failure to also probe the nature of failure (e.g., its impact in applications, the difficulty of correcting a failure). As in Hurst *et al.* [15], there are likely significant opportunities for hybrid approaches that combine the strengths of the accessibility API with the strengths of pixel-based methods. The contributions of this paper are a necessary step toward future characterizations of pixel-based methods, and our current validations are appropriate for this ongoing work.

Our interface customization demonstration dynamically re-renders a dialog box at a different size to create room for the "favorites" tab. This is possible because the nine-part prototype that detects the dialog box describes all of the pixels needed to generate it. To the best of our knowledge, we are the first to demonstrate pixel-based methods to create new widgets matching an existing interface. But not all Prefab prototypes necessarily have this property. The ability to seamlessly add new widgets to the interfaces of existing applications would dramatically extend pixel-based methods, and further examination of pixel-based methods is an additional opportunity for future work.

Our customization demonstration illustrates one approach to managing occlusion (using the hierarchy to maintain a memory of occluded components). Tab controls are perhaps the simplest case and this method may not immediately generalize to other forms of occlusion. For example, popup menus create less predictable occlusions that can span multiple nodes in a hierarchy (because they float above the hierarchy). Occlusion within a scrollpane also presents different challenges. We have shown that interface content and hierarchy provide a useful framework for reasoning about occlusion, and future work could examine more advanced methods building upon these initial insights.

CONCLUSION

This paper advances pixel-based systems by contributing new methods for hierarchical models of complex widgets, new methods for real-time interpretation of interface content, and new methods for real-time interpretation of the content and hierarchy of an entire interface. We validated our pixel-based methods in implementations of four applications: Stencils-based tutorials, Ephemeral Adaptation, interface translation, and the addition of customization support to an existing interface. Working only from pixels, we demonstrated these enhancements in complex existing applications created in different user interface toolkits running on different operating systems.

ACKNOWLEDGEMENTS

We thank Dan Grossman, Rick LeFaivre, Scott Saponas, and Dan Weld for discussions related to this work. This work was supported in part by a gift from Intel, by the UW CoE Osberg Fellowship, by the UW CSE Microsoft Endowed Fellowship, and by a fellowship from the Seattle Chapter of the ARCS Foundation.

REFERENCES

[1] Baudisch, P., Tan, D.S., Collomb, M., Robbins, D., Hinckley, K., Agrawala, M., Zhao, S. and Ramos, G. Phosphor: Explaining Transitions in the User Interface using Afterglow Effects. *UIST 2006*. 169-178.

[2] Bolin, M., Webber, M., Rha, P., Wilson, T. and Miller, R.C. Automation and Customization of Rendered Web Pages. *UIST 2005*. 163-172.

[3] Chang, T.-H., Yeh, T. and Miller, R.C. GUI Testing User Computer Vision. *CHI 2010*. 1535-1544.

[4] Dixon, M. and Fogarty, J. Prefab: Implementing Advanced Behaviors Using Pixel-Based Reverse Engineering of Interface Structure. *CHI 2010*. 1525-1534.

[5] Findlater, L., Moffatt, K., McGrenere, J. and Dawson, J. Ephemeral Adaptation: The Use of Gradual Onset to Improve Menu Selection Performance. *CHI 2009*. 1655-1664.

[6] Fujima, J., Lunzer, A., Hornbæk, K. and Tanaka, Y. Clip, Connect, Clone: Combining Applications Elements to Build Custom Interfaces for Information Access. *UIST 2004*. 175-184.

[7] Gaeremynck, Y., Bergman, L.D. and Lau, T.A. MORE for Less: Model Recovery from Visual Interfaces for Multi-Device Application Design. *IUI 2003*. 69-76.

[8] Greenberg, S. and Buxton, B. Usability Evaluation Considered Harmful (Some of the Time). *CHI 2008*. 111-120.

[9] Grossman, T. and Balakrishnan, R. The Bubble Cursor: Enhancing Target Acquisition by Dynamic Resizing of the Cursor's Activation Area. *CHI 2005*. 281-290.

[10] Hartmann, B., Wu, L., Collins, K. and Klemmer, S.R. Programming by a Sample: Rapidly Creating Web Applications with d.Mix. *UIST 2007*. 241-250.

[11] Hudson, S.E. Incremental Attribute Evaluation: A Flexible Algorithm for Lazy Update. *TOPLAS*, **13**(3). 315-341.

[12] Hudson, S.E., Mankoff, J. and Smith, I. Extensible Input Handling in the subArctic Toolkit. *CHI 2005*. 381-390.

[13] Hudson, S.E. and Smith, I. Supporting Dynamic Downloadable Appearances in an Extensible User Interface Toolkit. *UIST 1997*. 159-168.

[14] Hudson, S.E. and Tanaka, K. Providing Visually Rich Resizable Images for User Interface Components. *UIST 2000*. 227-235.

[15] Hurst, A., Hudson, S.E. and Mankoff, J. Automatically Identifying Targets Users Interact with During Real World Tasks. *IUI 2010*. 11-20.

[16] Kelleher, C. and Pausch, R. Stencils-Based Tutorials: Design and Evaluation. *CHI 2005*. 541-550.

[17] Lin, J., Wong, J., Nichols, J., Cypher, A. and Lau, T.A. End-User Programming of Mashups with Vegemite. *IUI 2009*. 97-106.

[18] Little, G., Lau, T.A., Cypher, A., Lin, J., Haber, E.M. and Kandogan, E. Koala: Capture, Share, Automate, Personalize Business Processes on the Web. *CHI 2007*. 943-946.

[19] Myers, B.A., Hudson, S.E. and Pausch, R. Past, Present, and Future of User Interface Software Tools. *TOCHI*, **7**(1). 3-28.

[20] Nichols, J. and Lau, T.A. Mobilizing by Demonstration: Using Traces to Re-Author Existing Web Sites. *IUI 2008*. 149-158.

[21] Olsen, D.R. Evaluating User Interface Systems Research. *UIST 2007*. 251-258.

[22] Olsen, D.R., Taufer, T. and Fails, J.A. ScreenCrayons: Annotating Anything. *UIST 2004*. 165-174.

[23] Potter, R. (1993). *Triggers: Guiding Automaton with Pixel to Achieve Data Access*. A. Cypher, eds. MIT Press.

[24] Rissanen, J. Modeling by Shortest Data Description. *Automatica*, **14**(5). 465-471.

[25] St. Amant, R., Lieberman, H., Potter, R. and Zettlemoyer, L.S. Visual Generalization in Programming by Example. **43**(3). 107-114.

[26] St. Amant, R., Riedl, M.O., Ritter, F.E. and Reifers, A. Image Processing in Cognitive Models with SegMan. *HCII 2005*.

[27] Stuerzlinger, W., Chapuis, O., Phillips, D. and Roussel, N. User Interface Façades: Towards Fully Adaptable User Interfaces. *UIST 2006*. 309-318.

[28] Takagi, H., Kawanaka, S., Kobayashi, M., Itoh, T. and Asakawa, C. Social Accessibility: Achieving Accessibility through Collaborative Metadata Authoring. *ASSETS 2008*. 193-200.

[29] Tan, D.S., Meyers, B.R. and Czerwinski, M. WinCuts: Manipulating Arbitrary Window Regions for More Effective Use of Screen Space. *CHI 2004*. 1525-1528.

[30] Wachenfeld, S., Klein, H.-U. and Jiang, X. Recognition of Screen-Rendered Text. *ICPR 2006*. 1086-1089.

[31] Yeh, T., Chang, T.-H. and Miller, R.C. Sikuli: Using GUI Screenshots for Search and Automation. *UIST 2009*. 183-192.

[32] Zettlemoyer, L.S. and St. Amant, R. A Visual Medium for Programmatic Control of Interactive Applications. *CHI 1999*. 199-206.

[33] Zettlemoyer, L.S., St. Amant, R. and Dulberg, M.S. IBOTS: Agent Control Through the User Interface. *IUI 1998*. 31-37.

Client TouchPoint Modeling: Understanding Client Interactions in the Context of Service Delivery

Aqueasha M. Martin
Clemson University
School of Computing
100 McAdams Hall
Clemson, SC 29634, USA
aqueasm@clemson.edu

Yolanda A. Rankin
IBM Research – Almaden
650 Harry Road
San Jose, CA 95120, USA
yarankin@us.ibm.com

Joe Bolinger
The Ohio State University
Department of Computer Science
and Engineering
Columbus, OH 43210, USA
bolinger@cse.ohio-state.edu

ABSTRACT

Service delivery organizations oftentimes overlook opportunities to cultivate client relationships due to a lack of awareness of the totality of touchpoints, or interactions, that occur between service delivery personnel and client personnel over time. To enable service delivery organizations to strategically manage their client relationships, we introduce the first phase of the Client TouchPoint Modeling (CTM) process in which service delivery teams create a touchpoint map of their collective interactions across a client account. Participatory design sessions with service delivery personnel informed the design of a CTM TouchPoint Map prototype. Through these sessions, we also discovered a more collaborative approach to CTM, one in which service delivery team members work together to co-construct a unified account map in a way that promotes team transparency and sensemaking of the service experience.

Author Keywords
Client touchpoints, Team situational awareness

ACM Classification Keywords
H.5.2 Information Interfaces and Presentation:

General Terms
Design

INTRODUCTION

Service delivery organizations recognize the distinction between fulfilling contractual obligations and meeting or exceeding the client's expectations [8]. Prior research implies that customer satisfaction is grounded in the client's perception of the service experience and such perception is directly correlated to complex, interpersonal relationships that develop between the client and the service provider over time [1,5]. Thus, each interaction, or touchpoint, represents an opportunity for the service provider to respond to the client's expectations and to proactively influence the client's perception of the service experience.

However, the sheer scale of touchpoints that occur between client and service delivery personnel makes it difficult for service delivery teams to have a shared global perspective of the client account. Not withstanding the managerial roles and the infrastructure for providing service, service delivery organizations need methods and tools to assist with strategically managing the client-provider relationship, specifically those touchpoints deemed to be critical by the client. Without well-defined processes and tools, service providers fail to realize new or existing opportunities to positively shape the customer experience and incur the risk of making uninformed decisions due to a lack of visibility into the delivery team's daily operations [1].

In response to this dilemma, we introduce the Client Touchpoint Modeling (CTM) process. CTM represents a three-step method for identifying, understanding and evaluating both formal and informal interactions between service delivery and client personnel as a means for gauging the customer experience. First, service delivery teams create an account map to promote evaluation of the customer experience from the service provider's perspective. Second, client personnel verify the account map to provide feedback about the service delivery team's performance. Third, the service delivery team and client personnel work together to identify opportunities (e.g. re-designing critical touchpoints) to improve the service experience. In this paper, we focus primarily on the first phase (the service provider's perspective) of the CTM process, eliciting service delivery personnel in the conceptualization of both the CTM process and the CTM TouchPoint Map prototype.

MOTIVATION FOR CTM: TEAM SITUATIONAL AWARENESSS

Prior research posits that team situational awareness involves more than just information sharing; it includes leveraging individual team member's expertise and contributions as a means for coordinating team performance [4]. Within the service delivery organization, team members have designated roles and responsibilities that are performed via typical service delivery processes, including execution of services, problem resolution, management of customer relationship, and development of new business opportunities [3]. We argue that team situational awareness extends beyond knowledge of team members' roles and responsibilities to understanding the context in which team members perform. Likewise, service delivery processes bound the service experience, promote the exchange of information between client and provider, and provide the means for evaluating team performance.

We concede that service delivery teams often do not share the same global perspective of a customer account and attribute the lack of team situational awareness to two key factors: 1. geographically distributed service delivery team members; and 2. informal yet significant client interactions that are unknown to other team members. Because of the complex and dynamic nature of teams, Sonnenwald [7] argues against the feasibility of an individual developing and maintaining the wealth of knowledge required for team situational awareness. While we concur with this impracticality, we suggest the need for appropriate technology that enables service delivery teams to develop a global perspective of the client account and maintain team situational awareness.

Shostack [5] emphasizes the need to pay particular attention to the people involved in delivering service as well as all encounters between employee and client. Service Blueprinting, one approach to developing a global perspective of the client account, distinguishes between customer-initiated interactions and service provider-initiated interactions and examines these interactions as inputs and outputs into the processes that define the service engagement [1, 6]. In contrast to the process driven approach of Service Blueprinting, CTM provides a finer level of granularity, examining each interaction between service provider personnel and client personnel in the context of a specific service delivery activity (e.g. attending softball game with client as a managing customer relationship activity).

CTM provides a seamless process for collecting touchpoint data across a client account and engaging service delivery team members in understanding their touchpoints from both an individual and team perspective. The CTM account map becomes a shared artifact that promotes a detailed, shared global perspective of what is happening on the client account. Without this perspective, team members cannot get a true sense of individual performance and contribution to the team. Because of the collaborative aspects associated with service delivery, support for information sharing and team situational awareness form the basis for conceptualizing the CTM prototype.

CONCEPTUAL DESIGN OF CTM

Initial Vision of the CTM Process

First, we identified the set of critical tasks for successful migration from individual awareness to team awareness and the technological support that would be needed to complete these tasks. To explore our initial assumptions, we chose a simple process as a starting point for CTM (See Figure 1). The process is as follows: 1. Each member of a service delivery team identifies her individual touchpoints with client personnel using a data collection instrument such as an online survey. 2. The focal point creates an aggregated account map of client touchpoints indicative of each team member. This task involves combining the touchpoint data, resolving redundant or shared touchpoints and any inconsistencies, and plotting the touchpoints on a map to create a visual representation of the touchpoints spanning the entire client account. 3. The focal point shares the account map with the service delivery team.

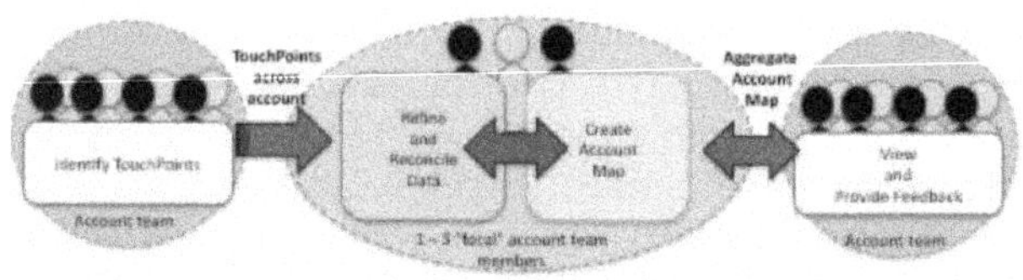

Figure 1. Initial Client TouchPoint Modeling Process.

METHODOLOGY

We intentionally engaged service delivery team personnel in the design process of CTM TouchPoint Map prototype to develop a better appreciation for the challenges service delivery organizations face in establishing and maintaining effective working relationships with customers. Five service delivery team personnel from two client account teams participated in the user study. Three participants served in managerial roles while two participants served in technical support roles on their respective accounts. Since no two participants shared the same location, user studies were conducted using video conferencing to record sessions and observe interactions with the three different progressive versions of the CTM Map prototype. All participants were given an explanation of the Client TouchPoint Modeling process along with the definition and examples of touchpoints. Each participant was instructed to identify and plot his or her touchpoints on the "CTM Map." Each participatory design session followed a semi-structured interview protocol that included questions about the UI design at each stage, and open-ended questions about the roles and responsibilities of service delivery team members; sessions lasted an average of 75 minutes for a total of 6.25 hours.

CTM Map Wireframe Prototype

We presented our initial design as a set of wireframes that consisted of a left sidebar of the categories (e.g. daily interactions with clients, social events with clients, etc.) of touchpoints and a 4 x 2 matrix of typical service delivery processes. (See Figure 2) The 4 x 2 matrix represented the CTM framework for understanding touchpoints and includes four columns indicative of critical service delivery processes --- service delivery (execution), resolving problems, managing customer relations and developing new business and two rows of temporal delineation --- planned and unplanned touchpoints [2]. The wireframes enabled users to drag touchpoints from the left sidebar and drop them in cells (e.g. Planned/Managing Customer Relations) on the map. Three individual touchpoint maps were created using the wireframe prototype design.

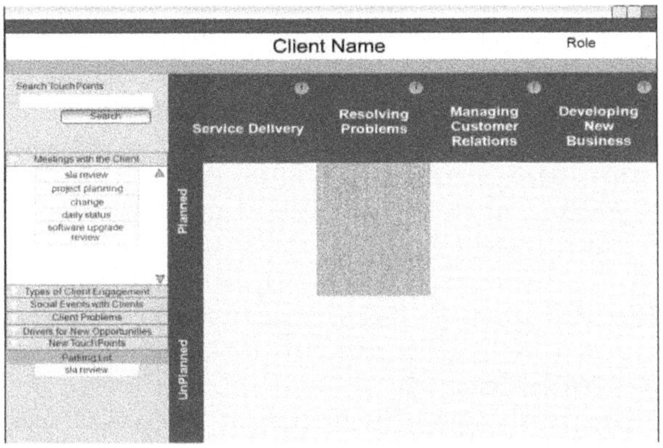

Figure 2. Wireframe of CTM TouchPoint Map application.

Web-Based CTM TouchPoint Map Prototype

As a result of the evaluating the wireframe version of the CTM Map, participants requested additional features that served as requirements for the web-based version of the CTM Map prototype. Additional functionality included the ability to create and delete touchpoints, provide contextual information about touchpoints (e.g. brief description, client personnel, etc.), and the capability to automatically save the map so users would not need to remember to do so. We also engaged participants in discussions regarding current client interactions, challenges in meeting client goals, and how the CTM process could be valuable to team members.

One service delivery team participated in a group session using the initial web-based CTM Map prototype to facilitate discussion and sensemaking of an account map. Four critical design requests came out of the both the initial web-based version and the group session: 1. the total number of touchpoints per category so users would know when the list was exhausted; 2. re-sizeable UI so that after the touchpoints are plotted on the map, the left sidebar can be eliminated and the map enlarged; 3. the coalescence of individual touchpoint maps into an aggregate client account map; 4. and a visual indicator of which role on the service delivery team created the touchpoint. To give all service delivery team members access to the account map and promote team situational awareness, we decided that CTM needed to include the ability to publish the account map once service delivery team members had created individual maps. These four design modifications were implemented in a second web-based prototype (See Figure 3).

Each round of user studies helped us to better understand how the technology could support users participating in the CTM process. In addition, through these sessions we were able to uncover a more realistic view of the CTM process.

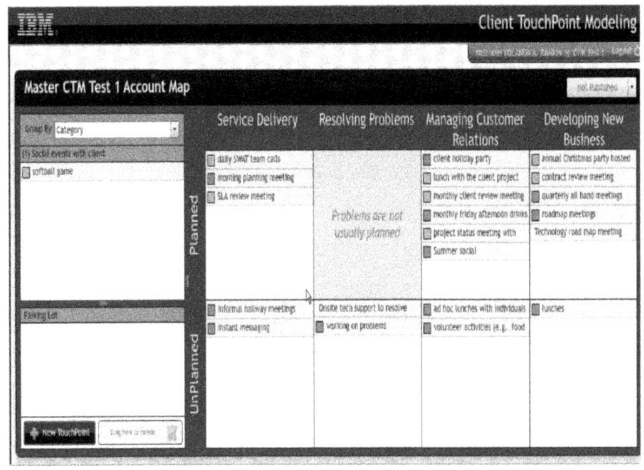

Figure 3. Example of an account map of aggregated service delivery team members' client touchpoints.

THE PERCEIVED VALUE OF CTM

Each session was recorded, transcribed, coded for recurring themes (e.g. transparency among team members) that were later identified as design criteria for the CTM tool. The goal of our evaluation was not to evaluate the CTM process or the tool but to gain feedback on the design.

Initially, we assumed that since the focal point has a managerial role on the service delivery team and is held accountable for ensuring customer satisfaction, the focal point should be responsible for organizing and reconciling the aggregated account touchpoint map. However, once we began to engage the two service delivery teams with the CTM Map prototypes, we began to revisit our assumptions and re-examine our vision of CTM (See Figure 4).

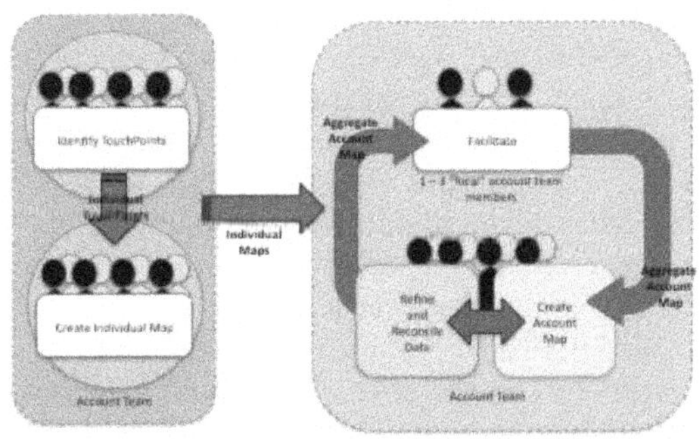

Figure 4. Revised Client TouchPoint Modeling Process.

The revised process supports self-accountability by introducing individual account maps. In addition, account team members become involved in sensemaking and creation of the account map, redefining the role of the focal point as facilitator of the construction of the account map.

Transparency that promotes team situational awareness

As a result of the data analysis, we made an interesting discovery. Though the purpose of the user study was to identify and validate the UI design, all five participants expressed an interest in viewing their teammate's maps.

P1: "... I would love to see a TouchPoint map of let's say everybody else on my account right, so I can say hey wait a second [Team Member], you built this TouchPoint map [and] there are things here that I didn't know you guys did or had an interface with the customer. How's that going? I mean is there any opportunities that are coming out of that? I mean it would help me to talk to my teams if I knew what their map look like and what kind of interactions that they had with the client."

This participant has a managerial role (service delivery manager) on the account team, and to some degree, he has some knowledge of the diffusion of touchpoints across the client account. After creating an individual touchpoint map, the user realizes that he is most likely unaware of his teammate's informal interactions and expresses that having such information enables him to gauge their efficacy and potential opportunities. It is this level of saliency that CTM offers that proves to be valuable to service delivery team members in managerial roles.

Co-Construction to Promote Distributed Accountability

Users' preferences to not only see their teammates' touchpoints but to participate in sensemaking of the account map speaks to the value of sharing the responsibility for providing quality service to the client. The act of constructing an individual map focuses the user's attention on self-accountability and the subsequent act of viewing the client account map shifts the user's focus to how her touchpoints impact the team's ability to provide quality customer support.

P2: "I would think from a brainstorming session, it would be good for everybody to go through it individually first, and then you come together and then go through it and finalize the data ..."

The aggregation of service delivery team members' individual maps creates an account map that visually depicts the density of client touchpoints. Thus, everyone who identified touchpoints and created individual maps can see what other team members are doing on the client account. One participant recognized that she was not very active in developing new business opportunities with the client in comparison to one of her teammates who had client touchpoints in the *developing new business* column on the map. This prompted her to consider how she could begin to pursue new business opportunities.

P2: " I can see that [Team Member] is doing all the New Business stuff and I am not doing much in that space."

We conclude that service delivery team members find value in constructing individual touchpoint maps that are automatically collated to create an aggregated account map. The account map offers a global perspective of service delivery activities and facilitates discussion and sensemaking of touchpoints.

CONCLUSION

Our current research emphasizes the first step in the Client TouchPoint Modeling (CTM) process---identifying each service delivery team member's interactions with client personnel to create an aggregated touchpoint map of the customer account. CTM promotes situational transparency among often geographically distributed service delivery organizations and facilitates team co-construction of a global perspective of the customer account. Future research efforts include further exploration of sensemaking of an account map to motivate design modifications to the CTM TouchPoint Map prototype and engaging client personnel in the verification and evaluation of the account map. As we engage more service delivery teams and client personnel in the CTM process, we can begin to identify similarities and differences between account maps and ultimately, best practices for positively shaping the customer experience.

ACKNOWLEDGMENTS

We appreciate Jeanette Blomberg and Melissa Cefkin for their efforts in making this work become a reality.

REFERENCES

1. Bitner, M. J., Ostrom, M. J., and Morgan, F. N. Service blueprinting: A practical technique for service innovation. *California Management Review*, 50 (2008), 66-94.
2. Blomberg, J., Cefkin, M., and Rankin, Y. Mapping and visualizing service provider and client interactions: the case for participation. *In Proc. Participatory Design Conf.* (2010), 294-296.
3. Endsley, M.R. Measurement of situation awareness in dynamic systems. *Human Factors.* 37, 1(1995), 65 – 84.
4. Salas, E., Prince, C., Baker, D.P., and Shrestha, L. Situational awareness in team performance: Implications for measurement and training. *Human Factors.* 37, 1 (1995), 123 – 136.
5. Shostack, L.G., Designing Services That Deliver. *Harvard Business Review*, (1984), 133-139.
6. Spraragen, S. and Chan, C. Service Blueprinting: When Customer Satisfaction Numbers Are Not Enough. *Int. DMI Education Conf*, (2008).
7. Sonnenwald, D. H., Maglaughlin, K. L., and Whitton, M. C. Designing to support situation awareness across distances: an example from a scientific collaboratory. *Info. Process Management,* 40, 6 (2004), 989-1011.
8. Stucky, S., Cefkin, M., Rankin, Y., Shaw, B, and Thomas, J. Business Value in Complex IT Service Engagements: Realization is Governed by Patterns of Interaction. *In Proc. HICSS 2010,* 1-10.

Using Predictive Human Performance Models to Inspire and Support UI Design Recommendations[1]

Bonnie E. John

IBM T. J. Watson Research Center
19 Skyline Drive. Hawthorne, NY 10532, USA
bejohn@us.ibm.com

Carnegie Mellon University
5000 Forbes Ave. Pittsburgh, PA, 15213, USA
bej@cs.cmu.edu

ABSTRACT
Predictive human performance modeling has traditionally been used to make quantitative comparisons between alternative designs (e.g., task execution time for skilled users) instead of identifying UI problems or making design recommendations. This note investigates how reliably novice modelers can extract design recommendations from their models. Many HCI evaluation methods have been plagued by the "evaluator effect" [3], i.e., different people using the same method find different UI problems. Our data and analyses show that predictive human performance modeling is no exception. Novice modelers using CogTool [5] display a 34% Any-Two Agreement in their design recommendations, a result in the upper quartile of evaluator effect studies. However, because these recommendations are grounded in models, they may have more reliable impact on measurable performance than recommendations arising from less formal methods.

Author Keywords
Human performance modeling, UI evaluation methods.

ACM Classification Keywords
H.5.2 User Interfaces: Evaluation/methodology.

General Terms
Human Factors

INTRODUCTION
Predictive human performance modeling, that is, using a computational model to predict what a human would do with an interactive system before it is built, is something of a "holy grail" in HCI. One step towards that ideal is the Keystroke Level Model (KLM, [2]), which predicts the time a skilled user will take to execute routine tasks with a UI. KLM and its more complex but more powerful relative, GOMS, has been extensively validated (e.g., [1] reports that 140 papers were in the GOMS bibliography, unfortunately no longer available on the web), but has not been used extensively in UI design practice. In the past decade, tools for constructing KLMs and GOMS models have arisen. Early anecdotal use of one of these tools, CogTool, showed a fourfold reduction in time to learn to model and an order of magnitude reduction for a skilled modeler to create a model [5]. Several studies have shown CogTool's accuracy improves on KLM's accuracy, reporting about a 10% deviation from empirical observations of skilled performance time [e.g., [5], [6]). A large study of novice modelers showed that CogTool reduced the coefficient of variance between the modeler's predictions from 22% to 7% [4]. This result increases the confidence of designers and developers that they can learn and use CogTool to get reliable quantitative predictions, because it is a tool embodying verified data and theory not an art transferred through extensive apprenticeship.

However, predictive human performance modeling has been traditionally used to quantitatively compare alternative design ideas, not to identify usability problems or make design recommendations. In contrast to previous modeling results (which were presented as a single quantitative time prediction and possibly a text trace of a complex underlying computer model), CogTool provides a timeline of what a user would see, think, and do to accomplish a task on a UI. These timelines allow differences between UIs to pop out as visual differences in patterns of colors, boxes and lines in the timelines, drawing the modeler's attention and simultaneously presenting the quantitative implications of these differences for the duration of tasks. This note investigates whether novice modelers can extract design recommendations from their CogTool models and support those recommendations with reference to the timelines.

THE STUDY
The study, detailed in [4], compared the predictions of novice modelers using CogTool to previously collected predictions of novice modelers using the original procedure for doing KLM [2]. The original KLM process

[1] Work done while the author was at Carnegie Mellon University.

was for a modeler to list the overt actions a user would have to take to accomplish a task (keystrokes, mouse movements, mouse clicks, etc.), place Mental operators using heuristics derived from user data, add system response time that makes the user wait, then sum up the times associated with these operations. In contrast, CogTool requires the modeler to build a storyboard of the interface, demonstrate the task on the storyboard (from which CogTool automatically creates a cognitive model), and hit a "compute" button. CogTool then runs the cognitive model to produce the numeric predictions and timelines. That study investigated whether CogTool reduced the variance between novice modelers' predictions, which it did, by 70%, from 22% to 7%. That study analyzed only the numerical predictions of the modelers, but qualitative data on design recommendations was collected in the CogTool condition as well.

Participants

The participants were students in the "HCI Methods" class at Carnegie Mellon University (Fall 2009), a required class for the bachelors and masters programs in HCI. All students in the class were either in an undergraduate major other than HCI (the BHCI is a 2nd-major), or already held a bachelors degree in another major. About ½ of the students were from a technical background, ¼ were from the behavioral sciences and ¼ had a background in design from a school of fine arts. The class included 101 students. One student had worked as a programmer on the CogTool Project the previous year and was removed from analysis because he had considerably more knowledge of the tool than the others, resulting in an N of 100. This assignment constituted 8% of each student's final class grade. Since no students included in the study had previous experience doing predictive human performance models or using CogTool, we will refer to them with the more descriptive term, "novice modelers."

Materials

These novice modelers were assigned to compare two web-based interfaces on three tasks, for a total of six models apiece. The interfaces were real-world web services for cataloging books and sharing collections on-line: Booktagger and LibraryThing. The tasks were (1) sign-in and add a book to your collection, (2) tag the book you just added, and (3) rate that book and sign-out. This assignment mimics what a UI designer might do in the real world to benchmark competitors' services before designing a new book-sharing service or the next release of an existing one.

These modelers were given step-by-step instructions of how to do each task on each interface with pictures of the screens that a user would encounter while doing the tasks. We believe this level of input is justified because we were looking for how well the modeling process allows the modeler to understand the effects of design elements on predictions of user performance time, not whether the UIs themselves were understandable. Furthermore, in the real world, a designer of a system should understand how their system or their competitors' systems, work; this detailed information mimics the real-world designer's knowledge.

Procedure

These modelers had one 1.5-hour lecture on predictive human performance modeling, about 20 minutes of which was how to use CogTool to storyboard a UI and generate predictions of skilled performance time. There was no instruction about how to use the timeline visualization to uncover usability problems or make design recommendations. There was a 3-hour working session where this author, a graduate student, and a CogTool developer were available to answer questions about the mechanics of using CogTool (e.g., "I accidentally closed my Project window, how do I get it back?" and "I have an old operating system on my Mac and CogTool's not working, what do I do?"), but not about decisions that would affect predictions. About two thirds of the modelers started the assignment during this session; all participants completed the assignment within one week.

The modelers had to create storyboards of the two websites using CogTool and demonstrate each of the three tasks on each of the storyboards. CogTool produced quantitative predictions of task execution by skilled users from these demonstrations and timeline visualizations of what a user would see, think, and do to accomplish the task. The modelers were asked to provide design recommendations, as follows.

> "Using what you learned from this modeling exercise, make recommendations for a new book-collection website that would be efficient for these three tasks. Include at least three recommendations in a bulleted list, being concise and precise. Here's an example:
>
> - **Recommendation:** Reduce system response time as much as possible.
>   **Justification from the CogTool Models:** In Booktagger, the user had to wait for the system to respond for XXX seconds (yyy% of the total time); in LibraryThing the user had to wait ZZZ seconds (www% of the total time).[2]
>
> **NOTE:** do not use reducing system response time as one of your recommendations."

RESULTS AND DISCUSSION

All 100 modelers submitted 6 predicted times (for 3 tasks on the 2 interfaces) and 98 modelers submitted recommendations (a total of 277 recommendations). I categorized these recommendations as (1) "correct and well supported" if they would decrease the predicted time

---

[2] xxx, yyy, etc. were used as placeholders in the instructions, because providing numeric values would give the modelers information as to whether their models were correct.

for frequent users of a collection website and if they were justified by correctly referencing specific portions of the models, (2) "vague or inarticulately argued" if the recommendation would decrease predicted time for frequent users but did not specifically reference the models, and (3) "incorrect" if the recommendation would increase time, prevent the website from working, or reduce the functionality of the website. For example, Figure 1 shows the timeline of what a user would see, think and do to tag a book with "dog" in both systems. The annotations call out differences in the timelines attributable to differences in the UI design. A well-supported recommendation is shown below the picture, referring to the extra steps called out in the top timeline. In contrast, an incorrect recommendation would be "do not use hover actions to tag a book." The annotation on the bottom left shows that Booktagger's hover interaction is actually faster than LibraryThing's click interaction as long as the pop-up on hover is immediate.

Figure 2 shows the most common recommendations. Two hundred eight were correct and well-supported, and additional 46 were correct but vague or inarticulately argued, for a total of 254 correct recommendations; 23 were incorrect. Thus, these novice modelers made an order of magnitude more correct recommendations than incorrect recommendations.

All 98 modelers who submitted recommendations provided at least 1 correct recommendation. Although 4 modelers did not argue convincingly for any of their recommendations, 94 provided a well-supported justification using the models for at least 1. However, 20 modelers did make at least 1 incorrect recommendation in addition to their well-supported correct recommendations.

As an example of how these recommendations would affect performance of skilled users, Figure 2 shows the first two recommendations involve the sign-in process. It may be obvious to CHI readers that putting the login field on the welcome screen with the cursor automatically in that field is a more efficient interface for frequent user than having to click through a splash screen and no auto-focus, but many existing websites do not include these efficient UI elements and Booktagger is one of them. These novice modelers were also novice UI designers, yet 66% were able to argue for putting the login on the welcome screen, which saves almost 2 seconds, and 57% argued for autofocus, which also saves about 2 seconds. 39% recommended doing both these things, for a saving almost 25% off the original time to sign in to Booktagger. These modelers could have generated qualitative recommendations from other methods taught in the class (e.g., Heuristic Evaluation) but they could not have argued quantitatively without time-consuming data collection (e.g., usability studies). On the other hand, only 3% of the modelers used their models to make the leap to recommending that users be allowed to stay signed in, a design that would save frequent users 12 seconds each time they used the site.

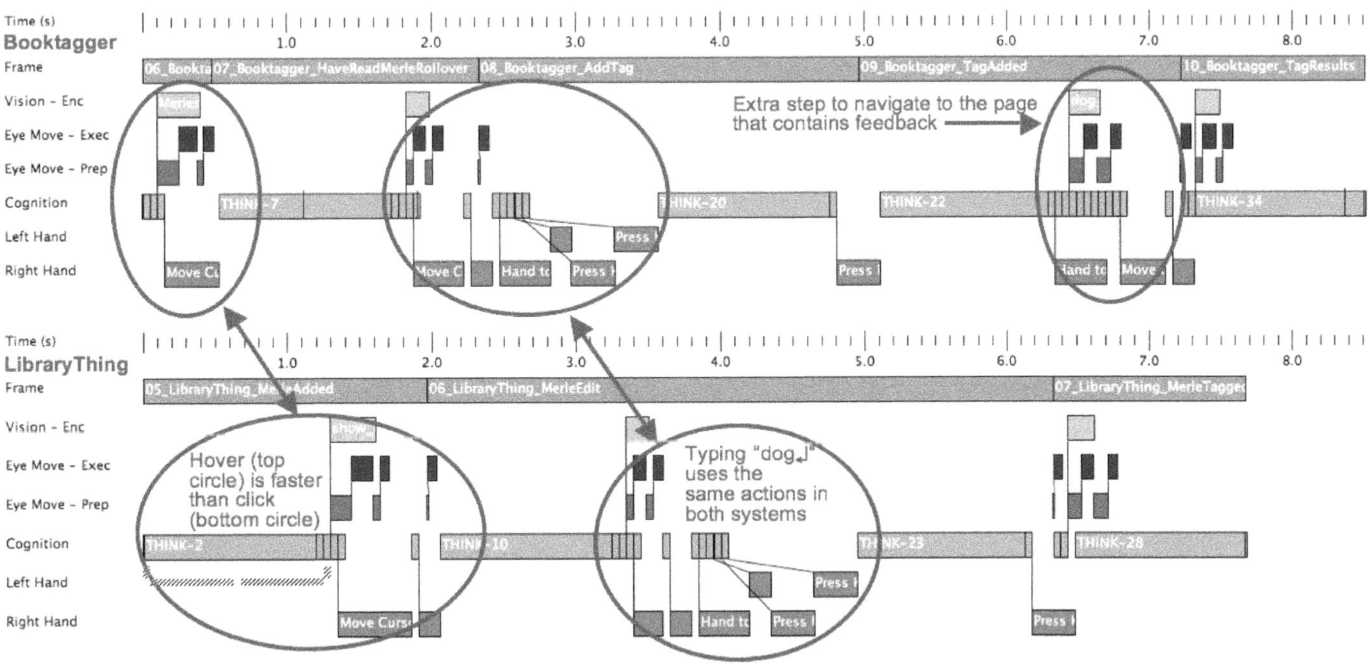

Recommendation: Provide visual feedback about the results of user actions on the page that follows that action.
Justification from the CogTool Models: In Booktagger, there was no visual feedback about which book was tagged and therefore the model-user had to do extra actions to make sure the right one had been tagged (see figure above). These extra actions would be eliminated if the page that resulted from tagging showed the book's name as well as the tag.

Figure 1. Example of a well-supported correct recommendation, using annotated timelines from CogTool as support.

Specific & Justified Recommendation	% of modelers making this recommendation	Time saved (s) in the instance given
Put the login on the welcome screen	66%	1.909
Put cursor in the login field automatically	57%	1.975
Give feedback for every action on the page that results from that action	38%	2.231
Targets as large & as close together as possible	32%	0.187
Eliminate a particular unnecessary step	5%	2.492
Allow user to stay logged in	3%	12.321
plus: 7 other specific and justified recommendations made by only 1 modeler apiece		
46 correct but vague or inarticulately argued recommendations from 34 modelers		
23 incorrect recommendations from 20 modelers		

Figure 2. Recommendations, how many novice modelers generated them, and how much time they would save.

As in [3], I calculated the Any-Two Agreement (A2A) rate for the 98 modelers. A2A is the number of problems two evaluators have in common divided by the number of problems they collectively detect, averaged over all possible pairs of two evaluators. 100% would be perfect agreement; the A2A for these evaluators using CogTool was 34%. Of the 12 studies for which A2A could be calculated by Hertzum and Jacobsen (Table 1 in [3], ranging in A2A from 5% to 65%), 9 studies had less than 34% A2A, putting this study in the top quartile. Of the three studies that did better, one was Cognitive Walkthrough (3 participants, 65% A2A), one was Heuristic Evaluation (77 participants, 45% A2A), and one was Think-Aloud (4 participants, 42%). All these methods were also represented in the set that performed worse than CogTool. Only 3 of the 12 studies had professional UI designers as participants and these were all worse than the current result (6%, 7% and 33% A2A).

Hertzum and Jacobsen posited three causes of the evaluator effect: vague goal analyses (i.e., different tasks being examined), vague evaluation procedures, and vague problem criteria. In this study, all modelers analyzed the same tasks, as was the case in five of the studies in [3], so we agree with Hertzum and Jacobsen that "the evaluator effect is not eliminated by giving the evaluators identical task scenarios" (p. 429). While the procedure for constructing the CogTool model is explicit, the modelers received no instruction in how to extract recommendations from the models, so vague evaluation procedures almost certainly plays a role in the evaluator effect in this study. However, the problem criterion was very explicit (and narrow): recommendations must decrease the time to accomplish the given tasks. More than 90% of the recommendations met that criterion, so perhaps if the modelers had been asked to produce all the recommendations they could identify (as in [3]), instead of only three, their A2A might have been higher.

CONCLUSIONS AND FUTURE WORK

This study of 100 novice modelers producing 600 models has shown that, in addition to producing quantitative predictions of skilled performance time with only 7% CV, they can also extract design recommendations that will increase efficiency for frequent users. Despite having no explicit instruction on how to do so, 96% of them could argue convincingly for adopting their recommendations with arguments grounded in validated theory of skilled human performance. Future work would include creating instructional materials to explicitly teach modelers to extract recommendations and supporting arguments, improve the timeline visualizations to help designers find opportunities for redesign, and extend to metrics beyond skilled execution time (e.g., novice exploration behavior with CogTool-Explorer [7]).

ACKNOWLEDGMENTS

This research was supported in part by funds from NASA and IBM. The views and conclusions in this paper are those of the author and should not be interpreted as representing the official policies, either expressed or implied, of NASA, IBM, or the U.S. Government.

REFERENCES

1. Brinck, T., Gergle, D., and Wood, S. D. (2002) *Designing Websites that Work: Usability for the Web.* Morgan Kaufman Publishers, San Francisco, CA.
2. Card, S. K., Moran, T.P. and Newell, A. (1983) *The Psychology of Human-Computer Interaction.* Lawrence Erlbaum Associates, Hillsdale, NJ.
3. Hertzum, M. and Jacobsen, N.E. (2001), The evaluator effect: A chilling fact about usability evaluation methods, *International Journal of Human-Computer Interaction, 13*(4), 421-443.
4. John, B. E., (2010) Reducing the variability between novice modelers: Results of a tool for human performance modeling produced through human-centered design. *Proceedings of the 19th Annual Conference on Behavior Representation in Modeling and Simulation (BRIMS)* (Charleston, SC, March 22-25, 2010).
5. John, B. E., Prevas, K., Salvucci, D. D., Koedinger, K. (2004) Predictive human performance modeling made easy. *Proceedings of CHI 2004* (Vienna, Austria, April 2004) ACM, NY. 455-462.
6. Luo, L. & John, B. E. (2005) Predicting task execution time on handheld devices using the Keystroke-Level Model. *Extended Abstracts of CHI 2005* (Portland, Oregon, April 2-7, 2005) ACM, NY, 1605 – 1608.
7. Teo, L. & John, B. E. (2008) Towards Predicting User Interaction with CogTool-Explorer. Proceedings of the Human Factors and Ergonomics Society 52nd Annual Meeting (NYC, NY, Sept 22-26, 2008).

Matters of Life and Death: Locating the End of Life in Lifespan-Oriented HCI Research

Michael Massimi
Department of Computer Science
University of Toronto
mikem@dgp.toronto.edu

William Odom
HCI Institute
Carnegie Mellon University
wodom@cs.cmu.edu

Richard Banks
Microsoft Research Cambridge
rbanks@microsoft.com

David Kirk
Mixed Reality Lab
University of Nottingham
dsk@cs.nott.ac.uk

ABSTRACT
Examining developmental periods of the human lifespan has been a useful tradition for focusing HCI research (*e.g.,* technologies for children or the elderly). In this paper, we identify the *end of life* as another period of the human lifespan that merits consideration by technology designers and researchers. This paper maps out current and future research in HCI at the end of life by first describing how this area raises questions concerning materiality and artifacts, social identities, temporality and methodologies. Having provided a description of the richness of this area, we then frame it against HCI traditions and practices in an orientation we term the *lifespan-oriented approach.* This paper maps early efforts in end of life research, structures and suggests areas for continued work, and situates the end of life among existing areas of HCI research.

Author Keywords
Death, dying, bereavement, lifespan, materiality, temporality, storytelling, ethics.

ACM Classification Keywords
H5.m. Information interfaces and presentation (*e.g.*, HCI): Miscellaneous.

General Terms
Design, Human Factors.

INTRODUCTION
Technology is increasingly part of the way we experience death, but to date, the topic has not been well-established in the HCI literature, even though the end of life acts as a crucible, transforming longstanding HCI issues in novel and interesting ways. While the HCI community has not addressed this topic in depth, there are numerous software companies, end of life service providers, and popular press articles that demonstrate the various ways that technology interacts with the end of life.

Software developers and end users alike increasingly apply technology to meet end of life needs. Technology helps us remember the dead through social networking and photo sharing sites such as Facebook and Flickr, and through a staggering array of memorial websites, such as Forever Missed [1]. Funeral homes and cemeteries augment traditional ceremonies with virtual condolence books and PowerPoint slide decks of photos of the deceased (see one such example at Ward Funeral Homes [2]). Technology helps us tell life stories in the face of fatal illness, and draws us closer to distant friends and family [24]. It guides hospital clinicians in drawing out advance directives [27], and enables therapists to counsel the bereaved through the Internet [26]. Sites like My Wonderful Life [3] can even provide preemptive options for planning your own funeral.

Concurrently, technology can complicate our experience of death. We may struggle to develop a will that accurately reflects the ever-shifting state of our digital assets (or use web sites like Entrustet [4] or Legacy Locker [5] to make this process easier). We may question why we were chosen to inherit certain digital possessions, reacting with confusion or resentment [53]. We may receive lingering misattributed emails or phone calls from the now deceased [46], or find disturbing system-generated recommendations to “reconnect” with dead friends on Facebook [67].

What remains certain is that technology is intersecting with the end of life in new and unexpected ways. As we have outlined above, it has the capability to ease suffering, or to disturb our sensitivities through its strangeness and irreverence. All the while, people are appropriating a wide range of publicly-available technologies – from blogs to electronic photo frames – to react to the eventuality, actuality, and aftermath of death.

Collectively, these trends help illustrate that issues related to the end of life are increasingly relevant, yet generally overlooked within the HCI community. The contributions of this paper are twofold. We begin by showing how HCI research addressing the end of life shares a *lifespan-oriented* approach that, in some ways, is similar – and can be productively linked – to work with the elderly or with children. Further, this approach precipitates a mapping of relevant stakeholder groups. Having framed the end of life among the lifespan-oriented approach in HCI research, we then set out to provide a critical review of research at the end of life to date. We begin by arguing that the end of life has a crucible effect – thinking about technology as applied to this domain adds new depth to existing HCI issues and introduces new directions for research. We map out thematic areas that can be useful tools for framing past, current, and future HCI research in this domain. We then conclude with a forward-looking discussion about opportunities for the HCI community to impact and potentially improve the complications associated with one's death and the social processes that unfold after a death occurs for all stakeholders involved.

THE END OF LIFE AS LIFESPAN-ORIENTED HCI

One way in which HCI research is commonly motivated and presented is through studying technology usage by people in a particular period of the human lifespan. For example, the interaction between children and computers is very different from the interaction that occurs when senior citizens are the primary user group. This approach to research, which we term *lifespan-oriented,* has proven to be beneficial to the HCI community by helping to identify prominent issues associated with a period in the lifespan. Childhood, for example, inspired and informed the HCI community regarding playfulness, creativity, and imagination [25, 28, 40]. Similarly, work with senior citizens foregrounds issues of accessibility [51], privacy and autonomy [15], health [12, 56], and cognitive decline [21]. Focusing on one part of the human lifespan at a time not only improves the quality of interaction for those in the developmental period in question, but as a secondary benefit, provides portable sets of design implications, artifacts, and methods that can improve interaction for users of all ages. It further helps researchers working in a particular space to share results, coordinate research efforts, and identify important problem spaces. By contextualizing a research project within a particular period of individual development, researchers may be better able to generalize to other people also at that stage of life. It holds fixed or mitigates differences in variables such as age, cognitive/physical capabilities, and interpersonal relationships. Applications targeted at users in a particular developmental stage may see higher rates of adoption due to a better fit with the desires and goals associated with that stage (*e.g.,* applications for teenagers [64]).

The lifespan has traditionally been taken up in HCI in an individual developmental context (with the notable exception of multi-lifespan design, which refers to systems applied over multiple generations to enduring human problems such as genocide [30]). While HCI has inherited many of the methodological and theoretical underpinnings of cognitive psychology [19], developmental psychology has also influenced a number of HCI research studies [69]. The developmental perspective makes explicit the idea that the passage of time influences the ways in which we think, feel, and use technology "from conception to death" [10]; this contrasts dominant user models and HCI discourse wherein the "user" is presumed to be static and eternal.

While the developmental orientation has had a reasonably well-accepted presence in the HCI literature, the end of life has remained conspicuously unexplored. Indeed, developmental psychologists have long considered the (natural) end of life to be a separate period of the lifespan from other parts of older adulthood [11]. If we think about an individual's lifespan in relation to his or her own death, then there are four distinct stakeholder groups through which he or she passes, starting from a vague awareness of one's own mortality, through to one's own death. The developmental perspective suggests an awareness of past and future stages of life as part of every other stage. Additionally, throughout the lifespan, the individual will be bereaved as family and friends die. In what follows, we explore each of these four stakeholder groups in turn.

The Living: Issues of mortality and death have been fundamental areas of concern across the humanities and social sciences for centuries [58]. While these discussions are well beyond the scope of this paper, one thing that is certain is that mortality is a key component of how people perceive themselves and how they choose to live their lives. While issues of what it means to be "mortal" are complicated, to say the least, there are a set of more tractable issues related to this condition that may very well have a computational or interactional component. One example is the issue of estate planning – software currently exists that is intended to help the user determine how to distribute assets upon his or her death. This activity (drafting a will) is commonly undertaken in middle-age, or when a significant life event (such as the birth of a child) prevails upon the individual that these plans must be made. In general, however, the issues of mortality are confined and rarely addressed publically [39, 63].

Dying: Individuals who have a clear prognosis or circumstances that indicate an imminent death have a unique set of concerns. With a limited timeframe for action bearing down upon the individual, spiritual and interpersonal issues frequently rise to the fore, such as simplifying daily activity, asking for forgiveness, waiting for forgiveness, and relinquishing dreams [35, 44]. The dying may also possess a limited ability to interact with other people or technologies due to unmet biological and emotional needs, such as: pain, cleanliness, problems breathing, fatigue, depression, anxiety, and loneliness [57]. These conditions may be exacerbated by psychosocial or environmental factors, such as being isolated from friends and family as a result of hospitalization or confinement to a retirement home [23]. How the dying appropriate technology is ill-understood, but it appears communication habits could be potentially influenced, and better supported, through technological means.

Dead: Interest in "life after death" has been a foundational concept of human history and meaning-making (*e.g.,*

Lazarus and Jesus's rebirth in the Bible, the Phoenix in ancient mythologies). Personal technologies that are now widely available make it possible for actions to be effected beyond the biological lifespan – for example, automation and recording systems may make the possibility of "telepresence after death" a reality [45]. The concerns and wishes of the deceased as a conceptual category may also be worth consideration for determining how data should be stored or destroyed, and how user profiles might change following death (*e.g.,* Facebook) [67]; however very few examples exist to date that take into account the needs and values of users beyond their own lives. The deceased are implicated as a stakeholder group insofar that the living use technology to continue to remember (or forget) them.

Bereaved: A final stakeholder group that also receives considerable attention in the death and dying literature is the bereaved. Loosely defined as the social network of people connected to someone who has died, bereavement research commonly focuses on understanding grief reactions, mourning, remembrance, and inheritance [62, 66]. This stakeholder group differs from the previous three because it is not an explicit developmental period of the lifespan, but rather a reaction to the death of a loved one. Further, the needs of the bereaved are more dynamic than those of the dying or dead; system usage and user needs change as time passes following a death [66]. Another differentiating feature is the possible inclusion of complicated or prolonged grief as a diagnosis in the upcoming fifth edition of the Diagnostic and Statistical Manual of Mental Disorders, recasting some grief reactions a mental health problem to be addressed, managed, and treated [55]. These issues, among others, are emerging in the HCI literature through qualitative studies involving bereaved people [46, 53].

Clearly there are other stakeholder groups that could be considered regarding system use at the end of life, such as funeral directors, clergy, medical staff, and so forth. However, these four categories emerge as the most salient stakeholders to immediately focus on for purposes of designing technology. Having provided this thumbnail of the primary stakeholder groups, we now trace the rise of end of life research in other disciplines, and subsequently map current and future opportunities for HCI research to productively engage end of life issues and stakeholders.

MAPPING OUT HCI RESEARCH IN THE END OF LIFE

Prior to describing HCI's interest in the end of life, we first briefly trace recent events in *thanatology* – the multidisciplinary study of death. Since the mid-20th century, there has been increasing interest in the end of life in medicine, social work, and psychology. Elizabeth Kübler-Ross's *On Death and Dying*, originally published in 1969, is often credited with bringing to public attention the unique experiences of dying people (and with it, the since-debunked "stage model" of denial, anger, bargaining, depression, and acceptance) [43]. Critical ethnographic analyses of hospitals and how death and dying are socially structured also appeared at this time, with notable studies from Sudnow [63] and Glaser and Strauss [34] casting light on how institutions manifested the "death-denying" tone of Western culture [39]. Fueled in part by these critical accounts, the hospice, palliative care, and supportive care movements took root and advocated dignity and compassion for those with long-term and fatal illnesses.

Despite the amount of public and academic interest in the end of life, researchers generally find it difficult to clearly articulate what is meant by "end of life," and when someone can be characterized as entering this part of their lifespan. For purposes of this paper, we refer to the end of life in the developmental, individualist sense outlined above: it is the period of a person's lifespan where there is an irreversible, downward progression in health and where biological death is imminent. While there are many problems with such a definition (it remains slippery like "childhood" or "old age"), we find that this term offers a useful conceptual handle for discussion.

The current state of research in this field is both behind the curve in terms of understanding how current technologies are appropriated, and simultaneously forward-looking insofar that new systems are being developed that interact with concepts in this space. These systems often draw upon existing topics in the HCI literature and re-apply them in this unique domain. In that sense, the end of life acts as a *crucible*: it draws into focus particular areas of HCI by destabilizing the interactional context (*e.g.*, how might a system respond if its intended user is dead?). It provides an arena in which long-accepted premises of interaction are no longer ensured, and opens up opportunities for research and design that meet human needs across the lifespan.

To demonstrate just how the end of life acts as a crucible, we map current research activities in this space, and show how they raise salient research questions and indicate potential design interventions. This mapping stems from our fieldwork and design work occurring in and across Europe, Canada, and the United States over the past 3-5 years, along with our consultation with researchers in the HCI community engaged with this topic at academic workshops and conferences [41, 48].

The mapping presented consists of four major themes that have been continual discussion topics at these workshops and conferences: materiality, identity, temporality, and research methods and ethics. We find these four themes compelling because they are so consistently found in various research projects; at the same time, they are different enough from one another to provide a conceptual indication of what HCI research at the end of life entails. Of course, there is some overlap between these themes; however, thinking about them separately presents a productive way to articulate key issues. Following this mapping, we expand on their collective implications for future HCI research and practice at the end of life.

Materiality and artifacts

A key way social relationships manifest themselves is through the presence and use of things; people commonly pass down key artifacts they deem reflective of their own lives as well as those constituting social bonds with friends and family [29]. Artifacts represent key elements of their identity as well as familial history and heritage. The study of the role of artifacts before, during and after bereavement is not new and has been a classic area of inquiry across the social sciences and humanities (*e.g.*, [37, 49]). This extensive body of work can serve as a productive platform to develop sensibilities concerning how technology may shape processes through which users pass on their things.

Changing material properties

A key issue in general for the HCI community is the changing materiality of the things that we own and increasingly interact with [38]. As people continue to acquire, create, and archive collections of digital artifacts similarly representative of their lives and those of their friends and family, a range of new issues are emerging. It is clear many artifacts traditionally physical are also becoming virtual. For example, photographs previously taken in small numbers and printed on paper, are now taken in large numbers, some of which may never be physically reproduced (perhaps even viewed) during the original owners' lifetime. While there are well-established processes for dealing with—and inevitably dispossessing—the wealth of material artifacts often left behind in the wake of a loved one's death, it remains unclear how these processes will unfold in the context of the digital. For example, prior research [46, 53] has described a range of troubling experiences that occurred for the bereaved when they inherited computers full of their departed loved ones' personal files. These cases highlighted how complications unfolded as the bereaved were burdened by a sense of obligation to sort through archives of personal files, while having no established mechanism to do so. It was frequently the case that they hid these machines out of sight; simultaneously being unable able to dispose of them or effectively investigate their contents. In general, idiosyncratic file naming and structuring conventions, among other things, complicated these participants' efforts to construct a cohesive sense of what they had been left behind. How might new tools be designed to enable users to better contextualize their digital belongings for particular groups and pass them to receivers in more elegant and meaningful ways? Similar to other recent works questioning a life-logging perspective (*e.g.*, [61]), there seem to be significant opportunities for future research to investigate how interactive systems might be designed to enable people to craft and bequeath distilled sets of digital objects meaningful to particular individuals or groups. Nonetheless, while the quantity of digital content can be burdensome, it may also open new opportunities for reminiscence and reflection. For example, the artful representation of large stores of digital photos might create new relationships to content as rich experiences archived within them are experienced in spontaneous and serendipitous ways.

Additionally, key issues such as materialization and presence must be taken into account when considering how digital elements of departed loved ones might be leveraged to create assemblies embodying significant aspects of their lives or moments shared with them. Physical artifacts are often put on display in the home to honor a person's life in meaningful and persistent ways. Digital objects and collections clearly do not have the same enduring presence, but nonetheless could provide dynamic and expressive tributes. Moreover, a key quality of digital artifacts is their ability to be inscribed with diverse types of metadata, which could provide rich opportunities to thoughtfully contextualize collections of virtual possessions passed down as well as help alleviate miscommunications in exchanges of bequeathed items. Previous research [31] has illustrated the value of converging streams of commonly available online content, such as weather information, historical events, etc., onto digital artifacts to evoke meaningful experiences. We imagine both personally ascribed layers of metadata could be combined with various 'ready-made' streams to contextualize artifacts being passed down in much more fluid and rich ways; indeed, these new interactive assemblies may also serve as rich resources for reflection on and commemoration of the lives of departed loved ones.

Very recent work [65] is emerging that explores how new form factors of interactive technologies might support ritual practices of remembrance in the home. However, to date little is known about how these new types of digital artifacts might fit within actual domestic environments and intimate places. Moreover, the processes that unfold after a death are extremely heterogonous and unpredictable, making it difficult to anticipate how a user would react to these designs even years into the future. Could these kinds of technologies serve as evocative portraits of our departed loved one's lives? Or, would they become persistent, perhaps painful, reminders of those no longer with us, leaving little space to romanticize past experiences shared with them? Clearly more research is needed to understand the social, cultural and ethical boundaries of appropriateness and acceptability these emerging technologies and systems as we consider their potential place alongside us in our own lives, and perhaps in those of future generations beyond us.

Identity

In addition to reconciling the local storage and material presence of digital elements owing to departed loved one's lives, new complications are arising as practices of storing, presenting, and sharing digital artifacts expand to online places and social networking systems, such as Facebook. In what follows, we describe a small set of critical themes related to identity in this context, which are accompanied by opportunities for future HCI research.

As people expand their practices of storing and presenting digital objects (*e.g.,* photos) from local computers to personal and shared online places, new, often valued, opportunities have emerged to support and strengthen social connection among friends and loved ones. However, along with these shifts, several new unanticipated issues have resulted in complications for stakeholders as a departed loved one's social networking profile(s) – and their attendant content(s) – continue to persist after she or he has passed away. For example, prior research with bereaved participants [46, 53] has detailed how the persistence of deceased users' public online profiles led to them being transformed into ad hoc memorial sites in which, despite their social orientation to the departed, anyone in the deceased users' online social network were allowed to post public statements. In several cases, bereaved parties perceived these actions to uncomfortably violate boundaries of social entitlement characterizing who ought to be considered "bereaved", and the socially and morally appropriate actions that ought to follow suit. In these cases the bereaved were often unable to gain access to the departed's account to intervene. Participants in these studies also described disturbing instances in which they received messages from a departed loved one's online profile, which typically owed to a family member using the deceased's account to communicate with their social network (*e.g.*, invitation to a memorial service), or system-driven notifications of content aimed at catalyzing "reconnection" with now departed friends and loved ones.

To be clear, each of the cases comprising these data are diverse and by no means represent an exhaustive set of death-related complications emerging with social networking systems. What we want to draw attention to is how they are linked by a common underlying problem: in the physical realm rituals have occurred to mark the passing of loved ones, whereas online they persist in a *liminal* space [33], neither alive nor treated as dead, but lingering on not unlike any other user in the system. In this same selection, bereaved participants reported a range of responses when asked to reflect on how they desired their digital possessions stored online to be treated after they are gone. In some cases, participants wanted to have control over their account(s) and content(s), often explicitly desiring to grant (or restrict) access to different archives of digital artifacts to specific people. Whereas, others desired to immediately cede total control to their loved ones. Additionally, while prior work has indicated the crucial role "letting go" of artifacts plays in moving past painful life experiences and evolving aspects of one's self [49, 52], it is unclear how one might dispossess digital artifacts shared in online places, such as Facebook, which owe to the life of the departed. While recent changes have occurred in Facebook to enable deceased users' accounts to be 'pushed' into memorials [67], there are still no clear mechanisms in place to facilitate the transfer of account ownership (and attendant digital possessions) to the bereaved.

The complications across these instances typically owe to the often unanticipated persistence of departed loved one's digital identities. They collectively suggest a suite of tools could be designed and incorporated into existing social networking sites to encourage users to prospectively consider the lifespan(s) and destination(s) of their online accounts and contents, and who(m) ought to have rites to them. There may be similar opportunities in supporting user delineation of future ownership permissions by fluidly integrating this kind of functionality into privacy tools as they become more sophisticated and integrated facets of social networking systems. More research is needed to understand the extent to which new interventions would be effective in making the processes of passing on (or destroying) online content more transparent. Additionally, research is required to understand to what degree these kinds of interventions are valued, and, importantly, when they themselves may become socially inappropriate or unacceptable. We can imagine, even if subtle, prompts to prospectively reflect on the longevity of one's digital possessions beyond life may not be desirable. Further, it is important to consider if tools and systems for bequeathing one's digital possessions would provide expressive outlets to celebrate unique social bonds between specific people. Or, would they create nagging obligations to continually curate and manage digital things as the social relationships implicated in them grow and change?

Finally, as the HCI community continues to expand to non-Western contexts, new questions arise in terms of how technology and systems are affecting – and potentially complicating – the social, cultural and religious aspects of groups that have well-established practices for dealing with death. For example, how do members of a group that believe in reincarnation come to terms with the persistence of a deceased member's social networking profile? Very little research to date within the HCI community explicitly addresses these concerns. However, emerging work at the intersection of spirituality and computing [13] suggests a key area that can be built on in the future as techno-spiritual, social, cultural and death-related issues increasingly converge in contexts around the world.

Temporality

Concepts of time and pacing are useful for evaluating our experiences of moving towards and beyond death. They sensitize us to differing aspects of the experience highlighting avenues for further research. Taking such a temporal lens to an aspect of experience is familiar territory for HCI and is something that has recently been explored in a growing literature on "trajectories" of experience [14]. In taking this approach we consider four focal points along a trajectory towards and beyond death.

Orienting to a future death

For most people death occurs as a result of either old age or long term illness and as such its inevitability is something that most people consider at some point in their lifespan.

Consequently, there is value in understanding how people prepare for death and in designing supportive technologies. For some, especially the terminally ill, the use of social networking sites, online support groups and remote counseling has become a valuable (perhaps controversial) resource in developing preparedness for death [22]. There has been little pragmatic research however, into the efficacious design of such resources.

An alternative aspect of preparedness is more material in its concerns. As other sections of this paper discuss, there is a growing need to manage the digital resources and ephemera of one's life and herein there is much scope for the development of tools to support the adequate archiving and triaging of digital resources. This digital settling of affairs concerns not only the design of tools to literally bequeath digital artifacts, negotiating the complex social imperatives of bequeathing and inheritance practices, but also the design of tools for managing one's digital legacy – for making testament of one's intentions with regards such ephemeral things as the correct use and appropriation of various social networking sites, post-mortem.

How one's remains, physical and digital, are to be treated and how one orients towards death must be informed for many people by religious or spiritual sensibilities, as we briefly alluded to above. Consequently, technology design that works in this space will presumably also need to consider how such faith-based matters intersect with technology (*e.g.*, [13, 68]).

Constructing narratives

One way in which people orient towards death and come to deal with its emotional consequences (*i.e.*, come to terms with the event itself, support the pre-grieving and eventual grieving of others, settle affairs and unburden oneself), is to form some narrative account of a life [20]. Within the trajectories literature this concept resonates with the notion of developing "historical trajectories" [14], having an account of experiences generated through data collection. Technological advances in data capture offer new means for doing this and at differing scales. For example, data capture might record an entire life (as per the My Life Bits project [32]) or just significant moments and interactions of our life, recorded through our interactions with objects [6], for example. Such data of experience can then be repurposed for the development of these accounts.

As a means for bridging from preparedness to post-mortem, creating a narrative account has significant potential value. How artifacts are shared and how they are given meaning through narration is a rich source of current research in HCI [53]. There is much potential in understanding how digital technologies can support the construction of what we might term *narratives of dying*, for people who are approaching the end of life. Design in this space requires a solid understanding of the attendant concerns of the users of such memorial technologies. Building tools to allow narratives to be recipient designed and to be delivered in contextually appropriate times and through appropriate means is an imperative but complex challenge.

In the moments (passing)

For much research on dying (even amongst our own prior works), there is often little foregrounding of the moment itself. Technology will however increasingly intersect with these moments. This area becomes problematic for discussion because of the ways in which it so readily raises issues of personal control and agency in one's own demise (or put another way, raises the issue of assisted suicide). The act of controlling one's own death of achieving it in one's desired way with dignity and control, having a good death [9, 36], even for those not directly taking their own lives, could be (and is) much managed with technology. The use of ambient and embedded (and even embodied) technologies to manage one's sensory and emotional experiences at the ultimate moment is an area of valid concern and clearly a potential human-computer interaction of much significance. Research within such spaces however, must be done in awareness of attendant moral, ethical and political sensibilities that might be raised.

Legacies and monuments

Post-mortem, extending our temporal lens on death past the moment itself, the legacy we leave behind and the ways in which we are remembered materially (including the digital) are evident concerns. The notions of monuments and memorialisation have been considered extensively in other fields, such as anthropology and cultural studies. As we move into the era of ubiquitous computing, with mobile, situated and perhaps again bodily-embedded technologies, we will increasingly leave behind a contextual data footprint. There is a suggestion that such a data footprint might be repurposed and become some form of lasting monument to persons or groups of people [42]. As discussed above, we see signs of this repurposing of the digital in practices of Facebook memorialisation; and indeed, in addition to emergent complications, the ad hoc memorilisation of departed users' social networking profiles has also provided rich resources for reflection and some collective sense of closure [18]. But with increasingly complex uses of technology such data might become increasingly personal, offering strange new records of a life which can be archived. In addition to this there is growing interest in the use of digital technologies in funerary ware and shrines to the deceased [65]. The value-centered design of future physical-digital and pervasive memorials depends upon developing a deep understanding of the human value of and response to such concepts and technologies.

Research Ethics, Methods, and Design Considerations

Death and dying are parts of life that can cause great strife, trigger significant changes in family structures, and cause people to enter an emotionally raw state. Just as additional protections are warranted when conducting research with vulnerable populations, investigating mortality, dying, death, and bereavement requires special consideration of participants' well-being. For researchers interested in working on issues surrounding the end of life, we discuss ethical and methodological issues, which should be considered during study design and execution – an approach called *thanatosensitive design* [47].

Standards for professional conduct in this area have been developed by the Association for Death Education and Counselling. These standards govern behaviour for grief therapists, death educators, researchers, and so on [7]. While many of the tenets outlined are similar to those found in other professional associations (such as the ACM or APA), ADEC outlines unique circumstances end of life professionals face that HCI researchers rarely encounter. One tenet describes the need for professionals to present "various views of a death-related question" which respect the individual's preferences, needs, and background. Another one of their ethical standards discusses the need to refer clients to an appropriate professional if the individual shows signs of dangerous behaviour (*e.g.*, if a participant shows signs of suicidal behaviour). We detail some of the potential issues that HCI researchers and designers may want to consider when working at the end of life, and organize them by potential stakeholder group.

Bereaved

Working with the bereaved introduces a unique set of challenges. Immediately following a loss, the bereaved may be in heightened states of emotion or in shock; this raises ethical concerns and compromises data collection [8]. But should we design technologies for the newly-bereaved at all? While some hospital-based studies found that the bereaved would like to be offered professional services such as counselling immediately after the death of a loved one [50, 54], multi-site longitudinal studies found that intervention is often unnecessary and may even potentially interfere with an adaptive grief response [16, 60]. Given the lack of consensus surrounding bereavement counselling, it remains unclear whether or not technology-centred interventions would be appropriate for the bereaved immediately after a loss. Current best practice is to make technological support or resources available, but not necessarily included as a standard part of care. Further, the holiday season, along with important dates like birthdays, death dates, marriage anniversaries, and so on have been noted as particularly difficult times for the bereaved [17]. Additional social reconfigurations occur as time passes, with family structures shifting to adapt to the loss. Researchers should consider the richness and variety of relationships the bereaved might have to the deceased when determining who to involve in the research process; similarly, designers should create systems that address an evolving family unit.

Dying

Talking to the dying as a distinct group of individuals with a specific set of needs and lessons to teach began in earnest with Elizabeth Kübler-Ross's work interviewing dying patients [43]. Her work, like much of the work since then, has focused on individuals in hospital settings who are in palliative care or have been given a poor prognosis. In these settings, the complications of working in hospitals (*e.g.*, issues of access, consent, use of medical data) are exacerbated by the failing health and limited time of participants; fatigue, pain, or drowsiness may impinge upon participants' ability to understand questions or respond. Additionally, family and friends may be acting on behalf of the individual. While family members may act as surrogates for certain types of questions, the validity of their responses is likely to be poor [8]. Schulman-Green *et al.* suggest a set of alterations to standard interviewing techniques based on their work with dying patients and their families [59]. They note the importance of allowing the interviewee to lead the interview, and the need for additional time and patience when allowing the interviewee to respond. HCI researchers and designers can potentially innovate in this space by developing technologies that permit the dying to communicate their needs and perspectives at their own pace, rather than during a single sitting.

Dead

When designing systems, it is increasingly important to consider how the system might gracefully and respectfully present or use information associated with the deceased. The idea of using technology to prevent death entirely, or to "speak from beyond the grave" has been a motif in science fiction for decades, but has begun to actually occur in current systems. As noted, Facebook's "friend suggestion" function intimated that a dead person was interested in speaking with the user [67]. Similarly, Massimi and Baecker describe how highly personal technologies like caller ID serve to disorient and surprise the bereaved when they receive a call from a dead relative [46]. Interactive systems designers should consider how agency is attributed to the users of their systems, and how that agency might be represented when a user is actually dead.

This idea of agency ties into notions of consent and data maintenance. Researchers and designers in this space need to carefully acknowledge how data associated with a dead producer should be handled: does it die along with its owner, or remain? Is it included in analysis, or removed? How should access to the data change as a result of a death? Systems designers and researchers should have clear plans about what happens to research data if a participant dies during the study, and additionally, should consider ethical approval of using of secondary sources (*e.g.*, webpages, emails) of people who have died during research.

The Living

As we increasingly store meaningful information across multiple disks, accounts, and devices, some living users have begun to plan out what should happen to their data upon their own deaths. Websites like Entrustet [4] promise to safeguard data and release it upon the death of the user. However, this type of situation raises ethical questions surrounding ownership and replication of data, right to inherit, and the legal role of these systems in various jurisdictions. How do we design systems to allow the living to create and ensure post-death plans are executed properly?

DISCUSSION

As presented in the four themes above, the end of life offers opportunities for a wide variety of HCI research and design. By addressing this domain, we have also shown how it fits with existing lifespan-oriented approaches in its ability to act as a crucible. In this discussion, we wish to suggest broad, but tractable directions for the HCI community to make an impact on the quality of end of life situations. We first address research directions, and then design directions.

Research Directions

At the moment, there are many anecdotes, stories, and thought-provoking scenarios about technology use at the end of life, but very few rigorous studies. HCI researchers interested in the end of life can contribute in multiple ways.

Achieving a better understanding of how technology is currently used at the end of life. This understanding helps provide technologists and end of life professionals alike with a foundation for improving end of life experiences. As we discussed before, this could be "in the moments" of death, looking at issues of materiality following death, or crafting a narrative to cope with one's own mortality. A variety of methodologies – both qualitative and quantitative – could be applied to better characterize users of end of life systems. Example research questions include: What percentage of the population uses technology for memorialization purposes? For inheritance purposes? What are the factors that predict use or avoidance of technology? How do religious, cultural, and personal differences account for technology use? How do types, and settings, of death influence the way that technology is used?

Applying and extending existing HCI theories, principles, and technologies to this domain. Many current theories and principles in HCI could be extended to consider the eventuality of death. For example, distributed cognition has been a useful tool for describing how knowledge in organizations is stored, communicated, and reproduced; but how is the death, or removal, of an actor in such a system accounted for? What are the best principles for systems that successfully withstand the test of time such that they are able to be enjoyed by multiple generations of users? What are the ethical dimensions of various technologies for achieving the various goals at the end of life?

Scholarly discourse and interdisciplinarity. The field of thanatology has been long-established, but to date, has had little input from technology experts. Cultivating a stronger technology-oriented presence in this field of study can help us find partnerships, resources, and common ground with people from a wide variety of disciplines. Thanatologists working in the arts and humanities may already adopt technology as part of their practice, but lack the expertise to adapt the technology to handle the delicate social and processes associated with death. At the same time, the thanatology community can benefit from the unique opportunities that technology can provide in terms of data collection, intervention, and application.

Design Directions

The end of life has been a continual topic in art and design. Interaction designers, too, may find it a significant—if not unavoidable—domain to explore. Here we suggest further opportunities for interaction designers and researchers.

Designing to empower. As the assistive devices community has shown, systems can be designed in a way that empowers the end user to achieve his or her goals despite disabilities. For the dying, this might indicate an opportunity to give the user the chance to say goodbye in a unique or meaningful way through channels that are more accessible than writing or typing. For example, there may be an opportunity in designing technologies that enable the dying to communicate their wishes in a more personal or desirable way, perhaps through conveying more expressive messages to specific individuals or groups. However, as we have discussed, it is crucial to take into account how these digital materials might be received and treated by other stakeholders, such as the bereaved, and consider ways in which they could be embodied, stored or put to rest. At the same time, interactive technologies and systems could be designed that empower all of us, as mortals, to engage in end of life planning more readily, or to make arrangements more easily. And finally, we can consider how systems might empower people who have died to maintain a digital identity that preserves their integrity and desires in this life; or, to deliver messages for loved ones into the future.

Designing to ease the transition. Systems intended for personal use rarely consider the death of the user, or even a change in the user's power of agency. Interaction and system designers may consider how their products could, be (mis)used following a death. How will data from the device be retrieved? How will this change affect the larger network structure? Who might become the new user, and how does that change the use cases for the technology or service?

Making meaning and making strange. All people seek to achieve personal understandings of what life and death mean. Interactive technologies and systems can place viewers or users into immersive emergent situations and experiences that can open the space for this kind meaning-making to unfold. For example, systems that sensitively "reanimate" the dead or transcend the barriers of death may have powerful emotional and even therapeutic effects.

CONCLUSION

In this paper, we have laid out the foundation for future work in HCI at the end of life. We have done so by first situating the end of life as part of a larger tradition of *lifespan-oriented research*. Drawing on this tradition, we described how the end of life introduces a new set of challenges, while also helping us to reexamine long-standing HCI issues in a new light. In particular, we call to mind four stakeholder groups which have been, and will continue to be, central to work in this area: *mortals, the dying, the dead, and the bereaved.* Based on our fieldwork, examination of the literature, and experiences organizing and attending international workshops on this topic, we have suggested four thematic areas that begin to map out what research at the end of life might include: *materiality, identity, temporality, and research ethics/methods.* With these conceptual cornerstones in place, it becomes possible to construct a concrete foundation from which future work can productively leverage and grow. Finally, we have remarked on research and design directions that may be explored to achieve a better understanding of technology's role at the end of life, improved designs and interactional experiences, and, ultimately, a more meaningful, personal, and human experience for anyone as she or he inevitably encounters or experiences the end of life.

ACKNOWLEDGMENTS

Thanks to the participants of the CHI 2010 workshop on HCI and the End of Life.

REFERENCES

1. Forever Missed. http://www.forevermissed.com/.
2. Ward Funeral Home. http://www.wardfuneralhome.com/.
3. MyWonderfulLife. https://www.mywonderfullife.com/.
4. Entrustet. https://www.entrustet.com/.
5. Legacy Locker. http://legacylocker.com/.
6. TOTeM. http://www.youtotem.com/.
7. ADEC Ethics. http://www.adec.org/about/ethics.cfm.
8. Addington-Hall, J. and McPherson, C. After-Death Interviews with Surrogates/Bereaved Family Members: Some Issues of Validity. *Journal of Pain and Symptom Management 22*, 3 (2001), 784-790.
9. Anon c. 1450. *Ars Moriendi.* .
10. Baltes, P.B., Reese, H.W., and Lipsitt, L.P. Life-Span Developmental Psychology. *Annual Review of Psychology 31*, 1 (1980), 65-110.
11. Baltes, P.B., Reese, H.W., and Lipsitt, L.P. Life-Span Developmental Psychology. *Annual Review of Psychology 31*, 1 (1980), 65-110.
12. Becker, S.A. A study of web usability for older adults seeking online health resources. *ACM Trans. Comput.-Hum. Interact. 11*, 4 (2004), 387-406.
13. Bell, G. No More SMS from Jesus: Ubicomp, Religion and Techno-spiritual Practices. In *Proc. UBICOMP*. Springer-Verlag, 2006, 141-158.
14. Benford, S. and Giannachi, G. *Performing Mixed Reality*. MIT Press, 2010.
15. Birnholtz, J. and Jones-Rounds, M. Independence and interaction: understanding seniors' privacy and awareness needs for aging in place. *Proc. CHI*, ACM (2010), 143-152.
16. Bonanno, G. *The Other Side of Sadness: What the New Science of Bereavement Tells Us About Life After Loss.* Basic Books, 2009.
17. Bowlby-West, L. The impact of death on the family system. *Journal of Family Therapy 5*, 3 (1983), 279-294.
18. Brubaker, J. and Vertesi, J. Death and the Social Network. *Proc. CHI Workshop on Death and the Digital.*
19. Card, S.K., Newell, A., and Moran, T.P. *The Psychology of Human-Computer Interaction.* L. Erlbaum Associates Inc., 1983.
20. Carlick, A. and Biley, F.C. Thoughts on the therapeutic use of narrative in the promotion of coping in cancer care. *European Journal of Cancer Care 13*, 4 (2004), 308-317.
21. Carmien, S.P., Cavallaro, F.I., and Koene, R.A. 'Senior moments': loss and context. *Proc. International Workshop on Systems and Networking Support for Health Care and Assisted Living Environments*, ACM (2009), 1-4.
22. Chung, D.S. and Kim, S. Blogging activity among cancer patients and their companions: Uses, gratifications, and predictors of outcomes. *J. Am. Soc. Inf. Sci. Technol. 59*, 2 (2008), 297-306.
23. Costello, J. Nursing older dying patients: findings from an ethnographic study of death and dying in elderly care wards. *J. Advanced Nursing 35*, 1 (2001), 59-68.
24. Damianakis, T., Crete-Nishihata, M., Smith, K.L., Baecker, R.M., and Marziali, E. The Psychosocial Impacts of Multimedia Biographies on Persons With Cognitive Impairments. *The Gerontologist 50*, 1 (2010), 23 -35.
25. Dix, A. Being playful: learning from children. *Proc. IDC*, ACM (2003), 3-9.
26. Dominick, S.A., Irvine, B.A., Beauchamp, N., et al. An internet tool to normalize grief. *Omega 60*, 1 (2009), 71-87.
27. Don Murphy, G., Schenkenberg, T., Hunter, J.S., and Battin, M.P. Advance Directives: A Computer Assisted Approach to Assuring Patients' Rights and Compliance with PSDA and JCAHO Standards. *HEC Forum 9*, 3 (1997), 247-255.
28. Druin, A., ed. *The design of children's technology.* Morgan Kaufmann Publishers Inc., 1998.
29. Finch, J. and Mason, J. *Passing On: Kinship and Inheritance in England.* Routledge, 2001.
30. Friedman, B. and Nathan, L.P. Multi-lifespan information system design: a research initiative for the hci community. *Proc. CHI*, ACM (2010), 2243-2246.
31. Gaver, W., Boucher, A., Law, A., et al. Threshold devices: looking out from the home. *Proc. CHI*, ACM (2008), 1429-1438.
32. Gemmell, J., Bell, G., Lueder, R., Drucker, S., and Wong, C. MyLifeBits: Fulfilling the Memex Vision. *Proc. of MULTIMEDIA*, (2002), 235-238.
33. van Gennep, A. *Rites of Passage*. Routledge, 2004.
34. Glaser, B.G. and Strauss, A. *Awareness of Dying.*

Aldine Transaction, 1965.

35. Goldberg, S. The Hard Work of Dying. http://www.examiner.com/x-17609-SF-End-of-Life-Issues-Examiner~y2010m6d30-The-Hard-Work-of-Dying.
36. Green, J.W. *Beyond the Good Death*. University of Pennsylvania Press, 2008.
37. Hallam, E. and Hockey, J. *Death, Memory and Material Culture*. Berg Publishers, 2001.
38. Hallnäs, L. and Redström, J. From use to presence: on the expressions and aesthetics of everyday computational things. *TOCHI 9*, 2 (2002), 106-124.
39. Howarth, G. *Death and Dying: A Sociological Introduction*. Polity, 2006.
40. Kafai, Y.B. *Minds in Play: Computer Game Design as a Context for Children's Learning*. L. Erlbaum Associates Inc., 1995.
41. Kera, D., Graham, C., Foong, P.S., Aceti, L., Gibbs, M., and Rouncefield, M. *Afterlife & death in the digital age seminar*. National Univ of Singapore, 2010.
42. Kosem, J. and Kirk, D. Spomenik: Monument. *Proc. CHI Extended Abstracts*, ACM, 4477-4480.
43. Kübler-Ross, E. *On death and dying*. Routledge, London, 1989.
44. Kübler-Ross, E. *Death: The Final Stage of Growth*. Simon & Schuster, 1997.
45. Lombard, M. and Selverian, M.E.M. Telepresence after death. *Presence: Teleoper. Virtual Environ. 17*, 3 (2008), 310-325.
46. Massimi, M. and Baecker, R.M. A death in the family: opportunities for designing technologies for the bereaved. *Proc. CHI*, ACM (2010), 1821-1830.
47. Massimi, M. and Charise, A. Dying, death, and mortality: towards thanatosensitivity in HCI. *Proc. CHI Extended Abstracts*, ACM (2009), 2459-2468.
48. Massimi, M., Odom, W., Kirk, D., and Banks, R. HCI at the end of life: understanding death, dying, and the digital. *Proc. CHI*, ACM (2010), 4477-4480.
49. Miller, D. and Parrott, F. Loss and material culture in South London. *The Journal of the Royal Anthropological Institute 15*, (2009), 502-519.
50. Murphy, S.A. A bereavement intervention for parents following the sudden, violent deaths of their 12-28-year-old children: description and applications to clinical practice. *The Canadian Journal of Nursing Research 29*, 4 (1997), 51-72.
51. Mynatt, E.D., Adler, A., Ito, M., Linde, C., and O'Day, V.L. Learning from seniors in network communities. *Proc. CHI Extended Abstracts*, ACM (1999), 47-48.
52. Odom, W., Banks, R., and Kirk, D. Reciprocity, deep storage, and letting go: opportunities for designing interactions with inherited digital materials. *interactions 17*, 5 (2010), 31-34.
53. Odom, W., Harper, R., Sellen, A., Kirk, D., and Banks, R. Passing on & putting to rest: understanding bereavement in the context of interactive technologies. *Proc. CHI*, ACM (2010), 1831-1840.
54. Oliver, R.C., Sturtevant, J.P., Scheetz, J.P., and Fallat, M.E. Beneficial Effects of a Hospital Bereavement Intervention Program after Traumatic Childhood Death. *The Journal of Trauma Injury Infection and Critical Care 50*, 3 (2001), 440-448.
55. Prigerson, H., Bierhals, A., Kasl, S., et al. Complicated grief as a disorder distinct from bereavement-related depression and anxiety: a replication study. *Am J Psychiatry 153*, 11 (1996), 1484-1486.
56. Rege, R., Jung, H., Hazelwood, W., Orlov, G., Connelly, K., and Shankar, K. Exploring early evaluation techniques of ambient health promoting devices in home environments of senior citizens living independently. *Proc. HealthNet 08*, ACM (2008), 1-3.
57. Reynolds, K., Henderson, M., Schulman, A., and Hanson, L.C. Needs of the dying in nursing homes. *Journal of Palliative Medicine 5*, 6 (2002), 895-901.
58. Scholl, S. *Death and the Humanities*. Bucknell University Press, 1984.
59. Schulman-Green, D., McCorkle, R., and Bradley, E.H. Tailoring traditional interviewing techniques for qualitative research with seriously ill patients about the end-of-life: A primer. *Omega 60*, 1 (2009), 89-102.
60. Schut, H. and Stroebe, M.S. Interventions to enhance adaptation to bereavement. *Journal of Palliative Medicine 8 Suppl 1*, (2005), S140-147.
61. Sellen, A.J., Fogg, A., Aitken, M., Hodges, S., Rother, C., and Wood, K. Do life-logging technologies support memory for the past?: an experimental study using sensecam. *Proc. CHI*, ACM (2007), 81-90.
62. Stroebe, M.S., Hansson, R.O., Schut, H., and Stroebe, W., eds. *Handbook of Bereavement Research and Practice*. APA, 2008.
63. Sudnow, D. *Passing on: The Social Organization of Dying*. Prentice Hall, 1967.
64. Taylor, A.S. and Harper, R. Age-old practices in the 'new world': a study of gift-giving between teenage mobile phone users. *Proc. CHI*, ACM (2002), 439-446.
65. Uriu, D. and Okude, N. ThanatoFenestra: photographic family altar supporting a ritual to pray for the deceased. *Proc. DIS*, ACM (2010), 422-425.
66. Worden, J.W. *Grief Counseling and Grief Therapy*. Springer Publishing Co., Inc., 2008.
67. Wortham, J. As Older Users Join Facebook, Network Grapples With Death. *The New York Times*, 2010. http://www.nytimes.com/2010/07/18/technology/18death.html?_r=1&scp=1&sq=ghosts%20reach%20out&st=cse.
68. Wyche, S.P., Magnus, C.M., and Grinter, R.E. Broadening Ubicomp's vision: an exploratory study of charismatic pentecostals and technology use in Brazil. *Proc. UBICOMP*, ACM (2009), 145-154.
69. Wyeth, P. and Purchase, H.C. Using developmental theories to inform the design of technology for children. *Proc. IDC*, ACM (2003), 93-100.

I Said Your Name in an Empty Room: Grieving and Continuing Bonds on Facebook

Emily Getty, Jessica Cobb, Meryl Gabeler, Christine Nelson, Ellis Weng & Jeffrey T. Hancock
Cornell University, Ithaca, NY 14853
{erg29, jcc97, mag359, cln28, ew82, jeff.hancock}@cornell.edu

ABSTRACT

In response to the death of a close friend or relative, bereaved individuals can use technology as part of the grieving process. We present a study that analyzes the messages of the friends and family of the deceased to their Facebook profile before and after their passing. Our analysis reveals that mourners use profiles as a way to maintain a continuing bond with the deceased, as well as a way to accomplish specific front stage bereavement communication, such as sharing memories, expressing sorrow and providing social support. These observations may improve the design of social networking technologies so that they remain useful, sensitive tools for the bereaved.

Author Keywords

Death, grief, language, Facebook, memorialized

ACM Classification Keywords

H5.m. Information interfaces and presentation (e.g., HCI): Miscellaneous.

General Terms

Design, Theory

INTRODUCTION

The bitterest tears shed over graves are for words left unsaid and deeds left undone." –Harriet Beecher Stowe

The loss of a loved one is perhaps the most difficult experience a person can face. When people suffer this kind of loss they often come together to share their grief, express their emotions, and to console one another. Over time, mourners must also learn to live without the deceased, either learning to let go or finding a new place in their life for their lost one.

These grieving activities are now complicated by the presence of Social Networking Sites (SNS) that have profiles of members who have passed away. Recent work has begun to examine the use of profiles in SNS contexts for grieving [1] and more generally with the sensitive and respectful design of technology around death and dying [2]. In the present work we examine the language of the posts before and after the death of Facebook users in an effort to explore two important issues for the grieving process in the networked age.

The first is the expressing and sharing of grief and emotion on profiles of recently deceased individuals, and we refer to these as memorialized profiles. Here we draw on Goffman's notion of front and back stage communication [8]. The second concerns the relationship with the deceased, and here we draw on Continuing Bond Theory [4], which argues that individuals in the grieving process hold the deceased in loving memory, maintaining an inner representation of the deceased long after they have passed. This view stands in contrast to the dominant model that mourner's must "let go" in order to move on with their life.

We focus on language patterns in the profile posts for several reasons. Most importantly, language has repeatedly been shown to reveal social dynamics and psychological states of speakers [7], from depression to personality traits. Second, language analysis adhers to calls for research on death and technology to be sensitive and respectful to mourners and to the deceased's memory [6]. Analyzing extant posts on memorialized profiles is non-invasive - users are not questioned or otherwise contacted by researchers. As such, we believe that this approach can provide important insights into why people post to memorialized profiles that can build on theory and improve design while being non-invasive and sensitive to users.

A Dramaturgical Analysis of Mourning on Facebook

Goffman (and others, see [8]) conceptualized social life with the metaphor of drama, with individuals acting out their roles on a social stage in their day-to-day life. Some of these roles are enacted *front stage* and constitute performances designed for public expression, and others are *back stage* performances acted out in private. In [8], the authors examine the American funeral in terms of front and back stage, observing that while grief is traditionally a backstage emotion, individuals can experience a great deal of relief when this emotion is brought to the forefront as a part of religious and cultural practices. Such practices offer people a place to come together to publicly express their grief, to console one another, and to share stories about the deceased. After these ceremonies, this front stage expression of emotion and support becomes more difficult because ceremonies are tied to a specific time and place.

The emergence of memorialized profiles has created new spaces for the front stage aspects of grieving. For example, recent work suggests that group commemoration "is an important aspect of bereavement, and different technologies are used for this purpose" [5]. In our increasingly mobile society, social networking sites should provide an online space that is not bounded by space or time for grieving individuals to come together.

If people use posts to memorialized profiles for front stage grieving, then relative to their pre-death posts, we should expect posts to include more language related to expressing sorrow and grief [8]. Less obviously, we should also expect more socially oriented language that reflects the seeking and offering of support associated with public grieving [2]. Finally, we should see more sharing of positive memories or narratives of the deceased, reflected in a higher verb to noun ratio, which is indicative of narrative rather than expository writing [7], more past tense verbs and more positive emotion words.

Continuing Bonds or Letting Go?

Social networking sites offer an opportunity to communicate with loved ones who have passed away, as well as with other mourners. Previous work suggests that technology can provide the means to evoke a highly vivid and realistic online presence of the deceased, reminiscent of when they were alive [1,4].

This ability to write directly to a digital representation of the deceased opens up new opportunities in relating with lost ones and managing grief. Therapeutic approaches to managing this grief take two contrasting approaches. The dominant model for the last century argues that the mourner must come to grips with the loss by letting go of the deceased. People should move on from the death of a loved one by detaching themselves emotionally. Failure to do so is viewed as pathological grief.

Continuing Bond theory offers an alternative approach by arguing that maintaining a relationship with the deceased is beneficial to the grieving process. Death disrupts but does not need to end a personal relationship. A continuing relationship with the deceased represents a different kind of relationship situated in entirely changed circumstances.

Directly addressing a deceased individual in Facebook wall posts provides users with a novel way to work out one's new relationship with those who have died, either letting them go or continuing the bond. Indeed, previous work [6] suggests that many messages posted on deceased members' Facebook walls were addressed directly to the deceased individual.

One way to determine if these messages are directed at the deceased in an effort to let go or to continue the bond is to examine the level of psychological distancing in the language of the posts. Distancing, or detachment, is apparent in a well-validated linguistic device called *verbal non-immediacy,* in which individuals that are psychologically detaching themselves from a tragic event tend to use more articles and long words but fewer self-reference, words indicating discrepancy from reality (e.g., *would, could*), and present-tense verbs [2,7].

If these messages directed at the deceased are part of letting go, we should see increased non-immediacy in posts that come after death relative to prior. In contrast, if the messages are part of continuing the bond with the deceased, we should see more immediacy in their language.

METHODS

Profiles

Posts were collected from the Facebook walls of eleven deceased Facebook users. All of the profiles were "Facebook friends" of one of the authors. This convenience sample consisted of 10 males and 1 female, ranging in ages from 17-32. All of the individuals died suddenly, including one homicide, several accidents and suicides.

Post collection and analysis

Wall posts collected from the 11 profiles included posts up to one year prior to death and all posts after death up to April, 2010. Post-death time periods ranged from several weeks up to 3 years. Using a computer program written specifically for preprocessing the profiles, all items such as comments, notes, Facebook gifts, quizzes, status updates and recent activity were removed, leaving only individual wall posts in the corpus. The total number of posts collected was 3592.

These wall posts were analyzed using the Linguistic Inquiry and Word Count (LIWC) program, a text analysis program that counts and categorizes each word according to a dictionary of approximately 70 linguistic and psychological dimensions that have been extensively pre-tested. LIWC output provides the percentage of words for pre-death and post-death wall posts falling within a given word category (see [7]). For instance, the words "sad" and "grief" would both increase the percentage of negative emotion terms present in a given text. The average word count per post was 39.9 (SD = 89.72).

The data from LIWC were translated into several indices matching the predictions above (see [2,7]). The *Sorrow/Grief Index* indicates how many sad-related words were used (e.g., cry, grief, hurt) and was the LIWC *negemo* dimension. The *Social Orientation Index* indicates how often posts contained terms related to friends, family, sharing, talking and personal pronouns and was the LIWC *social* dimension. The *Positive Memory Index* indicated the level of story telling about the past and was calculated as the sum of the ratio of verbs to nouns, with a higher index indicating more narrative content, past-tense verbs and positive emotion terms (e.g., happy, joy). Finally, the *Non-Immediacy Index* measured psychological distancing and was based [2]'s established formulation of summing the number of articles (e.g., a, the) and six letter words (i.e., words six letters or longer) and subtracting first person singular (e.g., "I" "me"), discrepancy words (e.g., would, should) and present tense verbs (see also [7]).

The statistical analysis employed mixed models to account for interdependencies between posts addressed to the same profile holder, with post nested within profile holder. When poster was included as a random effects factor the results reported below were upheld.

RESULTS & DISCUSSION

Front Stage Grieving

We expected several dimensions of language to reflect front stage grieving in the posts after a death. The descriptive data for each of the indices related to front stage grieving are presented in Table 1.

First, and most obviously, we expected and found that post-death posts contained more words related to grief and sorrow $F(1,1350.9) = 185.0$, $p < .001$. Comments such as *"Still can't believe your gone... have so much I wanna tell you and it hurts to know your not there =(Miss you buddy,"* illustrate this index, and reflect perhaps the most important front stage grieving function of publicly expressing sorrow.

Second, the *Social Orientation Index* revealed a more collective orientation after the profile holder's passing than before, $F(1,2779.6)=283.2$, $p < .001$. Posters referred to other people more in their posts, consistent with the supportive aspects of front stage grieving. For example "*I was thinking about you... and then stupid facebook told me to send you a message.... but i guess writing this on your wall means that someone will read it... and know that they aren't alone in their sorrow..... i miss you so much... peace.*"

Third, the *Positive Memory Index* was higher in the post-death posts than pre-death, $F(1,434.9)=50.4$, $p < .001$, suggesting that post-death posts contained more emotionally positive narratives about the past, as in the following: *"Can't stop thinking about u right now! Or ever actually. Even tho my heart is broken I can't help but laugh at the memories I have with u...like u running out to the pool in ur speedo! Hahah everyone was cracking up! And as usual it was you who made us all laugh! I miss u! This is still sooo unreal. In my heart forever ."*

Taken together, the data are strongly supportive of the notion that the posts on memorialized profiles function as

Index	Pre-Death		Post-Death	
	M	SE	M	SE
Sorrow/Grief	.78	.27	3.83	.26
Social Orientation	20.69	1.31	34.23	1.27
Positive Memory	12.85	.61	17.51	.55

Table 1. Mean (M) and Standard Error (SE) percent of words per index

front stage grieving, much like the kind of communication observed at more traditional grieving events, such as funerals [8].

Continuing Bonds

Did people posting to memorialized profiles evidence non-immediate language indicative of distancing themselves from the deceased in an effort to let go? Or did they show increased immediacy indicative of a continuing bond with the deceased? As Figure 1 shows, the language of posts after a death were significantly more immediate than prior to death $F(1,2834.1)=28.3$, $p < .001$, a pattern that supports the Continuing Bonds Theory.

The fact that language was much more immediate after death suggests that posters were not psychologically distancing themselves, as would be expected if the posts were part of a letting go process. These data provide powerful support for how people can learn to have a new kind of relationship with a loved one that has passed on, and that memorialized profiles can provide an important venue for continuing that bond.

This post *"gym isnt same without the toughest training partner being there...but dont worry im gona win mr pittsburgh for ya and put that 1st place trophy in ur trophy room bro!"* is illustrative of how posters maintained a close

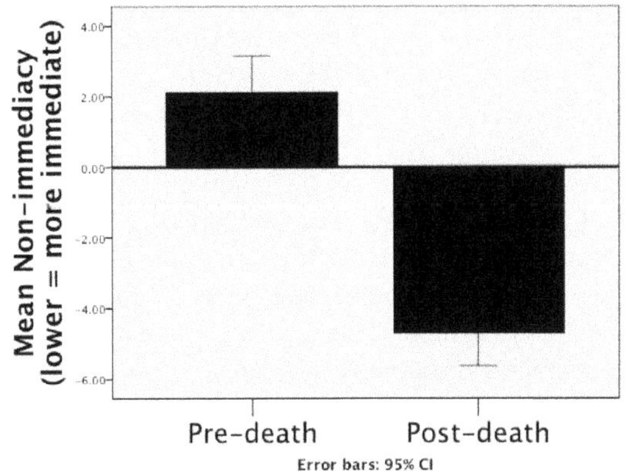

Figure 1. Mean level of non-immediacy per post before and after death

and intimate relationship with the deceased, an observation consistent with other recent work taking a qualitative approach [1]. If people are choosing to "let go" of the deceased, they do not appear to be using Facebook posts to do so.

DESIGN IMPLICATIONS

Our analysis suggests some important design insights for memorialized posts, including a need for connecting personally, for collective support, and a forum for sharing stories. Here we propose a number of design ideas for consideration.

First, instead of using one wall for posting it may be useful to include spaces in the profile for different purposes. One space could be dedicated to creating an environment where people are encouraged to remember and share stories about the deceased, ideally fostering a greater sense of community and facilitating the need for group commemoration.

Another space could involve a more personal setting for people to post messages directly to the deceased in a private space. Although the present data evidence a clear desire to maintain a strong continuing bond with the deceased, it is not clear that continuing the bond needs to be done in a private venue or if there is value to continuing the bond in a front stage space.

Other spaces could be dedicated to images sharing, for condolences directed to the family, and information about formal services that could facilitate the social support and communal commemoration aspects of the bereavement process. Users will know where to look for the sort of support they need or wish to offer, be it information about a memorial service or to engage with stories from others.

Importantly, however, any design implications must be considered carefully and in concert with the users of memorialized profiles. As recent controversies make clear [3], users have understandably strong feelings about memorialized profiles and the rules that govern them. Any design changes must be informed by research in the area and principles of laid out by [6] on respectful and sensitive design around technology and death.

LIMITATIONS

This study was subject to several important limitations. First, the results are based on a convenience sample and further, the sample consisted of premature deaths. These sample restrictions limit the generalizability of the results; those who die from chronic illness, for example, would be expected to have very different profile posts. Second, while this kind of computerized text analysis, in which words are categorized based on pre-defined dictionaries, can provide useful insights into overall statistical trends in large amounts of language, further content analysis with human coding is required to confirm these interpretations of the findings. Importantly, however, the present results are consistent with other qualitative work that involved close readings of the posts, such as [1]'s observation that posters often use language that is direct and psychologically close to the deceased. This kind of convergent evidence across methods is valuable for advancing our understanding of posts to memorialized profiles.

CONCLUSION

Our analysis of the language of Facebook posts indicate that mourners use memorialized profiles as a way to maintain a continuing bond with the deceased, as well as a way to accomplish specific front stage bereavement communication, such as sharing memories, expressing sorrow and providing social support. These observations may improve the design of social networking technologies so that they remain useful, sensitive tools for the bereaved.

ACKNOWLEDGMENTS
The authors are grateful to the students in the Comm/INFO 4500 class for their help, and to Natalya Bazarova for her comments on an earlier draft.

REFERENCES

[1] Brubaker, J.R. & Vertesi, J. Death and the Social Network. CHI2010 Workshop on *HCI at the End of Life* (2010).

[2] Cohn, M.A., Mehl, M.R., & Pennebaker, J.W. Linguistic Markers of Psychological Change Surrounding September 11, 2001. *Psych Science*, 15 (2010), 687-693

[3] Karas, T. (2010, February 5). The psychology of postmortem Facebook. Retrieved February 18, 2010, from http://www.dailynorthwestern.com

[4] Klass, D., Silverman, P., Nickman, S. (1996). *Continuing Bonds: New Understandings of Grief.* Philadelphia: Taylor & Francis.

[5] Lombard, M., & Selverian, M. E. M. Telepresence after death. Presence: Teleoper. Virtual Environ., 17 (2008), 310-325.

[6] Massimi, M., & Baecker, R. M. A Death in the Family: Opportunities for Designing Technologies for the Bereaved. In *Proc. CHI 2010*, ACM Press (2010), 1821-1830

[7] Tausczik, Y., & Pennebaker, J.W. The psychological meaning of words: LIWC and computerized text analysis methods. *Journal of Language and Social Psychology*, *29* (2010), 24-54.

[8] Turner, R. & Edgley, C. Death as theater: A dramaturgical analysis of the American funeral. *Sociology and Social Research, 60* (1976), *377-39.*

Dealing with Death in Design: Developing Systems for the Bereaved

Michael Massimi
Technologies for Aging Gracefully Lab
Department of Computer Science
University of Toronto
mikem@dgp.toronto.edu

Ronald M. Baecker
Technologies for Aging Gracefully Lab
Department of Computer Science
University of Toronto
ron@taglab.ca

ABSTRACT

Increasingly, systems are being developed and used in ways that involve end of life issues such as death, dying, and bereavement. Yet design considerations and guidelines for technologists working in this sensitive area are not well-established. We therefore report on exploratory fieldwork consisting of focus groups, observations, and consultation with bereavement experts aimed at understanding how technology might be designed to support bereaved parents. From this fieldwork, we derive a set of considerations useful for researchers and designers developing systems that deal specifically with bereavement, and with the end of life more broadly. These considerations focus on *interpersonal communication*, *new ways of being in the world*, and *materiality*. We conclude with a distillation of these considerations into practical design guidelines for working in this area.

Author Keywords

Bereavement, death, dying, social support, design, memory, thanatosensitive design.

ACM Classification Keywords

H5.m. Information interfaces and presentation (*e.g.*, HCI): Miscellaneous.

General Terms

Design, Human Factors.

INTRODUCTION

HCI research has a tradition of addressing distinct parts of the human lifespan, from childhood to old age. One part of the lifespan which is now emerging as a domain for interaction research and design is that of the *end of life* [26]. The end of life is a compelling domain for research for many reasons. It challenges ideas of user agency (*e.g.*, what if the user has died?). It draws together various strands of HCI research such as storytelling, personal information management, privacy, and lifelogging into an integrated experience with heightened stakes. It offers an opportunity to help people at an important time in their lives. Indeed, web sites have been deployed which can help users plan their own funerals [1], safeguard and distribute possessions [2,3], and publically mourn and remember the deceased [4,40].

But despite these initial examples of applying technology to end of life issues, working in this area can be intimidating. Encountering death is never an easy experience; and of course, this holds true for HCI designers and researchers. There is arguably no other human experience which challenges and engages us on a more fundamental level than death. Although death affects all of us on such a profound level, it retains a sense of taboo. Sociologists have repeatedly characterized Western culture as "death-denying" in numerous arenas from medical care to daily living [8,14,18,34]. While some critics argue that the frequent portrayal of death in the media runs counter to this characterization [7], end of life technology designers and researchers likely still have few authentic resources to draw upon beyond their personal, anecdotal experiences.

The goal of this paper is to provide HCI researchers and designers working on end of life issues with sensibilities for working with the bereaved. Based primarily on a series of focus groups with bereaved parents and our experiences participating in professional seminars and conferences on bereavement, we derive a set of empirically-grounded considerations that speak to issues in the HCI community. Structured into three broad categories – interpersonal communication, new ways of being in the world, and materiality – and illustrated with the results of our fieldwork, these considerations can help us better understand, interact with, and meet the needs of the bereaved. We conclude the paper with a discussion of how these considerations can translate into practical design guidelines. These guidelines may help HCI researchers and designers move into this space for future work, and develop a set of best practices for thanatosensitive design – that is, the creation of systems that actively engage with death as part of their concept [25].

RELATED WORK

While the end of life is a relatively new area for HCI, there has been some relevant work. In recent work in HCI on bereavement, Odom *et al.* provide a lens focusing on the death of a family member, showing how relationships with the deceased do not necessarily end once a person has died [29]. Based on interviews with 11 families, they describe how relationships change and become mediated by new rituals and inherited objects, and offer considerations for designing technologies that respect and engage this relationship. Massimi and Baecker offer a set of problem spaces derived from a survey and interview study conducted with bereaved family members [24]. They highlight a broad set of concerns – from the need for social support to inheritance of digital data – that reveal potential avenues for technology application and innovation for bereaved families. Massimi and Charise suggest that the HCI community address death in design through a humanistic approach called "thanatosensitive design," looking towards multiple forms of knowledge such as literature and film, in addition to empirical fieldwork, as ways of learning how to design systems that engage with death [25].

Design-oriented work has focused primarily on memorials and how they can be used as aids for remembering ancestry or the deceased. Uriu and Okude describe the design of ThanatoFenestra, a shrine developed to support Buddhist ancestor worship. The shrine displays and changes photographs of the deceased based on the flickering of a candle [35]. Kirk and Banks describe the concept of designing technology heirlooms [20] – devices crafted to respect and invoke social relationships and memories across generations through "deep storage" [21]. Van den Hoven *et al.* demonstrate design concepts such as handheld "memory stones" and tilting photo frames which are intended for bereaved people to help them communicate their grief in an abstracted way [37]. These examples demonstrate the interesting ways in which the HCI community has begun to move towards designing for the bereaved. At the same time, these projects rely heavily upon the designers' own experiences; they include very little fieldwork obtained from talking to the bereaved or professionals working in death education or care.

HCI researchers have also addressed issues which speak to end of life issues more tangentially. Friedman and Nathan describe multi-lifespan information system design as a unique type of design which addresses issues of profound human importance that are unlikely to be solved within a single generation [13]. Wyche, Magnus, and Grinter, in their account of Charismatic Pentecostals in Brazil, address religious understandings of the afterlife in their fieldwork and suggest that ICTs be designed to account for spirituality as well as the physical body as part of a supportive health paradigm [42]. Dimond, Poole, and Yardi also describe how death, among other forms of life disruption, impacts the ability for families to maintain home networks [11].

UNDERSTANDING BEREAVEMENT

Before presenting our design considerations, it is important to understand the research context. The goal of our research was primarily to better understand bereavement, and in particular, to do so from a technology design perspective. Based on prior work [24], we were interested in designing systems that provided social support. At the same time, we remained open to new possibilities and technological opportunities concerning bereavement more broadly – concerning, for example, issues of, remembrance, temporality, and emotion – because these topics influence, and are influenced by, the social setting in which grieving takes place. It is for this reason that in the considerations that follow, social support may be noticed as an underlying theme. Even so, the considerations presented are important for working with the bereaved regardless of domain. We briefly discuss social support tradeoffs to situate ourselves before describing how and where we studied it in the context of bereavement.

Research Domain: Social Support

The bereaved value social support and obtain it from a variety of sources [19,30]. Common sources include face-to-face support groups at community or religious centers, family and friends, therapists, and Internet discussion forums. However, each of these sources of support has tradeoffs. Family and friends are often supportive at first, but may become "burned out" in the long term; similarly, the bereaved worry about straining these relationships. Support group members may be a better source for long-term support, but are only available at a set number of weekly meetings. Therapists are similarly difficult to access and can be a costly option. Internet support groups are much more widely available, and can connect people who have suffered a particular kind of loss in ways that local groups cannot; however, it is difficult to ensure that these environments are trustworthy and credible. This array of options demonstrates how time plays an important role in selecting, accessing, and using various forms of support. In our fieldwork, we sought to better clarify this understanding of social support, and at the same time, learn about the "doing" and "being" of bereavement more generally.

Research Settings and Participants

Death is clearly a complex and immense topic, and unfolds in innumerable ways for people across the globe. In our investigation, we focused on bereavement in the secular context of the United States, Canada, and Western Europe. While of course cultural and religious elements are present in this (and any) study of death, we selected this context due to the widespread availability of computing resources and because we, as researchers, identify most strongly with this context. Positioning ourselves in this way allows us to better understand, reflect upon, and present the processes we observed, and permits us to center inquiry around lived experience with technology.

Middle-aged bereaved parents, in particular, were selected at the suggestion of a professional psychologist involved with several community groups in Ontario, Canada. We also chose to work with bereaved parents for two additional reasons: first, losing a child is so traumatic that parents are highly motivated to seek out support, and second, they represent a group familiar with technology and are therefore able to reflect on their own computing experiences.

Three focus groups took place at two different non-profit, secular community organizations: the COPING Centre in Cambridge, Ontario, and the Toronto branch of the province-wide organization called the Bereaved Families of Ontario. These focus groups involved a total of 24 bereaved parents who had completed a support group at one of these two organizations in the past 5 years[1]. Staff members from these organizations co-facilitated each focus group. These community organizations are of a peer-to-peer volunteer format; the group format does not involve a psychologist, therapist, social worker, or other type of professional.

To complement this first-person perspective with the perspective of bereavement experts, we participated in a 5-day bi-annual professional retreat in Germany organized by the International Working Group on Death, Dying, and Bereavement. Informal interviews were conducted with prominent international researchers and practitioners working in psychology, psychiatry, palliative/hospice medicine, nursing, sociology, social work, religion, the arts, family counseling, funeral services, and so on. These were accompanied by opportunistic observational field work in cemeteries in the United States and Germany, funeral homes in Canada and Germany, and a Buddhist shrine in Canada.

Throughout the design process, we kept notes about our experiences engaging with the bereaved, visiting field sites, and talking with professionals in the death, dying, and bereavement community. In our conceptual design, we draw upon many aspects of the process described by Wright and McCarthy where we draw upon shared narratives, dialogues with bereaved others, and our own human experiences [41]. Based on our notes, discussions, and lived experiences as designers, we present a set of considerations for working with the bereaved.

DESIGN CONSIDERATIONS

The considerations are grouped into three themes: *interpersonal communication, a new way of being,* and *materiality.* We find these themes house many of the design-oriented findings we uncovered from our fieldwork and research, and give purchase to a larger set of considerations that may fall within these spaces.

Interpersonal Communication

When a person dies, the surviving family members find themselves in a unique social situation both privately and publicly. If we examine the family unit's internal affairs, the death leaves a gap in the family structure. This gap results in a number of changes. Family members can find themselves in a new role (*e.g.*, a sibling becoming an "only child"). It has also been shown that family members frequently have different grieving styles: children, for example, often grieve through play. Men and women grieve differently, with men frequently demonstrating an instrumental style of grief which is focused on "doing," and women adopting an intuitive style which is more focused on "being." These variations in grieving styles may push family members apart; furthermore, bereaved family members may place anger or blame on other members. Studies show that the strain on marriage increases following the death of a child [31].

Concurrent with this private social restructuring within the family, the family is placed into a very *public* position. Friends, relatives, co-workers, and other people who knew the deceased will appear "out of the woodwork" to console this family and pay their respects. Considerable interpersonal interaction is required to maintain good relationships with condolers (such as returning phone calls, writing thank-you letters, or receiving guests into the home). These relationships can also become strained due to a gulf of misunderstanding surrounding the loss. For example, a boss might expect her employee to return to work within a particular period of time, even if the employee feels that they need more time to grieve. In addition, the bereaved family must work with hospitals, coroner's offices, funeral homes, cemeteries, lawyers, and other public institutions in order to properly handle the body and make arrangements for a memorial service.

As we can see, the social circumstances facing a bereaved person can be very busy and potentially overwhelming. When designing technologies for the bereaved, an appreciation of the messiness and scale of interpersonal relationships can help ensure that systems are designed appropriately. We describe here two considerations which designers should be aware of when designing systems for the bereaved, and in particular, communication systems.

Circles of Sympathy: Managing Communication Availability

In our fieldwork and research, we have found that bereaved parents frequently constricted their communicational availability and frequency. This might seem strange; in their emotionally devastated state, we often think that these vulnerable people may need substantial help and sympathy. While our participants and research demonstrates that bereaved parents appreciate the sentiment behind gestures of sympathy or compassion, the reality of receiving social support often plays out differently – it is far more nuanced. Bereaved parents described adapting their technology use and daily behavior to more tightly control *who* can contact them and *when* they are receptive to communication.

[1] Quotes in this paper are attributed to particular focus group sessions as FG1, FG2, or FG3.

One way to map out the social networks of bereaved people is as a set of concentric circles, with inner circles designating higher levels of openness and trust with respect to the loss (similar to the notion of communicational "clans" by Moncur [27]). For the bereaved parents at the grief support centers we observed, the highest levels of trust and support came not from siblings, children, or close friends – but from other people who had experienced a similar kind of loss.

Participants felt that others who had suffered a similar loss were less judgmental, and that they could be more open in their communication. For example, participants described being able to share moments of laughter with the other parents in their support group – an act that often surprises or offends outsiders who presume the bereaved to be constantly devastated. The shared experience of losing a child gave these parents more credibility in the eyes of other bereaved parents – they described being more likely to listen to their suggestions on helpful books, community resources, events to attend, and so on.

"At [this organization], it's nice to be with people that have lost a baby." – FG 1

While the support group setting permitted an opportunity to communicate unguardedly and openly, it only occurred for 2 hours each week, and over a period of 10-12 weeks. The majority of the bereaved parents' time was spent managing their contact with family and friends – a much more delicate act. Talking to these "outsiders" was difficult in part because it made parents feel responsible for alleviating the outsider's discomfort surrounding the topic.

"People want to find a way to talk to you and let you know they're thinking about you, but in a way that's not going to make them feel too uncomfortable." – FG 1

As a result, the bereaved parent may find themselves in a position where they are consoling the consoler, rather than the other way around. This added to the emotional stress associated with communicating with outsiders. Bereaved parents also described how conversation with outsiders was generally unhelpful – one study found that 80% of statements meant to support the bereaved are ultimately "unhelpful" [10]. Statements that were considered helpful tended to be open-ended and empathetic (*e.g.*, "Let's spend time together." or "Tell me how you're feeling."), rather than closed-form or observations of the situation (*e.g.*, "Time makes it easier." or "She led a full life."). The bereaved parents were well aware of how uncomfortable well-wishing condolers felt, but were unable to help them.

"Face-to-face was terrifying to people because... What do you say to someone?" – FG 1

Vale-Taylor, in her studies of families coping with a death, also noted the difficulties that the bereaved have with communicating with the outside world: "most interviewees said that they often sought to 'manufacture' reasons to get together with others to give them an opportunity to talk but found that after a while other people were embarrassed by this and they had to try to be careful not to risk losing friends" [36]. This highlights the tension between desiring to communicate, but ultimately being disappointed.

To alleviate this stress, bereaved parents will often purposefully distance themselves from outsiders who have not experienced a loss – one study found that "fathers experienced social isolation but also deliberately isolated themselves from human relationships" [6]. Parents achieved their desired levels of isolation in two ways: physically and technologically. By staying out of the workplace and public eye, parents could find a safe place to grieve.

"We hid out at home a lot, so there wasn't a lot of face to face with many people. Just mainly your spouse." – FG 1

Parents also availed themselves of technological forms of isolation – they described turning off their cell phones and using less personal media for communicating in order to prevent lengthy unwanted conversations.

"I didn't want to make phone calls, I didn't want to have that conversation. So, I'm writing an email telling people that I just lost my kids, and it felt weird at the time." – FG 1

It is also important to mention that levels of availability do change over time. People who are seen as extremely helpful in the short-term may be less available in the long-term. For example, many participants in our focus groups described how they continued to talk to some members of their groups past the end of their formal group sessions, but that their contact tapered off over time. In addition, we often think of bereaved parents needing a great deal of attention soon after the death, and less thereafter. However, as we have described above, parents needed time to grieve immediately following the death, and then – months later – found that the support that was once there was now lacking: the rest of the world had "moved on." Indeed, just as the bereaved parent became open and available, ready to talk about their loss, the rest of the world seemed to have closed off, much to their chagrin.

"You count on the cards, you count on the emails, and you count on people acknowledging your loss. And when it stops happening, it feels really empty. You feel really alone, and incredibly lonely." – FG 1

To sum up this consideration, while we often think of communication from the extended network as being desirable, reflecting on this design process has shown us that it sometimes can be unhelpful and potentially an additional burden. For designers working with the bereaved, an awareness of this shifting, complicated social world can be an asset. Technologies must be designed to accommodate an asymmetry in availabilities and a potential desire for isolation and periods of silence. To this end, we may also benefit from considering that not all kinds of support are treated with equal appreciation – graduated circles of trust and support exist. When communication does occur, it becomes important for systems to transmit sentiment appropriately, while potentially helping outsiders to relate to the vulnerable emotional state of the bereaved.

Storytelling, Narratives, and the Importance of Time

Sharing stories and memories is a key way in which bereaved parents review, share, and attach meaning to the loss they have experienced. Stories allow the bereaved to place structure around the life events of the deceased and relate those events to their own life. The power of stories is so strong that professionals may even involve them: "[in] narrative therapy, the story is treated as the basic unit of experience and serves to guide people in making sense of new experiences" [28]. In this clinical perspective, telling the story of the loved one's life, or the story of one's own loss, is a therapeutic activity of the first form.

Sharing stories with others serves multiple purposes. In the focus groups we conducted at support group centers, the creation and maintenance of a story is a precursor to subsequently sharing this story with supportive others. Being able to "tell the story" was seen as an important milestone in the grieving process. Outwardly, making a story visible to others helps to concretize the loss and affirms it in the public history. It says "my child existed." From this, there comes a sense that by existing in a collective conscious, the child is honoured and the memory "lives on." Over time, the acknowledgement and reaffirmation of the story by others helps to foster emotional closeness and the perception of support for the bereaved. A community of care springs up from the sharing of a story.

"I always think of this as a form of storytelling – group therapy. It's not that we come here as storytellers, but we can really tell the experience of our loss in detail." – FG 2

A second way that stories become powerful for the bereaved is in their ability to make meaning out of coincidence of the world. Like all people, grieving parents created stories not only to tell to others, but to tell to themselves. One mother described how the number 12 influences the way that she privately tries to make sense of her son's death.

"There are many [memory] triggers for us… and they do affect you. For me, the number 12. My son was a hockey player and he wore the number 12. He died on the 12th. So for me, so that number is a big thing. But to come up to you and say 'I saw the number 12 today,' you know, I don't talk about it, but I see it, and it connects with me." – FG 3

Storytelling also helps the bereaved explore potential "what-if" scenarios both concerning the circumstances leading up to the death, and how the deceased would be experienced today if he or she were still living.

"My wife did something wonderful, this is on his birthday, she wrote a book about two pages, about what [our son] would be like if he were still alive, how old, what he would be like as a one year old. And she talked about how he would be interacting with every other member of the family." – FG 1

Finally, storytelling activities such as those described above can be fruitfully supported by both existing and emerging technologies. Bereaved people are known to use Facebook, specialty memorial websites, and other web-based systems to share stories widely [24,40]. Emerging technologies such as ubiquitous computing devices for storytelling could also potentially be useful ways for bereaved people to tell the stories of their loved one's life and their own losses [16].

A New Way of Being

Grieving parents find their lives turned upside down by their loss; Buckle and Fleming's work with bereaved parents describes how "[t]he fracturing of one's assumptive world results in substantial psychological upheaval, and the reluctant recognition that the world is no longer safe, orderly, and fair leaves bereaved parents feeling fearful and vulnerable" [9]. As a result of the profound and enduring grief that parents experience, their daily routines and attitudes are changed forever. In the years that follow the loss, the bereaved parents may struggle to regain a sense of normalcy and routine. Working with bereaved people requires an acknowledgement of the profundity of grief, and the design of technologies for the bereaved must accommodate the ongoing, long-term needs experienced during grief. We present two considerations which speak to this set of needs.

Permanence and Continuity

In Western society, we rely heavily upon medicine for remedying the ills we experience both physically and psychologically. Perhaps in part due to this, many people expect grieving parents to "recover" from the loss at some point, and return to their pre-loss habits, attitudes, and feelings – as if the wound inflicted were a physical cut that would heal and, with time, be "good as new." Both our participants and clinicians reported that this concept of grief is increasingly being usurped by an understanding that grief is a *process* without a clear end [39]. In other words, it is a permanent change in worldview.

Acknowledging this perspective is a helpful way to work with the bereaved. In the focus groups we conducted, bereaved parents praised the format of the peer-support model offered by the community organizations, and the emphasis that the two organizations placed on "not fixing." Instead of trying to focus on improvement in mood or returning to a pre-loss sense of normalcy, these groups offered a time and place for parents to simply share and listen.

"For me it was a lifesaver because I could come here and talk about how I loved that baby. And you are the only people that could understand that. And because I could talk to everyone about how much I loved him, I could be less frustrated with everyone else and less angry at everyone else. And that's just tortured by the way that we don't get it

in our culture about how awful it is to lose a baby because babies aren't supposed to be lost. We just don't talk about that." – FG 2

This, in turn, allowed the parents the opportunity to acknowledge and accept the fact that their lives would never be the same again. One clinical psychologist described that in his practice he often likens the aftermath of losing a child to being like "an alien from Mars." While the bereaved can operate and function, there are many levels on which they feel they can no longer connect to others or their comparatively mundane concerns.

"So I just felt like their lives were... I was trying to act like my life was able to go on like theirs, like their day to day didn't change but mine did, and I couldn't find that connection with them. But here, I did." – FG 2

If grief is part of everyday life for a bereaved parent, then how do the parents accommodate the loss on a daily basis? One of the theories which has gathered support in the bereavement community is that of *continuing bonds* [22]. This perspective argues that instead of "getting over," or compartmentalizing the loss, the bereaved instead renegotiate the relationship they have with the deceased. They may still talk to their loved one, include them in family celebrations and rituals, and otherwise continue their relationship with the deceased. While professionals originally perceived this to be potentially a maladaptive response to grief, this perception is increasingly changing. Both the professionals we encountered and the bereaved we spoke with told us that the continuing bonds model rings true; it meshed well with the professionals' encounters in their practices, and with the lived experience of bereaved people in the focus groups and community centers.

As a designer of systems for the bereaved, it is important to share this same value: that the software being developed does not aim to "fix" or "restore" the person to their pre-loss state. We may too easily fall into the trap of designing systems which espouse a sort of medical-rehabilitative model, wherein the user is expected to "improve" over time. Rather, sensitivity to the permanence of the loss indicates that the bereaved would prefer open-ended systems that do not require consistent attention and are designed to operate for long periods of time.

Expression and Emotion – Finding "Something to Do"

So, if the bereaved are in a state where they are permanently changed in thought and emotion, there must be manifestations of this change to be found in their behaviour as well. Indeed, this is the case, as a growing body of research and accounts from the bereaved demonstrate.

The actions surrounding grief have been the subject of considerable study, and trace back to Freud's *Mourning and Melancholia* [12]. Freud argued that we invest life force – the *libido* – in our relationships with other people; upon death, the goal of grief was to divest and reclaim this energy in a process called *anti-cathexis*. More modern research captures this same notion, observed under more rigorous and verifiable circumstances, within the idea of "grief work" [33]. The "grief work hypothesis" suggests that grief requires, or is facilitated by, the performance of particular physical or mental actions such as crying, building a grave, or praying. These sentiments were echoed by participants in our focus groups:

"Now, I want to do something in memory of him, in honour of him." – FG 1

How might a bereaved person "do something?" What kinds of activities might be interesting for informing design? As noted by Vale-Taylor in her hospice-based study, "remembrance appears to be a journey made up of many small daily rituals, some of which are generic to bereaved people and some of which are highly individualistic" [36]. One way of considering these activities, for purposes of design, is as *group/prescriptive, group/creative,* and *individual/creative*. Note that these labels are simply useful devices for thinking about potential systems designs, and not representative of the entirety of activities a bereaved person might undertake.

Group/prescriptive types of grief activities are those which are shared among a larger social group and come with significant structure intact. The Chinese tradition of burning joss paper in honour of ancestors, for example, allows mourners to engage in a culturally-understood and sanctioned activity, and potentially experience a sense of community connection. Another example is a candlelight vigil, where a group of mourners all perform the same simple activity in solidarity. Religious activites like the Jewish tradition of "sitting shiva" are also similarly prescriptive and group-oriented. The mourner does not need to plan the activity. Instead, the steps and materials are prescribed by engaging in this ritual. The focus is on acknowledging that other people are experiencing the same kinds of feelings, and that there is communal support.

Group/creative grief activities maintain the same collective format, and offer bereaved people the opportunity to come together to recognize and support each other's grief. However, these types of activities involve significant individual creative processes in parallel and unison. One excellent example is the Mothers Against Drunk Driving (MADD) memorial quilt (*e.g.,* [5]) – each bereaved parent creates their own unique square of the quilt, which is then stitched together to form the whole. Other creative activities such as painting, writing, or crafting have been successfully used with children and adults as a therapeutic means of "working through" grief in a group format [33].

Individual/creative activities share the same emphasis on creativity and "working out" grief through self-expression. However, the steps or format of these activities are not handed down from an outside entity. Rather, they are created, maintained, and developed by an individual to serve his or her own needs. One example provided by a participant in our focus groups is a father who, in his grief, tore down the backyard shed and rebuilt it. Another example is a mother who writes extensively in her journal following her loss. In these cases, the activity's audience is unclear or non-existent; rather, the individual creates their own form of comfort from performing these activities.

Of course, it is important to note that not every bereaved person may find these kinds of activities beneficial or desirable. Instrumental grievers, in particular, may be more inclined towards these activities due to their pre-existing orientation towards externalizing and channeling grief into activities [23]. In addition, artists and other creative people may find the creation of a new work to be a fulfilling way to honor and remember the deceased. Figure 1 shows an art installation observed during our fieldwork at a funeral home in Germany. Created from the love letters of his deceased grandparents, the artist created this work as a way to grieve their deaths and symbolize their love for one another.

Examining these different ways of "doing," technology designers can find unique perspectives on how they might design their system. What types of interactive procedures are involved, and who will be able to view or interact with digital artifacts, becomes very important. Interacting with a system can be an opportunity to create and experience grief or other emotions, and in so doing, empower the user to make sense of their experience [17]. For those working in the domestic HCI space, there are rich opportunities: "informal rituals are far more important than the large planned events because the informal rituals occur and serve to sustain people in the context of their daily lives" [36]. Technologies could potentially fulfill a role similar to these rituals, or alter the way that existing home rituals occur.

Materiality

Thus far we have shown how the bereaved face complicated social and psychological worlds of which system designers and researchers should be aware. We now turn to the physical world, and examine more closely how special objects and places – the material "stuff" of life – is drawn into these psychological and social practices.

Heterogeneity, Sediment, and Upkeep

The ways in which bereaved people treasure and keep special possessions are elaborate and complicated. The professional death, dying, and bereavement community did not focus on these kinds of possessions until Volkan's 1972 paper on "linking objects" [38]. He describes encountering in his psychiatric practice a number of grieving individuals who formed troubling relationships with particular objects – perhaps a deceased lover's shirt, a handkerchief, watch, or some other trinket. Keeping these objects is not what troubled Volkan – rather, it was the way in which the griever's identity and relationship with the deceased were "bound up" in the object. If the griever lost or misplaced the linking object, it resulted in considerable anxiety or desperation – comparable to re-experiencing the death.

Figure 1.
"Reisegepäck I" by Ulrike Oerter.

Since then, additional work has examined how the material plays a role in grief and bereavement. Hallam and Hockey provide a sociological account of how objects mediate our relationships with the deceased, with ourselves, and with the living [15]. Recently, Odom et al. described how inheriting possessions functioned as a social act, influencing acts of communication, remembrance, and ritual performance [29].

While the literature demonstrates the importance of materiality in the lives of the bereaved, we would like to draw attention to the mechanics of working with these objects. In our observational fieldwork in cemeteries and funeral homes, we noted three thematic ways in which the bereaved related to their possessions: heterogeneity, sediment, and upkeep. These notions re-emerged during our focus groups with bereaved parents, and provide an orientation towards the building of "things" for the bereaved.

Heterogeneity refers to the wide variety of materials that are meaningful to the bereaved. From gravesites to the home, we saw how the bereaved's choice of meaningful objects was rarely of a singular type of object – for example, only photos or only clothing. Rather, many sizes, shapes, and materials came together in special places in order to scaffold together the memory of the deceased. One example from our focus groups came from a woman whose infant was stillborn; she described how she scrounged together the small amount of materials that testified to his life into a box:

"I guess it just gave me something to do. It's what I have left of my child. Like the items in it, for instance, I have the ultrasounds, I have pictures from the hospital when he was born, and blankets, a hat, cards – I keep all the cards people send me – and I think that's what I have in that box. I keep it in the living room. I just want to feel like he's still ***there****. And I keep fresh flowers near it." – FG 2*

The assemblage of these items was not a singular occurrence; rather, this collection bears traces of *sediment*. New items are added, while others may be removed, over a long period of time. The inclusion and removal of each item in the collection results in a "re-reading" of the other items, as the story of the grief unfolds. An excellent example of this comes from a bereaved father who described the "memory box" placed at his adult child's gravesite.

"At our daughter's grave, my son-in-law has a concrete box. It's for memories. People who come to the grave, friends, or whoever, leave a card or an object or a note...It's a memory box...To see that people who have been there, which of your friends, it's nice." – FG 3

We see here that it is not so much that the items are collected together at a single point in time, but that the items maintain their cohesion over time, and grow. We may also see similar examples in public memorials such as the one dedicated to Princess Diana [32].

However, over time, things wear away. Flowers die, letters and photos become torn, and weeds encroach upon the grave. While we may initially think of this as a problem, or a burden, which impinges upon the beauty of the collection, it in fact plays a key role in the life of the bereaved by allowing for the opportunity for *upkeep*. Maintaining the collection can be an act of love, and a renewed way to signal to oneself and to others that the deceased is remembered. One father described how important this process of upkeep was for him because it brought people together in a shared activity.

"The cemetery where [my son] was buried has a beautification day once a year in the summer, so everyone that's buried there can come, and it's a big get-together thing...everyone gets a butterfly in a box...and you open it up and the sun hits it, and they all fly." – FG 1

As designers of interactive technologies, bearing in mind these material processes can help create meaningful experiences for the bereaved. A system sensitive to these kinds of experience will allow for all types of media and materials to be juxtaposed together, allow for new material to be added over time, and realize that the upkeep and maintenance of the collection can be a treasured activity and not necessarily an unwanted burden worth automating.

Display and Control of Mourning Symbols

We have shown how materials play a role in social and psychological processes that the bereaved encounter – a final consideration is towards designing systems that enable the bereaved to control how much they wish to share, and how much they wish to hide, regarding their loss.

A death frequently results in a number of mourning signs. We may place flowers or wreaths, or invite people into the home for religious observation. A person may wear black for a period of time, based on religious traditions, or be expected to cry and otherwise appear saddened.

However, from talking to participants in focus groups, it became clear that there was an important choice involved in demonstrating mourning. Mourning – the outward expression of grief – is a socially mediated activity [12]. The bereaved may choose to express their grief openly and unreservedly in some situations, but choose to contain and hide those feelings in others.

This need to control the visibility of mourning was reflected in the way that items were worn or used in the home. This arrangement of items was a highly personal choice. One mother thought it was important to keep reminders of her child near her at all times.

"We have photos of him on every floor of the house, and I still sleep with his blanket. And I wear his picture around my neck so I always have him near me." – FG 2

Another participant in the same group chose to keep her mourning more private and hidden.

"The only thing we have to remember her is a petri dish and ultrasound pictures, so I keep that together and hidden away. I can't pull out a petri dish and show people that, but that petri dish means so much to us." – FG 2

Some participants fall somewhere in the middle; yet another mother in this same group described keeping photos and clothing in her living room for guests to see but kept the urn in her bedroom and hidden away from guests. When designing in this space, it is important to bear in mind that the bereaved must have a choice in demonstrating their mourning. There are situations that are made easier by trying to momentarily pass as being emotionally "normal" – for example, during professional dealings or when talking to unfamiliar people. Devices which are designed to be worn, placed in the home, or otherwise "displayed" need to be crafted in a way that allow the bereaved the opportunity to ignore or conceal the mourning symbol.

GUIDELINES

In presenting the considerations above, we have aimed to convey the richness to be found in designing systems with the bereaved in mind. From this account, we distill a set of practical guidelines that can be readily "picked up and used" by designers. Some of these guidelines may also be relevant for end of life situations besides bereavement – for example, systems which support the dying.

1. **Grief is not a problem to be solved.** Losing a loved one is a process, and a permanent change in worldview. Designing systems which seek to "fix" the person's grief as if it were a problematic medical condition – no matter how well-meaning the intention – can be potentially disrespectful and maladaptive.
2. **Communication is complicated**. We may often imagine the bereaved desire constant companionship and must "talk through" their feelings in order to achieve peace. While communication is important, designers must allow the bereaved to choose silence, disconnection, and isolation.
3. **Family and friends are not as helpful as one may think**. Friends and family may not be able to provide helpful support because of the complications of pre-existing relationships, or the inability to relate to the lived experience of the bereaved. When developing technologies that encourage communication during bereavement, consider extra-familial sources of support such as support groups, clergy, or grief counselors.
4. **Support storytelling.** Storytelling is a rich process for the bereaved, and serves many purposes: from recalling a fond memory, to trying to understand why the death occurred. New technologies can allow the bereaved to tell stories in ways they could not before: through photos, videos, or other forms of computer-mediated communication. Further, listening to these stories can be a productive way to imagine new opportunities for technological innovation (*e.g.,* through storyboarding and scenario development).
5. **Relationships don't die.** When a loved one dies, the relationship does not evaporate. Rather, a new asymmetry is introduced which changes the way that the relationship is conducted. Systems should acknowledge the reality of the relationship and the loss. In so doing, they can support the new form of relationship between the deceased and the bereaved.
6. **Make making meaningful.** For some people, taking action can be a powerful way to express grief, create meaning out of the death, and connect with supportive others. By offering users the opportunity to create, personalize, and build a meaningful artifact – be it digital or physical – systems can support bereaved people in a very practical and useful way. Include a range of prescriptive and creative activities, and allow them to be done either alone or in a group.
7. **Allow many things over time.** The bereaved use a wide range of cues – photos, clothing, jewelry, music, places, times of the year – to reflect on their loss. Systems seeking to support the bereaved in creating digital memorials or legacies should be built to accommodate this heterogeneity of materials, times, and places, and allow these reminders to be added slowly over time. Consider allowing users to engage with these cues in different ways (akin to the upkeep needed for a grave) as a continuing way to nurture the relationship.
8. **Control mourning symbols.** The bereaved must manage their outward appearance and control how much indication they give to others about their emotional state. In some situations, the bereaved do not wish to be seen as a person in mourning (*e.g.,* in professional dealings). Further, some mourning symbols are extremely private, while others are meant to be publicly viewed. When designing systems to be used by the bereaved, consider how the system could be easily ignored or omitted from daily interactions.
9. **Life goes on.** While losing a loved one is a tragic and emotional event, we must remember that the bereaved continue living their lives – just in a different form. System designers must remember the bereaved are still friends, relatives, employees, and neighbors; grieving is only one part of their lives.

CONCLUSION

Computing increasingly mediates the way that we approach end of life issues, and particularly the way that the bereaved live, grieve, and communicate. In this paper, we have reflected on our exploratory fieldwork examining the "doing" and "being" of bereavement from a technology design perspective. Our reflection on the design process has shown how many of our problem-solving assumptions about grief are less important to the bereaved than a sensitive orientation towards their needs. We have provided a set of considerations for researchers and designers working with the bereaved, and distilled these into potentially useful guidelines for the design of future systems. This exploration creates a foundation for technologists moving into this space, ultimately helping to create systems for the bereaved that meet their needs with sensitivity and respect.

ACKNOWLEDGMENTS

Thanks to the COPING Centre, Bereaved Families of Ontario, Dr. Stephen Fleming of York University, and the bereaved individuals who graciously shared their time, thoughts, and emotions with us.

REFERENCES

1. MyWonderfulLife. https://www.mywonderfullife.com/.
2. Legacy Locker. http://legacylocker.com/.
3. Entrustet. https://www.entrustet.com/.
4. Forever Missed. http://www.forevermissed.com/.
5. MADD Minnesota - Mothers Against Drunk Driving, http://www.maddmn.org/programs_quilt.html.
6. Aho, A.L., Tarkka, M., Astedt-Kurki, P., and Kaunonen, M. Fathers' Experience of Social Support After the Death of a Child. *American Journal of Men's Health 3*, 2 (2009), 93-103.
7. Bartalos, M.K. *Speaking of Death: America's New Sense of Mortality*. Praeger, 2008.

8. Becker, E. *The Denial of Death*. Simon and Schuster, 1997.
9. Buckle, J.L. and Fleming, S. *Parenting after the Death of a Child: A Practitioner's Guide*. Routledge, 2010.
10. Davidowitz, M. and Myrick, R.D. Responding to the bereaved: An analysis of "helping" statements. *Death Education 8*, 1 (1984), 1.
11. Dimond, J.P., Poole, E.S., and Yardi, S. The effects of life disruptions on home technology routines. *Proc. GROUP 2010*, ACM (2010), 85-88.
12. Freud, S. Mourning and melancholia. *Journal of Nervous and Mental Disease 56*, 5 (1922), 543-545.
13. Friedman, B. and Nathan, L.P. Multi-lifespan information system design: a research initiative for the hci community. *Proc. CHI 2010*, ACM (2010), 2243-2246.
14. Glaser, B.G. and Strauss, A. *Awareness of Dying*. Aldine Transaction, 1965.
15. Hallam, E. and Hockey, J. *Death, Memory and Material Culture*. Berg Publishers, 2001.
16. Helmes, J., Cao, X., Lindley, S.E., and Sellen, A. Developing the story: designing an interactive storytelling application. *Proc. ACM Tabletops and Surfaces*, ACM (2009), 49-52.
17. Höök, K., Ståhl, A., Sundström, P., and Laaksolaahti, J. Interactional empowerment. *Proc. CHI 2008*, ACM (2008), 647-656.
18. Howarth, G. *Death and Dying: A Sociological Introduction*. Polity, 2006.
19. Kaunonen, M., Tarkka, M., Paunonen, M., and Laippala, P. Grief and social support after the death of a spouse. *Journal of Advanced Nursing 30*, 6 (1999), 1304-1311.
20. Kirk, D. and Banks, R. On the design of technology heirlooms. *International Workshop on Social Interaction and Mundane Technologies 2008*, (2008).
21. Kirk, D.S. and Sellen, A. On human remains: Values and practice in the home archiving of cherished objects. *ACM Trans. Comput.-Hum. Interact. 17*, 3 (2010), 1-43.
22. Klass. *Continuing Bonds: New Understandings Of Grief*. Taylor & Francis, 1996.
23. Martin, T.L. and Doka, K.J. *Men Don't Cry - Women Do: Transcending Gender Stereotypes of Grief*. Psychology Press, 2000.
24. Massimi, M. and Baecker, R.M. A death in the family: opportunities for designing technologies for the bereaved. *Proc. CHI 2010*, ACM (2010), 1821-1830.
25. Massimi, M. and Charise, A. Dying, death, and mortality: towards thanatosensitivity in HCI. *Proc. CHI 2009 Extended Abstracts*, ACM (2009), 2459-2468.
26. Massimi, M., Odom, W., Kirk, D., and Banks, R. HCI at the end of life: understanding death, dying, and the digital. *Proc. CHI 2010 Extended Abstracts*, ACM (2010), 4477-4480.
27. Moncur, W. Providing affective information to family and friends based on social networks. *Proc. CHI 2007 Extended Abstracts*, ACM (2007), 2219-2224.
28. Nadeau, J.W. Meaning-Making in Bereaved Families: Assessment, Intervention, and Future Research. In *Handbook of Bereavement Research and Practice: Advances in Theory and Intervention*. American Psychological Association (APA), 2008, 511-530.
29. Odom, W., Harper, R., Sellen, A., Kirk, D., and Banks, R. Passing on & putting to rest: understanding bereavement in the context of interactive technologies. *Proc. CHI 2010*, ACM (2010), 1831-1840.
30. Oliveri, T. Grief groups on the internet. *Bereavement Care 22*, 3 (2003), 39.
31. Schwab, R. A child's death and divorce: Dispelling the myth. *Death Studies 22*, 5 (1998), 445-468.
32. Stone, L.D. and Pennebaker, J.W. Trauma in Real Time: Talking and Avoiding Online Conversations About the Death of Princess Diana. *Basic and Applied Social Psychology 24*, 3 (2002), 173.
33. Stroebe, M.S. Coping with bereavement: A review of the grief work hypothesis. *Omega: Journal of Death and Dying 26*, 1 (1992), 19-42.
34. Sudnow, D. *Passing on: The Social Organization of Dying*. Prentice Hall, 1967.
35. Uriu, D. and Okude, N. ThanatoFenestra: photographic family altar supporting a ritual to pray for the deceased. *Proc. DIS 2010*, ACM (2010), 422-425.
36. Vale-Taylor, P. "We will remember them": a mixed-method study to explore which post-funeral remembrance activities are most significant and important to bereaved people living with loss, and why those particular activities are chosen. *Palliative Medicine*, (2009), 537 -544 vol. 23:
37. Van den Hoven, E., Smeenk, W., Bilsen, H., Zimmerman, R., de Waart, S., and van Turnhout, K. Communicating commemoration. *International Workshop on Social Interaction and Mundane Technologies 2008*, (2008).
38. Volkan, V.D. The Linking Objects of Pathological Mourners. *Arch Gen Psychiatry 27*, 2 (1972), 215-221.
39. Worden, J.W. *Grief Counseling and Grief Therapy: A Handbook for the Mental Health Practitioner*. Springer Publishing Co., Inc., 2008.
40. Wortham, J. As Older Users Join Facebook, Network Grapples With Death. *The New York Times*, 2010. http://www.nytimes.com/2010/07/18/technology/18death.html.
41. Wright, P. and McCarthy, J. Empathy and experience in HCI. *Proc. CHI 2008*, ACM (2008), 637-646.
42. Wyche, S.P., Magnus, C.M., and Grinter, R.E. Broadening Ubicomp's vision: an exploratory study of charismatic pentecostals and technology use in Brazil. *Proc. UBICOMP 2009*, ACM (2009), 145-154.

Touch Input on Curved Surfaces

Anne Roudaut, Henning Pohl, and Patrick Baudisch
Hasso Plattner Institute, Potsdam, Germany
{anne.roudaut, henning.pohl, patrick.baudisch}@hpi.uni-potsdam.de

ABSTRACT
Advances in sensing technology are currently bringing touch input to non-planar surfaces, ranging from spherical touch screens to prototypes the size and shape of a ping-pong ball. To help interface designers create usable interfaces on such devices, we determine how touch surface curvature affects targeting. We present a user study in which participants acquired targets on surfaces of different curvature and at locations of different slope. We find that surface convexity increases pointing accuracy, and in particular reduces the offset between the input point perceived by users and the input point sensed by the device. Concave surfaces, in contrast, are subject to larger error offsets. This is likely caused by how concave surfaces hug the user's finger, thus resulting in a larger contact area. The effect of slope on targeting, in contrast, is unexpected at first sight. Some targets located downhill from the user's perspective are subject to error offsets in the *opposite direction* from all others. This appears to be caused by participants acquiring these targets using a different finger posture that lets them monitor the position of their fingers more effectively.

ACM Classification: H5.2 [Information interfaces and presentation]: User Interfaces: Input Devices and Strategies, Interaction Styles.

Keywords: touch, non-planar, targeting, curved, flexible, pointing, shape of device, industrial design, form factor.

General terms: Human factors.

INTRODUCTION

Recent advances in sensor technology have allowed touch-enabling *non-planar* surfaces. Examples include capacitive sensors in Rekimoto's *Smart Skin* [17] and in Apple's *Magic Mouse*, resistive sensors in the *UnMousePad* [18], and *FTIR*-based sensing in *Mouse 2.0* [24]. We also have started to see non-planar touch screens, such as *Sphere* [3].

For large touch surfaces, such as *Sphere*, surface curvature is comparably small. The smaller the device, however, the stronger the average curvature becomes, as illustrated by Figure 2. The surface of the DI-based *Mouse 2.0* corresponds to a Ø15cm sphere and by sensing touch through an optical fiber bundle, *FlyEye* [29] manages to touch-enable a Ø 4cm ping-pong ball. As sensing technology continues to evolve, it seems plausible that even smaller devices, such as watches or even electronic jewelry, might become touch sensitive in the near future, resulting in touch surfaces of extreme curvature.

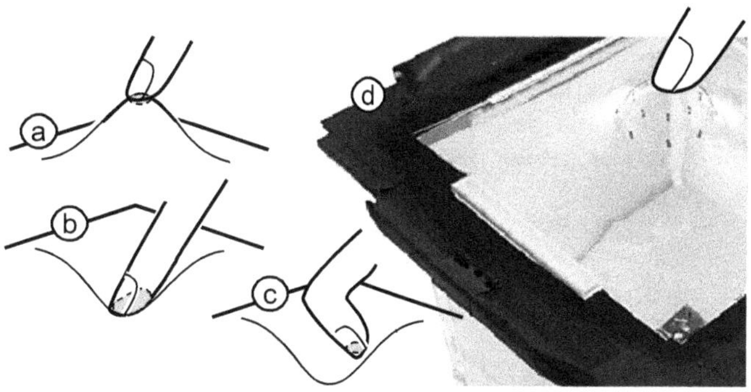

Figure 1: Summary of findings: (a) Surface convexity increases pointing accuracy and (b) concave surfaces are subject to larger error offsets. This is likely caused by how concave surfaces hug the user's finger thus resulting in a larger contact area. (c) When acquiring targets on a downhill slope participants employ a hooked finger gesture, which helps them target more effectively. (d) The FTIR–based prototype we used in our studies.

As researchers and engineers create these future touch devices, the question arises of how to design usable interfaces for them. Unfortunately, there is no empirical data about the human factors of touch on curved surfaces yet.

On *flat* surfaces, touch is comparably well understood. In particular, there is a series of studies investigating the factors responsible for the *inaccuracy* of touch, including the *fat finger problem* [26] and the *(generalized) perceived input point model* [26, 13]. While this paper is only a first step, our ultimate goal is to create similar metric for the usability of object surfaces of arbitrary shape and curvature. Such a metric would allow industrial designers to assess the usability of devices, similar to how the measurement of wind resistance has brought rigor to the design of the shape of cars.

Touch on arbitrary shapes is of very high dimensionality, because device, hands, and the way they can make contact are all of very high degree of freedom. As a first step, we select a tractable, self-contained subset of variables, namely, single touch on spherical shapes, as these already fit existing devices.

We present a user study in which participants acquired targets on surfaces of different curvature and at locations of different slope. We report how surface curvature affects pointing accuracy (preview in Figure 1). We provide minimum button sizes to help interface designers find the best location for their controls on a curved surface. We also report systematic error offsets that allow engineers to increase the accuracy of their devices by compensating for them [13].

RELATED WORK

The work presented in this paper is related to non-planar touch-sensitive objects and to research on touch input.

Non-planar touch devices

Curved touch devices include relative pointing devices, such as the aforementioned *Mouse 2.0* [24], and absolute pointing devices/touch screens, such as *Sphere* [3]. Devices can be touch-enabled using a range of technologies, such as capacitive (e.g., *Smart skin* [17]), resistive *UnMousePad* [18], and optical (e.g., *FTIR* [9, 24]). Many other sensor concepts could be adapted to non-planar surfaces, such as *GelForce*, a device that extracts directional pressure from touch [25].

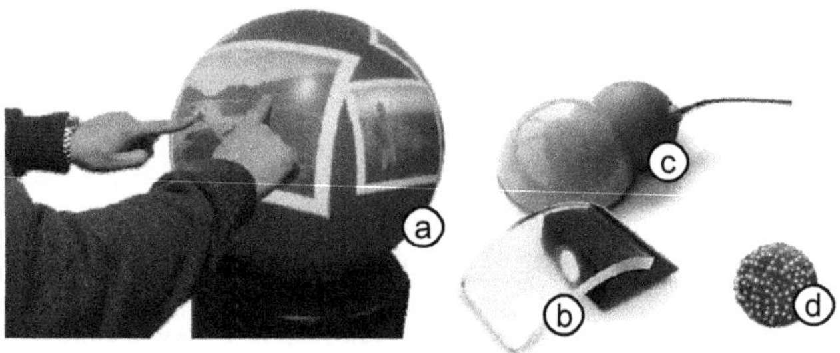

Figure 2: Selection of curved touch devices by decreasing curvature: (a) Microsoft Sphere, (b) FTIR-based and (c) DI-based Mouse 2.0, and (d) FlyEye (not to scale).

In addition to the rigid devices mentioned earlier, curved surfaces also occur as a side effect of *deformable* devices, including *Organic User Interfaces*, such as *Paper Windows* [12]. Objects may either be deformed by users, such as the optically sensed *PhotoelasticTouch* [19], Gummi [20], or even human skin (*Skinput* [11]), or objects may be deformed using a device, such as inflatable buttons [10].

While the majority of non-planar devices are still input-only, we are starting to see the first non-planar or deformable touch screens, to date primarily using projection [12].

Touch is related to (but different from) grasping, which is touch with the support by an opposing thumb. Examples of graspable interfaces include *Bar of Soap* [23] and *FlyEye* [29].

Understanding pointing and touch input

Modeling target acquisition has a long tradition. *Fitts' Law* models targeting time for one-dimensional targets [6]. Grossman and Balakrishnan's *probabilistic pointing* models two-dimensional target acquisition [8].

Touch screens were initially considered inherently inaccurate because of the softness of human fingertips and the occlusion of the target by the finger (*fat finger problem* [26]). Touch screens were, however, adapted to high-precision pointing using localized CD ratio adjustments (*high-precision touch screen* [21]) and extensions that prevent the user's finger from occluding the target (e.g., *offset cursor* [16], *shift* [26]).

While touch systems traditionally reduce contact areas to points [27], more recently researchers have proposed considering the entire contact area as input, such as *Shapetouch* [4] and *Sliding Widgets* [15].

Touch and angles between finger and surface

Several researchers have found systematic effects that cause a touch device to sense touch at an offset from the intended target. The *Shift* technique includes a corrective offset that compensates for differences between target location and the *perceived input point* [26]. Benko et al. noticed that the center of the contact area moves under pressure [2]. Forlines et al. found that touching a target using a flat finger angle leads to an offset input location [7]. Wang and Ren found that finger posture and motion impact the size of the contact area [27]. Holz and Baudisch found that differences in finger roll as well as differences in users' mental models result in additional offsets. They generalized the concept of offsets into the *generalized perceived input point model* [13]. Follow-up work by the same authors [14] explains error offsets as a conceptual mismatch between users and devices: users target by placing a fixed point located on top of their fingernail over the target. Touch devices, in contrast, determine the contact point as the center of the contact area between finger and device.

Measuring touch targeting error as *offset* + *spread*

Because of the presence of systematic offsets, researchers have started to specify touch inaccuracy using *two* variables, i.e., offset and spread [13] (also referred to as constant and variable error [5)). Since we use this metric to report our results, we discuss it in additional detail.

Each targeting interaction produces a *contact point*, generally computed as the center of gravity of all points in the contact area, e.g., the center of an oval fitted to the contact area (Figure 3a). All contact points together can now be summarized using two variables:

Error offset refers to the distance between the centroid of a cluster of contact points and the target, measured in millimeters (Figure 3c). Offsets can be compensated for by applying *corrective* offsets, which is a method for increasing the accuracy of a touch device. Offsets are therefore particularly relevant for device designers.

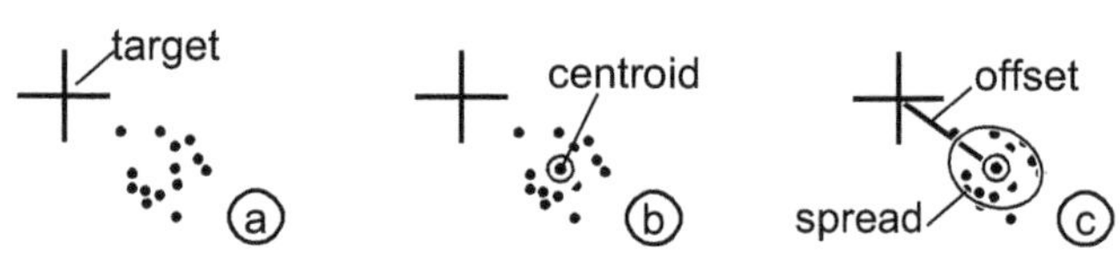

Figure 3: We report targeting error as offset and spread. (a) A series of trials results in contact points. (b) Contact points are aggregated into a centroid. (c) Offset is defines as the distance between the centroid and the target; spread is the size of the smallest button to contain 95% of all contact points.

Error spread is the remaining error after error offsets have been compensated for (Figure 3c). Spread is measured as a *minimum button size*, i.e., the diameter of the smallest circular button in millimeters that still contains 95% of all target acquisitions [13]. Note that this assumed button is centered on the centroid, *not* the target.

The findings in this paper allow us to extend this reasoning about offset and spread to curved surfaces.

GENERALIZING FROM FLAT TO CURVED SURFACES

In this section, we attempt to generalize what we know about touch on flat surfaces to curved surfaces. We use this to derive the hypotheses for our user study.

On flat surfaces, a finger of given posture always makes contact with the surface the same way. When we generalize to curved surfaces, the curvature of the surface affects the shape and size of the contact area. As illustrated by Figure 4, convex surfaces curve away from the finger, resulting in a smaller contact area. Concave surfaces, in contrast, hug the finger, which leads to a larger contact area.

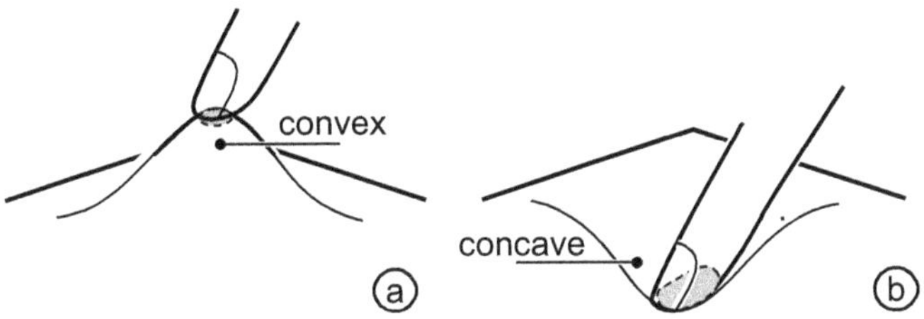

Figure 4: The contact area between finger and device (a) increases for concave and (b) decreased for convex surfaces.

In addition, the individual patches of a curved surface have different slopes, which causes the finger to make contact with the surface at different angles.

Our initial hypothesis was that users would maintain a constant finger posture, as shown in Figure 5a. For downhill slopes (from the user's perspective) this would have caused their fingers to form a flatter angle with the surface, yielding a larger contact area between finger and surface, and thus would have potentially caused larger offsets.

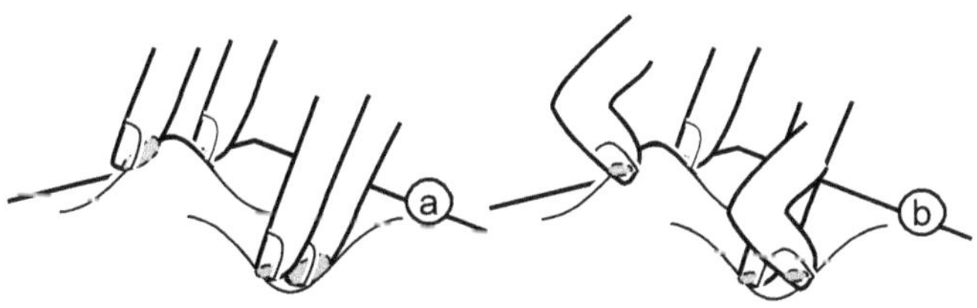

Figure 5: (a) Our initial hypothesis was that users would acquire all targets sing the same finger posture. (b) Piloting, however, revealed that most participants target downhill slopes using a hooked finger.

During piloting, however, we found that the finger contact area was *largely unchanged* across downhill and uphill facing slopes. Closer inspection revealed that our assumption about the finger posture was wrong. Instead, participants had targeted on downhill slopes with a hooked finger, as illustrated by Figure 5b. This posture allowed participants to hit the target surface at a roughly *constant angle*, which helped them *minimize the contact area* between their finger and the touch surface.

Hypotheses

Given that larger contact areas correlated with larger offsets on flat surfaces [13], we hypothesized that the same holds for curved surfaces. Because of the finger hugging property of concave surfaces we hypothesize

H1: Concavity increases offsets, convexity reduces it

For the same reasons we hypothesized

H2. Concavity increases *spread*, convexity reduces it

The observed variations in finger postures prevented us from formulating a clear hypothesis on surface slope—since flat surfaces offer nothing to reach around, hook-shaped finger postures had not been studied here. Which posture would lead to better targeting was hard to predict. Consequently, rather than formulating a hypothesis we decided to

Q1: Explore effect of uphill/downhill slope on offset

Q2: Explore effect of uphill/downhill slope on *spread*

CURVE TOUCH: STUDY PROTOTYPE BASED ON FTIR

To be able to analyze the impact of the factors discussed above, we needed a device that could observe the exact contact area between the finger and the touch surface in high resolution. Since diffuse illumination (e.g., [10]) delivers only vague contour data, and capacitive sensing (such as *Smart Skin* [17]) is hard to manufacture for high and non-interpolated resolution, we opted for a custom design based on FTIR [9], technology previously used, for example, in *Mouse 2.0* [24]. FTIR offers high resolution, a comparably crisp contact area outline, as well as reliable recognition of contact. On the flipside, FTIR starts bleeding out light with increasing curvature, which required us to make a series of modifications.

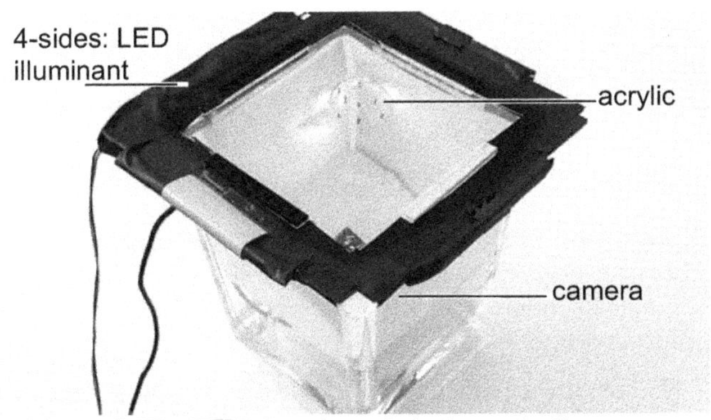

Figure 6: The FTIR-based touch device we built to sense touch on curved surfaces (*curve touch*).

Figure 6 shows our prototype device which we call *curve touch*. The basic FTIR design consists of the three familiar elements: (1) an acrylic touch surface, (2) a set of 8 bright white LEDs on each of four sides that inject light into the acrylic and (3) a high-definition web camera that observes the touch surface from below. As for all FTIR devices, a finger touching the surface causes the LED light to escape at the contact area, which is observed by the camera. We used a MS Lifecam (720p HD sensor, 30 fps). We processed the resulting image using OpenCV/Emgu.Cv.

Creating exact curvatures by stamping

To obtain exact surface curvatures, we deformed the acrylic using a series of stamps, as illustrated by Figure 7. We heated the acrylic locally using a heat gun (Figure 7a). Once malleable, we stamped shapes of the desired curvature into the acrylic (Figure 7b). Resting the acrylic on a larger ring allowed us to create the hemispherical target surface as well as a smoother transition to its periphery, which helped reduce light leakage (see next section). We obtained best results using 3mm acrylic sheets, which are thin enough to allow for easy deformation, yet still thick enough to allow for the injection of light.

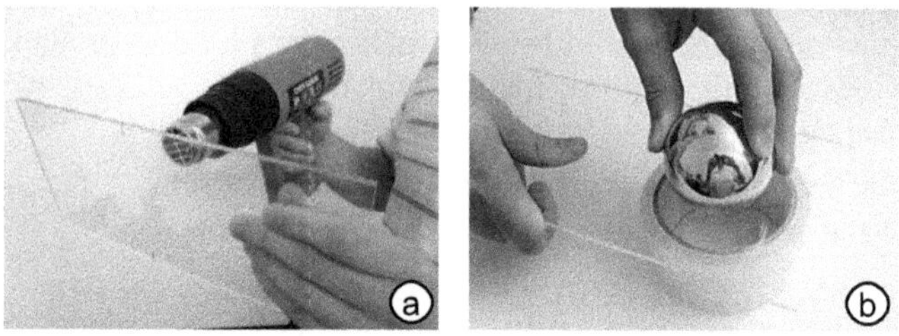

Figure 7: We created curved touch surfaces by (a) heating up the acrylic touch surface using a heat gun and (b) stamping curved objects (e.g. a silver sphere) into it.

Figure 8 shows six of the stamps we have experimented with. The four sizes we used in our user studies are highlighted in bold face.

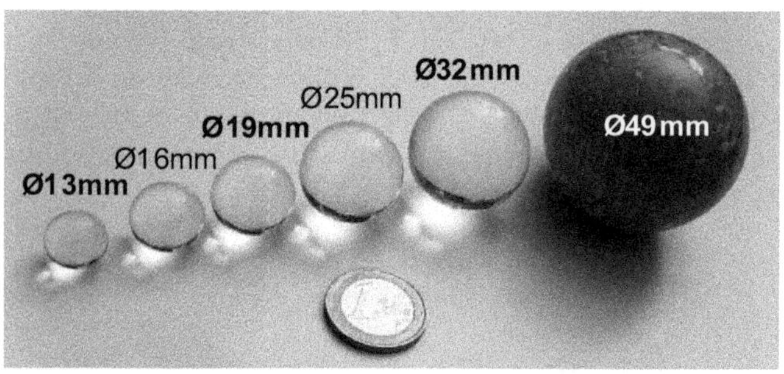

Figure 8: The stamps we used to make curved surfaces.

Design modifications for the curved touch surface

The necessity of distinguishing the light resulting from touch from other light sources required us to make some modifications:

1. No compliant surface: FTIR is most commonly used with a *compliant surface* layer to increase the frustration of light on contact. Unfortunately, the strong curvature of some of the shapes we used made it difficult to obtain accurately fitting compliant surfaces. We consequently dropped the compliant surface from our design. Instead, we used silicone spray to increase frustration when necessary.

2. Light leakage: Light leakage is inherent to all waveguides and only depends on curvature. It was not an issue at the actual bulge because the remaining light was strong enough and because we eliminated brightness differences by thresholding. At the *edge* of the bulge, it manifested as hotspots in the camera image (Figure 9b), because light was reflected off the opposite side of the bulge and into the camera as illustrated by Figure 9a. Smoothing the transition between bulge and periphery reduced the problem far enough that we could suppress it using thresholding.

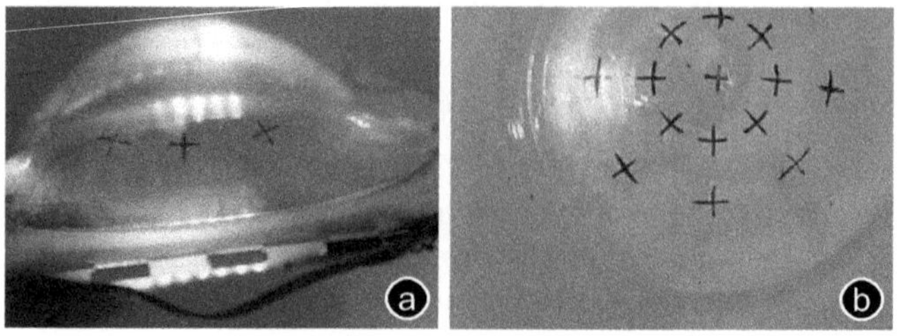

Figure 9: (a) Light injected from behind this bulge leaks at the transition from flat surface to bulge. (b) The same scene as seen by the built-in camera. The light injected from the right is reflected off the bulge and shows up as a hotspot on the left.

Exchangeable touch surfaces

To support multiple curvatures, we created different top units, each of which consisted of a differently deformed acrylic sheet with illumination (Figure 10). Snap connectors made from Lego bricks assured precise positioning of the top unit yet allowed replacing top units quickly. We also added a flat top unit to obtain a total of nine surfaces: a flat unit plus four curved units that could be flipped to serve as convex or concave shapes.

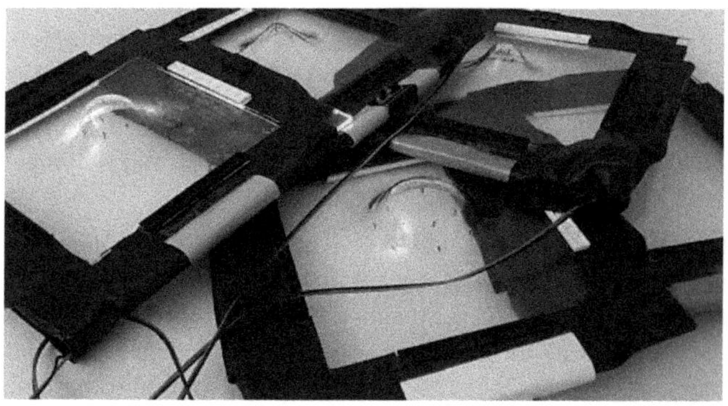

Figure 10: We implement different curvatures by using replaceable top units.

Compensating for optical distortion

The small fixed-focus lens offers a high depth of field, thus a clear image for all shapes. However, perspective effects make the curvature of the touch surfaces appear distorted. In particular, surface patches on convex bulges appear larger, because they are located further away from the camera; in addition, tilted surface patches appear deformed, because of foreshortening. A universally applicable correction for this distortion would require switching to a 3D representation of the surface.

Since we were only concerned with the relative position of contact points with respect to the target, however, we treated the respective patch of surface as if it were flat, which allowed us to scale with a simple linear transformation. We first restored the apparent size of the respective patch by scaling it proportional to its distance to the camera lens. We then stretched points by scaling them with the corresponding patch ratio.

USER STUDY: IMPACT OF CURVATURE ON ACCURACY

In this study, we investigated the impact of target curvature on touch accuracy. Participants acquired targets on the *curve touch*. Using different top units, we varied *curvature* in nine levels from convex to flat to concave. By using multiple targets placed across the curved surface we also varied *slope*. Our goal was to test the hypotheses discussed earlier, i.e., to determine how curvature and slope impact offsets and spread.

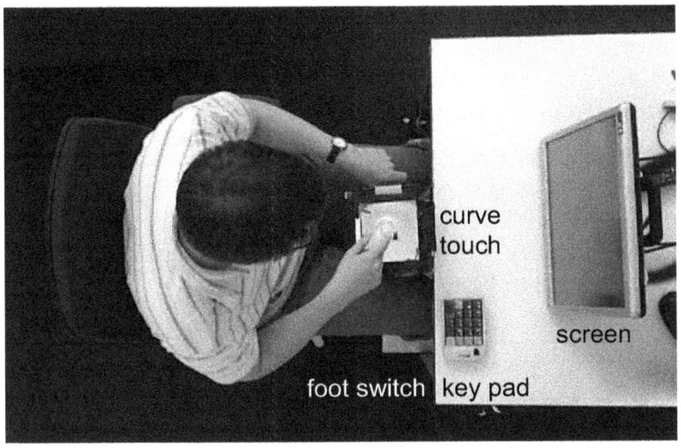

Figure 11: Apparatus: participant acquiring a target on the curve touch, here with a convex top unit.

Interface

Figure 11 shows the apparatus, consisting of the *curve touch* device, a screen presenting instructions, a numeric keypad for starting trials, and a foot switch for committing trials. To compensate for the depth of the curve touch device, it was mounted on a tripod, bringing its touch surface to the same height as the table. The screen was located 50cm behind the curve touch and the keypad 30cm behind and right of it. The *curve touch* device, screen, keypad, and foot switch were driven by a PC running Windows Vista.

Task

For each trial, participants were presented with a diagram illustrating the target to acquire (Figure 12a). Participants then pressed the enter key that was highlighted using red tape on the numeric keypad (Figure 12b) with their right hands and committed by pressing the foot switch (Figure 12c). We assured that all participants were seated so as to reach the device at a 45° angle as shown in Figure 11.

Participants then acquired the target on the curved surface with the same (right) hand (Figure 12d) and again committed by pressing the footswitch (Figure 12e). This completed the trial and played a sound.

When participants activated the footswitch twice, i.e. before a touch, the system discarded the input and played a sound. Participants then had to repeat the trial. Errors were rare in the study (< 10/participant).

As common in this type of study [13], participants did *not* receive feedback about the touch location registered by the device. This ensured that the participants acquired the target based on their own mental model of touch, rather than being trained by the device during the study.

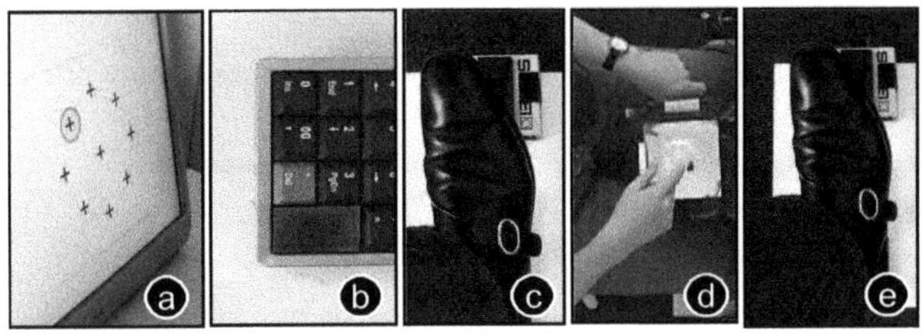

Figure 12: (a) The screen showed which target to acquire. (b) Participants pressed the start button and (c) committed using the footswitch. (d) Then they acquired the target with the same hand and (e) again committed using the footswitch.

We took the following three measures to minimize the impact of other potential factors. First, participants kept their heads in a fixed position above the touchpad, as shown in Figure 11, which controlled for parallax. Second, the use of a footswitch allowed us to avoid artifacts common with other commit methods, such as inadvertent motion during take-off. The unified button and target acquisition using the footswitch helped reduce participants' cognitive load. Finally, participants were told to focus on accuracy not on speed; consequently, we did not record task completion time.

Independent Variables: Curvature and Slope

Curvatures were implemented using the five top units (see in Figure 10). We varied slope by using targets at different locations on the curved surface. 8 targets were organized in a ring located at 45° zenith angle for each curved surface; in addition there was a single target at the apex.

To prevent participants from (unintentionally) biasing their targeting towards open space we added a second ring of unused/fake crosses further outside. In addition, participants were told that there was no penalty for getting close to other targets during targeting. Note that there was no reason to include real distracter targets though. Distracters have a major effect on *adaptive* input techniques, such as magnetic targets (e.g., [1]), but not on unmodified touch.

Experimental design

The study used a 9×9 within-participant design, with independent variables curvature (convex or concave Ø13mm, Ø19mm, Ø32mm and flat) and slopes (i.e. 8 targets in a ring at 45° zenith plus apex). Participants performed 6 trials for each curvature.

Curvature was counterbalanced within participants using a partial Latin Square design. The order of targets was randomized. Each participant completed all conditions: 9 curvatures × 9 target orientations × 6 trials = 486 trials per participant.

Participants performed 5 minutes of training before the experiment. They were allowed to take breaks every 54 selections. They completed the study in 45 minutes or less.

Participants

We recruited 12 right-handed participants (2 female) from our institution. They were between 20 and 32 years old. They received a small compensation for their time, and we awarded €20 to the most accurate participant.

Hypotheses

Our goal was to investigate our 4 hypotheses and questions:

H1: Concavity increases offsets, convexity reduces it

H2. Concavity increases *spread*, convexity reduces it

Q1: Explore effect of uphill/downhill slope on offset

Q2: Explore effect of uphill downhill slope on *spread*

In addition, we wanted to verify that this basic observation for flat surfaces continues to hold true on curved surfaces:

H0: Offsets are oriented along the user's finger

Results

Figure 13 shows the resulting raw data, i.e., all contact points by all participants as recorded during the study.

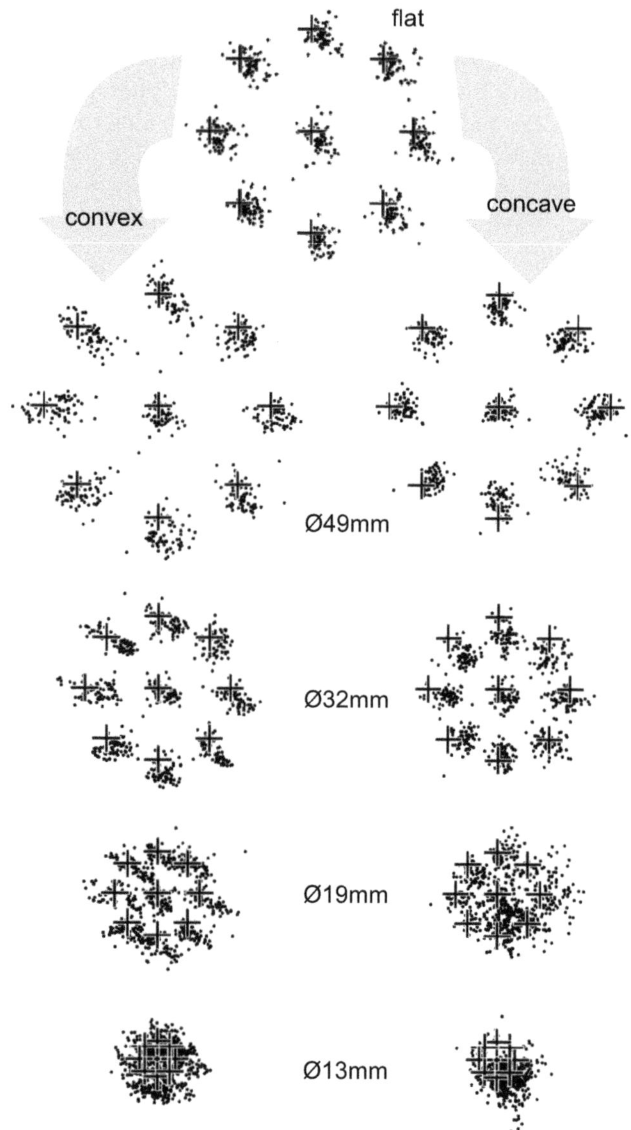

Figure 13: Raw data: all touch locations of all participants by curvature and target orientation/target.

H0: Offsets are oriented along the user's finger

All contact points of all targets combined showed an offset of 1.9mm. Its direction matched the direction of participant's fingers closely, i.e., it was off by only 5.1° clockwise from the 45° participant finger angle. This suggests that offsets are most likely the result of finger direction, rather than, say, head position, which should have produced a north/south oriented offset. This observation matches finger direction offsets previously observed on flat surfaces [13] and supports our hypothesis H0.

The overall effect shows reasonably clearly in Figure 13, where most contact point clusters are offset to the bottom right with respect to their target. An exception is the concave Ø49mm shape. Unlike any of the other curvatures, it showed virtually no global offset, but target-specific offsets towards the center. We discuss this effect in more detail below, and investigated it in a brief follow-up study, also presented in this paper.

H1: Concavity increases offsets, convexity reduces it

A one way ANOVA found a main effect of curvature on offset ($F_{8,88}$=5.24, p<.0001). Post-hoc comparison tests (using a Tukey's HSD test) indicated the significant differences shown in Figure 14a.

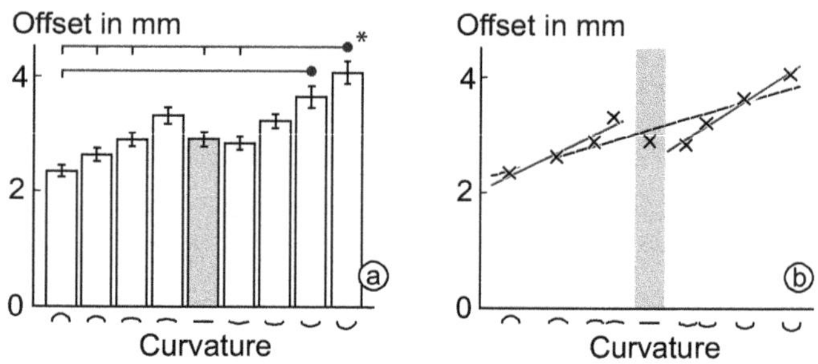

Figure 14: (a) Error offset by surface curvature (+/- 95% confidence, * significantly different) (b) Linear regression. The x-axis is curvature measured as 1/radius.

To understand this relationship better we performed linear regressions (Figure 14b). A single linear regression explains a significant portion of offset (r^2= .7768, $F_{1,7}$=24.36, p<.001) for the length of the projection vector: L = -.45 × curvature+ 3.1. Performing regression separately for convex and concave obtains a better fit: for convex (r^2= .9187, $F_{1,2}$=22.61, p<.04, L = -.76×curvature + 3.5) and for concave (r^2= .9752, $F_{1,2}$=78.77, p<.01, L = - curvature + 2.53).

These results support our hypothesis H1, i.e., error offsets indeed decreased with convexity and increased with concavity, as suggested by their differences in contact area (Figure 4). These findings integrate nicely with the related work on flat surfaces [13], while generalizing from flat to curved surfaces.

H2: Concavity increases spread, convexity reduces it

Figure 15 illustrates *spread* across curvatures. Note that we computed spread on a per-user basis. Intuitively, this means that each bar indicates how closely the contact points of a single user are collocated for a target on the respective curvature. For a device to exploit this it needs to employ a per-user calibration, as suggested by [13].

A two way ANOVA found a main effect of curvature on spread ($F_{8,88}$=7.62, p<.0001). Post-hoc multiple means comparison tests found the significant differences shown in Figure 15.

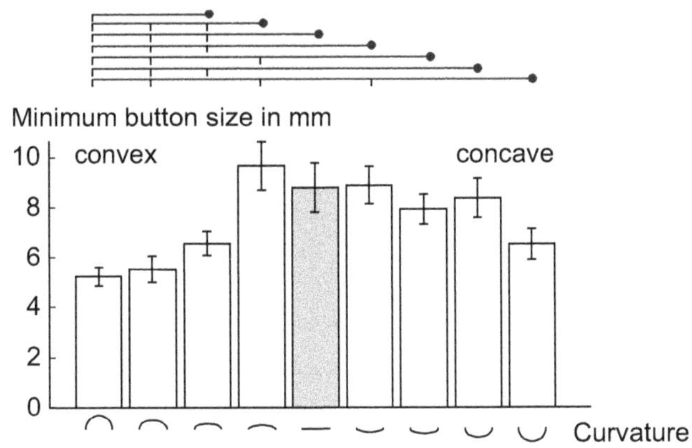

Figure 15: Spread in minimum button size by curvature (+/- 95% confidence).

The left half of Figure 15, i.e., the one depicting accuracy on convex shapes, is in general support of our hypothesis H2: spread indeed decreased with increasing convexity. The concave shapes, in contrast, came out unexpectedly. Rather than spread increasing further with concavity, spread eventually even *de*creased.

Figure 16 suggests one possible explanation for this effect. First, a tight cavity confines the finger, which provides users with tactile feedback that can help adjust the position of their finger. Second, the stronger the curvature, the shorter the part of the bowl that is actually concave. The space around the bowl has to be *convex* in order to connect the concave bowl to the rest of the surface. For very strong curvatures, users' fingers fill out the concave part, so that variations in finger posture lead to changes in the contact area on the convex part, where it leads to smaller changes in contact area, thus reduced spread.

This effect is inherent to the nature of curved surfaces: unlike flat surfaces, curved surfaces are finite and the stronger the curvature, the smaller the surface. This holds for concave, as well as convex, as illustrated also by the FlyEye shown in Figure 2.

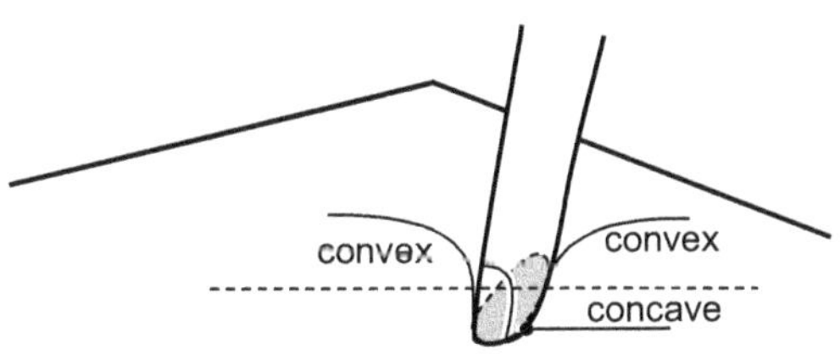

Figure 16: Strongly concave surfaces lead to lower spread. One possible explanation is that they provide tactile guidance. Another one is that they are framed by convex areas, where posture variations cause little variation in contact area.

Q1: Effect of uphill/downhill slope on offset

As illustrated by Figure 19, participants acquired different targets using different finger postures. For targets located on downhill slopes, participants were more likely to employ a hooked finger posture, while they were more likely to use a straight finger to acquire targets located on uphill slopes. When analyzing slope, we grouped target locations that resulted in similar finger postures, as shown in Figure 17.

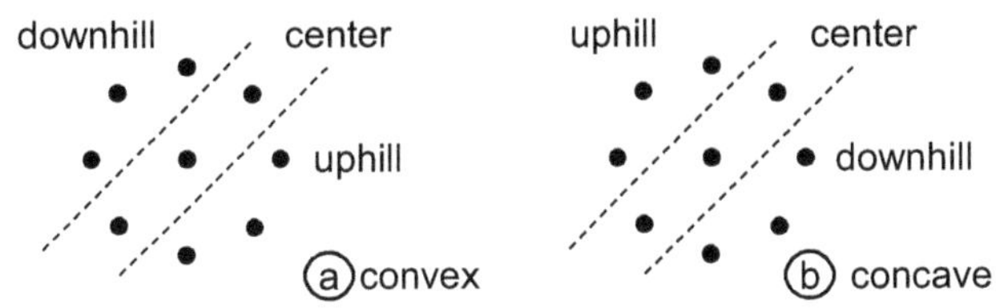

Figure 17: Targets were grouped by slope

A two way ANOVA found a main effect of curvature ($F_{8,88}$=5.25, p<.0001), slope ($F_{2,22}$=10.60, p<.001) and the interaction curvature×slope ($F_{16,176}$=7.02, p<.0001) on offset. Figure 18 shows pair wise differences.

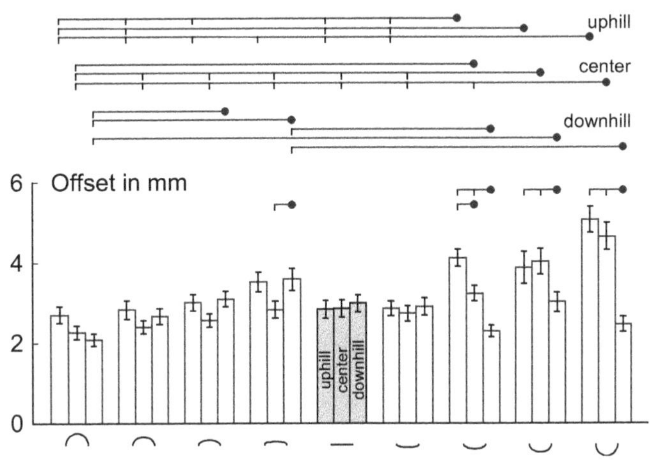

Figure 18: Error offset by curvature and slope: uphill, center, downhill (+/- 95% confidence)

Post-hoc multiple means comparison tests (using a Tukey's HSD test) found that the offsets of downhill slopes were generally smaller than the offsets of center slopes, which in turn were smaller than the offsets of uphill slopes. As apparent also in Figure 18, however, this effect was entirely caused by the concave surfaces.

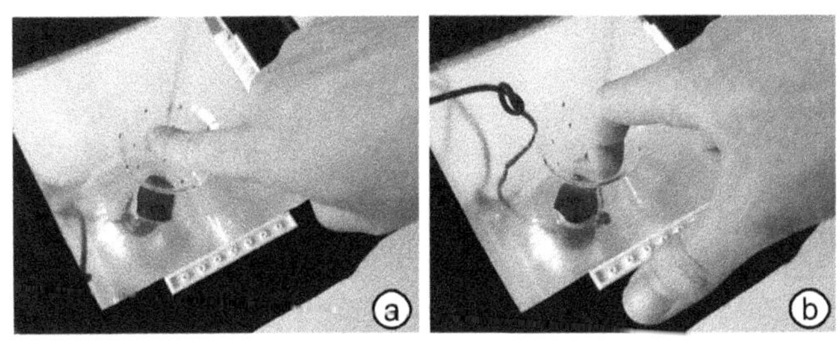

Figure 19: (a) When targeting with a straight finger, the soft bottom side of the user's finger is occluded. (b) Users can see it when targeting with a hooked finger.

One possible explanation for the smaller offsets on downhill slopes is differences in finger posture, i.e., that a hooked finger leads to smaller offsets than a straight finger. On flat surfaces, touch inaccuracy has been attributed to users' inability to monitor the soft fleshy bottom of the finger [26, 14]. As illustrated by Figure 19, users pointing using a hooked finger *can* see that bottom side. The now invisible side, i.e., the fingernail, is less malleable and thus suffers from the fat finger problem to a much lesser extent.

Q2: Effect of uphill downhill slope on spread

A two-way ANOVA found no significant effects of slope on spread.

Summary

In summary, by adding curvature as a factor, we have generalized the concept of *error offsets* from flat surfaces [13] to curved surfaces. We found that error offsets depend on curvature (H1) and slope (Q1). Both factors influence error offset, but there is an interaction and most of the error offset of concave targets comes from the uphill slope, where users are forced to target using a straight finger.

The effects of curvature on spread, in contrast, are moderate. There appears to be an effect for convex targets. For concave targets in contrast, multiple confounding factors compensate for each other.

FOLLOW-UP STUDY ON CONCAVE

As discussed earlier, we speculated that the smallness of the error offsets of the concave targets was caused by participants targeting using a hooked finger. To verify this assumption, we conducted an informal follow-up study with a small number of additional participants. Participants again repeatedly acquired crosshair targets of different orientations. Our main hypothesis was that the lack of offsets on concave surfaces was an artifact of participants employing different finger postures. To investigate this, we varied finger posture this time.

Interface & Apparatus & Task

We used the same *curve touch* device, screen, button, and footswitch setup as in the main user study (Figure 11). We limited the study to the Ø49mm concave surface, which had displayed the pattern most clearly. Participants performed the same task as before.

To obtain additional data for the slope variable, we broke the single target ring at 45° zenith angle from the previous study down into an *inner* ring at 30° and an *outer* ring at 60° zenith angle for an overall 8 outer + 8 inner + 1 apex = 17 targets.

Additional independent variable: Finger posture

(1) In the *fingertip* condition, participants were instructed to acquire all targets using their fingertip. This caused them to acquire targets using a straight finger for the uphill targets and to hook their finger for the downhill targets. (2) In the *flat finger* condition, they acquired all targets as with a flat finger. This forced them to use a straight finger also for downhill targets. (3) In the *free* condition participants acquired each target as they chose to—which corresponded to the first study. In order not to influence participants in the free condition, we ran the free condition first. We then counterbalanced the following *fingertip* and *flat finger* conditions.

Experimental design

The study used a 3×17 within-participant design, with independent variables finger posture (*fingertip*, *flat finger*, *free*) and slope (17 targets organized in two rings plus apex). Participants performed six trials for each finger posture and slope. The order of target orientations was randomized. Each participant completed all conditions, i.e., 3 finger postures × 17 target orientations × 6 trials = 306 trials per participant.

Participants performed 5 minutes of training before the experiment. They were allowed to take breaks every 34 selections. They all completed the study in 30 minutes or less.

Participants

We recruited 6 new right-handed participants (2 female) from our institution. They were between 24 and 30 years old. They again received a small compensation for their time and we awarded €20 to the most accurate participant.

Hypotheses

Our main hypothesis was that the unexpected lack of a *finger direction offset* of the Ø49mm surface would only happen in the free and fingertip conditions, but that the flat finger condition would still be subject to the offset.

H0: Offsets are oriented along the user's finger

Results

Figure 20 and Figure 21 show the raw data, i.e., all contact points obtained during the study by fingertip, flat finger, and free conditions.

As in the main study, the overall error offset of the free condition pointed towards the center rather than in the direction of the finger (the component of the error offset across all targets/slopes pointing in the direction of the finger measured only 0.8mm). This held across all targets including the additional ring of outer targets. For the fingertip condition the finger direction offset was equally small (0.9mm). In the flat finger condition, however, we did see a major offset in the direction of the finger (2.4mm).

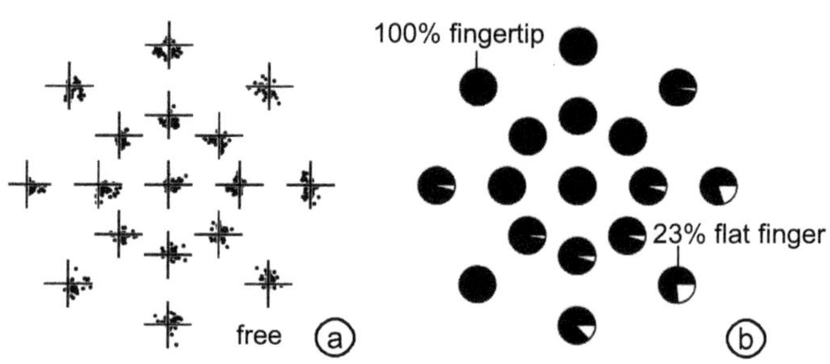

Figure 20: (a) Contact points in the free condition and (b) how much the free condition resembled the fingertip condition.

We reconstructed participants' finger posture in the *free* condition by comparing the contact area sizes for each touch with the *fingertip* and *flat finger* conditions. Figure 20b illustrates that participants effectively targeted with the fingertip throughout; a slight tendency towards using a flat finger in the bottom right was weak enough that it had little effect on the error offsets.

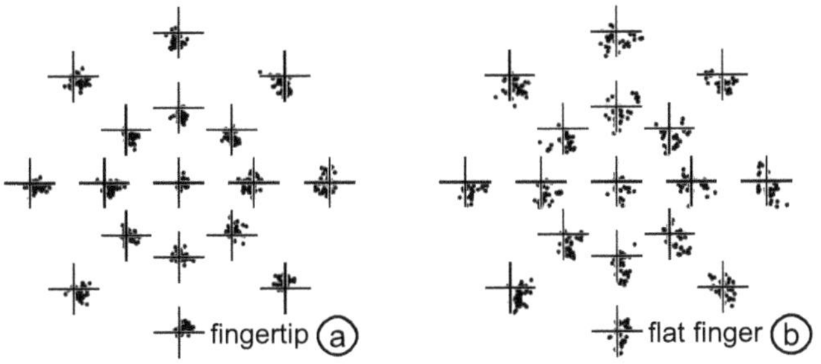

Figure 21: Contact points of (a) the fingertip and (b) the flat finger conditions.

Discussion

The results of this informal study indicate that the error offsets in the concave condition of the main study are indeed an artifact of finger posture. By switching between a straight and hooked finger, participants always targeted using the finger tip, thereby targeting more accurately in the sense that offsets were reduced.

What remains is the question why the more strongly curved concave conditions seemed to benefit less from the hooked finger posture (see also Figure 13). Figure 22 attempts to explain this by illustrating an effect we observed during piloting For strongly concave surfaces, a hooked finger posture introduces additional targeting errors when it accidentally touches the opposite side of the bowl (Figure 22a). Most pilot users avoided the issue by switching back to a straight finger posture. This avoids the accidental touches, at the expense of reintroducing the increased offset error of the straight finger.

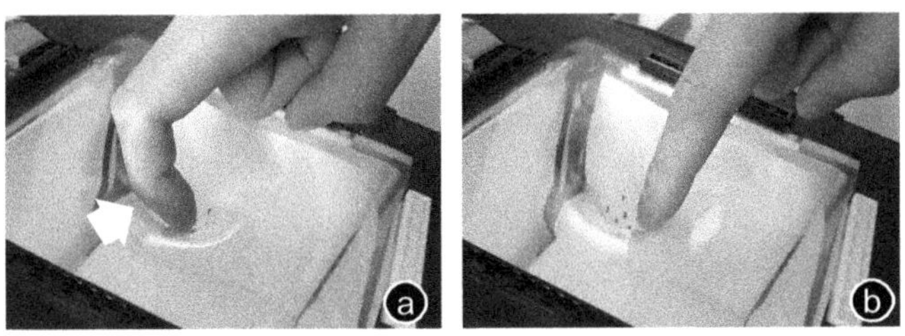

Figure 22: (a) A hooked finger accidentally touching the opposite side of the bowl. (b) Switching back to a straight finger posture avoids the issue at the expense of the increased error.

IMPLICATIONS FOR DESIGN

On the one hand, the findings presented in this paper are intended to deepen our understanding of targeting on non-planar surfaces. On the other hand, the same findings can be used to inform the design of curved touch devices as well as the design of interfaces running on such devices.

For device designers, we found two additional factors influencing error offsets, namely surface curvature and slope. Knowledge of these offsets allows engineers to compensate for these effects by coding corrective offsets into their device drivers, which will increase device accuracy (as demonstrated for flat surfaces by [13]).

For interface designers, minimum button sizes are relevant, because they help design usable interfaces. Our findings suggest placing targets on points of extreme curvatures in order to make them easier to acquire, so application designers might want to use them for frequently used functions.

CONCLUSIONS

Our findings indicate that the curvature of touch surfaces impacts targeting in terms of spread/minimum button size and in particular in terms of systematic offsets. This information can help designers of curved touch devices improve their devices.

As future work, we plan to study the impact of shape on more complex interactions, such as grasping. New findings in this space may one day provide the missing link between HCI and the disciplines that have discussed form factor and shape all along, such as industrial design.

ACKNOWLEDGMENTS

We thank Sean Gustafson and Christian Holz for valuable comments and help on statistics, and all participants of our studies for their time.

REFERENCES

1. Beaudouin-Lafon, M. and Mackay, W. E. Reification, polymorphism and reuse: three principles for designing visual interfaces. In *Proc. AVI'00*, 102–109.
2. Benko, H., Wilson, A. D. and Baudisch, P. Precise selection techniques for multi-touch screens. *Proc. CHI'06*, 1263–1272.
3. Benko, H., Wilson, A. D., and Balakrishnan, R. Sphere: multi-touch interactions on a spherical display. In *Proc. UIST'08*. 77–86.
4. Cao, X., Wilson, A. D., Balakrishnan, R., Hinckley, K. and Hudson, S. E. Shapetouch: leveraging contact shape on interactive surfaces. In *Proc. Tabletop'08*, 129–136.
5. Chapanis, A. Theory and methods for analyzing errors in man-machine systems. *Annals of the New York Academy of Sciences 51, Human Engineering* (1951), 1179–1203.
6. Fitts, P.M. 1954. The information capacity of the human motor system in controlling the amplitude of movement. *Journal of Experimental Psychology 47*, 381–391.
7. Forlines, C., Wigdor, D., Shen, C. and Balakrishnan, R. Direct-touch vs. mouse input for tabletop displays. In *Proc. CHI'07*, 647–656.
8. Grossman, T. and Balakrishnan, R. A probabilistic approach to modeling two-dimensional pointing. *TOCHI 12*, 3 (Sep. 2005), 435–459.
9. Han, J. Low-cost multi-touch sensing through frustrated total internal reflection. In *Proc. UIST'05*, 115–118.
10. Harrison, C. and Hudson, S. Providing dynamically changeable physical buttons on a visual display. In *Proc. CHI'09*, 299–308.
11. Harrison, C., Tan, D. and Morris, D. Skinput: appropriating the body as an input surface. In *Proc. CHI '10*, 453–462.

12. Holman, D., Vertegaal, R., Altosaar, M., Troje, N. and Johns, D. 2005. Paper windows: interaction techniques for digital paper. In *Proc. CHI '05,* 591–599.

13. Holz, C. and Baudisch, P. The generalized perceived input point model and how to double touch accuracy by extracting fingerprints. In *Proc. CHI'10,* 581–590.

14. Holz, C. and Baudisch, P. Understanding touch. To appear in *Proc. CHI'11,* 10 pages.

15. Moscovich, T. Contact area interaction with sliding widgets. In *Proc. UIST'09*, 13–22.

16. Potter, R., Weldon, L. and Shneiderman, B. Improving the accuracy of touch screens: an experimental evaluation of three strategies. In *Proc. CHI'88,* 27–32.

17. Rekimoto, J. SmartSkin: an infrastructure for freehand manipulation on interactive surfaces. In *Proc. CHI '02,* 113–120.

18. Rosenberg, I. and Perlin, K. The UnMousePad: an interpolating multi-touch force-sensing input pad. In *Proc. SIGGRAPH'09*, 1–9.

19. Sato, T., Mamiya, H., Koike, H. and Fukuchi, K. PhotoelasticTouch: transparent rubbery tangible interface using an LCD and photoelasticity. In *Proc. UIST'09,* 43–50.

20. Schwesig, C., I. Poupyrev, and E. Mori. Gummi: a bendable computer. In Proc. of *CHI'04,* pp. 263–270.

21. Sears, A. and Shneiderman, B. High precision touchscreens: design strategies and comparisons with a mouse. *Int. J. Man-Mach. Stud. 34*, 4 (Apr. 1991), 593–613.

22. Siek, K.A., Rogers, Y. and Connelly, K.H. Fat finger worries: how older and younger users physically interact with PDAs. In *Proc. INTERACT'05*, 267–280.

23. Taylor, B. T. and Bove, V. M. The bar of soap: a grasp recognition system implemented in a multi-functional handheld device. In *CHI'08 Extended Abstracts,* 3459–3464.

24. Villar, N., Izadi, S., Rosenfeld, D., Benko, H., Helmes, J., Westhues, J., Hodges, S., Ofek, E., Butler, A., Cao, X. and Chen, B. Mouse 2.0: multi-touch meets the mouse. In *Proc. UIST '09,* 33–42.

25. Vlack, K., Mizota, T., Kawakami, N., Kamiyama, K., Kajimoto, H. and Tachi, S. GelForce: a vision-based traction field computer interface. In *CHI'05 Extended Abstracts*, 1154–1155.

26. Vogel, D. and Baudisch, P. Shift: a technique for operating pen-based interfaces using touch. In *Proc.CHI'07*, 657–666.

27. Wang, F. and Ren, X. 2009. Empirical evaluation for finger input properties in multi-touch interaction. In *Proc. CHI'09*. 1063–1072.

28. Wigdor, D., Forlines, C., Baudisch, P., Barnwell, J. and Shen, C. LucidTouch: a see-through mobile device. In *Proc. UIST'07,* 269–278.

29. Wimmer, R. FlyEye: grasp-sensitive surfaces using optical fiber. In *Proc. TEI '10,* 245–248.

Audience Behavior around Large Interactive Cylindrical Screens

Gilbert Beyer[1], Florian Alt[2], Jörg Müller[3], Albrecht Schmidt[4], Karsten Isakovic[5], Stefan Klose[5], Manuel Schiewe[5], Ivo Haulsen[5]
[1]Ludwig-Maximilians-University Munich, Germany, gilbert.beyer@ifi.lmu.de
[2]University of Duisburg-Essen, Germany, florian.alt@uni-due.de
[3]Deutsche Telekom Laboratories, TU Berlin, Germany, joerg.mueller@tu-berlin.de
[4]VIS, University of Stuttgart, Germany, albrecht.schmidt@acm.org
[5]Fraunhofer FIRST, Berlin, Germany, name.surname@first.fraunhofer.de

ABSTRACT
Non-planar screens, such as columns, have been a popular means for displaying information for a long time. In contrast to traditional displays their digital counterparts are mainly flat and rectangular due to current technological constraints. However, we envision bendable displays to be available in the future, which will allow for creating new forms of displays with new properties. In this paper we explore cylindrical displays as a possible form of such novel public displays. We present a prototype and report on a user study, comparing the influence of the display shape on user behavior and user experience between flat and cylindrical displays. The results indicate that people move more in the vicinity of cylindrical displays and that there is no longer a default position when it comes to interaction. As a result, such displays are especially suitable to keep people in motion and to support gesture-like interaction.

Author Keywords
Cylindrical screens, digital columns, display formats, public displays, interactive surfaces, non-planar screens

ACM Classification Keywords
H.5.2. Information interfaces and presentation: User Interfaces.

General Terms
Human Factors.

INTRODUCTION
As display technology progresses and digital displays become cheaper, larger, and more robust, traditional displays in public spaces are being replaced by their digital counterparts. These digital displays can provide, among other benefits, interactivity, either by touch or by sensing the movement of the audience. Due to the deployed display technologies, nowadays the majority of displays are flat, rectangular, and framed. However, we learned from history, that there are many successful forms of non-planar displays.

One popular form were columns. Freestanding columns have the benefit of high visibility due to their concise and elevated shape, and can also provide more screen real estate on the same floor space. In addition, columns were extensively available inside buildings for structural reasons. Famous examples for ancient cylindrical displays are Trajan's Column in Rome (see Figure 1) or columns in the Hathor temple in Egypt. Even nowadays the most popular form of non-planar displays are cylindrical screens, such as cylindrical bulletin-boards, inflatable columns used at events, or street furniture columns used for cultural information, public announcements and ads (Morris or Litfaß Columns, see also Figure 1). With advances in technologies, bendable displays will allow for turning nearly any surface into a display and hence allow for creating displays of almost arbitrary shape and size for no additional costs compared to flat displays.

Figure 1: Examples of classical non-planar screens: (1) Trajan's Column with inscriptions in Rome (2) Replica of the first Litfaß Column in Berlin (3) Modern Citylight Column.

We opted to investigate cylindrical displays as one possible form of novel, arbitrary-shaped public displays. Hence we present a prototype of an interactive cylindrical display and report on a user study comparing user behavior in front of classical, flat displays and cylindrical displays showing the same content (we use the terms cylindrical display and column interchangeably). Our contribution is threefold:

- We present an interactive cylindrical display, which reacts to passers-by by adapting the content according to their movements.
- We show that people in front of cylindrical displays tend to move more and explore the content from a wider range of standing positions and discuss how this influences the way content should be designed.
- We discuss advantages and disadvantages of flat and cylindrical displays based on the findings of our study.

RELATED WORK

In recent years, a variety of prototypes of non-planar displays have been developed. Most public deployments, however, still use planar, framed displays and their designs are based on implicit assumptions that may not hold for non-planar displays. While a number of studies of audience behavior for planar displays exist, their results may not generalize to non-planar displays. Finally, the specific case of cylindrical displays introduces the new category of semi-framed displays.

Interactive and Public Displays

Inspired by early work such as Media Spaces [4] and the Digital Desk [29], a variety of interactive and public displays have been proposed. The Plasma Poster Network [7,8] was a network of touch enabled public displays installed in hallways supporting office communication. Similar to our approach, many of such displays used computer vision to enable interaction from a distance. The seminal work of Myron Krueger explored vision-based interaction with large displays where the displays reacted to the users' movements [15]. In ReflectiveSigns [22], a network of displays reacted implicitly to the audience's viewing behavior. The Intelligent Kiosk [6] was an early example of an interactive Avatar on a public display that reacted to passing people. Similarly, the AmiQuin [26] was a virtual mannequin in a shop window that reacted to the audiences' body movements. Finally, Malik proposed vision-based interaction techniques with multiple fingers for distant displays [19].

Designs of Non-Planar Screens

Organic user interfaces [12] have been proposed as computer interfaces that use non-planar displays for input and output. Lin et al. presented the i-m-Tube, an interactive tubular display [18]. The first version uses a single projector and a convex mirror to create a back-projected cylindrical display, which supports multi-touch. Benko et al. present Sphere [1], a multi-touch enabled spherical display. They discuss unique properties of spherical displays and multi-touch interaction techniques for such displays. Some of the properties for spheres are similar to properties of cylindrical displays (like that the user can not see the whole display at any time), while others are not (like a smooth transition between vertical and horizontal surfaces). Lee et al. [17] presented foldable displays like fans, newspapers, scrolls and umbrellas. Their prototypes were implemented using projection, infrared markers and the Nintendo Wii remote camera. They discuss affordances of different shapes and possible interaction techniques. Volumetric displays appear to show content inside the display volume. Grossmann et al. focus on such displays' unique properties and show how they can be used for collaborative applications [9,10].

Regarding cylindrical displays, a number of commercial designs exist. Many commercial cylindrical displays use rotating LED's (Kinoton, Dynascan), where the drive system has to be well adjusted to get a jitter-free image. Other technical solutions include static mechanical designs including rings of LED modules (Barco) and projection-based setups. In [2], Benko outlines challenges when designing gestural interactions with non-flat surface computing interfaces derived from the development of three prototypes (a gesture-enabled flat display, a sphere, and a dome). Challenges identified include walk-up-and-use functionality, linking heterogeneous devices, usability from multiple directions, and compelling applications.

Assumptions of Current Designs for Flat Displays

Most current deployments of interactive public displays use planar, framed displays enabling interaction either through touch or body gestures. The CityWall [24], for example, was a large multi-touch display installed in downtown Helsinki that supported browsing photo collections. Worlds of Information [14] was an extension of the same system to include touch interaction with 3D spheres of photos. Magical Mirrors [21] was a deployment in downtown Berlin where passers-by could see their own mirror image on a display and interact with virtual objects through body movements. Such designs for flat displays usually start from a number of implicit assumptions that need to be questioned for non-flat displays. Many designs assume that: 1) people stop walking before they interact, 2) users can perceive the content of the entire screen at any time, 3) users can see what other people do when interacting with the display, 4) shoulders are usually parallel to the display, 5) the position centrally in front of the display is preferred, 6) content is not distorted. For example, touch displays are obviously difficult to use while walking, and even for Magical Mirrors a walking user would quickly leave the camera view. For the CityWall, users could easily scale photos so big that they hide the view for others, which would be a problem if users cannot observe the effects of their actions on other parts of the screen. Similarly, users started to play 'soccer' by throwing photos around, which would be very different if one could not observe the actions of other users. Vogel [28] used a parallel shoulder position as an indicator of user interest, but it is not clear if this is valid for non-planar displays. Also, the distortion of content could render many current interfaces unusable on non-planar displays.

Audience Behavior in Front of Flat Displays

Any observations of audience behavior towards public displays have been conducted using planar displays, and it is unclear whether existing findings generalize towards non-planar displays. Scott et al. [27] explore how people use regions on round tabletops, which share some properties with cylindrical displays, but where the display itself is flat. Huang et al. [13] show that for existing planar displays, very few people look at them or stop in front of them. This may also be related to the fact that many flat displays are installed either on walls, orthogonal to walking direction, or above eye height. Cylindrical screens in contrast are often installed directly in the way of passers-by, such that they naturally appear in their field of view. Müller et al. [23] show that what people expect on public displays depends on the immediate surroundings, e.g. the apparent owner of a shop window where the display is installed. As columns are usually freestanding, expectations may differ. Brignull and Rogers [5] and Peltonen et al. [24] observed that users were waiting for their turn to access the display. For cylindrical displays, there is no central position where the user could 'own' the display, but all positions around the display are equal. Therefore, turn taking could be very different.

Influence of the Display Frame on Audience Behavior

A major difference between planar and non-planar screens may result from their frame. In this context Manovich [20] presents a theory of the imprisonment of the viewer's body by the screen apparatus on one hand and the requirements of the image perspective on the other hand. In cinema, e.g., the body of the viewer is confined to a seat and the head is aligned to forward view hence providing the best viewpoint. The same is true in classical arts (e.g., a painting in a museum) where the viewers seem to position themselves centrally at some distance in front of the screen. We show that this effect does not appear in front of non-planar screens. Another interesting conception of Manovich is the description of the screen's frame as a clearly defined rectangle, constituting a "viewing regime". Anything outside the frame can be ignored by the viewer, while immersing himself into the content inside the frame. Pinhanez and Podlaseck [25] discussed advantages and disadvantages of frameless displays, also claiming the significance of the frame to serve as a reference for the viewer to orient inside the scene and position himself accordingly. Cylindrical displays introduce a new category in between framed and frameless displays. It this case of semi-framed displays, a frame is provided on the top and bottom, but not left or right.

PROTOTYPE OF A CYLINDRICAL DISPLAY

For our research we developed a prototype of an interactive cylindrical display. Though our prototype is projector-based we envision that future versions will be based on bendable display foil. In the following, the hardware and software setup of this display is being described.

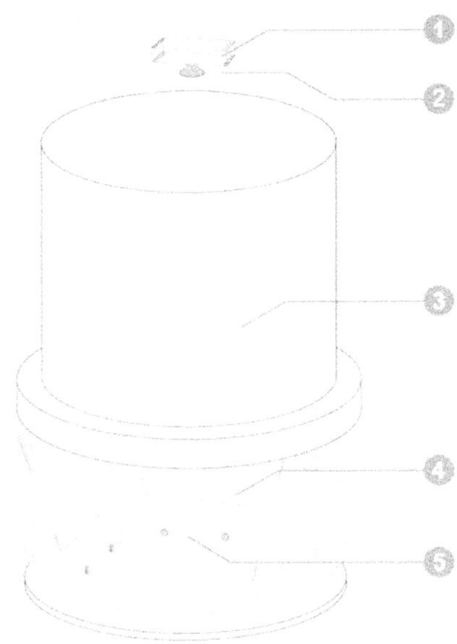

Figure 2: Prototype of a cylindrical display: (1) Camera sensor. (2) Fisheye lens. (3) Acrylic rear-projection screen. (4) 4 x Foil mirror. (5) 8 x Standard projector of 1024x768 pixels.

Figure 3: Cylindrical display with flower content for passing-by interaction as used in our user study.

Hardware

The prototype of the cylindrical display consists of a cluster of 8 standard projectors, 4 foil mirrors, 10 PCs, and a rear-projection screen. It has a height of 2.2 meters and a diameter of 1.5 meters. The 4:1 projection screen is 1.1 meters high, has a diameter of 1.3 meters and a resolution of 2048 to 512 pixels. Each cluster element projects onto a mirror reflecting the projection onto about one quarter of the screen. For a viewer independent image blending we use a special rear projection screen with a low gain factor. To detect position and movement of the passers-by around the column, a sensor interface is installed above the column consisting of a high-resolution camera and a 185° fisheye lens. The hardware setup is depicted in Figure 2.

Software

The raw projection on the cylindrical screen is heavily distorted due to the curvature of the screen and the projection angle. To correct these distortions we use the calibration technology described in [3]. This software is also used to resolve the blending function for the real time correction between overlapping regions of adjacent projectors. The visualization software for the displayed contents on the column screen is based on a distributed rendering system. To enable user interaction, we implemented a motion tracking software, using OpenCV. The motion tracker uses frame differencing to detect motion, and calculates the angle, speed, and pixel distance of moving blobs from the column. The Kalman filter is used to smooth these trajectories.

We also developed a VRML-based application framework that enables us to display the same kinds of interactive applications within the coordinate systems of flat as well as round screen shapes. For the interactive digital column different sample applications were designed (see Figure 4):

1. *Reactive animated typography.* In this application words appear on the column as the user walks around it. While moving around the column it's in principle possible to explore content from left to right as well as from right to left. To make the text readable while passing clockwise as well as counterclockwise, both the horizontal and vertical dimensions are used. In order that words don't collide when taking a shift in direction, the text is presented on a visual step-curve. To ensure viewers do not lose track of the text flow, the next appearing word is always announced by an animated dot.
2. *Direction of the viewer.* In this application items are flying "towards" the user in z dimension, following the user by adjusting their horizontal direction. For example, the crown of a soft drink bottle seems to fly from the inside to the outside of the column and target the viewer, who cannot evade the item as he is tracked by the camera sensor. Such content, where the viewer cannot disregard the information, can be used for presenting urgent or provoking messages in social conscience campaigns for example.
3. *Tales around the column.* In this application, an endless picture story of drinking up a soft drink bottle is told around the column. With the help of the camera sensor the application presents the first picture on the side where the viewer is approaching, and animates the viewer to move further around the column and proceed in the story by providing information stepwise only. In order to see the end of the tale, the user has to circle the column.

Figure 4: Developed applications for the cylindrical screen: (1) Reactive animated typography. (2) Direction of the viewer. (3) Tales around the column. (4) Movements of the viewer. (5) Reactive ambient column. (6) Interactive multi-player game (detailed descriptions below).

4. *Movements of the viewer.* In this application, the user paints a pattern of flowers or bubbles on the column by any kind of body movement. If the user stops the flowers slowly fade away, and the individual pattern that has been painted can't be seen any more. Yet, when moving on the flowers reappear and follow the user as he moves along the surface, so that he is encouraged to proceed moving.
5. *Reactive ambient column.* In this application, each person approaching the column is represented by "being served" a soft drink bottle, which appears in the direction the person is standing. The aim is to give information about the public gathering and creating a social atmosphere. There have been reactive media façades in the past that present ambient information about the weather or about what is happening inside a building (e.g., a train station). The round nature of the column also allows mirroring objects in the outdoor space around the column, while a flat screen would only be able to cover one spatial direction.

6. *Interactive multiplayer game.* This is a game where players are represented by individually colored bubbles on the screen appearing when moving fast, and have the task to burst all their opponents' bubbles. This game is making use of the fact that multiple users can interact with the round body of the column at the same time. In general all kinds of games are imaginable where teammates or opponents can chase each other around the column or hide behind it, like cops and robbers, hide and seek, etc.

Of these available applications, we chose application 4 for our study. This was because the application works for a single user and we were interested in user movement. The chosen application draws a flower pattern on the screen when the user moves, and he can influence the horizontal and vertical position of the flowers by walking left or right or by waving his hand. He can also influence the size of the flowers by moving faster or slower (see Figure 3).

HYPOTHESES

As no studies regarding user behavior towards cylindrical displays exist, first of all it is important to understand how people move and behave around them. This knowledge can then be used as a basis to develop applications that exploit the properties of the new format and investigate more elaborate topics such as multi-user interaction. As there are many (real-world) situations where only a single user is interacting, we decided to concentrate on single-user interaction only, leaving multi-user interaction for future work.

Based on informal observations of colleagues and visitors we posed three general hypotheses that characterize behavior around cylindrical displays. First, we assumed that users walk more when interacting with cylindrical than with flat displays. If true, this is an important property, as many flat displays are designed for people standing in front of them. Designs that work for people standing, with rather high complexity and small fonts, may not work for people walking. Second, we assumed that while users seem to have their shoulders parallel to flat displays, they would have their shoulders in a certain angle to columns. This would be an important property for gesture-based interaction, since while users can use both arms equally for flat displays, one arm would be turned away from a column, making symmetric gestures difficult. Further, it would be difficult to move any arm against the direction the user is facing, so a whole different gesture set would need to be designed. Finally, we hypothesized that due to the more active engagement users would spend more time interacting with columns.

Hypothesis 1: Users walk more when interacting with the cylindrical display.

1a: Users walk longer distances when interacting with the cylindrical display.

1b: Users spend more time walking when interacting with the cylindrical display.

1c: The position of users has a higher variance when interacting with the cylindrical display.

Hypothesis 2: Users position themselves with shoulders parallel to the flat display but not to the cylindrical display.

2a: The users' shoulder position is parallel to the display less often when interacting with the cylindrical display while walking.

2b: The users' shoulder position is parallel to the display less often when interacting with the cylindrical display while standing.

Hypothesis 3: Users spend more time overall interacting with the cylindrical display.

In addition, we had several hypotheses for the viewing behavior of participants. We hypothesized that participants would look more often at the cylindrical display, but for shorter bursts. We also hypothesized that participants would look at the left half of the column when walking clockwise and the right half when walking counterclockwise. While these hypotheses were formed before the design of the user study, we additionally conducted a post-hoc analysis of the data to explore further observations we made.

USER STUDY DESIGN

In order to test these hypotheses we conducted a user study comparing single users' behavior in front of interactive flat and cylindrical displays. The study was conducted at our lab over the course of two days. In the following chapter we describe the design and setup of our user study and report on the recruiting process as well as the study procedure.

We opted for a lab study due to the following reasons. (1) For the anticipated measurements, a highly controllable environment was required allowing for statistical data analysis. This would have been difficult to achieve in public due to a high amount of external influence and fragile, technical equipment. (2) To assess the users' behavior we used cameras during the study. This would have been a major issue in public due to privacy reasons. To create an authentic scenario we created a situation where participants were free to visit different rooms containing various exhibits. Hence we created a situation where (1) people behaved in a semi-natural way, (2) people were not aware what we were measuring in order to avoid influencing their behavior, and (3) we created a controllable, yet still realistic scenario.

Setup

For the study we prepared 4 rooms at our lab each of which contained a prototype. Two of the rooms contained "fake" prototypes, which were functional (one was an interactive flat screen with content that reacted to the viewers' head movements and facial expressions, the other one was a non-interactive dome projection and showed a movie) – however their only purpose was to create a more realistic situation and to distract from the displays under investigation.

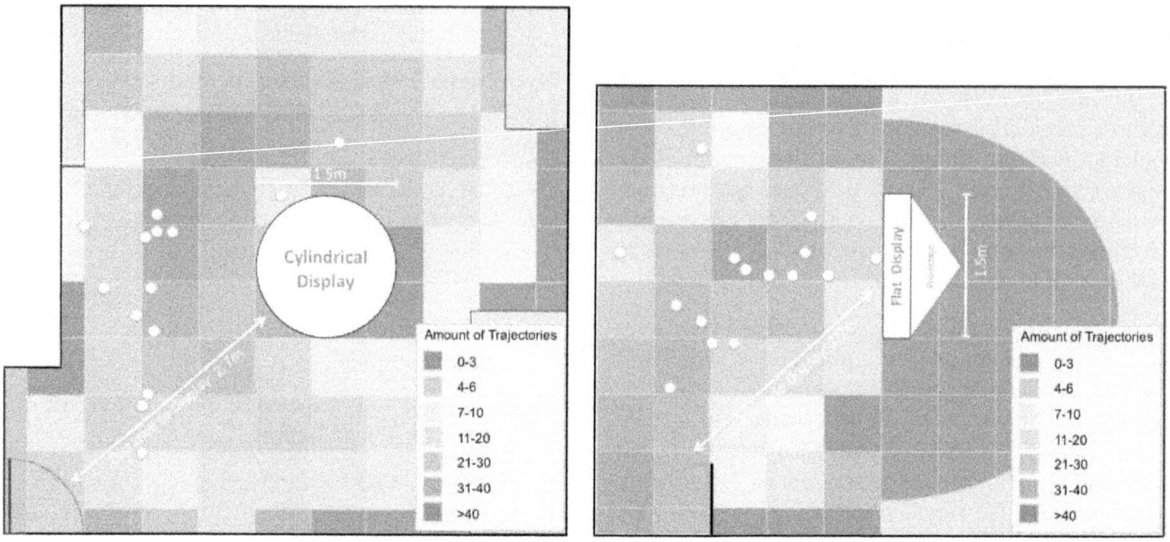

Figure 5: Room layout for the user study (1) Room with cylindrical display (2) Room with flat display. For the data analysis we separated the rooms into a grid consisting of 60x60cm^2 squares. The heat map shows the participants' trajectories of each square. (White dots indicate participants' first standpoint after entering the room.)

For comparing the flat and the cylindrical display we designed two similar rooms, one containing the cylindrical display, and one the flat display (Figure 5). We designed the two rooms as similar as possible while still preserving the situation in which a flat or cylindrical display would normally be deployed. The distance between door and displays was equal and both displays would be approached in the same angle. While the doors would open in different directions, both displays would visually appear at the same position in the room. The flat display is equipped with one standard projector and uses the same rear-projection material as the cylindrical screen. For the size of the flat display we had to choose between a display that has the same size as the visible display area of the column when a user is standing in front of it, and the total size of the cylindrical screen 'unrolled'. Being in the situation to choose whether to deploy a flat or cylindrical display one would usually have to choose between two displays that take the same floor real estate and be in the first situation. For this practical reason, we decided to test a flat display with the same size as the visible area of the column first and leave the second situation for future work. The flat display uses a webcam as a sensor. For user tracking we setup 4 webcams in each room, which allowed for detecting the user in each position of the room. From the webcams we created a synchronized, time-stamped video file using OpenCV. To be able to analyze and manually annotate the video files we attached markers to the floor hence creating a grid of 60x60 cm^2 squares.

Participants

We aimed for diverse participants as would normally be found in public spaces. People were recruited from bulletins in the surrounding neighborhoods (train stations, shopping malls, university campus, etc.) and mailing lists in the days prior to the study. In total, 15 people participated in the study (10 males, 5 females). The average age was 32.7 years; participants were students, artists, taxi drivers, office workers, and technicians.

Procedure

The participants were invited to the labs and asked to report to the doorman from where we led them to the laboratory. We started with an *initial briefing*. First, we had the participants fill in a demographic questionnaire (asking for age, gender, nationality, profession, and, if applicable, their major). Second, we explained them the setting of the study. They were told that there were 4 exhibition rooms containing different project works. We did not tell them which or how many expositions were to be found in each room. Instead, we asked them to simply walk through the rooms and spend as much time there as they wanted. We especially told them that there was no minimum and no maximum time we expected them to spend in each room, in order to minimize compliance effects. We told them that a one-page *questionnaire* was to be found after each room and asked them to fill it in once they finished their visit to the room. After that we wanted them to move on to the next room. Further we told them that several cameras were setup in the rooms, needed for the purpose of the study (we did not tell the participants that some prototypes were interactive).

After the initial briefing we guided the participants to the first room and explained them that arrows attached to the walls and floors would lead the way through and to further rooms. Though we surveyed the people in the different rooms (using webcams), we did not interrupt or talk to them during the study. Since we used a within-subject design (all participants saw all expositions) the order of the exhibits was counter-balanced among the subjects. Whereas the "fake" prototypes were always seen in the same order, we switched positions for the rooms containing the flat/cylindrical screens. After the participants finished the fourth questionnaire, we conducted a *semi-structured interview* with them. All semi-structured interviews were audio-recorded. Finally we debriefed the participants and explained them the purpose of the study. Participants were compensated with a small amount of money.

DATA ANALYSIS

Complete time-stamped and synchronized videos from four different perspectives of all user behavior were recorded in both rooms. All user positions were transcribed. A coding schema was devised containing codes for walking, shoulder angle, and head direction. The complete video recordings were coded by two independent raters using Mangold INTERACT coding software. In order to ensure inter-rater reliability, one video was coded by both raters and Cohen's Kappa was computed for all codes. Inter-rater reliability was satisfactory for walking (Kappa=.61) and shoulder (Kappa=.67) codes (we considered Kappa≥.61 substantial agreement [16]). Unfortunately, reliability was not satisfactory for head direction codes, such that we had to drop all hypotheses related to viewing behavior. In addition to the testing of the hypotheses, a post-hoc analysis of various variables of user behavior (e.g., duration of stops) was conducted. Because we could not ensure normal distribution for all dependent variables, all hypotheses were tested using the non-parametric Wilcoxon signed-rank test with paired samples using a level of significance of .05. The AttrakDiff questionnaire was evaluated using the associated software, and semi-structured interviews were partially transcribed to cover non-repetitive user statements.

RESULTS

In the following, we report on the results of our data analysis. An overview of the results is presented in Table 1.

Walking

All hypotheses regarding the walking behavior of participants (hypotheses 1a, 1b, and 1c) are supported by the data. Participants covered significantly more meters with the column screen (on average 47.3 m) than with the flat screen (21.2 m) (p<.003) (see Figure 9). With the column, participants spent most of their time walking (only 44.9% standing), while with the flat display, they spent most of their time standing (62.8%) (p<.027). Also, they covered many more different locations with the column. The variance of location in rows is more than twice as high (5.6) for the column than for the flat screen (2.3) (p<.001), and the variance in columns is more than three times as high (3.7) for the column than for the flat screen (.93)(p<.001).

Shoulders

The hypotheses of the angle of shoulders towards the display are partially supported. Overall, participants spent most of their time with their shoulders parallel to the flat display (69.5%) (see Figures 7 and 8).

Measure	Column (mean/std)	Flat (mean/std)
Distance walked (m)**	**47.3**/24	21.2/13.7
Time spent standing (%)*	44.9/25.9	**62.8**/16.6
Mean duration of stops (s)**	3.5/2.3	**9.9**/13.1
Max duration of stops (s)*	12.9/11.9	**38.7**/52.7
Total time spent (s)**	97.7/53.4	**172.8**/138.6
Time spent with shoulders parallel (%)***	41.5/21.3	**69.5**/17.2
Time spent with shoulders parallel while walking (%)***	22.1/10.6	**46.3**/16.1
Time spent with shoulders parallel while standing (%)	70.0/26.1	82.0/18.6
Stops per minute (1/min)	8.3/4.3	6.8/3.3
Mean distance from display (m)	1.5/.23	1.7/.41
Variance in location (Rows)***	**5.6**/1.4	2.3/.96
Variance in location (Columns)***	**3.7**/1.4	.93/.57

Table 1: All comparisons with Wilcoxon signed-rank test with paired samples (*=p<.05, **:p<.01, ***:p<.001)

Figure 6: Typical user behavior in front of cylindrical display (1) User gets engaged into interaction immediately. (2) User keeps waking around the display. (3) Shoulder position is mainly orthogonal throughout interaction phase.

Figure 7: Typical user behavior in front of flat display (1) User approaches display (2) User stops in front of display. (3) User maintains a parallel shoulder position, even during interaction.

In contrast, with the column participants spent most of their time with shoulders not parallel (only 41.5% parallel) (p<.001) (see Figures 6 and 8). If this data is divided by whether participants were walking or not, the picture is more diverse. When walking, participants spent 46% of their time shoulders parallel to the flat display, while this was the case for the column only 22% of the time (p<.001).

When standing, there is a trend towards participants having their shoulders parallel to the flat display more often (81%) than to the column (69%), however, this difference is not significant ($p<.069$). While hypothesis 2a is supported by the data, hypothesis 2b is not.

Time Spent for Interaction

Hypothesis 3 assumed that participants would spend more time with the column than with the flat display. This hypothesis is not at all supported by the data. Indeed, participants spent almost twice as much time with the flat display (2:53 min) than with the column (1:38 min). A post-hoc analysis shows that this is significant ($p<.002$) (Figure 9).

Post-hoc Analysis

When participants stopped for the first time in front of the flat display, most participants stopped in a very narrow area in front of it, while the locations of first stops were more diverse for the column (see Figure 5). The same figure also shows a heat map of where participants moved. This also nicely shows the "sweet spot" area in front of the flat display, which is much more spread out for the column. Also, participants spent slightly more time until they first stopped with the column (10.4s) than with the flat display (6.7s), and then continued walking sooner (after 5.7s) than with the flat display (22.5s). These differences however are not significant. Participants stopped slightly more often (per minute) with the column (8.3 stops) than with the flat display (6.8 stops), although this difference was not significant. However, if participants stopped, they stopped for more than twice as long (9.9s) with the flat display than with the column (3.5s), and this difference is significant ($p<.006$). The longest time participants spent without moving is even more extreme. While with the column, participants spent on average no more than 12.9s on a single location, with the flat display, participants spent up to 38.7s in a single location. Additionally, participants seemed to approach the column a little bit closer (avg. distance 1.5m) than the flat display (1.7m), however, these differences are not significant.

User Experience

To evaluate the user experience we had the participant fill in an AttrakDiff questionnaire [11] for both the flat and the cylindrical display. The results revealed that from a pragmatic as well as from a hedonic point of view the participants considered the cylindrical display to be of higher quality. Considering the attractiveness, the cylindrical display was rated very attractive whereas the flat display was rated medium attractive. All results from the questionnaire were not significant, which might have been caused by our rather small sample size.

Semi-Structured Interviews

The participants did not seem to feel bothered by the experimental setup: "As soon as you start to play around with the media, you forget that you are observed." (P2) Interestingly, many participants experienced the flat display like 'television' (e. g. P3, P4, P7), while they experienced the column as being more 'dynamic': "The flat was like a television feeling. The round was more dynamic. TV is more static." (P3) They also felt more passive in front of the flat display: "You stand in front of it like in front of a TV.

While with the column you are engaged more actively. It was more like a TV situation; you walk in front of it and think, what happens now. With the column, you immediately had the feeling, you do more with it." (P7) Some participants considered the column as more comfortable: "It was more spatial. [...] It is better if you can move around a fixed point than back and forth." (P1) "For me, round is more comfortable than square. It was more organic." (P3)

DISCUSSION

Our study revealed that single user behavior differs significantly between planar and cylindrical displays. Due to the setup of the study, there are certain limitations with regards to the generalizability of the results. (1) We only evaluated single user interaction. Hence no conclusion can be drawn towards behavior in multi-user scenarios. (2) Unlike in the lab, for real world deployments there are many factors influencing movement patterns, such as streets, buildings, or pedestrian traffic. However, as columns are often deployed in small free places, spatially similar to our lab setting, we believe that the observed movement patterns generalize to such situations. (3) With regard to the content, we believe that the findings are valid for most similar interactive content. Yet, very different content (e.g., a fixed framed video), unsuitable for the column, might lead to different results.

In the following we outline and discuss major findings.

Moving Around the Column

As opposed to a flat, rectangular display, a column does not provide any boundaries left or right. This lack of borders indeed seems to have the effect of making viewers move freely around the column (see Figures 5 and 6). Participants spent most of their time walking and covered significant distances, looking at the column from various locations and stopping quite often, but only for relatively short times, on average only 3.5 seconds. This led to much more diverse body postures as opposed to a flat display. Only about 30% of the time was spent with shoulders parallel to the display, and even when participants stopped, 30% of the time the shoulders were not parallel.

The Sweet Spot

The data shows that for flat displays, there is a relatively small area in front of the display where participants get themselves in a frontal position ('the sweet spot'). Though this looks like an obvious finding, we are not aware of any prior studies that support this assumption with data. This area was positioned centrally in front of the display, about 1.5 meters away from it. Participants seemed to approach this area quickly after entering the room, and stopped in this position with their shoulders parallel to the display, facing the display frontally (see Figures 5 and 7). From this position, they could see the entire screen from the best perspective, while the entire frame was still in the visual field. These observations are well aligned with the theory of Manovich [20]. Participants stopped in the same position for quite long times, on average for up to 39 seconds, with one participant not moving for more than three minutes. When they moved, almost half of the time they still had their shoulders parallel to the display, moving back- and forwards, or sideways without turning. Overall they spent most of their time standing and did not cover great distances.

Time Spent for Interaction

As opposed to the hypothesis, participants spent significantly more time with the flat display than with the column, almost twice as long. This is an interesting finding, which we believe is worthwhile to be investigated in more detail. As people stand still to identify with the screen image and ignore the real world, they might easily spend more time than if moving around, exploring also the physical space.

RECOMMENDATIONS

Based on these results we derive recommendations for designing content on planar and cylindrical displays.

Design for Walking Interaction

Cylindrical displays are most suitable to keep people in motion, even if they do not frontally face the display. Unlike flat displays where motion is often simulated in an unnatural way (e.g., "running" in the same spot in front of a flat display using Xbox Kinect Sports track-and-field), cylindrical displays provide a way to support real motion. Thus, columns and their content should be designed for walking, and be set up at sites where they can raise the attention of viewers by implicit interaction and encourage them to move on. A way to achieve this is to keep content simple, such that it can be perceived while passing by. Another good way is content that moves with the audience as they move around the column, adapting to the location of the viewer rather than requiring the viewer to adapt his location to the display. We propose that flat displays, because of their sweet spot, may be more suited for waiting situations and longer dwell times, and may support more complex content.

Place Columns in the Way of Users

Cylindrical displays are suitable to be located within the way of users and can better be used while passing by. For flat displays people tend to take a fixed standing position for interacting, probably blocking the way for others. In contrast, cylindrical displays allow users to avoid bumping into other people by keeping moving around the display. As a result, content on cylindrical displays should adapt to users passing by and could, e.g., attract them towards non-crowded areas around the display.

Enable Gesture-Based Interaction

Previous research showed that three interaction techniques are highly suitable for the use on public displays: touch, gestures/body position, and interaction through mobile phones. Whereas touch and mobile phone based interaction is applicable for flat displays where people stop in front, the motion-fostering character of cylindrical displays makes them more suitable for gesture-like interaction. We observed that almost 60% of the time, the viewers' shoulders were not parallel to the display, leading to that they could not use both hands equally well for interaction as one arm is constantly turned away from the display. It may be best to enable interaction with one arm alone, and not requiring movement of the arm against walking direction. As another difficulty, which arm is geared towards the display depends on walking direction and not on dominance of the hand.

Use Frameless or Semi-Framed Content

Digital columns are semi-framed. As a result they don't have a "sweet spot" any more, hence posing another difficulty since designers and audience can't use left or right frames to orient themselves anymore. Using framed content, like videos or images, on a column, of course can create a virtual frame (and thus probably another 'sweet spot'), but that may not put the cylindrical shape to its best use. As explained in [25], frames serve to create a distance between the content and the surface (in this case, the column), while frameless content integrates smoothly with the surface. In order to integrate well with the column and exploit the frameless nature, frameless content is ideally suited.

CONCLUSION AND FUTURE WORK

Non-planar, digital displays have the potential to change the experience of public displays in urban spaces. Presenting content on such displays, creating an engaging user experience, and exploiting the new properties of these screens requires us to rethink the way we design content and applications. Observations of users' behavior are a necessary first step to develop guidelines to design interactive columns.

In this paper we presented the same content on a cylindrical and a planar display and observed different user behavior. We found that users move more when interacting with cylindrical displays. The sweet spot of flat displays, where users tend to position themselves, does not exist for cylindrical displays. In our study, participants spent significantly more time interacting with the flat display than with the cylindrical display. These findings can inform the design of cylindrical displays in the following way. Content for cylindrical displays should be designed for audiences in motion. Further, they are suitable to be placed in the way of users. Gestural interaction should be possible, ideally using one hand only, because users may not have their shoulders parallel to the display. As they are only semi-framed, frameless content is best suited for cylindrical displays. If a design goal is that people spend little time engaging with the display (e.g., public display in a busy area) then cylindrical screens may be more appropriate than flat ones.

We see five important limitations of this study and areas of future work. First, for this study we decided to compare cylindrical displays to flat displays that cover the same floor real estate. A follow-up study should compare both displays to a flat display of the size of the cylindrical display unrolled. Second, multi-user scenarios are an obvious application area for cylindrical displays. Because there is no sweet spot, multiple users can approach the display on equal grounds and do not need to take turns. For this reason users may also feel less observed as if standing in an exclusively occupied spot. Third, while our experimental setup enabled the detailed investigation of motion behavior under lab conditions, behavior in public places might differ. A field study of the prototype will be the next step in investigating the properties of cylindrical displays. Fourth, in this study we compared display formats using one specific interactive application. It would also be interesting to evaluate user behavior with different applications. Fifth, we did not investigate gaze behavior or recall of content on the displays. It would be interesting to investigate whether the increased movement when interacting with columns leads to increased recall of content.

ACKNOWLEDGMENTS

The research leading to these results has received funding from the European Union Seventh Framework Programme under grant agreements no. 215893 and 244011.

REFERENCES

1. Benko, H., Wilson, A. D., and Balakrishnan, R. 2008. Sphere: multi-touch interactions on a spherical display. In Proc. UIST '08. ACM, New York, NY, 77-86.
2. Benko, H. 2009. Beyond flat surface computing: challenges of depth-aware and curved interfaces. In Proc. ACM Multimedia. MM '09. ACM, New York, NY, 935-944.
3. Biehlig, W., Deter, C., Dube, S., Hill, B., Helling, S., Isaković, K., Klose, S., Schiewe, M. 2004. LaserCave - Some Building Blocks for immersive Screens. VR AR Statustagung, Leipzig.
4. Bly, S. A., Harrison, S. R., and Irwin, S. 1993. Media spaces: bringing people together in a video, audio, and computing environment. *Commun. ACM* 36, 1 (Jan. 1993), 28-46.
5. Brignull, H. and Rogers, Y. 2003. Enticing people to interact with large public displays in public spaces. In Proc. INTERACT 03, Zürich, Switzerland, 17-24.
6. Christian, A. D. and Avery, B. L. Speak Out and Annoy Someone: Experience with Intelligent Kiosks. In Proceeding of CHI 2000, The Hague, Netherlands, 2000.
7. Churchill, E., Nelson, L., Denoue, L., Girgensohn, A. 20030. The Plasma Poster Network: Posting Multimedia Content in Public Places. In Proc. INTERACT 2003, Zürich, Switzerland.
8. Churchill, E., Nelson, L., Denoue, L. 2003. Multimedia fliers: information sharing with digital community bulletin boards, Communities and technologies, Kluwer, B.V., Deventer, The Netherlands.
9. Grossman, T. and Balakrishnan, R. 2008. Collaborative interaction with volumetric displays. In Proc. CHI '08. ACM, New York, NY, 383-392.
10. Grossman, T., Wigdor, D. and Balakrishnan, R. (2004). Multi-Finger Gestural Interaction with 3D Volumetric Displays. In Proc. UIST 2004. pp. 61–70.
11. Hassenzahl, M., Burmester, M., and Koller, F. 2003. AttrakDiff: A questionnaire to measure perceived hedonic and pragmatic quality. In J. Ziegler & G. Szwillus (Eds.), Mensch & Computer 2003. Interaktion in Bewegung, 187-196.
12. Holman, D. and Vertegaal, R. 2008. Organic user interfaces: designing computers in any way, shape, or form. Commun. ACM 51, 6 (Jun. 2008), 48-55.
13. Huang, E. M. Koster, A. and Borchers, J. 2008. Overcoming assumptions and uncovering practices: When does the public really look at public displays? In the Proc. Pervasive 2008. Sydney, Australia.
14. Jacucci, G., Morrison, A., Richard, G.T., Kleimola, J., Peltonen, P., Parisi, L., Laitinen, T. 2010. Worlds of information: designing for engagement at a public multi-touch display. In: Proc. CHI 2010, pp: 2267-2276.
15. Krueger, M., Gionfriddo, T., Hinrichsen, K. VIDEOPLACE — an artificial reality. SIGCHI Bull. 16, 4 1985, 35-40.
16. Landis, J.R., Koch, G.G. 1977. The measurement of observer agreement for categorical data. In Biometrics, 1977, Vol. 33, 159-174.
17. Lee, J. C., Hudson, S. E., and Tse, E. 2008. Foldable interactive displays. In Proc. UIST '08. ACM, New York, NY, 287-290.
18. Lin, J., Chen, Y., Ko, J., Kao, H., Chen, W., Tsai, T., Hsu, S., and Hung, Y. 2009. i-m-Tube: an interactive multi-resolution tubular display. In Proc. ACM Multimedia '09. ACM, New York, 253-260.
19. Malik, S., Ranjan, A. and Balakrishnan, R. 2006. Interacting with large displays from a distance with vision-tracked multi-finger gestural input. In Proc. SIGGRAPH '06. NY.
20. Manovich, L. 2001. The Language of New Media. Cambridge/Mass., MIT Press.
21. Michelis, D., Müller, J. 2010. The Audience Funnel: Observations of Gesture Based Interaction with Multiple Large Displays in a City Center. In: International Journal of Human-Computer Interaction.
22. Müller, J., Exeler, J., Buzeck, M. and Krüger, A. 2009. ReflectiveSigns: Digital Signs that Adapt to Audience Attention. In the Proc. Pervasive 2009, Nara, Japan.
23. Müller, J., Wilmsmann, D., Exeler, J., Buzeck, M., Schmidt, A., Jay, T. and Krüger, A. 2009. Display Blindness: The effect of Expectations on Attention towards Digital Signage. In the Proc. Pervasive 2009, Nara, Japan..
24. Peltonen, P., Kurvinen, E., Salovaara, A., Jacucci, G., Ilmonen, T., Evans, J., Oulasvirta, A., and Saarikko, P. 2008. It's Mine, Don't Touch!: interactions at a large multi-touch display in a city centre. In Pro. CHI '08, New York, 2008, 1285-1294.
25. Pinhanez, C. and Podlaseck, M. 2005. To frame or not to frame: The role and design of frameless displays in ubiquitous applications. In Proc. of Ubiquitous Computing, 340–357.
26. Reitberger, W., Meschtscherjakov, A., Mirlacher, T., Scherndl, T., Huber, H., and Tscheligi, M. 2009. A persuasive interactive mannequin for shop windows. In Proc. Persuasive '09, vol. 350. ACM, New York, NY, 1-8.
27. Scott, S. D., Carpendale, M. S. T., and Inkpen, K. M. 2004. Territoriality in Collaborative Tabletop Workspaces. In Proc. CSCW'04, NY, USA. ACM Press, 294-300.
28. Vogel, D. and Balakrishnan, R.: Interactive public ambient displays: Transitioning from implicit to explicit, public to personal, interaction with multiple users. In Proc. UIST '04, ACM Press, 2004, 137–14.
29. Wellner, P. 1993. Interacting with paper on the DigitalDesk. *Commun. ACM* 36, 7 (July 1993), 87-96.

MotionBeam: A Metaphor for Character Interaction with Handheld Projectors

Karl D.D. Willis [1,2] Ivan Poupyrev [2] Takaaki Shiratori [2]

[1] Computational Design Lab,
Carnegie Mellon University
5000 Forbes Avenue, Pittsburgh, PA 15213

[2] Disney Research Pittsburgh
4615 Forbes Avenue, Pittsburgh, PA 15213
{ karl, ivan.poupyrev, shiratori } @disneyresearch.com

ABSTRACT
We present the *MotionBeam* metaphor for character interaction with handheld projectors. Our work draws from the tradition of pre-cinema handheld projectors that use direct physical manipulation to control projected imagery. With our prototype system, users interact and control projected characters by moving and gesturing with the handheld projector itself. This creates a unified interaction style where input and output are tied together within a single device. We introduce a set of interaction principles and present prototype applications that provide clear examples of the *MotionBeam* metaphor in use. Finally we describe observations and insights from a preliminary user study with our system.

Author Keywords
Interaction metaphor, interaction techniques, handheld projector, pico projector, character, gesture, movement.

ACM Classification Keywords
H5.m. Information interfaces and presentation (e.g., HCI): Miscellaneous.

General Terms
Design, Experimentation, Human Factors, Theory.

INTRODUCTION
The vision of Augmented Reality (AR) is to seamlessly merge virtual content into the physical world [1]. Typical approaches to AR make use of intermediary displays through which the user views the augmented environment. Handheld projectors have the advantage of situating virtual content side by side with physical objects in almost any space. Their size allows users to grasp them in a single hand, attach them to their bodies, or move them from space to space. These qualities make them an ideal technology to realize the AR vision. Market research predicts as many as 39 million devices with embedded projectors on the market by 2014 [14]. Despite these significant predictions only a relatively small amount of research has focused on developing new applications and interaction techniques for handheld projectors. In particular the use of handheld projectors as an AR platform has yet to be fully realized.

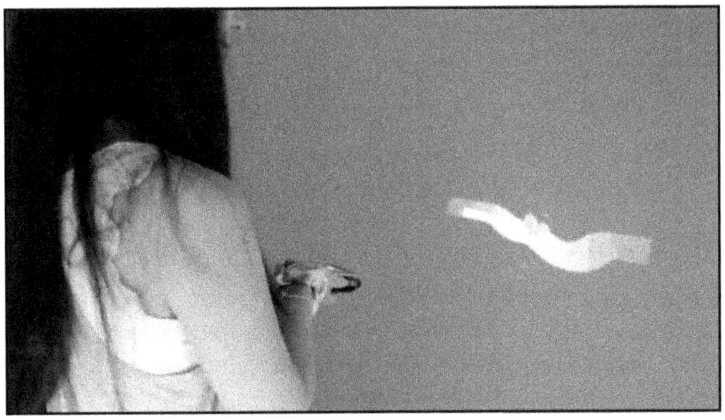

Figure 1. *MotionBeam* is a metaphor for character interaction with handheld projectors.

One of the major challenges when dealing with handheld projectors is to develop interaction techniques that accommodate movement. Projected imagery moves, shakes, and distorts with the user's every move. We present a novel interaction metaphor, labeled *MotionBeam,* which uses the movement of the projection device to control and interact with projected characters (Figure 1). Our work draws from the tradition of pre-cinema handheld projectors that use direct physical manipulation to control projected imagery. Rather than attempt to mitigate the effects of projector movement, we seek to encourage it by using the projector as a gestural input device. This creates a unified interaction style where input and output are tied together within a single device. To outline the use of the *MotionBeam* metaphor, we present a set of interaction principles, detail the implementation of several prototype applications with a custom device, and describe observations from a preliminary user study with our system.

Character interaction has applicability to a range of important domains such as games, educational software, virtual worlds, storytelling, and numerous other applications where an avatar is used to represent a user. The *MotionBeam* metaphor is a powerful tool to blend characters into the physical world; allowing them to perceive and react to the physical environment, as well as 'push back' on the world to actuate and control physical objects. In the long-term, the development of holographic, volumetric, and shape-changing displays will make character experiences even more convincing. Although future technologies will empower this area of research, we can build the foundations for richer interaction with virtual content in the physical world today.

This paper builds upon preliminary work [24] to present the following contributions:

1. We introduce the *MotionBeam* metaphor and interaction principles.
2. We present prototype devices and applications that illustrate the use of the *MotionBeam* metaphor.
3. We describe observations and insights from a preliminary user study with our system.

RELATED WORK

Pre-cinema Handheld Projection Devices

Starting in the pre-cinema era we can find a number of early projection devices that provide valuable insight into the possibilities offered by handheld projector interaction [23]. The *Magic Lantern* was an early projection device invented in the 17th century and used with the *Phantasmagoria* ghost show [19]. Although 'handheld' variations of the *Magic Lantern* did exist, they were impractical due to their metal enclosure and the heat generated from the light source (Figure 2).

In the early 19th century the *Magic Lantern* was adapted in Japan to a wooden form factor that insulated much of the heat generated from the light source. This Japanese *Magic Lantern* was used during *Utsushi-e* theater performances to act out stories with rear-projected images on a rice paper screen (Figure 3). *Utsushi-e* performers directly manipulated the device to change the size and location of the projected image. The performer could also switch between slides during the performance and use the physical movement of the device to produce relatively complex animated sequences [11].

Although technologically primitive by today's standards, the illusions and performances created by these early devices were extremely popular in the pre-cinema era. The role of the performer to control imagery with direct movement of the projector establishes a clear historical interaction precedent. Our work draws specifically from the use of these devices to control and animate characters. We build upon this work by focusing on interaction between virtual content and the physical environment.

Contemporary Research

Contemporary research with handheld projectors has explored a range of input methods such as on-device touch sensors [2], direct touch on the projected image [21], pen based sketching on the virtual environment [4], acoustic sensing on skin [5], and hand gestures [16]. In our work we focus on coupling together the movement of the projection device to the imagery projected. This approach avoids the problem of attention shift between input device and projected image by tying together input and output within a single device. Other areas with relevance to our work include research concerned with pointing-style interaction such as virtual reality ray-casting [3] and laser pointer based interfaces [10].

The issue of projector movement has been approached from several directions. Early research addressed the problems of image stabilization and distortion correction [18]. By dynamically correcting the image as the projector moves, conventional content can be viewed in a regular fashion. While a static projected image is well suited to numerous applications, the mobility of handheld projectors is one of the key affordances of the technology. We believe it is important to investigate interaction techniques that are suitable for use with movement. Other approaches that explore the movement of handheld projectors include systems such as *CoGAME,* where users interact to connect projected tiles together and form a path for a small robot [6], and *Twinkle,* where users guide a projected character to interact with objects in the environment [25]. These works present promising directions for augmenting environments with virtual content, but are only initial investigations.

A large portion of research has focused on the *spotlight metaphor* [4,17], where the projector reveals a section of a larger virtual environment that is tied to a physical space. The *spotlight metaphor* is primarily concerned with navigating a virtual *background* space. In contrast, our work is focused on interaction with characters in the *foreground.* We believe the two approaches are in fact

Figure 2. A belt-mounted *Magic Lantern* created by Phillip Carpenter, 1823, Huhtamo Collection.

Figure 3. Handheld projectors are directly held and positioned used during a Japanese *Utsushi-e* performance, 1800s.

complimentary and represent the primary metaphors for gestural interaction with handheld projectors.

There has been a significant amount of work on controlling and navigating on-screen characters with input modalities such as body movement [13], voice [7], sketching [22], and tangible interfaces [9]. However the use of handheld projectors to augment the immediate physical environment represents a largely different interaction scenario from fixed-screen systems.

MOTIONBEAM

MotionBeam is an interaction metaphor for controlling projected characters with user movement and gesture. It is part of our larger vision to seamlessly merge virtual content into the physical world. The essence of the *MotionBeam* metaphor involves the control of an object on the end of a metaphorical beam (Figure 4). The user has control over one end of the beam, while the object is linked to the opposite end. Moving the object up, down, left, and right is as simple as pointing the beam in the desired direction. The direct control of the projection device creates an immediate link between the device and the projected object. Physical movement and angling of the device draws upon our understanding of 'naive physics' and our 'body awareness and skills' [8].

Characteristics of the object can be changed dynamically based on how the user moves, gestures, and interacts with the *MotionBeam*. This can include the direction the object faces, animation of the object, size of the object, distance from the end of the *MotionBeam*, or viewing angle. These characteristics may also change when encountering other virtual and physical objects in the environment.

MotionBeam Components

The *MotionBeam* metaphor can be abstracted to a set of five core components.

- *User*. Moves, rotates, and points the *MotionBeam.*
- *MotionBeam*. A metaphorical beam that guides and controls the *MotionBeam* object.
- *MotionBeam Object.* A virtual object linked to one end of the *MotionBeam* and controlled by user interaction on the other end.
- *Virtual Objects.* Objects that augment the physical environment. Virtual objects can interact with the *MotionBeam* object.
- *Physical Objects.* Objects within the physical environment. Physical objects can interact with the *MotionBeam* object.

Interaction Principles

The interaction principles outlined in this section show how the *MotionBeam* metaphor can be applied using handheld projector based systems. To guide the design of these principles we have drawn from frameworks in related fields pertaining to animation [12] and sequential art [15]. This

Figure 4. Using the *MotionBeam* metaphor a character is controlled as if it is attached to the end of a virtual beam.

work deals directly with the use of imagery to illustrate the characteristics of animated characters and their interaction with other objects. We take a similar approach by defining principles that are not hard binding rules, but rather a toolkit for designing a wide variety of interactions with the *MotionBeam* metaphor. The interaction principles are not mutually exclusive and may be combined appropriately for each design scenario.

Local & Global Space

The *local space* is contained within the projected image and the *global space* encompasses the overall projection environment. Physical gesturing of the projection device translates the entire local space across the global space (Figure 5a). The existence of two spaces contrasts dramatically with the static display frame used throughout the history of moving image. The *MotionBeam* metaphor is designed explicitly to work with a moving screen. The *MotionBeam* object is tied to the middle of the *local space,* with the primary motion caused by the user moving the entire local space across the global space.

Movement

Movement is the change in location of the local space within the global space. Movement can be accentuated by displaying a motion trail left behind from past locations (Figure 5b). Sequential art utilizes numerous techniques to stylize movement including: zip ribbons showing a path traveled, multiple images depicting past object locations, and blurring akin to long exposure photography [15]. When using these techniques with the *MotionBeam* metaphor, the motion trails emerge from the *MotionBeam* object then flow out in the opposite direction from user movement. A path of motion is 'left behind' that maps out the most recent series of locations.

Physics

Physics is the simulation of physical properties to illustrate interaction between the *MotionBeam* object and other virtual objects, physical objects, and user gestures. Each interaction pair can utilize different physical properties to illustrate and emphasize the interaction taking place. Physics can often be depicted using simple translations

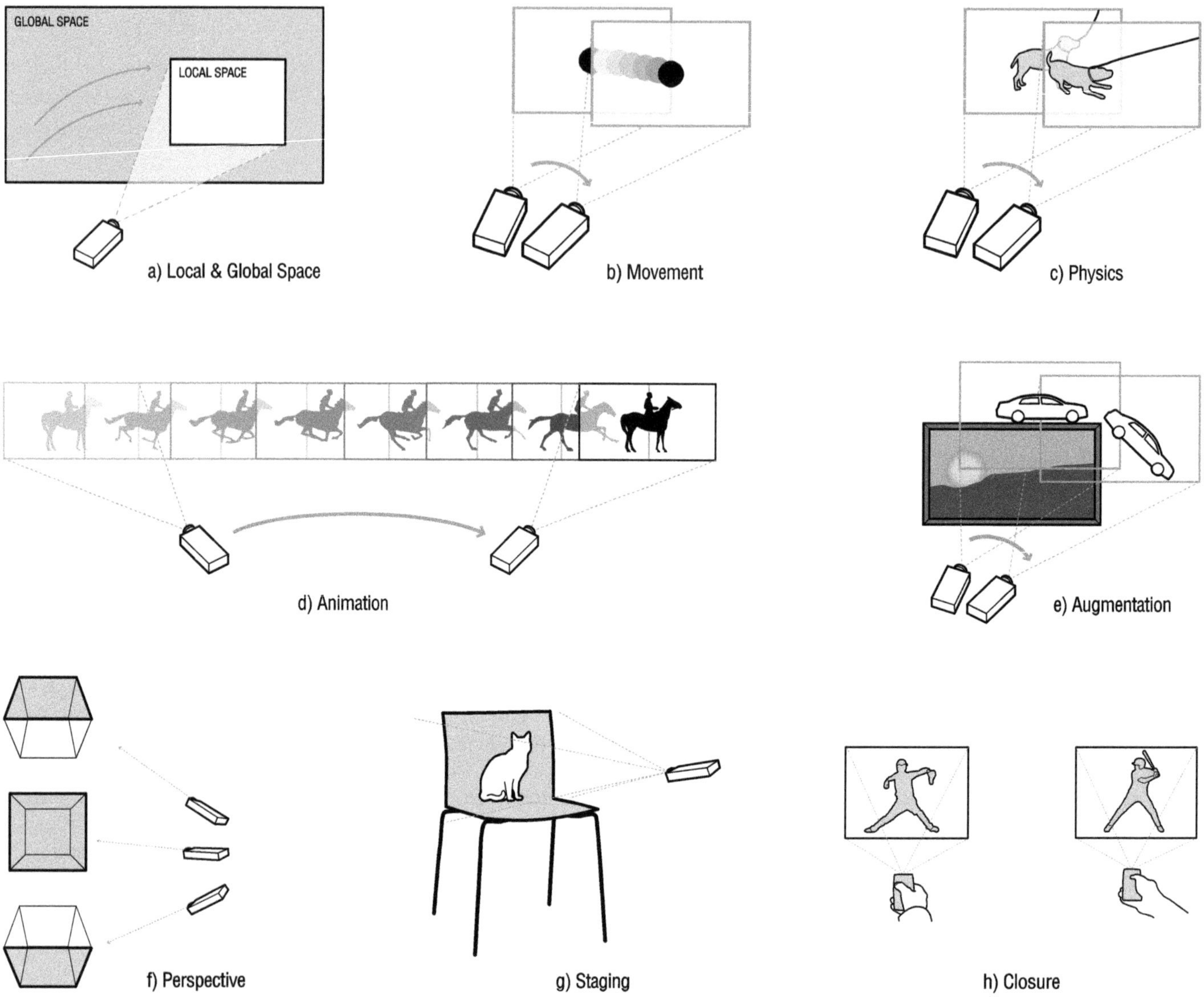

Figure 5. The *MotionBeam* interaction principles.

from the center of the local space. For example, a feeling of friction can be created if the object resists user movement and moves in the opposite direction (Figure 5c). The texture of a virtual or physical surface can also be illustrated by translating the object to depict a bumpy or smooth ride. The object can also be influenced by gravity; an upward flick motion can throw an object out of the screen, only for the object to return back again with gravity.

Animation

Animation is the depiction of changes in the state of the *MotionBeam* object over time. It can be depicted in a number of ways including rotation, deformation, transformation, or color change. Animation can be derived from movement within the global space, interaction with virtual and physical objects, character behavior, or user gestures. A fundamental form of animation is based on the heading and speed of the handheld projector. For example, the individual frames from Eadweard Muybridge's *The Horse in Motion* can be animated with a left to right motion. This leaves the impression of the horse galloping across the physical background (Figure 5d). Objects can also be animated to face the direction of movement. These approaches reflect to the user that the object is aware of the overall environment and responsive to user interaction.

Augmentation

Augmentation is the interaction between the *MotionBeam* object and physical objects. This relationship can flow in two directions; a physical object can affect the *MotionBeam* object or the *MotionBeam* object can 'push back' and affect the physical object. For example, a car driving along the top of a picture frame falls off when it reaches the end (Figure

5e). Conversely, the car could cause the picture frame to come ajar by landing on top of it with force.

Perspective

Perspective is the viewpoint of the *MotionBeam* object in relation to the projection device. The viewing angle of the *MotionBeam* object can be mapped to the angle at which the user is pointing with the projection device. For example when projecting a 3D cube, pointing the projector towards the ground displays the top of the cube; pointing the projector toward the ceiling displays the bottom (Figure 5f). *Perspective* mappings can create an intuitive correlation between the physical pose of the projector and the viewpoint of the projected object.

Staging

Staging is how the *MotionBeam* object is situated within the physical environment. In traditional animation staging aims to focus the attention of the audience by minimizing distractions in the frame [12]. An important aspect of staging is the use of silhouette to highlight the main point of focus. This is particularly important for handheld projectors that have limited image brightness and contrast; a strong silhouette will still be visible in conditions of high ambient light. The foreground object can be rendered on a black background to avoid displaying the rectangular projection frame. This strengthens the illusion of the object existing unframed within the physical environment (Figure 5g).

Closure

Closure is the relationship between actions performed in separate projection frames. The concept of closure is used in sequential art to infer meaning from a sequence of image panels [15]. By viewing one panel followed by another a single meaning emerges. For example, a panel of a shooting gun beside another of a speeding ambulance infers that someone has been shot. This same principle can be applied to interaction with multiple projection frames where only parts of a larger scene are revealed. Actions are shown sequentially in each frame to infer an overall meaning. For example, depicting a pitcher throwing a baseball from one frame, followed by a baseball entering a separate frame, infers that the ball has passed from one frame to the other (Figure 5h). The baseball may not have followed a perfect path or transitioned with perfect timing, but closure leads us to perceive it as the same object.

IMPLEMENTATION

We now describe the creation and implementation of a handheld prototype and several example applications. Their purpose was to firstly evaluate the feasibility of our approach – issues such as sensing accuracy, projection quality, and system latency; secondly, to explore and consider the possible application space; and finally, to better understand the usability of our system. We developed two example game applications and several smaller AR interaction scenarios. We chose games as they provide an ideal platform to explore a range of character interaction.

Prototype

Our prototype is implemented using an iPod Touch 2G, a Microvision ShowWX laser projector, and a microcontroller-sensor unit (Figure 6). The attached sensors include a 9DOF accelerometer/gyroscope/magnetometer board, an ultrasonic distance sensor (MaxSonar), and an infrared receiver. Applications run in real-time on the device and are written in a combination of C++, OpenGL, and Objective-C.

After a simple calibration sequence, the 9DOF sensor provides absolute orientation values. The distance sensor is used to determine if there is a projection surface within range. The infrared (IR) receiver is used to detect the presence of IR tags within the environment. These are small LEDs that emit IR light at timed intervals and are used to identify the location of physical objects in the environment. The device is also capable of communicating over Wi-Fi with other devices embedded in the environment. The iPod dock connector is used to communicate via serial with the sensor unit and send an S-Video signal to the projector. The touch screen can be used for input simultaneously with the projector. However due to the gestural nature of our interface we chose to limit touch screen interaction to a single 'Start' button. The size of the device is 164 x 62 x 32mm, and can be grasped by an average sized hand. System latency is almost unperceivable from a user standpoint. The response time between gestural motion and change in projected imagery is no more than the frame rate of approximately 25fps (40ms).

Character Game

In the character game the user guides a character through the game space by pointing with the projection device (Figure 7). Movement of the character is relative to other objects in the game space, allowing the user to lead the character towards or away from other game objects. Game play involves guiding the character along a trail of stars to collect points and increase the user's score. The user must try to avoid the 'bad-guy' character that chases them in an attempt to throw the character in the air and decrease their score. Once the user reaches the end of the trail they discover the goal – the character's missing car. The faster the user reaches this goal, the higher their score.

The mechanics of the character game are based on interpreting user movement of the device and mapping it to the projected image in real-time. Specific mappings are guided by the *MotionBeam* interaction principles. In keeping with the overall *MotionBeam* metaphor, the position of the character stays fixed to the middle of the projection frame. The *Local & Global Space* principle governs how transformations of the character are applied within the *local space* (the projection frame), while overall movement of the character across the physical environment is perceived in the *global space*.

The *Movement* principle is used to emphasize the motion of the character across the physical environment. A motion

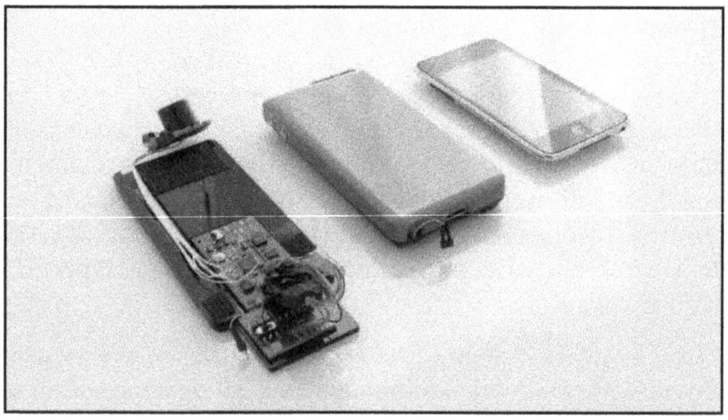

Figure 6. The components used in our prototype. From left to right, a sensor unit, a handheld projector, an iPod Touch.

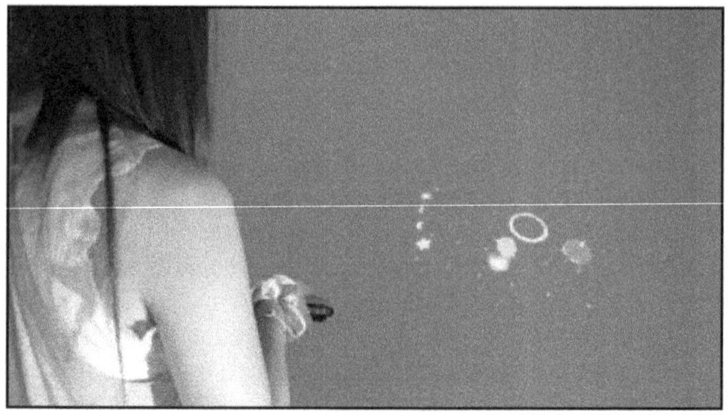

Figure 7. Users guide the character in our prototype game by physically moving and gesturing with the projection device.

trail is added behind the character to indicate the speed and direction travelled. We found that a simple implementation can be visually effective using only a short window of relative acceleration.

The *Animation* principle is applied by rotating the character to point in the direction of movement. This gives the impression that the character is attentive and aware of user input. Other simple animations include the character transitioning to riding its car when the two objects intersect.

The *Physics* principle is used when the character interacts with other objects in the game space. For example when the 'bad-guy' intercepts the character and sends it flying into the air (Figure 8, top), or when the character strays into an out-of-bounds area and falls from the game area. In both of these examples the character is displaced from the center of the local space to depict the physics based interaction.

The *Perspective* principle is used to change the viewing angle so display of the character is changed in relation to the environment. When projecting at a right angle to the wall, the character is viewed from a top-down perspective so it can easily be guided around in relation to other game objects. Tilting the device downward incrementally shifts the viewing angle so the character is viewable from the front. This adds depth to the game by allowing the character to be viewed in 3D form and also allows the user to view the game space from multiple perspectives.

Racing Game

In the racing game the user steers a character's vehicle to reach the end of a racetrack without falling off (Figure 1). By tilting the projector from side to side, the user controls the direction of the vehicle as it moves along the track. The speed of the vehicle is controlled automatically and gradually increases as the game progresses. The track also becomes more difficult as the game goes on, the user must navigate sharp turns, dead ends, and tunnels. If the vehicle does fall from the track it is repositioned after a short delay. As with the character game, the faster the user reaches the goal, the higher their score.

The racing game demonstrates a similar selection of interaction principles as the character game. These are implemented using variations of the algorithms from the character game. *Animation* is used to control the rotation of the vehicle so it faces in the direction of user input. *Movement* is used to emphasis the speed of the vehicle by displaying a motion trail. *Physics* interaction displaces the vehicle from the center of the projection frame when it

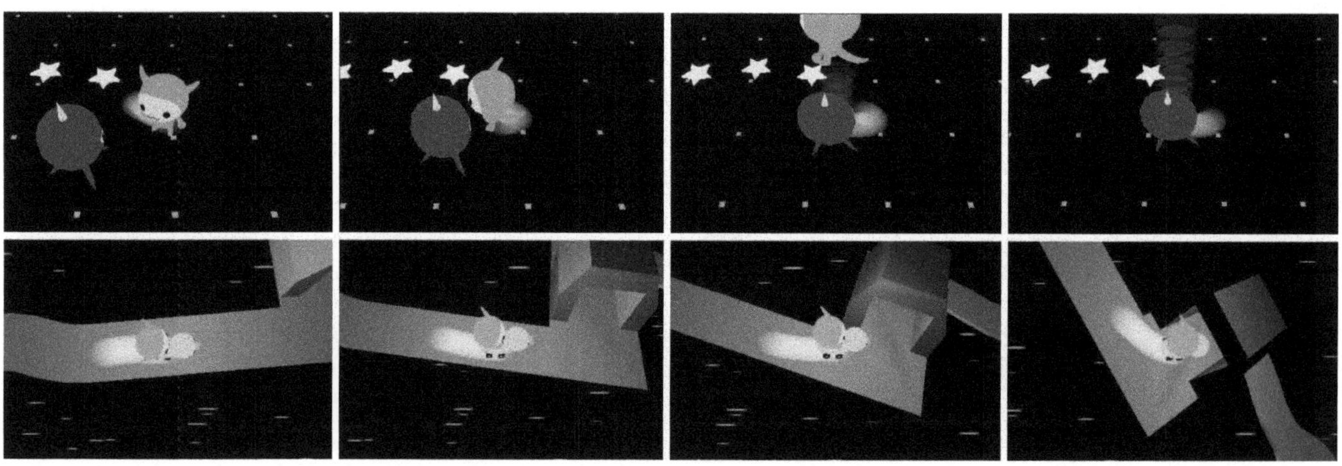

Figure 8. The *Physics* (top) and *Perspective* (bottom) interaction principles applied in our prototype games.

Figure 9. A projected character starts bouncing when it encounters a trampoline in the environment.

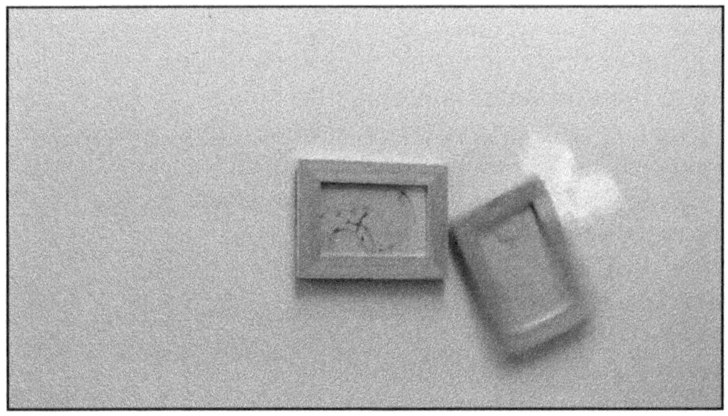

Figure 10. A projected character causes a picture frame to come ajar by jumping on it.

collides with an obstacle or falls from the track. *Perspective* is used to change the viewing angle of the game scene. When projecting at a right angle to the wall, a top view is displayed; by tilting the device downward the view gradually shifts to a front-on position. This enables the user to navigate through areas of the track, such as tunnels, that are not visible from the top view (Figure 8, bottom).

Augmentation Interaction Scenarios

In addition to the character and racing games, we have explored several interaction scenarios that link character interaction to the physical world. Augmentation requires physical objects to be perceived using a camera or a tagging system. Once the system understands the presence and location of these objects it can respond by either changing the projected imagery or actuating the objects themselves. We used an IR receiver attached to the device to detect the presence of IR tags embedded in the environment. Each tag functions much like a conventional TV remote control, by emitting IR light at timed intervals. When the receiver is in direct line of sight with the tag, it can respond based on the tag code being emitted.

To test this interaction with users we developed a standby screen for each of the two games. A character is projected that changes its behavior when located on an IR tagged sticker. The character starts bouncing when it finds the trampoline sticker (Figure 9), and the character's vehicle starts spinning when it drives over a puddle sticker. We developed a preliminary example demonstrating how the *MotionBeam* metaphor can be used to affect objects in the physical environment. In this interaction scenario the user 'drives' a character along the top of several picture frames. When the character jumps from one picture frame to the next, it jolts the picture frame out of place and causes the car to fall from the screen (Figure 10).

Our augmentation interaction scenarios further illustrate two *MotionBeam* interaction principles. *Staging* is used to situate the projected character with elements in the physical environment such as the trampoline sticker or the picture frame. We found the *Staging* technique to be most convincing when using laser based handheld projectors. These do not project light from black areas of the image, allowing the projection frame to completely disappear.

We used the *Augmentation* principle to make projected characters respond to physical objects in the environment, e.g. by jumping up and down on the trampoline or pushing the picture frame ajar. The ability to perceive and respond to the immediate physical environment is a key component of AR systems. Characters that respond by actuating the physical world further enhance the illusion of virtual content existing side by side in the 'real world'. The remaining interaction principle, *Closure*, has not yet been addressed in our implementation and is the subject of future work with a multi-user system.

USER STUDY

We now present details of a preliminary study we conducted to observe user interaction with our system and answer the following questions:

1. Does the amount of projector movement and distortion required by the *MotionBeam* metaphor make the screen difficult to watch?
2. How do users gesture with the device? How can we improve the interface for this interaction style?
3. At what range do users interact? For what reason?
4. What are the participant's impressions of the system?
5. What future studies are needed to better understand interaction with handheld projectors?

Participants & Procedure

We recruited eight participants (five female and three male) from the local area. Five were adults aged between 21-41 (mean 27.83) and three were children between 8-12 (mean 10). Participants played the game in pairs with the exception of two people who played individually due to cancellations. None of the participants had used the system before. Participants were first given a simple demonstration of the game and then invited to play it themselves. No time limit was set for interaction, rather participants were invited to replay the game at will. During the game play we observed interaction and filmed each participant for later analysis. We recorded data such as sensor readings, start/finish times, and game events. Participants then filled out a questionnaire to gauge their impressions of the interaction and the system as a whole. The questionnaire contained both open-ended questions and questions based on a 5 point Likert scale. This process was repeated once for each game and was followed by an interview where users commented on their experiences. The whole process took between 30-45 minutes.

Screen Movement and Distortion

One of the major concerns when dealing with a new type of interactive system is how easy it is for new users to adapt to its use. Systems using the *MotionBeam* metaphor differ significantly from fixed screen systems due to the heavy use of motion to guide characters. We were concerned with projector movement making the screen difficult to watch, acute projection angles causing distortion of the projected imagery, and imagery being projected onto surfaces that would make viewing difficult. This was the motivating factor behind question one.

To gain an idea of how often the projected image was moved into a distorted position we analyzed data recorded from the ultrasonic distance sensor on the device. This sensor uses time-of-flight readings to determine distance and is typically orientated in a perpendicular position to a surface. When the sensor is moved more than 40 degrees from perpendicular, readings time-out and a large value is returned. In our case this indicates that the projector has been orientated at an acute angle and the image is likely to be distorted considerably. We found that these large time-out values occurred with seven of the eight participants and represented 4% of the total readings recorded (Figure 11, values over 150cm). The character game requires more physical motion so had a greater number of time-out values compared to the racing game, with 5% vs. 2% of total readings respectively. This data suggests that users do orientate the device so that the projected image becomes distorted. We observed that the image is typically moved into a distorted position for only a short period of time, before quickly returning to a less acute viewing angle. Distortion of the projected image is typically coupled with quick movements of the device.

To understand how the distortion and movement of the projected image affected the user experience, we interviewed participants and asked them how difficult it was to watch the screen. Participant 8 described interaction with the projection device as 'natural' and was unaware of the screen because her focus was on controlling the character in the game. Participant 8 also stated that she only became aware of the projector when moving closer to the screen caused the image to shrink and vice versa. Participants 6 and 7 stated that they were unaware of the motion of the screen except for the rare instances when their screens would overlap. We noted that participants 5, 6, and 7 also projected onto the surrounding walls, but each

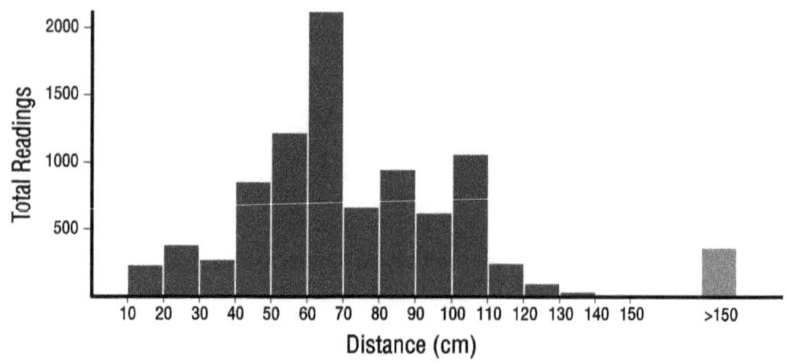

Figure 11. Distribution of distance values measured between the projection device and the projection surface.

responded this did not cause problems. Participants were finally asked in the questionnaire 'Was it difficult to watch the screen?' and scored on a 5 point Likert scale between *Really Difficult* (1) and *Really Easy* (5). The results for both games were the same with a median of 4.5 and a mode of 5. These results illustrate that watching the screen was not difficult; the overall consensus was that motion and distortion of the projected image was barely noticed.

Movement Styles

When seeking to address question two, we noticed two prominent styles of movement when interacting with our system: wrist movement and arm movement. The character game required the participant to lead the character in all directions, so was suited to full arm movement. Conversely, the racing game required the participant to orient a vehicle, so was better suited to finer wrist movement.

Participants who used arm movement with the character game, generally picked up the interaction quickly. Those who used wrist movement struggled initially as they tended to roll the device towards a given direction rather than point. However, when it was clear that the character was not responding as desired, these participants quickly adapted to arm movement. Although the device size was not overly large, creating a more compact and graspable form factor would afford more liberal movement of the device.

Projection Range

The handheld form factor of the projection device allowed participants to project at any distance from the projection surface. Figure 11 addresses question three by illustrating the distribution of distance values measured during the study. Table 1 shows the median and mode value calculated for each game. This data reflects the range at which participants felt comfortable interacting during the study. However, the brightness of the projector, the amount of

	Median	Mode
Character Game	72.39	62.23
Racing Game	66.68	62.23
Both Games	67.31	62.23

Table 1. Distance readings (cm) from the projection device to the projection surface.

ambient light, and the size of the projection surface are all factors that contribute to the user's chosen projection range. For AR systems that focus on merging virtual imagery together with physical objects, designing for a specific projection range is of increased importance. The differences in projection range we observed were relatively large. A change in distance from 50cm to 100cm results in the projected image doubling in size and losing considerable brightness. Several participants commented on their preferences: participant 6 preferred a larger image and therefore stood further back, while participant 7 preferred to stand closer for a brighter image.

Participant Impressions

To address question four, we asked participants to comment freely on the experience. We found that participant reactions to the session were very positive. Participants consistently described interaction with the character as 'natural' and 'easy'. Participants were allowed to replay the game as many times as they wanted, and we were surprised by their enthusiasm to play again and again. The character game, which was the shorter of the two, was played on average 8.75 times per participant, and the racing game on average 4.5 times per participant. We found that users responded well when the projected character would interact with the trampoline or puddle sticker. They quickly understood this simple interaction and were immediately engaged. Some users even pointed the device at a different sticker in an attempt to make the vehicle bounce on the trampoline or the character spin in the puddle. When asked: "Where would you play projection games like this one?" the preferred venue was *Home* (10 responses), followed by *Outside* (8 responses), then *Car* (6 responses). Participant 1 commented it would be possible to project onto people's backs on the bus and participant 4 suggested the game would be a fun social activity with a large screen and multiple players.

Future Studies

We address question five by identifying several directions for future studies. Firstly, we found that the motion and distortion of the screen was not a noticeable issue for participants in the study. A contributing factor may be the *willing suspension of disbelief*, as the user ignores imperfections in the presentation to follow the interaction. Although many handheld projector based systems utilize image stabilization and distortion correction, a future study may seek to determine if the user perceives a difference when these techniques are implemented and not. It is possible that the distortion of the image appears more 'natural' because it conforms to our naïve understanding of optics. Secondly, contrary to our experience with users of the system, we did find rare cases of spectators having trouble watching the screen. Informal comments suggested that viewing the screen was at times difficult and could even cause a very mild feeling of motion sickness. This can be likened to the motion sickness experienced by vehicle passengers, but not by drivers, when riding in a vehicle [20]. A more formal study is required to identify the specific circumstances when viewing a moving screen is problematic.

User Study Conclusion

By observing users interaction with our prototypes we concluded that participants did not find the high level of screen motion and distortion to be an issue. We were also able to observe how participants gestured with the device and at what range. These observations have real practical use for the design of projection devices or the environments in which they are used. Our study also identified several directions for future studies that can enhance our understanding of handheld projector based interaction.

CONCLUSION

We have presented the *MotionBeam* metaphor for character interaction with handheld projectors. Our work draws from the tradition of pre-cinema handheld projectors using direct physical manipulation to control projected imagery. Unlike the dominant direction of research that uses the spotlight metaphor to navigate a virtual *background* space, our focus is on establishing a complimentary interaction metaphor to control characters in the *foreground*. We believe these two approaches represent the primary metaphors for direct gestural interaction with handheld projectors.

Although the *MotionBeam* metaphor is applicable across a range of interaction scenarios, there are usage limitations:

- The metaphor is designed for the control of a single virtual object. It is unclear how the metaphor can be extended to control multiple objects simultaneously.
- The metaphor relies heavily on physical movement. It may not be appropriate for use in confined spaces or for users with limited mobility. Fatigue may be a factor when interacting for extended periods, but it is comparable to the use of video game motion controllers such as the *Wii*.
- The metaphor works at human scale. Using gesture and movement to control a miniature or oversized object may not be appropriate.
- Our current prototype is limited to the use of appropriate projection surfaces and ambient lighting conditions. However we have found that suitable environments are readily available and expect that advances in technology will continue to overcome this limitation.

We have detailed interaction principles that will aid other researchers to design using the *MotionBeam* metaphor. The prototype applications we developed provide a clear example of how the *MotionBeam* metaphor can be implemented using current technology. Further miniaturization of our prototype would allow a compact form factor akin to modern mobile phones. Such a device has the potential to establish a new 'game projector' platform for mobile and augmented reality gaming. Unlike existing portable game devices, a 'game projector' can use the real world as a playground and encourage direct interaction between multiple users.

Handheld projectors have the potential to seamlessly merge virtual content into the physical world. The ability to situate virtual content with physical objects *in any location* opens up numerous avenues for exploration. Future research will almost certainly focus on how to achieve tighter integration between the virtual and the real. We are now on the verge of being able to design our environments and interact with them like never before. With the continuing development of technologies to actuate and shape our environment, we will be increasingly able to design the physical world as well as the virtual. The challenge remains to imagine just how we want the world to be.

ACKNOWLEDGEMENTS

We thank Cheng Xu for assistance with the user study, Jill Lehman, Gabe Johnson, Carolyn Rose, and Chris Harrison for reading over early drafts of this paper, and Keiko Nakao for designing the game characters.

REFERENCES

1. Azuma, R.T. A Survey of Augmented Reality. *Presence: Teleoperators and Virtual Environments 6*, 4 (1997), 355-385.
2. Blaskó, G., Coriand, F. and Feiner, S., Exploring Interaction with a Simulated Wrist-Worn Projection Display. In Proc. *ISWC '05*, IEEE (2005), 2-9.
3. Bowman, D.A. and Hodges, L.F., An Evaluation of Techniques for Grabbing and Manipulating Remote Objects in Immersive Virtual Environments. In Proc. *I3D '97*, ACM (1997), 35-38.
4. Cao, X. and Balakrishnan, R., Interacting with Dynamically Defined Information Spaces using a Handheld Projector and a Pen. In Proc. *UIST '06*, ACM (2006), 225-234.
5. Harrison, C., Tan, D. and Morris, D., Skinput: Appropriating the Body as an Input Surface. In Proc. *CHI '10*, ACM (2010), 453-462.
6. Hosoi, K., Dao, V.N., Mori, A. and Sugimoto, M., CoGAME: Manipulation Using a Handheld Projector. In Proc. *SIGGRAPH '07 Emerging Technologies*, ACM (2007).
7. Igarashi, T. and Hughes, J.F., Voice as Sound: Using Non-verbal Voice Input for Interactive Control. In Proc. *UIST '01*, ACM (2001), 155-156
8. Jacob, R.J.K., Girouard, A., Hirshfield, L.M., Horn, M.S., Shaer, O., Solovey, E.T. and Zigelbaum, J., Reality-based Interaction: A Framework for Post-WIMP Interfaces. In Proc. *CHI '08*, ACM (2008), 201-210.
9. Johnson, M.P., Wilson, A., Blumberg, B., Kline, C. and Bobick, A., Sympathetic Interfaces: Using a Plush Toy to Direct Synthetic Characters. In Proc. *CHI '99*, ACM (1999), 152-158
10. Kirstein, C. and Mueller, H., Interaction with a Projection Screen Using a Camera-tracked Laser Pointer. In Proc. *MMM '98*, IEEE Computer Society (1998), 191-192.
11. Kobayashi, G. *Utsushi-e*. Chuo University Press, Tokyo, 1987.
12. Lasseter, J., Principles of Traditional Animation Applied to 3D Computer Animation. In Proc. *SIGGRAPH '87*, ACM (1987), 35 - 44.
13. Maes, P., Darrell, T., Blumberg, B. and Pentland, A. The ALIVE System: Wireless, Full-body Interaction with Autonomous Agents. *Multimedia Systems 5*, 2 (1997), 105-112.
14. Markets And Markets Global Pico Projector Market. 2010, http://www.marketsandmarkets.com/Market-Reports/pico-projector-market-196.html.
15. McCloud, S. *Understanding Comics*. Tundra Publishing, Northampton, MA, 1993.
16. Mistry, P., Maes, P. and Chang, L., WUW - Wear Ur World - A Wearable Gestural Interface. *Ext. Abstracts CHI '09*, ACM (2009), 4111-4116.
17. Rapp, S., Michelitsch, G., Osen, M., Williams, J., Barbisch, M., Bohan, R., Valsan, Z. and Emele, M., Spotlight Navigation: Interaction with a Handheld Projection Device. In Proc. *Pervasive '04*, Video Paper (2004).
18. Raskar, R., van Baar, J., Beardsley, P., Willwacher, T., Rao, S. and Forlines, C. iLamps: Geometrically Aware and Self-Configuring Projectors. *ACM Transactions on Graphics 22*, 3 (2003), 809-818.
19. Robinson, D., Herbert, S. and Crangle, R. *Encyclopedia Of The Magic Lantern*. The Magic Lantern Society, North Yorkshire, 2001.
20. Rolnick, A. and Lubow, R.E. Why is the Driver Rarely Motion Sick? *Ergonomics 34*, 7 (1991), 867-879.
21. Sugimoto, M., Miyahara, K., Inoue, H. and Tsunesada, Y., Hotaru: Intuitive Manipulation Techniques for Projected Displays of Mobile Devices. In Proc. *INTERACT '05*, Springer (2005), 57-68.
22. Thorne, M., Burke, D. and van de Panne, M., Motion Doodles: An Interface for Sketching Character Motion. In Proc. *SIGGRAPH '04*, ACM (2004), 424-431.
23. Willis, K.D.D. A Pre-History of Handheld Projector based Interaction. *Journal of Personal and Ubiquitous Computing*, Theme issue on Personal Projection (Forthcoming).
24. Willis, K.D.D. and Poupyrev, I., MotionBeam: Designing for Movement with Handheld Projectors. *Ext. Abstracts CHI '10*, ACM (2010), 3253-3258.
25. Yoshida, T., Hirobe, Y., Nii, H., Kawakami, N. and Tachi, S., Twinkle: Interacting with Physical Surfaces using Handheld Projector. In Proc. *VR '10*, IEEE (2010), 87-90.

3D Projection on Physical Objects: Design Insights from Five Real Life Cases

Peter Dalsgaard and Kim Halskov
Center for Digital Urban Living and CAVI, Aarhus University
Helsingforsgade 14, 8200 Aarhus N, Denmark
{dalsgaard, halskov}@CAVI.dk

ABSTRACT
3D projection on physical objects is a particular kind of Augmented Reality that augments a physical object by projecting digital content directly onto it, rather than by using a mediating device, such as a mobile phone or a head-mounted display. In this paper, we present five cases in which we have developed installations that employ 3D projection on physical objects. The installations have been developed in collaboration with external partners and have been put into use in real-life settings such as museums, exhibitions and interaction design laboratories. On the basis of these cases, we present and discuss three central design insights concerning new potentials for well-known 3D effects, dynamics between digital world and physical world, and relations between object, content and context.

Author Keywords
Design, projection, 3D, cultural heritage, exhibitions, architecture, visual effects, Augmented Reality.

ACM Classification Keywords
H.5.1 Multimedia Information Systems.

General Terms
Design.

INTRODUCTION
3D projection on physical objects is a nascent field of study, and engineers, designers, artists, and researchers have just started to explore the potential and characteristics of this type of technology. 3D projection may be construed as an evolutionary rather than a revolutionary technology, in that it is a further development and combination of existing technologies. Many of the uses of 3D projection borrow from more well-established forms of visual media, sometimes employing specific means of expression, sometimes tweaking them slightly and at yet other times, using juxtapositions of traditional visual expressions and 3D projection to create spectacular effects. As stated by Manovich: 'We will see that many of the principles [of new media] are not unique to new media, but can be found in older media as well.' [10:p50].

Broadly speaking, 3D projection on physical objects may be defined as a type of mixed reality [12], which refers to systems or installations that blend physical elements with digital, virtual elements. Milgram and Kishino [12] present a reality/virtuality continuum, with real environment at one end of the spectrum, on through augmented reality, augmented virtuality, and, eventually, virtual environment. With reference to this continuum, 3D projection is best defined as Augmented Reality (AR), since it consists of digital information that is projected onto physico-spatial structures. As such, 3D projection is related to an increasingly widespread type of visualization technology, namely AR that captures images of the physical environment and represents it, with added layers of data, on displays such as mobile phone screens [5]. This is used, for instance, by route-finding and locative services that combine video feeds captured by a mobile phone camera with information about nearby sites, by employing GPS data from the phone [15]. These systems can be construed as a further development of principles explored in see-through head-mounted AR displays [2].

3D projection on physical objects is distinct from these types of systems, since they display the virtual layer on top of the actual physical surroundings, and not on a representation thereof. As such, it falls within the category of spatial AR [13]. Since 3D projections rely on precise mapping of the physical spaces onto which they are projected – as opposed to 2D projections, which typically can be projected onto most flat surfaces – using Manovich's terminology [11], these installations may also be described as *augmented spaces*, which are defined as involving the embedding or overlay of layers of data onto the environment. In this respect, 3D projection on physical objects shares a number of traits with CAVE installations where the user is surrounded by projection surfaces [6]. This eliminates the need for mediating devices and places the spectator within the augmented environment. However, CAVE installations are closed, highly specialized stand-alone systems that use flat surfaces for projection, whereas the installations we introduce in this paper are positioned in other contexts (e.g. exhibition spaces) and use irregular projection surfaces that have been modeled in digital 3D.

In this respect, some 3D projections are also related to new kinds of displays integrated into the physical environment, such as media façades [7] and urban screens [17], insofar as 3D projections are sometimes employed to augment or transform the built environment.

In this paper, we present five cases in which we have developed installations that employ 3D projection on physical objects. These cases concern installations developed in relation to *The Mejlby Stone, Holger the Dane,* the *Architectons, Loop City* and *Expo 2010*. The installations are the outcome of three years of ongoing research and development into the field of spatial AR and 3D projection. The installations have been developed in collaboration with external partners and have been put into use in real-life settings such as museums, exhibitions and interaction design studios. On the basis of these cases, we discuss three central design insights concerning *new potentials for well-known 3D effects*, *dynamics between digital world and physical world*, and *relations between object, content and context*. The primary contributions of this paper are thus 1) the cases that exemplify how 3D projection can be used for various purposes and in various domains and 2) the design insights, which are a condensation of our findings from working with the cases.

RELATED WORK

During the past two decades, several research teams have been investigating 3D projections on physical objects from a technical perspective, in contrast to our interest in using the technology to support engaged communication. At an early stage, Raskar and his co-researchers [14] explored the use of projectors to graphically animate physical objects, and address technical issues such as the projection in relation to the physical object, intensity correction, and edge blending. In a related paper [13] Bandyopadhyay, Raskar, and Fuchs present an AR system, enabling the interactive painting and texturing of three-dimensional objects, and Lee et al. [9] have developed a setup that enables projection on a two-dimensional, handheld surface, which can be can be moved in physical, three-dimensional space. In continuation of the above-mentioned contributions, Bimber and Raskar [5] provides a thorough overview of the general principles and techniques of spatial AR.

Beyond such explorations of 3D projection, which primarily focus on the technical aspects of the technology, the most prominent examples of 3D projection are, arguably, the works of Pablo Valbuena. His series of installations entitled *Augmented Sculptures* [18] has been displayed at venues such as Ars Electronica, and has also attracted many views on Internet video services. Valbuena's installations are typically composed of very angular and clear-cut geometrical shapes that are camera tracked, and in conjunction with which 3D technology is used to create the illusion of light sources moving across the faces of the installations. There are also a growing number of installations that employ 3D projection to mimic the third dimension on a 2D surface. *555 Kubik* [16] is an example of such an installation. Projected onto the façade of Hamburg Kunsthalle, the installation employs visuals that in various ways create a sense of depth: the façade's tiles appear to move in and out of the façade, the interior of the building is revealed in perspective, and so forth. AntiVJ's installation, *Enghien* [1], employs similar forms of expression, but takes further steps to both underline and break down the illusion. Projected onto a building façade, the installation first mimics moving light sources to emphasize the 3D effect; then, starts copying and apparently moving the physical, architectural features, such as windows and balconies; finally, it deconstructs and eventually explodes these features of the building. Several other projects have used projections on buildings, but without fusing the projections and the forms of the buildings, for instance, *L.A.S.E.R. Tag* [8] and *The Climate Wall* [7]. These installations are either developed to explore technological potentials or for artistic reason. The artistically oriented installations primarily explore new means of expression, and may be defined as staged events for audiences. In relation to these installations, the work we present in this paper may be characterized as more functionally oriented, in the sense that the five systems we describe have been developed to support communication (in the cases of The Mejlby Stone, Holger the Dane, 3XN, and the Loop City project) or design practices (in the case of the Expo project). Furthermore, several of the systems also incorporate interactive elements that, to some extent, allow users to influence or control the content of the projections.

INSTALLATIONS

During the past three years, our research lab has developed a series of installations that explore the potential of projecting digital content on physical objects. The installations have been developed as parts of full-scale experimental projects, in collaboration with external partners, including museums and architectural firms.

In the main part of this paper we combine and condense the insights obtained from working with these installations, in order to establish a general understanding of the challenges and potentials of designing 3D projection on physical objects. In the following sections, we present five of these cases, which are also presented in the short video that accompanies this paper. The first example, The Mejlby Stone installation, in fact used 2D projection on a physical rune stone. We have chosen to include this installation because it was our first full-scale project using projection on physical objects and the findings from the project have informed the subsequent four installations and encouraged our use of 3D projection.

The installations are presented on the video accompanying this paper, throughout the paper we will refer to specific instances in the video in the following manner (video 2.35).

The Mejlby Stone installation

The Mejlby Stone installation is an augmentation of a Danish rune stone [4]. Rune stones are part of the cultural heritage from the Viking age in Scandinavia. More than 2300 stones tell of life in Scandinavia during the Viking Age period (AD 950–1050), through images and writing in the runic alphabet, which can only be read or understood by specialists. At museums, it is common practice to use exhibition labels to communicate the story told by the rune stones, but in the case of The Mejlby Stone, we have added a digital layer to the stone in the form of a projection, thereby fusing the physical artefact and the communication of information about the stone.

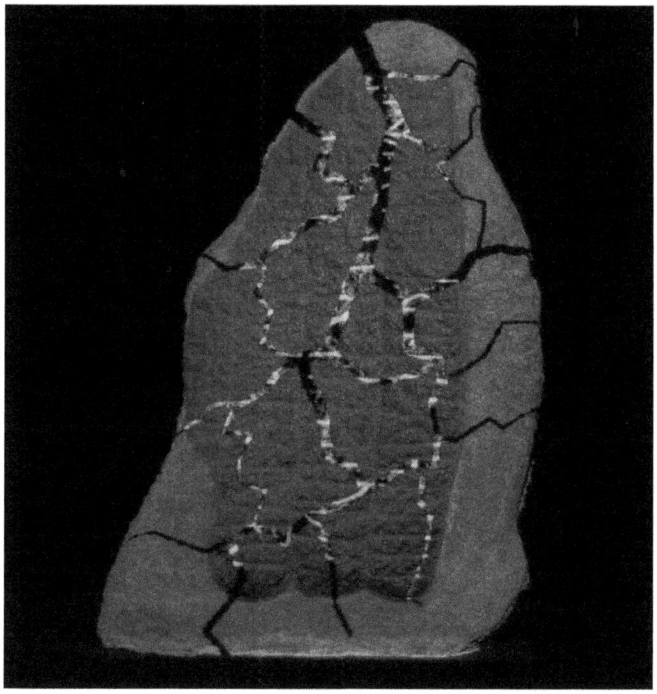

Figure 1. The Mejlby Stone Installation.

As reported in more detail in [4], the projection consists of five different elements presented cyclically: 1) when no visitors are near The Mejlby Stone the runes are lit up in red for about two seconds, at twenty-second intervals; 2) when someone passes within a few metres of the stone an animation appears on the stone. The animation tells the story of the events that led to the erection of The Mejlby Stone; 3) next the runes appearing on the stone as they are carved; 4) when all the runes are carved into the stone the passage of time is illustrated by visually exposing the stone to different kinds of weather. Rainstorms, frost, and lightning progressively efface the runes from the surface of the stone, see Figure 1; 5) in the final element, the runes first reappear on the stone in strong neon colours, then appear to tumble to the floor in front of the stone. Now the audience is supposed to kick the runes back onto the stone. When all the runes are back on the stone, they transform into Roman characters, legible to a present-day audience. The inscription reads: 'Åne erected this stone for his son Eskil who found death with Thore in Øresund'.

Since early 2009, The Mejlby Stone installation has been part of the exhibition at Randers Cultural Historical Museum in Randers, Denmark. Through a study in terms of interviews and observations we have investigated the effect on museum visitors. First of all, 34% of the recorded visitors spent between five and ten minutes in front of the stone. This indicates that the installation is capable of attracting attention and sustaining awareness of itself. We have observed extensive person-to-person interaction in terms of adults explain to children what happened in the story and in some instances people talk about subjects such as death and grief. Our study seems to suggest that the shift from passive watcher to interactively kicking the runes is difficult to decode. Moreover unintended use also emerged in the form of girls bringing themselves into the projection so that the projection falls directly on their bodies [4].

Holger The Dane installation

Holger The Dane is a mythical Danish figure, a statue of whom is found in the Castle of Kronborg, Denmark. Kronborg, also known from Shakespeare's *Hamlet*, is a renaissance castle close to 400 years old, and 100 years ago a statue of Holger The Dane was placed in one of the casemates in the cellar of Kronborg, see Figure 2. According to one of the myths about Holger The Dane, he will awaken and defend the country when an enemy from without threatens the kingdom of Denmark.

When visitors approach the statue the embers behind the feet of Holger The Dane gloves stronger and his life is told in terms of narrative segments. One of six fairies, which according to the legend gave special power to Holger The Dane, appears floated in front of the statue. The illusion is supported by a shadow of the fairy on the sculpture and by magic dust lighting up a part of the sculpture. Among the myths, we also read that he was held captive by *Karl den Store* (English: Charlemagne), that Holger The Dane is lawless, that fairies granted him magical powers, and that he fought the giant Burmand. The myths are visualized by abstract references to the myths: for instance, Holger The Dane's fight against Burmand is visualized by a shadow slowly covering the statue, to illustrate Burmand approaching Holger The Dane, followed by sounds illustrating the fight between the two, then a fairy arrives, giving Holger The Dane extra strength, enabling him to split the shadow, after which blood appears to sprinkle the shield and one of the feet's of the statue. In a final sequence Holger The Dane seems to have falling asleep indicated by the upper part of his body slowly moving in the rhythm of his breathing.

The statue is a very popular photographic subject and when a flash photographing is detected the visual style of the projection is changed.

Since October 2010 the installation has been in operation at the Castle of Kronborg and an initial study supplemented by interviews of visitors indicate that the installation creates an engaging experience. Most visitors who arrive at the room where the status is placed view the entire sequence, but only few notices the effect of flash photographing. Visitors' spontaneous exclamations indicate that visual effects make sense for them, for instance "now he is locked up" when grilles are projected on the statue (video 2.25). In particular the effect of splashing blood and the sleeping sequence triggers reaction from visitors. The interviews reveals that people are quit split when it comes to the overall concept and visual style: some find the installation a bit little too much Disney Worldish whereas others appreciated the mood and atmosphere created by the installation and also pointed out that the installation is powerful way of making younger generations interested in the myth of Holger the Dane. The manager of the Castle and the person in charge of cultural heritage communication were initially in the design process in favor of a more direct retelling of the myths but when seeing the final result found the atmosphere of the installation quit amazing.

Figure 2. The Holger the Dane Installation.

Loop City

Loop City is an installation presenting a proposed plan for a large-scale urban project that spans Copenhagen and Southern Sweden. The installation uses three projectors to present visuals on two walls set at a 90-degree angle in the corner of an exhibition room. Additionally, the installation presents visuals on the floor and on a solid elongated bridge volume that extends into the room from one of the walls.

The presentation is composed of three parts. The first part uses the two rear walls as a canvas for an introduction to the urban planning challenges, and the solution proposed by the architectural firm BIG. This part employs traditional 2D visuals, such as animated maps, diagrams, and text. At the end of this part, the visuals outline a future metro line, which suddenly extends onto a triangle that was previously in the dark. This initiates the second part, which employs 3D visuals centered around the bridge volume. Now, the walls serve as a backdrop, with additional information presented in 2D, but attention centers around a bridge volume, which displays both diagrams and specific proposals for metro lines. The floor is also brought into play, for instance when tiny images of people exit the metro lines and pour into the city, while buildings rise around them, see Figure 3. When these more specific instantiations have been visualized, the third part begins. This part returns to a 2D presentation, but now also incorporates the floor, to show a roller-coaster-inspired ride through Copenhagen on the new public transportation line.

Figure 3. The Loop City Installation.

Loop City was from August to November of 2010 part of the Danish Pavilion at the 2010 Venice Architectural Biennale in Italy. Through a study consisting of on-location observations and interview we investigated how the visitors reacted and responded to the installation. Since the installation was a kind of movie showed in an on-going cycle most of the visitors encountered the installation in the middle of the storyline. Out of 131 people 13% saw the movie from when they came in and until the narrative ended. 24% of the visitors saw the movie from when they entered the room and then saw it again from the beginning of the narrative till the point in the storyline, they saw when they arrived. 31% of the visitors entered the room and left immediately after only a short glance. Several of the visitors found it a very good idea to spatially communicate the spatial topic of urban planning but others did not pay particular attention to the 3D effects as such.

The Architecton installations

The Architectons are two digitally augmented sculptures that represent iconic features and façade elements of prominent buildings designed by 3XN Architects. We collaborated with a 3XN project team to develop 3D projections for the Architectons, which represented the headquarters of Saxo Bank, and the domicile of the Horten law firm. Both Architectons represented the buildings' distinct façades, which are composed of triangular and parallelogram-shaped elements assembled in a 3D structure, see Figure 4.

Figure 4. Scale model (1:4) of The Saxo Bank installation.

The Architectons were both approximately six meters wide, three meters tall and one meter deep. The two Architectons had different content projected onto them, but both had interactive zones in which the content would switch between three different loops, depending on viewer distance. The content projected on the first Architecton, that of the Horten firm, employed shifting positions of light sources, in order to emphasize the particular way in which elements of the façade appear to be either flat or protruding at various times of day, depending on the positions of the sun and the viewer. The content of the second Architecton, that of the Saxo Bank, emulated the context of the bank's headquarters, which has a glass façade and is positioned in the open; for these reasons, it often reflects the sky, see Figure 4. The three interaction zones therefore showed clouds, first moving across the sky in black and white, then in colour, and finally, to those standing in the innermost zone, the reflected clouds were supplemented by the reflection of the sun moving across the mirrored façade.

From February to May 2010, the Architectons were part of an exhibition at the Danish Architecture Center, entitled *Mind Your Behaviour*. The exhibition was composed of wall-mounted posters and scale models of buildings, as well as five Architectons, of which we worked with augmenting the two mentioned above. Our studies of the two Architectons in use both during the hectic launch event and on subsequent occasions, combined with feedback from the architects, revealed that the 3D visuals were only vaguely perceived by users, and consequently they did not explore the interaction zones as intended. In large part, we consider this to be a result of a late decision to increase the general lighting level in the exhibition area. Since we relied on projectors, this caused the visuals to fade in comparison to other elements of the installation. We thus consider the Architectons case to be the least succesful in regards in to using 3D projection to augment the experience and perception of the physical objects. A central finding that sprang from this case is therefore that designers must ensure that lighting conditions are adequate if 3D projection installations are to be effective.

The Danish Pavilion at Expo 2010

The Danish Pavilion at Expo 2010 (see Figure 5) is part of the world exhibition in Shanghai in 2010, during the period from 1 May to 31 October.

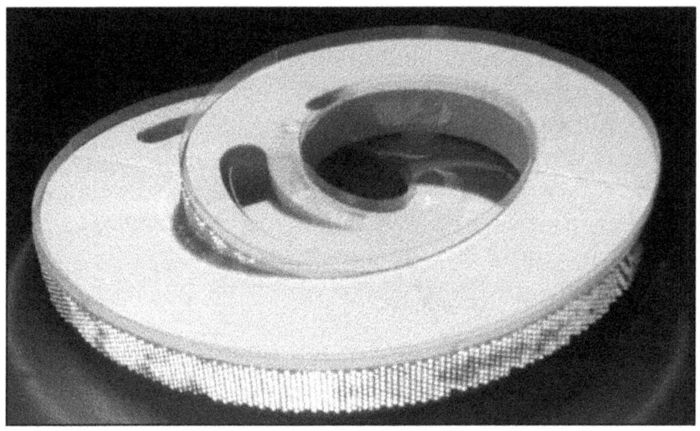

Figure 5. Scale model (1:100) of Expo Pavilion.

Its organic architecture was created by Danish architects at BIG, and our research laboratory participated in the design and implementation of the pavilion's media façade. The building is double-spiral, steel construction with an almost three-hundred-metre-long façade, see Figure 5.

The façade itself is perforated by 3600 holes of varying sizes, each containing a semi-translucent tube. With the addition of LED lighting fixtures behind each tube, the

	Rune stone	Holger the Dane	Architectons	Expo 2010	Loop City
Domain	Cultural heritage	Cultural heritage	Architecture	Design process	Urban planning
Object	Archaeological artefact	Statue	Model of façade element	Scale model of building	Walls, floor and bridge volume
Size (l,w,h) cm	80x50x170	110x110x190	600x100x300	60x60x40	340x340x200
Object structure	Organic	Organic	Complex, Planar	Complex, Non-planar	Simple geometry
Content	Animation Visual effects Narrative sections	Visual effect Narrative sections	Simulation of façade appearance	Simulation of façade appearance	Animation Text and graphics Narrative sections
Context	Museum exhibition	Castle casemates	Architectural exhibition	Design laboratory	Architectural exhibition
Interaction	Limited	Limited	Limited	Complex	None
Period	Permanent	Work in progress	3 months	4 months	2 months

Table 1. Overview of the installations.

façade becomes a large, low-resolution display, with tube-like pixels in an elongated, curved configuration. Because each pixel is a tube, they are less visible when viewed from the front than from an angle. In order to develop and test potential content for such a non-standard display integrated into a building, several custom-made design tools were developed. One such tool was a white, 1:100 scale model, combined with a projection setup, which enabled the visualization of potential content directly on the physical model.

Our evaluation of the installation is based on interviews with the interaction designers who used it during the design process. The installation was used by the design team on a regular basis - at least once a week, and often more frequently - for six months during the process. It was first intended to function as a simulation of how the final façade would appear; however, it turned out that the renderings of the interactive façade elements on the model were somewhat imprecise compared to how actual façade LEDs appeared in real life. For this reason, subsequent alterations had to be made on the Expo site. In spite of this, the installation turned out to be a useful instrument for the designers in several ways: first, it presented a way of visualising content on the very complex building structure which was not otherwise possible; second, it offered an straightforward way of understanding the coupling of the physical space with interactive content; third, it presented the designers with a tool for making on-the-spot alterations and experiments and see the immediate outcome; and fourth, it served as a pre-eminent boundary object for communicating with outside partners in the project.

Summary

Table 1 provides a structured overview of the five installations. The installations are diverse, both with regards to the domains for which they have been designed, with regards to their content, with regards to the size and complexity of the object onto which the content is projected, and with regards to the particular use situation that the installations affect.

ALIGNING DIGITAL MODELS AND PHYSICAL OBJECTS

Before we present and discuss our central design findings, we will give a brief overview of our strategies concerning the alignment of digital models and physical objects. In four of the five installations we had specific physical objects as our starting points for the installations, and in two of these four installations, The Mejlby Stone and Holger the Dane, we projected directly on the original object. In the case of the Architectons, we projected on full-scale models of fragments of two existing buildings, and in the case of The Expo Pavilion, we projected on a 1:6 scale model of a building under construction. The Loop City installation is different, in that the projection space is the corner of an exhibition room, together with a section of a bridge volume. For Holger the Dane, no digital model was readily available, so a scanning company assisted us in creating a digital model, which was subsequently used to create a 3D print in a scale of 1:4, enabling us to develop and test the installation without going to the castle. In all cases except that of Holger the Dane, we used more than one projector, creating a need for handling edge blending.

In the case of the Architectons, two existing buildings were the starting points for the process. First, a digital 3D model of a section of the façade was created, and from this, a physical model of the façade element was created. The content to be projected was produced using the 3D imaging software, and projecting the content on the physical model is simple in theory, but not in practice; several circumstances pose challenges, here. First, the physical model does not perfectly match the digital model, and the lenses in projectors are not perfect lenses, which causes distortion of the image; even small inaccuracies can be detrimental to the final result, since just a few pixels that 'spill over' their designated positions may be very obvious, depending on projection and viewing angles. To enable the match-up of the digital and the physical models, two custom-made tools were developed. The automatic calibration tool applies a heuristic algorithm that tweaks the position, rotation, field of view, and aspect ratio of the virtual camera, in order to compensate for the corresponding parameters of the projector, as well as discrepancies between the digital and physical models (video 3.26). The calibration process is initiated by informing the software tool of the positions of eight to ten predefined points on the physical model, coordinating and associating each of these points with the corresponding points in the digital models. Through a process that may last from 30 minutes to several hours, depending on the mismatch between the digital 3D model and the physical model, the camera's view of the digital model is tweaked, to compensate for the differences between the parameters of the virtual camera and those of the projector.

In addition to our automatic calibration tool, our lab has developed an interactive tool which works by selecting a portion of the physical area on the model where the projection of the digital 3D model does not match the physical model, then stretching the digital model to make the projection match the physical model (video 3.48).

The necessary calibration very much depends on the quality and complexity of the physical model. Both of the Architectons were made of cardboard glued together in a fairly complex and somewhat shaky structure, with some of the elements only connected to the rest of the model by a single edge, making the model vulnerable to physical stress. The Expo 2010 model, despite its organic form, was much more simple and physically stable, but both in this case and in that of the very plain model for the Biennale 2010, calibration is needed, when setting up the installation.

DESIGN INSIGHTS

In the following, we will present and discuss central findings from our work in the five cases with a particular emphasis on issues that may be of relevance to designers who wish to employ 3D spatial AR. Our presentation of these insights are based on our analysis of the cases in conjunction. Generally speaking, the use of 3D projection in spatial AR opens up for a range of effects and illusions that designers can make use of. Some of the effects are generic and may be employed in most spatial AR setups that make use of 3D, for example, variable light sources, particle systems and the introduction of virtual elements in the projection space. Other effects are highly context-specific, drawing on the physical properties of the place and projection surface, as well as on the ways in which people normally perceive the space that is being augmented. We will not offer a complete overview of these effects, but instead focus on three themes that we find particularly salient for the future design of 3D projection on physical objects: new potentials for well-known 3D effects, dynamics between digital world and physical world, and the relation between object, content and context.

New potentials for well-known 3D effects

In the five cases, we have to a large extent made use of standard visual effects that are part of existing 3D software (we have primarily used 3D Studio Max, but most the following techniques are available in other applications). Our findings from the five cases indicate that a number of these existing 3D techniques offer designers relatively straightforward means of creating intriguing effects and illusions when used in 3D projection of physical objects.

One of the most basic techniques afforded in 3D software is to establish the perception of depth by creating and moving light sources in the world of a digital model. This effect can be used in many installations involving 3D spatial AR and can be used to achieve a variety of illusions. For example, in the Architecton project, this effect was used to simulate the sun's movement across the sky, within a time frame of seconds; this caused the geometrical shapes of the Architectons to stand out, and visualized the way in which the buildings represented appeared at different times of day (video 4.00). Similarly, one of the reasons for employing spatial AR in the Expo 2010 project was that it allowed us to explore how the façade of the pavilion would appear at different times of day, as some parts of it would be in direct sunlight, and others in total shade (video 5.54). A related effect is the introduction of virtual objects casting shadow on the physical object causing them to appear in front of the physical object, like in the case of the fairies of the Holger the Dane installation (video 1.48).

Another common technique that can we have successfully worked with is the use of various particle systems, which can simulate for instance fire. Such particle systems can be placed in front of a model and create quite realistic effects, for instance in terms of reflections on the complex geometry of the physical object itself. In the Holger the Dane installation, particle effects such as fire are used extensively, for instance to animate the fairies that fly around Holger the Dane and grant him his magical powers (video 2.43).

A third technique that we have also used from 3D software is to employ various filters normally confined to the digital 3D world to create visual effects on the physical model. For instance we use the twirl filter to create he illusion that Holger the Dane is sleeping indicated by having the upper part of his body slowly moving in the rhythm of his breathing (video 3.06).

A fourth standard procedure that takes on new potentials is that of unwrapping the digital 3D model, thereby producing a digital 2D object corresponding to the surface of the digital 3D model, a process similar to that of making a 2D map of the world from a 3D globe. The 2D object may be processed in any 2D tool and wrapped back on to the 3D model. In this way, for instance, animations on the 3D model may be created, or video may be used as texture, which in turn transforms the surface of the physical object when projecting the digital model onto the physical model. In the case of the Expo model, we created custom software in order to map an elongated video feed onto the 3D models.

Although our focus here is on visual effects, we must emphasize that the use of audio can be a highly effective means for designers to achieve their intended objectives. For instance, when the runes on The Mejlby Stone are carved out, this is supplemented by the sound of a hammer striking a metal artefact on the stone (video 0.21), and when lightning illuminates the stone, peals of thunder complement the visual effects (video 1.06).

Dynamics between digital world and physical world

A second central insight from our work is that one of the most potent effects that designers can make use of is the interplay and dynamics between the digital world and the physical world.

One of the drawing powers of 3D spatial AR is that it has the potential to alter viewers' perceptions of physical structures. A visual effect that plays on this perception is that of shifting between 2D and 3D projection. In the Loop City project, we used this effect in the transition between two phases (video 4.29): the first phase, which employed traditional 2D visuals on the rear walls of the augmented space, and the second phase, which added 3D visuals to the presentation on the floor and the rectangular ramp in the centre of the space. In the first part, the floor and the bridge volume were not illuminated, and the viewer's gaze was attracted to the walls, until a red line denoting a metro line was suddenly projected onto the ramp, tracing the edges of the shape and connecting the 2D and 3D spaces (video 4.39). In this segment, the outline of the bridge is followed by projecting a series of arches on the solid bridge volume, which enables the illusion that cars can drive under the bridge through the arches and onto the floor in front of and behind the bridge volume (video 4.55). In this case, the introduction of a physical object in the augmented space (in the very simple form of the triangular bridge volume) proved highly effective. A related visual effect afforded by 3D projection is the ability to pick out and alter specific areas of a model, which can be used to demarcate or highlight designated areas of the physical model. This means that projections do not 'spill over' onto surrounding areas but can be concentrated on the physical objects or even specific parts of the object. In the case of the Architectons, which were both brought to life using two projectors, this emphasized the effect of moving light sources since this visual effect only appeared on the Architectons (video 4.00) and not on any other surfaces in the room; to the audience, this gave the perception of installations that stood out since they seemingly bended the laws of physics.

Operating in the digital 3D world also enables the designer to virtually project on specific elements of the physical model and thus pick out special areas that can augmented. In the case of Holger the Dane, this meant that we could focus the attention of the audience on the shield on the statue by isolating this in certain sequences (video 2.59). In the Expo case, we employed this effect to mimic the grid of embedded LEDs that made up parts of pavilion surface, while leaving other parts unprojected (video 5.45).

A further way of playing on the dynamics between the virtual and physical world is to emphasize the physical properties of the object(s) being augmented. This may be accomplished, for example, by tracing the outline of an object, as is done with the rectangular bridge volume in the Loop City installation (video 5.29). Often, this may be used to achieve spectacular results when combined with another visual effect, the transformation of physical properties, such as the textures or shapes of objects and surfaces. Often, these two effects are related to designers' intentions to emphasize or transform the semantic properties of objects in the augmented space. The Holger the Dane installation offers a good example of how the use of visual effects to emphasize and transform the physical properties may be combined with the emphasis or transformation of semantic properties: by the public, the Holger The Dane statue is perceived as rock solid, both literally, being cut from stone, and in terms of representing a firm and unyielding mythological warrior. In the installation, we emphasized this general perception by initially projecting an image of the statue onto the statue. The result is an increased contrast that emphasizes the physical properties, and makes it appear even more solid. However, at a later point in the unfolding narrative, we employ a visual filter on the projected image, which makes the statue appear to move and twist ever so slightly (video 3.05). This illusion plays into the viewer's perception of the physical structure, as well as the permanence of the mythological figure that now comes to life. The Mejlby Stone presents a different way of emphasizing and transforming the content of an augmented object: in several phases, the runes carved into the stone are highlighted. For example, at one point the stone is in darkness, but the runes are carved out, one by one, and appear in fiery red, underscoring the power of written language (video 0.21); later on, sets of runes are highlighted and visually transformed into translations, so they may be understood by present-day spectators .

An important point that arises in this presentation of visual effects and illusions is that spatial AR may be used to visualize both the actual and the imaginary; or in other words, it may be used to create the illusion of something real on a 'blank' object, or to create the illusion of something imaginary on an object that has specific properties. In the Expo 2010 project, our motivation was to simulate the real by approximating how the planned interactive façade would appear; in the Architecton projects, we sought to visualize in the exhibition space how the actual building façades would appear. In other cases, such as Holger the Dane and The Mejlby Stone, we employed spatial AR effects to visualize imaginary phenomena, such as the fairies that grant Holger the Dane his powers, or the story of the people mentioned on The Mejlby stone.

Relations between object, content and context

A unique challenge when designing projection-based, spatial AR is the development of content that is suited to the specific physical object or environment onto which it is projected. Therefore, this content must be developed with the complexity of the physical object in mind. Moreover, the context into which a 3D projection installation is placed is also a concern. Thus, the third central insight from our work concerns the connection and balance between object, content and context.

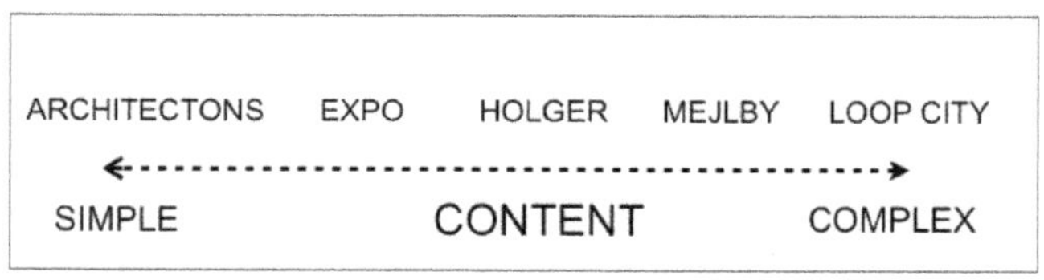

Figure 6. Complexity of content.

With regard to complexity of content, we have experimented with different communication strategies in the five projects. The projections in the Architectons case represent the simplest content of the five cases, in that they consist primarily of shifting light sources and intensities, as well as imagery of the sky's reflection on a façade. At the other end of the scale, we have very information-intensive projections, in the case of Loop City, in which both 2D and 3D graphics are used in combination with text and sound, to narrate the history of urban planning in the Copenhagen area, and envision the city's future. Between these two extremes we have Holger the Dane and The Mejlby Stone installations, which primarily employ visual effects and animation for communication, see Figure 6. In all five cases, excepting the EXPO 2010 case, the intention has been to use the installation to create awareness of the physical installation and the story behind it.

When developing content for 3D projection, designers must address the major design challenge posed by the geometrical complexity of the physical object onto which the content is to be projected. As illustrated by Figure 7 the objects may be positioned on a scale from simple to complex. Of our cases, the Loop City projection space represents the least complex physical projection surface, while The Mejlby Stone and the Holger the Dane statue are positioned at the other end of the spectrum. With regard to the relationship between content and object complexity, we have found that the very simple geometry of the Loop City projection space created an opportunity for quite complex content, whereas the organic forms and physical textures of the two cultural heritage objects (The Mejlby Stone and Holger the Dane) seemed better suited to visual effects that are less information-intensive. This is not to say that complex projection objects must rely on solely such effects – for example, animation and text have been employed with good results, in the case of The Mejlby Stone – but this information must be carefully integrated to fit the shape and expression of the object.

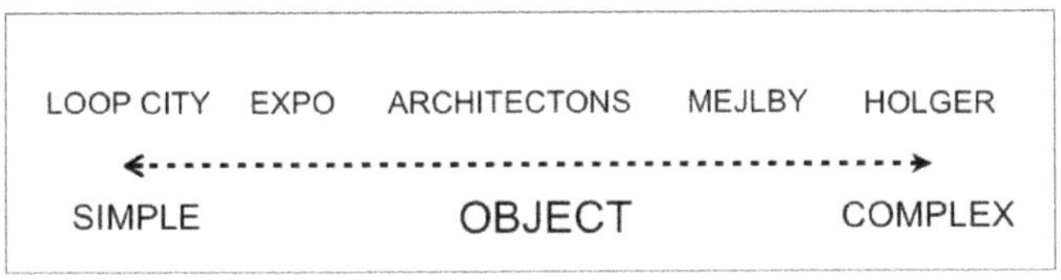

Figure 7. Complexity of projection objects.

An additional consideration in this regard is the complexity of the context of the projection space. In the five cases presented here, the complexity of the contexts has been quite diverse, as illustrated in Figure 8. The EXPO 2010 installation was set up in our laboratory, where we had full control over lighting conditions, and it was intended for use by a limited group of designers and stakeholders with the particular goal of evaluating and discussing specific design solutions. The two Architectons were parts of an architectural exhibition in which they competed for attention with other elements of the exhibition, such as back-lit, wall-mounted posters, which gave off so much light that they almost ruined the intended effect of the projections. The Loop City 2010 installation was also part of an architectural exhibition, but this space not as 'busy' as the setting of the Architectons case. The projection space for The Loop City installation was situated in the corner of a room, the entrance to the which led people quite naturally to the 'sweet spot' providing the optimal position for viewing the 3D effects. In contrast to The Mejlby Stone, which is positioned in a room that contains a number of other exhibition objects, the Holger the Dane Statue has its own confined space in the casemate of the castle, which provides a much more tranquil context for the installation.

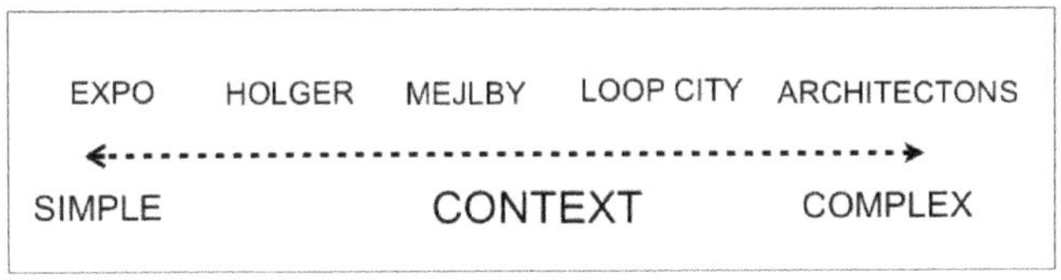

Figure 8. Complexity of context.

CONCLUSIONS AND FUTURE WORK

Recent years have seen a significant upswing in the presence of AR that layers digital information over representations of the physical environment', as smart phones and handheld devices now have sufficient processing power to support this technology [15]. Spatial AR, on the other hand, is still a nascent field for both practitioners and researchers. In the five projects discussed in this paper, we have begun to explore the potential and challenges of 3D projection within this field, through installations that have been implemented in real-life settings. In addition to general findings concerning the characteristics of 3D projection on physical objects, this approach has yielded valuable insights for the design of future systems that employ 3D projection on physical objects. We have focused in this paper on insights concerning new potentials for well-known 3D effects, dynamics between digital world and physical world, and relations between object, content and context.

In comparison to 'traditional' AR, such as that used by handheld devices, spatial AR using 3D projection presents interaction designers with unique opportunities as well as specific challenges, which are different from those encountered in AR using a mediating device like for instance a mobile phone. The most prominent advantage of using 3D projection on physical objects is, arguably, that it offers viewers an experience of immediacy and physical presence, which is different from what may be achieved with traditional AR using a screen as the mediating layer. 3D projection removes the screen as mediating layer and presents the virtual layer directly on top of the physical surroundings. This manoeuvre enables an experience of presence that is qualitatively different from screen-mediated AR, as explored in more detail by Zahorik & Jenison [19].

In addition to adding information to the physical environment, the use of various visual effects enabled by 3D projection allows the designer to alter the perception of physical structures. For this purpose, designers may employ standard visual effects that are included with 3D software, for example moving light sources and particle systems.

However, 3D projection on physical objects is also a complex process that presents the designer with a number of challenges. First, the process of developing a precise 3D model of the physical environment may be complicated, particularly when dealing with complex structures, such as the Holger the Dane statue. Second, content must be custom-developed for the specific environment; although standard effects from 3D software may be employed, other types of content must be carefully aligned with the physical environment. Third, successful implementation of 3D projection requires a large degree of control over the physical location in which the technology is employed. The projectors must be calibrated very precisely, the lighting conditions have to fall within specific parameters, and the physical environment must not be altered. This set of challenges is most likely the reason that related examples of spatial AR [1,13,14,18] are set up within controlled environments, either in lab settings or designated exhibition areas.

Given the emergent state of the field, there is a range of interesting research questions to pursue in future work. Extending the discussion of employing this technology in controlled settings, and technological explorations of how to accommodate shifting environments (e.g. continuous calibration of 3D models with moving physical objects, or calibration of light in accordance to changing light conditions in outdoor settings) might mitigate obstacles to implementation. Another topic, which we have only begun to explore, concerns which modes of interaction are particularly suitable to different types of 3D projection. In the cases we have explored, the interactive elements are limited. The EXPO 2010 case is an exception in this respect; however, the high level of customization of this installation is dependent on users being acquainted with 3D software. A related topic for future research is the exploration of which types of content are particularly suited to 3D projection. In many cases, the technology so far employed has presented relatively abstract visual imagery [1,18] or generic effects [14]. In cases such as The Mejlby Stone and Loop City, we have begun to explore more informative types of content; however, these are initial efforts that require further exploration.

ACKNOWLEDGMENTS

We would like to thank the partners involved in the production of the five installations: BIG, Kollision, DAC, 3XN, Randers Cultural Historical Museum, The Castle of Kronborg, Mark Film, The Animation Workshop, and Martin Professional. Moreover we would like to thank the many colleagues at CAVI who took part in the production of the five installations. Our research have been funded by the Danish Council for Strategic Research (Digital Urban Living, grant 09-063245), TEKNE, and The Central Region Denmark (MMeX and iKraft).

REFERENCES

1. AntiVJ. Enghien, http://www.antivj.com/enghien /index.htm (2009).
2. Azuma, R.; Baillot, Y., Behringer, R., Feiner, S.; Julier, S., MacIntyre, B. *Recent advances in augmented reality, Computer Graphics and Applications*, IEEE *21*, 6 (2001), 34-47.
3. Bandyopadhyay, D., Raskar, R., and Fuchs, H. Dynamic Shader Lamps: Painting on Movable Objects. Augmented Reality. ACM International Symposium on Augmented Reality, ACM Press (2001).
4. Basballe, D. and Halskov, K. Projections on museum exhibits – engaging visitors in the museum setting. *Proceedings of OzCHI 2010*, ACM Press (2010), 80-87.
5. Bimber, O. and Raskar, R. *Spatial Augmented Reality: Merging Real and Virtual Worlds*, A. K. Peters Publishing (2004).
6. Cruz-Neira, C., Sandin, D., DeFanti, T. A., Kenyon, R. V. & Hart, J. C. The Cave - Audio Visual Experience Automatic Virtual Environment. *CACM* 35, 6 (1992), 64-72.
7. Dalsgaard, P., Halskov, K. Designing Urban Media Façades: Cases and Challenges. *Proc. CHI 2010*, ACM Press (2010), 2277-2286.
8. Graffiti Research Lab. L.A.S.E.R. Tag, http://graffitiresearchlab.com/projects/laser-tag/, (2007).
9. Lee, J. C., Hudson, S. E., Summet, J. W., and Dietz, P. H. Moveable interactive projected displays using projector based tracking. In *Proceedings of the 18th Annual ACM Symposium on User interface Software and Technology*, ACM Press, (2005), 63-72.
10. Manovich, L. *The Language of New Media.* MIT Press: Cambridge, 2001.
11. Manovich, L. The poetics of augmented space, *Visual Communication 5*, 2 (2006), 219.
12. Milgram, P. & Kishino, F. A Taxonomy of Mixed Reality Visual Display. *IEICE Transactions on Information Systems 12* (1994), 1321-1329.
13. Raskar, R. Welch, G. & Fuchs, H. Spatially Augmented Reality. *Proceedings of the First IEEE Workshop on Augmented Reality* (IWAR'98). R. Behringer, G. Klinker and D. Mizell. San Francisco, CA, USA (1998), A.K. Peters Ltd.
14. Raskar, R., Welch, G., Low, K-L. and Bandyopadhyay, D. Shader Lamps: Animating Real Objects With Image-Based Illumination. *Proc. of the 12th Eurographics Workshop on Rendering Techniques* 2001. (2001), 89-102.
15. Roark, R. Hands-On: Android App 'Layar' Brings Reality's Unique Snowflakes to you Phone. *Wired Magazine*, http://www.wired.com/gadgetlab/2009/10/ layar-android-hands-on/ (2009).
16. Rossa, D. 555 Kubik, http://www.todayandtomorrow.net/2009/07/23/555-kubik-facade-projection/ (2009).
17. Struppek, M. The social potential of Urban Screens, *Visual Communication 5*, 2 (2006), 173- 188.
18. Valbuena, P. Augmented Sculptures, http://www. pablovalbuena.com/p05.htm (2007).
19. Zahorik, P. & Jenison, R. Presence as Being-in-the-World. Presence 7,1 (1998), 78-89.

The New Good: Exploring the Potential of Philosophy of Technology to Contribute to Human-Computer Interaction

Daniel Fallman
Interactive Institute Umeå
c/o Umeå University, School of Architecture
SE-90187, Umeå, Sweden
daniel.fallman@tii.se

ABSTRACT

As a result of the increased interest in issues such as engagement, affection, and meaning, contemporary human-computer interaction (HCI) has increasingly come to examine the nature of interactions between artifacts, humans, and environments through concepts such as user experience and meaning. In the transition from usability metrics to user experience, what appears lacking is a more explicit characterization of what it is HCI now strives for as a discipline—i.e. what constitutes a 'good' user experience? Through a detailed look at two contemporary philosophies of technology—Albert Borgmann's notion of the device paradigm and Don Ihde's non-neutrality of technology-mediated experience—this paper seeks to explore the potential of the philosophy of technology to contribute new insights and provide well-grounded conceptual tools for coming to terms with what may become HCI's 'new good'.

Author Keywords

Philosophy of Technology, Philosophy, Theory, Device paradigm, Non-neutral technology, Design.

ACM Classification Keywords

H5.m. Information interfaces and presentation (e.g., HCI): Miscellaneous.

General Terms

Design, Theory

INTRODUCTION

It is becoming increasingly difficult to ignore the impact that various digital interactive products, services, and systems have on the lives we live—our mobile phones keep ringing, our in-car navigation systems tell us to turn, our e-mail inboxes stack up and Twitter feeds roll by, and that we rather meet friends over Facebook than over a pint at the pub.

CHI 2011, May 7–12, 2011, Vancouver, BC, Canada.

Traditionally, analogue and mechanical technologies are also rapidly becoming enhanced with digital capacity, such as networking capabilities, 'smart' behavior, and interactive features. At the same time, a range of new pervasive technologies, such as Bluetooth, Wireless LAN, ANT, 3G, 4G, ZigBee, and RFID, are enabling this rich array of digital artifacts to communicate with each other, to create ad-hoc networks, negotiating handshakes, and exchanging information, while leaving us—formerly known as *users*—outside the loop altogether. Consequently, our world is rapidly becoming increasingly experienced only through these digital artifacts.

From the perspective of human-computer interaction (HCI), these trends, and their associated questions and uncertainties, pose a number of imperative questions whose reach we are currently struggling hard to grasp. For instance, first, while the concept of designing for user experience is rapidly catching on in HCI as an alternative to traditional usability metrics, few well-developed notions exist with regard to what would constitute a 'good' user experience. Second, the current pervasiveness of digital technology in our everyday life, including the Web and the mobile phone, further complicates this matter, as it is becoming increasingly difficult to distinguish a 'user experience' from any other kind of experience. Third, the trend towards networked digital artifacts primarily interacting with each other, and with computational power embedded in the environment rather than with human users, blurs and thus challenges the concept of 'user', which has been a crucial element of most methodological and theoretical approaches in HCI.

These three examples also illustrate that the kinds of problems with which HCI is concerned—in designing technology and in understanding the interactions that occur between technologies, humans, and environments—have become considerably more complex. This has shifted the kinds of investigation with which we are involved from reasonably well-defined, controlled problems, to what has been termed 'ill-structured' or 'wicked' problems in design research [49]. Such problems typically bring with them a range of concerns that seem to persist on a level beyond design, use, and evaluation—thus challenging not only our theoretical and methodological approaches, but also old truths in the field regarding its scope, purpose, and aim.

Ultimately, we argue, dealing in a structured way with these concerns—which are unavoidably ethical in nature—comes to threaten HCI's so far largely implicit notion of good and bad. It will make visible what we see as a current lack of a coherent and articulated vision of what HCI seeks to achieve as a field.

FROM USABILITY TO USER EXPERIENCE

Through the term usability, traditional HCI taught that interactive systems should be designed to be *effective, efficient, engaging, error-tolerant,* and *easy to learn.* By maximizing metrics constructed from these terms, usability sought to improve all interactive artifacts by enhancing their usability, i.e., making them more 'useful'. A shared technical terminology, a set of techniques, methods, and tools, and a common goal have been successfully constructed around these guiding notions. *Usability* is hence a collective term for a particular set of ideas developed primarily in HCI about the relationships between users, analysts, designers, artifacts, and the context in which design takes place.

To understand why usability developed this particular focus, it is necessary to briefly go back to the dawn of modern HCI —the early 1980s. At this time, there was substantial confidence in how cognitive psychology would come to contribute to the field of HCI [50]. Computers were difficult to learn and use, as users often had to strictly follow the computer's model of how to approach tasks. To improve the user's position, the accumulated corpus of knowledge and the credible, structured approach of cognitive science came to be seen as HCI's 'knight in shining armor'. Various information processing theories were adopted and adapted to advance new design principles and guidelines, methods, and analytic tools for the field. For instance, Norman's [44] theory of action focused on modeling people's goals and how they were met, while Card et al.'s [10] model enabled quantitative predictions about user performance that could be used to evaluate different kinds of interfaces and assess their suitability for a given task. Such predictive models became a keystone of the usability movement, allowing usability-driven HCI to "assess our designs and test our systems to ensure that they actually behave as we expect and meet the requirements of the user" [13]. Information processing can thus be seen as the theoretical foundation of HCI's 'first wave'.

HCI's Second Wave

Towards the end of the 1980s, however, questions were raised as to why the theories and approaches imported from cognitive psychology were found neither conceptually influential nor useful in the, at the time, rapidly expanding commercial practice of designing computers and interfaces [37]. Seminal books by Suchman [55] and Winograd & Flores [58] further revealed the limitations of information processing as the key theoretical approach to HCI.

Following what has been described as a theoretical crisis in the field [50], more encompassing theories and associated methodological approaches were proposed during the early 1990s, including participatory design [17], ethnography and ethnomethodology [31], phenomenology [15, 58], ecological psychology [26], distributed and external cognition [59], and activity theory [42].

The primary focus of these 'second wave' approaches was to move the center of attention away from the first wave's rather disembodied emphasis on a single user operating a single application; the focus was shifted to particular work settings, to well-defined communities of practice such as teams collaborating using a variety of applications, and to issues of context. Predicative models, rigid guidelines, and systematic testing were largely abandoned in favor of actively working together with users in participatory workshops, various forms of prototyping endeavors, and though contextual inquiry [5].

HCI's Third Wave

As computing and digital technologies started to become ubiquitous in our daily lives during the end of the 1990s however, the boundaries between public and private, as well as work and leisure, started to blur. Technology changed from being a tool for work to something through which the world could be experienced. In the early to mid-2000s, it became increasingly obvious and accepted that HCI could no longer just be concerned with Western people using technology at work. To remain relevant, HCI needed to broaden its scope substantially: it needed to study and design for technology use in a wide variety of contexts. However, how one would actually study and design for people that were not at work, who did not appear in distinguishable groups or other well-defined circumstances, who did not have well-defined tasks at hand, and who may have a completely different culture, was not entirely clear.

In the early 2000s, to find ways of tackling these new challenges (as well as to break with the theories and methodologies of the second wave), HCI became rapidly interested in issues such as meaning, complexity, culture, emotion, lived experiences, engagement, motivation, and experience—HCI's 'third wave' [5]. Theoretically, third wave HCI tends to relate and integrate technology design and incorporate more cultural analysis, critical theory, philosophy, values, and history than either sociological or psychological theories [1, 5, 23, 40, 52]. Through approaches such as Critical Design, Ludic Design, Reflective Design, Value-sensitive Design (VSD), and Value-Centered Design, third wave HCI has reacted against the second wave's strong commitment to users (and the consequential lack of emphasis on the designer) in favor of a more design-oriented, exploratory, interpretative, playful, ambiguous, and at times taken on an activist attitude [16, 25, 27, 28, 19, 20, 30, 4, 51, 11, 60].

IS THERE A NEED FOR A 'NEW GOOD'?

For the purposes of this paper, the underlying vision of early-day HCI is worth considering: what is a 'good design'? For what do we strive? When it comes to first wave usability, the answer is to construct a machinery to improve interactive artifacts by making them more useful. This can be regarded, admittedly somewhat simplified, as usability's concept of 'good', i.e., 'good' can be reduced to signify those designs that show high levels of usability.

When it comes to second wave HCI, the concept of a 'good design' becomes a little hazier. Participatory design, for instance, brings to the table the challenge of also incorporating political issues, as well as issues of labor and power, while other second wave approaches bring their own particular challenges and highlight other factors. Still, with its focus on well-defined professional teams with specific tasks at hand, on their particular work context, and on groupware as a typical solution, the concept of 'good' seems not that different from that of first wave approaches. The main difference is rather that second wave HCI tends to stress the human side, rather than the technological side. Here, 'good' is whatever enhances the group work process.

When it comes to third wave HCI, however, things get much less transparent. There are no easily distinguishable user groups and, because of the blending of public and private (as well as work and leisure), any clear-cut tasks to support are hard to find. For instance, people that are surfing the web can do so in order to find specific information, but they can just as well do it simply to pass the time.

Third wave approaches, however, tend to share an interest in meaning and in human experiences, momentary or long-term, of using or living with a digital product or service, often termed the 'user experience'. Despite the current boom of interest in the term, it has many different meanings. For instance, Colbert defines it as users' perceptions of interaction that constitute qualities of use [12], while Forlizzi & Battarbee characterize user experience as fluent, cognitive, and expressive [22]. Battarbee, on the other hand, emphasizes the social nature of user experience [2] and McCarthy & Wright discuss experience in terms of culture [40]. Picard [47] and Norman [43], however, highlight affective and emotional aspects. What currently appears lacking, especially in the light of recent third wave approaches, is a more explicit notion about what it is HCI now strives for as a field—what is the 'new good' that replaces the maximizing of usability metrics and improving group work processes? Put bluntly, what constitutes *a good user experience?*

While, for instance, Weiser's [56] vision of the disappearing computer provides an ideal for everyday computing [3], comparable coherent and articulated visions are yet to be established for the whole of HCI. The concept of direct manipulation [53] has come to play such a role, often as a de-emphasized background theme. While direct manipulation continues to be a strong ideal for much work in HCI to this day, it is questionable whether it can continue to function as a unifying, agreed-upon 'good', especially when taking into account the current broadening of HCI's scope, the new areas where HCI thinking is applied, and the multifaceted notion of the user in third wave HCI. Patel et al's [46] work with farmers in rural India is an excellent example of how third wave HCI may find it necessary to break with some of the ideals of direct manipulation.

It could of course be the case that the answer is entirely relativistic, i.e., that HCI has developed to a point where shared visions are neither possible nor required. It could also be that 'good'—given the broad scope of current HCI—has to come in many forms, depending on the particularities of the design situation. The argument of this paper is not necessarily that we will ever arrive at a single distinguishable 'good' for third wave HCI, but rather that there might be a danger in not paying any attention to the underlying vision of what we do, as we might then implicitly or explicitly come to inherit earlier visions of 'good'. If interactive artifacts are knowingly designed to provide users with the opportunity of having specific types of user experience, it is also necessary to develop guiding visions that provide the means—the ideas, concepts, models, and tools—for revealing, analyzing, and discussing the obvious implications (human, social, cultural, ethical, moral, ecological, and political) of these experiences, and how they foster particular relationships and dependencies. As argued by Cockton [11, p. 151], "HCI will not become a true discipline until it develops, expresses, discusses, agrees and integrates a set of core values".

This paper puts forward the proposition that, despite explicit attempts in other directions, the vision of usability still permeates HCI thinking. The second wave's interest in supporting groups and work did not cause problems (as usable artifacts are likely to also enhance, or at least not discourage, group work), but with the third wave's more radical interest in issues such as leisure, ambiguity, multiple interpretations, and activism, usability becomes problematic as an underlying 'good'. For instance, if one knowingly designs for ambiguity with the intent of creating room for experiences that should last or even grow for many years while remaining mysterious or partly unknown, usability may be counterproductive on many levels as an underlying theme: when the work is planned and carried out, when it is later evaluated, reviewed by peers, discussed at workshops and conferences, and eventually used in teaching.

TWO PHILOSOPHIES OF TECHNOLOGY

Given the perplexing challenges that questions of 'good' seem to raise in third wave HCI, we are in need of coherent intellectual frameworks that can help us address these challenges. Below, we propose the possibility of drawing on *the philosophy of technology* as a way to help us better articulate, understand, and illuminate the concept of 'good' in relation to technology. We will introduce two contemporary philosophies of technology that suggest a number of conceptual tools that operate on a level above design and evaluation, yet are often applicable to the technologies and technology relations that HCI suggests.

Ihde suggests that to qualify as a philosophy of technology, "the philosopher must make technology a foreground phenomenon and be able to reflectively analyze it in such a way as to illuminate features of the phenomenon of technology itself" [33, p. 38]. It was not until the 20th century, with John Dewey and Martin Heidegger, that such philosophies became distinguishable. The two accounts of philosophy of technology introduced below are both related to the pragmatism of Dewey and the existential phenomenology of Heidegger, and both were primarily developed during the late 1980s and 1990s. First, Albert Borgmann's [6,7,8,9] theory of the *device paradigm* will be introduced, followed by Don Ihde's [32, 33, 34, 35] notion of the *non-neutrality of technology-mediated experience*.

Albert Borgmann's Device Paradigm

In *Technology and the Character of Contemporary Life* [9], Albert Borgmann argues that technological development is generally focused on issues surrounding the usefulness of different kinds of technology, suggesting that while particular technologies may be both useful and good, some technologies that are useful for some purposes might be harmful in a broader context. Borgmann's work can thus be seen as a call to reconsider the often-assumed correspondence between 'useful' and 'good' in terms of technology. Rather than to mindlessly strive towards making all technologies more useful (as is the case with usability for instance), Borgmann argues that we must concentrate on those specific goods that are irreplaceably good, termed *focal things* and *practices*. In particular, he argues, we need to carefully nurture the focal things and practices that are currently threatened by the thoughtless employment of technology.

With the technological advancement of the world, comes a promise that liberation and enrichment will result from dominating nature, where technology "promises to bring the forces of nature and culture under control, to liberate us from misery and toil, and to enrich our lives" [9, p. 41]. This promise has led society to believe that a good life must be built on technological mediation and support. Borgmann questions this common belief that technology frees us to attend to other, more stimulating pursuits [54]. His argument is that rather that the technologies that surround us tend to turn us into passive consumers, increasingly disengaged from the world and from each other. According to Borgmann, a particularly dangerous aspect of technology in this respect is its strong seductive power, which seduces people to focus on material goods, quantitative thinking, commoditization, and disposability.

At the heart of Borgmann philosophy of technology is a separation between *devices* and *things*. *Things*, first, tend to engage mind and body, center our lives, and connect us with the world. Borgmann's most famous illustration of a focal thing is the role of the fireplace in a traditional country house, which he compares to a heart. The fireplace has strong centering powers, as it was the natural gathering point in the house and most activities either took place in its direct vicinity, including food preparation. The fireplace commanded presence, as the fire had to be built and maintained, and it preserved continuity with the world. To keep the house warm, trees had to be cut, split into wood, and dried. Taken together, the fireplace was inseparable from what inhabiting that country house meant: "Thus a stove used to furnish more than mere warmth. It was a focus, a hearth, a place that gathered the work and leisure of a family and gave the house a center. [...] It provided for the entire family a regular and bodily engagement with the rhythm of the seasons that was woven together with the threat of cold and the solace of warmth, the smell of wood smoke, the exertion of sawing and carrying, the teaching of skills, and the fidelity to daily tasks" [9, p. 42].

A typical attribute of focal things is that they put a number of demands on us. These demands generally require our presence, patience, endurance, skill, and some amount of resoluteness. Focal things are typically also continuous activities, things you *have* to do rather than things you can *opt* to do. To keep one's house warm during the winter, the fire must be maintained, even on days one would rather do something else. In this way, "a focal thing is not an isolated entity; it exists as a material center in a complicated network of human relationships and relationships to its natural and cultural setting" [54, p. 23]. A key characteristic is thus that focal things tend to unify means and ends, where achievement and enjoyment, individual and community, mind and body, and body and world are brought together.

Devices, on the other hand, are appealingly glamorous technologies, designed to be useful for a limited purpose. A characteristic of a device is that it only provides a commodity, only one aspect of the original thing it replaces. Borgmann illustrates how devices operate by describing the shift from wood-burning fireplaces to central heating systems. The central heating system (the device) provides a single commodity, namely warmth, which only represents a fraction of the fireplace (the thing) it replaces in terms of centering powers, the way in which it commands presence, and how it establishes continuity with the world. For this reason, Borgmann argues that most often, such devices turn out to be disengaging in their attempt to do this one thing for us. Because of their detachment from any larger context, devices are disposable, often mass-produced, and receptive to trends and fashion.

In switching from things to devices, Borgmann argues that human involvement simultaneously disappears and only disengaging commodities remain. Borgmann calls this the irony of technology. In this, humanity has become captive to the promises of modern technology, whose devices keep demanding less and less human input. The shift from being involved and engaged with focal things to disengaging consumption of devices, then, frustrates the deeper aspirations of life.

The term *the device paradigm* is used to give prominence to these ongoing transformations that Borgmann thinks contribute to modern life missing a natural center, a hearth, and thus also lacking a larger social and ecological context: "In this rising tide of technological devices, disposability supersedes commanding presence, discontinuity wins over continuity, and glamorous thrills trump centering experiences" [54, p. 24]. To explain why devices are disengaging, and our consumption of them ultimately disappointing, Borgmann notes that a device typically hides the mechanisms by which its commodity is produced. A device tends to split means and ends, whereas a thing tends to connect its means and ends. The user of a central heating system only experiences warmth as a technological foreground, while the commodity's background machinery, i.e., how that warmth is generated, brought into the house, and distributed, remains hidden and unknown; this means that users experience ends without knowing, caring for, or in any way getting involved with the means. Borgmann argues that such a separation between means and ends leads to disengagement, passive consumption, and disappointment. At the heart of Borgmann's philosophy of technology is thus the notion that modern technology tends to operate to deconstruct things and reconstitute them into devices, and that this transformation is accelerating with recent advances in information technology.

Borgmann has also focused specifically on aspects of information and communication technologies, and the way that they help shape people's experiences with reality [7]. According to Borgmann, there are three main types of information, each constituting a different connection between humans and reality: *natural* information, *cultural* information, and *technological* information. Natural information is information about reality. These are signs that directly inform us about the world we inhabit, making reality understandable for human beings. For instance, smoke tells us that there is a fire. Information can also be for reality, Borgmann argues, i.e., cultural information. Cultural signs cannot be found in nature, but acquire meaning by convention, such as written texts and musical scores. A quality of cultural information is that it realizes and shapes reality. A musical score, according to Borgmann, demands realization, it has to be played. Thirdly, technological information is fairly specific to recent advances in information technology—it is information as reality. The music we find on CDs, for instance, is a kind of information that is hyperreal, i.e., more real than reality itself, as the music on the CD is qualitatively superior to any actual reality. As opposed to both natural and cultural information, technological information does not provide access to reality but rather replaces reality.

Providing what could perhaps best be described as a neo-classical dystopian argument, Borgmann sees that technological information is increasingly being used as a substitute for reality and, through the mechanics of the device paradigm, "information is about to overflow and suffocate reality" [7, p. 213]. According to Borgmann, the virtual 'worlds' where people have started to live their lives, e.g. Second Life, World of Warcraft, and Facebook, are not sufficient alternatives to the first world as they lack the eloquence and engaging power of actual reality. In these hyperreal worlds, both reality and life become reduced to commodities: "Postmodern technology uses the hyper-reality of simulations to get rid of the limitations imposed by reality. The limit of postmodern reality is not the total objectification of nature, but the replacement of reality by virtual reality totally under our control. The objects of reality disappear to the extent that we as subjects gain control over them, but we are similarly reduced to 'a point of arbitrary desires'." [6, p. 108].

Through these examples, Borgmann tries to illustrate how information technology, rather than deepening our engagement with reality and with each other, often seeks to create new realities—hyperrealities—that are easier to control and experience, but which is parasitical to reality itself, and ultimately fails to engage us because of its lack of eloquence and engaging powers.

Don Ihde's Non-neutrality of Technology-mediated Experiences

Don Ihde was one of the very first philosophers in the US to make technology the subject of philosophical reflection, publishing his first of many books on the subject, *Technics and Praxis*, in 1979 [34]. In this work, Ihde focuses on optical technologies and shows how the early use of telescopes and microscopes helped reveal previously inaccessible worlds. But optical magnification did not only provide scientists with access to unknown worlds, it also irreversibly oriented scientific inquiry towards the worlds that these technologies exposed. This transformed not only what was seen, but also how it was seen in relation to technologically unaided vision, which Ihde proposes to be a structural component of all kinds of technologies, not only optical: "For every enhancement of some feature, perhaps never before seen, there is also a reduction of other features. To magnify some observed object, optically, is to bring it forth from a background into a foreground and make it present to the observer, but it is also to reduce the former field in which it fit, and—due to foreshortening—to reduce visual depth and background." [34, p. 111].

In his arguably most important book, *Technology and the Lifeworld: From Garden to Earth,* Ihde suggests that even seemingly ubiquitous technology, such as eyeglasses, have the same non-neutral mediating character [36]. Even though the transformation that comes from wearing eyeglasses (to turn blurry objects into sharp, distinct ones) is typically appreciated by the user, one must never forget that the transformation does not come without a price. The user needs to care for the mediating technology, which might come to affect both how people behave in certain situations as well as how others perceive them. Ihde also argues that when using glasses, the world inevitably comes to the user as 'enframed'. Subtle back glares, dust and water spots appearing on the glasses give eyeglass users a fringe awareness that the world as it appears to them through the eyeglasses is intruded upon by a technological intermediary: "for every revealing transformation there is a simultaneously concealing transformation of the world, which is given through a technological mediation. Technologies transform experience, however subtly, and that is one root of their non-neutrality" [36, p. 49].

From the point of view of HCI, the non-neutrality of technology reveals a number of issues currently neglected, implicit, or overlooked in the field. It points to elements that are typically outside of current understandings of user experience in HCI, but which congregate to make up a more complete experience. First, Ihde shows that just having a technology present imposes a number of behaviors, even without actually using it. Users may become more careful in terms of bodily engagement with the world, or by not risking ruining their expensive camera or scratching their new mobile phone. Also, carrying a large camera can be strenuous and may thus, often implicitly, come to influence what you do and where you actually go in the first place. Being surrounded by, or carrying, more or less expensive equipment also creates caution with regard to the possibility of theft and risk of bodily harm, thus influencing what one does, where one goes, and how one acts in the world. Finally, technology is also non-neutral when it comes to fashion; it is, for instance, not uncommon that people flash their new mobile phones in front of others as a sign of self-expression.

Optical technologies such as eyeglasses, telescopes, cameras, and microscopes, belong to a group of technologies that seek to enhance (and transform) our perceptual, experiential, and bodily experiences. Other kinds of technology, such as speedometers, clocks, and thermometers, seem not to have this enhancing or amplifying character; they seem to have a different mode of reference to observed objects, reliant on interpretation rather than mediation. While a pair of glasses amplifies seeing, using a speedometer in one's car is more of an interpretative act. There is still a world object being referred to—the speed of the vehicle—but this object is not perceptually represented but rather hermeneutically referenced. The speedometer must therefore be 'read'.

While the broader implications of this argument are clearly far beyond the scope of this paper (and indeed relevant to almost all computational contexts, as hermeneutical referencing of world objects is a key notion in computer systems and user interfaces in general), some of Ihde's insights in this area seem especially pertinent to current HCI. As all kinds of technology are non-neutral, so are hermeneutical representations. The translation that must occur between the signifier and the signified always comes to abstract, and hence significantly reduce, the referred-to phenomenon. What may be a rich, vivid, and heart-beating experiential experience (speed) becomes reduced to figure (miles per hour). This figure also requires that the user has previously acquired the skill to interpret, i.e., to read the instrument in order for it to have any meaning whatsoever. Technologies that provide hermeneutical relationships are hence highly dependent on the context in which they are designed and used; they must accordingly be understood as fully culturally embedded, and whose meaning is entirely constructed.

Ihde distinguishes between three types of human-technology relations: *embodiment*, *hermeneutical*, and *alterity* relations [36]. First, eyeglasses allow users to embody their praxis through the technology, in the sense that they get in between the wearer and the world, a relationship that Ihde thinks of as fundamentally existential. One experiences the world through the technology, and the technology inevitably becomes part of the way one relates to the world. While many technologies appear in between the user and the world, not all are embodied. For a technology to hold an embodiment relation it must be technically transparent, it must allow its user to 'see through' it. But the embodying of technology is also acquired or constituted; for users new to eyeglasses, there is typically a short period of time in which one notices their weight, experiences eyestrain, is annoyed by back glares, and has to compensate for and make adjustments in spatial motility. Once the skill of wearing and seeing through the eyeglasses has been acquired, however, they are more or less "taken into my own perceptual-bodily self experience" [36, p. 73], and withdraw into an embodied relation. The term *transparency* is used to refer to the degree to which an embodied technology recedes into the background of experience. The embodiment relation is not limited to optical technology, it may occur for any sensory dimension, including tactile motility through walking canes, hearing aids, etc.

Second, even though they also appear in between users and the world, speedometers and clocks are two examples of technologies that must be interpreted. When reading a speedometer, one's perceptual focus is not on the world but on the technological instrument, where one perceives the instrument itself rather than the object being referred to in the world. Hermeneutical instruments do generally neither enhance any of their users' innate capabilities or senses, nor are they meant to become invisible; quite the opposite, they are often designed to be objects of focus and, as a result, the world tends to withdraw from their users.

The hermeneutical relationship is thus referential in that it places users' immediate perceptual focus on the technology in between the user and the world. Typically, users of this kind of technology are not able to experience the object of reference experientially, for instance when checking the temperature in Tokyo on the Web, or when monitoring the core's temperature in a nuclear power plant. Rather, they are dependent on their own reading of the instrument, and it is therefore essential that they know how to properly read the instrument, and about its proper functioning. Thus, the instrument is only transparent, in a hermeneutical sense, if the user has acquired the skills necessary to read it. It can also be very difficult, and sometimes impossible, to know whether or not the instrument is operating properly, which means that users are accordingly forced to trust and depend on the instrument.

Ihde finds a third human-technology relation, termed *alterity*. It is not a mediated relation either with the world or with a referenced object in the world. Rather, it is primarily a relation to or with technology. The term alterity is used to describe a relationship between a human being and some otherness, albeit an otherness generally weaker than in the case of other people and animals, but stronger than our typical relation to objects. The spinning top, for instance, takes on a life of its own when put to use, seemingly defying gravity and moving unpredictably. Ihde sees traces of alterity in people's relations to computers. While many of the relations involved in, for instance, playing a computer game may be understood along an embodiment-hermeneutical continuum, some kind of otherness is often involved: "there is the sense of interacting with something other than me, the technological competitor … I must beat the machine or it will beat me" [36, p. 100-101]. When working with a word processor, the whole computer system functions as an almost transparent tool for manipulating the document. However, in the case of a serious breakdown, if a particular function cannot be activated or the application crashes, the transparency of the tool—"the quasi-love relationship" [36, p. 106]—is lost, the tool itself becomes conspicuous, and the relationship transforms into frustration and "quasi-hate" [36, p. 106], a kind of alterity human-technology relation. A comparable analysis of the differences between the state of flow (where attention is directed on the work being carried out) versus breakdowns (where attention focuses on the tool itself) has already been developed within the field of HCI by Winograd & Flores [58], drawing on Heidegger's description of tool use and breakdown.

To summarize, technologies mediate our experience of the world. They appear in between humans and the world and change our experiences, amplifying some aspects while reducing others. While a technology may enable one to act on the world, it simultaneously limits other ways of acting, enabling new experiences while closing down the potential for others. It is however important to realize that "no technology is 'one thing,' nor is it incapable of belonging to multiple contexts" [35, p. 47]. Technologies are thus *multistable*, as they can be embodied in various ways for various purposes.

DISCUSSION

The above outline of Borgmann's and Ihde's thinking is not intended to completely cover the rich field of philosophy of technology, which is clearly beyond the scope of this paper. A more detailed overview would also have covered work by Feenberg, Winner, Haraway, Hickman, Latour, Ellul, Mitcham, Verbeek, and many others, and even then the list would only account for contemporaries. The introduction has rather attempted to provide two instances of this kind of thinking in relation to technology and technological development in as unbiased a way as possible and, in doing so, try to keep some of the richness and context of their respective thinking. As noted by Bardzell [1], when HCI imports theory, it often borrows a single concept or idea and then directly attempts to apply that idea in design; this is not always an ideal process, as "the piecemeal appropriation of a single concept often strips much of its original analytic force, because concepts … are sensible inasmuch as they participate or are deployed in networks of other concepts, issues, and historical events" [1, p 2358]. Hence, the success or failure of such a borrowed new term, stripped from its original context, often somewhat paradoxically comes to depend on how well it resonates with the old paradigm (from which it may explicitly try to break free), and in the area of HCI its success then rather rapidly tends to become a matter of how well it provides implications for design [14].

Philosophy of Technology in HCI

Having described Borgmann and Ihde without much analysis, it is now time to discuss the potential of their work to contribute to contemporary HCI. First, compared with many other philosophers, they appear attractive to HCI in that they deal directly with today's technologies. At the same time, they sustain strong links to earlier philosophy, for instance in Borgmann's case with the dystopian undertones of Heidegger and Ihde's somewhat instrumental approach and the pragmatism of Dewey. This roots their thinking firmly within a larger philosophical setting. In different ways, Borgmann and Ihde can also be seen to attempt to reconcile the traditional dichotomy between utopian and dystopian accounts of the role of technology in our lives [41]. Both authors have also chosen to communicate their philosophical ideas in a legible form, rendering them fairly easy to understand without extensive philosophical training.

Rather than primarily discussing philosophically the existential effects of 'technology' as a whole, which was Heidegger's main concern, both Borgmann and Ihde address and deal with the same kind of technologies with which HCI is directly concerned. The distance between any particular HCI-related technology or circumstance and Borgmann or Ihde, is thus generally far shorter than the distance to Heidegger—yet the latter nevertheless tends be cited in passing far more often in the HCI literature. While the bulk of Borgmann's and Ihde's work is contemporary, with the shift from first to second wave HCI—i.e., late

1980s to mid-1990s—there has actually been very little interaction between them and HCI. This is rather surprising given HCI's willingness to adopt and adapt new theories and ideas from other fields.

Only in recent years a very modest body of literature in HCI has started to discuss their ideas. For example, Leshed et al. [39] use Borgmann to discuss issues such as commodification and de-skilling in and around use of in-vehicle GPS navigation systems. Odom et al. [45] use Borgmann in passing to discuss why people seem to preserve some things rather passionately while discarding others without much thought. Fallman [18] discusses how Borgmann's theory of the device paradigm raises some important social, cultural, ethical, and moral issues, with a bearing on new themes in HCI, such as sustainable interaction. Pierce [48] is inspired by Ihde's three human-technology relations as a framework when rethinking how to approach the design of everyday objects such as clocks.

The Non-Neutrality of Technology

With different approaches and with different goals in mind, Ihde and Borgmann demonstrate the *non-neutrality of technology*, i.e., that technologies are not simply neutral means for realizing human ends, but actively help to shape our experiences of the world. They are by no means the only philosophers that have arrived at such a conclusion (see e.g. [57]) and it has been explored in HCI-related literature before, e.g. [24, 23, 21], but the notion is still to be to be accepted by mainstream HCI—in part because of the rather persistent 'tool' perspective. Taking the non-neutrality of technology seriously has solemn implications for HCI however. In light of third wave HCI approaches, it needs to form a cornerstone.

Borgmann helps us see that technology should not simply be dismissed as a tool but could rather be seen as an inducement, often so strong that people find themselves unable to refuse it. Twitter feeds, Facebook, Web pages, GPS navigation systems, etc., are not only technologies that can individually be understood as good or bad. We also need to realize that human use of these artifacts coalesce into culture—into a way of life. This raises two concerns for HCI: first, it points to *the moral and ethical capacity of the technologies we design and evaluate*, which has remained largely deemphasized in HCI. Moreover, if our artifacts coalesce into culture and shape our lives, that also suggests that *this capacity goes beyond individual efforts of design and evaluation.*

These concerns can be partly explained through the strong historical association to cognitive psychology, whose goal at the time was to produce predicative models of human behavior. Ethical issues were not within the scope of such inquiry. If we believe that HCI's goal is to make all artifacts more usable, then it is only logical that ethical issues seem to be outside of our area of study. The absence of ethical concerns can also be explained by the rather strong commitment in HCI to the idea of technology as a 'tool', a thriving perspective to this day, which tends to make ethical concerns irrelevant as ethical agency is then solely placed in the hands of the user. In revealing the different relations humans have with technology and the world (Ihde) and the logic and machinery of the device paradigm (Borgmann), both authors illustrate the problems involved with assuming neutrality of technology, reducing it to inactive, dead matter; that technology is not 'just a tool'. While a gun, for instance, does nothing on its own, one's understanding of the situation changes radically when one approaches it from a perspective in which Ihde's human-technology relations are the primitive units of analysis. Using this theory, it can be seen that a human with a gun is very different from the human without a gun, i.e., the human-gun relation transforms the situation and comes to define it by offering specific possibilities for action [36].

The non-neutrality of technology also *challenges the assumed correspondence between 'useful' and 'good'* that through usability permeates HCI. Borgmann shows that such a focus is not enough, as some particular technologies may be both useful and good, while some technologies that are useful for a particular purpose might be harmful for another. As HCI is involved in designing artifacts that will come to play mediating roles in the actions and experiences of future users of these artifacts, we as designers are helping to shape ethical and moral decisions and practices.

The Role of Values and Ethics in HCI

In practice, values and ethical concerns came into view in HCI primarily through the adoption of user-centered design approaches, growing out of the Scandinavian design tradition and Participatory Design [5,17]. These approaches pointed to the importance of involving end users and paying attention to their thoughts, values, issues of labor, power hierarchies, and workplace politics, already from the very earliest stages of interactive artifact design. Since the late 1990s, Value-Sensitive Design (VSD) has been one of the few methodologies in HCI that has actively emphasized the role of values, ethics, and moral concerns in the design process [23]. What is more, VSD stipulates a set of core values with 'moral epistemic standing' [23] within a value-sensitive design, including human welfare, privacy, universal usability, and informed consent.

While Le Dantec et al. [38] note that these values largely echo 1960s US counterculture which was already an integrated part of information technology design, it is nevertheless interesting that VSD comes to illuminate the ethical and moral responsibility on the part of the *designer* rather than the *user*. The alternative suggested by Le Dantec et al. [38], i.e., to seek values locally within the confines of each particular design case, would again deemphasize the designer's role. In third wave HCI, the continued focus on the designer is needed as we wrestle with the problem of not always having easily distinguishable user groups to work with and that the groups we end up distinguishing are likely to have strong heterogeneous characters.

To the discussion on the role of values, ethics, and moral issues in HCI, philosophy of technology could contribute in numerous ways:

- **Offer new perspectives.** Theories such as Borgmann's device paradigm offer new perspectives on the role of values in technology design that tend to operate on a different level than those suggested by first, second, and third wave HCI approaches.
- **Connect specific values with a larger philosophical discourse.** As today's philosophers of technology deal with the same technologies as we do in HCI, we have through them access to a vast history of thinking around ethics and technology and to the different philosophical strands particular ideas belong.
- **Stimulate continued critical reflection on values.** Mainstream HCI tends to rather thoughtlessly connect technological development with societal progress and 'the good life'. Theories from philosophy of technology are often inherently reformist in nature and thus tend to stimulate reflection on values and ethics.
- **Provide guidance concerning how to incorporate specific values in design.** Theories from philosophy of technology may provide guidance as to how specific values might be incorporated into design even if they are not explicitly design-oriented. For instance, as in the case of Borgmann, how a number of specific values seem to foster engagement with reality [18].

CONCLUSIONS

A defining characteristic of third-wave HCI is the shift from a rather narrow task-orientation to the broader concern of trying to increase the quality of everyday experiences. This paper has recognized a need to establish a more explicit, shared notion of what it is HCI now strives for as a field. Further, it has been argued that if interactive artifacts are knowingly designed to provide users with specific user experiences, then guiding visions must be developed, which provide the means for revealing, analyzing, and discussing the obvious implications (human, social, cultural, ethical, moral, ecological, and political) of these experiences and how they foster particular relationships between users, designers, artifacts, and contexts. An extended discussion of these concepts would facilitate a sharpening, enrichment, and substantial deepening of the current discussion of the role of user experiences, engagement, motivation, and meaning in HCI design; it would also help to deal with and better understand *if*, *how*, and *why* some of the experiences we design for may be considered 'good' while others might perhaps be thought of as less so.

ACKNOWLEDGEMENTS

This research is supported by the Swedish Foundation for Strategic Research.

REFERENCES

1. Bardzell, J. Interaction criticism and aesthetics. *Proc. of CHI 2009,* ACM (2009), 2357-2366.
2. Battarbee, K. Defining Co-experience. *Proc. of DPPI,* ACM (2003), 109-113.
3. Bell, G. & Dourish, P. Yesterday's Tomorrows: Notes on Ubiquitous Computing's Dominant Vision. *Personal and Ubiquitous Computing*, 11, 2 (2007), 133-143.
4. Blythe, M. A. and Wright, P. C. 2006. Pastiche Scenarios: Fiction as a resource for user centred design. *Interacting with Computers* 18.5 (2006), 1139-1164.
5. Bødker, S. When second wave HCI meets third wave challenges. *Proc. of NordiCHI,* ACM (2006).
6. Borgmann, A. *Crossing the Postmodern Divide,* Univ. of Chicago Press (1992).
7. Borgmann, A. *Holding On to Reality: The Nature of Information at the Turn of the Millennium.* Univ. of Chicago Press (1999).
8. Borgmann, A. Reply to My Critics, in Higgs, E., Light, A., & Strong, D. (Eds.) *Technology and the Good Life?*, Chicago: University of Chicago Press (2000).
9. Borgmann, A. *Technology and the Character of Contemporary Life,* Univ. of Chicago Press (1984).
10. Card, S. K., Moran, T.P. & Newell, A. *The Psychology of Human-Computer Interaction.* Hillsdale (1983).
11. Cockton, G., Value-Centered HCI, *Proc of NordiCHI,* ACM (2004), 149-160.
12. Colbert, M. User experience of communication before and during rendezvous: Interim results. *Personal and Ubiquitous Computing,* 9.3, (2005), 134–141.
13. Dix, A., Finlay, J., Abowd, G. & Beale, R. *Human Computer Interaction,* 2nd Ed., Prentice Hall (1993).
14. Dourish, P. 2006. Implications for Design. *Proc. of CHI* (2006), 541-550.
15. Dourish, P. *Where the action is: the foundations of embodied interaction.* MIT Press (2001).
16. Dunne,A. Hertzian Tales: Electronic Products, Aesthetic Experience & Critical Design. Art Books (2000).
17. Ehn, P. *Work-Oriented Design of Computer Artifacts,* Arbetslivscentrum (1988).
18. Fallman, D. A Different Way of Seeing: Albert Borgmann's Philosophy of Technology and Human-Computer Interaction, *AI & Society,* 25.1 (2010) 53-60.
19. Fallman, D. Design-oriented Human-Computer Interaction, *Proc. of CHI2003,* ACM (2003), 225-232.
20. Fallman, D. The Interaction Design Research Triangle of Design Practice, Design Exploration, and Design Studies, *Design Issues,* 24.3, MIT Press (2008), 4-18.
21. Flanagan, M., Howe, D., & Nissembaum, H. (2008) Embodying Values in Technology: Theory and Practice.

In *Information Technology and Moral Philosophy,* Cambridge Univ. Press (2008) 322-353.

22. Forlizzi, J., & Battarbee, K. Understanding experience in interactive systems, *Proc.DIS,* ACM (2004), 261-268.

23. Friedman, B. & Kahn, P. H., Human Values, Ethics, and Design. In *The human-computer interaction handbook.* Lawrence Erlbaum (2003).

24. Friedman, B. & Nissenbaum, H. Bias in Computer Systems, *Trans. on Info. Systems,* ACM (1996) 330-347.

25. Gaver, B, Dunne, T, & Pacenti, E. Cultural probes. *interactions*, 6.1 (1999), 21-29.

26. Gaver, B. Technology affordances, Proc. of CHI1991, ACM (1991), 85-90.

27. Gaver, W, Hooker, B., & Dunne, A. The Presence Project. Royal College of Art (2001).

28. Gaver, W., Beaver, J. & Benford, S. Ambiguity as a Resource for Design. *Proc. CHI,* ACM (2003), 233-240.

29. Gaver, W.W., Dunne, T., and Pacenti, E. Cultural Probes. *interactions,* 6(1) 21-29, 1999.

30. Hallnäs, L., & Redström, J. Slow Technology: Designing for Reflection. *Personal & Ubiquitous Computing,* 5.3 (2001).

31. Heath, C. & Luff, P. Collaborative Activity and Technological Design: Task Coordination in London Underground Control Rooms, *Proc. of ECSCW,* Kluwer, (1991), 65-80.

32. Ihde, D. *Existential Technics.* State University of New York Press (1983).

33. Ihde, D. *Philosophy of Technology: An Introduction,* Paragon House (1993).

34. Ihde, D. *Technics and Praxis.* Reidel (1979).

35. Ihde, D. Technology and prognostic predicaments. *AI & Society,* 13, (1999) 44-51.

36. Ihde, D. *Technology and the Lifeworld: From Garden to Earth.* Indiana University Press (1990).

37. Landauer, T.K. Let's Get Real: A Position Paper on the Role of Cognitive Psychology in the Design of Humanly Useful and Usable Systems. In Carroll, J. (Ed.), *Designing Interaction: Psychology at the Human-Computer Interface.* Cambridge Univ. Pr. (1991), 60-73.

38. Le Dantec, C., Poole, E., & Wyche, S. Values as Lived Experience: Evolving Value Sensitive Design in Support of Value Discovery, *Proc.of CHI,* ACM (2009).

39. Leshed, G., Velden, T., Rieger, O., Kot, B., & Sengers, P. In-car GPS Navigation: Engagement with and Disengagement from the Environment. *Proc. of CHI,* ACM (2008) 1675-1684.

40. McCarthy, J., & Wright, P. *Technology as experience,* MIT Press (2004).

41. Mitcham, C. *Thinking through Technology: The Path between Engineering and Philosophy,* Chicago (1994).

42. Nardi, B.A.(Ed.) *Context and Consciousness: Activity Theory and Human-Computer Interaction.* MIT (1996).

43. Norman, D. A. *Emotional design: Why we love (or hate) everyday things.* Basic Books (2004).

44. Norman, D. Cognitive Engineering. In Draper, S. & Norman, D. (Eds.) *User Centered System Design,* Lawrence Erlbaum (1986), 31-61.

45. Odom, W., Pierce, J., Stolterman, E., and Blevis, E. Understanding why we preserve some things and discard others in the context of interaction design. *Proc. of CHI09* (2009) ACM 1053-1062.

46. Patel, N., Chittamuru, D., Jain, A., Dave, P., & Parikh, T.S. Avaaj Otalo: A Field Study of an Interactive Voice Forum for Small Farmers in Rural India, *Proc. of CHI,* ACM (2010).

47. Picard, R. *Affective Computing.* MIT Press (1997).

48. Pierce, J. Material awareness: promoting reflection on everyday materiality. *Proc. of CHI Extended Abstracts* (2009) ACM, 4459-4464.

49. Rittel, H. & Webber, M. Dilemmas in a General Theory of Planning, *Policy Sciences*, 4,Elsevier (1973) 155-169.

50. Rogers, Y. New Theoretical Approaches for Human-Computer Interaction. *Annual Review of Information, Science and Technology,* 38, (2004) 87-143.

51. Sengers, P. & Gaver, B. Staying Open to Interpretation: Engaging Multiple Meanings in Design and Evaluation. *Proc. of DIS,* ACM (2006), 99-108.

52. Sengers, P., Boehner, K., David, S., & Kaye, J. Reflective Design, CC'05, ACM (2005), 49-58.

53. Shneiderman, B. Direct manipulation: a step beyond programming languages, *IEEE Comp.* 16.8 (1983) 57-69

54. Strong, D. & Higgs, E. Borgmann's Philosophy of Technology, In Higgs, E. S., Light, A. & Strong, D. (Eds.) *Technology and the Good Life?* Chicago (2000).

55. Suchman, L. *Plans and Situated Actions: the Problem of Human-Machine Communication.* Cambridge (1987).

56. Weiser, M. The computer for the 21st Century. *Scientific American,* 265.3, (1991), 94-104.

57. Winner, L. Do Artifacts Have Politics? In *The Social Shaping of Technology,* Open Univ. Press (1985), 26-38.

58. Winograd, T. & Flores, F. *Understanding computers and cognition: a new foundation for design.* Ablex Publishing Corporation (1986).

59. Wright, P., Fields, R. & Harrison,M. Analyzing Human-Computer Interaction As Distributed Cognition. *Human Computer Interaction,* 51.1, (2000), 1-41.

60. Zimmerman, J., Forlizzi, J., & Evenson, S. Research through Design as a Method for Interaction Design Research in HCI, *Proc. of CHI,* ACM, (2007) 493-502.

Understanding Interaction Design Practices

Elizabeth Goodman
School of Information
University of California, Berkeley
Berkeley, CA 94720 USA
egoodman@ischool.berkeley.edu

Erik Stolterman
School of Informatics
and Computing
Indiana University, Bloomington
Bloomington, IN 47405 USA
estolter@indiana.edu

Ron Wakkary
School of Interactive Arts
and Technology
Simon Fraser University
Surrey, BC Canada V3T 0A3
rwakkary@sfu.ca

ABSTRACT
There is an undesirable gap between HCI research aimed at influencing interaction design practice and the practitioners in question. To close this gap, we advocate a theoretical and methodological focus on the day-to-day, lived experience of designers. To date, this type of theory-generative, experientially oriented research has focused on the users of technologies, not the designers. In contrast, we propose that HCI researchers turn their attention to producing theories of interaction design practice that resonate with practitioners themselves. In part one of this paper, we describe the mismatch between HCI research and interaction design practices. Then we present vignettes from an observational study of commercial design practice to illustrate the issues at hand. In part two, we discuss methodological and theoretical changes in research practice that might support the goal of integrating HCI research with interaction design practices. We then discuss current research methods and theories to identify changes that might enlarge our view on practice. In part three, we elaborate on our theoretically minded agenda and a kind of ideal-type theory.

Author Keywords
Interaction design, practice, theory

ACM Classification Keywords
H5.m [Miscellaneous]; K.4.3 [Organizational Impacts]

General Terms
Human Factors

INTRODUCTION
In many academic disciplines, one major research goal is influence on practice. The sharing of examples and theories of practice fuels education, research, and innovation in commercial activity. Indeed, human-computer interaction (HCI) researchers often describe HCI as an integration of academic practice and professional practices [3, 18, 32] – in particular, the new profession of interaction design.

Interaction design – the specification of digital behaviors in response to human or machine stimuli – is a complex discipline. Ideally, interaction designers combine knowledge of technological possibilities of the platforms and systems in play, skilled aesthetic judgment, and empirically informed empathy with potential users [28, 36]. Interaction designers as practitioners work in many arenas of technology development, from universities and research labs to business product groups and small start-ups.

Multiple studies have suggested that many frameworks and theories proposed in HCI research (ie, [34, 43]) have not fulfilled creators' goals of influencing professional design practice. We propose this disconnection in part emerges from a persistent failure to adequately address the lived complexity of design practices. HCI's research commitment to systematic analysis of how people make use of technologies is well-known. Yet there has been much less attention paid to understanding the diversity of environments in which design takes place. This inattention, we propose, results from an assumption that the social worlds and epistemological beliefs of the imagined "users" of HCI theories and frameworks — in particular, professional interaction designers — are largely identical to those of the researchers producing them.

Interaction design, as a profession, has its own distinct professional associations, publications and conferences[1]. If we as HCI researchers want to participate in this world, we will need to broaden our current research agenda. We cannot even assess the existence and nature of any gap without attending more closely to how professional designers actually work, and how they understand what constitute their competence, organizational, and professional roles. A broader research agenda could help HCI researchers understand and theorize what interaction design is, and present opportunities for HCI research to contribute to a broader range of practices.

In this paper, we contend there is a need to produce theories of designerly practice that are *resonant* with the everyday

[1] For example, the Interaction Design Association (IxDA) association and annual conference, the interactive track of the South by Southwest (SXSW) conference, and the American Institute of Graphic Arts (AIGA).

work of interaction designers. We believe that empirically grounded descriptions and critical analyses of design practice activities will offer frameworks for reflection on practices that designers can find useful. Such a research enterprise could then help create opportunities for HCI researchers to build longterm engagements with design practice that make sense to practitioners.

About this paper

The paper has three parts. In part one, we summarize two decades of publications that suggest a lack of synchronization between HCI research and interaction design practices. We then argue that many rational and scientific theories of design overlook the everyday practices of interaction design. We then move to three vignettes of everyday interaction design work to demonstrate how professionals negotiate research questions relevant to interaction design practice.

In part two, we discuss changes to the HCI research agenda that might better integrate HCI research and interaction design practices. We divide our discussion between methodological and theoretical concerns. We examine some current research methods and suggest how they could change to enlarge our views on practice. Moving to theoretical frameworks, we then draw out how some current theories suggest a kind of ideal-type theory.

In part three, we shift from the goal of researching interaction design practice to the aim of generating theories of practice. We elaborate the theoretically minded, practice-grounded agenda that we propose. We describe the opportunity for new theories to provide a language for discussing practice. Such a language would enable comparison of processes and projects, help support practitioners, influence the development of methods, tools and techniques for practice, and help evaluate the theories themselves.

We conclude with the notion that a research agenda for HCI practice oriented research would aim toward accounting for epistemological orientations, coherent principles that are open to critique and debate, and open methods to flexibility over prescriptions, and lastly but most importantly, mobilize theoretical ideas in a way that is accessible in practice and open to revision through practice.

DEFINING PRACTICE

The word "practice" has multiple meanings, and so we will clarify them before we continue.

The colloquial meaning of "practice," as employed by both HCI researchers and professional interaction designers, often refers to professional design activities intended to create commercial products, as in articles such as "CHI and the Practitioner Dilemma" [1]. This definition of "practice" assumes a division between the interests and perspectives of university and corporate research and those of professional practice. The social sciences, however, suggest more diverse notions of practice. This is particularly visible in research on professionalization [15, 19, 36].

Green recently argues for a definition of "professional practice" as four "senses" in which the concept can be understood and operationalized [15]. The first sense is when professional practice is seen as referring to the "practicing of a profession" as in 'practicing medicine', 'practicing law', etc. Secondly, the notion can refer to practicing professionalism, that is, it has a focus on what it means to be a professional, related to identity and position. Thirdly, it can refer to moral-ethical qualities of practice. Finally, professional practice can be opposed simply to amateur work. However, Green also argues that, in most definitions, regardless of "sense", it all comes down to a study and understanding of three aspects, and those are the *activities, experiences*, and *contexts* of practice. Practice becomes the composite of what practitioners do, what they experience, and the context where this takes place.

How then to think about analyzing that composite? We draw on the rich and extensive tradition of "practice theory" here. Studies of design work have often focused on specific and fairly well defined activities, for instance, the processes of idea generation through sketching and brainstorming (i.e., [5]). In studying the social shaping of technology, Mackay and Gillespie [25] refer to this orientation as a *micro* view. Among other approaches it tends to a constructivist understanding of interactions and activities. Alternatively, they propose a *macro* orientation that examines phenomena from an ideological framing and is broader in its consideration of socio-economic factors. However, a practice-based perspective on design need not oppose *macro* and *micro* analyses.

Drawing on Kimbell's application of practice theory in design [22], we can see interaction design practice as "carried by individuals" but constituted collectively. That is, looking at activities, experiences, and contexts requires that we look not just at individual minds and bodies, but also technical systems, organizational structures, tools, and knowledge [37]. Practice theory prompts us both to examine the embodied effort of designing technologies, using tools, and learning trades – but also how these activities are produced by and in turn sustain organizations, systems, and infrastructures.

HCI RESEARCH AND INTERACTION DESIGN

We are not alone in our concern that scholarly HCI research aimed at influencing professional design practitioners has fallen short of this goal; nor is this concern recent. Publications spanning the last two decades have identified various gaps between research — whether in universities or corporate laboratories — and non-research professional work. These publications have diagnosed three main problems. First, they have portrayed designers as relatively unaware of scholarly theories and methods [34]. One common complaint describes a lack of "knowledge transfer" between the HCI research community and that of design work [16, 23, 34]. Second, they have described designers as knowledgeable but unlikely to apply those theories or methods because of time, cost, or labor constraints [16, 43, 47]. Third, they have examined differences in scholarly researchers' and commercial practitioners' perspectives on similar problems, such as designing a user interface [1, 35].

Notably, in 2004, Rogers identified a "gap between the demands of doing design and the way theory is conceptualized" based on a study of practitioners in the UK and US that analyzed recognition and use of then-common HCI theoretical frameworks [34]. Assessing the influence of theoretical perspectives intended to inform HCI design, she shows that design practitioners have not taken up the complex analytic frameworks produced for them by researchers. Instead, what has persisted is "the pervasive use of a handful of high level concepts," such as "situatedness," "context," and "affordances." "Ironically," Rogers writes, "it appears that the analytic frameworks developed for use in HCI are not that accessible or easy to use." She continues: "It would seem that quite a different frame of reference is needed – one which focuses more on the *process* of design and how the different kinds of designers, themselves, want to be supported."

Another factor in the gap between HCI research and interaction design practices may lie in how some researchers define design complexity. Elsewhere, we have argued at length that HCI research mistakenly treats the complexities of design practice as a problem to be scientifically solved [43, 45]. In essence, many researchers assume that commercial designers can and should tackle the everyday experience of design complexity as they do — like scholarly scientists. This has led to a misapplication of scientific reasoning practices to design situations that in turn leads to results (methods, tools, and techniques) that design practitioners do not recognize as relevant.

In part, we believe that treating the complexities of different sorts of design practices as congruent to the work of scientists has rationalized away the need to closely examine actual design practice. And so it is no surprise that we have found so few rigorous, scholarly descriptions of the everyday work of interaction design, and even fewer of interaction designers' own understandings of what they do.

One set of existing descriptions aims not to represent the fullness of design practice, but to motivate the development and refinement of methods, techniques, or tools to support specific design tasks. These studies approach designers as potential technology *users* [8, 9, 31, 35]. While potentially very helpful in creating and refining task-specific tools, the focus on interaction design practitioners as users radically limits our perspective on how interaction designers motivate their own actions, decisions, and processes.

Another set of experimental studies aimed at understanding the cognition of designers (notably, [6]) has resulted in richly descriptive accounts of creative problem solving. Yet such studies often lack context by defining design situations as a well-bounded set of conversations internal to individual minds or within small teams. Ultimately, we believe that this focus on well-defined cognitive processes also crucially limits the analytic scope of the findings. We believe that this problem – of limiting one's perspective on where and how design complexity comes into play – also helps disconnect HCI frameworks and interaction design practice.

These factors suggest some reasons behind the continuing complaints within HCI of a division between "practitioners" and researchers. Without a shared set of references, HCI researchers may treat the complexities of design practice as inherent to a mysterious "black art" [46]. Alternately, designers may view HCI researchers as overly oriented to an objectivism anchored in science. Science is only one of many cultural languages and lenses one could use to construct an understanding of design practice. Designers themselves simply may not share the values of objectivity, lack of bias, and a-cultural thinking held by scientists.

A growing body of research (within and without HCI) has begun to produce a more practice-based perspective on design. Drawing on their own practice and on observation of others, researchers have described design as resting on a form of knowledge that differs from conventional notions of science. In this approach, successful designers often in practice value reflexivity, interpretation, and "judgment" above intellectual objectivity [28, 41]. Phrases like the *reflective* practitioner [38], *thoughtful designer* [24] *designerly knowing* [6] *mindful learner* [20], and *ambiguity* [12] instantiate similar notions of a form of knowing specific to design. Design reasoning may be seen as improvisation or "artistry," dealing with the particular, and only located "in action." Given this emergence from situated reflection, theorists often describe design as an act of particularity and contingency [22, 28, 38] rather than an implementation of objective principles or universal methods.

Our agenda for dealing with the complexities of design draws from this reflective perspective, rather than from a notion of design as set of objectively graspable problems. Design practice complexity should be understood as the complexity a designer *experiences* in a particular design *context* [43]. In this view, design complexity emerges within activities of designing, experienced through acts of reflection, decision, and judgment. Therefore, the "eye" of the practicing designer(s) defines it. This definition also resonates with the three core aspects of practice that Green proposes (as mentioned earlier), that is, activity, experience, and context. Design complexity is *experiential.* It cannot be exclusively an attribute of function, form, or performance, nor of the design problem alone, without considering the activities of designing and the contexts of designers' actions.

In summary, we locate the gap between HCI research and interaction design practice in researchers' distance from technology development practices that differ from their own. Design practice differs from scientific practice in valuing situated reflexivity and in locating complexity in experience. Some research tries to define and then solve the complexity of design practice through prescriptive frameworks. However, the complexity of design practice is emergent, experienced through reflection, judgment and practice in a manner that is synthetic and irreducible. A result of this distance is insufficient interest in and examination of the full complexity and richness of interaction design practice, and to even fewer attempts to theorize it. If we want a shared "frame of reference" between HCI theorizing and the practice of design, we will need more systematic and close attention to the experiences of the kind of practicing designers who are not already represented in HCI.

COMPLEXITY-IN-PRACTICE: STUDYING COMMERCIAL INTERACTION DESIGNERS

In this section, we provide an description and discussion of design practice that illustrates some of the ways that working designers grapple with complex questions of "good design." It draws on a six-month study of interaction designers in San Francisco's Bay Area.

The study included in-situ observation of three interaction design projects at two consulting companies, as well as interviews with eight designers outside the companies. The projects generally had one or more interaction designers, visual designers, and design researchers working alongside a project manager and perhaps (in consultancies) a client relationship manager, making a team of about three to five people. One project lasted six weeks; the other two lasted three months.

The participating consultancies were selected for recognized leadership in the interaction design professional community. They were also chosen as contrasts in organizational structure: a young, lightly staffed studio versus an older, larger firm. The interviewees were selected for individual breadth of technical experience as well as overall diversity of organizational location, including consultancies, start-ups, and in-house design teams. All had experience designing for computer-based applications (web and desktop software) as well as mobile applications. The majority of study participants were in the middle of their careers, with seven to 16 years of professional experience.

Many of the older designers had little formal training; they often described their first years as "learning on the job." Participants in their late 30s and 40s could often pinpoint a year in which they first used the phrase "interaction design" to describe what they did. Participants in their 20s and early 30s often had interaction design degrees, or had received early training through college internships. None attended — or wanted to attend — CHI or other ACM conferences, though one had an undergraduate degree in computer science. Their professional biographies echo the growth of interaction design in the 1990s and the solidification of a professional identity independent of computer science through the establishment of university programs, professional associations, and specialized conferences.

Despite differences in job description and organizational location, participants defined their work similarly: they saw themselves *producing representations to guide what will or could be built*. These representations included: interaction frameworks, task flows, sitemaps, wireframes, paper prototypes, textual descriptions, technical requirements, and product specification documents.

Participants typically differentiated themselves both from the visual designers who craft the "look and feel" of interfaces and deal with questions of emotionality and brand identity – and from the "devs" – the programmers and engineers who build applications and services. Many designers saw user research as a part of their job, but not the heart of it. The two types of work might take place in two project phases, or rely on different team members.

In both consultancies and corporations, interaction design is organizationally separated from software and hardware implementation. Designers often have to think like translators in creating representations accessible to people from different educational and professional backgrounds. However, the politics of translating those representations into functional products and services means successful designers do much more than make wireframes or write specifications. They "manage client expectations" through rounds of meetings, "get buy-in" from stakeholders on design decisions, negotiate technical decisions with developers, then "socialize" their deliverables by presenting them to relevant decision-makers.

Accounts of practice: understanding interaction design

What do practitioners themselves value in interaction design? In other words, how do they formally or informally validate practice; what language and terms come into play when considering "good and bad practice"; or how, within a design situation, do appraisals arise for "who is a good or bad designer"? The questions or learned lessons of interaction design deeply inform these kinds of everyday judgments. And understanding them is important if HCI researchers want to support designers' own aims for their work. In this section, we describe how these sorts of questions arise and get answered during the course of project work. We hope here to illustrate the importance of the workaday conversations and decision-making that currently rarely appear in HCI research.

Account One: Shortcut – optimal versus realistic

We begin at a workshop intended to prioritize features for a mobile rail ticket booking application. The project lead has scheduled an hour for her clients to place 50 post-it notes, each with a short description of a piece of functionality, on a whiteboard. The designers will use discussion about the positioning of the post-it notes to establish client priorities.

As the clients place post-its, the project leader leaves them to talk to the researcher. Unasked, she quietly explains the logic behind this exercise. For her, there is an "optimal way of doing things" and a "realistic" way. She would prefer to have the clients "sorting [potential features] by business and user priorities separately," and then sorting by technical feasibility. Instead, pressed for time by her clients' tight travel schedule, she took a "shortcut." This is, she points out, not the first shortcut she has had to take on this project:

> *Project leader: Sometimes you have to take some shortcuts just because it's hard not to.*
>
> *Researcher: Why?*
>
> *Project leader: Because of time constraints. But it doesn't get all the information we ideally could have gotten if everyone sat down and discussed it together.*

Ten minutes later, the prioritization exercise is complete. The project lead will use its results to generate a feature set for the application – which they hope will have thousands of users within three months.

Account two: A choice between two kinds of good design

A designer is discussing a weekly client "check-in":

> *Designer: I brought two options to the table – one that's more simple but utilitarian and one that we've been talking about. We wanted to show both to the client and get their reactions but the less utilitarian one might be a little more interesting and playful in the end.*
>
> *Researcher: And that's good?*
>
> *Designer: Yeah, that's* <pauses> *good. [...] I mean, I was erring on the very usable simple side but there's some question about whether that's the most appropriate thing.*
>
> *Researcher: Why?*
>
> *Designer: Just I mean I guess it has a little bit to do with the hooks and just kind of making this not feel like it's work.*

The "hooks" are the pleasurable and entertaining experiences that the project lead wants to induce at various points in the mobile rail ticket booking application. The lead is concerned, as the designer suggests, that the application will "feel like it's work" and not be enjoyable enough for users (likely be on vacation) to want to use.

Account three: Defining project-wide success

The team is sitting at a conference table. It is the second week of what will be a 12-week project. The lead designer has scheduled this meeting to answer a question raised by a colleague: "how do you measure success?" When asked, the lead designer realized that the team had never discussed metrics for evaluating the project. "Well," he begins, "besides making the client happy, which we're all assuming is a goal." As the other team members talk, he summarizes their points on the whiteboard: "makes client happy"; "having a solid point of view"; "looks hot"; "something they [the client] use." That last point prompts this exchange:

> *Lead designer: This could be a stepping-stone to lots of other projects. That could be a shared goal as well. This is a project to get more projects.*
>
> *Project manager: It's potentially about future work, additional work.*
>
> *Lead designer:* [to the team's user researcher] *You seem excited about this.*
>
> *User researcher: That should be the measure of success of all projects.*

Language and levels of practice

In *account one* it was so important for the designer to tell the researcher about how this workshop differed from the *ideal* method that she voluntarily stopped interacting with her clients. "Optimal" and "realistic" seem like objective concepts, but they actually refer to situational, negotiated judgments within the context of the project. What's optimal for one schedule may be more realistic for another. Thus, the shortcut draws on professional judgment about the importance of having a face-to-face negotiation with clients. To someone who does not share the lead's concern for satisfying client priorities while keeping the project on schedule, the rationale for her shortcut will be hard to see.

Where the designer in *account one* used precise, seemingly objective language to describe her situational tradeoffs, the designer in *account two* points to concepts that are tangibly present to him, but lacks precise language to explain them. In other words, he describes the relative qualities of the two options ("utilitarian" versus "interesting and playful"). But when it comes time to explaining what characteristics make one design more appropriate than another, he fumbles for words and uses an internal team metaphor – the "hooks." Of course, the actual disposition of the project – whether it takes the more utilitarian or the more playful direction – is not up to the designer. With the support of his team lead, he has presented two options to the clients to choose between.

The research orientation of the two accounts discussed above involves analyzing *what* designers make and *how* designers make within the day-to-day, lived experience of practice. *Account three* illustrates how factors beyond the daily activities of making things impinge on the problem-solving processes of design – thus interweaving what have been called *macro* factors. There, three people in different roles – interaction design, user research, and project management – agree that one of the main ways to evaluate the project's success is whether it wins the company more work. That is – the success of the project may not lie exclusively in what is designed but also in the organizational relationships forged by the design process.

Though formal evaluation and explicit theorizing were not often present in the design practices we studied, assessments occur regularly throughout the process of designing. Those assessments rest on *implicit theories of good design*. And theories, whether partially formed, ill informed or individually held. are always in operation. The question for HCI researchers is therefore not of generously providing theories to people with none. Instead, it is of how to study the work of interaction designers in order to inform both design practice and HCI research by making designers' existing theorizing external and visible.

Making design practice an object of HCI research along with technology use will help create explicit theorizing. It can help make accessible new forms of design evaluation or it can help articulate and demystify approaches like critiques or socio-economic factors. We do not mean theories that prescribe rigid guidelines of quality. Rather, we mean theories that would acknowledge the inseparable interpretive aspects of evaluation, which in large part rely on experiences and judgments of designers. Theories of practice would help lay the groundwork for interpretation by addressing the need for mutual intelligibility of language, terms and concepts that are the materials of debate in asking questions of quality.

RESEARCHING PRACTICE: EXTENDING HCI RESEARCH METHODS AND THEORIES

In this section, we look to current methods of research and theories related to practice and how we can extend and improve upon them.

Extending the methodology toolkit

Studying practice, especially professional practice, is not a straightforward endeavor; its complexity suits a range of approaches and methods. The methods we discuss are not entirely new to HCI – indeed, some are quite familiar. Our aim is to argue that these methods should be applied not just to study *user* experiences of technology but also interaction designers' experience of their own work. We are convinced that experiential approaches to user experience could and should be applied to the study of design practice.

We are not advocating any particular method. Instead we believe that interaction design practice as a new form of professional practice needs to a diverse set of research methods, each bringing complementary aspects and perspectives to an overall understanding.

Earlier, we cited Rogers's identification of a "gap between the demands of doing design and the way theory is conceptualised" based on a *survey* of practitioners in the UK and US [34]. Vredenburg et al published a similar study based on surveys that examined user-centered design and professional practice [47]. *Mixed method surveys* provide an empirical and quantitative picture of the state of the field of design practice, and as a method it holds clear credibility within the HCI community.

In our study of interaction design consultancies reported in this paper, we utilized *participant observation*. In-situ data collection similar to our own study is a mainstay approach to understanding the fullness of practice. It is a well-accepted method within HCI based on the contributions of CSCW and workplace studies (such as [8]) and so holds similar credibility within the community as mixed-methods surveys. Moreover, it can push the researcher to confront issues of belonging and expertise: to what extent can the researcher present himself or herself as a member of the design group being studied?

These two approaches can lead to significant findings on interaction design practices. However, we also advocate for an expansion to HCI's more usual methodological toolkit to include reported practice, anecdotal descriptions, and first-person research.

Reported practice

Reporting on practices by interviewing designers is a long-standing approach in the wider design fields. More recently, HCI and interaction design research venues have accepted it. For example, in an informal set of interviews [43], the authors observed how students used theories, methods, and instruments as tools for design. Additionally, Zimmerman et al based an analysis of research through design on interviews with a dozen HCI design researchers [48].

Anecdotes, stories, and cases

In some respects, descriptions of authors' design processes through descriptive anecdotes, stories or slightly more formal case studies have together contributed the most to giving insights into design practice in HCI. A good example is Gaver et al's account of the design of the *Prayer Companion*, an electronic resource for a group of cloistered nuns [13]. In another example, Wolf et al provide an account of their design of *Rendezvous*, a conferencing application as an illustration for how designers can communicate their "intellectual rigor to the CHI community" [46].

First-person research

This approach aims at an intentional accounting of practice that situates the designer reflexively as both the primary informant and researcher. For example, Wakkary provides a description and analysis of his own interaction design project *ec(h)o*, a tangible audio museum guide, as a way to explain design complexity [45]. Similarly, Gaver's first-person account of the design of *Video Window*, a video screen in his bedroom showing the skyline from outside his window, allowed the author through simultaneously living with and continually designing the system to analyze the intermingling aesthetic, utilitarian, and design issues of both creating and experiencing the system [13].

The approaches we suggest are by no means comprehensive. They are nascent in their evolution and use within HCI research. As part of the agenda to expand the repertoire of methods, we suggest some changes. *Reported practice,* as a method, raises questions about the status of the interview participants as experts. Should these designers remain anonymous, as is typical in user studies (i.e., [48]), or does identifying individual participants provide provenance and context for the data? Both are issues that affect credibility of the data. In *anecdotes, stories, and cases* how do we move from unintentional descriptions of practice to intentional and purposeful explanations that provide insights into research matters, as in the discussion Gaver et al provide with the *Prayer Companion*? And do designers themselves gain credibility to science-oriented audiences through a reflective, self-critical first-person account? This is a critical concern for first-person research.

However, research on design practice can draw from existing traditions of first-person qualitative research such as anthropology and phenomenology. Specifically, they can use techniques of *bracketing* or *epoche* [29] to make explicit the researcher's perceptions and expectations *prior* to commencing the research with the expectation of comparing these assumptions to the later findings. Researchers can explicitly consider how and why their perspective on the world is situated, embodied, and partial – not a "view from nowhere" but part of "working relations" that enable them to conduct and publish research [44].

Our discussion has centered on data collection methods, yet these methods bring with them researcher commitments aimed to ensure the integrity of the data and analysis, and to maximize the potential for translation of the findings to other similar situations of design practice. For example, participant observation commits to expressing the observations and findings in the informant's or studied group's *own language*. In many respects, this commitment to representing research participants on their own terms underlies all the methods we discussed, with the exception of the quantitative aspects of mixed methods survey.

Theorizing interaction design practices

We advocate for increased research into the practices of interaction design with the benefit of *explicit theorizing of the findings*. Research that leads to theory will help interaction design share a common intellectual foundation with HCI research and vice versa. Such theoretical foundations would make it possible for researchers to compare and contrast their findings. A theoretical foundation is by no means a monolithic solution. Instead we look forward to developing a shared "language" or frame of reference that would enable researchers to accept and/or advocate ongoing critical reflection and rethinking of foundational assumptions about design practice.

We have argued that there has been little theorizing of interaction design practices within HCI. However, it is important to remember that design fields, including interaction design, have often resisted the type of abstractions and formalizations that constitute theories. An earlier relationship to craft still heavily influences design practice [33]. Within the craft tradition, explicit theorizing about practice is not common or valued. The craft tradition treats hands-on, everyday practice as something that can only be understood by doing it, by being a practitioner [33].

We have also argued that the lack of theory generated from within interaction design practice leaves HCI's relationship to practice vulnerable. Without a set of frameworks against which to position their own contributions, scholarly research can easily assume an objectivity-oriented perspective we earlier described as ill suited to designers more focused on critical judgment and reflection. So what types of theories are better suited for interaction design practice? In this section we look at recent theories now largely used in HCI to examine the experiences of people with new technologies. While not fully serving the needs of a theory for interaction design practice, they are critical antecedents.

Activity theory, a theory of situated development and consciousness of the user, relates strongly to technology and informs design situations, its structures, and relationships. Though it does not provide a theory of practice, it can help us imagine a theory of interaction design practice. Kaptelinin and Nardi's *Acting with Technology* [21] is a good example of theory that aims to be descriptive, explanatory, and generative. Kaptelinin and Nardi discuss activity theory as a basis for revisionary critique of HCI. In it, they see the descriptive capacity to provide a new set of key concepts and definitions, and the explanatory capacity to redefine relationships and processes within HCI. They draw on Ben Shneiderman's notion [42] that generative theories facilitate creativity, invention, and discovery. Activity theory is generative in a theoretical sense in that it creates ongoing conceptual development within HCI. We see the need for theories of equal ambition that describe, explain, and ultimately generate ideas and actions of design practice that resonate with the activities of designers.

McCarthy and Wright's *Technology as Experience* [27], while also not a theory of interaction design, provides a pragmatist notion of generative theories that is potentially translatable to design practice. McCarthy and Wright's theory of user experience revises HCI theory by drawing on the pragmatist ideas of Dewey and the linguistics of novelist Mikhail Bakhtin. McCarthy and Wright re-theorize the notion of user experience to include the emotional, intellectual, and sensual aspects of interactions with technology, arguing in the pragmatist sense that we *live with* technology rather than simply use it. From a pragmatist viewpoint, theory is by definition generative. It is a systematic inquiry for imagining a possible future. For a pragmatist, theorizing is a necessary and practical consequence of living or approaching one's life such that theory changes one's world rather than represents it. McCarthy and Wright discuss how Dewey's criticism of scientific theory as retrospective, concerned with describing and explaining the world as it is, rather than prospective, concerned with how the world might become. The authors argue that their generative view is "valued not so much for whether it provides a true or false representation of the world as for whether it helps us think through relationships between for example, people, technology, and design." We believe that a similar approach to the specifics of design practice — instead of user experience — might be highly valuable.

Participatory design (PD) is perhaps the best example of a generative theory that attempts to take on design in its fullness, including everyday practice. Participatory design emerged from socio-technical concerns regarding the design and use of information systems in organizations [10, 17, 40]. Ehn's vision for technology development emphasizes embodied knowledge, mutual learning, and the active roles of different groups [10]. The basis of Ehn's notion of participation is a shared understanding of the design needs between designers and skilled workers. In order to create something new, designers must bridge the different languages, tacit knowledge, and past experiences that lie between them and stakeholders. Ehn phrased this as "the dialectics of tradition and transcendence – that is what design is all about."

Participatory design offers a set of theoretical tools for the practice of design and for the generation of design actions and outcomes. PD stands out as a relatively coherent and effective theory about and for design practice. Ehn in particular provides a theoretical context for PD based on Heidegger, Wittgenstein and Marx that offers a rationale and basis for further elaboration on techniques and principles incorporated into information systems design. The principles afford an articulation of techniques and goals for participatory design that mobilize the theory into a form serviceable in design practice – a *rationality resonance* between theory and practice [43]. PD focuses on the relationship between designers and end-users, devoting a large degree of its efforts on articulating how designers interact with end-users. It does not revise core concepts in how design occurs; rather it critiques scientific accounts of the user by offering a design perspective *from* users. It falls short of offering a mode of validation or self-reflection — ultimately the mechanism to critique and evolve theories. In consequence, it articulates little about the communication of PD research outcomes and PD's interactions with other disciplines. Yet it is a powerful precursor to thinking about practice in interaction design.

THEORIES OF PRACTICE?

Throughout this paper we have argued that research *into* interaction design practices can increase the practical relevance of HCI frameworks in general and lead to theorizing of interaction design practices. It will never be possible or desirable to establish an ideal, complete theory of interaction design practice. Nor is there agreement on what that would be like. Instead, the purpose of this section is to start the discussion about what would characterize a well-grounded and useful theory of practice.

To begin, we have drawn from previous theories the need for a theory to be descriptive, explanatory, generative and reflexive. If theorizing practice produces a unique type of theory, than the measures of success would differ as well. Theories for practice usually aim to be generative. In HCI research, theories often result in, or at least try to influence, changes in design practice and outcomes. However, this is hard to measure. Any form of validation would inevitably be interpretive and results would only be possible to measure over very long periods. Therefore, to detect, capture, and measure direct and immediate consequences of a new theory seems highly improbable. An ideal theory could however result in greater awareness of the utmost complexity and richness of design practice as a human endeavor. Therefore, the first measure of success for theorizing practice should *not* be changed practice. Rather, it should be a combination of goals: the degree to which design researchers can articulate and publish research on design practice, and the degree to which theoretical descriptions make design practice more accessible to interdisciplinary research, to critical and emancipatory examinations, to comparison and contrasting with other practices, and to professional reflection. Overall, we argue for the criteria of *rationality resonance* [43], in which theories are grounded and recognizable from the perspective within practice. Initially we propose:

Descriptive: We see descriptions of practice as the origin of theorizing practice. The aim is to provide legitimate, rich accounts of practice from which to begin developing a common language and identifying mutually intelligible areas of interests and needs. Accurate descriptions of practice benefit both core and broadly interdisciplinary researchers/practitioners whose interest is in design. We encourage active acknowledgement that practice is multi-leveled and can be understood along a constructivist to ideological continuum or *micro* to *macro* scale.

Explanatory: Drawing from the preceding discussion, an ideal theory for interaction design should establish critical concepts, principles and definitions. It should also provide an explanation of the relationships, actions, actors, and processes within interaction design. This form of theory enables deeper analytical work. Analytical rigor based in evidentiary reasoning is a necessary criterion. Explanatory research helps close the gap between HCI research and interaction design practice by strengthening clear, analogous, and like concepts, as well as establishing new knowledge as credible across the communities.

Generative: Coherent principles drawn from explanatory or descriptive approaches may guide the development of research methods, design methods, and evaluation methods. This creates flexibility and experimentation in methods that avoid the prescriptive approaches of the past. The philosophical difference in a generative form is that theorizing is a necessary and practical consequence of practice and focuses on how practitioners can shape the world through practice. A generative theory leads to an understanding of future possibilities or inventions in interaction design and guides us in determining the value of each possibility. The forward orientation is best suited for design and would move HCI theorizing away from exclusive reliance on retrospective accounts of interaction phenomena – a key benefit for the purpose of bridging HCI research and interaction design practice cultures.

Critical/reflexive: Make explicit and open to question epistemological orientations within the theorizing. An underlying philosophical grounding appropriate to design will guide the development of core concepts and defining principles. However, these concepts and principles need to constantly be open to critique and revisions. In addition, a reflexive theory grounded in practice will help mobilize theoretical ideas and actions in a way that is accessible in practice and open to revision through practice.

It is important to underline the interactions between the forms of theorizing in order to address practice. It will be more likely that theories of practice will be inclusive of all forms rather than separate theories with different approaches.

CONCLUSION

In this paper, we have argued that HCI lacks research and theorizing about interaction design practice. In response, we propose more frequent and more intensive studies of interaction design practice, development of theories of interaction design practice, and validation of new theories based on how well they resonate with existing practices.

We examined existing potential theories, and illustrated the intricacy and complexity of practice in three vignettes. We discussed the requirements from a methodological and theoretical point of view for the field to improve when it comes to understanding practice. We concluded by reflecting on the requirements for an "ideal" theory of interaction design practice.

In conclusion, we want to clarify what we see as the straightforward argument that this paper as its overall contribution: that a solid understanding of existing practice must ground research aimed at supporting interaction design practice. HCI research on users offers a clear counterpart that must be matched theoretically, otherwise interaction design practice will continue to be eclipsed and under-theorized. Underlying the theoretical depth of much HCI research is a shared epistemological grounding in science and empirical study. With agreement on core concepts, the concepts are open to revisions and subject to vigorous and critical debate that grows the field intellectually. This strength in focus and epistemology creates coherence around principles that in turn allow for flexibility and experimentation with methods of research, validation, and the means to verify claims. Further, HCI research has mobilized a theoretical understanding through communication and flexibility of methods. In many respects, interaction design practice research needs to match this standard in its own theory-making about its practice. An "ideal" theory can never exist – but our hope is that in raising an initial set of criteria, we can move closer to a theorizing that is useful to its potential constituencies: researchers and designers.

ACKNOWLEDGMENTS

Research contributing to this paper was funded by a National Foundation Graduate Fellowship and an Intel Corporation PhD Fellowship.

REFERENCES

1. Arnowitz, J. and Dykstra-Erickson, E. 2005. CHI and the practitioner dilemma. *interactions* 12(4), 5-9.
2. Bellotti, V. 1988. Implications of current design practice for the use of HCI techniques. In *Proc. 4th Conference of the British Computer Society on People and Computers*. Cambridge UP, 13-34.
3. Bucciarelli, L. 1994. *Designing engineers*. The MIT Press.
4. Carroll, John M. 2009. Human Computer Interaction (HCI). In Interaction Design Encyclopedia. Retrieved on June 6, 2010 from http://www.interaction-design.org/ encyclopedia/human_computer_interaction_hci.html.
5. Clemmensen, T. and Leisner, P. 2002. Community knowledge in an emerging online professional community: the interest of theory among Danish usability professionals. IRIS'25.
6. Cross, N. 2006. *Designerly ways of knowing*. Springer.
7. Day, C. 2000. Effective Leadership and Reflective Practice. *Reflective Practice: International and Multidisciplinary Perspectives*, 1(1), 113-127.
8. Diggins, T. and Tolmie, P. 2003. The 'adequate' design of ethnographic outputs for practice: some explorations of the characteristics of design resources. *Personal Ubiquitous Comput.*, 7(3-4) 147-158.
9. Dow, S., Saponas, T.S., Li, Y., and Landay, J.A. 2006. External representations in ubiquitous computing design and the implications for design tools. *Proc DIS '06*, ACM Press, 241-250.
10. Ehn, P. 1990. *Work-Oriented Design of Computer Artifacts*. Lawrence Erlbaum Associates.
11. Fallman, D. 2008. The Interaction Design Research Triangle of Design Practice, Design Studies, and Design Exploration. *Design Issues*. 24(3) 4-18.
12. Gaver, B., Beaver, J. and Benford, S. 2003. Ambiguity as a resource for design. In *Proc CHI'03,* ACM Press, 233-240.
13. Gaver, W. 2006. The video window: my life with a ludic system. *Pers. and Ubiq. Computing.* 10(2): 60-65.
14. Gaver, W., et al. 2010. The prayer companion: openness and specificity, materiality and spirituality. In *Proc. CHI '10.* ACM Press, 2055-2064.
15. Green, B. 2009. Introduction: Understanding and researching professional practice, in Green, B. (ed). *Understanding and researching professional practice.* Sense Publishers.
16. Green, T.R.G., Davies, S.P., and Gilmore, D.J. 1996. Delivering Cognitive Psychology to HCI: The Problems of Common Language and of Knowledge Transfer. *Interacting with Computers* 8(1), 89-111.

17. Greenbaum, J. and Kyng, M. 1991. *Design at work: Cooperative Design of Computer Systems.* Lawrence Erlbaum Associates.

18. Hewett et al. 1996. ACM SIGCHI Curricula for Human-Computer Interaction. Retrieved on September 21, 2010 from http://old.sigchi.org/cdg/cdg2.html.

19. Humphreys, M. & Hyland, T. (2002). Theory, Practice and Performance in Teaching: Professionalism, intuition, and jazz. *Educational Studies*, 28(1), 5-15.

20. Kelley, D. and Hartfield, B. 1996. The Designer's Stance. In *Bringing Design to Software.* Ed. Terry Winograd. Addison-Wesley. Retrieved on September 21 from http://hci.stanford.edu/bds/8-kelley.html.

21. Kaptelinin, V. and Nardi, B.A. 2006. *Acting with Technology: Activity Theory and Interaction Design.* The MIT Press.

22. Kimbell, L. 2009. Beyond design thinking: Design-as-practice and designs-in practice. Paper presented at the CRESC Conference, Manchester, September 2009.

23. Latour, B. 2008. A Cautious Prometheus? A Few Steps Toward a Philosophy of Design. Keynote lecture for the Design History Society. Falmouth, Cornwall.

24. Löwgren, J. and Stolterman, E. 2007. *Thoughtful Interaction Design: A Design Perspective on Information Technology.* The MIT Press.

25. Mackay, H. and Gillespie, G. 1992. Extending the Social Shaping of Technology Approach: Ideology and Appropriation. *Social Studies of Science* 22(4), 685 -716.

26. Mao, J., et al. 2005. The state of user-centered design practice. *Commun. ACM* 48(3), 105-109.

27. McCarthy, J. and Wright, P. 2007. *Technology as Experience.* The MIT Press.

28. Moggridge, B. *Designing Interactions.* 2007. The MIT Press,.

29. Moustakas, C.E. 14. *Phenomenological research methods.* Sage.

30. Nelson, H.G. and Stolterman, E. 2002. *The Design Way: Intentional Change in an Unpredictable World : Foundations and Fundamentals of Design Competence.* Educational Technology Publications.

31. Newman, M.W. and Landay, J.A. 2000. Sitemaps, Storyboards, and Specifications: A Sketch of Web Site Design Practice. *Proc. DIS 2000.* ACM Press, 263-274.

32. Preece, J; Rogers, Y. and Sharp, H. eds. 2002. *Interaction Design: Beyond Human-Computer Interaction.* John Wiley.

33. Risatti, H. 2007. *A theory of craft: function and aesthetic expression.* UNC Press Books.

34. Rogers, Y. 2004. New Theoretical approaches for Human-Computer Interaction. *ARIST.* 38, 87-143.

35. Rosson, M. B., Kellogg, W., & Maass, S. 1988. The designer as user: building requirements for design tools from design practice. *Commun. ACM,* 31(11), 1288-1298.

36. Saffer, D. 2006. *Designing for Interaction: Creating Smart Applications and Clever Devices.* Peachpit Press.

37. Schatzki, T.R. 2001. Practice theory. In *The practice turn in contemporary theory.* Theodore R. Schatzki, Karin Knorr Cetina, and Eike von Savigny (eds.), 10-23. Routledge.

38. Schön, D.A. 1983. *The reflective practitioner: how professionals think in action.* Basic Books.

39. Schön, D. 1987. *Educating the Reflective Practitioner.* Jossey-Bass.

40. Schuler, D. and Namioka, A. 1993. *Participatory Design: Principles and Practices.* Lawrence Erlbaum Associates.

41. Sengers, P. and Gaver, B. 2006. Staying open to interpretation: engaging multiple meanings in design and evaluation. In *Proc DIS '06*, ACM Press, 99-108.

42. Shneiderman, B. 2002. Leonardo's laptop : human needs and the new computing technologies. The MIT Press.

43. Stolterman, E. 2008. The Nature of Design Practice and Implications for Interaction Design Research. *International Journal of Design 2*(1), 55-65.

44. Suchman, L. 1994. Working relations of technology production and use. *Computer Supported Cooperative Work* 2(1-2), 21-39.

45. Wakkary, R. 2005. Framing Complexity, Design and Experience: A Reflective Analysis. *Digital Creativity.* 16(2), 65-78.

46. Wolf, T.V., Rode, J.A., Sussman, J., and Kellogg, W.A. 2006. Dispelling "design" as the black art of CHI. In *Proc. CHI '06.* ACM Press, 521-530.

47. Vredenburg, K., Mao, J., Smith, P. W., and Carey, T. 2002. A survey of user-centered design practice. In *Proc. CHI '02.* ACM Press, 471-478.

48. Zimmerman, J., Forlizzi, J., and Evenson, S. 2007. Research through design as a method for interaction design research in HCI. In *Proc CHI '07*, ACM Press, 493-502.

"Voluntweeters": Self-Organizing by Digital Volunteers in Times of Crisis

Kate Starbird
ATLAS Institute, Technology, Media & Society
University of Colorado at Boulder
Boulder, CO 80309-0430
starbird@colorado.edu

Leysia Palen
Department of Computer Science
University of Colorado at Boulder
Boulder, CO 80309-0430
palen@colorado.edu

ABSTRACT
This empirical study of "digital volunteers" in the aftermath of the January 12, 2010 Haiti earthquake describes their behaviors and mechanisms of self-organizing in the information space of a microblogging environment, where collaborators were newly found and distributed across continents. The paper explores the motivations, resources, activities and products of digital volunteers. It describes how seemingly small features of the technical environment offered structure for self-organizing, while considering how the social-technical milieu enabled individual capacities and collective action. Using social theory about self-organizing, the research offers insight about features of coordination within a setting of massive interaction.

Author Keywords
Computer-mediated communication, crisis informatics, crowdsourcing, disaster, emergency, microblogging, organizing, risk communication, self-organizing, volunteers

ACM Classification Keywords
H.5.3 Groups & Organization Interfaces—collaborative computing, computer-supported cooperative work, K.4.2 Social Issues

General Terms
Human Factors, Theory

INTRODUCTION
The new behaviors of mass interaction that information and communication technology (ICT) enable are affecting the way we seek and provide information, as well as the way we imagine our roles and responsibilities in such matters. Here we empirically consider the emerging role of the "digital volunteer" as an element of the phenomena popularly known as "crowdsourcing." We relate these behaviors to the social science theory of collective behavior [2,9], and show how microblogging platforms serve as a new arena for self-organizing.

We examine this phenomena in the context of disasters—specifically, the January 12, 2010 Haiti earthquake—when onset of the presence of such volunteers was rapid and their activities often remarkable. Previous research and development efforts have emphasized the potential for "crowdsourcing" via social media to increase situational awareness during crisis events [10,15]. However, use of the popular umbrella term risks both obscuring the underlying behaviors that constitute "crowdsourcing," and erroneously casting them as novel by-products of new media. Spontaneous volunteerism is not a new feature of crisis events [2,4,8,20]— disaster events in the pre-ICT era were places where such large-scale self-organizing phenomena could previously be seen. This paper attempts to unpack "crowdsourcing" in crisis response by applying an existing framework of self-organizing in disaster settings [9] to new digital volunteer behaviors. In so doing, it reveals new forms of volunteerism that were not previously possible.

This work extends previous research on the use of social media during crisis, e.g. [5,7,17,19,21]. We begin with an overview of a disaster-response initiative based on the Twitter platform—one that our group helped deploy. Though the initiative was not widely used, the innovation nevertheless served as an opening to seeing and subsequently studying the broader sphere of digital volunteerism. This overview then sets the stage for describing the multi-phased empirical study of digital volunteerism and self-organizing behavior.

TWEAK THE TWEET: INNOVATION AND DEPLOYMENT

A Brief Overview of Twitter Functionality
Twitter is a communication platform that allows users to broadcast 140-character messages (*tweets*) to groups of other users who subscribe to their accounts (*followers*). In turn, Twitter users (*twitterers*) receive tweets from the set of users they elect to follow. For twitterers whose accounts are not explicitly set as private, every tweet is also posted to a public, searchable timeline.

In a process of crescive adaptation, twitterers have developed a variety of linguistic conventions to meet communication needs, including addressed tweets, the retweet, and the hashtag. Twitterers began to use the @ sign preceding another user's account name as a way of mentioning or addressing tweets to that user. This convention, termed *addressivity*, allows users to engage in one-on-one, yet still public, conversation [6]. The retweet (`RT @` or `/via @`) emerged as a forwarding technique whereby twitterers pass on tweets with attribution to the original author. Promoted to enhance the searchability of tweets [12], the `#hashtag` convention is now used by twitterers to mark up tweets with thematic keywords of their choice.

An Emergency Micro-Syntax for Twitter

During the 2007 Southern California wildfires, Messina explained how hashtags could be particularly helpful during disasters [12]. Messina, Boyd and others have gone on to propose other microsyntaxes for increasing the information capacity of the 140-character tweet, some with specific application during emergencies [13].

The Tweak the Tweet (TtT) syntax is another entrant to the field of Twitter microsyntax proposals, designed to assist in computational filtering and classification of emergency-related information tweeted during an event [18]. The original TtT concept, generated in November 2009 at the *Random Hacks of Kindness* barcamp, proposed an extension to the role of the hashtag, encouraging users to mark up tweets in a way that would allow computers to easily identify and parse key pieces of information, such as the type of report, location, contact, etc. By placing specific hashtags preceding words related to those hashtags, the information can be automatically identified and parsed into a record.

The original TtT proposal suggested using accounts from formal response agencies and news media to distribute *prescriptive tweets*. The hope was that instructive tweets would teach twitterers how to use the syntax [18]:

```
proj_acct: To report a need: #eventtag #need [list your needs, like: rescue, or food and water] #loc [location or GPS coords] #contact [email, @ or #]
```

The 2010 Haiti Earthquake

On January 12, 2010, a 7.0 magnitude earthquake struck Haiti near its Port-au-Prince capitol. Due to the earthquake's intensity and shallow depth, as well as Haiti's vulnerable infrastructure, the destruction was catastrophic. Economic damage has been estimated at up to $13.9 billion [1] with 200,000 to 250,000 lives lost [14]. In the aftermath, thousands were trapped beneath collapsed structures, hundreds of thousands were injured, and nearly 1.5 million people had been displaced [14]. Relief agencies struggled to meet basic needs in this catastrophic event.

Tweak the Tweet Campaign in Response to Haiti

With a desire to assist the response in Haiti during a time of overwhelming need, and in collaboration with the CrisisCamp initiative (crisiscommons.org), our research group deployed the Tweak the Tweet (TtT) syntax on January 14, 2010 at 19:51 EST.[1] We activated a Twitter account to distribute prescriptive tweets at regular, automated intervals (hourly), in both English and French. At the same time, several team members began to tweet information from various sources, including other tweets as well as email messages from disaster-related lists, using TtT syntax. We used the dedicated account as well as personal accounts to maximize audience reach. We updated our project website to explain how the syntax worked, developed a web-based editor that helped people generate tweets in the syntax, and created how-to screencasts posted to YouTube. We issued a press release to encourage broad attention to and adoption of the syntax.

Though the effort to support syntax use continued for several weeks, we ended our active campaign and sent our last prescriptive tweet on January 24, due to the recognition that the syntax was hard to use from the ground, and that we could not assure users that TtT tweets were being channeled to people and agencies who could respond.

Unexpected Activity of Tweak the Tweet Translation

The TtT syntax was originally intended for use during a disaster by those directly affected by the event. We deployed the idea during the aftermath of the Haiti earthquake knowing that only a small percentage of the population of Haiti were Twitter users, and that using a syntax could be difficult, but hoping that the structured data format could nevertheless be useful in some fashion. Not surprisingly, few people used the syntax from "the ground."

However, what was unexpected were the many twitterers located around the world who emerged as "translators"—those who translated information from multiple sources into the syntax and tweeted it out to their followers. Previous research indicates that "synthetic" information activity—where users modify and synthesize information from multiple sources, including Twitter itself—is an important form of information production on Twitter [19]. We recognized this synthetic information generation in the activity of translation from raw, unstructured information to structured data forms as the basis for a new form of the volunteerism that pervades disaster response [2,4,8,16,20]. We initiated this study to investigate the behavior and motivations of the TtT translators.

Note that for this paper, *translating* and *translator* specifically refer to TtT syntax translation, though many digital volunteers contributed by offering classic language translation to assist in this international response.

METHOD

We employed a multi-step process for data collection, beginning with large-scale tweet data collection using Twitter APIs, then a preliminary tweet content analysis to identify the target study population, and finally email-based interviews with a sample of the population to understand their motivations and experiences while tweeting during the immediate aftermath of the Haiti earthquake.

Tweet Collection and Analysis

Twitter Data Collection

During the active TtT campaign period (January 14-24), we used the Twitter Search API to collect every tweet that contained both the `#haiti` hashtag and at least one specialized TtT hashtag (e.g., `#need`, `#offer`, `#loc`). On February 1, we identified every twitterer who had at least one tweet in that set and, using the Twitter REST API, captured their entire Twitter status update streams

[1] All times are reported in local Haiti time, which was Eastern Standard Time (EST) at the time of the quake.

(*contextual* streams) from January 10–February 1. These streams contain *all* of a user's public tweets, including public tweets addressed to other users. This initial data set consists of 339 twitterers, six of whom were from our research group, and a total 292,928 tweets.[2]

Qualitative Analysis and Coding of Tweets

We conducted an analysis of tweet content in the contextual streams to better understand the behavior of twitterers in our data set, and to identify how each was using TtT syntax. We manually coded every tweet that contained a TtT hashtag, excluding prescriptive tweets, as: 1) *original tweet* (a user putting her own offers or needs into the syntax); 2) *TtT retweet* (of another's TtT syntax tweet); 3) *translation tweet* (a user translating information from another source into TtT syntax); and, 4) *non-TtT tweet* (a tweet that contained one of these tags, but was not in the TtT format). Discerning between TtT translations and retweets could not be done computationally because some retweets are not "properly" credited using one of the known conventions, and because many of the twitterers in our sample generated *tag-added retweets*, meaning that they began with a conventional retweet, including the `RT @` marker, but then modified it by inserting TtT tags. Table 1 shows the number of tweets in each category, excluding those sent by our team. Of 2911 total tweets in the syntax, 1040 were translations of information found in other sources, including other, non-TtT tweets.

Total TtT tweets (not including from our team)	2911
Translated (including *tag-added* retweets)	1040
Original (from affected people & remote organizations)	39
Retweets of TtT tweets	1732
Unknown – cannot classify as RT or Translated	100

Table 1. Coding for TtT tweets

Identifying the Translators

This tweet coding differentiated people who were using TtT on their own behalf, those who were translating other information into TtT, and those who were only retweeting messages already in the syntax. Table 2 shows the frequency of the different TtT user types. Though only ten twitterers (four in Haiti) used TtT syntax for directly tweeting their own needs, 74 of the 333 twitterers were found to have translated at least one tweet into TtT syntax.

Other Remote Digital Volunteers

Though non-translators were not included in the interview portion of the data collection (described next), qualitative analysis of their tweet streams suggests that many exhibited similar remote volunteer behaviors as those in the primary participant pool. Many were members of the volunteer networks that we describe below and acted as remote operators during the event, directing the flow of critical information. It was these consistent, Twitter-abetted, volunteering behaviors that became the ultimate subject of this research, with the TtT syntax serving as one vehicle with which these new behaviors were exhibited.

Original twitterers - tweeting on their own behalf	10
Original twitterers located in Haiti	*4*
Original twitterers not located in Haiti	*6*
Retweeters	215
Translators	**74**
Our Own Research Team Members	6
Twitterers whose #hashtag use was not TtT	38

Table 2. Number of Twitterers by TtT user type

Interview Data Collection

Participants

The 74 translators were identified as candidates for the interview phase of the study, designed to better understand volunteer translating behavior. We attempted to contact participants through their Twitter accounts, the only available point of access, using "direct messages" ("DMs" are private person to person twitter messages) to those who were "following" our account (which is required for DMs), and publicly addressed tweets to those who were not. Between the Haiti earthquake and the commencement of the interview study in the summer, two accounts were deleted, and several others became inactive, making it likely that many of our addressed tweets went unread. 37 of the 74 twitterers responded; 27 of these consented to participate and 19 completed the full interview. Respondents were widely distributed across volume of TtT tweets, from one TtT tweet sent to 171 TtT tweets sent. The response rate among those who were reachable was 51%. Eight initial respondents did not complete the interview for reasons including ongoing involvement in Haiti relief efforts, illness, and others not specified.

Email Interview Instrument

The interviews were conducted via email for all participants, though participants were given the option of a verbal interview. Each participant was sent a message with the same set of open-ended questions.

There were six sections to the interview (which were untitled in the instrument): 1) general Twitter use; 2) Twitter use during Haiti; 3) use of TtT syntax; 4) awareness of Twitter followers; 5) other volunteer experience; and 6) further comment and suggestions for future use of social media during crises. The section themes and the questions within them were derived from the prior qualitative analysis of the contextual tweet streams.

Because our analysis began to reveal that Twitter connections served critical functions in volunteering behavior, respondents whose tweet streams showed interactivity with other translators were sent a follow up email inquiring about their twitter-related social connections. For several participants, this second round led to an ongoing exchange with unscripted follow-up questions, just as in a face-to-face open interview. Due to

[2] The Twitter API allows us to collect only the most recent 3200 tweets from each user. For some high-volume users (20 of the total and 2 from our interview set), we could not go back as far as Jan 10 for their contextual streams.

the back-and-forth nature of most exchanges, we felt the term "survey" was not representative of the data collection method and instead use the term "email interview."

A Note on Treatment of Data

For this paper, we have anonymized all interview response data. Because Twitter data is public and searchable, we have carefully disassociated the interview identities and responses from Twitter accounts and their data streams. For Twitter data reporting, we asked each participant to choose between three kinds of anonymity. We treat three participants under the default, using a pseudonym and altering the language of their tweets to reduce searchability. Two participants elected to use a pseudonym but maintain original tweet language. Fourteen participants indicated that they wanted their original tweet content attributed to their real Twitter account name. We also changed usernames for all twitterers who are mentioned in tweets but were not participants in this study.

FINDINGS

The Participants

We asked gender and age questions and used tweet analysis to capture basic demographics for our interview group and make comparisons to the larger group of TtT translators.

A majority of twitterers who translated information into TtT syntax tweets are women. In our interview pool, there are 17 females and two males. To determine if this breakdown is representative of all translators and not due to other factors, we coded each twitterer for gender by analyzing the name and photo associated with the Twitter profile and the content of the account owner's tweets. For the entire 74 TtT translators, we found 46 females, 16 males, one account that was operated by two people (one male and one female), and 11 accounts where gender could not be determined. Where we could determine and assign gender in the entire translator group, 74% are female.

Though most were located in North America during the event (nine in the US and six in Canada), our interview group includes one twitterer each from Turkey, Australia, Switzerland, and the UK. The average age is 40.1 years.

Previous Twitter Use

Figure 1 shows the date that each study participant joined Twitter. Three participants created their accounts after the earthquake, though one operates another account started nine months earlier. Two others joined Twitter earlier, but they did not send their first tweet until after the event. The remaining 15 interviewees were actively tweeting from their current accounts before January 12, 2010.

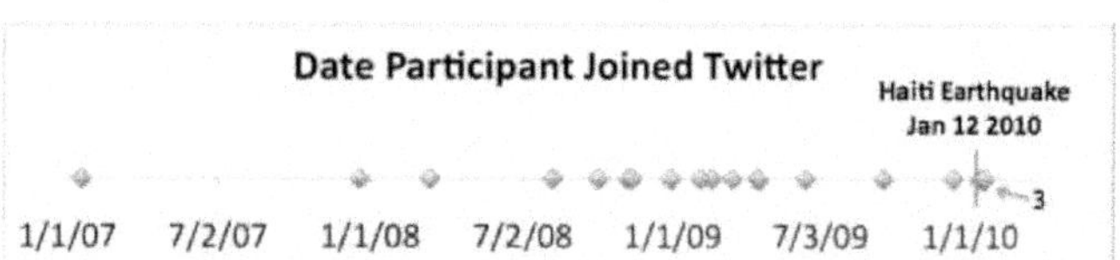

Figure 1. Twitter Join Date for Interview Respondents

The experienced twitterers in the study offer a variety of reasons for joining Twitter, including promoting a cause with which they are personally connected, and keeping up on pop culture and politics. Three report tweeting during previous disasters or crises and two of those specifically mention the political protests in Iran (June–December 2009) as their entry point to "crisis tweeting."

Personal Motivations for Haiti Tweeting

For those who began tweeting after the earthquake, all three cite personal connections to Haiti during the earthquake as motivation for creating accounts:

> *Emily: "My brother, a volunteer teacher in Port-au-Prince, had arrived in Haiti two days before the EQ. We... were not able to contact him and not sure where he was staying... As you know, the news was horrific and we were beyond worried. I joined Twitter approximately 12 hours after the EQ in order to try and communicate with surviving students from his school to find out if they had any news on him."*

Three other participants cite connections to people in or from Haiti as reasons for starting to tweet. Four of the five personally connected twitterers began with a single cause—a person or place with specific needs—and later branched out to communicating about other needs and issues.

Among those without personal connections, interview responses and tweet streams reveal the singular motivation of trying to help out, in any way possible:

> *Alena: "Why I did it? has no other explanation other than I had to. One part of the world was in pain and I could not sit back watch others do something when I had a little chance to send some drinking water to people if I could."*

> *Maria: "I think that's when I went on Twitter and started tweeting. Then I discovered a whole bunch of people tweeting for Haiti and started doing it myself and building up connections as much as I could in order to try to save some lives if possible. ... As you'll see some of us tweeted 16 hours a day or more... I just hoped what I was doing was helping. I'll never know if my tweets actually helped but that's ok as well."*

As these excerpts suggest, many of these people began tweeting for Haiti as a way of volunteering their time—sometimes entire waking days—from areas far removed from the event. Most, like Maria, entered the space with little direction or knowledge about how to help. Maria mentions that one of her first volunteer activities was to build up connections. We will return to these connections at length below to explain how volunteers were able to begin with little more than a Twitter account, yet end up helping in remarkable ways.

Using Tweak the Tweet Syntax

We asked participants where they first saw or heard about TtT syntax, why they decided to use it, and where they got the information that they translated into TtT tweets.

Discovering Tweak the Tweet

The majority of respondents learned about the TtT syntax from a tweet—many of these were prescriptive tweets from our team members' accounts found through hashtag searches, or seen in an RT from another twitterer they follow. Five participants report being directed to the syntax instructions by other twitterers in their networks and two mention receiving help from another twitterer who "explained" the format to them, or "taught" them how to use it. A few interviewees appear to have learned the format by mimicking its use in others' tweets. One of these did not realize she was using TtT syntax, though her tweet streams show that she began to use the `#location` and `#contact` data tags. Another explains that she discovered TtT when one of her tweets was retweeted in the format:

Emily: "Another Haiti volunteer on Twitter retweeted my post with the correct syntax, and I went to the "Tweak the Tweet" website, read up on it, and started using it for all my Haiti tweets and retweets except personal responses to people looking for information or offering help to [Haitian village] directly."

It is interesting that this respondent refers to the retweet of her information as being in the "correct syntax." This statement implies that the syntax was somehow more correct or more official than her original tweet. This theme shows up in several of the responses about TtT use.

Reasons for Adopting TtT Syntax

We asked all interviewees why they chose to use TtT, giving examples to each from their own Twitter stream. Several replied that it just "made sense":

Susan: "Because it standardized everything. It gave a SOP/ Standard Operating Procedure or MO/ Modus Operandi of doing tweets. I thought it made perfect sense."

The statement above suggests that this twitterer welcomed a standardized method for her tweeting and it echoes Emily's comment about "correct syntax." When these twitterers say that TtT made sense, they may not be talking about the rules of the syntax, per se. In fact, many of the same report that it was quite hard to use. What seems to appeal to them was the idea of standardization. The syntax itself became an object of authority—an organizing feature in the socio-technical milieu of Twitter activity. This is an idea we return to in the Discussion.

Some participants saw the syntax as a way to manually filter and identify key information for themselves, from within an inherently noisy information space:

Claire: "Myself having been searching using hashtags and keywords thought this was an excellent way to filter out (most likely) credible sources directly involved in the effort from possible citizens of Haiti or family members just sharing information and sorting through the chatter."

Some felt that using the syntax marked their own tweets as authoritative and helped their accounts rise above the fray:

Claire: "I realized my impression of those using the syntax was to take them more seriously, so once I had confirmed information it was translated into syntax."

A few noted that the format could be used as a way to make individual tweets more useful, regardless of back-end tools for filtering. By formatting or "syntaxing" their tweets in this way (as some came to call it), they made sure tweets had the necessary pieces of information. They could use the syntax as a way to instruct others to do the same:

Jenny: "I choose to tweet with the syntax because uniformity in messaging is essential in high pressure, emergency situations ... I also noticed that people ... spent a lot of time trying to decipher messages with missing info and what the source of the info was.... In short the time spent looking for missing parts to a message could be avoided by using TtT."

These responses suggest that some Haiti twitterers adopted TtT as another resource in their own volunteer work. The syntax helped them format tweets to include all the necessary pieces of information, such as contact number, location, and source. It was a signal they could give to say that the information in their tweets had been verified by someone who had experience in the space. ("Experience" might only amount to days worth, which can be enough to warrant credibility and even develop mastery relative to the newness of the volunteering tweeting phenomenon). TtT also helped some do manual filtering by allowing search on certain hashtags to identify important, actionable information, a topic we return to later.

Source Material for TtT Tweets

For their own translated TtT tweets, interviewees reformatted and passed on information from a variety of sources. Most report using other tweets as a key source. They first located tweets with key information that were not initially in TtT format, then added the TtT tags and retweeted them. Several mention verifying the content before passing it along. The example below shows how one twitterer took the information from a tweet she saw and translated it into TtT syntax, noting her source.

(Original) **`Delmon:`** `Marie Girard @ Institut FR, Ruelle Robin PaP needs food water 4 children, toddlers + pregnant woman 5555-5555`

(Translation) **`barbaraslavin:`** `#haiti #needs food H20 #name Marie Girard #loc Institut Franse, Ruelle Robin P-a-P #info 5555-5555 #source @Delmon TwT`

Participants also listed public blogs and Facebook posts, as well as DMs, emails and phone calls from contacts (some on the ground in Haiti), as sources for their TtT tweets.

Another key source for TtT tweets noted by six of our interviewees was Ushahidi. Ushahidi is a collaborative reporting environment that aggregates and maps information provided by citizens [15]. Originally developed during violent political unrest in Kenya in 2008, Ushahidi was used during the Haiti crisis in conjunction with an SMS shortcode to collect incident reports from the ground. Ushahidi organized and encouraged volunteers to help process the raw SMS messages into structured reports [10]. Some of our respondents monitored Ushahidi incident reports, identified new or newly verified information, and then tweeted it in TtT syntax. A few also directed these tweets to users they felt could act on the information.

Remote Operators: Mechanisms of Emergence

Analysis of interview responses revealed two types of digital volunteers within our translator group. The first was the type we identified at the onset of this research study, digital volunteers whose primary activity was the translation of other information into TtT tweets. For the other type, TtT was merely another resource adopted as part of a diverse tool set. In this second group, twitterers were not simply translating information, but instead were acting as *remote operators*, moving information between many sources using a variety of tools. TtT was only a small part of that activity. Many exerted considerable effort into building and leveraging connections to move information—and in some cases supplies—between affected people on the ground, response agencies in Haiti and abroad, and other volunteer crisis workers all over the world.

None of the twitterers in the second category were able to simply log on to their Twitter account and start acting like remote operators. Instead, they progressed from simple activities (e.g., retweeting or translating tweets) to more complex ones (e.g., verifying or routing of information).

Ushahidi was a key bridge between information-based activities (similar to TtT translation) and the more complex volunteer work of remote operators. Over time, some volunteers shifted from taking information from Ushahidi incident reports and tweeting it (sometimes in TtT syntax) to other activities, including verifying details, especially the origin date, and following up on contact email addresses and phone numbers to confirm reports. Others began to monitor Twitter by searching for certain hashtags, including TtT tags, and then used that information to create new Ushahidi reports or update existing ones. This shift between translating and pure data entry to information verification is one we see in several interview responses.

Though TtT translation and Ushahidi data entry were the primary entrance points to crisis tweeting for many, others began with different types of tweet-driven activities. One started her Haiti volunteer work by adding minutes to Haiti residents' cell phones as requested by other twitterers who were in Haiti or had connections to people there.

MelyMello (Jan 15 24:26): @ayitiJo we can top up your phone, can't we? add more minutes to it for you? Just need your phone #

MelyMello (Jan 16 17:38): @jean123 please let 50955555555 know that 630HTG were just added

deJacmel (Jan 16 ~19:00): @MelyMello Please Add min 2 ths cell numbers for me. They R helping Amer families to contact their haiti relatives.

MelyMello (Jan 17 13:11): @janeSM want to help? Help me add minutes to a WACK of phone numbers I have been sent!

MelyMello (Jan 17 14:32): @janeSM - please send any urgent request to help locals to @deJacmel - we're adding $ to cells of his local contacts to do just that

MelyMello (Jan 17 20:33): @Meira_Davi just emailed you the updated list - Paypal is almost empty again - have two more numbers to do - then we're at $0 :(

MelyMello (Jan 17 21:00): @deJacmel - can UR ppl help? At Brochette (Carrefour), 1500 ppl have nothing to eat or drink since Tues evening. Call 509.337-53-2154

As the sequence above describes, @MelyMello enlisted the help of other remote twitterers in her effort. She created a PayPal account and requested donations. She established digital relationships with other twitterers (@deJacmel) who had connections to people on the ground in Haiti. Later, she would use these contacts on the ground to get information on ground conditions, verify reports, and even request help for other needs she identified.

The interview excerpt below shows the evolution of isolated activity to a set of network connections and expanded set of activities:

Linda: In the beginning, I worked alone ... I started recognizing ppl who seemed to have good info and we would support each other, RT each other and help to find info for each other.

The exchange below, taken from the contextual streams of one of our translators and another twitterer in our initial 339 (the latter was not coded as a translator), demonstrates how some volunteers came to use connections and information on Twitter in combination with contacts on the ground to act as remote emergency operators.

CarolB (Jan 18 10:53): @IstanbulTWSTVL who needs the truck? What type of truck? Where in clercine?

IstanbulTWSTVL (Jan 18 11:04): @CarolB @janeSM Needs a truck by Clercine and help with & UN DRS that need ride at rue de l'enterrement #xx

CarolB (Jan 18 11:07): Okay made contact with someone should be sending truck.

IstanbulTWSTVL (Jan 18 11:21): @CarolB Second situation was stevePs people on the way to Clercine had no phone contact he has posted number @steveP is this solved

CarolB (Jan 18 11:27): @IstanbulTWSTVL It has been arranged. Truck has been arranged.

In this example, @IstanbulTWSTVL routes information gleaned from Twitter sources to @CarolB, who has a connection to people on the ground. Volunteer twitterers like @IstanbulTWSTVL would find information that had not yet been acted on through Twitter and Ushahidi reports, then act on it themselves in one of two ways. Some would follow up with contact numbers directly, calling affected people or responders on the ground in Haiti to confirm and update their reports. Others tried to find another twitterer to whom they could direct the information, getting it closer to those who could physically act on it.

Maria: "It didn't matter if I actually helped directly; the important thing was figuring out who to send the help requests to and depending who was online at the time..."

Connections Between Translators

The ability to leverage connections was a powerful part of the work process for the digital volunteers in this study. When we examine their contextual tweet streams, we see that the TtT translators were a highly interconnected group. Figure 2 shows a visualization of the entire network of translators (80), including our own research group members (in black). Edge thicknesses represent the (natural log of the) amount of interactions between each pair of twitterers as determined by *addressed tweets* or *mentions* within the contextual tweet streams. This is not a measure of Twitter *followers* and *followings*, but rather of who was publicly "talking" to whom during the January 10-February 1 time window. Four translators were *unconnected* to the network, translating tweets without direct interaction with other volunteer twitterers. Nine others were connected to one other twitterer within the group. The rest had direct interactions with multiple members of the network. The network is dense, with each translator connecting with, on average, 7.7 other translator-volunteers (excluding our researchers), and some of these connections are leveraged repeatedly, with over 40 mentions.

Our accounts (in black) are visible on the top right of the dense part of the network cluster. Note that we are not central to the network, and that the density exists elsewhere (in the lower left quadrant). In fact, when we create another graph removing all of our researchers from the network, the core of the network remains intact.

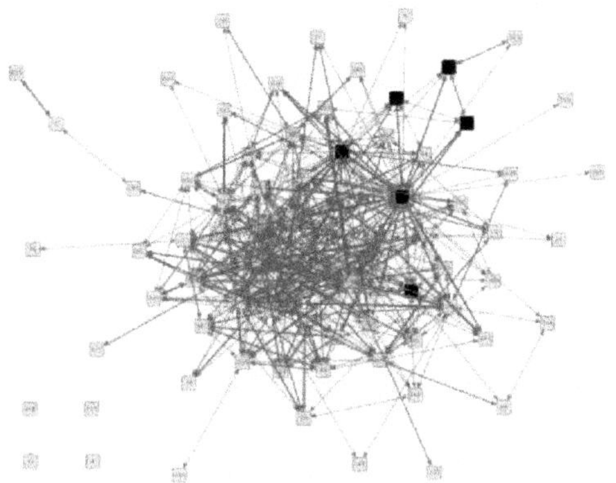

Figure 2. Connections between TtT Translators

To understand when and how these connections were formed, we sent each interviewee a list of all the other translators that they addressed a tweet to during the study time window in a follow-up email. We asked whether or not they knew each twitterer in real life or through Twitter prior to the earthquake. Though a few listed one or two previous connections, a clear majority replied that they had never previously connected with these other twitterers.

Julie: "We all came together by circumstance."

Karen: "All of these people I had never spoken with, prior to the Earthquake. I would have found all of them via the #Haiti #HelpHaiti or other Haiti hashtags, or occasionally a retweet from someone already in my Haiti network."

In the latter excerpt, Karen explains how she created her volunteer network, using hashtag searches to identify other twitterers with whom she wanted to connect, and sometimes used established connections to find new ones.

Karen: "I met many people through them whom I also came to trust. We worked on Twitter, Skype, Google Wave, Ushahidi & email - and during one emergency, on the phone when Skype failed us."

Features of Ad-hoc Communications Infrastructures

Participants we identified as remote operators incorporated a variety of social media and communication tools into their work practice, including email, Twitter, Skype, Google Wave, and Ushahidi. Within the Twitter platform, they used different affordances for different communication needs: public updates for broadcasting or seeking a wide range of help; addressed tweets for making connections, directing information, and challenging misinformation; DMs for moving resources, exchanging other contact info, and confronting possible hoaxers. Several cited the need to verify and manage misinformation as rationale for moving to tools with more access control, like Google Wave.

Sarah: "It was difficult to keep up with the stream at times, and some of us tried to branch [off] a "core" team to Google Wave, so we could have conversations without strangers butting in and confusing matters."

Without previous training, crisis tweeters cobbled together sophisticated, ad-hoc, digital infrastructures by appropriating existing tools.

Carla: "Social media will evolve to meet the needs that present during a crisis. ... Ppl say a crisis isn't the time to learn a new technology. That may be true but that's when solutions are inspired. Like meatball surgery in a war zone, you make do with what you have and along the way, you might invent a better way of doing something"

Volunteering through Tweeting: Role Identity, Momentum & Consequences

For many respondents, crisis tweeting during the Haiti event became and continues to be a significant part of their Twitter identities. Over half of interview participants report or have evidence in their recent tweet streams indicating continued volunteer tweeting during crises. Five still appear active in their Haiti tweeting (Aug 15-Sept 10) and seven have tweeted for other, more recent, crisis events. In their profile descriptions, @rachellehoude now refers to herself as a *voluntweeter*, @Meira_Davi claims to be a *crisis tweeter*, @MelyMello states that she is "heavily involved in Haiti relief via working w/ an amazing, effective, dedicated group of volunteers," and @cait proclaims that she "won't forget Haiti." Their crisis tweeting—a term we have adopted from the practitioners to describe this behavior—has come, in some ways, to define their Twitter personas.

Self-Identifying as a "Voluntweeter"

Between January 21 and January 23, twitterers throughout our translator dataset began to tweet or retweet updates with the terms "voluntwitter" and later, "voluntweeter."

`janeSM` (Jan 21): Am stunned-have gotten sups in-saved people fr rubble-brought them drs-we have best team! We R voluntwitters!

`rachellehoude` (Jan 21): I HEART VOLUNTWITTERS!

These tweets show a growing self-identification with the role of crisis tweeting as crisis tweeters, or voluntweeters. For those who embraced this role, the connection between their publicly enacted crisis tweeting behavior and their Twitter persona seems to contribute motivation for continued participation. A few participants displayed another layer of awareness, that these digital volunteer activities represented the birth of a new phenomenon.

@rachellehoude, from her blog: "Everyone over the past few weeks has felt that buzz, that collective energy flowing through each one of us, inspiring action and involvement. It's been incredible to be part of it and connect with like-minded people. It's been awesome to witness the birth social media's soul."

Long-standing research on the sociology of disaster suggests that the desire to help in times of crisis is age-old, and in fact is a behavior in disaster response that is critical to response and recovery [2,3,20]. Large numbers of people are known to converge onto the site in the wake of a disaster event to observe or to help [4,8]. Currently, novel forms of this phenomenon result from the affordances of social media tools, which allow more and remote people to contribute in ways not previously possible [16].

> *Kelly: "I don't have a lot of money and I'm not brave enough... to travel to Haiti, but this was an opportunity to get involved and, with the use of twitter, in a big way! I was already impressed with the reach twitter had, but seeing what it could do during a crisis like Haiti BLEW my mind away."*

Emotional Impact

In their initial responses, few interviewees mentioned the emotional impact from their digital volunteering. Follow up comments were far more likely to touch on this, even though we did not ask specifically about these experiences. Some remarked about rescue attempts that arrived too late and calls for help that went unanswered:

> *Maria: "It was horrid to hear all these cries for help; it haunts me to this day and I still have nightmares about it."*

One respondent told us that she had not continued crisis tweeting and remarked that she was not sure that she could do it again, because the work was too "emotionally draining." Another respondent, one who had participated in crisis tweeting during the political unrest in Iran, talked about how she backed away from her account after that event, before starting all over again for Haiti.

> *Carla: "During Iran, I got very caught up in it and was on twitter constantly. I dropped off after that when I changed my [Twitter] name. I kept my follower count low, stayed away from politics and emotional issues."*

Though we could not reach the people who had ceased tweeting from their Haiti-focused accounts, we can speculate that some, like Carla, had abandoned their Haiti-tweeting identities purposefully, suffering from emotional and perhaps also physical exhaustion.

Frustration with Formal Response

Another theme that emerged is a frustration that some volunteers began to feel towards the formal response effort:

> `rachellehoude (Jan 21): This is getting frustrating. I keep seeing the same calls for help, day after day. Can the NGOs at least HIRE us so we can do this for them?`

After over a week in the space, coordinating small-scale response using ad-hoc networks and over-the-counter digital infrastructures, this voluntweeter felt unappreciated and even obstructed when the "formal" response moved into place. Another explains how the new "organization" of response prevented them from accessing the resources that they had been using for their "informal" response activities.

> *Sarah: "...after that stage, it became clear that the larger NGOs were locking down streams of access for individuals. UN Cluster meetings were mandatory in order to obtain aid from the storage facilities. It became harder to help and our teams started to crumble due to feelings of powerlessness. It was a very frustrating time and most of my efforts turned more to shedding light on the broken system than trying to fight against it to get little done."*

In follow up comments, many participants said they hoped the formal response would learn how to better coordinate with social media volunteers in the future.

DISCUSSION

The activities of the crisis twitterers are a new form of previously recognized organizing behavior made possible through the availability of new media. Sociologists of disaster, including Dynes [2], call organizations that did not exist prior to a major disruption of the social order *emergent organizations*—groups of people that previously had no standing structure or defined tasks. (The other organizational types—*established*, *expanding*, and *extending*—have varying degrees of pre-existing structure and task definition.)

Emergent groups are usually self-organizing, and come about in disaster settings to meet some unmet need. *How* they come together is the subject of Kreps and Bosworth [9], who discuss a "theoretical tool" to explain collective behavior and organizing through a progressive manifestation of key features: Domains (D), Activities (A), Resources (R), and Tasks (T). Organizations can arise out of any sequential permutation of these mechanisms (though some arrangements are more common than others), as Kreps and Bosworth [9] empirically describe in a historical survey of accounts of emergent organizations in numerous disasters. Employing their framework to the behavior that many have come to call "crowdsourcing" we believe helps better explain and identify the underlying phenomena behind this term, including what makes it possible in disaster, and perhaps in other aspects of social life as well.

The temporal sequence that we believe best explains the behavior of the emergent voluntweeter population we studied is the $R \rightarrow A \rightarrow T \rightarrow D$ configuration of self-organization, with the Resources and Activities mechanisms of self-organizing being most developed, and with some indications of progression to the Tasks and Domain mechanistic stages. Groups that begin with Resources or Activities appear less often in Kreps and Bosworth's empirical taxonomy; this might be a type we see arising more often from today's ICT-supported environments. Note that not all emergent organizations endure long enough or organize completely enough to manifest all four attributes in their lifespans.

Resources (R) as Mechanisms of Self-Organization

For the "voluntweeters" in crisis events as described here, the means by which they began to work as volunteers in the Haiti event was the medium of Twitter. In other words, their initiation into the space was through the accessibility of *resources,* which are the "individual capacities and collective technologies of human populations" [9, p. 25].

Twitter was the gateway into an information space that itself contained resourceful features that helped would-be volunteers navigate within it, and begin to self-organize with others in an evolving practice of crisis tweeting.

Hashtags

Hashtags were used by many as an entrance into the space to find key information and identify the people participating in relevant conversations. Hashtags can be used to filter information to help narrow the focus of search. They were an important basis for the eventual organizing of activities (stage 2 in Kreps and Bosworth's organizing model). For example, `#rescuemehaiti` signaled a particular kind of help request, and became a tag around which people organized:

> *Alena: "One of them...proposed an idea; to use #rescuemehaiti hashtag. Promptly me and him made sure people asking for help would tag this word and within half hour everyone was following and using this tag. He said one day later officials contacted him and said this tag was very helpful so we should continue using it."*

Increasingly, it appears that the hashtag is employed as a mechanism for identifying useful social connections.

Syntax

Among our population, the TtT syntax also served as an organizing feature (though not the primary one) within the network of crisis tweeters. TtT added structure to tweet information; even when the syntax wasn't used in full, it helped voluntweeters to remember to include—and teach others to include—the necessary pieces of information into a single tweet to make it complete.

There was also indication that some saw the syntax as imparting a kind of authority because of its perceived rigor and assumptions about attention to accuracy by those using it. The manner in which some interviewees referred to the TtT syntax suggests an important structuring effect. One participant speaks about "syntaxing" as a task; another refers to the syntax as a kind of language, as in "translated into syntax." Though TtT syntax users may not fully understand what a syntax is, this co-opting of the term into language about voluntweeting suggests the syntax's role as an organizing feature.

Data Entry & Data Movement

"Individual capacities" are another resource that can initiate self-organizing, particularly among social action types of activities. Here, stepping into the Twitter space as well as the disaster volunteer role (typically for the first time), the basic activities of retweeting and entering data into a syntactical form using TtT, or entering data into Ushahidi's records, were the origins of a crisis tweeting practice.

Activities (A) as Mechanisms of Self-Organization

Activities are defined as "conjoined actions of individuals and social units" [9, p. 25], and we find this to be the second organizing mechanism in a large sector of the crisis tweeting network. It is in this stage when those drawn to Twitter, having discovered and used initial resources, begin to coordinate activities.

Data, Translation, Filtering, Verification, Cross-Referencing

The activities described in this paper—tweet translation, information filtering, information verification, as well as cross-referencing data records between Ushahidi and TtT-formated information—mark a graduation from data entry to coordinated activity with other people and groups.

Action Work

In addition, the hybrid virtual-physical "action" work of @Melymello, for example, who leveraged her Twitter social connections to obtain goods and services of direct benefit to those in Haiti, is an instance of conjoined action.

Conjoining Activities with other Organizations

A few notable organizations were entities to which the emergent band of voluntweeters began to connect. These included Ushahidi, Crisis Commons and Shaun King, an Atlanta, Georgia pastor of a faith-based organization. @ShaunKing's account was the most mentioned in our entire dataset. Thirteen of the 19 interview respondents mention or address him in their tweets, and two talk about him in their interviews. His activities began during the early aftermath of the quake and are ongoing in September 2010, with his aHomeInHaiti.org website serving as a place to coordinate donations and provide shelter for Haitians.

The self-organizing mechanisms of resources (R) and activities (A) seem to be clear in this emergence of a coherent, productive group of voluntweeters. In some cases, we begin to see introduction of division of labor—which in part describes tasks (T)—and some instances of movement to more formal collectives of domains (D).

Tasks (T) as Mechanisms of Self-Organization

Tasks are defined as "collective representations of a division of labor for the enactment of human activities" [9, p. 25]. As a core set of crisis voluntweeters gained experience with this emergent practice, some broke off to have extended and more private conversations elsewhere. These interviewees note that Skype and Google Wave became the means by which coordinated activity was discussed. Conversational excerpts provided earlier, including that between @CarolB and @IstanbulTWSTVL, demonstrate some division of labor, as does @MelyMello's activity of adding minutes to cell phones.

Some establishment of norms, especially with respect to how and when to retweet and verify information, begins to occur with the newly experienced, acting as mentors, pointing out to less experienced people what constitutes the most helpful tweeting behavior. Volunteers also began to challenge possible hoaxers, a Twitter behavior that Mendoza et al. recognize as occurring during the aftermath of the February 27, 2010 earthquake in Chile as well [11].

Domains (D) as Mechanisms of Self-Organization

Finally, for Kreps and Bosworth, domains are "collective representations of bounded units and their reasons for being" [9, p. 25]. For emergent, self-organizing groups, "bounded social collections" may or may not come about. Our investigation reveals some mix of consequences in social sub-groups of the broader crisis twitterer population.

There are volunteers who did a good amount of work for Haiti, but then fell away after a time. With Haiti as the sole focus of their Twitter use, their accounts go dormant or are even deleted entirely after their event participation ceases.

Still, others started reflecting on what it meant to be a good "crisis tweeter," and publicly identify as such. Though some of these multi-event crisis tweeters continued to work without affiliating with an organization, others found emerging organizations like *Humanity Road* as digital "places" to focus their volunteer activities. Humanity Road (humanityroad.org) is a virtual organization that was sparked by digital volunteering activities during the 2009 political unrest in Iran, but then formalized during the Haiti event [personal communication, Christine Thompson]. Its members, two of whom were interview respondents, describe themselves as performing crisis tweeting during disaster events, as well as mentoring crisis tweeters between events. The formation of Humanity Road represents the full culmination, as described by Kreps and Bosworth, of the graduation from resources and actions (for them, during the Iran unrest) to "domain"-driven features of organization (during the Haiti event).

CONCLUSION

The empirical examination of the products and motivations of crisis tweeters who emerged in the aftermath of the 2010 Haiti Earthquake reveals important features of self-organizing in a highly networked world. The broad attribution of social media-related behaviors to "crowdsourcing" can be more finely understood, in this case, as a collection of resources, capacities and a progression to increasingly more defined tasks and even organizational identity. In the matter of sudden and tragic events, the desire that some feel to help is newly enabled by resources like Twitter, where assistance can be provided remotely. Information creation and movement as the basis for social connection and subsequent collective action is at the core of these operations. The emergent ICT-abetted behaviors we have documented here and their consonance with knowledge about existing self-organizing mechanisms suggest that the digital volunteer will become a common and likely influential feature of social life.

ACKNOWLEDGMENTS

This work is supported by a US National Science Foundation Graduate Research Fellowship awarded to the first author, and NSF grants IIS-0546315 and IIS-0910586.

REFERENCES

1. Cavallo, E, Powell, A, & Becerra, O. Estimating the Direct Economic Damage of the Earthquake in Haiti. February 2010. *IDB Inter-American Development Bank.*
2. Dynes, RR. *Organized Behavior in Disaster*. Heath, 1970.
3. Fischer III, HW. *Response to Disaster: Fact Versus Fiction & Perpetuation, 2nd ed.* Univ Press of America, NY, 1998.
4. Fritz, C. E. & Mathewson, J. H. *Convergence Behavior in Disasters: A Problem in Social Control, Committee on Disaster Studies*, National Academy of Sciences, National Research Council, Washington DC, 1957.
5. Guy, M, Earle, P, Ostrum, C, Gruchalla, K & Horvath, S. Integration and Dissemination of Citizen Reported and Seismically Derived Earthquake Information via Social Network Technologies. *Advances in Intelligent Data Analysis IX, Lecture Notes in Computer Science*. 6065(2010), 42-53.
6. Honeycutt, C. & S.C. Herring. Beyond Microblogging: Conversation & Collaboration via Twitter. *HICSS 2009*, 1-10.
7. Hughes, A., L. Palen, J. Sutton, S. Liu, & S. Vieweg. "Site-Seeing" in Disaster: An Examination of On-Line Social Convergence. *Proc. of Information Systems for Crisis Response and Management Conference (ISCRAM) 2008.*
8. Kendra, J. M. & Wachtendorf, T. Reconsidering Convergence and Converger: Legitimacy in Response to the World Trade Center Disaster, *Terrorism and Disaster: New Threats, New Ideas: Research in Social Problems and Public Policy*, 11, (2003), 97-122.
9. Kreps, G. A. & Bosworth, S.L. *Organizing, Role Enactment, and Disaster: A Structural Theory.* Cranbury, NJ: Associated University Presses, 1994.
10. Liu, S. Iacucci, A.A., & Meier, P. Ushahidi Haiti & Chile: Next Generation Crisis Mapping. *American Congress on Surveying and Mapping (ACSM) Bulletin*, August 2010.
11. Mendoza, M, B Poblete & C Castillo. Twitter Under Crisis: Can we trust what we RT? *1st Workshop on Social Media Analytics. SOMA '10* (Washington, DC, July 25, 2010).
12. Messina, C. Twitter Hashtags for Emergency Coordination and Disaster Relief. Oct 22, 2007. Blog in: *FactoryCity.* http://factoryjoe.com/blog/2007/10/22/twitter-hashtags-for-emergency-coordination-and-disaster-relief/
13. Messina, C. Stowe Boyd Launches Microsyntax.org. May 16, 2009. Blog in: *FactoryCity*. URL: http://factoryjoe.com/blog/2009/05/26/stowe-boyd-launches-microsyntax-org/
14. New York Times. Haiti Earthquake of 2010. Sept 23, 2010. *The New York Times*. http://www.nytimes.com/info/haiti-earthquake-2010/
15. Okolloh O. Ushahidi, or 'testimony': Web 2.0 tools for crowdsourcing crisis information. *Participatory Learning and Action* 59 (2009): 65–70.
16. Palen, L & Liu, S. B. Citizen Communications in Crisis: Anticipating a Future of ICT-Supported Participation, *Proc. of CHI 2007*, 727-736.
17. Qu, Y., Wu, P. & Wang, X. Online Community Response to Major Disaster: A Case Study of Tianya Forum in the 2008 China Earthquake. In *Proc 42nd Hawaii Int'l Conf. on System Sciences, 2009*, 1-11.
18. Starbird, K. & Stamberger, J. Tweak the Tweet: Leveraging Microblogging Proliferation with a Prescriptive Syntax to Support Citizen Reporting. *Proc. of Information Systems for Crisis Response and Management (ISCRAM) 2010.*
19. Starbird, K, Palen, L, Hughes, A & Vieweg, S. Chatter on The Red: What Hazards Threat Reveals about the Social Life of Microblogged Information. *Proc. of CSCW 2010,* 241-250.
20. Tierney, K, Lindell, M, & Perry, R.W. *Facing the Unexpected: Disaster Preparedness and Response in the United States*. John Henry Press, Washington, DC, 2001.
21. Vieweg, S, Hughes, A, Starbird, K, & Palen, L. Micro-Blogging during Two Natural Hazards Events: What Twitter May Contribute to Situational Awareness *Proc of CHI 2010,* 1079-88.

Social Media Ownership: Using Twitter as a Window onto Current Attitudes and Beliefs

Catherine C. Marshall
Microsoft Research, Silicon Valley
1065 La Avenida
Mountain View, CA 94043
cathymar@microsoft.com

Frank M. Shipman
Department of Computer Science
Texas A&M University
College Station, TX 77843-3112
shipman@cs.tamu.edu

ABSTRACT
Social media, by its very nature, introduces questions about ownership. Ownership comes into play most crucially when we investigate how social media is saved or archived; how it is reused; and whether it can be removed or deleted. We investigate these social media ownership issues using a Mechanical Turk survey of Twitter users; the survey uses open-ended questions and statements of belief about realistic Twitter-based scenarios to give us a window onto current attitudes and beliefs. Our findings reveal that respondents take a liberal attitude toward saving and storing the tweets that they encounter. More caution is exercised with republishing the material, and still more with sharing the material among friends and associates. Respondents approach removal of this type of lightweight social media most cautiously. The material's provenance and the respondents' relationship to the material (whether they are the author or subject) has considerable bearing on what they feel they can do with it.

Author Keywords
Twitter, social media, information rights, survey, reuse.

ACM Classification Keywords
H4.3. Information Systems: Communications Applications.

General Terms
Design, Experimentation, Human Factors.

INTRODUCTION
Services such as Facebook, Twitter, and Flickr introduce new questions about the ownership and control of social media [16]. Although legal decisions, license agreements, and explicit policies address these issues, the people who use social media services may not be aware of them, nor adhere to them. Because social media may be created jointly and may document or record events involving many people [20,22], it presents design challenges for new digital services such as archiving or publishing.

What do people feel they can (and cannot) do with information created by others? We divide potential activities into four basic categories: (1) *saving* digital content; (2) *sharing* digital content with specified (and limited) groups of people; (3) *publishing* digital content so it is broadly accessible; and (4) *removing* digital content from its social media venue (and not necessarily deleting it from local storage, in line with reported behavior [21]).

CSCW applications have long demonstrated that users may not apply reciprocal standards to actions they feel they can take [5]. For example, they may want to see others without being seen, or they may want to have capabilities that are not offered to their peers. In this case, we investigate what respondents feel they should be able to do with microblog content they encounter, as well as probe what respondents feel that others can do with the respondent's content.

Finally, we are interested in scaling up our findings from individuals to public institutions: what do people feel that public institutions should be able to do with today's ephemera and everyday digital belongings? For example, some Twitter users were unhappy when the Library of Congress announced plans to archive public tweets; they felt strongly that the service offered them privacy through obscurity. How common is this sentiment?

Social media encompasses a number of different forms and genres. This study is the first in a series of studies we have designed to investigate peoples' attitudes (and in some cases, their reported practices) about social media ownership, archiving, and reuse. Because different types of social media have different properties—for example, emotional heft, creation ease, file size, and representational fidelity—we are limiting each study in the series to involve a single social media type.

This study is based on content from Twitter, a microblogging service in which users share short messages (140 characters or fewer) with a set of subscribers (although anyone may read the messages if an account's privacy settings allow them to). The messages, or tweets, may stand alone or they may be links to published material on the

Web (photos, blog posts, articles, etc.), or to content stored in sister services such as Twitpic.

If we are ultimately interested in persistent media, why look at Twitter first? Twitter tweets are largely categorized as lightweight bits of communication, and as such, are sometimes considered ephemeral. However, if we look more closely, tweets walk an interesting line between epigrams and microblog posts to news flashes and ambient pop culture material that is just 'in the air' at a particular time or place [3,8]. Yet people do save and reuse Twitter tweets (both their own, and those of others), and historians rely on this type of ephemera to characterize an era. We are beginning our series of studies with Twitter because tweets are an important point in the space of social media, and because people have already shown signs that they want to save them (see, for example, utilities like Twapper Keeper or BackupMyTweets).

In this paper, we present the results of a survey to probe the attitudes of social media-savvy people about who can save, share, publish, and remove tweets from a Twitter feed. In so doing, we explore issues associated with ownership, authoring and reuse, and privacy. The paper is organized as follows: At the outset, we summarize related work and present the method used to construct and disseminate the survey. Then we describe the respondents and their responses to open-ended questions about their Internet use, their concerns about sharing information, and the distinctions they make between publishing material and sharing it within a social network. We then discuss our findings, identifying trends in the data and areas of controversy and consensus. We conclude by discussing implications of these findings and by outlining future work.

RELATED WORK

There are three bodies of related work which form scaffolding for this study: (1) a growing literature about Mechanical Turk and techniques for using it to recruit and screen study participants and perform studies; (2) descriptive studies of Twitter and other social media in use; and (3) studies of the social side of personal archiving, and media reuse and remix.

In recent years, researchers have found that Mechanical Turk provides a convenient pool of respondents for studies, provided that emerging best practices are taken to heart. Kittur et al. recommend that verifiable questions should be included in surveys; that good-faith efforts should pay off; and that researchers should give themselves multiple ways to detect fraudulent responses [14]. In our study description, we outline how we have designed a survey that adheres to these suggestions; in designing our payment scheme and recruiting and screening techniques, we have also taken care to follow the pragmatic suggestions offered by Jakobsson [12] and Downs et al. [4] for screening participants and avoiding cheaters.

Unlike other studies intended to characterize microblogging as a phenomenon (primarily exemplified by Twitter) [3,7,8,13,15], its use in contexts such as education [6], conferences [20], emergencies [10], and the workplace [22], we are more interested in the long-term status and value of tweets as a representative (if limited) type of social media. Previous descriptive studies have found that people tweet for a variety of reasons, some of which do produce ephemera (such as 'daily chatter'), and others of which produce content of more enduring value (such as shared information) [13]. Studies also show that people who tweet may go to some effort to ensure their microblogging posts are not ephemeral (by using them to pass information [7] or opinions [8], or even by the way in which they capture crisis-related events [10]); by adhering to retweeting conventions, they ensure that authorship is respected [3].

Personal archiving is a social phenomenon that is becoming increasingly rooted in social media. Not only are some members of families or social groups more likely to curate the group's digital assets [19], the stewardship skills required to care for these assets are often held by different people than those with the necessary curatorial skills and motivations [18]. Considerable attention has also been devoted to the emergence of a broader digital content reuse and remix culture [16]. Both personal archiving and social media reuse are largely dependent on how the rights we discuss in this paper are resolved; the main contribution of this work is a survey of digital content ownership attitudes.

STUDY DESCRIPTION

We conducted a survey to determine participants' attitudes about saving, reusing, and removing Twitter tweets; the survey also gathered self-reported information about the participants' Internet use and publication practices.

We used Mechanical Turk to recruit and screen participants for our study, as well as to implement the survey itself. The survey took the form of a series of brief scenarios that embodied specific Twitter practices, statements about these scenarios for the participants to assess according to a seven point Likert scale, and a limited number of open-ended questions to ensure that the participants were reading carefully. Open-ended questions, coupled with multiple-choice responses, also enabled respondents to describe their own Internet use and publication practices.

There is a growing body of literature that describes best practices for performing studies using Mechanical Turk [4,12,14]. We carefully followed the advice offered in these papers, and used them to set our own expectations about what to include in the survey, and how to organize it effectively. Our strategy for using Mechanical Turk was generally successful.

We couched our screener and questionnaire as a Mechanical Turk Human Intelligence Task (HIT). The HIT was offered to Turkers from the United States who have proven themselves reliable in past work (i.e. 95% or greater HIT approval rate); the HIT was framed with a strongly worded statement that we were seeking participants who were fluent in English and were experienced Twitter users.

We double-checked these characteristics in the screener; data from respondents who appeared to have only a passing familiarity with Twitter were discarded. Respondents were paid at established rates for Mechanical Turk, which worked out to 50 cents/questionnaire; respondents were paid even if their data was eventually discarded.

The Mechanical Turk HIT consisted of 34 questions. Eight of the questions characterized the respondent; six questions were intended to measure the respondent's familiarity with Twitter; three questions tested the respondent's reading comprehension (a tactic other researchers have suggested to ensure that respondents are reading the survey before they fill in responses [14,12]); 16 questions were statements of belief for respondents to assess on a 7-point Likert scale; and the final question probed the respondent's willingness to participate in future surveys and interviews. Additional data (e.g. the respondent's work time) was collected by the Mechanical Turk infrastructure.

The Six Scenarios

The belief portion of the HIT consisted of six short scenarios or situations involving Twitter. In each, users either save, retweet, or reuse their favorite tweets in other venues. The scenarios are followed by statements of belief for respondents to assess. Each scenario is specific, and includes the actual tweets. By posing concrete situations, we hoped to put all respondents on a more even footing (so they envision similar situations) and to draw on their real experiences. We also hoped that specific content and details would help to mitigate gross inconsistencies between attitudes and behavior, such as those discussed at length in the privacy literature [1]; nonetheless, we are careful to note that the data we collected reflects attitudes and beliefs rather than behavior.

In Scenario 1, a Twitter user, Dave, collects humorous tweets posted by different people, including himself; in Scenario 2, Dave collects tweets that represent a conversation he is having with two other Twitter users. In Scenario 3, Dave encounters an offensive tweet about himself. In Scenario 4, the respondent has received Dave's list of funny tweets via email, and we investigate what he or she can do with the list subsequently. Scenario 5 covers the situation in which the respondent has removed his or her own tweet from the Twitter feed, but while it was still public, Dave has collected it, and is now posting it. Finally, in Scenario 6, the Library of Congress acquires the entire Twitter archive, and provides access to it under three different conditions.

Figure 1 shows a portion of Scenario 1, followed by an excerpt of the belief statements that followed the scenario.

Four Rights of Ownership

To design the scenarios and associated statements of belief, we assumed that different situations might elicit different responses. The data will indicate which situations can be distinguished from one another. It will also indicate trends in responses to individual questions: that is, do respondents tend to agree (or disagree) with the statement (is there a normal distribution of responses), or are they divided into communities at opposition (is there a bimodal distribution)?

Dave Sanders is one of your followers on Twitter. He tweets under the name @NewJerseyDave and you tweet as @SecretSquirrel. Dave keeps a list of his favorite tweets. This list includes some of his own tweets, some of your tweets, and some tweets posted by other witty folks. Part of the list looks like this:

> SecretSquirrel A city is only really home when you stop being mystified by its public transport and instead are just constantly angry at it.
>
> RedRabbit My personality results came back. They're negative.
>
> NewJerseyDave I'll go to the co-dependency workshop if you come with me.
>
> SecretSquirrel I might like the iPad better if it were red & furry.
>
> rrmutt I know how you feel, hon: "I'd stage-dive but I'm far too elderly"—Courtney Love
>
> NewJerseyDave Maybe the person in the car ahead of you isn't driving erratically because he's texting; maybe he's just knitting.

Dave should only be able to store his own tweets on his hard drive.
Dave has the right to post his list of funny tweets to his Facebook wall.
Dave has the right to publish his list of funny tweets in a blog post.

Figure 1. A portion of Scenario 1 exploring views about saving, sharing, and republishing a collection.

The following definitions of the four data ownership terms were provided to participants before they began the questionnaire to help ensure consistent interpretation:

> **Save** – to store the content on your own storage media. For example, you might ***save*** a photo to your local hard drive or burn it to a CD.
>
> **Share** – to make the content available to a limited set of friends or family members by using email or social media websites. For example, you might ***share*** a photo with your friends on Facebook.
>
> **Publish** – to make the content available to the public by uploading it to a website like Flickr, Blogspot, or YouTube. For example, you might ***publish*** a story to your blog or ***publish*** a video to YouTube.
>
> **Remove** – to 'unpublish' content; to delete content from a public website. For example, you might ***remove*** a photo from Flickr if you don't want everyone to see it.

Because we wanted the respondents to react to each scenario without perceiving a pattern and using it as a shortcut to fill in answers, we made concrete statements about the situation, and varied the ownership rights we tested. Again, refer to Figure 1 for examples.

Deploying the HIT

The HIT was deployed for two weeks; the bulk of the data was collected during the first week. We screened the responses based on a three point disqualification test, where a respondent must have fewer than three of the following disqualifying characteristics:

- respondent reported fewer than 5 followers on Twitter;
- respondent reported following fewer than 5 people;
- respondent reported posting fewer than 20 tweets;
- respondent spent less than 5 minutes (300 seconds) completing the survey;
- respondent answered an open-ended Twitter "how-to" question incorrectly;
- respondent answered either of two reading comprehension questions incorrectly (a third ambiguous comprehension question was discarded).

Our primary concern was that the respondents were sufficiently familiar with Twitter and its conventions to understand the scenarios and to respond to the hypothetical situations in ways that reflected their values. We were generally conservative about data quality and arrived at the formal criteria for disqualifying respondents only after we took a close look at the data we had collected to identify possible ways in which respondents had gamed the system.

At the end of two weeks, the HIT had been completed by 190 respondents; 173 passed the secondary screening criteria. Respondents took on average 8.7 minutes (8 minutes, 42 seconds) to complete the survey, which was sufficient to read and understand the scenarios and statements, and to complete the open-ended questions.

One measure of the HIT's success is that the answers to the open-ended questions were surprisingly rich; it was clear that respondents took the survey seriously, and offered us a real window onto their attitudes and their practices.

CHARACTERIZING THE RESPONDENTS

Eight initial questions were aimed at characterizing the study participants. From the screening, we knew the participants were familiar with Twitter, and because they were recruited from the Mechanical Turk worker population, we also knew that by some measure, they were Internet-savvy. Although there are characterizations of the Turk workforce [11], we thought it was important to describe the subpopulation of respondents.

Respondents were largely in their twenties (64%) and thirties (17%); 61% are female, 39%, male. This is unsurprising, given the characteristics of US Mechanical Turk workers. Table 1 breaks down the age and gender distribution of the participants in our study.

year born	before 1950	1950-1959	1960-1969	1970-1979	1980-1989	after 1990	declined to state	total
female	1	4	3	16	69	11	1	105
male	0	2	4	13	41	8	0	68
total	1	6	7	29	110	19	1	173

Table 1. Participant age and gender

The majority of the participants are college-educated—94 (54%) have a college degree—and almost all of them (152, or 88%) have at least some college education, including those who are still students. Unfortunately, we realized after the fact that we did not distinguish college dropouts from current students, but we assume that a significant portion of those who characterized themselves as having some college (58, or 34%) were probably current students. Twenty participants (12%) reported having a graduate degree.

Participants reported their familiarity with social media applications in multiple ways. They specified the number of years of Internet experience they had; selected which of a list of nine types of social applications that they use; and described in their own words how they use the Internet, what they spend the most time doing, and types of social media they create themselves.

Table 2 shows the distribution of application popularity; the ninth application was Twitter, which all qualified respondents reported using. Email and social networking are respondents' most commonly used applications.

Social media activity	# of respondents
Email	171
Social networking (e.g. Facebook)	161
Shopping (e.g. Amazon)	131
IM/chat	122
Online video sharing (e.g. YouTube)	110
Online photo sharing (e.g. Flickr)	84
Video conferencing (e.g. Skype)	60
Massively multiplayer online games (e.g. WoW)	37

Table 2. Popularity of applications among respondents.

Participants engage in a broad range of online activities; the majority have used the Internet for a long time, sometimes for a significant portion of their lives, and most engage is four or more social media activities (see Figure 2).

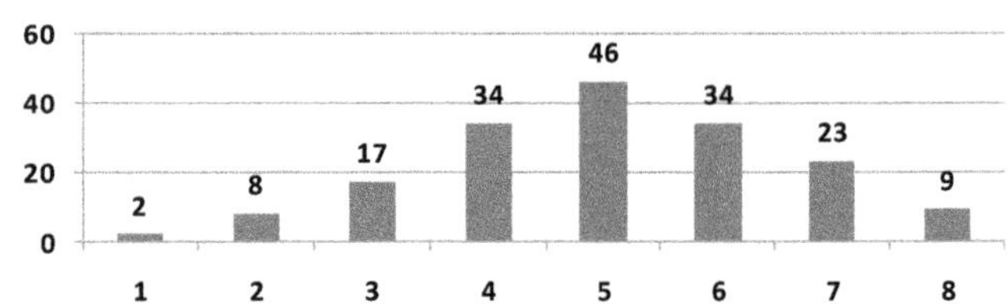

Figure 2. Number of social media activities (X axis) by number of respondents (Y axis).

Although the respondents were by no means homogenous, they seem to represent a type of Internet user—educated, fairly young, with a spectrum of attitudes about topics like privacy, and a range of Internet interests, from buying and selling in online marketplaces (e.g. Etsy and Craigslist) to playing multiplayer games to tracking news to participating in social networks (e.g. Facebook).

Internet Activities

Open-ended questions included a broad question about how respondents used the Internet, and what they spent the most time doing. Many of the respondents offered fairly detailed information about their extensive and varied Internet use; most cite communication-related activities as a principal preoccupation. For example, R77 said,

> "I use the Internet for things like communicating with friends and family (some nearby and some very far away) via email, IM, and social networking, I do research and shopping, I use it to streamline managing my finances, I follow hobby-related groups, and use it to pass the time when I'm bored. I'd say that I spend the most time communicating with friends and family on the Internet."

Respondents were also very specific about pursuits enabled by the Internet, often focusing on what they use the Internet for (growing as a Muslim [R159] or day-trading [R152]) rather than on applications they use or generic activities (communicating, browsing).

Unsurprisingly (since they are workers on Mechanical Turk), many respondents also report use related to some type of resourceful self-employment. For example, [R153] wrote, "As a web designer, much of my time spent online is work-related, either directly or indirectly (research)" and [R109] wrote, "I play the game SecondLife and use SL to make videos for my online business." Other respondents reported working as news aggregators (e.g. [R48]) or doing research in support of a non-Internet business, e.g. as a personal trainer [R75].

Publishing and Republishing

We asked respondents what types of information they published or shared on the Internet, with the thought that a broad framing would elicit informative responses. Although we had already brought up different types of applications, respondents went well beyond this limited range. In addition to saying that they shared photos of friends, and pictures they found, they also reported sharing things like "scans of my artwork" [R103], and republishing "pornography and videogames" [R167] and "information in Second Life" [R90].

Republishing arose in several contexts, sometimes as an offshoot of sharing articles and news stories, and in other cases as intentional piracy (e.g., when the respondent reported reposting porn and videogames).

Respondents reported creating social media, sometimes as a way of sharing their experiences with physical media ("I share projects I'm working on and helpful tips in the knitting community" [R132]; "I have a band, so I share songs pretty often" [R37]; "I write a lot of fanfiction and I use photoshop to create fanart" [R25]; "I write some game reviews and walkthroughs" [R64]).

Responses to this question included a number of new, evolving social media genres, including videogame walkthroughs, personal profiles, status updates, fan fiction and fan art, and links and blogs. The social marketplace of opinions, reviews, and Etsy and eBay postings is also well-represented in respondents' answers.

This diversity of use and sharing practices implies that respondents are conversant in social media, and are likely to have thought about the issues raised by the scenarios.

Sharing Personal Information

In both open-ended questions that preceded the scenarios, respondents volunteered concerns about sharing personal information via social media. These responses were not elicited by asking about privacy specifically; rather they arose organically in the course of respondents' reports of how they used the Internet or what they shared or published. While we cannot be certain that respondents did not try to ascertain our interests in administering this survey, there was nothing in the phrasing of the instructions that indicated that we were concerned with privacy.

From respondents' answers, it was evident that some divided social media into public and private information:

> "I try to publish/share information that would not offend my personal sense of privacy. While most stuff in my life is fair game (What I ate for dinner, what the score at the baseball was, etc.) some is not, such as how much I spent to attend the baseball game or on dinner, any information that may put someone (including myself) into legal, financial, or physical jeopardy, etc." [R77]

There was also a sense that some venues (e.g. Facebook) were more private than others (e.g. Flickr and Twitter):

> "I publish pictures and have a blog, but I don't share anything too personal. My facebook is very private only my close friends, but my flickr, twitter, and blog are public." [R158]

Other respondents expressed a sense of uncertainty and a fairly conservative outlook about life online:

> "I don't usually publish too much information about myself because I don't know who is going to look at it." [R39]

> "[I publish] As little information as possible for me to continue using the various sites that I am interested in." [R7]

> "I write articles on internet culture and technology. I tend not to write too much about my personal life." [R1]

On the other hand, some respondents indicated that they led a lively online life, that they had little concern for who encountered their personal postings:

> "I publish and share everything! Bad days, good days, what I make for dinner, when I go to bed I post goodnigts [sic], etc." [R41]

Respondents also indicated that they curated the information that they published online according to who they felt would see it; once they were publishing to a local audience, they felt they had to be meticulous. As the quotes above indicate, some respondents kept personal information to a minimum, providing only what was needed to meet the expectations of their audience and the requirements of the service. What they considered private varied, however:

> "I don't usually publish too much information such as location (city wise) and just recently I started privatizing my email address." [R5]

"Very highly curated information about my personal life; reviews of outside things, etc." [R98]

"Depends entirely on the trustworthiness of the person or site as demonstrated by time and consistently. Some know my name, address and phone number. Some only know my penname and e-mail." [R110]

FINDINGS AND DATA TRENDS

One of the aims of this survey was to tease apart closely related concepts. First, we investigated the nature of social media ownership. Who can archive a shared artifact? Ownership may be complicated by collaboration, by remix practices, and by reuse.

Next we probed the difference between publication and sharing: if a person has 500 Facebook friends, and their public blog is only read by 50 people, is there a difference between sharing and publication? And if there is a difference, what implications does it have? Furthermore, does it influence how people feel about institutional archiving of lightweight social media? If something has been published, people may have a reasonable expectation that it may be archived. Yet if it is just shared, people may still feel that it is part of a private realm, over which they may exercise the ultimate control.

Although there has been significant litigation centering on copyright infringement, we wondered whether social notions of reuse were deviating from codified laws and legal precedent. If a person collects social media—in this case tweets—does he or she have any authorial claim on the aggregate material? And what of material that was authored collaboratively, as a Twitter conversation would be—how far do reuse rights extend?

Finally, we examined how shared artifacts are unshared, and how published items are unpublished. Social media appears to deviate from the print/physical realm, where copies are more difficult to make, and media is thus less fluid and potentially volatile [17]. Teenagers are told to mind what they share on Facebook—that once something is shared, it cannot be unshared, or that a video posted to YouTube will 'live on forever on the Internet.' How do people feel about ownership and removal of social media?

We use five concepts to organize our findings:

- Social media ownership and control;
- Publication versus sharing;
- Reuse and republication;
- Removing social media;
- Institutional ownership and individual data rights.

We discuss each concept in turn. Although they are inexorably intertwined, we do our best to pull them apart, and discuss them from different perspectives.

Table 3 presents an overview of the respondents' reactions to statements about the scenarios. In the table, brief squibs that summarize the scenarios' basic premises are shown in bold. They are followed by statements that the respondents were asked to score on a seven point Likert scale. Mean and mode are shown for each statement; graphs later in this section present the full distributions.

Table 3 helps highlight statements that met with bimodal distributions of responses, and statements that are viewed in consistently favorable or unfavorable ways. For example, responses to statements about peoples' rights to store tweets, one's own or someone else's, were likely to be highly favorable (i.e. the mode value of these responses was 7, the most positive possible response). The distribution only became bimodal when we attempted to impose limits on which tweets people were allowed to store. Similarly, respondents displayed unfavorable responses to the right to delete tweets *about* oneself (see, e.g., Q12; Twitter allows users to delete tweets written *by* oneself). The Library of Congress scenario elicited bimodal responses, in particular, if the institution provides open access to the collection of tweets to the general public today (i.e. Q21). Attitudes about institutional archives appear to be very much divided; time delays (50 years in the future) and access limitations (access is granted to researchers only) ease respondents' discomfort with full public access to archived tweets.

Ownership and Control

Ownership and control over social media is an important foundation for designing many types of services. We are particularly interested in personal archiving—what will the long-term fate of social media be? Although social media is usually posted by a single author (or by a single identity), it is often mutually owned, and certainly it is often about a group or an event, or may refer to or depend on something else on the Web. The person who posts an item may not be the subject of the item, nor may the same person curate or maintain the media over time (e.g. see [19]). Who owns social media, and who controls it?

In this study, we are talking about something on the simple end of the spectrum, a tweet, a 140 character text string. Yet, as the scenarios posed in the survey illustrate, even something as simple as a tweet introduces considerable complexity. A tweet might be intensely personal; it might be plagiarized; it might be about someone else; it might refer to a social event; it might have a hypertext link that connects it to another, richer, piece of social media or external resource. In other words, it is difficult to make definitive statements about who owns and controls even lightweight social media.

The strongest positive reaction the survey elicited had to do with the storage and archiving of one's own tweets. Respondents felt strongly that they should be able to store their own Twitter conversations, especially the material that contextualizes what they have written (Q8). Although the reaction is not as strong, respondents seem to feel comfortable storing the tweets from their feed, regardless of who wrote them (Q3). (The tweets in the scenarios do retain attribution.)

Statement	*Mean*	*Mode*
Dave is one of your followers on Twitter. He keeps a list of his favorite tweets. This list includes some of his own tweets, some of your tweets, and some tweets posted by other witty people.		
Q3. Dave should have the right to store a copy of all of these tweets on his hard drive.	5.36	7
Q4. Dave should only be able to store a copy of his own tweets on his hard drive.	4.09	7
Q5. Dave hopes he can entice his friend Charlie to join Twitter and become one of his followers. Dave should have the right to post his list of funny tweets to his Facebook wall.	5.17	6
Q6. Dave should have the right to publish the list of funny tweets in a blog post.	5.36	6
Suppose Dave's list just contains tweets that are his own tweets and responses to them.		
Q8. Dave should have the right to store a copy of all of these twitter chats on his hard drive; after all, they're all either by him or about him.	5.75	7
Q9. Dave should only have the right to store a copy of his own tweets on his hard drive, not the responses written by other people, even if it makes it hard to understand the conversation.	3.38	2
Q10. Dave should have the right to post the entire conversation to his Facebook wall so his friends can see it.	5.01	6
Q11. Dave should have the right to publish this list of tweets—tweets that he wrote and responses to tweets he wrote—in a blog post.	5.27	6
Dave sees a tweet that claims he's gained 50 pounds; the tweet's author does not realize Dave is on Twitter and will see the tweet.		
Q12. Dave should have the right to delete the offensive tweet about him.	3.71	1
Suppose Dave emails his list of favorite tweets to you. They're hilarious. What can you do with the list?		
Q13. You should have the right to email the tweets to a friend without leaving Dave's email header on the forwarding.	4.45	7
Q14. You should have the right to publish the tweets in your public blog.	4.41	6
One of your tweets that's on Dave's list embarrasses you. You had deleted it from Twitter not long after you'd posted it, but Dave caught it while it was still part of the feed. Now he posts the whole list on Facebook.		
Q15. Suppose you can't delete only part of Dave's post. You should have the right to remove Dave's whole Facebook post to get rid of your bad tweet.	3.09	2
Q16. Suppose you can edit Dave's post. You should have the right to remove your bad tweet from Dave's published list. After all, you removed it from the Twitter feed.	4.32	6
The Library of Congress is acquiring the entire Twitter archive, dating back to its origins in 2006.		
Q20. The Library of Congress can give researchers access to the archive.	4.62	6
Q21. The Library of Congress can give everyone access to the archive.	4.10	1,6
Q22. The Library of Congress can give everyone access to the archive after 50 years has passed.	4.40	6

Table 3. Overview of the sixteen statements of rights and the Likert-scale responses to them.

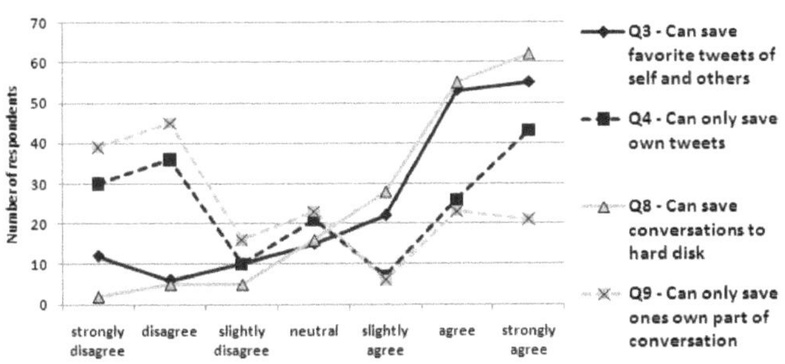

Figure 3. Views about saving favorites and conversations.

Publication versus Sharing

From its inception, social media introduced the idea that we don't just publish personal content to the open Web. Rather we share and build on existing content among our spheres of family, friends, colleagues, and acquaintances, making ever more nuanced distinctions between who sees what and what they are allowed to do with what they see [21]. Are people developing varied sensibilities about the distinctions between publication (posting social media on the open web) and sharing (controlling who sees what)?

In our Twitter scenarios, one way to investigate this question is to test statements about posting a collection of tweets to one's Facebook wall (as a form of controlled sharing), and publishing the same collection as a blog post. Note that the collection aggregates material from different sources: the tweets were written by different authors, and collected into a list of favorites.

A surprising finding is that respondents approach sharing on Facebook with more caution than they do publishing the same content on a blog. The difference between the scoring of the statements that embody this distinction is statistically significant ($0.02<p<0.05$, Wilcoxon Signed Rank Test) although the difference is not large (see the publication statements Q6 and the sharing statement Q5 in Table 3).

From the perspective of sheer exposure (the people who can see the Facebook post are necessarily a subset of the general Web-reading public who can see the published blog), this result is counterintuitive. We explain this difference cautiously, since there is nothing in the data that pinpoints the reason for it. We speculate two effects are at the root: (1) the Facebook audience is an audience of friends, and the blog audience is potentially an audience of strangers, and people are often more careful about what they share with a captive audience of Facebook friends (who may be more or less socially obliged to read the post, and may judge the person who posted it accordingly) and the self-selected audience of blog readers (who, the author may rationalize, are free to 'vote with their feet', and who may be less judgmental about whether the author has the right to publish the tweets) and (2) experience tells us that a blog may in fact have fewer readers than a Facebook wall post, a venue that suggests social engagement.

This result is consistent with one revealed by a second hypothetical situation involving a Twitter conversation rather than a collection of unrelated tweets (embodied by statements Q10 and Q11). Again, Facebooking the conversation was seen as an action to be approached with greater caution than simply publishing it broadly to the Web (as a blog post) ($p<.001$, Wilcoxon). These statements about sharing and publishing differed in a statistically significant way, while the pairwise comparison of the similar statements (sharing a collection vs. sharing a conversation and publishing a collection vs. publishing a conversation) were not significantly different using a Wilcoxon test ($0.05<p<0.1$ and $p>0.2$ respectively).

Thus our results raise a further question: is this a broad social media phenomenon? Where data ownership is concerned, is sharing really something to be approached in a more cautious, self-conscious way than publishing? In other words, do people actually worry more about their rights to post a photo to Facebook than they do to the open Web? This result seems worth further investigation; that a person would worry more about whether he or she actually has the right to post something in a social situation than he or she does in an abstract information environment makes sense; the effect may be even more dramatic when other types of media (such as photos) replace the lightweight (and often emotionally distant) media forms like tweets.

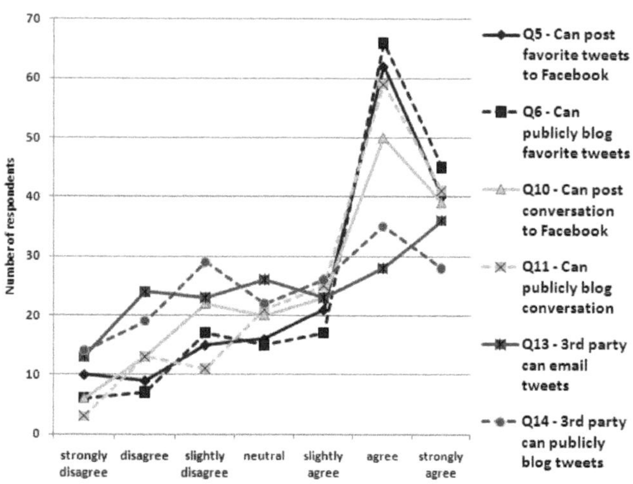

Figure 4. Views about sharing favorites and conversations.

Reuse and Remixing

Reuse and remixing represent emerging authoring practices for the Internet age [16]. Reuse and remix imply that the author is gathering media, excerpting desired portions, and putting them together in new and creative ways. There is a lingering feeling in some quarters that this practice edges on plagiarism; copyright law often reflects this sense of unease. But this feeling is by no means pervasive. We thought it was worth investigating reuse through our scenarios, and respondents brought up the issue themselves in the portion of the HIT that preceded the scenario-based survey statements and asked about respondents' practices.

For example, respondent R131 said, "Content I share is usually not my own, I just retweet, digg, or share it on facebook in hopes others will see in the piece the same thing I found." Others explained reuse in a less elaborate way; they unselfconsciously reported publishing or sharing:

- "Music, interesting or funny pictures I come across, videos, jokes" [R106]
- "sharing links/articles that I find interesting" [R159]
- "movies and videos. pornography and video games." [R167]
- "Pictures that I find in the internet." [R118]
- "I publish humor stuff on my network of web sites." [R59]
- "Information about ...deals I find, or interesting articles I come across." [R139]
- "previously published information" [R129]

It is then not surprising that respondents incorporated this right in their reactions to the scenarios (Q5, Q6, Q10, Q11, Q13, Q14). All of these scenarios involve either combining one's own material with tweets written by others, or simply reusing the kind of material that notoriously floats around the Internet as 'funny email', blog posts, tweets, or in other forums. The statements that involved sharing or publishing material without attribution to the collector who reused them (Q13 and Q14) scored significantly lower ($p<.001$, Wilcoxon for all comparisons) than the tweets that were attributed to their authors (but still republished without permission in venues other than Twitter) (Q5, Q6, Q10, Q11).

Removing Content

Constructive reuse (storing, publishing, sharing) was greeted less cautiously than removal. Instead of testing removal without any particular motivation, we introduced 'aboutness' to ownership: i.e. what are the limits of what you can do with material that is not by you but rather about you? People may feel they have a certain latitude to take action on materials that are about them, media documenting an event they attended, or using them as the subject. They feel free to tag themselves or other people they know in photos, for example, or they feel it within their rights to request that a photo of them be taken down (and surely in some cases, they would have taken it down themselves had they been able) [1].

Since tweets are so lightweight, we first tested removal using a sensitive topic, a tweet reporting that Dave looked as if he had gained 50 pounds. Can Dave remove such a tweet (as posed by Q12)? Responses to straightforward removal of this sort—when the tweet was about but not by oneself—revealed it to be a controversial action.

It would have been less controversial if the tweet was authored by the respondent, since this is a capability already offered by Twitter. We complicated this scenario (removing one's own tweets) by introducing the notion of a tweet that the respondent had already deleted using Twitter's delete function, but that had been reused by a follower before the deletion occurred. Did respondents feel they should be able to take matters into their own hands and make sure the delete propagated to the places where the tweet was reused? In other words, should the author be able to remove the reused tweet from the alternate contexts in which it now appears? In one of the situations we proposed, this removal could be performed surgically without further damaging the aggregate post that the author did not create. Respondents' scores trended mildly positive (see Q16 in Table 3). However, if the removal destroyed surrounding material too, the response trended negative (see Q15 in Table 3). This difference is significant ($p<.001$, Wilcoxon).

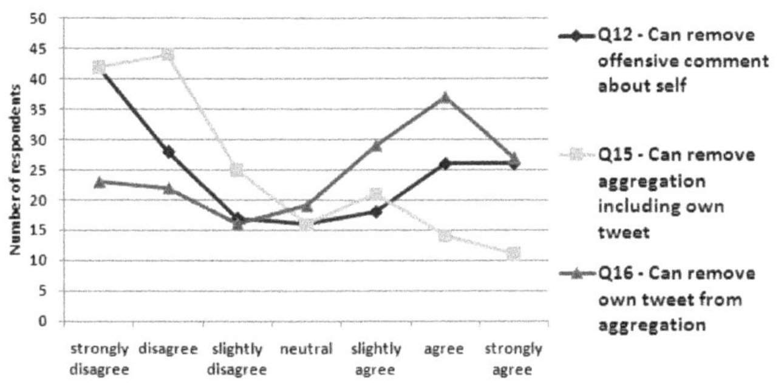

Figure 5. Views about removing tweets and aggregations.

Institutional Ownership and Individual Data Rights

Not long before we conducted this survey, the Library of Congress acquired the entire public Twitter database as part of an initiative to archive Web-based information. This acquisition was not without controversy: some Twitter users felt they had achieved a measure of privacy through obscurity, and although in principle their tweets were already available to the public, they were viewed and used in a known context, under an understood set of social mores. Yet it is part of the Library of Congress's mission to collect such ephemera, so that future scholars and historians have a window onto our time.

It seems worthwhile to investigate our respondents' attitudes toward the rights of public institutions to collect and archive social media such as tweets, so we posed the Library of Congress's actions as hypothetical, and in terms of access rather storage: Does the Library of Congress have the right to give the public access to this collection of tweets? What if the access were limited to researchers? What if public access were deferred for 50 years?

Interestingly, the most positive response was to the case that limited the access to researchers. This hypothetical limitation defined the context of use, and seemed to ease discomfort with the idea of full public access to tweets. The other two variations—full current access and full access in 50 years—elicited bimodal distributions of scores, although according to the mean scores, granting full access in 50 years and limiting access to researchers today fared similarly. The difference between Q20 (researcher access) and Q21 (full access) is significant ($p<.001$, Wilcoxon).

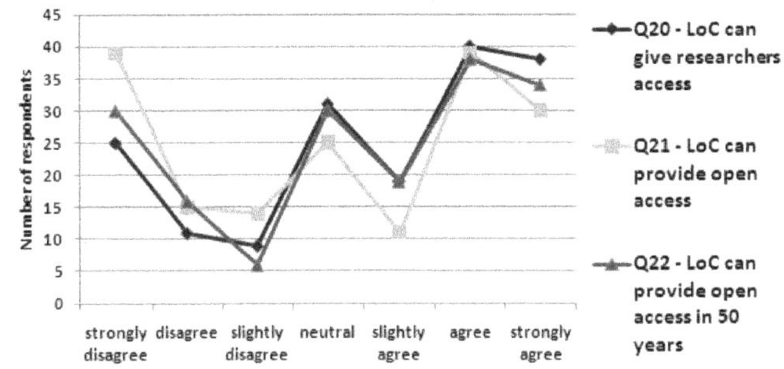

Figure 6. Views about institutional access to tweets.

CONCLUSION AND FUTURE WORK

What do these attitudes toward ownership rights tell us about Twitter content, and more generally, about social media? How should attitudes about social media ownership inform the design of collaborative services, especially services such as personal archiving? We approach this connection with a measure of caution, since we know there can be an important gulf between attitude and action, as demonstrated by privacy research (for example, [1]).

Yet we feel that attitudes are a good place to start, especially if they are coupled with investigations of existing behavior. For example, past studies tell us that people often approach the long term storage of their digital stuff with a strong tendency toward benign neglect [18]: if an archiving service were offered, where would the boundaries on stored content be? What would people be able to do with the contents of such a personal archive?

Much of the personal material that is on the Web is jointly owned—it is created collaboratively, records social settings and events, and is curated on the social Web. In other words, personal archiving is no longer a matter of creating a permanent copy of material from a personal computer's hard drive. In Twitter, a tweet may be written by one author, may refer to someone else (either about them or their content), and may implicate others as well (for example, as a retweet). Similarly, a photo on a photo sharing service may be taken by one photographer, be of several people in the foreground, and others visible in the background; it may further be described by metadata contributed by other people. In general, social media is a social endeavor, and hence it worthwhile to consider how this joint ownership affects its long-term fate.

There is some consistency to actions respondents feel they can take with lightweight social media like tweets. Certainly there is a sense that one can store almost any Twitter content that one encounters. More caution is exercised with publishing and republishing tweets, and more still with sharing the tweets among friends and associates. Finally, the most caution is exercised with the right of removal: deleting tweets seems to be seen as a potentially antisocial act. Even when it is not destructive, some respondents feel that they should exercise all due caution. It is important to know whether these findings extend to other types of social media, to begin to explore the ethos behind these beliefs, and to investigate the relationship between these attitudes and lived practice.

In this study, we found that the respondents' relationship to the material influences what they feel they can do with it. If they are cast as the author, they are the least cautious. They are slight more cautious if the tweets are cast as public (where there is no strong authorial claim laid to the material), which is in turn followed by tweets that reflect shared ownership. The most caution is associated with participatory content (e.g. Twitter conversations). Again, does this ordering hold for other types of social media?

Some ideas we posed in this survey seem to provoke disagreement or controversy. We uncovered three: (1) Respondents disagreed about limits that might be imposed on what you can store out of your twitter stream based on the individual tweet's role and provenance; (2) Respondents disagreed about whether public or governmental institutions should be able to provide universal access to public tweets; and (3) Respondents disagreed about whether individuals should be granted the power to remove tweets about themselves (tweets they did not write) that are potentially unpleasant or libelous.

Our future work will determine whether these belief patterns will hold for other social media types, particularly those that require more authorial effort or have greater emotional currency (e.g. family photos or videos). Further investigation will resolve whether these patterns of action (store, publish, share, remove) or authorial relationship (author, public content, shared content, participatory content) are meaningful in other social media contexts, and will identify potential gaps between attitudes and behavior.

REFERENCES

1. Acquisti, A. and Grossklags, J. Privacy Attitudes and Privacy Behavior, in J. Camp and S. Lewis (Eds.) *The Economics of Information Security*, Kluwer, Boston, pp. 165-178.
2. Besmer, A. and Lipford, H.R. Moving Beyond Untagging: Photo Privacy in a Tagged World. *Proc. CHI'10*, 1563-1572.
3. boyd, d., Colder, S., & Lotan, G. Tweet, Tweet, Retweet: Conversational Aspects of Retweeting on Twitter. *Proc. of HICSS*, 2010.
4. Downs, J., Holbrook, M., Sheng, S., & Cranor, L. Are your participants gaming the system?: Screening Mechanical Turk workers. *Proc. of CHI'10*. 2399-2402.
5. Dourish, P. and Bly, S. Portholes: supporting awareness in a distributed work group. *Proc. CHI '92*. 541-547.
6. Ebner, M. & Schiefner, M. Microblogging - more than fun? *Proc. of IADIS Mobile Learning Conference*, 2008, 155-159.
7. Galuba, W., Aberer, K., Chakraborty, D., Despotovic, Z., & Kellerer, W. Outtweeting the Twitterers - Predicting Information Cascades in Microblogs. *Proc. of Workshop on Online Social Networks*, 2010.
8. Honeycutt, C., & Herring, S. Beyond microblogging: Conversation and collaboration via Twitter. *Proc. of the HICSS 2009*. IEEE Press.
9. Huberman, B.A., Romero, D.M. and Wu, F. Social Networks that Matter: Twitter under the Microscope. First Monday, 14, 1, January, 2009.
10. Hughes, A.L. & Palen, L. Twitter adoption and use in mass convergence and emergency events. *Int. Journal of Emergency Management*. 6 (3/4) 2009, 248-260.
11. Ipeirotis, P. The New Demographics of Mechanical Turk. http://behind-the-enemy-lines.blogspot.com /2010/03/new-demographics-of-mechanical-turk.html
12. Jakobsson, M. (2009) Experimenting on Mechanical Turk: 5 How Tos. *ITWorld*, September 3, 2009.
13. Java, A., Song, X., Finin, T. & Tseng, B. Why we twitter: Understanding microblogging usage and communities. *Proc. ACM SIGKDD*, 2007.
14. Kittur, A., Chi, E., Suh, B. Crowdsourcing User Studies with Mechanical Turk. *Proc. CHI'08*. 453-456.
15. Krishnamurthy, B., Gill, P., & Arlitt, M. A Few Chirps about Twitter. *Proc. Workshop on Online Social Networks*, 2008, 19-24.
16. Lessig, L. *Remix: Making Art and Commerce Thrive in the Hybrid Economy*, Penguin, New York, 2008.
17. Levy, D. "Fixed or Fluid: Document Stability and New Media." *Proc. ECHT'94*, 1994, 24-31.
18. Marshall, C.C. Rethinking Personal Digital Archiving, Part 1: Four Challenges from the Field. *DLib*, 14, 3/4
19. Odom, W., Harper, R., Sellen, A., Kirk, D., Banks, R. Passing on & Putting to Rest: Understanding Bereavement in the Context of Interactive Technologies, *Proc. CHI'10,* pp 1831-1840.
20. Reinhardt, W., Ebner, M., Beham, G., & Costa, C. How People are using Twitter during Conferences. *Proc. of EduMedia*, 2009, 145–156.
21. Stutzman, F. and Kramer-Duffield, J. Friends Only: Examining a Privacy-Enhancing Behavior in Facebook. *Proc. of CHI'10*, 1553-1562.
22. Zhao, D. & Rosson, M.B. How and why people Twitter: the role that micro-blogging plays in informal communication at work. *Proc. of GROUP'09*, 243-252.

Fragile Online Relationship: A First Look at Unfollow Dynamics in Twitter

Haewoon Kwak, Hyunwoo Chun, and Sue Moon
Department of Computer Science, KAIST
291 Daehak-ro, Yuseong-gu, Daejeon, Korea
{haewoon, hyunwoo}@an.kaist.ac.kr, sbmoon@kaist.edu

ABSTRACT
We analyze the dynamics of the behavior known as 'unfollow' in Twitter. We collected daily snapshots of the online relationships of 1.2 million Korean-speaking users for 51 days as well as all of their tweets. We found that Twitter users frequently unfollow. We then discover the major factors, including the reciprocity of the relationships, the duration of a relationship, the followees' informativeness, and the overlap of the relationships, which affect the decision to unfollow. We conduct interview with 22 Korean respondents to supplement the quantitative results. They unfollowed those who left many tweets within a short time, created tweets about uninteresting topics, or tweeted about the mundane details of their lives. To the best of our knowledge, this work is the first systematic study of the unfollow behavior in Twitter.

Author Keywords
Unfollow, computer-mediated communication, Twitter, online relationship

ACM Classification Keywords
H.5.0 Information Systems: Information Interfaces and Presentation - General

General Terms
Human Factors

INTRODUCTION
Relationship formation and dissolution are two basic processes of relationship change and evolution in personal networks. Studies of relationship formation and dissolution mostly rely on surveys and interviews, both of which require considerable effort in terms of time and labour. Online social networks (OSN) aid researchers in at least two ways, such as (i) they contain a huge archive of human behavior related to online relationships, and (ii) they allow easy access. Studies of online relationship formation are straightforward, as most OSNs offer simple means of establishing online relationships, often referred to as a 'friend'. By contrast, research on the topic of online relationship dissolution has not been extensively conducted due to the lack of data; an online friend relationship remains rigid regardless of the actual relationship [28]. Researchers thus use proxies to represent the state of relationship dissolution. For example, a study of relationship dissolution in email networks assumes that the disappearance of online activities (the exchange of emails) reflects this type of dissolution [16]. However, a disappearance of communication cannot be directly translated to the dissolution of a relationship in most cases, because it is difficult to capture all communication means [23] and to regard the absence of an event as strictly intentional. The key insight behind this work is that unfollow in Twitter represents a user's explicit expression of the dissolution of an online relationship and breaks off the non-reciprocal online relationship.

Twitter has been redefining human behavior logging on the strength of worldwide popularity, brief text messages, and well-supported application programming interface (API) to access. Twitter allows a user to establish a one-way relationship known as *follow*. This is one of the most distinguishing features of Twitter, in contrast to the reciprocal friendship in most other OSNs, e.g., friends in Facebook. Literally, neither an invitation nor an acceptance is required for following; people can freely and easily follow others. When a user logs into Twitter, s/he sees tweets from those s/he follows (*followees*). The stream of followees' tweets is called a *timeline*. A user can easily stop following (*unfollow*) and needs no confirmation from the followee to do so. Unfollow, thus, is not a proxy but a verifiable action of breaking an online relationship. In the rest of the paper, we use unfollow both as a noun and a verb.

In this work, we analyze the dynamics of the unfollow behavior to understand online relationship dissolution. The two research questions explored here are: (i) what are the characteristics of the unfollow behavior? and (ii) why do people unfollow others? To address the first research question, we collected daily snapshots of the follow relationships of 1.2 million Korean-speaking users over the course of 51 days as well as their tweets. By comparing the daily snapshots, we confirm that unfollow is prevalent in Twitter. We have found that the reciprocity of the relationship, the duration of the relationships, the followees' informativeness, and the overlap of relationships are critical in the decision to unfollow. For the second research question, we conducted interviews with 22 users to determine their motivations behind the unfollow behavior. Our survey respondents answered that they unfollowed those who left many tweets within a short time, left tweets about topics uninteresting to them, or left tweets about mundane details of daily life. To the best of our knowledge, this work is the first systematic look at the unfollow behavior in Twitter.

For the rest of the paper, we first review the literature on friendship dissolution problems and state-of-the-art Twitter analyses. We then explain research questions and give the outline of this work. We describe our data collection methodology of crawling Twitter and interviewing Twitter users. We then demonstrate interesting unfollow patterns and factors that impact the decision to unfollow from large-scale data. Next, we present qualitative analyses of the underlying user motivation behind unfollow according to interviews with the Twitter users. We finally conclude by discussing implications for future research.

PREVIOUS LITERATURE

For better understanding this work, we review the literature on three different areas. We begin with the research on the topic of off-line relationship dissolution. Next, we introduce studies of the characteristics of user behavior in Twitter. Finally, we review models and empirical studies of the link dynamics in networks.

Friendship Dissolution

A few longitudinal studies have reported on off-line relationship dissolution. Mollenhorst have found that a half of adult friendships change over the period of seven years [25]. Two studies have observed that social networks among younger children have a higher retention rate [6, 12]. Homophily plays a decisive role in off-line relationship retention; several studies report that friendship is more stable when people are more alike [16, 30]. Homophily is a combined process of establishing friendships with those who are like you and acting like your friends [15]. Our interviewees confirm that they often stop following those who write tweets about topics uninteresting to them.

User Behavior Analysis in Twitter

Pioneering work by Java *et al.* has sampled $76,000$ Twitter users and found users to be clustered based on topics [14]. Kwak *et al.* have crawled the near-complete Twittersphere and collected profiles of 41.7 million users and 1.47 billion tweets of trending topics. They reported that Twitter carries the characteristics of a news medium rather than works as a typical online social network [18]. Other quantitative analyses of user behavior in Twitter also looked at the perspective of information delivery: homophily in terms of the shared interests [32], informational communication at work [33], and information propagation [20]. Facebook has been the focus of a good number of qualitative user behavior analysis [9, 19, 28], but few have covered qualitative analysis of Twitter yet. We study the unfollow behavior from the large-scale data and supplement with qualitative interviews for clear understanding of motivations behind unfollow.

Link Dynamics

From theoretical models to empirical studies of link dynamics in networks, link removal has been largely ignored due to lack of verifying data. The link prediction problem is "given a snapshot of a social network at time t, we seek to accurately predict the edges that will be added to the network during the interval from time t to a given future time t'" [22]. It deals only with newly added links but not removed links. The generative models in [3, 21] account only for link additions in the network evolution, and so are previous empirical studies [10, 17]. A recent study focuses on the structural predictors of tie formation particularly in Twitter [11]. Our study reports on the prevalence of link removal and major factors to affect link removal in the online relationship network of Korean Twitter users. It can aid researchers in creating new models and verifying the extensibility of conventional models.

THE GOAL OF THIS PAPER

Our goals are to observe the characteristics of the unfollow behavior and to understand why people unfollow.

R1: What are the characteristics of the unfollow behavior?

We reveal unfollow patterns through quantitative data analysis. We begin with the frequency of unfollow. We expect that unfollow is prevalent because: (i) follow relationships do not need to be reciprocal, (ii) Twitter does not notify unfollow to those who are unfollowed, and (iii) unfollow is done by just one click. We also find temporal correlation in the unfollow behavior. We then demonstrate the correlation between the frequency of interaction and the likelihood of unfollow. This shows the validity of general assumptions that the less frequency of interaction could be a sign of the dissolution of an online relationship.

Next, we analyze the stabilization of the relationships; do people tend to unfollow new followees or old ones? If older relationships are more broken, people continuously want the freshness in their timelines. Or if newer relationships are more broken, older followees mean that people are satisfied with them. If no correlation is observed, people unfollow a followee no matter how long a relationship has lasted. We also aim to find evidences that people tend to control the number of followees.

R2: Why do people unfollow?

Beyond the observations of the unfollow behavior, we answer what factors affect unfollow. We examine the motivations behind unfollow through not only the analysis of huge data but also user interviews.

First is the informativeness of a followee. Previous work highlighted the perspective of information delivery in Twitter. If the purpose of following is mostly subscribing to tweets, more informative followees could be hardly unfollowed.

Next, we study how the reciprocity of the relationships affects unfollow. We compare the likelihood of unfollow in reciprocal relationships to that in unreciprocated relationships. We also find the correlation between the overlap of relationships of two users and the likelihood of unfollow.

Then, we conduct interviews with 22 Korean users. We divide our questions into four categories: the motivation behind unfollow, the awareness of being unfollowed, the marketing campaigns driven by company accounts, and the ranking of followees in terms of the likelihood of unfollow.

DATA COLLECTION

The main challenge is to obtain traces of the unfollow behavior because Twitter does not offer the explicit records of unfollow. We solve this problem by comparing daily snapshots of each user's follow relationships and detecting any disappearance of a follow relationship as unfollow.

As of September 2010, the total number of Twitter users is close to two hundred million, too large for a few tens of crawlers to collect the entire user space within a short period of time. We had to choose a sampling strategy. Instead of choosing a random sampling methodology, we wanted a sample with a cohesive cultural and societal bound so that we could compare personal interviews in the same context. A typical choice in previous studies of online relationships would have been a university [19, 27, 29]. Thanks to the open API of Twitter, we could expand our sample from a university to a country bounded by the language.

We have chosen the exhaustive set of Korean-speaking users for the following reasons. First, it is like a miniature of the entire Korean society. Almost all walks of life are represented, such as politicians, sports stars, TV anchors, writers, students, housewives, labor unionists, etc., and relationships among them, such as celebrities and fans, political parties and their followers, and manufacturers and consumers. This offers relatively rich user behavior, in contrast to the limited scope of college life in previous studies. Further, we can get a longitudinal data with a fine-grained time resolution, as the pool of all Koreans is a manageable size to crawl in a single day. The other reason is authors are familiar with the culture of the online Korean community. We can grasp the context of tweets about almost every online or off-line issues in the Korean community.

We have collected the followers and followees of every Korean Twitter user. Any Twitter user who fell to one or more of the following four conditions was deemed Korean: (i) one wrote a tweet in Korean; (ii) one's biographical information was written in Korean; (iii) one's location was written in Korean; and (iv) one's screen name was written in Korean. We made daily snapshots of the entire Korean users from June 25th, 2010 to July 15th, 2010 and from August 2nd to August 31, 2010. We could not collect snapshots from July 16th to August 1st due to technical problems. In the rest of the paper we label social graphs from two isolated periods as *G(I)* and *G(II)*, respectively.

Next, we have crawled all tweets written by Korean users until the last day of *G(II)*, August 31st, 2010. Through the collected tweets, we can reconstruct who interacted with whom by a reply or a mention, and who acknowledged whom by a retweet or a favorite. The retweet has been typically considered as an indicator of the tweet's quality [18, 20], and we consider a 'favorite' as such an indicator as well.

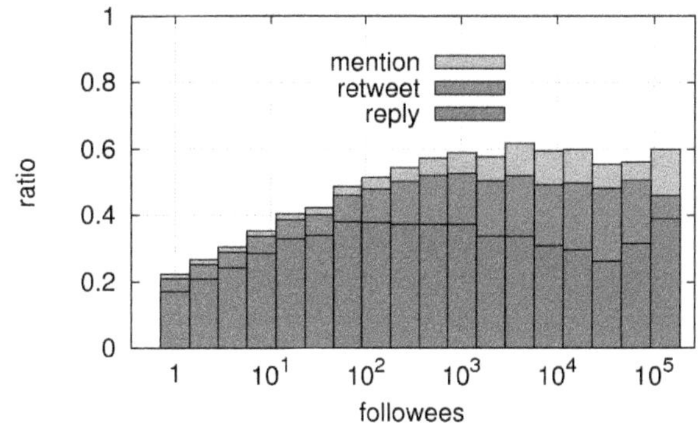

Figure 1. Proportion of tweets of each type

We note that the social and cultural norms about friendship, commitment, and online services might play out differently in Korea than in other countries. We thus need more data to show the generalizeability of our findings to non-Korean users. We plan to expand our dataset across both time and space for external validity in future work.

BASIC STATISTICS OF THE KOREAN TWITTER NETWORK

We first examine the basic statistics of Korean Twitter users. The number of Korean users in the last day of *G(I)* is $870,057$ and that of *G(II)* is $1,203,196$. The average number of new incoming users per day is $7,599$ in $G(I)$ and $8,515$ in $G(II)$.

We define the reciprocity of a network as the ratio of user pairs of mutual relationships over the total number of user pairs of either one-way or mutual relationships. Kwak *et al.* have reported a very low reciprocity of 22.1% in the near-complete Twitter network [18]. We find a quite high reciprocity among Korean users: in $G(I)$ we see 56-58% of reciprocity and in $G(II)$ 61-62%. It is still lower than the reciprocity observed in other services, such as 84% of Yahoo! 360 [17]. Interestingly, the reciprocity has increased slightly over time. We additionally discover that the average number of followees increases from 59.7 to 75.7 during the 51 days. These two observations illustrate a densification process in a directed network as similar as that reported in an undirected network [21].

A tweet can be classified into four categories by its purpose: a regular tweet, a reply, a mention, or a retweet. A reply and a mention are conversational, while a retweet is informational. How does a user utilizes the four categories vary depending on the number of followees? Figure 1 shows the average proportion of tweets of each type written by the users with the same number of followees. We omit the proportion of regular tweets in the figure. We read from the figure that the percentage of replies increases linearly to the

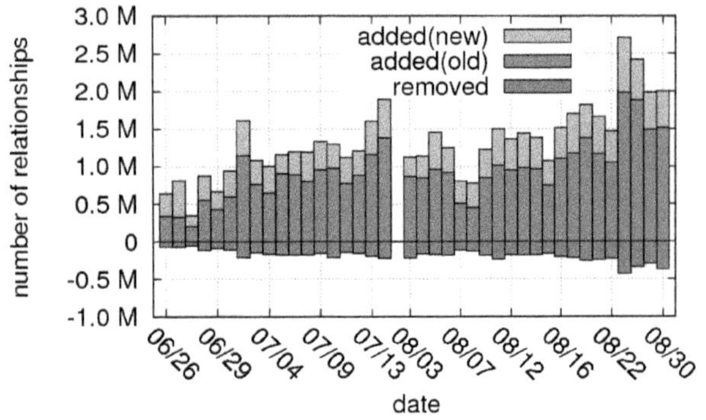

Figure 2. Number of relationship formation and dissolution per day

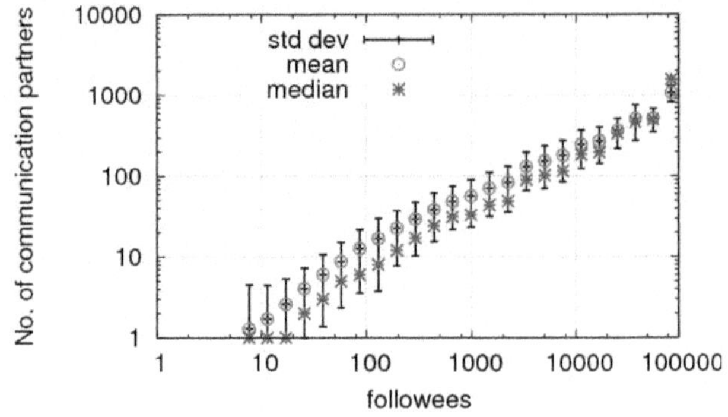

Figure 3. Number of communication partners vs. number of followees

number of followees up to 100, signifying that the more one follows, the more interactive one becomes. Once the number of followees exceeds 100, then the proportion of replies stays constant or decreases slightly, but that of retweets grows (the middle section in a bar expands from $x = 10^2$ to $x = 10^4$ and a little beyond). That is, the more followees one has, the more informational one becomes rather than conversational. We note that mentions are by far the smallest in ratio. Twitter offers buttons for a reply and a retweet, but none for a mention. The lack of a convenience feature can result in low usage of mentions, and the addition of the feature might increase the ratio in future.

QUANTITATIVE ANALYSIS OF UNFOLLOW BEHAVIOR

We demonstrate that the unfollow behavior is prevalent in Twitter and the low frequency of interaction cannot signify unfollows due to the passivity in most relationships. Especially, the latter shows the difficulty that low frequency of interaction is regarded as online relationship dissolution in Twitter. Then we discover some factors affecting the unfollow behavior, such as the mutuality of relationships, the duration of a relationship, the followees' informativeness, and the overlap of the relationships of two users.

Pervasive Unfollow

We begin with the network-wide statistics of unfollow. We count the number of relationship formation and dissolution by comparing snapshots from consecutive days and plot them in Figure 2. The lower bars labeled 'removed' represent unfollows and the upper bars are new follows. The new follow is divided into old and new: the former refers to relationship formation among existing users and the latter relationship formation with those users who newly joined on the day. We can see that the frequencies of follows and unfollows are strongly correlated with the Pearson correlation coefficient of 0.715 ($p \ll 0.0001$). Overall, 171,131 users in *G(I)*, 289,444 users in *G(II)*, and 360,321 users in *G(I)+G(II)* have stopped following at least once. During the 51 days about 30% of users had unfollowed at least once. If we filter out inactive users, who did not establish or break even a single relationship during the 51 days, the ratio increases to 43%. These numbers could increase if we could expand the time window of data collection. The average of unfollows per person is 15.4 in in $G(I)$ and 16.1 in $G(II)$. We conclude that unfollow is quite pervasive in Twitter.

Unfollows Frequent and Mostly Singular, But Often Clustered

To understand the temporal characteristics of the unfollow behavior, we analyze how many followees a user unfollow per day and how often a user unfollows. The resolution of our data is a single day for the interval of unfollow. We observe highly skewed unfollow patterns. About 66% of unfollows occurred singularly in a day, while 10% of unfollows occurred with at least other 5 unfollows. In addition, a few users who have many followees unfollow more than a hundred a day. We conjecture that they use some automatic tools to unfollow those who do not follow them back. We also observe that 90% of time intervals between days of unfollows of a user are less than 9 days.

In summary most unfollows are a singular event of the day, while the remaining unfollows appear clustered. Clustered or not, unfollows are a frequent event occurring once in 9 days for 90% of the cases.

Passiveness in Relationships

Unfollow is a much stronger expression of losing interest than diminished interaction between two people. Yet still, is unfollow an extreme form of diminished interaction? To paraphrase the question, can we predict an unfollow from the reduced interaction or not? This illustrates whether a proxy of frequency of interaction for online relationship dissolution is applicable in Twitter.

We first look at how many people a user actually interacts with. We define *communication partners* of a user as those who exchange tweets with the user reciprocally at least once by a mention, a reply, or a retweet. That is, a reply, a mention, or a retweet was sent from one user to the other and vice versa. This is a strong definition of communication in a network with a relatively low reciprocity. Figure 3 shows the correlation between the number of followees a user has and that of communication partners. For clarity of presentation we use log-scale in both x and y axes and log-scale bins for data points. At a first glance the plot exhibits a linear trend, but because the x-axis in log scale, a user is actually inter-

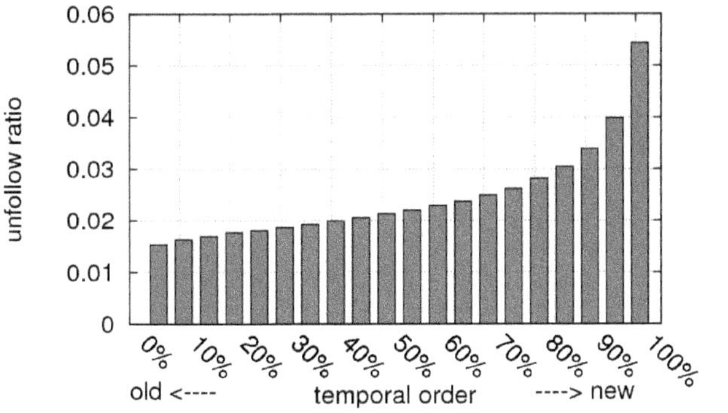

Figure 4. Aggregated number of broken relationships vs. temporal order of relationship establishment in a personal network

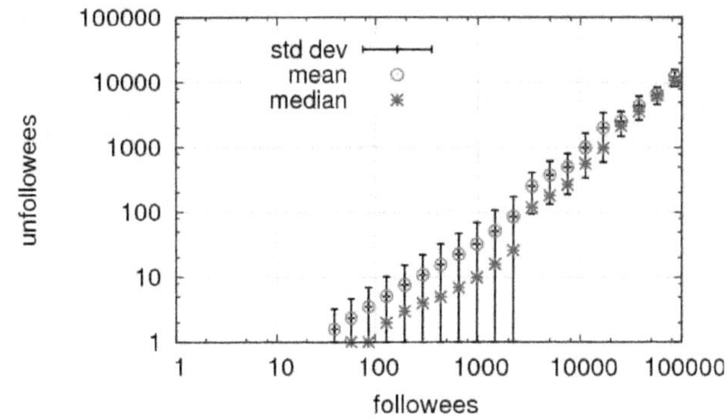

Figure 5. Number of followees vs. Number of unfollowees

acting with an order of magnitude smaller number of people than one's followees. The number of communication partners is positively correlated with the number of followees, as predicted, but its number is an order of magnitude smaller than that of followees. For example, users who follow 1000 people communicate with only about 70 people on average. This result shows that the majority of relationships do not result in social interaction in Twitter. Interestingly, we find a similar phenomena in other OSNs; Facebook users interact with a relatively small number of their own friends [8] as well as Cyworld users do [7]. These can be explained by the Dunbar's number, defined as 'the theoretical cognitive limit to the number of people with whom one can maintain stable social relationships'.

We observe the same level of low activity over most follow relationships. Out of $104,116,484$ follow relationships, 85.6% of relationships involve no activity at all and 96.3% of relationships involve 3 or fewer. This result reveals the very passive nature of follow relationships. People mostly just subscribe to followees' tweets, and they do not send a reply, a mention, or a retweet.

We compare the average numbers of sending tweets to those later unfollowed and to staying relationships. We find the difference is less than one tweet for the 99% confidence interval as most relationships are passive and incur no interaction. If we exclude passive relationships in calculation, broken relationships involve less activity than unbroken staying ones: the mean number of sending tweets is 4.107 for the former and 5.850 for the latter. The difference is statistically significant by the two-sample t-test ($p \ll 0.0001$).

Relationship Stabilization

Is a user less likely to unfollow those who the user has been following long enough? In order to gauge the duration of follow and correlate it with the likelihood of unfollow, we need to know when each relationship is established, but Twitter does not offer the information. Instead, Twitter offers the temporal order of the establishment of relationships in the personal network. We thus can recognize the relative order in relationship establishment of followees for each user. Now which relationship is more likely to be broken, old or new? We use 20 bins and put unfollows according to the ego-centric temporal ordering of relationship establishments. Because we choose the bin size of 20, we only consider users with more than 20 followees. For example, let us consider a user with 40 followees unfollowed the very first followee. Then the very first bin in Figure 4 would be incremented by one. Even though the y-axis in the graph is presented in likelihood, it is basically the same. We observe an increasing trend in likelihood of unfollow towards newer followees. The unfollow ratio increases significantly in the rightmost bin, which represents the most recent followees. The figure concludes that the longer the followee remains, the less likely the relationship is broken by unfollow.

No Cap in the Number of Followees

Here we inspect the overhead of managing online relationships based on the the number of followees a user has. We seek to find evidences whether people make an effort to maintain a manageable number of followees. We depict a correlation between the number of followees and that of unfollowees for each user in Figure 5. We do not find any evidence that people try to put a cap on the number of followees. Instead, the ratio of the number of followees to that of unfollowees remains between $1/12$ and $1/10$.

Reciprocity of Relationships

Reciprocal follow relationships can bring emotional closeness to both users and thus reduce the likelihood of unfollow. We compare the likelihood of unfollow in reciprocated relationships to one-way relationship. The likelihood that one of reciprocated relationships is broken is 0.0529, and that of one-way relationship is 0.1228. The one-way relationship is twice more likely to be broken than the reciprocated relationship. With a two-sample t-test, we see that the difference is statistically significant ($p \ll 0.0001$). We further investigate the likelihood of the remaining relationship to be broken after one of two-way relationships is broken. Interestingly, we observe that the likelihood increases to 0.2345. The remaining relationship is more likely to be broken than likelihood of one-way relationship to be broken. Note that 0.2345 is computed with the data for 51 days, and this likelihood can increase with the longer duration of data.

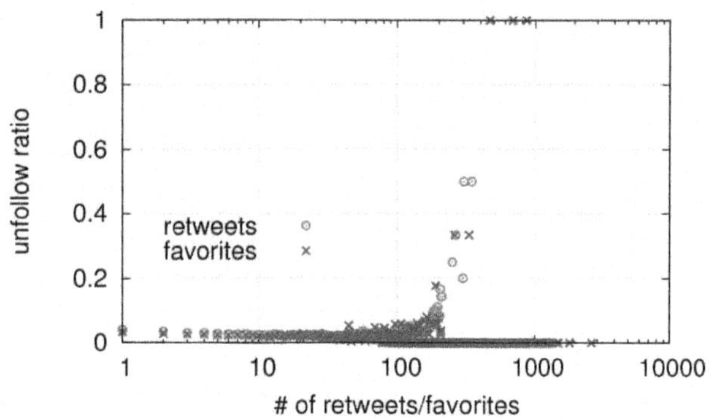

Figure 6. The correlation between followee's informativeness and the likelihood of unfollowing the followee

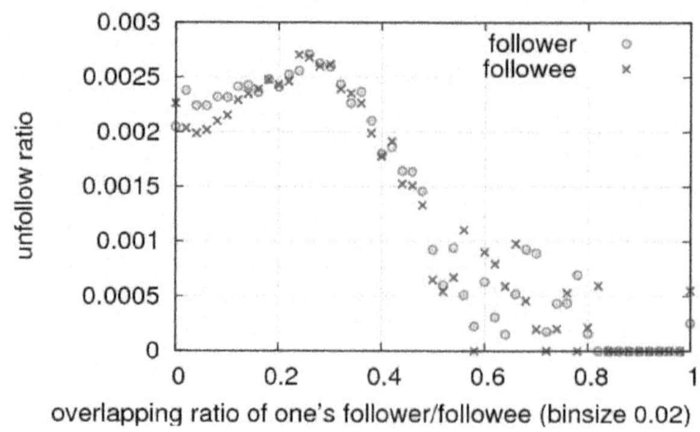

Figure 7. The correlation between the overlap of two users' relationships and the likelihood of the relationship between them to be broken

Followees' Informativeness

People can choose to unfollow a followee when they are no longer interested in reading the tweets of the followee. In other words, the informativeness of user's tweets can be the opportunity cost of unfollowing the user. The most common way to assess the informativeness of user's tweets is how many times user's tweets are retweeted [18, 32]. Similarly, it is possible to count how many people mark the user's tweets as their favorites. A helpful analogy for the favorites in Twitter is the bookmarks in web browsers; a user may mark a tweet as a favorite for future reading.

There is neither a common agreement nor the systematic study on which one of a retweet and a favorite is a better metric to evaluate informativeness, as a retweet and a favorite have different purposes and semantics. People retweet a followee's tweet to broadcast it to their own followers, whereas marking a favorite mainly for personal use. Here we consider both a retweet and a favorite as an indicator of user's informativeness and compare two results.

If we aggregate retweets and favorites of a followee by all the followers, we could inaccurately reflect the followee's informativeness to a user. For example, even if user A's tweets are marked as user B's favorites many times, user C may not regard user A as informative due to different interests. Therefore, we define informativeness strictly between a user and a followee; the informativeness of my followee to me is measured by only my retweets and favorites.

Figure 6 shows the correlation between a user's informativeness and the likelihood of being unfollowed. A few unfollow ratios above 0.2 are aberrant data points as only they represent only singular cases. We only focus on the majority of the cases that have the unfollow ratio lower than 0.1. It means that once a relationship involves either retweets or favorites, such relationship is less likely to be broken, while the probability of a relationship randomly picked is 0.114. The data points by the retweets are mostly under those by the favorites below for retweets and favorites under 100. It indicates retweets are a better metric than favorites in measuring informativeness: if one retweets a followee's tweet, the user is less likely to unfollow the followee than in the case of favoriting a tweet.

Shared Relationships

Onnela *et al.* find a positive correlation between the number of common friends of two users and the duration of calls between them in a large undirected mobile phone call network [26]. Similarly, in a directed network, outlink equivalence and inlink equivalence of two nodes are defined as the overlap in outlinks and inlinks of the two nodes, respectively [31]. In the domain of Twitter, the common followees map to outlink equivalence, and the common followers to inlink equivalence.

For every pair of users who have a follow relationship between them, we first compute the outlink equivalence of the pair. Then we normalize it by dividing the number of the union of followees of both users. This is basically the Jaccard coefficient for the two users' followees. We ignore the two users themselves in set operations. Unless we ignore two users in set operations, the maximum normalized value cannot reach 1 because a user cannot follow oneself. For the input equivalence, we normalize the values in the same manner. Figure 7 shows the correlation between the unfollow ratio of relationships and the normalized input and output equivalences. The unfollow ratio slowly increases up to 0.24 of the normalized outlink equivalence. In the rest of the graph, the unfollow ratio decreases while the normalized input and output equivalences increase. This result suggests that the overlap in followers or followees can be a proxy of tie strength in retaining relationships.

QUALITATIVE ANALYSIS - INTERVIEWS

In order to examine the motivation behind unfollow, we supplement interviews to this work. We recruited 22 survey respondents (11 males and 11 females). The age of study participants ranges from 22 to 36 years. Including the number of participants' followees, followers, and written tweets, we summarize the demographic breakdown of the 22 respondents in Figure 8.

We began an interview with a common question on their unfollow experience and proceeded with follow-up questions. The interviews lasted between 20 and 30 minutes for face-to-face interviews and between 30 and 40 minutes for Instant messengers, such as Google Talk. The difference in the

	Mean	Median	Min	Max	Std. dev.	Distribution
Age	27.3	27	22	36	3.7	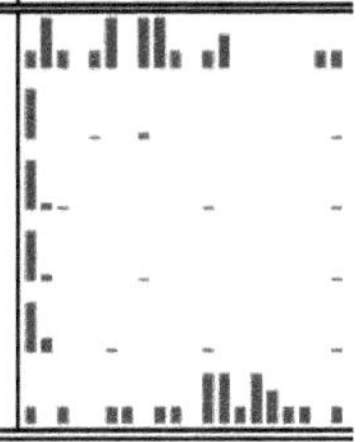
Favorites	80.7	1	0	851	199.0	
Followers	846.7	164.5	5	8,772	2,053.9	
Followings	600.4	144.5	5	7,103	1,562.7	
Tweets	3,325.8	583.5	5	30,639	7,220.5	
Registered days	449.2	471	14	766	179.1	

Figure 8. Demographic of 22 participants (11 males and 11 females)

interview duration comes mainly from the communication speed in speaking and typing. All face-to-face interviews were recorded by the digital camcorder and transcribed, and instant messenger interviews were recorded as client-side logs. All interviews were conducted in Korean and transcribed later by the first author. We transcribed the interview logs according to standard coding techniques reviewed by Miles and Huberman [24]. As having all tweets written by the participants, we minimized the informant accuracy led by retrospective data [5].

Our first question was why a participant decided to unfollow. Even though we had records of the participant's unfollow during $G(I)$ and $G(II)$, we did not explicitly mention it in order not to make the participants feel uncomfortable. Most participants easily recalled multiple reasons to unfollow, even without browsing one's own Twitter page. Our next question was whether the participant thought the unfollowee was aware of being unfollowed. If not, we asked whether the participant would have behaved differently if Twitter notified the unfollowee. Had the participant ever broken off a relationship on other OSNs, such as Facebook, and how would one compare the different services? We included a question about company accounts and their marketing campaigns in Twitter. If the participant ever followed corporate accounts, we inquired about their participation in the campaign. The final question was to choose ten users the interviewee would *never* unfollow. Who were they? Celebrities, offline friends, or informative sources? These are indirect answers behind why people use Twitter and how they use Twitter.

Motivation Category		Case
Burst (39)	Burst-only	13
	Uninteresting topics	10
	Mundane details of daily life	6
	Automatically generated	4
	Conversation	2
	Politics	2
	Different views	1
	Complains	1
Uninteresting topics (14)	Burst	10
	Uninteresting topics-only	4
Mundane details of daily life (11)	Burst	6
	Mundane details of daily life-only	5
Politics (8)	Different views	3
	Burst	2
	Strong opinion	2
	Politics-only	1
RT with no personality (4)	RT with no personality-only	4
Advertisement (4)	Advertisement-only	4
Automatically generated (4)	Burst	4
Different views (4)	Politics	2
	Different views-only	1
	Burst	1
Conversation (2)	Conversation-only	1
	Burst	1
Complains (2)	Complains-only	1
	Burst	1
Slang (1)	Slang-only	1
Dead account (1)	Dead account-only	1
Self-presentation (1)	Self-presentation-only	1
Language gap (1)	Language gap-only	1

Figure 9. Motivation behind unfollow for 73 unfollowees. Respondents answered multiple reasons for each unfollowee

Motivations behind Unfollow

The participants recalled 3.32 cases of unfollow, and some of them described multiple reasons for an unfollowee. We categorize respondents' answers in Figure 9.

Twenty out of 22 respondents reported that they unfollowed 39 people because of burst tweets. We break down these 39 into subgroups by the tweet contents. Very interestingly, respondents stated that they unfollowed 13 out of 39 because of the bursts no matter what their tweets were about. Next, respondents stated that tweets of 10 unfollowees were about uninteresting topics. The tweets of last 6 unfollowees were about the mundane details of daily life. We asked follow-up questions: why respondents did not like burst tweets? The top reasons behind the dislike of burst tweets were information overload. Respondents reported that they felt overwhelmed at the sheer amount of information of burst tweets. Also, too many tweets from a single followee often arrived back-to-back close in time, pushing other followees' tweets out of the timeline. Basically, it is similar to a Denial-of-Service (DoS) attack in computer networks. Some respondents said that they stopped following celebrities, although they remained big fans of those celebrities. One stated that s/he finally unfollowed a politician because of so many tweets, although s/he started Twitter to read the politician's tweets. Another respondent stated similar feelings:

> I'm a big fan of those celebrities, and I'm interested in what they talk about. But, they wrote burst tweets

> frequently, and their tweets filled my timeline. I finally unfollowed them. If they had not written too much, I would not have unfollowed them. (Respondent #8)

Four respondents counted the automatically generated log messages by third-party applications, such as Foursquare, as a cause of unfollow. Foursquare is a location-based social networking service [1]. Users with mobile phones *check in* at a venue and obtain points and badges like a game. Foursquare supports automatic transfer of user activity logs to Facebook or Twitter. The activity log typically consists of three-tuples: a short message, a location, and a Foursquare page URL. The trail of tweets by Foursquare describes a user's mobile trajectory over time. Respondents exhibited a distaste for automatically generated bursts of Foursquare logs. One respondent said:

> I unfollowed a user who frequently left Foursquare log messages. If not for the Foursquare logs [or similar reports], I would not have unfollowed him/her. I am really annoyed at Foursquare logs. (Respondent #1)

Apparently many users configured their Foursquare logs to be fed to their Twitter accounts [2]. With the prevalent use of this feature, other applications also have been launching a similar feature of leaving automatic tweets, such as a new record in iPhone game, a movie or song title in a streaming service, and even a shopping list in online shopping mall. Our survey shows that these features should be used with caution. Especially, a large number of tweets in a short time could trigger unfollows.

There were two respondents who did not unfollow in the face of burst tweets. They had a different approach to browsing Twitter. They said that they had given up reading all tweets of followees. Instead, they sometimes visited Twitter, looked over tweets of a few pages only, and checked for mentions and direct messages. They thus did not care much about burst tweets. Both participants have over 400 followees.

One major outcome from the discussion of burst tweets is the need for the user interface redesign. Even when a user follow others based on similar interest, s/he would unfollow in the presence of burst tweets. Our idea is to show only one latest tweet per user and hide the rest, and upon request (for example, by placing the cursor over a 'display all' button) the rest of the tweets are displayed. This interface ensures minimizing the stress on the user from burst tweets, particularly, tweets arrived back-to-back close in time. We asked a few respondents if such an interface would help deal with burst tweets and got positive answers.

Next, 11 respondents stated that they unfollowed 14 people because their tweets were about uninteresting topics, irrespective of the quality of the tweets. Here we cast the following question: Why did you follow the person at the first place? Respondents' answers can be put into two groups. First, when Twitter sent a notification email of a new follower, they followed back if the new follower did not look like a spammer. Respondents stated that they usually followed back a new follower. While previous work by Kwak *et al.* reports a low reciprocity of 22% in Twitter [18], our respondents surprised us: people followed back in return for being followed. The propensity for reciprocal following was developed into a solid relationship over time by shared interests, jobs, institutions, and so on. This we could call homophily in action. Second, respondents often found some tweets that appeared on their timeline via their followee's retweets and ended up following the original writer of a retweeted tweet. Retweets offered a chance to find people who wrote interestingly enough to be retweeted as social filtering. Recently, Twitter added an easy interface to retweet and now users view the retweet with the original writer's profile photo, the retweeter's name, and the total number of retweets. It helps identifying who the original writer of a retweeted tweet is.

Eight respondents replied that they unfollowed 11 people because their tweets were about the mundane details of daily life. One respondent stated:

> I think Twitter is a place to exchange ideas of certain quality, while it can also be a place to express personal feelings. I, of course, am not against emotional tweets. But, some tweets to just announce personal feelings, activities, or something. They are really about mundane details. "Oh, meat is good" is completely useless to me. It is different from "Meat is good, and I wonder how it eventually got delivered to my table." Don't you agree? (Respondent #14)

Six respondents gave political tweets as a reason to unfollow 8 people. Among them, 3 unfollowees wrote tweets of differing political views. This points at two interesting interpretations. While Weng *et al.* have reported people are likely to follow those who have similar interests based on cross-sectional data [32], our respondents showed a possibility of another scenario. Users readily followed back new followers. These relationships are not always formed based on shared interests but more on curiosity and habit, and thus homophily had not yet prevailed. After a while, people got to know each others' disagreeing opinions, in this case, on politics and eventually fell apart. Homophily eventually reigned in. The other is about positioning of Twitter as a soft news medium. Baum and Jamison argue that for politically unattentive citizens soft news are more effective than traditional news [4]. Both short messages and social interaction among users could establish Twitter as a soft news medium, but Twitter users did not seem to readily listen to different voices when it comes to politics. Thus, we claim that Twitter can be an effective medium to disseminate political messages to supporters, but not to conciliate opponents due to the lack of relationships to reach them.

Finally, 4 respondents stated that they unfollowed 4 people because they frequently retweeted seemingly on random topics. Also, the same number of respondents gave advertisements, automated messages, and differing views as a reason. The rest seem to reflect individual preference of respondents.

Awareness of Being Unfollowed

After the question about the experience of unfollow, we asked whether the participant thought the unfollowee was aware of being unfollowed.

A half of respondents stated that they thought unfollowees were aware of being unfollowed. Nevertheless, they unfollowed because: (i) they did not know unfollowees in person, (ii) they got used to unfollowing although they hesitated previously, and (iii) unfollow was easy. A few respondents stated that they unfollowed even off-line friends because they used Twitter as a tool for sharing information not keeping in touch. Two of them used the metaphor of an RSS reader. The RSS reader is used for reading new articles of blogs. People readily subscribe or unsubscribe blogs without any inhibition, and they so do in Twitter.

The other half of respondents thought that unfollowees were not aware of being unfollowed. Their reasons were: (i) unfollowees had too many followers to notice, (ii) Twitter did not offer a convenient interface to track it, and (iii) they themselves did not track who unfollowed them. Our follow-up question for these respondents is "If Twitter offers a feature to notify being unfollowed, would you still unfollow others?" Respondents replied that they would not be able to unfollow at least those who they knew in person.

We note that all respondents answered that they feel free to unfollow in Twitter compared to other OSNs, such as Facebook. Most respondents did not consider the followee's awareness seriously unless they were off-line friends or colleagues.

Company Accounts and Marketing Campaigns

Eight respondents answered that they have followed company accounts for marketing campaigns, and five of them kept following. The expectation for continual benefit was one of the reasons to keep following. One respondent stated:

> I love those events. I have followed a few company accounts. [After marketing campaigns end,] I do not unfollow them because they may do another marketing campaign in the near future. I unfollow company accounts only if they leave too many tweets. (Respondent #2)

Another reason was appreciation for an opportunity to win prizes. The rest of the three stated that they found no need to unfollow company accounts, because those accounts generated only a few tweets. All 5 respondents answered that they did not mind reading a few advertisement tweets occasionally, but all those users assured us that they would certainly unfollow company accounts if they leave burst tweets.

Twelve respondents answered that they have never followed company accounts conducting marketing campaigns. Their reasons were various. Some did not want to read even one advertisement tweet. They carefully chose whom to follow and did not want uninteresting tweets. Other respondents showed a strong sense of responsibility toward retweets. The most common form of a marketing campaign in Twitter is retweeting advertisement tweets, and respondents did not want to deliver an advertisement tweet to their own followers. These users retweeted only those tweets they deemed important enough to be disseminated broadly. Some of respondents stated that they did not like a lottery system for win prizes; they only participated in marketing campaigns where all participants received a gift.

Who Would You Unfollow Last

Finally we questioned participants on who would be the last ten people to unfollow. While Kwak *et al.* have highlighted that Twitter has the characteristics of news media rather than social networks, most respondents chose intimate friends as the last 10 people to unfollow. They wanted to read tweets of strong ties rather than those of informative sources. Even though the Korean Twitter network still has a low reciprocity hovering slightly over 50%, at its core the strong ties are what keeps the people connected. This evidence connects to the study of Huberman *et al.* [13]; they have revealed that each user has small number of friends, those who exchange at least two tweets, compared to declared followees. Some of respondents chose those who were role models to them, e.g. CEOs, politicians, and professors. They enjoy reading tweets capturing their role models' view. Only on Twitter they could access such information of their role models. Respondents stated that they found role models' tweets inspirational.

CONCLUSION

We have explored the dynamics of the unfollow behavior in Twitter. We collected daily snapshots of the online relationships of 1.2 million Korean-speaking users for 51 days and their all tweets. We observed the prevalent unfollow behavior in Twitter. We found that the major factors, including the reciprocity of the relationships, the period of the relationships, the followee's informativeness, and the overlap of the relationships, are crucial for the decision to unfollow. We conducted interview with 22 users to determine their motivation behind the unfollow behavior. The survey participants unfollowed those who left many tweets within a short time, created tweets about uninteresting topics, or tweeted about the mundane details of their lives.

ACKNOWLEDGEMENT

We are grateful to Hyunyoung Song, Alice Oh, Youn-kyung Lim, Sangjin Han, Seungyeop Han, Keon Jang, DK Lee, and Changhyun Lee for thoughtful feedback. We would like to thank all respondents for participating in survey. We also thank anonymous reviewers for their constructive and generous suggestions. This work was supported by the IT R&D program of MKE/KEIT [KI001878, "CASFI : High-Precision Measurement and Analysis Research"].

REFERENCES

1. Foursquare. `http://foursquare.com`.
2. Foursquare logs in Twitter. `http://twitter.com/#search?q=4sq.com`.

3. A.-L. Barabási and R. Albert. Emergence of scaling in random networks. *Science*, 286(5439):509–512, 1999.

4. M. Baum and A. Jamison. The Oprah effect: How soft news helps inattentive citizens vote consistently. *The Journal of Politics*, 68(4):946–959, 2006.

5. H. R. Bernard, P. Killworth, D. Kronenfeld, and L. Sailer. The problem of informant accuracy: The validity of retrospective data. *Ann. Rev. Anthropol.*, 13:495–517, 1984.

6. R. B. Cairns and B. D. Cairns. *Lifelines and Risks: Pathways of Youth in Our Time*. Cambridge, 1995.

7. H. Chun, H. Kwak, Y.-H. Eom, Y.-Y. Ahn, S. Moon, and H. Jeong. Comparison of online social relations in volume vs. interaction: A case study of Cyworld. In *Proc. IMC*, pages 57–70, 2008.

8. Economist.com. Primates on Facebook: Even online, the neocortex is the limit, `http://goo.gl/IxEsq`. *The Economist*, Feb 2009.

9. N. B. Ellison, C. Steinfield, and C. Lampe. The benefits of Facebook friends: social capital and college students use of online social network sites. *Journal of Computer-Mediated Communication*, 12(4):1143–1168, 2007.

10. Y.-H. Eom, C. Jeon, H. Jeong, and B. Kahng. Evolution of weighted scale-free networks in empirical data. *Phys. Rev. E*, 77(5):056105, 2008.

11. S. A. Golder and S. Yardi. Structural predictors of tie formation in Twitter: Transitivity and mutuality. *Proc. SOcialCom*, pages 88–95, 2010.

12. M. T. Hallinan and R. A. Williams. The stability of students' interraicial friendships. *American Sociological Review*, 52(5):653–664, 1987.

13. B. Huberman, D. M. Romero, and F. Wu. Social networks that matter: Twitter under the microscope. *First Monday*, 14(1-5), 2009.

14. A. Java, X. Song, T. Finin, and B. Tseng. Why we twitter: understanding microblogging usage and communities. In *Proc. KDD/SNA*, pages 56–65, 2007.

15. D. B. Kandel. Homophily, selection, and socialization in adolescent friendships. *American Journal of Sociology*, 84(2):427–436, 1978.

16. G. Kossinets and D. J. Watts. Origins of homophily in an evolving social network. *American Journal of Sociology*, 115(2):405–450, 2009.

17. R. Kumar, J. Novak, and A. Tomkins. Structure and evolution of online social networks. In *Proc. KDD*, pages 611–617, 2006.

18. H. Kwak, C. Lee, H. Park, and S. Moon. What is Twitter, a social network or a news media? In *Proc. WWW*, pages 591–600, 2010.

19. C. Lampe, N. B. Ellison, and C. Steinfield. Changes in use and perception of Facebook. In *Proc. CSCW*, pages 721–730, 2008.

20. K. Lerman and R. Ghosh. Information contagion: an empirical study of the spread of news on Digg and Twitter social networks. In *Proc. ICWSM*, 2010.

21. J. Leskovec, J. Kleinberg, and C. Faloutsos. Graphs over time: densification laws, shrinking diameters and possible explanations. In *Proc. SIGKDD*, pages 177–187, 2005.

22. D. Liben-Nowell and J. Kleinberg. The link-prediction problem for social networks. *Journal of the American Society for Information Science and Technology*, 58(7):1019–1031, 2007.

23. D. A. Menchik and X. Tian. Putting Social Context into Text: The Semiotics of E-mail Interaction. *American Journal of Sociology*, 114(2):332–370, 2008.

24. M. B. Miles and A. M. Huberman. *Qualitative Data Analysis: An Expanded Sourcebook*. SAGE Publications, 1994.

25. G. Mollenhorst. *Networks in contexts: How meeting opportunities affect personal relationships*. PhD thesis, University Utrecht, 2009.

26. J.-P. Onnela, J. Saramäki, J. Hyvönen, G. Szabó, D. Lazer, K. Kaski, J. Kertész, and A.-L. Barabási. Structure and tie strengths in mobile communication networks. *PNAS*, 104(18):7332–7336, 2007.

27. C. Steinfield, N. B. Ellison, and C. Lampe. Social capital, self-esteem, and use of online social network sites: A longitudinal analysis. *Journal of Applied Developmental Psychology*, 29(6):434 – 445, 2008.

28. S. T. Tong, B. Van Der Heide, L. Langwell, and J. B. Walther. Too much of a good thing? the relationship between number of friends and interpersonal impressions on facebook. *Journal of Computer-Mediated Communication*, 13(3):531–549, 2008.

29. Z. Tufekci. Who acquires friends hrough social media and why? "rich get richer" versus "seek and ye shall find". In *Proc. ICWSM*, 2010.

30. N. B. Tuma and M. T. Hallinan. The effects of sex, race, and achievement on schoolchildren's friendships. *Social Forces*, 57(4):1265–1285, 1979.

31. S. Wasserman and K. Faust. *Social Network Analysis: Methods and Applications*. Cambridge University Press, 1994.

32. J. Weng, E.-P. Lim, J. Jiang, and Q. He. TwitterRank: finding topic-sensitive influential twitterers. In *Proc. WSDM*, pages 261–270, 2010.

33. D. Zhao and M. B. Rosson. How and why people Twitter: the role that micro-blogging plays in informal communication at work. In *GROUP*, pages 243–252, 2009.

The Impact of Network Structure on Breaking Ties in Online Social Networks: Unfollowing on Twitter

Funda Kivran-Swaine, Priya Govindan and Mor Naaman
Rutgers University
funda@rutgers.edu, priyagn@cs.rutgers.edu, mor@rutgers.edu

ABSTRACT
We investigate the breaking of ties between individuals in the online social network of Twitter, a hugely popular social media service. Building on sociology concepts such as strength of ties, embeddedness, and status, we explore how network structure alone influences *tie breaks* – the common phenomena of an individual ceasing to "follow" another in Twitter's directed social network. We examine these relationships using a dataset of 245,586 Twitter "follow" edges, and the persistence of these edges after nine months. We show that structural properties of individuals and dyads at Time 1 have a significant effect on the existence of edges at Time 2, and connect these findings to the social theories that motivated the study.

Author Keywords
Social networks, tie breaks, social media, Twitter.

ACM Classification Keywords
H.5.0 [Information interfaces and presentation]: General

General Terms
Human Factors

INTRODUCTION
Many of today's popular Web applications and social media services, like Facebook, Twitter, or LinkedIn, are built on sets of contacts articulated by each user of the application. This contact list often drives the majority of user's activity in the system (e.g., users of *Social Awareness Streams* [12] like Twitter and Facebook see the stream of updates from their contacts when they log in). These contacts reflect various types of relationships, including friendship, kinship, common interests, attention, or information exchange. The aggregates of contact lists in each of these services result in immense, articulated *online social networks*. As these services shift the communication and information fabric of our society, the dynamics of the networks they support are important to understand and reason about in depth.

In particular, the articulated online social networks in these services change and evolve as individuals form new ties, or break existing ties to others. These structural changes, observed over time, are far from random, and depend on various factors that affect the relationship between the users. Most work in the Computer Science and HCI fields has focused on the dynamics and models of tie *creation* [5,9,13]. In particular, researchers considered the *structural* aspects of the social network that predict formation of ties [5,10,15]. Here, we also focus on the social network structure, but examine breaking and persistence of existing ties, rather than tie creation.

The topic of breaking and persistence of ties is exceedingly important. Tie breaks impact the dynamics and activity in online services over time, and, as we show below, are common on services like Twitter. Moreover, the act of "de-friending" in online social systems might impact social relationships within and beyond the online world, in part due to the articulated nature of the network, where the ties can be observed, and their nonexistence could be detected.

While a number of sociology studies have examined tie persistence and decay [1,2,11], the topic has not received enough attention even in the sociology field [1]. This gap is perhaps due to the lack of longitudinal data, or the fact that unlike online ties, social ties often decay rather than "formally" break, making measurement of the phenomena harder. The initial findings from sociology research, however, suggest that the structural aspects of individuals' social networks are strong determinants for persistence and decay of ties [1,11]. We now have an opportunity to examine these theories in online social networks, and at a scale that was not available before. The dynamics of these online networks may help us, then, to reason about other types of networks and social ties, and discover patterns that may shed light on social phenomena in different contexts.

We use two snapshots of the Twitter social network to study the breaking of ties. Twitter is founded on an articulated online network, and allows users to read updates from others that they "follow". Thus, users create a *directed* social network that reflects attention and transfer of information [5,7,12,13]. We borrow from sociology theory to frame our investigation of tie breaks and network structures using the concepts of tie strength, embeddedness as well as power and status. Our large-scale analysis uses information from 245,586 dyadic relationships on Twitter at Time 1, and the persistence or break of edges in these dyads by Time 2. The analysis aims to answer the following research question: *What structural social network properties of nodes and dyads predict the breaking of ties*?

THEORETICAL BACKGROUND

We build on several key sociology concepts that are likely to influence tie persistence and decay: *tie strength*, *embeddedness within networks*, and *power and status*. These concepts guide our choice of variables and models to use in the investigation. After providing the theoretical background, we explain the measurements and variables available from the Twitter data. We then connect the theoretic constructs to the results of the data analysis. Our examination is conducted in the context of a *dyad*: a relationship between two individuals A and B in the social network. However, note that we are interested in a *directed edge* in this dyad: an edge that indicates that one of the individuals in the dyad follows another.

Tie Strength Measures

Sociologists developed the concept of strength of ties [6] between individuals as a measure of their relationship. Stronger ties, such as family and close friends, offer emotional support and intimacy, while weaker ties may allow for exchange of novel information, or, for example, help in finding jobs. Tie decay is likely to be slower between people who share a strong tie [2]. As there are some indications that tie strength can be measured in social media data [4, 7], we expect the edges in dyads that exhibit greater tie strength to be less likely to break over time.

Embeddedness, Equivalence and Transitivity

In sociology, the *embeddedness* of a tie can be defined by the set of relationships that exists between the individuals in a dyad, through third parties (i.e., common friends). Embeddedness was shown to be a strong predictor of a tie's persistence over time in offline settings [11]. In addition, homophily plays an important role in retention of ties in networks [1], and homophily is connected to increased embeddedness as it is likely to manifest itself in dense, more transitive networks [13]. Related concepts to embeddedness for directed networks (like Twitter's) are inlink and outlink equivalence [14]. Measures of such equivalence are the common inlinks, people with direct ties to both individuals in the dyad, and common outlinks, people to whom both individuals in the dyad have directed ties. The common inlinks or outlinks suggest mutual interests [5], and support tie preservation.

Finally, the concept of transitivity captures another type of relationship individuals in the dyad have through third parties. Transitivity suggests that when individual A is connected to X, and X connects to B, it is likely that A and B will also be connected. The *triadic closure* is the process that drives transitivity. In the case of directed networks, A→X (e.g., A follows X on the Twitter network) and X→B, leads via the triadic closure process to A→B. Transitivity and triadic closure have been shown [5,10,13] to impact *creation* of ties on Twitter, and are likely to play a role in tie persistence as well. In summary, we expect the edges in dyads exhibiting greater embeddedness, inlink and outlink equivalence, or transitivity through third parties, to be less likely to break.

Power and Status

Dyadic relationships may exhibit different power relations [3], for example, due to different status or relative importance of the individuals (e.g., boss and employee). Status difference has been shown to effect tie persistence in work settings [1]. Online social networks may include both extrinsic and intrinsic measures of status and power relationships. For example, a boss and employee may be connected in an online social network (extrinsic); but two individuals may also be compared according to *prestige*, a status intrinsic to the online network and the activities within it. We anticipate the edges in dyads that exhibit greater difference in status or prestige to be more likely to break. We also expect for an edge to be less likely to break if the target individual in the edge holds greater prestige.

DATA

The key elements of our Twitter data are a set of randomly-selected seed nodes S, and, for each node $s \in S$, the nodes $f \in F_s$ that follow s on the Twitter social network. The dyads we examine are therefore (s, f) pairs of seeds and followers, where we know that an edge $s \leftarrow f$ (f follows s) existed in the Twitter network.

We consider two snapshots of the Twitter social network, from July 2009 (*Time 1*), and April 2010 (*Time 2*). The Time 1 snapshot is derived from complete Twitter social network as collected by Kwak et al. [8]. This snapshot was used to extract the ego-centric network data for the seed nodes in S, and the followers F_s for each node. The Time 2 snapshot was collected directly using the Twitter API, and was used to identify whether $s \leftarrow f$ follow relationships from Time 1 still exist, or whether f "unfollowed" s by Time 2.

The set S of seed nodes is described in [12] and includes 911 Twitter users that were randomly selected in April 2009, and who were identified as active, personal users of Twitter, not representing commercial entities or celebrities. We retrieved Time 1 and Time 2 data for 746 of these users whose Twitter profile was public at Time 2, and further removed users who had more than 5,000 followers or followees, reflecting our interest in the set of individuals that use Twitter for personal reasons. The final sample included 715 seeds, with a total of N=245,586 followers (343 per seed, on average). Out of these edges, 30.6% were dropped over the 9 months between Time 1 and 2. Seed nodes, on average, lost 39% of their original connections (SD=15%) demonstrating that the tie break phenomenon is significant in Twitter's online social network.

Computed Properties

As mentioned above, we focused our analysis on dyads where a seed s is followed by follower f ($s \leftarrow f$) in Time 1. We calculated the network properties of the seed, of the follower, and of the dyad as detailed next, and as listed in Table 1. We then examined how these properties affect the existence of the edge $s \leftarrow f$ at Time 2.

The *seed properties* include features such as the number of followers, the ratio of followers to followees, and the *reciprocity rate*: the ratio of connections the seed reciprocated to their followers. We also computed the seed's *follow-back* rate: the ratio of nodes followed by the seed that reciprocate a connection to them. The *follower properties* include the number of followers of *f*, and *f*'s ratio of followers to followees. In both seed and follower properties, we did not include the number of followees in the analysis as it is highly correlated with the number of followers. We calculated a number of *dyadic properties* for s and f. Reciprocity is a binary indicator of whether the connection between s and f was reciprocated, i.e. if the edge $s \to f$ was also present in the network in Time 1. For each dyad, we also counted the number of transitive relationships the two nodes belonged to with any third node X. For example, we use Right Transitivity to denote the number of nodes X such that there is a path $s \to X \to f$ at Time 1. The dyadic properties also include the number of common friends, followers, and neighbors between s and f. Finally, using the follower's perspective we calculated a simple "prestige ratio" between the two nodes in the dyad: the ratio of the number of followers of s to that of f.

METHOD

We use multilevel logistic regression to study the influence of the Time 1 properties of the seed, follower, and dyad on the breaking of the follow edge between follower and seed by Time 2. Our data includes many dyads that share the same seed node. In addition, various seed properties are unaccounted for, and may have a significant impact on likelihood of tie breaks (e.g., how "interesting" the seeds updates are). Therefore, we use multilevel logistic regression model, in which dyads *(s,f)* (level-1 units) are nested within seed nodes s (level-2 units). We calculated per-seed random intercept in order to account for seed nodes' inherent propensity to generate tie breaks. The analysis follows Golder & Yardi that used similar methods to investigate tie formation in experimental settings [5]. Importantly, we assume that beyond seed-level tendency, tie break decisions by different followers of the same seed are independent of each other; this assumption is likely to hold on Twitter where tie breaks are hard to detect by third parties. Finally, following [5], some variables had a power-law distribution and were log-transformed. We create three models to analyze the influence of the characteristics of seed, follower, and dyads on breaking of each follower-seed edge (our dependent variable). With Model 1 we look at the contribution of seed characteristics for explaining the tie breaks. We add follower properties as independent variables to construct Model 2, and the dyadic characteristics to create Model 3. The follower count of f is excluded from Model 3 as it had little effect in Model 2, and is directly determined by the newly added Prestige Ratio and s's followers count.

Results

The results are summarized in Table 1, reporting non-standardized coefficients, standard errors, and odds ratios for each model. Model 3 performed the best according to the Akaike's Information Criterion, and is our focus in the discussion below. Odds ratios are reported for easier interpretation of the magnitude of contribution of each variable. An odds ratio provides the increase in tie break odds for every one unit increase in the respective variable. For instance, odds ratio of 0.8 suggests that as the variable increases one unit, the odds of tie break decreases by 20% (e.g., from 1:2 to 1:2.5).

Predictors	Model 1		Model 2		Model 3	
Intercept	.80 *(.12)*	2.23 ***	1.63 *(.12)*	5.10 ***	.56 *(.13)*	.57 ***
Seed Properties						
^ Follower Count	-.30 *(.02)*	.74 ***	-.19 *(.02)*	.82 ***	.08 *(.02)*	1.08 ***
^ Ratio	-.09 *(.1)*	.91	-.08 *(.09)*	.92	-.07 *(.11)*	.93
^ Network Density	-.78 *(.07)*	.45 ***	-.55 *(.07)*	.57 ***	-.27 *(.08)*	.76 ***
Reciprocity Rate	-1.23 *(.19)*	.29 ***	-.70 *(.19)*	.49 ***	.50 *(.21)*	1.64 *
Follow-Back Rate	-.37 *(.16)*	.69 *	-.28 *(.15)*	.75 ◊	-.69 *(.17)*	.50 ***
Follower Properties						
^ Follower Count			-.06 *(.00)*	.94 ***	NA	NA
^ Ratio			-2.18 *(.02)*	.11 ***	-.81 *(.02)*	.44 ***
Edge (Dyad) Properties						
✦ Reciprocity					-.79 *(.01)*	.45 ***
^ Common Neighbors					-.33 *(.00)*	.71 ***
^ Common Followers					.05 *(.00)*	1.05 ***
^ Common Friends					.04 *(.00)*	1.04 ***
^ Right Transitivity					-.08 *(.00)*	.92 ***
^ Left Transitivity					-.03 *(.00)*	.97 ***
^ Mutual Transitivity					-.05 *(.00)*	.95 ***
^ Prestige Ratio					.06 *(.00)*	1.06 ***
Intercept Variance	.19 (SD=.44)		.17 (SD=.40)		.21 (SD=.46)	

◊ p<.10 * p<.05 ** p<.01 *** p<.001 (Standard errors are shown in parentheses.)
^ - variable was log-normalized ✦ - binary variable

Table 1. Effects (standardized coefficients and odds ratio) of seed, follower and dyadic properties on edge break (unfollow).

A number of variables had a negative effect on tie breaks in our results. Notably, the binary indicator for reciprocity had a large significant negative effect on tie breaks, the odds ratio indicating that s following back f decreases the odds of the breaking of the edge from f to s by 55%. (In the raw data, the break rate for reciprocated ties was 16.4%, while as many as 44.5% of unreciprocated ties broke by Time 2). The seed's follow-back rate also contributed significantly and negatively to all models, as well as the follower's follower-to-followee ratio. Further major negative effects were found for the seed's network density and the dyad's number of common neighbors.

The variables that had a positive affect on tie breaks included the seed's number of followers (the more followers s has, the more likely an edge to s is to be broken). However, that effect was minor and reversed from Model 1 and 2, suggesting that a negative effect of the number of followers might be mitigated by some of the dyadic features. Similarly, in Model 3 the seed's reciprocity rate had significant positive effect on tie break, reversed from Model 1 and 2, as the dyad-level reciprocity explains away reciprocity rate's negative effect. We discuss next what these findings suggest for our theoretical background.

DISCUSSION

Our results provide initial evidence that tie strength, status and embeddedness influence the breaking of ties.

A number of cues in our model illustrate the positive effect of tie strength on tie persistence. The large and negative effect of the dyadic reciprocity variable on tie break indicates that the reciprocity in dyadic relationship, which may indicate a stronger tie, is one of the most important factors for the persistence of the follower's edge. (We note, though, that while reciprocity *may* indicate strength of a tie [6], it is not a fully convincing measure in online networks [4, 7].) In addition, the results show that the odds of tie break decreases as *s*'s network gets denser. High density indicates intimate, tightly-knit networks, and ties between individuals in denser network are more likely to be strong.

Several indicators illustrate the connection between power and status, and breaking of ties. The prestige ratio between the follower and the seed contributes positively to the likelihood of a broken edge, pointing that the more "important" a follower is than the seed, the more likely the follower is to stop following that seed. The Follow-back rate is a potential measure of seed's status (in that users reciprocate connections to them), and its significant negative contribution in the final model suggests that the higher status of *s* mitigates tie break, even after controlling for *s*'s network size. Indeed, the negative effect of the follow-back rate on tie breaks may hint that this measure is a solid marker of status on Twitter. The two follower-to-followee ratio measures (for *s* and *f*) can also be considered proxies for status. While *s*'s follower-to-followee ratio did not significantly contribute to the model, the same ratio for *f* had a significant large negative effect, indicating that the higher the "status" of *f*, the less likely *f* is to break a tie, once he/she is already following *s*. Finally, a lack of a reciprocated edge to $f \leftarrow s$ may imply that *s* is in a more powerful location in the network than *f* (*s* may be an information source, or an authoritative figure). As reciprocity may be socially expected for relationships in Twitter, this imbalance might have even stronger consequences. The reciprocity effect, therefore, may also suggest that tie breaks are influenced by status differences between individuals in the dyad.

The influence of embeddedness on tie persistence is primarily marked by the effect of the common neighbors: the more common neighbors a dyad shares, the less likely the follow edge is to break. However, the effect of inlink and outlink equivalence is not quite evident, with minor and conflicting effects for the number of common followers and friends of the seed and follower. This outcome is perhaps due to the relationships between the equivalence measure variables. The minor, but significant negative effect of the transitivity variables may be because of other factors such as network density and reciprocity being more influential over tie breaks, and thus eliminating the effect of the various embeddedness and transitivity dyadic measures.

SUMMARY AND CONCLUSIONS

We have shown that network structure alone can significantly help explain the breaking and persistence of ties in Twitter's online social network. We connected these findings to sociological concepts that may be at the root of the tie break phenomenon, such as strength of ties and status. In future work, we would like to further explore the phenomenon of tie breaks using additional variables such as content characteristics, for a better operationalization of the sociological concepts. (We may even do a qualitative study!) At the same time, our findings already provide insights for systems or applications that build on online social networks, which account for a large proportion of activity on the Web today.

ACKNOWLEDGEMENTS

We would like to thank Scott Golder for his help and feedback. We also thank Yotam Margalit for support that cannot be quantitatively measured. This work is partially supported by a Google Research Award (thanks, Google).

REFERENCES

1. Burt, R. Decay functions. *Soc. Networks* 22:1–28. 2000.
2. Burt, R. Bridge decay. *Soc. Networks* 24:333–63. 2002.
3. Emerson, R.M. Power-dependence relations. *American Sociological Review*, 27(1):31–41. 1962.
4. Gilbert, E. and Karahalios, K. Predicting tie strength with social media. *Proc., CHI 2009*.
5. Golder, S. A. and Yardi, S. Structural predictors of tie formation in twitter: Transitivity and mutuality. *Proc., IEEE Social Computing 2010*.
6. Granovetter, M. S. The strength of weak ties. *American Journal of Sociology,* 78(6):1360–1380. 1973.
7. Huberman, B., Romero, D. M., and Wu, F. Social networks that matter: Twitter under the microscope. *First Monday*, 14(1). 2009.
8. Kwak, H., Lee, C., Park, H., and Moon, S. What is Twitter, a social network or a news media? *Proc., WWW 2010*.
9. Leskovec, J., Huttenlocher, D., and Kleinberg, J. Signed networks in social media. *Proc., CHI 2010*.
10. Liben-Nowell, D. and Kleinberg, J. The link-prediction problem for social networks. *J. Am. Soc. Inf. Sci. Technol.*, 58(7):1019–1031. 2007.
11. Martin, J. L. and Yeung, K.-T. Persistence of close personal ties over a 12-year period. *Soc. Networks* 28:331–362. 2006.
12. Naaman, M., Boase, J., and Lai, C.-H. Is it really about me? Message content in social awareness streams. *Proc., CSCW 2010*.
13. Romero, D.M., and Kleinberg, J. The directed closure process in information networks with an analysis of link formation on twitter. *Proc., ICWSM 2010*.
14. Wasserman, S. and Faust, K. Social network analysis: Methods and applications. Cambridge Univ. Press. 1994
15. Zheleva, E., Getoor, L., Golbeck, J., and Kuter, U. Using friendship ties and family circles for link prediction. *Proc., SNA-KDD 2008*.

Computing Political Preference among Twitter Followers

Jennifer Golbeck
Human-Computer Interaction Lab
College of Information Studies
University of Maryland
College Park, MD 20742
jgolbeck@umd.edu

Derek L. Hansen
CASCI, Human-Computer Interaction Lab
College of Information Studies
University of Maryland
College Park, MD 20742
dlhansen@umd.edu

ABSTRACT
There is great interest in understanding media bias and political information seeking preferences. As many media outlets create online personas, we seek to automatically estimate the political preferences of their audience, rather than of the outlet itself. In this paper, we present a novel method for computing preference among an organization's Twitter followers. We present an application of this technique to estimate political preference of the audiences of U.S. media outlets. We also discuss how these results may be used and extended.

Author Keywords
Twitter, politics, liberal, conservative, news, journalism

ACM Classification Keywords
H5.m. Information interfaces and presentation (e.g., HCI): Miscellaneous.

General Terms
Human Factors

INTRODUCTION
As major media outlets establish online presences in social media, understanding the characteristics of those audiences is an important task. It has implications for how information is presented in this environment where personalization is expected. Furthermore, it can provide valuable information to marketers and social media analysts.

As a first step toward understanding audiences, we present a technique for estimating audience preferences in a given domain on the microblogging service Twitter. We use U.S. politics as our motivating example by estimating the political preferences of media outlets' audiences.

BACKGROUND
While we are not studying media bias, but rather the political preferences of audiences, it is worth briefly discussing the extensive research on analyzing media bias.

A subset of this work uses automated methods to infer liberal/conservative bias of news stories and outlets. These automated methods do not depend on subjective measurements of bias, although the specific techniques used to infer bias can be problematic and are highly contested. One approach is to compute a media bias score based on citations in the news story – news outlets that cite "think tanks" that are also cited by Congressperson's with a known liberal bias are assumed to be more liberal [8]. Another approach is to compare keywords and phrases used by Congresspeople of known political persuasions with those used in news articles – news outlets that use terms like "death tax" and "illegal immigration" are more likely to be conservative [7]. A final approach assigns a liberal/conservative score to web documents based on the number of times they are co-cited with other web documents that have a known political bias [3].

In contrast to these approaches, we estimate the political preferences of news outlet audiences, not the news outlet content itself. Our strategy is similar to [8] in that we use Congresspeople's American for Democratic Action's (ADA) scores as a starting point for our scoring; however, we use Twitter Follow relationships rather than article citations. Using Follow relationships avoids the concern with [8] that results rely too much on the citation practices of journalists and Congresspeople. Our approach does not require coding of data (as in [8]) or access to large corpuses of news stories and congressional speeches; it relies instead on freely available and open access data from Twitter.

METHOD AND SAMPLING
Unlike [8], we are not interested in predicting media bias. Instead, we are interested in predicting the political preference of the *audience* of different media outlets and organizations by using sites like Twitter that embed social ties. Our examples and applications are in the political domain, but the technique is generalizable when the right background information is available. Our approach includes the following steps:

Step 1: Apply known scores to a seed group, in this case Congresspeople using Twitter. The base data of liberal/conservative scores are obtained from Americans for Democratic Action (ADA), who puts out an annual report that considers the voting record of members of Congress [1]. ADA defines a key set of votes that indicate liberal and conservative positions, and uses the Congressperson's voting record to assign each a score. The most liberal score is a 1.0, and the most conservative is 0.0. This is a widely accepted measure of political position. We apply the 2009 ADA ratings to the 111th Congress members.

Step 2: Map the scores of the seed group onto their followers. We collect the list of followers for each member of Congress on Twitter (i.e., Congress Followers). An inferred political preference score (P Score) for each Congress Follower is computed as the simple average of the ADA scores for all Congresspeople he or she follows. Our approach relies on the assumption that people's political preferences will, on average, reflect those of the Congresspeople they follow. Prior literature on "selective exposure" to political information suggests this assumption is reasonable since people seek after information from those with similar political views [4, 5]. We tested this assumption in the Twitter context by surveying a convenience sample (recruited via Twitter and email by the authors and friends) of 47 subjects who follow politicians on Twitter. Of those, 66% stated that the politicians they follow "mostly share [their] political views", while only 4% follow politicians who "mostly hold political views that oppose [their] own." The remaining 30% reported following a mix of both, with an average of 56% of the politicians they follow sharing their own views. Thus, overall, users tend to follow politicians with similar views; even when there is a mix of political views, those that match the user's views tend to dominate. These preliminary results suggest that our assignment of a P Score to congressional followers is a reasonable approximation of real political preference. An adjusted P Score could be computed based on data from more comprehensive surveys that compare self-reported liberal/conservative scores with inferred P Scores.

Step 3: Map the inferred scores of the seed group followers (i.e., Congress Followers) onto the target of the investigation, in this case the Twitter accounts of media outlets. A simple approach is to assign the average of the liberal/conservative scores of all Congress Followers who also follow the target media outlet. However, this approach raises a problem: Twitter users may not represent the population well.

Indeed, on Twitter Republican members of Congress significantly outnumber members who are Democrats (127 to 103), though Democrats outnumber Republicans in the 111th Congress. Furthermore, Republican Twitter users tend to have disproportionately more followers than Democrats. Even excluding John McCain, who has over 1.7 million followers as a result of the 2008 Presidential election (more than 30 times the next most followed member of Congress and nearly double the total number of followers of all other Congresspeople), the sum of Republican followers is 581,997, compared to 291,050 for Democrats. As a result, the pool of Congress Followers is significantly biased toward conservatives.

Without any adjustment, the audiences of news outlets will incorrectly appear more conservative. Our solution is to selectively sample Congress Followers so they more closely match the roughly equal ratio of Republicans and Democrats in the general population, minimizing the effect of the initial selection bias. John McCain was excluded as an outlier because his Presidential run makes him a particularly abnormal and overly influential data point.

Congresspeople were broken into groups by the number of followers they had: over 10,000, 5,000, 1,000, 500, 100, 50, and 10. Within each group, we randomly selected equal numbers of Republican and Democratic representatives until we had the maximum number for the least represented group. We chose equal numbers from each party since in recent elections there are roughly equal numbers in Congress. For each selected Congressperson, we randomly selected the number of followers equal to the group in which he was a member (e.g. for a Congressperson from the "over 1,000" group, we selected 1,000 random followers).

To compute the final media audience P Scores, we used a 10-fold validation; we drew 10 samples using this technique, computed the P Score for each media audience using each sample, and averaged the scores across samples.

CONGRESS FOLLOWER SCORES

Figure 1 shows a distribution of scores for all Congress Followers, as well as the distribution of ADA scores for all Congresspeople (not just those on Twitter).

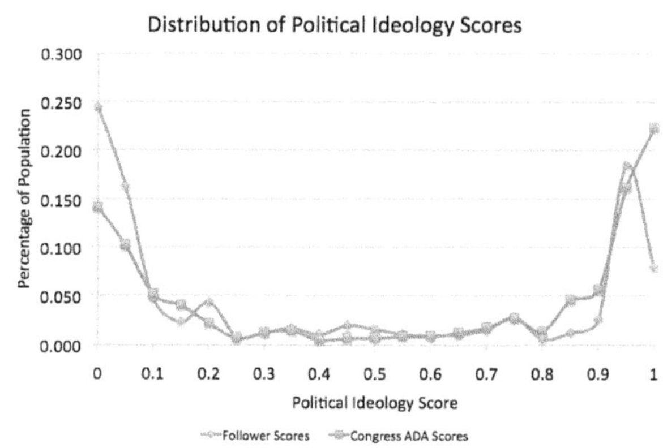

Figure 1. The distribution of P Scores among all Congress Followers and ADA scores for Congresspeople. A score of 0.5 is moderate, 0.0 is very conservative and 1.0 is very liberal.

The distribution of scores among the Congress Followers and the sampled follower population is strongly bimodal, since it is based upon the congressional ADA scores which are bimodal. This is in contrast to other evidence that suggests the distribution of political ideologies among the general public is a more normal distribution, with most of the population as moderate [6]. This discrepancy may arise from two sources. First, followers of Congresspeople may not share the views of those they follow, although our survey and prior "selective exposure" literature makes this unlikely.

Media Outlet	Twitter User ID	Total Followers	Avg. % of Total Followers sampled	Avg. P Score
Fox News	foxnews	266,121	7.33%	0.26
The Drudge Report	Drudge_Report	102,981	20.52%	0.27
Washington Times	washtimes	13,545	33.75%	0.29
Wall Street Journal	WSJ	392,332	5.75%	0.41
US News & World Report	usnews	7,836	28.60%	0.49
The L.A. Times	latimes	72,296	9.91%	0.51
USA Today	USATODAY	63,714	9.90%	0.51
Good Morning America	gma	1,698,875	0.72%	0.51
The News Hour	NewsHour	54,787	12.79%	0.52
CBS News	CBSNews	1,578,599	0.94%	0.53
Newsweek	Newsweek	1,256,536	1.25%	0.54
Washington Post	washingtonpost	154,400	9.51%	0.54
The Today Show	todayshow	629,088	1.89%	0.55
The Early Show	theearlyshow	12,628	11.16%	0.55
Time Magazine	TIME	2,134,411	0.99%	0.57
ABC World News	abcworldnews	12,973	14.93%	0.57
CNN Breaking News	Cnnbrk	3,314,716	1.40%	0.58
NBC Nightly News	nbcnightlynews	27,137	16.85%	0.58
The New York Times	nytimes	2,553,291	1.40%	0.60
Morning Edition (NPR)	MorningEdition	6,146	17.22%	0.66

Table 1. The average audience P Scores for the twenty popular media outlets studied in [8]. Averages are computed over 10 randomly drawn samples using the sampling method described above. Results are sorted from most conservative to most liberal.

Second, those who follow Congresspeople on Twitter may have more polarized political tendencies than the overall US population. This is likely the case, as those who actively decide to follow a Congressperson are likely more politically aware and active, characteristics that are often accompanied by more extreme political tendencies. If this is true, our estimated audience political preference scores for media outlets will rely on the Twitter follow practices of "politically savvy users" rather than the general population. This is not necessarily problematic, although it does impact the meaning of the P Scores. In our political example with the bi-modal distribution, the Avg. P Score for a media outlet is roughly equivalent to the ratio of "political savvy" liberals and conservatives that follow that news outlet.

MEDIA AUDIENCES' POLITICAL PREFERENCE

Our first application of this method was to estimate the audiences' political preferences, through their P Scores, of the same popular media outlets evaluated in [8]. Table 1 shows the audience bias scores along with the percentage of each outlet's followers who were considered when computing the value.

For traditionally conservative outlets [9], such as Fox News [2], we found audiences with correspondingly conservative P Scores: Fox News (0.256), the Drudge Report (0.265), and the Washington Times (0.290). There are no outlets with audiences that have P Scores that are liberal to the same extent that these are conservative, but some liberal preference is visible in the audiences of outlets like the New York Times (0.604) (considered to be liberal leaning [9, 11]) and NPR's Morning Edition (0.659).

The vast majority of these media outlets' audiences – 15 out of 20 – fall between the moderate scores of 0.4 and 0.6. Half are even closer to the midpoint, falling within 0.05 of the perfect moderate 0.5 value. This suggests that most media outlets audiences have roughly equal numbers of liberal and conservative Congress Followers.

Our findings of audience preference are similar to the estimates of political orientation of media outlets found in [3], which used co-citation of hyperlinks to infer political orientation of web documents and their associated news outlets. Although, the scales differ, like [3] we found that the Wall Street Journal and The New York Times equally deviated from the middle in opposite directions (conservative and liberal respectively). This similarity may come from the fact that [3] relies partially on news outlet audiences by using website linking behavior. Our method provides a more direct estimate of audience political preferences by focusing on follower relationships.

Note that these scores do not imply that the outlets themselves present news in a way that reflects their audience's political preferences.

DISCUSSION

There are a number of implications and areas for future work that follow from these results. Many users expect personalized web-based content. Some personalization comes from the structure of the services themselves (e.g. who users choose to follow on Twitter affects which tweets they see). However, there are many opportunities to further personalize and enhance the way information is presented.

Understanding the political preference of an audience can be important for presenting tailored information (including or excluding information according to the user's tastes) and personalizing the user's experience (e.g. through recommender systems). For example, an audience's political preference can be used as input into recommender systems. In collaborative filtering systems, items are recommended by finding people with tastes similar to the user and recommending things those people like. In this context, if we know a user's political preferences, we can find media outlets that have audiences with a similar preference, mimicking the basic idea behind collaborative filtering. Tweets (or information provided on other social media sites) can be highlighted, filtered out, or sorted based on the similarity of their audiences' political preferences to those of the user. Alternatively, our method could be used to help recommend tweets commonly read by people on both sides of the political spectrum reducing homophily [10]. Finally, marketers and analysts can use our method to measure their Twitter reach within different political markets to see if they are reaching their intended audience.

Outside of personalization, this technique may have applications for studying media bias in social media. While we have set out to estimate audience political preference, not media bias, previous work has shown that news consumers have a significant preference for like-minded media outlets [4, 5] and use new social media tools to actively seek out those with similar views. This implies that people may choose a media outlet because its presentation of the news reflects their own political beliefs, and thus the preference of an audience may generally reflect the bias of the outlet. While we do not have evidence to support this connection, predicting media bias based on audience preferences is an area for future research.

Finally, while we have used political preference and media outlets as our example case, we believe this technique is applicable in other domains. We have begun to use this technique to estimage the political preferences of Twitter audiences of government agencies, think tanks, political organizations, and individuals. It could also be used for non-political analysis. For example, a similar analysis could be done using the Green Scores that rate how environmentally responsible companies are. These could be used to create an environmental score for Twitter followers of organizations, politicians, and other Twitter accounts.

CONCLUSION

In this paper, we have presented a technique for estimating the political preferences of Twitter account followers. Using the political domain as our motivating example, we present a method that uses the follower connections in the Twitter network to propagate liberal/conservative scores from members of Congress to Congress Followers and then to audiences of media outlets. Our results show that the estimated political preferences of media outlets' audiences reflect the liberal/conservative leanings of the media outlets as presented in prior literature.

The results have potential applications for motivating new interface personalization techniques, understanding media bias, and for detecting other types of audience preferences in different domains. There is much future work to be done in this space and we hope this initial work serves as motivation to pursue those issues.

ACKNOWLEDGMENTS

Thanks to members of the University of Maryland's Human Computer Interaction Lab (HCIL) for their helpful comments on an earlier draft.

REFERENCES

1. Americans for Democratic Action. Annual Voting Records, 2009. Available at http://www.adaction.org/

2. DellaVigna, S. and Kaplan, E. The Fox News Effect: Media Bias and Voting. *Quarterly Journal of Economics, 122*, 3 (2007), 1187-1234.

3. Efron, M. 2004. The liberal media and right-wing conspiracies: using cocitation information to estimate political orientation in web documents. In *Proceedings of CIKM'04.* (Washington, D.C., November 2004), ACM Press, 390-398.

4. Frey, D. Recent research on selective exposure to information. *Advances in experimental social psychology*, 19, 1986.

5. Garret, K. Politically Motivated Reinforcement Seeking: Reframing the Selective Exposure Debate. *Journal of Communications, 59*, 4 (December 2009), 676-699.

6. Gelman, A. *Red state, blue state, rich state, poor state: why Americans vote the way they do*. Princeton Univ Press, Princeton NJ, 2008.

7. Gentzkow, M. and Shapiro, J. What drives media slant? Evidence from US daily newspapers. *Econometrica, 78*, 1 (2010), 35–71.

8. Groseclose, T. and Milyo, J. A Measure of Media Bias. *The Quarterly Journal of Economics, 120*, 4 (2005), 1191–1237.

9. Mondo Times: The worldwide news media directory. Available at http://www.mondotimes.com

10. Munson, S. A. and Resnick, P. 2010. Presenting diverse political opinions: how and how much. In *Proceedings of CHI'10*. (Atlanta, GA, April 2010). ACM Press, 1457-1466.

11. Puglisi, R. Being the New York Times: The Political Behaviour of a Newspaper. Available at SSRN: http://ssrn.com/abstract=573801

Online Contribution Practices in Countries that Engage in Internet Blocking and Censorship

Irina Shklovski
IT University of Copenhagen
Rued Langgaards Vej 7
2300 Copenhagen S, Denmark
irsh@itu.dk

Nalini P. Kotamraju
IT University of Copenhagen
Rued Langgaards Vej 7
2300 Copenhagen S, Denmark
kotamraju@itu.dk

ABSTRACT
In this article we describe people's online contribution practices in contexts in which the government actively blocks access to or censors the Internet. We argue that people experience blocking as confusing, as a motivation for self-censorship online, as a cause of impoverishment of available content and as a real threat of personal persecution. Challenging ideas of blocking as a monolithic, abstract policy, we discuss five strategies with which Internet users navigate blocking: self-censorship, cultivating technical savvy, reliance on social ties to relay blocked content, use of already blocked sites for content production as a form of protection and practiced transparency. We also discuss strategies that forum owners and blogging platform providers employ to deal with and to avoid blocking. We conclude by advocating for more research that acknowledges the complexity of the contexts in which all Internet users contribute to the Internet and social media.

Author Keywords
Internet censorship, blocking, motivation, contribution, government, Internet non-use, Internet use, lurkers, online communities, social media, ethnography

ACM Classification Keywords
K.4 [Computing Milieux] Computers and Society; H.5.m [Information Systems and Presentation] Miscellaneous

General Terms
Human Factors

INTRODUCTION
The Internet's very existence depends on people's contributions of words, images, and video. Many popular social media–blogs, discussion forums, image, music and video-sharing sites like Flickr or YouTube, and, of course, Wikipedia–rely on people's willingness and ability to contribute content. People's contributions are the backbone of user-generated content sites and much of the Internet.

However, the importance of the small fraction of Internet users who are active contributors to social media places them at the center of research about how people use online communities, and engage in blogging and other digital practices. Understanding the reasons and contexts in which people contribute to social media is of utmost importance to people who design, provide content for, and use the Internet and social media. The individualized motivations of active contributors have been studied across a range of domains in a diverse set of social media, most often drawing on theories of psychology and communication.

Individualized approaches to understanding contribution practices tend to be insensitive to context. They tend to assume that contributors face few, if any, structural consequences as a result of their contributions. People's willingness and ability to contribute to social media, however, are also shaped by their contexts, and, in particular, their relationship to the state. In countries with strong protection of freedom of speech and relatively democratic legal systems, the negative potential consequences are relatively slight: loss of a job for inappropriate postings or merely social embarrassment. For much of the rest of the world, however, the negative potential consequences–whether actual or perceived–are far greater.

In this article we describe people's contribution practices in contexts in which the state actively censors Internet use through blocking access to Internet resources. Blocking of Internet web sites is commonly discussed as a technical phenomenon, using techniques such as DNS tampering and IP and URL blocking using a proxy [17]. Our research, however, indicates that people who live in countries with extensive Internet censorship, experience blocking as a complex phenomenon that shapes their decisions about and attitudes toward contributing to social media.

In many countries where populations are just recently starting to utilize the Internet, state governments tend to see the development of locally grown Internet resources as national projects. Governments make investments into the infrastructure and fund Internet entrepreneurship, supporting the development of locally relevant social media tools that often depend on user contributions to survive. At the same time, many governments monitor the content produced by their citizens and engage in extensive censorship. These mixed signals usually do not deter Internet users in these countries from accessing the Internet, but we argue that such state actions influence what Internet users access and how and whether they contribute online.

WHY PEOPLE CONTRIBUTE (& NOT) TO SOCIAL MEDIA

Research about why people contribute to social media does not coalesce into a coherent, definitive list. The significance of individual and social motivations–both intrinsic and extrinsic–differ, as others have noted [26], along numerous axes. The form of social media (e.g., video vs. web blog [22]), the nature of an initial encounter with a social network [1], the technology's ease-of-use [8], the content domain (e.g. contributions in medical versus technical support online groups [15]), whether contributions on an online encyclopedia are directed between users or to the community at large [12], and, of course, people's socio-economic characteristics [6], have all been identified as explanatory variables in people's contribution practices.

Most users of the Internet do not contribute content or material. By default most people participate in social media as recipients or consumers of content created by other people. In fact, in most social media, a minority of people creates the majority of the content or contributes most actively. A small number of members or participants in online discussion groups post messages [19], a minority create content for user-generated encyclopedias [12], more people read blogs than have them, and following on Twitter is far more common than sending tweets.

Research about why people do not contribute on the Internet [15,19], as well as what it means to be a user of the Internet [20,21,23,25,28] has appropriately added complexity to the understandings of contribution, sharing, and the very idea of a participatory culture. Empirical research has dispelled [15,19] the idea that people who participate in but do not post in online communities–nonpublic participants [15] or so-called lurkers–are simply selfish free riders. Rather, people choose not to contribute for myriad reasons, including wanting more information about the group first, shyness, feelings that they have nothing worth contributing or, often, the sense that reading and browsing satisfies their goals and needs [15,19].

The majority of Internet (and social media research) assumes that people make decisions to contribute in contexts in which they are free, willing and voluntarily able to do so, with few non-psychological consequences. The typical theories (e.g., uses and gratifications theory) and survey questionnaire items reflect and reinforce this assumption.[1] We argue that what has also regularly been overlooked in research about online contribution is that any decision to contribute to social media takes place in a context shaped not only by individual and organizational motivations, but also by the laws and policies of states, often in tandem with technology and telecommunication companies. For people in countries with strong legal protection of speech and ideas, this fact has gone unnoticed and unremarked upon. People in these contexts, for the most part, feel "free" to contribute to the Internet, and the negative repercussions to their lives are slight and rare, such as dismissal from a job or legal fines. For an increasing number of people worldwide, however, their social media contribution practices are less free from repercussions and are shaped by another force: the practice of censorship through the blocking of web sites by the state.

[1] One challenge to these assumptions is research highlighting possible structural obstacles to contribution and participation, such as the continuing existence of a digital divide in terms of access or in terms of digital skills [23] or digital literacy [5].

BLOCKING & CENSORSHIP

The practice of blocking

Blocking is beginning to receive some attention by research communities. As a research object, blocking is most often approached in three ways: as a technical practice, as a policy-level phenomenon, or in connection with political activism online. From a technical viewpoint, blocking is discussed as existing techniques to restrict access to web sites and to circumvent these restrictions [17]. At a policy level, blocking is often construed as part of State media policies, control practices and legislative frameworks [11,16]. Another approach highlights how people circumvent blocking usually in the name of political activism, using technologies to stage or facilitate government protests [2,13,14,30]. Regular users' practices under such conditions–how they experience and navigate blocking–are rarely discussed in the literature, though for many people censorship is a common factor in their Internet use. As countries worldwide add the Internet to their list of capabilities, they bring with them their own ideas and ideologies about how their own citizens ought to navigate the Internet [10]. Many of these ideas and ideologies get translated into methods of control, censorship and site blocking reminiscent of the much-debated approaches used in the Middle East [7] or China [13,14,29,30]. In this article we discuss our findings about how people experience blocking "on the ground" and how blocking and censorship figure into online contribution practices.

Note on Ethics of this Research Study

Issues of blocking and censorship are sensitive topics often seen as inappropriate for discussion in countries where such practices are prevalent. The data reported here are derived from an ongoing project in a country where these practices are present but are perceived as politically sensitive and inexpedient for open discussion. In the course of data collection, all participants were provided with a study information sheet and were informed of potential risks from participating in the study. We had intended to follow the accepted confidential treatment of the data by anonymizing participants in the course of publication. However, the IT community under study was sufficiently small where by simply identifying the fieldsite, we would have violated collective anonymity [24], making it simple for community members to identify individual respondents despite accepted anonymization practices.

In an effort to protect the respondents who graciously agreed to be a part of this project and the integrity of the project itself, we have chosen to anonymize the name of the country described in these pages and to call it The Country. We do not cite any of the local news and scholarly sources in The Country that, while providing support for some of the statements made in this article, would immediately identify the location in question. We realize that such anonymization efforts do not completely protect the authors or the people involved, however a good faith effort can produce sufficient barriers to limit potential harm.

The National Context Under Study

The country under study can be construed as a digitally nascent State [27] with less than 30% of the population on the Internet, although technology adoption is rapidly growing due to decreases in prices for broadband and mobile access. With increases in user base, The Country is quickly developing its own Internet infrastructure and resources in languages spoken by its population.

Internet users in The Country tend to perceive the Internet as a series of differentiated nationalistic spaces with themselves located in the local national Internet space. The government of The Country engages in a broad effort to support what it sees as the development of the national space on the Internet, funding products and services that are locally produced. From the user's point of view, the national Internet space is defined through the country-code top-level domain (ccTLD)[2] and through local content and its visibility. The localness can also be signaled by some part of the URL outside the ccTLD as sites often sport either a city- or the country name somewhere in the URL.

According to the official domain name registration rules of The Country, a site that has a second-level domain within the national Internet address space has to be hosted on the territory of The Country. Each country designs the specific policies under which it administers ccTLDs[3]. The resources available in what is considered the national Internet space signal their affiliation either through obtaining a URL with the relevant ccTLD or, if they are not granted the ccTLD usually for reasons of blocking, history or content, by other indications in the URLs and through presentation of local content. For example, several oppositional news sources are housed on servers in other countries. These resources have not been able to obtain the relevant ccTLD due to government resistance and threats of persecution. However, these news sources retain the name of The Country as part of their URLs to signal their affiliation.

Although no official list or a clear set of rules establishes which sites are allowed or disallowed in The Country, the blocking of sites is rampant and known to the users. A popular worldwide blogging platform is currently the only site that is officially blocked by a court ruling. Other sites are often blocked for arbitrary periods of time by the main Internet provider, which is owned by the state-controlled telecom. For example, a popular video sharing site and a microblogging site were blocked with no warning or explanation for about 2-3 days in 2010 and then unblocked just as swiftly.

While blocking and censorship have been discussed in the literature on the technical, policy, and political activism [4,12,14,29] little of this research has considered how users that live in countries that censor the Internet might develop strategies to deal with blocking and how the twin threats of blocking and censorship may affect their online content contribution practices.

METHOD

The research presented here is part of an ongoing research project that investigates how people in The Country use the Internet and other communication technologies for communication and information seeking purposes and how these technologies are being integrated into everyday practices. The first author conducted semi-structured interviews, focus groups and many hours of informal conversations and observations in three different cities in The Country over the course of seven weeks in the spring of 2009 and in the spring of 2010. Interview and focus group participants were recruited using snowball sampling initially seeded through personal contacts or encounters in Internet cafés and public spaces. The interviews were conducted in the native language, and lasted between 30 and 60 minutes each, usually in a location of the interviewees choosing. Informal conversations and observations were conducted in the course of visiting and participating in IT-related and educational events in order to get a sense of discussions around IT-related issues and online contributions. The majority of conversations centered on communication and information seeking practices as well as any contributions in the form of blogging or posts on discussion forum spaces. We focused on urban centers, as levels of Internet penetration in rural areas at this time were negligible. Thus the results of this research apply to urban population only.

Participants

Our sample of 49 included 38 individual interviews and two focus groups. Nineteen of the interviewees were directly engaged in IT-related activities or policy debates, and the rest were people of varying socio-economic status and backgrounds with no direct professional connection to the IT industry. We interviewed IT professionals and Internet

[2] Each country has a unique two-character abbreviation which is appended at the end of the domain name (eg .us for US, .de for Germany, .uk for United Kingdom, .cm for Cameroon, etc)

[3] See the IANA TLD Delegation Practices Document (ICP-1) http://www.icann.org/icp/icp-1.htm

resource developers, prominent local bloggers, forum moderators and Internet policy advisors. The sample included 25 men and 24 women, aged 18 to 62 (average 35). All but two were native to The Country.

In the course of the fieldwork a pattern emerged wherein participants and informants tended to talk more openly about blocking and their fears about online contributions, as well as engaged in more political discussions once the recorder was turned off and the notebook was put away. These observations, informal conversation and post-interview discussions were noted and paraphrased in memos and field notes after the fact and constitute part of the data on which we base our analysis.

Data Analysis

All interviews were audio-recorded and transcribed. Following the methods of qualitative data analysis suggested by Emerson and colleagues [3] we developed a coding scheme based on open coding of transcripts, memos and field notes. Our initial purpose was to investigate the strategies users develop to deal with State blocking of Internet resources, whether or not they contributed content online and how fears of State persecution may figure into their decision making and Internet use practices. Relevant references from each transcript were combined and summarized to form a coherent narrative for each theme. These summaries then provided an analytical overview. All quotes presented here were translated. Names and initials were changed to a random numbering of respondents in order to preserve confidentiality. Given the sensitivity of the topics discussed, we do not present additional information about respondents, such as their location at the time of interview, background or occupation.

EXPERIENCES OF BLOCKING AND CENSORSHIP

Participants in our study experienced blocking and censorship in a variety of ways: as something confusing and difficult to comprehend, as something that inspired self-censorship online, as a cause of an impoverishment of available content and as a threat of real personal persecution. Some of these experiences were shared across respondents and some were unique, depending on where they lived and what activities they engaged in on the Internet. Moreover, owners of forums and blog platforms experienced blocking and censorship as reasons for instituting oversight and heavy moderation on their sites. We begin this section however, with discussing how State blocking and censorship practices were in part responsible for delineating State boundaries online and for the creation of a national Internet space that was clearly identifiable to the state citizens.

National Internet space

In 2009 the agency of information and communication of The Country released an official report that made recommendations to develop resources in the national internet space, recognizing the importance of local content, improvements in telecommunication infrastructure and reduction of the digital divide through education and promotion. A large proportion of government support went toward two specific projects – implementation of the electronic government, and promotion and development of resources and content in the national Internet space through provision of support to internet-based businesses (*from field notes*). In early 2010 the agency was disbanded and management of internet-related issues moved under the umbrella of the Ministry of Information. As a result the government took an even more overtly active role in promotion and control of internet-related issues. A newly appointed minister conducted formal meetings with entrepreneurs and owners of leading Internet businesses in The Country and participated in a series of open forums discussing the issues faced by the developers of local content in the national Internet space.

These actions did not simply increase government involvement, but they were a response to something the majority of people we spoke to in the course of this study pointed out time and again: "*You know,* [national Internet space] *is simply empty. There is nothing there, just torrents and downloads*." (R1)

The government and the businesses involved realized that in order to accomplish the development of what they and the users saw as the national space on the Internet, they had to encourage regular Internet users in The Country to produce content. However, the government also pursued a conflicting goal of controlling certain types of speech on the Internet. Mixed signals from the government–encouraging and yet controlling content–generated a fair bit of skepticism among Internet users in The Country about the viability of this national Internet project.

As one active blogger commented: "*No, they want it so that everything is in the* [National] *domain. On one hand that's a good thing, that's development of* [national Internet space]*, but they should make it worth our while*." (R2)

"They" in the quote above, of course, refers to the government and its stated goals. The question remained, however, how the government might make being part of the national Internet space "worth their while" for people who make up the fledgling participatory culture in the region. The mixed signals of participation promotion and censorship resulted in the opposite effects. In the course of one interview a participant commented: "*The information space of* [The Country] *is impoverished, simply impoverished. It is objectively like that*." (R3)

He further explained: "*Well there are such things as freedom of speech and censorship. We don't have the former and we have the latter – there are some disallowed topics. So there is nothing interesting to read*." (R3)

Many activists, bloggers and IT professionals shared the view that the national Internet space lacked anything "interesting" to read. One of the major reasons for this evaluation was the fact that the government and the government-controlled Internet provider engaged in content control by blocking offending sites. However, not all users experienced technical blocking equally as several areas of The Country accessed the Internet through channels outside the main government-controlled pipeline. In these areas, the stories about blocking, control and finding interesting things to read were more abstract and similar to the kinds of ideas about blocking that one might encounter in most Western countries because although people had heard about blocking, they had not experienced it first-hand.

Blocking as an Abstract Concept

In the course of fieldwork, it became obvious that blocking in The Country was going to be difficult to pin down and define analytically, given that the users we spoke to communicated a fair amount of confusion about this government practice. Blocking tended to be variable, inconsistent and mostly manifested as a sudden inability to connect to certain web sites. However, in locations where many places have spotty Internet connections it was sometimes difficult to tell whether a site was blocked or simply inaccessible for technical reasons. The fact that several small independent Internet providers exist, offering limited services in some areas of the country, and choose not to block sites, added to the complication of figuring out whether a site was in fact blocked. Internet users in The Country at times tested sites with different settings and attempts at access through different providers, and then posted results of such experimentation on forum discussions or swapped information through text messaging among groups of friends. Those that lived in areas where blocking was minimal encountered it far less often, but certainly heard of the practice from their friends.

"*Some of my friends said, they tried to access some site and they were basically told that access to the site is blocked for people from* [The Country], *but I never experienced that.*" (R4)

Such stories of friends or acquaintances encountering blocking were often confusing and difficult to interpret for users who were new to the Internet. If they lived in areas where blocking was absent, it was clearly difficult to conceptualize what that might mean for their Internet use and how that might even be experienced.

"*Yeah we heard about blocking but we get everything here, no problem. Here, see I can access* [blogging platform blocked in the rest of The Country] *no problem.*" (R5)

We also noted that where blocking was not rampant or particularly evident, the idea of starting a blog or contributing to a forum was a less daunting prospect although the likelihood of doing so was still fairly low given the lack of popular examples of such content production.

"*Well I had lots of time and I was alone there* [studying abroad] *and I have so many relatives and everyone wants to chat and everyone wants attention. So I decided blogging would be better and I will put up photos and everyone will know what I am up to.*"(R6)

In these areas the idea of contribution was attractive and reluctance to contribute had more to do with more familiar reasons, such as lack of time, lack of technical knowledge, caution about saying something that might generate conflict at work or at home or simply being intimidated by the existing conversations.

"*Yeah I should start a blog I think, or something like that. I mean my friends think I should but I am not sure. I don't actually know anyone who does it.*" (R4)

Although the perceived immensity of already available information on the Internet discouraged many interviewees from considering online contributions, those that did think about creating content were often deterred not only by the common reasons of shyness or technical limitations, but also due to other more specific reasons. For example, even when the content in question would seem benign and largely unthreatening to a State that actively polices the local Internet space, many respondents described caution and tentativeness about putting up photos and content that were either too explicit or creatively unique:

"*Who knows who might see photos of me on the beach!*" (R6)

Even without the threat of blocking, the worry of being seen by an unknown audience and the kinds of potential unintended consequences were some of the most common reasons. Users in The Country did not seem seduced by the idea of anonymity on the Internet, as many similar users in the West had been. The practice of self-censorship has been observed in other contexts where State surveillance was openly present in the everyday lives of citizens [16]. This kind of self-censorship also belied a lack of trust in online audiences that their contributions could attract, as users were worried about having their original work somehow stolen and appropriated.

"*Well these are my photographs and I don't want people to steal them.*" (R7)

Blocking as an Experienced Reality

Yet in most areas of The Country blocking was evident as a central fact of life for many users. Effects of blocking could often be detrimental to the sites affected:

"*People are leaving that site* [a news discussion and oppositional site], *blocking didn't do them any favors and such and so people are no longer reading it.*" (R3)

Blocking as delineating state boundaries online

As sites got blocked, being a part of the national Internet space was seen as problematic. The probability of the national telecommunication company suddenly blocking one's blog or website was largely unknown and unclear. Web sites were sometimes taken down through denial of service (DOS) attacks initially and eventually blocked outright if the site owners were able to deal with the DOS attacks. Patterns of blocking were erratic and largely incomprehensible. Moreover, many respondents related stories of observed persecution as reasons for not being part of the national Internet Space.

"[Oppositional news site] *moved to Tuvalu,* [Newssite].*tv now. They were constantly getting DOS'ed and their commentaries page was always getting blocked so they moved out*" (R8)

Impoverished content

Technically savvy and politically active respondents often cited these kinds of forced relocations as the main reason why even though many "interesting" conversations and information happened on the Internet, they were not to be found in the national Internet space:

"*So basically, if there is an interesting conversation happening online, really interesting intellectual discussion, it gets blocked. That's why they get blocked, if they are interesting.*" (R8)

Even if "interesting" conversations were available outside of the national Internet space, there were plenty of forums and even a recently developed blog-platform available in The Country, ostensibly for the purpose of fostering interesting conversations in the local space. Yet here as well, censorship was faulted for lowering the quality of contributions:

"*Yeah you can contribute on the* [locally-developed blog-site], *but it's all childlike. You know girls writing about poetry and long walks on the beach and you get deleted as soon as you start saying anything interesting*" (R8)

Blocking as persecution

Aside from observations of other conversations getting blocked or removed, there were also plenty of examples of personal access to the Internet being actively monitored. Experience with such forms of surveillance on the part of government, or more often, the employer who provided Internet access in the first place:

"*I wouldn't access* [oppositional news site], *because that's oppositional. Or if it is government supported then it is ok, because you know at work, they will know.*" (R6)

If just reading an oppositional site could elicit persecution in the workplace, then the thought of actually posting on a forum or a blog seemed unthinkable and even irresponsible to those users who observed their co-workers' experiences:

"*We have one guy at work, they took away his Internet for a week and fined him for using* [local forum]. *So I looked and I won't post there again.*" (R9).

Blocking as cause for oversight and moderation

Blocking and monitoring were actively discussed not only by Internet users but also by IT professionals who developed and maintained sites and businesses that relied on user contribution to survive. In these cases, the owners of forums freely admitted that there were government national security agents whose job it was to monitor discussions on the sites. Forum owners made no secret about this monitoring to their users as well, often reminding them that the Internet was monitored and not anonymous. Forum owners knew how many such watchers there usually were and even when they logged in to monitor. Thus forums and discussions sites of every stripe employed a range of paid and volunteer moderators to manage submitted content in order to limit their own exposure for the content their users produced and to reduce the perceived danger of getting censored and blocked.

STRATEGIES TO DEAL WITH/HANDLE BLOCKING

As Internet users in The Country encountered blocking, evidence of monitoring and being monitored, they developed a range of strategies for Internet use. These strategies varied depending on the goals of the users and the kinds of content they were interested in producing online. Overall, we recognized five strategies that individual respondents used for dealing with blocking and censorship. These strategies were self-censorship, technical savvy, reliance on social ties to relay blocked content, use of blocked sites for content production as a form of protection and practiced transparency. Our respondents often utilized several of the strategies we discuss here to varying degree. However, we separated these concepts for analytical purposes. We also discuss how forum owners and blogging platform providers dealt with blocking and what strategies they employed to avoid having their sites blocked.

Individual strategies

Self-censorship

Bloggers who wrote on non-political topics and themes were generally cautious about what they posted. Although they still expected that they would probably get blocked at some point, they tried to minimize that possibility by engaging in forms of self-censorship and careful attention to both the content they produced and the commentary they received. Despite taking care to control their speech, many bloggers and forum posters were worried that they might get blocked or deleted anyway at any moment.

"*I check every day, you know we are afraid of getting blocked again. We don't know why we got blocked last time, but it can always happen*" (R10)

The quote above illustrates the fear of being blocked, because such blocking could be detrimental for smaller sites with readership leaving to seek non-blocked content elsewhere. The distinct uncertainty over why one might get blocked meant that the fear remained regardless of the topics discussed on the site.

"*Well that site opens now but at some point it was blocked. We are still a bit scared that we will get blocked again. Because many of the bloggers are getting really active. More active than official sites.*" (R2)

Having been blocked once, a community of bloggers that discuss local IT and national language issues came up with reasons for why they might get blocked again. Their explanations often centered on steadily increasing levels of activity among bloggers who were interested in the national language and ethnic identity issues. In the course of one discussion with a small group of these bloggers it became clear that they felt the simple increases in posting frequency and local audiences made them more visible and exposed to the government that may or may not have approved of their discussions. This exposure was largely imagined because none of the blogs usually received more than a few hundred hits a day and most received just a few dozen a week. Yet this imagining of visibility as a cause for being persecuted both technically (through blocking) and physically (through direct government action) were based in the visible reality of sites getting blocked and in the second-hand or even first-hand stories of legal persecution and individuals experiencing direct government pressure:

"*So* [news discussion site], *they* [the government] *took away their domain* – [sitename] *and so they moved to the .net space cause then the government can't get to it* [the physical server], *but they still don't want to get blocked so they have toned down what they say.*" (R8)

In the course of the fieldwork we heard stories of people being asked to remove their comments by some form of authority. In one story, repeated by several sources, an opinion leader on a local forum was suddenly seen posting announcements in which he uncharacteristically reneged on everything he expressed in a series of prior posts lamenting particular aspects of government financial policies. He subsequently stopped posting entirely on the forums under the pre-text of having too much work. People relating this story to us usually concluded that the opinion leader was either banned from the Internet or arrested. Some suggested that he might have decided a few comments on a forum were not worth losing too much over and that was probably a smart move on his part. While people relating these stories intended, in part, to shock the interviewers, at the same time, they also clearly regarded the consequences as a normal and logical outcome of one's activity online.

Technical Savvy

Despite the erratic nature of the blocking and the shadowy evidence of persecution, technical savvy and knowledge of efficient workarounds such as proxy servers or anonymizers was important for getting access to blocked content. These were utilized by a wide range of users and were especially important for those who produced content and those who were determined to access oppositional resources and blocked blogging platforms.

"*Well so it got blocked, so whatever ... Today it got blocked, tomorrow it will get unblocked or I will access it through an anonymizer or some other way, through some other browser and that's all.*" (R8)

Reliance on social ties

When users in some areas of The Country could not access a blog post or a news site for whatever reason, users who did have access to these resources because they either were technically savvy or happened to live in areas without blocking, simply pasted the information into email or reposted it on their social network site profiles for their friends to read. Thus many users were able to circumvent some forms of blocking without much technological savvy, but instead relying on social ties to people who lived in areas with unfettered access to the Internet.

Blocked sites as a form of protection

Armed with technical savvy of navigating proxies and anonymizers, many users in The Country continued to actively post on blocked blogging platforms, forming well-defined intellectual communities behind the firewall. Although a few did so because they intentionally blogged for friends or family who lived outside The Country, some clearly produced content that was local and directed at an audience inside The Country. For content producers that blogged on sites that were officially blocked, and especially for those that produced politically charged content, blocking was at times perceived as a form of protection from potential persecution by the government.

"*Government put itself into a stupid* position [by officially blocking a site]. *So if they say "You wrote this and that and the other on your blog?" and I will say "I am sorry, but all of these blogs are blocked according to this court decision. That's all – they don't exist and they are officially inaccessible to citizens of* [The Country]*." So what are they going to do then?*" (R8)

The scenario described above was produced in full seriousness and with the expectation that this, in fact, was something likely to happen – an expectation of persecution that was part and parcel of political blogging in The Country. Given this environment, the prominent and prolific bloggers and forum participants talked openly about expecting to have their phones tapped and their online conversations followed.

"*I wouldn't go get a blackberry. I could go down the street and get one, but I wouldn't because they [the government] can't crack that encryption and they would just get suspicious. Cause they listen to me and listen to me and then suddenly I am encrypting and so that means I am really saying something they don't want me to.*" (R8)

Practiced transparency

There was a resignation to being watched and an acceptance of this as a practice where personal transparency would be the best policy and best protection. Many prominent bloggers and IT professionals practiced transparency as a policy of self-preservation. They limited their use of encryption and made sure to post commentary on sites outside their own blogs in a manner that clearly indicated their identity. In interviews and conversations these kinds of practices were often pitched as a form of bravado and yet at the same time described with clear and calculated detail. Practiced transparency also removed any illusions of anonymity one might harbor when interacting online. Nearly every respondent was careful to explain that nobody was anonymous on the Internet, but that sometimes people tried to hide behind temporary handles anyway.

Forum owner and platform provider strategies

The data presented in this portion of the article includes few representative quotes because these stories were told in confidence and the interviewer was explicitly asked not to record and not to take notes. In order to protect our participants we give no detailed information and present this data in general terms.

The fear of persecution and the experience of surveillance were not unique to people producing content in public space, but also to those providing platforms for such contribution. In fact the onus of control and censorship often fell to blog, discussion and forum platform operators as the initial level of control. The owners of blog and forum spaces felt they were required to do active surveillance, in some cases surrendering information about their clients that could identify them to the government. They developed a range of practices to give their users a chance to take back untoward commentary and to adjust behavior. The owners did so in order to protect their users from persecution, to create a space where online contributions were encouraged despite the censorship and to protect the site from being blocked by the government.

For example, small forum owners or private bloggers monitored comments on their sites by hand and sent reminders that there is no such thing as anonymity on the Internet, offering people a chance to remove or augment the offending commentary. This was only tenable, however, if the audience and readership of the site was small. In one example, the owner of a local forum realized that he no longer had time to sleep because his site had gained popularity and saw swift increases in traffic and comments.

Larger sites promoted some of their frequent users to volunteer moderators of online conversations and sometimes even hired people to moderate. The way the moderators dealt with offenders on the sites was largely similar. The most common strategy for the administrators and moderators of online discussion spaces was first to warn, always pointing out that the feeling of anonymity on the Internet was deceptive and that in reality anonymity did not exist. Users of the forum or blog were given a chance to revise their statements and if these same people did not heed the advice, their information was eventually handed over to the relevant government agencies.

Forums with very large audiences and readership developed sets of rules to govern posting and moderator activities. These rules were often so lengthy and detailed that when the moderators cited a reason for a warning or a deletion of a comment, it looked as if they were referring to a part of a fully-fledged legal codex. Owners, employees and moderators on these forums worked 24 hours a day, tirelessly reminding users that they were responsible for keeping the conversation civil and for treading carefully around problematic topics. The idea that online and offline worlds are somehow separate was combated with reminders that no matter what was said online – the people responsible for the words could be held accountable in their all too physical realities. The users often loudly complained of unfair moderators and bickered over the details of the rules, but by and large they understood the reasons and motivations for such control:

"[a local forum] *has huge amounts of information but you have to be careful and they moderate because you know, they have to.*" (R11)

These strategies illustrate a tricky balancing act that both the audience and contributors of the sites and the site administrators had to manage. The threats of blocking and persecution were all too real for the owners and administrators, and they did their best to relate the reality of these threats while at the same time managing to retain an environment that fostered online content contributions for their users. Forum users, in turn, understood and, to some extent, supported that the forum and blog owners had to moderate and control what was said on their web sites.

DISCUSSION

The goal of this research was to explore how blocking and Internet censorship may be implicated in people's decisions about and attitudes toward contributing online. Our findings illustrate the complexity of Internet experiences for people who live in a country that censors the Internet through site blocking and persecution of individuals and content and platform providers. Such government actions served as opportunities for state monitoring and surveillance, and served as a reason for people responsible for social media sites to moderate and oversee user-generated content produced there. Blocking and Internet censorship shaped people's experience of the Internet by delineating state boundaries online, and often resulted in impoverished content online. Our findings also reveal specific strategies that people in The Country used to navigate blocking and Internet censorship. Individuals engaged in self-censorship, used technically savvy workarounds, relied on social ties for access to blocked content, co-opted government blocking and monitoring, and practiced transparency in their everyday activities. In addition, forum owners and platform providers also engaged in strategies to handle blocking and censorship, primarily by monitoring and controlling user-generated content on their sites and platforms and by consistently reminding their users about the lack of anonymity on the Internet.

Despite the reliance on a single fieldsite, our findings provide a clear opportunity to address more broadly the existing literature about user-generated content and Internet censorship. In particular, our findings speak to the importance of considering macro-level social contexts in user-generated content, the cultural specificity of issues such as anonymity and privacy in the practice of contributing online, the need to conceptualize blocking as more than merely a technical phenomenon, and the importance of a richer understanding of people's overall strategies to create and consume online content.

First, our research project demonstrates that research on user-generated content would benefit from paying more attention to and making more explicit the broader social, macro-level context in which such practices take place. National-level, state-sponsored actions of blocking and censorship permeated people's Internet practices, shaping actions of resistance such as accessing oppositional news web sites, but also creating an environment of caution that trickled down to concern about posting holiday photographs or a blog for family. These sources of concern run counter to much of the existing research on user-generated content that focuses solely on individual-level or group-level motivations–whether intrinsic or extrinsic–to create content. Considerations of the kinds of real repercussions that practices of content creation may bring about are important and overlooked aspects of participatory culture.

Regardless of geographic location, everyone makes decisions about whether to contribute or what to contribute in a context determined by legislation and regulations enacted by governments and companies. In democratic countries contributory practices occur in a framework that guarantees free speech (whose implementation and definition varies between countries), but this context should be explicitly acknowledged in research in such places. Our communal understanding of user-generated content will only be enriched if we are to explore more carefully, or at least acknowledge and make explicit the circumstances in which people create such content.

Second, our findings underline the cultural specificity of the concepts intrinsic to user-generated content, most notably anonymity. A premise underlying much of the current research on user-generated content is that people, if they possess sufficient technical skills, are able to manage their anonymity online by controlling how or whether they are personally identifiable, for example, as the reviewer of a product or a particular contributor to a mailing list. Our findings demonstrate the degree to which that was not true. The people to whom we spoke did not assume that anonymity was possible, rather they tended to accept a lack of anonymity as a fact of life and not as particularly onerous or unfair given their expectation of state surveillance. Recurring in our conversations with respondents ranging from political bloggers to photograph-posting vacationers was a pervasive attitude of caution about making oneself visible or expressing opinions, an attitude that pre-dates and encompasses more than the Internet. Individuals regularly engaged in self-censorship when it came to creating user-generated content. Similarly, political bloggers and forum owners worked under the assumption of a lack of anonymity. This findings provoke additional questions about the ways in which people across a variety of circumstances–including those with less censorship and blocking–may also self-censor in their online contribution practices and expose further reasons for non-use of technology [20,21]. The insight that anonymity, much like privacy [18], is a culturally specific concept that is experienced and valued differently across contexts, is particularly relevant to user-generated content research.

Third, through discussions of the complexity of blocking and Internet censorship, our findings underscore the need for a more nuanced conception of the online experience in censored environments. In practice, blocking is more than simply a technical construct involving IP addresses, URLs, and DNS. Blocking and censorship must be understood as socially framed and experienced phenomena rather than merely forms of blackouts of information or as direct and logical forms of persecution by a repressive State. Our respondents described an uncertain environment in which blocking and censorship happened haphazardly and inconsistently. Respondents who were not IT professionals, for example, expressed confusion about whether particular sites were blocked officially or were simply inaccessible for an innocuous technical reason. Forum owners and moderators accepted and expected that items related to political issues or even personal blogs might be periodically monitored, censored and eventually blocked. Many forum and public discussion board users commented that they were largely comfortable with the heavy involvement of moderators in their conversations because they knew this was a way to keep valuable resources available.

Fourth, our findings add to the growing body of literature that illuminates the rich, contingent, and multi-modal strategies that people use to create online content. While the strategies used by our respondents for online content creation emerged from a context of more blocking and censorship than in some parts of the world, they speak to greater understanding of how people make decisions about whether to contribute content online, what to contribute and how. Our findings imply that it might be fruitful to go beyond considerations of individual motivations in the study of online contributions and to explore the broader political and social circumstances under which people make their decisions. It is quite possible that some of the specific strategies that emerged in this study, such as self-censorship and the use of social ties as alternative information sources or communication paths, might well be relevant to user-generated content practices in less censored contexts.

CONCLUSION

Our research findings challenge conventional research on how, when and why people contribute online by highlighting the complexity and sophistication of people's contribution practices. While all online contributors produce content in environments shaped by state-policies, much of the research about online contribution tends to assume a Western democratic context. Recent high-profile events, such as India's consideration of banning Blackberry service, the negotiation around Google's activity in China and Wikileaks actions, have highlighted that many people use the Internet in contexts that look quite differently. Of course, one does not have to live in a society that openly censors Internet access in order to experience repercussions from making online contributions. Yet, the ways that people in The Country experience blocking and censorship and the strategies they use to navigate the Internet underscore the urgent need to better understand how people in a broad variety of contexts experience and navigate blocking and censorship when making decisions about online contributions.

ACKNOWLEDGMENTS

We are indebted to all of our respondents for their generous participation in our study. We thank J. Vertesi, D. Struthers and anonymous reviewers for constructive commentary. This research was funded by the NSF grant IIS-0917401. Any opinions, findings, conclusions or recommendations expressed in this material are those of the authors and do not reflect the views of the National Science Foundation.

REFERENCES

1. Burke, M., Marlow, C., and Lento, T. Feed me: motivating newcomer contribution in social network sites. *In Proc. CHI2009*, ACM Press (2009), 945-954.
2. Castells, M., Fernández-Ardèvol, M., Qiu, J.L., and Sey, A. *Mobile communication and society: A global perspective*. MIT Press, Cambridge, USA, 2007.
3. Emerson, R.M., Fretz R.I., Shaw L.L. *Writing ethnographic fieldnotes*. University of Chicago Press, Chicago, 1995.
4. Goldsmith, J. L. and Wu, T. *Who controls the Internet? Illusions of a borderless world*. Oxford University Press, New York, 2006.
5. Hargittai, E. An update on survey measures of web-oriented digital literacy. *Social Science Computer Review*, 27, **1**, (2009), 130-137.
6. Hargittai, E., & Walejko, G. The participation divide: Content creation and sharing in the digital age. *Information, Communication & Society*, 11, 2, (2008), 239-256.
7. Howard, P.N. *The Digital Origins of Dictatorship and Democracy: Information Technology and Political Islam*. Oxford University Press, Oxford, UK, 2010.
8. Hsu, C, and Lin, J. Acceptance of blog use: The roles of technology acceptance, social influence and knowledge sharing motivation. *Information & Management*, 45 (2007), 65-74.
9. Jenkins, H. *Convergence culture: Where old and new media collide*. NY University Press, NY, USA, 2006.
10. Kogut BM. *The global internet economy*. MIT Press, Cambridge, MA, USA, 2003.
11. Lacharite, J. Electronic decentralisation in China: A critical analysis of Internet filtering policies in the People's Republic of China. *Australian Journal of Political Science*, 37, 2, (2002), 333-346.
12. Lampe, C., Wash, R., Velasquez, A. and Ozkaya, E. Motivations to participate in online communities. *In Proc. CHI2010*, ACM Press (2010), 1927-1936.
13. MacKinnon, R. China's Censorship 2.0: How companies censor bloggers. *First Monday, 14*, 2, (2009).
14. MacKinnon, R. Flatter world and thicker walls? Blogs, censorship, and civic discourse in China. *Public Choice*, 134, (2008), 31-46.
15. Nonnecke, B., Andrews, D. and Preece, J. Non-public and public online community participation: Needs, attitudes and behavior. *Electronic Commerce Research*, 6, 1 (2006), 7-20.
16. Ognyanova, K. Careful what you say: Media control in Putin's Russia – Implications for online content. *International Journal of E-Politics*, 1, 2, (2010), 1-15.
17. OpenNet Initiative. http://opennet.net.
18. Philips, D.J. From Privacy to Visibility: Context, Identity, and Power in Ubiquitous Computing Environments. *Social Text*, 23 (2005), 95-108.
19. Preece, J., Nonnecke, B. and Andrews, D. The top five reasons for lurking: improving community experiences for everyone. *Computers in Human Behavior*, 20 (2004), 201-223.
20. Satchell, C. and Dourish, P. Beyond the user: Use and non-use in HCI. *In Proc OZCHI2009*, ACM Press (2009), 9-16.
21. Selwyn, N. Apart from technology: understanding people's non-use of information and communication technologies in everyday life, *Technology in Society*, 25, (2003), 99-116.
22. Stoeckl, R., Rohrmeier, P. and Hess, T., Motivations to produce user generated content: Differences between webloggers and videobloggers. *In Proc. BLED 2007*. Paper 30, (2007).
23. Van Deursen, A.J.A.M. and Van Dijk, J.A.G.M. Measuring Internet skills. *International Journal of Human Computer Interaction*, 26, 10, (2010), 891-916.
24. Van den Hoonaard, W.C. Is Anonymity an Artifact in Ethnographic Research? *Journal of Academic Ethics*, 1, 2, (2003) 141-151.
25. Van Dijck, J. Users like you? Theorizing agency in user-generated content, *Media Culture & Society, 31*, (2009), 41-58.
26. Van Velsen, L. and Melenhorst, M. Incorporating user motivations to design for video tagging. *Interacting with Computers 21*, 3 (2009), 221-232.
27. Wei, C.Y. and Kolko, B. Resistance to globalization: Language and Internet diffusion patterns in Uzbekistan. *New Review of Hypermedia and Multimedia*, 11 (2005), 205-220.
28. Wyatt, S. Non-users also matter: The construction of user and non-users of the Internet. In *How users matter: The co-construction of users and technology*. MIT Press, Cambridge, USA, 2003.
29. Yang, G. Activists beyond virtual borders: Internet-mediated networks and informational politics in China, *First Monday*, 7 (2006).
30. Zittrain, J. and Edelman, B. G., Internet filtering in China. *IEEE Internet Computing*, March/April, 2003

Real-time Collaborative Editing Behavior in U.S. and Japanese Distributed Teams

Lauren Scissors[1], N. Sadat Shami[2], Tatsuya Ishihara[3], Steven Rohall[2], Shin Saito[3]

Northwestern University[1]
2240 Campus Drive,
Evanston, IL, 60208, U.S.A
l-scissors@northwestern.edu

IBM TJ Watson Research Center[2]
1 Rogers St.,
Cambridge, MA 02142, U.S.A
{sadat,steven_rohall}@us.ibm.com

Tokyo Research Lab, IBM Japan[3]
1623-14 Shimo-tsuruma
Yamato-shi, Kanagawa-ken, Japan
{tishihara, shinsa}@jp.ibm.com

ABSTRACT
While there are tools that allow distributed teams to collaboratively edit in real time, little work examines this practice among real teams doing real work. Even less is known about how teams from different countries make use of real-time collaborative editing tools. The current work highlights results from a qualitative user study of real-world Japanese and U.S. distributed work teams who used LiveDeck, a real-time slide editing and whiteboarding tool. Through the implementation of various novel features used as probes, differences in behavior and attitudes between team members were uncovered. Differences in the use of slide navigation options, anonymity features, and pop-up 'emotes' representing nonverbal gestures are discussed.

Author Keywords
CSCW, collaborative editing, distributed teams, cultural differences, computer-mediated communication

ACM Classification Keywords
H5.3. Group and Organization Interfaces: Computer Supported Collaborative Work

General Terms
Human Factors

INTRODUCTION
Collaborative software that is popular in one country may not always be adopted in another. This may be due to the fact that certain collaborative tools may not fully support aspects of communication emphasized by a particular country (e.g., [27]). Yet, even when technologies are adopted across countries, they are not always adopted for the same reasons (e.g., [23,34]) or in the same ways (e.g., [19]). Little empirical research, however, has examined in depth how distributed teams use real-time collaboration tools for their actual day-to-day work, and fewer studies have examined whether use of these tools differs across countries. That some recent tools intended to support real-time communication and collaboration, such as Google Wave, have been unpopular with consumers [7] seems to contribute to even more uncertainty over what features users desire from real-time collaboration tools.

Various aspects of communication and culture may contribute to whether a distributed team uses a given tool. For instance, the emphasis on nonverbal communication in some countries might make individuals less likely to adopt technologies that minimize nonverbal cues. Or, individuals from countries where independence and uniqueness is valued may be less likely to use technologies that emphasize group control. Yet the extent to which one's cultural background relates to behaviors and preferences for certain real-time editing features is largely unknown.

Understanding how individuals in different countries use real-time collaboration tools is important for two main reasons. First, understanding which technology features are preferable in different countries may allow designers and developers to understand which features may be adopted globally and which features are important to tailor to specific audiences. Second, understanding how individuals use various features may help us better understand whether cultural differences identified by a large body of empirical research persist in a distributed, collaborative environment.

In this paper, we address the research question: How do Japanese and U.S. distributed work teams use real-time collaborative editing tools? In order to examine the usage of different real-time collaboration features in Japanese and U.S. teams, we conducted an exploratory study of Japanese and U.S. distributed work teams' use of LiveDeck, a system that supports real-time collaborative editing of presentation slides. Using LiveDeck, a nascent prototype, we inserted various features as "cultural probes" [2,5] in order to understand usage patterns in both Japan and the U.S. Results reveal how Japanese and U.S. participants differ in their use of various novel LiveDeck features, including group vs. independent slide navigation, anonymity features, and pop-up 'emotes' that represent select nonverbal behaviors. In addition, results suggest that Japanese and U.S. participants differ in their attitudes and rationale behind their use of various features.

In the following related work section, we review some of the literature that shaped our exploratory processes. We used the previous findings to inform both the probes that we built into LiveDeck and the themes that we explored.

RELATED WORK

Collaborative Content Creation & Editing

When collaborating at a distance, individuals must negotiate the process of coordination and deal with issues such as miscommunication and awareness of group members' behavior. Early tools like ShrEdit [14] allowed users to work on different parts of a document in parallel, and more recent tools like CoWord and CoPowerpoint allow users to work collaboratively within out-of-the-box software platforms [35]. How one navigates through a document or set of slides is important for real-time collaboration and is often examined from an awareness perspective (e.g., [16,17]). Yet, navigation control, or who controls what the group sees, is also important. While many slide-sharing tools typically assign a "leader", where one person navigates through the slides for the group, other systems (e.g., [17]) allow users to move from slide to slide on their own. It is unclear, however, whether these or additional options might be better suited to the work styles of individuals from different backgrounds.

One commonly discussed issue for distributed teams who collaborate online is the lack of nonverbal cues during distributed collaborations. This can be troublesome for teams (see [12] for a review) and may be especially hard on individuals who rely heavily on nonverbal communication for understanding. Proxies for nonverbal communication, such as emoticons, are often present in web conferencing software and may help promote friendship formation [36] or satisfaction with a tool [30]. It is unclear, however, whether these findings hold for distributed work teams as emoticons may be interpreted as unserious. There is also no clear consensus on how representations of other nonverbal behaviors like gestures may be interpreted in a real-time collaborative environment.

Another issue for distributed teams is conflict. Previous research has indicated that distributed teams experience more conflict than collocated teams (e.g., [11]). Issues of conflict may be especially significant for teams that place emphasis on maintaining social harmony. However, certain features of a tool may help to mitigate conflicts, maintain social harmony, and may be more effective for teams from certain countries. For instance, being able to communicate anonymously may make it easier for group members to make contributions during meetings (e.g., [14]) or to provide constructive criticism [37]. Or, anonymity might make individuals less likely to participate since they cannot be as easily held accountable. However, issues such as how easily a message sender can hide her identity or how strongly the message recipient wishes to identify the sender may influence how anonymity features are adopted [28].

In order to better understand how teams in Japan and the U.S. might use real-time collaborative editing tools, we review the differences between these two cultures.

Japanese & American Culture

Across disciplines and within the field of HCI, numerous conceptualizations of culture have been put forth (e.g., [13]; see [25] for a review). One definition conceptualizes culture as concepts, values, and schemata that are developed from experiences and that are specific to certain contexts [33]. While there are many levels of culture including the accepted norms and schemas held by people in a particular job role or team (e.g., [3,18]), the current work focuses on national culture, as defined by geographic location. Though we do not assume that every Japanese or American individual is alike, a vast body of empirically supported literature has identified several differences in how individuals from these two cultures behave and communicate. Different cultural dimensions, however, may become more or less salient depending on the social context or situation [6], suggesting the need for an investigation of the role of culture in novel environments.

One cultural difference between Japanese and American individuals is how they define the self. Japanese individuals typically have a sense of self that is interdependent, or defined by their relationships with others. Interdependent societies emphasize one's membership in a group, as well as the promotion and maintenance of interpersonal harmony (e.g., [22]). In a work setting, consensus is emphasized, and Japanese individuals often exert much effort to gain group consensus during decision-making processes [15]. Alternatively, individuals in the U.S. typically identify with an independent sense of self, which emphasizes being unique from others and promotes the expression of unique ideas and opinions, even at the risk of threatening social harmony (e.g., [22]).

Another difference identified in previous research is the use of nonverbal communication. Japanese individuals tend to rely on (often subtle) nonverbal behaviors, such as eye movements, smiles, and other facial expressions for social feedback [9,15] while Americans tend to rely more on language when communicating [8]. Additionally, Japanese and Americans often differ in their focus on hierarchies. While Americans recognize social hierarchies, individuals in Japan tend to be more cognizant of hierarchies in interpersonal interactions, and place high value on respecting people in leadership roles [31]. In one study, Japanese individuals perceived greater differences in verbal (e.g., length of sentences, volume of speech) and nonverbal (e.g., smiling, using eye contact) behavior based on status/hierarchy than did Americans [20].

Japanese and American individuals may also differ in their strategies for expressing opinions. For instance, one study of the Japanese and U.S. versions of Slashdot, an online news community, found that Japanese users were more likely to post their opinions anonymously than were U.S. users [24]. In fact, researchers have debated the extent to which Japanese individuals are able to express their true feelings in anonymous questionnaires and note that individuals in Japan may be more likely to say one thing but mean another in order to publically present themselves in the right way (see [10] for a review). Yet, these findings may not hold in situations where individuals are acquainted

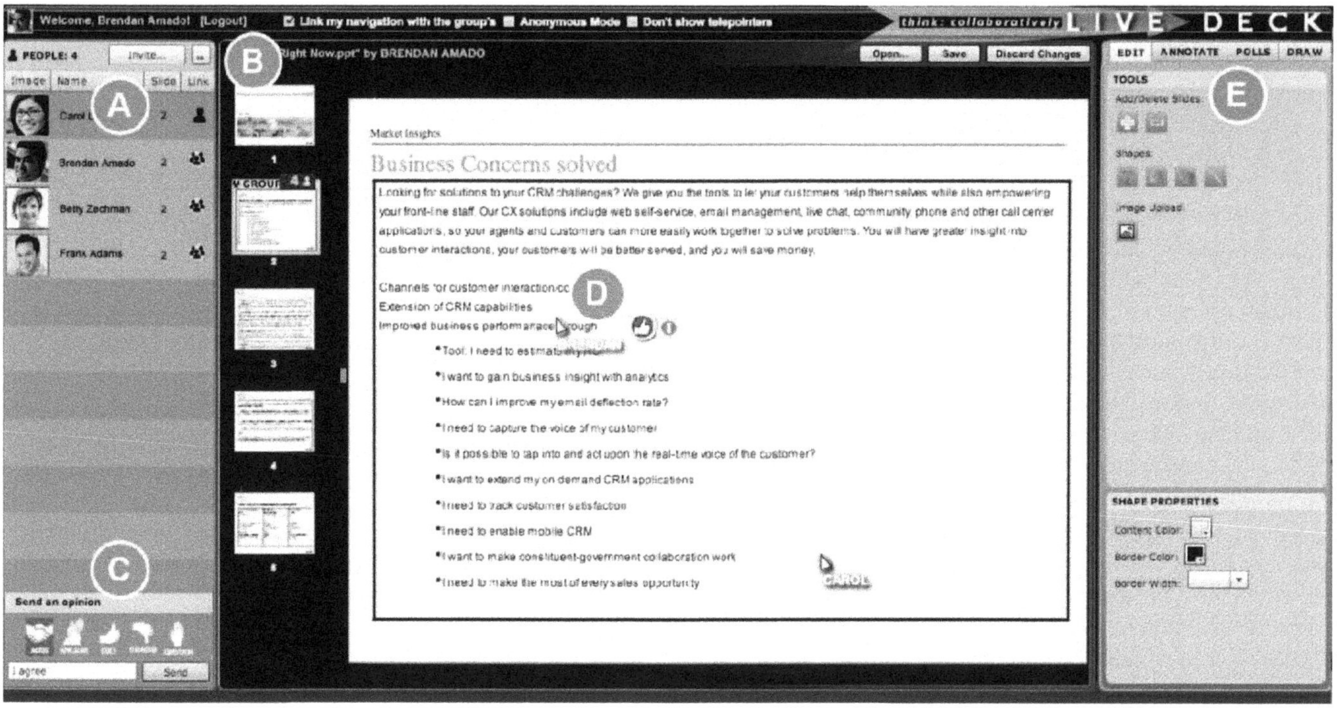

Figure 1. The LiveDeck interface as viewed by the user 'Brendan Amado' (names have been changed to preserve privacy). (A) Meeting participant list. The list shows the slide number participants are on and whether they are in 'group' (highlighted in yellow) or 'independent' navigation mode. (B) Slide thumbnails allow users to navigate slides and show the number of people viewing a slide. Here, all participants are viewing slide 2. (C) 'Emotes' allow users to send a pre-generated or custom message. (D) Slide content showing a telepointer of a user and a minimized 'thumbs up' sticky note. (E) Editing tab. Other tabs allow users to use 'sticky notes', create polls, and draw freehand.

or plan to have non-anonymous interaction in addition to anonymous interaction.

Cultural backgrounds may influence the extent to which equal participation and collaboration within groups is achieved. For instance, in Japan where a hierarchical structure is salient, workers may feel uncomfortable making suggestions in front of their superiors and peers for fear of disrupting social harmony. While this respect likely works for some types of work, it may be problematic in a collaborative exercise where more participation across group members might yield more and varied ideas. Yet, another central aspect of eastern cultures like Japan is that individuals should act for the good of the group [4]. Making suggestions in the form of constructive criticism may ultimately benefit the group yet the concern for respecting and not embarrassing others seems at odds with this goal. Therefore, it is unclear how Japanese individuals may use anonymous features during collaborative work.

In the current work, we are interested in examining how these cultural differences may affect how distributed teams behave and communicate in a real-time collaborative editing environment. While cultural differences have been studied extensively across various disciplines, there has been little empirical work examining how individuals from different cultures use real-time collaborative tools. Furthermore, the majority of work on this topic has looked at how randomly assigned teams complete arbitrary tasks in a laboratory setting. While there are benefits to this type of methodology, little is known about how real-world distributed teams in different countries use real-time collaborative tools for real work.

LIVEDECK

LiveDeck is a web-based, real-time, synchronous slide editing / whiteboarding tool. It is built using Adobe Flash [1] and supports both Microsoft PowerPoint and Open Document Presentation formats. Users can work on an existing slide deck or create a new one using templates available from within LiveDeck. Users invite others to join them for real-time collaboration by sending them the unique meeting URL LiveDeck creates for each slide deck. Below we describe the main features of LiveDeck, including those used to probe certain topics. Figure 1 provides a screenshot of the complete LiveDeck interface.

Group vs. Independent Navigation

There may be many reasons why users want to navigate a slide deck independently, as opposed to passively viewing what the presenter is showing. In a presentation meeting, users that arrive late may want to view content that they missed. Others may want to skip ahead. In brainstorming or collaborative editing meetings, users might want to form subgroups to work on separate slides. LiveDeck supports all of these scenarios. By default, when users log in, they are in 'independent' navigation mode. They can group their navigation with others by clicking a checkbox at the top left of the LiveDeck interface. In LiveDeck we did not want to have users rely on a moderator who assigns privileges such

Figure 2. An 'applause' emote from 'Carol Li'.

as controlling slide navigation. Thus, when any user in 'group' navigation mode moves from one slide to another, all other users that are grouped together move with her. There is only one group and users may not force other users into the group; users must self-select into the group. These navigation options allowed us to probe how one's sense of self (interdependent vs. independent) [22] might influence individuals' preferences for slide navigation options.

Anonymous mode

Based on findings that hierarchy and group harmony are more salient in Japanese culture than in the U.S. [10,31], we implemented an anonymous mode as a probe to determine if anonymity makes a difference in expressing constructive criticism. Users can choose to be in anonymous mode by checking the 'anonymous mode' checkbox at the top of the interface. When a user is in anonymous mode, her telepointer, annotations created, and emotes sent are not associated with her identity.

Emotes

To explore how findings that Japanese individuals focus on nonverbal behavior in face-to-face conversation [9] might be manifested in an online setting, we included a set of five "emotes" or expressions with pre-determined sayings ('Agree', 'Applause', 'OK!', 'Disagree', and 'Question'). A corresponding picture of a gesture accompanied each saying. We confirmed that these gestures held the same meaning in Japan and in the U.S. Users can customize the message by typing in the text box in the emote window. Sending an emote causes a pulsating square to appear around a user's picture (see Figure 2). All emotes except 'Question' disappear after 3 seconds. The 'Question' emote stays active until the user who sent it cancels it.

Annotations

We wanted users to be able to quickly provide comments on aspects of a slide that would persist and could be saved as metadata. For example, a user might want to remark that she does not agree with a particular point in the slide, with the intention of revising it later. We thus allow LiveDeck users to input six types of 'sticky notes': 'Plain', 'Thumbs up', 'Thumbs down', 'Important', 'Question', and 'Bookmark'. There is also an annotations tab, along with a log that lists what annotations have been created on what slide. The log items are hyperlinks, allowing users to easily navigate to the slide containing the annotation. Users can also reply to an annotation, similar to chat.

Polls

To allow users to get quick feedback on an issue and to further explore issues of anonymity, we implemented polls in LiveDeck. From the polls tab, users can create a slide-specific or global poll. A slide-specific poll is shown in the poll tab on that slide whereas global polls are shown regardless of the slide a user is on. Users can specify whether the poll requires a yes/no response or a choice from multiple options. Users receive a pop-up message when a poll gets created, requesting them to participate. The poll creator can see how many people have voted and can end the poll, though all votes are cast anonymously.

Team	*Country*	*Size*	*Task Type*
Team 1	Japan	12	Brainstorming
Team 2	Japan	4	Reporting project updates
Team 3	Japan	4	Review slides with feedback
Team 4	Japan	4	Project planning, minute taking
Team 5	USA	3	Reporting project updates
Team 6	USA	5	Brainstorming
Team 7	USA	4	Review slides with feedback
Team 8	USA	8	Review slides with feedback

Table 1. Summary of Teams Observed.

METHOD

Participants

Participants (*N=44*) were employees at a large international technology organization who volunteered to use LiveDeck with their teams. 44 individuals across 8 teams participated in a LiveDeck meeting and 31 volunteered to participate in a follow-up interview. 18 were male and 13 were female. Participants had on average 11.5 years of full-time work experience. Participants were fairly familiar with their team members, and reported an average familiarity of 6.9 on a scale of 1 to 9 (1=*not at all familiar*, 9=*extremely familiar)* Teams ranged in job role (e.g., sales, product development), size, and task type (see Table 1 for a summary). The average meeting lasted 67 minutes.

Procedure & Analysis

The researchers contacted team leaders to see if they would be interested in using LiveDeck as part of a user study. Teams were chosen based on the fact that they were distributed, that members all worked in different locations in the same country, and that they had regularly scheduled meetings for collaborative activities. The LiveDeck interface was internationalized, and teams worked on tasks in LiveDeck in their native language. The researchers did not assign tasks; tasks were already on teams' agendas. Team members communicated via telephone while they used LiveDeck and the researchers recorded these calls.

A demo was provided to the teams that agreed to use LiveDeck. This allowed team members to become familiar with the tool. We do not report any data from the demos. The data reported in this paper is from the meeting where LiveDeck was used for real work following the demo. After that meeting, participants were contacted via email to see if they would participate in a 30-minute individual interview.

A semi-structured interview script was developed based upon a thorough literature review on various topics related to collaborative editing and cultural differences between individuals in Japan and the U.S. Although we intended to explore certain themes identified in the interview script, the semi-structured nature allowed participants to tell us what they thought was relevant, which allowed for the possibility of additional themes to emerge. The interview script was originally crafted in English and later translated to Japanese. Extensive discussion of the interview items occurred between the American and Japanese researchers in order to keep the two interview guides as semantically similar as possible. In addition, a researcher outside the immediate team fluent in both languages reviewed the two interview scripts to ensure that the meaning of the English questions was accurately transferred.

American participants were observed and interviewed by the American members of the research team and Japanese participants were observed and interviewed by the Japanese members. The researchers logged into LiveDeck and observed the meetings and accompanying audio calls as a 'fly on the wall'. Researchers were not co-located with any of the participants during the meetings. Audio recordings and screenshots of the meetings were made during the observations and interviews, which were conducted via telephone. These were recorded with the permission of participants and later transcribed in the language they were conducted. Japanese interviews were then translated into English by the Japanese members of the research team, who are fluent in both English and Japanese. In addition, all actions performed in LiveDeck were captured in a log.

Conducting observations and interviews in the participant's native language reduces the potentially harmful effects of a language barrier, such as second language anxiety [32], in cross-cultural research. In other words, Japanese participants did not have the strain of answering questions in English, which likely allowed them to be more clear and thorough. U.S. and Japanese members of the research team discussed the interview data in English.

English language versions of the interviews were coded using HyperResearch [29], a qualitative analysis software tool, to identify themes related to the use of LiveDeck's various features. We used an iterative process, reading through interviews and field notes several times, applying initial codes, and then reevaluating and changing codes as we delved deeper into the data. Transcripts were tagged with codes related to themes identified from the previous literature and to topics that interviewees brought up themselves. Some codes were more general (e.g., "likes emotes") while others were more specific (e.g., "likes emotes – friendly"; "likes emotes – easy to interrupt"). As patterns began to emerge, the interview script was altered to reflect these discoveries. Additionally, follow-up interviews were conducted with some participants to further explore emergent topics of interest. After the interviews were coded, we focused on the more frequently occurring codes to develop themes related to the use of the probes. Ultimately, we identified three themes related to LiveDeck features that represented our sample.

RESULTS

While numerous interesting aspects emerged from our exploratory research, we will mainly focus on three: *group vs. independent navigation, emotes (proxies for nonverbal behavior),* and *anonymity features.* We note that our study was not a formal evaluation of LiveDeck. Rather, it was an attempt to understand real-time collaborative editing behavior in Japan and the U.S., using LiveDeck as a probe.

Group vs. Independent Navigation

Participants in Japan and the U.S. used the navigation features differently. While U.S. participants primarily used independent navigation, Japanese participants used group navigation about 41% of the time of the entire meeting and independent navigation about 59% of the time (across teams), noting the usefulness of both. On the one hand, using the group navigation option seemed to help Japanese groups stay connected to their leaders:

"Linking with the moderator's page is very important because we have to see the same page as the moderator. Sometimes I need the moderator's command, so the 'link with group' option is important." ***(Interviewee 9, Japan)***

On the other hand, some Japanese participants also liked the ability to move freely through the slide deck:

"I think both of these modes will be necessary. Basically, it is usual that everyone watches the same slide at the same time. But sometimes I want to go back to the previous chart, or want to see the following slides. In such cases, it will be convenient to use this function to go to other slides separately." ***(Interviewee 17, Japan)***

However, some Japanese participants wished there was less control for each group member over the slide navigation and more control for one person who would be in charge. For example:

"I think it is better if LiveDeck has a function to lock other people's operation. If freely editing slides interrupts the progress of the meeting, it is better if a moderator can prevent the editing of slides." ***(Interviewee 1, Japan)***

Alternatively, most U.S. participants (82%) responded well to the fact that there was no one leader in charge of navigating the slides for the group. For example:

"I liked the fact that there was not just one person running the meeting who had to hand off control to everybody else. I thought that made for a much more interactive and lively meeting." ***(Interviewee 12, USA)***

Many U.S. participants liked the fact that they could look at different slides but still be a part of the meeting. For instance, one participant noted that she…

"...felt comfortable that if people were on different pages, they could still contribute to that conversation."

And further mentioned:

"It felt like we were in a real meeting and someone would just flip over a piece of paper." ***(Interviewee 13, USA)***

In fact, several U.S. participants explained that monitoring the movement of others actually contributed to a greater sense of awareness. Taken together, these observed differences in preferences for group vs. independent navigation may be related to previous work suggesting that individuals in the U.S. tend to value independence while individuals in Japan tend to value interdependence.

Emotes

As previously discussed, a menu of 'emotes' or pop-up features representing various nonverbal expressions and gestures such as "Agree" or "OK!" was implemented. Japanese participants used these emotes overwhelmingly more often than did U.S. participants. While there were 91 instances of emote use across Japanese teams, only 7 instances of emote use occurred in two U.S. teams; the other U.S. teams did not use the emotes at all. Of Japanese participants who used the emotes, 93% rated them favorably. Japanese participants liked the emotes for various reasons. For instance, one participant explained:

"The functions we used were the Applause, OK, and Question buttons. We cannot nod in a telephone conference, so this function is good because we can casually send our opinions." ***(Interviewee 6, Japan)***

In addition to replacing nonverbal behavior like nodding which may be typical of face-to-face meetings, Japanese participants felt that the emotes promoted a level of friendliness that is often difficult to achieve over the phone. For instance:

"The pictures of hands [emotes icons] *were very good for me. They were very friendly. So it is easy to send my opinion by using the pop-up message and also I'm happy to receive opinions by pop-up message. So it is not cold. I think it is a good balance."* ***(Interviewee 9, Japan)***

Japanese participants also used the emotes as a way of communicating without disrupting the main conversation during the meeting. For instance, one participant explained:

"When it is hard to ask a question, especially in the case of a remote meeting, it is good to ask a question by using the left side button without interrupting the discussion." ***(Interviewee 8, Japan)***

Another Japanese participant echoed these sentiments:

"When I say something by telephone, I interrupt the talking. If I want to say 'I think this is good' or make an agreement, and do not have something to say in detail, I do not have to interrupt by using this button. So it is convenient." ***(Interviewee 4, Japan)***

Alternatively, U.S. participants did not view the emotes as a way to communicate without disturbing the discussion. About 55% of U.S. participants attributed their lack of emote use to the size of the group, and could see how the emotes might be useful in larger meetings. For instance:

"Sometimes when you have a big meeting with 20, 25, 30 or even 40 people ... the head nodding and hearing people say, 'yes this looks fine', that sort of pulse of where the audience is, it's useful to get that. If you only have 5 people on the call, you can just ask. People will talk and give you that. I think it's [the emotes] *useful when it's impractical for each person to speak individually. ... I think it's useful for large groups to see what the general mood and temperature is."* ***(Interviewee 12, USA)***

While group size may be the moderating factor behind emote use for U.S. teams, it may not be for Japanese teams, since Japanese teams that were similar in size to the U.S. teams did use the emotes. Interestingly, a few U.S. participants saw emotes as beneficial to the extent that they reduce or omit other nonverbal cues that may exist in web meetings. One participant explained:

"The agree/disagree buttons you have, it takes away the verbal inflection of the voice. You can have somebody that agrees with something who is very polite about it, and somebody who agrees with something who is very rude about it. So it kind of gives you the chance to be neutral." ***(Interviewee 11, USA)***

For this participant, neutrality could minimize the harmful effects of a team member who is being negative or dominant and bringing down the morale of the team.

About 34% of emotes sent by Japanese participants were accompanied by custom messages such as "Great", "Cheers for good work", and full-sentence questions to accompany the Question emote. One participant explained:

"I wanted to show my activeness with my words. I can provide my meaning to the moderator by using the custom message." ***(Interviewee 9, Japan)***

This feedback suggests that using pictorial descriptions of feedback such as "Applause" or "OK!" may not express sufficient meaning in some circumstances, and further clarification is needed. Furthermore, the fact that some Japanese participants inserted their own messages may be an example of an adaptation to overcome certain limitations of the technology. Overall, however, Japanese participants thought that the emotes enhanced their meetings:

"It makes the meeting more alive." ***(Interviewee 25, Japan)***

Anonymity Features

In addition to the group vs. independent navigation option and emotes, we included features to allow participants to behave and communicate anonymously in their meetings. The main feature for this was "anonymous mode" which was an opt-in choice that rendered all comments and behavior (e.g., switching slides, telepointer movement on the slide screen) unlinked to one's identity. One reason for including an anonymous mode, as suggested by a fellow researcher in Japan, was to explore whether or not Japanese participants would be able to express unique ideas and opinions more comfortably under the guise of anonymity.

Somewhat surprisingly, Japanese participants did not use anonymous mode in their meetings other than trying it out to see how it worked. Furthermore, a vast majority (90%) of Japanese participants noted that anonymous mode was not appropriate for meetings where team members are acquainted with one another or for meetings where the team is relatively small. Participants revealed several explanations for these preferences. For instance:

"If I say something by anonymous mode, other people will think 'who is it?' and will not take it seriously. If I write a comment, people cannot understand who wrote it, and they cannot determine how important it is." ***(Interviewee 8, Japan)***

Participants also said that they would not make a comment anonymously, *especially* if it was constructive criticism.

"When we talk about criticism, the meeting does not work if we do not know who says the criticism. An anonymous opinion does not have much meaning." ***(Interviewee 5, Japan)***

While we might have expected that criticism would be easier to say if it could be done without the potential threat to one's standing with one's teammates, it seems that criticisms without knowing the source would be meaningless to the Japanese participants in our study.

This feedback reveals two important aspects of why anonymity does not work in the types of meetings we observed. First, team members might try to guess who made the anonymous comment, which may be distracting to the team and could ultimately disrupt group harmony. Second, this participant's feedback highlights the importance of the context of the message. Knowing who said a comment may influence how to interpret the comment or determine its importance.

Japanese participants, however, did not reject all of the anonymity features. The polling feature, which allows any user to create a poll and send it to the team for an anonymous vote, was used and liked by Japanese participants. An average of 2.2 polls was created per Japanese team. 80% of participants felt that the polls were a convenient way to gather opinions from the group and liked that one's vote was anonymous. For example:

"Hiding results until voting finishes is also good because we do not change our opinions by watching other people's opinions." ***(Interviewee 2, Japan)***

As opposed to anonymous comments that Japanese participants wanted to be able to attribute to a particular individual, the anonymous polls, which were used in order to gather opinions across the group, enabled Japanese participants to express their unique opinions without being influenced by the opinions of others. Furthermore, this feature was popular since it allows individuals to express themselves without obviously standing out from the group, which may disrupt group harmony and threaten one's standing in the group.

U.S. participants did not use anonymous mode, nor did they use the polling features. In order to gather opinions, U.S. participants used the audio channel rather than the polling feature. For instance, one participant in Team 5 asked the group if there was a website they looked at everyday, and each group member took his turn on the audio channel giving his response. Furthermore, U.S. participants were not concerned about their identity being tied to their comments or behavior, nor were they concerned about disrupting group harmony. In addition, U.S. participants felt that these features neither encouraged nor hindered the ability to express their opinions.

Most Japanese participants (85%), however, noted that they could see a use for anonymous mode in certain circumstances. The first is when one is participating in a meeting with a large group (e.g., greater than 20) where individuals do not have much or any previous experience with each other. In this type of meeting, many Japanese participants felt it would be difficult to make a unique or slightly critical comment if it was attached to their identity. One participant noted that the option to use anonymous mode in this type of meeting …

"...would reduce the psychological burden when I say something that is totally different from what we are talking about." ***(Interviewee 4, Japan)***

Another Japanese participant explained why he would use the anonymous mode in a meeting where people do not know much about each other:

"The reason is, I do not want to give a negative impression by saying a negative opinion. In our case, we knew about each other. If participants know about the personality of each person, we will acknowledge negative opinions." ***(Interviewee 3, Japan)***

This participant's comments reveal an interesting distinction about how critiques are received. Making negative remarks in front of people one knows well is considered acceptable because it will not reflect poorly on one's character or 'face'; one's character is already known to the group. Making comments in front of people that one does not know well may lead those others to conclude that the person is divisive and would disrupt social harmony.

Similarly, some Japanese participants said that anonymous mode would be helpful for meetings with customers. For instance:

"When customers are participating, it is good to have anonymous mode to make it easy for customers to say opinions. But I think it is not necessary as an internal tool. ... From my experience, customers cannot say opinions by raising their hands. Because I think they especially have difficulties saying counterarguments, it will be useful. ... It is difficult for customers to say counterarguments, like negative opinions about our product, with saying their names." ***(Interviewee 26, Japan)***

Another situation where anonymous mode could be helpful is when communicating with one's superior. Several Japanese participants explained that anonymous mode would be useful for expressing opinions where they might be reticent to do so. For instance:

"I think [anonymous mode] *is necessary to say critiques ... in some cases, for example, in the case that it is difficult to say an opinion to your boss."* ***(Interviewee 7, Japan)***

Some U.S. participants (45%) could also see some use for anonymous mode, though their examples were based on personality rather than relationships or group context. For example:

"I think where it [anonymous mode] *may work - for people who are quieter and maybe don't like to talk as much - it may give them the opportunity where they could post a comment or pose a question."* ***(Interviewee 13, USA)***

While Japanese participants thought of different contexts, U.S. participants mainly thought of a different personality type for which anonymous mode might be useful.

DISCUSSION

By introducing specific features into a real-time collaborative editing environment, we were able to uncover both behavioral and attitudinal insights about how Japanese and American distributed work teams communicate and collaborate. The first feature or probe was the option for group vs. independent navigation in the slide deck. Japanese participants saw a use for both the group and independent navigation while U.S. participants almost always used the independent navigation. Interestingly, both U.S. and Japanese participants noted that feeling a part of the group was important. However, U.S. participants still felt part of the group without actually linking to the group navigation, while Japanese participants tended to attribute feeling connected to the group to joining the group navigation. It seems that while the goal of feeling connected to the group was shared across Japanese and U.S. teams, the way the teams achieved the goal was different. This finding suggests that explicit interface indications of being "in the group", such as our group icon indicating those in the shared navigational state, may be especially useful in cultures that promote an interdependent sense of self.

Yet, the lack of a leader was problematic for some Japanese participants. This may be due to the fact that typical business meetings in Japan are formal, contain a fair amount of structure, and emphasize social roles or hierarchies. Accordingly, several Japanese participants suggested we implement a 'presenter mode' as a third navigation option. This option would appoint a 'leader' who would control the slide navigation, similar to the way many web meeting presentation tools operate. Interestingly, this mode was requested not for traditional slide sharing but for collaborative editing and brainstorming activities, suggesting that an environment with no leader may not be ideal for activities that are traditionally thought of as egalitarian. On the other hand, American culture tends to place more of an emphasis on freedom, such as the freedom to express an idea even if it disrupts social harmony [22]. This may help to explain why U.S. participants tended to use the independent navigation option.

Japanese participants' reasons for using the emotes suggests that ethereal, relatively innocuous messages which represent nonverbal behaviors that might occur in a face-to-face meeting help to create a feeling of friendliness among team members. Furthermore, these emotes served as a way of contributing to the meeting swiftly but without interrupting the main flow of the meeting, reflecting previous findings that Japanese individuals are concerned with maintaining group harmony. And while U.S. participants said small meeting size was the reason they did not use emotes, similarly sized Japanese teams did choose to use emotes. Japanese participants may prefer to use emotes because they remind them of "kawaii", an aspect of Japanese culture that refers to cute things that evoke positive emotions and feelings of social affiliation [26]. Or, they may have felt more comfortable providing their input through emotes than through other channels.

The inclusion of the anonymous features (anonymous mode, anonymous voting in polls) revealed differences among Japanese and U.S. participants in terms of how they might use such tools across various business situations. While Japanese participants felt that anonymous mode was inappropriate for meetings with their familiar teams, they pointed out various instances where anonymous mode might be useful. Alternatively, U.S. participants could not easily see a use for anonymous mode. That anonymous mode, a feature we thought might aid in maintaining harmony, was problematic for teams reflects the inconsistent findings in the literature about the benefits of anonymity in group work [21], and suggests that we may need to reevaluate the link between group harmony and anonymity. In addition, our findings suggest that different types of anonymity features may be more or less successful in actually disguising one's opinion. Though anonymous mode does not connect comments and edits with one's name, participants suggested that it might be possible to discern the identity of the content creator through other cues. Not only would this practice be distracting, it might make others unwilling to use anonymous mode for fear that it would not actually mask one's identity.

The anonymous polls, however, seemed to thoroughly disguise participants' opinions, and Japanese participants liked this feature. There seemed to be a difference with the sort of opinions participants wished to gather via a poll vs. the opinions participants wished to gather through text-based comments or over the telephone. With a poll, the information is collected to gain an understanding of how the group feels at an aggregate level. Individual comments, however, typically come attached with meaning based on the individual's identity, which carries information such as status or personality. That individual comments would lack this contextual information was problematic for participants working with familiar co-workers. Taken with previous research [10,24], our data suggest that the appropriateness of acting anonymously differs across situational contexts. While anonymous behavior may be appropriate in online communities or even with unfamiliar clients, acting anonymously within one's familiar work team may be awkward or even problematic.

These observed differences across Japanese and U.S. teams suggest that the usability of the system was at some level influenced by cultural distinctions in the interpretations of features. In addition, our findings indicate that knowledge of cultural differences at the aggregate level cannot simply be mapped onto the design of collaborative software to improve usage across cultures. Rather, specific aspects of culture, such as the desire to maintain social harmony or the tendency to communicate through nonverbal behavior, must be explored across different scenarios in order to understand how one's background may influence how one uses collaborative software. Accordingly, our findings suggest that designers of collaborative software should include multiple options for features like slide navigation and anonymity so that users can choose the best option across situations. Furthermore, designers can use insights not only about how but *why* certain features work in order to further expand on these features in the right direction.

Limitations & Future Work

While our work provides new insights into how Japanese and U.S. distributed work teams use real-time collaborative editing tools, there are limitations to our work. First, the number of teams examined was relatively small, and teams were not identified a priori for variables such as task type or team size. While we examined a variety of team sizes and task types, we did not focus on these variables, which have been shown to influence team dynamics and outcomes. Our data revealed that team size and task type might influence Japanese participants' use of LiveDeck. In particular, observing the use of anonymous mode in Japanese teams might be more appropriate for larger teams where participants can more easily hide amongst their fellow teammates or in teams who work with clients. Future work could examine a wider variety of group sizes, including very large teams, to further explore our findings on the use of anonymity, as well as navigation options and emotes. Second, while we examined teams in two different countries, all participants were employed by the same global organization, so findings might be different if individuals from other organizations were included. Finally, since we did not examine teams' use of LiveDeck over time, certain findings may be influenced by the novelty of LiveDeck to users.

Because of these limitations, we are unable to know for sure whether geographic location is at the root of the differences we observed. However, we feel that this in-depth investigation of real teams doing real work can help to inform hypothesis generation for more structured or experimental studies that could potentially isolate the effects of geographic location.

CONCLUSION

In this study, we attempted to gain a deeper understanding of how Japanese and U.S. teams use real-time collaborative editing tools. As real-time collaborative editing software evolves, it is important to understand what features work for individuals with different cultural backgrounds and in different contexts. By exploring the different features that enhance friendliness, participation, or the ability to express one's opinions, we can continue to unravel the relationship between cultural backgrounds and online collaboration.

ACKNOWLEDGMENTS

We acknowledge the helpful contributions of Di Liu and Akihiro Kosugi in programming different features of LiveDeck. We are grateful for the useful conversations and ideas from Andrew Sempere, Hironobu Takagi, Susumu Harada, and Chen-Hsiang Yu regarding the design of LiveDeck and its use in a cross-cultural context. We thank Saeko Nomura, Darren Gergle, and William Barley for their insightful comments on prior drafts of this paper.

REFERENCES

1. http://www.adobe.com/products/flash
2. Boehner, K., Vertesi, J., Sengers, P., & Dourish, P. (2007). How HCI interprets the probes. In *Proc. CHI 2007*, ACM Press, 1077-1086.
3. Erez, M. & Gati, E. (2004). A dynamic, multi-level model of culture: From the micro level of the individual to the macro level of a global culture. *Applied Psychology: An International Review, 53*(4), 583-598.
4. Fiske, A.P., Kitayama, S., Markus, H.R., & Nisbett, R.E. (1998). The cultural matrix of social psychology. In D.T. Gilbert, S.T. Fiske, & G. Lindzey (Eds.), *Handbook of social psychology.* New York: Oxford University Press.
5. Gaver, B., Dunne, T., & Pacenti, E. (1999). Cultural probes. *Interactions, 6*(1), 21-29.
6. Gibbs, J.L. (2009). Culture as kaleidoscope: Navigating cultural tensions in global collaboration. In *Proc. IWIC 2009*, ACM Press, 89-98.
7. http://googleblog.blogspot.com/2010/08/update-on-google-wave.html
8. Gudykunst, W.B., Matusmoto, Y., Ting-Toomey, S., Nishida, T., Kim, K., & Heyman, S. (1996). The influence of cultural individualism-collectivism, self-construals, and individual values on communication styles across cultures. *Human Communication Research, 22*, 510-543.
9. Hasada, R. (1997). Some aspects of Japanese cultural ethos embedded in nonverbal communicative behavior. In F. Poyatos (Ed.) *Nonverbal Communication and Translation* (pp. 83-103). Philadelphia, PA: John Benjamins Publishing Co.
10. Heine, S.J., Takata, T., & Lehman, D.R. (2000). Beyond self-presentation: Evidence for self-criticism among Japanese. *Personality and Social Psychology Bulletin, 26*(1), 71-78.

11. Hinds, P.J., & Bailey, D.E. (2003). Out of sight, out of sync: Understanding conflict in distributed teams. *Organization Science, 14*(6), 615-632.
12. Hinds, P.J., & Kiesler, S. (Eds). (2002). *Distributed work: New research on working across distance using technology.* Cambridge, MA: MIT Press.
13. Hofstede, G. (1984). Dimensions of national cultures in fifty countries and three regions. In J. Deregowski, S. Dzuirawiec & R. Annis (Eds.), *Expectations in Cross-Cultural Psychology.*
14. Hymes, C.M., & Olson, G.M. (1992). Unblocking brainstorming through the use of a simple group editor. In *Proc. CSCW 1992*, ACM Press, 99-106.
15. Ishii, H. (1993). Cross-cultural communication and CSCW. In L.M. Harasim (Ed.) *Global networks: Computers and international communication.* Cambridge, MA: MIT Press.
16. Junuzovic, S., Dewan, P., & Rui, Y. (2007). Read, write, and navigation awareness in realistic multi-view collaborations. In *Proc. CollaborateCom,* 2007: IEEE.
17. Kam, M., Wang, J., Iles, A., Tse, E., Chiu, J., Glaser, D., Tarshish, O., & Canny, J. (2005). Livenotes: A system for cooperative and augmented note-taking in lectures. In *Proc. CHI 2005*, 531-540.
18. Karahanna, E., Evaristo, R.J., & Srite, M. (2006). Levels of culture and individual behavior: An integrative perspective. *Journal of Global Information and Management, 13*(2), 1-20.
19. Kayan, S., Fussell, S.R., & Setlock, L.D. (2006). Cultural differences in the use of instant messaging in asia and north america. In *Proc. CSCW 2006,* ACM Press, 525-528.
20. Kowner, R., & Wiseman, R. (2003). Culture and status-related behavior: Japanese and american perceptions of interaction in asymmetric dyads. *Cross-Cultural Research, 37*(2), 178-210.
21. Kraut, R. (2003). Applying social psychological theory to the problems of group work. In J.M. Carrol, (Ed.) *HCI models, theories and frameworks: Toward a multidisciplinary science* (325-356). Morgan Kaufman, New York, NY.
22. Markus, H.R., & Kitayama, S. (1991). Culture and the self: Implications for cognition, emotion, and motivation. *Psychological Review, 98*(2), 224-253.
23. Miyata, K., Boase, J., Wellman, B., & Ikeda, K. (2005). The mobile-izing Japanese: connecting to the internet by PC and webphone in Yamanashi. In M. Ito, M. Matsuda, and D. Okabe (Eds.) *Portable, personal, pedestrian: Mobile phones in Japanese life.* Cambridge, MA: MIT Press.
24. Morio, H., & Buchholz, C. (2009). How anonymous are you online? Examining online social behaviors from a cross-cultural perspective. *AI & Society, 23*(2), 297-307.
25. Myers, M.D., & Tan, F. (2002). Beyond models of national culture in information systems research. *Journal of Global Info. Management, 10*(1), 24-32.
26. Nittono, H. (2010). A behavioral science framework for understanding kawaii. *In Proc. of the Third International Workshop on Kansei*, Fukuoa, Japan, 80-83.
27. Olson, J.S., & Olson, G.M. (2003). Culture surprises in remote software development teams. *ACM Queue, 1*(9), 52-59.
28. Rains, S.A., & Scott, C.R. (2007). To identify or not identify: A theoretical model of receiver responses to anonymous communication. *Comm. Theory, 17,* 61-91.
29. http://www.researchware.com/
30. Rivera, K., Cooke, N.J., & Bauhs, J.A. (1996). The effects of emotional icons on remote communication. In *Proc. CHI 1996.*
31. Samovar, L.A., Porter, R.E., & McDaniel, E.R. (2009). *Communication between cultures.* Boston, MA: Wadsworth.
32. Setlock, L.D., Fussell, S.R., Ji, E., & Culver, M. (2009). Sorry to interrupt: Asian media preferences in cross-cultural collaborations. In *Proc. IWIC 2009*, ACM Press, 309-312.
33. Sieck, W.R. & Mueller, S.T. (2009). Cultural variations in collaborative decision making: Driven by beliefs or social norms? In *Proc. IWIC 2009*, ACM Press, 111-117.
34. Staub, D., Keil, M., & Brenner, W. (1997). Testing the technology acceptance model across cultures: A three country study. *Information & Management, 33*(1), 1-11.
35. Sun, C., Xia, S., Sun, D., Chen, D., Shen, H., & Cai, W. (2006). Transparent adaptation of single-user applications for multi-user real-time collaboration. *ACM Transactions on Computer-Human Interaction, 13*(4), 531-582.
36. Utz, S. (2000). Social information processing in MUDs: The development of friendships in virtual worlds. *Journal of Online Behavior, 1*(1).
37. Valacich, J.S., Dennis, A.R., & Nunamaker, J.F. (1992). Group size and anonymity effects on computer-mediated idea generation. *Small Group Research, 23*(1), 49-73.

Cultural Differences on Visual Self-Presentation through Social Networking Site Profile Images

Chen Zhao
Microsoft Research Asia
No.49 Zhichun Road, Beijing, China
chzha@microsfot.com

Gonglue Jiang
Harvard University
24 Everett St, Rm 207, Cambridge, MA, USA
gjiang@gsd.harvard.edu

ABSTRACT
A profile image is one of the most important personal attributes on social networking sites (SNSs). The current study examines whether self-presentation on SNSs is related to national culture and how forms of self-presentation differ between American and Chinese users. We accomplish this by analyzing profile images on two social networking sites, Facebook in the US and Renren in China. Our findings indicate that self-presentation is sensitive to national culture: Chinese users are more likely to customize their profile images than Americans. Our study suggests that there is a need to design social networking website features that better support profile construction for international users.

Author Keywords
Cultural differences, self-presentation, social networking sites, profile images.

ACM Classification Keywords
H5.m. Information interfaces and presentation (e.g., HCI): Miscellaneous.

General Terms
Human Factors.

INTRODUCTION
One of the values provided by Social Networking Sites (SNSs) is the opportunity for self-presentation, which is usually conveyed in the form of online profiles. SNS profiles often consist of a profile image, a self-description, (e.g., demographics) and lists of various interests. These profiles play a significant role in "users' ability to initiate, develop and maintain personal relationships" [1].

There are a variety of ways that online self-presentation can be characterized. Most previous studies have looked at profile pages with a focus on textual elements. We focus on a common element to all SNS profile pages: The profile image. The profile image usually appears in a noticeable part of the profile page and is a primary piece of identification in a user's profile. Why is it interesting to study profile images? The profile image, which shows physical appearance, is "the most remarkable feature for self-presentation" according to Leary [2].

In this paper, we examine the cultural differences in the forms of self-presentation of the SNS profile image. Our results identified different profile image styles between Chinese and American users. Chinese, compared with American users, are more likely to customize their profile images by using, for example, digital effect photos. American users are more likely to show group photos in their profiles, contradicting our original hypothesis. We discuss how these findings provide implications for designing specific features on SNSs for users who are not from Western cultures and have particular preferences for their self-presentation on SNSs.

Self-presentation and Photos as Visual Profiles in SNS
Self-presentation is "the process by which people convey to others that they are a certain kind of person or possess certain characteristics" [2]. Tufekci pointed out that self-presentation is regarded as "a minimum" requirement for participation on SNSs by users and one of the most important pieces of SNSs [3]. Much of the previous research concerning SNSs' user profiles has examined different perspectives. Stecher and Counts explored aspects of online impression formation and discussed the crucial role of user profiles in this process [4]. A study conducted by Pempek et al. found that participants find self-presentation one of the most interesting things about Facebook and 62.64% of Facebook users consider posting photos as a way to express who they are to other users [5]. Strano studied what kind of photos people choose for their profile images on Facebook and found that gender and age affect what photos people choose for their profiles [6]. Here we consider only how national culture affects the form of self-presentation on SNSs.

Cultural Differences on Self-Presentation
Culture is one of the major influences on self-presentation [6]. In general, the terms "individualism" and "collectivism" are used to understand how cross-cultural differences shape self-presentation. Collectivists, such as

the Chinese, tend to emphasize the results of their actions on members of their in-groups. They also tend to be interdependent with in-group members. Individualism in western nations, such as the United States, reflects a tendency to respect individual entities, rather than group entities [7]. Chinese and Americans, for example, have different self concepts in relation to others. Marcus and Kitayama described the Chinese as having *interdependent* self-construals and Americans as having *independent* self-construals [8]. A person with an interdependent self-construal sees him/herself as defined by the relationships and contexts s/he inhabits. A person with an independent self-construal, in contrast, sees him/herself as unique, with dispositional attributes that are independent of the relationships and contexts in which s/he is embedded.

This cultural difference has implications for the ways in which people from different cultures might choose to present themselves to others, in part because the concept of "self" varies by culture. Since an interdependent self-conception is desirable in collectivism cultures, we hypothesize that users from this culture might choose to present their social group memberships when presenting themselves online, because relating to others is part of their self concept. Therefore, we form the following hypothesis:

H1. *Chinese SNS users, as compared with Americans, will be more likely to use group photos in their profile images.*

Here we define a group photo as an image showing a user with one or more other people.

In recent cultural psychology research, researchers have proposed a bicultural self theory for contemporary Chinese individuals, encompassing two main components: The individual-oriented self and the social-oriented self. The social-oriented self is rooted in a traditional Chinese conceptualization, whereas the individual-oriented self has, in recent years, emerged and developed under Western influences, along with modernization. Prior research has found that the individual self of the Chinese gets developed and grows in some situations, such as the workplace [9]. Some research has examined how self-presentation has changed online and found that more flexibility is provided for users in how they construct their self-presentation [10]. Users are provided with a totally new channel and have more freedom when presenting themselves on SNSs when compared with a face to face condition. We believe that the bicultural self in contemporary Chinese individuals can also be reflected in their self-presentation on SNSs. We propose that Chinese SNS users would be more likely to customize their photos in a profile image in a variety of ways, which infers Chinese bi-self concepts when compared to Americans.

H2. *Chinese SNS users, when compared with American users, will be more likely to customize their profile images.*

We categorized the methods of customization into several classifications: (1) Self photos with digital effects, edited by programs such as Photoshop; (2) Photos of celebrities: Sports stars, movie stars, successful businessmen etc.; (3) Photos of a Baby, Animal, Landscape and Fine arts. (4) Photos of Objects: Phone, computer, car, etc. Figure 1 shows several examples of customized profile images.

Figure 1. Examples of Customized Profile Images.

METHOD

Participants

This study is based on data collected from Renren[1] and Facebook. The participants of the study came from a list of students at eight top universities (four each in China and the US) who were referred by members of the researchers' social networks in China and the US. We restricted our sample using two filter questions: Where the student was born and raised, and what language(s) they spoke fluently before the age of 10, to make sure the cultural identity of each participant in this study was strictly either Chinese or American. There were 114 subjects sampled from China and the US in total (57 participants from each country; among the 57 participants, 31 male and 26 female from each country). The average number of friends for each participant was 398 for the Chinese (ranging from 31 to 1608) and 377 for the Americans (ranging from 56 to 2276). All of our participants opened their profile photos for public viewing.

Data Analysis

The profile photos were independently coded by two researchers for group photo (coding interliability: 0.98) and customized photo, including customization type (coding intereliability: 0.89).

RESULTS

An independent sample T-test was conducted to examine the number of SNS friends and showed no significant difference between the Chinese and American participants (t(101)=.30, sig.=.77). We examined the gender effect with a binary logistic regression and found no significant

[1]Renren (www.renren.com) was launched in 2005, and has 100 million users as of Aug 2010. It is the most popular SNS in China.

Category	Customization	American		Chinese	
		Count	Percent	Count	Percent
Group photo	N/A	20	35.09%	0	0%
Customized photo	1. Self with digital effect	6	10.53%	11	19.30%
	2. Celebrities	0	0%	2	3.51%
	3. Baby	0	0%	1	1.75%
	4. Animal	1	1.75%	3	5.26%
	5. Landscape	1	1.75%	1	1.75%
	6. Fine Arts	0	0%	4	7.02%
	7. Objects	1	1.75%	2	3.51%
	In total	9	15.79%	24	42.11%

Table 1. Photo choices for Profile image.

difference on group photo (β = -.09, p=.87) and customized photo (β = -.72, p=.10).

We used the 2-Independent Sample Mann-Whitney Test to test our first hypothesis. For H1, we predicted that Chinese, compared with American participants, will be more likely to use group photos in their profile images. Interestingly, our data showed that 35% of the Americans (20 out of 57 participants) used group photos and none of the Chinese participants had group photos in their profile images; the opposite of our H1 is supported (z=-4.9, p<.001, two-tailed). We used binary logistic regression to test our second hypothesis. Our H2 predicted that Chinese participants, when compared with American participants, will be more likely to customize their profile images. A significant effect of national culture was detected here (β= 1.14, p<.05), suggesting significantly more Chinese (42.1%) customized their profile photos compared to American participants (15.8%). See Table 1 for the customization details.

DISCUSION

This study examined self-presentation differences across Chinese and US users of social networking sites. Results suggest that in the SNS scenario, more Chinese users tend to customize their profile photos than American users do. Nevertheless, American users tend to present profile photos that contain more people, contradicting the "western-individualism, eastern-collectivism" theory.

First we would like to compare the designs of Facebook and Renren in order to verify if our findings are caused by cultural differences, as we hypothesized, or by the different designs of Facebook and Renren. We found both similar and different features. Both Facebook and Renren provide Friend's news feeds, profile, friend suggestion, status attachment, and privacy settings. There are also interesting different features when comparing Facebook and Renren. With regards to sharing features, Renren provides a set of emotion facial icons alongside Videos, Links and Photos; Facebook provides Status updates, Questions, Photos, Links and Video. Asian users' preference on emotion icons was identified by previous cross culture research. Kayan et al's Instant Message survey found that emotion icons were significantly used more in Asia than in North America [12]. Another different feature is that Renren provides a set of rich features for users to decorate their profile pages and photos, including skin templates, photo frame templates and animations. To the best of our knowledge, neither Facebook nor Renren provides features for users to customize their profile images or encourages this behavior. In fact, Renren actually ranks the users who do not use real personal photos for profile images lower, which actually discourages Chinese users' customization behaviors. Therefore, there is a reason to believe our findings would be more strongly supported if we take into consideration the design differences of Facebook and Renren.

Facebook profile images can be seen as a form of "implicit" identity construction in which users display personal characteristics through images [13]. Zhao et al. found through a content analysis of 63 college student Facebook accounts that users rely heavily on implicit modes of self-presentation. Our results echo these findings but we also found that Chinese and American users have different "implicit" presentations: Chinese users tend to choose customized images that show "polished" images of the self and Americans tend to choose group photos. We articulated possible reasons why Chinese users prefer to customize their profile image in our hypothesis. Collectivism oriented Chinese culture tends to value looking proper in front of social groups; external objects (such as a nice car, a mobile phone, etc.) implicitly shows the status of an individual. It might also be attributed to a concern of identity disclosure as research shows that Chinese disclose themselves less than Americans [14]. It is surprising to find that more American participants (35%) compared with Chinese participants (0%) choose a group photo, as it is contrary to previous culture difference theories. We can speculate about two possible interpretations for this finding. All of our participants are undergraduate and graduate university students. Is there a possibility that the new Chinese generation is more individualistic than the new American generation? This would form interesting exploration in future work. Another reason could be that social activity plays more important roles for Americans when compared to Chinese. Additional research, with additional and more focused measures, can help provide a firm conclusion.

There are also limitations in our study. First, our participants were identified via our own social network and could have led to a limited demographic. Second, Strano found that age affects users' profile image choices [6]. We do not know if our results can be generalized for other age groups. In future research, we plan to examine a larger range of online behaviors and user backgrounds by taking into account the role of age in self-presentation and examining multiple forms of online self-disclosure.

CONCLUSION

We are interested in how people use their profile photos to constitute the self image in different cultures. These findings will help the community to get a more holistic view on how SNSs are used in different cultures given that the majority of current SNS research has been performed on Facebook or MySpace in the US. Moreover, the findings could also have implications for SNS design in achieving cultural sensitivity. Are customization features necessary for the success of SNSs? Currently, Renren does not have any special features for users to better customize their profile images. However, it does have special features to support users in decorating and personalizing their homepage. The homepages on Renren are diverse in terms of background and visual design, suggesting customization or personalization needs of Chinese users. Additionally, another excellent example is Tencent (www.tencent.com), which is currently the third largest internet company in the world and known for localized design features for Chinese users. Tencent provides a number of features to support users in customizing their avatars and homepages, such as virtual clothes, profile image patterns, and many templates for personal pages. Cultural differences in self-presentation have implications for the design and use of social networking sites. Graphical applications and tools can be incorporated into existing sites such as Facebook to provide more ways for users to visually present themselves in particular for non-Western users.

ACKNOWLEDEMENTS

We thank Matt Callcut, Desney Tan and James Landay for helping edit this paper, Huiting Zhang and Ilana Diamant for their early participation in this work, and the anonymous CHI reviewers for their thoughtful comments.

REFERENCE

1. Toma, C.L. Affirming the self through online profiles: Beneficial effects of social networking sites. In Proc. CHI 2010, ACM Press (2010), 1749-1752.
2. Leary, M.R., Tchividijian, L.R. and Kraxberger, B.E. Self-presentation can be hazardous to your health: Impression management and health risk. Health Psychology, 13, 6 (1994), 461-470.
3. Tufekci, Z. Can You See Me Now? Audience and Disclosure Regulation in Online Social Network Sites. Bulletin of Science, Technology & Society, 28, 1, (2008), 20-36.
4. Stecher, K., Counts, S. Thin Slices of Online Profile Attributes. In proc. ICWSM'08, American Association for Artificial Intelligence, (2008).
5. Pempek, T.A., Yermolayeva, Y.A. and Calvert, S.L. College students' social networking experiences on Facebook. Journal of Applied Developmental Psychology, 30, 3 (2009), 227-238.
6. Strano, M.M. User Descriptions and Interpretations of Self-Presentation through Facebook Profile Images. Journal of Psychosocial Research on Cyberspace, 2 (2008).
7. Triandis, H.C. The self and social behavior in differing cultural contexts. Psychological Review, Vol. 96, No. 3, (1989), 506-520.
8. Markus, H.R., Kitayama, S. Culture and the self: Implications for cognition, emotion, and motivation. Psychological Review 98, 2 (1991), 224-253.
9. Lu, L. The Individual-Oriented and Social-Oriented Chinese Bicultural Self: Testing the Theory. J. Soc. Psychol., 148, 3 (2008), 347-374.
10. Huffaker, D.A. and Calvert, S.L. Gender, identity, and language use in teenage blogs. Journal of Computer--Mediated Communication, 10, 2 (2005), 1.
11. Scott, C., and Stecher, K. Self-presentation of personality during online profile creation. In Proc. ICWSM '09, American Association for Artificial Intelligence, (2009).
12. Kayan, S., Fussell, S. R., and Setlock, L.D. Cultural Differences in the Use of Instant messaging in Asia and North America. In Proc. CSCW 2006, ACM Press (2006), 525-528.
13. Zhao, S.Y., Grasmuck, S., and Martin, J. Identity construction on Facebook: Digital empowerment in anchored relationships. Journal of Computers in Human Behavior. 24 (2008). 1816-1836.
14. Chen, G.M. Differences in self-disclosure patterns among Americans versus Chinese: A comparative study. Journal of Cross-Cultural Psychology 26, 1 (1995), 84-91.

MonoTrans2: A New Human Computation System to Support Monolingual Translation

Chang Hu[1,2,3], Benjamin B. Bederson[1,2,3], Philip Resnik[1,3,4] and Yakov Kronrod[3,4]
[1]Computer Science Department, [2]Human-Computer Interaction Lab,
[3]Institute for Advanced Computer Studies, [4]Department of Linguistics,
University of Maryland
{changhu, bederson}@cs.umd.edu, resnik@umiacs.umd.edu, yakov@umd.edu

ABSTRACT
In this paper, we present MonoTrans2, a new user interface to support monolingual translation; that is, translation by people who speak only the source or target language, but not both. Compared to previous systems, MonoTrans2 supports multiple edits in parallel, and shorter tasks with less translation context. In an experiment translating children's books, we show that MonoTrans2 is able to substantially close the gap between machine translation and human bilingual translations. The percentage of sentences rated 5 out of 5 for fluency and adequacy by both bilingual evaluators in our study increased from 10% for Google Translate output to 68% for MonoTrans2.

Author Keywords
Monolingual, translation, translation interface, human computation, distributed human computation, wisdom of crowds, crowd-sourcing, machine translation.

ACM Classification Keywords
H5.m. Information interfaces and presentation (e.g., HCI): Miscellaneous.

General Terms
Design, Human Factors, Experimentation

INTRODUCTION
Monolingual translation, or translation by people who speak only the source or the target language, has been proposed as a way to solve the problem of translating between rare languages, or to achieve more cost effective, high quality translation at a large scale [2][3]. At the core of monolingual translation are protocols in which the human participants (monolingual source or target language speakers) work together to make sense of machine translations. Since monolingual translation does not depend on bilingual humans, it enables translation between uncommon language pairs where a bilingual translator is hard to find. In addition, monolingual translation can be supported by a larger population, and thus it is likely to result in higher throughput. In scenarios where bilingual participants are still required to guarantee quality, it can transform their role into a combination of translation checking and translation creation, rather than just the latter.

Our previous monolingual translation system, MonoTrans, showed promising results [2]. However, we encountered a number of limits to its scalability. First, MonoTrans requires users to participate in a strictly alternating sequence, thus requiring the presence of speakers on both sides for a sustained period for a successful and timely translation. Second, to successfully complete translations, users need to understand the different roles of source and target language speakers, which can be confusing.

These limitations render the system impractical, because participant populations are usually imbalanced. There can be many source language speakers and very few target language speakers, or vice versa. Those users may have vast differences in their schedules and motivations; e.g., some may only intend to spend too short a time to understand the translation UI.

Drawing upon this experience, we present MonoTrans2, a new monolingual translation system, with two goals:

1) Participation in parallel: Enable every participant to take part in the translation process at any time.

2) Minimal context: Decrease the amount of contextual knowledge required to participate.

We performed an experiment in which MonoTrans2 was deployed to translate children's books in the International Children's Digital Library (www.childrenslibrary.org, ICDL). The results show a dramatic improvement in the production of high quality translations (as determined by bilingual evaluators), without relying on any human bilingual expertise.

RELATED WORK
Monolingual translation is a fairly new idea. Previous systems include MonoTrans [2] and the Language Grid system [3]. These are examples of *Human Computation*, systems that connect people and computers to solve problems not easily addressable by either one alone [4]. In these systems, a machine translation channel connects one or more source language speakers with target language speakers. On each side, the users perform actions such as *edit*, *accept*, *reject*, and/or *attach extra information*. The source and target speakers try to make sense of the (usually

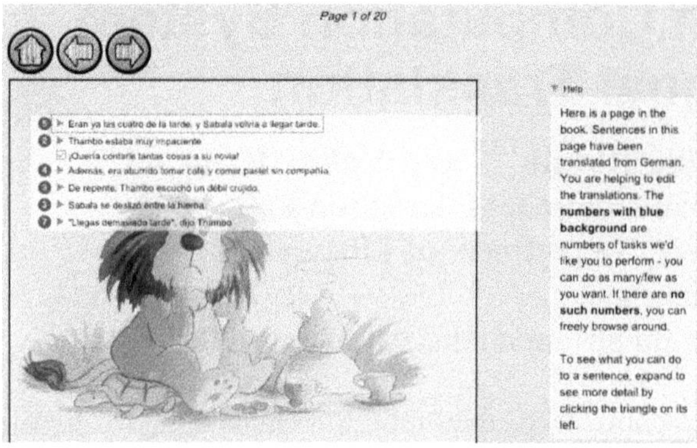

Figure 1. The MonoTrans2 UI for the target language speakers. Notice 1) the number in a blue circle indicating tasks before sentences; and 2) the contextual help on the right. The background image is a scan of the actual book (with original text removed) to provide context.

noisy) machine-translated sentences and progress toward a correct target translation.

The Language Grid experimental system [3] is based on a two-phase synchronous protocol involving two users. In the first phase, the source language speaker repeatedly rephrases the sentence being input to the MT system until the target language speaker indicates that the machine translation can be understood. Then the protocol enters the second phase, in which the target language speaker proposes one rephrasing of the machine translation at a time, until the source language speaker decides that the translation is sufficient by comparing the back-translation with the original. The Language Grid system assumes that users are online and that the same pair (or pairs) of users are working on the same sentence extensively until it has been translated.

MonoTrans [2] was based on a different iterative protocol. Similarly, the source sentence is first automatically translated into the target language and given to the target language speaker. Then, at each step, the source and the target language speaker take turns to edit or attach extra information to the translation (or its back-translation). Monotrans has a clearly defined back-and-forth process where each side's task must be completed before the next step of work can be done.

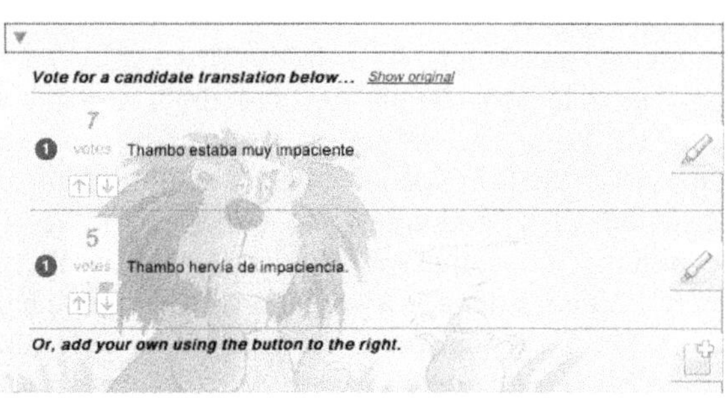

Figure 2. The list of candidate translations for the target language speakers.

Source Side	Target Side
Vote on a candidate	Vote on a candidate
Give explanation to marked "error" phrases	Mark a phrase in the candidate as "error"
Rephrase the source sentence	Suggest a new translation candidate

Table 1. Tasks in MonoTrans2

MONOTRANS2 UI

We designed MonoTrans2 (Figure 1) to support participation in parallel as well as tasks with minimal context. Like all the previous systems, MonoTrans2 still connects two (groups of) users through a machine translation channel. However, it allows translation or back-translation to be edited by multiple users on the same side simultaneously. The edited (back-)translations are then sent to users on the other side in parallel. Compared with translation in MonoTrans, the biggest difference is that now there are multiple parallel threads of translations/back-translations for any one sentence. This enables multiple users to participate at the same time without waiting.

To deal with multiple parallel translation threads, candidates and voting are introduced. The simultaneous edited (back-)translations are presented in MonoTrans2 as translation candidates. Target language speakers propose translation candidates (Figure 2). These candidates are back-translated and presented to the source language speakers in parallel with each other. Source language speakers, in turn, can propose a rephrasing of the original sentence at any time, and the rephrased source sentences become candidates, which are then translated and presented to the target language speakers. To identify the best candidate, MonoTrans2 allows users to vote for or against any candidate. Voting not only helps to identify the best candidate in a cumulative manner, but also provides casual users with a very short and intuitive task.

There are six tasks in MonoTrans2, three tasks for each side (see Table 1.) During the design of these tasks, special attention was paid to minimizing users' need for context. For example, we redesigned the mechanism that allows users to attach clarifying information (such as an image or URL) to parts of a sentence. In an initial design of MonoTrans2, target language speakers asked questions about the parts they felt needed clarification, and source language speakers attached clarifying information as answers. This design created a tension for casual users who use MonoTrans only once on the target side, because they either send questions for which they will never see an answer, or receive answers for questions they did not ask. To avoid this problem, this functionality was refactored so that target language speakers only mark parts of sentences that need clarification (without asking a specific question), which is a very simple and intuitive task, and source language speakers see which parts of the source sentence were confusing and choose the clarification type and content.

EXPERIMENT

We evaluated MonoTrans2 by translating content from children's books (intended reader's age 6-9) from the ICDL. We had volunteers work on translating four Spanish books into German, and one German book into Spanish. All translations started from the language in which the book was originally published. Machine translation was done using the Google Translate Research API.

Participants were recruited from a database of ICDL volunteer translators, soliciting people who spoke German or Spanish (but not both). Sixty (60) fluent Spanish speakers and 22 fluent German speakers participated. In four days, participants edited/voted on 162 sentences. We estimate 20 words per typical sentence, so on average, roughly 800 words were translated per day, which is close to half the speed of professional translators.[1]

Two fluently bilingual evaluators unfamiliar with the project were recruited to assess translation quality for fully automatic output of Google Translate (as a baseline) and for the output of MonoTrans2 (using Google Translate as the translation channel). They were paid for their work. Systems were identified only as Systems A and B, and evaluators were not told which outputs came from which system. For each output (target sentence) paired with its corresponding source sentence, the evaluator's task was to rate the target sentence's fluency and adequacy on a 5-point scale, where fluency of 5 indicates complete fluency and adequacy of 5 indicates complete preservation of meaning [1]. Bilingual assessments were obtained for all five books.

In addition, two native Spanish speakers, both unfamiliar with German, rated quality for translations of the German book into Spanish. They also were independent of the project and paid for their time. They were given ground-truth Spanish translations for reference. The evaluation results are shown in Table 2.

Fluency		1	2	3	4	5	Total
B1	G	2	8	69	28	55	162
	M2	4	7	6	14	131	162
B2	G	5	52	55	25	25	162
	M2	3	11	11	22	115	162
S1	G	11	6	6	15	34	72
	M2	3	3	1	11	54	72
S2	G	6	9	12	20	25	72
	M2	1	1	2	18	50	72

Adequacy		1	2	3	4	5	Total
B1	G	6	33	38	23	62	162
	M2	2	7	6	5	142	162
B2	G	5	52	55	26	24	162
	M2	4	10	11	21	116	162
S1	G	9	7	7	20	29	72
	M2	7	1	4	8	52	72
S2	G	14	12	6	19	21	72
	M2	6	4	14	25	23	72

Table 2. Distribution of fluency scores (top) and adequacy scores (bottom) by evaluator. Each column shows the number of sentences receiving that rating. B1 and B2 are bilinguals; S1 and S2 are Spanish speakers; G: Google Translate; M2: MonoTrans2

Figures 3 and 4 summarize the results. Unsurprisingly, MonoTrans2 produced large gains in fluency compared with raw machine translation output.[2] Crucially, however, note the shift in adequacy in Figure 4: using MonoTrans2, the peak of the adequacy distribution has been shifted from 3 to 5. We ran four two-tailed paired t-tests, between scores of MonoTrans2 and scores of Google Translate for both fluency and adequacy for each bilingual evaluator (Table 4). We also ran chi-square tests for the scores (both for individual evaluators, and for the evaluators in aggregate). The p values are well under .001 (Table 5). These results show that MonoTrans2, using only monolinguals, significantly improved translation fluency and adequacy over Google Translate.

	Google	MonoTrans2
Sentences with fluency = 5	21 (13%)	112 (69%)
Sentences with adequacy = 5	17 (10%)	118 (73%)
Sentences where BOTH = 5	17 (10%)	110 (68%)

Table 3. Number of sentences with maximum possible fluency and adequacy. Number of sentences, N = 162.

Table 3 conveys our experiment's bottom-line results more strikingly. On the very conservative criterion that a translation output is considered *high quality* only if *both* bilingual evaluators rated it a 5 for *both* fluency *and* adequacy, Google Translate produced high quality output for 10% of the sentences, while the MonoTrans2 process improved this to 68%.

We also elicited subjective reactions from our monolingual translation participants. In the fifteen written comments, the greatest concern was that we might simply publish the translations created through our process without bilingual review; as ICDL volunteers, these participants were deeply committed to attaining 100% bilingual-translator quality. In followup correspondence, their concerns were alleviated

[1] Generally, professional translators' speed is 2000 words per day. We hired a translation firm to translate the same books. They took four days.

[2] Improvements in fluency are to be expected given that the last step of output is always produced by a human, as is the heavy non-bell-curve skew toward top fluency.

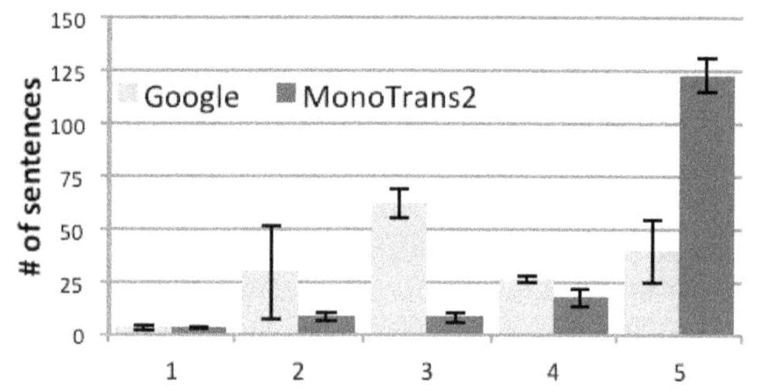

Figure 3. Fluency distribution of edited sentences with two bilingual evaluators (1=worst, 5=best)

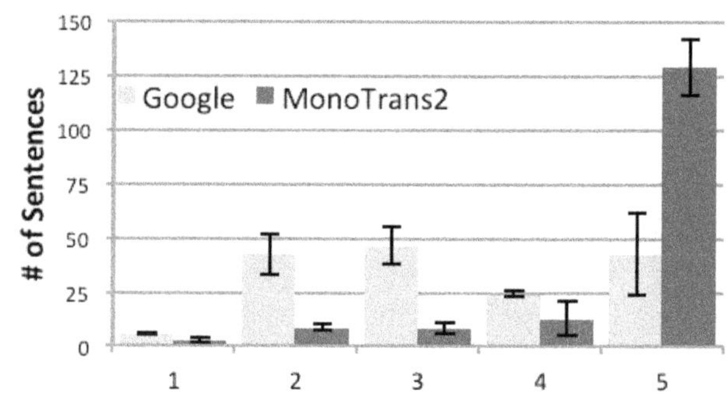

Figure 4. Adequacy distribution of edited sentences with two bilingual evaluators (1=worst, 5=best)

once they understood that in the real-world ICDL use case, the results suggest MonoTrans2 could potentially convert 68% of bilingual translators' time to validation rather than full translation, but the role of those bilinguals would remain necessary.

Evaluator	Fluency	Adequacy
B1	63e-16	3e-19
B2	5e-27	6e-27

Table 4. T-test results (p values)

Evaluator	Fluency	Adequacy
B1	89.4	85.1
B2	115	115
Both	192	192

Table 5. Chi-square test results (F values, DOF=4)

DISCUSSION

MonoTrans2 users appeared to finish more work in the same amount of time than users of the original MonoTrans.[3] However, there were a number of differences in these studies, so this should be taken only as a rough comparison. While one might expect finer-grained comparisons between the two systems, the value of such a comparison would be unclear, since MonoTrans2 is not an incremental revision, but rather a new design inspired by, and drawing on the old design. So much has been changed that a direct comparison with MonoTrans would not provide the ability to isolate particular dimensions of the design, and the processes are so different that they do not offer any obviously comparable user-level measures. In this paper, the key, bottom-line result is the comparison between fully automatic translation and the new process: a dramatic improvement in the production of high quality translations, without requiring *any* human bilingual expertise.

[3] In an unpublished study of MonoTrans, 22 participants translated 12 sentences in 4 days.

CONCLUSION

This paper presented MonoTrans2, a new monolingual translation system that supports participants working in parallel with minimal context. Our experiment confirmed that tasks in a translation process can be designed so each user performs tasks independently of the others, rather than working synchronously with another monolingual user as in every previous monolingual translation system. Breaking the monolinguals' tasks down and shortening them ensures that there are always tasks available for all users, making the approach more scalable and more attractive to participants regardless of their intended time commitment. In comparison with state of the art automatic machine translation, MonoTrans2 obtains dramatic improvement in the production of high quality translations, *without* relying on any human bilingual expertise. The approach shows significant promise for use cases like ICDL, where bilingual costs and effort must be kept to a minimum. In addition to fully integrating bilingual post-processing in the ICDL scenario, we also plan to evaluate the approach in other scenarios where bilingual validation simply cannot be expected.

ACKNOWLEDGMENTS

This research is supported by NSF contract #BCS0941455 and by a Google Research Award.

REFERENCES

1. Dabbadie, M., Hartley, A., King, M., et al. A hands-on study of the reliability and coherence of evaluation metrics. *Workshop at the LREC 2002 Conference*, Citeseer (2002), 8.
2. Hu, C., Bederson, B.B., and Resnik, P. Translation by iterative collaboration between monolingual users. *Proceedings of Graphics Interface 2010 on Proceedings of Graphics Interface 2010*, Canadian Information Processing Society (2010), 39-46.
3. Morita, D. and Ishida, T. Designing Protocols for Collaborative Translation. In *Principles of Practice in Multi-Agent Systems*. 2009, 17-32.
4. Quinn, A.J. and Bederson, B.B. Human Computation: A Survey and Taxonomy of a Growing Field. *In Proceedings of SIGCHI* 2011, in press.

Culture or Fluency? Unpacking Interactions Between Culture and Communication Medium

Leslie D. Setlock, Susan R. Fussell
Department of Communication, Cornell University
Ithaca, NY 14850 USA
lsetlock, sfussell@cornell.edu

ABSTRACT
In this paper we describe two studies intended to replicate earlier work comparing American and Chinese communication in a negotiation task using several different media. In the earlier studies, the participants all spoke in English, raising the question of whether differences in fluency rather than differences in cultural background explained the results. We replicated the earlier studies using materials translated into Chinese, a native Chinese-speaking experimenter, and native Chinese participants. Counts of Chinese characters in each media show nearly the identical pattern found in the earlier studies, suggesting that cultural differences in communication styles, rather than fluency, account for the earlier findings. We describe implications of this work for tools to support intercultural communication.

Author Keywords
Computer-mediated communication, CMC, collaborative work, intercultural collaboration, cultural differences

ACM Classification Keywords
H5.m. Group and Organization Interface: Computer-supported cooperative work

General Terms
Human factors; Experimentation

INTRODUCTION
The increasing globalization of the workplace, home life, and education has led to increasing communication and collaboration among people from a variety of geographical locations around the world, usually via computer-mediated communication (CMC) technologies. Studies have shown that these interactions often face problems arising from cultural differences in communication styles, task orientation, power structures, and a host of other factors [e.g., 1, 3].

In recent years, researchers have tried to isolate the specific ways in which culture affects CMC, both in culturally homogeneous and culturally heterogeneous groups [e.g., 7, 8, 9, 10, 11]. These studies typically use laboratory paradigms in which the task can be specified in advance and comparisons can be made across cultures in terms of efficiency, task performance, the relative emphasis on task completion vs. relational development, liking for partners, and the like. Virtually all such studies have found differences between Western cultures and other cultures, as well as interactions between culture and medium.

For example, Setlock and colleagues conducted two studies comparing American dyads, Chinese dyads, and mixed American-Chinese dyads performing a decision-making task via different media. In their first study [7], they found a significant interaction between culture and medium: Chinese participants talked significantly longer face-to-face than in Instant Messaging (IM), whereas American participants talked very little in both media conditions. Intercultural pairs lay intermediate to these same-culture pairs. In their second study [8], they found that mixed culture pairs talked significantly more using audio or video conferencing than did either American or Chinese same-culture pairs. In both studies, mixed culture pairs reported liking each other less than same-culture pairs.

There are numerous theories which attempt to explain cultural variation, and each has its supporters and critics. This study utilizes observed behavior to clarify one specific theoretical concern: that observed behavioral differences often attributed to culture may be caused by fluency issues. Hall [4]'s theory proposed that low-context cultures, such as that of the United States, tend to emphasize the words people use to communicate, whereas high context cultures, such as that of China, tend consider the entire situation of communication in understanding a message. The affordances of a medium [1] may make it more or less appropriate for communicators from different cultural backgrounds. In particular, people from cultures with high context communication styles may make more use of affordances of richer media, whereas people from cultures with low context communication styles may find rich and lean media equally suitable for their needs.

In Setlock et al.'s studies, as well as many similar studies, all pairs interact in English. This was done to ensure comparability across the different conditions, and is reasonable given that English is often used as a lingua franca in international discourse. However, it raises the question of whether the communication patterns of the Chinese participants might have been due to issues of fluency rather than culturally shaped styles of communication. This is an important issue, because it informs the design of new tools to support intercultural communication. If observed differences between groups stem from fluency, machine translation-based CMC tools [e.g., 5] alone may be sufficient to facilitate communication across nations and groups. If observed differences stem from cultural factors, however, CMC tools may also need to adapt to cultural differences in communication styles and help bridge gaps that arise in mixed-culture groups.

The purpose of the current studies is to assess fluency as an alternative explanation for the findings reported by Setlock and colleagues, by replicating the Chinese condition of both studies entirely in Chinese. All materials for both studies, including consent forms, etc., in addition to the task materials, were translated into Mandarin Chinese by a native Mandarin speaker (an instructor of Chinese at an American University). Materials were back-translated into English to ensure appropriateness. The sessions were likewise run entirely in Mandarin Chinese, by a native Mandarin speaker, from the time participants entered the lab. As will be shown, the results of these two studies closely parallel those by Setlock et al., suggesting that cultural differences in communication styles rather than fluency in a second language explain the earlier results.

STUDY 1

Method

Pairs of participants performed a modified version of two decision-making tasks (the Desert Survival Task and the Arctic Survival Task). Participants performed one task face-to-face and the other via Instant Messaging.

Participants. Twelve pairs (24 participants) of native Mandarin Chinese speakers born and raised in the People's Republic of China (PRC) participated in the study (mean age 28.5; age range 22-37, 54% male). Participants were drawn from two universities in the eastern United States. They had been studying in the U.S. for fewer than two years. All were fluent in spoken and written English, to ensure comparability with Setlock et al., although English was not used at any point in the current study.

Materials and equipment. Materials and equipment were identical to those used by Setlock et al. [7], with the exception that we used MSN as an IM client rather than AIM because it is better suited to typing in Chinese.

Participants collaborated on two tasks, the Desert Survival Task and the Arctic Survival Task. The goal of these tasks is to rank salvaged items in order of importance for the survival of the team. Participants completed the tasks in pairs. First, they ranked the items individually, then negotiated and completed a joint ranking, and finally completed a second individual ranking. Items included a "gallon can of maple syrup" and a "hand ax" (Arctic Survival Task) and "Book 'Edible Plants of the Desert'" and "loaded .38 caliber pistol" (Desert Survival Task.) Items were ranked from 1 (most important item for survival in this simulation) to 6 (least important item for survival in this simulation.)

Participants also completed a post-task questionnaire following each task, which assessed their experience with the communication media and partner. The questionnaire included such items as "This method of working together was effective," and "We disagreed often." Items were rated from 1 (strongly disagree) to 7 (strongly agree). At the end of the study, they completed a post-experimental questionnaire which asked about their demographic characteristics (age, gender, major, country of birth, years in the United States). The post-experimental questionnaire also included the Schwartz value inventory [6].

Procedure. All sessions were run entirely in Mandarin Chinese, by a native Chinese speaker. Participants were brought to the laboratory and instructed about their task and the media (lapel microphones and the AIM program) used in each condition. Following the brief instructions, they were situated in the correct location for their first trial, either in the same section of the room (for the Face-to-Face condition) or separated by a divider (for the IM condition). They completed the individual item ranking, had 20 minutes in which to complete the joint ranking (a single, mutually agreed-upon ranking), and then completed the final individual ranking. Each trial was followed by a post-task questionnaire. After both trials were completed, participants completed the post experimental questionnaire. They were then debriefed and compensated.

Results

Conversational efficiency. The audio recordings from the face-to-face condition were transcribed and then translated by a native Mandarin Chinese speaker. We then calculated the Chinese characters per task (roughly equivalent, though not identical, to words per task in English) as well as the translated English words per task for the two media conditions. We ran all analyses twice, once using Chinese character counts and once using the number of English words after translation. The pattern was identical, so here we report significance values using the Chinese character counts.

Figure 1 shows characters per task from the current study compared to words per task from Chinese participants in Setlock et al. [7]. As can be seen, the Chinese language results replicate the English findings. Pairs used a mean of 1088.92 (SD = 618.73) Chinese characters per task in the face-to-face condition in comparison to only 456.50 (SD =159.38) Chinese characters per task in the IM condition. A repeated measures ANOVA using the pair as the unit of analysis showed this difference to be highly significant ($F [1, 11] = 8.34$, $p < .005$).

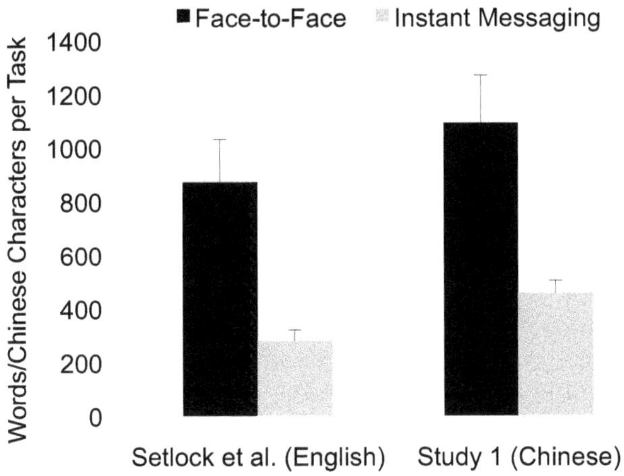

Figure 1. Results from Chinese participants speaking in English in Setlock et al. [7] (left) and Chinese participants speaking in Chinese in Study 1 (right). The measures are not exactly equivalent (words in English; characters in Chinese) but the pattern of findings is nearly identical.

Outcome measures. On the whole, the participants rated the quality of their interaction with their partner highly (Ms = 6.22 and 6.08 for the face-to-face and IM conditions, respectively). These ratings are comparable to the mean rating of 6.5 provided by the Chinese pairs speaking in English in Setlock et al. [7]. The data was analyzed in a 2 (trial) by 2 (media condition) Mixed Models ANOVA in which participant within pair was the random variable. No main effects or interactions were found for trial or media (all $F < 1$).

Persuasion was measured by summing the absolute difference between pair members' individual rankings both pre- and post-discussion. With this measure, smaller scores indicate closer agreement between pair members' rankings. Differences between participants' pre-discussion averaged 8.5 (SD = 3.53) in the face-to-face condition and 7.17 (SD = 3.66) in the IM condition. Differences in post-discussion individual ranks also did not differ between media condition (M = 1.42 for the face-to-face condition and 1.50 for the IM condition; $F\ [1, 12] < 1$, *ns*.). The high agreement between partners after discussion is not quite as great as found in the earlier study (where Chinese pairs speaking in English averaged .56 difference between their final rankings) but is greater than American (M = 2.88) and mixed culture pairs (M = 4.50) in the earlier study.

Discussion

The results from this study, in which Chinese participants communicated in their native language, closely parallel those from Setlock et al. [7], in which they communicated in English. Thus, the interaction between culture and medium reported by Setlock et al. does not appear to be due to the fact that the Chinese participants were speaking in a second language.

STUDY 2: AUDIO VS. VIDEO CONFERENCING

Method

The design of Study 2 replicated Setlock et al. [8]. Pairs performed two survival tasks, one via audio conferencing and one via video conferencing. Tasks and media were counterbalanced across pairs.

Participants. Twelve pairs (24 participants) of native Chinese speakers born and raised in the People's Republic of China participated in Study 2 (mean age 29.04; age range 22-35, 54% male). All had lived in the U.S. for two years or less, were studying at a local university, and spoke English as a second language.

Materials and equipment. The materials were identical to those used in Study 1. In the video condition, web cameras located above each participant's monitor sent a head and shoulders view of that participant to his/her partner. Video was displayed full-screen on a color 13-inch monitor located directly in front of each participant. Sony wireless microphones were used to record and transmit audio in both conditions.

Procedure. The procedure was identical to Study 1. The study was conducted entirely in Mandarin Chinese.

Results

Conversational efficiency. Consistent with the results reported by Setlock et al. [8], there was little difference between conditions in terms of how many Chinese characters pairs used to come to their joint rankings (for audio, M = 729.67, SD = 409.17 ; for video, M = 757.75, SD = 470.59; $F\ [1, 11] < 1$, *ns*). Means per condition are shown in Figure 2.

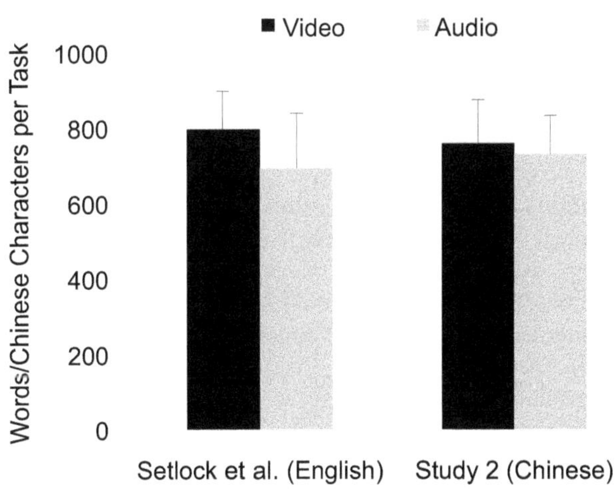

Figure 2. Results from Chinese participants speaking in English in Setlock et al. [8] (left) and Chinese participants speaking in Chinese in Study 2 (right).

Outcome measures. There were no effects of media condition on any of our outcome measures. Participants' ratings of the quality of their interaction were high for both conditions (for audio: 6.24 on a scale of 1-7 [SD = .66]; for video: 6.23 [SD = .72]; $F < 1$, ns). Persuasion, as indicated by the difference between partners' post-task individual rankings, was 1.17 (SD = 1.99) for the audio condition and .67 (SD = 1.30) for the video condition ($F [1, 11] < 1$, ns). This low score indicates high agreement and is consistent with Chinese pairs' persuasion scores in previous studies.

Discussion

The results for Chinese pairs conversing in Chinese are very similar to those for the Chinese pairs conversing in English reported by Setlock et al. [8]. In both cases, there was no evidence that adding visual cues to the auditory channel improved conversational efficiency, subjective evaluations of the success of the collaboration, persuasion, or task performance. In Setlock et al., gaze coding suggested that participants did not make use of the video channel for establishing mutual gaze. We consider the same may have happened in this study.

GENERAL DISCUSSION

The results from Experiment 1, in which Chinese participants communicated in their native language either face-to-face or via IM, parallel those Setlock et al.'s [7] similar study in which they communicated in English. The results of Experiment 2, in which Chinese participants communicated in their native language using audio or video conferencing, likewise parallel those of Setlock et al.'s second study [8]. Thus, the interaction between culture and communication medium, found in the previous experiment do not appear to be due to the fact that the Chinese participants were speaking in a second language. In addition, participants' scores on the outcomes measures (liking for each other, persuasion) were similar to the scores of Chinese pairs in the previous studies. This suggests that the main effects of culture reported in those studies are likewise not due to fluency issues. Chinese pairs enjoy working together and successfully persuade one another, regardless whether they interact in Chinese or English.

Our results are limited in that we only replicated two of the many previous studies in which native Chinese speakers were asked to communicate in English. Possibly, replications of other studies using quite different kinds of tasks [e.g., 9, 11] would show some effects of non-native language use. Similarly, our results are limited in that we could not, due to the lack of available participants, replicate the American condition in Setlock's studies using native English speakers fluent in Chinese. It would be very interesting in the future to see if Americans speaking in Chinese adopted a more high-context communication style.

One implication of these findings is that solutions to intercultural communication that rely exclusively on machine translation are unlikely to lead to successful interactions. Yamashita and colleagues have already demonstrated how small errors in translation can lead to confusion [12, 13]. Our results suggest that even if machine translation were perfected, cultural differences in communication styles will continue to create barriers that need to be overcome if we are to maximize the success of intercultural collaborations.

ACKNOWLEDGMENTS

This material is based upon work supported by the National Science Foundation under Grants #0803482, #0325087 and #0329077. The authors thank Ying-Ying Shih for translating the materials and running the sessions.

REFERENCES

1. Adair, W. L., & Brett, J. M. (2005). The negotiation dance: Time, culture and behavioral sequences in negotiation. *Organizational Science, 16,* 33-51.
2. Clark, H., & Brennan, S. (1999). Grounding in communication. In L. B. Resnick, J. M. Levine, & S. D. Teasley, *Perspectives On Socially Shared Cognition* (pp. 127-149). Washington D.C.: APA.
3. Cramton, C., & Hinds, P. (2007). Intercultural interaction in distributed teams: Salience of and adaptations to cultural differences. *Proc. Academy of Management Annual Meeting, Best Papers*.
4. Hall, E. 1976/1981. *Beyond Culture*. New York, NY: Doubleday/Anchor Books.
5. Ishida,T. (2006). Language Grid: An infrastructure for intercultural collaboration. IEEE/IPSJ Symposium on Applications and the Internet (SAINT-06), 96-100.
6. Schwartz, S. (1992) Universals in the content and structure of values: Theoretical advances and empirical tests in 20 Countries. In M. Zanna (Ed) *Advances in Experimental Social Psychology*, *25*, 1-65.
7. Setlock, L. D., Fussell, S. R., & Neuwirth, C. (2004). Taking it out of context: Collaborating within and across cultures in face-to-face settings and via instant messaging. *Proc. CSCW 2004* (pp. 604-613).
8. Setlock, L. D., Quinones, P. A., & Fussell, S. R. (2007). Does culture interact with media richness? The effects of audio vs. video conferencing on Chinese and American dyads. *Proc. HICSS 2007.*
9. Vatrapu, R. & Suthers, D. (2009). Technological intersubjectivity in computer supported intercultural collaboration. *Proc. IWIC 2009* (pp. 155-164). NY: ACM.
10. Veinott, E., Olson, J., Olson, G. & Fu, X. (1999) Video helps remote work: Speakers who need to negotiate common ground benefit from seeing each other. In *Proc. CHI 1999* (pp. 302-309). NY: ACM.
11. Wang, H-C., Fussell, S. R. & Setlock, L. D. (2009). Cultural difference and adaptation of communication styles in computer-mediated group brainstorming. *Proc. CHI 2009* (pp. 669-678). NY: ACM.
12. Yamashita, N. & Ishida, T. (2006). Effects of machine translation on collaborative work. *Proc. CSCW 2006* (pp. 515-523). NY: ACM Press.
13. Yamashita, N., Inaba, R., Kuzuoka, H., & Ishida, T. (2009). Difficulties in establishing common ground in multiparty groups using machine translation. *Proc. CHI 2009* (pp. 679-688). NY: ACM Press.

Skim Reading by Satisficing: Evidence from Eye Tracking

Geoffrey B. Duggan
Department of Computer Science,
University of Bath
Bath BA2 7AY, UK
g.duggan@bath.ac.uk

Stephen J. Payne
Department of Computer Science,
University of Bath
Bath BA2 7AY, UK
s.j.payne@bath.ac.uk

ABSTRACT
Readers on the Web often skim through text to cope with the volume of available information. In a previous study, Duggan and Payne [11] tracked readers' eye movements as they skimmed through expository text under time pressure. This article presents novel analyses of these eye-movement data. Results indicated that readers were able to explicitly direct attention to the most important information in the text and that this improved performance on a subsequent test of memory for the meaning of text. We suggest readers achieve this by *satisficing* – reading through text until the rate of information gain drops below threshold and then skipping to the next section of text. Further analyses of gaze patterns for paragraphs and pages supported this explanation. Combining satisficing with some form of scanning or sampling behaviour could explain patterns of reading found on the Web. A greater understanding of the way that text is read on the Web would assist many producers of online content.

Author Keywords
Skimming, reading, speed reading, information foraging, time allocation.

ACM Classification Keywords
H5.4. Information interfaces and presentation (e.g., HCI): Hypertext/Hypermedia.

General Terms
Experimentation, Theory.

INTRODUCTION
One of the most important and widespread interactions between humans and computers is the reading of text online. Descriptive studies suggest that there are a number of ways that reading on the Web differs from other forms of reading but one of particular importance is the tendency for online readers to *skim* text. Because of the sheer volume of text on the Web, and its interlinked and searchable nature, the amount of easily accessible information often outstrips the time available to read it. To compensate for this, it is commonplace to employ some form of rapid, selective reading strategy such as omitting words, paragraphs or pages [1,19,21]. Presumably, the purpose of such skimming is to maximise the information gained by focusing on the most useful sections of text.

Background Literature
Until recently the literature on text skimming provided limited support for the idea that, when there was insufficient time to read all the text available, readers could effectively focus on the most important parts of the text. Masson [20] varied the duration for which texts were presented to participants and then tested recognition performance for important and unimportant sentences from the texts. As reading rate increased, scores on the recognition test deteriorated roughly equally for important and unimportant information. Similarly, other studies [5,12,18] found that the comprehension of important and unimportant information from a text was equally degraded by an increase in reading rate. Thus, it is unclear from this work whether skimmers really can improve their understanding of the most important elements of a text by skipping over less important sections of text.

One limitation of these studies of skimming was the length of the texts used – typically around 500 words. To effectively focus on more important sections of text, the reader must be able to make inferences about the content of parts of the text before they are read (so as to know whether to skip over them). Assumptions of continuity and coherence may allow such inferences, but these processes may be more effective for larger amounts of text – as are found on the Web. In previous work [11] we have tested this suggestion by presenting readers with texts of over 3000 words for a constrained amount of time and comparing skimming with linear reading at normal pace. Because both conditions had the same amount of reading time, this design tested the *improvement* in understanding that could be attained through skimming unlike the other studies of skimming that tested the *decrease* in understanding due to a reduction in reading time. Moreover, this design was more representative of the typical situation on the Web where readers have a limited amount of time and must decide to either read a smaller section of text at normal pace or skim a larger section of text.

After reading, participants in Duggan and Payne [11] were tested on their understanding of the text in the same way as in [20]. Important and unimportant sentences from the text were presented one at a time to participants. Some of the sentences had their wording changed so as to contradict their original meaning and participants had to categorise each sentence as either consistent or inconsistent with the text. Duggan and Payne [11] found that memory for the meaning of the important sentences was better in the skimming condition than in the control condition in which some of the text was read through at normal speed. There was no difference in memory for the unimportant sentences. This result was found for pages structured linearly and for a hierarchical Website-like arrangement of pages.

To our knowledge [11] is the first empirical demonstration that skimming can improve readers' understanding of important information given a fixed budget of time. However, the advantage of skimming was not apparent when compared with conditions in which linear readers read half of every paragraph [11]. This raises the possibility that skimming is effective primarily because it distributes attention across a document. Important information plays a major role in the macrostructure of a text [17] and thus may often be inferable from neighbouring sections. For example, reading any text within a section on the medical applications of hypnosis could be a useful clinical technique. This account is quite different to the suggestion that skimmers are able to deliberately direct attention to important parts of the text.

Extensions to Eye tracking Analyses

These alternatives are tested for the first time by analysing gaze location and duration, recorded by tracking eye-movements during skim reading. This approach enables us to test directly the extent to which skimmers focused on the most important text and skipped over text that was less important. Understanding the effectiveness with which skimmers can focus on the most important elements of a text has clear practical relevance as it can guide writers as to the proportion of a text that should contain important information and also the extent to which this information needs to be signposted using headings or other highlighting tools.

The second purpose of the analyses of eye-tracking data that are presented here is to examine the process of skim-reading and contribute to the development of an account of the way that skimmers manage their time allocation whilst reading. This goal has even greater applicability, as an understanding of *how* users choose which to text to skip over can facilitate the creation of text and Websites that specifically cater for the methods of readers with limited time. The importance of this topic has already been recognised by Nielsen who has argued that text online is read differently to text elsewhere and that writers should take account of these differences [21].

Skim Reading Strategies

An important feature of Nielsen's description of online reading is that it is sensitive to the limitations in time to read material on the Web. Observations of eye-movements while browsing the Web have led him to conclude that readers typically scan web pages in an "F-shape" [22]. That is, a horizontal movement is made along the top of the page, followed by another horizontal movement of shorter length further down the page and then finally a vertical scanning movement down the left side of the page. Reading text in an F-shape is one potential method that skim readers could use to allocate their time. This strategy provides an easily executable technique for sampling a portion of text from a page before moving to a different page.

Another strategy for allocating time across a text is to use a strategy identified by Reader and Payne [28], that they termed *satisficing* (see also [30]). The description of this strategy is derived from an information foraging approach to browsing [24] in that it assumes that readers are sensitive to some proxy for "information gain" and use this as a basis for their behaviour. When satisficing, readers set a threshold of satisfaction and linearly read through a unit of text as long as the rate of information gain remains above this threshold. When a unit of text has been read or current satisfaction drops below threshold readers move to the next unit of text. During skimming it might be expected that the satisficing threshold be rather high, meaning that the threshold was often unmet. The theory does not specify the size of the unit of text that readers evaluate, however, data from [28] and [11] suggest that the paragraph may be an appropriate unit of text, not least because it is the most perceptually salient unit of text that is smaller than a page.

Some support for satisficing was found by [11]. They reported that skim-readers spent more time reading the first half of each paragraph, presumably because when the rate of information gain was low, participants skipped over the second half of the paragraph and started the next paragraph. Duggan and Payne [11] also reported that skimmers spent more time reading paragraphs that were earlier in a page. This indicates that they may have been evaluating the page as a unit of text as well as the paragraph. Judging (and deciding whether to abandon) units of text at more than one level complicates the account of satisficing but seems plausible – when a paragraph is judged uninformative perhaps the page or Website that contains the paragraph are also being judged as uninformative.

These results were derived from eye-tracking data from the participants in Experiment 2 from [11]. Here we report more in depth, finer grained analyses of this data that allow new hypotheses to be tested. All of the analyses reported in this paper are novel and were not included in [11].

To test whether participants focused on the most important text while skimming we compare total gaze duration for the important and unimportant sentences from the test of memory for meaning. These sentences were classified as important or unimportant by a separate group of participants. We predict that important sentences should be more likely to be read than unimportant sentences. However, with units of text as small as a sentence, given a font-size that was chosen with ecological validity in mind more than eye-tracking accuracy, there is a danger of fixation measures being made noisy by eye-tracker error. Such noise is not confounded with our hypothesis, but it necessarily weakens the test.

Consequently, we also consider the larger units of text – line and paragraph – that embed important versus unimportant sentences. Fixation measures of such larger units will be less affected by eye-tracker error. Furthermore, within well-written text, consecutive sentences will deliberately contain shared referents to improve coherence [31] meaning that the information surrounding an important sentence should also be more likely to contain important information. Thus, we predict that lines and paragraphs that contain important sentences should also be more likely to be read than lines and paragraphs containing unimportant sentences.

A further test of the extent to which actually reading text produced any improvements in understanding is to compare sentences that were answered correctly and incorrectly during the test of memory for meaning that followed skim-reading. We predict that gaze duration during skimming should be longer for sentences that were answered correctly than for sentences answered incorrectly.

The eye-tracking analyses reported in [11] do not clearly decide between Nielsen's description of F-shaped browsing and satisficing. The two horizontal movements across the page described by Nielsen could produce the increased reading time for the first half of a paragraph relative to the second half of a paragraph. Here though, we test reading time for each individual line within a paragraph. If readers make a simple horizontal movement then scan down the page, reading times for each line within a paragraph should decrease in a step function. In comparison, satisficing predicts that reading time per line, averaged over a group of readers or a set of paragraphs, should decrease over the course of a paragraph but this decrease should be gradual as the rate of information gain will decrease at different rates for different paragraphs. Indeed, where important information is contained within a paragraph, readers may read all of a paragraph. We also test the extent to which skim-readers scan down the left hand side of the page by measuring gaze duration in vertical stripes across the width of the page.

METHOD

Participants

Participants were 10 male and 18 female students from the University of Manchester. The mean age was 20.93 years (SD = 2.24). These were all the participants that were successfully eye tracked in Experiment 2 from [11] – data for the remaining 4 participants from that experiment could not be used due to technical difficulties in achieving accurate calibration.

Apparatus

A Tobii 1750 binocular eyetracker monitored participants' eye movements while they read. The eyetracker consisted of a high-resolution camera embedded in a 17-inch monitor. A PC was connected to the eyetracker and the stimulus materials were presented on the eyetracker monitor. The fixed wide-angle camera allowed data to be recorded from a freely moving person with approximately 20 cm of freedom on each side. The screen resolution on the monitor was set to 1024 x 768 pixels and the sampling rate was 20 ms. Participants were seated 61 cm from the monitor.

The application ClearView was used to export the eye-tracking data. The fixation filter from this package determined the start and end of a fixation. Thus, a fixation was deemed to start when the distance between each successive gaze point remained within a specified number of pixels for a specified period of time. A fixation ended when the distance between successive gaze points exceeded the threshold. The fixation filter size was set to 40 pixels and the minimal fixation duration was 80 ms. Analyses were conducted on "Total Gaze Time" which was the sum of all fixation durations in a region regardless of order.

Materials

Two texts were adapted from Scientific American articles on Hypnosis (3134 words) and Attention-Deficit Hyperactivity Disorder (3252 words). The two texts were restructured into 11 pages of approximately equal length (Page length in words: ADHD, M = 292.64, SD = 75.42; Hypnosis, M = 281.73, SD = 87.20). Page boundaries were selected so that the content within each page addressed a distinct topic that could be summarised using a single heading. A separate heading was devised for each page. There were 30 paragraphs in the ADHD text and the mean number of lines per paragraph was 7 (SD = 1.93). The Hypnosis text contained 28 paragraphs with a mean length of 6.90 lines (SD = 2.62).

From each text, 36 target sentences were selected for the test of readers' memory for meaning. These sentences were categorised following a procedure used in [20]. A group of 20 undergraduates who did not participate in the main study rated the sentences for their importance to the general meaning of the text. The 18 most highly rated sentences were used as the "important" sentences and the 18 lowest rated sentences were used as the "unimportant" sentences. For the test of memory for meaning, half of the important sentences and half of the unimportant sentences had their meaning changed so as to be semantically incongruent with the original statement. Because results from the memory for meaning are not analysed here, we shall not distinguish between sentences that did or didn't have their meaning changed during the test of memory for meaning.

The different sentence types were distributed approximately evenly across the different pages in the text with all pages containing at least one target sentence. The mean number of target sentences per page was 3.27 (SD = 1.39). The mean number of words between the start of the text and the target sentence was 1467 (SD = 958) for the important sentences and 1571 (SD = 898) for the unimportant sentences. This

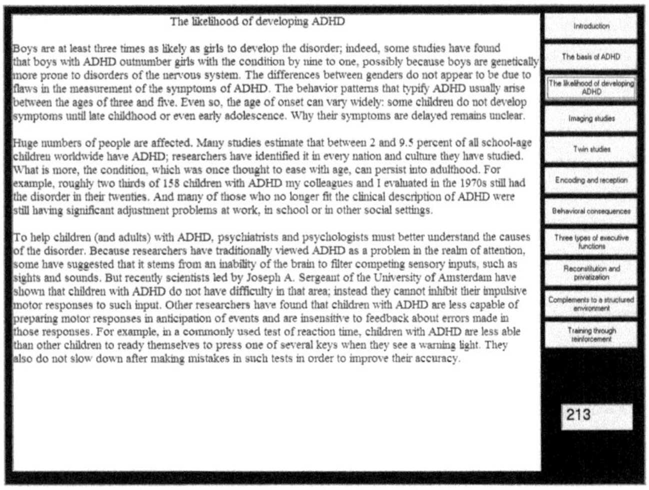

Figure 1. Screenshot showing the presentation of the texts.

difference was not significant ($t < 1$). Across both texts there were 36 important sentences and 36 unimportant sentences, these were distributed so that in total in the first half of a text there were 21 important sentences and 19 unimportant sentences.

Important and unimportant sentences were approximately evenly distributed across paragraphs (Mean number of target sentences per paragraph = 1.24, SD = .80). Target sentences were equally distributed across both halves of a paragraph within both texts. Thus, across both texts there were 18 important sentences and 18 unimportant sentences in the first half of a paragraph and the same number in the second half of a paragraph.

A purpose-built program presented the texts and the subsequent test of memory for meaning. The texts were presented one page at a time in a large box that filled most of the screen (see Figure 1 for a screenshot). Participants could navigate back and forth through the text by clicking on one of 11 buttons from a column down the right hand side of the screen (top to bottom in page order). Each button was labelled with the heading from the corresponding page. The texts were presented in font size 12, with up to 106 characters fitting on each line. Text was single line spaced and there was an empty line of text between paragraphs. In the bottom right hand corner of the screen a clock counted down the remaining number of seconds before the text was removed.

Procedure

Participants were instructed that they would be presented with a text on either Hypnosis or ADHD for a limited period of time before being tested on their understanding of the whole text. They were also told that there was not enough time to read through the text at normal reading speed but that they should allocate their time while reading so as to maximise performance on the subsequent test of memory for meaning. The ADHD text was presented for 325 seconds and the Hypnosis text was presented for 313 seconds which meant participants would have to read at 600 words per minute to read through the complete text (normal reading speed is approximately 225 words/minute – [20]).

When the time for reading had elapsed participants were required to complete the test of memory for meaning. Target sentences were presented serially in the centre of the screen in a randomised order. Participants categorised each sentence as either consistent or inconsistent with the text they had just read.

RESULTS

Reading Times for Important and Unimportant Text

The time spent looking at the target sentences, the lines containing the target sentences and the paragraphs containing the target sentences are given in Table 1. These total gaze times are given per character to aid comparison across sections of text that differ in length. (Total time spent fixating on an area of text was measured and then divided by the maximum number of characters that could have fitted into the area.) Means were calculated first within participants and then between participants. All means and standard deviations reported in this article reflect the average of the individual means across all 28 participants. All times were log transformed before analysis, although this made no difference to the pattern of significance. (See [26] for justification of the use of transformations upon latencies.)

Table 1 indicates that important sentences were read for longer than unimportant sentences, $t(27) = 4.52, p < .001, d = .55$. This effect was replicated when the areas of text that contained important and unimportant sentences were compared. Thus, lines that contained important sentences

	Important Sentences		Unimportant Sentences	
	M	*SD*	*M*	*SD*
Sentences	13.26	6.98	8.95	3.98
Lines containing sentence	10.12	4.58	6.76	2.84
Paragraphs containing sentence	9.60	3.94	6.76	3.33
Correct sentences	16.86	11.35	10.51	5.63
Incorrect sentences	9.20	4.76	7.27	4.69
Proportion correct	.73	.13	.66	.12

Table 1. Total gaze time per character (ms) for target sentences and for lines and paragraphs that contain target sentences. Target sentences are either important or unimportant sentences from the text. Target sentence total gaze times per character also provided split according to whether the target sentence was correctly or incorrectly categorised during the test of memory for meaning. Final row includes proportion of important and unimportant sentences correctly categorised in test of memory for meaning from [11].

were read for longer than lines that contained unimportant sentences, $t(27) = 4.99, p < .001, d = .59$, and paragraphs that contained important sentences were read for longer than paragraphs that contained unimportant sentences, $t(27) = 3.92, p = .001, d = .57$. (Paragraphs that contained both sentence types are excluded from the means in Table 1 and these analyses.) Overall mean fixation duration for all areas containing text was 160.61ms.

Reading Times for Correctly and Incorrectly Remembered Text

A key goal for this study was to test whether memory for the meaning of a sentence was related to the time spent looking at the sentence. For each participant, target sentences were categorised as correct or incorrect according to performance on the test of memory for meaning. For the purposes of comparison, the proportion of important and unimportant sentences correctly classified on the memory for meaning test from [11], are reproduced in Table 1. Total gaze times per character for sentences answered correctly and for sentences answered incorrectly are also provided in Table 1. These times were analysed using a 2 (Memory for Meaning: Correct or Incorrect) × 2 (Sentence Type: Important or Unimportant) within participants ANOVA.

Total gaze time was longer for sentences that were answered correctly than for sentences that were answered incorrectly, $F(1, 27) = 17.25, p < .001, \eta^2_p = .39$. There was also a main effect of sentence type which replicated the analysis reported above that important sentences were read for longer than unimportant sentences, $F(1, 27) = 17.24, p < .001, \eta^2_p = .39$. The interaction between sentence type and memory for meaning performance was not significant ($F < 1$) indicating that the longer total gaze times for sentences answered correctly applied to both important and unimportant sentences.

The standard deviation of gaze time for important sentences that were answered correctly was noticeably higher than the other standard deviations in Table 1. This appears to reflect a tendency for participants to sometimes dwell for a relatively long period of time on important material. This is consistent with a satisficing account of skim-reading. Statistical outliers did not cause the high variance – only one data point was greater than 2 standard deviations from the mean and removing this value did not affect the pattern of statistical significance.

The results presented above indicate that participants were successful at allocating their time to more important parts of the text and that this aided their memory for the meaning of important sentences from the text. We now turn our attention to the question of *how* participants managed to focus their attention on more important parts of the text. Analysis of the pattern of reading over the course of a paragraph provides a starting point to address this question.

Reading Strategy within a Paragraph

Mean total gaze times per character for all lines from first to eleventh within each paragraph were computed and are shown in Figure 2. As for the previous analyses, where there was an incomplete line at the end of a paragraph, gaze time was only measured for the area containing text. Figure 2 indicates that total gaze time decreased over the course of the paragraph. A one way within participants ANOVA found that this decrease over lines within a paragraph was significant, $F(1, 27) = 44.78, p < .001, \eta^2_p = .62$. Figure 2 indicates that this was a gradual decrease rather than a step function and that for 10 of the 11 lines total gaze time was more than half the total gaze time for the first line. Only 5 paragraphs had more than 10 lines, so we consider the time for the 11th line to be unreliable (excluding the data from the 11th line made no difference to the pattern of significance). The analysis supports and extends the finding from [11] that the first half of a paragraph was read for longer than the second half. Although the line in Figure 2 looks somewhat curved, a linear regression predicted 81% of the variance in total gaze time, and this was not improved significantly by adding a quadratic term.

The means for each line in Figure 2 were averaged across all paragraphs that contained the particular line. However, because paragraphs differed in length ($M = 6.95$ lines, $SD = 2.32$), some paragraphs did not contribute data to the later lines. This means that the figure reflects the distance of each line from the start of the paragraph but does not clearly represent the distance of a line from the end of the paragraph. Moreover, it seems plausible that the distance from the end of a paragraph may affect reading time. To account for this each paragraph was divided into 7 equal intervals following a procedure used by Jacoby *et al.* [15]. Where there were more than 7 lines some intervals represented the mean of more than one line and where there were fewer than 7 lines some intervals were left empty. All paragraphs contributed a value for the first and last interval. This transformation of the data did not affect the result and

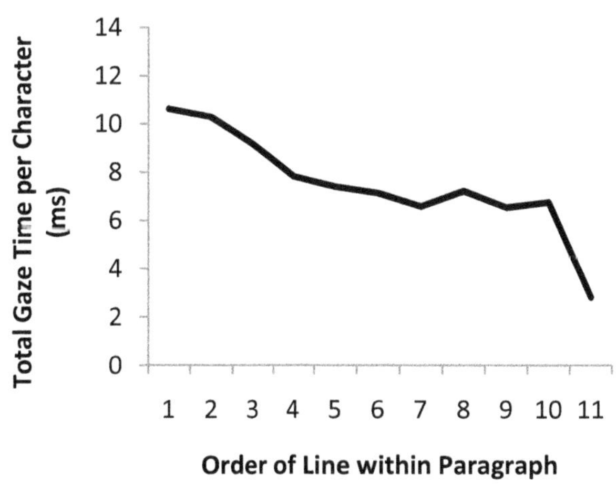

Figure 2. Total gaze time per character for each line within a paragraph.

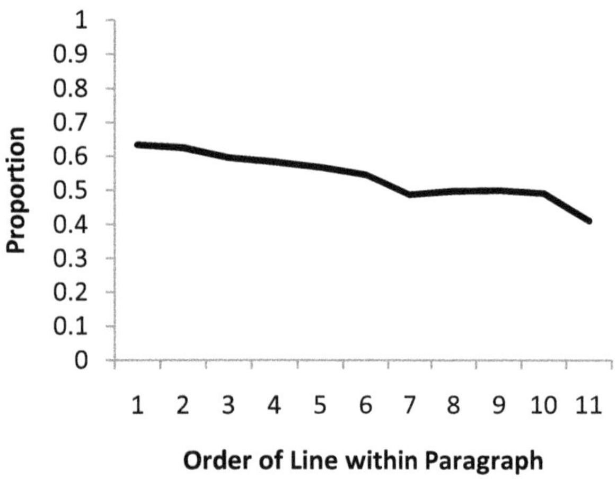

Figure 3. Proportion of times each line in a paragraph was fixated upon at least once by each participant.

there was a decrease in total gaze time over the course of the paragraph, $F(1, 27) = 40.76, p < .001, \eta^2_p = .60$.

The total-gaze-time-per-line data were also used to plot the proportion of times that each line was fixated upon at least once by each participant. These proportions were calculated for every paragraph for each participant and are shown in Figure 3. The figure shows that lines earlier in the paragraph were more likely to be fixated upon than lines later in the paragraph, $F(1, 27) = 8.20$, $p = .008$, $\eta^2_p = .23$. More importantly though, the figure indicates that most lines were fixated upon at least once and, typically, participants did not just read the first line or two of a paragraph. This is consistent with a satisficing strategy where participants read each paragraph and then skip to the next paragraph when the rate of information gain falls below threshold. We next assess the pattern of reading times over the course of a page.

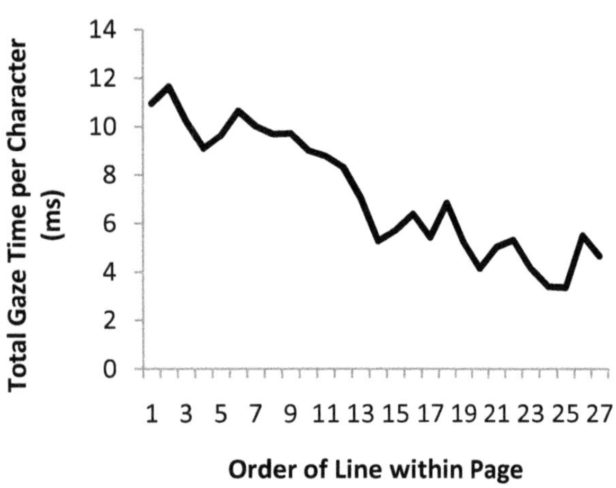

Figure 4. Total gaze time per character for each line within a page.

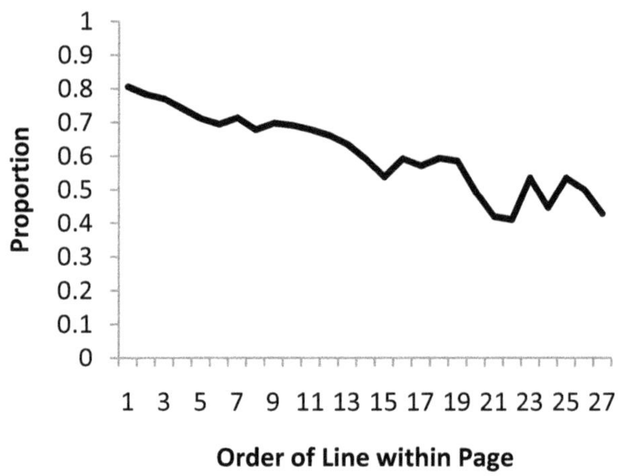

Figure 5. Proportion of times each line in a page was fixated upon at least once by each participant.

Reading Strategy within a Page

Mean total gaze times for each line within a page are provided in Figure 4. Blank lines between paragraphs were excluded from the figure and analyses. The means in Figure 4 suggest that total gaze time decreased over the course of a page. This effect was reliable when tested using a one way within participants ANOVA, $F(1, 27) = 44.90, p < .001, \eta^2_p = .62$. As for the paragraph analyses, the decrease was gradual rather than a step function. This analysis is consistent with the finding in [11] that paragraphs toward the top of the page are read for longer than paragraphs towards the bottom of the page. Linear regression predicted 87% of the variance in total gaze time, and this was not improved significantly by adding a quadratic term.

The proportion of times that each line within a page was fixated upon at least once by each participant is given in Figure 5. This figure shows that lines towards the top of the page were more likely to be fixated upon than lines towards the bottom of the page, $F(1, 27) = 19.62, p < .001, \eta^2_p = .42$. As for the paragraph analyses, the figure also shows a high proportion of lines were fixated upon at least once. The gradual decrease over the course of a page indicates that, in addition to the paragraph, participants may have treated the page as a unit of text over which they satisfice.

Gaze times were also analysed according to their position across the page. The page was divided into ten equal-width stripes and total gaze time for each stripe was measured. Only areas of the screen containing text were included and times were calculated per tenth of a line of text. Figure 6 shows total gaze times for each stripe (tenth of the screen) in order from left to right. Time spent looking in each stripe was approximately equal except for the first stripe which had a slightly longer total gaze time and the final tenth which had a much shorter total gaze time. The decrease in

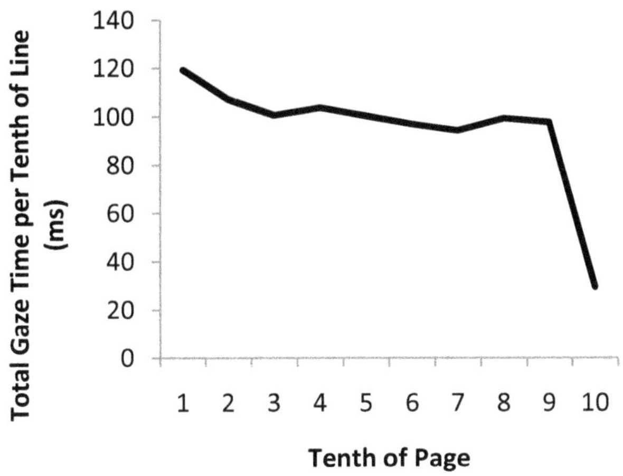

Figure 6. Total gaze time for each tenth of a page divided into equal-width vertical stripes across the width of the page. Tenths are ordered from left to right and reported as tenths of a line.

total gaze time from left to right was significant, $F(1, 27) = 97.58$, $p < .001$, $\eta^2_p = .78$. The higher total gaze time for the leftmost tenth of the page is consistent with a pattern of scanning down the left hand side of the text; however, the size of the difference is not large and a technical explanation for this effect is provided in the discussion below. The result for the final tenth is attributable to the text not being justified to the right margin of the page – this meant the text finished a number of characters before the end of most lines.

DISCUSSION

Overall, the results suggest that skim-readers can successfully focus on important text and that they achieve this by satisficing. Eye tracking analyses indicated that sentences, lines and paragraphs containing important information were read for longer than sentences, lines and paragraphs containing unimportant information. Furthermore, these differences improved readers' understanding, as better memory for the meaning of a sentence was associated with longer reading time for that sentence. The results enable us to discount the idea that the benefits for skimming reported by [11] were due to simply reading a more distributed selection of text. Skim readers' strategies were more sophisticated than that – they read important text and skipped over unimportant text.

Support was also found for the use of satisficing as a strategy to help readers focus upon the most important text. Average reading time for each line decreased gradually over the course of a paragraph, as did the proportion of times a line was fixated upon at least once. Therefore, lines toward the end of a paragraph were more likely to be skipped over than lines towards the start of a paragraph. This is consistent with a satisficing account that states skimmers begin every paragraph and continue reading until the rate of information gain drops below a threshold whereupon they skip to the beginning of the next paragraph.

Satisficing also provides an explanation for the rather smooth rate of decrease in reading time over the course of a paragraph. If important information is distributed equally throughout a paragraph, then the rate of information gain is equally likely to fall below threshold at any point and the probability that a participant has skipped to the next paragraph will increase at a consistent rate throughout the paragraph. Results also showed that almost all lines were read for at least half as long as the first line and the proportion of times a line in a paragraph was fixated upon at least once was always 0.4 or greater, suggesting that many paragraphs were read in their entirety. Assuming the threshold at which participants leave a paragraph was not too easily attainable this is, again, consistent with satisficing behaviour.

The reading times for each line within a page decreased over the course of the page. This suggests that participants also evaluated pages when satisficing and may have monitored rate of information gain within both areas of text while reading. That is, readers may simultaneously assess whether useful information is provided within the current page overall and also within the particular paragraph being read. Because paragraphs started and finished throughout a page it is difficult to be clear about reading patterns just due to the page. As well as generally adding variance to the page level analyses a tendency to skip information towards the end of paragraphs could also be partly responsible for the decrease in reading time over the course of the page. However, [11] simultaneously analysed within and between paragraph effects. They found that paragraphs towards the top of a page were more likely to be read for longer and that differences in reading times between the first and second halves of a paragraph could not be explained by the position of the paragraph on the page. Therefore, the most likely explanation for the data is that readers evaluate both the page and the paragraph when satisficing.

The relatively high reading times for lines late in a paragraph and a page suggests some or all pages of text were not read in an F-shape such as that suggested by Nielsen [22]. It seems unlikely that a horizontal movement across the start of the paragraph would incorporate information 11 lines from the start of the paragraph. The results for reading times across the width of the screen provided limited support for a scanning pattern down the left hand side of the screen. Reading time for the vertical stripe that was the leftmost tenth of the screen was marginally higher than for the rest of the screen. This difference was not large though and could be easily caused by corrections to eye movements after the relatively long traversal between words at the end of one line and the start of the next [27]. Finally, the reading times for each line within a page showed that text towards the end of a page was often read. We do not interpret these results as strong evidence against a general tendency to read in an F-shape. The pattern was observed by Nielsen under reading conditions that differed in many ways from those in our study and below we discuss the importance of some of these factors. Nonetheless, for the specific set of constraints within our experimental paradigm, satisficing provided a better account of the data.

Applicability to the Web

The texts and target sentences used in this experiment were carefully selected and matched to enable the study of skimming versus reading at normal speed and the processing of important versus unimportant information. The alternative method of allowing readers to browse the Web freely is confounded by the amount of text on a page, the density of important information, the quality of the writing, the structure of the page and the location of information within it, the presence of graphics and other multimedia, the intrusive effect of adverts, the number and type of links from a page etc. Similarly, the task completed (e.g. searching for specific information rather than general browsing) and factors relating to the readers (motivation, background knowledge) are likely to affect reading strategies. Therefore, as a first step, we believe the control in our design was necessary to focus on the behaviour of interest – skim-reading. Notwithstanding this, key features of our method are representative of reading situations on the Web and were designed to promote similar reading behaviours. For example, participants were allowed to freely navigate through a number of pages of text that were linked together and the task was simply "To learn as much as possible in the time available". Naturally, the next step is to attempt to generalize our findings to other reading materials and task constraints. With a view to this future research, we shall now discuss factors of particular relevance to reading on the Web.

In our study, participants had more than twice the amount of text than they could read in the time available. This proved sufficient to discriminate between skimming and reading at normal pace but arguably is less extreme than typical reading conditions on the Web. The sheer size of the Web means there can be a near limitless supply of text and there is always the option of continuing to search for more text. Moreover, quality and type of text was relatively constant in our experiment whereas text on the Web comes from a variety of different sources and, despite the efficiency of search engines, can be of limited relevance [13]. Thus, skimming online may be different from the skimming observed here due to a different ratio of time to text and higher variance in the quality of text. Studies of Web usage support this argument, as page visits are often very short indeed [6,7,32]. For example, Weinreich, *et al.* [32] report that 25% of all pages were displayed for less than 4 seconds, and 52% of all visits were shorter than 10 seconds. However, they also found that 10% of all page visits were longer than 2 minutes. This suggests that Web users engage in some rapid evaluative behaviour not observed in our study but it also implies that less cursory reading, potentially including satisficing, was also common. Indeed, although these longer visits were fewer in number they accounted for a high proportion of the total time users spent on the Web.

The frequency of rapid visits to Web pages suggests that users may be engaging in some form of "sampling" behaviour that acts as a precursor to satisficing or normal reading ([28]; see also research on "document triage", e.g., [2,3,8]). Sampling involves reading a small part of a document and using that to evaluate its content before reading further. Typically, users might be expected to sample a number of different documents before deciding upon one to read but, in principle, users could evaluate each individual sample against a pre-existing baseline and make an immediate decision. Sampling will be more efficient when there is high variance in quality between the available texts – as is often the case on the Web. The scanning of pages in an F-shape, as described by Nielsen, may be one such sampling behaviour and the absence of sampling in our experiments could explain the absence of an F-shaped reading pattern.

From an applied point of view, we believe that both satisficing and sampling are important. Website designers need to capture users' attention relatively quickly during the sampling phase to prevent them leaving and sampling an alternative site. However, it is the users that stay for the longest periods of time that are likely to be the most important visitors to a site, and our research indicates that when navigating within fairly homogenous pages, such as those found within the same Website, users are more likely to satisfice than sample.

The high proportion of rapid visits reported by Weinrech *et al.* may be in part a reflection of the type of pages visited in that study. Unconstrained use of the Web entails visiting pages, such as homepages and lists of content, that are simply navigated through to reach more useful content. It also seems plausible that, unlike the text in this study, such pages may be read in an F-shape [22]. The materials used in this study were not designed to encourage such reading behaviour. Although such rapid visits are frequent it does not follow that they are correspondingly important for an understanding of skimming behaviour. We seek to understand how skimming allows gains in information. Focusing on text that has some relation to the user's goal has enabled us to study how readers allocate their time to the most important text within a generally relevant document.

Implications for Design

This discussion and the results from our study suggest several conclusions about skim reading that have relevance for producers of text on the Web.

Locating information at the start of paragraphs and pages increases the likelihood that it will be read. Therefore, writers should ensure that information early in a page should grab and hold the reader's attention. This is the most straightforward conclusion and is not new, following on from general guidelines for writing [31] and specific advice for writing on the Web [21]. Our contribution is to provide supporting data using a controlled experiment and a theoretical account of how this pattern of reading comes about.

Information that is later in a text is still relevant to time-pressured readers. Figures 2-5 indicate that information towards the ends of paragraphs and pages was read by a significant proportion of participants. Writers should not be afraid of including important information after the first line or two provided the preceding text is likely to sustain the reader's attention. Clearly, this will depend on the purpose of the text but the writer's goal need not be to frontload the text with all the major points. Beyond an initial sampling phase readers will satisfice and general principles of writing such as maintaining coherence and explaining causal relations are important to support the comprehension of the text [17].

Readers simultaneously evaluate the current paragraph and the current page. Readers appear to evaluate different sized units of text when deciding whether to keep reading or not. Therefore, writers must anticipate the units of text most relevant to the particular circumstances and structure their text accordingly. This could include inserting section headings and altering the length of paragraphs and/or pages to ensure that if readers do move to the next unit of text, information that is important to the writer is not skipped over.

Skimming can be effective. Although less effective than reading at normal pace [5,12,18], skimmed text can still be understood and remembered. In particular, when satisficing the sections of text that people choose to read may be read for the same amount of time and understood as well as when read without time pressure. This means that complex information can be included within text online and that this information may well be recalled and used at a later date.

Related Work and Future Directions

Finding information on the Web is, of course, not just a question of deciding whether to continue reading text or not. Both search and navigation online have been extensively investigated [e.g. 10,16,24] and a full account of their relationship to skim reading is beyond the scope of this article. Nonetheless, another experiment in [11] provided some insight into the importance of the links between pages. They arranged pages of text in a hierarchical Website-like structure and varied the links between pages to manipulate the ease with which participants could navigate through the text. Subsequent tests of text understanding found the advantage for skimming over reading at normal speed was dependent on the ease with which readers could navigate between pages.

Work investigating the links to a page of text highlights another issue not touched on here – the depth of understanding achieved by skim reading. Requiring users to click on a link to access a page of instructional text can increase the amount read each time the text is accessed and the subsequent level of understanding achieved [9]. Similarly, Salmerón *et al.* [29] demonstrated that the different strategies adopted by readers of hypertext did not affect their understanding of features of the text, but did affect their deeper understanding of the meaning of the text. We have shown that skimming is an effective method for quickly grasping the most important points of a text but writing text that exclusively supports rapid reading may marginalise the more sophisticated processes present in slower reading. Just such a phenomenon has already been anecdotally observed elsewhere [4,25].

Finally, we note that a measure of readers' perceptions of their progress while reading would help understand the decisions taken by readers on the Web. The theory of satisficing supposes, after information foraging [24], that behaviour is moderated by rate of information gain but currently it is difficult to measure this rate. It is possible to answer similar questions about currency-dependent foraging by investigating tasks in which the currency is more readily available [14,23], and thus to test particular heuristics underlying local decisions to switch from one activity to another. But for understanding skim reading *per se*, this rather sidesteps the issue. It remains for future work to investigate whether any indirect measures of information gain (e.g. subjective reports) allow similarly sophisticated analysis of the local satisficing decision to stop reading and skip to the next unit of text.

REFERENCES

1. Agosto, D. E. Bounded rationality and satisficing in young people's web-based decision making. *Journal of the American Society for Information Science and Technology, 53* (2002), 16-27.
2. Buchanan, G., & Loizides, F. Investigating document triage on paper and electronic media. *Euro. Conf. on Digital Libraries* (2007), 416–426.
3. Buchanan, G., & Owen, T. Improving skim reading for document triage. *Proc. International Symposium on Information Interaction in Context* (2008), 83-88.
4. Carr, N. Is Google making us stupid? http://www.theatlantic.com/doc/200807/google (2008).
5. Carver, R. P. Rauding theory predictions of amount comprehended under different purposes and speed reading conditions. *Reading Research Quarterly, 19* (1984), 205-218.
6. Catledge, L. D. & Pitkow, J. E. Characterizing browsing strategies in the World-Wide Web. *Computer Networks and ISDN Systems, 27* (1995), 1065-1073.
7. Cockburn, A., & McKenzie, B. What do web users do? An empirical analysis of web use. *International Journal of Human-Computer Studies, 54* (2001), 903-922.
8. Cockburn, A., Savage, J., & Wallace, A. Tuning and testing scrolling interfaces that automatically zoom. *Proc. CHI '05,* ACM Press (2005), 71–80.
9. Duggan, G. B. & Payne, S. J. Interleaving reading and acting while following procedural instructions. *Journal of Experimental Psychology: Applied, 7* (2001), 297-307.
10. Duggan, G. B., & Payne, S. J. Knowledge in the head and on the web: Using topic expertise to aid search. *Proc. CHI '08*, ACM Press (2008), 39-48.

11. Duggan, G. B., & Payne, S. J. Text skimming: The process and effectiveness of foraging through text under time pressure. *Journal of Experimental Psychology: Applied, 15* (2009), 228-242.

12. Dyson, M. C., & Haselgrove, M. The effects of reading speed and reading patterns on the understanding of text read from screen. *Journal of Research in Reading, 23* (2000), 210-223.

13. Hölscher, C., & Strube, G. Web search behavior of internet experts and newbies. *Computer Networks, 33* (2000), 337-346.

14. Hutchinson, J. M. C., Wilke, A., & Todd, P. M. Patch leaving in humans: Can a generalist adapt its rules to dispersal of items across patches? *Animal Behaviour, 75* (2008), 1331-1349.

15. Jacoby, J., Jaccard, J., J., Currim, I, Kuss, A. Ansari, A., & Troutman, T. Tracing the impact of item-by-item information accessing on uncertainty reduction. *Journal of Consumer Research, 21* (1994), 291-303.

16. Jansen, B. J., & Pooch, U. A review of web searching studies and a framework for future research. *Journal of the American Society of Information Science and Technology, 52* (2000), 235-246.

17. Kintsch, W. *Comprehension: A paradigm for cognition.* New York: Cambridge University Press (1998).

18. Kiwan, D., Ahmed, A., & Pollitt, A. The effects of time-induced stress on making inferences during text comprehension. *Euro. Conf. Educational Research* (2000).

19. Liu, Z. Reading behavior in the digital environment. *Journal of Documentation, 61* (2005), 700-712.

20. Masson, M. E. J. Cognitive processes in skimming stories. *Journal of Experimental Psychology: Learning, Memory and Cognition, 8* (1982), 400-417.

21. Morkes, J., & Nielsen, J. Concise, SCANNABLE, and Objective: How to write for the Web. http://www.useit.com/papers/webwriting/writing.html (1997).

22. Nielsen, J. F-shaped pattern for reading Web content. http://www.useit.com/alertbox/reading_pattern.html (2006).

23. Payne, S. J., Duggan, G. B., & Neth, H. Discretionary task interleaving: Heuristics for time allocation in cognitive foraging. *Journal of Experimental Psychology: General, 136* (2007), 370-388.

24. Pirolli, P. (2007). *Information foraging theory: Adaptive interaction with information.* Oxford: Oxford University Press (2007).

25. Pitts Jr., L. Leonard Pitts Jr: Is Google making us stupid? http://www.contracostatimes.com/columns/ci_9583256 (2008).

26. Ratcliff, R. Methods for dealing with reaction time outliers. *Psychological Bulletin, 114* (1993), 510-532.

27. Rayner, K. Eye movements in reading and information processing: 20 years of research. *Psychological Bulletin, 124* (1998), 372-422.

28. Reader, W. R., & Payne, S. J. Allocating time across multiple texts: Sampling and satisficing. *Human-Computer Interaction, 22* (2007), 263-298.

29. Salmerón, L., Cañas, J. J., Kintsch, W., Fajardo, I. Reading strategies and hypertext comprehension. *Discourse Processes, 40* (2005), 171-191.

30. Simon, H. A. Rational choice and the structure of the environment, *Psychological Review, 63* (1956), 129-138.

31. Strunk, W., & White, E. B. *The Elements of Style.* New York, NJ: Macmillan (1979).

32. Weinreich, H., Obendorf, H., Herder, E., & Mayer, M. Not quite the average: An empirical study of web use. *ACM Transactions on the Web, 2,* (2008).

Older Web Users' Eye Movements: Experience Counts

Robin Hill[1], Anna Dickinson[2], John Arnott[2], Peter Gregor[2], Louise McIver[2]
[1] Visual Cognition Laboratory, Psychology, University of Edinburgh, Edinburgh, EH8 9JZ, Scotland, UK.
[2] School of Computing, University of Dundee, Dundee, DD1 4HN, Scotland, UK.
[1] r.l.hill@ed.ac.uk, [2] {adickinson, jarnott, pgregor, lmciver}@computing.dundee.ac.uk

ABSTRACT
Eye-tracking is a valuable tool for usability research. Studies into the effect of age on eye-movement behavior tend to indicate a propensity for slower viewing and longer times spent examining information. This pattern is usually attributed to the general physiological and cognitive slow-down associated with normal aging. In this paper, however, across three different tasks based on computer and internet use (free-viewing, visual search, and browser interaction), we show that among older adults (n=18, age range: 70-93) computer experience appears to be a highly important factor in eye-movement behavior. We argue that as a consequence of the experimental environment used in modern eye-tracking studies, characteristics such as familiarity and experience with computers should be taken into account before conclusions are drawn about the raw effects of age.

Author Keywords
Ageing, eye-tracking, experience, web usability.

ACM Classification Keywords
H5.m. Information interfaces and presentation; H.5.2 User interfaces: *evaluation/methodology*.

General Terms
Experimentation, Measurement, Performance, Human Factors.

INTRODUCTION
Eye-tracking is widely used as a tool in usability and HCI evaluations. It has the potential to be especially useful when participants are older or lack contextual knowledge about computer systems, offering an unobtrusive means of examining cognitive and attentional processing. Research so far has seemed to demonstrate that older adults are slower and display different eye movement behaviors from those of younger people. The research reported here explores the link between experience and older adults' eye-movements in web usability research. Experimental data are provided (see below) which suggest that differences in eye movement behavior may be more strongly associated with experience than with age as a physiological process.

EYE-TRACKING AND HCI
Interest in eye-tracking as an evaluation method in web usability has been enthusiastic. There are now courses for practitioners (e.g. at City University in London and De Montford University in Leicester), and the presentation of results by such specialists as Jakob Nielsen [22] as well as numerous academic articles [e.g. 11,16,31] demonstrate the popularity of the methodology.

This popularity in monitoring eye movements is hardly surprising: as Nielsen and Pernice point out in their 2009 book [22], recent developments have meant that the technology is now relatively inconspicuous, with no need for the uncomfortable bite bars and chin rests previously required to ensure accuracy and reliability. Moreover, eye-tracking, by giving the researcher a direct insight into where the user's attention is focused, allows direct access to usability flaws that are more likely to emerge from eye-tracking data than from discussions with users themselves. Essentially, the entire cognitive journey and time-course of a task, from start to finish, can be unwrapped and analysed; not just the end result.

Measures such as where a participant first fixates on a page, whether they notice the object they are seeking, and the way in which their gaze travels across the page are all useful measures of their interaction with the stimuli. A particularly useful measure of cognitive effort is fixation duration: the longer a participant spends looking at something, the more effort they are expending trying to recognize or understand it.

Eye-tracking is a powerful means of investigating cognitive processing by offering a spatio-temporal record of visual attention. There is however a danger of over-simplifying or ignoring some of the more valuable measures. The results can be difficult to analyze; heatmaps, for example, while providing interesting information at a glance, can run the risk of over-simplifying, as descriptive statistics can. This paper warns that eye-tracking results may have encouraged misleading conclusions about cognition and ageing.

Older adults, web usability and eye-tracking
An especially valuable application of eye-tracking usability is its use with older adults: older adults, particularly novices, are likely to have more problems than younger

ones with conventional usability methods [see [14] for a review]. This is an issue in terms of cognitive focus (think aloud), memory (retrospective think aloud) and simply in terms of familiarity with terminology and "alien" technology. Conscious critique of a usability experience is very complex for an inexperienced user of computer systems. Ageing, as evinced by cognitive change, poorer motor control and sensory deficits, impacts on the ability to use computers [14]. The central focus of this research area has been the differences between older and younger adults in terms of visual behavior on websites. Despite the advantages that eye-tracking offers for research with older adults, the field is currently small and research reports are rather scattered. A small number of web usability studies have been carried out with older adults (people over 50).

One of the earliest studies involves an eye-tracking examination of railway timetables [15]. In the study, the authors classified younger (mean: 22.5) and older users (mean: 67) into 'beginner' and 'intermediate' groups. They concluded that older people made longer fixations, but that this was due to visual difficulties reading small text (point 10). Older users were also more vulnerable to usability flaws, which impacted significantly on the time it took to complete tasks.

A similar finding emerged from two studies looking at expert older users working at the investment company, Fidelity. The first study reported examined the behavior of expert older adults (50-69) in work who used the web daily, compared to their younger colleagues (20-39) [30]. Older adults spent longer viewing web pages and longer looking at navigation areas than their younger colleagues. Evidence from heatmaps suggests that the older participants also distributed their gaze more widely across the pages and read more of the text than younger users did. The second study, using the same eye-tracker, and examining preferences for web page presentation, reported that older users (the study looked at "baby boomers" (44-62) working at Fidelity) tended to fixate for longer on large images and search bars [5].

Zaphiris and Savitch [32] compared older (58-87) and younger (19-27) web users browsing health information sites of varying depth of hierarchy, and concluded, like [30], that older adults looked at more of the page and spent longer considering which link to choose. Notably, the researchers found no significant difference in reading speeds, suggesting that older adults were not simply slower than younger ones.

Josephson and Holmes [18], however, compared four age groups, children (mean age 10), teenagers (mean age 18), younger adults (mean age 38) and older adults (mean age 58), all of whom were experienced and regular web users, on a visual search task and found no differences between the groups. They suggest that "older adults who are avid Internet users are able to rapidly and accurately find information", with the implication that many of the differences that are categorized as due to "ageing" are likely to be, in fact, due to experience. It is also worth noting that their "older adults" were relatively young (range: 55-65).

There is scope for further and more detailed research in this area. Some of the existing studies show results in the form of heatmaps, rather than giving detailed spatio-temporal eye-movement metrics such as fixation duration and location. The eye-trackers used had relatively low sample rates, ranging from 30 Hz [15] to 60 Hz [18]. The older adults are defined in these studies as people older than 50 (indeed, older than 44 in [5]). Only one study had participants with a wide range of ages, including one participant of 87 [32]; because means are absent, however, the overall age distribution of their group is unclear.

Despite the small number of reports, outcomes have been relatively consistent. With one exception [18], researchers conclude that older adults are slower [5,15,30,32].

Older adults and eye-tracking in psychological studies

This conclusion fits with much of the existing psychological data that concludes that older adults exhibit age-related slowing that affects their eye-movement behavior: psychological eye-tracking literature has reported general slowing and decline with age [4]. This work should be viewed in context, however: a lot of the evidence (particularly in the earliest studies) was from reflexive saccades, which are essentially automatic and involve no higher order control. Older adults were slower to react to stimuli (reviewed in [1]). In terms of physiological and oculomotor behaviors, older adults are slower and their performance is more variable [1].

From an eye-tracking perspective, there is less data on older people's higher order cognitive control on real world information processing tasks. This is particularly significant as these are the sort of tasks where compensatory strategies might be expected to reduce the differences related to physiological slowing, and the sort of tasks that have real relevance for daily life.

In reading research, an area of higher order behavior where there has been preliminary research with older participants, older adults make more fixations, longer fixations (a mean of 260ms compared to 246ms for younger readers [26]) and more regressions (backwards movements to re-read text). These differences do not necessarily have a dramatic impact on reading performance and (at least where reading is "easy") are of little functional significance [20]: in other words, older adults are performing at a reasonable level (that is, they are successfully reading) but similar texts demand more effort, as demonstrated by longer fixation durations.

The web usability research is less established than the psychological research and it is difficult to quantify what increased cognitive effort might look like for older people using web pages. In existing web usability research with older adults, however, one study explicitly reports that older adults have longer mean fixation durations [15], although without supporting figures for these. Other research does not report fixation durations, although [5] gives "fixation data" which are presumably fixation durations (based on the background discussion of eye-tracking measures). It is indicated that fixations on screen elements such as large images and search bars were longer for older participants, although total mean durations and other statistical results are not presented.

Typical mean fixation durations

Previously reported mean fixation durations tend to be judged from work with younger adults, very often university students. Table 1 displays a summary of the "typical" mean fixation duration data over various tasks. Specific times depend on the complexity of the task and the stimuli, so in some cases the data are presented as a range rather than a single figure.

	Mean Fixation Duration
Silent reading	225-250 ms
Oral reading	275-325 ms
Visual search	180-275 ms
Static scenes	287 ms
Dynamic scenes	358 ms
Films	453 ms
Joint collaborative tasks	322 ms
Web search	230-293 ms[1]
General browsing (including instructions to remember content)	353-377 ms

Table 1. "Typical" mean fixation durations derived from previous research [6, 17, 23-25, 27, 28]

The summary information in Table 1 is provided to show contextualising times for fixation durations on different tasks. As the table shows, mean fixation durations range from 180ms on straightforward visual search tasks to 453ms when participants are looking at films. Web-based tasks tend to come between these two extremes, with free-viewing (when the participant is also trying to remember what they see) between 353 and 377ms, and search tasks ranging between 230 and 293ms.

[1] Note: Cowen et al. report mean fixation durations for their study of mobile phone homepages [8]. The range reported is 394-553ms, undoubtedly an outlier in terms of other research data, suggesting that the stimuli were very complex – or that Cowen et al. are using a slightly different definition of the term.

Why are there differences between older and younger web users?

Although mean fixation duration differences between older and younger adults are commonly taken to reflect age-related cognitive slowing or other fundamental aspects of ageing, it has not been demonstrated that this is actually the case. As Loos and Mante-Maijer point out in their review of the literature [21], it is unclear whether the differences between older and younger adults looking at web pages exist because of age or because of some other factor such as cultural background, education or experience which studies have not controlled for. So far, older adults have been treated as a homogeneous group in the research, despite evidence that they are, in fact, extremely diverse [see [7] for example].

Indeed, many of the differences between older and younger adults appear to be experience-related [18]. The psychological literature demonstrates that observed differences may vanish with practice: for example, well-practiced younger and older adults perform similarly in anti-saccade tasks (where participants must deliberately suppress automatic behaviors) [13]; poor visual search strategies in older adults can be rectified with simple instructions and minimal practice [2], and reading efficiency training can greatly improve performance in older adults [29].

Thus 'difficulty' appears to be a function of situation novelty and amount of practice in tasks for older adults [3]: unfamiliar tasks are likely to benefit younger participants when compared to older people, but a relatively small amount of practice minimizes – and potentially removes – this advantage.

These conclusions from the psychological literature, as well as the findings of Josephson and Holmes [18] and the issues raised by Loos et al. [21], raise the question of the extent to which experience plays a role in older adults' eye movement behavior on websites: might the slowing observed in the literature be a function of experience as much as of age?

THE STUDY: BEGINNERS AND NOVICES LOOKING AT WEB PAGES

As discussed above, while several studies have examined the differences between older and younger adults, no one has yet looked at differences between older adults. In this paper we report the first study which has examined the eye-tracking behavior of older adults in terms of computer experience and begin the process of unpicking the differences caused by experience to add to the research data that looks at ageing.

In this study, complete novices are compared to people who have a small amount of computer experience in order to begin to explore whether experience makes a difference.

Participants

18 participants (mean age: 77.5 years; range 70-93) were recruited through a local charity for older adults. All attended a single two-hour session at the laboratory. An interview on computer knowledge was used to divide participants into two groups. There were 12 novice computer users, people who had minimal, if any, experience with a computer and had not attained any level of independent computer use (mean age: 77; range 71-93). The remaining 6 participants (mean age: 78.5; range 70-90) were more experienced; they had enough experience to use at least one application independently. People in this group had some email experience or had used a word processor or had accessed the Internet. It is important to emphasise that they were in no sense "expert" users. All participants had normal or corrected-to-normal vision. Refreshments and transport were provided but there was no monetary compensation for participation.

Apparatus

An SR Research Eye-link II head-mounted eye-tracker (see Figure 1) running at a sample rate of 500Hz was used to monitor participants' eye movements. Screen shots were presented on a 19-inch CRT monitor at a resolution of 1024 x 768. A digital dictaphone with a table-mounted microphone recorded the auditory data.

Figure 1. SR Research Eye-link II Eye-tracker.

Procedure

A brief interview was conducted outside the laboratory to confirm participants' age and computer inexperience. Once inside the laboratory, the apparatus and procedure were explained and participants read and signed a consent form. Participants were required to sit at a normal viewing distance from the monitor and to wear any spectacles they would normally use for reading at that distance. A test screen of words in different sizes was presented to ensure minimum levels of eyesight proficiency and a test was used to identify participants' dominant eye. The head-mounted eye-tracker was then placed on their head. Although only the dominant eye was tracked, participants' vision remained binocular and normal viewing behavior was unimpeded.

Task requirements were reiterated and participants were informed that the basic instructions would be repeated before each experimental trial was initiated. Participants were also able to rest or take a break between trials. The experiment began with a manual calibration procedure that involved looking at a series of nine points which formed a 3 x 3 grid across the screen. The Eyelink software then re-presented these points in a different random order to validate the accuracy of the system. If this failed, the entire calibration was repeated until a successful validation was obtained. Each trial was initiated by a central fixation marker to ensure that the calibration remained accurate and representative; if inaccuracies were detected during the experiment then the calibration process could be repeated whenever necessary.

After successful calibration, a random colour pattern was presented for 2 seconds, encouraging the free movement of eyes around the screen and removing the bias of starting from a central position because of the fixation marker. These visual "white noise" screens also help limit any lingering working memory contamination arising from the previously displayed page.

Stimuli

This study is part of a larger project looking at the effects of browser interface design alterations on older novice viewing behavior. Participants saw two interface designs: a conventional Internet Explorer interface, and an experimental system consisting of a smaller toolbar placed at the bottom of the screen (minimal distraction and interface clutter). Full rationale and results for the beginner group (first stage) have previously been reported [9,10].

Building on previous eye-tracking research, which demonstrates the importance of content layouts in influencing eye movement behavior [e.g. 23], three different content designs were used. Screens from the Web were selected as stimuli. While the screen designs were standard, their content changed, so users had new information to look at and try to understand each time a new screen was presented. The three content structures were: Amazon search results, Google search results and ITV news stories.

These screens provided a range of characteristics, including a varying proportion of image and text, varying density of content, and varying placement of navigation controls. In order to avoid possible interference from the rest of the Windows set up, all screens were maximised so that the Windows toolbar/Start button was not shown on the screen.

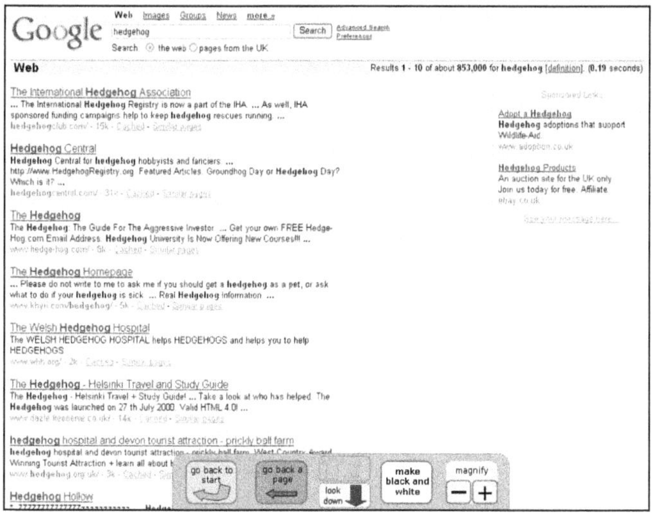

Figure 2. Example page from the study with novel browser interface (half of the pages were displayed with a conventional browser interface).

Each participant saw 42 unique screens; half of the screens displayed were shown with the Internet Explorer browser (7 of each content design), and half with the experimental interface (also 7 of each content design). An example is shown in Figure 2. Presentation was pseudo-randomised to control for any order effect. There were no differences between experience groups in terms of screens viewed.

Tasks

Participants completed three separate series of tasks: "free-viewing" tasks, search tasks, and browser tasks. The tasks were chosen to explore how older adults interacted with web pages. The free viewing task was intended to represent the first time that a participant saw a page, and their initial effort to make sense of what they were looking at. The search task represented a web user seeking items of relevance on the page. Finally, the browser tasks were used to explore the extent to which users understood the role of the browser interfaces, and the possibilities for changing text attributes or for using the browser to navigate. These tasks were all relatively 'naturalistic' in that they reflected the sort of behavior that a web user might display.

Task series 1: free-viewing

The first series of tasks that participants were asked to undertake involved looking at the screen silently for 20 seconds then re-examining the screen for a further 30 seconds while describing what they saw. The distinction between the initial examination and the subsequent description was intended to separate the cognitive effort of understanding from the cognitive effort of describing the screens [14]. Josephson and Holmes considered a 15-second exposure to be adequate time for a user to completely examine a web page [19]. The time was extended in this study by 5 seconds because participants, as older inexperienced computer users, were expected to respond more slowly to the screens presented.

To ensure that each participant understood the procedure there were three practice screens. The practice screens were composed of both pictures and text. As with the genuine experimental items, participants saw them for 20 seconds and then described them for 30. Neutral images rather than web pages were used in order to avoid introducing experimental items during the practice session. The experimenter or the participant could raise any difficulties or questions during the practice session. Following the practice session, there were twelve experimental screens.

Task series 2: search

The second series of tasks consisted of searches. Participants were asked to find a target word or image on the screen and to say whether the target was at the top or the bottom. Search tasks ranged from basic recognition (e.g. "is the word "education" on the next screen?") to tasks requiring more processing ("Do any of the birds mentioned on the next page end up in Britain?"). There were 18 screens in total and in half of the screens the target being sought was not present. Participants had 40 seconds to decide whether the target was present or not.

Task series 3: browser tasks

The third task series concerned overall impressions of the screen and browser tasks. Participants were asked six questions over twelve screens (each question was asked twice). Questions covered browser-relevant topics such as "What would you do if you wanted to make the text larger?" and "What would you do if, after you had been exploring the web for a while, you wanted to go back to where you started from?". Participants had 30 seconds in which to answer the question.

RESULTS

Both groups of participants completed all the tasks. Following the studies, mean fixation durations were calculated in order to explore cognitive effort over the three task series. Distinct differences emerged between the 'experienced' and 'inexperienced' groups.

An additional dependent variable is included in the results tables for comparative purposes: saccade amplitude. This is a measure of the size of the eye movements between steady fixations. Thus a large amplitude may reflect more global scanning behavior as found in scene perception (about 4°) while a smaller amplitude is more similar to reading-like behavior (about 2°) [25]. However, for the purposes of this paper the focus of discussion will remain on the fixation duration results.

Two sets of analyses were performed to confirm statistical reliability. The first involved fitting a Linear Mixed Effects Model for each task, treating the Experience Grouping variable as a Fixed Effect and participants as a Random

Effect. The second set involved a more conventional Repeated-Measures Analysis of Variance approach to ensure that individual differences did not skew the overall group profiles.

Plots and descriptive statistics for the entire distribution of data obtained during free-viewing task (19482 and 31961 observations for two participant groups) are in Figure 3.

The LME model, detailed in Table 2, treats the novice group as the baseline and indicates that when participants were asked to look at a screen and try to understand it, there was a 53ms facilitation on average per fixation for the experienced participants [$t(15.982) = -3.918$; $p=0.001$]. There was no evidence of a difference in saccade amplitude (the size of the movement of the eyes between fixations) between groups, however [$t(15.977)=-0.131$; $p=0.897$].

Figure 4 shows the distribution of fixation durations for the two groups of older users during a web-based search task, along with a summary of their eye-movement data.

Task series 1: free-viewing

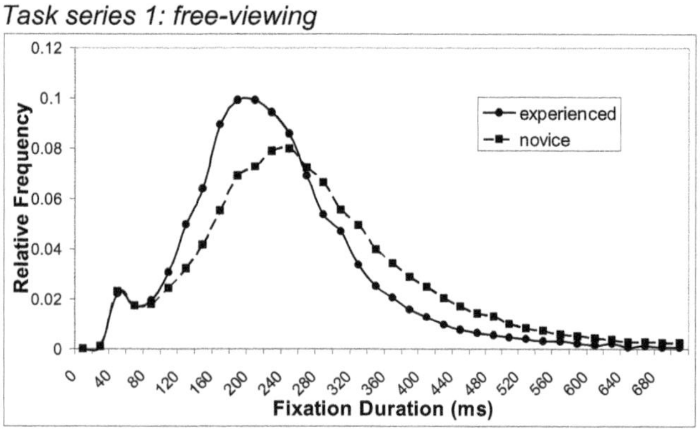

	Fixation duration		Saccade amplitude	
	Exp	**Novice**	**Exp**	**Novice**
Mean	221ms	273ms	4.23°	4.28°
Median	204ms	244ms	2.65°	2.60°
St. Dev.	116ms	155ms	4.68°	4.69°
N	19482	31961	19171	31311

Figure 3. Data summary for Free-viewing Task

			95% C.I.				
Parameter	**Estimate**	**Std. Error**	**Lower Bound**	**Upper Bound**	**df**	**t**	**Sig.**
Intercept	275.1	7.8	258.6	291.5	16.022	35.443	.000
Experienced	-52.6	13.4	-81.1	-24.1	15.982	-3.918	.001
Novice	0	0	.	.	.	.	.

Table 2. LME output for Free-viewing Task (milliseconds)

Task series 2: search

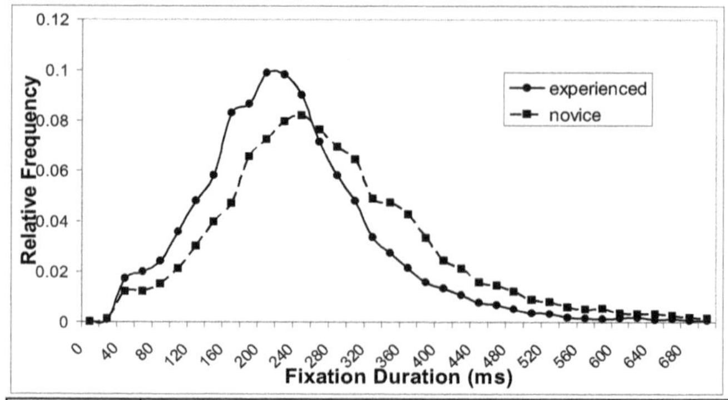

	Fixation duration		Saccade amplitude	
	Exp	**Novice**	**Exp**	**Novice**
Mean	221ms	272ms	4.43°	4.17°
Median	208ms	248ms	2.57°	2.64°
St. Dev.	111ms	144ms	6.49°	4.63°
N	7900	15423	7703	15025

Figure 4. Data summary for Search Task

			95% C.I.				
Parameter	**Estimate**	**Std. Error**	**Lower Bound**	**Upper Bound**	**df**	**t**	**Sig.**
Intercept	273.2	7.8	258.6	291.5	16.010	35.029	.000
Experienced	-53.0	13.5	-81.1	-24.1	16.006	-3.926	.001
Novice	0	0	.	.	.	.	.

Table 3. LME output for Search Task (milliseconds)

Task series 3: browser tasks

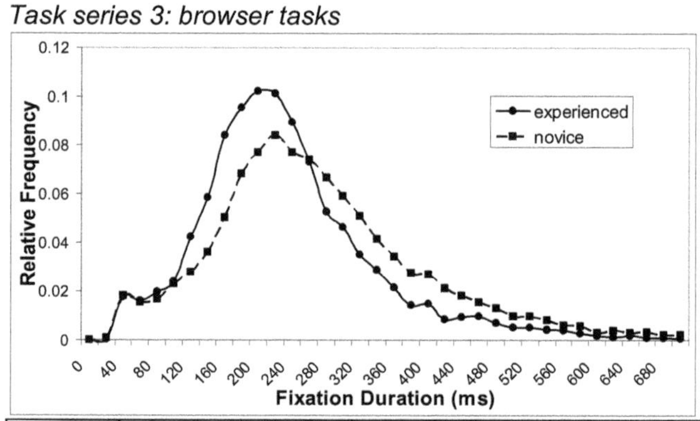

	Fixation duration		Saccade amplitude	
	Exp	**Novice**	**Exp**	**Novice**
Mean	229ms	276ms	5.12°	4.66°
Median	212ms	248ms	3.07°	2.75°
St. Dev.	119ms	166ms	5.88°	5.32°
N	6193	13461	6065	13195

Figure 5. Data summary for Browser Interaction Task

For search tasks, the LME model (Table 3) reveals a 53ms mean difference between experienced participants and novices [t(16.006)=-3.926; p=0.001]. The slightly longer "jumps" between fixations on average for the more experienced were accompanied by a higher variance (the median was lower) and the difference was not reliable [t(15.983)=0.462; p=0.650].

The differing shapes of the distributions for the two samples of data obtained during the Browser Interaction Task can be seen at the top of Figure 5.

Parameter	Estimate	Std. Error	95% C.I. Lower Bound	95% C.I. Upper Bound	df	t	Sig.
Intercept	278.3	8.9	259.6	297.1	16.042	31.399	.000
Experienced	-49.4	15.4	-82.0	-16.9	16.065	-3.217	.005
Novice	0	0	.	.	.	.	.

Table 4. LME output for Browser Interaction Task (milliseconds)

For the browser interaction, the model (Table 4) estimates a 278ms fixation duration, reduced by 49ms if a participant is classified as more experienced [t(16.065)=-3.217; p=0.005]. Again, the slightly longer jumps between fixations for experienced participants were actually highly variable in extent and non-significant [t(15.988)=0.799; p=0.436].

As a check to ensure that these findings were not explicitly due to stimuli being webpages, the viewing task (mirroring Task 1 above) for the practice materials was also analysed. These materials consisted of three normal photographs which had no computer-related or internet context, but were displayed using the same apparatus as the experimental stimuli. The results are entirely consistent with those found for Task 1 and hence the rest of the experiment: means of 223ms vs. 270ms for the two groups [LME difference t(15.879)=3.488; p=0.003]. There is therefore no evidence that our findings are restricted to webpages alone.

Combined statistical analysis

A second ANOVA was carried out to test across the mean fixation durations for each participant to ensure that the overall results were not skewed by individual differences. A 2 (Experience [between variable]) x 3 (Task [within variable]) repeated measures ANOVA was carried out. A main between-groups effect of Experience [F(1, 16)=15.720, p<0.01] indicates a reliable difference between the novice and experienced groups throughout the experiment. A lack of a main Task effect [F(2, 32)=0.073, p=0.930] confirms that the participant performance is consistent across all three tasks. Similarly, there was no interaction between the variables [F(2, 32)=0.592, p=0.559], confirming that the overall findings were not driven by one or two cells in the experimental design alone: individual novice durations were similar on all three tasks; more experienced participants also had similar durations across the tasks; but novices had reliably longer fixation durations compared to more experienced participants.

Summary

Overall, the results show that novice older users made fixations that were approximately 50ms longer (a 20-25% increase) than those made by (modestly) experienced older users, across all three conditions. The graphs also indicate that the difference is not just a simple shift in means, but that the two participant groups clearly have different overall distributions of fixation durations. The more experienced group has a much stronger leftwards skew and tighter spread, matching the general profile reported for younger adults; whereas the novice group had a more random appearance, with a lower, wider peak and greater symmetrical variance. This pattern is remarkably consistent across all the tasks performed. While more experienced users had slightly longer average saccade amplitudes when they were given a specific objective to carry out (Tasks 2 and 3), these distributions were too varied to verify the adoption of a more efficient scanning strategy. The close value for the saccade amplitude statistics implies that the size of the movements between fixations is homogeneous for the two groups, i.e. participants made similar movements around the screen regardless of experience. What was different was the length of time they remained stationary before moving on again.

DISCUSSION

Inexperienced older adults displayed an "older" profile in these eye-tracking tasks. Previous research has demonstrated that such a profile is associated with ageing [1,26] but it is also classically associated with confusion and uncertainty. Unpicking the interaction between ageing and inexperience needs significantly more research, but these results indicate that further research is desirable: inexperience is likely to be an important factor, possibly as important as age itself. Further investigation is necessary to explore the relative importance of age and experience, and to explore whether the basic level of experience reported here is sufficient – as these preliminary results suggest – to allow older adults to utilise the sort of compensatory strategies that ameliorate the age-related differences as reported in other higher order processing tasks [2,13,20,29].

For unconstrained free-scanning, experienced older users had an average fixation duration of 221ms, compared to novices' 273ms. Both groups had significantly lower mean fixation durations than the participants in Pan et al.'s [23] study (see Table 1), a difference that is likely to be attributable to the stimuli, as well as to the instruction to Pan's participants to remember what was on the screen. An alternative is to compare free-viewing in our study with silent reading in the existing eye-tracking research, for which "typical" fixation durations range from 225-250ms [24] and which place the more experienced group at the lower end of the scale, whereas the beginners are off the scale at the higher end.

Similarly, "typical" visual search fixation durations (including those for extremely complex tasks) range from 180-275ms, with web search apparently more complicated, ranging from 230-293ms: novices on both the reported search tasks (page search and browser interaction search) had mean fixation durations of 272 and 276ms, at the upper limits of the "typical" data [24], comparing to 221 and 229ms for the more experienced participants, at the lower end of the range.

The pattern is highly consistent through the three tasks: where contextualising data exists, a relatively small amount of computer experience is sufficient to produce a "typical" mean fixation duration – indeed, one that is at the lower end of the established range. By comparison, although the differences in time may not look dramatic at first (in relative terms it is a 20% to 25% difference, however, with 50ms being large in terms of neural activity and also longer than the duration of most saccadic eye movements), inexperienced older people were consistently at the higher end of the range of mean fixation durations.

Many details and differences in viewing behavior can sometimes be obfuscated by analysis techniques that over-aggregate the data. Heatmaps, for example, can reveal areas of high vs. low total viewing times, but do not show the order in which areas of the screen were attended, whether objects were re-fixated or held the eye for longer when initially encountered, etcetera. The heatmaps in Figures 6a and 6b do not reveal the differences reported earlier, for example. A more fine-grained spatio-temporal approach to analysing eye movements, such as distinguishing between patterns of individual fixations, offers a much richer understanding of what is going on inside a computer user's head. Different patterns will manifest for features that are attention-grabbing, attention-holding, ambiguous or perhaps just generally more interesting.

It is well established that practice on eye-tracking tasks can reduce, and even remove, the difference between older and younger participants [2,13,29]. Older people have less computer experience on average than younger people do, and many older adults have none. These results suggest that it is important to control for computer experience in eye-tracking tasks, since inexperience can increase task difficulty and misleadingly imply the presence of age-effects. Even indirect experience and familiarity, such as non-specific computer use, may have a profound effect on data collection.

The importance of this finding for usability research is considerable: where older people do self-paced tasks, the effect of even a small amount of computer experience could be substantial. The difficulty inherent in unfamiliar tasks brings greater cognitive load, but the level of experience necessary to overcome such difficulty is surprisingly small. Apparent age-effects may in some cases simply reflect inexperience, and with a little experience, compensatory strategies and other cognitive skills come into play. This underlines the importance of avoiding prejudicial judgment about the effects of ageing.

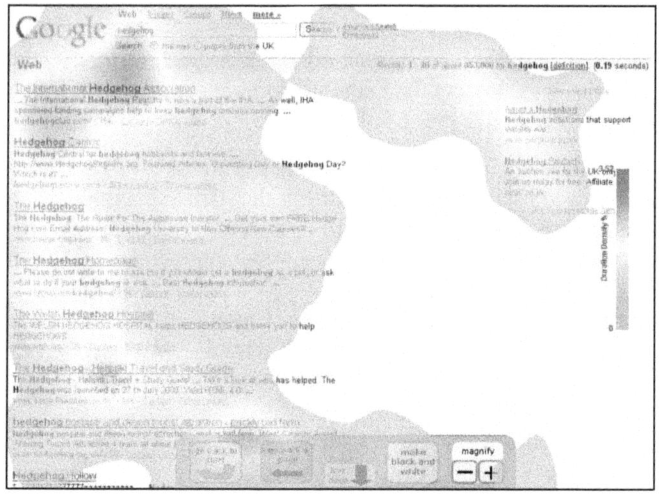

Figure 6a. Aggregate heatmap for experienced participants viewing search results for "hedgehog" (1146 fixations in total)

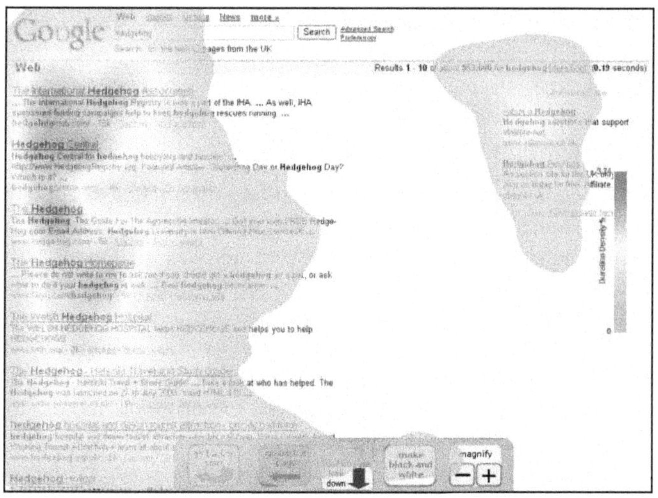

Figure 6b. Aggregate heatmap for novice participants viewing search results for "hedgehog" (2016 fixations in total)

For practitioners, it underlines the dangers of 'snapshot' studies where participants are only evaluated on one occasion. Since novices will behave in unique idiosyncratic ways there is a danger that this behavior will become equated with "older people". To rely on older participants with computer experience is one alternative, but it does effectively mean depending on a relatively small subset of the potential user group. It may be advisable to explore more longitudinal evaluation strategies with this user group instead.

Further, it is clear from these results that initial views of unfamiliar interfaces are associated with significant cognitive effort for older people; this emphasizes the relevance of work on familiarity in interfaces, and scaffolding and layering approaches to encourage older adults to gain a level of experience which will support further exploration and development of computing skills. For interface designers, applications need to facilitate the development paths that older people require to expand and consolidate their computing abilities.

As Fairweather notes in his analysis of users' problem-solving strategies, "...some of the effects of age, strong as they may appear, result from the level of knowledge these users had about how to solve the assigned problem using the web." [12]

CONCLUSION

Overall, our data suggest that having just a little experience of computer use is associated with a user's eyes moving around a computer monitor faster but without altering how far apart the eye movements were. In other words, even a small prior exposure to computers is linked with individuals not needing to spend so long looking at any location on the screen. This behavior was exhibited independently across tasks of varying complexity and cognitive demand, and where no formal training or familiarisation was involved.

In conclusion, on three web-viewing tasks, marginally experienced older adults displayed eye-movement behaviors consistent with "typical" behaviors, as measured by mean fixation durations. By contrast, less experienced computer users of similar ages displayed eye-movement behaviors that have generally been regarded as characteristic of all older people. This study suggests that behaviors previously identified as characteristic of ageing might be related instead to other factors, such as experience, and challenges assumptions about the effects of age as opposed to other aspects that divide the older age group. Age and personal experience remain highly correlated properties, which questions the merit of any over-simplified approach to improving the user experience for the older demographic.

ACKNOWLEDGMENTS

The authors would like to thank the participants who took part in this research, and Mr. T. Nind for assistance with programming. The research was funded by a gift from IBM. Author Dickinson was funded by the Royal Society of Edinburgh / Lloyds TSB Foundation for Scotland.

REFERENCES

1. Abel, L.A., Douglas, J. Effects of age on latency and error generation in internally mediated saccades. *Neurobiology of Aging 28,* 4 (2007), 627-637.
2. Becic, E., Boot, W.R., Kramer, A.F. Training older adults to search more effectively: Scanning strategy and visual search in dynamic displays. *Psychology and Aging 23,* 2 (2008), 461-466.
3. Bojko, A., Kramer, A., Peterson, M.S. Age equivalence in switch costs for prosaccade and antisaccade tasks. *Psychology and Aging 19,* 1 (2004), 226-234.
4. Bono, F., Oliveri, R.L., Zappia, M., Aguglia, U., Puccio, G., Quattrone, A. Computerized analysis of eye movements as a function of age. *Archives of Gerontology and Geriatrics 22,* 3 (1996), 261-269.
5. Capozzo, D., Groezinger, R.L., Ng, K.-F.F., Siegel, M.J. *Appeal of Web Page Layout and Characteristics Based on Age: Usability Research through Eye Tracking at Fidelity Investments Inc.* Worcester Polytechnic Inst., Worcester, MA, USA, 2008.
6. Carletta, J., Hill, R.L., Nicol, C., Taylor, T., Ruiter, J.P.d., Bard, E.G. Eyetracking for two-person tasks with manipulation of a virtual world. *Behavior Research Methods 42,* 1 (2010), 254-265.
7. Carmichael, A. *Style guide for the design of interactive television services for elderly viewers.* Kings Worthy Court, Winchester, England: Independent Television Commission, 1999.
8. Cowen, L., Ball, L., Delin, J. An eye movement analysis of Web page usability. In *Proc. People & Computers XVI: Memorable yet invisible,* (2002), 317-335.
9. Dickinson, A., Gregor, P., McIver, L., Hill, R.L., Milne, S. The Non Browser: helping older novice computer users to access the web. In *Proc. Accessible Design in the Digital World Conf.,* British Computer Society (2005).
10. Dickinson, A., Hill, R.L., Gregor, P., McIver, L., Milne, S. Making sense of content: eye-tracking older, novice users to evaluate an alternative web browser design. *Journal of Eye Movement Research 1,* SI: ECEM13 (2005), 87.
11. Ehmke, C., Wilson, S. Identifying web usability problems from eye-tracking data. In *Proc. BCS-HCI '07: 21st British HCI Group Annual Conference on People & Computers,* British Computer Society (2007), 119-128.
12. Fairweather, P.G. Influences of age and experience on Web-based problem solving strategies. In: Stephanidis, C., editor. *Universal Access in Human-Computer Interaction: Addressing Diversity, Pt I, Proceedings: Addressing Diversity.* Springer-Verlag Berlin, Berlin (2009), 220-229.
13. Fischer, B., Biscaldi, M., Gezeck, S. On the development of voluntary and reflexive components in human saccade generation. *Brain Research 754,* 1-2 (1997), 285-297.
14. Fisk, A.D., Rogers, W.A., Charness, N., Czaja, S.J., Sharit, J. *Designing for Older Adults: Principles and Creative Human Factors Approaches.* Second ed., CRC Press, Boca Raton, FL, 2009.
15. Fukuda, R., Bubb, H. Eye tracking study on Web-use: Comparison between younger and elderly users in case of search task with electronic timetable service. *PsychNology Journal 1,* 3 (2003), 202-228.

16. Guan, Z., Cutrell, E. An eye tracking study of the effect of target rank on web search. In *Proc. CHI 2007*, ACM Press (2007), 417-420.

17. Jay, C., Stevens, R., Glencross, M., Chalmers, A. How people use presentation to search for a link: expanding the understanding of accessibility on the web. In *Proc. 2006 International Cross-Disciplinary Workshop on Web Accessibility (W4A): Building the mobile web: rediscovering accessibility?,* ACM Press (2006).

18. Josephson, S., Holmes, M.E. Age differences in visual search for information on web pages. In *Proc. Eye Tracking Research & Applics.,* ACM Press (2004), 62.

19. Josephson, S., Holmes, M.E. Visual attention to repeated internet images: testing the scanpath theory on the world wide web. In *Proc. Eye Tracking Research & Applics.,* ACM Press (2002), 43-49.

20. Kliegl, R., Grabner, E., Rolfs, M., Engbert, R. Length, frequency, and predictability effects of words on eye movements in reading. *European Journal of Cognitive Psychology 16,* 1-2 (2004), 262-284.

21. Loos, E., Mante-Meijer, E. User-centred websites: The (ir)relevance of age. In *Proc. Include 2009 International Conf on Inclusive Design,* RCA, London (2009).

22. Nielsen, J., Pernice, K. *Eye-tracking Web Usability.* New Riders, Berkeley, CA, 2009.

23. Pan, B., Hembrooke, H.A., Gay, G.K., Granka, L.A., Feusner, M.K., Newman, J.K. The determinants of web page viewing behavior: an eye-tracking study. In *Proc. Eye Tracking Research & Application,* ACM Press (2004), 147-154.

24. Rayner, K. Eye movements and attention in reading, scene perception, and visual search. *Quarterly Journal of Experimental Psychology 62,* 8 (2009), 1457-1506.

25. Rayner, K. Eye movements in reading and information processing: 20 years of research. *Psychological Bulletin 124,* 3 (1998), 372-422.

26. Rayner, K., Reichle, E.D., Stroud, M.J., Williams, C.C., Pollatsek, A. The effect of word frequency, word predictability, and font difficulty on the eye movements of young and older readers. *Psychology and Aging 21,* 3 (2006), 448-465.

27. Rele, R.S., Duchowski, A.T. Using eye tracking to evaluate alternative search results interfaces. In *Human Factors & Ergonomics Society Annual Meeting Proc 49,* (2005), 1459-1463.

28. Smith, T., Henderson, J. Attentional synchrony in static and dynamic scenes. *Journal of Vision 8,* 6 (2008), 773.

29. Solan, H.A., Feldman, J., Tujak, L. Developing visual and reading efficiency in older adults. *Optometry and Vision Science 72,* 2 (1995), 139-145.

30. Tullis, T.S. Older adults and the web: Lessons learned from eye-tracking. In *Universal Access in Human Computer Interaction: Coping with Diversity, Pt 1 (Lecture Notes in Computer Science), 4554,* (2007), 1030-1039.

31. Yesilada, Y., Jay, C., Stevens, R., Harper, S. Validating the use and role of visual elements of web pages in navigation with an eye-tracking study. In *Proc. 17th International Conf. on World Wide Web,* ACM Press (2008), 11-20.

32. Zaphiris, P., Savitch, N. Age-related differences in browsing the Web. In *SPARC Workshop on "Promoting independence through new technology",* Reading, England, UK, 2008.

Retrospective Think-Aloud Method: Using Eye Movements as an Extra Cue for Participants' Verbalizations

Sanne Elling
Utrecht University
Utrecht Institute
of Linguistics OTS
Trans 10, 3512 JK Utrecht
The Netherlands
S.Elling@uu.nl

Leo Lentz
Utrecht University
Utrecht Institute
of Linguistics OTS
Trans 10, 3512 JK Utrecht
The Netherlands
L.R.Lentz@uu.nl

Menno de Jong
University of Twente
Faculty of Behavioral Sciences
Department of Technical and
Professional Communication
P.O. Box 217, 7500 AE Enschede
The Netherlands
M.D.T.deJong@utwente.nl

ABSTRACT
The retrospective think-aloud method, in which participants work in silence and verbalize their thoughts afterwards while watching a recording of their performance, is often used for the evaluation of websites. However, participants may not always be able to recall what they thought, when they only see few visual cues that help them remembering their task execution process. In our study we complemented the recording of the performance with a gaze trail of the participants' eye movements, in order to elicit more verbalizations. A comparison was made between the traditional retrospective think-aloud protocols and the variant with eye movements. Contrary to our expectations, no differences were found between the two conditions on numbers of problems, the ways these problems were detected, and types of problems. Two possible explanations for this result are that eye movements might be rather confronting and distracting for participants, and the rather generic way of probing we used. The added value might be stronger when specific questions are asked, based on the observed eye movements. Implications for usability practitioners are discussed in the conclusions of this paper.

Author Keywords
Retrospective think-aloud protocols, verbalization, eye-tracking, usability testing.

ACM Classification Keywords
H.5.2. Information interfaces and presentation (e.g., HCI). User interfaces: Evaluation/methodology.

General Terms
Experimentation, Human Factors, Measurement.

INTRODUCTION
The think-aloud method is often used to evaluate the quality of websites [18, 19, 21]. Two variants of this method are concurrent think-aloud protocols (CTA), which involves participants who verbalize their thoughts while performing certain tasks, and retrospective think-aloud protocols (RTA), in which participants verbalize their thoughts afterwards while watching a recording of their performance. An RTA evaluation has the advantage that the participant can be observed working on the website in silence in a natural way [29]. The verbalizations that are gathered afterwards can complement the observations, which results in a comprehensive diagnosis of the participants' obstacles on the website. However, RTA participants may not be able to remember everything they thought during their task performance, which may lead to fewer, incomplete, or reconstructed verbalizations of their thoughts. This may especially occur with website evaluations, because websites may provide only few visual cues that can help participants to remember what they were doing and thinking [29]. If, for example, a participant thoroughly scanned the homepage, the recording afterwards shows a static image of the homepage for a long time. A possible solution for this problem can be found in the combination of eye-tracking and thinking-aloud. Complementing the recordings of the performance with a replay of the participants' eye movements, may provide cues that support the verbalization task [1, 6, 11, 14, 25]. Instead of looking at a static homepage, participants will see a gaze replay that, for example, moves from the main menu, to a picture, to the news items. Hence, there is a considerable increase in the number and detail of the cues participants receive, which may have a positive effect on the participants' memory and thus on the number and/or types of verbalizations. We will call this think-aloud variant retrospective think-aloud

protocols with eye movements (RTE). In the present study, we compare the traditional RTA method with RTE. Does seeing a gaze replay of the eye movements indeed lead to more or different verbalizations?

This study aims at providing a better understanding of the retrospective think-aloud method, and possibly increasing the quality of this method by adding a recording of the eye movements. In addition, this study explores one of the possible uses of eye-tracking in usability testing. Although eye-tracking is used more and more in a usability context, it remains difficult to really exploit the strengths of this method. Confronting participants with their eye movements and eliciting thoughts about the processes behind these movements might be a fruitful combination of methods.

Research on the practical use of thinking-aloud

There is a wide range of research on the use of think-aloud protocols, focusing on three main topics. First, there are many studies about the practical use of the think-aloud method [2, 8, 12, 17, 20, 21, 23]. These studies focus on the way participants should be instructed, which probes should be used to stimulate participants to verbalize their thoughts, how often this should be done and to what extent methodological variations used in practice affect the results of an evaluation. The theoretical framework of the think-aloud method was developed by Ericsson and Simon [8]. The underlying idea of the method is that verbalizations provide an accurate representation of participants' thought processes. Ericsson and Simon proposed a procedure for collecting valid and reliable think-aloud data, in which a facilitator should not interfere with the subjects' cognitive processes. Many studies showed that Ericsson and Simon's protocol is not used as intended in usability practice [2, 12, 17, 20, 21], and that alternative protocols should be studied. Boren and Ramey [2] proposed a more effective think-aloud procedure for a usability context, based on speech-communication theory. They advised facilitators to behave as active listeners and to create a natural dialogue between speaker and listener. A facilitator should do this by using phrases and sounds indicating to the speaker that the listener is paying attention and is engaged with what is being said, the so called 'acknowledgement tokens'.

In several studies, different think-aloud protocols have been compared, varying from the strict classical way to more 'relaxed' approaches in which the facilitator actively intervenes in the participant's task processing. Relaxed forms of thinking-aloud seem to affect behavior during task processing [12, 17, 21], but not the number of problems detected [17]. In sum, different think-aloud instructions may be used and they seem to influence the results of an evaluation. It is therefore important that researchers and practitioners carefully document the type of think-aloud protocols they used, to facilitate comparisons across studies.

Comparison of variants of the think-aloud method

Besides differences in instructions and probing, there are also variants of the think-aloud method that differ in the moment and/or setting of verbalizing. A second line of research compares different variants of the think-aloud method. Van den Haak et al. [27] compared concurrent think-aloud (CTA) and retrospective think-aloud (RTA) in an evaluation of an online library catalogue. They found that concurrent and retrospective think-aloud protocols revealed comparable sets of usability problems. However, participants in the RTA condition performed better than the CTA group and experienced fewer observable problems. This result can be explained by the double cognitive workload in the concurrent condition, also called reactivity, which makes it more difficult to complete tasks adequately. In three other studies [28, 29, 30], Van den Haak et al. compared the CTA, RTA and a third condition, called constructive interaction, which involves two users working on the website together. These three variants were compared on number and types of problems, the relevance of the problems detected, the task performance, and participant experiences. In these studies only minor differences were found between the three variants in terms of output, which makes them largely interchangeable. Ummelen and Neutelings [26] compared concurrent thinking-aloud with the click-and-read method and a silent condition, focusing on reactivity. The different conditions had no effect on information selection and knowledge. However, there was an effect on judgments, think-aloud participants being more positive about proposals in the text.

In sum, we can conclude that different variants of thinking-aloud hardly seem to influence the task performance and the output of the evaluation. However, sometimes reactivity can occur in the concurrent think-aloud studies, which makes the retrospective condition, in which participants work in silence, the most natural of the three think-aloud variants.

Combining eye-tracking and the think-aloud method

The third group of studies combines thinking-aloud and eye-tracking. Eye-tracking is increasingly used in usability research and has the potential of providing useful contributions to the field of usability evaluation [9]. The methodology is based on the idea of a direct relationship between what people are looking at and what they are thinking, the so called eye-mind hypothesis of Just and Carpenter [16]. However, it is not easy to interpret eye-tracking data and to elicit useful information for a usability context [15, 22]. Questions are still open how to exploit the strengths of eye-tracking and minimize its weaknesses [24]. Eye-tracking does not seem to be a complete usability method by itself, but seems particularly useful in a broader usability context, in combination with other methods [3, 4, 15]. The combination most often used is that of eye-tracking and thinking-aloud.

In some studies eye-tracking is used to elicit more information about the think-aloud method, for example about the question to what extent participants are able to adequately verbalize their thoughts. Cooke and Cuddihy [5] used eye-tracking to address limitations in concurrent thinking-aloud, answering the question what users do when they are not verbalizing their thoughts. They found that the think-aloud method may overlook some subtle cues about participants' expectations of information and link location and about their confidence in link names. Guan et al. [10] focused on retrospective thinking-aloud and compared subjects' verbalizations with their eye movements. Their study showed that RTA is a valid method that provides an accurate account of participants' task processing.

Other studies have taken the opposite perspective, using think-aloud data to obtain more information about eye movement patterns. Ehmke and Wilson [7] defined a set of problems collected with think-aloud protocols and connected these problems to eye-tracking patterns. In this way they tried to relate eye movement patterns to specific usability problems.

Finally, the combination of thinking-aloud and eye-tracking can be applied as a think-aloud variant in which eye movements are used as an extra cue for participants who retrospectively verbalize their thoughts (RTE). Russo [25] found that a retrospective condition with replay of eye movements yielded more output than concurrent and retrospective conditions. Hansen [11] compared two retrospective conditions, cued by a video recording or a recording of eye movements. He concluded that the types of verbalizations differed in the two conditions, with more comments on physical actions in the video cued condition and more comments on visual actions in the eye cued condition. However, both studies have limitations concerning the number of participants, the eye tracking equipment, and the design, which makes it difficult to apply the results to the current practice of usability testing. More recent research, with better eye tracking equipment, is described by Ball et al. [1]. They used the so called PEEP method (post-experience eye-tracked protocols) in commercial practice as a promising technique to elicit usability problems. Their method resembles what we call the RTE method. Eger et al. [6] aimed at validating this retrospective think-aloud variant. They compared retrospective thinking-aloud cued by eye movement replay (which they call "retro eye cue"), with concurrent think-aloud, and with the traditional form of retrospective think-aloud cued by a recording of screen events ("retro screen cue"). A total number of 24 participants performed a search task on two search engines (Google and Infomagnet). The retro eye cue variant elicited more usability problems than the concurrent condition. The two retrospective conditions did not differ on the overall number of problems identified. There was, however, an interaction between reporting method and search engine, with retro eye cue being particularly good at detecting usability problems with the unfamiliar and more complex browser Infomagnet. Hyrskykari et al. [14] also combined thinking-aloud and eye-tracking and compared CTA with RTE. In this study RTE produced more verbal data, that were more informative and of better quality than the CTA data. However, only eight participants took part in the study and they conducted simple fact finding search tasks.

In sum, RTE might be a promising new variant of thinking-aloud, but research is needed to gain more knowledge on this method. It is important to test with larger numbers of participants, on different types of websites, and with tasks that include more than just searching for information. We therefore developed a study in which the two retrospective think-aloud variants were compared to each other in a comprehensive scenario task.

Research questions and hypotheses

In our study participants were asked to verbalize their thoughts in two conditions:

- Retrospective thinking-aloud (RTA): participants verbalize their thoughts retrospectively after task completion, cued by a dynamic screen replay of their actions (pages visited and mouse movements).
- Retrospective thinking-aloud with eye-tracking (RTE): participants verbalize their thoughts retrospectively, cued by a dynamic screen replay of their actions, complemented with a dynamic gaze replay of their eye movements.

Do the eye movements serve as an extra cue that supports participants remembering what they did, resulting in more verbalizations? To what extent does adding the eye movements to the retrospective condition result in differences in:

- the total number of usability problems detected?
- the way the problems are detected: (1) through observation of the behavioral data and eye tracking patterns, (2) through verbalization by the participant or (3) through a combination of observation and verbalization?
- the types of usability problems detected: navigation, content and design?
- participants' opinions about their participation?

We expected that the RTE method would elicit a higher number of verbalized usability problems, in line with the results of Russo [25] and to a certain extent Eger et al. [6]. Participants receive more cues, which helps them to better remember what they thought, and to verbalize more of these thoughts. Hence, we expected significantly more verbalizations in the RTE condition, which would lead to a higher total number of problem detections, a higher number of problems detected through verbalization, and a higher number of problems detected through a combination of observation and verbalization (since in the RTE condition more observed problems will also be verbalized). As a result, we expected fewer problems that are detected only through observation in the RTE condition.

We had no concrete hypotheses concerning the types of problems detected. Seeing the eye movements may elicit other memories than just seeing a recording of the performance, which might result in different types of verbalizations [11]. Eger et al. [6] found no main effect on types of problems.

Our hypothesis with regard to the user opinions was that RTE participants will judge their participation more positively. We expected that they would find it easier to verbalize their thoughts afterwards and that they would evaluate their participation more positively than RTA participants.

EXPERIMENTAL METHOD

The independent variable in this study was the think aloud variant, with two conditions: RTA and RTE. The dependent variables were: numbers of usability problems, the way the problems are detected (verbalization, observation or combination of these two), the types of problems detected, and the opinions of participants.

Test object

The test object we used in this study was the municipal website of Apeldoorn (www.apeldoorn.nl), a city in the Netherlands with 155.000 inhabitants. This website provides information and services to the citizens of Apeldoorn and to other interested users, such as tourists and businesses.

Participants

A total number of 40 participants took part in the study, 20 in each condition. They were recruited by a specialized agency that maintains an extensive database with potential candidates. Participants received a financial compensation for taking part in the study.

Condition	RTA (N=20)	RTE (N=20)
Age:		
18-29	5	5
30-39	3	5
40-54	6	4
> 55	6	6
Gender:		
male	11	11
female	9	9
Education:		
low	6	6
middle	7	7
high	7	7

Table 1. Characteristics of participants.

All participants indicated they used the Internet at least once a week. We selected participants with different characteristics on gender, age and educational level. Educational level was divided into three levels: (1) low: ranging from elementary school to junior general secondary professional education, (2) middle: intermediate vocational education, senior general secondary education or pre-university education, or (3) high: higher vocational education or university. Table 1 shows how the participants were spread over the two conditions. Characteristics were mixed in such a way that, for example, all age groups consisted of equal numbers of men and women and of different educational levels.

Task scenario

Participants conducted three tasks on the website, of which the first task was analyzed for this study. For this task we were sure that none of the participants had prior knowledge about the website and there was no influence on user experiences from former tasks on the website.

The task provided ample data for answering our research questions, as it was a comprehensive task with three sub sections that included searching for information, as well as reading, understanding, and applying the relevant information to the described scenario. The task was introduced with a scenario that described the relevant context and details that were necessary to perform the task. Participants were asked to imagine themselves in this scenario and to act as if they really wanted to find the information. The task concerned obtaining a subsidy that the government offers to support people buying a house for the first time in their lives. Participants were asked to answer three sub questions: (1) what is the name of this subsidy; (2) do you meet the requirements for this subsidy; and (3) what should you do to make a request for this subsidy? The shortest navigation path to this information consisted of six links, the last of which was a link to a pdf-file with information about all kinds of possible subsidies for buying or renovating a house. Participants were not allowed to use the search engine, so they needed to navigate to the information.

Questionnaire

Participants' opinions on the thinking-aloud procedure were measured at the end of a session with four questions on a five-point Likert scale, ranging from strongly disagree, to strongly agree. We asked participants about the ease of verbalizing afterwards, the support they experienced from seeing the recording, and to what extent they liked seeing back their performance and to verbalize afterwards what they thought. Appendix A gives an overview of the questions. Questions 1 and 4 were the same in both conditions, questions 2 and 3 focused on the recording of the performance (with or without eye movements) and were therefore slightly different in both conditions.

Figure 1. Fragment from gaze replay of the eye movements.

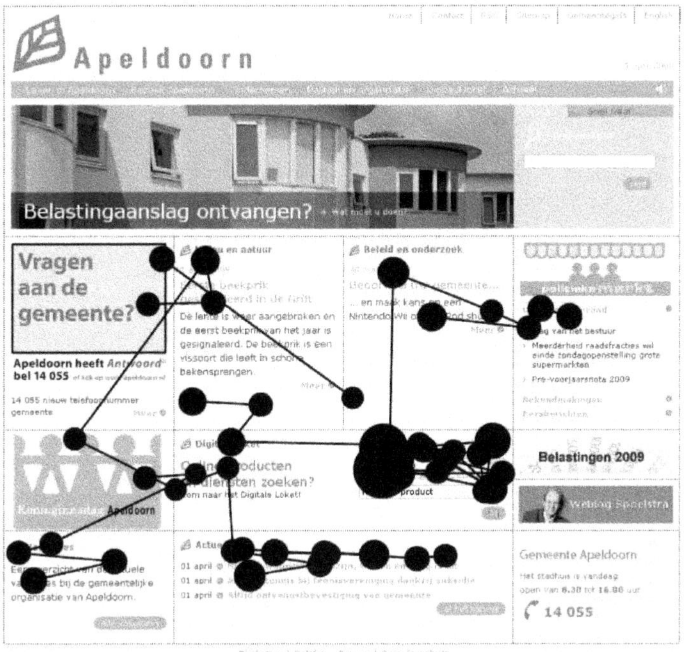

Figure 2. Gaze plot of the eye movements.

Equipment

Data were collected with a remote Tobii 1750 eye-tracker with Tobii Studio 1.2 software. A flat monitor was used to display the website, with a resolution of 1024x768 pixels, with 16-bit color depth. Another monitor showed the facilitator simultaneously what the participant was doing, by projecting the following elements: the stimulus, the gaze overlay, the real time tracking status, and the user camera image. The replay for the participants in the RTE condition was projected in a grey color that was slightly transparent. The fixation radius was set on 70 pixels and the fixation duration on 100 ms, which resulted in a gaze replay that was rather steady.

Figure 1 shows a screenshot with a fragment from a gaze replay of the eye movements. The dots represent fixation points (the longer the fixation, the larger the dot), and the lines show the scan path. Participants saw these lines and dots moving over the screen. The gaze plot in figure 2 displays a static view of the whole scan path of a participant on one screen. In our study participants looked at a dynamic and slightly transparent replay, so they saw the scan path moving over the screen in approximately half a minute (depending on the time they spent on this page during task processing).

Procedure

The study consisted of 40 individual sessions of approximately one hour. The sessions started with a short instruction in which participants were invited to perform three tasks on a municipal website. We asked them to imagine themselves in the described situations and to carry out the tasks in the same way they would do it at home. Then, the eyes were calibrated with a nine point calibration and the participants started their tasks, working in silence. Participants who had not found the information after five minutes, were directed to the right web page on which they could read the information and answer the scenario questions.

The facilitator observed the performance of the participants on a monitor in another room. Sometimes the eye movement recording was disrupted, for example because the participant moved too much. In these cases the facilitator tried to correct the position of the participant between tasks. Participants with incomplete eye tracking recordings, were put in the RTA condition. In this way we made sure that all RTE participants would see an adequate recording of their eye movements. Of course, we took care of a balanced distribution of demographic variables in both groups.

After task completion, the participants were instructed about the remaining part of the session. They were asked to verbalize the thoughts they had during task performance, while looking at a recording of their actions. To prepare them, they were shown an example of a recording: in the RTA condition a dynamic screen replay of pages visited and mouse movements, in the RTE condition the same replay, complemented with the dynamic gaze trail of the eye movements. Subsequently, they received an explanation about thinking-aloud. We asked them to verbalize everything they thought during task execution, while looking at the recording of their performance. We emphasized that it was the website that was being tested and not themselves, so they could verbalize really everything they thought. We explicitly asked them not to describe actions that were already visible on the screen (for example, 'I clicked on link x'), but to verbalize as much as possible the thoughts, reflections, and motives they had while performing these actions (for example, 'I was not sure which link to choose, but I chose link x because I thought it was the best match with the information I was looking for').

After the instruction, the participants took a seat in front of the computer, and the replay of the recording of their performance was started. When participants fell silent for more than five seconds, they were probed with a neutral prompt, such as 'Please, keep verbalizing what you thought', 'What did you think at this moment', and 'Please, can you say what you were thinking'. At the end of the session, participants filled out the questionnaire.

Data analysis

We started the data analysis with analyzing the recordings of the participants' task performance. In order to extract observations that pointed to usability problems, we developed a task model that described all necessary steps to complete the task successfully. Examples of relevant steps are: clicking on a link that leads to the required information, reading the paragraph in the pdf-file that contains the information about the subsidy, and interpreting this information correctly, resulting in the right answer to the question. Deviations from this task model were reported as observed usability problems. After that, the verbalizations were analyzed, again on the basis of the task model. A problem could be either only observed, or observed as well as verbalized, or only verbalized. The problem set that resulted from this analysis contained all problem detections from all participants. This means that problems in this set can occur several times, since the same problem might have been experienced by several participants. We therefore also looked at the number of different problems in each condition and the overlap between the two conditions, taking together the problem detections that point to the same problem. This matching procedure is not straightforward and can be done in more strict or more liberal ways [13]. We used a rather strict matching procedure in which two problems were only considered the same if they (1) occurred at the same page, (2) concerned the same object on that page (for example, a menu, an illustration, or a text block), (3) were coded as the same problem type, and (4) had the same cause and result.

For each problem the problem type was determined. We distinguished four problems types: navigation, content, design, or other. The navigation category contains all problems that are related to finding the required information on the website, for example a poorly organized home page, unclear link labels, and problems with the structure. The content category consists of problems on the target pages on which the information can be found. Examples are problems with understanding the information, incomplete information, or inaccurate information. The design category involves everything that relates to the functionality of the design, such as an illegible font, or an unclear lay out. The "other" category consists of problems that do not fit into the three categories, for example technical issues.

Finally, the four questions on opinions about working in RTA or RTE were analyzed. Differences between the conditions on all these results were analyzed using independent samples t-tests.

RESULTS

Task performance

Results between the two conditions can only be compared meaningfully if the participants in both conditions showed equal task performance in the 'pre-think-aloud phase'. The average task times did not differ significantly between the conditions: 325 sec. (sd 113) in the RTA condition versus 362 sec. (sd 101) in the RTE condition ($t(38) = 1.12$, p = .27). Also, the percentage of users directed to the right web page did not differ significantly in the two conditions: 30% in RTA versus 15% in RTE ($\chi^2(1) = 1.29$, p = .26).

Number of problems

In total, 292 usability problems were found in the 40 sessions: 149 (51%) in the RTA condition, and 143 (49%) in the RTE condition. The mean number of problems per participant was 7.5 in the RTA condition and 7.2 in the RTE condition, which means that there were no significant differences between the methods on the number of problems found (t(38) = .33, p = .74).

We also looked at the number of different problems detected in each condition, for one problem can be found by several participants. In the RTA condition 98 different problems were found, and in the RTE condition 88. A number of 36 problems were found in both conditions (37% of the RTA set and 41% of the RTE set).

Ways of detection

How were the problems detected in both conditions? Table 2 shows the mean number of problems per condition, found through observation, verbalization, or a combination of both.

There were no significant differences between the conditions in the ways the problems were detected: through observation (t(38) = .43, p = .67), verbalization (t(38) = -.94, p = .35), and both (t(38) = 1.51, p = .14).

Way of detection	RTA Mean (sd)	RTE Mean (sd)
Observed	2.2 (1.7)	2.0 (1.3)
Verbalized	1.8 (1.0)	2.3 (2.2)
Observed and verbalized	3.6 (1.3)	3.0 (1.2)
Total	7.5 (2.6)	7.2 (3.1)

Table 2. Mean number of usability problems detected per participant in the two conditions, split for the way they were detected (through observation, verbalization or both).

Types of usability problems

What are the types of problems found in the two conditions? Table 3 shows the distribution of the problem types: navigation, content and design over the two conditions.

No significant differences were found between the two conditions for navigation (t(38) = 1.05, p = .30), content (t(38) = -.88, p = .38), design (t(38) = -.53, p = .60), or other (t(38) = 1.61, p = .12). In both conditions most problems were found on navigational issues, but there were also many problems on content and design.

Problem type	RTA Mean (sd)	RTE Mean (sd)
Navigation	3.6 (2.2)	2.9 (1.7)
Content	1.9 (1.1)	2.3 (1.4)
Design	1.7 (1.5)	2.0 (1.5)
Other	0.3 (0.7)	0.1 (0.2)
Total	7.5 (2.6)	7.2 (3.1)

Table 3. Mean number of usability problems detected per participant in the two conditions, split per dimension.

Participants' experiences

How did the participants experience their participation in the study? Table 4 shows the opinions on four topics, for the two conditions (the complete questions can be found in Appendix A).

Only for question 3 a significant difference between the conditions was found (t(38) = -2.7, p = .01). This means that the RTE participants liked seeing back the replay (with eye movements) more, than the RTA participants did. However, no differences were found on the ease of verbalizing retrospectively (t(38) = -.94, p = .35), on remembering the thoughts (t(38) = -.99, p = .33), or on the extent to which participants liked to verbalize their thoughts retrospectively (t(38) = -1.65, p = .11).

Question	RTA Mean (sd)	RTE Mean (sd)
1. 'Easy to verbalize'	3.5 (.89)	3.8 (.79)
2. 'Recording supported remembering'	3.9 (.67)	4.1 (.60)
3. 'Liked seeing task recording'	3.8 (.97)*	4.5 (.76)*
4. 'Liked verbalizing'	3.8 (.77)	4.2 (.77)

Table 4. Participants' experiences (*p < .05). Note: Scores are measured on a 5-point Likert scale, on which 5 is most positive.

Summary of results

To summarize, no differences were found between the two retrospective conditions on numbers of problems, the ways these problems were detected, and the types of problems. The participants in the RTE condition liked seeing back the recording of their performance (with eye movements) more than the participants in the RTA condition. No other differences in opinions about the procedure were found.

DISCUSSION

Contrary to our hypothesis, we did not find any differences in output between the two retrospective think-aloud conditions. We expected that showing the eye movements would provide extra cues that stimulated participants to verbalize their thoughts. A first explanation for the results of our study might be that the eye movements not only supported participants, but also distracted them. Most participants had never seen eye movements before. Although we prepared them with an example recording and elaborately explained to them what they would see, we observed that it was often confronting for participants to see a gaze replay of their eye movements. In spite of the rather smooth settings we chose, a dynamic gaze replay moves rather quickly over the screen. Moreover, it was a new and intriguing discovery for participants to learn that it is possible to represent what they just looked at in lines and dots. Eger et al. [6] have not reported observations on how participants reacted to their eye movements. They report, however, results of a questionnaire that participants filled out after their experiment. These results show no significant differences on user experience between the retrospective conditions, which partly corresponds with our questionnaire results. We know of no other studies that describe how users experience being confronted with their own eye movements. It would be useful to do more research on this topic and to reduce the potentially negative effects of seeing back the eye movements. If participants receive more training in interpreting eye movements and get more used to looking at gaze replays, the effects of the eye movement cues might be stronger. Other solutions might be to slow down the replay speed [14], or to allow users to pause during the replay.

Eger et al. [6] concluded in their study that, for the complex search engine, RTE elicited more problems than the other think-aloud conditions. The difference between our results and the former study may be explained by differences in probing. We used a rather strict way of probing, while Eger et al. seem to have used a less strict way of thinking-aloud. A less strict way of probing and asking questions possibly leads to more additional verbalizations because the facilitator can ask specific questions based on the observed eye movements.

In sum, we conclude that in our study the eye movements did not have additional value. This brings this research in line with other studies in which no differences between think-aloud variants were found [26, 28, 29, 30].

CONCLUSIONS AND FUTURE RESEARCH

Ball et al. [1] reported promising results from the retrospective think-aloud variant cued by eye-movement replay, which they applied in commercial practice. Our study did not confirm the additional value of showing participants their eye movements: the output of the two variants we compared did not differ. Moreover, seeing their own eye movements might be rather confronting and distracting for participants, although they report afterwards that they enjoyed seeing back their eye movements. Based on our study, we would advise practitioners to choose the RTA method in which participants verbalize on a recording of their performance, for adding a gaze replay of the eye movements does not result in more verbalizations.

This result does not mean however, that eye tracking data have no added value in usability testing. When evaluators observe the eye movements, they might have a better understanding of the participants' experiences and they might be better able to ask relevant questions that help to diagnose the usability problems. Hence, the interaction between the facilitator and the participants might improve. To shed more light on this matter a systematic comparison should be conducted between strict and relaxed ways of probing in both retrospective think-aloud conditions.

We consider RTE an interesting addition to the range of usability methods. Moreover, this method can be a step towards better exploiting the merits of eye-tracking. We encourage further work on this method, to better exploit the merits and address the limitations. Future research may focus on evaluations of other websites and other (types of) tasks than we used in this study, since Eger et al. [6] have shown that the task complexity can influence the output of the retrospective methods. Also, research is needed on the effects of training participants more intensively on interpreting eye movements. In future studies a systematic comparison should be made between conditions with different levels of replay speed and pausing options. Another interesting line of research concerns the extent to which user characteristics influence the way participants verbalize and react to their eye movements. There may be interaction effects between sex, age, or educational level and the way of cueing retrospective verbalizations. For example, higher educated participants might benefit more from seeing their eye movements than lower educated participants. In preliminary analyses on our dataset we did not find any significant differences between the different groups. However, larger groups of participants should be compared to obtain adequate answers on this topic.

The combination of the think-aloud method and eye tracking may result in relevant knowledge that can be used to further improve the quality of usability testing. Our study showed no positive effect of the RTE method in comparison to RTA. However, this study can be used as a first step to further explore the merits of this method.

ACKNOWLEDGEMENTS

This paper is based on a research project financed by the Dutch Organization for Scientific Research (NWO). It is part of the research program Evaluation of Municipal Websites. We would like to thank Ineke Waas, Master's student at Utrecht University, who contributed to the study in this article.

REFERENCES

1. Ball, L.J., Eger, N., Stevens, R., Dodd, J. Applying the PEEP method in usability testing. *Interfaces, 67* (2006), 15-19.
2. Boren, T., and Ramey, J. Thinking aloud: Reconciling theory and practice. *IEEE Transactions on Professional Communication 43*, 3 (2000), 261-278.
3. Cooke, L. Is eye tracking the next step in usability testing? *International professional communication conference* (2006), 236-242.
4. Cooke, L. Eye tracking: How it works and how it relates to usability. *Technical Communication 52*, 4 (2005), 456-463.
5. Cooke, L., and Cuddihy, E. Using eye tracking to address limitations in think-aloud protocol. *IEEE international professional communication conference proceedings* (2005), 653-658.
6. Eger, N., Ball, L.J., Stevens, R., and Dodd, J. Cueing retrospective verbal reports in usability testing through eye-movement replay. *Proceedings of the 21st British CHI group annual conference on HCI 2007: People and computers XXI: HCI... but not as we know it, Volume 1*, British Computer Society (2007), 129-137.
7. Ehmke, C., and Wilson, S. Identifying web usability problems from eye-tracking data. *Proceedings of the 21st British CHI group annual conference on HCI 2007: People and computers XXI: HCI... but not as we know it, Volume 1*, British Computer Society (2007), 119-128.
8. Ericsson, K.A., and Simon, H.A. *Protocol analysis: Verbal reports as data* (Revised ed.). MIT Press, Cambridge, MA, 1996.
9. Goldberg, J.H., and Wichansky, A.M. Eye tracking in usability evaluation: A practitioner's guide. In: *The mind's eye: Cognitive and applied aspects of eye movement research.* Hyönä, J., Radach, R., and Deubel, H., eds. Elsevier (2003), 493-516.
10. Guan, Z., Lee, S., Cuddihy, E., and Ramey, J. The validity of the stimulated retrospective think-aloud method as measured by eye tracking. *Proceedings of the SIGCHI conference on human factors in computing systems.* Montréal, Québec, Canada. ACM (2006), 1253-1262.
11. Hansen, J.P. The use of eye mark recordings to support verbal retrospection in software testing. *Acta Psychologica 76* (1991), 31-49.
12. Hertzum, M., Hansen, K.D., and Andersen, H.H.K. Scrutinising usability evaluation: Does thinking aloud affect behaviour and mental workload? *Behaviour & Information Technology 28*, 2 (2009), 165-181.
13. Hornbæk, K. Dogmas in the assessment of usability evaluation methods. *Behaviour & Information Technology 29*, 1 (2010), 97-111.
14. Hyrskykari, A., Ovaska, S., Räihä, K., Majaranta, P., and Lehtinen, M. Gaze path stimulation in retrospective think-aloud. *Journal of Eye Movement Research 2*, 4 (2008), 1-18.
15. Jacob, R.J.K., and Karn, K.S. Eye tracking in human-computer interaction and usability research: Ready to deliver the promises. In: *The mind's eye: Cognitive and applied aspects of eye movement research.* Hyönä, J., Radach, R., and Deubel, H., eds. Elsevier Science BV (2003), 574-605.
16. Just, M.A., and Carpenter, P.A. Eye fixations and cognitive processes. *Cognitive Psychology 8*, 4 (1976), 441-480.
17. Krahmer, E., and Ummelen, N. Thinking about thinking aloud: A comparison of two verbal protocols for usability testing. *IEEE Transactions on Professional Communication 47*, 2, (2004), 105-117.
18. Lewis, C., and Mack, R. Learning to use a text processing system: Evidence from "thinking aloud" protocols. *Proceedings of the 1982 conference on Human factors in computing systems.* New York, USA. ACM (1982), 387-392.
19. Molich, R., and Dumas, J. Comparative usability evaluation (CUE-4). *Behaviour & Information Technology 27*, 3 (2008), 263-281.
20. Nørgaard, M., and Hornbæk, K. What do usability evaluators do in practice? An explorative study of think-aloud testing. *Proceedings of the 6th conference on designing interactive systems ACM.* (2006), 209-218.
21. Olmsted-Hawala, E.L., Murphy, E.D., Hawala, S., and Ashenfelter, K.T. Think-aloud protocols: A comparison of three think-aloud protocols for use in testing data-dissemination web sites for usability. *Proceedings of the 28th international conference on human factors in computing systems ACM.* (2010), 2381-2390.
22. Poole, A., and Ball, L.J. Eye tracking in human-computer interaction and usability research: Current status and future prospects. *Encyclopedia of Human Computer Interaction* (2005), 211-219.
23. Ramey, J., Boren, T., Cuddihy, E., Dumas, J., Guan, Z., Van den Haak, M. J., and De Jong, M. D. T. Does think aloud work? How do we know? *CHI'06 extended abstracts on human factors in computing systems ACM.* (2006).
24. Renshaw, J.A., Finlay J., and Webb, N. Getting a measure of satisfaction from eyetracking in practice. *CHI'06 extended abstracts on human factors in computing systems ACM.* (2006).
25. Russo, J.E. A software system for the collection of retrospective protocols prompted by eye fixations.

Behavior *Research Methods & Instrumentation 11* (1979), 177-179.

26. Ummelen, N., and Neutelings, R. Measuring reading behavior in policy documents: A comparison of two instruments. *IEEE Transactions on Professional Communication 43*, 3 (2000), 292-301.

27. Van den Haak, M.J., De Jong, M.D.T., and Schellens, P.J. Retrospective vs. concurrent think-aloud protocols: testing the usability of an online library catalogue. *Behaviour & Information Technology 22*, 5 (2003), 339-351.

28. Van den Haak, M.J., De Jong, M.D.T., and Schellens, P.J. Employing think-aloud protocols and constructive interaction to test the usability of online library catalogues: A methodological comparison. *Interacting with Computers 16*, 6 (2004), 1153-1170.

29. Van den Haak, M.J., De Jong, M.D.T., and Schellens, P.J. Evaluation of an informational web site: Three variants of the think-aloud method compared. *Technical Communication 54*, 1 (2007), 58-71.

30. Van den Haak, M.J., De Jong, M.D.T., and Schellens, P.J. Evaluating municipal websites: A methodological comparison of three think-aloud variants. *Government Information Quarterly 26*, 1 (2009), 193-202.

APPENDIX A

Questionnaire for measuring participants' experiences.

1. I found it easy to verbalize my thoughts after I completed the tasks.

2a. (RTA) Seeing back the recording of the pages I visited supported me in remembering what I thought.

2b. (RTE) Seeing back the recording of my eye movements supported me in remembering what I thought.

3a. (RTA) I liked seeing back the recording of my performance.

3b. (RTE) I liked seeing back the recording of my eye movements.

4. I liked it to subsequently verbalize the thoughts I had during task performance.

Triggered Think-Aloud Protocol: Using Eye Tracking to Improve Usability Test Moderation

Beverly Freeman
PayPal
2211 North 1st Street
San Jose, CA 95131, USA
bfreeman@paypal.com

ABSTRACT

Usability practitioners often rely on research participants' verbal reports to better understand the user experience. These reports can be collected either during or after task execution, with each approach entailing unique benefits and limitations. This note presents a framework for using eye tracking data to "trigger" when and how moderators probe participants for verbal comments during task execution to supplement or elaborate participant-initiated comments. A preliminary case study suggests that this approach affords a level of efficiency and effectiveness difficult to achieve with retrospective verbalization or without the use of eye tracking. The hope is that practitioners will be encouraged to use and refine this method for the benefit of the field.

Author Keywords

Eye tracking, usability, verbal protocol, think-aloud protocol, concurrent think-aloud protocol, retrospective think-aloud protocol.

ACM Classification Keywords

H.5.2 User Interfaces (D.2.2, H.1.2, I.3.6).

General Terms

Human Factors.

INTRODUCTION

Concurrent Think-Aloud Protocol

In usability research, it is common among practitioners to employ the concurrent think-aloud (CTA) protocol, in which research participants verbalize their thoughts during the execution of a task. Many practitioners rely on CTA to better understand how and why participants approach tasks the way they do. For example, verbal comments enabled Lewis and Mack [5] to make the distinction between unintentional task failures (due to interface design flaws) and deliberate task refusals (due to inaccurate assumptions influenced by past experiences).

While popular (Jakob Nielsen has called the think-aloud protocol "the single most valuable usability engineering method" [6]), CTA is not without its limitations. As outlined in Eger et al. [2], the resulting verbal account may be inaccurate (since explanations may be fabricated in order to justify behavior), incomplete (since many cognitive processes are unconscious), or interfering (since talking aloud may either positively facilitate performance or degrade it due to the increased cognitive demand of continuous reporting). Furthermore, in the context of eye tracking research, Pernice and Nielsen [7] observed that "surveying" behavior (i.e., scanning a webpage thoroughly) is common during CTA studies, possibly because participants feel the need to familiarize themselves with the interface before commenting.

If verbal reports are useful for understanding behavior, can they be elicited with minimal impact on behavior?

Retrospective Think-Aloud Protocol

Verbal reports can be valuable in usability research, but they need not necessarily be collected during task execution. Retrospective think-aloud (RTA) entails collecting verbal comments after the task, which removes potentially biasing effects talking has on task behavior [2]. Additionally, there is evidence that the CTA experience can be perceived as less pleasant than the RTA experience because participants are prompted to talk even when they have nothing to state [2]. However, RTA's primary challenge is the increased chance of memory decay due to its reliance on long-term memory [1]. Additionally, although the verbal account cannot retroactively alter behavior, participants can still provide a fabricated account of prior behavior [9] or explain their actions in a manner that reflects a more rational approach than was actually taken [4]. The delay between behavior and commentary in RTA presents increased opportunity for participants to formulate a heavily interpreted account of behavior.

Different Ways of Cueing RTA

There are a variety of ways to elicit a retrospective account. Participants might be asked to do so based solely on memory. Alternatively, their account can be cued by video – that is, they can watch a video replay of their task execution, and describe what they were thinking during each step of the process. Eye tracking technology may also provide an additional memory aid by showing participants where they were looking while completing the task. Gaze-cued RTA uses a video of the task execution, with the gaze data (eye fixations and saccades) superimposed over the stimulus. Eger et al. [2] found that gaze-cued RTA revealed more usability issues compared to CTA, and eye tracking technology provider Tobii Technology suggested that gaze-cued RTA yielded more quality comments and revealed more usability issues than did other retrospective cueing methods [8].

Controversies Surrounding Gaze-Cued RTA

Despite the benefits of gaze-cued RTA, a few prominent usability professionals recommend that practitioners *not* include the gaze overlay when cueing RTA with the video replay. As reported in the Nielsen Norman Group guide on eye tracking methodology [7], the fact that usability participants were often "shocked, sometimes nervous, and at the same time, enamored with the gaze replay" interfered with the collection of verbal reports. Ultimately, the guide stated, "We typically do not recommend using retrospective [protocol] in [eye tracking]." (The guide mentioned the option of showing the video replay without gaze data, but adds that it is difficult for participants to follow.) The sentiment is echoed by usability firm Bunnyfoot, which pioneered the Post Experience Eyetracking Protocol (PEEP) [1]. In its original incarnation, PEEP involved cueing RTA using gaze video. The method was supported by Eger et al.'s study, which suggested the incremental benefits of the gaze cue over video alone [2]. However, Bunnyfoot has since modified its approach in an effort to avoid the disruption caused by participants' fascination with eye tracking technology. They now employ a post-task interview in lieu of gaze-cued RTA [10].

Regardless of how RTA is cued, it still suffers from limits of long-term memory; though participants can use gaze data to see *where* they were looking at a given moment, they are still at risk of forgetting *why* they looked there, or what they were thinking. If gaze data is beneficial to moderators for formulating thoughtful follow-up questions, can moderators use it to maximize insights during task execution instead of waiting until after? Can this be accomplished with minimal impact on task behavior?

TRIGGERED THINK-ALOUD PROTOCOL

Motivated by the unique benefits and limitations of the CTA and RTA protocols, triggered think-aloud (TTA) was proposed as a modified form of CTA. With TTA, the moderator uses gaze data from an eye tracker to determine when and how to probe participants for verbal comments during task execution. A key difference between TTA and the traditional CTA protocol is that participants are not given a directive to continuously think aloud during the task. Though participants are encouraged to talk aloud if they have something to share, they are not explicitly asked to do so, thereby mitigating the influence that talking has on task behavior. Another key difference between TTA and CTA is that the moderator probes the participant based on what is observed in the gaze data, rather than prompting based on predetermined periods of silence. With TTA, moderators can use gaze data to determine what questions are relevant, and when to ask them.

Initial Instructions

The following is a condensed version of instructions given to participants to situate them for participant-moderator interaction in the TTA framework:

Please start working on the task on your own. Approach it as you would if you were at home. At any time, if you would like to share something with me that would help me better understand what you're experiencing, feel free to do so. From time to time, I may ask you a question or two to better understand what you're experiencing. Please keep in mind that there are no right or wrong answers.

For participants who are generally less talkative, these instructions are intended to alleviate social pressure to talk simply to fill silence. For participants who are generally more talkative, these instructions are intended to give them explicit freedom to talk if they would have been inclined to do so anyway.

Using Gaze Data to Determine Probes

A critical component of TTA is the judicious use of probes, triggered by gaze data. By studying the gaze data in real time, the moderator can avoid asking questions like "What are you looking at now?" The moderator can guide verbal reports to focus on questions that can only be answered through verbalization. The decision to refrain from or engage in conversation with the participant is based on the goals of the study and the aspects of the experience that are of greatest consequence to the research goals.

Gaze data can be used to help moderators determine when to probe and when to refrain. If the gaze data shows that the participant is reading text that is not central to the study, the moderator can decide to refrain from probing the participant. However, if the participant is spending a significant amount of time scrutinizing a design element of particular interest to the study, the moderator can choose to ask what the participant is thinking while the initial interpretation is still fresh in his/her mind. Alternatively, the moderator may note that a design element was visually attended, and decide not to probe until the participant returns to it later. This could be especially useful for subtle design elements or changes that may require repeat exposure prior to achieving awareness, and ultimately usage. The spirit of this approach is similar to that of Bunnyfoot's current approach to RTA to use "highly skilled practitioners, capable of multitasking and thinking on their feet" [10]. The difference is that the Bunnyfoot approach leverages skillful moderation to guide post-task interviews, while the TTA approach leverages skillful moderation to guide discussion during task execution.

In TTA, eye gaze data provides an additional data point to help moderators formulate probes. The types of comments we wish to reduce are those that merely broadcast observable actions (e.g., "I'm typing in my password.") and those that alter behavior (e.g., "Talking about it makes me wonder if I should try this link here."). To that end, the neutral "keep talking" prompt proposed by Ericsson and Simon [3] does not give the moderator the freedom to dynamically move away from or toward certain topics in order to better serve the research goals.

In order to maintain an active yet neutral role in shaping the conversation, moderators can use carefully formed probes. Some probes appropriate for TTA include:

- *How would you describe what you're seeing here?*
- [After the participant has moved away from a page of interest] *I'd like to ask you to pause for a second. How would you describe what just happened [or what has happened so far]?*
- *Is there anything else you can share that would help me better understand what you're experiencing?*

The purpose of these probes is to capture thoughts while they're still fresh and less subject to decay or alteration, while still being vague enough so as not to lead the participant. Based on the participant's responses to these open-ended questions, the moderator can direct the line of questioning as necessary and probe for clarification.

TTA: A PRELIMINARY CASE STUDY

The TTA method was used to inform the redesign of product pages on eBay.com. These pages display products' stock photos, specifications, and buying options (see Figure 1). The "buying options" module (indicated with an overlaid dashed line) summarizes which sellers carry the product, and how much they charge for it.

A key research question was how successfully users would discover and use the buying options module, as this was the first time this type of summary was provided for each product. Several participants were observed to look at the top part of the page (i.e., the photo and product name), and then immediately skip to the product description, thus bypassing the buying options module (see example gaze plot in Figure 1). Upon observing this behavior, the moderator refrained from probing, with the desire to see whether repeat exposures to the page would lead to eventual discovery of the module. This approach helped the team avoid premature conclusions about discoverability based on initial exposure. Additionally, the moderator was able to eventually understand through careful probing why some participants repeatedly overlooked the module.

For participants who did look at the module, the moderator was able to probe on participants' interpretations and expectations for the information in the module without delay. Had it not been for the use of gaze data in the moment, it would have been a greater challenge for the moderator to determine if and when to probe without artificially drawing attention to the module.

Figure 1. Example gaze plot showing lack of visual fixations on the "buying options" module (indicated with dashed line).

TTA Compared to Other Approaches

Key qualitative differences have surfaced between TTA and more traditional approaches used at eBay, largely due to the complex nature of the online shopping experience.

TTA helped the moderator be more informed about when to probe for comments compared to CTA. eBay users spend significant effort reviewing item descriptions and sellers' policies. The real-time gaze data made it possible to tell the difference between reading a paragraph of text (an action typically not interrupted by a probe) and looking at various sections of a page (an action that might lead the moderator to explore whether the participant is looking for a particular piece of information). With CTA, participants would often read aloud text on sellers' listing pages in order to fulfill the request to talk. With TTA, they were not compelled to this behavior, and the moderator was less likely to interject when not necessary.

Compared to gaze-cued RTA, TTA allowed participants to easily report their shopping strategies because they did so as those strategies evolved, rather than retrospectively by memory. In gaze-cued RTA studies, participants sometimes commented that they simply could not remember what they had been thinking at the time, having had browsed so many different items from so many different sellers throughout the course of the session.

TTA may therefore be especially beneficial for studying experiences with dynamic content that involve a wide range of user situations and strategies.

CONSIDERATIONS

Not all usability research situations may benefit equally from TTA. One factor to consider is the goal of the research. TTA would not be appropriate for benchmarking eye tracking data because in such cases, the act of talking has been shown to influence behavior, impacting metrics such as task completion rates and task times [2]. However, TTA has tremendous potential for formative studies in which the aim is to reveal issues for the purpose of design iteration.

Another factor is participant characteristics. TTA could be particularly useful for less-talkative participants, as well-timed probes could elicit valuable comments without the need for continuous verbalization. Indeed, thinking aloud may be especially difficult for non-westerners who come from cultures that do not emphasize self expression [4]. Other people, however, may find it quite natural to talk continuously; for them, there may be less risk of CTA interfering with their behavior.

CONCLUSION

There is no one-size-fits-all solution when it comes to research methods, including think-aloud protocols. However, when the goal is to understand how participants perceive the experience in the moment, TTA can help moderators more strategically formulate and administer their probes with the help of eye gaze data. It can equip them to better understand participant behavior, and to know when to be silent and when to elicit additional or clarifying comments. The desired end result is better informed moderation that leverages observed behaviors to facilitate the collection of valuable verbal reports.

Since TTA is an extension of existing think-aloud protocols, the hope is that this note will spark additional examination and refinement of the TTA method. One promising avenue is experimental research that investigates how verbal comments and task behaviors are impacted by variations in think-aloud protocol, type of product or service being tested, and degree of participant talkativeness.

ACKNOWLEDGMENTS

I am grateful to Mike Katz and Aga Bojko for their valuable feedback on this paper.

REFERENCES

1. Ball, L. J., Eger, N., Stevens, R., and Dodd, J. Applying the PEEP method in usability testing. *Interfaces, 67*, (2006), 15-19.
2. Eger, N., Ball, L., Stevens, R., and Dodd, J. Cueing retrospective verbal reports in usability testing through eye-movement replay. *Proc. BCS-CHI 2007*, ACM Press (2007), 129-137.
3. Ericsson K. A. and Simon, H. A. *Protocol Analysis: Verbal Reports as Data.* MIT Press, Cambridge, MA, USA, 1993.
4. Hyrskykari, A., Ovaska, S., Majaranta, P., Räihä, K.-J., and Lehtinen, M. Gaze path stimulation in retrospective think-aloud. *Journal of Eye Movement Research, 2*,4:5 (2008), 1-18.
5. Lewis, C. and Mack, R. Learning to use a text processing system: Evidence from "thinking aloud" protocols. *Proc. CHI 1982*, ACM Press (1982), 387-392.
6. Nielsen, J. *Usability Engineering.* Morgan Kaufman, San Francisco, CA, USA, 1993.
7. Pernice, K. and Nielsen, J. (2009). Eye tracking methodology: How to conduct and evaluate usability studies using eye tracking. http://www.useit.com/eyetracking/methodology/.
8. Retrospective think aloud and eye tracking. (2009). http://www.tobii.com/archive/files/20342/RTA_and_eye tracking_tobii_whitepaper.pdf.aspx.
9. Russo, J. E. A software system for the collection of retrospective protocols prompted by eye fixations. *Behavioral Research Methods and Instrumentation, 11*,2 (1979), 177-179.
10. Stevens, R. (2009). Why I'm not in love with eye tracking. http://thinkeyetracking.com/Blog/?p=331.

Learning Patterns of Pick-ups and Drop-offs to Support Busy Family Coordination

Scott Davidoff, Brian D. Ziebart, John Zimmerman, Anind K. Dey
Carnegie Mellon University
{ scott.davidoff | bziebart | johnz | anind } @ cs.cmu.edu

ABSTRACT
Part of being a parent is taking responsibility for arranging and supplying transportation of children between various events. Dual-income parents frequently develop routines to help manage transportation with a minimal amount of attention. On days when families deviate from their routines, effective logistics can often depend on knowledge of the routine location, availability and intentions of other family members. Since most families rarely document their routine activities, making that needed information unavailable, coordination breakdowns are much more likely to occur. To address this problem we demonstrate the feasibility of learning family routines using mobile phone GPS. We describe how we (1) detect pick-ups and drop-offs; (2) predict which parent will perform a future pick-up or drop-off; and (3) infer if a child will be left at an activity. We discuss how these routine models give digital calendars, reminder and location systems new capabilities to help prevent breakdowns, and improve family life.

Author Keywords
Sensing, machine learning, data mining, statistical models, graphical models, GPS, mobile phones, routines.

ACM Classification Keywords
H.m Information Systems: Miscellaneous.

General Terms
Algorithms, Human Factors.

INTRODUCTION
Parents are often responsible for planning, coordinating, and executing the transportation of their children to and from their many activities. One coping strategy dual-income parents employ is to develop routines. As parents repeatedly perform similar sequences of actions around each pick-up and drop-off, a routine emerges, significantly reducing the attention required to complete the task.

When tasks unfold in a routine fashion, coordination requires minimal attention to detail. However, when families must deviate from their routines – *e.g.* when one parent must travel for work, schedule an orthodontist appointment, plan a new carpool, or remain home with a sick child – the likelihood that some part of their plan will break down significantly increases.

One these days, effective logistics can often depend on knowledge of the routine location, availability and intentions of other family members. Interestingly, families rarely document routine events on their home calendars [13]. Even when they do, descriptions are incomplete, missing key information, like which parent will drive. Without a resource to provide needed information on routines, family members must recall details of other members' routines (or their own), and here errors can take place. Plans for new events or reactions to unanticipated situations can result in double-booked schedules, missed events, and even children being left at events [10, 11], and, or course, stress and anxiety for parents [19, 37].

This paper explores how sensing and modeling can provide computational access to family transportation routines, and how these learned models function as an *enabling technology*. Specifically, we demonstrate how location data from standard mobile phones can be used to:

1. Detect if a pick-up or drop-off has occurred
2. Predict which parent has responsibility for a future pick-up or drop-off
3. Infer if a child will forgotten at an event

We also discuss how these learned models can create new resources that enable end-user applications, for example:

1. Awareness systems can know when pick-ups occur
2. Calendars can display implicit routine data like where and when pick-ups and drop-offs will occur
3. Location systems can show what pick-up and drop-off responsibilities family members have
4. Reminder systems can alert parents about children left at activities without explicit reminder creation

In this paper, we describe the design and evaluation of our learned models of family routine. Our goal is to develop a proof-of-concept while providing insights on how to improve technical performance. We provide an overview of our previous research and situate our contribution within the field; we describe the design and performance of our learning systems; and we discuss how learned models can enable end-user applications, and ultimately, families.

PREVIOUS RESEARCH

Our focus on routine models emerges from three years of fieldwork on the needs and values of dual-income families.

While many domestic research projects envision technology to provide people more control over home devices, our first yearlong ethnography of dual-income families showed that *more than control of their devices, families desire more control of their lives* [11]. Next, a year Speed Dating design concepts highlighted that parents' often feel seriously out of control as they decide how to transport their children to and from their activities [12]. A third yearlong field study to understand how families manage transportation illustrated how and why coordination breakdowns occur [13].

These breakdowns cut across families, parents, coordination styles and economic class. Parents would commit their spouses to tasks they could not do given the spouse's current routines. Even when known in advance, we saw parents go to a routine place to pick-up a child when the child was at another location. We family members neglect to inform one another when their routines changed. Finally, on multiple occasions, we witnessed well adjusted, responsible parents forget to pick-up their children, leaving them at their activity locations for as long as 40 minutes.

Routines are at once central to many coordination problems, and at the same time not documented (on calendars or elsewhere), so unavailable to family members and coordination support applications.

Since family members currently do not record their routine information, we developed a vision where learned models of routine could create new resources to help families with:

1. **Planning** – Using our models, calendaring systems like LINC [27] and DateLens [29] could display implicit routine events, event times, pick-ups and drop-offs that parents don't document but are critical to making effective plans for and that affect others. Family members could see an entire day's plan, helping make unresolved and conflicting responsibilities salient.
2. **Coordinating** – Using our models, location systems like Motion Presence [6] and the Whereabouts Clock [8] could display where people are with implicit routine information like future pick-ups and drop-offs, helping remind family members what they need to do, and alerting others as days happen as planned.
3. **Improvising** – Using our models, applications could update plans in real-time, helping parents make more reliable decisions. As pick-ups happen, reminder systems like comMotion [25] and PlaceMail [24] could suppress potentially annoying reminders.
4. **Protecting** – Using our models, reminder systems could infer that a required pick-up is not happening, and remind parents without their explicit creation of a reminder, creating a new kind of safety net to guard families against this uncommon but stressful outcome.

BACKGROUND

Existing research has highlighted the value of routines in support of everyday living, while observing limits to that support when people depart from their routines.

Many successful routines serve important organizational and social purposes. A form of habituated memory, routines free up people's attention, creating a tacit knowledge that constrains and directs activity [26]. Successful routines help to scaffold and streamline the decision-making process [38]. However, as their performance becomes more automatic, people cannot recall the details of what they do, making routines difficult to transfer between people [34]. Also, since people often default to routines when faced with limited information, deviations from routine (planned and unanticipated) can cause plans to break down [32].

Dual-income families, in particular, rely heavily on routines to support their dynamic schedules [10, 37], providing them with a feeling of control (*cf.* Bandura [3]) over the environment [38]. But because dual-income families also experience many deviations from routine – *e.g.* rained out games, holidays, scheduled school closings and half-days, doctor and dental checkups, forgotten items and sick children – their plans are often susceptible to breakdowns [5, 10], leading to increased stress [37]. Even the thought that a non-routine day might occur, such as a child showing signs of getting sick, can cause parents stress [10, 37].

During non-routine days, information about the routines of others would often help improvise appropriate responses. Despite this value, routines themselves rarely are documented – they do not appear on calendars [14]. Our work explores the use of machine learning and data mining to learn routines in order to make this information available to families and to family support systems.

The routine is emerging as a useful computational abstraction across a variety of domains. It has been used, for example, to improve the classification of domestic activities [21, 35] and to create opportunities for workplace communication [5]. GPS has provided a gateway to many of those capabilities. Researchers have used GPS data to model geographic mobility [20], social networks [15], individual one-step destination [22, 39], and navigation for the cognitively impaired [23].

Our work builds upon these findings, extending them into the complex and highly nuanced context of family coordination. We model a family as a group of collaborating dependents, not independent individuals (*e.g.* [20, 22, 23, 25]), With multiple people, we can introduce models of collaborative family goals, like when parents pick up and drop off children, and whether a pick-up might be forgotten. Currently, the only extant notification mechanism we know for forgotten children arrives as phone calls from impatient day care managers [19], embarrassed friends [10], or irritated spouses [11]. Notification of this event in any form would present a significant contribution to family life, and create a new kind of safety net.

APPROACH

The goal of this paper is to provide an initial demonstration of the feasibility of our underlying technical approach in a realistic setting. It is also important to note that we in no way claim that our approach is optimal. Instead, the reader should consider the approach in this paper a demonstration of what is possible, and food for thought about other capabilities that knowledge of routines can offer.

First, to operate with a shared vocabulary, we offer a set of definitions. Since we are relying on GPS as our primary sensor for learning routines, we developed a place-centric view of coordination. A person's day can be described as an ordered list of the places they go. We call the transition between each place a *ride*. In our families, each ride has a *driver* (the parent) and possibly a *passenger* (the child). A *drop-off* is a ride given to a place, and a *pick-up* is a ride given from a place. A *plan* is an ordered list of pick-ups and drop-offs, each with an *ideal time*, when the parent intends it to occur, and an *actual time*, when it actually does occur. As a plan unfolds, the family *coordinates*, acknowledging completed rides, and reflecting on the need to modify their current plan for future rides. Families *improvise*; they dynamically modify and even generate new plans based on unanticipated situations that challenge the current plan. Collectively, we refer to planning, coordinating and improvising as family *logistics* (also known as coordination in other literature). Children participate in *activities* like violin and swimming lessons Parents give children rides to *events*, which are instances of the activities.

With this shared vocabulary, the remainder of this section describes the construction of three models of routine, their relationships, and how they can help families plan, coordinate and improvise; creating a new kind of protection against logistical breakdowns. Figure 1 depicts our modeling approach graphically, with arrows indicating the flow of data and inference. Models are constructed from two data sources: interviews, and GPS (Figure 1, top). Our GPS data set follows the movements of 23 people in 5 dual-income families across approximately six months, and is labeled with data collected from nearly 1,000 surveys, over 500 phone interviews, and over 100 home visits (collection reported in [13]). Leveraging previous work on automated place discovery [1, 25], we assume that all models include a set of known locations (taken from our interviews). Interviews provide a ground truth about which activities occur each day, and the ideal pick-up and drop-off times. We combined this information with GPS, and designed a series of three models, each recombining and building on the output of the previous model, and each supporting family logistics in different ways.

First, we apply a temporal logic to our GPS data streams, and compare the location and driving state of separate individuals to *recognize when rides occur and who participated in the rides*. Participation allows us infer which parent drives which kid to which activity. In the most basic sense, this is part of the routine that families almost never record on their calendar. The output from this model can begin to fill in the empty calendar spaces for the things people do every day.

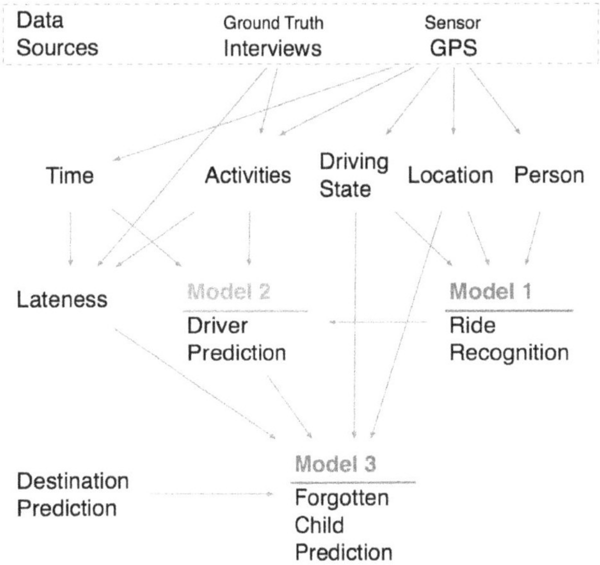

Figure 1. Interviews provide each activity's location and each event's intended pick-up time. All other knowledge is inferred from low-level GPS, creating unsupervised models that (1) sense rides; (2) predict the driver for the next event; and (3) predict if parents will arrive late for pick-ups. End-user coordination applications can use any model's output as a new data source to help families plan, coordinate and improvise. Model 3 can work with reminder svstems to create a new kind of safetv net.

Second, the ride recognition model provides seed data to learn the probability distribution that each parent will be driving a child to an activity (Figure 1, Model 2). We can use this distribution to *predict future drivers*, which, when compared with observations in real time, can offer an indicator of when events are happening in non-routine ways [31]. Because non-routine events are those most likely to lead to logistical breakdowns, early detection of non-routine rides can help propagate that information to coordinating family members, and, when appropriate, allow them to respond earlier, and to make plans in response to these situations with a more complete overall picture.

Third, the driver prediction model, along with real-time location and driving state, a learned distribution on lateness, and a driver destination model, feeds into a higher-level inference machine to detect when *parents forget a child* at an activity (Figure 1, Model 3).

We demonstrate that our approach is practical by conducting this work under legitimate sensor and modeling constraints. Since families literally rely on their phones, battery-heavy GPS sampling is limited to once per minute instead of the more common rates upwards of once per second. Models are then trained using an online approach, meaning we use only the data that would be available at any given point in time, and not the entire data set.

MODEL 1: RECOGNIZING RIDES

The routine rides family members take every day are one of the basic units of undocumented family logistics. The automatic capture of rides introduces the possibility of computational support while requiring minimal behavioral changes. Each sensed ride includes a driver, a passenger, a place and a time, providing information that can be immediately shared with calendaring and awareness systems, as well as creating a source of labeled data with which computing systems can perform further reasoning. In this section, we describe a method for recognizing rides and examine its performance.

How are rides recognized?

To recognize when rides occur, we apply a simple temporal logic to the synchronized, discretized GPS data. We define three states for a person (see Eq. 1). A person is always either at a location, L_n, or traveling, T, which we define as the unique location occupying the space between all known places. Two family members are said to be co-traveling, *CoT*, if during the same time, t_i they are both traveling and are located at a Euclidian distance of less than 500 meters apart. Any remaining states (*e.g.*, no sample, outliers) are collectively labeled *else*.

$$States = \{L_n, T \mid CoT, else\} \quad (1)$$

We examine each parent-child combination separately, and refer to parent as *P*, and child as *C* (see Eq. 2)

$$People = \{P, C\} \quad (2)$$

We define a pick-up as the conjunction of states of a parent, *P*, and a child, *C, over time* (See Eq. 3). At time t_1, the child is at location L_n. At time t_2 both parent and child are at location L_n. Lastly, at time t_3, both parent and child are co-traveling, *CoT*. This definition is broad enough to cover two cases of pick-ups. In the majority of cases, a parent comes from a different location to the child's location and they drive off together. We also consider a pick-up in the case where a parent is already at the child's location, and they depart together. Drop-offs are the inverse of the sequence for pick-ups (see Eq. 4).

$$\left.\begin{array}{ll} \text{a.} & (t_1, P, \neg CoT) \wedge (t_1, C, L_n) \wedge \\ \text{b.} & (t_2, P, L_n) \wedge (t_2, C, L_n) \wedge \\ \text{c.} & (t_3, P, CoT) \wedge (t_3, C, CoT) \end{array}\right\} \textit{Pick-up} \quad (3)$$

$$\left.\begin{array}{ll} \text{a.} & (t_1, P, CoT) \wedge (t_1, C, CoT) \wedge \\ \text{b.} & (t_2, P, L_n) \wedge (t_2, C, L_n) \wedge \\ \text{c.} & (t_3, P, \neg CoT) \wedge (t_3, C, L_n) \end{array}\right\} \textit{Drop-off} \quad (4)$$

Our method to detect rides is based directly on the definitions. We parse the GPS streams from all members of a family and predict that a ride is occurring for each example that meets all three requirements of our definition.

Accuracy of ride-sensing

To evaluate the performance of our ride-sensing method, we compare its predictions with the ground truth taken from our interviews.

Aggregate interviews report 3283 rides, or roughly one ride per day per family. Real-world constraints on phone use (*e.g.*, forgotten phones, dead batteries, school mandates) place 1721 beyond the reach of sensor data collection. We report on the 1562 rides accessible to sensing. Across all families, for both pick-ups and drop-offs, our simple temporal model performs well. 90.1% of the events the model identified were in fact rides (see Table 1, Precision), and 95.5% of all rides were sensed (see Table 1, Recall).

Family	***Precision***		***Recall***	
	How many of the sensed rides are right?		*How many of the total rides are sensed?*	
	Pick-up	*Drop-off*	*Pick-up*	*Drop-off*
A	.991	.987	.912	.910
B	.966	.962	.979	.981
C	.913	.824	.971	.921
D	.878	.873	.980	.944
E	.931	.684	.959	.985
Average	.936	.866	.960	.950
	.901		.955	

Table 1. Evaluation of our temporal logic model for sensing when children are picked up and dropped off.

Precision and recall measures between families are also consistent, with a variance of 0.072. This variance measure is dominated by the precision value of 0.684 for family E drop-offs, the only value below .80. Three factors appear responsible for this low drop-off precision value. First, for family E, false positive drop-offs, where a drop-off was detected but did not occur, are five times as likely to occur at home than at any other location. Second, false positive errors at home occur almost exclusively in the late afternoon. Third, false positive errors in the afternoon at home occur almost entirely between their 10-year-old daughter (D10) and Mom.

Narratives from our interviews help explain the meaning behind these numbers. In family E, D10 walks to and from school. Family E's Mom, a doctor, arrives home from some hospital shifts at around the same time as D10 arrives home from school. Our temporal logic correctly identifies that parent and child are at the same location (Eq. 4b), and not co-traveling (Eq. 4c). Our temporal logic, however, mistakes arrival at home within the same minute for co-travel (Eq. 4a). Both Mom and D10 are correctly labeled as traveling, and are within 500 meters of one another, but are *not* traveling together, causing the false positive errors.

MODEL 2: PREDICTING DRIVERS

With a capable ride recognition model providing reliable information on the driver, passenger, place and time of each ride, we can combine this information gleaned from sensed rides with low-level GPS data, derive a set of features, and use this to train a model of driver prediction.

Modeling which parent drives

To model the online probability distribution of which parent drives, at each point in time, we create a labeled set of rides using the ride detection model's output. For each row, or prediction example, we build a feature vector, *f*, containing:

Name	*Meaning*	*Values*
L_n	Location of pick-up or drop-off	Place ID
RType	Ride type	Pick-up, Drop-off
DoW	Day of week	0,1,2,3,4,5,6
ToD	Discretized time of day (15 min)	1,2,3…96
$driver_{t\text{-}j}$	Driver for the last 5 rides to L_n	Mom, Dad
ϕ	Driver distribution model	[0,1]

Table 2. Feature vector for predicted rides.

We define the driver distribution for rides of type *RType*, on day *DoW*, at location L_n, to be the following:

$$\phi = \frac{\sum_{L_n, Rtype, DoW} driver = P_1}{\sum_{L_n, Rtype, DoW} driver = P_1 + \sum_{L_n, Rtype, DoW} driver = P_2} \quad (5)$$

For each example, we assign the label, *y*, as -1 if Dad was detected as the driver, and +1 if Mom was detected. Our goal is to create a classifier to determine the probability that each parent is driving. Because the shape of the decision boundary is unknown, we use a decision tree classifier, which performs well with both linear and non-linear boundaries. Because previous research on family routines observes frequent deviations from the intended family schedule [10, 37], before classification we chose to use local weighting to reduce the impact of these non-routine outliers [2]. For each labeled example *q, we calculate a new label d(y) as a function of the old label y and the features f:*

$$d(y)^q_{LW} = \frac{\sum_{i \in labeled\ data, i \neq q} y_i e^{-\sqrt{\sum_j (x_i^j - q^j)^2}}}{\sum_{i=q} e^{-\sqrt{\sum_j (x_i^j - q^j)^2}}} \quad (6)$$

This transformation pushes the labels for deviation examples closer to 0 and non-deviation examples closer to the original -1 or 1. The closer the label to 0, the less impact it has on the accuracy of the classifier. The overall classification process combines local weighting with a binary decision tree, creating a locally weighted decision tree (LWDT) to predict which parent drives for each ride.

Driver prediction accuracy

The ride model's treatment of the output class (Mom or Dad) as a nominal variable leaves only two cases for evaluation: (1) a prediction of Mom when Mom drives or Dad when Dad drives is correct; and (2) a prediction of Mom when Dad drives or Dad when Mom drives is incorrect. With no case that can lead to false positive or false negative, we cannot evaluate using precision or recall. Instead, we look at accuracy: how many times out of the total did the classifier predict mom *or* dad correctly.

We then train the model using a sliding window, and test on the week immediately following the training period, a common technique used with time-series data [30]. Searching for an optimal window size, we vary the size of the sliding window from one to 24 weeks, and analyze the results. Across all families, when the model is trained using only one week of training data (Figure 2, top left), the model correctly predicts the driver 72.1% of the time, showing that a deployed system might be able to provide useable data after just a single week in the field. The optimal window size is four weeks, which predicts the driver correctly 87.7% of the time.

At test weeks twelve (June 1) and eighteen (July 13), nearly every graph in Figure 2 shows a steep drop in performance, correctly predicting the driver only marginally better than chance. These dips correspond to significant changes in family routines at test week eleven (May 25), when all our families transitioned from school to a new summer schedule, and at test week seventeen (July 6), when camps ended (families D, E), families vacationed (Families A, C), and summer sports ended (family B). Poor performance during these weeks is consistent with previous findings that routines are least stable during transition times [13, 37].

Changes in routine that occurred in weeks eleven and seventeen would not appear in the training data until weeks twelve and eighteen, which exactly overlap the drops in performance. Looking more closely, the changes in routine at weeks eleven and seventeen also influence the outcome of our driver model optimization.

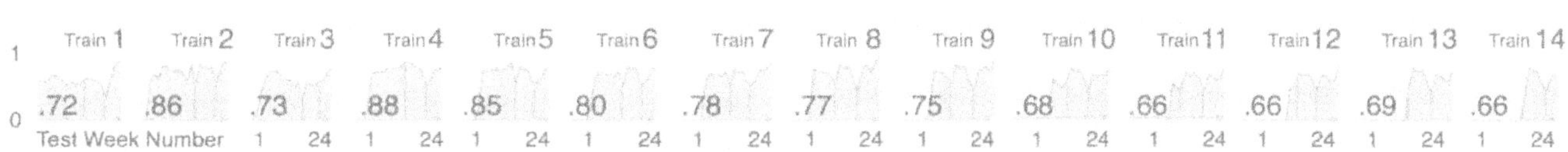

Figure 2. Accuracy (vertical axis) of our driver prediction model across all families, plotted by test week number (horizontal axis), varying the amount of training data provided to the model from one (left) to fourteen (right) weeks. No matter how much training data is used, accuracy drops at weeks 12 and 18 (vertical lines).

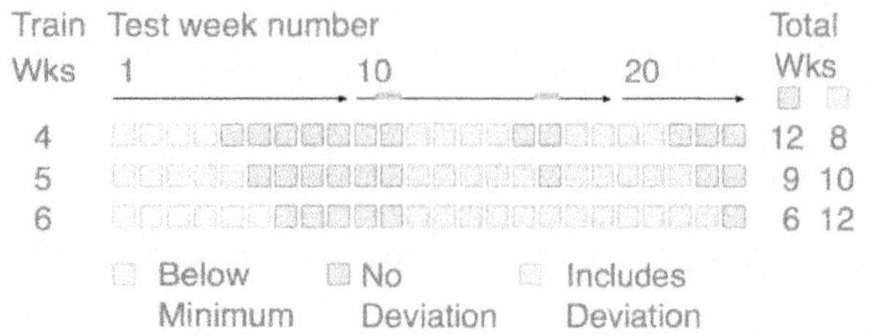

Figure 3. Performance drops of the driver prediction model at weeks 12 and 18 occur as transitions from the routines of school to into summer (week 11), and from the routines of camp to back-to-school prep (week 18) first appear in training data. Because these changepoints are separated by five weeks, models using five weeks or more of training data will include one of these aberrant weeks.

Figure 3 shows the relationship between the size of the training data sets, and the number of times they include an aberrant week. Since five weeks separate the routine changes, training data sets that include five weeks of data or more will include one of these aberrant weeks more often than not, providing them with noisier training data, and lowering their accuracy. In fact, four weeks of training data marks the turning point, when training data sets do not include aberrant weeks more often than they do, explaining why it is the optimal number of weeks of training data to use in the driver prediction model.

Lastly, despite poor performance at test weeks twelve and eighteen across the variations in size of the sliding window, performance makes a sharp turnaround in weeks thirteen and nineteen. This suggests that the model is able to make correct predictions with only one week's data from the new routine, adding support to the belief that a deployed model could recover quickly and again provide useful data even after facing changes in routine.

FORGETTING CHILDREN

In this section, we explore the feasibility of a system that can predict when a parent will forget to pick a child up from an activity at an agreed-upon time, using only GPS trace information for family members. The fear of being late and forgetting a child is a constant source of stress and anxiety for dual-income families [4, 11, 18]. Such a prediction system could create a new kind of safety net, reducing anxiety and increasing feelings of safety.

Modeling forgotten children

Forgetting is an ambiguous term. It can mean that a parent never goes to get a child, or that a parent failed to remember at the appropriate time and thus began the pick-up task later than expected. Relying on GPS for all our information, we develop a time- and place-centric definition of forgetting. We say that a parent wants to arrive at an ideal time, t_{ideal}. We say a parent forgets a pick-up when their actual arrival time, t_0, is more than ten minutes after t_{ideal} (we defer the explanation for the choice of the 10 minute threshold to the discussion). From within the set of 1562 sensed rides, we apply this rule to the 813 pick-ups, and identify 83 instances of parents forgetting pick-ups.

Building upon our earlier driver prediction model, and relying on our GPS data set, we designate the following features to help us detect these incidents of forgetting:

Name	***Meaning***	***Values***
R	Whether the parent remembers	True, False
J	Driver prediction model	Mom, Dad
T	If the parent is traveling	True, False
λ	*Empirical cumulative distribution(ecdf)* of on-time arrivals to L_{child} at time $T_{now}T_{ideal}$	[0,1]
L_{child}	Location of the child	Place ID
L_{start}	Starting location of a parent	Place ID
L_{curr}	Ending location of a parent	Place ID
D	Destination of a parent	Place ID

We assemble these features into a Bayesian Network (see Figure 4). The Bayesian network captures the complex dependencies shared by coordinating parents. Here, we use the term *dependency* as used in probability theory to mean the outcome of an event makes its dependent event more or less likely. It can be read as *influences*. Each side of the symmetrical model represents the state of one parent (Mom on the left, Dad on the right). Mutual dependencies are represented at the crossover nodes in the graph's center. For example, the location of each parent depends on (is influenced by) the location of the child, L_{child}, and whose job the pick-up is, J.

Other dependencies are mirrored for each parent. For example, according to the model, whether or not a parent is traveling, T, depends on their location, L_{start}, the location of the child, L_{child}, how often they have been late in the past, λ, and if they remember the pick-up, R. The model also shows that a parent's destination, D, depends on the location of their child, L_{child}, their current location, $L_{current}$, and if they remember the pick-up, R. The driver prediction model appears in the network as node J, predicting which parent has the job to make the pick-up. We can see that according to the network, if a parent remembers the pick-up, R depends on whether or not the pick-up is their job, J.

Starting 30 minutes before every late pick-up, we ask the network to make *two* predictions. First, we see if the non-driver *is not* going to be late. Second, we look to see if the driver *is* going to be late. We repeat these calculations at each minute until the actual time of the late pick-up, and see how early we can make the correct predictions.

We use the properties of the network structure to derive the formulas that will provide us the prediction values. To see if Dad remembers, we calculate the posterior probability R_{dad}, and then repeat the calculation for Mom.

$$P(R_d \mid L^d_{start}, L^m_{start}, L^d_{curr}, L^m_{curr}, L_{child}, T_d, T_m, \phi) \quad (7)$$

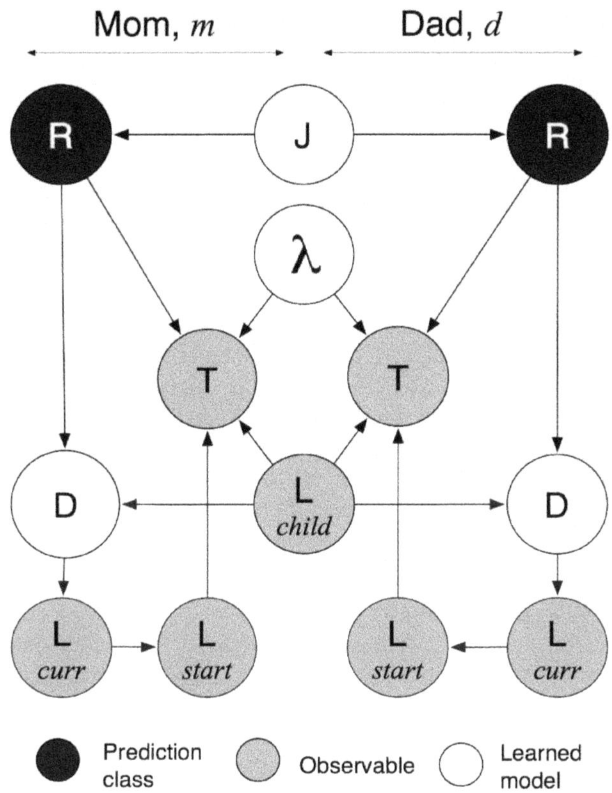

Figure 4. A Bayesian Network used to predict if a parent remembers to make a pick-up. Each side of the symmetrical model represents the state of one parent. At each point in time the model makes two predictions: (1) does the parent who drives remember the pick-up; and (2) does the other parent not remember the pick-up.

Performance of the forgotten child model

To evaluate the forgotten child model, we first learn the optimal distributions for the remaining learned model nodes – λ, and D. Using four weeks of training data for the driver prediction model, *J* (our learned optimum) we vary the amount of training data to λ and D, and compare the output. Ten weeks of data gives optimal values for both λ, and D.

To calculate the output of the entire network, we use the Maximum Entropy Inverse Optimal Control algorithm [39] to compute *D*, destination, and starting thirty minutes before each forgotten pick-up, compute values for R_{mom} and R_{dad} at one-minute intervals, until we arrive at t_{ideal}+10, ten minutes after the ideal pick-up time, when the parent is late (by our definition).

Given the unequal distribution of forgotten pick-ups (83 examples of forgotten children out of 1562 sensed rides – majority of these are parents arriving late but some are instances of parents actually forgetting their children), a model based on no data, but that simply always predicted on-time arrival would be right 0.885 of the time. Evaluation using precision and recall would output high values, but would lack a way to distinguish how much of that number comes from the excellence of the model, and how much simply from the sheer number of negative examples.

As an alternative, we evaluate the model using a technique from signal processing [30] called the receiver operating characteristic (ROC), which is a more conservative measure of performance [16]. Figure 5 shows two ROC plots. For each plot, the y-axis shows correct predictions, and the x-axis shows incorrect predictions. The points inside each square represent different ratios of correct predictions to incorrect predictions. Points along the diagonals mean the ratio is even, and the model is performing no better than a coin flip – for every one correct prediction, there is one incorrect prediction. The upper left corner is perfection, with all correct predictions and no mistakes.

We can use this property of ROC curves to visualize how a notification system would balance the desire of the parent to never miss a pick-up, against the cost of sending wrong information (*e.g.*, an unnecessary reminder). For any given number of correct predictions, an ROC curve indicates how many incorrect predictions the model will also produce. At t_{ideal}-30 (Figure 4, right, dark pink line), for every 6 correct predictions the model makes 5 incorrect predictions. When viewed as percentages, every rate of accurate predictions between 0 and 1 has a corresponding rate of inaccurate predictions between 0 and 1, producing a smooth curve. If we continue to follow this curve up and to the right, we can see that the ratio improves little. At t_{ideal} (light orange line), for every 8 correct predictions the model makes 2 incorrect predictions. At t_{ideal}+10 (dark orange line) for every 8 correct predictions the model makes only 1 incorrect prediction.

We can also measure the area beneath an ROC curve to describe a model's cumulative performance across all confidence values. At thirty minutes before t_{ideal}, the area under the ROC curve is 0.649 (Figure 4, pink area). The performance gradually rises as the pick-up time approaches, and is highest t_{ideal}+10, at 0.826.

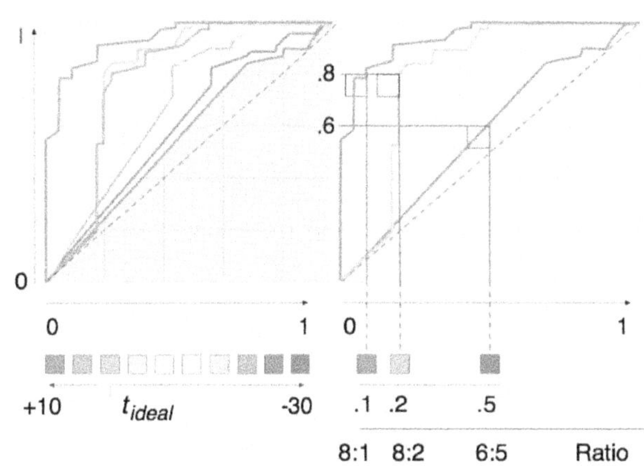

Figure 5. Forgotten child model performance. At left, ROC curves show performance improving from 0.640 at t_{ideal}-30 to 0.826 at t_{ideal}+10. At right, the values demonstrate the relationship between right and wrong guesses.

DISCUSSION

This paper describes a successful initial demonstration of the feasibility of our approach to the sensing and modeling of pick-ups and drop-offs, and hopes to spur investigation of routine as a versatile and enabling abstraction. In this section, we discuss possible directions, and identify ways to continue towards optimal performance. As a broad reaching proof-of-concept, this work required many simplifications. In this section we discuss their impact, and extensions to the work as a whole.

Building on the ride model

Our ride detection model provides ample evidence that the large scale detection of rides is within reach. Still, across all families, the model overlooks about ten percent of rides (false negatives), and makes incorrect detections (false positives) around ten percent of the time. Because our hierarchical approach to modeling means that errors in ride detection propagate to downstream models, causing further errors, improvements in ride detection will pay threefold, helping to improve driver and forgotten child prediction as well.

A variety of ways exist to improve upon our ride detection. Because we sample GPS only once per minute, pick-ups, or examples of co-location that happen on a faster time scale are simply missed. In our fieldwork, we observed busy families carrying out pick-ups and drop-offs below this detection threshold. An intelligent approach to sampling would increase rates during times when data collection would be more valuable (*i.e.*, when a person is moving), and lower the sampling rate during periods of stasis, avoiding battery depletion. This approach would require the integration of other low-level sensors into the model (*e.g.*, accelerometer, noise or light). The addition of Bluetooth could also improve co-location and co-travel accuracy by providing additional proximity cues to the model.

Missed rides are also caused by the model's simple ride representation. We defined travel in terms of one parent, one child and one car. The model has no representation of other modes of transport, causing it to miss common activities like walking, riding bicycles, and taking the bus. For simplicity we limited our observations to the nuclear family, but in reality families plan and coordinate with their extended families, friends and carpoolers, all whom were outside the scope of this investigation. The model also requires that activities occur while people are at a location. Activities like paper routes, however, occur over a wide area that contains home, neighbors, and schools, making it appear to the model as an unusual occurrence of travel.

Building on the driver prediction model

The driver prediction model learns parental responsibilities at more than 70% accuracy with only one week of training data, and about 85% accuracy with four weeks of training data. These are satisfactory numbers when seen as a technical problem. A deployed system, however, will face unknown scrutiny from coordinating parents during stressful times. Even small errors may deter adoption, encouraging examination of ways to achieve better results with less training.

While we explored a general-purpose algorithm for use across all families, we know that there is great variation in the ways families plan, coordinate and improvise. Even within families, as children grow, parents age, interests, even entire geographies, evolve. Exploration remains to find algorithms both for family style, and for attending to and integrating to the inevitable changes.

The driver prediction model also showed a remarkable potential for detecting large-scale transitions in routine. Because families experience the most stress during times of large-scale routine change, an algorithm tuned to this class of events could effectively function as a seasonal boundary detector, offering an index of routineness to other models providing services to families, helping the driver prediction model identify seasonal boundaries in training data and achieve better learning faster.

Building on the forgotten child model

Because end-user evaluation metrics will vary with application context (e.g. missed pickups for a reminder application will be less tolerable than incorrect event times in a calendar application), a precise assessment of its performance requires a field deployment. Instead, we presented an ROC analysis, which quantifies performance tradeoffs as confidence values. End-user application designers can define the behavior of systems that implement the model by calculating a future expected value based on model confidence, and the costs and benefits as defined by their domain.

Unfortunately, without a field deployment, we can only estimate costs and benefits. The ROC analysis, for example, showed that the model has about sixty percent accuracy at thirty minutes before a parent forgets a child. With about twenty actual incidents of forgetting children per family, this would equate to forty alerts over six months, or about 1.5 per week. Given the stress caused by forgetting a child, would this number of alerts constitute an annoyance, or prompt a parent to take a moment and double-check their plan and their assumptions?

This question is further complicated by the question of information delivery. It is unknown how early a forgotten pick-up needs to be detected in order to be of use. A message that comes too late to enable a parent to arrive on time might be marginally helpful, but the real goal is to make this detection early enough to ensure prevention of the event.

Improved models will also need to address the temporal complexity of coordinating parents. In some families, ten minutes late might be considered on time. In others, it might constitute abandonment. A range might more faithfully represent an ideal time than any particular minute. Also, if a parent plans to be late, then their late arrival time is their ideal time, and not the one the model assumes.

Applications of models of routine

The haphazard introduction of learning systems into the home has been a subject of concern to researchers. Their caution reflects an understanding of the technical challenges that idiosyncratic human behavior could present to modeling [32, 34], a sensitivity to the unintended consequences of technology in the home [9], a concern over the appropriate role of domestic technology [33], all which threaten to take away autonomy from families.

Ultimately, we distinguish a belief that aspects of family life can be *modeled* from the belief that family life should be *automated*. We advocate a measured approach where intelligence is applied in such a way that it does not take on the role of parent and does not conflict with the social structure within the family.

Our work does not focus on optimizing the work of families in order to allow an ever-increasing number of activities to be performed. Instead, our intention is to help family members more elegantly and effortlessly perform their role within the family by providing the resources they need to better understand what they do and what they plan to do.

Our technical models of routine support this decisively human need by acting through existing research family support systems, allowing them to better address the situations they were originally designed for. Calendaring systems like LINC [27] and DateLens [29] could display implicit routine events, event times, pick-ups and drop-offs that parents don't document but are critical to making effective plans for and that affect others. Location systems like Motion Presence [6] and the Whereabouts Clock [8] could display where people are with implicit routine information like future pick-ups and drop-offs, helping remind family members what they need to do, and alerting others as days happen as planned. Applications could update plans in real-time, helping parents make more reliable decisions. As pick-ups happen, reminder systems like comMotion [25] and PlaceMail [24] could suppress potentially annoying reminders. Reminder systems could infer that a required pick-up is not happening, and remind parents without their explicit creation of a reminder, creating a new kind of safety net to guard families against this stressful outcome.

CONCLUSION

In this paper, we demonstrated that dual-income family transportation routines could be sensed and modeled without any supervision using the GPS available on commodity mobile phones. Towards that end, we gathered a large data set of family location, and of pick-ups and drop-offs. Using simple heuristics and statistical models, we demonstrated that pick-ups and drop-offs can be sensed, and their drivers predicted. We also demonstrated a model that can predict when parents are going to forget to pick-up their children at activities before these damaging events happen.

We provided examples of how learned models of family routines can function as an *enabling* technology. We described how they could be added to digital calendars to help families make better plans, to reminder systems and to location systems to help families coordinate on routine days, and to function as a safety net, helping observe and prevent incidents where children are forgotten at their activities.

Future work

We intend this work to stimulate discussion around the broad applicability of routine as an enabling abstraction. Considering our choice of exploration over optimization, a significant amount of the modeling space remains open to investigation. Additionally, the use of routine in various application domains brings with it a series of questions. Identifying appropriate ways to visually represent implicit information, or entire learned routines, presents challenges to the visualization community. And ways to repair and amend incorrect implicit information presents challenges to the interaction techniques community.

Because routine as a computational abstraction is able to capture and model events that are meaningful but ephemeral, the algorithms developed in this work could be applied across other domains. In the workplace, for example, best practices could be described as a form of routine. Their modeling, visualization, and communication would represent another significant research opportunity.

ACKNOWLEDGMENTS

The authors would like to thank Google for their financial support. This work was funded by NSF grant IIS-1017429.

REFERENCES

1. Ashbrook, D. & Starner, T. (2002). Learning significant locations and predicting user movement with GPS. *Proc. ISWC 2002*, 101-108.
2. Atkeson, C. G., Moore, A. W. & Schaal, S. (1997). Locally Weighted Learning. *Artificial Intelligence Review*, 11:11-73.
3. Bandura, A. (1997). *Self-efficacy: The exercise of control*. New York: Freeman.
4. Beech, S. *et al*. (2004) Lifestyles of working parents: Implications and opportunities for new technologies, HP Tech report HPL-2003-88 (R.1).
5. Begole, J., Tang, J.C. & Hill, R. (2003). Rhythm modeling, visualizations and applications. *Proc. UIST 2003*, 11-20.
6. Bentley, F. & Metcalf, C. (2007). Sharing motion information with close family and friends. *Proc. CHI 2007*, 1361-1370.
7. Brdiczka, O., Makoto Su, N., Begole, J. (2009). Using temporal patterns (t-patterns) to derive stress factors of routine tasks. Proc. *CHI 2009 Ext. Abst.*, 4081-4086.

8. Brown, B. *et al.* (2007). Locating family values: A field trial of the Whereabouts Clock. *Proc. UbiComp 2007*, 354-371.
9. Cowan, R. S. (1985). *More work for mother: The Ironies of household technology from the open hearth to the microwave.* New York: Basic Books
10. Darrah, C.N., Freeman, J.M. & English-Lueck, J.A. (2007). *Busier than ever: Why American families can't slow down*, Palo Alto: Stanford University Press.
11. Davidoff, S., Lee, M.K., Yiu, C.M., Zimmerman, J. & Dey, A.K. (2006) Principles of smart home control. *Proc. UbiComp 2006*, 19-34.
12. Davidoff, S., Lee, M.K., Dey, A.K. & Zimmerman, J. (2007). Rapidly exploring application design with Speed Dating. *Proc. UbiComp 2007*, 429-446.
13. Davidoff, S., Zimmerman, J. & Dey, A.K. (2010). How routine learners can support family coordination, *Proc. CHI 2010*, 2461-2470.
14. Dey, A.K. & Abowd, G.D. (2000). CybreMinder: A Context-Aware System for Supporting Reminders. *Proc. HUC 2000*, 172-186.
15. Eagle, N. & Pentland, A. (2006). Reality mining: Sensing complex social systems, *Personal and Ubiquitous Computing*, 10(4): 255-268.
16. Fogarty, J., Baker, R. S., & Hudson, S. E. (2005). Case studies in the use of ROC curve analysis for sensor-based estimates in human computer interaction. *Proc GI 2005*, 129-136.
17. Fiese, B.H. *et al.* (2002). A review of 50 years of research on naturally occurring family routines and rituals: Cause for celebration? *Journal of Family Psychology*, 16(4): 381-390.
18. Frissen, V.A.J. (2000) ICTs in the rush hour of life, *The Information Society*, 16: 65-75.
19. Gneezy, U. & Rustichini A. (2000). Pay enough or don't pay at all. *Quarterly Journal of Economics*, August 2000: 791-810.
20. González, M.C., Hidalgo, C.A. & Barabási, A.-L. (2008). Understanding individual human mobility patterns, *Nature*, 453, 479-482 (2008).
21. Huynh, T., Fritz, M. & Schiele, B. (2008) Discovery of activity patterns using topic models. *Proc. UbiComp 2008*, 10-19.
22. Krumm, J. & Horvitz, E. (2006). Predestination: Inferring destinations from partial trajectories. *Proc. UbiComp 2006*, 243-260.
23. Liao, L., Patterson, D.J., Fox, D., & Kautz, H.A. (2007). Learning and inferring transportation routines. *Artificial Intelligence*. 171, 311-331.
24. Ludford, P. J. *et. al* (2006). Because I carry my cell phone anyway: Functional location-based reminder applications. *Proc. CHI 2006*, 889-898.
25. Marmasse, N. & Schmandt, C. (2000). Location-aware information delivery with ComMotion. *Proc. Handheld and Ubiquitous Computing*, 64-73.
26. Medved, C.E. (2004) The everyday accomplishment of work and family: Exploring practical actions in daily routines, *Communication studies*, 55(1): 128-145.
27. Neustaedter, C., Brush, A. J. & Greenberg, S. (2009). The calendar is crucial: Coordination and awareness through the family calendar. *ToCHI*, 16(1): 1-48.
28. Pentland, B.T., Haerem, T. & Hillison, D.W. (2009). Using workflow data to explore the structure of an organizational routine, in M.C. Baecker & N. Lazaric (Eds.) *Organizational routines: Advancing empirical research* (pp. 47-67), Cheltenham: Edward Elgar.
29. Plaisant, C et al. (2006). Shared family calendars: Promoting symmetry and accessibility. *ACM ToCHI*. 13(3): 313-346.
30. Roberts, S. W. (1959). Control chart tests based on geometric moving averages. *Technometrics*,1, 239-250.
31. Simpson, R.C., Schreckenghost, D., LoPresti, E.F, Kirsch, N. (2006). Plans and planning in smart homes, J.C. Augusto & C.D. Nugent (Eds.), *Designing Smart Homes: The Role of Artificial Intelligence*, 71-84.
32. Suchman, L. (1983). Office procedures as practical action: Models of work and system design. *ACM ToIS*, 1(4): 320-328.
33. Taylor, A. S. *et. al* (2007). Homes that make us smart. *Personal and Ubiquitous Computing*. 11(5): 383-393
34. Tolmie, P. *et al.* (2002). Unremarkable computing. *Proc. CHI 2002*, 399-406.
35. Van Laerhoven, K., Kilian , D. & Schiele, B. (2008). Using rhythm awareness in long-term activity recognition, *Proc. ISWC 2008*.
36. Wakkary, R. & Maestri, L. (2007). The resourcefulness of everyday design. *Proc. Creativity and Cognition 2007*, 163-172.
37. Wolin, S.J. & Bennett, L.A. (1984). *Family rituals. Family Process*, 23: 401-420.
38. Zerubavel, E. (1981). *Hidden rhythms: schedules and calendars in social life*, Chicago: The University of Chicago Press, 1981.
39. Ziebart, B.D. *et. al* (2008). Navigate like a cabbie: Probabilistic reasoning from observed context-aware behavior, *Proc. Ubicomp 2008*, 322-331.

Mediated Parent-Child Contact in Work-Separated Families

Svetlana Yarosh
Georgia Institute of Technology
School of Interactive Computing, GVU Center
85 5th Street NW, Atlanta GA 30332, USA
lana@cc.gatech.edu

Gregory D. Abowd
Georgia Institute of Technology
School of Interactive Computing, GVU Center
85 5th Street NW, Atlanta GA 30332, USA
abowd@gatech.edu

ABSTRACT

Parents and children in families living with regular separation due to work develop strategies to manage being apart. We interviewed 14 pairs of parents and children (ages 7 – 13) from work-separated families to understand their experiences and the strategies that they use to keep their family together. Parents focus on combining scheduled synchronous and spontaneous asynchronous communication to maintain a constant presence in the life of the child. Children, on the other hand, focus on other sources of support, on other activities, and on the eventual reunion. Both the remote parent and the child rely heavily on a collocated adult to maintain awareness and contact. We compare work-separated families with other types of separation and highlight opportunities for new designs.

Author Keywords

Parents, children, computer-mediated communication

ACM Classification Keywords

H5.2. Information interfaces and presentation (e.g., HCI): User Interfaces. *User-centered design.*

General Terms

Human Factors

1. INTRODUCTION

Families are increasingly living with the challenge of regular separation due to work. Taking the United States as an example, 3.6 million Americans live in a different city from their partner due to work, a 53% rise since 2003 [3]. Additionally, many families with young children are affected by long-term separation due to military deployment [8]. Increasingly, work-separated families look to communication technology to support continued contact during the separation [3] and there has been a great deal of interest in the HCI community in designing for family communication [5,9,16,19,22,23]. However, there has been relatively little work exploring the current parenting practices of work-separated families, especially taking into account the perspectives of both the parent and the child. We conducted a qualitative investigation of the experiences of work-separated families with 14 pairs of parents and children. Two research questions drove our work:

- How do parents and children respond to work separation?
- What are the strategies used by these families to stay in touch and what are the limitations of these strategies?

Aside from addressing these questions, there are two other goals in this work. First, we want to expand our current understanding of the experiences of separated families, particularly in contrasting work-separated families with other types of separation. Second, by highlighting the limitations of current strategies, we hope to point out opportunities for new designs that are grounded in existing practices.

We begin by reviewing the previous studies of parent-child separation, communication technology in the home, and designs for supporting parent-child contact. Next, we describe our interview methods and participants. Then, we present the results of our study with regard to our two research questions. Finally, we discuss the results of this work in the context of previous work in this field and point to opportunities for both research and design.

2. RELATED WORK

Parent-child separation has been investigated both in HCI and in other domains. However, HCI researchers have particularly focused on collocated parent-child closeness, how specific existing technologies are used for communication in the home, and on how to design new communication technologies for separated parents and children.

2.1. Parent–Child Separation

Studies of parent–child separation have often focused on the effects of military deployment. Kelley et al. have shown that children in deployed families are more likely to exhibit clinical psychological problems [12]. Another study of separation has also showed it to be a cause of short-term distress for both the parent and the child [20]. However, this previous work points out that temporary separation from either parent does not lead to permanent negative consequences for children. In supporting work-separated families, we are focusing on addressing the in-the-moment distress that separation causes for families. These previous studies were conducted to investigate correlations between separation and children's outcomes. In contrast, in our study we are interested in examining the qualitative experience of separation for parents and children and the specific strategies that these families use to manage separation. Dalsgaard et al. looked at the characteristics of parent-child closeness and how intimacy is built in families [4]. While this paper looked at in-person contact, our work is focused on understanding closeness during physical separation.

There have been three relevant qualitative investigations of technology's role in parent-child separation. Yarosh et al. [24] and Odom et al. [18] investigated the needs of parents and children in divorced families. We want to apply a similar methodology to examine how the needs of divorced and work-separated families may differ. Modlitba [16] interviewed business travelers who have toddlers and found a significant need to support communication during separation. One of our goals is expanding this understanding of work-separated families by including the perspectives of not only the parents, but also the children involved in the separation. To be able to speak to the children about their experience, we are focusing on an older age range (7 – 13).

2.2. Studying Communication Technology in the Home

Several studies examine how established communication technologies are used by families to maintain connectedness. Ballagas et al. showed that the telephone is not an effective technology for communicating with children, as children face cognitive, social, and motivational challenges to audio-only communication [2]. Several studies of videoconferencing pointed to the great potential that this technology has for keeping families connected, because it enables show-and-tell and sharing daily activities [1,11]. Studies of text messaging (SMS) and instant messaging (IM) have shown both to be particularly important communication technologies for older children [10]. We focus on the entire ecology of communication tools used by the family rather than any specific technology. We want to identify the specific strategies that work-separated families have developed around communication technologies, but also point out the limitations of those strategies in the hope of identifying opportunities for new designs.

2.3. Designing for Parent-Child Separation

A number of novel systems focus on connecting adults and children remotely. Collage [22] and eKiss [5] are two systems that support children and parents posting photos from a mobile device to an in-home display or blog. Virtual Box [6] and Globetoddler [16] focus on supporting children and parents in playing asynchronously while apart. ShareTable [23], Family Story Play [19], and Video Play [9] focus on expanding the interaction afforded by video chat by providing opportunities for synchronous play and reading together. Sesame Workshop has recently shown interest in supporting remote families with the release of Family Connections[1], a private social networking site for families. Globetoddler [16] and Family Connections were the only two of these systems explicitly targeted at work-separated families, but all of these projects could be potentially applied to this domain. We return to these projects in the discussion section to highlight how such technologies relate to existing practices of work-separated families.

3. METHODS

We conducted in-depth semi-structured interviews with parents and children from work-separated families.

3.1. Participants

We interviewed parent–child pairs from 14 different families separated by work, speaking to the traveling parent and one of their children (selected by the parent) between the ages of 7 and 13. We wanted the children to be old enough to be able to reflect on their experience, yet young enough to be considered a child rather than a teenager. We looked for families that spend on average at least five nights per month apart or had recently (less than six months ago) returned from a separation that was longer than two months. Recruiting was done through word-of-mouth, ads on craigslist.org, and through local military support organizations. Table 1 contains detailed descriptions of our participants. Throughout this paper, we attribute quotes to specific individuals by using the family number followed by 'P' for parent or 'C' for child. We continued recruiting families until we felt that we had approached a point of data saturation. A *post-hoc* detailed analysis of the interviews revealed that all of the major themes pertaining to our research questions were represented in the first seven interviews, thus there is some support for the claim that we did indeed reach data saturation for our purpose.

3.2. Procedure

We conducted hour-long semi-structured interviews with each participant. All of the interviews were conducted in-person in a location familiar to the participant (typically, their home) with the exception of interview 13P, which was conducted over videoconferencing. Parents and children were interviewed separately, though in eight out of the 14 families the parent remained in the vicinity of the interview and was able to hear the child's responses, which may have potentially affected the child's answers. The questions focused on the participants' general experiences with the separation, how they manage contact during separation, and how they use technology to stay in touch. We also asked each participant to talk about whether he or she was generally happy with the amount of contact they had with their partner. Lastly, we asked a series of more specific questions about their experiences with the two most common technologies they use. We found that participants had no trouble

[1] http://www.sesamestreetfamilyconnections.org

#	Interviewed Parent (Traveling)	Children [Interviewee]	Collocated Adult	Periodic Separation	Long-Term Separation	Most Used Technologies
1	37F - Recruiter	6M, **[7M]**, 13M	Father	3 days/week	-	phone + video chat
2	43F - Personal Assistant	3M, **[13F]**	Adult Cousin	2-4 days/week	-	phone + SMS
3	36F - Army Pilot	**[9F]**	Father	-	1 year	phone + email
4	39M - Army	**[10M]**, 17M	Mother	-	1-2 years	phone + email
5	39M - National Guard	**[8F]**, 10M	Mother	1 week/month	1 year	phone + SMS
6	48F - Research Scientist	**[12F]**, 15F, 16M	Brother	6-8 weeks/year	-	phone + video chat
7	48M - Professor	7F, 10M, **[12M]**	Mother	3 weeks/year	5 months	phone + video chat
8	44M - Marketer	**[11M]**, 14M	Mother	10 days/month	-	phone + SMS
9	42M – Manager	6F, 6M, **[8F]**, 10M	Mother	1-2 weeks/month	-	phone
10	51M - Manager	**[10F]**	Grandmother	10-20 days/month	-	phone + video chat
11	46F - Manager	**[11F]**, 13M, 14M	Father	1-4 days/week	-	phone + SMS
12	42M - Military Tech	5F, 6M, **[9F]**	Mother	1 week/month	1 year	IM + video chat
13	47M - Student	12F, **[13M]**, 15M, 17M	Mother	-	2 years	phone + SMS
14	40M - Instructor	**[11F]**	Mother	-	1 year	phone + IM

Table 1. Work-separated families participating in the study, including the ages and genders of participants. We specify whether the family experienced periodic separation, long-term separation, or both.

reflecting upon their long-distance communication routines and practices explicitly, because many of these involved problem solving and complex coordination by the families. Nonetheless, we acknowledge that an inherent limitation of the interview method is that it may not get at some of the more tacit communication routines in the home.

3.3. Analysis

All interviews were audio-recorded and transcribed by the lead author. The interview transcripts were analyzed by creating thematic connections using a data-driven approach [21]. Statements of interest were extracted from each interview and grouped together by theme. With each pass through the interview data, these were refined until a set of distinct themes emerged. The analysis was conducted by the lead author. To demonstrate that an independent rater would code the data in a similar fashion, we computed an inter-rater reliability metric. The lead author and an independent coder coded three randomly-selected segmented interviews for these themes. The Cohen's Kappa value of agreement between the two coders was 0.85 (for 76 statements), which is classified as outstanding agreement [13]. Any disagreements on codes were discussed until consensus was reached. The lead author then proceeded to code the rest of the interviews using the agreed-upon scheme.

4. RESULTS

Our results focus on two research questions. How do parents and children respond to being separated by work? What strategies do these families use to manage separation and when do these strategies fail?

4.1. Responding to Separation

Parents and children respond to the separation in different ways. For the parents, the focus is maintaining an active role in the child's life, while children try to spend time with collocated adults and focus on the eventual reunion.

4.1.1. Parents Seek Active Contact Remotely

Nine out of the 14 parents made comments about wanting to remain an important, active part of the child's life while away.

> *"I guess just try and let your kids know that you're still there; you're still a part of their lives; that you haven't really gone; not to worry about you." (4P)*

> *"Just 'cause they know that you're there and you still care and that you're part of their life. 'Cause they get busy too and they'll – out of sight, out of mind." (8P)*

Parents maintain contact by initiating either synchronous or asynchronous communication (we discuss this in more detail in 4.2.1 and 4.2.2). They describe their most meaningful conversations while apart as having to do with learning about the child's day and finding opportunities to provide support:

> *"She was complaining about something her teacher had done. And I called to say that I hope her day gets better." (6P)*

Additionally, parents spent much of their time away thinking and talking to others about their children:

"I talked about her a lot. I would talk to other people about her. It just made me think of her more." (3P)

"I got into the habit of quite liking thinking about what to buy them ... I suppose it's a way of thinking about them when I'm away." (9P)

Nine other parents also mentioned acquiring physical and digital artifacts during their travels to share with the child. It seems that while away, parents dedicate a lot of thought and energy to the separation.

However, it is also important to acknowledge the experiences of the other five parents, who did not emphasize the importance of contact while apart. For all five of these families, separation lasted no more than a week. These parents mentioned relying on the collocated adult to take care of all childcare matters while they were away, but spending more time with the children upon their return. Interestingly, this strategy seems to be more in line with the way children manage separation, as we discuss next.

4.1.2. Children Focus on In-Person Interaction

Unlike the parents, children think of separation in terms of the eventual in-person reunion, rather than focusing on maintaining instrumental contact while apart. The most meaningful conversations for children were ones that focused on the reunion:

"What we were going to do when he got home, planning different restaurants that he hadn't been able to go to, what games he hadn't been able to play with us, stuff that he hadn't been able to do that was one of the first things we wanted to do when he got home, looking forward to getting home." (12C)

Ten out of 14 children mentioned being comforted by "counting down the days" (3C) as the most important topic of conversation with the remote parent while they were away.

Physical objects representing the remote parent seemed to be a big component of how children handle moments when they miss their parent.

"He gave me a medallion with a picture of us before he left, so I can know that he's right next to me ... I wore it all the time." (4C)

"We had daddy dolls. One that was a pillow that was actually a human shape that had a full body picture of him. And so I would sleep with those at night or whatever when I missed him." (12C)

As an interview strategy, we asked the interviewees how they would advise other children in handling separation from their parents. Rather than dealing with the separation by advising actively seeking a connection to the remote parent, children advised focusing on the eventual reunion, spending time with other family members, or finding other distractions:

"I'd probably tell them that they're not going to work there indefinitely because that helped a lot." (3C)

"You should spend time with your mom when your dad's away and spend time with your dad when you mom is away." (9C)

"Maybe try to like think about other stuff. Like try not to think about that. Sometimes like watching TV gets my mind off of it." (8C)

Perhaps because children's way of managing separation is not focused on direct contact, children were more likely than adults to be satisfied with the amount of contact during travel. Nine out of 14 children were satisfied with the current contact, compared to only four out of 14 adults. Three of the children in our study expressed some level of displeasure about being obligated to maintain contact with their parent while they travel, because it takes them away from other activities.

"Evenings is my free time and I'm usually busy with my own things. I don't really like to spend time to chit-chat. It's just not who I am." (7C)

Several parents confirmed that often children are not motivated to take the time to speak to them.

"I'm calling from Iraq and he's like, 'Dad, my friend is here. I need to go play.'" (4P)

Again, it is important to acknowledge the experience of the four out of the 14 children, all over the age of 10, who did manage separation by actively maintaining contact. Three of these children had been living with regular separation due to work for more than two years. We saw evidence that willingness to actively communicate is related to the personality of the child, his or her age, and the opportunity to practice communicating while apart.

4.2. Strategies for Managing Separation

Through our interviews we identified five specific strategies used by parents and children to manage separation due to work. For each of these strategies we will discuss the reasons for employing this strategy, the number of families in our study that have attempted this strategy and the number that use it regularly, and the limitations of this strategy that may be addressed with new technology.

4.2.1. Scheduled Synchronous Contact with the Home

It is not surprising that all of the families in our study maintained contact through synchronous technologies like the phone and video chat. Our contribution is identifying two specific characteristics of this synchronous contact that were shared by many families: the contact was scheduled and it consisted of the remote parent contacting multiple members of the household in a single call. For most of the families we spoke to, typical synchronous communication consisted of the remote parent contacting multiple members of the household during a pre-established window of time by either calling the house phone or contacting the collocated adult first.

> *"I'll call home every night and then it just kind of depends on who's here." (9P)*

> *"I'll call and see whoever answers, and they'll say, 'Oh, do you want to talk to so and so,' and I'll talk to each one for a little bit. But if somebody can't talk, that's okay." (6P)*

Only two families reported that their typical synchronous contact that did not exhibit these characteristics—family 13 only made sporadic unscheduled contact and family 8 contacted each household member individually rather than calling the house.

There are three advantages of this strategy. First, it allows the remote parent to schedule the interaction at a time that doesn't interrupt their work.

> *"A lot of times I feel like I'm interrupted, you know. Like I'm in the middle of something and the phone rings and I'm like, 'Oh geez, I've got to answer.' I'm much more of 'Okay, we're going to talk at this time. Set it up.'" (7P)*

Second, it limits interruption of individual activities of those at home, because only those who are available to talk participate.

> *"They also have lots of activities, so it's too hard to try to figure out when they might be available. I just call at a certain time and whoever can talk talks." (6P)*

Lastly, it allows multiple members in the household to participate in the conversation at the same time, which leads to a sort of synergy and generally a more fun experience:

> *"Whenever someone else is talking, like my sister or my brother, we all just have fun, like sometimes I put rabbit ears in front of the other person to make my mom laugh and stuff." (6C)*

> *"We'll say something like an inside joke, and she'll laugh. And my brother, he'll say something weird. We don't know what he be saying, but we just laugh."(2C)*

However, there are also three limitations that this strategy creates. First of all, because the interaction is driven by the parent, the child sometimes does not feel empowered to initiate contact:

> *"She usually calls us because we don't know what kind of meeting she's in right then or something." (6C)*

Second, it put the remote parent into the difficult position of coming up with regular topics for conversation:

> *"They don't like me to call every day because I ask the same questions ... I'm forcing myself to be a part of their life when they don't really have anything new to talk about." (4P)*

Lastly, four of the 14 households no longer had a communication device shared by the household (e.g., house phone) so the act of "calling home" must be mediated by the collocated adult. This can reduce contact with the child if the collocated adult is unavailable or unwilling to talk. We discuss this issue in more detail in 4.2.3.

4.2.2. *Spontaneous Asynchronous Phatic Communication*

Thirteen out of the 14 families attempted to supplement the scheduled synchronous contact with spontaneous asynchronous communication over mail, email, or SMS. Eleven of these 13 families used asynchronous communication regularly. Eight of the parents explicitly mentioned that sending an asynchronous message was the way they dealt with moments when they miss their child. Asynchronous communication was usually targeted individually at the child:

> *"I'll flood her box with a bunch of e-mails and send her animation things. And sometimes, I may just overnight her something in the mail. I mean, to get something with her name on it blows her away." (10P)*

Rather than focusing on instrumental concerns, asynchronous contact was usually *phatic* in nature—focused on reinforcing the social bond rather than providing information [14]. Two children describe their emails to their parents:

> *"I always use big letters and say I love you. They take up like half of the page. I used to make these little smiley faces and I'd put them on there. Then I'd put like a little background." (3C)*

> *"I wouldn't talk about how I'm feeling, I would just use a lot of those smiley face pictures."(4C)*

SMS messages were often focused on conveying a sense of connection rather than practical information exchange.

> *"Oh, I'll send her little smiley faces or little messages. Little special, you know, songs or little gifts through the phone." (2C)*

> *"I'll just send him a text and say, 'Hey, I'm thinking of you. Hope you're having a good day' type thing." (4P)*

Phatic communication was the rule for most of the families who communicated asynchronously (except families 6, 8, and 11, who also used asynchronous communication for instrumental purposes).

There are two limitations of this strategy. First of all, the only form of asynchronous communication available for individual use with younger children is mail, because they often do not have phones or email accounts. That makes it difficult for parents with younger children to enact this strategy. Four parents mentioned struggling with the idea of buying their child a cell phone to allow them to send messages to each other, but not feeling that the child was ready for the responsibility of owning a phone. The second issue is that asynchronous communication offers limited opportunities for emotional expressiveness—a major limitation since it is mostly used for phatic messages.

> *"...with email, sometimes you will sanitize it a bit; like you're feeling really sad but you don't want the person to know how sad you are." (3P)*

> *"... you can't really, like, feel someone's emotion that they're, like, feeling. Like if they don't want to talk about it then you don't know what we're going through." (8C)*

4.2.3. Enlisting the Aid of a Collocated Adult

All of the families in our study talked about seeking help from a collocated adult during the separation. For children, this was the most listed strategy for managing separation:

> *"If one of your parents is gone and stuff, then start to talk more to the other parent too about how you feel and stuff." (6C)*

> *"She would, you know, would be there and like talk to me, tell me that he'd be home soon, that it's all right."(12C)*

For parents, the collocated adult is not only a source of emotional support, but also the major mechanism by which they stay in touch with the child. The collocated adult serves as an awareness system about the event in the child's life and encourages the child to speak to the remote parent:

> *"It's [my wife] I'm always phoning ... she'd always make sure that they come to the phone, you know, talk a little bit ... And she recounts what's been going on, especially if there's anything around school or behaviors or something." (9P)*

> *"If something comes up, she'll just normally send it to me on email while she's thinking about it. And then when I get to email, I'll have four, five, six emails waiting on me, and just get caught up that way" (5P)*

Additionally, the collocated parent supported technology use by helping set up any technology involved in the communication and motivating its use:

> *"He would make videos with her, so he would actually set up the camera and everything and they would make videos together to send to me, which she couldn't have necessarily done on her own at that time because she was little."(3P)*

However, two of the families in our study were unable to use this strategy routinely: one (family 2) because the collocated adult was a distant relative unmotivated to maintain contact and one (family 4) where there was frequent marital conflict between the parents. These examples point to the limitations of this strategy. Even in families that are usually cooperative, there may be times that the collocated adult may be unwilling to participate fully:

> *"There were times when, if my husband and I weren't getting along ... he was short in answer and so then I'm only able to email with her and that was very upsetting." (3P)*

In other situations, the collocated adult may be willing to support the communication but may not have the technical competency to do so in the most effective way:

> *"...because of her lack of technology awareness, she hasn't really helped too much..." (4P)*

Lastly, in six of the families parents expressed concern over the additional responsibilities that their absence introduced to the collocated adult and wanted to limit this overhead.

4.2.4. Using Video Chat

We discuss the practices of using video chat separately from the synchronous communication practices highlighted in 4.2.1, because using video chat had a different effect on satisfaction with contact than other types of communication. We did not explicitly recruit for families that use video chat, yet nine of the 14 families had attempted to do so and five out of those families used it regularly. As in the previous investigations of videoconferencing [1], our participants described a number of advantages over the phone, such as being more emotionally expressive, leading to longer conversations, and allowing show-and-tell:

> *"She's always showing me something new she got, something she made in school. So it's really, really fun." (10P)*

The availability of video seemed particularly important to parents during longer separations:

> *"If I had not done the video, it would have been when I left in June till December when I saw everybody ... So I don't know that I would have recognized them if it hadn't been for the video as often as it was." (12P)*

Video chat seems to be an effective strategy for staying in touch. Eight out of 10 participants who used video chat routinely were satisfied with their overall contact with their remote partner, whereas only six out of 18 of those who didn't use video chat reported being satisfied with the overall level of communication (80% vs. 33%). So, why is it that so few families use it routinely? We discovered three major limitations of video chat that prevented it from becoming used routinely. First of all, setting up video chat is still a major barrier for families because it requires at least one knowledgeable user at each location who is willing to deal with the setup overhead:

> *"You know if I was to be here and try to get a video call done ... I just know that it's gonna be fraught with problems. It's not gonna be simple. Something's gonna be wrong ... It doesn't just have an on, off button." (9P)*

Second, for a relatively large number of families video chat was simply unavailable because they did not have the necessary infrastructure such as a computer (family 2) or a reliable Internet connection (families 3, 4, 5):

> *"When we were deployed, the bandwidth wouldn't support it and it would lock up, and you'd end up getting*

madder about the whole thing. We tried to use it and it just wasn't reliable. So that's the only experience I've had with it." (5P)

Lastly, whether for technical or social reasons video chat requires a dedicated time and place for the interaction. Several families mentioned that they used the phone more than video chat because it supports multitasking:

"If I'm on the phone I could be washing the dishes, or doing other things that are mindless; whereas with Skype I can't be doing that because they'll notice." (13P)

"I can walk with [the phone]. That's what I can't do as easily while I'm Skyping." (6P)

For others it was because the video-chat-enabled computer was often placed in a location usually used for work or rest rather than a living room.

"I think it's because she has to be upstairs in her bedroom ... And she's not in her bedroom unless she's going to bed." (10P)

"We're supposed to be on the computer at the same time, which usually can't happen because I'm not in the [home] office that much." (13C)

Many families viewed video chat as something only worth attempting on special occasions. For casual communication, they did not want to "make a big meal of it" (9P) and often used the phone instead.

4.2.5. Playing Online Games

Four out of the 14 families attempted to incorporate some form of online gaming into their contact while apart, but only two families used online gaming regularly. Three of these families tried synchronous casual online games and one tried asynchronous gaming through Facebook.

Family 12 found online gaming to be so important that they switched video chat clients to one that provided a larger variety of games. The games that they played online became part of their in-person interaction as well:

"We would play backgammon or Chinese checkers ... That was excellent. We even bought a Chinese checkers game after I got back home." (12P)

However, there are a number of challenges to incorporating online gaming into long-distance interaction. First of all, children do not necessarily want to see their parents involved in every game space:

"I don't want to play online games with my dad. I more like to play on my own." (14C)

One avid World of Warcraft player rejected the idea of using it to stay in touch with his dad:

"That'd be kind of weird. I would feel like he's watching over me." (4C)

Second, when gaming is a synchronous interaction, multiple children may want to participate at the same time. However, currently multiplayer games are usually set up to allow only one player per computer. So, while children will often *talk* to their parent all at the same time, they have to take turns in order to *play* with their parent.

"I think there was a couple of games where you could play with more than two players ... But we didn't do that often, because we don't have another computer at home." (12C)

Lastly, when playing in-person, parents often have the responsibility of motivating the game and guiding the younger players. This is very difficult to do with online games, so younger children may quickly lose interest in the game:

"I try to do some kind of chess play you know, that kind of thing, but with them is a little difficult because they are still learning ... we tried to do a monopoly game one day but it was very slow, the thing is he gets bored." (1P)

There was less interest in playing online games together than may have been observed in previous work (e.g., [17]).

5. DISCUSSION

In this section, we put our investigation in context of other work in this field and point out some opportunities to further investigate and support work-separated families.

5.1. The Unique Situation of Work-Separated Families

While work-separated families share some challenges and needs with other types of parent–child separation, there are some unique aspects to their situation. We considered the results of interviews with divorced families [18,24] to better understand the similarities and differences between divorced and work-separated parent–child contact.

On first examination, the situation of work-separated families is not in as much need for intervention as the situation for divorced families. In work-separated families, reintegration is assumed, so many families are willing to put up with non-optimal communication technologies as a temporary solution. At least some of the parents and the majority of the children are willing to minimize long-distance interaction with the understanding that a forthcoming reunion will provide better opportunities for staying in touch. Overall, nine of the children and four of the adults in our study were satisfied with the currently available methods of communication. However, there is a class of families that seems to be consistently unhappy with the available options for communication. Out of the eight military family interviewees, only one was satisfied with the amount of contact during the deployment. So, while the overall level of satisfaction with current contact is higher for work-separated families than for divorced families, there are a clearly opportunities where additional interventions would be welcome.

The second difference between divorced and work-separated families is the greater expectation of conflict in the former. Work-separated families make greater use of the collocated adult, whose cooperation is expected. The presence of this ally makes the work-separated situation easier to handle. However, our interviews revealed that even in intact work-separated families, conflict between the remote and collocated adult can limit interaction with the child. In divorced families, this conflict is anticipated and families implement strategies to minimize the effect of this conflict on the relationship between the remote parent and the child. Work-separated families do not usually prepare alternative routes of communication and strategies for managing conflict. In this way, when the conflict does occur, its effects may be more serious.

Lastly, a big difference between separation due to work and other types of parent–child separation is the relative lack of control by the remote parent over their environment. In divorced families or other permanent separations, the parent may be more able to invest in the necessary infrastructure to support richer forms of interaction. Work-separated families may not have access to the necessary infrastructure or the influence to create such infrastructure either because their relocation is short-term or because they are in an infrastructure poor location (as is often the case for military families [8]). Additionally, work-separated parents may have less control over their time while away for work and fewer opportunities to develop permanent social strategies for maintaining contact with their children. In essence, while divorced families may sculpt their permanent environment to support maintaining contact, work-separated families must often make do with temporary solutions that they can bring into the situation with them.

5.2. Non-Consensus in Work-Separated Families

Studies of communication technologies for the home often emphasize families that seek out more opportunities to communicate. It is a common trend in discussing domestic communication technology to focus on harmony and consensus. However, recent work in the HCI domain points out that conflict, disruption, and non-consensus are also part of family life and the way families use technology [7]. To contribute to this conversation, we want to highlight the finding that there is often a lack of consensus between parents and children in work-separated families as to what constitutes "enough" communication.

Our study showed that the need to increase contact is a characteristic common of travelling parents, but less commonly seen in children. Spending more time communicating with the remote parent may in fact interfere with the strategies used by children to cope with the separation. To them, the time is better spent connecting with a collocated adult and focusing on things other than being apart. While only three children expressed displeasure with excessive contact from their traveling parent, a number of parents expressed frustration with short conversation and single-word replies. At least one previous project has considered giving the child the power to determine the amount of communication—the eKiss system allowed only the child to send messages to the system and did not provide the parent with any means of prompting for a communication [5]. They found that children did not share as much as the researcher had expected or as much as their parents had hoped. This is additional evidence that children are not as motivated to communicate as their parents may be.

In designing new communication technologies for families, we are implicitly supporting the desires of the typical parent over the desires of the typical child. Perhaps, we are justified in making this design decision in the spirit of meeting the *needs* rather than satisfying the desires of the child. However, it is important for designers to consider the obligation to communicate that their system may impose on the child and what may happen if the parent's expectations for communication are not met.

5.3. Opportunities in Designing for Separation

There are three clear opportunities in designing for work-separated families that emerged from our interviews: designing for synchronous communication with multiple children, designing for direct asynchronous communication between the parent and child, and designing for infrastructure-poor environments.

Synchronous communication in work-separated families often occurs between the remote parent and multiple members of the household simultaneously. Video chat supports participation by multiple individuals and is reportedly used this way quite frequently [1]. However, the synchronous communication technologies that we have been designing as a community seem to focus on contact with one child at a time [9,19,23]. In our interviews, families talked about the synergy that occurs when multiple children are able to talk to their parent together. We should consider placing a greater emphasis on designing to support this configuration.

Though there have been several previous projects looking at asynchronously sending photos from a mobile device to a public display or blog [5,15,22], there is an opportunity to explore designing devices that allow the parent and child to exchange asynchronous messages directly. Our study showed that though synchronous communication tends to occur "with the household," asynchronous communication is often targeted directly to the child. Parents mentioned that sending a message just to the child is a way of making him or her feel special. Though cell phones currently fulfill this functionality for older children, mail is often the only available form of asynchronous contact with younger children—a clear opportunity for new designs. In creating novel methods of asynchronous communication, it is important to keep in mind that such a system would be most helpful if it provided opportunities for including color, images, and animations. Our participants emphasized that these are important to the way that children express themselves in asynchronous messages.

Perhaps the biggest need in designing for work-separated families is in supporting military parents. These families face a combination of three challenges that make the separation particularly difficult: the separation is usually long-term, there is usually a significant time zone difference, and there is usually very limited access to communications infrastructure [8]. Using video chat is a key strategy for other work-separated families, but one that is often denied to this group. These families have found creative ways of appropriating communication technologies that are otherwise not very child-friendly, such as email. There is a clear opportunity to provide expressive, low-bandwidth means of communication for these families. Some of these prospects are being explored by Sesame Workshop's Family Connections, but there are still many opportunities for future work.

5.4. Opportunities in Investigating Separation

There are two directions for future investigation: studying the role of the collocated adult and further investigating the role of games in staying in touch.

The collocated adult plays a key role in work-separated families. Aside from serving as emotional support, a human awareness system, and encouraging communication, they are in the difficult position of reconciling the sometimes conflicting strategies for managing separation enacted by the child and the remote parent. Though our interviews revealed some of the responsibilities of these individuals, a follow-up study looking specifically at collocated adults in work-separated families would allows us to better understand the challenges they face, the strategies they use, and how we could support them in their role.

Our interviews revealed a tension in how families use online games to stay in touch. While two families found it helpful, others rejected the idea of playing games together for various reasons. This seems contrary to the previous suggestion that activities together are a more natural way for parents and children to stay in touch than simply talking [24] and to previous accounts of families playing together online [17]. As a community, designing for remote play between parents and children has been a key approach taken by several projects [6,9,16], but all of these system presented only preliminary evaluations so it is what would happen in a longer deployment. Our assumptions as a community about the benefit of games for connecting parents and children may not reflect the reality of long-distance parent–child interaction, so we should investigate this in more detail. What aspects of games contribute to families adopting online gaming as a strategy for staying in touch? In what situations can online gaming be an effective strategy and in what situations do families reject it?

6. CONCLUSION

When separated by work travel, parents and children adopt strategies for managing being apart. Parents often turn to synchronous and asynchronous communication technologies in order to maintain a consistent presence in the child's life. Scheduled synchronous communication with the entire household is supplemented with spontaneous asynchronous contact with each child individually. Video chat is a successful strategy for staying in touch when it is used, but is often unavailable or impractical for regular use. Unlike their parents, children often do not seek out communication but rather focus on managing separation by spending more time with a collocated adult. It is often up to the collocated adult to balance the gap in motivation to communicate between the parent and child. Current communication practices are meeting the needs of many work-separated families, but not the needs of military families. A designer focusing on work-separated families should consider the tension between the amount of contact desired by the parent and child, the role of the collocated adult, supporting existing synchronous and asynchronous communication practices, and designing for situations with limited infrastructure.

ACKNOWLEDGMENTS

We thank Jane Kim, Fatima Boujarwah, all of the members of the UbiComp Lab at Georgia Tech, and the many readers of this paper, whose feedback was invaluable. Lastly, we want to acknowledge the support of Nokia University Funding Award which paid for this research.

REFERENCES

1. Ames, M.G., Go, J., Kaye, J., and Spasojevic, M. Making Love in the Network Closet: The Benefits and Work of Family Videochat. *Proc. of CHI*, (2010).
2. Ballagas, R., Kaye, J.', Ames, M., Go, J., and Raffle, H. Family communication: phone conversations with children. *Proc. of IDC*, ACM (2009), 321-324.
3. Conlin, J. Living Apart for the Paycheck. *The New York Times*, 2009.
4. Dalsgaard, T., Skov, M.B., Stougaard, M., and Thomassen, B. Mediated intimacy in families: understanding the relation between children and parents. *Proc. of IDC*, ACM (2006), 145-152.
5. Dalsgaard, T., Skov, M.B., and Thomassen, B.R. eKiss: Sharing Experiences in Families Through a Picture Blog. *Proc. of British HCI*, (2007), 67-75.
6. Davis, H., Skov, M.B., Stougaard, M., and Vetere, F. Virtual box: supporting mediated family intimacy through virtual and physical play. *Proc. of OZCHI*, (2007), 151-159.
7. Dimond, J., Poole, E., and Yardi, S. The Effects of Death, Divorce, and Life Disruptions on Home Technology Routines. *Proc. of GROUP*, (2010), To Appear.
8. Drummet, A.R., Coleman, M., and Cable, S. Military Families under Stress: Implications for Family Life Education. *Family Relations 52*, 3 (2003), 279-287.

9. Follmer, S., Raffle, H., Go, J., Ballagas, R., and Ishii, H. Video play: playful interactions in video conferencing for long-distance families with young children. *Proc. of IDC*, ACM (2010), 49-58.

10. Grinter, R.E., Palen, L., and Eldridge, M. Chatting with teenagers: Considering the place of chat technologies in teen life. *ACM ToCHI 13*, 4 (2006), 423-447.

11. Judge, T.K. and Neustaedter, C. Sharing conversation and sharing life: video conferencing in the home. *Proc. of CHI*, ACM (2010), 655-658.

12. Kelley, M.L., Hock, E., Smith, K.M., Jarvis, M.S., Bonney, J.F., and Gaffney, M.A. Internalizing and externalizing behavior of children experiencing military-induced separation. *American Academy of Child and Adolescent Psychiatry 40*, 4 (2001), 464-471.

13. Landis, J.R. and Koch, G.G. The Measurement of Observer Agreement for Categorical Data. *Biometrics 33*, (1977), 159-174.

14. Malinowski, B. The Problem of Meaning in Primitive Languages. In C.K. Ogden and I.A. Richards, eds., *The Meaning of Meaning*. London, 1923, 146-152.

15. Markopoulos, P., Romero, N., van Baren, J., Jsselsteijn, W., de Ruyter, B., and Farshchian, B. Home and away with the ASTRA awareness system. *Proc. of CHI*, ACM Press (2004), 1351-1354.

16. Modlitba, P.L. Globetoddler: Enhancing the experience of remote interaction for preschool children and their traveling parents. Masters Thesis. MIT. 2008.

17. Nardi, B. and Harris, J. Strangers and friends: collaborative play in world of warcraft. *Proc. of CSCW*, (2006), 149-158.

18. Odom, W., Zimmerman, J., and Forlizzi, J. Designing for dynamic family structures: divorced families and interactive systems. *Proc. of DIS*, (2010), 151-160.

19. Raffle, H., Ballagas, R., Revelle, G., et al. Family Story Play: Reading with Young Children (and Elmo) Over a Distance. *Proc. of CHI*, ACM (2010).

20. Rutter, M. Parent-Child Separation: Psychological Effects on the Children. *Journal of Child Psychology and Psychiatry 12*, 4 (1971), 233-260.

21. Seidman, I. *Interviewing as Qualitative Research: A Guide for Researchers in Education And the Social Sciences*. Teachers College Press, New York, 1998.

22. Vetere, F., Davis, H., Gibbs, M., and Howard, S. The Magic Box and Collage: Responding to the challenge of distributed intergenerational play. *Intl J of Human-Computer Studies 67*, 2 (2009), 165-178.

23. Yarosh, S., Cuzzort, S., Mueller, H., and Abowd, G.D. Developing a Media Space for Remote Synchronous Parent-Child Interaction. *Proc. of IDC*, (2009), 97-105.

24. Yarosh, S., Chew, Y.C., and Abowd, G.D. Supporting Parent-Child Communication in Divorced Families. *J of Human Computer Studies 67*, 2 (2009), 192-203.

Hello, is Grandma there? Let's Read!

StoryVisit: Family Video Chat and Connected E-Books

Hayes Raffle[1], Glenda Revelle[2], Koichi Mori[1], Rafael Ballagas[1], Kyle Buza[1], Hiroshi Horii[1], Joseph 'Jofish' Kaye[1], Kristin Cook[3], Natalie Freed[1], Janet Go[1], Mirjana Spasojevic[1]

[1] Nokia Research Center
955 Page Mill Rd, Palo Alto CA 94306
hayes.raffle | koichi.mori | tico.ballagas | hiroshi.horii | jofish.kaye | janet.go | mirjana.spasojevic @nokia.com

[2] Human Environmental Sciences
University of Arkansas
Fayetteville, AR 72701
grevelle@uark.edu

[3] Sesame Workshop
One Lincoln Plaza
New York, NY 10023
kristin.cook @sesameworkshop.org

Abstract

StoryVisit allows children and long-distance adults to experience a sense of togetherness by reading children's story books together over a distance. StoryVisit combines video conferencing and connected books: remote grown-up and child readers can see and hear each other, and can also see and control the same e-book. We report on research with 61 families – over 200 users including parents, children and long-distance readers – who used StoryVisit in their homes with a long-distance reader for at least one reading session. In addition, we report qualitative findings regarding nineteen of the families who participated in telephone interviews and four families who were monitored and interviewed by researchers at home. Results show that connected e-book video chat sessions last about five times as long as the typical video chats reported in previous research on families with young children. Moreover, the addition of an animated character increased session lengths by another 50%. StoryVisit usage peaked for families with three year olds, showing that sustained distance interactions with very young children are possible if communication technologies incorporate joint activities that engage children and adults.

Author Keywords

Reading, children, literacy, video conferencing, agent, dialogic reading, family communication

ACM Classification Keywords

H.5.2. Information interfaces; H.4.3. Communications Applications: Computer conferencing, teleconferencing, and videoconferencing

General Terms

Design, Human Factors

Figure 1. A three-year-old and her father read an e-book with Grandma over video chat

INTRODUCTION

Today's families are becoming increasingly dispersed, and loved ones are often far from each other. For instance, more than half of the grandparents living in North America are over 200 miles from their grandchildren [5], and working parents increasingly travel away from home for professional reasons [3]. And while children and elders often have the most time and motivation to connect over a distance, they have the fewest tools to help them create a sense of togetherness. A series of recent studies has addressed how telecommunications technologies and media are used by families to maintain their relationships over a distance [1, 2, 11, 13, 15]. Tools like phone calls, SMS, or email are not appropriate for families with young children, because they do not always make sense to children or elders. Video chat services like Skype® are growing in popularity because video allows children to express themselves through action as well as words, and (once connected) the video medium is more equally shareable and accessible to the young and old. However, video conferencing technologies require significant technical and social work to use, and families with younger children still struggle to use these technologies to create meaningful emotional connections over a distance [1].

Our previous research in family communication [2, 14] has indicated that while video conferencing allows family members to see and hear each other, they need something to talk about, or even better, something to do together. When adults interact with young children, they do not converse – they play. The challenge is to facilitate playing together at a distance.

Our results with Family Story Play [2, 14] showed that coupling shared book reading and video conferencing could support family communication at a distance. StoryVisit (Figure 1) builds on that research, and uses larger-scale, in-situ data to reveal what works and what doesn't work for shared family activities in the real world. Research goals of this work include (1) evaluating the viability of a co-reading system in ecologically-valid environments, (2) identifying the strengths and weaknesses of such a system relative to prior lab results, and (3) evaluating how different design elements such as reading tips and use of an interactive character may affect families' success in building meaningful connections over a distance.

RELATED WORK

The idea of helping families to connect through images and video has been addressed in HCI over the years. Technology Probes suggested that a sense of togetherness could be built with always-on photo sharing devices situated in people's homes [9], and Yarosh et al. have conducted a series of studies of children's sense-making of video conferencing technologies. They state, for example, that equally sized windows for children and adults in a video chat UI will help children understand the perspective of the distant partner [17] and that shared (often physical) activities like playing board games or reading books can help families feel better connected over a distance [19]. With Video Play, Follmer et al. [7] extended these ideas by presenting a series of shared activities that are integrated in a video chat UI. While not fully implemented, their designs explore how open ended games or books can help distant family members play together and have a sense of shared context. Our previous work showed that traditional paper books, coupled with mobile video conferencing and interactive content, can help families have a sense of togetherness over a distance [2, 14]. That research also showed that children's learning and family communication are complementary goals, since talking with children about books while you read them can improve children's literacy as well as helping intergenerational family members have things to talk about.

The StoryVisit project builds on these explorations of activity-based family video conferencing in the home, and adds an examination of ways in which certain features of children's content (e-books with reading tips and with an interactive character) may help families engage in longer and richer interactions over a distance. The reading tips are based on research in "dialogic reading" [16, 20] which is a style of reading picture books with young children in which adults ask children questions and engage them in conversation about what is happening in the book while they are reading together. Adults often engage in these kinds of conversations while reading traditional picture books [12] and online storybooks [6]. When they do, it facilitates children's

Figure 2. StoryVisit UI

language and vocabulary development [20], as well as helping children and adults converse at a distance [14]. Laboratory trials have shown that adults can learn dialogic techniques through training in a research setting [17].

Our approach to incorporating an interactive character in the reading session is informed by research with older children [10, 13] that shows that including interaction with social agents can improve student learning in educational contexts. In StoryVisit, we use Elmo® from Sesame Street® as an interactive social agent both to support child engagement and to model/scaffold dialogic reading techniques for adults.

In parallel with that research, a series of new web applications are also addressing how rich online media can help families connect over time and distance via story reading. AStoryBeforeBed.com is a website where grown up readers can record themselves reading an e-book, and then send that recording via email to a child who may watch the reading session later. An asynchronous sharing model sidesteps the logistical challenges families confront with synchronous video chat. However, a one-way model does not provide means for the reader to get feedback about how the child enjoyed being read to, and thus provides a more limited social connection. Readeo.com introduced shared e-book reading alongside video conferencing, and implemented a system similar to StoryVisit. Our research design addresses how two specific aspects of content – an interactive character and reading tips – might help both children and adults achieve successful distance communication, and provide rich communication channels that help families feel connected even when they are apart.

STORY VISIT

StoryVisit is a collaborative web application designed to give children and long-distance adults a sense of togetherness by enabling them to read children's story books together over a distance. The system combines browser-based video conferencing and connected books: remote grown-up and child readers can see and hear each other, and can also see and control the same story book (Figures 1, 2). When a grown-up turns the page, the child's page turns along with it, and if the child clicks on something on his screen, the grown-up can see that on her screen too. Five titles were adapted from the Sesame Street library of illustrated e-books, which were authored for children ages 2-5 years old. We wanted to build an application that was simple and fun for children and adults to use together. We believe that reading ought to be an enjoyable activity for children and adults alike, because children who learn to love reading as preschoolers are well positioned to succeed later in school and in life.

System Features

Pointing: In addition to video and book synchronization, StoryVisit allows for a sense of "shared pointing" — if one user points to (by clicking on) something on the page, the other user will see a large hand-icon appear where the book has been clicked (Figure 2). This allows children or adults to point to things in the book they are talking about.

Tips: Reading tips were written for every page of every book in the system, giving suggestions regarding questions the Reader might ask on that page. Since the tips were designed as an aid for the long-distance adult Reader, they were viewable only by the Reader, and not by the Child. The tips were introduced to Readers with a 5 minute video explaining how adults can read to children in a "dialogic" manner.

Interactive Social Agent: Interactive video footage of Sesame Street's Elmo character was overlaid on e-books (Figure 2). Elmo could be triggered by the Reader to talk about the book in a dialogic style, for example prompting Elmo to ask a question or make a comment about what was happening on that page of the book. The Reader could also make Elmo laugh, or answer yes and no questions. Elmo's actions, like the rest of the book content, were synchronized for both the reader and child, but the controls were available only to the adult Reader. Because controls for Elmo are hidden from the child's view, the Reader can create the illusion that the character is part of the family's ongoing conversation about the book. For instance, the Reader may ask Elmo "What's happening on this page," and then click *Talk* to make him comment on the story. Character dialogue was produced for every page of every book, so Elmo can ask children contextually relevant questions and draw a child's attention to aspects of the story. Elmo does not ever read the book, but instead asks questions in the spirit of "dialogic reading" that invite children and adults to engage in conversation with him and with each other.

Shared Family Accounts: User accounts were designed as shared family accounts with a "Reader" half and a "Child" half that were automatically paired for co-reading. This design allowed a single family member to set up an online account for the whole family and then share login credentials with distant family members via email or a phone call. We adopted this design to simplify sharing online, taking cues from previous work on shared accounts for the desktop environment [4]. This model also removes (as much as possible) the technical complexities of calling, authentication and handshaking that families have described as pain points in the process of making video calls [1]. The resulting design is different from many conventional phone or video calling services in that there is no "call" or "hang up" button in the UI - families are automatically connected - and are provided with no means to connect to other people outside one's own family account. Our goal was to simplify the video calling portion of the UI, as well as to ensure a sense of privacy and safety in the system.

UI Flow: When an adult logs in for the very first time, s/he is directed to a series of introductory pages that explain the shared account model, present a demographic survey to the user, and present appropriate instructional videos. Then, the user is directed to the default view, which is a "library" showing covers of five children's e-books. Clicking on a book opens that book in a content pane that sits alongside two equally sized video panes (Figure 2). When users return to the site, they will see the last view that either they or their reading partner has viewed. For example, if a user closed the browser on page 5 of "Abby in Wonderland," returning to the website will take them back to that page.

A note about Video: Prior to this design, we experimented with a much simpler design, which used only an audio communication channel and simple animations of Elmo. After limited trials, we found the system to be rather unsuccessful: a strong sense of emotional connection and child engagement was hard to achieve between reading partners without the video conferencing, and the animated character elements had a limited presence when displayed as simple 2-D animations. We found video conferencing created a stronger sense of emotional connection between co-readers, and video of Elmo brought the book to life in a more convincing way.

USER STUDY

StoryVisit was launched as a research-based e-book prototype with a limited-time trial. In response to promotion of the research project on the Sesame Street web site and in a Sesame Street Family Newsletter, 260 families registered to use the system for a period of 4 weeks. Sixty-one families became "active" users, using the system for at least one reading session with a long-distance reader, representing nearly 25% uptake. Families generally had at least three members (at least one child, co-located parent and remote reader) and often had more (siblings and multiple parents), resulting in a pool of over 200 individual users.

For all 61 families, basic usage data (amount of time spent per session, number of books read per session, etc.) was logged. All participants completed a pre-survey and 19 of those families volunteered in their post-survey to complete a telephone interview with a researcher.

In order to get richer qualitative insights into system usage, four of the 61 families were recruited for "home visits" by the research team. The home visits included technical support, as well as observation and recording of video and audio streams during book-reading sessions and in-depth semi-structured interviews.

First we will report on quantitative usage data for the 57 families who did not have home visits and, separately, the quantitative usage data for the four families who had home visits. Next, we will report on the qualitative observational and interview data for the 4 home visit families, along with the phone interview data from the 19 families who volunteered to be interviewed as part of their post-surveys. Finally, we will discuss relationships between the quantitative usage data and the qualitative observational and interview data.

Quantitative Findings

The goal of this part of the research was to test StoryVisit in an ecologically-valid manner with a large number of families and see how the system might succeed or fail in people's homes under naturalistic circumstances, with neither the technical support nor the extrinsic motivation typically provided to users who participate in lab trials. We also hoped to gain some understanding regarding the relative strengths and weaknesses of various design elements, including the basic interactive book design, the dialogic reading tips (Tips) and the interactive character as participant and model (Elmo). When a family registered for StoryVisit, they were randomly assigned to one of four conditions: Elmo+Tips, Elmo Only, Tips Only, or No Elmo/No Tips. All families received video conferencing alongside shared e-books with the pointing feature. Users completed a demographic survey before using the service.

Analysis

Fifty-seven non-home-visit families engaged in at least one reading session with a remote partner. A reading session was defined as use of StoryVisit by two parties at different locations that lasted more than 30 seconds with at least 3 book pages viewed. Data only includes times that families were engaged in co-reading with books; data does not include times that families may have used the system for video conferencing alone, or times the site may have been used for eBook reading alone (e.g. co-located reading, ignoring the video conferencing feature).

In the pretest survey, families were asked to report the age (in years) of the child who would be using StoryVisit. Four families did not report the child's age, so these families were omitted from all analyses involving age as a factor. The distribution of children's ages for the 53 families who reported age was as follows:

Age	1 yr	2 yrs	3 yrs	4 yrs	5 yrs	6+ yrs
# children	4	21	13	6	3	6

For purposes of analysis, children were divided into three Age Groups: Under Age 3 (N=25), 3 year olds (N=13), and Over Age 3 (N=15).

Families were evenly distributed across the four Study Conditions with Elmo+Tips (N=14), Elmo Only (N=12), Tips Only (N=16), No Elmo / No Tips (N=15).

Analyses of variance were performed to examine the effects of Age Group and Condition on the following dependent variables:

- Number of Reading Sessions
- Average Reading Time per Session
- Total Reading Time Across all Reading Sessions
- Total Number of Pages Read Across all Reading Sessions
- Average Reading Time per Page
- Average Amount of Pointing per Page
- Average Number of Elmo Activations per Page (for Elmo and Elmo+Tips Conditions)
- Average Number of Reading Tip Activations per Page (for Tips and Elmo+Tips Conditions)

Results

Number of Reading Sessions. The 57 participating families averaged about 1½ reading sessions across the four week time period of the study. Thirty-eight families engaged in just one reading session, fifteen had two sessions, three had three sessions and one family had five sessions. There were no significant differences in number of reading sessions by Age Group or by Study Condition.

Average Reading Time per Session. Families spent an average of 12 minutes per reading session. There were no significant differences in the length of reading sessions by

	Total Reading Time (mins)			Total Number of Pages Read		
Age Group	Mean	Std Dev		Mean	Std Dev	N
Under 3	11.2	6.3		27.4	14.3	25
3 year olds	28.6	22.5		52.1	47.4	13
Over 3	17.2	17.7		29.7	23.6	15
Total	17.2	16.4		34.1	29.5	53

	Total Reading Time (mins)			Average Reading Time per Session		
Condition	Mean	Std Dev		Mean	Std Dev	N
Elmo Only	30.2	22.7		18.4	10.2	12
Elmo+Tips	14.7	8.3		11.2	8.2	14
Tips Only	14.6	15.1		7.9	5.1	15
No Elmo / No Tips	11.4	10.6		10.5	11.3	16
Total	17.1	16		11.7	9.5	57

Table 1. Total Reading Time, Total Number of Pages Read and Average Reading Time per Session across all reading sessions by Age Group and Condition

Age Group, but there were significant differences by Condition ($F_{3,56}$=3.22, p<.05). Tukey post hoc analysis indicated that families in the Elmo Only Condition had significantly longer reading sessions than families in the No Elmo/No Tips Condition. Means and standard deviations for this and all other significant effects are shown in Table 1.

Total Reading Time Across all Reading Sessions. In analyzing a sum of all reading sessions for each family, we found a significant effect of Age Group, ($F_{2,52}$=5.67, p<.01) and Tukey post hoc analysis showed that the only statistically significant difference was between 3 year olds and those younger than 3, where families with 3 year olds spent a significantly greater amount of time engaging in StoryVisit reading sessions than families with children under three. This indicates that families with 3-year-olds were a demographic "sweet spot" among StoryVisit users. We also found a significant effect of Condition ($F_{3,56}$=4.14, p<.01). Tukey post hoc analysis indicated that families in the Elmo Only Condition spent significantly more time engaging in StoryVisit reading sessions than families in any of the other three Conditions.

Total Number of Pages Read Across all Reading Sessions. We found a significant effect of Age Group, ($F_{2,52}$=3.54, p<.05). Tukey post hoc analysis showed that, once again, the only statistically significant difference was between families with 3 year olds and those younger than 3, with families of 3 year olds reading significantly more pages across all their StoryVisit reading sessions than those with children under three, further indicating StoryVisit's effectiveness among families with children age 3.

Reading Time per Page. Families spent an average of 32 seconds per page across all books read in all reading sessions. There were no significant differences in reading time per page by Age Group or by Study Condition.

Pointing. Overall, the occurrence of clicking on something on the page to point to it was low: only about half of the pages read had a point by the remote adult, and less than a quarter of the pages read had a child point.

Elmo activations. Elmo or any of the Elmo controls were clicked on an average of once per page. There were no significant differences in Elmo Activations per page by Age Group or by Study Condition.

Reading Tip Activations per Page. Overall, Readers clicked on the Reading Tips infrequently. For the Conditions in which Tips were present, they were clicked on less than 5% of the pages read. That said, those families that had Elmo+Tips activated the Tips significantly less frequently than those who had Tips Only ($F_{1,29}$=4.33, p<.05). Families in the Elmo+Tips condition clicked on Tips on only about 2% of the pages, whereas those in the Tips Only condition clicked on Tips about 7% of the time. An examination of whether Tips were ever clicked at all yielded a similar but even more striking pattern: 75% of the Tips Only families clicked on Tips at least once, whereas only 20% of those with Elmo+Tips ever clicked on Tips at all.

Key Take Aways that we will return to in the Discussion section include (1) relatively low rates of repeat usage of the system, with only four of the 57 families engaging in more than two reading sessions, (2) a sweet-spot for families with 3 year olds, (3) families in the Elmo Only condition spent significantly more time with the system, and (4) Readers didn't use tips, especially if Elmo was present.

Quantitative Findings — Home-Visit Families

Four families participated in "home visits," including observation sessions in the home context, in-depth interviews, and video recording of their use of the system in exchange for compensation. Three of these families were recruited prior to the beginning of the larger scale "in-situ" study, and were assigned to the Elmo+Tips condition so that all software features could be tested prior to the larger launch of the study. A fourth family (that happened to have been assigned to the Tips Only condition) volunteered to participate in home visits after signing up for the larger scale study.

Teams of two of our researchers made an initial visit and observed during setup of the software, taking notes, videotaping the process, and offering advice when it was requested. Families used their own computers in parts of the home they chose. Three families moved laptop computers to public areas such as dining and living rooms, and the fourth family used a desktop computer in their home office. We observed an initial StoryVisit session with a remote Reader and requested that families use the system at least once a week. We then telephoned the family two weeks later to get initial feedback. Four weeks after the initial visit we visited families again, observed a reading session, and interviewed them. We also encouraged families to contact us directly if they had any problems in the course of the study.

Results

The only striking difference in usage patterns for the home-visit families was in the total number of reading sessions in which they engaged over the course of the four weeks. This pronounced difference could be attributed to biasing effects of compensation, awareness of monitoring, follow-up, or initial technical support. The characteristics of their individual reading sessions, however, were not strikingly different.

As seen in Table 2, one of the home-visit families (F22) was clearly an outlier with regard to the total number of reading sessions, average time per session, and average number of pages read per session. Not counting that family, the home visit families engaged in at least four times as many reading sessions as the families who only had the web experience. For the Average Reading Time per Session and the Average Number of Pages Read per Session, the averages for the non home-visit families are in the range of the 3 non-outlier home visit families. With regard to all of the other usage measures logged (e.g. #pointings/page, #tips/page, #Elmo Interactions per page), the non home-visit averages were comparable to the home visit averages across all home visit families.

Condition	Child Age(s)	# Reading Sessions	Avg mins / session	Avg # pages / session
F22: Elmo+Tips	3, 5	15	41	67
F25: Elmo+Tips	3	8	13	23
F26: Elmo+Tips	4	6	16	20
F73: Tips Only	4	6	21	33
Avg. Non H-V	3	1.5	12	24

Table 2. Total # Sessions, Home-Visit vs. Non Home-Visit families

Qualitative Findings - Emergent Patterns of Behavior

Children drive usage, but it's a family affair

Within each individual family there were different perspectives on technology and different attitudes towards adoption. A big barrier for many families was convincing other family members to use StoryVisit. Often, it seemed it was children's attraction to the system that motivated families to use it. Initially, a few home-visit families expressed skepticism about the system. For example the mother in Family 22 (Elmo+Tips) expressed that she would not trust her child to touch her computer. But after showing StoryVisit to her 5 year old - who was able to abide by her instructions - she let both her children (3 and 5) use the system repeatedly, about 15 times over a one-month period. Many other families' positive comments about the system stemmed from their children's enjoyment of it.

While parents were the social bridge connecting children to others outside the home, they could also be seen as gatekeepers for system usage, and family dynamics seemed to play a major role in who was allowed to read with children and in how people did or did not choose to use StoryVisit. The Mother in family 22 struggled with the idea of reading with her father-in-law, and was relieved when she learned she could instead connect with her brother in China, with whom she and the children were close. Grandparents were well-aware that parents were gatekeepers to the children; one grandparent pointed out that even if she wanted to read with her grandkids again, she'd have to set it up with her daughter. *We're here in St. Louis and they're in Oregon, and it's a 2 hour time difference. It depends on what they have time for and are inclined to do. They are the ones to initiate it.* (Family 27, No Elmo/No Tips)

Beyond gatekeeper, the co-located parent's role

Parents supported children in different ways, consistent with other findings [1, 14] of family video conferencing. Parents did technical setup and logistics such as arranging the call, but the UI was designed to be simple enough so that children could be left to read without a parent present. This did happen sometimes, but even when parents walked away from the computer, they consistently would keep an ear or an eye open to help children or remote readers get along. Most often, though, parents sat with their children while the book was read to them. Family 73 mentioned, *A lot of times she (distant aunt) would say things and he wouldn't understand them the first time, so I would repeat them.* And one anonymous user commented online: *My 3 1/2 yr-old son loves using StoryVisit with his Grandparents and Aunt. He has no trouble with the mouse and likes to be the one to turn the pages. I definitely need to hang around in case he needs help or doesn't hear something the first time but in general he can do whatever he needs to himself and the grown-up on the other end can do the rest.*

When parents are present, they can connect children's experiences with StoryVisit to everyday family life. Some families in the study reported using recipes from one of the books, cooking together with their children after a StoryVisit reading (Figure 3). The aunt, who was the distance Reader in Family 73 (Tips Only) discussed with her nephew's parents:

Aunt: *You guys tried these, right? (referring to the recipe on the page)*

Father: *We did try this, yeah, yeah, many times. Banana, strawberries and yogurt.*

Aunt: *mmm*

Mother: *Yeah, we made those last week. Was that prompted by this?*

Father: *Yeah that's what started that bananas and strawberries. It was a good idea.*

Aunt: *Sounds like a delicious snack*

Father: ... *and healthy too!*

Figure 3. Smoothie recipe, from Child's perspective.

StoryVisit seemed to be supporting family togetherness by facilitating shared activities and memories that families could remember and discuss later.

Elmo — bringing the book to life

The inclusion of the interactive Elmo character almost doubled the Total Reading Time (Table 1). Many families expressed positive feelings toward Elmo and found him to be an important participant in the book reading sessions, sometimes requesting more Elmo features: *I like the different story choices and the fact that Elmo can ask comprehension questions about things on each page. It would be great if he could have more than one question/comment for each page. My son really liked to say, "Let's hear what Elmo says!" after his relative finished reading each page.* (Family 75, Elmo Only)

Some families thought Elmo was in the way, but recognized him as an important draw for children: *That night I was mad at the webcam for not working so I was like I don't even care about this little Elmo guy, I just want to get them to read the story. So I didn't even take the time to figure it out that night, `cause I had other things on my mind. In the future I can see using it, because Leila really likes Elmo.* (Family 101, Elmo+Tips)

The design for Elmo was based on his role in Family Story Play [14], with a major difference being that Readers had a greater degree of control over when and how Elmo would participate in the reading conversation. Children often seemed delighted that Elmo appeared to be joining their conversations, and even answering their questions as if he were alive.

We were surprised to find that families in the Elmo Only condition engaged in so much more reading than those who had Elmo+Tips. The data did not provide a clear cause—perhaps StoryVisit just got too complex for Readers when Elmo and Tips were both present.

Tips

While the presence of Tips did not have a significant effect on reading times, some users found them to be helpful. For the remote Reader in Home Visit Family 73 (Tips Only), the tips became "how to be a good aunt instructions," because they prompted her to ask age-appropriate and engaging questions of her niece:

Aunt: *What part of these boats should you not eat?*

Son: *Fruit letters(?). HAHAHA!*

Aunt: *That was one of the questions they suggest.*

Father: *What's that? Oh, it suggests a question to you?*

Aunt: *Uh hmm.*

Father: *Oh, I didn't know it was telling you what to read.*

Aunt: *Well, like the question on "what do fireworks sound like?", I wish I had thought of that myself, but.*

Father: *Oh, oh!*

Aunt: *It says offer general and specific praise and encouragement.*

Father: *Oh, oh, oh it's giving you instructions. You mean this hasn't been really you at all, it's just been...*

Aunt: *it's been "how to be a good aunt" instructions.*

Father: *That's good*

Aunt: *No it is actually really helpful.*

Father: *Some people don't have the knack for it that you do.*

Tips were hidden from the children and co-located parent. On one hand, this may have been a mistake, in that parents were not able to coach remote readers about the use of tips or help their children understand what was being asked of them. On the other hand, tips may have helped empower Readers to be more engaging than they would otherwise.

Home visit Family 22 (Elmo+Tips) provided an unexpected reversal of our designed use-case; it was the children who would explain the book content to the Reader, who was a native Mandarin speaker not fluent in English. Their Chinese uncle would read and ask a question, and the children, ages 3 and 5, would translate for him or explain in English what was going on. This suggests opportunities for content in other languages and support for language learning - in one's native language or otherwise - with systems like StoryVisit.

In future systems, it may be preferable to show tips to both Reader and Child so that the parents could view and make use of the tips themselves. In general, Tips may not have been accessible enough. Although we created a video to explain dialogic reading to Readers, the length (over 5 minutes) may have been too much for some viewers, and some participants reported they didn't notice Tips at all.

The design of the tips and the video are based on prior research in dialogic reading [17] and our data point to a big difference between experimental research results (parents being in a lab and doing what they're told), vs. parents in their homes doing it by choice. While not conclusive, our data suggested that each aid (tips and Elmo character) may have succeeded best on their own and may not have worked so well in combination.

Technical Difficulties

Technical complexity came up as a general issue for our users. Our video conferencing infrastructure, based on Adobe Flash Media, was the best browser-based solution we could find, yet it was flawed with audio echo and feedback problems that plagued users and severely compromised the experience for many families. It is tempting to conclude that the large difference in usage patterns between home-visit and other users was due (at least in part) to technical difficulties, because home-visit families had more technical support than others. Needless to say, video conferencing is still a rapidly evolving technology that introduces real challenges to users. This observation has been made before [1], and suggests that experiences like StoryVisit will likely not receive wide appeal until video chat infrastructure is more reliable and easy to use.

Touching the screen — children and interface usability

Standard computers are not well designed for children's use. Children routinely touched the pages of the book on-screen and many parents suggested that touch-screen computers would be better. While some parents indicated a general preference for their children to control the computer interface themselves, others were more hesitant to hand control over to their 3-year-olds. One mother wrote on her blog: *One issue for us: Touchpad vs. Touchscreen confusion. My three-year-old daughter prefers to touch the screen than use the touchpad to direct the cursor. (Seems as though they are confusing my laptop for my iPhone!) I really need to introduce a mouse to my kids, but have not gotten around to buying one yet. What makes matters worse, the website encourages "touching" parts of the "page" (in other words, the screen), and even shows a finger popping up when you click on an object with the mouse. Really this product would be best put on a touchscreen device.*

E-books or Paper Books?

Some families missed the familiarity and tangibility of paper books. *With IChat we can use the same book at both ends of the phone. The experience is more personal. (Fam. 140, No Elmo/No Tips).* However, most families saw real benefits to the connected e-books. Family 75 (Elmo Only) called it a *unique experience that was a step up to our usual Skype conversations.* Another family compared StoryVisit to Skype: *I have a specific memory of my mother [son's grandmother]. Yes once definitely reading to him over Skype...where grandma was holding a physical book up to the camera and turning pages. It was cumbersome and hard to follow, but it was an interesting precedent.... Obviously with StoryVisit the book is not jiggling around, turning pages. Talking about details on the page with StoryVisit is much easier. I guess arguably less lively than when mom read to him... but the fact that the book page stays in focus, you can really study it and notice things yourself, and have more control. I think those are big pluses. When my mom was holding the book for the camera, it moved around, he had trouble looking at the details. (Family 138, Tips Only).*

Similarly, Family 101 (Elmo+Tips) reported, *It's a lot easier than just trying to read a story over Skype. Otherwise the other person has to have the same copy of the book you have. [You] don't have to do gymnastics to get everything on the screen.... Bedtime reading with Daddy is such an important part of the day for our daughter, so we were grateful for the opportunity to continue the tradition even when he had to be away for a few days.*

The symmetrical control of page turning allowed families to choose how to control pacing of book-reading sessions. Sometimes, families would let children turn the pages. Other times, Readers alone turned the pages in order to control the pacing of the reading session.

A Skype Alternative

We observed emergent use of the system as a Skype alternative with book reading being just a part of the communication session. In one of our home visit families (Family 22, Elmo+Tips) over half of sessions (8/15) were longer than 30 min, and the longest was 2 hours, 41 min. Closer observation of video recordings of the sessions indicated that much of the time adults were using the system for video conferencing, and children would pop in and out to read a book with a relative or chat, smile and exchange conversation. Book reading sessions with children were interspersed throughout the longer video session.

Some other families reported video communication as their primary use. The father from Family 53 (Tips Only) read to his daughter, *at lunchtime, while I was at work talking with my 2 Y.O. daughter at home. ACTUALLY we left it on all day and I could "pop-in" and see what was happening at home. It was nice to see her playing.*

A parent from Family 90 (Tips Only) elaborated, *I'd suggest marketing StoryVisit as one piece of a long-distance call between a child and a long-distance family member. We only have the opportunity for a webcam call every few weeks, and we'd like to spend most of the call catching up and letting our son have a conversation with his grandparents and dance, sing or do whatever he wants to do. StoryVisit is a nice part of such a call, but it should be thought of as one component, as opposed to the entire reason for having the call.*

These patterns suggest a design that is balanced between video conferencing and other child-appropriate activities, including storybook reading.

Overall Feelings about StoryVisit

Overall, many families saw an improvement in their experience when compared to existing communications means. Family 26 (Tips Only) wrote *It certainly is an incredible way to spend time with a child in another town.* And in the final home-visit, Family 73 (Tips Only) explained *There is clearly a lot more control than a [phone] conversation where he might be talking about whatever comes to mind. It was really fun to read a book with him. I enjoy that because it allows us to really interact more. When I ask him a question about school, he answers it and we can have a conversation, but the book sort of facilitates a little bit, within the narrow confines of the topic of the book, but still it's fun.* While not perfect, the system is beginning to meet our design goals of facilitating family communication around shared activities and content.

DISCUSSION

For most families who used StoryVisit, the system seemed to create a sense of social and emotional togetherness. Families in our home-visit group used the system repeatedly, with one requesting to keep using it past the study deadline to maintain their new family ritual. Previous work makes it clear that for families, a sense of togetherness is hard to create, and most communications media fall short of meeting young children's needs. StoryVisit seemed to provide that sense of togetherness for most of the families in our study. In this section, we'll return to the discussion items we noted earlier: the value of Elmo in video conferencing with children (and lack of value of Tips), the particular value of our system for 3 year olds, and the challenge of providing a system sufficiently engaging to encourage repeated usage.

Richer Interactions

While StoryVisit does not necessarily make home video conferencing easier for families (in terms of technicalities and logistics), it does seem to make them richer. This is evidenced, to a degree, by how much time people spent with the system. Prior ecologically-valid research on home video conferencing reported typical child engagement times of 2-3 minutes on a Skype call [1]. Families who used StoryVisit engaged in distance activities for an average of ~12 minutes, with average session length rising to 18 minutes when Elmo was present. (We note again that the presence of tips to encourage dialogic reading did not increase session times.) This indicates quite a change in families' abilities to engage young children in using video conferencing technologies. This is a long time for a preschooler to engage in *any* activity – even typical ones like co-located reading or playing with blocks – and is especially surprising considering their reading partner was not physically present.

Is such long use of a communications system sustainable for a preschooler and adult partner? We believe so, although it happened only for a few families in our trials. While many families in the web trial group stopped using the system after only a few sessions (reportedly due to technical issues such as audio quality), all families in our home study - who had technical support available - used the system repeatedly, with one family using it almost every other day for a month, and continuing to use it after the study had concluded. We believe that the combination of a more accessible interface for children and improved video conferencing infrastructure could lead to wider acceptance and effectiveness of these kinds of family communication tools.

Distance Communication for Three Year Olds

Another surprising finding is that the data makes it clear that age plays an important role in families' uptake and use of the system. A demographic sweet spot for families with children age 3 is both understandable and surprising; on the one hand, the content provided at StoryVisit was geared towards children ages 2–5, and three-year-olds were an ideal audience. But on the other hand, we are aware of only limited lab trials that indicate that sustained distance interactions with such young children is generally *possible* [14]. The fact that usage peaked for families with children age 3 shows that it is possible for families with even very young children to create meaningful connections over a distance.

Researchers have noted that children's developmental issues provide clues as to why young children are not adept with use of communications technologies [8, 14, 18]. Challenges include children's nascent theories of mind and resulting inabilities to envision other people's perspectives, as well as their preferences for action over words as means of expression. It has also been noted that the primary way to communicate with preschoolers is play, not conversation. These findings influenced our design choices in concrete ways. For example, synchronized views between Child and Reader allow the child's perspective to be consistent with the remote adult's, and the video windows of the Child and Reader are the same size to help children understand how the Reader may see them. Also, the UI is designed to be simple and appealing to adults, but also to be fun for children. Content is bright and bold, use of text is limited, and technical setup screens and supporting pages are hidden from the Child's view.

Ongoing User Experience Challenges

Despite our efforts to improve the user experience of family video conferencing, we did not do enough; families cited software, hardware and network problems, all typical for home video conferencing [1]. Logistics provided another key issue preventing more usage. And while technology problems may be solvable through better engineering or design, logistical problems can probably not be solved by technology. Apart from the home-visit families, families typically did only one or two reading sessions, and only one family had more than three reading sessions. Clearly, more can be done to make using systems like this not only more appealing but also more easily accessible.

Design Guidelines for shared family activities

Through the design and evolution of StoryVisit, we have experimented with different approaches to designing synchronous family activities over a distance. Many features seemed successful enough to use again for other activities:

- creating a fun and playful UI
- automatic reconnection upon launch
- display of content is symmetrical and synchronized
- single user can setup accounts for the whole family
- content structures activity, and layers of content can be used flexibly by adult

Content can have big influence on who uses the system, and how often it is used. Our e-books draw on characters and story lines scripted for 2-5 year olds, and our character is most popular with 2-3 year olds. Families cited content as a major factor in their use of the system. Allowing families to add their own content or connect to existing digital content libraries would likely expand the age range and usage of such a system, since it's important to have a rich library of content to share and to have that library feel personally meaningful.

We are inspired by the rich and personal family activities reported in previous studies, like a grandchild playing the trumpet for her delighted grandmother, and families kissing goodbye after a Skype call [1]. Grandparents appreciate these moments, no matter what. Can there be digitally distributed activities that all members of intergenerational families look forward to? StoryVisit is approaching the kind of activities that children request and can initiate themselves and that grandparents and other adult relatives already enjoy doing with their young relatives. We have already had children requesting books, turning book pages, and actively making choices about how they used the system. Children often touched the screen, indicating a need for more direct interfaces, with touch-enabled e-reader devices seeming the obvious platform for systems like StoryVisit. As high-bandwidth and high-performance computers are more commonly handed to children under age five, we may find that new forms of content and communications mean that young children are driving technology uptake and bringing others - perhaps even their distant adult family members - to computing technologies.

CONCLUSION

Our goal with this research has been to apply findings from studies of family video conferencing [1, 11] and shared book reading in the research lab [2, 14] to shared family activities in the real world. We have conducted in-depth qualitative interviews with four families, telephone interviews with an additional nineteen families, and have analyzed quantitative usage data about how a larger number of families "in the wild" might adopt and use such a system. By pursuing an ecologically valid, in-situ test of StoryVisit, we have begun to understand how shared activities might be brought to the real-world homes of families with young children.

Our results show that engaging young children in shared activities over a distance is possible, and that technology can help increase family engagement. Content plays a key role, with reading books together accounting for a 5-fold increase in usage times compared to prior reports of family video conferencing, and the addition of an interactive character contributing another 50% increase in usage times. Usage of this system content peaked for families with 3-year-olds, demonstrating that shared activities over a distance can be quite salient even for families with very young children. While such a result had previously been demonstrated in a lab setting with simulated "distance" [2, 14], this study shows that distance communication with very young children is possible "in the wild" with technologies that families already own today, albeit with limited repeat usage in our study. One implication of this work is that communications technologies, when designed to consider young children's developmental needs and the needs of their families, can facilitate a rewarding and sustainable experience for both the young and old.

REFERENCES

1. Ames, M., Go, J., Kaye, J. 'J.', Spasojevic, M. "Making love in the network closet: the benefits and work of family videochat." *Proc. CSCW 2010,* 145-154.
2. Ballagas, R., Raffle, H., Go, J., Revelle, G., Kaye, J., Ames, A., Horii, H., Mori, K., and Spasojevic, M. "Story time for the 21st century." *IEEE Pervasive Computing*, 9:28–36, 2010.
3. Conlin, J. "Living Apart for the Paycheck." *The New York Times*, Jan. 4, 2009.
4. Egelman, S., Brush, A.J., & Inkpen, K. Family accounts: A new paradigm for user accounts within the home environment. In *Proc. CSCW 2008,* 669-678.
5. Davies, C., Williams, D. "The Grandparent Study 2002 Report." AARP, 2002.
6. Fisch, S. M., Shulman, J., Ackerman, A., Levin, G. . "Reading between the pixels: Parent-child interaction while reading online storybooks." *Early Education and Development,* 13(4), 435-451, 2002.
7. Follmer, S. Raffle, H., Go, J., Ballagas, R., Ishii, H. "Video play: playful interactions in video conferencing for long-distance families with young children." *Proc. IDC 2010,* 49-58.
8. Freed, N., Burleson, W., Raffle, H., Ballagas, R., Newman, N. "User interfaces for tangible characters: can children connect remotely through toy perspectives?" *Proc. IDC 2010,* 69-78.
9. Hutchinson, H., Mackay, W., Westerlund, B., Bederson, B. B., Druin, A., Plaisant, C., Beaudouin-Lafon, M., Conversy, S., Evans, H., Hansen, H., Roussel. N., Eiderbäck, B. "Technology probes: inspiring design for and with families." *Proc. CHI 2003,* 17-24.
10. Johnson, W., Rickel, J., and Lester, J. "Animated pedagogical agents: Face-to-face interaction in interactive learning environments." *Int'l J. of Artificial Intelligence in Education*, 11(1):47-78. 2000.
11. Judge, T. K. and Neustaedter, C. Sharing conversation and sharing life: video conferencing in the home. *Proc. CHI 2010*, 655-658.
12. Kerr, B. M., & Mason, J. M. (1994). Awakening literacy through interactive story reading. In F. Lehr & J. Osborn (Eds.), *Reading, language, and literacy: Instruction for the twenty-first century*, (pp. 133-148). Hillsdale, NJ: Lawrence Erlbaum Associates, Inc.
13. Lester , J. Converse , S., Kahler , S., Barlow, T., Stone, B. & Bhogal, R. "The persona effect: affective impact of animated pedagogical agents." *Proc. CHI 1997,* 359-366.
14. Raffle, H., Ballagas, R., Revelle, G., Horii, H., Follmer, S., Go, J., Reardon, E., Mori, K., Kaye, J., Spasojevic, M. "Family Story Play: reading with young children (and Elmo) over a distance." *Proc. CHI 2010,* 1583-1592.
15. Vutborg R., Kjeldskov J., Vetere F., & Pedell S. "Family Storytelling for Grandparents & Grandchildren living apart." *Proc. NordiCHI 2010,* 531-540.
16. Whitehurst, G. J., Falco, F. L., Lonigan, C. J., Fischel, J. E., DeBaryshe, B. D., et al. (1988). "Accelerating language development through picture book reading." *Developmental Psychology, 24*(4), 552-559.
17. Whitehurst, G. J., Arnold, D. S., Epstein, J. N., Angell, A. L., Smith, M., & Fischel, J. E. (1994). "A picture book reading intervention in day-care and home for children from low-income families." *Developmental Psychology, 30*, 679-689.
18. Yarosh, S, Inkpen, K.M., Brush, A.J. "Video playdate: toward free play across distance." *Proc. CHI 2010,* 1251-1260.
19. Yarosh, S. Cuzzort, S. Müller, H., Abowd, G.D. "Developing a media space for remote synchronous parent-child interaction" *Proc. IDC 2009*, 97-105.
20. Zevenbergen, A. A. & Whitehurst, G. J. (2003). "Dialogic reading: A shared picture book reading intervention for preschoolers." In van Kleek, Stahl and Bauer (Eds.), *On reading books to children: Parents and teachers.* Mahwah, NJ: Lawrence Erlbaum Associates, pp. 177-200.

Family Portals: Connecting Families Through a Multifamily Media Space

Tejinder K. Judge[1], Carman Neustaedter[2], Steve Harrison[1], Andrew Blose[3]

Virginia Tech[1]
2202 Kraft Drive
Blacksburg, VA, USA

Simon Fraser University[2]
250-13450 102nd Avenue
Surrey, BC, Canada

Kodak Research Labs[3]
1999 Lake Avenue
Rochester, NY, USA

tkjudge@vt.edu, carman_neustaedter@sfu.ca, srh@vt.edu, andrew.blose@kodak.com

ABSTRACT

Video conferencing allows distance-separated family members to interact somewhat akin to being together at the same place and time. Yet most video conferencing systems are designed for phone-like calls between only two locations. Using such systems for long interactions or social gatherings with multiple families is cumbersome, if not impossible. For this reason, we wanted to explore how families would make use of a video system that permitted sharing everyday life over extended periods of time between multiple locations. We designed a media space called Family Portals that provides shared video between three locations and deployed it within the homes of six families. Results show that the media space increased feelings of connectedness and the focus on a triad, in contrast to a dyad, caused new styles of interaction to emerge. Despite this, families experienced new privacy challenges and non-adoption by some family members, not previously seen in dyadic family media spaces.

Author Keywords

Media space, domestic, families, awareness, video.

ACM Classification Keywords

H5.3. Information interfaces and presentation: Group and Organization Interfaces – *Computer-supported cooperative work*

General Terms

Design, Experimentation, Human Factors.

INTRODUCTION

Many families are separated by distance due to job or educational opportunities in different cities or simply because of lifestyle preferences. Despite this, most family members still want to remain connected and aware of each other's lives [13,21,24]. For instance, grandparents want to see their grandchildren grow up and parents want to know about the well being of their adult children [1,12,14]. People also typically want to participate in multifamily gatherings such as holiday events or birthday parties, but this is difficult to do unless one is able to travel.

Video conferencing (VC) is one technology that is increasingly being used by families to stay in contact over distance [1,12,14]. However, the inclusion of multiparty video calls in VC systems—connections between more than two sites [6]—is still in its infancy. Multiparty video calls are important for they can allow people to connect with more than a single family at one time, thereby modeling face-to-face situations even more. Yet there are also potential challenges. We do not yet have a good understanding of how such systems can support family routines, including varied privacy expectations, sharing needs, and relationship dynamics [27].

Given this, we wanted to see how we could allow multiple families to easily connect over distance with a VC system to maintain an awareness of one another, participate in shared activities, and, ultimately, feel connected by actually seeing each other. Here we turned to media spaces given their potential to easily fit into domestic life and permit long-term sharing [13]. Media spaces have been studied for dyadic (two family) connections and shown relative success [5,9,28]. What is not clear is if and how media spaces might extend beyond this to support multifamily connections.

As a first step in this direction, we explored three-way connections or triads, as the simplest multifamily case. This builds on our previous work on the Family Window [13] by moving from dyadic to multifamily connections.. We designed a three-way domestic media space called Family Portals and evaluated it through a field deployment in six families' homes. Our results illustrate the ways in which a multifamily media space changed family interaction dynamics to increase feelings of connectedness and awareness and the design features that led to this activity. We also describe the challenges faced by families in terms of privacy and non-adoption by certain family members.

RELATED WORK

Awareness of Family and Friends

People have a strong need to gather an awareness of multiple family members, loved ones, and friends' *activities*, *locations*, and *status* (e.g. health) [21,24,27]. Knowing this information helps people feel close and connected to others [21,24,27]. Preference for this awareness varies though. People like to know very detailed information about the people they live with, labeled *home inhabitants,* and those with whom they have a close relationship, called *intimate socials* [21]. Yet they desire less information about their extended contacts [21]. This information is shared using everyday technologies such as email, the telephone, or instant messaging when people are unable to meet and share information in person [21,27].

Researchers have also investigated new systems directed specifically at supporting this type of awareness sharing. Several focus on dyadic exchange between only two households [5,20,24]; however, it is not clear if and how they systems might extend to multifamily sharing (the focus of this paper). In contrast, there are also systems that directly focus on multifamily awareness. For example, messageProbe [10] and Wayve [17] supported multifamily drawing and messaging. While beneficial, neither system allowed families to participate in shared activities like they might in face-to-face situations or over VC systems [12,13].

In recent years we have seen people migrate to using social networking sites such as Facebook or Twitter to remain connected to a multitude of friends and family members all at the same time [2,11,15,16]. Studies of college students showed that users can, in theory, keep track of hundreds of contacts through one system by monitoring status messages, wall posts, and uploaded media, a process labeled as *social searching* [16]. Again, this is beneficial, however we hypothesize that such sites do not provide family members with true feelings of intimacy and closeness given the large number of contacts that one can follow and the broadcast nature of the information being exchanged.

Video in the Home

VC has also been explored in the home as a technology for supporting family communication and awareness. Studies have shown that VC allows families to easily communicate and share activities in real time and increase feelings of connectedness [1,12,14]. Yet VC systems are not typically used without challenges. Ames et al. [1] describe the work that goes into a video call: *technical work* to schedule and establish calls, *presentation work* to make family members presentable, *behavioral work* to manage children's behavior during video calls, and *scaffolding work* to aid children in participating in the video call. This additional "work" can make existing VC systems difficult for families to use.

Recently media spaces have been studied in terms of their ability to support dyadic family connections [13,23,28]. Here we differentiate between two types. First, there are media spaces used for interactions over short durations, akin to phone calls. In this category, we place media spaces like the Share Table [30] and Family Story Play [25] which both aim to support specific activity instances (e.g., reading, playing). Second, there are media spaces that are left *always-on* to provide awareness over time and sharing everyday life. Our interest falls in this category. Always-on media spaces have the potential to reduce the technical work [1] needed to establish connections since connections are ongoing. This also means that extended activities such as social gatherings are easily shared [13].

The closest media space to our current efforts is our previous work on the Family Window [13], an always-on dyadic video media space. Using it, families were able to gain availability awareness in order to time interactions and subsequently shared daily activities [13]. The Family Window saw very few privacy concerns arise, which is surprising for always-on video broadcasting from the home [13]. We found this to be true because of the close relationships shared by participant households [13].

Multiparty Media Spaces in the Workplace

Media spaces have been studied in the workplace for over two decades as a means to promote awareness and communication between non-collocated colleagues [3]. The first media space at PARC supported only a dyadic connection; however, several systems following on from this investigated multiparty connections. First, multiparty media spaces were designed to support workplace awareness and informal interactions. For example, Portholes showed updating video snapshots of media space participants and allowed users to send *targeted* messages to individuals or *broadcast* messages for all [8]. Community Bar [19] extended this to support the creation of ad-hoc groups within a larger group setting.

Second, multiparty media spaces were used for collaborative work and real time meetings between colleagues. CAVECAT [18] allowed users to interact with four colleagues simultaneously by viewing four video feeds on a split screen. Hydra [25] replaced each participant in a meeting with a video surrogate created by a camera, monitor and speaker. LiveWire [26] used voice activation to determine who was speaking and automatically represented the speaker in a "full screen" mode. According to Buxton et al. [6], multiparty VC systems in the workplace were limited in their ability to support parallel conversations and in allowing participants to selectively listen to different, parallel conversations.

This paper builds on the history of multiparty media spaces in the workplace by exploring them in the context of the home and domestic life. Here we explore targeted *vs.* broadcast messaging, full screen *vs.* screen split viewing, and varying group dynamics created by multiple families.

DESIGN OF FAMILY PORTALS

Our first step in this exploration was to design and implement a multifamily media space. We call this media space Family Portals (FP) as it contains "portals" into distant families' homes (Figure 1).

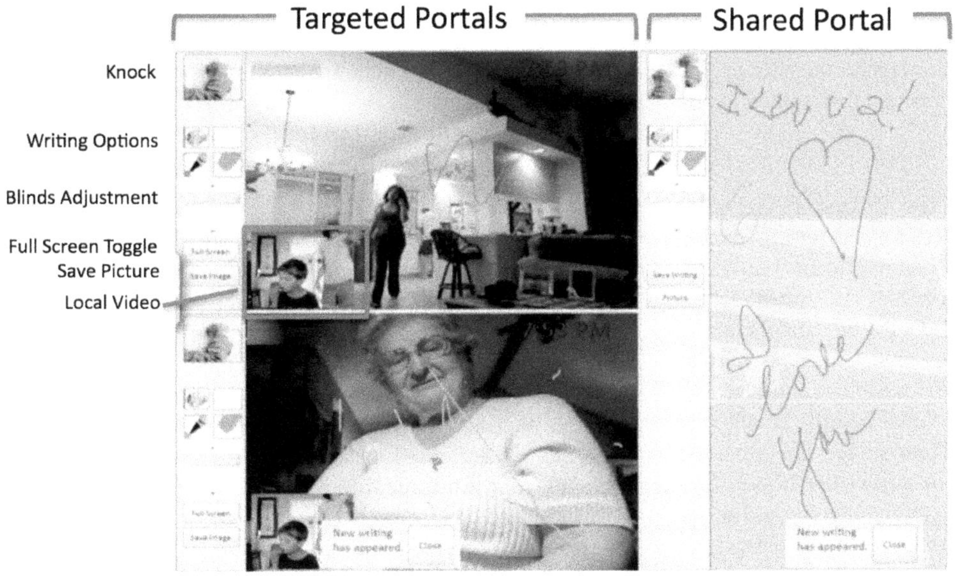

Figure 1. Family Portals.

Figure 2. Blinds halfway down at night in one home.

Figure 3. Full screen view.

Basic Design

FP is an always-on media space that provides a continuous video connection between three households. We omitted audio because we wanted to focus our investigation on video for awareness and focus on asynchronous interaction (eg. writing). Although audio is a rich medium for communication, studies have shown that audio is often more privacy intrusive than video [9,13]. As such, we focused on features that were potentially less intrusive.

FP was prototyped on a touch and pen-sensitive Tablet PC with an external webcam to simulate the idea of it being a dedicated information appliance as opposed to a computer used for multiple tasks. The dedicated device means that FP can be easily moved throughout the home depending on where family members want to share activities.

Although FP is designed to connect three families, we did not expect the families to have the same relationship with each other. For instance, a daughter connecting to both her *mother* and *sister* might not want to share the same amount and type of information with both of them. Thus we decided to provide two types of interactions–*targeted interactions* and *shared interactions*–to allow families to share information in a dyadic manner vs. a triadic manner. For this reason, as seen in Figure 1, the screen is divided into two areas: Targeted Portals on the left, and a Shared Portal on the right. We describe these next.

Targeted Portals

The left side of the screen in Figure 1 shows two Targeted Portals (top and bottom), one for each family that a local user is connecting to. The Targeted Portals are intended to allow families to interact and share information with *one* of their two remote families in a dyadic manner. This is similar to the concept of *directed* in Portholes [8]. Interactions within each Targeted Portal affect only the remote family that is associated with that Portal. Each Portal is identical in terms of its features.

Always-On Video. The main portion of each Targeted Portal shows video from the remote family's home. Video is transmitted over the Internet at a rate of one frame per second with 320 × 240 resolution, using a client-server architecture. Latency issues made it difficult to maintain a continuous connection with higher frame rates. The bottom left corner of each Targeted Portal shows the local family's video feed as seen by the remote family. This provides feedback of what is shown of one's home. Family members can obscure their video feed, as seen in Figure 2, by adjusting slate blinds using a slider on the left side of *each* Targeted Portal. This allows families to provide a different view for each remote family, if they so desire. The slow frame rate also creates an unintended privacy filter by not broadcasting in full fidelity.

Initiating Interaction. Studies of the use of video conferencing in the home noted that families need an easy and unobtrusive way to determine if the distant family is available for a video chat [12]. Users can click a *Knock* button in the top left corner of the Targeted Portal and this produces a knocking sound in the local and remote home.

Messaging. Users can leave handwritten messages for specific families by writing on top of the video in each Targeted Portal using either the stylus or one's finger. Only the target family sees the writing; thus, it is a private writing space for the two families. A notification appears in the remote home when a new message is written. Users can pick ink colors and erase writing using the icons on the left side of the Portal.

Full Screen. We also expected families to want to focus their attention on one remote family at a time, e.g., if the third family isn't home. To enable this, users can toggle between *Full Screen* and *Split Screen* views by clicking a button on the left of the Portal. In Full Screen mode, the Portal expands to cover the entire screen, as shown in Figure 3. The third family's video is minimized and displayed at the bottom right corner.

Shared Portal

The right side of Figure 1 shows the Shared Portal. It provides shared interactions intended for the entire triad. Dourish et al. [8] called this type of interaction *broadcast,* where all users of the system have access to all information. The main portion of the Shared Portal displays a whiteboard to support triadic interactions. Users can write on it to leave messages for *both* remote families. A multifamily knocking feature lets a local family knock on both remote families' portals simultaneously. The Shared Portal also contains a slider that will adjust the blinds for the local family's video. Blinds adjustments performed here affect the video that is transmitted in *both* of the Targeted Portals. This allows families to quickly show the same video feed to both remote families.

Comparison to Existing Systems

The design of FP draws from existing systems and extends them to support multifamily interaction in a media space. Family Window's knocking feature [13] and CoMeDi's blinds [7] are extended to include multifamily versions of these in the Shared Portal. CommuteBoard, messageProbe and Wayve [9,10,17] all provided a shared writing space like our Shared Portal. However, we extended this by also providing a private message board for each family in the Targeted Portals. The appropriation of these features in combination with our understanding of domestic communication, existing domestic media spaces, and multiparty workplace media spaces led to the design of FP.

FIELD EVALUATION OF FAMILY PORTALS

Following the design and implementation of FP, we conducted a field evaluation to learn how families would use the system in their daily lives, what communication and awareness practices would emerge, and what privacy concerns they would face. We recruited families using snowball sampling and advertisements in local mailing lists and web sites. Potential participants completed a screening questionnaire that asked about their communication with extended family and whom they wanted to connect to using a futuristic VC system. We selected six families (two triads) from the USA who would provide interesting and different relationship dynamics. Participating households were composed of young families, blended families, a divorcee, and retirees. Families received gift cards for participating.

Initial Interview and Setup. We first visited each family's home and interviewed them about their existing communication practices with their extended family and, more specifically, about the families they were going to connect with using FP. One family lived outside driving distance and was interviewed using Skype. At the conclusion of this interview, families were walked through the initial setup of FP on their home wireless Internet connection, asked to select a location for FP and use it as they naturally saw fit. All families were given a Tablet PC with FP application, a stand for the Tablet PC and webcam for the duration of the evaluation. The initial interview lasted 2 to 3 hours and setup took 1 to 2 hours.

Deployment and Interviews. All six families had FP within their homes over a period of eight weeks. We visited families throughout the deployment and conducted six semi-structured contextual interviews with them during this time period. The one distant family, again, was interviewed using Skype. Adults were interviewed individually (when possible) and children were interviewed with parents present. Questions focused on families' usage of FP, changes in communication, connectedness and awareness with remote families, as well as privacy concerns. Interviews occurred weekly with the exception of weeks two and four; technical difficulties discussed below caused families to not be connected with the system during these two weeks. Each family was given a diary for self-reports between interviews. We also sent emails and phoned between interviews to check for technical difficulties and to help troubleshoot problems. After the final interview at the end of eight weeks, we removed FP from families' homes.

Post-Deployment Interview. We conducted a final interview two weeks after FP had been removed from the families' homes. Questions focused on communication, connectedness and awareness of remote families compared to the eight weeks families had FP in their home.

Data Collection and Analysis. Usage data was collected through the interviews as well as self-reports in diaries given to each family. The limitation of interviews and self-reports is that participants may self-censor responses and omit details. We were able to sufficiently overcome this limitation by comparing responses between family members. All interviews were audio-recorded and handwritten notes were taken to aid analysis. In total, we acquired data from approximately 108 hours of interviews and observations across all six families. Usage of features (e.g. blinds, full screen) was logged throughout the study. Snapshots of writing on FP were also taken by the system. We used open coding to analyze the interviews and diary entries and generated codes that reflected a variety of usage patterns. These codes were combined to create themes that are reported in our results.

Caveats. Although FP was placed in families' homes for eight weeks, families were only able to use the system for an average of five weeks. Despite rigorous testing before deployment, numerous technical issues related to connectivity arose. Such issues have also been reported in other field evaluations in the home [9,24]. Nonetheless, we found that five weeks of usage was sufficient for participants to overcome novelty factors, develop patterns of use, and incorporate the system into their daily lives.

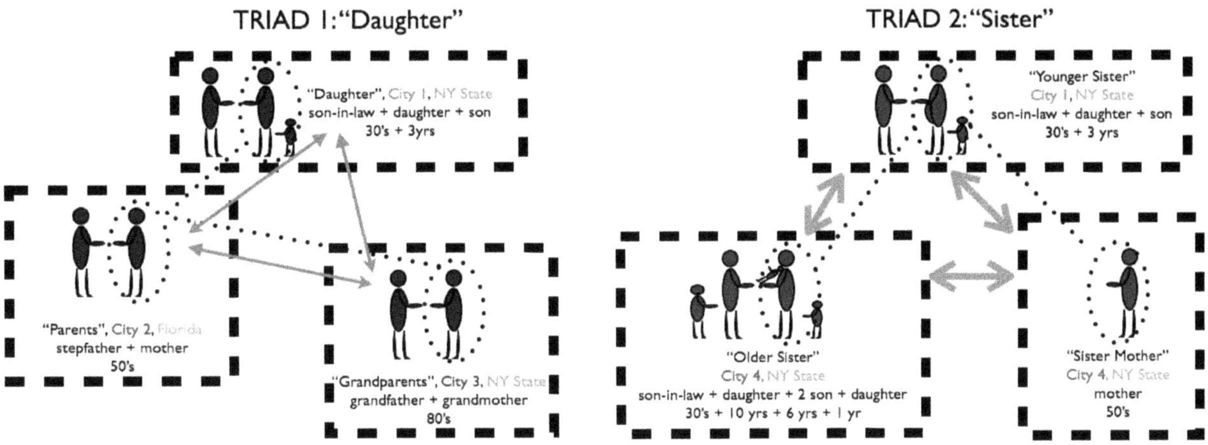

Figure 4. Participants in Triad 1 and 2. Primary users are circled and connected with dotted lines. Numbers refer to ages.

Participants. Figure 4 illustrates our participant families. Relationships are described from the point of view of the *seed family* (e.g., "Daughter", "Sister") who responded to the advertisement of the study. A seed family is connected to two *remote families*.

Triad 1 consisted of the *Daughter family*, composed of two parents and a 3-year-old son. They used FP to connect with the wife's mother and stepfather who we call the *Daughter Parents family,* and to her maternal grandparents who we call the *Daughter Grandparents family*. All three families placed their FP in their family room.

Triad 2 consisted of the *Younger Sister family*, composed of two parents and a 3-year-old son. The wife in this family was in the 8th month of her pregnancy when we started the field evaluation. They were connected to the wife's mother who we call the *Sister Mother* and to her older sister and family who we call the *Older Sister family*. Younger Sister placed her FP on their dining table, Older Sister in the home office and Sister Mother in her family room. All six families had experience using dyadic communication such as email, telephone, video chat and IM but none had experience with multiparty interactions with these tools.

RESULTS

We begin by describing the communication patterns between families prior to using FPs. Next we describe the interesting patterns of usage that occurred with FP and discuss design features that led to and supported these routines. We also discuss the features that did not meet users' needs, thereby causing workarounds to be used. Given the similarity between FP and the Family Window [13], we directly compare usage between the two systems.

Communication Prior to Using Family Portals.

Triad 1. The wife in the Daughter family and her mother were very close to one another. They phoned and emailed almost daily. She also used Skype every weekend to allow her parents to interact with her son. Although she lived within an hour's drive from her grandparents, she only communicated with them over the phone once a month, but felt guilty for not communicating more with them. The wife in the Daughter Parents family was the oldest daughter of the Daughter Grandparents. She phoned her father every morning while commuting to work and spoke to her mother once a month. The Daughter Grandparents did not like to phone their children or grandchildren because they knew they had busy lives and did not want to disturb them. They also preferred face-to-face interactions over the telephone.

Triad 2. The wife in the Younger Sister family and her mother spoke on the phone once a week and conversed via text or IM messages daily. Sister Mother lived in the same city as the Older Sister family, met them in person at least three times a week, and used IM daily. Younger Sister and Older Sister did not communicate much due to scheduling difficulties. The sisters spoke on the phone once a month and emailed or IM once a week. Both sisters wanted to communicate more with each other.

Basic Usage and Reactions

Families left FP running continuously throughout the field evaluation with the exception of downtime due to technically difficulties. Over time, FP became the focus of communication between most families. In comparison to dyadic communication, families said they preferred the three-way video provided by FP because they could connect to more families simultaneously and if one family was not available, the other would be. This provided ample opportunities for interaction. Families reported that their communication (using FP and other technology such as phone) increased during the study. Once FP was removed, communication returned to its previous pattern and families felt less connected as they could no longer see each other.

Usage and Non-Usage

The primary users in each triad were the women of the families. In Triad 1, this was the daughter, mother and grandmother. In Triad 2, it was the younger sister, older sister and their mother. This is consistent with the findings from [9], which show women are generally the "household communicators." It is also important to note that one woman in each triad answered the advertisement for our study and determined who they would like to be connected to using FP. Surprisingly, the husband in the Daughter family (Triad 1) was also a heavy user of FP. He worked from home on a daily basis and liked having people to interact with while his wife was at work and his son was at daycare. Secondary users in each household were the families' children. Younger children (3 years and younger) used FP under their parents' supervision for the first week and then on their own when they wanted to after that.

One might expect that certain individuals may not like always-on video being broadcast from their home. Findings from the Family Window showed this type of privacy concern to be of little issue when families shared a close relationship [13]. For these reasons, we were both surprised *and* not surprised, to find out that not all members of our participant households used FP or even wanted it in their home. Three adults and one child (aged 6) did not want to use FP or did not want to be captured in the video feed. We saw four reasons for this:

Intrusion. The husband in the Younger Sister family and live-in boyfriend in the Older Sister family avoided FP because they did not want to be seen by their in-laws all the time. They tried not to be captured in the video feed or moved the camera to face a different direction when in the same room as FP. Although both of them were cordial with their in-laws, they did not want to see them all the time and thought the always-on video was intrusive.

"It is like someone is staring at me all the time. Even if no one is there, I still think someone is staring at the back of my head while I am on the computer [FP is placed opposite the computer]" – Interview with Boyfriend in Older Sister family

Fear of Technology. The grandfather in the Daughter Grandparents family did not use FP because he was intimidated by the technology. After technical problems with the system, he was afraid to use FP because he was concerned he "might break it". He did, however, occasionally look over his wife's shoulder while she interacted with the remote families. Over time, he overcame his fear and sporadically "peeped," as he called it, into FP to see the remote families but he never interacted.

Satisfaction with Communication. The grandfather in the Daughter Grandparents family also told us that he was satisfied with the amount of communication he had with the remote families and did not need additional communication using FP:

"When you have 5 children, 7 grandchildren and 12 great grandchildren, you have a lot of family to keep up with." – Interview with Grandfather from Daughter Grandparents family

Lack of Closeness. The only child who did not use FP was the second child in the Older Sister family. He was Older Sister's stepson who lived with them during the weekend and with his mother on weekdays. To him FP was a connection to his *step*mother's family who he met a few times a year and was not close to.

Despite the non-adopters, we saw heavy usage by the primary and secondary users. We describe this next.

Sharing Everyday Life and Providing Awareness

The most prominent pattern of usage for FPs across all six families was to share information about each other's daily life. This emerged in two ways. First, families used the *video* feed to share information and participate in each other's daily activities. For instance, Older Sister moved FP to their kitchen one night, to allow her mother to watch her and her son work on an art project (Figure 5). Younger Sister, on the other hand, used the video to show her mother and sister the progression of her pregnancy. Because the video was always on, it was easy for her to walk up to the display and show her baby bump to her remote family.

Figure 5. Sister Mother watching Older Sister and her son work on an art project.

"They like seeing how big I am getting." – From Interview with Younger Sister

This type of sharing was also found with the Family Window [13] due to the always-on nature of the video feed.

Second, families used the shared whiteboard to share information about their *location*, *activities* and *status*, all awareness types articulated by [21]. This type of sharing was done by adults in the families. In terms of *location* and *activities*, this meant, for example, leaving messages saying where family members were going and what they planned to do that day. For *status*, it meant describing how their day was going, how they were feeling, etc. For example:

"Hi [Younger Sister]. How are you doing? What's going on? I'm seeing a Doc for gall bladder issues too. Had a sonogram. Waiting 4 results." – Older Sister's note on shared whiteboard to Younger Sister

When asked about this sharing, Older Sister commented that she would not normally share this level of detail with her sister because, by the time they had their monthly phone call, she would have forgotten the specifics. Other family members said this type of information was typically not shared with distant family members using other technology (e.g., phone, email) because it was thought of as mundane and not of interest to others [27]. The fact that it became something they *did* talk about suggests families do place value in knowing this level of detail. The increased *frequency* of information exchange led to the adults in all six families (except non-adopters) feeling more connected.

Playful Interactions

Families also had fun with FP by engaging in playful activities. This was surprising since it was not found with the Family Window [13]. Both the video feed and writing capabilities supported families' playful activities. They drew pictures, doodled, made faces, and simply had fun with each other. For instance, Older Sister who was an artist regularly drew pictures of sunsets and other scenery. The grandmother in the Daughter Parents family drew planets for her grandson who was learning about the solar system. Such activities were made possible by the shared whiteboard and multiple ink colors that families could use.

Figure 6. Children in Triad 2 interacting.

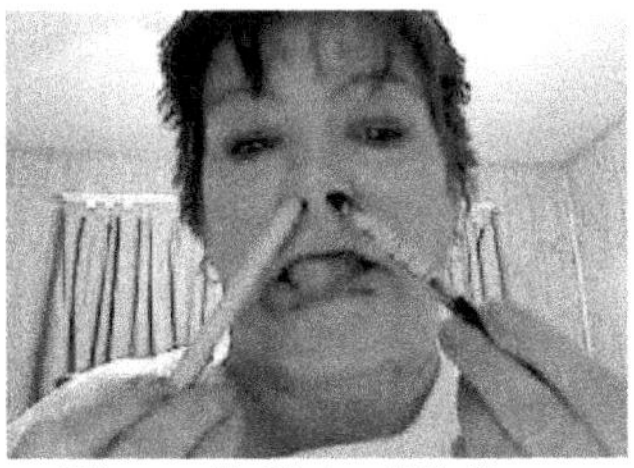

Figure 7. Sister Mother interacting with grandson.

The writing feature also provided a fun and easy way for younger children to communicate via drawings. Children in the families, such as Younger Sister's 3-year-old son, used FP to interact with his 10-year-old cousin (Older Sister's son) by drawing (Figure 6). This is similar to the way families used Wayve [17] for play, however, families said the video feed in FP enhanced this experience by allowing family members to *see* each other while interacting. This type of interaction was especially important for children as it kept them engaged long enough to interact with distant family members. This provides one solution to the problem of keeping children engaged while using VC systems [1].

Playful activities were also common between grandparents and grandchildren. For example, Sister Mother drew pictures and made funny faces while interacting with her grandson (Figure 7).

"My nanna [Sister-Mother] makes faces. She was a walrus that day. I draw on her face and she looks funny. I also drew octopus" – Interview with Older Sister's 10-year-old son

Synchronous Communication

We had designed and expected that FP would be mostly used for ambient awareness and asynchronous interactions (e.g., "checking in" on families every now and then), especially because the device was always running and available. Indeed we saw this, as previously described. However, more surprisingly, we also found that families would move into episodes of synchronous interaction where FP became the focal point for real-time communication.

Dyadic Communication

Despite FP being designed for a triad of families, as one might expect, there were many occasions where only two families were around and available for synchronous communication. Thus, a prominent use for FP was dyadic communication. These sessions were not meant to exclude the third family but typically happened serendipitously or were scheduled based on two households' availability.

There were three patterns of dyadic communication. First, families used the video in FP to see each other and supplemented the video with a phone call. This is similar to the way families used the Family Window [13]. However, the addition of a third family in the media space led to members of the third family inadvertently feeling left out on occasion. For example, the grandmother in Triad 1 occasionally saw her daughter and granddaughter talking to each other on the phone. She sometimes tried to inconspicuously get their attention by waving, but they were usually too engrossed in their conversation to notice her. This made her feel left out. This suggests design features to notify families who are conversing that another family is around and possibly available for communication.

Second, families chose to use the shared whiteboard for synchronous "chats". This is similar to findings from the Family Window [13] where families had synchronous chats by writing on the video feed. For example, the daughter in Triad 1 and her grandmother routinely had conversations this way. This was surprising because the grandmother complained about the difficulty she faced writing on FP due to her old age and left-handedness (this was awkward because the shared drawing space was on the right side). Despite that, she participated because she said it was a fun way for her to communicate with her granddaughter.

Third, we saw families starting conversations by writing on FP and then migrating the conversation to IM. This was done by families in Triad 2 who primarily communicated via IM prior to using FP. They told us it was easier for them to have long conversations via IM because they could type faster than they could write on FP.

We had expected that most dyadic communications would involve families using the full screen feature, but this happened only occasionally. Across triads, the mother in the Daughter Parents family was the primary user of the full screen feature. She used it to interact with her grandson almost every night. She enjoyed watching him play and have his bedtime snack. Interestingly, when not engaged in synchronous communication, families always left FP in split screen mode because it allowed them to see both families simultaneously. That is, they were interested in seeing *both* families throughout the day.

Multifamily Communication

As stated, serendipitous opportunities for multifamily communication are rare given a variety of schedules and likelihood of everyone being available at the same moment. Thus, most *multifamily* communication that participants told us about was asynchronous, with families responding to each other's messages throughout the day (described above). Despite this, there were several routines that emerged around multifamily synchronous communication.

Synchronous multifamily communication in Triad 1 involved video from FP supplementing three-way phone calls. These typically involved the Daughter Parents family and the Daughter Grandparents family interacting with the child in the Daughter family and happened 1-2 nights a week. The daughter and mother scheduled three-way phone calls ahead of time and informed the grandmother about these by leaving a note on the shared whiteboard. They did this because they felt they needed to make an effort to include the grandmother in their interactions. However, despite the scheduled sessions, the grandmother sometimes forgot about them.

Synchronous multifamily communication in Triad 1 also included chat sessions on the shared whiteboard between the daughter, mother and grandmother. These sessions were typically impromptu. They reported that this happened 1-2 nights a week and that their chats lasted around 30 minutes. These chat sessions usually happened at night after the child in the Daughter family was asleep. According to them, they did this because it was a fun activity for them to engage in with each other, it was relaxing after a long day and they could combine this activity with other household chores such as preparing lunches and folding laundry.

"It is nice to have an adult conversation with my mother and grandmother without being distracted by [son]" – Interview with Wife from Daughter family

"It is fun and relaxing to write back and forth. Sometimes I sit down the whole time and other times I am around the kitchen making lunches [for the next day]" – Interview with Mother from Daughter Parents family

On the other hand, Triad 2 only had multifamily interactions twice during the entire evaluation. The first time was when there was an earthquake and the younger sister, older sister, and their mother wrote back and forth on FP about the tremor. The second instance was impromptu when the older sister saw both her younger sister and mother on FP. This triad did not have many multifamily interactions because their schedules were simply too varied.

Privacy

Throughout their use of FP, families did not tell us they were concerned about the always-on video or multifamily connection being an infringement on their privacy (except for the non-adopters). This was because they picked the families that they wanted to connect to and families who they had close relationships with. By choosing who to connect to, families were regulating their *autonomy* [4]. There were, however, instances of intrusion on family members' solitude and confidentiality, even for adopters.

Solitude

Although families typically used the always-on video or availability messages to determine a remote family's availability for interaction, there were instances of intrusion on a family's solitude (as defined by Boyle et al. [4]). For example, one evening, the Older Sister in Triad 2 was cooking dinner when her 1-year-old daughter started crying. She was trying to pacify her daughter and prevent food on the stove from burning when Sister Mother started knocking incessantly on FP. Sister Mother had just arrived home from work and wanted to interact with Older Sister's family. Sister Mother was annoyed because nobody responded to her knocks when she knew they were home and wrote on FP,

"STOP ignoring me" – Note from Sister Mother to Older Sister

Older Sister continued ignoring the knocks but was annoyed at her mother. A few hours later, when the kids were in bed and she was no longer annoyed, she called her mother and explained the situation.

"If there was sound [audio] in the system I would have yelled at my mum. How does she expect me to handle so many things at once?" – Interview with Older Sister about Sister Mother

Such incidents are not easily avoidable if one family has the expectation that the other family is home at a certain time and thus available. The location of FP could help in this instance. Older Sister placed her FP in the home office, which is separated from the kitchen by the family room. If she had placed her FP in the kitchen, her mother could have seen that she was busy and might not have interrupted. Yet this would have only worked for situations in the kitchen.

Confidentiality

An always-on media space leads to privacy risks over confidentiality: remote families seeing more that one may intend [4]. However, families were able to control what the remote families were viewing by determining the location of FP and the position of the camera. For example, Younger Sister placed FP on their dining table with both the tablet and webcam facing the wall. She would occasionally move the webcam to point towards the family room when she and her son were in there. She did not report privacy concerns with FP because the location she picked, consciously or unconsciously, regulated her confidentiality. It is also interesting to note that both Younger and Older Sister, whose respective husband and boyfriend were not adopters of the system, placed FP in a non-central location in their home (i.e. dining table & home office). The remaining four families placed FP in their family room.

Families preferred hardware options to control confidentiality instead of the software option provided in FP (Figure 2). All families used the blinds less than three times during the field evaluation. Instead, when concerned about confidentiality, some families moved the webcam or placed inanimate objects in front of the webcam. This happened most often in Triad 2. For instance, when Older Sister and Sister Mother complained that they only saw the wall in Younger Sister's home, she started placing objects such as her son's new toy or a bowl of cherries so they would have something to look at. While Younger Sister may have done this intentionally for playful purposes, the unintentional effect was that she was regulating her and her family's confidentiality by selecting objects that would be visible to the remote families.

Although there were mixed reactions about FP not containing audio, families speculated that always-on audio would be overly intrusive and would have resulted in them not leaving FP turned on all the time. They were concerned about remote families overhearing conversations about topics such as finances and health or even conversations regarding the remote families. Families wanted the option to turn audio on and off as desired. Yet even with this option, there was concern that people might forget to turn the audio off which could result in remote families overhearing private conversations.

DISCUSSION AND CONCLUSIONS

This research has revealed key routines surrounding the use of a multifamily media space. First, we found that, as expected, a multifamily media space supports the same primary routine as a dyadic family media space [14]: providing an awareness of families' lives and sharing of activities. Yet the addition of a dedicated writing area in FP resulted in families writing more about their daily life and sharing more information. This suggests that domestic awareness systems are best when coupled with video, which permits implicit sharing of life, with interaction techniques that allow explicit sharing (e.g., writing).

We also saw different patterns of usage emerge that were not found with always-on dyadic media spaces [14]. The most striking was that not all family members adopted and used the system. The successful adoption of FP in a household was greatly dependent on the relationship between members of each household. We had expected family members to form a closed circle of contacts where all wanted to stay in contact with one another. Instead, this naïve assumption proved false. Even within a closed network of families, there will be certain family members with differing awareness and communication needs. This was exposed by having more families connected as part of a media space (as compared to [14]).

We found that adopters were comfortable with and valued increased degrees of awareness beyond selective information. Initially, the adopters could be labeled as intimate socials as defined by [23]. However, while using FP, the adopters started sharing more information and even started participating in activities in each other's homes. This changed their relationship to resemble inhabitants of the same home, which is a remarkable change in families' patterns of communication, awareness, and connectedness. Even though the adopters in our families liked this, we expect that some families may find this to be overwhelming at times and unnecessary.

The previous study of the Family Window did not find that playful activities were a common occurrence for family pairs [13]. Our observation of such activities could simply be because of idiosyncrasies of the families or differences in demographics, yet we also believe it was, at least in part, due to the introduction of a third family. Even though the majority of ludic interactions were dyadic, because there were more users, there were more opportunities for interaction and a more playful environment arose. This may be similar to differences in social dynamics when comparing a two-person conversation to a multi-person gathering, which typically has more banter and interactions.

Compared to a dyadic media space like the Family Window [13], triadic synchronous communication did not happen often in FP due to families' varied schedules and availability. Multifamily synchronous communication needed to be scheduled and was not typically impromptu. This contrasts the use of workplace media spaces which encourage impromptu and serendipitous communication. It also suggests design features are needed in a multifamily media space to better support availability awareness. This is difficult because families aren't usually in one location the way they might be at work. Providing multiple media space links throughout the home is a potential solution, yet this would increase privacy risk. Another possibility is to provide additional information such as calendars to determine likely availability as opposed to simply video feeds. Either way, more investigation is needed.

Interestingly, there was no difference in what families shared with each of the two remote families through video. Families left the video going nearly all the time and both remote families saw the same thing, despite options to obscure one family's feed and not the other's. Families also left the video in split screen mode most of the time. Families reported issues over confidentiality breech as a result of the video capturing, but this was not particular to one remote family over the other. Such breeches were not found in prior dyadic media space studies [13]. To circumvent these issues, families utilized everyday objects and changed the camera's direction rather than using our software approach of blinds. This suggests that hardware privacy controls are more suitable for the home as opposed to software fixes such as blinds, blur filters, or avatars [7,22]. Given this preference though, what we don't know is if multiple cameras were present (one per remote family), would families choose the same camera view for each remote family. We suspect this to *not* be the case given our results, but it suggests further exploration.

We have studied triadic multifamily connections as a first step in exploring multifamily media spaces. We expect that our results generalize to other triadic family connections, in particular to those situations where each family has at least one member who has a strong need and desire to connect with the other families. Cases where two of the families do not have a reason to connect, despite sharing a need to connect with the same third family, will present different situations, likely with exacerbated privacy challenges. For example, imagine an adult child's family connecting with parents *and* in-laws where the two sets of parents have no need to connect. We also expect that moving beyond a triad to connect four or more families will present even more privacy challenges and, in these situations, the need to focus video on a subset of families will increase. This should be studied in future explorations.

ACKNOWLEDGMENTS

This research was generously funded by Kodak. We thank Rodney Miller, Andrew Kurtz, Elena Fedorovskaya, Manuel Perez, Dennis Kafura, Deborah Tatar, and Andrea Kavanaugh for valuable feedback on this work. We also thank all the families involved in the evaluation for sharing their experiences with FP and for their valuable feedback.

REFERENCES

1. Ames, M.G., Go, J., Kaye, J.J. and Spasojevic, M., Making love in the network closet: the benefits and work of family videochat. *Proc. CSCW 2010*, ACM.
2. Barkhuus, L. and Tashiro, J., Student Socialization in the Age of Facebook. *Proc. CHI 2010*, ACM.
3. Bly, S., Harrison, S. and Irwin, S. Media Spaces: Bringing People Together In A Video, Audio, And Computing Environment. *Communications of the ACM, 36* (1), (1993).
4. Boyle, M., Neustaedter, C. and Greenberg, S. Privacy Factors in Video-Based Media Spaces. In *Media Space: 20+ Years of MediatedLife*, Springer, (2009).
5. Brush, A.J., Inkpen, K. and Tee, K., SPARCS: Exploring Sharing Suggestions to Enhance Family Connectedness. *Proc. CSCW 2008*, ACM.
6. Buxton, W., Sellen, A. and Sheasby, M. Interfaces for multiparty video conferencing. In *Video-Mediated Communication*, Lawrence Erlbaum Associates, Mahwah, New Jersey, (1997).
7. Coutaz, J., Bérard, F., Carraux, E. and Crowley, J., Early experience with the mediaspace CoMedi. *Proc. IFIP Working Conference on Engineering for Human-Computer Interaction (EHCI 98).*
8. Dourish, P. and Bly, S., Portholes: supporting awareness in a distributed work group. *Proc. CHI 1992*, ACM.
9. Hindus, D., Mainwaring, S., Leduc, N., Hagstr, A. and Bayley, O., Casablanca: designing social communication devices for the home. *Proc. CHI 2001*, ACM.
10. Hutchinson, H., Mackay, W., Westerlund, B., Bederson, B., Druin, A., Plaisant, C., Beaudouin-Lafon, M., Conversy, S., Evans, H., Hansen, H., Roussel, N. and Eiderback, B., Technology probes: inspiring design for and with families. *Proc. CHI 2003*, ACM.
11. Joinson, A.N., 'Looking at', 'Looking up' or 'keeping up with' People? Motives and Uses of Facebook. *Proc. CHI 2008*, ACM.
12. Judge, T.K. and Neustaedter, C., Sharing Conversation and Sharing Life: Video Conferencing in the Home. *Proc. CHI 2010*, ACM.
13. Judge, T.K., Neustaedter, C. and Kurtz, A., The Family Window: The Design and Evaluation of a Domestic Media Space. *Proc. CHI 2010*, ACM.
14. Kirk, D.S., Sellen, A. and Cao, X., Home video communication. *Proc. CSCW 2010*, ACM.
15. Lampe, C., Ellison, N. and Steinfield, C., A Face(book) in the Crowd: Social Searching vs. Social Browsing. *Proc. CSCW 2006*, ACM.
16. Lampe, C., Ellison, N.B. and Steinfield, C., Changes in Use and Perception of Facebook. *Proc. CSCW 2008*, ACM.
17. Lindley, S., Harper, R. and Sellen, A., Designing a technological playground: a field study of the emergence of play in household messaging. *Proc. CHI 2010*, ACM.
18. Mantei, M., Baecker, R., Sellen, A., Buxton, W., Milligan, T. and Wellman, B., Experiences in the use of a media space. *Proc. CHI 1991*, ACM.
19. McEwan, G. and Greenberg, S., Supporting social worlds with Community Bar. *Proc. GROUP 2005*, ACM.
20. Mynatt, E., Rowan, J., Craighill, S. and Jacobs, A., Digital Family Portraits: supporting peace of mind for extended family members. *Proc. CHI 2001*, ACM.
21. Neustaedter, C., Elliot, K. and Greenberg, S., Interpersonal awareness in the domestic realm. *Proc. OzCHI 2006*, ACM.
22. Neustaedter, C., Greenberg, S. and Boyle, M. Blur filtration fails to preserve privacy for home-based video conferencing. *ACM ToCHI 13* (1), (2006).
23. Raffle, H., Ballagas, R., Revelle, G., Horii, H., Follmer, S., Go, J., Reardon, E., Mori, K., Kaye, J. and Spasojevic, M., Family Story Play: reading with young children (and Elmo) over a distance. *Proc. CHI 2010*, ACM.
24. Romero, N., Markopoulos, P., Baren, J., Ruyter, B., Ijsselsteijn, W. and Farshchian, B. Connecting the family with awareness systems. *Personal Ubiquitous Computing, 11* (4), (2007).
25. Sellen, A., Buxton, B. and Arnott, J., Using spatial cues to improve videoconferencing. *Proc. CHI '92*, ACM.
26. Sheasby, M. Brady Bunch and the LiveWire engine: Peripheral awareness in video conferencing, *MSc thesis*, Dept. of Computer Science, University of Toronto, (1995).
27. Tee, K., Brush, A.J. and Inkpen, K. Exploring communication and sharing between extended families. *Int. Journal of Human-Computer Studies, 67* (2), (2009).
28. Yarosh, S., Cuzzort, S., Mueller, H. and Abowd, G.D., Developing a media space for remote synchronous parent-child interaction. *Proc. IDC 2009*, ACM.

The Information Flaneur: A Fresh Look at Information Seeking

Marian Dörk, Sheelagh Carpendale, Carey Williamson
Department of Computer Science, University of Calgary, Calgary, Alberta, Canada
{mdoerk, sheelagh, carey}@ucalgary.ca

ABSTRACT
We introduce the information flaneur as a new human-centred view on information seeking that is grounded in interdisciplinary research. We use the metaphor of the urban flaneur making sense of a city as an inspiring lens that brings together diverse perspectives. These perspectives shift information seeking towards a more optimistic outlook: the information flaneur represents curious, creative, and critical information seeking. The resulting information-seeking model conceptualizes the interrelated nature between information activities and experiences as a continuum between horizontal exploration and vertical immersion. Motivated by enabling technological trends and inspired by the information flaneur, we present explorability as a new guiding principle for design and raise research challenges regarding the representation of information abstractions and details.

Author Keywords
Information seeking, human-computer interaction, flaneur.

ACM Classification Keywords
H.5.2 Information Interfaces and Presentation: Miscellaneous

General Terms
Design, Human Factors.

INTRODUCTION
The World Wide Web has stimulated social and technological transformations that are arguably comparable to those from the invention of the printing press. Both inventions have triggered strikingly similar reactions. Scholars of that historical era were worried about keeping up with the rapid publication of books, yet were also intrigued by growing information access [45]. Today's overabundance of digital information—as exemplified by our email inboxes, news feeds, and web search results—can be viewed similarly, as both overwhelming information overload and fascinating information access. This issue is triggering research across a wide variety of fields such as cognitive science, psychology, library information science, human-computer interaction, and information visualization.

In this paper, we draw upon this wealth of related research to conceptualize a new approach to information seeking. While our paper is philosophical in flavour, many of the ideas are well-grounded in prior inter-disciplinary research, which we highlight and quote throughout the paper. We also argue that many of the trends in the Web today, including increased browser functionality, enriched media formats, semantic data, and user mobility, provide the enabling technologies for a fresh approach to information seeking, particularly one that better utilizes human perceptual and cognitive skills.

Information seeking research strives for a human-centred understanding of the search process [4, 14, 35, 48, 63]. However, even though information seeking research is intentionally focused on the human aspects, they are typically contextualized along tasks—considering utilitarian goals of overcoming information needs, knowledge gaps, uncertainty, and problems [5, 14, 35, 48]. Despite the use of casual terms like 'surfing', traditional information seeking is predominantly a 'serious' endeavour, where factors such as accuracy and efficiency are crucial. Besides a few studies [21, 46], 'casual' perspectives that incorporate play and pleasure, for example, are rarely considered in information seeking research.

Research on everyday [40, 48], serendipitous [18, 46, 62], and exploratory [39, 61] information seeking suggests that it is time to go beyond keyword search and '10 blue links' [7]. To make this shift, a holistic and positive perspective on information seeking is needed that brings together the mind, heart, senses, and soul of the information seeker. Recent work on aesthetics in human-computer interaction [57] and visualization [44] provides such a perspective, highlighting experience, imagination, and reflection as important factors in interface design. We aim to explore these experience-based considerations in the context of information seeking.

In this work, we introduce the *information flaneur* as a new way of thinking about information seeking. The information flaneur is informed by three human-centred perspectives and inspired by the literary figure of the urban flaneur. The human-centred perspectives provide established insights about cognitive, perceptual, and affective aspects of information seeking. The flaneur is an urban wanderer, who leisurely walks through streets and squares interpreting and re-imagining the city [6]. Following the flaneur's attitude toward the city, the information flaneur sees beauty and meaning in growing information spaces. By envisioning the information flaneur as a curious, creative, and critical persona, we promote a shift from negative concepts such as needs and problems towards positive information experiences [30].

As concrete examples, consider reading news, following microblogs, and exploring a library catalog. How could interfaces be designed to support open-ended and enjoyable interaction with overviews of entire information spaces and details of particular resources? The information flaneur provides a vision to design such interfaces. We formulate a model for information seeking that conceptualizes interaction with information spaces at varying levels of exploration and immersion. Motivated by enabling technological trends and inspired by the information flaneur, we present explorability as a new guiding principle for design and raise research challenges regarding information abstraction and detail.

PREMISES

We first outline three basic premises that guide this work. Since information spaces form the backdrop of many human activities today they have a dual complexity, concerning both their technical realization and their social adoption. On the one hand, growing information spaces raise technological challenges around scale, heterogeneity, and dynamics that are driving many innovations in computer science. On the other hand, growing information spaces imply a social complexity with regard to communities and their representation, which is typically addressed in the humanities and social sciences. This dual nature between technical challenges and social implications is seldom considered in concert. For example, search can be seen as an engineering challenge to optimize precision and recall, yet it is important to realize that rankings can also have embedded values with social or political ramifications [23]. Following from this, we posit that *information spaces and their interfaces are not inevitable technical solutions, but cultural artefacts that need to be open for reflection, critique, and appropriation.*

To develop a holistic view of information seeking, we take aesthetics as an analytical basis. While there is no universal definition, a literature survey of aesthetics in computer science by Udsen and Jørgensen reveals four main approaches: 'cultural', 'functionalist', 'experience-based', and 'techno-futurist' [57]. The experience-based approach generally rejects the primacy of utilitarian considerations in favour of a wider angle that includes emotions of enjoyment and surprise. In the context of information seeking, where problem-oriented paradigms such as Kuhlthau's information search process [35] are prevalent, aesthetic considerations have been largely absent. *Information seeking is an inherently complex human experience that includes a wide range of emotions and motivations beyond a particular problem or need.*

The Web, arguably the most significant information space today, is undergoing considerable transformations that enable entirely new ways for information seeking. In particular, developments around web-based semantics, graphics, and interaction allow new ways for exploring information. More and more structured data are embedded into existing web pages [33] and even entire information spaces such as the Wikipedia [3] are exposed as semantic information spaces. With the HTML standard maturing [58], rich interactive graphics (bitmap and vector) are becoming natively supported by web browsers. The Web is increasingly accessed via mobile devices [51], so that input methods are diversifying considerably, including touch input and implicit input such as location and orientation. While it will take some years until these developments affect the majority of web users, *these ongoing and projected technological trends on the Web enable the design of novel interfaces for exploring growing information spaces* (see Figure 1).

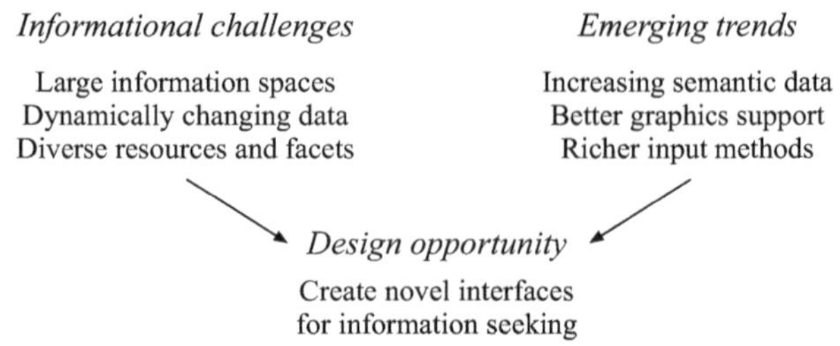

Figure 1. Emerging trends in the Web and the informational challenges of growing information spaces provide a unique design opportunity.

THE FLANEUR

The computing and information sciences are shaped by analogies derived from work settings such as offices and libraries. This leads to an emphasis of corresponding metaphors such as the desktop with its files and folders and databases with indices and keys. Our goal is to reach beyond these analogies and develop a new perspective that highlights curiosity, reflection, and imagination. For this, we assume that cities can be places of creative exploration and borrow the concept of the flaneur from cultural studies as an inspiring, human-centric perspective that can help us envision novel interfaces that are more playful, pleasurable, and provoking.

Observer and Painter of the Modern City

Curious Explorer

Derived from the French masculine noun 'flâneur', the flaneur is an urban character who makes himself at home in the boulevards, arcades, and cafes of Paris in the 1840s [6]. The flaneur appears to have no goal; rather, experiencing city life is his primary aim. Without becoming fully part of it, he passes through squares and crowds making sense of the city. While the cityscape may be teeming with crowds and commerce, the flaneur opens his senses and paints his own picture of the city [6]. The growing disparity between the large city population and the individual makes it unlikely to meet personal acquaintances by chance [6]. While city life becomes more accelerated, the flaneur keeps a leisurely pace, resisting the growing speed of emerging capitalism. The flaneur moves "through space and among the people with a viscosity that both enables and privileges vision" [29]. He explores the city following "whatever cue, or indeed clue, that the streets offer as enticement to fascination" [29].

Critical Spectator

The flaneur also has a critical side that allows him to create his sense of what is happening around him. Fascinated by the commercial spectacle, he is also aware of the accompanying social realities [6]. The approach of the flaneur toward the city can be seen as a critical method of seeing modernity, "an analytic form, a narrative device, an attitude towards knowledge and its social context" [29]. The flaneur can be seen as a contradictory figure torn between fascination and rejection. While he sees poetry and beauty in the urban landscape, he is also a cultural critic resisting the commercialization and acceleration by taking his time and "walking out of step" [29]. One can see in him the growing opposition to the late-modern city that becomes more "rational, predictable, visually coherent, but emotionally alienating" [22].

Creative Mind

The flaneur's critique of urban alienation is accompanied by a creative "aestheticisation of everyday life" [29]. Viewing the urban story as epic heterogeneity, the flaneur is an interpreter making the "urban landscape legible and meaningful" [22]. While there was no particular flaneur who came to fame for his artistic works, one can see in the flaneur a collective "spectator and depicter of modern life" [29]. An avant-gardist interpretation of the flaneur sees in him "radical creativity" dismantling, re-assembling, and re-imagining the urban form, while being "deliberately selective in focus and aestheticizing in technique" [22]. Instead of turning the world into a set of categories, the flaneur has the unique "capacity to relate to the world through multiple facades" [22].

The Flaneur and Information Seeking

There are several striking similarities between growing cities of the 19th century and today's information spaces, especially with regard to the relation between the individual and the whole (see Figure 2). As cities have become the cultural backdrops of daily activities for the majority of people in the world, digital information spaces increasingly assume a similar role. In the following, we briefly highlight growth, significance, and struggles as important commonalities:

- *Growth.* The city of the flaneur and today's information spaces continuously grow. In both cases, there is a significant discrepancy between the individual and the disproportionately large—urban or digital—environment.
- *Significance.* Like the late-modern city can be seen as a grandiose cultural artefact, information spaces arguably form the culturally significant phenomenon of our times. They are becoming an important context for our daily activities as part of work, play, and community.
- *Conflict.* Cities and information spaces are also contexts for social struggle and negotiation. Urban issues such as acceleration and alienation do not remain uncontested. Similarly, information spaces pose issues such as copyright, network neutrality, and information poverty.

Considering these parallels between cities and information spaces, we see the flaneur as a lens through which to envision new perspectives on information seeking. We are particularly interested in his exploratory mindset. In order to experience the city, the flaneur does not methodically navigate streets, checking each edifice like a building inspector in search of code violations. Nor does the flaneur hastily interrogate each city-dweller, like a police officer in search of a thief. Because the flaneur does not accurately scrutinize everything that crosses his path, he is able to sense what city life is about. The flaneur is the embodiment of exploration and serendipity, while the police officer and building inspector personify traditional search and browsing.

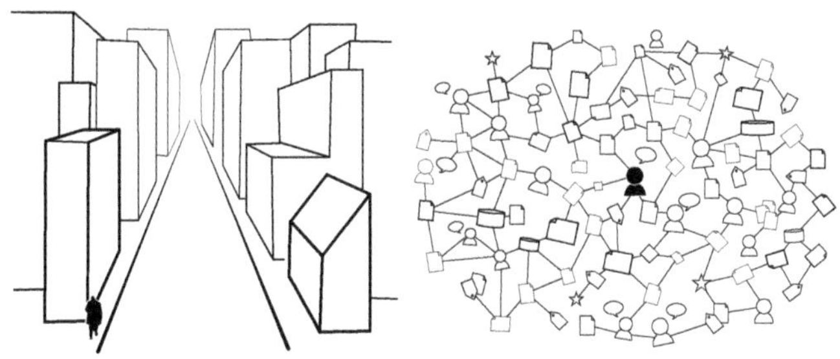

Figure 2. The relationship between a flaneur and the large city (left) bears some similarity to the relation between information seekers and growing information spaces (right).

HUMAN-CENTRED PERSPECTIVES

In order to gain a better understanding of information seeking, we draw upon interdisciplinary research on cognitive, perceptual, and affective perspectives. We are particularly interested in empirical insight informing novel interfaces.

Information Behaviour

Information seeking has been conceptualized using a range of models. An early attempt to describe information seekers was the analogy of the *informavore*, a living being whose "mind survives by ingesting information" from the surrounding world [41]. Dervin's notion of *sense making* focuses on the interaction with such a world through situations and structures [14]. Important premises are that "reality is neither complete nor constant" and that information is not "independent of and external to human beings" [14]. Information seekers are creators of the world engaging in a "circling of reality" including a multitude of observations and perspectives. Central to Dervin's approach are discontinuities in the real world and gaps in the knowledge of the information seeker. The challenge is to help information seekers turn information gaps and discontinuities into sense-making opportunities. Bates characterized interaction with online information systems as berrypicking, an evolving search using a wide variety of sources and techniques [4].

Since early on, *searching and browsing* were identified as basic forms of information seeking. While the former is typically characterized as purposeful and goal-directed the latter is seen as more open and casual. This distinction finds resemblance in different types of reading as either locating information towards a certain task or open-ended reading for general comprehension [25]. In order to support varying degrees of goal orientation in the browsing of online information, a retrieval system needs to provide adequate information structures and interaction techniques [12]. Conceptually browsing can be seen as "movement in a connected space" [37] and as the "scanning [of] its content (objects or representations) and/or structure, possibly resulting in awareness of unexpected or new content or paths" [9]. Toms has shown how a retrieval system's information representation and an information seeker's needs are highly influential on the browsing process [54, 55].

Kuhlthau's *information search process* is a linear model that describes information seeking as a progression of stages for the information seeker's feelings, thoughts, and actions [35]. In an information search process, a person starts out with vague thoughts and feelings of uncertainty, and then moves towards clearer, more focused thoughts and feelings of confidence and satisfaction. Kuhlthau highlighted a conceptual mismatch between a person's information problems ("uncertainty and confusion") and a system's view of information ("certainty and order"). Based on an interview study of 45 interdisciplinary researchers, the linear nature of information seeking has been disputed and contrasted with a non-linear model capturing three cognitive processes: opening, orientation, and consolidation [19].

Another line of research considered the costs involved in sense-making tasks, in particular with regard to the use and cost of external representations [47]. Following from this, *information foraging* describes how the searcher weighs the cost of retrieving a given resource against its perceived information value [43]. One approach to indicate the potential value of information is to enrich result lists with visual cues, such as *information scents* [10], which guide the information seeker from one resource to the next. Other forms of information seeking include monitoring and recommending information (via a system or person). Information streams on community sites such as Digg and Twitter allow for hybrids between recommending and monitoring.

Orientation

An important aspect of information seeking is having a sense of *orientation* (i.e., where one is, and where one seeks to go next). The notion of orientation combines a sense of overview (having an idea of the lay of the information landscape, in a map-like fashion) and direction (having an idea of where one has been, how to move forward, and how to return). In an information space, this notion of map and directionality typically refers to an information need or interest. A diary study on email, file, and web search revealed *orienteering* as an information seeking style in its own right that includes small situated steps toward a target [53]. Situated information seeking required less cognitive effort than explicit search, and also provided the searcher with a sense of context, control, and trust. This finding suggests that stepwise interactions can help information seekers gain a greater sense of orientation. However, existing search interfaces often exhibit abrupt changes of context between result lists. The challenge is to design search interfaces that help information seekers gain and maintain a sense of orientation.

Serendipity

Occasionally, we find interesting and inspiring information by accident. That is, we did not explicitly look for it, or expect to find it. This property is referred to as *serendipity*. In several studies on people's information practices, it has been observed that serendipitous information encountering constitutes a key component of acquiring relevant information and resources. For example, a study on the information practices of 202 elderly people revealed how participants typically learned important information from family, friends, and media without actively seeking it [62]. A study of 194 people reading books for pleasure has shown how book readers actively monitored libraries, magazines, and their friends, in order to increase the probability of information encounters [46]. A study on the information practices of interdisciplinary researchers has shown how 45 researchers regarded serendipity as a purposive activity [20]. The authors suggest that information systems should help the information seeker develop a mind that is open towards new information, encouraging people to "step back and take a broader view" [20]. These studies provide interesting insight into how people engage in open-ended information practices that help keep them informed, while encountering new information, and cultivating an open mind. However, existing interfaces centred around keyword search and filtering have been identified as a threat to such serendipitous information encounters [20, 49]. Approaches to designing for serendipitous information encountering include similarity-based suggestions [54] and visual information surrogates [32].

Exploratory Search

Exploratory search is an attempt to broaden information seeking from simple lookup towards knowledge building [39], aiming to support "users [to] explore, overcome uncertainty, and learn" [60] without specific questions or tasks in mind. The issue is how to create interfaces that help the searcher freely engage in information exploration. While there are few interaction techniques or approaches that are explicitly designed to support exploratory search, faceted navigation is a notable exception. *Faceted navigation* could be viewed as an exploratory search technique because it provides the searcher with multiple ways to navigate an information space without entering explicit search queries [17]. A comparative usability study with 32 art students has shown higher levels of confidence, satisfaction, and recall with a faceted versus a search-based interface [66]. Researchers observed how the facets on the start page would provide "ideas about what to search for". In another study, eye gazing information from 18 university students using a faceted library interface indicated that the facets were crucial during the exploration process [36]. The faceted interface helped the study participants to orient themselves in an unfamiliar information space, and provided guidance for proceeding with their search.

Everyday Life

Information seeking is often portrayed as an activity carried out by knowledge workers interacting with information systems. However, there is a wider range of information practices in everyday life. An interview-based study with 11 workers and 11 teachers from Finland has revealed interesting insights into everyday information seeking [48]. Participants sought both *orienting* and *practical* information, with the former referring to finding appropriate or relevant sources and the latter consuming the actual information. A study on the information practices of 19 women pregnant with twins has shown how participants engage in two information seeking stages: *connecting* and *interacting* [40]. During the connecting stage, participants established an association with people, locations, and institutions, which gradually led into the interacting stage, during which they actually requested or encountered information. One can see parallels between these two studies, considering the connecting stage as a way to find orienting information and the interacting stage to access practical information. An interesting question is how novel interfaces could support this dual nature found in everyday information seeking.

Visual Perception

While our perceptual system was trained by our distant ancestors looking for food and predators, we are now exploring how to utilize our vision for today's challenges.

Element Detection

An interesting aspect of visual perception is the ability to rapidly discern certain elements based on different visual features. Early research attributed this ability to *preattentive* processing, which functions across the whole visual field in parallel, followed by attentive processing that works serially on individual locations [56]. More recent research associates preattentive processing with higher-level more attentive functions, as part of a two-way mechanism [64]. Experiments utilizing our preattentive capabilities for visualization show that certain perceptual tasks can be accelerated, such as element detection, grouping, and value estimation [27]. Further studies on reaction time during visual search have shown that previously scanned locations within a scene have a slower response time than those not yet attended [34]. This phenomenon, called *inhibition of return*, explains how our perceptual system relishes novel information, and thus facilitates visual foraging behaviour [59]. These studies on preattentive processing and inhibition of return provide important insight into how our perceptual system favours both visually salient and newer elements. This has interesting implications for the design of novel information seeking interfaces.

Visual Momentum

Search interfaces are characterized by several discrete display changes. That is, a changed query is often followed by a blank screen, and then another screen with the new search results. The cognitive experience of display changes can be examined using visual momentum as the reciprocal of "mental effort required to place a new display into the context of the total data base and the user's information needs." [65]. Higher levels of visual momentum, i. e., less mental effort, can be achieved by providing more gradual display transitions, helping the viewer to comprehend the new display state more quickly. Current search interfaces have low visual momentum, since they require a lot of mental effort to relate successive displays. Recurring results are only indicated if they were actively visited, which does not include those items that a searcher has already mentally discarded on a previous screen. Relatively established techniques such as animated transitions, detail-on-demand overlays, and zoomable interfaces improve visual momentum.

Information Visualization

Result listings typically convey a ranking, which is often opaque to the information seeker, who does not know the criteria behind the ordering of selections portrayed. On the other hand, information seeking interfaces could benefit much more from our perceptual capabilities to help distinguish and relate resources. Building on our perceptual capabilities, information visualizations are "computer-supported, interactive, visual representations of abstract data to amplify cognition" [8]. Important functionalities to be supported in information visualization include overviews, zooming, filtering, and detail-on-demand [50]. Considerable research has been devoted to the use of visualizations during information seeking, however, they are still centred around search queries and results. For example, several techniques have been developed to explore the use of interactive visualization for query formulation [52] and result representation [28]. For the exploration of databases, it has been shown how interactive sliders can act as visual filters that are tightly coupled with visualizations [2]. Subsequent research has shown how a web-based multiple-view interface can be used for filtering and visualization of blogs and photos along time, location, and tags [15]. Considering growing information spaces and diverse information interests, the challenge is to represent a range of perspectives and venture beyond the query-response paradigm. For example, horizontally-centred stacked graphs of topics over time can be used to represent topical development of news topics [26] and ongoing backchannel conversations during events [16]. Initial attempts have been made to introduce aesthetic considerations to visualization design and research [44], however, more work (and play!) is needed to understand the role of aesthetics in representing and exploring growing information spaces.

Emotion and Motivation

In addition to information behaviour and visual perception, information seeking involves a wide range of emotional experiences and personal motivations. A small selection of the relevant literature is discussed in the following.

Higher Things in Life

The typical starting point of information seeking is the information need, also known as 'anomalous state of knowledge' [5] or knowledge gap [14]. These negative notions characterize the information seeker along two deficiencies: inadequate knowledge to solve a problem, and an inability to specify the information need itself. Kuhlthau follows this deficiency-oriented approach, and sees confusion and uncertainty at the beginning of an information search process [35]. However, recent research suggests that this emphasis of deficiencies is not representative for a wide range of information practices. It can be argued that information seeking research emphasizes "lower things of life" such as problems. In contrast, Kari and Hartel suggest a greater emphasis of "higher things in life", which they see as "positive human phenomena, experiences, or activities that transcend the daily grind with its rationality and necessities" [30]. Within the set of higher things, they distinguish between "the pleasurable", such as art, fiction, and play, and "the profound", such as creativity, ethics, and personal growth.

Pleasure and Leisure

Pleasure constitutes a particularly underrepresented aspect of information seeking. A study of avid readers choosing books for leisurely reading reveals a diversity of perspectives and motivations for selecting the next book—including its title, blurb, and cover, as well as the reader's competencies, preferences, life experiences, and mood [46]. The study participants saw their reading as a way of making sense of themselves and the world. They found that "wide and frequent reading" helped them answers current problems without engaging in deliberate information seeking [46]. A study of 24 hobby genealogists reveals how feelings of enjoyment, enthusiasm, and dedication were an integral part of their information seeking experience [21]. Instead of feeling anxious or uncertain, the genealogists saw unfamiliarity with a topic as an inviting challenge to increase their knowledge. The researchers observed how positive emotions further increased "confidence with an evolving information landscape" [21].

Flow and Curiosity
The aforementioned genealogists often found themselves immersed in the hobby "to the point of losing track of time" [21]. Such levels of absorption have been referred to as "flow", a mental state in which a person is fully immersed in an activity that brings a sense of harmony and satisfaction [13]. A survey of 288 college students and their opinions of the Web revealed a similarly deep involvement with information technologies, but accompanied by high levels of playfulness [1]. Based on multiple studies, Kashdan et al. formulate a model of curiosity that links perceived novelty and challenge with opportunities for personal growth [31]. The curiosity model consists of two complementary tendencies: 1) exploration: "tendencies to seek out new information and experiences", and 2) absorption: "tendencies to become fully engaged in these rewarding experiences" [31]. These two tendencies have some similarities with the previously discussed dual nature of everyday information seeking, in that they also have a sense of higher-level navigation and lower-level interaction. The challenge is to envision interfaces that support both broad and deep interaction with information spaces.

ENVISIONING THE INFORMATION FLANEUR

With the *information flaneur* we propose a human-centred model for positive information practices neglected by previous information seeking approaches. It is inspired by the literary character of the urban flaneur, and grounded in empirical research on the cognitive, perceptual, and affective aspects of information seeking. While the practices of the information flaneur have been observed in several studies, they are not well considered in the design of interfaces and systems. It is not our intention to propose a comprehensive theory for information seeking, but instead a fresh vision for future interfaces that support a range of information activities and experiences. The model consists of a poetic persona, an interaction schema, and an illustrative scenario. We also compare it with existing information seeking models.

The Information Flaneur as a Poetic Persona

We see the information flaneur as a poetic persona inspired by a literary figure and informed by empirical research. Congruent with personas in interaction design [11], the information flaneur is a descriptive model of a user that is based on extensive research. The information flaneur does not represent all forms of information seeking, but a particular class of practices, goals, and motivations involving exploration, reflection, and imagination. In this sense, we do not 'invent' the information flaneur, but observe and characterize emerging information practices that are underrepresented by existing models. We are using the urban flaneur as a lens to view exploratory attitudes of information seekers and characterize a coherent persona (see Figure 3). We describe the information flaneur as vividly as possible to engage the empathy (and creativity) of designers and researchers.

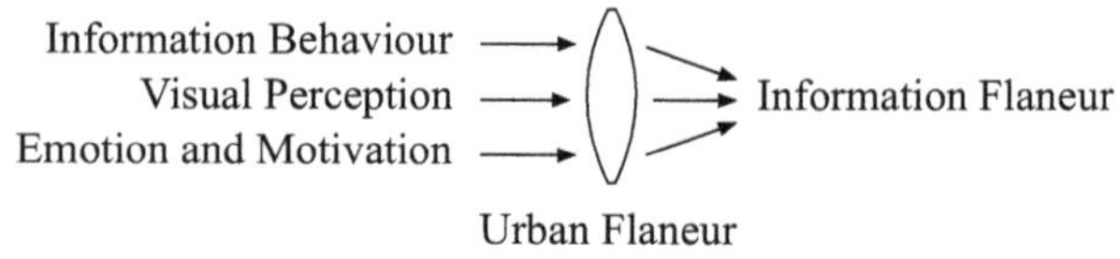

Figure 3. The information flaneur is grounded in prior research on information practices (left). Gathering these perspectives, the urban flaneur serves as a lens that brings out the information flaneur.

Exploration
Similar to the urban flaneur's appreciation of the city [6], the information flaneur is intrigued by "evolving information landscapes" [21]. While the urban flaneur feels at home in boulevards and cafes [6], the practices of the information flaneur are embedded into her daily activities and environments [48]. She monitors her surroundings to pursue her interests [21, 46], encounter new information [18, 31], and stay informed [62]. As the urban flaneur perceives "the world through multiple facades" [22], the information flaneur explores unfamiliar information using several tools and facets [4, 36, 66]. Sometimes she navigates information spaces using step-wise interactions toward information targets [53]. At other times, she uses visualizations that make use of her perceptual capabilities [8] providing her with perspectives that are related to the privileged views of the urban flaneur [29]. Visualizations allow her to detect salient and novel elements in information landscapes [27, 59].

Reflection
Resisting the growing specialization and acceleration of modern capitalism [6], the urban flaneur becomes a cultural critic and chooses to walk "out of step" [29]. Similarly, the information flaneur's practices run counter to common emphases on gaps, problems, and uncertainty. Instead, she foregrounds 'higher things in life', such as pleasurable and profound experiences [30]. As the urban flaneur confronts a city that becomes more predictable and rational [22], the information flaneur avoids interfaces that constrain serendipitous information encounters through excessive filtering and ranking [20, 49]. Instead, she enjoys "bumping into information" [18]. Similar to how the urban flaneur is not blinded by the spectacle to ignore the social realities of capitalism [6], the information flaneur cultivates an "open and questioning mind" as a strategy to find "hidden connections" [20].

Imagination
Analogous to the urban flaneur recognizing the real and imagined character of the city [29], the information flaneur scans her real and fictional environment to make sense of herself and the world [46]. By engaging in "wide and frequent reading", the information flaneur finds answers to problems without actively engaging in information seeking [46]. The urban flaneur's "amusement, excitement, adventure and enchantment, unavailable to ordinary spectators" [22] resembles the information flaneur's enjoyment and personal meaning in exploring unfamiliar information spaces [21]. As she experiments with novel technologies [1] and becomes deeply engaged with new information discoveries [31], she loses a sense of time, yet gains a sense of fulfillment [13].

	Information Behaviour	*Visual Perception*	*Emotion and Motivation*
Horizontal Exploration	explore information space along several facets	gain sense of overview and orientation	follow interest, mood, and clues for new information
↕	↕	↕	↕
Vertical Immersion	make sense of information space and resources	see details of information space and resources	engage in pleasing, profound, and/or provoking experiences

Table 1. Two dimensions of the experience-based interaction schema: experience (top) and activities (left).

An Experience-based Interaction Schema

The information flaneur's exploratory behaviour is not captured by current information seeking models. Our goal is to gain a better understanding of her information practices on the basis of empirical research and inform the design of new interfaces. To that end, the following schema uses evidence from previously discussed studies that examined people's information practices in the context of everyday life [40, 48] and curiosity [31]. Furthermore, the schema draws on established insights about orientation, visual momentum, serendipity, and perception during information seeking. The interaction schema has two dimensions: experience and activity (see Table 1). The experience dimension resembles the three human-centred perspectives on the cognitive, perceptual, and affective aspects of information seeking. The activity dimension contains two intertwined information activities: horizontal exploration and vertical immersion, between which the information flaneur gradually shifts depending on information encounters and personal interests.

Horizontal exploration is a broader type of information activity during which the information flaneur monitors and explores information spaces on a high level. This activity is based on the 'connecting' stage [40] when 'orienting' information [48] was accessed in studies on everyday information seeking. Furthermore, in the context of the curiosity model, horizontal exploration corresponds to an information flaneur's tendency to "seek out new information and experiences" [31]. During horizontal exploration the information flaneur makes use of interactive visualizations to gain overviews of information spaces and see information patterns [50]. Exploring diverse facets and perspectives on information spaces [4, 14], the information flaneur follows her own personal inclinations and is guided by visual cues along the way [27, 59]. The information flaneur cultivates her desire to find both inspiring and challenging information by following a playful approach to information seeking [1, 20, 31]. When a visualization reveals a particularly interesting piece of information, the information flaneur may gradually shift into the information activity of vertical immersion.

Complementing the higher-level activity of horizontal exploration, *vertical immersion* is a more absorbing activity during which the information flaneur follows her interest or curiosity at a more detailed level. This activity corresponds to the everyday information practices of 'interacting' with 'practical' information [40, 48]. In the context of the curiosity model, vertical immersion represents the tendency "to become fully engaged" in enjoyable experiences [31]. Practically, this means that the information flaneur accesses detailed views [50] of resources and actively makes sense of information [14] in the context of an information space. This may include randomly flipping through the pages of a book to get a sense of what it is about [46] or the challenging, yet pleasing interaction with a new insight [21].

Vertical immersion and horizontal exploration form a continuum as intertwined activities that support each other. For certain sub-activities the information flaneur shifts from vertical immersion to horizontal exploration to find related information or make connections between new and previously visited resources. Shifting between exploration and immersion may involve step-wise navigation [53] and gradual display changes that sustain visual momentum [65].

Scenario

In order to illustrate the persona of the information flaneur and the interaction schema, we are going to describe an example scenario of an information flaneur called Frances.

For Frances, a range of information spaces provide the context for making sense of the world. She particularly enjoys exploring the daily news and her friends' status updates by looking at topical patterns over time using interactive visualizations. Sometimes she links weather and mood information from different data sources providing unique views of occasionally interesting relationships; for example, she noticed the other day how people complain less about work when it rains. Frances is fascinated by digital information spaces, yet, she criticizes the commercialization of information spaces and rejects centralized collection of personal data. However, she is very engaged in demanding the release of data concerning environmental pollution and public spendings. Furthermore, she is not only an information consumer, but she typically shares her own opinions on current issues, public discourse, and works of art. While the default views created by professional interface designers give her basic ways to access information, Frances enjoys creating her own visualizations that are based on her own preferences and perspectives. She regularly explores the personal data patterns of her friends, which they share with her privately, in order to receive personal data paintings in return.

Sometimes when exploring the news, Frances encounters information about issues she is passionate about. One evening, she finds unsettling information about a recent oil spill that was close to her city, detailing the companies involved and their environmental track records. After some investigation, Frances finds incident logs from one of the implicated companies. Employees concerned about their company's environmental practices anonymously leaked these logs, revealing several critical incidents in the recent past. Frances is outraged that the company has not informed the public. Getting more absorbed by the issue, she decides to write an opinion piece and create a mashup visualization of the incident data with photos of the oil spill. When she sends her article to an environmental community blog, she is surprised to notice that it is already well past midnight.

Comparison with Previous Models

Building on top of prior information seeking research and related domains, the information flaneur constitutes a move away from models based on deficiencies and tasks towards positive traits and information practices.

Most information seeking approaches model the information seeker as a person with information needs [4, 5], the need to survive [41], knowledge gaps [14], and feelings of uncertainty [35] weighing resource value against sense-making cost [43, 47]. However, studies on serendipitous [18, 20, 62], leisurely [21, 46], and everyday information seeking [40, 48] have shown that many information practices are driven by interest, desire, and an open mind. Based on this evidence and the mindset of the urban flaneur we conceptualized the information flaneur with positive attitudes and experiences such as exploration, reflection, and imagination, i. e., as a mirror image of how information seekers are typically portrayed.

It is generally assumed that searching and browsing co-occur in a complementary fashion as part of an evolving [4], multifaceted [9], linear [35] or non-linear [19] information seeking process. The duality of searching and browsing describes a gradient between directed and undirected information seeking. However, in studies on everyday-life information seeking [40, 48] and curiosity [31] another distinction emerged, namely between high-level, exploratory and low-level, immersive activities. The interaction schema of the information flaneur is the first attempt to conceptualize exploratory and immersive information experiences at multiple levels of interaction with information spaces. Regardless whether driven by specific goals or general curiosity, the information flaneur shifts between high-level and low-level activities that are not supported by today's information seeking interfaces.

IMPLICATIONS FOR RESEARCH AND DESIGN

The experiences of the information flaneur cannot be designed and our model is not a recipe to induce certain behaviours. Instead, we see the information flaneur as a visionary model inspiring innovation. Well-grounded in research, the information flaneur suggests a shift towards a positive notion of the information seeker engaging in horizontal exploration and vertical immersion. In the following, we outline a high-level recipe for future work by providing concrete design goals and research challenges, in the hope that researchers and designers find new ways for the information flaneur to make sense of growing information spaces.

Explorability

A new set of guiding principles is needed to guide innovative design of information seeking interfaces. We pose explorability as an umbrella goal that integrates principles that have evidence for supporting the information flaneur in cultivating her curiosity, reflection, and imagination. As an initial set of explorability principles, we suggest the consideration of orientation, visual momentum, and serendipity—concepts that can directly inform interface design.

- *Orientation* within an information space denotes having a sense of overview and direction. Orientation can be supported through situated navigation, faceted navigation, and information visualizations.
- Higher levels of *visual momentum* need to be supported in order to ease the shifting between horizontal exploration and vertical immersion. Visual momentum can be increased through a range of techniques including animated transitions, zoomable interfaces, and detail-on-demand.
- Opportunities for *serendipity* could be increased by juxtaposing resources that share unusual facets or relate to one's previous interactions. The visual saliency or novelty can be used to emphasize a resource in the display.

Explorability deliberatively lacks established usability principles [42]. While they are important and should be considered in later design phases, we share the concern that they may impede the initial creation of novel interfaces [24]. Furthermore, usability typically centres around specific goals and tasks, a perspective that may constrain the possibilities for finding innovative interfaces for information seeking.

Figure 4. In order to support horizontal exploration and vertical immersion, novel interfaces need to bring together abstraction and detail.

From Gaps to Continuities

Information spaces considered for information seeking are typically discrete data sets containing individual resources with possibly inconsistent metadata. Novel interfaces in support of the information flaneur need to be designed to expose commonalities. By using reoccurring facets and data patterns, information visualizations can represent discrete, inconsistent information spaces as continuous information landscapes. Such visual information landscapes should be designed to be as inviting, inspiring, and informative as possible. The challenge is to integrate the abstract nature of information visualization with the detail of visual previews. Analogous to the continuum between horizontal exploration and vertical immersion, abstraction and detail should not be seen as discrete and separated. We need to find new interaction and representation techniques that bring these two views of information spaces and resources closer together, supporting a more integrated information experience. As illustrated in Figure 4, we suggest that the space between abstraction and detail can be designed as a gradual continuum.

- *Abstraction:* At the level of conceptual representation, entire information spaces can be shown as visualizations. Representation techniques could be timelines, maps, and graphs, depending on the facets of interest.
- *Detail:* Literal presentations provide detailed previews of

a few information resources, using thumbnails, movie trailers, and audio snippets, for example.

While previews provide higher level of detail, there are limits to the number of resources that can be shown. Abstract visualizations, however, can summarize large sets of resources along interesting facets, while sacrificing some level of detail. The challenge is to make visualizations that encourage horizontal exploration and provide a diverse range of facets and representations that invite vertical immersion.

CONCLUSION

Information seeking is a complex human activity and as such it is a great challenge to design powerful interfaces to support it. Considering growing information spaces, technical advances, and positive information practices, we have developed new ways to think about information seeking by making the following contributions:

1. First use of the urban flaneur's mindset towards the city as an inspiring analogy for information seeking.
2. An interdisciplinary literature survey on cognitive, perceptual, and affective aspects of information seeking.
3. A human-centred model for positive information practices featuring a poetic persona, a novel interaction schema, and an illustrative scenario.

There are some caveats with our approach, among which we briefly discuss two here. First, the comprehensive consideration of interdisciplinary research provided us with a broad view. However, such a wide angle may have sacrificed the depth and completeness for those perspectives. We tried to compensate for this by focusing on information experiences that inform a positive approach to information seeking. Second, we 'borrowed' the urban flaneur from cultural studies as an inspiring lens. This poses the risk of constraining the understanding of a phenomenon to its analogy [41] and reducing a rich philosophical school of thought [38]. We attempted to retain both the complex and critical aspects of the urban flaneur in our vision of the information flaneur.

We see this work as part of an emerging trend towards better understanding of and support for positive information practices. The information flaneur poses many exciting challenges of which we outlined a few with regard to interactive explorability and issues of representation. We ultimately need novel ways to support the practices embodied by the information flaneur in curiously and critically moving through information landscapes and creatively constructing meaning.

ACKNOWLEDGEMENTS

We thank the InnoVis group at the University of Calgary for their ideas and advice, and Lindsay MacDonald, Nicolai Marquardt, and David Monteyne for their feedback on drafts of this paper. We are also very grateful to the reviewers for their constructive feedback and suggestions. Funding was provided by SMART Technologies, NSERC, and AITF.

REFERENCES

1. R. Agarwal and E. Karahanna. Time flies when you're having fun: Cognitive absorption and beliefs about information technology usage. *MIS quarterly*, 24(4):665–694, 2000.
2. C. Ahlberg and B. Shneiderman. Visual information seeking: Tight coupling of dynamic query filters with starfield displays. *Proc. of ACM CHI*, pp. 313–317, 1994.
3. S. Auer, C. Bizer, G. Kobilarov, J. Lehmann, R. Cyganiak, and Z. Ives. DBpedia: A nucleus for a web of open data. *Proc. of International Semantic Web Conference*, 2007.
4. M. Bates. The design of browsing and berrypicking techniques for the online search interface. *Online Information Review*, 13(5):407–424, 1989.
5. N. Belkin, R. Oddy, and H. Brooks. ASK for information retrieval: Part I. background and theory. *Journal of Documentation*, 38(2):61–71, 1982.
6. W. Benjamin. *Charles Baudelaire: A Lyric Poet in the Era of High Capitalism*, chapter The Paris of the Second Empire in Baudelaire: II The Flâneur, pp. 35–66. NLB, 1973.
7. A. Broder, E. Churchill, M. Hearst, B. Pell, P. Raghavan, and A. Tomkins. Search is dead!: long live search (panel). *Proc. of WWW Conference*, pp. 1337–1338, 2010.
8. S. Card, J. Mackinlay, and B. Shneiderman. *Using Vision to Think*, chapter 1: Information Visualization, pp. 1–34. Morgan Kaufmann, 1999.
9. S. Chang and R. Rice. Browsing: A multidimensional framework. *Annual review of information science and technology (ARIST)*, 28:231–76, 1993.
10. E. Chi, P. Pirolli, K. Chen, and J. Pitkow. Using information scent to model user information needs and actions and the web. *Proc. of ACM CHI*, pp. 490–497, 2001.
11. A. Cooper and R. Reimann. *About Face 2.0: The Essentials of Interaction Design*. Wiley, 2003.
12. J. Cove and B. Walsh. Online text retrieval via browsing. *Information Processing Management*, 24(1):31–37, 1988.
13. M. Csíkszentmihályi. *Flow: The psychology of optimal experience*. Basic Books, 1997.
14. B. Dervin. An overview of sense-making research: Concepts, methods and results to date. *International Communication Association annual meeting*, 1983.
15. M. Dörk, S. Carpendale, C. Collins, and C. Williamson. VisGets: Coordinated visualizations for web-based information exploration and discovery. *IEEE Transactions on Visualization and Computer Graphics (TVCG)*, 14(6):1205–1212, Nov/Dec 2008.
16. M. Dörk, D. Gruen, C. Williamson, and S. Carpendale. A visual backchannel for large-scale events. *IEEE TVCG*, 16(6):1129–1138, Nov/Dec 2010.
17. J. English, M. Hearst, R. Sinha, K. Swearingen, and K. Yee. Flexible search and navigation using faceted metadata. *Proc. of ACM SIGIR Conference*, pp. 11–15, 2002.
18. S. Erdelez. Information encountering: It's more than just bumping into information. *Bulletin of the American Society for Information Science*, 25(3):25–29, 1999.
19. A. Foster. A nonlinear model of information-seeking behavior. *Journal of the American Society for Information Science and Technology*, 55(3):228–237, 2004.
20. A. Foster and N. Ford. Serendipity and information seeking: An empirical study. *Journal of Documentation*, 59(3):321–340, May 2003.
21. C. Fulton. The pleasure principle: the power of positive affect in information seeking. *Aslib Proceedings: New Information Perspectives*, 61(3):245–261, 2009.
22. M. Gluck. The flaneur and the aesthetic: Appropriation of urban culture in mid-19th-century paris. *Theory, Culture & Society*, 20(5):53–80, 2003.
23. E. Goldman. Search engine bias and the demise of search engine utopianism. *Web Search*, 14(III):121–133, 2008.

24. S. Greenberg and B. Buxton. Usability evaluation considered harmful (some of the time). *Proc. of ACM CHI*, pp. 111–120, 2008.
25. J. Guthrie and P. Mosenthal. Literacy as multidimensional: Locating information and reading comprehension. *Educational Psychologist*, 22(3):279–297, 1987.
26. S. Havre, E. Hetzler, P. Whitney, and L. Nowell. ThemeRiver: Visualizing thematic changes in large document collections. *IEEE TVCG*, 8(1):9–20, 2002.
27. C. Healey, K. Booth, and J. Enns. High-speed visual estimation using preattentive processing. *Transactions on Computer-Human Interaction*, 3(2):107–135, 1996.
28. M. Hearst. TileBars: Visualization of term distribution information in full text information access. *Proc. of ACM CHI*, pp. 59–66, 1995.
29. C. Jenks. *Visual Culture*, chapter 8 Watching Your Step: The history and practice of the flâneur, pp. 142–160. Routledge, 1995.
30. J. Kari and J. Hartel. Information and higher things in life: Addressing the pleasurable and the profound in information science. *Journal of the American Society for Information Science and Technology*, 58(8):1131–1147, 2007.
31. T. Kashdan, P. Rose, and F. Fincham. Curiosity and exploration: Facilitating positive subjective experiences and personal growth opportunities. *Journal of Personality Assessment*, 82(3):291–305, 2004.
32. A. Kerne, E. Koh, S. Smith, A. Webb, and B. Dworaczyk. combinformation: Mixed-initiative composition of image and text surrogates promotes information discovery. *TOIS: Transactions on Information Systems*, 27(1):5:1–5:45, December 2008.
33. R. Khare and T. Çelik. Microformats: a pragmatic path to the semantic web. *Proc. of WWW Conference*, pp. 865–866, 2006.
34. R. Klein. Inhibition of return. *Trends in Cognitive Sciences*, 4(4):138–147, 2000.
35. C. Kuhlthau. Inside the search process: Information seeking from the user's perspective. *Journal of the American Society for Information Science*, 42(5):361–371, 1991.
36. B. Kules, R. Capra, M. Banta, and T. Sierra. What do exploratory searchers look at in a faceted search interface? *Proc. of ACM/IEEE Joint Conference on Digital Libraries*, pp. 313–322, 2009.
37. B. Kwasnik. A descriptive study of the functional components of browsing. *Proc. IFIP TC2/WG2.7 Working Conference on Engineering for Human-Computer Interaction*, pp. 191–203, 1992.
38. L. Leahu, J. Thom-Santelli, C. Pederson, and P. Sengers. Taming the situationist beast. *Proc. of ACM Conference on Designing Interactive Systems*, pp. 203–211, 2008.
39. G. Marchionini. Exploratory search: From finding to understanding. *Communications of the ACM*, 49(4):41–46, 2006.
40. P. McKenzie. A model of information practices in accounts of everyday-life information seeking. *Journal of Documentation*, 59(1):19–40, 2003.
41. G. Miller. *The Study of Information: Interdisciplinary Messages*, chapter Informavores, pp. 111–113. Wiley-Interscience, 1983.
42. J. Nielson. *Usability Engineering*, chapter 2: What is Usability, pp. 23–48. Morgan Kaufmann, 1993.
43. P. Pirolli and S. Card. Information foraging in information access environments. *Proc. of ACM CHI*, pp. 51–58, 1995.
44. Z. Pousman, J. Stasko, and M. Mateas. Casual information visualization: Depictions of data in everyday life. *IEEE TVCG*, 13(6):1145–1152, Nov/Dec 2007.
45. D. Rosenberg. Early modern information overload. *Journal of the History of Ideas*, 64(1):1–9, 2003.
46. C. Ross. Finding without seeking: the information encounter in the context of reading for pleasure. *Information Processing & Management*, 35(6):783–799, 1999.
47. D. Russell, M. Stefik, P. Pirolli, and S. Card. The cost structure of sensemaking. *Proc. of ACM CHI*, pp. 269–276, 1993.
48. R. Savolainen. Everyday life information seeking: approaching information seeking in the context of "way of life". *Library & Information Science Research*, 17(3):259–294, 1995.
49. m. c. schraefel. Building knowledge: What's beyond keyword search? *Computer*, 42(3):52–59, 2009.
50. B. Shneiderman. The eyes have it: A task by data type taxonomy for information visualizations. *Proc. IEEE Symposium on Visual Languages*, pp. 336–343, 1996.
51. A. Smith. Mobile access 2010. Technical report, The Pew Research Center, 2010. `http://pewinternet.org/Reports/2010/Mobile-Access-2010.aspx`.
52. A. Spoerri. InfoCrystal: A visual tool for information retrieval. *Proc. IEEE Conference on Visualization*, pp. 150–157, 1993.
53. J. Teevan, C. Alvarado, M. Ackerman, and D. Karger. The perfect search engine is not enough: a study of orienteering behavior in directed search. *Proc. of ACM CHI*, pp. 415–422, 2004.
54. E. Toms. Understanding and facilitating the browsing of electronic text. *International Journal of Human-Computer Studies*, 52(3):423–452, 2000.
55. E. Toms. Information interaction: Providing a framework for information architecture. *Journal of the American Society for Information Science and Technology*, 53(10):855–862, 2002.
56. A. Treisman and G. Gelade. A feature-integration theory of attention. *Cognitive psychology*, 12(1):97–136, 1980.
57. L. Udsen and A. Jørgensen. The aesthetic turn: unravelling recent aesthetic approaches to human-computer interaction. *Digital Creativity*, 16(4):205–216, 2005.
58. W3C. HTML5: A vocabulary and associated APIs for HTML and XHTML: Editor's Draft 12 January 2011. `http://dev.w3.org/html5/spec/Overview.html`.
59. Z. Wang and R. Klein. Searching for inhibition of return in visual search: A review. *Vision research*, 50(2):220–228, 2010.
60. R. White, B. Kules, S. Drucker, and m.c. schraefel. Supporting exploratory search: Introduction. *Communications of the ACM*, 49(4):36–39, 2006.
61. R. White and R. Roth. *Exploratory Search: Beyond the Query-Response Paradigm*. Number 3 in Synthesis Lectures on Information Concepts, Retrieval, and Services. Morgan & Claypool Publishers,
62. K. Williamson. Discovered by chance: The role of incidental information acquisition in an ecological model of information use. *Library Information Science Research*, 20(1):23–40, 1998.
63. T. Wilson. Information behaviour: An interdisciplinary perspective. *Information Processing & Management*, 33(4):551–572, 1997.
64. J. Wolfe. Moving towards solutions to some enduring controversies in visual search. *Trends in Cognitive Sciences*, 7(2):70–76, 2003.
65. D. Woods. Visual momentum: A concept to improve the cognitive coupling of person and computer. *International Journal of Man-Machine Studies*, 21(3):229–244, 1984.
66. K. Yee, K. Swearingen, K. Li, and M. Hearst. Faceted metadata for image search and browsing. *Proc. of ACM CHI*, pp. 401–408, 2003.

No Clicks, No Problem: Using Cursor Movements to Understand and Improve Search

Jeff Huang
University of Washington
Seattle, WA 98195 USA
chi@jeffhuang.com

Ryen W. White
Microsoft Research
Redmond, WA 98052 USA
ryenw@microsoft.com

Susan Dumais
Microsoft Research
Redmond, WA 98052 USA
sdumais@microsoft.com

ABSTRACT
Understanding how people interact with search engines is important in improving search quality. Web search engines typically analyze queries and clicked results, but these actions provide limited signals regarding search interaction. Laboratory studies often use richer methods such as gaze tracking, but this is impractical at Web scale. In this paper, we examine mouse cursor behavior on search engine results pages (SERPs), including not only clicks but also cursor movements and hovers over different page regions. We: (i) report an eye-tracking study showing that cursor position is closely related to eye gaze, especially on SERPs; (ii) present a scalable approach to capture cursor movements, and an analysis of search result examination behavior evident in these large-scale cursor data; and (iii) describe two applications (estimating search result relevance and distinguishing good from bad abandonment) that demonstrate the value of capturing cursor data. Our findings help us better understand how searchers use cursors on SERPs and can help design more effective search systems. Our scalable cursor tracking method may also be useful in non-search settings.

Author Keywords
Cursor movements, clicks, implicit feedback, Web search.

ACM Classification Keywords
H.3.3 [Information Storage and Retrieval]: Information Search and Retrieval–*selection process, relevance feedback*

General Terms
Experimentation, Human Factors, Measurement.

INTRODUCTION
Understanding how people interact with Web sites is important in improving site design and the quality of services offered. The Web provides unprecedented opportunities to evaluate alternative design, interaction, and algorithmic methods at scale and *in situ* with actual customers doing their own tasks in their own environments [19]. Such studies typically involve measuring clicks which can be obtained easily at scale. However, they fail to capture behaviors that do not lead to clicks (e.g., which items are attended to, in what order, etc.) or subjective impressions. Gaze-tracking studies with participants present in the laboratory can provide more detailed insights but on a smaller scale. In this paper we consider how mouse movements, which can be collected remotely on a large scale, can be used to understand richer patterns of behavior.

We focus on understanding cursor activities in Web search behavior. People conduct Web searches to satisfy information needs. Their interaction with search engines begins by issuing a search query, then reviewing the search engine results page (SERP) to determine which, if any, results may satisfy their need. In doing so, they may move their mouse cursor around the page, hovering over and possibly clicking on hyperlinks. Small-scale laboratory studies have observed participants making many uses of the cursor on SERPs beyond hyperlink clicking [1,21,25]. These uses include moving the cursor as a reading aid, using it to mark interesting results, using it to interact with controls on the screen (e.g., buttons, scroll bars), or simply positioning the cursor so that it does not occlude Web page content. However, studying such behaviors in small-scale laboratory settings is limited in terms of what inferences can be made.

Tracking mouse cursor movements *at scale* can provide a rich new source of behavioral information to understand, model, and satisfy information needs. Recent research has shown that cursor movements correlate with eye gaze [6,13,25,26], and may therefore be an effective indicator of user attention. We believe that cursor data, like click data [18], can provide signals that reveal searcher intent and may be useful in improving the search experience. Cursor data can be used to complement click data in several ways. First, cursor data can be captured for uncommon queries where strong indicators of relevance such as result clicks may occur less frequently or not at all. For example, analyzing click logs for a query that has been issued several times but never clicked may provide limited relevance information, but cursor behavior on the SERP associated with the query may provide insight about relevance. Second, in cases of so-called *good abandonment* [20], where the content on the SERP satisfies the user's information need directly, a search result click may be unnecessary. Thus the lack of a click should not always be interpreted as a search failure. Cursor behavior may help in distinguishing between good and bad search abandonment.

The research questions that we ask are: (i) to what extent does gaze correlate with cursor behavior on SERPs and non-SERPs? (ii) what does cursor behavior reveal about search engine users' result examination strategies, and how does this relate to search result clicks and prior eye-tracking research? and (iii) can we demonstrate useful applications of large-scale cursor data? Answers to these questions help us determine the utility of cursor tracking at scale, and ultimately inform search system design and improve the experience for users of search engines.

RELATED WORK

One line of related research has explored the use of cursor movements, clicks, and gaze as *implicit indicators of interest* on Web pages. In early work, Goecks and Shavlik modified a Web browser to record themselves browsing hundreds of Web pages [11]. They found that a neural network could predict variables such as the amount of cursor activity on the SERP, which they considered surrogate measurements of user interest. Claypool et al. [7] developed the "curious browser," a custom Web browser that recorded activity from 75 students browsing over 2,500 Web pages. They found that cursor travel time was a positive indicator of a Web page's relevance, but could only differentiate highly irrelevant Web pages. Surprisingly, they also found that the number of mouse clicks on a page did not correlate with its relevance. Hijikata [15] used client-side logging to monitor five subjects browsing a total of 120 Web pages. They recorded actions such as text tracing and link pointing using the cursor. The findings showed that these behaviors were good indicators for interesting regions of the Web page, around one-and-a-half times more effective than rudimentary term matching between the query and regions of the page. Shapira et al. [27] developed a special Web browser and recorded cursor activity from a small number of company employees browsing the Web. They found that the ratio of mouse movement to reading time was a better indicator of page quality than cursor travel distance and overall length of time that users spend on a page.

In the search domain, Guo and Agichtein [12] captured mouse movements using a modified browser toolbar and found differences in cursor travel distances between informational and navigational queries. Furthermore, a decision tree could classify the query type using cursor movements more accurately than using clicks. Guo and Agichtein also used interactions such as cursor movement, hovers, and scrolling to accurately infer search intent and interest in search results [13]. They focused on automatically identifying a searcher's research or purchase intent based on features of the interaction. Buscher et al. investigated the use of gaze tracking to predict salient regions of Web pages [2] and the use of visual attention as implicit relevance feedback to personalize search [4].

Another line of research examined the *relationship between eye gaze and cursor positions*. An early study by Chen et al. [6] measured this relationship in Web browsing by recording 100 gaze and cursor positions from five subjects browsing the Web. They showed that the distance between gaze and cursor was markedly shorter in regions of encountered pages to which users attended. Liu and Chung [21] recorded cursor activity from 28 students browsing the Web. They noticed patterns of cursor behaviors, including reading by tracing text. Their algorithms were capable of predicting users' cursor behaviors with 79% accuracy.

More recent work has focused on the relationship between cursor and gaze on search tasks. In a study involving 32 subjects performing 16 search tasks each [25,26], Rodden et al. identified a strong alignment between cursor and gaze positions. They found that the distance between cursor and gaze positions was longer along the x-axis than the y-axis, and was generally shorter when the cursor was placed over the search results. Rodden et al. also observed four general types of mouse behaviors: neglecting the cursor while reading, using the cursor as a reading aid to follow text (either horizontally or vertically), and using the cursor to mark interesting results. Guo and Agichtein [14] reported similar findings in a smaller study of ten subjects performing 20 search tasks each. Like Rodden et al., Guo and Agichtein noticed that distances along the x-axis tended to be longer than the distances along the y-axis. They could predict with 77% accuracy when gaze and cursor were strongly aligned using cursor features.

The research presented in this paper extends previous work in a number of ways. Our analysis of the cursor-gaze relationship (Study 1) involves more search tasks than prior studies, compares SERP and post-SERP Web pages, and confirms earlier results with a large study using the same SERP layout that we use in the remainder of the paper. More importantly, we develop a scalable approach to capturing cursor data that enables us to analyze real user activity in a natural setting for more than 360 thousand searches from an estimated 22 thousand searchers (Study 2). Finally, using two case studies, we show how cursor data can supplement click data on two search-related problems.

STUDY 1: GAZE-CURSOR RELATIONSHIP

We begin by replicating and extending prior laboratory experiments on the relationship between gaze and cursor activity using the same SERP layout deployed in our large-scale cursor study (Study 2, see Figure 2). Study 1 also involves more tasks and participants than prior laboratory studies, and measures the relationship between gaze and cursor position on SERP and on non-SERP pages.

Data

We used a Tobii x50 eye tracker with 50Hz tracking frequency and 0.5° visual angle on a 1280 × 1024 resolution 17 inch monitor (96.42dpi) and 1040 × 996 resolution Internet Explorer 7 browser. Cursor and gaze coordinates were collected in an eye-tracking study of 38 participants (21 female, 17 male) performing Web searches. Participants were recruited from a user study pool. They ranged in age between 26 and 60 years (mean = 45.5, σ = 8.2), and had a wide variety of backgrounds and professions.

Each participant completed 32 search tasks on the same search engine, with the same SERP layout template, as used for the large-scale cursor study described in the next section (see Figure 2). Half of the tasks were navigational (i.e., they had to find a specific Web page) and half were informational (i.e., they had to find factual information). Each task started with a description of what participants should look for on the Web. Gaze and cursor positions were recorded for each SERP as well as subsequent Web pages (i.e., pages visited after clicking on a search result). In total, we collected data for 1,210 search tasks, 1,336,647 gaze positions, and 87,227 cursor positions. Gaze-specific findings on this data set, unrelated to cursor behavior, have been reported by others [5,10]. Those researchers granted us access to their data so that we could examine the relationship between gaze and cursor behaviors.

Gaze and cursor positions were extracted from the eye-tracking logs. In our data, the gaze positions were recorded approximately every 20ms, whereas cursor positions were recorded approximately every 100ms. Since cursor and gaze events did not always have identical timestamps, a gaze position was interpolated for every cursor position. Interpolation was performed by calculating gaze x and y coordinates weighted by the coordinates of the nearest gaze coordinates before and after the cursor position. For example, the interpolated x-coordinate for eye gaze is calculated as $x_0 + (x_1 - x_0)((t_c - t_0)/(t_1 - t_0))$ where t_c is the time for the corresponding cursor position, x_0 is the gaze's x-coordinate preceding the cursor position, recorded at time t_0, and x_1 is the gaze's x-coordinate following the cursor position, recorded at time t_1. To reduce noise, cursor positions were only captured if they occurred between gaze positions that were at most 100ms apart.

Findings

Figure 1 shows the frequency distribution for different values of Δx (distance between cursor x-coordinate and gaze x-coordinate), Δy (distance between cursor y-coordinate and gaze y-coordinate), and Euclidean distance between cursor and gaze coordinates, i.e., $\sqrt{(\Delta x)^2 + (\Delta y)^2}$. The solid lines in Figure 1 show the distances for SERP pages. As can be seen, cursor and gaze positions are quite similar for both x and y values, their deltas peaking near 0, when the gaze and cursor positions are in the same place. The mean Euclidean distance between cursor and gaze is 178px (σ = 139px) and the median is 143px. The most common offset for the cursor is +3px (to the right) for the x-coordinate and +29px (lower) for the y-coordinate. That is, the cursor is most likely to be just below where the user is focusing with their eyes. We also observed that the differences are greater in the x than y direction (average 50px in the x direction and 7px in the y direction), similar to other studies [14, 25]. Possible explanations for the difference between Δx and Δy include: (i) users may place the cursor to the left or right of their gaze to prevent it from obscuring the text as they read up or down, and (ii) computer screens are usually wider, offering more horizontal space for the cursor.

The dotted lines in Figure 1 represent post-SERP landing pages. Distances between the gaze and cursor on the landing pages were greater than those on the SERP (215px vs. 178px), perhaps due to greater variance in the layout and the content of those pages, as has already been suggested by earlier gaze analysis [2]. Thus the cursor is a better proxy for user attention on the SERP than post-SERP pages. Monitoring cursor behavior on SERPs may help estimate which results or features users attend to and when, and we now turn to a large-scale study of this.

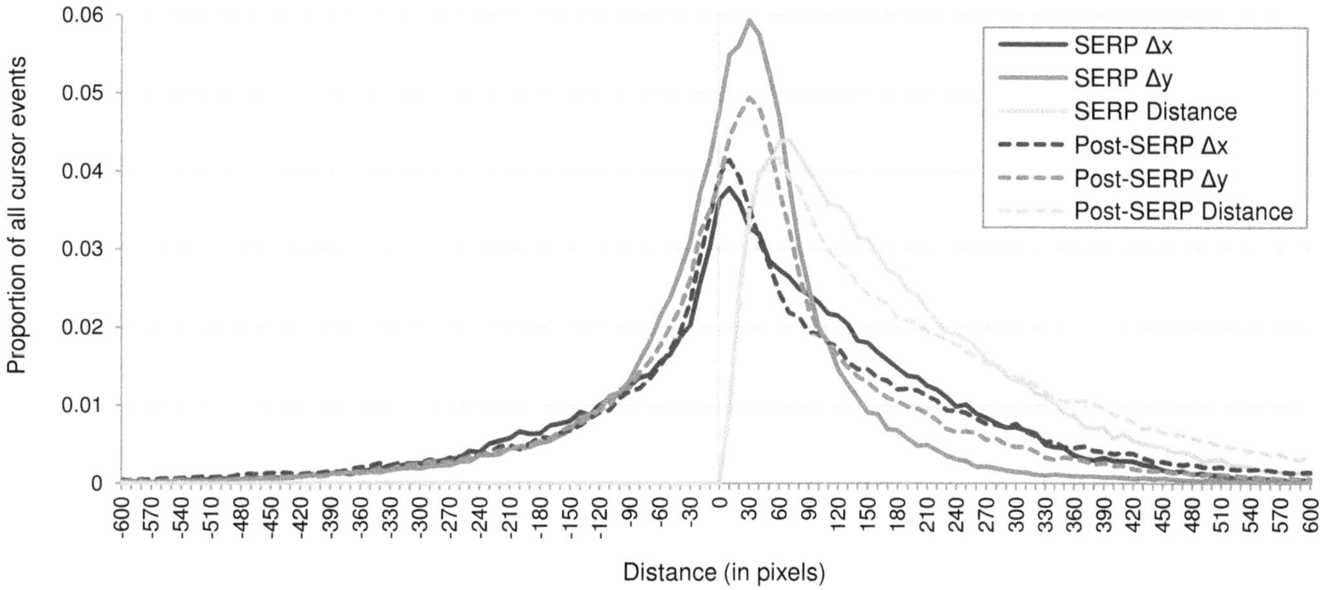

Figure 1. Δx, Δy, and Euclidean distance plotted in a frequency distribution for SERP and post-SERP pages. Solid lines represent these distances gathered on the SERP, while dashed lines represented distances gathered on post-SERP pages (landing pages).

STUDY 2: LARGE-SCALE CURSOR TRACKING STUDY

Following on from the eye-tracking study, we instrumented cursor tracking on the SERP of the Bing search engine, deployed as an internal flight within Microsoft. Cursor tracking at scale involves careful instrumentation of the SERP to address issues with page load latencies associated with the cursor capture script, and the need to remotely record the large volumes of data generated from cursor behavior. We now describe the method that we devised to capture cursor movement data on SERPs at scale.

Method

We wanted to collect cursor data without requiring additional installation. To do this, we instrumented the search results page using client-side JavaScript embedded within the HTML source for the results page. The embedded script had a total size of approximately 750 bytes of compressed JavaScript, which had little effect on the page load time. The script recorded users' cursor interaction within the Web page's borders relative to the top-left corner of the page. Since cursor tracking was relative to the document, we captured cursor alignment to SERP content regardless of how the user got to that position (e.g., by scrolling, or keyboard). Therefore this approach did not constrain other behaviors such as scrolling or keyboard input.

In previous cursor tracking studies, cursor position was recorded at particular time intervals, such as every 50 milliseconds (ms) [13] or every 100ms [25]. This is impractical at a large scale because of the large amount of data to transfer from the user's computer to the server. One alternative is to record events only when there is activity, but this is still problematic because even a single mouse movement can trigger many mouse movement events. We devised a different approach by only recording cursor positions after a movement delay. From experimentation, we found that recording cursor positions only after a 40ms pause provided a reasonable tradeoff between data quantity and granularity of the recorded events. This approach recorded sufficient key points of cursor movement, e.g., when the user changed directions in moving or at endpoints before and after a move; occasionally, points within a longer movement were also captured if the user hesitated while moving. All mouse clicks were recorded since they were less frequent. The events were buffered and sent to a remote server every two seconds and also when the user navigated away from the SERP through clicking on a hyperlink or closing the tab or browser; this was typically 1-3 kilobytes of data. The pseudo-code below summarizes this logic.

```
onCursorMove:
  loc = getCursorPos()
  wait(40 milliseconds)
  if loc == getCursorPos(): // cursor stable for 40ms
    buffer.add(time,loc,getRegion(loc),"position")
onCursorClick:
  buffer.add(time,loc,getRegion(loc),"click")
onTick, onPageClose:
  send(buffer)
  clear(buffer)
```

A server-side process aggregated data from multiple pageviews belonging to the same query (e.g., from returning to SERP using the browser "back" button or viewing multiple result pages), to facilitate query-level in addition to pageview-level analysis. All analysis presented in this paper is at the query level. Table 1 describes the fields present in each record. We identify *regions* that the cursor hovers over using attributes in the HTML, and use two such regions in subsequent analyses (result rank, link id).

Table 1. Fields in data recorded by cursor tracking script.

Field	Description
Event	Cursor move or click
Cursor Position	x- and y-coordinates of the cursor
Timestamp	Time that the event occurred
Region	Result rank or link id
QueryId	Unique identifier for each query
CookieId	Unique identifier for each cookie
Query	Text of the issued query
Result URL	URL of clicked result (if any)

The large volume of data collected using the method described in this section allowed us to examine a number of aspects of how searchers use their cursors on SERPs. For this purpose, we use the query-level data, comprising all clicks and cursor movements for a query instance. In addition to the location of cursor positions, we summarize the total amount of cursor activity for a query using *cursor trails* (i.e., complete contiguous sequences of cursor movements on the SERP). As we show later, these trails are useful in situations where no clicks are observed.

Data were accumulated from a random sample of Microsoft employees' searches on the commercial Web search engine used between May 12, 2010 and June 6, 2010. In total, we recorded 7,500,429 cursor events from 366,473 queries made by 21,936 unique cookies; the actual number of users may be fewer since multiple cookies could belong to a single user. Although we realize that employees of our organization may not be representative of the general Web searcher population in some respects, e.g., they were more technical, we believe that their interaction patterns can provide useful insights on how SERPs are examined.

We now summarize our results on general cursor activity, evidence of search result examination patterns, and the relationship between click and cursor hover activity. We then present two applications demonstrating the potential utility of gathering cursor data at scale.

General Cursor Activity

We begin by determining where on the SERP users click and move their mouse cursors. This offers some initial insight into differences between click and movement data.

Figure 2 shows heatmaps for clicks and cursor movement activity for the same query aggregated over all instances of the query *[lost finale explanation]* (in reference to the final episode of the US television series "Lost") observed 25 times from 22 different users in our data. Heavy interaction

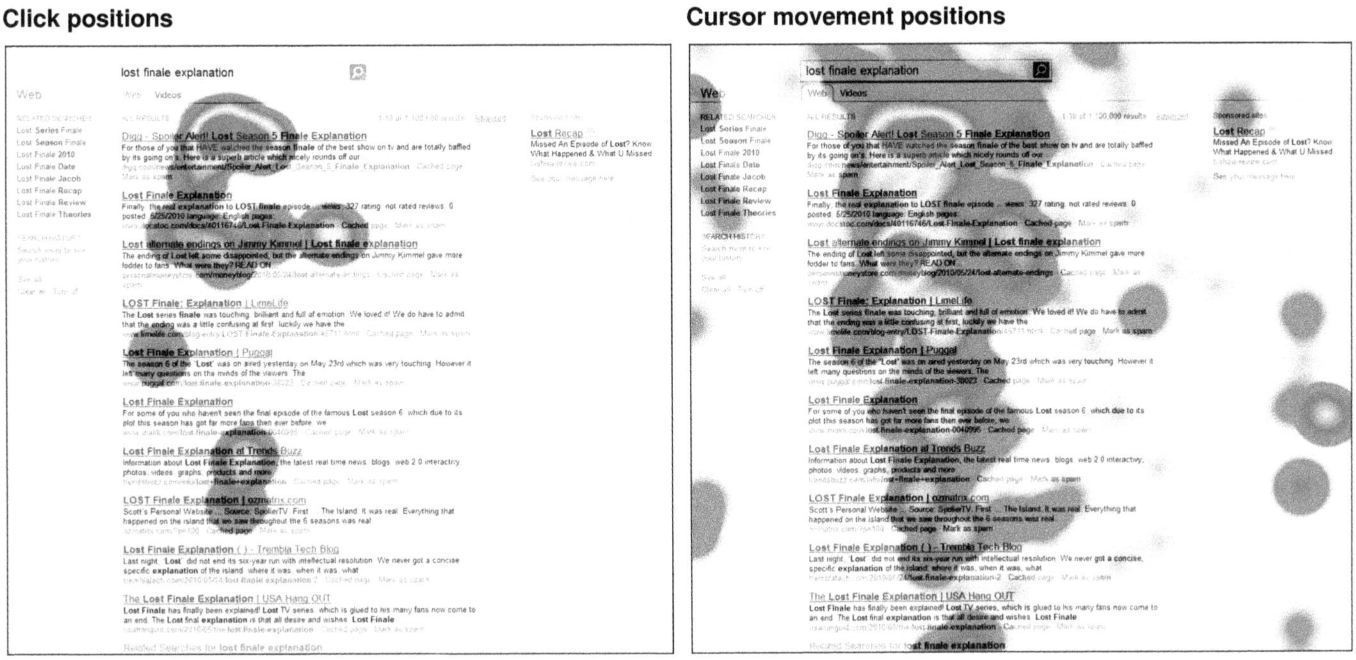

Figure 2. Heatmaps of all click positions (left) and recorded cursor positions (right) for the query *[lost finale explanation]*. Heavy interaction occurs in red/orange/yellow areas, moderate interaction in green areas, light interaction in blue areas.

occurs in red/orange/yellow areas, moderate interaction in green areas, and light interaction in blue areas. Most of the clicks occur on results 1, 3 and 7, and this is also seen in the cursor activity. However, there are some interesting differences as well. For example, there is considerable cursor activity on result 4 even though it is not clicked. The cursor heatmap also shows some activity on query suggestions (on the left rail) and advertisements (on the right rail) although there are no clicks on these regions. Across all queries, cursor positions are more broadly distributed over the SERP than clicks. Thus cursor movement can provide a more complete picture of interactions with elements on the SERP. Such information may be useful to search engine designers in making decisions about what content or features to show on search result pages.

Search Result Examination

In addition to monitoring general cursor movement activity on the SERP, we can also summarize cursor movements that reflect how people examine the search results. Previous work on gaze tracking demonstrated differences in the length of time that users spend reading each of the results based on its position in the ranked list [9]. In a similar way, we were interested in whether the time participants spent hovering over the search results was related to the position in the ranked list. To reduce noise caused by unintentional hovering, we removed hovers of less than 100ms in duration. In Figure 3 we present a graph of the average time spent hovering over each search result title (shown as bars; corresponding scale shown on the left side), and the average time taken to reach each result title in the ranked list (shown as circles connected with lines; corresponding scale on the right side). Error bars denote the standard error of the mean (SEM).

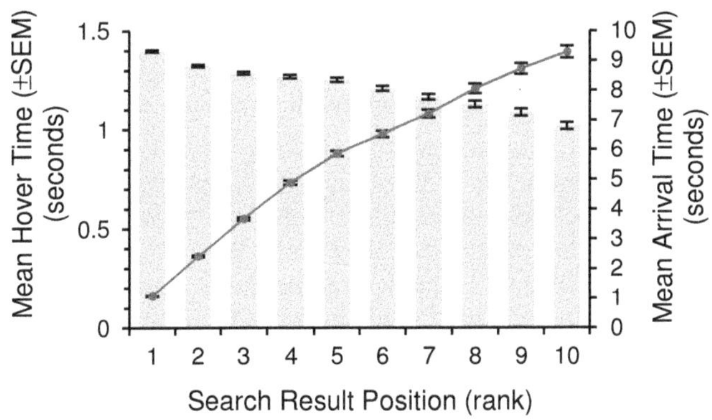

Figure 3. Mean title hover duration (bars) and mean time for cursor to arrive at each result (circles).

The figure shows that time spent hovering on the results decreases linearly with rank and that the arrival time increases linearly with rank. The results are generally similar to gaze tracking findings reported in previous literature [5,9,18]. Hover time decreases with rank as was previously reported; however, cursor hover time drops off less sharply than gaze duration. This difference may be because we miss some of the rapid skimming behavior on low ranks that has been observed previously [5,9,18] since we only recorded hovers after a 40ms pause (to reduce data payload) and filtered out hovers of 100ms or less (to reduce cases of capturing accidental hovers). As expected, search results that are lower ranked are entered later than higher ranked results due to the typical top-to-bottom scanning behavior [8]. The arrival time is approximately linear, suggesting that users examine each search result for a similar amount of time.

We also examined which results were hovered on before clicking on a result, re-querying, or clicking query suggestions or advertisements. This provides further information about how searchers are using their cursor during result examination and again allows us to compare our findings with prior eye-tracking research from Cutrell and Guan [9]. Figure 4 summarizes our findings. This figure shows the mean number of search results hovered on before a click as blue lines, and clicks as red circles. The data are broken down by result position (1-10), and separately for clicks on query suggestions, clicks on ads, and re-queries.

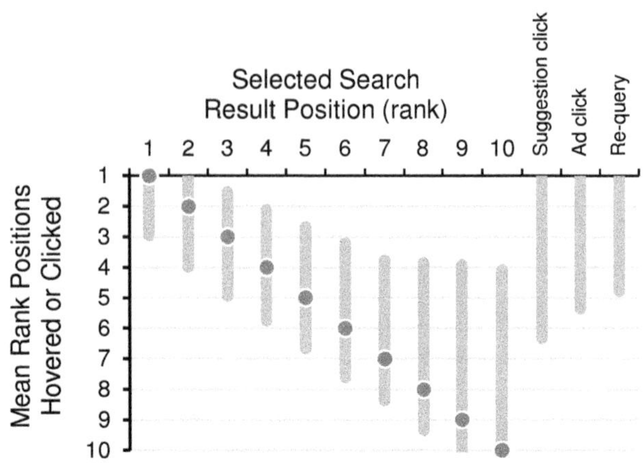

Figure 4. Mean number of search results hovered over before users clicked on a result (above and below that result). Result clicks are red circles, result hovers are blue lines.

Figure 4 shows that prior to clicking on a search result, people consider the surrounding search results. For example, before clicking on result 1, people also hover on results 2 and 3 on average; when they click on result 2 they also hover on results 1, 3, and 4; etc. The findings are similar to those reported by Cutrell and Guan [9], but differ in that the search result hovers do not appear to extend as far *above* the clicked search result in cases where a result is clicked on far down the list (in positions 6–10). This may be because queries where low-ranked clicks are observed may have clearly irrelevant results in top ranks, and by excluding hovers of less than 100ms we miss rapid skims over such irrelevant results.

The findings also show that users consider many results prior to turning their attention to the additional SERP features: on average six results in the case of query suggestions, five results in the case of advertisements, and around four results prior to re-querying. This behavior is similar to that reported in [9], at least in terms of re-querying, which is examined in both studies. Cutrell and Guan do report inspection further down the list (up to rank position 8) prior to re-querying, whereas we find that users hover on around 4 results. One explanation for the difference is that the cursor does not track well with eye movements in situations where users rapidly skim low-ranked search results. An alternative explanation is that in naturalistic non-laboratory settings, users may only consider the top-ranked search results prior to trying another query by clicking on a query suggestion or re-querying.

In the next section we compare the distributions of search results clicks and search result hovers.

Comparing Click and Hover Distributions

Prior studies have presented data on click distribution [18,24] or gaze distribution for the search results [5,18]. These distributions tell us how much attention is given to each result because of its rank and other features such as snippet content [9]. Some theoretical models of behavior depend on accurate models of these distributions, e.g., [16] assumes the frequency with which users review a search result is a power law of its rank, while [28] assumes the frequency with which a search result is clicked follows a geometric distribution of its rank.

In this experiment, we show a cursor hover distribution, and compare it with the corresponding click distribution. Figure 5 shows both the number and proportion of cursor hovers and clicks that occur on each of the top ten search result links. Bars representing absolute counts are scaled by the primary *y*-axis (on the left), e.g., there are approximately 240,000 occurrences of the cursor hovering on the first search result. Circles representing percentages are scaled by the secondary *y*-axis (on the right), e.g., 50% of result clicks occur on the first search result.

As is typical in SERP interactions, users interact more with top-ranked search results since they are in a more accessible location and are generally more relevant. However, Buscher et al. [5] reported that the distribution of clicks does not always reflect the relative distribution of visual attention (measured by gaze in their study). Similarly, we find that hovers are more evenly distributed across the top-ten results than clicks, and the *hover rate* is higher than clickthrough rate for all ranks beyond the first position. There are proportionally more clicks than attention on the top-ranked result, which is consistent with previously-reported bias towards selecting one of the top organic results [18,22]. This suggests that for lower-ranked search results, result hovers may correlate with clicks more than at top ranks.

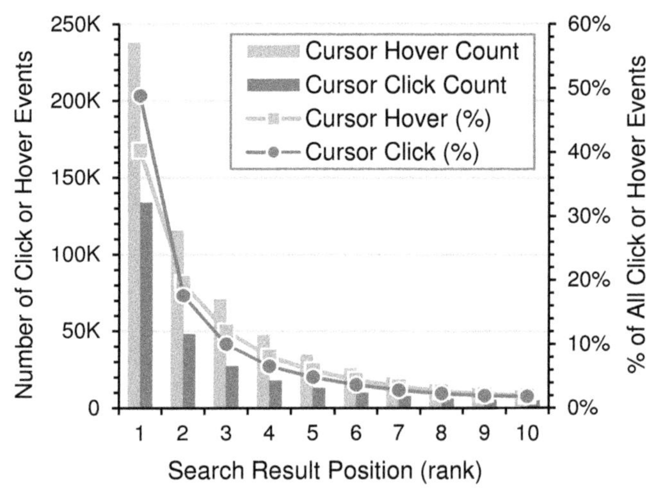

Figure 5. Frequencies and percentages of cursor hovers and clicks occurring on the search results. Percentages reflect the proportion of hover or click events over all ten results.

Unclicked Hovers

Finally, we are interested in seeing if hovering over a result but not clicking on it can be a useful signal of user interest. To examine this, we define an *unclicked hover* as an instance of the cursor hovering over a link but not clicking that link before being moved to another location on the page. Table 2 shows the number of unclicked hovers on a search result and the percentage of times that it was subsequently clicked by the same user. Result clicks can occur without an unclicked hover when the user does not hover over the result for at least 100ms and go to another location on the page before coming back and clicking the result.

Table 2. Percentage of unclicked hovers for which the hovered search result was eventually clicked.

# unclicked hovers	0	1	2	3	4	5
Result clicked	7.0%	16.7%	19.0%	22.4%	23.3%	25.2%

When there are no unclicked hovers, the result is not very likely to be clicked (only 7% of the time). Observing one or more unclicked hovers dramatically increases the likelihood of a result click, perhaps because it demonstrates that the user has attended to it. The more unclicked hovers the more likely the user will ultimately return to the result and click it. The Pearson correlation between the number of unclicked hovers and the percentage eventually clicked is strong (r =0.84), when considering up to 10 unclicked hovers. Thus the number of unclicked hovers on a result may help predict result clickthrough or perhaps result relevance.

Segmenting the unclicked hovers by the search result rank shows that result rank significantly affects unclicked hover behavior. Figure 6 shows the proportion of each result rank that is eventually clicked after an unclicked hover.

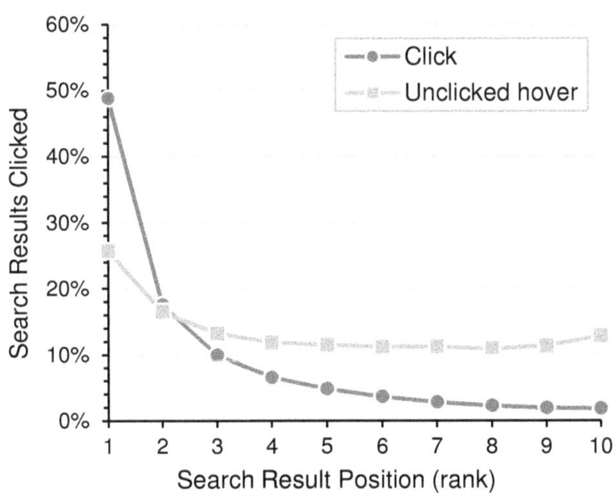

Figure 6. Proportion of search results that are eventually clicked after an unclicked hover, plotted against the click distribution from Figure 5.

The blue squares show that a search result is eventually clicked after an unclicked hover around 25% of the time for the top-ranked result and less than 15% for low-ranked results. However, when we consider that low ranked results typically have a low clickthrough rate, an unclicked hover on a low ranked result may actually provide implicit feedback that the result is relevant. To show this, we overlay the click distribution on the chart to compare the probability that an unclicked hover results in a later click (blue squares) with the original probability that the search result will be clicked (red circles). We see that whether an unclicked hover is a positive or negative indicator depends on result rank. To quantify the degree of this effect we compute the phi correlation (φ) across all queries. For the first search result, the presence of unclicked hovers negatively correlates with result clicks ($\varphi = -0.47$), but for results at lower ranks, unclicked hovers positively correlate with clicks ($\varphi = 0.59$).

In this section we examined characteristics of cursor behavior during search result examination using data from a large-scale study involving more than 20 thousand people and 360 thousand queries. We now turn to applications of this data for improving our understanding of search.

APPLICATIONS OF CURSOR DATA

There are a broad range of possible applications of large volumes of cursor tracking data, from query classification to search interface enhancements. In this section we present two applications mentioned earlier in this paper: estimating search result relevance and distinguishing good abandonment from bad abandonment. The first application makes use of features from search result hovers, whereas the second uses features derived from cursor trails.

Estimating Search Result Relevance

One useful application of cursor movement data is for estimating search result relevance. At scale, these data could be used as an additional data source to train search engine ranking algorithms and boost retrieval performance. We conducted a study in which we gathered human relevance judgments for query-URL pairs, and examined the correlation between features of the cursor movements and the human relevance judgments. In addition, we examined the value that cursor movements provide compared with search result clicks, the more traditional source of behavioral data used to estimate search result relevance.

We obtained human relevance judgments for thousands of queries as part of an ongoing evaluation of search engine quality. Trained judges assigned relevance labels on a five-point scale—*Bad*, *Fair*, *Good*, *Excellent*, and *Perfect*—to top-ranked pooled Web search results for each query. This provided hundreds of relevance judgments for each query. We intersected the judgment data with our cursor data, resulting in 1,290 query-result URL pairs for which we had both explicit relevance judgments and cursor activity. These pairs formed the basis of our analysis. We computed the following features for each pair:

- **Clickthrough rate:** Fraction of the times that URL was clicked when the query was issued (and URL returned).
- **Hover rate:** Fraction of times that URL was hovered over when the query was issued (and URL returned).

- **Number of unclicked hovers:** Median number of times for which the query was issued and the URL is hovered on but not clicked, per the earlier definition. We selected the number of unclicked hovers as a feature because we found that it was correlated with clickthrough in our previous analysis.
- **Maximum hover time:** The maximum time that the user spent hovering over the result per SERP instance. We take the maximum as this indicates the point where the user was most interested in the result.

As stated earlier, the clickthrough rate is commonly used to estimate the relevance of a URL to a query from behavioral data [18], and is included in this analysis as a baseline.

We computed the Pearson correlations between each feature and the human relevance judgments (represented numerically as a five-point scale ranging from 0 to 4 inclusive) independently and in combination using linear regression. Table 3 summarizes the findings, grouped by whether results were clicked for the query. All correlations and differences between correlations are significant at $p < 0.02$ using Fisher's z' transformations where appropriate.

The results of this analysis show that the use of cursor tracking data can improve estimates of search result relevance. Result hover features correlate better with human relevance judgments than clickthrough rates (0.46 vs. 0.42), and they lead to an improved model when combined with clickthrough (0.49 vs. 0.42). In addition, even when there are no clicks for a query, hover features show a reasonable correlation with human judgments (0.28). This is particularly important since many queries occur infrequently, resulting in little or no clickthrough data. Further analysis on the impact of query-URL popularity shows that hover features provide most value over clickthrough rate when query-URLs are less popular. There are large and significant increases in the correlation for query-URL pairs with fewer than five instances in our cursor data (0.45 hover vs. 0.35 click) and small and not significant for pairs with five or more instances (0.59 hover vs. 0.58 click). Thus cursor data appears to be especially useful when click data is less plentiful, which allows relevance estimates to be made for a much larger range of queries.

The correlations between human judgments and unclicked hovers and hover time are interesting as well. For clicked queries, unclicked hovers and hover time are negatively correlated with relevance judgments. This appears to contradict previous findings which suggested that hesitation over a result is a positive indicator of relevance [21,23]. This may be because clicks often occur on top-ranked results, where unclicked hovers are negatively correlated with clickthrough (as shown in Figure 6). For unclicked queries, we find small positive correlations between judgments and all measures. Unclicked queries have fewer relevant results, leading to more exploration lower in ranked list (where unclicked hovers are positively correlated with clicks).

Table 3. Correlations between click and hover features and relevance judgments for queries with and without clicks.

Result clicks or no clicks	Feature source	Correlation with human relevance judgments
Clicks (N=1194)	Clickthrough rate (c)	0.42
	Hover rate (h)	0.46
	Unclicked hovers (u)	-0.26
	Max hover time (d)	-0.15
	Combined[1]	**0.49**
No clicks (N=96)	Hover rate	0.23
	Unclicked hovers	0.06
	Max hover time	0.17
	Combined[2]	**0.28**

[1] $y = 2.25 - 0.1c + 1.38h - 0.08u - 0.12d$; [2] $y = 0.36 + 0.80h + 0.22u + 0.30d$

In this section we showed that the correlation between explicit relevance judgments and search activity increases when cursor actions are added to clicks, especially when clicks are infrequent or unavailable.

Differentiating Between Good and Bad Abandonment

A second application of cursor information is to distinguish between different types of abandonment. Abandonment occurs when searchers visit the search engine result page, but do not click. As noted in previous research [20], abandonment can suggest that users are dissatisfied with the search results (bad abandonment) or that they have found the answer directly on the SERP (good abandonment). For example, for queries like *[Vancouver weather]* or *[WMT stock price]*, answers are typically shown on the SERP so there is no need for people to click through to other pages. We now examine whether features of SERP cursor behavior can distinguish between good and bad abandonment.

As reported in [20], it may be straightforward to estimate good or bad abandonment for queries where search engines offer special interface treatment (e.g., weather updates or stock quotes). A more challenging scenario is determining whether observed abandonment for other queries is good or bad. To study this we focused on selected queries from our log data that were short questions (ending in a question mark) which could be answered by SERP snippets. A similar query class was also studied in earlier abandonment research [20]. To identify examples of likely good abandonment in such cases, we performed some hand labeling.

To determine whether these short questions were answered, one of the authors reviewed the SERPs returned to users and identified whether an answer appeared in the snippet text of results. Judgments were made for results which were hovered on for at least 100ms, indicating that they had been attended to but not clicked on. Of the 859 queries for which the SERPs were visually inspected, 184 (21%) contained the answer in the snippet content and hence were identified as likely examples of good abandonment. The remaining 675 queries were classified as bad abandonment.

We computed summary measures that reflect how the cursor was used on the SERPs. Specifically, we looked at cursor trail length, cursor movement time, and cursor speed for each SERP, defined as follows:

- **Cursor trail length:** Total distance (in pixels) traveled by the cursor on the SERP.
- **Movement time:** Total time (in seconds) for which the cursor was being moved on the SERP.
- **Cursor speed:** The average cursor speed (in pixels per second) as a function of trail length and movement time.

Table 4 shows the mean (M) and SEM for each measure.

Table 4. Features of cursor trails for queries associated with likely good and bad abandonment.

Feature	Abandonment Type			
	Good		*Bad*	
	M	SEM	M	SEM
Cursor trail length (px)	1084	98	1521	71
Movement time (secs)	10.3	0.9	12.8	0.6
Cursor speed (px/sec)	104	9	125	5
Number of queries	184		675	

As can be seen from the table, our preliminary analysis reveals differences in trail length, movement time, and the speed with which users moved their mouse cursor in good and bad abandonment queries. Cursor trails were shorter in cases where good abandonment was likely, compared to instances of bad abandonment. Searchers also spent less time moving the cursor, and moved the cursor more slowly when answers were in the snippet (good abandonment). All differences between the measures for good and bad abandonment were significant using independent measures t-tests (trail length: $t(857) = 2.58$, $p = .01$; movement time: $t(857) = 2.20$, $p = .03$; cursor speed: $t(857) = 2.17$, $p = .03$). It appears that when the answer appears on the SERP, users need to consider fewer results, and move the cursor more slowly as they examine snippet content in detail. These findings show that features of cursor trails, such as length, duration, and speed, are different for good and bad abandonment. Further research will examine the extent to which these differences in feature values can be used to predict good and bad abandonment in operational settings for a broader set of queries.

We now discuss the implications of these and other findings presented in this paper for the design of search systems.

DISCUSSION AND IMPLICATIONS

In this paper we explored how cursor data, which can be easily collected at scale, can be used to augment more commonly-used click measures to provide a richer picture of how searchers interact with search result pages. In Study 1 we extended previous work on the relationship between gaze and cursor using a large laboratory study. In Study 2 we developed and deployed a system to collect much larger-scale cursor data, and summarized search result examination patterns evident in cursor activities. Finally, we presented two applications of these cursor data to improve estimates of search result relevance and distinguish good from bad search abandonment. We believe that these results are quite promising, but can be extended in several ways.

Our analyses report aggregate data averaged over all users and all queries. Some laboratory studies have shown differences in search strategies for different people [2,10]. We would like to examine the extent to which such individual differences are also reflected in large-scale cursor behavior. Additionally, page layouts for SERPs are constantly changing and differ between queries. We would like to better understand how SERP features such as advertisements, query suggestions, or snippet presentation methods, as well as general component layout, influence cursor behavior. There is also a need to study the effect of different methods of scrolling (e.g., via the scrollbar or mouse scroll wheels) on the cursor tracking data. Finally, we would like to extend our research to other search engines and a broader range of users from outside Microsoft Corporation.

We demonstrated two applications of cursor tracking data at scale: estimating search result relevance and distinguishing good from bad search abandonment. In both cases, we showed clear value from leveraging large amounts of cursor tracking data. We showed that cursor features were useful for queries with result clicks (where cursor data augment click data) and for queries without result clicks (where cursor data can be a reasonable substitute). We believe that cursor features may also be used for other search-related tasks such as query classification or search ranking, and for a variety of other Web-based applications. .

Cursor data has qualitative uses as well. Usability tools that use cursor behavior (e.g., [1]) may be useful to search quality analysts. For aggregate analysis of mouse movements, heatmaps (such as those in Figure 2) can show where the interaction took place for different SERP features or queries. Heatmaps allow analysts to quickly see aggregate behavior across multiple query sessions or queries. This may be useful for determining whether users notice new features and how cursor behavior changes following their introduction.

We are also interested in continuing to explore methods for summarizing cursor activity that incorporate interesting characteristics of search behavior but can also be collected at large scale. Our current approach of only recording movements after a 40ms pause precludes analysis of cursor metrics such as acceleration. There may be alternative approaches for sampling cursor movement such as identifying sub-movement boundaries [17]. Exploring efficient methods to tune the trade-off between performance and data granularity is an important next step.

CONCLUSIONS

We described a study of mouse cursor behavior on SERPs combining eye-tracking findings with analysis of large-scale cursor data. We: (i) show that cursor and gaze position are correlated especially on search result pages, confirming and extending previous findings, (ii) develop a scalable approach to capturing cursor movements at scale and analyze search behavior evident in these data; and (iii) demonstrate the value of cursor features in two applications (estimating search result relevance and distinguishing good and bad search abandonment). Our study adds to the general understanding of how users examine search results, which is typically difficult to study in naturalistic settings on a large-scale, and demonstrates utility of these data in search-related applications. Future work will explore enhancements to the applications presented and investigate the applicability of our general approach to recording cursor movements at scale in settings beyond search.

ACKNOWLEDGMENTS

We thank Danny Bain, Craig Miller, Sarvesh Nagpal, and other members of the Bing team, for help with the development and deployment of the cursor tracking code.

REFERENCES

1. E. Arroyo, T. Selker, and W. Wei. Usability tool for analysis of web designs using mouse tracks. *Ext. Abstracts CHI '06*, 484–489.
2. A. Aula, P. Majaranta and K-J. Raiha. 2005. Eye-tracking reveals personal styles for search result evaluation. *Proc. INTERACT '05*, 1058–1061.
3. G. Buscher, E. Cutrell., and M.R. Morris. What do you see when you're surfing? Using eye tracking to predict salient regions of web pages. *Proc. CHI '09*, 21–30.
4. G. Buscher, A. Dengel, and L. van Elst. Eye movements as implicit relevance feedback. *Ext. Abstracts CHI '08*, 2291–2996.
5. G. Buscher, S. Dumais, and E. Cutrell. The good, the bad, and the random: An eye-tracking study of ad quality in web search. *Proc. SIGIR '10*, 42–49.
6. M.C. Chen, J.R. Anderson, and M.H. Sohn. What can a mouse cursor tell us more?: correlation of eye/mouse movements on web browsing. *Ext. Abstracts CHI '01*, 281–282.
7. M. Claypool, P. Le, M. Wased, and D. Brown. Implicit interest indicators. *Proc. IUI '01*, 33–40.
8. N. Craswell, O. Zoeter, M. Taylor, and B. Ramsey. An experimental comparison of click position-bias models. *Proc. WSDM '08*, 87–94.
9. E. Cutrell and Z. Guan. What are you looking for?: An eye-tracking study of information usage in web search. *Proc. CHI '07*, 407–416.
10. S. Dumais, G. Buscher, and E. Cutrell. Individual differences in gaze patterns for web search. *Proc. IIiX '10*, 185–194.
11. J. Goecks and J. Shavlik. Learning users' interests by unobtrusively observing their normal behavior. *Proc. IUI '00*, 129–132.
12. Q. Guo and E. Agichtein. Exploring mouse movements for inferring query intent. *Proc. SIGIR '10*, 707–708.
13. Q. Guo and E. Agichtein. Ready to buy or just browsing? Detecting web searcher goals from interaction data. *Proc. SIGIR '10*, 130–137.
14. Q. Guo and E. Agichtein. Towards predicting web searcher gaze position from mouse movements. *Ext. Abstracts CHI '10*, 3601–3606.
15. Y. Hijikata. Implicit user profiling for on demand relevance feedback. *Proc. IUI '04*, 198–205.
16. J. Huang and A. Kazeykina. Optimal strategies for reviewing search results. *Proc. AAAI '10*, 1321–1326.
17. R.J. Jagacinski, D.W. Repperger, M.S. Moran, S.L. Ward, and B. Glass. Fitts' law and the microstructure of rapid discrete movements. *J. Exp. Psychol. [Hum. Percept.]*, 1980, 6(2), 309–320.
18. T. Joachims, L. Granka, B. Pan, H. Hembrooke, F. Radlinski, and G. Gay. Evaluating the accuracy of implicit feedback from clicks and query reformulations in Web search. *ACM Trans. Inform. Syst., 25(2)*, 2007.
19. R. Kohavi, R. Longbotham, D. Sommerfield, and R.M. Henne. Controlled experiments on the Web: Survey and practical guide. *Data Mining and Knowledge Discovery, 18(1)*, 2009, 140–181.
20. J. Li, S. Huffman, and A. Tokuda. Good abandonment in mobile and PC internet search. *Proc. SIGIR '09*, 43–50.
21. C. Liu and C. Chung. Detecting mouse movement with repeated visit patterns for retrieving noticed knowledge components on web pages. *IEICE Trans. Inform. & Syst.*, 2007, E90-D(10), 1687–1696.
22. L. Lorigo, B. Pan, H. Hembrooke, T. Joachims, L. Granka, and G. Gay. The influence of task and gender on search and evaluation behavior using Google. *Inform. Process. Manage., 42(4)*, 2006, 1123–1131.
23. F. Mueller and A. Lockerd. Cheese: Tracking mouse movement activity on websites, a tool for user modeling. *Ext. Abstracts CHI '01*, 279–280.
24. G. Pass, A. Chowdhury, and C. Torgeson. 2006. A picture of search. *Proc. InfoScale '06*, 1.
25. K. Rodden and X. Fu. Exploring how mouse movements relate to eye movements on web search results pages. *Workshop on Web Information Seeking and Interaction at SIGIR '07*, 29–32.
26. K. Rodden, X. Fu, A. Aula, and I. Spiro. Eye-mouse coordination patterns on web search results pages. *Ext. Abstracts CHI '08*, 2997–3002.
27. B. Shapira, M. Taieb-Maimon, and A. Moskowitz. Study of the usefulness of known and new implicit indicators and their optimal combination for accurate inference of users interests. *Proc. SAC '06*, 1118–1119.
28. K. Wang, T. Walker, and Z. Zheng. PSkip: Estimating relevance ranking quality from web search click-through data. *Proc. KDD '09*, 1355–1364.

Enhancing Credibility Judgment of Web Search Results

Yusuke Yamamoto
JSPS Research Fellow and Kyoto University
Yoshida-Honmachi, Sakyo, Kyoto, Japan
yamamoto@dl.kuis.kyoto-u.ac.jp

Katsumi Tanaka
Kyoto University
Yoshida-Honmachi, Sakyo, Kyoto, Japan
tanaka@dl.kuis.kyoto-u.ac.jp

ABSTRACT
In this paper, we propose a system for helping users to judge the credibility of Web search results and to search for credible Web pages. Conventional Web search engines present only titles, snippets, and URLs for users, which give few clues to judge the credibility of Web search results. Moreover, ranking algorithms of the conventional Web search engines are often based on relevance and popularity of Web pages. Towards credibility-oriented Web search, our proposed system provides users with the following three functions: (1) calculation and visualization of several scores of Web search results on the main credibility aspects, (2) prediction of user's credibility judgment model through user's credibility feedback for Web search results, and (3) re-ranking of Web search results based on user's predicted credibility model. Experimental results suggest that our system enables users — in particular, users with knowledge about search topics — to find credible Web pages from a list of Web search results more efficiently than conventional Web search interfaces.

Author Keywords
Web search, credibility analysis, credibility feedback

ACM Classification Keywords
H.5.4 Hypertext/Hypermedia; H.3.3 Information Search and Retrieval: Search process.

General Terms
Design, Human Factors.

INTRODUCTION
Today, the Web is becoming important information source in our daily life. A large amount of information is uploaded on to it, varying from lightweight readings like product information to serious readings that affect our daily life like news, product information, medical information, and so on.

Users can freely obtain and publish information on the Web, but most information is not fact-checked before it is uploaded, unlike in other media. Therefore, Web information is not always accurate or correct. For example, Sillence et al. reported that there are more than 20,000 medical Web sites on the Web, but over half are not checked by medical experts [23]. Denning et al. warned about the credibility of Wikipedia, which is one of the most popular websites [4]. On the other hand, some researchers reported that a lot of Web users trust Web information to some extent [15]. In particular, for Web search engines, which are used as gates to vast Web information, many users perceive their search results to be somewhat credible, and some users think that the Web search engines rank Web pages on the basis of credibility [16]. If users obtain Web information without caring enough about its credibility, they can be easily misled by incorrect Web information. In the worst cases, users can suffer from actual harm in their daily lives. Therefore, it is important to measure the credibility of Web information and to help users judge the credibility of Web information.

There has been a lot of research into evaluating Web information in terms of information retrieval. However, most has focused on ranking a set of data on the basis of relevancy or popularity by analyzing similarity between query and documents, link structures [3], and user-behavior data [12]. Recently, researchers have started to discuss information quality, and some have argued that the importance of credibility is a factor in information quality [21, 20]. However, research into information quality has only just started, and few studies have measured Web information credibility.

In the research area of communication and social psychology, credibility researcher has been an important topic since 1950s [11, 9, 14]. However, in those research fields, few researchers have developed practical methods to measure information credibility. In library science, some researchers developed a guideline to evaluate information credibility [13]. However, despite the presence of ready guidelines, it is difficult for many users to appropriately assess the credibility of Web information. This is partly because in contrast to traditional publishing, Web pages often lack clues to judge their credibility such as the credentials, names of authors, references to information sources, and evidence information. Consequently, few users rigorously judge the credibility of obtained information. Therefore, automatic tools for helping users judge Web information credibility are becoming increasingly necessary.

The aim of this paper is to bridge the gap between credibility theory in social psychology and search technology in Web information retrieval. In this paper, we propose a system to help users judge the credibility of search results that Web search engines provide and find credible Web pages. Information credibility is a subjective quality that differs depending on the users obtaining the information [9, 24]. Therefore, search systems should not measure the credibility of Web pages and provide search results while ignoring users. Our system's goal is to help users obtain credible Web search results while users judge the credibility of Web search results on the basis of their own credibility criteria.

Currently, Web search results contain only the information representing content of Web pages like titles, snippets, and URLs. These do not give enough clues to enable the credibility of Web pages to be judged. Therefore if users are not careful about the credibility of Web information, and even if Web pages in a list of Web search results are not credible, the non-credible Web pages are difficult for users to detect. On the other hand, even if users are careful about the credibility, it takes too long for them to judge the credibility of Web search results. This is because there are few clues to judge credibility of Web pages, and users need to compare them with other Web pages or to search for information to judge credibility. For example, when for credibility criteria users want to know whether a target Web page describes content similar to those of many other Web pages, users need to check a large amount of Web pages and compare them with the target Web page. Also, opaque ranking algorithms of Web search engines are a big problem when users judge the credibility of Web search results. Ranking algorithms of Web search engines do not always match users' criteria for credibility judgment. If users' credibility criteria do not match ranking algorithms of search engines, it is difficult to efficiently search for credible Web pages. For example, when users wish to obtain credible Web pages that are often updated and not biased by their authors, but conventional Web search engines provide more popular, but less credible Web pages.

If a system provides additional information for credibility judgment of Web search results and ranks Web search results considering the factors users think to be important in judging credibility, users can obtain more credible Web search results. To achieve such a system, we propose the following three functions as an extension system for Web search engines:

- Analysis and visualization of scores of Web search results on the main credibility factors.
- Prediction of users' credibility judgment model through users' credibility feedback for Web search results.
- Re-ranking of Web search results based on a predicted users' credibility model.

In the field of Web searches, a lot of researchers have focused on searching for Web pages relevant to users' information needs, but few researchers have discussed Web searches from the viewpoint of Web page credibility. Our proposed system enables users to do credibility-oriented Web searches.

In summary, the contributions of this paper are:

- We address the new concept of credibility-oriented Web searches and necessary requirements for achieving systems to help users do credibility-oriented Web searches.
- We introduce and implement three functions to help users judge the credibility of Web search results and to search for credible Web pages.
- We examine how our system affects users' credibility judgment of Web search results. We show that our proposed system enables users to find credible Web pages from a list of Web search results more efficiently than conventional Web search interface.

RELATED WORK

Credibility has been studied in communication and social psychology since 1950s [11]. In these fields, credibility is defined as a perceived quality and acceptance by receivers of messages or senders of the messages. Generally, people often think of the credibility of information as an objective quality like authenticity or accuracy. However, researchers in the above fields indicate that information credibility is a subjective quality, and its interpretation depends on the receivers and types of information [9, 24, 14]. In communication and social psychology, a main research topic of credibility is to reveal the mechanisms of or factors that affect credibility judgment. Many factors concerned with credibility are grouped into two key components: expertise and trustworthiness [9]. Some researchers focus on Web information credibility. Fogg et al. conducted a large-scale survey to investigate what factors affect users' perception of the credibility of Web sites [8]. Metzger et al. surveyed how college students check the credibility of Web information [15].

In the field of information science, some researchers developed methods to analyze the credibility of specific Web contents (such as Wikipedia, Q&A contents, and people on social networks) from specific credibility aspects. Vuong et al. developed a method to find controversial Wikipedia articles [28]. Adler et al. considered sentences that remain unedited as credible, and they developed an algorithm to evaluate the credibility of sentences in Wikipedia articles by analyzing edit histories [1]. Research aimed at evaluating the credibility of Q&A contents like those on Yahoo! Answers[1] is becoming more popular. Suryanto et al. focused on expertise of answerers on Q&A sites to evaluate answers posted on them [26]. Agichtein et al. evaluated authority and hub scores of users by using a graph structure representing the interactions between the users and then evaluated the quality of answers on the basis of those users' scores [2]. Guha et al. developed a framework to predict trust between two people on a large trust network through link analysis [10]. These studies focus on specific aspects to measure the credibility, but as mentioned before, information credibility varies in accordance with users and types of information. Therefore, credibility aspects for measuring the credibility of information must change depending on users and information types.

[1]http://answers.yahoo.com/

There have been some studies focusing on helping users judge credibility. Ennals et al. developed DISPUTE FINDER, the system that searches the Web for counter sentences when users specify questionable sentences on browsed Web pages [6]. Suh et al. developed WIKIDASHBOARD, a system to visualize edit histories on Wikipedia articles [25]. Pirolli et al. used WikiDashboard to study how the system affects users' credibility judgments on Wikipedia articles [19]. For support systems to judge the credibility of Web search results, Nakamura et al. developed a prototype system [16], but they did not evaluate its effectiveness for judging the credibility of Web search results.

SYSTEM DESIGN

Our goal is to realize a system to help users judge the credibility of Web search results like those on Google and Yahoo! so that users can find more credible Web pages more efficiently by themselves. In this section, we first summarize system requirements and then explain the approach for system implementation.

Requirements

As already mentioned, information credibility is a subjective quality, and its criteria depend on the users and types of information. Search results should contain clues to judge the credibility from various viewpoints, so that users can judge the credibility of Web search results. However, conventional Web search results contain only titles, snippets, URLs, and ranking orders. Therefore, users need to manually collect clues to judge the credibility of Web search results by browsing or comparing other Web pages, but it takes too long to make a solid credibility judgment. For these reasons, systems have to automatically collect and aggregate the information necessary to judge a Web page's credibility from various viewpoints, so that users can easily know how credible it is.

The goal of credibility-oriented Web searches is to obtain more credible Web pages from the large amount of Web pages relevant to a given query. To efficiently obtain credible Web pages, Web pages must be ranked in accordance with viewpoints of their credibility. Credibility criteria depend on the users and types of information. For example, as for Web pages about Apple products, some users think that unbiased Web pages are credible, and other users think that Web pages which Apple enthusiasts appreciate are credible. Therefore systems should not rank Web search results by using a pre-defined credibility-oriented ranking function. The important thing is to rank Web pages on the basis of users' credibility judgment model. To achieve this, systems need to predict users' credibility judgment model in some way.

To achieve the above requirements, in this paper, we propose the following three functions on our system:

- Analysis and visualization of scores of Web search results on main aspects to judge the credibility.
- Prediction of users' credibility judgment model through users' credibility feedback for Web search results.

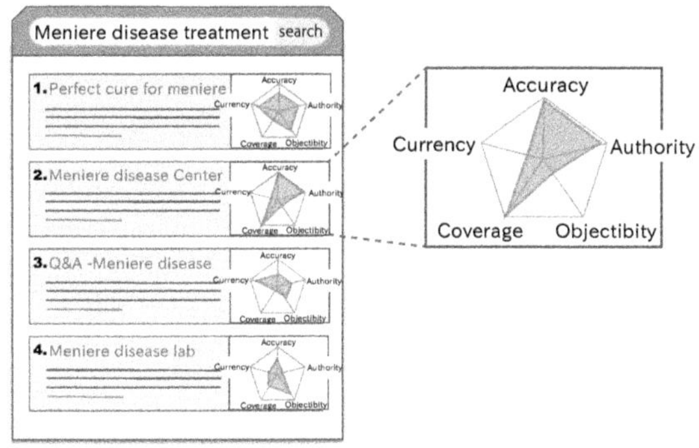

Figure 1. Visualization of scores for each of the main credibility aspects.

- Re-ranking of Web search results based on predicted users' credibility model.

Analysis and visualization of scores of Web search results for each of the main credibility aspects

In communication and social psychology, researchers have developed various taxonomies of credibility factors [5, 14]. In this paper, we selected the following five criteria, which many researchers mentioned, as the main factors to judge the credibility of Web search results [13]: accuracy, objectivity, authority, currency, and coverage. Accuracy means how accurate the Web information is, and it is measured, for example, by checking the number of errors, accuracy of links, the existence of sources, and so on. Objectivity means how biased the Web information is or is not. Authority is a criterion about the author of the Web page, and it is measured by reputation for the author and ability of the author to create contents, and so on. Currency is measured by checking when Web pages were last updated or whether Web pages are kept up to date. Coverage means how complete and comprehensive the Web information is.

Given a query and Web search results for it, our proposed system calculates scores of Web search results for each of the five aspects above. Each score is normalized by considering the distribution of the scores of all Web search results. This normalization of scores makes it easier to understand relative order of each Web search result from a specific aspect, and to compare the score of a Web page on one aspect with that on another aspect. To make users intuitively understand the scores of Web search results for each of the five credibility aspects, the system visualizes the scores as radar charts like in Figure 1. Visualization of such radar charts makes users aware of the credibility of Web search results. Furthermore, it enables users to intuitively judge the credibility of Web search results from various credibility aspects.

Prediction of user's credibility judgment model

To re-rank Web search results on the basis of users' credibility judgment criteria, we propose that the system predicts users' credibility judgment model through users' credibility feedback for Web search results. In this paper, we define the user's credibility judgment model as representation of how important the user think each of main credibility aspects to

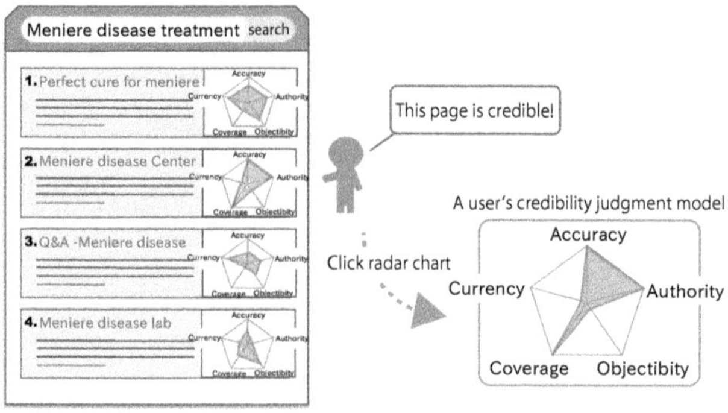

Figure 2. Prediction of user's credibility judgment model through credibility feedback for Web search results.

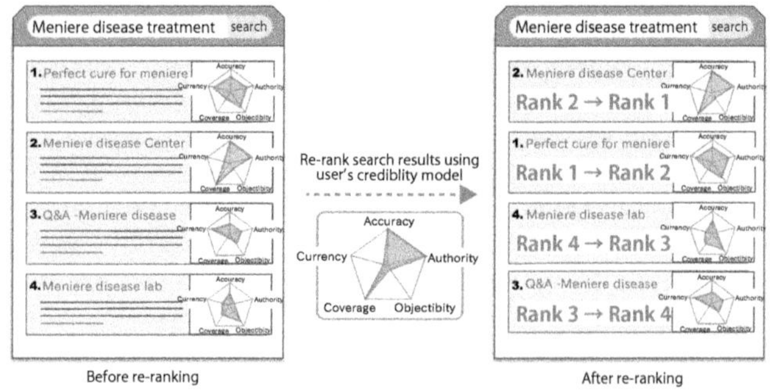

Figure 3. Re-ranking of Web search results using predicted user's credibility judgment model. Web search results are ordered in terms of accuracy, authority, and coverage.

judge the credibility of Web search results is. Users' credibility judgment model is represented by weights for main credibility factors. Users check a radar chart indicating credibility scores of a Web search result, and then they send feedback to the system by specifying the Web search result if they judge the Web search result to be credible, as shown in Figure 2. The system predicts the aspects that users consider important for judging credibility of Web search results, analyzing the scores of Web search results that users have fed back on each of the main credibility aspects. A predicted users' credibility model is shown as a radar chart on a Web browser in Figure 2, and the radar chart helps users check the predicted credibility model. In the case of Figure 2, the system predicts that the user think accuracy, authority, and coverage are the most important credibility aspects because the search result that the user specified has very high scores for these three aspects. Users can give credibility feedback to the system several times. Every time they do so, the system modifies the users' credibility judgment model that has been already predicted.

Re-ranking of Web search results using user's credibility judgment model

Our system re-ranks Web search results using a predicted users' credibility judgment model. The system analyzes credibility scores of Web search results in accordance with users' credibility judgment model and re-ranks Web search results. To calculate credibility scores of Web search results, the system uses scores of each Web search result for each of five credibility aspects and the predicted users' credibility judgment model. Every time users give credibility feedback to the system, the system re-ranks Web search results. Figure 3 illustrates an example in which the system re-ranks Web search results for the query "meniere disease treatment" by using the user's model predicted in Figure 2.

In information retrieval, a lot of researchers have developed methods for relevance feedback [22] or personalized searches [27]. These methods focus on optimizing Web search ranking for users just as our approach does. However, relevance feedback and personalized search focus on relevance of search objects for users' information needed to enhance search ranking. Also, in the two approaches, only the data that search objects contain in themselves is used to enhance relevance-oriented searches. The goal of these studies is different from that of our research because our research focuses on credibility-oriented search ranking. Our proposed system enables users to re-rank Web search results in accordance with users' credibility model and to efficiently search for credible Web pages, by analyzing content data and meta-data of Web pages.

CREDIBILITY ANALYSIS OF WEB SEARCH RESULTS FOR EACH OF THE MAIN CREDIBILITY FACTORS

In this section, we describe a method to measure accuracy, authority, objectivity, coverage, and currency of Web search results. There can be various factors related to these five aspects, but we can practically measure only a portion of them. In this work, we focus on the following possible six factors for measuring the main five credibility aspects:

- Accuracy: referential importance of Web page
- Authority: social reputation of Web page
- Objectivity: content typicality of Web page
- Coverage: coverage of technical topics on Web page
- Currency: freshness and update frequency of Web page

Our system provides users with each score for each of the above factors as referential importance, social reputation, content typicality, topic coverage, freshness, and update frequency, respectively.

Referential importance

We assume that accurate Web pages are often linked to by other Web pages as references, and we define referential importance as one of criteria to measure accuracy of Web pages. In many cases, referential importance of Web pages is often measured by PageRank algorithm, HITS algorithm, and so on. In our implementation of our prototype, we used scores of PageRank provided by Google[2].

Social reputation

We assume that if a lot of people believe or highly regard certain Web pages, the Web pages are authoritative, and we

[2] http://djangosnippets.org/snippets/221/

define social reputation as one criterion to measure authority of Web pages. We use numbers of social bookmarks for Web pages as scores of social reputation. Our prototype system uses Hatena Bookmark service[3] to obtain the number of social bookmarks for Web pages.

Content typicality

We assume that if a Web page is similar to many other Web pages about a given query, the Web page is objective. Thus we define content typicality about a given query as one criterion to measure objectivity of Web pages. We use the LexRank algorithm to calculate content typicality [7]. The LexRank algorithm summarizes text contents. By using the algorithm, a graph is created from text contents where text contents are nodes and textual similarity between text nodes is the weight of the edge, and centrality of text nodes is calculated by using the graph. In our study, the system measures content typicality of Web pages by creating textual feature vectors of Web pages and applying the LexRank algorithm to a set of Web pages about a given query.

Topic coverage

To measure how Web pages in a list of search results cover technical topics about a given query, we use the method to search Wikipedia for technical terms that Nakatani et al. developed [17]. This method focuses on bias of the links among Wikipedia articles, and extracts the terms that Wikipedia articles only in specific categories link to as technical terms. Our system measures topic coverage of a Web page to calculate the number of technical terms on the Web page.

Freshness and update frequency

To measure freshness and update frequency of Web pages, we obtain a list of updated dates of Web pages using the Wayback Machine of Internet Archive[4]. The Wayback Machine archives versions of Web pages across time. Next, we denote a set of dates when a Web page was updated, by $T = \{t_1, t_2, \ldots, t_n\}$ $(t_1 < \cdots < t_n)$. Our system calculates freshness and update frequency of the Web page as $C - t_n$ and $|T|$, respectively (C is a constant).

RE-RANKING OF WEB SEARCH RESULTS THROUGH CREDIBILITY FEEDBACK

Scores of Web search results on each of six credibility factors are visualized by radar charts. When users check credibility radar charts of Web search results, if users judge some Web search results to be credible, users can feed them back to our system by double-clicking the radar charts of the credible Web search results. The system predicts users' credibility judgment model through users' feedbacks, and then the system re-ranks Web search results in accordance with the predicted model. In this paper, we use the six kinds of scores mentioned in the previous section, to represent the features of Web search results and users' credibility judgment model. Here we denote the feature vector $\boldsymbol{v}(p)$ of Web page p by $\boldsymbol{v}(p) = (s_1(p), s_2(p), \ldots, s_6(p))^{\mathrm{T}}$, where $s_i(p)$ means a normalized score of p on credibility factor i. When the user judges Web page p as credible and sends a credibility feedback to our system, the system predicts the user's credibility judgment model $\boldsymbol{u} = (u_1, u_2, \ldots, u_6)^{\mathrm{T}}$ using $\boldsymbol{v}(p)$. Model $\boldsymbol{u}$ represents how important the user thinks each of the six credibility factors to be.

Where a set of Web pages that the user judges to be credible is denoted by $P = \{p_1, p_2, \ldots, p_n\}$, we define the n-th degree of the user's credibility judgment model $\boldsymbol{u}$ as

$$u_n = \left(\frac{1}{n}\sum_{p \in P} \frac{s_n(p)}{|\boldsymbol{v}(p)|}\right)^3. \quad (1)$$

Here $|\boldsymbol{v}|$ is a norm of vector $\boldsymbol{v}$. The system cubes the arithmetic average of Web pages' scores for each credibility factor because we wish to emphasize scores for credibility factors that users think important/unimportant.

The system re-ranks Web search results in accordance with the predicted user's credibility judgment model $\boldsymbol{u}$. Web search result p is scored by the following ranking function:

$$\mathrm{rank}(p) = \boldsymbol{u}^{\mathrm{T}} \cdot \boldsymbol{v}(p) = \sum_{k=1}^{6} u_k s_k(p) \quad (2)$$

PROTOTYPE SYSTEM

We implemented our prototype system as an extension of Safari Web browser[5]. We used Javascript to implement the following three functions on Safari browsers: visualization of radar charts of credibility analysis, credibility feedback to the system, and re-ranking of Web search results. Also, we implemented the function to calculate scores of Web search results on each of the credibility factors on our server by using Python and Sqlite3.

When users run the system on Google's search engine result pages, (1) the system inserts radar charts that illustrate scores of Web search results on each of credibility factors into search results, and (2) users can re-rank the search results in accordance with their credibility judgment model by double-clicking radar charts of credible Web search results and sending feedbacks for the credible Web search results to the system. Immediately after running the system, Google's original ranking is directly presented. Figure 4 shows an example where a user uses our system for Web search results for "meniere disease treatment".

EXPERIMENT

To examine how using our system affects users' credibility judgments of Web search results, we conducted experiments using our prototype system.

Experiment #1: Online user study

We conducted an online user study (1) to investigate which factors are important for users to judge the credibility of Web search results about specific topics, and (2) to investigate how different the consistency of credibility judgment is depending on users' familiarity with search topics when

[3] http://b.hatena.ne.jp/help/api

[4] http://www.archive.org/web/web.php

[5] http://cowsearch.hontolab.org/ (Web service version)

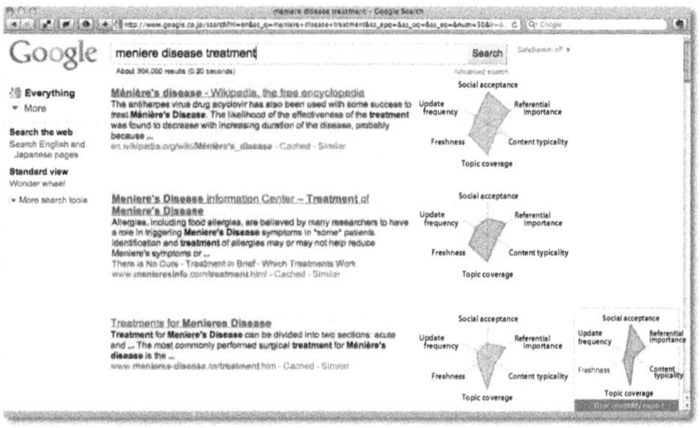

Figure 4. Screenshot of our system. In this example, a user uses our system for search engine results for "meniere disease treatment".

Table 1. Query set.

Topic	Query set A	Query set B
Disease	Meniere disease treatment	Parkinson disease treatment
Politics	Dual surnames problem	Child allowance problem
Science	Global warming cause	Earthquake cause
Health	Effective dieting	Reduce blood pressure
Sightseeing	Osaka famous place	Sendai famous place
Economics	Forex risk	Futures contract risk
Goods	Camera comparison	Video camera comparison
Food	Margarine risk	Genetically-modified food risk
History	Yamataikoku location	Kamakura shogunate formation year
Law	Personal bankruptcy procedure	Succession of property procedure

users judge the credibility of Web search results by checking their surface information (title, snippet, and URL) and their scores on various credibility factors.

Materials

We manually selected ten topic categories and prepared two queries (and tasks) for each category by considering topics whose credibility is important to examine Web pages about. A set of the prepared queries and topics is shown in Table 1. We randomly selected ten relevant Web search results and their actual Web pages for each query from Google search results before this experiment and presented them to participants in the experiment.

Participants

A total of 960 participants were recruited via an online questionnaire company. The participants were recruited so that their sex and their age (from 20's to 50's), spread evenly. The participants were randomly assigned to one of 20 groups. The participants received $2 as compensation for their time.

Procedure

The participants joined this experiment through the Internet. In the experiment, the participants of each group conducted two tasks for each topic category in Table 1.

Before starting tasks, the participants were asked to answer two questions. The first question was about (1) how important they thought each of nine factors was to judge the credibility of Web information about one specific topic of the ten topics on a 5-point Likert scale (from -2="strongly not unimportant" to 2="strongly important"). The nine factors are *content expertise*, *social reputation*, *update frequency*, *content freshness*, *authority of page creator*, *content typicality*, *evidence presentation*, *objectivity*, and *accuracy*. The second question was about how familiar the participants were with the topic on a 3-point Likert scale (1="familiar", 2="neutral", and 3="unfamiliar").

After answering the two questions, the participants performed two tasks. Immediately before starting each task, we showed a brief description about the tasks like:

> *Suppose you or one of your family has meniere disease. You are now searching for Web pages. We will show some Web pages or Web search results about meniere disease. Please evaluate the credibility of them.*

In the first task, the participants rated each of 10 Web search results for either of two queries in the specific topic using the interface where credibility radar charts for Web search results were presented on Google search interface (called the +chart interface) on a 7-point Likert scale. They rated how credible they perceived each of the search results to be (from 1="strongly not credible" to 7="strongly credible"). In this process, the participants were limited to check the presented information to rate the credibility of Web search results without following their URL links. Next, as the second task, the participants were asked to rate each of actual Web pages for the Web search results in the same way. These tasks had no time limits for rating Web search results and their actual Web pages.

In this experiment, we controlled (1) topic categories, and (2) queries in each topic category to use for two tasks, to split them equally for participants. As a result, we divided the 960 participants into 20 groups of 48 people.

Results

First we report which factors the participants thought as important to judge the credibility of Web pages about the specific ten topics. Table 2 shows the average weights of multiple credibility factors for participants who were familiar with the topics (called knowledgeable participants) and those for participants who were not (called unknowledgeable participants). According to the table, for all topics, unknowledgeable participants thought accuracy as the most important credibility factor. Also, we found that they were not so confident about factors to judge the credibility (weight $<$ 1). On the other hand, the most important credibility factor for knowledgeable participants depended on the topic categories. Furthermore, knowledgeable participants thought several credibility factors to be very important in the six categories other than science, health, economics, and food (weight $>$ 1). In some topic categories, unknowledgeable participants thought a specific factor to be a little important while knowledgeable participants thought it to be a little unimportant (e.g. social reputation in economics), and vice versa (e.g. authority in food). In this way, credibility judgment models of knowledgeable participants and unknowledgeable participants differed.

Table 2. Average weights of factors to judge the credibility of information about topics in specific categories. Weight values range from -2 (strongly unimportant) to 2 (strongly important). Numbers without/with parenthesis are weights of factors for participants familiar/unfamiliar with specific topics. Bold value means the most important factor in specific topic. In (category x factor) with gray background, unknowledgeable participants' thoughts conflict with knowledgeable participants' thoughts.

Topic	Content expertise	Social reputation	frequency	freshness	Authority of page creator	Content typicality	Evidence presentation	Content Objectivity	Content Accuracy
Disease	0.923 (0.413)	0.231 (0.217)	0.077 (0.196)	0.923 (0.543)	0.923 (0.152)	0.154 (0.239)	**1.231** (0.413)	1.153 (0.500)	0.929 **(0.935)**
Politics	0.857 (0.419)	0.357 (0.210)	0.357 (0.081)	0.643 (0.306)	0.357 (0.016)	0.286 (0.177)	0.929 (0.613)	**1.000** (0.500)	**1.000** **(0.726)**
Science	0.800 (0.175)	0.200 (0.079)	0.300 (0.048)	0.900 (0.444)	-0.300 (-0.206)	0.200 (-0.063)	0.800 (0.333)	0.400 (0.317)	**1.300** **(0.730)**
Health	0.440 (0.353)	0.100 (0.382)	0.400 (0.265)	0.720 (0.441)	-0.600 (-0.118)	-0.140 (0.029)	0.440 (0.324)	0.480 (0.088)	**0.980** **(0.588)**
Sightseeing	0.667 (0.440)	0.400 (0.100)	0.800 (0.400)	**1.333** (0.720)	0.000 (-0.600)	0.133 (-0.140)	1.000 (0.440)	0.533 (0.480)	1.133 **(0.980)**
Economics	0.429 (0.397)	-0.071 (0.293)	0.214 (0.259)	0.571 (0.379)	0.071 (-0.017)	-0.214 (0.121)	0.071 (0.345)	0.071 (0.328)	**0.643** **(0.793)**
Goods	0.800 (0.508)	0.500 (0.220)	1.000 (0.220)	0.900 (0.542)	0.300 (-0.017)	0.400 (0.152)	**1.400** (0.458)	0.900 (0.492)	1.200 **(0.881)**
Food	0.659 (0.160)	0.561 (0.040)	0.463 (0.160)	0.756 (0.400)	0.146 (-0.200)	0.244 (0.040)	0.707 (0.480)	0.756 (0.440)	**1.000** **(0.680)**
History	1.000 (0.308)	0.200 (0.077)	0.650 (0.128)	1.100 (0.462)	0.150 (0.077)	0.200 (-0.026)	1.100 (0.359)	1.150 (0.205)	**1.450** (0.538)
Law	**1.136** (0.441)	0.455 (-0.088)	0.545 (0.294)	1.000 (0.618)	0.273 (0.029)	0.409 (0.206)	1.045 (0.676)	0.955 (0.382)	**1.136** **(0.912)**

Table 3. Mean number of consistent credibility judgments for different familiarity levels.

Familiarity level	Consistent credibility judgment: Good-Good or Bad-Bad	Neutral--Neutral	Total
Not familiar (470 people)	2.95 (2.15/0.80)	3.55	6.51
Neutral (309 people)	2.72 (1.94/0.78)	3.76	6.48
Familiar (181 people)	4.00 (3.00/1.00)	2.50	6.50

Next we focused on the participants' credibility ratings to examine whether the credibility judgments of Web pages were consistent or not when the participants checked the crediblity of Web pages when using the +chart interface and when viewing the pages' content only. "Good-Good" means that participants judged a Web page as credible (rate = 5, 6, 7) on both the +chart interface and its own URL. In addition, "Bad-Bad" means that participants judged a Web page as not credible (rate = 1, 2, 3) on both the +chart interface and its own URL. "Neutral-Neutral" means that participants judged the credibility of a Web page as unknown (rate = 4) on the +chart interface and its own URL. The larger the number of "Good-Good", "Bad-Bad", and "Neutral-Neutral" judgments, the more consistent credibility judgment for Web pages when checked on the +chart interface and on their own URLs. That is, we can assume that the +chart interface enables users to judge the credibility of Web pages in a list of Web search results more consistently without checking them on their own URL.

We examined the mean number of consistent credibility judgments per 10 Web pages for each participant, for different levels of participants' familiarity to topics. Table 3 shows the results focusing on the familiarity with search topics. According to the table, as for the total number of "Good-Good", "Bad-Bad", "Neutral-Neutral" credibility judgments, there was no statistically significant difference depending on the participants' familiarity with search topics (not familiar: 6.51, neutral: 6.48, familiar: 6.50). However, we made an interesting finding in the analysis on different types of consistent credibility judgment. Focusing on the total number of "Good-Good" and "Bad-Bad" credibility judgments (that is, black-and-white judgments), that of the participants who were familiar with the search topics was significantly larger than that of the participants that were not so familiar with the topics (familiar vs. not familiar: $4.00 > 2.95$, $t(649) = 3.316$, $p < 0.001$) (familiar vs. neutral: $4.00 > 2.72$, $t(488) = 3.915$, $p < 0.001$). This suggests that if users familiar with search topics use the +chart interface, they can make a consistent and clear judgment on the credibility of Web search results, while users unfamiliar with the topics often make an unclear credibility judgment.

Experiment #2: Laboratory study

One of our system's expected advantages is that users will be able to find credible Web pages from Web search results more efficiently. To evaluate search efficiency of our system, we compared how many credible Web pages could be selected from search results within a limited time using our system with the number obtained using a conventional Web search interface. In addition, we investigated how users use our system to search for credible Web pages.

Design and materials

Across Web search results for two queries in the same topic category, we contrasted the participants who used our system + Google interface against a baseline condition involving just the original Google search interface. Participants were asked to select credible Web pages from Google's results for one query of a category using one interface and to select credible Web pages from search results for the other query in the category using the other interface.

We used the same query set as the previous online study and

prepared two tasks for each of the ten topic categories to check the credibility of Web search results.

Participants

We recruited ten students from our university as participants: three undergraduates, and seven postgraduates. The participants received $20 as compensation for their time. We randomly assigned them to either of group 1 or 2.

Procedure

Participants did our experiment individually. We briefly introduced credibility judgment tasks and our system. The participants also practiced answering a task by using our system on their own PC for Web search results for a sample query.

After the task introduction and the practice, the participants went through 10 tasks using our system + Google and 10 tasks using only Google. Before starting each task, we briefly described the task like this:

> *Suppose you or one of your family has meniere disease. You are now searching for Web pages that Google returned for "meniere disease treatment". Please select as many credible Web pages as possible within three minutes.*

After the participants read the description and started each task, the system automatically showed the top 50 Google Web search results for a prepared query about the task. The participants were asked to select as many credible Web pages as possible within three minutes by using the normal Google search interface or our system + Google interface (we fixed which interface users used for each query in advance). If necessary, participants were allowed to follow links from search results. We asked the participants not to modify the query. In this experiment, if the participants found credible Web pages from search results, they were asked to double-click their search results. When search results were double-clicked, the experimental system changed their background color. When three minutes passed, the participants stopped performing the task and the experimental system stored the information about selected Web search results. In using our system, the participants' credibility feedback was stored for analysis of users' behavior to judge the credibility later.

The experimental system assigned twenty tasks to the participants in the same order and alternated between query set A and B (disease A $\rightarrow$ disease B $\rightarrow$ politics A $\rightarrow$ politics B $\rightarrow \cdots \rightarrow$ law B). The five participants in group 1 performed the tasks for query set A and B using only Google and then Google + our system, respectively. The five participants in group 2 performed the tasks for query set A and B using Google + our system and then only Google, respectively.

Results

Table 4 presents the mean and the standard deviation of the number of credible Web pages the participants selected by using the two different interfaces (only Google vs. our system + Google). According to the table, the mean of the number of selected credible Web pages in using our system + Google were significantly larger than when using only Google ($t(99) = 3.703$, $p < 0.01$). This result suggests that our system enabled the participants to find larger number of credible Web pages than Google interface within a limited time.

Table 4. Mean and standard deviation of number of selected credible Web pages within three minutes.

	Interface type	
	Google	**Our system + Google**
Mean	4.07	5.21
SD	2.44	3.13

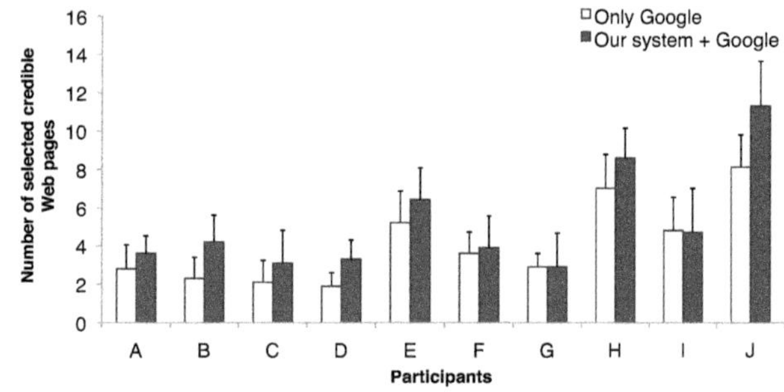

Figure 5. Mean number of credible Web pages each participant selected from a list of search results within three minutes.

Figure 5 presents results of the same analysis for each participant. According to this figure, in the results for participants F, G, and I, only Google and our system + Google do not differ significantly, but most participants could use our system + Google to find larger number of credible Web pages within a limited time than when using only Google. From the results of Table 4 and Figure 5, we found that our system can help users to find credible Web pages from a list of Web search results more efficiently or more quickly than conventional Web search interfaces.

We analyzed credibility feedback logs to examine how the participants used our system to select credible Web pages from a list of Web search results. In the experiment, the ten participants sent credibility feedbacks a total of 121 times, meaning the average per participant was 12.1. Participant A did not re-rank Web search results by sending credibility feedback. We analyzed the credibility judgment model of each participant through his/her credibility feedback logs. Table 5 presents the results. In the table, each number represents the weight of each factor for credibility judgment. If a specific factor's weight is high on the credibility judgment model of a participant, we presume the participant considered the factor as important to judge the credibility of Web search results. The table shows the factors important to judge the credibility of Web search results vary among participants. For example, the important factor for participants B and C was social reputation, while those of participant G and J were update frequency and freshness of Web pages.

Like participant A, sometimes users might be able to find credible Web page efficiently from a list of Web search re-

Table 5. Predicted credibility judgment model of each participant. SR, RI, CT, TC, CF, and UF mean social reputation, referential importance, content typicality, topic coverage, content freshness, and update frequency, respectively. Bold numbers are the most important aspects for each participant. Participant A sent no credibility feedback.

Pariticapnt	SR	RI	CT	TC	CF	UF
B	**0.1004**	0.0636	0.0601	0.0630	0.0514	0.0477
C	**0.0929**	0.0653	0.0466	0.0631	0.0543	0.0605
D	0.0650	**0.0781**	**0.0722**	0.0588	0.0545	0.0609
E	0.0641	**0.0843**	0.0651	0.0499	0.0587	0.0669
F	0.0609	**0.0747**	0.0262	0.0187	0.0384	0.0447
G	0.0509	0.0675	0.0561	0.0547	**0.0772**	**0.0875**
H	**0.0767**	0.0555	0.0651	**0.0777**	0.0654	0.0524
I	**0.0885**	**0.0700**	0.0484	0.0441	0.0659	0.0651
J	0.0530	0.0535	0.0421	0.0489	**0.1068**	**0.0927**

sults by only checking credibility radar charts of Web search results without using the re-ranking function. However, it is difficult sometimes to find many credible Web pages in a visible list of Web search results by only using the information on radar charts. In such cases, the re-ranking function becomes more important. We checked the participants who sent less feedbacks to the system than the average (12.1): participants F(4), G(5), and I(7). We know from Figure 5 that they found almost the same number of credible Web pages within the limited time using either only Google or our system + Google. From this, we think that users can find credible Web pages from the vast Web more quickly and efficiently by checking credibility radar charts and using the re-ranking function through credibility feedbacks.

DISCUSSION

We found from experiment #1 and #2 the following results:

- If users are familiar with search topics, the additional information about scores of Web search results on credibility factors as radar charts is useful for them to consistently make a black-and-white judgment about their credibility. On the other hand, if users are not familiar with the topics, users often cautiously judge the credibility of Web search results as "unknown" by checking the additional information on the Web search results.
- Our system enables users to find credible Web pages from a list of Web search results more efficiently than conventional Web search interfaces.

These results suggest that our system can be more useful for users — particularly those familiar with search topics — to search for credible Web pages in a list of Web search results from the viewpoint of efficiency than conventional Web search interfaces.

Our system is also useful for users who are not familiar with search topics to search for credible Web pages. However, the results of experiment #1 indicate they cannot judge the credibility of Web pages as clearly as users who are familiar with the topics. In real life, users often search for Web pages to learn about topics with which they are not familiar. Therefore it is very important to help such users judge the credibility of Web search results more clearly and obtain credible Web search results more efficiently.

According to ELM theory proposed by Petty et al. [18], if people have enough knowledge to understand information about a topic, they often pay attention to it. On the other hand, if people do not have enough knowledge to understand information about the topic, they often determine whether to accept the information or not with poor judgment. Considering this ELM theory and the results of the experiments, unknowledgeable users can make a consistent but poor credibility judgment on Web search results about search topics. In the worst case, they can be misled, if their credibility criteria are different from those of knowledgeable users. To avoid this, we need to think about providing help such as recommending knowledgeable users' credibility judgment models to unknowledgeable users so that unknowledgeable users can judge the credibility of Web search results more appropriately and obtain credible Web pages.

CONCLUSION AND FUTURE WORK

In this paper, we proposed the system to help users judge the credibility of Web search results and find credible Web pages from a list of Web search results. The proposed system has the following three functions for credibility-oriented Web searches: (1) visualization of score of Web search results on each of credibility factors, (2) prediction of users' credibility judgment model through users' credibility feedback for Web search results, and (3) re-ranking of Web search results according to predicted users' credibility judgment models.

We conducted two experiments to evaluate our system. Experimental results shows that our system is more useful for users — particularly users who are familiar with search topics — to efficiently find credible Web pages from a list of Web search results than conventional Web search interfaces. However, we need to consider about some issues. First, we need larger-scale experiments for more rigorous evaluation of our system. Then we also need controlled experiments where images in Web pages are eliminated, because visual designs of Web pages often affect participants' quality judgment as Zheng et al. pointed out [29]. The second issue is about making it easier for users to provide credibility feedbacks for Web pages. As in the case of participant A in experiment #2, some users are unwilling to explicitly send credibility feedbacks. Therefore it is important to think about designing better interfaces to promote users' credibility assessments or implicit credibility feedbacks for Web pages.

For users who are not familiar with search topics, we have to think about additional help for more appropriate credibility judgments of Web search results. As one possible solution, we plan to study recommending credibility judgment models of users who are familiar with the specific topics by analyzing other users' credibility feedbacks. We also think search technology for evidence information is also important as well as analysis of Web pages on the main credibility factors, so that users can make a final judgment of Web page's credibility.

To safely and efficiently obtain Web information from the vast Web, search systems focusing on credibility will become more important in the future, as well as conventional relevance-oriented and popularity-oriented ones. We believe our proposed system can contribute to credibility-oriented Web searches.

ACKNOWLEDGEMENTS

This work was supported in part by the following projects and institutions: Grants-in-Aid for Scientific Research (No. 18049041) from MEXT of Japan, a Kyoto University GCOE Program entitled "Informatics Education and Research for Knowledge-Circulating Society," the National Institute of Information and Communications Technology, Japan, and Grants-in-Aid for Scientific Research (No. 09J01243) from JSPS.

REFERENCES

1. B. T. Adler and L. de Alfaro. A Content-Driven Reputation System for the Wikipedia. In *Proceedings of the 16th international conference on World Wide Web (WWW 2007)*, pages 261–270, 2007.
2. E. Agichtein, C. Castillo, D. Donato, A. Gionis, and G. Mishne. Finding High-Quality Content in Social Media. In *Proceedings of the international conference on Web search and web data mining (WSDM 2008)*, pages 183–194, 2008.
3. J. Cho, S. Roy, and R. E. Adams. Page Quality: in Search of an Unbiased Web Ranking. In *Proceedings of the 2005 ACM SIGMOD international conference on Management of data (SIGMOD 2005)*, pages 551–562, 2005.
4. P. Denning, J. Horning, D. Parnas, and L. Weinstein. Wikipedia Risks. *Communication of ACM*, 48(12):152–152, 2005.
5. M. Eisend. Source Credibility Dimensions in Marketing Communication—A Generalized Solution. *Journal of Empirical Generalisations in Marketing Science*, 10(2):1–33, 2006.
6. R. Ennals, B. Trushkowsky, and J. M. Agosta. Highlighting Disputed Claims on the Web. In *Proceedings of the 19th international conference on World wide web (WWW 2010)*, pages 341–350, 2010.
7. G. Erkan and D. Radev. LexRank: Graph-based lexical centrality as salience in text summarization. *Journal of Artificial Intelligence Research*, 22(2004):457–479, 2004.
8. B. J. Fogg, J. Marshall, O. Laraki, A. Osipovich, C. Varma, N. Fang, J. Paul, A. Rangnekar, J. Shon, P. Swani, and M. Treinen. What Makes Web Sites Credible? A Report on a Large Quantitative Study. In *Proceedings of the SIGCHI conference on Human factors in computing systems (CHI 2001)*, pages 61–68, 2001.
9. B. J. Fogg and H. Tseng. The Elements of Computer Credibility. In *Proceedings of the SIGCHI conference on Human factors in computing systems (CHI 1999)*, pages 80–87, 1999.
10. R. Guha, R. Kumar, P. Raghavan, and A. Tomkins. Propagation of Trust and Distrust. In *Proceedings of the 13th international conference on World Wide Web (WWW 2004)*, pages 403–412, 2004.
11. C. Hovland and W. Weiss. The Influence of Source Credibility on Communication Effectiveness. *Public Opinion Quarterly*, 15(4):635–650, 1951.
12. Y. Liu, B. Gao, T.-Y. Liu, Y. Zhang, Z. Ma, S. He, and H. Li. BrowseRank: Letting Web Users Vote for Page Importance. In *Proceedings of the 31st annual international ACM SIGIR conference on Research and development in information retrieval (SIGIR 2008)*, pages 451–458, 2008.
13. M. Meola. Chucking the Checklist: A Contextual Approach to Teaching Undergraduates Web-Site Evaluation. *portal: Libraries and the Academy*, 4(3):331–344, 2004.
14. M. Metzger, A. Flanagin, K. Eyal, D. Lemus, and R. McCann. Credibility for the 21st century: Integrating perspectives on source, message, and media credibility in the contemporary media environment. *Communication yearbook*, 27:293–336, 2003.
15. M. J. Metzger, A. J. Flanagin, and L. Zwarun. College student Web use, perceptions of information credibility, and verification behavior. *Computer & Education*, 41(3):271–290, 2003.
16. S. Nakamura, S. Konishi, A. Jatowt, H. Ohshima, H. Kondo, T. Tezuka, S. Oyama, and K. Tanaka. Trustworthiness Analysis of Web Search Results. In *Proceedings of the 11th European Conference on Research and Advanced Technology for Digital Libraries (ECDL 2007)*, pages 38–49, 2007.
17. M. Nakatani, A. Jatowt, H. Ohshima, and K. Tanaka. Quality Evaluation of Search Results by Typicality and Speciality of Terms Extracted from Wikipedia. In *Proceedings of the 14th International Conference on Database Systems for Advanced Applications (DASFAA 2009)*, pages 570–584, 2009.
18. R. Petty and J. Cacioppo. The elaboration likelihood model of persuasion. *Advances in experimental social psychology*, 19(1):123–205, 1986.
19. P. Pirolli, E. Wollny, and B. Suh. So You Know You're Getting the Best Possible Information: A Tool that Increases Wikipedia Credibility. In *Proceedings of the 27th international conference on Human factors in computing systems (CHI 2009)*, pages 1505–1508, 2009.
20. S. Rieh and D. Danielson. Credibility: A Multidisciplinary Framework. *Annual Review of Information Science and Technology*, 41(1):307–364, 2007.
21. S. Y. Rieh. Judgement of Information Quality and Cognitive Authority in the Web. *Journal of the American Society for Information Science and Technology*, 53(2):145–161, 2002.
22. G. Salton and C. Buckley. Improving Retrieval Performance by Relevance Feedback. *Journal of the American society for information science*, 41(4):288–297, 1990.
23. E. Sillence, P. Briggs, L. Fishwick, and P. Harris. Trust and Mistrust of Online Health Sites. In *Proceedings of the SIGCHI conference on Human factors in computing systems (CHI 2004)*, pages 663–670, 2004.
24. J. Stiff and P. Mongeau. *Persuasive communication*. Guilford Publications, 2002.
25. B. Suh, E. H. Chi, A. Kittur, and B. A. Pendleton. Lifting the Veil: Improving Accountability and Social Transparency in Wikipedia with WikiDashBoard. In *Proceeding of the twenty-sixth annual SIGCHI conference on Human factors in computing systems (CHI 2008)*, pages 1037–1040, 2008.
26. M. A. Suryanto, E. P. Lim, A. Sun, and R. H. L. Chiang. Quality-Aware Collaborative Question Answering: Methods and Evaluation. In *Proceedings of the Second ACM International Conference on Web Search and Data Mining (WSDM 2009)*, pages 142–151, 2009.
27. J. Teevan, S. T. Dumais, and E. Horvitz. Personalizing Search via Automated Analysis of Interests and Activities. In *Proceedings of the 28th annual international ACM SIGIR conference on Research and development in information retrieval (SIGIR 2005)*, 2005.
28. B.-Q. Vuong, E.-P. Lim, A. Sun, M.-T. Le, and H. W. Lauw. On Ranking Controversies in Wikipedia: Models and Evaluation. In *Proceedings of the international conference on Web search and web data mining (WSDM 2008)*, pages 171–182, 2008.
29. X. S. Zheng, I. Chakraborty, J. J.-W. Lin, and R. Rauschenberger. Correlating Low-Level Image Statistics with Users' Rapid Aesthetic and Affective Judgments of Web Pages. In *Proceedings of the 27th international conference on Human factors in computing systems (CHI 2009)*, pages 1–10, 2009.

Augmenting Web Pages and Search Results to Support Credibility Assessment

Julia Schwarz
HCII, Carnegie Mellon
Pittsburgh, PA, USA
julia.schwarz@cs.cmu.edu

Meredith Ringel Morris
Microsoft Research
Redmond, WA, USA
merrie@microsoft.com

ABSTRACT
The presence (and, sometimes, prominence) of incorrect and misleading content on the Web can have serious consequences for people who increasingly rely on the internet as their information source for topics such as health, politics, and financial advice. In this paper, we identify and collect several page features (such as popularity among specialized user groups) that are currently difficult or impossible for end-users to assess, yet provide valuable signals regarding credibility. We then present visualizations designed to augment search results and Web pages with the most promising of these features. Our lab evaluation finds that our augmented search results are particularly effective at increasing the accuracy of users' credibility assessments, highlighting the potential of data aggregation and simple interventions to help people make more informed decisions as they search for information online.

Author Keywords: Credibility, Trustworthiness, Web

ACM Classification Keywords
H.5.4 **Information Interfaces and Presentation** – Hypertext/Hypermedia: *User issues*.

General Terms: Human Factors.

INTRODUCTION
The internet is increasingly becoming a primary source of information for people around the world. While there is a great deal of useful information online, misleading and incorrect Web pages continue to proliferate. Assessing the *credibility* of Web pages is therefore becoming an increasingly important aspect of information literacy [25], albeit one that many end-users struggle with [17].

The difficulty of assessing Web sites' credibility manifests itself in several problematic phenomena. For instance, providing account information to malicious sites masquerading as authentic ones, as in phishing attacks, results in the loss of billions of dollars annually [7], despite the integration of phishing toolbars into mainstream browsers [33]. The presence of misleading, questionable, and factually incorrect information on the Web is yet another source of concern. For instance, misinformation campaigns portraying U.S. President Barack Obama as a member of the Muslim faith have resulted in substantial confusion among American voters [29]. This latter issue of incorrect information is the focus of this paper. *Non-credible* Web pages of this type can have serious consequences when people use information found online as the basis for decisions in critical domains such as politics, finance, and health.

Naïve user populations, such as school-age children, may be particularly at risk for being misled by such content; hence, credibility assessment is considered a high-priority topic by educators. Jenkins [21] names Web search as one of several key "new media literacies" for students, and identifies *judgment* ("the ability to evaluate the reliability and credibility of different information sources") as a key part of that process. Leu and Zawilinski [25] note that "online reading" has altered the meaning of literacy to include Web-related skills such as discerning credibility. This challenge extends beyond childhood – even college-educated adults tend to visit non-credible Web pages when searching, because of a tendency to conflate high ranking in search result lists with credibility [17].

In this paper we present visualizations to augment search results and Web pages in order to help people more accurately judge the credibility of online content. After first discussing our creation of a public dataset of credibility-labeled URLs, we identify several page and site-specific features that are currently difficult or impossible for end-users to assess, and quantify their relationship with credibility. We then present two visualizations designed to assist users in their credibility judgments. Finally, we present findings from a user study that evaluates our visualizations' effectiveness in increasing credibility assessment accuracy. Our findings suggest that augmenting search results with information about expert user behavior is a particularly effective means of enhancing users' credibility judgments, resulting in a doubling of judgment accuracy.

RELATED WORK
Due to the dire economic consequences of phishing scams and malware sites, a great deal of effort has gone into increasing end-users' awareness of insecure Web sites that steal users' personal information or spread computer viruses (e.g., [7, 33]). In this paper, we consider the issue of *credibility* as separate from *security* (other researchers, such as Lazar et al. [24], make a similar distinction); hence, we do not focus on sites that actively perpetrate criminal activities, but rather on sites that contain questionable, misleading, or fac-

tually incorrect information. Such non-credible sites may be particularly problematic for naïve Web consumers such as children and teens [21, 25], as well as for adults seeking critical information in unfamiliar domains.

Prior research on Web credibility includes research on understanding users' mental models when assessing credibility and on the development and evaluation of interventions to help people better judge credibility online.

Mental Models

Organizations put considerable effort into appearing credible to gain customers' trust. The field of captology [12] studies how technology can be designed to persuade end-users. Much prior work in the area of credibility approaches the topic from a captology perspective, with a goal of understanding how people evaluate credibility so as to help Webmasters and designers create sites that will appear more credible (regardless of their true information quality), e.g., Schneiderman's guidelines for designing trust online [30] and Ivory and Hearst's tool for high quality site design [19].

This line of prior research has shown that users consider many different pieces of information to help them evaluate the credibility of Web pages. Fogg categorizes this information into four types of credibility [12]:

1. *Presumed credibility* is based on general assumptions in the users' mind (e.g., the trustworthiness of domain identifiers like *.gov*).
2. *Surface credibility* is derived from inspection of a site, is often based on a first impression that a user has of a site, and is often influenced by how professional the site's design appears.
3. *Earned credibility* refers to trust established over time, and is often influenced by a site's ease of use and its ability to consistently provide trustworthy information.
4. *Reputed credibility* refers to third party opinions of the site, such as any certificates or awards the site has won.

Fogg et al. conducted large-scale studies to determine what factors people use to evaluate credibility [11, 14], ultimately determining that in practice the "look and feel" of a site has the greatest impact on users' credibility assessments. McKnight and Kacmar [27] also found that professionalism of site design heavily influences credibility perceptions.

Hargittai et al. [17] found that search result ranking is often interpreted by end-users as a key credibility indicator, despite that fact that search engine rankings primarily reflect keyword relevance, not factual correctness, and are influenced by factors like search engine optimization businesses [26] whose aims may be at odds with credibility. More than two-thirds of American internet users think search engines are a "fair and unbiased" information source [9].

Educational institutions, consumer watchdog groups, and libraries offer guidance to users on techniques for credibility assessment, such as directing readers to consider a Web page's accuracy, authority, objectivity, currency, and coverage [22]. Whether users take the time to follow such advice, assuming they are aware of it, is influenced by factors such as the nature of their task [28].

Fogg proposed Prominence-Interpretation Theory [13] to model how people assess credibility online. P-I Theory posits that the impact an element has on perceived credibility is a product of its prominence (how likely it is to be noticed) and interpretation (what value or meaning people assign to that element). Factors such as user involvement [10], user task [28], and experience affect prominence, while a user's assumptions, knowledge level, and context affect interpretation [13]. Hilligoss and Rieh [18] present a framework which identifies aspects of credibility assessment independent of media, information type, and environment. This framework identifies three levels of credibility judgment: construct, heuristics, and interaction. Similar to P-I Theory, Hilligoss and Rieh observed that people repeatedly refine their credibility judgments as they are viewing a Web page.

Interventions

In addition to understanding how people evaluate credibility, there have also been efforts toward improving people's credibility assessment accuracy. Three main approaches are content analysis, prediction, and informing end users.

Content Analysis

One approach to helping people find factually correct content is to automatically identify false facts. Extracting factual information from the Web is an active research area. An example of such work is Open Information Extraction [1]. However, natural language approaches are not yet reliable or comprehensive enough for use on the open Web.

Some researchers have applied content analysis approaches to specific aspects of credibility. For instance, Dispute Finder [8] identifies contentious topics by looking for text such as "X is disputed," and BLEWS [15] provides insight into online news by analyzing the content and sentiment of blogs referencing particular articles.

Predicting Credibility

Developing algorithms to predict the credibility of a page is another promising approach. Two of the better known algorithms, TrustRank [16] and CredibleRank [4], use the link structure of the Web to determine a credibility score. However, these algorithms define non-credible pages in terms of Web spam, not in terms of information quality.

Informing End-Users

A third approach is to show end-users information that may help them form more accurate impressions of a page's quality. Examples of this type of intervention include augmenting Wikipedia pages with a visualization of edit history [23], and creating certifications or whitelists for trustworthy sites (such as HON certification [www.hon.ch]). A challenge of this approach is designing interventions that impact user behavior; for example, studies of anti-phishing browser toolbars have found them to be ineffective because people don't notice or pay attention to the toolbar [33].

Our present work follows the "informing end users" approach. Since content-analysis and prediction approaches are not yet accurate enough to rely on for credibility analyses, this approach of supporting a user's reasoning process avoids the risk of incorrect classifications by automated techniques. This approach also permits more nuanced interpretations of credibility (e.g., situations where there is not a single accepted truth, or in which quality judgments may differ based on cultural norms). Another potential benefit of this approach is that informing end-users might encourage reflection on credibility, potentially enhancing users' credibility assessment skills over the long-term.

DATA SET

Creating and testing interventions for improving users' credibility assessments requires a data set of Web pages that have been labeled with a "ground truth" credibility score. To our knowledge, no such data set is publicly available. The following sub-sections describe our process for creating such a data set.

Page Selection

Hand-labeling Web pages for credibility is a time-consuming process (requiring several minutes to read the contents of each page plus time to look for additional information from other sources to support the assessment in cases where the factual correctness of a page was unclear). We chose 1,000 Web pages as the size of our data set to balance the desire to have a large sample size with the time constraints of generating meaningful credibility ratings.

To balance topical breadth and depth, we selected five topics by browsing directory headings and sub-headings in the Open Directory Project [dmoz.org], with the aim of selecting topics known to have substantial amounts of both credible and non-credible coverage online. The five topics selected were Health, Politics, Finance, Environmental Science, and Celebrity News. We then used Google Zeitgeist [google.com/zeitgeist] to identify more specific information needs in each of these areas, based on recent popular search trends. Based on the Zeitgeist trends, we developed five queries within each topic area (Table 1). We then issued these queries to a popular search engine, and used the URLs for the top 40 search results for each query as the URLs to label for our data set. This resulted in a total of 1,000 URLs (5 topics x 5 queries each x 40 results each).

Credibility Ratings

We associated a five-point Likert scale rating with each URL in our data set, with a score of 1 for "very non-credible" and a score of 5 for "very credible." Based on a synthesis of the research literature [11, 14, 18, 22, 24, 27, 28], we used the following definition to operationalize credibility for the purposes of assigning a score: *A credible webpage is one whose information one can accept as the truth without needing to look elsewhere. If one can accept information on a page as true at face value, then the page is credible; if one needs to go elsewhere to check the validity of the information on the page, then it is less credible.*

Using this definition as a guide, one author of this paper rated all of the 1,000 pages in our data set. This rater is an expert Web user who interacts with the Web and search engines on a daily basis, holds a bachelor's degree in computer science, is enrolled in a graduate degree program in a related field, and is familiar with suggested pedagogies for credibility assessment (e.g., [22]). This process took approximately 20 hours. To ensure reliability, another author of this paper, with similar background and credentials, rated 50 randomly selected URLs from the data set. A Spearman correlation test to measure inter-rater reliability indicates high agreement for this overlapping sample ($\rho(50) = 0.7$).

To further ensure reliability, we solicited additional ratings from topic experts for the subset of 21 pages ultimately used in our evaluation sessions. As discussed in the "Evaluation" section, this subset consisted of 7 pages each on the topics of Finance, Politics, and Health. For the reliability check, we recruited two experts in each of these topic areas, and gathered their credibility scores for the pages in their topic. The finance experts were both professionals working in the banking and investment industry, the political experts were both volunteers on presidential political campaigns, and the health experts were both medical doctors. Agreement was calculated by averaging the two experts' scores for each page, and then comparing these to the ground truth scores using Spearman correlation. Agreement between the average of the experts' ratings in each domain and our ratings was $\rho(7) = 0.6$ for Finance, $\rho(7) = 0.7$ for Politics, and $\rho(7) = 0.9$ for Health.

In the remainder of this paper, we refer to the scores we assigned as the credibility "ground truth" for these 1,000 Web pages. Although we used a rater with high general expertise regarding credibility and the Web, the reader should bear in mind that assigning credibility ratings is to some extent a subjective process. However, our comparisons with a sample of topical specialists' ratings indicate that our ground truth ratings are a fair approximation of expert opinion on the credibility of Web pages. We have made our labeled data set available at http://research.microsoft.com/credibility to enable readers to assess the quality of our labels, as well as to build upon this data for future research.

FEATURE EXPLORATION

As discussed in the "Mental Models" section, prior research on users' credibility assessment practices indicates that people typically make credibility judgments based on features such as a page's search result ranking [17] and visual design [14]. We hypothesized that, in addition to these readily apparent features that people currently rely on, there are many features which are difficult or impossible for users to reflect on when viewing a Web page, but that might help them better judge credibility. We explored several such features, each of which fell into one of three categories: on-page, off-page, and aggregate features.

Following each feature description, we report how it correlates with our ground truth labels. We used a non-parametric

Topic	Query Terms	Expert URL Filters	# of Users
Health	Atkins diet effectiveness P90x exercise program H1N1 vaccine side effects Alzheimer's genes Autism warning signs	ncbi.nlm.nih.gov/pubmed pubmedcentral.nih.gov	254,175
Finance	Is it a good time to invest in gold? What mutual funds to invest in Reduce personal debt Mortgage refinancing Is it a good time to invest?	bloomberg.com edgar-online.com hoovers.com sec.gov	201,014
Politics	Iran election rigged Cash for clunkers eligibility Obama birthplace Death Panels Tea Party	foreignaffairs.com theatlantic.com foreignpolicy.com hir.harvard.edu economist.com	66,155
Celebrity News	Lady Gaga Adam Lambert Nadya Suleman Floyd Landis Michael Jackson	ew.com usmagazine.com people.com	692,611
Environmental Science	Renewable energy Green jobs Climate change Cap-and-trade Organic Eating	pewclimate.org epa.gov rff.org nrdc.org whitehouse.gov/administration/ceq	83,476
All Users		*(none)*	*50,473,520*

Table 1: Our data set contained 1000 URLs – 200 in each of 5 topics, consisting of the top 40 search results for each of the 5 topical query terms). The "expert URL filters" for each topic are the sites used to heuristically identify topical experts. The final column shows the number of users in one month's worth of browser toolbar data identified as experts by these filters.

correlation measure (Spearman's ρ) since our credibility labels were subjective and not continuous.

On-Page Features

On-Page features are present on a page but are difficult or time-consuming for a person to quantify or attend to.

Spelling Errors: We computed the number of spelling errors by writing a program to screen-scrape and spell check each URL in our data set. (ρ[1000]=0.01)

Advertising: Our program computed the number of advertisements on a page by searching the HTML for script tags from several popular advertisers such as Google AdWords [adwords.google.com] and DoubleClick [doubleclick.com]. (ρ[1000]=-0.20)

Domain Type: Because users tend to focus on the page contents rather than the browser's address bar [33], the domain type (.com, .gov, etc.) of a page may not be salient; we collected this as a categorical feature. (ρ[1000]=0.19)

Off-Page Features

Off-page features require the user to leave the target page and look elsewhere for supplementary data.

Awards: We collected information about what awards and certifications sites had received from three agencies. A Webby Award is "the leading international award honoring excellence on the internet" [webbyawards.com]. We counted the number of Webby Awards a site had received for the year 2009. Alexa [alexa.com] (an organization that monitors internet traffic) publishes a list of the top one million most popular sites on the internet. We used the Alexa rank of a site as another feature. Health on the Net (HON) [www.hon.ch] promotes reliable health information online, and certifies reliable health-related Web sites. We treated the presence or absence of a HON award as a binary feature for the "Health" subset of our URLs. (Alexa rank: ρ[1000]=-0.15, number of Webby awards: ρ[1000]=0.11, HON certification: ρ[200]=0.35)

PageRank: A Web page's PageRank [3] is not generally visible to end-users, unless they install browser toolbars or look up URLs on dedicated sites such as those run by search engine optimization companies [26]. We gathered the PageRank of each URL in our data set. When the PageRank for a particular page was unavailable, we used the rank of its parent site. A related feature we also gathered was a major search engine's ranking of the URL for the queries used in generating our data set. (ρ[1000]=0.30)

Sharing: We also gathered information about how frequently a URL was shared using publicly available sharing and click information from Bit.ly [bit.ly]. We obtained the number of times a link to a Webpage was shared, liked, commented on, and clicked from Facebook, as well as the number of times a shortened version of the URL (commonly used when sharing links on Twitter) was clicked. We also counted the number of users that bookmarked a URL [del.icio.us]. (bookmarks: ρ[1000]=0.22, bit.ly clicks: ρ[1000]=0.17, Facebook shares: ρ[1000]=0.29)

Aggregate Features

Aggregate features are not generally available to end users, though they could be made available by companies such as search engines who often log user behavior via browser toolbars. Our aggregate features were computed from one month's worth of anonymous browsing data (June 2010) from 50,473,520 users who opted to provide data via Microsoft's browser toolbar.

General Popularity: To calculate overall popularity, we counted the number of unique user IDs visiting the page in the time period covered by our logs. (ρ[1000]=0.38)

Geographic Reach: To approximate the popularity of a page among a broad demographic, we computed the number of different geographic locations visitors to the site originated from using zip code information. (ρ[1000]=0.32)

Dwell Time: We computed the average length of time users kept a URL open in their browser as a proxy for the amount of time spent viewing a page. (ρ[1000]=0.001)

Revisitation Patterns: Returning to a page can be considered an implicit vote for its quality. We calculated on average how much each page was re-visited. (ρ[1000]=0.36)

Expert Popularity: Fogg's classification of credibility into presumed, surface, earned, and reputed [12] suggests that not everybody is able to evaluate credibility equally well. For example, people unfamiliar with a topic, such as medicine, have little opportunity to evaluate the *earned credibility* of a given medical site because they have spent little time on medically-related websites. Indeed, research comparing search strategies of experts and non-experts in topics such as health reveal that topic experts are more effective searchers in their expertise area because they use previously-encountered, high-quality URLs as starting points in the information-seeking process [2]. Therefore, behavior of experts within a particular domain may provide an especially useful source of information regarding credibility.

Based on the approach described by White et al. [31], we classified each of the fifty million user IDs in our log data with regards to expertise in the five topic areas in our URL data set. White et al. [31] found that a heuristic-based approach to defining expertise (users who visit a set of white-listed URLs identified by a professional in the target topic area) is effective at differentiating users according to several standards of expert behavior used in the information retrieval community (e.g., [2, 32]). Using this approach with whitelists from [31] (health, finance) and discussions with topic professionals and enthusiasts (politics, environmental science, and celebrity news), we labeled users who visited any of the whitelisted sites in a particular topic area more than ten times to be "experts" in that topic (Table 1). Using this metric, we then calculated the number of topic experts who had visited each page in our data set in the period covered by our log data. (health: ρ[200]=0.5, politics: ρ[200]=0.4, environment/celebrities/finance: ρ[200]=0.3)

Feature Selection

While showing users all the features we gathered for each page would contain the most information, Prominence-Interpretation theory suggests that showing a user all of this information may not help people evaluate credibility. Not only would each of the features be less prominent, but the inevitable clutter that would result from so much information would make our entire augmentation less prominent on a page. Additionally, such an information-heavy intervention may distract users from their primary intent. Consequently, we reduced the size of our feature set by first measuring how well each feature correlated with our ground truth. As expected based on the difficulty of predicting nuanced concepts such as credibility [4, 16], the highest of these correlations were in the "moderate" range of ρ = .3 to ρ = .5. These moderate correlations indicate that predicting an objective credibility score using the features above would lead to only moderate success; however, they also indicate that these features contain signals that can inform end users in their interpretation of a page's credibility.

We then selected a few features that we felt would be intuitive to end-users, would support an interesting visualization, and that correlated well with ground truth. Features such as spelling errors were omitted due to low correlation, and features such as awards, though sparse, were included because of relatively high correlation. The features we chose were: overall popularity of a Website; popularity of a site among domain experts; the number of zip codes people accessed a site from; receipt of awards and certifications; and PageRank. We then used these features to create visualizations for augmenting Web pages and search results.

VISUALIZATIONS

Prior work indicates that subtle cues (such as color changes to indicate safety levels in anti-phishing toolbars [33]) may not be salient enough to alter users' perceptions of a Web page. However, work on augmenting Wikipedia pages with visualizations of edit history [23] has succeeded in altering users' opinions, perhaps due to the more salient nature of the latter visualizations. Hence, we decided to create a rich visualization to represent our chosen features to end users.

In addition to presenting the features adjacent to Web pages themselves, we created a second, more compact version of the visualization to augment search results. We felt that augmenting search results was particularly important given recent findings that many users make determinations of credibility based on search results pages [17]. Such assessments are particularly in need of assistance, due to the limited information scent [4] of search results as compared with Web pages. We hypothesized that a search result visualization might also have more impact than one on the Web page itself, since the sparseness of search results pages would boost the likely impact of such visualizations according to Prominence-Interpretation theory [11], and since once users have seen a Web page itself, it is difficult to overcome the first impressions they form based on the professional appearance of a page's design [14, 27].

We built a Web application to augment the Web pages and search result snippets for the 1,000 URLs in our data set. The Web page visualization (Figure 1) appears adjacent to the Web page, so that it is visible regardless of scroll positioning. The increasing popularity of wide-screen displays and multi-

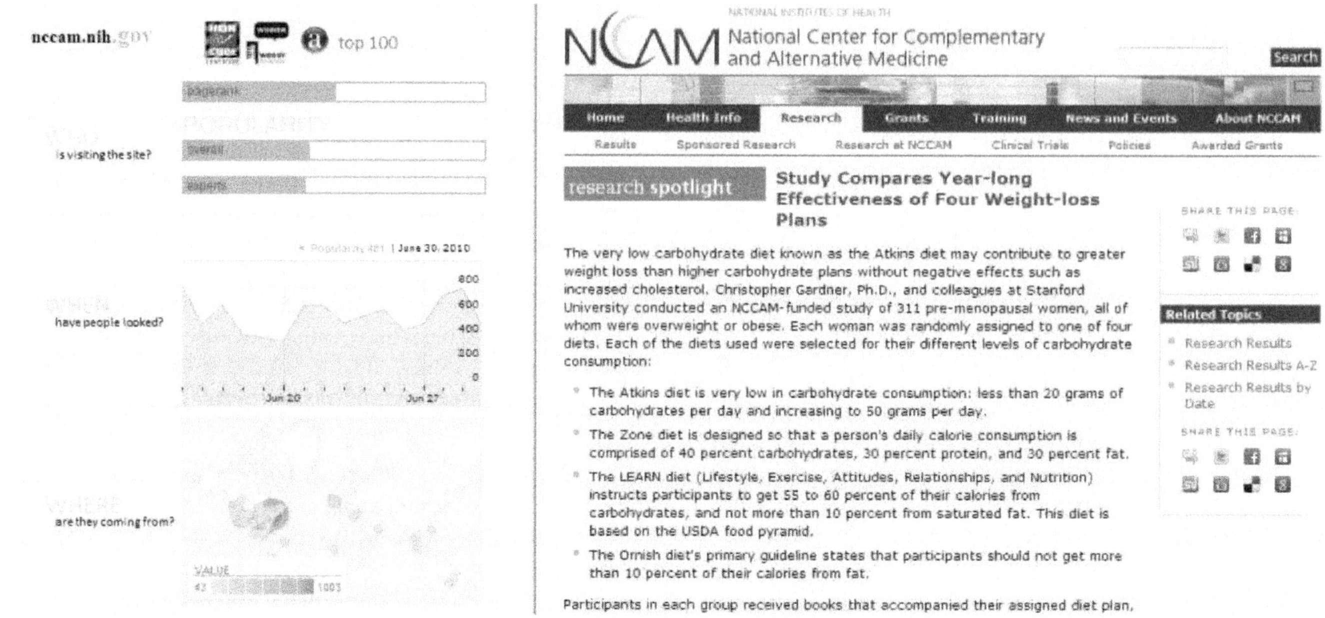

Figure 1. Web page augmented with our visualization.

monitor setups facilitates this horizontal expansion of the browser footprint. The visualization uses color and font size to draw attention to a page's domain type, and includes icons to indicate whether a page has received a Webl Families HON certification, or high (top-10, top-100, or Alexa ranking. Horizontal bars indicate the relativ the current page's PageRank, general popularity, larity among experts for the page's topic (normali on the minimum and maximum values in our data s all popularity is further broken down to reveal ten geographic patterns in separate charts. These indi grouped thematically according to the interrogative questions "who," "when," and "where."

The search result visualization (Figure 2) is more compact than the Web page visualization, to reflect the space constraints of search result pages. Only items from the "who" category are shown in this condensed view.

EVALUATION

In addition to assessing users' subjective reactions, we also sought to evaluate the following hypotheses:

H1: Users' credibility ratings will be more accurate when the visualizations are available to them.

H2: Users will feel more confident in the accuracy of their ratings when the visualizations are available to them.

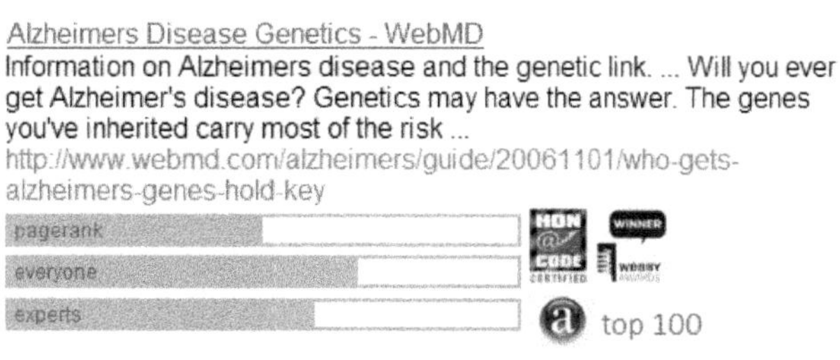

Figure 2. Search result augmented with our visualization.

H3: The impact (on both accuracy and confidence) of augmenting search results will be greater than the impact of augmenting Web pages.

agers' ratings will receive more benefit from these ons than adults' will.

cted a within-subjects experiment to evaluate our s. We recruited 26 paid participants (13 female) Seattle metropolitan area. Participants came to our ne-hour session to complete the study. Participants' ed from 13 to 40 (mean = 21). 15 of our participants were middle-school or high-school students. Adult participants had a variety of occupations unrelated to programming, Web design, or usability. Occupations included freelance photographer, sales representative, and graphic artist. All participants had experience browsing the internet and using search engines (most used them daily).

From our data set of 1,000 credibility-labeled URLs, we selected 21 URLs for evaluation in our study. These 21 URLs were selected by choosing seven URLs associated with each of three queries (Politics: "Obama birthplace", Finance: "Is it a good time to invest in gold?", and Health: "H1N1 vaccine side effects"). For each of these three queries, we selected the seven URLs (from the 40 available) in a manner that enabled us to achieve broad coverage of search result rankings and ground-truth credibility ratings for each query. As discussed earlier in the "Credibility Ratings" section, the ground-truth ratings for these 21 URLs were verified for agreement with ratings from experts in these three topic areas. The Web pages and associated search result snippets for our data set were cached at the time of ground truth data collection to ensure consistency.

Block	Condition	Topic
1	Basic Search Results	Politics
2	Basic Search Results	Finance
3	Augmented Search Results	Politics
4	Augmented Search Results	Finance
5	Basic Web Page	Politics
6	Basic Web Page	Health
7	Augmented Web Page	Politics
8	Augmented Web Page	Health

Table 2. Study Design. The seven URLs within each block were shown in random order.

For each participant, the experimenter first provided a tutorial session using URLs that were not part of the evaluation set to demonstrate both visualizations and explain the meaning of each visualization component in appropriate terms (e.g., "PageRank measures how many other Web pages link to this page."; "Expert popularity measures how many people who visit specialized sites on a topic also visit this page."). The experiment procedure was explained in detail, including the rating scale and definition of credibility discussed earlier in the "Credibility Ratings" section.

The study was organized into 8 blocks, with 7 URLs per block (Table 2). The order of URLs within blocks was randomized to reduce order effects. The order of blocks was constant for all participants. Counterbalancing conditions was not desirable, due to the progressively increasing level of information revealed by varying conditions. For instance, it would not make sense to ask a user to rate the credibility of a given URL in the "basic Web page" condition if they had already rated that same URL in the "augmented Web page" condition, since they may remember the additional information revealed by the visualization. Similarly, rating the credibility of a URL in either of the "search result" conditions after already having viewed the full Web page would present a confound.

To enable comparisons on the relative influence of the visualization on search results versus Web pages, the URLs from one topic (Politics) were repeated in all four conditions. Consequently, for the Politics URLs, information is introduced and later removed (between the "augmented Search result" and "basic Web page" conditions). To mitigate this potential learning effect on our data, we tested the other two sets of URLs in one condition rather than cross-conditions, using Finance for search results and Health for Web pages. Additionally, we alternated topics with each block to facilitate forgetting of previously seen URLs.

At the beginning of each block, participants were reminded of the query associated with the current topic, and were instructed to pretend they were conducting that query, in order to contextualize their credibility judgments in a realistic task. Then, for each of the seven URLs on the current topic, participants viewed either the basic search result, augmented search result, basic Web page, or augmented Web page, according to the current condition. They rated the target page's credibility on a five-point Likert scale, as well as their confidence in their credibility assessment (also on a five-point Likert scale).

Type	Feature	Rating
Search Result	*Expert Popularity*	4.5
	Summary	4
	URL	3.9
	Awards	3.9
	Title	3.8
	Result Rank	3.5
	PageRank	3.2
	Overall Popularity	3.1
Web Page	Factual Correctness	4.5
	Expert Popularity	4.4
	Citations	4
	Familiarity with Site	3.9
	Title	3.8
	Domain Type	3.8
	Look & Feel	3.7
	Author Information	3.6
	Awards	3.5
	PageRank	3.3
	Overall Popularity	3.3
	Popularity Over Time	2.8
	Number of Ads	2.6
	Where People Are Visiting From	2.5

Table 3. Mean Likert ratings of relative feature usefulness in the credibility assessment process, including features of our visualizations (in *italics*) and features deemed important by prior studies of credibility perceptions.

To enable completion within participants' one-hour lab visit and to simulate realistic circumstances (in which users rarely devote substantial time to credibility assessment [28]), there was a limited time to view the contents: 20 seconds for a search result and 60 for a Web page. These timings were selected based on prior findings [6] that users typically spend 10 seconds reading search results. Once the time expired, the content disappeared and the participant was forced to make a rating. Participants rated pages before time expired 90% of the time in the basic search results condition (μ=12 sec.), 94% of the time with augmented search results (μ=9 sec.), 97% of the time with the basic Web page (μ=18 sec.), and 99% of the time with the augmented Web page (μ=13 sec.). Each participant completed 56 ratings.

At the conclusion of the session, participants completed a short questionnaire about the usefulness of the visualizations, utility of different features, and demographics.

RESULTS

We collected a total of 1456 credibility ratings, 1456 confidence ratings, and 26 questionnaires from our study. Using these data, we revisit our initial hypotheses and questions. Due to the subjective (and potentially non-equidistant) interpretations participants may attribute to Likert scales, and the fact that ratings were not normally distributed, we use non-parametric tests when analyzing Likert responses. Specifically, we used Spearman's ρ to measure inter-rater reliability between user ratings and ground truth, and Wilcoxon tests to evaluate differences in ratings between conditions.

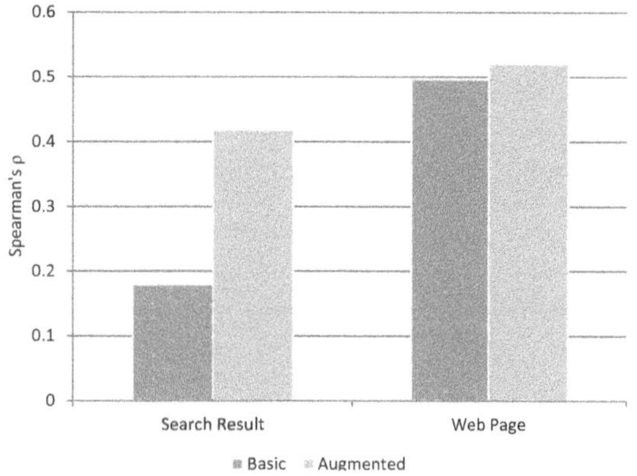

Figure 3. Agreement between participant ratings and ground truth.

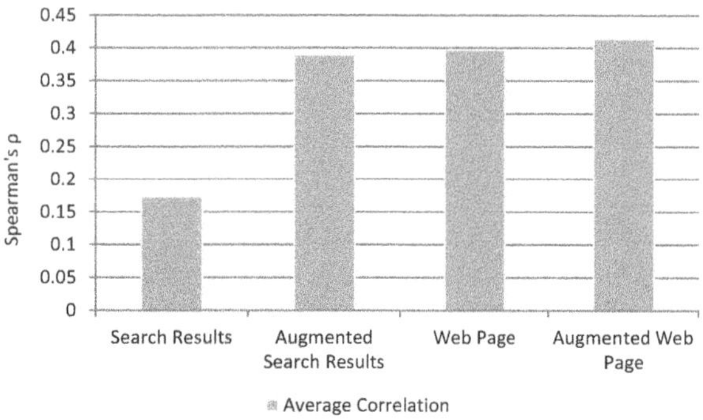

Figure 4. Agreement between participant ratings and ground truth for the subset of URLs (Politics) that were present in all conditions.

Questionnaire Data

Table 3 summarizes the credibility-assessment-utility participants reported for several features of search results and Web pages. In addition to attempting to judge the correctness of a page's contents, users found the expert popularity to be most helpful both when viewing full Web pages and also search results. For instance, P18 mentioned "The expert bar was very useful in finding credible information. I would be very happy to have one on search engines I use." P17 said "I really like the experts bar…this is because if experts don't use the site…then it must be wrong."

Performance Data

Not only did our visualization *seem* useful (receiving a mean utility score of 5.9 on a 7-point Likert scale), our data suggest that our visualization made a significant impact on participants' ability to evaluate credibility. We present our results in the context of our initial hypotheses:

H1: Users' credibility ratings will be more accurate when the visualizations are available to them.

Our data supports this hypothesis for search results. To assess accuracy, we first measured the distance (absolute value of the difference) between users' credibility ratings and ground truth for a Webpage. We also measured the correlation between participant ratings and our ground truth.

Distance from Ground Truth

Our results indicated a significant improvement between the basic search results and augmented search results condition, ($z = -2.50$, $p < 0.05$). The mean distance between credibility and ground truth in the basic search results condition was 1.25; this distance was reduced to 1.09 in the augmented search results condition. There was no significant difference in the basic Web page (0.84) and augmented Web page (0.92) conditions. These results indicate that the visualization significantly impacted people's ratings when viewing search results but not a Web page.

Agreement with Ground Truth

Not only did our visualization decrease the distance from ground truth in the search result condition, it also improved participants' agreement with the ground truth by a factor of two (Figure 3). The average agreement in the search results condition was 0.17, while the average agreement in the augmented search results condition was 0.42. This difference is statistically significant ($t(25) = -4.75$, $p < 0.01$).

Not only does our visualization significantly improve users' ability to evaluate the credibility of Web pages when viewing search results, it makes users as accurate as if they were viewing the entire page. Figure 4 shows average agreement between participant ratings and ground truth for the seven "Politics" URLs that were shown in all four conditions. A repeated measures ANOVA test ($F(3) = 2.97$, $p < 0.05$) and follow-up pairwise t-tests indicated a significant difference between the basic and augmented search results ($t(25) = -2.38$ $p < 0.05$) as well as the basic search result and augmented Web page ($t(25) = -2.21$, $p < 0.05$) and (marginally) the basic search result and basic Web page ($t(25) = -1.93$, $p = .07$), while showing no support for differences between any of the other conditions.

Although not statistically significant, the general trend in our data was that people tend to overestimate the credibility of non-credible pages, and underestimate the credibility of credible pages, and our visualization helped them correct for this over/underestimation.

H2: Users will feel more confident in the accuracy of their credibility ratings when the visualizations are available to them.

Participants consistently felt somewhat confident in their ratings across all conditions. The mean confidence rating (using a five-point Likert scale) across all conditions ranged from 4.1 to 4.3, and there was no correlation between confidence and accuracy. The discrepancy between participants' confidence scores and their actual accuracy further highlights the importance of helping people evaluate information credibility because people trust their judgments regardless of whether they are correct or not.

H3: The impact (on both accuracy and confidence) of augmenting search results will be greater than the impact of augmenting Web pages.

Our data indicates that the impact of augmenting search results is greater than that of augmenting Web pages in terms of accuracy but not confidence. As discussed above, augmenting search results significantly improves credibility accuracy, while augmenting Web pages has little effect, and participant confidence was high in all conditions.

H4: Teenagers' ratings will receive more benefit from our intervention than adults' will.

We found no significant differences in accuracy improvements between teenagers and adults. However, teens found expert popularity to be more helpful than adults when viewing search results. Teens rated expert popularity as more important, on average, than adults ($z = -2.74$, $p < 0.01$).

DISCUSSION

Our findings suggest that augmenting search results with additional features can help users make more accurate assessments about the credibility of the target Web pages. Aggregate information about topical experts' visitation patterns appears particularly promising in this respect.

While our visualization significantly improved users' ability to evaluate credibility when viewing search results, it had little effect on page-level credibility assessment. The increased impact of the visualizations in the search results context harmonizes with the predictions of Prominence-Interpretation theory [13]. It is particularly striking that that the augmentation of search results increased users' credibility assessment performance to the same level as viewing an entire Web page, demonstrating that our visualizations added valuable information scent [4] to search results. Improving the utility of search results for credibility assessment is particularly important, as users increasingly use search engines as their entry point to the Web [9] and already attempt to infer credibility from search engine result lists [17].

The lack of additional benefit of our visualization in the Web page condition is disappointing, but not altogether surprising in light of the large influence a page's visual design has on credibility assessments [14, 27] and prior findings in related areas such as the effectiveness of anti-phishing toolbars [33]. Prominence-Interpretation theory would suggest that, given the amount of information competing for attention when viewing a page, our visualization was not sufficiently salient. The visualization did not detract from performance, however, and therefore may be valuable to retain for cases in which users are making critical decisions (e.g., medical choices) whose motivations are difficult to simulate in laboratory studies, but which have been shown in prior work to influence users to devote additional time and attention to credibility assessment [28].

Educators' emphasis on the need for students to be taught about Web credibility (e.g., [21, 22, 25]) led us to believe that the teens in our study would be less accurate in their credibility assessments (and therefore benefit more from our visualizations) than adults; however, their performance was comparable. Overall, both teens and adults had room for improvement in their credibility assessment skills (and both groups were overconfident in the correctness of their ratings), suggesting that credibility assessment education and interventions may need to be directed to the population at large rather than only to youth.

Our results indicate that search engine companies could add value to their services by augmenting search results with visualizations that reflect features indicative of credibility that are typically not available to end-users, but which are available in aggregate in the opt-in log data such companies already collect. In particular, our participants indicated that page popularity among topical experts was one the most informative aspects of our visualization. Due to the desire of many search engines to fit as many results "above the fold" as possible, and to represent results compactly so as to reserve space for advertising, even our condensed visualization may be prohibitively large for real-world deployment. Reducing the footprint of the visualization further by only showing the "expert popularity" bar that participants found most persuasive may be a reasonable compromise. For highly motivated users (e.g., [28]), revealing the other aspects of the visualization upon hover may be acceptable.

In addition to displaying credibility-correlated features (particularly expert behavior) to end-users, search engine companies might consider integrating such data into their ranking algorithms, particularly given user mental models that already assume that ranking is a proxy for credibility [17]. Alternatively, credibility visualizations could be used as interactive advanced query operators, enabling users to sort and filter search result lists by criteria they deem important (e.g., indicating minimum popularity criteria for search results returned, or that they would like to see pages popular in specific regions of the world, or pages that have won certain award categories).

In order to realize these design visions on arbitrary Web pages and search result sets, further research is required on algorithms for automatically determining the topic of a Web page (a partial solution could involve reverse lookup in labeled sets such as the Open Directory Project [dmoz.org] or crowdsourced efforts such as tagging via social bookmarking tools). Improving upon the heuristic method of identifying topical experts proposed by White et al. [31] is another direction for future research. Their whitelist approach, though simple, provided value to the participants in our study; more sophisticated expertise identification algorithms may further enhance users' credibility assessments.

Long-term assessments of search result augmentation in ecologically-valid settings are also an important area for further research, in order to answer questions such as whether exposure to such visualizations helps users learn over time to be more discerning Web consumers, or whether augmented search results will change users' tendency to predominantly click through to the top-ranked result [20].

The objective versus subjective nature of truth is a topic of extensive philosophical debate, which extends far beyond the scope of this paper. Our approach navigated this nuanced space by creating an "objective" credibility score that has some additional perspectives as sanity-checks (ratings by outside professionals in health, finance, and politics for the pages in our test set), and then using an "informing end-users" approach (as opposed to a predictive approach) to present this data to users in order to support subjective interpretations. However, our definitions of expertise and choice of expert raters may inherently reflect a particular worldview that is not shared by all Web searchers. The fraught politics of defining credibility may make mainstream search engines hesitant to explicitly promote such indicators; implicitly incorporating expertise information into ranking algorithms or displaying it only on educational search portals may be more expedient.

CONCLUSION

Assessing Web page credibility is an increasingly important literacy as people turn to the Web for information in a variety of critical domains. In this paper, we made several contributions toward the goal of enhancing users' ability to assess Web page credibility, including (1) creating a publicly available data set of 1,000 Web pages with associated credibility ratings, (2) identifying features not readily available to end-users that relate to credibility, and quantifying the degree to which they do so, (3) designing visualizations to augment Web pages and search results that convey the most promising of these features, (4) evaluating the effectiveness of these visualizations in a laboratory study, and (5) offering design suggestions and future research directions based on these findings.

Our findings indicate that visualizing features not readily available to most users (particularly page popularity among topical experts) on search results is an effective way to improve the accuracy of users' credibility assessments. Augmenting search results in this manner makes users' credibility judgments as accurate as if they were viewing the target page in its entirety. These results demonstrate that a simple visualization can help people make more informed decisions as they search for content online, and point the way for future research addressing this important issue.

REFERENCES

1. Banko, M., Cafarella, M.J., Soderland, S., Broadhead, M., and Etzioni, O. Open information extraction from the Web. *IJCAI 2007*, 2670-2676.
2. Bhavnani, S. Domain-Specific Search Strategies for the Effective Retrieval of Healthcare and Shopping Information. *CHI 2002 Extended Abstracts*, 610-611.
3. Brin, S. and Page, L. The anatomy of a large-scale hypertextual Web search engine. *ISDN 1998*, 107-117.
4. Cavarlee, J. and Liu, L. Countering Web spam with credibility-based link analysis. *PODC 2007*, 157-166.
5. Chi, E., Pirolli, P., Chen, K., and Pitkow, J. Using information scent to model user information needs and actions and the Web. *CHI 2001,* 490-497.
6. Cutrell, E. and Guan,Z. What are you looking for? An eye-tracking study of information usage in Web search. *CHI 2007*, 407-416.
7. Dignan, L. Gartner Puts Phishing Tab at $3.2 Billion. *ZDNet.* Dec.17, 2007.
8. Ennals, R. Byler, D., Agosta, J.M. and Rosario, B. What is Disputed on the Web? *WICOW 2010*, 67-74.
9. Fallows, D. Search Engine Users. *Pew Internet and American Life Project*, 2005.
10. Ferebee, S. An examination of the influence of involvement level of Web site users on the perceived credibility of Web sites. *PERSUASIVE 2007*, 176-186.
11. Fogg, B.J. Marshall, Laraki, O., Osipovich, A., Varma, C. Fang, N., Paul, J., Rangekar, A., Shon, J., Swani, P., and Treinen, M. What makes Web sites credible?: A report on a large quantitative study. *CHI 2001*, 61-68.
12. Fogg, B.J. Persuasive Technology: Using Computers to Change What We Think and Do. *Morgan Kaufmann*, 2002.
13. Fogg, B. J. Prominence-interpretation theory: explaining how people assess credibility online. *CHI 2003 Extended Abstracts,* 722-723.
14. Fogg, B.J., Soohoo, C., Danielson, D.R., Marable, L., Stanford, J., and Tauber, E.R. How do users evaluate the credibility of Web sites?: A study with over 2,500 participants. *DUX 2003*, 1-15.
15. Gamon, M., Basu, S., Belenko, D., Fisher, D., Hurst, M., and Konig, A.C. BLEWS: Using Blogs to Provide Context for News Articles. *ICWSM 2008.*
16. Gyongyi, Z., Molina, H.G., and Pederson, J. Combating Web spam with TrustRank. *VLDB 2004*, 576-587.
17. Hargittai, E., Fullerton, F., Menchen-Trevino, E. and Thomas, D. Trust online: young adults' evaluation of Web content. *International Journal of Communications*, 2010.
18. Hilligoss, B. and Rieh, S.Y., Developing a unifying framework of credibility assessment: construct, heuristics, and interaction in context. *Info. Processing &Management,* 44(4), 2008, 1467-1484.
19. Ivory, M. and Hearst, M. Statistical profiles of highly-rated Web sites. *CHI 2002*, 367-374.
20. Joachims, T., Granka, L., Pan, B., Hembrooke, H., and Gay, G. Accurately interpreting clickthrough data as implicit feedback. *SIGIR 2005*, 154-161.
21. Jenkins, H. Confronting the Challenges of Participatory Culture: Media Education for the 21st Century. 2006.
22. Kapoun, J. Teaching Undergrads WEB Evaluation: A Guide for Library Instruction. *C&RL News*, July/August 1998, 522-523.
23. Kittur, A., Suh, B. and Chi, E. Can you ever trust a wiki?: Impacting perceived trustworthiness in Wikipedia. *CSCW 2008*, 477-480.
24. Lazar, J., Meiselwitz, G., and Feng, J. Understanding Web Credibility: A Synthesis of the Research Literature. *Foundations and Trends in HCI*, 1(2), 2007.
25. Leu, D.J. and Zawilinski, L. The New Literacies of Online Reading Comprehension. *New England Reading Assoc. Journal*, 43(1), 2007, 1-7.
26. Lohr, S. This Boring Headline is Written for Google. *The New York Times*, April 9, 2006.
27. McKnight, D. and Kacmar, C. Factors and effects of information credibility. *ICEC 2007*, 423-432.
28. Metzger, M. J. Making sense of credibility on the Web: Models for evaluating online information and recommendations for future research. *Journal of the American Society for Information Science and Technology*, 58(13), 2007, 2078-2091.
29. Pew Research. Growing Number of Americans Say Obama is a Muslim. August 18, 2010.
30. Schneiderman, B. Designing trust into online experiences. *CACM,* 43(12), 2000, 57-59.
31. White, R., Dumais, S., and Teevan, J. Characterizing the influence of domain expertise on Web search behavior. *WSDM '09*, 132-141.
32. White, R. and Morris, D. Investigating the querying and browsing behavior of advanced search engine users. *SIGIR 2007*, 255-262.
33. Wu, M., Miller, R., and Garfinkel, S. Do security toolbars actually prevent phishing attacks? *CHI 2006.*

Using Fast Interaction to Create Intense Experiences

Joe Marshall, Steve Benford
Horizon Digital Economy Research, Sir Colin Campbell Building
University of Nottingham Innovation Park, Triumph Road, NG7 2TU, Nottingham, UK
{jqm,sdb}@cs.nott.ac.uk

ABSTRACT
Several emerging strands of HCI involve connecting physical exercise activity with digital interactive systems to create intense combined experiences, for example pervasive games, GPS based exercise games and 'exertion interfaces'. Many of these systems are mobile, used outside in public, whilst moving quickly through the environment. In this paper, we argue that the combination of moving fast and interacting with a digital system allows us to create a powerfully intense experience for participants, and that key to this is careful attention to the way in which movement is combined with digital content.

We study an interactive art experience in which a person runs whilst listening to poetry. Based on this study and other HCI research, we present a framework for mixing physical and interactive content, based on 3 dimensions, which describe ways that a movement activity may itself create intense experiences, followed by a set of tactics for combining intense movement and interactive content.

Author Keywords
Intensity, exertion, mobile, running, full body interaction.

ACM Classification Keywords
H5.m. Information interfaces and presentation (e.g., HCI): Miscellaneous.

General Terms
Design

INTRODUCTION
Connecting physical exercise activity to computer systems used for entertainment is increasingly common, with games such as Dance Dance Revolution [12], and Wii Fit [21] encouraging people to dance or do aerobics in to interact with a computer game. Further to this, capability of mobile platforms to detect position and speed has created a genre of 'pervasive games', games played on mobile devices whilst outside in a public place. Several of these involve fast movement, such as running to keep your heartbeat within a certain range [3], cycling around a city [25] and racing to beat other people's time around a course [17]. As well as games, exercise tools have been developed which use mobile technology to enhance exercise experience, for example by allowing runners to 'run together' in different places using devices connected by a network link [18], or to log exercise and allow people to compete with friends to do more exercise in a particular time period [7].

We argue that a key aim of interactive entertainment is to provide people with intense experiences, in the sense of a notable or unusual experience which provokes a strong reaction in the participant, and that encouraging moving fast while interacting ('fast interaction') is one possible way of intensifying the reaction of participants. Mueller et al's experiments [19] suggest that the combination of hard physical activity and interactive content in an 'exertion interface' creates a more intense experience for participants than a purely computer based experience. As well as the exertion of a physical activity, we argue that taking part in an activity outdoors in public further enhances the intensity of their experience. To explore this, we created a simple interactive movement activity, an art experience called 'I Seek the Nerves Under Your Skin' ('I Seek'), in which a poem alters based on the running of a participant. 'I Seek' is designed to create an intense experience, whilst being simple to understand and lightweight enough to deploy in a variety of settings. It is designed to elicit an interesting range of responses from participants and be compelling to them. We ran 'I Seek' with 82 participants at various artistic events, using a combination of data logging and interviews to explore people's experiences.

The key contribution of the paper is in two parts; firstly, we extract a set of dimensions from the study to describe ways in which exertion can be intense and mentally demanding:

i) Speed and level of exertion of the activity.

ii) Terrain and environment where the activity is taking place.

iii) Novelty of the activity and setting .

Secondly, we present a set of 8 tactics which take these dimensions into account. These tactics allow us to create extremely intense experiences by mixing fast physical movement with interactive content.

Whilst we wish to create very intense experiences, which may be scary for some participants, we usually do not want to expose participants to risks other than the normal risk of taking part in a physical activity. We finish this paper with a discussion of how we may ensure safety for participants in this kind of intense fast moving experience.

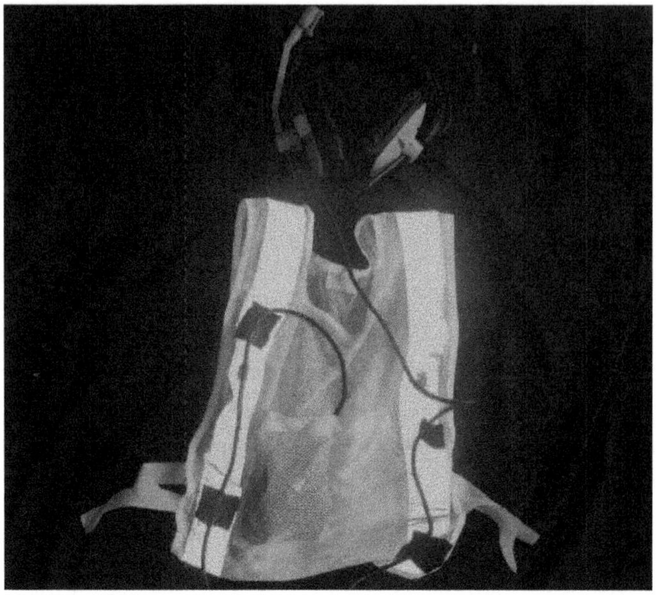

Figure 1. I Seek the Nerves Equipment

I SEEK THE NERVES UNDER YOUR SKIN

This section describes 'I Seek' both from a participant's perspective and also in terms of the technology that runs it, and the data that we gathered from the experience.

Experience

When a person takes part in 'I Seek', they are given a fluorescent jacket and a pair of headphones (Figure 1). When they put on the jacket and start to walk, a poem starts playing in the headphones (the poem used is 'Babelogue', by Patti Smith [29], a punk poem performed by her in a full on, spitting, swearing manner). If the person continues just to walk, the poem fades out. However, if they increase in speed, the poem continues playing for longer. Through the poem, the performer of the poem gets increasingly agitated, shouts louder and louder in the headphones, an audience to the poem starts a rhythmic clapping in the background and cheering, and everything gets a lot more intense. In order to hear the whole poem, the runner must accelerate continually, with the increase in intensity of their running mirroring the crescendo of the poem. If the runner does not go fast enough, the poem fades out gradually and restarts.

The runner must accelerate relatively quickly to reach a very fast sprinting pace by the end of the poem. This is very difficult, only a third of people managed to hear the full poem. Running this hard is a very intense experience, even for the short time required to hear the poem (99 seconds).

When the runner has had enough, they take off the jacket and headphones, and the equipment is immediately ready for another person to have a go. People take part in 'I Seek' outdoors, in public, running freely, wherever they like.

Design & Implementation

When designing 'I Seek the Nerves', we wanted a quick and reliable response to changes in running speed, and to be able to very quickly fit the equipment to people and take it off. We chose to base the system around a mobile phone (Nokia N95), using the built in accelerometer to detect speed – this is significantly faster to respond and gives a better indication of speed than the GPS on the phone. The phone is in the front pocket of the fluorescent jacket, with a wire coming out to the headphones.

The 'I Seek' software on the phone (written in Mobile Python [26]) runs throughout an event. In its idle state, it waits until it detects a certain threshold level of movement, and then starts the poem. While the poem is playing, the threshold level slowly increases. If the level of movement is below threshold, the poem begins to fade, until it has completely faded out, at which point the phone returns to idle state (and restarts if further movement occurs). Figure 2 shows how this threshold alters through the poem.

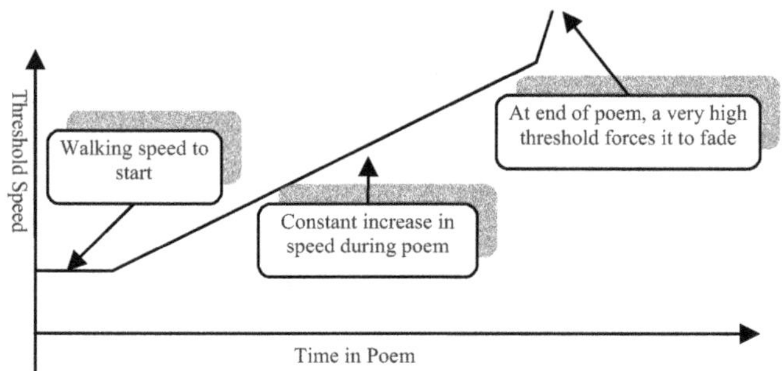

Figure 2. Speed Threshold in I Seek the Nerves

The current running speed is calculated using a scale based on the variance of the last .5 seconds of the total magnitude of the phone's built in accelerometer. This measurement was chosen as it is not affected by the angle of the phone. It also offers a more nuanced & fast reacting value than the step count value used in a pedometer, but is still easy to calculate. The relationship between actual speed and the speed value detected by the phone is roughly linear, but differs slightly between people, with longer legged people who take longer strides needing to go slightly faster to get the same detected speed. This is not a problem for the experience, as the change in threshold is far more than the difference between people. Essentially it just makes things slightly more even between short people and tall people.

Because there is no screen based interaction, the phone can be hidden in the pocket so it is not obvious. This both aims to stop people characterising the experience as a mobile phone game or similar, and also reduces the chance of the phones being stolen either by participants or onlookers. We also avoid the safety problems of looking down at screens whilst moving through cities which have caused danger to participants in several previous mobile experiences [1,3].

Running I Seek the Nerves

After initial testing with friends and colleagues, 'I Seek' has been run in three phases. Firstly, we ran a test of the system at an arts festival in Liverpool, UK. This was held in a run-down industrial area, on a dark and rainy winter night, with 30 participants. At this event, runners ran on small streets, and had to watch out for traffic, and deal with bad weather, potholes etc. We collected some observational data at this event, but primarily used it to fine tune the difficulty of the system and to get a rough idea of what people did with it.

The second event was at another art festival, held at Berkeley Art Museum, Berkeley, CA, with 41 participants. This event was run in the grounds of the museum, a complex modernist building, surrounded by ramps, terraces, and multiple different surfaces that runners had to negotiate. At this event we briefly interviewed all participants and collected log data from the system which describes how they ran. As all participants in this event ran in the same environment, much of the comparative data presented in the following sections is from this event.

We have three jackets, so up to three people were running at any one time at these events. At both the art events, as well as the runners, there were quite a few other bystanders. For the final phase of running 'I Seek', we wished to get a greater understanding of how it worked in different places, so we ran it individually for 11 participants, at the place of their choice, again following each run with an interview. Participants ran in a range of terrains, ranging from a tiny village, to a university campus, a town park, and a running event in a hilly country park.

We deliberately did not tell people what 'I Seek' was about, allowing them to make their own judgements as to what they felt it was for, and what the concept of the work was. This meant that people treated it very differently, with some seeing it as a game or challenge to be completed, others seeing it as a work of art to be explored, and a few seeing it more as a potential training tool for improving running. We were inspired in this by Sengers and Gaver's work on leaving interpretation up to users [27], which suggests that if no explicit interpretation is placed upon a system, either by telling people what it is for, or by implying it in the design, people will create their own story to describe the meaning and purpose of the system. The full body interaction and slightly odd social situation that the system is part of also helps in our aim to create an intuitive, visceral, intense experience, perhaps aiming for what Isbister & Höök describe as '*beyond the cognitive/rational level of the standard GUI interface*' [11].

Studying I Seek the Nerves

To study 'I Seek', we collected two forms of data about participants' experiences. Firstly, we logged the speed of the participants throughout the experience, along with data describing how far through the poem they were. Secondly, we interviewed participants afterwards, to get some idea of their subjective experience of 'I Seek'. We also collected demographic data from participants.

Figure 3 shows the speed log for one participant. The jagged lines show detected running speed, and the straight slowly rising lines show the threshold speed, dropping back close to zero each time the poem restarted and the runner had another try. By combining these graphs and the interviews, we are able to see what the system was doing and how people experienced it.

The scale shown is the raw speed estimate calculated by the device, which as mentioned previously has a roughly linear relationship to speed within a single participant, but does not compare across participants exactly – due to this the vertical scale is shown in device units, as it cannot be exactly converted into a real world unit. The jaggedness on the detected speed graphs is due to the uneven nature of the speed detected as people take steps while running – this is not a problem in the software as the fading out of the poem is quite gradual, essentially smoothing out the signal, meaning that if the person is generally above the threshold, they will still hear the poem, even if noise in the signal makes it sometimes go below threshold.

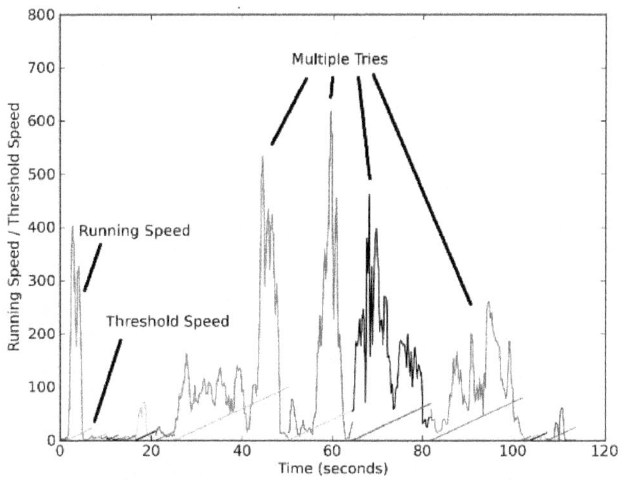

Figure 3. One Participant's Speed Graph

EXPERIENCES OF I SEEK THE NERVES

All participants who we interviewed reported that they enjoyed taking part in 'I Seek the Nerves'. Almost all participants had multiple tries at listening the poem, with a few trying it for over 10 minutes, a long time to take part in such a short experience (the poem is 99 seconds long).

People also reported that 'I Seek' was a very intense experience, as one member of a local running club said – "*yeah [I enjoyed it] … not what I'd call relaxing though, quite stressful*", "*that's like that movie Crank, or whatever it is, where you're going to die if you don't keep going faster.*" In this section we describe the different elements that come together to make running in a public space whilst wearing the 'I Seek' equipment such an intense and exciting experience. This will be illustrated with quotes from participants and graphs showing how they ran during their experience of 'I Seek'.

'I Seek' was intense both for people who run regularly, and those who do not, although there were differences between runners and non runners. 15 of 52 participants in the last two experiments were runners (about a third).

The Innate Difficulty of Running Fast and Pacing

Only a third of the participants actually heard the full poem through to the end (13 of 41 runners at Berkeley, where all runners were running on similar terrain, so the difficulty level is roughly comparable). Making the experience difficult was a deliberate design choice, as we wished to mirror the fact that performing live poetry well is a challenging activity, by putting the participant in a challenging situation. A lot of this was just because it is very hard to run in the way that the experience demands.

Running fast is itself a difficult an intense thing to do. In 'I Seek', it is made particularly hard by the need to constantly increase speed. A big part of what makes this hard in 'I Seek' is that it only gives feedback when a person is going too slow, so people found it hard to pace themselves so that they did not run out of energy too quickly, one participant noticed this and actually altered their behavior to hear the end of the poem the next time - '*I think I at one point I probably accelerated more than I needed to, because at one point I was getting really out of breath and then I slowed down a bit and found it was still going, I think I made it harder*'. Interestingly, looking at the speed data, a lot of participants were able to reach the maximum speed, but were unable to keep it up. This inability to pace themselves was not just amongst non runners, because this is very different to how a runner would normally run – "*I found that really hard to do, because I think I'm used to running at a more consistent, constant pace, rather than running at a gradually building pace*". Several runners also likened the way in which 'I Seek' encourages an unexpected type of pacing to 'fartlek' or 'speed play' training, a form of running training which involves a mix of slow running interspersed with intense sprints of varying lengths. This is particularly true when a person cannot get to the end of the poem, as it will keep fading out and restarting, causing repeated cycles of slowing down and accelerating.

We can see pacing issues people had in the speed graphs, Figure 4 shows a runner who achieved a very fast speed, fast enough to complete the experience if they could keep it up, yet was unable to keep their speed up for long enough to hear the whole poem, and had to slow down. As well as poor pacing, quite a few people were just unable to reach the speed required by the system, so accelerated well to start with, then ran out of extra speed (Figure 5).

Interestingly, of those who completed the poem, there were also two distinct groups, mostly people paced themselves to beat the poem by gradual acceleration, but a few extremely fit people just went extremely fast for the full length of the poem and finished it (Figure 6). This was clearly hard, only 2 out of 41 participants at Berkeley managed it.

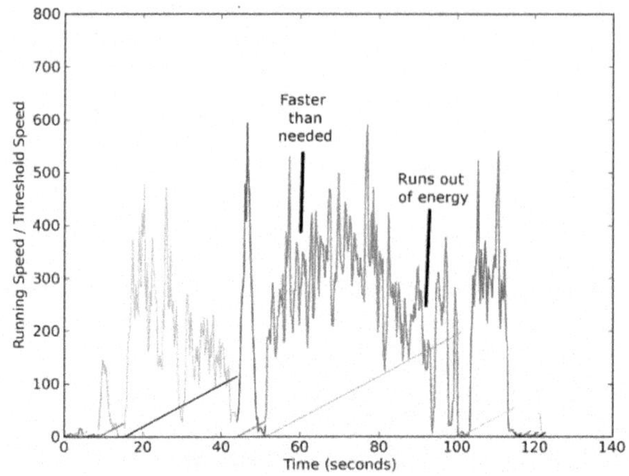

Figure 4. A runner who paced themselves badly

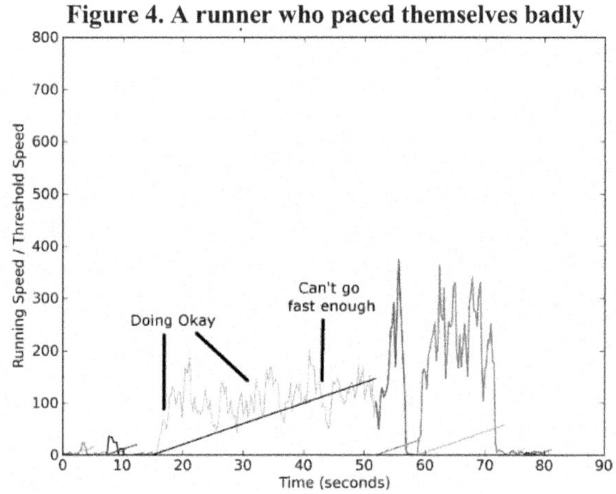

Figure 5. A participant who just couldn't go fast enough

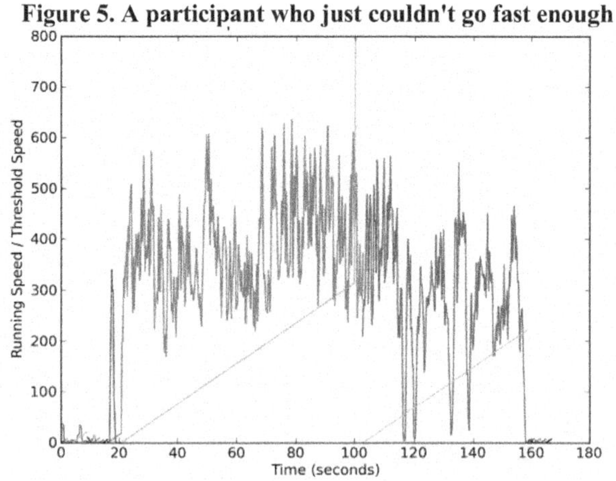

Figure 6. Constant fast running to complete the poem

Environment & Terrain

At Berkeley, the environment people were running in was complex, containing a lot of ramps, terraces, several different surfaces, such as grass, concrete and earth, and a lot of large metal pillars that people had to run around (Figure 7). It was also somewhat constrained, as it was at a ticketed event, so no one was allowed to run outside the grounds of the museum. This meant that whilst running, people had to deal with the challenges of dealing with their environment in addition to adjusting their speed and listening to the poem in their headphones. Just running in this environment was a complex task - "*I was going down the hill, I was going up the hill, ah, there were poles, I was navigating through the poles*"; often people would come to a sudden halt due to the terrain (Figure 8 shows an example of a runner who got stopped by the terrain). Interestingly, several participants felt that dealing with the terrain was not a negative and actually added to the excitement and intensity of the experience – "*that actually added to the overall sensation, it added to the whole thing, if I was just running down a dirt road or something it'd be different, because it wouldn't be such a challenging environment*".

Figure 7. The complex running environment at Berkeley

One interesting element of terrain was that as well as slowing people down and getting in the way, participants reported making positive use of the terrain, for example one participant reported using a downhill to allow them to gain speed and get to the end of the poem -"*well, I saved myself up for the downhill bit, knowing it was going to get harder and I thought, well the downhill would give me a boost ... so I ran round in circles up there.*", this extra acceleration on the downhill can be seen in their speed graph (Figure 9).

Interestingly, the terrain seemed to be much less of a problem for people who regularly ran. Potentially this may be because they are used to taking account of terrain at high speed. In one example, one of the authors ran along with a runner, who was running through their local village, and observed the runner maintaining speed as they went round a blind corner, saw a car coming, timed their crossing of the road to avoid the car, and then ran past a group of people. Afterwards, when asked, the runner said that there was nothing in the terrain or the environment that they were running in that was in the way, and appeared unaware of the complex process of observations and avoidance that they had used to get through the area.

Regular runners also made use of their knowledge of the terrain they were running in and of how long it would take them to get somewhere in order to improve their chances - "*like if I could go down here, and then I could keep it going till the pub, and then down the really steep bit of hill when I was getting to the really tough bit*".

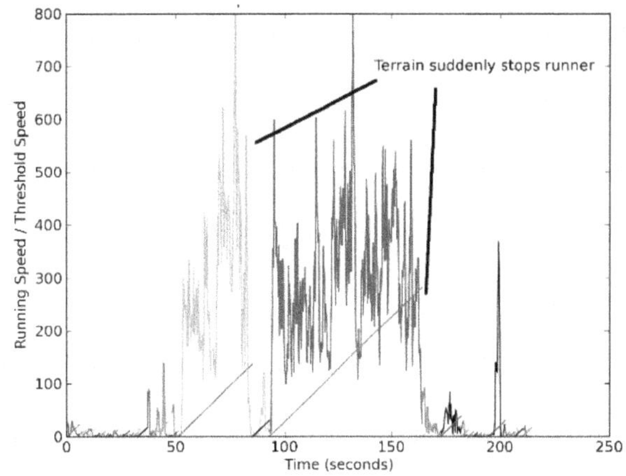

Figure 8. Runner stopped by the terrain

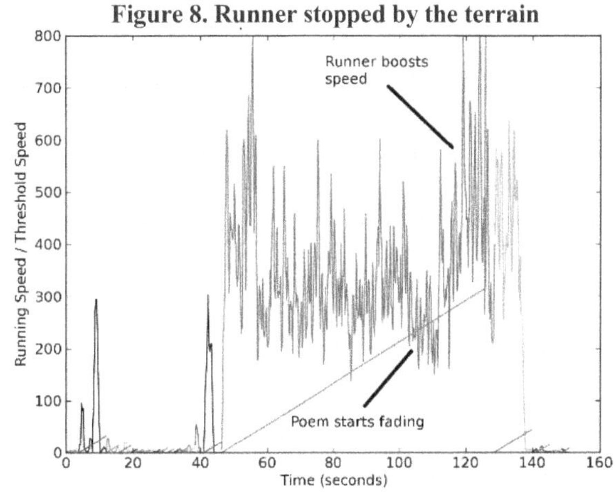

Figure 9. Using a downhill to boost speed

Other People

The design of 'I Seek' is what Reeves et al.[23] describe as a 'suspenseful' interface, with the effects of the interaction (the poem) being private to the participant, as they are only heard on their headphones, whilst the running with which the person interacts with the system is highly visible, made even more so by the fluorescent jackets and large headphones that are being worn. This is designed to act as an advertisement for the experience, making it very visible. It also appeared to make it more intense for people taking part – "*and er, and er.. because of this .. context .. you feel a little bit weird you know, running around, around the other people?*". Other people who were also doing the experience also had an effect on runners. For example a group of three who ran together found it reduced the oddness – "*I prefer going in a group, maybe because you feel a bit silly doing it, if you're in a group you don't feel so silly*". This group also found themselves competing to get as far through the poem as possible, which clearly added intensity to their shared experience.

Other people also made the experience more intense as they became obstacles to runners, slowing them down. This occurred both in terms of people physically getting in the way, as with objects in the terrain, but also politeness sometimes made people slow down when close to other people, meaning the poem stopped - "*[I] slow down when I pass by, and then it's like "oh wait, no, don't stop*". One runner even described how they found themselves running differently because a friend chased them – "*somebody started to chase me, I had to run away from him, he started chasing me again, I had to run away again*".

Split Attention – Mixing Running and Poetry

Testing with a local running club, we discovered a significant minority of the runners completely refused to take part, as they did not believe it was 'right' to run with headphones on. One runner described this – "*I never wear headphones while running … I like to be aware of the environment*". This appeared not to be for safety, but more due to wanting to focus purely on the place in which they were running; there was a general disdain for 'joggers' who run wearing headphones without paying attention to where they are running. 'I Seek' deliberately splits this focus, forcing people to pay attention to both the environment in which they are running and the poem on their headphones. This leads to some interesting conflicts as the increasingly intense running requires more and more concentration.

For example, one runner described how whilst having multiple tries at completing the poem, they started trying to listen to the poem carefully, in order to be able to know exactly how far they had got through each time, however, the act of doing this made them lose concentration and run less well - "*I was thinking 'what was that they said then?' and I was listening a bit more carefully to what she was saying, and then I wasn't concentrating on my pace*".

Several runners described how they were unable to pay attention to the poem, particularly once they got running fast - "*[I heard] only the beginning, then after that, the, the err, the sort of the thudding of the running and the beating of the heart took over*". Others described how whilst they did not listen in enough detail to remember whole sentences, they still felt the poem added to the experience – "*I heard pieces of the poem, but I don't, I don't feel like I really heard a narrative, I heard a mood, there's an energy*"

The transition away from detailed listening, to focus more on the experience of running is also enhanced by the way in which running impinges on the audio – with the large headphones insulating people from other outside noise, the sound of their feet hitting the ground comes through their body and can be heard, mixing in with the rhythmic clapping in the background of the poetry performance - "*hearing my footfalls as like, bass* [in the headphones] *It was rhythmic, and I was trying err, you know, to keep up and do my thing*", "*I could really hear my feet, running, and that was really interesting to me, so the text became more background*". As described in the quote above, when doing hard exercise with your ears covered by headphones, you can hear your heart beating as blood is pumped faster around the body, which also becomes mixed in with the poetry to create an intense mix of replayed and live audio.

Control

The poetry track was deliberately chosen to fit in with the style of running encouraged by the work; this helped give people a feeling of control. For example, part way through the poem, an audience begins to clap rhythmically, slowly increasing in speed towards the end – a combination of this with the beat from their running led people to feel that they had more control of the soundtrack than the simple playback system provides, "*towards the end, there's quite a lot of beats, and you can actually, the faster you run, the faster the beat of the music is*". People reported surprise at being able to control the poem - "*I was thinking 'No, don't stop, don't stop, I wanna hear that', then 'oh, I can actually go faster'* ".

Whilst some participants simply tried to 'beat' the experience by getting to the end, many seemed to enjoy playing with the control afforded by their running. These two differing strategies are perhaps a key way in which the interpretation of the work is left up to runners themselves. We can see the two extremes of these approaches in the two graphs shown in Figure 10. The first runner started running, accelerated smoothly to finish, slowed to a stop, walked back and returned the equipment.

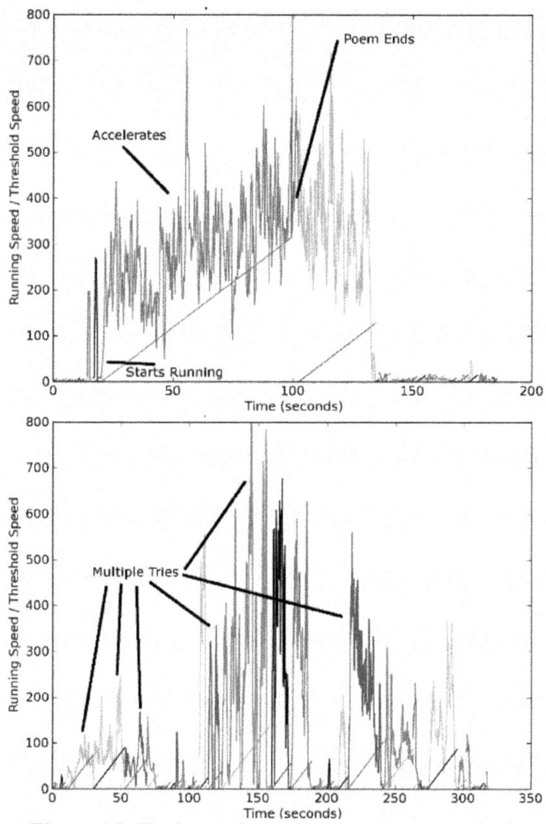

Figure 10. Trying to beat the experience vs playing

In contrast the other runner put on the equipment, danced off whilst wearing it, and took more playful approach to the experience – "*I found myself running for the sake of running, like, running in, around the building, just, running in all kinds of weird places. ... experimenting, to see if different movements would, err, get another kind of feedback. That was fun*".

DISCUSSION: HOW TO CREATE INTENSE EXPERIENCES USING FAST INTERACTION

In this section, we discuss ways of using fast movement to create intense interactive experiences, based on the lessons learnt from deploying 'I Seek the Nerves'. From experience of running 'I Seek', we believe that key to this is the way extreme physical activity increases mental load on the participant, making them only focus on the essential aspects of the activity. Potentially this may create experiences in which the physical activity and the interactive content are seen as a single 'flow activity' [6], where people are unable to focus in on particular aspects of the situation such as running or interactive content, and instead become immersed in the experience as a single combined activity.

We first consider the ways in which physical activity may be intense, as a set of 'dimensions'; an increased difficulty in any of these dimensions creates intensity. The activity of running in 'I Seek' exploited aspects of all these dimensions to create an extremely intense experience.

The dimensions are followed by a set of tactics, which are ways to exploit the intensity of fast movement described by the dimensions in combination with interactive content to create intense interactive experiences.

Dimensions: How Fast Movement Can be Intense

Dimension 1: Exertion and Speed

The key thing that is used in 'I Seek the Nerves' to create intensity is making people run quickly. As we saw in people's experiences, accelerating and running at a high speed requires a large amount of concentration. The faster people go, the more they exert themselves, the more they have to focus on the running. The fact that exertion makes for more intense interaction is noted in previous work, for example in explorations of adding exercise to networked games to provide a more intense social experience [19], or adding real punching to a boxing game [10]. As the boxing game shows, exertion has multiple aspects – 'I Seek' focuses on very short, fast running, however there are also other ways in which exercise may be made intense, such as lifting heavy weights, performing exercises for an extended length of time, or performing difficult balance activities.

Dimension 2: Environment and Terrain

Where the physical activity takes place also has a major effect on how intense it feels. As we discussed above, obstacles (and people in the way) clearly make an experience require more focus on movement. When people are moving quickly, hills have much more impact on their movement than for slower experiences – something that has previously also been noted for cycling based experiences [25], where it was also argued that individual variations in fitness mean hills make a lot more difference, as the range of speeds possible are much greater. Downhills and uphills, as well as impacting the difficulty of exertion, may also change how much people have to focus, for example a downhill may allow you to run very fast, but that fast running may require far more concentration to avoid obstacles, Types of terrain also make a difference, for example in 'I Seek', people found it required more focus to run in woodland, with a lot underfoot, than in a flat field.

Weather and time of day also have a visceral effect – when 'I Seek' was run in Liverpool, it was a dark evening in a poorly lit area of the city, and there were several rain storms during the event. Even in the flat area in which it was run, people found the act of running to be an intense experience.

Bystanders are also part of the environment in which people move. Taking part in a fast experience around other people may well involve doing something visible to spectators which a person is not used to. This element of performing ones actions to bystanders can make an experience more intense – particularly when a strategy of exposing the interface to spectators is used [23]. Bystanders may also be in vehicles, or also running, which may make the situation require more concentration. Clearly putting people into situations with traffic requires careful design; for example in the cycling game Rider Spoke [25], riders were only allowed to interact with the computer system when stopped.

Because of the many challenges of real world outdoor environments, we would argue that outdoor experiences have the potential to add a new dimension of intensity compared to purely exertion based experiences using treadmills or other stationary equipment.

Dimension 3: Novelty of the Activity and Setting

People for whom a physical activity is a more novel skill will find it more intense compared to those who have trained extensively. For example at the various events where 'I Seek' was run, we encountered a large variety of running ability and skill. For some people, running was a regular activity, for others it was something they were not accustomed to at all. John Hockey [9] discusses the way in which skilled regular runners have a very rich knowledge of terrain in which they run, and analyse and respond to it quickly as they run; this domain knowledge appeared in 'I Seek' to make quite a difference to how much of their attention people have to give over to their running.

Hockey's work also highlights how much people know about the areas in which they run regularly – this can be seen in the example of the runner discussed above, who managed to navigate through a complex junction and a traffic situation in their local village, whilst still paying attention to their overall strategy of using the hilly terrain to their advantage. This made a big difference when running 'I Seek' with people in places familiar to them, compared to the events in Berkeley and Liverpool, where most people were running in areas that they had never visited before.

Tactics for Matching Physical & Interactive Experiences

In this section, we present 8 tactics which allow us to utilize the intensity created by physical exertion (and described by the dimensions above) within an interactive experience.

Tactic 1: Overload attention

People only have a limited ability to process information. This means that if people perform multiple tasks simultaneously, they are potentially distracted from one task by another task which is taking more of their attention. Overloading people's attention is typically seen as a problem in HCI. For example, avoiding computer interfaces distracting people away from the visual task of driving has been a particular focus of HCI research, due to the obvious safety implications [22]. Clearly we do not want to endanger participants by taking their mind off their running. However, the inverse, making people perform intense physical activity and making it hard for them to pay attention to interactive content may be a useful strategy when trying to create intensity in an interactive experience. For example, runners in 'I Seek' reported how once they ran fast, they could not entirely concentrate on the poem. Some suggested that this added to the experience, with the poem being heard as more of a 'mood' underlying their experience, rather than them consciously listening to it.

Tactic 2: Exploit Partial Attention

The way in which people are distracted from the audio by the running creates a situation where they can only pay partial attention to the audio. As shown in 'I Seek', creating this kind of partial attention has the potential to make audio or other outputs less clear, leading to people interpreting it in interesting ways, such as the person who felt that the speed of the music was directly reacting to them in 'I Seek', when in fact it was just the natural progression through the poem coupled with their acceleration in order to be able to hear it. We would argue that the knowledge that people were unable to fully listen to the poem made the experience more intense – ie. Running fast whilst not quite managing to listen to poetry is a more intense experience than either just running fast or listening to poetry while stopped.

Tactic 3: Create Transitions in Attention

The transition from a state in which the person is fully able to pay attention into partial attention is also interesting, as it creates the feeling of loss of ability to handle all the stimuli that are being thrown at the participant in an experience. This transition could be used when planning an experience by deliberately exploiting factors such as increased speed (Dimension 1), orchestrating experiences so that people arrive at hills or other terrain features at the same time as digital content which we wish to be obscured (Dimension 2), or making interactive content less distinct by moving the experience out of people's comfort zone, for example by making them increasingly lost or encouraging them to perform increasingly complex movements (Dimension 3).

Tactic 4: Match interactive and physical content

Mueller et al. [19] describe how simply taking an existing sport and making it an interactive game does not really work, and how physical 'exertion interfaces' and the games or experiences they are used in must be designed to work together. For example, in 'I Seek', care was taken choosing the short, explosively intense poem to fit with the relatively short burst of intense running required by the system, and fitting the threshold used in the system to the timing of the poem. This was not just about the matching the tempo of the poem with the running, but also about finding a poem that was performed in an increasingly loud and intense manner, so that in the most intense points of the running, the poem was also extremely intense in tempo, volume and the general agitation of the person performing it.

Deliberate matching between content and movement in 'I Seek the Nerves' is purely about speed and exertion level (Dimension 1), as that is all the experience is able to measure. The way in which terrain (Dimension 2) affects choice of content in has been discussed in previous work relating to cycling based audio experiences [25], where designers may wish audio placed on uphills (when people are working hard, but moving slowly) to be very different to that placed on downhills (where people are not pushing themselves, but are moving quickly). Also, in cycling (or other exercise) different fitnesses of rider can have a very different experience [25]. This means that interactive content may need to adapt itself to match the skill, experience and fitness people taking part (Dimension 3). 'I Seek' sidesteps this slightly, by deliberately being a difficult experience, which it is expected unfit or poorly skilled people will not be able to finish, rather than attempting to adapt for different fitness levels.

Tactic 5: Exploit Sensory Overlaps

The matching between poem and running is encouraged by the way that people's senses are overloaded not just visually, but also by the way sounds created by the system and sounds generated by people's running overlap. The matching between interactive and physical content is not just about matching the mood and tempo of the content to the running, it is also enhanced by the way in which the beat of the person's feet as they run mixes in with the poem, making a combined audio soundtrack which feels more intense to participants than purely listening to the audio track alone. Interestingly, sports science research has demonstrated that people actually run significantly faster if audio they are listening to is in synchronization with their running [28], meaning that this kind of matching may in itself encourage people to push themselves harder, thus making their experience more intense.

Tactic 6: Encourage Intense Physical Behavior with Content

In order for the tactics described here to work, we must have some way of encouraging people to push themselves to reach a desired level of physical intensity. In 'I Seek', this is done by using a very basic mapping, which requires a constantly increasing intensity of running in order to hear the content at all. In combination with compelling content, which people wish to engage with, this very simple method of removing the content unless someone performs the desired level of exertion is very effective. Several other 'exertion interface' [19] based systems use biological measures as a proxy for exercise intensity, such as measuring the heart rate of participants [3], and again reward people for keeping these measures within particular ranges. A particularly interesting system is 'Pulse Masters Biathlon' [20], which measures two aspects of fitness, first a cross country skiing minigame which rewards intense effort and high heart rates, then a shooting minigame, played directly after the skiing game, where it is easier to aim if one has a lower heart rate, rewarding ability to recover from exercise. As well measuring how hard or fast physical activity is (Dimension 1), we can also consider the other two dimensions that make things intense. Terrain (Dimension 2) can make a big difference, potentially systems can take into account the particular terrain people are running over, as is done in the sport of orienteering, where higher points are awarded for crossing more rough terrain, or going up large hills. As well as purely physical terrain, the particular social environment in which an experience is run can also be rewarded – for example the drug smuggling game Blowtooth [14] rewards players for (pretending to) smuggle drugs through real airport security zones, something which clearly makes the game more intense than if it were played in a less charged environment or purely online. Similarly, Rider Spoke [25], creates rewarding experiences for those who are willing to navigate complex city traffic on a bicycle.

Tactic 7: Encourage Performative Actions

The visible and unexpected nature of actions in 'I Seek' also encourages an intense experience, in that people were rewarded for running fast and effectively performing in front of other people (Dimension 2). Running was particularly unexpected at busy art festivals. Other projects have also used large, visible movements such as spell casting [1] to create increased intensity. It may also be useful when aiming to design this kind of performative gesture and encourage intensity by making people do things that feel out of the ordinary, to deliberately work outside HCI guidelines for what gestures are felt to be normal or socially acceptable when performed in public [24].

Tactic 8: Encourage Unexpected Actions

With 'I Seek', we created something which even for runners was an odd experience, which encouraged them to move outside their accustomed running styles (Dimension 3). We also encouraged a lot of people to run in places where they were unlikely to have run before, and non runners to run fast, something which many had not done since childhood. Rewarding people for moving outside their comfort zone is a useful tactic, and has been used in other experiences, for example the pervasive game 'Uncle Roy All Around You' began by asking people to leave their possessions behind, including maps, which intensified the experience - *"Players were asked to leave all possessions at the ICA so I had no watch, mobile or map. This worried me because I didn't know the area and when directed to Pall Mall or other places, I had no idea where these were and unfortunately, the people I asked for directions got it wrong resulting in me heading in the wrong direction. This, however, didn't detract from the experience."*[2]. This deliberate encouragement and rewarding of disorientation and doing things that are out of the ordinary may be a very useful way of creating intensity even when people are not being made to move fast.

SAFE MIXING OF INTERACTIVITY AND MOVEMENT

Whilst we wish to create intense, often dark and perhaps scary experiences, when creating experiences in which people move fast it is important to keep participants alive. This is particularly true when people mix with traffic (such as in cycling [25] or car based experiences [4,8]), or encounter challenging terrain (such as interactive climbing walls [13]). We need to ensure that when we push people to a point where they are unable to concentrate on everything that is happening to them, they are still able to pay attention to things likely to harm them. Key to this in 'I Seek the Nerves' is the purely audio interface, as when people are moving fast, vision is a key sense that allows them to navigate and avoid danger (a similar approach has been discussed in car based computing [5]). We also performed site surveys on locations before we ran 'I Seek', to check whether there was any danger nearby that we needed to warn participants about. One must also be careful about health when encouraging people to push themselves – 'I Seek' is deliberately short, and also does not penalize stopping and resting, or multiple tries and is unlikely to cause any medical problems, but in longer experiences if care is not taken to avoid pushing people too hard for too long, there is a potential health risk (e.g. marathon running can increase risk of heart attacks [16]).

When considering safety, we need to take into account all three dimensions which may all make a difference. For example how hard people are asked to run (Dimension 1: Speed and Exertion) may be less important if the people in question are experienced runners (Dimension 3:Novelty). Safety may also depend on where people are asked to run (Dimension 2:Environment and Terrain), and how well they know that particular environment, and how skilled a runner they are (Dimension 3: Novelty).

CONCLUSIONS

In this paper, we have described the study of a mobile interactive experience combining poetry with running. This was a very intense experience for people taking part. By interviewing participants and collecting logs of their running, we have been able to explore the factors which make this an intense experience.

Based on the study, we described ways in which physical activity produces an intense experience, and a set of tactics for integrating hard physical activity within interactive experiences in order to create very intense experiences.

These dimensions and tactics may be particularly useful to those developing systems such as games involving fast movement or extreme physical exertion (eg. [3, 10,13,20,25]), and in making novel exercise support systems (eg. [7,18,19]) more compelling for users. One interesting point to make, is that whilst here we measure physical activity by measuring speed, a growing number of projects use biological sensing as a measure of physical exertion. Our tactics are also applicable in such a situation, but use of bio-sensing to create intense experiences may also create further interesting feedback loops between participant and system, as the biological signals are not purely representative of physical activity, they are also affected by the stress of an intense experience. We explore an example of combined physical and emotional feedback in our research into breathing controlled thrill rides [15].

ACKNOWLEDGEMENTS

This work is supported by Horizon Digital Economy Research, RCUK grant EP/G065802/1. We would also like to thank all those who went running for us during testing and deployment of 'I Seek the Nerves.'

REFERENCES

1. Ballagas, R., Kuntze, A., and Walz, S.P. Gaming tourism: Lessons from evaluating rexplorer, a pervasive game for tourists. *Proc. Pervasive* 2008.
2. Benford, S. Crabtree, A. et al. The frame of the game: blurring the boundary between fiction and reality in mobile experiences. *Proc CHI 2006.* 427-436
3. Boyd Davis, S., Moar, M., Jacobs, R., Watkins, M., Riddoch, C., and Cooke, K. Ere be dragons: Heartfelt gaming. *Digital Creativity 17 (*3).
4. Brunnberg, L. The Road Rager: making use of traffic encounters in a mobile multiplayer game. *Proc. 3rd Conf. Mobile Ubiquitous Media* (2004), 33-39
5. Burnett, G. and Porter, J. Ubiquitous computing within cars: designing controls for non-visual use. *Int. Jnl. Human Computer Studies* 55(4) (2001), 521-531
6. Csíkszentmihályi, M. *"Flow: The Psychology of Optimal Experience"*, Harper and Row (1990)
7. *Endomondo* (2009), http://www.endomondo.com
8. Hertz, G. OutRun: perversive games and designing the de-simulation of eight-bit driving, *Proc. 5th Conf. Foundations of Digital Games* (2010)
9. Hockey, J. Knowing the route: Distance runners' mundane knowledge. *Sociology of Sport Online* 7 (1), (2004), 1-10
10. Höysniemi, J., Aula, A., Auvinen, P., Hännikäinen, J., and Hämäläinen, P. Shadow boxer: a physically interactive fitness game. *Proc. of NordiCHI 2004*
11. Isbister, K., Höök, K. On Being Supple: In Search of Rigor without Rigidity in Meeting New Design and Evaluation Challenges for HCI Practitioners, *Proc CHI 2009*
12. Konami, *Dance Dance Revolution.* (1998)
13. Liljedahl, M., Lindberg, S., Berg, J. Digiwall: an interactive climbing wall. *Proc. ACE 2005*, 225-228
14. Linehan, C., Kirman, B., Lawson, S. and Doughty, M. Blowtooth: pervasive gaming in unique and challenging environments. *Ext. Abstracts CHI 2010.*
15. Marshall, J., Rowland, D., Rennick Egglestone, S., Benford, S., Walker, B., McAuley, D. Breath Control of Amusement Rides. *Proc CHI 2011.*
16. Möhlenkamp S, Lehmann N, et al. Running: the risk of coronary events : Prevalence and prognostic relevance of coronary atherosclerosis in marathon runners. *European Heart Journal* 29(15), (2008) 1800-1802
17. Mopius *RealReplay.* (2005) http:// mopius.com/
18. Mueller, F., O'Brien, S. and Thorogood, A. Jogging over a distance: supporting a "jogging together" experience although being apart. *Extended Abstracts CHI 2007*
19. Mueller, F., Stevens, G., Thorogood, A., O'Brien, S., and Wulf, V. Sports over a distance. *Personal Ubiquitous Comput. 11*, 8 (2007), 633–645
20. Nenonen, V., Lindblad, A., Häkkinen, V., Laitinen, T., Jouhtio, M. and Hämäläinen, P. Using heart rate to control an interactive game. *Proc. CHI 2007*, 853-856
21. Nintendo, *Wii Fit*. (2007)
22. Pettitt, M., Burnett, G., Stevens, A. An extended keystroke level model (KLM) for predicting the visual demand of in-vehicle information systems. *Proc CHI 2007* 1515-1524
23. Reeves, S., Benford, S., O'Malley, C. and Fraser, M. Designing the spectator experience. *Proc. CHI 2005*
24. Rico, J and Brewster, S. Usable gestures for mobile interfaces: evaluating social acceptability. *Proc. CHI 2010.*
25. Rowland, D., Flintham, M., Oppermann, L., Marshall, J. et al. Ubikequitous computing: designing interactive experiences for cyclists. *Proc MobileHCI 2009.*
26. Scheible, J. Mobile phone programming for multimedia. *Proc Multimedia 2007.*
27. Sengers, P. and Gaver, B. "Staying open to interpretation: engaging multiple meanings in design and evaluation". *Proc DIS 2006.*
28. Simpson, S.D. and Karageorghis, C.I. The effects of synchronous music on 400-m sprint performance. *Journal of Sports Science 24* (2006), 1095–1102.
29. Smith, P. "Babelogue", *Easter*, Arista Records, 1978

A VJ Centered Exploration of Expressive Interaction

Jonathan Hook[1] David Green[1] John McCarthy[2] Stuart Taylor[3] Peter Wright[1] Patrick Olivier[1]

[1] Culture Lab, School of Computing Science, Newcastle University, UK

[2] People and Technology, Dept. of Applied Psychology, University College Cork, Ireland

[3] Socio-Digital Systems, Microsoft Research Cambridge, Cambridge, UK

{j.d.hook, d.p.green, p.c.wright, p.l.olivier}@ncl.ac.uk john.mccarthy@ucc.ie stuart@microsoft.com

ABSTRACT
This paper identifies key themes of expressive interaction for VJs. VJs are visual artists who use digital media to express themselves to an audience during a live audio-visual performance. Those designing for the expressive use of technology can gain insight from an articulation of expressive interaction from the perspective of VJ practice. This is developed using a novel qualitative methodology designed to be sensitive to the subtle and tacit nature of expression. We detail our methodology, present the results of its application to a group of VJs and conclude with a discussion of the implications our findings may have for those wishing to design for VJs, or those in related domains that involve expressive interaction with technology.

Author Keywords
Creative response, dialogue, documentary film, expressive interaction, methodology, thematic analysis, VJ.

ACM Classification Keywords
H5.m. Information interfaces and presentation (e.g., HCI): Miscellaneous.

General Terms
Design, Human Factors.

INTRODUCTION
Expression, *"the action of making known one's thoughts or feelings"* [22], relates to the conveyance of ideas and emotion through the manipulation of a medium. In music for example, expression inhabits the nuances of a performance and is often associated with communicating emotion, or evoking an emotional response, in the audience [4, 23]. Similarly in art, a work is said to be expressive if, for an observer, it arouses a particular feeling or emotion [18]. Hence, if it is to contribute to the design of expressive interaction, HCI needs methods that are sensitive to the more nuanced spaces of user activity that expression inhabits. Moreover, a deeper understanding of expressive interaction would assist those wishing to design for the growing body of expressive and creative users of technology and would provide a distinct standpoint from which novel ideas about interaction may be developed.

In this paper we make two contributions to the field of expressive interaction. We provide an analysis of the important qualities of interaction for one group of users for whom expressivity is pivotal, video-jockeys[1] (VJs). Our findings provide a novel perspective on expressive interaction, which has the potential to inspire and guide future discussion of the topic in HCI. The methodology we developed to explore expressive interaction for VJs involved a novel twist on qualitative research methods that responds to the creative nature of the group involved. The methodology used combines two well-known approaches to qualitative research, documentary film [25] and Focus Groups, and includes a novel *Creative Response* activity. As well as helping us to understand VJ practice, our methodology may also be a useful mechanism for exploring other creative and expressive settings.

EXPLORING EXPRESSIVE INTERACTION AMONG VJS
VJs adapt and appropriate technology in order to attain expression through visual media. Indeed, it might be helpful to consider them as pragmatic designers [7] who in the development of a performance evaluate technology primarily in terms of expression. By studying the qualities that underpin the VJ's relationship with technology we sought to uncover insights from a novel perspective that will assist in the understanding of expressive interaction. We also believe that this approach will help to inform the development of expressive interfaces for both the VJ and potentially those in related disciplines such as electronic music.

VJing and other creative performance domains have been considered previously in an interaction design context. A primary concern of this research was the relationship between performer and audience. Interactive surfaces have been designed to make the audience aware of a VJ's actions using enhanced visibility [17] and collaboration [32]. Empirical studies have also explored aspects of this relationship [9] and addressed issues including the spectator

[1] The VJ is a visual artist whose practice is based upon the live performance of visual media such as video or computer generated imagery; a comprehensive description can be found in [8].

CHI 2011, May 7–12, 2011, Vancouver, BC, Canada.

experience [29] and audience participation [30]. Furthermore, Engström et al. explored the integration of VJs' aesthetic, interface and social preferences into a participatory scenario using mobile devices [6]. Our work is distinctive as we consider VJing from the explicit standpoint of expressive interaction. Aspects of our findings do touch upon the performer-audience relationship; in these cases we hope to provide novel insight that will further its understanding as a concept in HCI.

Expressive interaction, in a practice such as VJing, is a challenging concept to study from an interaction design perspective. Being expressive is not a distinct action or task that can be isolated for study, but rather a phenomenon that arises as a consequence of how an action is completed. Consider two methods of playing the same musical note: plucking a guitar string and clicking on a sound file. The former involves qualities such as control over timbre that make it, at least to the guitarist playing the note, a more expressive act. For this reason we must take a more holistic approach in our investigation that not only captures *what* the VJ does, but also the nuances and contexts of action that define *how* they do it.

The qualities of interaction in an expressive practice will likely be subtle and many of the features that define expression in VJing may be tacit [24]. When investigating tacit elements we expect to encounter the *"say-do problem"* [1] where the difficult task of adequate articulation results in a gulf between the VJ's account and their practice. Therefore, our methods must be sensitive to not only the face value of an action but also the deeper, less easily described, concepts that underpin it. Suitable methods are likely to involve the kinds of personal responses and interpretations of data that require a great deal of reflection and critical analysis. We therefore see our findings as provisional, as a contribution to a conversation on expressive interaction that results in an inter-subjective understanding [5] with the VJ about their practice and relationship with expression.

In response to these challenges we have developed an approach to engaging with, and understanding, VJs and other expressive users of technology. Our methodology begins with the creation of a documentary film [25], which forms the basis of a multi-stage dialogue with the VJs.

Documentary Film-making

In the first stage of the process a documentary film is created about a small group of VJs. The documentary is produced by a professional filmmaker who is accompanied and assisted by one of the researchers. We follow the VJs as they prepare, practice and perform their work. In addition to gathering footage for the film, this process acts as our initial inquiry and leads to our first interpretation of the subjects' practices. This understanding develops as we view, analyze, select, and edit footage to produce the film.

The role of documentary film in our process extends beyond a video ethnography. When analyzing a concept as intricate as expressive interaction in VJ performance, we resolve what we observe into a personal interpretation. The creation of a documentary film produces an artifact that can be used to communicate this interpretation to the VJ and hence form the basis of a reflective dialogue through which our understanding may evolve. Film captures and portrays the *"elusive details"* of situations [3] that other methods of presentation, such as a vocal or textual description, may miss. As such we are able to illustrate our interpretations of expressive interaction in the detailed context of the practice from which they arise. Moreover, film places the viewer, in this case the VJ, in a situation from which they may witness the reality perceived by the filmmaker [26]. By presenting our ideas through film we therefore enable the VJs to observe their practice from our point of view and consequently engage with and discuss it with this perspective in mind.

Exchange

In the next stage we initiate a conversation about the portrayal of each VJ in the film. A Focus Group is held and attended by one of researchers, the filmmaker, and the VJs, who will be referred to from here-on as participants. The film, which comprises short vignettes describing each VJ performance, is shown. Following each vignette a discussion is held. We intend the topics of discussion to be primarily guided by the participants in reaction to the film. However, at times the researcher may ask for comment on a particular aspect of the vignette.

The principal aim of the Focus Group is to elicit data from the participants that will advance our interpretation of their practices. The film plays a significant role in this activity for three key reasons. First, the film communicates our interpretation to the subject so they may challenge or affirm it. Second, by presenting the participants with a portrait of their practice that may not match their personal viewpoint, we hope to inspire them to reflect on their work and thus consider and discuss the issues that shape it from novel perspectives. Finally, video footage has been shown to enable the re-experience of tacit skill in a manner more conducive to understanding and reflection [27]. Therefore the film will assist in the articulation and discussion of tacit elements of VJ practice tackling the *"say-do problem"*.

As a methodology, Focus Groups are highly appropriate for fostering self-reflection amongst participants. Group discussion of a topic allows participants to explore and clarify their ideas; and therefore advance and change them in response to the views and experiences of others [15]. Thus, the participants will be provoked to reflect on issues of their practice as they are discussed from alternate perspectives and depicted in the practices of others. Furthermore, Focus Groups give participants a better opportunity to control how topics are addressed by *"generating their own questions and pursuing their own priorities"* [16]. As a result, participants will use their expert knowledge of the domain to question each other about issues that differ from those broached in the film.

Focus Groups also have disadvantages in the current context as they have been found at times to stifle the opinions of individual participants in favor of views held more widely in a group [15]. As such it may be difficult to gather the whole spectrum of opinions on an issue and differentiate the views of individuals from those enforced by the group. This dilemma is particularly relevant in the context of expressive practice where a homogenized group opinion may not capture the rich variety of views about an issue. For this reason, each of the participants is interviewed individually following the Focus Group. Each interview lasts approximately 20 minutes and follows a script that is derived from the topics discussed in the Focus Group. As a result, we hope to examine those issues considered important by the group from the perspective of each participant's individual practice.

Creative Response

The final phase of our methodology is a novel *Creative Response* activity. The activity makes use of the participants' standing as creative practitioners by asking them to create a short re-edit of our documentary film, which emphasizes their response to a particular issue (or range of issues) that arose from our film or during the Focus Group. Participants are provided with the raw footage of the film and digital video editing equipment. They are then given a period of around two hours to produce a response that is approximately 2-3 minutes in length. On completion, each response is presented by its creator(s) to the other participants and the researcher. The presentation of the response is coupled with a short vocal rationale that explains its content.

We envisage that there exist elements of expressive interaction that are so intertwined with a practice that reflection on them, and their articulation, outside of its context is particularly challenging. Hence, the retrospective discussion of the Exchange phase may not be sensitive to particular aspects of the participants' practices. The *Creative Response* activity responds to this challenge by using the creative act of film-making to afford both contextual communication and reflection amongst the participants.

Film provides a language through which the participants may incorporate elements of their practice directly into the discussion of an issue. By selecting particular clips, the VJs may demonstrate concepts such as the significance of their personal visual aesthetic that might have proved difficult to articulate during the earlier stages of the methodology. Furthermore, the creative process of making a short film presents the participants with the opportunity to reflect about their practice in a detailed and methodical manner. As footage is edited to respond to individual issues, the participants are given the opportunity to examine, and reflect upon, the account they are hoping to convey in the detailed context of practice from which it arises. Moreover, the Creative Response activity will be approached by the VJs with the ideas raised by our film and the Focus Group in mind. Hence, the participants may be inspired to cross examine their practices from these novel perspectives, and feed insights from this further reflection into their response.

Figure 1. The featured performances (clockwise): (a) 3D Disco, (b) Electro-Flamenko, (c) Kinetxt, (d) Tron Lennon.

AN APPLICATION OF THE PROCESS

In the following sections we describe an application of our process that studied the practices of four VJs/VJ collectives. The study of four performances allowed time for a much deeper investigation than would have been possible with a broader sample size. The documentary film that would provide the focus for the exploration was produced by a filmmaker and the first author during a month long audio-visual arts festival. The film, which featured each subject's performance, had a total duration of approximately 12 minutes and was divided into four vignettes that were on average three minutes in length.

A montage style was adopted where interview footage, shot throughout the film-making process, was placed alongside relevant scenes of the subject at work or in performance. This approach was chosen to create a film that portrayed our interpretation of the performer as a reality or truth that was depicted with their words and actions alone. As a consequence we hoped to evoke a much stronger response than if we had actively spoken our ideas with the addition of a narration track. An abridged version of the film can be seen in [11].

Over the following sections we give a quick introduction to each of the featured performances and briefly describe the interpretation of the work that we wished to convey in the film. As VJ practice is both public facing and personally significant, with their explicit permission, we use the participants' real names in our analysis and discussion.

3D Disco

The 3D Disco is a performance which takes place in a night club setting. The piece is produced by a large collective of VJs, two of whom (Andrew and Elliot) took part in our exploration. The performance consists of 3D images that are projected around a venue; audience members wear special glasses in order to see an anaglyph 3D effect. The visual materials are created prior to the performance in the studio and are then divided up into short clips that are triggered by the VJ in a semi-scripted sequence together with a soundtrack. Figure 1 (a) shows an audience member silhouetted against a screen during the 3D Disco.

The vignette emphasizes the relationship between audience enjoyment and the theme and content of the 3D Disco. We stress how the technical challenge posed by the presentation of 3D visuals limits the ability of the VJ to improvise and experiment in the moment of performance. We contrast this discussion with footage of audience members reveling in the atmosphere of the event and an interview of the VJ just after leaving the stage, where he recalls his enjoyment and satisfaction with the performance. Accordingly, we hope to question whether or not the audience's experience is negatively affected as a consequence of the reduced scope for improvisation and experimentation posed by the pre-rendered visuals.

Electro-Flamenko

Electro-Flamenko is a band that fuses traditional Flamenco and electronic music. The band consists of musicians, singers, dancers and a VJ (Alasdair), who is the primary subject of the vignette. Alasdair performs on stage alongside the other members of the band. He manipulates video clips using a MIDI controller[2] and the commercial VJ software Modul8 [20]; the resulting images are then projected at the rear of the stage. Electro-Flamenko can be seen in Figure 1 (b).

The vignette highlights the holistic nature of Electro-Flamenko and consequently that Alasdair's visuals are intertwined with, and hence less meaningful without, the other visual and sonic elements of the band. Footage of the differing elements of the band is shown alongside interview footage of Alasdair speaking about his idea of a complete audio-visual artwork and the importance he places on the link between image and sound. We bring to light Alasdair's requirement for an interface that allows for powerful manipulation of visual material but is also portable enough to accompany him on tour. Therefore we hope to ask whether an interface must be complex and bespoke in order to be expressive, or if something simpler is adequate.

Kinetxt

Kinetxt is an interactive visual performance, created by two VJs (Toby and Andrew), that is held in venues ranging from galleries to nightclubs. Audience members enter passages of text using computer terminals that are situated around the performance space. Using a Nintendo Wii [35] controller, a performer creates a narrative from these passages, which is then displayed on a large panoramic screen. In addition, this narrative is illustrated by a graffiti artist whose sketch pad is projected behind the passages. The audience responds to this evolving narrative by entering further passages of text; as such a dialogue develops between the performer, graffiti artist and the audience. Figure 1 (c) shows the panoramic screen during a performance.

By showing a collage of the elements of Kinetxt from the perspective of an audience member, we hope the vignette stresses how the performance surrounds and immerses the viewer. We include interview footage of Toby giving an in-depth walkthrough of the technical infrastructure behind the performance. We hope as a result to expose the role technology plays in creating an environment conducive to a particular experience, of immersion in a dialogue, rather than as a tool of manipulation or presentation as in the other vignettes.

Tron Lennon

Tron Lennon is a collaboration between two improvisational electro-acoustic musicians (John and Paul), who describe their performance as an experiment into the inclusion of visuals into an exclusively musical practice. Paul has a background as a turntablist whilst John has a background as a guitarist. In their visual practice they extend the capabilities of their instruments in order to improvise with video material. Paul uses the MsPinky digital vinyl system (DVS) [21] to scrub through video clips using a turntable, whilst John augments his guitar with a range of camera feeds that are manipulated in response to his guitar and effects units. Figure 1 (d) shows John surrounded by his equipment during a performance.

The vignette emphasizes the contrast between the practices of John and Paul. We hope to show that rather than co-creators of a single practice they are two performers, with well-defined practices of their own, in collaboration. Interview footage of Paul speaking almost exclusively about his desire for finite control and powerful manipulation of video content is set next to John's discussion of the adaptation and misappropriation of technology. Footage of Paul and John's visuals are shown in isolation to illustrate the contrasting aesthetics that are combined to produce the final visual output. We hope through the isolation and juxtaposition of aspects of both practices to enquire about the reasoning for, and consequences of, their collaboration.

ANALYSIS OF THE VJS' EXPRESSIVE INTERACTION

The Exchange phase of our methodology revealed insights that lead to a thematic articulation of the qualities of expressive interaction among VJs. The Focus Group and interview sessions combined, produced a data set consisting of approximately 4 hours of video footage. After transcription, a Thematic Analysis was applied according to guidelines set-out by Braun and Clarke [2]. The transcripts were first open coded to highlight potential trends in the participants' discussion of their expressive practices.

[2] *MIDI controller* refers to hardware control devices typically used by performers to interact with software based instruments and tools.

Following this, an iterative process was completed whereby the initial trends were grouped into categories, and these refined. We followed an *inductive* rather than a *theoretical* Thematic Analysis and therefore the coding and categorization process was not guided by any pre-determined theoretical frameworks or hypotheses.

Although a thematic analysis was carried out, there is not space to present the full account here. Instead, we present sufficient analysis and quotations to explain those themes that are most relevant to the aims of this paper. When taken together with insights from the *Creative Responses*, the reader should be able to gain an insight into the VJs' practices and experiences to a depth which is sufficient to understand how the results inform and inspire the design of expressive interfaces for them.

Aspirational

The first key thematic category was the range of desires and intentions that shaped each of the participants' practices. These conceptual aspirations inspired and guided both the structure and content of a piece and its live performance.

Evocative

Andrew and Toby discussed a desire to evoke particular experiences within the audience. Andrew explained how the 3D visuals in his performance were designed to stir up feelings of astonishment or amazement. Toby spoke about how Privy (a performance mentioned in comparison to those featured in our film) was designed to create an emotional experience for those witnessing it:

"Privy is kind of this very kind of dream like thing where if you sit back and let it wash over you it is a very emotional experience." (Toby)

In other extracts, Andrew described how he aimed to create immersive experiences, through audience participation. He also spoke of how intentionally ambiguous materials could create thought provoking experiences:

"A bit of footage will be very blurred and you will just get a sense of what's happening and it's all about building up your own sort of thoughts about what's happening or what the story is about." (Andrew)

Evolving

The drive to evolve and develop was seen as essential to many of the participants' practices. Andrew spoke of the enjoyment of trying out new possibilities and conversely how something as simple as boredom could compel the VJ to push their work forward.

"The most enjoyable aspect of it is to create new things. It's all about creating new pieces of work, or new elements [...] it's very easy to get bored by a lot of stuff, so it's keeping fresh and keeping new." (Andrew)

New technological possibilities seemed to go hand in hand with the aspiration for evolution. Elliot remarked upon the inspiration he gains from new types of sound reactive visuals for example:

"Oh yeah, I am completely technology driven, I love reactive visuals and I am trying to develop that further." (Elliot)

Meaningful

Significant weight was attributed to the desire for a meaningful performance. Alasdair described how he hoped to create and communicate new meaning by re-contextualizing found footage. Toby recounted a rite of passage whereby the VJ begins to explore something beyond *"pretty pictures"* and endeavors to instill a performance with something deeper:

"After a while you go: 'I am happy controlling this screen for X hours, pretty pictures whatever that I do that I am happy with' and then you kind of go 'ahhhh so what's next?' There are a few different avenues to go down and for me narrative is the most interesting." (Toby)

As highlighted above, the predominant form of meaning discussed was narrative. Interestingly there was an apparent resistance against prescribed or set narratives. Andrew spoke of how he wished to explore the *"random"* nature of a live show to create something that differs from a film. Moreover, Paul referred to intentional disruption of narrative in his practice:

"The really strong theme that's running throughout this is trying to create some narrative in what you are doing; whereas a lot of the stuff I'm actively trying to do is actually trying to fracture narrative as well, and that's where the needle dropping thing comes from." (Paul)

Pride-worthy

The participants spoke of how pride in their work inspired them to produce high quality performances. Elliot described how, despite being able to do just enough to get paid, he always tries to perform at the highest standard.

"You can turn up and be really blasé about it, and just be there just to get a bit of pocket money, but sometimes you really want to be there because the people are watching what you're doing, and your name is on a list on the line-up, and you want people to look at your work and say, 'Hey actually he's quite good!'" (Elliot)

The fear of mistakes, and the resulting degradation of audience experience, was also a key issue. Andrew described how the successful elements of a performance may go unnoticed whilst the simplest of mistakes can make the visuals noticeably jarring to the audience.

Interaction

Methods of interacting with digital technology were particularly prevalent topics of discussion, much of which focused on the effect that particular characteristics of interaction had on the participants' practices.

Constraining Interaction

Technologies which limited the VJ were often discussed in beneficial terms. Constraining interaction was described as playing two key roles. Firstly, it prevented the VJ from becoming overwhelmed by a sea of possibilities, and therefore provided focus:

"Working in tight knit spaces is really useful, just exploring one small area. I'm never going to explore all of the possible areas but at least I might get somewhere with something." (John)

Secondly, constraints were praised for their function as a mechanism for creativity. For example, in one of Elliot's performances, based around the manipulation of nothing but a white cube, simplicity was said to inspire new ideas.

"I manipulate a white cube on the fly [...] every set it's entirely different, with the same sort of feeling but you know it, you are constantly coming up new ideas all of the time, because you are just working with one white cube." (Elliot)

Haptically Direct

Participants spoke of wanting to *"get hold of"* and *"grapple with"* media. This implies a desire for interaction that provides a sensation akin to being in direct contact or touching and molding media as if it were an artifact in the physical world. Toby noted negatively how the mode of interaction afforded by the controller he uses is disconnected from the video media that it allows him to manipulate:

"I want something that I can directly grapple with the media that I'm dealing with. At the moment I have a planar flight deck of buttons and knobs and that has got nothing to do with video flowing in real time." (Toby)

Paul illustrated an existing device that affords Haptically Direct interaction. He compared how the turntable gives him the sense of touching and feeling the sound in the videos he is manipulating:

"I've got this really gestural interface that is a turntable I can really feel the sound in the video, whereas if you've got something that's plastic, costs about 80 quid and you are trying to, I dunno. You don't get the same kind of feel, experience, interaction." (Paul)

Immediacy

An immediate response to an action was considered essential to many. Paul spoke of plans to move away from the DVS he uses to control video due to the unacceptable latency it introduces:

"The latency, well it's not ideal especially for scratching so I'm trying to move away from time-coded vinyl." (Paul)

Immediacy was also discussed in terms of predictable and modeless interaction. Andrew described how MIDI controllers presented him with a consistent one to one mapping of control that enables a desired function to be found and utilized instantly; as opposed to a generic control device such as a mouse:

"With a mouse and pad, you can do a million things with it but you've got, it changes each time; but you know you can hit a key, or hit the Kaos pad like that, you know what you are going to do straight away and its immediate." (Andrew)

Manipulable Media

A desire for powerful and varied manipulation of media was evident from the participants' comments. Toby, for example, stated a desire for as much control as possible:

"The key thing is, giving yourself the maximum potential for effecting and controlling what you want to do." (Toby)

In relation to this, participants showed frustration with media that requires rendering prior to, but is immutable during, performance. This illustrated how the participants wanted to manipulate their materials at the microscopic level as opposed to simply collaging clips. Interestingly, there was much discussion of devices that mimicked audio-synthesizers:

"We need something like synthesizers, you know electronic synths. When synths came through, like drum machines and things, you were creating things on the fly; you were creating things from nothing really." (Andrew)

Such devices would allow new content to be generated during a live performance and as such break away from the restricted manipulation associated with rendered sequences of video clips. Finally, Paul discussed his desired manipulation in terms of granularity, stating that the low frame-rate of video made his attempts to control it with small, nuanced, gestures futile.

Parallel Interaction

Parallel or concurrent interaction was seen as an important aspect during a performance. MIDI controllers were mentioned as exemplifying such parallel interaction:

"I need to bring down 10 different things at a time, when I perform I can have two cross faders instead of one that do two slightly different things, and I can only do that with external physical controls." (Toby)

Conversely, Toby warned that parallel control was only beneficial to a certain degree; the performer may not have the physical or mental capacity to interact with too large an array of controls:

"I have 20 buttons, 8 sliders, a few knobs, um, a few rotary controllers, and I only have ten fingers and two hands, and I can only think about so many things at the same time!" (Toby)

Reconfigurable Interfaces

The ability to reconfigure interaction to suit a VJ or a particular performance was said to be important. For example, Toby described a hardware device that consists of physical controls that could be laid out in any configuration:

"It gives you Lego blocks which are the controller bits, so you can literally go 'I want three sliders in a row, and I want this button, and I want that' and so you really can lay

it out. And then you just close your suitcase and turn up. It really did seem like the perfect thing." (Toby)

Reconfigurable interfaces were not just referred to in the context of hardware prototypes. Alasdair described how the interface of the desktop VJ program he uses (Resolume [28]) could be to be tailored to suit his practice.

Visible Interaction

Participants believed interfaces or controllers should be manipulated in such a way that the performer's interaction is visible to the audience. Alasdair described how the visibility of interaction with a controller is essential, even if visibility doesn't equate to an understanding of that interaction:

"If you are on stage they will see you doing something; you know they will see you playing a keyboard or interacting with an interface or whatever. Whether they understand that what you are doing is live visuals, in the context of a band I mean, I guess that doesn't really matter, as long as they are seeing you on stage performing, and they get a sense that something special is happening" (Alasdair)

Toby hoped the audience would not only see, but understand, his interaction. He envisioned a future technology that would externalize the decision process that guided his interactions:

"If we had an interface that was, that really was transparent to the audience, in the sense that your actions, your decision process, everything like that is as obvious to the audience as it is to you as you kind of go through it; then absolutely you have a very compelling reason to be on the stage." (Toby)

Live

The final thematic category notes the importance that the participants placed on their performances being live events. Situating the presentation of visual media in a live context was described as having a range of consequences that set the act of VJing apart from other forms of visual media such as film.

Improvisational

A live performance was described by the VJs as providing the opportunity to experiment and improvise with the creation and manipulation of visual media. Improvisation was described in wholly positive terms by participants who associated it with satisfaction, interest, play and artistic freedom:

"There are lots of opportunities to be quite improvisational, which is a good thing because it's quite satisfying and gives you a sense of artistic freedom" (Alasdair)

Digging deeper, improvisation appeared to be more than a satisfying and interesting trait of a practice but rather a mechanism for creativity inspired by the performer's exploration of his aspirations and materials. Participants spoke of how the act of experimentation would inspire ideas in the moment and future directions in a practice as a whole:

"So with my live cinema piece, which is basically an hour long, say, I basically performed that for about eight hours straight, and tried every combination with everything else, with all these different things, you know, and discovered a thousand things that I never would have come across if I was a film-maker." (Toby)

Responsive

Participants described how a live performance allowed them to incorporate a range of stimuli from the environment into their practice. These included the music played by a DJ, live camera feeds, and active participation from the audience. This concept was of particular importance to Elliot who described how the incorporation of the environment into his performance is the key reason for the VJ to play live:

"The argument about why it is live, should you 'press play' has been raging essentially forever, and it will continue to rage, but before we couldn't do this live feedback, the event back into itself that we can do now, and that puts VJs centre stage and gives them a reason to be there." (Elliot)

Unique

Andrew spoke of how playing live made each performance a unique event that is different for each audience. He associated the unique element of performance to both of the aforementioned factors of live improvised manipulation and responding to the performance environment:

"If the elements that you are doing are controllable by the environment you are in some way [...] it gives some feeling of specialness, or one-off-ness, or individualism." (Andrew)

He also spoke of the personal significance of a performance that is presented just once to an audience:

"This is our thoughts, this is our ideas, this is the thing that we are trying to convey; and it's almost like telling a story or telling something... you tell a story to someone in a pub and then you tell someone else, it's always going to be different, almost that personal thing." (Andrew)

FURTHER INSIGHTS FROM CREATIVE RESPONSES

The *Creative Response* phase of the workshop lead to insights which further developed the themes of expressive interaction among VJs. Four short videos were created that each responded to one of the vignettes. Each response was created by participants featured in the corresponding vignette; as Andrew was featured in two of the vignettes he contributed only to the 3D Disco response. Three of the responses were short re-edits of the footage from our film, whilst the Kinetxt response was an ad-hoc performance. In the following sections we describe each of the responses, alongside the rationale that the performers provided, and present a brief analysis of how they clarify, contrast, and extend the themes defined in the previous section.

3D Disco

The 3D Disco response begins with footage of the performers preparing audio and visual material in their studio. The performers are shown quietly concentrating at their laptops whilst a heartbeat like rhythm plays in the background. These scenes continue for nearly two and a half minutes until the final 40 seconds of the response where footage of the performance is shown. When discussing their response Andrew and Elliot commented that by creating an imbalance in the footage of pre-production and performance, they hoped to emphasize the hours of work that are spent preparing materials compared to the relatively short duration of the live show. Andrew attributed this to the anaglyphic visuals, which must be perfectly produced in order for 3D effect to work.

By commenting upon the imbalance of manipulation between pre-production and performance, the response stresses that the limitations Andrew and Elliot face in terms of *Manipulable Media* are rooted in the format of the visual materials which they utilize rather than, say, methods of control. Furthermore, the response demonstrates that, despite these limitations in terms of manipulation, the performers are able to achieve their goals of a *Pride-worthy* piece that is *Evocative* of audience enjoyment. Hence, the response suggests that for the VJ's interaction with digital technology to be expressive, it need not embody all of the themes defined in the previous section. Rather, an appropriate combination or selection may suffice.

Electro-Flamenko

The response commences with shots of musicians and dancers alongside Alasdair as he performs. Over these scenes Alasdair speaks a monologue that describes his desire to share the links between sound and image, which he holds in his mind, with an audience. Following this, a two minute sequence of visuals is played. The visuals quickly skip and loop in synchrony along to the sound of a recording by Electro-Flamenko. Alasdair stated that the first half of the response captured the different strands of music and dance that together with his visuals entwine to produce the Electro-Flamenko performance and as a result illustrate what it means to VJ in a live band. He described the second half as a live demonstration of his work and stressed the importance of it being produced with only the tools he utilizes in his actual live sets. He hoped that this would express how essential it is that his work is live and how he could never *"just turn up and press play"*.

The response presents a new perspective from which to consider the concept of a *Meaningful* performance. Prior discussion noted that performances may be augmented with meaning such as narrative to make them more interesting and conceptually meaningful for the performer. Alasdair's monologue however suggests that the communication of links between sound and image is an activity otherwise impossible without participation in VJ practice. Hence, the externalization of meaning may be a much more central driving force for expressive interaction in VJ performance than first thought.

Kinetxt

Toby presents a short performance of Kinetxt on his laptop. The Kinetxt environment is configured to present passages of a script, which Toby reads as they arrive on the screen as contributions from an imaginary audience. Initially the passages describe the desire to create a show that embraces the environment and the moment of the performance and as such create something that is *"beyond broadcast"*. Next passages are spoken, from the imaginary voice of Kinetxt, that talk of its existence as an entity or actor that creates an immersive environment by responding to the audience, the performer and the drawings of graffiti artists. Toby stated that, as Kinetxt is an experimental live performance, he made the response in an experimental and live way. He described Kinetxt as a *"story telling experiment"* and said that if Kinetxt cannot tell its own story then somehow he and Andrew fail.

Toby's desire to perform an instance of Kinetxt, rather than re-edit one captured on film, suggests that he believes to truly understand Kinetxt one must witness it in action as it facilitates storytelling in response to the environment it inhabits. This suggests we must consider the theme *Responsive* in a new light. Rather than just providing new sources of inspiration, the incorporation of environmental aspects into a performance may instill it with contextual significance and meaning that distinguishes it from any form of recorded practice. Moreover, this suggests that a *Responsive* performance may go hand in hand with a *Unique* one.

Tron Lennon

Throughout the response short sounds play and loop in tandem with video clips of both John and Paul manipulating their instruments and controllers. At points the sound stops and footage of the pair speaking about the turntable as a tactile controller is shown. At one point visuals are scrubbed through in time with a video of a Paul's hand scratching a record. The response concludes with a clip of a man speaking about the unison between the sound of his speech and the moving image, throughout which the audio is out of sync. Paul emphasized the importance of tactility in their performance through the response. He hoped that footage of interaction with his equipment cut with simple movements and fades of visuals would illustrate his desire for a mapping between physical gesture and video. John hoped that by looping short video clips and sound samples together he could demonstrate his desire to create rhythmic patterns of video as he does when improvising with audio.

Paul and John's response highlights a desire for controllers that afford a strong relationship between physical gesture and manipulation of visual media. This is referred to as tactility and relates to the notion of *Haptically Direct* interaction. The most interesting aspect of the response was the choice to utilize the video editing equipment to mock-up the forms of interaction that were desired, but not yet possible, with video. For example, physical gestures tightly synchronized with the manipulation of video demonstrated the *Immediacy* and *Visible Interaction*, that although present in the pair's audio practice, were thus far unattainable in the visual arena.

DESIGN IMPLICATIONS

Our account of expressive interaction relates to abstract characteristics of the relationship between VJs and interactive technology. In order to guide those wishing to design in response to our findings we discuss our results in terms of relevant techniques and theories from the literature.

Tangible user interfaces (TUIs) bridge the gap between the intangible bits of a computer and the perceptible atoms of the physical world [14]. Consequently, TUIs would seem to naturally lend themselves to the realisation of *Haptically Direct* interaction. By giving the underlying content of a VJ performance a tangible manifestation, the feelings of holding and grappling with media may be attained. Furthermore, TUIs strive to replicate the natural union of physical gesture and effect that we find when manipulating physical objects. Wensveen et al. describe such interaction as being *"naturally coupled"* and note the effect where results, and feedback, occur instantaneously alongside an action [33]. Hence, TUIs present an interesting avenue of exploration into the realisation of *Immediacy*. Additionally, the visible relationship between physical action and effect afforded by such naturally coupled interaction makes the manipulation of TUIs highly conducive to *Visible Interaction* [13].

Interfaces based upon metonymy [1] move away from the abstraction of interface metaphors. As a consequence, they allow users to better understand the relationship between their action and the underlying function of a system. For example, a musical synthesiser based on metonymy would allow the user to directly manipulate a waveform as opposed to clicking a virtual piano key. If we consider *Haptically Direct* interaction not in a physical sense, but in terms of probing an object's characteristics, metonymy arises as a compelling design option. By exposing the underlying qualities of software, metonymy may allow the user to sense and *"grapple with"* them in a virtual context. Hence, an alternative approach is suggested for realising a sense of *Haptically Direct* interaction suited to the case where the direct association of underlying software functionality with physical form (of the TUI) may be inappropriate or impractical.

Shneiderman proposed that interfaces that support creative users should have *"high ceilings and wide walls"* [31]. That is, they should provide the user with a wide range of functionality which is complex enough to permit skill development amongst advanced users. Similarly, discussion of electronic musical instruments and interfaces highlights that limitations imposed on skill development are unacceptable [34]. The theme *Manipulable Media* supports this proposal and suggests that when designing for the VJ it may be appropriate to provide a more complex space of control possibilities. McCullough describes such interaction in terms of *"density"*, and envisions control where *"between any two states there exists still another"* [19]. The value of providing an un-bounded space of control is however questioned by the theme *Constraining Interaction*. Participants noted how too large a space of possibilities could overwhelm, and limitations were in many cases useful features that give rise to creative acts. As such the VJ may benefit from complex interaction possibilities that are contained within a well-defined space. *Reconfigurable Interfaces* (e.g. [12]) pose an interesting method for the provision of both *Manipulable Media* and *Constraining Interaction*. If the user is presented with a complex space of manipulation possibilities, but is able to reconfigure the interface to voluntarily impose limitations on that space, they may find a personal balance that affords both complexity and constraint.

We return to the definition of expression given at the outset of this paper: *"the action of making known one's thoughts or feelings"* [22]. The theme *Improvisational* suggests that it is essential for the VJ to partake in a practice for it to develop. Therefore we consider *"making known"* not only to refer to the communication of ideas to an audience, but rather their formation and development through practice and experimentation with interactive technology. McCullough [19] describes how a craftsperson must participate in a practice to develop a relationship between their expressive intent and their materials. If we look at our results though such a lens, expressive interaction among VJs can be considered as a dialogue through which, over time, the *Aspirational* elements that underpin a practice are given form in the context of technology. Hence, designers may do well to consider work such as that by Hallnäs and Redström which explores how artifacts develop a longitudinal presence in the life of the user [10].

DISCUSSION

Whilst many of the techniques utilized in our methodology are well established, our *Creative Response* activity is novel and as such we reflect upon its application. Participants primarily utilized the responses to reflect on a single or small number of issues. As opposed to the Focus Group, where discussion could quickly dart between topics, the *Creative Response* required a sustained period of engagement in order to produce a video artifact. Consequently, participants were pushed to prioritize issues and therefore regard only the most salient in terms of their practice. As a result of this more involved stance, we found participants tended to broach their personal relationship with the issues at hand. Alasdair, for example, utilized the response to elaborate upon his individual interpretation of meaning in a VJ performance. A particularly interesting, yet unexpected, consequence of the method arose as John and Paul used the response to give form to future aspirations for their practice. In this case, the *Creative Response* afforded a means of experiencing aspects of a practice that have yet to exist.

The *Creative Response* method may prove to be a valuable mechanism for exploring creative practices are not video-based. Video can capture actions and effects of a practice and as such could form the basis of an engaging reflective activity even if the focus of expressive interaction is a different medium. In this case however, the creative skill and experience of the participant with their medium will not be directly leveraged in the making of the response. Therefore, it may be necessary to adapt the method for each use-case, so that the participant may express their response to using the medium of their practice; for example a musician with music or a sculptor with clay.

ACKNOWLEDGEMENTS

This work was funded by an EPSRC Doctoral Training Award and the RCUK Digital Economy Research Hub SiDE: Social Inclusion through the Digital Economy.

REFERENCES

1. Bertelsen, O. W., Breinbjerg, M., & Pold, S. Instrumentness for Creativity Mediation, Materiality & Metonymy. In *Proc. C&C'07*, ACM, 233-242.
2. Braun, V & Clarke, V. Using Thematic Analysis in Psychology. *Qualitative Research in Psychology*, 3, 2 (2006), 77-101.
3. Brun-Cottan, F., & Wall, P. Using Video to Re-present The User. *Commun. ACM*, 38, 5 (1995), 61-71.
4. Dobrian, C., & Koppelman, D. The 'E' in NIME: Musical Expression with New Computer Interfaces. In *Proc. NIME'06*, IRCAM, 277-282.
5. Dourish, P. *Where The Action Is: The Foundations of Embodied Interaction*. MIT Press, 2004.
6. Engström, A., Esbjörnsson, M., & Juhlin, O. Mobile Collaborative Live Video Mixing. In *Proc. MobileHCI'08*, ACM, 157-166.
7. Fallman, D. Design-oriented Human—Computer Interaction. In *Proc. CHI'03*, ACM, 225-232.
8. Faulkner, M. *VJ: Audiovisual Art + VJ Culture*. Laurence King, 2006.
9. Gates, C., Subramanian, S., & Gutwin, C. DJs' Perspectives on Interaction and Awareness in Nightclubs. In *Proc. DIS'06*, ACM, 70-79.
10. Hallnäs, L., & Redström, J. From Use to Presence: On the Expressions and Aesthetics of Everyday Computational Things. *TOCHI*, 9, 2 (2002), 106-124.
11. Hook, J., Green, D., & Olivier, P. A Short Film about VJs: Using Documentary Film to Engage Performers in Design. In *Ext. Abs. CHI'09*, ACM, 3491-3492.
12. Hook, J., Taylor, S., Butler, A., Villar, N., & Izadi, S. A Reconfigurable Ferromagnetic Input Device. In *Proc. UIST'09*, ACM, 51-54.
13. Hornecker, E., & Buur, J. Getting a Grip on Tangible Interaction: A Framework on Physical Space and Social Interaction. In *Proc. CHI'06*, ACM, 437-446.
14. Ishii, I., & Ullmer, B. Tangible Bits: Towards Seamless Interfaces between People, Bits and Atoms. In *Proc. CHI'97*, ACM, 234-241.
15. Kitzinger, J. The Methodology of Focus Groups: The Importance of Interaction between Research Participants. *Sociology of Health & Illness,* 16, 1 (1994), 103-121.
16. Kitzinger, J. Introducing Focus Groups. *British Medical Journal,* 311, 7000 (1995), 299-302.
17. Lew, M. Live Cinema: Designing an Instrument for Cinema Editing as a Live Performance. *In Proc. NIME'04*, NUS, 144-149.
18. Matravers, D. *Art and Emotion.* Oxford University Press, 1998.
19. McCullough, M. *Abstracting Craft: The Practiced Digital Hand.* MIT Press, 1998.
20. Modul8 VJ software. http://www.modul8.ch.
21. Ms Pinky's Playhouse. http://www.mspinky.com.
22. Oxford Dictionary. http://oxforddictionaries.com.
23. Poepel, C. On Interface Expressivity: A Player-Based Study. In *Proc. NIME'05,* NUS, 228-231.
24. Polanyi, M. *Personal Knowledge: Towards a Post-Critical Philosophy*. University of Chicago Press, 1958.
25. Raijmakers, B., Gaver, W., & Bishay, J. Design Documentaries: Inspiring Design research Through Documentary Film. In *Proc. DIS'06*, ACM, 229-238.
26. Raijmakers, B. Design Documentaries: Using Documentary Film to Inspire Design. *PhD Thesis,* Royal College of Art, 2007.
27. Raingruber, B. Video-Cued Narrative Reflection: A Research Approach for Articulating Tacit, Relational, and Embodied Understandings. *Qualitative Health Research*, 13, 8 (2003), 1155-1169.
28. Resolume VJ Software. http://www.resolume.com.
29. Reeves, S., Benford, S., O'Malley, C., & Fraser, M. Designing the Spectator Experience. In *Proc. CHI'05,* ACM, 741-750.
30. Sheridan, J., Dix, A., Lock, S., & Bayliss, A. Understanding Interaction in Ubiquitous Guerrilla Performances in Playful Arenas. In *Proc. BCS-HCI'04*, Springer-Verlag, 3-18.
31. Shneiderman, B. Creativity Support Tools. *Commun. ACM,* 45, 10 (2002), 116-120.
32. Taylor, S., Izadi, S., Kirk, D., Harper, R., & Garcia-Mendoza, A. Turning the Tables: An Interactive Surface for Vjing. In *Proc. CHI'09*, ACM, 1251-1254.
33. Wensveen, S., Djajadiningrat, T., & Overbeeke, K. Interaction Frogger: A Design Framework to Couple Action and Function through Feedback and Feedforward. In *Proc. DIS'04*, ACM, 177-184.
34. Wessel, D., Wright, M., & Schott, J. Problems and Prospects for Intimate Musical Control of Computers. *Computer Music Journal*, 26, 3 (2002), 11-22.
35. Wii at Nintendo. http://www.nintendo.com/wii.

Placing a Value on Aesthetics in Online Casual Games

Erik Andersen, Yun-En Liu, Richard Snider, Roy Szeto, and Zoran Popović
Center for Game Science
Department of Computer Science & Engineering, University of Washington
{eland,yunliu,mrsoviet,szetor,zoran}@cs.washington.edu

ABSTRACT
Game designers frequently invest in aesthetic improvements such as music, sound effects, and animations. However, their exact value for attracting and retaining players remains unclear. Seeking to estimate this value in two popular Flash games, we conducted a series of large-scale A/B tests in which we selectively removed aesthetic improvements and examined the effect of each component on play time, progress, and return rate. We found that music and sound effects had little or no effect on player retention in either game, while animations caused users to play more. We also found, counterintuitively, that optional rewards caused players to play less in both games. In one game, this gameplay modification affected play time three times as much as the largest aesthetic variation. Our methodology provides a way to determine where resources may be best spent during the game design and development process.

Author Keywords
games, aesthetics, analytics, A/B testing

ACM Classification Keywords
H5.0. Information interfaces and presentation: General.

General Terms
Experimentation, Human Factors

INTRODUCTION
Game designers must decide how to focus limited resources on various aspects of their games. Aesthetic elements such as music, sound effects, and animations, for example, are believed to be crucial components of the video game experience. Schell [9] argues that good aesthetics can make the player more likely to tolerate imperfections in game design, and can draw a player into a game they might have otherwise ignored. However, the exact effect that aesthetic quality has on how long players play games is unknown. Discovering this information would be of considerable use to game designers, in order to focus their effort on the areas of their games with the greatest impact.

Performing large-scale experiments to test the effects of these game elements on player behavior can be difficult. However, the rise of online casual and "indie" games [12] gives researchers a cheap and attractive option for gathering massive amounts of experimental data. Kongregate, one of the most popular websites for free online games, attracts 10 million players who collectively spend 23 million hours playing games per month [1]. The popularity of these websites and the ease with which a new game can be uploaded and distributed makes them an ideal testbed for experimentation. Game companies have started to gather data about player behavior remotely through internet analytics and beta testing; unfortunately, most of this data remains unpublished. A well-known advocate for such testing is the social games company Zynga, who used a metrics-driven approach [4] to bring FarmVille to a peak of almost 88 million users [2]. By instrumenting our games to record player behavior, we also are able to measure player engagement quantitatively on a large scale.

In this study, we evaluate the importance of aesthetic quality in two Flash games, Refraction and Hello Worlds, that we developed and uploaded to Kongregate. Through A/B testing, we varied these elements one by one and measured how much progress players made in the game, how long they played, and how likely they were to return. We expected to find that each of these aesthetic improvements significantly increased player retention; however, we found no significant effects for music and sound effects in either game. Animations caused players to play significantly longer. In contrast to what is commonly believed, we also found that the presence of optional rewards decreased play time. Further research is necessary to determine whether these results generalize to other games.

In contrast to in house playtesting, our experiments are conducted "in the wild" where players do not know they are part of an experiment. This gives us the advantage that players are playing under their own motivation and that our findings are based solely on their observable behavior; however, there is also the disadvantage that we cannot know what players are thinking or feeling. These quantitative measurements can be used in conjunction with other quantitative and qualitative data to provide strong empirical reasoning for design decisions. Our methodology can help determine where resources should be spent during the game development process, and also suggests a new way of gathering huge numbers of participants for answering research questions relevant to games and user interfaces.

	Hello Worlds	Refraction
Music	eleven alternating songs	title screen, intro and ending movie, song for each of the 7 worlds
Sound	picking up a coin using a door and error sound on unusable doors applause at end of each level bouncing on trampoline	picking up and placing pieces on the board navigating the menu fireworks and spaceship flyaway at the end of each level overpowered, underpowered, satisfied, and unsatisfied targets
Animation	walking, jumping, climbing ladder, falling, turning left and right fading between stages counting points and fireworks on level finish combination view gliding rewind bar projector animation on worlds picking up coins and stars unusable door quake	intro and ending movies, intro level penguin animation laser splashes and pulses animated piece description when player hovers over the piece fireworks and spaceship flyaway at the end of each level animated title screen, moving title bar, level select screen zooming arrows, blinking animations, and moving pieces in tutorials magnifying glass

Figure 1. Description of various aesthetic additions in Hello Worlds and Refraction that we removed to evaluate their importance. Removing music and sound had no significant effect in either game. Removing animations had negative effects on player progress, time played, and return rate in Refraction, and time played and return rate in Hello Worlds.

AESTHETICS

The word "aesthetic" has multiple meanings in the context of games [8]. Here, we are concerned with content that adds style and artistic depth to the player experience. Aesthetics can also be used to create a sense of theme; however, our goal is to evaluate our investment in aesthetics, not to determine whether our particular choice of art or theme was optimal. Others have studied the effects of aesthetics on user behavior. In user interfaces, Kurosu and Kashima [6] and Tractinsky [11] showed that the aesthetic quality of an interface can affect how usable the interface is perceived to be. In games, surround sound [10] and music [7, 3] have both been shown to increase enjoyment and sense of presence.

LARGE-SCALE A/B TESTING

To collect data on a large scale, we rely on A/B testing and player metrics. In A/B testing, researchers present two conditions randomly to users in the same population and see how they respond, allowing them to assign quantitative values to different aspects of their systems. For example, Amazon uses various metrics to discover which version of a website layout will maximize sales [5]. The same method also applies to games; Zynga, for example, used this approach to find that pink fonts caused players to click on an advertisement for PetVille far more often [4].

For our tests, we used two Flash games that we developed. Hello Worlds is a puzzle-platformer game in which the player's character inhabits as many as four worlds at the same time. Hello Worlds has been played over 900,000 times on Kongregate since its release in May 2010. The game was developed by a team of undergraduate computer science students and an artist as part of a game design capstone course. The visual style of the game is relatively simple, but the game contains music, sound effects, and some animations. The music and sounds were taken from free audio websites. A list of the aesthetic elements that we examined can be seen in Figure 1.

Refraction is a puzzle game in which players use pieces to split and redirect lasers in order to satisfy targets that all want some specific fraction of the laser. A team of graduate and undergraduate computer science students created this game as part of a larger games for learning project. Refraction was released to Kongregate in September 2010, and has been played over 100,000 times. The game features extensive artwork and animations created by three artists. Similar to Hello Worlds, and probably to most Flash games, the music and sound effects were selected from websites for audio under the Creative Commons license. Figure 1 also shows the aesthetic qualities that we examined for Refraction.

METHODOLOGY

To evaluate the importance of music, sound effects, animations, and other game-related aesthetic variables, we conducted a series of A/B tests over a two week period. For each experiment, we changed the versions of Hello Worlds and Refraction on Kongregate, each time replacing the game with a version that tested a single aesthetic variable. In each trial, the uploaded game would remove the target aesthetic variable with 50% probability. We also removed all of the components that suggested the presence of that aesthetic, such as buttons for toggling on and off sound.

We tracked players with variables stored in the local Flash cache. We focused solely on new players; veteran players who had already played the game were not included. There is always some possibility that a player might clear the cache or use a different computer and be treated as a new player.

We measured player engagement in three ways. First, we counted the number of levels that each player completed during their first run-through of the game. Second, we measured the amount of time that each player spent during this first run-through. Since players occasionally idle for long periods while playing Flash games, we aggregated moves the player made in 30-second intervals. If two or more consecutive intervals (a full minute) had no player actions, this time was discounted from the total play time. Finally, the third measure of engagement that we used was return rate. If the player loaded the game again within a day after the first play session, we counted them as a returning player.

DATA ANALYSIS AND RESULTS

Our data was not normally distributed; for example, user play times exhibited a spike near 0 and a long falloff (Fig-

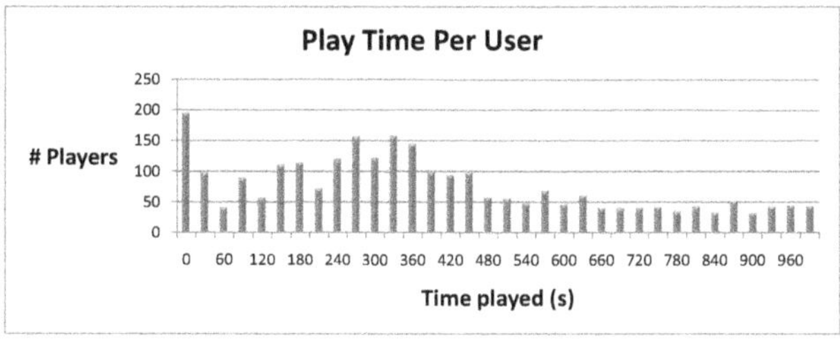

Figure 2. Typical user play times for their first play of Refraction. Many people quit immediately after loading the game. The data is not normally distributed, so we must rely on nonparametric tests.

ure 2). We therefore relied on a nonparametric test, the Wilcoxon / Kruskal-Wallis 2-sample test, to analyze levels completed and time played. For return rate, we used Pearson χ^2 analyses to compare the percentages.

Music and Sound Effects

The first experiment evaluated the importance of music. In Hello Worlds, 4915 people played the game, 2491 with music and 2424 without. There was no significant change in the median number of levels completed (M = 7 levels) (Z = 1.293, p = 0.20), nor was there an effect in the time played comparing those with music (M = 458 seconds) and those without (M = 450 seconds), (Z = 1.061, p = 0.29). No significant effect was found for return rate, $\chi^2(1, 4915) = 0.18$, p = 0.67, with 16.7% of those with music returning, and 16.25% of those without music. In Refraction, 3883 people played the game while testing music, 1939 with music and 1944 without. No significant effect was found for levels completed (Z = -0.502, p = 0.62); players with and without music completed the same number of levels (M = 10). Players with and without music played the same amount of time (M=540), (Z = -0.446, p = 0.66). Finally, no significant effect was found for return rate, $\chi^2(1, 3883) = 2.67$, p = 0.10, with 11.6% of those with music returning, compared to 9.9% of those without music.

Next, we evaluated the importance of sound effects. In Hello Worlds, 4984 people played the game, 2491 with sound effects and 2493 without. Players with sound (M = 7) did not complete significantly more levels than those without (M = 6), (Z = 0.193, p = 0.85). No significant effect was found for time played (Z = 0.265, p = 0.27) between those with sound (M = 450) and those without (M = 390). 16.9% of players with sound returned, compared to 16.7% without, which was not significant $\chi^2(1, 4984) = 0.03$, p = 0.86. In Refraction, 3892 people played the game during the experiment, 1951 with sound and 1941 without. No significant effect was found for levels completed (Z = -0.568, p = 0.57) between those with sound (M = 11) and those without (M = 10). No significant effect was found for time played (M = 600 for both groups), (Z = -0.720, p = 0.47). Finally, no significant effect was found for the return rates of 8.2% with sounds and 7.5% without, $\chi^2(1, 3892) = 0.531$, p = 0.47.

We found little payoff for our investment in music and sound effects, as we did not observe significant effects on player retention. It may be the case that many players are playing with their audio turned off, perhaps because they are in a location where sound would disturb others, such as at work or school. We unfortunately cannot know remotely if players are listening to the audio. Although music tempo has been shown to affect player enjoyment in racing games [3], our games do not rely heavily on audio feedback, potentially reducing any effect on player behavior.

Figure 3. Example of animation in Refraction. Removal of the animations in an A/B test caused significant decreases in level completion, play time, and return rate.

Animation

In Refraction, 7765 people played the game while testing animations, 3938 with animations and 3827 without. Figure 3 shows one such animation. A significant effect was found for levels completed (Z = -2.473, p = 0.01). Players with animations (M = 11) completed more levels than players without animations (M = 9). A significant effect was also found for time played (Z = -5.973, $p < 0.0001$). Players with animations (M = 570) played longer than players without animations (M = 480), a difference of almost 20%. Finally, the return rate dropped from 13% to 11% for players without animations $\chi^2(1, 7765) = 5.046$, p = 0.02. In Hello Worlds, 5050 people played during this experiment, 2493 without animations and 2557 with animations. The median levels completed was 6 for both groups, and was not significant (Z = -1.302, p = 0.19). However, people played longer with animations (M = 390) than without (M = 330), and this was significant (Z = -2.851, p = 0.004). Players also returned significantly more with animations (19.2%) than without (16.5%), $\chi^2(1, 5050) = 6.35$, p = 0.01.

Animations serve an integral purpose, as they are the primary means of feedback about game state. Removing them makes it more difficult for the player to evaluate what is actually happening. Animation is also often used to give the user hints about how different objects in the game world work. It is therefore not surprising that the lack of animation would cause players to quit because gameplay and usability were negatively impacted.

Modifying Gameplay

We also compared the effect of aesthetic and gameplay variations. Most levels of Hello Worlds have optional coins scattered throughout the level that the player can collect to gain a higher score. Similarly, many levels of Refraction contain coins that present an additional challenge for each level. Refraction also rewards the player with cards for certain achievements. Prior to this experiment, we believed that these optional rewards helped to keep players hooked and feel a sense of accomplishment, similar to the achievements that have recently become popular in online games. Therefore, they would encourage players to play longer and return more often. Removing these optional rewards, however, had the opposite effect. During this experiment, 4162 people played Hello Worlds without coins and 4207 people played with them. Removing the coins increased the median number of levels that players complete from 6 to 9, ($Z = -10.382$, $p < 0.0001$). Since removing coins might cause players to focus more on completing the levels rather than collecting optional rewards, this is not surprising. However, the median player played about 50% longer without coins ($M = 510$) than with coins ($M = 330$), ($Z = 4.652$, $p < 0.001$). We also found a significant effect on return rate, $\chi^2(1, 8369) = 11.98$, $p < 0.01$. 20.2% of players without coins returned, compared to 17.2% with coins.

The same effect was observed in Refraction. 2294 people played Refraction without coins and 2281 people played with them. Removing the coins increased the median number of levels that players complete from 11 to 17, ($Z = -11.469$, $p < 0.0001$). Users also played about 20% longer without coins ($M = 690$) than with coins ($M = 570$), ($Z = -3.004$, $p = 0.003$). We did not find a significant effect on return rate, $\chi^2(1, 4575) = 1.10$, $p = 0.295$. 10.6% of players with coins returned, compared to 9.6% of players without.

Further experimentation is necessary to explain why optional rewards do not improve player retention in our game in the way that we expected. Perhaps players try to complete these challenges even when they are difficult, and instead of giving up and continuing to play, they become frustrated and quit. Or, the presence of large numbers of achievements or optional challenges cause players looking for a quick, fun experience to go elsewhere, because the game looks more complex and difficult than it really is. Regardless, even modifying this non-essential gameplay mechanic affected player behavior more than any of our aesthetic experiments. In Hello Worlds, removing coins affected play time three times as much as animation, the strongest aesthetic effect.

CONCLUSION

We used large-scale A/B testing in two online casual games and found that music and sound had little effect on player behavior, while animations caused users to play more. We also found that a minor gameplay modification affected player retention more than aesthetic variations, although understanding the reasons for these effects and how they generalize to other games and genres requires further research. Our methodology can be used by other game designers to evaluate game prototypes and to determine the best use of resources. One can envision a development process that first tests the importance of key costly parts of the game as soon as the basic game mechanics are worked out, and then proceeds with development based on the findings of those tests.

We believe that games are valuable for gathering large numbers of participants for HCI research, as large-scale data is often expensive to collect. While creating games can be expensive, once they exist, they can attract large numbers of users at low cost. Since players are not aware that they are being experimented on, results obtained this way match more closely to their "true" behavior. For these reasons, experimentation within games may help researchers discover principles of player behavior and motivation. We have only scratched the surface of this potential by studying aesthetics and optional rewards in two online Flash games, and more nuanced tests in a wider variety of games will help develop more general theories.

ACKNOWLEDGMENTS

We thank Kongregate and the additional creators of Refraction and Hello Worlds: Ethan Apter, Brian Britigan, Eric Butler, Seth Cooper, Michael Eng, Mai Dang, Happy Dong, Jeff Flatten, Justin Irwen, Christian Lee, Marianne Lee, Emma Lynch, Stephen Sievers, and Blake Thompson. This work was supported by an NSF Graduate Fellowship, NSF grant IIS0811902, DARPA grant FA8750-11-2-0102, the University of Washington Center for Game Science, Adobe, Intel, and Microsoft.

REFERENCES

1. L. Alexander. Gamestop buys social gaming hub kongregate. *Gamasutra*, 2010.
2. E. Caoili. Farmville, top facebook games continue to shed users. *Gamasutra*, June 2010.
3. G. Cassidy and R. A. MacDonald. The effects of music on time perception and performance of a driving game. *Scandinavian Journal of Psychology*, 51:455–464, 2010.
4. K. Graft. Dice 2010: Zynga's reynolds on 'social' first and foremost. *Gamasutra*, 2010.
5. R. Kohavi, R. M. Henne, and D. Sommerfield. Practical guide to controlled experiments on the web: listen to your customers not to the hippo. In *KDD '07: Proceedings of the 13th ACM SIGKDD international conference on Knowledge discovery and data mining*, pages 959–967, New York, NY, USA, 2007. ACM.
6. M. Kurosu and K. Kashimura. Apparent usability vs. inherent usability: experimental analysis on the determinants of the apparent usability. In *CHI '95: Conference companion on Human factors in computing systems*, pages 292–293, New York, NY, USA, 1995. ACM.
7. S. D. Lipscomb and S. M. Zehnder. Immersion in the virtual environment: The effect of a musical score on the video gaming experience. *Journal of PHYSIOLOGICAL ANTHROPOLOGY and Applied Human Science*, 23(6):337–343, 2004.
8. S. Niedenthal. What we talk about when we talk about game aesthetics. In A. Barry, K. Helen, and K. Tanya, editors, *Breaking New Ground: Innovation in Games, Play, Practice and Theory: Proceedings of the 2009 Digital Games Research Association Conference*, London, September 2009. Brunel University.
9. J. Schell. *The Art of Game Design: A Book of Lenses*. Morgan Kaufmann Publishers, Burlington, MA, 2008.
10. P. Skalski and R. Whitbred. Image versus sound: A comparison of formal feature effects on presence and video game enjoyment. *PsychNology Journal*, 8(1):67, 2010.
11. N. Tractinsky. Aesthetics and apparent usability: empirically assessing cultural and methodological issues. In *CHI '97: Proceedings of the SIGCHI conference on Human factors in computing systems*, pages 115–122, New York, NY, USA, 1997. ACM.
12. D. Wesley and G. Barczak. *Innovation and Marketing in the Video Game Industry: Avoiding the Performance Trap*. Gower Publishing Ltd., Farnham, Surrey, England, 2010.

Kinetic Tiles

Hyunjung Kim **Woohun Lee**
Dept. of Industrial Design, KAIST
291 Daehak-ro, Yuseong-gu, Daejeon 305-701
{rroseoscar, woohun.lee}@kaist.ac.kr
+82-42-350-4559

ABSTRACT
We propose and demonstrate Kinetic Tiles, modular construction units for kinetic animations. Three different design methods are explored and evaluated for kinetic animation with the Kinetic Tiles using preset movements, design via animation toolkit, and design via direct input. It is expected that the Kinetic Tiles, as a new design and architecture material, will assist designers to introduce kinetic expressions to the surfaces of everyday objects and spaces.

Author Keywords
Kinetic design, Kinetic interaction, Kinetic design material.

ACM Classification Keywords
H5.2. User Interfaces: Prototyping.

General Terms
Design.

INTRODUCTION
Due to recent advances in technology and increased demand for new interactive experiences, there has been an increasing interest in using physical kinetic motion in the fields of interaction, architecture, and product design [8, 9]. By setting physical movement as a new aesthetic factor, kinetic design encourages designers to explore the animation of products and spaces [4]. In order to generate and control movement for kinetic design, designers not only combine materials and actuators to create dynamic forms, but also choreograph movements. However, for product and environment designers, it is not simple to devise moving mechanisms using actuators and to program kinetic motions appropriate to their purpose. Even though Kinetic Sketchup has been demonstrated as a pioneering tangible method for motion prototyping [7], studies on developing design tools and materials for kinetic design remain in the beginning stages of development.

We present Kinetic Tiles, modular construction units of physical tiles with a kinetic motion. Unlike existing kinetic displays, Kinetic Tiles can be used as a novel design material for physical kinetic animations. Similar to decorating walls and surfaces with ordinary tiles, people can assemble and animate the Kinetic Tiles through simple tangible-touch interaction with the modules. Three design methods for kinetic animation using Kinetic Tiles are explored and evaluated.

IMPLEMENTATION
The current prototype of Kinetic Tiles is shown in Figure 1[1]. Kinetic Tiles consists of tile modules and an actuation platform. The actuation platform consists of a matrix of electromagnets [2] and a driver board. Electromagnets separate the actuation platform from the tile modules and conceal it behind the object surfaces. Thus, users are unaware of the actuators and interact solely with the tile modules, which enable quick construction and manipulation of various compositions through tactile interactions.

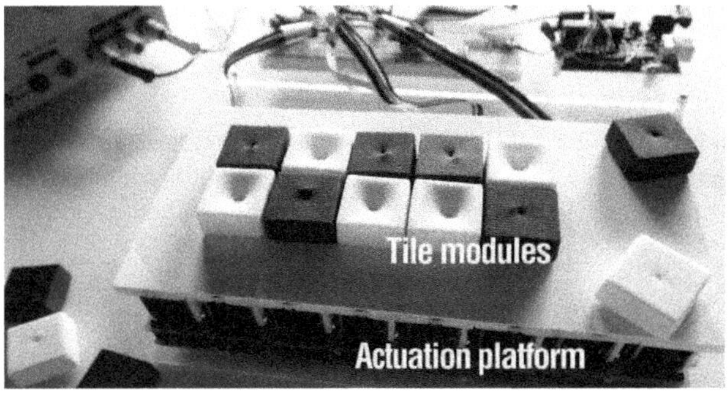

Figure 1. Kinetic Tiles prototype.

Among many possible movements, the current tile module employs a vertical linear motion generated by deforming the surface of the elastic fabric (e.g. [6]). Figure 2(a) illustrates the detailed structure of the tile module. The tile module is topped with spandex; inside the module, a magnet is attached to the back of the fabric layer. The external electromagnetic force generated by the actuation platform drives the magnet to move up and down. When the magnet is pulled down, a concave dip is created on the tile surface (see Figure 2(b)). Each tile is an 11 mm-thick square sized 25 mm × 25 mm. The deformation depth is approximately 7 mm. (See [5] for more information on the structure and the operating mechanism of the tile.)

[1] To see how the prototype works, please refer to our movie file uploaded along with this paper.

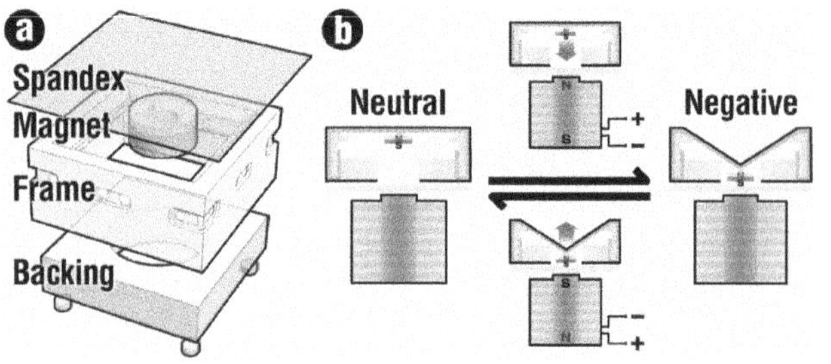

Figure 2. (a) Detailed structure of the tile module. (b) Moving mechanism of the Kinetic Tiles.

DESIGN METHODS FOR KINETIC ANIMATION USING KINETIC TILES

Kinetic Tiles constructs a physical kinetic animation that includes a foreground graphic and a background actuation. The foreground graphic is an initial picture drawn by arranging the tiles. The background actuation is a programmed performance of the electromagnets. The background actuation itself is invisible; however, combined with the foreground graphics, it becomes visible and tangible through the movements of the tiles. Then, how can the background actuation be programmed? How can kinetic animation be created and edited using Kinetic Tiles? We designed three design methods for kinetic animation using Kinetic Tiles based on different programming methods for background actuation. The first method, using a preset actuation, provides an initially fixed background actuation without allowing users to edit. The second method, design via an animation toolkit, uses a tangible kit for scripting the background actuations; while the third method, design via direct input, actuates tiles directly through finger input. Each method is described in detail as follows.

Use of preset actuation

The user designs only the foreground graphics that will operate in a fixed background actuation. For example, a row-by-row actuation with a 500 ms delay is given in the following user workshop (see Figure 3(b)).

Design via animation toolkit

Frame-by-frame animation enables designers to freely create foreground graphics and background actuation, and thus precisely demonstrate their ideas. Inspired by Pixel Materiali [3], a system for creating pixel animations, a tangible frame animation toolkit was designed (see Figure 3(c)). The toolkit represents the current Kinetic Tiles prototype and is composed of 8 × 4 blank frames, timeline grids, and four types of tiny tiles that have two different colors (white and brown) and two different status (flat and dented). The user designs individual frames with the tiles, and then places them on a timeline to create an animation sequences (see Figure 3(d)).

Design via direct input

After constructing a foreground graphic, users can actuate individual tiles via direct finger input. In order to detect and record the location and status of the tile, a hall sensor array is embedded in the top of the actuation platform. The sensor array interacts with the magnet inside the tile module and provides feedback to the control system. Several reported kinetic displays can react to input such as touch (e.g. Lumen [10]), light (e.g. Aperture [1]), and sound (e.g. Murmur [12]). However, the reactions are temporary without recording and editing for further use. Inspired by Topobo [11], a constructive system with kinetic memory, Kinetic Tiles provides recording and playback modes. In the recording mode, the user presses the tiles to be activated in the playback mode and registers the tiles in the control system (see Figure 3(e)). In the playback mode, the pressed tiles play a preset motion in the order in which they were pressed (see Figure 3(f)).

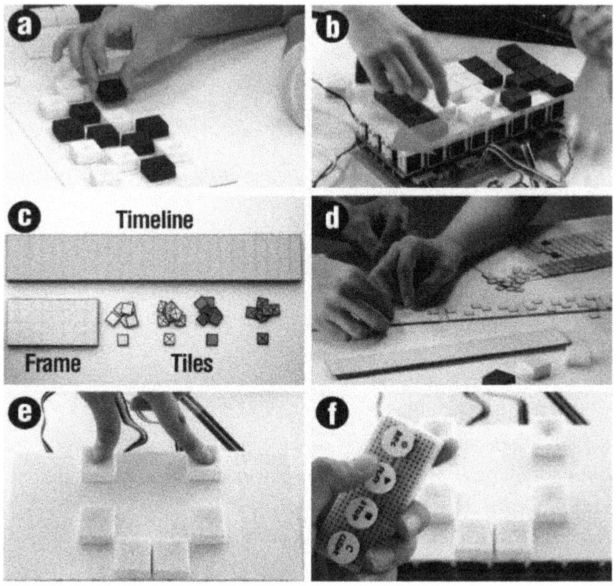

Figure 3. (a) Conventional design with static tiles. (b) Kinetic design with preset actuation. (c) Frame animation toolkit. (d) Kinetic design with the toolkit. Kinetic design with direct input in (e) the recording mode and (f) the playback mode.

EXPLORATORY USER WORKSHOP

To test the feasibility of the Kinetic Tiles as a new design material and to evaluate the three design methods for kinetic animation, a workshop-based user study was conducted. Six industrial design students (two graduates and four undergraduates) participated in this study. The workshop sessions were held twice and three students were involved in a session. Each session lasted approximately ninety minutes.

The session began with a pattern design task. First, the participants were provided with the tile prototypes (hereinafter, static tiles) instead of the Kinetic Tiles and were asked to design tile patterns without using actuation (see Figure 3(a)). Secondly, the participants tested the Kinetic Tiles using an 8 × 4 actuator matrix, which was pre-programmed to be actuated row-by-row with a 500 ms delay (see Figure 3(b)). The participants created kinetic patterns on the preset background actuation. Thirdly, the participants were asked to design animation sequences using the frame animation toolkit (see Figures 3(c) and 3(d)). At the end of the session, the method of designing via direct input using the Wizard of Oz method was demonstrated (see Figures 3(e) and 3(f)). The study was concluded with a written survey asking the participants about their opinions and suggestions for each of the methods and tasks.

DISCUSSION

Although the participants had never used kinetic design material prior to the workshops, they were able to quickly adapt to using the Kinetic Tiles. The technical aspects of the Kinetic Tiles are aesthetically hidden behind the shape of the tile module and its tactile feeling. Therefore, the participants could readily use the Kinetic Tiles as ordinary tiles. The participants responded that the fabric cover of the tiles gives a warm and soft feeling; they even compared the tiles to chocolate cubes.

The outcomes from the tasks show that the Kinetic Tiles motivate the participants to add character and liveliness to their designs. With static tiles, the participants tended to create abstract geometric patterns, whereas with the Kinetic Tiles, they depicted specific objects with dynamic movements such as a swimming fish and a wiggling tadpole. The participants evaluated their designs using the Kinetic Tiles as more eye catching, emotionally engaging, and informative. More results and findings from the tasks that explored the three design methods for kinetic animation are discussed in the following.

Use of preset movements

The participants explored and created diverse foreground graphics that fit the preset background movement in the row-by-row sequential actuation mentioned above. Figure 4 shows an example of the designs produced by the participants: a lightning bolt. Other designs were depictions of lively objects, such as a swimming fish, sailing clouds, and the launching of a rocket. The works that were designed were not only descriptive, but also informative such as scrolling texts. It is notable that the participants verified that their designs were in harmony with the movement and repeatedly revised them.

The participants evaluated this method as simple and an instant way to produce kinetic animations. However, they indicated that the fixed movement limited their expression. To mitigate this problem, they proposed an interface that enables simple modification of the direction and speed of the background actuation, as well as the selection of the background actuation from the preset actuations. In addition, adding non-magnetic passive tiles, which do not react to external actuation, was proposed. The passive tiles remained static, whereas the active tiles moved. Thus, more sophisticated design is available without specific modifications of the background movement.

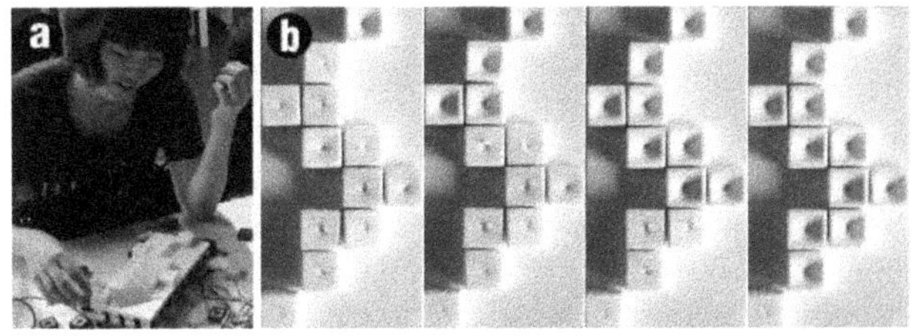

Figure 4. Depiction of a lightning bolt from the preset movement method. (a) Participant assembling tiles on the actuation platform. (b) The actuated design.

Design via animation toolkit

The participants validated that frame-by-frame animation enables designers to express their ideas precisely by scripting freeform movements and controlling the time interval between the frames. The participants quickly became familiar with the toolkit, since the interface of the toolkit is analogous with that of traditional 2D animation software. Figures 5(a) and 5(b) describe a wiggling tadpole with a customized actuation. Figures 5(c) and 5(d) describe waves spreading out radially. It is worthwhile noting that the participant expressed acceleration by gradually shortening the time interval.

With the toolkit, the participants tended to produce long and complicated animations. However, they were bored with the repetitive work of producing frames and wanted to copy and paste the frames. In addition, the participants mentioned that it was inconvenient for them to view the animation only after they built all sequences. To address these problems, they suggested the development of a software program that enables quick editing and preview of the animation.

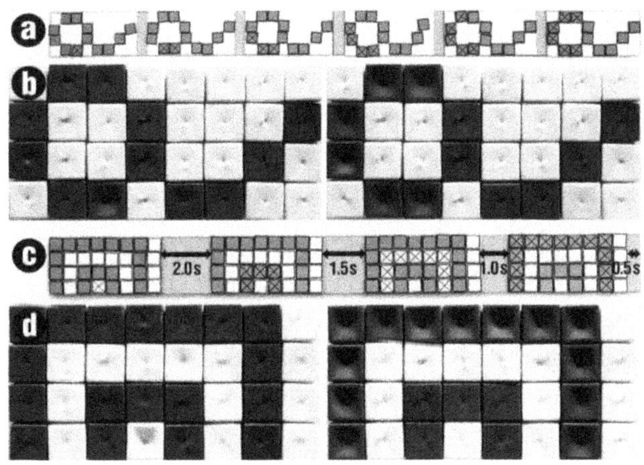

Figure 5. Design outcomes using the animation toolkit method. Depiction of (a, b) a wiggling tadpole, and (c, d) a radial wave. (a, c) The designed animation sequences. (b, d) The first and last frames using the Kinetic Tiles.

Design via direct input

Finally, after the demonstration of the design method using direct input, the participants responded that this is most intuitive and pleasurable method. However, they mentioned it has limitations in designing complicated animations. For example, the issue of the limited number of tiles activated at one time by finger input was raised in the discussion. Figure 6 illustrates examples of the designs produced: a space invader with blinking eyes and digestion in the intestine.

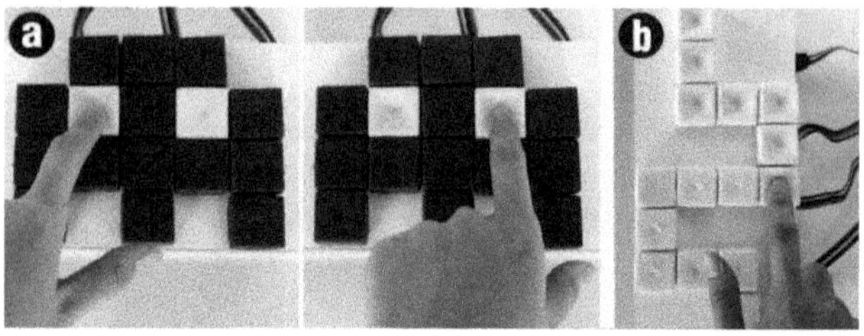

Figure 6. Design outcomes using the direct input method: (a) a space invader with blinking eyes, and (b) digestion in the intestine.

FURTHER WORKS

The Kinetic Tiles need further engineering and design refinement. Future development of the Kinetic Tiles will aim to support higher resolution as the current 8 × 4 scripting platform restricts the designers in the full expression of their ideas. The platform itself is designed to be scalable. However, producing a sufficient number of tile modules requires much time and effort because the tiles were sewn one-by-one to attach the fabric and the magnet to the tile. Modification of the tile design will allow the extension of the platform.

In addition, to enrich the designs which are possible to be created using the Kinetic Tiles and to realize various applications, surface materials (e.g. color, shape, and texture), kinetic motion mechanisms (e.g. linear, rotational, and radial movements), and tile size should be further explored.

CONCLUSION

Kinetic Tiles, modular construction units for kinetic animations, have been proposed and demonstrated. Users can assemble and animate the Kinetic Tiles through simple tangible-touch interactions with the modules. Three different design methods were explored and evaluated for kinetic animation with the Kinetic Tiles using preset movements, design via animation toolkit, and design via direct input. The participants of the exploratory user workshop preferred the design using the animation toolkit method for professional contexts and creation of complicated and precise animations, and design using the direct input method for pleasurable creation of simple animations. In addition, the addition of different types of tiles, such as passive tiles, was suggested as a simple way to produce more sophisticated designs. It is expected that the Kinetic Tiles, as a new design and architecture material, will assist designers to introduce ambient and pleasurable kinetic expressions to the surfaces of everyday objects and spaces.

ACKNOWLEDGMENTS

This work was supported by National Research Foundation of Korea – Grant funded by the Korean Government (NRF-2009-327-G00046) and the BK21 program of the Ministry of Education, Science and Technology, Korea.

REFERENCES

1. Aperture. http://www.fredericeyl.de/.
2. DKC DSD-06A (DC24V). http://www.dkcair.co.kr/.
3. Drori, T. and Rinott, M. Pixel Materiali: a system for creating and understanding pixel animations. In *Proc. of IDC '07*, ACM Press (2007), 157-160.
4. Kinetic Design and the Animation of Products. http://www.core77.com/blog/featured_items/kinetic_design_and_the_animation_of_products_by_ben_hopson_12642.asp.
5. Kim, H. and Lee, W. Kinetic Tiles: Modular Construction Units for Interactive Kinetic Surfaces. *UIST '10 Posters*, ACM Press (2010)
6. Kim, H. and Lee, W. Shade Pixel. *SIGGRAPH '08 Posters*, ACM Press (2008), n. 34.
7. Parkes, A. and Ishii, H. Kinetic sketchup: motion prototyping in the tangible design process. In *Proc. of TEI '09*, ACM Press (2009), 367-372.
8. Parkes, A., Poupyrev, I., and Ishii, H. Designing kinetic interactions for organic user interfaces. *Communications of the ACM*, 51, 6 (2008), 58-65.
9. Poupyrev, I., Nashida, T. and Okabe, M. Actuation and tangible user interfaces: the Vaucanson duck, robots, and shape displays. In *Proc. of TEI '07*, ACM Press (2007), 205-212.
10. Poupyrev, I., Nashida, T., Maruyama, S., Rekimoto, J. and Yamaji, Y. Lumen: interactive visual and shape display for calm computing. *SIGGRAPH '04 Emerging technologies*, ACM Press (2004), 17.
11. Raffle, H., Parkes, A., Ishii, H. Topobo: a constructive assembly system with kinetic memory, In *Proc. of CHI '04*, ACM Press (2004), 647-654.
12. Rydarowski, A., Samanci, O. and Mazalek, A. Murmur: kinetic relief sculpture, multi-sensory display, listening machine. In *Proc. of TEI '08*. ACM Press (2008), 231-238.

SandCanvas: A Multi-touch Art Medium Inspired by Sand Animation

Rubaiat Habib Kazi[1], Kien-Chuan Chua[1], Shengdong Zhao[1], Richard C. Davis[2], Kok-Lim Low[1]

[1]Computer Science, National University of Singapore
13 Computing Drive, Singapore 117417
{rubaiat, chkch, zhaosd, lowkl}@comp.nus.edu.sg

[2]SIS, Singapore Management University
80 Stamford Road, Singapore 178902
rcdavis@smu.edu.sg

Figure 1: A user interacting with *SandCanvas* (left), and images created with *SandCanvas* (right).

ABSTRACT
Sand animation is a performance art technique in which an artist tells stories by creating animated images with sand. Inspired by this medium, we have developed a new multi-touch digital artistic medium named *SandCanvas* that simplifies the creation of sand animations. *SandCanvas* also goes beyond traditional sand animation with tools for mixing sand animation with video and replicating recorded free-form hand gestures. In this paper, we analyze common sand animation hand gestures, present *SandCanvas*'s intuitive UI, and describe implementation challenges we encountered. We also present an evaluation with professional and novice artists that shows the importance and unique affordances of this new medium.

Author Keywords
Sand animation, multi-touch, tabletop computing, creativity

ACM Classification Keywords
H5.m. Information interfaces and presentation (e.g., HCI): Miscellaneous.

General Terms
Design, Experimentation, Human Factors

INTRODUCTION
Sand animation, also known as sand art, is a form of visual storytelling in which an artist dexterously manipulates fine granules of sand to produce images and animations. The process begins by applying sand to a lighted surface, after which images are rendered on the surface by drawing lines and figures with bare hands. It is an increasingly popular medium for performances and stop-motion animation [14].

Two characteristics combine to make sand animation a unique art form. First, because it is a performance medium, its attraction and aesthetics are closely tied to the creation process as well as the finished artwork [16, 18]. The creation process in performance media is improvisational, fast, continuous, and often accompanied by other forms of performance art, like music, choreography, drama, and dance. The sand animator's task is to unfold a narrative through a progression of visual images produced with a seamless stream of physical gestures.

Second, sand animations are formed through a powerful and expressive vocabulary of physical interactions between artist's hands and small granules of sand. In contrast with sketches or paintings, which are produced with discrete pen or brush strokes, sand animation leverages the delicate structure of the artist's whole hand (often both hands). These hand gestures are easy to learn, quick to perform, and economical to correct, which makes this medium suitable for exploration and brainstorming in addition to storytelling through live performance.

Sand animation has increasingly attracted audiences and artists because of its innovative and expressive graphic style [14, 24]. However, sand-animation performance spaces are difficult to set up and maintain [1], which prevents many novices from getting started. This led us to create *SandCanvas*, a new digital artistic medium inspired by sand animation. *SandCanvas* adds undo and recording features that make sand animation easier to produce, it allows easy experimentation with colors and textured backgrounds, and it adds new capabilities that go beyond traditional sand animation, such as recorded gestures and video mixing.

The increased availability of multi-touch display surfaces has removed some of the technical obstacles to creating a digital sand animation medium, but we still faced significant challenges. Multi-touch UI toolkits do not currently capture all the richness in human hand gestures [21]. In particular, they do not attempt to map touch regions in the current time step to touch regions in the previous time step. This required us to devise a new, fast approach to performing this mapping. Also, simulating the physical behavior of sand in real time is still a major challenge. We achieved real-time performance by optimizing an existing technique [28] and using graphics hardware acceleration.

In this paper, we make the following contributions:

- We introduce a new digital artistic medium that leverages the expressiveness of hand gestures on a multi-touch platform to provide a visual experience that goes beyond physical sand animation.
- We analyze the sand animation process, highlighting common pouring and manipulation techniques and developing a taxonomy of hand gestures.
- We present *SandCanvas*'s intuitive UI design and its enhanced digital capabilities.
- We describe our implementation, which employs new techniques for performing real time sand simulation in response to gestural input.
- We evaluate *SandCanvas* with 1 professional artist, 4 amateur artists and 2 novice users to gain insight into the importance and unique affordances of this medium.

RELATED WORK

SandCanvas is inspired by new media interactive installations and recent advances in interactive surfaces. We divide related work into three sections. First, we briefly summarize recent work in technologically enhanced static and performance art creation systems in general and for multi-touch surfaces. We then describe related systems and algorithms for sand motion simulation. Finally, we discuss systems closely related to *SandCanvas*.

Technologically Enhanced Art Creation Systems

Performance art has a rich history that spans hundreds of years [17]. Myron Krueger's *Videoplace*, developed between 1969 and 1975, was an early interactive artwork that incorporated computer vision [15]. Since Videoplace, numerous audio-visual performance systems have been driven by human gestures [18, 27]. Examining numerous audio-visual performance systems, Levin derived a set of design goals for new performance art systems [18]. According to him, successful systems should be predictable, instantly knowable and indefinitely masterable. We pursued similar goals when designing *SandCanvas*.

In recent years, researchers have produced 2D animation by demonstration systems that could be used for performance art. K-Sketch [9] is a general purpose and informal sketch based 2D animation tool that allows novices to create animation quickly and easily, but all interaction must be done through a single point. In Video Puppetry [4], artists record simultaneous manipulations of multiple physical puppets to create animation. Researchers have also explored the use of multiple touch points to record real-time deformation of characters [13].

Researchers have also produced notable multi-touch painting systems. Project Gustav attempts to create a realistic painting experience [22], while I/O brush [25] allows artists to paint with patterns and movements "picked up" from everyday materials. Fluid Paint [30] and IntuPaint [31] use the entire region of contact between brush and surface to model brush strokes. *SandCanvas* also captures the entire region of contact between the surface and the artist's hand to model interactions with sand.

SandCanvas bears a resemblance to each of the art creation systems presented here. It is a medium for performance art where the final performance is a kind of 2D animation. Instead of animating a fixed set of characters, however, the artist creates characters in sand using rich gestures that cannot be represented adequately with a set of discreet points. *SandCanvas* also has unique creative tools like recorded gestures that aren't found in any of these systems.

Physical Sand Simulation

Since the sand particles used in sand animation are very fine, the number of sand particles is potentially huge. Hence, physically accurate interaction with sand is particularly challenging. Li and Morshell devised one simulation approach, but it assumes that sand is moved by convex objects only [19], which prevents touch regions of arbitrary shape from interacting with sand. Bell and colleagues devised a sand simulation method that handles arbitrary shapes [5], but it models each grain as a discrete element and will not produce real-time simulations on the scale needed for sand animation.

Summer and colleagues developed a faster technique that still falls short of real-time performance [28]. Onoue and colleagues sped it up by assuming that only rigid objects would interact with sand [23]. Our method is also based on Summer's, but we do not assume objects are rigid, because an artist's hand can change as it moves across the canvas.

Sand Art for Storytelling

We have found few sand art systems worth noting. Hancock and collegues' sandtray therapy system allows storytelling on a sand background, but users manipulate figurines instead of sand [11]. Ura and colleagues developed a tool for painting with simulated sand, but it reduces input to discrete points [29]. iSand[1] is an iPhone application for sand art that shares this limitation, and its sand granules are much larger than those used in traditional sand animation.

In contrast, *SandCanvas* captures rich human hand gestures in multiple areas instead of multiple points. It also preserves the expressive and playful nature of sand animation and adds new capabilities that go beyond traditional sand animation, such as recorded gestures and video mixing.

[1] http://itunes.apple.com/us/app/isand-sand-particle-painting/id346966446?mt=8

SAND ANIMATION ANALYSIS

To better understand the special requirements of our new medium we sought to enumerate the gestures commonly used by sand animators. After a meticulous observation of 30 sand animation videos, we identified a set of sand animation techniques commonly employed by artists.

Common Sand Animation Techniques

Sand animation has pouring and manipulation techniques.

Pouring Techniques

Pouring is an additive technique that varies depending on how much of the canvas is affected. *Canvas pouring* is used to set the texture and initial context for painting (Fig. 2 *left*), or, to change context while storytelling. *Skinny pouring* is used to draw tiny details, lines, and shapes (Fig. 2 *right*).

Manipulation Techniques

Sand manipulation techniques move sand rather than adding it. We classified these techniques by how the artist's hand interacts with sand. *Fingertip drawing* traces out lines with the tip of one or more fingers (see Figure 3 *left*). While, *finger carving* (see Figure 3 *right*) uses the whole finger, typically the index finger, small finger, or the outside of the thumb, for drawing and fine tuning shapes.

Artists do not use their fingers exclusively. Palms are often used to create semi-elliptical, or spiral like patterns, such as clouds. We call this technique *palm rubbing* (see Figure 4 *left*). Whole hands are often used to make big sweeps to clear the canvas and set up a new context for the animation, which we termed *hand sweeping* (see Figure 4 *right*).

One final technique that bears mentioning is actually a special version of other techniques. Sand animators will sometimes use both hands simultaneously to quickly draw or pour *symmetrical* patterns in sand (see Figure 5). This technique, which is quite rare in other artistic media, is very common in sand animation.

These techniques can be combined to fluidly transform one image into another (see Figure 6), creating surprise and conjuring emotion. Here lies the beauty of sand animation.

Taxonomy of Sand Animation Gestures

After listing common sand animation techniques, we saw many similarities and differences between them. To better compare and contrast these techniques, we created the low-level taxonomy of gestures found in Table 2. While there are other gesture taxonomies in the literature [10, 33], we needed one that was created specifically for multi-touch art work like sand animation.

Pouring	**Manipulation**
Canvas	Fingertip draw
Skinny	Finger carve
	Palm rub
Symmetrical	Hand Sweep

Table 1: Common sand animation pouring and manipulation techniques. *Symmetrical* is a modifier that can apply to both pours and manipulations.

We manually classified gestures along five dimensions: *mode*, *form*, *precision*, *hands* and *actuation*. **Mode** separates *pouring* gestures from *manipulation* gestures. **Form** indicates any motion in the gesture. In *static* gestures, the hand is held in one position and one configuration, while dynamic gestures change the position or configuration of the hand. (This is similar to the *pose* and *path* concepts in Wobbrock et al.'s gesture taxonomy [33]) The **precision** of the gesture can be *coarse* or *fine*, and the **hands** dimension indicates the number of hands involved in a gesture: one (*uni-manual*) or two (*bi-manual*).

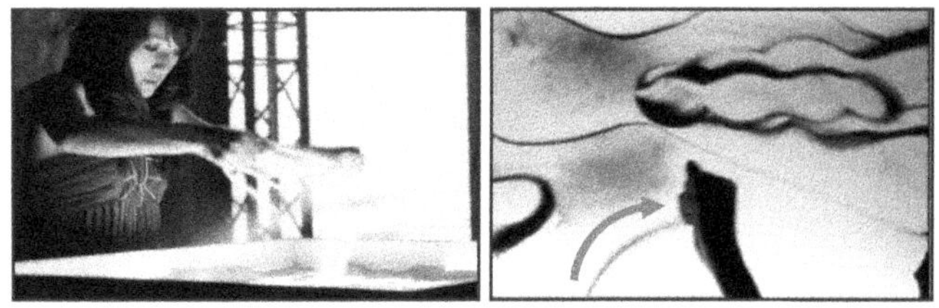

Figure 2: *Canvas pouring* (left) creates background textures, while *skinny pouring* (right) is for drawing lines.

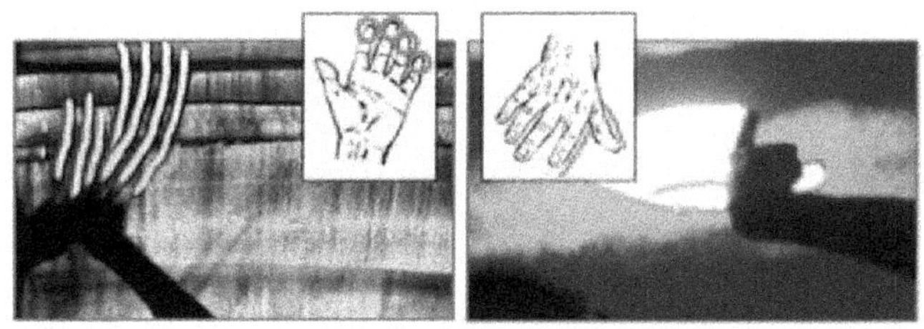

Figure 3: *Fingertip drawing* (left) and *finger carving* (right) to create and manipulate shapes.

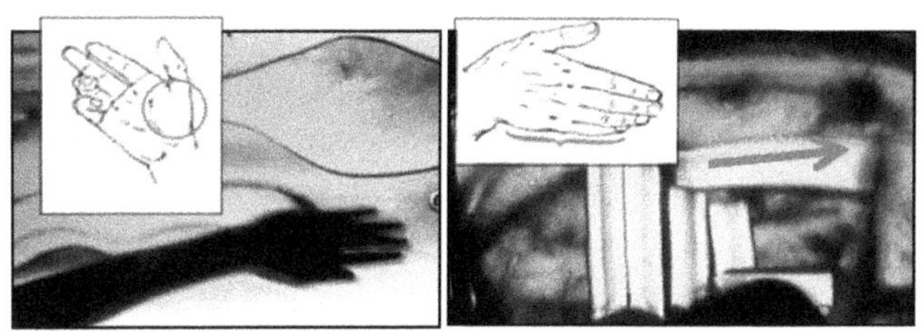

Figure 4: A palm rub (left) draws cloudy patterns, and a *hand sweep* (right) clears part of canvas.

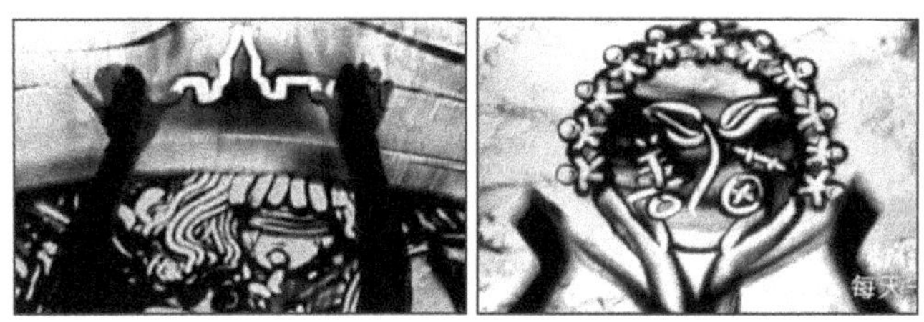

Figure 5: *Symmetrical hand sweep* (left) & *skinny pour* (right).

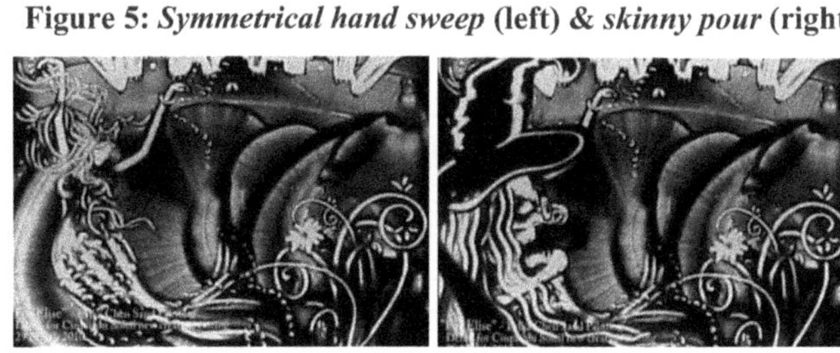

Figure 6: Fluid transformation of images.

Finally, **actuation** indicates the portion of the artist's hand that interacts with sand: a *single finger*, *multiple fingers*, the *palm* (without fingers), or the whole *hand* (both palm and fingers). When using one or more fingers, we distinguish between the finger *tips* and the *side* of the finger. We also note when artists use *tangible* objects to interact with sand.

We can classify common sand animation drawing techniques within our taxonomy to gain a more detailed understanding of these gestures (see Table 3). For example, we found the canvas pour technique uses the pouring mode (p); the form can be either static or dynamic (s/d); the precision is coarse (c); it can be done either by one hand (u) or two hands (b), and it leverages the whole hand (h) instead of the other parts to perform the sweep.

This analysis of sand animation gestures helped us to understand the range of interactions that sand animators

Dimension	Categories	Description
Mode	*Pouring*	Pouring on surface
	Manipulation	Manipulating on surface
Form	*Static*	Hand held in one position
	Dynamic	Hand moved
Precision	*Coarse*	Gesture has low precision
	Fine	Gesture has high precision
Hands	*Uni-manual*	Use one hand
	Bi-manual	Use both hands
Actuation	*Single fingertip*	Use single fingertip
	Single finger side	Use side of a single finger
	Multi-fingertip	Use multiple fingertips
	Multi-finger side	Use side of multiple fingers
	Palm	Use palm without fingers
	Hand	Use both palm and fingers
	Tangibles	Use other objects

Table 2: Taxonomy of sand animation gestures. The underlined letter(s) in each category indicate the abbreviation used for that category in later tables.

	Canvas pour	Skinny pour	Fingertip draw	Finger carve	Palm rub	Hand sweep	*Symmetrical
Mode	p	p	m	m	m	m	p/m
Form	s/d	s/d	s/d	s/d	s/d	s/d	s/d
Precision	c	f	f	c/f	c/f	c	f/c
Hands	u/b	u/b	u/b	u/b	u/b	u/b	b
Actuation	h	h	st/mt	ss/ms	p	h	all

Table 3: Classification of common sand animation drawing techniques. Each column shows the categories of gestures that we observed for that technique. Category abbreviations are found in Table 2.

need in *SandCanvas*. The following section explains how we designed and developed a UI to support these gestures.

DESIGN AND IMPLEMENTATION OF *SANDCANVAS*

SandCanvas is designed to run on an interactive surface based on the principle of diffused illumination [2]. Our table uses a 29cm by 21cm white acrylic surface as a diffuser and projection screen for a rear-placed LCD-projector. An array of 140 infrared LEDs also shines on the surface from below, and objects touching the surface reflect this infrared light back on a 320 by 240 pixel infrared video camera. Our software was written with OpenFrameworks[2], a C++ toolkit for graphic applications with image processing tools. This software runs on a 3.0 GHz Intel Core2 Duo CPU E8400 running Windows Vista with 4GB RAM and a graphics card with an nVidia GeForce 9500 GT2 GPU.

Sand Simulation in *SandCanvas*

Real-time simulation of sand movement in response to rich hand gestures is a challenging problem. Here we describe all the steps in our simulation process.

Tracking and Modeling Contact Shapes

As our multi-touch platform was vision-based, we used standard image processing techniques for contact shape detection. We used dynamic background subtraction to remove the background from the current frame, thresholding to adjust the level of acceptable tracked pixels, Gaussian blur for smoothing and filtering out random noise, and highpass filter to amplify edges. The resulting contact shapes are represented as 2D polygons. We then use the Community Core Vision[3] tools to correspond touch regions with one another across successive frames.

Sand Modeling

Although particle systems and voxels are commonly used for modeling the motion of granular materials, they are computationally expensive and cannot handle a very large number of sand granules. Instead, *SandCanvas* uses a discrete height field that is often used to model ground surfaces [23, 28]. The height field has a resolution equal to the screen resolution, thus, each pixel has a height value (16-bit float), which we call a *column*.

Given a set of hand contact shapes and a grid of sand columns, we compute the sand deformation in three steps:

- First, when a contact shape moves on the surface, we find the columns of sand that collide with the path of this contact shape.
- Second, sand within those columns is pushed outward towards the surrounding columns.
- Finally, by detecting steep slopes, sand is moved from higher columns to lower columns, producing realistic sand settling motion or *sand erosion*.

[2] http://www.openframeworks.cc

[3] http://ccv.nuigroup.com

Computing the Collision Region

When a contact shape first touches the surface, the collision region is the polygon that represents the contact shape itself. However, when a contact shape moves on the surface (Figure 7(c)), the first part of our algorithm computes the region swept by the contact polygons across successive frames. Sand within this *collision region* need to be pushed on the surface. Figure 7(d) shows the contact polygons for the current frame (f_{t+1}) in orange and the previous frame (f_t) in grey. We must now compute the collision region from these two polygons.

Our first step is to compute the point-to-point correspondences between the two polygons. An iterative-closest-point method [6] could be used to compute these correspondences, by rotating the polygons until they are closely aligned. While this gives accurate results, the iterations take a long time. Instead, we simply align the centers of the two polygons and examine each point in the f_{t+1} polygon to find its closest neighbor in the f_t polygon (see Figure 7 (e–f)).

In our second step, we construct a graph, which consists of the polygon in f_{t+1}, the polygon in f_t, and the correspondence edges (see Figure 7(g)). We then compute all the line segment intersections and create a DCEL (doubly-connected edge-list) for this graph (see Figure 7(h)). Finally, we compute the outline of the graph by finding the lexicographically minimal point and walking along the outside edges until we reach our starting point (see Figure 7(i)).

Volume-Conserving Sand Displacement

Now that we have found the columns that collide with the user's hand, we need to push the sand (as shown in Figure 7(j)) from the previous frontier (grey edges) towards the new frontier (black edges). To do this, we calculate the Euclidean distance transform [8] within the collision region from the center of the previous polygon f_t (this center is the "x" in Figure 7(j)). In the resulting distance map (illustrated in Figure 7(k)), for pixels surrounding the collision region, their distance values are set to a very high distance value (higher than any value computed in the distance transform). To propagate the sand, the sand in each column within the collision region is evenly distributed to its neighboring columns that have higher distance values. We use the algorithm in [26] to perform the distance transform and the propagation efficiently on the GPU, which we implemented using OpenGL Shading Language fragment shaders.

Sand Erosion

Our method to simulate the settling motion of the sand around the collision region is based on the algorithm described in [28]. Our method is implemented for the GPU using OpenGL Shading Language fragment shaders. In the first pass, the slopes of each pixel with the eight neighboring columns are examined. If a slope is larger than a threshold value, excess sand is distributed from the higher column to the lower column using a gathering approach in the second pass. The two passes are performed every rendering frame, and the sand erosion takes many frames to complete, producing the realistic effect of sand rolling down the slope over time. To produce the asymmetric erosion caused by the temporary obstruction of the hand, unlike [28], we simply do not distribute sand into any collision region that might exist during a frame.

Performance

Our system runs at interactive rates (20–35fps). For a single finger, the average fps is 35, while for 7–8 fingers manipulating at the same time, the average fps is 20–25. With these frame rates, sand movement does not significantly lag behind hand movements, and users are able to feel immersed in the sand animation experience.

Exploring the design space for sand pouring

In addition to developing the algorithm to simulate sand manipulation, another essential component of Sand Animation is sand pouring. Most sand animators begin new scenes in their animations by quickly pouring sand on the canvas to set a background texture. We considered using computer vision techniques to distinguish pouring from manipulation gestures, but we quickly determined computer vision was not up to the task, given the variety of gestures and lighting conditions. Building a 3D deformable mesh model of the user's hand would achieve the highest fidelity, but it is difficult to build this model in a robust way [32].

Instead, we designed a bi-manual touch interface for pouring. Users touch a pouring button with their non-

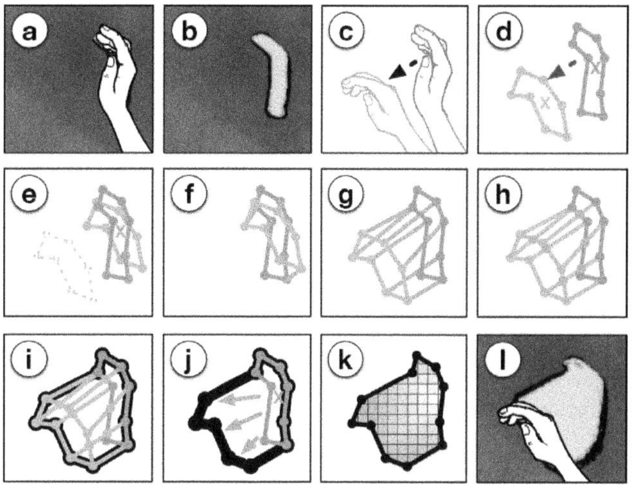

Figure 7: A step-by-step illustration of computing the collision region and pushing the sand. (a) The hand first touches the surface. (b) The sand is pushed to the boundary of the contact shape. (c) The positions of the hand in two successive frames. (d) Their contact polygons. (e) The two polygons are aligned at their centroids. (f) Point-to-point correspondences are computed between the two polygons. (g) A graph is constructed consisting of the polygons and the correspondence edges. (h) The intersections of the edges are computed. (i) The boundary of the whole graph is computed. (j) Sand is to be pushed from the grey frontier to the black outline. (k) A distant map is constructed and sand is pushed from the lighter pixels to the darker pixels until it reaches the boundary of the collision region. (i) Final rendering of the new sand height map (after some sand erosion).

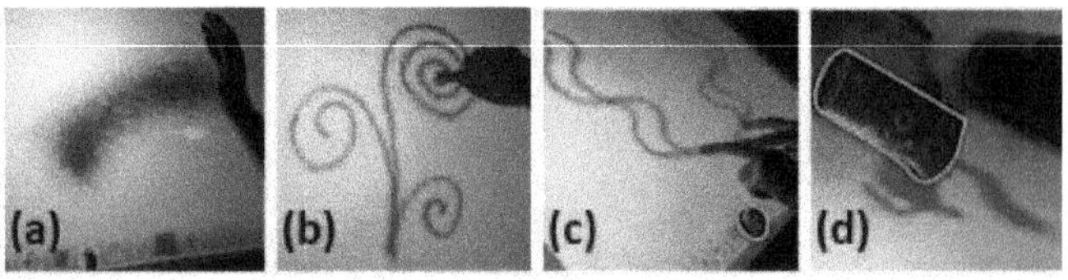

Figure 8: Pouring with touch and tangibles. (a) Canvas pour with whole hand. (b) Skinny pour with fingertips. (c) Symmetrical pour, tangible on button. (d) Pour with tangible.

dominant hand while specifying a pouring region with their dominant hand. This style of interaction avoids mode error. It has been shown to be effective [20] and has been used successfully in several systems [9, 12]. Users distinguish *canvas pouring* from *skinny pouring* by the size and shape of the pouring region. Sweeping through the canvas with the whole hand results in *canvas pouring* (Figure 8(a)), while pointing or tracing a path with a fingertip results in *skinny pouring* (Figure 8(b) and 8(c)). Users can place tangible objects on the pouring button if they wish to pour with both hands (Figure 8(c)).

We also allowed users to pour sand using tangible objects such as jars, thinking that this would provide a more natural feel (Figure 8(d)). In vision based multi-touch systems like ours, bright objects can be detected even when they do not touch the surface. We attached a piece of white paper to the face of a black jar so that it would pour sand when brought close to the surface in pouring mode.

SandCanvas User Interface

Before designing *SandCanvas*'s user interface, we interviewed two professional sand animators to learn how they would like to enhance sand animation in the digital form. We first interviewed Sheh Meng, a professional practitioner with 10 years of experience in performing and teaching sand animation. According to him, most sand animators record video clips of their animations and edit them in a post-production step. Post production also allows animators to play with colors, saturation, and contrast. Hence, a desirable system should provide these capabilities. Sheh Meng also asked for features that allow new types of expression. He suggested a tool for recording gestures and saving them for future reuse.

Second, we interviewed Erika Chen, the winner of "Impresario the Open Platform" 2010. Erika is the world's first singer sand animator, having unique, extensive collaborations with drama, dance and live musicians. She was mostly interested in mixing sand animation with other media, such as clip art or ink drawings.

Our final user interface for *SandCanvas* is the toolbar shown in Figure 9. This toolbar appears at the bottom of the canvas, and it can be reduced to include only the sand pouring and expand UI buttons if the artist desires more canvas area. Based on our interviews, we put the following tools into this toolbar.

Record Session. Users can record their animation as video for later editing.

Undo and Redo. Users can undo and redo up to five operations. This number can be increased at the cost of additional memory.

Change Texture. Users can start with an empty canvas or they can choose from a set of predefined sand textures. Some textures are computer generated, while others are images of real sand.

Reset. Change the surface to the initial state of the texture.

Record Gesture. Users can press a button to begin recording a sequence of pouring or manipulation gestures. Pressing the button a second time stops recording and places a new gesture button icon in the toolbar (see Figure 10). The recorded gesture can be played back by touching this gesture button with one hand and touching the canvas with the other hand. Each touch plays the gesture starting at that touch point. This enables users to play gestures in parallel in different parts of the canvas.

Capture Frame. Users can capture snapshots of the canvas to use as frames in a stop-motion animation (see Figure 11). After pressing the *capture frame* button, it changes to show a thumbnail of the image that was captured.

Change Color. In film and animation production, color is used to create specific moods [3]. For example, a love scene will need different colors than a suspense scene. In *SandCanvas*, users can create a sequence of color gradients before a performance and cycle through them by pressing the change color button.

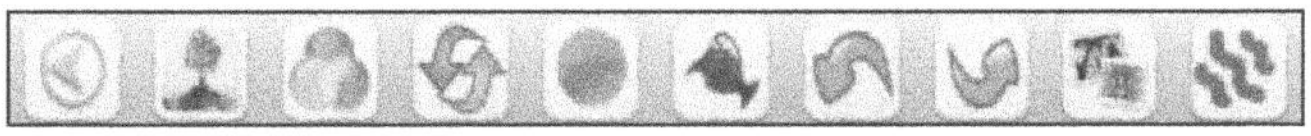

Figure 9: The user interface panel. From left - hide UI panel, change texture, change color, reset, record session, pour, undo, redo, capture frame and record gesture.

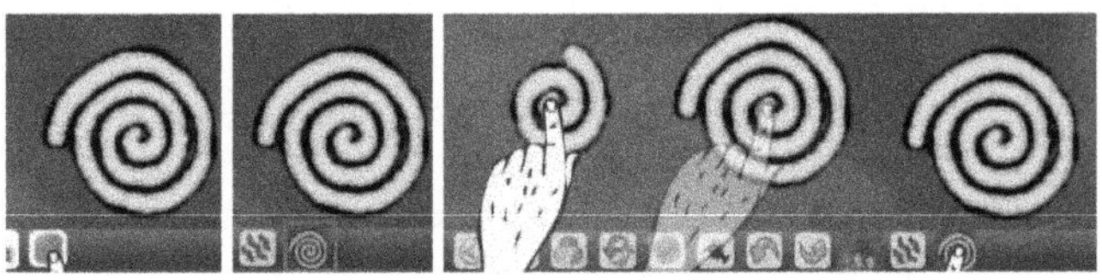

Figure 10: Steps of Gesture recording and playback after pressing the gesture record button (a) User draw a gesture and stop recording (b) An icon having the gesture appears in the UI panel (c) By pressing the recorded gesture button with non-dominant hand and touching by another hand initiates the gesture in different parts of the canvas.

Figure 11: Three key frames for stop-motion animation.

Enabling Mixed Media. In film production and storytelling, *mixed media* refers to the mixing of images from separate sources [3, 24]. *SandCanvas* allows users to define a set of still images and video clips that will appear underneath sand during a performance. These images and clips are placed in sequence with color gradients and are also accessed through the *change color* button.

As soon as our system was implemented, we wanted to evaluate it to establish its usability and to understand the importance and the unique affordances of this artistic medium. The details of our evaluation are described below.

USER EVALUATION

Before our final study, we performed a pilot study with three users who gave us qualitative feedback which we report here with other data. Our final study with seven users was both qualitative and quantitative, using a formal protocol designed to answer the following questions:

Q1. How do users evaluate the realism, fidelity and intuitiveness of Sand Canvas?
Q2. Do users find the novel features of SandCanvas useful, and can they apply them effectively?
Q3. Can we gain further insight into the expressiveness of this new medium by analyzing gestures that users employ?
Q4.Is there evidence that SandCanvas facilitates creativity?

Participants and Environment

Our formal study had seven participants, all males ranging from 24 to 29 years old (*M*=26, *SD*=1.63). Among them, one is a professional artist, four are amateur artists, and two are novice users. 4 out of 7 users reported that they create artistic works once a week. Our pilot study participants were three females aged 26 to 29. One is a professional artist with prior sand animation experience and the other two are amateur artists. All evaluation sessions took place in a university laboratory using the tabletop system described previously in our design and implementation section. Lighting in the room was dim to give the surface maximal tracking accuracy. Each user received $25 for their participation.

Method

The formal evaluation process was conducted in the following four steps.

1) *Exploration: 10 minutes*. In this step, users were given no explanation of the system, and were told to play with *SandCanvas* while thinking out loud. This step helped us gauge the initial learnability of the system and users' initial impressions.

2) *Training: 10–15 minutes*. In this step, users were given a brief description and demonstration of the features they didn't discover in step one. We asked users to recreate a sequence of five drawings, each designed to teach sand animation techniques (Figure 12). Users first recreated all five drawings in their own way. After this, a facilitator demonstrated an easy way to create each drawing, and asked the user to try again.

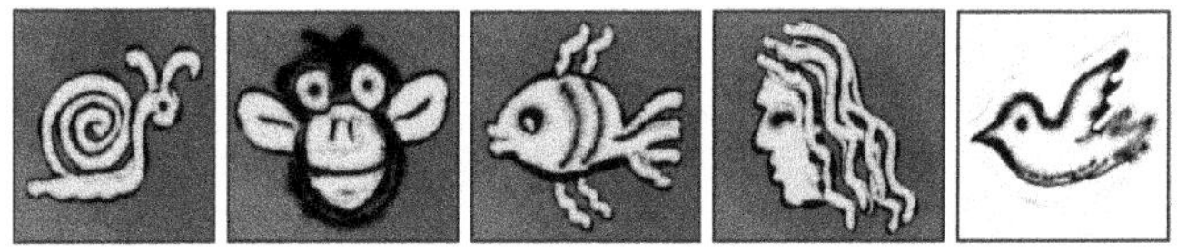

Figure 12: Pictures given to users in step 2 (training).

3) *Guided task: 10–15 minutes*. In this step, users were asked to create an animation sequence based on three key frames provided (see Figure 11). This step allowed us to compare user performance on a fixed task.

4) *Free task: Up to 30 minutes*. In the final step, users were asked to use their own imagination and create the best sand animation they could. This step helped us assess users' preferred techniques, and it allowed us to observe creative use of *SandCanvas*.

At the end of the study, users were given a questionnaire and interview. The entire study took about 90 minutes.

Results and Discussion

Users' overall reaction was very positive. They found *SandCanvas*'s UI intuitive and they were able to create meaningful artworks in the time they were given. The medium was a pleasure to use; as one user reported, "*The ability to play with sand itself is the most interesting part.*"

Q1. How do users evaluate the realism, fidelity and intuitiveness of SandCanvas?

Most of our users felt that the behavior of virtual sand in *SandCanvas* closely mimics the feeling of physical sand. They often perform gestures on *SandCanvas* as if they were playing with real sand: 3 users piled sand in the middle of the canvas and observed its spreading behavior. In the post-study questionnaire, users rated the realism of *SandCanvas* as 4.4 on a scale of 1 (not realistic) to 5 (very realistic). However, one user commented that it has yet to achieve the fluidity of real sand. We believe this is because our current implementation does not model sand grain momentum.

Users commented that they liked the look and feel of *SandCanvas* and indicated that it was very easy to learn: average rating 4.6 on a scale of 1 (extremely difficult) to 5 (extremely easy). In the initial exploration step, five functions *(undo*, *redo*, *reset*, *change texture*, and *change color)* were discovered by all users. All but one user discovered *capture frame* and all but three guessed the purpose of the *record session* button. No users discovered how to pour sand or record gestures, but we expected that these bi-manual functions would require training. After the training step, all users understood all features. One user commented, "*After going through the instructions once, the functionalities are quite obvious*".

Q2. Do users find the novel features of SandCanvas useful, and can they apply them effectively?

To better understand the relative merits of our novel features, we recorded the number of times each feature was used in the free task step. Our seven participants spent a total of 159 minutes on free tasks, during which we logged 380 feature usages (average 2.39 features per minute).

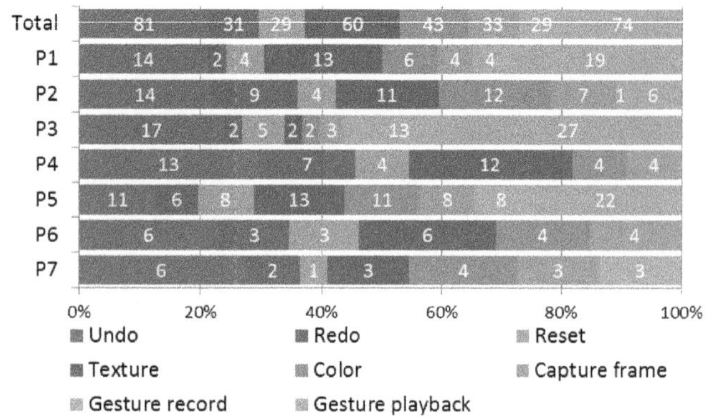

Figure 13: Feature usage counts among participants.

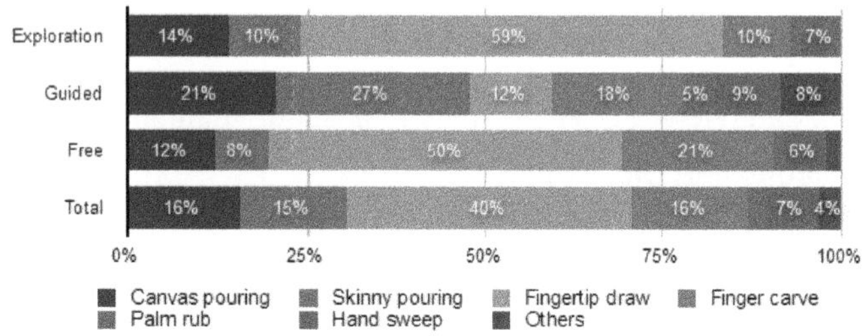

Figure 14: Overall usage of techniques in evaluation steps 1 (exploration), 3 (guided task), and 4 (free task).

Figure 13 summarizes feature usage. Each user made moderate use of most features, though *undo* and *change texture* stood out, accounting for 81 (21%) and 60 (16%) occurrences of all feature usages logged. Only four users took advantage of *gesture playback,* but they made heavy use of this feature (74 times or 29% of all feature usage). We also note that no users took advantage of the *record session* function, because post-production was outside the scope of this study.

The fact that almost all users used most of the features multiple times indicates that users found them useful in creating art works on *SandCanvas*. We are also encouraged to find out a number of users (3 of 7) embrace the more advanced gesture record functionalities and frequently used it in their art creation process.

Q3. Can we gain further insight into the expressiveness of this new medium by analyzing gestures that users employ?

In addition to our feature analysis, we wanted to enhance our understanding of the unique affordance of *SandCanvas* by analyzing the gestures employed by users. We analyzed the video tapes of the user evaluation and classified all 3580 gestures they performed in steps 1 (exploration), 3 (guided task), and 4 (free task). Note that step 2 was for training purpose only; therefore it is not included in the analysis. Step 1 is included because it demonstrates users' the initial reaction to *SandCanvas*, which can be contrasted with later stages when they become more experienced.

Figure 14 shows the breakdown of common sand animation techniques used in the three evaluation stages. Overall, pouring accounted for 31% of gestures and manipulating accounted for 69%. The most common technique was *fingertip draw* (40% of gestures). *Finger carve*, *canvas pour*, and *skinny pour* are the next most popular techniques (each contains 15-16% of all gestures). *Hand sweep* (7%) and palm rub (2%), were used less frequently, but they did play a role in drawing. Finally, we note that tangibles were also used occasionally (4%).

We also observed two approaches to creating artworks in *SandCanvas* (Figure 15), each with a different distribution of drawing techniques. In the free task, five users took a subtractive approach, in which sand is manipulated to create shapes. Two users took an additive approach, in which shapes are made by pouring sand onto the canvas.

Different stages of our experiment also showed different distributions of drawing techniques. The guided task requires uses to take an additive approach, in which shapes are made by pouring sand onto the canvas. In the free task, however, 5 of 7 users took a subtractive approach, in which shapes are created by drawing in sand. Because of this, pouring was used much more frequently in the guided task (48% of gestures) than in free tasks (18% of gestures). However, the beauty of Sand Animation is that users are free to switch between these approaches, making smooth and seamless transitions to create interesting and often surprising effects, such as Figure. 6.

In addition to high level techniques, we analyzed gestures according to our low-level taxonomy to get a detailed sense of how users employed their hands. Almost all gestures (99%) were dynamic rather than static, which helps to justify our efforts to support dynamic gestures. Precision was more or less evenly split between coarse (42%) and fine (59%), indicating the variety of gestures performed. 7% of gestures were bimanual, and almost all of these were performed by three participants drawing symmetrical shapes. This confirms our intuition that bimanual interaction would be an essential part of this medium.

Figure 16 shows the hand actuation dimension of our taxonomy for gestures performed in the exploration, guided task, and free task steps of our experiment. This data shows that *SandCanvas* truly leverages many parts of the hand. The most common gestures were single fingertip (46%), followed by single finger side, multi-fingertip, and hand gestures (19%, 18%, and 11%, respectively).

Tangible gestures were less common (4%), but played a vital role in the artworks where they appeared. One user

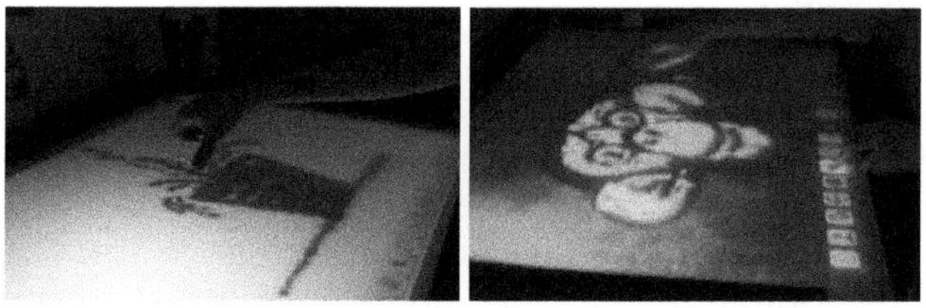

Figure 15: Drawing and animating with pouring (*left*) and manipulation (*right*).

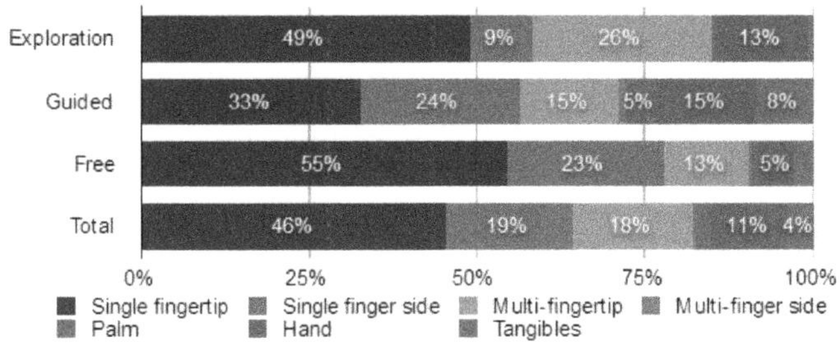

Figure 16: Another dimension of gestures we are particularly interested in is the distribution of different parts of hand (or actuation) in creating art works.

used a sheet of paper to pour over a very large area, and another used a sharp object to draw a star shape. Palm gestures were rare (2%) and served the same purpose as hand gestures. We have noted elsewhere, however, that palm gestures are useful for creating cloud-like shapes. Finally, this hand actuation data highlights the importance of capturing the full region of contact between the user's hand and the drawing surface. Single finger side and hand gestures together accounted for 30% of all gestures. None of these gestures could have been captured by a system that reduced users' input to a set of points.

The gesture analysis presented here demonstrates that *SandCanvas* truly capitalizes on the expressive vocabulary of hand gestures found in sand animation. This was possible only because our implementation captures the full area of contact with the surface, and because it carefully balances sand simulation speed and accuracy. All parts of the hand can be used to produce creative works of art.

Q4. Is there evidence that SandCanvas facilitates creativity?
We found four classes of evidence to support this. The richness of gestures captured by *SandCanvas* provides some initial evidence that it facilitates creativity. As one user put it, *"[The] use of different parts of hand for direct manipulation inspires creativity."* This rich input inspired users to envision radically new uses that go beyond performance art. As another user reported, *"I like the instant gratification of it. I would like to use it for brainstorming and story prototyping, because it's so easy and quick to create."* Because these gestures are more intuitive than the complex tools in conventional interfaces, SandCanvas may also reduce memory demands, making it easier for users to enter a state of creative flow [7].

Second, the variety of artworks produced by users during the free task is also evidence that *SandCanvas* facilitates creativity. In the 159 minutes our 7 users spent on this task, they were able to create 13 different artworks, with 161 distinct drawings (about 1 drawing per minute). Among the 13 artworks, eight of these were performance artworks, four were stop motion animations, and one was a static image. The subject of these artworks ranged from portraits to dynamic landscapes to action sequences with multiple characters. The ability of users to create such a collection of art work in a short time demonstrates the potential of *SandCanvas* as a creative medium.

Third, we observed users devising creative strategies for producing similar effects. For example, one training task asked users to draw a snail. Figure 17 shows two users' approaches to drawing the spiral shape: one used a finger carve gesture, while the other used his whole hand.

Finally, we found that *SandCanvas*'s novel gesture recording feature inspired particularly creative uses. Many users took advantage of gesture recording to clone objects on the canvas, (e.g., to quickly create a crowd of people). One user recorded several drawings of words and played them back all at once to give an impression of many simultaneous speakers. Another user interleaved playback of ring-shaped pouring and drawing gestures that produced a complex interplay between gestures. Finally, one user combined gesture playback with undo to produce stop-motion animation. He recorded the drawing of a spaceship and moved it across the canvas with a sequence of capture frame, undo, and play gesture operations. These unexpected and creative uses of *SandCanvas*' gesture recording function show that *SandCanvas* is truly a creative medium that goes beyond traditional sand animation.

The evaluation we have presented here has demonstrated the intuitiveness of *SandCanvas* and the effectiveness of our approach to modeling real-time interactions between hand and sand. But it does much more. It has also given us a deeper understanding of the affordances of this new medium, particularly the variety of gestures at users' disposal. Finally, it has shown how *SandCanvas*'s modeling approach, novel creative tools, and intuitive UI combine to produce an important new creative medium.

LIMITATIONS AND FUTURE WORK

SandCanvas works well overall, but it has a few limitations. Like most other diffuse illumination multi-touch tables, sometimes it triggers just before the finger touches the canvas. The system is also dependent on surrounding ambient light. We hope to improve our hardware and eliminate these problems.

Our study users suggested adding a gesture library to *SandCanvas*, giving them access to a larger collection of their own gestures and others created by fellow users or artists. Users also suggested making gesture recording hierarchical, so that complex gestures can be composed from simple ones. One of our users, a professional artist, commented that such library would allow novice users to quickly learn expressive sand animation techniques.

In the future, we plan to integrate video editing and special effects capabilities into *SandCanvas* to enable complete

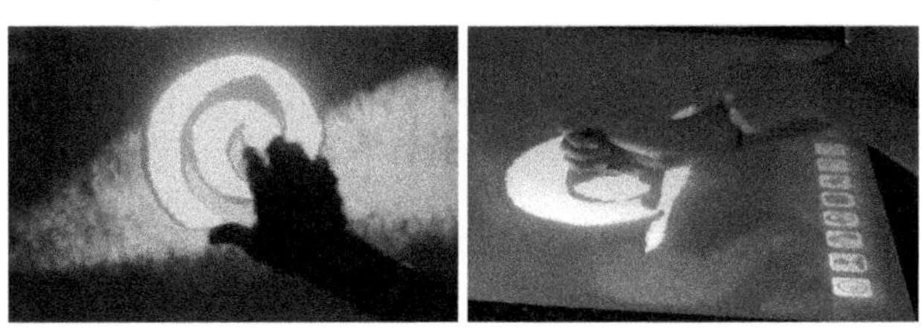

Figure 17: Two users' approaches to the same training task.

production work. Finally, with the increasing popularity and ubiquity of multi-touch devices (such as iPad), we plan to deploy *SandCanvas* to smaller multi-touch devices so that it can soon be used by more creative hands.

CONCLUSION

The elegance of sand animation lies in the seamless flow of expressive hand gestures that cause images to fluidly evolve, surprising and delighting audiences. While physical sand animation already possesses these properties, *SandCanvas* enhances them. *SandCanvas*'s color and texture features enable faster, more dramatic transitions, while its mixed media and gesture recording features make it possible to create entirely new experiences. Session recording and frame capture complement these capabilities by simplifying post-production of sand animation performances.

Producing this new artistic medium required us develop a new approach to real-time sand simulation that strikes a balance between speed and realism. It also required a simple and intuitive UI that would enable users to employ our new features effectively. Our evaluation of *SandCanvas* shows that we succeeded. When we analyzed it with respect to common sand animation techniques and our own taxonomy of gestures, we found it to be a genuinely rich artistic medium that enhances both professionals' and novices' opportunities for creative expression.

ACKNOWLEDGMENTS

We thank the professional sand animators who provided interviews, insightful comments, and permission to use sand animation images: Erika Chen (Figures 2, 3 left, 4 left, 5, and 6) and Sheh Meng (Figure 4 right). We thank Yi Bo, Haimo and other members in the NUS-HCI lab for their support. This research is supported by National University of Singapore Academic Research Fund R-252-000-375-133.

REFERENCES

1. Sand Animation: Interview with Cako. http://www.sandanimation.com/page.php?2.
2. (Ed.) CM-T, *Tabletops - Horizontal Interactive Displays*. Springer, 2010.
3. Bacher HP, *Dream Worlds: Production Design for Animation*. Focal Press, 2007.
4. Barnes C, et al. Video puppetry: a performative interface for cutout animation. In. *ACM SIGGRAPH Asia 2008 papers* 2008, ACM (2008), 1-9.
5. Bell N, Y.Yu, and P.J.Mucha. Particle Based Simulation of Granular Materials. *SIGGRAPH* 2005.
6. Besl PJ and McKay ND. A Method for Registration of 3-D Shapes. *IEEE Trans. on Pattern Analysis and Machine Intelligence* 1992; 14(2): 239-256.
7. Csikszentmihalyi M, *Flow: The Psychology of Optimal Experience*. (1st edition). New York: Harper and Row, 1990.
8. Danielson P-E. Euclidean distance mapping. *Computer Graphics and Image Processing* 1980; 14: 227-248.
9. Davis RC, Colwell B, and Landay JA. K-sketch: a 'kinetic' sketch pad for novice animators. In. *Proceeding of CHI* 2008, 413-422.
10. Efron D, *Gesture and Environment*. New York: King's Crown Press, 1941.
11. Hancock M, Cate T, Carpendale S, Isenberg T. Supporting Sandtray Therapy on an Interactive Tabletop. *Proceeding of CHI* 2010.
12. Hinckley K, et al. Design and Analysis of Delimiters for Selection-action Pen Gesture Phrases in Scriboli. *Proceeding of CHI* 2005, 451-460.
13. Igarashi T, Moscovich T, and Hughes JF. As-rigid-as-possible shape manipulation. In. *ACM SIGGRAPH 2005 Papers*, 1134-1141.
14. Kenyon H, *Animating under the Camera*, in *Animation Magazine*. 1998.
15. Krueger MW, Gionfriddo T, and Hinrichsen K. VideoPlace—an artificial reality. *SIGCHI Bulletin* 1985; 16(4): 35-40.
16. Lakin F. A performing medium for working group graphics. *Proceedings of the CSCW 1986*, 255-266.
17. Levin G, *Audiovisual Software Art: A Partial History*, 2009.
18. Levin G, *Painterly Interfaces for Audiovisual Performance*, in *Media Laboratory, School of Architecture and Planning*. 2000, Massachusetts Institute of Technology
19. Li X and J.M.Morshell. Modelling soil: Realtime dynamic models for oil slippage and manipulation. *SIGGRAPH* 1993.
20. Li Y, et al. Experimental Analysis of Mode Switching Techniques in Pen-based User Interfaces. *Proceedings of CHI* 2005, 461-470.
21. McCullough M, *Abstracting Craft: The practiced Digital Hand*. MIT Press, 1998.
22. Nelson Chu WB, Li-Yi Wei, and Naga Govindaraju. Detail-preserving paint modeling for 3D brushes. *Non-Photorealistic Animation and Rendering* 2010.
23. Onoue K and Nishita T. An Interactive Deformation System for Granular Material. *Computer Graphics Forum* 2005; 24(1): 51-60.
24. Richard T, *The encyclopedia of Animation Techniques*, 1999.
25. Ryokai K, Marti S, and Ishii H. I/O brush: drawing with everyday objects as ink. In. *Proc. of CHI* 2004, 303-310.
26. Schneider J, Kraus M, and Westermann Ru. GPU-Based Real Time Discrete Euclidean Distance Transforms with Precise Error Bounds. *VISAPP* 2009(2009).
27. Snibbe SS and Levin G. Interactive dynamic abstraction. In. *Proc. of the 1st international symp. on Non-photorealistic animation and rendering* 2000, ACM (2000), 21-29.
28. Summer RW, Brien JFO, and Hodgins JK. Animating Sand, Mud and Snow. *Eurographics* 1999(1999).
29. Ura M, et al. A Paint Tool for Image Generation of Sand Animation Style. *IEICE Tech* 2009(2009).
30. Vandoren P, et al. FluidPaint: an interactive digital painting system using real wet brushes. In. *Proceedings of the ACM International Conference on Interactive Tabletops and Surfaces* 2009, ACM (2009), 53-56.
31. Vandoren P, et al. IntuPaint: Bridging the Gap between Physical and Digital Painting. *IEEE TABLETOP* 2008(2008).
32. Wilson AD, et al. Bringing Physics to the Surface. *ACM UIST* 2008(2008), 67-76.
33. Wobbrock JO, Morris MR, and Wilson AD. User-defined Gestures for Surface Computing. *ACM CHI* 2009(2009), 1083-1092.

Evaluating Effects of Structural Holds on Pointing and Dragging Performance with Flexible Displays

Rob Dijkstra, Chris Perez and Roel Vertegaal
Human Media Lab
School of Computing, Queen's University
Kingston, Ontario, K7L 3N6, Canada
{dijkstra,perez,roel}@cs.queensu.ca

ABSTRACT
In this paper, we present a study of the effects of structural holds and rigidity of a flexible display on touch pointing and dragging performance. We discuss an observational study in which we collected common holds used when pointing on a mockup paper display. We also measured the force patterns each hold generated within the display surface. We analyzed this data to produce 3 force zones in the display for each of the four most frequently observed holds: the *grip* zone, *rigid* zone, and the *flexible* zone. We report on an empirical evaluation in which we compared the efficiency of pointing and dragging operations between holds, and between structural zones within holds, using a real flexible Lumalive display. Results suggest that structural force distributions in a flexible display affect the Index of Performance of both pointing and dragging tasks, irrespective of hold, with rigid parts of the display yielding a 12% average performance gain over flexible areas.

ACM Classification H5.2 [User Interfaces]: Interaction styles.

Author Keywords Organic User Interfaces, Flexible Displays, Fitts' Law.

General Terms Experimentation, Human Factors.

INTRODUCTION
With the recent development of flexible display technologies, such as Flexible E Ink [3], Flexible Organic LEDs (FOLEDs) [1] and Lumalive displays [9], come new challenges for the development of touch screens. While touch input in rigid Liquid Crystal Displays (LCDs) has matured to mass-market adoption, issues exist, both technical and user-related, that may impede adoption of touch in flexible displays. One immediate issue is that flexible displays, unlike rigid screens, give way: flexible displays may not always provide a sufficient normal force to support the fingers when touching. A second, and related, issue is that the distribution of normal forces in a flexible display may depend on the way the display is held: different supporting holds may produce different force curves in the display. Such curves may provide structural support during pointing tasks on flexible substrates, such as paper. A compounding issue here is the presence of a bezel. In rigid tablet PCs, such as the Apple iPad, large bezels are used to prevent the holding hand from spuriously activating the touch inputs while holding. Because holding a bezel of a flexible display may not provide an evenly distributed normal force throughout the display, users might need to hold the screen beyond its bezel, potentially triggering spurious touches. One question then, is whether users of flexible displays can produce a sufficient distribution of normal forces in the display surface while holding only the edges of the display. Despite the above issues in developing touch inputs for flexible display interfaces, we believe there is one compelling reason why flexible displays, particularly, Flexible E Ink, will be adopted: they allow for user interfaces that closely mimic the easy of use of paper documents. According to Sellen and Harper [13], there are a number of distinct advantages of paper documents over traditional windowed computer interfaces. The superior contrast and infinite battery life of paper documents aside:

(1) Paper is thin, low-weight, yet rugged, allowing superior portability over any current mobile computing form factor.

(2) Paper can have many different form factors and sizes. This allows for distinct physical affordances [8] that relate to specific functionalities: reading a newspaper serves a different purpose than reading a product label, and these distinctions are evident through those form factors.

(3) Paper is flexible in shape, which provides ergonomic benefits and adjustment of screen real estate size to the context of use. Users are adept at reading paper documents in different physical contexts, independently of the size of the document. This is because they can fold paper documents such as a maps or newspapers into a size or form that befits space limitations.

(4) Most rigid UIs, the iPad no exception, also rely on input that is dependent on visual rather than tactile cues. By contrast, paper is both tactile and kinesthetic.

(5) In Graphical UIs, input is typically limited to a single display, making interleaving, retrieving and organization of information relating to multiple tasks a sequential process. By contrast, paper documents can have many *"displays"*, with each display pertaining only to a specific and physically delineated task context.

Paper does have one obvious downside: it cannot be dynamically rewritten. Flexible display technologies such Flexible E Ink are now changing this, allowing the navigational benefits of paper documents to be combined with the dynamical display characteristics of computers. But before digital paper receives widespread market adoption, we will need to advance our techniques and technologies for (multi)touch input on flexible screens.

In this paper, we present a first step in this direction: an empirical study aimed at exploring the relationship between flexibility of the display and the efficiency of pointing at specific locations on the display. We examine these aspects in light of different holding patterns producing force differentials in the display that alter its rigidity, and thus its performance.

RELATED WORK

There is a significant body of research on flexible sensors, but there appears to be little work on evaluations of their performance. SmartSkin by Rekimoto [10] was one of the first papers to demonstrate the potential for capacitive (multi)touch sensors in flexible form factors. Rosenberg et al. [11] discuss the unMousePad, (now Touchco [14]), a touch-sensitive flexible surface capable of measuring multi-touch pressure signatures. It is one of only a few flexible multi-touch input devices available on the market. Another capacitive flexible touch technology is Displax [2], which has mostly been applied to rigid displays. To our knowledge, these technologies have yet to receive formal usability assessments as flexible input devices.

Flexible Computers

Schwesig et al. [12] produced one of the first mockups of a small credit-card sized computer that involved physical deformation of its surface. Navigation was achieved through bending the display, e.g., to zoom in and out of information. Authors did not provide an evaluation. In PaperWindows, Holman et al. [5] simulated the use of flexible display surfaces for page navigation by augmenting real paper with projected images. This was accomplished by tracking the shape and location of paper documents as well as fingers using Vicon motion capture. While their system and tracking techniques are very similar to those deployed in our work, the authors did not report on a quantitative study. Lee et al. [6] discussed one of the few user studies of deformable (mockup) displays. In their experiment, they asked users to create and perform bend gestures for future flexible displays, using paper, plastic and textile mockups. They found a significant time difference in planning time for gesture design between cloth and plastic displays. They also found that the non-dominant hand played a supporting role, while the dominant hand performed most interactions on the middle of the right side of the material. We were inspired by this work for our first study. Similar in nature, Watanabe et al. [16] discussed Bookisheet, a set of flexible input devices made out of sheets of thin acrylic augmented with bend sensors. Bookisheet could simulate the turn of pages through bends. However, their evaluations focused on the use of various bend gestures for interactions, rather than pointing.

Fitts' Law for Display Evaluation

We cannot possibly do justice to the large body of work on Fitts' Law in this review. However, much of the work is geared towards gauging effects of input devices on pointing and dragging performance [7]. In one of the original evaluations of dragging performance, MacKenzie et al. [7] found values of 4.5 bits/s for pointing, as compared to 4 bits/s for dragging with a mouse. We did not find related work on Fitts' Law evaluations comparing areas of display. Zhai [17] discusses differences in performance between manipulations of the fingers, hand and wrist in an experiment where he utilized a glove and a FingerBall in a six degree of freedom VR docking task. He concluded that small muscles groups, such as fingers, have performance advantages over large muscle groups. Wang et al. [15] evaluated finger input for multitouch interactions. Their work centers on the "fat finger" problem: the size of the finger in relation to the accuracy of touch. Wang found that the index, middle and ring finger give a higher input precision than other fingers. Guiard [4] explained differences between non-dominant and dominant hand performance with his Kinematic Chain theory. According to him, the non-dominant hand typically provides the context to the dominant hand, e.g., by holding a piece of paper, or a display, while the dominant hand provides the action component, e.g., pointing at the display.

STUDY 1: OBSERVATIONAL STUDY

In order to better understand how the non-dominant hand provides support for pointing on flexible surfaces, and to obtain insight into the kind of supporting holds that exist, we designed an observational study into the ways in which users might hold flexible displays in various tasks.

Observing Holds

Our study was designed as a field study in which users were asked to perform representative tasks in real world conditions. We wanted to introduce as little technology as possible, so as to allow as rich an environment for discovering potential holding behavior as possible. To avoid damage to our flexible display, we deemed the use of a simple printed paper mockup sufficient for this open-ended study. We did require some electronic way to record various holding patterns during the field study, as the use of video alone was insufficient: Camera placement was an issue, and video would not allow us to record force differentials in the display surface between holds. To be able to reliably measure holds and folds on the display surface, we deployed a pressure sensitive film called Touchco [14] in most tasks, details of which are outlined in the *Apparatus* section.

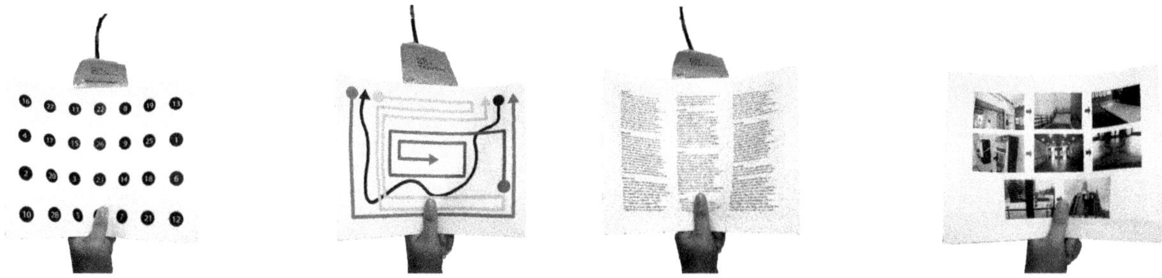

(1) Pointing (2) Tracing (3) Reading (4) Mobile Navigation

Figure 1. Four tasks, printed on a paper mockup display mounted on a Touchco flexible multitouch pressure sensor.

Selecting Tasks

In selecting task scenarios for our observational study we were inspired by mobile applications. We wanted our tasks to be generalizable, yet sufficiently specific for users to be familiar with. For this reason, we included a basic pointing task in our observational study, in which users were asked to point at a random number, printed on a mockup paper display (Fig. 1.1). A second basic task was dragging. Dragging involves pointing at a target, selecting it by touching, moving the finger to a second target location, then releasing. The simplest way to model this task without interactive graphics was to print lines on paper, asking participants to trace these lines from start to finish (Fig. 1.2). Since tablets are commonly used for reading, we wanted to include a reading task as well (Fig. 1.3). Finally, we decided to include a way-finding task in which participants needed to hold the display while walking through a building (Fig. 1.4). A requirement for the first study was that tasks were executed in a number of different postures, in particular, while standing, sitting and walking. Because of the logistics involved, and because our participants spent a significant amount of time in this locale, we chose a public lounge with large leather couches, hardwood chairs, soft leather study chairs, soft foam cushions, and carpeted areas, rather than a participant's home.

Apparatus

We used a printed US Letter paper mockup display sandwiched with a sheet of 8.5" *x* 11" Touchco (see Figure 1) [14]. Touchco is a pressure sensing flexible multitouch device consisting of 5 layers: a layer of parallel wires, a Force Sensing Resistor (FSR), a layer of air, another FSR and a second layer of parallel wires that are perpendicular to the top layer. It is approximately 0.25 mm thick. Touchco has a resolution of 100 dpi and is capable of sensing forces from .05 N to 50 N. We used this information to create a pressure map for each hold. A video camera was used to record additional footage of the participant holding the mockup display. In the mobile task, we used a head mounted camera to observe the participant holding the display, while a second camera recorded the 3rd person view. During each of the tasks, we marked recordings every time a unique holding gesture or change in posture occurred, which eased subsequent analysis of both video and Touchco data. A rigid backing that could easily be attached and removed was used to check for differences in holding styles between flexible and rigid displays. Note that the Touchco had to be held in landscape mode because of the connector interfering with holds; we corrected for any potential skew this caused in our data for our second study.

Tasks

Figure 1 shows each task printed on a different sheet of paper. Participants conducted each task, in random order, in both rigid and flexible conditions.

(1) Pointing

For this task, the Touchco was overlaid with a sheet of 28 printed numbers, as shown in Fig. 1.1. Participants were asked to listen to an audio file listing a series of random numbers. They were instructed to touch the display in the location associated with each number. During the task, we instructed the participants to hold the interface in the most comfortable way, while standing.

(2) Tracing

To simulate dragging, we asked participants to trace a line from a circle to a triangular symbol printed on the mockup paper display overlaid on the Touchco (Fig. 1.2). These lines covered all areas of the screen in several orientations (left, right, up, down, diagonally, straight and curved). As in the first task, the participants were instructed to hold the display comfortably while standing.

(3) Reading

The third task was a reading task (Fig. 1.3). In this task, we instructed the participants to find a location in the room and make themselves comfortable while seated, to read a single page of Shakespeare's *Sonnets* off of a mockup paper display overlaid on the Touchco.

(4) Mobile Navigation

We requested participants to walk through a building while holding the mockup display. They were required to navigate to a series of locations indicated by a set of pictures on the display (Fig. 1.4), and asked, as a distractor task, to copy down a number placed in those locations on a notepad with a pen. The path was approximately 150 *m* long and started indoors and ended outside. It utilized one

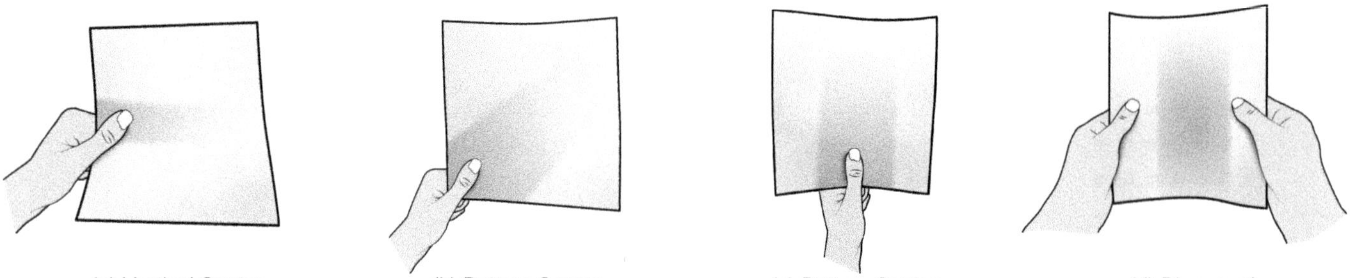

(a) Vertical Center (b) Bottom Corner (c) Bottom Center (d) Bi-manual

Figure 2. The four common holds observed using a mockup display during our first study: (a) hand in the vertical center, (b) hand at the bottom corner, (c) hand in the bottom center, and (d) bi-manual. Gray zones indicate corresponding structural forces.

staircase and three doors. We did not measure force patterns with Touchco in this task as it was insufficiently portable.

Participants

We used 8 participants, mean age 21.3, 4 females, 4 males.

OBSERVATIONAL STUDY: DISCUSSION

We analyzed Touchco data, with video recordings serving as a visual reference to identify holds, between markers in our data recordings. We then calculated frequency of use of each hold for each task as a mean percentage of overall hold time during which that hold was deployed. The 5 most frequently deployed holds are listed below, with frequency of use per task, for both flexible and rigid conditions:

a) **Vertical Center** (Fig 2*a*). Left or right non-dominant hand holding the center of the display, left or right. Pointing *(rigid 10%),* Tracing *(flexible 27%, rigid 21%),* Reading *(flexible 30%, rigid 30%)* and Mobile Navigation *(flexible 17%);*

b) **Bottom Corner** (Fig 2*b*). Left or right non-dominant hand holding the bottom corner of display, left or right. Pointing *(flexible 9%, rigid 17%),* Tracing *(rigid 15%),* Reading *(flexible 13%)* and Mobile Navigation *(flexible 30%, rigid 38%);*

c) **Bottom Center** (Fig 2*c*). Left or right non-dominant hand holding the bottom center of display. Pointing *(flexible 87%, rigid 47%),* Tracing *(flexible 73%, rigid 31%),* Reading *(flexible, 12%, rigid 12%)* and Mobile Navigation *(flexible 49%, rigid 55%);*

d) **Bi-manual** (Fig 2*d*). Both hands holding vertical center of the display on each side. Pointing *(flexible 3%, rigid 10%),* Reading *(flexible 33%, rigid 51%),* Mobile Navigation *(flexible 6%, rigid 6%);*

e) **Flat** (not shown). Display placed on surface of the flat left or right non-dominant hand. Rigid only, Pointing *(8%),* Tracing *(31%).*

Differences Between Tasks

There were some marked differences in the use of holds between tasks. Most notably, in pointing and tracing all holds were one-handed. E.g., the reading task frequently involved *Bi-manual* holds, while in mobile navigation tasks users preferred a *Bottom Center* hold.

(1) Observations in the Pointing Task

In the flexible condition, 87% of the holds used in pointing consisted of a hold in which the display was held up with the non-dominant hand at the *Bottom Center* (Fig 2*c*). We believe the prevalence of this hold was due to it producing a relatively pronounced structural fold through the y-axis of the display, which radiates an even normal force through the horizontal center of the display. At 9%, the second most popular flexible hold was with a non-dominant hand in the *Bottom Corner* (see Fig 2*b*). Here, force fields radiate diagonally through the display. A *Bi-manual* hold (see Fig 2*d*) was performed in 3% of cases, alternated with one of the one-handed holds. In the rigid condition, participants used *Bottom Center* 47% of cases. A *Bottom Corner* hold was used in 17% of cases, and *Vertical Center* (Fig 2*a*) and *Bi-manual* holds each in 10% of cases. They also deployed a *Flat* hold in 8% of cases, where the display was placed on top of a flat non-dominant hand. We observed more variety and alternation of holds in the rigid condition, with participants moving back and forth between a bi-manual hold and a one-handed hold between trials, presumably due to fatigue. Infrequently, when the target was located near the bezel, we observed participants alternating a *Bi-manual* hold with a pinch gesture to select the target without releasing the display.

(2) Observations in the Tracing Task

In our tracing task, we observed participants using three different holds. In the flexible condition, at 73%, the most frequent hold was the non-dominant hand holding the *Bottom Center.* At 27%, the second most frequent hold was at the *Vertical Center.* In the rigid condition, results were evenly split. In 31% of cases participants used the non-dominant hand holding the side of the display at the *Bottom Center.* In 31% of cases, participants used a hold in which the display was placed on top of a *Flat* non-dominant hand. In 21% of cases participants held the display at the *Vertical Center*, and in 15% of cases at the *Bottom Corner.* Some participants deployed a bimanual hold between traces, likely to provide a force counteracting friction on the display surface. When a drag interfered with a hold, participants either relocated their thumb or switched holds.

(3) Observations in the Reading Task

At 33% of flexible and 51% of rigid cases, the most frequently observed hold while reading was a *Bi-manual* hold in which the display was held in the vertical center on both sides. We believe this hold provided the most stability with the least energy expenditure. We found participants

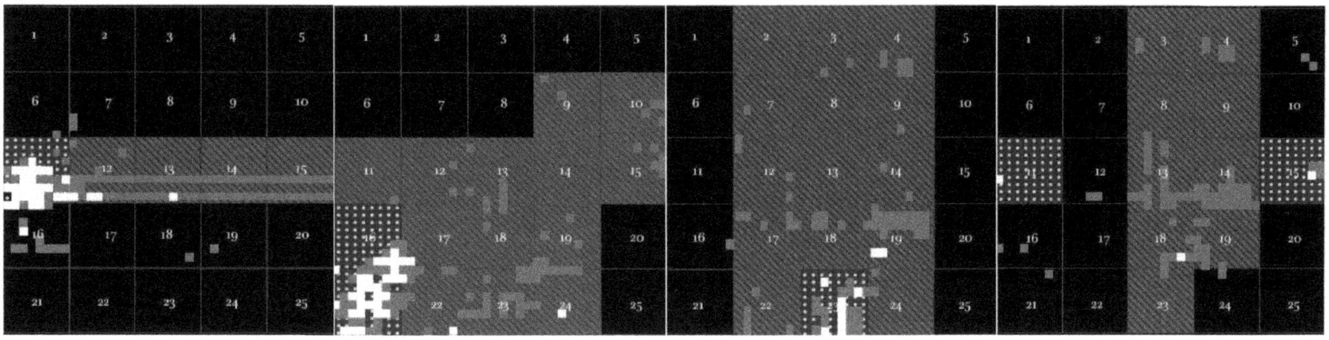

(a) Vertical Center *(b) Bottom Corner* *(c) Bottom Center* *(d) Bi-manual*

Figure 3. Force heat maps for the 4 most common holds found in the observational study: Vertical Center, Bottom Corner, Bottom Center, and Bi-manual. White, gray and black areas respectively indicate high, medium and low-pressure zones measured over all tasks. Dotted (*red*), hatched (*green*) and black areas indicate grip, rigid, and flexible structural zones for which performance was compared in our second, controlled study. Numbers correspond to locations used as targets in pointing tasks.

resting elbows, and bottom parts of their display, on their lap or table while holding, in both rigid and flexible conditions. For both conditions, at 30%, the second most frequent hold was the non-dominant hand placed at the *Vertical Center*. For flexible, the *Bottom Corner* hold was also used in 13% of cases. For both flexible and rigid conditions, *Bottom Center* was used in 12% of cases. Participants with flexible displays deployed a larger variety of holds and postures. Participants sitting at a table, in an upright position, preferred to hold the display bi-manually. Participants sitting in a lounge chair in a more relaxed position tended to hold the display with a non-dominant one-handed hold, while using a body part to prop up the other side of the display.

(4) Observations in the Mobile Navigation Task

In our mobile navigation task, the participants were given complete freedom of movement. The majority of our participants were, however, consistent in the way they held their paper display, irrespective of rigidity. At 49% of flexible and 55% of rigid usage cases, the most frequently observed hold was where the non-dominant hand held the *Bottom Center* of the display. The *Bottom Corner* hold was the second most popular at 30% of flexible and 38% of rigid cases. In flexible conditions, 17% of cases was a *Vertical Center* hold. Bimanual holds were observed in 6% of cases for both rigid and flexible. When taking notes, participants changed holds. In the rigid condition, participants used the display as a surface for their notepad. In the flexible display condition, they would hold the display either with the same hand as the note pad, while letting it dangle, or they would put the display in their pocket.

STUDY 2: EXPERIMENT DESIGN RATIONALE

For our second study, we designed a controlled experiment that measured the effect of the identified holds, as well as differences in structural integrity caused by these holds, on pointing and dragging tasks using a real flexible display.

Selecting Holds for the Experiment

Together, the five observed holds accounted for over 93% of all observed hold cases. Since the *Flat* hold only occurred with rigid displays, we selected the other four holds for our second study. Since all of the participants in the second study were right-handed, and applications of holds appeared identical, but mirrored, for left and right-handed versions, we selected only left-handed versions of holds. This led to a shortlist of the four holds in Figures 2 and 3: *Vertical Center; Bottom Corner; Bottom Center;* and *Bi-manual.*

Relating Holds to Structural Areas of the Display

After classifying Touchco data as pertaining to one of these four holds, we calculated the average force deployed by each of the four holds, for each of 25 locations on the Touchco, over all participants. Numbers identify these 25 locations laid out as a square in Figure 3. We performed a linear geometrical transformation along the horizontal axis to fit the 8.5"*x*11" Touchco grid into an 8.5"*x*8.5" square, such that it would correspond to the dimensions of the flexible display used for our second study. For each hold, Touchco force differentials provided us with insights as to the normal forces generated, allowing us to identify where the display was being held, and where the areas with the highest rigidity and flexibility might be. Figure 3 shows force heat maps for each hold across the 25 locations. We thresholded Touchco pressure data, averaged across participants, to produce three distinct force levels: 0-33% of maximum force (black in Fig. 3); 33%-66% of max. force (gray in Fig. 3) and 66%-100% of max. force (white in Fig. 3), where maximum force was normalized over all recordings. We then overlaid the 25 locations, assigning locations to structural zones of the display as follows: locations with more than two white pixels were tagged as *grip zones*, i.e., where the thumb was holding the display (dotted/red areas in Fig. 3) and locations with more than 2 gray pixels as *rigid zones*, i.e., where structural folds occurred (hatched/green areas in Fig. 3). The remaining locations were tagged as *flexible zones* of the display (black areas in Fig. 3), for each hold. We used this assignment of structural areas for each hold to analyze the performance of rigid vs. flexible areas of the display in our second experiment.

Flexible Display

To study the effect of holds in the proper context of an interactive display, we needed to deploy a real flexible display in this experiment. Rather than simulating a flexible display through projection, we chose the Philips Lumalive [9] LED display. This display was the only available flexible display technology approximating US Letter size that was available at the time of this study. One of the drawbacks of Lumalive over other methods is its relatively slow response time, and relatively low resolution. However, we believed the results of the study would be more generalizable by using an actual flexible display.

Task Selection

We decided against using the reading task, as it did not involve any real interactivity. We also could not use the mobile task as it was too difficult to obtain measurements while users were walking through a space. We thus limited our empirical study to tasks 1 and 2, pointing and tracing (i.e., *dragging*), two of the most basic tasks performed in GUIs [7].

Problems with Flexible Touch Input

We also decided not to use Touchco as an input device in the second study. While Touchco works well for identifying holding patterns that exert sufficient pressure on the material, the normal forces exerted by the Lumalive display were not sufficient to obtain a reliable signal from the pressure sensitive surface during pointing. A second flexible touch technology that we considered was Displax [2]. Displax consists of a capacitive touch film that is extremely thin, transparent and flexible. It is extremely sensitive to any single touch. When tested, it was very difficult to hold the display without also triggering input on the Displax. Additionally, sensitivity to the supporting hold rendered large parts of its input grid unusable. A bezel would not have solved this problem as the capacitive field was too strong to shield effectively.

Input on Flexible Displays is Inherently 3D

Another important consideration in determining a suitable tracking technology for our formal study was the observation that finger movement on flexible displays is mostly not two-dimensional: When a finger moves across a bent screen its path is three-dimensional. Moreover, the shortest distance between locations on the screen is not necessarily along the surface of the screen. We therefore decided to measure the three-dimensional movement of the fingers, not just their movement across the surface of the display. For this reason, we decided to use a Vicon 3D motion capture system [5] to measure finger movement as well as movements by the flexible display.

Not a Reciprocal Tapping Task

We specifically did not design our pointing task in the second study to be a Fitts' Law reciprocal tapping task, for good reason: such tasks feature targets between *two* locations on a screen and the outcome is a Fitts' Law model of the throughput of the interaction, across the entire amplitude of the display [7]. One reason to use point targets was our need to determine the speed and accuracy with which users could point at any *one* location on the display. A second reason was the low resolution of the Lumalive display, which did not allow for a wide variety of target widths. We therefore designed a task in which users were asked to point at single point targets distributed across the entire flexible display surface. As our second task, we included a dragging operation. This provided us with a second elementary UI action that related performance to structural integrity of the display [7]. To be able to precisely tie performance in the dragging task to the underlying 25 target areas on the display, we again purposefully did not vary the width in this task, but we did vary the amplitude with two target lengths: one at the full width of the display, and one at half the width.

Because of the 3D nature and potential curvature of the display, we observed that users often rested their pointing finger in mid-air, away from the display, between movements. To increase real-world validity of our experiment, and because it is non-trivial to define a specific 3D starting location in mid-air in front of the screen that is similar between holding gestures, we allowed users to choose their starting location freely. We then corrected for 3D distance of the path to target after the fact by calculating Fitts' Law's Index of Performance (IP) [7] per target location, allowing us to isolate time/accuracy tradeoffs for each location. Note that we would have had to correct for various distances to target even if we had defined a specific 2D starting location on the surface of the screen, as this was *not* a Fitts' Law reciprocal tapping task.

STUDY 2: METHODS & APPARATUS

For our experimental apparatus, we used an 8.5"*x*8.5" Lumalive flexible display consisting of 196 LEDs woven into a 14*x*14 pixel grid on a flexible plastic substrate. This substrate is normally sewn into a fabric pillow designed to be worn on the body. We modified the display to be more paper-like by removing it from its pillow, then covering it with a layer of thick 110 *g* paper, which also acted as a diffuser (see Fig. 4). The images shown on the Lumalive display were controlled via a remote control attached to an Arduino Mega microcontroller. Since this solution was not fully wireless, we designed a simple pulley apparatus that allowed the display as well as its battery to be balanced off its cable with a counterbalancing weight of 510 *g*. This allowed subjects to move the display freely in threespace without producing significant forces on the display surface.

Tracking

We tracked the hands and the movement of the display using a *Vicon MX 4* motion capture system [5]. Markers were attached to the four corners of the display, with a fifth marker on the cable to distinguish orientation. The hand was tracked by 2 markers on a wristband, with 1 marker on a finger cap (see Fig. 4). The communication between the Vicon, Arduino, and the storage of all the data was

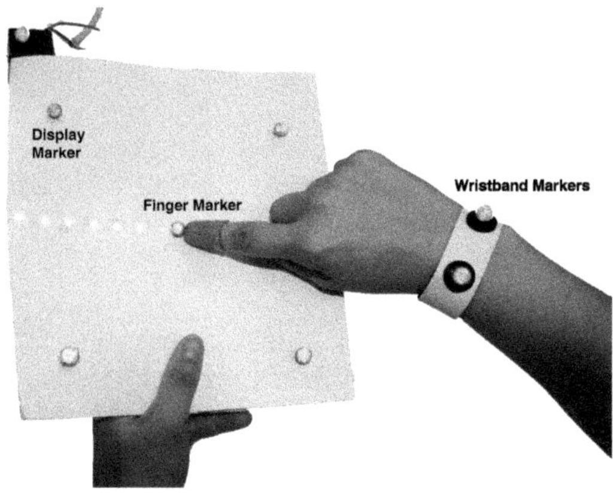

Figure 4. Flexible display with paper coating and 5 markers; wrist-band with 2 markers, finger cap with 1 marker.

managed in software. We modeled the shape of the paper by calculating Bezier curves between the four points on the display. A touch was registered whenever the marker on the tip of the finger was within 5 *mm* from the display surface. This meant the Vicon simulated a perfect capacitive touch surface that required no pressure to register a touch, with no crosstalk between holds and touches.

Tasks, Measurements and Procedure

For each task, we instructed participants to hold the display in each of the four holds obtained during the first study (see Figure 2).

Pointing Task

For the pointing task, we then asked participants to point at one of 25 randomly illuminated LEDs on the display, corresponding to the center of the 25 squares in Fig 3, as fast as possible without trading off accuracy. Each target was repeated 3 times. We trained users until their performance leveled off below 10% improvement in movement time (*MT*). Between trials, we asked participants to choose a position above the display, and hold their finger steady. We started *MT* measurements when users moved their finger more than 25 *mm* in threespace after presentation of the target on the display. We ended measurements when users were both within 5 *mm* of the display surface, taking into account its curvature, *and* within a two-dimensional radius of 7.5 *mm* from the target pixel. Trials where users were within 5 *mm* of the surface but outside the radius of the target area were flagged as error cases and discarded. Note that the mean error of Vicon measurements was below 3 *mm*.

Dragging Task

For the dragging task, because of the limited interactivity of the Lumalive, we asked participants to trace lines of illuminated LEDs on the display: a grid of 5 vertical and 5 horizontal lines of 19.5 *cm* evenly distributed across the entire screen, in each direction, and a plus formation of 2 vertical and 2 horizontal lines of 9 *cm* from each edge of the display to its center, and back. Each line was repeated 3 times, with a random order of presentation of lines. Training and instruction was similar to that in the pointing task. This dragging task was a compound task, in which the first component was a pointing task to acquire the beginning of the target, and the second part the actual dragging to the second target across the surface of the display. Participants were provided with an auditory stimulus after reaching the first target, and visual feedback upon reaching the second target. Since the first part was identical to pointing, we only analyzed the second part of this task. Measurement of *MT* started when users moved their finger more than 1 *mm* from the first target (after having successfully acquired that target). We ended measurement when users were within a two-dimensional radius of 7.5 *mm* from the target pixel. Trials where users moved their finger further than 5 *mm* from the display surface, while outside the radius of the target area, or stopped for longer than 80 *ms* before reaching the target, were flagged as error cases and discarded.

Experiment Design and Participants

We used 15 participants (mean age: 25.1; 9 males, 6 females). Participants were paid $10 for their participation. All participants in our study were right-handed.

For the pointing task, we used a fully factorial 4*x*25*x*3 within-subjects repeated measures design with two factors: hold (4 levels: *Vertical Center; Bottom Corner; Bottom Center* and *Bi-manual*) and location (25 levels, locations evenly distributed across the Lumalive display), and 3 trials per location. Order of presentation of holds was counterbalanced using a Latin square design.

For the dragging task, we used a within-subjects repeated measures design with three factors: hold (3 levels: *Vertical Center; Bottom Corner* and *Bottom Center*), amplitude (2 levels: 19.5 cm and 9 cm) and location (14 levels, evenly distributed across the display), with 3 trials per location. All conditions were counterbalanced for order using a Latin square design. Data for *Vertical Center* holds was discarded for 1 participant due to a system malfunction. The *Bi-manual* hold was not replicated in the dragging task because it approximates a one-handed *Vertical Center* hold.

For both tasks, we aggregated results for single locations into 3 levels pertaining to the structural areas from the first study (see Fig. 3): *grip* zone; *rigid* zone; and *flexible* zone, rendering a 4*x*3*x*3 fully factorial design for our pointing task and a 3*x*3*x*3 fully factorial design for our dragging task.

Analysis: Index of Performance

Although our experiment did not involve a classic Fitts' Law task, to calculate performance for each of the 25 target areas on the Lumalive display independently of the distance of the finger to the target, we treated each trial as having a Fitts' Law target with a certain bandwidth using the following formula:

(1) $$MT = a + b\log(A/W + 1)$$ [7]

Hold	Vertical Center	Bottom Corner	Bottom Center	Bi-manual
Total excl.	9.7	8.9	9.1	6.3
Grip Zone	(.76)	(.60)	(.49)	(.30)
Error *(s.e.)*	2%	1%	3%	3%
Grip Zone	7.2	5.5	5.6	5.2
IP *(s.e.)*	*(.84)*	*(.58)*	*(.76)*	*(.35)*
Rigid Zone	10.1	9.4	9.9	6.5
IP *(s.e.)*	*(.76)*	*(.68)*	*(.54)*	*(.32)*
Flex Zone	9.3	8.3	8.3	6.1
IP *(s.e.)*	*(.80)*	*(.57)*	*(.50)*	*(.30)*

Table 1. Pointing Task: Mean IP and Error Rates for each of three structural zones for each of four holds.

The log component of this equation is called the Index of Difficulty (*ID*), while the *a* in this equation constitutes response time (*RT*) [7]. For the pointing task, each of the 25 target areas had a variable distance (*A*), freely determined by the participant, and a fixed target size (*W*) of 1.5 *cm*, the distance between pixels on the Lumalive display. We calculated *b* by dividing movement time (which excluded *RT* or *a* after accounting for display latency) by the *ID* for each trial. Note that in this calculation, only the movement time and the target distance (*A*) varied. We then calculated the Index of Performance (IP) for each of the 25 target areas by taking the reciprocal of *b*. While we only used this analysis procedure to correct our measurement for any differences in distance between conditions, conveniently, this produced a true measure of performance for each of the 25 target areas.

Assignment to Structural Areas

As per the heat maps obtained during Study 1, for each hold, we then assigned each of the 25 target areas to one of three structural zones within the hold: grip (dotted/red), rigid (hatched/green) or flexible (black). This process is illustrated in Figure 3. For pointing, per hold, we then averaged the IP value for the dotted/red squares to obtain the IP of the grip zone, and the IP of the hatched/green squares to obtain the IP of the rigid zone. The average of the remaining black areas constituted the IP for the flexible zone. We used a similar way of relating structural zones to dragging performance. First, we calculated the IP per participant for each of the 28 (2 sizes; 14 locations) dragging stimuli by dividing *MT* by ID of the task. We calculated ID using line length (19.5 *cm* or 9 *cm*) as the amplitude and 1.5 *cm* as the width. We then assigned each dragging stimulus to the subset of 25 areas on the display that were crossed. Our final data set consisted of 25 areas, with as a value the average IP taken over all dragging stimuli that crossed that location. These 25 areas were then mapped to the same 3 structural areas: grip, rigid and flex zones as per the above.

Questionnaire

After each trial, participants were given a questionnaire that asked about their enjoyment and efficiency ratings using positive statements, with agreement measured on a 5-point Likert scale (1 Strongly Disagree – 5 Strongly Agree). To reduce the time taken to answer questions, we used a larger grid of 9 areas on the display. Answers were mapped to the underlying 25 target areas and related to the same 3 structural areas: grip, rigid and flex zones, as per the above.

STUDY 2: RESULTS

We tested overall differences between conditions using a repeated measures Analysis of Variance ($p<.05$). Where pairwise comparisons were conducted, we used Bonferroni corrected posthoc t-tests ($p<.05$, one-tailed).

Pointing Task

Table 1 shows the total mean IP and error rates for each of the four different holds in the pointing task, grip zone data excluded. Overall differences in performance were significant between holds ($F(3, 42)=14.3$, $p<0.001$) as well as structural zone ($F(1,14)=27.8$, $p<0.001$). There were significant interaction effects between holds and structural areas ($F(3, 42)=2.9$, $p<0.05$). Pairwise comparisons show the *Bi-manual* hold to be the only significant outlier compared to all other hold conditions (Bonferroni, $p<.01$). Error rates were within 4%, with no significant differences between holds ($F(3,42)=2.3$, n.s.). Table 1 also shows the mean IP per hold for each of the three structural zones in the Lumalive display: the grip zone, rigid zone, and flexible zone. Differences in IP were significant between structural zones for all holds: *Vertical Center* ($F(2,28)= 6.4$, $p<0.01$); *Bottom Corner* ($F(2,28)= 37.5$, $p<0.001$); *Bottom Center* ($F(2,28)= 19.2$, $p<0.01$) and *Bi-manual* ($F(2,28)= 16.7$, $p<0.001$). Pairwise comparisons show structural zones to be significantly different from one another for all holds (Bonferroni, $p<0.05$).

Dragging Task

Table 2 shows the total mean IP and error rates for each of the three different holds in the dragging task, grip zone data excluded. For the dragging task, overall differences in performance were significant between structural zones ($F(2,28)=29.8$, $p<0.01$) but not between holds ($F(2, 28)=2.6$, n.s.) We found a significant interaction between holds and structural area ($F(4, 28)=7.4$, $p<0.01$). Error rates were again well within 4%, with no significant differences between holds ($F(2,28)=.55$, n.s.). Table 2 also shows mean IP and std. error per hold for each of the three structural zones of the display in the dragging task: grip zone, rigid zone, and flexible zone. Differences in IP were significant between structural zones for two out of three holds: *Vertical Center* ($F(2,26)= 6.0$, $p<0.01$) and *Bottom Center* ($F(2,28)= 4.3$, $p<0.05$). Pairwise comparisons showed these differences to lie between the rigid and flexible zones for both holds (Bonferroni, $p<0.05$). Differences between structural zones were not significant for the *Bottom Corner* hold ($F(2,28)= 2.4$, n.s).

Questionnaire and Participant Comments

When analyzed by structural zone, respondents considered the rigid zone of the display significantly more efficient for pointing than the flexible zone for the *Bottom Corner* (77% vs. 69% $Z=2.14$, $p<0.05$), *Bottom Center* (71% vs. 50% positive answers, $Z=1.72$, $p<0.05$) and *Bi-manual* (86% vs. 64%, $Z=1.75$, $p<0.05$) holds. When analyzed by structural

Hold	Vertical Center	Bottom Corner	Bottom Center
Total excl. Grip Zone	5.9 (.57)	5.5 (.50)	5.8 (.53)
Error (s.e.)	2.9%	2.7%	2.4%
Grip Zone IP (s.e.)	6.3 (.53)	5.9 (.49)	6.1 (.65)
Rigid Zone IP (s.e.)	6.4 (.67)	5.6 (.52)	6.2 (.49)
Flex Zone IP (s.e.)	5.3 (.48)	5.5 (.48)	5.5 (.57)

Table 2. Dragging Task: Mean IP and Error Rates for each of three structural zones for each of three holds.

zone, respondents considered the rigid zone of the display significantly more enjoyable during pointing than the flexible zone for the *Bi-manual* hold only (86% vs. 57% positive answers, Z=2.27, $p<0.05$). Results on this question were not significant for other holds. When analyzed by structural zone, respondents considered the rigid zone of the display significantly more enjoyable for dragging than the flexible zone for the *Bottom Center* (87% vs. 73%, Z=1.73, $p<0.05$) and *Bi-manual* (86% vs. 57%, Z=2.09, $p<0.05$) holds only. As for comments, in the pointing task, many participants commented the target was difficult to see *"when it was underneath my thumb"*. Participants in the dragging task indicated *"It was awkward when a line passed under my thumb"*. Sometimes, *"the view of a target was blocked by my right hand, while waiting for the next target"*. One participant commented that *"the further from the hold, the harder it was to touch"*. Many participants commented that they did not enjoy the *Bi-manual* hold because they had to switch hand position during the task.

STUDY 2: DISCUSSION

Results were largely in line with expectations. When pointing, the flexibility of the display surface material negatively impacts performance. However, when provided with an optimal touch sensitive surface that does not require a force to register touch, users were able to produce a sufficient normal force in the surface of the display for pointing and dragging operations, through structural folds. While the type of hold did affect the distribution of the structural forces in the display, with the exception of the *Bi-manual* hold, different holds produced similar performance. We surmise this was because of the way we selected holds from our first study: they were the most frequently deployed holds, presumably because they were the most useful. However, with the exception of the Bi-manual hold, holding preferences from the first study did not translate into significant performance differences in our second study. Instead, performance differences were due to differences in rigidity between structural zones *within* holds. This is true more so for pointing then for dragging operations, as the direction of the movement in relation to the fold lines in the display appeared relevant, as will be discussed in more detail below.

Pointing Task

For the pointing task, the only hold that negatively impacted performance was the *Bi-manual* hold. This was due to the fact that this was the only hold that required users to reposition their hand. A compounding issue may have been that this was also the only gesture in which the structural integrity of the display surface changed while pointing. Our main finding, however, is that the structural forces in a flexible display affect the Index of Performance of pointing operations. This meant that the measurements of rigid vs. flexible structural zones in a flexible display from our first study were successfully translated to our second study. We were able to predict, using data obtained with a Touchco pressure-sensitive flexible multi-touch device, which areas are affected by folds that increase rigidity, or structural integrity, of the display. We were able to show how zones with higher rigidity, on average over all holds, yielded a 12% higher Index of Performance over flexible zones, in pointing tasks. Results show users were able to radiate normal forces throughout the display through holds at the bezel. Grip zone, the area where the display was held, did have a significant effect on performance, for two reasons. Firstly, when the target was inside the grip zone it was, in some cases, obscured by the thumb. This *"fat thumb"* problem was confirmed by participant comments: we could not, and did not want to control *exactly* how users would hold the display over time, despite instructing participants on the way in which they were to hold the display. Secondly, the grip zone interfered, in some cases, with pointing activity. Observations showed users resolving this by moving the grip slightly, which may have negatively affected performance as well. We isolated this problem by excluding data from grip zones when comparing overall performance. Overall, holds did not have a significant effect on error rates, which were well within the margins typically reported in pointing experiments.

Dragging Task

Our results for the dragging task mimicked those for pointing, but with lower IP values, which is consistent with the literature [7]. Again, areas with higher rigidity produced approximately 12% higher performance in the dragging task than areas that were more flexible, with the actual hold not having a significant effect. There was, however, a significant interaction effect between hold and structural area: this was likely due to the *Bottom Corner* hold, which produced results in this task that appeared different from the other holds. The likely reason for this was that the structural forces in this hold ran diagonally across the screen, whereas the target lines were presented either vertically or horizontally. This meant that many of the horizontal and vertical dragging targets obtained performance gains while crossing this area, benefits that were then carried over across the entire drag zone during analysis. This likely removed differences between structural zones in this condition. This also means that orientation of the dragging stimulus may have an effect on performance. It is likely that, for dragging tasks that are diagonally laid out across a flexible display, the other holds would not have yielded a significant difference. This means that dragging performance is likely similarly affected by the rigidity of a structural zone as pointing performance, in that performance is boosted whenever the finger hits an area of high rigidity. There is, however, no easy way to analyze this effect, as dragging tasks typically cross both rigid and flexible zones. We see proper analysis of effects of directionality on dragging performance in flexible displays as a future direction of this work, but conclude that, at least in our task situation and with our horizontal and vertical target sets, structural integrity of the display surface mattered. Again, holds did not have a significant effect on error rates, which were well within the margins typically reported. As opposed to the pointing task, however, the grip zone had no discernable effect on the dragging task, with similar performance between grip and rigid zones of the display. This was likely because visibility of targets was not affected by grip zone in this task: targets were a line rather than a single pixel. Furthermore, the grip zone is one of the most rigid areas in the display, and would be expected to have the highest performance of all areas as long as there is no *"fat thumb"* problem.

Design Recommendations

Our study shows that there are issues to be resolved before flexible touch technology becomes viable as a source of input for flexible displays. E.g., Touchco is pressure-sensitive, which is problematic for flexible areas of the display. As for the capacitive Displax film, the presence of a thumb in the grip zone interfered with sensing in the rest of the surface. Our study does provide guidance on design. Firstly, while flexibility of the display negatively impacts performance in pointing and dragging tasks, users are capable of achieving good levels of performance. This is due to the structural support provided by holds that curve the display. Designs for flexible display hardware need to accommodate for such structural folds. Secondly, we recommend that, like rigid tablet PCs, flexible touch screens use a bezel to avoid *"fat thumb"* problems in grip zones. This could take the form of a paper-style margin. Thirdly, interactive graphics in flexible parts of the screen could be enlarged to allow for bigger targets, or could move to rigid areas of the display, depending on the kind of hold.

Limitations

Our study was limited to right-handed participants. We believe results would be mirrored for left-handed individuals. Results pertain to displays with the rigidity of Lumalive. However, given measurements from our 1st study yielded significant performance differences in our 2nd study, we believe observations would translate to paper and other more flexible displays. Display and hand size may impact results, because of its impact on structural forces. Results may have been different had we used a flexible touch screen instead of a Vicon. Finally, direction of dragging may have limited generalization of our 2nd task: for omnidirectional drags, effects on IP may be more evenly spread across structural areas of the display.

CONCLUSIONS

We presented a study of the effects of structural holds and rigidity of a flexible display on touch pointing and dragging performance. We collected commonly used holds with a mockup paper display, along with data on forces these holds generated within the display surface. We analyzed this data to produce 3 force zones for each of the four most frequently observed holds: the *grip* zone, *rigid* zone, and the *flexible* zone. Our empirical evaluation compared the efficiency of pointing and dragging operations between holds, and between structural zones within holds, using a flexible Lumalive display. Results suggest that the force characteristics of folds in a flexible display matter. Performance in pointing and dragging tasks is, on average, 12% better in rigid than in flexible parts of the display.

ACKNOWLEDGEMENTS

We thank Tovi Grossman, Autodesk Research and *fuseproject* for their support. This work was supported by Ontario Research Fund & NSERC Strategic Project Grants.

REFERENCES

1. Chwang, A.B. et. al. Thinfilm encapsulated flexible organic electroluminescent displays. *App. Physics Letters*, 83(3) (2003).
2. Displax, Inc. *http://www.displax.com/*
3. E Ink Corporation. Flexible E Ink. *www.eink.com*
4. Guiard, Y. Asymmetric division of labor in human skilled bimanual action: The kinematic chain as a model. *Journal of Motor Behavior*, 19, (1987), 486-517.
5. Holman, D., et al. Paper windows: Interaction techniques for digital paper. In *Proc. CHI 2005*. ACM: New York, (2005), 591-599.
6. Lee, S., et al. How users manipulate deformable displays as input devices. In *Proc. CHI 2010*. ACM: New York, NY, (2010), 1647-1656.
7. MacKenzie, I. S., Sellen, A., and Buxton, W. A. A comparison of input devices in element pointing and dragging tasks. In *Proc. CHI 1991*. ACM: New York, NY, (1991), 161-166.
8. Norman, D. A. *The psychology of everyday things*. New York: Basic Books, 1988.
9. Philips, Inc. *Lumalive. http://www.lumalive.com/*
10. Rekimoto, J. SmartSkin: an infrastructure for freehand manipulation on interactive surfaces. In *Proc. CHI 2002*. ACM, New York, NY, (2002), 113-120.
11. Rosenberg, I. D., et al. IMPAD: An inexpensive multi-touch pressure acquisition device. In *Proc. CHI 2009*. ACM: New York, (2009), 3217-3222.
12. Schwesig, C., Poupyrev, I., and Mori, E. Gummi: A bendable computer. In *Proc. CHI 2004*. ACM: New York, NY, (2004), 263-270.
13. Sellen, A.J. and Harper, R.H. *The Myth of the Paperless Office*. MIT Press: Boston, MA, 2003.
14. Touchco Inc. Touchco. *http://www.touchco.com/*
15. Wang, F. and Ren, X. Empirical evaluation for finger input properties in multi-touch interaction. In *Proc. CHI 2009*. ACM: New York, NY, (2009), 1063-1072.
16. Watanabe, J., et al. Bookisheet: Bendable device for browsing content using the metaphor of leafing through the pages. In *Proc. UbiComp 2008*. ACM: New York, NY, (2008), 360-369.
17. Zhai, S., Milgram, P., and Buxton, W. The influence of muscle groups on performance of multiple degree-of-freedom input. In *Proc. CHI 1996*. ACM: New York, NY, (1996), 308-315.

PaperPhone: Understanding the Use of Bend Gestures in Mobile Devices with Flexible Electronic Paper Displays

Byron Lahey[1,2], Audrey Girouard[1], Winslow Burleson[2] and Roel Vertegaal [1]

[1] Human Media Lab
School of Computing, Queen's University
Kingston, Ontario, K7L 3N6 Canada

[2] Motivational Environments Research Group
Arizona State University
Tempe, Arizona, AZ 85281, USA

{lahey,audrey,roel}@cs.queensu.ca, winslow.burleson@asu.edu

ABSTRACT

Flexible displays potentially allow for interaction styles that resemble those used in paper documents. Bending the display, e.g., to page forward, shows particular promise as an interaction technique. In this paper, we present an evaluation of the effectiveness of various bend gestures in executing a set of tasks with a flexible display. We discuss a study in which users designed bend gestures for common computing actions deployed on a smartphone-inspired flexible E Ink prototype called PaperPhone. We collected a total of 87 bend gesture pairs from ten participants and their appropriateness over twenty actions in five applications. We identified six most frequently used bend gesture pairs out of 24 unique pairs. Results show users preferred bend gestures and bend gesture pairs that were conceptually simpler, e.g., along one axis, and less physically demanding. There was a strong agreement among participants to use the same three pairs in applications: (1) side of display, up/down (2) top corner, up/down (3) bottom corner, up/down. For actions with a strong directional cue, we found strong consensus on the polarity of the bend gestures (e.g., navigating left is performed with an upwards bend gesture, navigating right, downwards). This implies that bend gestures that take directional cues into account are likely more natural to users.

Author Keywords

Flexible Displays, E Ink, Bend Gestures, Organic User Interfaces

ACM Classification

H.5.2. User Interfaces

General Terms

Human Factors, Experimentation

INTRODUCTION

While research in the domain of flexible display interfaces has been ongoing for the better part a decade, there is, to our knowledge, little to no user interface research where actual flexible displays were deployed. Most of the display technologies used in prior studies were either based on simulations using projection on paper [10], rigid LCD displays on a flexible substrate [20] or paper mockups [13]. These methods of simulating real flexible displays potentially introduce biases for the evaluation of interactions. By using real flexible displays and integrated bend sensing we achieve interactions that align with the performance characteristics of devices that could be commercially available in the immediate future. While there may be suggestions that bending of a flexible display can be as effective and efficient an input technique as button controls in rigid displays for tasks like paging, the case for the use of flexible over rigid screens is not necessarily based on the superior efficiency of interactions. Indeed, much work is required for flexible touch screens to become as effective as rigid ones. However, while rigid screens may continue to have the edge in terms of interaction efficiency for some time, we believe there are sufficient practical and interactional reasons for flexible displays to achieve mass adoption. The likely reason for adoption of flexible displays is that they may closely approximate the look and feel of paper documents. Sellen and Harper [21] describe some characteristics

Figure 1. The PaperPhone prototype with flexible E Ink display features bend gesture input recognition.

of paper documents that may explain their continued popularity. Rigid Graphical User Interfaces (GUIs) often feature input that is indirect, one-handed, and dependent on visual cues. By contrast, paper documents, and presumably flexible displays, may:

1. Be very thin, low-weight, yet rugged, allowing superior portability over any current mobile computing form factor.
2. Have many form factors. This allows for distinct physical affordances that relate to specific functionalities: reading a newspaper serves a different purpose than reading a product label, and implies a different form factor.
3. Provide variable screen real estate that fits the current context of use.
4. Have many physical pages, each page pertaining only to a specific and physically delineated task context.
5. Use physical bend gestures with strong tactile and kinesthetic feedback for efficient navigation.

Prior simulations of flexible displays [8, 9, 10, 13, 20] have already produced a library of paper-like interaction styles, most of which focus on the use of bend gestures. A bend gesture is the physical, manual deformation of a display to form a curvature for the purpose of triggering a software action. In this paper, we present an evaluation of user preferences for bend gestures in executing a real set of tasks, using an actual flexible display. We designed a study in which users were asked to design their own bend gestures using a thin film E Ink display with integrated bend sensors. This approach has two distinct advantages over prior work: (1) visual feedback is provided directly on the display itself, and (2) dynamic material characteristics of bending layers of sandwiched flexible electronics were included.

In the first part of our study, we asked participants to define 8 bend gesture pairs. In the second part, we asked them to evaluate the appropriateness of their bend gestures for use with multiple actions. Finally, users were asked to use and evaluate bend gestures in the context of complete tasks (e.g., operating a music player). Results showed that users selected individual bend gestures and bend gesture pairs that were conceptually simpler and less physically demanding. There was a strong agreement among participants to use 3 bend gesture pairs in applications: (1) side of display, up/down (2) top corner, up/down (3) bottom corner, up/down. There was also strong consensus on the *polarity* (physical bend direction: up or down) of bend gesture pairs for actions with clear *directionality* (e.g., navigating left and right to select an icon).

RELATED WORK

We will first discuss work related to the development of flexible display interfaces, after which we will address empirical work on the design of bend gesture sets for multi-touch and flexible display user interfaces.

Understanding Interactions with Flexible Displays

Balakrishnan et al. [2] explored the use of ShapeTape, an input device that senses bend and twists, as a tool for 3D modeling. They emphasized the significance of the sensor affordances and the abilities of the user. They classified this input device as a high dimensional device, with more than three simultaneous degrees of freedom. We believe that flexible displays using deformation as an input modality will typically fall into this class of device, and are subject to user challenges arising from the associated complexity.

Schwesig et al. discuss Gummi, a bendable computer prototype. They demonstrated the feasibility and potential benefits of compact, flexible mobile computing form factors [20]. Gummi was designed with flexibility as an affordance, allowing both discreet events, considered at a maximum bending threshold, and analogue events, by measuring continuous transition states between thresholds. Navigation was achieved through bending the display. The interface was implemented using a rigid form factor display and a flexible sheet of acrylic augmented with resistive bend sensors. They proposed that such devices should have different interaction styles than traditional GUIs.

In PaperWindows, Holman et al. [10] created a projection based windowing environment that simulated fully wireless, full-color digital paper. Holman merged the properties of digital media with those of physical paper, allowing for input and output directly on the flexible display. They demonstrated use of gestural inputs such as hold, collate, flip, bend, point and rub [8, 10]. Augmenting this work, Gallant et al. [8] designed Foldable User Interfaces, a prototyping tool for flexible displays that uses Foldable Interaction Devices, sheets of paper augmented by infrared retroreflectors. They argued that physical page bends are effective metaphors for document navigation, an argument congruent with findings by Lee and Herkenrath [9, 13].

Twend was a hardware prototype developed by Herkenrath et al. that allowed complex navigations using twisting and bending [9]. Twend was constructed out of 8 optical bend sensors to recognize a wide variety of contortions. Similar in nature, Watanabe et al. [17] discussed Bookisheet, a set of flexible input devices made out of sheets of thin acrylic augmented with bend sensors. Bookisheet could simulate the turning of pages through bends. The interface changed between discrete jumping and continuous scrolling modes based upon the degree of bend between two sheets of cardboard. Similarly, Lee et al. [12] used image projection on foldable materials to simulate flexible displays with variable form factors and dimensions. They did not conduct an evaluation of this system, but suggested that devices of this nature may have advantages in mobile contexts and will afford new interaction styles.

Designing Gestures

Wobbrock et al. [19] investigated user-defined gestures for tabletop computing using the Microsoft Surface through a participatory design and a *guessability* session [18]. They

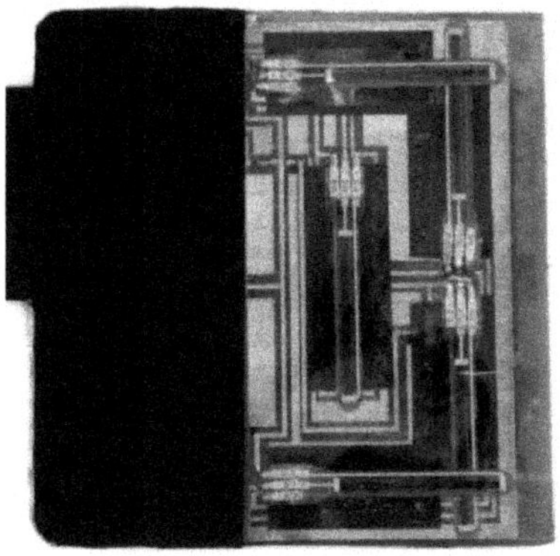

Figure 2. The back of PaperPhone, showing a Flexible Printed Circuit featuring an array of bend sensors.

asked non-technical users to perform gestures for 27 typical computing actions. They used a measure of agreement between users to define a gesture set for each action. In a follow up study, Morris et al. [15] compared gestures for the Surface defined by users to those defined by interaction designers. They concluded that users preferred gestures that were generated by larger groups and generally favored the gestures created by users, as these tended to be conceptually simpler and less physically demanding. For our evaluation, we borrowed heavily from the basic methodology used in these papers, allowing users to generate, test and rank gestures for mobile computing tasks.

Lee et al. [13] conducted a study to generate a set of interaction gestures for mockup deformable displays as input devices. In this study, participants were given A4-sized paper, plastic and elastic cloth as imaginary displays. The participants were given 11 specific interaction tasks, such as zooming or navigating to the next page, and were instructed to deform the displays in ways that would execute these tasks. They found that users preferred pairings of closely related but opposite actions and gestures. This observation informed the design of our study.

PAPERPHONE: A FLEXIBLE SMARTPHONE

We anticipate that one of the first major commercial applications of flexible displays will be in handheld mobile devices [16]. There are several reasons for this. First, the flexible displays that arrive on the market will be limited in size for technical reasons. Second, many of the benefits of flexible displays, such as portability, are ideally suited for mobile form factors. Third, mobile devices benefit most from the power efficiency of electrophoretic displays. For these reasons, we developed PaperPhone, a smartphone prototype designed around a 3.7" electrophoretic display. PaperPhone features an array of thin film bend sensors on the back of the display (see Figure 2) that allows triggering of software actions on the device. Our prototype was designed to allow users to build their own bend gesture vocabulary, allowing us to study their preferences for mapping specific bend gestures to specific actions on the flexible display.

Apparatus

PaperPhone consists of an Arizona State University Flexible Display Center 3.7" Bloodhound flexible electrophoretic display, augmented with a layer of 5 Flexpoint 2" bidirectional bend sensors [6]. The prototype is driven by an E Ink [5] Broadsheet AM 300 Kit featuring a Gumstix [7] processor. The prototype has a refresh rate of 780 ms for a typical full screen gray scale image.

An Arduino [1] microcontroller obtains data from the Flexpoint bend sensors at a frequency of 20 Hz. Figure 2 shows the back of the display, with the bend sensor configuration mounted on a flexible printed circuit (FPC) of our own design. We built the FPC by printing its design on DuPont Pyralux flexible circuit material with a solid ink printer, then etching the result to obtain a fully functional flexible circuit substrate. PaperPhone is not fully wireless. This is because of the supporting rigid electronics that are required to drive the display. A single, thin cable bundle connects the AM300 and Arduino hardware to the display and sensors. This design maximizes the flexibility and mobility of the display, while keeping its weight to a minimum. The AM300 and Arduino are connected to a laptop running a Max 5 [14] patch that processes sensor data, performs bend gesture recognition and sends images to the display.

Recognizing Bend Gestures

PaperPhone has a training mode during which the user designs and records bend gestures, and an operating mode in which the system uses currently defined bend gestures to trigger software actions. In the training mode the bend sensor data is recorded and used to train a k-Nearest-Neighbor (kNN) algorithm with k=1. kNN assigns the label of the most similar examples (the closest neighbor) to the example to classify. In our case, the examples are vectors from the live values of the 5 bend sensors. We trained the system to recognize the flat shape as the baseline, or a neutral state. In the operating mode, in which trained bend gestures trigger software actions, a bend gesture is recognized when the display is bent to a curvature that is closer to a recorded shape than a flat shape. This recognition algorithm requires only a single training input for each gesture, making it ideal for rapid programming of user defined bend gestures.

To minimize the unintended triggering of actions by false positives, an additional stage of filtering was implemented immediately after the raw kNN classification output. The software takes a sample of the recognized bend gesture alternatives, reporting the mode value from this set as the recognized bend gesture. The window size of the sample ranged from 5 to 40 samples depending on the number of candidate bend gestures and on the similarity of these bend gestures to one another. This window size was manually defined based on observations of system performance. The final stage of the Max program maps the recognized bend gestures to a set of actions on the flexible display. For this purpose, we designed a state machine in Max that takes recognized bend gestures as inputs and produces states as output. The state data includes the specific action to be executed (such as placing a phone call), and the next state the state machine should be in on the next cycle (such as a menu for icon navigation). This information is transmitted to the Gumstix computer, which renders the appropriate images on the flexible display of PaperPhone. The state machine allows bend gesture pairs to be used in isolation and applied to all the individual actions, or used in concert to perform compound tasks. Although PaperPhone is fully flexible, the current design contains a number of fragile connectors on the left side of the display that may be damaged while bending. We protected these connectors by affixing a less pliable plastic board to this side. The right side of the PaperPhone display allows bends up to 45 degrees. Our bend gesture recognition system requires a minimum bend of 10 degrees for proper detection of bend gestures.

DEFINING BEND GESTURES

We defined a bend gesture as the physical, manual deformation of a display surface to form a curvature for the purpose of triggering an action on a computer display. To aid in the design of our study, we developed a simple classification scheme for bend gestures based on the physical affordances of the display, the sensing data available from the bend sensor array, and the PaperPhone bend gesture recognition engine. We classify the bend gestures our users could perform according to two main characteristics: the *location of the force* exerted on the display, and the *polarity* of that force. The rigid bezel allowed three fundamental locations of the force that can be exerted on the display: Bend gestures could be located on either right corners, or along the side of the display. Individual bend gestures could be of two sorts: a single bend or a compound bend. A single bend gesture contains only one fold, and is generated by applying a force to a single location. A compound bend consists of more than one fold, and is generated by applying forces to multiple locations simultaneously, e.g., bending both corners of the display. For each bend location, the *polarity* of a bend gesture could be either up (towards the user) or down (away from the user). Note that we recognize alternative criteria, such as the amount of force exerted on the display, the number of repetitions of bends, the velocity of movements, continuous vs. discrete use of bends and the orientation of the screen (portrait or landscape). However, given the constraints of our hardware, and in order to limit the overall time spent by participants designing bend gestures, we decided against investigating these in the present study.

BUILDING A FLEXIBLE INTERACTION LANGUAGE

We wanted users to build a simple interaction language for bend gestures: one that is both sufficiently general to be used universally, yet at the same time personalized and easy to reconfigure. In this language, bend gestures trigger individual actions on the PaperPhone system. We defined actions as the lowest verbalizable activities in the PaperPhone user interface [4]. Examples included selecting, navigating menu items, and ending a phone call. One of the goals of our study was to evaluate whether users would associate bend gestures with actions in a way that would approach the formation of a general interaction language, satisfying criteria of orthogonality, consistency, polymorphism and directionality [3, 22].

Orthogonality

Orthogonality, at a basic level, means that one bend gesture can be recognized as independent from another bend gesture, thus allowing each to map to a single action in a way that is combinatory [3]. We were particularly interested to see whether, at a semantic level, users associate orthogonal bending gestures to orthogonal actions of similar meaning. A design implication of this criterion is that orthogonal bend gestures can be conducted concurrently leading to predictable actions, e.g., the combination of two orthogonal bend gestures will result in a predictable outcome that is the direct combination of the two actions. When a right top corner up bend gesture moves the cursor to the left and a right bottom corner up bend gesture moves the selection point up, will users define a combination gesture that moves the selection point diagonally to the upper left corner?

Consistency

Orthogonality also leads to the question of consistency: a consistent design uses the same, or similar, bend gestures to trigger the same, or similar, actions across different applications. We were interested in whether users would, e.g., use the same bend gesture for moving down through a list of menu items as they would use to move down a selection of application icons.

Polymorphism

We were interested to see whether the same bend gesture would be used in a consistent manner, to trigger *different* actions that were related *semantically*. For example, if one chooses to bend the right side of the display down for a page forward action, would they choose it again to go to the next song? We examined whether polymorphism would reduce the diversity of gestures to a smaller set of favorites.

Directionality

Directionality refers to the spatial relationships defined or implied by the application (e.g., navigating *up* or *down* to select an icon). Directionality may be explicit, as is the case when icons are spatially distributed on a screen, or implicit, such as when navigating between pages of a document. Transitional animation effects can make implicit directionality explicit. We wondered whether users would, for example, associate an *up* action with bend gestures performed at the top of the display, and a *down* action with bends at bottom of the display, or if they would instead associate this with the polarity of the bend gesture, such as performing an upwards bend of the top corner for the *up* action, and a downwards bend of the same corner for the *down* action.

Polarity and directionality are distinguished by the item they relate to: polarity always refers to the physical deformation of display, bent towards (up) or away from (down) the user's body, while directionality always refers to either

Applications	Action Pairs	# Pairs	Session
Icon Navigation	Left – Right		2 3
	Up – Down	3	2 3
	Open – Close		2 3
Contacts	Up – Down		- 3
	Open – Close	3	2 3
	Call – Drop		2 3
Music Player	Play – Pause	2	2 3
	Next – Previous Song		2 3
Book Reader	Next – Previous Page	1	- 3
Map Navigation	Zoom In – Out	1	- 3

Table 1. Mobile applications and associated 10 action pairs, to which bend gesture pairs were mapped by participants.

a spatial relationship on a screen (e.g., between icons) or mental model (e.g., previous/next page could be up/down, left/right).

USER-DEFINED BEND GESTURES STUDY

To determine what sets of bend gestures users would find appropriate as inputs for various actions in PaperPhone, we asked participants to define, design and evaluate bend gestures for specific functions in the context of a number of mobile applications. Our methodology was based on studies by Wobbrock et al. [19] and Lee et al. [13] on the participatory design of gestures for multi-touch tabletops as well as flexible display mockups.

Our study consisted of three sessions. In the first, we asked users to define a set of 8 bend gesture pairs. In the second session, we asked users to evaluate the appropriateness of each of these bend gesture pairs for each one of seven action pairs pertaining to three applications. They then selected their favorite bend gesture pair for each action pair. In the third session, users were asked to perform all available actions in each application.

Participants

10 participants volunteered for this study (3 females). The participants were between the age of 19 and 36 (average of 23.7 years old). All participants were university students, and received $20 for their 2 hours of participation.

Applications and Action Pair Design

We selected five typical applications that are commonly performed on a mobile phone: navigating through icons, selecting contacts and making phone calls, playing music, reading a book, and navigating a map (see Table 1). Figure 3 shows four of the screen layouts on our PaperPhone prototype. Many user actions have a symmetrical correlate. We call such symmetrical actions *action pairs.* We identified 20 actions (10 action pairs) for the five applications.

(a) Icon Navigation

The user was required to navigate a series of twelve application icons distributed in a 3*x*4 grid pattern (see Figure 3a). They were asked to perform these actions by going *left*, *right*, *up* and *down*. *Opening an application* led to a splash

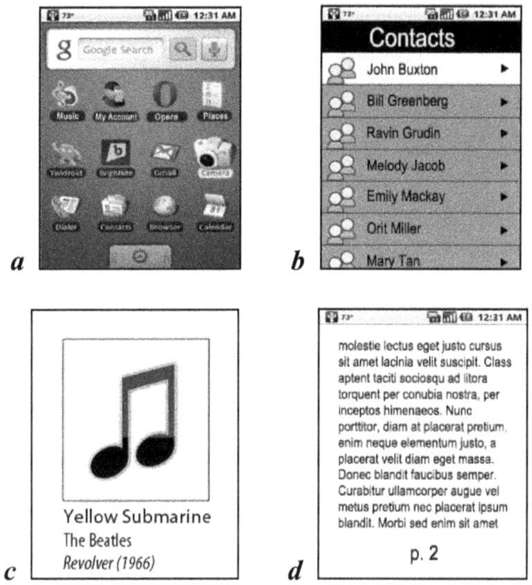

Figure 3. Screenshots of 4 of the applications: Icon Navigation, Contacts, Music Player, and Book Reader.

screen. The user could *close the application* which returned the interface to the set of application icons.

(b) Contacts

The user was asked to navigate *up* and *down* a list of contacts (see Figure 3b). Once the user had chosen a contact, she could *select* it to view the contact details. The user could *close the contact details* and return to the main list, or *call the contact.* When calling, the user could *drop the call.*

(c) Music Player

The user was asked to *play* and *pause* a song, and select the *previous* or *next song* (see Figure 3c). To minimize bias, we provided no visual or verbal cues of the directionality of these actions. When the *play* or *pause* action was performed, the state of the action was displayed on the screen. When new songs were selected, the name of the song and performer was also visible.

(d) Book Reader

The user was asked to navigate to the *previous* or *next page* (see Figure 3d). We again avoided introducing directional bias by not asking users to *page up, down, left* or *right.* We limited actions for this application to a single action pair to allow us to observe the user's orthogonality considerations in applying this mapping.

(e) Map Navigation

The user was asked to *zoom in* or *zoom out* (not shown in Figure 3). Because of the limited refresh rate of the display, zooming was implemented as a discrete action. We again limited this application to a single action pair.

Procedure

Before starting the experiment, users were provided with minimal instructions to prevent damage to PaperPhone. We physically demonstrated a single bend gesture (Figure 4A), emphasizing the degree to which the display could be bent without damaging the device. We instructed the users to

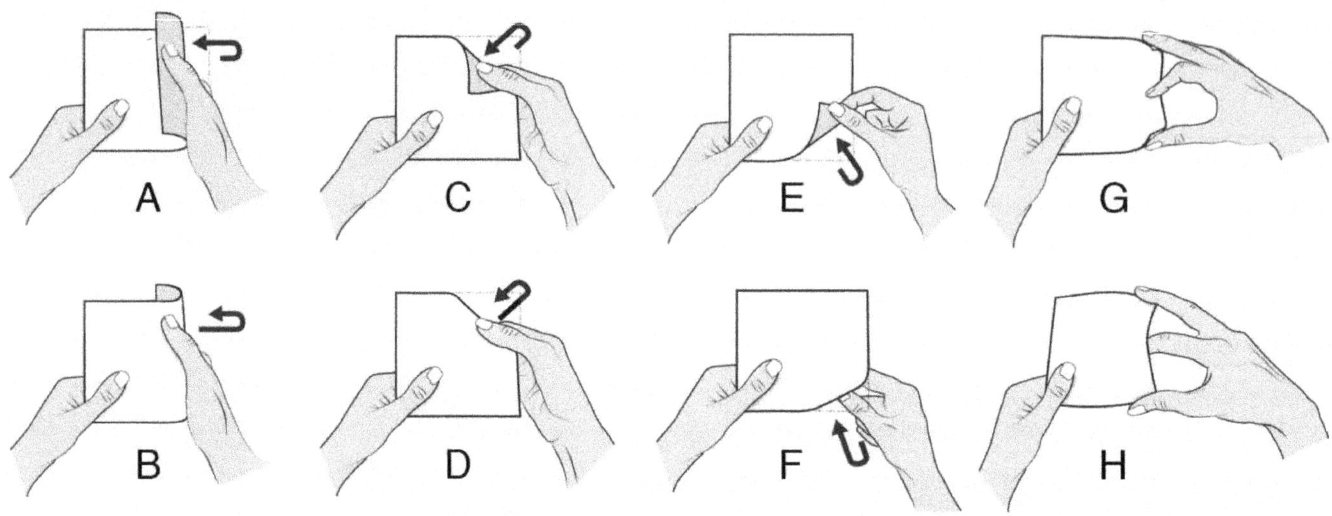

Figure 4. The eight participant defined individual bend gestures used in bend gesture pairs.

avoid bending directly on the left edge of the device, where the electrical contacts were located. We guided the participants to hold the display as if it were wireless, and to ignore and not hold the connecting ribbon cables. Participants were informed that the system would only recognize discrete bend gestures. Aside from this, we did not instruct participants on bend gestures. Throughout the experiment, participants were encouraged to think aloud, so as to verbalize their thought processes.

Session 1: Defining Bend Gestures

To encourage users to consider a wide variety of bend gestures, their first assignment was to design 8 unique pairs of bend gestures. We derived 8 as the number of bend gesture pairs empirically from a pilot study: a high enough number to challenge beyond obvious choices, while allowing completion within 2 hours. Participants were allowed to reuse individual bend gestures in different pairs, as long as the resulting pairs were not identical. First, the user executed each bend pair once to train PaperPhone's bend recognition system. After the system was trained, it executed an action whenever the bend gesture was performed. To emphasize that each bend gesture was going to be associated with an individual action, and to encourage participants to create comfortable bend gestures, we gave the users the opportunity to try out their bend gesture with an abstract action. Here, the display turned either to black or white when the user performed a bend gesture pair successfully. This continued until they had defined all 8 pairs.

Session 2: Assigning Bend Gestures to actions

The second part of the experiment let users test out each bend gesture pair with each individual action pair. We selected 7 unique action pairs from the list of 10 (Table 1). The *up/down* action pair from the Contacts application was not repeated, as it is a duplicate of the *up/down* action pair in the Icon Navigation application. To examine orthogonality, we reserved the Book Reader and Map Navigation applications for evaluation in session 3. In the Icon Navigation application, users moved *left, right, up, down through icons, opened* and *closed the application.* In the Contacts application, users *opened* and *closed a contact, called the contact* and *dropped the call.* In the Music Player, users *played* or *paused*, and selected the *next or previous song.*

Users first assigned the mapping of each bend gesture to an action, meaning that they selected which bend gesture components of the previously designed bend gesture pair would trigger the individual actions in the action pair. The user was then able to try out each bend gesture pair/action pair mapping, after which they rated the appropriateness of the bend gesture pair for this action pair using a 5-point Likert scale of agreement (1 Strongly Disagree-5 Strongly Agree). This was repeated for all 8 bend gesture pairs. The participants were then asked to determine their favorite bend gesture pair for the action pair. When a user suggested an alternative bend gesture pair, we would record this pair and add it to our total count of bend gesture pairs. Users each tested 56 mappings of bend gesture pair to action pairs (8 bend gesture pairs x 7 actions pairs). The presentation of bend gesture pairs for each action pair, as well as of action pairs, was counterbalanced using a Latin-square design.

Session 3: Using Bend Gestures across Applications

For the final part of the study, the users were instructed to try out the full suite of top ranked bend gesture pair/action pair mappings, in each of the five applications. In the previous part, each action pair was performed individually. In this session all of the action pairs for the active app were available at once, allowing users to perform them in any order, independently of the pairs. Users were free to assign any bend gesture pair to any action pair, with any polarity, whether previously used or not. Users were reminded of their favorite bend gesture/action mappings for each application and were instructed to determine whether there were any conflicts between these bend gestures. In the case of orthogonality conflicts, the user was invited to revise their choice of bend gestures to eliminate any conflicts. For each

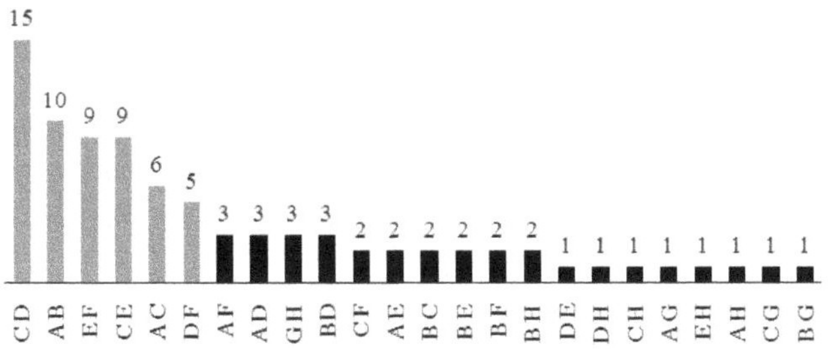

Figure 5. The 24 unique bend gesture pairs generated and frequency (Letters refer to individual bend gestures from Fig. 4. Gray indicates six most frequently used pairs).

Applications	Action Pairs	CD	AB	EF	CE	AC	DF
Contacts	Call - Drop	3.5	4.4	3.1	3.3	3.2	3.0
	Open - Close	3.8	4.9	4.0	3.5	4.2	3.6
Music Player	Next - Previous	4.1	4.3	4.2	3.6	2.8	3.6
	Play - Pause	4.1	4.0	3.7	3.1	3.2	4.2
Icon Navigation	Left - Right	3.6	4.1	3.8	1.9	2.2	2.4
	Open - Close	3.7	4.1	3.7	3.1	3.8	3.2
	Up - Down	4.0	3.6	4.3	4.4	2.0	4.6

Table 2. Appropriateness scores per action pair (1-5 scale, 5 being most appropriate). Gray cells highlight the action pairs with the highest appropriateness value.

app, the system was trained with the selected bend gestures and the user was allowed to freely test and evaluate the interaction experience. Before ending the experiment, users were asked to identify situations where they would prefer to use bend gestures over other input techniques.

RESULTS

The first session in the experiment generated 8 bend gesture pairs per participant, for a total of 80 bend gesture pairs. A few participants created bend gesture pairs in the 2nd session (7 additional bend gesture pairs), for a total of 87 pairs (174 individual bend gestures). We first identified high-frequency individual bend gestures. Four HCI researchers grouped each bend gesture, according to the location and polarity of the force exerted on the display, such that each group only contained identical bend gesture. The same procedure was repeated for bend gesture pairs. We did not consider the order of the bend gestures in the pair. A total of eight individual bend gestures were identified out of a possible set of ten: six single bends and two compound bends, illustrated in Figure 4. Individual letters identify individual bends (e.g. *A*). Bend gesture *C* was the most frequent used at 20.9% (36 out of 172 individual bends). The other five single bend gestures obtained an average frequency of 14.1% (24/172). Two compound bends constituted 8.7% of the total individual bend gestures (15/172). A total of 24 unique pairs were identified, from a possible set of 45. Pairs of letters indicate which individual bend gestures constitute each bend gesture pair (e.g. *AD*). Their composition and frequency is shown in Figure 5. Six bend gesture pairs obtained a frequency of five or more, meaning they were performed by at least half of the participants: *(CD, AB, EF, CE, AC* and *DF)*. We consider those six bend gesture pairs to be our *most frequent used bend gesture pairs*. The six bend gesture pairs are identified with a gray color in Figure 5. We focused our analysis of session 2 on these six bend gesture pairs.

Applications	Action Pair	Agreement	Unique Bend Gesture Pairs
Contacts	Open - Close	0.52	5
	Call - Drop	0.28	4
Music Player	Next - Previous	0.38	3
	Play - Pause	0.26	5
Icon Navigation	Left - Right	0.44	3
	Open - Close	0.24	6
	Up - Down	0.16	7

Table 3. Agreement for each action pair from the users' favorite bend gesture pairs.

Session 2: Bend Gesture Pairs for Action Pairs

For each bend gesture pair defined in the first part of the experiment, users rated their appropriateness for a series of action pairs. Table 2 shows the frequency distributions of these appropriateness ratings per action pair.

Agreement on Favorite Bend Gesture

To identify the best bend gesture for each action, we looked at the bend gesture pairs identified by each participant as their favorite for that action pair. For each action pair, we calculated a measure of agreement, as defined in Wobbrock et al. [18, 19]. The agreement score reflects the degree of consensus among participants. An agreement score of 1 indicates that all the participants selected the same bend gesture pair as their favorite, while an agreement of 0 indicates that every participant selected a different bend pair. Table 3 shows this agreement score for every action pair. Agreement was highest for *open-close* in Contacts (A_{OC}=.52) and *left-right* in Icon Navigation (A_{LR}=.44).

Polarity of Favorite Bend Gestures

We observed the polarity of the individual bend gesture in each pair as it related to each individual action. In the case of two identical polarities (e.g. two upwards bend gestures), we define polarity as the location of the bend (top, side or bottom of the display). The *left/right* action pair in the Icon Navigation application had a 100% polarity agreement, with all users performing an upward bend gesture for *left*, and a downward bend gesture for *right*. Nine out of ten participants associated the *open* action in Icon Navigation with an upward bend gesture, and the *close* action with a downward bend gesture. We observed that the *up* action corresponded to either an upward bend gesture (6 participants), or a top (location) bend gesture (3 participants), while a *down* action corresponded with either a downward bend gesture (5 participants) or a bottom bend gesture (3 participants). For the remainder of the applications, the actions were approximately equally distributed between two polarities.

Applications	Action Pair	Agreement	Unique Bend Gesture Pairs
Book Reader	Next - Previous	0.42	3
Contacts	Call - Drop	0.26	5
	Open - Close	0.66	3
	Up - Down	0.30	4
Map Navigation	Zoom in - out	0.42	4
Music Player	Next - Previous	0.38	3
	Play - Pause	0.40	5
Icon Navigation	Left - Right	0.38	3
	Open - Close	0.30	4
	Up - Down	0.28	5

Table 4. Agreement for each action pair from the users' application bend gesture pairs.

Session 3: Bend Gestures for Applications

Agreement on Bend Gestures in Applications

We calculated the agreement among participants for each of the 10 action pairs. Table 4 shows the agreement score for every action pair.

Orthogonality in Applications

We extracted the bend gesture pairs used in applications by each participant, creating either sets of 2 pairs (for the Music Player), or 3 pairs (for the Contact and the Icon Navigation application). We counted the frequency of those pairs, and calculated the agreement score. We observed a higher consensus in applications with three action pairs: the majority of participants selected the trio of bend gesture pairs *AB, CD,* and *EF* in the Icon Navigation applications (A_{IN}=0.66, 8 participants), and the Contacts applications (A_C=0.40, 6 participants). The Music Player obtained an agreement score of A_{MP}=0.32, as participants selected either the set of bend gesture pairs *AB* and *CD* (5 participants), or *CD* and *EF* (2 participants).

Polarity of Bends in Applications

The majority of the bend gesture pair/action pair mappings were consistent in terms of their polarity. 10 (out of 10) participants selected downward bend gestures for the *right* action and upward bend gestures for the *left* action in the Icon Navigation application. 8 participants selected a downward bend gesture for *zooming in* and an upward bend gesture for *zooming out*. 8 participants selected an upward bend gesture for *calling*, and 7 participants selected a downward bend gesture for *dropping* a call.

DISCUSSION

The results show that participants express strong agreement when designing individual bend gestures as well as bend gesture pairs. However, they agreed less on the assignment of bend gesture pairs to action pairs. Specifically, we found a cohesive set of bend gesture pairs with high frequency, and a cohesive set of individual bend gestures, indicating agreement. However, the consensus on the mapping of those bend gestures to actions was overall low, showing that each participant had his or her own preference. This has strong implications for the design of flexible display user interfaces that use bend gestures as a source of input.

Cohesive Set of Bend Gestures and Bend Gesture Pairs

When examining the bend gestures and bend gesture pairs in isolation, without their action mappings, the set of six most frequent gesture pairs are all composed of simple individual bend gestures. From the six identified bend gesture pairs, we can identify a subset of three that were both the most frequently designed (in session 1), and the most frequently assigned in applications (in session 3), with high agreement. We believe that those three bend gesture pairs (*AB*: side of display up/down, *CD*: top corner up/down and *EF*: bottom corner up/down) likely form a good foundation for a simple bend gestural interaction language. The three bend gesture pairs both consisted of the simplest individual bend gestures, and were also orthogonal to one another. We also observed their repeated and consistent use amongst different applications in session 3. We believe that individual bend gestures and bend gesture pairs that are conceptually simpler, and less physically demanding, were purposefully selected by users with higher frequency and appropriateness, an observation similar to that of Wobbrock et al. [19] with their set of gestures for multitouch input.

Overall Favorite Bend Gesture Pair

When assigning appropriateness scores for bend gesture pair/action pair mappings, we found that the bend gesture pair *AB* was rated the highest for the majority of action pairs (5 out of 7). The appropriateness of bend gesture pair *AB* was even higher for the contacts application. This indicates that *AB* was the favorite bend gesture pair amongst participants in this study. Note, however, that it was also considered the least appropriate for the *up/down* action pair in the Icon Navigation application. One likely reason for this is that the *AB* bend gesture pair was the least spatially ambiguous, as the bend gesture was on a vertical axis. Additionally, we observed that the Contacts *open* and *close* action pair had the highest agreement score both in the second and third session. In both cases, the large majority of participants mapped this action pair to the *AB* bend gesture pair (70% and 80% of participants, respectively).

Building a Bend Gesture Interaction Language

We proposed four criteria required when creating a bend gesture interaction language. We were interested in determining whether participants would naturally integrate each criterion in their assignment of bend gestures to actions in applications when more than one mapping was required.

Orthogonality

In terms of *orthogonality*, users did understand and respect the need to associate a unique bend gesture to each action. If their mapping of bend gesture pairs to action pairs in the second session was not orthogonal when applying them to applications in the third session, they updated those mapping to find a set that was orthogonal. Approximately 42% of all mappings changed for this reason.

Consistency

We found no strong evidence of *consistency* among the action pairs present in more than one application (i.e. *open* and *close* action pair in the Contacts and Icon Navigation applications). Only with the action pair of moving *up* or *down* did a majority (6 participants) choose the same bend gesture pair in both Contacts and the Icon Navigation applications. This is partly due to the fact that orthogonality plays a large role in assigning a bend gesture pair to an action pair. We believe this has implications for the design of flexible user interfaces in that designers may be better able to preserve consistency amongst applications than users.

Polymorphism

Polymorphism, which dictates the use of a bend gesture across different actions, did not reveal any consensus. Two action pairs with similar meaning, the page forward and backward, and skipping to the next or previous song, obtained little to no agreement in the bend gestures associated with them. Because the design of the study dictated the use of action pairs, we did not include a *symmetry* criterion, which would require symmetrical bend gestures to be used with symmetrical actions. However, participants still considered the relative symmetry of actions and the bend gestures used to trigger these actions. One user in particular described not liking using, what he considered, symmetrical bend gestures for actions he did not consider symmetrical. He observed that when bend gestures were symmetrical, it was more difficult to recall the polarity of his mappings.

Redundancy

Redundancy is a criterion where multiple bend gestures may be programmed to activate the same action. Our experiment was not designed to test for redundancy. However, because users evaluated many bend gestures for a single action in the second part of the study, we can extrapolate that it would be possible, and suitable, to provide the user with redundant bend gestures. For instance, the appropriateness scores were very close for three bend gesture pairs in action pairs in the music player application. Selecting the *previous* or *next* song can be accomplished with bend gesture pairs *AB*, *CD* or *EF* with similar appropriateness results. *Playing* or *pausing* the music yielded comparable scores whether mapped to *AB*, *CD* or *DF*. All appropriate bend gestures could be redundantly assigned to these actions, when available.

Directionality

Spatial and *directional cues* did play an important role in the mapping of bend gestures to actions. The Icon Navigation application included actions with a clear spatial relationship *(up/down/left/right)*. For other actions, such as *opening* and *closing* applications, spatial relationships appeared based on mental models constructed by the participants. In particular, participants described the action of opening an item as pulling the information towards them, or opening a door. As actions with strong directional cues showed consensus on the polarity of the associated bend gestures, we believe bend gestures that take directionality into account will likely seem more natural to users [11]. Bend gestures were mapped to directionally signified actions in a variety of ways. However, the *directionality* of actions was not clearly defined from our data. We did observe a similar scenario with the polarity of bend gestures in application actions as we did with individual actions. Selecting an icon *left* was strongly coupled with an upwards bend gesture, and the *right* action with a downwards bend gesture. Bend gestures performed on either corner (diagonal axis) were logically mapped to both *up* and *down* actions. Had the entire display been flexible, with equivalent bend gestures on all corners and sides, we would expect to see more opportunities for the criteria to be addressed.

Physical Affordances of PaperPhone

Users consistently reported that bending the corners of the display was easier than bending the whole side of the display. Three users reported bending the lower right corner down to be a more comfortable gesture than bending the same corner up, as the result of the angle of their wrist when holding this corner. They had more range of motion in one direction than the other, and needed to change their grip to compensate. Gestures such as bending two corners at once were also described as requiring more physical effort. Few participants generated, preferred, or used compound bend gestures in complex applications (below 9% overall). In addition, while the recognition engine supported it, no user defined compound bend gestures with opposite polarities as they were physically challenging. One user specifically commented about how it seemed natural to use bend gestures on PaperPhone to navigate *left* and *right* but found it challenging to find bend gestures that seemed appropriate to navigate *up* and *down*. This user preferred bending the entire vertical side of the display up and down to navigate *left* and *right*. Because it was not possible to bend the top or the bottom side of the display in the same way, this user could not chose an equivalent bend gesture to navigate upwards and downwards. Several users spoke about how much it would help to have the entire display be flexible and could clearly see how this would afford more input options. One user said that they would have preferred to use the device in a landscape orientation if one edge had to be kept rigid so that they could make bend gestures with both hands on left and right corners.

Mental Models

Users described how mental models of the actions and of the display affected the bend gesture pairing and polarity choices. These mental models were influenced by metaphors, such as: Viewing the display as a book; Prior experiences with GUI layouts; Physics models, such as inclined planes on which icons slide; and iconic representation of actions such as the right pointing arrow used for play on music players. Several users specifically described liking bend gestures for navigating the pages of a book because of the physical similarity to flipping pages in real books. The *zoom-in* action was commonly defined with bending the display in a convex shape in relation to the user. Users explained this by observing that with this bend gesture, the middle of the display was moving towards them. Several users described mental models in which more complex or physically challenging bend gestures would be reserved for applications that were performed less frequently or had a higher psychological significance, such as dropping a phone call. One user who used a compound bend gesture to drop a call described the bend gesture as "crushing the call".

Making the Case for Bend Gestures

Users saw potential for the use of bend gestures when wearing gloves, which inhibit touch screen interactions. They also imagined usage by people with motor skill limitations that prevented the use of other input systems. Bend gestures were recognized as potentially usable without visual engagement with the device and when one was interacting directly with the display but needed to avoid occluding areas of the display. Users reported bend gestures as appropriate for navigating pages in a book reader, which could take advantage of the analog properties of the bend gesture to allow for variable speed scrolling based on the degree of bend. Zooming in and out of a map was also noted, but several participants specifically described wanting this function to be implemented as a continuous analog control.

Limitations and Future Directions

The main limitation of this work resides in the physical engineering of the prototype display, which restricted bending to one side of the display. This reduced the number of bend gestures available for consideration. We believe this limitation did not outweigh benefits of being able to evaluate a functional flexible display, with results representing a significant subset of findings for a full flex display. While it was possible for us to detect continuous (analog) bend gestures, the slow refresh rate of flexible E Ink delayed visual feedback, making real-time animation impossible. Effects of display size on the use of bend gestures may be answered through future studies: We believe that with appropriate material qualities, bends could apply from small to large form factors. We expect touch input to complement bends and recognize the challenges this presents: current flex touch input options are limited. In addition, our study proposed a maximum of six actions per application, which was the max number of single bend gestures available given our constraints. An important step to validate our bend gesture set would be to test compound applications with four action pairs or more. Finally, it would be interesting to perform a follow-up study that compares user generated bend gestures mappings with those produced by designers [15].

CONCLUSION

In this paper, we presented PaperPhone, a smartphone with a functional flexible electrophoretic display and 5 integrated bend sensors. We studied the use of user-defined bend gestures for triggering actions with this flexible smartphone. Results suggest a strong preference for 6 out of 24 bend gesture pairs. In general, users selected individual bend gestures and bend gesture pairs that were conceptually simple and less physically demanding. There was a strong agreement among participants to use 3 particular bend gesture pairs in applications, bending the: (1) side of display, up/down (2) top corner, up/down (3) bottom corner, up/down. For actions with a strong directional cue, there was strong consensus on the polarity of the bend gestures. Results imply that gestures with directional cues are preferred. Results suggest bend gestures form a useful addition to interaction modalities of future flexible computers.

ACKNOWLEDGMENTS

We thank Jann Kaminski & Nicholas Colaneri of the ASU Flexible Display Center, Seth Bishop & Michael McCreary of E Ink Corporation, *fuseproject* and Autodesk Research for their support. This project was funded by the Ontario Research Fund and by an NSERC Strategic Project Grant.

REFERENCES

1. Arduino. http://www.arduino.cc.
2. Balakrishnan, R., Fitzmaurice, G., Kurtenbach, G., and Singh, K. Exploring interactive curve and surface manipulation using a bend and twist sensitive input strip. In Proc. Interactive 3D Graphics. I3D '99 (1999), 111-118.
3. Bowdon, E., Douglas, S. and Stanford, C. Testing the Principle of Orthogonality in Language Design. Human-Computer Interaction (4) 2 (1989), 95 – 120.
4. Card, S.K.; Thomas, T.P.; Newell, A. The Psychology of Human-Computer Interaction London: Lawrence Erbaum (1983).
5. E Ink Inc. http://www.eink.com
6. Flexpoint Inc. http://www.flexpoint.com
7. Gumstix Inc. http://www.gumstix.com
8. Gallant, D.T., Seniuk, A.G., and Vertegaal, R. Towards more paper-like input: flexible input devices for foldable interaction styles. In Proc. UIST '08 (2008).
9. Herkenrath, G., Karrer, T., and Borchers, J. Twend: twisting and bending as new interaction gesture in mobile devices. CHI 2008 Extended Abstracts (2008).
10. Holman, D., Vertegaal, R., Altosaar, M., Troje, N., and Johns, D. Paper windows: interaction techniques for digital paper. In Proc. CHI '05 (2005), 591-599.
11. Jacob, R.J., Girouard, A., Hirshfield, L.M., et al. Reality-based interaction: a framework for post-WIMP interfaces. Proc. CHI'08 (2008), 201–210.
12. Lee, J.C., Hudson, S.E., and Tse, E. Foldable interactive displays. In Proc. UIST '08 (2008), 287-290.
13. Lee, S. et al. How users manipulate deformable displays as input devices. In Proc. CHI '10 (2010), 1647-1656.
14. Max 5. http://www.cycling74.com
15. Morris, M.R., Wobbrock, J.O., Wilson, A.D. Understanding Users' Preferences for Surface Gestures. Proc. of Graphics Interface (GI '10) (2010), 261-268.
16. Readius. http://www.wistron.com
17. Watanabe, J., Mochizuki, A., and Horry, Y. Bookisheet: bendable device for browsing content using the metaphor of leafing through the pages, Proc. UbiComp (2008), 360 - 369.
18. Wobbrock, J.O., Aung, H.H., Rothrock, B. and Myers, B.A. Maximizing the guessability of symbolic input. Ext. Abstracts CHI '05 (2005), 1869-1872.
19. Wobbrock, J.O., Morris, M.R., and Wilson, A.D. User-defined gestures for surface computing. In Proc. CHI '09 (2009), 1083-1092.
20. Schwesig, C., Poupyrev, I., and Mori, E. Gummi: a bendable computer. In Proc. CHI '04 (2004), 263-270.
21. Sellen, A. J. and Harper, R. H. The Myth of the Paperless Office MIT Press (2003).
22. Stroustrup, B. The C++ Programming Language Special Edition. O'Reilly Media, Inc. (2000).

Pinstripe: Eyes-free Continuous Input on Interactive Clothing

Thorsten Karrer **Moritz Wittenhagen** **Leonhard Lichtschlag**
Florian Heller **Jan Borchers**
RWTH Aachen University
52062 Aachen, Germany
{karrer, wittenhagen, lichtschlag, flo, borchers}@cs.rwth-aachen.de

ABSTRACT
We present Pinstripe, a textile user interface element for eyes-free, continuous value input on smart garments that uses pinching and rolling a piece of cloth between your fingers. The input granularity can be controlled in a natural way by varying the amount of cloth pinched. Pinstripe input elements physically consist of fields of parallel conductive lines sewn onto the fabric. This way, they can be invisible, and can be included across large areas of a garment. Pinstripe also addresses several problems previously identified in the placement and operation of textile UI elements on smart clothing. Two user studies evaluate ideal placement and orientation of Pinstripe elements on the users' garments as well as acceptance and perceived ease of use of this novel textile input technique.

Author Keywords
smart textiles, wearable computing, eyes-free interaction, continuous input.

ACM Classification Keywords
H5.2 Information interfaces and presentation: User Interfaces—*Haptic I/O*

General Terms
Experimentation

INTRODUCTION
'Smart clothing' incorporates electronic circuits in garments, whether to control devices, to take measurements, or to output information. It is often viewed as a branch of the more general 'wearable computing' characterized by the fact that the controls or even the complete systems are tightly integrated into fabrics or garments and more closely related to their functionality. One early example of smart clothing was introduced by Rantanen et al. in 2002; their arctic suit [17] incorporates a wearable computer with a control element

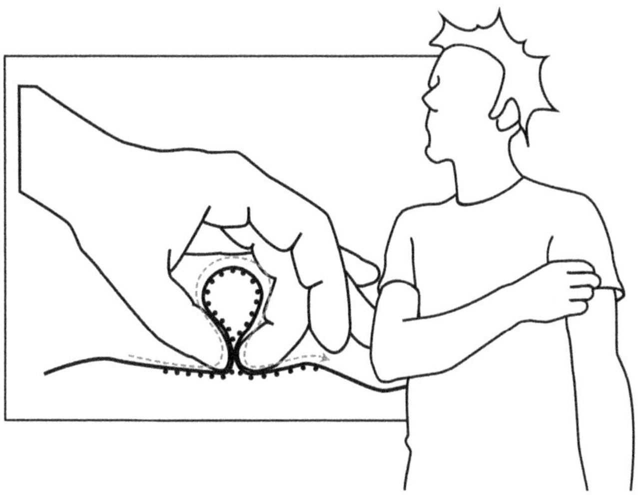

Figure 1. To use Pinstripe, you pinch and roll a fold of your garment between your fingers. This easy gesture allows you to control a linear value on a mobile device.

that was designed specifically for the wearable context and integrated in the garment itself.

Closely related to Mark Weiser's vision of ubiquitous computing [21], smart clothing makes computing invisible and, in the very sense of the word, part of the fabric of everyday life [11]. Garments containing electronic circuits or controls can be made to be visually unobtrusive and interacting with them has a chance to be socially more acceptable than openly fiddling with the interface of mobile devices such as cell phones or music players [20]. Current smart clothing systems range from DIY approaches [1] to a small number of commercially available textile music player controls (e.g., Rosner mp3blue[1]) and specialized systems in the areas of health care or sports (e.g., the 'Nike + iPod' system[2,3]).

Still, designing user interface elements for such e-textiles is hard which may be one of the reasons for the relative absence of commercial success [10] (with the notable exception of the systems mentioned above). A multitude of challenges presents itself when trying to design, engineer, and manu-

[1] http://www.mp3blue.de
[2] http://nikerunning.nike.com/nikeplus
[3] http://www.apple.com/ipod/nike

facture smart clothing which can be roughly divided into the following four areas:

Wearability, although several definitions exist, commonly demands that the electronic component of smart clothing should not influence the main functionality of the clothing itself. This includes—but is not limited to—wearing comfort, body temperature distribution and insulation, or breathability of the fabric [11, 12, 13]. A more thorough discussion on wearability and a set of guidelines for the design of wearable systems is given by Gemperle et al. [2].

Fashion compatibility asks for the electronic and interactive components in clothes not to interfere with the visual aesthetics of the garment or, ideally, to be invisible altogether [4, 14, 11, 20].

Durability is another quality that is crucial for the success of smart clothing. Just as regular garments are engineered to withstand many cycles of staining, washing, and drying, smart clothes have to exhibit the same resilience towards this kind of regular use [10].

Most importantly though, the *interaction* with control elements on smart clothing poses a set of challenges by itself [12]. They should not activate involuntarily [9], and since their surface area is delimited, they need to be easy to detect on the clothing through visual or haptic cues [4]. Their position on the body frequently shifts with changing body posture and with movement, and users on the move often require eyes-free, one-handed operation [4]. Existing systems, however, mostly resemble buttons that activate on touch; as such they are difficult to operate eyes-free and support discrete input only.

We propose Pinstripe, a textile UI element that builds upon the natural affordances of cloth and textiles and which addresses these challenges. Pinstripe lets users pinch and roll a fold of their garment between their fingers to to input continuous values (Figure 1).

RELATED WORK

Holleis et al. [4] already identify many of the problems described above. The paper presents a valuable set of guidelines to the design of wearable control elements and is one of the relatively few works to include user studies. It emphasizes the need for eyes-free, one-handed interaction and methods to ensure that commands cannot be initiated accidentally. The paper also discusses the importance of where to place control elements across the body and that these positions may change with body posture. While these results are being supported by a number of studies, the paper only takes capacitive (textile) buttons as input elements into account. Thus, we conducted a similar user test to verify the findings in case of the Pinstripe UI element.

Schwarz et al. [18] use the headphone cord of an MP3 player as an input device that can be twisted and tugged. The design is also based on the deformation of a flexible piece worn on the user's body, making the interaction gesture similar to Pinstripe, although its location is constrained to the length of the cable. The paper also mentions the requirement of wearable systems to be suitable for eyes-free operation. The system, however, is not textile-based or designed as an invisible part of a garment.

Recently, Gilliland et al. [3] explored conductive embroidery for user input widgets, most notably the 'electronic pleat'. It consists of a row of folds in the textile which detect if bend to the left or right. Similar to Pinstripe, the user can give directional and continuous value input depending on the amount of pleats folded, but the pleats change the surface structure of the garment.

Komor et al. [9] propose a chording button interface to reduce involuntary activations of textile controls. While effective, it required a higher mental effort and was slower to use than standard textile buttons. Their paper also discusses the influence of body posture on the users' ability to locate and operate control elements and reports on the difficulties that arise from the observation that different locations of the interface on the garment may afford very different interaction gestures. Our first study tries to support and complement these observations with regard to Pinstripe.

Strachnan et al. [19] present BodySpace, a portable device to build a UI element that changes its control dimension according to which position on the body it is located at that moment. Holding the device at the hip and tilting it changes the volume of a music player; holding the device next to the ear that gesture is mapped to switching tracks. Although this method solves the problem of requiring the user to find and acquire an input element that is fixed to a potentially moving position on the body or garment, it requires an external control device. Pinstripe adopts the concept of mapping functionalities to coarser body areas and being laxer about precise control positioning. At the same time, similar to BodySpace, the control gesture itself has much more expressiveness than a button press.

Kim et al. [8] performed a Wizard-of-Oz study to explore the suitability of a plethora of wearable objects for controlling a music player. Participants were given free choice as to the location and precise nature of the control gestures they were applying to the different pieces of clothing. Apart from the inspiration that can be drawn from many of the observed interactions, one important result is the difficulties users had in differentiating between the directions of symmetric control mappings (e.g. volume up/down) where no natural mapping was evident. This problem also applies—to a lesser extent—to techniques like Pinstripe as we found out in our studies .

Jung et al. [6] built a working prototype of a wearable music player that is controlled via a textile keypad. The main focus of their work lies with the demonstration of the feasibility to engineer and build such a system. Together with the work done by Post et al. [15] and Quirk et al. [16] and the experiments by Linz et al. [10], they provide valuable insight into the process and caveats of manufacturing electronic components that are embedded into textiles.

An outline of this work has been accepted as a non-archival poster submission [7] for the ACM UIST 2010 conference.

SYSTEM DESIGN

The key idea of Pinstripe is to build upon two characteristic affordances of textiles: grasping and deforming. Most clothes exhibit loose folds in different areas when worn, and Pinstripe makes use of this fact: It lets wearers provide input by pinching a part of their clothing between their thumb and another finger, creating a fold in the garment, and then rolling this fold between their fingers (Figure 1). This rolling movement changes the relative displacement of the two sides of the fold, which is measured by conductive threads sewn into the fabric, and interpreted as a continuous change in value.

This design allows us to counter the *interaction* problems mentioned above: Pinstripe is operated one-handed, and since it is not necessary to create the fold at an exact location on the garment (control is *non-local*), Pinstripe is particularly well-suited for eyes-free operation. These non-local controls also make Pinstripe highly robust against the garment shifting relative to the body during movement. While a button implemented as a local capacitive touch sensor, for example, may change its position from the back of the wrist to its side when the sleeve of the garment twists, Pinstripe works equally well no matter which part of the general wrist area the input gesture is applied to. Also, Pinstripe does not directly activate when being touched, greatly reducing the problem of involuntary activation. The user first has to pinch a fold into the garment, a gesture which is quick and easy to perform but rarely done accidentally. Body areas like the joints, where involuntary garment folding is common or desired, are, of course, less suited for Pinstripe.

The active areas thus do not need to be highlighted on the garment, and since the conductive threads only run along the inside of the textile, their impact on *fashion* is minimal. The *wearability* of the garment is not impaired either; the sensor is flexible and the threads are spaced apart enough to allow breathability and preserve other engineered properties of the fabric. Running the conductive lines across the garment is possible, potentially allowing to house the necessary electronic components, a microcontroller and a power supply, inside a seam or button. Pinstripe can be constructed as a *durable* textile interface as modern conductive yarns and flexible printed circuit boards (PCBs) and interconnects between the two are becoming increasingly robust and can withstand aging and washing [10].

Continuous Value Input

Continuous value input elements usually exhibit an inherent problem of domain scaling. A GUI slider, e.g., can only produce as many distinct values as it occupies pixels on the screen. Zooming sliders as proposed by Hürst et al. [5] are often used to mitigate that problem, for example in the Apple iOS video player. Pinstripe implements a similar approach: pinching a large fold in the textile allows coarse control over a wide range of values. Pinching a smaller fold yields more fine-grained control (Figure 2).

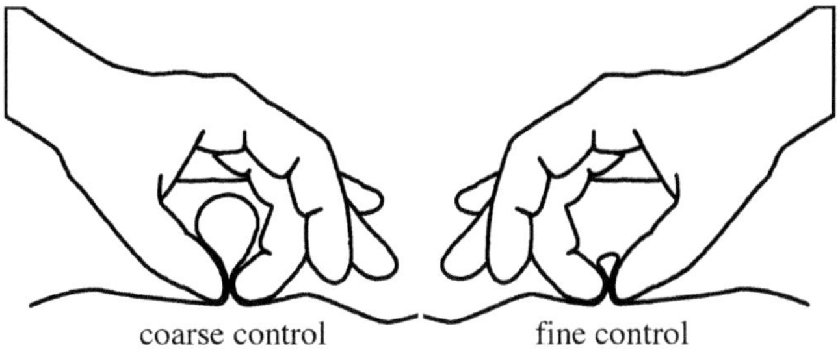

Figure 2. Pinching and rolling deeper or smaller folds of the textile provides different granularities of control.

Menu Navigation

Pinstripe can also be used to navigate linear or nested menu structures, e.g., a music player's playlist. In this scenario, rolling the cloth between the fingers moves the current selection across the list. Feedback can be given by either an auxiliary display or by auditory icons. Different pinching depths let the user navigate the list by individual items (small pinch) or by some hierarchical semantic structure (large pinch) as, e.g., different albums in a list of songs. Several techniques to issue confirmation and cancellation commands without additional control elements are possible: 'dwell time', 'activate-on-release', and 'grab-and-crumple' are the ones most suitable for use with Pinstripe. 'Dwell time' confirms a selection if the current pinch is held for a time of a few seconds and cancel the current command if the fabric is released before reaching the confirmation dwell time. Although it is easy to implement, we chose not to utilize this approach because time based interfaces are well known to negatively affect usability. 'Activate-on-release' confirms a selection implicitly when the user releases the pinch. In this case, an explicit cancel item has to be included in the list of possible selections, preferably at either end. 'Grab-and-crumple' allows the user to grab the fold in the garment with her full hand, crumpling the textile in her fist, to issue an activation command; this is easy to distinguish from the normal Pinstripe navigation gesture, both for the sensor and for the user.

Applications

Possible applications of Pinstripe are situations where users want to control mobile devices without the need to take the device out of the pocket and without the need for eye contact. Music player and mobile phone controls that can be integrated into sports apparel or street fashion are not only more comfortable to use in mobile contexts but are also often socially more acceptable [20]. Safety-critical situations like road traffic or extreme sports are other examples, where eyes-free, one-handed controls like Pinstripe may be beneficial. Finally, since the Pinstripe sensor can be integrated to the inner layer of a garment it is well-suited for use in protective clothing that requires tight sealing.

PROTOTYPE

For our first Pinstripe prototype [7], we sewed 18 lines of *Statex 117/17* 2-ply conductive thread, spaced 2mm apart, to the inside of a T-shirt sleeve (Figure 3). For the outer (visible) counterthread, we used standard black cotton. Each line

Figure 3. Lines of conductive thread sewn into the sleeve of a T-shirt and connected to a microcontroller board (left: outside, right: inside). Lines are spaced approx. 2mm apart. On the outside, the lines are also painted on for demonstration purposes—normally the black outer cotton thread would be invisible.

was connected to a digital I/O pin of a LilyPad[4] Arduino microcontroller board. The Arduino was tethered to a computer to do the signal processing.

To determine which lines are connected to each other, the microcontroller pulls one line at a time to ground level voltage, connects all other lines to 5V via internal pull-up resistors, and then checks their voltage level. If any of those lines report a level near 0V, they are recorded into a binary matrix as having a connection to the current ground line at this time. Even though the inside conductive thread directly touches the skin, skin conductance is low enough to not impede our sensor readings. The process is then repeated using the next line as the ground line, thus yielding the next row of the connection matrix (Figure 4).

The complete matrix is sent via a serial connection to a computer, where it is filtered to remove noise before being searched for a connected area of positive entries. The location and size of this 'blob' along the secondary diagonal of the matrix indicates the size of the fold the user has pinched. When the user rolls the fold, the blob changes its position along the main diagonal (Figure 4).

This information can now be used, e.g., to change the volume of a mobile MP3 player, to adjust the temperature of a garment with built-in heating, or to navigate through graphical or auditory menus on a device. For this prototype, we implemented part of the processing chain on a desktop computer to facilitate rapid prototyping. Industrial microcontrollers, however, are already powerful enough to perform these computations directly, so that future versions of Pinstripe can run untethered.

INTERACTION WITH PINSTRIPE ACROSS THE BODY

To find out where a textile sensor like Pinstripe should ideally be placed on the users clothing we conducted a user study. The goal of the experiment was to find out, which of these areas are found to be most conveniently accessible and what position, angle, and direction the users would use for pinching and rolling the fabric of their clothing. While by design Pinstripe sensors do not require exact positional placement, it is crucial to know the *angle* at which users will perform the interaction gesture. If, for example, a Pinstripe element is used perpendicular to its intended operation angle, nothing is detected because the conductive threads just fold back on themselves and do not interconnect.

[4]http://www.arduino.cc/en/Main/ArduinoBoardLilyPad

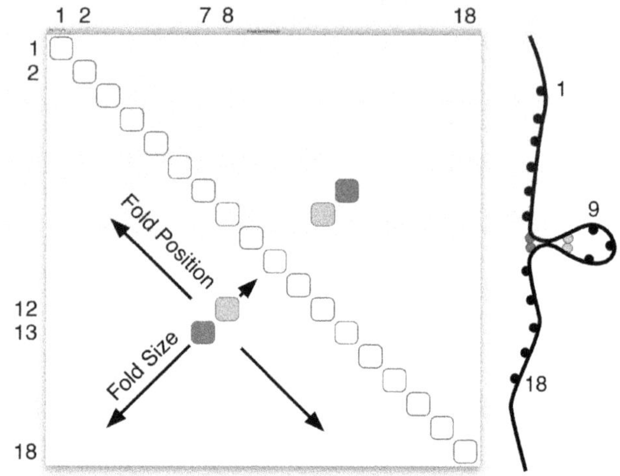

Figure 4. The connection matrix (filtered to remove outliers) and a corresponding fold. Entries in the connection matrix show which lines are currently connected through pinching. The 'blob' of all connection entries in the matrix indicates the size and placement of the fold across the conductive threads. Here, lines 7 and 13 (blue) as well as 8 and 12 (violet) are connected; the user has formed a small fold for fine-grained control. Note that the matrix is always symmetric.

First Study

We identified 16 potentially suitable areas on the human body (Figure 5) where a Pinstripe element could be conveniently placed. The grayed out areas in Figure 5 were left out on purpose as they seem socially unsuited for Pinstripe interaction. Body areas that are usually not covered by normal clothing (head, hands) or otherwise difficult to reach (feet) were also excluded. Before each trial, the Pinstripe gesture of pinching and rolling was demonstrated by the experimenter on an 'off-body' pice of cloth. This was done to avoid influencing the participants in how they would perform the gesture on their garments. Since we only wanted to study the interaction gesture itself, we did not use an actual working Pinstripe system for the experiment.

The experiment was conducted under three distinct body posture conditions (between groups, 30 users each): sitting, standing still, or walking. In each trial, participants assumed the assigned posture—in the walking condition the experimenter walked with the user—and we asked them to perform the Pinstripe gesture on each of the 16 body areas respectively, using their own clothing. Users were free to choose which hand they used for each of the areas. If a user's clothing would not permit using Pinstripe in one ore more areas, these areas were excluded from the trial (e.g., forearm while wearing a t-shirt, sternum while wearing a shirt with a low neckline). Also, to get an idea of the social impact of using Pinstripe, we allowed participants to reject body areas for social or personal reasons. No further reason for rejecting the area had to be given by the participant in this case.

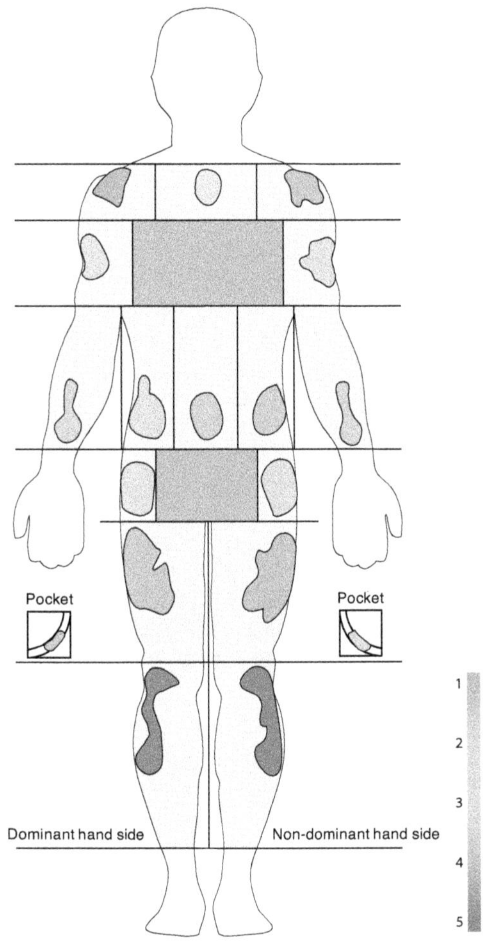

Figure 5. We selected 16 areas from the front of the human body where textile UI elements could be placed. Some areas were left out deliberately. The two 'pocket' areas were added after the study to account for an observation we made during the experiment. The 'blobs' outline the parts of each area where study participants grabbed a fold. Each 'blob' is colored according to the average grade given to the respective area.

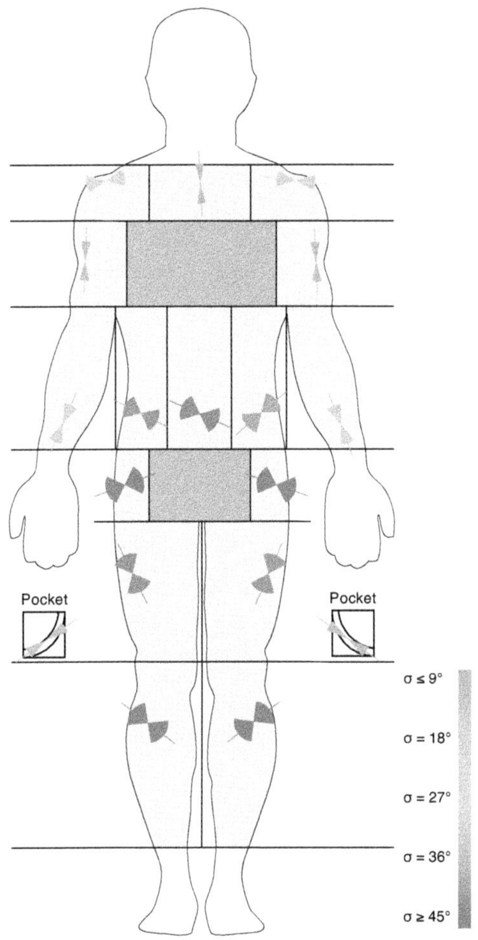

Figure 6. Visualization of the mean and standard deviation for the gesture angle distribution in each area. The colors correspond to the standard deviation; areas that are technically well suited for Pinstripe are shown in green, less suited areas are drawn in red.

For each area, participants were asked to grade how conveniently they could perform the pinch-and-roll gesture. Grades were collected on a 5-point Likert scale (1 being 'very convenient' and 5 being 'very inconvenient'). The experimenter also recorded the position and angle of the fold by drawing a mark on a template sheet (similar to Figure 5) which was vectorized later, and he noted down the use of the dominant or non-dominant hand. After the trial, participants were asked to name the one single body area they would most prefer to use Pinstripe at. We also asked users for their preferred orientation of the control gesture, i.e. mapping an inwards motion of the thumb to an increase in the controlled value or a decrease. This information was only collected for the preferred body area the user had named.

Observations

We performed the study asking people on the campus of our university and around the city to participate. Of the 90 participants, 15 were female, 75 were male. 13 participants were left handed, the rest right handed. No ambidextrous person took part in this study. 8 persons wore tight fitting clothes, 9 wore loose clothing and the rest wore regular fitting clothes. Because we conducted the study during the summer, only 16 participants wore long sleeves.

Table 1 shows an overview of the tested areas. For each area, we calculated the median grade, lower and upper quartiles of the grade, and the standard deviation of the angle of the control gesture (Figures 5, 6). Five regions received a median grade of 2, six regions received a median grade of 3 and six regions received a grade of 4 or 5. The standard deviation of the angles reach from 11.7% at the sternum to 44.7% for the lower leg. The regions with the smallest spread in gesture angles are the sternum, the pockets, and the upper as well as the lower arms. These regions also show only one mode in the distribution of gesture angles. Most of the other areas show several modes, typically two, which correspond to different ways in which users held their hands when performing the gesture in these areas. Figure 7 shows the angular distribution of the middle waist area as an example where 23

area	combined			sitting			standing			walking		
	n	$M[Q]_{grade}$	σ_{angle}	n	$M[Q]_{grade}$	σ_{angle}	n	$M[Q]_{grade}$	σ_{angle}	n	$M[Q]_{grade}$	σ_{angle}
pocket (d)	17	2 [1, 2]	14.4°	3	2 [1, 4]	20.2°	4	2 [1, 3]	17.4°	10	2 [1, 2]	4.3°
forearm (nd)	16	2 [1, 2]	20.2°	4	3 [2, 3]	2.3°	7	1 [1, 2]	9.9°	5	2 [2, 2]	33.1°
upper arm (nd)	84	2 [2, 3]	13.6°	30	2 [1, 3]	16.3°	27	2 [1, 2]	1.5°	27	3 [2, 4]	16.3°
pocket (nd)	17	2 [2, 3]	13.9°	3	2 [1, 4]	18.3°	4	4 [3, 4]	15.6°	10	2 [2, 3]	3.6°
forearm (d)	16	2 [2, 3]	19.5°	4	2 [2, 3]	4.3°	7	2 [1, 3]	9.9°	5	3 [2, 3]	30.0°
sternum	77	2 [2, 3]	11.7°	26	2 [2, 3]	14.9°	26	3 [2, 3]	10.8°	25	2 [2, 3]	7.7°
hip (d)	74	3 [2, 4]	44.8°	27	3 [2, 4]	38.4°	26	3 [2, 4]	46.4°	21	2 [2, 3]	43.6°
upper arm (d)	84	3 [2, 4]	13.6°	30	3 [2, 3]	16.2°	27	3 [2, 4]	2.3°	27	3 [3, 4]	16.3°
waist (d)	88	3 [2, 4]	39.1°	28	3 [2, 4]	36.7°	30	3 [2, 4]	38.7°	30	3 [2, 4]	41.0°
hip (nd)	74	3 [2, 4]	43.2°	27	3 [2, 4]	34.9°	26	3 [2, 4]	46.6°	21	3 [2, 4]	44.6°
waist (center)	89	3 [3, 4]	40.7°	29	3 [2, 4]	38.7°	30	3 [3, 4]	43.7°	30	3 [2, 4]	37.8°
waist (nd)	88	3 [3, 4]	36.1°	28	3 [3, 4]	32.7°	30	3 [3, 4]	40.0°	30	4 [3, 4]	33.7°
shoulder (nd)	86	4 [3, 4]	23.5°	30	4 [2, 4]	28.8°	29	4 [3, 4]	21.1°	27	4 [3, 5]	16.6°
thigh (d)	82	4 [3, 5]	40.0°	28	3 [2, 4]	43.3°	28	5 [4, 5]	40.8°	26	5 [4, 5]	30.4°
thigh (nd)	82	4 [3, 5]	38.9°	28	3 [2, 4]	44.0°	28	5 [4, 5]	38.8°	26	5 [4, 5]	29.7°
shoulder (d)	86	4 [3, 5]	26.2°	30	4 [3, 4]	35.3°	29	4 [4, 5]	16.3°	27	5 [3, 5]	16.8°
lower leg (d)	37	5 [5, 5]	43.9°	15	5 [4, 5]	43.7°	12	5 [5, 5]	44.0°	10	5 [5, 5]	41.1°
lower leg (nd)	37	5 [5, 5]	44.7°	15	5 [4, 5]	45.6°	12	5 [5, 5]	44.3°	10	5 [5, 5]	41.0°

Table 1. Count (n), median and quartiles (M[Q]), and standard deviation of the angle (σ_{angle}) for all areas and conditions. Areas are subdivided by their position on the dominant (d) or non dominant (nd) hand side of the body. The rows printed in bold denote areas that were most often chosen by the users as their preferred area. The table is sorted by the combined median grade. Smaller values are better.

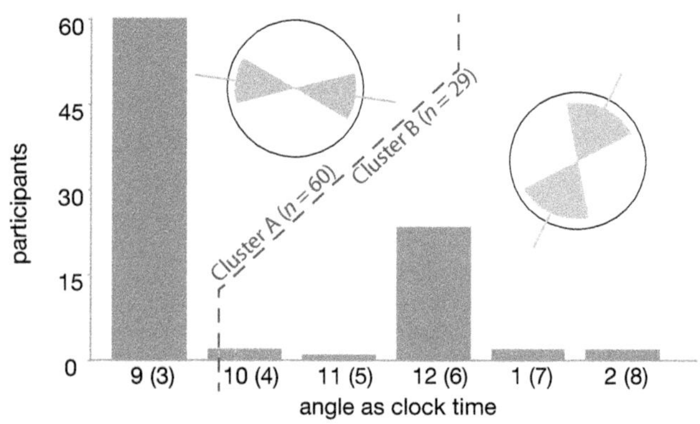

Figure 7. Histogram of angles used for the Pinstripe control gesture at the waist and visualization of two clusters obtained by k-means clustering.

people grasped a vertical fold, holding their hands horizontally, and 59 participants grasped a horizontal fold, holding their hands with the fingers pointing downwards.

Note that, since the procedure to capture the angles involved visual judgement on the side of the experimenter, we can expect the data to contain measurement noise up to ±7.5° determined by the performance of human angular perception. Even so, the current implementation of Pinstripe starts reporting wrong positions or fold sizes only when the control gesture deviates from the axis by more than ±19.8° allowing us to base out design decision on the presented data.

Participants rejected areas for social or personal reasons in 36 cases. The areas most often rejected were the lower legs (6 participants), thighs and waist (4 participants each). Some users commented that they felt uncomfortable bending down (lower leg) or touching their belly (waist) while potentially being watched by others.

Figure 5 shows the positions of the Pinstripe gesture on the garments. Positional spread is largest at the thigh area and the lower leg. The areas above and including the waist exhibit a smaller spread in position. Most of the participants (67) preferred a mapping of an outward motion of the thumb (Figure 8) to an increase in values.

As table 1 shows, the grades and angles vary with the different body postures, like we expected. While the upper arm is a rated very highly for standing and sitting, was only graded with a median of 3 for the walking condition. The forearms display the smallest spread in the sitting and standing conditions but exhibit a high increase in the walking condition.

When asked for the area with the highest preference after the test, the upper arm of the non dominant hand was mentioned most frequently (27.8%) followed by dominant hip (13.3%), pocket (12.2%) and sternum (10.0%). Only 16 people wore long sleeves allowing them to perform the gesture on the forearm, but seven chose it as the best position. Of the people who wore long sleeves 43% preferred the forearm of the non dominant hand and 25% preferred the upper arm of the non dominant hand.

Unexpected observations

When asked to perform the gesture on their hip or thigh 18 participants chose to perform the gesture using their trousers' pockets, placing their thumb inside the pocket and the fingers outside the pocket pointing down their leg. We had not foreseen Pinstripe to be used in this manner; nevertheless, twelve (≈ 67%) of these users rated it as the best position to use Pinstripe (in contrast to [20]). This is especially no-

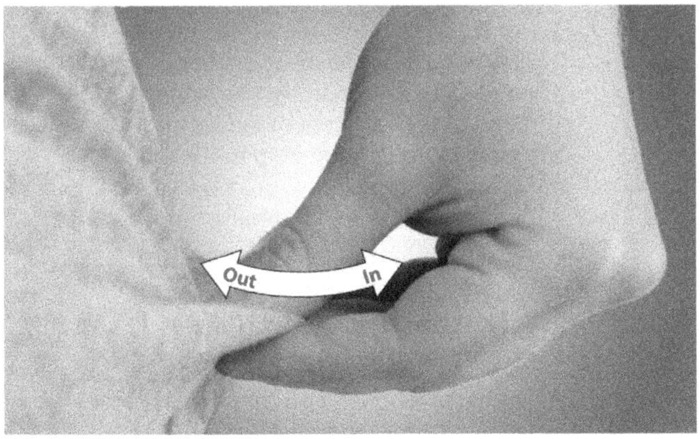

Figure 8. Typical Pinstripe gesture. Most users associate moving the thumb in the 'out' direction with an increase in value.

ticeable in the walking condition where 'pocket' even is the strongest preference. Because of this, we decided to add the pockets as areas 17 and 18 (see Figures 5 and 6) to our evaluation.

Conclusions

The study reveals several feasible positions for the Pinstripe input technique. Since Pinstripe works best when the variations in angle stay small, an area is only feasible for Pinstripe when the respective σ_{angle} is small. This is especially important for mass production of Pinstripe enabled shirts since the position of the control element has to be fixed for a larger population. In that regard, the best positions for Pinstripe are the upper arm, the sternum, and the forearm.

The overall best suited areas are the upper arms. The dominant upper arm is highly preferred and the standard deviation of angles stay consistently low. For our next prototype we chose to use the right arm to accommodate for the larger part of right handed people in the population.

The forearm seems to be a good solution for with long sleeved garments. Most people are already used to interact with watches in that area and the forearm is usually easily reachable.

The sternum received high marks by the study participants and shows the lowest standard deviation in the angle used. However, 73% of the female participants in our study wore clothes with a low neckline that would not allow interaction in that area. Additionally, two participants flagged it as an area that is socially unacceptable for interaction. We still believe that the sternum is a promising area when only looking at a part of the population. Especially in the walking condition the area was received very well which we attribute to the fact that it, compared to the arms, exhibits less movement while walking. It is likely that we would observe similar results while running. This would make the sternum well suited for a textile control to be used during sports, e.g., to control a music player during jogging.

Hips, waist, and thighs seem to be less suitable for Pinstripe. Besides some mentions of social unacceptability, the area is less restrictive in terms of hand position which increases the spread in angles used in these areas. This reduces the applicability of Pinstripe since the system can only work in one direction.

Although the shoulders show a lower spread in angle the area is harder to reach, and thus received worse grades. Additionally, seven participants complained that it would not be possible to use the system in that area when wearing a backpack.

Our study results differ from the results of the study conducted by Holleis et al. [4]. Especially the thigh was highly preferred by users in their study while receiving bad grades in our study. We think that these differences are related to the input devices evaluated in the two studies. It is more comfortable to press a button located on the thigh than trying to grasp a fold and moving it. In that regard, the grading results presented in our study are not necessarily generalizable to other input devices. However, our results regarding the social acceptance and the positions that are used for interaction may be applicable to other devices.

USING PINSTRIPE IN A REAL-WORLD SCENARIO

Based on our experience with the first prototype and our findings from the first study we created a second Pinstripe prototype. We created a larger Pinstripe sensor patch (24 threads) in the left upper arm region of another shirt; this region was identified as highly preferred in our first study for right handed people. In contrast to the first prototype, we slightly changed the position of the sensor on the sleeve from the front of the arm to its side to better match our observations of how people typically pinched their shirts in that area during the first study.

We also further reduced the noise in the detected connections by modifying the low pass filtering. A simple median-of-three filter removes outliers and the mean position and loop size are smoothed using an exponential filter. This already greatly reduces the effect of a jittering connection between two threads. Instead of the original LiliPad Arduino, we used an AVR ATmega1280[5] micro controller which has a higher clock speed (16 MHz instead of 8 MHz), thus allowing for a higher sample rate (¿5 KHz instead of 2.6 KHz for the cross-connection matrix entries) to reduce the lag caused by the filtering.

As a real-world example, we implemented a simple music player application that utilizes Pinstripe to either control volume or the current track in a playlist. We also implemented a mode unrelated to music playback where users can navigate through a graphical menu and select items from it to test the systems viability as a more general input device.

When interacting with the system, each new pinching gesture resets the origin of Pinstripe's internal coordinate system. Subsequent rolling of the fabric then applies the result-

[5] http://www.atmel.com/products/avr/

ing change in position as a relative offset to the value that is currently controlled (selected menu item, track number, or volume level). To allow coarse and fine grained control, the size of the grasped fold is used as a scaling factor for these offsets. Creating the smallest detectable fold in our implementation means pinching off a length of 2mm on the fabric (only two neighboring conductive threads connect), the largest fold is detected when the outermost conductive threads connect (cf. Figure 2). For volume control, moving the fold 2mm (distance between two threads) changes the volume by 1% for the smallest and 33% for the largest fold size. When switching through the list of tracks, 'next track' and 'previous track' commands are issued every time a threshold is crossed which happens approximately every 4mm.

Many portable music players apply volume changes directly while for track changes they first give audio feedback in the form of a beep before they switch over. In the music player mode, our system copies this behavior and additionally plays a different sound when reaching either end of the playlist. In the graphical menu mode, moving the selection mark inside the graphical menu works similar to changing tracks but no audio feedback is given. To activate the selected menu item we adopted the 'grab-and-crumple' technique described earlier. This gesture is detected when 35% of all possible thread connections are active. All of these settings were derived in a small pilot study performed beforehand with members of our lab.

Second Study

Using this second prototype, we conducted a short user test where the participants used the Pinstripe UI element to control our test application in three modes: graphical menu, music player volume, and playlist controls. We wanted to get a qualitative impression on how well people would understand the interaction and be able to use the control in a series of real-world tasks. For this experiment the participants wore the prototype Pinstripe shirt over their own short-sleeved garments. The playback software was running on a small notebook computer carried in a backpack.[6]

Before the tests, the interviewer gave a brief introduction to the Pinstripe input method and demonstrated it on his own shirt. Afterwards, people had five minutes to become familiar with the system where we asked them to think aloud. During the main part of the study, testers were asked to perform several tasks using Pinstripe (Table 2): changing tracks in a playlist of 15 songs, adjusting the volume, and navigating through the graphical menu which was displayed on an iPod touch. At the end of the trial we conducted an informal interview where we encouraged the users to share their general thoughts about Pinstripe.

Observations and Lessons Learned

From the 14 people that participated in this second study 12 were male, 2 were female. Their ages ranged from 21 to 31; only one participant was left handed. When being introduced to the Pinstripe garment most users expected touch functionality—similar to touchpads or interactive surfaces—at first. After being shown by the experimenter and a short initial learning phase, however, all participants were able to successfully use Pinstripe.

[6]A version of the control circuit currently under development will be able to directly control an iPod portable music player, making the computer unnecessary.

menu mode	1	move to the next item in the menu
	2	move back to the previous item
	3	move ahead 3 items in the menu
	4	skip to the last item in the menu
	5	go back to the first item in the menu
	6	select the item "flower" in the menu
	7	deselect the item "lightning" in the menu
volume mode	8	adjust the volume to a suitable value
	9	adjust the volume to minimum
	10	adjust the volume to maximum
	11	adjust the volume to a suitable value
playlist mode	12	move to the next item in the playlist
	13	move back to the previous item
	14	move ahead 3 items in the playlist
	15	go back to the first item in the playlist

Table 2. Tasks to be performed during the qualitative study

Sensor location and angle

In accord with our findings from the first study, the angle at which people pinched the sleeve was in alignment with the sensor lines and very consistent across all participants. At the same time, the absolute location of the interaction on the shirt sleeve could be observed to vary strongly between different users. Some pinched the cloth on the outside of the arm, others performed the control gesture on the inside. This supports our argument that non-local controls like Pinstripe have an advantage over capacitive buttons and similar designs. However, since our prototype was technically limited in the number of conductive lines and thus the size of the sensor patch, some participants still happened to 'slip off' the Pinstripe sensor during the interaction. This can be easily remedied, though, by using a larger flexible PCB as a breakout board for the microcontroller, allowing for a full-size sensor which spans the full circumference of the sleeve.

Ease of use

All participants felt that navigating the graphical menu using Pinstripe was easy. Activating menu items by grabbing the fold with the full hand and crumpling the textile was also immediately understood and performed without difficulty. Most people felt more at ease when using the menu condition—which was the only condition with graphical feedback—than using the music player controls that only gave auditory feedback.

Variations in gesture

Interestingly, none of the participants experienced problems to switch to the next track or turn the volume up but some struggled with the opposite direction. We found that, on closer observation, these users performed the Pinstripe gesture in a way that resulted in asymmetric forward and backward finger motions. They would hold the thumb against the index finger when performing the forward gesture, and then move the fold by bending and stretching the index finger while holding the thumb steady. This is similar to the way the instructor performed the demonstration gesture (Figure 9 left). When going backward they would do the opposite and bend the thumb against the steady index or middle finger. This latter movement is restricted by the smaller angular range of the thumb joint. Users performing the gestures in this way usually felt that reaching the threshold for, e.g., skipping to the previous song required a larger movement of the thumb in contrast to the index finger although the threshold is currently equal in both cases. Some participants, however, made the gesture in a totally different way: such that the thumb and fingers were parallel to the cloth fold (Figure 9 right). Instead of bending the fingers, they would form a flat surface with their fingers and then slide the thumb sideways across it. These users perceived no difference in the amount of movement required to issue forward and backward commands, presumably because the thumb can be slid sideways in both directions equally well. However, they generally felt that the distance they had to move their thumb to reach the next piece or menu item was too large.

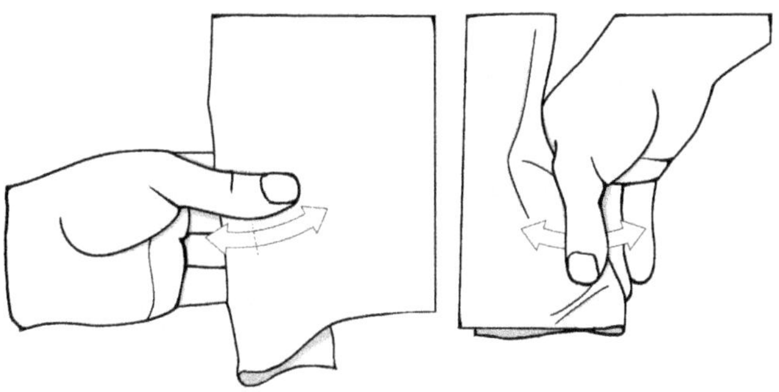

Figure 9. Alternative Pinstripe gestures. Left: This Pinstripe gesture is commonly used and has an asymmetric range. Right: This allows moving the thumb in both directions equally well but has less total range than the first gesture.

The movement direction that users expected to be associated with 'forward' commands was consistent with our predictions based on the first study. For 79% of the participants, the system's behavior matched their expectations, the rest found the mapping to be more natural the other way around.

The observations related to gesture and preferred directions indicate that Pinstripe should either allow some amount of personalization or adapt to the user. Both approaches seem feasible as clothes usually are personal items that are not commonly shared between people. A future version of our algorithm will implement this technique.

Different granularities of control

When controlling the music volume, all testers understood the domain scaling feature of Pinstripe and were able to change the volume in different levels of granularity by using smaller or deeper folds. However, some participants performed the gesture in a way that rolling the cloth between their fingers to change the position of the fold also resulted in a change of its size. This problem, which we had not not encountered in our pilot tests, made controlling the volume more difficult for these users. A possible solution would be to determine the size of the fold only when it is initially formed by the pinching gesture. This, however, would then require two interactions when a user wanted to change the scale for more fine grained navigation, e.g. first selecting a music album and then a specific song in it.

SUMMARY

Pinstripe is a continuous value input technique for smart garments that utilizes the affordances of cloth—grasping and deforming—instead of adopting known input techniques, like touch buttons, to the textile domain. This way, Pinstripe can address many of the challenges that UI elements for smart garments face: it can be operated quickly and easily in an eyes-free fashion, it is robust against involuntary activation and garment shift, and it implicitly allows to input values in different granularities. The design of Pinstripe facilitates its wearability, durability, and fashion compatibility—all important considerations when creating smart clothes.

In a first user study we identify locations on users' clothes that are suitable for Pinstripe interaction, both from the viewpoint of the system (low variance in gesture angle) and the user (acceptance and preference). We also discuss how and to what extent other textile input methods may benefit from the results of this study.

To demonstrate the applicability of our approach, we report the results of a qualitative second user study where participants interact with a Pinstripe prototype in a real-world scenario. Users were able to use Pinstripe to control the volume of a music player application in different granularities and to change tracks, as well as navigate through a graphical menu on a mobile device. From our observations during the test, we got valuable insights into how users experience the interaction with Pinstripe. Also, we learned that different users interact with Pinstripe using different gestures; a fact we will account for in future iterations of our prototype.

FUTURE WORK

For our current prototypes we are sewing each sensor line individually into the shirts. This process is laborious and prone to inaccuracies that limit the sensor's performance. Conductive lines that are directly woven into the fabric of clothes may provide a much more consistent line spacing, higher density, and larger sensor surfaces while at the same time boosting durability and manufacturability. Also we are creating an untethered, self-contained version of a Pinstripe shirt that can directly control, and is powered by, an iPod mobile music player.

Apart from the sensor locations on the upper and lower arms, we will investigate the promising concept of placing textile input elements inside the pockets as users commented positively on the perceived convenience and the low negative social impact of that position. This, of course, requires a modification of the algorithm because the two sides of the 'fold' always touch; the system would only look at deviations from a default pattern in the cross-connection matrix.

Further experiments are needed to verify the consistency of Pinstripe gestures for single users over a larger timeframe, not only for a population of users over a single trial as we did in this paper. Also, we are planning to perform a more detailed analysis of the influence of different cuts and fabrics of clothing on the applicability of Pinstripe.

ACKNOWLEDGEMENTS

This work was partially funded by the German B-IT Foundation and by the German Government through its UMIC Excellence Cluster for Ultra-High Speed Mobile Information and Communication and its HumTec Human Technology Center at RWTH Aachen University.

REFERENCES

1. L. Buechley. A construction kit for electronic textiles. In *Proc. ISWC '06*, pages 83–90, 2006.
2. F. Gemperle, C. Kasabach, J. Stivoric, M. Bauer, and R. Martin. Design for wearability. *Proc. ISWC '89*, page 116, Jan 1998.
3. S. Gilliland, N. Komor, T. Starner, and C. Zeagler. The Textile Interface Swatchbook: Creating graphical user interface-like widgets with conductive embroidery. In *Proc. ISWC '10*, pages 1–8, 2010.
4. P. Holleis, A. Schmidt, S. Paasovaara, A. Puikkonen, and J. Häkkilä. Evaluating capacitive touch input on clothes. *Proceedings of the 10th international conference on Human computer interaction with mobile devices and services*, pages 81–90, Jan 2008.
5. W. Hürst, G. Götz, and P. Jarvers. Advanced user interfaces for dynamic video browsing. In *Proc. MULTIMEDIA 2004*, pages 742–743, 2004.
6. S. Jung, C. Lauterbach, and W. Weber. A digital music player tailored for smart textiles: First results. In *Avantex Symposium, Frankfurt, Germany*, Jan 2002.
7. T. Karrer, M. Wittenhagen, F. Heller, and J. Borchers. Pinstripe: Eyes-free Continuous Input Anywhere on Interactive Clothing. In *Proc. UIST '10 EA*, pages 429–430, 2010.
8. K. Kim, D. Joo, and K.-P. Lee. Wearable-object-based interaction for a mobile audio device. In *Proc. CHI EA '10*, pages 3865–3870, Apr 2010.
9. N. Komor, S. Gilliland, J. Clawson, M. Bhardwaj, M. Garg, C. Zeagler, and T. Starner. Is It Gropable? — Assessing the Impact of Mobility on Textile Interfaces. In *Proc. ISWC '09*, pages 71–74, Jan 2009.
10. T. Linz, C. Kallmayer, R. Aschenbrenner, and H. Reichl. Embroidering Electrical Interconnects with Conductive Yarn for The Integration of Flexible Electronic Modules into Fabric. In *Proc. ISWC '05*, pages 86–91, Jan 2005.
11. D. Marculescu, R. Marculescu, N. Zamora, P. Stanley-Marbell, P. Khosla, S. Park, S. Jayaraman, S. Jung, C. Lauterbach, W. Weber, T. Kirstein, D. Cottet, J. Grzyb, G. Troster, M. Jones, T. Martin, and Z. Nakad. Electronic textiles: A platform for pervasive computing. *Proceedings of the IEEE*, 91(12):1995–2018, Jan 2003.
12. A. Martin, R. Hurford, J. McCann, and D. Smith. Designing Wearables: A Brief Discussion. In *Proc. The Role of Design in Wearable Computing, Workshop of ISWC '07*, page 2, Jan 2007.
13. J. McCann, R. Hurford, and A. Martin. A Design Process for the Development of Innovative Smart Clothing that Addresses End-User Needs from Technical, Functional, Aesthetic and Cultural View Points. In *Proc. ISWC '05*, pages 70–77, Jan 2005.
14. R. O'Donnell. Prolog to Electronic Textiles: A Platform for Pervasive Computing. *Proceedings of the IEEE*, 91(12):1995–2018, Jan 2003.
15. E. Post, M. Orth, P. Russo, and N. Gershenfeld. E-broidery: Design and fabrication of textile-based computing. *IBM Systems Journal*, 39(3–4):840, Jan 2000.
16. M. Quirk, T. Martin, and M. Jones. Inclusion of Fabric Properties in the E-Textile Design Process. In *Proc. ISWC '09*, pages 37–40, Jan 2009.
17. J. Rantanen, J. Impio, T. Karinsalo, M. Malmivaara, A. Reho, M. Tasanen, and J. Vanhala. Smart clothing prototype for the arctic environment. *Personal and Ubiquitous Computing*, 6(1):3–16, Jan 2002.
18. J. Schwarz, C. Harrison, S. Hudson, and J. Mankoff. Cord input: an intuitive, high-accuracy, multi-degree-of-freedom input method for mobile devices. In *Proc. CHI '10*, pages 1657–1660, Apr 2010.
19. S. Strachan, R. Murray-Smith, and S. O'Modhrain. Bodyspace: inferring body pose for natural control of a music player. *CHI EA '07*, page 2006, Apr 2007.
20. A. Toney, B. Mulley, B. Thomas, and W. Piekarski. Social weight: designing to minimise the social consequences arising from technology use by the mobile professional. *Personal and Ubiquitous Computing*, 7(5):309–320, 2003.
21. M. Weiser. The computer for the 21st century. *Scientific American*, 272(3):78–89, 1995.

Grips and Gestures on a Multi-Touch Pen

Hyunyoung Song[1,3,4], Hrvoje Benko[1], François Guimbretière[3,4], Shahram Izadi[2], Xiang Cao[2], Ken Hinckley[1]

[1]Microsoft Research
One Microsoft Way
Redmond, WA 98052

[2]Microsoft Research Cambridge
7 JJ Thomson Avenue
Cambridge CB3 0FB, UK

{benko,shahrami,xiangc,kenh}@microsoft.com

[3]University of Maryland
Computer Science
College Park, MD 20742
hsong@cs.umd.edu

[4]Cornell University
Information Science
Ithaca, NY 14850
francois@cs.cornell.edu

ABSTRACT
This paper explores the interaction possibilities enabled when the barrel of a digital pen is augmented with a multi-touch sensor. We present a novel multi-touch pen (*MTPen*) prototype and discuss its alternate uses beyond those of a standard stylus, such as allowing new touch *gestures* to be performed using the index finger or thumb and detecting how users *grip* the device as a mechanism for mode switching. We also discuss the hardware and software implementation challenges in realizing our prototype, and showcase how one can combine different grips (tripod, relaxed tripod, sketch, wrap) and gestures (swipe and double tap) to enable new interaction techniques with the MTPen in a prototype drawing application. One specific aim is the elimination of some of the comfort problems associated with existing auxiliary controls on digital pens. Mechanical controls such as barrel buttons and barrel scroll wheels work best in only a few specific hand grips and pen rotations. Comparatively, our gestures can be successfully and comfortably performed regardless of the rotation of the pen or how the user grips it, offering greater flexibility in use. We describe a formal evaluation comparing MTPen gestures against the use of a barrel button for mode switching. This study shows that both swipe and double tap gestures are comparable in performance to commonly employed barrel buttons without its disadvantages.

Author Keywords
Digital stylus, digital pen, multi-touch, grip detection.

ACM Classification Keywords
H5.2 [Information interfaces and presentation]: User Interfaces- Graphical user interfaces.

General Terms
Design

INTRODUCTION
Digital pens and styli are popular input devices for digital tasks, such as annotating and drawing, due to their ability to leverage the fine precision of a pen tip and the dexterity of human hands. Beyond this fine control of a physical pen, digital pens also support common interface tasks such as mode switching and scrolling. However, current commercial digital pens offer limited additional input capabilities, mainly consisting of mechanical buttons or scroll wheels mounted on the barrel of the pen [16, 27]. These options provide *explicit* controls and are simple to operate, but are limited in number and fixed in location and size. The use of mechanical buttons and wheels also leads to many usability challenges. Due to different hand sizes or different tasks, users often wish to hold their pens in different ways, and the need to access these mechanical controls greatly restricts the variety of grips that can be used. In addition to these grip restrictions, some grips can result in users mistakenly triggering buttons when simply intending to ink. Some grips require users to rotate or reposition the pen to acquire a physical button on the stylus when wanting to access on-screen context menus.

Figure 1. Our MTPen prototype. Inset image shows touch data imaged by the multi-touch sensor around the barrel.

Previous studies suggest using other dimensions of a digital pen such as rolling [4] or tilting [25] as alternative explicit controls [4, 23, 25] required by digital interfaces. Additionally, researchers have demonstrated that grip can be leveraged as an *implicit* dimension that conveys some user intention (or state) as users interact with a device [14, 24, 29]. This can also be applied to a pen. There are many instances where the way in which the pen is being held can convey information. For example, when a user holds the pen using the conventional tripod grip [13] (Figure 1), this may indicate that she requires precision for a task such as inking or drawing. Clearly the use of grips could become an important cue in increasing the input vocabulary of pen users.

In this paper we explore the possibilities of broadening the gestural language of the digital pen through multi-touch sensing along the pen barrel. We demonstrate how this novel combination allows for sensing of both the handgrips for implicit controls, and finger-based touch gestures for explicit controls, all while preserving the symmetric nature of a normal pen. We provide the following four contributions:

First, we present a custom-built and novel digital pen prototype called *MTPen* with a capacitive multi-touch sensor wrapped around an off-the-shelf stylus (Figure 1).

Second, we demonstrate the implementation of a recognizer that can distinguish different hand grips using the contact data from fingers resting on the multi-touch sensor. This recognizer also detects finger-based touch gestures such as horizontal or vertical swipes and double taps with the thumb or index finger. We further discuss the challenges in building such a recognizer, in particular interpreting contact data on a pen device of curved cylindrical nature coupled with the close proximity of fingers resulting in many merged contact points.

Third, we demonstrate how the sensed grips and gestures on the MTPen device can be combined into novel interaction techniques to provide the ability to switch modes, adjust continuous parameters, and issue customized commands within a sample drawing application.

Finally, to confirm the viability of our finger gesture approach, we conduct a formal evaluation to compare our pen with an existing mode switching technique, the pen barrel button. We found that the performance of our proposed finger gestures, swipe or double tap, are comparable to mechanical barrel button without its disadvantages.

RELATED WORK

Our work builds upon three distinct areas of prior research that are covered in turn in this section. The first is the body of work that investigated adding additional input controls to the digital pen. The second is work that explored the use of touch sensing on the surface of existing input devices to extend interaction vocabulary. The third covers studies in grips and pen design in ergonomics.

Additional Input Controls on Digital Pens

Digital pens have been augmented with auxiliary hardware controls such as one or two buttons or a scroll wheel (e.g. Wacom's Airbrush) to manipulate the pen's properties or on-screen widgets. However, Li et al. [15] performed a comparative study of five mode switching techniques and concluded that clicking a mechanical button on a digital stylus was not the optimal solution. Inspired by their study, we use the same methodology to compare our new gestures on MTPen – the swipe and double tap – with the de facto standard barrel button implementation.

Some researchers have proposed solutions to mode switching such as using a distinct gesture in the hover zone above the tablet to change the modality [8, 22], and redesigning the entire pen interface to use ink crossing [1] or pigtail strokes [10].

Another line of research for pen control is to utilize other pen parameters such as rolling [4], tilting [25], pressure [19], and combined rolling and motion [23] that can be used for changing modes or providing further single handed input mechanisms. Pen rolling [4] at a resolution of 10 degrees around its longitudinal axis can be used to control a mode change and multi-parameter input. The *Tilt Menu* [25] is a technique to generate secondary input by tilting the angle of the pen to select one of the eight pie menus. *Pressure widgets* [19] demonstrated how six levels of pressure can, with appropriate visual feedback, improve selection tasks. Suzuki et al. [23] explored pen rolling and shaking as an interaction technique. Our approach in enabling finger touch gestures on a pen adds a new perspective to this body of research.

Extending Device Capabilities through Touch Sensing

While the MTPen is the first prototype to utilize a multi-touch sensor on the outer barrel of a pen, multi-touch sensing technologies have been demonstrated on many other input devices to extend interaction capabilities. Most recently, *Mouse 2.0* [26] showed a series of re-designs of the traditional mouse to support touch sensing on the outer casing.

Researchers have also attempted to understand the user's intention (or mode switch) by capturing the *implicit input* that occurs in the ways people hold their devices [14, 24, 29]. For example, *Graspables* [24] demonstrated how a coarse grid of capacitive sensors can be wrapped around various form-factors and shapes to allow different grips to be recognized and utilized for input. Our work extends this approach and uses a much finer grained multi-touch sensor to understand the movements of the user's fingers while grasping a pen.

Combining a multi-touch table surface with pen-based usage scenario has also been explored in recent years [5, 12, 31]. These projects explored bimanual techniques that support multi-touch input with the non-dominant hand, whilst supporting pen-based interaction using the dominant hand. Such interactions have been employed for drawing [5], annotation in active reading environment [12], and even solving math problems [31]. In comparison, our MTPen provides touch directly on the barrel of the pen and explores a novel way for touch and pen to be combined in a single hand.

Grips and Pens in Ergonomics

Fields such as ergonomics and surgery have been exploring the dynamics of the hand and grips for digital [30] and physical pen design [20], particularly in the context of drawing and writing. Goonetilleke [20] investigated how different barrel shapes (triangular, square, elliptical, hexagonal, octagonal, circular) of the pen can offer improved drawing and writing performance.

In prior studies, Napier [18] provided valuable observations that we found our work on. First, according to Napier, *"during a purposive prehensile action, the posture of the hand bears a constant relationship to the nature of that activity"*. Napier also lays the foundation for our postulation that while griping the pen, the majority of the hand is used to stabilize the grasp while only certain fingers remain free to carry out a gesture. These insights have been valuable in designing and developing our research prototype.

Figure 2. Different grips observed in our pilot investigation: (a) Tripod grip is used for precise writing or drawing, (b) relaxed tripod grip is frequently used for less precise tasks. (c) Sketch grip, (d) tuck grip, and (e) wrap grip is an example of a grip not frequently used with digital pens but is often used with physical tools.

MOTIVATING INVESTIGATION

To help better understand the limitations of current digital pens in everyday computing scenarios, we conducted an observational design study with expert users of digital pens. We interviewed four regular digital pen users (2 male, 2 female) aged 27–35. Each used a digital stylus for more than half of their computing time on a regular basis. The participants were long-term pen users (ranging 5–15 years) and were industrial designers and artists by profession. All participants used Intuos/Cintiq Grip pens [27], which feature two buttons on the barrel, a pressure sensitive tip, and a pressure sensitive eraser (Figure 2b-d). We asked them to fill out a questionnaire (with ratings on a 7 point Likert scale) before the interview, which asked about their everyday pen usage. We then observed how they use their digital pens in their work environment and conducted one-on-one interviews that focused on understanding two issues: a) the extent to which the current pen design supports changing the pen grip while inking, gesturing, or relaxing, and b) how users access the mechanical buttons on the pen.

While all our users expressed that they would prefer to hold the pen in different ways depending on the task, they commented that the fixed button location makes changing the grip difficult. As a result, three of our participants adapted their grips in order to be able to activate the buttons, e.g., we observed that P3 – who has been using digital pens for over 15 years – had developed an awkward style for griping the Wacom pen so that both buttons were always underneath his finger. P4 commented, "*While digital drawing applications excel in replicating other physical drawing tool properties, the design of digital stylus is not only limited to replicating a pen but even constrains how we actually hold the pen.*"

When asked about the different pen grips that the users currently employ or would like to use, the most common grip for all our four designers was the *tripod* grip [13] (Figure 2a). It is a type of a precision grip [18] that is most commonly used in writing and drawing. P2 demonstrated a relaxed version, i.e., a *relaxed tripod* grip (Figure 2b), used not only to draw and write but also to manipulate their general software controls. P1 mentioned that she would relax her tripod grip when less precision is required such as using a marker for highlighting documents. P3 demonstrated a *sketch* grip which is used to create long and consistent strokes especially when the tablet was angled (Figure 2c). When transitioning between different input controls, P1 adjusted their grip to balance the pen in between the fingers such that the pen was tucked underneath the middle finger (*tuck* grip, Figure 2d). Finally, P4 showed a *wrap* grip that they would use to hold a crayon, a stamp, or a brush, or when a drawing tool is being transported (Figure 2e).

While participants all agreed that they would appreciate more controls (buttons or scroll wheels) for interacting with their pen (*I would like more control while holding the pen* averaged 6 - on the 7 point Likert scale) they all complained that the current barrel button was difficult to access (*The button is the right size* averaged - 2.25 on the Likert scale, and *the right location* averaged – 3). This is likely due to the one-size-fits-all design of the barrel button which does not account for the diversity in hand sizes and grips. P1 and P4 pointed out that they put down and re-grasp their pens when they have to change input devices (e.g. keyboard or other auxiliary controls on the tablet). This frequent transition makes the acquisition of the button difficult for them, as the button is often not directly under their finger when they retrieve the pen. Other participants resonated highly with that sentiment in their answers (*I change my pen grip to access the barrel button* – 6.75, *I rotate the pen to access the barrel button* – 6.75). At the same time, users would often "hide" the button by rotating the pen when drawing to reduce accidental activations, then rotate the pen back in order to use the button again later (*I sometimes press the barrel button accidently when I don't intend to* – 5.75).

In addition to these hardware design limitations, our participants complained that a single (or two) button input is very limiting given that their drawing software is overloaded with numerous options and controls. While the scroll wheel on Wacom Airbrush pen affords a bit more in terms of continuous input, P4 expressed the desire to manipulate more controls while inking, which is currently difficult even with additional inputs using the non-dominant hand (e.g., keyboard or side buttons on the tablet). All of these observations demonstrate a need to increase the interactive potential of the pen by supporting different grips and alternative input techniques.

MULTI-TOUCH PEN IMPLEMENTATION

Motivated by the feedback from the experts, we chose to redesign the standard digital pen to activate mode switching regardless of user hand posture, while allowing for a diversity of hand grips. We designed a custom pen which does not employ discrete mechanical buttons, but instead uses a touch-sensitive barrel as a means to explore a new approach to the problem. MTPen allows for sensing of different hand *grips*, and enables auxiliary controls via touch *gestures* along the barrel. In addition, our design opens up possibilities to combine grips and gestures that allow access to greater number of interactions than are available using the standard pen models with mechanical buttons.

Hardware Design

Our prototype is built around a standard Wacom Intuos/Cintiq grip pen which is augmented with a custom capacitive sensor (Figure 3). We designed a plastic cylindrical enclosure around the pen onto which we overlaid a flexible matrix of capacitive-sensing electrodes to track the image of user's hand. Our enclosure eliminates access to the barrel button and makes the pen completely smooth and cylindrical. The length of the pen is 175 mm with a diameter of 16mm.

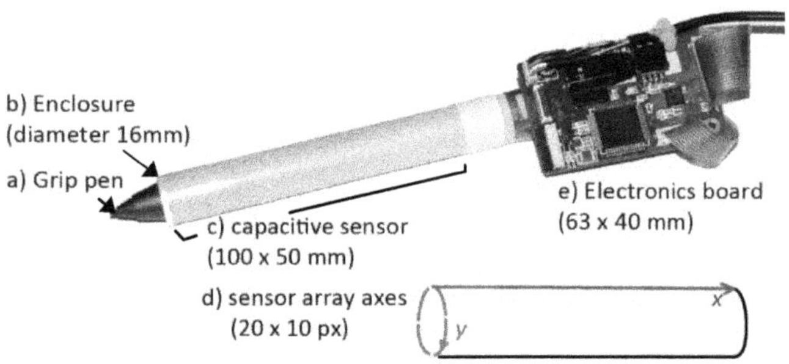

Figure 3. MTPen hardware prototype

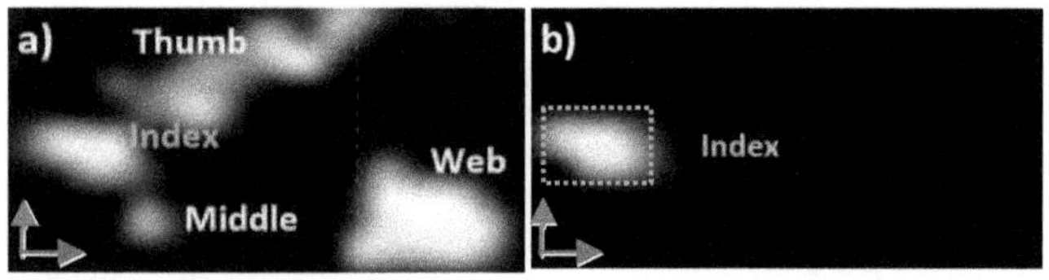

Figure 4. Touch and gesture sensing. (a) Raw sensor image captures the ambiguous hand parts. (b) We segment *the dynamic contacts* (Index) from the rest of the *static contacts*. Notice that the vertical (red) arrow that corresponds to the longitudinal (x) axis and the horizontal (blue) arrow that corresponds to the circumference (y) axis of the pen from Figure 3.

The sensor is positioned 10mm from the tip of the pen, and covers an actual sensed area of 50mm x 100mm which is roughly 2/3 of the pen's barrel area. This is sufficient to sense many of the typical hand contacts while using the pen. The capacitive sensor is covered with a thin protective coating (architectural velum) to prevent direct electrical contact between the user's fingers and the sensor. We chose architectural velum as its surface properties made it comfortable to both hold the pen and to slide the fingers to perform gestures.

The sensor is capable of tracking multiple simultaneous contacts on a 20x10 grid of sensing elements printed on a flexible substrate using conductive ink. The raw capacitive sensor values are reported as 20x10 pixel grayscale images (Figure 1) at 100Hz, and processed to extract and track individual touch contacts. Note that the figures show interpolated grayscale images for clarity and smoothness; however, all processing is performed on the 20x10 grid.

We affixed the PCB (63mm x 40mm) at the rear end of the pen, which controls the sensor, captures raw capacitance values, and communicates these to a computer via USB. While the electronics board is exposed in our current hardware prototype, integrating it into the pen itself and using wireless communication in the future should make the pen easier to handle.

Sensor Data Processing

Compared to the typical fingertip use of the traditional touch-screen, our multi-touch sensor captures contacts from different sections of the hand (e.g. finger tips and sides, web of the thumb, palm, etc.). As such, we share similar problems as described in the Mouse 2.0 project [26] in that our device needs to be held while interacting. Thus, any touch-gesture recognition not only needs to focus on specific contacts and their movement, but also to tolerate the existence of numerous additional contacts in order to support the user grasping the device.

In addition, due to the small size of the pen and the nature of the hand grip, contacts closely group together and often merge into larger connected blobs. In response to these challenges, we alter standard computer vision touch processing techniques (e.g., Rekimoto's Holowall [17]) that determine separate connected components in the image and track them frame-to-frame.

We classify contacts into two categories based on their temporal characteristics: *static* and *dynamic*. The static contacts (Figure 4a) do not exhibit much movement and mostly remain in constant size and location. These static contacts are usually mapped to the parts of the hand sustaining the majority of the pen weight (e.g., thumb, middle finger, and web of the thumb). The dynamic contacts (Figure 4b) exhibit more movements and usually correspond to the agile finger (e.g., index, thumb) that is used for versatile purposes (e.g., gesturing, precision control, or pushing a button).

We extract these two types of images to detect grips and gestures on the surface of the pen. First, we process the static sensor image to detect the handgrip. Then, we segment out the dynamic contacts and process them to detect gestures.

$$\text{DynamicImage}(x,y) = \text{Signal}(x,y) - \text{Baseline}(x,y); \quad (1)$$
$$\text{Baseline}(x,y) = \text{Signal}(x,y) * \alpha + \text{Baseline}(x,y) * (1 - \alpha);$$

To obtain the dynamic image, we employ a decay function (Equation 1) over the entire image, which preserves only the moving elements, while the static contact areas are effectively removed. To compute this *DynamicImage*, the capacitive signal value is compared with the baseline value at each pixel location (x,y), which in turn is updated given a decay value ($\alpha = 0.03$). We track the connected components in this decayed image and thus report only moving contact points for the gesture recognition.

This simple approach works well in practice to segment moving contacts from the rest of the hand while the user maintains a stable grip; however, when the user acquires the pen, puts the pen down, or simply repositions the pen in her hand, many dynamic contacts can temporarily occur on the surface. We detect these re-griping events by observing the size of the bounding box fitted around all the pixels present in the dynamic image (Figure 4b, green rectangle). During the grip changes, the size of this bounding box is fairly large since many contacts are moving (Figure 5). When only a single finger is moving, the bounding box is considerably smaller. By focusing on small overall movements, we can isolate the movement of the single finger and use that information to detect finger gestures regardless of how the user holds the pen. The overall amount of contact pixels (i.e., their pixel sum) can be used to easily detect when the pen is being held or not.

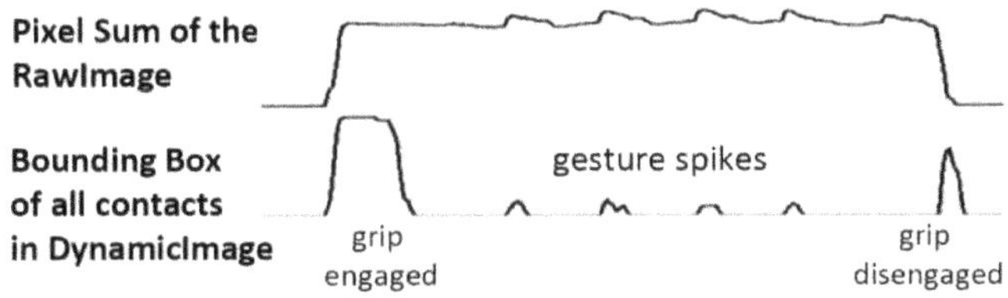

Figure 5. Temporal sequence of acquiring the pen, performing four finger swipes followed by the release of the pen.

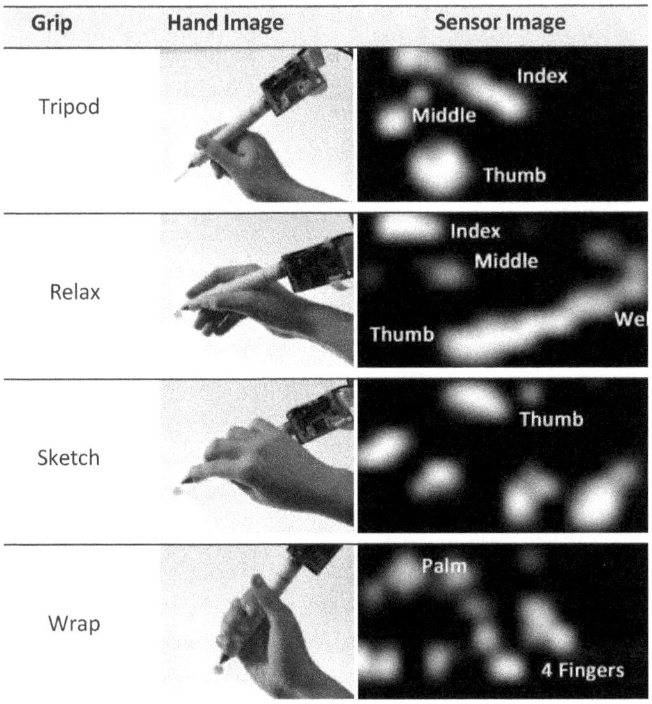

Figure 6. Different grips we recognize and their corresponding static sensor images.

Grip Recognition

To support the recognition of different hand grips, we track the entire shape of the hand using the static sensor image. When users are maintaining a stable grip, we match it against a grip image database using the Naïve Bayes classifier. Taylor and Bove have showed that this classifier provides a good trade-off between accuracy and speed of classification [24].

Since we need to detect hand grips regardless of how the user orients the pen in their hand, we extract features that are rotationally invariant along the pen's cylindrical axis. The position of finger or hand contacts is not rotationally invariant, so instead we use features that include the number of the contacts, their sizes, orientation, and eccentricity in our recognition algorithm. We currently disambiguate between four different types of grips: tripod, relaxed tripod, sketch, and wrap (Figure 6).

To gauge the effectiveness of our initial recognizer, we used a traditional *training and testing* approach. We trained the recognizer for each individual user while adding more training images for faulty grips. We then collected data from ten pilot users who each provided 2000 recordings per grip. The recognition rate for four grips was 87% when using each user's training data individually. The wrap grip was the most problematic grip to recognize due to the great variability of the grip between grasps of the same user. Removing the wrap grip and reducing the set to three grips improves our overall recognition to 94% success rate.

Gesture Recognition

In addition to different grips, we recognize two types of finger gestures on the MTPen: *double tap* and *swipe*. Both gestures are simple to perform, and simple to detect in our dynamic sensor image (as described previously).

Double tap: If two consecutive taps are reported within a threshold distance (d<5mm), and time span (t<200ms), they are recognized as a *double tap*. These thresholds were chosen after testing distinguishable thresholds on several pilot users with different hand sizes. Our recognizer also reports the location of each double tap.

Swipe: This gesture is performed when the user slides their finger along the barrel of the pen. The distance of the trail (> 0.5 mm), and the ratio of the width to the height of the bounding box (>3) are used to recognize a swipe. The recognizer reports the following: the coordinate of the starting point and the current point, the direction and the distance of the movement. As such, swipe can be used to control a simple mode switch or a continuous parameter.

MTPEN INTERACTION TECHNIQUES

Combining our gestures and grips in interesting ways opens up a large set of possible interactions for the MTPen users. We highlight these possibilities in a sample drawing application. Throughout these interactions, we assume that the base grip is the tripod grip, and note when other grips are required.

Automatic Focus Control using Engagement of the Pen

MTPen can detect whether the pen is being held or engaged. Observed in our interviews, designers frequently alternate back and forth between pen and other input devices (keyboard, mouse, etc). When MTPen detects that the user's hand is in contact with the pen, the input focus changes to the drawing area. When the user puts down their pen, the focus is passed onto non-pen-based interface components. Similar "engagement" interaction has previously been suggested by Hinckley and Sinclair [11].

Double Tap Color Picker

Once the double tap is detected, a color picker marking menu is brought up to easily change the color of the pen. Since changing the color of the ink is one of the most frequent tasks, we decided to map it to the double tap (Figure 7a).

However, as double tapping is a simple mode switch, it can also be mapped to trigger other interactions such as mouse right click or bringing up other menu widgets.

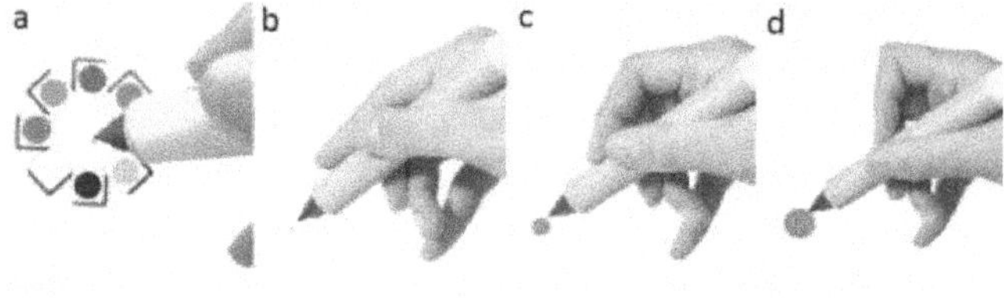

Figure 7. User controls mapped to finger gestures: (a) Control widget (e.g., color palette) pops up when double tap gesture occurs. (b-d) Continuous parameter such as the pen tip size is mapped to our swipe gesture.

Continuous Pen Size Control using Swipe Gesture

Our swiping gesture also provides the capability to control continuous parameters. Users can change the size of the pen tip by swiping their index or thumb. When swiping occurs during inking (pen-down state), users can create a single stroke of varying width.

Although pressure of the pen tip is frequently mapped to the width of the pen stroke, users can neither control the parameter using the pressure nor lock it at a certain value. Comparatively, our approach provides a scroll wheel-like control that can be accessed explicitly regardless of where and how the user is holding a pen (Figure 7b-d).

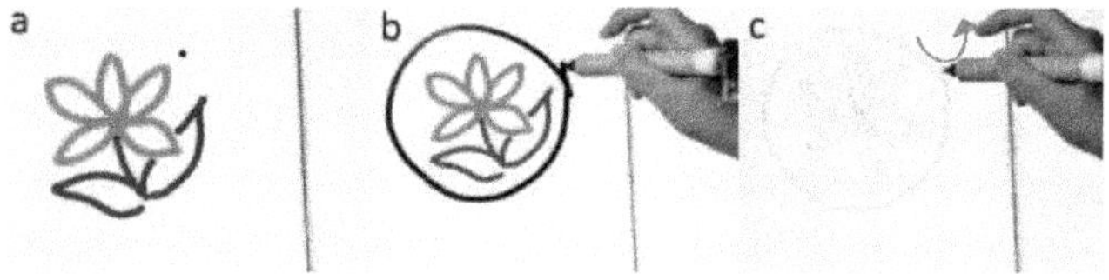

Figure 8. Swipe lasso selection: When the index finger (or thumb) swipes the barrel of the pen after a self-intersecting ink trace, the ink turns into a gesture ink, hence selecting the contents inside.

Swipe Lasso Selection

Another frequent operation that occurs in a drawing application is selection and repositioning of objects on the canvas. If a swipe gesture is detected after a self-intersecting ink stoke, the stroke turns into a lasso selection [10] (Figure 8), allowing the specified object to be moved on the canvas.

In this specific example, we demonstrate h*ow finger gestures* (e.g., a swipe meant to activate the resizing of the pen tip and one meant to lasso a selection) combined with *ink strokes* can be distinguished by the nature of the stroke. When the swipe occurs without a self-intersecting stroke, the magnitude of the finger swipe is used to change the pen tip width, while when the swipe occurs after a self-intersection, it indicates a lasso selection.

When a user swipes to change the current ink to become a selection ink, the mode is retroactively applied to the entirety of the stroke. Synchronizing controls and inks at the same time is a well identified problem in pen-based interfaces [15], and our approach is similar to that of Guimbretiere where the synchronization is relaxed between ink and a mode switch [9]. In our prototype, we relax the time period in which users can "mode" the current ink via finger gestures. Such design alleviates the burden of ensuring that every decision is made before starting their ink.

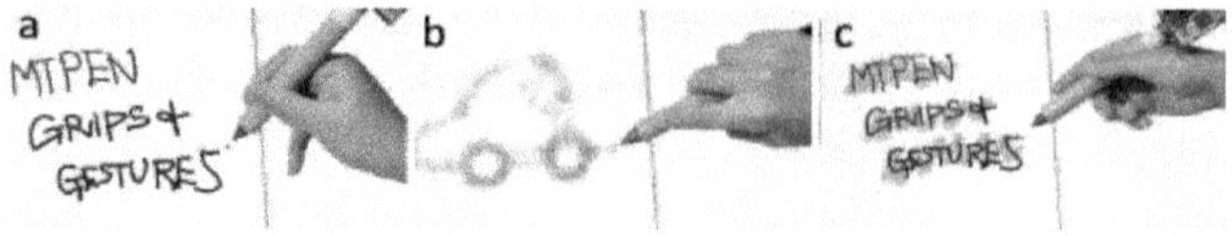

Figure 9. Pen selection based on grip: (a) Pen ink for the tripod grip, (b) paintbrush for the sketch grip, and (c) highlighter for the relaxed tripod grip.

Grip-based Pen Selection

In our painting demonstration application, we apply different pen grips to different pen types: tripod grip is mapped to a normal pencil, sketch grip is mapped to a paintbrush, and relaxed tripod grip is mapped to a highlighter (Figure 9). Thus the user can implicitly change modes, simply by changing their grip.

Page Selection using Wrap Grip and Swipe Gesture

Touch gestures on the pen's barrel can be detected and used when the pen is not directly in contact with the tablet surface. One example of this is to perform page flipping (forwards and backwards) by holding the pen in the wrap grip outside of sensing range of the tablet and using the thumb to swipe against the top of barrel. Depending on the direction of the horizontal swipe, the notebook flips to the previous or next page (see Figure 10).

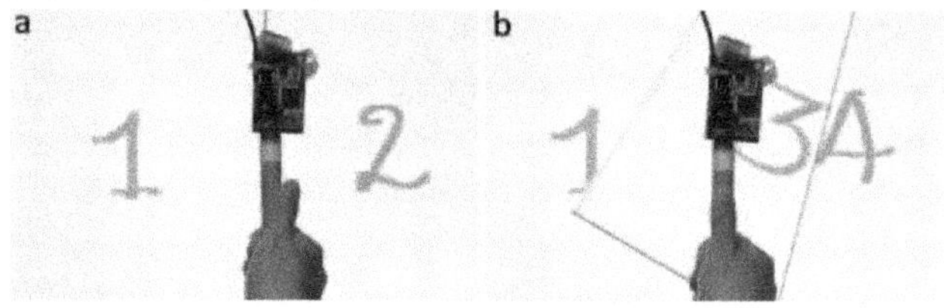

Figure 10. Page flipping interaction is triggered when users hold the pen in a wrap grip and performs a horizontal swipe (right to left in this image).

USER EXPERIMENT

In the previous section, we showed how our finger gestures and grips can be used to design novel interactions using the MTPen. We ran a formal experiment to test how *quickly* and *reliably* the gestures can be used for mode switching. In particular, we were interested in comparing our gestures to the conventional barrel button. In particular, we introduced a lower bound and an upper bound for the barrel button conditions based on our observation from earlier interviews. These confirmed that barrel button activation time should factor in the time to acquire a button, in addition to activating a button. We were also interested in the false positive and the false negative rate of our gesture recognizer. To answer these questions, we used a setting similar to Li [15] in which we created a pie crossing task that requires users to alternate between ink and command stroke to identify the cost of mode switching.

Mode Switching Techniques

We compare the swiping (SW) and the double tap (DT) techniques described above to two barrel-button baseline conditions. In the first baseline condition (BB1), the users switch the mode using a barrel button, but we do not force the user to acquire the button (i.e. users could have their finger directly over the button for the duration of the experiment). This is the standard setting used by Li [15].

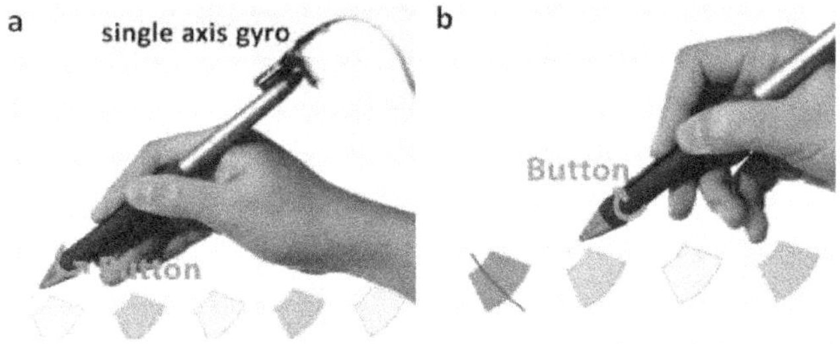

Figure 11. The BB2 condition requires rotation of the pen in order to acquire the button: (a) Button faces down when inking. (b) Button faces up in order to activate it. The arrows show the button location.

Second barrel button (BB2) condition reflects the cost of button acquisition (similar to homing in the KLM model [6]). In this condition, users are forced to acquire the button before clicking it. To simulate 90–180 degrees rotation that occurs often before clicking the button, we require the users to place the button facing down as an initial setup. When we require the user to click the button, users must rotate the pen so that the button is facing up, to activate the button. To ensure the pen rotation in our trials, we installed a single axis gyro to the rear end of the regular pen (Figure 11). Our software required the user to rotate the pen by 120 degrees before the button could be activated.

In SW and DT condition, if users issue a finger gesture while inking, the gestural state is retroactive to the beginning of the stroke similar to our swipe-based selection technique. This recommendation was also supported by Li's study [15], which showed that relaxing synchronization between ink and mode switch improved the user's performance.

Compound and Baseline Task

Users were asked to complete two pie-crossing tasks (Figure 12). In the baseline task (Figure 12, top), the user does not need to switch modes, but simply cross through all five pie slices in the desired direction. When the corresponding stroke intersects both arcs (inner and outer) of each pie, the color becomes darker, allowing the user to progress onto the next slice.

In the compound task (Figure 12, bottom), the user needs to switch modes when proceeding to each new pie slice. Participants were asked to cross blue slice with blue ink and red slices with red ink. In order to switch ink color, users have to change the mode using one of the four mode-switching techniques described previously. Blue ink is the default and the red ink is only available with a mode switch (a touch gesture on the MTPen or a barrel button press on a standard stylus). In the BB2 condition, users must rotate their pen before activating the button because blue slices must be crossed with the button facing down (Figure 11a), and red slices must be crossed with the button facing up while pressing the button (Figure 11b).

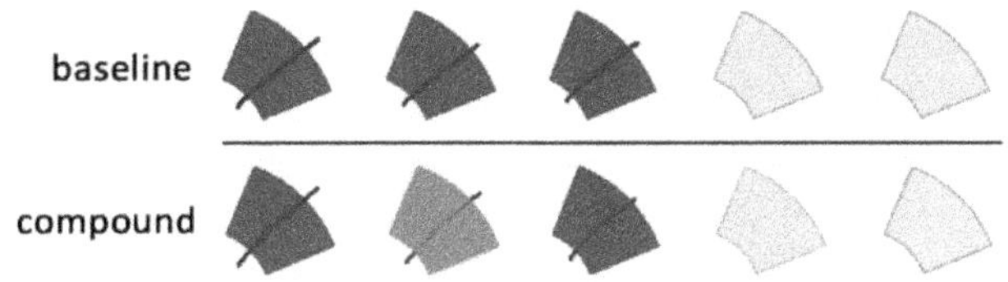

Figure 12. Baseline and compound pie crossing tasks are performed left to right. Successfully crossed slices are darker. Note: slices in this trial need to be crossed in NE direction.

To evaluate hand positions and wrist movement in different inking scenarios, each compound and baseline block is repeated in eight different directions (N, NE, E, SE, S, SW, W, and NW). A full set included all repetitions of both the baseline and the compound blocks in all eight different directions consisting of 80 pie crossings (2x5x8=80) in total.

Participants

Twelve participants (aged 22–35, right-handed, five male and seven female) were recruited from a university campus. Among them, one participant used a digital stylus on a regular basis, four participants claimed to have digital stylus experience in the past, while the rest had never used a digital stylus before.

Procedure

The study consisted of a training phase and an evaluation phase for each of the four techniques: BB1, BB2, DT, and SW. In the training phase, participants were asked to complete four sets of compound tasks. All participants completed the training set right before the evaluation phase for each of the conditions. The overall order of trials was counterbalanced using Latin square across users.

During the evaluation phase, participants had to go through four full sets (baseline and compound blocks in 8 directions). The first set was used to help users get used to the baseline and compound conditions, hence the data was discarded. The data from the next three sets was used for our analysis. The participants could take a break between sets. Since there are 16 mode switch cycles in a single set (eight directions, two mode-switch cycles per direction), users completed 64 mode switch cycles and 320 pie crossings (eight directions, two blocks, five pies per block) per condition (total of 1280 pie crossings in the evaluation stage).

Time Measurement

To give us a measure of how long it took our participants to mode switch in each of our conditions, we logged the timestamps of all pen-up events that occurred after successfully crossing a pie slice. Pen-up events are events generated when the pen loses contact with the surface.

Since the only difference between the baseline and compound tasks were the mode-switches, we computed the average mode-switching time by comparing the specific time intervals in both the compound and the baseline blocks. We illustrate this in Figure 13.

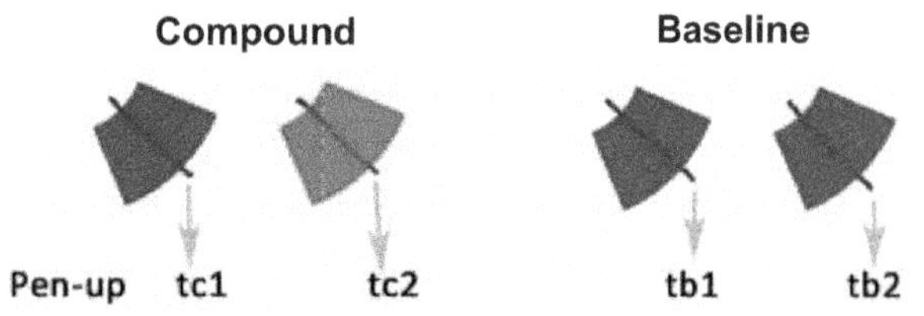

Figure 13. We measure the average time (ms) it took participants between two pen-up events in both compound (tc2-tc1) and baseline tasks (tb2-tb1). The difference between these two time stamps is the mode switch time.

In essence, we measure the average time it took the participants to issue two specific pen-up events. In our example illustrated in Figure 13, that is accomplished by computing *tc2-tc1* for the compound task, and *tb2-tb1* in the baseline. The difference of those two timings provides the mode switching time. While Dillon [7] calculates the mode switching time using the pen-up of the previous stroke and the pen-down event of the current stroke, we use the pen-up events in both cases since our mode switching condition can occur before or during the entire stroke. Note that in the BB2 condition, the button acquisition time is captured within the net mode switching time.

Error Measurement

In addition to mode switching times, we logged two different types of errors: false negatives and false positives. The *false negatives* can occur only in the compound block when the mode-switch is not recognized (i.e. mode engagement failed). If a mode switch is detected in the baseline block, the gesture or the button is triggered accidently and is the cause of *false positives*.

Results

We analyzed our data using repeated measure ANOVA, and Bonferroni corrections were used for multiple comparisons.

Mode Switching Time Analysis

We first discuss the mode switching time. A one-way repeated measure ANOVA showed a significant main effect of technique ($F(3,33)=22.447$, $p<.001$, partial $\eta^2=.67$). Pairwise comparison revealed that the BB2 condition was significantly slower than all other conditions, while there were no significant differences in other conditions (Figure 14). Overall, this result suggests that the MTPen gestures (especially SW) performed comparably to the best-case barrel button scenario (BB1) and drastically better than the sub-optimal use of the barrel button (BB2). Since BB1 (lower bound) and BB2 (upper bound) cover the two extreme ends of the pen button use spectrum, typical usage falls somewhere in between those two values.

Error Rate Analysis

We also analyzed the error rate. There was a significant main effect on *false negative errors* between different type of techniques ($F(3,33)=8.91$, $p<.001$, partial $\eta^2=.448$). Swipe (M=5.3%, SD=2.51%) and double tap (M=6.8%, SD=1.97%) suffered more from this error compared to both barrel button conditions (BB1: 0% and BB2: 1.3 %) mostly due to the gesture recognition errors.

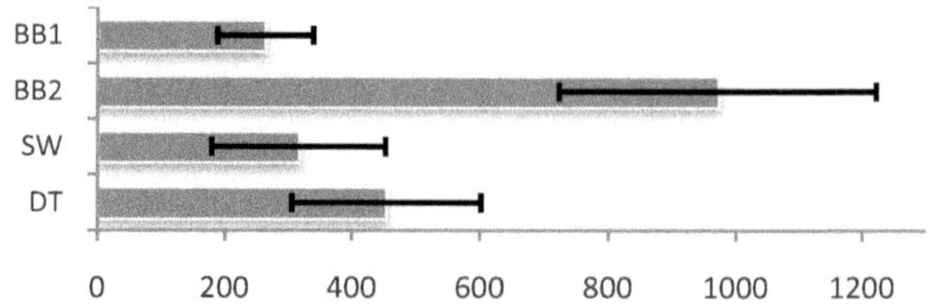

Figure 14. Mean mode switching time (ms) and confidence levels (α=.05) are shown in error bars.

In terms of the swipe gesture, some users could not maintain finger contact when the pen tip came into contact with the screen. Since the swipe gesture requires a continuous touch trace, this had a negative impact on performance. With the double tap gesture, the second tap would sometimes shift location with respect to the first tap, resulting failure to detect the gesture. However, increasing the distance threshold for double tap wasn't an ideal solution either; for some users, neighboring fingers of the index (thumb or middle) would be registered as a second tap because the threshold was too big.

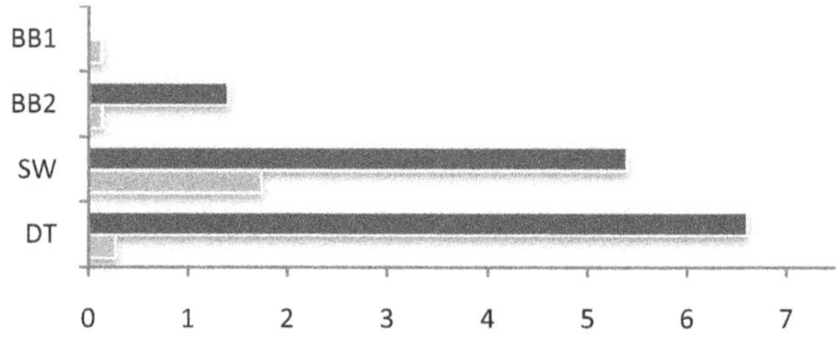

Figure 15. False negatives (black) and false positives (gray) for each condition. The values show percentages (%).

We also measured the *false positives* during the baseline block. Accidental double taps (1.7%) occurred more frequently than the swipe gesture (0.2%). Accidental double taps occurred when users mildly re-adjusted their entire hand for a better grip, contact points that are mapped to web of the thumb or the middle finger would rub against the sensor surface and trigger double tap. Similarly, we observed that for one user the web of the thumb would travel a long distance while readjusting the grip which triggered false positives of swipes. Figure 15 illustrates the false positives and false negatives errors.

Given the occurrence of false positive in the baseline condition, we analyzed the effect of each condition on the baseline performance. A one-way repeated measure ANOVA found a marginal effect of technique on the baseline time ($F(3,33)=2.595$, $p=.069$, partial $\eta^2=.19$) with BB1 (M=482.5, SD=142.18), BB2 (M=516.3, SD=112.0), SW (M=567.9, SD=152.2), DT (M=614.9, SD=152.1).This variation is partially attributable to a false positive trigger, which may have a slight impact on the mode switch time computation. However, several participants noted that the bulk of the prototype MTPen makes it more difficult to handle, which could account for some false positives. This issue equally affects the baseline and the compound conditions, and therefore does not influence the timing difference.

DISCUSSION

In this section, we reflect on the feedback from our study participants and from the four professional pen users that tried out our prototype drawing application.

Gestures

The ability to perform gestural mode switching on MTPen depends on a variety of ergonomic and technical issues. In terms of the ergonomics, the performance depends on how a user's hand is shaped (especially the index finger). For example, swipe gesture proved to be asymmetrical in terms of the swiping direction. Although we enabled swipe in both directions along the barrel, our participants used the flexion (curving the straight finger along the barrel) much more often than the extension (straightening the curved finger along the barrel).

When our professional designers used the swipe gesture to change the pen tip width, swipe gesture was better supported by our recognizer for the flexion than the extension. Since we modeled the contact points based on the centroid of their contact area, when the tip of the finger transitions to being flat as users extend their finger, the centroid actually travels in the opposite direction. As the result, it was harder to control the pen tip width during extension. From this observation, Wang's [28] touch point model that predicts the shape and orientation of the contact point was later added to replace use of the centroid with that of the tip of the finger. Our gesture recognizer also had limitations in detecting swipe when the finger trace was perpendicular to the pen's axis (e.g., in the page flipping interaction). As noted by Benko [3], the non-flat shape of the touch surface definitely presents challenges when doing touch interactions. In our case, the effects of the non-flat surface are especially noticed when using thumbs for the horizontal swipes. As thumbs are bound to the hand, they leave traces in an arc instead of straight line.

We further discovered that non-finger part of the hand can also be used as a dynamic contact point: The possibility of using the web of the thumb as a dynamic contact point to control interactions was mentioned both during the user experiment and during designers' feedback sessions. While we did not design such feature or demonstrate it to our users, some designers discovered this option and used it to control the pen width, instead of using their index fingers. Designers also mentioned that while transitioning between the tight tripod grip (Figure 2a) and a relaxed tripod grip (Figure 2b), the web of the thumb is bound to swipe across the barrel. As such, it is great way to capture squeezing movement of a hand which is yet another hidden dimension of the hand movement.

Hardware Design

When compared to the current industrial digital pens, MTPen's performance was generally hindered because of the larger diameter (16mm), extra weight, imbalance (from the electronics board and the wire), and its low-friction surface which negatively affected the stability required for gesturing. All of these issues are primarily due to the prototype nature of our device. However, even with such clear disadvantages, MTPen performed well in our user study despite that gesture-based input has higher error rate than mechanical input in general.

One of our expert designers also commented about extending sensor coverage area in both directions. The edge of the barrel, which starts tapering near the tip, plays a big role in pen interactions. If this front part was also covered with the sensor, finger tip movement would be better modeled. Similarly, extending the sensor to the rear end of the pen may open up opportunities for bimanual interaction with the device.

FUTURE WORK

Grip Recognition

We have started investigating ways to improve the grip recognition. In a different multi-touch hand-held device, adding an accelerometer has been shown to improve the grip detection by 10% [14, 24]. One of our preliminary experiments indicates that using additional sensor readings to reliably detect the rotation of the hand may improve grip recognition by reducing the task to a generic statistical pattern-matching problem. Alternatively, combining our capacitive sensor with a resistive pressure sensor is another possibility [2] as each has its pros and cons in sensing hand movement. We observed, for example, that a resistive sensor [21] may be better at reliably detecting grips due to extra dimension that reflects the force of a grip.

Sensor Fusion

Another promising future work is to leverage the benefit of sensor fusion. In this work, our primary goal was to assess the benefit of a multi-touch sensor for recognition of grips and gestures. However, there is likely further contextual information to be gained through other sensors (e.g., roll [4], tilt [25], pressure [19], and motion [23]), that can be combined with the sensor image of a hand to enable new set of foreground interaction techniques. With respect to the sensor technology, we have already experimented with using a resistive sensor to sense pressure and enable new squeezing interactions.

Longitudinal Study

We also plan to extend the drawing application to observe how changes in grips and gestures affect the recognizer while users annotate and sketch. We intend to study the effect of false positives and false negatives of the recognizer on the users' pen-holding behavior.

Reaching beyond designers

This work was primarily motivated by our observations of the expert designers who use electronic pens on a daily basis in their workflow. Much work remains to be done to investigate specific interactions tailored to other domains. For example, MTPen can be combined with small slate computers, or a paper-based digital pen [16]. In addition, it may prove interesting to explore the use of MTPen in game scenarios where the pen would be used for writing or as a "magic" remote controller.

CONCLUSIONS

In this paper, we presented a new input device that combines a multi-touch sensor array and a digital stylus. We describe the technical challenges and solutions in detecting gestures and grips on our custom-designed prototype. Hand grips and touch gestures can be combined to support a rich set of interaction techniques. Lastly, our user experiments showed that MTPen finger gestures provide a mode switch comparable to mechanical barrel buttons without their limitations. We believe that MTPen prototype opens a large area for design of novel interactions with a digital pen. Furthermore, the lessons learned from building and testing our prototype will be applicable to future research in enabling multi-touch sensing on input devices.

ACKNOWLEDGEMENT

This research was supported by the National Science Foundation under Grant IIS-0447703. We thank our study participants and anonymous CHI reviewers. We also thank Tomer Moscovich, Otmar Hilliges, Tom Yeh, Shenwei Liu and Adam Bender for their help.

REFERENCES

1. Apitz, G. and F. Guimbretiere. CrossY: A Crossing-Based Drawing Application. In Proc. *UIST'04*. ACM Press. p. 3 - 12
2. Baudisch, P. and G. Chu. Back-of-device interaction allows creating very small touch devices. In Proc. *CHI'09*. ACM Press. p. 1923-1932
3. Benko, H. Beyond flat surface computing: challenges of depth-aware and curved interfaces. In Proc. *Multimedia'09*. ACM Press. p. 935-944
4. Bi, X., T. Moscovich, G. Ramos, R. Balakrishnan, and K. Hinckley. An exploration of pen rolling for pen-based interaction. In Proc. *UIST'08*. ACM Press. p. 191-200
5. Brandl, P., C. Forlines, D. Wigdor, M. Haller, and C. Shen. Combining and Measuring the Benefits of Bimanual Pen. In Proc. *AVI'08*. ACM Press. p. 154-161
6. Card, S.K., T.P. Moran, and A. Newell, The keystroke-level model for user performance time with interactive systems, in *Communications of the ACM*. 1980. p. 396 - 410.
7. Dillon, R.F., J.D. Edey, and J.W. Tombaugh. Measuring the true cost of command selection: techniques and results. In Proc. *CHI'90*. ACM Press Press. p. 19 - 26
8. Grossman, T., K. Hinckley, P. Baudisch, M. Agrawala, and R. Balakrishnan. Hover widgets: using the tracking state to extend the capabilities of pen-operated devices. In Proc. *CHI'06*. ACM Press. p. 861-870
9. Guimbretiere, F., Fluid Interaction for High Resolution Wall-size Displays. 2002, Stanford University. p. 157.
10. Hinckley, K., P. Baudisch, and F. Guimbretière. Design and Analysis of Delimiters for Selection-Action Pen Gesture Phrases in Scriboli. In Proc. *CHI'05*. ACM Press. p. 451-460
11. Hinckley, K. and M. Sinclair. Touch-sensing input devices. In Proc. *CHI'99*. ACM Press. p. 223-230
12. Hinckley, K., K. Yatani, M. Pahud, N. Coddington, J. Rodenhouse, A. Wilson, H. Benko, and B. Buxton. Pen + touch = new tools. In Proc. *UIST'10*. ACM Press. p. 27-36
13. Jones, L.A. and S.J. Lederman, Human hand function. 2006: Oxford University.
14. Kim, K.-E., W. Chang, S.-J. Cho, J. Shim, H. Lee, J. Park, Y. Lee, and S. Kim. Hand grip pattern recognition for mobile user interfaces. In Proc. *Innovative applications of artificial intelligence*. AAAI Press. p. 1789-1794
15. Li, Y., K. Hinckley, Z. Guan, and J.A. Landay. Experimental analysis of mode switching techniques in pen-based user interfaces. In Proc. *CHI'05*. ACM Press. p. 461-470
16. LiveScribe, http://www.livescribe.com/
17. Matsushita, N. and J. Rekimoto, HoloWall: designing a finger, hand, body, and object sensitive wall, in *UIST'97*. 1997, ACM: Banff, Alberta, Canada. p. 209-210.
18. Napier, J.R., The prehensile movements of the human hand. Journal of Bone and Joint Surgery. **38**(B): p. 902-904.
19. Ramos, G., M. Boulos, and R. Balakrishnan. Pressure Widgets. In Proc. *CHI'04*. ACM Press. p. 527 - 534
20. Ravindra S. Goonetilleke, Errol R.Hoffmann, and A. Luximon, Effects of pen design on drawing and writing performance. Applied Ergonomics 2009: p. 292-301.
21. Rosenberg, I. and K. Perlin, The UnMousePad: an interpolating multi-touch force-sensing input pad, in *SIGGRAPH 2009*. 2009, ACM. p. 1-9.
22. Subramanian, S., D. Aliakseyeu, A. Lucero. Multi-layer interaction for digital tables. In Proc. *UIST'06*. p. 269-272
23. Suzuki, Y., K. Misue, and J. Tanaka. Stylus Enhancement to Enrich Interaction with Computers. In Proc. *HCII'07*. LNCS 4551 Press. p. 133-142
24. Taylor, B.T. and J. V. Michael Bove. Graspables: grasp-recognition as a user interface. In Proc. *CHI'09*. p. 917-926
25. Tian, F., L. Xu, H. Wang, X. Zhang, Y. Liu, V. Setlur, and G. Dai. Tilt menu: using the 3D orientation information of pen devices to extend the selection capability of pen-based user interfaces. In Proc. *CHI'08*. ACM Press. p. 1371-1380
26. Villar, N., S. Izadi, D. Rosenfeld, H. Benko, J. Helmes, J. Westhues, S. Hodges, E. Ofek, A. Butler, X. Cao, and B. Chen. Mouse 2.0: multi-touch meets the mouse. In Proc. *UIST'09*. ACM Press. p. 33-42
27. Wacom Technologies, http://www.wacom.com/index.html
28. Wang, F. and X. Ren. Empirical evaluation for finger input properties in multi-touch interaction. In Proc. *CHI'09*. ACM Press. p. 1063-1072
29. Wimmer, R. and S. Boring. HandSense: discriminating different ways of grasping and holding a tangible user interface. In Proc. *TEI'09*. ACM Press. p. 359-362
30. Wu, F.-G. and S. Luo, Design and evaluation approach for increasing stability and performance of touch pens in screen handwriting tasks. Applied Ergonomics, 2006. **37**: p. 319-327.
31. Zeleznik, R., A. Bragdon, F. Adeputra, and H.-S. Ko. Hands-on math: a page-based multi-touch and pen desktop for technical work and problem solving. In Proc. *UIST'10*. ACM Press. p. 17-26

WYSIWYF: Exploring and Annotating Volume Data with a Tangible Handheld Device

Peng Song **Wooi Boon Goh** **Chi-Wing Fu**
Nanyang Technological University, Singapore
{song0083, aswbgoh, cwfu}@ntu.edu.sg

Qiang Meng **Pheng-Ann Heng**
The Chinese University of Hong Kong
{qmeng, pheng}@cse.cuhk.edu.hk

ABSTRACT
Visual exploration of volume data often requires the user to manipulate the orientation and position of a slicing plane in order to observe, annotate or measure its internal structures. Such operations, with its many degrees of freedom in 3D space, map poorly into interaction modalities afforded by mouse-keyboard interfaces or flat multi-touch displays alone. We addressed this problem using a ***what-you-see-is-what-you-feel*** (WYSIWYF) approach, which integrates the natural user interface of a multi-touch wall display with the untethered physical dexterity provided by a handheld device with multi-touch and 3D-tilt sensing capabilities. A slicing plane can be directly and intuitively manipulated at any desired position within the displayed volume data using a commonly available mobile device such as the iPod touch. 2D image slices can be transferred wirelessly to this small touch screen device, where a novel fast fat finger annotation technique (F^3AT) is proposed to perform accurate and speedy contour drawings. Our user studies support the efficacy of our proposed visual exploration and annotation interaction designs.

Author Keywords
User interaction, volume data, data exploration, visual annotation, multi-touch, accelerometer, handheld devices.

ACM Classification Keywords
H.5.2 User Interfaces: [Interaction Styles]; I.3.6 Methodology and Techniques: [Interaction techniques].

General Terms
Design

INTRODUCTION
Technological advances in data acquisition and computational simulation have made the visualization of 3D volume data a common and integral part of many scientific disciplines. Examples include quantum chemistry simulations [23], medical volume data [19], volumetric flow data [34], as well as large-scale galaxy structure simulations [13]. Since volume data has internal structures that could be highly complex, visualization and interaction methods are needed to accentuate occluded structures and their relationships.

Despite the immense research effort and progress in volume visualization techniques, interactions with such applications are still very much through mouse-keyboard controls, or relatively large and expensive virtual-reality apparatus such as the virtual workbench and haptic devices. In this paper, we describe our efforts in developing an affordable volume data visualization and interaction system that uses interaction devices that are widely available in the consumer market. Our system employs a standard upright multi-touch display, which can be a custom-made multi-touch display (as in our case, see Figure 1) or a multi-touch LCD display, together with a handheld device with multi-touch and 3D-tilt sensing capabilities, like the iPhone or iPod touch, for example. By combining the strengths of both devices into a seamless integrated system, we are able to provide direct and tangible manipulation of volume data in ways that are intuitive, efficient and easy to use.

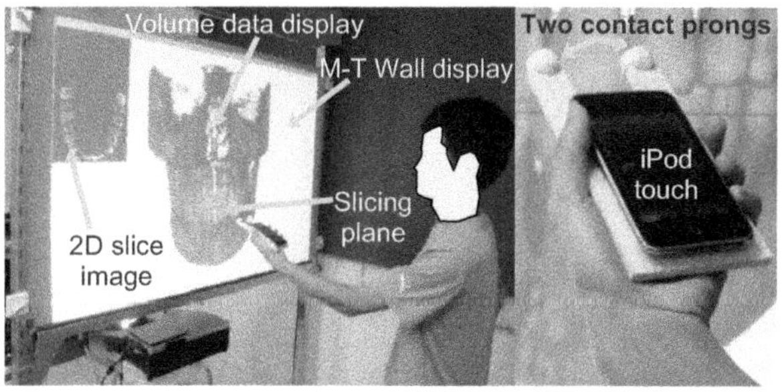

Figure 1. The WYSIWYF approach: the iPod touch in the user's hand provides natural control of a slicing plane against a reference 3D volume display on the multi-touch wall display.

To our knowledge, this is the first visualization system that fully integrates a commodity handheld device (with multi-touch and 3D-tilt sensing) and an upright multi-touch display to support direct and tangible exploration and annotation of volume data. We present several novel interaction methods that provide efficient exploration and annotation of volume data on this WYSIWYF system [37]. They are summarized as follows:

- **Direct Tangible Volume Slicing**. Firstly, we propose using a tangible handheld device such as an iPod touch to slice the volume data displayed on the upright multi-touch screen. By directly touching the wall display with the handheld device, we can initialize a 3D slicing plane at the very locality of the touch. Using the tilt sensing capability of the iPod touch, we can also synchronize the slicing plane's orientation to that of the handheld device during the contact. In the same way, the slicing plane can be translated by directly sliding the device over the wall display, with the visible volume data acting as a useful reference image. Such direct manipulation provides an intuitive and efficient means to walk through various cross-sections in the volume data.
- **Remote Tangible Volume Slicing**. We extended the WYSIWYF design principle further to allow the user to remotely manipulate the slicing plane on the wall display. A combination of local fingers and tilt gestures on the handheld device allows near full 3D control of the slicing plane. Being able to move a distance away from the large multi-touch wall display helps alleviate the problems of limited viewing angle, hand occlusion and annoying pixilation artifacts (due to projector resolution).
- **Constrained Rotation of the Slicing Plane**. A unique feature implemented in our system is the ability to use the multi-touch capability of the handheld device to anchor carefully chosen point and line constraints about which the slicing plane can be rotated in 3D space. Such constrained rotation is helpful in simplifying the complex manipulation of a plane with many degrees of freedom.
- **Efficient Visual Annotation on Small Touch Screen**. Lastly, with the ability to transfer 2D sliced images to the small screen on the handheld device, users can draw simple visual annotations on these images and have these annotations transferred immediately back to the volume data visualization on the wall display. To support this feature, we proposed a novel technique for fast and accurate finger tracing of smooth continuous contours in a 2D image that is displayed on a small touch screen.

RELATED WORK

Interaction with Volume Data

According to Ratti et al. [24], interaction approaches for exploring 3D data sets can be classified as graphical interfaces, virtual reality interfaces, augmented reality interfaces, and tangible interfaces. Since this work relates more to the virtual reality and tangible aspects in this scheme, we review mainly these two categories:

Virtual reality approach. This approach focuses on immersing users in a virtual environment with the 3D volume data and optionally some 3D user interface elements and virtual simulation tools. To support the user interaction, various virtual reality devices such as position or head tracking and stereoscopic viewing are required. Avila and Sobierajski [2] proposed a haptic interaction approach for volume visualization; they simulated a virtual tool by using the position and orientation provided by a haptic device. Szalavári and Gervautz [32] introduced the Personal Interaction Panel system consisting of a tracked simple clipboard and pen; this setup enables a natural two-handed interface for assorted applications. Aliakseyeu et al. [1] developed the Visual Interaction Platform (VIP) for navigation and manipulation of 2D and 3D data; it is an augmented reality platform for different natural interaction techniques. Subramanian et al. [31] employed this platform to show that hybrid 2D and 3D interfaces can offer better performance than 3D or 2D interfaces alone. Their work supports constrained rotation on 3D objects by inserting a virtual pin on the 2D workspace via a digital pen.

Unlike [1], we do not require a passive prop and its associated tracking system. Instead, we integrated various functionalities available on off-the-shelf handheld devices, such as the multi-touch screen and tilt-sensing, to perform volume data annotation and manipulation. Similar to [31], we also support constrained rotation of a slicing plane by direct specification of up to two rotation points, but we use touch inputs on handheld device's multi-touch display.

Tangible approach. Tangible interfaces seek to interact with virtual objects by manipulating tracked props in physical space. Hinckley et al. [15] proposed one of the first tangible 3D interfaces to support continuous clipping interaction in 3D space; it allows surgeons to use passive interface props to explore a patient's anatomy data by interactively generating cross-section views of the data.

Fröhlich et al. [10] built the Cubic Mouse system that embeds a six-degree-of-freedom tracker in a cube-shaped box; users can manipulate this tangible device to transform and slice 3D objects. Qi and Martens [22] investigated the problem of positioning a slicing plane within a volume data set by using a wooden cube and a pen/frame in physical space; tracked by a vision-based system, the wooden cube controls the volume data orientation and zoom factor while the pen/frame controls the orientation and position of the clipping plane. Bonanni et al. [5] proposed the Handsaw system to explore cross-sectional cuts in a volume data set, either by projecting a luminous line or by holding an outstretched hand at the desired cut location; related sectional information can be shown on an adjacent display. Couture et al. [7] designed the GeoTUI system, a tangible user interface specifically for geophysicists; it employed a tabletop vision-projection setup for the selection of cutting planes on the geographical data. Spindler et al. [29] developed the PaperLens system that tracks and projects on a sheet of paper in physical space over a tabletop surface; we can move the paper to navigate and slide a virtual 3D data volume, and freely move and orientate the paper in a tangible manner.

The use of tracked props in existing works of this approach requires users to switch visual foci between the hand-manipulated tangible interface and the computer screen. Our use of a large interactive surface for both image display and user interaction with a tangible interface provides a single visual focus for both visualization and interaction, thus removing the stressful time-shared visual foveation. Moreover, the use of a computation-capable tangible device with a built-in multi-touch surface enables instantaneous transfer of desired 2D slice images for volume data annotation and portable take-away storage.

Tangible approach with handheld devices. Today, many consumer handheld devices come with built-in accelerometers to sense 3D tilting. These devices enable us to develop a low-cost system for volume data exploration. Gallo et al. [12] employed the Wiimote controller to manipulate and select 3D medical data with two system states: pointing state to use the Wiimote like a laser pointer, and manipulation state to use the Wiimote to rotate, translate and scale a 3D object. Zsaki [38] made use of a two-axis accelerometer as a tangible input to slice a given volume data set in a natural manner. Besides using the tangible device to slice volume data, the tangible interface in our system is able to receive and display the 2D sliced images. These reference images displayed on the handheld device are useful for supporting visual annotation as well as allowing users to locate and specify anchor point(s) for constrained point and line rotation of the slicing plane.

Handheld Devices and Large Displays

There are numerous works that involve interaction between handheld devices and an assortment of display systems.

Handheld devices as remote controllers. Similar to TV and VCR remote controllers, handheld devices equipped with multi-touch and 3D-tilt sensing capabilities can also serve as remote controllers for supporting user interaction with a co-located display system. Kela et al. [17] explored gesture commands with accelerometers in design studio setting to control devices such as TV and VCR, while Ballagas et al. [3] presented a structure of taxonomy to examine the interaction paradigm of using smart phones to control contents on a digital display. Later, Boring et al. [6] proposed and compared three different interaction methods, called scroll, tilt, and move, for using a mobile phone to continuously control a pointer on a large display. Dachselt and Buchholz [8] proposed the throw and tilt gestures on handheld devices to interact with a large display. Kim et al. [18] controlled the virtual navigation in a CAVE™ setup by using multi-touch on an iPhone/iPod touch. More recently, Katzakis and Hori [16] applied the accelerometer and magnetometer on smart phones to manipulate the rotation on 3D virtual objects.

Applications with handheld device interaction. Wilson and Sarin [36] developed an interactive surface called BlueTable; it can automatically connect to mobile devices, allowing us to conveniently transfer photos and show them on the table. Since mobile devices have higher visual and input resolution than local regions on large displays, Olwal and Feiner [20] suggested tracking mobile devices over large displays to take advantage of mobile devices to support better graphics and user interaction. Similarly, Voida et al. [33] proposed using an iPod to perform interactive lensing in focus+context visualization on a tabletop surface. Another application class that often integrates handheld/mobile devices and large displays is multi-player games. Shirazi et al. [28] designed and implemented the Poker Surface, which combines a multi-touch table and mobile phones for an interactive card game. Various natural interactions such as throwing, touching the table, tilting and shaking are explored in this work. Echtler et al. [9] studied a new paradigm of multi-player game (using the Sudoku game) with public display on a tabletop and private display on one's own mobile phone.

Contacting handheld devices on upright displays. Directly touching a display with a mobile device as a form of interaction is a relatively new concept. Hardy and Rukzio [14] proposed using such a touch action to perform position selection, data picking or dropping over a large display. Schöning et al. [25] studied the authentication issue for this interaction scenario when using handheld devices to interact with a public multi-touch surface and proposed using the camera flash with an infra-red camera to identify the touch action. Steinicke et al. [30] explored the potential of using a multi-touch mobile device with stereoscopic displays.

Compared to these works, the main novelty of our work is the use of a direct touch contact between the handheld device and upright multi-touch display to enhance the control of the slicing plane during the exploration of the volume data. The convergence of these two types of interactive devices allows the design of useful interactive features such as the ability to initiate constrained slice plane rotation and fast visual annotation from a remote multi-touch display on the tangible interface.

SYSTEM SETUP

Our system setup consists of an iPod touch (tangible interface), a large vertical multi-touch wall display, a wireless router and a server PC (see Figure 2). Wireless connection with low-latency UDP is used to transmit sensor data and files between the iPod touch and server. The multi-touch wall display transmits touch information to the server through UDP over wired Ethernet link.

Multi-touch Wall Display and Tangible Device

This work employs a vision-based whiteboard-style multi-touch display system (see Figure 1). The interactive surface uses the infrared laser light plane (LLP) emitters to detect the multiple finger contact points. For the tangible device, we used an iPod touch for rapid prototyping, and employed many of its built-in features, which include a 3-axis accelerometer, multi-touch screen, wireless network, and 3D graphics capability.

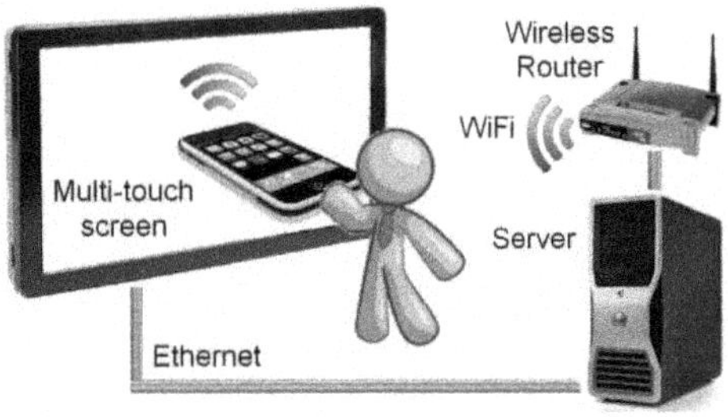

Figure 2. The system setup.

Server Program on Server PC

Our volumetric data visualization application uses the Visualization Toolkit (VTK) [26] to render the volume data. A small pop-up window on top-left of the screen shows sliced image as we manipulate the slicing plane, see Figure 1. An integrated interaction module receives and processes input data both from the multi-touch wall display and the remote handheld device. Wall display interaction-sensing is implemented as a thread, which records all multi-touch events and stores them in a linked-list data structure shared with the application thread. The iPod touch interaction-sensing is implemented as another thread that receives and processes user input from the mobile device, as well as sends 2D sliced image data to the device upon request.

Client Program on Handheld Device

The iPhone SDK is used to build a client program to sense the touch and tilt events, and transmit them to the server PC. At the same time, the client program also receives and displays the small-sized 2D sliced image received from the server program. Since the iPod touch is used for slicing plane manipulation and also visual annotation, the client program on the mobile device operates under three modes: *remote control*, *image manipulation* and *annotation*. In remote control mode, the device sends both accelerometer and multi-touch signals to the server for controlling the slicing plane. Moving-window low pass filtering is used on the device to reduce the jitter inherent in the accelerometer signal. 2D sliced images can be automatically loaded to the device when the tilt activation button (see Figure 4) is released. The image manipulation mode allows the 2D sliced image to be translated, rotated and scaled using simple finger gestures on the device's multi-touch screen. Finally, the annotation mode allows users to quickly draw outlines or contours on the 2D sliced image and to send their sketches back to the server PC for visualization.

VOLUME DATA EXPLORATION AND ANNOTATION

Our volume data exploration and annotation system integrates the natural user interface of a 2D interactive multi-touch wall display with the physical 3D manipulative dexterity afforded by a handheld device with multi-touch and tilt sensing capabilities. In our usage configuration, the large multi-touch wall display is employed for general volume data visualization purposes. Its large screen format is amenable to group viewing, such as when a doctor is teaching human anatomy to a small group of medical students. Basic 3D data manipulation operations can be done on this display using finger gestures. The handheld device, e.g., an iPod touch, is used as a tangible interface that allows the user to interactively position a slicing plane, control its orientation, and perform visual annotations. The next section details the different groups of interaction designs involved in realizing this integrated system.

Volume Data Manipulation on Multi-touch Wall Display

For completeness, we briefly describe how the volume data is manipulated on the multi-touch wall display. These wall-display-based operations help set the reference of the volume data image to a convenient 3D orientation so that the user can begin to use the tangible handheld device to specify the desired slicing plane. Since the interactive surface is essentially 2D, a combination of single finger, two-finger and multiple–finger gestures are required to perform objected-centered rotation, scaling, and translation operations, respectively, as summarized in Figures 3(a-c).

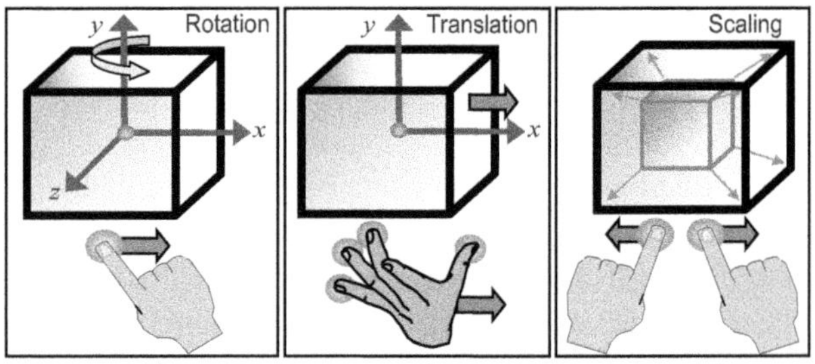

(a) (b) (c)

Figure 3. Basic volume data manipulation on the wall display. (a) Rotation about the data-centered origin using a one finger swipe gesture, (b) translation in the x and y directions using a 4-5 finger panning gesture, and (c) scaling using two-finger drag-in, drag-out or pinch (two fingers of one hand) gestures.

Volume Data Slicing

Visual exploration of volume data often requires a user to manipulate the position and orientation of a slicing plane in order to observe, annotate or measure internal structures within the 3D volume data. The flexible and direct manner by which this slicing plane can be manipulated would greatly enhance the exploratory power of the visualization system. The primary strength and novelty of our system is the combined use of a multi-touch wall display and a tangible tilt-aware interface. We describe novel and intuitive interaction design afforded by this system.

Positioning and rotating the slicing plane

Imagine being able to specify the slicing plane's position and orientation (on the x and y plane) by just drawing a line over a volumetric display in front of you. This is exactly the type of direct manipulation afforded by our system. The physical contact between the mobile device and the volume data that is being visualized on the multi-touch display provides an intuitive way for a user to specify the initial position and orientation of a slicing plane within the 3D data. In order to enable a standard multi-touch wall display to detect the contact of the tangible device, we attached a simple wooden base to the iPod touch, thus providing it with two rounded protruding prongs (see Figures 1 and 4). These prongs allow the mobile device to contact the multi-touch display with a simulated two-finger touch gesture of fixed Euclidean spacing *d*, which the application has been calibrated to detect. The slicing plane's new position on the *x*-*y* plane can be specified by directly touching the wall display at any desired location with the mobile device (the *z*-axis position remains unchanged).

Once in contact with the wall display, the user can press the tilt activation button (see Figure 4) on the mobile device to inform the client program to continuously transmit tilt sensor data to the server. The orientation of the slicing plane can now be computed, and will follow the iPod touch as the device is rotated against the wall display. This way of controlling the slicing plane is intuitive and gives the user the sense that he is holding a physical slicer in his hand.

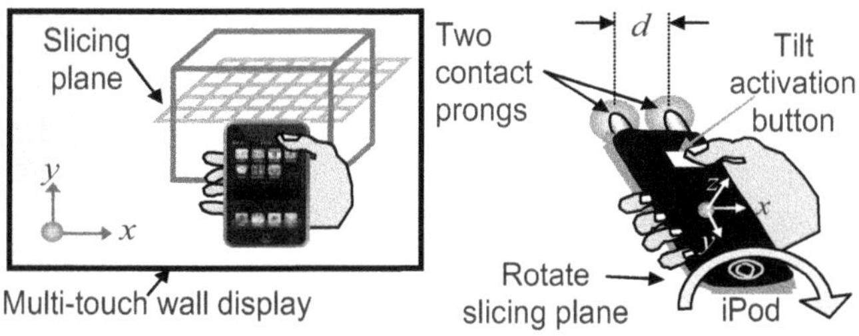

Figure 4. Position a slicing plane by touching the wall display with a modified two-prong contact (attached to the handheld device) and controlling *x*-*y* orientation of plane by pressing the tilt activation button and rotating iPod touch.

Translating the slicing plane

The slicing plane is a virtual window with boundary in the 3D space, corresponding to what is shown on the handheld device screen. The slicing plane can be translated either along its own coordinate axes (x', y', z') or the wall display coordinate axes (x, y, z). Incremental translation about the slicing plane coordinate system is more intuitive and has proven useful when there is a need to move the slicer to a precise position to acquire a 2D image slice for geometric measurements. Figure 5a shows how the multi-touch capability of the mobile device is used as a convenient remote interface for controlling the slicing plane translation. One finger gesture on the mobile device's multi-touch screen translates the slicer in x'-z' plane while two fingers moving gesture translates the slicer along the y'-axis. However, a more intuitive and speedy way to move the slicer is by using direct manipulation of the iPod touch on the multi-touch wall display. Making two-pronged touch contact and moving the iPod touch along the wall display's *x*-*y* plane will translate the slicer on its x'-y' plane (see Figure 5b). The flexibility of our integrated system also provides users the option of positioning the slicing plane by translating the 3D volume data on the wall display using the panning gesture (see Figure 5c).

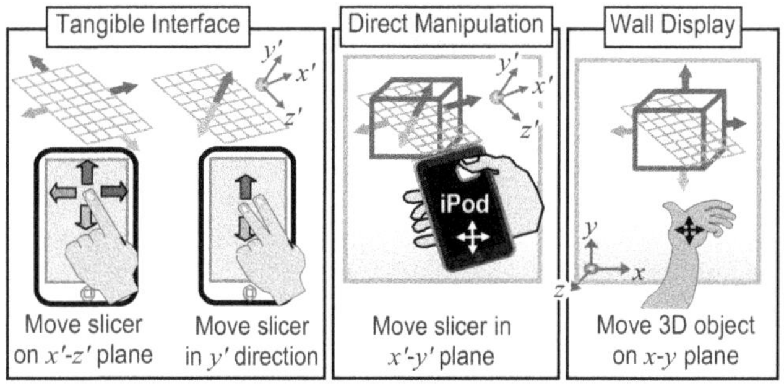

(a) (b) (c)

Figure 5. The translation of the slicing plane about its coordinate system can be done by (a) remotely using various finger gestures on the iPod touch and/or (b) sliding the iPod touch against the wall display. (c) Multi-touch manipulation of the wall display can be used to move the 3D volume data relative to the slicing plane.

Constrained rotation about slicing plane normal

The handheld device's 3-axis accelerometer is unable to detect rotation about the *z*-axis (see Figure 4) since no gravitational force change is experienced by the device's inertial sensor when it is held horizontally and facing up. In order to perform constrained rotation about the slicing plane normal, manipulation of the reference volume data on the wall display is needed. This is achieved when one finger is held stationary on the multi-touch surface while another finger moves. The direction of the moving finger determines clockwise or counterclockwise rotation.

Tangible constrained 3D rotation of slicing plane

The slicing plane's 3D orientation can be manipulated by performing corresponding tilt gestures on the handheld device, while the tilt activation button is being touched. The slicing plane in the virtual space will rotate in unison with the tangible interface, matching angle for angle, axis for axis. Unfortunately, a horizontally held iPod touch cannot detect rotations about it *z*-axis (see Figure 4) since no gravity changes occur. Thus, the slicing plane can only be rotated along the *x* and *y* axes. The constrained rotation of the 3D object about the slicing plane normal, which can be performed using finger gestures on the wall display (described earlier) can compensate for this limitation.

By default, the slicing plane will rotate around an anchor point located at the mid-point of the slicing plane's edge that is the closest to the iPod touch when contact was made with the wall display. A novel and powerful feature provided by our interaction design is highlighted in Figure

6, which shows a user trying to orientate the slicing plane such that it flushes and touches the sloping cut surface of a 3D cylindrical object. Due to the many axes of freedom in controlling the 3D orientation of a plane in free space, this is not an easy feat to achieve for a novice. By providing the ability to interactively shift the anchor point about which the constrained plane rotation can occur, this greatly simplifies the exploratory process required to tilt the slicer to the desired 3D orientation. Once the slicer has intersected a strategic position in the 3D object, the user merely needs to use the multi-touch screen on the iPod touch to visually move an anchor ball on the slicing plane to any desired 2D location on the plane. As far as we are aware, this is the first interactive volume visualization system that uses a single tangible device to provide tangible slicing plane manipulation and the ability to interactively shift the point of constrained rotation.

An additional feature of our interaction design is the ability to sequentially place (two) anchor points on the slicing plane, thereby allowing constrained rotation about a line. This is especially useful in the visualization of fabricated 3D machine parts where line geometry is prevalent. Once the slicing plane is in position and the relevant 2D slice image data is acquired, the next task that may be performed is visual annotation.

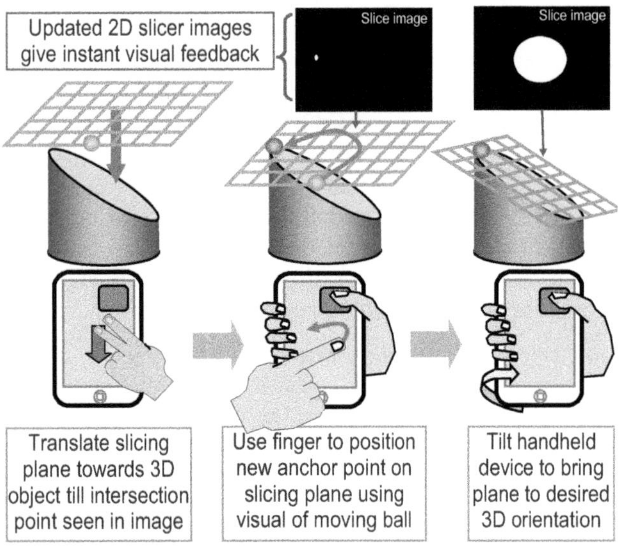

Figure 6. Easy manipulation of slicer to desired 3D orientation using a novel multi-touch technique for specifying an arbitrary point on the slicing plane, about which the constrained plane rotation can be performed. With one finger touching the tilt activate button, another finger from the other hand can be used to slide the anchor ball to a new location (orange ball) from its initial default location (green ball).

Volume Data Visual Annotation

The ability to visually annotate 3D volume data provides the user with a powerful tool to visualize and communicate structural relationships between embedded objects. Figure 7 illustrates an example where simple planar outlines drawn on two teeth, one on the upper jaw and one on the lower jaw, can allow a dentist to quickly communicate to the patient why dental braces are needed to correct the teeth misalignment caused by malocclusion.

Releasing the tilt activation button on the iPod touch after manipulating the slicing plane will wirelessly transfer the 2D sliced image data. With the 2D image conveniently in the hand of the user, he can now perform the visual annotation operation remotely while seated comfortably away from the wall display. Tracing annotation outline over the slice image on a small multi-touch screen can be inaccurate and tedious. We next discuss the issues related to this problem and propose a novel technique to perform fast visual annotation on a small multi-touch screen.

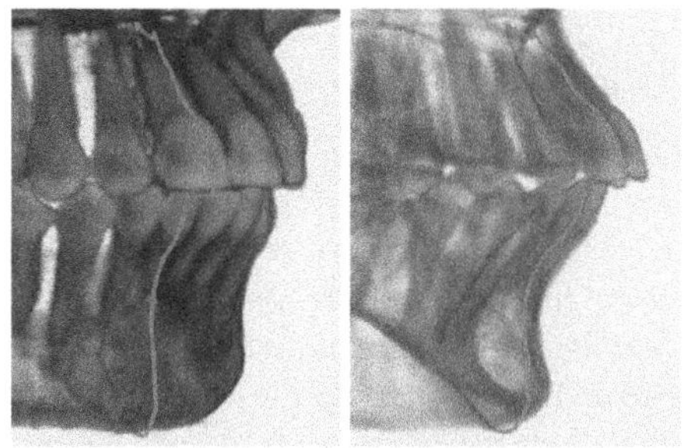

Figure 7. Examples of planar outline annotations showing the extent of malocclusions in a dental patient.

The fat finger problem

The fat finger problem [4, 21, 27, 35] is a well-known problem related to the difficulty to accurately locate a desired point on a touch display by using one's finger. Unlike a pen or stylus that has a sharp tip, the human finger is soft and compresses to a large blob-like contact point when pressed against a multi-touch surface. The centroid of this detected blob may not coincide with the point on the image where the user wishes to draw the desired outline. Using cross-hair visual feedback does not help because of the occlusion of the human finger over the visual area of interest. The two finger technique of Benko et al. [4] is not appropriate here since a single finger is needed to do boundary tracing. An interesting solution to the fat finger problem is *LucidTouch* by Wigdor et al. [35]. By sensing finger touches from behind the display and augmenting the screen visuals with point cursors and pseudo translucent shadow fingers, users can select accurate screen locations without finger occlusions. Unfortunately, this is not currently a solution on the ubiquitous iPhone or iPod touch.

In fact, the simplest way to alleviate this problem is to zoom up the visual region of interest so that the object boundary region where the outline is to be drawn is now of size commensurate to that of the human finger tip (see Figure 8a). However, this image zooming gives rise to another problem. In order to complete the outline drawing of the entire shape, the user has to go through many individual zoom-up sections of the image (see Figure 8b).

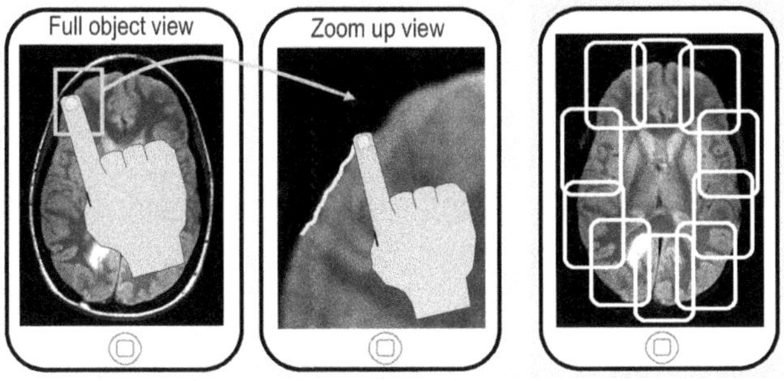

(a) (b)

Figure 8. The fat finger problem. (a) Image zooming helps alleviate this problem. (b) But the object boundary is now spread over many overlapping image zoom-up segments.

Single finger down drawing

There are basically two interaction modes during visual annotation (see Figure 9a). The PAN mode allows the user to pan the image to reveal out-of-view regions that may require visual annotation. A thick green boundary around the image is used to indicate PAN mode. The DRAW mode allows the user to annotate by tracing an outline along the desired object boundary in the image. In this mode, the image remains stationary and a yellow line is drawn under the sliding finger. The DRAW mode is indicated by a thick red boundary around the image. The users can switch between the two modes by touching the thick red or green border with the same tracing finger (one-handed) or with the non-gripping thumb of the hand that is holding the handheld device (two-handed). Our user performance evaluation on the visual annotation task shown in Figure 12 revealed that the two-handed switching technique is on average about 28% less accurate and 15% slower than the one-handed technique. Moreover, some users complained that coordinating repeated PAN-DRAW switching using two hands was confusing and their finger that performs the mode switching sometimes occlude relevant image regions.

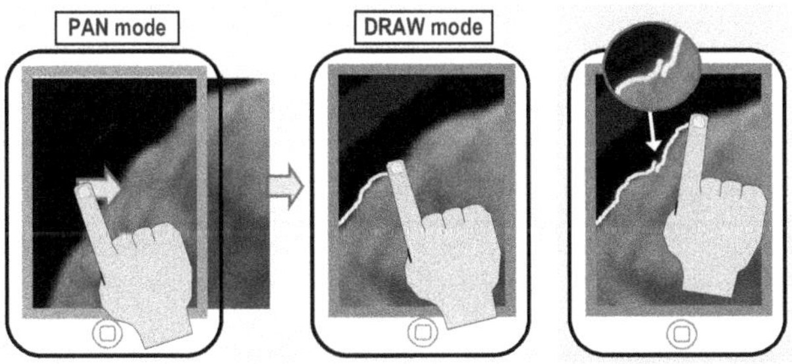

(a) (b)

Figure 9. (a) The basic PAN and DRAW annotation modes. (b) Overlap and discontinuity in the outline when the finger is lifted up and placed down again to resume the drawing.

To address the fat finger problem, the complete outline to be drawn is now spread over many zoomed-up image sections. This requires the user to perform countless image panning and drawing actions thus switching between PAN and DRAW modes repeatedly. If the superior one-handed technique is adopted, this requires the drawing finger to be lifted up to perform the switch between the PAN and DRAW modes. When the user removes his finger to switch mode and then places it back to continue the drawing from where he last stopped, overlaps and small discontinuities in the outline can result due to the inaccurate placement of the user's finger over the last drawn point (see Figure 9b).

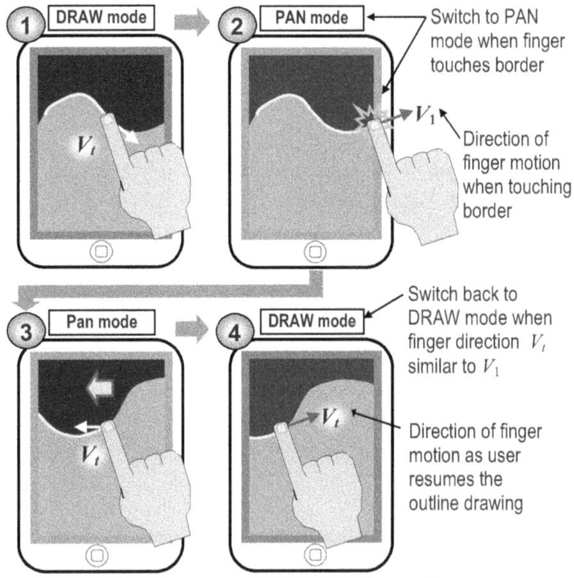

Figure 10. The basic steps in the Fast Fat Finger Annotation Technique (F^3AT). Steps 1-4 are repeated until the entire contour along the boundary of the object is drawn or whenever the user decides the outlining is done.

The Fast Fat Finger Annotation Technique

We propose a novel technique called the Fast Fat Finger Annotation Technique (F^3AT) to address this problem. The user normally starts annotation with an image view that displays the complete object boundary. When he touches the boundary area where he wishes to start the drawing, the image can automatically zoom up (to a resolution preset by the user) so that enough visual resolution is now available to avoid the fat finger inaccuracy when drawing. The image is now in DRAW mode. Figure 10 illustrates the various steps in using F^3AT. One finger is used to trace the desired outline along the boundary (step 1) until it reaches the red border (step 2), where no more drawing can be done since the remaining boundary in the image is out of view. At this instant (when finger touches red border), the annotation mode automatically switches to PAN mode (step 2). The border changes its color to green, indicating to the user that he can freely pan the image in the opposite direction to the drawing direction to reveal more image boundary region to draw (step 3).

The main novelty in the proposed F^3AT is the constant monitoring of the direction of finger movement during the image pan. As soon as the panning direction of the user's finger returns to the general drawing direction, given by the vector V_l in (step 2), DRAW mode resumes (step 4). The trigger for automatically switching back to DRAW mode determined by the dot product of two vectors given by

$$V_l \cdot V_t > 0$$

where V_l is the motion vector of the finger when it last touched the red border and V_t is the current motion vector of the finger in PAN mode. Essentially, any motion vector with an angular difference of ±90° from V_l is sufficient to trigger a switch back to DRAW mode.

The main advantage of using the F^3AT to trace lines on a small touch screen is the fact that the user can complete the contour drawing along the boundary of a large image region without lifting up the drawing finger even once. This avoids overlaps and discontinuities in the outline (see Figure 9b). Additionally, since the F^3AT automatically switches between PAN and DRAW mode based on the context of the user's finger position (touching red border) and motion direction (last drawing direction), this allows the user to perform annotation more speedily than the traditional approach of manual toggling between PAN and DRAW mode as is evident from our user study results.

USER STUDY

Two series of user studies were conducted. A total of 10 participants (6 males, 4 females) aged between 22 and 30 were involved. Prior to the trial, none of the participants have used the systems in our study. To remove biases arising from task familiarization, equal numbers of participants used one technique first to complete the required task and then the other and vice-versa.

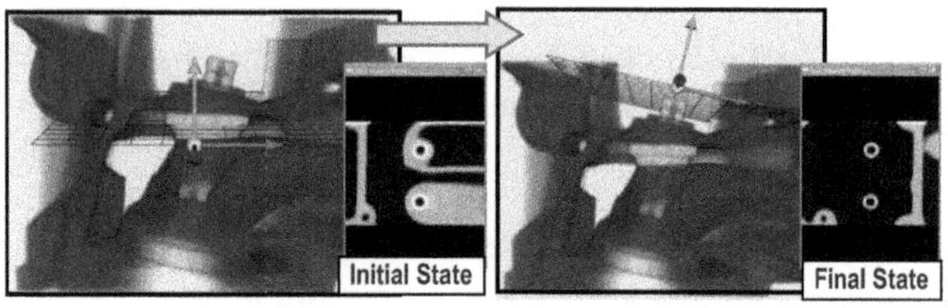

Figure 11. Task 1 requires the user to manipulate the position and orientation of the slicing plane from the initial state shown on the left to the final state shown on the right.

Manipulating the Slicing Plane

The goals of this study are to observe how well users of the proposed interface are able to transfer their practice skills on one task to another new task and the variability in the acquired competency level among a small population of naive users. A traditional mouse-and-keyboard interface was used to obtain a set of baseline timing measures that allows us to gauge the quantum of improvement afforded by our proposed WYSIWYF approach.

The study compares the speed performance in manipulating the position and orientation of the slicing plane from an initial state to a new one. The 2D slicer image is shown pictorially to the user (see Figure 11, right side) to allow him to judge if the plane is in the required position and orientation. The task completion time using the WYSIWYF system is compared to a traditional keyboard-mouse system, which uses a combination of mouse (to manipulate the volume data) and keyboard control (to translate and rotate slicer about its various axes). A graphical depiction of the keyboard and mouse functions was made available for user reference. Users could practice performing task 1 with the interface currently under trial for up to 5 minutes. After the practice, the slicing plane was reset to its initial state and the time taken to perform task 1 was recorded. The user was then given another task 2 without the possibility of practice to see if they can transfer their newly acquired slicer manipulation skills to a novel situation.

Table 1 summarizes the mean timing results μ and their respective variances δ. As expected, the direct and tangible 3D manipulation of the slicing plane afforded by our system allowed the user to perform the tasks much more speedily. For the familiar task 1, it was 97% faster and for unfamiliar task 2, it was 142% faster. The increase of about 15s when moving from task 1 to task 2 using the proposed system compared to a much longer 42s using the mouse-keyboard approach suggests that users are better at transferring the practice skills to another new task using the WYSIWYF approach. The intuitive and direct manner in which the slicing plane can be positioned (by touching the screen with the device) and orientated (by tilting the device) makes it easier for the users to figure out how to perform the necessary operations to manipulate the slicing plane to the target. The comparatively lower variances in timing for our proposed system also suggest that the more intuitive integrated WYSIWYF mode of interaction allows a larger cross-section of users to acquire similar level of competency with limited usage exposure on the system.

Method	Complete Task 1		Complete Task 2	
	μ (sec)	δ (sec^2)	μ (sec)	δ (sec^2)
Keyboard + Mouse	26.4	112	68.6	960
Wall display + iPod touch	13.4	27	28.3	187

Table 1. Comparative results of the slice plane manipulation study between the proposed and a keyboard-mouse system.

Visual Annotation

The second user study compares the timing performance in doing contour tracing on a small touch screen device (iPod touch) using the manual approach of toggling between PAN and DRAW modes with one hand and the novel F^3AT.

Table 2 shows that the proposed F^3AT method is 49% faster than the manual method. Every single user drew the required contour faster using F^3AT. In fact, the significantly lower variance in average task completion time for F3AT suggests that this method of visual annotation is probably more intuitive and easily adopted. User comments on F3AT were all positive, praising its speed and convenience. The F3AT accuracy in following the required trace path is also slightly better than the manual mode.

Method	Average timing (sec)	Variance of timing (sec^2)	Average tracing accuracy (pixel)
Manual	111.8	0.16	0.88
F3AT	75.1	0.09	0.78

Table 2. Comparative results of the visual annotation user study between the one-handed manual and F3AT method.

In fact, our observations were that for faster drawing speed, which F3AT affords, the more likely it is that the user gets negligent in keeping to within the stipulated line trace width. However, the greatest advantage of F3AT is its ability to draw an entire outline without lifting one's finger. The benefits are clearly illustrated in comparison of the visual quality of drawings produced by the two techniques (see Figure 12b-c). The contour drawn using F3AT is smooth and continuous while that drawn using the manual method has many overlaps and discontinuities.

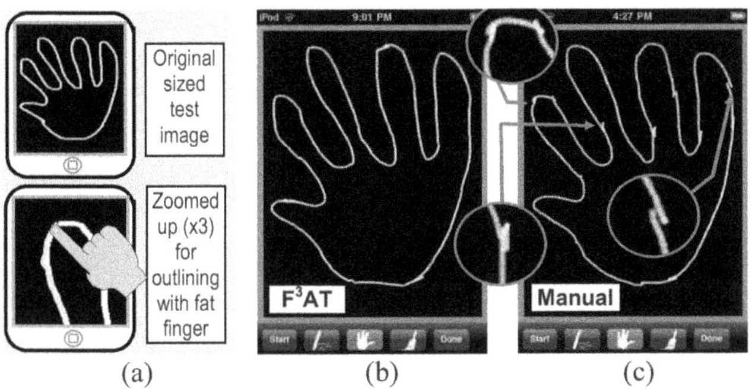

Figure 12. Visual annotation user study. (a) Test image used was zoomed up by 3 times for user to outline. (b) A user's sample result for the F3AT and (c) one-handed manual trials.

CONCLUSIONS

We have described a novel interactive visual exploration and annotation system that combines the strengths of a standard upright multi-touch display and a commonly available handheld device that acted as an intuitive tangible interface. We described how the WYSIWYF concept was realized using the 3D-tilt sensing and multi-touch capability on the handheld device. A novel feature of this concept is the ability to directly and efficiently manipulate a slicing plane on the multi-touch wall display by making direct contact with the handheld device. We can also use this same handheld device to remotely manipulate the slicing plane while activating the constrained rotation capability to selectively reduce the degree of freedom of the slice plane. Finally, we also proposed a fast and accurate contour drawing technique so that small touch screen devices can be efficiently used to perform remote visual annotations. User studies conducted support the efficacy of our proposed visual exploration and annotation interaction designs. In future, we also would like to explore our interaction techniques in astrophysical visualization settings [11].

Acknowledgment. We thank all reviewers for the valuable comments and we express our gratitude to those who participated in our experiments; this work is supported by A*Star SERC grant (No. 092 101 0063) and Hong Kong RGC General Research Fund (Proj. No. CUHK 412510).

REFERENCES

1. D. Aliakseyeu, S. Subramanian, J.-B. Martens, and M. Rauterberg. Interaction techniques for navigation through and manipulation of 2D and 3D data. In *Eurographics Workshop on Vir. Env.*, 79-188, 2002.
2. R. S. Avila and L. M. Sobierajski. A haptic interaction method for volume visualization. In *IEEE Visualization*, 197–204, 1996.
3. R. Ballagas, J. Borchers, M. Rohs, and J. G. Sheridan. The smart phone: A ubiquitous input device. *IEEE Pervasive Comp.*, 5(1):70–77, 2006.
4. H. Benko, A. D. Wilson, and P. Baudisch. Precise selection techniques for multi-touch screens. In *CHI 2006*, 1263–1272, 2006.
5. L. Bonanni, J. Alonso, N. Chao, G. Vargas and H. Ishii. Handsaw: Tangible exploration of volumetric data by direct cut-plane projection. In *CHI 2008*, 251–254, 2008.
6. S. Boring, M. Jurmu, and A. Butz. Scroll, tilt or move it: Using mobile phones to continuously control pointers on large public displays. In *OZCHI 2009*, 161–168, 2009.
7. N. Couture, G. Rivière, and P. Reuter. GeoTUI: A tangible user interface for geoscience. In *TEI 2008*, 89–96, 2008.
8. R. Dachselt and R. Buchholz. Natural throw and tilt interaction between mobile phones and distant displays. In *CHI 2009*, 3253–3258, 2009.
9. F. Echtler, S. Nestler, A. Dippon, and G. Klinker. Supporting casual interactions between board games on public tabletop displays and mobile devices. *Personal and Ubiquitous Comp.*, 13(8):609–617, 2009.
10. B. Fröhlich, J. Plate, J. Wind, G. Wesche, and M. Göbel. Cubic-mouse-based interaction in virtual environments. *IEEE Computer Graphics and App.*, 20(4):12–15, 2000.
11. C.-W. Fu, W.-B. Goh, and J. Ng, Allen. Multi-touch techniques for exploring large-scale 3D astrophysical simulations. In *CHI 2010*, 2213-2223, 2010.
12. L. Gallo, G. D. Pietro, and I. Marra. 3D interaction with volumetric medical data: Experiencing the Wiimote. *International conference on Ambient media and systems*, 2008. Article No.: 14.

13. J. D. Genetti. Volume-rendered galactic animations. *Communications of the ACM*, 45(11):62–66, 2002.
14. R. Hardy and E. Rukzio. Touch & interact: Touch-based interaction of mobile phones with displays. In *Proceedings of MobileHCI '08*, 245–254, 2008.
15. K. Hinckley, R. Pausch, J. C. Goble, and N. F. Kassell. Passive real-world interface props for neurosurgical visualization. In *CHI 1994*, 452-458, 1994.
16. N. Katzakis and M. Hori. Mobile devices as multi-DOF controllers. In *UIST 2010*, 139–140, 2010.
17. J. Kela, P. Korpipää, J. Mäntyjärvi, S. Kallio, G. Savino, L. Jozzo, and S. D. Marca. Accelerometer-based gesture control for a design environment. *Personal and Ubiquitous Comp.*, 10(5):285–299, 2006.
18. J.-S. Kim, D. Gracanin, K. Matkovic, and F. Quek. iPhone/iPod touch as input devices for navigation in immersive virtual environments. In *IEEE Virtual Reality*, 261–262, 2009.
19. M. Levoy. Display of surfaces from volume data. *IEEE Computer Graphics and App.*, 8(3):29–37, 1988.
20. A. Olwal and S. Feiner. Spatially aware handhelds for high-precision tangible interaction with large displays. In *TEI 2009*, 181–188, 2009.
21. R. Potter, L. Weldon, and B. Shneiderman. Improving the accuracy of touchscreens: An experimental evaluation of three strategies. In *CHI 1988*, 27–32, 1988.
22. W. Qi and J.-B. Martens. Tangible user interfaces for 3D clipping plane interaction with volumetric data: A case study. In *International Conference on Multimodal Interfaces*, 252–258, 2005.
23. W. Qiao, D. S. Ebert, A. Entezari, M. Korkusinski, and G. Klimeck. VolQD: Direct volume rendering of multi-million atom quantum dot simulations. In *IEEE Visualization 2005*, 319–326, 2005.
24. C. Ratti, Y. Wang, B. Piper, H. Ishii, and A. Biderman. PHOXEL-SPACE: An interface for exploring volumetric data with physical voxels. In *DIS 2004*, 289–296, 2004.
25. J. Schöning, M. Rohs, and A. Krüger. Using mobile phones to spontaneously authenticate and interact with multi-touch surfaces. In *AVI 2008, Workshop on designing multi-touch interaction tech. for coupled private and public displays*, 2008.
26. W. Schroeder, K. Marti, and B. Lorensen. The Visualization Toolkit: An object oriented approach to 3D graphics. *Kitware Inc., 4th ed.*, 2006.
27. A. Sears and B. Shneiderman. High precision touchscreens: Design strategies and comparisons with a mouse. *International Journal of Man-Machine Studies*, 34(4): 593–613, 1991.
28. A. S. Shirazi, T. Döring, P. Parvahan, B. Ahrens, and A. Schmidt. Poker surface: Combining a multi-touch table and mobile phones in interactive card games. In *MobileHCI '09*, 1–2, 2009.
29. M. Spindler, S. Stellmach, and R. Dachselt. PaperLens: Advanced magic lens interaction above the tabletop. In *ITS 2009*, 69–76, 2009.
30. F. Steinicke, K. Hinrichs, J. Schöning, and A. Krüger. Multi-touching 3D data: Towards direct interaction in stereoscopic display environments coupled with mobile devices. In *AVI 2008, Workshop on Designing Multi-Touch Interaction Techniques for Coupled Public and Private Displays*, 46–49, 2008.
31. S. Subramanian, D. Aliakseyeu, and J.-B. Martens. Empirical evaluation of performance in hybrid 3D and 2D interfaces. In *INTERACT*, 916-919, 2003.
32. Z. Szalavári and M. Gervautz. The personal interaction panel - A two-handed interface for augmented reality. In *Computer Graphics Forum*, (Proc. of Eurographics '97), 16(3): 335-346, 1997.
33. S. Voida, M. Tobiasz, J. Stromer, P. Isenberg, and S. Carpendale. Getting practical with interactive tabletop displays: Designing for dense data, "fat fingers," diverse interactions, and face-to-face collaboration. In *ITS 2009*, 109–116, 2009.
34. D. Weiskopf, T. Schafhitzel, and T. Ertl. Texture-based visualization of unsteady 3D flow by real-time advection and volumetric illumination. *IEEE Tran. on Vis. and Comp. Graphics*, 13(3):569–582, 2007.
35. D. Wigdor, C. Forlines, P. Baudisch, J. Barnwell, and C. Shen. LucidTouch: A see-through mobile device. In *UIST 2007*, 269–278, 2007.
36. A. D. Wilson, R. Sarin. BlueTable: Connecting wireless mobile devices on interactive surfaces using vision-based handshaking. In *Graphics Interface*, 119–125, 2007.
37. Y. Yokokohji, R. L. Hollis, and T. Kanade. WYSIWYF display: A visual/haptic interface to virtual environment. *Presence: Teleoperators and Virtual Env.*, 8(4): 412-434, August 1999.
38. A. M. Zsaki. Cutting | Plane: An interactive tool for exploration of 3D datasets via slicing. In *C3S2E 2008*, 167–171, 2008.

Eden: A Professional Multitouch Tool for Constructing Virtual Organic Environments

Kenrick Kin[1,2] Tom Miller[1] Björn Bollensdorff[3] Tony DeRose[1]
Björn Hartmann[2] Maneesh Agrawala[2]
[1]Pixar Animation Studios Emeryville, CA, USA
[2]University of California, Berkeley Berkeley, CA, USA
[3]Technische Universität Berlin Berlin, Germany

ABSTRACT
Set construction is the process of selecting and positioning virtual geometric objects to create a virtual environment used in a computer-animated film. Set construction artists often have a clear mental image of the set composition, but find it tedious to build their intended sets with current mouse and keyboard interfaces. We investigate whether multitouch input can ease the process of set construction. Working with a professional set construction artist at Pixar Animation Studios, we designed and developed *Eden*, a fully functional multitouch set construction application. In this paper, we describe our design process and how we balanced the advantages and disadvantages of multitouch input to develop usable gestures for set construction. Based on our design process and the user experiences of two set construction artists, we present a general set of lessons we learned regarding the design of a multitouch interface.

Author Keywords
eden, multitouch, object manipulation, camera control, gestures, gesture design, set construction

ACM Classification Keywords
H.5.2 Information Interfaces and Presentation: User Interfaces—*Graphical user interfaces, Interaction styles*

General Terms
Design, Human Factors

INTRODUCTION
The production of computer-animated feature-length films, such as Pixar's *Toy Story* and DreamWorks' *How to Train Your Dragon*, consists of many distinct stages, commonly referred to as the production pipeline. One of these stages is the construction of virtual sets. Similar to a physical set for live-action films, a virtual set is the environment in which animated films are shot. Set construction artists select and position geometric models of objects, such as furniture and props to build manmade environments, and vegetation to build organic environments.

CHI 2011, May 7–12, 2011, Vancouver, BC, Canada.

Today, many animation studios use off-the-shelf modeling and animation packages (e.g. Maya, 3ds Max) for set construction. Despite more than a decade of interface refinement, the process required to build a set using these mouse and keyboard interfaces is long and tedious. An artist commonly places hundreds if not thousands of 3D objects in the set, but is usually limited to placing one object at a time. Moreover, to properly place a single object in 3D space, the artist often performs several individual 3D manipulations, such as translation, rotation, and scale. However, the mouse only has two degrees of freedom, so the artist cannot manipulate more than two spatial parameters of the object at a time. In addition, existing interfaces introduce significant overhead: the artist must manage modes, select small manipulators, and traverse long distances with the mouse.

In this work we investigate whether *Eden*, a new organic set construction application that leverages multitouch input, can address these concerns. We focus on direct-touch multitouch workstations, which support the use of two hands on a screen where display and input are co-located. With two hands, the artist can work in two different parts of the screen at the same time, thereby reducing the need to travel back and forth between spatially distant screen regions. The artist may also become more efficient by performing simultaneous operations, one with each hand. Furthermore, multitouch workstations can sense the position of each finger and thus two hands provide many degrees of freedom of input. Multitouch interfaces can use these many degrees of freedom to allow users to specify both target object and operation, while manipulating more than just two of the object's spatial parameters at a time. As a result, the application can reduce the number of modes and the number of individual steps needed to complete the placement of a single object.

Despite these advantages, building a multitouch application presents design challenges, such as choosing gestures that are efficient, memorable, and comfortable to perform. There are many different ways to map multitouch sensor data to operations, and the best gesture for a given task is often not obvious. An application might also require a large set of operations, and in order for the application to unambiguously interpret the user's actions, no two gestures can be the same. Finally, touch input has several drawbacks that can reduce the user's efficiency, including imprecision due to the fat finger problem [25] and occlusion of content by the hands [30].

To address these challenges, we built Eden while working in close collaboration with our co-author (TM), a veteran set construction artist at Pixar Animation Studios. We relied on his feedback and experience to create a set construction application suitable for professional-level use. From our design process, we found that restricting Eden to support one operation at a time allowed us to design simple, easy to learn gestures that split the workload across two hands. Using Eden, TM has built a set for an upcoming feature film, and found the system to be more efficent and more pleasant than his current toolset. We believe the general lessons we learned from our design process and the evaluations by TM and a novice user will be informative to researchers and application developers designing multitouch applications for professional users.

RELATED WORK

Prior research has examined new interface techniques for professional tasks. Such case studies include: *Proteus* – a personal electronic journal [9], *ButterflyNet* – a digital field journal for biologists [41], and *ILoveSketch* – a sketching interface for creating 3D curve models [2]. Similarly, we investigate a new multitouch interface technique for professional set construction. We focus on two main areas of related work.

Multitouch Interactions

Researchers have done extensive work on the use of multitouch devices in recent years. They have explored the utility of different attributes of touch, such as shape [7] and orientation [32], as well as simulating physics with touch [35].

Other researchers such as Wu et al. [38, 39] have developed task-oriented multitouch applications including a room planning application to investigate multi-user interaction and an annotation application to investigate gesture design. Brandl et al. [5] developed a sketching application to investigate touch and pen interaction. However, these applications primarily served as testbeds for multitouch interaction design. Researchers have also deployed applications designed for casual users outside of a lab setting, including a senior citizens center [12] and a public city center [24].

Few researchers have explored the use of multitouch for producing professional work. One notable exception is the work of Wigdor et al. [34], which investigated the long term use of a multitouch workstation for office-related tasks. However, the authors used multitouch as a mouse emulation device for pre-existing mouse and keyboard interfaces, whereas we designed and implemented a professional-level set construction application specifically for a multitouch workstation.

Researchers have also recently examined user-defined gestures. Wobbrock et al. [36] combined gestures designed by 20 end-users to create a gesture set for 22 commonly used commands. Follow-up work by Morris et al. [21] found that users preferred gestures designed by end-users and researchers over those designed by researchers alone, seemingly because researchers proposed more physically and conceptually complex gestures than end-users. Thus, we designed our gestures with the help of a veteran set construction artist, one of our target users.

Figure 1. An organic set in Pixar's *Up*. Copyright Disney/Pixar.

3D Object Manipulation

Research in object manipulation and set construction has a long history, but most prior work has developed techniques to improve the mouse and keyboard interface for object manipulation by using constraints, pseudo-physics, and semantic information [6, 16, 23, 29, 40, 42]. In constrast, we examine whether a completely new multitouch interface is a better alternative to the mouse and keyboard interface.

The mouse's limited degrees of freedom (DOF) has motivated research on input devices with more DOFs. Higher DOF input devices such as the *Data Glove* [43], the *Bat* [33], *GlobeFish* and *GlobeMouse* [11], and the commercially available *SpaceBall* were developed for object manipulation. Multitouch workstations also provide many input DOFs, and we designed our application specifically for this input.

In more recent work, Hancock et. al. [15] and Reisman et al. [27] investigated using multitouch for object manipulation. These researchers leveraged direct-touch and the many DOF input of multitouch for this isolated task. In addition, Cardinaels et al. [8] developed a multitouch application for conceptualizing scenes for televison productions. Their application, however, was designed for pre-visualization, while our application is designed for final production.

ORGANIC SET CONSTRUCTION

Set construction is the process of selecting and positioning virtual objects to build a virtual environment inhabited by characters of a computer-animated movie. Before building a set, the set construction artist first works with the story and art departments to determine the aesthetics and rough layout of the set. Then the set construction artist works with the layout department, which is responsible for placing the foundation of the set by positioning the terrain and any key architectural elements that help dictate the action in the scene. The set construction artist then populates the sets with the geometric objects built by the modeling department to flesh out the world. The layout department also provides the set construction artist with shot cameras, which are used to make the final renders. Using the shot cameras, the set construction artist "constructs to camera," to avoid building sections of the set that will not be seen in the final film. Throughout this process, the set construction artist continues to work iteratively with the story, art, and layout departments to fi-

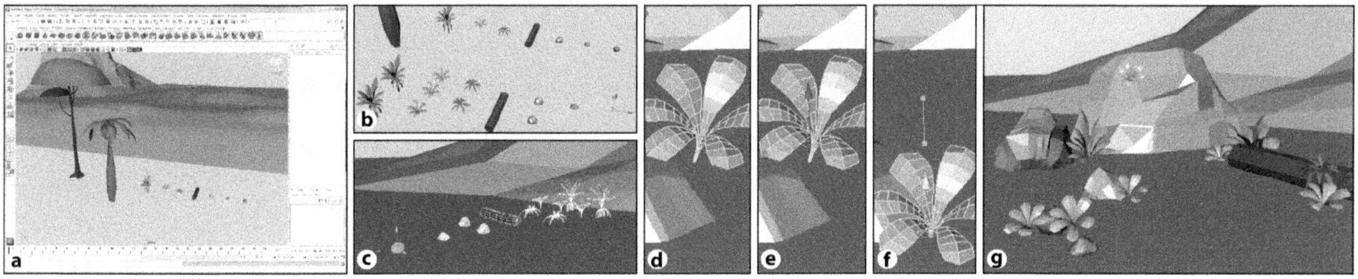

Figure 2. Constructing a set with Maya: a) The set artist creates a model catalog by lining up the models he plans on using away from the terrain. b-c) He then makes duplicates of the objects and translates them to the region of the terrain where he is constructing the set. d-f) To translate an object he first selects the object, then switches to translation mode with a hotkey, and finally picks and drags the arrow manipulator. g) He translates, rotates, and scales objects one by one until he completes the set.

nalize the set. Once the director approves the set, it is then sent to the animation department.

To gain a better understanding of the set construction process, we observed TM, who has over 10 years of set construction experience at Pixar Animation Studios. TM specializes in building organic sets, such as forests and parks, and other outdoor environments consisting primarily of vegetation (Figure 1).

To build a set, TM traditionally uses Autodesk Maya [1], a 3D modeling and animation package. His workflow, whether for manmade or organic sets, typically proceeds as follows (Figure 2). First, TM loads the objects he plans to use for a set and lines them up in a location away from the terrain. These objects serve as his *model catalog*. To add objects to the set he duplicates them in the model catalog area and moves them into the region of the set he is working on. Then using the Maya translation, rotation, and scale manipulators, he positions and orients each object into place. To translate an object, for example, he selects the object, hits the 'W' hotkey to enter translation mode, and picks the appropriate arrows on the translation manipulator (Figure 2e,f) to drag the object into position. He can inspect the set by using the default Maya camera controls: while holding the 'alt' key, a left mouse button drag performs arcball rotation, a middle mouse button drag translates the camera along the view plane (truck and pedestal), and a right mouse button drag moves the camera forward and back (dolly). He also uses the shot cameras to construct to camera. He repeats this process, working region by region, until he completes the set.

Our original intent was to build a multitouch application for general set construction. However, we found that the imprecision of touch makes the construction of manmade sets particularly difficult. Manmade environments are often structured and rigid. They contain highly regularized elements like furniture arrangements, books on a shelf, or city streets. The positions and orientations of objects often depend precisely on the positions and orientations of other objects. Placing these objects requires precision and fine-tuning, which is problematic as touch is imprecise and the artist's hands can obscure the content being manipulated.

Instead we chose to first target organic set construction, since it is less affected by precision issues. According to TM, he is less concerned about precision when constructing organic sets because he places vegetation coarsely compared to manmade objects. In addition, he often places a large amount of vegetation in an organic set, so he can frequently make use of the fast coarse targeting of direct-touch [10, 18, 28] to indicate the positions of vegetation. The experience we gain from designing a multitouch application for organic set construction might help us with the more involved task of designing a multitouch application for building general sets.

Figure 3. The interface of Eden consists of the main content view, a drawer containing the model catalog and stroke pad overlaid on the left, and two matching columns of buttons.

EDEN

The interface of Eden (Figure 3), our multitouch set construction application, is composed of a main view, a virtual drawer, and two columns of buttons. The main view presents the scene through a perspective camera and the artist can directly manipulate objects through this view. We designed the view to take up virtually the entire screen to help keep the artist's focus on the content. On the left side of the interface is the *drawer*, which houses the model catalog and the stroke pad. The model catalog consists of objects available to the artist for a given session. On the stroke pad, the artist can draw single-stroke symbols that execute infrequent commands. If the artist wants to maximize the content area, he can slide the drawer closed. In addition, we provide two matching columns of buttons that map to additional set construction commands. We repeat the buttons on both sides of the interface to allow either hand to invoke them.

TM's process for building a set with Eden typically proceeds as follows (Figure 4): TM starts a new session by loading the terrain and key architectural elements provided by the layout department into the set. He then creates a model catalog

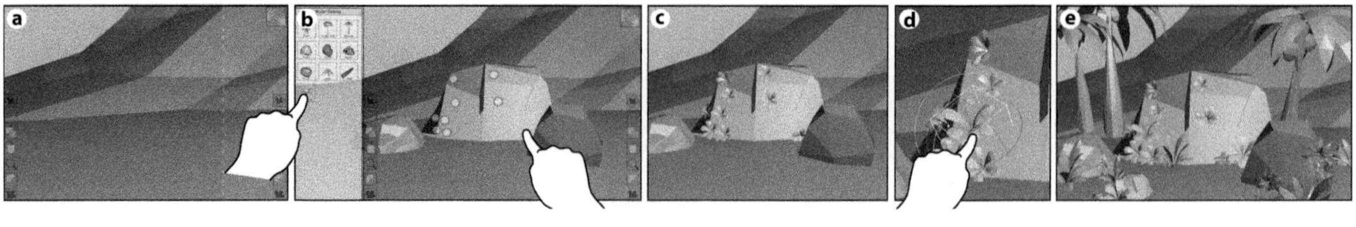

Figure 4. Constructing a set with Eden. a) The set construction artist starts with the empty terrain. b-c) Using the model catalog in the drawer, the artist can touch one finger on the model, and with a second hand touch the locations for where to place copies of the model. He taps several times on the boulder to quickly add nine bromeliads. d) He makes additional adjustments to each bromeliad by performing an arcball rotation for example. e) He continues adding and manipulating objects until the set is complete.

by drawing an 'L' in the stroke pad to open a panel, from which he chooses the geometric objects he wants to add to the model catalog. After building the catalog, he adds objects into the set. He might touch a tree in the model catalog and make multiple taps on the terrain to indicate the locations at which to plant each tree. If he is dissatisfied with how a tree looks he can translate, rotate, or scale the tree by performing the corresponding gesture, which we describe in the object manipulation section. In addition to using the default camera to inspect the quality of the set, TM also loads in shot cameras via a stroke command so he can construct to camera by checking the quality of the set through the shot cameras' views. TM continues to place objects and adjust them until he is satisfied with the set.

Design Principles

Our multitouch workstation can sense the positions of the artist's ten fingers, providing many degrees of freedom of input. Our challenge is to design gestures that map these degrees of freedom to operations and their parameters. To help us design gestures for object manipulation and camera control, we developed several design principles:

Use simple gestures for frequently used operations
Gestures that require fewer touches and fewer movements require less coordination and are faster to perform. We bind such simple gestures to the more frequently used operations to increase overall efficiency.

Conjoined touch as a modifier
To increase the size of the gesture space while keeping gestures simple, we introduce the *conjoined touch* into our gestures. A one-touch is a standard touch where a single finger touches the screen and yields a single 2D contact point. We detect a conjoined touch whenever two touches are adjacent to each other. Specifically, the two touches are combined into a single instance of a conjoined touch where the centroid of the two touches serves as the 2D contact point for the conjoined touch. Thus, two fingers on the same hand can represent three static states: one-touch, a pair of one-touches, and a conjoined touch (Figure 5). We can use a conjoined touch instead of a one-touch to differentiate two operations similar in function, while maintaining the same underlying motion of the hands.

One operation at a time
We initially designed one-handed gestures for object manipulation so the artist could perform two operations simultaneously, one with each hand. However, we found that TM concentrates on manipulating a single object at a time and seldom requires the ability to manipulate two objects at a time. According to Raskin [26], a person only has a single locus of attention, and thus can only focus on the position of one object at time, making the simultaneous manipulation of two objects mentally difficult. Moreover, allowing only one operation at a time reduces the ambiguity of interpreting touch input. For instance, if we had permitted simultaneous gestures, then the application could interpret two touches as either two simultaneous one-touch gestures or a single gesture that uses two touches.

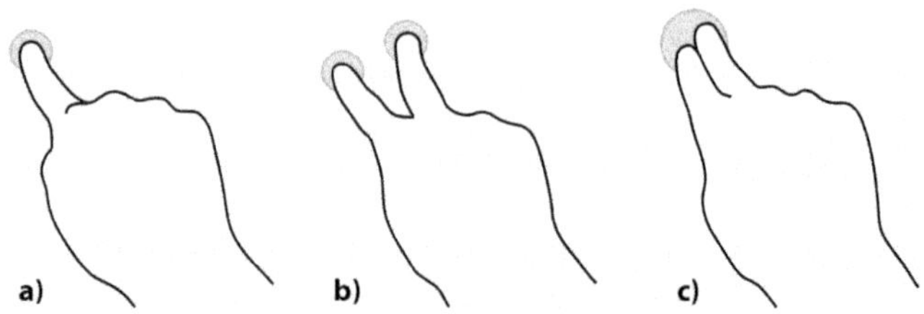

Figure 5. a) One-touch using a single finger. b) Two one-touches using two fingers. c) Conjoined touch using two fingers next to each other.

Split touches across both hands
Since we only support one manipulation at a time, we split the touches of a single gesture across both hands for two reasons. First, fingers on separate hands are not constrained by the palm, which makes them more mobile than fingers on the same hand. This increased mobility makes performing complex motions easier and more comfortable. Second, assigning touches to a second hand can reduce the amount of occlusion of the object being manipulated as the second hand can perform movements in an indirect fashion away from the object.

Use at most two fingers from each hand
Although a single hand supports up to five touches, anatomical constraints of the hand limits the flexibility of each touch. For example, the middle and index fingers on the same hand cannot move arbitrarily far apart. The more fingers a gesture requires, the more complicated and uncomfortable the gesture can become. Therefore, we designed gestures that limited the number of fingers used to at most two per hand.

Interchangeability of hands
For bimanual interaction, Guiard assigns fixed roles to the hands in his Kinematic Chain Model [13]: the non-dominant

hand sets the frame of reference while the dominant hand performs the primary action. We, however, permit the artist to begin an operation with either hand. Since an object can be located anywhere on the screen, interchangeability of the hands allows the artist to choose the most convenient hand to manipulate an object.

Motion of gesture reflects the operation
If the motion of the gesture is similar to the effect of the operation, then the artist can more easily guess how the gesture will affect the target object. Also, the association between motion and operation can help the artist recall gestures.

Combine direct and indirect manipulation
An attractive quality of performing direct manipulation with direct-touch is the sensation of moving a virtual object as one would in the physical world [27]. However, including indirect manipulation can improve efficiency. Using indirect manipulation, the artist can perform movements away from the target object. As a result, the artist does not need to select the object with the manipulating hand and thus the hands occlude less of the object.

Control at most two spatial parameters at a time
We had intended to design gestures that allow an artist to manipulate more than two spatial parameters of an object at a time. However, TM prefers having more individual control of these spatial parameters, so each of our gestures controls just one or two spatial parameters of an object. Research has also shown that even with a six degree of freedom input device, users perform translation and rotation separately [20].

Object Manipulation

Eden supports eight operations for object manipulation that utilize two types of touches: one-touch and conjoined touch. In Eden, the world is oriented such that the x and y axes correspond to the horizontal ground plane, and the z-axis corresponds to the up direction. As shown in Figure 6, the object manipulation operations and gestures consist of:

- x-y translation – a conjoined touch on the object, then drag
- z translation – a conjoined touch on the object, together with a one-touch drag up and down
- arcball rotation – a one-touch on the object, then drag
- local z rotation – a one-touch on the object, together with a second one-touch drag left and right
- world z rotation – a one-touch on the object, together with a conjoined touch drag left and right
- uniform scale – a one-touch on the object, together with a two-touch pinch
- one-dimensional scale – a one-touch on the object, together with a conjoined touch drag on the bounding box face perpendicular to the local scaling axis
- throw-and-catch – a one-touch on the object, and a second one-touch tap at another location

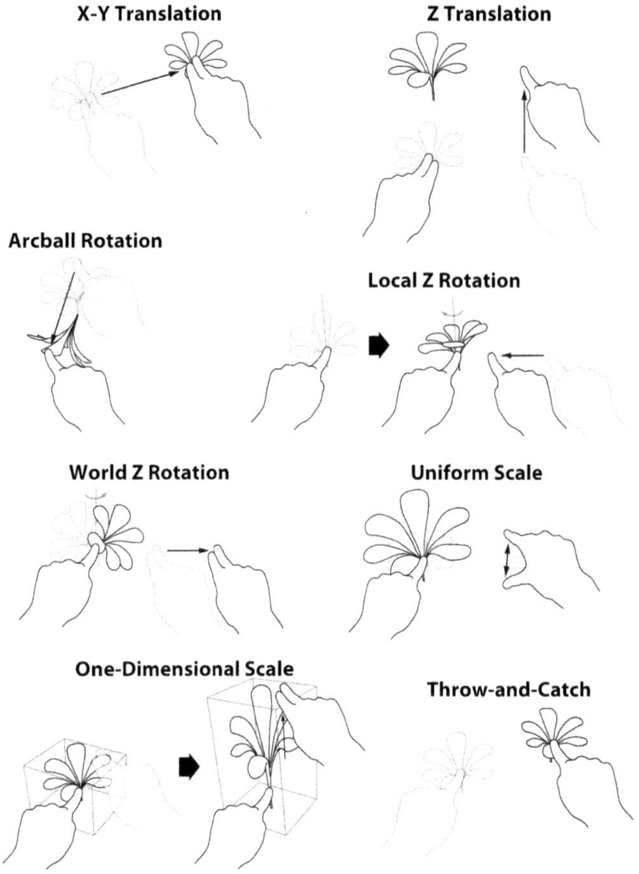

Figure 6. Set of object manipulation gestures.

We tailored the set of operations for organic set construction to support the operations most useful to TM. A set construction artist typically uses separate x and y translations to carefully align manmade objects with each other. For organic objects, however, TM finds controlling both of these translational degrees of freedom at the same time to be more efficient. Thus, we support simultaneous x-y translation, instead of separate x and y translations. We also provide a separate z translation to give TM full 3D positional control.

In addition to positioning each object, TM also adds variation to each object by rotating and scaling it. For example, he can build a grove of oak trees replicating just one oak tree model, and rotate and scale each copy to make it appear different from the other trees. TM needs just enough rotational control to tilt each object off the world z-axis and spin it about its local z-axis to make the object appear unique. Therefore, arcball rotation and z rotation are sufficient for specifying the orientation of an organic object. For some objects such as rocks that do not have a natural orientation, we provide world z rotation. We also include both uniform and one-dimensional scaling along the object's local axes, to provide additional methods to add variation to an object.

To help TM transport objects across long distances, we provide the *throw-and-catch* operation. Mouse-based interfaces often require dragging to transport an object from one location to another, as typically exhibited in the *drag-and-drop* technique. The *Boomerang* [19] technique for use with a mouse allows the user to suspend the dragging component by using a mouse flick gesture to *throw* the object off the screen. The user can later *catch* the object to resume dragging. With multitouch throw-and-catch, TM teleports an object by specifying the source and target locations simultaneously, thus eliminating the time needed to drag the object.

The gestures bound to object manipulation operations all require the artist to first select an object for manipulation with either a one-touch or a conjoined touch. The most frequently used operations should be the simplest to perform, so arcball rotation and x-y translation only require the first touch and then a drag. For the remaining gestures, the artist uses both hands with no more than two fingers per hand. He selects the object with one hand, and then with the second hand, he adds touches away from the object to perform indirect manipulation. For each object manipulation gesture, the artist needs only to select the object and place any additional touches eyes-free to specify the object, operation, and parameters. In Maya, however, the artist needs to select a mode and sequentially target the object and manipulator.

To help make these gestures easy to remember, we used the first touch to indicate the category of manipulation. A conjoined touch on the object always begins a translation and a one-touch on the object begins either a rotation or a scale. When possible, we designed the motion of a gesture's second or third touch to reflect the motion of the object being manipulated. For example, translation along the z-axis moves an object up and down in screen space, so the second touch of the z translation gesture moves in an up and down motion. The second touch of the z rotation gesture moves side to side, which provides the sensation of spinning the object about a vertical axis. The second hand of the uniform scale gesture performs a pinching motion, which is commonly used for resizing photos on multitouch devices.

Camera Control

Camera control is an important component to set construction as the artist must be able to inspect the scene from different angles. To control the camera, the artist first holds down the camera button, which invokes a *quasimode* [26] in which Eden interprets any additional touches as a camera control gesture. This technique is analogous to holding down the 'alt' key in Maya to invoke camera control. We designed our camera control gestures to be similar to object manipulation gestures so they would be easier to remember. A one-touch drag rotates the camera in an arcball fashion, as it does for object manipulation. A conjoined touch drag translates the camera along the view plane (truck and pedestal), which is the same gesture for the planar translation in object manipulation. Lastly, we used the two-touch pinch gesture to move the camera forward and back (dolly), which is similar to the pinch used for scaling an object. We also included view direction rotation (roll) using the same two touches as dolly, as the orientation of the two fingers maps well to the camera's orientation. While holding the camera button, the artist can also choose a custom camera pivot by tapping on the scene or the artist can *frame* on an object (i.e. position the camera to provide a close-up view of the object) by tapping the object with a conjoined touch.

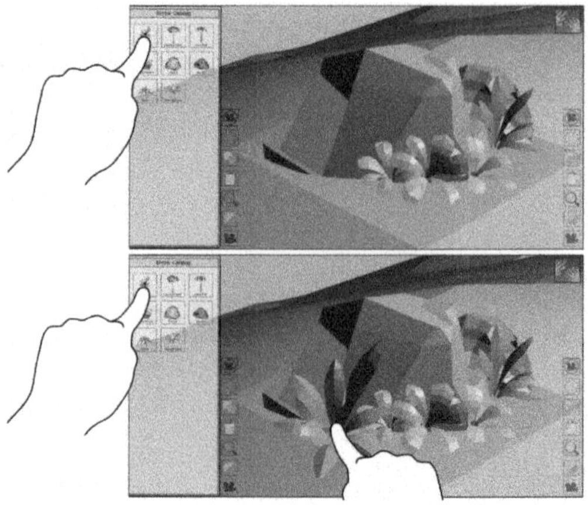

Figure 7. To add an object using throw-and-catch, the first finger selects the model and the second finger taps the position to place it.

In an early iteration of Eden, we distinguished camera control from object manipulation not by a quasimode, but by the touch locations. If the touches did not hit an object, then the system interpreted the touches as a camera control gesture, otherwise it interpreted the touches as manipulating the touched object. However, this method had a major flaw as objects could easily fill the entire view, making camera control impossible.

Adding Objects

The artist can add an object to the set using throw-and-catch. Specifically, he selects and holds the object in the model catalog to throw with one finger and specifies the destination to catch the new object instance by tapping with a second finger (Figure 7). The base of the new object rests directly on the terrain or the closest object underneath the touch. This technique allows the artist to quickly drop a pile of shrubs onto the terrain, for example. The artist can even use all five fingers to place five new objects with one action, although in practice it could be difficult to position all five fingers in the desired configuration. Since no two objects are identical in nature, if the user selects an object in the model catalog with a conjoined touch, we add a small amount of randomness in scale and orientation to the placed object.

In addition to adding objects from the model catalog to the set, the artist can throw a copy of an object from the set into the model catalog. To store a new object, the artist holds an object in the scene with one finger and then taps inside the drawer with a second finger. Adding objects into the model catalog allows the artist to set the size and other parameters of the object and save it for future use. For example, he can scale up a rock object to the size of a boulder and then save it to the model catalog using this throw-and-catch technique.

Additional Commands

We incorporate quasimodes and stroke-recognition to support additional set construction commands.

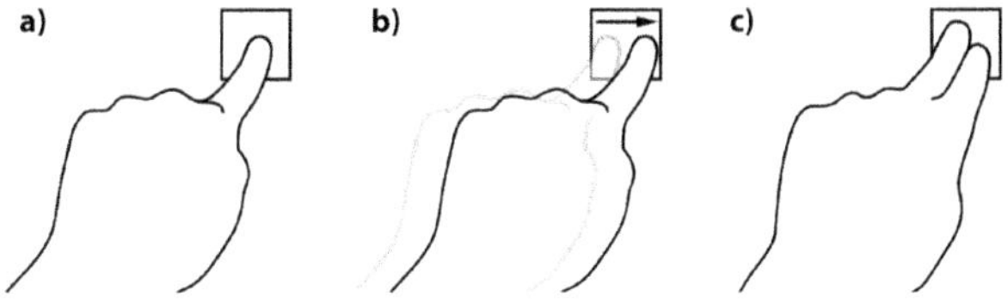

Figure 8. a) One-touch to invoke quasimode. b) Swipe on button triggers secondary action. c) Conjoined touch to make mode explicit.

Quasimodes and Buttons

Quasimodes in our application have the general advantage of keyboard-based quasimodes: the muscle tension needed to hold a key or button down reminds the user that a mode is currently invoked. In addition to camera control, we use quasimodes for various secondary operations that TM finds useful for organic set construction. Although we intended to avoid modes, quasimodes allow us to reuse simple gestures thereby keeping gestures easy to perform. The simplest gesture is a tap, and touch-based interfaces are particularly good for tapping on objects [10, 18, 28]. By holding down one of the quasimode buttons (Figure 3), the artist can simply use another finger to tap on objects to freeze/unfreeze, delete, duplicate, or group select them.

We augment our buttons in a number of ways. We place descriptive icons on the buttons so the artist can recognize the icon, whereas with a keyboard the artist would need to memorize key bindings. More importantly, a user can perform gestures directly on the icon. For example, if we have saved camera positions, a swipe through the icon (Figure 8b) can cycle back and forth between the saved cameras in a manner similar to Moscovich's *Sliding Widgets* [22]. In addition, a conjoined touch tap on the camera icon (Figure 8c) can activate persistent camera mode, where the application only recognizes camera control gestures even if the camera button is not held down. Although we avoided regular modes, we provide camera mode so the artist can keep a hand free when only inspecting a set.

To make the buttons easy to access, we carefully considered their layout. Our multitouch screen sits almost horizontally, so in order to minimize the reach needed to hit buttons, we placed the buttons towards the bottom of the screen. Moreover, we put the same set of buttons on both sides of the screen to allow either hand to initiate a quasimode. We also made our buttons larger than the width of a finger to provide easy targeting.

Stroke Commands

In mouse and keyboard interfaces, commands are typically executed with hotkeys and menus. To keep the artist's focus on the content, we avoided cluttering the interface with buttons or requiring the artist to navigate through menu hierarchies. Instead, the artist can execute commands by drawing single-stroke symbols in the stroke pad of the drawer (Figure 9 left). For example, drawing an 'L' opens a load model panel, whereas drawing a left arrow performs undo. The stroke pad interprets any touch as a potential stroke command, which allows the artist to execute single-stroke commands that do not conflict with default object manipulation operations. Since the stroke pad is large and always in the same location, the artist can easily target the pad and draw a stroke with the left hand. Strokes can be difficult to remember, so the artist can define his own strokes for the supported commands, using a stroke binding panel (Figure 9 right). We use the dollar gesture recognizer [37] for stroke recognition.

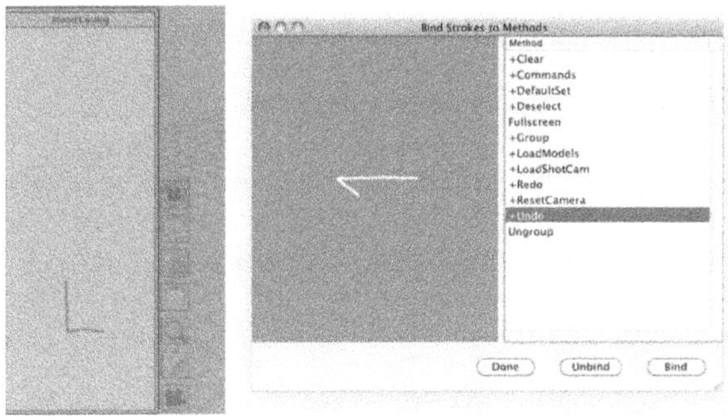

Figure 9. Left: Stroke pad. Drawing a stroke executes the corresponding command. Right: Stroke binding panel. The left panel displays the stroke bound to the highlighted command in the right panel. The artist can choose his own stroke by drawing a new stroke in the left panel.

QUALITATIVE EVALUATION

We asked TM to evaluate his experience using Eden to build a set for an upcoming feature film. We also asked a second set construction artist who has not previously used Eden to evaluate the system from the perspective of a novice user.

Apparatus

Eden runs on a multitouch workstation that we built using the frustrated total internal reflection technique of Han [14]. The size of the screen is 72.5 cm x 43.5 cm with a resolution of 1280 x 768 pixels. The device is patterned after a drafting table and is capable of detecting an arbitrary number of simultaneous touches. The artist interacts with the table by standing in front of the screen, which is mounted at a 23 degree incline. For text entry the artist uses a keyboard connected to a terminal next to the multitouch workstation. Text entry is reserved for infrequent actions such as naming a new set before saving it.

Veteran User Experience

Over the course of two 30-minute sessions, TM used Eden to build a set consisting of 136 trees for an upcoming feature film. He had built the same set previously in Maya, but he and his supervisor found no difference in quality between the two sets. We summarize his experience and evaluation of the system.

Object manipulation

According to TM, the rotation and scaling gestures on Eden are particularly effective because he does not need to first select the object to manipulate and then carefully pick a small manipulator to adjust the object as he does with Maya. In Eden, both the object and the operation are specified by the gesture. For rough placement, x-y translation in Eden is faster than in Maya. However, TM needs more precision when fine-tuning object positions, and x-y translation is cumbersome on a small object because the conjoined touch obscures the position of the object. Also, TM occasionally needs to dolly close to an object in order to select it, because distant or partially occluded objects have small target areas making them difficult to select. In working with Eden, TM did discover an unintended but positive side effect: in certain situations our implementation permits him to switch between operations without lifting the finger selecting the object. For example, if TM first performs an x-y translation, he can then fluidly transition to z translation by adding a one-touch with a second hand, without lifting the conjoined touch used for x-y translation.

Camera control

For TM, the Eden camera controls have slight usability advantages over Maya. Clutching a mouse is a physical annoyance for TM as he sometimes inadvertantly slides the mouse off the working surface, which is not an issue with direct-touch. However, TM finds framing on an object difficult with Eden, because it often requires tapping on a small object, which is imprecise with the conjoined touch.

Adding objects

TM finds adding objects to a set with Eden is more efficient than with Maya. Using the throw-and-catch technique he can tap directly where a new object should roughly be positioned. The visual icons in the model catalog also help remind him what each model looks like. Maya does not provide preview icons.

Additional commands

TM considers quasimodes to be effective for accessing additional commands. Quasimodes permit the reuse of simple gestures, which makes the corresponding commands easy to invoke. The icons on the buttons help him remember which quasimodes are available. TM also finds strokes are as effective as keyboard shortcuts for executing simple commands such as undo and redo.

Repetitive Stress Injury

Over the years building sets, TM has developed repetitive stress injury (RSI) and currently wears a wrist protector on the hand he uses to control the mouse. To prevent his RSI from worsening, he takes regular breaks and finds other ways to exercise his wrist. TM finds that using two hands with Eden better balances the load between both hands. However, we do not have enough experience to know if different RSI problems will arise from multitouch interaction.

TM estimates that he is 20% faster building a set with Eden than with Maya. These results suggest that we have succeeded in providing an expert set construction artist a fully functioning multitouch application that is more efficient than an industry-approved application that has been refined over many years.

Nevertheless there is still room for improvement in both the interface and hardware of our system. According to TM, coarse placement is sufficient for the majority of the organic set construction task. But, if we can address the occlusion problem for x-y translation and the precision problem for selecting small objects with techniques such as Shift [31] or FingerGlass [17], then we can provide a better overall experience for TM. Our hardware also limits the effectiveness of Eden. Our multitouch sensor only runs at 30 Hz and our touch detection system has a small delay when responding to input, which makes Eden less responsive than Maya. Also, detection for conjoined touch is not 100% robust, so the application may at times interpret TM's intentions incorrectly.

New User Experience

We designed Eden using the input from one set construction artist. To gain a better understanding of Eden's potential, we asked TP, a set construction artist with two years of experience, to use Eden for three, 45-minute sessions.

In the first session, we introduced Eden to TP, explaining its operations and features. He spent the second half of the session exploring and familiarizing himself with the interface by constructing a few small sets. His biggest early frustration was camera control, as the sensitivity did not match the Maya controls he was used to.

At the start of the second session we asked TP to recall the object manipulation gestures and the camera control gestures. He was able to perform each one without help, with the exception of world z rotation and one-dimensional scale. These two operations tend to be the least frequently used for object manipulation. After spending 20 minutes warming up and refamiliarizing himself with the interface, he was ready to construct a set. In 15 minutes he was able to build the set shown in Figure 3. At this stage, TP claimed he was "having fun" and building organic sets with his hands "feels like gardening." By the end of session two TP felt he was over the initial hump of learning the gestures.

TP returned for the third session three days after session two. Despite the break, TP was able to recall all the object manipulation and camera control gestures. He remembered the quasimode functions as well as the stroke commands for loading models, performing undo, and resetting the camera position. After ten minutes of practicing the various gestures, he spent the remaining time constructing a set.

Overall, TP found that Eden provided a more immersive experience than Maya, because he felt like he was "sculpting a space" with his hands and could "forget about the technology," which made him feel like he was sketching. In addition to enjoying the tactile quality of interacting with the objects, he found that using both hands to quickly transport objects in and out of the drawer was effective and efficient. We are encouraged that TP was able to learn and remember all of the object manipulation and camera control gestures after just two sessions, suggesting that our gestures are easy to learn and recall. Like TM, TP also discovered that he could perform fluid transitions between operations without lifting the selecting finger. He used fluid transitions frequently.

Although TP had a positive experience overall, he found certain operations difficult to perform with Eden. While he could control the camera, he was uncomfortable with the gestures. He found that camera roll mapped to two fingers was confusing as he would inadvertently roll the camera when he wanted to only perform a dolly. Although the dolly gesture has enough degrees of freedom to also specify roll, we could separate the two operations or remove roll entirely. Also, his interpretation for the pinch motion to perform dolly was inverted from its intended use. When he spread two fingers apart he thought he was pushing the set away, so he expected the camera to dolly away from the set; instead, the camera dollied towards the set. We could resolve this difference in interpration by giving TP a method to customize gestures. For the majority of the organic set construction process, TP did not find precision to be an issue. However, like TM, when TP wanted to fine-tune the positions of a few objects, he had to dolly in close, otherwise he found selecting and manipulating small or distant objects difficult.

As we observed with TM, our hardware has room for improvement. TP felt he had to apply heavy pressure on the screen when performing gestures, making them slow and possibly straining on the hand. If we improve the hardware to recognize lighter touches and be more responsive, then we can provide a more comfortable and seamless experience.

LESSONS LEARNED

Based on our experiences designing a complete multitouch application and our interviews with professional set construction artists who used it, we summarize the following lessons:

- **Justify simultaneous interactions** – Determine how often users will use simultaneous interactions, if at all. If the benefits of simultaneous interactions do not outweigh the complexity of handling simultaneous interactions and the cognitive difficulty for a user to perform them, then support just one interaction at a time.
- **Balance gestures across both hands** – Split the touches across both hands in order to reduce the number of touches per hand and increase mobility. Fewer touches per hand makes gestures faster and more comfortable to perform.
- **Reuse gestures via modes** – As the number of operations increases, the more complicated the gestures generally become. Although we sought to reduce modes, quasimodes allow resuable gestures, which keep gestures simple.
- **Interpret gestures based on location** – Reduce conflicts by interpreting gestures made in one location (e.g. stroke pad) differently than gestures made in other locations.
- **Identify low precision tasks** – Evaluate the proposed application and consider whether precision will be a major factor. Techniques that compensate for touch imprecision [3], may slow the user's performance and limit the effectiveness of a multitouch interface.
- **Factor in occlusion** – Consider designing gestures that use indirect manipulation, so the user can perform manipulations away from the object and reduce hand occlusion, or allowing the user to release static touches once a gesture is recognized [39]. In addition, consider augmenting the interface to be occlusion-aware [30].
- **Throw objects** – A mouse cursor cannot be in two places at once, whereas a user's hands can. Pass objects between the hands to reduce travel times. Consider integrating a flick gesture to indicate a throw.
- **Design fluid transitions between gestures** – If two operations are often performed in sequence, design corresponding gestures that smoothly transition between the two. For example, a one-touch gesture can transition to a two-touch gesture with the application of a second touch.

EXTENSIONS

Eden primarily supports the rough placement of objects for organic set construction. For general set construction, we need to augment Eden with more precise interaction techniques. An artist should be able to adjust a single spatial parameter of an object without affecting the others, so we need additional gestures that control each spatial parameter separately. We could also incorporate existing techniques such as snap-dragging [4] to help the artist precisely align and position manmade objects found in general sets. In addition, a better hardware setup could improve precision by increasing touch resolution and reducing latency. Aside from object manipulation, we expect Eden's basic interface for camera control, adding objects, and setting modes to be sufficient for general set construction.

In addition to general set construction, our design decisions should transfer well to other single-user multitouch applications. By restricting applications to support only one operation at a time, developers can design simple, two-handed gestures that are easy to remember and comfortable to perform. Quasimodes allow the reuse of simple one-handed gestures, and when applicable, throw-and-catch eliminates the need for dragging.

CONCLUSION

We have developed and presented Eden, a multitouch application for organic set construction. A veteran set construction artist has used Eden to construct a scene for an upcoming feature film at Pixar Animation Studios. He found the tool to be more efficient than Maya, which demonstrates that multitouch is a viable option for producing professional level work for at least one workflow. From our design process, we found that focusing on supporting one operation at a time allows us to design simple gestures that split the workload across two hands. These gestures are easy to learn and remember as demonstrated by the experience of a set construction artist new to Eden. Despite focusing on organic set construction, our artists have some trouble with precision and occlusion issues. We believe that with further development we can address these issues to provide not only a better interface for organic set construction, but to begin supporting general set construction as well.

FUTURE WORK

When building Eden, we quickly discovered the difficulty in managing the variety of different gestures. Adding a gesture would require careful design and implementation to avoid conflict with preexisting gestures. A practical avenue of future work is to develop a framework that helps programmers and interaction designers manage large gesture sets. Another area of future work that is important to the investigation of multitouch for professional use is to understand the long-term physical effects and potential RSI issues. Other areas include exploring more aspects of multitouch input, such as using finger identification to reduce the number of modes, and investigating how multitouch widgets should differ from mouse-based widgets, such as Sliding Widgets [22] and our buttons that interpret multitouch input.

ACKNOWLEDGMENTS

We would like to thank Kurt Fleischer, Dominik Käser, Tony Piedra, Craig Schroeder, and Allison Styer for their invaluable input. This work was partially supported by NSF grant IIS-0812562.

REFERENCES

1. Autodesk Maya. `http://www.autodesk.com/`.
2. S. Bae, R. Balakrishnan, and K. Singh. ILoveSketch: As-natural-as-possible sketching system for creating 3D curve models. *Proc. UIST 2008*, pages 151–160, 2008.
3. H. Benko, A. Wilson, and P. Baudisch. Precise selection techniques for multi-touch screens. *Proc. CHI 2006*, pages 1263–1272, 2006.
4. E. Bier. Snap-dragging in three dimensions. *Symposium on Interactive 3D Graphics*, 24:193–204, 1990.
5. P. Brandl, C. Forlines, D. Wigdor, M. Haller, and C. Shen. Combining and measuring the benefits of bimanual pen and direct-touch interaction on horizontal interfaces. *Proc. AVI 2008*, pages 154–161, 2008.
6. R. Bukowski and C. Séquin. Object associations: a simple and practical approach to virtual 3D manipulation. *Symposium of Interactive 3D Graphics*, pages 131–138, 1995.
7. X. Cao, A. Wilson, R. Balakrishnan, K. Hinckley, and S. Hudson. ShapeTouch: Leveraging contact shape on interactive surfaces. *Proc. Tabletop 2008*, pages 129–136, 2008.
8. M. Cardinaels, K. Frederix, J. Nulens, D. Van Rijsselbergen, M. Verwaest, and P. Bekaert. A multi-touch 3D set modeler for drama production. *Proc. International Broadcasting Convention 2008*, pages 330–335, 2008.
9. T. Erickson. The design and long-term use of a personal electronic notebook: a reflective analysis. *Proc. CHI 1996*, pages 11–18, 1996.
10. C. Forlines, D. Wigdor, C. Shen, and R. Balakrishnan. Direct-touch vs. mouse input for tabletop displays. *Proc. CHI 2007*, pages 647–656, 2007.
11. B. Froehlich, J. Hochstrate, V. Skuk, and A. Huckauf. The GlobeFish and the GlobeMouse: two new six degree of freedom input devices for graphics applications. *Proc. CHI 2006*, pages 191–199, 2006.
12. S. Gabrielli, S. Bellutti, A. Jameson, C. Leonardi, and M. Zancanaro. A single-user tabletop card game system for older persons: General lessons learned from an in-situ study. *Proc. Tabletop 2008*, pages 85–88, 2008.
13. Y. Guiard. Asymmetric division of labor in human skilled bimanual action: The kinematic chain as a model. *Journal of Motor Behavior*, 19(4):486–517, 1987.
14. J. Han. Low-cost multi-touch sensing through frustrated total internal reflection. *Proc. UIST 2005*, pages 115–118, 2005.
15. M. Hancock, S. Carpendale, and A. Cockburn. Shallow-depth 3D interaction: design and evaluation of one-, two- and three-touch techniques. *Proc. CHI 2007*, pages 1147–1156, 2007.
16. S. Houde. Iterative design of an interface for easy 3-D direct manipulation. *Proc. CHI 1992*, pages 135–142, 1992.
17. D. Käser, M. Agrawala, and M. Pauly. FingerGlass: Efficient multiscale interaction on multitouch screens. *Proc. CHI 2011*, 2011.
18. K. Kin, M. Agrawala, and T. DeRose. Determining the benefits of direct-touch, bimanual, and multifinger input on a multitouch workstation. *Proc. GI 2009*, pages 119–124, 2009.
19. M. Kobayashi and T. Igarashi. Boomerang: Suspendable drag-and-drop interactions based on a throw-and-catch metaphor. *Proc. UIST 2007*, pages 187–190, 2007.
20. M. Masliah and P. Milgram. Measuring the allocation of control in a 6 degree-of-freedom docking experiment. *Proc. CHI 2000*, pages 25–32, 2000.
21. M. Morris, J. Wobbrock, and A. Wilson. Understanding users' preferences for surface gestures. *Proc. GI 2010*, pages 261–268, 2010.
22. T. Moscovich. Contact area interaction with sliding widgets. *Proc. UIST 2009*, pages 13–22, 2009.
23. J. Oh and W. Stuerzlinger. Moving objects with 2D input devices in cad systems and desktop virtual environments. *Proc. GI 2005*, pages 195–202, 2005.
24. P. Peltonen, E. Kurvinen, A. Salovaara, G. Jacucci, T. Ilmonen, J. Evans, A. Oulasvirta, and P. Saarikko. It's mine, don't touch!: interactions at a large multi-touch display in a city centre. *Proc. CHI 2008*, pages 1285–1294, 2008.
25. R. L. Potter, L. J. Weldon, and B. Shneiderman. Improving the accuracy of touch screens: an experimental evaluation of three strategies. *Proc. CHI 1988*, pages 27–32, 1988.
26. J. Raskin. *The Humane Interface*. Addison Wesley, 2000.
27. J. Reisman, P. Davidson, and J. Han. A screen-space formulation for 2D and 3D direct manipulation. *Proc. UIST 2009*, pages 69–78, 2009.
28. A. Sears and B. Shneiderman. High precision touchscreens: design strategies and comparisons with a mouse. *International Journal of Man-Machine Studies*, 34(4):593–613, 1991.
29. M. Shinya and M. Forgue. Laying out objects with geometric and physical constraints. *The Visual Computer*, 11(4):188–201, 1995.
30. D. Vogel and R. Balakrishnan. Occlusion-aware interfaces. *Proc. CHI 2010*, pages 263–272, 2010.
31. D. Vogel and P. Baudisch. Shift: A technique for operating pen-based interfaces using touch. *Proc. CHI 2007*, pages 657–666, 2007.
32. F. Wang, X. Cao, X. Ren, and P. Irani. Detecting and leveraging finger orientation for interaction with direct-touch surfaces. *Proc. UIST 2009*, pages 23–32, 2009.
33. C. Ware and D. Jessom. Using the Bat: a six-dimensional mouse for object placement. *IEEE Computer Graphics & Applications*, 8(6):65–70, 1988.
34. D. Wigdor, G. Perm, K. Ryall, A. Esenther, and C. Shen. Living with a tabletop: Analysis and observations of long term office use of a multi-touch table. *Proc. Tabletop 2007*, pages 60–67, 2007.
35. A. Wilson, S. Izadi, O. Hilliges, A. Garcia-Mendoza, and D. Kirk. Bringing physics to the surface. *Proc. UIST 2008*, pages 67–76, 2008.
36. J. Wobbrock, M. Morris, and A. Wilson. User-defined gestures for surface computing. *Proc. CHI 2009*, pages 1083–1092, 2009.
37. J. Wobbrock, A. Wilson, and Y. Li. Gestures without libraries, toolkits or training: a $1 recognizer for user interface prototypes. *Proc. UIST 2007*, pages 159–168, 2007.
38. M. Wu and R. Balakrishnan. Multi-finger and whole hand gestural interaction techniques for multi-user tabletop displays. *Proc. UIST 2003*, pages 193–202, 2003.
39. M. Wu, C. Shen, K. Ryall, C. Forlines, and R. Balakrishnan. Gesture registration, relaxation, and reuse for multi-point direct-touch surfaces. *Proc. Tabletop 2006*, pages 185–192, 2006.
40. K. Xu, J. Stewart, and E. Flume. Constraint-based automatic placement for scene composition. *Proc. GI 2002*, pages 25–34, 2002.
41. R. Yeh, C. Liao, S. Klemmer, F. Guimbretire, B. Lee, B. Kakaradov, J. Stamberger, and A. Paepcke. ButterflyNet: a mobile capture and access system for field biology research. *Proc. CHI 2006*, pages 571–580, 2006.
42. R. Zeleznik, K. Herndon, and J. Hughes. Sketch: an interface for sketching 3D scenes. *Proc. SIGGRAPH 1996*, pages 163–170, 1996.
43. T. Zimmerman, J. Lanier, C. Blanchard, S. Bryson, and Y. Harvill. A hand gesture interface device. *Proc. CHI 1987*, pages 189–192, 1987.

2D Touching of 3D Stereoscopic Objects

Dimitar Valkov, Frank Steinicke, Gerd Bruder and Klaus Hinrichs
Visualization and Computer Graphics Research Group
University of Münster, Einsteinstr. 62, 48149 Münster, Germany
[dimitar.valkov, fsteini, gerd.bruder, khh]@uni-muenster.de

ABSTRACT
Recent developments in the area of touch and display technologies have suggested to combine multi-touch systems and stereoscopic visualization. Stereoscopic perception requires each eye to see a slightly different perspective of the same scene, which results in two distinct projections on the display. Thus, if the user wants to select a 3D stereoscopic object in such a setup, the question arises where she would touch the 2D surface to indicate the selection. A user may apply different strategies, for instance touching the midpoint between the two projections, or touching one of them.

In this paper we analyze the relation between the 3D positions of stereoscopically rendered objects and the *on-surface touch points*, where users touch the surface. We performed an experiment in which we determined the positions of the users' touches for objects, which were displayed with positive, negative or zero parallaxes. We found that users tend to touch between the projections for the two eyes with an offset towards the projection for the dominant eye. Our results give implications for the development of future touch-enabled interfaces, which support 3D stereoscopic visualization.

Author Keywords
Touch screens, multi-touch, stereoscopic displays.

ACM Classification Keywords
H.5.2 Information Interfaces and Presentation: User Interfaces – Input Devices and Strategies, Evaluation / Methodology.

General Terms
Experimentation, Human Factors

INTRODUCTION
Two different technologies have dominated recent tech exhibitions and the entertainment market: multi-touch surfaces and 3D stereoscopic displays. These two orthogonal technologies, i. e., multi-touch is about *input*, 3D stereoscopic visualization about *output*, have recently been combined in different setups [3, 27, 29], and first commercial systems that support stereoscopic display and multi-touch interaction are already available [2]. Furthermore, interdisciplinary research projects address the question how users interact with stereoscopic content on a two-dimensional surface [3, 4]. This combination has the potential to provide more intuitive and natural interaction setups with a wide range of applications, e. g., geo-spatial applications, urban planning, architectural design, collaborative tabletop setups, or 3D desktop environments [2, 27]. However, until now these systems are mainly used for navigation purposes whereas the interaction with the stereoscopically displayed objects is supported rather rudimentarily.

The ability to directly touch and manipulate graphical elements without using any unnatural input devices has been shown to be very appealing for novice as well as expert users [7]. In particular, passive haptics supplied by direct-touch devices and multi-touch capabilities have the potential to considerably improve the user experience. Therefore, the FTIR (frustrated total internal reflection) and DI (diffused illumination) technologies and their inexpensive footprints [14, 22] have led to the widespread usage of multi-touch on large displays. These setups detect direct touch contact and thus provide tangible feedback without requiring any further user instrumentation. Since humans in their everyday life usually use multiple fingers and both hands for interaction with their real world surroundings, such techniques have the potential to build intuitive and natural interfaces.

Stereoscopic visualization has been known for decades, but recently it has been reconsidered again due to the rise of 3D motion pictures and the upcoming 3D television. With stereoscopic display, objects might be displayed with different parallaxes, i. e., negative, zero, and positive, resulting in different stereoscopic effects. Objects rendered with *zero parallax* appear attached to the projection screen and are perfectly suited for touch interaction, especially if 2D input is intended. Until recently, multi-touch interaction research was mainly focused on those monoscopically rendered 2D or 3D data sets.

In this paper we present first steps to analyze the users' approaches to touch stereoscopically rendered virtual objects on a multi-touch enabled projection screen. Interaction with stereoscopically displayed content in such a setup opens new research challenges. In contrast to objects rendered with

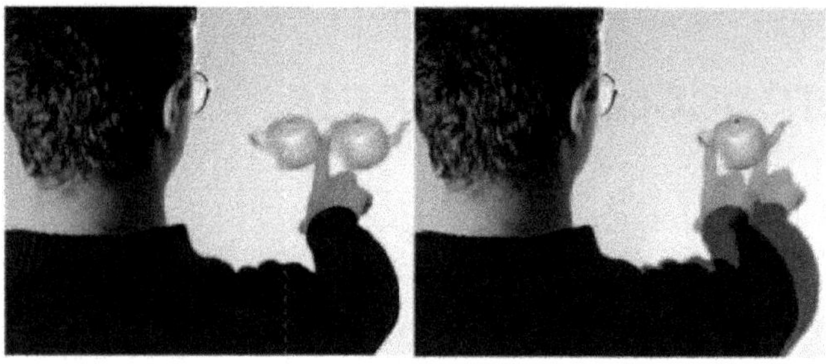

Figure 1. Illustration of the main problem for touch interaction with stereoscopic data. The user is either focused on the finger, which makes the selection ambiguous, or on the object, which disturbs the visual perception of the finger.

zero parallax, objects displayed with *positive parallax* appear behind the projection screen and cannot be accessed by direct touch interaction, since the screen surface limits the user's reach [13]. While one can use indirect selection and manipulation techniques for such objects [15, 23, 25], it is difficult to apply these techniques to objects in front of the screen. In fact, objects that appear in front of the projection screen, i. e., objects with *negative parallax*, introduce the major challenge in this context. When the user wants to interact with such an object by touching, she is limited to touch the area behind the object, since most touch sensitive screens capture only direct contacts, or hover gestures close to the screen. Therefore the user has to penetrate the visual objects to reach the touch surface with her finger. If the user penetrates an object while focusing on her finger, the stereoscopic effect for the object would be disturbed, since the user's eyes are not accommodated and converged on the projection screen's surface. Thus the left and right stereoscopic images of the object's projection would appear blurred and could not be merged anymore (Figure 1 (left)). However, focusing on the virtual object would lead to a disturbance of the stereoscopic perception of the user's finger, since her eyes are converged to the object's 3D position (Figure 1 (right)). In both cases touching an object may become ambiguous. However, as suggested by Valkov et. al. [29], users are insensitive to observe discrepancies between visual penetration and touch feedback when they try to touch stereoscopic objects which are displayed close to the surface. In particular, they found that users are less sensitive to discrepancies between visual and tactile feedback, if objects are displayed with negative parallax.

In the monoscopic case the mapping between an *on-surface touch point* and the *intended* object point in the virtual scene is straightforward, but with stereoscopic projection this mapping introduces problems. In particular, since there are different projections for each eye, the question arises where users touch the surface when they try to "touch" a stereoscopic object. In principle, the user may touch anywhere on the surface to select a stereoscopically displayed object. However, according to observations we have made, it appears most reasonable that users try to touch

- the midpoint between the projections for both eyes (so called *middle* eye projection),
- the projection for the *dominant* or *non-dominant* eye, or
- the orthogonal projection of the stereoscopic object onto the touch surface (i. e., the object's "*shadow*").

A precise mapping approach is important to ensure correct selections, in particular in a densely populated virtual scene. In order to allow the user to select arbitrary objects, a certain area of the touch surface, which we refer to as *on-surface target*, must be assigned to each object.

In this paper we present the results of an experiment that we have performed in order to determine the on-surface targets for objects stereoscopically rendered at different 3D positions. The results of this experiment provide guidelines how this mapping can be applied in future applications.

RELATED WORK

Recently many approaches for extending multi-touch interaction techniques to 3D applications with *monoscopic* rendering have been proposed [15, 21, 25, 33]. For instance, Hancock et al. [15] have presented the concept of *shallow-depth 3D*, i. e., 3D interaction with limited depth, in order to extend the interaction with digital 2D surfaces. They have developed intuitive interaction techniques for object selection and manipulation in this context. Extending the interaction space beyond the touch surface has been investigated by Hilliges et al. [16]. They have tested two depth sensing approaches to enrich the multi-touch interaction on a tabletop setup with monoscopic projection. Interaction with objects with negative parallax on a multi-touch tabletop setup is further addressed by Benko et al. [5]. The proposed *balloon selection* metaphor supports precise object selection and manipulation for augmented reality setups.

Nevertheless, direct touch interaction with *stereoscopically* rendered scenes introduces new challenges, as described by Schöning et al. [27]. In their work an anaglyph- or passive polarization-based stereo visualization was combined with FTIR-based touch detection on a multi-touch enabled wall, and approaches based on mobile devices for addressing the formulated parallax problems were discussed. A similar option for direct touch interaction with stereoscopically rendered 3D objects is to separate the interactive surface from the projection screen, as proposed by Schmalstieg et al. [26]. In their approach, the user is provided with a physical *transparent prop*, which can be moved on top of the object of interest. This object can then be manipulated via single- or multi-touch gestures, since it has almost zero parallax with respect to the prop. Recently, multi-touch devices with non-planar touch surfaces, e. g., cubic [8] or spherical [6], were proposed, which could be used to specify 3D axes or points for indirect object manipulation. The parallax problem described in the introduction is known from the two-dimensional representation of the mouse cursor within a stereoscopic image [28, 31]. While the mouse cursor can be displayed stereoscopically on top of objects [28] or monoscopically only for the dominant eye [31], movements of real objects in the physical space, e. g., the user's hands, cannot be constrained such that they appear only on top of virtual objects. Grossman and Wigdor [12] provided an extensive review of the existing work on interactive surfaces and developed a taxonomy for classification of this research. This framework takes into account the perceived and the actual display space, the input space and the physical properties of an interactive surface. As shown in their work 3D volumetric visualizations are rarely being considered in combination with 2D direct surface input.

Even on monosopic touch surfaces, the size of the human fingers and the lack of sensing precision can make precise touch screen interactions difficult [7, 17]. Some approaches have addressed this issue, for example, by providing adjustable [7] or fixed cursor offset [24], by scaling the cursor motion [7] or by extracting the orientation of the user's finger [17].

The kinematics of point and grasp gestures and the underlying cognitive functions have been studied by many research groups [11, 19, 32]. For instance, it has been shown that total arm movement during grasping actually consists of two distinct component phases: (1) an initial, *ballistic phase* during which the user's attention is focused on the object to be grasped (or touched) and the motion is basically controlled by proprioceptive senses, and (2) a *correction phase* that reflects refinement and error-correction of the movement, incorporating visual feedback in order to minimize the error between the hand or finger, respectively, and the target [18]. Furthermore, Mac Kenziea et al. [19] have investigated the real time kinematics of the limb movements in a Fitt's task and have shown that, while Fitt's law holds for the total limb-movement time, humans usually start sooner decelerating the overall motion, if the target seems to require more precision in the end phase. The changes of the kinematics and control of the reaching tasks within virtual environments have been investigated by Dvorkin et al. [9] or Viau et al. [30]. Valkov et al. [29] have shown that users are, within some range, insensitive to small misalignments between visually perceived stereoscopic depth and the sensed haptic feedback when touching the object. They proposed to manipulate the stereoscopically displayed scene in such a way that the objects are moved towards the screen when the user reaches for them. However, the problem is that objects have to be shifted in space, which might lead to a disturbed perception of the virtual scene for larger manipulations.

EXPERIMENT

In this section we describe the experiment in which we have analyzed where users would touch the surface of the projection wall for objects at different 3D positions in space rendered stereoscopically with positive, negative and zero parallax. We have also examined if the stereoscopic parallax impacts users' performance time or the kinematics of the touch gestures.

Experimental Setup

For the experiment we used a multi-touch enabled passive stereoscopic back projection system. The prototype is illustrated in Figure 2. The multi-touch technology of this surface is based on the *Rear-DI* [22] principle. We use a $200cm \times 161cm$ projection screen as touch surface, and a

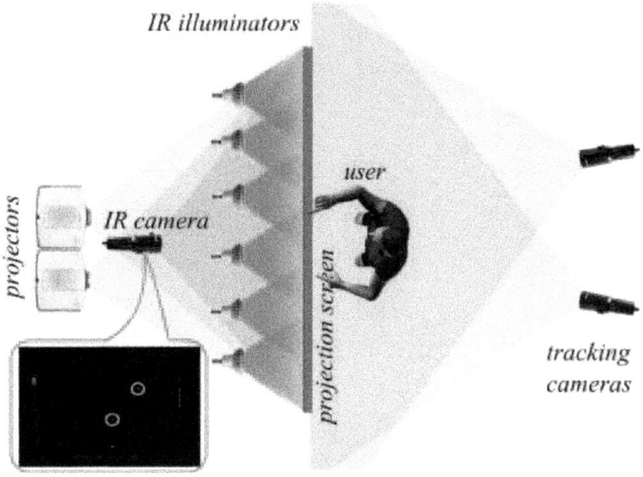

Figure 2. Illustration of the multi-touch-enabled stereoscopic projection wall used in the experiment. The inset shows a screenshot of the touch IR camera for touch recognition.

total of six infrared (IR) illuminators (i. e., high power IR-LED lamps) for back-lighting this surface. Since our projection screen is made from a mat, diffusing material, we do not need an additional diffusing layer for it. A digital video camera (PointGrey Dragonfly2) equipped with a wide-angle lens and a matching IR band-pass filter is mounted at a distance of $3m$ from the screen and captures an 8-bit monochrome video stream with a resolution of 1024×768 pixels ($2.81mm^2$ precision on the surface) at 30 frames per second (fps). For visualization we use passive stereoscopic back projection with circular polarization. Two DLP projectors with a resolution of 1280×1024 pixels ($1.56mm$ effective pixel-width, brightness 2800 $ANSIlumen$) provide stereo images for the left and right eye of the user. In order to perceive a stereoscopic image, subjects wear circular polarization glasses. For detection of the touch input we use a modified version of NUI Group's CCV software. The software needed for the experiment runs on a computer with Intel Core i7 @ $2.66GHz$ processor, $6GB$ RAM and nVidia GTX295 graphics card. As illustrated in Figure 2, an optical tracking system tracks the position of the user's head in order to provide view-dependent rendering. However, during the experiments subjects were not moving in front of the projection wall, and therefore head tracking was not used. All participants were recorded with a video camera (640×480 @ $30fps$) during the experiment.

Materials and Methods

We have used the *Porta test* and the *Dolman test* to determine a subject's *sighting dominant eye* [20]. Subjects exhibiting differing eye dominance in the two tests were excluded from the experiment. Next, subjects judged in a *two-alternative forced choice* [10] task the parallax of four small shapes displayed stereoscopically on the projection wall (two with positive and two with negative parallax) in order to verify their ability of stereoscopic vision.

Subjects were positioned in front of the projection screen in such a way that they could conveniently perform all touch

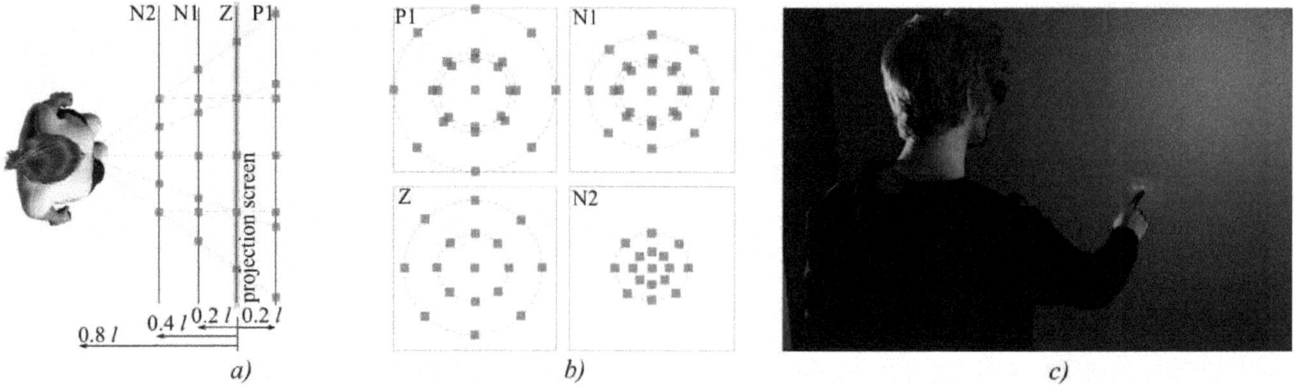

Figure 3. Experiment design; (a) top view of the object arrangement; (b) object arrangement for each parallax plane; (c) photo of a subject while participating in the experiment.

gestures during the experiment with their dominant arm. In a pilot experiment we determined an optimal distance to the projection screen of about 0.8 the subjects arm-length (l). This distance provided an operational radius of $r = 0.6 \cdot l$ around the projection of the subject's head position on the wall (see Fig 3(a)). We marked the corresponding position for each subject on the floor. Subjects were told to remain in this position during all trials of the experiment. If both stereopsis and eye-dominance tests were accomplished successfully, a written task description of the experiment was presented via slides on the projection wall.

For the experiment we have used the method of constant stimuli. In this method the object positions are not related from one trial to the next, but presented randomly and uniformly distributed. For visual stimuli we have used small spheres with a size of $1.5cm$, which ensured a clearly visible target with a reasonable stereoscopic impression; the center of the sphere indicated the exact position subjects should touch. For each trial, the sphere was surrounded by a semi-transparent box to provide additional depth cues (such as perspective distortion, texturing, etc.) to the user. As illustrated in Figure 3(c), we adjusted the color of the box and sphere as well as the background in such a way that stereoscopic crosstalk between the stereoscopic images for the left and right eye was minimized.

In each trial, the subject's task was to touch the center of the sphere, hold her finger at the same position until the object disappeared ($200ms$ after the touch was detected) and then release her finger from the touch wall. $200ms$ after subjects moved their fingers away from the touch surface a new object was displayed, which indicated the beginning of the next trial.

As illustrated in Figures 3(a) and (b), the objects used in the trials were arranged in concentric circles on four different planes parallel to the projection plane at $z = 0$ in a left-handed coordinate system. Since users are more sensitive to discrepancies between visual and tactile feedback if objects are display with positive parallax not accessible for direct touch interaction (cf. [29]), we have focused in this research primarily on objects exhibiting negative parallax. Therefore we have tested two parallax planes, called N1 and N2, with negative parallax at distances $z = 0.2 \cdot l$ and $z = 0.4 \cdot l$, respectively. In addition, we have tested one plane P1 with positive parallax at $z = -0.2 \cdot l$, and the plane Z aligned with the projection plane ($z = 0$), i. e., with zero parallax. The plane P1 was chosen to be relatively close behind the projection surface. If the plane has been chosen to be further behind, it would have been more likely for the subjects to accidentally hit the projection screen while still in the ballistic phase of the motion. The arrangement in concentric circles was used to provide symmetrical view conditions for the objects on the same plane, i. e., with same stereoscopic parallax. As mentioned above, for the $z = 0$ plane we have chosen the radius of the outer circle to match the maximal (convenient) reach distance r of the user, i. e., $0.6 \cdot l$. The inner circle had half the radius ($0.3 \cdot l$). On the planes N2, N1 and P1 the radii of the circles were selected in such a way that corresponding objects across all planes were positioned on a line of sight extending from the user (see Figure 3(a)), thus the users' hand movement distances were the same across all conditions. In addition to these locations, we have added on each plane circles with a constant radius of $0.3 \cdot l$ in order to test also different stimuli that depend only on the stereoscopic parallax, i. e., differ only in their z values.

Participants

13 male and 9 female subjects (age 22-29, $\varnothing : 25.4$; height $163cm{-}196cm$, $\varnothing : 179.9cm$) participated in the experiment. All subjects were right-handed. We determined for 15 subjects that their right eye was dominant (8 male and 7 female), and for 7 subjects (5 male and 2 female) that their left eye was dominant. All had normal or corrected to normal vision. 11 of the subjects wore glasses or contact lenses and none of them reported amblyopia or known stereopsis disruptions. 11 subjects had experience with stereoscopic projections, and 9 had already participated in a study in which stereoscopic projections were used. All subjects were naïve to the experimental conditions. The total time per subject including pre-questionnaire, instructions, training, experiment, breaks, and debriefing took 35 minutes. Subjects could take a break at any time. In addition, after each 45 trials subjects had to take breaks of two minutes in

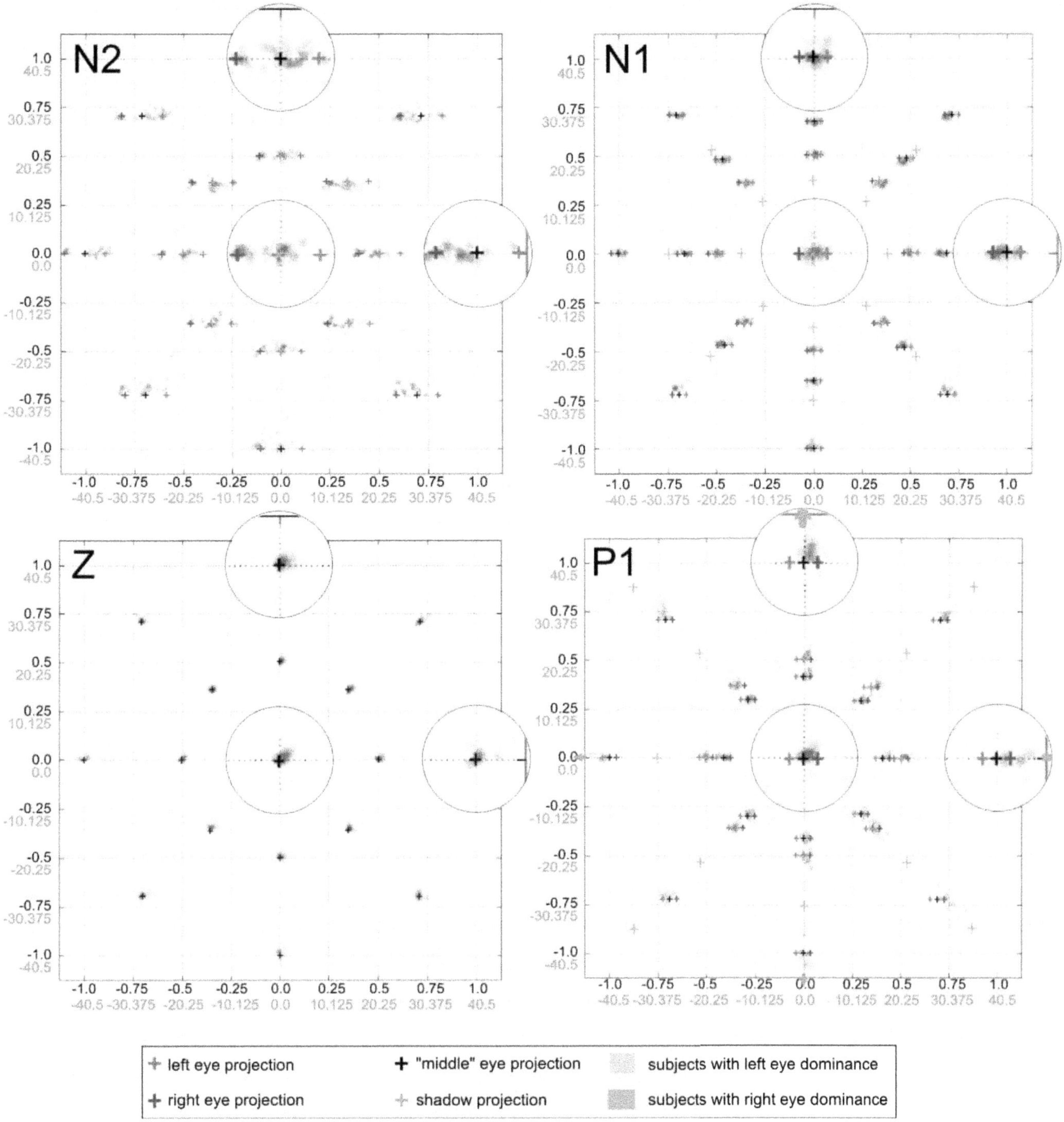

Figure 4. Individual touch results for all trials from the experiment: (top left) shows the touch locations for the subjects in condition N2, (top right) for condition N1, (bottom left) for condition Z and (bottom right) for condition P1. The crosshairs illustrate the position of the different touch targets: (blue) corresponds to dominant eye, (red) corresponds to non-dominant eye, (black) corresponds to the center, and (green) to the shadow projection of the stereoscopic object. The green numbers show the corresponding values in centimeters calculated for subject with $180cm$ body height. The insets show zoomed by factor $\times 2$ views for some of the clusters.

order to minimize errors due to exhaustion or poor concentration. Subjects were students or members of the departments of computer science, mathematics and psychology. Some subjects receive class credits for their participation.

RESULTS

In this section we summarize the results in terms of the touch points and time. For one subject we observed differing eye dominance in the *Porta test* and the *Dolman test*, and therefore excluded this subject from the experiment.

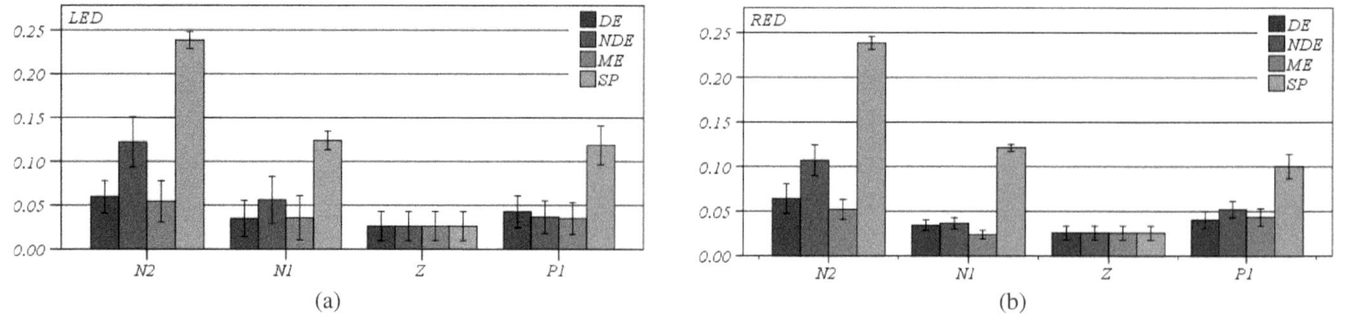

Figure 5. Mean distances from the target points for different parallax surfaces for subjects from (a) Group LED and (b) Group RED. The vertical bars show the standard error.

Touch Points

Since the objects in our experiment were arranged in concentric circles centered at the subject's eye level, we define the focus point on the projection wall as the origin of a 2D coordinate system, with the y-axis running from bottom to top, and the x-axis running from left to right. As units for both axes we have chosen the subject's maximal (convenient) reach distance $r = 0.6 \cdot l$ (cf. Section *Materials and Methods*). We express the coordinates of all touches performed by the subject in terms of this coordinate system. Since the coordinate systems used for the different subjects take into account the differing arm lengths and body heights of the subjects, the coordinates of the touch points are already normalized and can be compared directly among all subjects.

The individual touch locations for all trials are plotted in Figure 4. The crosshairs illustrate the positions of the different touch targets, i. e., blue corresponds to the projection for the dominant eye (DE), red to the projection for the non-dominant eye (NDE), black to the midpoint point between both projections (middle eye, ME), and green to the orthogonal "shadow" projection (SP) of the stereoscopic object.

We have not found a significant difference in the data for male and female participants (two-sided t-test, $p = 0.932$ for the x-coordinate and $p = 0.637$ for the y-coordinate), so we have pooled the results for all subjects. We have calculated for each tested object the corresponding unified coordinates for the four considered touch targets, i. e., DE, NDE, ME and SP, and determined the distances between the performed touches and the corresponding target points using a 2D Euclidean metric. With a two-sided t-test we found a significant difference between the mean distances for subjects with left eye-dominance and for subjects with right-eye dominance ($t(20) = 2.174, p = 0.042 < 0.05$). Mean distance for the left-dominant subjects was $0.094 \cdot r$ ($SD = 0.0284$), and for the right dominant subjects it was $0.075 \cdot r$ ($SD = 0.0135$). Thus, we split the results for the two groups, i. e., left eye dominance (LED) group and right eye dominance (RED) group, in the subsequent analysis.

Figure 5 (a) shows a bar plot of the distances from the target points for different parallax surfaces for the group LED. We have calculated the mean distances to each target point for the four different parallax planes for each subject of the LED group. Those mean values were then analyzed with a factorial analysis of variance (ANOVA), testing the within-subjects effects of target point and stereoscopic parallax. The analysis revealed a significant main effect for the parallax ($F(3, 96) = 59.61, p < 0.001$) as well as for the target point ($F(3, 96) = 69.69$, $p < 0.001$). Post-hoc analysis with the Tukey test showed that subjects touched significantly closer to an object that is displayed on the surface with zero parallax compared to objects displayed with positive or negative parallax ($p < 0.001$ for P1, N1 and N2). Furthermore, there was a significant difference between the touch targets for objects displayed with strong negative parallax N2 and objects displayed with other parallaxes ($p < 0.001$ for P1, Z and N1). We have not found a significant difference between planes P1 and N1 ($p = 0.919$). The post-hoc analysis also showed that the touch points were significantly farther away from the SP target than from all other targets ($p < 0.001$ for DE, NDE and ME). Furthermore, subjects from group LED touched significantly further away from the NDE target in comparison to the targets DE ($p = 0.034 < 0.05$) or ME ($p = 0.01 < 0.05$), but significantly closer than to the target SP ($p < 0.01$). For the LED group, we have not found a significant difference between the two targets, which were closest to the subjects' touch points, i. e., DE and ME ($p = 0.973$).

Figure 5 (b) shows a bar plot of the distances from the target points for different parallax surfaces for the group RED. The mean distances were then analyzed with a factorial analysis of variance (ANOVA), testing the within-subjects effects of target point and stereoscopic parallax.

Again, we calculated the mean distances to each target point for the four different parallax planes for each subject of the RED group and performed a factorial ANOVA to test the within-subjects effects of target point and stereoscopic parallax. The analysis revealed a significant main effect for the parallax ($F(3, 224) = 230.68$, $p < 0.001$) as well as for the target point ($F(3, 224) = 254.19$, $p < 0.001$). Post-hoc analysis with the Tukey test showed that it was also significantly easier for subjects from group RED to touch an object with zero parallax compared to all other parallaxes ($p < 0.001$ for P1, N1 and N2), and there was a significant difference between strong negative parallax N2 and all other

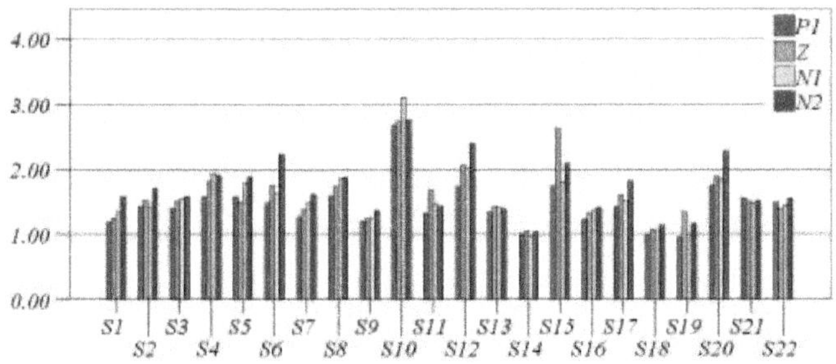

Figure 6. Performance times per subject and parallax.

parallaxes ($p < 0.001$ for P1, Z and N1). As for the LED group, we have not found a significant difference between planes P1 and N1 ($p = 0.463$). Similar to subjects from group LED, subjects from group RED touched significantly farther away from the SP touch target in comparison to all other targets ($p < 0.001$ for DE, NDE and ME). Furthermore, subjects touched significantly farther away from the NDE target in comparison to the targets DE ($p < 0.001$) or ME ($p < 0.001$), but significantly closer than to the target SP ($p < 0.001$). As for the group LED, we found no significant difference between the ME and the DE targets ($p = 0.491$).

Performance Time

Figure 6 shows the mean time elapsed until a subject touched a corresponding object, for each subject and parallax planes P1, Z, N1, N2. We have analyzed the results with a one-way ANOVA, testing the within subject effect of stereoscopic parallax on the mean performance time. We have not found a significant main effect ($F(3, 18) = 1.489$, $p = 0.223$), i. e., the subjects performance time is almost the same for objects on planes P1, Z, N1 and N2. The estimated mean value for the performance time on the parallax plane P1 is $1.446s$ ($SD = 0.3599$), for the Z plane is $1.608s$ ($SD = 0.4287$), for plane N1 $1.575s$ ($SD = 0.4467$) and for plane N2 $1.710s$ ($SD = 0.4359$).

Again, we have not found a significant difference between male and female subjects (two-sided t-test, $p = 0.07$). The mean time for the female subjects was $1.73s$ ($SD = 0.352$) and for the male subjects $1.91s$ ($SD = 0.532$).

DISCUSSION

In general, the results for the LED and RED group show the same qualitative behavior and differ only in quantity. Right-handed subjects with right eye dominance perform significantly more precise touch gestures than right-handed subjects with left eye dominance. However, subjects from both groups tend to choose the same strategy to select a stereoscopic object on a two-dimensional touch surface.

As it can be seen in Figure 4, the touch points for planes N2 (top left), N1 (top right) and P1 (bottom right) are more scattered than the touch points on the Z plane (bottom left), although the size of the projected images for objects on P1 is smaller the size of the projections for objects on the Z plane. Furthermore, the touch points on planes N1 and P1 are comparably scattered, although the projected images for objects on N1 are greater then those on P1. This indicates that touching objects displayed with positive or negative stereoscopic parallax on a 2D surface induces more imprecision than touching objects with zero parallax. The touches on the N2 plane are more scattered compared to those on all other parallax planes and, as described in the section *Results*, the calculated distances to the target points are significantly larger than those for the planes N1, Z and P1. Thus, imprecision increases with stereoscopic parallax, in particular for objects displayed with negative parallax.

As described in the section *Results*, we have not found a significant difference between the per-subject performance times for different parallaxes. Nevertheless, Figure 6 shows that most of the users performed more slowly for objects on the N2 plane than for other objects. The inverse tendency can be seen for objects displayed stereoscopically with positive parallax, i. e., the objects on P1. An analysis of the video records that we made during the experiment revealed that for the objects on N2 and N1 most users perform a "usual" point gesture until they reach the visual representation of the object and then move the finger slowly through it until it reaches the interactive surface, which may be an explanation for the increased performance times. In contrast, some of the users reported that they were "surprised by the surface" while performing some of the touch gestures in order to select objects behind the surface. This also may have had an impact on the decreased performance times and precision, since in these cases, the gesture ended prematurely, without users fully executing the slower and more precise *correction phase* (cf. Section *Introduction*). Furthermore, since the motion of a user's arm during a touch gesture may differ very much among users and for different object positions, the prematurely ended gestures may have led to the "random touches", i. e., outliers, on P1, as may be seen in Figure 4.

None of the subjects complained about touch difficulties, for example, accidentally recognized touches, during the experiments. Most of the subjects have observed the parallax problem described in the introduction (see Figure 1) and reported that for objects displayed with negative stereoscopic parallax it was difficult to get a stereoscopic impression when touching the surface behind the object with the finger. None of the subjects evaluated this effect as a strong distraction from the interaction, and some of the subjects, in particular those with lower performance times, have not noticed it at all. Interestingly, some of the subjects reported difficulties to merge the objects on the N2 plane, although they were within the wide accepted maximal distance for positive parallax. This may be due to the fact that the participants were relatively close to the projection wall and thus were more sensitive to small mismatches due to resolution or illumination constraints.

DESIGN IMPLICATIONS

Even though our analyses show that the ME and DE targets are best guesses for the location of the on-surface touch targets for stereoscopic objects, the calculated mean distances to the actual touch points are still rather large. For instance, the mean distance between the DE targets and the corresponding touch points is 0.0656 (for group LED) and 0.0493 (for group RED), which corresponds to $2.65cm$ (group LED) respectively $1.99cm$ (group RED) for a user with a height of $180cm$. Furthermore, the video recordings of the subjects during the experiment reveal that during most of the trials they neither touched the DE nor the ME target, but rather a point "in-between" both touch targets.

We can express this new *intermediate* target point (IMD) as:

$$\text{IMD} = \text{ME} + \alpha \cdot (\text{DE} - \text{ME}) \tag{1}$$

The parameter $\alpha \in [0, 1]$ determines the position of the point IMD according to the segment (DE – ME). For instance, for $\alpha = 1$ the IMD coincides with DE, whereas for $\alpha = 0$ it coincides with ME. One can find the optimal value of α with an optimization algorithm, minimizing the mean distance between the touch points and the IMD target.

Let $P_i \in \mathbb{R}^3$ be the position of the i-th tested object, with $i = 1, \ldots, n$ and $T_{ij} \in \mathbb{R}^2$ is the actual touch point of the j-th trial ($j = 1, \ldots, m$) for the object at P_i. Then the optimization could be expressed as:

$$\min_{\alpha \in [0,1]} \left(\frac{1}{m \cdot n} \sum_{i=1}^{n} \sum_{j=1}^{m} \| T_{ij} - \text{IMD}_i \| \right) \tag{2}$$

Using Equation 2 the optimal α value for the LED group is 0.551 with mean error $\epsilon = 0.0266$, i. e. $1.07cm$ for a subject with $180cm$ body height. For the RED group we have determined $\alpha = 0.165$, $\epsilon = 0.0365$ ($1.47cm$), which suggests that the subjects in the RED group choose a slightly different strategy than the subjects from the LED group.

Apparently, the optimal α may be influenced by several parameters such as the parallax, the users' handiness, performance speeds and preferences. Nevertheless, the reported values could be used to optimize the selection of a stereoscopically rendered virtual object on an interactive surface if the user's eye dominance is known. We expect even greater improvements by using parallax and eyedness dependent α values, which will be addressed in future works.

CONFIRMATORY STUDY

In this section we describe a confirmatory study in which we applied the results of our experiment in a real-world application. The test application has been developed in the scope of the AVIGLE project [1], which explores novel approaches to remote sensing using a swarm of *Miniature Unmanned Aerial Vehicles (MUAVs)*, equipped with different sensing and network technologies. At the end of the pipeline the currently available sensor data from the MUAVs and their status are displayed to a human operator, while new data continuously arrive. The user can interact with this visualization, for instance, by changing the viewpoint to the virtual environment. In addition, she can define new positions for each MUAV moving their visual representation in the virtual environment (see Figure 7). Since MUAVs within a swarm usually fly at different altitudes, stereoscopic visualization is essential to provide additional depth cues. In order to select the correct MUAV from the swarm, it is important to determine the exact touch target for each virtual MUAV as described above. The goal of the confirmatory study was to verify if operators of the AVIGLE system perform better with the touch targets that we determined in the experiments in comparison to the other approaches.

Procedure

8 expert operators of the system participated in this study (6 had right eye dominance and 2 had left eye dominance). In a within-subject design experiment, we placed the operators in front of the stereoscopic multi-touch surface used in the experiment (cf. Section *Experimental Setup*). The visual stimulus was a typical scene of our application showing a view with a swarm of 12 stereoscopically displayed virtual MUAVs (see Figure 7). We tested a subset of 42 locations from our initial experiment for the swarm. The position of each MUAV within the swarm and its altitude was randomized in each trial with respect to the minimal and maximal inter-MUAV distances. In each trial a MUAV was highlighted and the operator's task was to select it. We gave visual feedback about the selection, so that the operator could retry until the highlighted MUAV was selected. We tested two different on-surface targets, i. e., DE and ME, against the IMD (as explained from Section *Design Implications*). In order to simplify the confirmatory study, we averaged the IMD across both groups and rounded the IMD to 0.4. The swarm's position and the on-surface targets were randomized and uniformly distributed. To determine if a MUAV had been selected we constructed a ray with origin at the position of the dominant eye (for DE), or at the camera's position (ME), or shifted by $0.4 \cdot (\text{IOD}/2)$ towards the dominant eye (IMD) and the actual touch point; IOD denotes the interocular distance. A collision test between a cone around the ray with radius $0.03 \cdot l$ ($1.21cm$) at the projection wall and the mesh of each drone was used to determine the selection. The radius $0.03 \cdot l$ ($1.21cm$) was half the standard deviation (cf. Section *Results*). We measured the number of errors in terms of the number of repetitions required to select the correct MUAV, as well as the time required to perform the task.

Results

The mean number of touches the operators required to select the correct MUAV was 2.15 ($SD = 2.291$) for the touch target DE, 2.10 ($SD = 1.951$) for the touch target ME, and 1.73 ($SD = 1.634$) for the touch target IMD. We have analyzed the mean number of touches for each target and subject with a one-way ANOVA over all trials. We have found a significant main effect ($F(2, 1005) = 4.47$, $p = 0.12 < 0.05$) of the touch target on the number of touches required to hit the correct MUAV. Post-hoc analysis with the Tukey test showed that operators required significantly less touches to hit the correct MUAV, when we used the IMD touch target instead of the touch targets DE ($p = 0.018 < 0.05$) or ME ($p = 0.042 < 0.05$). We have not found a significant difference between the number of touches required to hit the MUAV when the touch target was ME or DE. Operators required approximately 1.7 touches to select the highlighted MUAV using our approach. This large value is caused by

Figure 7. Multi-touch interaction with a swarm of virtual MUAVs flying over a virtual city model.

the small radius of the touch target as explained above. However, in a swarm of several MUAVs, touch targets may overlap if their radii are chosen too large.

The mean time the operators required to select the correct MUAV was $2.77s$ ($SD = 2.819$) for the touch target DE, $3.93s$ ($SD = 7.836$) for the touch target ME, and $2.65s$ ($SD = 4.421$) for the touch target IMD derived from our experiments. We have analyzed the mean performance time for each target and subject with a one-way ANOVA over all trials. We have found a significant main effect ($F(2, 1005) = 5.687$, $p = 0.012 < 0.05$) of the touch target on the time required to hit the correct MUAV. Post-hoc analysis with the Tukey test showed that operators required significantly more time to hit the correct MUAV, when we used the ME touch target ($p < 0.05$ for both IMD and DE). We have not found a significant difference between the time required to hit the MUAV when the touch target was DE or IMD ($p = 0.958$).

CONCLUSION AND FUTURE WORK

In this paper we have made some first steps to analyze the relation between 3D positions of stereoscopically rendered objects and the *on-surface touch point*, where the user touches the surface. We performed an experiment in which we determined the positions of the users' touches for objects which are displayed with different parallaxes. The results of the experiment show that users tend to touch between the projections for the two eyes with an offset toward the dominant eye's projection. We gave guidelines to set the on-surface touch points for stereoscopically displayed objects on a multi-touch surface. These guidelines depend on the user's head position as well as eye dominance; we explained how both can be easily determined. We have verified these guidelines in a real-world application and showed the benefits in terms of task performance over other approaches. Our results give novel implications for the development of future touch-enabled interfaces which support stereoscopic visualization.

While these initial findings provide useful insights into how users touch 3D stereoscopically displayed objects on a 2D touch surface, further studies are required to fully understand users' strategies in such setups. First, the scope of the experiment can be expanded to include varying user positions and orientations, as well as objects displayed with larger parallaxes or different projection sizes. Furthermore, we will more deeply consider the impact of handedness as well as eye dominance. The question arises if the IMD point be expressed in a model considering all these factors. We will extend this research and consider also other stereoscopic multi-touch surfaces such as table-top or mobile devices.

The combination of multi-touch technology and stereoscopic display provides an enormous potential not only for simple selection tasks, but also for richer interaction such as 3D manipulations of or collaborative interactions with stereoscopically rendered virtual scenes. These and similar research questions and challenges will be addressed in the future in the scope of the iMUTS project.

ACKNOWLEDGMENTS

The work was partly supported by grants from the Deutsche Forschungsgemeinschaft (DFG) in the scope of the iMUTS project. The AVIGLE project is part of the Hightech.NRW initiative funded by the Ministry of Innovation, Science and Research of the German State of North Rhine-Westphalia. We acknowledge the cooperation of the subjects as well as expert operators, which participated in the experiments and the confirmatory study.

REFERENCES

1. AVIGLE - Avionic Digital Service Platform. http://www.avigle.de/.
2. Immersion SAS. http://www.immersion.fr/.
3. iMUTS - Interscopic Multi-Touch Surfaces. http://imuts.uni-muenster.de/.
4. InSTInCT - Touch-based interfaces for Interaction with 3D Content. http://anr-instinct.cap-sciences.net/.
5. H. Benko and S. Feiner. Balloon selection: A multi-finger technique for accurate low-fatigue 3d selection. *IEEE Symposium on 3D User Interfaces (3DUI)*, pages 79–86, 2007.
6. H. Benko, A. D. Wilson, and R. Balakrishnan. Sphere: multi-touch interactions on a spherical display. In *ACM Symposium on User Interface Software and Technology (UIST)*, pages 77–86, 2008.
7. H. Benko, A. D. Wilson, and P. Baudisch. Precise selection techniques for multi-touch screens. In *ACM Proceedings of Human Factors in Computing Systems (CHI)*, pages 1263–1272, 2006.
8. J.-B. de la Rivière, C. Kervégant, E. Orvain, and N. Dittlo. Cubtile: a multi-touch cubic interface. In *ACM Symposium on Virtual Reality Software and Technology (VRST)*, pages 69–72, 2008.

9. A. Y. Dvorkin, R. V. Kenyon, and E. A. Keshner. Reaching within a dynamic virtual environment. *Journal of NeuroEngineering and Rehabilitation*, 4(23), 2007.

10. J. Ferwerda. Psychophysics 101: How to run perception experiments in computer graphics. In *SIGGRAPH core*, 2008.

11. L. Geniva, R. Chua, and J. T. Enns. Attention for perception and action: task interference for action planning, but not for online control. *Experimental Brain Research*, 185(4):709–717, 2008.

12. T. Grossman and D. Wigdor. Going deeper: a taxonomy of 3d on the tabletop. In *IEEE TABLETOP '07.*, pages 137 – 144, 2007.

13. T. Grossman, D. Wigdor, and R. Balakrishnan. Multi-finger gestural interaction with 3d volumetric displays. In *ACM SIGGRAPH '05*, pages 931–931, 2005.

14. J. Y. Han. Low-cost multi-touch sensing through frustrated total internal reflection. In *ACM Symposium on User Interface Software and Technology (UIST)*, pages 115–118, 2005.

15. M. Hancock, S. Carpendale, and A. Cockburn. Shallow-depth 3d interaction: design and evaluation of one-, two- and three-touch techniques. In *ACM Proceedings of Human Factors in Computing Systems (CHI)*, pages 1147–1156, 2007.

16. O. Hilliges, S. Izadi, A. D. Wilson, S. Hodges, A. Garcia-Mendoza, and A. Butz. Interactions in the Air: Adding Further Depth to Interactive Tabletops. In *ACM Symposium on User Interface Software and Technology (UIST)*, pages 139–148, 2009.

17. C. Holz and P. Baudisch. The generalized perceived input point model and how to double touch accuracy by extracting fingerprints. In *ACM Proceedings of Human Factors in Computing Systems (CHI)*, pages 1165–1174, 2009.

18. G. Liu, R. Chua, and J. T. Enns. Attention for perception and action: task interference for action planning, but not for online control. *Experimental Brain Research*, 185:709–717, 2008.

19. C. L. MacKenziea, R. G. Marteniuka, C. Dugasa, D. Liskea, and B. Eickmeiera. Three-dimensional movement trajectories in fitts' task: Implications for control. *The Quarterly Journal of Experimental Psychology Section A*, 39(4):629–647, 1987.

20. A. P. Mapp, H. Ono, and R. Barbeito. What does the dominant eye dominate? a brief and somewhat contentious review. *Perception & Psychophysics*, 65(2):310–317, 2003.

21. A. Martinet, G. Casiez, and G. Grisoni. The design and evaluation of 3d positioning techniques for multi-touch displays. In *IEEE Symposium on 3D User Interfaces (3DUI)*, 2010.

22. C. Müller-Tomfelde, J. Schöning, J. Hook, T. Bartindale, D. Schmidt, P. Oliver, F. Echtler, N. Motamedi, P. Brandl, and U. Zadow. Building interactive multi-touch surfaces. In C. Mller-Tomfelde, editor, *Tabletops - Horizontal Interactive Displays*, Human-Computer Interaction Series, pages 27–49. Springer London, 2010.

23. J. Pierce, A. Forsberg, M. Conway, S. Hong, R. Zeleznik, and M. Mine. Image Plane Interaction Techniques in 3D Immersive Environments. In *ACM Interactive 3D Graphics*, pages 39–44, 1997.

24. R. L. Potter, L. J. Weldon, and B. Shneiderman. Improving the accuracy of touch screens: an experimental evaluation of three strategies. In *ACM Proceedings of Human Factors in Computing Systems (CHI)*, pages 27–32, 1988.

25. J. L. Reisman, P. L. Davidson, and J. Y. Han. A screen-space formulation for 2d and 3d direct manipulation. In *ACM Symposium on User Interface Software and Technology (UIST)*, pages 69–78, 2009.

26. D. Schmalstieg, L. M. Encarnaç ao, and Z. Szalavári. Using transparent props for interaction with the virtual table. In *ACM Interactive 3D graphics '99*, pages 147–153, 1999.

27. J. Schöning, F. Steinicke, D. Valkov, A. Krüger, and K. H. Hinrichs. Bimanual interaction with interscopic multi-touch surfaces. In *IFIP TC13 Conference on Human-Computer Interaction (INTERACT '09)*, pages 40–53, 2009.

28. F. Steinicke, T. Ropinski, G. Bruder, and K. Hinrichs. Interscopic User Interface Concepts for Fish Tank Virtual Reality Systems. In *IEEE Proceedings of VR2007*, pages 27–34, 2007.

29. D. Valkov, F. Steinicke, G. Bruder, K. Hinrichs, J. Schöning, F. Daiber, and A. Krüger. Touching floating objects in projection-based virtual reality environments. In *Joint Virtual Reality Conference of EuroVR - EGVE - VEC*, pages 17–24, 2010.

30. A. Viau, A. G. Feldman, B. J. McFadyen, and M. F. Levin. Reaching in reality and virtual reality: a comparison of movement kinematics in healthy subjects and in adults with hemiparesis. *Journal of NeuroEngineering and Rehabilitation*, 1(11), 2004.

31. C. Ware and K. Lowther. Selection using a one-eyed cursor in a fish tank vr environment. *ACM Transactions on Computer-Human Interaction*, 4:309–322, 1997.

32. D. Whitney, D. A. Westwood, and M. A. Goodale. The influence of visualmotion on fast reaching movements to a stationary object. *Letters to Nature*, 423:869–873, 2003.

33. A. D. Wilson, S. Izadi, O. Hilliges, A. Garcia-Mendoza, and D. Kirk. Bringing physics to the surface. In *ACM Symposium on User Interface Software and Technology (UIST)*, pages 67–76, 2008.

TZee: Exploiting the Lighting Properties of Multi-touch Tabletops for Tangible 3D Interactions

Cary Williams[1], Xing-Dong Yang[3], Grant Partridge[1], Joshua Usiskin-Miller[1], Arkady Major[2], Pourang Irani[1]

[1]Dept. of Computer Science
University of Manitoba, Canada
{umwill22,umpartr3,ummillaj, irani}@cc.umanitoba.ca

[2]Dept. of Electrical and Computer Engineering
University of Manitoba, Canada
a_major@umanitoba.ca

[3]Dept. of Computing Science
University of Alberta, Canada
xingdong@cs.ualberta.ca

ABSTRACT
Manipulating 3D objects on a tabletop is inherently problematic. Tabletops lack a third degree of freedom and thus require novel solutions to support even the simplest 3D manipulations. Our solution is *TZee* – a passive tangible widget that enables natural interactions with 3D objects by exploiting the lighting properties of diffuse illumination (DI) multi-touch tabletops. TZee is assembled from stacked layers of acrylic glass to extend the tabletop's infrared light slightly above the surface without supplemental power. With TZee, users can intuitively scale, translate and rotate objects in all three dimensions, and also perform more sophisticated gestures, like "slicing" a volumetric object, that have not been possible with existing tabletop interaction schemes. TZee is built with affordable and accessible materials, and one tabletop surface can easily support multiple TZees. Moreover, since TZee is transparent, there are numerous possibilities to augment interactions with feedback, helpful hints, or other visual enhancements. We discuss several important design considerations and demonstrate the value of TZee with several applications.

Author Keywords
Input device, TUI, 3D UI, multi-touch surface.

ACM Classification
H5.2 [Information interfaces and presentation]: User Interfaces. Input devices and strategies.

General terms
Design.

INTRODUCTION
Tabletops are ideal devices for direct interaction with 2D virtual objects, such as digital pictures and documents. Interactive surfaces provide easy access to any two dimensions, much like conventional graphical user interfaces or paper-based workspaces. The introduction of a third dimension, however, raises a number of interesting problems [11]. For example, common interaction techniques, like pinching and flicking, cannot be easily extended to support free three-dimensional manipulations.

Researchers have recently gained interest in displaying and providing interactions with 3D content on tabletop surfaces [5, 11, 13, 26, 30]. The unique affordances of tabletop computers have led to a number of interesting approaches for the manipulation of 3D objects. These include the use of pressure [5], multiple fingers [11], or layers above the surface [26, 13] to interact with the third dimension. These techniques have their own disadvantages, however; for instance, in the case of multiple fingers [5] or specialized hardware [26], users must learn a special gestural syntax.

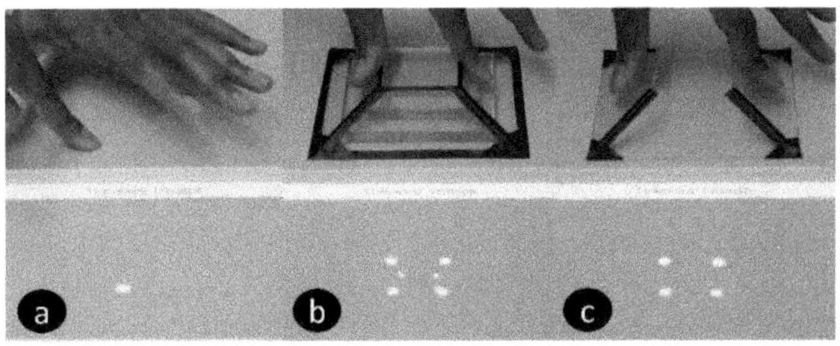

Figure 1 – TZee uses the lighting properties of DI tabletops to map gestures on its tilted faces to three-dimensional interactions. (a) Fingers above the surface that could not be detected by the camera are (b) now visible when placed upon TZee. (c) Without the acrylic kernel, touch cannot be detected.

To address these weaknesses, we introduce TZee, a tangible widget that benefits equally from the characteristics of common touch tabletops and natural interaction strategies. TZee – which stands for *tangible z-axis*, referring to the interactions it supports – is a clear, palm-sized block in the shape of a truncated pyramid, or *frustum*. When placed upon a diffused illumination (DI) surface, the widget funnels some light to its five faces without additional power. TZee can be manipulated with one hand, leaving the other to create mixed bi-manual interactions on the tabletop surface. TZee is simple to create and offers capabilities previously restricted to powered devices like CubTile [24]. Since it is easy to build and requires no wires or power source, TZee is a cost-effective method for interacting with 3D objects on tabletops that scales to accommodate multiple users. Moreover, it is compatible with common tabletop hardware. This makes it an extremely useful and accessible tool for designers to work with 3D content.

Our contributions in this paper are as follows. First, we introduce TZee, a novel passive tangible device that allows manipulations of objects in 3D. We outline a set of gestures that facilitate both common and complicated 3D interactions. Finally, we discuss several important factors in the design of TZee, and based on its limitations, we outline some promising approaches to improve this class of device.

RELATED WORK

Our work builds upon a multitude of prior results for interacting with 3D objects. We review related literature on 3D manipulation with 2D devices, above the surface interactions, and tangible interfaces for 3D control surfaces.

Exercising 3D control on 2D interactive surfaces

Researchers have often explored the use of multi-touch systems for interacting with 3D objects [11, 33]. Davidson and Han [5] suggested that motion in the *z*-direction could be controlled using pressure. Their approach maps light pressure to lifting the object up and towards the surface and heavy pressure for pushing the object down and away from the surface. Shallow-Depth [10] enables smooth single-finger 2D rotate-and-translate, while 3D operations, such as pitch and roll, can be performed by holding down the first touch and gesturing with a second touch [19]. Hancock et al. [11]'s approach requires users to define a rotational axis using two fingers and then perform the rotation with a third finger. A pinching gesture is commonly proposed [10, 11] for motion along the *z*-axis, which is conceptually related to zooming in and out.

A drawback of these sorts of 3D tabletop interaction is that they rely upon explicitly indirect control of at least one dimension (typically the *z*-axis). As a result, the techniques cited above can be considered less natural [13], since they do not directly resemble the ways we manipulate objects in the real-world. Additionally, such techniques suffer from ambiguity issues in the interpretation of user input [22].

Above the surface interactions

To overcome the aforementioned limitations, developers have combined 3D motion sensing devices with tabletop computers [4, 26]. Cutler et al.'s [4] system accepts users' hand or finger gestures above the surface via gloves or a stylus equipped with 6DOF sensors. Subramanian et al. [26] suggested dividing the space above the tabletop into horizontal layers and associating each layer with a different set of commands. Benko et al. [2] proposed using muscle sensing techniques to detect mid-air finger gestures. Their system could detect pinch gestures to pick up or drop off a virtual object. However, due to the difficulty of accurately mapping muscle sensing to depth information, complex operations could not be supported in the z-direction.

Recently, optical depth-sensing techniques have been introduced to resolve some of these concerns [3, 32]. These methods capture 3D hand motions and map them to depth interactions. Hence, 3D interactions on tabletops have become somewhat easier and more natural for users [3, 13]. Nonetheless, optical techniques still suffer from several issues, which make them unreliable for precise 3D interactions. For instance, current depth-sensing cameras have relatively low sensing resolution, suffer from disruption by finger occlusion, and lack visual and haptic feedback to facilitate 3D interactions. Other problems, such as arm fatigue from constant interaction above the surface, can make such solutions less practical in real-world settings [13].

Tangible user interfaces

Tangible user interfaces (TUI) [16] provide intrinsic haptic feedback through a more direct mapping between the user's input and the digital world. Studies have suggested that TUIs offer improved performance over typical graphical user interfaces for many tasks [15, 12, 6, 27]. Furthermore, using TUIs for 3D interactions can be more intuitive, since they preserve the manner that we manipulate physical objects in the real-world. TUIs have been developed for numerous purposes. For instance, ActiveCubes [18] are cubic TUIs that are used for constructing and interacting with virtual cubes. Magic Cube [35] has a built-in orientation sensor supporting richer interactions with tilt. Graspable UIs [7] are physical gadgets that can be dynamically coupled to virtual objects to serve as physical handles or controls. Many of these TUIs support a few of the most common gestures, but due to limited degrees of input freedom, they lack support for useful operations, including constrained stretching along a fixed axis.

Due to their particular benefits, TUIs have recently appeared as supplementary devices for tabletop computers. Fiebrink et al. [6] augmented a tabletop with physical controls to support precise parameter adjustment. Other developments include using TUIs on a tabletop to control robots [9], to work as musical instruments [17], to augment graphical information displays [23], and to represent parameters inside a software application [21]. Many TUIs need to be powered through a tether or batteries. This can limit the size and the number of the TUIs that can be used on a tabletop, and also increases the development and maintenance costs, making them less accessible for general use.

Because of these reasons, there has been increased attention given to developing unpowered TUIs for tabletop interactions. To date, most of these are built upon computer vision technology. Gallant et al. [8]'s foldable user interface is a flexible physical widget made of construction paper augmented with IR reflectors, the shape of which can be tracked by a video camera. Bending the widget into different shapes manipulates objects in the virtual world. PhotoelasticTouch [25] supports interaction with virtual objects via deformation of its transparent, elastic body. SLAP widgets [31] are physical sliders, buttons and knobs with reflective markers on their undersides that can be seen by the same camera that detects touches upon the table's surface.

TZee is primarily inspired by two recent TUI developments: Lumino [1] and CubTile [24]. Lumino are building blocks made of glass fiber bundles that pass light from the table to the block's top and vice versa. This allows several blocks to be stacked while allowing the system to detect the blocks on top. Lumino was primarily designed for detecting stacked objects. It was not designed for 3D interactions, and since the sides of a Lumino are not sensitive to touch input, it offers no support for *z*-axis transformations [1].

CubTile, on the other hand, was designed especially for 3D interactions on large vertical displays. CubTile is a cubic device with five multi-touch faces (all but the bottom). Its four vertical surfaces enable easy motion in the *z*-direction. However, it is less than ideal for typical tabletop scenarios. First and foremost, CubTile requires a power source. Also, its size restricts portability and the number of devices that can be used simultaneously in one application. In addition, CubTile requires users to use both hands in order to interact on two faces of the device, which limits its usability. TZee borrows the best of both worlds by enabling a cost-effective solution with an unpowered (passive) tangible interface for multi-touch 3D interaction. TZee blocks can be created in a few hours and operate on DI tabletops without modifying any underlying hardware.

TZEE

In this section we describe how the design of TZee evolved and explain how it operates. We also demonstrate how to construct a TZee with easily accessible materials.

Design of TZee

We designed TZee with three key ideas in mind. First, we decided that one-handed operation is important to keep the second hand free to perform other gestures. We also strived to mimic real-world interactions. Most importantly, the device had to effectively channel light from the table.

One- vs. two-handed constraints. Each face of TZee is a multi-touch surface. Therefore, multi-finger interactions can be easily carried out with one or both hands. Two-handed input provides more contact points, providing the potential to support richer interactions. For instance, a natural way to stretch an object is to use both hands to pull in opposite directions, which works well with TZee (see Figure 11). However, we wanted to make sure users could perform the most common gestures with one hand.

Shape. Candidate shapes for our tangible widget include a cylinder, a cube, a sphere or a pyramid, since objects of these shapes have vertical or inclined surfaces that can be easily distinguished from input on the *x-y* plane. A cube has four such faces at right angles, clearly defining *x* and *y* axes. A square pyramid has the same properties. This arrangement of symmetric opposing faces also enables useful gestures like grasping (Figure 9). To facilitate input in the *x-y* plane, we truncated the pyramid, removing its tip and leaving a flat top. This also has the advantage of providing a convenient surface upon which images can be displayed through the device from the display below (discussed further in the section below labeled *Widget as display*).

To acquire rapid feedback on the ergonomics of the two shapes, we built a preliminary prototype for both design options. The cube was made by gluing 5 USB touchpads (2 × 2.5 inches each) together on a hard base panel (Figure 2 left). The touchpads were connected to a desktop computer via a USB hub and allowed us to test some basic interaction techniques on each face of the cube. The result was a device much like the CubTile [24], though at a size appropriate for tabletop use. Each of the four inclined faces of the pyramidal device were shaped like a trapezoid. We made the latter prototype 4.5×4.5×1.25 inches in size using a polyurethane mixture (Figure 2 right). At this early stage we were only interested in whether these shapes support easy and comfortable gesturing by using one and two hands.

Figure 2 – Left: cube made from touchpads. Right: polyurethane pyramid allowing some light to pass through the object.

After five people evaluated both prototypes, we found that gestures can be easily carried out on both the cube and pyramid with two hands. However, when used with one hand, the pyramid was easier to use than the cube. This effect was particularly obvious with gestures that required two fingers to move on the two opposite faces (Figure 3). Since these gestures require users to apply pressure on the two symmetric faces of the cube, this would accidently cause the cube to be rotated or otherwise displaced from its resting position. Gesturing upon opposing faces of the pyramid, on the other hand, transferred force downward and prevented accidental motion. Certain gestures that were tricky with the cube like sliding two fingers up and down in the *z* direction (Figure 3 right), were easier with the pyramid because of its slope. Overall, our observations suggested that a pyramid offered both better ergonomics, and was thus selected for the physical shape of our device.

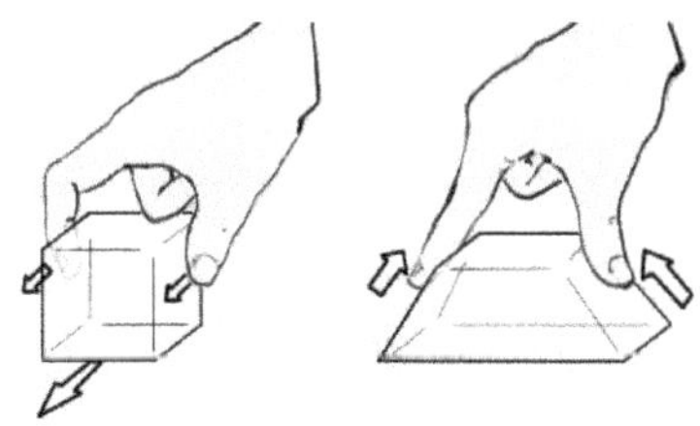

Figure 2 – Left: carrying out gestures on two parallel faces often accidently moves the cube. Right: the tilted faces make it easy to perform a pinch gesture. Force applied to the tilted faces keeps the pyramid in place upon the tabletop.

Lighting optics and construction

Our choice of shape also simplified the device's optics. Recognition of finger gestures on TZee relies on infrared light being transferred through the tabletop surface and into the widget. A passive cube TUI would require a solution to redirect light to its vertical faces. A pyramid differs because the tabletop's camera can directly detect touches upon the device's angled faces.

For this purpose, we required a system based on Diffused Illumination (DI) similar to [20]. Much like Lumino [1], TZee allows the image of objects above the surface to be clearly seen by the table's built-in camera. To accomplish this, it must be made from an appropriate material to minimize light loss in transmission. One of our main challenges was finding the most suitable material to construct TZee to meet our requirements. In short, our mission was to combine a suitable material with an appropriate design to reliably transmit finger motions above the surface to the tabletop's built-in camera. Loss of signal during a gesture may cause undesired behaviors (e.g. inadvertently finishing a gesture), impairing the system's performance.

First Attempt: fiber bundles. Our initial solution was based on a fiber optic bundle as proposed in [1]. Fiber bundles can fit in blocks of different shapes. In addition, the bundle can be banded or cut into different angles to accommodate the slope of TZee's tilted faces. However, due to the round cross-section of optical fibers, it is difficult to bind them seamlessly, as this creates tiny gaps between the thin fibers. These gaps impair the resolution of gesture images. In a preliminary system test, we were not able to reliably transmit finger touches using a 1.2×1.2×1.2 inch bundle. This implied that if we chose to use fiber bundles, large parts of TZee's surface, especially those parts closer to the edges and the corners, could not detect gestures accurately.

Second attempt: solid silicone block. We built our second prototype by pouring a silicon-based mixture – polydimethylsiloxane, or PDMS – into a frustum-shaped mould. PDMS is transparent, light and flexible. The PDMS prototype was created in an air-tight chamber to avoid the intrusion of air bubbles upon solidification that could result in additional loss of light via scattering. Interestingly, upon testing this prototype by shining a red laser pointer beneath it, we found that much of the light was reflected back toward the light source rather than passing through the widget, owing to the phenomenon of total internal reflection (TIR). As a result, finger touches upon the angled faces of the device could not be registered. This encouraged us to further investigate the physical and material properties demanded by our objectives, leading to the third prototype.

TZee: stacked acrylic. Enhanced light transfer is possible using a piece of acrylic, a light-weight transparent material that is often used in DI and frustrated total internal reflection (FTIR) tabletop systems. In our experiments we found that the intensity of light at a fixed height above the tabletop surface could be increased by simply placing a piece of flat acrylic panel on the tabletop surface. This effect can be explained by considering the characteristics of the light radiation profile above the tabletop surface and its refraction in materials with relatively high (>1) refractive index (please note that the refractive index of air is ~1). Each point upon the surface of the tabletop (at the interface defined by the diffuser placed atop it) acts like a light source with a Lambertian radiation profile [29]. Figure 4.a schematically represents each point upon the table and, as defined by Lambert's cosine law, the spherical pattern that describes the light intensity at each angle. As can be seen, the intensity of light is gradually reduced above the table and at a certain height the image of the object above the surface will be blurred and eventually become undetectable. Placing an acrylic panel on the tabletop surface modifies the Lambertian profile, reducing the spread inside the acrylic panel and therefore effectively increasing the transmitted light intensity versus an equivalent amount of air. This variation in transmissibility is a result of light refraction at the surface of the acrylic. When passing through two media of different refractive indices, light refracts at the interface between them according to Snell's law [29] (see Figure 4.b). The ray in the higher-index material (in our case acrylic with ~1.49) is closer to the normal of the interface. This translates into a more narrow radiation profile, corresponding with an increase of the transmitted light intensity. Therefore, for a given intensity, light can be brought to a slightly higher position above the surface of the DI table using this simple mechanism (Figure 4.b).

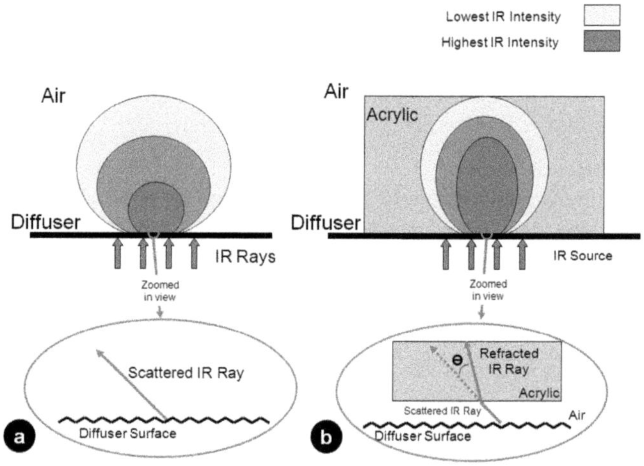

Figure 4 – Left: at each point upon the tabletop surface where the light reaches the diffuser, the light is dispersed according to a Lambertian profile. The microscopic view beneath shows one ray among countless others being scattered. Right: when a piece of acrylic is placed on top of the diffuser, the rays deviate due to refraction. This alters the Lambertian profile, causing it to spread less within the acrylic panel and increasing the light intensity at a certain height above the table.

Upon light's exit from the acrylic block, it resumes its original propagation direction and continues to spread in a Lambertian fashion. Due to refraction inside the acrylic panel, however, the spot size at which light emerges from the panel will be smaller than if the light had travelled to the same height solely through air. The smaller spot size corresponds to a higher intensity of light (i.e. less spread). It is worth mentioning that since the light intensity at the top of the acrylic panel is higher, a higher intensity of light reflecting off the object will be captured by the IR camera. The resulting light pattern inside the acrylic panel(s) will be a superposition (via interference) of all individual Lambertian sources created by the diffuser under the acrylic panels. Therefore, the net effect of placing the acrylic panel on the tabletop's diffuser will be similar, i.e. it will result in overall increase of light intensity above the panel.

To support our claim, we performed two separate tests to detect the increase in light intensity once the acrylic panel is placed on the tabletop. In one case, we used a reflective marker above the table for the sake of consistency. When placed at a fixed height without the acrylic panel, the IR camera registered a bright spot corresponding to the image of our marker. Once the acrylic panel was inserted between the marker and the table, the spot became appreciably larger; this is because more pixels in the processed signal had an intensity exceeding the threshold defining surface activity. This indicates that the camera within the table detects more reflected light from the marker, which implies the effectiveness of the acrylic in preserving light intensity. The degree of change in the blob's size depended on the height of the reflective marker and on the number of acrylic panels, though in all cases, we clearly detected the same effect (Figure 5).

In the second test, we used a silicon (Si) photodiode operating in the photovoltaic regime to quantitatively measure the intensity of light above the table. Similar to the first test, the photodiode was placed at various heights and its signal was registered on an oscilloscope. Note that, when the detector is above the surface, its sensing area is larger than its physical size. Therefore, some light rays from the DI surface are refracted towards the detector while others are refracted outside of it. This is particularly the case for rays from point sources that lie on the periphery of the detector's sensing area. To overcome this unwanted effect we masked a portion of the DI table with a dark tape and left a small opening that was similar in size to the detector's physical size. In this case the detector sees no peripheral light. When the acrylic panel was introduced between the photodiode and the table's diffuser surface, the signal became stronger. For example, with a single panel and a photodiode placed just above it, we detected a 10–15% increase in transmitted light intensity. As expected, intensity gains (versus equivalent amounts of air) diminished as new panels were added. This was caused by spreading of light as well as additional losses introduced by multiple Fresnel reflections at the edges of the panels.

We made our TZee prototype using a stack of acrylic pieces (Figure 5.a), which can be easily found in hardware stores. The prototype is approximately 1.2 inches high, consisting of 3 layers of square acrylic pieces, each 0.4 inches thick (Figure 5, top left). The acrylic pieces measured 4×4 inches, 3×3 inches and 2×2 inches from bottom to top. We polished the cut edges of each acrylic piece. A thin plastic cover (<0.05 inches thick) covers the slope of the steps to provide four tilted surfaces for fingertip contact (Figure 5.b).

We noticed a glowing halo along the edges and joining seams of the device's outer casing, so we covered these joints with black electrical tape. This helped to prevent false blob detections while the user's hand was hovering above the device. The tape also served the purpose of a handle, so that users could hold onto that part of the device if needed and not have the touch detected.

TZee has four reflective markers upon its bottom corners (Figure 5.c), which allows the tabletop's vision system to detect the region occupied by the tangible block, as well as its orientation. Our system thus interprets the gestures and assigns them appropriately to actions, regardless of TZee's orientation or position on the tabletop. Any actions detected within the boundary of the reflective markers are registered as touches upon TZee.

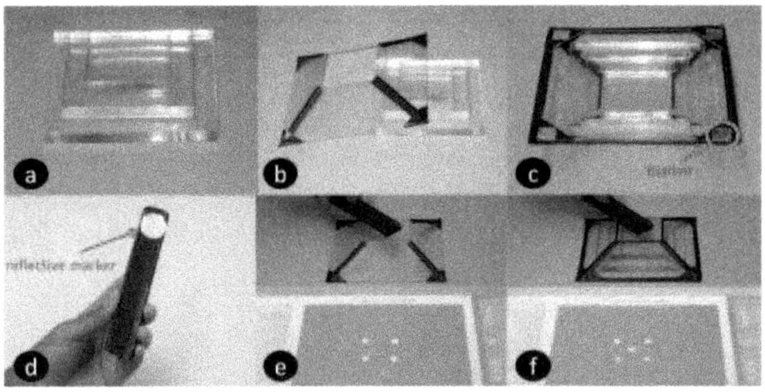

Figure 5 – (a) TZee's kernel consists of a stacked pile of 3 acrylic pieces. (b) a thin plastic cover allows fingers to slide upon the stepped sides. (c) reflective markers and their detection allows us to gauge the space for interacting with TZee. (d) a reflective marker for the test. (e) with the reflective marker above the shell without the device's internals, light is not reflected strongly, (f) but when the marker is at the same height above the acrylic blocks, the camera can detect the reflection.

SYSTEM TEST

To assess TZee's ability to transmit signals, we conducted a system evaluation. Since prior work has already demonstrated advantages for tangibles versus virtual controls [6, 12, 15], we were mainly interested in knowing whether continuous gestures could be reliably carried out at all points upon the surface of TZee. We also collected informal feedback from participants on the characteristics of TZee's gestural support. However, additional studies (beyond the scope of this paper) are required to ascertain under which conditions a TUI such as TZee works better than a virtual control for 3D tasks.

Apparatus

We used a custom-built diffuse illumination (DI) tabletop system with dimensions 20 in. (length) × 26 in. (width) × 36 in. (height). The diffuser placed upon the tabletop was made from vellum and had a thin silicone coating on the side facing the acrylic tabletop surface. The tabletop used infrared LED lamps emitting light at a wavelength of 850 nm using a 12 volt power supply. The table's built-in IR camera captured the input image at a resolution of 320×240 pixels and at a rate of 15 fps. The experimental platform was implemented using the TUIO protocol with the Community Core Vision tracker [28], and ran upon a 1.86 GHz Core 2 Duo PC running Windows XP.

Participants

Ten participants (9 male) between the ages of 25 and 35 were recruited from a local university to participate in this study. Every participant was a daily computer user, but only two had previous experience with tabletop systems. All of our participants were right-handed.

Task and design

We evaluated TZee using a series of 2D docking tasks. Participants were required to interact with objects displayed upon the device. Users performed sliding gestures upon the TZee using one or two fingers at a time to move objects from an initial position to a marked target. This task allowed us to assess whether all the signals were being captured reliably by our system. A failure in docking could be attributed to a loss of signal. The experiment consisted of two tasks. In the first task, participants were asked to drag the object using their index finger on the top and side surfaces as follows (see Figure 6 left):

TOP SURFACE	(1) left-to-right on the top face;
	(2) back-to-front on the top face;
SIDE SURFACES	(3) front-to-back on the top of the a side;
	(4) front-to-back in the middle of a side;
	(5) left-to-right on the bottom of a side;
	(6) top front-to-bottom back on a side;
	(7) up-to-down on a side.

In the second task, participants were asked to (8) use their thumb and index fingers simultaneously to drag two objects from left to right on the front and back faces (Figure 6 right). This would allow us to evaluate the system's performance with multiple simultaneous gestures.

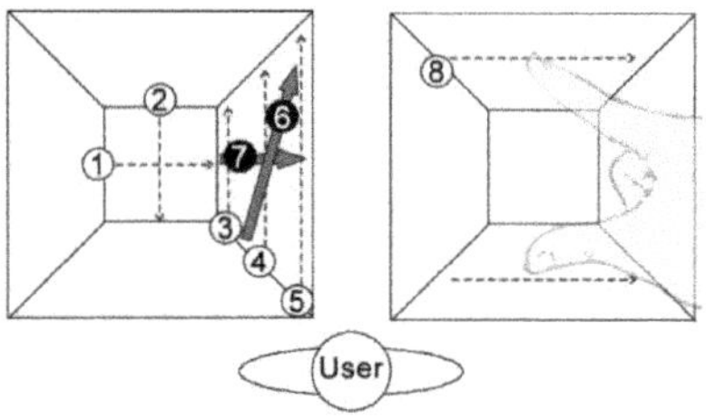

Figure 6 – Left: the direction of movement used in the docking tasks with the index finger. Right: the motion of the docking task with the thumb and index fingers.

Each condition was repeated 10 times. A trial was completed if participants successfully docked the object. Otherwise, they had to try again until they succeeded. Participants were given an unlimited number of attempts for each trial. The object to be dragged and the target were each large enough (0.6 inches) to ensure that the task was easy to perform. Thus, most of the failure was attributed to the loss of the tracking signal. TZee's control-display (CD) ratio (only for this experiment) was set to 1:1, so the distance between the object's initial position and target position was the same as the finger's dragging distance. Both the object and target dock were displayed underneath the TZee, clearly visible due to the device's transparency.

Results

Accuracy and number of attempts were recorded for analysis. A failed attempt happened when the drag action was not detected by the system. Therefore the accuracy rate refers to the percentage of time that the system was able to detect the entire gesture (from start to end) without losing the signal. Participants performed the task with an overall average accuracy rate of 76.5%, i.e. in 76.5% of all trials the system detected the entire drag signal. Results show that sliding on the top face attained an average 76% accuracy rate. Accuracy sliding with two fingers (each on opposing faces) had the lowest accuracy (69%). Sliding on the side faces achieved a 78% accuracy rate, except that the performance when sliding on the top (condition 3 in Figure 6) edges of a side face was relatively low (Figure 7 left; around 66%). We found that this usually occurred when users accidentally slid their fingers onto the tape used to hold the faces of the cover together. On the lower ends of each side face, accuracy rates approached 90%.

Participants had an average of 1.43 attempts per trial. The number of attempts was higher with tasks that required sliding along the top and sliding with two fingers (Figure 7 right). This is consistent with the corresponding accuracy rate. Tasks with higher accuracy (e.g. 4, 5 and 6 in Figure 7) also had fewer repeated attempts. Further analysis reveals that most of the attempts were made during the first few trials with the task, suggesting a learning trend.

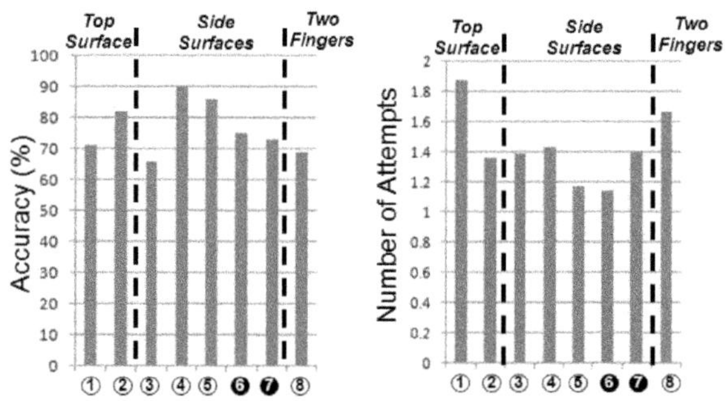

Figure 7 – Y-axis shows accuracy rate (left) and average number of attempts (right). X-axis shows different docking conditions described in Figure 6.

Overall, our results show that TZee can reliably detect several gestures. Furthermore, the results were largely uniform across all of TZee's regions, albeit without a 100% accuracy rate. It is noteworthy that the results were obtained with minimal amount of training to our participants. The tests were performed using raw camera data. These rates can be improved by applying filters or properly extrapolating points between samples. We did not implement such algorithms as we wanted to obtain a raw performance measure.

Next, we describe some basic 3D interactions, such as translations and rotations that can be carried out on TZee with gestures exploiting natural metaphors. Additionally, we show a set of object manipulations that cannot be easily accomplished with existing devices, but are now possible with TZee using simple gestures.

INTERACTIONS WITH TZEE

Once TZee is placed on the table, a simple calibration routine assigns a unique F-ID (Face Identifier) to each face of the widget (Figure 8). To accommodate input independently of the device's orientation, TZee defines its own local coordinate system. The base square of the TZee pyramid establishes the x and y axes. The z-axis lies perpendicular to the base, extending up and into the table.

TZee can be linked to one or more virtual objects. Once linked, TZee serves as a tangible handle for controlling the object(s). Although we do not explicitly recommend a particular mechanism for linking an object to TZee, we envision two potential methods. The first, Symmetrical Bimanual Synchronous Tapping [31], is similar to that used in SLAP widgets. It pairs an object with the tangible block by double tapping on TZee and the object simultaneously. The second method could allow the user to 'bump' the tangible device against a desired object, as exemplified by [14].

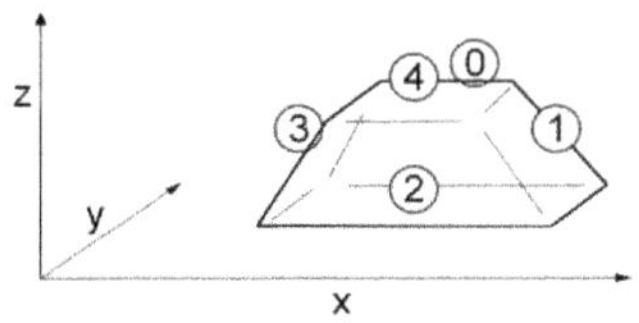

Figure 8 – Faces of TZee are given a unique F-ID, or face identifier, according to the degree of parallelism between a face and the x, y and z axes of the table.

Object manipulations on TZee are aided by the gesture recognition engine. The gesture recognizer requires at least 3-4 detected input samples from a given face to recognize a gesture. Once the gesture is identified, the engine continues the transformation (such as a rotation) until the touch is lifted from the device. This allows for smooth object movements, which compensates for the device's limited input resolution. We assigned a different CD ratio to the sides than the top face of TZee, as our results show that the signal is weaker on the top. In the rest of the paper, we showcase the capability of TZee with a few simple interactions. An investigation of their efficiency and intuitiveness is worthwhile for a future study.

Translation, scaling, and rotation (TSR)

Basic 3D transformations, i.e. translation, scaling, and rotation on the x, y, and z axes, can be easily accomplished with TZee in a natural manner. All of the gestures performed upon the device are interpreted in the context of the widget's local coordinate system.

Translation. Translation along a particular axis can be accomplished by sliding two fingers across two opposite faces. For instance, translation in the z direction can be made by sliding straight up or down on faces 1 and 3 (Figure 10). Sliding up moves the object towards the user; sliding down pushes the object away. A horizontal slide on faces 0 and 2 will result in translation in the x direction. Similarly, sliding horizontally on faces 1 and 3 will translate in the y direction. Sliding TZee across the tabletop also translates the object along the x-y plane.

Note that TZee is an indirect input device. One strong benefit of using indirect input for translation is that it allows users to move the object to an area that is unreachable by direct touch. Using indirect input for translation in the z direction is necessary, since z-axis motion cannot be performed directly upon a 2D surface.

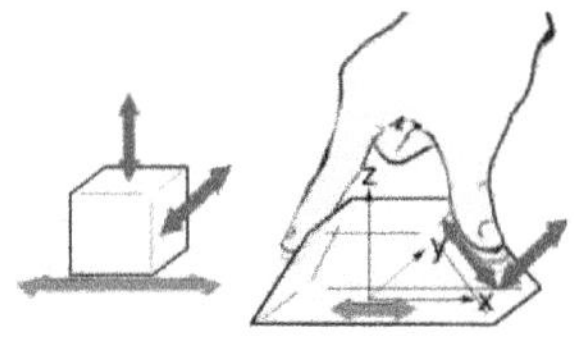

Figure 10 – Illustration of translation using TZee.

Scaling. Scaling can be achieved with two hands. By placing four fingers on two opposite sides of TZee, the user can stretch the virtual object along that axis. A similar pulling-apart or pushing-together gesture makes stretching in the z direction possible (Figure 11). Alternatively, this can be achieved using one hand, and a modifier "key". With the index finger resting on the top face as a modifier (face 4), scaling in the x direction can be accomplished by sliding fingers horizontally on faces 0 and 2. These metaphors replicate our natural actions: scaling requires an origin, represented by the top face touch, plus a spread or contraction, defined by the other two fingers moving in opposition. Scaling is similarly achieved in the y and z directions.

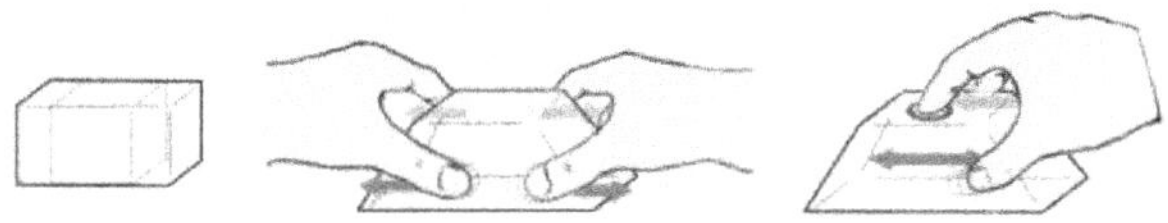

Figure 11 – Illustration of scaling in the x-axis using two hands (middle) and one hand (right).

Rotation. A horizontal flick gesture on any of the tilted faces (F-IDs 0–3) will result in a rotation about the z-axis. In addition, turning the widget will also rotate the associated object around the z-axis. A vertical flick gesture on faces 1 and 3 will rotate the virtual object about TZee's y-axis. A vertical flick gesture on faces 0 and 2 rotates the object about TZee's x-axis (details in Figure 9).

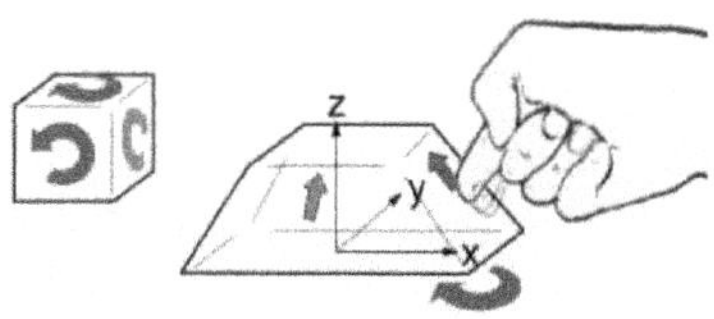

Figure 9 – Illustration of rotation along each of the three axes using TZee. The interactions map naturally to how one would rotate a physical object along these axes.

Beyond TSR

In addition to the basic functions supporting translation, scaling, and rotation, TZee can support a variety of novel interactions. These have not been demonstrated with prior tabletop 3D interaction systems. In this paper, we discuss only a few of them, and leave the design space to be built upon by future application designers.

Stretching across axes. With TZee, virtual objects can be stretched across two axes at a time. To do this, the user can slide the thumb and index fingers towards the edge of two adjacent faces. The corresponding part of the object is stretched out (Figure 12).

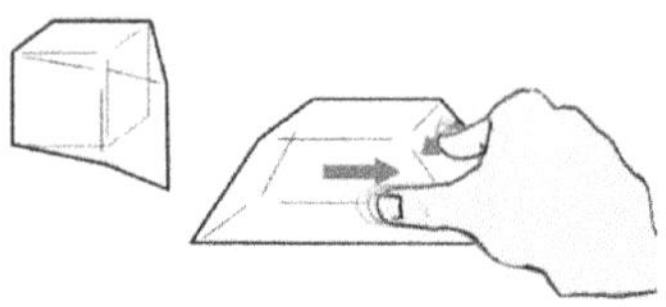

Figure 12 - Illustration of stretch on two adjacent faces using thumb and index finger.

Modifier key. As demonstrated by the scaling operation, TZee supports the use of a modifier key metaphor to extend the functionality of fundamental gestures. Alternate modes are triggered by holding one or more fingers on any of the tangible faces. We demonstrate an example of using a modifier key to invoke a *cut* operation. A virtual object can be sliced into two pieces by cutting it. This task is not uncommon when interacting with 3D volumetric data. The slice action is accomplished with a translation gesture with the addition of a finger held on a tilted face as a modifier (Figure 13). In this case, the translation gesture defines the position and the orientation of a cutting plane.

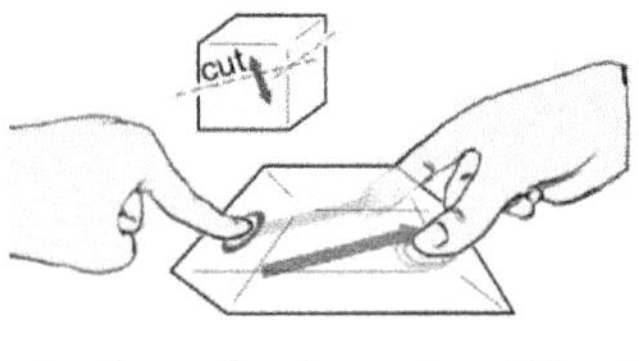

Figure 13 – Illustration of using a 'modifier key' to "cut" an object with different cutting planes.

Widget as display. Since TZee is transparent, images on the surface beneath the widget can be clearly seen through it. This enables a wide range of possibilities. For instance, novice users could benefit from the availability of guides much like our sketches that demonstrate how gestures are performed. Alternatively, to support more sophisticated modes of interaction, various options or parameters for a transformation might be displayed upon the device. At the very least, the usual contents of the tabletop will be visible through the device.

DISCUSSION

We presented an accessible tangible device capable of supporting numerous useful 3D interactions. Here we summarize our findings. There are also a few limitations in the current design, however, that need to be addressed carefully in future studies.

Summary of results

The development of TZee was multi-faceted. In the first step, we identified the necessary ergonomics of the device that would suit our objectives. This in turn led us to create prototypes with materials consisting of fiber, silicone, and finally settle on stacking acrylic blocks and covering them with a thin transparent shell. All of our tests confirmed that this allowed light from the tabletop setup to travel at a height slightly higher than what would be possible in air alone. We leveraged this property to create interactions that were intuitive and that mapped naturally (to the extent possible) to interactions in 3D.

Our system test showed that we can reliably detect a complete sliding action, along the sides of TZee, over 75% of the time. This is impressive given that we did not apply any noise reduction algorithms (other than what was available through the TUIO protocol) to the raw camera images. With such algorithms, we expect accuracy rates to improve, whereby lost signals could be extrapolated from samples that were already collected. Since TZee is an indirect input device, it can use the most suitable control-display ratio for smooth input. This can allow designers to extend the physical space available on the sides to create rich interactions.

Despite these favorable properties that make TZee a viable tool for rapid 3D manipulation tasks, certain limitations need to be considered in its construction.

Limitations

Touch area. The ability to detect a signal with TZee is sensitive to the size of users' touch points. The effectiveness of the device also varies with the pressure exerted by users. The skin tissue at the tips of the fingers flattens out when pressed against the sides of TZee. This forms a larger touch area that reflects more light than a comparable curved surface. If a user placed two fingers together to create a single large touch point on the top surface, for example, signals could sometimes be detected more reliably. The TZee shell was also important in this regard. It not only gave users a smooth surface upon which to glide their fingers on, but also flattened the finger tips as they touched it.

Resolution. TZee's effectiveness of supporting precise gestures is limited by the size of the device, combined with the resolution of the tabletop's camera. Our system used a 320x240 camera resolution, with which we were able to reliably detect the direction of users' gestures. However, detecting the precise amplitude of each gesture is difficult with such a low resolution. The effect of this can be mitigated using fixed-rate transformations rather than controlling the rate with the gesture amplitude. We intend on using higher-resolution cameras that support quick frame rates to improve the resolution limitation. In its current design, TZee can only recognize two finger touches per side. There must also be space between each touch point, or else the software will detect a single large blob rather than two smaller ones. A larger surface area for each can resolve this issue, but in all our informal feedback from users, none were concerned about the use of only two touches per face.

Light loss. Like other optical tangible widgets [1], TZee is also vulnerable to issues of light loss during the transmission from the LEDs beneath the surface of the tabletop, through the surface itself, and into the device. The current prototype is made of 3 layers of acrylic pieces and a thin acrylic cover. This setup introduces a maximum of 8 reflective surfaces (two per piece) before the light reaches the user's finger. During the transmission of the light from the tabletop surface to the surface of TZee, each ray passing through an acrylic piece gets refracted twice. This increases the amount of loss, and therefore reduces the intensity of the light above the table. Furthermore, the air between the acrylic steps and the cover also introduces a fair amount of light spread. This is a result of change of direction when the light enters or leaves the air (since air has a smaller refractive index than acrylic). These issues limit the vertical distance that light can travel within the TZee. With our prototype, we were unable to detect steps reliably through more than three layers unless the touch points were increased beyond the size of human fingertips (although two finger tips together would provide a large enough area to enable detection with four blocks). On the other hand, the loss at the interfaces can be minimized by manufacturing a monolithic acrylic device or by joining the acrylic panels with optically transparent adhesives with an index of refraction close to that of acrylic. Alternatively, higher light intensity can be achieved by employing panels of transparent materials with higher (>1.5) refractive index. This would result in stronger bending of rays, and thus a more pronounced "narrowing" of the light's radiation profile.

Lighting conditions. To obtain optimal input, we needed to find the appropriate balance between light intensity, noise and blob size threshold. Like all diffuse illumination systems, TZee requires a certain degree of calibration that could vary slightly based on the lighting conditions available. We are further investigating methods of limiting the noise that can sometimes result from improper light settings.

Slope of tilted faces. The slope of the tilted faces is largely dependent upon the size of the open step surfaces in each acrylic layer (Figure 14 left). A steeper slope presents a smaller surface to the camera. To obtain a preliminary understanding of the effects of slope on signal transmission, we built several TZee prototypes, each with a different slope. We tested the performance of these prototypes, and found that finger gestures can be reliably detected on tilted surfaces of slopes up to 39°. Past this limit, the size of each slanted face (when projected upon the tabletop from the perspective of the camera) is not sufficiently large to capture the gestures reliably. Additionally, the number of acrylic layers and their thickness determines the size of the open space on each layer. Therefore, it is important for designers to be aware of the balance between these factors in designing TZees with different slopes.

Alternative designs. The limitations of the current prototype can be resolved to some extent by using different methods to construct TZee. For instance, one approach might be to embed a reflective area (mirror) inside a TZee facing the tabletop surface (Figure 14 right). This design allows the slope of tilted faces to be independent of the open space in each layer; such a device could potentially support the construction of steeper devices or other shapes altogether. These approaches may have potential and more work is needed to verify these possibilities.

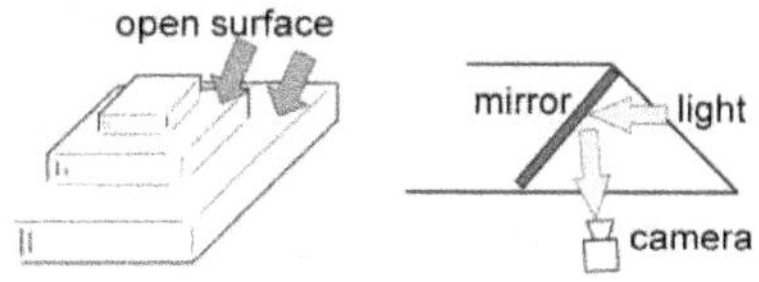

Figure 14 – Left: open surface on each acrylic layer causes some loss of light, but was necessary to avoid total internal reflection; Right: using a reflective surface such as a metallic mirror to bring the image from tilted faces to the camera may also be possible. However the ability to manipulate objects using face #4 would be negatively affected.

CONCLUSION AND FUTURE WORK

We introduce TZee, an accessible and cost-effective tangible widget designed for natural 3D interactions on tabletop systems. TZee is an unpowered device that works by exploiting the lighting sources of the tabletop. Its acrylic medium allows IR light to be transferred to its faces above the surface without major intensity loss. This allows finger motions carried out on the faces of TZee to be captured by the tabletop's integral camera. In our system evaluation, we show that even with a low resolution webcam (320×240, 15 fps), TZee can reliably extend input above the surface of the table. We demonstrate that TZee can be easily built by using cost-effective materials such as acrylic pieces.

Because of TZee's angled faces, 3D object interactions that were previously not natural on tabletop systems can be carried out intuitively. This has the added benefit of avoiding some of the ambiguities that lessen the effectiveness of previous gestural systems. We demonstrated that basic transformations such as translation, rotation, and scaling can be easily accomplished with TZee. In addition, the widget facilitates both one- and two-handed interactions, thus enabling a large design space for novel bi-manual interactions. Future work will be focused on evaluating different hardware designs so that the limitations of our prototypes can be resolved. In addition, we will develop software packages to integrate TZee with real-world applications. We also plan to explore the use of TZee in collaborative settings.

ACKNOWLEDGEMENTS

We thank Saravanan Nandagopal, Francis Lin and Jing Li for their help with PDMS block fabrication. We also thank NSERC for funds.

REFERENCES

1. Baudisch, P., Becker, T., and Rudeck, F. (2010) Lumino: Tangible Blocks for Tabletop Computers Based on Glass Fiber Bundles. *CHI'10*, 1165-1174
2. Benko, H., Saponas, T. S., Morris, D., and Tan, D. (2009). Enhancing Input On and Above the Interactive Surface with Muscle Sensing. *ITS'09*.
3. Benko, H. and Wilson, A. (2009). DepthTouch: Using Depth-Sensing Camera to Enable Freehand Interactions

On and Above the Interactive Surface. *Microsoft Research Technical Report MSR-TR-2009-23*. 2009.

4. Cutler, L. D., Fröhlich, B., and Hanrahan, P. (1997). Two-handed direct manipulation on the responsive workbench. *i3D'97*, 107-114.
5. Davidson, P. L. and Han, J. Y. (2008). Extending 2D object arrangement with pressure-sensitive layering cues. *UIST'08*, 87-90.
6. Fiebrink, R., Morris, D., and Morris, M. R. (2009). Dynamic mapping of physical controls for tabletop groupware. *CHI'09*, 471-480.
7. Fitzmaurice, G. W., Ishii, H., and Buxton, W. A. S. (1995). Bricks: laying the foundations for graspable user interfaces. *CHI'95*, 442-449.
8. Gallant, D. T., Seniuk, A. G., and Vertegaal, R. (2008). Towards more paper-like input: flexible input devices for foldable interaction styles. *UIST'08*, 283-286.
9. Guo, C., Young, J. E., Sharlin, E. (2009). Touch and toys: new techniques for interaction with a remote group of robots. *CHI'09*, 491-500.
10. Hancock, M., Carpendale, S., and Cockburn, A. (2007). Shallow-depth 3d interaction: design and evaluation of one-, two- and three-touch techniques. *CHI'07*, 1147-1156.
11. Hancock, M., Cate, T., and Carpendale, S. (2009). Sticky Tools: Full 6 DOF Force-Based Interaction for Multi-Touch Tables. *ITS'09*, 145-152.
12. Hancock, M., Hilliges, O., Collins, C., Baur, D., and Carpendale, S. (2009). Exploring tangible and direct touch interfaces for manipulating 2D and 3D information on a digital table. *ITS'09*, 85-92.
13. Hilliges, O., Izadi, S., Wilson, A. D., Hodges, S., Garcia-Mendoza, A., Butz, A. (2009). Interactions in the air: adding further depth to interactive tabletops. *UIST'09*, 139-148.
14. Hinckley, K. (2003). Synchronous gestures for multiple persons and computers. *UIST '03*, 149-158.
15. Huang, C. (2004). Not just intuitive: examining the basic manipulation of tangible user interfaces. *CHIEA'04*, 1387-1390.
16. Ishii, H. and Ullmer, B. (1997). Tangible bits: towards seamless interfaces between people, bits and atoms. *CHI'97*, 234-241.
17. Jordà, S, Geiger, G., Alonso, M., and Kaltenbrunner, M. (2007). The reacTable: exploring the synergy between live music performance and tabletop tangible interfaces. *TEI'07*, 139-146.
18. Kitamura, Y., Itoh, Y., Masaki, T., and Kishino, F. (2000). ActiveCube: A Bi-directional User Interface using Cubes. *KES'00*, 99-102.
19. Kruger, R., Carpendale, S., Scott, S. D., Tang, A. (2005). Fluid integration of rotation and translation. *CHI'05*, 601-610.
20. Microsoft Surface, http://www.microsoft.com/surface/
21. Patten, J. and Ishii, H. (2007). Mechanical constraints as computational constraints in tabletop tangible interfaces. *CHI'07*, 809-818.
22. Reisman, J. L., Davidson, P. L., and Han, J. Y. (2009). A screen-space formulation for 2D and 3D direct manipulation. *UIST'09*, 69-78.
23. Rekimoto, J., Ullmer, B., and Oba, H. (2001). DataTiles: a modular platform for mixed physical and graphical interactions. *CHI'01*, 269-276.
24. Rivière, J., Kervégant, C., Orvain, E., and Dittlo, N. (2008). CubTile: a multi-touch cubic interface. *VRST'08*, 69-72.
25. Sato, T., Mamiya, H., Koike, H., and Fukuchi, K. (2009). PhotoelasticTouch: transparent rubbery tangible interface using an LCD and photoelasticity. *UIST'09*, 43-50.
26. Subramanian, S., Aliakseyeu, D., and Lucero, A. (2006). Multi-Layer Interaction on Digital Tables. *UIST'06*, 269-272.
27. Tuddenham, P., Kirk, D., Izadi, S. (2010) Graspables revisited: multi-touch vs. tangible input for tabletop displays in acquisition and manipulation tasks. *CHI'10*: 2223-2232.
28. TUIO (tracker). http://www.tuio.org/.
29. Uiga, E. (1995). Optoelectronics. Prentice-Hall, pp. 352. ISBN 0-02-422170-8.
30. Vlaming, L., Collins, C., Hancock, M., Isenberg, T., and Carpendale, S. (2010). Integrating 2D mouse emulation with 3D manipulation for visualizations on a multi-touch table. *ITS'10*, 221 – 220.
31. Weiss, M., Wagner, J., Jansen, Y., Jennings, R., Khoshabeh, R., Hollan, J. D., and Borchers, J. (2009). SLAP widgets: bridging the gap between virtual and physical controls on tabletops. *CHI'09*, 481-490.
32. Wilson, A. (2007). Depth-Sensing Video Cameras for 3D Tangible Tabletop Interaction. *Tabletop'07*, 201-204.
33. Wilson, A., Izadi, S., Hilliges, O., Garcia-Mendoza, A., and Kirk, D. (2008). Bringing physics to the surface. *UIST'08*, 67-76.
34. Yang, X. D., Mak, E., McCallum, D., Irani, P., Cao, X., and Izadi, S. (2010). LensMouse: Augmenting the mouse with an interactive touch display. *CHI'10*, 2431-2440.
35. Zhou, Z., Cheok, A. D., Li, Y., and Kato, H. (2005). Magic cubes for social and physical family entertainment. *CHIEA'05*, 1156-1157.

Guess Who? Enriching the Social Graph through a Crowdsourcing Game

Ido Guy[*], Adam Perer[**], Tal Daniel[*], Ohad Greenshpan[***], Itai Turbahn[****]

[*]IBM Research-Haifa, Mt. Carmel, Haifa 31905, Israel {ido, taldan}@il.ibm.com
[**]IBM Research, One Rogers Street, Cambridge, MA 02142, USA adam.perer@us.ibm.com
[***] School of Computer Science, Tel-Aviv University, Tel Aviv 69978, Israel ohadgree@tau.ac.il
[****] MIT, 77 Massachusetts Avenue, Cambridge, MA 02139, USA itai@mit.edu

ABSTRACT
Despite the tremendous popularity of social network sites both on the web and within enterprises, the relationship information they contain may be often incomplete or outdated. We suggest a novel crowdsourcing approach that uses a game to help enrich and expand the social network topology. The game prompts players to provide the names of people who have a relationship with individuals they know. The game was deployed for a one-month period within a large global organization. We provide an analysis of the data collected through this deployment, in comparison with the data from the organization's social network site. Our results indicate that the game rapidly collects large volumes of valid information that can be used to enrich and reinforce an existing social network site's data. We point out other aspects and benefits of using a crowdsourcing game to harvest social network information.

Author Keywords
Crowdsourcing, Games, Social Networks, Human Computation

ACM Classification Keywords
H5.m. Information interfaces and presentation (e.g., HCI): Miscellaneous.

General Terms
Design, Experimentation, Human Factors, Measurement

INTRODUCTION
As social network sites (SNSs) gain popularity, more people are connecting to their colleagues, family, and friends in these online spaces. Such relationships allow users to stay up-to-date with their peers and perhaps exploit their social network for many tasks, including finding a job [17], ideation [8], getting answers to questions [29], and more. Data mining and information retrieval algorithms can also use social network information to enhance their functionality (e.g., [26]). However, there are several drawbacks to relying on online social network information for these human and machine information discovery tasks.

Relationships on social network sites are often incomplete. Many populations are not active in SNSs for various reasons, including privacy concerns, uneasiness with the technology, limited access to the technology, or simply a lack of time. Relationships may also be outdated or frozen [6]. Often, people connect online with new people who come into their lives, but tend not to disconnect online even when a relationship no longer exists offline. Finally, online social network relationships are typically unweighted [16]. This means all online relationships are treated equally, even though a variety of strengths exist across all connections.

Incomplete, outdated, or unweighted information suggests that discovery tasks performed by both people and computational algorithms may suffer from this imperfect data. In this paper, we propose using crowdsourcing games to help fill the gaps in social network information and improve the representation of the overall social network.

We introduce GuessWho, a crowdsourcing game for the enterprise, where users enter knowledge about their peers to enrich the organizational social network. The advantage of using a game, rather than a tool, is that it rewards people for contributing valuable information with a fun experience. We show that inviting 'the crowd' to compete in entering social network information can produce high-quality data.

While crowdsourcing games have been used in the past to gather tags about peers [4], our game focuses on collecting data about relationships. As past research indicates that the crowd can generate tags that enhance user profiles that may be incomplete or frozen, GuessWho also supports people tagging by the crowd. This also allows us to compare the relationship information collected through the game with previously studied tag information. However, this paper's main novelty lies in the collection of social relationships through a crowdsourcing game. These relationships can affect the social graph in a more global way, bridging previously disconnected clusters of people, which can lead to a dramatic improvement in tasks and algorithms for recommender systems, search engines, or expertise locators.

Existing literature offers a variety of motivations and potential uses for the kind of information collected by GuessWho. Social relationship information can be used for a wide range of enterprise applications, such as recommending people and content [21,22], finding paths to experts [11], producing dynamic contact lists [18], and personalizing search results [9]. Other studies have focused on the use of tags in the enterprise, for example, to infer expertise and interests [12] and build communities [13].

We allow users to play GuessWho on both explicit and implicit ties. We refer to explicit ties as ones that have been articulated in a formal way, such as a connection within an SNS or a manager-employee relationship within the organizational chart. We infer implicit ties from social media activity, such as people who co-edited the same wiki page or shared a file with one another. Previous research [19] has shown that these mined relationships indeed reflect people with whom the user is familiar. Thus, our approach extends beyond existing "friendsourcing" techniques [4], since we allow players to input information about implicit ties, for which they may have knowledge that can be useful as part of the crowd's input.

We evaluated our results by comparing the data generated by GuessWho to the relationships and tags on the organization's existing widely-used enterprise SNS, which supports relationships (via "friending") and people tagging. Our analysis suggests that data generated via the GuessWho game is of significantly higher quality than data already existing within the SNS, and thus can be used to enrich, expand, and validate it.

The main contributions of this work are (1) suggesting a novel approach to elicit social relationship information using a human computation game, by having players input people's names as opposed to tags, (2) providing a large-scale evaluation in the enterprise, which includes a comparison to a widely used system that does not apply a gaming approach, and (3) introducing a novel scoring scheme that aims to balance the validity and diversity of the input, and can serve as a subject for future research.

Our paper begins with a reflection on related work, where we discuss crowdsourcing and human computation games. We then briefly describe the enterprise SNS we used as a benchmark, and its usage within the organization. We follow with a detailed description of GuessWho. Next, we describe the deployment of GuessWho in a large organization where almost 2,000 players generated over 80,000 items of social network data. We then describe our evaluation of 132 participants, where we compared data generated by the game to data generated by the enterprise SNS. The evaluation suggests that data generated by the GuessWho game is of significantly higher quality than the SNS data. Finally, we discuss different aspects of our work, and then conclude.

RELATED WORK

Crowdsourcing [23] is an emerging paradigm that harnesses masses of users to construct knowledge bases, perform various types of tasks and solve problems [7,24,1]. Crowdsourcing applications have been recognized as a powerful tool for taking advantage of the "wisdom of the crowd" [30] in various domains, e.g., distribution of programming tasks [3], enhancement of search engines [14], or machine translation [1].

Luis von Ahn introduced Games with a Purpose (GWAP) [31,32], a framework for motivating crowdsourcing through games. Participants play a game, have fun, compete with others on the web, and at the same time help computers solve problems through the data they enter as part of the game. The ESP game [33] was the first game of this kind, soliciting players to label images with descriptive tags. The ESP game is typically played by two players simultaneously. They both receive an image as input and need to "agree" on as many tags as possible that describe the given image. These tags are used to enhance image search, as they enrich images' textual metadata. Following the ESP game, many other games have been developed by Von Ahn et al., harnessing the power of *human computation* (thus often referred to as *human computation games*). Most of these games focus on annotating non-textual media, such as images, music, or video.

Von Ahn et al. [31] classify the ESP game as an *output-agreement* game, in which both players are given the same input and each tries to produce the same output as their partner. GuessWho is also an output-agreement game, in which the input is a person and the output is either the name of another person or a tag. Other classes of games include *input-agreement* games, in which players are given inputs and are prompted to produce descriptive outputs, so their partners can asses whether their inputs are the same or different. An example for such a game is TagATune [27], in which players are given a musical pitch, asked to describe it with tags, and then prompted to assess, based on their partner's tags, whether they both received the same tune or different ones. In *inversion-problems* games, one player is the describer and the other is the guesser. The describer is given an input and is asked to provide outputs that help the guesser produce the original input. For example, in Peekaboom [35], a game for locating objects in images, one player is given an image along with a word related to it and must reveal parts of the image for the other player to guess the correct word. Verbosity [34] is a game for collecting common-sense facts. The describer provides short structured facts about a given input word (e.g., it is a kind of X, it is used for Y) so that the guesser can infer it.

Human computation games have also been studied by other authors in different domains. For example, Curator [36] is a two-player game for creating collections of items that fit together. Given a set of items, the players need to group them into collections and are rewarded for matching collections. PageHunt [28], a single-player non-collaborative game, challenges the user to guess search queries that would yield a given web page among their top five results. The data received through the game is used for improving the search results of a commercial search engine. Arase et al. [2] describe a multi-player game for inferring image geographical relevance. Through an analysis of the game logs, they confirm that geographically relevant objects can be derived and that their game-based method can significantly improve image search results and enhance application in domains such as image location recognition. Finally, like GuessWho, the Dogear Game [10], is an enterprise single-player human computation game. The player is presented with a bookmarked web page and needs to guess the colleague to whom the bookmark belongs. Incorrect answers are used to produce human-sourced bookmark recommendations for users of an enterprise social bookmarking system. In all of these games, the input is an artifact such as an image or a web page, while in GuessWho, it is the name of an individual person.

The closest research project to GuessWho is Collabio [4], a Facebook application that encourages friends to tag one another with descriptive terms through a game. As in our case, the game application needs to make sure the player is familiar with the individuals who appear as input. Collabio does so by allowing people to tag only their Facebook friends. Ultimately, since the tag cloud for a given person is not created by the general public, but rather by that user's set of Facebook friends, Collabio is referred to as an example of *friendsourcing* rather than crowdsourcing [4]. Apart from being an enterprise game, GuessWho is different than Collabio, as it supports building the social network itself, rather than just annotating people within the social network. As opposed to Collabio and many other human computation games, the input players provide is not only in the form of tags, but also in the form of relationships. Other differences lie in the way the game is played, for example, how the people who appear as input are selected, and how scores are calculated. We discuss in detail the commonalities and differences between Collabio and GuessWho later in this work.

LOTUS CONNECTIONS

Lotus Connections (LC)[1] is a social software application suite for enterprises. It includes various enterprise social software applications, such as a blogging system, a wiki system, a social bookmarking system, a file sharing system, and more. LC's Profiles application is an enterprise version of a social network site (SNS). It allows employees to reciprocally connect to one another by sending and receiving invitations. This paper utilizes the deployment of LC in a large, global IT company, where the system has been available for over three years. Overall, in this organization, 175,000 relationships have been formed between 80,000 employees. The basic profile of a user (name, job title, email address, etc.) is based on the corporate directory. In addition, employee profile pages are enriched with their activity within LC. In particular, LC includes an enterprise people tagging application that allows employees to tag one another with descriptive tags [12]. Those tags are presented as part of the profile page of each employee within LC. In the organization, 9,500 users have tagged 55,000 other individuals, with 170,000 tags.

[1] http://www.ibm.com/software/lotus/products/connections/

GUESS WHO

GuessWho is a crowdsourcing game, in which users enter knowledge about their peers to enrich the social network with additional relationships and tags. In this section, we describe the game in detail, including the person selection process, the scoring calculation, and the user interface.

Person Filtering

In GuessWho, the *object* for which players are required to provide input is a person. In addition to soliciting person-to-person relationships, we wanted to examine how people tags are collected through the game; this has been previously inspected in a non-enterprise context [4]. Hence, for each round of the game, the input type of either relationships or tags, is randomly drawn. Each round lasts one minute, during which the player must specify as many relevant relationships or tags as possible, in order to gain points.

Because the object in each round is a person, a filtering stage is required to make sure players are familiar, at least to some extent, with the person for whom they are entering information. To this end, we use SONAR [18], an enterprise social network aggregation system that collects and aggregates social network information from various sources across the organization; these sources include an enterprise SNS, a file sharing system, a wiki system, a paper and patent database, the organizational chart, and more. SONAR extracts both explicit relationships, such as being connected on an SNS or having an employee-manager relationship by the organizational chart, and implicit relationships, such as co-editing a wiki page or co-authoring a paper. These relationships are all aggregated to create a ranked list of the people most familiar to a given user. More details on SONAR, its data sources, and score calculation can be found in [18,19,20].

At the beginning of the game, the *object list* for a given player, i.e., the list of people on whom they can play, consists of the top 100 related people as returned by SONAR for that player. For each round of the game, a person is drawn at random from this list, and, as mentioned before, the input type (relationships or tags) is also decided at random per round. To allow more options for playing, we dynamically update the object list of a player any time they add the name of a new person as input; we assume that

player / round	p1	p2	p3	p4	p5	p6	p7	p8	p9	p10
r1	**0**									
r2	12	**9**								
r3	25	19	**14**							
r4	50	38	28	**21**						
r5	100	75	56	42	**32**					
r6	50	38	28	21	16	**12**				
r7	25	19	14	11	8	6	**4**			
r8	12	9	7	5	4	3	2	**2**		
r9	6	5	3	3	2	1	1	1	**1**	
r10	3	2	1	1	1	1	1	1	1	**1**

Table 1. GuessWho scoring scheme for a given answer.

specifying a person as input indicates some level of familiarity between that person and the player. In this way, the object list grows dynamically as the player continues with the game and provides more people as input.

Score Calculation

GuessWho is played in a single-player mode, in which the player's input is matched against previous input on the same person by other players. We opted for a single-player mode, as it is unlikely that two players will have enough people they both know to play simultaneously.

The GuessWho scoring function aims at encouraging original, yet valid, answers. Thus, an answer that has already been given by many other players would not yield as many points as an answer that has been given by only few players. We also apply a concept of *dividend points*. These are points accumulated **after** the input has been provided by the player, when more players note the same input—thereby corroborating the information. Most dividend points are granted for an original answer that was not given previously, but is later noted by many individuals.

Collabio [4] also uses an accumulating point mechanism, giving *i* points to the *i*-th player who mentions a tag, as well as to all preceding players who mentioned the same tag for the same person. This method rewards popular answers, while our scoring system aims at eliciting non-popular answers. The ESP game applies Taboo Words [33] as a means to disallow very popular answers. However, we felt that this method would not suffice, since it can only eliminate a limited number of very popular answers.

Table 1 describes the GuessWho scoring scheme for a specific answer. Each column shows the scores of the *i*-th player ($i \in [1,10]$), while the *i*-th row refers to the round in which the *i*-th player provided the answer. The top number in each column (bolded in blue) shows the immediate points the player gets, while the rest of the numbers in the column show the dividend points given to the player in case other players mention the same answer later on. For example, when the first player (*p1*) gives the answer, s/he gets 0 points, as the answer is not valid yet, and we want to avoid encouraging arbitrary answers. When the second player mentions this same answer, s/he immediately gets 9 points, while *p1* gets 12 dividend points. The highest amount of points is given when a fifth player provides the same answer. This player then immediately gets 32 points, granting the first player who provided the answer with 100 dividend points, the second with 75, the third with 56, and the fourth with 42. The eleventh player to specify an answer does not get any points, and does not grant dividend points to previous players. This method encourages diversity and prevents players from specifying the most popular answers.

We note that this scoring scheme has various parameters that control the way it behaves. Optimization of the scoring scheme is beyond the scope of this work and is left for future research.

User Interface

Figure 1 shows the GuessWho welcome page, presented once a player logs in with his organizational username and password. This page gives a short description of the game instructions and shows the leaderboard with the 15 players who scored the most points thus far. The bottom of the page indicates the number of people who played during the past week and prompts the player to join them. The player's overall points, ranking within the overall scoring list, and number of dividend points accumulated since the last login are also shown. Finally, a tip showing the number of points required to pass the next player on the list (i.e., improve the ranking by 1) is highlighted as another means to motivate players. By clicking "Start Game", the player begins a new round in GuessWho.

Figure 2 depicts the main user interface of GuessWho. Figure 2a shows a relationship round (required input is related people) and Figure 2b shows a tag round (required input is related tags). At the center, a person who is familiar

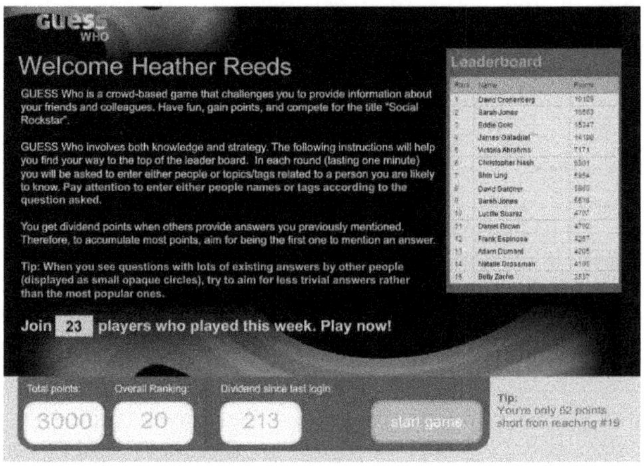

Figure 1. After players log in to GuessWho, they are greeted with instructions, their current points and ranking, a leaderboard, and motivating tips to raise their ranking.

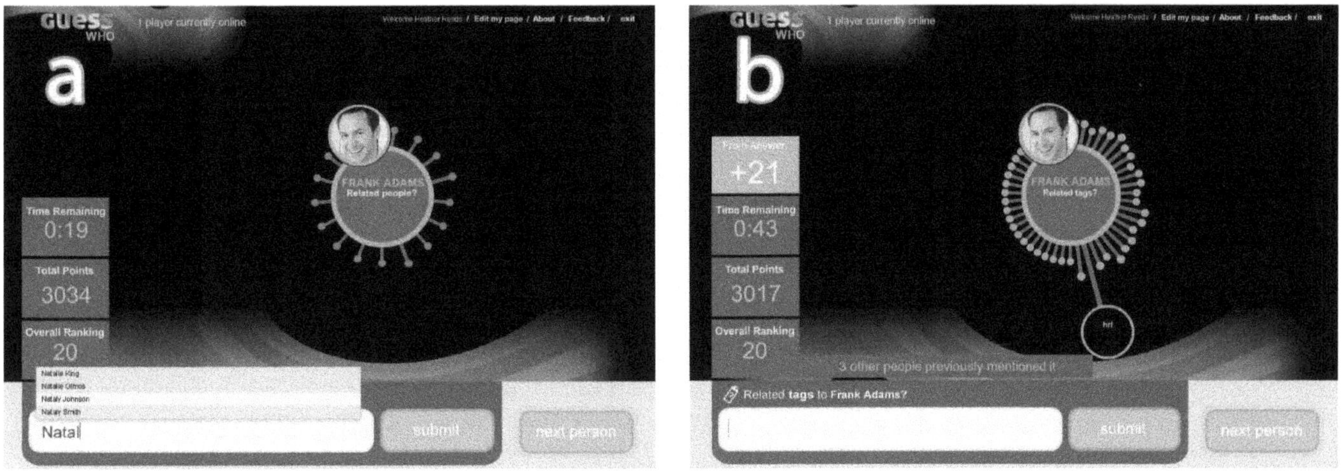

Figure 2. a) A GuessWho relationship round, where players input people related to the person in the center (Frank Adams). When a name is being entered, the auto-complete service suggests completion options. b) A GuessWho tag round, where players input tags related to the person in the center. In this example, a related tag has just been entered that was previously mentioned by 3 other players.

to the player is presented by their name and photo, and the player is asked to specify people or tags related to that person. Answers already given by the player for that person, if any exist, are highlighted in circles coming out of the central circle (as in Figure 2b). The small opaque circles denote answers given by other players for this person. The remaining time (starting from 60 seconds and decreasing to 0), current total points, and overall ranking, are indicated on the left. The bottom of the screen includes an input box where the player can enter the answers. Above the box, a text repeats the current requested input (e.g., "related tags to Frank Adams"). A representative icon to the left of this text also indicates whether the required input is a relationship or a tag. As long as the remaining time is greater than zero, the player can submit answers. The player can also choose to move to the next person before the allotted time expires, at the cost of 1 point.

If the required input is a related relationship, a name auto-complete service is used to facilitate identifying a person by their name. This service makes use of the corporate directory to suggest unique identities based on the prefix entered by the player. Figure 2a shows an example of suggestions made by this service, just above the input box. If the input is a tag, a spell-checking service is used. This service matches the answer submitted by the player with answers previously entered (by all players); it also uses the Yahoo! Spelling Suggestion API[2] to offer alternative spellings, when appropriate. Once the player enters an answer, a text line pops up indicating the number of players that already gave this answer. Then, another green box pops up, indicating how many points the player just received for the current answer. For example, Figure 2b indicates that the answer provided was already mentioned by three other individuals, and that the player gained 21 points for this answer.

At the top of the page, the user can see how many other players are currently playing. In case dividend points are added due to answers given by other users playing at the same time, the player will receive a popup notification indicating dividend points were won in real-time. Users can also choose to edit the data entered on then. Clicking that option loads a profile editing page, as demonstrated in Figure 3. The page presents two separate lists of tags and people that were assigned to the user by players of the game, each sorted alphabetically. Each person or tag on these lists includes a count, indicating how many players provided it, without naming these players. The user can remove each of these people or tags, which would indicate to us that s/he does not want this data exposed to other

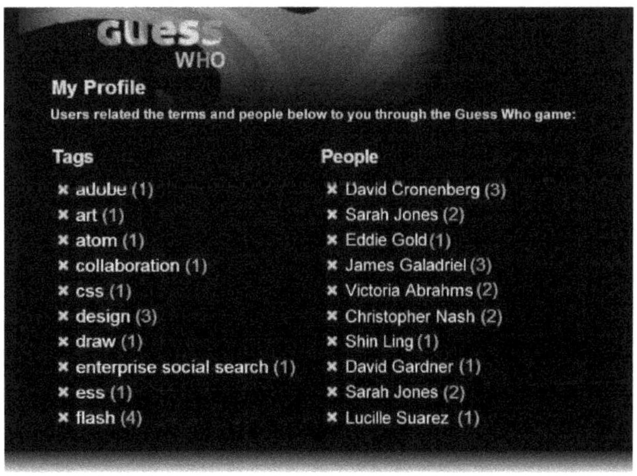

Figure 3. GuessWho profile editing page, where users can choose to remove sensitive or inaccurate information mentioned about them.

[2] http://developer.yahoo.com/search/web/V1/spellingSuggestion.html

services. The game, however, would not be affected by this action, i.e., in case another player enters this tag/relationship again, points will be given as if the tag/relationship has not been removed. A similar concept of editing your own tags has been applied in Collabio [4].

The GuessWho application sends weekly update emails to all people who ever provided input through the game. The email message includes the user's total points, current ranking, point missing for moving one ranking up, and the Top-15 leaderboard. In addition, the email lists up to 10 relationships/tags that yielded most dividend points to the user in the past week. For example, an item in this list looks like 'Frank Adams->"design": 112 points (3 new mentions)'. This way, we aim to take advantage of the dividend point mechanism to highlight for users their most successful answers and motivate them to engage in more rounds of GuessWho. The email message includes a link to the game and also a link that would unsubscribe the user from getting further GuessWho updates.

RESULTS

The GuessWho game was deployed in a large, global IT organization for a period of one month starting June 2010. Initially, 2000 active social media users spanning different countries and organizational divisions were invited to play the game. Further game participants were then recruited based on the social data played on by these initial users. In total, 1915 users from 52 different countries played the GuessWho game, generating data on 16,764 unique people in 61 countries across the company.

Relationships

During the game's deployment, 42,487 relationships between 13,957 people were specified by users playing the game. Of these, 22,741 were unique relationships. On average, each relationship was entered 1.87 times, with 14,614 relationships (64.26%) verified by at least two players.

Only 4,053 of the 22,741 unique relationships generated by GuessWho already existed on LC (17.82%). This shows that the game was able to generate many relationships previously missing from the enterprise social graph.

An interesting trend in the data suggests that the more times a relationship was verified by GuessWho players, the more likely the relationship already existed in LC. As Figure 4a shows, the higher the verification, the greater the chance the relationship already exists on LC (e.g., there is a 58% chance the relationship exists on LC if it was verified 10 or more times).

Tags

During deployment, GuessWho players entered a total of 38,768 tags about 7,499 peers. Of these, there were 35,657 unique person-tags. Only 2,221 of these person-tags were verified 2 or more times (6.23%), resulting in high tag diversity. On average, each person-tag was entered 1.09 times by players of the game.

Only 3,598 of the 35,657 unique person-tags generated by GuessWho already existed on LC (10.09%). This shows that the game was able to generate many new tags about people, resulting in a much richer overall data.

Similarly to the trend with relationships, the data suggests that the more times a tag was verified by GuessWho players, the more likely the tag already existed in LC. As Figure 4b shows, the higher the verification, the greater the chance the tag already exists on LC (e.g., there is a 55% chance the tag exists on LC if it was verified 5 or more times).

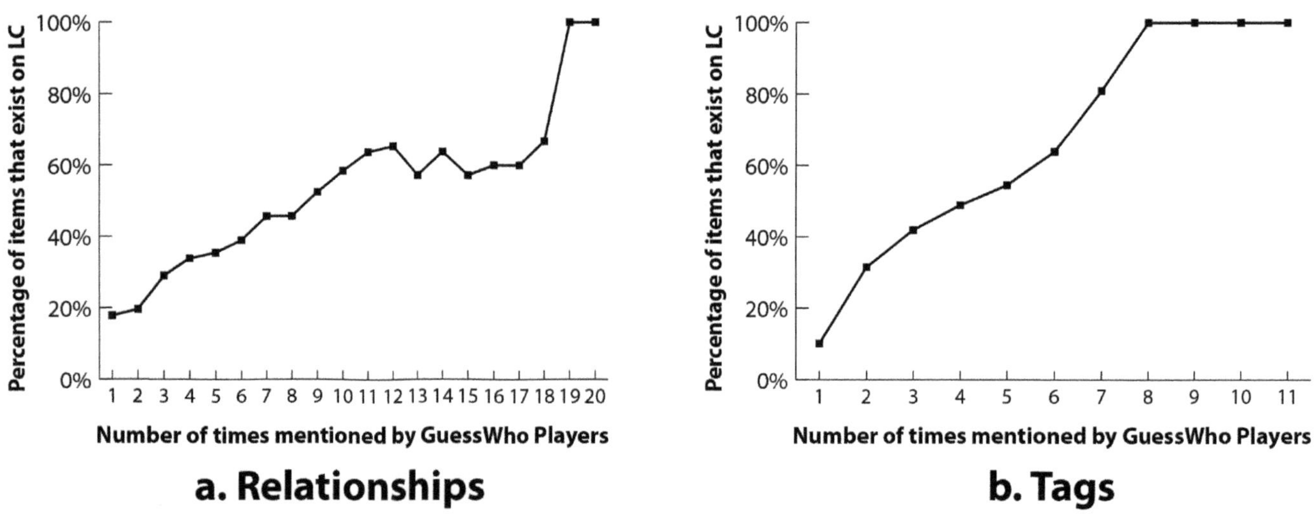

Figure 4. A correlation exists between the number of times items were mentioned by GuessWho players and the probability that the item exists on the enterprise social network, LC.

Privacy

As users are not in control of the data being entered about them in GuessWho, users were able to remove any data about them that they might find undesirable or inaccurate. Only 455 items (0.006%) of the 81,255 user-generated tags and relationships were marked to be deleted by users. Of the hidden items, 295 were relationships and 160 were tags. 224 users out of all 1,915 GuessWho users did opt to hide at least 1 item mentioned about them.

EVALUATION

In order to better understand the quality of data produced by the GuessWho game, we invited 332 people to rate the data generated about them. These 332 people were chosen based on having a sufficient amount of data generated by the game, as well as having sufficient data on LC, to generate 10 relationships and 10 tags for evaluation. This is explained in the following paragraphs.

Each of the players were sent an email invitation to a within-subjects survey, in which they were asked to rate the quality of up to four randomly chosen tags and four randomly chosen relationships that were generated uniquely by the GuessWho game. In order to generate a baseline, four random tags and relationships were also extracted from LC. Participants were also asked to rate up to two tags and two relationships that existed on both systems. Of the 332 invitations, 132 people (39.76%) opted to take the survey.

Relationships

After a set of brief instructions, participants were shown a list of 10 people. Next to each person's name was a set of radio buttons representing an ascending Likert scale from 1 to 5. Participants were asked to rate the strength of the relationship between themselves and that person (where 1 indicates no relationship and 5 represents a strong relationship). The set of 10 people was chosen as follows: 2 of the people were listed as relationships on both GuessWho and LC, 4 of the people were only listed on GuessWho, and 4 were listed only on LC. Comparing relationships mentioned in GuessWho to those listed on LC allowed us to understand the quality of data entered in a crowdsourcing game. The 10 people were presented in a randomized order and participants were not told the sources of the data to avoid any biases.

As the first row of Table 2 shows, participants gave an average score of 3.84 to relationships that originated only from GuessWho. Relationships from LC only were given a less favorable rating, with an average score of 3.56. Finally, relationships that existed in both systems were given a rating of 4.25. A one-way ANOVA indicates that ratings across the three conditions are significantly different, $F(2,1230)=28.297$, $p<0.001$. This suggests that data gathered by the GuessWho game is significantly better than friending data from the LC SNS, indicating the very real potential of our crowdsourcing technique.

	LC	GuessWho	Both
Relationships	3.56	3.84	4.25
Tags	4.14	4.35	4.78

Table 2. Participants rated tags and relationships generated in LC and GuessWho. Data generated in GuessWho was rated significantly higher than LC data, on an ascending Likert scale. Data that was present in both systems was rated even higher.

	Mentioned 1 time in GuessWho	Mentioned 2 or more times	Mentioned 3 or more times
Relationships	3.62	3.96	4.31
Tags	4.34	4.63	4.81

Table 3. The quality of data generated by GuessWho increases based upon the number of times items were mentioned by separate players.

There is also a correlation between the number of times a relationship was entered by multiple players in GuessWho and the quality of the data. As Table 3 shows, relationships that were entered only once got an average rating of 3.62, whereas relationships that were entered by two or more players got an average of 3.96. This rating rose to 4.31 when three or more players all verified the same relationship.

Tags

Similarly, participants were also asked to rate how well 10 tags describe themselves using a Likert scale of 1-5, where 1 means 'not at all', and 5 means 'very well'. Tags were extracted in a similar manner to relationships (4 unique GuessWho tags, 4 unique LC tags, and 2 that were entered in both systems). As the second row of Table 2 shows, tags extracted from GuessWho resulted in an average rating of 4.35. Similar to relationships, tags from LC were rated lower than the GuessWho tags, with an average score of 4.14. Once again, tags that existed on both systems performed even better, with a rating of 4.78. A one-way ANOVA indicates that ratings across the three conditions are significantly different, $F(2,1238)=29.209$, $p<0.001$. Thus, tags entered on GuessWho were significantly better than tags that existed on LC, suggesting that crowdsourcing games are indeed a good source for tag knowledge as well.

As with relationships, a correlation exists between the number of times a tag was mentioned by multiple players in GuessWho and the quality of the data. Table 3 shows that tags that were only entered once got an average rating of 4.34, whereas tags that were entered by two or more players received an average of 4.63. This rating increases to 4.81 when three or more players all verified the same tag. The Collabio study [4] showed that tags entered by more players were rated higher than tags entered by fewer players. Our analysis reinforces these results for both tags and relationships in the enterprise.

DISCUSSION, LIMITATIONS, AND FUTURE WORK

Our evaluation indicates that harnessing the crowd to enrich the social network with relationships and tags can be highly beneficial. The information harvested through GuessWho contributed many new relationships and tags that did not exist before in LC. Ratings of these new relationships and tags indicate that their validity is higher than existing LC data, even if entered only once. Yet, the more mentions an answer gets, the higher its rating is likely to be. In addition to contributing plenty of new data, the GuessWho answers can be used to reinforce and validate existing LC data. Our survey indicates that answers that appear both on LC and GuessWho receive especially high ratings. Because relationships in LC (as in most other SNSs) are unweighted, GuessWho relationship data can be used to rank them, according to the number of people who mentioned these relationships. In practice, GuessWho can be tuned to give priority to collecting data for individuals whose information is sparse or suspected as being stale, by boosting these individuals within the user's object list.

Our scoring function aims at flattening the distribution of answers and yielding more original yet valid answers. Indeed, the diversity of received answers was high, as each item was only repeated an average of 1.39 times overall. In fact, only 55 answers were given more than 10 times (the area of no awarded points in our scoring function). On the other hand, the validity of the answers was also high, as reflected in the survey's results. This may imply that the scoring function indeed helps produce diverse yet valid results. Future work should explore how optimizing the scoring function can further improve the results; this should also consider factors such as the number of expected players, their level of engagement, the number of possible objects and possible valid answers per object, and more.

The fact that the game-based data was fresher than the LC data may offer one explanation for the higher rating the former received in our survey. This fact was pointed out in several of the comments we received from survey participants. For example:

"The one thing I noticed looking at both the relationships and tags was the staleness of some of them. In many cases, I once had strong relationships with the people that have waned over time. The same is true for tags where, because of, for example, job changes, the tags are no longer as relevant as they once were."

While the data in LC could be filtered by timestamp to make it fresher, it would also make it much sparser. Moreover, it is hard to infer which relationships and tags are stale and which have been maintained or developed even though entered a few years ago. GuessWho, or a variant of the game, can serve as a means to validate the freshness of the data in LC. As indicated in our results, the data that appeared on both GuessWho and LC was rated very positively by the users, with relationships rated 4.25 on average, and tags getting an extremely high average rating of 4.78.

Tag diversity was substantially higher than relationship diversity. On average, each tag-answer was repeated 1.09 times, as compared to 1.87 for a relationship-answer. The percentage of answers that were verified by two users or more is much smaller for tags than for relationships (6.2% vs. 64.3%). This can be attributed to the fact that the set of possible inputs for people is smaller than for tags. Moreover, relationship input is made through a unique identifier (given by the name autocomplete service), while tags may have different forms and synonyms. Hence, people-answers are easier to validate.

There was also a difference between relationships and tags with respect to the improvement of GuessWho answer ratings compared to LC data. The rating raise was higher for relationships than for tags (7.9% vs. 5.1%), indicating, again, the efficacy of crowd-based relationship extraction.

In summary, we observe several unique advantages of the relationship version of the game, compared to the tag version: (1) Since people in the enterprise have unique identifiers, there is no need for canonization, stemming, or synonym merging; thus validation of results is easier. (2) As opposed to people tags, which can be entered in LC by any other person, relationships can only be formed when one of the two parties initiates the connection. Our crowd-based approach allows others to point at a relationship between two other individuals and hence may reveal relationships between people who are not active in social media and will not initiate the connection. (3) The increase in average rating compared to LC data is higher for relationships than it is for tags (7.9% vs. 5.1%). (4) LC relationships are unweighted, while the crowd-based relationships can be weighted by the number of players who mentioned them. (5) The game revolves around three entities: the player, the object, and the input. The relationships among these entities are reflected throughout the course of the game: person filtering using SONAR determines the initial player-object relationships; the object list dynamically grows based on player-input relationships; and, the social graph is enriched through object-input relationships. Furthermore, this symmetry allows us to potentially infer relationships not only based on object-input relationships, but also based on player-input relationships. Future research should compare the data that can be extracted through these two types of relationships.

The volume of the data collected through the game was impressive. In the period of just one month, over 24% of the overall LC relationships and 22.5% of the LC tags were generated by the GuessWho game (LC has been deployed in the organization for over three years). In fact, over 50% of this data was produced in the first week of the game, while in subsequent weeks we witnessed a constant decrease in data production. These findings indicate that a crowdsourcing game can be an effective means to extract large volumes of data in a very short period of time. Keeping up the pace of data production is a great challenge with such a game, as with other non-monetary incentive mechanisms [14]. Weekly emails with motivating personalized statistics are one method we applied to keep players engaged. Yet, as mentioned, a rapid decay of contribution was inevitable. Future research may examine new ideas (e.g., other incentives such as organizational rewards) and whether they can enhance longer-term participation in crowdsourcing games.

One limitation of the game approach and its evaluation here stems from this challenge of keeping the game's data fresh. It could be that the "novelty effect" of the game, leading many people to try it out early on, is the main reason for its data being of higher quality than the LC data. Ultimately, as the novelty wears off, these differences may fade. Future work should inspect whether the findings of our evaluation hold over a longer period of time.

After deploying the game, we received many comments by email or through the enterprise blogosphere. For example, one user wrote in his status update:

"Tried out GuessWho. Fun way to encourage tagging!"

And another wrote:

"For me watching the clock tick down definitely added pressure to the game! Whew! I'm exhausted...I think I need a long weekend!"

We also received quite a few emails expressing surprise that we asked people to play games inside the enterprise. This suggests that initiating a game culture inside the enterprise can be difficult, even when both the players and the community at large benefit. Showing the value games like GuessWho in enterprises can help create an organizational culture that is more receptive of such games.

Privacy concerns were also raised by a few of the game's participants. While crowd-based people-tagging in the enterprise was introduced a few years ago and found to be appropriately used [12], GuessWho introduces a paradigm in which a relationship between two individuals can be pointed out by others. As one user expressed:

"What if I don't want to be known for knowing or interacting with people because of a troubled project, secret project or different internal job offers?"

The profile editing enablement, which allows individuals to remove any relationship others have indicated, tries to mitigate privacy issues. Further means should be examined to help protect privacy, such as allow editing the profile in interfaces other than GuessWho or sending notifications whenever a new relationship or tag about the employee has been indicated by others. Our results indicate that relationship data might be more sensitive than tags data, since more relationships were removed than tags (295 vs. 160). Additional exploration of employee sensitivity to others making input about their relationship information should also be studied in more detail.

We also received many suggestions for enhancing the game, including dynamic updates of the player's object list with other players who mentioned him, rather than just with players he mentioned; allow players to correct an input they entered by mistake; extend the game to allow annotating relationships with labels indicating why two individuals are linked (e.g., boss of, worked on the same project, etc.); and allow players to indicate they do not know the person they received as the object in a specific round, so this person will not appear again in future rounds. This would also help us learn about relationships that do **not** exist, and potentially amend SONAR.

We note that aside from using the SONAR system to create the initial object list, GuessWho can also serve as a data source for SONAR, feeding back the relationships it collects to the SONAR aggregation system.

Implementing an equivalent version of GuessWho outside the firewall can be valuable in many ways, for example to maintain and enrich the social graph within an SNS or an online community, or even build a network from scratch within a social site. The challenge in producing high-quality and valid results is bigger in this case, as the accountability for one's ID is not as high as within the organization.

Crowdsourcing as a whole often raises a controversy around the quality of the data it produces. This controversy may even grow when the subject is as sensitive as unveiling relationships and areas of expertise. One of our users hypothesizes:

"My favorite relationships are those I select myself, rather than those others might choose for me."

While this may be true, we believe many latent relationships still exist that can be positively utilized. The results of this work show that the data stemming from a crowd-based game during one month is more representative than the user's own relationships within an SNS, accumulated over more than three years.

CONCLUSION

We introduced an approach that utilizes a crowdsourcing game to expand and enrich the enterprise social network. The game allows players to indicate relationships and tags related to a given person. We compared the data collected through a one-month deployment of the game with the data of a well-established enterprise SNS. Results indicate that the game can rapidly extract large amounts of relationships and tags that are both diverse and valid. Validity of the data rises as more people mention an answer, yet even an answer given just once is rated higher, on average, than a relationship/tag taken from the SNS. While tags have been previously used as input within crowdsourcing games, relationship input is novel. We point out several advantages of a game that collects relationships as input in comparison to tags. In addition, the game introduces several unique mechanisms, such as a scoring function that includes dividend points and the dynamic update of the player's object list based on people s/he has previously mentioned. Future work should explore ways to exploit the data collected through the game; investigate refinements of the scoring function, means for longer-term engagement, and methods for privacy preservation; and examine whether this game-based approach can be applicable outside the firewall.

REFERENCES

1. Ambati, V., Vogel, S., & Carbonell J. 2010. Active learning and crowd-sourcing for machine translation. *Proc. LREC'10.*
2. Arase, Y., Xie, X., Duan, M., Hara, T., & Nishio, S. 2009. A game based approach to assign geographical relevance to web images. *Proc. WWW '09*, 811-820.
3. Archak, N. 2010. Money, glory and cheap talk: analyzing strategic behavior of contestants in simultaneous crowdsourcing contests on TopCoder.com. *Proc. WWW '10*, 21-30.
4. Bernstein, M., Tan, D., Smith, G., Czerwinski, M., & Horvitz, E. 2010. Personalization via friendsourcing. *ACM Trans. Comput.-Hum. Interact.* 17, 2 (May. 2010), 1-28.
5. Bonhard, P. & Sasse, M. A. 2006. 'Knowing me, knowing you' -- Using profiles and social networking to improve recommender systems. *BT Technology Journal* 24, 3 (Jul. 2006), 84-98.
6. Boyd, D. & Heer, J. 2006. Profiles as Conversation: Networked Identity Performance on Friendster. *Proc. HICSS '06.*
7. Brabham, D.C. 2008. Crowdsourcing as a model for problem solving: An introduction and cases. *Convergence* 14, 1, 75–90.
8. Burt, R. S. 2004. Structural Holes and Good Ideas. *American Journal of Sociology*, 110(2), 349–399.
9. Carmel, D., Zwerdling, N., Guy I., Ofek-Koifman, S., Har'el N., Ronen, I., Uziel, E., Yogev, S., & Chernov, S. 2009. Personalized Social Search based on the User's Social Network. *Proc. CIKM '09*, 1227-1236.
10. Dugan, C., Muller, M., Millen, D. R., Geyer, W., Brownholtz, B., & Moore, M. 2007. The dogear game: a social bookmark recommender system. *Proc. GROUP* '07, 387-390.
11. Ehrlich, K., Lin, C. & Griffiths-Fisher, V. 2007. Searching for experts in the enterprise: combining text and social network analysis. *Proc. Group'07*, 117-126.
12. Farrell, S., Lau, T., Nusser, S., Wilcox, E., & Muller, M. 2007. Socially augmenting employee profiles with people-tagging. *Proc. UIST '07*, 91-100.
13. Farrell, S., Lau, T., & Nusser, S. 2007. Building communities with people-tags. *Proc. INTERACT '07*, 357-360.
14. Farzan, R., DiMicco, J., Millen, D. R., Dugan, C., Geyer, W., & Brownholtz, E. 2008. Results from deploying a participation incentive mechanism within the enterprise. *Proc. CHI '08*, 563-572.
15. Ganjisaffar, Y., Javanmardi, S., & Lopes, C. 2009. Leveraging crowdsourcing heuristics to improve search in Wikipedia. *Proc. WikiSym '09.*
16. Gilbert, E. & Karahalios, K. 2009. Predicting tie strength with social media. *Proc. CHI '09*, 211-220.
17. Granovetter, M. 1974. Getting a Job: A Study of Contacts and Careers. *University Of Chicago Press.*
18. Guy, I., Jacovi, M., Shahar, E., Meshulam, N., Soroka, V., & Farrell, S. 2008. Harvesting with SONAR: the value of aggregating social network information. *Proc. CHI '08*, 1017-1026.
19. Guy, I., Jacovi, M., Meshulam, N., Ronen, I., & Shahar, E. 2008. Public vs. private: comparing public social network information with email. *Proc. CSCW'08*, 393-402.
20. Guy, I., Jacovi, M., Perer, A., Ronen, I., and Uziel, E.: Same Places, Same Things, Same People? Mining User Similarity on Social Media. *Proc. CSCW'10*, 41-50.
21. Guy I., Ronen I., & Wilcox E. 2009. Do You Know? Recommending People to Invite into Your Social Network. *Proc. IUI'09*, 77-86.
22. Guy, I., Zwerdling, N., Carmel, D., Ronen, I., Uziel, E., Yogev, S., & Ofek-Koifman S. 2009. Personalized Recommendation of Social Software Items based on Social Relations. *Proc. RecSys '09*, 53-60.
23. Howe, J. 2006. The rise of crowdsourcing. *Wired Magazine* 14, 6 (June 2006).
24. Huberman, B. A., Romero, D. M., and Wu, F. 2009. Crowdsourcing, attention and productivity. *J. Inf. Sci.* 35, 6 (Dec. 2009), 758-765.
25. Kempe, D., Kleinberg, J., & Tardos, É. 2003. Maximizing the spread of influence through a social network. *Proc. KDD '03*, 137-146.
26. Kautz, H., Selman, B., & Shah, M. 1997. Referral Web: combining social networks and collaborative filtering. *Commun. ACM* 40, 3 (Mar. 1997), 63-65.
27. Law, E. & von Ahn, L. 2009. Input-agreement: a new mechanism for collecting data using human computation games. *Proc. CHI '09*, 1197-1206.
28. Ma, H., Chandrasekar, R., Quirk, C., & Gupta, A. 2009. Page hunt: improving search engines using human computation games. *Proc. SIGIR '09*, 746-747.
29. Morris, M. R., Teevan, J., & Panovich, K. 2010. What do people ask their social networks, and why?: a survey study of status message q&a behavior. *Proc. CHI '10*, 1739-1748.
30. Surowiecki, J. 2004. The wisdom of crowds: Why the many are smarter than the few.
31. Von Ahn, L. & Dabbish, L. 2008. Designing games with a purpose. *Commun. ACM* 51, 8 (Aug. 2008), 58-67.
32. Von Ahn, L. 2006. Games with a purpose, *IEEE Computer Magazine* 39, 6 (June 2006), 92-94.
33. Von Ahn, L. & Dabbish, L. 2004. Labeling images with a computer game. *Proc. CHI '04*, 319-326.
34. Von Ahn, L., Kedia, M., & Blum, M. 2006. Verbosity: a game for collecting common-sense facts. *Proc. CHI '06*, 75-78.
35. Von Ahn, L., Liu, R., & Blum, M. 2006. Peekaboom: a game for locating objects in images. *Proc. CHI '06*, 55-64.
36. Walsh, G. & Golbeck, J. 2010. Curator: a game with a purpose for collection recommendation. Proc. CHI '10, 2079-2082.
37. Yang, J., Adamic, L. A., & Ackerman, M. S. 2008. Crowdsourcing and knowledge sharing: strategic user behavior on taskcn. *Proc. EC '08*, 246-255

PhotoCity: Training Experts at Large-scale Image Acquisition Through a Competitive Game

Kathleen Tuite
University of Washington
ktuite@cs.washington.edu

Noah Snavely
Cornell University
snavely@cs.cornell.edu

Dun-Yu Hsiao
University of Washington
dyhsiao@u.washington.edu

Nadine Tabing
University of Washington
nadine@cs.washington.edu

Zoran Popović
University of Washington
zoran@cs.washington.edu

ABSTRACT
Large-scale, ground-level urban imagery has recently developed as an important element of online mapping tools such as Google's Street View. Such imagery is extremely valuable in a number of potential applications, ranging from augmented reality to 3D modeling, and from urban planning to monitoring city infrastructure. While such imagery is already available from many sources, including Street View and tourist photos on photo-sharing sites, these collections have drawbacks related to high cost, incompleteness, and accuracy. A potential solution is to leverage the community of photographers around the world to collaboratively acquire large-scale image collections. This work explores this approach through PhotoCity, an online game that trains its players to become "experts" at taking photos at targeted locations and in great density, for the purposes of creating 3D building models. To evaluate our approach, we ran a competition between two universities that resulted in the submission of over 100,000 photos, many of which were highly relevant for the 3D modeling task at hand. Although the number of players was small, we found that this was compensated for by incentives that drove players to become experts at photo collection, often capturing thousands of useful photos each.

Author Keywords
games with a purpose, real-world games, data collection, crowdsourcing, photography, 3D modeling

ACM Classification Keywords
H.8.0 Information Systems : General – Games

General Terms
Design

INTRODUCTION
Imagine having a huge collection of georegistered photos taken from every corner of a city, inside and out, at many different times of day, different seasons, across many years. Such a photo collection would have many applications. You could give your faraway friend a tour, or scope out a new part of town before going there. For any location, you could see it during the day, at night, during summer or winter, and from any angle. If a building was torn down or rebuilt, a snapshot of how it once was would be preserved. These localized photos could be used to enable dozens of new augmented reality applications, could help in monitoring and analyzing building infrastructure, and could aid in urban planning and analysis of changes in cities over time. The photos could even be used to build a detailed 3D model of the entire city using computer vision techniques [21, 6].

While large sets of urban photos exist in very structured (e.g., Google Maps and Street View) as well as unstructured (Flickr, Facebook, Picasa) collections, these existing collections have a number of drawbacks in the context of such mapping and analysis applications. The structured collections (usually captured by commercial enterprises, most famously Google) are quite expensive to acquire, only available in certain areas, and typically capture only certain areas such as city streets and popular footpaths. These structured collections tend to be "refreshed" infrequently and thus photos may often be out of date; similarly, only a single time of day or year is usually available. On the other hand, unstructured collections (e.g., the millions of photos of Rome on Flickr) are captured "for free" by thousands of people (many of them tourists) walking around everyday with cameras. However, only landmarks, such as the Colosseum and Trevi Fountain, are well-represented, and most of the rest of the world is very sparsely photographed. For instance, in recent work in computer vision, 150,000 Flickr photos of Rome were downloaded and automatically reconstructed into a set of 3D models spanning the city [6], but these models only represent disconnected pockets of 3D structure corresponding to famous landmarks. Less popular areas such as side streets were not photographed enough times to be modeled.

What if there was a way to effortlessly and cheaply collect the vast number of 'missing' photos—without special equipment and with the effort distributed among millions of photographers in the community? We have developed PhotoCity to crowdsource the gathering of these photos in a fun and effective way, focusing on the application of 3D city modeling. PhotoCity is a game played by simply taking photos. The game processes the captured photos using computer vision techniques and uses them to incrementally expand 3D models; players 'capture' virtual flags and castles as they contribute to digital 3D replicas of real buildings. The result of the game is a set of detailed 3D models and a large set of photos that densely cover an entire area from many different angles. A preliminary version of the game is described in [22], with attention on the design of a game that enables players to collaboratively construct 3D models by taking photos. In this paper, we apply PhotoCity to the real task of modeling two university campuses, demonstrating what the game can accomplish with a small group of expert players who have been trained by playing the game. We seek to determine whether the game dynamics we designed for PhotoCity are conducive to large-scale distributed data collection. We present the detailed results of a field study to determine the effectiveness of our game PhotoCity, as well as present design changes made as we received feedback from this experiment.

PhotoCity, like other games with a purpose (GWAPs), provides incentives and game mechanics that drive people to perform a useful task, in this case, to capture missing photos needed for 3D modeling. However, a unique challenge in PhotoCity is to find ways to take people's normal behavior when taking photos—i.e., to take a few well-composed shots from "canonical" viewpoints of the fronts of buildings—and change them so that they take a larger, more useful set of photos for the task at hand. PhotoCity addresses this through a map-based user interface design and competitive game mechanics, but we still found that it often takes some time for users to warm up to how to play the game. To be a viable mechanism for large-scale data collection, the game must engage the interest of enough players for long enough for them to "learn" this new photo-taking behavior and collect a sufficiently complete set of photos.

To evaluate whether PhotoCity is an effective way to collect a comprehensive set of photos of a large area, we held a competition between two universities. The competition brought in over 100,000 photos; compared to photos of the same areas available on Flickr, the PhotoCity collection provides much greater geographical coverage, and is much more effective for 3D reconstruction.

These 100,000 photos were contributed by a relatively small number of players (forty-five). Despite this small number, the game was engaging enough for these players to capture a very sizable collection of useful data, and the results suggest that crowdsourcing is a viable mechanism for large-scale acquisition of visual data.

In this paper, we will briefly outline the basic mechanics of PhotoCity and the ways in which we guide players' actions towards the purpose of the game. We will then describe enhancements made to the game along the way to focus player efforts (on completing buildings) and increase player engagement (by organizing a competition between two universities). Finally, we will discuss the outcome of our university competition: that the success of PhotoCity depends on the participation of highly-motivated expert players who become so involved in the game that they play for an extended period of time, are able to hone their skills, and contribute thousands of photos each.

A key contribution of this paper is the design and evaluation of a game for large-scale, targeted data collection. An overarching lesson is that the success of such a game is not necessarily dependent on the number of players. What is most important is focusing player effort and providing competitive or exciting situations that lure people in long enough to turn them into expert players.

RELATED WORK

GWAPs

A game with a purpose (GWAP) is a means of extracting useful output from a human player in a game setting in a way that is fun for the player. Many GWAPs are designed to have humans perform tasks that are difficult for computers, such as labeling images and folding proteins. Our GWAP leverages humans for the physical activity of going outside and taking a picture (or set of pictures) in a specific place.

In their seminal work on the ESP game [24], von Ahn and Dabbish designed a game for the purpose of labeling Internet images with relevant textual tags. The general idea of the ESP game is that two players who can see the same image try to come up with matching tags. The players are paired randomly and have no way to communicate with each other, so if they want to earn points, they must type words that are relevant to the image—words that make good tags. PhotoCity uses automatic vision techniques as a verification mechanism, only rewarding players for verifiably useful input.

The key to labeling large numbers of images with the ESP game is to have a lot of people play, for minutes or hours each. Accordingly, the game is very simple and quick to play, with rounds lasting two minutes, making it ideal for an audience of casual gamers. In contrast, we found that PhotoCity could achieve its goals with a small player base, which is fortunate because the game is significantly more involved and time consuming than the ESP game.

Foldit [9] is a GWAP designed for human-assisted protein folding, taking advantage of humans' innate spatial reasoning abilities. To play, players manipulate digital 3D protein structures, trying to find a configuration with the most tightly packed (and lowest energy) shape for each protein. Foldit is designed to have a wide appeal, with colorful proteins and gentle introductory levels, but all that is needed to find the best protein configuration is one or a few experts. The problem is that no one knows what constitutes such an expert, so Foldit must attract many of players on the off chance that one of them discovers he or she is a protein-folding savant. PhotoCity similarly relies on a small group of highly motivated, expert photo-takers.

Finally, another relevant GWAP is the photography game EyeSpy of Bell et al. [8]. The purpose of EyeSpy is to collect photos and tags that would be useful for navigation and giving someone directions around a city based on easily recognized landmarks. To play, a player walks around with a cell phone taking photos, entering tags, and trying to locate the photos or tags of other players. Like PhotoCity, this game focuses on producing usable output, specifically photos that are useful for a specific navigation application, as well as of places that people would not ordinarily photograph. The difference is that EyeSpy photos are used for navigation purposes and have different requirements than PhotoCity photos, which are used for 3D modeling.

Collaborative mapping and modeling tools

A number of recent systems have utilized collaboration from large numbers of people to generate large-scale public goods related to online maps (following an altruistic incentive model, like Wikipedia [5]). Most relevant to our work is OpenStreetMap [3], an online system that allows people to contribute GPS traces and edit maps in the service of creating a open map of the entire world, complete with street networks, parks, building outlines, and many other features. Our work is complementary, seeking to supplement such maps with dense sets of ground-level photos contributed by the community (as well as 3D models resulting from processing these photos with computer vision techniques). A related project, Wikimapia [4], allows users to draw overlays and annotate regions on aerial photos, resulting in more semantically rich maps; the LabelMe system [18] provides similar functionality for Internet photos. Google has also released several tools for individuals to create 3D models of real-world buildings, including SketchUp [2] and Building Maker [1]; the goal is to use these models to populate city maps. These tools have grown out of work on interactive modeling in the CAD and computer graphics communities [25, 11, 20, 16]. Unlike all of these systems, our work explores the use of competition in a game setting to provide incentives for users to contribute content.

3D Reconstruction

PhotoCity is designed around the goal of acquiring photos for use in 3D modeling, and uses as a back end recent work in computer vision for automatic 3D reconstruction from 2D images. This computer vision technology used stems directly from the work of Snavely et al. on Photo Tourism [21] (also incorporated into Microsoft's Photosynth), as well as the multi-view stereo work of Furukawa and Ponce [13]. This technology takes a set of photos and automatically reconstructs the viewpoint (position and orientation) from which each photo was taken, as well as a "point cloud" representation of the scene; example 3D point clouds are shown in Figures 3, 4 and 8. PhotoCity exposes these models to players through a map-based interface, one for each building in play, and actively encourages players to capture views that extend and expand these models. Unlike Photosynth, where each model is built by a single user, PhotoCity players collaborate to reconstruct the world. These computer vision techniques can also be run on large collections of user-contributed photos on sites like Flickr. However, PhotoCity encourages *new* photos to be taken, whereas the tourist photos on photo-sharing sites are largely concentrated around a small number of viewpoints and landmarks. While this data is extremely useful for understanding and visualizing where people take photos and reconstructing famous landmarks [19, 15, 17, 10], in our context we seek a much more complete set of photos for our task. Even extremely large sets of Flickr photos are insufficient for reconstructing *complete* models of buildings and cities [6, 12].

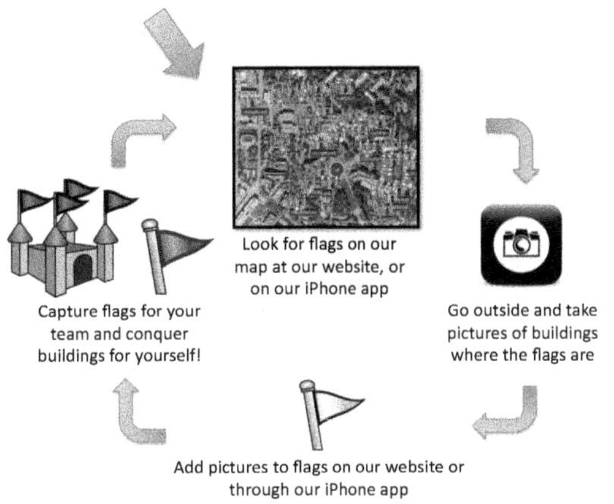

Figure 1. Gameplay cycle: players look for flags to capture on the map, go outside and take photos, upload the photos, and then capture flags and conquer buildings.

In contrast to scraping the web for images, the Wiki-based city modeling approach [14] of Irschara et al. solicits photos from the users in much the same way as PhotoCity. By contributing their photos to a central repository, wiki users (and PhotoCity players) are helping to build a 3D model of a location of shared interest. The difference is that PhotoCity provides additional incentives for players to upload their photos, such as capturing virtual flags and scoring points.

GAME DESCRIPTION

A description of a preliminary version of PhotoCity and the underlying computer vision technology is given in [22], but we recap and expand on it here. The core mechanic of our game involves players inspecting the state of the game world on a map, taking photos at locations of promising in-game value, uploading the photos to the PhotoCity website, and then observing the results of their play. Through repeated cycles of this process, summarized in Figure 1, players introduce new photos of the game world into play, which in turn expand the 3D "point cloud" models stored on the servers. The geometric points in these point clouds correspond to points on the surfaces of buildings, trees, and other objects, and also to the game "points" that players accumulate through the course of the game.

The Game World

The game world of PhotoCity is a map of the real world overlaid with virtual castles and virtual flags, as shown in Figure 2. By contributing photos in certain locations, players can capture and control these castles and flags. Each castle

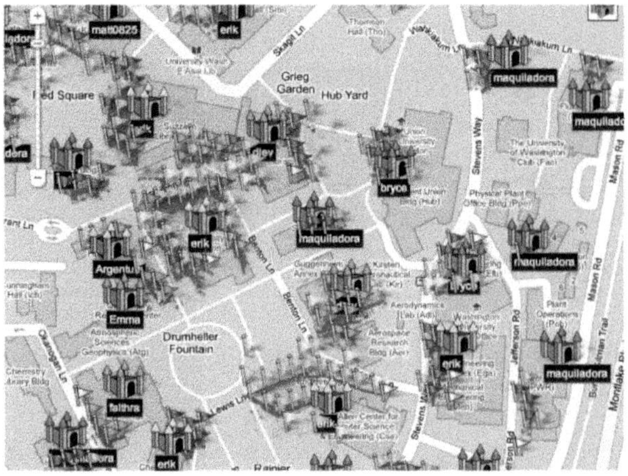

Figure 2. PhotoCity map with castles and flags at University of Washington. Different teams (at the same school) have different colored flags and castles. When a player captures a flag, the flag becomes the color of her team. When a player captures a building, her name appears under the castle icon.

corresponds to one partially reconstructed 3D model of a real-world building. If a player adds the most points to the school library, for example, that player "captures" the building, and his name appears next to the library's castle icon on the map. Flags correspond to specific map locations in the real world, and are automatically placed along building walls to guide players to more lucrative, missing viewpoints. A player controls a flag when her photos contribute the most points to that one section of wall. As models grow larger, more flags appear along the edges of the model.

Basics: Earning Points and Capturing Flags

Every virtual model in the game is represented as a dense point cloud, like the one pictured in Figure 4. When a player adds a photo to a model, our back end server estimates the 3D pose of that photo with respect to the current 3D model, then matches pixels in that photo to existing, nearby photos, in order to triangulate new points—in essence, each photo acts similar to a "laser scan" captured at a particular viewpoint, with geometry created by matching points in that photo to other views. This process literally adds new 3D points to the model, and the player earns one game point for each new 3D point.

To play the game, the typical player looks at the map of the game, identifies the flags she wishes to capture, and then takes photos of that portion of the building. For a photo to earn points, it must (1) overlap with enough existing points in the model and (2) overlap the empty space next to a model. The first requirement allows the photo to connect with the model and have its position within the model automatically calculated. The second requirement, that the photo look beyond the existing model, allows new points to be added to that void as soon as there are enough other photos to triangulate the 3D positions of those features. A photo can add up to several thousand new points.

Instead of taking a nice photo of the front of a particular building, an area that is likely already saturated in photos,

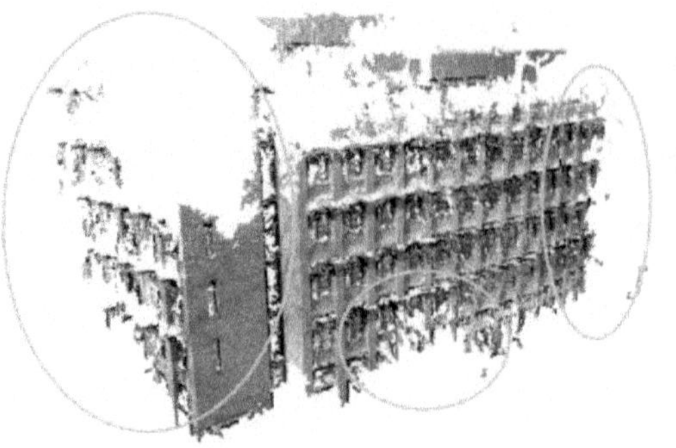

Figure 3. A seed made from 30 photos. Players take photos to fill in the missing holes (indicated in this image by the ovals) and to expand this seed from a single facade to the entire building.

the player can earn many more points (and capture flags) if he goes to the *edge* of the virtual model and takes entirely *new* photos there. This basic game mechanic accomplishes two things towards the purpose of PhotoCity: (1) Photos are not just of the 'popular' locations, but include many different locations and many different viewing angles of each location. (2) Every photo that a player earns points for has already been determined by the game to be useful.

A verification mechanism is built into the game. Every photo is compared against a 3D model when it is uploaded, and the only photos that earn points are photos that overlap with or fit into an existing model. If a player uploads an irrelevant photo, of a different building or of a flower for example, that photo will fail to match the 3D model and the game will mark it as 'unsuccessful'. The game performs this matching in a matter of seconds and then the player views which photos failed and which worked. They can use this information to modify their approach to taking pictures. Occasionally, a photo of of the correct building fails to match because the virtual model of that building is not yet large enough to incorporate that photo. The system automatically retries each photo three times, but if a photo repeatedly fails to match (because the model has not grown enough), players are free to re-upload photos. When they do, the game considers these as entirely new photos.

Advanced Technique: Seeds

In addition to playing PhotoCity by growing existing models, players can also seed their own models.

Every model in PhotoCity starts off as a seed generated from a small batch of photos of the real building. The number of photos used to make a seed is between 20 and 200. Models in their starting state usually only span one face or one corner of a building and have rough edges and large holes where data for the building has yet to be captured. Figure 3 shows the size of a seed made from thirty photos. Once a seed has been generated, it is aligned with the map and added to the set of active, under construction models in the game.

If a player wants to take pictures of a particular building but that building is not already in the game, that player can seed

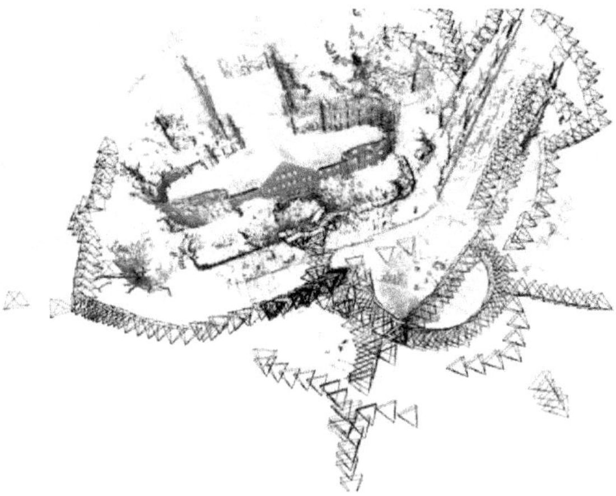

Figure 4. A near-complete model with camera positions shown as black triangles around the model. The game requires a different style of photography, one that favors quantity and variety over artistic composition. In order to expand a model, players must take photos that overlap the existing model, and then move to a new area, taking many photos along the way.

that building herself. To do so, she takes a starting set of photos that capture just one side or corner of a building from all possible angles. Then she uploads those photos through a separate web interface and waits for the game to generate the model using the techniques of [21] and [13]. This can take up to several hours, depending on the number of photos. It can also fail to work if the building is too shiny or featureless (e.g. a building with large glass windows). If the seed generation was successful, the player then aligns an overhead view of the model with a map and waits for the game developers to approve her seed and her alignment. We make sure that each seed meets a minimum quality requirement and is neither offensive nor irrelevant.

Letting players start seeds themselves is beneficial to the game's purpose and to the player. It is impossible for the game designers to seed a large number of buildings, especially if they are not physically present where PhotoCity is taking place. But it is easy for players to start seeds anywhere and everywhere, and earn many points for each seed. Players can choose buildings that have personal meaning to them or are convenient to photograph. Having so many models active in the game gives other players variety for where to go and take photos.

PhotoCity-style Photography

The photography style required in PhotoCity is different from ordinary photography. Van House [23] examines the types of photos posted on Flickr and finds that most represent a way of 'life chronicling' and self-representation. Baber et. al. [7] point out that "much 'tourist photography' represents a special form of image capture" in which tourists tend to gravitate towards the best vantage points to take their own versions of photos seen in brochures. PhotoCity requires a more utilitarian approach to photography than the artistic approach seen on Flickr, but also requires more creativity than normal 'tourist photography' to get away from canonical views and capture a scene from entirely new angles.

Instead of carefully composing a single shot, the key to PhotoCity is to take as many photos as possible from many different angles. The ideas of quantity over quality, and sweeping the camera around a scene, are probably the most radical notions that people new to PhotoCity have to learn. Figures 4 and 11 show camera/photographer positions and how players walked around a particular model taking photos every few steps. This is but one dimension on which to change how players take photos, favoring quantity and variety over nice composition. In the end, the photos taken for PhotoCity should have the coverage, density, and variety to essentially blanket an entire location in photographs.

FIELD STUDY

In our setting, the main challenge is to acquire a different and much larger set of photos than what people normally take and post online. This set of photos should also be large enough and comprehensive enough to be completely "cover" a target area (and in particular yield complete 3D reconstructions of buildings). This could be accomplished either by having many players stray slightly from their ordinary behavior and do a small amount of work, or having fewer players drastically change their photographic style and each contribute a large amount.

We designed PhotoCity to have a variety of different incentives, and deployed it as a competition against two universities to evaluate its success and find whether the game solicits many new users, a few passionate users, or something in between.

New Incentive: Competition

In the Spring of 2010 we instigated a rivalry between two schools. For six weeks, split into two three-week rounds, Cornell University and the University of Washington in Seattle played PhotoCity and competed to see which school could reconstruct the "best" model of its campus. Players could view the PhotoCity map for each school, or track the game on a single competition webpage. Anyone at either school could sign up online and start contributing photos. We advertised though school newspapers, department mailing lists, and temporarily ran an advertisement on Facebook targeted at students interested in photography.

The competition was not just between schools, but also between players (within and across schools). The competition page featured a leader board where players were ranked by number of points and by number of successful photos. There were also five 'titles' that one player at each school could hold: Kingdom Overlord (owning the most models), Expert Expander (spawning the most new flags), Expert Seeder (starting the most new seeds), Master Flag Conqueror (most flags captured), and Best Recruiter (players could invite their friends to play and get recruiter credit). Finally, within each school there was also a team competition; players could select from four teams (red, green, blue, yellow) to join, and the webpage provided a ranking of each team by score.

We awarded prizes after the competition: T-shirts for the top 15 players (based on points), Flickr Pro accounts for the title-holders at each school, and 3D laser-etched trophies of models built during the game for the top player at each school.

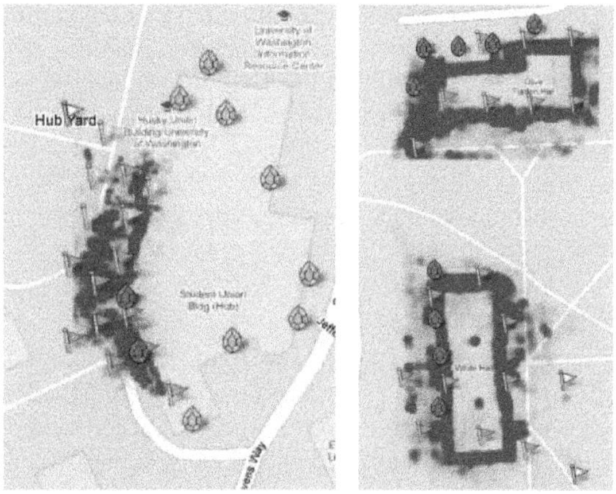

(a) (b)

Figure 5. Collectable PhotoCity gems entice players to complete buildings. 5(a) shows gems on the unfinished side of a model while 5(b) shows gems on two completed models.

New Mechanic: Gems

The competition took place in two rounds. The first round lasted three weeks and players played with the game mechanics described above, seeding and expanding models. We discovered at the end of the first round that while players seeded many buildings throughout each campus, most reconstructions were not complete.

The theme of the basic PhotoCity mechanics, and of holding the competition, is to focus player efforts to get something productive done. For the second round, we expanded on this theme by adding a new mechanic designed to entice players to complete buildings.

This new mechanic was collectable gems. Gems are very similar to flags in that they represent specific locations on the map. But unlike flags, which are automatically placed on existing building walls, gems are manually placed (by the designers) on the far sides of buildings. Unlike flags, which different players can contribute points to, capture, and steal from each other, gems are *collectable*. The first player to grow a model into the vicinity of a gem collects that gem and no other player can steal it from the first. Figure 5(a) shows a building with a seed started on one side of the building and gems placed around the far side. Gems turn from gold to purple when they are collected. Figure 5(b) shows two buildings that were completed during the second round with the gem mechanic.

RESULTS

In total, forty-five players played PhotoCity for the six weeks of the competition and submitted over 100,000 photos. There were 26 students from University of Washington and 19 students from Cornell who participated, mostly recruited through department mailing lists and word-of-mouth. Figure 9 shows

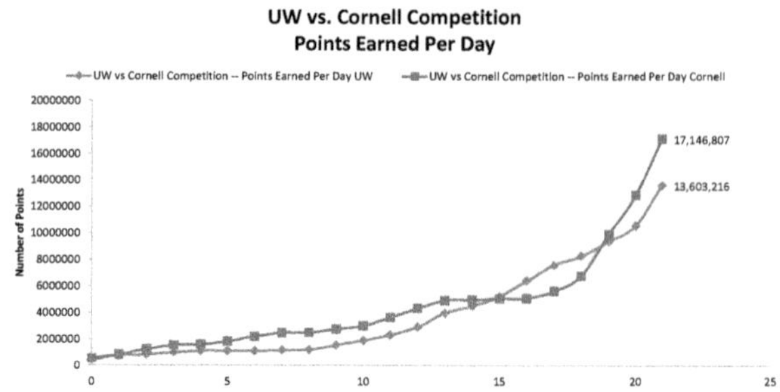

Figure 6. A plot of the points earned by UW and Cornell over the first round of the competition, demonstrating that competition made a significant impact in effort exerted by players. Cornell's points are shown in red and UW's points are shown in blue. Cornell held the lead for the first two weeks, and when threatened by UW at the start of the third week, defended their first place position.

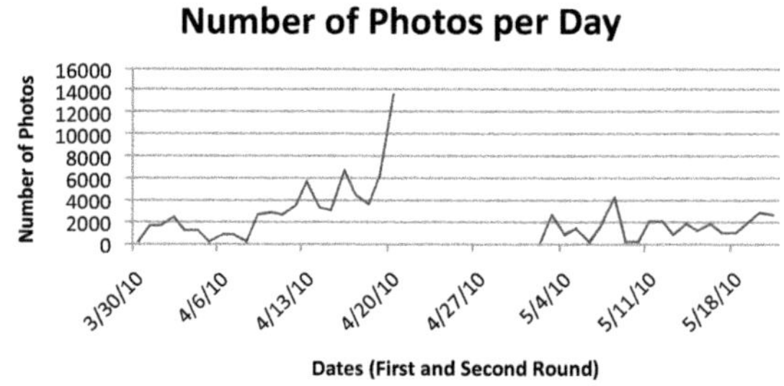

Figure 7. This graph shows the total number of photos submitted per day by students at both schools during the first and second rounds of the competition, each of which lasted for three weeks. Daily photo-submission is higher in the first round, especially towards the end, because there are over 50 active buildings per campus instead of the 10 active buildings per campus in the second "gem-collecting" round.

the number of players who were "active" and submitting photos on any given day, while Figure 7 shows the total number of photos submitted on each day of the competition. Activity and enthusiasm at both schools was roughly equal, though Figure 6 shows Cornell maintaining a lead in the number of points for most of the first round, despite having fewer players.

The first round started with four seeds at each zone, and by the end, players had started 64 seeds at University of Washington and 55 seeds at Cornell, totaling 119 new seeds. Figure 11 gives an idea of the distribution of seeds at the University of Washington. The top two seeder players began 26 and 20 seeds respectively.

During the first round alone, players submitted over 76,000 photos. During the entire competition, players submitted over 109,000 photos. Players were able to re-upload photos that initially failed to match, and 31% of the final photo count were resubmissions. About 68,000 photos of those photos registered, amounting to about 500 photos on average per model. Three completed models from the game are shown in Figure 8. We now compare our photo set against Flickr to see if the game accomplishes its goal.

(a) Lewis Hall (UW) (b) Sage Chapel (Cornell) (c) Uris Library (Cornell)

Figure 8. Buildings reconstructed in detail during the PhotoCity competition.

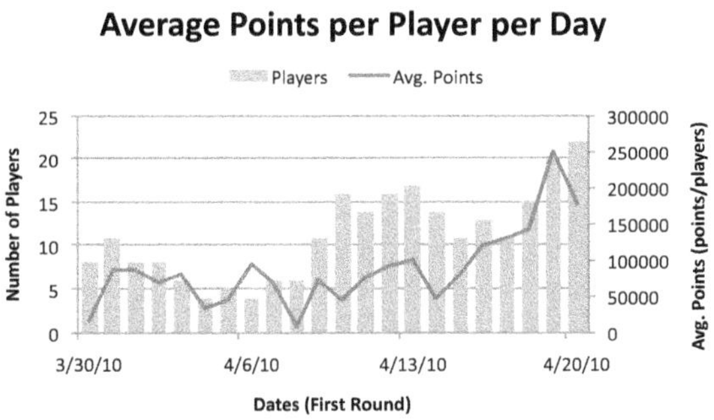

Figure 9. This graph shows the number of active players who submitted photos each day, and the average number of points per active player each day (total number of points scored that day divided by active players). Towards the end of the first competition round, players had learned how to take effective photos and earn more points per day: 100,000-250,000 points on average (and generating the same number of geometric 3D points).

Versus Flickr Photos

PhotoCity collected 109,000 photos divided between University of Washington and Cornell. In contrast, the Rome in a Day project used 150,000 photos in its Rome reconstruction. We totaled up the photos of each of the connected components of Rome (the largest of which contained 2,106 photos) and calculated that around 10% of the 150,000 photos were used in any 3D model. The rest do not usefully contribute because they are of people, interiors, or other kinds of photos meant to provide some personal value to the photographer.

In contrast, 60% of PhotoCity photos are used! Furthermore, while some of the unused photos are definitely unrelated, many are still likely to be of school buildings. They did not overlap a model when they were added, but may have overlapped at the end of the game if retried.

Again compared to Rome, the largest connected reconstruction has 2,106 photos in it. Our largest single model is of the Cornell Arts Quad with over 4,000 photos and 8,000,000 points. Each campus reconstruction consists of several multi-thousand photo/multi-building reconstructions.

We found PhotoCity photos to be significantly more useful for 3D reconstruction than Flickr photos of a popularly photographed city of Rome. Of a less popularly photographed location such as a university campus, this difference was even more striking. Figure 10 shows 35,000 PhotoCity photos densely packed across University of Washington campus and there are only about 30,000 geotagged photos on Flickr, most of which are not suitable for modeling the campus buildings.

Even though there were only 45 players, these players took thousands of photos of *views that had never been captured before* and covered their campuses much more thoroughly than an unorganized effort could reasonably achieve. Another round of PhotoCity could fill in the remaining gaps or even chronicle the campus changing over time. This conclusively demonstrates that PhotoCity is an effective way to collect large, dense photographs of places previously not thoroughly photographed.

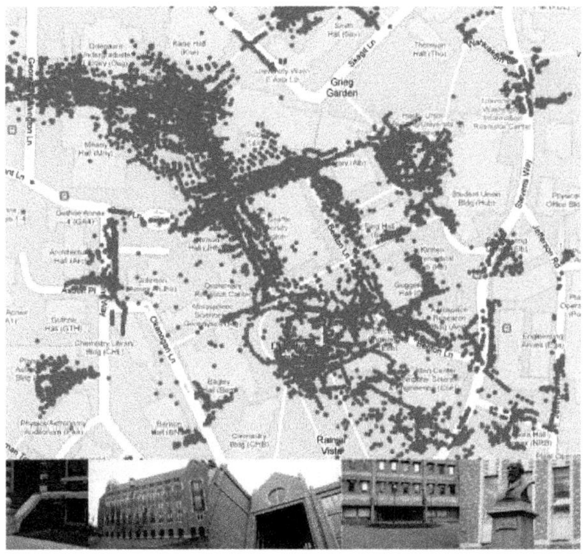

Figure 10. Locations of PhotoCity photos (where the photographer was standing) on a map of UW. Photos densely cover the parts of campus active in the game, especially walkways and open areas between buildings. Real photos from the game shown below the map.

DISCUSSION

The results of our experiment show that it only took a small group of players to capture a large amount of data. We now discuss what motivated these players to participate so enthu-

Figure 11. The walls of a building are shown in black and camera positions are shown as colored circles, colored in the order they were taken and submitted to the game, with blue being the oldest photos and yellow being the newest photos. The top-left (north-western) faces of the building were photographed first, then a very straight and deliberate path of photos was taken slightly closer to the building, and finally, photos were taken from completely new viewpoints (from the south and east) as the building grew.

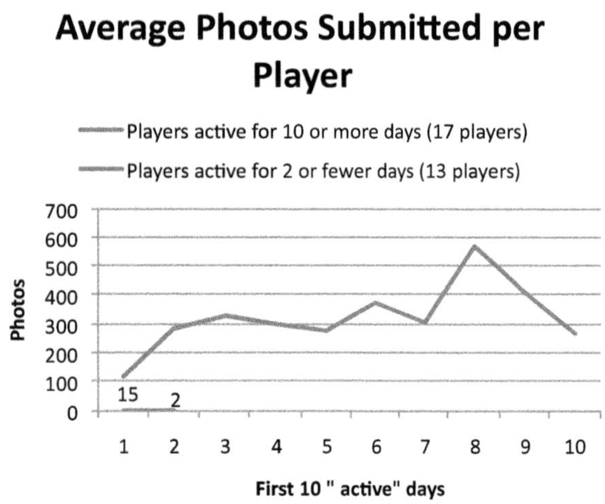

Figure 12. The most striking difference between players who became heavily involved in the game and played for many days (10 or more) was simply the number of photos each group took on their first few active days. Players who played very little (one or two days only) took very few photos their first day. Players who wound up playing a lot (10 or more active days) took almost 10 times as many photos their first day, and even increased the number of photos they took each day for the first several days, until leveling off.

siastically, how they became so effective, and what positive outcomes they experienced personally.

Player Motivation

At the end of the competition, we presented players with a survey that included questions about what motivated them to start playing and keep playing, and what strategies they developed to gain a competitive advantage. Twenty-two players responded. While this survey mainly captured the opinions of those who played through the end of the competition, the responses were in line with what we observed during the study: that competition was a good motivating factor and that most people who played were also interested in the resulting 3D models.

There were different types of competition: competition between schools, rivalries between players, and players trying to climb to the top of the leader board or earn one of the five titles (e.g. "Expert Seeder"). The graph in Figure 6 shows evidence of the competition between schools having an impact on play. Cornell, in red, held the lead for the first two weeks of the competition. When University of Washington temporarily surpassed Cornell, Cornell quickly stole back its lead. In talking to students at both schools, Cornell students were more interested in winning the competition, while University of Washington students were interested in competing among themselves. Most of the top players at the University of Washington were friends and spent their time trying to outdo each other.

Players also cared about the game's purpose. More than half of survey responders cited it as a reason for trying PhotoCity initially. Unlike Photosynth, PhotoCity produces dense, detailed 3D models of real world locations and allows for people to collaborate and improve models. The popularity of Photosynth (over 400,000 synths created in the first year[1]) suggests that people want to thoroughly capture the meaningful things around them in photos.

The main de-motivator of players, especially novice players who did not submit very many photos to begin with, was when their photos were rejected by the system. Observing Figure 12, we suspect players have to take more than 10 or 20 photos to reap benefits like seeing a model actually grow, which make the game fun.

Players Becoming Experts

The majority of point contributions (80%) during the university competition came from the top 10 players. The top player alone contributed 20% of the total number of points. PhotoCity appears to be a game for experts, with the best players taking significantly more photos and earning significantly more points than novice players.

The difficulty for new players stems from the need to adopt a different photography style and to learn (from the map) what to take photos of. Most of the players who end up

[1] http://blogs.msdn.com/b/photosynth/archive/2009/08/18/photosynth-turns-one-year-old.aspx

playing PhotoCity a lot start off with a reasonable idea of how to play (take lots of photos) and then get even better with experience. The top line in Figure 12 shows players who played 10 or more days taking gradually more photos each day over the first few days. The bottom line in the same figure shows players who only played for one or two days taking very few photos to start out with, and then apparently being so discouraged or uninterested that they took even fewer photos the next day. A possible improvement to the game is to encourage a new player to take many photos (at least 20, though 50 or 100 might be better) right away, (a) so that they can make a sizable contribution, and (b) so that they can earn a large number of points right away and feel inspired to play again.

Expert Strategies

Further evidence of players' deep involvement in the game is the strategies they described to us in the survey. Different strategies involved playing with a different game mechanic, finding the most lucrative types of buildings, or optimizing for time of day, but each was developed to give the player a competitive advantage.

Regarding what types of buildings were most lucrative:

> "Targetting buildings without huge slabs of glass/windows works best. Buildings that have plain facades are tough to get points on. Buildings with stone exteriors, especially rough hewn stone, have tonnes of points. Brick buildings can give lots of points if the grout is especially thick."

Players mentioned that the corners of buildings and trees planted next to buildings were especially difficult to navigate around. One player described how to tackle corners, while another mentioned an alternate strategy for earning points that avoided dealing with corners.

> "I've been trying to work out my corner strategy, and mostly it consists of taking a lot of pictures of that corner from a lot of angles."

> "I thought that since it seemed to be very hard to mesh around corners, I would make lots of seeds and try to get points that way."

Some strategies optimized over lighting and time of day.

> "The third strategy was to try and approximate the time of day and the lighting that some pictures were taken; this would help prevent rejection by the game. With that said, cloudy days were the best by far when dealing with corners because less contrast helped the game figure out the geometry from my pictures."

> "When it was sunny, I utilized my camera's anti-shake features to allow myself to take photos while walking around a particular zone. This allowed me to take crisp photos while not having to stop my stride. Also bonus: less people stared at me!"

Finally, several of the players mentioned how they planned their photo-taking sessions and kept their photos organized.

> "Taking many pictures of one building with 5 megapixel camera, then coming home to submit, sometimes up to 5 gigs on a weekend shoot, was primary photo capture strategy. Organizing photos on external hard drive folders by campus region, building, then face of building provided good hierarchy to structure uploads."

> "I used my ipod while on campus to help me pin-point uncaptured flags. I would then write out a checklist of places to go to take photos (kind of like a photo-route) If unsure, I would just check it again. It was pretty nifty."

Positive Outcomes for Players

Although the primary purpose of PhotoCity is to collect photos, players experienced personal benefits through the game play. In the survey, we asked players whether they felt they got to know their campus better. Twelve of the 22 participants surveyed said yes. We also asked whether they took photos as part of their daily routine or went out of their way to take photos. Thirteen people responded, 'I went out of my way to take photos,' eight said, ' I didn't stray far from my normal route, but did seek out new vantage points,' and only one participant responded with 'I only took photos where I was already going.' We can conclude that PhotoCity made many of the participants more physically active than their default state.

Only a small group of players participated, but they still contributed a surprising amount of data. Given time to gain expertise and incentives to become deeply involved in the game, players can become extremely effective.

CONCLUSION

The problem we set out to address was to gather enough photos of a certain location, such as a university campus, to be able to thoroughly reconstruct that location in 3D. We have demonstrated that our game, PhotoCity, is capable of bringing in many thousands of highly relevant photos–photos of buildings from a diverse set of angles and viewpoints. During a competition between the University of Washington and Cornell, players took over 100,000 photos, over 60% of which were used in the resulting 3D models. It only took 45 players to collect this data. To achieve such success with a small number of players, we designed various game mechanics that made players' in-game actions productive and beneficial to our purpose, and motivated our players through competitions, prizes, and a leader board. Some players became so deeply involved in the competition that they submitted many thousands of photos apiece, most of them usefully contributing to a 3D model of that player's campus. To verify that our players' photos had more coverage and completeness than existing community photo collections, we compared our dataset to a Flickr set of Rome reconstructed by Rome in a Day, and to Flickr photo counts of each campus. The photos collected by PhotoCity are vastly more relevant to our purpose of 3D modeling than Flickr photos, especially of underrepresented locations like school campuses.

The message we hope to impart on others is that even with a small player base, games with a purpose can still take on large-scale problems, provided the players are trained to make efficient and massive contributions to the game.

ACKNOWLEDGEMENTS

This work was supported by DARPA grant FA8750-11-2-0102, the University of Washington Center for Game Science, Intel, Google, and Microsoft.

REFERENCES

1. Google Building Maker. http://sketchup.google.com/3dwh/buildingmaker.html.
2. Google SketchUp. http://sketchup.google.com/.
3. OpenStreetMap. http://www.openstreetmap.org/.
4. Wikimapia. http://www.wikimapia.org/.
5. Wikipedia. http://www.wikipedia.org/.
6. S. Agarwal, N. Snavely, I. Simon, S. M. Seitz, and R. Szeliski. Building Rome in a day. *International Conference on Computer Vision*, 2009.
7. C. Baber, J. Cross, T. Khaleel, and R. Beale. Location-based photography as sense-making. In *BCS-HCI '08: Proceedings of the 22nd British HCI Group Annual Conference on People and Computers*, pages 133–140, Swinton, UK, UK, 2008. British Computer Society.
8. M. Bell, S. Reeves, B. Brown, S. Sherwood, D. MacMillan, J. Ferguson, and M. Chalmers. Eyespy: supporting navigation through play. In *CHI '09: Proceedings of the 27th international conference on Human factors in computing systems*, pages 123–132, New York, NY, USA, 2009. ACM.
9. S. Cooper, F. Khatib, A. Treuille, J. Barbero, J. Lee, M. Beenen, A. Leaver-Fay, D. Baker, Z. Popovic, and F. Players. Predicting protein structures with a multiplayer online game. *Nature*, 466(7307):756–760, August 2010.
10. D. Crandall, L. Backstrom, D. Huttenlocher, and J. Kleinberg. Mapping the world's photos. In *Proc. Int. World Wide Web Conf.*, 2009.
11. P. E. Debevec, C. J. Taylor, and J. Malik. Modeling and rendering architecture from photographs: A hybrid geometry- and image-based approach. In *SIGGRAPH Conf. Proc.*, pages 11–20, 1996.
12. J.-M. Frahm, P. Georgel, D. Gallup, T. Johnson, R. Raguram, C. Wu, Y.-H. Jen, E. Dunn, B. Clipp, S. Lazebnik, and M. Pollefeys. Building Rome on a cloudless day. In *Proc. European Conf. on Computer Vision*, 2010.
13. Y. Furukawa and J. Ponce. Accurate camera calibration from multi-view stereo and bundle adjustment. *Int. J. Comput. Vision*, 84(3):257–268, 2009.
14. A. Irschara, C. Zach, and H. Bischof. Towards wiki-based dense city modeling. pages 1 –8, oct. 2007.
15. L. Kennedy, M. Naaman, S. Ahern, R. Nair, and T. Rattenbury. How Flickr helps us make sense of the world: Context and content in community-contributed media collections. In *Proc. Int. Conf. on Multimedia*, 2007.
16. L. Nan, A. Sharf, H. Zhang, D. Cohen-Or, and B. Chen. Smartboxes for interactive urban reconstruction. In *SIGGRAPH Conf. Proc.*, 2010.
17. T. Quack, B. Leibe, and L. V. Gool. World-scale mining of objects and events from community photo collections. In *Proc. Int. Conf. on Content-based Image and Video Retrieval*, pages 47–56, 2008.
18. B. C. Russell, A. Torralba, K. P. Murphy, and W. T. Freeman. LabelMe: A database and web-based tool for image annotation. *Int. J. of Computer Vision*, 77(1-3):157–173, 2008.
19. I. Simon, N. Snavely, and S. M. Seitz. Scene summarization for online image collections. In *Proc. Int. Conf. on Computer Vision*, 2007.
20. S. N. Sinha, D. Steedly, R. Szeliski, M. Agrawala, and M. Pollefeys. Interactive 3d architectural modeling from unordered photo collections. In *SIGGRAPH Asia Conf. Proc.*, 2008.
21. N. Snavely, S. M. Seitz, and R. Szeliski. Photo tourism: Exploring photo collections in 3d. In *SIGGRAPH Conference Proceedings*, pages 835–846, New York, NY, USA, 2006. ACM Press.
22. K. Tuite, N. Snavely, D. Hsiao, A. M. Smith, and Z. Popovic. Reconstructing the world in 3d: Bringing games with a purpose outdoors. In *FDG '10: Proceedings of the 5th International Conference on Foundations of Digital Games*, Monterey, CA, USA, 2010. ACM Press.
23. N. A. Van House. Flickr and public image-sharing: distant closeness and photo exhibition. In *CHI '07: CHI '07 extended abstracts on Human factors in computing systems*, pages 2717–2722, New York, NY, USA, 2007. ACM.
24. L. von Ahn and L. Dabbish. Labeling images with a computer game. In *CHI '04: Proceedings of the SIGCHI conference on Human factors in computing systems*, pages 319–326, New York, NY, USA, 2004. ACM.
25. R. C. Zeleznik, K. P. Herndon, and J. F. Hughes. Sketch: An interface for sketching 3d scenes. In *SIGGRAPH Conf. Proc.*, pages 163–170, 1996.

Cooks or Cobblers? Crowd Creativity through Combination

Lixiu Yu
Stevens Institute of Technology
Castle Point on Hudson, Hoboken NJ 07030 USA
lisayu1103@gmail.com

Jeffrey V. Nickerson
Stevens Institute of Technology
Castle Point on Hudson, Hoboken NJ 07030 USA
jnickerson@stevens.edu

ABSTRACT
A sketch combination system is introduced and tested: a crowd of 1047 participated in an iterative process of design, evaluation and combination. Specifically, participants in a crowdsourcing marketplace sketched chairs for children. One crowd created a first generation of chairs, and then successive crowds created new generations by combining the chairs made by previous crowds. Other participants evaluated the chairs. The crowd judged the chairs from the third generation more creative than those from the first generation. An analysis of the design evolution shows that participants inherited and modified presented features, and also added new features. These findings suggest that crowd based design processes may be effective, and point the way toward computer-human interactions that might further encourage crowd creativity.

Author Keywords
Crowdsourcing, creativity, conceptual combination, human based genetic algorithms, social computing, design sketches.

ACM Classification Keywords
H5.3. Group and Organization Interfaces

ACM General Terms
Design

INTRODUCTION
Can a crowd design well? On the one hand, diversity of thinking should lead to creativity, as expressed in a Chinese proverb: Three cobblers combined make a genius mind. On the other hand, conflicting styles may lead to chaos: Too many cooks spoil the broth.

Scientific research on social creativity reflects this division: for example, brainstorming has been shown by some to be a powerful technique for encouraging ideas and by others as a waste of time [21, 25, 27]. Technology has played a role in the debate: some of the problems encountered in brainstorming, such as production blocking, can be mitigated by the use of computer-based tools [26].

Indeed, the creativity tool landscape is diverse. Among these, automated design tools often make use of blind variation, followed by selection: several random choices are made, and the results evaluated [6]. Of particular note are genetic algorithms: computer simulations of evolution in which gene-like representations are altered and combined in a search for optimal solutions [7, 11, 15]. Such algorithms, however, don't work well if the candidate solutions cannot be formally represented and computationally evaluated. Because of this, *human based* genetic algorithms have been proposed; these algorithms allocate many or all of the combination and evaluation functions to human labor [19].

Until recently, large-scale experiments to test human-based algorithms were prohibitively complex. But web technologies, and the organizational structures provided by crowdsourcing marketplaces now make it feasible to coordinate large numbers of people: Participants can collaborate with each other by working on parts of an overall task, facilitated by crowdsourcing processes and technology [1, 4, 9, 16, 17, 22, 23]. Some of these techniques are designed so that each member of the crowd functions like a processing node in a computer system [20, 29].

These techniques may not work, because computers and humans are so different. Computers execute the instructions of an algorithm without complaint or caprice. In contrast, while human beings can bring a wealth of alternative perspectives to any task, they may also choose to ignore algorithmic instructions. Will humans participating in such systems be productive, like the cobblers, or destructive, like the cooks?

We answer this question by performing an experiment, based on a system we have built. This sketch combination system is a variant of a human-based genetic algorithm: one crowd creates a first generation of sketches, and then successive crowds create additional generations by combining the sketches made by the previous crowds. A total of 1047 participants played a variety of roles, leading to the creation of 80 third-generation design sketches.

The contributions of this research are two-fold. First, the effectiveness of the sketch combination system is demonstrated: the creativity of later design sketches increased significantly, compared to the initial sketches. This sketch system has the potential to be applied to design problems in many fields. Second, this system provides evidence for the role of combination in creativity. Specifically, designers inherit and modify existing features and also added new features when combining the given designs. In addition, the affordances of the drawing tool affect the emergence of features. The work has practical implications—the system can solve design problems—and theoretical implications—the crowd can function as a combination process.

In the following sections of the paper, the sketch combination system is described, along with an experiment illustrating its use. First, previous research on combination and creativity is discussed.

COMBINATION AND CREATIVITY

The combinatorial conjecture of creativity and related theories claim that new ideas come through combination [6, 35, 40]. Combination is also central to the success of genetic algorithms [15]. But such algorithms express combination in a very specific way.

Genetic algorithms start with a population of genes. A gene can be imagined as sequence of bits that represent features. Once a population is ranked for fitness, parents are picked to produce offspring. As in natural selection, the fit parents are more likely to produce offspring than the unfit parents. The children are created by crossover: some proportion of the bits will come from the first parent, and the rest from the other parent. Thus, new combinations are produced. Prior to this combination step, the population undergoes a mutation stage, in which some parents are altered by flipping their bits [7, 11, 15]. In practice, some genetic algorithms rely mainly on crossover, others mainly on mutation [37]. Whatever operator is being used, the search space is bounded. That is, the bits in a genetic algorithm represent a finite if large search space, and the crossover operation can only produce a child by combining the bits of the parents.

Human conceptual combination shares some similarities with machine combination. Simonton sees scientific creativity as a kind of natural selection: ideas are combined at random, and some of them lead to discoveries [35]. We don't have direct access to combinatory processes in the brain, so when a fortuitous combination occurs, we are not sure if it is the result of a directed search to find complementary ideas, or instead the result of many blind trails run below the level of consciousness [6]. Thagard claims that inference processes guide search [40]. In the design community, a variety of computer based and human assisted genetic algorithms have been used successfully [10].

But human combination processes also differ from machine processes in important ways. The search space of human processes is not neatly bounded: in combining ideas our minds have access to many past experiences and present perceptions, not just the representations at hand (c.f. [24]). Consequently, even if instructed to combine two ideas, a person may associate the presented ideas with any of a vast number of other ideas, remembered or constructed on the fly. These other ideas may or may not be as good as the presented ideas. Thus, we could argue either that human based genetic algorithms will work, because the human process is close enough to the machine process, or will not work, because there will be too much variability in the human based process. We predict that the human combination process will work much like a genetic algorithm – that even if there is more variability, it will often be to advantage. In the end, the designs evolved through a human based genetic algorithm will be judged more creative than the initial designs.

In testing this through experiment, we will ask the participants to sketch. Sketches play a strong role in design. On the one hand, they are used as a way of refining ideas, and work as stimuli to elicit creativity [12, 38]. On the other hand they can constrain ideas: that is, designers will fixate upon seeing a sketch, and likely fail to design something original. This fixation has been described as conformity to the sketches just seen [36]. If designers fully conform to the provided sketches, then the proposed combination system will result in a reshuffling of the initial feature set. In contrast, if the instructions are ignored, and ideas are generated through free association, then the algorithm will play little role in the final designs. To our knowledge there has been no empirical research on human based genetic algorithms that has addressed this issue. Because of human variability, we predict that there will be mix: there will be some cases of conformity to the features in parent ideas, and some cases of modification of these features, or introduction of new features outside the two given ideas, a process we call augmentation.

People may conform to or augment the features of the given designs during the combination process. Then how will features move through the generations of the combination process? Atypical features are attended to more, remembered better [28, 34], and selected more often than typical features [14]. Extending this idea to the context of a genetic algorithm, we predict that atypical features will occur more often in the third generation than in the first, and that typical features will occur less often in the third generation than in the first.

The drawing tool should exert an additional influence on combination and the eventual creativity of the sketches: participants may produce only what the tool makes easy to produce, or may associate one shape with another shape based on the options the tools provide.

In sum, we make several testable predictions. The sketch combination system will produce more creative designs in the last generation than the first. Atypical features will increase more often than typical features. Combination will include instances of conformity and augmentation.

METHOD

Problem Definition

Sketches provide a rich way to study design: sketches are the way conceptual designs are developed and shared with others [38, 41]. We looked for a design problem that both novices and experts could accomplish, and decided to use a problem that has been the focus of previous creativity research [12]: the design of chairs for children. Chairs are objects that are universally understood, but allow for a range of variations. Moreover, in the psychological literature, chairs are considered a basic level category [31], and thus have a recognizable prototypical shape, which might make it easier for participants to evaluate the originality of design alternatives. Children's chairs are not necessarily different from adult chairs in anything but size, but in practice are often more whimsically designed and utilize a wide range of geometries, which may encourage variation in the designs.

The Measurement of Creativity

Innovation is generally believed to be the successful implementation of creative ideas [3]: In the current study, we focus on the creativity of the designs, and will leave the study of their implementations to future research. A creative idea should be both novel and potentially useful [3]. Operationally, this leads to a binary measure of creativity: Creative designs are designs that exceed a certain threshold on both the scales of originality and practicality [8]. Thus in our study, the designs are evaluated on two scales: originality and practicality. The designs will then be classified as being creative or not based on the their scores on the two scales.

The Sketch Combination System

We brought together a crowdsourcing marketplace, design tools, and organizational processes to create a sketch combination system. We will look at each in turn. Briefly, the technology was an integration of the Amazon Mechanical Turk platform [2] and the Google Docs drawing platform [13]. The organizational process was based on the idea of a genetic algorithm [11, 15] implemented with human participants [19].

The crowdsourcing marketplace

Amazon Mechanical Turk was used by participants in this study. There are two types of users in Amazon Mechanical Turk: requesters and workers. Requesters post their tasks by creating HITs (Human Intelligence Tasks) and workers perform tasks in return for compensation. Previous studies have described the characteristics of these workers [18, 32].

The design software

Google Drawing was the tool used by participants to produce designs. The drawing tool provides options to perform freehand sketching, vector line drawing, text entry, and shape drawing. Participants were directed to a Google document page already opened as a drawing. Such a page, in later generations, presented the designs to be combined. Participants had access to all the features of that drawing tool. In the combination tasks, the presented sketches were rasterized, so that participants were required to generate the new features they saw in the images.

The organizational process

In order to clearly specify the sketch combination system, we first need to describe the way a genetic algorithm works. Such an algorithm starts with a first generation population, and performs a fitness ranking. Then, members of the population are selected to become parents of the next generation. Most often, tournament selection is used: two parents are selected at random, and the fitter chosen. Another two parents are chosen, and the fitter chosen. The two chosen parents then produce offspring through a combination procedure. These offspring serve as a new population, which is then ranked, and the process repeats. Because combination can sometimes take the worst features of highly ranked parents, and thereby degrade the available genetic pool, a set of the strongest parents are promoted into the next generation without change, an aspect of the algorithm referred to as *elitism* [7].

The sketch combination system was based on the above description, and designed to run for three generations, as summarized in Figure 1.

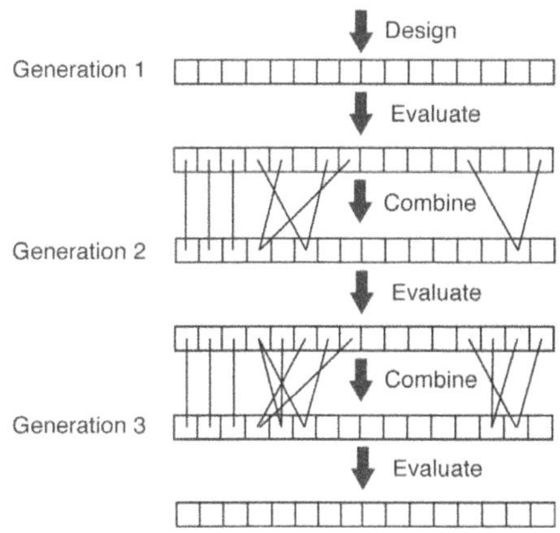

Figure 1. The generations of the experiment.

Below, we elaborate how the six steps in Figure 1 were implemented during the experimental test of the sketch combination system.

Generation 1 design

Eighty randomly selected participants were instructed to generate the population of the first generation:

Please design a chair for children.

Generation 1 evaluation
Two hundred different participants, randomly selected, then evaluated the designs generated by generation 1. Each participant rated 12 randomly selected designs on originality and practicality using 7-point Likert scales, as shown in Figure 2.

In response to a request to design a chair for children, your fellow workers created the following chairs for children. Please evaluate the originality and the practicality of each design based on the given scales.

Not original at all	○1	○2	○3	○4	○5	○6	○7	Extremely original
Not practical at all	○1	○2	○3	○4	○5	○6	○7	Extremely practical

Figure 2. The evaluation prompt.

Generation 2 combination
Tournament selection was used to select sixty pairs of generation-1 designs to serves as parents for generation 2. Participants combined the pairs:

The designs on the right are from your fellow workers. Please create a new chair for children by combining aspects of the two chairs shown.

The twenty highest-rated chairs from generation 1 were automatically promoted to generation 2.

Generation 2 evaluation
All 80 chairs were evaluated by a new set of 247 participants in the same way generation 1 was evaluated.

Generation 3 combination and evaluation
Again, tournament selection produced sixty pairs of generation-2 designs that a new crowd of sixty participants combined to create new chairs for Generation 3. In addition, the twenty top-rated chairs from Generation 2 were also promoted into generation 3. Then, 400 new participants rated the originality and practicality of all designs from all generations. Each participant rated 10 designs, including four from generation 1, three from generation 2, and three from generation 3.

RESULTS

Overall, there were 1047 participants involved in the experiment. Eighty participants took part in generation 1 design, 200 participants in generation 1 evaluation, 60 participants in generation 2 combination, 247 participants in generation 2 evaluation, 60 participants in generation 3 combination, and 400 participants in the overall cross-generation evaluation. Among all participants, 47% were female, 59% were native English speakers and 79% had earned college or graduate degrees. Ages ranged from 19 to 60 with a mean age of 28. Among the 200 participants who created or combined the chairs, 20% claimed 1-3 years of design experience.

Overall, 200 sketches of chairs were collected. They varied in many aspects, including shape and color. Participants made use of the menu choices of the Google Docs drawing tool to draw the chairs–some sketched freehand, and others started with shape stencils. Some sketches portray everyday chairs. Others depict unusual chairs, including child-attractive features, such as smiley faces, animal figures, and heart shapes. Several example chairs are shown in Figure 3.

Figure 3. Examples of the chairs.

The Generational Effect

Are designs from the last generation better than the first generation? Participants had been asked to rate the practicality and originality of both generation 1 and generation 3 designs. Figure 4 shows a scatter plot of generation 1 and generation 3 designs with respect to originality and practicality.

As discussed in the previous section, we used a binary measure of creativity that includes only designs that exceed a certain threshold on both the scales of originality and practicality [8]. We chose the approximate mean value of the ratings across all designs, 4.0, as that threshold. The dots in the upper right quadrant of Figure 4, with positions above and to the right of (4, 4), qualify as creative designs. From the figure, we can see that generation 3 designs tend to be shifted toward more creative side than generation 1 designs. The proportion of creative designs per generation is shown in Figure 5.

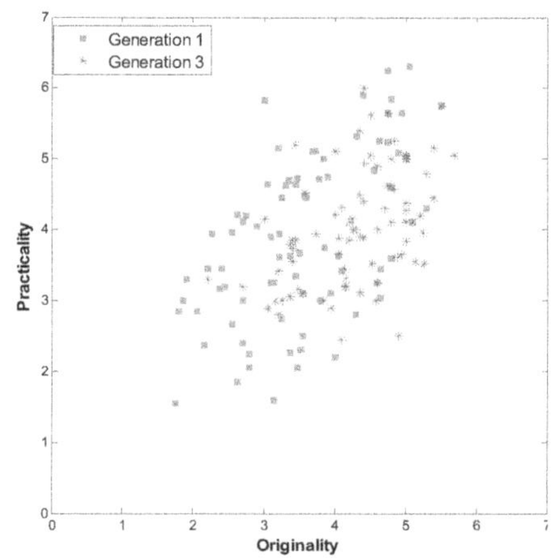

Figure 4. The originality and practicality of all designs from generation 1 and generation 3.

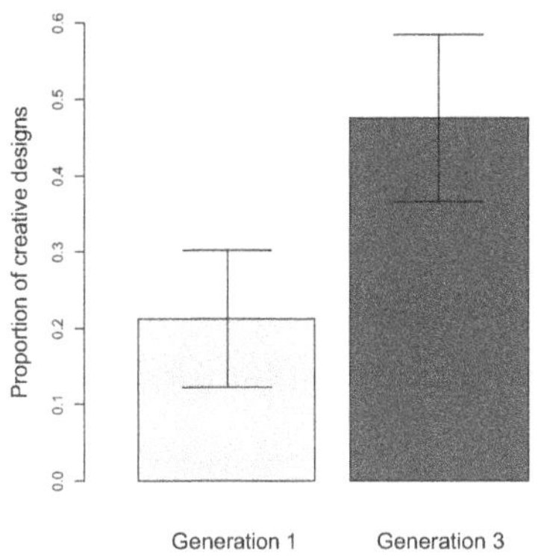

Figure 5. Proportion of creative designs. Error bars represent 95% confidence intervals.

The proportions are significantly different (x^2(1, N=160)=11.08, P<0.01). The difference is not an artifact of elitism: only five of the 20 elite chairs from generation 1 are still present in generation 3, and, if they are removed, the difference between the generations remains significant (x^2(1, N=155)=6.55, P<0.01).

This result is encouraging for the future of human based genetic algorithms. Any genetic algorithm needs to produce some children that are superior to their parents; otherwise the population regresses. Here not only do the children not get worse, the number of top children increases significantly. At the end of any design process one can expect implementation of only the best few designs, so a design process that generates a few high quality designs and many poor ones is preferable to a process that generates all medium quality designs.

We next compared the means of originality and practicality across all designs in the first and last generation. T-tests confirmed that originality increased significantly from generation 1 to generation 3 (t(158)=5.67, P<0.01) while practicality did not (t(158)=1.04, P=0.15) (see Figure 6).

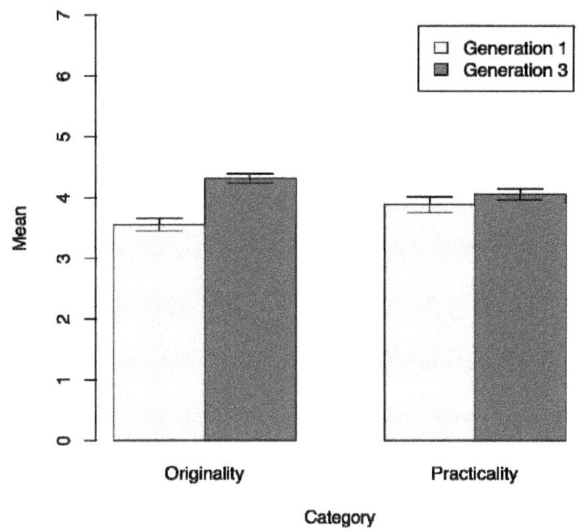

Figure 6. The originality and practicality of all chairs in generation1 and generation 3. Error bars represent standard error.

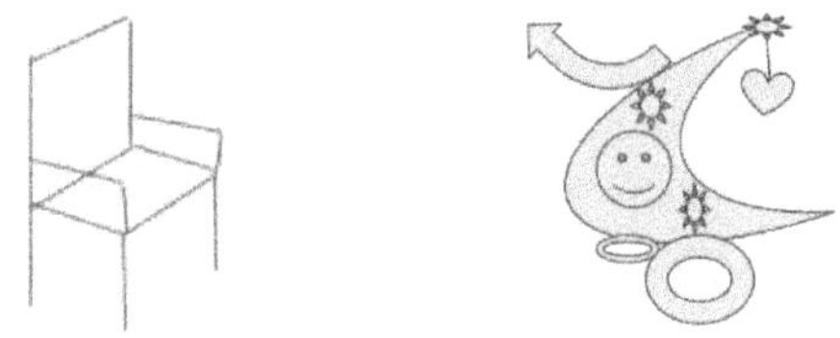

Figure 7. Two chairs rated with low creativity, from generations 1 and 3.

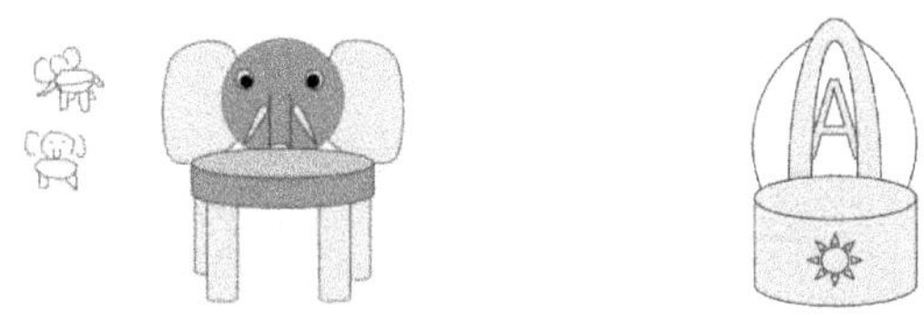

Figure 8. Two chairs rated with high creativity, from generation 1 and 3.

Participants' Ratings

Are the participants performing well on the combination and rating tasks? The designs shown in Figure 7 are example chairs with low creativity. The left chair is rated relatively high in practicality but low in originality. The right chair, high in originality, low in practicality. The designs in Figure 8 are example of chairs rated as creative designs. Participants do appear to perform well on the combination and rating tasks: their ratings appear to capture the originality and practicality of the design, and at least some participants carefully combine features from one generation to the next.

The demographics of the participants were examined to exclude the possibility that the designers' characteristics might have determined the difference in creativity between generation 1 and generation 3. No significant correlations between gender, education, and age were found with the originality or practicality of the sketches produced. The language spoken (classified as English vs. non-English) did correlate with creativity, but there was no difference in the proportion of participants with respect to this language distinction in generation 1 and 3.

How Participants Combine Designs

By looking at the way the designs were combined we might gain insight into the sources of increases in creativity. We may also learn how to improve the system in order to amplify this increase.

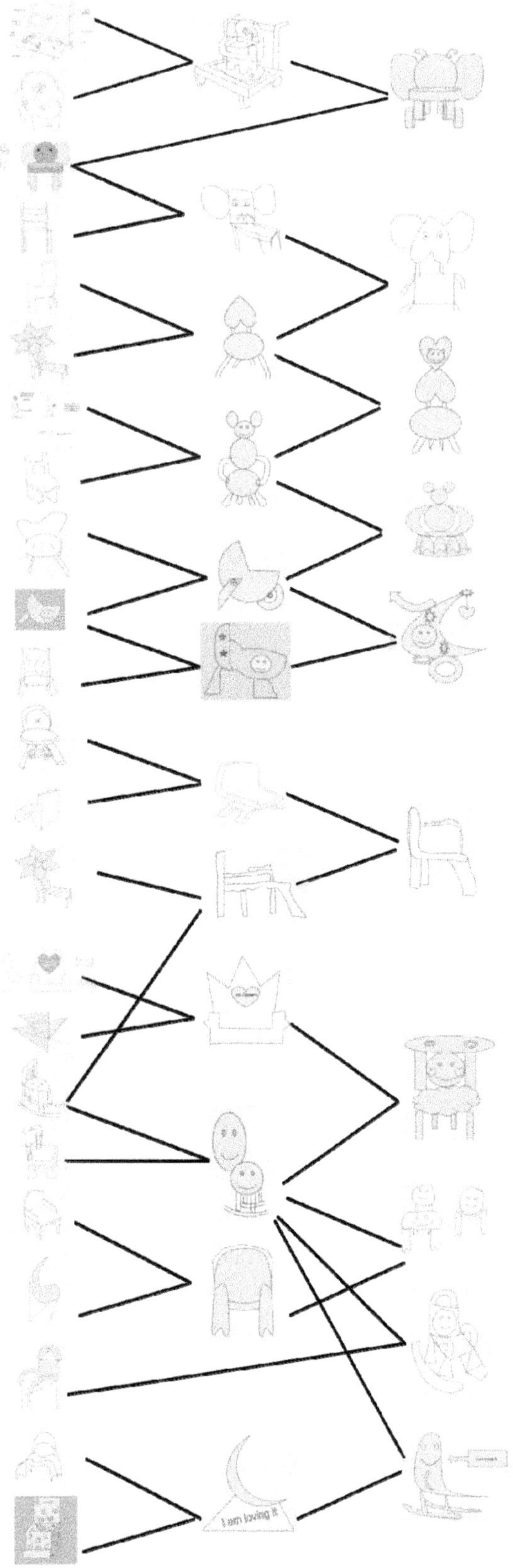

Figure 9. Evolution of several chairs.

Participants combined the given designs in many different ways, as shown in Figure 9. On the left are the chairs created in generation 1. In the middle are the chairs of generation 2, created through combining the chairs of generation 1. On the right are the generation 3 chairs, combined from generation 2. The lines indicate parent-child relationships.

As predicted, there appear to be two forces at work in the combination process. The first is conformity: the designers faithfully create a new chair by combining features of the provided chairs. The second is augmentation: the designers modify features inherited from the given chairs, or add features not present in the given chairs.

Figure 10 shows an example of conformity. The chair inherits features from parent chairs in a direct way. In addition, the designer explicitly describes the features that were combined:

> *The chair is more similar in design to the second than the first, with the straight armrests and the legs, but has the cushioning that the first seems to have. It also has some of the fun shapes that the first chair had.*

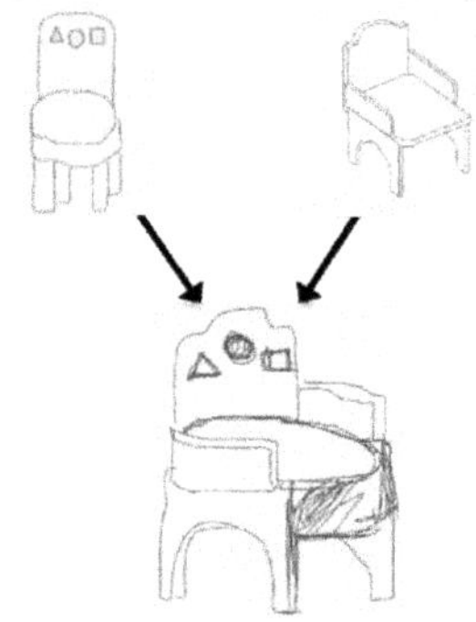

Figure 10. An example of conformity.

In contrast, the evolution tree shown in Figure 11 is an example of augmentation.

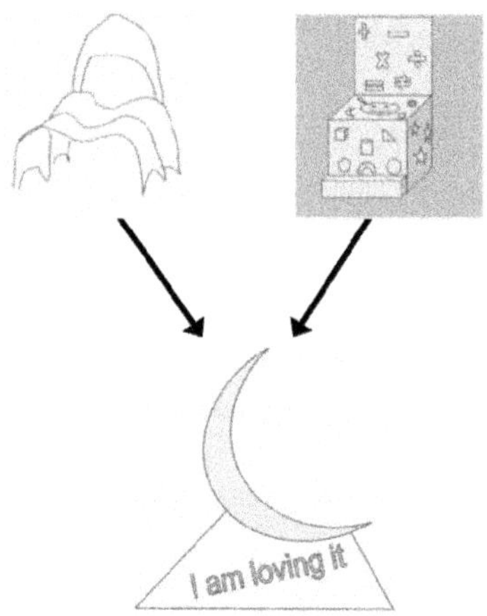

Figure 11. An example of augmentation.

			G1	G3
Typical legs	Four straight legs	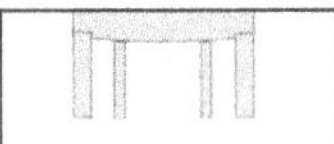	44	22
	Four straight legs with crossing bars	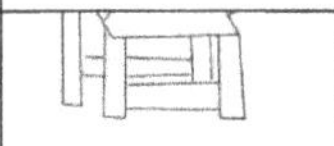	5	3
	Two straight legs	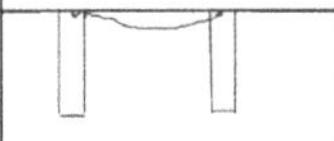	8	4
Atypical legs	Pointing legs		1	2
	Rocking chair legs	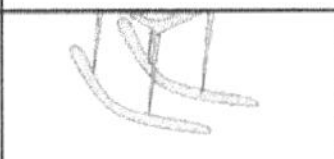	2	6
	Animal legs		0	5
	Flower legs	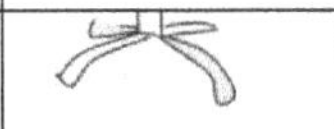	0	3
	Wheel legs		4	10
	Crossing legs	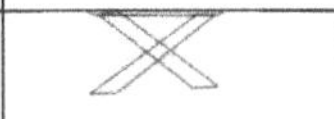	0	1
	Ball legs	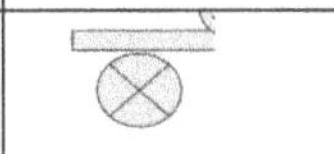	0	1
	Triangle legs	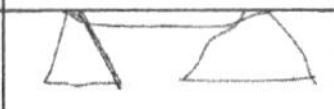	0	1
	Semi-circle legs		0	1
	Curly legs		0	2
	Goblet legs	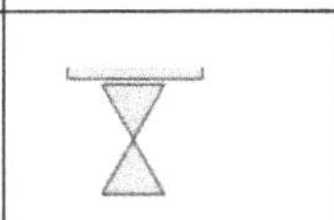	0	2
	Base legs	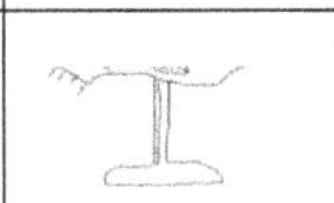	1	1
	Three legs	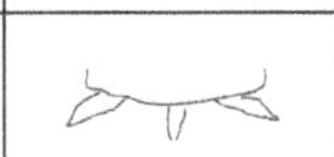	0	1
Legless			15	15

Table 1. Chair legs.

One small feature of the right parent, a crescent moon, is amplified into a major feature. And text is added to the chair inside a new legless base. The explanation of the designer doesn't mention the parent chairs:

It is a round chair which will allow the child to relax on it. The legs are straight to give the chair a firm and stable bottom. The half moon like shape makes the chair attractive and fun for the child to use.

The Evolution of Features

The typical features of the chairs are those that occur in prototypical chairs [31]. For example, prototypical chairs have four straight legs, a typical feature. A non-prototypical chair might have legs that are designed to look like the legs of animals, an atypical feature. We predicted that such atypical features would be more likely to increase in subsequent generations than typical features. In order to test this, the legs of the chairs were examined. Coding of the legs was accomplished by two raters by first determining a set of distinct categories, and then classifying all chairs into those categories. These include 17 different categories that are summarized in Table 1. The chair legs were then coded into three major categories: typical, atypical, and legless by the two raters. Inter-rater reliability, measured by a Kappa score, is 0.82.

We contrast the proportions of atypical legs and typical legs in Figure 12. We found that atypical features increase significantly in frequency ($x^2(1, N=160)=19.59$, $P<0.01$), at the same time as typical features decrease significantly ($x^2(1, N=160)=13.30$, $P<0.01$) in generation 3.

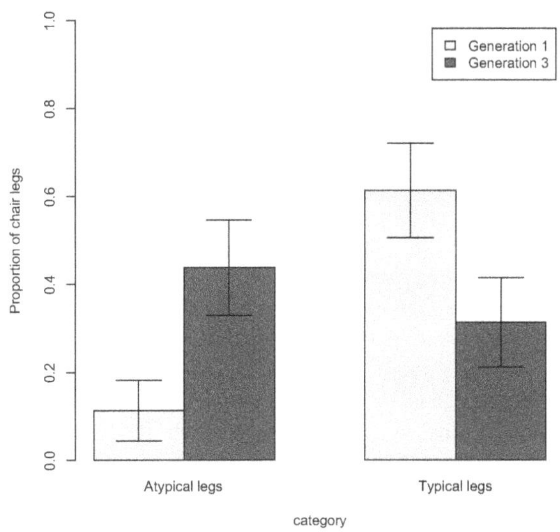

Figure 12. The evolution of chair legs from generation 1 to generation 3. Error bars represent 95% confidence intervals.

Affordances of the Tool

The Google Docs drawing tool provides several options for drawing sketches, including a pull-down shape palette, as shown in Figure 13. There are two ways the tool appears to be affecting the sketches.

Many participants made use of the shapes shown in the palette to design their chairs. In our experiment, we asked participants to use the scribble freehand drawing function when designing their chairs. However, many participants didn't comply, and used shapes instead. Specifically, we found that 17 sketches out of 80 in generation 1 used the shapes palette to design their chairs, while 40 sketches out of 80 in generation 3 used the shapes palette. This difference is significant according to a proportion test ($x^2(1, N=160)=13.19, P<0.01$). Many of the shapes used from the palette are atypical with respect to chair design, so one possible explanation for the increase is that these atypical features tend to be noticed, and are carried over into the next generation, just like the atypical chair legs.

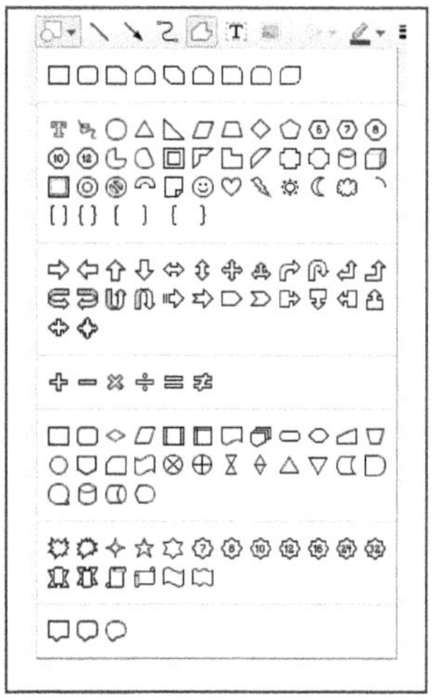

Figure 13. Pull-down shape palette in the Google Docs Drawing application.

Another explanation is that the palette serves as source of association [24]. For example, the number of hearts, smiley faces, crescent moons, circles, cloud and suns is high in the sketches. These all occur in the same section of the palette. Of the 57 sketches that use any shapes, 25 sketches have at least two of the mentioned shapes as decorations or as the shapes of the seat, back or arms. For example, Figure 14 shows a combined chair with multiple shapes as decorations, while the parent chairs only have the sun as decoration. Perhaps a participant pulled down the shape palette to add one shape, and decided to also add several neighboring shapes. This conjecture might be tested through experiments that provide different palettes and measure the frequency of shapes used in relation to their distance from each other on the palettes.

FUTURE RESEARCH

The described system affords future studies that might contrast different tool and processes. Future research might extend the reported experiment in three ways. First, the evaluation of the designs was done by a general population, recruited through Amazon Mechanical Turk. Other populations, and in particular expert or specialist populations, might have different perceptions of creativity. They may be especially skilled at assessing pragmatic issues such as manufacturing costs. Moreover, if indeed experts do have different perceptions, then it might be important to involve them in not just the evaluation but also the generation of the designs.

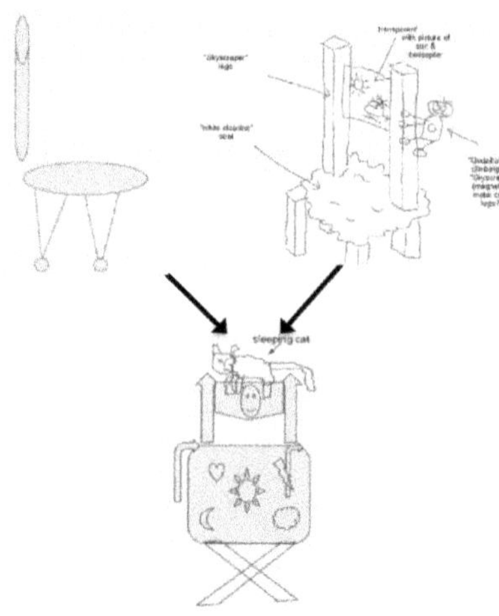

Figure 14. A combined chair with shapes.

Then, the design problems could contain more constraints that experts are more likely to be familiar with: time to market, materials, labor costs. Because it is difficult to assemble a crowd of experts, those that can be assembled might be given different tasks or their work assigned different weightings, as has been practiced in other domains [30]. Such experiments would need to be designed in domains where there are a sufficient number of experts to allow for multiple conditions and multiple trials.

Second, another important test of a creative design happens after it is implemented. That is, eventually the consumer or user evaluates the product for purchase and ongoing use. How could such tests be run? For many products, such as the chair example here, production tests are probably infeasible. But there exist sites that specialize in customized manufacturing and online sales of inexpensive objects (e.g. [5]), and so artifacts might be designed by the crowd and offered for sale in those environments.

Third, the system might extend its use of collaborative mechanisms: The coordination between participants provided in the current system is minimal. That is, no participant interacts directly with another. Instead, only some participants see the previous work of two others: all coordination is mediated through the designs. The independence of the participants makes possible large-scale parallel efforts, and guards against the many problems of tightly coupled collaborations, as described in studies of brainstorming [21, 25, 26]. But more interaction might be useful – for motivation, for clarification, and for deeper idea integration. Thus future studies might try a variety of ways of linking participants to each other: for example, through game-like interfaces that allow for two-way interaction (e.g. [1]), or through structured dyadic conversation (e.g. [42]), or through the communication patterns used in open source environments (e.g. [9, 33, 39]).

CONCLUSIONS

We asked if the crowd functions as a set of cooks or cobblers. We conclude that the systems' users were more like cobblers: they combined with each other to form a creative mind. That is, the generation 3 designs were significantly more creative than the generation 1 designs. The sketch combination system also provided a way to study the interrelations between creativity, combination, and tools. We showed that atypical features were favored in combinations, and that a drawing tool influences the evolution of these features.

That we can perform large-scale experiments related to creativity, and contemplate much larger ones, is perhaps the most important general message of this work. Collaboration necessarily takes place beyond the individual: in this case, it took place among over a thousand individuals, mediated entirely through the designs they produced. Such crowd-based systems are built in the hopes of catalyzing new kinds of collective minds.

ACKNOWLEDGMENTS

Funding for this research was provided by the National Science Foundation, awards IIS-0855995 and IIS-0968561. We are thankful for the suggestions of our colleagues Yasuaki Sakamoto and John Voiklis. This paper is taken in part from a dissertation to be submitted in partial fulfillment of the requirements for the Ph.D. degree at Stevens Institute of Technology.

REFERENCES

1. von Ahn, L. and Dabbish, L. Labeling images with a computer game. In *Proc. CHI 2004*, ACM Press (2004), 319-326.
2. Amazon Mechanical Turk. https://www.mturk.com/mturk/welcome.
3. Amabile, T. M., R. Conti, H. Coon, J. Lazenby, and M. Herron. Assessing the work environment for creativity. *Academy of Management Journal*, 39 (1996), 1154 – 1184.
4. Benkler, Y. *The Wealth of Networks: How Social Production Transforms Markets and Freedom*. Yale University Press, New Haven, CT, USA, 2006.
5. Brabham, D. Moving the crowd at Threadless: Motivations for participation in a crowdsourcing application. *Information, Communication & Society,* 13 (2010), 1122 - 1145.
6. Campbell, D. T. Blind variation and selective retention in creative thought as in other knowledge processes. *Psychological Review*, 67 (1960), 380 - 400.
7. Deb, K. *Multi-Objective Optimization using Evolutionary Algorithms*. Wiley, Chichester, UK, 2001.
8. Finke, R., Ward, T., and Smith, S. *Creative Cognition: Theory, Research, and Applications*. MIT Press Cambridge, MA, USA, 1996.
9. Fischer, G. Social Creativity: Turning Barriers into Opportunities for Collaborative Design. In *Proc. PDC2004*, 152-161.
10. Gero J. S., and Maher M. L. (eds) *Modeling creativity and knowledge-based creative design*. Lawrence Erlbaum, Hillsdale, NJ, USA, 1993.
11. Goldberg, D. E. *Genetic Algorithms in Search, Optimization and Machine Learning*. Kluwer Academic Publishers, Boston, MA, USA, 1989.
12. Goldschmidt, G, and Litan Sever A. From text to design solution: inspiring design ideas with texts. In *Proc. ICED 2009.*
13. Google Docs Drawing Application. http://docs0.google.com/demo/edit?id=scACRQaIm3t83kVISWPhWfrqx#drawing.
14. Heit, E. Influences of prior knowledge on selective weighting of category members. *Journal of Experimental Psychology: Learning, Memory, and Cognition*, 24 (1998), 712-731.
15. Holland. J. H. *Adaptation in Natural and Artificial Systems.* University of Michigan Press, Ann Arbor, 1975.
16. Hu, C., Bederson, B.B., and Resnik, P. Translation by iterative collaboration between monolingual users. *In Proc. of Graphics Interface 2010*, Canadian Information Processing Society (2010), 39-46.
17. Kittur, A. Crowdsourcing, collaboration and creativity. *XRDS: Crossroads*, December (2010).
18. Kittur, A., Chi, E. H., and Suh, B. Crowdsourcing user studies with Mechanical Turk. In *Proc. CHI 2008*, ACM Press (2008), 453-456.
19. Kosorukoff, A. Human based genetic algorithm. In *Proc. IEEE Conference on Systems, Man, and Cybernetics,* 2001, 3464-3469.
20. Little, G., Chilton, L. B., Goldman, M., and Miller, R. C. Exploring iterative and parallel human computation processes. In *Proc. of the ACM SIGKDD Workshop on Human Computation* (2010), 68-76.
21. Lorge, I., Fox, D., Davitz, J., and Brenner, M. A. Survey of Studies Contrasting the Quality of Group Performance and Individual Performance, 1920-1957, *Psychological Bulletin* 55, 6 (1958), 337-372.
22. Maher, M. L. Design Creativity Research: From the Individual to the Crowd. *Design Creativity* 2010.
23. McDonald, D. W. Social Computing: A Research Topic in Search of Disciplinarity. *In the Research Directions for Social Computing Workshop at the ACM* International Conf. on Supporting Group Work (2007).

24. Mednick, S. A. The associative basis of the creative process. *Psychological Review* 69, 1962, 220-232.

25. Mullen, B., Johnson C. and Salas E. Productivity Loss in Brainstorming Groups: A Meta-Analytic Integration, *Basic and Applied Social Psychology* 72, 1 (1991), 3-23.

26. Nunamaker, J., Dennis, A. R., Valacich, J. S., Vogel, D. R. and George, J. F. Electronic Meeting Systems to Support Group Work, *Communications of the ACM* 34, 7 (1991), 40-61.

27. Osborn, A.F. *Applied imagination: Principles and procedures of creative problem solving (3rd Edition).* Scribners, New York, USA, 1963.

28. Palmeri, T. J., and Nosofsky, R. M. Recognition memory for exceptions to the category rule. *Journal of Experimental Psychology: Learning, Memory, & Cognition,* 21 (1995), 548-568.

29. Quinn, A. J., and Bederson, B. B. Human Computation: A Survey and Taxonomy of a Growing Field, *CHI 2011,* ACM Press (2011).

30. Raykar, V. C., Yu, S., Zhao, L. H., Valadez, G. H., Florin, C., Bogoni, L., and Moy, L. Learning from crowds. *Journal of Machine Learning Research.* 11, 7 (2010), 1297-1322.

31. Rosch, E. H. Principles of categorization. In E. Rosch and B. Lloyd, eds. *Cognition and Categorization.* Lawrence Erlbaum Associates, 1978, 27-48.

32. Ross, J., Irani, L., Silberman, M. S., Zaldivar, A., and Tomlinson, B. Who are the Crowdworkers? Shifting Demographics in Mechanical Turk. *Ext. Abstracts CHI 2010,* ACM Press (2010).

33. Sack, W., Détienne, F., Burkhardt, J-M., Barcellini, F., Ducheneaut, N., and Mahendran, D. A methodological framework for socio-cognitive analyses of collaborative design of Open Source Software. *Distributed Collective Practices Workshop at CSCW,* (2004).

34. Sakamoto, Y., and Love, B. C. Vancouver, Toronto, Montreal, Austin: Enhanced oddball memory through differentiation, not isolation. *Psychonomic Bulletin & Review,* 13 (2006), 474-479.

35. Simonton, D. K. Scientific creativity as constrained stochastic behavior: The integration of product, person, and process perspectives. *Psychological Bulletin,* 129 (2003), 475-494.

36. Smith, S. M., Ward, T. B., and Schumacher, J. S. Constraining effects of examples in a creative generation task. *Memory & Cognition,* 21 (1993), 837-845.

37. Spears, W. M. *Crossover or Mutation? In Foundations of Genetic Algorithms 2.* L.D. Whitley (ed). Morgan Kaufmann, CA, USA, 1993.

38. Suwa, M. and Tversky, B. What do architects and students perceive in their design sketches? A protocol analysis. *Design Studies* 18, 4 (1997), 385-403.

39. Tech Guru, *Open Source Cars,* http://www.techquark.com/2010/05/ open-source-cars.html, May 26, 2010, accessed January 10, 2011

40. Thagard, P. *Conceptual revolutions.* Princeton University Press, USA, 1992.

41. Tversky, B. and Chou, J. Creativity: depth and breadth. *ICDC 2010.*

42. Voiklis, J. *A Thing Is What We Say It Is: Referential Communication and Indirect Category Learning*, Ph.D. dissertation, Columbia University, New York, USA, 2008

Human Computation: A Survey and Taxonomy of a Growing Field

Alexander J. Quinn[1,2], Benjamin B. Bederson[1,2,3]
University of Maryland, College Park
Human-Computer Interaction Lab[1] :: Computer Science[2] :: Institute for Advanced Computer Studies[3]
College Park, Maryland 20740
{aq, bederson}@cs.umd.edu

ABSTRACT
The rapid growth of human computation within research and industry has produced many novel ideas aimed at organizing web users to do great things. However, the growth is not adequately supported by a framework with which to understand each new system in the context of the old. We classify human computation systems to help identify parallels between different systems and reveal "holes" in the existing work as opportunities for new research. Since human computation is often confused with "crowdsourcing" and other terms, we explore the position of human computation with respect to these related topics.

Author Keywords
Human computation, crowdsourcing, taxonomy, survey, literature review, social computing, data mining

ACM Classification Keywords
H5.m. Information interfaces and presentation (e.g., HCI).

General Keywords
Theory

INTRODUCTION
Since the birth of artificial intelligence research in the 1950s, computer scientists have been trying to emulate human-like capabilities, such as language, visual processing, and reasoning. Alan Turing wrote in 1950:

> *"The idea behind digital computers may be explained by saying that these machines are intended to carry out any operations which could be done by a human computer."* [62]

Turing's article stands as enduring evidence that the roles of human computation and machine computation have been intertwined since the earliest days. Even the idea of humans and computers working together in complementary roles was envisioned in 1960 in Licklider's sketch of "man-computer symbiosis" [37]. Only recently have researchers begun to explore this idea in earnest [21,50,53].

In 2005, a doctoral thesis about human computation was completed [64]. Four years later, the first annual Workshop on Human Computation was held in Paris with participants representing a wide range of disciplines [28]. This diversity is important because finding appropriate and effective ways of enabling online human participation in the computational process will require new algorithms and solutions to tough policy and ethical issues, as well as the same understanding of users that we apply in other areas of HCI. Today, the field of human computation is being advanced by researchers from areas as diverse as artificial intelligence [35,38,58], business [41,56,29,72], cryptography [64], art [16,31], genetic algorithms [32], and HCI [2,3,5,etc.].

As this area has blossomed with an ever-expanding array of novel applications, the need for a consistent vocabulary of terms and distinctions has become increasingly pronounced.

This paper presents a classification system for human computation systems that highlights the distinctions and

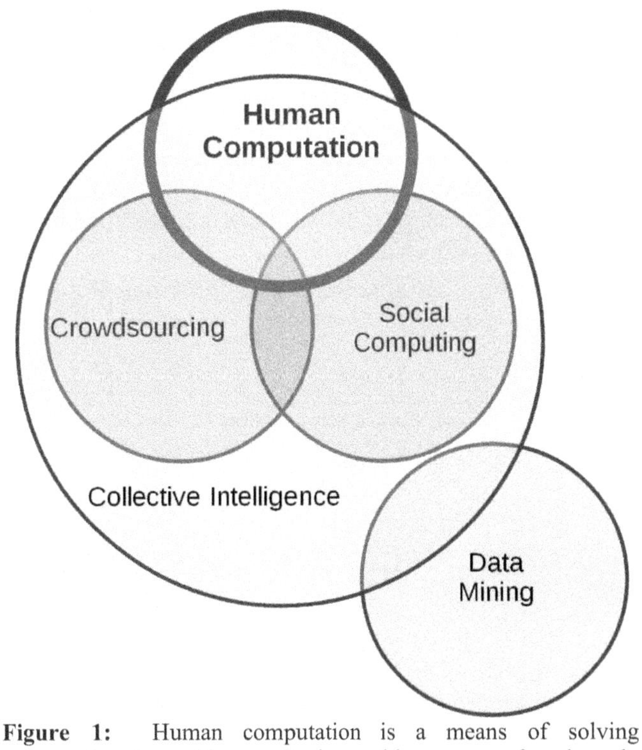

Figure 1: Human computation is a means of solving computational problems. Such problems are found only occasionally in crowdsourcing and social computing applications.

similarities among various projects. The goal is to reveal the structure of the design space, thus helping new researchers understand the landscape and discover unexplored or underexplored areas of opportunity.

The key contributions can be summarized as follows:

- Human computation is defined concretely and positioned in the context of related techniques and ideas.
- We give a set of dimensions that can be used to classify and compare existing human computation systems.
- We explain how to apply the system to identify open opportunities for future research in human computation.

DEFINITION OF HUMAN COMPUTATION

There have long been many interesting ways that people work with computers, as well as ways they work with each other through computers. This paper focuses on one of them. Human computation is related to, but not synonymous with terms such as *collective intelligence*, *crowdsourcing*, and *social computing*, though all are important to understanding the landscape in which human computation is situated. Therefore, before introducing our human computation taxonomy itself, we will define a few of these terms, each on its own and in the context of human computation. This is important because without establishing the boundaries of human computation, it would be difficult to design a consistently applicable classification system. Since we have no particular authority over these definitions, we will defer to the primary sources wherever possible.

Human Computation

The term *human computation* was used as early as 1838 [69] in philosophy and psychology literature, as well as more recently in the context of computer science theory [62]. However, we are most concerned with its modern usage. Based on historical trends of its use in computer science literature (Figure 2) as well as our examination of citations between papers, it appears that the modern usage was inspired by von Ahn's 2005 dissertation titled "Human Computation" [64] and the work leading to it. That thesis defines the term as:

> *"...a paradigm for utilizing human processing power to solve problems that computers cannot yet solve."*

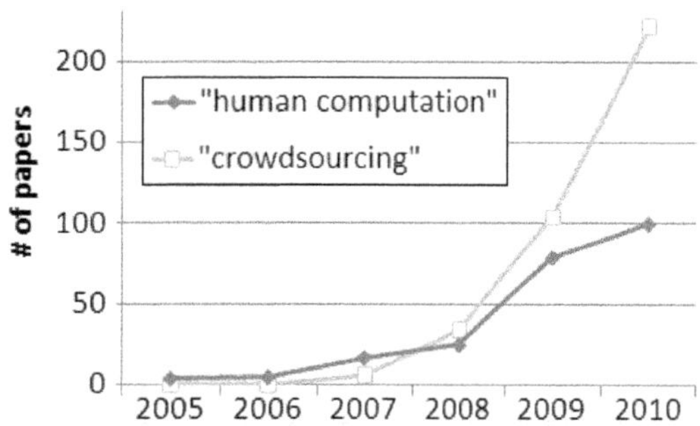

Figure 2: Use of the terms "human computation" and "crowdsourcing" in the computer science literature has been steadily increasing. Search results for the two terms in the ACM Guide to the Literature were counted on January 14, 2010 and may not include all publications from late 2010.

This seems compatible with definitions given elsewhere by von Ahn (co-author on the first one) and others (the rest):

> *"...the idea of using human effort to perform tasks that computers cannot yet perform, usually in an enjoyable manner."* [33]

> *"...a new research area that studies the process of channeling the vast internet population to perform tasks or provide data towards solving difficult problems that no known efficient computer algorithms can yet solve."* [9]

> *"...a technique that makes use of human abilities for computation to solve problems."* [8,74]

> *"...a technique to let humans solve tasks, which cannot be solved by computers."* [54]

> *"A computational process that involves humans in certain steps..."* [73]

> *"...systems of computers and large numbers of humans that work together in order to solve problems that could not be solved by either computers or humans alone"* [50]

> *"...a new area of research that studies how to build systems, such as simple casual games, to collect annotations from human users."* [34]

Most other papers using the term do not define it explicitly. From these definitions, taken together with the body of work that self-identifies as human computation, a consensus emerges as to what constitutes human computation:

- The problems fit the general paradigm of computation, and as such might someday be solvable by computers.
- The human participation is directed by the computational system or process. (This is discussed more below.)

COMPARISON WITH RELATED IDEAS

The definition and criteria above do not include all technologies by which humans collaborate with the aid of computers, even though there may be intersections with related topics. For example, human computation does not encompass online discussions or creative projects where the initiative and flow of activity are directed primarily by the participants' inspiration, as opposed to a predetermined plan designed to solve a computational problem.

We further argue that editing Wikipedia articles is excluded, though the distinction is subtle. An encyclopedia purist might argue that an online encyclopedia should contain no creative content and could be interpreted as a very advanced search engine or information retrieval system that gathers existing knowledge and formulates it as prose. Such is the goal of Wikipedia's "neutral point of view" policy [71]. If realized fully and perfectly, perhaps Wikipedia might reasonably be considered an example of human computation. However, Wikipedia was designed not to fill the place of a machine, but as a collaborative writing project in place of the professional encyclopedia authors of yore. The current form of Wikipedia is created through a dynamic social process of discussion about the facts and presentation of each topic among a network of the authors and editors [30]. When classifying an artifact, we consider not what it aspires to be, but what it is in its present state.

Perhaps most notably, the very choice of which articles to create is made by the authors, the people who would be counted as part of the computational machinery if Wikipedia editing were considered computation. A computer with free will to choose its tasks would cease to be a computer [62]. Therefore, Wikipedia authors cannot be regarded as merely performing a computation.

Crowdsourcing

The term *crowdsourcing*, first coined in a Wired magazine article by Jeff Howe [22] and the subject of his book [23], was derived from *outsourcing*. Howe's web site offers the following definition, which frames it as a replacement for roles that would otherwise be filled by regular workers:

> Whereas human computation replaces computers with humans, crowdsourcing replaces traditional human workers with members of the public.

> *"Crowdsourcing is the act of taking a job traditionally performed by a designated agent (usually an employee) and outsourcing it to an undefined, generally large group of people in the form of an open call."* [24]

There is some overlap between human computation and crowdsourcing where computers and humans already had established roles performing the same type of task. However, the center of gravity of the two terms is different.

The intersection of crowdsourcing with human computation in Figure 1 represents applications that could reasonably be considered as replacements for either traditional human roles or computer roles. For example, translation is a task that can be done either by machines when speed and cost are the priority, or by professional translators when quality is the priority. Thus, approaches such as our MonoTrans project [2,25], which provides a compromise solution with moderate speed, cost, and quality, could be considered members of both sets.

Social Computing

Technologies such as blogs, wikis, and online communities are examples of *social computing*. The scope is broad, but always includes humans in a social role where communication is mediated by technology. The purpose is not usually to perform a computation. Various definitions of social computing are given in the literature:

> *"... applications and services that facilitate collective action and social interaction online with rich exchange of multimedia information and evolution of aggregate knowledge..."* [48]

> *"... the interplay between persons' social behaviors and their interactions with computing technologies"* [15]

The key distinction between human computation and social computing is that social computing facilitates relatively natural human behavior that happens to be mediated by technology, whereas participation in a human computation is directed primarily by the human computation system.

Data Mining

Data mining can be defined broadly as:

> *"the application of specific algorithms for extracting patterns from data."* [17]

Since these algorithms are often used to extract patterns from human-created data, some might think of them as a form of human computation. We argue that data mining software in itself does not constitute human computation.

As an example, consider Google's PageRank web indexing algorithm, which mines the structure of hyperlinks between web pages to estimate the relevance of web pages to search queries [47]. Many of the pages were indeed created and linked together by humans. However, the work that the humans did in linking the pages was not caused or directed by the system and, in fact, may have taken place before the PageRank algorithm was even invented. Thus, the system cannot be said to have harnessed their processing abilities. Furthermore, the humans created the pages out of free will, so they cannot be said to be part of a computation.

In general, the use of data mining software does not encompass the collection of the data, whereas the use of human computation necessarily does. Thus, no data mining software system can be human computation, and vice versa.

This distinction matters because if data mining were considered as human computation, our taxonomy would need to be as applicable to data mining applications as it is to the rest of the ideas included in human computation. For example, challenges common to all human computation systems (i.e., resistance to cheating, motivation, etc.) do not make sense when discussed in the context of data mining.

Collective Intelligence

Encompassing most of the territory discussed so far is the overarching notion that large groups of loosely organized people can accomplish great things working together. Traditional study of collective intelligence focused on the inherent decision making abilities of large groups [36,42]. However, the view most relevant to human computation is that expressed in Malone's taxonomical "genome of collective intelligence." It defines the term very broadly as:

> *"... groups of individuals doing things collectively that seem intelligent."* [41]

Malone's work scope explicitly includes the PageRank algorithm, as well as virtually any group collaboration, even including "families, companies, countries, and armies." Therefore, as Figure 1 illustrates, collective intelligence is a superset of social computing and crowdsourcing, because both are defined in terms of social behavior. Data mining crosses the circle because some applications benefit from groups while others do not (i.e. mining climate data).

The key distinctions between collective intelligence and human computation are the same as with crowdsourcing, but with the additional distinction that collective intelligence applies only when the process depends on a group of participants. It is conceivable that there could be a human computation system with computations performed by a single worker in isolation. This is why part of human computation protrudes outside collective intelligence.

We are unaware of any well-developed examples of human computation that are not collective intelligence, but it is conceivable and might be a basis for some future work. Suppose a solitary human translator operates an on-demand, mechanized translation service. It is human computation because it utilizes the human translator's abilities to do a computation, translating text from one language to another. It would not be considered collective intelligence because there is no group, and thus no group behavior at work.

CLASSIFICATION DIMENSIONS

The common denominator among most human computation systems is that they rely on humans to provide units of work which are aggregated to form an answer to the request. Still, that leaves a wide range of possible structures and algorithms that can (or could) be utilized.

The classification system we are presenting is based on six of the most salient distinguishing factors. These are summarized in Figure 3. For each of these dimensions, we provide a few possible values corresponding to existing systems or notable ideas from the literature. Part of the job of researchers and technologists working to advance human computation will be to explore *new* possible values to address unmet needs, such as better control over speed and quality, efficient use of workers' time, and positive working relationships with the humans involved.

To develop the dimensions, we started by performing a review of the human computation literature and notable examples found in industry. Within those examples, we searched for groupings that tend to cite each other, use a common vocabulary, or share some obvious commonality. For example, there is a large cluster in the literature relating to games with a purpose (GWAPs).

For the taxonomy to be valid and useful, every dimension must have at least one (and ideally only one) value for each human computation system. To that end, we identified the underlying properties that these groupings have in common, expressed in a way that would be relevant for any of the examples seen in the initial review. For example, all GWAPs use enjoyment as their primary means of motivating participants. These properties formed three of our dimensions: *motivation*, *human skill*, and *aggregation*.

To ensure that the dimensions could be used to gain new insight into the field of human computation, we also looked for properties that cut across the more obvious groupings. For example, a certain cross section of human computation systems has in common that all involve dividing up a single source request into small slices (i.e. pages of a book, sections of an image, frames of a video, etc.), and issuing each slice as an individual task, even though the rest of the system design and problem domain may be completely different. In this way, three more properties were formed: *quality control*, *process order*, and *task-request cardinality*.

Motivation

One of the challenges in any human computation system is finding a way to motivate people to participate. This is eased somewhat by the fact that most human computation systems rely on networks of unrelated people with connected computers in their homes or workplaces. They need not go anywhere or do anything too far out of their ordinary lives to participate. Even so, since the computations frequently involve small unit tasks that do not directly benefit the contributors, they will only participate if they have a motivation—a reason why doing the tasks is more beneficial to them than not doing them. Unlike a traditional job, which almost always pays with money, human computation workers may be motivated by a number of factors. Still, some workers are paid, so we start there.

Pay

Financial rewards are probably the easiest way to recruit workers, but as soon as money is involved, people have more incentive to cheat the system to increase their overall rate of pay. Also, because participants are usually anonymous, they may be more likely to do something dishonest than they would if they were identified.

Mechanical Turk [44] is an online market for small tasks (computational or not) that uses monetary payment. Developers can write programs that automatically submit tasks to be advertised on the site. The tasks are completed by a network of workers, usually directly through the Mechanical Turk web site. Prices are driven by an open market with about 90% of tasks paying $0.10 or less [27].

Another example that uses financial motivation is ChaCha [7], a search service that uses humans to interpret search queries and select the most relevant results. LiveOps [40] is a company that employs workers online to handle phone calls for businesses, as a sort of distributed call-center. The workers follow scripts, which makes the job analogous to an automated telephone system, a role that might otherwise be filled by a computer. An older example was the Cyphermint PayCash anonymous payment kiosks [49,18], which used remote human workers to help verify the user's identity.

In some cases, the pay need not be money. CrowdFlower is a company that acts as an intermediary for businesses wanting to take advantage of crowdsourcing or human computation [4]. Businesses send tasks to CrowdFlower, which works with a variety of services for connecting with and compensating workers (i.e., Mechanical Turk, Gambit, Prodege/SwagBucks, TrialPay, etc.). Workers may be paid in money, gift certificates, or even virtual currency redeemable for virtual goods in online games.

Dimension	Sample values	Example
Motivation	Pay	Mechanical Turk [44]
	Altruism	helpfindjim.com (Jim Gray) [19]
	Enjoyment	ESP Game [63]
	Reputation	Volunteer translators at childrenslibrary.org
	Implicit work	reCAPTCHA [68]
Quality control	Output agreement	ESP Game
	Input agreement	Tag-a-tune [33]
	Economic models	(see [18])
	Defensive task design	(see [6])
	Redundancy	reCAPTCHA
	Statistical filtering	(see [10,29])
	Multilevel review	Soylent [3]
	Automatic check	fold.it (protein folding game) [14]
	Reputation system	Mechanical Turk
Aggregation	Collection	reCAPTCHA
	Wisdom of crowds	Kasparov-World chess game [45]
	Search	helpfindjim.com (Jim Gray)
	Iterative improvement	Monotrans [2,25] and [39]
	Genetic algorithm	(see [32])
	None	VizWiz [5]
Human skill	Visual recognition	ESP Game
	Language understanding	Soylent
	Basic human communication	ChaCha [7]
Process order	Computer ➔ Worker ➔ Requester	reCAPTCHA
	Worker ➔ Requester ➔ Computer	ESP Game
	Computer ➔ Worker ➔ Requester ➔ Computer	FACTory [60]
	Requester ➔ Worker	VizWiz
Task-Request Cardinality	One-to-one	ChaCha
	Many-to-many	ESP Game
	Many-to-one	helpfindjim.com (Jim Gray)
	Few-to-one	VizWiz

Figure 3: Overview of our classification system for human computation systems.

Altruism

Do good. It may sound easy to trust in people's desire to help, but it can only work if participants actually think the problem being solved is interesting and important.

When the computer scientist Jim Gray went missing during a sailing trip in early 2007, thousands of online volunteers combed through over 560,000 satellite images [19] hoping to determine Gray's location. Sadly the effort was not successful, but the heroic efforts of these volunteers nevertheless demonstrated that people will expend significant time and effort for the right cause.

Enjoyment

The abundance of time-consuming, entertainment activities on the Internet attests that even simple forms of entertainment have value to many web users. By making a task entertaining, either as a game or some other enjoyable activity, it is possible to engage humans to do tasks that contribute to a computational goal.

Games With A Purpose is a strategy where you create a game that requires players to perform some computation in order to get points or succeed. People play because they enjoy it. If the game is fun, they may play for a very long time and supply a lot of computational power. However, it can be difficult to turn computational tasks into games that are truly fun to play [65]. Furthermore, it is important to be able to prove that the game will yield correct results, much like designing a computer algorithm [66]. Some views of human computation are centered on the use of games [74]. Games have been created for a variety of computations, including image labeling [63], protein folding [14], and music recognition [33].

Reputation

Where the problem is associated with an organization of some prestige, human workers may be motivated by the chance to receive public recognition for their efforts. This strategy has been implemented by the International Children's Digital Library to recruit volunteer translators.

Implicit work

It is sometimes possible to make the computation a natural part of some activity the users were already doing. However, examples are scarce because it is very difficult to match a task to an existing activity.

ReCAPTCHA [52,68] is a human computation system for transcribing old books and newspapers for which OCR is not very effective. It takes advantage of the pre-existing need for CAPTCHAs, the distorted images of text that are used by websites to prevent access by automated programs. When a user goes to a website (i.e. a webmail service), instead of seeing computer generated distorted text, they see an image of a word from an old book or newspaper, for which the OCR software could not identify the content. By typing the letters in the course of visiting the website, the user provides computational power to help with the transcription effort.

Quality control

Even if the users are motivated to participate, they may try to cheat or sabotage the system. Workers may also be acting in good faith, but misunderstand the directions or make mistakes due to personal bias or lack of experience with the subject matter. Ipeirotis used expectation maximization to estimate the quality, and also infer some characteristics of the types of errors [29].

Output agreement [66]

Epitomized by the ESP game [63] (a game for labeling images), two or more contributors work independently and simultaneously in different locations. The answer is only accepted if the pair can agree on the same answer.

Input agreement [66]

This is almost the converse of output agreement. Two humans working independently and simultaneously in different locations are given inputs that may or may not be the same. They are asked to describe the inputs to one another and then try to decide whether they are looking at the same input or different inputs. If both participants agree, then the description is deemed to be correct.

Input agreement was introduced by Law with the Tag-a-Tune game [33], which collects descriptions of music clips. The players each listen to a sound file and type descriptions. If both players agree on whether or not the other's descriptions seem to be describing the same clip, then the descriptions are deemed to be relevant.

Economic models

When money is used as a motivating factor, it may be possible to use different incentive structures to elicit more good quality work for less money [43]. Gentry et al proposed to pay according to a game-theoretic model of the worker's rating, reducing the incentive to cheat [18].

Defensive task design

More practically, several solutions have been developed to improve the accuracy of results from paid services like Mechanical Turk [44]. One approach is to design tasks so it is no easier to cheat than to do the task [6].

Reputation system

In some systems, users may be motivated to provide quality answers by a reputation scoring system. With Mechanical Turk, a worker who frequently submits bad work can be blocked from accessing future tasks or, more positively, given special access to more desirable tasks.

Redundancy

By finding more contributors, you can have each task done by multiple workers, and use a voting scheme to identify good answers. This in turn helps you identify consistently poor workers so that their work can be removed so it does not affect the final quality. In our experience using Mechanical Turk, a large proportion of bad work comes from a small number of human workers.

Ground truth seeding

A common approach used by users of Mechanical Turk is to start with a small number of tasks for which ground truth has been provided by a trusted source. By mixing in questions with known answers, the system can identify workers who are deliberately submitting useless answers, or perhaps just confused by the instructions.

Statistical filtering

Filter or aggregate the data in some way that removes the effects of irrelevant work. For example, Chen discounts results that do not fit an expected distribution [10].

Multilevel review

One set of workers does the work, and a second set reviews the work and rates its quality. It is like output agreement, except that the work need not be done synchronously. More elaborate multilevel schemes are possible, such as the *find-fix-verify* pattern demonstrated by Soylent, a word processor that uses workers on Mechanical Turk to help writers improve their text [3].

Expert review

A trusted expert skims or cross-checks contributions for relevance and apparent accuracy. For example, with Mechanical Turk, people who post tasks may review the work and choose whether to pay or not.

Automatic check

Some problems are much easier to verify than compute. This class of problems lends itself to automatic checking. For example, in automated planning, a subfield of AI, it is difficult for a computer to generate a plan that gets from the start state to a desired end state, but given a plan as input, it is easy to test if it is correct. In the foldit game, users use a graphical interface to predict protein structures, an important problem in biochemistry. The game uses *Rosetta energy* a property of protein structures, to identify the most useful results [14].

Aggregation

Part of the process of human computation is to combine all of the contributions to solve the global problem. The means of doing this partly determines the class of problems a system or strategy can be applied to.

Collection

A knowledge base of discrete facts or a hierarchical ontology is collected. A contribution may either add a new fact or improve quality by correcting, refuting, or confirming existing facts in the knowledge base.

Knowledge Collection from Volunteer Contributors (KCVC) is kind of human computation that uses the collection method of aggregation. KCVC is summarized in [13]. The goal is to advance artificial intelligence research by using humans to build large databases of common sense facts. The idea is that humans, by way of their child development and adult lives, acquire a great deal of common sense knowledge (i.e. "People cannot brush their hair with a table."). Several efforts have demonstrated ways of using volunteer contributors to provide such facts, either by using games (e.g. the FACTory [60], Verbosity [67], 1001 Paraphrases [12]) or by plain volunteerism (e.g. Learner [11], Open Mind Common Sense [58]). The collected facts are often used to improve on the results of automated attempts at extracting the information. As such, the practice of KCVC is important to AI research and has been the topic of dedicated workshops and symposia.

Statistical processing of data

Consider a game where hundreds of people try to guess the number of jelly beans in a large jar. It turns out that under normal circumstances, the average of the guesses will be very close to the actual count.

In the book, The Wisdom of Crowds, Surowiecki explains how aggregating answers from a decentralized, disorganized group of people, all thinking independently can yield surprisingly accurate results to questions that would be difficult for one person to answer alone. It works only if the individual errors of each person are uniformly distributed, which in turn requires individual judgments to be made independently [59].

Several online polling web sites and prediction markets harness this concept to not only determine a group opinion, but to try to predict future events [72] (e.g. Ask500People [1], News Futures [46], and Iowa Electronic Markets [26]). While prediction markets are not examples of human computation, they are one of the most commonly cited examples of Wisdom of Crowds.

Iterative improvement

For some applications, it makes sense to give each worker the answer given by previous workers for the same task. As a test of this strategy, Little asked workers on Mechanical Turk to try to read some text that had been severely distorted for purposes of the experiment [39]. Initially, the image of distorted text was given to two workers. Next, a third worker (or small group of workers) examined the transcriptions from the first two workers, and chose the best one, which was given to the fourth worker as a starting point. They found that iterative improvement had the potential to yield very high quality results, but that the quality was less consistent than the control method they compared with.

Active learning

In machine learning, classifiers are software modules that can be trained to recognize certain patterns in data (i.e., outlines of common objects in an image, fraudulent credit card transactions, spoken words, etc.). The simplest way to train a classifier is to input a large quantity of example patterns along with annotations (answers) for it to learn from. Sometimes when obtaining enough annotations would be especially labor-intensive, the active learning approach can be employed to reduce the number of annotations needed to train. The classifier is given a large number of example patterns without annotations. Then, it analyzes them to identify which examples would have the most training benefit if annotations were made available [61]. Human participants then create the annotations, which are given as input to the classifier.

Essentially, the annotations contributed by the human participants are aggregated by the classifier to compute the internal classifier state that will eventually be able to recognize the patterns automatically.

Search

Several projects have used large numbers of volunteers to sift through photographs or videos, searching for some desired scientific phenomenon, person, or object.

For example, the Space Sciences Laboratory at the University of California at Berkeley used human computation to search for tiny matter from space as part of the Stardust@home project [70]. The particles had been mixed into an aerogel collector from the Stardust spacecraft. Contributors searched through photographs of the aerogel for traces of the particles. This recognition problem was much too difficult for computer vision algorithms or even untrained humans. Therefore, participants had to complete an online training program to learn how to identify the tiny particles before they could contribute. With this aggregation method, the only contributions that are of value are the one(s) that contain the target (e.g., photo of Jim Gray or trace of a particle).

Genetic algorithm

Genetic algorithms are used in computer science to solve search and optimization problems. The Free Knowledge Exchange is a site where users work together to evolve answers to freeform questions. While not actually a computation, it demonstrates how users can perform the key functions of initialization, mutation, and recombinant crossover [32]. A simpler example is PicBreeder, where users evolve interesting graphical patterns by choosing among computer-generated choices [55]. This is probably not computation either, since the choices are subjective.

None

Some human computation systems need no aggregation at all, but simply use humans to perform a large number of small tasks which are independent of one another.

Human Skill

Depending on the application, human computation may leverage a variety of skills that are innate to nearly all humans or, in some cases, special knowledge or abilities held by only some (e.g., can read and write Chinese). When designing a solution that uses human computation, it is helpful to be very specific about what skill is being used, in order to factor out other aspects of the problem that could just as easily be done by a computer. For example, to improve an image search engine, one could imagine employing an extremely large number of humans to search through images exhaustively for every query. It is far more efficient to have them simply associate text descriptions with images, and then have a computer search the text.

Process Order

In any human computation system, there are three roles: the requester, worker, and computer. The requester is the end user who benefits from the computation (i.e., someone using an image search engine to find something). A subtle distinction among human computation systems is the order in which these three roles are performed. We consider the computer to be active only when it is playing an active role in solving the problem, as opposed to simply aggregating results or acting as an information channel. Many permutations are possible.

Computer ➔ Worker ➔ Requester (CWR)

With reCAPTCHA [68], a *computer* first makes an attempt to recognize the text in a scanned book or newspaper using OCR. Then, words which could not be confidently recognized are presented to web users (*workers*) for help. Their transcriptions become part of the transcription of the book or newspaper for use by users (*requesters*) reading or listening to it.

Worker ➔ Requester ➔ Computer (WRC)

Players (*workers*) of image labeling games [63, etc.] provide labels for images, which are then aggregated by a computer to remove labels believed to be irrelevant. When a web user (*requester*) visits the image search site and enters a query, the *computer* searches the database of labels to find matches.

Computer➔Worker➔Requester➔Computer (CWRC)

The Cyc system (*computer*) has inferred a large number of common sense facts by analyzing text. To improve the quality of the facts in the database, they use FACTory [60], a game with a purpose. Facts from the database are presented to players (*workers*) who can confirm or correct them, thus improving the quality of the Cyc database. When an user (*requester*) of Cyc performs a query that requires AI functionality, the system (*computer)* make inferences using facts in the database.

Requester ➔ Worker (RW)

Mechanical Turk [44] allows a *requester* to submit tasks, such as audio transcription or text dictation, for which no additional computation is necessary. For small jobs, quality can be confirmed by spot checking.

Task-request cardinality

When an end-user uses a service powered by human computation, there may be many human workers involved in producing the result, especially if a lot of aggregation is required. In other cases, just one or a handful of workers may suffice. This depends on the structure of the problem, and thus is a key dimension in classifying human computation systems, as well as analyzing the financial or time requirements of any given system.

One-to-one

With ChaCha's web search a single human worker would handle the entire search. (Recently, ChaCha changed to a multi-stage process for their SMS mobile search service.)

Many-to-many

Image search engines use tagging done by many humans to annotate each image in the search index, which is then used to process any number of search requests. Without receiving several annotations for each of a very large number of images, it would be impossible to return results for any single query.

Many-to-one

In the search for Jim Gray, over 12,000 [57] volunteers attempted to find just one image out of over 560,000.

Few-to-one

VizWiz [5] is a mobile application that lets a blind user take a photo (i.e., restroom doors) and ask a question (i.e., Which is the men's room?). A few workers on Mechanical Turk give redundant answers to each query.

OPENINGS FOR GROWTH

Up to this point, we have described a classification system that can be used to understand human computation systems in the broader context of what exists. We are now ready to use the dimensions to presuppose some possible areas for future exploration. The examples mentioned so far occupy specific points in the design space, but by combining the dimensions in other ways, it is possible to imagine new kinds of systems that could be used to solve other problems.

Consider new dimension pairs

For researchers looking for new avenues within human computation, a starting point would be to pick two dimensions and list all possible combinations of values. For example, considering motivation and aggregation shows that input agreement has not been applied with paid labor or any motivation other than enjoyment. Similarly, combining cardinality with motivation reveals that there are no known examples of one-to-one human computation motivated by altruism. One might imagine a service like VizWiz that used trusted volunteers so that redundancy was not needed.

Invent new values for dimensions

Another way to use a classification system is to consider if there are other possible values that could be used for a given dimension. For example, one might look for human skills that have not yet been well-explored. The foldit protein folding game made use of humans' spatial manipulation abilities, a skill that still has not been well utilized in other human computation systems [14].

Classify new work and consider variations

When encountering new work, it may be helpful to think of the applicable values for each dimension of the system. Doing this may help identify ways in which the novel aspect of the system could be combined with other ideas. For example, when encountering the VizWiz mobile application, one might note that it uses pay for motivation, few-to-one cardinality, and a Requester➔Worker (RW) process order. Changing the process order to (CRW) might yield an interesting application that uses the mobile device's CPU to do more meaningful processing before the request is ever entered into the phone. Perhaps it could use situational awareness to suggest possible requests.

CONCLUSIONS

Our motivation in developing this classification system was to stimulate new directions of research in human computation. Many researchers and practitioners are excited about this new area within HCI, but there can be a tendency to focus on just one style of human computation, potentially missing more suitable solutions to a problem.

Beyond new algorithms and designs, there is also a pressing need to address issues related to ethics and labor standards. It is possible that as technology obviates the jobs of some unskilled workers, future human computation systems may offer a viable employment option for them. The current state of human computation has a tendency to represent workers as faceless computational resources. As designers, we have the power to orient our systems to encourage positive working arrangements and fair pay as the default.

Finally, the first two sections addressed distinctions between terms in some detail. While it is important as a community to agree on a vocabulary, it is equally important to consider what is left out. Perhaps future incarnations will be more social in nature, while still maintaining their purpose as systems for performing computations.

ACKNOWLEDGMENTS

We gratefully acknowledge the advice and support of Lise Getoor, Chang Hu, Pete Kelleher, Oded Nov, Ben Shneiderman, Alexander Sorokin, and Yan Xu.

REFERENCES

1. Ask 500 People. http://www.ask500people.com
2. Bederson, B.B., Hu, C., & Resnik, P. Translation by iterative collaboration between monolingual users. *GI'10*
3. Bernstein, M., Miller, R.C., Little, G., Ackerman, M., Hartmann, B., Karger, D.R., & Panovich, K. Soylent: A Word Processor with a Crowd Inside. *Proc. UIST 2010.*
4. Biewald, L. Massive multiplayer human computation for fun, money, and survival. *XRDS* (Dec. 2010), 10-15.
5. Bigham, J.P., Jayant, C., Ji, H., Little, G., Miller, A., Miller, R.C., Miller, R., Tatrowicz, A., White, B., White, S., & Yeh, T. VizWiz: nearly real-time answers to visual questions. *UIST 2010*, ACM (2010), 333-342.
6. Callison-Burch, C., & Dredze, M. Creating Speech and Language Data with Amazon's Mechanical Turk. *Workshop on Creating Speech And Language Data With Amazon's Mechanical Turk NAACL HLT,* (2010), 1-12.
7. ChaCha search engine. http://www.chacha.com.
8. Chan, K. T., King, I., & Yuen, M. Mathematical modeling of social games. *Proc CSE 2009*, 1205-1210.
9. Chandrasekar, R., Chi, E., Chickering, M., Ipeirotis, P. G., Mason, W., Provost, F., Tam, J., von Ahn, Front matter. *Proc. SIGKDD HCOMP 2010.*
10. Chen, K., Wu, C., Chang, Y., & Lei, C. A crowdsourceable QoE evaluation framework for multimedia content. *Proc MM 2009*, ACM, 491-500.
11. Chklovski, T. Learner: a system for acquiring commonsense knowledge by analogy. *Proc. K-CAP '03.*
12. Chklovski, T. Collecting paraphrase corpora from volunteer contributors. *Proc. K-CAP'05*, ACM (2005)
13. Chklovski, T. & Gil, Y. Towards Managing Knowledge Collection from Volunteer Contributors, *KCVC 2005.*
14. Cooper, S., Khatib, F., Treuille, A., Barbero, J., Lee, J., Beenen, M., Leaver-Fay, A., Baker, D., & Popovic, Z. Predicting protein structures with a multiplayer online game. *Nature*, 466:7307, (Aug. 2010), 756–760.
15. Dryer, D.C., Eisbach, C., & Ark, W.S. At what cost pervasive? a social computing view of mobile computing systems. *IBM Systems Journal*, (Dec 1999).
16. Edmunds, P. SwarmSketch. http://swarmsketch.com/.
17. Fayyad, U., Piatetsky-Shapiro, & P Smyth, P. Knowledge Discovery and Data Mining: Towards a Unifying Framework. *Proc. KDD 1996.*
18. Gentry, C., Ramzan, Z., & Stubblebine, S. Secure distributed human computation. *Proc EC* 2005, 155-164
19. Gonçalves, D., Jesus, R., & Correia, N. A gesture based game for image tagging. *CHI 2008 EA.*
20. Help Find Jim. http://www.helpfindjim.com
21. Horvitz, E. & Paek, T. Complementary computing: policies for transferring callers from dialog systems to human receptionists. *User Modeling and User-Adapted Interaction 17*, 1-2 (Mar. 2007), 159-182.
22. Howe, Jeff. The Rise of Crowdsourcing. *Wired. Jun'06.*
23. Howe, Jeff. *Crowdsourcing: Why the Power of the Crowd is Driving the Future of Business.* Crown (2008).
24. Howe, Jeff. Crowdsourcing: A Definition http://crowdsourcing.typepad.com
25. Hu, C., Bederson, B.B., & Resnik, P. MonoTrans2: A New Human Computation System to Support Monolingual Translation, *Proc. CHI 2011.*
26. Iowa Electronic Markets. http://www.biz.uiowa.edu/iem
27. Ipeirotis, P.G. Analyzing the Amazon Mechanical Turk Marketplace. *XRDS* 17:2, ACM (Dec. 2010), 16-21.
28. Ipeirotis, P.G., Chandrasekar, R., & Bennett, P. Report on the human computation workshop. *HCOMP 2010.*
29. Ipeirotis, P.G., Provost, F., & Wang, J. Quality management on Amazon Mechanical Turk. *HCOMP'10.*

30. Kittur, A., Suh, B., Pendleton, B.A., & Chi, E. He says, she says:conflict and coordination in Wikipedia. *CHI'07*
31. Koblin, A. Sheep Market. http://thesheepmarket.com.
32. Kosorukoff, A. Human based genetic algorithm. *Trans. on Systems, Man, and Cybernetics,* 5:3464, IEEE (2001)
33. Law, E. & von Ahn, L. Input-agreement: a new mechanism for collecting data using human computation games. *Proc. CHI 2009*, 1197-1206.
34. Law, E., West, K., Mandel, M., Bay, M., Downie, J. S. Evaluation of algorithms using games: the case of music tagging. *Proc. ISMIR 2009*, 387-392.
35. Lenat, D. B. CYC: a large-scale investment in knowledge infrastructure, *CACM,* (Nov. 1995), 33-38.
36. Levy, P. *Collective intelligence: Mankind's emerging world in cyberspace*. Perseus, Cambridge, MA, 1997.
37. Licklider, J.C.R. Man-computer symbiosis. *IRE Transactions on Human Factors in Electronics, vol. HFE-1* IEEE (Mar. 1960), 4-11.
38. Lieberman, H., Smith, D., & Teeters, A. Common Consensus: a web-based game for collecting common-sense goals. *Proc. IUI 2007.*
39. Little, G., Chilton, L.B., Goldman, M., and Miller, R.C. Exploring iterative and parallel human computation processes. *Proc. HCOMP 2010*, 68-76.
40. LiveOps. http://www.liveops.com
41. Malone, T. W., Laubacher, R., & Dellarocas, C. N. Harnessing crowds: Mapping the genome of collective intelligence. MIT Sloan Research Paper 4732-09, (2009)
42. Mataric, M.J. Designing emergent behaviors: from local interactions to collective intelligence. *Proc of Animals To Animats 2,* MIT Press (1993), 432-441.
43. Mason, W. & Watts, D.J. Financial incentives and the "performance of crowds". *SIGKDD Explorations Newsletter.* 11:2, ACM (May 2010), 100-108.
44. Mechanical Turk. http://mturk.com.
45. Nalimov, E.V., Wirth, C., & Haworth, G.M. KQQKQQ and the Kasparov-World Game. *ICGA J.*,(1999)195-212
46. News Futures. http://www.newsfutures.com
47. Page, L., Brin, S., Motwani, R., & Winograd, T. The PageRank citation ranking: Bringing order to the Web. Tech. report, Stanford Digital Libraries Project (1998).
48. Parameswaran, M. & Whinston, A.B. Social Computing: An Overview. *CAIS* 19:37, (2007), 762-780
49. Peha,J.M. & Khamitov,I.M. PayCash: a secure efficient Internet payment system. *Proc. ICEC 2003*, 125-130.
50. Quinn, A. & Bederson, B.B. A Taxonomy of Distributed Human Computation. Tech. Rep. HCIL-2009-23, University of Maryland, (2009).
51. Quinn, A., Bederson, B.B., Yeh, T., & Lin, J. CrowdFlow: Integrating Machine Learning with Mechanical Turk for Speed-Cost-Quality Flexibility. Tech. Rep HCIL-2010-09, Univ. of Maryland, (2009).
52. reCAPTCHA. http://recaptcha.net.
53. Resnik, P., Buzek, O., Hu, C., Kronrod, Y., Quinn, A., & Bederson, B.B. Improving Translation via Targeted Paraphrasing, *EMNLP 2010*, ACL (2010), 127-137.
54. Schall, D., Truong, H., & Dustdar, S. The Human-Provided Services Framework. *CECANDEEE 2008.*
55. Secretan, J., Beato, N., Ambrosio, D.D.B., & Rodriguez, A., Campbell, A., Stanley, K. O. Picbreeder: evolving pictures collaboratively online. *Proc CHI 2008.*
56. Sheng, V., Provost, F., & Ipeirotis, P. Get Another Label? improving data quality and data mining using multiple nosy labelers. *KDD 2008*, 614-622.
57. Silberman, S. Inside the High Tech Hunt for a Missing Silicon Valley Legend. *Wired Magazine*. (Jul. 24, 2007). http:// wired.com/techbiz/people/magazine/15-08/ff_jimgray
58. Singh, P., Lin, T., Mueller, E. T., Lim, G., Perkins, T., & Zhu, W. L. Open Mind Common Sense: Knowledge Acquisition from the General Public. *Lecture Notes in Computer Science*, v. 2519, Springer (2002), 1223-1237
59. Surowiecki, J. *The Wisdom of Crowds*. Anchor (2005).
60. The FACTory. http://game.cyc.com.
61. Tong, S. & Koller, D. Support vector machine active learning with applications to text classification. *J. Mach. Learn. Res.* 2 (Ma. 2002), 45-66.
62. Turing, A.M. Computing Machinery and Intelligence. *Mind*, 59:236, Oxford University Press (1950), 433-460.
63. von Ahn, L. & Dabbish, L. Labeling images with a computer game. *Proc CHI 2004.*
64. von Ahn, L. *Human Computation*. Doctoral Thesis. UMI Order Number: AAI3205378, CMU, (2005).
65. von Ahn, L. Games with a Purpose. *Computer*, 39:6, IEEE Computer Society (Jun 2006), 92-96.
66. von Ahn, L. & Dabbish, L. Designing Games with a Purpose. *CACM*, 51:8, (Aug. 2008), 58-67.
67. von Ahn, L., Kedia, M, & Blum, M. Verbosity: a game for collecting common-sense facts. *Proc CHI 2006.*
68. von Ahn, L., Maurer, B., McMillen, C., Abraham, D., & Blum, M. ReCAPTCHA: human-based character recognition via web security measures. *Science*, 321:5895, (Sept. 12, 2008), 1465-1468.
69. Wayland, F. *The Limitations Of Human Responsibility*. Applewood Books, Bedford, Massachusetts, (1838).
70. Westphal, A.J., Butterworth, A.L., Snead, C.J., Craig, N., Anderson, D., Jones, S.M., Brownlee, D.E., Farnsworth, R., Zolensky, M.E. Stardust@ home: A Massively Distributed Public Search for Interstellar Dust in the Stardust Interstellar Dust Collector. *Thirty-Sixth Lunar and Planetary Science Conference* (2005).
71. Wikipedia. http://en.wikipedia.org/wiki/Wikipedia:5P
72. Wolfers, J. & Zitzewitz, E. Prediction markets. *Journal of Economic Perspectives*, 18:2, (2004), 107-126.
73. Yang, Y., Zhu, B.B., Guo, R., Yang, L., Li, S., & Yu, N. A comprehensive human computation framework: with application to image labeling. *Proc. MM 2008.*
74. Yuen, M., Chen, L., & King, I. A Survey of Human Computation Systems. *Proc CSE* 2009.

The Times They Are A-Changin': Mobile Payments in India

Deepti Kumar
Department of Computer Science and Engineering
Chennai, India
deepti@lantana.tenet.res.in

David Martin, Jacki O'Neill
Xerox Research Centre Europe
Grenoble, France
{firstname.lastname}@xrce.xerox.com
+33 4 76 61 50 50

ABSTRACT
We report on an ethnographic study of payment and banking practices in India. Currently a mobile payment mechanism is being developed in India and we were interested to see how it would fit with various current payment systems for various types of users. Therefore we studied a variety of current payment situations and gained an understanding of the banking and payment practices and needs of a diverse community. Our aim was to inform the development of interface elements, applications and services that would support the needs we uncovered. We describe our findings and the design ideas they provoked.

Author Keywords
Mobile payments, ethnography, payment practices, India, interaction, ecosystem, services, financial inclusion

ACM Classification Keywords
H 1.2 Information systems, models and principles, user/machine systems, human factors

General Terms
Human factors, design

INTRODUCTION
In recent years the CHI community has shown an increasing interest in previously neglected countries such as the BRIC nations (Brazil, Russia, India and China) where rapid economic and technological development is underway. The local specificities of these countries are less understood in the West and this is also often coupled with a desire to aid social improvement. It is a phenomenon which is sometimes known as 'design for the other 90%' [17]. Recently research and academic articles have focused on innovation in these places [10,14,15]. From a research perspective these new areas are interesting for a number of reasons: various technologies – most notably the mobile phone – have been reconfigured in an innovative fashion to suit local needs and requirements in different ways to Europe or North America; some modern technologies in 'developing countries' are relatively inexpensive and may be widely available, while at the same time elements of large scale economic and technological infrastructure may be relatively undeveloped; the widespread take up of technologies is happening in different orders and at different rates than in the west. This different usage, customization and adoption of technologies offers new opportunities for innovation and design. Against this backdrop, we report on the findings of a series of ethnographic studies of current payment situations and practices, undertaken by the first author as part of a project on the design of a mobile payment (m-payment) standard for India. These studies were carried out to understand how an m-payment system might fit into the Indian market. The results are not simply a series of design implications, although we certainly discuss what might be needed to make the system work, plus possible value-added services to encourage system take-up (i.e. where the system offers advantages over current payment mechanisms). However, we also consider m-payments in a wider context: how might they fit into current payment workflows, where might they work easily and what might their problems be, and could they even aid financial inclusion?

BACKGROUND
In India, a large scale m-payment initiative is being undertaken by a public-private consortium – the Mobile Payment Forum (MPF) of India [16]. The members are banks, telecom companies, payment providers, credit card companies, plus academic institutes such as IIT Madras. Together they are developing standards for a system which enables people to make merchant or person-person payments using their mobile phone, without the need for credit or debit cards, whether they have high or low end phones. A key aim behind the system is financial inclusion; providing electronic payments to those who currently do not have access to them. The mobile phone seems to be the ideal tool. Given the widespread penetration of mobile phones in India, the idea is that people, such as small merchants, auto-drivers, etc. will be able to use the system without having to purchase costly additional equipment or infrastructure. Since the Indian financial market is highly regulated, the Government of India has mandated that

mobile payments will have to be routed through banks [16] (see figure 1 below). This means that the system is necessarily different in both set-up and use from systems which use only telecoms providers such as M-PESA [5]. System take-up will be limited by the number of bank accounts, which at present is approximately 400 million. Whilst de-linking mobile payments from the banking network does have advantages given the large number of unbanked in India, it carries the risk of default by mobile payment service providers. In India many people on low incomes or in rural areas have difficulty getting bank accounts for a variety of reasons, including travel distance, their perceived unsuitability by banks and so on. For example, a study by a microfinance organization looking at spending patterns of auto-rickshaw drivers and cab drivers found that none of them had bank accounts [1]. They did however have small amounts of money to spare suggesting there is spare capacity for banking services if they could be conveniently and beneficially provided. Similarly in the study reported here we interviewed two waiters at a guest house in Delhi. Neither had a bank account, although they were in the wage bracket to be served by one (Rs 5-15,000 per month). They reported that they have a full day (9am to 9pm) job and by the time they finish the banks are closed.

In parallel with the development of m-payments, the Indian Government has instigated a large scale financial inclusion program to bring banking to the unbanked through, for example, enabling shopkeepers to set up as bank agents. In combination, m-payments and schemes to increase banking penetration promise opportunities for financial inclusion. Thus the motivation for introducing m-payments is twofold. Firstly its potential impact on society, in terms of financial inclusion, can be pervasive, and secondly, it has enormous business potential. Even amongst bank account holders, debit and credit card penetration is relatively low and it is envisaged that m-payments will be a cheaper form of electronic transaction that is simple to use (even for those with poorer literacy), convenient and secure. On the business side m-payment is envisaged as a low-charge service for many daily (or micro) purchases, as well as allowing person-to-person transfers. The idea is to allow payments up to the price of a domestic airline ticket (~ Rs 10,000). The hoped for convenience and amount of transactions mean that even a very small charge per transaction can make it a good business opportunity due to market size.

Mobile phone use in India

One reason that m-payment systems offer such promise in the Indian market is the widespread penetration of mobile phones. In the last ten years the subscriber base has reached 450 million with an approximate growth of 9 million a month [18]. More Indians own a mobile phone than a PC, thus technology adoption is likely to be more 'wireless' than PC centric. Hence it may be the mobile phone and not the PC that has the maximum potential to bridge the digital divide between the rich and the poor. If m-payments are to be accessible to the poorer sections of the population, however, the system needs to be easily usable, including for non- or semi-literate users. Studies looking at mobile phone use in the non-literate population of India [3,7] found that non-literate users can call but cannot message or use address books. They also face problems in dialing national or international numbers because of the extra digits. In comparison semi-literate users can enter and manipulate numbers. This is likely due to exposure to number-based data formats and tools such as calendars and calculators [4]. That number literacy outstrips literacy was a motivator for the MPF to design a system which requires at minimum only entry and reading of numbers. However, studies like [3] also point out that non-literate mobile phone users are unwilling to explore the functionalities in the phone as they are concerned about making mistakes and having to pay etc. From these studies we can infer that although the semi-literate and non-literate user groups are the ones who are greatly in need of a banking service, they might have some problems with m-payment systems unless (and perhaps even) if they are very well designed. However, another study [13] which showed that technology use in slum areas was often facilitated by a neighbour or family member, offers hope of use in these communities. *Intermediation* enables persons for whom technology is inaccessible due to non-literacy, lack of skills, or financial constraints, to benefit through digitally skilled users, thus expanding the reach of technologies. Certainly any m-payment system with the goal of financial inclusion needs to work on both high and low end phones, meaning that whilst many high-end services might be offered for the wealthy a more basic service is also required. This need for both low and high end functionality makes an interesting design challenge.

Finally, there has been some preliminary work examining the conditions for acceptance and usage of mobile payment procedures [2,5,6,8]. Amongst other findings these studies have identified essential conditions like cost, security and convenience. However, there has been no work describing in detail the features that an 'easy-to-use' and 'convenient' system should have. We will partially address this here.

INDIA'S M-PAYMENT SYSTEM

The chosen architecture for the m-payment system is shown below in figure 1:

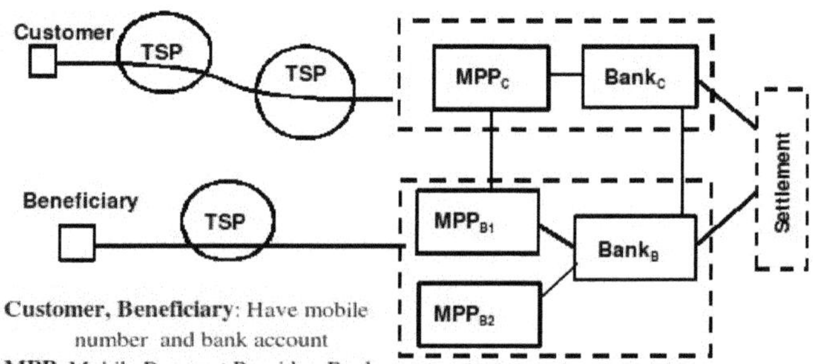

Customer, Beneficiary: Have mobile number and bank account
MPP: Mobile Payment Provider, Banks may act as own MPPs or use 3rd party MPP's services
TSP: Telecommunication Service Provider

Figure 1: Mobile payment entities

As well as payers and beneficiaries it involves Banks, Telecom Service Providers (TSP's) and Mobile Payment Providers (MPPs). It will function according to the following workflow: The customer C pays the Beneficiary B by entering the mobile phone number of B, the Bank Identifier Number of B's bank and B's account identifier digits. The transaction is carried by the Telecom Service Provider's network to the MPP/Bank. C's Bank transfers funds to B's Bank and the settlement happens later during the day. The architecture provides flexibility for the transaction to be initiated by either party. MPPs are likely to be the entity that provides value added services. The first author is involved in the MPF consortium and lived through a number of changes in the standards, such as payments only requiring the entry of numerals to support the semi-literate. Yet added security concerns and the need to support people with multiple bank accounts (a different population to the semi-literate) meant that more and more numbers were added. Currently around 20 numbers need to be entered to make a m-payment. Often when the user population was being invoked to make choices about standards and so on, it was based on conjecture. We therefore decided to use ethnography to try to understand what might be involved in creating a really usable m-payment system for a variety of users in various situations.

METHOD

As m-payments of the type being designed are not already in use, the ethnographic studies covered a range of existing payment practices and situations to understand how they are played out in practice. The aim was to understand how m-payments *might fit* into various pre-existing payment situations, or not, and *how they might be delivered or supported* in order to work (or stand a good chance of working) in various settings for various types of user. M-payments will have to be made at home in the world of buying, selling and paying [12]. Consequently the first author carried out a series of ethnographic studies [9] in order to understand how current payment situations unfolded. The studies involved participant-observation of various payment situations; on buses and auto rickshaws (low cost motorbike taxis), in railway stations, supermarkets, different shops, roadside vendors and so on. Some situations were more *participant* and others more *observational*, at times she accompanied informants as they e.g. went shopping, dining, etc. The data was analysed ethnomethdologically [9]. To further understand peoples' experiences with banking and payment situations and technologies, unstructured one-to-one interviews with open-ended questions were also conducted for example with workers such as waiters, carpenters and so on. Such workers fall into the income bracket of Rs 5–15k and as such *should* be able to access banking, and are a key target grouping for mobile payments. The study covered semi-urban areas such as Gutkar, Mekal and Mandi in Himachal Pradesh and urban areas including New Delhi and Lucknow in the north and Chennai in the south. We wanted to cover a large variety of payment situations across lower, middle and upper middle class families. Thus the studies covered a range of locations, environments and people.

FIELDWORK FINDINGS

Paying for a good or service is a sequential, ordered interaction which can glossed, in many cases, as follows: customer arrives at point of sale ready to pay (perhaps with product in hand or ready-to-buy, or having already partaken of the service e.g. dinner!), the seller totals up the price, the customer hands over either cash or a credit card, the seller in the case of cash may give change, for a credit card may ask for a signature or PIN number. Terminating the transaction, the seller often hands over a receipt and the customer is free to leave. This ordered interaction, of course, takes place in a wider workflow and the exact way in which the order plays out in the service workflow varies across situations: even for a particular type of activity, such as buying food there are a number of ways in which the workflow might be ordered (just think about the difference between going to a fast food drive-in and a posh restaurant). We will first look at some features of what we might call payments 'in the narrow', before considering the wider payment workflow and how different payment mechanisms fit into and influence that. Finally, since m-payments are also intended to be used for person to person payments we consider some features of current payment practices as they relate to this. To illustrate our points in the following sections we have selected a number of vignettes from the various studies we carried out that show interesting features of various payment situations, and that can be relevant to design requirements.

Payments 'in the narrow'

As might be expected in a country with so many people, payment situations are often pressured and time critical and this is keenly oriented to by the service provider. For example, on the bus a conductor collects fares. When the bus is not too full, he will move up and down the aisle, giving prices, collecting the money and exchanging it for tickets. As shown in figure 2 the conductor keeps notes between his fingers and tickets in his hand to facilitate rapid processing of each fare.

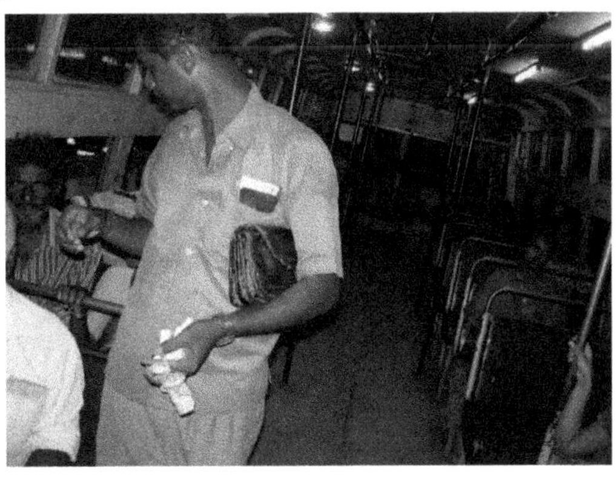

Figure 2: Bus conductor with notes between his fingers

When the bus is too full for the conductor to navigate the aisles, passengers will shout up the aisle to find out fares then pass the money up the bus via other passengers – whilst keenly watching the progress of the money and the return of any change and the ticket. When busy, successfully managing payments on the bus relies on the conductor's observation, memory and rapidity but also knowing cooperation and a degree of trust within the crowd. That it can be observed helps ensure the moral and practical order of the emergent queue which is not based purely on a spatial order. This suggests to us that in mobile payment situations with similar features, where payments may arrive in a 'disorderly' manner (i.e. not sequentially visible or clearly observably traceable to payers) attention will need to be paid to how they can be attributed to specific individuals. This may of course be achieved technically (e.g. tagging, recognition) or organizationally (ensuring visibility and tracking via a workflow). Furthermore, two types of ticketing were observed on the buses: manual ticketing where the conductor had a book of tickets of different values and ripped out the right one and a ticket machine where the conductor entered the information and the machine printed a ticket. There is no doubt that the first is quicker than the second, however the conductor with the ticket machine preferred it because it saved him considerable time in cashing up at the end of the day.

There were many situations where queuing was commonplace and as such the service provider attempted to deal with each customer in a timely fashion. For example, at both the railway reservation counter and mobile phone bill counter, the assistants left the money in a largely unordered mess on their desks – both coins and notes intermixed, because 1) the time between each customer was so short and 2) this provided them with convenient access to the money. When they had short periods of quiet they would order the notes and change (Figure 3).

Figure 3: Organising the notes when there are no customers at the counter

Thus, although cash *can be* convenient to access, keeping it in order and cashing up can take considerable work, whether during or at the end of the day. However, it is frequently undertaken outside of the buyer-seller interaction where the focus is on the speed of processing customers. A clear feature of cash payments is that change can be a problem, especially where the transaction frequency is high and transactions are micro in nature, or may come to random amounts, e.g. in supermarkets. Customers and shopkeepers orient to the problem of change by for example 1) keeping a workable 'float' i.e. a reasonable amount of coins and small denomination notes, or 2) trying to ensure that less complex change is required (comprising fewer coins and notes). This is an occasioned practice, instigated by either party according to particular circumstances, the most obvious being when a merchant asks for more exact tendering of money. In other circumstances customers clearly use shopping as a means of specifically getting change themselves, e.g. to 'break' a higher denomination note or to get specific change for a purpose. Excerpt 1 and the discussed examples demonstrate some of these 'change management' practices.

Excerpt 1: *A lady was getting her purchase billed. She had shopped for her household, the bill amount was Rs 320 and she gave the cashier Rs 400.*

`Cashier: Please give change. Give me Rs 20.`
Lady (digs in her bag for 2 mins. Looks upset as she has to dig in her big bag)

`Lady: I don't have any change`
Cashier (looks into his cash drawer again and comes up with change)

Excerpt 1 reveals the cashier's orientation towards his float. He has not asked for Rs 20 because he is unable to give change, rather he is orienting towards keeping a reasonable float for future transactions. Commonly the customer *was* able to provide the money such that a round amount of change could be given, which might even mean two or three rounds of cash exchange. For example, where the bill amount was Rs 56 and the customer gave Rs 60, the cashier returned Rs 5 and the customer gave the cashier Rs 1. In other situations, the customer has to wait for the right change even after the billing has been done. We observed in situations like the railway station that customers were even asked to step out of the queue and go and find change (e.g. from family members) before having their transaction completed. In some situations, if a customer has the exact amount of change for the purchase they may jump the queue ahead of someone with problematic change (i.e. they can help to ameliorate the change problem), or even jump the queue full stop. In a Chennai supermarket queue jumping was occasionally observed when customers had the exact amount for payment, often for a single item. The cashier would take the purchase and bill it (keeping the entitled customer on hold). These situations show that customers, too, orient to the issue of change, and to the privileges (or the avoiding of inconveniencies) that having the correct change may give you! Indeed many of these features are widespread cross-culturally and may well be already familiar to the reader.

Having the correct money and carrying change is also a problem in other situations. During an interview with a textile company in Chennai that employs networks of workers in rural areas we found out that paying and distributing salaries to the field force, who are unbanked, was a major task. The salary amount (for 60-70 workers) is transferred to the unit manager's bank account in the village. The unit manager withdraws the cash from the bank and pays it to the workers. Salary disbursement in this way is not only time consuming but also potentially insecure as the manager must carry a sack-full of coins and low denomination notes worth Rs 10,000 so all the individual wages can be paid exactly. To provide this the bank has to be informed in advance.

We can see then that speed and convenience are key features of payment situations and the workers have developed practices which enable them to smoothly and quickly complete the transactions. Both workers and customers orient to the tangible and finite nature of cash. In the last situation where the payment is for payroll the requirement to use cash is a major logistical burden.

THE WIDER PURCHASING WORKFLOW

Payment practices (to merchants) are part of a service or goods provision workflow. It is important for m-payment design to understand this workflow and its implications. What constraints might it impose on m-payments and conversely are there places where m-payments can offer added value over other payment mechanisms? A good illustration of this wider workflow comes from the railway reservation counter in Lucknow where ticket officers provide a valuable service in enabling customers to get the 'correct' reservation. In theory, customers simply complete a reservation form in advance and then the ticket officer would issue the ticket and take payment. In practice the form in many cases serves only as a initial draft and orienting device which begins a conversation that refines the selection. In Excerpt 2 we see an example of the valuable service they provide in highlighting potential common mistakes in proposed bookings, thus allowing customers to double check:

Excerpt 2: *A person hands the reservation form in which the date of departure is 16th. The officer looks at the reservation form given to her.*

```
Officer: The train is at 12:30 AM so do you
want the ticket for 16th night or 17th
night?
Person: 16th night
Officer: Then change the date in the form to
17th because it is at 12:30 AM
```

Officer hands over the form to him, he changes the dates and returns it.

In Excerpt 3 we see another important service being provided – helping customers navigate through the slightly labyrinthine system of trains and possible reservations:

Excerpt 3: *Another passenger in the queue hands over his form to the officer sitting at the reservation counter. The officer enters the details of the form in the computer and gets the status.*

```
Officer: Waiting 106

Person: Check in this other train which goes
from Lucknow to Ghaziabad at time 2:00 PM. I
only know the source and the destination,
don't know the train name.

Officer [checks in the computer]: The name
of the train is Neelachal Express but it
doesn't run on the dates you want to go

Person: Check for this other train, name
Sadbhawana Express

Officer: It has no 'sleeper' class, only Air
Condition class(AC)

Person: Check in Tatkal
```

(late reservation option)

```
Officer: The status in all the trains
running from the source and destination on
that date is this [gives status of trains]
Person: Do it in the one with the least
waiting
```

Officer hands over the form and he changes it.

Different trains of different names run the same route so the customer relies on the officer being able to identify the correct train. Furthermore, express trains in India offer various 'class' options as well as 'waiting' (with 'waiting' you may be able to board a train with a ticket, but you are not guaranteed a seat) that the officer can help the customer navigate through to a preferred choice. Interestingly this is clearly a customer who knows the system to some extent but still requires help to work up the best option. In this study the vast majority of customers needed some sort of assistance in purchasing their tickets, often in the form of several question and information exchange 'rounds'. What this material makes clear is that when buying tickets customers do not necessarily know in advance just what it is they want or what the best solution would be – they need help in choosing, refining and checking. They are not in a position to successfully purchase their tickets unless supported in some way and although taking payments and issuing tickets is an important part of the reservation clerk's job it is by no means the main part.

A second example can be seen when we look at the various functions of receipts in purchasing workflows. Certainly receipts are not one single thing serving one single purpose. If we think of the payment as one activity within a wider exchange of goods and/or services that has contractual elements (whether socially and morally defined in informal situations e.g. with roadside vendors, or more explicitly defined in more formal situations e.g. buying off the Internet, where we 'sign up' to agreements) we can see the importance of the receipt in marking out contractual rights and obligations. Receipts, whether printed or written, often serve as a proof of payment/purchase, after the fact of buying and receiving goods. As such, we saw them used in two fashions – proof of purchase in the light of a problem with the goods or services or as a means of claiming expenses. In different types of purchasing models the orderings and temporal relations between receiving receipts and receiving goods or services alter. For example, buying something off the Internet, you will often receive the digital (though printable) receipt (for payment) in advance of the purchased good – in which case it serves as a promise to deliver, and then once delivered as a proof of purchase. Receipts can also serve as tickets (or vice versa) as observed on the buses where the payment is made and the ticket is collected. The paper ticket serves as a (a) ticket (b) receipt/proof of payment (c) potentially as a bill for expense claims. The receipt-as-ticket may also have corresponding timestamp, alighting and destination information.

Another interesting example comes from observations in a Chennai restaurant, Tiffany's. Here, people go to the counter, order, pay and get a receipt (listing food ordered, amount paid etc.) which then acts as a token. The receipt/token is handed in by the customer at the service counter, where the order is prepared (here this consists of putting pre-cooked food onto trays according to the combination ordered). Once ready the dish is called out and the customer, who usually hangs about in the vicinity takes his tray. In one situation a customer wanted their receipt/token back for an expense claim, but this was not particularly easy since the server had to find it amongst the pile of unordered tokens on his table. This example reminds us that receipts are designed and deployed as organising elements in *workflows*. Tiffany's is a fast food restaurant and managing the customer flow is aided by the way the service is ordered through the receipt. People pay up-front then go to the service counter where the token triggers the preparation of the meal, which is then called out for the customer. The receipt features in efficiently and relatively dependably dealing with many customers in a quick-fire manner. Here the potential need for the receipt to be returned to the customer is not well catered for. When claiming expenses, the receipt that was part of the paying for goods 'workflow' becomes part of another workflow within the employer's human resource systems.

Bargaining and haggling

In the final set of examples in this section we examine practices of haggling and bargaining. In many transactions in India – fares for autos, roadside shopping and even in larger stores prices can be flexible. The price of the commodity/service often varies and getting the best or the correct price can rely on local knowledge. Excerpts 4-6 all come from 'haggles' with auto drivers that illustrate some interesting features of the activity. Firstly, auto drivers invariably, unsurprisingly, try to get the best price for themselves, which mostly involves setting it initially high (see 4 and 5). However, the success of this tactic relies on the customer lacking the local knowledge to spot the inflated fare, or whether they can be bothered to bargain or are willing to accept a higher price. In excerpt 4 Rs60 is accepted even though is a bit high, in Excerpt 5 the customer simply declines the haggle and the auto.

Excerpt 4: *During the study the ethnographer observed: 'While coming back from Besant Nagar, the time was 9.15 PM. I thought we'll take a bus but Professor suggested we take an auto. We stopped an auto going on the other side of the road. He crossed the road to meet us at the other end'.*

```
Prof: IIT Gate
Auto: 90
Prof: Too much, 40
Auto: Night time sir
Deepti: You don't even have to take a U-turn
Prof: We came in 40.  Okay, how about 50?
Auto: No sir 60 is okay
```

'I think Prof was either tired or he did not want to bargain more so he said okay'.

Excerpt 5: *During a study the ethnographer stopped an auto. The destination from the place of boarding was 5 km away.*

```
Deepti: IIT Gate?
Auto: 90
Deepti: No
```

Without bargaining or saying anything more the ethnographer walks away for the requested amount is so unreasonable it is not worth negotiating. The ethnographer stopped another auto.

Looking again at excerpts 4 and 5 we can see that there are *tolerances* to haggling. In 5 we see that the customer does not even bother because the initial price is too high. Indeed this is common in India where autos are readily available and if one deems the initial price to be too high, it is often not worth continuing. Tolerances include the possibility of overpaying but only within reasonable amounts, for example, Rs 10. Of course different people have different tolerances! Another feature of haggling is the notion of how it should proceed – that initial positions should be taken that are reasonable (within tolerances for both) and that the haggle should proceed rapidly and reach a mutually accepted mid-point quickly. There is, however, an asymmetry in relation to initial positions as to the *what next* action if either party deems these to be inappropriate; while the buyer will often just walk away, the seller may well exhibit his consternation but will mostly continue within the haggle. Excerpt 4 illustrates a fairly classic pattern while 6 really shows features of a 'good haggle' – brevity and rapid concordance:

Excerpt 6: *The ethnographer stopped a running auto.*

```
Deepti: IIT Gate
Auto: 50
Deepti: 40?
Auto: No
Deepti: Okay
```

The ethnographer did not bargain a lot with him because in the first go the auto driver quoted a decent price.

The ability to haggle effectively and quickly relies heavily on the knowledge and experience of the participants, because this sets out what customarily good starting points are, what a reasonable tolerance may be and so forth. This can pose as much a problem for Indians moving city as for foreigners as there is not a clear standard fare across the country. Returning to the theme of change introduced above, getting change is a known problem when catching autos, particularly where a fare has been bargained down from say Rs 100 to Rs 90, where drivers will frequently withhold the Rs 10 change under the pretext of it being a long ride, rush hour etc. Consequently it is common that people prepare for auto rides by having a variety of notes and change. Although keeping the extra money is a form of cheating it is within *socially acceptable limits*. It may provoke some annoyance but little more. Drivers never seem to try to keep much more than a few rupees, presumably as otherwise this would provoke a more extreme reaction. Hence, there are unsaid norms which are maintained by both the payer and the payee, and there is a moral dimension to haggling.

A haggle is to some extent a social activity in itself – like a kind of greetings exchange – it is not simply about final price. The next examples further show this social and moral dimension. In the first situation the ethnographer stopped at a roadside coconut vendor to buy a coconut. When he quoted it as Rs 20, she asked for a cheaper one and he showed her one for Rs 15 and began to cut it. While she was looking for Rs 15 in her wallet she realised she didn't have enough money so immediately asked him to stop. The vendor asked her how much she had and she showed him Rs 9.5. She was searching for a couple of more coins in the bag and wallet but couldn't find anything. The vendor said Rs 9.5 was fine and didn't even count the money when he got it. Due to the way the activity was conducted, with the ethnographer sincerely searching for more coins, the shopkeeper trusted her. This 'unintentional haggle' was accepted because it appeared genuine and trustworthy – i.e. not as some kind of ruse. Conversely, if haggles 'go wrong' people may be offended. The ethnographer sometimes visits a small roadside footwear shop in Chennai. One time when she visited she had a problem with the shopkeeper. He initially quoted a price of Rs70 for a pair of slippers but quickly changed it to Rs 60 without a haggle. But, he would not reduce the price further for a bulk buy of 6 pairs. The haggle degenerated so she left. Conversely, when she returned after 6 months and the shopkeeper's father was in charge he quoted a price of Rs 80 a pair. When he was told that she would buy 6 pairs he reduced the price to Rs 70 a pair. Even though the slippers were more expensive the second time, due to the fact that the haggling proceeded in the 'correct' manner, i.e. a discount *should* be given for buying multiples, a successful transaction was concluded.

PERSON TO PERSON PAYMENT PRACTICES

The Indian m-payment system is not just being designed for merchant payments, it may also be used for transferring cash between people, we therefore briefly consider a couple of current practices which we believe relevant to this function, namely transferring money to family members and sharing of credit/debit cards.

It is common practice for family members with jobs, often in the cities to transfer money home to the family, who remain living in rural areas. Sending money home is an expensive and insecure affair for the unbanked who often come from the poorer villages to earn money in big towns and cities. Most people send money by informal networks such as (a) an agency, where the sender pays the money to a broker/agent in his/her city. The agent calls up another agent in the beneficiary's town/village and asks him to deliver the required amount. The agent charges 10-12% of the total amount; (b) *Angandia service*, which is a kind of a courier service where the sender pays the money to a person who travels to the beneficiary's town and delivers the money. The charge in this case is 15-20%. (c) Post office transfer, which is a government provided service where the postman transfers the money to the beneficiary. The problem in this case is that the postman does not pay all the amount in one go, he will pay the beneficiary in installments and will keep rotating the money in the market. Sometimes they even charge a commission of another 15% to deliver the amount to the intended beneficiary. (d) Informal/black market networks with money lenders/intermediaries. E.g. one of our interviewees, working in a hotel sent money home regularly through an acquaintance who then transferred the money to a distant relative in his home village who would then pass on money to his parents. These types of money transfer are very common amongst 'migrant' workers who need to send money back to their families but transfers like this are fraught with risks and many have tales of losing money.

Of relevance when we think of the implications of a new m-payment system on the above activities is that sharing of debit/credit cards is common practice amongst the banked in India. For example, our studies and interviews of students and people above 40-45 years of age, found that (a) they had their friends' card details with them and would use them anytime after informing the owner of the card; (b) the owner of the card would give their card details to someone else (a son or a daughter) and ask them to book tickets/services with the cards; and (c) the settlement between the owner of the card and the user happens in cash or in kind, depending upon the relationship. Implications for m-payment systems of the sharing of payment mechanisms and our other findings are discussed below.

DISCUSSION

Although understanding payment situations might seem rather straightforward, their very routine nature can mean that the order inherent in these day-to-day practices disappears for us as we live them. Through ethnographic study we are able to begin to address a number of questions central to the design of an m-payment system:

1) How might we go about designing elements of the interaction model for mobile payments?

2) What is the *ecosystem* required to support mobile payments? We introduce the notion of ecosystem here as it emerged as an important idea in our study. It was clear that enabling an m-payment system to work is not simply about standards or interaction design. We need to think about the interaction of the core payment system with a number of other 'elements' to be successful. That is, what types of hardware, software and services, in what sort of configuration would be required to support different types of mobile payments for different users in different settings? This is the *ecosystem*. In part, this is an infrastructure question. For example, it involved envisioning how to handle m-payments for booking railway tickets or paying an auto fare, both from the payee and the payer sides.

3) How might mobile payments work in two markets? These are encapsulated by two types of phone – a middle to upper-middle class audience, more technically savvy, more likely to have an Internet enabled phone, and a lower class audience, more likely to have a more basic phone, less educated and less technically savvy? Of course, these groups are 'glosses' but from a design point of view, useful. The former allows us to think about more state-of-the-art solutions, while the latter allows us to think about basic and simple solutions that go towards aiding financial inclusion.

Interaction elements of mobile payments

Payment situations are often hurried and both buyers and sellers adopt practices to deal with the need for speed e.g. the bus driver with notes between his fingers or customers preparing the right change in advance. They also entail a socially understood moral and practical order. In the next sections we consider how the system could be designed to deal with money efficiently and effectively, how m-payments may impact social aspects of transactions, and what added value services may be attached to m-payments.

1) Number Entry: The current m-payment system requires the entry of around 20 numbers to make a payment and this is likely to be a major barrier to use as it will take time (and concentration). Hence good number entering solutions are key. Number entering might be eased through a number of possibilities for high end phones: Bluetooth could be used for example in shops, where the customers can scan their phone past a pay-point near a till and receive all the numbers relevant to the shop (phone number, account details and so on). The additional infrastructure requirements here mean that initially this would be likely in India only for users of high-end phones shopping in high-end shops. Lower-end merchants could consider printing business cards with a data glyph or bar code which could be read by a phone with the required application and a camera. Customers would still need high-end phones but the infrastructure costs for the merchant would be much less. Speech to text for converting spoken numbers is also a possibility, as well as to pre-fill numbers of regular merchants from a payments address book stored on the phone. However, there are many fewer options to manual number entering for low end phones, verbal number entry is one possibility, either via IVR or human operators in a dedicated call centre. The transaction would then be completed over the call centre computer system. For low-end phones or when paying merchants without extra infrastructure, beyond the call centre option, customers will currently have to manually enter the numbers. Where this can be done when queuing or riding an auto it might be less of a burden, certainly one can imagine the seller posting a board with the details of his phone number, bank identifier and account identifier in a visible location to enable the customer to prepare in advance. A simple design requirement then for m-payments is that the amount payable should be the last thing entered to enable preparation by the customer.

2) Cash and Cashing Up: While cash can often be quickly exchanged in busy situations, potentially making it preferential to m-payments there is a burden to ordering the change and cashing up – currently this is often done outside of the customer interaction (although, e.g. in supermarkets, the ordering of cash is done at the time through use of tills). However, if the m-payment system can be designed such that it reduces the burden of cashing up there might be incentive for merchants to adopt it even if it makes the payment interaction a little slower (as for example with the bus conductor's automatic ticket machine). Thus being a little slower or more difficult to use is not a complete block for adoption of the m-payment system as long as it offers added-value to customers and/or merchants. This added-value could simply be from paying electronically in places where you currently cannot, e.g. the auto. The m-payment system avoids the problem of having to have the right change and, in the case of the autos, would mean you could bargain for a fare and then pay exactly the right amount, avoiding the chance to be cheated. There is a fine balance between ease of use and added-value that will affect adoption of the technology and it is not possible to specify in advance where it lies. However, what we can do is describe potential problems and opportunities, as we understand them from our studies, to enable the m-payment system designers to take them into account during design.

3) Tangibility & the Social Order of Payments: Cash is a tangible, physical object which is exchanged for goods during the payment interaction. Its tangibility is both useful (both parties know it has been exchanged; the available amount can be made available to both parties as a part of bargaining e.g. with the coconut seller) but it can also be problematic (can run out, problem of change). With m-payment the exchange is 'virtual', which has similarities to credit cards. However, when we consider the buyer-seller interaction with credit cards, we see that although the actual exchange of money is virtual (going on behind the scenes, digitally) the payment interaction still involves the transfer of the card from the buyer to the seller, who runs it through their system and demands verification from the customer. The purchasing interaction is a tangible, ordered exchange from individual buyer to individual seller. M-payments change this since the transfer of money is virtual and involves no physical exchange (of cash or card). The m-payment system is currently being designed such that both buyer and seller will receive a notification (by SMS or USSD) containing either 1) the phone number of the person making the transaction and the amount or 2) the phone number of the person to whom the transaction is made and the amount, depending on whether you are (payee/payer). This notification is to serve as verification of payment. It is important that this notification is fast, otherwise the merchant is unlikely to be willing to let the customer leave until it has been received. If it arrives quickly, in one-on-one interactions it is probably adequate, e.g. the small shop keeper or auto-driver will be satisfied they have been paid if they receive prompt notification of the amount arriving into their account. However it could introduce problems for situations with many buyers as in the bus example. Customers could be treated sequentially as a conventional queue but this would not be innovative or efficient. It would be much better to allow payments from multiple customers at once but this raises the issue of how do you easily identify the customer and match them to the payment? We will discuss the latter possibility below.

4) Added Value Services: In terms of added value, one of the key things that the mobile phone offers as a payment channel which is not offered by most existing channels is that communication (and document) services can be offered hand-in-hand with the payment mechanism. Only the Internet offers this but in India it is less available in a private or mobile manner and most online payment is through credit cards. In the current design of the system, the customer only receives a simple notification, yet we have described how receipts are central parts of many interactions. There is certainly an opportunity for m-payment providers to provide receipts through the mobile phone – whether simple SMS receipts, containing details such as merchants name, products purchased, etc., so as to be useful to the customer (rather than just a list of notifications with phone numbers and amounts), or more complex document services linked into invoicing and so on.

Initial ideas for m-payment ecosystems

We mentioned above the issues surrounding transactions when there are numerous customers paying at the same time. This is partly an infrastructure issue. When thinking about one-pay-point-to-one-customer situations, the minimum m-payment system does not require additional infrastructure for it to work. All it requires is that both buyer and seller have a mobile phone and bank account (and have registered with the service). However, once there are multiple payers and/or pay points it becomes more complex. Let us take for example a grocery chain store with five check-outs. The cashiers might well have their own mobile phones, but certainly the grocery would not want the money being directed to the cashiers account! Rather they are likely to have a central account into which the payments go. We then have a number of options, all which require additional infrastructure: 1) a mobile phone is purchased for each till point, all linked to the same account 2) a computer system is purchased to handle m-payments 3) only one till accepts m-payments, using either a phone or a computer system. We should note at this point that the majority of grocery stores visited in India, even of large chains did not have computerised tills, so purchasing in a computer system for each store could be a prohibitive investment and apart from option three there is still a problem of associating the customer at your till with the payments being made on the system. The Bluetooth number entering system described above could address this, since information exchange could be two way, however as mentioned this is only feasible in high end stores for customers with high end phones so more innovation to refine this clearly possible.

Now let us consider another situation, requiring a different ecosystem – railway ticket reservation. Ticket booking is one of the most important online services offered in India. Booking a ticket involves looking up the various options and then choosing the most suitable one, this means a lot of displays and selections. Since ticket availability is rapidly changing it requires a fast real-time connection to the booking system. Remote ticket reservation then is an option on high end phones with Internet connectivity. A potential value-added service is to provide the ticket on the mobile phone, initially this is likely to be through a notification with a number which enables customers to print out a paper ticket, but one could imagine wholly digital tickets in the future. For low end phones other options are required, for example kiosks where selections can be made and then payment is simply by entering you mobile phone number and then pin number. Such kiosks could enable printing out of receipts and tickets. They also offer possibilities for sharing m-payment services amongst family members, since users would just need to know the mobile phone number and the pin number, rather than actually to carry it around with them. There is a question mark however around whether such kiosks would really take off in India, given that even in internet cafes intermediaries may be used to do the actual ticket selection and payment.

The situation where m-payments might seem to work best is in one-on-one payment situations, such as the auto or small merchant (fruit seller, shopkeeper) etc. Currently there is no alternative payment mechanism to cash for these situations, thus they might benefit from an electronic payment mechanism. It could reduce problems around change and the numbers could be entered during the ride or wait. It would not require additional infrastructure, but is likely to require either manual or IVR number entering.

M-payments for financial inclusion

To wrap up we would like to say a few words on the topic of financial inclusion. If we imagine that good ecosystems and services are put in place for number entering and so on then the most likely immediate users of the system might well be literate, middle class, professionals with high end phones. This population already has access to debit/credit cards, but we can imagine that m-payments will be able to offer added value through a range of services e.g. receiving tickets on the phone, notifications when payments are due and so on. For all populations, person to person payments offer a real value add as these are often difficult now, unless through cash, involving creating arrangements for individual people to be able to transfer money between different bank accounts. If handled correctly and in parallel with new banking programs, m-payments can help new communities achieve financial inclusion. It is unlikely that there will be immediate widespread adoption amongst the poorest and least educated communities. Even those who have basic number literacy might struggle with the entering of so many digits, however dedicated call centres/voice services could help, although they might also push up the transaction cost. However, for the currently unbanked communities between the very poor and the middle class there is real potential. For these markets though there needs to be a simple system to be used on low end phones. For example a simple SMS could be sent to a 'generic payment number' e.g. 777 containing <beneficiaries phone number, bank ID, account code, amount>. Although this requires a lot of number entry, given the cost and insecurity of transferring money by current routes, it would offer a considerable value-add that might encourage adoption. Sharing and intermediaries [13] in the community could also enhance the reach of the service into the poorest communities e.g. only one family member in the rural home need have a bank account for all to benefit.

CONCLUSION

We have reported on a series of ethnographic studies of payment practices in India and have described some of the arising implications for m-payments, not just in terms of interaction and functionality design, but also how m-payments might fit into or impact existing payment workflows. We also consider how m-payments could impact financial inclusion. These ideas do not represent the final say in design and should be seen as a first exploration of possibilities. As m-payments develop we are bound to see unexpected innovations and changing practices but balancing creativity while looking at how they might work in reference to today's practices seems a good place to start.

ACKNOWLEDGEMENTS

We would like to thank Professor Timothy A. Gonsalves of IIT Mandi, Himachal Pradesh, India for his assistance in facilitating and carrying out the work reported in this paper.

REFERENCES

1. Study of Auto-Rickshaw Drivers. Internal Commonwealth Microfinance India Limited Report. http://www.commonwealthmf.com/
2. Chen, L., (2008) A model of consumer acceptance of mobile payment. *Int. J. Mobile Communications*. 6(1), pp. 33-52, ISSN 1470-949X.
3. Chipchase, J. (2005). *Understanding Non-Literacy as a Barrier to Mobile Phone Communication*. http://research.nokia.com/bluesky/non-literacy-001-2005/index.html (16/09/08)
4. Ghosh, K., Parikh, T.S. Chavan, A.L. (2003) Design considerations for a financial management system for rural, semi-literate users, *CHI '03*. 824 - 825
5. Hughes, N. & Lonie, S. (2007) M-PESA: Mobile Money for the "Unbanked" Turning Cellphones into 24-Hour Tellers in Kenya. *Innovations: Technology, Governance, Globalization*. 2 (1-2). 63-81. MIT Press
6. Kumar, D., Gonsalves, T., Jhunjhunwala, A. & Raina, G. (2010) Mobile Payment Architectures for India. *National Conference of Communication,* Chennai, Jan 2010. 1-5
7. Medhi, I., Nagasena, G.S.N., and Toyama, K. (2009) A Comparison of Mobile Money-Transfer UIs for Non-Literate and Semi-Literate Users. *Proc. CHI'09*. ACM
8. Pousttchi, K. (2003) Conditions for Acceptance and Usage of Mobile. Payment Procedures. *Proc. of the* M-*Business Conference 2003*
9. Randall, D., Harper, R. & Rouncefield, M. (2007). *Fieldwork for Design: Theory and Practice*. Springer Verlag, New York
10. Rangaswamy, N. (2007). Representing the Non-formal: the Business of Internet Cafes in India. *Proc. of EPIC, 2007*. Keystone, CO, USA, October 3-6, pp. 115-127
11. Roberson, J. and Nardi, B. (2010). Survival Needs and Social Inclusion: Technology Use Among the Homeless. *Proc. of CSCW 2010*. 445-448
12. Sacks, H. (1992) "A single instance of a phone-call opening", *Lectures on Conversation* (ed. Jefferson, G.), vol. II. 542-553, Oxford: Blackwell.
13. Sambasivan, N., Cutrell, E., Toyama, K. & Bonnie, N. (2010). Intermediated technology use in developing communities. *Proc. of CHI '10*. 2583-2592
14. Sambasivan, N. Rangaswamy, N., Cutrell, E. & Nardi, B. (2009) UbiComp4D: Infrastructure and Interaction for International Development—the Case of Urban Indian Slums. *UbiComp 2009*. 155-164
15. Sambasivan, N., Rangaswamy, Toyama, K. & Nardi, B. (2009). Under development: Encountering Development Ethnographically. *Interactions*. 16 (6). 20-23
16. www.mpf.org.in
17. http://other90.cooperhewitt.org/
18. http://www.coai.com/statistics.php.
19. Reserve Bank of India mobile payments information http://www.rbi.org.in/Scripts/bs_viewcontent.aspx?Id=1365

Folk Music Goes Digital in India

Neha Kumar
School of Information
UC Berkeley
Berkeley, CA 94720
neha@ischool.berkeley.edu

Gopal Singh
Self-Employed
Bikaner, Rajasthan
gopalbkn1@gmail.com

Tapan S. Parikh
School of Information
UC Berkeley
Berkeley, CA 94720
parikh@berkeley.edu

ABSTRACT
Folk music forms in India are rich and diverse, varying from region to region across the Indian landscape. The recent explosion of new media technologies (e.g. DVDs, CDs, mobile phones) in both rural and urban India is changing how oral folk music is being performed, produced, distributed, and shared. To further understand this impact, we conducted an extended field study across four field sites in India that are rich in folk music tradition and activity. Through a process of interviews, participant observation, focus group discussion, and content analysis with a varied group of stakeholders – including folk musicians, listeners, retailers, and radio show producers – we found that 1) there are a diverse set of motivations for performing and listening to folk music, 2) new media technologies are helping folk musicians become more popular, while reducing some streams of revenue, particularly for businesses engaged only in music production and distribution, and 3) as expected, piracy is widely tolerated by musicians, both out of apathy, and an interest in reaching new audiences with their message, while increasing their own fame and associated patronage. Based on these findings, we propose some implications for the design of an appropriate folk music sharing and distribution service that addresses these various motivations of the musicians and listeners.

Author Keywords
ICTD, Entertainment, Media, Sharing, Folk Music, Copyright, Piracy

ACM Classification Keywords
H5.m. Information interfaces and presentation (e.g., HCI): Miscellaneous.

General Terms
Human Factors

INTRODUCTION
Folk music forms in India are rich and diverse, varying from region to region and even district to district across the Indian landscape. Oral folk traditions have been passed down for generations and have served many purposes in the lives of villagers. Greene writes of village music in the Indian state of Tamil Nadu:

> "...villagers sing folksongs on numerous occasions and for many purposes. Women and men working in the fields sing worksongs to take their minds off of their arduous labor. At the end of the day, men gather at tea shops and sing epic ballads or other songs for entertainment. [...] Villagers feel free to change the words to reflect the concerns of their particular village, local village deities, and also personal concerns [14]."

The relevance of folk music in the rural context, where it is mostly practiced, goes beyond entertainment alone. Studies on folk media in the developing world (and India in particular) show that folk music is frequently used in mass awareness and publicity campaigns [12][26]. Local fairs, puppet shows, street theatre, songs and ballads are used in support of local development schemes for generating health and political awareness [21][28][30]. Folk media plays a key role towards increasing social awareness of important developmental issues. According to a Food and Agricultural Organization (FAO) study on folk and traditional media for rural development:

> "If we are to properly communicate with rural communities, we must learn more about and better understand how to channel our development work through those communities' traditional communication channels [27]."

The recent explosion of new media technologies (e.g. DVDs, CDs, mobile phones) in rural and urban India is changing how oral folk music is being performed, produced, distributed, and shared. To understand the impact of these trends, we conducted an extended field study across four field sites in India that are rich in folk music tradition and activity. Through a process of interviews, participant observation, focus group discussion, content analysis with a varied group of stakeholders – including folk musicians, listeners, retailers, and radio show producers – we find that 1) there are a diverse set of motivations for performing and listening to folk music, 2) new media technologies are helping folk musicians become more popular and reach new audiences, while also reducing some streams of revenue, particularly for businesses engaged only in music production and distribution, and 3) as expected, piracy is widely tolerated by musicians, both out of apathy and an interest in reaching new audiences, thereby increasing the reach of their message, and their own fame and associated patronage.

The rest of this paper is organized as follows. The next section provides some necessary background information, while summarizing the prior research results most relevant to our study. The following section describes our research methodology, including a description of the four field sites that we visited. The next three sections summarize our main findings, including 1) the motivations for listening to and performing folk music, 2) the impact of new media technologies on the performance, production, sharing and distribution of folk music, and 3) the impact of widespread piracy. The next section provides some implications for the design of an appropriate music sharing and distribution service motivated by these findings, followed by our conclusions.

BACKGROUND AND RELATED WORK

Before recording technology was available in rural India, music was performed and listened to primarily in live concert settings. The trend towards new media adoption in rural India began with the widespread use of audio cassettes approximately 25 years ago, when most people were first able to listen to music at will [24].

Johnson's study [18] explores the social environment of village life and the role that television plays in the ever-changing landscape of rural India, looking at the lives of villagers and their evolving relationship with TV, and the role of television in the dynamics of social change.

> "Though television began in India as a limited developmental tool with programming orchestrated by the government, the medium today has blossomed into one of the largest competitive entertainment industries in the world. Villagers are not simple peasants passively waiting to be manipulated and prodded into action by their government, but are active members of a vibrant society using the media for their own advantage."

Among other studies on mass media and how it impacts folk arts in rural India, Sharma has studied how television, VCDs, and audio cassettes have impacted the *Nautanki* folk theater art form, concluding that both continue to coexist, and the popularity of *Nautanki* remains unaffected, though its content has evolved over time, especially because of its relevance to the contemporary rural context [36].

Especially within the last 5-10 years, new media technologies such as DVDs, CDs, and mobile phones have gained considerable popularity in rural areas, offering many people in villages a personal device that they can use to listen to their choice of content. Even many low-end phones have FM radio, audio players, and recorders. Among other changes, this has allowed folk musicians to reach out to wider and more geographically-distributed audiences [22]. This transition to digital media has been facilitated by the mobile phone. As Bellman says [3]:

> "In the furthest reaches of India's rural heartland, the cellphone is bringing something that television, radio and even newspapers couldn't deliver: Instant access to music, information, entertainment, news and even worship."

Smyth et al. [37] show in their recent paper that entertainment is a major motivating factor driving mobile media-sharing in urban India. Our findings are in line with theirs on content access and distribution, although they studied urban low-income users while we explored the rural space, in addition to discussing the practices surrounding content generation. Frohlich et al.'s [38] paper on mobile digital storytelling emphasizes the importance of user-generated content and text-free interfaces. Our findings support this emphasis on user-generated content, as we discover the widespread access to locally produced mobile media.

Several research efforts in the emerging field of Information and Communication Technology and Decelopment (ICTD) have investigated how the introduction of various new media technologies have affected education, health care, agriculture, and entertainment in India. Kam et al. explore the potential of mobile learning in the lives of underprivileged children in rural India [20]. Ramachandran et al. study how mobile video messages can impart beneficial health information in India [34]. Patel et al. [31] and Gandhi et al. [11] look at the potential of audio and video technologies, respectively, for providing farmers in rural India with timely and relevant agricultural advice.

METHODOLOGY

This paper presents the results and analysis of a set of formal and informal semi-structured interviews, sessions of participant observation, group discussion, as well as recorded feedback sessions from four sites in India. All data collection was conducted between December 2009 and August 2010.

The sites we studied and the qualitative methods we used are detailed below. These sites were selected not only because they have traditionally been (and continue to be) rich in folk music culture, but also because they are experiencing rapid adoption of new media technologies (along with the rest of India).

Field Sites

The sites below were chosen because they housed active folk music communities where the music is listened to and shared on a frequent basis, and live performances are regularly held and widely attended. The study participants included folk musicians, community members who actively listen to local folk forms, and the local retailers of this music.

Malwa (Madhya Pradesh)
Malwa is a region in the west of Madhya Pradesh (with a population of almost 19 million in 2001 [6]) that has traditionally been known for its rich folk culture. The site we focused on for our study includes the small town of Maksi and the village Luniyakhedi which borders Maksi. One of the best-known folk musicians of Malwa lives in Luniyakhedi, which makes this village a frequent venue for performances large and small [22]. The community here is primarily agricultural. Literacy rates hover around 40% [6]. Recent ICT penetration is significant, with almost every household owning at least one mobile phone.

In Malwa we conducted interviews with 6 musicians, in addition to conversing with 20-25 local residents of Luniyakhedi and neighboring villages. We also explored the commercial market areas of Maksi and interviewed 10-12 shop owners who were involved in the production and sales of folk music (along with other popular music). Our subjects were mostly literate with 6-8 years of schooling, although others ranged from being illiterate (some of the local residents) to being a middle-school teacher (one of the artists).

Figure 1: A folk artist with his family in a village near Bikaner.

Bikaner (Rajasthan)
Bikaner is a small district in the north-west of Rajasthan with a wide listenership of folk music. Festivals with folk performances and concerts are regularly held here and in neighboring villages, and are well attended. There is an increasing trend towards using digital media for listening to and sharing music.

In Bikaner, we interviewed 4 local musicians, some of who lived in the town of Bikaner, while the others lived in a village called Pugal about 40 km from Bikaner. We also spoke with 20-25 active listeners of folk music (these were from Bikaner as well as neighboring villages such as Pugal), and 3-4 distributors (all from Bikaner) who have been involved in the sales of folk music – many of them transitioning all the way from selling audio cassettes to using current digital technologies.

Gurgaon (Haryana)
The demographics of Gurgaon are starkly different from those of the Malwa region and Bikaner. It is more urban, due to its close proximity to New Delhi. As such, it has a large low-income migrant worker population that actively listens to folk music, including several local folk musicians who regularly perform here. In Gurgaon, we worked with the *Gurgaon ki Awaaz* [15] community radio initiative that began in 2009 and is actively involved in seeking out and recording local musicians, and soliciting regular feedback from its listenership.

The data we collected here includes informal interviews and focus group discussions with 6-8 members of staff and local volunteers at the radio station, as well as 10 listeners and 6 musicians. It also includes analysis of recordings of prior feedback sessions with listeners (approximately sixty) over the previous year.

Most of the radio station's listeners are uneducated local Haryanvi residents, but many migrant workers also call in regularly to request songs and/or provide feedback. The occupations of the callers ranged from farming to carpentry, tailoring, driving taxis, and other odd jobs.

Bundelkhand (Uttar Pradesh & Madhya Pradesh)
In the Bundelkhand region, which runs across the border of Uttar Pradesh and Madhya Pradesh states, we visited *Radio Bundelkhand*. This is a community radio initiative that began in 2008 and now caters to approximately 120,000 people across 120 villages [33]. Like *Gurgaon ki Awaaz*, the staff here is intimately connected with the local community, conducts frequent field visits, and has encouraged the growth of folk music and musicians in this region by catering to the musical interests of the local community.

Here we conducted informal interviews and discussions with the entire staff of 14-15 people, observed recordings of 3-4 folk performances as conducted by them, and also interviewed 3 local musicians.

Qualitative Methods
Several factors dictated the use of methods, including the geographic setting, level of access and comfort with the community, and the nature of the musical practices. There was a continual need to improvise on the modes of data collection based on the availability and accessibility of subjects and other resources, as well as available infrastructure for sharing music. Different methods worked for different sites. At the community radio station sites, it was more beneficial to hold interviews at the radio station itself because this allowed us to sample a range of musicians and listeners, considering the large geographical spread of participants. At the other sites, interviews were based on personal contacts of local musicians, who in turn were contacted via our several partner organizations. One-

on-one interviews were possible in certain other contexts. In other places, informal group discussions were conducted.

Data Analysis

The data we collected was in the form of audio recordings and written field notes. All interviews and discussions were conducted in Hindi (both the first and second authors are fluent in Hindi). We then transcribed these recordings and translated them to English. Due to the mix of methods, sites, and participants, we ran our data through several passes of coding, repeatedly consolidating to arrive at the findings we present in this paper. Our overall aim was to follow a grounded theory approach, as advocated by Glaser & Strauss [39].

Our focus was on observing and understanding the themes at play within the realm of folk music listening and sharing practices. By iteratively analyzing our data, three main questions of interest emerged for consideration:

(i) *What are various motivations underlying the sharing and listening of folk music within these communities?*

(ii) *How are new media technologies influencing these practices and supporting these motivations?*

(iii) *How do considerations of piracy interact with these changes?*

These questions guided subsequent data analysis, and the resulting findings are elaborated upon in the following sections.

MOTIVATIONS AND BENEFITS

In order to understand the listening and sharing practices within the folk music communities in each of these sites, we first focused on the underlying motivations for and benefits obtained from listening to this music. Why do people listen to this music? What do they think they have gained from it? Did our participants only listen to it for entertainment? Did it also serve as informal education – either in the form of spiritual guidance or by inspiring a more socially conscious conduct? The answers we received to these questions are summarized below.

Entertainment

We observed in our study that entertainment plays a key role in folk media sharing in rural India. This is in line with Smyth et al.'s findings in urban India [37]. Folk music is one of the major local and accessible sources of entertainment, and families spend significant portions of their time listening to or performing it. A participant from Malwa claimed that in every local household, entire families watched folk music VCDs/DVDs for at least 1.5 hours every evening. In Gurgaon, a local tailor shared that he listened to folk music on community radio from morning to night – either on his radio at home, or on his mobile phone through his work hours. *Radio Bundelkhand* even designed a local version of a popular talent-hunt show, called *Bundeli Idol* – seeking to identify upcoming folk musicians in the region – which generated considerable public interest [7].

Spiritual Education

Folk songs have varying flavors across the Indian landscape. In the performances we observed at Malwa, almost all songs had a significant spiritual bent. Along with singing, musicians were equally engaged in sharing with the audience the spiritual lessons they had gleaned from these songs. Within the smaller concerts we observed (*satsangs* [22]), the audience was often engaged in two-way discussions on these topics. In Malwa, one of the locally revered folk musicians we interviewed shared that, over time, these discussions were "most certainly" successful in bringing about positive change in the character and mindset of the listener. Another musician from Malwa shared his experience of working with the *Kanjar* caste, an ostracized community infamous for its crime rate [35]. According to this musician, in the months that he practiced and taught music around them, the spiritual content of the music led the people of this caste to gradually adopt a more peace-filled and harmonious approach towards life.

> "In 1991, I worked with the *Kanjar* folk, who are known to have a high crime rate. There we did many *satsangs* and I felt that the music brought about a positive change (*parivartan*) in them. Those who brought themselves in the company of this music, they quit smoking, drinking and of course, robbery. My goal was to sing songs that would coerce them to think for themselves, not to preach any kind of conduct… this brought about a change in about 40% of their community of 15-20,000."

Communal and Regional Harmony

In Pugal, a village near Bikaner, we interviewed a family of locally well-known folk musicians. They said that in their village, Hindus and Muslims had never had problems with each other, because the local music traditions that were secular in nature had brought these communities closer together. One of the artists in the family shared:

> "Before the rains came, the Hindus and the Muslims in the village came together to hold *satsangs* in the local temple. Everyone gets together."

In Gurgaon, the local (Haryanvi) dwellers were initially resistant towards the community radio station airing music from other regions (e.g. Bihar, Rajasthan, Gujarat) because migrant workers came from these regions and requested the music from these traditions. This led to several disturbed and resentful phone calls to the station's hotline. As Rajni, a member of the local staff, assured a local caller:

> "Just as you like to listen to songs from your tradition, they [the migrant workers] like to listen to songs from their traditions. Just as they also listen to songs from your tradition without any complaints, you too should listen to their songs and learn to accept their different style of music."

Over time, according to the community radio staff, local Haryanvi listeners have become more accepting towards different folk traditions and, as a result, towards the migrant worker community coming from other Indian states.

Classroom Education

With traditionally low rates of literacy among women, efforts have been initiated to focus on the education of the girl child. In Dewas, a small town in Malwa, there is an ongoing project (across twelve schools) that uses spiritual folk music to inspire girl children to pursue their ambitions, and encourages their families to support their education. Run by two local folk musicians, the project teaches folk songs to the schoolchildren, encouraging them to discuss these teachings and ask questions. The project also aims to create a syllabus using folk songs that inspires children to stay in school [16].

In a concert we observed in Luniyakhedi (Malwa), a local artist (who was also hosting the event) sang songs, gave an inspiring speech to the girl children in the audience, and invited other women in the audience to impress upon the girls and their families the importance of education. In our interview with him, he also explained that although he would have liked to devote himself to his music, teaching brought him fulfillment because it allowed him to work with and inspire girl children (he teaches at a girls' school) - who were at an impressionable age – to study further and "make something of their lives".

Social, Cultural, and Environmental Awareness

Our interviews with up and coming folk musicians at Bundelkhand and Gurgaon revealed that the songs they sing are not just limited to oral traditions that have been passed down generations but also include new compositions with contemporary references. They are written to address local needs that are often social, environmental, agricultural, or health-related. As a Bundeli artist shared – he composes songs based on the occasions/settings where he has been asked to sing. Not only does he sing these himself, but he also composes new songs for other local Bundeli musicians who pay him Rs. 200 ($4-5) per song.

In Gurgaon, Meghna – who runs the community radio initiative – shared that they had recently played a *ragini* (composition) that had been written by its Haryanvi artist on the theme of female infanticide. As Meghna shared, the radio station received several feedback calls from individuals who were moved by this piece and claimed that it had "opened their eyes".

In general, the data we collected at each of our sites showed that many musicians are keen on singing songs that can have a strong social impact, encouraging people to lead better and more socially aware lives.

USE OF NEW MEDIA

Our second question focused on the changes in folk music production and dissemination brought about by the influx of new media technologies, from the point of view of three main actors: the musicians, members of the listening community, and the local businesses who engage in the sales of this music within the rural context.

We found that the last two decades, in particular, have seen increased and widespread access to new media in the form of television, CDs, VCDs/DVDs, community radio, and mobile phones. With high penetration of these technologies, especially in some of the more developed portions of rural India, villagers have the option of listening and sharing their music in more forms and ways than ever before.

Acquiring Mobile Content

In the last 3-5 years, mobile phones have become increasingly prevalent in rural India. Just as the advent of audio cassettes further popularized folk music [24], the use of mobile phones appears to have increased listenership considerably, making folk music (as well as other music) far more accessible among villagers than before. At a folk music festival in Luniyakhedi (Malwa) that was attended by 2-3,000 people from neighboring villages, we observed hundreds of people in the audience holding their phones up high and pointing them at the stage (where 30-40 folk troupes from the Malwa region were taking turns performing from 6 pm to 4 am). This was done, as we later found, to make both audio and video recordings of the performances that could be later listened to on demand. On further questioning, we discovered that instead of the attendance at live performances going down, these recordings served as 'advertisements' for local musicians, keeping the listenership alive and growing.

To understand the mobile media use of these communities, we conducted interviews at 5 of approximately 10 mobile phone outlets in the neighboring town of Maksi. Not only do these businesses engage in the sales of mobile phones, they also often house a desktop computer that serves as a media library (of approx. 150-200 GB). A customer will often receive a full allotment of music as a perk for buying a phone, or for obtaining some other product or service.

In each of the shops we visited, we found that the shop assistants who operated the media library were about 15-20 years old, male, and had minimal technical training. They were well versed, however, in compiling various thematic assortments of media, maintaining directories of 1GB/2GB audio and video collections, which they would download onto various phones. Charges ranged across the shops from Rs. 20 to Rs. 80 ($0.5 to $2) for 2GB of content. There were no clear answers received for why this wide a range existed. One of the shop assistants said, however:

> "I have good knowledge of music. That is why I charge a greater price. Because quality is better."

Figure 2: A shop in Maksi (Malwa) that claims to fulfill every electronic need of its customer.

Since there was no Internet access available in Maksi, we were eager to know how the shop owners obtained their media libraries. We found that all of these came via physical storage media from shops (of relatives or family friends) in either Ujjain or Indore – the two major cities in Malwa. To further augment their collections, they often uploaded the content from a customer's mobile phone onto their own computer before downloading new content. Phone owners received no compensation or consideration for this practice.

Transition to Digital Stored Media

Most of these shops were previously electrical goods or photo-printing outfits, transitioning to become mobile phone outlets in the last 3-5 years, to address a rising demand for devices and music downloads. The transition from cassettes and CDs to mobile stored content has been steady. As one of the shop owners informed us:

> "We stopped keeping tapes [audio cassettes] four years ago. No one wants CDs anymore. Only mobile."

This transition to digital media was visible at other sites as well. At the community radio sites of Gurgaon and Bundelkhand, we found that the listeners frequently use their mobile phones to listen to the radio content (on speaker mode). One participant in Gurgaon shared that before the community radio station was launched, he did not have regular access to music.

> "Before *Gurgaon ki Awaaz*, I did not own any CDs or audio cassettes. Now, I listen to music of my choice [folk songs] all the time [on my phone], when possible even through the night."

In Bikaner, we observed pilgrims who walk 200 KM to attend the annual Ramdevra festival – in honor of Baba Ramdev, their spiritual deity. (The festival draws a crowd of around 1-1.5 million, of which 500-600,000 choose to walk.) Nearly all of these pilgrims listen to devotional folk songs on their mobile phones as they walk (with earphones attached). More pilgrims are choosing to walk, we were told, also because they have this constant source of entertainment with them.

Decline of Audio Shops and Recording Studios

While businesses that distribute music in the form of mobile downloads have multiplied in recent years, recording studios and audio-only shops appear to be on the decline. One of the shop owners we interviewed in Bikaner, who had been in this business for many years, said:

> "The market of CDs and audio cassettes has gone down by 85% in the last 3-5 years, ever since the mobile phone gained widespread use. People no longer want to listen to cassettes or CDs. They prefer mobile modes of listening."

His shop used to produce albums of folk musicians but he no longer earns a profit from this. He now rents his studio space to musicians and lets them take responsibility for their own distribution. This, however, requires an investment by the artist and has therefore not been a very successful business model thus far.

A Shared Experience

Our interviews indicated that almost every household – in each of our field sites - has one if not several mobile devices. The mobile phone acts not just as a personal listening device, but also a communal one. The desire to share musical experiences with one's friends and families was a common theme among the listeners we spoke to. One of our respondents from Gurgaon shared:

> "We listen mostly in groups. There are [usually] 2-3-4 of us. Kids also listen. Adults also listen. We listen together."

When asked how they share songs with their loved ones who may be away (at the time), one of the Gurgaon respondents said that he would call his friends and tell them to turn on and listen to the radio, or else he would record the piece using the audio recorder on his mobile phone.

From Audio to Video

Many listeners we interviewed across sites shared an increasing motivation to transition from audio content alone to video as well. Be it on the small screen of their mobile phones or on their DVD players at home, listeners like to watch video recordings of the musicians. One of the Malwa folk musicians we interviewed said:

> "Five years back, people were only interested in listening to music on cassettes, radio and CDs, but

> now people are demanding music with video. They don't buy if you don't give them songs recorded with video."

Some shop-owners work with local musicians to help them produce video recordings to address this demand.

PIRACY

A discussion about the production and distribution of music at our four sites would be incomplete without talking about piracy and how different segments of the community have responded to it.

The most straightforward and transparent approach to music distribution that we observed was at the community radio stations. The stations have low-tech recording studios of their own, and play only those songs that have been recorded there. For every recording, they sign an agreement with the musicians that, in return for allowing the musicians to record themselves live, they obtain the rights to air that recording on their station when they choose. In exchange, *Gurgaon ki Awaaz* provides the troupe of musicians with a CD of the recording that they can duplicate and share as they like.

We found that well-known and older folk musicians who could previously afford to sell their audio cassettes and CDs have lost a substantial portion of their potential earnings due to the widespread sale of pirated recordings. Lesser-known musicians do not have the notoriety or resources to obtain recordings in the first place. As a result, the folk music market is currently dominated by local individuals and businesses who use low-cost recording devices to obtain recordings from live performances and sell them at low cost to interested listeners, almost always without permission from the musicians.

We asked several folk musicians to share their views on this practice, and on piracy in general. The strongest opinion we heard against piracy was from one of the musicians in Bundelkhand who said:

> "The voice should have a price."

When asked to share their views on how this practice made them feel about their music – the fact that their CDs were reproduced without their earning the revenue from the sales – the general view was one of passive acceptance. A musician from Malwa said:

> "What can we do if a robber comes, steals our goods and runs away? It is not in our control."

When asked if they approved of the practice, musicians appeared convinced that it was unfair, but nevertheless, their primary interest was still in spreading the word of the great poets and saints from the folk traditions, whether or not they received remuneration for their art. As a result, many of the musicians' own opinions about piracy were ambivalent. One such artist from Bikaner offered a refreshingly positive outlook:

> "There is no solution for piracy. You just can't stop people from copying music and law doesn't work in this case. This kind of access to music for the common man shows that *music is priceless*. Now we can listen to one thousand songs by paying just Rs. 100 [$2]. Do you think we are paying for music? The shopkeeper is not charging for music; he is charging for the software in which he has invested."

Piracy leads to illegal but wider distribution of music and therefore also serves to extend the popularity and fame of many musicians. This could be an opportunity for increasing the remuneration for musicians through live performances– even for up and coming musicians who are not already well known. Echoing this sentiment, one Bikaner artist said:

> "Singers are still on the safe side because when people record our music on their mobile devices at any live performance, it spreads like fire. People get to know about our good performance only through these devices and we get publicity as well as more shows to perform at. On the one hand, the CD and cassette business has gone down, but on the other, the demand for our live performances is rising."

In general, illegal duplication of media content ("doubling") appears to be widespread and socially accepted. Local businesses that we interviewed in Malwa and Bikaner did not offer any resistance in sharing the details of their business with us. On the contrary, they were proud of showing off their large media libraries and how they obtained them. Listeners also benefited from cheap and ubiquitous access to folk content.

IMPLICATIONS FOR DESIGN

We summarize the key design implications resulting from our study here.

Money ~~versus~~ *and* Fame

Our interviews show that it is not one or the other, but both money *and* fame that are important to folk musicians. While they would certainly like to receive remuneration for their art, they do appreciate the patronage they receive on account of widespread (but illegal) distribution of their works.

Empowering Musicians with Technology

With the availability of low-cost and easy-to-use recording devices, the technological skills and capacity required for producing and distributing music need not be limited only to local businesses. Musicians and/or their troupes and families can be empowered to create, share, and market their own recordings. This would allow more musicians (and not just the more famous ones) to get their music into the market.

In this vein, one of the musicians we interviewed at Pugal (near Bikaner) shared his personal success story with us. Although folk music had run in his family for generations, he had performed only in his village and in Bikaner until four years ago when his talent was discovered by an outside filmmaker who produced a documentary that included his music [19]. Since then, he has had the chance to perform in several locations within India and even overseas, and earns enough from his music practice to have built a *pukka* (permanent) house and to put his children through school.

Audio and Video are Both Desirable

The influx of new media technologies such as DVDs, VCDs, and mobile phones has fueled the desire of users to partake of video as well as audio content. As a participant said, "Now we can see what we are listening to." This trend appears to please some while it makes others unhappy. An artist from Bikaner shared:

> "I don't like the way folk is presented on a television screen. Folk on television does not appear *jivant* (live). It is not good to see music instead of listening with proper attention."

Musicians Need Copyright Protection

The standard copyright procedures in India are both cumbersome and expensive. As a result, for the average folk artist, this is not worth the effort. If simpler and more affordable means for protecting content and compositions are made available to musicians, they may explore this possibility. The head of one of the community radio stations that we visited brought up this issue. He showed us a printout of the Copyright Act of India from 1957 [8]:

> "According to the Act, the artist has to pay Rs. 400 ($10) for every CD[1] that he wants to copyright. That is so expensive. Why will he do that for every CD will not sell in the local market for more than Rs. 20-30 ($0.5)?"

On the other hand, excessive protection and enforcement might limit the spread of folk music, limiting its spiritual reach and musicians' opportunities for patronage through live performances and other appearances. In that case, a Creative Commons type of license, which maintains attribution and provides certain relaxed protections against unauthorized profiting, might be more appropriate [9].

Managing and Appreciating Large Media Libraries

Due to the increase in piracy and low-cost distribution, the quality of music the community is listening to has also suffered. Access to a much wider variety of musicians, recordings and recording qualities may also lead to a less cultivated sense of taste and thoughtful listening. As an artist from Bikaner stated:

> "Those who have 500 songs in their mobiles are constantly changing songs without paying attention to any particular song. They don't know what to listen to."

[1] It costs Rs. 50 to copyright a single song. Assuming there are at least 8 songs on a CD, it would take Rs. 400 to copyright a CD.

CONCLUSION

Our research study focused on the emergence of new mobile media sharing practices related to folk music in the communities of Malwa, Bundelkhand, Bikaner, and Gurgaon. Through the use of a combination of qualitative methods at each of these sites, we sought answers to three main questions:

(i) *What are various motivations underlying the sharing and listening of folk music within these communities?*

(ii) *How are new media technologies influencing these practices and supporting these motivations?*

(iii) *How do considerations of piracy interact with these changes?*

Our findings show that 1) there are a diverse set of motivations for performing and listening to folk music, 2) new media technologies are helping folk musicians become more popular and reach new audiences, while also reducing some streams of revenue, particularly for businesses engaged only in music production and distribution, and 3) as expected, piracy is widely tolerated by musicians, both out of apathy and an interest in reaching new audiences, thereby increasing the reach of their message, and their own fame and associated patronage. Based on these findings, we propose some implications for the design of an appropriate folk music sharing and distribution service that addresses these various motivations of the musicians and listeners.

ACKNOWLEDGMENTS

We thank the *Kabir Project*, *Gram Vaani*, *Gurgaon Ki Awaaz*, and *Radio Bundelkhand* for their assistance and guidance along the way. We also thank the folk musicians, local patrons and retailers who took the time to participate in our study and share their experiences.

REFERENCES

1. M. H. Allen. Tales Tunes Tell: Deepening the Dialogue between "Classical" and "Non-Classical" in the Music of India. *Yearbook for Traditional Music* 30:22-52. 1998.
2. R. C. Allen and A. Hill. *The Television Studies Reader.* Routledge. 2003.
3. E. Bellman. Cellphone Entertainment Takes Off in Rural India. *The Wall Street Journal*. November 22, 2009.
4. R. Bharucha. *Rajasthan: An Oral History: Conversations with Komal Kothari*. Penguin Books, New Delhi, 2003.
5. G. Booth. Religion, Gossip, Narrative Conventions and the Construction of Meaning in Hindi Film Songs. In *Popular Music 19 (2)*. Cambridge: Cambridge University Press, pp. 125-145. 2000.
6. *Census of India*, 2001.

7. *Community Radio in India Includes Report on Eclipse, 'Bundeli Idol'* http://www.pbs.org/idealab/2009/08/community-radio-in-india-includes-report-on-eclipse-bundeli-idol219.html
8. *Copyright Act of India 1957* http://copyright.gov.in/Documents/CopyrightRules1957.pdf
9. *Creative Commons License* http://creativecommons.org
10. A. Dutta. Nation, Liberalisation and Film Songs: Technology and Hybridisation in Contemporary Hindi Film Music. *Widescreen.* 2009. http://widescreenjournal.org/index.php/journal/article/viewArticle/14/12
11. R. Gandhi, R. Veeraraghavan, K. Toyama, and V. Ramprasad. Digital Green: Participatory video for agricultural extension. In *Proceedings of IEEE/ACM Conference on Information and Communication Technology and Development* (Bangalore, India), December 2007.
12. I. Grandin. Music and Media in Local Life: Music Practice in a Newar Neighbourhood in Nepal. Linkoping University, Department of Communication Studies. 1989.
13. P. D. Greene. *Cassettes In Culture: Emotion, Politics, and Performance in Rural Tamil Nadu.* PhD dissertation, University of Pennsylvania. 1995.
14. P. D. Greene. Authoring the Folk: the crafting of a rural popular music in south India. *Journal of Intercultural Studies*, 22: 2, pp. 161 – 172. 2001.
15. *Gurgaon Ki Awaaz* http://www.trfindia.org/community_radio.php
16. L. Hess. Kabir in Schools: Pilot Project in Dewas & Ujjain Districts of Madhya Pradesh. *Final Report.* April, 2010.
17. H. Jenkins. *Convergence Culture: Where Old and New Media Collide.* NYU Press. 2006.
18. K. Johnson. *Television and Social Change in Rural India.* Sage Publications. 2000.
19. *The Kabir Project* www.kabirproject.org
20. M. Kam, A. Kumar, S. Jain, A. Mathur, and J. Canny. Improving Literacy in Rural India: Cellphone Games in an After-School Program. In *Proceedings of IEEE/ACM Conference on Information and Communication Technology and Development* (Doha, Qatar), April 17-19, 2009.
21. H. Kumar. Folk Media and Rural Development. *Indian Media Studies Journal*. 1:1. 2006.
22. N. Kumar and T. S. Parikh. New Media and Folk Music in Rural India. In *CHI 2010: Extended Abstracts on Human Factors in Computing Systems* (Atlanta, Georgia), April 10-15, 2010.
23. S. Marcus. Recycling Indian Film-Songs: Popular Music as a Source of Melodies for North Indian Folk Musicians. *Asian Music (24) 1.* Austin: University of Texas Press, pp. 101-110. 1992.
24. P. Manuel. *Cassette Culture: Popular Music and Technology in North India.* University of Chicago Press. 1993.
25. B. Meyer and A. Moors. *Religion, Media, and the Public Sphere.* Indiana University Press. 2005.
26. D. Mukhopadhyay. Folk Arts and Traditional Media for Peace, Education and Conflict Resolution. 2008.
27. J. L. Ng'ombe. The communication model and folk media in development. *Sustainable Development Dimensions* http://www.fao.org/sd/CDdirect/CDan0029.htm, Food and Agriculture Organization. 2000.
28. R. Obregón, K. Chitnis, C. Morry, W. Feek, J. Bates, M. Galway. Achieving polio eradication: a review of health communication evidence and lessons learned in India and Pakistan. *Bulletin of the World Health Organization.* 87:624-30. 2009.
29. A. Paige. Acoustic Entanglements: Negotiating Folk Music in Naiyanti Melam Performance. *Indian Folklore Research Journal.* 2009.
30. S. Panford. Using folk media in HIV/AIDS prevention in rural Ghana. *American Journal of Public Health.* 91:1559–1562. 2001.
31. N. Patel, D. Chittamuru, A. Jain, P. Dave, T. S. Parikh. Avaaj Otalo: A Field Study of an Interactive Voice Forum for Small Farmers in Rural India. In *Proceedings of ACM Conference on Human Factors in Computing Systems* (Atlanta, Georgia), April 10-15, 2010.
32. *Piracy Costs Indian Music Industry 325 Million* http://www.radioandmusic.com/content/editorial/news/piracy-costs-indian-music-industry-325-mn-ey#story
33. *Radio Bundelkhand* www.devalt.org/radio.pdf
34. D. Ramachandran, J. Canny, P. D. Das, E. Cutrell. Mobile-izing Health Workers in Rural India. In *Proceedings of ACM Conference on Human Factors in Computing Systems* (Atlanta, Georgia), April 10-15, 2010.
35. *Saarthak* http://www.saarthakindia.org/index_files/Page382.htm
36. D. Sharma. Nautanki vs. Mass media: Exploring the Role of Community Folk Performances in the Age of New Media Forms and Technology. *NCA 93rd Annual Convention.* Chicago, Illinois. November 14, 2007.
37. T. Smyth, S. Kumar, I. Medhi, K. Toyama. Where There's a Will There's a Way: Mobile Media Sharing in Urban India. In *Proceedings of ACM Conference on Human Factors in Computing Systems* (Atlanta, Georgia), April 10-15, 2010.

38. D. M. Frohlich, D. Rachovides, K. Riga, R. Bhat, M. Frank, E. Edirisinghe, D. Wickramanayaka, M. Jones, and W. Harwood. StoryBank: mobile digital storytelling in a development context. In *Proceedings of ACM Conference on Human Factors in Computing Systems* (Boston, Massachusetts), 2009.

39. B. Glaser and A. Strauss. *The discovery of grounded theory: Strategies for Qualitative Research.* Chicago, IL: Aldine De Gruyther, 1967.

Designing for Emerging Rural Users: Experiences from China

Elisa Oreglia*, Ying Liu†, Wei Zhao†

School of Information, UC Berkeley*
Berkeley, CA 94720
elisa@ischool.berkeley.edu

IBM Research China†
Beijing, China 100193
{aliceliu, weizhao}@cn.ibm.com

ABSTRACT
As part of IBM's Smarter Planet initiative, we studied information-sharing practices in rural Northern China to understand if and how ICT can help rural residents improve their lives. Interviews and participant observation in two villages showed a profusion of ICT devices, as well as an abundance of face-to-face information exchanges, but a shortage of localized and easily accessible information, and a deep dependence of many rural residents on 'information brokers' such as agricultural extension workers and shop owners. Can ICT support existing practices of information sharing among rural residents, when these practices are largely based on face-to-face encounters and passive reception of information? We argue that in such an environment, ICT should build on existing social habits even if less than ideal, rather than trying to transform them, and we outline a possible way to do so.

Author Keywords
Rural users, developing regions, methods, information-sharing, information brokers.

ACM Classification Keywords
H5.m. Information interfaces and presentation (e.g., HCI): Miscellaneous.

General Terms
Human Factors.

INTRODUCTION
In the past fifteen years, the Chinese government has invested heavily to extend the infrastructure to secure access to Information and Communication Technologies (ICT) in rural areas, in order to support the adoption and use of ICT among rural residents [15]. The fast-increasing number of Internet users (420 million as of June 2010, 364 million of whom use broadband) [2] and of mobile phone sets (more than 539 million in 2009) [8] is therefore taking place in an environment that has been intentionally designed to encourage and support such growth.

Within the context of its Smarter Planet initiative, centered around the idea that data captured by interconnected digital devices can be used to create more efficient and intelligent systems, IBM Research China is seeking to better understand the living conditions of rural Chinese residents, in order to develop innovative solutions for 'smart villages.' Rural residents are the fastest growing segment of ICT adopters [2], so in January 2010 we began a project to study ICT use in rural Shandong through secondary source analyses, ethnographic field work, identification of existing problems and opportunities, as well as possible solutions. This paper describes the methods we used to define our scope and to identify areas with a potential for ICT to support existing social practices, as well as a scenario that builds on our findings. As the system that we envisioned for improving the efficiency of information exchanges is still under development, we only describe some of its key features as far as they are related to our findings.

RELATED LITERATURE
Given our focus on the economic conditions of rural residents, we concentrated on two aspects of rural life: existing practices of information gathering and sharing, and the current state of ownership and use of ICT. First we referred to work on the rural conditions in Shandong, in order to get basic data about farming practices, agricultural activities, farmers, and other actors such as small traders, small entrepreneurs, agricultural extension workers, etc [4, 6, 10]. Then we looked at research on Human-Computer Interaction for Development (HCID), whose main concerns are summarized in [3]. The focus on 'community-centered design' rather 'user-centered design' advocated by HCID practitioners was well-taken, although 'family-centered' ended up being more appropriate to our circumstances. This was a useful discovery, because many if not most rural families have members who migrated to urban areas and who can provide a link to urban resources, as suggested also by research on Chinese migrant workers and ICT [5, 7]. [12] discussion of orality versus literacy provided a key to understand the preference for face-to-face information exchanges (discussed below) even in a context where most people have basic literacy skills. Another important theme in HCID is 'intermediated technology use,' where people who cannot use ICT on their own because of illiteracy, lack of appropriate skills, lack of access, etc, can still benefit from it by relying on third parties [11]. India has been a testing ground for projects meant to facilitate intermediated technology use [9, 11, 13], but their findings

are not directly applicable to China, where there is a high level of literacy. This means that 'intermediated use' is often a temporary phase that can lead to independent use, unlike the scenarios highlighted in much HCID literature, that require long-term intermediated access. Moreover, compared to other emerging regions, China has a much more stable and developed infrastructure, eliminating many of the problems highlighted in [1, 3] and others. At the same time, the country faces many of the same challenges that emerging regions do, in the inefficiency of its markets, in a vast rural population of semi-skilled small-hold farmers, poor quality schooling, and quite simply, poverty of a magnitude that does not exist in countries that are more evenly developed economically. In fact, the peculiar situation of China in relation to ICT and, to a certain extent, to the challenges that China poses to HCI has been the subject of a handful of papers. The use of ICT in the Chinese countryside has been explored by [14, 16, 17, 18, 19]; with the exception of [19], which is a broad survey undertaken in different regions, all the other papers are small-scale qualitative case studies, useful for seeing the details of use and understanding local conditions. These studies all agree that information-sharing practices among farmers are mostly based on face-to-face encounters, even when more convenient, reliable, and cheaper alternatives exist.

RESEARCH FINDINGS

We did our field work in two villages in north-west and south-west Shandong, and in the course of eight months, we visited each twice, from one to two weeks. We lived in local residents' houses, conducted participant observation sessions that included helping farmers in the fields, and carried out open-ended and semi-structured interviews with 28 people. Interviews were transcribed and coded. Each visit was followed by extensive debriefing and further literature review. We found that there is:

1. Abundance of information, but scarce localization

Agricultural information, information about markets, weather forecasts, information about policies relevant to the countryside are all widely available, but this can hide the fact that the more specialized and more localized information that farmers need is not easy to discover or access, and is usually not available in the form preferred by farmers. On one side there is an abundance of websites and publications about markets, weather conditions, pests, subsidies, etc. On the other, there are farmers who for the most part do not read nor use the Internet, get most of their information from oral sources (e.g. face-to-face or television), and are not familiar with or have forgotten the use of *pinyin* (the system used to input Chinese characters on mobile phones or computers). Getting reliable information is therefore a laborious task:

> *"First I watch the national weather report on television; then I watch the local one; then I compare them with the weather forecast I get on my mobile. Then I analyze this information and come up with my forecast, and it's 70% reliable" (Farmer Liu, Village A)*

2. Abundance of ICT, but under-utilization

Mobile phones are very widespread: in many rural families, adults each had their own. However, they were substantially under-utilized. In particular, the most commonly used functions were making and receiving calls, (with a rather low use of text messaging on the part of people older than 40), and the radio, common on Chinese mobile phones, which people found good company when they were working in the fields. In general, when asked what other functions their mobiles had, older people often did not know and sometimes just handed their mobile to the researchers to find out for themselves. It is also very common to see people carry around small address books where they write down phone numbers, because they don't know how to input them directly on the phone, and are afraid of losing precious contacts.

Computers (with broadband internet connections, available even in villages) are increasingly popular, although for now generally limited to young couples (it is becoming a common wedding gift), or families with children of school age. Use is mostly geared towards entertainment, although younger people, often returned migrants, are beginning to experiment with different types of use. For example, the 27-year-old owner of a rural 'computer hospital' in Village A has just opened his own virtual shop on Taobao.com, an online market similar to ebay. He is not sure how he is going to use it, but he is sure that some form of e-commerce is important in order to expand his business. However, ownership often does not equate with usage: the owner of a seed shop has a computer, and excitedly told us that if farmers have problems with their crop, they can bring the concerned plants to his shop and he can get in touch via video-conference with the experts at the headquarters of the seed company. On our second visit, though, he admitted that this was something he saw when he participated in training organized by the seed company, and that in fact his computer was not connected to the internet and seldom used. Nonetheless, he thought it gave his customers a good impression of his shop.

3. Prevalence of oral/face-to-face information exchange

The main sources of information about all aspects of life are neighbors, traders, shop-keepers, local government officials (often through village-wide loud-speakers), agricultural extension workers, and television. The way farmers sell wheat, which we witnessed during our field visit in June, is illustrative. Buyers travel to villages, on small trucks. They stop at a well-trafficked corner, and announce their arrival through a loud speaker. Farmers gather and ask what is their offer, mostly to double-check the price, which they already know from neighbors, or from the national index, or, in one case in Village B, from a neighbor who checked online. Everybody concurred that price is not a real issue in their decision. The window to sell wheat is not very long: if the weather is hot and dry, the wheat dries up and weighs less; if it's raining, then it risks mold. Farmers hold out for a few days to see if better offers come, but then sell for a price that is usually the same as the one offered by the first buyer.

They do not establish long-term relations with buyers, and they do not travel themselves to markets in bigger villages or in cities, even though the roads are good, because the trouble involved is not considered worthwhile. Mrs Yang, in Village B, calculated that the difference between selling to a random buyer in the village and going to the county market would amount to about 60 Renminbi, or 9 US$, which she did not consider worth the time and hassle necessary. It is worth noting that for most of the families we interviewed, farming was only one source of income, supplemented by seasonal work in nearby cities or remittances from children in the city.

Even when farmers can and do access directly information, they still rely on their existing social infrastructure, which includes public officials such as the village head or agricultural extension workers. Historically, the relationship between farmers and government officials has not always been felicitous, but current policies to develop the countryside are beginning to rebuild some trust between the state and farmers, at least in the areas we surveyed. When asked what was the event that most changed their lives in the past 10 years, many farmers answered that it was the abolition of the agricultural tax in 2006, and the introduction of farming subsidies. People in various positions of power are very much part of the information-sharing process, and are not necessarily or entirely distrusted: in fact, many farmers are aware of specific individuals' biases, and take them into account when evaluating the information they receive. For example, two farmers said that they knew that their agricultural extension officer was getting money on the side from the company that made the seeds he was telling them to buy, but they thought that his advice on crop diseases was valid.

4. Lack of crop diversification

In the areas we surveyed, the main crops are wheat, corn, sweet potato, peanuts, apples. Farmers favor them because the sale prices are stable, although low, and predictable:

> *"This year the price of garlic is 5RMB per jin! (US$ .75 per pound) And I'm not growing any! I grew garlic four years ago, because they said I would make money. That year it sold for 2 mao per jin (US$0.03) and I lost money. Now I just grow wheat and corn, at least it's safe." (Farmer Cui, Village B)*

Many farmers have heard about more lucrative crops, but they are uncertain on how to switch, and they do not know if there are ways to manage risks. The only farmer we interviewed who grew an unusual crop did so because an agricultural extension worker came to her village, trained the farmers, and connected them to a buyer in the city.

DISCUSSION

The most interesting challenge to emerge from our field work is illustrated in the answer farmer Liu gave when asked what he does if his crop has a problem:

> *"I ask the neighbors, but if they don't know, we wait for the agricultural extension worker to come and tell us, and if it is a really big problem, we see if it is on television. Otherwise, we have to put up with it, there's no other way."*

He owns a mobile phone, and has two university-educated daughters who can use the internet and could help him. In fact, he is well aware of the possibilities offered by the internet, because when he decided to buy a new refrigerator he asked his daughters to check the price online, to see if he was getting a good deal. However, he does not think the Internet can help with farming: he thinks he is too old to learn, and his daughters not knowledgeable enough to look things up on his behalf. Our main research question then became: can current ICT, still heavily text-based, increase opportunities for rural residents used to face-to-face information exchanges and to being told information from television and experts – rather than asking for it?

We found that rural ICT users tend to fall into one of three categories. The first are *independent users*, typically younger people, who can use mobiles and/or computers without constant help from outsiders, and who can learn new tasks and functions by themselves, or from their peers. Few farmers belong to this category, because young people tend to migrate to urban areas and those left behind are older, but their children often do. Belonging to the second category are *dependent users*, who can use mobiles and sometimes computers, but only under the tutelage of other people, like their children or spouses. These users learn a limited number of tasks by repeating the instructions their 'tutors' provide, but are very unlikely to explore further functions by themselves, out of fear of 'breaking the machine.' Finally, there are *proxy users*, that is people who do not own computers and have never used the internet directly, but are aware not only of its existence, but also of the possibilities it offers. These people will, on occasion, mobilize their helpers to find information online on their behalf, as Farmer Liu did with his daughters. This taxonomy can be further extended, as suggested by [11], and we may well do so when we reach the pilot phase. What is important now is the differentiation between users who can progress from intermediated to independent use, and users who are likely to remain dependent. The existing village organization supports a certain amount of interaction among the three categories, and 'information brokers,' i.e. people who either have access to more or better information, or are more proficient in using ICT and can therefore help end users find the information they want, play a particularly important role. These 'information brokers' can be family members, who live in the village or who have migrated to urban areas and remain in touch through mobile phones, but also institutional figures, such as agricultural extension workers; university graduates, who spend up to three years in the countryside as support to local administrators and whose job is often to find information on the internet; shop owners like the one in Village B who sells computers, but is also de facto consultant for 'all things internet' for his rural clients, including occasionally finding agricultural information.

'Information brokers' can typically use ICT proficiently, but do not always know what kind of information farmers need, or how to evaluate what they find online; the rural residents they help also use ICT, but do not have the technical knowledge to use them well. We believe that it is possible to use ICT in a more effective way to connect different types of users and their different types of knowledge and skills. The system we are designing would allow 1. multiple access points to existing information, so that, for example, information can be accessed on a computer by an agricultural extension worker and then sent to farmers through text messages, or accessed directly by farmers; 2. multi-device access; 3. localization: interviewees stressed the importance of getting information on market prices nearby, or local weather forecasts; 4. the development of third-party services so that there can be a commercial as well as a government-supported source of content. With such a system, an agricultural extension worker could check the system for information useful for farmers, which is collected from websites he and his office know and trust. To spread information more efficiently, he can ask all the farmers who come to visit him in person to subscribe to a weekly SMS service, so they can receive updates on the most important issues he comes across. Every week, he composes an SMS with information such as localized weather report; pests; changes of prices in the agricultural products of the area; new rules that concern farmers. Thus, the information received by the farmers is screened by an expert, and is localized. Moreover, if the information is useful, farmers are ready to pay for it, as proven by the popularity of weather report SMS subscriptions, which cost about 3 RMB per month (US$ .4).

CONCLUSION

ICT have the potential to expand the opportunities of rural residents, especially in an information-rich environment such as China. However, the majority of semi-literate middle-aged rural residents is unlikely to learn to find and evaluate this information by themselves. Existing social practices are usually based on partially mediated access to information, and if information brokers often may act as gate-keeper, they can also enable people who would not be able to access information to at least partially do so. The use cases we are developing aim at improving the quality of and access to information for all parties, and at supporting farmers in choosing, evaluating, and acting upon information in an incremental rather than sudden way.

REFERENCES

1. Brewer, E. et al. The challenges of technology research for developing regions. *IEEE Pervasive Computing 5*, 2 (2006), 15-23.
2. CNNIC. *The 26th survey report on the Internet development in China.* 15 July 2010.
3. Dearden, A. User-centered design considered harmful. *ITID 4*, 3 (2008), 7-12.
4. Huang J. et al. Markets, specialization and China's agriculture. *Working paper for Food and Agricultural Organisation*, Center for Chinese Agricultural Policy, Chinese Academy of Sciences, Beijing, China, 2005.
5. Lang X. et al. Social practices and mobile phone use of young migrant workers. In *Proc. MobileHCI2010*, ACM Press (2010), 59-62.
6. Li, B. Shandong agricultural products exports. *International Journal of Business and Management 4*, 3 (2009), 62-65.
7. Liu X. et al. Design for China's migrant workers: A case of user research and mobile product concepts development. In *Proc. HCD09*, Springer-Verlag, Berling, Heidelberg, 482-491.
8. MIIT. Statistics on fixed phone users by Province as of January 2010. March 8, 2010.
9. Parikh, T. et al. Understanding and designing for intermediated information tasks in India. *IEEE Pervasive Computing 5*, 2 (2006), 32-39.
10. Rozelle, S. The nature of China's food economy. Presentation at the Inclusive Business in Agrifood Markets. Beijing, China, March 5-6, 2008.
11. Sambavisan N. et al. Intermediated technology use in developing communities. In *Proc. CHI2010*, ACM Press (2010), 2583-2592.
12. Sherwani J. et al. Orality-grounded HCID: Understanding the oral user. *Information Technologies and International Development 5*, 4 (2009), 37-49.
13. Sukumaran, A. et al. Intermediated technology interaction in rural contexts. In *Ext Abstracts CHI 2009,* ACM Press (2009), 3817-3822.
14. Ulrich, P. Poverty reduction through access to information and communication technologies in rural areas. *The Electronic Journal on Information Systems in Developing Countries 16*, 7 (2004), 1-38.
15. Xia, J. Linking ICTs to rural development: China's rural information policy. *Government Information Quarterly 27*, 2 (2010), 187-195.
16. Zhang, M. et al. Knowledge, attitude, and home Internet adoption in rural China: A case of Hubei, *China Media Research 5*, 4 (2009), 1-12.
17. Zhao, J. ICT4D: Internet adoption and usage among rural users in China. *Knowledge, Technology & Policy, 21*, 1 (2008), 9-18.
18. Zhao, J. Integrating the Internet into farming activities: A study of farmer users in Shandong Province, China. *Science Technology & Society* 13, 2 (2008), 325-244.
19. Zhong, Y. Information services in rural China: Field surveys and findings. *RAP Publication*, 2004/03. Bangkok, FAO, 2004.

Adapting Usability Testing for Oral, Rural Users

Trina Gorman[1], Emma Rose[2], Judith Yaaqoubi[2], Andrew Bayor[1], Beth Kolko[2]

[1]Literacy Bridge
1904 Third Avenue, Suite 733
Seattle, WA 98101, USA

[2]Department of Human Centered Design & Engineering
Box 352315, University of Washington
Seattle, WA 98195, USA

trina@literacybridge.org, ejrose@uw.edu, judithy@uw.edu, andy@literacybridge.org, bkolko@uw.edu

ABSTRACT

Traditional usability methods are of limited use when evaluating systems designed for distant, diverse populations. In this paper, we describe a study conducted in two Ghanaian villages that evaluated an audio computer designed for people living in oral cultures. Informed by ICTD and orality-grounded HCID, we modified existing usability testing practices and we reflect on the utility of these adaptations. We found that conducting a culturally appropriate study often meant forgoing more traditional approaches in favor of flexible, opportunistic methods. We acknowledge the challenges of adapting traditional usability methods for oral, rural users. However, we found that by implementing strategic modifications led by local staff, our study produced valuable, actionable results.

Author Keywords

user-centered design, usability testing, standards, illiteracy, oral cultures, methodologies, audio technology, ICTD.

ACM Classification Keywords

H.5.1. Information interfaces and presentation: Multimedia Information Systems.

General Terms

Design, Experimental, Human Factors, Languages

INTRODUCTION

There is a growing acknowledgement that technology can assist with poverty alleviation efforts. However, as products are created by an eclectic group of people—from nonprofit organizations and for-profit companies to academics—designers face new obstacles in being able to iterate and evaluate for distant populations [1]. Distance, in this regard, can be geographic, cultural, or cognitive, and operative gaps can include issues of language, literacy, disability, and others. Techniques like usability testing become especially challenging when working with people who are distant in one or more of these ways. Usability testing is an accepted method in Human Computer Interaction (HCI) research used to determine how well a product works for its intended users and how it can be improved. While usability best practices and standards are well established [2, 3], what is lacking from the literature is a thorough understanding of how these approaches translate into diverse contexts. Furthermore, the little research that has been done suggests that many traditional approaches either do not transfer well within these settings [4, 5] or have to be modified [5, 6].

What follows is a summary of a study we conducted with oral, rural people. This work is informed by Information and Communication for Development (ICTD) literature including orality-grounded HCID as proposed by Sherwani, et al [5]. Sherwani is among the small group of researchers who stress the challenges of designing for oral users [7-9]. In particular, Sherwani says it is arguable whether traditional usability methods are of much analytical value.

Below we discuss traditional usability approaches and how our study differed. We then elaborate on where the adaptations were successful (or ineffective) and what we learned as a result. Our intention is that lessons learned will be instructive to others conducting usability research with oral users, rural communities, and when devices are shared among users. We use the term 'oral' instead of 'illiterate' because it highlights a person's ability. Or, as Sherwani says, because "terms like 'illiterate' devalue the identity and knowledge of oral cultures by implicitly suggesting that lack of literacy is equivalent to 'backwardness.'"

USABILITY STUDY: THE TALKING BOOK

To share locally relevant information with and among oral people who live without electricity, Literacy Bridge created the Talking Book (Figure 1). The Talking Book is a handheld, durable, battery-powered device that enables users to create and listen to recordings and copy recordings between devices. To access recordings, users are guided by audio prompts, to which they respond with key presses. For instance, right and left arrows navigate through categories (e.g. health, agriculture, stories) and once in a category, the up and down arrows rotate through individual messages.

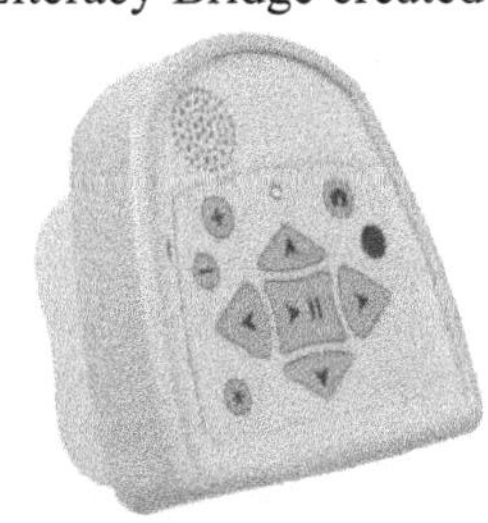

Figure 1: The Talking Book

Our study took place in two Ghanaian villages (Charia and Ving Ving), which are representative of Literacy Bridge's target population. Each village has between 1000 and 1500 residents, almost all residents are farmers, and literacy levels are low (~10%). In terms of infrastructure, Charia has intermittent electricity and mobile network connectivity; Ving Ving has no electricity and weak mobile connectivity in a few areas.

Goals

Our goal was to improve the Talking Book to make it easier for oral people to use. Specific research questions included: 1) Are the audio system instructions unclear or hard to follow? 2) Which button icons are more difficult to decipher and navigate with? 3) What tasks or parts of the information architecture are more challenging for users?

Challenges

Conducting usability studies for the Talking Book presented a variety of challenges. First, the target users for the device are oral and therefore think, learn, and process information differently compared to those who have been taught to read and write [5]. This meant that while conducting the study and considering solutions, we had to try to understand the thought processes of oral people, which can be radically different from our own. Second, the target users also have limited exposure to technology. As a result, most users needed a detailed introduction as well as training prior to the study—making it difficult to determine if a usability problem was the result of the device or the training method. Third, this device was designed to fill the global need of getting verbal information to people in developing regions. Therefore, we could only consider changes that would benefit the entire targeted demographic. Lastly, we had a diverse team including members with local expertise and members with usability expertise, but no members with both skillsets.

To overcome these challenges, Literacy Bridge's staff from the United States worked with usability researchers to create an initial plan that considered traditional approaches. We then altered those approaches using existing literature and our field experiences [1, 5, 12]. Next, we worked with local staff who live and work in the region to adapt our plan to be culturally appropriate.

ADAPTED METHODOLOGIES FOR USABILITY TESTING

Study team

In traditional usability methods, trained facilitators ensure sessions are consistent and that data is collected in a systematic way. In our study, we asked local staff who had no previous usability experience to facilitate sessions [5]. We trained them on basic usability techniques, the goals of our study, and on orality-grounded HCID. Local staff then took ownership of the study while we played more of an advising role. We chose to favor cultural appropriateness over methodological expertise. This helped us ensure the findings were based on problems with the device and not on the misinterpretation of cultural norms.

Location and Test Equipment

Usability studies are often conducted in a lab that mimics a familiar location, such as an office or a home. Labs enable researchers to repeat conditions consistently and to use equipment (such as one way mirrors) to collect data. For our study, a "familiar" location meant outside in a village, typically under a tree or in a common area (Figure 2).

Figure 2: Typical setting for a usability study

This setting made it more difficult to ensure privacy. Passersby would sometimes stop to see what we were doing, which was at times distracting to both facilitators and participants. However, the location also created unique learning opportunities. For example, one day we had too many participants who wanted to be involved and it was inappropriate to ask them to leave. After brainstorming as a team, we split up and were able to explore more scenarios with a more diverse group compared to our initial plan. This setting also meant that our data collection methods (video, note taking) were visible to users—a practice that is commonly avoided. We stopped using a still camera almost immediately as it was disruptive. However, using a small, inconspicuous video camera was less noticeable and enabled us to view the study after the fact. In the future we plan to use the Talking Book to capture keystrokes as well.

So while there were drawbacks to this uncontrolled setting, we found that being creative with existing resources ensured our team had an effective work setting and our participants were in a familiar environment.

Participants and Testing in Groups

Typically, in more developed regions, users are given a single product to use and sessions are conducted 1:1 so the facilitator can view the user's progress without other influences. However, in Literacy Bridge's programs, users often share Talking Books and teach one another how to use them. Therefore, we conducted our sessions in groups to simulate how users experience the device in practice. Our groups included men and women between the ages of 20 and 35. None of the adults we worked with were literate; all were farmers and had little to no access to technology. We also worked with smaller numbers of students and the elderly. To recruit these groups, we approached the village chief to discuss our plans and gain his support. Not only was this necessary to show respect, but we also learned of existing rivalries in the village; his involvement meant we did not exacerbate problems by favoring one group over another. Working with the chief also helped us assemble participants who knew each other, which proved to have pros and cons. For example, having users from the same social group (family, close friends) helped ensure they were comfortable—participants interacted socially, joking and laughing at times. However, one woman was teased by her husband because he thought she should be learning more quickly. She became self-conscious and lost confidence in her ability. When forming groups, researchers should anticipate negative consequences like this, particularly for those who tend to be marginalized, such as women.

Introduction and Training

It is common practice for facilitators to give users only a brief introduction to a product and limit training. Since our users were unfamiliar with technology, including the Talking Book, we needed to thoroughly introduce the device and train users on how to use it.

As Sherwani et al., point out, oral people do not internalize new information the same way as literate people. Based on our experience conducting studies in other developing contexts, we have also seen firsthand participants struggle with abstract introductions and scenarios. Therefore, the facilitator explained the device as a concrete solution to a local problem [5]. For example, the facilitator spoke of how complicated farming can be; participants agreed that each crop variety required detailed instructions. The facilitator then asked if they were satisfied with extension visits; participants said no, officers did not come often enough. The facilitator then explained how they can get relevant information from the officer through the Talking Book—at which point they saw value in the device and were interested in learning more.

In addition, we found that a compelling introduction was important because it affected a person's desire to use the device and therefore how quickly they learned. For example, one elderly woman appeared unmotivated and did not even seem to try. Following the session, she said she did not need to learn because her grandson could relay the information to her. Therefore, specifically tailoring and/or personalizing introductions was important—particularly for those who were intimidated by technology.

After introducing the device, we tried two training methods—both of which were centered around repeated practice and apprenticeship, which is how oral people learn [5]. First, the facilitator taught interactively through demonstration. After performing the task repeatedly and explaining each step, he/she asked a participant to perform the task as the others watched. The facilitator repeated until all tasks had been covered and all users had used the device. Second, we tried ways of having participants adopt the role of trainer: users trained each other in front of the group; users trained each other privately; users took the devices home after our session to continue practicing and learning from each other.

While each approach had drawbacks, we had success with both facilitator and peer training methods. Peer training away from the facilitators proved to be particularly successful. This could be because participants felt more comfortable in their homes or away from the team. When we led the training, it was necessary to continually adapt. For example, when requesting that a participant perform a task, it was important to alter the task so users did not just memorize button presses. The method that was least effective was having new users train each other in front of the group—perhaps because of performance anxiety or because the selected users were simply not strong teachers. In the future, we will try 'training the trainer' to see if brief guidance would improve their training methods. Peer training and facilitation need more investigation, but are promising techniques for others to consider.

Facilitation

Typically, to elicit naturalistic behavior, facilitators avoid intervening when a user struggles with a task. During our study, we often did the opposite and encouraged users to help each other, which aligns with how devices are used in practice. While this approach made it difficult to track the learning pace of users, it had various benefits. For example, it allowed the facilitator to learn a better way to explain something. Peer assistance also revealed when participants did not fully understand the device when he/she offered incorrect assistance. When it was necessary for the facilitator to intervene, he/she did not just offer minimal prompts as is typical, but rather thoroughly taught the task as before—explaining it in a slightly different way or adding a helpful tip. Since redundancy is an important part of oral communication [5], it is likely that the repetition of the training and facilitation method helped users to learn.

The think aloud protocol (TAP) is a common technique, but one that was not feasible in our study for a variety of reasons. We were concerned that thinking out loud would make participants uncomfortable since they would be expected to articulate confusion in front of peers. This would be the case for any device that is shared among users. In addition, Talking Book users must listen to the instructions to operate it. Having users talking while the device was talking would have been chaotic—an important realization for orally-delivered information technology.

Data Collection

In this study, collecting data was more difficult than in traditional studies not only because of the location, as previously mentioned, but also due to the varying skillsets of our team: local staff did not have usability experience; staff from the United States did not speak the local dialect. To work around these restrictions, local staff took notes in English focusing primarily on qualitative measures (underlying reasons for problems, meaningful social dynamics). English speaking staff found it particularly helpful when note takers wrote down verbatim quotes from users. They also found that success indicators were often unnecessary because they could typically follow a user's progress through facial expressions and tone of speech. Another technique that helped bridge the language divide was when facilitators made brief comments in English during the session or when English speaking staff asked questions to clarify something that had occurred. This helped ensure all staff were involved in learning and could help alter plans to take advantage of learning opportunities.

CONCLUSION

What worked well in our study was working with local staff to alter methods in two primary ways. First, we mimicked how the device is used in practice by incorporating familiar surroundings, group interaction, and peer training. Second, we prioritized cultural appropriateness over avoiding bias in how we facilitated sessions and collected data.

Many of the adaptations we chose meant our study was less controlled than a traditional study. Although the adaptations had drawbacks, users consistently struggled with the same issues, which over time revealed the ways the device could be improved. Through this work, we made the system instructions slower in pace and more conversational where the tone was too computerized. We also simplified the information architecture to be more consistent and less hierarchical. As we anticipated, users had difficulty locating the button icons for which there was not a word in their dialect. However, agreeing on new icons among users was more challenging than we envisioned. More research is needed to be sure any changes are indeed an improvement compared to the existing design.

In terms of our methodology, our experiences show that common best practices like 1:1 training, strict adherence to consistency, and TAP need to be reevaluated according to setting constraints. This study also made us question whether researchers should redefine the variables used to measure success in these contexts. For example, we propose the following two variables for others to consider:

- **Memory retention**. How do we evaluate a user's success when we are less concerned with efficiency (such as time on task) and more concerned with the extent to which the user remembers how to use a product? Should future usability studies collect longitudinal data and, if so, how?
- **Training methods**: How do we understand what helps users learn and how such findings can improve the product itself? Should we accept flexible training methods, and if so, how can we maximize what we learn about the product's usability while ensuring valid results?
- **Testing in groups:** How do we train and test when users use devices in group settings?

We conclude that usability studies need to be localized to suit each unique context, especially for products like the Talking Book that are designed for a global audience. As usability research progresses in this area, studies will be effective to the extent they are driven primarily by local staff, based on a thorough understanding of orally-grounded HCID, and when researchers implement flexible, opportunistic approaches to best adapt to the local setting.

REFERENCES

1. Putnam, C., et al., "Adapting User-Centered Design Methods to Design for Diverse Populations," Information Technologies & International Development, vol. 5, 2009.
2. Dumas, J. and Redish, G., A Practical Guide to Usability Testing. Exeter, UK: Intellect, Ltd. , 1999.
3. Barnum, C., Usability Testing and Research. New York: Longman, 2002.
4. Winschiers, H., Fendler, J., "Assumptions Considered Harmful," in Usability and Internationalization, ed Berlin: Springer, 2007, pp. 452-261.
5. Sherwani, J., et al., "Orality-Grounded HCID: Understanding the Oral User," Information Technologies and International Development, vol. 5, pp. 37-49, Dec 16 2009.
6. Medhi, I., Sagar, A., and Toyama, K., "Text-free user interfaces for illiterate and semiliterate users," Information Technologies and International Development, vol. 4, pp. 37-50, 2007.
7. Sambasivan, N., et al., "Intermediated technology use in developing communities," Proceedings of the 28th international conference on Human factors in computing systems, pp. 2583-2592, 2010.
8. Medhi, I., Prasad, A., and Toyama, K., "Optimal audio-visual representations for illiterate users of computers," Proceedings of the 16th international conference on World Wide Web, p. 882, 2007.
9. Medhi, I., Gautama, S., and Toyama, K., "A comparison of mobile money-transfer uis for non-literate and semi-literate users," Proceedings of the 27th international conference on Human factors in computing systems, pp. 1741-1750, 2009.
10. Putnam, C., Kolko, B., Rose, E. & Walton, R. (2009). , "Mobile phone users in Kyrgyzstan: A case study of identifying user needs and requirements," in Proceedings of International Professional Communication Conference (IPCC '09), Honolulu, Hawaii, 2009.
11. Kolko, B. E., Wei, C, and J.H. Spyridakis. , "Internet Use in Uzbekistan: Developing a Methodology for Tracking Information Technology Implementation Success," Information Technologies and International Development, vol. 1, pp. 1-19, 2003.
12. Schmidt, C., Gorman, T., Gary, M., Bayor, A. "Impact of Low-Cost, On-Demand Information Access in a Remote Ghanaian Village." Information Technologies and International Development 2010. London

Evaluating Video Visualizations of Human Behavior

Mario Romero[1], Alice Vialard[2], John Peponis[2], John Stasko[1], Gregory Abowd[1]

[1] School of Interactive Computing
Georgia Institute of Technology
{mromero, abowd, staskso}@cc.gatech.edu

[2] School of Architecture
Georgia Institute of Technology
avialard3@gatech.edu, john.peponis@ca.gatech.edu

ABSTRACT

Previously, we presented *Viz-A-Vis*, a **VI**suali**Z**ation of **A**ctivity through computer **VIS**ion [17]. Viz-A-Vis visualizes behavior as aggregate motion over observation space. In this paper, we present two complementary user studies of Viz-A-Vis measuring its performance and discovery affordances. First, we present a controlled user study aimed at comparatively measuring behavioral analysis preference and performance for observation and search tasks. Second, we describe a study with architects measuring discovery affordances and potential impacts on their work practices. We conclude: 1) Viz-A-Vis significantly reduced search time; and 2) it increased the number and quality of insightful discoveries.

Author Keywords

Information Visualization, Video, Behavior, User Studies.

ACM Classification Keywords

H.5.2 **[Information Interfaces and Presentation]**: User Interfaces-Graphical user interfaces. Evaluation / Methods.

General Terms: Human Factors.

INTRODUCTION

Many disciplines spend considerable resources studying behavior. Methods range from qualitative pen-and-paper observation to automatic video content analysis. We present a semi-automated method where a network of overhead cameras captures behavior. The images are processed and visualized for rapid search and visual pattern analysis. Overhead video has the temporal and spatial resolution to potentially open new insights into everyday behavior by objectively revealing its invisible spatiotemporal structures. If analyzed thoroughly, it may function as a window into how people relate to each other and how they appropriate natural spaces and the objects within. Overhead video has potential for new analytical applications in multiple domains. For example, it may capture and evaluate the long-term effects of behavioral therapy in especial classrooms. It may track developmental progress in a baby's nursery. It may provide objective, long-term, and continuous physical therapy reports in natural places beyond the doctor's office. It may trace factory operations to increase industrial productivity. It may uncover subtle customer behaviors to boost retail space marketability. In this paper, we explore two domains: Behavioral Analysis and Architecture. Behavioral analysts track the topography (physicality and context) and the function (goal) of target human behaviors [8]. Architects analyze the relationship between the environment and people's behavior to evaluate designs and gain lessons for theory [16].

Previously, we developed *Viz-A-Vis*, a **VI**suali**Z**ation of **A**ctivity through computer **VIS**ion [17]. Viz-A-Vis captures behavior using overhead cameras, it processes the video with simple and robust computer vision, and it visualizes behavior as aggregate motion over the places of observation. Video Figure 1 demonstrates Viz-A-Vis.

Here, we evaluated Viz-A-Vis through two complementary user studies. A *performance* study measured its low-level usability and a *discovery* study measured its impact on high-level analysis. The performance study compared task-based user preference and performance against two systems. It determined that the tool is superior for some of the most critical tasks of behavior analysis. More importantly, it set a foundation that simplified the discovery study, where we did not test low-level usability. The discovery study reports Viz-A-Vis's clear positive impact on the practices of a group of architects, including increased opportunities for the discovery of actionable insights.

Additionally, we briefly discuss our lessons learned in evaluation design. While measuring performance in the laboratory is a bounded effort, the typical field study of a system's impact is not. We argue that our two-part evaluation may approximate the findings of a field study.

This paper's sections present related work in visualizations and evaluations, Viz-A-Vis's system architecture, the performance study, the discovery study, a discussion on the evaluation design, and its conclusions and future work.

RELATED WORK

Video Visualizations of Behavior

The first image sequences visualizing action and behavior are the beautifully pioneering photographs of Muybridge and Marey from the 1880s [10]. The first 3D space-time representation of a video cube (VC) is the 1970s work on motion by Ullman [20]. Fels et al. were the first to describe interactive cutting planes for visually filtering a VC [7].

Daniel and Chen present one of the first abstract visualizations of behavior in video [5]. They visualize motion in a translucent space-time cube by mapping greater motion to greater opaqueness, thus enabling an operator to see through inactive regions. Ivanov et al. present a visualization of the history of living spaces [9]. The authors provide 2D visualizations of motion sensor and raw video data. Through motion detection they visualize contextual paths and provide detail through strategic camera views. Botchen et al. present a 2D time lapse video visualization with highlighted abstractions of target objects and activities [1]. We propose similar goals and techniques to these papers, except our video has a near one-to-one correspondence with architectural space that naturally supports space-centric queries.

TotalRecall visualizes long-term video from real environments [13]. The main difference from Viz-A-Vis is that TotalRecall visualizes video in a 2D representation that introduces ambiguity between time and space. It slides frames like cards spread out from a deck. The visual effect is that each 2D location in the visualization is an ambiguous combination of multiple spatiotemporal coordinates.

Due to our image-to-space correspondence, we were inspired by GeoTime [11], which vertically maps temporal data as linear paths above a 2D geography. However, unlike GeoTime, Viz-A-Vis visualizes dense 2D layers of activity over 3D space. While the visualization is more challenging, the result is a more thorough view of activity across the entire space for each time frame.

Evaluations of Video Visualization Systems

While the number of video visualization systems is considerable, there are alarmingly few rigorous evaluations. Daniel and Chen's work has a follow-up publication that describes a rigorous study validating very specific usability claims of visual signatures [4]. Chen et al. argue that video analysis without human input is impossible for unbounded sequences and that a human must be in the loop of decision making. The role of video visualization is to fill in the gap between vast data sets that humans cannot practically search linearly and automation that is not computationally tractable. By placing the human in a critical role, the authors recognize the intrinsic need of user studies for video visualizations. In their study, the authors use computer graphics to carefully synthesize a clean video for evaluation that only models translations of one sphere. While this study rigorously answers questions about users' ability to interpret the visual signatures of the synthetic video, its level of artificiality fails to answer the ecologically-valid questions raised by the complexities of real data and tasks. In both of our studies we provided participants with real data and ecologically valid tasks.

Wang et al. developed a spatially contextual video representation that was based on requirements gathering and on understanding current security operator tasks [21]. They conclude with an informal user study based on tasks and usage patterns. In a follow-up, Wang et al. present a rigorous user study comparing performance through path

Figure 1. Viz-A-Vis visualizing two people cooking and eating on the activity cube (AC), map (AM), and table (AT).

reconstruction tasks [22]. They compare two contextualized video design factors and two levels of knowledge in participants. We gathered our requirements and tasks from interviews with domain experts, both in Behavioral Analysis and Architecture, and from the domain literature [8, 16]. Also, we trained participants until they self-reported proficiency in 3D navigation and filtering. Finally, we compared three experimental conditions.

Our performance study measured the user's preference and performance through time-to-task completion, precision, recall, coverage, and exit surveys. Numerous authors have proposed similar methods for evaluating information visualizations [2, 3]. In particular, Plaisant categorizes the types of evaluations based on the tasks, users, and goals [15]. Our performance study is an instance of a laboratory experiment comparing three tools: 1) the commonplace – a video player (VP); 2) the state-of-the-art – a video cube (VC); and 3) our experimental prototype and the central element of Viz-A-Vis – the *activity cube* (AC). Plaisant characterizes the fundamental problem of matching tasks, tools, users, and relevant high-level goals. Furthermore, her recognition that discovery requires real expertise, needs, context, and prolonged exposure to occur is central to the design of the two studies. There are a number of discovery-focused field studies that perform the costly evaluations we approximate [6, 18, 19]. In the performance study, participants execute predetermined tasks with correct answers. In the discovery study, users pose and answer novel questions creating a discovery loop. The discovery study goes deeper into questions of analytic insight.

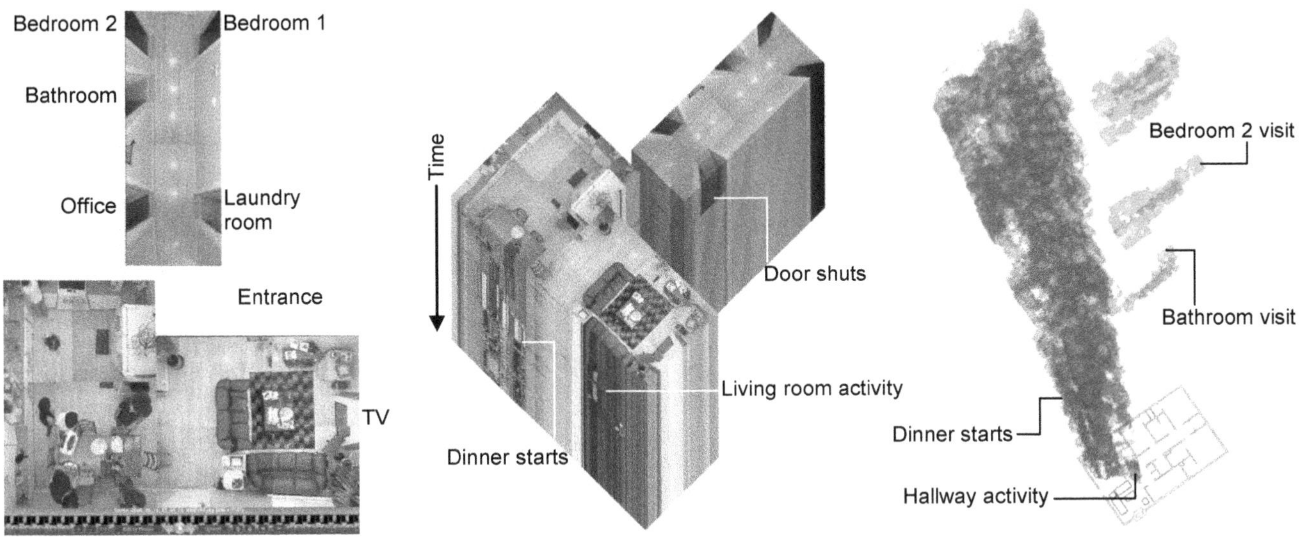

(a) Video Player (VP) (b) Video Cube (VC) (c) Activity Cube (AC)

Figure 2. Three experimental conditions visualizing behavior from overhead video mapped onto architectural space.

VIZ-A-VIS SYSTEM ARCHITECTURE

Viz-A-Vis stands for **VI**suali**Z**ation of **A**ctivity through computer **VIS**ion [17]. Primarily, it is a capture-and-access system for the analysis of human behavior. In this paper's instantiation, the capture module is a synchronized network of overhead cameras that provide full coverage over the kitchen, dining room, living room, and hallways of the Aware Home [12]. Each frame results from un-warping, scaling, translating, rotating, stitching, and cropping overhead images to match pixels with locations. The result resembles a single orthographic projection (see Figure 2a). Ten wide-angle cameras collect 24-bit color, 320-by-240-pixel JPEG files at 2 Hertz. We continually captured over 200 hours in the life of a married couple and their guests.

Viz-A-Vis combines 2D and 3D histograms and heat maps of aggregate motion (see Figure 1). We compute motion through frame differencing and we aggregate it over regions and periods of interest. The main overview structure is the *activity cube* (AC). AC is a volumetric geographic information system (GIS), where the geography is the home's floor plan. Time maps to the vertical axis. The heat maps doubly-encode aggregate motion into color and translucency – the more opaque and red the area, the more active. Users navigate and filter AC by rotating, zooming, and translating the cube and by placing cuts along the sub-volumes of interest, respectively. The cube includes an index to the original frames that allows the user to reify hypotheses about its visible patterns of behavior.

The *activity map* (AM) is a 2D aggregate summary of the activity cube. The user defines a period of aggregation from pre-computed aggregates, from a few seconds to a few hours. Also, the user can zoom and translate the map.

The *activity table* (AT) is a 2D array of aggregate motion across space (rows) and time (columns). In this version of Viz-A-Vis, the system presents manually pre-define regions of interest and aggregates motion over the regions across a window of time. A future version of Viz-A-Vis will allow dynamic region definition by the user and automatic region definition by the system. A cell on the table holds the value of the spatiotemporal aggregate of motion, which maps to a 2D color histogram equivalent to the heat maps (greater motion maps to red). The user can zoom and filter AT and index original frame sequences in the video. We implemented the backend of Viz-A-Vis in C++ and Matlab and the frontend in Ruby as a plug-in for Google Sketchup.

CONTROLLED LABORATORY PERFORMANCE STUDY

Preference and Performance Study Design

Our research question is: what are the task-based user preference and performance operating the Activity Cube (AC) compared to a video player (VP) and a video cube (VC) as measured by exit surveys, time-to-task-completion, precision, recall, and coverage? To answer it, we designed a counterbalanced-order, within-subject user study. We intentionally simplified this user study by evaluating only the activity cube and not the table (AT) or map (AM). First, it is a natural progression to go from a video player, which uses time to view time, to a video cube, which uses space to view time, to an activity cube. The activity cube also uses space to view time, but its view of activity goes deeper into the cube at a loss of detail. Second, training users to understand and operate the activity table and map would have tripled the resources necessary for this study, without much further insight into Viz-A-Vis's usability. Finally, the activity table and map are not as natural progressions from the video player and cube as the activity cube is.

We recruited 24 participants (18 male, 22.9 average age) with normal vision from two classes, HCI and CogSci, where they received 1% extra credit on the final grade as compensation. Given the within-subject design, we measure 24 data points per condition-task pair. Through an initial survey, we determined that most participants were computer scientists and considered themselves experts at interfaces (some at 3D navigation), good at programming, and experienced with data analysis and visualizations. On the other hand, most participants had never analyzed behavior and had no experience with Picasa or Sketchup.

Condition 1, VP, provides standard video playback functionality. We use Google Picasa Image Viewer to browse the raw JPEG frames (see Figure 2a). Condition 2, VC, provides a 3D structure of frames across time with interactive cutting surfaces to remove occluding volumes and standard 3D navigation tools (see Figure 2b). Condition 3, AC, provides the same 3D structure and interaction model, except it visualizes a stack of translucent heat maps of aggregate motion (see Figure 2c).

We evaluated the three conditions in counterbalanced order for each participant during three one-hour sessions on separate days. For each condition, participants trained until they self-determined proficiency. Training times varied across conditions. On average, the training required for VP was 3 minutes, for VC, 18 minutes, and for AC, 23 minutes. We placed an upper time limit on tasks and most participants completed them before reaching the limit.

We conducted this study in a usability laboratory. The computer had two 19-inch monitors, a 2.4 GHz Intel Core 2 CPU, 4 GB of RAM, and a necessary NVIDIA GeForce GTX 280 GPU for the visualizations to flow without lag.

We collected a dataset ripe with target events for this study during a four-hour dinner party. Eight friends in their 30s prepared food, had dinner, cleaned up, and played a board game (see Figure 6). There were 3 married couples, 2 single males, 7 Latin Americans, and 1 American. The first author and his wife hosted. All signed consents and were aware of the recording. We stated our goal: "to visualize natural human behavior." We asked them to act naturally, which they did within a few minutes. We purposefully included two activities into the soirée: a raclette and a game of Cranium™. A raclette is an electric grill surrounded by raw ingredients at the table and people cook their own meal. Cranium is a board game where two teams compete by performing a number of tasks, some very physical (acting, sculpting, and drawing) and some not (spelling backwards).

We carefully split the data into three scenes and showed a different scene during each experimental condition to avoid data learning effects. The scenes contained equivalent targets for each condition. We always presented the scenes in chronological order, regardless of the condition. Scene one, presented on the first session of participation, includes arriving, preparing dinner, setting the table, and starting the raclette. Scene two includes ending the raclette, cleaning up, and preparing and eating dessert. Scene three includes ending dessert, cleaning, moving to the living room, and starting Cranium. All scenes include bathroom visits.

While behavioral analysis tasks routinely include high-level statistical comparisons, for instance, they also include low-level tasks. Our study focuses on nine typical low-level, evidence-gathering tasks of behavior observation:

- **Interacting** is operating the application's low-level controls (clicking & dragging, filtering, navigating).
- **Overviewing** is verbalizing a shallow narrative of behavior and its context across an entire dataset.
- **Describing** is verbalizing the details and context of the behavior of all subjects during a target event.
- **Tracking** is following the location and describing the actions of one target subject during a target event.
- **Searching** is spatiotemporally locating sporadic and brief target behaviors and events.
- **Counting** is enumerating the repetitions of recurrent and brief target behaviors and events.
- **Finding transitions** is locating the periods where the entire group switches between activities.
- **Short-bounding** is finding the tight spatiotemporal boundaries of activities lasting a few seconds.
- **Long-bounding** is finding the tight spatiotemporal boundaries of activities lasting minutes or hours.

For all conditions, we carefully presented each task through a script that clearly defined it, provided examples, set a time limit, and asked participants if they had any questions. We also invited participants to formulate a strategy before starting the task in order to model expert users.

For all datasets, participants overviewed, described, tracked, short-bounded, and found transitions by choosing their own targets. We tasked participants to search for bathroom visits in all datasets. We asked participants to count raclette reaches, ice scream spoonfuls, and game board reaches in the first, second, and third dataset, respectively. Finally, we tasked participants with long-bounding dinner, dessert, and game play. For this task, we asked participant to define the boundaries. Through pilots, we determined, for example, that dinner starts for some participants when all are at the table and, for others, when someone starts eating. We needed a concrete a-priori definition to consistently measure performance, yet we wanted to observe the process of defining very concrete boundaries and let the users experience it as well.

We measured preference through an exit survey. We asked participants to rank the three conditions based on how well they support each task. We also asked them to design a hypothetical analysis system for an airport where the goal is to understand typical behavior and learn to discover outlier behavior. The design had to be based on at least one of the conditions and at most be any combination of the three.

We measured performance through time-to-task-completion (TTC), precision, recall, and coverage. *TTC* is a bounded period between the start and end of a task, including repetition until user satisfaction. *Precision* is the percentage of correct targets in the set of retrieved items. *Recall* is the percentage of retrieved targets from the set of possible targets. *Coverage* is the percentage of the dataset reviewed.

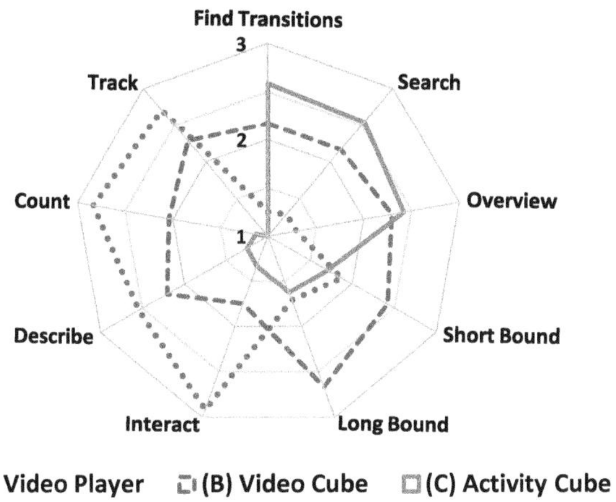

Figure 3. Task-based user preference: VP, VC, and AC.

Not every task lends itself to all measures of performance. Interacting, overviewing, describing, tracking, and finding transitions present subjective and variable definitions of the quality of the results, thus precision and recall do not apply.

For analysis, we summarized the data as mean ± standard error. We conducted a one-way repeated measures analysis of variance (ANOVA). We used the Tukey test to conduct pair-wise comparisons between conditions and considered differences at $p < 0.05$ to be statistically significant.

Preference and Performance Study Results

We present the preference results first and we use these to frame the performance results. The target users of Viz-A-Vis are expert analysts and their preferences are paramount to the success of the tool. Figure 3 presents a radar plot that visualizes the average of the 24 participants' ranking of the three conditions across the nine tasks. The radial scale of the graph goes from 1 to 3, where 3 is preferred. We sorted the plot clockwise in decreasing preference for AC. The first observation is that there is a clear complement between VP and AC, except for bounding, where VC is preferred. Second, participants preferred some conditions for certain tasks: VP – tracking, counting, describing, and interacting; VC – long and short bounding; AC – finding transitions, searching, and overviewing. We expected most of these results (tracking, counting, describing, and interacting). It is clear that VP is not only simpler to use, but actually required for its detailed and controlled video traversal. We expected AC to outperform in the other tasks, including bounding. Though there was the extra cost of performing cuts, participants preferred VC for bounding because it unambiguously visualized activity boundaries. With AC, users were not sure they could clearly interpret boundaries.

Given the design of the study and its metrics of performance, it is possible to compute performance for counting, long-bounding, and searching only. Since people simply could not count with AC, because long-bounding was difficult, and in the interest of space, we only present the statistical analysis of searching performance.

We analyze the results visualized in Figure 4. With

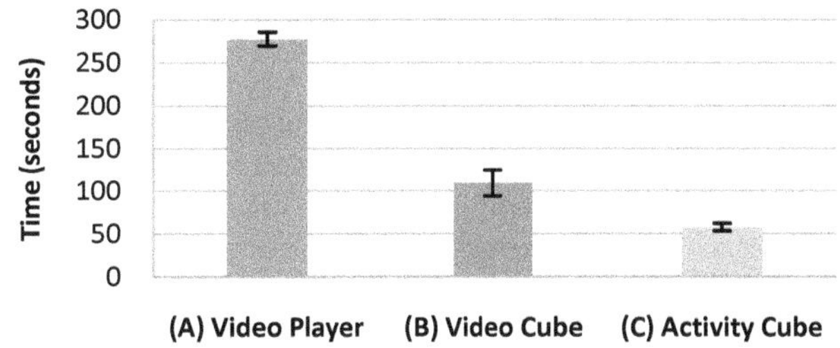

Figure 4. Search time-to-task completion: VP, VC, and AC.

statistical significance ($p<0.01$), AC's average time to *search* completion (57 seconds) outperformed the video player (278 seconds) by nearly 5-to-1 and the video cube (110 seconds) by nearly 2-to-1, while maintaining precision and recall at 100% and increasing coverage from VP's 78% to 100%. This is particularly relevant since, according to our interviews with professional behaviorists, their most time-consuming task is searching. Furthermore, since we limited task execution time to five minutes, we restricted the improvement factor. Without restriction, we extrapolate the improvement to be 8-to-1. Moreover, as 3D navigation and interpretation proficiency increase and as sequences lengthen, the improvement factor may grow further.

As a dramatic example, one participant, an extreme outlier, searched in 2 seconds. He orbited AC to its side, detected the relevant patterns, pointed to each target event, and said: "there!" His two-second search of random targets buried in over 7000 frames measured 100% precision, recall, and coverage, while managing to avoid two subtle false positives – an improvement factor of 139!

Finally, we present the results of the hypothetical design question and relevant comments. First, AC was the only condition unanimously chosen, always in complement with VP or VC, though. Users cited overviewing and searching for outlier behavior as the primary tasks of AC. Also, participants stated that AC could help learning the shape of normal patterns, thus outliers would easily stand out. Participants highlighted the importance of privacy in designing behavior capture systems but noted the tradeoff between security and privacy, for instance. They volunteered a number of applications: tracking disabilities in the home, monitoring child development with a baby-cam, observing social behavior for gender studies, tracking behavioral changes in children with autism in classrooms, performing ubiquitous computing and augmented reality studies, where physically observable behavior is part of systems' experience, and studying body language in group dynamics. To finish, all twenty-four participants expressed admiration and found value in both 3D models:

> *Wow! I get the illusion that I see the scene from different perspectives. It feels like I'm moving the [capture] camera! Although I know it's not true, I feel I can see faces better when I look from the side [of VC].*

> *The activity clouds show where the action is and the type of action by the amount of activity. You lose who is doing what, but you get to see longer periods of time and where things happened.*

DESIGN STUDIO & FOCUS GROUP DISCOVERY STUDY

Discovery Study Design

Our research question is: can the visualization of behavior raise opportunities for discovery and change work practices and outcomes for a domain-specific application? To answer it, we devised a two-group design studio and focus group with architects. The control group used current methods to inform their design and the experimental group augmented those practices with Viz-A-Vis. They viewed the activity cube (AC), the activity table (AT), the activity map (AM), and indexed original frames with the video player (VP).

Environmental psychologists are architects who formulate design choices through the systematic study of the relationships between space and behavior. Their data gathering and analysis methods are arduous. For example, architects gather flow and occupancy by observing and manually counting or by interviewing and surveying.

During a design studio, we observed two groups consisting of five and six doctoral architecture students each. Their task was to renovate the interior public spaces of the Aware Home given a number of constraints and requirements as stipulated in writing and verbally by fictional clients. Each architect worked individually, but shared the work space, the delivery of the requirements, and the clients' answers to the questions posed by other architects in the same group.

The study had two sessions on separate days for each group. The first session was a five-hour design studio. The second session was a two-hour focus group. The design and the focus group sessions took place, respectively, in the dining room and the living room of the Aware Home.

The design studios consisted of the delivery of the design program, the fictional clients' requirements statement, questions from the architects, sketching, a second round of questions, refinements, and the architects' presentation of their designs. For the experimental group the presentation of the requirements and current patterns integrated Viz-A-Vis visualizations. The client requirements included supporting a mutual sense of presence during parallel activities and providing space for entertaining friends, shelving books, watching movies, and listening to music.

From the start, both groups were aware of the general goal of the study: "to understand your current design practices and to determine the efficacy of a software tool aimed at supporting part of those practices." The control group was aware of the existence of the tool and they knew they would not see it until the focus group, where we showed them a number of episodes from daily living in the home and asked them to relate the visualizations back to their original design. We also motivated them to project how they could use the visual data in future designs.

We started the experimental group with a presentation and discussion of the system. We visualized a number of episodes from the everyday life of the fictional client occupying the home during a period of nine days and asked the participants to input queries into the system, for example, "what does typical cooking look like?" Figure 1 shows the result of this query with some context around it. Notice in AM the regions of highest activity around the kitchen and in AT, the period of dispersed activity, cooking, focused activity, eating, and dispersed again, cleaning.

Participants asked questions that would then be answered with visualizations. We displayed the results of the queries to all participants and let them verbally guide the interactive views, allowing them to interpret the data. To sidestep training the participants and to exert a uniform impact, we delivered the queries through a dedicated technician instead of hands-on participant interaction. We were not testing the controls of the interface in this study. Rather, we tested whether participants could interpret and utilize the visualization to support their design task.

The experimental group had equal time limits to complete their design and shared the same deliverables. We presented to the experimental group the results of the individual queries mid-way through their design and we collected their deliverables at the end. On a separate day, we conducted a focus group with emphasis on what worked, what did not work, what influenced their design, what was missing from the tool, and how they could use it to inform future designs.

We observed, recorded, and transcribed the design studios and the focus groups. We collected questions, comments, suggestions, and critiques, as well as the presentations of their design in visual, verbal, and textual media.

It is important to expose a potentially confounding factor in our study. The first author played four roles during the design studio and one more role during the focus group. First, he created the system. We did not hide this fact in order to motivate the participants by providing them with the real opportunity to have impact on the tool. Second, the first author and his wife played the fictional clients. They lived in the home and recorded the nine days of activity visualized during the study. We modeled the fictional clients' behavior closely based on the real life behavior of the couple. Third, he was part of the team observing the architects during their practices. The observation included taking notes, photographs, and video recording. It did not include questions during the design studio. During the presentation of the designs of the architects, the author played both the role of the client and the role of the observer when asking questions. Fourth, for the experimental group, the author played the role of the technician. He collected the queries, asked enough questions to eliminate any ambiguity, executed the queries, and presented the results being careful not to interpret them. Finally, the first author also moderated the focus groups.

To mitigate the impact of these factors, we took a number of steps. First, the study included five observers, three of whom are professional architects. Second, we carefully modeled and practiced playing the clients in order to deliver exactly the same descriptions and return equivalent answers

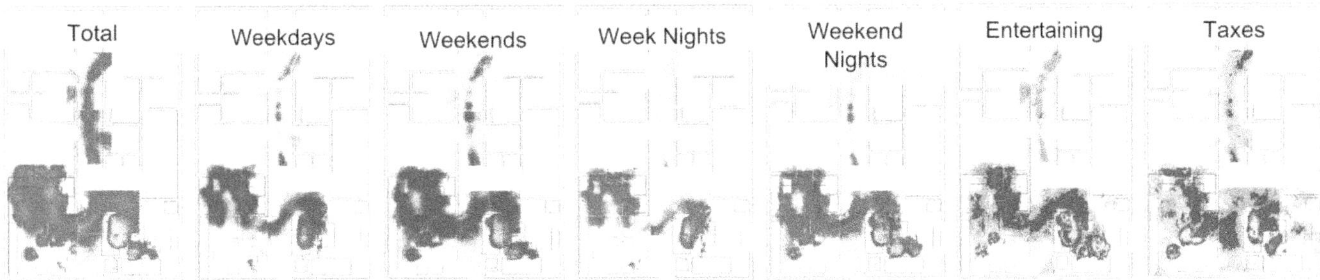

Figure 5. Activity maps showing aggregate motion heat maps presented as examples of everyday living episodes.

to similar questions. Third, we carefully controlled the technician's role. His task was only to deliver the results of the query. We avoided including behavioral interpretations of the results. Fourth, we rapidly established an amicable environment where we constantly encouraged criticism.

The two groups' previous design experience differed. While the control group had a 10-year design experience on average, the experimental group only had a 5-year experience. Participants were randomly divided into the groups based on their availability. While this difference is significant, we were less concerned about its impact because it was the control group with more experience. The experimental group, if anything, was at a disadvantage.

We defined the same task and schedule for both groups. They were in charge of renovating the kitchen, dining room, living room, foyer, media closet, coat closet, south end of the main corridor, and balcony. Both groups had 30 minutes for initial data gathering, 120 minutes for initial sketches, 15 minutes for further data gathering, 60 minutes for final sketches and presentation material, and 5 minutes per architect for the presentation of the final design. The total running time for the control design studio was 4 hours and 20 minutes and for the experimental design studio, it was 4 hours and 50 minutes. The extra time of the experimental group was due to the additional architect and the 25-minute presentation of the system at the beginning of the session. For the data gathering sessions, we balanced the time of showing query results with the time of clients delivering their verbal accounts of their lifestyle. We kept it in the same time limits of 30 and 15 minutes each.

We observed the practices and evaluated the product of design employing a technique called *architectural moves*, which analyzes the design's impact on the elements, features, and programs in the layout. A program is the set of intended uses of a space together with the architectural affordances. During the design studio, we observed participant questions, comments, critiques, descriptions, and presentations of their designs.

During the focus groups, we collected the architects' reflective evaluation based on any new information provided by Viz-A-Vis, their interpretations and use, if any, of the visualizations, their critiques of the technology, and proposed future improvements and applications. We used focused coding for the analysis of the results [14].

Discovery Study Results

We present the results through five themes: 1) discovery of patterns of behavior; 2) architectural moves; 3) creation of a new spatiotemporal ontology of behavior; 4) creation of behavioral design sketches; and 5) comments and critiques.

The first theme is *discovery of patterns of behavior*. Figure 5 shows activity maps summarizing behavior across multiple days and events. We presented these samples of daily living to the experimental group at the start of their design studio and to the control group during their focus group. Both groups discovered a number of behavioral patterns, some of which the clients were not aware of. In the interest of space, we present the most striking pattern.

During the control focus group discussion, one of the architects (A) remarked: "[the clients] seem to be introverted." The moderator, who was also one of the clients and who did not believe it, replied: "What do you mean?" A: "Well, [the clients] always stay away from the windows [pointing at Figure 5]. When I'm at my house, I like to have coffee by the window and watch the world outside." After an extended discussion and analysis of the evidence, we concluded that the clients were not introverted. They were avoiding Atlanta's 10th Street, which is crowded, polluted, noisy, and public. Living in this home was different from their regular home, which bordered on the Chattahoochee River National Park. There, the clients would spend many hours by the windows. But at the Aware Home, the clients avoided the outside at all cost. The most striking aspect of this discovery is that the clients were not aware of this behavior – it simply happened. It required an extended discussion grounded on the objective evidence provided by the visualization to arrive at this conclusion.

The second theme, *architectural moves*, refers to the designed changes in form or function of the architectural space. We synthesized five types of architectural moves from the eleven designs: 1) the inclusion of the balcony into the indoor space; 2) the creation of a foyer, an entrance; 3) the establishment of visual links between the public spaces; 4) the bounding of spaces with half walls or furniture; and 5) the creation of a space solely dedicated to media consumption. Between the control and the experimental group, we only observed a significant difference in the fifth architectural move, the creation of media spaces. All the other four architectural moves had roughly the same number of instantiations for both groups.

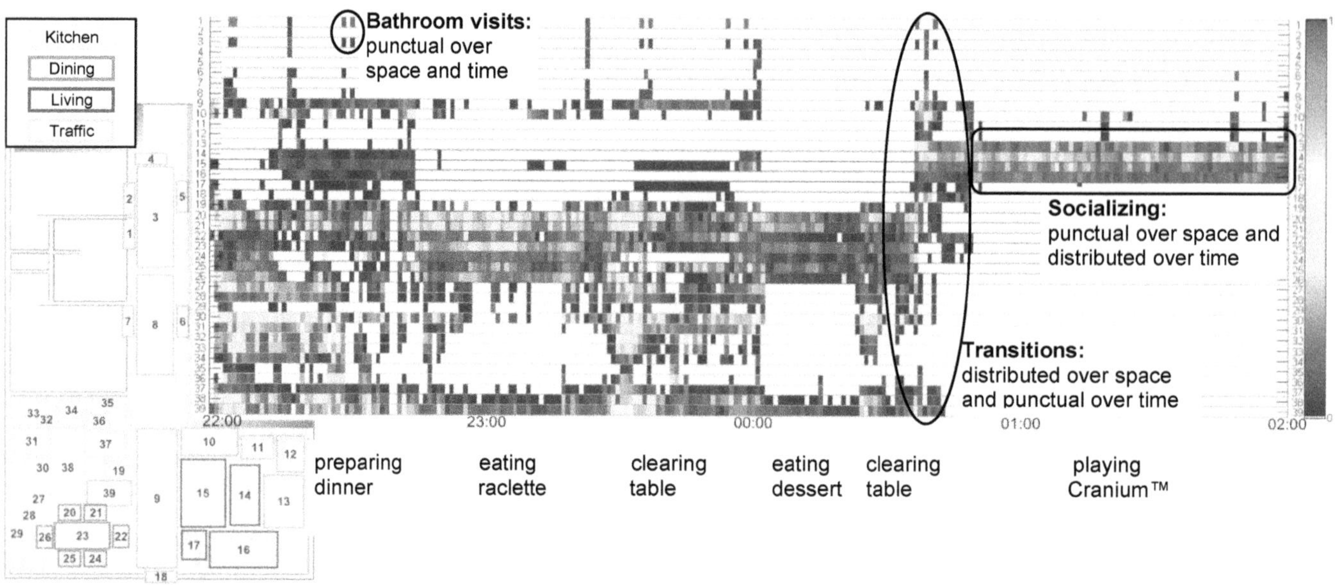

Figure 6. Architects used this activity table (AT) of a dinner party to create a spatiotemporal ontology of behavior.

While none of the more experienced architects in the control group created a dedicated media space, four out of the six architects in the experimental group created it. The experimental group discovered and used a behavioral pattern of extreme media consumption in the "Taxes" visualization on the right-hand side of Figure 5. The activity map depicts the clients preparing their tax returns. It shows activity in the living room and in the dining room. After an inquiry from the architects, the wife explained that they started filing their taxes electronically in the living room. When they attempted to electronically submit the return, the "free" service charged a $50 fee. The clients moved into the dining room to redo their returns on paper. The unexpected behavior, visible in the map, is that the clients sat on the far side of the table. After prompting from the architects, the wife answered that they were watching Spiderman 2 and they needed to sit on the far left to continue to view the television on top of the fireplace on the far right.

The third theme is the *creation of a new spatiotemporal ontology of behavior*. Figure 6 presents an activity table with the data presented in the controlled performance study. The clients invited a group of six friends to a dinner party. We presented the table to the control group during their focus group. We did not label the activities, yet the architects were able to describe the sequence of events. They found the table very insightful. It allowed them to quickly understand "density of occupancy" and "patterns of flow." As they discussed the image, they started creating a new vocabulary to describe behaviors in relation to space and time. One of the architects stood up and, in front of the screen, stated: "these bathroom visits are punctual over space and time, these periods of transition are distributed over space and punctual over time, this socializing is punctual over space and distributed over time, and this preparing dinner is distributed over space and time." She outlined four broad behavioral categories for the use of space and time and created a spatiotemporal ontology of behavior and a new vocabulary to describe it. After further discussion, the group's senior architect agreed that this new ontology was worth exploring in Architectural Theory. He imagined an example where a museum curator would be interested in distinguishing between three patterns of patron behavior: 1) "translation," going from one place to another in the museum; 2) "vibration," staying in one place but moving a lot, like during a conversation; and 3) "contemplation," remaining relatively static and contemplating a compositional space within the museum where several exhibition pieces create one visual statement.

The fourth theme is the *creation of behavioral sketches*. The architects in the control group did not create any type of sketches that outlined behavior over space. During their focus group discussion, we established that it is not part of their practice. On the other hand, two of the six architects in the experimental group created sketches that depicted a model of behavior the architects had extracted from the visualizations (see Figure 7). When we queried them, they explained that they analyzed the relationship between behavior and space, abstracted some patterns from the old space, and instantiated the abstractions into their designs. In other words, they ran a thought simulation partly motivated by the data driven visualizations. The sketches on figure 7 depict lines of communication from particular points in the floor plan. On the left, yellow depicts inward communication and red depicts outward communication.

The fifth theme compiles the most relevant *comments and critiques* from the architects. First, the architects found the activity table and the activity maps more useful to their analysis than the activity cube. They had a hard time visualizing a summary of activity from the 3D structure. We did not expect it, but in retrospect it is clear. Architects are not as interested in the sequence of events as behaviorists are. Architects focus on the event-based relationship between space and time. The 2D

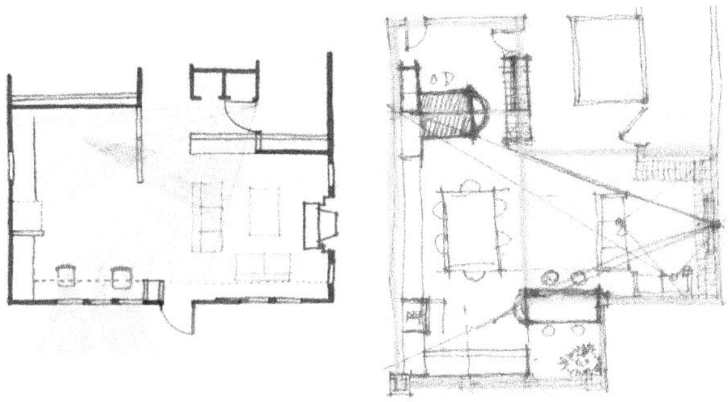

Figure 7. Behavioral sketches for architectural design.

representations provided these summaries clearly and succinctly. One caveat is that they did not have to search for the temporal windows of aggregation. The interaction with the activity cube is crucial for these searches.

Second, architects stated that visualizing household activity was not the most justified use of the powerful tools provided by Viz-A-Vis. A house, in their opinion, is a place of relative simplicity, where at least one dweller understands the overall pattern of occupancy. They stated that more complex environments, where no single individual understands the overall patterns of activity, would dramatically highlight the virtues of our system and would undoubtedly have an impact on the theory, the practice, and the product of Architecture. They volunteered a number of complex spaces for using the tool at its potential: nurses' desks, hospitals, plazas, museums, ground and air terminals, and public transportation lines.

Third, they stated that it would be of great benefit to their practice to include identity in the visualization. Viz-A-Vis is intentionally simple; it only visualizes motion. Individuals are indistinguishable in this visualization. A reification step, indexing original frames, is necessary to understand individual behavior. Blob tracking is considerably more complex and less reliable than motion aggregation and we purposefully avoided it for this stage of our research, but the point is well taken.

DISCUSSION

We did not set out to contribute to evaluation methodologies of visualizations. Nevertheless, we learned a number of lessons that we consider can be applied to future evaluations and we report these here.

The ultimate goal of visualizations is to promote discoveries that support actionable insights. This is difficult to evaluate. It typically requires long-term field studies that determine current practices and products and the visualization's impact on both. The studies occur in the workplace with relevant datasets. Participants typically require extensive training and monetary incentives. Field deployments consume thousands of human-hours [18, 19].

Through our performance and discovery studies, we informally approximate the results of a field study at a fraction of the cost. In the lab, we test the low-level usability performance of the system compared to the state-of-the-art and the commonplace: a three-condition, within-subject, counterbalanced-order study. The performance study consumed approximately 80 hours for testing and 140 hours for analysis. Testing includes one participant and one researcher, thus its total cost is roughly 300 human-hours.

Prior to the discovery study, we answer the foundational questions: "can participants use and understand the visualization and can they be more effective or more efficient than with regular and advanced tools?" In the discovery study, we focus on high-level and domain-specific questions of insightful discovery. We tested two groups: a control and an experimental group. To optimize the time of engagement with highly-skilled domain experts, we do not train participants on the low-level operations of the visualization. The performance study established this usability. Rather, we present the interpretative affordances of the visualization. Next, we use our own datasets and, together with a domain expert, we designed a work exercise aimed at closely mimicking real practices. Familiarity with the datasets facilitates rapidly answering search queries. The key is to avoid interpreting the query or the results. The technician must clarify the query beyond ambiguity and must present the results without any interpretation. In a sense, this approach is a Wizard-of-Oz intelligent interface.

Through this approach, we compress what typically takes many days of regular work per person into a five-hour period with each group. By parallelizing domain expert participation, we not only optimize time, we standardize within-group conditions. Every participant in the group consumes exactly the same sequence of queries and contributes and benefits from the group discussion interpreting the information. It is important to stress that participants work independently to maintain plurality. Each participant uses the same information differently for individual work goals. On the other hand, the efficiency tradeoff comes at a cost. We can't claim to have five statistically independent data points. The designs are not fully independent because the query results informing the designers are consumed by all the members of one group.

Excluding study design, the discovery study took 18 hours and consumed 90 researcher-hours and 99 participant-hours. The analysis consumed approximately 72 researcher-hours. The approximate cost is 261 human-hours.

CONCLUSIONS AND FUTURE WORK

We presented a two-part evaluation of the preference, performance, discovery, and impact of an information visualization of human behavior in everyday environments called Viz-A-Vis. We presented the complementary results of these evaluations with respect to our visualization. From the performance study, we highlight that our system greatly out-performed the other conditions for the critical task of searching for target events. The performance study also clearly establishes system usability, a necessary condition for acknowledging the discovery study's results. From the discovery study, we emphasize that we cost-effectively provided multiple and conclusive evidence of the visualization's support for the discovery of actionable insights in the real practices of domain experts. Finally, we discussed the principles we learned for the general design of cost-effective evaluations of the visualization's power to raise opportunities for insightful discovery.

Our future work includes three venues. First, we are testing blob tracking algorithms and identity visualizations. That was the most unanimous unfulfilled requirement from participants in both studies. Second, we are recruiting domain experts from different fields and collecting data from significantly more complex spaces. As stated by the architects, the virtues of the visualization should become more apparent as the full complexity of the observation environment escapes human understanding. Finally, we are planning to run performance and discovery evaluations alongside long-term field deployments in order to compare the quality of the results with the justifiability of the costs.

ACKNOWLEDGEMENTS

This work was funded in part by the NSF Expeditions Award 1029679. We thank the contributions of architect Julie Zook to the discovery study. We thank our friends who donated their frank behaviors in the Aware Home during our data capture. We thank the 33 participants of our two user studies. Mostly, the first author thanks his wife, Dr. Natalia Landázuri, for her relentless support of this research, including donating over 200 hours of her private life to the data capture. Finally, Dr. Mario Romero dedicates this work to the memory of his mother.

REFERENCES

1. Botchen, R.P., Schick, F., and Ertl, T., Action-Based Multifield Video Visualization, in *Visualization and Computer Graphics, IEEE Transactions on*, 2008. 14(4): p. 885-899.
2. Card, S., Mackinlay, J. and Shneiderman, B., *Readings in Information Visualization: Using Vision to Think*. The Morgan Kaufmann Series in Interactive Technologies. 1999, San Francisco, Calif. Morgan Kaufmann.
3. Chen, C. and Yu, Y., Empirical Studies of Information Visualization: a Meta-Analysis. *International Journal of Human Computer Studies*, 2000. 53(5): p. 851-866.
4. Chen, M., Botchen, R., Hashim, R., Weiskopf, D., Ertl, T., Thornton, I., Visual Signatures in Video Visualization, in *Visualization and Computer Graphics, IEEE Transactions on*, 2006. 12(5): p. 1093-1100.
5. Daniel, G. and Chen, M., Video Visualization, in *Proceedings of the 14th IEEE Visualization 2003 (VIS'03)*. 2003, IEEE Computer Society.
6. Fayyad, U., Grinstein, G., and Wierse, A., *Information Visualization in Data Mining and Knowledge Discovery*. 2002, San Francisco, CA: Morgan Kaufmann.
7. Fels, S., Lee, E., and Mase, E., Techniques for Interactive Video Cubism. *Proceedings of ACM Multimedia*. 2000.
8. Grant, L. and Evans, A.N., *Principles of Behavior Analysis*. First ed. 1994, New York: HarperCollins College Publishers.
9. Ivanov, Y., Wren, C., Sorokin, A., Kaur, I., Visualizing the History of Living Spaces, in *Visualization and Computer Graphics, IEEE Transactions on,* 2007. 13(6): p. 1153-1160.
10. Jaschko, S., Space-Time Correlations Focused in Film Objects and Interactive Video, in *Future Cinema: The Cinematic Imaginary after Film*. 2003, MIT Press.
11. Kapler, T. and Wright, W., GeoTime Information Visualization, in *Information Visualization, INFOVIS 2004*. 2004. Austin, Texas.
12. Kidd, C., et al., The Aware Home: a Living Laboratory for Ubiquitous Computing Research. *Proceedings of the Second International Workshop on Cooperative Buildings*—CoBuild - 1999.
13. Kubat, R., DeCamp, P., Roy, B., and Roy, D., TotalRecall: Visualization and Semi-Automatic Annotation of Very Large Audio-Visual Corpora, in *Ninth International Conference on Multimodal Interfaces (ICMI 2007)*. 2007.
14. Lofland, J. and Lofland, L., *Analyzing Social Settings: A Guide to Qualitative Observation and Analysis*. 3rd ed. 1995: Wadsworth Publishing Company.
15. Plaisant, C., The Challenge of Information Visualization Evaluation, in *Proceedings of the working conference on Advanced Visual Interfaces*. 2004, ACM: Italy.
16. Proshansky, H., *Environmental Psychology: People and Their Physical Settings*. 2nd ed. 1976: Holt McDougal.
17. Romero, M., Summet, J., Stasko, J., Abowd, G., Viz-A-Vis: Toward Visualizing Video through Computer Vision, in *Visualization and Computer Graphics, IEEE Transactions on,* 2008. 14(6): p. 1261-1268.
18. Saraiya, P., North, C., and Duca, K., An Evaluation of Microarray Visualization Tools for Biological Insight, in *IEEE Symposium on Information Visualization, 2004. INFOVIS 2004*. 2004, IEEE: Austin, TX.
19. Shneiderman, B. and Plaisant, C., Strategies for Evaluating Information Visualization Tools: Multi-Dimensional In-depth Long-term Case Studies, in *Proceedings of the 2006 AVI workshop on Beyond Time and Errors: Novel Evaluation Methods for Information Visualization*. 2006, ACM: Venice, Italy.
20. Ullman, S., *The Interpretation of Visual Motion*. 1979, Cambridge, MA: MIT Press.
21. Wang, Y., et al., Contextualized Videos: Combining Videos with Environment Models to Support Situational Understanding, in *Visualization and Computer Graphics, IEEE Transactions on,* 2007. 13: p. 1568-1575.
22. Wang, Y., et al., Effects of Video Placement and Spatial Context Presentation on Path Reconstruction Tasks with Contextualized Videos, in *Visualization and Computer Graphics, IEEE Transactions on*, 2008. 14(6): p. 1755-1762.

Sizing Up Visualizations: Effects of Display Size in Focus+Context, Overview+Detail, and Zooming Interfaces

Mikkel Rønne Jakobsen & Kasper Hornbæk
Department of Computer Science, University of Copenhagen, Denmark
mikkelrj@diku.dk, kash@diku.dk

ABSTRACT
Whereas the literature is clear on the benefits of large displays and visualizations, little is known about their combination, that is, how display size affect the usability of visualizations. We describe a controlled experiment where 19 participants used focus+context, overview+detail, and zooming techniques with varying display sizes (13.8, 1.5, and 0.17 megapixels). Participants navigated geographical maps to find specific locations, compare items, and follow routes. Results show that for multi-scale navigation, classic interactive visualization techniques did not benefit from being scaled to a large display: In contrast to the literature we find similar performance on medium and large displays. Across display sizes, overview+detail works the best, in particular for comparing items. Focus+context is relatively more difficult to use at a small display size. We explain these findings and discuss the design of interactive visualization techniques for large displays.

Author Keywords
Large high-resolution displays, information visualization, multi-scale navigation, user study

ACM Classification Keywords
H.5.2 [Information interfaces and presentation]: User Interfaces—Graphical user interfaces (GUI)

General Terms
Experimentation, Human Factors

INTRODUCTION
Interactive visualization techniques aim to help users navigate large information spaces that do not fit within the display. However, their usability has mostly been investigated for a narrow range of display size (roughly corresponding to Figure 1, b). Meanwhile, the range of display sizes in common use is increasing, from mobile devices to large high-resolution displays. This paper investigates how classic interactive visualization techniques perform with larger and smaller displays (Figure 1, a and c).

Large high-resolution displays allow more information to be shown at a time, and have been found to improve task performance and user satisfaction [e.g., 14, 35]. Similarly, visualization techniques have been shown useful for many tasks [e.g., 11, 13]. The combination of large displays and visualizations, however, raises new questions: Can we expect the performance gains of visualization approaches for smaller displays [10] to scale to large displays? Does the finding that overview+detail visualizations improve task completion time and satisfaction [13] hold on displays with enough pixels to give an overview? Which tasks are most effectively solved with visualizations on a large display?

North and colleagues have given answers to some of these types of question [1, 3, 36, 37]. They have shown how physical navigation improves performance on large displays and that comparison of visualizations' performance gives similar results across display sizes. However, they have argued that questions about what happens when "the data/pixel count scales up" and how "different navigation strategies, such as overview+detail, and focus+context, affect high resolution visualization" remain unanswered [3].

This paper contributes empirical data on the effect of display size on the usability of visualization techniques for navigating multi-scale information spaces. We investigate three classic interactive visualization techniques (focus+context, overview+detail, and zooming), using tasks and data similar to previous studies. In contrast to most work by North and colleagues, we investigate interactive visualizations and look at their usability for navigating the same, large information space. In contrast to work on visualization for small displays [e.g., 10], we compare across all display sizes of Figure 1. The intended benefit of this line of work is to understand better how to design and adapt visualizations for small and large displays.

Figure 1: How do visualization techniques perform at different display sizes such as (a) 13.8, (b) 1.5, or (c) 0.17 megapixels?

RELATED WORK

Increasing display size has been shown to improve performance across tasks as different as 3D navigation [35], office work [14], map navigation [3, 6], sensemaking [1], and collaboration [23]. Large displays have also played important roles in systems such as Prairie [34], iLand [33], Stanford Information Mural [16], and Liveboard [15]. Several mechanisms behind the improvements promised by large displays have been proposed, including that they (a) provide a wider view of data, allowing peripheral awareness of context and better spatial orientation [35], (b) ease window management and navigation [14], and (c) prompt physical navigation in front of the display, reducing the need for virtual navigation [5].

Similarly, information visualizations are well researched, and much is known about the relative performance of different visualizations [e.g., 11, 32]. For instance, overview+detail visualizations have been shown to increase subjective satisfaction and improve performance for both complex tasks, like essay writing [22], and simpler tasks [8]; Cockburn et al. recently reviewed these benefits [13]. Different terms are used for these interface approaches that transform the view of a visual structure [11]: We use the term visualization technique, as used in previous research [e.g., 7, 17, 22].

Few papers, however, have studied the relation between information visualization and display size. Next we review empirical studies of information visualization where display size played a central role; Figure 2 shows the size of display used in these studies. Unless otherwise noted, we focus on the displays' pixel counts (rather than their physical size or dots-per-inch).

Baudisch et al. [7] presented focus+context screens. They surrounded a 17.3-inch monitor with a cardboard frame onto which a projected image gave low-resolution context to the information on the monitor. Focus+context screens were found superior to zooming and overview+detail

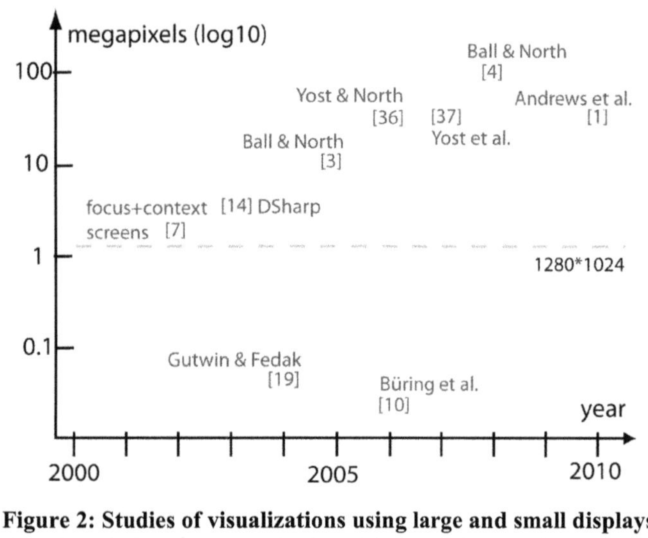

Figure 2: Studies of visualizations using large and small displays. Numbers in brackets may be found in the reference list, and the axes indicate the year of publication and pixel count of displays.

techniques. Other studies have used focus+context effects on large displays (e.g., Spotlight [25]), but have not attempted to generalize findings across display sizes or to other focus+context designs. We are unaware, for instance, of papers studying fisheye lenses on large displays. Several studies of small displays, however, have focused on focus+context techniques. Büring et al. [10] compared zooming and fisheye interfaces on small screens. Based on preferences for the fisheye interface, they suggested that users might value the navigational context in a fisheye interface higher when using a small screen. Gutwin and Fedak [19] compared interface techniques on displays about the size of mobile devices and typical desktop monitors. For small displays, they found that two-level zoom (an overview and a detail view) and a fisheye lens performed well with most tasks, even though users of the fisheye interface experienced overshooting. DateLens, a fisheye calendar interface, was found superior to an existing calendar application on PDA-sized devices [9].

North and colleagues have provided the most extensive empirical data on how visualizations work on large displays. Ball and North [3] compared simple navigation tasks using a zoom+pan interface with one, four and nine tiled monitors. Data images fit the largest display. Thirty-six participants performed tasks faster and felt less frustration with nine monitors than with one monitor. Also, participants engaged in more physical navigation and less virtual navigation with nine monitors than with one monitor. Later studies provided further evidence for the importance of physical movement for solving map tasks on a 100 megapixel display [4]. Yost and North [36, 37] investigated how visualizations that provide more pixels than visual acuity improved performance and showed that data density could be increased significantly with larger displays with only a modest increase in task completion times. The visualizations tested were small multiples of bar charts and graphs. In these studies by North and colleagues, the information space is significantly larger for the large displays, although not in [5]. For instance, [37] compared three interfaces that increased pixel counts by a factor of four (2, 8, and 31.5 megapixel displays); the number of data points was similarly increased (5488, 23548 and 94192 data points). The increases in task completion time on large displays were less than a factor of four, supporting the conclusion that "performance on most tasks was more efficient and sometimes more accurate because of the additional data that could be displayed" [37, p. 101].

In sum, most studies on visualization have been made on standard-sized displays. Data on the general performance of visualizations on other sizes of display are thus lacking. Specifically, the literature on the relation between display size and visualization technique mainly concern static visualizations. For some interactive visualization techniques (e.g., overview+detail) few results exist; for others (e.g., focus+context) results are positive for small displays, but it is unclear if the technique is useful on large displays. Finally, studies that investigate the effect of display size typically keep the size of the data set constant [e.g., 3, 5] or varied relative to display size [e.g., 4, 36, 37]. The scale factor between an overview of the entire data set and the lowest zoom level varies if data size is kept constant, which can impact the performance of different visualization techniques. The scale ratio can be kept constant if the data set size is varied, but because data and tasks differ across display sizes, performance cannot be compared in absolute measures. Instead, conclusions are based on whether increases in completion time are lower than increases in data set size. In the experiment presented next, we use the same size information space for different sizes of display and different interactive visualizations.

EXPERIMENT

We conducted an experiment with three interfaces for navigating maps using three different sizes of display. Our aim is to understand better the relation between usability of interactive visualization techniques and display size.

The guiding principle behind the design of the experiment is to build on existing work on visualization. Thus, the interfaces implemented three widely used visualization techniques: focus+context, overview+detail, and zooming. The implementations resemble those typically used in the literature so as to extend earlier results, in particular from comparisons of visualization techniques. For this reason we did not use improvements such as speed-coupled flattening or high-precision magnification lenses [2, 28]. Further, participants solved tasks similar to previous research on visualizations or large displays. This choice means that our aim is not, initially, to adapt visualizations for a particular display size, but rather to bring about the empirical data that would inform such adaptations.

Method

A within-subjects design was used in which three factors were varied: display size (Small, Medium, Large), interface (Focus+Context, Overview+Detail, Zooming), and task type (Navigate, Compare, Trace). Participants performed all types of task in each of nine blocks. Each block used a unique combination of display size and interface. We systematically varied the order of the combinations across participants using a Greco-Latin square so as to reduce the influence of learning effects. Also, the order of task types was varied randomly across blocks. In total, 21 repetitions of tasks were made in each block (10 Navigate, 9 Compare, 2 Trace), giving 189 data points for each participant (3×3×21).

Participants

Nineteen volunteers (five female), 19-38 years old, participated in the experiment. Participants were recruited by word of mouth and were provided no compensation.

Apparatus

Participants used a 13.8 megapixel (5760x2400) display (shown in Figure 3). The display consisted of six 24" LCD monitors, each with a maximum resolution of 1920x1200, arranged in a 3x2 grid. The monitors were positioned at a 135° horizontal angle relative to each other, so that they are curved around the user, as suggested by [31]. The monitors were operated by a Radeon HD 5870 Eyefinity card.

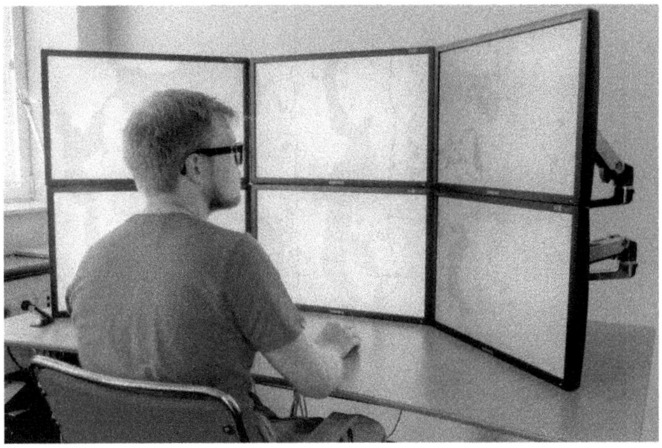

Figure 3: The six-monitor setup used in the experiment.

Three display sizes were used in the experiment containing 1/81th, 1/9th, and all of the display's pixel area (see Figure 1). Thus, the aspect ratio could be kept constant at 2.4:1 across display sizes. The Small condition used 640x267 pixels of the upper-center panel; the Medium condition used 1920x800 pixels. The Large condition used the full 5760x2400 of the display. The display contained 94 pixels per inch in all conditions.

For input, participants used a Logitech LX8 wireless laser mouse with a scroll-wheel. The default mouse settings in Windows 7 were used. Touch input is becoming common for small-screen devices. However, we chose a mouse as input across conditions for experimental control. Also, mouse is the input device most frequently used for the visualization techniques we study.

Interfaces

Three interfaces allowed users to navigate the maps. The interfaces were implemented in Java using a modified version of the ZVTM library [27]. We optimized the interfaces so that the screen updated at a minimum of 15 frames per second, which was found acceptable in informal evaluations with users.

Focus+Context

The focus+context interface (see Figure 4) shows the entire map at the lowest possible scale (i.e., map pixels per display pixels, see Table 1). A Gaussian lens using an L(2) radial metric [12] magnifies the focus region at the mouse cursor. The lens has a diameter of 50% of the display height

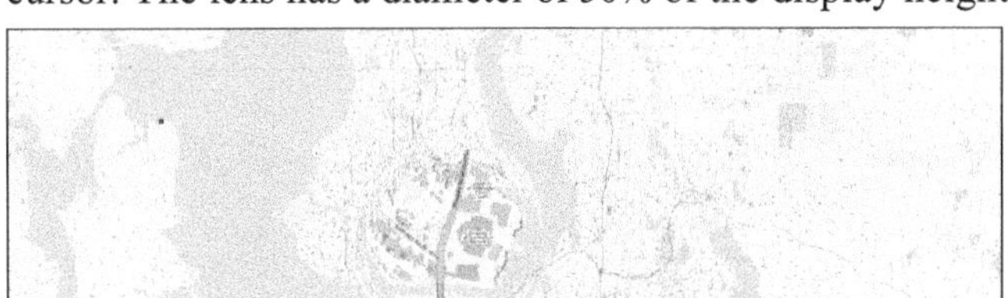

Figure 4: The focus+context interface at Medium display size.

Figure 5: The overview+detail interface at Medium display size containing an overview window in the upper-right corner.

and thus covers 12% of the total display area. The lens has a flat top that shows the focus area at constant magnification, with a diameter of 30% of the display height. The magnification in the focus area varies between 3x in Large, 9x in Medium, 27x in Small so that the lens shows the map at the lowest scale (1 map pixel per display pixel, see Table 1).

Our aim was for the focus+context interface to resemble the implementations used in previous research. We reviewed 14 papers reporting empirical studies of fisheye interfaces published between 2000 and 2009 [e.g., 10, 17, 18, 20]. A flat-top lens was most frequently used and most often with a diameter around 30%.

Overview+Detail

The overview+detail interface (see Figure 5) includes a detail view that can be panned to show different parts of the map at lowest scale. To pan the view, the user clicks and drags the mouse opposite the panning direction (i.e., the map follows the mouse). The interface also includes an overview window, located in the upper right corner of the detail view, which shows the entire map at a higher scale (see Table 1). The user can click and hold the left mouse button to drag a field-of-view box in the overview in order to pan the detail view. Also, the user can click on a point in the overview outside the field-of-view box to center the detail view on that point. We used 10% of the display area for the overview widget. This size was found by reviewing 13 studies mentioned in [13] and choosing the median size overview; the field-of-view and the interaction facilities working on it were also typical among the reviewed studies.

Zooming

The zooming interface (see Figure 6) includes a view that can be panned in the same way as the detail view in

		Small	Medium	Large
F+C	Focus / Context	1 / 27	1 / 9	1 / 3
O+D	Detail / Overview	1 / 85	1 / 28	1 / 9
Z+P	Highest / Lowest	1 / 27	1 / 9	1 / 3

Table 1: Scale (map pixels per display pixels) in the focus and surrounding context of focus+context (F+C), detail and overview windows of overview+detail (O+D) and at highest and lowest zoom level in zooming (Z+P). For instance, maps are 7200 pixels high, the overview window at Small 84 pixels, requiring 85 map pixels per display pixel.

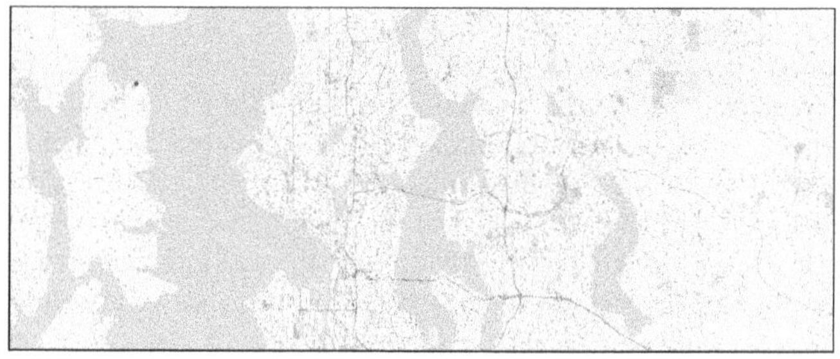

Figure 6: The zooming interface at Medium display size.

overview+detail. Additionally, the user can zoom the view to show the map at different scales. Zooming is constrained between the lowest scale of 1 map pixel per display pixels and the scale at which the entire map fits in the display (see Table 1). The user scrolls the mouse wheel up to zoom the map to a lower scale, and scrolls down to zoom to a higher scale; transitions between scales are animated. The zoom rate was adjusted so that zooming from the highest to the lowest scale (or vice versa) could be done in 300ms. The mouse cursor is used as the center of zooming, which is familiar to users of widespread map interfaces (e.g., Google Maps, maps.google.com).

Information Spaces and Tasks

Participants performed geospatial tasks using maps of large cities. Nine maps were used, all generated from OpenStreetMap (www.openstreetmap.org) at zoom level 16 for which most street names are visible. Each map was 17280 x 7200 pixels, which is the same aspect ratio as the display. Participants completed a block of 21 tasks with each interface × display size combination. Each block was completed with a different map.

All tasks involved targets superimposed on the maps. Targets are smaller at higher levels of scale (see Table 2). To make targets perceptible at high levels of scale on the small display (especially in the overview) and with the wide field-of-view of the large display, an animated halo was shown (increasing radius in one-second repeating loop) around each target. Three tasks were used:

For *Navigate* tasks, a single target was shown on the map that participants had to select by clicking it using the mouse. The target could only be selected at the lowest level of scale, at which the target representation would change so as to indicate that it could be selected. Clicking on the target completed the task. Targets were 40x40 map pixels and were placed at distances of 3500 or 7000 map pixels

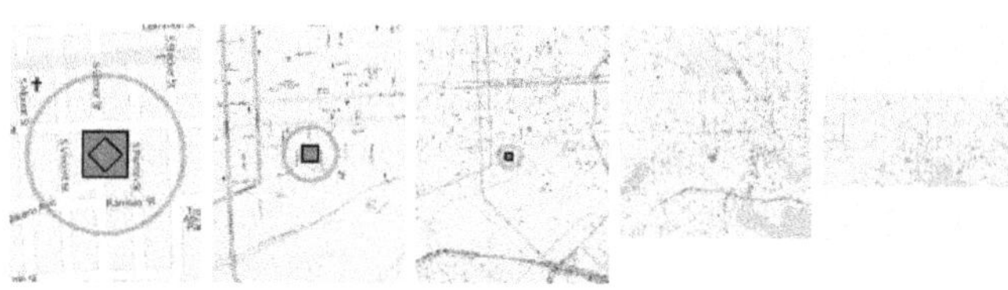

1 3 9 27 85

Table 2: Map containing a Navigate target, shown at different scales. The lowest scale (left) is 1 map pixel per display pixel and, the highest scale (right) is 85 map pixels per display pixel (only used in the overview window at Small display size).

(about 50% and 100% of the map height) from the center of the map; their angle to the center was varied at random.

For *Compare* tasks, three targets representing fictional houses were shown on the map, placed equidistant to each other. Participants were asked to compare the dollar amount of the targets and select the target with the highest amount. The amounts were only visible at the lowest level of scale and also, similar to Navigate tasks, targets could only be selected at the lowest level of scale. Clicking on a target finished the task. A similar type of task was used by Ball and North [4]. Targets were 40x40 map pixels. The distance between targets varied between 1440, 3600, and 5760 map pixels (20%, 50%, or 80% of the map height).

For *Trace* route tasks, the start and end point of a route were indicated as a green triangle and a red circle on the map. The routes used in the tasks were sections of roads about 3000 map pixels in length. We selected major roads (e.g., interstate highways) that were distinguishable at all levels of scale for all display sizes. Participants had to follow the route, clicking on all overpasses along the route with the mouse. This task resembles that used by Shupp et al. [31]. Mouse clicks were logged for later analysis. Participants finished the task by clicking on the red circle that indicated the end point of the route.

Dependent variables

Dependent variables were time to complete tasks, measures of accuracy, and subjective measures of mental effort. We automatically recorded task completion times, accuracy, and data describing participants' interaction with the interfaces. Following the advice of Sauro and Dumas [30], we used the Subjective Mental Effort Questionnaire (SMEQ, see [38]). SMEQ consist of a graphical rating scale, annotated with descriptions of effort. It is easy for participants to use, and could thus be administered after each task type. Thereby we get a more fine-grained, and thus more valid, assessment of participants' mental effort, based on SMEQ measures for each of the 27 display size × interface × task type combinations.

Procedure

Participants sat in a chair with their face at a distance of about 67cm from each of the monitors. The field-of-view angle varied between 16° for Small and 135° for Large.

Participants were first given an introduction to each of the interfaces, using the medium display size. The three types of task used in the experiment were then explained. Next, participants performed training tasks of each type using each of the nine display size × interface conditions. After the introduction, participants completed nine blocks of 21 tasks using a different display size × interface condition to complete the tasks in each block. Tasks were presented in a window that cued participants to continue when they were ready. Immediately after participants clicked 'start', targets were added to the map and the mouse cursor was automatically placed in the center in the display. An electronic version of SMEQ was administered to participants after completing all trials of a particular type of task. After completing all tasks, participants were asked to comment on their use of the interfaces at different display sizes. The experiment lasted on average one hour and 15 minutes for each participant.

Expectations

Although we consider the experiment exploratory, we did form some hypotheses before running the experiment. Overall, we expected users to perform tasks fastest using the Large display condition, because less virtual navigation is required. This is suggested by results from earlier research [3, 5, 36, 37].

For focus+context, we expected relatively faster performance with a larger display. Increasing the display size results in lower control-display ratio in the lens and thus problems of acquiring targets are less severe. Also, the size of the lens is larger, resulting in (1) less compression in transition between focus and context, and (2) more information shown in detail. It was not clear a priori whether the positive findings from earlier research on small-display focus+context techniques would transfer to our setup, because earlier research would make extensive adaption of techniques to suit the small displays.

For overview+detail, we were unsure whether to expect faster overall performance with larger display because a larger area can be viewed in detail. Nevertheless, we expected comparison tasks to benefit from the difference in ratio between scales in overview and detail views, because of decreased motor effort.

For zooming, we expected comparable performance across display sizes, although the zooming functionality and the accuracy with which you can zoom towards a point is likely to hurt performance in the Small display condition.

RESULTS

We performed a 3 (display size) × 3 (interface) × 3 (task type) repeated measures analysis of variance on the task completion times and the SMEQ ratings. To correct the skew and to reduce the influence of outliers, the completion times were logarithmically transformed. We examine significant effects using Bonferroni-corrected pairwise comparisons. Unless otherwise noted, differences are significant at the $p < .001$ level.

Accuracy was uniformly high ($M = 99\%$, $SD = 10\%$) and is not analyzed further.

Task completion times

Average task completion times with the different display sizes and interfaces are shown in Figure 7. We found a main effect for interface, $F(4, 36) = 118.05$, $p < .0001$. Overall, pairwise comparisons showed that overview+detail ($M = 7.9$s) was faster than zooming ($M = 9.6$s), $p < .05$, which in turn was faster than focus+context ($M = 14.9$s). However, an interaction between interface and task type was found, $F(2.65, 47.69) = 13.666$, $p < .0001$. Figure 8 summarizes task completion times for the different task

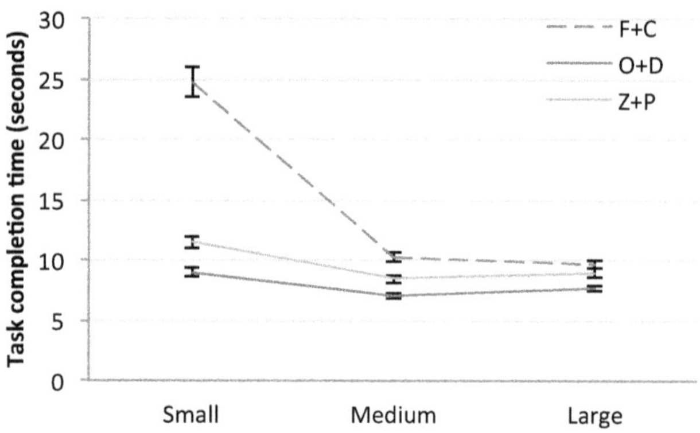

Figure 7: Average task completion times with focus+context (F+C), overview+detail (O+D), and zooming (Z+P) at different display sizes. Error bars show standard error of the mean.

types. As the figure suggests, overview+detail (M = 9.1s) was faster than zooming (M = 12.9s) for Compare tasks, but was not faster for Navigate or Trace route tasks. It is likely that overview+detail only performed better in Compare tasks because participants could bring the three targets into view with low physical effort, once they had moved the mouse to the overview; in zooming, participants had to either pan or zoom to navigate to each target.

We also found a main effect for display size, $F(4, 36) = 167.59$, $p < .0001$. Participants performed tasks faster with Large (M = 8.8s) and Medium (M = 8.6s) compared with Small (M = 15.1s). Contrary to our expectations, Large was not faster than Medium, but slightly slower, $p < .05$; however, the difference is small (2.5%). As suggested by Figure 7, this finding is related to differences between interfaces, which we analyze below. Despite the qualifications below, this finding is a key result because the expectation raised by the literature would be a strong effect in the opposite direction.

A significant interaction between display size and interface was found, $F(4, 72) = 38.904$, $p < .0001$. Post-hoc comparisons showed a significant increase in time for all interfaces when moving from Medium to Small display size, $p < .0001$ (see Figure 7). The largest differences between interfaces are found for the Small display; in particular, participants spent 173% more time with focus+context (M = 24.7s) compared with overview+detail (M = 9.1s). Possible explanations for the exceptionally poor performance of focus+context at the Small display size are that (1) the very small lens top together with the increased compression in the transition between focus and context make focus targeting more difficult and (2) the high control-display ratio makes it hard to acquire targets.

One explanation behind the observation that Medium slightly outperforms Large could be that participants with the large display initially had to spend more time searching for targets, offsetting other performance benefits of that display. We thus analyzed the initial search time, that is, task completion times minus the time spent before participants moved the mouse more than a threshold distance. The average initial search time was 0.8s (SD = 1.1s). Adjusting the times for initial search did not change the overall result, but reveals an interface-specific finding: the poorer performance with focus+context and zooming in the Large display seems due to slower initial search for targets. First, in Table 3, which shows initial search times as percentage of total task time for each interface, we see an increase in time spent searching with focus+context and zooming, but not with overview+detail. By comparing Figure 8 with Figure 9 (in which initial search times are excluded) we see that this increase in initial search time accounts for the decreased performance with focus+context and zooming for Navigate tasks; the performance decrease with overview+detail, in contrast, seems unrelated to search time. The reason participants spent more time searching with focus+context and zooming is probably because of the wider field-of-view that needs to be searched; with overview+detail, participants could likely find targets faster in the overview. The increase in search time on large displays has less impact on the relatively longer task times for Compare and Trace route tasks (see Table 4).

Subjective ratings of effort

Participants rated each interface × display size × task type using SMEQ; higher values of SMEQ indicates higher effort. Figure 10 shows average ratings for the different display sizes and interfaces. There was a main effect for

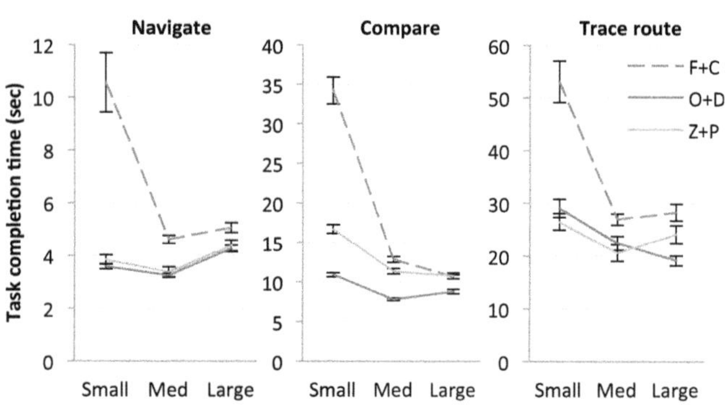

Figure 8: Average completion times for the three task types with focus+context (F+C), overview+detail (O+D), and zooming (Z+P) at different display sizes. Error bars show standard error of the mean.

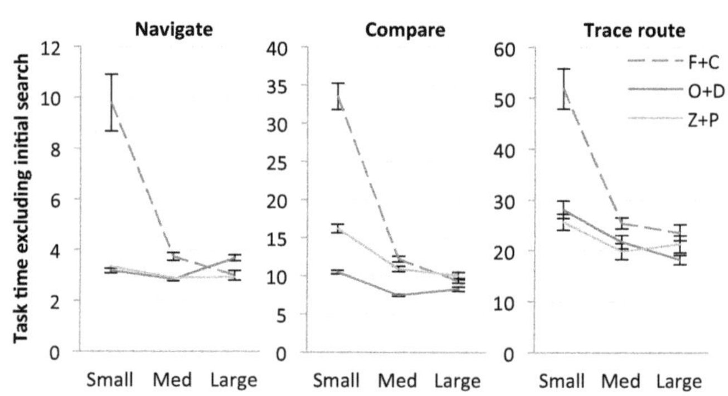

Figure 9: Average completion times without initial search time for the three task types with focus+context (F+C), overview+detail (O+D), and zooming (Z+P) at different display sizes. Error bars show standard error of the mean.

	Small	Medium	Large
Focus+context	4%	10%	23%
Overview+detail	6%	7%	8%
Zooming	6%	7%	17%

Table 3: Percentage of task time initially spent searching for targets with different interfaces and display sizes. A noticeable increase between Medium and Large is found for focus+context and zooming, but not for overview+detail.

display size, $F(2, 32) = 91.178$, $p < .0001$. Participants found tasks "fairly hard" to "rather hard" to do ($M = 48.9$) with Small, a significantly worse rating than both Medium ($M = 22.5$) and Large ($M = 19.9$). There was no overall difference in ratings between Medium and Large, $p = .396$.

We also found a main effect for interface, $F(2, 32) = 71.438$, $p < .001$. Participants found both overview+detail ($M = 18.4$) and zooming ($M = 21.2$) easier to use than focus+context ($M = 51.7$) but ratings did not differ between overview+detail and zooming, $p = .569$.

A significant interaction of display size × interface was found, $F(4, 64) = 57.629$, $p < .0001$. Participants found overview+detail more difficult to use on Large ($M = 18.3$) than Medium ($M = 12.0$), $p < .05$, whereas focus+context was found less difficult on Large ($M = 25.0$) than Medium ($M = 37.9$), $p < .01$. No difference was found for zooming.

Participants' comments

Participants commented on their use of the interfaces after the experiment. Supported by informal observations we made during the experiment, these comments help explain the results.

Overall, most participants expressed preference for overview+detail; the overview helped finding targets and moving them into the detail view. Focus+context was the least preferred, especially with the Small display; common reasons given were that targets were difficult or impossible to see in the transition area and that the pointing precision in the lens was poor. We saw participants employ different

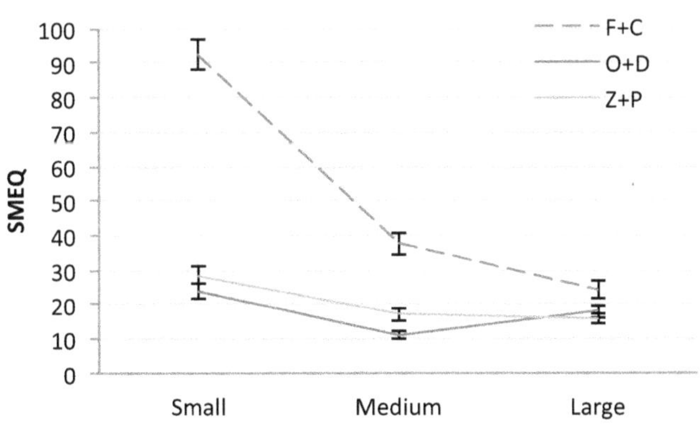

Figure 10: Average Subjective Mental Effort Questionnaire (SMEQ) ratings with focus+context (F+C), overview+detail (O+D), and zooming (Z+P) at different display sizes. Higher values indicate higher effort. Error bars show standard error of the mean.

	Small	Medium	Large
Navigate	9%	16%	30%
Compare	3%	5%	9%
Trace route	3%	4%	12%

Table 4: Percentage of time initially spent searching for targets for different types of task and different display sizes.

strategies for overcoming these problems (e.g., steering in a straight line toward the target or by geographical features or landmarks).

Overall, Medium was the display size that most participants preferred. At least two participants said they liked that the Medium display fit into their field of view. In contrast, participants said that the Large display required more visual search and too much movement (head or mouse). Specifically about overview+detail with the Large display, a few participants gave comments suggesting that it was difficult to coordinate the overview and the detail view because the detail view was so large. This might explain why participants found tasks more difficult to complete with overview+detail in Large compared with Medium.

Participants commented that the bezels could be disruptive when, occasionally, targets ended up between two display panels. From informal observations, the bezels seemed particularly problematic for the fisheye lens in route tracing tasks; the map moves inside lens across bezels, which might be confusing – we saw participants move the lens back and forth across bezels in trace route tasks.

Interaction

We analyzed the data collected during the experiment so as to understand differences in how participants used the interfaces at different display sizes. We discuss two activities in participants' interaction with the interfaces: (1) mouse movement and (2) virtual navigation (zooming, panning, and use of the overview) in the overview+detail and zooming interfaces.

First, we examined the effect of display size on physical mouse movement. To do so, we calculated the Euclidian distance between coordinates of the mouse pointer at each mouse event. We found a main effect of display size on the mouse travel distance, $F(1.25, 22.46) = 281.51$, $p < .0001$. Overall, the average mouse travel distance in pixels increased 73.4% from Small ($M = 1755$) to Medium ($M = 3043$) and 93% from Medium to Large ($M = 5874$). Figure 11 shows how the average mouse travel distance varied between display sizes and across interfaces and tasks. We note three differences between interfaces. First, the focus+context interface required the least mouse movements across tasks. Second, overview+detail required relatively more mouse movements for Navigate and Trace route tasks than the other interfaces, but less movements than the zooming interface in Compare tasks. Third, the mouse movements required by the zooming interface seems to scale proportionally with display size.

We also analyzed how much time participants spent on virtually navigating in the maps using the interfaces: Figure 12 shows how much of the time participants spent on zooming and panning with the zooming interface; Figure 13 how much of the time participants spent on using the overview and on panning with overview+detail. Time spent on zooming was the time from participants started scrolling the mouse wheel to the animated transition ended. Time spent on panning included periods where participants dragged the mouse with the button pressed. We found a main effect of display size on the amount of time participants spent navigating using Overview+Detail, $F(1.24, 22.39) = 27.366$, $p < .0001$, and Zooming, $F(2, 36) = 121.62$, $p < .0001$. Overall, participants spent less of the time zooming and panning with Large (M = 22.9%) compared with Medium (M = 32.8%) and Small (M = 35.3%). Time spent using the overview included periods where the mouse cursor was inside the overview window. Also, relatively less time was spent on using the overview and on panning with Large (M = 52.1%) than with Medium (M = 62.7%) and Small (M = 63.2%).

In sum, although virtual navigation was reduced on larger displays, as indicated by the reduction in panning, zooming, or interaction with the overview, there was an increase in physical mouse movements.

DISCUSSION

Our study has shown that users perform surprisingly similar with multi-scale navigation techniques used for simple visualizations on medium and large size displays. The larger display increases mouse movement and affects visual search time, possibly offsetting other performance benefits such as lowered virtual navigation. The difference between a small display and a medium display was significant, both in terms of task completion time and subjectively perceived effort. Overview+detail performed the best, was preferred by participants, and provided useful support for navigation through its overview widget. The focus+context technique worked very poorly at small displays, but required the least movement for large displays. We found strong effects of task, both on the interaction between display size and visualization technique and on how participants interacted with the interfaces.

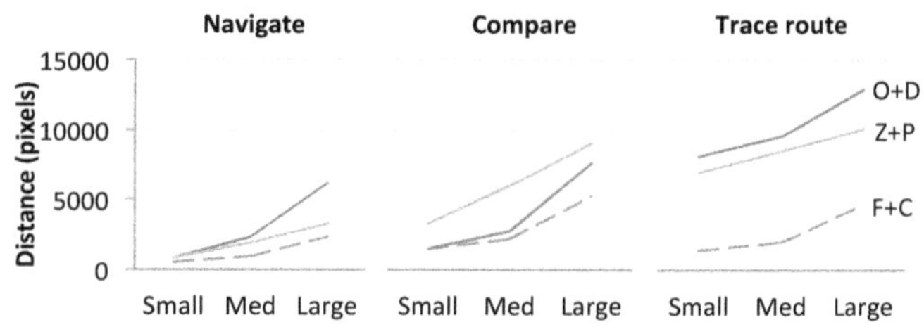

Figure 11: Average distance participants moved the mouse to complete tasks using focus+context (F+C), overview+detail (O+D), and zooming (Z+P) at different display sizes.

The main point for discussion is why the benefits that we would expect from large-display research [e.g., 14, 35] do not materialize in the present study. Whereas the wider-view-argument for large displays presented in the section on related work has extensive empirical support, a wider view negatively interferes with our techniques. First, if targets are visible at all levels of scale, then much more visual search has to be done on a large display compared to the smaller displays. Second, for interactive visualization techniques like zooming and overview+detail, most of the contents of the display changes when the user zooms or pans. The experienced optical flow is thus much higher and may potentially add to the perceived mental effort (as measured by SMEQ). This is the case, for instance, for overview+detail where SMEQ increases from Medium to Large display sizes.

Our results are particularly disappointing given the work of North and colleagues [1, 3, 5, 6, 36, 37]. Ball et al. [6] found that "find" and "trace route" tasks were performed faster when display size increased from 1 through 4 to 9 monitors. In their study, however, no interaction with targets was required. Our results show reduced virtual navigation, but potential benefits are offset by the need for more mouse movement. Other work by North and colleagues emphasize the role of physical navigation [5]. One difference in our approaches—that may explain why North et al. found performance improvements with large displays while we did not—is that target search time was excluded from their navigation tasks (find a particular house and related information), whereas search was included in our tasks. Also, physical navigation was

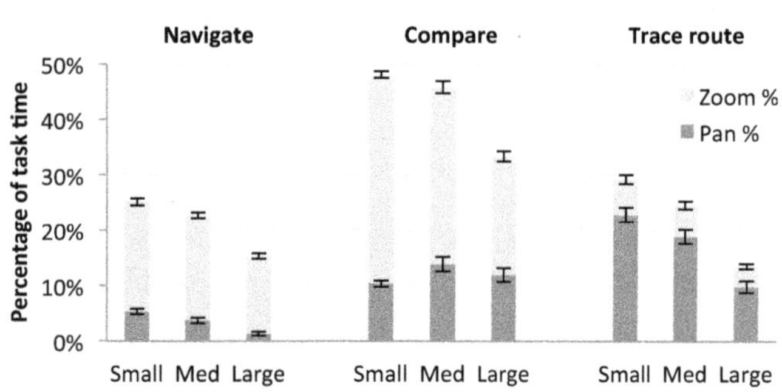

Figure 12: Time spent on zooming or panning with the zooming interface at different sizes. Error bars indicate standard error of the mean. Overall, time spent on zooming and panning actions tend to fall as display size increases.

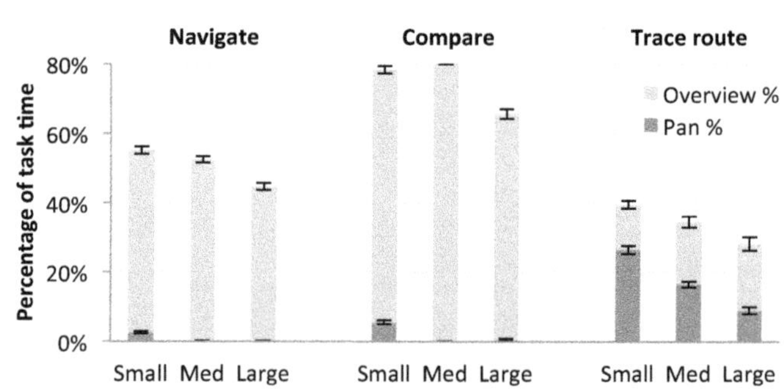

Figure 13: Time spent using the overview or panning with the overview+detail interface at different sizes. Error bars indicate standard error of the mean. Overall, time spent on navigation actions tend to fall as display size increases.

beneficial in [5], but our setup restricted physical navigation to head movements. Nevertheless, the difference in time to find a particular known object on the smallest display varies a lot between their study (about 17 seconds) and ours (about 4 seconds with overview+detail or zooming). It seems that more work is needed to define and explain these differences in methodology and results.

The inferiority of a small display to a medium display is clear, both in terms of task completion time, subjective assessments of effort, and comments after the evaluation. In particular, the relation between changes in motor space and the corresponding changes in display space poses many difficulties to participants. Earlier work [10, 19] suggested that focus+context is a particularly viable technique for small displays; in our case, focus+context performs considerably poorer than the alternatives. Key differences are (a) the size of the information space relative to the display, (b) the specialized nature of the focus+context implementations in earlier work.

Our results may also be discussed as a comparison of three visualization techniques, about which much is already known. We find overview+detail relatively robust across display sizes, in agreement with reviews [13] and empirical studies on medium-sized displays [8, 22]. Pietriga et al. [29] similarly found a preference for overview+detail, but also found that focus+context outperformed zooming; this is not the case in our experiment. One important difference is that Pietriga used an adjustable magnification factor between 2 and 12, whereas ours were fixed. Also, the zoom factor in our experiment was high. Gutwin and Skopik [20] found a focus+context interface to perform better than both overview+detail and zoom+pan interfaces in steering tasks. In the large display condition, our focus+context interface used a similar magnification factor (they used 2 and 4), but performance in trace route tasks that are similar to the steering tasks of [20] was relatively worse.

Another important point of discussion is the view that visualization techniques could not be expected to scale to larger (or smaller) displays directly; adaptations of such techniques would be needed to make them work well. In this view, the expectation that three classic interactive visualization techniques would work on large (and small) displays is overly optimistic. Several design choices in the present experiment have influenced performance. First, we restricted the allowed zoom levels, so that participants could not zoom in or out too much (as done also by for instance [21, 29]). This is often seen as a benefit, helping users avoid "desert fog" [24], but it means that participants are restricted from using approaches they might use with other zooming interfaces. Second, the field-of-view in the overview+detail was a fixed size, and the detail view thus at a constant zoom level (as done by [8, 26], though not in for instance [21]). This forces users to relatively much virtual navigation (see Figure 13). Third, other focus+context techniques could perform better than our implementation, particularly for the Small display size: speed-coupled blending lenses [22] make focus targeting easier; high-precision magnification lenses [2] help acquire targets at magnification factors as high as 27x. Fourth, the optical flow on large displays with for instance overview+detail could be reduced in future adaptations of visualization techniques (e.g., by using coordinated windows).

The experiment that we presented has some obvious limitations that should be addressed in future work. First, we used fixed-sized information spaces: As already argued, this approach differs to that of many papers by North and colleagues. Our approach may have favored larger displays in that the information space was kept constant across display sizes; it also results in higher magnification factors on small displays (which might especially impact focus targeting and target selection in focus+context). Future work should compare fixed information spaces (as we have used) to information spaces whose size scale with the size of the display. Second, the tasks we used are limited. Tasks focused on navigation in geographical maps where targets are visible at all levels of scale. None of the tasks required extensive use of information at multiple levels of scale. Third, our purpose in this paper has not been to model the differences in navigation across displays and visualization techniques. A more focused experiment using Fitts's style task and modeling (as in [29]) might help further characterize navigation on large and small displays.

CONCLUSION

Much research has documented the benefits of large displays and those of visualizations, but we know little about their combination. We have investigated the usability of classic interactive visualization techniques (viz., focus+context, overview+detail, and zooming) across three sizes of display, used by 19 participants to navigate maps.

The results show that interactive visualization techniques work comparably for multi-scale navigation across large and medium sized displays in terms of task completion time and subjective satisfaction; visualizations on small displays performed the worst. We find strong interactions of display size and visualization technique. Also, task type significantly influences the display conditions under which a particular technique performs the best.

Our findings stand in contrast to most other studies of visualizations on large displays. Key differences concern whether visualizations are interactive or not, whether physical navigation is possible or not, and the size and contents of the data sets tested. Nevertheless, we argue that adaptation of interactive visualization techniques for large display is needed, and that further work needs to investigate both the possibilities and the limitations of large displays for interactive visualizations.

ACKNOWLEDGMENTS

We thank the reviewers for helping us improve this paper. Also, we thank Aurelien Tabard, Jakob E. Bardram, Juan Hincapié Ramos, and colleagues at our department for comments on earlier drafts of this paper. Last, we thank Chris North for advice on the setup of large displays.

REFERENCES

1. Andrews, C., Endert, A. and North, C. Space to think: Large, high-resolution displays for sense making. In *Proc. CHI 2010*. ACM Press (2010), 55-64.
2. Appert, C., Chapuis, O. and Pietriga, E. High-precision magnification lenses. In *Proc. CHI 2010* (2010), 273-282.
3. Ball, R. and North, C. Effects of tiled high-resolution display on basic visualization and navigation tasks. In *Proc. Extended Abstracts, CHI 2005*. ACM (2005), 1196-1199.
4. Ball, R. and North, C. The Effects of Peripheral Vision and Physical Navigation on Large Scale Visualization. In *Proc. GI 2008* (2008), 9-16.
5. Ball, R., North, C. and Bowman, D. A. Move to improve: promoting physical navigation to increase user performance with large displays. . In *Proc. CHI 2007* (2007), 191-200.
6. Ball, R., Varghese, M., Carstensen, B., Cox, E. D., Fierer, C., Peterson, M. and North, C. Evaluating the Benefits of Tiled Displays for Navigating Maps. In *Proc. IASTED International Conference on Human-Computer Interaction* (2005), 66-71.
7. Baudisch, P., Good, N., Belotti, V. and Schradley, P. Keeping things in context: a comparative evaluation of focus plus context screens, overviews, and zooming. In *Proc. CHI 2002*. ACM Press (2002), 259-266.
8. Beard, D. B. and Walker, J. Q. Navigational Techniques to Improve the Display of Large Two-Dimensional Spaces. *Behaviour and Information Technology*, 9, 6 (1990), 451-466.
9. Bederson, B. B., Clamage, A., Czerwinski, M. P. and Robertson, G. G. DateLens: A fisheye calendar interface for PDAs. *ACM Transactions on Computer-Human Interaction*, 11, 1 (2004), 90-119.
10. Büring, T., Gerken, J. and Reiterer, H. User Interaction with Scatterplots on Small Screens - A Comparative Evaluation of Geometric-Semantic Zoom and Fisheye Distortion. *IEEE transactions on visualization and computer graphics* 12, 5 (2006), 829-836.
11. Card, S. K., Mackinlay, J. D. and Shneiderman, B. *Readings in Information Visualization*. Morgan Kaufmann, San Francisco, CA, 1999.
12. Carpendale, M. S. T. and Montagnese, C. A framework for unifying presentation space. In *Proc. UIST2001*. ACM Press (2001), 61-70.
13. Cockburn, A., Karlson, A. K. and Bederson, B. B. A review of overview+detail, zooming, and focus+context interfaces. *ACM Computing Surveys*, 41, 1 (2008).
14. Czerwinski, M., Smith, G., Meyers, B., Robertson, G. and Starkweather, G. Towards characterizing the productivity benefits of very large displays. In *Proc. Interact'2003*. IOS Press (2003), 9-16.
15. Elrod, S., Bruce, R., Gold, R., Goldberg, D., Halasz, F., Janssen, W., Lee, D., McCall, K., Pedersen, E., Pier, K., Tang, J. and Welch, B. Liveboard: a large interactive display supporting group meetings, presentations, and remote collaboration. In *Proc. CHI'92* (1992),
16. Guimbretière, F., Stone, M. and Winograd, T. Fluid interaction with high-resolution wall-size displays. In *Proc. UIST 2001* (2001), 21-30.
17. Gutwin, C. Improving focus targeting in interactive fisheye views. In *Proc. CHI 2002*. ACM Press (2002), 267-274.
18. Gutwin, C. and Fedak, C. A comparison of fisheye lenses for interactive layout tasks. In *Proc. GI 2004*. Canadian Human-Computer Communications Society (2004), 213-220.
19. Gutwin, C. and Fedak, C. Interacting with big interfaces on small screens: a comparison of fisheye, zoom, and panning techniques. In *Proc. GI 2004*. Canadian Human-Computer Communications Society (2004), 145-152.
20. Gutwin, C. and Skopik, A. Fisheye views are good for large steering tasks. In *Proc. CHI 2003*. ACM (2003), 201-208.
21. Hornbæk, K., Bederson, B. and Plaisant, C. Overview+Detail and Zoomable User Interfaces: An Evaluation of Navigation Patterns and Usability. *ACM Transactions on Computer-Human Interaction*, 9, 4 (2002), 362-389.
22. Hornbæk, K. and Frøkjær, E. Reading patterns and usability in visualizations of electronic documents. *ACM Transactions on Computer-Human Interaction*, 10, 2 (2003), 119-149.
23. Jeremy P. Birnholtz, Tovi Grossman, Clarissa Mak and Balakrishnan, R. An exploratory study of input configuration and group process in a negotiation task using a large display. In *Proc. CHI 2007* (2007), 91-100.
24. Jul, S. and Furnas, G. W. Critical zones in desert fog: aids to multiscale navigation. In *Proc. UIST'98*. ACM (1998), 97-106.
25. Khan, A., Matejka, J., Fitzmaurice, G. and Kurtenbach, G. Spotlight: directing users' attention on large displays. In *Proc. CHI 2005* (2005), 791-798.
26. Nekrasovski, D., Bodnar, A., McGrenere, J., Guimbretiére, F. and Munzner, T. An evaluation of pan & zoom and rubber sheet navigation with and without an overview. In *Proc. CHI 2006*. ACM Press (2006), 11-20.
27. Pietriga, E. A Toolkit for Addressing HCI Issues in Visual Language Environments. In *Proc. VL/HCC'05* (2005), 145-152.
28. Pietriga, E. and Appert, C. Sigma lenses: focus-context transitions combining space, time and translucence. In *Proc. CHI 2008* (2008), 1343-1352.
29. Pietriga, E., Appert, C. and Beaudouin-Lafon, M. Pointing and beyond: an operationalization and preliminary evaluation of multi-scale searching. In *Proc. CHI 2007* (2007), 1215-1224.
30. Sauro, J. and Dumas, J. Comparison of three one-question, post-task usability questionnaire. In *Proc. CHI 2009* (2009), 1599-1608.
31. Shupp, L., Andrews, C., Dickey-Kurdziolek, M., Yost, B. and North, C. Shaping the Display of the Future: The Effects of Display Size and Curvature on User Performance and Insights. *Human-Computer Interaction*, 24, 1&2 (2009), 230-272.
32. Spence, R. *Information Visualization: Design for Interaction. Second Edition*. Prentice Hall, Harlow, UK, 2007.
33. Streitz, N. A., Geißler, J., Holmer, T., Konomi, S., Müller-Tomfelde, C., Reischl, W., Rexroth, P., Seitz, P. and Steinmetz, R. i-LAND: an interactive landscape for creativity and innovation. In *Proc. CHI'99*. ACM Press (1999), 120-127.
34. Swaminathan, K. and Sato, S. Interaction design for large displays. *interactions*, 4, 1 (1997), 15-24.
35. Tan, D. S., Gergle, D., Scupelli, P. and Pausch, R. With similar visual angles, larger displays improve spatial performance. In *Proc. CHI 2003*. ACM (2003), 217-224.
36. Yost, B. and North, C. The perceptual scalability of visualization. *IEEE Transactions on Visualization and Computer Graphics*, 12, 5 (2006), 837-844.
37. Yost, B., Haciahmetoglu, Y. and North, C. Beyond visual acuity: the perceptual scalability of information visualizations for large displays. In *Proc. CHI 2007* (2007), 101-110.
38. Zijlstra, F. *Efficiency in work behavior. A design approach for modern tools*. Delft University Press, Delft, The Netherlands, 1993.

The Impact of Social Information on Visual Judgments

Jessica Hullman, Eytan Adar
University of Michigan, School of Information
Ann Arbor, MI, USA
{jhullman, eadar}@umich.edu

Priti Shah
University of Michigan, Department of Psychology
Ann Arbor, MI, USA
priti@umich.edu

ABSTRACT
Social visualization systems have emerged to support collective intelligence-driven analysis of a growing influx of open data. As with many other online systems, social signals (e.g., forums, polls) are commonly integrated to drive use. Unfortunately, the same social features that can provide rapid, high-accuracy analysis are coupled with the pitfalls of any social system. Through an experiment involving over 300 subjects, we address how social information signals (social proof) affect quantitative judgments in the context of graphical perception. We identify how unbiased social signals lead to fewer errors over non-social settings and conversely, how biased signals lead to more errors. We further reflect on how systematic bias nullifies certain collective intelligence benefits, and we provide evidence of the formation of information cascades. We describe how these findings can be applied to collaborative visualization systems to produce more accurate individual interpretations in social contexts.

Author Keywords
Graphical perception, information visualization, social proof, social influence, Mechanical Turk.

ACM Classification Keywords
H5.m. Information interfaces and presentation (e.g., HCI): Miscellaneous.

General Terms
Experimentation, Human Factors, Measurement.

INTRODUCTION
More individuals are generating and analyzing interactive data visualizations online than ever before, thanks to a growing number of social visualization sites like ManyEyes [43] and Swivel [40]. The need for such systems is in part driven by the ample availability of open data and the strong belief that collective analysis of this data might produce better understanding of this information. Social interaction, through visualization annotation, is suggested to be a primary motivator of use [20, 46, 44]. This leads researchers and system designers to consider how they might further increase users' engagement in these environments through design features that support and encourage social interaction. Such features include active and passive collaboration tools that range from threaded discussions, social embedding, tagging and other social annotation schemes. The most evident impact of these designs is that the visualization artifact is no longer considered independently of social content as prior members' responses and observations become attached to the visualization. This represents a significant shift from traditional visualization representation where any commentary or annotation was limited to a small group.

Online visualization communities may generate useful insights into data sets, under conditions that lead to the majority answer being more likely to be correct than any individual response [37, 39]. It is also possible that visualization users may misinterpret data when one or more prior users within the community have made errors in their interpretations of data. Of particular concern is the possibility of an erroneous information cascade in which initial members seed a discussion with inaccurate interpretations that get further distorted over time. A viewer new to a complex set of data with numerous options for creating visualizations may rely on the visualizations and interpretations that prior users have generated to constrain the search space. This is not unlike studies on patterns of bias arising from *social proof* in cultural markets like music downloading websites, where the popularity of artifacts becomes unpredictable and subject to a "rich get richer" dynamic [34, 17].

The principle of social proof—which suggests that actions are viewed as correct to the extent that one sees others doing them—falls under the larger category of social influence effects: those where a subject's feelings, thoughts, or behaviors are influenced based on observations of others' behavior in a similar situation. Studies of how social influence and conformity affect decision-making date back to the 1950's and earlier. In the context of visual perception, Asch's line experiment famously showed that the subject's responses for a simple length judgment task can be influenced by the answers first supplied by confederates [2]. Many new experiments have since identified different types of social influence and the contexts in which they are effective [9, 5, 49].

Interpreting a data visualization involves a complex set of cognitive and perceptual processes that have been identified by psychological research on graph comprehension (see [36]). Psychological models of graph interpretation focus on how the visual properties of a graph (e.g., it's color, size, format, and so forth) influence how easily different information can be encoded from a data set (e.g., [11]). Although there is some evidence that prior beliefs and expectations have an influence on graph interpretation (e.g., [35]), the focus of research has been on an individual's own prior beliefs rather than the effect of beliefs of others. The work presented here seeks to extend graphical comprehension models to take into account social influences so that these models are appropriate for describing data interpretation in the context of social visualization systems. At the basis of any interpretation from visualization is an underlying graphical perception task. While we hope to eventually close the gap between basic graphical perception tasks and the higher-level interpretations that they lead to, our goal here is to provide initial evidence for the possibility for social influencers like social proof to occur in graphical settings.

We begin by modifying Cleveland and McGill's original experiments on the accuracy of visual judgment types (as executed by Heer and Bostock's Amazon Mechanical Turk implementation [19]). By including socially-derived signals (e.g., histograms of putative previous answers), and testing for other potential effects (e.g., anchoring), we are able to assess the impact of social influence by adjusting the bias in these signals towards or away from the "true" answers. Our work illustrates how social proof with an *unbiased* signal results in *more* accurate estimates_but that a *biased* signal results in *less* accuracy. Additionally, we extend the classical experiments to include a more difficult, and arguably more realistic task, that of judging linear associations between variables in a scatterplot. We also provide evidence that biased collective estimates for a graphical perception task can emerge in social environments through information cascades. We use the insights gained from our experiments to identify the implications for social visualization systems and discuss the impact of social proof and other forms of social influence on visualization research.

RELATED WORK

Social visualization environments have captured the attention of researchers in visualization, HCI, and CSCW who seek to understand the features of successful social data analysis systems. Heer, Wattenberg, Viegas, and others have completed a series of works aimed at describing the space [20, 43, 44, 46]. Motivated by work in various fields with socio-organizational bents, the authors of [18] present design considerations for asynchronous collaboration in visual analysis environments, highlighting issues of work parallelization, communication and social organization.

While highlighting many useful design considerations, the tone of these investigations is optimistic in that pitfalls that may stem from social processes, individual biases, and their combination are rarely considered. Instead, researchers discussing socially-related challenges tend to focus the most on the tendency toward imbalances in contributions among members [29]. There remains little work beyond Asch's classical experiments that attempts to combine perception and social influence tasks. We briefly summarize the two areas as they motivate our thinking and experimental design.

Graphical Perception

Graphical perception is a mainstay of visualization research [11, 41, 7, 45] due to its potential to improve the efficiency of automatic presentations of data [26]. Graphical perception can be affected by both design and data characteristics, warranting its continued investigation. A recent set of experiments executed by [19] demonstrated the use of Amazon's Mechanical Turk (MTurk) as a means for replicating prior studies and producing new knowledge in this area. Statistically comparable results are demonstrated despite the lack of control over screen resolution and other technical conditions. Qualification tests consisting of sample questions for a target task help control for workers' prior experience with graph interpretation and statistical literacy. For example, Heer and Bostock replicate one experiment from Cleveland and McGills's seminal study ([11]) to rank visual variables such as length, area, and color for encoding quantitative data. A proportion judgment task executed on bar, stack bar, and pie charts (among others), is used to rank the dominant visual variables on which the chart types are based. Heer and Bostock's results match the original authors' ranking of visual judgment types and add rankings for additional chart types. Though MTurk experiments do not address social influence, they do demonstrate a type of collective intelligence applied to perception tasks (see also [24]). As Heer and Bostock and others have suggested [33], Mechanical Turk offers a greater diversity of subjects, scalable experimentation, and rapid responses.

An important point with regard to our study of influence is that many graphical perception tasks are based in intuitive judgment, such as scanning a plot to form an impression of the underlying distribution. Intuitive judgments are typically faster, require less effort, and are less subject to over-thinking than analytic reasoning [1, 23]. They can benefit the perceiver of a graph, by displaying properties of the data that remain hidden when only the statistical parameters are computed [27]. However, they can also mislead an observer's interpretation of a stimulus [1, 23]. Hence, the fact that graphical perception results are replicable in some cases does not mean that subjects' answers are always correct. In some cases, systematic biases at the individual level may affect responses (see [36] for a compilation). Proportion-judging, for example, has been cited as one task where systematic biases can occur [38, 36]. In such cases, rather than errors distributing evenly in both directions from the actual answer, such biases may lead to potentially "bad" social signals.

Linear association estimation is another task subject to numerous biases and considered relatively difficult for humans [15]. Intuitive estimates have in many cases been

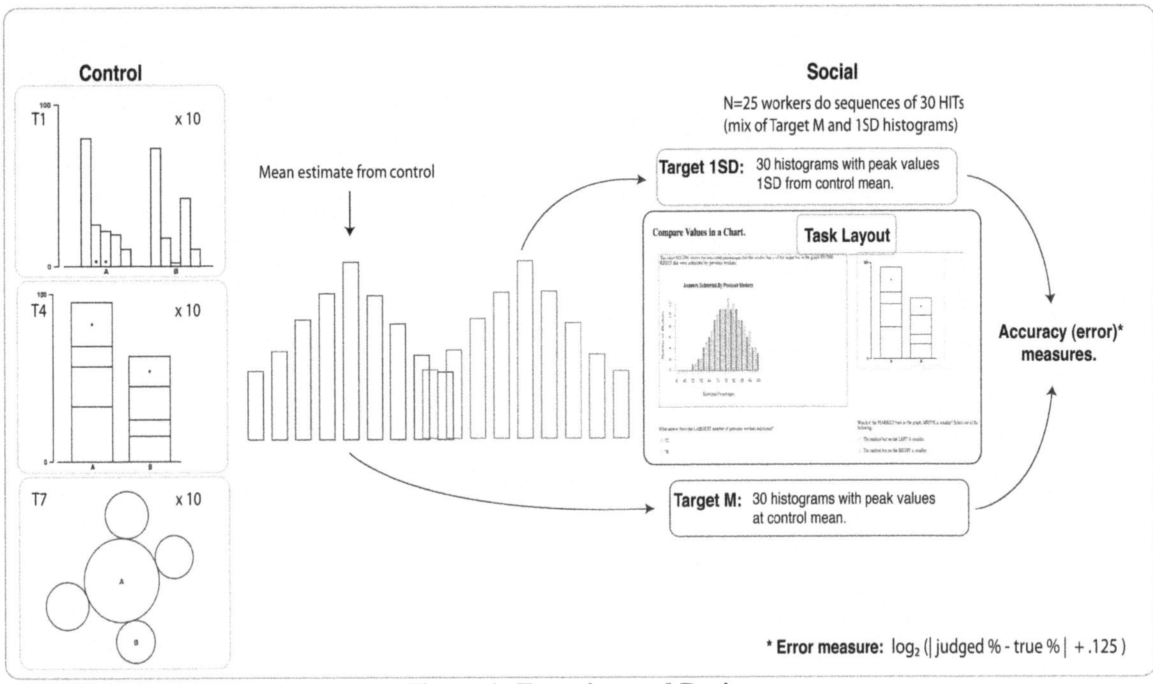

Figure 1: Experimental Design

found to be lower than the statistical coefficient *r* [28]. Further, estimates can be affected by manipulating visual characteristics, complicating the accurate judging of an association. While social data analysis from visualizations often involves further interpreting these underlying visual relationships, errors at the perceptual level undoubtedly play a role in determining the ultimate analyses.

Social Influence and Social Proof

Social psychologists use the term *social influence* to describe the tendency to respond in certain ways to the behaviors of others. For example, *conformity* refers to changing one's behavior to match responses of others. In analyzing conformity, social psychologists typically distinguish between *informational motivations,* arising from a desire to form accurate interpretations, and *normative motivations* deriving from a desire to obtain social approval [14]. This distinction is important in framing our work's focus on influence as applies to visualization perception to prior influence experiments that utilize perception tasks. Asch's well-known line judgment experiment [2] showed that individuals asked a simple visual judgment question (to identify which of three lines drawn on a blackboard matches a target line) responded differently depending on the answers first reported by other individuals in the room. The powerful support provided that elementary visual judgments can be subject to social influence inspired various replications and extensions (surveyed extensively in [5]). In the Asch paradigm, identifiability and social presence—normative social factors—characterize the setting [30]. However, subsequent experiments [5] suggest that a controversy with this experimental set-up is the difficulty of replication within different cultures or time periods. Our work avoids some of these pitfalls by concentrating on informational rather than normative influence.

Under conditions when others' opinions are expressed as quantitative estimates and "judge" and "advisor" are equally well-informed, averaging represents an optimal strategy for accurate estimation because it cancels out errors [37]. Yet in the case of social environments where multiple individuals view and interpret a visualization, can displaying information on prior responses lead to social signals that are biased, thus negating the effectiveness of averaging? Our work is motivated by exploration of the multiple ways in which social information might be represented in interactive visualizations, including comments, bar and pie graphs, and graphical annotations [48]. We make use of a histogram as a concise representation of social information to avoid the additional complexities of comments that might confound our experimental objectives.

While not targeted at information visualization, recent studies on the social dynamics of online cultural markets motivate some of the design of the present work. The concept of social or observation learning [3, 4] describes cases where an abundance of options leads to conditions where popularity is taken as a signal of quality. This theory has motivated experiments that simulate information cascades in social environments in which individuals motivated to make informed choice use social signals. Experiments on online music downloading markets [34] and collaborative tagging such as bookmarking [17] find that success in online cultural markets is difficult to predict but can be described through a stochastic urn model based on social influence signals restricted to information on others' behavior. Similarly, work in recommender systems provides evidence that recommendations can change users opinions, where users tend to rate toward the system's predictions [12]. With regard to online reviews [49], it is shown that exposure of previous opinions induces trend following and ultimately the expression of increasingly extreme views. The cost of expressing an opinion when other previous views are known tends to lead to a selection bias that softens the extreme views.

This form of influence, arising from information on the prior decisions of other community members, is similar to online collaborative visualization environments, where prior responses are commonly provided to the viewer (sometimes as text or numerical summaries and sometimes depicted with yet another visualization). As in the music downloading environments described by [34], the number of possible visualizations calls for a natural heuristic for dealing with the choice overload, and people may benefit through interaction, and notions of commonality when they coordinate their choices with others.

These results echo the concept of social proof, which states that a behavior is viewed as correct in a given situation to the extent that others are performing it, and that more people, more ambiguous situations, and an increased sense of similarity to others increases the power of the influence [8].

STUDY OBJECTIVES

For this work we conducted a number of large-scale experiments using Amazon's Mechanical Turk (as well as additional validation experiments). We specifically tested the following main hypotheses:

- H1: Adding a social information signal on prior workers' behavior (responses submitted for a graphical perception task) will directly influence subject's accuracy on the task at hand.
  - H1a: If the social signal is an accurate representation of the true answer (i.e., unbiased), errors will decrease for those witnessing that signal.
  - H1b: If the signal is inaccurate (i.e., biased), errors will increase.
- H2: Biased responses can emerge through information cascades and initial conditions
  - H2a: Accuracy will be significantly affected, in the same direction as the social signal.
  - H2b: For an increase in the number of people included in the social signal *(n)* there will be a concurrent increase in the weight of the social signal on the judgment of person $n+1$.

Below we describe the main experiments used to test these hypotheses. The first extends Cleveland and McGill's seminal study of visual judgment types by examining how social proof affects visual judgments. The second, which adds another layer of task difficulty, is informed by work in the estimation of linear associations [10, 32, 28]. We then describe an experiment for simulating an information cascade in order to determine the likelihood that biased collective estimates for a graphical perception task might to naturally emerge in online social environments.

EXPERIMENT 1: PROPORTION JUDGMENT

Method

Control. Our first experiment was designed to ascertain the impact of social information on classical graph perception tasks. As a control, we began by adapting Heer and Bostock's 1a experiments [19] using Mechanical Turk. We limited our replication to three chart types distributed across their reported ranking of visual judgment types: a bar graph representing the high accuracy encoding type position along a common scale (T1), a stack bar graph representing primarily length encoding (T4), and a bubble chart representing relatively low accuracy circular area encodings (T7). We depict these within a representation of our experimental design (Figure 1).

Workers who accept the task examine a graph such as a bar or pie chart where two bars or sections of the graph are marked and then answer two questions: 1) "Which of the two MARKED bars is larger?" and 2) "Make a quick visual judgment on what proportion the smaller is of the larger." Like Heer and Bostock, we used the first question to verify responses and required workers to first pass a qualification test of several examples with multiple-choice questions. Each of the 30 unique chart versions was launched as an individual HIT to be completed by 50 workers for a reward of $0.05. This was raised to $0.08 to increase completion speed [27].

Social Conditions. Using the control data we implemented two social conditions through a social signal. Specifically, a *social histogram* showed a distribution based on 50 previous answers for the same judgment task. For each chart of the 30 charts, two social histograms were generated: Target M was set to the mean answer found in the control, and Target 1SD was set to one standard deviation from the mean in the direction of the greatest density of the control distribution (ranging from 3.15 to 14.8). We chose this particular target in order to test the case where the more incorrect social information might still be relatively believable. In all situations, Target M means were closer to the true proportion values than Target 1SD. In generating the histograms, we required that the value with the highest count in the histogram fall within three of the control mean used to generate the sample. The task required the worker to first identify 1) "What answer the LARGEST number of previous workers submitted?" followed by the two questions in part 1A. The task layout can also be seen in Figure 1.

Because participants saw a mix of biased (Target 1SD) and unbiased (Target M) histograms, one possibility was that whatever version they saw in their first HIT would influence subsequent HITs. Stated another way, if a biased histogram was shown first, was the subject less likely to rely on the social signal for subsequent HITs? To insure that a worker's judgments were not affected by ordering,

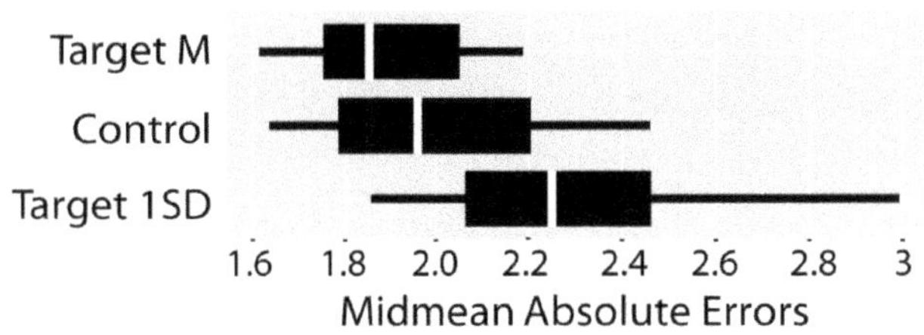

Figure 2: Mean log absolute error measures for control, Target M, and Target 1SD conditions of proportion task.

we ran several pilot experiments consisting of three chart tasks per HIT with half the 50 subjects first seeing the Target 1SD histogram and the other half the Target M (with the second and third charts randomly assigned). We saw no statistical difference ($p > .05$) between perception errors in the subsequent charts, indicating that whether the first observed social histogram was accurate or inaccurate does not appear to impact how subsequent histograms were perceived.

We launched the 60 chart/histogram combinations in sets where each worker could do 30 unique chart tasks, with equal numbers of Target M and 1SD histograms and HIT order counterbalanced by the Mechanical Turk. All workers taking part in the social condition completed a qualification task, as before, with the addition of several example and practice histogram reading tasks, presented separately from the proportion judgment portion of the qualification.

Results

Control. A small majority (56%) of the workers accepted all 30 available HITs. We included in analysis all workers who had completed HITs regardless of the number (sensitivity analysis described below). We used the verification question to exclude workers with incorrect responses. Because we were concerned with the bias that outliers might lead to in the worst case scenario of charts with a large standard deviation in responses, we removed outliers by defining a range around the actual proportion for each chart (+/- 40) based on approximately 3x the largest standard deviation for a chart and omitting values outside of this range (a total of 6.0% of responses removed as outliers). To validate our control experiment, we use the midmeans of log absolute errors (i.e., the mean of the middle two quartiles or MLAE) using $\log_2(|judged\_percent - true\_percent| + .125)$ for each chart and bootstrapping (following [11]). We find that the ranking of judgment types is preserved and that the rough shape and ranking of visual judgment types by accuracy are preserved (relative to [19] and [11]).

Social Conditions. An average of 22% of workers completed all 30 tasks in a sequence. We again considered all HITs for analysis regardless of the number done by individuals, removing outliers and those who didn't understand the task according to the procedure for the control. We also excluded HITs where the histogram verification question was answered incorrectly. A total of 7.2% of HITs were removed. As above, we calculated the MLAEs for each of the 60 unique chart/histogram pairs. Ignoring the particular chart type, we grouped all calculated MLAEs by experiment (i.e., control, Target M and Target 1SD). Figure 2 shows boxplots of the means from the control data and each of the social conditions. After doing an ANOVA ($p < .001$) we used a Tukey HSD test to compare the MLAEs across all three conditions. We found a significant difference for Target M and 1SD ($p < .001$). The lowest errors appear in the Target M condition (mean: 1.886, stdev: 1.210), followed by the control (mean: 1.989, stdev: 1.197), then Target 1SD (mean: 2.267, stdev: 1.173). A significant difference also exists between Target 1SD and the control ($p < .001$), although not between the Target M condition and the control ($p = .1792$). These results are consistent with our hypothesis 1 (the further the social signal, the less accurate the estimate).

Sensitivity Analysis. To control for the mix of between- and within-subjects data we conducted two sensitivity analyses: collapsing errors by individual by condition (reanalyzing the difference between the Target M and 1SD conditions while controlling for within-subjects variance by computing average mean error scores for the M and 1SD conditions for each individual), and controlling for effects of particular individuals on results by re-running the ANOVA and Tukey test using a systematic leave-one-out design. In both cases, final t-tests yielded significant results (p-values $< .05$) for all but the Target M and control comparison.

EXPERIMENT 2: LINEAR ASSOCIATION ESTIMATION

Method

Control. In a second two-part experiment similar to 1, we pseudo-randomly generated 30 correlation values to use in generating scatterplots (10 unique values under .5, 10 values between .5 and .8, and 10 values over .8). We chose these bins after the suggestion ([47]) that many statisticians see $|r|$ values below 0.5 as "small", and values of $|r|$ as "large" only when they are 0.8 or greater. For each correlation we generated 100 pseudo-random x values from a Gaussian distribution as well as pseudo-random y values for each. We transformed these (x, y) pairs by adapting

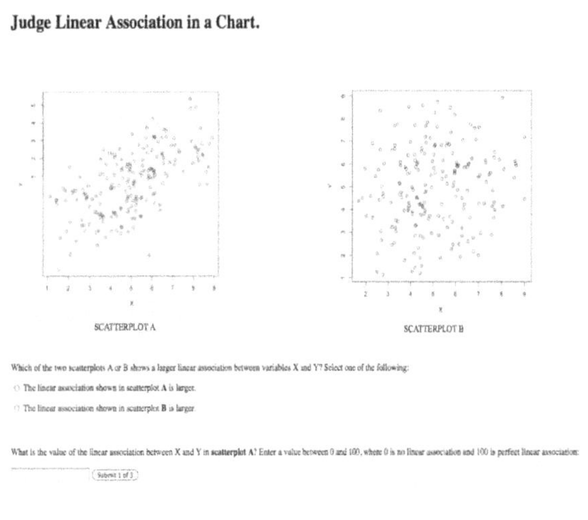

Figure 3: Layout for linear association task.

[32]'s method to generate only positive linear associations, resulting in a final 30 scatterplots, one depicting each of our original correlations. In the individual tasks, the worker is shown a labeled scatterplot of the two variables X and Y and asked to estimate the value of the linear association between them on a scale of 0 and 100, the scale chosen after [10]. As in experiment 1, the 30 unique plots were launched as 30 individual HITs with N=50 assignments.

Each HIT (see Figure 3) consisted of two radio button verification questions: 1) "Which of two scatterplots [A and B shown side by side in the HIT] shows a larger linear association between variables X and Y?", and 2) "Would you describe the linear association in scatterplot A as high, medium, or low? Assume high is over 80, medium is from 50 to 80, and low is less than 50." The workers were then asked to enter a value between 0 and 100 describing the linear association in scatterplot A, where 100 represented perfect linear association and 0 represented no association. Each worker first took a qualification test showing examples of 100 and 0 association plots plus two additional examples and three practice tasks. Due to the relative difficulty of accurately estimating correlations, we allowed subjects to pass the qualification given 11 out of 12 correct answers. The B scatterplots used for comparison to the A plot in the first question of each HIT had an average difference of 61 from the true value of the A scatterplot.

Social Conditions. We modified the control as in experiment 1, adding two social influence conditions for each of the 30 scatterplots, where the target guess used to generate the distribution for the histograms of previous answers is the actual mean guess in one condition (M) and one standard deviation in the other (1SD) which ranged in practice from 3.07 to 22.2. In order to keep the presentation of the scatterplots A and B the same as in the control, we presented the histogram and histogram question beneath the two plots and question 1. Question 3, which asked the worker to estimate the association, was below the histogram and question 2. The 60 chart/histogram pairs were launched as individual hits in sets of up to 30 unique charts, with equal numbers of M and 1SD histograms and order counterbalanced between workers.

Results

Control. Under this condition, 75% of the workers accepted all 30 HITs in a sequence, yet we considered all completed HITs for analysis (sensitivity analysis described below). We used the verification questions to validate that subjects understood the task, excluding HITs with one or more wrong answers. We also excluded from analysis outliers that were more than 50 off from the actual correlation in the scatterplot (a total of 7.9% were removed), defining this boundary using approximately 3x the largest chart standard deviation. For each of the scatterplots, we calculated the mean estimated linear association and standard deviation.

We compared the pattern of results from our experiments to those of prior work in linear association estimation [10, 32]. Figure 4 shows the actual pattern

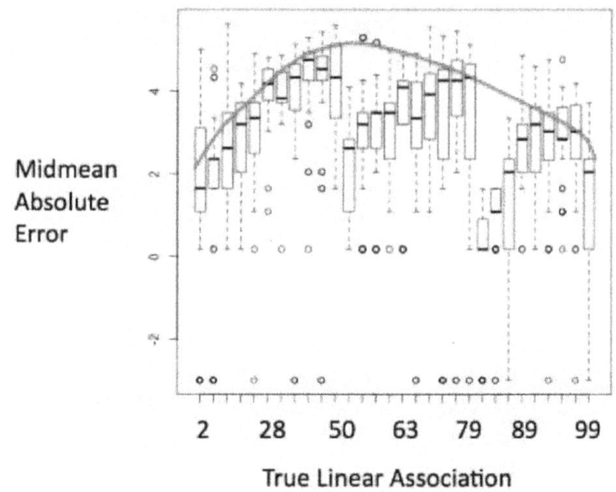

Figure 4: Log absolute errors across 30 linear association tasks (pre-bootstrapping), with expected pattern in red.

observed (with a hand drawn line, in red, illustrating the expected patterns given previous literature that demonstrated maximum errors at "medium" correlations). We first noted that accuracy, as defined by the log absolute error of estimates, dipped at linear association levels of 50 and 80, then jumped back to the more expected trend. We attribute these jumps to the anchoring effect of the question text on the page. Recall that 50 and 80 were used to describe the transitions from low to medium to high correlations. Because this may have led to a slight bias in utilizing these answers, when the correlation was in fact 50 or 80, error was reduced. In future experiments we hope to eliminate these types of signals. However, this is not critical for the current experiment as we are not seeking to compare errors by task difficulty and data is aggregated for all correlation types. Additionally, outside of this difference, our pattern of log absolute errors accuracy measures matched prior results, in that the accuracy of estimates of association declined as the actual linear association moved closer to 50.

Social Conditions. An average of 58% of the workers accepted all 30 HITs in a sequence though we again considered all HITs in analysis, removing those that qualified as outliers using the procedure described for the Control. We also excluded HITs where the histogram verification question was answered incorrectly (a total 10.8% was removed between the two conditions). We calculated the midmean log absolute error accuracy measure as in Experiment 1 (including bootstrapping) for each of the 60 unique chart/histogram pairs, and ran an ANOVA ($p = 0.4506$). In this case, the log absolute error means for the three conditions were quite close (Target 1SD mean: 3.010, stdev: 1.122; control mean: 3.040, stdev: 1.128; Target M mean: 3.319, stdev: .8436). The lack of significance of the ANOVA and the relatively high errors from the Target M condition led us to consider the assumptions behind the hypothesis that as a social signal becomes more biased, errors will increase.

If we assume that the Target M histogram value is always between the actual answer for the task and the Target 1SD value (as it was in Experiment 1), then this

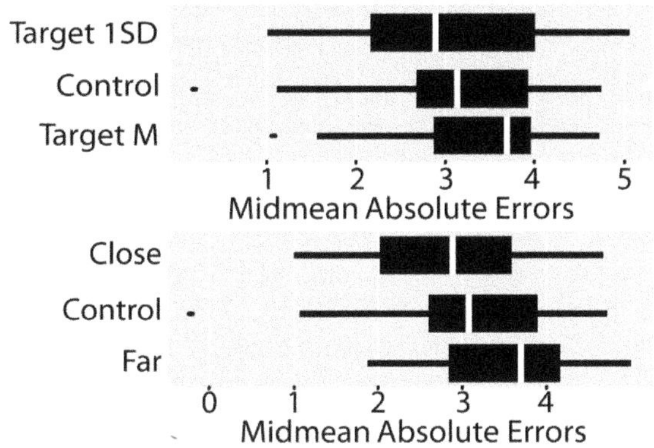

Figure 5: Mean log absolute error measures for control, Target M, and Target 1SD conditions of linear association task (above), and regrouped Farther and Closer conditions.

pattern goes against our hypothesis that as a social signal becomes more biased, errors will increase. In looking closer at the data, however, we realized that the results remained unclear with regard to H1, because in 16 of the 30 cases, the Target 1SD histogram value was in fact closer to the truth. Considering that prior research has shown humans to be relatively bad at linear association estimation, this outcome is plausible. Yet because the ordering is random, this confuses our relationships.

To overcome this complication, we regrouped the data based on which of the two histograms displayed a mean answer that was closer to the actual association (which we re-termed the Closer condition) versus the histogram that was farther from the actual association (Farther condition). With this measure, our previous observation—that the farther the social signal is from the actual, the less accurate the estimate—holds. An ANOVA yielded significance ($p < .01$). Tukey's HSD test showed no significant difference between the Control and Closer condition ($p = 0.5391$), nor between the Control and Farther condition ($p = 0.1113$). However, we saw a significant difference between the Closer and Farther condition ($p < .01$). Figure 5 depicts the ordering of mean absolute errors (Close mean: 2.767, stdev: .9533; control = 3.040, stdev: 1.128; Far mean: 3.561, stdev: .7740). We discuss these results further in the discussion section.

ANCHORING EFFECTS

Before going further to investigate the possibility that "bad" social signals might naturally emerge in a social visualization environment, we validate that the results of experiments 1 and 2 did in fact represent social influence rather than non-social influences. As examples of the latter, anchoring and adjustment [42] are psychological heuristics that subconsciously influence the way people intuitively assess probabilities. A subject starts with an implicitly suggested reference point (the "anchor"), and makes adjustments to that number based on additional information. Anchoring, which is related to priming, is the general activation of a particular idea or ideas based on associations between a stimulus and that idea(s).

To test for anchoring we ran a validation experiment that displayed the social histograms as in Experiment 1 but labeled them as something unrelated to the chart (which was itself labeled). For example, the histogram might be labeled "Temperature Recorded at Location 11" and a bar chart as "Employee Salary in Company R" (a set of unrelated labels that nonetheless made sense in the context of histogram and the different chart types were manually selected). This condition also made a clear delineation using different colored backgrounds behind each sub-task in the single HIT. We ran the conditions as 30 HIT sequences for $.10 a HIT with N=25 unique workers who had not yet done any of our prior tasks.

Prior to this we used a paired t.test to confirm that adding a label to the proportion-judging chart itself would not affect responses, by rerunning our control experiment with (N=25) but with a label (e.g. "Salaries of Employees in Company R" for a bar chart) above the chart ($p = 0.1214$).

Under the social condition with delineation, 72% of workers accepted all 30 HITs in the sequence (2.4% of responses were omitted in processing the results). After performing an ANOVA ($p < .05$), we used Tukey's HSD test to find that the delineated Target 1SD MLAEs were not significantly different than the control ($p = .1594$). As the same non-delineated Target 1SD histograms *were* different from control in the social task ($p < .001$), we can infer that anchoring is likely not contributing to increased errors as the histogram shifts from the "true" value.

EXPERIMENT 3: INFORMATION CASCADE AND INITIAL CONDITIONS

Method

Although the previous experiments clearly demonstrate that *if* an individual is presented with social histograms their judgment will change, it is not entirely obvious that *different histograms* would emerge from the *same social process* (e.g., an information cascade or initial conditions). Stated another way, we seek to establish whether judgments of the $n+1^{th}$ person are influenced by the number of previous judgments (n) and the distribution of those judgments. If an individual over-utilizes the judgments of others, one might expect that a) the initial condition would impact all subsequent judgments (e.g., if the first person is really off, everyone after them will be really wrong) and that b) the more individuals providing the estimate, the more "trusted" that social signal would be (e.g., person 31 relies more on the estimate than person 5).

If such a cascade pattern holds, an initial bad estimate may grow or become more entrenched as more and more people contribute their estimates. To simulate an iterated process we presented 1500 HITs that displayed histograms with varying n's and displaying a histogram with different means. An indication informing the participant that they were person $n+1$ in a series of individuals was made in 3 places on the interface (the histogram caption, question text, page heading, all in bold). Histogram means were centered at one standard deviation to the left (based on the control data), one standard deviation to the right, and at the mean of the control experiment (yielding 3 charts). The n variable was varied from 1 to 37 in steps of 4. Note that the control experiment serves as a test at n=0 (i.e., the participant is the first to make a judgment). In total, we produced 30 histograms per chart. This was done for all 10 circular area plots (chart type T7) yielding 300 total variants, which we launched as 10 HIT sequences at $.08 per HIT with 5 workers per variation (total of 1500 HITs).

We constructed a number of linear models to test for the relationship of actual answer (the Turker's judgment) against histogram mean, n, and the true proportion. Specifically, the model:

$$Answer_{n+1} = b_0 + b_1 * true\_proportion + b_2 * histogram\_mean + b_3 * histogram\_mean * n + e$$

attempted to capture the increasing effects of n on the answer as well as the participant's personal evaluation of the true proportion. Sensitivity analyses with robust standard errors were performed using generalized estimating equations in *R* to account for the repeated measures per person. These findings were robust to control for the correlation induced by collecting multiple measurements per study subject.

Results

Modeling the main effects of the actual value and the suggested histogram mean on the answer produced an adjusted r^2 of .8122. Both the actual value and histogram mean were positively associated with the person's answer with a slightly large effect for the true proportion (effect=0.65, standard error = 0.27, $p < .001$) than the histogram mean (effect=0.439, standard error = .033, $p < .001$). Interestingly, we could find no significant effect of n in this model or any other we used for sensitivity analysis.

The results of this experiment suggest that hypothesis H2b does not hold. In other words, the opinion of 5 people counts the same as that of 30, and the first judgment, erroneous or not, sets the stage for all subsequent answers. For the sake of completeness we discuss below several potential limitations of our experimental conditions that might partially affect the results.

DISCUSSION

Findings and Implications

The main finding in this work is the evidence we provide that responses to online graphical perception tasks can be subject to influence from socially-derived information signals such as social proof via prior responses, and that such biased signals are possible given a situation where any $n+1$ person can see the responses of the n individuals who saw a graph before him or her.

Social Errors. In the proportion judgment experiments, we observed a clear difference between the individuals exposed to Target 1SD histograms over Target M. Furthermore, because biased histograms like our Target 1SD might emerge from a cascade process there is a need for any system utilizing such social signals to be highly aware of this possibility, and to potentially mask social signals in situations where this type of bias might happen.

Systematic Bias. To mitigate information cascades, a designer might have the intuition to mask the social signal (e.g., hide the histogram) until a sufficient number of samples is obtained. However, as demonstrated by the lack of significant difference between Target M and the control, there does not appear to be any benefit (or conversely, harm) in displaying this information. This result is only surprising if one assumes that graphical perception lacks systematic bias. However, because individual judgments are wrong, and generally wrong in the same "direction," the overall collective opinion does not appear to be any better than the individual one. Worse, in situations such as the linear estimation task, when systematic bias and estimation errors were so high that Target 1SD histograms were equally likely to be closer to the true correlation as Target M (16 of the 30), there is a clear indication that the social signal, even the individually-derived one, has a negative impact on perception. This observation indicates that caution is necessary—or at least awareness—when designing systems in domains with systematic bias.

Social Influence and Future Work

Social influence, construed more broadly, is known to be a result of multiple features. In this study we have targeted a specific type of social influence, one centered around social proof, which we believe can serve as a jump-off point for future work.

One opportunity for future work is to address the reasons why, as in our Experiment 3, the number of previous responses (n) did not impact the model. Given that the results of our social conditions did appear to be based on the socially-derived signal, we would expect that more responses would result in a stronger social information signal, exerting a greater effect. Effects of this sort have been validated in other contexts by [34, 12]. Yet this was not suggested by our data. We hypothesize that it may be that the MTurk environment did not support the type of systematic processing that may have been required for a worker to sufficiently understand the relationship between the total count in the histogram and the potential value of the social signal. Utilizing a true iterated experiment (e.g., through [25]) may yield a different result. In addition, while we chose a one standard deviation difference in order to investigate cases where the social signal remains believable, future work might offer more insight into how biased a social signal can be while still exerting similar effects.

We also note that our study is not designed to induce normative social influence stemming from a desire for social approval. The histograms are informational in nature. Because the decisions of workers in our experiments were not witnessed in the presence of others, workers may have felt more confident in deviating from the distribution. While some recent research suggests that anonymity need not always degrade social influences effects in computer-mediated environments, it is suggested that a sense of social identity must be in place for influence to occur [31]. Furthermore, social influence is also known to be stronger when signals come from others whom the subject deems similar to her/himself [8]. The extent to which a person identifies with message source (majority or minority) is a significant factor in determining information processing strategies plus outcome of influence attempt [13]. Such theories indicate that stronger influence might be achieved had the presence of the other workers and their similarity to the subject been emphasized. Because users of social visualizations sites are not commonly designed around anonymity, additional normative effects may lead to more significant effects on judgments within these frameworks.

Another future inquiry might further investigate the effects of task difficulty on influence, as the relative difficulty has been cited to have an effect on the degree to which people accept advice [16]. Because the distance between the Target M and 1SD histograms in our experiment was defined relative to the variance of the control data (e.g. standard deviation), our results did not allow us to cleanly analyze whether task difficulty affected the level of influence. Yet such knowledge would offer designers of social visualization systems further insight into the particular types of situations where the risks of social influence are most heightened.

The contributions we make to social visualization system design are based on experiments that focus on a narrow type of task and environment. However, our results indicate that graphical perception, a key first step in the interpretation of visual information, can be influenced by social signals that may be present in collaborative visualization systems. Clearly, actual systems like ManyEyes are complex environments. Factors such as expertise and interest in the content, prior experience with graph interpretation and statistical literacy (see [36] for others), undoubtedly play a role in such systems. Such environments present individuals with graph comprehension tasks of varying difficulty, and may also present situations that fall along a continuum of objectivity with regard to the pattern being visualized. For example, while the tasks we investigate here have objective answers in the true proportions and linear associations that are visualized, there are many tasks where an objectively true answer might not be possible, such as graph aimed at visualizing an evaluation formed by subjective sentiments on a topic. These may still serve as important points of discussion and collective analysis, and thus potential distinctions in social influence patterns as determined by objectivity may offer further insight for designers.

CONCLUSION

In this paper, we have presented evidence suggesting that responses to graphical perception tasks online may be subject to social influence. We demonstrate through a large-scale study that social proof has an impact on visual judgment, and with it, perceptual accuracy. By modifying classic graphical perception tasks on proportion judgment and linear association estimation, we found a clear indication that an erroneously biased social signal will result in more errors and conversely that a less-biased one will lead to fewer errors. However, we also identify that systematic bias makes many socially derived signals (e.g., a histogram of individually-collected results) erroneous on the whole, and these signals do not commonly provide a definite benefit over individual assessments. This calls into question some of the benefits of "collective intelligence" and highlights a number of design risks. We also identify that initial seeds in social signals (e.g., the first person to contribute to the histogram) allow information cascades to rapidly take hold and impact all future answers. Collective visualization systems hold a great deal of promise for the great influx of data experienced today. However, previous work on visualization systems frequently ignores social effects, treating visualization interpretation as an individual process. As our study highlights, there is a need to form new theories and models that explain the impact of social processes on community-driven visualization environments and lead to new systems.

ACKNOWLEDGEMENTS

We thank Jeff Heer and Mike Bostock for making their materials and experimental details available. We are grateful to Sara Adar, Tom Finholt, Paul Resnick, Eytan Bakshy and Erin Krupka for their comments and advice.

REFERENCES

1. Alter, A.L., Oppenheimer, D.M., Epley, N., and Eyre, R.N. Overcoming intuition: Metacognitive difficulty activates analytic reasoning. *J. of Exp. Psyc.-General 136*, 4 (2007): 569–576.
2. Asch, S.E. Effects of group pressure upon the modification and distortion of judgment. In *Groups, leadership and men*. Edited by H. Guetzkow. Pittsburgh, PA., 1951.
3. Banerjee, A.V. A Simple Model of Herd Behavior. *The Quarterly J. of Economics 107*, 3 (1992): 797-817.
4. Bikhchandani, S., Hirshleifer, D., & Welch, I. (1992). A theory of fads, fashions, customs, and cultural change as information cascades. *J. of Pol. Econ.*, 100(5): 992–1026.
5. Bond, R., and Smith, P. Culture and Conformity: A Metanalysis of Studies Using Asch's (1952b, 1956) Line Judgment Task. *Psych. Bulletin* 119, 1, (1996): 111-137.
6. Bresciani, S., Blackwell, A. F. and Eppler, M. "A Collaborative Dimensions Framework: Understanding the mediating role of conceptual visualizations in collaborative knowledge work," in *HICSS*, (2008),: 364.
7. Card, S.K., Mackinlay, J., and Shneiderman, B. *Readings in Information Visualization: Using Vision to Think*. Morgan Kaufmann, 1999.
8. Cialdini, R.B. *Influence: Science and Practice*. Allyn & Bacon, 2000.
9. Cialdini, R. B., and Goldstein, N. J. "Social Influence: Compliance and Conformity," *Ann. Rev. of Psych.* 55, no. 1 (2, 2004): 591-621.

10. Cleveland, W. S., Diaconis, P., and McGill, R. "Variables on scatterplots look more highly correlated when the scales are increased," *Science* 216, no. 4550 (1982): 1138–1141.
11. Cleveland, W.S. and McGill, R. Graphical perception: Theory, experimentation, and application to the development of graphical methods. *J. Am. Statistical Assoc.*, 79, (1984): 531-554.
12. Cosley, D., Lam, S.K., Albert, I., Konstan, J.A., and Riedl, J. Is seeing believing?: how recommender system interfaces affect users' opinions. *CHI'03*, (2003): 585-592.
13. David B, Turner JC. Majority and minority influence: a single process self-categorization analysis. In *Group Consensus and Minority Influence: Implications for Innovation*, ed. CKW De Dreu, NK De Vries,. Malden, MA: Blackwell (2001): 91–121.
14. Deutsch, M., & Gerard, H. B. A study of normative and informational social influences upon individual judgment. *The J. of Abnormal and Soc. Psych.* 51 (3, 1955): 629-636.
15. Doherty, M., Anderson, R., Kelley, A., Albert, J. Probabilistically valid inference of covariance from a single x,y instance when univariate characteristics are known. *Cog. Sci.*, 33 (2009): 183-205.
16. Gino. F. and D. Moore. "The Effects of Task Difficulty on Use of Advice." *J. of Behav.Decision Making*, 20 (2007): 21-35.
17. Golder, S. A. "Usage patterns of collaborative tagging systems," *J. of Info. Sci.* 32, no. 2 (4, 2006): 198-208.
18. Heer, J., and Agrawala, M. Design considerations for collaborative visual analytics. *Information Visualization, 7*, 1 (2008), 49-62.
19. Heer, J. and Bostock, M. "Crowdsourcing graphical perception: using mechanical turk to assess visualization design," in *SIGCHI'10*, (2010), 203–212.
20. Heer, J., Viégas, F.B., and Wattenberg, M. Voyagers and voyeurs: Supporting asynchronous collaborative visualization. *Communications of the ACM* 52, 1 (2009), 87–97.
21. Henrich, J., Heine, S.J., and Norenzayan, A. The Weirdest People in the World? SSRN eLibrary, (2010).
22. Kittur, A., Suh, B., and Chi, E.H. Can you ever trust a wiki?: impacting perceived trustworthiness in wikipedia. *CSCW '08,* (2008): 477–480.
23. Klein, G. *Streetlights and Shadows: Searching for the Keys to Adaptive Decision Making*. MIT Press, 2009, 76-100.
24. Kosara, R. and Ziemkiewicz, C. Do Mechanical Turks Dream of Square Pie Charts? *BELIV '10* (2010): 373–382.
25. Little, G. TurKit: Tools for iterative tasks on mechanical turk. , *IEEE VL/HCC'09* (2009): 252-253.
26. Mackinlay, J. Automating the design of graphical presentations of relational information. *ACM Trans. Graph. 5*, 2 (1986): 110-141.
27. Mason, W., and D. J. Watts, "Financial incentives and the 'performance of crowds," Workshop on Human Computation *SIGKDD '09* (2009): 77-85.
28. Meyer, J., Taieb, M., and Flascher, I. Correlation estimates as perceptual judgments. *J. of Exp. Psych., Applied*, 3 (2005): 3-20.
29. Noel, S. and Lemire, D. On the Challenges of Collaborative Data Processing. 0906.0910 (2009).
30. Postmes, T, Spears, R, Sakhel, K, De Groot, D. "Social influence in computer-mediated communication: The effects of anonymity on group behavior," *Personality and Soc. Psych. Bulletin* 27, (10, 2001): 1243.
31. Reicher, S.D, Spears R., Postmes T. A social identity model of deindividuation phenomena. *Eur. Rev. Soc. Psychol.* 6 (1995): 161–98.
32. Rensink, R., and Baldridge, B. The Perception of Correlation in Scatterplots. *Computer Graphics Forum*, 29, (2010): 1203-1210.
33. Ross, J., Irani, I., Silberman, M. Six, Zaldivar, A., and Tomlinson, B. (2010). "Who are the Crowdworkers?: Shifting Demographics in Amazon Mechanical Turk".*CHI EA '10* , (2010): 2863-2872.
34. Salganik, M. J., Dodds, P. S., and Watts, D. J. "Experimental Study of Inequality and Unpredictability in an Artificial Cultural Market," *Science* 311, no. 5762 (2, 2006): 854-856.
35. Shah, P., and Freedman, E. (in press). Bar and line graph comprehension: An interaction of top-down and bottom-up processes. *Topics in Cognitive Science.*
36. Shah, P., Freedman, E., & Vekiri, I. The comprehension of quantitative information in graphical displays. In P. Shah and A. Miyake, (Eds.). *The Cambridge handbook of visuospatial thinking*. New York: Cambridge University Press, (2005): 426-476.
37. Soll, J. B., & Larrick, R. P. (2004) Strategies for revising judgment: How, and how well, do people use others' opinions? Unpublished manuscript.
38. Spence, I. Visual Psychophysics of Simple Graphical Elements. *J. of Exp. Psych.: Human Perception and Performance 16*, 4 (1990): 683-692.
39. Sunstein, C. R. *Infotopia: How Many Minds Produce Knowledge*, annotated edition. Oxford University Press, USA, 2006.
40. Swivel, Inc. (2007). Swivel. Retrieved September 18, 2010, from http://www.swivel.com.
41. Tufte, E. R. *The Visual Display of Quantitative Information.* Graphics Press, Cheshire, Conn., 1983.
42. Tversky, A. and Kahneman, D. Judgment under Uncertainty: Heuristics and Biases. *Science 185*, (4157, 1974): 1124-1131.
43. Viegas, F. B., Wattenberg, M., van Ham, F., Kriss, J., and McKeon, M. 2007. ManyEyes: a Site for Visualization at Internet Scale. *IEEE TVCG* 13, (6, 2007), 1121-1128.
44. Viegas, F.B., Wattenberg, M., McKeon, M., Van Ham, F., and Kriss, J. Harry potter and the meat-filled freezer: A case study of spontaneous usage of visualization tools. *HICSS '08,* (2008): 159.
45. Ware, C. *Information Visualization, Second Edition: Perception for Design.* Morgan Kaufmann, 2004.
46. Wattenberg, M. and Kriss, J. "Designing for social data analysis," *IEEE TVCG* (2006): 549–557.
47. M. B. Wilk. Bell Laboratories Technical Memorandum. Bell laboratories, Murray Hill, N.J., 1966.
48. Willett, W., Heer, J., and Agrawala, M. Scented widgets: Improving navigation cues with embedded visualizations. *SIGCHI '07*, (2007): 51-58.
49. Wu, F. and Huberman, B. How public opinion forms. *Internet and Network Economics*, (2008): 334-341.

Directing Attention and Influencing Memory with Visual Saliency Modulation

Eduardo Veas[1], Erick Mendez[1], Steven Feiner[2], Dieter Schmalstieg[1]

[1]Institute for Computer Graphics and Vision
Graz University of Technology, Graz, Austria
{veas, mendez, schmalstieg}@icg.tugraz.at

[2]Department of Computer Science
Columbia University, New York, USA
feiner@cs.columbia.edu

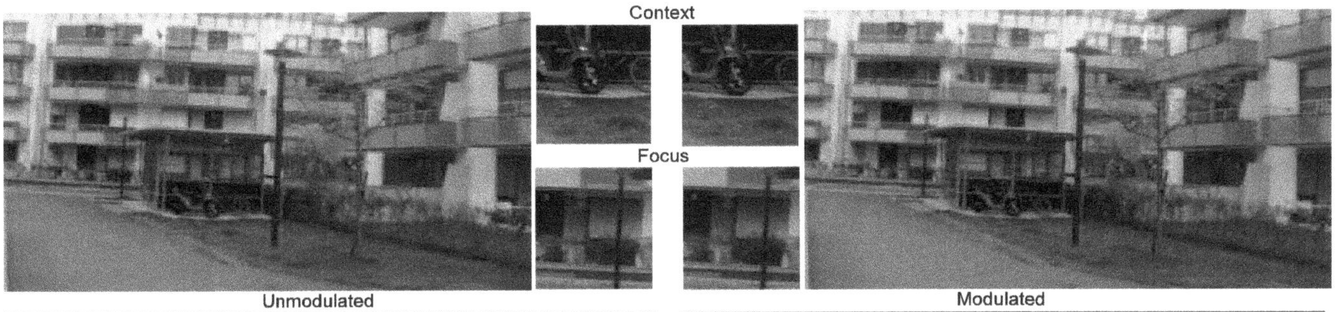

Figure 1. Comparison between modulated and unmodulated video. (Left) Frame and details from an unmodulated video. (Right) Same frame and details after modulation. Differences may be seen when compared side by side, but evidence of modification is difficult to see when viewing the modulated version in isolation.

ABSTRACT
In augmented reality, it is often necessary to draw the user's attention to particular objects in the real world without distracting her from her task. We explore the effectiveness of directing a user's attention by imperceptibly modifying existing features of a video. We present three user studies of the effects of applying a saliency modulation technique to video; evaluating modulation awareness, attention, and memory. Our results validate the saliency modulation technique as an alternative means to convey information to the user, *suggesting* attention shifts and *influencing* recall of selected regions without perceptible changes to visual input.

Author Keywords
Saliency, Visual Attention, Augmented Reality.

ACM Classification Keywords
H.1.2 [**Models and Principles**]: User/Machine Systems—*Human information processing*; H.5.2 [**Information Interfaces and Presentation**]: User Interfaces—*Screen design (e.g., text, graphics, color)*; H.5.m [**Information Interfaces and Presentation**]: Miscellaneous; I.4.3 [**Image Processing and Computer Vision**]: Enhancement.

General Terms
Human Factors, Experimentation.

INTRODUCTION
Augmented reality (AR) applications intended to call attention to real objects often do so by overlaying on the real world highlighting effects or virtual objects such as arrows. At times, it would be desirable that these effects were more subtle, in part to avoid exacerbating perceptual issues inherent to AR (such as depth perception, occlusion and visual clutter), but mostly in cases where the objects highlighted are secondary to the user's task. In many cases, the application needs to appeal to post-perceptual processes, to tell the user that a particular object is somehow related to their current task, but without alerting or interrupting the user's workflow. For example, an environmental scientist visualizes simulation results overlaid on a mountain landscape, and the application wants to highlight the sensors that contributed data to the simulation. Similarly, a user watching a remote video feed from a multi-camera system needs to be reminded of the locations of the viewing camera, of other cameras, and of interesting objects [19]. Or, a panoramic 3D system for navigation may need to draw a tourist's attention towards buildings or landmarks along a path.

The technique presented in this paper offers an alternative means to convey information to the user. We investigate its effectiveness to 1) direct attention to a selected region of the visual input and 2) influence the recall rate of certain objects, 3) without the user becoming aware of any modifications. The literature on psychology and vision identifies saliency as a model of attention [8]. Moreover, attention influences memory at different stages of processing [1]. Thus, we assume that by manipulating the saliency of a region in the visual input, we can potentially influence attention and memory. We apply a saliency modulation technique (SMT) to modify videos so that a region of our selection contains the highest saliency. The SMT enables an AR approach known as "mediated reality," in which existing features of the real-world image are modified, instead of adding discrete new objects. Our primary contribution is to show, by modulating prerecorded video in a lab setting, the potential for developing AR user interfaces that imperceptibly direct a user's attention toward other parts of their environment that are auxiliary to the user's task.

We performed three studies, measuring modulation awareness, attention, and memory. The *modulation awareness* study finds the largest amount of modulation we can apply that is imperceptible to the viewer. The *attention* study evaluates whether this modulation threshold shifts attention towards selected regions of videos. The *memory* study evaluates whether it increases recall for selected objects. Our results indicate that regions modulated with the SMT will draw a first fixation faster than without modulation. Moreover, modulation can increase recall for selected objects. In summary, the SMT can significantly shift attention to selected areas and influence memory of selected objects from a video in a way that is imperceptible to the viewer.

RELATED WORK

Visual salience (or *visual saliency*) is the distinct subjective perceptual quality that makes some items in the world stand out from their neighbors and immediately grab our attention [8]. It refers to the evolved process in primates and other animals that restricts complex object recognition to small areas or objects at any one time that are analyzed serially. Saliency is commonly agreed to have bottom-up and top-down factors. *Bottom-up*, (memory-free, stimulus-based) factors refer to pure sensory information, such as a bright light suddenly appearing in front of us. *Top-down* (memory-bound, goal-based) factors involve a conscious effort, such as ignoring more salient stimuli while carefully scanning a book index. This paper focuses on *bottom-up* factors, which announce to the organism whether a location differs enough from its surroundings to warrant attention.

Measurements of the attention process of an organism are typically focused on stimulus-only factors. The most influential work on understanding this was done by Treismann and Gelade [18], and by Koch and Ullman [11]. Koch and Ullman, in particular, proposed the idea of a single map that is a combination of individual salient contributions; the normalized result is referred to as the *saliency map*. They state that the saliency at a given location is determined primarily by how different this location is from its surround in properties such as color, orientation, motion, and depth.

Saliency and Visual Attention

There is much evidence indicating a correlation between visual attention and the saliency map. Ouerhani et al. [14] and Santella et al. [16] used an eye tracker to confirm the relationship between the saliency map and human visual attention. Lee et al. [12] went one step further by using the saliency map to track objects being attended to by the user.

Practically any change made to an image will modify its saliency map. Blurring, (de)saturating, harmonizing, and distorting are operations that implicitly change the saliency of an image. Recent research has focused on directing attention through saliency manipulation for volume rendering [9], non-photorealistic stylization [16], and geometry [10]. These works concentrate on creating salient features; in contrast, our work receives an *existing* image as input and outputs a modified image whose saliency is manipulated without adding new features.

Closest to our intentions is the work by Su et al. [17] on de-emphasizing distracting image regions and by Bailey et al. [2] on subtle gaze direction. Su et al. focused on so-called second-order saliency by modulating variations in texture to redirect the user's attention to specific locations. Bailey et al. apply first-order modulations to the focus, only when the user is not looking there, as determined by an eye tracker. In contrast, our technique works with dynamic live video and can thus support augmented reality applications with arbitrary scenes and without requiring an eye tracker.

Saliency and Memory

There is a two-way relation between attention and memory that has been widely studied in the past [1][7][4]. Awh et al. [1] identified experiments leading to the conclusion that attention influences processing during both early sensory and post-perceptual stages. They also collected evidence supporting that the same attentional processes that facilitate early sensory identification of new information are recruited for active maintenance of information in memory. Two recent studies have proven the influence of saliency in memory, albeit with different results regarding the reasons. Berg and Itti [3] concluded that salience contributes to memory by influencing overt attention. They had participants examine a shopping-related scene for 2s and then asked if a target item was contained in the scene. They found that fixation times, but not saliency, influenced performance. Fine and Minnery [5] found that the influence of saliency extends beyond oculomotor behavior to higher order centers involved in spatial working memory. They presented participants with maps that included a number of icons to memorize. After a pause, participants had to drag each icon to its original position. They found that participants attended to icons equally regardless of their saliency (quantified using the model from Itti et al. [6]), but errors in placement were significantly reduced for salient icons. Thus, results could not be explained by a biasing of overt attention. Both cases support the fact that saliency influences memory. We assume that by actively modifying an object's saliency, we can influence memory.

SALIENCY MODULATION TECHNIQUE

We apply a recently developed SMT capable of manipulating the saliency of a video [13]. The SMT works at interactive framerates. For each frame, the SMT computes a saliency measure on every fragment according to a hierarchical multi-channel contrast measure [6]. It then modifies the image, changing contrast in lightness and color to have the highest attention salience inside a designated focus region. Changes are applied so that spatial and temporal coherence are respected.

In detail, the SMT works by analyzing and modulating conspicuities in three dimensions: lightness (L), red–green color opponents (O_r), and blue–yellow color opponents (O_b). Each frame is first converted to CIE L*a*b space, thereby obtaining the values for each dimension $k \in \{L, O_r, O_b\}$. A pyramid of images is created with p levels. Modulation progresses from coarse levels to fine levels of the image pyramid. This allows changes affecting a large region to occur early in the process, while later steps progressively refine the result, thus introducing less noticeable artifacts. For each level, *analysis* and *modulation* steps are carried out iteratively for each dimension k.

Saliency analysis. During this step, the conspicuities of the image are computed to measure the naturally salient objects in the scene. A conspicuity is given as a signed sum of the center–surround differences at multiple scales of an image pyramid. The conspicuity c_k is the defined as:

$$c_k = \frac{\sum_{n=0}^{n=2}\sum_{m=n+3}^{m=n+4} k_n - k_{n+m}}{p},$$

where $p = 6$, and k_i is the conspicuity $k \in \{L, O_r, O_b\}$ at mipmap level i.

The conspicuity c_k is normalized using the global conspicuity maxima [12]. The normalized conspicuity $\hat{c}_k$ is:

$$\hat{c}_k = \frac{c_k}{\max(c_k)},$$

where $k \in \{L, O_r, O_b\}$.

Saliency modulation. Given a dimension $k \in \{L, O_r, O_b\}$, let $\hat{c}_k$ be the normalized conspicuity of a location and t_k be the threshold of the conspicuity, a floating point number that governs the amount of modulation. A modulation adjustment m_k is calculated for this location as,

$$m_k = \begin{cases} 0 & \hat{c}_k < t_k \\ \hat{c}_k - t_k & \text{otherwise} \end{cases}.$$

For a feature value f_k of a location, the modulated value f'_k is calculated by applying the modulation m_k in order to increase the conspicuity of the focus, and correspondingly decrease that of the context. Thus,

$$f'_k = \begin{cases} f_k + m_k & \text{if the location is marked as focus} \\ f_k - m_k & \text{otherwise} \end{cases}.$$

Modulation is performed in the order of sensitivity of the human visual system [20]: first, lightness is modulated, then red–green opponents, then blue–yellow opponents. Note that other contributors to saliency remain unaffected (e.g., motion, size, and orientation). Finally, the image is converted from CIE L*a*b to RGB. See Mendez et al. [13] for implementation details. Our contribution is in applying thresholds so that modulation is imperceptible.

METHODOLOGY

To prepare the stimuli for the awareness and attention studies, we recorded ~10h of video under various situations (indoors, outdoors, night, day, with moving objects, free moving camera, panning camera). The idea was to have a manageable variety of videos that represented day-to-day situations. From these, we extracted clips, each lasting ~10s, with the restriction that no human body parts appear in the clips because they represent a high attention sink. Videos were recorded at a resolution of 1280×720 at 29.97fps and presented without resizing and uncompressed to avoid interpolation artifacts by the graphics card. For each experiment, we recruited a balanced number of participants from the university population and the general public. All participants had normal or corrected to normal vision, and were screened for color-sensitivity deficiencies by an on-screen Ishihara test. We used an SMI desktop-mounted eye tracker, operating at 60 Hz. Stimuli were presented on a 19″ monitor at 70cm from the participant. A chin rest was used to limit head movements. All studies were performed in an empty office with lights off, and windows and doors closed, to minimize attention distracters.

Focus regions (FR) for the awareness and attention studies were chosen by analyzing the videos and selecting low salience regions. The selection methodology is presented in the next section. Each clip contained one or more FR. Each FR was visible for at least 2s.

EXPLORATORY STUDY: MODULATION AWARENESS

In the SMT presented above, the *amount* of modulation is governed by a threshold (t_k) for each modulation dimension. Thus, the SMT can be configured to produce different modulation thresholds (see Figure 2). Our initial concern was how to apply the SMT so that the viewer is unaware of the manipulation. In other words, we were seeking the *maximum* modulation that is imperceptible to the viewer. To investigate viewers' attitudes towards modulation, we conducted a series of studies on modulation awareness.

A threshold is a floating point value in the [0...1] range. To reduce the search space, we discretized this range into a set of seven samples. Additionally, we used the extreme values 0 (no modulation) and 1 (full modulation), for a total of nine thresholds. We performed three studies to investigate the appropriate modulation threshold. A challenge in these studies is that participants need to evaluate different modulation thresholds for videos by actively checking for visual manipulations in them, a goal-based task. This type of task is known to modify the gaze path of participants and suppress stimulus-based attention. Thus, analysis of attention cannot be performed at the same time as the study on awareness of modulation.

First Pilot Study

Our intention for the first pilot was to identify and discard thresholds for which modulation is clearly perceivable, thus reducing the search space for a subsequent formal study. The stimulus was a series of 18 clips, two for each of the nine modulation thresholds, lasting ~10s each.

Figure 2. Modulation thresholds. Frame from a video modulated to emphasize a window using different modulation thresholds. From left to right, modulation thresholds zero (no modulation), three, four, five, eight (full modulation).

Three people (all male, ages 28, 33, and 35) participated in this study. Participants were requested to look at the videos and verbally rate each of them on a 7-point Likert scale for naturalness (where 1=natural corresponded to *the video is as it came from the camera*, and 7=unnatural meant *the video has been manipulated to such an extent that it feels unnatural*). The videos were shown in randomized order, in two sets of nine with a short break in-between. It is important to note that participants had to judge each video in isolation and the videos for each modulation threshold were different. Therefore, participants were not given the chance to compare a modulated video with the original version.

Analysis and Results

We did not perform any statistical analysis in this set due to its small sample size. We confirmed, however, that the higher the modulation threshold; the higher the score given by the participants (see Figure 3 top). Thresholds 0–5 scored below the middle of the scale (*somewhat unnatural*). In fact, thresholds 0 and 4 had an average score of 3.

Second Pilot Study

In the first pilot study, participants judged each modulation threshold in isolation. This raised the doubt of whether they would detect a difference if they were given the chance to see both modulated and unmodulated versions of the same stimulus. The goal of this pilot was to verify whether participants could notice a difference between modulated and unmodulated images. We randomly selected screenshots from the stimulus videos. These were presented in pairs with a change-blindness break in between, following the setup suggested by Rensink et al. [15]. For each pair, the images were presented in the order FBFBSBSB, where F corresponds to first image shown for 240ms, B to blank image shown for 320ms, and S to second image shown for 240ms. There were nine change-blindness sets, one for each threshold considered. We modulated two images for each of the nine modulation thresholds, totaling 18 image pairs.

Three participants took part in this study (2 male, 1 female, ages 28, 29, and 24). They were instructed to observe the images and state whether or not the images were different. Each participant saw each of the 18 image pairs once. The presentation of the image pairs was randomized. As suggested by Rensink et al., each change-blindness pair was presented for 60s. Participants, however, had the possibility to interrupt the sequence by stating a judgment.

Analysis and results

We did not perform statistical analysis for this set due to its small sample size. Figure 3 (bottom) shows responses for this study as stacked bars. We interpreted each affirmative response as a value of 1, and each negative response as a value of 0. As shown in the figure, the pair zero–zero was always correctly judged as being unmodulated (it never received an affirmative response). Pairs zero–seven and zero–eight were also always correctly judged as being modulated (6 affirmative responses each). Intriguingly, pair zero–four was graded higher than zero–five and zero–six.

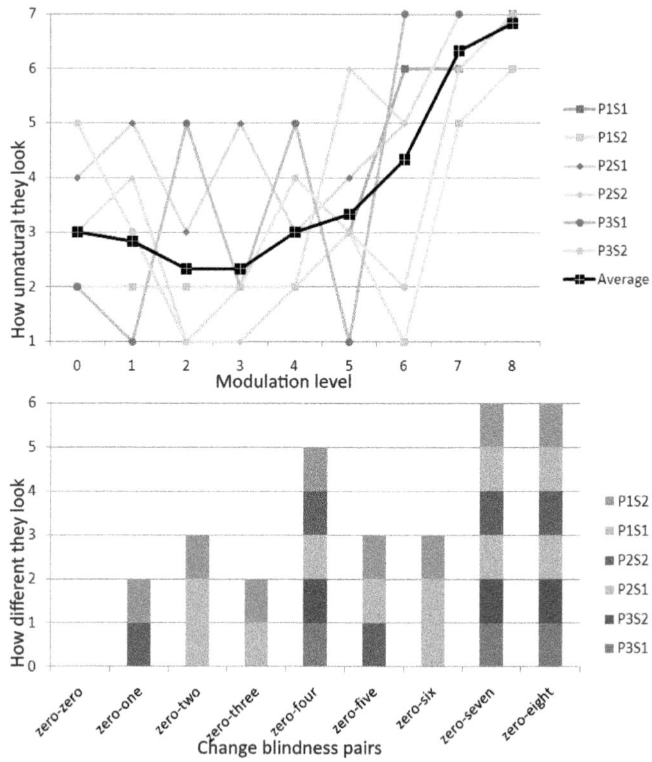

Figure 3. Responses of both pilots. (Top) Responses corresponding to the first pilot study. (Bottom) Responses corresponding to the second pilot study. Notation *PmSn* means *Participant m, set n*. Notation *zero–number* means a pair with the same image unmodulated and modulated at threshold *number*.

Formal awareness study

Building on the pilot studies, we conducted a formal study to further evaluate the reaction of people to modulation thresholds 3–5. Our aim was to verify that the threshold used in later experiments was imperceptible.

Method

The stimuli for the awareness study were obtained using the same 20 clips used in the attention experiment presented below. Therefore, three candidate thresholds (3, 4, and 5) plus the control (no modulation) times the 20 stimulus videos resulted in 80 video–threshold pairs. We arranged the videos so that each video–threshold pair was seen by four participants. Each participant watched each video with a randomized modulation threshold. No participant watched the same video twice with different modulation thresholds.

We recruited 16 participants for this study (12 male, 4 female, 18–35 years old, $\overline{x}$=27.8), none of whom participated in the subsequent experiments. The procedure and instructions were the same as those described for the first pilot.

Analysis and Results

To analyze results, we considered the four modulation thresholds (0, 3, 4, and 5) as related samples. We then conducted three Wilcoxon signed tests for two related samples, to determine whether participants noticed significant damage to the videos compared to the ground truth. Our pair samples were zero–three, zero–four, and zero–five. We applied a Bonferroni correction to account for the number of pair samples and keep the α level below .05. The analysis showed no significant difference for any of the pairs. Thus, there was no evidence that the general population would be able to distinguish which videos had been modulated and which had not. However, we decided to take a somewhat conservative approach and use threshold four for our modulation procedure. Figure 1 illustrates the results of modulation. The left image was obtained from the unmodulated video (first condition). The right image was obtained from the video modulated with threshold 4 (second condition). When comparing both images side-by-side, changes are barely perceptible. If, however, one is allowed to see only the modulated video in isolation, the changes become imperceptible. The insets in Figure 1 show a detailed comparison of the changes. Observe that the focus after modulation has slightly more vivid colors and more contrast, while the context has slightly duller colors and less contrast.

ATTENTION EXPERIMENT

The goal of this study was to verify, through use of an eye tracker, whether the SMT can direct the visual attention of participants to selected regions. Here, we assume that a participant's visual attention can be characterized by their eye gaze. As stimuli for this experiment, we selected 20 clips lasting roughly 10s each.

Hypotheses

H1: The time before the first fixation on the FRs will be smaller for the videos modulated with our procedure than for the original unmodulated videos.

H2: The fixation time in the FRs (i.e., sum of durations of all fixations on the focus) will be higher for the videos modulated with our procedure than for the original unmodulated videos.

H3: The percentage of participants that have at least one fixation on the FR will be higher for the videos modulated with our procedure than for the original unmodulated videos.

Method

Since we wanted to compare eye-gaze for regions between unmodulated and modulated versions of a video, we used a between-subjects, repeated measures design with independent variable *modulation* (unmodulated, modulated), and dependent variables *time before first fixation*, *fixation time* (i.e., sum of durations for all fixations on the focus), and *percentage of participants with at least one fixation*.

We recruited 40 participants to take part in this experiment. They were divided into two conditions for the between-subjects setup (20 in the unmodulated condition, 20 in the modulated condition): (20 regions × 20 participants) = 400 trials per condition = 800 trials total.

Twenty participants (14 male, 6 female, 24–52 years old, $\overline{x}$ =31.4) took part in the first (unmodulated) condition. Each participant was provided with the following instructions:

You will sit in front of a computer screen. We will display a series of short video clips. All you have to do is look at the clips. That's it!

This test is divided into two parts so you can have a break in between. Your eye gaze will be tracked with a non-wearable system. It will be using an infrared camera and light placed in front of you. Infrared light is invisible to the eye and poses no harm to you.

Care was taken not to mention the number of video clips in order to avoid counting (which would trigger a top-down task). It was emphasized that there was no task and that all that was required was to watch the clips. The eye tracker was calibrated for each participant before the stimuli were presented. Each participant watched each of the 20 unmodulated videos once, in random order. Between videos, a blank slide was shown for 2000ms.

By analyzing eye-gaze data from the first condition, we determined a visually unattended region for each clip in the unmodulated stimuli. We define *unattended regions* as those that have fewer than five fixations by less than twenty percent of the participants. These unattended regions were then designated as the FRs of the study. To increase the saliency of FRs for the second condition, the clips were modulated with the SMT at threshold 4, as suggested by the awareness study. The clips derived through this process were used as stimuli for the second condition.

Twenty participants (14 male, 6 female, 25–42 years old, $\overline{x}$ =32.1) took part in the second (modulated) condition. They went through the same procedure as in the first condition, the only difference being that the stimuli were modulated.

Analysis

Analysis was performed with independent samples *t*-tests whenever our data satisfied the condition of normality and with Mann–Whitney *U* tests otherwise. In both cases, tests were one-tailed. Two-tailed tests would be able to indicate whether there is a significant difference between both conditions, but not whether this difference is in the intended direction (increasing attention). A Shapiro–Wilk test indicated that the data for H1 and H3 satisfied normality. However, the data for H2 did not. We adjusted α levels using a Bonferroni correction to ensure a level of .05.

Results for H1. The results of the one-tailed *t*-tests indicate that the mean values of the second condition (modulated) were significantly smaller than the mean values of the first condition (unmodulated), t (35) = 2.916, p < .01. Therefore, the mean duration before the first fixation on the FRs for participants in the second condition (M = 9231.58, SD = 468.16) was significantly smaller than that of the participants in the first condition (M = 9638.86, SD = 363.10).

Results for H2. There is no significant difference in total fixation time between the unmodulated (M=26.79) and the modulated (M=43.31) conditions (Mann–Whitney *U*=99.0, n1=17, n2=20, p=.3, one-tailed). Despite the lack of normality of the data for this hypothesis, we performed a *t*-test confirming the results t (35) = –2.117, p = .02. Therefore, the mean total fixation time for participants in the second condition (M = 43.31, SD = 24.32) was not significantly different from that of the participants in the first condition (M = 26.79, SD = 22.82).

Results for H3. The results of the one-tailed *t*-tests indicate that there is no significant difference in the number of participants that had at least one fixation between the unmodulated and the modulated conditions, t (35) = –2.028, p = .05. Therefore, the mean number of participants with at least one fixation in the second condition (M = .13, SD = .08) was not significantly higher than that of the participants in the first condition (M = .08, SD = .06).

As can be seen, H1 proved statistically significant; however, we were unable to find significant differences for H2 and H3. We further examined the gaze data of our participants to try to find consistent failures in our modulation procedure. By visually analyzing heat maps of our videos in the second condition, we found what seemed to be a consistent pattern where our modulation procedure failed: whenever the camera panned directly away from the FR, the technique seemed to be unable to attract fixations. This did not happen on videos where the camera was static, or whenever the panning was not directly away from the FR. Subsequently, we filtered out the information from FRs that fit this criterion (5 regions out of 29 were excluded). Then we repeated the analysis. Once again, we performed a Shapiro–Wilk test to verify the normality of our filtered data. The results indicated that the filtered data for H1 and H3 satisfied normality, but the filtered data for H2 did not.

On the filtered data for H1, the results of the one-tailed *t*-tests indicate that the mean values of the second condition (modulated) were significantly smaller than the mean values of the first condition (unmodulated), t (35) = 3.386, p < .01. Hence, the mean duration before the first fixation on the FRs for participants in the second condition (M = 9126.98, SD = 499.44) was significantly smaller than that of the participants in the first condition (M = 9616.66, SD = 352.59). On the filtered data of H2, results showed a significant difference in the total fixation time between unmodulated (Mean=14.03) and modulated (Mean=23.23) conditions (Mann–Whitney *U*=85.5, n1=17, n2=20, p< .01, one-tailed). Despite the lack of normality of the data for this hypothesis, we performed a *t*-test, which confirmed the significant difference in total fixation time between conditions t (35) = –2.659, p < .01. Consequently, the mean total fixation time for participants in the second condition (M = 49.52, SD = 26.04) was significantly higher than that of the participants in the first condition (M = 27.65, SD = 23.55). On filtered data for H3, the results of the one-tailed *t*-tests indicate that the mean values of the second condition were significantly higher than the mean values of the first condition, t (35) = –2.478, p < .01. Consequently, the mean number of participants with at least one fixation in the second condition (M = .15, SD = .09) was significantly higher than that in the first condition (M = .08, SD = .06).

Discussion of Attention Experiment

As can be seen from the analysis, we could always draw the eye gaze of participants significantly sooner with our modulation technique. However, once we filtered out situations in which the camera panned directly away from the FR, analysis revealed additional effects of the SMT in the modulated condition. On filtered data, the average duration before the first fixation on the FRs was significantly shorter. We could also retain the visual attention of participants for a significantly longer time. And finally, the number of participants with at least one fixation on the FRs of the modulated videos was significantly larger than for the unmodulated videos. It is difficult to illustrate the accumulated fixations on a region in a video, since the fixations on a region are spread out throughout the duration of the clip. Nevertheless, Figure 4 illustrates one frame of one video in both conditions, showing eye fixations accumulated over multiple frames, in which the effects of the SMT are clear. The image on the left comes from the unmodulated video and the image on the right from the modulated video. A white outline denotes the position of the FR. In the general case, however, the effect is not this apparent throughout the entire duration of the video.

Figure 4. Heatmaps of the user studies. (Left) Unmodulated condition. (Right) Modulated condition. This is a handpicked example chosen to illustrate the effect of the SMT.

The technique was not always effective for each of the video clips, nor for each of the participants in the tests. In the general case, the SMT will draw a first fixation faster than without modulation. In cases where the camera is not moving away from the focus regions, the number of participants that had at least one fixation in the focus region also increased, and the fixation time was significantly higher. Thus, we can state that attention direction with SMT was successful.

MEMORY EXPERIMENT

The goal of this experiment was to assess whether the SMT increases recall of selected objects in the video without suppressing recall for others. With the aim of comparing recall for regions between unmodulated and modulated videos, we used a between-subjects, repeated measures design with independent variable *modulation* (unmodulated, modulated), and dependent variable *recall hits*.

In order to prepare the stimuli, we recorded ~ 2h video in a furniture store and extracted two clips (identified as video *A* and video *B*) lasting 1m each. These clips include people walking by, but no faces. The choice of location ensured the appearance of many different objects in the videos.

Hypotheses

H4: There is no significant difference in recall hits between the first condition (unmodulated) and the second condition (modulated) for recalled objects.

H5: There is a significant difference in recall hits between the first condition (unmodulated) and the second condition (modulated) for non-recalled objects.

Hypothesis H4 concerns losses caused by the technique in the normal condition in terms of suppressing recall of normally recalled regions. H5 concerns gains due to the technique in terms of increasing recall of selected regions.

Prerequisites: Recall Study

The memory experiment requires a set of regions that appear in each video from which participants would select those they remember. These regions are associated with objects and are regarded as objects for the rest of the discussion. We expected to be able to determine the set of objects by examining the videos using Itti's model for saliency, but the results were mostly coarse, and would not help identify individual objects. We then decided to use a mixed approach in which we preselected some regions based on visual inspection and validated them by means of a pilot study. Thus, we visually examined the videos and selected scenes containing both low and high salience objects. Factors for scene selection included being clearly visible for an acceptable amount of time (about 2s), and that the objects in it be clearly distinguishable. We selected 18 scenes in total and, for each we extracted one object with high saliency and one with low saliency. Pictures of these objects were printed on 36 cards, each 11cm × 10cm.

To refine the set of objects, we carried out an exploratory study with six participants (5 male, 1 female, ages 25–35), who did not participate in any subsequent test. The procedure and apparatus were the same as those for the formal memory experiment. Based on eye-gaze analysis and on recall hits, seven scenes were removed, and three objects were changed in the remaining scenes resulting in deck *A* with 10 cards from video *A*, and deck *B* with 12 cards from video *B*. We classified five objects from deck *A* and seven from deck *B* as highly salient. The remaining objects were classified as having low saliency. This classification served as a control, as the experiment assumes that objects with high saliency will have high recall hits. We added five and six distracter objects to decks *A* and *B*, respectively, to assess whether a participant was picking cards randomly.

Method

The same 40 individuals that participated in the attention experiment took part in the memory experiment. Participants were divided into two conditions for the between-subjects setup (20 unmodulated, 20 modulated): (22 objects × 20 participants) = 440 trials per cond. = 880 trials total.

For each condition, videos *A* and *B* were shown in interleaved order; so that 10 participants experienced video *A* first and 10 participants experienced video *B* first. Before starting the experiment, participants were instructed to:

Observe the video and try to memorize the objects that you see. At the end you'll be presented with a deck of cards picturing objects printed from the video and you'll be asked to select those that you remember. Be careful, the deck of cards also contains objects that did not appear in the video.

Participants experienced the first video, and were subsequently presented with the corresponding deck of cards from which they could pick those objects that they remembered. A recall hit was recorded for an object if it was selected by a participant. After a short break, the same procedure was applied for the second video. For each video, participants answered a questionnaire in a 7-point Likert-scale format to assess the difficulty of the task. After finishing the procedure for the two videos, they answered general questions about the naturalness of the videos.

Based on analysis of the first condition, we classified objects as high recall (HR, recall higher than 60%) or low recall (LR, recall lower than 40%). The 40% and 60% thresholds were arbitrarily selected based on results of the first condition. Visual inspection of recall hits for this condition showed a gap in results: no object scored between 40% and 60%. Decks *A* and *B* had four HR objects each, totaling eight HR objects, all of which had been classified as highly salient. Three objects that had been classified as highly salient had low recall in the first condition, whereas objects classified as having low saliency all had low recall hits. In preparation for the second condition, videos *A* and *B* were modulated using the SMT to increase the salience of objects in LR. For the second condition, the only difference was the modulated stimulus; the procedure was the same.

Analysis

A Shapiro–Wilk test proved that the data for recall did not satisfy the condition of normality; the data are binary and not interval-scaled. Analysis was performed with Mann–Whitney *U* tests, due to their robustness under these conditions. Since our hypotheses focus on one side of the distribution, all the tests are one-tailed. We adjusted α levels with a Bonferroni correction to ensure a level of .05.

Results for H4. For objects $o \in HR$, mean recall hits in unmodulated (M=.69) and modulated (M=.68) conditions show no statistical difference (Mann–Whitney U=1.1272e^4, n1=n2=160, p=.46, one-tailed). The result supports H4.

Results for H5. For objects $o \in LR$, the mean recall hits for unmodulated (M=.19) and modulated (M=.22) conditions show no statistical difference (Mann–Whitney U=3.78e^4, n1=n2=280, p=.15, one-tailed). There is not enough evidence to support H5.

To further analyze these results, we classified LR objects into those that increased in recall hits in the second condition, and those that did not show any change or showed a decrease in recall. We first confirmed the relationship between recall and attention, correlating recall with fixation count r(878) =.35, p<.001; and with fixation time r(878) =.666, p<.001. Then, we analyzed features of these objects that contribute to saliency and how they affect recall. We found moderate correlations between recall and size (in pixels) r(878) =.449, p=.032, and the average size in time of the region (% coverage × % visible time) r(878) =.428, p=0.042. We observed that objects $o \in LR$ that decreased in recall in the second condition were either < 2e^{4}px or appeared for less than 2s. Since the SMT cannot control contributions to saliency due to size or spatial frequency, we filtered data in LR based on these criteria, yielding two datasets: $LR' = o \in LR, size(o) > 2e^4px$ and $MR = LR - LR'$. Subsequently, we analyzed the filtered data.

Object	o1	o2	o3	o4	o5	o6	o7
Unmodulated	2	2	3	2	8	1	8
Modulated	6	6	5	3	13	2	11

Table 1. Recall differences for objects in LR'

On filtered data for H5, objects $o \in LR'$, the mean recall for unmodulated (M=0.19) and modulated (M=0.31) conditions differed significantly (Mann–Whitney U=1.128e^4, n1=n2=160, p=.008, one-tailed). The result supports H5, meaning that objects that had low recall hits in the first condition significantly increased in score when modulated with the SMT (see Table 1). Furthermore, objects $o \in MR$ did not suffer a significant reduction in recall from unmodulated (M=.18) to modulated (M=.11) (Mann–Whitney U=6.660e^3, n1=n2=80, p=.05, one-tailed).

The results support H4 in the general case. This means that the SMT does not suppress recall for objects with otherwise high recall. The results did not provide enough evidence to support H5 in the general case. Nevertheless, for objects that cover more than 2e^{4}px and come into view for over 2s, the results showed a significant increase in recall. This suggests that the SMT increases recall of regions > 2e^{4}px with durations > 2s, without a significant loss to other regions.

Discussion of Memory Experiment

Exit interviews showed no difference in mean difficulty of the task between the first (M=5.28, STD=.987) and second conditions (M=4.98, STD=1.250), t(40)=1.190 p=.237 (2-tailed *t*-test). Furthermore, there was no difference in mean difficulty between video *A* (M=5.25, STD=1.171) and *B* (M=5.00, STD=1.086), t(40)=.990 p=.325 (2-tailed *t*-test).

The main contribution of this work is to show that the SMT introduces imperceptible changes to a video that increase recall of selected objects, without significantly reducing recall of others. The resource addressed, namely memory, is limited. In this study, participants in both conditions tended to remember the same number of objects, χ^2 (1, N = 880) = .39, p = .53. There is a tradeoff where the recall of some objects is reduced, while that of others is increased. In practice, our observations showed that a participant would recall on average five objects (at most eight) with certainty.

Figure 5. Scene extracted from the modulated condition. The high salience object (top left) had equally high recall hits (12) in both conditions. The low salience object (bottom left) had a score of 8 (LR) in the unmodulated condition and achieved a score of 13 (HR) in the modulated condition.

Some objects in HR decreased in recall, but not significantly (H4). Conversely, objects that were filtered out (objects $o \in MR$) also decreased in recall, albeit not significantly. In comparison, recall of objects $o \in LR'$ significantly increased. This comparison is between scores for the same object; it does not mean that we can increase recall hits of an object over those of another object. In particular, it does not mean we can increase recall hits of an inconspicuous object over those of a conspicuous object. The results merely show that the SMT increases the chances of an object being remembered. Having clarified this, there were two cases where the scores of an object in LR' increased to equal those of its scene counterpart in HR (Figure 5 shows one example). In both cases, recall hits in the first condition for the LR objects were at the 40% limit.

GENERAL DISCUSSION

The results presented in this paper indicate that the SMT can significantly shift attention to selected areas of a video, and it can increase recall of selected objects, without the viewer becoming aware of any manipulation. This provides strong evidence that the technique can influence the viewer's experience of a video at different levels of processing: it has applications in stimulus-based conditions (bottom-up) and task-based conditions (top-down).

Experiment Design

Since our main motivating field is AR, the studies were performed in videos, rather than still images. Using still images would not prove that the SMT works in videos, which contain motion, a contributor to saliency that the SMT cannot control. All videos used in these experiments are available for download[1]. Figure 6 shows the stages of each experiment and the order of their implementation. Two issues are important: the attention and memory experiments were carried out simultaneously with the same participants, and the formal study on awareness was carried out right after the first condition of the combined attention/memory experiment. Regarding the latter, to generate the stimuli for the formal awareness study, we needed the FRs for each video clip. Conveniently, this is exactly the outcome of the first condition of the attention experiment. On the other hand, the result of the formal awareness study is a single modulation threshold needed to prepare the stimuli for the second condition of the combined attention/memory study. The participants of the awareness studies did not take part in any of the other studies. Thus, there is no risk in interleaving these experiments. Concerning the combination of the attention and memory experiments, all participants received the instructions and performed the memory experiment after completing the attention experiment. The attention experiment evaluates stimulus-based responses and requires that the participant is not given a task. In contrast, the memory experiment was conceived to evaluate a task-based response, requesting participants to remember objects. The duration of the combined experiment was roughly 30 min.

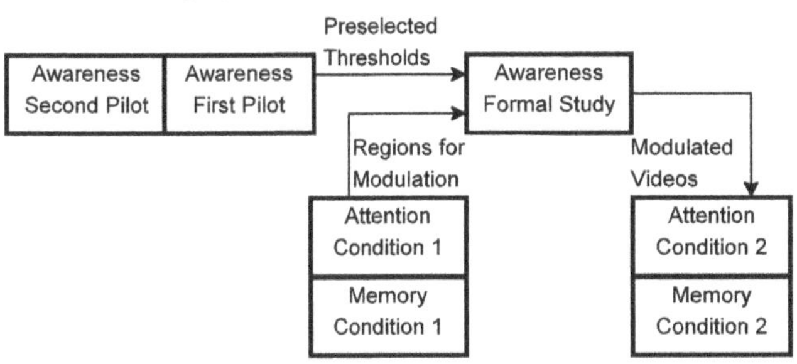

Figure 6. Stages of each experiment in chronological order.

Limitations

The restriction that no faces/hands appear in the clips seems to impact generalizability. However, in our experience, AR applications in non-urban areas easily meet this requirement, and even urban AR applications often involve users looking at equipment without seeing people. We believe the restriction is a reasonable way to control this potential confound now, prior to addressing it in future research.

The results of our experiments do not guarantee that every viewer will attend to and/or remember the selected objects, but that they are more likely to, as compared to the original unmodified condition. However, thresholds can be adjusted interactively by passing a parameter to the SMT implementation (e.g., in response to eye tracker feedback). So, if an application needs to make the effects of the SMT perceptible, it only needs to increase the modulation threshold.

[1] http://hydrosys.icg.tugraz.at/media_files/Saliency

Several factors have been identified that contribute to saliency (e.g., see Wolfe and Horowitz [20]). Of these, the SMT controls contributions in lightness, red–green color opponents, and blue–yellow color opponents, while other factors remain unaffected. In our studies, factors such as motion and size negatively affected results. Future research will need to address how contributors to saliency not controlled by the SMT affect its application. Meanwhile, the effectiveness of the SMT depends on the balance of these factors throughout the input. Avoiding extremes (e.g., small objects) can help in using the SMT successfully.

The main limitation of this approach is registration: how do we decide that a certain portion of the video frame corresponds to a real world object that we want to emphasize. Vision-based object recognition can provide an answer to this question, albeit with limitations of its own.

Outlook

The SMT is implemented in a GPU shader program, and runs at interactive rates on a desktop PC. We are currently experimenting with implementations on an ultramobile PC.

That the modulation is imperceptible is a crucial contribution of our technique. Exit interviews from the attention/memory experiment showed that the mean perceived alteration of videos was equally low for the first (M=2.0, STD=1.214) and second conditions (M=1.7, STD=.801), $t(40)=.922$ $p=.362$ (2-tailed *t*-test). Choosing the right modulation threshold is a key requirement for the SMT to work imperceptibly and effectively. For the experiments presented in this paper, thresholds have only been studied empirically. A thorough study of thresholds for each modulation dimension and their effect on visual attention could greatly improve the selection of modulation threshold.

Our main motivation for developing and experimenting with the SMT is AR, in particular, information-rich visualizations. One idea for mobile devices is to use the SMT as an aid to navigation. We would like to suggest objects related to landmarks and explore whether a navigator would recall having seen them along a path. Our results foster experimentation in this direction. Furthermore, we are aware that the SMT has applications beyond AR; for example, in training, the SMT could be used to suggest that a trainee shift attention towards areas of interest in a scene. A surgeon during training surgery might be reminded of sensitive organs near the work area without visually overlaying any information on the video feed. By varying the modulation thresholds, one could even support using more subtle levels for advanced trainees. Alternatively, physicians following a procedure in real-time could each have the SMT applied to different aspects, depending on a user profile.

CONCLUSIONS

The results of our studies validate the SMT as an alternative means to convey information to the user, *suggesting* attention shifts and *influencing* recall of selected regions without perceptible changes to visual input. These results represent fundamental research and, by no means, cover all the requirements of our motivating scenarios. Still, our experiments address two processes common in HCI: Stimulus-based attention guides the user in the exploration of visual input, playing an important role in tasks such as visual search. Memory is involved in user tasks at several stages (e.g., navigation and visual search). To our knowledge, we are the first to interactively modify videos so that a region we selected contains the highest saliency and experimentally validate its application. We presented three experiments that validate the SMT as an alternative means to convey information to the user. An awareness experiment certifies a modulation threshold that is imperceptible to the user. An attention experiment warrants that regions modulated with the SMT draw a first fixation significantly faster than without modulation. A memory experiment supports that modulation increases recall for selected objects without significant loss in recall for others. In summary, the SMT can significantly shift attention and influence memory to selected areas of a video without the viewer becoming aware of any manipulation. We believe that the results provide sufficient evidence to justify further experimentation in tasks that better match real-world conditions.

The SMT presents an alternative means of attention direction by modifying existing features of the real-world image, instead of adding traditional augmentations (such as pointing arrows or frames). The SMT enables mediated reality, since its premise is modifying the existing video input instead of adding virtual artifacts to it. One advantage inherent to this approach is that it protects context. While the saliency of the context is diminished as that of the focus is increased, the context does not suffer any other degradation. Perceptual issues arising from visual clutter or differences in depth between virtual and real objects are also prevented.

While other approaches to draw attention or influence memory exist, most lack the subtlety of the SMT. The suitability of this technique depends on the application, and also raises ethical issues. In many applications, it will be essential to inform the user that salience modification is being used. Nonetheless, it is our hope that these results provide motivation to contemplate this technique when attempting to design unobtrusive user interfaces.

ACKNOWLEDGEMENTS

This work is partially funded by the EC 7th Framework project HYDROSYS (224416, DG-INFSO). We thank Andreas Duenser for his insight on statistical analysis.

REFERENCES

1. Awh, E., Vogel, E., and Oh, S. Interactions between attention and working memory. *Neuroscience 139*, 1 (2006), 201-208.
2. Bailey, R., McNamara, A., Sudarsanam, N., and Grimm, C. Subtle gaze direction. *ACM TOG 28*, 4 (2009), 1-14.
3. Berg, D. and Itti, L. Memory, eye position and computed saliency. *Journal of Vision 8*, 6 (2008), 1164.
4. Chun, M.M. and Turk-Browne, N.B. Interactions between attention and memory. *Current opinion in neurobiology 17*, 2 (2007), 177-184.
5. Fine, M.S. and Minnery, B.S. Visual salience affects performance in a working memory task. *Journal of Neuroscience 29*, 25 (2009), 8016-21.
6. Itti, L., Koch, C., and Niebur, E. A Model of Saliency-Based Visual Attention for Rapid Scene Analysis. *IEEE Transactions on Pattern Analysis and Machine Intelligence 20*, 11 (1998), 1254-1259.
7. Itti, L. Models of bottom-up attention and saliency. *Neurobiology of attention 582*, 1980 (2005), 576-582.
8. Itti, L. Visual salience. *Scholarpedia 2*, 9 (2007), 3327.
9. Kim, Y. and Varshney, A. Saliency-guided Enhancement for Volume Visualization. *IEEE TVCG 12*, 5 (2006), 925-932.
10. Kim, Y. and Varshney, A. Persuading Visual Attention through Geometry. *IEEE TVCG 14*, 4 (2008), 772-782.
11. Koch, C. and Ullman, S. Shifts in selective visual attention: towards the underlying neural circuitry. *Human Neurobiology 4*, 4 (1985), 219-227.
12. Lee, S., Kim, G.J., and Choi, S. Real-time tracking of visually attended objects in interactive virtual environments. *ACM VRST*, (2007), 15-24.
13. Mendez, E., Feiner, S.K., and Schmalstieg, D. Focus and Context in Mixed Reality by Modulating First Order Salient Features. *Int. Symp. on Smart Graphics*, (2010), 232-243.
14. Ouerhani, N., Wartburg, R.V., Hugli, H., and Muri, R. Empirical validation of the saliency-based model of visual attention. *Electronic Letters on Computer Vision and Image Analysis 3*, 1 (2004), 13–24.
15. Rensink, R.A., O'Regan, J.K., and Clark, J.J. On the Failure to Detect Changes in Scenes Across Brief Interruptions. *Visual Cognition 7*, 1-3 (2000), 127-145.
16. Santella, A. and DeCarlo, D. Visual interest and NPR: an evaluation and manifesto. *NPAR*, (2004), 150.
17. Su, S.L., Durand, F., and Agrawala, M. De-emphasis of distracting image regions using texture power maps. *Texture 2005: Proc. 4th ICCV Workshop on Texture Analysis and Synthesis*, (2005), 119-124.
18. Treisman, A.M. and Gelade, G. A feature-integration theory of attention. *Cognitive psychology 12*, 1 (1980), 97-136.
19. Veas, E., Mulloni, A., Kruijff, E., and Schmalstieg, D. Techniques for View Transition in Multi-Camera Outdoor Environments. *Graphics Interface 2010 (GI2010)*, (2010), 193-200.
20. Wolfe, J.M. and Horowitz, T.S. What attributes guide the deployment of visual attention and how do they do it? *Nature reviews. Neuroscience 5*, 6 (2004), 495-501.

Freed: A System for Creating Multiple Views of a Digital Collection during the Design Process

Philip Mendels, Joep Frens and Kees Overbeeke
Designing Quality in Interaction, Department of Industrial Design
Eindhoven University of Technology
Den Dolech 2, 5612 AZ, Eindhoven, The Netherlands
{p.mendels, j.w.frens, c.j.overbeeke}@ tue.nl
+31 40 247 5924

ABSTRACT
In this paper Freed is presented, a system that enables design students to spatially organize their digital collection, define relations between collection content and reflect on it. The system features a force-based layout that allows to explore spatial organizations, and hence to gain new insights. Its main advantage over existing software, is that it empowers the students to create different views of their digital collection. A view is a spatial organization of a selection of the collection content and its relations. It can e.g. be used for a specific design activity or project phase, for organizing work around a specific topic, or for explaining the perspective of a given student or stakeholder. Feedback of design students working with Freed during their design projects, and results from a workshop as measured by a questionnaire, show positive prospects for adoption of the system during the design process.

Author Keywords
Design process, reflection, digital collection, multiple views, force-based layout

ACM Classification Keywords
H.5.4 Information interfaces and presentation: Hypertext/Hypermedia. H.5.2 Information interfaces and presentation: User Interfaces: Interaction styles

General Terms
Design

INTRODUCTION
In the Industrial Design Department at the Eindhoven University of Technology, students spend 60 percent of their time working in semester-long design projects, often for real clients. Students collect a lot of diverse digital content. Examples of collection content include plannings, requirement lists, related or inspiring work, ideas, sketches, interaction scenarios, client and expert feedback, prototyping tutorials, CAD models, programming code, photos or videos of prototypes, information from user tests, presentations and reports. As design teachers, we have observed that our students mainly organize and browse this digital content within standard hierarchical file browsers (e.g. Windows Explorer or Mac OSX Finder).

These standard file browsers do not do justice to the visual nature of design work, and are not designed to define and see relations other than hierarchical ones, such as associations, comparisons and temporal relations. They also do not integrate well with different software-based activities, such as making a mood board, a map of ideas, a scenario or a presentation. This fragments the collection because the same content that is used in multiple activities is imported in different files or copied to different folders.

This fragmentation and the lack of easily visible relations make it difficult for the students to reflect on their work and process, and to communicate these to others. Reflection is important, after and during the design process. Schön describes design as a dynamic explorative process during which the design problem is explored and refined [1], in contrast to Simon's rational problem solving approach in which the design problem is fixed at the start of the design process [2]. In our department we strongly embrace Schön's ideas, which fit the competency-based learning system that is used, in which students learn by doing and in which equal weight is given to knowledge, skills and attitudes. We also want students to develop a vision about how our world could be like and to become designers that can transform our world, not that only solve existing problems. Therefore in our department the Reflective Transformative Design Process is developed [3,4].

To fit such a dynamic design process, and to resolve the shortcomings of standard file browsers, we see a need for a collection system that enables students to easily switch between different visual-spatial representations of their work. To avoid fragmentation of the collection this system should integrate various design related activities (e.g. mapping ideas, presenting).

In what follows we first describe related work. We continue by explaining the current state of Freed. Then we discuss the feedback of design students working with the system during part of their design projects, and results from a workshop with accompanying questionnaire. We conclude with our plans for improving the system and validating it during semester-long student design projects.

RELATED WORK

In this section we describe related work in three parts:

- digital collections during the design process
- spatial organization and automated layouts
- multiple views

We end with a discussion on how Freed combines several aspects of the related work, and how it differs.

Digital collections during the design process

Many systems that have been developed to support design, focus on how designers can combine their digital and physical artifacts [5,6]. Such systems often add extra, large devices to the designers' workspace, and the focus is often not on how designers can organize their digital work.

In a recent study on professional designers' knowledge management practices, is found that reuse of prior design knowledge is highly valued during early design activity, but seldom performed. Also, designers indicated that they want to know more about the stories associated with artifacts and want to reflect on past processes. An inquiry into designers' organization strategies showed that besides the physical note/sketch book, *digital* folders were clearly the most used organization strategy. These folders were generally described as 'messy' [7].

The Digital Scrapbook is an online tool that is discussed in a recent article on design's processional character [8]. The tool is developed in-house in the Interaction Design department of the Royal College or Art. It was developed to enable tutors to gain insight in their students' design processes, which was difficult because students had troubles with documenting their process. The tool automatically gathers mainly visual content from students' project blogs, online photo sites, and online video sites, and aggregates this content of different people in a minimalistic grid-based interface. The tool is valued by both staff and students for looking at each other's work and for drawing inspiration, for the way it represents the dynamic and haphazard nature of the design process, and for the way it reflects the creative nature of the department as a whole.

Spatial organization and automated layouts

Free spatial organization allows for mapping the many possible relations that can exist between collection content and the complexity of the design process. It also allows for differences between individual design students and between projects. Additionally, it supports free association between collection content. Free association is important for drawing inspiration during the creative process [9] but also for reflection. A design student might for example find a new direction for the project by comparing or clustering his/her ideas.

Prezi is an online software application [10] that can be used to create interactive maps and animated presentations. We have observed several of our students using it for creating presentations. Its canvas is zoomable, so that major topics can be presented much larger than more detailed topics. To create a presentation, a presentation path has to be generated on the canvas. When playing back this presentation, the application smoothly zooms, pans and rotates across the canvas. *The Visual Understanding Environment (VUE)* is a concept and content mapping software application that like Prezi features a digital canvas and the possibility to create presentation paths [11]. Presentation slides are however not an integral part of the canvas, but are independent entities that are linked to items (image nodes and text nodes) on the canvas. These slides can be edited separately without influencing the content map on the canvas.

When the amount of items and relations in a collection grows, it becomes increasingly harder for the user to find a satisfying layout. A solution is to offer a (semi-) automated layout. An example of an application that shows the strengths of a semi-automated layout is *Vizster*, a tool for exploring online social networks [12]. Vizster represents a network as a node-link diagram and features a force-based layout. This means that the links between nodes behave as springs. The user can directly interact with the nodes, and the layout tries to keep related nodes close to each other and avoids the nodes from overlapping.

Product World is a software application specifically geared at industrial designers, that features a semi-automated layout [13]. It is a tool for creating and exploring a collection visually, based on similarity between the collection content. A designer enters product samples into the collection by positioning them into a two-dimensional area in such a way that their relative positions express their perceived similarities regarding a specific criterion. An example of such a similarity criterion is 'form'. When all the samples are entered, the collection can be explored. By 'clicking' positions between the samples an object is retrieved from the collection that 'fits' in this position relative to the other samples.

Multiple views

An overview of research into coordinated and multiple views is given in [14]. Views can be predefined by the developer, or generated by the user. Often used in exploratory visualization, they allow the user to 'understand trends, locate anomalies, isolate and reorganize information, compare and make clear any differences or similarities between datasets'. The user can interact with the data while examining the results in multiple views. A common approach to this is *brushing*, during which elements are selected in one view, and concurrently the same information is highlighted in other views.

Less seems to have been written about the use of multiple views in relation to digital collections or personal information management. *Compendium* is an example of a tool that combines multiple views with design rationale [15]. Each view is an argument map and can contain multiple nodes such as ideas, questions, arguments, images and documents. The user can create as many maps as s/he wants. A node can have instances in multiple maps, but this is not necessary. A number above each node shows how many maps the node is used in, and by clicking on this number a popup menu is shown through which the user can open (some of) these other maps if they are currently closed.

Discussion

Although we recognize that physical artifacts are part of designers' collections, and that digitizing physical content is an issue, our current focus is on the organization and use in software. This overview of related work supports our observations that a new system to document the design process is needed. We think that an automated collection system such as the Digital Scrapbook can be useful for aggregating parts of individual digital collections, but that it does not cater for the *entire* design process in our department, and that is our goal.

We discussed several examples relating to spatial organization, semi-automated layouts and multiple views. We see value in combining these aspects, as they can strengthen each other. Relations do not only serve the purpose of association and reflection (this could also be supported by spatial organization alone), but they also play a crucial role in enabling the force-based layout by behaving as springs, and in exploring the collection. The latter is done by showing (or hiding) content that is *related* to specific content. This showing and hiding, in combination with the easy reorganization possibilities of the force-based layout, help to explore spatial organizations and selections and hence to create different views. We see value in the way Compendium integrates multiple views. We consider it however to be more suitable for argument mapping of more rational and structured design processes, requiring users to specify whether a new node is for example a question or argument, while we seek a quicker and more playful way of organization to support dynamic creative design processes.

Some of the discussed examples show the integration of additional activities besides making a spatially organized collection. We explained that Product World enables designers to compare content based on a similarity criterion such as form. We imagine that this can also be useful for mapping ideas or concepts to for example requirements. Although we see it as an interesting addition for future work, we currently do not focus on these activities, as it requires the student to set specific distances between content or specify weights for the relations in a force-based layout. This might decrease the spontaneity of the interaction, i.e. it might make building the collection a too cognitive and perhaps too complex process. *Prezi* and *VUE* feature the possibility to create presentations. We do integrate this activity, because formal but especially informal presentations (e.g. showing the project progress to a project coach) occur often throughout the entire design process. More about this is explained in the next section in which the current state of Freed is explained.

FREED: CURRENT STATE OF THE SYSTEM

Our system is called *Freed*, because it gives design students the freedom to position and relate content freely, to quickly spatially reorganize their content, to create multiple linked views, and to integrate different activities (e.g. presentation). Freed is a work-in-progress that is developed during the PhD project of the first author. It is however functional, and is and has been used by students during their design projects. In this section we will describe the main functionality of the system as it is now. It is not possible to explain all functionality of Freed within this paper. For getting a sense of the dynamic qualities of the system, we refer the reader to the video that accompanies this paper.

System overview

Freed is in its current state a standalone single-user software application created in Java using the Processing libraries [16] within the Eclipse development environment. The application can run in normal and openGL hardware accelerated mode, the latter being clearly the preferred choice because it operates much smoother. It currently works in Windows and Mac OS X and is used by design students on both operating systems.

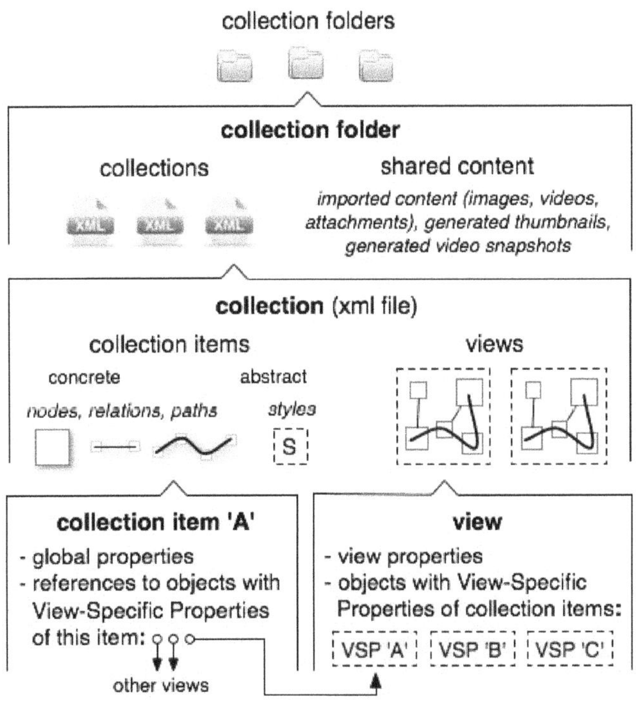

Figure 1: The structure of the system

The application supports text, image and video content. A collection is saved as an xml-file in a collection folder. All imported content is copied to a shared content folder within that collection folder. Multiple collection files can exist within a collection folder (e.g. saved iterations of the same collection), and they can share (part of) the shared content. The structure of the system is explained in figure 1.

Graphical interface

The interface of Freed consists of two main parts: the canvas and the panels. The canvas (figure 2a) is the place where the main action takes place. Here the designer creates a visual-spatial organization of the collection content. The canvas can be zoomed and panned seamlessly, and individual content or selections of content can be easily zoomed to fill the screen. In the main panel (figure 2b) several tools can be chosen to interact with the content, as well as several actions that are applied immediately to selected content. From the main panel, several floating panels can be opened and closed, such as a panel for controlling the properties of the collection items, and a panel for controlling the force-based layout.

Views and multi-view presentations

The designer can switch between views and create new views from the 'views panel', which can be opened from the main panel. Views are not separate files; they are part of a collection file (figure 1). View switches are animated: The content that is in both views is gradually moved and transformed to its new position and size. The other content either fades in or out. These animations help seeing the relations and differences between views. They can be also be useful when giving a presentation consisting of multiple views (i.e. views are used as slides). We do not yet provide a thumbnail overview of views (or slides), and grouping of views into presentations is not yet supported, although we think that these can be useful features. In the current implementation of the system there can only be one view open at a time. Enabling multiple views to be open at the same time to support brushing (see related work) or copying content between views is planned for future work.

Collection items

The main collection items are *nodes*. Graphical nodes (figure 2d) can be created by dragging one or more images and/or videos from a file browser onto the canvas. Thumbnails of various sizes are automatically created, and are automatically loaded into or out of memory depending on the current display size of the node. Text nodes (figure 2c) are created by clicking anywhere on the canvas with the text tool. The background color and font of a text node can be changed specifically for each view. Graphical nodes can be unified with text nodes so that the text appears as a description below the graphical content (figure 2e). Content that cannot be viewed within freed, such as documents, animations or CAD files, can be included as a clickable attachment to a node. Also hyperlinks to online websites can be attached to a node. Besides being resizable, nodes can be minimized (figure 2i), after which they are presented as little dots. Possibly attached relations and paths stay connected. The dot serves as a visual reminder that there is something to show.

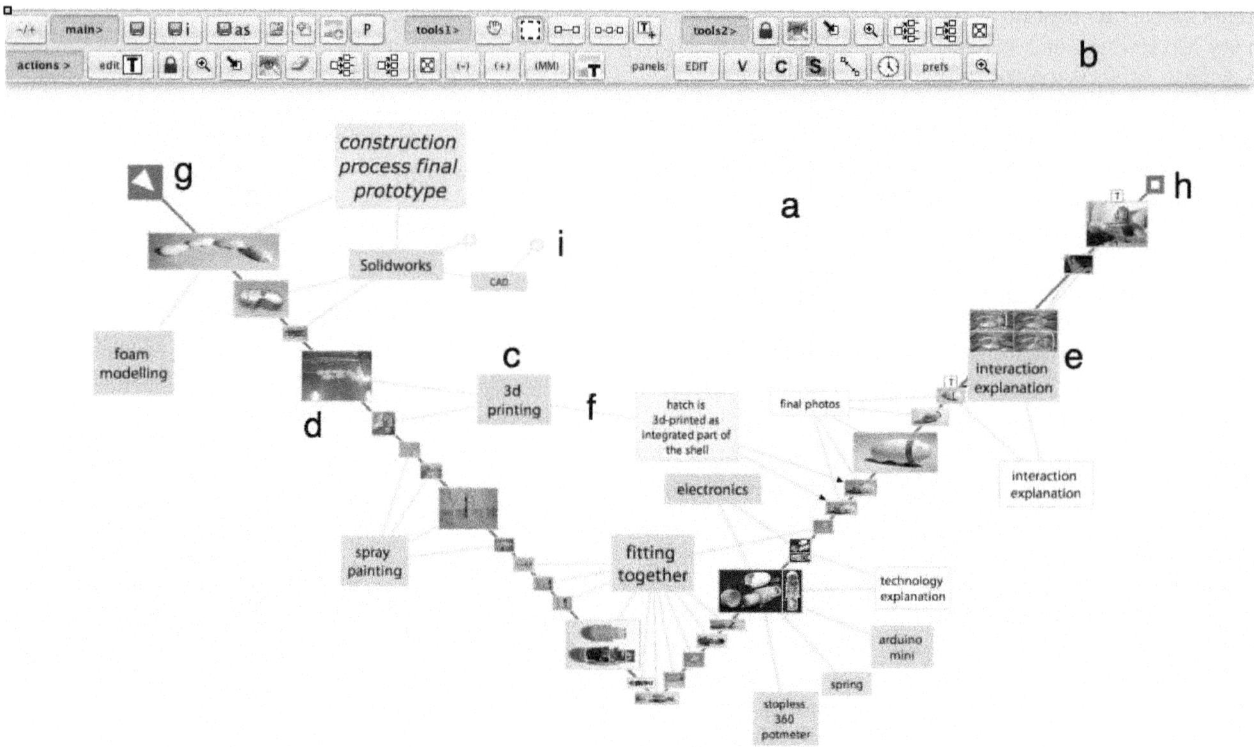

Figure 2. Different elements within Freed. a: canvas, b: main panel, c: text node, d: graphic node, e: combined text-graphic node, f: relation, g: start of a path, h: end of a path, i: minimized node

Besides nodes, there are three other types of collection items: *Relations, paths and styles*. A *relation* (figure 2f) is a visual link between two nodes. We call it relation rather than link, because students confused the latter with hyperlinks to websites. A relation can be created by clicking on multiple nodes in succession. The first-clicked node stays selected so that it is easy to quickly relate many nodes to that specific node (making it the center of a cluster). Text can be added to relations, and global visual properties of the relation can be changed (e.g. arrow type, directionality).

A *Path* (figure 2 g-h) is a linear sequence of nodes. It can be created by clicking on multiple nodes sequentially with the path tool. A path can be useful for showing a linear process (e.g. construction process of a prototype), a scenario, or for preparing an informal presentation of nodes within the view (which differs from a multi-view presentation). Paths are independent of relations: A path is not a linear group of relations. Paths and relations can overlap (i.e. the same node can be part of both a relation and a path). Multiple paths can also overlap. In the current implementation, paths cannot branch. For branches, new paths or relations have to be used.

When playing back a video within Freed, snapshots of the video can be created. These snapshots are image nodes that are automatically related to the video node. Additionally, a path is automatically created that orders the snapshots chronologically.

Styles are the only abstract collection items, and are designed to make it easier to control the visual appearance of nodes. They have properties such as 'node background color' and 'font-style'. A style can only be set as global property of a node. For each view, the designer can choose whether to use the view-specific appearance properties of the node, or whether its appearance is controlled by its global style. To add even more flexibility, styles have view-specific properties too. This can help the designer to for example quickly choose a different color simultaneously for all the nodes with the style 'comment' in the current view.

Force-based layout

The force-based layout avoids nodes from overlapping and keeps linked nodes close to each other, so that it is easy to reposition and resize the nodes. By slightly pulling a node, the user gets feedback about its connectivity, because connected nodes will also start to move. The designer can also explore connectivity by placing the mouse over a node or relation: Connected nodes or relations are then highlighted (figure 3). The main purpose of the force-based layout is to make it easy to adapt the spatial organization, and hence to create new views. It helps the designer to create a rough initial spatial organization. S/he can then lock one or more nodes to gain full control over their positions and fine-tune the spatial organization. The force-based layout uses two view-specific user-definable distance settings: distance between nodes and distance between clusters. The latter is implemented similarly as in Vizster (see related work): Clusters are not specifically defined by the user, but depend on the amount of relations between nodes. By using a relatively small distance between nodes, and by using a relatively high distance between clusters, clusters of nodes become apparent (figure 3).

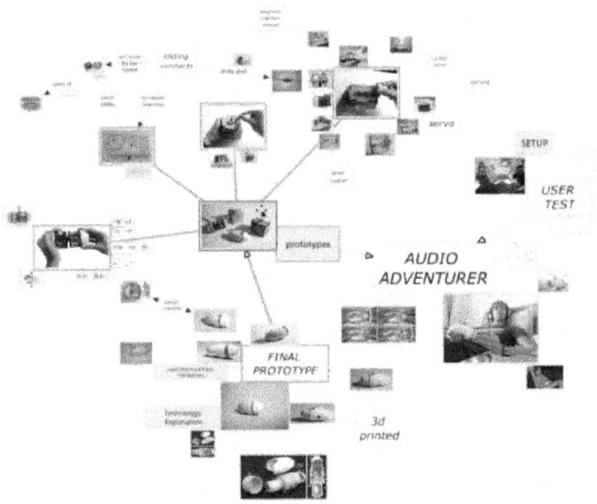

Figure 3: Distance settings can help to keep the visual information relatively dense while still seeing clusters. When the mouse cursor is placed over a node or relation, all connected nodes and relations are highlighted.

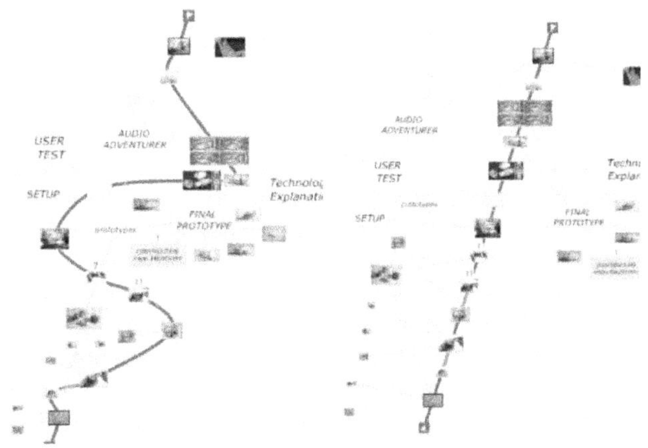

Figure 4: Two times the same path but with different path settings. Left: A curved path with a small straighten-force. Right: A straight path with a high 'space around path' setting.

Force-based paths

Paths in Freed differ from paths in related work, because they are force-based. A path can be straight or curved (figure 4). The straight setting can be used if the student wants to focus on the path and wants to see how the other nodes in the view (if any) relate to the path. The curved setting is useful if the student wants to focus on the organization of the nodes in the view, and wants to see how the path flows through this organization. The curviness of the path can be gradually controlled, using its 'straighten force' slider in the path properties panel. This straighten-force competes with the general force-based layout. The student can also gradually control the distance between the path and the other nodes in the current view, to make it stand out more. The straighten-force of the path and the distance around it are view-specific settings.

Force-based timeline

Also the timeline function in Freed differs from related work, because it is force-based. This timeline can help design students to organize the nodes within a view chronologically, after which they can for example make a process overview (figure 5). They can add directional relations that show how different content has inspired each other. A time-align force slider allows the user to gradually mix the linear organization by time with the two-dimensional categorization of the force-based layout. Different timestamps can be used, such as the time the node was created, the time the file was last modified at time of import (for an image or video node), or a user defined time. The latter can be set by dragging the anchor of a node on the timeline.

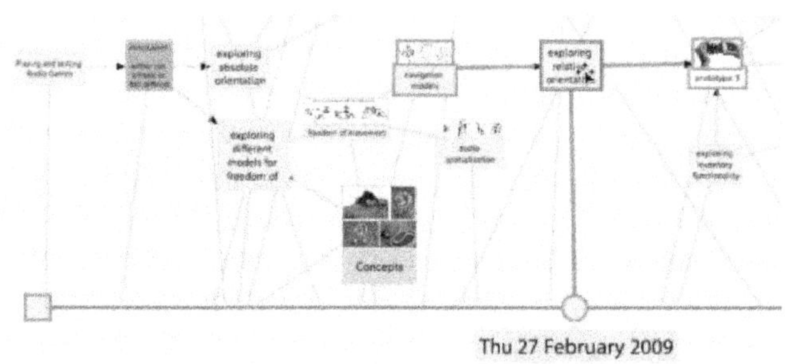

Figure 5: Small cutout of a process-overview, made with the force-based timeline

Showing and hiding content

To focus or to reduce visual clutter, nodes can be hidden (besides minimizing them). This can be done directly, or by hiding all the leaf-nodes (nodes that have no other relations) related to a specific visible node at once. Hidden content can be shown in two distinct ways: By showing it from the collection panel (which shows all the content in the collection and has search and filter options), or by showing it through related content that *is* visible in the current view. The latter is much quicker. Above each node that is visible in the current view, a button is displayed with a number that indicates the amount of invisible related nodes (except if zero). When clicking on this button, all these nodes are immediately shown. When placing the mouse cursor over a node that has any hidden related nodes, also another button is shown above it. When clicking this button a special panel is shown at the bottom of the screen from which these hidden related nodes can be shown individually (figure 6).

When placing the mouse cursor over a node that is visible in the current view, all hidden relations to other nodes that are visible in the view are shown as dotted lines. When clicking on such a line, the relation is shown.

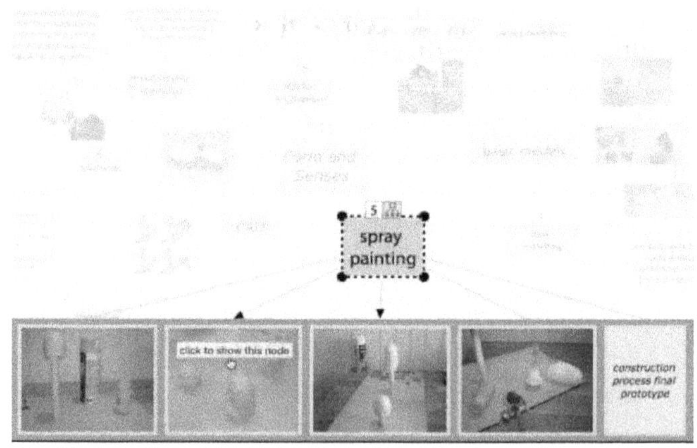

Figure 6. The panel for showing hidden related nodes. The hidden relations between the selected node and its hidden related nodes are temporarily shown when this panel is open, and all the items in the view except for the selected node are partly faded out.

EVALUATION

In this section we discuss two evaluations of Freed. The first is a longitudinal evaluation during which 4 students worked with Freed between March 2010 and June 2010. This was the first time that Freed was used by students. The second evaluation is a 3-hour workshop held with 14 students in September 2010. This evaluation included a questionnaire about the students' general collection and reflection practices during the design process, their first reactions to Freed during the workshop, and their intended use of Freed. It is not our intention here to present a highly detailed discussion of usability issues. We describe our first experiences with the use of Freed by students. Besides discussing how both evaluations influenced and will influence the design of Freed, we will focus on:

- Freed as a tool for documentation
- Freed as tool for exploration and reflection
- Freed as a tool for additional activities
- General comments and challenges for acceptance

Longitudinal evaluation

Freed was tested with four industrial design students (two male, two female) during the last three months of their semester-long individual final bachelor project. The students were asked to participate directly by the first author, who was the only researcher involved in the evaluation. At the start of the evaluation, the students were provided with the software and an illustrated digital manual. Additionally, the researcher demonstrated some of the main features, such as adding and relating content, using the force-based layout, and using multiple-views. At that point some features were not yet implemented, namely: the timeline, adding attachments and hyperlinks to nodes, changing the color of nodes, and adding video nodes. During the course of the evaluation, the researcher continuously worked on Freed and made several updates available, partly based on student request. Information about each update and how to install it was e-mailed to the students. They were not forced to install the updates. The students were not instructed to use the software in a specific way or with a specific frequency.

During the evaluation, the researcher contacted the students about every three weeks to ask them if they agreed to have a one-and-a-half our meeting with the researcher, to discuss their work using Freed. These meetings were loosely structured interviews during which the students showed their work using Freed, and the researcher asked questions about how Freed was used, things that were unclear, bugs and missing functionality. He also demonstrated functionality that was unclear, unknown or new. Two students used the system respectively two and three times, which resulted in respectively two and three meetings with the researcher. The other two students (one male, one female) used it on a more regular basis, about every two weeks. The researcher had four meetings with each of these two students.

Documentation

All students created a relatively similar main view in which they organized their design process horizontally in a chronological way. They locked the main nodes of this process (e.g. 'concept 1' or 'interim presentation'), and let the related content (e.g. different sketches of concept 1) for a large part unlocked so that it was easy to reorganize the view by dragging the main nodes. They made these main nodes bigger to show their importance. They then created relations, mostly associations or causal relations (e.g. 'inspired by'), between the content of the different phases. Three students also created additional views that gave a more detailed overview of selections of the process (i.e. to show *all* the ideas in one view). One student used the path tool to connect the main project phases in a chronological way. He used a curved path and used it for its visual properties (a clear thick line) and not for its quick reorganization possibilities (e.g. by using a straight path) or its full screen presentation possibilities.

Exploration and reflection

During the projects, the students did not use Freed for dedicated reflection. They mainly used it to document or communicate their work. They however felt that documentation and preparing informal presentations in Freed helped them to revisit previous work and to gain a better overview of their project process. These activities were therefore seen as part of reflection. They indicated that exploration during these activities was enforced by the playful nature of Freed.

Two students used the collection that they had built in Freed at the end of the project, when they had to create their educational portfolio on which they are assessed. They mainly used it to explore all the work that they had done, and to gain a better overview. They felt that Freed helped them to do this, but they did not change their collection during this process (e.g. add comments/reflections, relations, new views).

Additional activities

Besides documentation, exploration and reflection, Freed was mainly used for communication. The two students who used Freed on a more regular basis used it to explain their progress to their project coach (about every two weeks). They used it mainly as an informal presentation tool; they did not add coach comments to the collection during these meetings. One of these two students made a new view for most coach meetings. This view then included the entire collection (it was not a selection), but the student used the path tool and the size of the nodes (making them bigger) to 'highlight' what he wanted to show to his coach. The student mentioned that the advantage of having all content in the view was, that it was easy for the coach to see what they discussed in the previous meeting (i.e. the student could show the new work in the context of the old work). He used the path for its visual properties (a clear thick line) and for the possibility of quickly browsing through the nodes of the path in full screen using the arrow keys.

The two students that used the system on a more regular basis made screen captures (still images) of their main view. One student used these on a large poster at the education exhibition where he had to show the final outcome of his work (figure 7), the other student used them in her report.

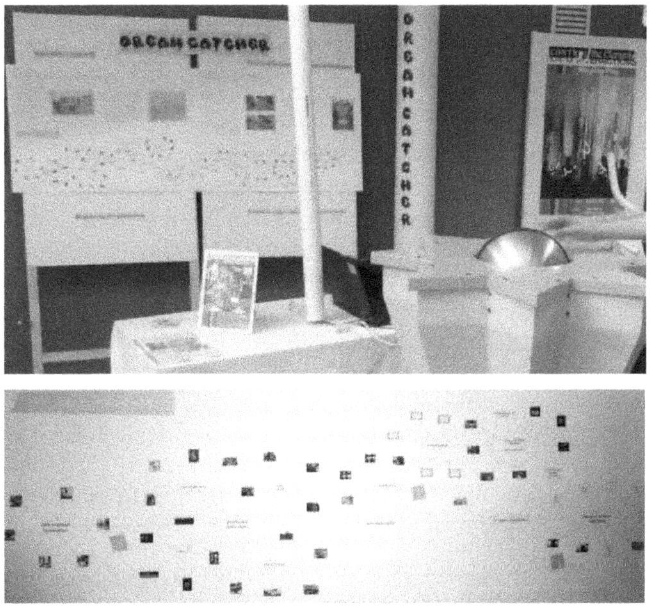

Figure 7: Top: An exhibition stand of a design student with at the back a poster with a process overview made in Freed. Bottom: The left half of the process overview.

General comments and challenges for acceptance

The students mentioned that they did not find the time to explore all the functionality of the system during their busy projects, but that they would probably have used the system more if they had learned to work with the system from the start of the project in a gradual way. An important relating problem was the lack of explanation or tutorial videos. A quite lengthy manual with lots of images was provided, but all students mentioned (independently and without asking) that they were missing explanation videos. Finally, two missing features (different colors for nodes and adding attachments/hyperlinks to nodes) were experienced as barriers for using the software more often. Nevertheless, all students were enthusiastic about the freedom that the system gave them. They liked the quick way of organizing and reorganizing their work, and although not used extensively, they liked the ability to create multiple views.

Changes made to Freed

In response to the students' requests, the researcher added functionality for adding colors, attachments and hyperlinks to nodes and created a website with tutorial videos. These developments were already planned, but were prioritized due to the requests. Additionally, the researcher added styles (for quickly changing the appearance of multiple nodes), support for playback of video, and the timeline functionality.

Workshop and questionnaire

After the previously described evaluation, a three-hour workshop was held with fourteen industrial design students, followed by a questionnaire returned by thirteen of these participants. All students never used the system before. Seven students (three female, four male) were Bachelor students in their final third year. The seven other students (one female, six male) were Master students in their final second year. All students had experience with many semester-long design projects, as well as keeping a design and education portfolio

During the 3-hour workshop, the students were provided with the system, explanation videos of the main functionality, and an example collection that they could explore. The students were asked to bring as much digital content as possible from previous projects and their just-started current project, and to spend half of the time working with the former and the other half with the latter. They were explicitly told that they should include everything in one collection and that they were allowed to make previous and current work overlap. Roughly the first 45 minutes were spent exploring the explanation videos and example collection, so about 2 hours and 15 minutes were spent with their own work.

The questionnaire was divided in three parts: Questions about the students' general collection and reflection practices during the design process (6 questions), questions about the use of Freed during the workshop (19 questions) and questions about the students' intention to use Freed and required changes or improvements (9 questions). The majority of the questions was open.

Documentation

The students' physical collections mainly exist out of their sketch/note book, loose sketches and physical models or prototypes. They sometimes use their physical work as visual references for inspiration and communication purposes in their workspace (e.g. on the walls), and also print out digital work for this sake. All students indicated that they use the main file browser of their operating system (e.g. Windows Explorer) for managing their digital work during the design process. They create folders with the main activities or project phases. Some organize these chronologically by numbering them. One student mentioned that he used a blog in some projects to document his work and to communicate to his team and client. One other student creates a video log. Some other students use weekly to-do and have-done lists to document their work.

All students create a portfolio including reflections, as this is required to pass their semester. None of the students mention that they work on this portfolio before the end of the semester. All students indicated that they feel that it is important to keep a well-structured digital collection during the project, but seven students mention that they do not or only partly succeed to, and that it is especially hard during project phases with a lot of time-pressure. In such phases the collection becomes more chaotic and less physical content is digitized. One student specifically mentions that he does not keep a complete digital collection because he does not know which part of his physical work (e.g. notes, sketches) will be relevant to have in digital form later (e.g. for reflecting, reporting or presenting). Three students perceive it as a problem that they have no software for creating a collection that will be compatible with the portfolio that they have to create in the end of the semester. Most students make these portfolios using an HTML WYSIWYG editor or Adobe Flash. These are not used to keep a collection during the entire project. Apart from the time pressure and the time it takes to digitize physical work, most students mention the lack of freedom and exploration possibilities, and the lack of a visual overview, as key-problems during their digital collection process.

During the workshop, seven students did not plan in advance how to structure their content and were inspired while working with the system. The six others mentioned that it was a combination of planning and being inspired while working. The following answer is an example of the latter:

"During the process, I got inspired by the option of multiple views. While I was going through my collection, I realized that in different situations, you need different 'views' on your collection. In my case I figured that there are situations where you want to present your specific skills as a designer and there are situations where you want to focus more on your projects." (figure 8)

Most students, in particular the ones that did not plan ahead, started with dragging many images onto the canvas, and then started 'playing' supported by the force-based layout. Two students were somewhat overwhelmed by the large amount of images that they had imported, but this improved when they started scaling, minimizing and hiding content. It is important to note however, that this will be different when introducing the system from the start of a design project, because then less content at a time will be imported, and perhaps with clearer goals in the context of an activity within the design process.

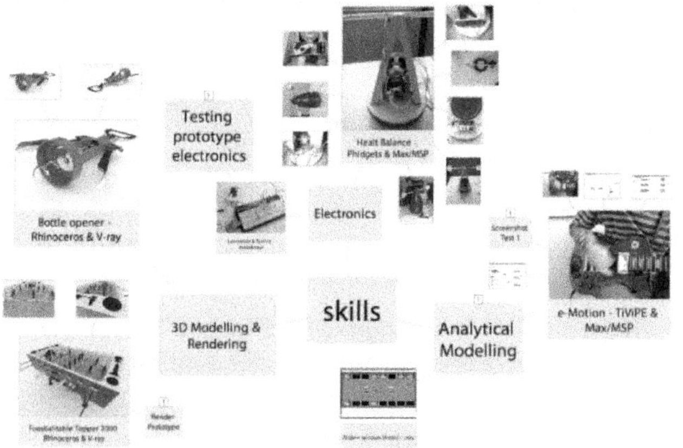

Figure 8: One student made a view about skills.

Two of the students did not create multiple views. One explains that he was too busy organizing his imported content in his one and only view, the other mentions that she had no inspiration during the workshop for a new view. Five of the students that created multiple views, created at least one view that was a categorization of work, and another view that was a more chronological organization of the same work. Some used the timeline feature for the latter, but most used the path feature. Three students each created multiple views that were different categorizations of the same work, e.g:

"The first view is hierarchical to show my activities during a semester, where each activity can have subgroups. This view was an overview to see what kind of media I have created for these activities. The second view was to visualize my activities linked to competencies that I need to work on for my education."

Exploration and reflection

The students indicated that reflection is often postponed until the end of the project, when they have to make their educational portfolio. At this point, it is a lot of work to review all the details of the project. Also deciding what to focus on and creating a coherent story are mentioned as problems at this point.

One student mentions that she prints out digital work such as ideas and requirements so that she can try out different physical mappings of these on her desk, and reflect on that. One other student mentions that he explores different overlapping representations of his project work in software, but that this is a lot of work:

"The various representations of my output are tedious to produce as most of the time it involves recreating part of a previous representation. The difference between these kind of representations are key to gaining insight, however the representations of the current software I use (OmniGraffle, Photoshop, Visio) are too static."

Besides general insights such as '*the workshop made me again aware of the importance of visual documentation*', or '*I was inspired to new visual styles for presenting my work in the future*', two students mentioned that they gained new insights in their work. One concerned a possible direction for a project, and one concerned skills, as was described under 'documentation' and shown in figure 8. The other students mention the limited time of the workshop, and the focus on learning the system, as the reason for not gaining new insights. They expected to gain new insights when using the system over a longer period of time in a more relaxed setting.

Additional activities

Many students create small 'collections' for specific design activities, such as a planning, mood boards, mind maps or brainstorms, mappings of ideas and concepts (sometimes mapped against requirements), reports, presentations, and process overviews. Sometimes these small collections are physical and exist within the workspace, but they are mostly digital. The students indicated that these collections are not well integrated with each other.

Besides documenting work based on previous and current activities (as students would normally do in their standard file browser), several other activities were observed during the workshop: Making a visual chronological overview of work (nine students), organizing work based on competencies or skills (four students), making a mindmap of the current project (two students), mapping related work (benchmark) of the current project along two dimensions (one student), mapping prototypes along two dimensions (one student), making a stakeholder overview for the current project (one student) and making a geographic overview of work (one student).

General comments and challenges for acceptance

All students except one praised the freedom that the system gave them and the multiple view functionality. This one student had doubts that the system was too free/open for him, because he knows that he needs a lot of structure during his design process. He said that he might not know what to do with it and preferred to have some templates for structuring, or tutorials. Most of the other students answered that they explicitly did not want templates and prefer freedom.

Nine of the thirteen students said that they were intending to use the system during their design process (of which five thought they would use it structurally, perhaps weekly), the four others had doubts or conditions: One of these four was the just-described student that desired more structure. Another student thought that the system might require him to digitize too much physical content that he would not really need later. Another student thought that the flexibility and playfulness might make him spend too much time with it. Finally, one student answered that he *required* the system to drag and drop PDF documents, and to be able to preview these documents within Freed. Drag and drop of files (other than images and videos which was possible already), such as documents, Flash, Illustrator and Photoshop files, was also requested by most of the other students. Other much requested features were to have multiple views open at the same time so that it is possible to quickly switch between views without thinking about saving, to see the views as visual tabs, and to switch to a view from *within* another view: e.g. switching to a view about the final prototype by clicking on a node that shows the final prototype (like in Compendium, see related work).

CONCLUSION AND FUTURE WORK

Although we feel that Freed can also be useful for practicing designers (especially since our education is modeled to a professional context), our current focus is on design students. The evaluations confirmed our observations regarding students' documentation and reflection practices, and the need for a system such as Freed. The ease of exploration and reorganization and the possibility to create multiple views and integrate different activities, which we consider the key features of our system, were well appreciated. This, combined with the use of Freed by two of the students during the longitudinal evaluation and combined with the students' answers regarding intended use of Freed, gives us good hopes for acceptance of Freed during the design process.

Freed is however a work in progress, and there are instruction and usability aspects that need to be improved (most notably tutorial improvements and GUI/menu improvements) and features to be added (most notably regarding switching views and supporting the drag and drop of additional file types). Additionally personal differences between students will keep playing a role. Some students might require a more structured way of documentation and reflection than Freed offers. Also, it differs per student how much content originates in digital form and how much energy is put in digitizing physical content.

Besides improving Freed, we need to do a longitudinal study that captures the *entire* design process. It is important to see how the different activities in the different stages of the design process integrate with the system. We also need to analyze how the more advanced features of the system, such as paths and the timeline are used, and how the system supports reflection. We have currently started this longitudinal study. Ten of the students that participated in the workshop take part in the study. We will examine the use of the system by each student for the whole semester. After that, we will try to adapt Freed for use in a group setting.

ACKNOWLEDGEMENTS

We would like to thank the students that participated in the evaluations.

REFERENCES

1. Schön, D.A. *The Reflective Practitioner*. Basic Books, 1982
2. Simon, H. A. *The Sciences of the Artificial*. MIT Press, Cambridge MA, 1969.
3. Hummels, C. and Frens, J. The reflective transformative design process. *Ext. abstracts CHI 2009*. ACM press (2009), 2655-2658.
4. Hummels, C. and Frens, J. Designing for the unknown: A design process for the future generation of highly interactive systems and products. In *Proc. EPDE 2008*, 204-209.
5. Keller, I. *For Inspiration Only*. Doctoral Dissertation. Delft University of Technology, the Netherlands
6. Martens, J., Parthesius, F., Atasoy, B. Design TeamMate: a platform to support design activities of small teams. In *Proc. AVI 2010*. ACM(2010), 119-126.
7. Sharmin, M., Bailey, B.P., Coats, C., Hamilton, K. Understanding knowledge management practices for early design activity and its implications for reuse. In *Proc. CHI 2009*, ACM press (2010)
8. Swan, L., Tanase, D., Taylor, A.S. Design's processional character. In *Proc. DIS 2010,* ACM press (2010), 65-74.
9. Ben Shneiderman. Creating creativity: user interfaces for supporting innovation. *ACM Trans. Comput.-Hum. Interact. 7*, 1 (2000), 114-138.
10. http://prezi.com/. Accessed September 2010.
11. Kumar A., Saigal R. Visual understanding environment. In *proc. JCDL 2005*. ACM Press (2005), 413.
12. Heer, J., Boyd, D. Vizster: Visualizing Online Social Networks, Proc. IEEE Symposium on Information Visualization, IEEE Press (2005), 33-40.
13. Pasman, G., Stappers, P.J. ProductWorld, an Interactive Environment for Classifying and Retrieving Product Samples. In *Proc. 5th Asian Design Conference*
14. Roberts, J.C. State of the Art: Coordinated & Multiple Views in Exploratory Visualization. In *Proc. CMV 2007*, 61-71
15. Buckingham Shum, S.J., Selvin, A.M., Sierhuis, M., Conklin, J., Haley, C.B., and Nuseibeh, B. Hypermedia Support for Argumentation-Based Rationale: 15 Years on from gIBIS and QOC. In *Rationale Management in Software Engineering*. Springer-Verlag (2006), 111-132.
16. Reas, C., Fry, B. Processing: a learning environment for creating interactive Web graphics. *In Proc. SIGGRAPH 2003*, ACM press (2003)

Teenagers and Their Virtual Possessions: Design Opportunities and Issues

William Odom, John Zimmerman, Jodi Forlizzi
Human-Computer Interaction Institute
Carnegie Mellon University
{wodom, johnz, forlizzi} @cs.cmu.edu

ABSTRACT

Over the past several years, people have increasingly acquired *virtual possessions*. We consider these things to include artifacts that are increasingly becoming immaterial (e.g. books, photos, music, movies) and things that have never traditionally had a lasting material form (e.g. SMS archives, social networking profiles, personal behavior logs). To date, little research exists about how people value and form attachments to virtual possessions. To investigate, we conducted a study with 21 teenagers exploring the perceived value of their virtual possessions, and the comparative similarities and differences with their material things. Findings are interpreted to detail design and research opportunities and issues in this emerging space.

Author Keywords

Virtual Possessions, Teenagers, Interactive Systems Design

ACM Classification Keywords

H5.m. Information interfaces and presentation (e.g., HCI): Miscellaneous.

General Terms: Design

INTRODUCTION

Many parents confess a strong attachment to books they read to their children at bedtime; often keeping and cherishing these books long after their children have left home. If e-readers replace physical books, will parents who read digital stories to their children instead develop an attachment to a particular device, or digital file?

We live in a world increasingly filled with *virtual possessions*. We characterize virtual possessions to include the many objects that are losing their lasting material form, such as books, music, photos, plane tickets, and money. In addition, we also consider them to include things that never traditionally had a material form, such as video game avatars; electronic messages including email, SMS, IM and status updates; social networking profiles; personal behavior logs, such as purchase histories; visited locations from services such as brightkite.com; and a listing of activities, such as jogging routes from MapMyRun.com. It appears that the convergence of social and cloud computing, along with the growing presence of mobile media players and networked mobile phones/computers has produced a world in which people both carry and ubiquitously access large collections of virtual possessions.

Research on material practices [e.g. 10, 24] and on material possession attachment theory [e.g. 6, 21] both describe the importance of material artifacts and the activities they support. Through the use of their things, people create meaning in their actions and construct an individualized sense of value for their things. The HCI community has learned the importance of understanding the practices and activities of users in the process of designing digital artifacts intended to augment more traditional material practices [e.g. 19, 29]. In many cases, HCI researchers and practitioners have focused on how the digital can improve performance in terms of efficiency and effectiveness. However, rarely has the HCI community investigated how the form and presentation of an immaterial thing might modify its value.

This research project takes a step towards better understanding the perceived value of virtual possessions. Specifically, we conducted a field study looking at practices of teenagers. This paper makes two contributions. First, it offers a designerly perspective of virtual possessions as a resource for people's value construction activities; a perspective that draws on the theories of material practices and material possession attachment. Second, it details three opportunity areas around value construction with immaterial things: value in accrual of social metadata; value in placelessness and presence; and value in curation and presentation of self to multiple audiences; along with these design opportunities, we note several key concerns to help critically frame future work in this emerging area.

BACKGROUND AND RELATED WORK

Related work falls into three areas: product attachment and material culture; teenager bedroom culture; and intersecting HCI research.

Studies on material possessions describe attachment as arising from meaning making that emerges as objects are integrated into one's life and help form idealized future goals [9]. Material culture researchers have explored how possessions shape everyday practices and the construction of social values, relationships, and meaning [e.g. 24]. A strand of material culture research has been particularly concerned with how new value emerges as people personalize artifacts in everyday life [e.g. 10]. Here, material possessions provide a key resource that people use to make sense of the world, demarcate social relationships, and assign value to people, places, and things. This work illustrates how consumptive practice has a key moral component driven by utilitarian needs, personal values, and socio-cultural, economic and political structures [1].

A key strand of consumer behavior research investigates the ways in which people develop a deep love for their possessions. Meaningful attachment can emerge through the process of *self-extension*, where people attribute important aspects of their self to the persons, places, things and events symbolized by their possessions [6]. Consumption of material goods offers continuous opportunities to perform, affirm and mange the self [also see 14]. Through these interactions over time and in the presence of other social groups and environments, people develop a reflective sense of self and establish deeper attachments to their things [6, 21].

Research on attachment has also focused on the importance of the home as a place where people can manifest a presentation of self. Researchers have reported that teenagers often feel the strongest attachment to their bedrooms [8]. Here, teens surround themselves with precious possessions as they experiment with their identity through display of self to parents and peers [32]. Teens particularly tend to draw on displays of music, movies, celebrities, etc., as a way of authoring their space and communicating values [3].

With the emergence of the Internet, people have begun to create digital selves. Social networking sites enable people to create personal online places where they can design and reformulate experimental selves. In contrast to earlier work exploring identity experimentation among anonymous users in online environments [e.g. 35], recent studies have drawn attention to how performances of identity in social networking sites are unfolding in largely 'anchored' social relationships, where members of social groups are typically bound by offline relationships [2]. With these new modes of self-expression comes production of new kinds of virtual possessions, reflecting key elements of the past as well as future idealized goals [31]. While adults have large collections of material and immaterial things, teenagers have emerged as rapid adopters of technology and are growing up in a time when their possessions are increasingly virtual [17, 27, 34].

The HCI community has a rich tradition of investigating human relationships with material artifacts to productively inform the design of new interactive technologies [e.g. 18, 20 25, 29]. Recently, researchers have begun to explore implications surrounding the increasing virtualization of material artifacts, such as currency [22], music [4] and familial possessions [19]. More generally, the issue of how to approach designing digital artifacts largely characterized by immaterial qualities has been an area of ongoing interest in HCI [e.g. 16, 36].

There is also emerging HCI research describing how people develop sentimental attachments to digital artifacts. Kirk and others [19, 20] present a values-oriented approach to designing tools to support archiving of cherished digital artifacts. Durrant et al. [11] explore how the curation of digital photos could open an expressive space for intergenerational interaction in the home. Others have explored how physical mementos can inform the design of systems aimed at creating digital mementos capable of triggering reflection on past experiences [e.g. 25, 29]. Finally, Peesapati et al. [28] designed and implemented a system re-presenting social networking content back to users specifically to evoke reminiscences.

Additionally, there is growing interest in exploring the ways in which designers consider the values of their users throughout the design process [e.g. 12, 18, 34, 36, 37]. Outside of HCI, the processes through which value and values are constructed on individual, cultural and societal levels have been a fundamental area of inquiry in the social sciences and humanities [e.g. 1, 10, 14, 15, 23].

Our work attempts to bring these different strands of research together within the purview of HCI. We want to investigate how people construct value with their immaterial things and provide designers and researchers with insights on how they might create technologies and systems that enable people to find new (or increased) value with their virtual possessions.

FIELD STUDY METHOD

We recruited 21 'tweens' and teenagers from a mid-sized city in the United States, ranging in age from 12-17; 9 female and 12 male. We chose this group for three reasons: they are deeply occupied with the process of constructing their identities [32]; they are heavily engaged in digital media, online communication, and use of interactive technologies [e.g. 17]; and they are on the vanguard of social and cloud computing, embracing these emerging technologies and

Figure 1. Left to right: (a) John's walls deeply reflected his current interests, (b) Michelle's mobile phone served as a portal to online places, (c) Julia's Jonas Brothers shrine now stored in the closet, (d) Bill extended digital copies of physical drawings to friends online.

actively defining the behavior and social mores of these products and services [e.g. 7, 34]. Participants hailed from middle and upper-middle class families, and typically had direct access to the Internet. It is important to note, our teenage participants clearly had less time to acquire massive archives of virtual possessions as compared with older populations, and we in no way mean to indicate that they are the "best" or only group to investigate. We see them as an important group and one that prior research indicated would likely be productive to study; as such, they are the first group we chose to focus on.

We conducted semi-structured interviews in participants' bedrooms that lasted 1.5 to 2 hours. Interviews aimed to develop an understanding of participants' everyday lives, common activities, technology-usage trends and cherished physical and virtual possessions. The bedroom elicited reflections about participants' relationships with material possessions, provided a basis of comparison to their virtual possessions, and revealed how participants access, engage with and organize their virtual and material possessions. We asked participants to give us a tour of their material possessions both stored in and on display in their bedroom, and to describe their relationships with these artifacts. This was typically followed by a tour of participants' virtual possessions, where we observed virtual artifacts on their personal computer, phone, media player, etc.

We videotaped all interviews and took field notes and documentary photographs. Following [33], the research team repeatedly reviewed field notes, video and photographs, and drew out underlying themes. Textual documents were coded using these themes. We also created conceptual models and affinity diagrams to reveal unexpected connections across participants. Very early findings of a pilot study were reported in [26]; in this paper we increased our participant pool and expand extensively on the collected field evidence and resulting design issues and opportunities. In what follows, we refer to each participant with a pseudonym followed by his or her age.

FINDINGS

Interviews and observations in teenagers' bedrooms revealed a range of 'precious' material possessions. These included photographs of family and friends, artifacts such as collages created by friends, and mementos and symbols of personal achievement, such as academic and athletic awards. The display of these possessions matches findings from research on teenage bedroom culture [e.g. 3, 32].

Discussions revealed diverse collections of virtual possessions, including but not limited to several years worth of homework assignments, blog entries, status messages from social networking systems, archived SMS messages, digital video, various self-made digital artworks, and expansive archives of digital music (often with accompanying artwork). Participants generally were frequent users of digital media, including music and video they owned and that they accessed through services such as youtube.com and hulu.com. Digital photos surfaced as a major category. Photos roughly broke down into images of family, friends and social events; photographs as art; and photographs specifically taken to document cherished material possessions such as items made by friends.

In many cases, our participants conveyed a general trend of moving away from shared home computers towards use of individually owned personal computers in their bedrooms: However, in some cases participants reported also using shared family computers from time to time. Additionally, all but one of our participants owned a mobile phone and/or media player, which emerged as common devices through which virtual possessions were accessed, made and managed.

In the following sections, we present several examples taken from field observations that capture the emerging themes: storage of virtual possessions; how virtual possessions are curated and displayed to manage presentation of self; how social metadata can be a crucial part of virtual possessions; and how artifacts transition between material and virtual forms.

Storage of virtual possessions: drive for accessibility

In general, interviews with participants indicated a strong trend away from storage on local computers to a reliance on and preference for cloud computing. Below, we describe instances in which mobile devices emerged as temporary storage centers; how movement towards the cloud shaped participants' interactions; and how email was drawn on to more easily move possessions from place to place.

We observed participants kept many things on personal computers, mobile phones, digital cameras, and media players, and to a lesser extent on other forms of physical media. In addition, participants both expressed desires for their virtual possessions to be immediately accessible in and outside of the bedroom. Devices that restricted the transfer of virtual possessions often complicated this goal. As a coping mechanism, we found several participants conveyed a strong preference for storing their things on a range of cloud services. For example, Suzy-17 reflects on her 3-year old archive of photos, nearly all now stored online, "*I have to have* [access to] *them wherever I'm at ...on my bed or at the mall. ...I've been uploading all of* [my photos] *online. Obviously I can't look at them all and that's not the point. I like knowing that they'll be there if I want them.*"

In fact, several participants described their mobile devices as portals to online places: "*...the biggest change is I use my phone all the time to check things like Facebook and change my status, add new information and photos, and leave comments. ...it's as much a gateway to all my stuff online as* [it is] *a phone*" (Bill-17).

In addition to being seen as portals to personal collections, key cases emerged in which mobile devices appeared to function as temporary storage centers. In several cases, participants reported storing photos on their devices, while waiting for the opportunity to transfer them online. "*If I take photos on my phone, I upload them right away and then usually delete* [the local copies]. *...It's better because I feel like I know where they're at ...and they're always available*" (Michelle-16).

In general, participants perceived online services as providing unlimited and enduring storage: "*I store everything online. It's much safer than keeping it all on my computer. I mean it* [computer] *could just die, but if they're online, they'll be there forever unless I decide to take them down*" (Sherry-16). Interestingly, in a few cases, participants described how the transition to cloud storage resulted in a perception that they would require less storage on their mobile devices. For example, Derek-15 describes his decision to not to upgrade to a larger iPod, "*I was going to get a 32GB iPod but I don't really need the space. ...I stream music and movies from the web more now and upload most of my photos, so I thought I wouldn't fill it up.*"

Evidence of participants' transition to the cloud also emerged when they discussed file management strategies. Bill-17 describes his shift in management practices: "*I still have my old folders where I keep things like homework assignments, music, photos, my diary... but aside from music and sometimes photos ...I've been putting most new stuff online for the past couple years.*" Several younger participants had never adopted concrete practices for organizing local files: "*I always try to get my files and stuff online first. Then I delete them or put* [files] *in a folder where I kind of keep them all ...I don't go back there* [in local folder]" (John-14). Similar to John, it was apparent in several cases that participants maintained only a single or small subset of local backup folders in which their varying types digital content was inconsistently dumped together.

Participants both implicitly and explicitly expressed desires to be able to move their digital possessions to the next place they were going to be; several drew on their email accounts as a workaround to transport things such as photographs and accompanying annotations, video, personal artwork, personal notes and diary entries, presentation slide decks, homework assignments, and, in a few cases, personally meaningful text messages. For example, Chris-16 reflects on how self-emailing provided the opportunity to privately access his journal, music files, and homework across school, home and friends' houses, "*it's the only way to know I have something saved and only I can access it. ...I'll email myself journal entries in Gmail and later tag and archive them. ...I'll send music files so I can play them at a friends' house if I don't have my iPod or I want to give them* [the songs]. *...all of my friends and me, we email our homework assignments to ourselves. ...*[this way] *I can work on them for a while, like on at school, and then later at someone's house or on my laptop at home.*"

Digital technologies and presentation of self

Most of our participants regularly interacted with their virtual possessions in order to manage their presentation of self to multiple audiences. In what follows, we describe how value emerged through redecoration; how the curation focused on different audiences; and tensions around constructing multiple digital selves for different audiences.

The display and organization of possessions in teenagers' bedrooms play significant roles in shaping their evolving sense of self. The presentation of trophies, photo collages, and posters of popular culture icons, among other things, shape teens' perceptions of who they are and who they might become [32]. In this way, the bedroom presents a material infrastructure that teenagers can exert control over in order to experiment with their identity. For example, Julia-14 had an equestrian theme permeating her room, where many of her possessions (including bedroom wallpaper) directly related to riding horses. However, she had recently lost interest in horses and made plans to redecorate her room in a more "mature" way. She also had constructed a shrine to the teen celebrity Nick Jonas that had moved from being present in her room to being inconspicuously stored in her closet. Most participants shared stories of how their shifting tastes created a continuing re-authorship of their bedroom.

Several cases emerged in which participants shared how they customized mobile phone, personal media player, gaming console and personal computer display backgrounds to reflect their shifting tastes. We observed a diverse collection of background images including friends and family members, celebrities, music and popular culture imagery, personal avatars from online games, and physical artifacts symbolic of favorite hobbies. In contrast to the relatively slow rate of change in display of material possessions, in several cases virtual possessions populating backgrounds appeared to change frequently (from weekly to, in a few cases, several times a day): "*My laptop background is usually something really important to me, like a picture of my girlfriend, or right now it's an image of where I want to go* [to college]. *It's like that because I'm the only one that looks at it. Same with my phone. ...but my Playstation, that I download new skins for all the time. ...since I play* [it] *with my friends. ...It's usually some kind of skin that's from a game or a movie we all like*" (Bill-17). Similarly, Sarah-13 described a habitual practice of reflecting on her mood and recent likes and dislikes, and subsequently searching several bookmarked popular culture and graphic design websites to find new backgrounds for her computer and mobile phone weekly. She claimed that, "*everything on my technology must represent me. ...I change what I like and how I feel a lot, so they change too.*"

While the bedroom was a key site for identity experimentation, the presentation of some key possessions conflicted with the social and moral structure of the home, and several participants discussed their inability to display posters or to listen to music their parents found to be in conflict with family rules and values. However, several key instances emerged in which participants described feeling considerably more control over social networking sites. Michelle-16: "*...in my parents' home, there are things I can't* *exactly put up in my room. ...and things that've caused problems when I've tried* (laughs). ...[like] *photos of me and my boyfriend. He's older and my parents don't like it, so they won't let me have photos of us here* [bedroom]. *...but on Facebook I have control over what goes up about me and what it says. ...and I recently added lots of photos with my boyfriend there.*" She further elaborates on how Facebook provides a place to store and present contraband digital objects, "*Almost everything here* [bedroom] *is important. It all represents me. ...but there's also stuff that I could never have here ...Mom would kill me. ...a lot of it ends up on Facebook: photos and messages of* [myself and friends] *out being ourselves. ...I put it there because it's me, but a part of me I don't need to share with everyone.*"

These reflections help illustrate how of the display of virtual possessions in online places enabled some of our participants to experiment with crafting and presenting different aspects of their self to different audiences. In these cases, participants frequently used the services' privacy settings to demarcate groups, allowing particular possessions to be viewed by certain audiences. Many participants reflected on how making their status messages and specific groups of photos accessible to only friends (e.g. as opposed to parents) shaped the way they framed their online content. For example, Suzy-17 stated: "*I have lots of Facebook 'friends' like my friends' parents and random people I meet. But only my close friends get access to everything. ...I would like other people to see some of my stuff or updates, and there's a way to do that, but it's hard to figure out and I don't trust it, so I have to choose one* [group] *and with them* [close friends] *I'm most my self.*"

We also encountered instances in which participants indicated information they made available to everyone (e.g. parents, family, etc.) on their social networking sites was frequently shaped to reflect relatively mundane aspects of self. For example, Frank-16 describes his decision to only contribute new material perceived to be 'safe' in the context of all his social groups: "*I want my relatives and other people to still know some things about me so I made my* [status] *updates public and end up posting pretty harmless stuff...*[like] *cheering for a sports team or 'passed my test'.*" Despite efforts like this, we encountered other participants that described tensions emerging from accidently sharing personal information too broadly. A classic case of this is reflected in Bill-17's description of his mother and grandparents viewing inappropriate images of him at a late-night party, "*I got tagged in some pics from a party. ...they were full of things that would've been fine for my other friends to see. But, it was terrible for like my mom and grandma to see them. ...I had to stop going out for a while and I stopped using Facebook for a long time. ...it totally affected my social life.*" Laura-16 reflected on how the emergence of photos of her and her new boyfriend complicated other relationships: "*...it's a big step to be tagged together in photos* [on Facebook]. *...I put some* [photos of self and new boyfriend] *up and thought they were restricted to* [us]*, but they ended up being visible to lots of people like my ex and a lot of his friends that we'd see together. They all were unhappy. ...I untagged myself from most of the photos and ended up deleting some*"

We also observed tensions around boundaries of social appropriateness, such as when parents added comments to their children's social networking pages. For example: " *I can try to control who see's what I put on my wall, but it's hard to control who sees the posts and comments from different people. ...My Mom posts on my wall all the time and I don't want my friends to see it. ...I guess I don't always want her to feel like she can't Facebook me. ...but my wall, where everyone can see, isn't the right place. I usually delete* [Mom's posts] *when I see them*" (Mary-16). Similar to Mary, a handful of other cases emerged in which participants reported deleting posts or comments from family members (usually Mom or Dad) and in some instances later contacting them through the phone or email.

The ability to fluidly craft a targeted presentation of self through privacy permissions emerged as a rich resource to strengthen a sense of social connectedness among several of our participants and members of their different groups. At the same time, a lack of more usable and sophisticated privacy considerations resulted in numerous embarrassing and regrettable experiences. These instances tended to amplify the tensions among social groups in participants' networks, which often motivated them to remove or, in some cases, permanently dispossess certain virtual possessions by deleting them.

Personal and group attributions of social metadata

Metadata emerged as a defining aspect of virtual possessions. It provided a platform for users to collaboratively and individually personalize a possession, as well as relationally link multiple types of virtual possessions together. Below we describe how value emerged as virtual possessions acquired metadata.

In some cases, new value emerged as photos documenting a specific event or experience, once shared online, accrued social metadata; the ability to create metadata appeared to support collective reconstruction and revisitation of shared experiences with friends and family members. For example, Kate-16 describes how this activity served her desire to develop a more 'real' representation of an event: "*I bring my camera with me whenever I go out with my friends. We take lots of pictures. ...When I get home I upload them. Then I tag most of my friends* [in the photos]. *...and we all tag and untag other people and post comments. ...*[we] *delete the ones that we don't need ...the ones that don't get a lot of comments or don't seem as good as the others.*" She continued to describe how this attributed a layer of realness, "*It feels like a more authentic representation of the event ...we comment and agree on everything together. ...then there's a shared sense of what happened.*"

We also observed how participants used the "tag" function in Facebook to define a set of friends that extend beyond the people in a specific photo. "*We tag people that aren't in our photos all of the time. ...it's a way to get their attention and get them to comment on the photo or, if they don't, at least linking you all together. ...you're showing something happened that made you think of them. ...maybe when you were there, or maybe it reminds you* [of them] *later when you see it online*" (Mary-16). These comments collectively highlight key ways in which value appeared to surface through the use of metadata. For Kate it involved a deeper sense of authenticity that emerged from collaborative curation, while for Mary, value came from reinforcing an affiliation through sharing. In both cases, value emerges from the creation of the metadata instead of the creation or exchange of the initial artifact.

In addition to photos, participants engaged with metadata related to music. Interestingly, several instances emerged in which participants described giving and receiving musical playlists as gifts, and sometimes modified metadata as a part of the gifting practice. For example, Frank-16 described his practice of replacing album art images with photos from events he attended with his girlfriend, "*Now, before I give her a mix* [CD] *of songs, I go in the info and put a photo of us together. ...at least it'll come up on her iPod and it makes it different in her library from everything else.*" Derek-15 also reported editing mp3 metadata to include personal notes in playlists given to his girlfriend in hopes that one day "*she would look there and find something special.*" These reflections highlight the challenge of making a gifted virtual possession standout among an ever-increasing collection of similar things, as well as strategies employed to make gifted music more unique and particular to the receivers.

Finally, we encountered various cases in which participants' music collections encompassed all of the music they had ever owned, and, in some cases, expressed strong reluctance to delete songs or albums they no longer listened to. Despite our population's young age, these kinds of collections typically represented several different life stages, at times evoking experiences of reflection on past taste and current preferences. They also to some extent mimic the collections of data common to adults who have vast backups of email, etc. In this case, the systems created metadata detailing when and how often songs had been played; metadata participants could use to examine who they were. For example: "*...I have stuff I listened to when I was really young and what I was listening to in middle school, and I'm what listening to now. ...the things I like change and I change too, and it's interesting to see how you've changed through how often you listened to things and when you last did*" (Kate-16). In contrast to Kate's case, a few participants described how these archives and records evoked reflection on more melancholy aspects of past experiences. Nonetheless, across these cases, machine-produced metadata did appear to provide rich resources for reflection on one's self and for re-visitation of past selves.

Transition between material and virtual forms

We observed several examples of possessions transitioning between material and virtual forms. In what follows, we first describe how participants physically displayed their virtual possessions. We then present examples of how material possessions took on a digital form in order to move beyond the constraints of a single bedroom.

A key factor differentiating virtual and material possessions is that virtual possessions lack a lasting material form. Interestingly, we observed some participants compensated for this by keeping their computers, mobile phones and media devices always on and connected to their collections of virtual things. There appeared to be several related motivations to this behavior. Kristen-16 described methodically encoding albums in her music collection with the appropriate artwork and always projecting these images through her computer screen to amplify the material presence of her digital songs, "*so it feels like it's more than an mp3 ...it's there reminding you what it is. ...but you can easily ignore it too, like anything else around* [my bedroom]." Suzy-17 similarly kept her desktop monitor on to display photo collections stored on Facebook: "*They're different from the ones on my computer* [hard drive] *because online they have what my friends' said and the links they posted. ...that's all part of the* [photos] *now and I want it all there together.*" James-16 describes his desire to be on Facebook as frequently as possible; when in his room he reported often simultaneously accessing his account through his phone, iPad and laptop: "*I like to be logged in to my laptop and iPad so I know when something happens, like someone writes on my wall or a photo or tags me. ...I want to see it around me. ...way better than getting a text* [message] *or an email about it later. ...it keeps me up to date with everything going on.*" Collectively, these practices highlight several of our participants' desires to fluidly move between the material and virtual world.

We also encountered instances in which participants printed and displayed their virtual possessions within their bedroom. In particular, numerous participants had printed out cherished photographs from Facebook, often constructing large collages. For example, Kate-16 compares her previous practice of making collages with photos she had taken to her current practice of compiling assemblies from various shared albums online: "*I like them better because my friends' personalities come out in their pictures. ...sometimes I'll be looking at one and think about what I wrote or what my friends' wrote* [on them online]." In a rather extreme instance, Michelle-16 described printing and archiving her favorite Facebook photos in a scrapbook, often along with notes documenting the associated metadata, "*I pick the best ones* [photos] *from an album ...usually they have comments on them. ...*[I] *write them down on notes next to the photos* [in the scrapbook]. *When my friends come over we look through it and add new things when we feel like it.*" We also encountered an interesting case in which Derek-15 had printed excerpts of his friends' status messages and chats to display in his room; he conveyed a desire to be surrounded by them as, "*they represent my friends and much as my photos.*" In these instances, participants reported these virtual-made-material possessions had served as focal points for reminiscence with friends or family when in the bedroom.

We encountered other instances in which participants used photos to make digital copies of material possessions that were typically constrained to the bedroom. These material-made-virtual possessions could accrue additional value through socially constructed narratives that emerged outside of the home; examples included trophies and certificates, artifacts associated with hobbies, and self-made artworks. Bill-17 provided a exemplary case in his description of uploading digital copies of several hand drawings he made of his Halo avatars: "*Lots of people 'liked' and commented on them ...the digital* [copies] *are different because you can't hold them, but it's meaningful because all these other people never would've seen them and wrote on them. ...some people left comments about how it's so 'me' to draw my characters ...some gave me artistic advice;* [they] *like left links for me to look at, and some just thought they were cool. ...those things, what people posted, are important. ...now I think about them when I look at* [the original drawings] *in my room ...they're definitely something I'll keep.*" Instances we encountered, such as Bill's, highlight how interactions across social groups in online places jointly inscribed valued records of metadata into collections of possessions; and, similar to this case, shaped how material possessions themselves were perceived.

DESIGN OPPORTUNITIES AND ISSUES

Our findings show how virtual possessions and online places create new opportunities to support identity construction and experimentation, to re-enforce old and shape new social connections, to develop deeper meaning through shared and personalized use, and to support re-visiting perceptions of one's past as a way of reflecting on the current self. We also found several participants fluidly moved themselves and their things between online and material environments without needing to clearly demarcate boundaries between the two. These findings suggest several opportunities that can aid designers in generating new forms for virtual possessions and new interactive systems to engage with these things. They also raise a range of potential unintended consequences and paradoxes [23] that could easily emerge if designers blindly make new products and services. Through repeated discussion and modeling sessions of our findings, we identified three specific opportunity areas for investigation by researchers and practitioners: *accrual of metadata, placelessness and presence,* and *presentation of selves.* We also highlight several potentially negative consequences that should be considered when working in this emerging space.

Accrual of metadata

One unique quality of virtual possessions is their ability to accrue metadata over time. In some cases, metadata itself became a valued virtual possession; in others, it appeared to be an element indivisible from the original artifact. Across all these instances, value appeared to emerge as different types of metadata enabled participants to craft and keep social histories; something that had been considerably less explicit in a world filled only with material things.

Prior research [e.g. 9] has described how material artifacts take on particular qualities that make them meaningful, such as the books parents read to their children at bedtime and grow attached to. On the surface, this seems less achievable for virtual things as they are infinitely reproducible and lack an inherent ability to gather a patina from age and use. Interestingly, we observed participants encoding new elements into virtual possessions (e.g. music collections, digital photos, textual annotations), to make them more uniquely self-expressive, or to share experiences with others. We also found machine-produced metadata (e.g. timestamps, frequency of use) provided a valued resource for connecting a thing to particular experiences. These instances suggest an opportunity to design technologies that enable users to encode a more diverse range of content into virtual possession metadata, which could shape the resulting digital artifact to be more reflective of an individual or group. For example, virtual possessions associated with a particular event could be encoded with things such as the aggregate status updates of a person when last in the event location, songs most frequently listened to during the event, or perhaps personal messages or other forms of content associated with the event that would emerge as these digital objects are interacted with over time. We imagine interactive systems could also provide richer ways of contextualizing experiences associated with virtual possessions through aggregating various types of metadata from online resources, such as weather information, or local and historical news events associated with the place in which the event was held. Previous research [e.g. 13] has illustrated the value in converging streams of 'ready-made' online information onto collections of digital objects to evoke rich, personally meaningful experiences. In general, there appears to be a large opportunity in combining human and machine-created metadata to construct more expressive assemblies of virtual possessions that evolve over time.

We also found the ability to attribute different types of metadata to virtual possessions in shared online places in some cases supported practices aimed at developing a more 'authentic' collective understanding of an event. New value also appeared to emerge as metadata was used to extend an artifact beyond its original content, such as linking it to other people, places, possessions and experiences. These instances illustrate how storage and presentation of virtual possessions in online places opens a space for new value to emerge from sharing, editing and, ultimately, the collaborative construction of social histories focused on virtual things. These practices collectively model Belk's [5] notion of *sharing in*, where people share within a social group as a way of strengthening bonds. Importantly, similar to how people can extend their sense of self through possessions, this process of extending permissions to present and edit (or collectively 'own' rights to edit) particular possessions with others plays a key role in extending individual sense of self *through* other people [5, p. 726]. Offering the opportunity for collaborative curation of virtual possessions in more nuanced and extensible ways appears to be a rich space for further investigation.

Finally, the value of social metadata is not limited to only virtual possessions. We observed some cases in which participants virtualized their material things to make them available to targeted audiences beyond their bedrooms. At times, these things appeared to increase in value through accruing metadata; interestingly, as in the case of Bill's Halo avatar drawings, they seemed to shape some participants' perceptions of the material artifact. This suggests a significant opportunity area for designing systems for managing virtual proxies of material artifacts. These systems could collate information related to a particular artifact (e.g. locations, time and frequency of use, social audience(s) present, social metadata) to create rich personal or shared histories of a thing. We imagine they could provide valuable virtual resources shared across members as families expand and heirlooms are fragmented across multiple homes, as well as enduring social records of treasured material possessions forever lost or destroyed. Future research could scaffold and extend recent work exploring tangible interactions with digital copies of familial artifacts [18] and digitally augmented physical mementos [25, 29] to investigate how virtual proxies (and virtual possessions in general) could be embodied to support interactions with individuals and groups, as they move in and between virtual and material environments.

Placelessness and presence

One clear value for many material possessions comes from the fact that people can display them, such as a collection of books on a shelf in a bedroom. We observed it was difficult to make virtual possessions' presence dynamic and enduring in a physical place; however, they could be made temporarily present in nearly any location. This quality of placelessness provided teenagers with a feeling that their collections of virtual possessions could travel with them across social and physical contexts. While our population had less time to acquire expansive archives of virtual possessions as compared to older populations, it was clear many had a significant desire to ubiquitously access and amplify the presence of their virtual things. Several of our participants drew on social networking sites and email accounts to move and access their virtual possessions as they moved about their day; several also appeared to frequently use mobile devices as portals to their online places. In general, our participants reported valuing the ability to ubiquitously draw on their virtual things across contexts, and instances emerged in which they appeared to use this ability to breakdown boundaries between material and virtual worlds, and to move fluidly between them.

Clearly, current services for uploading, storing, and interacting with virtual possessions are insufficient. The breakdowns shared by our participants collectively point to a desire for a new kind of cloud computing that unites disconnected services, making it easier to move and access virtual possessions stored in different online repositories. There also appears to be an opportunity for designing storage systems that enable a single virtual possession to be more easily shared and made present across multiple places, and which stores archives of multiple layers of metadata as these virtual things acquire new annotations. Issues for designers include how to communicate the size of virtual possessions, and changes that have taken place as they acquire new history. For example, a digital photo frame could explicitly show metadata associated with an image; this kind of display could provide a map of a virtual possession's shifting statuses as it acquires "digital patina" through new attributions. Past research has speculated that as digital collections grow, more meaningful experiences will likely arise from collating and contextualizing smaller groups of content, as opposed to archiving every aspect of a person's digital life [29, 30]. We think it pertinent to design tools to support the cultivation of virtual possessions into valuable and accessible assemblies as collections expand.

Finally, several of our participants' practices of uploading and accessing their virtual things through multiple online places and devices contrast to some extent earlier work investigating how meaning emerged for teens through the ritual exchange of text messages and their embodied presence on a specific phone [34]. As virtual possessions like archives of SMS messages, social media content, and digital photos are stored in various online places and accessed through multiple devices, key opportunities lie in exploring how new form factors and expressive materials might extend embodied interactions across platforms and environments in meaningful ways. In general, this area suggests more research is needed into understanding people's immaterial practices with and perceptions of virtual possessions across space, time and technical platforms; and how this knowledge might shape how virtual things are given form in material environments.

Curation and presentation of self to multiple audiences

We observed a range of ways in which our participants drew on virtual possessions to personalize technology and to project shifting tastes and identities to different audiences. Background images on mobile devices were frequently modified; in some cases, new content was actively searched to reflect evolving interests. Social networking services such as Facebook appeared to function more as a "place" where participants exhibited fluid control over expression and curation of different aspects of their identities. In several cases, the ways in which virtual possessions were framed and presented varied depending on the social group(s) that had access to them. These findings highlight how the management and presentation of virtual possessions in online and offline places offers key opportunities for creative experimentation with one's sense of self. In particular, the ability to attribute access privileges to specific virtual possessions appeared to be desirable. In several cases, this strengthened social connections to members of different groups by highlighting unique social bonds. However, significant complications also emerged from the accidental presentation of virtual possessions to a social group (or groups) they were not intended for.

These findings suggest an opportunity to design environments that are socially reactive to the groups that are present, or to create better ways to select aspects of self to project to these different groups. For example, a system could respond to the audience present and context in which it is being used to automatically generate an appropriate display. More broadly, it is clear that current tools people use to manage online privacy are deeply underdeveloped. Opportunities exist to design systems that enable end users to create displays of multiple aspects of self to be delivered to different audiences, which extend far beyond the current model of managing permissions. This could lead to more complex and expressive assemblies of virtual possessions that, in turn, project more socially appropriate and meaningful aspects of self to particular audiences.

We also found several participants fluidly moved between material and virtual environments and appropriated various everyday materials in attempts to breakdown barriers separating these two worlds. We imagine there may be opportunities in leveraging the relatively more flexible nature of online places within intimate material environments. For example, we envision one context to explore the potential consequences of this direction is through the design of a socially reactive bedroom that enables teens to easily display and curate virtual possessions and attendant metadata; that enables them to create new metadata and see when it is created by others; that transforms displays based on people present in a room, surfacing things they have in common, or perhaps making the room "Mom Approved" when a parent is nearby. We imagine a series of technology probes in this area could produce new knowledge into dimensions of social appropriateness of this opportunity area, and open the space for richer exploration in and beyond the bedroom.

Probing potential paradoxes and consequences

While there are many opportunities to re-imagine the forms of virtual things to increase their perceived value, it is important to critically consider possible negative outcomes. As form givers of technical systems, HCI researchers and practitioners must recognize requirements emerge from complex interplay between technology and users, as opposed to pure technological advancement [12, 23, 34]. When approaching this space the community should keep in mind the complexities of dispossessing virtual things and persistent virtual records, as well as potential negative social obligations and expectations that could emerge.

People actively reinvent themselves by selecting which elements of their past to keep and which to let go [21, p. 9]. While virtual possessions can play a potentially important role in supporting identity construction processes, how one might *dispossess* a virtual thing is unclear. For example, shared (and co-curated) possessions could pose problems, as consensus is required across various members on dispossession. Users will need to be able to richly experience sharing their virtual things with different social audiences, while having the flexibility to retain control over rites to (dis)possession. Moreover, the persistent archiving of virtual possessions over time offers new opportunities to support reflection on life experiences; however it also creates an exacting history of who we are, leaving little space for romanticizing about the past and forgetting experiences we no longer wish to relive.

While virtual possessions can increase a sense of social connectedness across individuals and groups, they could also work to amplify differences and reinforce cliques. New technologies for presentation of virtual possessions could provide people with valuable portraits of their identity; however, they equally could promote self-obsession through creating the ongoing obligation to curate multiple selves. Accrual of metadata opens a new space to construct virtual possessions more uniquely reflective of particular experiences, while also possibly creating new social expectations to continually create these attributions. These issues must be considered and could serve as productive framing mechanisms for future research as researchers and practitioners move forward in critically determining socially appropriate and beneficial design interventions.

CONCLUSION AND FUTURE WORK

We have explored how our teenage participants perceive, value and form attachments to their growing collections of virtual possessions. A goal of our paper is to surface key issues and opportunities related to our audience's interactions with virtual possessions to critically consider the benefits and potential dangers of designing new technologies that might enable people to find more value in their virtual things. Our fieldwork presented several complications participants faced when presenting and interacting with their virtual possessions in online spaces, and key strategies employed to engage with their virtual stuff in valued ways. Based on these findings we proposed *accrual of metadata, placelessness and presence, curation and presentation of self to multiple audiences*, and *probing paradoxes and consequences* as an opportunity map to guide future research and practice in the HCI community.

A clear limitation of our study is that all of our participants had frequent access to technology and hailed from middle and upper middle class families in the United States. Participants from different socio-cultural and economic backgrounds represent significant populations and would potentially produce alternative results. This suggests opportunities for future cross-cultural investigations into how different groups construct value with their virtual things; and how these processes unfold within populations representing different ages and economic backgrounds. Our findings do raise several issues about the social appropriateness of new technologies. We are currently developing technology probes based on these opportunity areas to critically explore such issues. Ultimately, we hope this study inspires future research into how technologies could be designed to engage people with their virtual possessions in more valuable and values-oriented ways.

ACKNOWLEDGMENTS

This work was partially supported by NSF grant IIS-1017429 and by Google. We thank Hajin Choi, Lee Hillman, James Liu, Kami Neumiller, Amritha Prasad, Aditya Sharma, and Alena Tesone for their assistance in data collection.

REFERENCES

1. Appuradai, A. 1988. Commodities and the politics of value. *The social life of things: Commodities in a cultural perspective*, p. 3-63 Cambridge University Press.
2. Barkhuus, L., Tashiro, J. 2010. Student socialization in the age of facebook. In *Proc. of CHI '10*, 133-142.
3. Bovil, M., Livingstone, S. (Eds.) 2001. *Children and their changing media environment.* London: Erlbaum.
4. Brown, B., Sellen, A. 2006. Sharing and Listening to Music. in *Consuming music together: social and collaborative aspects of music.* p. 37-56. Springer press.
5. Belk, R. 2010. Sharing. *Journal of Consumer Research*, 36, 715-734.
6. Belk, R. W. 1988. Possessions and the Extended Self. *Journal of Consumer Research*, 15, 2, 139-168.
7. boyd, danah. 2007. Why Youth (Heart) Social Network Sites: The Role of Networked Publics in Teenage Social Life. *Youth, Identity, and Digital Media Volume*, 1-26.
8. Chawla, L. 1992. Childhood Place Attachments. In Altman, I. (ed.). *Place Attachment.* Plenum, 63-86.
9. Csikszenthmihalyi, M., Rochberg-Halton, E. 1981. *The Meaning of Things: Domestic Symbols and the Self.* Cambridge University Press, Cambridge.
10. Douglas, M., Isherwood, B. 1979. *World of Goods.* New York: Basic Books.
11. Durrant, A., Frohlich, D., Sellen, A., Lyons, E. 2009. Home curation versus teenage photography: Photo displays in the family home. *Int. J. Hum.-Comput. Stud.* 67(12): 1005-1023.
12. Friedman, B. 1996. Value-sensitive design, *interactions*, v.3 n.6, p.16-23.
13. Gaver, W. et al. 2008. Threshold Devices: Looking Out From The Home. In *Proc. of CHI '08*, 1429-1438.
14. Goffman, E. 1959. *The Presentation of Self in Everyday Life.* Penguin Books.
15. Graeber, D. 2001. Toward an anthropological theory of value: the false coin of our own dreams. Palgrave.
16. Hallnäs, L., Redström, J. 2002. From use to presence: on the expressions and aesthetics of everyday computational things. In *TOCHI , 9, 2*, 106–124.
17. Ito, M. et al. 2010. *Hanging Out, Messing Around, Geeking out: Kids Living and Learning with New Media.* MIT Press.
18. Kaye, J. et al. 2006. To have and to hold: exploring the personal archive. In *Proc. of CHI '06*, 275-284.
19. Kirk, D, Izadi, S., Sellen, A., Taylor, S., Banks, R., Hilliges, O. 2010. Opening up the family archive. In *Proc. of CSCW '10*, 261-270.
20. Kirk, D., Sellen, A. 2010. On human remains: Values and practice in home archiving of cherished object. *ACM Trans. Comput.-Hum. Interact.* 17, 3, Article 10.
21. Kleine, S., Baker, S. 2004. An Integrative Review of Material Possession Attachment. *Academy of Marketing Science Review.* 1-39.
22. Mainwaring, S., March, W., and Maurer, B. 2008. From *meiwaku* to *tokushita*!: lessons for digital money design from japan. In *Proc of CHI '08*, 21-24.
23. Mick, D., Fournier, S. 1998. Paradoxes of Technology: Consumer Cognizance, Emotions, and Coping Strategies. *Journal of Consumer Research*, 25, 123-143.
24. Miller, D. 1987. *Material Culture and Mass Consumption*, New York: Blackwell.
25. Nunes, M., Greenburg, S., Neustaedter, C. 2008. Sharing digital photographs in the home through physical mementos, souvenirs, and keepsakes. In *Proc. of DIS '08*, 250-260.
26. Odom, W., Zimmerman, J., Forlizzi, J. 2010. Virtual Possessions. In *Proc. of DIS '10*, 368-371.
27. Odom, W., Zimmerman, J., Forlizzi, J. 2010. Designing for dynamic family structures: divorced families and interactive systems. In *Proc of DIS '10*, 151-160.
28. Peesapati, S., Schwanda, V., Schultz, J., Lepage, M., Jeong, S., Cosley, D. 2010. Pensive: supporting everyday reminiscence. In *Proc. of CHI '10*, 2027-2036.
29. Petrelli, D., Whittaker, S., Brockmeier, J. 2008. AutoTopography: what can physical mementos tell us about digital memories? *CHI '08*, 53-62.
30. Sellen, A., Whittaker, S. 2010. Beyond total capture: a constructive critique of lifelogging. *Commun. ACM* 53, 5, 70-77.
31. Siddiqui, S. et al. 2006. Extending the self in a Virtual World. *Advances in Consumer research*, vol. 33, 647-648.
32. Steele, J., Brown, J. 1995. Adolescent room culture: Studying media in the context of everyday life. *Journal of Youth and Adolescence*, 24, 5, 551-576.
33. Strauss, A., Corbin, J. 1990. *Basics of Qualitative Research: Grounded Theory Procedures and Techniques.* Newbury Park, CA: Sage.
34. Taylor, A., Harper, R. 2002. Age-old practices in the 'new world': a study of gift-giving between teenage mobile phone users. In *Proc. of CHI '02*, 439-446.
35. Turkle, S. 1995. *Life of the Screen: Identity in the Age of the Internet.* New York: Simon and Schuster.
36. Wright, P., Wallace, J., McCarthy, J. 2008. Aesthetics and experience-centered design. ACM Trans. Comput.-Hum. Interact. 15, 4, Article 18.
37. Zimmerman, J. 2009. Designing for the self: making products that help people become the person they want to be. In *Proc. of CHI '09*, 395-404.

Life Editing: Third-Party Perspectives on Lifelog Content

Daragh Byrne[1], Aisling Kelliher[2] and Gareth J.F. Jones[1]
[1] Centre for Digital Video Processing, School of Computing,
Dublin City University, Glasnevin, Dublin 9, Ireland.
[2] School of Arts Media and Engineering, Arizona State University, Tempe, AZ 85281.
daragh.byrne@computing.dcu.ie

ABSTRACT
Lifelog collections digitally capture and preserve personal experiences and can be mined to reveal insights and understandings of individual significance. These rich data sources also offer opportunities for learning and discovery by motivated third parties. We employ a custom-designed storytelling application in constructing meaningful lifelog summaries from third-party perspectives. This storytelling initiative was implemented as a core component in a university media-editing course. We present promising results from a preliminary study conducted to evaluate the utility and potential of our approach in creatively interpreting a unique experiential dataset.

Author Keywords
Lifelog, SenseCam, storytelling, sensemaking, editing

ACM Classification Keywords
H.5.1. Multimedia Information Systems: *Evaluation/methodology;* H.1.2. User/Machine Systems: *Human information processing*

General Terms
Human Factors, Experimentation

INTRODUCTION
We document our daily lives using a variety of forms and processes, including diaries, photographs, movies, status updates, and tweets. These captured moments and reflections allow us to engage with Socrates' exhortation to examine, interrogate, and reason about life events. The construction and exchange of stories about our everyday experiences is one of the primary sensemaking methods we use to find meaning in our lives. For some, this process is supported by professional third parties such as therapists, lawyers, and biographers who help us piece together fragments of our existence into coherent narratives.

Online social platforms such as weblogs, Facebook, and Twitter allow us to document our daily lives using new digital techniques. These digital formats demonstrate rich potential for considering our life experiences at whole new levels of scale and time, where we can receive near-instantaneous feedback from a global audience. Small form factor digital devices such as cellphones or Flip video cameras provide the means for easily capturing impromptu content, while experimental technologies such as the Microsoft SenseCam [13] introduce the possibility of extensive everyday documentation. Lifelogging technologies like the Sensecam have been employed in a variety of scenarios to offer the collection owner benefits in terms of self-examination, reflection, reminiscence, and sharing of past experiences [8,9,10,16]. Personal capture technologies and the lifelog data they collect clearly offer profound opportunities for insightful self-exploration [15]. The level of richness and detail contained within such collections also offer opportunities for learning and discovery by third parties, whether interested general audiences or motivated individuals situated across a range of professional practices [4]. Such an investigative scenario is the focus of our research, where we examine the direct or indirect value of lifelog collections to third parties.

Within this paper, we present an analysis of third-party exploratory and interpretive practices with lifelog data sets using a custom-designed storytelling tool. Storytelling provides a commonly understood framework for making sense of experiences and in this case, is proposed as a useful lens for exploring and interpreting a unique experiential dataset. We first explore how a diverse set of individuals can help us understand a variety of unbounded responses to a unique lifelog dataset. Findings from this investigation can then provide recommendations for the potential design and development of interpretive systems for specific types of professional or everyday practice,. In our research, we evaluate the examination and construction of storied interpretations of lifelog data in a provocative learning environment where the pedagogical focus is the construction and consideration of digital, media artifacts.

In this paper we describe the use of a custom-designed storytelling tool as a core component in an undergraduate media editing class. We present findings from a preliminary user study, including examination of the processes' of data selection and story construction, together with analysis of the reflections of study participants. We conclude with design recommendations, suggestions for future avenues of research, and discussion of the general applicability of this work to archives of personal content.

BACKGROUND

Lifelogging

Lifelogging technology enables the capture of rich personal life histories through digital means and it has demonstrated utility in a wide range of domains [7,8,10,16]. Lifelogs contain huge volumes of data gathered from one or more modalities through a variety of complimentary techniques, tools and technologies [11]. These include SenseCam (see below); mobile and desktop content; geo-location; contextual sampling; explicitly captured photos or videos; and online social media, such as Twitter. While lifelogs show much promise in a variety of applications, they carry a number of practical challenges. The most obvious of these is their voluminous nature and as such, much of the research effort to date has focused on the management of vast repositories of past experience [9,11].

SenseCam

The SenseCam is a major tool for lifelogging research. Developed by Microsoft Research in Cambridge, UK, it is a small wearable device that passively captures a person's day-to-day activities as a series of photographs [13]. At a minimum the SenseCam will automatically take a new image approximately every 30 seconds, but onboard sensors can trigger more frequent photo capture. It captures the day indiscriminately resulting in voluminous collections which often contain undesirable artifacts such as blurring, noise or lensing effects [11]. Due to its orientation and continuous mode of capture, it tends to offer a distinctive and unusual viewpoint on personal activities [12,16]. The objective, and chronological account of past action may also facilitate new appreciations of the habitual and everyday [12].

Storytelling and Lifelogs

Storytelling has been previously explored within lifelog collections in a number of small-scale studies, for example [10]. Harper et al. [12] conducted a study with six participants manually composing narratives using one-week's worth of their SenseCam images, highlighting usefulness in reflection and reminiscence. In a follow-on study Lindley et al. have employed SenseCam archives in family based explorations in which small stories were co-created to explore a social context of use [16].

Given the relative novelty of the lifelogging domain, there are not many fully developed and comparable tools for narration, with much of the work to date relying on simple implementations or tangible, paper-based methods. There are however a number of related projects within the space of digital storytelling. The Confectionary application allows the construction of everyday rich-media narratives from content co-opted from a variety of sources [18]. It has notable parallels with the lifelog solution we employ, as it provides an authoring environment for the creation, arrangement and layout of two-dimensional spatial stories. Two-dimensional space provides a familiar and instinctual story composition fabric, and is a well-established form of both traditional and digital narrative [22]. Confectionary, like our tool, exemplifies this approach by providing a spatial canvas for creating patterned stories from aesthetically-presented media fragments. Appan et al. [1] explore the composition of digital narratives for everyday experiences using media such as photos, gathered during the user's day-to-day activities. They also provide a tool for everyday storytelling, however, unlike Confectionary, the presentation and authoring of that narrative is simultaneous; evolving through interactive exploration of the content [1].

Storytelling and Sensemaking

Storytelling is described by Walter Benjamin as the ability to exchange experiences [3] while Richard Kearney defines stories as the transformation of time from '*an impersonal passing of fragmented moments into a pattern, a plot*' [17]. Constructing patterned stories based on the experiences of another requires the development of a distributed framework that acknowledges the emergence of individual and social identity from the entire knowledge flow experience, including notes taken, media consumed, friends consulted etc. [5]. French philosopher J. –B Pontalis once wrote that "*one shouldn't write one autobiography, but ten of them, or a hundred because, while we have only one life we have innumerable ways of recounting that life to ourselves*" [21].

Such a monumental recounting exercise can be undertaken with the support of a third party, as evidenced in the practice of psychotherapists, biographers, lawyers and anthropologists. Designing tools and mechanisms for third parties to engage in active, constructive reflection on personal digital archives has strong potential utility in supporting such professional practice. A storytelling framework that embraces the *act of mimesis* helps to provide a breach between actual life experiences and life-stories allowing for the possibility of alternative perspectives through reflection. Kearney suggests that mimesis involves both "a free-play of fiction and a responsibility to real life", as the action moves from the text and back again in a way that enriches our understanding [17]. Our approach situates storytelling as the ideal sensemaking mechanism for tackling vast archives of disparate personal mediated experiences, and proposes an editorial approach of judicious selection, composition and framing as a purposeful creative constraint.

Pedagogical Context

Digital storytelling as a pedagogical approach occupies a significant place in learning environments, where the combination of creative and analytical inquiry provides a flexible avenue of exploration [14, 23]. Studies indicate that digital storytelling integrates significant student-centered learning techniques such as deep engagement, considered reflection and project-based learning [2]. In creating a computational tool for composing rich-media stories from personal lifelog data, considerable technical, aesthetic and ethical challenges must be addressed. Integrating these challenges as meta-components in a learning curriculum provides a powerful scaffold for students to think beyond the specifics of their personal experiences towards a

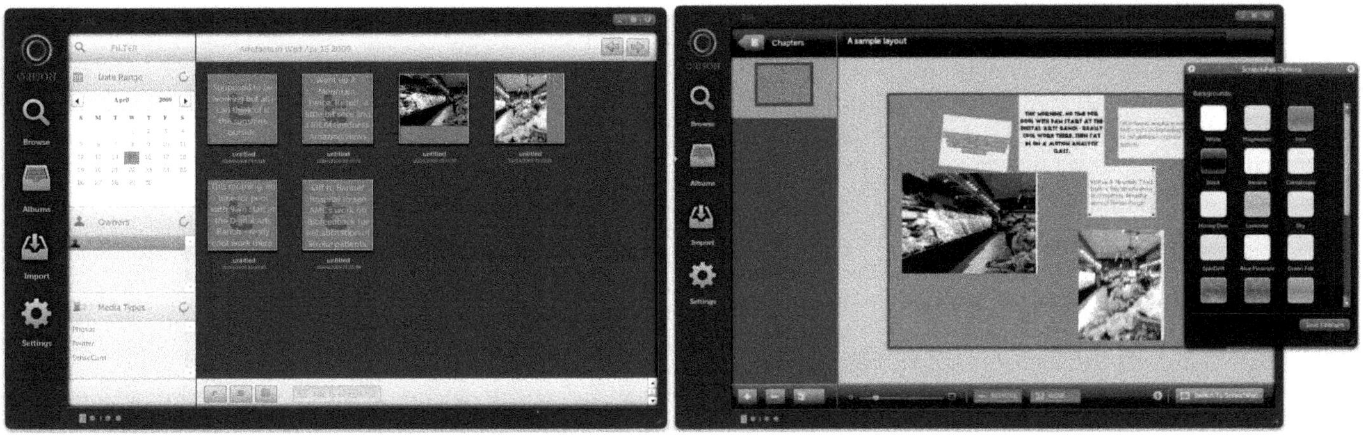

Figure 1. a) The browsing screen and b) the story chapter editing and layout screen.

broader understanding of what it means to be human in a digitally captured world.

COLLECTION AND TOOLS

The third-party participants in this investigation were provided access to a lengthy lifelog dataset and a custom-designed storytelling tool developed as part of an ongoing research investigation into long-term multimodal lifelogs.

Lifelog Collection

Data from a previous lifelog collection effort was employed within this work [7]. While there are a number of content and contextual sources available for use within this research, it was decided to constrain the amount and types of information provided to class participants. From a much broader collection, three main content streams were chosen for use within this work, namely: passively captured SenseCam images, explicitly captured digital photos, and Twitter status updates. The decision to constrain a 2-year multimodal lifelog was dependent on issues of privacy and manageability. The duration was fixed at 9 months and the modalities limited to those most critical as the participants only had a concentrated amount of time to complete their work and it was felt providing the entirety of the collection would be excessively overwhelming. Several of the original modalities (e.g. SMS, call histories, email) contained direct or private communications with third parties and their inclusion raised potential breach of privacy issues for all corresponding parties. This was deemed an unnecessary risk by the institutions ethical review boards and the dataset was therefore constrained to those modalities considered most critical. A subset of 9 months provided participants a reasonably large, yet manageable dataset, where creative responses could still be developed within the timeframe of the study. While constrained it represents a more authentic set being broader in duration and available modalities compared with most previously employed lifelogs.

The content from a single long-term lifelog collection owner was provided with consent to the participants. The archive contained content between the 12th of March and the 21st of November 2009 inclusive, as follows:

SenseCam images: A set of passively captured images (sampled every 20-40 seconds) gave a rich visual diary of the individual's day-to-day activities. Over half a million frames were available but to avoid overwhelming the participants with repetitious images [11], the dataset was temporally skimmed to every 10th image. In total 53,000 images were provided to the participants. It should be noted that due to recording issues during the collection period, images were not available for much of August (5-24th incl.) and September (7th-23rd incl.).

Digital Photographs: To compliment the SenseCam images, a set of 301 digital photographs were also provided. The majority were captured in April 2009 where the collection owner had been traveling for three weeks.

Twitter status updates: A set of 'tweets' taken from the collection owner's public timeline were also provided to the participants. These 140-character text messages can be viewed as contextual annotations about items of interest or activities the collection owner engaged in.

Storytelling Tool

A storytelling tool developed as part of ongoing work [7] was provided to all participants within this investigation. The tool, dubbed Orison, supports the exploration of lifelog content and its arrangement into a story-based layout. It offers a complete cross-platform desktop application. The system was fully implemented having all of the expected behaviors and functionality of a media-editing tool from single click installation, to export and import which facilitated sharing of completed stories.

The software was designed based on initial probative and exploratory studies with the scrapbooking community and the method of digital storytelling enabled closely resembled that observed in these studies: album based two-dimensional layouts. Additionally, the tool's workflow was intended to parallel their observed patterns and creative practices, albeit in a digital environment. Three primary actions were identified: locating information for inclusion in a layout (*browsing*); the arrangement of content into a working layout (*composition*); committing that layout to an album and situating it appropriately (*placing*). There are three major sections within the application, each relating to one of these functions.

When creating an Orison composition, the user first visits the browsing screen (see Fig 1a.) where they can locate content from the lifelog data by selecting a day of interest, and/or filter the content to display a single modality. The browsing options are deliberately kept straightforward and the presentation of content is kept conventional. Once the user finds content for their composition, they can move it to a working-space known as the scratchpad (see Fig 1b.) Within the scratchpad, they are given options to manipulate the content to create a desired spatial layout. They may for example, move and reorder content, adjust its size and rotation, apply a caption to the content, and style its appearance. The tool affords a large degree of control over the presentation of content, allowing any text to be resized or displayed in one of over 20 typefaces, and content to be bounded with either a customizable simple solid border or a predefined frame. When satisfied with their story layout, the user can move it from the working space of the scratchpad into an album, where it becomes a chapter. Each album can contain one or more chapters, which can be re-ordered as desired. A title can be specified and the arrangement of its elements can be adjusted at any point. Some layout examples can be seen in Figures 2 and 3.

INTEGRATION INTO PEDAGOGICAL CONTEXT

A new multidisciplinary undergraduate course in media editing at a large US state school provided an ideal learning context for evaluating the Orison tool. One of the authors developed and taught the course, which aims to move beyond tool teaching (e.g. a Photoshop class) towards a critical approach to the conception, production, publication and interpretation of diverse media artifacts. Students use a wide variety of free, commercial, open-source and custom designed software to tackle course assignments, in so doing, understanding the constraints and affordances that each tool brings to their process. Given the diverse disciplinary makeup of the class cohort, the course is designed to scaffold over a semester accommodating different student proficiencies and interests.

The class explores the core concepts of media editing (e.g. form, composition, rhythm, pattern, etc.) through 6 integrated modules (graphics, audio, movies, networks, interfaces, experiential) of increasing complexity. The final 'Experiential Editing' module provides students with a unique opportunity to take on the role of *life editor*, where in the words of master film editor Walter Murch they become 'the ombudsperson for the audience' [19], selectively revealing the salient life events of another. Using the Orison software and the provided lifelog collection, this assignment presents students with complex computational, artistic and moral challenges.

LIFE EDITING STUDY

Participants

15 study participants (13 male, 2 female) from the media editing course cohort agreed to participate in our study. Participation meant granting permission to the researchers to use their assignment content, descriptions of their work and analysis of such in external presentations. The participants represented students from all four years of undergraduate education and derived from a wide variety of disciplines including design (6), engineering (1), liberal arts (3), art (4) and film (1).

The participants were given some general information about the collection owner, but they had no extensive prior knowledge of the collection owner's life, friends, associates, or places in which he regularly spends time. A single participant had coincidentally attended a talk by the collection owner a year previously at the study site and data from this event was included in the collection.

The module assignment was used to evaluate our approach and was a required element for all students in the class, regardless of their study participation. All students were informed that participation was completely voluntary and had no impact on final grades.

Experiential Editing Module

At the beginning of the Experiential Editing module, participants were introduced to the concept of 'life editing' through a screening of the 2004 movie, '*The Final Cut*'. *The Final Cut* is set in the not-to-distant future where an implanted chip captures a complete audiovisual record of a person's life experiences. The main character, a 'cutter', is hired to review and edit this captured footage into a cogent movie summary upon an implantee's death. The Final Cut movie introduced the concept of life capture and editing, and also highlighted many of the features and considerations of life capture, such as being able to subvert lifelogging technology and the revision or re-conception of personal histories. Building on these ideas, participants were also assigned a variety of readings including [6]. Ideas expressed in the movie and assigned readings were used to seed discussion during a follow-up class seminar.

Methods

Participants were instructed on the setup and use of the Orison software during a classroom session. The participants were given one week to complete the following assignment: "*You will be "The Cutter" of someone's life experience. Using the data collected by an individual over a 9-month period, you will create an album(s) demonstrating insight into this person's life. Who are they, what have they done, how can we interpret their everyday encounters, how might they be remembered?*"

The instructor gave the participants a broad overview of the data collection, including how and when it was collected.

General details about the collection owner were introduced. In addition to submitting their edited works, the participants were asked to provide a written reflection of their experience completing the assignment. The participants presented and discussed their work in a class critique session. The collection owner was present via video-conference, offering feedback and clarification about the validity and creativity of the students' story compositions.

Ethical Considerations and Practices

Given the highly personal nature of the supplied lifelog collection, a number of considerations for ethical best practice were put in place within this study. Many of these considerations were directly embedded within the software the students employed during this study. The system was designed to securely provide access to the content, and users were required to authenticate for each session of use. They were additionally required to formally agree not to publish or redistribute the content in any medium beyond the confines of the classroom.

Sharing lifelog content in this manner raises questions about privacy, both for the owner and captured third parties. We endeavored to minimize exposure through many implemented considerations. While not discussed at length here, deeper reflection of these issues is available in [20].

RESULTS AND DISCUSSION

The stories created by the students ranged in number, type, composition, style and strategy, reflecting the variety of competencies, skills and background of the participants involved. The 15 students produced 27 album-based compositions in total, with an average of 1.8 albums submitted per student (max 5). An album contained an average of 3.52 chapters (max 13.) In total 95 chapter compositions were created, of which 62 were given an explicitly title by the author. Each chapter employed approximately 8.36 artifacts from the lifelog, with a maximum of 32 items being used in a single layout. 66 photos (max 9, avg. 0.7), 672 SenseCam images (max 32, avg. 7.1), 56 tweets (max 10, avg. 0.6) were used, totaling 794 elements employed. 738 of those were unique, meaning only a small number of elements were repeatedly used across layouts.

General Findings

We discuss the types of stories created and then present the findings of the evaluation: we first explore *browsing*, discovery and exploration; next *ideation and composition* of a working layout; and finally the *placement* of a layout, framing within a story and reflection on completed works.

Types of Compositions Created

The created stories varied widely in terms of the aspects of the collection owner's experiences chosen and the storytelling point of view adopted. Not only was there a variety in the execution but also in the types and topics of the created stories. These were broadly classified into 4 major groups:

Time: Several albums examined chronological or focused accounts of a specific day or isolated episodes within the lifelog. These included for example, a detailed exploration of a 'typical' day, traveling and sightseeing. See Fig. 2a.

Biographical: These higher-level accounts examined the collection owner's life broadly from psychological and social perspectives or through exploration of evident trends and recurrent themes. They often considered encounters with people, places, objects or technologies and typically included authorial narration through captioning which exposed reflections on the owner's lifestyle. See Fig. 2b.

Expressive: These stories moved beyond the life of the individual in some way. They considered the aesthetics of the captured content, playing on colors and forms found in the lifelog content. In 2 cases, participants layered entirely new narratives on top of the existing content. In these cases the content and the real-world actors and settings were repurposed and re-conceived from the storyteller's perspective to tell a fictive account of an imagined happening. They also served as an allegorical reflection on aspects of the collection owner's life. See Fig 2c.

Investigative/Critical: These highly analytical and reflective compositions provided commentary on either the nature of the medium, the data or experience-editing project. These accounts used captioning to present explicit narration of the author's position. See Fig 2d.

Exploration of the Content

36% of all content used in the participant's compositions came from the first month within the collection (March 2009.) With 73% of all employed content being drawn from the first three months of the provided lifelog; 288, 176 and 121 artifacts originating in March, April and May 2009 respectively. While this appears to indicate limited exploration with participants emphasizing the earlier portions of the collection, this is not necessarily the case. These months were particularly busy for the collection owner with a lot of travel in April and thereby contained more non-habitual, and perhaps more novel content for use within compositions. As October 2009 – a month with travel and large amount of non-habitual activity - was the next most employed month (111 artifacts), this seems to reinforce that content was selected based on interesting activities rather than just shallow exploration. Additionally, the layouts were composed of artifacts spanning an average of 38.99 days (max 234 days.) This indicates that the participants were not just choosing easily assessable material, but carefully considering the media for inclusion, often surveying reasonably broad time-spans to identify the content appropriate to their story.

Observed Strategies for Way-finding and Sensemaking

The participants clearly perceived the volume of content to be a barrier to understanding and working with the collection. One participant commented that "*It was a little tough for me to get into because it was almost overwhelming to have such a wealth of information*

Figure 2. The types of story created. a) ***Time*** **– A chronology of a single day; b)** ***Biographical*** **- An exploration of observed eating habits; c)** ***Expressive*** **– A fiction layered on the real world content; d)** ***Investigative/Critical*** **- reflections on technology**

available to you and having to make sense of it and present it in a cohesive and logical way", while another remarked "*Never before have I been given the opportunity to look at someone else's life in such detail. It was a bit staggering at first.*" While students often identified the topic of their story early on, they still experienced challenges in terms of locating content relevant and appropriate to their story: "*the only real struggle I had with the project was meticulously scrolling through each day-trying to find the right images I wanted to use with the project.*"

Participants employed a variety of strategies to help them navigate the voluminous lifelog content and three predominant strategies emerged. First, and most simply, the participant heavily constrained the task by limiting the duration of exploration to a few days or a particular month of interest. This focused the task making it easier to find content. By doing so however, they consequently constrained the story they could tell to simpler forms and chronological accounts. The second approach was to randomly or in a semi-guided fashion jump to a location in the collection, with one student commented that this strategy worked well for his particular compositions: "*...randomly looking through them did however help me stumble on the abstract images...*". Finally and the seemingly predominant approach to locating content, was to explore the lower frequency modalities first (tweets and photos), ignoring the voluminous SenseCam images. This allowed the participants to build up an understanding of the events and identify the location of interesting items within the collection. One of the participants explains: "*I realized that by scanning through all the regular pictures, which were much fewer in numbers would be easier and most likely have more importance as they were actually chosen by the 'cuttee'. This turned out very effective...*" The tweets and photos - occurring relatively sparsely within the corpus - enabled the users to navigate to potential points of interest. In addition, the Twitter text content not only allowed for way-finding but allowed the users to gather a deeper understanding of the activity, its significance and its context: "*Some of the data was immediately obvious as far as what it was communicating however in other instances it was helpful to have access to the tweets to make sense of what was happening.*"

Ideation and Composition

"Figuring out what to do with all of these images was the hardest part of this project by far."

In this section, we explore the very different approaches adopted by participants in their compositions, arrangements and in the focus and subjects of the stories they produced.

Patterns and Themes: Recurrent themes and patterns often formed the basis of the participant's stories. They examined the relationship of the collection owner to people, places and things encountered and the significance or bearing of them. Such stories were typically composed as an exploratory process, first identifying the major and salient themes within the archive and then identifying the most suitable elements for inclusion. The authors took care to minimize repetition and to carefully select content based on its aesthetics and appeal. One participant explains: "*As I was browsing through all the files on Orison, I found certain patterns...I decided to divide the albums into these three sections to make up the idea of this person.*"

On-the-Fly Creation: While some of the participants conceived their story upfront, several of the students took a less directed approach and ideated their story dynamically. The story iteratively evolved and was opportunistically crafted based on interesting items stumbled upon through exploration. One participant elaborates: "*I found it fairly difficult to do much planning because I honestly had little idea where I wanted to go with it. The challenge with this then was sifting through information as I went along and simultaneously determining what I wanted and how to build a narrative with it on the fly.*"

Aesthetics: The authors gave careful consideration to the attractiveness of the compositions, considering all visual aspects of content added to a layout: "*I tried to find the moments that 'looked the best' - images that captured smiles, or maybe interesting lighting, and also images that contained the most people in one shot.*" Many of the authors additionally spent a great deal of time applying background, frame, and text styles to the content within a layout (see Fig 3.) This was often done to visually reinforce the narrative being communicated. For example, in Fig. 2c a comic-book style was applied to underpin the fictive nature of the story.

Authorial Captioning: 65.3% of the created chapters were given an explicit title and 13% of the artifacts were given a caption. They allowed the participant to communicate their perspectives: "*I used mostly [SenseCam] pictures, and then wrote my interpretation... and why they might have been important to that person.*" In some cases, the author considered what that individual might have said and placed the caption in a first-person voice, thereby adding to the weight of the narration. The existing Twitter content, being authored directly by the collection owner, was used in place of captioning on occasion to achieve similar effect: "*Sometimes the tweets adequately framed what I wanted to express...Other times I did a little of my own interpretation of the provided images and added my own captions.*"

Integrity: For some of the participants the honesty, objectivity and integrity of the account was of paramount concern. They took on the mantle of the 'ombudsman of the audience', desiring to create an undistorted, unembellished and representative account of the life experiences. This had bearing on the compositions created, limiting them in the scope of what they could create and compose from the content. One explained: "*I finally decided on telling a simpler story that was more conceptual in nature. It seemed like the best way to present the data in a way that wouldn't skew or misinterpret it at all. Keeping integrity in the truth of his life was a major motivation for me.*"

Identification with and understanding of the collection owner

The high volume of content contained within a lifelog can be a significant obstacle to third-party understanding, however, it appears surmountable. Several participants reported a perceived understanding of who the collection owner was ("*...the more I considered it the more I felt it captured a decent amount of who I perceived [the collection owner] to be*"), with one of the participants correctly deducing roles and relationships of encountered individuals, thereby indicating some level of understanding can be built through exposure to the content. One participant initially offered that "*the sheer volume of SenseCam images picturing his desktop computer gives us a pretty good idea of how he spends the majority of his waking hours*" but later offers the following conflicting perspective "*there's no real way I'm going to know who this person is based solely on a few pictures, several tweets and a whole bunch of SenseCam images*". They suggest that while a lifelog can offer an objective account of activity, from which actions can be metricated and settings, scenes or actors discerned, truly understanding the owner at a deep level is challenging.

There are clearly open questions about how fully a life can be understood through objective data alone, how complete that data must be, and how much it can truly and honestly reflects the life, personality and traits of the individual in question. While, the question of a lifelog's ability to convey the nature of that person is open, we believe in order for the participants to have creatively, competently and reflectively transformed the information into a meaningful story, they must have demonstrated at least some holistic understanding and appreciation of that person's life.

Case Study

From the 15 students, we have chosen to highlight one of the participants in particular as we feel they exemplify many of the works, processes and considerations involved. The student in question was additionally selected, as they were themselves a scrapbooker. As the tool was oriented towards this community, this made them an ideal candidate for more detailed exploration. The participant was clearly intrigued and engaged by the task and produced 4 albums, containing a total of 16 chapter-based compositions. They employed 164 items from the lifelog (130 SenseCam images, 26 tweets, and 8 digital photos) spanning the full range of the collection, indicating it had been well explored.

Artistic Opportunities

"The opportunities for simply creating something artistic out of his experiences was intriguing." The participant was motivated by the opportunity to create aesthetically pleasing compositions which juxtaposed playful, experimental and artistic layouts with considered and reflective thoughts on the nature of the medium, the notion of life capture and the aspects of the collection owner's life communicated via the data (see Fig 3.) This observation is similar to that of Harper [12] and Lindley [16] who noted the construction of 'creative views' and the potential for playfulness in the compositions.

The Nature of the Media

Within the album 'Obscure' the participant ruminates on lifelogged media. In particular the compositions reflect many of the unique aspects of the SenseCam. Seemingly undesirable low-quality features of the SenseCam are well documented and include blurring, noise, light lensing effects and poor capture in low light conditions. Many of the students' compositions similarly noted this, but the participant does not just simply highlight but instead capitalizes upon the 'strangeness' [16] that can be seen in the SenseCam frames. These unusual artifacts of the capture technology facilitate creative compositions and were explored in chapters entitled *'Mystery'* (blurring), *'The Effects of Light'* and *'Colours in the Dark'* (see Fig 3.b).

The SenseCam may additionally highlight seemingly innocuous things making them more apparent. In the album 'Awareness: I Can See Myself!' the participant explored this in great detail; choosing to focus on 'Busy Hands' (see Fig 3.c). The position and infrared trigger of the SenseCam emphasizes capture of conversational hand gestures. The participant, noting this, dedicates an entire composition them. This again complements the findings of Lindley and Harper [12,16] that the medium allows for new appreciations of the ordinary and the everyday. Not only is there opportunity for understanding of the individual from lifelogs but by leveraging the unusual aspects of the medium wholly creative exercises and studies can also be enabled and empowered.

Thoughts on Life Capture

"*I feel as though I have insight into a stranger's private existence and I'm conflicted as to whether or not that is ok.*

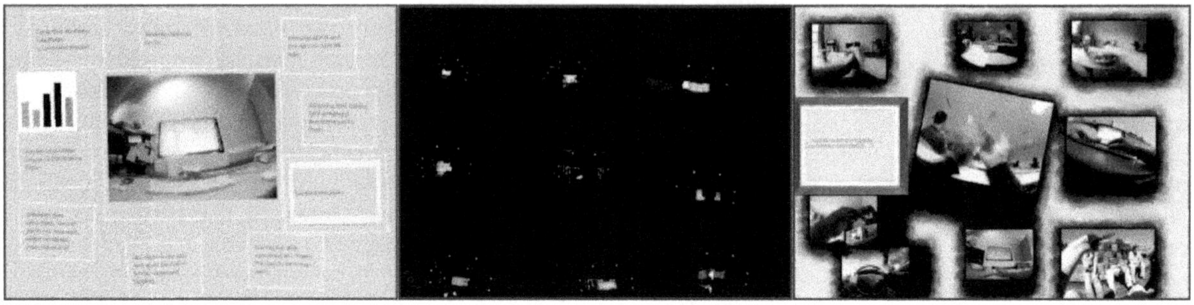

Figure 3. Samples from the case study participant a) What would we do without the web - *The center of the universe*; b) Obscure - *Colours In The Dark*; c) Awareness I Can See Myself - *Busy Hands*

But I do feel like I know him after these hours I have spent with him in his car, office and house."

Despite the participant's keen insight and careful consideration of both the technology and the medium, they seem to have grappled with the moral and ethical implications of the technology. This is reflected in the compositions produced; which contemplate awareness of others within the space around the collection owner, the degree to which the owner might be aware of this, and the number of people encountered, while another explores missed experiences as a result of gaps in recording.

Significant Happenings

"It occurs to me that the reason for editing the events of one's life can be summed up in one word: significance. Different people will find different things about [the collection owners]'s life significant..."

From the point of view of the third party, it is not always about being faithful to an objective account of the individual's life, but the role of the ombudsman is to tease out what they perceive to be important and meaningful. The participant notes that this will undoubtedly change from person-to-person based on their values, perspectives and interests. The album *'Snipettes of a Life Well-lived'* is singularly focused on this idea, and the participant has distilled a number of events they perceive to be especially meaningful from their perspective. For example, the thoughtfully titled *'Only God Can Make a Tree'* appreciates the simple pleasure and beauty in a day spent in the park, *'Night Gems'* explores being indoors on a rainy day from an aesthetic standpoint, while *'We All Need Somebody to Lean On'* explores the importance of people in our lives and the regularity at which we encounter them.

Life Editing and the Learning Experience

This assignment was designed as the semester's most challenging and time consuming and the students responded in kind with evident enthusiasm and curiosity. Certainly, the novelty of the media and the custom-designed software piqued their interest, but their engagement in thoughtfully discussing the ethical, conceptual and technological implications of the exercise was beyond that experienced by the instructor in prior modules. A student described in his reflection text how his understanding of the scope of the endeavor developed over time noting "*what seemed like a simple project at first really turned into something profound once it was looked deeper into. We weren't just stringing pictures together to tell a story. We were actually given the ability to take someone's recorded life and reorganize it all in any way that we saw fit. Never before have we been given such an opportunity to take control of someone's life like this and manipulate the truth.*" Recognition of the editor's level of responsibility to the material and the complex issues of power and control engendered were evident in several of the student's comments, with students writing that it '*was interesting to have control of the narrative of someone's life'* and yet another *"it was interesting that the program did allow us to sort of "cut" someone's life. It's still kind of a weird concept to me'*. Consideration of their comfort level with the role of life editor was a provocative topic of online and in-class discussion, as noted earlier in the case study.

In thinking more broadly about the Orison tool, one student noted their impression that the class cohort was *"more amazed about being able to use such a tool, and what it could develop into later on"* and how *"It is staggering to imagine what effects this will have on social development and interaction... Will things get to a point where it won't be necessary for people to physically update things themselves; their computers will be automatically updating for them?"* This form of reflection and projection closely aligns with the overall learning goals of the class, demonstrating ability to think beyond the tool and situating their constructions in a broader socio-cultural context.

DESIGN REFLECTIONS & RECOMMENDATIONS

In this section we reflect on the findings of this study and offer some recommendations both on how this and related tools might be improved to better support third-party use.

Ethical Considerations

Providing personal content to third parties requires a coherent ethical framework to protect the privacy of the individuals contained within the content.

Provoked Responses: Many of the study participants grappled with the ethical implications of accessing personal lifelogs. Such dimensions should be fully considered and feedback channels to address concerns provided.

Information Exposed: Careful consideration of what personal content and communications are exposed and how is required. It should also be remembered that while a collection owner may provide consent, consent must also be obtained from all parties as many private communications and encounters are captured in lifelog data.

Mediating Access: Any solution must address ethical and privacy considerations by mediating and restricting access to content. We currently facilitate this through automatic roll-down of content updates and through a remote authenticated server architecture.

Lifelog Content, Affordances and Constraints

The study lifelog content was initially perceived as overwhelming. The continuously capturing SenseCam provides a detailed overview of ordinary day-to-day encounters. The SenseCam data volume, while unwieldy, facilitates a rich understanding of the everyday and enables patterns and routines to be discerned. Lower frequency modalities, like Twitter and photos are however captured with intent and remark on a moment of significance or interest to the collection owner. They each offer interesting and valuable opportunities for sensemaking from lifelogs and bring different fluencies and capabilities in contextualizing experiences and composing stories.

Data Discovery And Exploration

The Orison tool offered deliberately simple browsing strategies in order to facilitate this investigation. There is much need to better support content discovery and exploration.

Scaffold Understanding: The participants noted the utility of the lower frequency modalities in both identifying periods of interest and in contextualizing the activities. This feature should be exploited to support data discovery by scaffolding understanding through these modalities.

Highlight Interest: Ideation of the stories often emphasized particular times of interest, where non-habitual activities occurred. In order to facilitate data discovery, it would be helpful to explicitly highlight these as well as periods of particularly active or unusual capture.

Associate and Recommend: Stories were often conceived around a specific topic or theme but some participants struggled to identify content aligned to this concept. Computational techniques could associate content and enable suggestion of related content in response to a variety of requirements (aesthetics, relevance, similarity, contrast).

***Aggregation*:** Many of the participants described being overwhelmed by the volume of content, so reducing its complexity would be advantageous. Presenting content aggregated around particular activities or centered on lower frequency content would significantly help in this regard.

Story Creation And System Support

Categories and Approaches: Four story types were observed (time, biographical, expressive, critical). The time and biographical formats took broadly similar approaches in the creation and composition of spatial narratives. As such, a third party could benefit from the provision of authorial support through programmatically provisioned guidance during their construction. The expressive and critical compositions, however, tend to be more unique in topic, arrangement, and visual style. Consequently, these compositions would be difficult to provision explicit authorial support for.

Planning and Ideation: Authors tended not to ideate a single layout in isolation, but rather explored for content relating to multiple compositions in parallel. While a working space is useful, the single container scratchpad provided failed to support the strategies of the users and needs revision to better support the observed behaviors.

Reflection and Captioning: The provision of narration is desirable requiring the third party to reflect on compositions under construction. Captioning was, however, used irregularly despite utility in communicating the end construct. It should be encouraged to increase narration and reflexivity in compositions. Currently captions are tied to content and more flexible support would be advantageous.

Templates: Many of the created works, and in particular the chronological accounts, repeatedly employed similar visual aesthetics and patterns of arrangement. Templates should be integrated to facilitate rapid layout of content in the regularly observed arrangements.

Applications and Domains of Use

Coarse Tool: We have investigated an unbounded tool suited to exploration by a diverse mix of participants. Unlike our study, most third-party explorations tend to be situated within a professional community of practice, for example, cultural anthropology, biography editing, therapy, etc. The tool could be used to stimulate, mediate and build personal, cultural and societal understandings within these domains with suitable provision and support for the strategies, practices and workflows which apply.

A useful tool for the everyday user: Equally there is the possibility to explore the potential of more conventional and prevalent personal content in third-party explorations. The low frequency modalities showed utility in organizing, contextualizing and sense-making with life experiences. Employing content from online social sources may offer enormous and more immediately accessible potential for motivated parties to explore individual, societal and cultural understandings with the Orison tool.

Artistic and Creative Potential: Our case study highlights the creative and artistic opportunities latent within third-party explorations of lifelog content. Unconstrained deployments could yield exciting possibilities in this regard.

BIGGER PICTURE & NEXT STEPS

We have explored the use of lifelog collections and content in a life-editing task set within a learning framework. This study represents a first of its kind exploration of the use of lifelogs with third parties and there are a number of potential avenues for future exploration. We will conduct a repetition of this study to gather additional evidence of utility in an educational context and to further establish the comprehensibility of lifelog content to third parties. We also intend extending the evaluation framework to allow for comparison between the first- and third-person experience-editing. To do this, we will enable the Orison tool to allow participants use their own digital content.

In addition to this, there are many scenarios relating to third-party use of lifelog content that may be studied further as part of future work. These exciting possibilities include working with historians, archivists, genealogists and cultural anthropologists, who operate at a broader societal and cultural level, probing, identifying and preserving moments of significance from a third-party perspective. In the modern digital age, there is much need for novel tools to support these practices. Finally, at a personal level, the use of digital lifelog content in combination with narrative editing techniques may additionally offer new modes of support to professional third parties such as lawyers, therapists and documentary editors who already help us negotiate our past and imagine our futures.

CONCLUSION

In this paper we present a custom-designed storytelling application for constructing third-party stories from lifelog collections. Storytelling provides an ideal sensemaking framework for interpreting life experiences, whether as part of everyday or professional practice. We evaluated our implemented approach as a creative and analytical assignment in a university media-editing course. Study participants successfully constructed diverse, meaningful story compositions from a very large data collection and within a constrained time frame. This demonstrates the potential of our approach. The application of this research in a variety of professional interpretive life practices represents a promising future direction.

ACKNOWLEDGMENTS

We would like to thank the Irish Research Council for Science, Engineering and Technology. We also would like to extend our sincere thanks to the participants of this research effort and to the members of the CHI community for their feedback and advice on this work and its future directions.

REFERENCES

1. Appan, P., Sundaram, H., Birchfield, D.: Communicating Everyday Experiences, In Proc. SRMC 04, ACM, New York, NY, 2004, 17-24.
2. Barrett, H. Researching and evaluating digital storytelling as a deep learning tool. In C. Crawford et al. (Eds.), Proc. SITE 2006, Chesapeake, VA, 647–654.
3. Benjamin W. The storyteller. In *Illuminations*.Transl. H Zohn, New York: Schocken, 1968, 83-109.
4. Berry E., Byrne D., Doherty A.R., Gurrin C., Smeaton A.F. Proceedings of. SenseCam 2010.
5. Bruner, J. Autobiography and Self, *Acts of Meaning*. Cambridge: Harvard University Press, 1990.
6. Bush, V. As We May Think, *In The Atlantic Monthly*, 176, 1, (July 1945), 101-108.
7. Byrne, D., Jones, G.J.F. Towards Computational Autobiographical Narratives through Human Digital Memories. In Proc. SRMC 2008, Canada, 2008.
8. Byrne, D., Jones, G.J.F.: Creating Stories for Reflection from Multimodal Lifelog Content: An Initial Investigation, In CHI 2009 Workshop on Designing for Reflection on Experience, Boston, 2009
9. Doherty, A.R., Smeaton A.F. Automatically Segmenting Lifelog Data into Events, Proc. WIAMIS 2008.
10. Gemmell, J., Aris, A., Lueder, R.: Telling Stories with MyLifeBits, In Proc. ICME 2005, 2005, 1536-1539
11. Gurrin, C., Smeaton, A.F., Byrne, D., O'Hare, N., Jones, G., and O'Connor, N. An Examination of a Large Visual Lifelog. In Proc. AIRS 2008, Harbin, China, 2008.
12. Harper R., Randall, D., Smyth N., Evans, C., Heledd, L., Moore, R. Thanks for the Memory, In Proc. BCS HCI 2007, Vol. 2. 2007, 39-42.
13. Hodges S., Williams, L., Berry E., Izadi S., Srinivasan J., Butler A., Smyth G., Kapur N., Wood K. SenseCam: a Retrospective Memory Aid. In Dourish and A. Friday (Eds.): Ubicomp 2006, LNCS 4206, 2006, 177–193
14. Leon, S.M. Slowing Down, Talking Back, and Moving Forward: Some reflections on digital storytelling in the humanities curriculum, *Arts and Humanities in Higher Education*, 7, 2, 2008, 220-223
15. Li, I., Forlizzi, J., and Dey, A. Know thyself: monitoring and reflecting on facets of one's life. In Proc. CHI 2010. CHI, ACM, New York, NY, 2010, 4489-4492.
16. Lindley S., Randall D., Sharrock W., Glancy M., Smyth N., and Harper R., Narrative, memory and practice: Tensions and choices in the use of a digital artifact, In Proc. BCS HCI 2009, 1-9.
17. Kearney, R. On Stories. New York, Routledge, 2002.
18. Kelliher, A., Davenport, G. Everyday storytelling: supporting the mediated expression of online personal testimony. In Proc. HCI International, In J. A. Jacko, (Ed.) LNCS. Springer-Verlag, 2007, 926-933.
19. Murch, W. The Cutting Edge - The Magic of Movie Editing, 2005.
20. O'Hara, K., Tuffield, M., Shadbolt, N. (2009) Lifelogging: Privacy and Empowerment with Memories for Life. Identity in the Information Society, 1 (2).
21. Phillips, A. *On Flirtation.* London: Faber, 2007.
22. Ryan, ML. Narrative Across Media. London: U of Nebraska Press. 2004.
23. Tsou, W., Wang, W., Tzeng, Y. Applying a multimedia storytelling website in foreign language learning. *Computers & Education*, 47, (2006), 17–28.

Metrics for the Evaluation of News Site Content Layout in Large-Screen Contexts

Michael Nebeling
Institute of Information Systems, ETH Zurich
CH-8092 Zurich, Switzerland
[lastname]@inf.ethz.ch

Fabrice Matulic
Institute of Information Systems, ETH Zurich
CH-8092 Zurich, Switzerland
[lastname]@inf.ethz.ch

Moira C. Norrie
Institute of Information Systems, ETH Zurich
CH-8092 Zurich, Switzerland
[lastname]@inf.ethz.ch

ABSTRACT
Despite the fact that screen sizes and average screen resolutions have dramatically increased over the past few years, little attention has been paid to the design of web sites for large, high-resolution displays that are now becoming increasingly used both in enterprise and consumer spaces. We present a study of how the visual area of the browser window is currently utilised by news web sites at different widescreen resolutions. The analysis includes measurements of space taken up by the article content, embedded ads and the remaining components as they appear in the viewport of the web browser. The results show that the spatial distribution of page elements does not scale well with larger viewing sizes, which leads to an increasing amount of unused screen real estate and unnecessary scrolling. We derive a number of device-sensitive metrics to measure the quality of web page layout in different viewing contexts, which can guide the design of flexible layout templates that scale effectively on large screens.

Author Keywords
Web Design Guidelines, Web Site Adaptation to Large Screens, Technical Tools for Usability Evaluation

ACM Classification Keywords
H.5.2 Information Interfaces and Presentation: User Interfaces—*Screen design*

General Terms
Design, Human Factors

INTRODUCTION
The popularity of hand-held devices with web browsing functionality has prompted media publishers to design special, accessible web sites for these devices. Online news sites in particular have striven to address customer demand in delivering content that can be consumed on smartphones and the like. However, at the other end of the spectrum, little is being done to cater for the range of large-display surfaces that are now in widespread use in offices, homes and public spaces.

As shown by recent reports from the market research firm DisplaySearch[1], average screen dimensions and resolutions are increasing; moreover, the trend is towards displays with a 16:9 format, especially for notebook computers. In recent years, there has also been a growing number of other types of large-display devices such as wall screens, digital tabletops and projected surfaces, all predominantly geared towards horizontal, wide-format aspect ratios. This change in the browsing device landscape requires adaptations of many web site layouts where the often strongly vertical orientation at fixed width seems a poor design choice for such device characteristics. Also, with higher resolutions, the text becomes physically smaller and therefore less readable. Some web sites attempt to alleviate this problem by including a function allowing users to change the size of the font, an effect that can also be achieved using zoom features available in modern browsers. Another common function is a printer-friendly view where only the main content is shown with minimal or no layout constraints so that text can flow freely to fill the available space. However, those are only minor improvements of the user experience and the fact that they require user intervention is not always convenient.

We therefore decided to investigate both the technical and design issues raised by adaptation to large-display devices, which poses new challenges such as the efficient 'upscaling' of content, not to waste valuable screen real estate and impose unnecessary scrolling on the user. We argue that it is necessary to provide flexible screen layouts that make appropriate use of the higher amount of screen space available on large displays and, as a first step, we have developed a set of metrics that can be used to assess the presentation of content in different widescreen settings and hence to inform web page design also for large, high-resolution screens. The proposed metrics are grounded in a comprehensive study of existing news web sites to see how the browser viewport is currently utilised by different news content elements at viewing sizes larger than 1024x768 and to identify key issues. In this paper, we present the results of this study and the proposed metrics as well as how these can be implemented based on

[1]http://www.displaysearch.com

native web technologies to provide developers with the technical tools for evaluating web page layouts in terms of the spatial coverage of content in different widescreen contexts.

RELATED WORK

Many different usability evaluation methods have been specifically crafted for the web [11], e.g. design inspections to examine the hypertext specification, web usage analysis to understand user behaviour, and heuristic evaluation of prototypes at different design stages as well as of the final web site [18]. Given today's proliferation of web-enabled devices, the usability of a web site is also determined by its ability to adapt to the specific device in use. Much attention has been paid to the adaptation of web content for mobile phones and other kinds of small-screen devices. A number of automatic methods for partitioning web pages into smaller, semantically related units that fit into the screen of a mobile device have been proposed, e.g. [3, 10]. On the other hand, for large screens that are now increasingly used in enterprise and also consumer spaces, techniques to aggegrate content from multiple related pages into a single view might be welcome to reduce unnecessary navigational overhead. However, optimal design for large-display viewing contexts remains largely unexplored. Research in HCI currently seems to focus on new interaction techniques on such devices where touch and gesture-based modalities seem to be predominant, but efforts to design user interfaces that make appropriate use of the greater amount of screen real estate are minimal. We believe that, as a first step, some sort of device-sensitive web design metrics are required that can inform current web design processes so that they also cater for the characteristics of large-display devices.

Early research proposed several metrics to quantify usability factors such as the total word count in a page, the number of links and media as well as the spectrum of colours and font styles employed [13]. It was also found that web design is a moving target and that many of the established guidelines change over time [12], which may explain the lack of concrete thresholds for a wider class of quantitative web page measures. Existing guidelines such as WCAG, the Web Content Accessibility Guidelines[2] by W3C, consist of a set of recommendations on making content accessible, primarily for disabled users, with only some advice on designing for highly limited devices such as mobile phones. Their web site also includes a list of many different evaluation and issue reporting tools, but none of them address design deficiencies related to the spatial coverage of content with respect to different viewing contexts.

While several productivity benefits have already been characterised for large-display environments, e.g. in [4, 23], there is still a lack of concepts and tools to take advantage of large screens [20]. Due to the many fixed designs with often a vertical flow, using web sites in widescreen contexts generally does not bring any real advantages to users, which is why large screens at this stage still seem to be primarily suited for multi-task scenarios. For a single application to capitalise on the greater amount of screen space, various forms of adaptation would be required that are currently not supported by most web sites. Research has shown that selecting and placing different versions of text and media to display only the relevant parts on small screens or a much higher level of detail on large displays is generally possible [1, 14, 21], but requires substantial technical overhead, especially if one was to rely on native web technologies. One can hope that a flexible segmentation of content will become easier and more popular if W3C's proposals to include new tags in HTML5[3] for the annotation of page elements as well as multi-column layout in CSS3[4] are adopted and implemented in all major web browsers. However, our ongoing experiments with these new technologies show that even the latest additions to HTML and CSS are insufficient for effective adaptation of content and presentation using only features of those web standards.

One of the key challenges for adaptive layouts is to reduce the amount of scrolling required by fitting most of the content on the screen area above the fold (i.e. the screen space that is visible at first without scrolling), while, at the same time, not overloading the page with too much information. Directly related to this aspect is the physical layout of text which is found to have a considerable impact on the on-screen reading experience [5]. There is an increasing number of relevant tools, such as Instapaper[5] or Apple's Safari Reader technology, that extract long text paragraphs from web pages and show these using font settings and a display format optimised for reading, but also they provide poor results in large-screen environments due to the common one-column, fixed vertical layout that only makes use of a minimal portion of the screen in wide-format settings.

To generally improve users' reading comfort and efficiency, many findings suggest the use of multiple text columns and some even argue for horizontal scrolling, e.g. [8, 2]; however, this brings up two important issues. The first problem is that current support for multi-column layout in popular browsers is at best experimental and subject to change, as this is a feature proposed to be included only with the upcoming CSS3 modules. The current workaround among web developers is to specify adaptive layouts with the help of JavaScript libraries such as jQuery Masonry[6], which can allow the content to be spread in multiple columns, the number and size of which depends on the dimensions of the target viewing size. However, while such flexible layout engines based on automatic methods are also desirable for printer-friendly versions of news articles to improve on the simple sequential positioning of content used by most current browsers, they give less control over the concrete design in a particular viewing context and customisation of the layout mechanisms generally requires considerable programming skills. The second issue is that vertical scrolling is predominant on most web pages and further compounded by the fact that there is often only a vertical mouse wheel, so a com-

[2] http://www.w3.org/TR/WCAG20/

[3] http://www.w3.org/TR/html5/

[4] http://www.w3.org/TR/css3-multicol/

[5] http://instapaper.com

[6] http://www.smashingmagazine.com/2009/06/09/smart-fixes-for-fluid-layouts/

plete change to horizontal scrolling would be rather radical and require many users to change their browsing habits.

In view of these problems, we have started to investigate the technical and design challenges for developing adaptive web interfaces that also cater for large-display, high-resolution devices while building on established standards. Our first results comprise the metrics presented in this paper that we have derived from an empirical study of current news site designs and how these adapt in different widescreen settings. The proposed metrics mark the first step of our effort to build a research framework that seeks to establish design guidelines as well as to form sound technical tools for the development of flexible web interfaces that also adapt to novel forms of large displays, i.e. not only larger desktop screens, but also digital TVs, tabletop systems or wall-size displays.

The study presented in the next section provided important input for developing the metrics following this. Many other studies have been conducted to understand users' browsing habits and identify patterns of navigation on the web, e.g. [22]. Several studies have also investigated the visual aesthetics of web sites as perceived by users [15] and how framing effects may influence users' web site quality judgement [9]. However, the effects of different device characteristics in terms of screen size and resolution and their potential impact on the browsing experience have so far played only a minor role in studies and have primarily been investigated for small-screen devices, e.g. [6]. For large screens, there is still only limited insight obtained from a few formative evaluations of user expectations when browsing web pages on high-resolution, wide-format displays [7]. The results there also suggest the use of constraint-based liquid layout for web pages to automatically fill larger portions of the screen as more space becomes available. However, an important factor that has not received enough attention is a definite strategy to specify suitable constraints for those adaptive layouts as these are key for such layout mechanisms to be effective. In that sense, we believe that our work is complementary and makes an important step forward, as the metrics and visual tools presented in this paper are devised to inform web page design and help developers find device-related layout constraints.

STUDY

Our study aimed at providing numbers on the status quo of text-centric web content layout and window space occupation in widescreen environments. In that regard, the closest to our study is [16] that presents a detailed breakdown of the different web page elements to relate the relative page coverage taking into account text, images and other embedded objects. However, their content analysis does not address spatial distribution of content elements at different viewing sizes, nor does it resolve the different semantics of content, for example, to differentiate actual content from ads.

The choice of news articles over other types of web sites was motivated by their relative homogeneity in terms of structure and appearance and the fact that online newspapers and magazines can be easily compared to their print counterparts. Moreover, news web sites are backed by companies that have a vital interest in delivering an optimal reading experience to their customers in order to keep up their businesses.

Methodology

In order to assess the spatial distribution of web content for a news page, we approached the problem by first identifying the major functional categories of structural elements that typically appear on a page showing a full news article. However, since the purpose of the study was to measure space occupation rather than establishing the full portrait of a web page, we decided to limit ourselves to four categories: background, article content, ad and web interface, the latter including links to other news items related or not related to the current article. The idea was then to calculate the positions and combined areas of these elements in several viewing contexts and based on those results compute a number of indicators to present the overall situation.

The web pages were all viewed and analysed on Firefox using standard settings and a set of extensions to perform the measurements. To obtain meaningful results reflecting a sufficiently representative collection of news articles, the 50 most popular news web sites as ranked by Alexa were considered[7], excluding news aggregators that only show short text snippets for each news item. For each site, a sample article was chosen and using a customised version of the Aardvark extension[8], the DOM elements of the page were marked manually according to their semantic function. Typically, the main structural blocks in a news web page have their own HTML container elements with identifying id or class attributes that are consistent across the whole web site. Those attributes were used to associate marked areas with their semantic function so that other articles retrieved from the same web site could then be broken down and tagged automatically. All pages that were marked in this way were subsequently viewed by the authors to check for inconsistencies and discrepancies that would distort the measurements. Some web sites split long articles over several pages and, in those cases, values were added or averaged as appropriate to match the criteria used for single-page layouts. Any reader comments were also hidden or removed as they do not belong to the article per se, although technically an integral part of the page.

The measurements consisted of determining the position and length of marked blocks and calculating the combined area that they covered in the page. Each article was loaded simultaneously in five independent browser windows set to different sizes. The dimensions were chosen based on browser resolution statistics provided by W3Counter[9]. The three most popular widescreen resolutions were selected along with the reference 1024x768 resolution for 4:3. The resolution 1680x 1050 was also reversed for one measurement set so as to give the window a vertical orientation in order to simulate a rotating monitor in portrait mode. Since the study focused on raw, pixel-based space occupation, the physical screen

[7] http://www.alexa.com/topsites/category/Top/News

[8] http://karmatics.com/aardvark

[9] http://www.w3counter.com/globalstats.php

size did not come into consideration at that point. The latter is however important when taking into account subjective, user-dependent criteria such as reading comfort and needs to be addressed when designing web pages for large screens.

Each browser window was left in its default appearance with only the navigation and bookmark toolbars. This means that the actual dimensions of the browser viewport were $w - 6px \times h - 136px$, including possible scrollbars. The sizes reflect a situation where the browser window is maximised or set to full screen, which according to many user studies (e.g. [22]) is what the majority of users adopt. For situations where the browser is run in windowed mode and hence at intermediate user-defined window sizes, it should be easy to extrapolate from the results for the considered resolutions.

Results

The vast majority of news web sites currently adopt a two or three-column layout with one or more headers and footers, and the article content itself in the left or central column. Navigation items such as menus, buttons and links to related content typically appear in sidebars surrounding the article, at the top and directly below it in the footer(s). Frequently, floating blocks also appear inside the main article causing breaks in the article's text flow and formatting. As for the ads, while their content frequently changes between loads, they are generally placed at fixed locations and have fixed dimensions for a given web site. No particular design rule seems prevalent as to where the ads should appear. Ad banners and inserts can be embedded in virtually any of the aforementioned elements, including within the article text itself. With only a few exceptions, the web page content is centred, except perhaps for some footers, headers or background elements that are made to stretch to the whole width of the window. The area covered by the article content itself in the selected pages averaged 42% of the total web area and the space taken up by ads roughly 12%. This perhaps contrasts with blogs and other user content-intensive sites, where entries are typically appended one after the other inside a long column (and where possibly there is even more space lost due to sub-optimal layout strategies).

Figure 1 shows the average percentages of the areas covered by web, article content and ad elements in the client space, i.e. the total area of the browser window, including visible and invisible parts. As the resolution increases, the amount of space used by actual web content decreases, except when the window is set to vertical mode (1050x1680). A side effect of this phenomenon is the appearance of margins on each side that become larger as the viewport width increases, as illustrated in Fig. 2. The margin lengths are computed by taking the leftmost and rightmost pixels of the first and last solid elements of the web document (i.e. non-background) at each scanline and determining the distances to the left and right edges of the viewport, respectively. (If the document width is larger than the viewport then the margin is negative). The average margin width is then calculated for the whole page. This means that pages with long articles extending beyond their flanking sidebars would see their line margin widths significantly increase if columns are static and content is not reflowed inside them. At screen widths around 1024 pixels, the margin is minimal and there is a jump above 1200. This is due to the fact that many web sites are currently designed for a target resolution of 1024x768. But, even at this size, the margin average is more than 10% due to unbalanced column heights. As a matter of comparison, the amount of white space used by a page of a regular print newspaper is roughly 10% of the paper surface (mostly covered by margins).

Another consideration which perhaps matters to publishers and editors is what users see when the web page is first loaded in the web browser and the topmost portion of it ap-

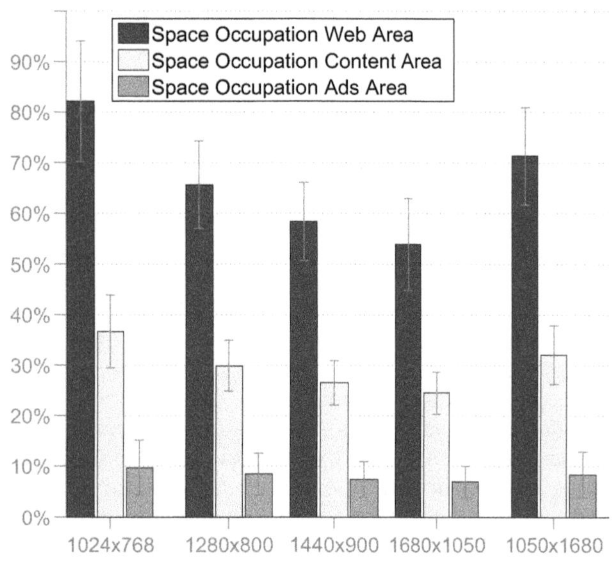

Figure 1. Area coverage in whole client space

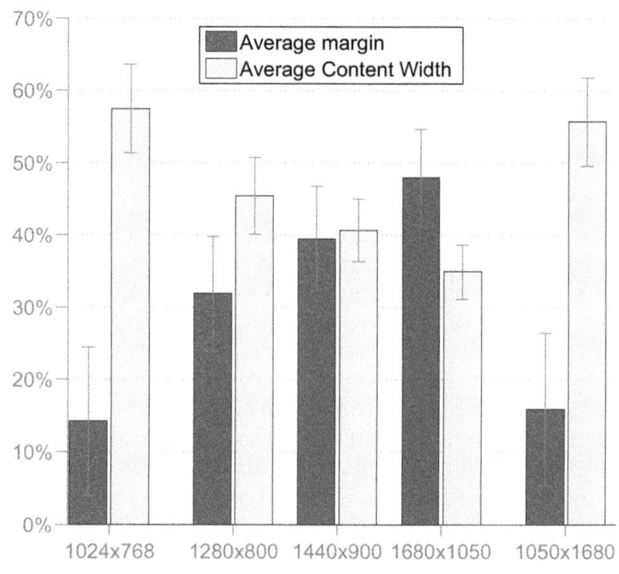

Figure 2. Average margin and content widths as percentage of the total viewport width

pears in the window. Too many extraneous elements, ads and too much background might indeed frustrate readers who are mostly interested in viewing the article. For publishers sustaining their business through advertisements, the placement of ad containers on the web page might be an important design factor. If ads are located in areas which readers never come to see, then this represents a potential loss of revenue. As it turns out, a significant proportion of ads are placed below the article (about 28% of the total ad surface), a zone that may never be exposed to users that do not scroll that far.

Figure 3 depicts the area distribution of the different categories visible on the area above the fold (or 'first screen'), where the 'nav' area is the area that remains after content and ad areas have been subtracted. Figure 4, on the other hand, shows the extent of surface coverage by the web page's elements on the first screen as a percentage of the total space they occupy in the whole web document (here 'web area' includes article content and ad areas). The figures show once again that, as widescreen resolutions increase, the browser window is mainly filled with background pixels at the detriment of content. At 1680x1050, the user only sees less than 1.5 times the amount of a page's content than at 1024x768 on average, although there is more than 2.2 times as much available space. Viewing the page at 1050x1680 yields much better results, as the user is able to see more than half of the web page and almost 60% of the article content without scrolling.

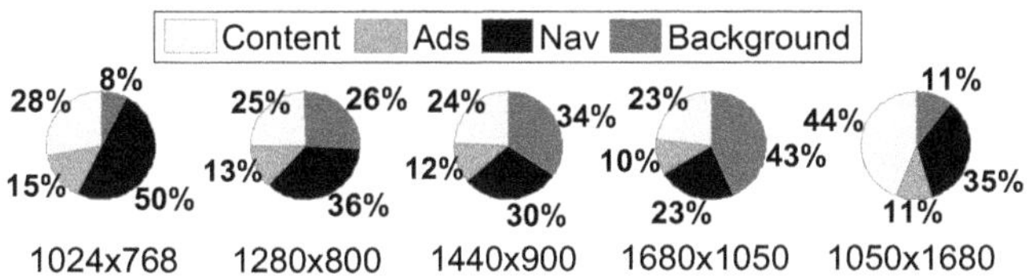

Figure 3. Area distribution on first screen client space

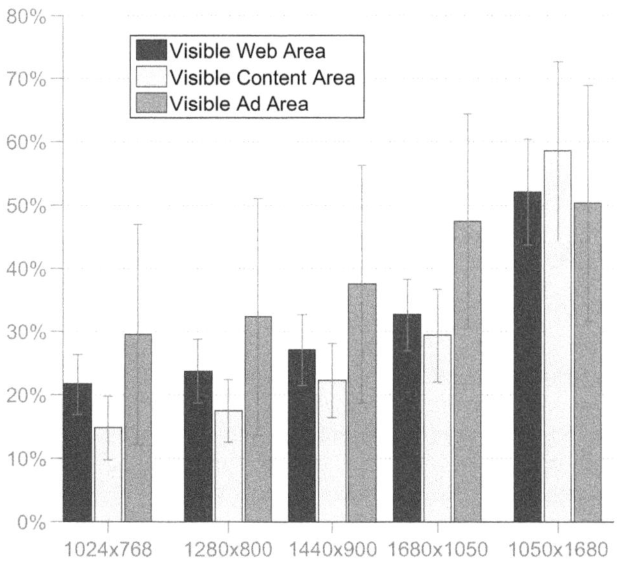

Figure 4. Percentage of visible elements on first screen from total surface in page

The same effect can be observed with ads, which generally do not adapt well to higher amounts of screen real estate. While they still occupy 15% of the first screen at 1024x768, the visible ad area decreases to 10% at 1680x1050. Even though much more content becomes visible at its counterpart resolution of 1050x1680, the visible ad area only slightly increases to 11%.

A simple metric to measure how much space could be saved if screen real estate were used with maximum efficiency is to compare the amount of scrolling needed to view the whole page as rendered with the amount required to display the document's foreground elements when optimally filling the available space. Figure 5 shows the scroll factors of the two theoretical fills (web and article content) vs. that of the actual rendering expressed as the number of viewports needed to show the total area of the considered categories. A value

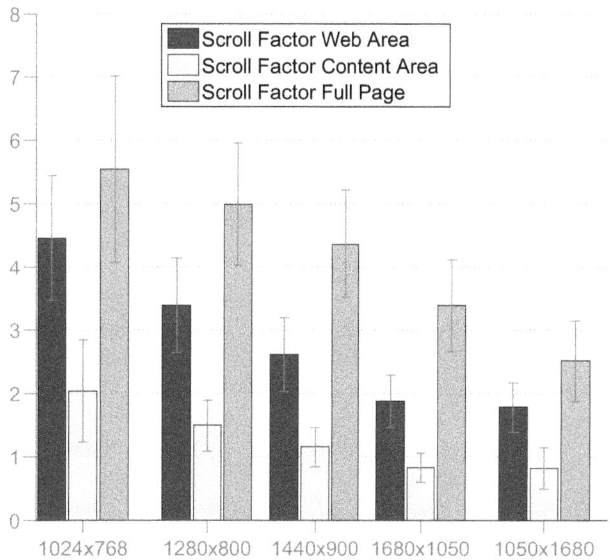

Figure 5. Scroll factor for optimal web and content coverage vs. actual rendering

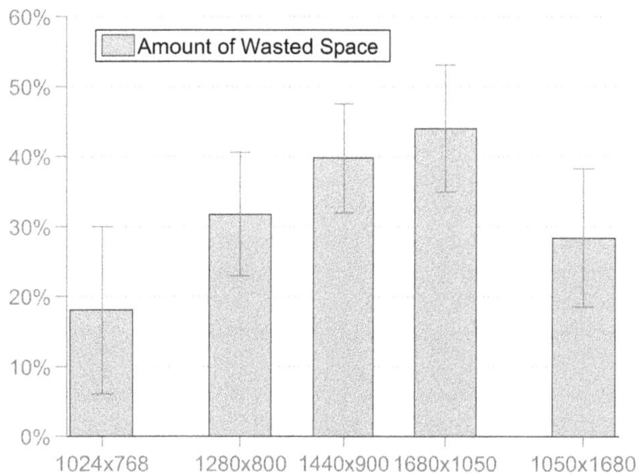

Figure 6. Amount of space that could theoretically be saved by optimal use of screen real estate

lower than 1 means that the entire area can be displayed in the viewport and no scrolling is required. The results for the content areas reflect a hypothetical case where only the actual content of the article itself is shown on the screen, similar to printer-friendly renderings.

Juxtaposing the theoretical scroll factors with the values for the actual renderings reveals increasing gaps between the optimal and real measures. At higher widescreen resolutions, more and more unnecessary scrolling is imposed on the user to view the page's entire content. The amount of space that is potentially 'wasted' is summarised in Fig. 6. Once more, the data shows a clear increase of unused screen real estate in high-resolution horizontal contexts, as web pages generally fail to adapt to the change of rendering environment.

Discussion

Obviously, web design is more than simply optimising space usage and the costs of leaving much of the screen bare on a large display are not as critical as those associated with wasting paper in a print newspaper where costs are real. One could even say that the penalty of a web page with an ill-suited layout is only the fact that it involves more scrolling and clicking for the reader. However, as the diversification of browsing clients further expands, the need for more flexible layouts to accommodate more demanding users will no doubt arise.

Discussions of the respective merits of static layouts versus flexible or liquid layouts have sparked lively debates among designers. Proponents of the former point out the ease and convenience of designing for an area with fixed dimensions, while the advocates of the latter argue that accessibility should be the prime factor in content presentation [17]. Print newspapers and magazines make near-optimal use of the available paper surface using columns and separations, but their template sizes are fixed and the appearance of the final product is determined at printing time. To achieve optimal surface occupation without sacrificing aesthetic considerations of layout design on digital surfaces, whose dimensions and resolutions are unknown at creation time, is a non-trivial engineering challenge.

One argument against flexible layouts is that they often allow text column widths to stretch without limit, thus producing excessively long lines that impose cognitive strain on the reader when trying to follow on to the next line. Among the reviewed web pages, the maximum number of characters per line for article columns with fixed widths was on average 94. This already exceeds the recommended 70 characters per line for pleasant and efficient reading [19], and increasing column widths, and hence line lengths, further would detract from readability and the overall user experience.

Another decisive factor that heavily influences readability is typography, i.e. font type and size [5]. News sites tend to adopt either modern-looking sans-serif fonts, mostly Arial, or a serif font such as Georgia or Times New Roman. The latter seem to be particularly favoured by traditional newspapers such as The New York Times and The Washington Post, perhaps to retain a distinctive print-like look to assert their identity. The typical font size of paragraphs in news articles tends to be between 13 and 15 pixels, regardless of the viewing resolution. As mentioned in the introduction, there are several ways to compensate for text that is rendered too small by default, but they typically require user intervention. While one can imagine site-specific text-display settings optimised for a particular viewing environment, it should be possible for web sites to automatically adapt the default font settings based on thresholds relative to the increase in resolution even with no user preferences set.

METRICS

The problems identified in our study essentially relate to three major aspects of web layouts: (1) the overall use of the screen, (2) the proportions between different content elements and (3) the readability of larger amounts of text. We can trace the cause of the observed problems to the following design issues.

- Many web layouts have been designed for a fixed width only. In widescreen contexts, the greater amount of screen space is therefore potentially wasted as it gets mostly filled with background content.
- Text and font characteristics such as font weight and size, number of columns and column widths as well as line spacing are often optimised for the 'standard' screen resolution of 1024x768 and typically hard-coded. As a consequence, text flow and style hardly scale with larger resolutions to maintain readability in widescreen contexts.
- Media resources such as images, videos and animations are often available only in one size and embedded with fixed dimensions. As a result, the embedded media do not scale well in widescreen contexts. For instance, ads that make extensive use of animated GIFs or Flash animations to draw the attention of the user consequently lose high proportions of the visible area on the first screen in comparison to the text.
- While web sites generally attempt to place the most important content elements on the first screen, the amount of information presented to the user at larger viewing sizes often increases substantially as more content becomes visible at once. Particularly for the navigation options, this can lead to an overflow of visible links, which makes it harder for users to find a particular navigation point.

In order to quantify these issues, we have defined the metrics shown in Table 1. The basis for these metrics build the window area, web area and content area. Similar to our study, the window area is the browser viewport and therefore the room available for the content elements to be visible without scrolling. The web area is the space that all foreground and background content elements in the document require to be viewed at the same time. The content area refers to the space occupied only by the foreground content elements. Depending on individual web site requirements, it can be helpful to divide the content area into groups of semantically related content elements in order to compare how often elements of

Table 1. Metrics to measure the quality of web layouts with respect to the viewing context

Metric	Description
Document-window ratio = $\frac{\textit{Web area}}{\textit{Window area}}$	Determines how many viewports are required to fit the whole document. This ratio can be divided into vertical and horizontal scroll factors determined by height and width ratios, respectively. Web sites at larger viewing sizes should approach a value closer to 1. A value less than or equal to 1 means that no horizontal and/or vertical scrolling is required, but very low values mean that most of the available space is not used.
Content-window ratio = $\frac{\textit{Content area}}{\textit{Window area}}$	Determines how many viewports are required to fit the foreground or actual content only. Significantly different values between the document-window and content-window ratios for larger viewing environments hint at potentially 'wasted' screen real estate, as the space that becomes available would primarily be consumed by background content.
Wide text ratio = $\frac{\textit{Wide text area}}{\textit{Total text area}}$	Determines how much of the total text area contains lines longer than the aforementioned 70 characters per line. While static layouts tend to waste much screen space at larger viewing sizes, more flexible layouts often produce excessively long lines that detract from readability. Particularly text-intensive sites should keep the wide text area at a minimum to allow for efficient reading of longer text in widescreen contexts.
Small text ratio = $\frac{\textit{Small text area}}{\textit{Total text area}}$	Determines how much of the total text area is likely to appear too small on high-resolution displays. There is no such general guideline for what constitutes potentially too small a font on devices with wide-format aspect ratios. Many screen designs have been optimised for a particular resolution, but the small text area should be kept minimal and not substantially increase with higher resolutions.
Visible text ratio = $\frac{\textit{Visible text area}}{\textit{Total text area}}$	Determines how much of the total text area is visible in the viewport. Larger displays should potentially show more text, but too much text at once can overstrain the user. Particularly on the first screen, it is most important to balance out text and media in order to keep the user interested in reading even if continuing requires scrolling.
Visible links ratio = $\frac{\textit{Visible links}}{\textit{Total links}}$	Determines how many of the total navigation options are visible in the viewport. Web sites generally attempt to place as many controls and navigation options as possible in the top navigation area. Larger viewing environments potentially display more links at once and are likely to cause an overload on navigation options.
Media-content ratio = $\frac{\textit{Visible media area}}{\textit{Visible content area}}$	Determines how much of the visible content area is filled with media. Larger viewing sizes should not only fit more text, but scale embedded media accordingly to keep the reading experience interesting. In the case of ads, it may be to the frustration of the user if larger viewports only fill with more ads and to the disadvantage of the advertiser if their ads do not scale with the page's remaining content.

a particular kind occur and the space on the screen that they occupy and use effectively.

The ratios defined in Table 1 directly relate to the problems we have identified in our study. The document-window and content-window ratios assess how efficiently the available screen space is used and how much scrolling is required to view the whole document. The wide text and small text ratios target the overall readability, while the remaining ratios are related to the visibility and spatial distribution of different content elements. The visible text and link ratios hence give further indication of the web site's readability and operability depending on the viewport. Finally, the media-content ratio and possible derivatives track the proportions of text, media and, for example, ads at different viewing sizes.

We note carefully the correlation between the different metrics as optimal results for some of them may have a negative impact on others. For example, higher visible text ratios may be preferable not to impose too much scrolling on users, however the wide and small text ratios should be the constraining factors. The same is true in combination with the media-content ratio as images related to the content will need to be aligned and scaled with the text to keep the reader interested. Finally, an optimal content-window ratio of 1 is a desirable goal in theory, but may come at the expense of aesthetic considerations where the appropriate use of white space can often play an important role to support the overall usability of a web site and improve the user experience.

It follows that optimising web layouts along the defined metrics means to balance out the measured values, as it is impossible to achieve optimal numbers for all considered factors at the same time. Depending on the particular content and purpose of a web site, developers may put more emphasis on some aspects of the layout at the expense of others. The main purpose of online newspapers, for example, is to deliver news content to the screens of their users and support them in accessing this text-heavy information. Special emphasis should hence be on all factors concerning readability on the screen. This may in return mean lower values for the media-content ratio compared to, for example, more artistic web sites where information is mainly conveyed through images and not text. Furthermore, how accurate the obtained values will be depends on how fine-grained the measurements are performed. If we only measure by means of rectangular shapes, it can be rather difficult to approach the effective text area when the actual shape of the text may be significantly different after white space caused by wrapping is removed. Also care has to be taken to avoid content elements being measured twice, for example, due to a media area being embedded in text. We show how we implemented the proposed metrics and discuss the encountered problems in the next section.

IMPLEMENTATION

The proposed metrics were implemented on top of the popular jQuery JavaScript library[10] to ease development and maintain cross-browser compatibility. Using jQuery, the document-window ratio is represented by the product of the computed width and height for *$('body')* divided by the respective product for *$('window')*. We need to mark content elements with an empty CSS class *isContent* so that the content area is the sum of all areas determined for the jQuery selector *$('.isContent')*. Putting the content area into proportion with the window area gives the content-window ratio. Because media can be either embedded using *img*, *object* (e.g. for Flash animations) or the new HTML5 *video* tag, the media-content ratio is computed for *$('img,object,video')* under two conditions. First, one has to make sure that only elements with a non-zero width and height are considered (i.e. they actually fill space somewhere in the page). Second, the element's offset must lie within the current viewport and only the visible part of the bounding box counts towards the area (i.e. only the space they effectively fill in the current viewport is measured). Counting the links in the content area via *$('.isContent a')* in proportion to those that are currently visible yields the visible links ratio.

Considerably more effort has to be expended to compute the various text ratios that we have defined. While there are several difficulties due to the way in which browsers interpret font sizes specified using CSS and although it is not possible to count the characters per line in JavaScript per se, relatively accurate results can still be obtained with the following procedure. Many web sites make use of predefined semantic markup such as *h1* to *h6* for headings and *p* to mark paragraphs of text. As the nesting of these elements is not meaningful and therefore discouraged by the HTML specification, we can measure distinct text areas for the elements returned by *$('h1,h2,h3,h4,h5,h6,p')*. To assess areas of small text, we need to convert the font size of each text element from *px* to *cm* to resolve the physical character height on the screen; however, this requires taking into account the current screen's DPI. It turns out that all major browsers directly work with the system DPI of usually 96, which can be significantly different from the current display's actual DPI. In our tests, a square specified at 10cm by 10cm using CSS actually measures between 7.46cm on a 15.4" notebook with 128 DPI at 1650x1080 and 9.47cm on a 30" screen with 101 DPI at 2560x1600. Our current workaround is to prompt the developer for the screen diagonal (a value which cannot be obtained via the *screen* object in JavaScript). In combination with the current screen's resolution, we can calculate the pixels per inch and extrapolate the effective character height when converting to centimeters. Currently, we consider elements with a font size lower than 0.4cm to be part of the small text area. As there is no general threshold for what constitutes small text, this value has been determined by an informal experiment where three members of our research group were separately asked to select the one paragraph that is still comfortable to read from a number of paragraphs of the same text in various font sizes from 0.1 to 0.6cm. As for wide text areas, we can base our implementation on available research results and currently count in particular paragraph elements whose width is greater than that of a hidden *span* created dynamically at run-time to fill 70 characters using the respective font. In the last step, we remove the summed up area for *$('img,object,video', p)* for each measured paragraph *p* in order to exclude any media that may have been counted towards the text area.

[10]http://jquery.com/

Based on this implementation of the proposed metrics, we have started to develop a visual tool that can be loaded into existing web pages at run-time to perform on-the-fly measurements in the browser as shown in Fig. 7. It then allows the user to select content elements (and their child elements) to be included in the measurements by hovering and double-clicking the respective areas in the web page. That way our implementation does not have to rely on the accuracy of automated methods and designers have full control over fine-grained measurements based on the visual representations of the content elements rather than their hypertext specification. The tool draws an outline around all content elements that were considered in the performed measurements. As illustrated in Fig. 7, we carefully chose visual annotations such as outlines, not borders, and coloured overlays not to break the layout and flow of the original page which is the case with many other evaluation tools. Because the viewing context plays an important role in our evaluations of the web layout, the evaluation method is not only sensitive to changes regarding the visible web area (e.g. resizing of the browser window), but in order to react to potential adaptations of content and presentation, also automatically performs recalculations when content is dynamically added or updated in the web page, e.g. via AJAX menus or tab-based navigation controls that essentially toggle the visibility of page elements.

To compare the results obtained for a number of different viewing sizes, the visual tool also allows individual measurements to be captured and restored by clicking the respective links. For each setting that is captured, a new link will be added, showing the window dimensions, the document-window ratio and the difference to the content-window ratio. For example, the first measurement shows that even a maximised window at 2560x1600 still requires users to scroll down 3.47 pages to view the whole article as large amounts of screen space left and right are filled with background. The +2.21 in this case means that only slightly more than one viewport should be required to fit the actual content.

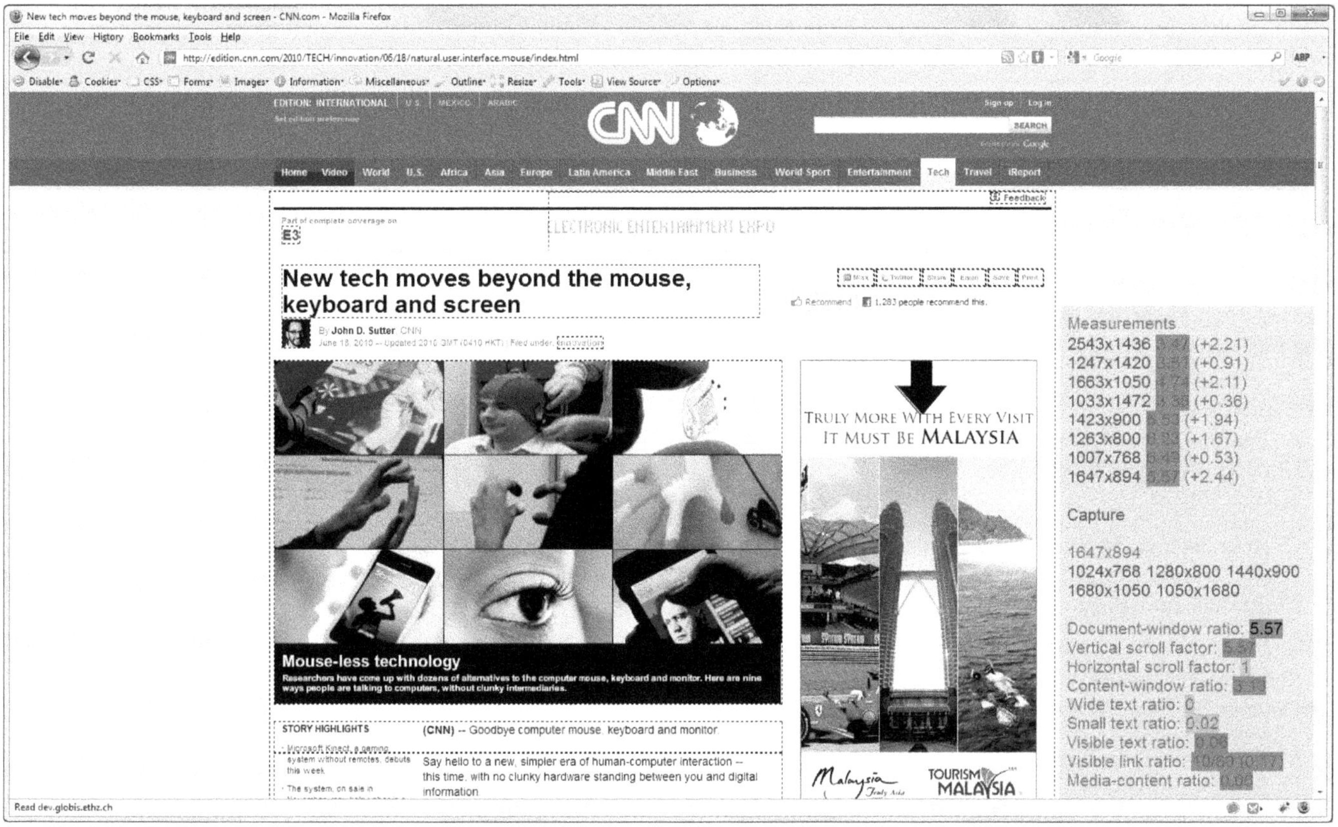

Figure 7. Measuring the quality of a CNN article's layout for a number of different viewing sizes on a 30" screen at a resolution of 2560x1600

The colouring of the obtained values is based on several valuation methods for the different metrics. For example, we say that the document-window ratio is better the closer it is to 1 and expect it to come much closer to this value with increasing viewing sizes. We have defined a number of thresholds for near-optimal, tolerable and poor-quality values based on which the measured values can be assessed and highlighted, for example, in green, yellow and red. However, as the current range of values is largely experimental, we will scrutinise these in another study. The goal at this stage was to show that the metrics we have defined can be implemented in a way that is feasible, with the focus being on the methods required to provide visual feedback for developers so that they can see fairly quickly where adaptations are required. The tool is available for download from our web site[11].

CONCLUSION

In an attempt to set new directions for research in web design where large, high-resolution displays have so far received little attention, we have presented an analysis and comparison of screen usage by text-centric web sites viewed in different widescreen contexts. The results show that the spatial distribution of content elements does not scale well and leads to an increasing amount of unused screen space and no reduction in scrolling. Based on our study, we have proposed several metrics to quantify the critical aspects of screen layouts and have shown how they can be implemented and applied to existing web sites. There are of course many more factors to be considered and directly measuring the quality of web sites in a way that is consistent with how users perceive it is very difficult. For the same reason, it is problematic to define universal guidelines such as ideal values or thresholds and alert levels for the numbers computed by our tool. While we can argue that a small text ratio of 0.02 measured by our tool is worse than one of 0, realistic thresholds and definite alert levels depend on the particular type of web site under development. With the study presented in this paper and the proposed metrics, it will be interesting to correlate any numbers produced by the tool with data collected in user studies in order to scrutinise some of the more experimental and informally determined placeholder thresholds currently used in our implementation of the metrics.

Despite our study being based on a significant number of web sites, the approach could still be criticised for focussing on a specific type of web sites. We intentionally chose online newspapers in order to compare a relatively homogeneous set of web pages and focus on quality aspects that are directly related to the common task that the reviewed web sites were designed for, namely delivering text-centric content to the screens of their readers. Furthermore, we believe that many of our findings can be generalised to news sites and aggregators not considered in the study and potentially to other prominent classes of modern web applications that

[11] http://dev.globis.ethz.ch/jqmetrics

also display large amounts of textual information, such as blogs, wikis and discussion forums.

Our future work will mainly follow two directions. First, we plan to design and implement an adaptive screen layout for news web sites based on the proposed metrics while exploring different forms of context-aware adaptation including the use of multi-column layouts and different scrolling mechanisms. Second, we want to conduct user studies to be able to compare how users actually perceive the quality attributes assessed by our tool and to learn which web site adaptations bring real benefits in widescreen contexts.

REFERENCES

1. A. Borning, R. Lin, and K. Marriott. Constraint-Based Document Layout for the Web. *Multimedia Systems*, 8(3), 2000.
2. C. Braganza, K. Marriott, P. Moulder, M. Wybrow, and T. Dwyer. Scrolling Behaviour with Single- and Multi-column Layout. In *Proc. WWW*, 2009.
3. Y. Chen, W. Ma, and H. Zhang. Detecting Web Page Structure for Adaptive Viewing on Small Form Factor Devices. In *Proc. WWW*, 2003.
4. M. Czerwinski, G. Smith, T. Regan, B. Meyers, G. Robertson, and G. Starkweather. Toward Characterizing the Productivity Benefits of Very Large Displays. In *Proc. INTERACT*, 2003.
5. M. Dyson. How physical text layout affects reading from screen. *Behaviour & Information Technology*, 23(6), 2004.
6. L. Findlater and J. McGrenere. Impact of screen size on performance, awareness, and user satisfaction with adaptive graphical user interfaces. In *Proc. CHI*, 2008.
7. J. H. Goldberg and J. I. Helfman. Evaluating User Expectations for Widescreen Content Layout. In *Proc. UPA*, 2007.
8. J. H. Goldberg, J. I. Helfman, and L. Martin. Information Distance and Orientation in Liquid Layout. In *Proc. CHI*, 2008.
9. J. Hartmann, A. De Angeli, and A. Sutcliffe. Framing the User Experience: Information Biases on Website Quality Judgement. In *Proc. CHI*, 2008.
10. G. Hattori, K. Hoashi, K. Matsumoto, and F. Sugaya. Robust Web Page Segmentation for Mobile Terminal Using Content-Distances and Page Layout Information. In *Proc. WWW*, 2007.
11. E. Insfran and A. Fernandez. A Systematic Review of Usability Evaluation in Web Development. In *Proc. WISE Workshops*, 2008.
12. M. Ivory and R. Megraw. Evolution of Web Site Design Patterns. *ACM Trans. on Information Systems*, 23(4), 2005.
13. M. Ivory, R. Sinha, and M. Hearst. Empirically Validated Web Page Design Metrics. In *Proc. CHI*, 2001.
14. C. Jacobs, W. Li, E. Schrier, D. Bargeron, and D. Salesin. Adaptive Grid-Based Document Layout. *ACM Transactions on Graphics*, 22(3), 2003.
15. T. Lavie and N. Tractinsky. Assessing dimensions of perceived visual aesthetics of web sites. *Int. J. of Human-Computer Studies*, 60(3), 2004.
16. R. Levering and M. Cutler. The Portrait of a Common HTML Web Page. In *Proc. DocEng*, 2006.
17. P. Lynch and S. Horton. *Web Style Guide, 3rd edition: Basic Design Principles for Creating Web Sites*. Yale University Press, 2008.
18. M. Matera, F. Rizzo, and G. Carughi. Web Usability: Principles and Evaluation Methods. *Web Engineering*, 2006.
19. A. Nanavati and R. Bias. Optimal Line Length in Reading–A Literature Review. *Visible Language*, 39(2), 2005.
20. G. Robertson, M. Czerwinski, P. Baudisch, B. Meyers, D. Robbins, G. Smith, and D. Tan. The Large-Display User Experience. *IEEE Computer Graphics and Applications*, 25(4), 2005.
21. E. Schrier, M. Dontcheva, C. Jacobs, G. Wade, and D. Salesin. Adaptive Layout for Dynamically Aggregated Documents. In *Proc. IUI*, 2008.
22. H. Weinreich, H. Obendorf, E. Herder, and M. Mayer. Not Quite the Average: An Empirical Study of Web Use. *ACM Transactions on the Web*, 2(1), 2008.
23. B. Yost, Y. Haciahmetoglu, and C. North. Beyond Visual Acuity: The Perceptual Scalability of Information Visualizations for Large Displays. In *Proc. CHI*, 2007.

YouPivot: Improving Recall with Contextual Search

Joshua Hailpern[1], Nicholas Jitkoff[2], Andrew Warr[2], Karrie Karahalios[1], Robert Sesek[3], Nikita Shkrob[4]

[1]University of Illinois
Urbana, IL USA 61801
(jhailpe2, kkarahal)@cs.uiuc.edu

[2]Google
Mountain View, CA USA 94043
(alcor, andywarr)@google.com

[3]Boston University
Boston, MA USA 02215
rsesek@bu.edu

[4]University of Waterloo
Waterloo, Ontario, Canada N2L 3G1
nshkrob@uwaterloo.ca

ABSTRACT
According to cognitive science literature, human memory is predicated on contextual cues (e.g., room, music) in the environment. During recall tasks, we associate information/activities/objects with contextual cues. However, computer systems do not leverage our natural process of using contextual cues to facilitate recall. We present a new interaction technique, **Pivoting**, that allows users to search for contextually related activities and find a target piece of information (often not semantically related). A sample motivation for contextual search would be, "what was that website I was looking at when *Yesterday* by The Beatles was last playing?" Our interaction technique is grounded in the cognitive science literature, and is demonstrated in our system **YouPivot**. In addition, we present a new personal annotation method, called **TimeMarks**, to further support contextual recall and the pivoting process. In a pilot study, participants were quicker to identify websites, and preferred using YouPivot, compared to current tools. YouPivot demonstrates how principles of human memory can be applied to enhance the search of digital information.

Author Keywords
Search, Human Memory, Contextual Cue, Interface, Contextual Search, Pivoting, Pivot, Time Mark, YouPivot

ACM Classification Keywords
H5.2. Information interfaces and presentation: User Interfaces.

General Terms
Design, Human Factors

INTRODUCTION
"What was that PDF I was looking at yesterday? The name escapes me, but I know that AC/DC was playing when I was reading it," or "I know that I read it during that meeting last week." Many people have had moments like this. They occur when trying to retrieve a document, website, or file, when the semantic information (name, url, system path, etc.) cannot be recalled, but environmental factors can. A user may remember the song that was playing, their physical location, a phone call that interrupted them, or even other files or websites that were open at the same time. These temporally related activities are referred to as **contextual cues**.

Contextual cues are a key component of human memory. Consider the advice given when someone loses their car keys: "retrace your steps since the last time you know you had them." People are told to remember the context, and often the lost item is uncovered. We can define a *contextual cue* as any event/object that has a temporal relationship to a search target. For example, consider a Twitter message (a "Tweet") that a user sent while working on a document. If she searches for that Tweet in order to locate her document, the Tweet is a *contextual cue*. We define search based on contextual cues as **Contextual Search**[1]. It is important to note that a *contextual cue*, and thereby the contextual search, does not have to match semantically to the search target. Consider the earlier example of searching for a song playing while a document is open. The song's name and content is unlikely to be a semantic match to the document the user is working on.

While using contextual cues is a natural method of recall, [5] modern computers (and their extensive search applications) do not yet support this form of contextual search. Moreover, research in cognitive science has shown that leveraging context improves speed and accuracy in recall tasks [3]. At present, personal file history search is limited to file metadata (e.g., file name, last date accessed, file size, file type and sometimes file content). If a user does not know this information, she cannot search for and find a file. Without a form of contextual search, users cannot leverage the natural process of recall. We do not know how pervasive the desire for contextual search on computers is or could be, because modern systems to not support it. Working from the extensive theoretical background on memory, it stands to reason that search based on contextual cues will enhance recall and computer usability.

We present **YouPivot**, a contextual history based search tool that bridges the gap between the literature on human memory/recall and search. YouPivot leverages our natural method of recall by allowing a user to search through their

[1] While the term "contextual search" is used in the IR community (e.g. query context), we draw our usage from the psychology research on human memory, which relies on contextual cues.

digital history (e.g., files, URLs, physical location, meetings, and events) for the context they *do* remember. The user can then **Pivot**, or see everything that was going on while that context was active. Further, YouPivot displays a visualization of the user's activity, providing another method for finding context. By visually browsing their own computer usage, a user can find key moments in time by identifying "landmarks" of activity (e.g., browsing Facebook while working in Photoshop). Lastly, YouPivot introduces a new annotation method for contextual recall called **TimeMarks**, in which a user marks a moment in time as being important. This effectively leaves a temporal landmark for later contextual recall. Because YouPivot logs a user's personal activity, TimeMarks effectively bookmarks all the user's activity at that moment (open webpages, files, songs, physical location etc.) for easier recall.

We discuss how YouPivot builds on existing tools for facilitating search. We then present YouPivot's features and implementation, followed by a preliminary pilot study comparing YouPivot with current tools. We conclude by discussing future work, features, and experiments.

CONTEXTUAL MEMORY AND RELATED WORK

We describe the underpinnings of human memory, how we facilitate and leverage it, and describe how our work builds upon and extends tools that examine searching/collecting a person's digital data/activities.

Human Memory and Contextual Cues

"It would be hard to overstate the importance of understanding the profound influence of environmental context on human memory." [5] Consider the difficulty in recalling a person's name when we encounter them in an unexpected situation. Yet by "placing" their face in the original context, we are able to more easily recall the individual's name and personal information about them [30]. Human memory functions by activating these contextual cues [5]. The probability that the human mind recalls a piece of information is a function of the strength of the association between the context used for recall, and the target information [5]. Therefore the richer the set of contextual cues available to an individual, the higher the probability of successful recall.

Consider the example of two groups of students being taught material in room A. If tested on the material, those students who take the exam in the same room (A) have better recall and perform better, than students who take the exam in a different room (B) [5,30]. In 1979, Smith demonstrated that recalling even the context of the room can improve performance on a recall test [31]. Additional research has shown that as we increase the number of contexts in which information is acquired (studying for a test in 5 rooms vs. 2 rooms), performance on recall tasks also improve. This performance increase is due to the influence of room context on recall, or the ability of individuals to remember information based on their environment. The greater the variety of environmental artifacts (e.g., room setup, music playing, etc.) the greater number of "links" or associations that human memory can leverage during recall [4,15].

In short, contextual cues aid human memory; users can remember events/items in their environment, even if they cannot immediately remember the item in question. By following this preverbal "trail" of cues, we remember. And in the computer age, people more often recall non-title information (e.g. associated events) [6]. As our digital lives become increasingly complex and dispersed [3], facilitating search based on contextual cues could be one way to improve information recall in our digital lives.

Data Aggregation and File Management

To create a rich set of cues to draw upon, computer systems must collect disparate sets of user data. One notable project in the domain of data aggregation and file management is MyLifeBits [14]. This groundbreaking work challenged researchers to explore computers that have the capability to store and archive all the data in which we encounter, perceive, and interact. MyLifeBits demonstrated that computers, simply through data collection, can provide a meaningful narrative to our digital and physical lives. A major contribution was developing a collection infrastructure to manage and store the diverse set of data MyLifeBits collected, while also providing a user interface (UI) to facilitate browsing of this data. However, this project did not explore the rich set of interactions needed for contextual search.

MyLifeBits was not the only foray into new techniques to store and represent personal data activity. Poyozo [26] sought to aggregate all of a user's web-activity into one central location. Lifestreams [13], TimeScape [28] and others [25,27,29] have explored displaying and organizing personal activity (both digital and real-world) chronologically, rather than the traditional directory-based organization method. DejaView takes [24] another temporal-based approach by treating desktop activity as a video that can be replayed. While all of these approaches advance personal file organization, they do not, nor is it the purpose of these systems to, address a user's need to search for items based on semantically unrelated contextual cues.

Other Search Techniques

Other research has examined the creation of robust techniques for searching through personal data. Haystack [23] implements a "fuzzy text" search allowing users to locate semantically related files/events. Balakrishnan [1] and others [2,22] examined search and organizing based on semantically identified tasks/activities. Similarly, Connections [32] allows a user to find semantically related files that were open at the same time. Horvitz identifies key landmarks in a user's history based on calendar activity [20]. Jensen has explored document provenance as a technique for tracking file relationships [21]. Most notably, a number of approaches provide additional related (e.g. semantic) meta-data to files or websites, that is not in the file/

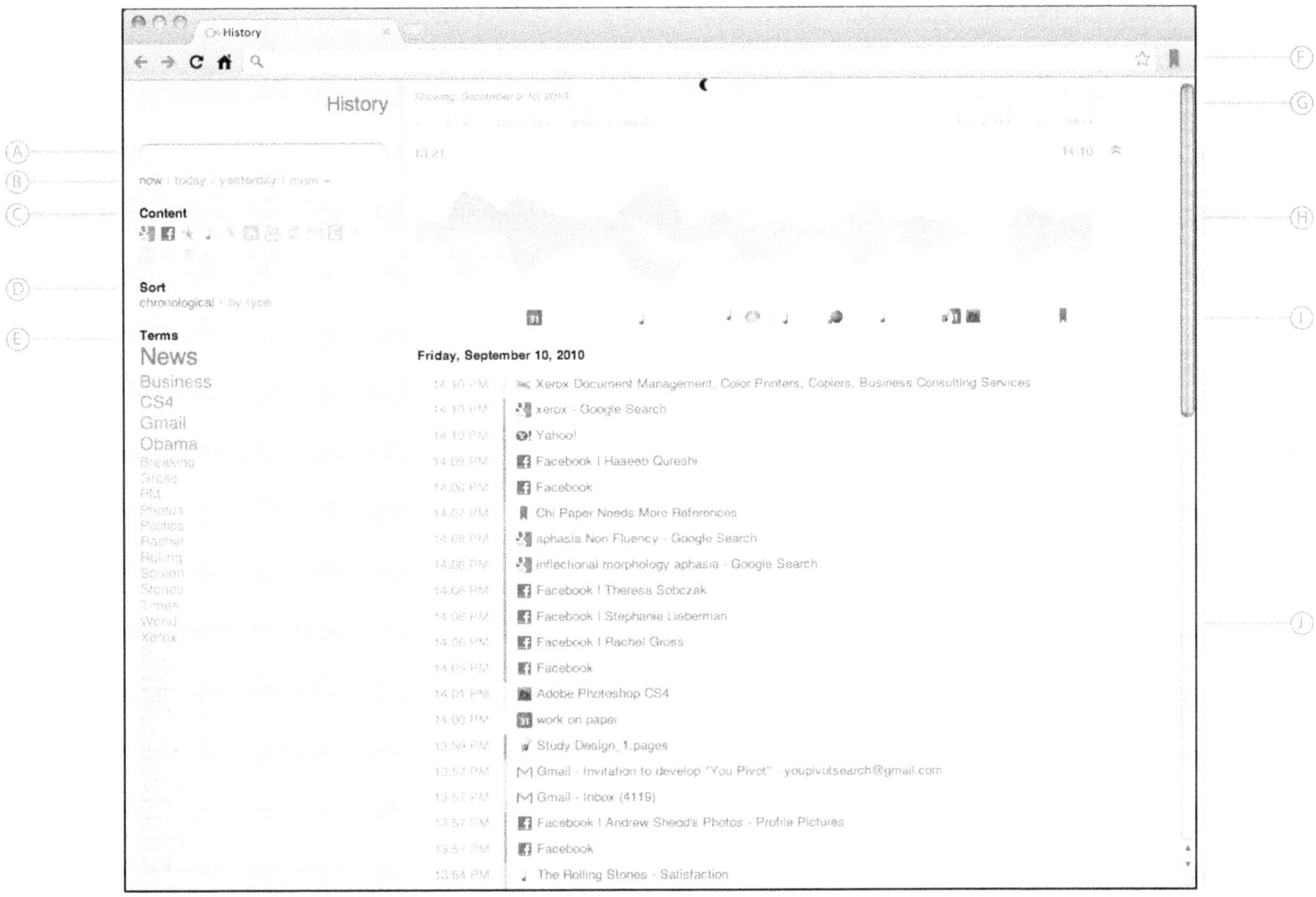

Figure 1. YouPivot Interface and Its Elements

*A) search box **B)** date selector **C)** source list represented by icons whose opacity is based on the frequency of their occurrence in the currently viewed time period **D)** sort history elements by type or chronologically **E)** key term list whose opacity and size is based on the frequency of their occurrence in history elements in the currently viewed time period **F)** create TimeMark button **G)** 24 hour visualization **H)** detailed Modeled Activity Visualization **I)** detailed NonModeled Activity Visualization **J)** History List*

website itself (Feldspar [9], Stuff I've Seen [12], CWH[34], Faceted Metadata [35], Phlat [11]). Thus, a user has the ability to search based on the visual structure of a web page, or execute queries such as, "who emailed me this file?"

These techniques provide new and innovative approaches to personal history but do not facilitate searches based on contextual cues to find semantically unrelated items in a user's activity history. We have developed YouPivot to support this need.

YOUPIVOT

Given the strong evidence from researchers in the cognitive sciences, we envision computer systems (desktop, portable and mobile) that augment and leverage the natural recall methods of the human mind. While personal data collection (e.g., MyLifeBits) and storage is not a modern problem, the creation of efficient and timely retrieval techniques and interfaces is central to leveraging this near flawless memory stores of computers [3].

To this end, we have developed **YouPivot**, a novel system that directly addresses and demonstrates how computers can implement contextual search. At the heart of our system is the ability for a user to shift their point of view to that of a file, website, or some other activity in their own digital history. From that perspective, they can see everything else that was active during that period of time. Because access to websites, songs, files, other digital activity and physical location is temporal (not just a split second moment, but with start and end times), a user can now think of search in terms of the context of a file rather than just a meta-data title, or keyword.

We illustrate the features and functionality of YouPivot through a scenario of Sarah, a graphic designer. Through her interactions with YouPivot, we will highlight the interface, interactions, and use cases therein. To illustrate the breadth of YouPivot's features, we present the following overly extensive scenario to cover multiple approaches to YouPivot search. In practice, users can apply any subset of the following search techniques at any time or in any order depending on their contextual cue. Providing users with

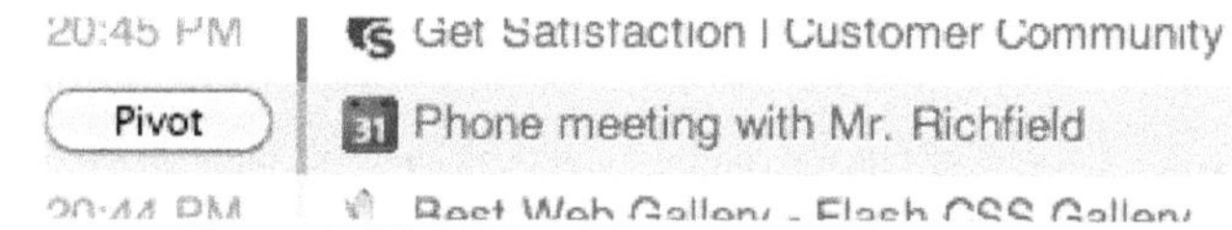

Figure 2. Highlighted Row in the History List

On hover, rows highlight and users are presented with a Pivot button that allows them to switch their context to see everything that was active while the selected item is open

flexibility in leveraging contextual cues is a key strength of YouPivot.

Sarah is developing a new website layout presentation for the WeSaySo Cooperation. As Sarah is working on her presentation for WeSaySo, she realizes that it would benefit with screen shots of websites on which she is basing her design. She first needs to find the websites.

Search and Pivoting

At first, Sarah attempts to recall the target website's name. She cannot remember the title, domain or even when she last saw the webpage. A traditional web history cannot aid her - there are far too many items and the titles in the history do not help her find the one she wants. The only relevant information Sarah recalls is that she last viewed the website around the same time of her last meeting with the CEO of WeSaySo, Mr. Richfield. Sarah launches her YouPivot interface (Figure 1), and searches for Mr. Richfield (Figure 1A). YouPivot returns a list of history/activity (replacing the content in Figure 1 section J) that match her semantic query. Finding the meeting she is thinking of, she hovers over the entry (Figure 2), which highlights the row and brings up a Pivot button. When Sarah presses the Pivot button, a new history list loads (in Figure 1J) and shows approximately 38 minutes of data. When Sarah entered her meeting with Mr. Richfield into her calendar, she listed it as being 30-minutes long. YouPivot used the calendar entry's lifespan as the pivot time period (plus a small buffer on each side for temporal context).

The updated history list now displays all of Sarah's activity that occurred during her meeting with Mr. Richfield. This includes any websites that were open on Sarah's computer, local files or applications open, Tweets sent, etc. If a website or file was opened *before* the visible time period, it would still appear in the history list so long as it was not closed prior to the start of the meeting. With a revised and shorter history list at hand, Sarah can now check to see if her target website is listed, and if found, open it.

Temporal Context: Before, During and After

A review of the history of activities during her meeting with Mr. Richfield reveals that the website in question was not actually open during the meeting, so Sarah thinks it must have been open a short while before or after the meeting. Running along the top of the YouPivot interface is a 24-hour visualization of Sarah's activity (Figure 1G). We

Figure 3. Selectable Region in 24 Hour View

*A) The selectable, resizable, draggable "in focus" region in the 24 hour view is denoted by a white box with a gray border **B**) red sympathetic highlighting in the 24 hour view indicating all the times when a particular website was open and how important*

used area graphs for this purpose as they have been proven to allow users to easily identify overall trends through visual analysis [10].

Much like visualizations of stock data, this 24-hour view has a draggable and resizable region (Figure 3A) representing the time range over which Sarah is seeing data. She can easily resize, drag and reposition the selected area to adjust the amount of data she sees in her history list.

Sarah notices that to the left and right of the selected region (representing the meeting with Mr. Richfield), there are approximately three hours of high activity. She resizes the selection area to encompass the active time before and after her meeting with Mr. Richfield.

Visualization of Activity

After quickly scanning the list of activity she has selected, the website Sarah is looking for still has not jumped out at her. The six hour time range selected has too much data. As she racks her brain, she remembers that at the time she saw this website, she was accessing many Gmail and Facebook

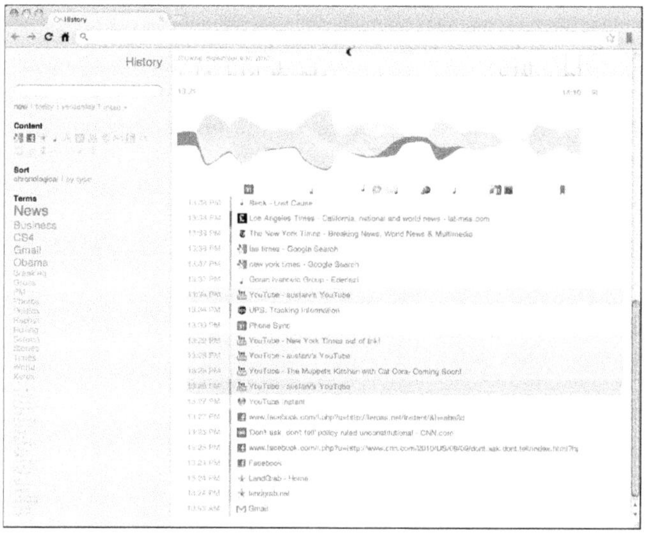

Figure 4. Sympathetic Highlighting

YouTube 13:28 is highlighted with other websites from YouTube having a lighter colored background. The visualization highlights the change in activity of the selected YouTube history element.

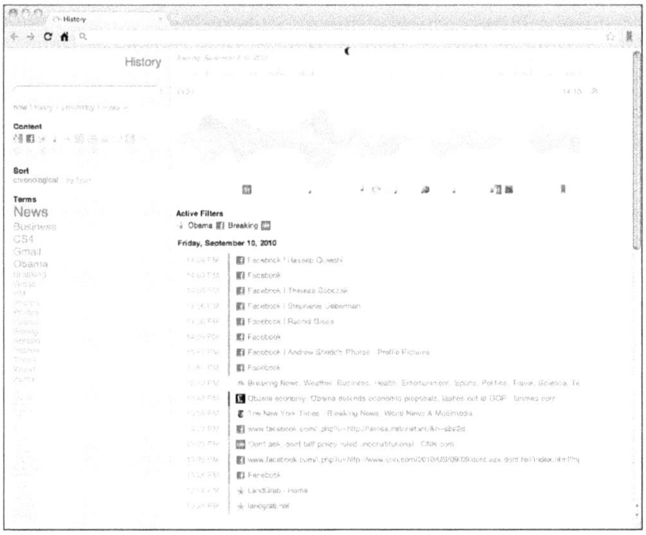

Figure 5. Live Filter List

When users filter on terms of sources, those filters appear above the history list. Clicking on filters them removes them

pages. Sarah needs a way to identify a context based on surrounding sources of activity.

Directly under the 24-hour visualization, is a more detailed representation[2] (Figure 1H) of the selected region in the 24-hour visualization. This visualization (Figure 1H) shows each history item's activity over time within a stream graph. We used a stream graph for this data, because users can more easily identify and quantify individual layers, offering a more enhanced and legible version of a stacked area graph [8,19,33]. [17] illustrated that visualizations of user activity over time can serve as recall cues, allowing a user to identify their own activity from only the visualizations. Each history item is a different color based on the dominant color in the icon associated with its source (the source icon). YouPivot extracts color, using K-means, from the favicon of websites, file icons of local files, or representative icon from other sources (e.g., music, calendar, etc.). This allows connections to be made between colors in the visualizations and history items.

Sarah can easily see a large swatch of blue (for Facebook's icon), and a large swatch of red (for Gmail's icon). When Sarah hovers over the blue area in the visualization, the individual layer highlights (Figure 4), while also highlighting the corresponding row in the history list (Figure 2). Further context is provided by highlighting that history element in the 24-hour visualization (Figure 3B). For a website like Facebook, the 24-hour highlight is a small blip. If Sarah highlights Gmail (whose webpage is open all day long), it highlights during multiple periods of time.

At this point, Sarah can resize and refine her viewable area using the 24-hour visualization, or can Pivot on one of the

Figure 6. TimeMark

When the TimeMark icon next to the omni box is clicked, users can enter their TimeMark descriptions

Facebook webpages she visited (discussed at the beginning of this chapter). Either way, Sarah refines her time frame, and examines her activity in the context of the time period when she was browsing Facebook and answering a lot of emails on Gmail. If her target website is listed, she can open it.

Ambient Context Display & Filtering

When Sarah refocuses to her new context, she sees almost a "sea of blue," with the amount of activity at Facebook. For websites which display new content with pageloads, or when users open many files at the same time (e.g., picture browsing), they generate a lot of activity that can muddle and cloud a history list.

Running along the left side of the YouPivot interface, Sarah browses a list of the source icons[3] (Figure 1C) and key terms extracted from the pages (Figure 1E) that represent all the activity during the displayed time period. Order and opacity of each source icon and key-word vary based on the occurrence count within the visible time-range. For the key-term list, size also changes.

By looking at her list of terms and domains, Sarah can quickly see that terms on *gardening* and *finance* are large, not opaque, and high on the term list. Sarah remembers, the websites she was looking for were from banking and gardening websites.

Sarah clicks on the terms in the list, dynamically applying them as filters on her data (source icons can also be used as filters). Now only activity that had the words gardening or finance are displayed (Figure 5). Sarah quickly opens all the websites she found in new tabs, and locates her desired website.

As she is opening her links, Sarah notices a Microsoft Word document that matched the filters in her list. She forgot that while doing research on website layouts, she had started a Word document with notes to herself. She

[2] The visualization represents change in website's utility to the users based on the modeling work of [16]. Discussion of website utility is covered in more detail later in the paper.

[3] Websites icons originate from their domain, local files from the application that open them (e.g. word documents), other sources (e.g. calendar or music) are grouped by source.

proceeds to open the document by clicking the element in the YouPivot history list.

TimeMarks

After she has the Word document and all her websites open, Sarah wants to make she she can find all these resources again. Bookmarking 20+ websites is a time consuming task, and she would need to organize them in a manner she could easily find again. In addition, there is no way to bookmark local files, or non-web activity.

Sarah leverages the YouPivot pivot architecture to resolve this problem and creates a TimeMark. **TimeMarks**, are a new mechanism to allow a user to decide that "this moment" is worth remembering. By clicking the TimeMark button (Figure 1F), the user is presented with a window asking them for a description about that moment (Figure 6). YouPivot then stores that TimeMark in their history, creating a custom contextual cue.

Sarah creates a TimeMark, and labels it "Website Layout Inspiration for WeSaySo." Now Sarah can easily locate all these files and websites again by browsing or search for this TimeMark (example in Figure 1 at time 14:07). She can then Pivot, and reclaim this movement from her past, and the full context that comes with them.

YOUPIVOT ARCHITECTURE

YouPivot natively supports a handful of data types (Twitter, LastFM, ICS calendar data, and web activity), in addition to logging user physical location, local file and application activity. We now discuss the more technical aspects of the YouPivot system, its client-server architecture, and implementation.

Interface

The YouPivot interface is constructed using web technology (CSS, HTML5, Javascript, Python) and the Protivis visualization toolkit [7]. It can therefore be accessed on any standards-compliant web browser, regardless of OS or make of computer.

The visualizations of user activity, within the YouPivot interface, represent the change in "importance" of individual tabs/websites in a web browser over time. YouPivot leveraged and adapted the work of Hailpern, et. al. [16] who created models that can quantitatively predict the utility of a given application on a scale from 1 (high utility) to 0 (low utility). According to [16], at a given point in time, users can have multiple applications, websites, and documents open, but only a small subset of them are considered "important." They termed this subset of important applications "high utility applications." Further, visualizations of changes in utility can provide a meaningful interface for recalling daily activity [17].

We likewise use visualizations of website utility to allow a user (e.g., Sarah) to easily identify trends in activity. As each website has more and less utility to the user, its thickness grows and shrinks. A website like Gmail (that is open all day) will have thick moments, when the user is actively responding to email, and thin moments when Gmail has not been recently used. The 24-hour visualization (Figure 1G) represents the sum of all importance values, easily highlighting lulls in activity (e.g., sleep, or lunch), while the detailed visualization (Figure 1H) allows users to find source specific trends in activity.

In a realistic representation of real world data, not all data types have, or will have, models of utility level. Therefore YouPivot appropriately handles activity that does not have a model. While activity that does not have utility values cannot be visualized in a stream graph, these events can act both as contextual cues and temporal landmarks in the user's daily activity (e.g., seeing activity relative to a phone call or a meeting). We therefore locate them under the visualization (Figure 1I) by placing their icon at the correct time. In this manner, the visualization shows the user when these contextual cues are accessed in relation to each other and in relation to the modeled user activity (Figure 1H).

Backend

Users' web activity is logged via the Chrome Extension and sent to the YouPivot server. The YouPivot server also pulls LastFM and Twitter data from the services' open APIs; and retrieves calendar data via public ICS files.

YouPivot's default storage system uses Google's AppEngine. This provides secure authentication through a user's Google account, as well as secure cloud-based storage, and a dynamic and fast architecture. This infrastructure does not store the user's activity (the actual files), rather it retains a record of the occurrence (and its associated metadata). This further improves performance speed, security, and privacy.

Multiple Device History

By using cloud-based storage, a user with multiple devices can send all her data to a central repository. Thus the user's contextual history can be far richer than one based on the history of a single device. YouPivot shows each user their history from all submitting devices.

Ubiquitous Access to Contextual Data

Because YouPivot is based in the Cloud, it can be accessed on any standards-compliant web browser (desktop or mobile). With the YouPivot storage system living in the cloud, a user's context effectively travels with them. Even when on a mobile device, a user can search their own history based on contextual cues. In addition, The YouPivot interface can be accessed via an extension in Chrome browser/ OS, that replaces the default Chrome history page with YouPivot.

Communication Protocol

Whenever a user would like to look at their history, they simply log into their Google account. This provides a secure method for viewing and interacting with their data. All data is transferred over secure HTTP (HTTPS).

To log data *into* YouPivot, applications send the data via secure web GET requests. When a user first signs up for YouPivot, they are assigned a unique alpha-numeric string. This string is used by any application wishing to log data into YouPivot, by passing the alpha-numeric sequence with a submission request.

Extensibility & 3rd party data support

While YouPivot natively can log multiple types of data, many users may wish to log additional data for contextual search or to act as additional contextual cues. While some of these data types may be more universal (e.g., local file access), others may be unique to the individual or their profession (e.g., actions in CAD for architects, or statistical tests run in STATA for epidemiologists).

Custom third-party logging software can easily be written to extend the data contained within YouPivot. Developers/users simply need to write the appropriate logging software that sends a secure GET request to the server with the data to be logged and the user's identifying alpha-numeric string. Thus, YouPivot is neither limited by the initial data feeds, nor access to the YouPivot source code.

We developed two such third-party desktop logging applications. The first logs a user's geographic locations using Mac OS X's CoreLocation; and the other logs a user's local file and application access.

PILOT STUDY

To show the benefit of YouPivot we conducted a preliminarily pilot study to test if YouPivot could support and improve recall given some contextual cues, compared to existing tools. This experiment should be viewed a first piece of a larger set of possible studies that could be conducted to evaluate the effectiveness and value of the contextual history. It was not the purpose of this experiment to prove the use of contextual cues to support recall. Rather, the purpose was to demonstrate that YouPivot could support and improve recall given some contextual cues, compared to existing methods.

Dependent and Independent Measures

This experiment followed a within subject design that manipulated one independent variable, the browser's history, which consisted of two levels:

1. The traditional browsing history user interface condition (referred to as *Traditional Condition*)
2. The contextual browsing history user interface condition (referred to as *Contextual Condition*)

The dependent variable measured was the time taken to identify a website given a contextual cue. It was hypothesized that participants would be able to identify website(s) quicker with YouPivot, than using the traditional browsing history user interface in Chrome. In addition to this measure, we also administered a questionnaire to understand user satisfaction and preference.

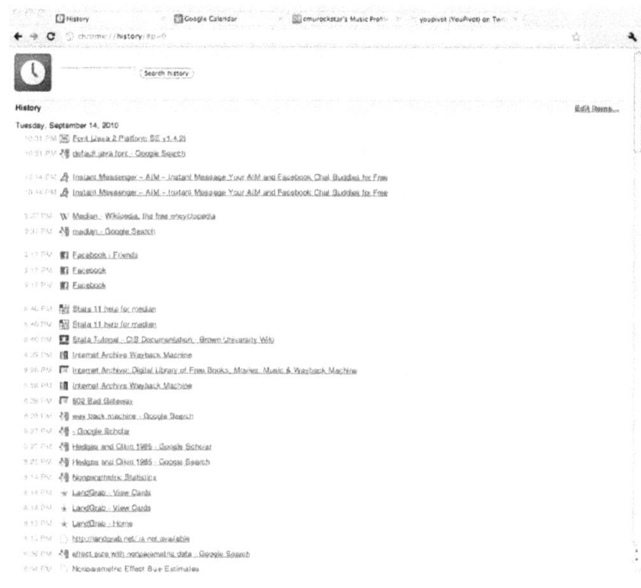

Figure 7. Traditional browsing history user interface set-up

Participants

Seven participants (four female and three male, aged 18 - 44) took part in this study. Participants were volunteers from a variety of backgrounds (e.g., research and development, consumer operations, finance and sales) at a large software corporation. Furthermore, all participants recruited were frequent users of the Internet, who used Chrome to browse the Internet. None of the participants had prior knowledge or experience with YouPivot. Participants received a $40 gift card for participating in the study.

Set-up

Participants used a 15" MacBook Pro laptop running the Chrome web browser. In the *Traditional Condition*, a Chrome web browser window was open with 4 open tabs (see Figure 7):

1. The Chrome browsing history - allowing the participants to see their browsing history.
2. Google Calendar - allowing the participant to see their appointments/meetings
3. LastFM - allowing users to see the music they listened to.
4. Twitter - allowing users to see the tweets they posted.

In the *Contextual Condition*, a Chrome web browser was open with a single tab displaying the YouPivot interface (see the YouPivot section for more information).

The data used in this experiment (i.e., browsing history, appointments/meetings, music and tweets) was not the participant's real data, but was rather constructed by the experimenters for the purpose of this experiment. While a fictitious dataset would not be appropriate for recall tasks, the goal of this study was to test if users, when given a specific cue, can find an experimental target. Therefore using a consistent dataset across participants is essential for an objective analysis of interface performance. We do envision a future study test the effectiveness of YouPivot in recall tasks (see future work).

Methods

Each participant was assigned to one of the two conditions. The assignment of conditions was counterbalanced across participants to mitigate ordering effects. The procedure in each condition is detailed bellow.

Participants were demonstrated either the traditional browsing history user interface, or the contextual browsing history interface, depending on the condition assigned to them. Then they were given time to explore it on their own. Following their self exploration of the interface, participants were asked to perform a 15 tasks. For example, some tasks used in the experiment were:

- What website were you viewing before you watched the New Kindle Pool Ad on YouTube?
- What websites were you viewing when listening to the song Jack's Mannequin - Dark Blue?
- What website did you view after writing your last tweet?

Tasks required participants to identify a website(s) viewed (if any) based on different types of contextual cues: websites viewed, music listened to, tweets posted, and appointments/meetings. In addition, different contexts of use were included: before; during; after. In addition to identifying the website(s) in the browsing history, each participant was given an additional three tasks that asked them to identify a website (or websites) that were not in the browsing history - for all tasks, the participant did not know if the website(s) existed or not. This was to address if the user interfaces could support a user identifying when something did not exist, and thereby reducing wasted time. Tasks were administered randomly between conditions and participants to mitigate ordering and learning effects.

It should be noted, that while the YouPivot interface could have been used to identify items other than websites (e.g., music playing when viewing a website, or files open while at a meeting), these questions were not asked. These types of queries are not answerable with traditional browsing history user interfaces, and would not be meaningful to compare YouPivot against something traditional history could not accomplish.

After completing all tasks for a condition, each participant was asked to complete a questionnaire about their experience with the browsing history user interface. Upon completing the questionnaire, the participant repeated the experiment in the other condition. As noted above, conditions were counterbalanced across participants to mitigate ordering effects. Once the participant had completed both questionnaires, the participant was asked to compete a third questionnaire about their experience with both browsing history user interfaces.

RESULTS & DISCUSSION

While the primary goal of this experiment was intended to elicit qualitative feedback, some quantitative measures were taken (e.g. time taken to identify website). Due to the scale of the study, these findings are preliminary.

For each participant, the total time to identify a website(s) for all tasks was calculated, thereby control for any potential systematic differences between tasks. Tasks with the traditional history had a mean time to identify a website(s) of 569.00 seconds ($\sigma = 61.07$) while contextual search had a mean time of 451.86 seconds ($\sigma = 96.77$). Statistical significant differences were found (Student's t-test) between the traditional history user interface condition and the contextual history user interface condition ($p = 0.01$). Suggesting that YouPivot performs faster than traditional history.

Participants were asked to rate their satisfaction with each of the browsing history user interfaces on a scale of 1 (very dissatisfied) to 5 (very satisfied). The mean satisfaction rating for the traditional browsing history user interface was 2.29 ($\sigma = 0.95$); and the mean satisfaction rating for the contextual browsing history user interface was 3.43 ($\sigma = 1.33$). The data was analyzed using a Wilcoxon signed rank test. Statistical significant differences were found between participants satisfaction ratings for the traditional history user interface condition and the contextual history user interface condition ($p = 0.03$). Therefore, participant were more satisfied with the contextual history user interface condition, compared to the traditional history user interface condition. Further, five out of the seven participants reported that they preferred the contextual browsing history user interface.

Qualitative feedback tended to focus on having all the information in one place. Participants also liked being able to search and sort their information in different ways;

> *It's really helpful to be able to sort based on website. It's also nice to be able to see what you were looking at when you were doing another activity. Searching by time period is also super useful. This one seemed more all-encompassing than traditional history.*

> *I like the different search functions with the contextual history which made it easier to search through the data.*

The two participants that preferred the traditional history user interface focused on speed and simplicity;

> *I prefer the simplified UI and lack of clutter, despite my hatred for the 'Older' link and inability to pivot on websites*

fast, simple, though the visualization [in the contextual history user interface] was cool!

This suggests that future tools must allow users to have a simplified view, and run as fast as traditional history systems built into web-browsers. Yet overall, our initial study suggests that participants were quicker identifying websites, more satisfied and preferred using the contextual browsing history user interface.

FUTURE WORK

YouPivot is not intended to be the perfect incarnation of contextual search. Rather, it is the first demonstration of how computer systems can leverage human memory to enhance recall and recovery of personal information, such as files access and other computer-related activity. As a result, there are many avenues of further exploration into contextual search.

Applications Beyond Personal Search

While YouPivot focuses on personal data/computer usage, contextual search may also be applicable to many other domains, augmenting the capacity of human memory. Consider a doctor who sees a patient who reminds her of another case she had. A contextual search-based computer system would allow the doctor to search on the context (symptoms) of other patients, thus discovering diagnoses, treatments and other relevant information. This could lead to faster diagnoses and treatment. Similarly, lawyers could leverage a context search tool based on cases, allowing them to search on client name, arguments made, resources cited, and then seeing the contexts in which they were applied.

Long Term Use

As the literature in cognitive psychology suggests, the more contextual cues users can leverage, the greater the ability for recall. While a controlled lab study that forces users to leverage their own contextual cues is difficult to design. Diary studies could provide a unique insight into the real world use of a contextual search tool like YouPivot. We propose testing YouPivot over a long period of time to see how contextual search can integrate into the daily functioning of users.

CONCLUSION

We leveraged theory in cognitive psychology to motivate how contextual cues can greatly improve the quality and speed of recall. We developed a novel system called YouPivot that addresses the need for personal file and activity search through digital history based on the context users remember. A core part of our work is the ability of users to Pivot, and change their point of view to that of a file, website, or some other activity in their own digital history. From that perspective, they can see everything else that was active during that period of time. As a result, a user can now think of search in terms of the context of the activity surrounding a file or website rather than just the title, keywords, or other meta-data.

We also introduce a new method of personal annotation called TimeMarks, which bookmarks a moment in time, allowing a user to access all activity that was ongoing at a particular moment rather than manually keep track of individual files, websites, and conventional bookmarks.

Results from a pilot study suggest that participants were quicker to identify websites, and preferred using YouPivot, compared to current history tools. This research demonstrates how principles of human memory can be applied to enhance the search of digital information.

ACKNOWLEDGMENTS

We would like to thank our reviewers, participants, family and friends for their support. In addition, we want to thank Jason Hong, Vicki Hanson, Shari Trewin, Fernanda Viégas, Craig Tashman and Tessa Lau who have been supportive of this research, and the project that led to it [18].

REFERENCES

1. Balakrishnan, A. D., Matthews, T., and Moran, T. P. Fitting an activity-centric system into an ecology of workplace tools. In CHI '10 (2010). ACM, Atlanta, Georgia, USA New York, NY, USA.
2. Bellotti, V. et al. Taskmaster: recasting email as task management. In CSCW Workshop: Redesigning Email for the 21st Century (2002). ACM, New Orleans, Louisiana.
3. Benjamin, A. S. Memory is more than just remembering: Strategic control of encoding, accessing memory, and making decisions. Psychology of Learning and Motivation, 48, 2007, 175-223.
4. Bilodeau, I. M. and Schlosberg, H. Similarity in stimulating conditions as a variable in retroactive inhibition. Journal of Experimental Psychology, 41(3), 1951, 199-204.
5. Bjork, R. A. and Richardson-Klavehn, A. On the puzzling relationship between environmental context and human memory. In Current issues in cognitive processes: The Tulane Flowerre Symposium on cognition. Hillsdale, NJ: Lawrence Erlbaum Associates (1989).
6. Blanc-Brude, T. and Scapin, D. L. What do people recall about their documents?: implications for desktop search tools. In Proc. of the international conference on Intelligent user interfaces (2007). ACM,
7. Bostock, M. and Heer, J. Protovis: A graphical toolkit for visualization. IEEE Transactions on Visualization and Computer Graphics, 2009, 1121-1128.
8. Byron, L. and Wattenberg, M. Stacked graphs-geometry & aesthetics. IEEE Transactions on Visualization and Computer Graphics, 2008, 1245–1252.
9. Chau, D. H., Myers, B., and Faulring, A. What to do when search fails: finding information by association. In Proc. CHI '08 Conference (2008). ACM, New York, NY.

10. Cleveland, W. S. and McGill, R. Graphical perception: Theory, experimentation, and application to the development of graphical methods. Journal of the American Statistical Association, 79(387), 1984, 531–554.

11. Cutrell, E. et al. Fast, flexible filtering with phlat. In Proc. CHI'06 (2006). ACM,

12. Dumais, S. et al. Stuff I've seen: a system for personal information retrieval and re-use. In Proc. International ACM SIGIR Conference (2003). ACM,

13. Freeman, E. and Gelernter, D. Lifestreams: a storage model for personal data. ACM SIGMOD Record, 25(1), 1996, 80-86.

14. Gemmell, J., Bell, G., and Lueder, R. MyLifeBits: a personal database for everything. Commun. ACM, 49(1), 2006, 88–95.

15. Greenspoon, J. and Ranyard, R. Stimulus conditions and retroactive inhibition. Journal of Experimental Psychology, 53(1), 1957, 55-59.

16. Hailpern, J. et al. The CLOTHO Project: Predicting Application Utility. In Designing Interactive Systems (2010). ACM, Aahus Denmark.

17. Hailpern, J., Karahalios, K., and Jitkoff, N. Clotho and Lachesis: Building, Optimizing and Validating Models to Predict Important Applications in a Real-World Context. Universit of Illinois Computer Science Research and Tech Reports, http://hdl.handle.net/2142/17091, September, 2010.

18. Hailpern, J. WISE: a wizard interface supporting enhanced usability. In Proceedings of ASSETS 2006 (2006). ACM, Portland, OR.

19. Havre, S., Hetzler, B., and Nowell, L. ThemeRiver: Visualizing theme changes over time. In InfoViz 2000 (2000). IEEE Computer Society,

20. Horvitz, E., Dumais, S., and Koch, P. Learning predictive models of memory landmarks. In Proceedings of the CogSci 2004: 26th Annual Meeting of the Cognitive Science Society (2004). Citeseer,

21. Jensen, C. et al. The life and times of files and information: a study of desktop provenance. In CHI '10 (2010). ACM, Atlanta, Georgia, USA New York, NY, USA.

22. Kaptelinin, V. UMEA: translating interaction histories into project contexts. In Proc. CHI '03 Conference (2003). ACM, New York, NY.

23. Karger, D. R. et al. Haystack: A customizable general-purpose information management tool for end users of semistructured data. In Proc. 2005 CIDR Conference (2005). Asilomar, CA.

24. Laadan, O. et al. Dejaview: a personal virtual computer recorder. ACM SIGOPS Operating Systems Review, 41(6), 2007, 292.

25. Lamming, M. and Flynn, M. Forget-me-not: Intimate computing in support of human memory. In Proc of the FRIEND 21: International Symposium on Next Generation Human Interfaces (1994). Tokyo, Japan.

26. Moore, B., Van Kleek, M., and Xu, C. Poyozo make life make sense. http://mypoyozo.com/, 2010.

27. Prante, T., Sauer, J., and Lotfy., S. Personal Experience Trace: Orienting Oneself in One's Activities and Experiences. In Extended Abstracts of SIGCHI CHI 2010 Conference (2010). ACM, Atlanta, GA.

28. Rekimoto, J. Time-machine computing: a time-centric approach for the information environment. In Proceedings of the 12th annual ACM symposium on User interface software and technology (1999). ACM,

29. Ringel, M. et al. Milestones in time: The value of landmarks in retrieving information from personal stores. In NTERACT'03 (2003). Ios Pr Inc, Zurich, Switzerland.

30. Smith, S. M. 1988 Environmental context-dependent memory. In Memory in context: Context in memory, G. M. Davies and D. M. Thomson,Eds New York: Wiley.

31. Smith, S. M. Remembering in and out of context. Journal of Experimental Psychology, 5(5), 1979, 460-471.

32. Soules, C. A. N. and Ganger, G. R. Connections: using context to enhance file search. In SOSP '05 (2005). ACM, Brighton, United Kingdom.

33. Viegas, F. B. et al. Manyeyes: a site for visualization at internet scale. IEEE Transactions on Visualization and Computer Graphics, 13(6), 2007, 1121.

34. Won, S. S., Jin, J., and Hong, J. I. Contextual web history: using visual and contextual cues to improve web browser history. In Proc. SIGCHI CHI '09 Conference (2009). ACM, New York, NY.

35. Yee, K. P. et al. Faceted metadata for image search and browsing. In Proc. of the CHI'03 (2003). ACM, Fort Lauderdale, FL.

An Examination of Two Delivery Modes for Interactive Search System Experiments: Remote and Laboratory

Diane Kelly
University of North Carolina
Chapel Hill, NC USA
dianek@email.unc.edu

Karl Gyllstrom
Katholieke Universiteit Leuven
Leuven, Belgium
karl.gyllstrom@cs.kuleuven.be

ABSTRACT

We compare two delivery modes for interactive search system (ISS) experiments: remote and laboratory. Our study was completed by two groups of subjects from the same population. The first group completed the study remotely and the second group completed the study in the laboratory. We compare differences in participants, participation behaviors, search behaviors and evaluation behaviors. Overall, for most measures no significant differences were found, but there were some notable differences. Greater variance was observed in time taken and number of documents opened and saved by remote subjects. Lab subjects provided more favorable responses to exit questionnaire items and reported significantly higher satisfaction. Lab subjects also provided significantly longer responses to open questions, while remote subjects provided more null responses. These results suggest that many behaviors do not change significantly according to study mode and that results from remote ISS experiments are similar to those from laboratory experiments.

Author Keywords

Study mode, remote usability study, online experiment, interactive search system evaluation.

ACM Classification Keywords

H.5.2 [**Information Interfaces and Presentation**]: User Interfaces – *Evaluation/methodology, Theory and methods.*

General Terms

Experimentation

INTRODUCTION

The laboratory was once the primary location where researchers studied interactive search systems (ISS). Today, researchers are increasingly using different delivery modes to gather data from human subjects. Researchers use services such as Amazon's Mechanical Turk [3] to gather relevance assessments and survey data [1, 2, 24], online games such as ESP [11] to generate training data for classifiers [30], and remote usability testing to interact with geographically dispersed clients [4, 7, 12, 13, 19].

One of the benefits of conducting a laboratory study is that the researcher has increased control over the study situation. Many sources of variance can be identified and controlled, and the researcher can ensure that a standard protocol is followed and that subjects are not engaged in extracurricular activities. When studies are conducted remotely, the researcher is no longer able to fully monitor the subject and cannot even be certain that there is a human subject. It is also difficult to ensure that subjects follow the experimental protocol. However, remote studies allows researchers to study a wider range of more diverse users and researchers do not always have to be present when subjects are participating.

While new evaluation models are starting to emerge, little empirical work has been conducted comparing differences in the quality of data generated using each model. In this paper, we review different study modes that have been used in ISS evaluations and in other related research areas. We present results of an ISS evaluation experiment that was completed by two sets of subjects from the same population: the first set completed the study remotely and the second completed the study in the laboratory. We compare differences in the behaviors and performances of subjects in each set, as well as their responses to open-ended questionnaire items.

BACKGROUND

While there are many different kinds of studies that comprise the interactive information search literature, many studies are evaluations of one kind or another. Scriven [26] defines an evaluation as the systematic determination of the quality or value of something. The 'something' can be indexing, retrieval or ranking algorithms, user interfaces or interactive techniques. Although an experiment is just one way a researcher might conduct an evaluation, this is generally accepted as the standard method. The initial innovations in information retrieval (IR) evaluation were rooted in a systems-centered perspective and continue with the work of the Text Retrieval Conference (TREC) [23, 32].

CHI 2011, May 7–12, 2011, Vancouver, BC, Canada.

While users were involved in some early IR evaluations, the Interactive Track at TREC established one of the most used laboratory models for ISS evaluations with users [10]; this model is the focus of our study.

The basic components of ISS evaluation are described in [15, 27, 28]. There are generally three methods used to conduct an ISS evaluation: experiment, usability test and/or log analysis. ISS evaluation experiments typically involve both a baseline and experimental system, with the two differing in only a small, but systematic way. Two important characteristics of true experiments are that there are at least two things being compared on a set of outcome measures, and that some control takes place. For instance, a researcher might control which system a subject uses and/or in what order. Control is critical in experiments to ensure that the results are caused by variations in the experimental stimulus rather than spurious factors.

Usability tests are also a common type of evaluation method in ISS. Traditional usability tests are usually conducted with a single version of a system, with the goal of identifying potential usability problems. The researcher might control some aspects of a usability test. For example, the researcher might control the collection users search, the tasks users are asked to complete, the order in which users complete tasks and the order in which instruments are administered. However, the researcher is not able to demonstrate how much better users perform or how their behaviors and interactions have changed since there is no point of comparison. Usability studies with single systems are characterized as pre-experimental [8], although this does not diminish their importance. They are very useful for identifying usability problems and improving systems.

A final method used to conduct evaluations, especially those of real-world systems, is log analysis. In early IR research, transaction logging was a popular method for evaluating operational systems in natural environments and has continued to be an important source of data for those managing operational information systems, such as search engine companies and digital libraries. While logging is part of many ISS evaluations, it can also be the sole source of data in studies where the researcher does not interact with users. This includes situations where a researcher passively observes user activity and situations where a researcher pushes alternative interfaces or search results to select users (c.f., 5, 21). This latter type of study can be considered an Internet experiment, assuming users have been randomly selected to receive the alternative version.

Alternative Models of Evaluation

One alternative to traditional models of evaluation is remote evaluation where participants are geographically and temporally removed from the researcher. Participants might be known or unknown to the researcher and the evaluations might occur synchronously (where the researcher is separated from the subject spatially, but not temporally) or asynchronously (where the researcher is separated from the subject spatially and temporally) [13].

Remote Usability Studies

A number of studies have been published that evaluate remote usability tests [4, 7, 12, 13, 19, 25]. Hartson, et al. [13] defined remote evaluation as "usability evaluation wherein the evaluator, performing observation and analysis, is separated in space and/or time from the user" (p. 228). Hartson, et al. identified advantages and disadvantages of several types of remote evaluations and presented results of case studies exploring two remote modes, including teleconferencing. McFadden, et al. [19] provided an overview of remote usability evaluation with a focus on collaborative software for facilitating synchronous evaluation. More recently, Andreasen, et al. [4] provided a classification of literature describing different types of remote usability tests and found that the majority have focused on synchronous usability evaluations using audio communication and video capture. Andreasen, et al. also conducted an empirical evaluation of several usability test modes, including the classic laboratory, remote synchronous and remote asynchronous, and found that the results from the remote synchronous were similar to those of the classic laboratory mode. Finally, Bruun, et al. [7] compared three methods for remote synchronous usability testing (self-reported critical incidents, forum-based reporting and diary reporting) with a traditional laboratory-based think-aloud protocol and found that in the remote conditions subjects only identified about half the problems of those in the traditional condition, although the cost of administering these studies was much less.

Many of the studies investigating the remote usability test mode have found results favorable to the remote synchronous mode, but results regarding the asynchronous mode have been mixed. Furthermore, it is important to point out that these studies focus on usability testing, not experiments where the researcher is interested in isolating the effects of test variables and attempts to control the experience of subjects. Many of the methods investigated in these studies involve usability inspections and cognitive walkthroughs (usually via think-aloud), which are important types of usability tests, but not as relevant to ISS evaluation experiments. Furthermore, none of these studies focused on experimental information search systems.

Toms, et al. [29] proposed WiRE, a prototype system for conducting ISS experiments online. While WiRE was designed to support remote ISS experiments, Toms, et al. evaluated it within a university computer laboratory, not remotely, so the findings are preliminary. However, they found that many subjects desired personal contact and were unhappy with the amount of instructional reading. Toms, et al. observe that ISS experiments are often quite complex and require much instruction and researchers conducting remote evaluations need to consider this as an important part of study design.

Online Psychology Experiments

Psychologists have been conducting experiments on the Web for quite some time [6]. In 1995, the *Web's Experimental Psychology Lab* was established and the first two experiments were run from this lab in September of the same year [6, 22]. Birnbaum [6] provides an extensive discussion of the benefits and limitations of conducting psychology experiments on the Web. Some of the positive aspects of online experiments include access to a broader range of more diverse participants, the ability to do targeted recruitment and recruitment of larger samples at lower costs. Birnbaum also discusses positive aspects related to subjects being studied in their natural environments including less artificiality, subject familiarity and comfort, and no travel time. Finally, Birnbaum discusses the potential lessening of demand characteristics and experimenter effects. Demand characteristics occur when subjects form an impression of the purpose of the study and then behave accordingly. This includes behaving in a way that is aligned with how the subject thinks the experimenter wants them to behave, but can also include situations where the subject tries to sabotage an experiment by purposely acting in a way that is counter to what they think is being studied. Experimenter effects are caused by the experimenter; for example, the experimenter might provide subtle clues about how the subject should act.

Birnbaum [6] also discusses limitations of Web experiments, many of which are related to lack of control. These issues include cheating and fraud, multiple submissions, fake data, collaboration with others and imitation of treatments. Another difficulty is ensuring that subjects experience the study in a similar way. Subjects' potential lack of understanding of what they are meant to be doing, interruptions, consulting other sources for help (e.g., dictionaries), multi-tasking, and environmental distractions all pose potential problems. Self-selection bias, attrition and technical variance can also be issues. Birnbaum's work shows that a remote study mode can introduce a host of issues that simultaneously threaten and enhance the validity and reliability of the study results. He also cites empirical studies investigating the impact of the remote mode on psychological experiments which have found few differences. However, given that ISS evaluation experiments are typically more complex than psychology experiments, it is an outstanding question if these results generalize to this domain.

Crowdsourcing

One popular alternative approach that leverages online participation is the use of crowdsourcing through systems such as Amazon's Mechanical Turk (AMT) [3] and online games, such as ESP [11]. The most common rationale given for using this approach is to increase participation and reduce costs. Many recent studies in IR have used crowdsourcing and/or AMT [c.f., 1, 14] and several studies in HCI have investigated participant demographics and data quality issues, which are two major concerns [9, 17, 24]. Ross, et al. [24] found that a large number of AMTurkers are young, well-educated Indian workers. Ross, et al. raises some compelling questions about labor issues, the fairness of compensation and worker exploitation. Quality is also an issue. Kittur, et al. [17] examined the quality of AMT workers' responses to a task where workers were asked to evaluate the quality of select Wikipedia articles. They found widespread data integrity issues with 58% of subjects' evaluation ratings being flagged as potentially invalid and 48% of free-text responses being considered uninformative. Downs, et al. [9] used screening questions in an AMT study and found that 39% of respondents either did not answer the questions correctly or skipped them.

RESEARCH QUESTIONS

In this study, we focus on ISS evaluation experiments and remote study methods. We do not consider alternative sampling methods such as crowdsourcing, but focus instead on subjects from the same population who participate in the same study either remotely or in-person. The basic research question we seek to address is: "To what extent do subjects' participation behaviors, search behaviors and evaluation behaviors differ according to study mode?" Regardless of the outcome of the study, the results should be useful since they will provide some evidence about whether remote ISS evaluation experiments produce different results from laboratory ISS evaluation experiments.

METHOD

The basic design of the study had two set of subjects participating in the same evaluation of an experimental ISS system, but in two different modes: remote and laboratory. Subjects in the remote mode completed the study online at the time and location of their choice, while subjects in the laboratory mode came into the laboratory and completed the study with an experimenter. This latter mode represents the baseline mode since this is one of the standard ways in which ISS evaluation experiments are conducted.

Experimental Design

Subjects used a query suggestion interface and a term suggestion interface (Figure 1). From these interfaces, subjects could view documents they had saved, their past queries and the current search topic. The query suggestion interface presented clickable query suggestion which, when clicked, would replace the current query and generated a new list of search results. The term suggestion interface presented a list of clickable terms which subjects could click to add to their queries. The interfaces were piloted to ensure that they could be operated without instruction.

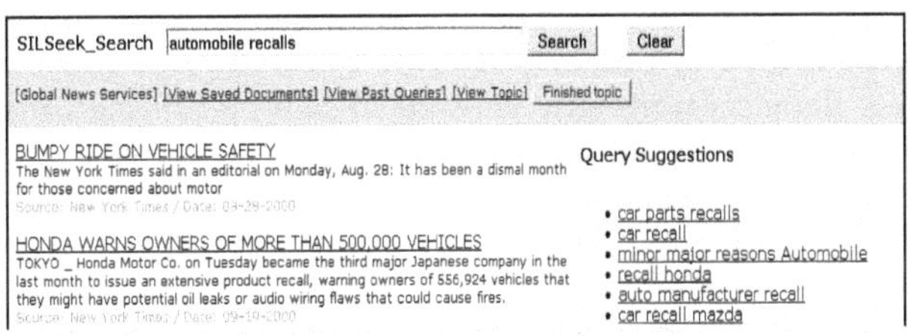

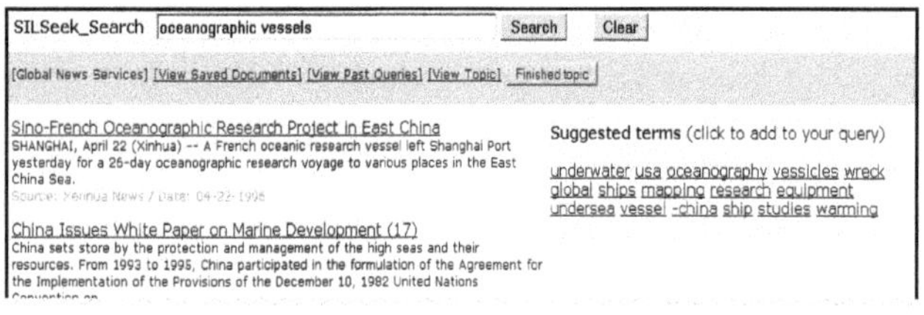

Figure 1. Interfaces for Query and Term Suggestion Systems

The Lemur [18] toolkit was used for indexing and retrieval, with KL-divergence as the principle retrieval method. The suggestion features were based on a combination of semantic clustering and pseudo-relevance feedback. A more detailed description of the system is available in [16] (while this core system has been used in two previous studies, data reported in this paper are from a unique study). The system ran on a local Web server and only 3 subjects were able to login at any one time. A TREC test collection [31] containing over one million newspaper articles was used.

Twenty test topics from the TREC collection were used; each subject completed four of these. The search task was open-ended and exploratory with the basic objective to find as many relevant documents as possible. This task type was chosen because it represents the classic search task used in ISS experiments and many ISS experiments use TREC collections. An example search task is presented in Figure 2. Topics were rotated and counter-balanced across subjects and systems. Each subject completed two topics with each system. System order was counterbalanced.

Title: automobile recalls

Identify documents that discuss the reasons for automobile recalls. A relevant document will specify major or minor reasons for automobile recalls by car manufacturers. Documents that discuss truck recalls are not relevant.

Figure 2. Example Search Task

Recruitment

Subjects were recruited by sending an email solicitation to all undergraduates at our university. The solicitation announced the different studies and let students self-select into the remote or laboratory modes although no indication was given that this was the variable under study. Rather, the invitation introduced "a series of studies investigating search systems." The other difference articulated in the solicitation was a difference in time commitment and compensation. The remote study was estimated to take about 1 hour and the compensation $10.00, while the other studies were estimated to take about 1.5 hours and the compensation $20.00. The differences in compensation were justified by the differences in effort to participate and time. Subjects were only allowed to sign-up for one of the studies. While self-selection can present problems with respect to equivalence of groups, we felt it would be fairer to allow students to choose.

Instruments and Protocol

Subjects participating remotely were sent a URL, username and password via email to access the online search system. In this email, subjects were also provided additional instructions which asked them to complete the study on a standard size machine (e.g., laptop or desktop) and not on a mobile device such as an iPhone. Subjects were also told that they should complete the study in one uninterrupted session, close all other applications on their computers and not multi-task. Subjects were also asked not to answer their cell phones and/or read/send text messages. It was emphasized to subjects that following these instructions would help maintain the integrity of the research and that the researchers were relying on them. Of course, ultimately, researchers have no control over how subjects experience remote studies (which is perhaps one of the biggest threats to validity), so there is no guarantee that any of these requests were honored in our study.

These instructions were also presented to remote subjects as soon as they logged in. Additional guidelines were provided about how subjects should complete the study, reiterating what was presented in the earlier email. Subjects were asked to only use a single browser window and were informed that we would log their keystrokes. Subjects were told they would have up to 15 minutes to search for each topic and they should search as they normally would although they should only use the experimental system. We informed them that the system would keep track of the time for them and alert them when 15 minutes had passed. Finally, subjects were told that the system would automatically log them off after a 10 minute period of inactivity and they would not be able to resume the study later. It is noted that crafting and piloting these instructions took quite a bit of time. The importance of clear, well-written instructions and the time it takes to create them should not be underestimated by researchers (this was one of the main findings of Toms, et al. [29]).

For subjects in the lab mode, a researcher was present to greet the subject, provide an overview of the study, answer any questions during the session and distribute compensation. The researcher sat at a workstation near subjects while they completed the study.

When subjects logged into the system, they completed a consent form, demographic questionnaire and search experience questionnaire. Before subjects started searching, the computer displayed a Pre-Search Questionnaire. After completing the questionnaires, subjects clicked a button to begin searching. Subjects had up to 15 minutes to find and save documents relevant to the information described in the topic. After completing four search topics, subjects completed the Post-Search and Exit Questionnaires. Subjects' interactions with the system were logged. Several pilot tests were conducted to ensure that the instructions, tasks, interfaces and questionnaires were understandable to those in both conditions.

At the end of the study, lab subjects were compensated, while remote subjects were given information about how to collect compensation. An online calendar displayed times when compensation could be collected and a unique identification number which was required to collect the compensation. A researcher was available about 5 hours per day for several weeks during and after the study and subjects could also schedule a time to collect compensation.

RESULTS

Participation Behaviors

Sixty-nine subjects completed the study: 39 remotely and 30 in person. Four remote subjects started the study, but did not finish it. Data from these subjects are not included in the analysis. There were 8 remote subjects who completed the study, but did not collect compensation.

The majority of remote subjects were female (n=32; males=7), while those in the lab condition were more evenly split (females=17; males=13). The differences in these distributions was significant [$\chi^2(1, 69)=5.308$, $p=0.021$]. Subjects' majors were classified into five categories: science, social science, humanities, professional and undecided. There were no differences in these classes across the two sets of subjects [$\chi^2(4, 69)=3.77$, $p=0.437$]. Remote subjects' ages (M=20.28, SD=1.36) were similar to lab subjects' (M=21.17, SD=4.48); these differences were not significant [$t(67)=-1.17$, $p=0.247$].

The self-reported search experience of remote and lab subjects were also compared. Subjects responded to a question asking them to describe their overall ability to search and locate information on the Web. Subjects responded using a 5-point scale where higher values indicated greater experience. The mean search experience for remote subjects was 5.51 (SD=0.91), while the mean for lab subjects was 5.40 (SD=0.97). This difference was not significant [$t(67)=0.50$, $p=0.622$].

Time taken to complete the study was also compared across the two groups (Table 1). Remote subjects took less time (M=33.13; Med.=31.08) than lab subjects (M=38.50; Med.=36.72). Despite these differences, a t-test showed this difference was not significant [$t(66)=-1.28$, $p=0.205$]. There was greater variance in the times for remote subjects, but a Levene's test for homogeneity of variance showed the variances did not significantly differ [$F(1,66)=1.12$, $p=0.295$].

	Mean	SD	Med.	Max.	Min.	Ran.
Remote	33.13	18.31	31.08	68.60	5.23	63.37
Lab	38.50	15.56	36.72	66.77	15.12	51.65

Table 1. Description of time spent completing study for remote and lab subjects (SD=standard deviation; Med.=median; Max.=maximum; Min.=minimum; Ran.=range).

Search Behavior

Several search behaviors were compared: number of queries issued, number of documents opened and saved, and use of the suggestion features. Tables 2 and 3 display the descriptive statistics for these measures. These values are at the study level: for example, remote subjects issued an average of 19.23 queries for four search topics (or about 5 queries per topic). For all three measures, the mean and median values for remote subjects were less than those for lab subjects. Remote subjects issued fewer queries, opened fewer documents and saved fewer documents. T-tests showed no significant differences [Queries: $t(67)=-0.795$, $p=0.429$; Opened: $t(67)=-0.525$, $p=0.602$; Saved: $t(67)=-0.188$, $p=0.852$].

	Mean	SD	Med.	Max.	Min.	Ran.
Queries RS	19.23	12.58	16.00	60	4	56
LS	21.70	13.04	18.50	52	4	48
Opened RS	39.36	30.93	29.00	164	4	160
LS	43.07	26.50	35.00	111	11	100
Saved RS	31.10	26.74	24.00	152	0	152
LS	32.17	17.98	25.00	77	10	67

Table 2. Description of search behaviors (RS=remote subjects; LS=lab subjects; SD=standard deviation; Med.=median; Max.=maximum; Min.=minimum; Ran.=range).

There was also more variability in remote subjects' search behaviors. For each measure, the standard deviations and ranges for remote subjects were greater. In particular, the range of saved documents for remote subjects was over twice as large as the range for lab subjects, although the mean values were similar. Levene's tests were conducted to evaluate if the variances different significantly. These tests showed no significant differences [Queries: $F(1, 67)=0.053$, $p=0.818$; Opened: $F(1, 67)=0.213$, $p=0.646$; Saved: $F(1, 67)=0.770$, $p=0.383$].

Subjects' uses of the suggestion features were also investigated. Because there was great variability in use of the features (i.e., some subjects used the features a lot, while many did not use them), a simple 3-level measure of usage was taken, where 0 indicated no use, 1 indicated at least one use of one feature (query or term) and 2 indicated at least one use of each feature. Overall, there was little difference in use of the suggestion features between groups as shown in Table 3. These differences were not significant [$\chi^2(2, 69)=4.07$, $p=0.131$].

Usage:	0	1	2
Remote	16 (41%)	18 (46%)	5 (13%)
Lab	16 (53%)	7 (23%)	7 (23%)

Table 3. Use of suggestion features (0=no use; 1=at least one use of one feature; 2=at least one use of both features).

We used the baseline relevance assessments that accompanied the test collection to evaluate the relevance of the documents saved by subjects. Table 4 shows these results. Lab subjects saved on average more relevant documents (22.45 vs. 19.36) and fewer non relevant (7.66 vs. 8.85). These subjects also saved more documents without baseline relevance assessments (5.62 vs. 4.90). T-tests were used to evaluate the differences between all of these values, but none were significant.

	Remote	Lab	t-tests
Relevant	19.36 (14.35)	22.45 (11.83)	$t(66)=-0.94$, $p=0.348$
Non relevant	8.85 (11.65)	7.66 (4.92)	$t(66)=0.52$, $p=0.607$
No assessment	4.90 (7.68)	5.62 (6.17)	$t(66)=-0.42$, $p=0.678$

Table 4. Mean (SD) number of relevant, non relevant and unassessed documents saved.

Evaluation Behavior

Pre-Search Questionnaire

The Pre-Search Questionnaire contained five questions that asked subjects to indicate their knowledge of the topic (knowledge), how often they have searched for information about the topic in the past (search experience), how difficult they expect searching will be (expected difficulty), how relevant the topic is to their lives (relevance) and how interested they are to learn more about the topic (interest). Subjects responded using 5-point scales; higher values indicated more of whatever the item asks (e.g., more knowledge, more difficult, more relevance).

Subjects' mean responses are displayed in Table 5. For all questions but one (difficulty), the mean responses of lab subjects were slightly higher than those of remote subjects. These differences were not significant except for the item about interest in learning more about the topic.

	Remote	Lab	t-tests
Knowledge	1.97 (1.06)	2.13 (1.04)	$t(274)=-1.30$, $p=0.196$
Search Experience	1.29 (0.60)	1.37 (0.65)	$t(274)=-1.06$, $p=0.291$
Expected Difficulty	3.06 (1.09)	3.03 (1.08)	$t(274)=0.18$, $p=0.854$
Relevance	1.83 (1.00)	1.98 (1.05)	$t(274)=-1.14$, $p=0.255$
Interest	2.37 (1.08)	2.68 (1.12)	$t(274)=-2.39$, $p=0.018$

Table 5. Mean (SD) responses to Pre-Search Questionnaire.

Post-Search Questionnaire

The Post-Search questionnaire contained three questions that asked subjects to describe their experience searching for information about each topic: difficulty finding relevant documents (difficulty), personal skill and ability to find relevant documents (personal ability) and system's abilities to find relevant documents (system ability). These items were assessed with 5-point scales. For difficulty, higher values indicated more difficulty and for personal and system ability, higher values indicated better ability. This questionnaire also contained three items related to the experience of flow during each search: how enjoyable the search experience was (enjoyable), level of engagement (engagement) and ease of concentration (concentration). These items were assessed with 5-point scales, with higher values representing greater enjoyment, more engagement and greater ease concentrating. Subjects' mean responses to these items are displayed in Table 6. For many items, there were virtually no differences between the means. There were some small differences for three items: remote subjects indicated that it was slightly more difficult to find relevant documents and rated the system's abilities slightly better than lab subjects. Lab subjects, on the other hand, indicated that their experiences were slightly more enjoyable. None of these differences were significant.

	Remote	Lab	t-tests
Difficulty	2.86 (0.59)	2.67 (0.50)	$t(67)=1.37$, $p=0.177$
Personal Ability	3.19 (0.74)	3.13 (0.74)	$t(67)=0.33$, $p=0.774$
System Ability	3.05 (0.89)	2.97 (0.66)	$t(67)=0.44$, $p=0.664$
Enjoyable	2.61 (0.84)	2.80 (0.70)	$t(67)=-.097$, $p=0.336$
Engagement	2.76 (0.95)	2.74 (0.89)	$t(67)=0.66$, $p=0.948$
Concentration	3.22 (1.05)	3.23 (0.91)	$t(67)=-.003$, $p=0.998$

Table 6. Mean (SD) responses to Post-Search Questionnaire.

Exit Questionnaire

After completing all four searches, subjects completed an Exit Questionnaire. The Exit Questionnaire consisted of three major types of items: 11 statements asked subjects to rate the two systems along several dimensions using 5-point scales, where 1=strongly disagree and 5=strongly agree; 3 questions that asked subjects to indicate their preferences by selecting a system; and five open-response questions.

Ratings

Subjects responded to 9 items that described various properties of the system and the suggestion features (see Table 7) and 2 items to elicit their overall ratings of system effectiveness and satisfaction (*Overall, the system was effective in helping me complete the search tasks* and *Overall, I am satisfied with my performance*).

A factor analysis was conducted to reduce the 9 items to a smaller number of factors. The two statements assessing overall perceptions were not included in the factor analysis because they asked subjects to evaluate their total experiences and were likely a function of the individual nine items as well as other aspects of the user experience that were not evaluated by any item. Bartlett's Test of Sphericity was used to evaluate the linearity assumption [20]. This test showed that the relationship among the 9 items was linear [$\chi^2(36)=451.56$, $p<0.001$]. The Kaiser-Meyer-Olkin Measure of Sampling Adequacy (KMO) was used to determine if the data would factor well. The KMO was 0.800 which was more than adequate [20].

A principal components analysis with varimax rotation was used to extract the factors. The 9 items loaded on two factors after three iterations. The factor loadings are displayed in Table 7. The factors had eigenvalues of 3.63

and 1.80 and explained 40% and 20% of the variance, respectively. The solution was fairly strong and easy to interpret. Seven items loaded on Factor 1; these items asked subjects about the suggestions. Two items loaded on Factor 2; these items focused on system performance. Subjects' responses for each factor were averaged for use in subsequent analysis.

	Factor	
Questionnaire Item	**1**	**2**
The suggestions made things I wanted to accomplish easier to do.	**0.595**	-0.138
The suggestions helped me modify my queries.	**-0.633**	0.247
The suggestions helped me think of new approaches to searching.	**0.779**	-0.093
The suggestions helped me better understand the topics.	**0.823**	0.194
The suggestions were easy to use.	**-0.676**	0.417
It was hard to understand how the suggestions related to the search topics.	**0.653**	-0.285
The quality of the suggestions was poor.	**0.824**	0.100
It was hard to find relevant documents with the system.	-0.170	**0.810**
It was hard to understand why some documents were retrieved in response to my queries.	0.025	**0.867**

Table 7. Results of Principal Component Analysis of 9 items from Exit Questionnaire.

A general linear model (GLM) was used to evaluate the main and interaction effects of study mode and system type (query vs. term suggestion) on Factors 1 and 2, and the two items assessing the overall experience. Of primary concern was the main effect for study mode, but an evaluation of the effect of system type and the interaction between study mode and system type were also conducted. Subjects' mean responses to the four items are reported in Table 8. The data show that remote subjects consistently provided higher ratings than lab subjects. However, the GLM showed no significant main effects for system type or the interaction between study mode and system type. These results are not presented here because of space limitations. The GLM showed a main effect for study mode for overall satisfaction [$F(1, 138)=5.90$, $p=0.016$], with remote subjects indicating less satisfaction (M=3.00) than lab subjects (M=3.43). The non-significant results for study mode and the other outcome measures were: [$F(1, 138)=1.79$, $p=0.184$], [$F(1, 138)=0.25$, $p=0.618$] and [$F(1, 138)=1.44$, $p=0.233$].

Study Mode	Factor 1	Factor 2	Overall System Effectiveness	Overall Satisfaction
Remote	2.74 (0.53)	3.08 (0.98)	2.91 (1.12)	3.00 (1.02)
Lab	2.85 (0.49)	3.16 (0.90)	3.15 (1.21)	3.43 (1.05)

Table 8. Subjects' mean (SD) responses to Exit Questionnaire items according to study mode.

Preferences

Subjects responded to three preference questions (Table 9). The first asked subjects to indicate which were more useful to them while they searched: suggested terms or suggested queries (useful). The second asked subjects to indicate which of the two systems was easier to operate and integrate into their searching (operate). The last asked subjects to indicate which system they preferred overall (overall). Two remote subjects and one lab subject did not respond to these questions.

Useful	**N**	**Terms**	**Queries**	**Equally useful**	**Equally useless**
Remote	37	12 (32%)	7 (19%)	4 (11%)	14 (38%)
Lab	29	6 (21%)	12 (41%)	1 (3%)	10 (35%)
Operate		**Terms**	**Queries**		
Remote	37	23 (62%)	12 (38%)		
Lab	29	14 (41%)	17 (59%)		
Overall		**Terms**	**Queries**	**Neither**	
Remote	37	16 (43%)	8 (22%)	13 (35%)	
Lab	29	9 (31%)	12 (41%)	8 (28%)	

Table 9. Subjects' responses to preference questions.

For the first question, more remote subjects selected the system that presented suggested terms as their preference (32% or n=12), while more lab subjects selected the system that presented suggested queries (41% or n=12). It can also be seen that many subjects indicated that the two systems were equally useless (Remote: n=14; Lab: n=10, with a slightly larger percentage of remote subjects selecting this option (39%) than lab subjects (34%)). These differences were not significant [$\chi^2(3, 66)=4.89$, $p=0.180$].

For the second question, 62% of the remote subjects preferred the term suggestion system (n=23), while only 43% of the lab subjects preferred the term suggestion system (n=12). The majority of lab subjects preferred the query suggestion system (59% or n=17). Again, as with the previous preference question, these differences were not significant [$\chi^2(1, 66)=2.82$, $p=0.093$].

For the last question, the results were similar to those for the other questions. A larger majority of remote subjects selected the term suggestion system (n=16; 43%) while a larger majority of lab subjects selected the query suggestion system (n=12; 41%). More remote subjects indicated no preference (13; 35%) than lab subjects (n=8; 27%). As with the differences for the other preferences, these were not significant [$\chi^2(2, 66)=3.03$, $p=0.220$].

Responses to Open Questions

Five open response questions were asked on the Exit Questionnaire. Three of the open response questions followed the preference questions and asked subjects to explain their preferences, while the other two questions asked subjects to describe the major differences between the two systems and additional situations for which term and/or query suggestion would be useful. Subjects' responses were analyzed in two ways: first by taking a raw count of the length of the responses (total number of terms) and second by determining the quality of the responses. The latter approach includes evaluating the number of empty and redundant responses, and response completeness.

The lengths of subjects' responses are displayed in Table 10. For all 5 responses, the average lengths of remote subjects' responses were shorter. All of these differences were significant except for the first item.

	Remote	Lab	t-tests
Differences	17.79 (15.61)	25.03 (18.78)	$t(67)=-1.75$, $p=0.085$
Pref: Useful	19.08 (11.78)	24.90 (13.23)	$t(67)=-1.93$, $p=0.058$
Pref: Operate	15.31 (11.73)	21.50 (13.49)	$t(67)=-2.04$, $p=0.046$
Pref: Overall	12.41 (9.75)	20.13 (17.72)	$t(67)=-2.15$, $p=0.037$
Situations	17.87 (16.73)	30.03 (23.76)	$t(67)=-2.49$, $p=0.015$

Table 10. Mean (SD) lengths of responses to open questions.

To examine the quality of the responses, each of the 345 responses (69*5) was first clustered according to question and then labeled with a random number to ensure that the researchers did not know from which study mode the response originated. The responses were then coded into 10 classes which are displayed in Table 11 along with their descriptions. Completeness was divided into three levels to reflect thoroughness since there was quite a bit of variability in subjects' completed responses. Completeness 1 was when the subject provided a single fragment or statement (e.g., "they were helpful"), Completeness 2 was when the statement included an explanation or rationale (e.g., "they were helpful because they gave me ideas for queries") and Completeness 3 was when the subject provided multiple statements and explanations. Redundant responses only included those where the subject typed responses such as "see above."

The distributions of subjects' responses into the various categories are displayed in Table 12. Statistical tests were not used to compare these distributions since the matrix is too sparse to allow for reliable results. There were not many differences in number of complete, incomplete, incomprehensible and redundant responses. However, some notable differences are shaded within the no response and not addressed categories. There were many more remote subjects providing these types of responses. A large number of subjects in both groups did not address the preference operate question, which suggests that the question itself may have been problematic.

C1	Complete 1	Response considered complete in that subject addressed question. The numbers correspond to the relative thoroughness of the response, with 1=less thorough.
C2	Complete 2	
C3	Complete 3	
IN	Incomplete	Response only partially addresses question.
I	Incompre-hensible	Response does not make sense.
N	None	No response provided or consists of "no" or "none."
R	Redundant	Response was redundant, e.g., "see above," "same as above"
NA	Not Addressed	Response was provided, but did not address the question asked.
DU	Didn't Use	Subject indicated they did not use feature.

Table 11. Codes used to analyze responses to open questions.

	Codes								
	C1	C2	C3	IN	I	N	R	NA	DU
Differences RS	3	9	3	4	3	9	0	8	0
LS	9	8	5	1	2	2	0	3	0
Pref: Useful RS	10	16	1	0	2	2	0	1	7
LS	7	11	2	2	1	1	2	2	2
Pref: Operate RS	3	2	0	0	5	3	2	19	5
LS	4	6	0	0	4	1	2	12	1
Pref: Overall RS	10	12	0	1	2	5	4	4	1
LS	9	6	2	1	3	2	3	3	1
Situations RS	5	10	2	6	3	11	0	2	0
LS	4	8	5	5	2	3	0	3	0

Table 12. Classification of open responses into quality codes (see Table 11 for description of codes) (RS=remote subjects; LS=lab subjects).

DISCUSSION & CONCLUSION

This study investigated the extent to which subjects' participation behaviors, search behaviors and evaluation behaviors differed according to study mode. While several studies have compared the results of online, remote study modes in the context of usability testing and psychology experiments, no study has investigated this in the context of ISS evaluation experiments. We used two groups of subjects from the same population: one group completed the study remotely and the other completed the study in the laboratory. Overall, we found few significant differences between groups, which indicate that at least for the measures used in this study the remote study mode produced similar results to the laboratory mode. However, there were some interesting differences and some important study limitations that are worth discussing.

With respect to differences in participant demographics, participants were similar on most variables, but there were significantly more females in the remote mode than in the lab mode. Overall, we expected more females since our university has a larger female population; however, one would expect differences between groups to be about the same. Students self-selected into groups and there was a limit to how many students could enroll in each group, so it might be that more females were online when the initial solicitation circulated. Remote subjects reported higher search experience than lab subjects; given that they completed the study online and the study was about online searching, this may have heightened their sense of search efficacy, or it may be a demand characteristic where they felt they should report higher search expertise since they elected to complete the study in this mode.

With respect to search behaviors, it was found that there was no significant difference in the amount of time taken by subjects to complete the study, although there was much greater variance in the times of remote subjects. Lab subjects opened and saved more documents. As with time, there were also greater variances observed for remote subjects for number of documents opened and saved. It may be the case that subjects on the low and high ends of the distribution were not working as faithfully and carefully, but we found no significant differences in the numbers of relevant and non-relevant documents saved, or those without relevance assessments between groups, so subjects on the high end of the distribution may have just been working harder. Those on the low end may have decided to take less time, but they were at least working diligently in those few minutes. Although there were no significant differences in the quality of the documents saved, there was huge variance in the average number of non-relevant documents saved by remote subjects, so there may in fact be some subjects who blindly saved documents. There are a number of different ways that we might further analyze this data on a much finer level of granularity (e.g., by looking at individual subjects and the correlation between time and performance) which we plan to do in the future. Finally, with respect to search behaviors, it was found that 59% of the remote subjects used at least one of the experimental features once, while only 46% of the lab subjects did. One might expect the laboratory setting to 'demand' the subject to use the experimental features with greater frequency, but this did not happen in this study.

Subjects' evaluation behaviors were examined in a number of ways. First, it was found that lab subjects had more favorable responses than remote subjects for all but one item on the Pre-Search Questionnaire and for one item (interest in learning more about the topic), this difference was significant. This was also the case for the Exit Questionnaire items: Lab subjects' mean responses were consistently higher than remote subjects', and significantly so for a question asking about overall satisfaction. One possible explanation is demand characteristics: because of the immediacy of the experimenter, lab subjects may have been more eager to be positive. Alternatively, given Toms, et al.'s results [29], these subjects may have genuinely enjoyed the experience more because of the interaction with the researcher. Subjects who come into the lab have more investment in the experience and therefore might show greater interest, engagement and/or enjoyment.

The results regarding preferences were puzzling, especially since the log data showed that many subjects did not use the experimental features. For the first two preference questions, more remote subjects selected the term suggestion system than the query suggestion system, while the finding was reverse for lab subjects. Again, we might consider if these differences are a characteristic of demand, where lab subjects 'guess' that the query suggestion system was the 'new' one and select accordingly to please the researcher; however, it was the case that a greater percentage of remote subjects indicated that the two systems were equally useful (perhaps the most diplomatic response). It is also the case that many subjects in both groups indicated that both systems were equally useless.

With respect to subjects' responses to the open-ended questions, we found that lab subjects provided significantly longer responses, but we did not detect any major differences in quality. However, our quality assessment (completeness) was quite coarse and looking more closely at these responses might reveal differences. We also observed that more remote subjects provided null responses. One important limitation of remote, asynchronous study designs is that exit interviewing is not possible. The absence of this type of qualitative data which can provide context to subjects' responses is an important consideration. Finally, a few remote subjects made mean-spirited responses. Lack of face-to-face contact with the researcher likely encouraged some subjects to say things that they might not say otherwise. We should note that by 'mean-spirited' we do not mean responses criticizing the system – there were plenty of those made by both groups – but rather, uncivil comments.

In conclusion, this study demonstrated that there were no major differences in participation behaviors, search behaviors and evaluation behaviors of subjects from the same population who completed the same ISS evaluation experiment remotely or in the laboratory. Although many ISS researchers have discussed remote testing (and probably also tried it out), there have not been any studies to our knowledge that have evaluated this study mode empirically. While most of the results of this study were not significant, this does not diminish the usefulness of the study since even these null findings provide evidence which researchers can consider when planning remote ISS experiments. Future research should continue to investigate alternative methods of ISS experiments; as new methods emerge it is important that they are thoroughly evaluated before being adopted.

Before closing, it is important to acknowledge study limitations and the possibility of Type II errors. We choose to closely replicate the classic model of ISS evaluation (including the protocol, tasks and outcome measures); this choice may have prevented us from identifying differences in study mode. For example, the task we studied (find as many relevant documents as possible in a given time period) may have been too easy, which in turn, may have resulted in subjects giving inflated system ratings (essentially exhibiting a ceiling effect and preventing us from detecting differences). Instructing subjects to be more selective, giving them more focused and/or more difficult tasks or placing greater restrictions on search time may have produced different results. We also did not include any additional measures beyond the ones used in the classic ISS evaluation model. Additional measures may have allowed greater insight into subjects' behaviors and experiences. Future studies might include a more extensive exit questionnaire which elicits feedback from subjects about, for instance, their motivation, level of effort, engagement and/or enjoyment.

ACKNOWLEDGMENTS
We thank Earl Bailey for helping with data collection and the reviewers for their useful suggestions.

REFERENCES
1. Alonso, O. & Mizzaro, S. Relevance critieria for e-commerce: A crowdsourcing-based experimental analysis. In *Proc. SIGIR 2009*, ACM (2009), 760-761.
2. Alonso, O., Rose, D. E., & Stewart, B. Crowdsourcing for relevance evaluation. *SIGIR Forum, 42*(2) (2008).
3. Amazon Mechanical Turk. https://www.mturk.com/
4. Andreasen, M. S., Nielsen, H. V., Schrøder, S. O., & Stage, J. What happened to remote usability testing? An empirical study of three methods. In *Proc. CHI 2007,* ACM Press, (2007), 1405-1414.
5. Anick, P. Using terminological feedback for web search refinement: A log based study. In *Proc. SIGIR 2003,* ACM Press, 2003, 88-95.
6. Birnbaum, M. H. *Psychological Experiments on the Internet.* London, UK: Academic Press, 2000.
7. Bruun, A., Gull, P., Hofmeister, L. & Stage, J. Let your users do the testing: A comparison of three remote asynchronous usability testing methods. In *Proc. CHI 2009*, ACM Press (2009), 1619-1628.
8. Campbell, D. T. & Stanley, J. C. *Experimental and quasi-experimental designs for research.* Chicago: Rand McNally, 1966.
9. Downs, J. S., Holbrook, M. B., Sheng, S., & Cranor, L. F. Are your participants gaming the system? Screening Mechanical Turk workers. In *Proc. CHI 2010*, ACM Press (2010), 2399-2402.
10. Dumais, S. T. & Belkin, N. J. The TREC Interactive Tracks: Putting the user into search. In *TREC: Experiment and Evaluation in Information Retrieval* (pp. 123-153), Cambridge: MIT Press, 2005.
11. ESP Online Game. http://www.gwap.com/gwap/gamesPreview/espgame/.
12. Hammontree, M., Weiler, M. & Nayak, N. Remote usability testing. *Interactions 1*(3) (1994), 21-25.
13. Hartson, H. R., Castillo, J.C., Kelso, J., & Neale, W. C. Remote evaluation: The network as an extension of the usability laboratory. In *Proc. of CHI 1996*, ACM Press (1996), 228-235.
14. Kazai, G., Milic-Frayling, N. & Costello, J. Towards methods for the collective gathering and quality control of relevance assessments. In *Proc. SIGIR 2009*, ACM Press (2009), 452-459.
15. Kelly, D. Methods for evaluating interactive information retrieval systems with users. *Foundations & Trends in Information Retrieval, 3*(1-2) (2009), 1-224.
16. Kelly, D., Gyllstrom, K., & Bailey, E. (2009). A comparison of term and query suggestion features for interactive searching. In *Proc. of SIGIR 2009*, ACM Press (2009), 371-378.
17. Kittur, A., Chi, E. H., & Suh, B. Crowdsourcing user studies with Mechanical Turk. In *Proc. CHI 2008*, ACM Press (2008), 453-456.
18. Lemur IR Toolkit. http://www.lemurproject.org/.
19. McFadden, E., Hager, D. R., Elie, C. J., & Blackwell, J. M. Remote usability evaluation: Overview and case studies. *International Journal of Human-Computer Interaction, 14*(3-4) (2002), 489-502.
20. Mulaik, S. A. *Foundations of factor analysis*. Boca Raton, FL: CRC Press, 1972.
21. Radlinski, F., Kurup, M. & Joachims, T. (2008). How does clickthrough data reflect retrieval quality? In *Proc. of CIKM 2008*, ACM Press (2008), 43-52.
22. Reips, U.-D. *The Web's Experimental Psychology Lab.* http://iscience.deusto.es/archive/ulf/Lab/WebExpPsyLab.html, 1995.
23. Robertson, S. E. On the history of evaluation in IR. *Journal of Information Science, 34*(4) (2008), 439-456.
24. Ross, J., Irani, L., Silberman, M. S., Saldivar, A., & Tomlinson, B. Who are the crowdworkers? Shifting demographics in Mechanical Turk. In *Proc. CHI 2010*, ACM Press (2010), 2863-2872.
25. Scholtz, J. Adaptation of traditional usability testing method for remote testing. In *Proc. HICSS 2001*, 1-8.
26. Scriven, M. *Evaluation thesaurus (4th edition).* Newbury Park, CA: Sage Publications, 1991.
27. Spärck-Jones, K. *Information Retrieval Experiment.* London, UK: Butterworths & Co. Ltd, 1981.
28. Tague-Sutcliffe, J. M. The pragmatics of information retrieval experimentation, revisted. *Information Processing & Management, 28*(4) (1992), 467-490.
29. Toms, E. G., Freund, L. & Li, C. W*ISS*E: The Web interactive information retrieval experimentation system prototype. *Information Processing & Management, 40*(5) (2004), 655-675.
30. von Ahn, L. Games with a purpose. *IEEE Computer Magazine*, June 2006, 96-98.
31. Voorhees, E. M. Overview of the TREC 2005 Robust Retrieval Track. *Proc. of TREC-14* (2006).
32. Voorhees, E. M. & Harman, D. K. *TREC: Experiment and Evaluation in Information Retrieval*, Cambridge, MA: MIT Press (2005).

Review Spotlight: A User Interface for Summarizing User-generated Reviews Using Adjective-Noun Word Pairs

Koji Yatani, Michael Novati, Andrew Trusty, and Khai N. Truong
Department of Computer Science
University of Toronto
Toronto, ON M5S 3G4, Canada
{koji, atrusty, khai}@dgp.toronto.edu, michael@novati.ca

ABSTRACT
Many people read online reviews written by other users to learn more about a product or venue. However, the overwhelming amount of user-generated reviews and variance in length, detail and quality across the reviews make it difficult to glean useful information. In this paper, we present the iterative design of our system, called Review Spotlight. It provides a brief overview of reviews using adjective-noun word pairs, and allows the user to quickly explore the reviews in greater detail. Through a laboratory user study which required participants to perform decision making tasks, we showed that participants could form detailed impressions about restaurants and decide between two options significantly faster with Review Spotlight than with traditional review webpages.

Author Keywords
Summarization, user interface, user-generated reviews, natural language processing, word pairs

ACM Classification Keywords
H5.2. Information interfaces and presentation (e.g., HCI): User Interfaces.

General Terms
Human Factors

INTRODUCTION

Online review websites offer users a wealth of perspectives about products that can be purchased or locations that can be visited (which we will refer to as reviewed entities). However, the number of reviews for any given entity often extends well beyond what users can read quickly. User-generated reviews also vary greatly in length, detail and focus in comparison to ones written by professional editors. These issues make it difficult for users to quickly and easily glean useful details about the entity, as described in the following way by a participant in our study:

The problem with all these reviews is they put a lot of really useless information there. For example, this guy included a dialogue he had with a waitress... [That] makes it difficult when you actually try to quickly find something.

There are several ways to provide a brief overview of user-generated reviews. For example, often reviewers are asked to rate their overall impression (usually from 1 to 5) of an entity. Although this rating gives the reader a quick understanding of how much the reviewer liked or disliked the entity, it does not offer information about why that rating was given. Several websites also allow readers to rate the usefulness of posted reviews, and order reviews by this usefulness rating. These features allow the user to browse reviews in a way that differs from needing to read them all. However, browsing in this manner may result in the user missing information that she could find to be important to her (*e.g.*, comments in recent reviews).

In this paper, we describe our iterative design of Review Spotlight—a system which provides a quick overview of user-generated reviews. Figure 1 shows the concept of Review Spotlight. The system displays a list of adjective and noun word pairs that appeared most frequently in the review text. It also performs a sentiment analysis on the extracted word pairs and uses different font colors to represent the level of positivity or negativity of each word

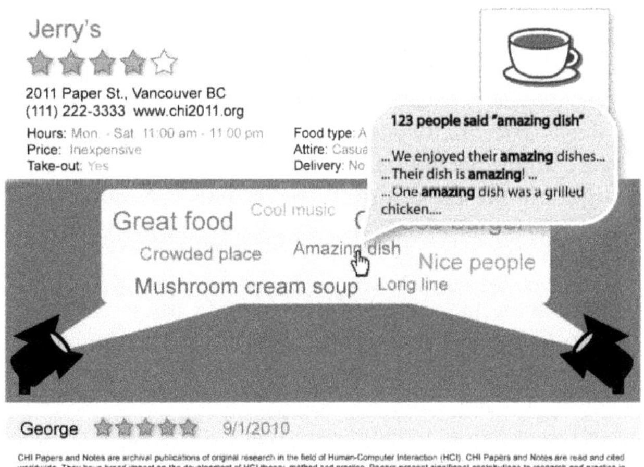

Figure 1. The Review Spotlight concept. Review Spotlight can be integrated into any review webpage, and shows some of the most frequently-mentioned word pairs in the reviews.

pair. Review Spotlight also allows the user to click on a word pair to see additional contexts in which it is used in the original review text. The user interface does not arrange word pairs in a specific order so that the user can serendipitously acquire information even from word pairs with small fonts. Through our user study, we found that while using Review Spotlight, participants could form detailed impressions about reviewed entities and decide between two options significantly faster than when reading traditional review webpages.

RELATED WORK

The Review Spotlight interface is based on a tag cloud, a visualization using a set of words (or "tags"). The size and color of each tag are associated with the importance or relevance in the original text. The use of natural language processing can improve the efficiency and accuracy of extracting the tags that best represent the original document. However, this work primarily examines the user requirements for an interface that displays a summary of user-generated reviews, and not the process of efficiency of generating tag cloud. Thus, we mainly review research focused on interfaces for review summarization and the effects of a tag cloud on different tasks.

User Interfaces for User Review Summarization

Although user review summarization has been investigated well in computational linguistics [11], user interfaces employing it have not been studied extensively. One approach for user review summarization is to collect opinions on different features in an entity (*e.g.*, food or service in a restaurant review). Liu *et al.* developed a system to visualize how many positive or negative reviews were posted about features of an entity using bar graphs, but the system was not evaluated from the user interface perspective [17]. Carenini *et al.* used a Treemap visualization to show the information extracted from user-generated reviews organized in a tree structure based on the features [3]. However, their user study showed that the participants were often confused by the Treemap visualization, and preferred text-based summarization. They also developed a system similar to Liu *et al.*'s work [17], but they specifically designed it to allow the user to compare multiple entities [4]. Their user interface shows the distribution of positive and negative reviews along different features. However, they did not formally study the efficacy of their user interface.

A computational linguistics method often used for summarizing user-generated reviews is a sentiment analysis, which determines the semantic orientation of a given text. Turney [24] and Pong *et al.* [18] applied a sentiment analysis technique to analyze review text. Both systems used machine learning techniques to identify the semantic orientation of the phrases extracted using n-gram methods.

There are several systems that have applied sentiment analysis for tag cloud visualization. Dave *et al.* built a system to extract the tags from product reviews and display a sentiment score calculated based on those tags [6]. Lee *et al.* developed a system in which the user can manually add tags to an entity, and can rate whether the added tag contains a positive or negative sentiment [16]; the rated positivity/negativity of the tag is visualized using the font. Ganesan *et al.* incorporated emoticons into a tag cloud visualizing eBay seller feedback [9]. For example, a smiley face is automatically added to a tag that their system recognized as a positive tag. Although the effect of word sentiment visualization has not been studied in detail previously, we believe that incorporating a sentiment orientation into a tag cloud visualization could be useful for the user to quickly understand how positively or negatively the entity is reviewed.

Effects of a Tag Cloud on Different Tasks

Rivadeneira *et al.* categorized four user tasks for which a tag cloud could be useful [19]: *searching* (finding a particular term, often as a means to navigate to more detailed information about the term); *browsing* (casually exploring information without seeking any specific term); *impression formation* (building an impression about the entity that the tag cloud visualizes); and *recognizing* (providing additional information about the entity to support the user in identifying the entity she is seeking).

Several studies have been conducted on *searching* and *browsing*. In their study of the usefulness of tag clouds in information-seeking tasks, Sinclair *et al.* [22] concluded that such an interface is more useful for *browsing* tasks than for *searching* tasks. Kuo *et al.* demonstrated how a tag cloud displaying the search results of biomedical text at PubMed helped the user find the correct answers to simple medical questions [14]. They also found that a tag cloud was better for answering general questions (*e.g.*, whether a certain factor is transcriptive), but was not helpful for finding specific details (*e.g.*, the names of the genes involved in a particular biological process).

However, there still exist open research questions related to understanding how a tag cloud visualization could be useful and should be designed for beyond *searching* tasks. Viégas and Wattenberg [25] discussed the use of tag cloud visualizations for analytical purposes. These purposes are closely related to *impression formation* and *recognizing*, but the effect and design of a tag cloud visualization for these purposes have not been deeply studied. Although Review Spotlight can support *searching* or *browsing* for user-generated reviews, we are most interested in how Review Spotlight can support *impression formation*.

Effects of Tag Cloud Visual Features

The visual features of a tag cloud can impact the user's performance on *searching* tasks. For example, Rivadeneira *et al.* studied how many words people could recall after reading a tag cloud with different visual properties [19]. They discovered that words in larger font and those located at the upper-left corner of the tag cloud were easier to recall.

Bateman *et al.* examined the effect of nine visual properties of a tag for the task of determining the most important words based on visual appearance [2]. Their study revealed that the font size and font weight had strong effects on the word selection—but not the color.

The visual organization of a tag cloud also impacts user performance on *searching* tasks. Halvey and Keane studied the effect of three different layouts (a tag cloud, a linear list with vertical and horizontal alignments) with random and alphabetical ordering on *searching* tasks [10]. They found that the alphabetical ordering contributed to faster user performance than the random ordering in all layouts. In Schrammel *et al.*'s study of how a tag cloud word order affected the identification of specific tags and tags related to a particular topic [21], they showed that an alphabetical ordering was significantly faster than the other three ordering methods for searching for a specific tag. However, they did not find a significant difference in performance time when searching for tags related to a particular topic. These studies did not go beyond *searching* tasks whereas our focus in this study also includes *impression formation* tasks.

FORMATIVE STUDY

We conducted a formative study to learn about the types of information that users typically focus on and glean about a reviewed entity, and specific challenges they have with the user interface for user generated-reviews. We recruited 8 normal computer users who regularly did web browsing (4 males and 4 females between the ages of 20 and 50). They were likely to visit review websites in the past, but, like other normal computer users, it is unlikely that they frequently posted online reviews. In the formative study, we asked them to perform a think aloud as they read webpages with user-generated reviews (referred as "review pages" throughout the rest of this paper) to glean information about venues. We used four different review pages (two restaurant reviews from Yelp.com and two hotel reviews from TripAdvisor.com), each with more than 30 reviews at the time of the study. We instructed the participants to read the reviews as they normally would and to stop reading when they had drawn conclusions about that location. We then asked them to describe their impressions of the location as they would do for a friend who is considering visiting it. The entire session was audio-recorded and transcribed for analysis.

We found two important user behaviors from this study:

- **Formulating and adjusting an impression**: We found that the majority of the participants formed an initial impression about a location using the overall rating, the rating distribution, and photographs at the top of the page. The participants would then skim through the reviews to identify comments frequently repeated about the location by different reviewers, often noting the frequency with which those comments were expressed. Participants tended to notice and read reviews with remarks that differed from the commonly-expressed opinion, and then adjust their impression if necessary.
- **Verbalizing impressions with short phrases**: The participants also tended to verbalize their impression with short phrases, with descriptive information about the venue (*e.g.*, "Asian food") or subjective opinion statements (*e.g.*, "good steak").

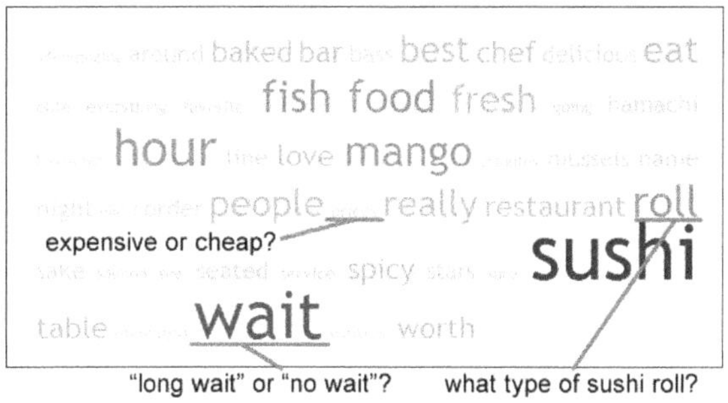

Figure 2. A tag cloud of user-generated reviews using single words. It is possible to learn the general information about the restaurant, but details are hard to overview.

These findings offer several design implications. First, our system should help the user gain a quick overview of the comments frequently mentioned about an entity. It is important for this overview to represent how many times reviewers commented on a particular aspect of the entity in their reviews (*e.g.*, whether "good food" is mentioned repeatedly by many reviewers or just once). The system should also allow the user to further evaluate the context in which those comments were made in order to support her in refining her impression about that entity. As participants skimmed the reviews, they often gleaned short phrases that captured the essence of each reviewer's comment. Thus, showing short phrases could accelerate the formation of impressions and decision making.

Based on the findings from our formative study and literature survey, we decided to use a tag cloud for our interface. Tag clouds already have been integrated into many websites, and have been familiar to many users. Thus, users are less likely to have problems with understanding the information displayed in the tag cloud and interacting with it. This is an important design aspect because we wanted our interface to be designed for casual users, and not for professionals who would examine the data deeply [5].

REVIEW SPOTLIGHT PROTOTYPE

We developed the Review Spotlight interface to help users quickly obtain information about a reviewed entity.

High-level Design

From our literature survey and observations made in the formative study, we decided to explore a tag-cloud-like interface. However, a standard tag cloud is not necessarily appropriate for our purposes. Figure 2 shows a tag cloud simply based on the frequency of words appearing in reviews for a restaurant. Although it is possible to learn general information about the restaurant from this tag cloud (*e.g.*, it is a Japanese restaurant, and the meals are probably good), the details that may be important for decision making are hard to overview. For instance, "roll" is a term mentioned frequently, but it is not clear what type of sushi rolls reviewers frequently mentioned. This finding motivated us to use a word pair as a meaningful chunk of information. Using word pairs is also in line with one of the design implications gained from our formative study (*i.e.*, using short phrases).

Figure 3 shows the interface of the Review Spotlight prototype. Although other tag cloud visualizations have also used word pairs extracted using n-gram methods [6], based on our findings in the formative study, we focused on adjective-noun pairs frequently mentioned in the reviews. The font size of each word pair is set to be proportional to the number of word pair occurrences. Review Spotlight also uses color to visualize the sentiment of each word, which will be discussed later.

When the user moves the cursor over an adjective-noun pair, Review Spotlight shows as many as four adjectives that are most frequently paired with that noun. In the example shown in Figure 3a, Review Spotlight shows "ridiculous," "worth," "bad," and "terrible" when the cursor is over the word pair "long wait." When the user clicks adjectives, the interface displays the number of occurrences of that adjective-noun word pair, and the sentences in which it appears in a separate textbox (Figure 3b). Thus, Review Spotlight supports quick examination of review details to enable the user to test her impressions.

Implementation

To generate a summarization from the review text, Review Spotlight performs the following four steps: 1) extracts adjective-noun word pairs; 2) counts each word pair's occurrences; 3) performs a sentiment analysis of each word pair; and 4) displays the word pairs.

Review Spotlight first extracts adjective-noun word pairs from the review text. Using a part-of-speech (POS) tagger developed by Tsuruoka and Tsujii [23], our system labels the part of speech for the words in the review text. This allows Review Spotlight to identify the locations of the adjectives and nouns. Review Spotlight then pairs a noun with the closest adjective modifying it. Review Spotlight also extracts a word pair from a sentence with the "to be" verb. For instance, if Review Spotlight parses a sentence "The food is great," it extracts the word pair "great food." In addition, by focusing on adjective-noun pairs, Review Spotlight intrinsically removes noise introduced by common trivial words, such as articles and prepositions.

Review Spotlight then counts the number of occurrences of each word pair and groups word pairs by nouns. The system then eliminates the word pairs that only appear once in the original review text. It then calculates the font size for the extracted adjectives and nouns. The font size for a noun is determined linearly by its number of occurrences. The font size for an adjective is determined linearly by the number of occurrences of the word pair consisting of it and the associated noun. We set the minimum and maximum font sizes to 10 and 30 pixels, respectively.

Next, Review Spotlight performs a sentiment analysis on the word pairs using SentiWordNet [8], a context-free, word-based sentiment analysis tool. A sentiment value provided by SentiWordNet for each word consists of three scores (*i.e.*, positivity, negativity, and objectivity), and it is defined for each common use of the word. Review Spotlight first calculates the sentiment value for an adjective by taking the average of its sentiment values for all the use contexts. It then calculates the sentiment value for a noun by taking the average of the sentiment values of all paired adjectives weighted by the number of occurrences. It maps the sentiment value into the color scheme in which shades of green, red, and blue represent positive, negative, and neutral meaning, respectively; the darkness of the shade conveys the sentiment strength. Through a preliminary

Figure 3. Screenshots of Review Spotlight for reviews on the same restaurant used in Figure 2 (the name of the restaurant is masked in this figure): a) The user can see frequently-mentioned adjective-noun word pairs. She can also move the cursor over the word pair to see more adjectives that are paired with the noun; b) When she clicks an adjective (*e.g.*, "long"), Review Spotlight displays the original sentences from which the clicked word pair came.

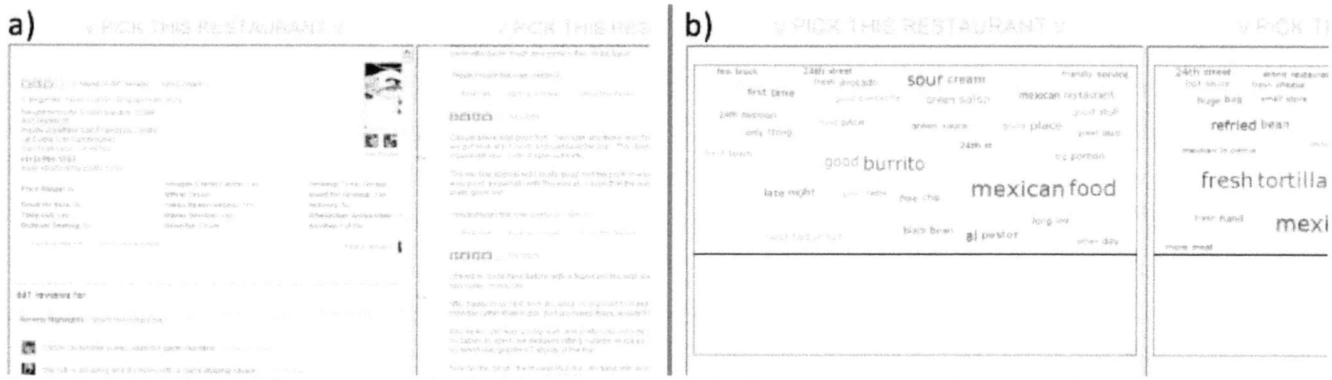

Figure 4. Screenshots of the pages used in the laboratory user study. Two restaurant reviews were displayed side-by-side: a) Review pages (the name of the restaurant is masked in this figure); b) Review Spotlight.

experiment with the prototype system, we determined that users preferred the noun coloring based on this weighted average over the coloring based on the average of the sentiment values defined in SentiWordNet.

After the sentiment analysis, Review Spotlight performs a spatial allocation function to place the extracted word pairs within a given space (600 x 250 pixels by default, but the dimensions can be adjusted). Because Review Spotlight prioritizes larger word pairs in the allocation, an optimal layout (*i.e.*, the layout that accommodates as many word pairs as possible) can be accomplished by the greedy algorithm described by Kaser and Lemire [14]. However, we found that an optimal layout is visually complex, and large word pairs placed towards the top of the layout often attracted much more attention than other word pairs.

Review Spotlight instead places the word pairs randomly so that the user is not biased to any specific terms based on their placement position. Review Spotlight also adds padding around each word pair that is relative in size to the bounding box of the word pair. Although the resulting layout is much sparser than the optimal layout, our pilot studies showed that participants preferred it over the optimal layout because it was less visually complex. Review Spotlight performs this spatial allocation, starting with the largest word pair to the smallest, until it cannot find a location for a new word pair which does not cause an overlap on any other word pairs that have been placed already. Review Spotlight then combines as many four adjectives that are most frequently paired with the noun. These adjectives become visible when the user moves the cursor over the word pair.

The efficiency of the summarization process and the accuracy of the extracted word pairs are outside the scope of this paper. We have not experimented with these aspects of Review Spotlight in depth.

LABORATORY USER STUDY

We conducted a laboratory study to evaluate how Review Spotlight addresses user requirements for an interface summarizing user-generated reviews compared to traditional review pages. Although a comparative study against other interfaces is one possible type of user study, our intention here was to examine in depth how Review Spotlight supports *impression formation*, as defined by Rivadeneira *et al* [19].

Procedure

At the beginning of the study, we introduced the participant to a sample Review Spotlight interface and review page used in the study (Figure 4), and allowed the participants to explore both interfaces. After the participants became comfortable with the systems, we presented them the reviews for two restaurants side-by-side. Both reviews were displayed using either the Review Spotlight interface or the review pages. By separating the interfaces, we could differentiate the effects on the participants' decisions caused by the two different user interfaces. The participants were then asked to examine the reviews and decide which restaurant they would like to visit by clicking the link above each restaurant review. The system recorded all the mouse hover and click events on word pairs in Review Spotlight, and the time the participants spent making their decision between each restaurant pair. We also asked them to rate how strongly they preferred the selected restaurant over the other, and to provide the reasons for their decision verbally. The entire session was audio-recorded and transcribed.

We selected eight pairs of the restaurants that were located in a region unfamiliar to the participants and had more than 50 reviews on Yelp.com. Each restaurant within a pair offered similar cuisine, was of similar price range, and was from the same part of a city. Four pairs of restaurants had similar overall review ratings (PA1–PA4), and the rest consisted of pairs of restaurants in which one had a high overall rating and the second had a low overall rating (PB1–PB4). To examine the effect of Review Spotlight on impression formation in comparison to normal review pages, we presented four of the pairs (PA1, PA2, PB1, and PB2) to participants through both the Review Spotlight interface as well as the normal review page. To prevent participants from knowing that those four restaurant pairs were presented to them with both interfaces and from using predetermined decisions, we used the remaining four restaurant pairs (PA3, PA4, PB3, and PB4) as distracters. We presented PA3 and PB3 to participants using only the Review Spotlight interface; and we presented PA4 and PB4 to participants through the normal review pages. Thus, each participant viewed 6 Review Spotlight and 6 review page interfaces in the study. The presentation order of these twelve interfaces was randomized for each participant. The resulting Review Spotlight interfaces contained 26 word pairs with 66 hidden adjectives on average. We noticed that some word pairs were noises (*e.g.*, meaningless word pairs). However, we did not perform any manual filtering of the word pairs because we wanted to test our system in a natural manner.

Apparatus

All the Review Spotlight summarizations and review pages were prepared before the experiment, and stored on the computer used in the experiment. We cached all the pages on the computer before the study to minimize their loading time. We used a laptop running Windows Vista with a 30.5 x 19.0 cm, 1280 x 800 pixel display. The screen was sufficiently large for the participants to comfortably read the reviews for two restaurants side-by-side. We also provided the participants with a mouse.

Participants

Ten individuals (5 male and 5 female between the ages of 20 and 50) with a variety of backgrounds (such as students, system administrators, a retail manager, a home maker, and an accountant) participated in this study. None of them participated in our formative study. All participants regularly did web browsing, but none of them had any significant experience of writing and posting online reviews. The study lasted approximately 50 minutes. The participants were compensated with $20 cash.

LABORATORY STUDY RESULTS

Performance Time

We examined the data for the four restaurant pairs that were presented in both the Review Spotlight interface and the review pages (*i.e.*, the non-distracters) to compare the time that participants took to make a decision. Our unpaired Welch's t-test revealed that the participants spent less time with the Review Spotlight interface (122 seconds on average, SD=49) than the review pages (157 seconds on average, SD=63; $t_{73}=2.75$, $p<.01$). This finding is in line with the qualitative evidence we gathered from the study.

It's faster. Instead of like going through reading so much non-sense, [I can] just pick up important things right away.

Forming Detailed Impressions Using Review Spotlight

In 30 out of the 40 cases, the participants chose the same restaurants with both user interfaces. The participants often cited the ratings and the number of reviews to explain their decision when viewing the review pages whereas they used specific details about the restaurants (*e.g.*, food or service) to explain their decisions with Review Spotlight. For example, one participant picked the same restaurant using different reasons as follows:

***With the review pages**: This one has more reviews and more positive [reviews]. Overall rating is higher too.*

Rating	Same Choice		Different Choice	
	RP	RS	RP	RS
Average (SD)	2.8 (0.75)	2.9 (1.0)	3.0 (1.0)	2.2 (1.0)

Table 1. The results of the self-rated preferences on the choices through the review pages (RP) and Review Spotlight (RS). A higher value (between 0 to 4) means a stronger preference. Same Choice represents the 30 cases in which the participants chose the same restaurants with both interfaces, and Different Choice represents the other 10 cases.

***With Review Spotlight**: I know that people say even though the wait is long, it's worth it. Usually I don't like waiting for food, but it must be good. And the price is reasonable. [The other restaurant] seems like ok too, but some people say the portion is really really small.*

Even in the ten instances where participants chose different restaurants between the two interfaces, they still provided a greater level of detail to support their decision when using Review Spotlight. In seven of these cases, the participants selected a restaurant with weak preference over the other restaurant. For example, one participant selected one restaurant with the review pages by focusing primarily on the ratings it received.

Everyone seems to think the restaurant on the left is very average, like there is nothing wrong there, but it wasn't fantastic. People on the right generally seem to think...it was average and some people thought above average, but the reviews generally seem to be more positive.

However, he chose the other restaurant with the Review Spotlight interface because he thought that the restaurant he chose with the review pages may offer a small portion of food. In this case, Review Spotlight helped the participant uncover specific information that was important to his decision from the review text.

People on the left generally seem like they are happy with the food and the portion, and price. People on the right, ...they mentioned what they ate, and seems like some people were happy with food, but some people thought the portion is small, so I was more sure that people thought more positively about the restaurant on the left.

Quantitative Analysis of Review Spotlight Usage

Our system recorded the number of mouse hover events over word pairs in the Review Spotlight interfaces. Halvey and Keane's study indicated that the user typically scans the tag cloud rather than reads it while performing *searching* tasks [10]. To study whether the participants only scanned word pairs, we first removed the 3008 hover events that lasted 200 milliseconds or less from the 7240 hover events recorded in all 12 Review Spotlight interfaces (including the four distracters) as unintentional hover events. We determined this time threshold from the fact that the average reading speed is 200–240 milliseconds/word [13]. Although this cutoff does not mean a perfect separation of intentional and unintentional hover events (and furthermore, it might be too conservative), we believe that this is still a good approximation. As a result, we had 4232 intentional hover events, and the average number of intentional hover events per Review Spotlight page per participant was 35.3 (SD=2.5). This implies that the participants tended to read the word pairs in our experiment because they needed to examine what words appeared in Review Spotlight in order to form their impressions.

Our system also recorded the number of mouse click events on word pairs. We had a total of 1200 click events in the Review Spotlight interfaces. This means that the average number of click events per Review Spotlight page per participant was 10.0 (SD=1.3). 658 clicks (54.8%) occurred on the adjectives that appeared by default, and the rest of the clicks occurred on the hidden adjectives. Furthermore, we found that 28.4% of the intentional hover events resulted in a click. These numbers indicate that Review Spotlight encouraged the participants to explore more details about how the words were used in the actual reviews.

We were unable to analyze the types of word pairs which the participants tended to view. One reason for this is that some word pairs, such as "good food", were displayed by the Review Spotlight more frequently than other word pairs. The same word pairs also were displayed with different font sizes at different locations in the twelve Review Spotlight summarizations. We leave a quantitative analysis of the types of word pairs that the users typically look at to form their impressions about the restaurants for future work.

Qualitative Analysis of User Strategies

We did not provide the overall rating in Review Spotlight because we found that it does not always match word pairs that appeared in the interface. But participants successfully gained an idea of how positive or negative the reviews about the restaurant were. Although the word pair coloring based on the sentiment analysis was intended for this purpose, nine of the participants rather looked at the words themselves, their font sizes, and their exact numbers of occurrences to obtain their general impression.

> *I more used words that were used, and secondly the size of the words... and then I would read similar comments, and then I would look for [details of] where people say bad things, just to have a comparison of how strongly they say they were bad or good, and how often... I completely forgot about the color.*

Another common strategy was to focus on particular adjectives, such as "good", "great", or "poor". The participants also looked at how many times each word pair was mentioned in the original review page.

> *The first thing I would do usually is [look at] the biggest one. Then I checked things that seem relevant, like,... if I saw "best" or "worst," I would definitely check that. Also specific dishes...I see how many times they say that. Like if one side mentioned "best" twice, and the other side mentioned 20 times.*

The participants generally liked the ability to view a word pair in its original review. Half of the participants explicitly mentioned that this feature reduces the effort needed to read the reviews in order to find detailed information about what they were interested in.

> *I like that they are just short sentences that got right to the point of what I was looking for... It was neat to just click it and see what people had to say about. How many times it was mentioned, I also really liked.*

> *The thing I like the most was if I was only interested in food or service..., you can click that and see all comments about one particular aspect... Pick up one thing you're more interested in instead of reading through the reviews.*

DISCUSSION

One aspect we wanted to focus on in our study was how Review Spotlight could help users perform tasks which required what Rivadeneira *et al.* described as *impression formation* [19]. The participants often (30 out of 40 times) were able to choose the same restaurant with nearly the same level of preference using both the Review Spotlight interface and current review pages (see Table 1). However, our participants were able to make this decision significantly faster with Review Spotlight. Furthermore, their decisions were always guided by more detailed impressions than ones formulated when they used the traditional review webpage interface, even when the participants chose different restaurants.

Providing a More Consistent Presentation

Four participants explicitly commented on the presentation of the word pairs. Because the system places the word pairs without following any particular layout, it causes an inconsistency in the presentation. For example, one participant had trouble finding particular information that she wanted to know in Review Spotlight. Another participant described that the Review Spotlight interface was harder to find particular information that he was seeking because he often could not tell quickly whether that information was actually displayed.

> *Information may be there if you are looking..., but it's hard [to determine] if it's missing or not... You may be looking for price range, or attire, or whether they deliver. [On review pages,] it's easier [to find] just from looking at the top, but here (on Review Spotlight) [such information] may or may not be there.*

We decided to use a random ordering instead of a specific word ordering. This seemed to cause problems when the participants were looking for a particular word. However, the participants generally could identify words that are important or interesting to them quickly.

> *If you're looking for something, looking for wine, or..., it's easy to spot whereas [on the review page], you have to look for it, search for it.*

Random word ordering resulted in accidental learning and facilitated the *impression formation* tasks defined by Rivadeneira *et al* [19]. That is, presenting the user with different word orderings mitigates the problem of biasing them towards particular word pairs.

> *The good thing about [Review Spotlight] is that I came across the things like specific dishes that would've been harder to see in [the review pages]... Like people, if they mention mac 'n' cheese a lot or best burrito, you would be able to see that [in Review Spotlight].*

Participants also mentioned the inconsistency of the size of the word pair. Because the size of each word pair was determined based on its number of occurrences within the review text for one entity (in this case, a restaurant), the same font size across multiple Review Spotlight summarizations does not necessarily mean that the word pair has the same number of occurrences. This can be confusing when the user wants to compare multiple entities, as the participants did in this experiment.

In addition to user reviews, every review page provides a summary of basic information about the restaurant (*e.g.*, the hours, price range, and atmosphere) and visual elements (*e.g.*, a photo or a graph). The user may use these elements to quickly compare two restaurants. As seen in Figure 1, we envision integrating Review Spotlight into the original review page instead of replacing it completely. In this manner, the user would be able to obtain the general information about a restaurant that is typically found in a review page, but still be able to obtain an overview of the reviews with Review Spotlight.

Graceful Recovery from Linguistic Analysis Problems

As expected, the participants noticed and commented on errors caused by the natural language processing we used. Participants noticed that some word pairs did not make much sense and that the color of the fonts did not often match to what they thought (*e.g.*, "impeccable" has a high negativity value in SentiWordNet). This type of problem could be addressed by incorporating a more sophisticated method of determining the relevant information and sentiment in the review [12]. Another linguistic analysis problem is that the meanings of some word pairs were context-dependent. For example, if one reviewer commented "Last time we went, we had and loved the grilled chicken," and another commented "I will avoid their grilled chicken next time," the current Review Spotlight implementation would detect that "grilled chicken" is a common pair despite the contrasting reactions. Similarly, the current Review Spotlight implementation does not accurately extract the word pairs that appeared in negative sentences (*e.g.*, "This is not a good restaurant").

Review Spotlight allows the user to click on an adjective-noun pair to see the original review text containing that word pair so that she can learn additional information about the reviewed entity. But our user study showed that this feature also gracefully compensated for imperfect word pair extractions.

> *Something that I wouldn't notice is that someone says "this place was not very good," so they changed the positive word into the actual negative review about it, so that's why I found that it was important for that word, in particular, that I actually clicked on that in every review that I looked at... That's how it kind of differentiated if it's actually a good place to go to or NOT good place to go to.*

Improvements on the accuracy of the word pair extraction and sentiment analysis could contribute to a better review summarization. However, user-generated reviews, in general, are hard to parse automatically because they do not follow any particular format and they are not always grammatically correct. The findings from our study suggest that providing the user with a way to obtain additional contextual information about the word pairs is a useful way to recover from the errors caused by the linguistic analysis.

Controlling Displayed Word Pairs

Some participants suggested a feature to allow the user to adjust which word pairs are displayed. For instance, Review Spotlight could have a scale widget to tune the percentage of positive/negative word pairs to appear in the interface. Based on participant comments, we also found two interesting parameters that could be adjusted by the user in order to enhance the usefulness of Review Spotlight.

Subjective-Objective Parameter

One interesting adjustment parameter is the degree of subjectivity or objectivity in the word pair. One participant told us that she wanted to have more objective (descriptive) words than subjective (evaluative) words to understand what the restaurant is like and what it offers. She explained the aspect that she did not like in the prototype Review Spotlight interface as follows:

> *These words [subjective word pairs shown in Review Spotlight], it's like somebody's opinions of the restaurants, not compared to "hot source" or "sweet potato", like description of the actual food or service. So, it's like you have mixed [subjective] comments as well as [a] description of type of food.*

However, subjective words were still useful for many participants to make decisions. Therefore, allowing the user to adjust the amount of subjective/objective words appeared in the interface could improve Review Spotlight.

Time Parameter

Another interesting improvement could be to display word pairs based on their post date, as the trend of the reviews often changes over time. For example, reviews might change dramatically after a food poisoning incident or the

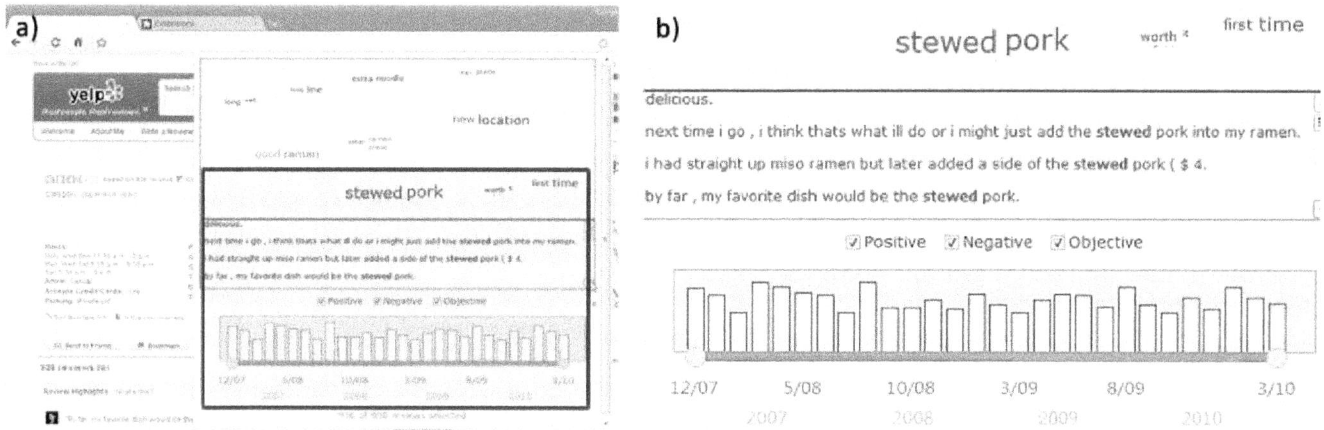

Figure 5. The Google Chrome extension of Review Spotlight. The histogram indicates the number of the reviews over time, and the user can control which sentiment types to be displayed: a) the whole view of our extension; b) the enlarged view of the highlighted area in Figure 5a.

start of a new chef. Allowing the user to filter reviews from before and after an influential incident could enable them to better understand the entity as one participant commented:

> *One good thing about [the review page] is that you tend to read only the recent reviews... Maybe things change,... like if they... improve the service... the recent reviews indicate that as opposed to old reviews [in which] people complain about the service... So maybe if you have some sort of a time bar on the top you can sort of drag it and see how tags change from recent to oldest.*

Such a feature has been included in different web-based systems. The Zoetrope interface allows the user to examine how a portion of a particular webpage has changed over time [1]. Dubinko *et al.* developed an algorithm to show the most salient tags that were posted by users in Flickr for a given time interval [7]. Thus, this feature could also be beneficial in Review Spotlight.

REVIEW SPOTLIGHT EXTENSION

Based on the findings from the laboratory study, we revised our Review Spotlight interface and developed a Google Chrome extension which resembles what we illustrated in Figure 1. This Review Spotlight extension supports reviews available on Amazon.com as well as Yelp.com.

Figure 5 shows the revised Review Spotlight interface. We added several features suggested by participants in our laboratory study. First, the interface includes a histogram showing the number of reviews entered for a given entity along a timeline; this gives the user an overview of how the number of the reviews changes over time. The sliders below the histogram allow the user to specify the time period for which Review Spotlight should summarize the reviews. Finally, the new interface also provides checkboxes for selecting sentiment types. This feature allows the user to specify whether positive, negative, and subjective word pairs should be displayed by clicking the corresponding checkboxes.

We made our Review Spotlight extension available to anyone in our website and Google Chrome Extension Gallery for three months. To enable the extension, the user had to consent with our data gathering of their usage of the extension. We did not extensively recruit the users for our extension because it was still a research prototype. Eleven users volunteered to use our extension. Our log showed that on average the users accessed 29.0 different webpages (SD=38.0) on which Review Spotlight could have been used; and on average they used Review Spotlight 19.9 times on average (SD=25.7). Thus, 68.6% of the user's visits to Yelp or Amazon webpages (for which the Review Spotlight was available) resulted in its use. This indicates that our users did use Review Spotlight to view a summary of user-generated reviews provided by Review Spotlight. Because we implemented the extension to only log information when the user visits a Yelp or Amazon webpage for which it can summarize, it is not possible for us to know if a user still has the extension installed or has removed it. Thus, we can only report how many days after first installing the extension was a user's most recent use. On average, participants' most recent use of the extension came 35.7 days after they installed it (SD=29.8). This indicates that participants saw value in the tool and continued to use it.

CONCLUSIONS AND FUTURE WORK

The overwhelming number of user-generated reviews and their inconsistent writing style often require a significant amount of time and effort to read, and can result in important information being obscured from the user. To counter such challenges, we developed Review Spotlight, a user interface that helps users with impression formation by summarizing user-generated reviews using adjective-noun word pairs. Our interface provides a quick overview of the reviews and allows the user to explore the details of reviews in which word pairs are mentioned. Our laboratory user study with Review Spotlight showed that participants could form detailed impressions about restaurants from examining an overview of the reviews and the original context of the word pairs that interested them. The participants could also choose their preferred restaurant with Review Spotlight significantly faster than with traditional review webpages.

We do not claim that Review Spotlight would outperform other kinds of interfaces or visualizations. However, this study revealed that Review Spotlight has the potential to support the quick formation of an impression of the reviewed entity. We plan to perform a comparative evaluation between different kinds of interfaces which summarize user generated reviews.

One concern with using user-generated reviews is their reliability. The current Review Spotlight did not do any filtering of word pairs or review text. Thus, it could provide false impressions if the original reviews were posted under malicious motivations (*e.g.*, a reviewer posted false information or negative comments to decrease the venue's popularity). We can address this issue by adding more weight to reviews from highly-rated reviewers (*e.g.*, top 100 reviewers) or reviews other users found useful.

The current interface only supports reviews written in English. Adopting an international POS tagger like TreeTagger [20] would enable the system to extract adjective-noun pairs from the text and display the review written in a different language in the same way as that it currently does with English text. However, adjective-noun pairs might not be the best way to summarize review pages in other languages. Thus, an investigation on what users would find to be more appropriate in other languages is necessary for internationalization.

ACKNOWLEDGEMENTS

We would like to thank members of the DGP, Fanny Chevalier and Elaine M. Huang for their comments on this paper. We also thank all the participants in our user studies.

REFERENCES

1. Adar, E., Dontcheva, M., Fogarty, J., and Weld, D. S. Zoetrope: Interacting with the ephemeral web. In *Proc. of UIST 2008*, ACM Press, 239-248.
2. Bateman, S., Gutwin, C., and Nacenta, M. Seeing things in the clouds: the effect of visual features on tag cloud selections. In *Proc. of HT 2008*, ACM Press, 193-202.
3. Carenini, G., Ng, R. T., and Pauls, A. Interactive multimedia summaries of evaluative text. In *Proc. of IUI 2006*, ACM Press, 124-131.
4. Carenini, G. and Rizoli, L. A multimedia interface for facilitating comparisons of opinions. In *Proc. of IUI 2009*, ACM Press, 325-334.
5. Chevalier, F., Huot, S., and Fekete, J. D. WikipediaViz: conveying article quality for casual wikipedia readers. In *Proc. of PacificVis2010*, IEEE, 215 – 222.
6. Dave, K., Lawrence, S., and Pennock, D. M. Mining the peanut gallery: opinion extraction and semantic classification of product reviews. In *Proc. of WWW 2003*, ACM Press, 519-528.
7. Dubinko, M., Kumar, R., Magnani, J., Novak, J., Raghavan, P., and Tomkins, A. Visualizing tag over time. *ACM Transactions on Web 1*, 2 (2007), 7.
8. Esuli A., and Sebastiani F. SENTIWORDNET: a publicly available lexical resource for opinion mining. In *Proc. of LREC 2006*, ELRA, 417-422.
9. Ganesan, K. A., Sundaresan, N., and Deo, H. Mining tag clouds and emoticons behind community feedback. In *Proc. of WWW 2008*, ACM Press, 1181-1182.
10. Halvey, M. J. and Keane, M. T. An assessment of tag presentation techniques. In *Proc. of WWW 2007*, ACM Press, 1313-1314.
11. Hu, M., and Liu, B. Mining and summarizing customer reviews. In *Proc. of KDD 2004*, AAAI, 168-177.
12. Jo, Y., and Oh, A. Aspect and sentiment unification model for online review analysis. In *Proc. of WSMD 2011* (to appear).
13. Just, M. A., and Carpenter, P. A. *The psychology of reading and language comprehension.* Allyn & Bacon, Boston, 1987.
14. Kaser, O., and Lemire, D. Tag-cloud drawing: algorithms for cloud visualization. In *WWW 2007 Workshop on Taggings and Metadata for Social Information Organization 2007*, ACM Press.
15. Kuo, B. Y., Hentrich, T., Good, B. M., and Wilkinson, M. D. Tag clouds for summarizing web search results. In *Proc. of WWW 2007*, ACM Press, 1203-1204.
16. Lee, S. E., Son, D. K., and Han, S. S. Qtag: tagging as a means of rating, opinion-expressing, sharing and visualizing. In *Proc. of SIGDOC 2007*, ACM Press, 189-195.
17. Liu, B., Hu, M., and Cheng, J. Opinion observer: analyzing and comparing opinions on the Web. In *Proc. of WWW 2005*, ACM Press, 342-351.
18. Pong, B., Lee, L., and Vaithyanathan S. Thumbs up? sentiment classification using machine learning techniques. In *Proc. of EMNLP 2002*, ACL, 79-86.
19. Rivadeneira, A. W., Gruen, D. M., Muller, M. J., and Millen, D. R. Getting our head in the clouds: toward evaluation studies of tagclouds. In *Proc. of CHI 2007*, ACM Press, 995-998.
20. Schmid, H. Probabilistic part-of-speech tagging using decision trees. In *Proc. of NEMLP 1994*, 44-49.
21. Schrammel, J., Leitner, M., and Tscheligi, M. Semantically structured tag clouds: an empirical evaluation of clustered presentation approaches. In *Proc. of CHI 2009*, ACM Press, 2037-2040.
22. Sinclair, J., Cardew-Hall, M. The folksonomy tag cloud: when is it useful? *Journal of Information Science 34*, 1 (2008), 15-29.
23. Tsuruoka Y., and Tsujii, J. Bidirectional inference with the easiest-first strategy for tagging sequence data. In *Proc. of HLT/EMNLP 2005*, ACL, 467-474.
24. Turney P. Thumbs up or thumbs down? semantic orientation applied to unsupervised classification of reviews. In *Proc. of ACL 2002*, ACL, 417-424.
25. Viégas, F. B. and Wattenberg, M. Tag clouds and the case for vernacular visualization. *Interactions 15*, 4 (2008), 49-52.

Making Spaces: How Design Workbooks Work

William Gaver

Interaction Research Studio
Goldsmiths, University of London
w.gaver@gold.ac.uk

ABSTRACT
In this paper, I discuss *design workbooks*, collections of design proposals and related materials, both as a method for design and as a design methodology. In considering them as a method, I describe a number of examples of design workbooks we have developed in our studio and describe some of the practical techniques we have used in developing them. More fundamentally, I discuss design workbooks as embodiments of a methodological approach which recognises that ideas may emerge slowly over time, that important issues and perspectives may emerge from multiple concrete ideas, potentially generated by multiple members of a team, rather than being theory-driven, and that maintaining the provisionality and vagueness of early proposals can be useful in supporting a quasi-participatory design approach that allows participants to interpret, react to and elaborate upon the ideas they present.

Author Keywords
Interaction design, research through design, ideation, design proposals, conceptual design, design spaces

ACM Classification Keywords
H5.m. Information interfaces and presentation (e.g., HCI): Miscellaneous.

General Terms
Design

INTRODUCTION
In this paper, I discuss the creation, collection and use of *design workbooks* in our practice. Workbooks are collections of design proposals and other materials drawn together during projects to investigate options for design. They can be used at various points in the design process, but in this paper I will focus mainly on workbooks created during the early stages of projects. As I will describe, at din the turn from considering background research towards possible designs, are produced from an array of resources and using a range of techniques, describe design ideas to greater and lesser degrees of resolution, address a number of audiences, and take a variety of forms. What they share, I will suggest, is not just the description of a design space but its creation: through the multiplicity of design ideas they contain they implicitly suggest important issues, approaches and options that might be considered in designing for a given situation, and in their provisional nature show those ideas, approaches and options in the making and still malleable to change.

CHI 2011, May 7–12, 2011, Vancouver, BC, Canada.

Design workbooks can be considered as a design method, and I discuss some of the practical techniques we use in our team to develop them. More fundamentally, however, workbooks are also evidence of, and a tool for, a methodological approach which recognises that ideas may develop slowly over time, that important issues and perspectives may emerge from multiple concrete ideas, potentially generated by multiple members of a design team, rather than being theory-driven, and that when the provisionality of early ideas is maintained in their expression, design workbooks can support a quasi-participatory design approach as people interpret, react to and elaborate upon the ideas they present.

Finally, design workbooks are also interesting for their own sake, as explorations of topics and approaches that extend beyond the eventual outcomes of design projects. This paper does not describe any particular workbook in enough detail to explore an associated design space in depth, but the illustrations I use may still be of interest for the domain-specific ideas they convey.

Of course, the use of design workbooks is hardly unique to our practice[1]. Producing and collecting proposals in one form or another is a fundamental process in design work. My purpose in reflecting on our practice here is two-fold: first, I hope to help other designers reflect on their practices by articulating our own, and second, by sharing this way of working more broadly I hope to help in 'dispelling the black art of design' [13] to those working within other methodological traditions.

[1] The proposals shown here were developed by various design teams with whom I have worked; see the acknowledgements.

TWO WORKBOOKS

To ground the discussion, in this section I describe two early workbooks. These serve to illustrate the roles that workbooks can serve in the design process, and also some of the basic techniques that can be used in developing them. Later I will describe more recent examples, as I focus more closely on how workbooks can be constructed.

The Alternatives Workbook

The first workbook was compiled as part of a project on 'information appliances', a then-voguish concept of computational products specialised to offer one or a few functions with simplicity and elegance (e.g. [11]).

Dissatisfied with current examples of what such devices might be like, I spent some holiday time putting together about a dozen very rough collages of alternative devices that explored a range of personal and idiosyncratic possibilities. The images were constructed from pictures of household goods scanned from a catalogue before leaving on holiday, and thus were extremely limited in range and quality. For example, Figure 1 shows the image used to introduce the idea of an 'Objective View' camera. This was an idea for a device that could be launched tens of meters into the air to capture an image of the user in his or her surroundings, counter-acting the normal self-centred view of whatever troubling situation might be bothering them. Constructed from a picture of a corkscrew arranged over one of a bowl, the notion was that the swirling tail might indicate flight, and the indentation of the bowl could suggest a data receiver. Though crude, images such as this one seemed to work well when accompanied by relatively extensive descriptions to convey ideas that were, at the time, relatively unusual.

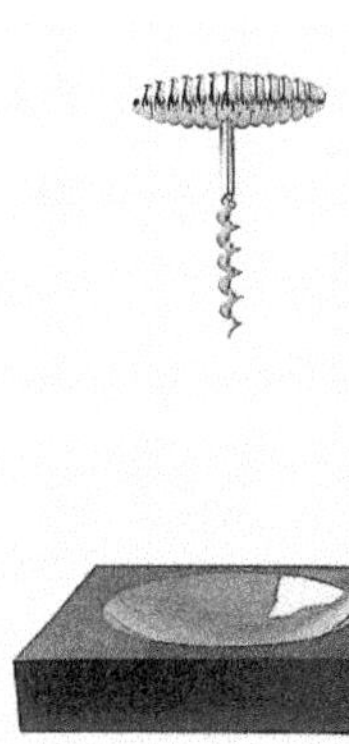

Figure 1. The Objective View proposal from the first, in-house Alternatives workbook.

This sketchy, quickly-produced workbook first evoked a rather bemused response from my partner on the design team, but ultimately proved effective in generating discussion and design explorations of other possible devices. As these progressed we decided to capture them in a more visually finished workbook for circulation to our sponsoring collaborators. Though still relatively simple to produce, the images used in this workbook included a number of new features: background images, electronic displays superimposed on everyday objects, and wholly constructed elements, all of which reflected both a greater range of available visual resources and more time spent using software tools such as Photoshop™ to develop images. For example, Figure 2 shows part of the image used to accompany a proposal for Placeholders, small electronic screens that could present information in the home independently from the computers that might feed them. Though centred on an image of a postcard holder, similar to the everyday artefacts used in the first workbook, it is substantially augmented with a background image of a table and crockery, as well as constructed imagery of possible screen contents.

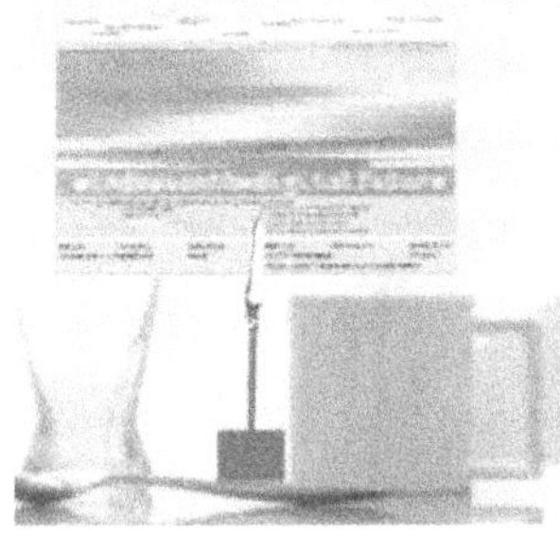

Figure 2. Detail of the Placeholder proposal from the second Alternatives workbook.

The completed Alternatives workbook included ten proposals, each presented on a double-page spread in A4 landscape format, bound together to form a small booklet. We distributed the workbooks to our partners on the project and described the ensemble in a meeting and presentation before leaving them behind. This was a key event in the project: the workbook made clear a domain of interest and a style of work that clearly influenced the rest of the project (for examples of later work, see [10]).

In addition, the workbook itself became the subject of a publication in its own right [6], in which we described the individual proposals and the overall design space they created. Perhaps most telling, for the purposes of this paper, was the argument that the proposals served similarly to a collection of prototypes, providing relatively concrete 'devices' that viewers could mentally simulate and critique as they might ones that were physically realised.

WORKBOOKS IN THE DESIGN PROCESS

As these examples indicate, workbooks can play an important role, both functionally and experientially, in early stages of the design process. In this section I treat them as a method for design, arguing for the benefits of making and using them.

A Turning Point

One of the most valuable roles for design workbooks is as a fulcrum in the transition from initial background research to the generation of designs to be developed. This stage of design is often a daunting one, when attention turns from the richness of an existing situation to the blank page of a design sketchbook. There are a number of ways to go wrong in making this turn. It can be tempting to develop ideas quickly and commit to the first one that seems satisfactory; or, alternatively, design teams may become suspended in diffuse discussions of situations and general possibilities they offer. Design ideas can be trapped in iterative versions of the status quo, or dislocated by technical possibilities that may have little to do with the context for design. Design workbooks can help to overcome and even profit from many of these challenges.

Buying Time

Resolving to produce a workbook at the outset of a design process makes clear that the object of coming up with ideas is not to define a final design directly, but to understand the nature of problems and possibilities to be addressed in a given domain. This means that a given idea does not have to bear the full weight of a project's expectations, but there is still an obligation to act, and a requirement to concretise ideas, which are crucial in moving beyond vague notions of possibility. Considering whether specific proposals might work allows a clearer sense of promising design directions to be gained. In effect, workbooks are a tool in developing from initial research towards a brief for design.

Design workbooks are a mechanism to compel 'safe' creative activity (though often this encourages exploration of relatively 'risky' possibilities) but they also have the advantage of ensuring that this does not happen too swiftly. This is particularly appropriate for research through design projects, where the responsibility is to create original perspectives and possibilities, without many of the time pressures of commercial design projects. Producing workbooks can take days, weeks, even months, particularly when care is taken over the quality of images and text within them. Both the time taken to create proposals, and their treatment as contributions to a collection of ideas rather than a representation of final designs, can help in avoiding premature commitment to particular notions or even broad design directions. Moreover, a side effect of the time and effort needed to produce workbooks is the tendency to filter out unpromising ideas and to allow broad themes to emerge and grow. Effort follows enthusiasm: there is a tendency to represent the most intriguing ideas first, during which time other ideas may lose interest while new ones, based on the first, start to develop. This filtering can happen within a team as well as individually as proposals are shared and discussed. In this way, the process of developing a workbook is not just a matter of producing a physical artefact but also the ideas within it and a shared ground within the design team.

Externalising Ideas

Using images and text to express design ideas often entails developing those ideas. Creating workbook proposals is not a matter of externalising internal visions: trying to turn an idea into a proposal often reveals just how woolly and incomplete that idea is, and in developing the proposal one is likely to be forced to resolve certain of the its details in order to proceed. As I will discuss later, the kinds of representations used in developing proposals can usefully maintain ambiguity and provisionality, so that not all—indeed, not many—details need be resolved. Nonetheless, the requirements of capturing a design idea in images and text can be useful in forcing its further consideration.

Externalising ideas in the form of proposals acts as the first step towards realising them as independent entities, apart from their creator. Sometimes proposals can take on a life of their own, for example when the resources used to externalise them shape their details in unanticipated directions (as, in an extreme instance, the limited images used in creating the first Alternatives workbook shaped those proposals; see Figure 1). Even when proposals develop in a way that conforms comfortably with the original notion behind them, their independent existence gives the designer an opportunity to view and assess them as if found rather than owned. Can I imagine this device / system / service existing in the world? Would it be engaging? What's good about it? What would be annoying?

Moving an idea into the world also allows it to be seen in an external context, whether literally against a setting used in depicting the proposal or implicitly in its relationship to other products, prototypes and proposals that surround it. This process of de-identification with design possibilities, and of integrating them with the world, is valuable in allowing them to be assessed independently from an individual designer's likes and dislikes. They emerge from their creator's voice to take on their own,

Projecting Futures

Implicit in the move from appreciating an existing situation to considering possible designs is a turn from understanding the past and present towards anticipating possible futures. Most of our proposals are not 'futuristic', instead exploring possibilities that could already have existed at the time of their creation. Nonetheless, they point to a future, even if it is a future differentiated from the present by their realisation, and invite viewers to imagine what that future might be like.

Contrast with Design Scenarios

Many techniques exist for exploring the potential futures of proposed systems, many of which can be grouped under the broad category of design scenarios (e.g. [2]). Taking the form of storyboards, videos, or simple text descriptions, scenarios usually create narratives about people using the proposed system in different contexts.

Design scenarios can be very useful in allowing designers to work out and communicate how they imagine the systems they propose would be used. Moreover, developing scenarios can be a useful mechanism for working out the details of designs, just as externalising design proposals can motivate the development of the ideas behind them. In practice, design scenarios often share two characteristics, however, that can limit their utility. First, the majority present largely positive accounts of the experience and effects of using the systems they consider. This is not surprising, given that the work to develop design scenarios is usually motivated by enthusiasm for the systems they describe, and, insofar as scenarios are to be used to communicate the possibilities to other stakeholders, their authors want to convey that enthusiasm effectively. But it can be unfortunate, because a focus on intended use can divert attention from potential problems or overlooked issues, some of which may even lead to new and more promising ideas (c.f. [4]). The second characteristic that design scenarios often share is that of presenting a unitary vision of a proposed system's future. By creating a detailed scenario of use, there is a tendency to collapse the space of possibilities suggested by a design idea, curtailing a fuller exploration of its implications.

Few of our design proposals include detailed scenarios of their intended use. Instead, they indicate what a system might do and establish, often implicitly, the 'needs' it might address, usually without including details of how this would be achieved technically or accessed by an interface. In their reticence, they invite viewers to speculate about these prospects themselves. It is not uncommon for people seeing our proposals—including, importantly, ourselves—to generate multiple stories of how the devices they describe might be used. These stories may include dystopian possibilities as well as positive ones (though rarely scenarios in which the devices are simply ignored), they may trace multiple, alternative paths, explore various technical and formal implementations, lead to suggestions for qualitatively different alternatives, and invoke different values (e.g. aesthetic or ethical) at different times. By avoiding the specification of detailed design scenarios, proposals can trigger speculation that opens the design space rather than closing it, which is often of great benefit in the early stages of design.

Creating Design Spaces

I have suggested that a single design proposal, when expressed with a requisite openness, can hint at a range of possibilities as it occasions people's speculation about the functions it might offer, how it might be realised, the circumstances in which it might be used, and the sorts of experiences and values it might serve. The power of design workbooks is in creating a much larger landscape for exploring such concerns by exploiting the combinatorial explosion of similarities and differences among many such proposals.

Consider, for instance, the Alternatives Workbooks described earlier [6]. The proposals they contained included two proposals for how information might be displayed in the home, a suggestion for an audio-only city guide that might lead you on unusual routes to your destination, a proposal for an artificially-intelligent birdfeeder that would train local songbirds to sing tunes of the user's choice, a device allowing people to influence their partners' dreams, another that would allow people to exercise their psionic powers, and one that would allow people to transmit their voices directly into space, whether as a form of electronically augmented prayer, or in an attempt to capture the attention of passing aliens.

Each of these proposals was potentially desirable and technically plausible, and indeed we later developed several of them further. Their real utility for the project, however, was in delineating a range of possibilities, technically, topically, and experientially, and in helping us to think about them ourselves and communicate them with our partners. For instance, the technologies they indicated ranged from displays and projectors to handheld devices, sensors, public displays, and so on. They simultaneously opened up a variety of technology we might consider, while implicitly suggesting that others, most notably those involving traditional arrangements of computers and monitors, were less interesting. In terms of topics, they brought into play issues of how information enters and is displayed in the home, how and why people navigate in the city, the importance of spirituality and non-traditional beliefs, our relationship with wildlife and each other, etc.

If the differences among the Alternatives pointed to a range of options for further investigation, equally important was what they had in common. Most fundamentally, all of the Alternatives proposals explored forms of engagement marked by curiosity, exploration and wonder rather than by the utilitarian pursuit of tasks. By presenting relatively concrete examples of technologies expressing such values, they simultaneously allowed the inductive definition of a genre of *design for ludic engagement* and provided a number of quasi-existence proofs that such an approach might be possible and interesting.

The notion of a 'design space' is a valuable metaphor for the way design workbooks can affect designers' perceptions of possibility. On the one hand, insofar as the similarities amongst the proposals they contain allow them to be seen as an integrated collection, workbooks pick out a particular configuration of concerns from amongst the vast range of possibilities open to design. On the other hand, their differences imply a kind of dimensionality that allows for other ideas—room to move around a central set of concerns and among the particular possibilities suggested by the proposals.

Of course, like any metaphor, the notion of a design space can be misleading. To begin with, variations among a reasonably sized set of proposals are not likely to reduce to a few dimensions, nor is it always useful, or even possible, to locate all proposals along all dimensions of contrast. One implication of this is that it is naive to think that simply looking in the 'spaces' between proposals can be a mechanism for generating new ideas. Instead, like a 'landscape' (rather than abstract Euclidian space), there may be areas that are impenetrable or uninhabitable. One of the challenges of design, from this perspective, is to identify the areas within a design space that can be successfully developed.

Design *creates* the spaces in which it operates. They do not pre-exist their manifestation, whether as undiscovered design ideas or as the abstract and rationalised parameter spaces that some of those who follow Simon [12] might suggest. Design workbooks are helpful in the process of elaborating a design space because in their multiplicity and simplicity they can allow the creation of a wide and complex territory relatively quickly, and in their provisionality they can invite the exploration of that space to discover particularly fertile areas within it.

In sum, constructing design workbooks can be valuable in turning from appreciating *what is* towards speculating about *what might be*. They ease the pressure of designing the 'right thing' [14], allowing designers to consider a range of external options and imagine how these might evolve, and to create and explore a space of designs before choosing to develop a particular option. In the next part of this paper, I describe another two design workbooks before turning to a discussion of the techniques for constructing proposals in this way.

TWO MORE WORKBOOKS

The Alternatives workbooks used a fairly limited set of techniques in their construction, largely involving collage, product visualisation and textual descriptions. In this section I describe a pair of more recent workbooks to illustrate a number of other techniques we have used in developing design proposals, as material for a more detailed discussion of techniques to follow.

Equator Workbook 1

The second two workbooks were produced in the course of developing designs within the Equator Interdisciplinary Research Collaboration, which brought together seven UK university groups to explore how computational technologies can blur the boundaries between electronic and physical worlds in everyday life (www.equator.ac.uk/). Within Equator, our group focused on home technologies.

With such an open-ended brief, an integral part of developing specific designs was to decide for ourselves how to orient to the home, what sorts of topics and activities our designs might address, the overall perspective we might take in addressing those topics and values, and the technologies that might help us do so. We set the stage with a Domestic Probes study of London households [8], as well as through eclectic research into possible views on the home ranging from previous work in HCI, sociology and the arts to psychoanalytic accounts of the home, descriptions of the home as a hiding place for contraband, and popular news articles about unusual domestic activities.

As our research matured, we moved to a phase of developing sketch proposals for the home in an improvised, inspiration-driven manner. The four members of the design team developed the proposals relatively independently, with frequent informal discussions in the studio to share ideas and coordinate development. After several months of developing our ideas we grouped the proposals into categories in a post hoc fashion, and gathered them together in a workbook of about 50 more-or-less distinct proposals and related treatments printed in A4 landscape format.

The individual team members each had their own techniques and approaches for expressing design ideas, so proposals varied in their visual appearance and use of text (see Figure 3). An overall shared style did emerge, however. The images used a variety of resources: found imagery, diagrams, and computer-generated images that themselves ranged from the clearly hand-constructed (e.g. Sailor's Return on the bottom right of Figure 3) to the more impersonal (e.g. Product Wars in the bottom centre). Nonetheless, the overall graphical style of this workbook is more open than the second Alternatives workbook, with more white space and a lack of background images. In addition, the spreads are looser, often juxtaposing images to

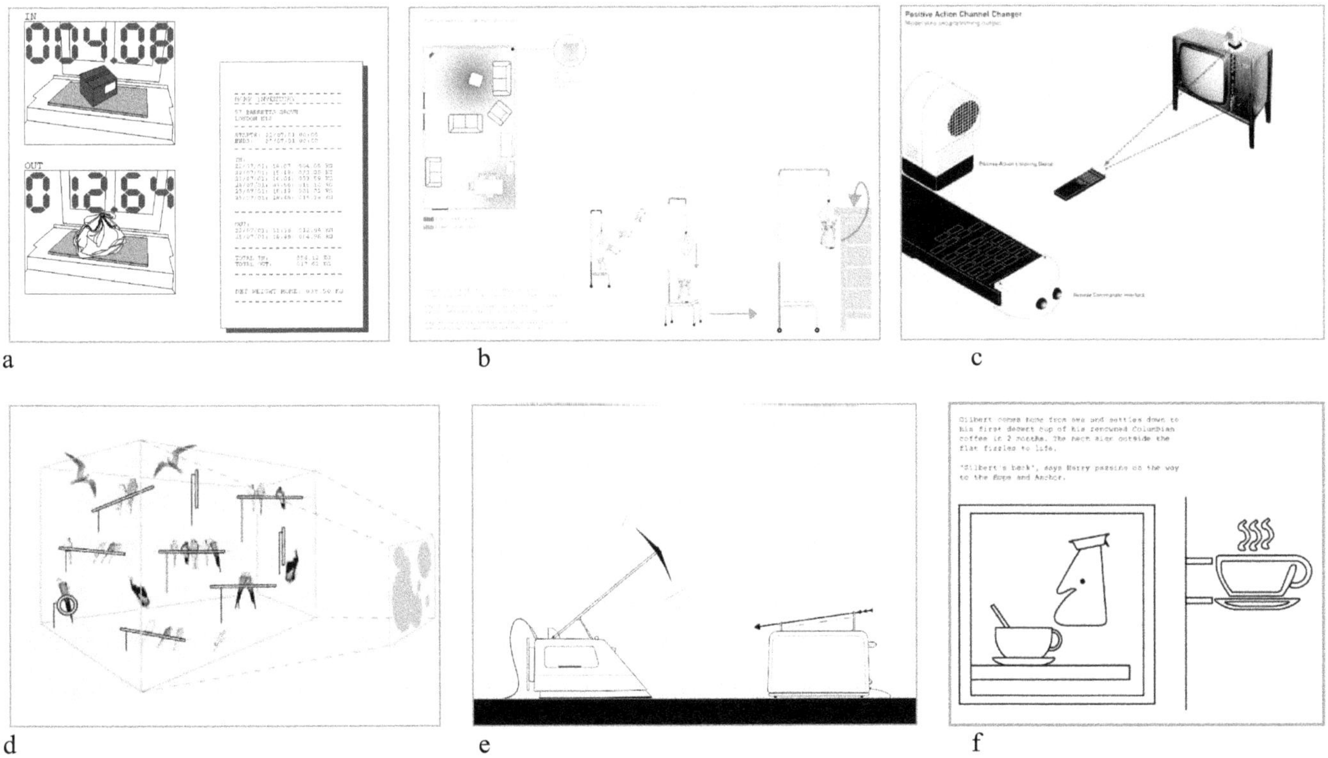

Figure 3. Proposals from Equator Workbook 1.

provide multiple views on an idea rather than presenting a single visual scenario.

The text of Equator Workbook 1 is also sparser than that of either Alternatives workbook. Many of the proposals include only a title and a line of explanation, with only a few using slightly longer explanations. For instance, the 'Sailor's Return' proposal shown on the bottom right of Figure 3 recounts a short narrative:

> ***Gilbert comes home from sea and settles down to his first decent cup of his renowned Columbian coffee in 2 months. The neon sign outside the flat fizzles to life.***
>
> ***"Gilbert's back", says Harry passing on his way to the Hope and Anchor.***

The text here conveys the essential idea of the proposal both technically and in terms of its most obvious intended social impact with humour and economy. Other proposals are much drier descriptions that leave the sociocultural implications implicit. For instance, the text accompanying the 'Nonessential Object Autosort' proposal at the top centre of Figure 3 reads:

> ***Step 1: A network of sensors monitors room activity in order to determine a hierarchy of space.***
>
> ***Step 2: Place any non-essential objects—ornaments, curios, unwanted gifts etc—in the trolley.***
>
> ***Step 3: The trolley then moves the objects around the home and finds unused space for them to live.***

Finally, a number of proposals consisted only of a single image and title. For example, the proposal at the bottom centre of Figure 3 is simply entitled 'Object Wars.' Such proposals point to a possible issue to be developed or situation to be explored while leaving both technologies and sociocultural implications completely unspecified.

We produced Equator Workbook 1 as a resource for our in-house design work, but also to distribute to our partners from other universities to indicate the direction of our work, share ideas, and invite collaboration. One group reviewed the workbook page by page in a meeting, and later told us that their attention was particularly caught by a proposal that suggested measuring the "Net Weight of the Home" by recording the total mass of all items entering or leaving the premises, thus allowing inhabitants to track whether their home was gaining or losing weight over time. According to their accounts at the time, this inspired the group to investigate how to equip surfaces ranging from floors to shelves with load-sensors to enable tracking of objects upon them. Their research in this area in turn led our group to consider applications of load-tracking technologies, which led to our first tranche of prototypes produced in the project [5].

Equator Workbook 3

Several years were occupied in developing the designs and field trials that resulted from Equator Workbook 1. As this phase ended we started to consider the new directions our design research might take. We did not feel the need to undertake more research on homes, given how much we had learned from our original research and through the field trials of the prototypes we had developed. Instead, the task was to develop new perspectives and approaches that might be productive for our designs.

Once again, producing a workbook was an important stage in developing the ideas that eventually led to a set of new prototypes. Similarly to the first Equator workbook, this was produced over several months by the team working individually with occasional informal meetings to discuss progress. The workbook comprised about 40 pages in A5 portrait format, and was divided into four sections: 'Tracking Objects In The Home', 'Storage And Display: How Our Stuff Is Represented', 'Links To The Outside World', and 'Imaginary Extensions'.

Workbook 3 contrasts visually with Workbook 1 in using fewer diagrammatic treatments and including more contextualised images. More interesting for the sake of this discussion, however, is the way it mixes different presentations of ideas. Some of the pages (e.g., Figure 4a) describe project ideas as was done in the earlier workbook.

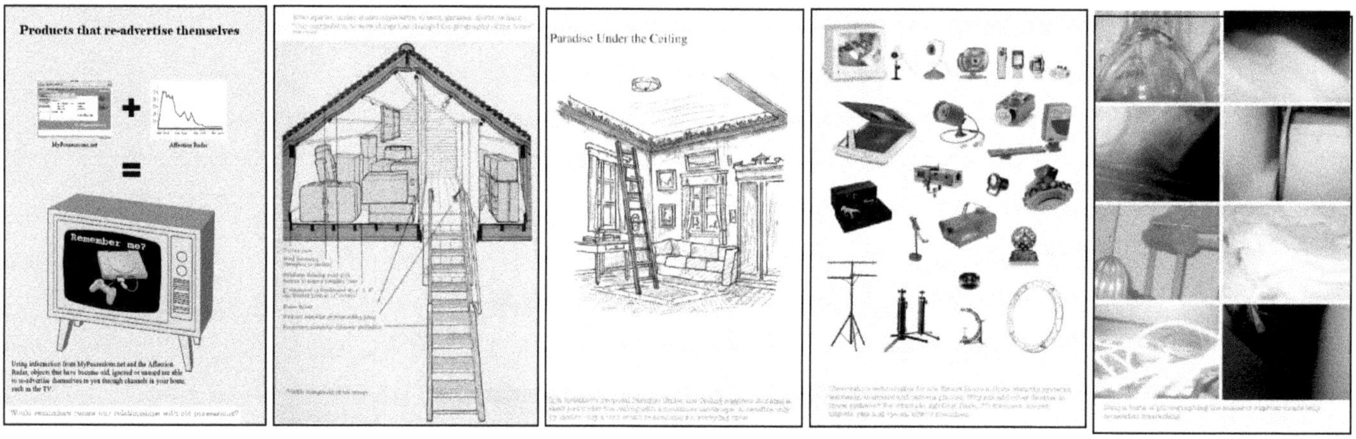

a b c d e

Figure 4. Pages from Equator Workbook 3.

Other pages, in contrast, explore more general issues. Figure 4b, for instance, highlights the proportion of space in our homes dedicated to storage. Others show images of artworks we found inspiring or directly suggestive of possible designs. Figure 4c, for example, shows Ilya Kabokov's 'Paradise Under the Ceiling', which suggests that inaccessibility may lead to a sense of wonder [9]. Still other treatments show illustrations of technical equipment that are suggestive without being directly relevant. For instance, 4d shows samples of movie-making equipment helpful in considering dramatic presentations of stored objects. Finally, some images showed results of our own design explorations. Figure 4e, for example, shows photographs taken of seldom-considered details of one of our homes. Similar mixtures of general considerations, artistic landmarks, external resources, experiments and proposals were used to explore a variety of topics.

Workbook 3 was again distributed to our project partners, but the primary intention in producing it was to advance our own design thinking. Over the following months, our development focused on one of the main themes of the workbook, having to do with the information thresholds of the home, culminating ultimately in the development of three deployed prototypes [7].

CONSTRUCTION TECHNIQUES

The four workbooks illustrate a range of techniques for constructing design proposals. In this section, I reflect on our practice, both to share methods that have been effective and, in particular, as a way of articulating the implicit intentions behind expressing ideas in particular ways.

Making Images

Few design proposals are described in words alone. Images are invaluable in expressing ideas for several reasons. They afford communicating an object's form or relationship with other components, as for example in Figure 3f. They allow a design to be appreciated both as an integrated whole and as a collection of more detailed parts, as in Figure 3c. Even if unable to fully convey complex ideas, images can serve as summaries or reminders, as in Figure 3d, or as shorthand representations of the basic issues, as in Figure 3e.

Images also tend to compel a degree of resolution about details of design ideas, which entails benefits and risks. This applies not only to the specification of functional aspects of a design, but also to the emotional or aesthetic tone it might convey. On the one hand, the specificity of images can be useful in encouraging consideration of aspects that might otherwise be left vague or overlooked altogether. In addition, the concreteness of images allows the ideas they represent to be approached as if they have an autonomous reality, independent from a particular imagination, which is useful in developing a disinterested stance towards them. However, their concreteness and detail can be dangerous in encouraging ideas to be treated as fixed, leading to designers becoming reluctant to explore alternative concepts or forms, or alternatively to objections to general ideas based on particular treatments. One of the aims in creating images for proposals, then, is to achieve a useful balance between resolution and indication, between actualising a design idea and leaving it open to change.

Collage and Found Images

Existing images can be a useful resource in constructing design proposals. They are appealing both for pragmatic and expressive reasons. On the one hand, they offer an appealing alternative to other forms of image creation insofar as they only require selection rather than creation (although a great deal of time may be spent finding and processing digital images, e.g. for use in collages). They can be used to imply that a proposed design might embody a similar form and scale, use similar materials, and perhaps involve similar technologies. In short, found images can sometimes be used as fairly literal representations of proposed designs.

More interesting, however, is the use of found imagery as indicative rather than representative. Images carry with them a host of information about materials, styles, kinds of people and places, aesthetics and cost that vivify them beyond their literal depiction of form and scale, and this can all be used to indicate features of proposed designs. The images used in Figure 1, for example, do not represent the intended appearance of an Objective View device, and it seems unlikely they would be interpreted as such. Instead, features of the image may trigger associations that can inform further design. The corkscrew's ridged handle, for instance, might resemble a cloud, indicating that the camera is to be launched high overhead, while the curling blade might symbolise the radio waves that would beam an image to the waiting receiver/bowl, or perhaps look like flight lines tracing the device's trajectory. Perhaps the corkscrew as a whole looks like a thundercloud, symbol of the stormy moods in which the device is to be used. Or perhaps it simply looks like a relatively high-priced gewgaw. Thoughts such as these, transient, speculative, hardly attended to, may be elicited by found imagery without requiring explication or commitment; often, found images may be chosen simply for the unexpected, difficult to control connotations they carry.

Collages build upon the suggestive potential of found imagery. They can be used relatively directly as building blocks to construct new images, but equally their power can lie in the combination and contrast of different parts. This can complicate the set of associations they make available, but equally, it can simplify interpretation by reinforcing some elements and not others. The Prayer Device (Figure 5), from the second Alternatives workbook, is an example of a collage, designed to form a single coherent image, which works in these ways. It was constructed by joining an image of a snorkel to part of an image of a floorlamp, whose glass shade has been inverted. Used to visualise a device that would transmit one's voice to the heavens, the bowl suggests an upwards-facing transmitter (rather than a source of illumination) while the mouthpiece indicates not only a place that one might speak (rather than breathe), but that speaking would be a intimate and potentially uncomfortable affair.

Found imagery can also be a useful resource in suggesting new ideas for design. Collecting, juxtaposing and relabeling (c.f. [3]) existing images while attending to their connotations and associations can be a fruitful source of inspiration. On these occasions, constructing proposals can merge with ideation itself.

Figure 5. The Prayer Device is represented by a collage.

Diagrams and Renderings

Found images and collage can lead to richly evocative images, but finding appropriate images can be difficult, and the results can lead in undesirable directions. A more controlled technique for constructing proposals is to produce imagery directly, in the form of diagrams, drawings and renderings at various degrees of finish. Most of the proposals in Figure 3, from the first Equator workbook, are constructed in this way. They range from the fairly literal renderings of the Positive Action Channel Changer shown in 3c, in which the televisions' audio signal would be monitored and the channel automatically changed in the case of inappropriate content, to the illustrations resembling cartoons (3e) or caricatures (3f).

The degree of detail of a diagram or rendering can be useful in indicating how developed a design is thought to be. Very simple, untextured, geometric renderings can give a basic indication of form and scale while clearly avoiding further commitment (e.g. 3d). However, detailed renderings are not necessarily to be taken as resolved. For instance, the Nonessential Object Autosort system shown in 3b indicates the functional requirements of a robot designed to stow 'non-essential' possessions using a fairly detailed, but highly improbable, image—the exaggeration here (as well as the title) clearly indicating that the idea needs developing. Similarly, the warring appliances in 3e are detailed but intended to illustrate a concept, not an actual design, a fact which their absurdity as well as their lack of texture and background all help to indicate.

Hybrid Images

Often diagrams and renderings are used with found images. For instance, a photograph of an existing setting may be overlaid with a diagram of a system to be designed, the different styles of imagery clearly distinguishing the real from the imaginary. The Placeholder proposal in Figure 2, for example combines a realistic backdrop with an image of a proposed device that itself combines collage with rendering. The simple block-and-clip picture-holder that represents the device's base simultaneously indicates its small size and simple form as well as the casual flexibility and perhaps low cost it is intended to have, while the rendered screen above is a more literal interpretation of the digital content it might display. Similarly, the untitled proposal in Figure 3d suggests that we might install sensors into a room, which one of our participants devoted to the keeping of about twenty birds, and use the resulting data to somehow visualise the birds' agitation as an indication of the household's overall well-being. The notional nature of this proposal is conveyed by the use of only the most diagrammatic indication of the room and display, while photographs of birds indicate that they, at least, are real.

Sketching

While reviewing our workbooks and proposals to develop this paper, I found that sketches (of the traditional, hand-generated sort) almost never appear within them. This is somewhat surprising given that in our studio we all actively sketch ideas throughout the design process as a way of visualising possibilities, working out problems, and communicating with one another—as writers such as Buxton [1] have pointed out, sketching is a fundamental technique through which designers think. In fact, many of our workbook pages are the result of a sketching process, in which we use sketches to develop both the design ideas and their presentation.

On reflection, there seems to be several reasons that we avoid reproducing sketches in our workbooks. First, they are too clearly authored to achieve the autonomy we require of them. Individual sketching styles are clearly identifiable, which makes merging proposals produced by different team members into an integrated collection difficult. In addition, traces of individual authorship may inhibit willingness to critique or suggest changes to the ideas they present, and this may be exacerbated when it is clear that a great deal of care has been put into their production. On the other hand, other methods of image generation also give evidence of the time taken to produce them, including the degree of conscious reflection about how to best represent an idea, that sketching may not indicate. Whereas sketches may be developed continuously from the first idea to the final drawing, other forms of production imply a pause for thought.

In sum, the lack of sketches in our notebooks reflects the properties we desire for the proposals they include. Design proposals should convey ideas as independent entities, able to be considered as separate from their authors and as part of an integrated collection. In addition, proposals should clearly have matured beyond their first conception, yet retain a requisite degree of provisionality to bring the ideas into play for speculation, development and inspiration of new ideas. In short, design workbooks are neither sketchbooks nor specifications, but in between the two, and the techniques used to create them reflect this.

Text

Images are almost always used to convey design proposals, but text usually plays a significant role as well. The balance between text and imagery in clarifying ideas can vary widely. Sometimes images serve to illustrate proposals explained largely through text, while in other examples text merely clarifies how to read an image. I describe these extremes separately to clarify the role that text plays and some of the writing techniques that are useful.

Text as Primary

In the Alternative workbooks, proposals relied on extensive text descriptions with images serving largely as illustrations to convey a sense of aesthetics and emotional tone. For example, the following text is from one of the proposals:

> **Intimate View**
>
> **The objective nature of text, words, even video images is not only unsatisfactory for supporting distant love relationships, but even seems to interfere with the deeper, more subtle forms of interaction that create intimacy.**
>
> **The Intimate View seeks to build a visual connection between lovers, but constrained so that shared perceptions, rather than visual facts, become the object. This is achieved by transmitting images from a tiny macro camera, or personal scanner, worn on the body.**
>
> **By sharing only tightly focused portion of the local environment--the veins of a leaf, a drop of water, the corner of one's smile--the system would encourage partners to join together in a moment of highly focused mutual perception. Used playfully, aesthetically, or erotically, the device would permit rich new forms of loving communication to exist even over great distances.**

Like most of the Alternatives proposals, this text takes the form of a short essay. The first paragraph sets out a perspective and identifies a problem from this point of view. The second conveys the proposal itself, in terms of a desired effect and how this might be accomplished technically. The third suggests the anticipated implications of the system.

These proposals may appear specific in the problems and solutions they describe, but they were intentionally written to be more ambiguous than they appear. For instance, they describe the technologies to be used in enough detail to seem plausible, but without over-specifying either a technical implementation or a particular interaction model. More fundamentally, important to the effect we tried to achieve was the tone we adopted in the writing. It is slightly over-earnest and yet deadpan, expressing a point of view clearly but without reflection or doubt. This adoption of an almost fictional voice—inspired in part by the artist Kabokov's [9] presentation of proposals as the inventions of fictional teachers, brick-layers and plumbers—appears effective in encouraging readers to approach the ideas from a critical remove, much as the exaggerated images described earlier invite scepticism.

Text as Subordinate

Many of our design proposals are expressed primarily through images, with text serving mainly to clarify them. Captions, titles and labels may be used with extreme economy to great effect. For example, the Positive Action Channel Changer is explained using merely the title, a subheading ('moderates programming output') and two labels ('Positive Action Listening Device' and 'Remote Commander Interface'). These four phrases, in conjunction with the images, serve to communicate the proposal adequately within the design team, and moreover, by echoing a phrase used by one of the Probe participants, give an indication of the kind of person for whom the device is intended, and the values it is meant to support.

Text is useful not only in explaining a proposed technology, but in setting its context and indicating the values that inform it. For example, the proposal for Products that Re-Advertise Themselves in Figure 4a contains a relatively lengthy description of how the system would operate, but also a simple caption: 'Would reminders renew our relations with old possessions?' that assumes a state of affairs (we neglect old possessions), a set of values (this neglect is undesirable) and a proposed solution (reminders), all in the form of a question inviting readers to think about their own position on the issues.

In addition, text can be used to transform material uncovered from background research into design proposals in their own right. For instance, a collection of movie-making equipment shown in Figure 4c becomes a proposal with the addition of a caption:

> **Observation technologies for the Smart Home include security systems, webcams, scanners and camera phones. Why not add other devices to these systems? For example, lighting, flash, 3D scanners, scopes, tripods, rigs and special effects machines.**

Used in this way, simple captions can invite readers to extrapolate beyond the material included in a design proposal. Rather than pointing to a reified idea, proposals like these establish a starting point for further speculation, serving as seeds for further design work.

DISCUSSION

The different forms proposals take—the images and text used to construct them—can convey a great deal of information about their nuances and the ways they are to be approached. Humour, for instance, can open an idea for play without undermining the insight it suggests (e.g. Figures 3b, e and f). Nonetheless, design workbooks also depend crucially on a community of practice that informs their interpretation and use. Many of the images and captions used in our proposals gain meaning within our team because they recall previous projects, conversations with volunteers, art and design work with which we are familiar, and cultural references that we share. Much as a conversation among old friends may be difficult for an outsider to comprehend, many of our proposals require explanation when used to communicate with project partners or the audiences for our design.

Constructing design workbooks to rely on our community of practice has advantages, however. Most fundamentally, we share an understanding that everything in a design workbook should be addressed as a proposal: that is, as indicating a direction and course of action for design. Increasingly, this applies to materials that we include in our workbooks that do not appear to be proposals at all. For example, the cut-away view of a house's storage spaces in Figure 4b points to a direction for design to address the amount of 'dead space' this represents. The image of Kabakov's 'Paradise Under the Ceiling', in 4C, suggests finding ways to revivify stored possessions as objects of rarity and wonder. Finally, the movie-making equipment in 4D, and the snapshots of disused spaces in one of our homes in 4E, both serve as explorations of how this might be achieved. These implications and connections are only hinted at by the images and text of the workbook itself; it is our established understanding of the role and purpose of workbooks that allows us to use them as they are intended.

Design workbooks, in our group, also express and depend on an underlying methodological approach that stresses the importance of initial design explorations. Workbooks such as the ones described here often take weeks or months to construct. They defy the assumptions of brainstorming sessions as traditionally understood, in which valuable design ideas are thought to emerge from quick, uncritical sessions of free association. Instead, they reflect the labour and care we feel necessary to establish new design spaces successfully. At the same time, the workbooks we produce often contain dozens of proposals and treatments, the vast majority of which will not be developed. By serving as archives of a thought process that may extend over a long period, sketchbooks ensure that we do not discard unused ideas, but may return to them years later. Most fundamentally, then, the workbooks, and our profligacy with ideas, reflects the fact that what we value in the process is not just the specific ideas themselves, but the space of opportunities to which they give access.

There can be problems in developing workbooks, of course. They are time-consuming to develop, and it can be seductive to over-produce them—that is, to craft their appearance beyond what is necessary to explore and convey a set of ideas. The proposals shown here were largely developed by experienced designers, but as Figure 1 indicates, they can also be realised effectively in a more amateurish style. In addition, workbooks are printed documents, which has several advantages (portability, ease of annotation, the ability to control formality) but means that representing dynamic interactions can be difficult (though indications are still possible). Finally, the mix of resolution, openness and provisionality that makes the workbooks effective within our established design culture can make them confusing for outsiders. These potential pitfalls need to be negotiated as projects develop.

More importantly, my description of developing myriads of proposals over long periods of time may make them appear unsuitable for commercial practice. This reflects our use of workbooks at the outset of open-ended research through design projects, when it is important to access a broad design space for investigation. In a commercial setting, however, such workbooks, developed across several projects, could be useful in establishing an ongoing sense of group identity, direction and style. We have also developed workbooks at later stages of projects, moreover, and for communicating ideas to participants and collaborators. Having already focused on a direction for design, our proposals tend to be fewer and more detailed, and the production time shorter, making these workbooks more similar to those that might be developed within commercial projects. Even in these more constrained situations, the commitment to multiplicity and provisionality the workbooks embody is useful in avoiding commitment to the first idea that seems feasible: workbooks still work to encourage exploration of rich and non-obvious spaces of opportunity.

ACKNOWLEDGEMENTS

My thanks to Andy Boucher, Andy Law, Heather Martin, Sarah Pennington, and Brendan Walker, who developed most of the proposals shown here. Thanks also to Andy Boucher, David Cameron and Nadine Jarvis for insightful comments on this paper.

REFERENCES

1. Buxton, B. *Sketching User Experiences*. Morgan Kaufmann Publishers Inc, 2007.
2. Carroll, J. *Making Use: Scenario-Based Design of Human-Computer Interactions.* MIT Press, Cambridge, MA, 2000.
3. Djajadiningrat, J, Gaver, W, & Fres, J. Interaction re-labelling and extreme characters. Proc. DIS '00, 2000, 66-71.
4. Dunne, A. *Hertzian Tales*. MIT Press, Cambridge, MA, 2006.
5. Gaver, W, Boucher, A, Bowers, J & Law, A. Electronic furniture for the Curious Home. IJHCI, 2007, 119-152.
6. Gaver, W. & Martin, H. Alternatives. Proc.CHI'00, 2000, 209-216.
7. Gaver, W., Boucher, A., Law, A., Pennington, S., Bowers, J., Beaver, J., Humble, J., Kerridge, T., Villar, N., & Wilkie, A. Threshold devices. Proc. CHI'08, 2008, 1429-1438.
8. Gaver, W., Boucher, A., Pennington, S. & Walker, B. Cultural Probes and the value of uncertainty, Interactions, 2004.
9. Kabokov, I. *A Palace of Projects*. Artangel, London, 1998.
10. Martin, H. and Gaver, W. Beyond the snapshot: From speculation to prototypes in audiophotography. Proc. DIS'00, 2000, 55-65.
11. Norman, D. *The Invisible Computer*. MIT Press, Cambridge, MA, 1998.
12. Simon, H. *The Sciences of the Artificial*. MIT Press, Cambridge, MA, 1969.
13. Wolf, T, Rode, J, Sussman, J, & Kellogg, W. Dispelling "design" as the black art of CHI. Proc. CHI'06, 2006, 521-530.
14. Zimmerman, J, Forlizzi, J, & Evenson, S. Research through design as a method for interaction design research in HCI. Proc. CHI '07, 2007, 493-502.

Inspirational Bits
Towards a Shared Understanding of the Digital Material

Petra Sundström[1], Alex S. Taylor[2], Katja Grufberg[1], Niklas Wirström[1], Jordi Solsona Belenguer[3], Marcus Lundén[1]

[1]Mobile Life@SICS
Box 1263, SE-164 29 Kista
{petra, katja, niwi, mlunden}@sics.se

[2]Microsoft Research
7 JJ Thomson Avenue
Cambridge, CB3 0FB, UK
ast@microsoft.com

[3]Wireless@KTH
Electrum 229
SE-164 40 Kista
jordisb@kth.se

ABSTRACT
In any design process, a medium's properties need to be considered. This is nothing new in design. Still we find that in HCI and interactive systems design the properties of a technology are often glossed over. That is, technologies are black-boxed without much thought given to how their distinctive properties open up design possibilities. In this paper we describe what we call *inspirational bits* as a way to become more familiar with the design material in HCI, the digital material. We describe inspirational bits as quick and dirty but fully working systems in both hardware and software built with the aim of exposing one or several of the dynamic properties of a digital material. We also show how they provide a means of sharing design knowledge across the members of a multi-disciplined design team.

Author Keywords
Digital materials, Design, Design materials, Design approach, Multi-disciplined design teams, Bluetooth, RFID, Accelerometers, Wireless sensor networks, Sensor nodes, Radio communication, Radio signal strength

ACM Classification Keywords
H.5.m Miscellaneous

General Terms
Design

INTRODUCTION
As a research group tasked with designing interactive systems, we are made up of an eclectic assortment of differently skilled individuals - a multi-disciplined arrangement that now arguably typifies a significant proportion of R&D groups in HCI. Not only do our members consist of the prerequisite software engineers and interaction designers. We also have people skilled in hardware, experimental psychology, qualitative fieldwork and even choreography.

Assembled in this way, one issue the group regularly faces is how to work, collectively, to imagine new interaction possibilities and different applications of emerging technology. Too often we find ourselves reverting to the established sub-divisions of social science, design and engineering, and conforming to a design approach where insights into users' experiences are applied to drive design and development. We may use lab-based or in-the-field studies of people's activities to inform an interactive system's design, or use evaluations of working prototypes to shape new design iterations. However, the actual building of the technical systems, even when iterative, is bracketed off.

Although this approach will be familiar to many and recognized as one that has produced valuable outcomes, we have found it troubling on two counts. First, it feels that much of the emphasis at the early stages of design exploration is placed on what users do and, consequently, attention is directed away from exploring and thinking imaginatively about the technologies. Often the technologies are chosen to solve a user need or support some experience before thoroughly examining their distinctive properties and how they might open up the design possibilities. In effect, the technologies are treated as black boxes, configured to enable predefined interaction scenarios.

Second, we find it leads to a largely linear and one-directional form of communication within our group. At best, the ideas used to open up the design possibilities flow from the studies of users to those who build the interactive systems. The actual implementation of a system remains closed; as a group, we rarely get a sense of the technologies until they are an integral part of a working prototype. Thus, there is little discussion between the skill sets in the group about what the properties of the technologies are and, again, whether they might open up new possibilities. In short, there are few chances in the design process to simply explore the technology, collaboratively.

In this paper, we present our recent and ongoing efforts to address these two concerns. We describe an approach to interactive systems design using *inspirational bits* that aims to foreground technologies as design materials early on in the design process. We see the approach as complimenting the design strategies many of us in HCI have become familiar with and, importantly, encouraging dialogue within multi-skilled interaction design teams. What we hope to convey in reporting our own experiences is that inspirational bits might be seen as a generally applicable method, relevant to groups involved in interactive systems design other than ours.

BACKGROUND

To address what we have felt to be our group's lack of collaborative experimentation with technology, we have in a number of recent projects attempted various strategies to expose and experiment with the properties of technologies. That is, we have sought to identify some of the defining features of a technology and then informally experiment with their configurations. We have found this technological un-blackboxing, if you will, has provided us with a richer set of possibilities when designing interactive systems; in effect, exposing the properties of the technology has opened us up to discovering new and in some cases unexpected directions for our designs.

A recent example is a project in which we used wireless, motion sensors to capture and display the emotional character of a community's physical movements [16]. Initially, we had hoped to use the radio signals from the sensor devices to triangulate location and then visually display the physical proximity between people alongside a visualization of their movements. However, we found this location detection to be far too unreliable because of the manner in which radio signals travel. Instead, through a series of experiments with radio and the sensors, we found we were able to detect and reliably communicate concurrent movements between people. This allowed us to cluster common kinds of movements and visually present them to the users, enabling them to interpret both the kinds of emotions being physically expressed and the prevalence of the expression in real-time.

One lesson we drew from this project was that in starting with a particular end goal in mind we found ourselves thwarted by the particular constraints of radio transceivers - constraints that only became apparent as we sought, unsuccessfully to determine location and physical proximity. Instead of viewing these constraints as a barrier to progress, however, we decided to take a different starting point. In short, we chose to think of the constraints as basic properties of the technology and to purposefully exploit them. Rather than stick to a predefined design and user experience to be achieved with a chosen technology, the system emerged by starting with a treatment of the technology as a material, alongside the other factors shaping the work. The final design came about because we eventually allowed the properties of the technology to play a stronger role in shaping the outcome and be a formative resource driving the overall design process.

On the face of it, such a process may seem unremarkable. Yet, what has struck us in looking back is how this particular treatment of technology as a design resource is not something we have really pursued with deliberate intent, nor regularly brought up in shared discussions among the interdisciplinary members of our design team. Indeed, in our experience the default position has often been to think of the technology as a means to solve a defined problem such as detecting location. It has been only when we have started getting our hands dirty, so to speak, that we have found ourselves tweaking the underpinnings of a technology and almost accidently arriving at some promising possibility. Consequently, such an exercise has not been pursued as a systematic component, where it is deliberately used as a resource for expanding or *"opening up the play of possibilities for design"* (to borrow a phase from another context [2]).

In articulating this, we want to be careful to distinguish our reflections from the conventional forms of techno-centric innovation that HCI has made it its business to address. We see this re-centering of technological concerns as remaining very closely tied to user and design concerns, and human centered/experience-oriented design, specifically. However, in bringing together the user, design and technological concerns, what we aim to explore in this paper is whether we might start from different points of entry – and in this particular instance, from the material and architectural properties of the technology (cf [5], [6]).

RELATED WORK

Most of us will readily accept that algorithms, databases, hardware, communication standards, etc. have their own limitations and possibilities. Embedded in each are properties that are more or less fixed, even though the possibilities for combining them are almost endless [11]. Also, development work rarely starts from scratch; instead, we build using existing libraries, established communication protocols etc. each with their own pre-defined properties.

In this vein, Vallgårda and Redström talk of *computational composites*, alloys made up of a combination of digital material that impose particular properties [18]. Thus, they explain that it is almost impossible to work with the digital material in its most raw form, at the granularity where technology *"handles only voltage according to stored sequences of (practically) discrete voltage levels and maybe input streams likewise of (practically) discrete voltage levels"* (p. 516). Components such as accelerometers, short-range communications etc. build on top of this basic level, and, in turn, become subsumed into yet more abstract interactive systems, such as PCs, mobile phones, etc. Because of this layering of technology, what we find in HCI and interactive systems design is that the particular properties of low-level technologies are often glossed over.

This appears to stand in stark contrast to the techniques and approaches that permeate studio-based and creative design practices [3]. Through sketches, mock-ups and early prototyping, traditionally schooled designers engage in a *conversation with materials* [15]. In the formation of a new idea the materials are worked with is such a way that they start to *talk back*, revealing new opportunities and challenges. It seems, however, that computing technology is a more complicated material for many designers to work with [8]. It is a material that evolves over both space and time [7]. It is not enough to touch and feel this material in any given moment and thereby get to know its properties and potentials; instead; the digital material has to reveal itself and its dynamic qualities when put together into a running system.

One popular approach to supporting developers and designers building interactive systems has been to work on so-called support tools. Yet, most of these systems aim to support designers in the processes of visualizing and refining an interactive system's design (e.g. [9], [13]), not to handle and explore the digital material. There are also a range of systems that enable designers to rapidly reconfigure the construction of their designs, such as varying the color, form and overall build of an object, and also visualize previous versions of a design (e.g. [17]), but still this does not provide access to the full range of possibilities the digital material might offer. The designer remains, in some fashion, removed from the actual technology.

The range of *plug and play* building block solutions provide an alternative, hands-on approach to building systems and, in doing so, go some way towards solving the immediacy problem. These systems, such as Phidgets[1] and Arduino[2], let the amateur hardware developer/maker handle and come to understand more of the digital material's potentials, making the material more open to what Schön refers to as *reflection in action* [15]. But, they still compartmentalize and blackbox basic building blocks such as RFID, Bluetooth, accelerometers, etc. Arguably, this is intended in their design and the basis of their success.

In the following, we thus present a strategy or approach to support the creative and collaborative experimentation with technologies that are usually embedded and thus taken for granted in the design process. As we have suggested, this approach has emerged through our own varied experiences of designing interactive systems in a multi-disciplined group. For example, it builds on our efforts to learn from designers and their use of sketches, storyboards and mock-ups to open up a design space and how they find inspiration in a range of new design ideas. It also draws on the attempts we have made to design *hand in hand* with the digital material [16]. It has been informed too by the increasing number of experiences we have had with hardware kits such as Arduino and Phidgets. Rather than using the kits to build specific solutions, however, our experiences have been centered on getting to know the workings of the technologies and their peculiar properties. Last but not least, it hinges on our processes of engaging all members/disciplines of our group in the generative stages of design thinking.

For the purposes of this paper, the phrase we have adopted to articulate this roughly circumscribed and still evolving approach is inspirational bits. Our idea is for an inspirational bit to offer the basic elements of a technology in a shape that allows all members of a design team to *look* at it, *feel* it and experience it over time and space - exposing all or some of the properties of the technology as a material. The inspirational bits approach thus involves the design team's attempts to work with and handle the technology; exposing its parts, and figuring out how it really works. To communicate the properties of the material to the design team, a fun and inspirational application of the technology is then used. The examples we present are made up of a range of quick and dirty games as we had the idea that the incentives people naturally have to understand the rules of a game would be helpful in conveying technological limitations and properties.

More specifically, this paper describes how we started out to explore Bluetooth as a design material and how we used the feedback we received in our continuous work refining the approach as well as going on to build bits using RFID, accelerometers, and wireless sensor networks. It also describes a two-days workshop to which we invited designers from both research and industry to introduce them to the idea of using inspirational bits in design. From this workshop, we describe how the feedback from one of the more experienced designers has helped us to be clearer about what we want the inspirational bits to be.

INITIAL EXPLORATIONS

Something that contributed early on to this idea of inspirational bits was an exploration we undertook into Bluetooth. Bluetooth was chosen as a technology for a number of reasons. Broadly, we were attracted to the ubiquity of Bluetooth and its status as a standard for wireless, short-range data communication. We felt this provided us with a technology that is often seen as a closed system or black box with numerous taken for granted properties. Again, the intention was not to solve a specific problem using Bluetooth or to achieve some predefined endpoint. It was rather to see whether a focused investigation into Bluetooth, as a design medium, might open us up to anything different and/or unexpected—that is, to find what could be inspirational in this technology.

One thing we found interesting was how a Bluetooth device cannot search and listen at the same time. One device needs to be searching and one needs to be listening for two devices to find each other. Incidentally, this is a property of Bluetooth that is problematic when it comes to peer-to-peer connectivity as both systems may be searching or listening at the same time and therefore not find each other (as in e.g. the MobiTip system [14]). BluePete is an inspirational bit we have built that aims to expose this material property of

[1] www.phidgets.com
[2] www.arduino.cc

Figure 1. BluePete; on the left a device having him and on the right a device about to get him (being this close)

Bluetooth and also in order to show how it can be played with that the Bluetooth technology needs two clients to be in different modes in order for them to find each other. In this quickly implemented game searching devices "carry" BluePete and listening devices are in danger of "catching" him, which can happen when the two devices are close enough, see Figure 1. Playing this game allows a design team to experiment with the relationship between proximity, connectivity and exchange (e.g. sneaking up on someone, physically hold on to them or taking their phone). Playing the game also allow all parties of an multi-disciplined design team to think of new ways of exploiting these Bluetooth properties and other scenarios where the properties might add to the experience of a system's design.

BTScore is another of our Bluetooth bits. The BTScore bit reveals the Bluetooth devices that are nearby and of what kind they are, e.g., headsets, printers, mobile phones, etc. The bit thereby helps to explain what information one Bluetooth device will send to another, such as device class, services provided and more, and thus reveals a property that might be used for the purposes of design. In BTScore a device's class number allocates a predefined point value when a connection is made with it. To increase their scores users thus have to run around looking for potential Bluetooth devices to connect to. Coincidently, the device class numbering scheme for Bluetooth devices works well with this game design as rare devices tend to have a higher number than common devices, such as 7936 for an Bluetooth Arduino board versus 512 for a smart phone. The bit, then, conveys something of the practical details and the real-world workings of the Bluetooth protocol and, specifically, how devices differentiate themselves through connections and communication.

These examples hopefully capture some of the key ideas we think to be of value in the inspirational bits approach. First and foremost they illustrate the understanding of the material one can get from using them. They show too how this can be achieved with quick and simple systems. For example, BTScore was built in a day or two and relies on a crude graphical interface to convey details about the device class numbering in Bluetooth. Also by presenting the two examples, we hope they capture the experimental quality of the approach. It should be clear that different features of the technology led to different strategies for exposing and working creatively with the properties and constraints. In this way the approach is seen as open-ended and relatively unstructured. Again, the aim is to be generative and to let the material's properties serve as a guide in this creative process.

BITS EXPOSURE

To introduce other designers and researchers to the inspirational bits approach and to get their perspectives on working with technologies as design materials we have presented our Bluetooth bits at two workshops: the Materialities workshop[3] at the Designing Interactive Systems conference 2010 and at the Artifacts workshop[4] at CHI 2010. At both workshops we received very positive feedback. Broadly, the responses suggested the approach was seen as valuable in helping to understand technologies as a medium for design and in generating new design ideas.

At the Artifacts workshop the Bluetooth bits were the starting point for a design exercise; the workshop participants, having used the bits, were told to brainstorm around Bluetooth technology and develop design sketches. In total, a broad range of ideas was generated. Here though we wish to focus on the workshop participants' impressions of using inspirational bits to inspire design. One overall impression was how the ideas that came about seemed to be more grounded in the material. This in comparison to ideas that came out of a similar exercise in the workshop using inspirational pictures of various kinds.

We have also used the Bluetooth bits as a starting point for a design project in the Affective Interaction course given at Stockholm University. Here, the students showed a fascination with the bits. They said they liked how the technology had been transformed into experiences, and how it was the experiences—in this case of Bluetooth, such as the experiences of hunting or being pushed something—that inspired them. However, the students reported struggling to develop their own designs recounting how it was one thing to understand and another to recreate/make use of the bits.

This latter result, in particular, got us thinking about the principal intention of the bits approach. It had never been our intention that the bits would explain how to work with the material; our aim was to use inspirational bits to promote a greater familiarity with the technology and to communicate this knowledge within the design team. In contrast to plug and play toolkits, such as Arduino and Phidgets, we hoped for users of the bits not to become individually accomplished system engineers. Rather, we intended for the design team itself to mark out time to build and come to understand some provided bits and then communicate this knowledge to all members of the team

[3] http://sites.google.com/site/materialitiesdis2010/

[4] http://people.cs.vt.edu/~swahid/chi2010-artifacts/

and subsequently use this knowledge in the design process. We also imagined this to be a cumulative process where teams and individuals in the teams retained skills and knowledge around particular technologies and their bits.

GOING BROAD

With this early indication that we were on to something useful and something design teams possibly want, we decided to expand our exploration to include other digital materials. In the following, we describe our application of the inspirational bits approach using RFID, accelerometers, and wireless sensor networks, further detailing the approach as well as showing how it has evolved. For each technology we first give a short summary of some of the characteristics and properties of the technology and then mention just a few of the bits we built using the technology. Each section ends with a summary of the bits discussed and what property they aim to convey. The presented examples have been chosen, in part to convey the diversity of bits that can come from working with quite different digital materials and how such a diversity can be the source of creativity. Our hope is the range and variety of bits may help to communicate the underlying notion of this work, that the digital material really is a *material*, and a material we need to consider in design like any other.

RFID

Radio Frequency Identification (RFID) is a material that has been experimented with in the past (e.g. [12]). In the work we present, however, the distinctive intention has been to consider what happens when the technology's properties are exposed in the design process and to design teams.

RFID is a technology that uses radio waves for sending and reading information at a distance. This communication occurs between a reader and a tag. The angle of a tag's antenna with respect to the reader's antenna is critical for a tag to be read. The diZe is an inspirational bit that was designed to convey this property. This bit is a board game that consists of a high frequency RFID reader with a very large antenna and a dice with pockets on each side, see Figure 2. In this bit, the reader's antenna defines the area of the game board. A player chooses one of the pockets of the dice for a RFID tag and then throws the dice onto the board. This only gives the tag a one-in-three chance of being read. Because of the direction of the magnetic flow that the reader's antenna creates, current will be induced only when the antenna's tag is perpendicular to the magnetic flow. With these properties in mind, the game can be introduced as it is or in a context chosen for a design task specifically.

RFID might not be as complex as a design material as perhaps some of the other materials presented in this paper. But the diZe in a very good way exemplifies how a bit does not need to be complex. How a bit, in fact, can be something very simple. Through something as easy as varying the size of a familiar technology can make its workings intelligible but also open it up for new ways of thinking about its use. But also how a deeper knowledge in materials offers us the possibility of twisting and tweaking the underpinnings of that material to open up for more innovative ideas. But, in order to be inspirational the question is, if this bit is enough? We will return to this question later in the paper, but what we see here is a possible difference between bits that are designed to explain and bits that are meant to inspire. What we see though is that it may be a range of bits that is in fact what is needed to fully understand the range of possibilities of a material.

Another slightly more complicated bit we developed using the large RFID antenna is our strategic game, inteRFere. This is a two-player game where each player has a set of three tags and must role them in such a way that their tag is the last one read. The game is designed to demonstrate the properties of antenna interference, variations in magnetic field strength and that readers can only communicate with one tag at the time. For example, this bit reveals how two tags on top of one another can cause interference and also that there is an inverse relationship between magnetic field strength and the distance between the tag's and reader's antennae.

To emphasize the diversity of the bits we have built, before continuing we also want to briefly mention BendID. BendID is a game that aims to break away from the conventions of handheld technologies and, in the case of RFID, the common assumption of one-tag-per-user. In

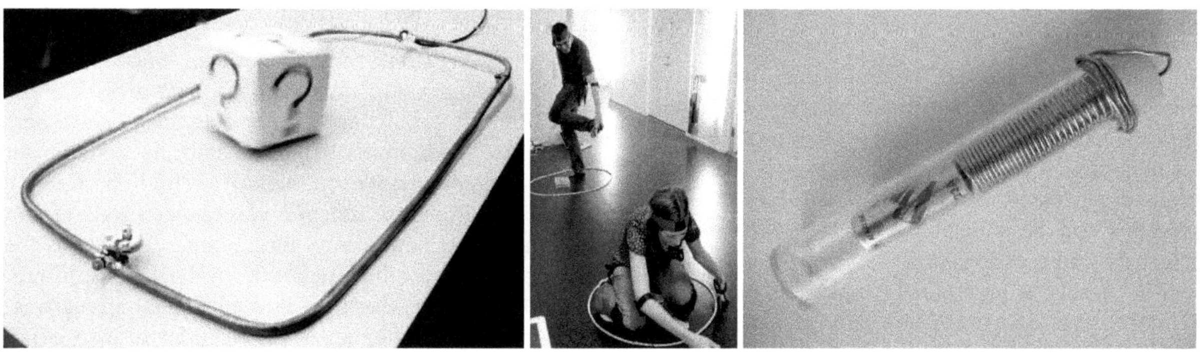

Figure 2. The diZe – a playful presentation of the reading angle of RFID; BendID – a bit where the user wears tags over her whole body; A mechanical model of an accelerometer showing how gravity always is a factor

BendID each user has tags placed over her body. When a game master calls a specific body part the aim is to be the first player to have that body part read without stepping out of a small circle on the floor, where the reader is placed, see Figure 2.

To summarize:

- diZe – demonstrates how the relationship between the tag's and reader's antennae is critical;
- InteRFere – demonstrates the properties of antenna interference, variations in the magnetic field and how a reader can only communicate with one tag at a time; and
- BendID – plays with the conventions of hand held technologies, in this case with several RFID tags distributed over the body.

The Accelerometer

The accelerometer is a sensor that measures change of velocity (acceleration) relative to freefall (or zero gravity) and transforms this measure into a proportional electric signal. The device is usually attached to an object, the acceleration of which one wants to measure.

To visualize the basic mechanics of an accelerometer and also to show how gravity continuously acts on the acceleration that is measured, we found that we needed something as basic as a mechanical model. This model consists of a transparent tube, a mechanical spring and a small weight. One end of the spring is attached to the top of the tube, and the other is attached to the weight. When the tube is moved, the displacement of the weight corresponds to the acceleration that is affecting it. With this tube we wanted to show how it really is acceleration and not movement that an accelerometer captures, something one would think is obvious, but as the accelerometer is used very often to capture movements and also does so rather well [16] the misunderstanding is common. Our test tube, so to speak, also illustrates how accelerometer measurements are always influenced by gravity, as it reveals that when turned towards the ground an effect is apparent even though it is being held perfectly still (see Figure 2). A combination of three such test tubes visualizes the same characteristics of a three-dimensional accelerometer.

Another interesting property we found was how accelerometers in fact sense movement slightly differently, even when moved together. This is a typical issue that can become frustrating in a design situation if it is exact data that is wanted/needed. With our WaveRave bit we aim to show how this can be a design feature. WaveRave is a multiplayer game where the aim is to follow the movements of a leader as closely as possible. To make this game a full body exercise, the accelerometers are attached to the players' chests rather than held in the hand, where it is easier to control the accelerometer using small hand gestures. Players must thus "follow" the physical movements of the leader as best they can. Scores are continuously updated depending on the similarity between a player's accelerometer readings and the leader's. However, imperfect measurements and imperfectly calibrated devices add an extra dimension to the pleasure of playing this game. Players' devices can also be attached differently than that of the leader. For example, by turning the leader's device upside down, players are forced to perform movements that are inverted to that of the leader.

To summarize:

- The mechanical model - visualizes the basic mechanics of an accelerometer and how gravity always acts on the measured acceleration; and
- WaveRave – shows how imperfect devices can be inspiration to a game and in a way the game feature.

Wireless Sensor Networks

Wireless sensor networks consist of sensor nodes that can communicate and share data with each other in various ways. Each sensor node is a small electronic system containing a transceiver, a microcontroller and different kinds of sensors. For the following bits we have been working with sensor nodes communicating over radio. More specifically, we have been working with electromagnetic radiation, radio waves that propagate in space and travel at the speed of light.

In several of our previous designs we have encountered problems with wireless sensor networks and radio (e.g. [16]). The fact is that radio signal strength is currently one of the most common ways to perform outdoor and indoor positioning. This works relatively well outdoors, but indoors the technology is susceptible to interference from many sources. For this reason, we have found radio particularly hard to think through and design with in the multi-disciplined teams we have worked in. In short, the very immaterial characteristics of this material accentuate the problems; even though the sensors can be seen and their use can be discussed in various scenarios, it is not always easy to see/feel how the radio communication works, and why it is so hard to calculate distance and position (indoors). Therefore, in starting our design exploration into sensor networks, we first set out to try to make this problem more visible, more material.

We built two bits for this purpose, one turning the radio signal strength into sound and one into graphics. The sound bit, RadioSound, consists of two sensor nodes where one is equipped with a small speaker emitting a single tone. The tone increases with the signal strength between the two nodes. Using these sensor nodes one can walk around in the environment noting how the volume changes as the signal is affected by other materials, walls and furniture. Using this bit one can also hear how the signal strength is greatly affected by the human body. In order to also explain how the signal strength measurement is difficult to measure for fast moving and moving sensor nodes, we also decided to build a bit using a graphical representation of the radio signal strength. In this second bit, that later evolved into the GoldRush game, the size of a graphical circle visualizes signal strength. As the circle sometimes disappears, completely, this graphical representation very clearly shows the fluctuations in the signal strength measurement when a node is moving quickly in relation to a receiver node and how a signal stabilizes when holding it still. Also the circle flickers more if the two nodes are far apart.

As one of the intentions with the bits is to turn limitations into possibilities, we explored using these thought of limitations of the radio material as possible features. In GoldRush, for example, a sensor node is hidden, and then looked for by the game's players using a combination of another sensor node and the graphical representation described above. This hide-and-seek game is made more challenging by giving the four players their own sensor nodes and graphical representations of the hidden node. This demands that players cooperate by, for instance, asking others to stand back not to lessen the interference cause by their bodies or sharing their individual graphical representations to find the hidden sensor node faster.

Playing with this bit, we also found that we could use the flickering of the circle as an indicator of whether a sensor node was moving slow or fast. This we used in a second game, Gymkhana, in which the aim is, initially, to move as fast as possible to disturb the signal reception as much as possible and thereby gain points. Players then aim to limit the amount of points they lose by moving between a set of distributed sensor nodes, undetected.

To summarize:

- RadioSound – visualizes the radio signal strength between sensors and how it is affected by the environment and the human body;
- GoldRush – turns the difficulty of using radio signal strength for positioning into a game feature; and
- Gymkhana – visualizes and plays with how the measurement of radio signal strength is different/difficult to measure correctly when there is a lot of movement in the room.

WORKSHOP @ MOBILE LIFE

Our most recent activity targeted at exploring the inspirational bits process has centered on a workshop in which we wanted to get feedback about both the bits and the approach as a whole.

In August 2010 we invited our colleagues and partners at the Mobile Life centre to a two-day workshop where we allowed everyone to experience and learn more about the materials we had worked with so far. Approximately twenty designers and researchers took part in this event. To allow everyone to handle, experience and play with the bits, we divided them into three smaller groups and gave each group time to work with the RFID hardware, accelerometers, and sensor nodes. Each material session lasted for approximately two hours. The first day each group got two such material sessions and one the day after. The second day we also gave each group a design exercise to find out if they felt they could apply what they had learnt.

For this paper, we have asked one of the workshop participants, Anna Karlsson from BORIS design studio[5] in Hong Kong for her thoughts on the idea of using inspirational bits in design and also on the workshop in general. We chose to solicit feedback from Anna for a number of reasons. One important reason was that she does not usually work as a researcher but rather as a professional designer in an international design firm. With her extensive experience in doing design and also working both in multi-disciplined design teams and in collaboration with other stakeholders in a design process we regarded Anna a good person to ask for feedback. Anna has also worked with us on a number of occasions on different projects, and held the role of design research consultant with us. We present Anna's feedback, below, not as a formal evaluation of the idea of using inspirational bits in design, but instead as a means to convey how the idea was responded to in practice, and also as a resource to better articulate our own ideas on this matter.

Below, we have chosen to focus on three themes Anna raised in her feedback: *the idea in general*, *a categorization of the bits*, and *a template for constructing bits*.

The idea in general

First a quote from Anna's feedback to the general idea:

"The inspirational bits approach is about play; it is a positive way to approach a technology. During the play you will learn certain things about the material and the learnings are something you will bring with you to the next step in the design process. Keeping the bits intact could though have the opposite effect for the design team, the team can get stuck on the initial ideas and not be able to move on to the next step. It is therefore important as I see it to point out that after experiencing the bits they should be broken down into their basic material parts; these are what you can use as the foundation for innovation.

The inspirational bits approach is a good way to start a complex project, it helps the team to get a better idea of the material's properties, possibilities and limitations and it also lays the ground for more equal discussions within the group. This is maybe one of the most important aspects you can get from using the inspirational bits approach.

The inspirational bits can also help the design process to become less linear. By integrating construction and production at the start of product development, this cross disciplinary way of working creates a common platform of knowledge for the whole team."

[5] www.borisdesignstudio.com

A categorization of the bits

In her feedback, Anna also explained how she experienced the bits to be quite different to each other and was therefore compelled to categorize them. She explained how a categorization of the bits would help her and others decide what category of bits that should be used in different projects, or different phases of a project. This is something we had started to contemplate ourselves. We had begun to categorize the bits in terms of whether they served some explanatory role or whether a particular property served as inspiration. From this in mind, we found Anna's feedback as an outsider to the approach to be particularly interesting. In effect, we have found it to provide a useful counter-position to our own.

Anna's categorization consists of four categories; *core bits*, *educational bits*, *boundary bits* and *beyond bits*.

Core Bits - "Give it to me in one sentence or 3 secs"

These are bits that can be described in one sentence or quickly grasped in three seconds, Anna explains. An example of such bit is the oversized mechanical model of the accelerometer.

"Using these bits the approach is similar to a design method where you establish the very basics of things as a way to inspire innovation. It is similar to the task of designing a chair where one had to explain what a chair is in one sentence, a sentence that really grasps the concept of a chair. One such sentence could be: 'A horizontal plane big enough for one person to sit'. This explanation opens up for innovation rather than frames you in an idea of what a chair is. The core bits as I see them are about explaining technology in that very same way and thus opening up for innovation."

Educational Bits - "Explain it to me, I am an idiot"

Anna explains how these are bits that share a focus on learning, they convey the basics of a technology. The fewer aspects of the material that are highlighted the better and the easier the bit is to grasp. There should be no value *vis-à-vis* a final design when creating an educational bit. An example of an educational bit is the diZe. The level of complexity in this bit is low, it is immediately or very quickly understood.

Boundary Bits - "Show me the Limits"

The boundary bits are about highlighting a downside to the technology. They serve to break pre-defined ideas about a material and to start group discussions. An example of such a bit is the RadioSound bit.

"The boundary bits are similar to the educational bits as the defining characteristic is learning. The boundary bits are powerful in the way that the whole team gets a full understanding of the limitations of a material before proceeding with a design conceptualization. Another great advantage of the boundary bits is the time that could be saved in the development process of a new service or product: 'show me the limits so that I can avoid traps.'"

Beyond Bits - "Turn the limitation into a feature"

The last of Anna's four categories she calls "beyond bits". This category she explains are bits that are very creative and can trigger a lot of spin-off ideas. They thus tackle the limitations of a material and turn them into features. A good example here is the Gymkhana bit.

"To summarize the first three categories, they are all about understanding a technology, here refereed to as the material. These bits should be built and explained by those who know the material well. The fourth category is slightly different and could be used as the subsequent phase, after presenting bits in the first three categories. The beyond bits could work as a good kickoff in the concept design phase in a development project where the developers get together with the rest of the team to take things one step further. The beyond bits are about making use of the things the design team all learnt from the earlier bits."

We are very grateful to Anna for giving us this extensive feedback; it has helped us to be clearer about what we want the bits to be. We find her categorization useful because it captures the diverse role bits can play at various levels of applicability and complexity; we see how some are more inspirational and others better explain the basic elements of a material. Anna's categorization scheme offers an approachable way of understanding the bits in these terms.

We also agree with Anna that the bits need to be picked apart before using them in design, and that some of them might fit better than others in a specific project and in specific stages in the design process. We are slightly more cautious, however, about Anna's next suggestion, which is about defining the purpose of the bits *a priori*. If we tried to shape the approach into something more structured, we feel we might sacrifice what we see as a fundamental aspect of the approach; that is, its dynamic and open approach to experiencing and exploring technologies and design materials.

A template for constructing bits

What Anna suggests is a template for how to construct bits, a helping guide in creating them. Anna described how she wanted the different types of bits to be well defined. She says: *"before building a bit it should be clear what purpose the bit should have. Should its purpose be to highlight a problem or show a specific characteristic? The template should work as a guideline and checklist but also as an inspirational trigger for developers."*

As a response to this suggestion we want to point out how the digital materials in fact are very different from each other. One can think of the processes of uncovering materials as very structured, where a designer/engineer simply thinks of and builds one bit at a time. And also that the first bits that appear to him or her are the most simple bits and that they, throughout the process, become more complex. Our impression, however, is that it should be quite the opposite. In fact, it is most often in what Anna refers to as the beyond bits, her last category, that we start this kind of process and it is in fact through building these more playful and perhaps more "designed" bits that we begin to understand the material better and begin to pin down the more basic properties of the material. For this to happen it is essential, though, that the process is kept explorative and open ended. It is not that there is a specific set of bits to find. What bits there will be depend on who in the design team participates in the process, the potential limitations/directions, previous experiences and more. In these terms, it is most beneficial if the process can be unconstrained for a short period of time. And, also as Anna suggests, the bits can always be picked apart later on and not all bits need to be used. Most important is that someone in the design team gets to develop a deeper knowledge of the material, or perhaps expands her previous knowledge of that material, and is able to better communicate some of this knowledge to the rest of the design team—something we in fact believe we accomplished in the workshop Anna attended.

CONCLUSION

Inspirational Bits

In summary, the work we report on above has, hopefully, conveyed our experiences with technologies as materials—what we refer to as inspirational bits. We also hope the paper has painted a clearer picture of what we think inspirational bits to be. In short, we see the inspirational bits as a rough way of seeing the technology that allows us to *look* at it, *feel* it and experience it over time and space, exposing all or some of the properties of a material. As we have come to understand them, inspirational bits can be used as one of the initial steps in a design process, making them similar to a technology-driven design process or to Ljungblad's and Holmquist's work on grounded innovation [10] (alt. 1 in Figure 3). In addition, they can also be used to inform a design team about the properties of the materials that might be used in a project (alt. 2 in Figure 3). In any case, we see inspirational bits as something to be used in the early stages of a design process or as early as possible. Also, importantly, we do not see them being used in the first stages of a potential prototype that is to be extended into a full-blown system. Nor do we see them as narrowing down options as in the case of structured methods or design patterns [1]. Rather, they provide a way to produce quick and dirty but fully working sketches with the primary aim of exposing the properties of the material. We have also

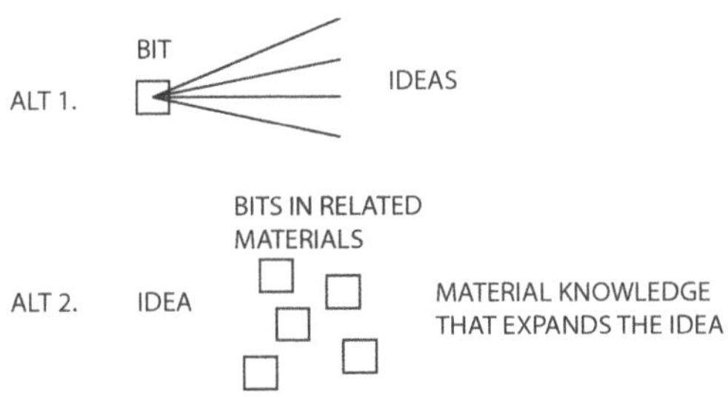

Figure 3. A schematic diagram for how/when the inspirational bits idea can be used, and what for

found that it helps to work with inspirational bits in a playful way to open up the possibilities of a material and not focus as much on its limitations.

However, inspirational bits should be quick to build. While building the first bit in a material may take longer time, most of the digital materials are very adaptable and from our experience the second and third bit will take much less time to build. This also means that using these or other inspirational bits in a design workshop they can to some extent be changed there and then to fit with ideas the design team come up with while using them. The idea is to move some of the time and effort we in a design situation at some point anyway will have to spend getting to know materials, to the more early stages of a design process when it can have an effect on the overall idea. By doing so we also believe the total amount of time it takes to build interactive systems in fact will be shorter, in that we will stay away from fighting our material and instead working with it working out the design concept.

Moreover, taking a longer-term perspective, we see the approach having an impact on the longer lasting skills and expertise within a design team. Thus technologies would not need to be repetitively subject to the same investigation, but rather the materials might be added to and taken from a growing repository of bits.

General themes

To conclude, we want to foreground several themes we believe have some general importance to interactive systems design:

Technologies as design materials

Overall, we think there is value in treating a technology as a material in the design process. In our examples, we hope to have shown that unpacking a technology like Bluetooth and exposing at least some of its properties, we can produce some productive tools for a design process.

Design inspiration

We also hope to have shown that there is inspiration to be found in exploring the properties of a technology. Critically, we believe the approach we have taken differentiates itself from a techno-centric perspective. As opposed to the technology driving a design (and, as frequently happens, the resulting solution "looking for a problem"), we have shown that exposing a technology's properties can open up design possibilities and inspire a space for creative thinking. In short, working with a technology as a material does not just limit you to solving problems, it can also be a source of creative inspiration.

Constructive limitations

We think a *technology-as-material* approach provides inspiration because it encourages a constructive view of the technology's limitations or constraints. When technologies are used to solve user-defined problems or achieve technology-defined criteria, their limitations or constraints are usually seen as things to be overcome or worked around. In our examples, we have hopefully shown that the limitations of a few digital materials can be regarded as constructive properties that can inspire design ideas.

Material sketches

We hope the work above illustrates the value of open-ended prototyping or sketching around a technology. In much the same way as Fallman [4] and Buxton [3] describe sketching in design, sketching we see that using technology-as-material opens up the creative options. We find it is also a way to expose the properties of a technology that are frequently overlooked or taken for granted.

System descriptions

Finally, while we recognise the publishing constraints most research is subject to, we feel that a design community could benefit from system descriptions that were more explicit about the properties of the technologies used and how/if they severed as building blocks in the design process?

In sum, then, we believe we have provided some details about Bluetooth, RFID, accelerometers and wireless sensor networks as design materials and also raised some general themes broadly relevant to the interaction design community. Our implications are modest in so far as we recognise the sources of creativity and inspiration in design are many and varied. Nevertheless, we hope to have contributed somewhat to, as Vallgårda and Sokoler express it, a "*better understanding of the space of possibilities.*" ([19], p. 4152).

ACKNOWLEDGMENTS

The research was done in the Mobile Life centre, funded by VINNOVA, Ericsson, Sony Ericsson, TeliaSonera, Microsoft Research, Nokia and Stockholm City Municipality, and at Microsoft Research in Cambridge.

Thanks to all our colleagues at the Mobile Life Centre, Microsoft Research and elsewhere, whom have helped us clarify the idea of using inspirational bits in design.

REFERENCES

1. Alexander, C., Ishikawa, S., et al. (1977) A Pattern Language, New York: Oxford University Press.
2. Anderson, R. J. (1994). Representations and requirements: the value of ethnography in system design. Human-Computer Interaction, 9(1), 151-182.
3. Buxton, B. (2007) Sketching User Experiences - Getting the Design Right and the Right Design. Morgan Kaufmann.
4. Fallman, D. (2003) Design-oriented human-computer interaction. CHI'03, Ft. Lauderdale, Florida, USA.
5. Gellersen, H. et al. (2005) UbiPhysics: Designing for physically integrated interaction. Ubicomp'05, Tokyo, Japan.
6. Greenberg, S. and Buxton, B. (2008). Usability evaluation considered harmful (some of the time). CHI'08. Florence, Italy.
7. Hallnäs, L. and Redström, J. (2006). Interaction Design - Foundations, Experiments, The Interactive Institute, The Swedish School of Textiles, and University College of Borås.
8. Kursat Ozenc, F. et al. (2010) How to support designers in getting hold of the immaterial material of software. Proceedings of the 28th international conference on Human factors in computing systems. Atlanta, Georgia, USA, ACM.
9. Landay, J. and Myers, B. (2001). "Sketching Interfaces: Toward More Human Interface Design." Computer 34(3): 56-64.
10. Ljungblad, S. and Holmquist, L. E. (2007). Transfer Scenarios: Grounding Innovation with Marginal Practices. CHI 2007, San Jose, CA, USA.
11. Löwgren, J. and Stolterman, E. (2004). Thoughtful Interaction Design: A Design Perspective on Information Technology, The MIT Press.
12. Marquardt, N., Taylor, A., et al. (2010) Rethinking RFID: awareness and control for interaction with RFID systems. Proceedings of the 28th international conference on Human factors in computing systems. Atlanta, Georgia, USA, ACM.
13. Richard C. et al. (2008) K-Sketch: A "Kinetic" Sketch Pad for Novice Animators. In Proc. of CHI, ACM Press, 413--422.
14. Rudström, Å. Höök, K. and Svensson, M. (2005). Social positioning: Designing the Seams between Social, Physical and Digital Space. HCII'05, Las Vegas, USA.
15. Schön, D. A. (1983). The Reflective Practitioner: How professionals think in action. London, Temple Smith.
16. Sundström, P. and Höök, K. (2010) Hand in hand with the material: designing for suppleness. Proceedings of the 28th international conference on Human factors in computing systems. Atlanta, Georgia, USA, ACM.
17. Terry, M. and Mynatt, E. (2002) Recognizing Creative Needs in User Interface Design. In Proc. of C&C, ACM Press, 38--44.
18. Vallgårda, A. and Redström, J. (2007). Computational composites. Proceedings of the SIGCHI conference on Human factors in computing systems. San Jose, California, USA, ACM.
19. Vallgårda, A. and Sokoler, T. (2009). A material focus: exploring properties of computational composites. Proceedings of the 27th international conference extended abstracts on Human factors in computing systems. Boston, MA, USA, ACM

Don't Drop It! Pick It Up and Storyboard

Shahtab Wahid, D. Scott McCrickard, Joseph DeGol[1], Nina Elias[2], Steve Harrison
Center for Human-Computer Interaction, Virginia Tech, Blacksburg, VA
Dept. of Computer Science & Engineering, The Pennsylvania State University, University Park, PA[1]
Dept. of Writing, Rhetoric, & American Culture, Michigan State University, East Lansing, MI[2]
swahid@cs.vt.edu, mccricks@cs.vt.edu, jmd5352@psu.edu, eliasnin@msu.edu, srh@cs.vt.edu

ABSTRACT
Storyboards offer designers a way to illustrate a narrative. Their creation can be enabled by tools supporting sketching or widget collections. As designers often incorporate previous ideas, we contribute the notion of blending the reappropriation of artifacts and their design tradeoffs with storyboarding. We present PIC-UP, a storyboarding tool supporting reappropriation, and report on two studies—a long-term investigation with novices and interviews with experts. We discuss how it may support design thinking, tailor to different expertise levels, facilitate reappropriation during storyboarding, and assist with communication.

Author Keywords
Storyboard, reappropriation, design tradeoffs

ACM Classification Keywords
H5.2. User Interfaces: Prototyping.

General Terms
Design, Human Factors

INTRODUCTION
An integral part of creating and sharing ideas involves the creation of visual narratives in the form of *storyboards*. Originally used by those creating cartoons, movies, and commercials, they excel at highlighting the most important aspects of a narrative [7,8]. Storyboards depict actors engaging in a series of actions with an intended purpose in mind—often in the form of simple sketches. *Wireframes*, another form of prototyping, focus on the look, content, and connections for an interface [2]. While both are different in content, presentation, and use, researchers in human-computer interaction (HCI) and user experience (UX) professionals greatly benefit from using storyboards and wireframes to illustrate how users interact with a system [2,3,19]. Both are powerful when used to communicate current practices and/or those newly introduced.

In making a storyboard, consideration must be given to major artifacts, such as technologies or settings, used to depict a narrative for a design. Different and more specific artifacts, such as widgets and controls, come into play when creating a wireframe. In doing this, designers often try to identify new ideas leading to novel solutions through creative efforts. Encompassed in artifacts, solutions can be collected and connected to each other to illustrate a series of key actions. These artifacts reflect vital functionality and therefore, can be critical to how a system is designed.

We also recognize practitioners often turn to ideas that stand the test of time. For example, the basic design elements of microwave keypads, spreadsheets, and webpage layouts maintain the same principles. While new iterations are produced, designers continue to naturally *reappropriate* ideas from the past and incorporate them into new designs—providing motivation to build upon previous work [27]. Improvements on prior work can enable designers to potentially continue to maximize successes while avoiding or mitigating pitfalls and lowering costs. HCI has focused on the methods for reppropriating design components often in the form of design knowledge [5,10,12,21] and has shown its benefits for usability [26].

Storyboarding and wireframing are supported by academic and industrial tools such as DENIM [17], SILK [13], Illustrator, Visio, Axure, and OmniGraffle. We notice the tools can be grouped as those that focus on sketching capabilities for storyboarding and those that encourage depicting the look and feel for wireframing. In these tools, sketches can be highly creative ways of elevating core *ideas* while reducing emphasis on details that are unimportant in storyboards. Wireframing tools for the visual aspects of software, some *incorporating* components from widget collections, highlight details closer to production. Our goal is to reappropriate core ideas in creating what is a hybrid of storyboards and wireframes—filling an unaddressed void.

Thus, the research trajectory leading to this paper focuses on the notion of reappropriating ideas represented as artifacts. We want to emphasize both the use of imagery and design reflection when using artifacts that might serve the purposes of a design. For simplicity's sake, we refer to this hybrid approach as storyboarding due to its emphasis on imagery. Previous work focused on creating a card-based artifact set that combines both inspiring imagery and design tradeoffs [25]. The cards could be sequenced together to create storyboards depicting new systems [24].

With this work, we aim to contribute the idea of storyboarding through reappropriation of artifacts and their design tradeoffs. As advocates, we prioritize collecting and sharing artifacts and their tradeoffs within a community—an aspect mostly overlooked by other tools. We introduce a storyboarding tool, called *PIC-UP*, as an example of how one could enable such an approach. We present two studies in which we were concerned with not *what* can be designed, but *how* one might reappropriate and share while storyboarding toward situating PIC-UP within the tool space. We deliberately focus on studying how to enable reappropriation and not on the creativity or quality of the storyboards. In our first study, we deployed the tool for two months within a community of novice designers to observe storyboard creation and artifact sharing. We then present interviews conducted with expert designers to identify an appropriate target user group and possible uses. Finally, we review the results and discuss PIC-UP.

RELATED WORK

Storyboarding is typically illustrated as a creative process of describing a user's interaction with a system over a span of time through a series of pictures, often sketches, and a textual narrative. Truong et al. mention the portrayal of time, the use of people and emotions, the inclusion of text, and the level of detail as key aspects of storyboards [22]. They are used to depict the flow of a story, reduce costly elements of design, and propose ideas to stakeholders [3,18]. Thus, they are early low-fidelity prototypes.

On the other hand, some product features might come about as a result of previously existing solutions. The reappropriation of existing design solutions has been researched by many to reduce development time and costs [6]. Its value has been seen in industry in different situations. For example, the IDEO Tech Box serves to collect and store objects that can inspire and improve the design of products [3]. Designers often refer to examples that could be intergrated into their work [9]. Patterns, knowledge structures that incorporate contexts of use, conflicting forces, and potential solutions, are adopted by HCI as a form of design rationale [5]. The Yahoo! Patterns Library is an example of a repository that stores components to be reappropriated for web design [28]. Claims, are another form of design rationale emphasizing the consideration of a feature's design tradeoffs [4] and can also be utilized in repositories [21].

Tools from academia such as SILK [13], DENIM [17], and DEMAIS [1] facilitate storyboarding early in design while emphasizing their visual nature. These tools have a heavy focus on sketching capabilities for the prototypes being created. Damask [14] is a recent storyboarding tool meant to support design pattern reappropriation. It does not necessarily support growing the collection of patterns to further future reappropriation. Within industry, tools such as Visio, Axure, and Omnigraffle are used to build wireframes. Even these tools do not strictly adhere to the key tenets of storyboarding—excluding aspects like actors, emotions, and narratives. While they might have a library of components used to create storyboard elements, they are not meant to evoke explicit design tradeoffs consideration.

The IDEO Method Cards [11] and Friedman's Envisioning Cards [16] are card sets aiming to inspire through stunning imagery and provoke thought about the design process through nuggets of informative textual descriptions. More recently, the IDEO Method Cards were released again as a mobile phone application to share easily—demonstrating a trend toward digitizing such card-based approaches. A card set integrating pictures of possible design features on the front with tradeoffs on the back was also researched as a possible method for creating storyboards [25].

The work presented in this paper seeks to blend the issues mentioned. We carve a new direction by taking advantage of the visual and storytelling capabilities of storyboards while enabling the reappropriation of existing solutions through explicit design tradeoff consideration.

REAPPROPRIATING AND STORYBOARDING IN PIC-UP

Previous investigations on the use of physical card decks for storyboarding and reappropriation and a review of design tools, led us to consider how software leveraging cards could extend this activity [24]. Based on an analysis of what designers did, we created a digital tool called PIC-UP (Figure 1). We aimed to provide designers exposure to a collection of artifacts and their associated tradeoffs, mechanisms for searching for appropriate artifacts, guidance through basic design principles, and ways of contributing artifacts to share with others.

Artifacts as Cards

Each artifact or feature in PIC-UP uses a *card* metaphor. Cards have a *label* and an *image* on the front and associated *design tradeoffs* on the back (see 1 in Figure 1). Users can flip cards to see both sides—inspiring both creativity and rational thought. We intend for the images to serve as mechanisms to attract attention to cards and inspire new ways for how they can be reappropriated in a storyboard. We also encourage designers to consider the impact of using the artifact by referring to the advantages and disadvantages. A storyboard is created by gathering and sequencing cards to illustrate a *scenario* of use in a series of frames. Each frame contains one or more cards.

The storyboard with generic images, tradeoffs, and a narrative is non-traditional as it forgoes sketching—a tenet of storyboarding [3]—but actors and emotions are still included in the narrative. Because the images are high-fidelity representations of objects that may be used, it also borders wireframing—a visual skeleton depicting content and navigation [2]—but does not focus on the final look of the system being designed. Because we believe the

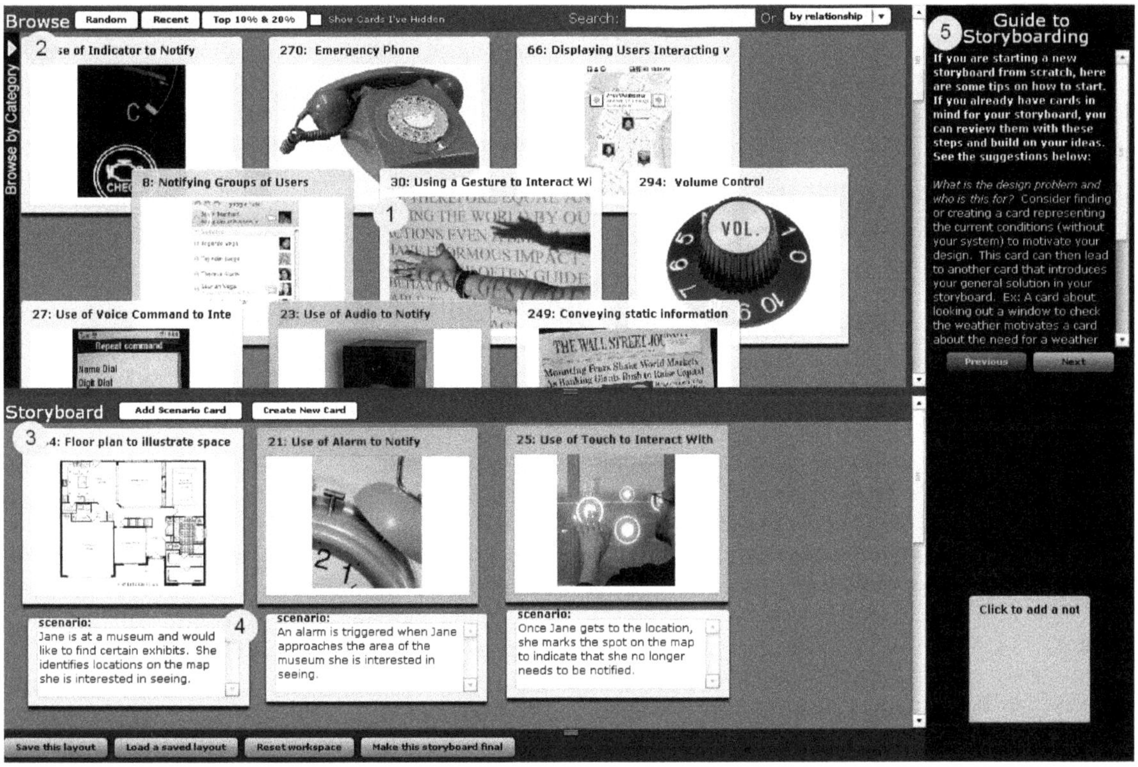

Figure 1. PIC-UP is a storyboarding tool supporting the reappropriation of design ideas in the form of cards. Users look for cards in the browse space. Cards are collected and sequenced in the storyboard space. A narrative is added to complete the storyboard.

majority of characteristics most closely resemble a storyboard, we choose to use this term.

PIC-UP leverages cards collections from targeted areas or domains. The cards focus on a class of systems called *notification systems*—products built to manage dual-task situations and the interruptions that might occur [15]. Users are encouraged to contribute new cards to facilitate growth and sharing. A designer must provide a label, picture, and short description of a feature and its positive and negative tradeoffs to make a card. We deliberately chose to keep the structure simple by using a list of design tradeoffs—instead of Damask's approach of using patterns [14]—to reduce the burden on users. Cards can be edited to suit needs. When created or edited, it is only available to the creator. We believe the need for new cards is established once it is integrated into a storyboard. We avoid storing temporary cards and retain them in saved files. After a storyboard is submitted through a finalization process, the new or edited cards are permanently stored for others to see.

Card Spaces

PIC-UP uses two spaces in which cards are manipulated: browse and storyboard. Cards are dragged from the browse space, containing the card collection, and dropped into the storyboard space, an area for storyboard assembly.

Browse Space

The browse space has several methods of searching and filtering through cards (see 2 in Figure 1). Apart from a *keyword search*, users can view a *random* set of 30 cards. This view provides initial exposure to the collection for possible inspiration. The *recent view* displays the last 10 new cards created by the community so that users are aware of new additions. Users can also view cards that belong to certain *categories* related to specific kinds of notification systems—giving a way to find what might be appropriate while also familiarizing users with the domain.

The browse space also allows cards to be seen in a *detailed view* mode (Figure 2). This shows both the front and back of cards together and the number of times it was used by others. In addition, it shows all cards that share a *relationship* with the selected card. There are 8 relationships that are semantic connections [23] established between cards by users of the system. (The relationships are described later.) Clicking on a related card allows one to navigate to it—offering a browsing mechanism for discovery of other relevant cards to reappropriate. Users can also choose to see cards with a certain relationship by using a *relationship search*.

Because of user generated content, some cards may be more useful than others because of language, scope, applicability, and imagery. We anticipated needing to elevate cards that offer strong solutions. This could be done through expert reviews or voting, but currently we use the number of times a card is previously used to indicate a measure of strength since we believe usage implies some perceived benefit. For the scope and size of our collection, this reduces the need

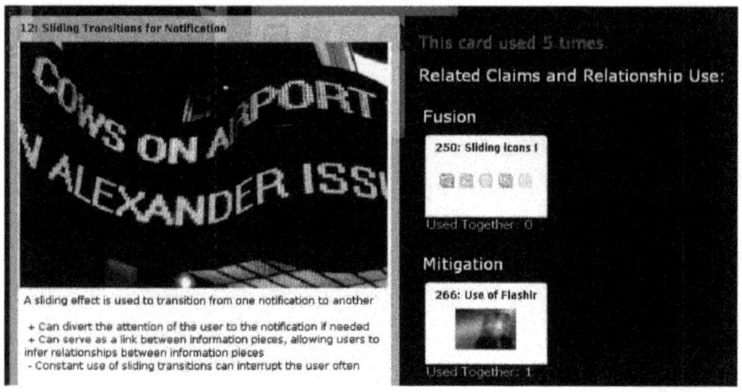

Figure 2. The detailed view shows the label, image, and design tradeoffs of a card. It also shows how many times the card was used and links to related cards through relationships.

for moderation or explicitly collecting information from others. The top 10% and 20% view shows the most used cards, indentifying cards that emerge in importance over time. These cards are color-coded with shades of green indicating their usage throughout PIC-UP.

Storyboard Space

This section provides a canvas for collected cards (see 3 in Figure 1) so they can be sequenced to create a task flow representing the progression of a story. One can then add *scenario cards* to write a narrative for each storyboard frame (see 4 in Figure 1).

Designers often realize the need for artifacts that might not be available as the scenario is formed. Cards included in this space can be edited to fit the context of the storyboard. Additionally, cards can also be created and stored for others to see when the storyboard is finalized.

While the storyboards are non-traditional because of the lack of sketches, it is possible for one to edit a card and include a sketch as an image, but this is perhaps unlikely to occur. However, aspects such as the passage of time and the use of a narrative are maintained. Actors and any possible emotions are included in the narrative.

Storyboarding Guide and Relationships

Just as DENIM [17] and Damask [14] chose to guide designers through a tailored style of storyboarding—from overview to finer details—we adopted an approach that would tailor to the nature of our cards. We included a storyboarding guide to aid designers who may be unfamiliar with design concepts, storyboarding, and PIC-UP features (see 5 in Figure 1). Each of the seven steps in the guide probes the user with a question to consider about their design and offers suggestions on what can be done and which card relationship to use to find a card (Figure 2).

The first step asks the designer to identify the problem being solved. It then suggests including an actor in the narrative. Since the postulation relationship is established between a card representing a problem, such as checking the weather, and one offering to a solution, such as using a weather ticker, it suggests using the relationship to find a card that motivates the storyboard. The other steps probe the designer about information presentation and interaction techniques, alternative solutions, combining artifacts to create new ones, accounting for the negative consequences of cards, and broader or narrower scopes of the cards. The relationships associated with these steps are called execution/evaluation, translation, fusion, mitigation, and generalization/specification respectively. Mitigation, for example, connects to other cards that resolve a specific downside of a card.

The last step suggests iterating and finalizing. During finalization users have a chance to add relationships between storyboard cards for others to see in the detailed view.

STUDYING PIC-UP IN USE

We conducted a study over 2 months by deploying PIC-UP to a group of aspiring designers to evaluate how it could serve a community. Our goals were to observe the creation of multiple storyboards, artifact selection processes, use of the guide and relationships, contribution of new cards, and impact of previous card usage.

Participants

Our group of aspiring designers consisted of nineteen graduate students who were all taking a usability engineering course (CS 5714) at Virginia Tech. The course is an introduction to design and evaluation methods in HCI. Their previous experiences with design and HCI varied widely. Some students were engaged in HCI research. Seven students said their previous experience was limited to HCI coursework. Three students were exposed to HCI and design work through both courses and previous jobs. Three others mentioned they did UI work before in work settings, but did not take any classes. Of all that had some experience, only three specifically had storyboarding knowledge. The remaining six had no previous experience.

Procedure

Participants were asked to use PIC-UP to design three different systems in three phases during the study. We changed some requirements for phases to observe behaviors in PIC-UP usage. Each phase asked them to turn in a storyboard containing 4-7 frames, but we did not enforce the frame requirement. All subjects worked in pairs except for one.

PIC-UP was freely available to participants throughout the study. In phase 1 they were given 1.5 weeks outside of class to design a notification system to alert airline passengers of flight status information. This phase gave them a chance to familiarize themselves with PIC-UP. In phase 2 we asked them to design a system to alert building occupants of an emergency and guide them out. We asked all the subjects to only work on the storyboard during an hour-long observed session where they could be videotaped. Following the session, we conducted a semi-structured interview to gather thoughts on the storyboard, card selection, the guide and relationships, card creation, and previous card usage. This phase allowed us to observe how certain artifacts can be shared within a community when solving a common problem. In phase 3 we allowed the subjects to choose what to build over 1.5 weeks outside of class, but required them to follow the guide in PIC-UP. This last phase gave us insight into the growth of the collection and the effects of structuring the design process. After all phases, we conducted semi-structured interviews with fourteen of the students to hear final comments on the experience and longer-term impact.

Data and Analysis

For each phase we gathered storyboards, logs, and design journals providing system descriptions, notes on how storyboards were created, and reflections on PIC-UP. During the observed sessions and interviews, we made video and audio recordings. We analyzed the storyboards, journals, and interviews based on the open coding technique [20] which led us to identify categories related to card selection approaches, guide usage, design learning, card creation, and identification of highly used artifacts. The videos were consulted when transcripts referred back to events during the observed session. Logs were mined to gain an overview of key actions and collection growth.

PIC-UP Prior to Deployment

Before the study PIC-UP contained 54 cards created by us and others during a series of small-scale deployments. There were 53 relationships established between the cards with some cards being more connected than others.

Results

We now turn to the results of our study with our aspiring designers. We aim to present the range of activity that took place when reappropriating during storyboarding and comment on the impact of PIC-UP.

Construction Approaches

There were 11 storyboards produced for phase 1, and 10 for phase 2 and 3 (see Figure 3). Overall, we found the size of the storyboards remained mostly constant, indicating no drastic change took place. In phase 1, the storyboards contained 5-14 total cards, averaging 6.9 total cards and 1.46 cards per frame. Phase 2 had a total number of cards ranging from 4-13 with an average of 7.1 and 1.61 cards per frame. In phase 3, there were between 4-13 cards with a total average of 7 and 1.52 per frame.

We found there were two approaches to choosing cards: taking a *card-first* approach and creating a scenario out of what is available or a *scenario-first* approach where a predetermined scenario drives the selection and creation of cards in the storyboard. This was illustrated when a participant posed a choice during the observed sessions: "*How do you want to start...by looking at the cards first or by writing down some ideas?*" In response, her partner said, "*I was going to say we discuss some stuff and try to come up with some vague idea for what our system is.*"

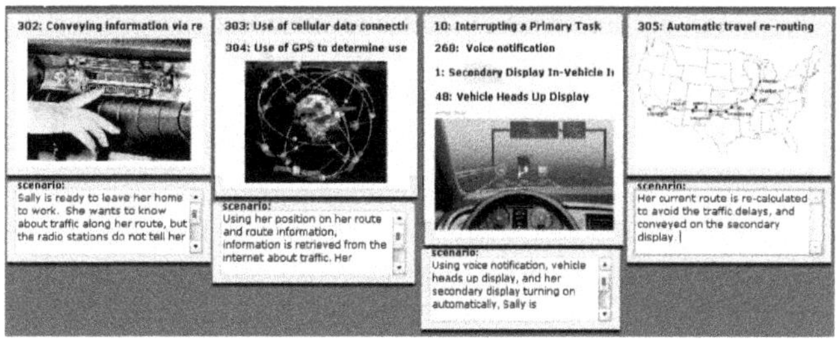

Figure 3. An example of a phase 3 storyboard with 4 frames and 8 cards. Each frame has a scenario card.

We found a majority of the storyboards followed the scenario-first approach. During the observed sessions an average of 4 minutes were spent determining the scenario. The pairs would agree on the basic ideas for the design by discussing possibilities. One student described the initial brainstorming: "*We would typically do pen and paper prototyping first and do a rough sketch and do a stick figure drawing and that's when we would hash out stuff and spend time on the system.*" Another pair chose to record ideas in PIC-UP during phase 2: "*My partner and I started by thinking about the design of an emergency notification system and then by writing the scenario cards for our design. This helped us clarify our ideas and identify what could be improved. This also helped us choose all the different cards to illustrate our scenarios.*" Students then proceeded to choose cards by mapping them to the scenario.

When asked about the card-first approach, respondents generally agreed it did not seem to be the ideal approach: "*I remember flipping through the cards and trying to apply different scenarios to the cards. It was very inefficient because I was matching a scenario to a card instead of the card to a scenario.*" We found some examples of the approach in phase 1 and only one example in phase 2. Previous work showed a card-first approach was chosen more with a finite set of physical cards [24]. PIC-UP, with a larger collection, might be causing such a change, but a scenario driven approach is what traditional storyboarding would advocate and we are encouraged by this.

Inspiring New Ideas for Reappropriation

PIC-UP can inspire new thoughts while following a scenario-first approach. In looking for artifacts to reappropriate, a participant explained plans often changed: "*We came across other cards that, while not what we were searching for, turned out to be applicable to our project, and we altered our envisioned system to reflect the new ideas that we had generated based on the cards.*" The images often played a key role in attracting attention and inspiring certain ideas during the search, but it is often checked by referring to the design tradeoffs. A student explained this by saying: "*The image I think just helps us to catch our attention at first 'cause there were cases...we flip through the [tradeoffs], maybe the image might semi-work, but when we saw the [tradeoffs] we're like 'ok no this isn't the type' so ultimately it really would probably be the [tradeoffs]. The image we can always alter.*"

Reappropriation of cards can be highly dependent on how relevant their tradeoffs are. This is prominent when designers are faced with choices: "*When we were trying to decide which card to use when there were two similar cards we flipped each card over and compared the [tradeoffs] on the back. After comparing the two, we decided on which one was more [like] what we had envisioned for the system, and then chose to add that one to the system.*" Participants flipped cards 126, 115, and 88 times in phases 1, 2, and 3 respectively. Participants acknowledged this is an important activity when seeing cards initially. We believe it decreased due to increased card familiarity over time.

Searching for Cards

Based on journal entries, card-first approaches used the random view. The view was not used as much in the scenario-first approach. When looking for a very specific kind of feature related to notification systems (such as an alert method) participants referred to the category view since cards were organized by type. The final interviews found this served to illustrate core concerns of notification systems, better familiarizing users with the class of systems.

Interesting issues came up when we looked more closely at the recent and top 10% and 20% views. The recent view, showing the 10 newest cards, played an important role in phase 2. Since everyone was working on the same problem, designing a system for building evacuations, new cards had the chance of being relevant to other storyboards. An example of a card shared and reappropriated within the community was one called *lighted directional path*. The artifact was about using lights along a path to guide people during an emergency. The picture showed emergency lights along the aisle of an airplane. Many individuals had thought of similar ideas and when one person looked at the recent view and saw that it was already made, he reacted by saying, "*Someone made that for us! Sweet.*" As others used it, the card broke the threshold and acquired a green status, placing it in the top 10% and 20% view. This example shows reappropriation can directly benefit efforts to solve a problem. However, this also illustrates the recent view may only be useful when everyone works on the same problem.

Impact of Previous Reappropriation

We wanted to see how knowing the number of times a card was previously used impacted reappropriation. The top 10% and 20% view led participants to express different opinions. Since this shows the most reappropriated cards, it elevates those that stand the test of time. We believed the view and green cards would let designers quickly identify cards of higher perceived value. One participant who thought similarly said, "*Highly [reappropriated] cards could provide a starting point for designers, in that those cards could contain high level ideas applicable to a wide range of products.*" Another student explained the benefit for him: "*I used the most frequently used cards as a starting point for my exploration of options in the ideation stage. The most popular cards were usually applicable in some way to the system I was tasked to create. Also, looking through the cards that other users had chosen gave me an idea of how they solved the design challenges.*" On the other hand, we found previous use is not necessarily a key factor: "*Just 'cause they use it a lot doesn't necessarily mean that it's going to fit with what you're doing.*"

We realized there were a lot of strong views about whether something should be used just because it was reappropriated by others as we probed further into this last comment. One respondant in our phase 2 interview explained it this way: "*Yeah, I don't even like allowing [previous use] to influence...I mean honestly I could even imagine myself being biased in the other direction...just wanting to use cards that haven't been used much before so I don't feel like I'm doing the same thing that everyone else did.*" Another informant gave an example of how this notion might negatively impact them: "*While considering popular cards can be efficient, it can often hinder creativity and sometimes cause designers to implement the wrong type of system for a designer problem. For example...we immediately looked to implementing a mobile system because that card was most used...after thought, we realized that a mobile system would not be [appropriate].*" Even though the ability to reappropriate artifacts in new designs is not being challenged, it seems there is discomfort regarding a potential loss of innovation if users feel they are reappropriating the same solutions over and over again.

Guide and Relationship Use

We observed a different way of impacting reappropriation in phase 3 with the guide requirement. The guide was previously ignored because either they felt they knew what to do or did not notice it. Only 4 pairs showed limited activity with the guide in phases 1 and 2. In phase 3, all pairs used all the steps of the guide. We found the overall impact of the guide was to give a sense of targeted reappropriation. When discussing overall thoughts, one participant said, "*One benefit of the guide was that it prompted users to think about things that they may not have thought of before. For example, we never really considered adding additional things in our storyboard that may help explain the system we are designing.*"

Each step prompted them to consider reappropriating certain types of cards. For example, in the first step a subject wrote in his journal that they, "*...wanted a card that presented the problem of blind spots which subsequent cards would solve.*" For the second step, in which they were asked to consider information display methods and interaction techniques, a participant said, "*Here we identified that we wanted to deliver the information as text with links to more information.*" In the fifth step, where negative design tradeoffs are identified and resolved, a student wrote, "*Originally, we had not thought of any possible negative outcomes until we looked through the mitigation cards. Then we realized that there was a chance the user might not hear the verbal notification.*" We notice these kinds of actions were only mentioned in phase 3. They are indicative of a form of design learning that took place—especially considering they initially saw no utility in the guide. However, based on feedback, we also see the guide may only be used initially and ignored later, once the core lessons are understood, to avoid its prescriptive nature.

Relationship usage depended on the conditions of the phase. In phase 1, logs indicated users followed relationships 9 times in total and used the relationship search 46 times. In phase 2, the numbers were 59 and 22, indicating a greater reliance on following relationships. In phase 3, it was 17 and 81, this time favoring the relationship search. One informant described his reaction to following relationships in the phase 2 interview: "*It's nice that they're categorized by the relationship, but usually I'm just clicking on it to see what other cards are associated with it 'cause that's not exactly what I'm looking for but close...*" Most participants initially used relationships to browse without grasping their full potential.

In phase 3 they began to see what relationships were really capable of since each relationship was tied to the guide—explaining the increase in the relationship searches. This change in thinking was portrayed by one participant: "*The guide introduces you to the power of the relationships. Not in a sense of finding more cards, but a power in the sense that the relationships help you make sure you cover all the spectrums for your storyboard. You don't want multiple cards when you could generalize. You don't want a postulation card without its solution card. You don't want a card without using its mitigation card because this minimizes the cons of your storyboard.*" It is notable the role each artifact plays in the design is considered.

Participants mentioned they did not always find what they needed due to the small number of relationships. We did, however, see the number of relationships created grow over time. The relationship count went up by 30, 47, and 26 over the three phases. For example, the *lighted directional path* card was eventually connected to 5 other cards. There was a sharp increase in new relationships in phase 2, but this fell in phase 3 despite a larger number of new cards. We believe many new relationship assignments that may not have been strong were added. We posit the number fell in phase 3 because the participants better understood the concepts and only created relationships that matched their description in the guide. This may indicate the guide should be consulted the first time to better explain the relationships.

Creating Cards

We also looked closely at card creation as it is a large part of reappropriation and sharing. The number of cards grew by 3, 6, and 14 in phases 1, 2, and 3 respectively. All the participants created a card at some point. A participant explained there was one sole reason for trying to create a card: "*...the fact that we couldn't find a card with the right kind of [tradeoffs] for what we had in mind.*" When deciding to make a new card, we observed participants taking other cards as examples and learning from how they were scoped and worded. An informant described how he created a new artifact: "*We took our time in creating our card, making sure that it contained the kind of information that would help us in this specific instance, but also making the [tradeoffs] broad enough so that others could use it in the future. We also included a fair number of [tradeoffs]... since we came across some cards that were lacking...*" In one instance, we came across a pair in the observed session that decided to use a card they created in phase 1. When deciding to do so, one of the partners said, "*Hey if we keep using this, this will eventually go up and...get green status.*" These examples demonstrate that the novice designers strive to balance how generic or specific a card is to maintain its applicability—often intertwined with a sense of ownership for their cards. It must also be mentioned that we are cautious about new cards since the utility of PIC-UP might rely heavily on the number of new cards being contributed and, particularly, on the quality of those cards.

INTERVIEWS WITH DESIGN EXPERTS ON PIC-UP

Our first investigation painted a picture of how novice designers could learn storyboarding elements and reappropriation while appreciating the value of design tradeoffs. As we were encouraged by some of the positive impacts the tool had, we wanted to find out who else this form of storyboarding could tailor to and how it might be used. To that end, we conducted interviews with experts about their work and thoughts on PIC-UP.

Seven informants were recruited from both academia and industry. We talked to a UX researcher, a UX designer, a UX manager, 2 professors (one of whom spent significant time as a designer in industry), a director of a usability consulting group, and a researcher at a large corporation.

The one-hour sessions were carried out via phone and screen sharing. Audio recordings were made. We first conducted semi-structured interviews about their background and existing design practices. They were then asked to read instructions and follow a sample task taking them through designing a notification system for museum visitors in PIC-UP. The task was designed to illustrate all the system features. Their actions were observed through screen sharing. Once completed, they were interviewed about their storyboarding practices and reactions to the tool.

Results

We report on the findings from our interviews. We first provide a short description of current practices and then focus on who might use PIC-UP and how communication might be facilitated.

Current Practices

We first wanted to gain a sense of how designers initially start their work on design. The professor who had a background in industry explained designers, "*start with sketching the stories of people, generally with scenarios and the construction of people and places and [them] doing something...*" In brainstorming sessions, it was mentioned a whole team might use whiteboards or post-it notes to record ideas and storyboard during design charettes.

The UX manager explained his approach to problems in new areas: "*Over time a series of different sessions of design research and just talking and looking at...best practices.*" The director said she would try to find out what had been done before. When discussing tools, informants mentioned prototypes could be pitched using Illustrator, Omnigraffle, Dreamweaver, Flash, and PowerPoint.

When discussing reappropriation, five informants mentioned some form took place in their work. This could appear as styles, templates, and practices to maintain consistency. The UX researcher specifically advocated sharing designs and practices. A professor explained that there is no creativity without some kind of reappropriation. On the flip side, the researcher mentioned reappropriation was not an option because research demanded novelty.

Use Based on Expertise

We were encouraged to find PIC-UP may offer value to users of different expertise levels in varying roles. It was believed experts could use PIC-UP *after* the initial problem exploration since it is a solution-oriented system. Participants believed it has the potential to make brainstorming more comprehensive. The UX manager described the impact of having a storyboard at this stage of the design process: "*The idea of having an artifact to respond to...makes a huge difference for brainstorming.*" He added that the storyboard, "*might be a deliverable for an initial brainstorming phase where we might work through...a round of revisions and think about some of the pros and cons.*" PIC-UP can be a resource during brainstorming. For example, the UX designer mentioned: "*I think it would be a good resource for discovering methods of interaction or usability that I hadn't necessarily thought of. It's just a good way of exploring ideas or opportunities.*" Similar thoughts were also expressed by the UX manager: "*If we had an easy way to view a lot of prior work...it might help us by putting it in one visual field, to be able to review ideas...and say does this apply and be more comprehensive about the brainstorming.*" Such comments lead us to believe that experts might use PIC-UP in the appropriate design phase in addition to existing practices—most of its utility being in facilitating brainstorming.

Reasons for using PIC-UP might change for the less experienced. The UX designer suggested, "*for somebody less familiar with design, this could be their step one...a non-designer could start more from the ground up with a tool like this.*" We found that for some non-designers such as developers, managers, or clients, the sketching that comes so easily to experts can be an obstacle. The UX researcher explained the problem this way: "*A lot of the designers...they always start with sketching and that's a really uncomfortable place to start for somebody that's not comfortable with sketching.*" Although we cannot confirm, perhaps this same obstacle may exist in DENIM [17] and SILK [13] since they emphasize sketching too. Additionally, PIC-UP may offer a way to synthesize initial concepts. One person stated, "*this could help those people who weren't so familiar with UI concepts and design and things like that and give them a starting place and a method for illustrating their ideas.*" In putting these ideas together, the UX researcher noted, "*because it is a storyboard, it necessitates thinking about workflow which is something that can get lost a lot...especially with somebody who isn't thinking about design all the time.*" For novices or non-designers, PIC-UP may reduce initial hurdles by offering the utility of generic images and a way to communicate design concepts.

Design teams with mixed levels of expertise might leverage PIC-UP too. For them it can serve as a record of work: "*This seems like a way to keep a collaborative team up to date...about what happened in a design session.*" Groups might also have to identify what the best practices are for a new class of systems. For this situation, the UX manager explained, "*this tool is a way to rapidly move towards a solution that builds in some awareness of what you've already done to analyze the problem, but also...on best practices in that area. So if you are unfamiliar...this tool seems like a resource to turn to...*" This strategy of learning from other work is useful for both the experienced and inexperienced designers working with unfamiliar systems.

Communicating Through Storyboards

Some interviewees mentioned communication gaps that can exist during design. We found PIC-UP might be able to make the communication more effective in certain situations. One of the professors mentioned: "*What I want to know every time I see a designer argue for a choice is show me the user centered evidence that supports that choice.*" This may be facilitated by the explicit tradeoffs in each card. Another way PIC-UP could be used in an organization was explained by the UX researcher: "*We could sort of build cards based on the needs of our own organization...because right now, that information lives in people's heads, and if it lives in people's heads, then it looks a little bit differently in the other person's head, which means there's not a common enough understanding even though there definitely should be.*" She continued by saying: "*The notification examples you've put together here sort of represent what we as a department have talked about wanting to do for a long time, which is creating a UI pattern library.*" We find that the reasoning for design choices and the sharing of these ideas can play an important role—placing greater importance on PIC-UP's use of design tradeoffs and its reappropriation capabilities.

DISCUSSION

We were able to identify a range situations where PIC-UP could be used and activities that occur. We found that PIC-UP may tailor to designers of mixed expertise levels, supplement design activities, follow scenario-driven approaches, encourage design thinking and learning, and facilitate reappropriation of artifacts during storyboarding. With these findings in mind, we discuss PIC-UP.

We understand certain pitfalls may exist. Exposure to high fidelity images may have a negative impact on creativity since too many unnecessary details might come into play at an early stage, taking focus away from the overall problem and leading to unwanted feedback. Integrating sketching could provide a different creative avenue. The quality of cards may be an issue over time. Just as good ideas may propagate, lesser ideas may also spread throughout a collection. Furthermore, the storyboard quality is unknown. The small number of cards and relationships may have a negative impact. Perhaps quality might be aided with social navigation, but its scalability is unknown. Issues related to the top 10% and 20% or other search methods may emerge with a significantly larger collection of artifacts.

On the other hand, the nature of PIC-UP—its reliance on tradeoffs, elements such as the guide, an emphasis on scenarios, and the storyboard—positions it as one that may encourage design learning and thinking. We are heartened by reports from our novice participants stating they found use for PIC-UP and storyboarding in their own research and jobs because it changed the way they were thinking about design. PIC-UP may reinforce lessons of workflow, focus thoughts on potential users, and encourage early consideration of problems to be solved—effects observed as a result of the guide. The guide prescribes a process, but student designers or non-designers in organizations may find value in initially following some suggestions. Even if one cannot find a card using a relationship in a step, we consider the actions taken to be better than inaction since they indicate the overall structure of the design is being considered—leading to reappropriation not for the sake of having a solution, but also to satisfy tradeoffs, scenario discrepancies, and task flow.

We believe PIC-UP could eventually tailor to three user groups. First, as both our studies outlined, our tool can be beneficial to the *novice and non-designers*. The interviews with academics lead us to believe they may be enthusiastic about exposing students to interaction, workflow concepts, and solutions that can be reappropriated. PIC-UP can provide students a chance to utilize technology and interact with it the way designers might. Non-designers such as developers, managers, and clients who might be involved with a design project can find ways to express their thinking. Second, our work can aid *diverse practitioner groups* that may be unfamiliar with a certain class of systems. PIC-UP can facilitate group brainstorming sessions for UX teams by inspiring ideas when starting a new project—especially for areas in which they have not worked. However, we acknowledge expert designers might resist fully adopting PIC-UP as they might prefer their existing storyboarding or wireframing methods. Third, an *organization with a vested interest collecting and sharing design practices* can take advantage of PIC-UP's reappropriation and sharing capabilities. Such an effort can evangelize practices across an organization and help bring new designers onboard. This requires the artifacts be tailored to the needs of the organization and its practices.

Our approach to storyboarding is novel in that we embed design tradeoffs into the process. PIC-UP demonstrates reappropriation and storyboarding are not at odds with each other. Instead, they can both function together hand-in-hand. However, unlike storyboarding in SILK [13] and DENIM [17], we focused not on sketching, but reappropriation. The advantage of reappropriating existing solutions into a storyboard is that it is being done within the context of a design—similar to some of the sentiments in Damask [14]. This approach is in sharp contrast with isolated instances of reappropriation that might occur with patterns libraries, such as the Yahoo! Patterns Library [28], where a prototype is not being constructed at the same time. Additionally, wireframing tools like Axure, OmniGraffle, and Visio, with access to widget libraries to create prototypes, do not encourage explicit design tradeoff consideration. They also do not focus on narratives for context. These differences uniquely position PIC-UP in the array of storyboarding and wireframing tools. As portrayed, collections of artifacts can be beneficial in certain situations, but we also acknowledge that tensions can always arise. It is our opinion that the very presence of *tension between creativity and reappropriation is an advantage as it promotes debate about the utility and viability of the artifacts* in question.

Although the storyboard is non-traditional, we are compelled to argue there is utility in constructing this kind of storyboard for learning and communication. It tries to retain the main characteristics of traditional storyboards [22]. Elements such as the motivation, problem, key features and design tradeoffs, and the associated scenario—all contained within a PIC-UP storyboard—show potential in jumpstarting conversations about a product. It serves as a method to deliver ideas to others, such as clients or team members, early in the design process. Furthermore, it shows potential in bridging the divide between the experts and inexperienced—*allowing novices to build solutions containing the basic elements of design while overcoming potential obstacles and enabling experts to quickly pitch ideas to a non-designer audience.*

CONCLUSION

This paper investigates how storyboards can be constructed by reappropriating previous ideas—a direction unaddressed by tools currently available. We introduced a storyboarding tool, PIC-UP, that allows for a collection of artifacts, along with their associated design tradeoffs, to be reappropriated during storyboard construction. Through two studies conducted with novice and expert designers, we explored how PIC-UP might be used and the behaviors exhibited when deployed within a community of designers. We found PIC-UP may encourage sharing and reappropriating features for storyboards, support design learning, tailor to both experienced and inexperienced users, and facilitate communication with others involved in design projects.

ACKNOWLEDGMENTS
This work was partially funded by the National Science Foundation (IIS-0851774). We thank the reviewers and ACs for their comments.

REFERENCES

1. Bailey, B. P., Konstan, J. A., & Carlis, J. V. DEMAIS: designing multimedia applications with interactive storyboards. *In Proc. MULTIMEDIA 2001*, (2001), 241-250.
2. Bryan-Kinns, N & Hamilton, F. One for all and all for one?: case studies of using prototypes in commercial projects. *In Proc. NordiCHI 2002*, ACM Press (2002), 91-100.
3. Buxton, B. *Sketching User Experiences: Getting the Design Right and the Right Design*. Morgan Kaufmann, San Francisco, CA. 2007.
4. Carroll, J. M., & Kellogg, W. A. Artifact as theory-nexus: Hermeneutics meets theory-based design. *In Proc. CHI 1989*, ACM Press (1989), 7-14.
5. Dearden, A. & Finlay, J. Pattern languages in HCI: A critical review. *Human-Computer Interaction*, 21, 1 (2009), 49-102.
6. Dusink, L. & van Katwijk, J. Reuse Dimensions. *In Symposium on Software Reusability*, (1995), 137-149.
7. Finch, C. *The Art of Walt Disney: From Mickey Mouse to the Magic Kingdom*. Harry Abrams, New York. 1973.
8. Hart, J. *The Art of the Storyboard: Storyboarding for Film, TV, and Animation*. Focal Press. 1998.
9. Herring, S. R., Chang, C., Krantzler, J., & Bailey, B. P. Getting inspired!: understanding how and why examples are used in creative design practice. *In Proc. CHI 2009*, ACM Press (2009), 87-96.
10. Hughes, M. A pattern language for user assistance. *Interactions*, 14, 1 (2007), 27-29.
11. *IDEO Method Cards*. [S.I.]: IDEO. 2003.
12. Landay, J. A. & Borriello, G. Design Patterns for Ubiquitous Computing. *Computer*, 36, 8 (2003), 93-95.
13. Landay, J. A. & Myers, B. A. Interactive sketching for the early stages of user interface design. *In Proc. CHI 1995*, ACM Press (1995), 4-50.
14. Lin, J. & Landay, J. A. Employing patterns and layers for early-stage design and prototyping of cross-device user interfaces. *In Proc. CHI 2008*, ACM Press (2008), 1313-1322.
15. McCrickard, D. S., Chewar, C. M., Somervell, J. P., & Ndiwalana, A. A Model for Notification Systems Evaluation—Assessing User Goals for Multitasking Activity. *Transactions on Computer-Human Interaction (TOCHI)*, 10, 4 (2003), 312-338.
16. Nathan, L., Friedman, B., & Hendry, D. SUSTAINABLY OURS: Information system design as catalyst: human action and environmental sustainability. *Interactions*, 16, 4 (2009), 6-11.
17. Newman, M., Lin, J., Hong, J., & Landay, J. A. DENIM: an informal web site design tool inspired by observations of practice. *Human-Computer Interaction*, 18, 3 (2003), 259-324.
18. Rosson, M. B. & Carroll, J. M. *Usability Engineering: Scenario-Based Development of Human Computer Interaction*. Morgan Kaufmann Publishers, San Francisco, CA. 2002.
19. Sharp, H., Rogers, Y., & Preece, J. *Interaction Design: Beyond Human-Computer Interaction*. John Wiley & Sons Ltd., West Sussex, England. 2007.
20. Strauss, A. & Corbin, J. *Basics of qualitative research: Grounded theory procedures and techniques*. Sage Publications, Inc., Newbury Park, CA. 1990.
21. Sutcliffe, A. G. & Carroll, J. M. Designing Claims for Reuse in Interactive Systems Design. *International Journal of Human-Computer Studies*, 50, 3 (2000), 213-241.
22. Truong, K. N., Hayes, G. R., & Abowd, G. D. Storyboarding: an empirical determination of best practices and effective guidelines. *In Proc. DIS 2006*, ACM Press (2006), 12-21.
23. Wahid, S. Allgood, C. F., Chewar, C. M., & McCrickard, D. S. Entering the Heart of Design: Relationships for Tracing Claim Evolution. *In Proc. SEKE 2004*, (2004), 167-172.
24. Wahid, S., Branham, S. M., Cairco, L., McCrickard, D. S., & Harrison, S. Picking Up Artifacts: Storyboarding as a Gateway to Reuse. *In Proc. INTERACT 2009*, Springer-Verlag (2009), 528-541.
25. Wahid, S., Branham, S. M., McCrickard, D. S., & Harrison, S. Investigating the Relationship Between Imagery and Rationale in Design. *In Proc. DIS 2010*, ACM Press (2010), 75-84.
26. Wania, C. *Examining the impact of an information retrieval pattern language on the design of information retrieval interfaces*. Ph.D. Dissertation, Drexel University, 2008.
27. Whittaker, S. Things to talk about when talking about things. *Human–Computer Interaction*, 18, 1 (2003), 149-170.
28. Yahoo! Patterns Library. developer.yahoo.com/ypattern.

Rock & Rails: Extending Multi-touch Interactions with Shape Gestures to Enable Precise Spatial Manipulations

Daniel Wigdor[1], Hrvoje Benko[1], John Pella[2], Jarrod Lombardo[2], Sarah Williams[2]
[1]Microsoft Research, [2]Microsoft
One Microsoft Way, Redmond, WA
{dwigdor | benko | jopella | jarrodl | sarahwil}@microsoft.com

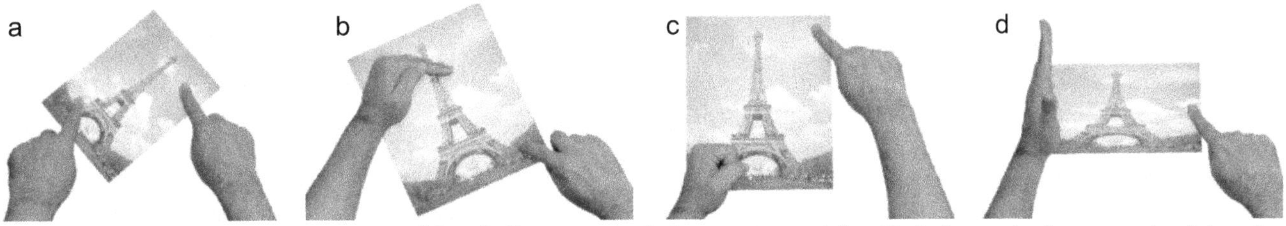

Figure 1 Rock & Rails augments traditional direct-manipulation gestures (a) with independently recognized hand-postures used to restrict manipulations conducted with the other hand (b: rotate, c: resize, d: 1-d scale). This allows for fluid selection of degrees of freedom and thus rapid, high-precision manipulation of on-screen content.

ABSTRACT
Direct touch manipulations enable the user to interact with the on-screen content in a direct and easy manner closely mimicking the spatial manipulations in the physical world. However, they also suffer from well-known issues of precision, occlusion and an inability to isolate different degrees of freedom in spatial manipulations. We present a set of interactions, called *Rock & Rails,* that augment existing direct touch manipulations with shape-based gestures, thus providing on-demand gain control, occlusion avoidance, and separation of constraints in 2D manipulation tasks. Using shape gestures in combination with direct-manipulations allows us to do this without ambiguity in detection and without resorting to manipulation handles, which break the direct manipulation paradigm. Our set of interactions were evaluated by 8 expert graphic designers and were found to be easy to learn and master, as well as effective in accomplishing a precise graphical layout task.

ACM Classification: H5.2 [Information interfaces and presentation]: User Interfaces. - Graphical user interfaces.

General terms: Design, Human Factors

Keywords: Shape gestures, fluid, precise multi-touch interactions, interactive surfaces, separation of constraints.

INTRODUCTION
Using multiple points of input to perform direct manipulations on virtual objects allows users to rapidly specify affine transformations (e.g., [14]). For example, in the typical multi-touch scenario, the user can translate, rotate and scale a virtual photograph with a single gesture consisting of simultaneous movement of two fingers. The advantages of such direct-touch interactions are twofold: they have the potential to increase the speed of complex manipulations by eliminating the need to perform the operations sequentially, and they resemble real object manipulations in the physical world which makes them both intuitive [36] and easily interpreted [22].

Despite these benefits, there are numerous tasks (e.g., graphic layout) where simultaneous control of multiple degrees of freedom can be detrimental. Such tasks usually require high precision and the ability to isolate the degrees of freedom (DOF) for each manipulation. For example, when precisely aligning an image, the user might want to adjust only the rotation of the object, but not its position or scale. Furthermore, they might want to have a fine control of the movement gain, to allow them to precisely position an object. Enabling such fine explicit control in multi-touch interfaces is challenging, particularly if trying to preserve the direct manipulation paradigm (i.e., the idea that the movement of the fingers is directly affecting the content underneath them) and thus not resorting to on-screen handles [3, 23] or introducing specific movement or velocity thresholds to constrain the interactions [23].

To address this, we developed a set of interaction techniques, called *Rock & Rails* (Figure 1), which maintain the direct-touch input paradigm, but enable users to make fluid, high-DOF manipulations, while simultaneously providing easy in-situ mechanisms to increase precision, specify manipulation constraints, and avoid occlusions. Our toolset provides mechanisms to rapidly isolate orientation, position, and scale operations using system-recognized hand postures, while simultaneously enabling traditional, simple direct touch manipulations.

The guiding principle of Rock & Rails is similar to that described by Guiard – that the non-dominant hand be used as a reference frame for the actions of the dominant hand [13]. In our interactions, the hand pose of the non-dominant hand sets the manipulation constraints, and the fingers of the dominant hand perform direct, constrained manipulations with the content. Further, we exploit the physical principle of leverage, affording quick hand adjustments to increase the precision of manipulations.

In this paper, we describe Rock & Rails interactions and present evidence of their utility in enabling expert use in a graphical layout tasks. First, we review related work, with an emphasis on precise interaction using touch and multi-touch. Second, we discuss the hand shapes which enable our interactions, and present the Rock & Rails interaction techniques in detail. Third, we describe the results of an expert user evaluation conducted among designers at a major software vender, which showed strong advantages and preferences for our interactions in the graphical layout task compared to current multi-touch input and the mouse-based methods they currently employ. Finally, we discuss design recommendations and conclusions of the present work.

RELATED WORK

This work builds upon three distinct areas of previous research. The first is a body of work which has demonstrated methods and the utility of maintaining a direct-touch and manipulation paradigm when interacting with digital content. The second is made up of other techniques which attempt to achieve independence of transforms while maintaining a direct-manipulation metaphor. The last is the use of posture differences to differentiate input modes. We review each in turn.

Direct Touch and Manipulation

Controlling a graphical user interface using touch input offers several advantages over mouse input. For example, gestural commands physically chunk command and operands into a single action [7], and gestures can also be committed to physical muscle memory which can help users focus on their task [19].

Several projects have demonstrated that multi-touch interaction is best supported through a *direct manipulation* mapping. It has been demonstrated that bimanual interaction is better supported by direct than by indirect input, since bimanual coordination and parallelism are both improved [9]. Furthermore, Tan found that direct manipulation is superior to indirect in promoting spatial memory [30], while Morris et al. found that it aided group coordination and task awareness [21]. Finally, in a pair of results found that direct manipulation was the only universally discoverable gesture [36], and that it was also the only gesture that users could observe and identify without any information about the system state [22].

The litany of advantages demonstrated by direct manipulation makes it attractive as the basis for the design of user interfaces for direct, multi-touch input. Before this can be adopted more broadly, however, fundamental disadvantages with the technique must be addressed. Perhaps the most critical is that direct manipulation supports rapid coarse adjustments, but fine manipulations are difficult. We attribute the difficulty to three factors. The first is the fixed control/display (C/D) gain that direct manipulation necessitates. The second is the occlusion of the content created by direct touch. The third is the interdependence of multiple unit affine transformations. Overlaying rotation, translation, and scale allows for rapid coarse manipulation, but makes it more difficult to adjust any one in isolation.

Rock & Rails addresses all three of these issues. It includes an expanded mechanism for achieving variable C/D gain while maintaining direct manipulation which builds on previous techniques. It provides a method of quickly offsetting manipulations from their target, reducing occlusion. Finally, it includes several fluid mechanisms for achieving independence of rotation, translation, and scaling transforms.

Explicit vs. Implicit Transform Independence

Previous attempts have been made to provide fluid mechanisms for transform independence with direct manipulation [3,23]. These can be broadly characterized as implicit and explicit mechanisms. Explicit mechanisms place the burden on the user to perform some action that is consciously different from a regular manipulation in order to enter a mode to achieve independence. In the realm of the traditional mouse-based user interface, a common explicit mechanism is a set of manipulation handles, thus differentiating mode by the location of the mouse pointer at the time the user presses the button. Another common mechanism is to mode the mouse manipulation using key presses on a keyboard, such as requiring utilization of modifier keys to select a transform type. In multi-touch toolkits, manipulation handles have also been demonstrated [14, 23, 28]. Popular toolkits commonly differentiate between modes based on the number of contacts. Manipulating with a single finger can provide translation only, or translation and rotation simultaneously (e.g., the *RNT* technique [14]). In most instances, manipulating with two or more fingers simultaneously rotates, translates, and scales, though in some instances rotation is omitted entirely (e.g., Apple iPhone).

Implicit mechanisms attempt to infer the user's intention through differentiation of the input/mode mapping by some non-explicit means. The *RNT* technique, for example, allows the user to simultaneously translate and rotate an object by dragging it with a single finger. The magnitude of rotation is proportional to the distance of the finger from the centre of the object, intending to map to naïve physics. A consequence of this mapping is that drags initiated at the precise geometric centre of the object apply only translation. To ensure this can be easily achieved, implementations may exaggerate the size of this central area [18, 14].

In contrast, the *DiamondSpin* technique imposes the constraint that objects be oriented towards the nearest outer edge of the display. To achieve this, they are rotated automatically as the object is moved [28]. A logical extreme of this technique is that employed by the iPhone toolkit, where objects remain aligned to the bottom of the display.

Solutions that mix explicit and implicit actions are described by Nacenta et al. [23]. They propose two approaches that permit the user to limit the number of simultaneously engaged transformations by either filtering the movements of small magnitude or by classifying the overall user's input into a likely subset of manipulation gestures. Both of those approaches require the user to change the nature of the overall interaction, e.g., in order to be able to perform even the smallest amount of scaling with Magnitude Filtering technique, they user needs to first perform a rather exaggerated stretching motion to enable that transformation.

Although explicit mechanisms provide easier control of mode, they typically require additional control surfaces, such as a keyboard or dedicated UI. In contrast, implicit mechanisms eliminate this need, but trade-off for less reliable detection of user intent or reduced expressiveness. Rock & Rails seeks to leverage the advantages of both approaches: allowing the user to unambiguously and explicitly specify mode, without the need for additional control surfaces. To accomplish this, Rock & Rails utilizes mappings based on actions of the non-dominant hand. In effect, the posture and position of the non-dominant hand is a mode selector for the dominant hand.

Non-Dominant Hand as Mode Indicator

Utilizing the non-dominant hand to mode the actions of the dominant is a common technique. In mouse UI, this typically is accomplished by pressing keys on the keyboard while manipulating with the mouse. Mac OS X relies on the use of a function key to differentiate clicking actions; Microsoft Windows differentiates file drag actions based on held modifier keys; and Adobe Illustrator utilizes an elaborate set of modifiers, such as specifying manipulations of the canvas while holding the space bar.

The domain of gestural user interfaces also contains examples of using non-dominant hand to select the interaction mode. For example, several pen + touch projects each have different methods of moding pen input with the dominant hand via multi-touch posture performed by the non-dominant hand [6,15,35]. Grossman et al. also utilized the non-dominant hand to mode input of the other hand [12].

In Rock & Rails, we use the shapes of the non-dominant hand to constrain manipulations performed by the dominant hand. A contribution of Rock & Rails is that symbolic moding gestures are mapped onto postures which are intended to extend the direct manipulation metaphor. Furthermore, we strictly adhere to the interaction recipe where different shapes specify the mode and fingertips perform manipulations, to reduce the ambiguity and activation errors among users. This also ensures that Rock & Rails can live alongside the language of standard direct manipulation, without adding any on-screen affordances or reducing the expressiveness of the language.

Shape vs. Finger Input

There are three general schools of thought as regards touch input with various contact shapes. The first, and most common approach, is to ignore the contact shape and to treat all contacts equally, recognized typically as points of contact. Hardware limitations sometimes make this a necessity, but oftentimes this is simply a result of the shape information being ignored by the software platform (e.g., Apple iOS and Microsoft Windows 7). Gestural techniques which act solely on points of contact have been presented, such as *BumpTop* [2], as well as multi-point manipulation, such as work demonstrated by Igarashi et al. [16], and techniques designed for the pen, such as described by Geißler [11].

At the other extreme is the notion that no shape, fingertip or otherwise, should be treated specially, and instead all input is allowed to pass unfiltered. *SmartSkin* [27] demonstrated the use of hand contours to "drive" objects. *ShapeTouch* explored the idea that contacts' area and motion fields can be used to infer virtual contact forces to enable interactions with virtual object in a physical manner; e.g., a "large" contact provides a bigger force and moves objects faster than using a "small" contact [8]. Wilson et al. modelled human touches based on their outline to simulate real world physics using a physics game engine [33]. These approaches should not be confused with others which use shapes for visualization purposes alone, but continue to perform interactions based on touch points alone (e.g., *LucidTouch* [32]).

Somewhere between these two extremes lies a large group of projects which distinguish between various shapes through a recognition step. Off of the surface of a device, *Charade* defined a large set of hand postures and movements which mapped onto system functions [4]. In the area of surface computing, an early example of this is the *RoomPlanner* interface [34], which assigned specific functions to specific hand shapes, e.g., using a 'karate chop' shape to reveal hidden content. A simpler use of shape is the *SimPress* technique [5], which assigns two states to a touch ("light", and "pressed") based on the area of contact, allowing the user to press-down on the surface to transition between states. Finally, Freeman et al. strictly delineate between shape contacts and point contacts in defining their taxonomy of surface gestures [10].

In such systems, shapes other than fingertips do not tend to perform manipulations, but can be used to provide a different kind of input (e.g., invoke a toolbar or define an editing plane [34]). Rock & Rails occupies this same middle ground by making a distinction between fingertips and other shapes and using this distinction to enable novel interactions. In so doing, Rock & Rails provides solutions to problems of C/D gain, occlusion, and transform interdependence by providing an explicit method to allow the user to select modes meant to address each of these problems. Furthermore, it enables fluid interaction, allowing users to quickly engage and disengage these modes.

ROCK & RAILS INTERACTION TECHNIQUES

Rock & Rails enables improved user control by addressing each of the three limitations of direct manipulations: it reduces occlusion, provides a variable C/D gain, and provides mechanisms to isolate unit-transformations.

Shape Gesture Vocabulary

Rock & Rails interactions depend on detecting the vocabulary of three basic shapes: *Rock*, *Rail*, and *Curved Rail* (Figure 2). Rock is a hand shape that the user makes by placing a closed fist on the table; Rail is a flat upright hand pose similar to a "karate chop" [34], and Curved Rail is a slightly curved pose, somewhere between a rock and a rail.

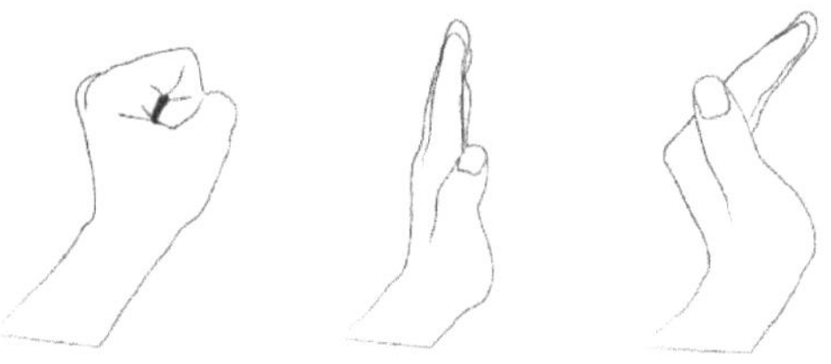

Figure 2. Three hand shapes used in Rock & Rails interactions. From left: Rock, Rail, and Curved Rail.

In our prototype, these hand shapes were recognized simply by examining the eccentricity and the size of the ellipse detected by the Microsoft Surface: a rounded shape detected as Rock, thin long shape as Rail, and in-between shape for Curved Rail. While simple, this eccentricity-based detection works reliably in our prototype; however, more elaborate solutions might be necessary if greater robustness is desired. In the following sections we describe how each of these basic shapes can be combined with fingertip input to allow for novel interactions, summarized in Table 1.

Shape	*Outside Object*	*Inside Object*
Rock	Create proxy	Uniform scale
Rail	Create ruler: 1D translation & object alignments	Non-uniform scale
Curved Rail	(Not currently used)	Rotation about centre only

Table 1. Input/Mode mappings of our three hand shape gestures. The gestures can be performed with either hand, typically the non-dominant.

Reducing Occlusions via Proxies

Direct-touch systems increase occlusion, as was long ago noted by Potter et al. [25]. Several solutions have been proposed, most of which optimize for selection. These include the *Precision-Handle* [1], *Shift* [31], and *Escape* [37] techniques. However, these techniques fail to provide a mechanism for reduced occlusion for manipulations, since they require reassigning on-screen movement from manipulations to a second phase of their respective selection techniques.

The Rock & Rails approach for alleviating occlusions is to allow the user to quickly define a proxy object, which acts as a kind of *voodoo doll* for the original object [24], such that manipulations performed on the proxy are applied to both the proxy and its linked object(s).

Proxies are created by making a Rock gesture outside of an on-screen object, and linked by simultaneously holding a proxy and touching on-screen objects. They can be relocated convenience without affecting linked content by dragging them with a Rock. Proxies are also transient, in that they can be quickly created and deleted, without affecting any of the linked objects. In our implementation, proxies are visualized as simple semi-transparent blue rectangles and they can be removed via an associated on-screen button. Figure 3 illustrates the basic use of proxies.

Proxies can also be set to a many-to-many relationship to linked objects, so that any one object can be joined to more than one proxy, and each proxy can be joined to multiple objects. The effect of this is that proxies can act as a sort of ad hoc grouping mechanism.

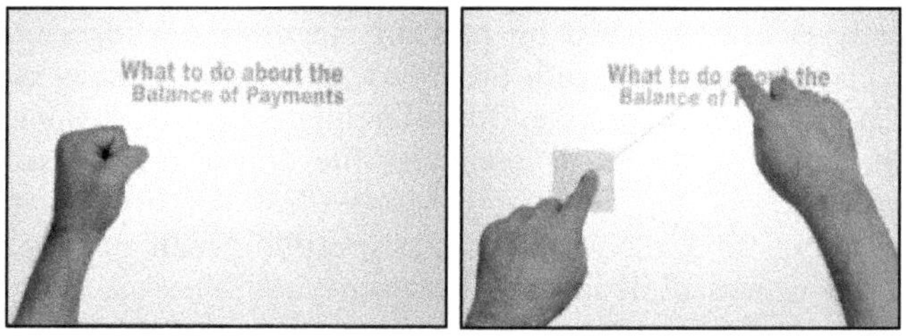

Figure 3. Left: the Rock gesture creates a proxy. Right: a text object is linked to the proxy by holding it and tapping the object.

The many-to-many relationship between proxies and objects varies from traditional groups in three ways. First, a proxy object is a de facto icon for each group, making each group visually apparent to the user, and serving as a target for direct manipulation. Second, proxy links can overlap, unlike groups and sub-groups which traditionally follow a tree structure. Third, objects can be quickly and easily manipulated without affecting other objects linked to the same proxy simply by manipulating the object rather than the proxy, thus not requiring the user to group and ungroup to choose the scope of their manipulations. Figure 4 illustrates many of the elements of these differences.

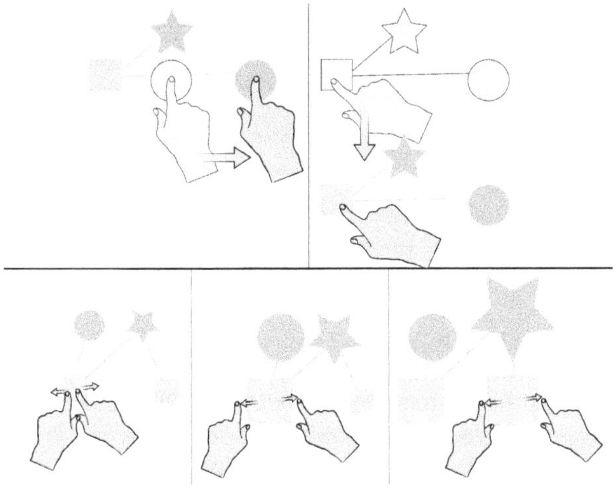

Figure 4. Top: objects linked to proxies can still be manipulated independently without affecting the link. Bottom: proxies exist in a many-to-many relationship with objects.

Variable C/D Gain

In a basic manipulations (as in Newtonian physics), when rotating an object about a pivot point, C/D gain is proportional to the distance of the manipulating hand from the pivot. Thus, finer control can be achieved by moving the manipulating hand farther from the pivot. Commercial devices have demonstrated the extension of this notion to other manipulations. In the Apple iOS, for example, C/D gain of the manipulator of a slider is proportional to the distance of that manipulator to the slider. To achieve finer-grained adjustment, the user slides their finger away from the track of the control. Traditional unconstrained direct manipulation systems are unable to leverage this principle, however, because the movement of the manipulator away from the centre of rotation is mapped to a scale and rotation operation.

Rock & Rails extends this idea to allow the user to vary the C/D gain of all manipulation transformations once they have been isolated using one of the Rock & Rails hand gestures. As we describe each manipulation individually below, we also explain how one can finely adjust the C/D gain during the interaction.

Fingertips Manipulate, Hand Shapes Constrain

As we have discussed, input contacts classified as fingertips operate as manipulators of on-screen content. Hand postures sensed by the device (Rock, Rail, and Curved Rail), in contrast, are identified and used to apply constraints to those manipulations. These shapes were selected by roughly matching physical properties to their perceived effect to a user's understanding of naïve-physics, as advocated by Jacob et al. [17]. We now review how these shapes are used to constrain various manipulations.

Isolated Uniform Scale

Uniform scale is achieved by placing a Rock gesture on an object. The object is locked in place and prevented from rotating, thus eliminating all the unwanted compound effects present when uniformly scaling an object with two or more fingertips. The object is scaled proportionally to the change in distance between Rock and the manipulating finger, i.e., Rock acts as one control point of the scale, the finger as the other. To adjust C/D gain, the user can change the direction of movement, reducing the contribution of motion to the distance between Rock and finger. While complex in theory, the visual feedback loop ensures an apparent linkage between user action and the resulting increase in precision. Figure 5 illustrates.

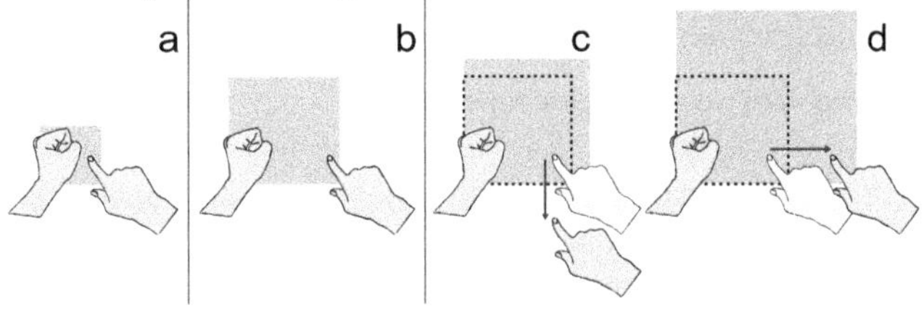

Figure 5. Placing a Rock gesture on an object (a) allows for uniform scaling (b) without rotations or translations. A user can either change the angle of movement to adjust C/D gain (c), or continue along the same path to maximize manipulation speed (d).

Isolated Non-Uniform Scale

Non-uniform scale is achieved by placing a Rail gesture within an object, and sliding a manipulation fingertip perpendicular to the palm of the hand. Given a bounding box of an on-screen object, the Rail gesture placed on top of the object will be associated with the closest edge of the bounding box (as illustrated in Figure 6). This allows the user to quickly isolate the scaling dimension to manipulate. Furthermore, C/D gain is adjusted by moving the finger parallel to the track of the Rail.

Isolated Rotation

Isolated rotation (without scale or translation) is achieved using the Curved Rail gesture. The user places a curved-rail gesture on an object, and an additional manipulating fingertip rotates the object around its centroid. C/D gain is adjusted by moving the finger closer to or farther away from the centre of the object Figure 7 illustrates.

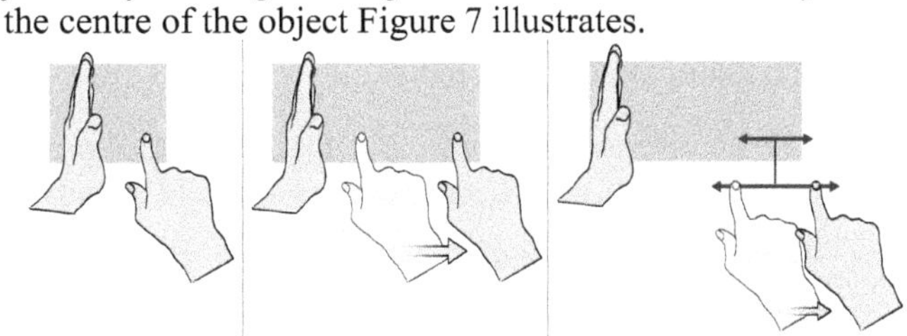

Figure 6. Left, centre: sliding a finger away from Rail within an object scales that object in the axis perpendicular to the rail. Right: C/D gain is proportional to the distance from the object.

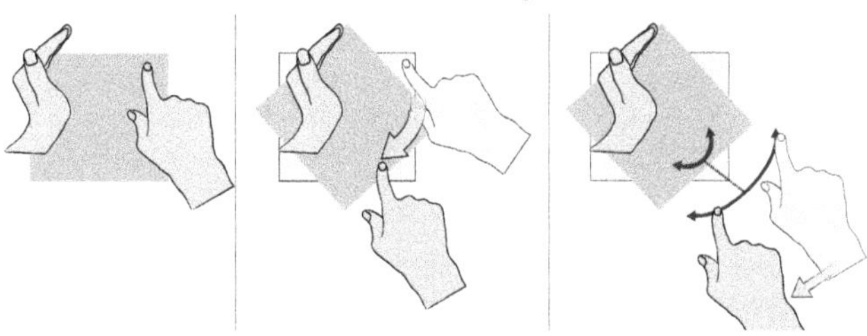

Figure 7. Left, centre: placing a curved rail over an object locks it to rotate about the objects' centre. Right: distance of finger from centre adjusts gain.

Isolated 2D Translation

We achieved isolation of 2D translation by simply eliminating the RNT effects of one-finger translation [14, 18], i.e., when using Rock & Rails, objects are not allowed to rotate when moved in 2D using only a single finger contact. While we did not intentionally provide a means to adjust the C/D gain of 2D translations, one of the participants in our user study discovered a method for achieving this, as we will later describe.

Isolated 1D Translation via Rulers

The user may wish to further constrain the object's movement and translate in one dimension only. 1D-constrained translation is accomplished by placing a Rail gesture on the screen next to the object of interest. The Rail gesture then invokes a helper object, called a *ruler,* which is used to constrain the manipulations (Figure 8). The concept of the ruler has been directly adapted from the architecture drafting tables, which often feature large movable rulers (or straight edges). They differ from traditional guides found in graphics packages in that they can be quickly placed at arbitrary orientations and locations. In our prototype, rulers are created on-demand via a Rail gesture and they can be placed at arbitrary positions and orientations.

Figure 8. Placing a Rail outside of any object creates a ruler parallel to the hand.

If an object is selected (via fingertips), the ruler placed proximal in both position and orientation to an object's bounds is snapped to that boundary. Figure 9 illustrates. Similarly to the proxy object invoked with a Rock gesture, rulers are visualized as long semi-transparent blue rectangles that extend beyond the screen's boundaries. Rulers can also be easily removed with an associated on-screen button.

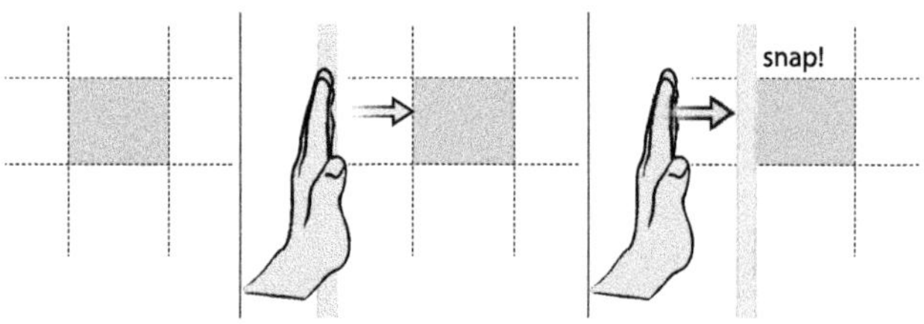

Figure 9. Left, centre: rulers can be placed anywhere on the screen by making a Rail gesture. Right: placing a ruler near an active object will snap the ruler to that object's bounds.

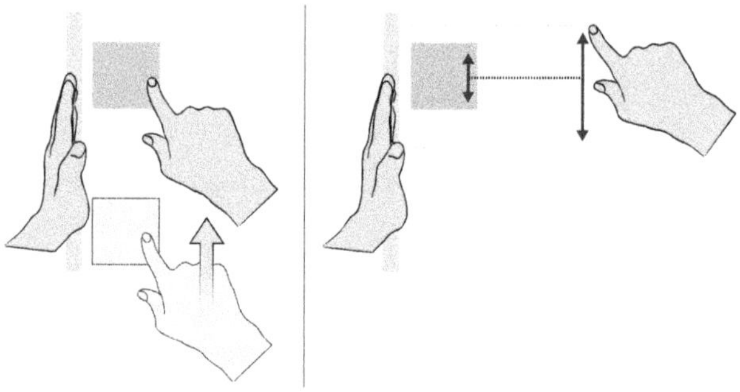

Figure 10. Left: once a ruler is snapped to an object, movement of that object is limited to the axis defined by the ruler. Right: moving the manipulating finger away from the ruler adjusts C/D gain.

An object snapped to the ruler can be translated along it in one dimension only (Figure 10). Furthermore, by moving the manipulating fingertip away from the ruler, the user is able to adjust C/D gain, similarly to the slider control manipulations in Apple iOS interfaces. Figure 10 illustrates.

Rapid Alignment

An additional use for the ruler is to enable the user to rapidly and easily align multiple objects against it. This is achieved by instantiating a ruler on one object's bounds, and then translating other objects towards the ruler. Once they collide, objects will not translate across a ruler, and will rotate as they are pushed against the ruler so that they align with it. This use of bimanual input and ruler, illustrated in Figure 11, is similar to the *alignment stick* [26].

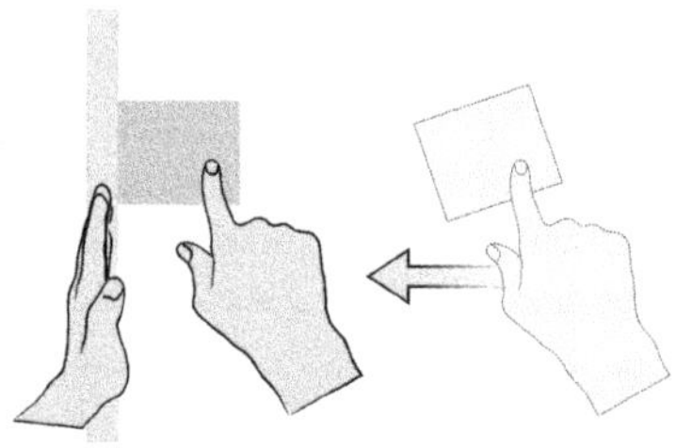

Figure 11. Rulers serve as obstacles to translation. Once abutting the ruler, further movement will cause the object to rotate towards the ruler.

In order to allow users to align objects with the same ruler repeatedly, we allow users to pin them to the canvas by tapping them. Once pinned, a ruler can be *active* or *inactive*. An active pinned ruler acts as a regular transient ruler, serving as a barrier to translation, and serving as a guide for rotation. Alternatively, when the user lifts their hand from the ruler and it becomes inactive, it has no effects on the moving objects as seen in Figure 12.

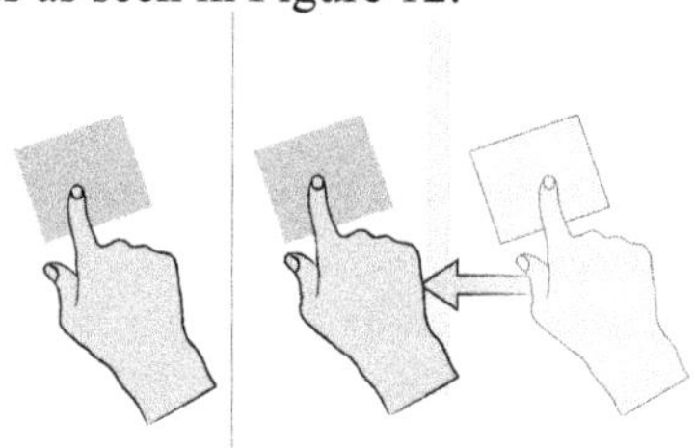

Figure 12. An inactive ruler does not serve as an obstacle to translation.

USER STUDY: EXPERT REVIEW

The Rock & Rails techniques are able to achieve the goals of reduced occlusion, variable C/D gain, and manipulation constraint / transform independence with the introduction of three simple spatially-recognized postures: Rock, Rail, and Curved Rail. To gauge their effectiveness, we invited eight real-world designers to evaluate them within a prototype image layout application developed for Microsoft Surface. Given the simplicity of the implementation of our recognizer, it was fully expected that issues in usability would be encountered by the participants. The primary goal of the evaluation was to collect information on *usefulness*, rather than the usability of the features, and to gain overall feedback about the use of a touch system equipped with Rock & Rails vs. traditional, mouse-based methods to perform more layout tasks. We also recorded each participant session in order to observe interesting behaviours which might suggest future feature sets or capabilities.

Implementation

We implemented Rock & Rails as an application running on a Microsoft Surface multi-touch table using the Microsoft Surface SDK 1.1, running under WPF. We relied on the contact processing capabilities of Microsoft Surface to disambiguate between fingertips and hand shapes, and classified each of the required three shapes using the aforementioned contact ellipse eccentricity method.

Procedure

Participants were given an introduction to Rock & Rails, and the experimenter gave a demonstration of its use. When participants understood the various functions, they were then presented with an image of a completed book cover, and told their task would be to reproduce it given an array of the graphical elements laid out on the table. The elements were arranged in a row at the top of the screen, and were each rotated and resized such that all would require each of the unit affine transforms to be applied in order to complete the task. An image of the application before and after the completion of the task is shown in Figure 13.

Figure 13. User evaluation setup. Left: objects were randomly arranged, and resized and shaped as small squares. Right: final completed layout.

To reduce novelty effects, participants were required to complete the layout to their satisfaction. While they performed the task, the experimenter observed and noted interesting behaviours, and would intervene if the participant encountered difficulty or asked questions.

Instrument

The questionnaire was composed of Likert-scale questions designed to collect the experts' response to the usefulness of the system. In order to help separate usefulness from usability, usability questions were also asked, but not reported. The questionnaire also included open-ended questions which focused on the usefulness of the various functions of the Rock & Rails system. Participants were asked to consider the alternative of using traditional methods for completing this task using a mouse and keyboard and their preferred graphics software.

Participants

Eight participants began the review. One participant was unable to complete the review for personal reasons. Of the remaining 7, 6 were male, 1 female, and all were professional designers. All were highly experienced with graphical layout using various software applications. The designers were all employees of the same software company. Participants were not specifically compensated for their participation in the experiment.

Results

Reported results are of a 7-point Likert scale, with 1 labelled "strongly disagree" and 7 labelled "strongly agree". Overall, participants responded that the Rock & Rails system would be useful to them in performing a layout task on a multi-touch device, as compared with traditional methods. Five participants rated their agreement with the statement "The system you used today was helpful in completing the task" as 5/7, the remaining two 6/7. To the question "I would want a system like this in a real product", two participants rated 5/7, one 6/7, and the remaining four 7/7. Free form comments reinforce the utility of the technique: "*I dig it and would really like to see this evolve and make its way into design-related applications*". One commented that the system would be useful for multi-touch tables in general, aside from graphics applications: "*some people can't stand having things be just a few degrees off, so this really piqued my curiosity*".

Transform Independence

Participants were asked specifically to rate the usefulness of Rock & Rails' isolation of each of the transforms. It was again pointed out to them that all operations are possible using traditional methods. There was significant agreement that the ability to do so using direct manipulation was valued, as shown in Table 2. A participant noted: "*As a designer I really liked the rails, or how I saw them, as T-Squares. I preferred that over moving a guide with a mouse. I really enjoyed manipulating the content with my hands, I seems like I just feel it more.*"

Useful Compared to Traditional Methods			
Transform	Agree	Neutral	Disagree
Rotation	5	1	1
Resize	6	1	0
Translate	7	0	0

Table 2. Participant-reported ratings on the usefulness of isolating each transform using Rock & Rails versus traditional methods.

Occlusion & Precision

Participants each noted the utility of the proxies as a desirable feature. When asked to note differences from traditional methods that they preferred in Rock & Rails, 5/7 noted the use of proxy objects as a desirable innovation. One participant noted that they would prefer the inclusion of proxies even for mouse-based systems, as a method of rapid creation of ad hoc overlapping groups.

Although all participants were made aware of the use of leverage to increase precision of their tasks, few participants made use of it. Only 4/7 surveys include mention of this feature. We attribute this failure mostly to inexperience with the concept and hypothesize that more extended use would lead to more extensive use of this feature.

Observed Behaviours

In addition to explicit feedback, we noted several interesting behaviours. One such behaviour was the use of a combination of proxies and rulers: the participant would link multiple objects to a proxy, and then align them with one another by pushing the group over a ruler. This was especially noteworthy because it contradicts the normal behaviour of groups in traditional mouse-based systems. This behaviour is illustrated in Figure 14.

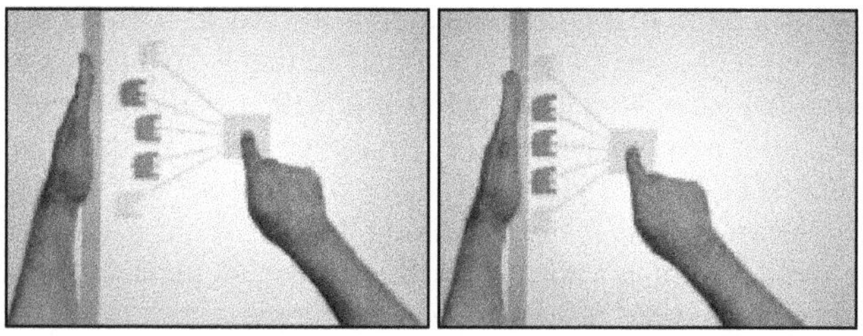

Figure 14. A user aligns multiple objects by pushing their shared Proxy towards a Ruler.

Another interesting behaviour developed out of a missing element of our system – there is no intended mechanism to adjust the C/D gain for 2D translations. We had presumed that users would perform two consecutive 1D manipulations to complete this. Instead, one user developed the innovative approach of linking two proxies to an object, and manipulating it with both proxies simultaneously. By holding one of the proxies still, the user effectively halved the gain of the manipulation applied by moving the other proxy. This is illustrated in Figure 15.

Figure 15. A user achieves higher precision 2D translation by holding one proxy and moving the other.

One participant who made extensive use of proxies noted that they indicate their linked objects only when touched (intended to reduce visual clutter). To compensate, she performed a non-proportional resize on each proxy object before linking it, rendering them visibly distinctive. Further, participants were observed replacing proxies repeatedly. We realized this occurred because the proxies were changing size and shape as manipulations were applied, often becoming too small or narrow to be useful. We also observed that many participants would arrange several inactive ruler objects on the screen, creating layout guides.

Finally, it was also interesting to note that participants tended to use a subset of gestures which spanned the needed degrees of freedom and precision. For example, the participant who disagreed that isolated rotation using the Rock was useful (Table 2), chose instead to rotate using traditional manipulations and correct using the remaining Rock & Rails techniques.

Requested Features

Participants requested several features not included in our prototype. Many of these are features that would likely be included in an application implementing the Rock & Rails technique, such as *undo* and a fixed grid. Two types of requests in particular were noteworthy. Three participants requested a mechanism to numerically specify transforms "*just to be sure*" that a specific value were reached. Participants also noted the lack of a zoom function in Rock & Rails – both who observed this attributed this desire to verify the precision of their actions. Like other functions noted above, we anticipate an application utilizing Rock & Rails might include these capabilities. In these two cases, however, we believe that better feedback to show users the precise numeric values may alleviate much of the need.

Discussion

The results of the study demonstrate the utility of the feature set of Rock & Rails, and point to its advantages over traditional mechanisms. Particular feedback from designers points towards the perception that this set of gestures extends the direct-touch input paradigm, despite the offset of the proxy object. It is also clear from observed behaviours that the designers were able to extend the functionality of the system, suggesting the cohesiveness of the set of operations. As for improvements, the specific method of achieving 2D gain control illustrated in Figure 15 was clearly overly elaborate, and a mechanism to achieve 2D gain control through simpler means is a clear candidate for future work. The requested features we note above have a common theme of overcoming a lack of feedback. Maintaining a UI-free screen when not touching was a design goal; however, a clear area for future work is an exploration of feedback mechanisms to better support these operations.

Finally, we attribute the tendency of participants to perform subsets of available operations to our experimental task. Because it always began with objects requiring all unit transforms applied, whichever transformation was applied first needed not be isolated, since any spill-over from a more coarse gesture would be corrected at the same time as the user undid the initial setting.

FUTURE WORK

A focus for future work will be further design of the proxy objects. Observed user behaviours suggest the need for a mechanism to render each visibly distinctive, as well as to allow repeated manipulation without changing the shape of the proxy object itself. Further work is also required to find the correct balance of the transient nature of the proxies and rulers. A primary goal of this project was that no on-screen UI be necessary to complete the set of operations. None the less, these two objects themselves represent an addition of UI elements. While we and many of our participants viewed these as residual gestures rather than as objects unto themselves, it remains a rich area for future exploration. Also worthy of consideration is the combination of these residuals into compound residual gestures.

Learnability and feedback are also ripe for future exploration. While our gesture set was iteratively designed and intended to mimic direct manipulations and naïve physics, we make no claim that users would quickly learn this language without help. Work in the area of gesture teaching would serve as a useful starting point for this work [10]. Further, providing feedback mechanisms before, during, and after each operation will ultimately be a necessary.

While the Rock & Rails technique showed promise in isolation, a clear avenue for future work is its integration into a larger system. Observation of its use in contexts where the primary task is not alignment, but rather where alignment is only an occasional task might be particularly interesting. We also plan to explore the abstraction of the modes achieved in our gestures, to explore alternative gestures, or the use of physical objects to create them.

The directions we have discussed here would best be implemented through user-centric iterative design, and would also benefit from further comparisons with traditional tools. Methods such as coordination measures could be used to evaluate the efficacy of the gesture language [38].

CONCLUSIONS & DESIGN RECOMMENDATIONS

Based on the success the expert review, we recommend continuing to explore the use of shape gestures to build the set of traditional direct manipulation gestures. While we did not explore usability of our system, the particular set of gestures we selected was quickly learned by the participants in our study, and thus forms a reasonable basis for future work.

We also recommend the use of shape gestures to create a distinct break from direct manipulation and constraints on those manipulations, as it does seem to afford easy, flexible use without the need for extensive on-screen elements. An element of Rock & Rails not highlighted earlier is that rulers and proxies can be moved by placing the appropriate hand shape (Rock, Rail respectively) over them and sliding, and such movement does not affect any adjacent or linked objects – this is the final element in a rule which seems to make Rock & Rails successful: *fingertips manipulate, shapes constrain*. Any movement of a shape on the surface of the device will not affect underlying content in any way, unless objects are directly linked to it.

The distinction between shapes and fingertips is a success also in that the language could be immediately applied to any direct-manipulation-based system, without conflicting with existing gestures.

One key benefit of Rock & Rails is that while each of the interactions is rather simple on their own, it is easily possible to combine them into more complex combinations. This has already yielded many unexpected solutions in our user evaluations, for example, when a several objects are aligned simultaneously with a ruler simply by dragging them all together via a common proxy. It is this ability of easy composition, which makes our rather simple vocabulary of interactions powerful and useful in accomplishing a real world task.

Finally, it is worth noting that while we claim that Rock & Rails does not require on-screen elements, the proxy and ruler objects are represented graphically. The distinction we draw is that these objects are residuals of user actions, rather than on-screen elements created by the designer. While a fine line, we suspect a designer implementing a visual language for Rock & Rails would be well served to represent these elements in that way.

ACKNOWLEDGEMENTS

We thank Paul Hoover and Kay Hofmeester for their help during the design process, as well as the many designers who participated in our expert review. We also thank Brad Carpenter and the Surface team for their support with the project.

REFERENCES

1. Albinsson, P. and Zhai, S. 2003. High precision touch screen interaction. *CHI* '03. p. 105–112.
2. Agarawala, A. and Balakrishnan, R. 2006. Keepin' it real: Pushing the desktop metaphor with physics, piles and the pen. In *Proc. of ACM CHI '06*. p. 1283–1292.
3. Apted, T., Kay, J., and Quigley, A. 2006. Tabletop sharing of digital photographs for the elderly. *CHI '06*. p. 781–790.
4. Baudel, T., and Beaudouin-Lafon, M. 1993. Charade: remote control of objects using free-hand gestures. *Communications of the ACM, 36(7)*. p. 28–35.
5. Benko, H., Wilson, A. D., and Baudisch, P. 2006. Precise selection techniques for multi touch screens. In *Proc. of ACM CHI '06*. p. 1263–1272.
6. Brandl, P., Forlines, C., Wigdor, D., Haller, M., and Shen, C. 2008. Combining and measuring the benefits of bimanual pen and direct-touch interaction on horizontal interfaces. In *Proc. of Advanced Visual Interfaces (ACM AVI '08)*. p. 154–161.
7. Buxton, W. 1986. Chunking and phrasing and the design of human-computer dialogues. In *Proc. of the IFIP World Computer Congress*. p. 475–480.
8. Cao, X., et al. 2008 ShapeTouch: Leveraging contact shape on interactive surfaces. *ITS '08,* p. 129–136.

9. Forlines, C., Wigdor, D., Shen, C., and Balakrishnan, R. 2007. Direct-touch vs. mouse input for tabletop displays. In *Proc. of ACM CHI '07*. p. 647–656.

10. Freeman, D., et al. 2009. ShadowGuides: Visualizations for in-situ learning of multi-touch and whole-hand gestures. *ITS '09*. p. 165–172.

11. Geißler, J. 1998. Shuffle, throw or take it! Working efficiently with an interactive wall. *CHI '98*. p. 265–266.

12. Grossman, T., Wigdor, D., and Balakrishnan, R. 2004. Multi-finger gestural interaction with 3-D volumetric displays. In *Proc. of ACM UIST '04*. p. 61–70.

13. Guiard, Y. 1987. Asymmetric division of labor in human skilled bimanual action: The kinematic chain as a model. *Journal of Motor Behavior, 19(4)*. p. 486–517.

14. Hancock, M. S., et al. 2006. Rotation and translation mechanisms for tabletop interaction. *ITS '06*. p. 79–88.

15. Hinckley, K., Yatani, K., Pahud, M., Coddington, N., Rodenhouse, J., Wilson, A., Benko, H., and Buxton, B. 2010. Pen + Touch = New Tools. *UIST '10*.

16. Igarashi, T., Moscovich, T., Hughes, J.F. 2005. As-rigid-as-possible shape manipulation. *ACM Transactions on Computer Graphics, 24(3), ACM SIGGRAPH '05*. p. 1134-1141.

17. Jacob, R., Girouard, A., Hirshfield, L.M., Horn, M.S., Shaer, O., Solovey, E.T., and Zigelbaum, J. 2008. Reality-based interaction: A framework for post-WIMP interfaces. In *Proc. Of ACM CHI '08*. p. 201–210.

18. Kruger, R., Carpendale, S., Scott, S. and Greenberg, S. 2003. How people use orientation on tables: comprehension, coordination and communication. In *Proc. of ACM SIGGROUP '03*. p. 369–378.

19. Kurtenbach, G. *The Design and Evaluation of Marking Menus*. Dept. of Computer Science, U Toronto. 1993.

20. Malik, S., Ranjan, A., and Balakrishnan, R. 2005. Interacting with large displays from a distance with vision-tracked multi-finger gestural input. In *Proc. of ACM UIST '05*. p. 43–52.

21. Morris, M.R., Paepcke, A., Winograd, T., and Stamberger, J. 2006. TeamTag: Exploring centralized versus replicated controls for co-located tabletop groupware. In *Proc. of ACM CHI '06*. p. 1273–1282.

22. Morris, M.R., Wobbrock, J., and Wilson, A. 2010. Understanding users' preferences for surface gestures. In *Proc. of Graphics Interface (GI '10)*. p. 261–268.

23. Nacenta, M. A., Baudisch, P., Benko, H., and Wilson, A. 2009. Separability of spatial manipulations in multi-touch interfaces. In *Proc. of Graphics Interface (GI '09)*. p. 175–182.

24. Pierce, J.S., Stearns, B., and Pausch, R. 1999. Two handed manipulation of voodoo dolls in virtual environments. In *Proc. of Interactive 3D Graphics (I3D '99)*. p. 141–145.

25. Potter, R.L., L.J. Weldon, and B. Shneiderman. 1988. Improving the accuracy of touch screens: an experimental evaluation of three strategies. In *Proc. of ACM CHI '88*. p. 27–32.

26. Raisamo, R., Raiha, K.-J. 1996. A new direct manipulation technique for aligning objects in drawing programs. *UIST 1996*, 157-164.

27. Rekimoto, J. 2002. SmartSkin: An infrastructure for free-hand manipulation on interactive surfaces. *CHI '02*. p. 113–120.

28. Shen, C., Vernier, F. D., Forlines, C., and Ringel, M. 2004. DiamondSpin: an extensible toolkit for around-the-table interaction. *CHI '04*. p. 167–174.

29. Shneiderman, B. 1983. Direct manipulation: a step beyond programming languages. *IEEE Computer* 16(8) (August 1983). p. 57–69.

30. Tan, D., Stefanucci, J.K., Proffitt, D., and Pausch, R. 2002. Kinesthesis Aids Human Memory. *Extended Abstracts ACM CHI '02*. p. 806–807

31. Vogel, D. and Baudisch, P. 2007. Shift: A technique for operating pen-based interfaces using touch. In *Proc. of ACM CHI '07*. p. 657–666.

32. Wigdor, D., Forlines, C., Baudisch, P., Barnwell, J., Shen, C. 2007. LucidTouch: A see-through mobile device. In *Proc. of ACM UIST '07*. p. 269–278.

33. Wilson, A. D., Izadi, S., Hilliges, O., Garcia-Mendoza, A., and Kirk, D. 2008. Bringing physics to the surface. In *Proc. of ACM UIST '08*. p. 67–76.

34. Wu, M. and Balakrishnan, R. Multi-finger and whole hand gestural interaction techniques for multi-user tabletop displays. In *Proc. of ACM UIST '03*. p. 193–202.

35. Wu, M., Shen, C., Ryall, K., Forlines, C., and Balakrishnan, R. Gesture registration, relaxation, and reuse for multi-point direct-touch surfaces. *ITS'06*. p. 183–190.

36. Wobbrock, J.O., Morris, M.R. and Wilson, A.D. 2009. User-defined gestures for surface computing. In *Proc. of ACM CHI '09*. p. 1083–1092.

37. Yatani, K., Partridge, K., Bern, M., and Newman, M. W. 2008. Escape: a target selection technique using visually-cued gestures. In *Proc. of ACM CHI '08*. p. 285–294.

38. Zhai, S., Milgram, P. 1998. Quantifying coordination in multiple DOF movement and its application to evaluating 6 DOF input devices. CHI '98, 320-327.

Multi-touch Document Folding: Gesture Models, Fold Directions and Symmetries

Patrick Chiu, Chunyuan Liao, Francine Chen
FX Palo Alto Laboratory
3400 Hillview Avenue, Bldg. 4, Palo Alto, CA 94304, USA
{chiu, liao, chen}@fxpal.com

ABSTRACT
For document visualization, folding techniques provide a focus-plus-context approach with fairly high legibility on flat sections. To enable richer interaction, we explore the design space of multi-touch document folding. We discuss several design considerations for simple modeless gesturing and compatibility with standard Drag and Pinch gestures. We categorize gesture models along the characteristics of Symmetric/Asymmetric and Serial/Parallel, which yields three gesture models. We built a prototype document workspace application that integrates folding and standard gestures, and a system for testing the gesture models. A user study was conducted to compare the three models and to analyze the factors of fold direction, target symmetry, and target tolerance in user performance when folding a document to a specific shape. Our results indicate that all three factors were significant for task times, and parallelism was greater for symmetric targets.

Author Keywords
Multi-touch screens, gesture input, document visualization.

ACM Classification Keywords
H5.2. [Information interfaces and presentation]: User Interfaces - Input devices and strategies.

General Terms
Design, Experimentation, Human Factors.

INTRODUCTION
Multi-touch displays are becoming more widely used and appealing: in addition to the iconic Apple iPhone & iPad devices and the compelling Perceptive Pixel systems, other mobile phones, desktop PCs and large flat panels with multi-touch hardware have been productized by Google, HP, Smart Technologies, etc. Another trend is the increasing utilization of 3D graphics on personal computers and operating systems such as the Mac OS and Windows 7. These technologies are providing opportunities and challenges for the development of new applications and interaction techniques for multi-touch 3D graphical user interfaces.

(a) (b)

Figure 1. Examples of multi-touch document folding gestures: (a) Symmetric-Parallel, (b) Asymmetric-Serial.

In this paper, we focus on the use of these technologies for the problem of interactive document visualization that enables viewing part of one or more document pages simultaneously, but in context. Toward this end, an effective principle of information visualization is that of focus-plus-context, where the content in a focus region is rendered at high fidelity with minimal distortion, and the content in a peripheral context region is rendered with a certain amount of distortion to make efficient use of screen space or computational resources.

A well-known example of a focus-plus-context technique is the fisheye view. However, this works poorly for documents due to legibility problems, as the fisheye view transforms straight lines into curves.

A better focus-plus-context approach for visualizing documents is to use folding. The idea is to render the objects or pages in 3D so that the focus regions are flat and parallel to the screen without distortion, and the context regions are folded off to the sides with perspective distortion. An early example is the Perspective Wall [16], which has a center wall facing the user and two walls angled off each side. A more recent visualization, Melange [9], uses a 3D space folding metaphor with multiple focus regions parallel to the screen and the rest of the space folded up.

Although these systems effectively address the visualization aspect, good techniques for interacting with folding

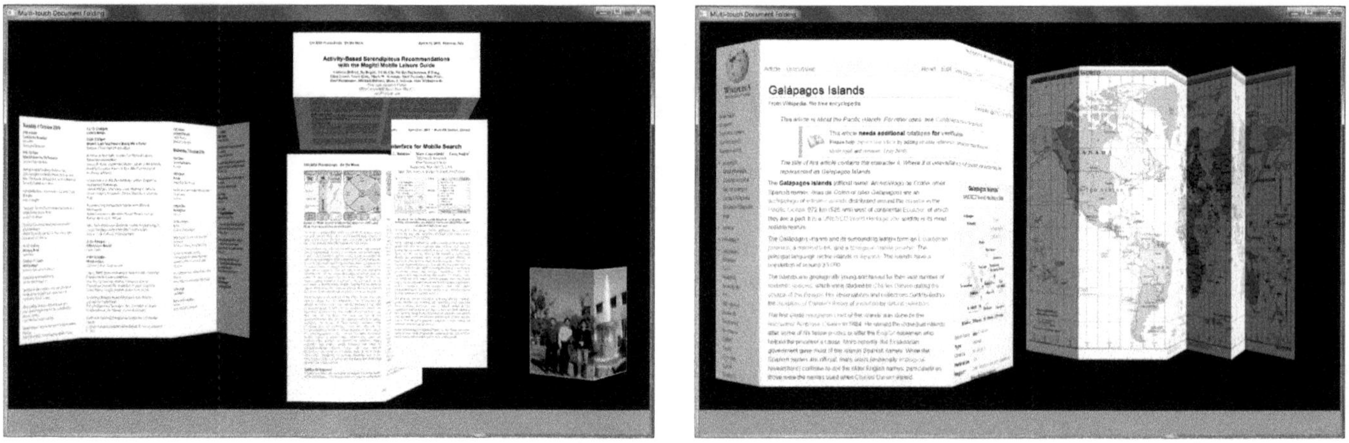

(a) (b)

Figure 2. Screenshots of application with folded documents.

visualizations are still lacking. With the Perspective Wall [16] and Melange [9], a standard mouse and keyboard setup is used. Even going to a more direct style of interaction on a touch screen with a single input point would not be very natural—in the real world, folding a piece of paper is usually done with more than one finger and with two hands.

Our approach is to employ multi-touch screens, supporting more natural and direct interaction by allowing fingers from both hands to be used together. It is worth pointing out that for the folding task, multi-touch technology can be utilized to enable new forms of interaction that are simpler and modeless, and not just to perform tasks that can be done serially in a more efficient way (e.g. combinations of positioning-scaling and scrolling-selecting [3], selecting multiple targets [14]).

To frame the problem better, we will discuss several design considerations for simple gesture interfaces and for compatibility with standard multi-touch gestures. We then present two practical multi-touch gesture models for folding document page objects, along with a more general categorization based on the characteristics of Symmetric/Asymmetric roles of the hands and Serial/Parallel use of the hands.

For exploring gesture interaction techniques, we have developed a prototype for folding document page objects in a 3D visualization. See Figure 1 and Figure 2. Useful types of folds for document visualization will be described including basic folds and accordion folds. We will also explain different ways of mapping the 2D gestures into folding actions in 3D space.

For understanding the performance of multi-touch gesture folding interactions, we have identified several factors and measures. Some of these, such as target tolerance and parallelism, have been studied in the context of bimanual interaction (e.g. [3], [11]) and the asymmetry between preferred[1] and non-preferred hands (e.g. [1], [10], [13]). Hence, we focus on those factors that are relatively less understood and pertain to folding, such as the folding direction and target symmetry.

A user study was conducted to compare the multi-touch gesture models given by our categorization, and to analyze the various factors involved. We found many of the factors to be significant. The study also suggests that both of our practical gesture models are viable, with tradeoffs that can make one more suitable than the other depending on the requirements of the specific application.

RELATED WORK

We have already mentioned Perspective Wall [16] and Melange [9] as systems that visualize information using folding techniques. Our interface also differs from these systems in the geometry used. While the Perspective Wall has a fixed geometric structure with changeable content rendered on it, our 3D page objects have a more dynamic geometry. And unlike Melange, our folding is performed on the objects and not on the space.

Another interface, Roller [21], uses an effect similar to folding for displaying information targeted for small displays on mobile devices. It has a trigonal prism with sections wrapped around it, and rolling and unrolling it allows the sections to be revealed or hidden.

Multi-touch interaction has been the subject of much research (e.g. see [4], [22]). It has been applied to origami folding, which has somewhat different goals than folding for document visualization. In origami, sections are often folded flat against each other and diagonal folds are common; whereas in document folding, sections need to be folded independently and not always completely. In the Origami Simulator system [5], combinations of touch points of two different sizes (finger and knuckle) correspond to origami functions which are not really suitable for document folding. For example, a 1-touch knuckle gesture results in an action that folds two sections completely together with animation.

[1] The *preferred hand* is also known as the *dominant hand.*

There are other interactive origami visualization systems at various stages of development, and the general computation problem is hard [15]. Most of these systems are not focused on supporting fluid interactions. For example, in Foldinator [19], performing a fold requires several operations with buttons and mouse strokes.

Other systems with related interactive folding techniques include the following: folding windows [2], paper flyer metaphors [7], Fold-and-Drop [8]. None of these support multi-touch. In contrast, LiquidText [20] is a multi-touch system that has a feature to collapse parts of the text via 2D interline compression. And the Microsoft Research physics-based system for interactions on surfaces [23] supports multi-touch operations for deforming and folding cloth-like meshes.

Since our gesture models are bimanual, the research in this area provides motivation and guidelines for designing interaction methods. For asymmetric methods with respect to the roles of the two hands, Guiard's Kinematic Chain theory [10] provides three principles that can be applied to our designs: the non-preferred hand helps delineate frames for the task, the preferred hand is more suitable for higher precision actions, and the non-preferred hand naturally starts before the preferred hand. For symmetric methods, a study on symmetric bimanual interaction [1] explores the visual integration of targets in a tracking task. In this paper, a different factor that we explore is the symmetry of targets; in particular whether these can be performed with greater parallelism and lower task times. Other relevant work in this well-studied area include: [3], [6], [11], [13], [14], [22].

GESTURE MODELS FOR FOLDING

In this section, we discuss some design considerations for gesture models, two practical models, and a categorization along two characteristics. We also describe several mappings of 2D gestures into 3D folding actions.

Design Considerations

For ease of use and to minimize gesturing errors, it is a good idea to use extremely simple gesture shapes such as those that have been successfully deployed on commercial products (e.g. iPhone/iPad and Windows 7).

To make it easier for novice users to learn, we avoid more sophisticated techniques involving complex gestures in which a single gesture path can be parsed into several gestures, such as detecting certain geometric features or other delimiters in the gesture (e.g. [12]). These complex gestures can be used for performing multiple selections and commands with a single gesture, but can be deprecated with multi-touch technology, which enables support of separate gesture paths using different fingers.

Modes should be avoided if possible, as they can be a source of interaction errors in software systems. For a gesture interface, having modes (e.g. one for translation and scaling, another for folding) would make the interaction less fluid. Furthermore, on larger screens, having to reach for buttons or menus to control the modes is awkward and interrupts the task.

Another important consideration is compatibility with standard gestures popularized in commercial products like the iPhone/iPad and Windows 7. Two important ones are the "Drag" and "Pinch" gestures. With the Drag gesture, using a single finger to drag on an object moves it along the drag direction.

With the Pinch gesture, touching an object with two fingers and moving them together or apart results in a scaling operation. We note that some implementations are more lax than the specification: moving just one finger (while holding the other finger still) is sufficient to perform a Pinch gesture. For our designs, however, we will be stricter and a gesture is interpreted as a Pinch gesture only if *both* fingers move together or apart. This will enable a richer supply of gestures.

There are other standard multi-touch gesture operations, but except for the Pinch gesture, these will not conflict with our gesture schemes for folding. We mention one other operation, which is part of the fundamental rotate-scale-translate operations. For translate and scale operations, we have already described the Drag and Pinch gestures. For the rotate operation, one common gesture in Windows 7 is to touch with two fingers and turn them simultaneously. Alternatively, the user can rotate by orbiting a finger around another stationary finger. The rotate operation is useful for tabletop displays where orientation matters, but it is not always needed for applications on vertical displays like desktop and wall displays.

To summarize our design considerations:

D1. Avoid complex gestures.
D2. Avoid modes.
D3. Compatibility with standard gestures.

Two Practical Gesture Models for Folding

Based on the above design considerations, we developed two practical multi-touch gesture models for folding. Depending on the requirements of the target application, one model and its variations may be more suitable than the other. Also, some variations may be quicker to perform than others or may be more compatible with existing standard gestures.

Symmetric-Parallel (SP)

In a simple multi-touch gesture model for folding, which we call *Symmetric-Parallel* (or *SP* for short), the user employs a finger from each hand to touch and select two sections of the document page object, and then drags the fingers to fold the sections about the crease between the two sections. This is illustrated in Figure 3.

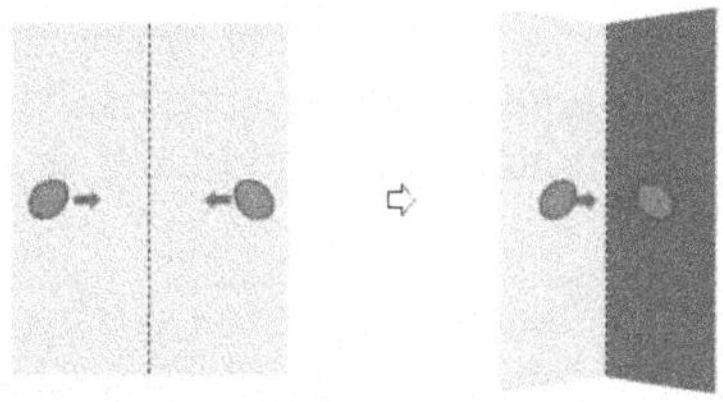

Figure 3. Symmetric-Parallel gesture model: A folding operation in which contact points can move simultaneously.

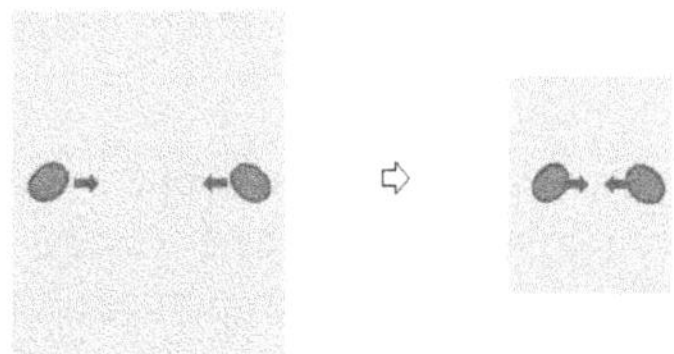

Figure 4. A standard Pinch gesture operation for scaling.

The operation is *symmetric* in the sense that both finger touch events are interpreted in the same way: touching a section selects it, and dragging a touched section folds it. Another way to think about it is that both hands are assigned identical roles [1]. It is *parallel* because both fingers can move simultaneously.

While conceptually simple, in practice this SP gesture model can be a bit difficult to use for novice users. We prototyped and informally tested this model on a few users and discovered that they had difficulties performing basic folding tasks with it. One task we tested is that given a target wireframe, the user had to fold two sections along a fixed crease of the document page object to match the target wireframe. Our observations were that users had difficulty moving the two sections simultaneously, or at least had to concentrate very hard. One reason could be that the users had trouble focusing on doing two things at once. For an expert user (e.g. project members who have spent many hours with the prototype), the SP model was not difficult to use. As we will see in the user study section below, users can be relatively fast but the perceived mental effort under this gesture model is greater.

Another design issue with the SP model is that it may violate our design considerations *D2* or *D3*, depending on how it is adopted. It is not compatible with the standard multi-touch Pinch gesture for scaling an object because the two contact points are moving simultaneously toward or away from each other. Compare Figure 3 and Figure 4. In order to employ the Symmetric model, extra mechanisms would be required such as providing modes or supporting more than two touch points—which further complicates the system and usability.

Thus, the SP model may be more appropriate for specialized applications like a dedicated origami application. A reasonable design for the origami application is to let the folding be the main interaction handled with gestures, and let the scaling be a secondary operation that can be handled with a slider widget.

Asymmetric-Serial (AS)

To address the deficiencies of the SP model, we developed a second gesture model that we call *Asymmetric-Serial* (or *AS*). It is motivated by how people often work with physical objects, and is consistent with Guiard's theory on asymmetric bimanual action discussed above. For example, when cutting an orange with a knife, the non-preferred hand holds the orange and does not move, while the preferred hand cuts the orange by moving the knife. For folding a document page object, our AS gesture model uses a finger from the non-preferred hand to touch a section and hold it fixed, followed by the use of a finger from the preferred hand to touch and drag a second section to perform a folding action. See Figure 5 to Figure 7.

With the AS gesture model, one hand is always held fixed while the other hand moves. In preliminary informal testing, this seemed easier for novice users to manage and requires less coordination than the SP gesture model.

A design advantage of the AS model is that it satisfies our design consideration *D3* since it is compatible with standard multi-touch gestures. It does not produce the same sequence of touch input events as the Pinch gesture.

A Categorization of Gesture Models

The two bimanual multi-touch gesture models described above can be viewed as belonging to a categorization along two sets of characteristics: {Symmetric, Asymmetric} and {Serial, Parallel}. See Table 1.

The Symmetric/Asymmetric characteristic refers to how the two hands function. The Serial/Parallel characteristic refers to whether simultaneous gesturing by both hands is enabled.

The categorization yields a third gesture model, *Symmetric-Serial* (*SS*). This model is not very practical because there is no reason to limit the user from moving both hands simultaneously since they function independently. Nevertheless, the SS model provides a good benchmark for comparing with the SP and AS models, as it differs from each along one characteristic.

The last case, *Asymmetric-Parallel*, is not possible because our definition of asymmetric is based on the non-preferred hand staying still while the preferred hand is moving.

We note that one can imagine using a single hand with two contact points to fold a document page object, but there are several drawbacks. While it is easy to move the fingers in a coupled manner like the Pinch gesture, it is much more difficult to move the fingers independently to manipulate two sections of a page to different positions, especially when trying to precisely position each section. Another problem is that sometimes the fingers need to be placed at locations that are far apart on the page object, which may be impossible to do with one hand (e.g. see Figure 8).

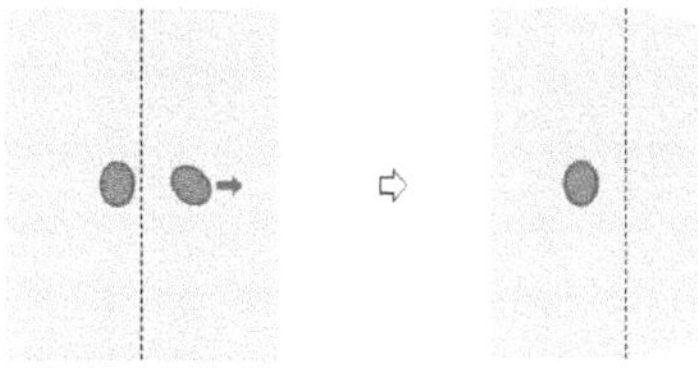

Figure 5. Asymmetric-Serial gesture model: A folding operation in which one contact point is held fixed, and another contact point is moved.

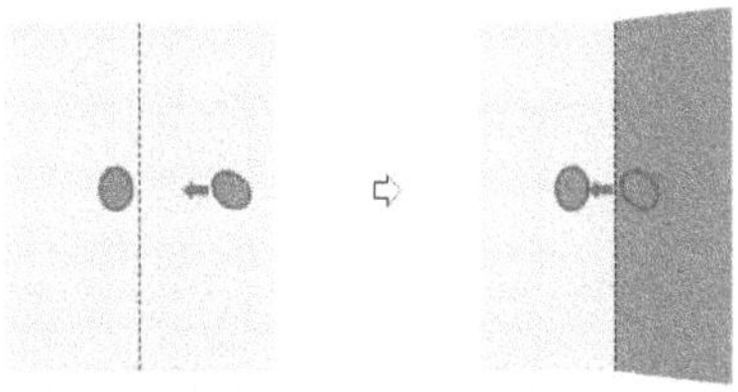

Figure 6. Another instance of Figure 5 where the folding is in the opposite direction.

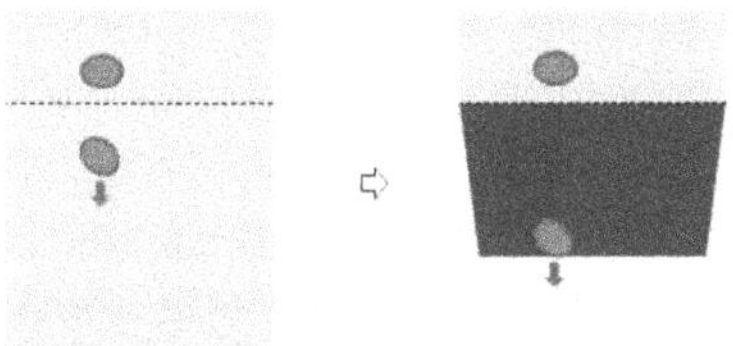

Figure 7. Another instance of Figure 5 where the folding is with respect to a horizontal crease.

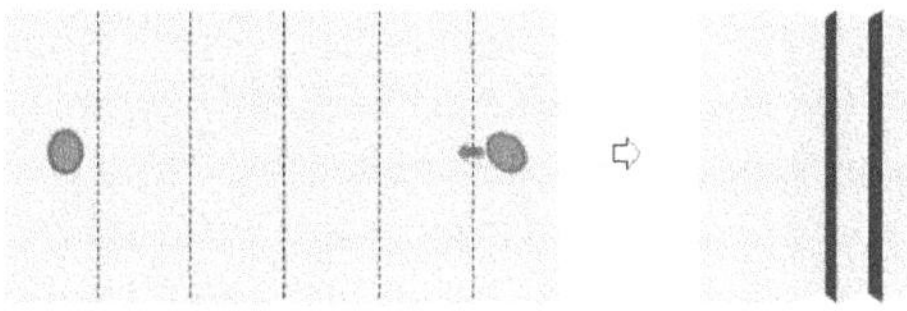

Figure 8. An accordion fold.

Mapping 2D Gestures into 3D Folding Actions

The direction and amount of folding, which is sampled every few milliseconds and dynamically rendered, are determined by the moving gesture paths. There are different ways to map the gesture path events, and we describe three possibilities:

- *Logical*: The amount of gesture movement perpendicular to the projection of the crease onto the screen is mapped to the fold angle. The fold direction is governed by a convention such as the "right hand rule" from vector geometry.
- *Directional*: The fold direction is based on whether the two fingers are moving toward each other or moving apart. The fold angle is based on the amount of movement.
- *Contact Point Constrained (CPC)*: The contact point of the finger on the screen corresponds to a point on a section via the projection of the section in 3D space onto the 2D screen, and this point on the section follows the movement of the finger so that it is always under the contact point.

The Logical mapping is easy for the user to understand; the finger motion is like moving a slider that controls the amount of rotation or bending. From the system standpoint, the Logical mapping is well-defined and simple to implement. Figure 5 and Figure 6 illustrate the Logical mapping, with the crease defining a fold axis vector that points upward. Dragging to the right rotates the section into the screen (a "Mountain" fold, Figure 5), and dragging to the left rotates out toward the screen (a "Valley" fold, Figure 6).

	Serial	Parallel
Symmetric	SS	SP
Asymmetric	AS	n/a

Table 1. A categorization of bimanual gesture models for folding.

For the user, the Directional and CPC might be more intuitive in some ways. With these two mappings, however, there is one problem that happens to occur at the most common configuration where the page object is completely flat and facing the user. If the user moves a finger in a straight line toward the other finger, the folding operation is not well-defined because there is an ambiguity: the section can be either a Mountain or Valley fold. Therefore, the gesture must encode more information to specify which way to fold. One solution for the Directional mapping is to angle the gesture upward for a Mountain fold and downward for a Valley fold.

The CPC mapping requires solving non-linear equations and takes a relatively large amount of computation. Furthermore, induced by the constraints, it can exhibit strange behaviors (e.g. rotating and scaling in unexpected ways); these subtle and complicated issues are studied in the Perceptive Pixel work [18] for the basic rotate-scale-translate manipulation of a generic 3D object in a multi-touch system. Since folding introduces more constraints, the CPC mapping will be less robust.

The CPC mapping must also deal with the frequently occurring Mountain-Valley ambiguity problem described above. The above solution for the Directional mapping would not work because under the CPC mapping, the additional vector component is interpreted as a rotation about a horizontal axis parallel to the screen. More clever solutions are required. One approach is to use momentum by having the system initially pick an arbitrary direction, and if the fold does not go the intended way, the user quickly reverses the gesture direction and the momentum carries the section pass the point with the ambiguous state. Another approach is to use pressure (not commonly supported on touch displays) by sensing a hard press and mapping that to a mountain fold into the screen.

FOLD TYPES AND EXAMPLES

For interactive document visualization, a basic fold that bends a page object about a single axis is the main type of fold. Basic folds include Mountain or Valley folds. Some examples are shown in Figure 2a above, where the three pages in the middle and the photo on the right are each folded with a basic fold. By folding the two page objects in the center, the figures in those pages can be compared side-by-side.

In Figure 2b, the Web page object has been folded twice, to achieve a Perspective Wall effect. The navigation section on the right and the side section on the left have been de-emphasized. This also makes more efficient use of screen real estate.

The accordion fold is a useful fold inspired by folded maps. Both the SP and AS gesture models can be used. An accordion fold is activated when there is at least one section between the two sections touched by the fingers. See Figure 8. As the user moves a contact point, the intervening sections will fold in or out like an accordion. By holding one contact point fixed (required under the AS gesture model), the fixed contact point's section remains stationary. This has the benefit that a folded up object can be easily selected and manipulated; otherwise, the object or its sections may become too narrow and thus difficult to select with a fingertip (i.e. the "fat finger" problem).

An example shown in Figure 2b is a map consisting of 6 sections. It has been folded twice: (1) an accordion fold with a fixed contact point on the 2nd section and a moving contact point on the rightmost section, (2) a basic fold bending the leftmost section into the screen.

Another example in Figure 2a is the schedule on the left with four sections that have been similarly folded with an accordion fold and a basic fold, except that the basic fold bends the leftmost section out toward the screen.

More complex origami style folds involving a series of folds can also be considered. These can be sequences of folds about horizontal and vertical creases, or a fold about a diagonal crease, with the added complexity that the creases themselves may be folded over. An example is folding a page in half vertically until it is completely flat, and then folding that in half horizontally. Due to legibility issues, these complex folds are not as useful for document visualization applications as the basic and accordion folds. We have not yet implemented these complex folds, which we leave for future work.

PROTOTYPES

To explore multi-touch document folding interactions, we built the document workspace application shown above in Figure 1 and Figure 2. We also built a special version for performing user studies, which is described further below. These were developed as 3D applications on the Windows 7 platform, and run on HP TouchSmart desktop and laptop/tablet PCs with multi-touch screens.

In the 3D visualization, each document page object appears to be a single artifact (see Figure 2). Each page object actually consists of a 3D model with an underlying

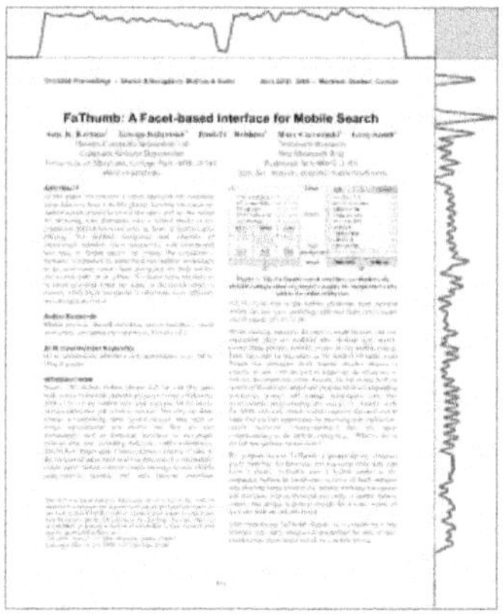

Figure 9. Projection profiles of a page image.

triangular mesh geometry, and the document page image is texture mapped onto the mesh geometry. In our implementation, folding occurs at the edges where two page sections meet. These edges are a subset of the edges of the mesh geometry.

The sections are specified by metadata. Currently, we hand-label the metadata to describe the columns or sections of a page. We are also exploring automatic computation of the sections using document analysis algorithms [17]. For example, in Figure 9, the horizontal and vertical projection profiles of a page image are shown, and the "dips" in the profiles can be used as candidate crease locations. In particular, the deep dip in the vertical profile indicates a two column layout and the center of the dip is a good location for a crease. To interact with fold lines, one possible method is for the user to perform a Hold gesture to bring up a context menu to select and adjust, delete, or create a new fold line. The local minima ("dips") in the projection profile can help the user snap to a good location, mitigating the "fat finger" problem.

As a document workspace application, standard gestures for moving and scaling the page objects are supported in our prototype. The Drag gesture is used for moving, and the Pinch gesture for scaling. These gestures are integrated with the folding gestures. For compatibility, the AS gesture model is employed. For simplicity, the Logical mapping of gestures into folding actions is used. A custom gesture recognizer was built to interpret the user's multi-touch input events, bypassing the Windows 7 gesture recognizer.

This prototype enabled us to explore various designs for the gesture models, and designs for the mesh geometries with document page images. Working with the prototype had a great impact on the design process; for example, this is how we noticed that the SP gesture model may not be easy for some users and led to the development of the AS model.

USER STUDY

We conducted a controlled experiment to compare the three bimanual multi-touch gesture models in Table 1, and to learn about the various factors that affect the performance and the degree of parallelism of the two hands.

Experiment Task

To be general, we focus on the folding gestures without integration with others such as Drag and Pinch. We asked each participant to perform a basic folding task on a multi-touch screen, under different parameters and using each of the three gesture models in Table 1: SS, SP, AS.

We built a specific testing system, where there is only one object representing a blank sheet of paper with a vertical crease down the middle, along with a target wireframe (see Figure 10). The target wireframe represents a desired location with a specified tolerance, and is rendered as two wedges, one for each section of the object. At the beginning of a trial task, the sheet is flat and facing the user. The target wireframe is presented to the user, and the task is to fold the two sections so that they are placed inside the wedges.

When a section is inside a wireframe wedge, the wedge changes color (from blue to red). For the serial gesture models (SS and AS), the user always manipulates the section on the preferred-hand side first, and the other target wireframe wedge is grayed out until the first side is completed. All three gesture models were implemented along with the Logical gesture mapping.

The device employed for the user study was a HP TouchSmart tx2 tablet (convertible laptop). It has a multi-touch capacitive screen (12.1", 1280x800 resolution).

Hypotheses

We examine the factors that have significant impact on the user performance of folding and that have been less studied in the literature. In particular, we consider the gesture models, fold directions, target symmetry, as well as the more customary target tolerance.

First of all, the gesture models (SS, SP and AS) certainly play a key role in user performance. We hypothesize that SS is slower than SP because it does not have the time savings from simultaneous action, and SS is slower than AS because the preferred hand is faster despite having to move that hand from one section over to the other. For SP vs. AS, it is not clear which is faster because there is a tradeoff between simultaneous action and preferred hand dexterity.

Second, different fold directions, i.e. Mountain (Figure 11a) or Valley (Figure 11b), involve different interactions that may affect user performance. We did not consider other folding tasks in which one section bends into the screen and the other section out, as this is not a common type of fold. The Mountain fold may be more difficult than the Valley fold due to the 3D perspective projection. Since the Mountain target wireframes are "behind the screen" and farther away from the user, the widths of the rendered targets are smaller in screen coordinates. Another issue is the partial occlusion of the Mountain wireframe (see the left section in Figure 11a), but in a pilot study this was not observed to be a problem. On the other hand, the Valley fold has the potential of the fingers obstructing each other as they move.

Third, the symmetry of the targets is an interesting factor. Although two hands are used, if the participant can coordinate and mentally "couple" both hands so that they move in unison, the task time can be decreased through this kind of parallelism.

Finally, the target tolerances will affect the task times, which can be predicted by Fitts' law. Our aim is not to focus on or to verify Fitts' law, but we expect the results to be consistent with it.

To summarize our hypotheses:

- *H1.* SS takes longer to perform than either SP or AS.
- *H2.* For fold directions, the Valley fold takes less time than the Mountain fold.
- *H3.* (a) Symmetric targets take less time than asymmetric targets. (b) Symmetric targets are performed with more parallelism than asymmetric targets.
- *H4.* A small target tolerance takes more time than a large tolerance.

Independent Variables

To test the hypotheses, we chose the above four key factors as the independent variables and examined the impact of different factor values. For gesture models, all the three possible settings (SP, SS, AS) were tested.

For fold directions, participants were given an equal number of Mountain and Valley folding tasks for all four combinations of two different angles (30 and 60 degrees) on the left and right sides. The aggregate distance covered

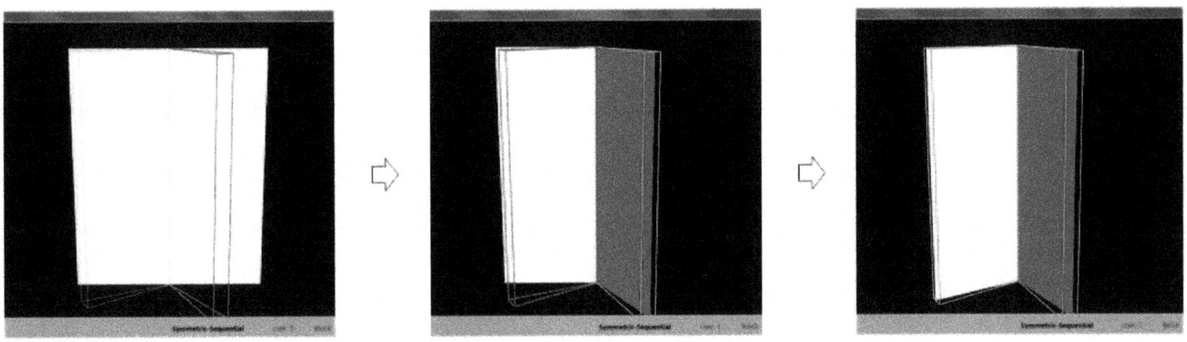

Figure 10. Folding on the user study testing application (the left and right sides of the screenshots cropped for space).

(a) (b)

Figure 11. (a) An example of Mountain fold. (b) Symmetric target with small target size.

by each direction type is the same over the set of tasks (and also over subsets with the other factors' levels held fixed).

For target symmetry, half the tasks were symmetric targets and half were asymmetric. As with the fold direction, the aggregate distance covered by each task symmetry type is the same over the set of tasks.

We tested two target tolerances: small (wedge size of 4 degrees) and large (10 degrees). The size of the small target was tuned in a pilot study (with three participants) so that it was not too small to be frustrating.

Measurements

Our primary measurements were *task time*, *parallelism* and *perceived workload*. The task time is the duration from the first touch event on the screen to the last lift event of both fingers from the screen with the two document sections inside their target wireframes.

Parallelism indicates the degree to which both hands move in parallel. It can be computed using the Error-Reduction bimanual parallelism measure formulated in [1], which is defined as follows: First, for each hand's gesture path, the percentage of error reduction (%ER) per time step is defined as the magnitude of the movement towards the target divided by the movement required to reduce the error to zero. Then the amount of parallelism at each time step is the ratio of the two hand's %ER values, with the larger value in the denominator to normalize the result between 0 and 1. We then take the average, weighted by the time step lengths, to be the parallelism score for the task.

The perceived workload is measured with the standard NASA-TLX questionnaire. Users were asked to rate on a scale of 1 to 7, various types of workloads: mental effort, physical effort, temporal demand, performance, overall effort, frustration level.

Procedure

The study used a repeated measures design. The within-subjects factors were the gesture model types (SS, SP, AS), fold direction (Mountain, Valley), target symmetry (Symmetric, Asymmetric), and tolerance (Small, Large). The between-subjects factor was gender (Male, Female). Each participant used all the gesture models in one sitting, and the order was counterbalanced across the participants. For each gesture model, a participant performed one practiced block of trials (excluded from analysis), followed by 4 blocks. Each block of trials consisted of one instance for each of the 16 combinations of fold directions, target symmetries, and target tolerance. Users were instructed to perform the tasks as fast as they can. Within a block, the trials were presented in randomized order. Between blocks, participants were given a rest period of 10 seconds. The total time for a session was about 45 minutes. At the end of the session, users were given a questionnaire about the perceived workload, with space for writing down open-ended comments.

Results and Discussion

We recruited 12 unpaid participants in our laboratory, who were lab members and interns not involved in this project. All participants were familiar with touch screens, and one participant had not used a multi-touch screen before. All were right-handed, half were females.

The total number of (non-practice) trials for the study was 12 *participants* × 3 *conditions* × 4 *blocks* × 16 *trials* = 2,304. The data was pre-processed to remove outliers, defined as trials with a task time greater than 3 standard deviations away from the mean time of the trials with the same set of parameters. In total, 14 (0.6%) of the trials were removed for the following analysis. Unless otherwise noted, we used Greenhouse-Geisser correction to account for deviations from sphericity, and Bonferroni corrections for all post-hoc tests.

Task Time Performance

We first examined the learning effect by running a 2-way repeated measures ANOVA on the factors of gesture model and block, with task time as the dependent variable. The analysis indicates that block is not a main effect, and there is no *model* × *block* interaction. Therefore, the presentation order of the models in the experiment did not significantly affect the user performance; since there was no learning effect, we ignored the factor *block* for the following analyses.

We then ran a 4-way repeated measures ANOVA on the factors of gesture model, fold direction, target symmetry, and target tolerance, with task time as the dependent variable. We found gesture model (*model*) to be a main effect (Table 2). Post-hoc pairwise comparison showed that SS was significantly slower than SP ($p < 0.01$) and AS ($p < 0.05$), but there was no significance found between SP and AS (Figure 12-aggregated). This confirms hypothesis *H1*.

There was an interaction between gesture model and target tolerance (*model*×*tolerance*) (Table 2). Further examination reveals that with the small tolerance, model SS is significantly slower than SP and AS, with $p < 0.01$ for both; with the large tolerance, SS and AS are significantly slower

Factor	*F*-statistic	Significance	Partial η^2
model	$F_{2,22} = 9.99$	$p < 0.01$	0.48
direction	$F_{1,11} = 14.99$	$p < 0.01$	0.58
target symmetry	$F_{1,11} = 6.87$	$p < 0.05$	0.38
tolerance	$F_{1,11} = 202.44$	$p < 0.01$	0.95
Interacting Factors	***F*-statistic**	**Significance**	**Partial η^2**
model × tolerance	$F_{2,22} = 10.86$	$p < 0.01$	0.50
direction × tolerance	$F_{1,11} = 13.90$	$p < 0.01$	0.56
model × direction × tolerance	$F_{2,22} = 6.64$	$p < 0.01$	0.38

Table 2. Significance values of the factors.

than SP, with $p < 0.05$ for both (Figure 12). This suggests that AS allows users to achieve comparable performance to SP in fine-grained folding (i.e. small tolerance), but it is slower than SP in coarse-grained folding (i.e. large tolerance). On the other hand, SP is not compatible with the Pinch gesture. Therefore, the folding interface designer should take into account the targeted folding precision and possible integration with other gestures.

Fold direction (*direction*) was also observed to be a main effect (Table 2). Post-hoc pairwise comparison indicates that Mountain folding is significantly slower than Valley folding (Figure 13), and thus supports our hypothesis *H2*. We also observed a *direction* × *tolerance* interaction (Table 2). A further *t*-test shows that Mountain folding is significantly slower than Valley folding at the small tolerance ($t_{11} = 4.54$, $p < 0.01$), but there is no significant difference between the two directions at the large tolerance. This interaction may mainly be attributed to perspective projection: a target with a small tolerance appears smaller for the Mountain fold as the target is farther away; the small tolerance is more sensitive to this difference.

Although we did not find a *model* × *direction* interaction, the analysis did reveal an interesting *model* × *direction* × *tolerance* 3-way interaction (Table 2): There exists a *model* × *direction* interaction with the small tolerance ($F_{2,22} = 4.03$, $p < 0.05$, partial $\eta^2 = 0.27$), while there is no such interaction with the large tolerance. This result further indicates that user performance is dependent on required folding accuracy.

The analysis revealed target symmetry to be another main

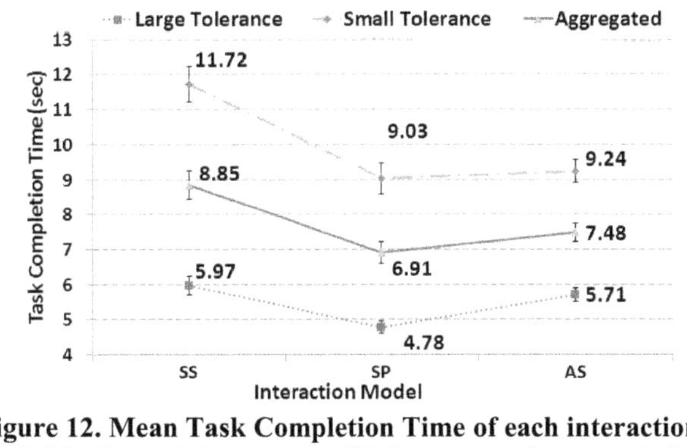

Figure 12. Mean Task Completion Time of each interaction model for large tolerance, small tolerance and aggregated over tolerances (bars show standard error).

effect (Table 2). The asymmetric targets took longer to perform than the symmetric targets (Figure 13). This result supports hypothesis *H3(a)* and suggests the lower cognitive load for symmetric hand movement. Application designers thus may prefer to use symmetric folding as much as possible.

Consistent with Fitts' law, target tolerance *(H4)* is a main effect (Table 2). The small tolerance took longer to perform than the large one (Figure 13).

There were no other 2-way, 3-way and 4-way interactions. We also analyzed task time with gender as a between-subject factor. Our data did not show gender to be a main effect ($F_{1,10} = 2.42$, $p = 0.15$).

Parallelism

The parallelism score only applies to the SP gesture model. Using only the data in this condition, we ran a *t*-test on the factor of target symmetry with parallelism as the dependent variable. The test shows that the asymmetric targets ($M = 0.15$, 95%CI = [0.12, 0.17]) yielded significantly less parallelism than the symmetric targets ($M = 0.22$, 95%CI = [0.18, 0.25]) with $t_{11} = -6.21$, $p < 0.01$. This supports hypothesis *H3(b)*.

This result indicates that the participants were able to move their fingers simultaneously toward the targets for a larger portion of the symmetric targets. Lower parallelism on asymmetric targets also indicates that the users were not able to coordinate the two fingers to move at *different* rates, proportional to the distances to the target so as to arrive at the targets at about the same time. This is quite difficult to do, especially for novice users.

Perceived Workload

To gather perceived workload data, users rated on a scale of 1 to 7 (1 is least effort) various types of workloads: *mental effort*, *physical effort*, *temporal demand*, *performance*, *overall effort*, *frustration level* (see Figure 14). A 1-way repeated measure ANOVA on the data found gesture model to be a main effect on mental effort ($F_{2,22} = 4.211$, p < 0.05). Post-hoc pairwise comparison with Bonferroni correction found that SP model ($M = 4.92$, 95%CI = [4.35, 5.48]) causes marginally more mental effort than AS ($M = 3.75$, 95%CI = [2.95, 4.55]) with $p = 0.068$, and it is similar to SS ($M = 4.92$, 95%CI = [4.26, 5.58]). There was no significant difference between the other pairs.

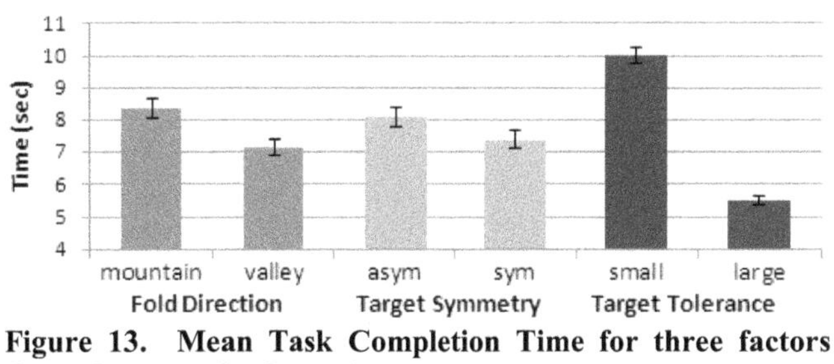

Figure 13. Mean Task Completion Time for three factors (bars show standard error).

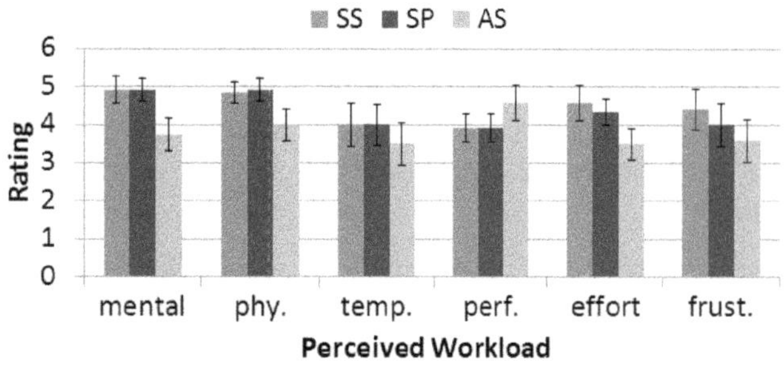

Figure 14. Means of perceived workload (bars show standard error).

Moreover, during the user study we did not observe any serious usability problems. As for the understandability, the participants readily understood the different models when they were explained and we did not observe any confusion between them. These qualitative results, combined with the previous quantitative analysis, suggest that the two practical models SP and AS are both viable, with some tradeoffs. The SP model is faster, but not significantly faster; while the AS model requires marginally less perceived mental effort. Comments from the participants reinforce this finding: "[SP] natural but inaccurate", "[SP] takes a lot of coordination and concentration", "[AS] more like operating physically".

One interesting finding from the SS model is a "wobbly finger" problem. Three participants commented that they had difficulty keeping the right finger still after they shifted their attention to moving the left finger. The problem was that with the small tolerance, when the user completed the left side, the right side occasionally drifted out of the target.

CONCLUSION & FUTURE WORK

We presented an exploration of document folding using multi-touch gestures. Our main contributions in this paper are identifying design considerations for simple folding gestures and providing a categorization of gesture models (Symmetric/Asymmetric, Serial/Parallel), developing two practical gesture models and a document workspace prototype, and conducting a user study which indicated that the factors (model, direction, target symmetry, tolerance) affect folding performance. Another finding was the higher parallelism for symmetric targets.

For future work, we plan to develop the aforementioned complex folds and to enable users to specify creases in document pages by gesturing and dynamically modifying the underlying mesh geometry. We also plan to explore the design of folding gestures with more than two contact points.

REFERENCES

1. Balakrishnan, R., Hinckley, K., Symmetric bimanual interaction. *Proc. CHI 2000*, pp. 33-40.
2. Beaudouin-Lafon, M. Novel interaction techniques for overlapping windows. *Proc. UIST 2001*, pp. 153-154.
3. Buxton, W. Myers, B. A study in two-handed input. *Proc. CHI 1986*, pp. 321-326.
4. Buxton, B. "Multi-touch systems that I have known and loved" (ver. Oct. 2009). http://www.billbuxton.com/multitouchOverview.html
5. Chang, S. H-H., Stuart, L. and Plimmer, B. Origami Simulator: A multi-touch experience. *CHI 2009 Extended Abstracts*, pp. 3889-3894.
6. Cutler, L.D., Fröhlich, B., Hanrahan, P. Two-handed direct manipulation on the Responsive Workbench. *Proc. I3D 1997*, pp. 107-114.
7. Denoue L., Nelson L., Churchill, E.F. A fast, interactive 3D paper-flier metaphor for digital bulletin boards. *Proc. UIST 2003*, pp. 169-172.
8. Dragicevic, P. Combining crossing-based and paper-based interaction paradigms for dragging and dropping between overlapping windows. *Proc. UIST 2004*, pp. 193-196.
9. Elmqvist, N., Henry, N., Riche, Y., Fekete, J.D. Melange: Space folding for multi-focus interaction. *Proc. CHI 2008*, pp. 173-176.
10. Guiard, Y., Asymmetric division of labor in human skilled bimanual action: the kinematic chain as a model. *J. of Motor Behavior*, 19 (4): 486-517, 1987.
11. Hinckley, K., Pausch, R., Proffitt, D., Patten, J., Kassell, N. Cooperative bimanual action. *Proc. CHI 1997*, pp. 27-34.
12. Hinckley, K., Baudisch, P., Ramos, G., Guimbretiere, F. Design and analysis of delimiters for selection-action pen gesture phrases in Scriboli. *Proc. CHI 2005*, pp. 451-460.
13. Kabbash, P., MacKenzie, I.S., Buxton, W. Human performance using computer input devices in the preferred and non-preferred hands. *Proc. CHI 1993*, pp. 474-481.
14. Kin, K., Agrawala, M., DeRose. T. Determining the benefits of direct-touch, bimanual, and multifinger input on a multitouch workstation. *Proc. Graphics Interface 2009*, pp. 119-124.
15. Lang, R.J. Computational origami: from flapping birds to space telescopes. *Proc. Symp. Computational Geometry 2009*, pp. 474-481.
16. Mackinlay, J.D., Robertson, G.G., Card, S.K. The Perspective Wall: Detail and context smoothly integrated. *Proc. CHI 1991*, pp. 173-176.
17. O'Gorman, L., Katsuri, R. *Document Image Analysis*. IEEE Computer Society Press, 1995.
18. Reisman, J.L., Davidson, P.L., Han, J.Y. A screen-space formulation for 2D and 3D direct manipulation. *Proc. UIST 2009*, pp. 69-78.
19. Szinger, J. The Foldinator modeler and document generator. *Proc. Origami 3 (2002)*, pp. 129-135.
20. Tashman, C. LiquidText: active reading through multitouch document manipulation. *CHI 2010 Doctoral Consortium.*
21. Wang, L., Sajeev, A.S.M. Roller interface for mobile device applications. *Proc. AUIC 2007*, pp. 7-13.
22. Westerman, W. *Hand Tracking, Finger Identification, and Chordic Manipulation on a Multi-Touch Surface.* PhD Dissertation (1999), U. of Delaware.
23. Wilson, A.D., Izadi, S., Hilliges, O., Garcia-Mendoza, A., Kirk, D. Bringing physics to the surface. *Proc. UIST 2008*, pp. 67-76.

FingerGlass: Efficient Multiscale Interaction on Multitouch Screens

Dominik Käser[1,2,4]
dpk@pixar.com

Maneesh Agrawala[1]
maneesh@eecs.berkeley.edu

Mark Pauly[3]
mark.pauly@epfl.ch

[1] University of California
Berkeley, CA 94720
United States

[2] ETH
8006 Zürich
Switzerland

[3] EPFL
1015 Lausanne
Switzerland

[4] Pixar Animation Studios
Emeryville, CA 94608
United States

ABSTRACT
Many tasks in graphical user interfaces require users to interact with elements at various levels of precision. We present *FingerGlass*, a bimanual technique designed to improve the precision of graphical tasks on multitouch screens. It enables users to quickly navigate to different locations and across multiple scales of a scene using a single hand. The other hand can simultaneously interact with objects in the scene. Unlike traditional pan-zoom interfaces, FingerGlass retains contextual information during the interaction. We evaluated our technique in the context of precise object selection and translation and found that FingerGlass significantly outperforms three state-of-the-art baseline techniques in both objective and subjective measurements: users acquired and translated targets more than 50% faster than with the second-best technique in our experiment.

ACM Classification Keywords
H.5.2 Information Interfaces and Presentation: User Interfaces (D.2.2, H.1.2, I.3.6)—*Interaction Styles*

General Terms
Design, Performance

INTRODUCTION
We interact with our environment in many different scales. For example, creating a painting requires us to work on its global composition as well as its finest details. The physical world provides a natural way of transitioning between different scales by allowing us to move our viewpoint towards or away from our objects of interest.

Some computer applications operate on virtual scenes or artboards. Examples are graphical content creation systems such as Adobe Illustrator or map browsing tools like Google Maps. In contrast to the physical world, their user interfaces are limited in size and resolution and therefore encompass a small range of scales. Such systems typically overcome this limitation by providing zoom controls that redefine the current viewport. However, when a user performs a zoom, there is a loss of contextual information. In addition, the input of such tools has usually been limited to single-point input devices such as the mouse, and repeatedly switching back and forth between navigation and interaction with the same input device is time-consuming.

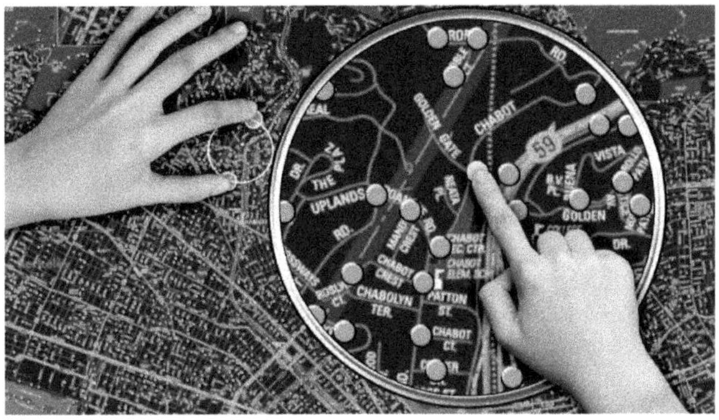

Figure 1: Interaction with *FingerGlass*: The user specifies an area of interest with one hand and interacts with the magnified objects with the other hand. During the interaction, a new area of interest can be defined. Releasing all fingers makes the tool vanish.

Multitouch workstations provide more degrees of freedom than single-point input devices. They also reduce the mental effort required for interacting with virtual objects by removing the indirection of an external pointing device. These advantages come at the cost of screen occlusion and reduced precision. Nonetheless, Forlines et al. [13] showed that touch-based devices can achieve faster task completion times and comparable error rates to a mouse, given sufficiently large targets.

The precise selection of small on-screen targets has been well-studied. However, with the recent advent of multitouch-based content creation applications such as Eden [22], we require tools for more complex interactions than just selection. In this work, we focus on developing a more general technique enabling users to quickly navigate through the space of potential viewports while selecting and translating targets.

We propose *FingerGlass*, a technique that lets the user define a viewport using one hand. The other hand can simultaneously interact with objects in the scene. At all times, the contents of this viewport are shown twice on the screen: once in a global zoomed-out view stretched out across the entire screen, retaining contextual information, and once as

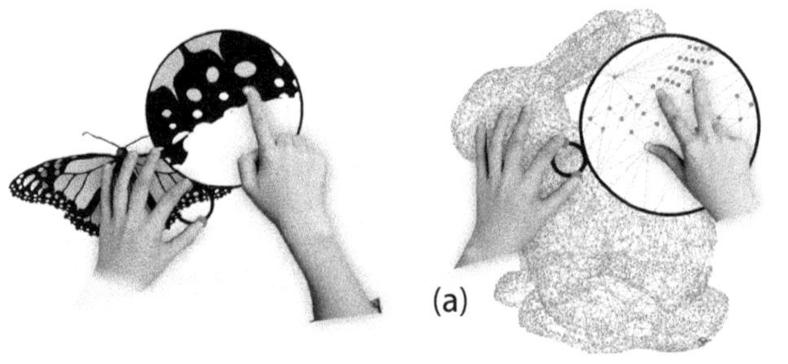

Figure 2: Two fictional example applications employing *FingerGlass*: (a) Translation of a 2D shape in a vector graphics application. (b) Translation of vertices in a multitouch 3D modeling system.

a magnified copy on top of the zoomed-out view. We call the latter the *magnified view*. Any interaction with objects in the scene takes place in the magnified view. This way, fingertips do not occlude the area of interest in the zoomed-out view. Figures 1 and 2 show sample applications of FingerGlass.

We evaluated FingerGlass and its variant, *FingerMap*, in the context of precise object selection and translation. Our formal user study shows that FingerGlass significantly outperforms three state-of-the-art techniques: with FingerGlass, users acquired targets more than 50% faster than with PrecisionGlass, the second-fastest technique in our experiment. Translation times were between 40% and 100% faster than the second-fastest technique for distances between 2.7mm and 350mm. Users also subjectively preferred using FingerGlass than the other techniques.

Participants also responded positively to the ergonomics of our tool: FingerGlass requires only individual taps to perform precise selection. For translations, the amount of physical dragging is limited to local corrections.

RELATED WORK

Two distinct areas of research are relevant for our work: multiscale navigation and interaction with virtual scenes, and precise target interaction on (multi-)touch screens.

Multiscale Navigation and Interaction

For the exploration of two-dimensional scenes, researchers developed zoomable user interfaces (ZUIs) such as *Pad++* [4] or *Speed-Dependent Zooming* [20]. However, ZUIs inherently suffer from context loss and are hard to navigate once zoomed in. Researchers have addressed this in a variety of ways: Pook et al. [27] and Hornbaek et al. [19] provide global context information in small overviews or extra layers. Other focus+context approaches include *Fisheye Views* [14], *Perspective Wall* [23], *Document Lens* [30], *Melange* [8] or *High-Precision Magnification Lenses* [2]. *DTLens* [12] is a similar technique for multitouch screens. Furnas and Bederson introduced the *Space-Scale Diagram* [15], an analytical framework for analyzing multiscale navigation interfaces such as the ones discussed here. None of these systems consider manipulations of the scene but are limited to navigation. *Magic Lenses* [6] allow users to place virtual lenses using one hand and interact with the scene using the other hand. However, they are not designed to be fast and there are no time measurements provided.

Precise Touch-Screen Interaction

Precision and occlusion issues associated with touch-based input devices are an active topic of research. Researchers have evaluated their solutions on the task of target selection. *Offset Cursor* [28] was the first technique addressing occlusion by remapping the physical touch location to a non-occluded screen location. *ThumbSpace* [21] and *Dual Finger Offset* [5] extend this concept. Instead of remapping the touch location, *Shift* [34] displays an offset copy of the occluded area. While these techniques address occlusion, they do not increase precision.

To address precision, *PrecisionHandle* [1] enhances the control-display ratio by giving the user a lever-like widget at hand. Correctly placing this widget requires additional time and taps. A simpler technique doubling the control-display ratio is *Dual Finger Midpoint* [5]. Researchers have proposed a number of content-sensitive techniques to solve input precision problems. *Bubble cursor* [16], *MagStick* [32] and *Semantic pointing* [7] increase the target size in motor space. *Escape* [35] assigns different directional vectors to targets lying next to each other. To select a target, the user swipes over it in a target-specific direction. *Sliding Widgets* [25] provide a generalization of this technique to a wider scope of widgets. *Enhanced Area Cursors* [10] let the user specify a coarse area in the first phase. Then, in a second phase, they invoke an angular menu containing all available targets in this area.

All these techniques are designed for selection tasks: after the initial touch, the user performs corrective dragging movements or disambiguation gestures. Selection is then usually triggered by releasing the finger. This makes extensions to translations or complex multi-finger gestures non-trivial. A few techniques remedy this problem for single-point dragging operations by offering both a tracking and a dragging state: *DTMouse* [9] works similarly to Dual Finger Midpoint [5], and *Pointing Lenses* [29] are pen-based precision enhancement techniques. In addition to being limited to single-point, they still require corrective dragging movements which are relatively slow to perform and can be uncomfortable. Furthermore, none of the techniques above serves for visual exploration.

Visual exploration is addressed by *Zoom Pointing* [1], *TapTap* [32] and *Rubbing and Tapping* [26] which let the user redefine their viewport by zooming. *Dual Finger Stretch* by Benko et al. [5] gives the user the option to perform unaided target selection, and to summon an in-place magnifying glass using a second finger to facilitate corrective movements. The technique by Mankoff et al. [24] displays an in-place magnification if and only if the first tap was ambiguous. All these techniques suffer from a loss of context after zooming in since the original area of interest is occluded.

Researchers evaluated the above techniques only on target selection, but not on translation tasks which comprise a large part of our interaction with GUIs. Context-sensitive techniques to facilitate dragging operations over long distances are *Drag-and-Pop* and *Drag-and-Pick* [3]. These techniques distort geometrical relationships and assume that there is a small discrete set of possible destinations for a scene object.

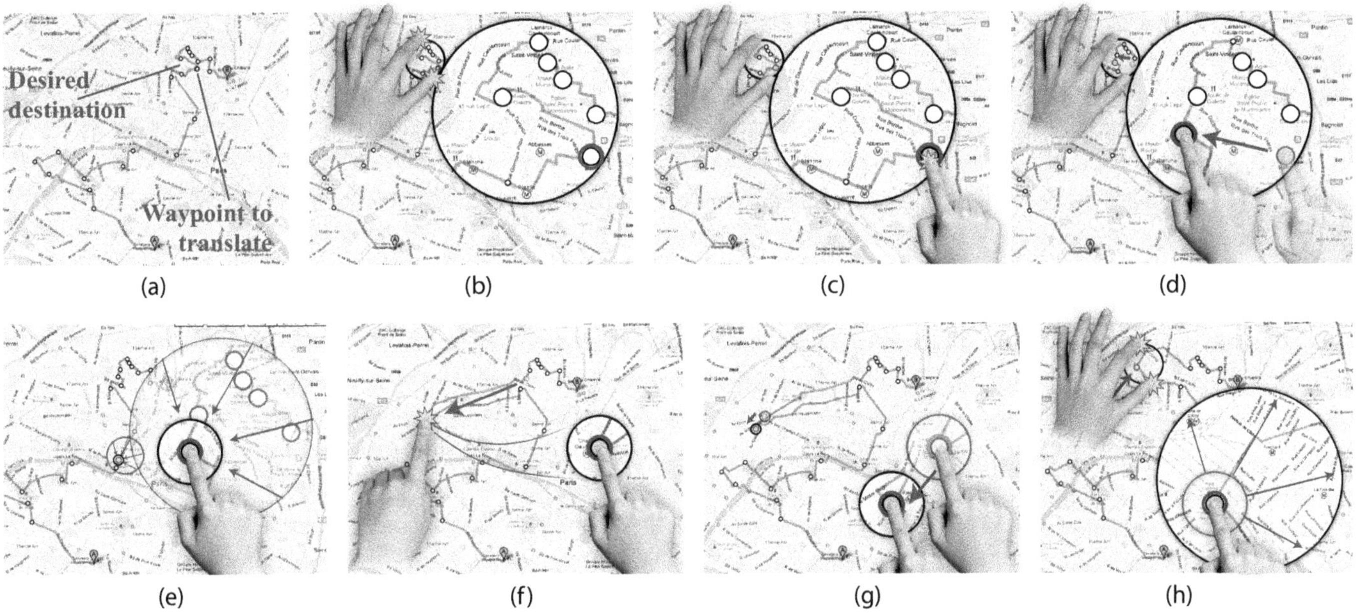

Figure 3: Interaction with Google Maps using *FingerGlass*: (a) Task description. (b) Once the user defines the area of interest, the magnified view appears. (c) The user selects the waypoint in the magnified view and (d) translates it. (e) After releasing the coarse hand, the magnified view shrinks. (f) If the user taps at a location in the original viewport, FingerGlass translates the waypoint to this location. (g) FingerGlass applies any translation of the fine hand to the waypoint on a smaller scale. (h) If the user specifies a new area of interest, the magnified view grows again.

FINGERGLASS

Figure 3 shows a walkthrough of *FingerGlass* in a trip planning application: the user would like to move the marked waypoint (Figure 3a) to a different street intersection in the same neighborhood. At the initial scale the waypoint is too small to be selected by a finger, and street names are not visible. To get a close-up view of the waypoint and its surroundings, the user touches the screen with two fingers. Their tips span a circle which we call the *area of interest*. FingerGlass immediately displays an enlarged copy of this area which we call the *magnified view* (Figure 3b). We call the fingers spanning the area of interest *defining fingers*, their hand *coarse hand* and the other hand *fine hand*. Based on Guiard's studies on human bimanual action [17], we suggest that users use their non-dominant hand as the coarse hand.

The magnification ratio of the magnified view is prescribed by the application. Developers are advised to use a ratio that enlarges the smallest pickable targets to about the size of a fingertip. If the magnification ratio is too large, small translations require too much physical movement by the fine hand. If it is too small, selection of small targets can be difficult. For our street map application, ratios between 4x and 6x have worked well. The magnified view is always tangent to the area of interest. A placement algorithm determines its position such that the prescribed zoom ratio can be achieved as closely as possible and that the fine hand can comfortably interact with its contents. As the user moves his coarse hand, the magnified view follows. Once the user releases his coarse hand, the magnified view vanishes.

To translate the waypoint, the user touches it inside the magnified view (Figure 3c) with a finger on his fine hand. He then drags it to the desired destination (Figure 3d). FingerGlass translates the waypoint in the zoomed-out view accordingly in real-time. This behavior allows users to focus on the original viewport during dragging operations in order to judge their effect in a global context. While the fine hand is translating objects in the magnified view, the area of interest is locked and any movement of the coarse hand has no effect.

The destination of the waypoint might lie outside the current area of interest. The user can release his defining fingers while retaining the finger of the fine hand on the screen. The magnified view then centers around the selected waypoint and shrinks down to a size encompassing just the object's immediate surroundings. The area of interest shrinks accordingly to maintain the zoom ratio (Figure 3e).

A finger of the coarse hand then taps on the desired destination in the original viewport. The selected waypoint immediately moves to the location of the tap (Figure 3f). The fine hand can then refine its position: FingerGlass applies any movement of the fine hand to the waypoint, scaled down by the magnification ratio. The magnified view follows the finger and its content continues to display the current neighborhood of the waypoint (Figure 3g). If the desired destination in the original viewport is occluded by the magnified view, the user can first move the magnified view by dragging his fine hand, and then tap at the desired destination.

The user might want to explore the neighborhood of the desired destination before finishing the translation. To do so, he defines a new area of interest by pressing and holding two fingers of his coarse hand. The magnified view then grows again to accomodate the size of the new area of interest while maintaining the zoom ratio. FingerGlass translates

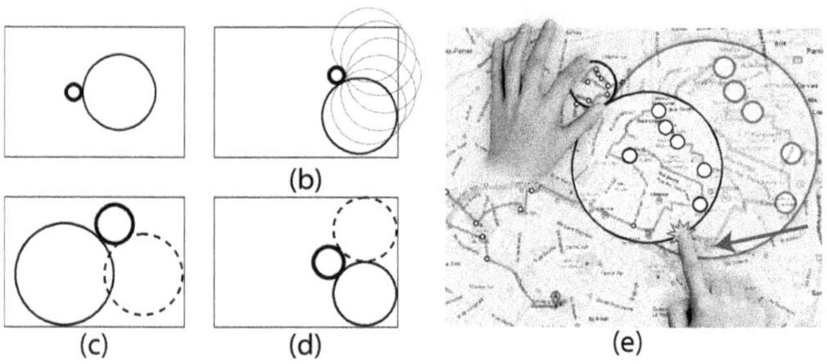

Figure 4: (a)-(d) Placement of the magnified view, assuming a right-handed user: (a) Optimal placement. (b) FingerGlass searches for compatible configurations along the border of the area of interest. (c) Tradeoff between shrinking the magnified view or moving it further away. (d) Ambiguous configuration. (e) By touching the screen outside of the magnified view, the magnified view can be manually defined.

the waypoint to the new area of interest. To determine the exact location of the waypoint, we use its relative position at the time before the magnified view shrunk (Figure 3h). The interaction then continues as in Figure 3d, except that the area of interest and the magnified view are detached. The translation operation ends once both hands are released.

Automatic Placement of the Magnified View

In this section, we assume a right-handed user. We noted in the previous section that FingerGlass computes a suitable size and location for the magnified view. We developed an optimization algorithm with the following three goals.

- **Minimal eye movement**: In the course of an interaction, the eye has to travel from the area of interest to the magnified view and back. Thus, FingerGlass only considers configurations in which the magnified view is adjacent to the area of interest.
- **Comfort for fine hand**: In our setup, we configured FingerGlass to place the magnified view as far to the right as possible. The right hand can then comfortably interact with objects in the magnified view while the left hand specifies the area of interest.
- **Usage of prescribed magnification ratio**: Developers provide a recommended magnification ratio with their application. FingerGlass will try to use this ratio if possible, but resort to smaller ratios if necessary.

Figures 4a-d show areas of interest in different scenarios, and the magnified view as determined for a right-handed user by our algorithm. Without any boundary restrictions, FingerGlass places the magnified view to the right of the area of interest (Figure 4a). If the magnified view would thereby extend beyond the screen boundaries, we call this location *incompatible*. FingerGlass then searches for compatible locations along the boundary of the area of interest (Figure 4b). Our system also tries to shrink the magnified view to obtain more compatible locations. There can be a tradeoff between reducing the magnification ratio and shifting the magnified view further to the left (Figure 4c). We control this tradeoff with a parameter in our code. If there are multiple locations with very similar qualities, a term for temporal coherence prevents the magnified view from jumping back and forth (Figure 4d).

Manual Adjustment of the Magnified View

In some cases, the user may not be satisfied with the placement of the magnified view. For example, the placement algorithm is unaware of the current position of the fine hand as it hovers over the screen. Hence, there may be cases in which the magnified view opens up in a place that would require the fine hand to travel a large distance or to make uncomfortable movements. In other cases, the user may want to employ a different magnification ratio than the prescribed one. For example, the scene may contain objects with a wide variety of sizes, and small objects need a higher magnification ratio than large ones.

FingerGlass allows users to redefine the size and location of the magnified view: once the user touches the screen outside of the current magnified view, FingerGlass will reposition the magnified view such that it lies exactly between the area of interest and the touching finger (see Figure 4e).

FINGERMAP

FingerGlass occludes a significant portion of the screen and requires users to shift their attention to the magnified view to interact with scene objects. Although we minimized the required eye movement with careful placement of the magnified view, performing many interactions could still lead to fatigue. *FingerMap* is an alternate design without magnified views which follows the interaction model underlying FingerGlass as closely as possible. FingerMap is optimized for situations in which the user wants to maintain his focus on the area of interest at all times.

Figure 5 shows an abridged walkthrough of FingerMap in the same trip planning task we used in Figure 3. As with FingerGlass, the user specifies the area of interest with his coarse hand. Then he touches the screen with a finger of his fine hand anywhere outside of the area of interest. We call this finger *tracking finger*. FingerMap then displays a selection cursor at the center of the area of interest (Figure 5a). The shape of the cursor is a cross surrounded by a circle, and its radius is the radius of an average fingertip (e.g. 10mm), scaled down by the magnification ratio. As an extension, we made the magnification ratio dependent on the distance from the initial touch of the tracking finger to the area of interest: a larger distance leads to a bigger magnification ratio.

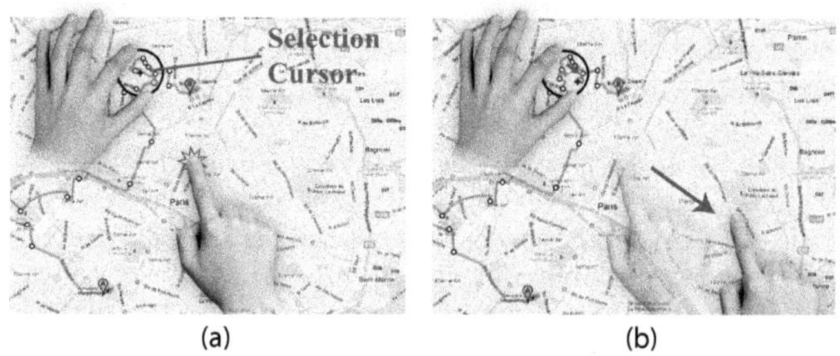

Figure 5: Interaction with *FingerMap*: The coarse hand specifies an area of interest. (a) The user touches the zoomed-out view with the tracking finger, and a selection cursor appears in the center of the area of interest. (b) FingerMap applies any translation of the fine hand to the cursor on a smaller scale. Once the cursor overlaps with the desired waypoint, the user selects it by releasing the coarse hand.

As long as the tracking finger remains pressed, it operates as an indirect control for the selection cursor: FingerMap applies any movement of the tracking finger to the selection cursor, scaled down by the magnification ratio (Figure 5b). Once the cursor overlaps with the desired waypoint, the user selects it by releasing the coarse hand. To translate the waypoint, the user keeps the tracking finger pressed. This finger then indirectly controls the position of the selected waypoint, scaled down by the magnification ratio. The remaining interaction works analogously to FingerGlass in Figures 3f-h.

The initial world space position of the tracking finger is always at the center of the area of interest. To minimize corrective dragging movements, the user should choose the area of interest such that its center is as close as possible to the desired target. This makes target selection using FingerMap somewhat similar to *Dual Finger Midpoint* [5], but adds small-scale corrective movements. Pilot testers of our system stated that acquiring targets using FingerMap feels similar to capturing them with a lasso.

DESIGN PRINCIPLES

Based on the techniques presented above, we establish design principles for bimanual interaction techniques on touch screens that enable users to efficiently navigate to objects and manipulate them across different scales. Our principles should be general enough for various types of multi-scale interaction scenarios. Most touch devices report both the time stamp and the two-dimensional location of touch events. These events comprise, at a minimum, *press*, *move* and *release*. In order to design for a wide range of multi-touch systems, we will not make use of any other input information. In particular, we do not use pressure [31] or touch area [5] information to implement a tracking state.

Bimanual Interaction

(P1) *The nondominant hand should set the reference frame for subsequent actions performed by the dominant hand.*

In his study on the division of labor in human bimanual action, Guiard [17] noted that the two hands assume very different roles and strongly depend on each other in the vast majority of everyday tasks. The nondominant hand defines a frame of reference and performs coarse granularity actions. Subsequently, the dominant hand performs fine grain interactions within this frame. Hinkley et al. [18] showed that this concept is applicable to human interaction with digital user interfaces as well. More recently, Schmidt et al. [33] used this insight to let the non-dominant hand define user-specific private areas on multi-user touch screens for dexterous interactions by the dominant hand.

Redefining Viewports

(P2) *When operating on a small scale, the user should be able to quickly redefine the viewport to any other location.*

Many target selection tools in the literature provide an increased zoom ratio to enhance precision and to facilitate selection of small targets. However, this approach is not sufficient for tasks that go beyond target selection. A large zoom ratio implies that the tool maps fingertip positions from a large screen area (domain) to a much smaller area (range). The choice of this mapping is crucial for translation tasks: if the range does not contain both target and destination, a translation can not be completed without altering the mapping. Such a change is slow and the user needs to reorient himself. Yet, if target and destination are far apart, this change may be necessary to keep the zoom ratio large and should be well supported by the tool. For example, FingerGlass lets the user specify the range and determines a well-suited domain that does not intersect with the range.

From Selection To Translation

(P3) *Once an object is acquired, no further events should be necessary to start transforming it.*

Translation operations with objects in graphial user interfaces are a two-stage process. In the first stage, the user specifies the object of interest. In the second stage, he continuously translates this object. The transition into this second stage can be seamless: some mouse-based interfaces allow users to hit an object and to immediately transform it by translating the mouse. Other interfaces may require the user to first release the input controller in order to complete the selection process before the transformation can begin. For an efficient interaction technique, we suggest a seamless transition from the selection to the transformation phase.

Ambiguities

(P4) *Contact area interaction should be used for acquisition tasks. No target should be acquired in ambiguous cases.*

Moscovich [25] pointed out that direct screen touches by a fingertip should not be interpreted as if only one single pixel was touched. Doing so would ignore ambiguities and inappropriately resolve them in an unpredictable way. Rather than selecting one single point in a somewhat arbitrary fashion when multiple points are touched at once, the system should perform no selection and indicate all points under the finger to the user. Thus, the user can navigate to a smaller scale and retry. This strategy addresses our goal of designing a tool with minimal error rates. Another advantage of contact area interaction is that the effective width of a target is increased, making selection easier in scenes with a sparse distribution of small objects.

EXPERIMENTAL EVALUATION

Our design process aimed for an efficient tool to navigate through virtual scenes and to select and translate objects. Navigation is a task which is difficult to quantify and to formally evaluate. However, the feedback from our pilot testers using FingerGlass in a map browsing application showed that our technique is a very promising alternative to the existing baseline tools for navigation.

For the selection and translation of targets, we conducted a lab experiment in which we measured the performance of participants for every technique.

Participants also answered a questionnaire in which they subjectively ranked the techniques according to different criteria such as personal preference or ease of learning. In addition, they were asked to compare a multitouch screen employing their favorite technique to a pen- and a mouse-based interface. The questionnaire also contained some space for written comments and suggestions.

Release-Tapping

We compared FingerGlass and FingerMap to three existing techniques from the literature. However, while they all facilitate precise target selection, none of them support subsequent translation: they let users first approach the desired target by corrective dragging movements and then complete the selection task by releasing their finger. This behavior is not extensible to subsequent translation operations without violating principle (P3). However, since our device could not sense pressure or touch area to introduce a tracking state, we had to implement the baseline techniques in a way that employs an additional discrete event to start the translation.

To this end, we created a technique we call *ReleaseTapping* (RT) that works as follows: once the user releases his finger, the system displays a semi-transparent solid circle around the selected target. This circle remains on-screen for a given time before it disappears. In order to translate the target, the user can touch this circle, keep his finger pressed and translate the target by dragging. For the radius of the circle, we used the radius of the target object plus 20mm. Regardless of whether or not the user hits the circle, tapping on the screen makes the current circle vanish immediately. We measured the time users spent for performing RT.

Baseline Techniques

In this section, we discuss the three techniques to which we compared our tools in the study. For fair comparison, we extended these techniques as follows:

- *Dual Finger Stretch* [5]: The user specifies an initial anchor location by pressing and holding his primary finger. Then he uses a secondary finger to scale a screen portion around the anchor location. The zoom ratio is proportional to the distance between the two fingers. We added Release-Tapping: performing RT with the primary finger starts the translation. Releasing the secondary finger makes the scaled portion vanish, and the user can enlarge new screen portions. The translation ends once the user releases the primary finger.

- *Shift* [34]: Once a finger touches the screen, the system displays a call-out copy of the occluded region with a cursor denoting the current finger position. The user can then refine this position by dragging. We added Release-Tapping: performing RT will start translation. The authors of Shift discuss CD gain as an extension, hence we added this functionality in the spirit of Dual Finger Slider [5]: by touching the screen with a second finger and dragging towards or away from the primary finger, Shift will magnify or de-magnify the offset view and modify the CD ratio accordingly.

- *PrecisionGlass*, a variation of PrecisionHandle [1]: The original technique enables the user to deploy a virtual handle on the screen. Any translation performed by the finger at the end of the handle will be applied on a smaller scale at the tip, thus increasing precision. Since the other two techniques offer visual magnification, we altered the technique to display a magnifying glass instead of a handle. After deploying the magnifying glass on the screen, it will remain on the screen for one second. During this second, the user can press and hold a target to start the translation. Our pilot studies showed that PrecisionGlass performed better than the original PrecisionHandle. As with our version of Shift, the user can change the zoom and CD ratio using a secondary finger.

Task and Stimuli

We asked participants to complete a series of target translation tasks with all 5 techniques – *FingerGlass*, *FingerMap*, *Dual Finger Stretch*, *Shift*, and *PrecisionGlass*. Depending on the current technique, each task consisted of two or three phases. Initially, the system presented two circular targets of width 7 pixels (2.0 mm) on the screen, separated by a given distance. The first touch event then started the *acquisition phase*, during which participants had to acquire the yellow *source target* as quickly and accurately as possible. For Dual Finger Stretch and Shift, this was followed by the *Release-Tapping phase*. Finally, during the *translation phase*, participants had to translate the selected yellow target onto the blue *destination target*.

We considered the acquisition phase successful if the user acquired the correct target. In the case of failure, the system did not proceed to subsequent phases. Instead, it presented a new pair of targets and the acquisition phase was repeated with the same parameters until successfully completed. The translation phase was considered successful if the source target and the destination target overlapped after releasing. In the case of failure, the entire task was repeated with the same parameters until successful completion.

At the beginning of each phase, a shrinking circle visually highlighted the corresponding target. The system displayed targets in front of a high-resolution street map in order to facilitate orientation in magnified views. In addition to the two targets in the task definition, 1500 red distractor targets were distributed uniformly at random across the screen. These distractors made it impossible to reliably acquire targets without assistive tools.

Apparatus

The experimental apparatus was *M2256PW*, a prototype 22" LCD touch screen manufactured by 3M. Its active display area is 476 x 295 mm, running at 1680 x 1050 pixels resolution with a pixel size of 0.28 x 0.28 mm. Our experiment used an area of 1371 x 914 pixels (388 x 257 mm) for the scene interaction, the remaining space was reserved for feedback about the completed tasks (see Figure 6). The refresh rate of the screen was set to 59 Hz. Participants were allowed to choose a tilt angle and desk height that was comfortable for them.

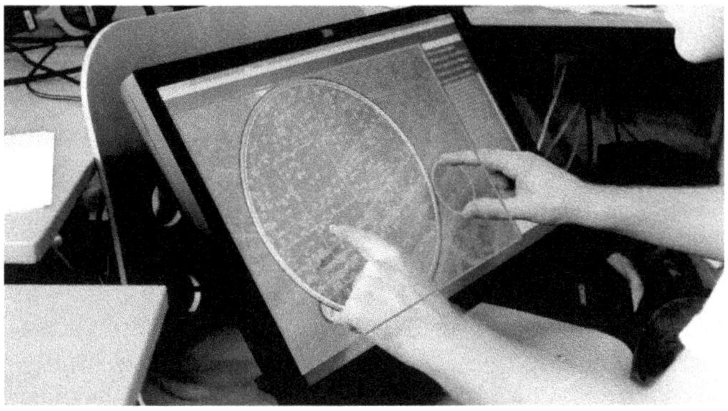

Figure 6: Our user study took place on a commercially available and freely tiltable 22" multitouch screen. The red area marks the portion of the screen we used for the interaction.

We implemented the techniques *FingerGlass*, *FingerMap*, *Dual Finger Stretch*, *Shift* and *PrecisionGlass*. We assumed a fingertip diameter of 10mm for contact area interaction. For the techniques FingerGlass and PrecisionGlass, the prescribed zoom ratio was 6x, thus leveraging the effective target size from 2mm to 12mm.

Our implementation was written in C++ using the Qt and OpenGL APIs. We chose to make use of graphics hardware acceleration in order to ensure maximal framerates in our test scene with thousands of targets displayed on top of a 4096×4096 texture. Running on a single-core CPU with an ATI Radeon HD 2600 card, we obtained frame rates consistently above 30fps.

Dependent Variables

In accordance to our design goals, the basic dependent measures for all phases of the task were completion time and error rate. The completion times of the individual phases are denoted *acquisition time*, *Release-Tapping time* and *translation time*. Their sum is denoted *total time*. For timing measurements, we took only successful attempts into account. In a similar fashion, we define the error rate for each subtask: the *acquisition error rate* is defined as the number of failed acquisitions divided by the number of total acquisitions. The *translation error rate* is obtained by dividing the number of failed translations by the number of total translations.

Independent Variables

We used a repeated measures within-subject factorial design for the study. The independent variables were *Technique* and *Distance*. We chose 8 values for *Distance* on a logarithmic scale. The longest chosen distance was 350 mm. To obtain the other distances, we successively divided by a factor of two. Hence, the other values were 175 mm, 87.5 mm, 43.75 mm, 21.87 mm, 10.94 mm, 5.47 mm and 2.73 mm. For the translation subtask, the combination of our target size with the chosen distance results in a range of index of difficulty (ID) values in Fitts' law terms [11], from 1.2 to 7.5 bits.

Techniques were presented to each participant in random order. For every technique, 12 blocks had to be completed. Each block contained a random permutation of the 8 distances. We collected a total of 5 (techniques) x 12 (blocks) x 8 (distances) = 480 successful trials from each participant.

Participants

10 volunteers (4 female) with a mean age of 22.9 years participated in the experiment. All of them had some experience with touch screens from automated teller machines. All participants have used multitouch based phone or PDAs before, 5 participants use them on a daily basis. Only one participant has ever operated a multitouch workstation before. All participants were right-handed. We gave a $10 gift card to every participant as a reward.

Hypotheses

Unlike *Dual Finger Stretch*, *Shift* and *PrecisionGlass*, *FingerGlass* supports high-precision selection without the cost of any dragging operations. Both *FingerGlass* and *FingerMap* support subsequent and fast multiscale translation operations according to our principles (P2) and (P3). Therefore, we hypothesize:

- **(H1) Acquisition Time** – *FingerGlass has significantly shorter task completion times than the three baseline techniques when acquiring small targets ($r = 2mm$).*
- **(H2) Translation Time** – *FingerGlass and FingerMap have significantly shorter task completion times than the three baseline techniques when translating targets.*

RESULTS

We performed repeated measures analysis of variance on both trial completion time and error rate for the tasks of acquisition and translation. We classified timing results outside of 3 standard deviations as outliers. This way, we removed 126 (2.62%) and 116 (2.42%) trials for the tasks of acquisition and translation, respectively. In this section, we summarize our data analysis. More detailed results and figures can be found on the project website[1].

To verify if we could aggregate across the independent variable *Block*, we investigated the effect of this variable on task completion time. Participants significantly improved their total task completion time over their 12 trial blocks ($F_{11,99} = 9.37$, $p < .0001$). Concerned that the learning effect could influence the results of our study, we removed the first two trial blocks after visually inspecting the data. Although *Block* had no significant main effect on task acquisition time anymore ($p = 0.182$), it still had some on translation time ($p < 0.01$). However, there was no interaction between *Block* and *Technique*, neither for acquisition ($p = 0.889$) nor for translation ($p = 0.552$). We are mainly interested in a quantitative comparison of the different techniques, rather than in their absolute measurement. Therefore, it is sufficient to know that no tool is at an unfair advantage due to learning effects.

Task Completion Time

Figure 7 shows the total times for acquiring and translating a 2mm target across the screen. For *Shift* and *Dual Finger Stretch*, the time for Release-Tapping is added as well.

[1] http://www.fingerglass.com

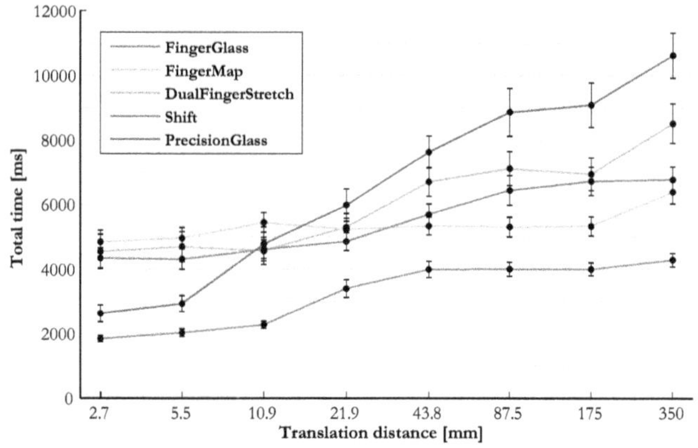

Figure 7: Total time (acquisition, Release-Tapping, translation) with respect to translation distance. Error bars represent the standard error of the mean.

Acquisition Time

Technique had a significant effect on acquisition time ($F_{4,36} = 7.6$, $p < 0.001$). Paired samples t-tests show that *FingerGlass* was significantly faster than any other technique (all $p < 0.02$) for the selection of 2mm sized targets. This observation confirms our hypothesis H1. The second-fastest technique for this task was *PrecisionGlass*. The differences in acquisition time between *FingerMap* and all three baseline tools were insignificant (all $p > 0.1$). Table 1 lists the acquisition times for all techniques and comparison to *FingerGlass*. The mean completion time for the subtask Release-Tapping was 211ms (SD = 213ms). This time is not included in the acquisition time.

Translation Time

For translation, we performed a 5×8 (*Technique* × *Distance*) within subjects ANOVA aggregated across *Block*. We found significant main effects for both *Technique* ($F_{4,36} = 360.61$, $p < 0.001$) and *Distance* ($F_{7,63} = 473.94$, $p < 0.001$). However, most relevant is the significant *Technique* × *Distance* interaction ($F_{28,252} = 49.44$, $p < 0.001$). For the verification of our hypothesis H2, we were interested in post hoc multiple means comparisons. Paired samples t-tests showed that *FingerGlass* was significantly faster than the three baseline techniques for all distances equal to or greater than 10.9mm (all $p < 0.03$). For the smallest two distances, *FingerGlass* was significantly faster than *Dual Finger Stretch* and *Shift* (both $p < 0.03$), but not significantly different from *PrecisionGlass*.

These results for translation time confirm our hypothesis H2 for *FingerGlass* for all distances greater or equal to 10.9mm, but not for the two shortest ones. We reject the hypothesis for FingerMap: even at a distance of 350mm, the difference to Shift in translation time is insignificant ($p = 0.376$).

Paired samples t-tests on *Total Time* show that *FingerGlass* outperforms any other tool at any distance (all $p < 0.02$).

Effect of Translation Distance

For *Shift*, performance time increases smoothly over ascending distances. All other techniques operate differently for long distances than they do for short distances. This is reflected by a slope change in the curve at the threshold distance at which techniques change their behavior. With FingerGlass, some participants started redefining the area of interest during translation for distances 21.9mm and 43.8mm. For distances equal to or greater than 87.5mm, this was almost impossible to avoid: with an area of interest encompassing both the source and destination targets, the zoom ratio was often limited to 2x or less. Note that the threshold distance is about twice as large for *FingerGlass* than for *PrecisionGlass*: FingerGlass allows users to define the area of interest in a way that both the source and the destination of the dragging operation just barely fit in the magnified view, making full use of its space.

Total Acquisition Time [ms]				
Finger-Glass	*Finger-Map*	*Dual-Finger-Stretch*	*Shift*	*Precision-Glass*
1271 (×1.00)	**2571** (×2.02)	**2905** (×2.28)	**2194** (×1.73)	**2077** (×1.63)

Table 1: Time required for selecting a target with a diameter of 2mm. Factors in parentheses compare the respective tool to *FingerGlass*.

Manual Control of CD Ratio

Extending *PrecisionGlass* and *Shift* with a virtual slider for changing the CD ratio proved to be inefficient. With Shift, where users did not need to use the slider, this feature was hardly ever employed. With PrecisionGlass, changing the CD ratio was the only possible way to accomplish long-distance translation tasks. Thus, although PrecisionGlass performed very well for short distance translations, the timings were poor for medium- and long-distance ones. A closer analysis of the recorded performances showed that users often overshot or undershot the destination target after changing the CD ratio. The reason for this is that users chose a different CD ratio in every trial and thus could not predict the required distance in motor space. Thus, we conjecture that techniques addressing multiscale translation by varying the CD ratio should use a few (e.g. two) discrete levels so users can get accustomed to them quickly.

FingerMap

The performance of *FingerMap* did not meet our expectations: acquisition times were about twice as long as those of *FingerGlass*, and translation times were worse for all distances. For selecting targets, FingerMap sacrificed direct touch selection in order to minimize eye movement. Our result indicates that this does not lead to better task completion times. Whether or not it reduces fatigue would be subject to further research. For translation, the users might confuse the role of their hands without visual feedback, resulting in worse performance. Our performance logs show that participants often tried to move their fine hand, which only applies relative movements, towards the absolute position of the target. In addition, the design of FingerMap suffered from the same problem as our extension of PrecisionGlass: participants hardly made any strategic use of the controllable CD ratio. More often, they were overshooting or undershooting targets during both acquisition and translation.

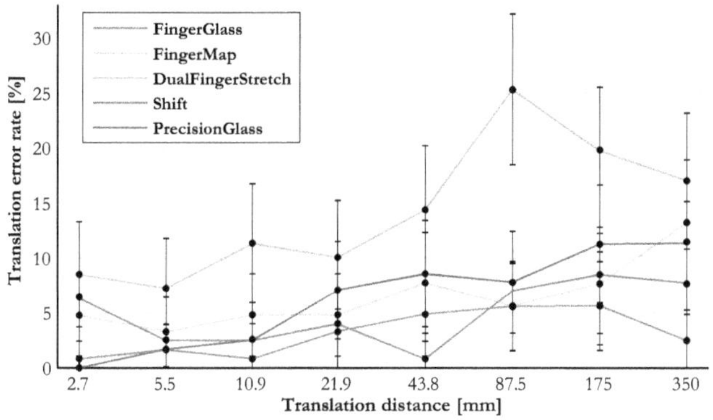

Figure 8: Error rate for the translation subtask with respect to distance. Error bars represent the standard error of the mean.

Effect of Target Location

We noticed that targets in the right half of the screen were somewhat harder to interact with than those in the left half. In some cases, the magnified view must be placed on the left side of the interest circle. Because all our subjects were right-handed, they had to either cross their arms or perform interactions in the magnified view with their non-dominant hand. To investigate this effect, we created a new grouping variable *XPos* indicating whether the source target was placed in the left, middle or right third of the screen. A 3×5 analysis of variance (*XPos*×*Technique*) on acquisition time and translation time revealed that there is a significant effect of the horizontal target position on translation time ($F_{2,18} = 17.15$, $p < 0.001$), but not on acquisition time ($F_{2,18} = 0.96$, $p = 0.38$). Similarly, the interaction between *XPos* and *Technique* was borderline significant for translation time ($F_{6,54} = 2.29$, $p = 0.032$), but not for acquisition time ($F_{6,54} = 0.39$, $p = 0.88$). FingerGlass had an average total time of 3214ms in the left, 2957ms in the middle, and 3561ms in the right third. As all other tools have a total time of over 5000ms in all thirds, this effect changes little about the relative performance of the tools.

Error Rate

To investigate selection and translation errors, we created variables *AcquisitionFail* and *TranslationFail* which measured the error rates for every condition (*Technique*, *Distance*, *Block*), aggregated across subjects. Note that there were more than $5 \times 8 \times 12$ trials for this analysis since subjects had to repeat erroneous attempts. The error rates are plotted in Figure 8.

Technique had no significant effect on *AcquisitionFail* ($F_{4,36} = 1.9$, $p = 0.128$), but had a significant effect on *TranslationFail* ($F_{4,36} = 10.81$, $p < 0.001$). *Distance* also had a significant effect on *TranslationFail*, but there was no interaction between *Technique* and *Distance*. Paired samples t-tests showed that *Dual Finger Stretch* had higher error rates than other tools with borderline significance. It had significantly higher error rates than both *FingerGlass* and *Shift* for distance 87.5mm, and than *Shift* for 43.8mm (both $p < 0.05$). By replaying the performances, we determined that many of the translation errors in Dual Finger Stretch happened in cases where users released the secondary finger before the first finger to end the translation. This reset the interface to the unmagnified state and moved the selected target to the absolute position of the primary finger. Subsequently releasing the first finger dropped the target in the wrong location.

We noticed that our touch device sometimes reported erroneous touch release events. This resulted in targets getting released early in translation operations and yielded false translation errors. To discard these cases, we used the event log to compute the velocity of a touch point immediately before its release event. We then removed trials with a higher release velocity than a threshold we determined by visual inspection of the data. To compute the velocity of a touch point, we averaged the pairwise distances of the last 5 touch move events. Using this method, we removed 201 translation attempts (3.16%).

	Dual-Finger-Stretch	Finger-Glass	Finger-Map	Shift	Prec.-Glass
acquisition	2.4	4.6	2.3	2.0	3.7
short drag	2.7	4.5	1.9	2.0	3.9
long drag	2.2	4.9	3.3	2.6	2.0
easy to learn	3.0	3.9	2.4	3.8	1.9
preference	2.5	4.5	3.4	2.3	2.3

Table 2: Mean subjective ranking, from 1 (worst) to 5 (best). Short dragging operations were defined to have a range of less than 5cm.

Subjective Evaluation

In the post-study questionnaire, participants were asked to rank the five techniques according to their preference for performing everyday tasks on their hypothetical personal multitouch workstations. Of the ten subjects, eight preferred *FingerGlass*. When asked to compare their preferred technique to a pen-based interface, users preferred the multitouch technique (3.3 out of 4 points, 4 being strong preference for multitouch). Comparison to a mouse yielded similar results (3.0 out of 4 points).

We also asked users which tool they find easiest to learn. The results show that *FingerGlass* was considered almost as easy to learn as *Shift*: 5 subjects would recommend *Shift* as the easiest technique to learn, 4 persons would recommend *FingerGlass*.

Finally, the participants ranked the tools by their subjective impression of the performance in object acquisition, short-distance dragging (5cm or less) and long-distance dragging (more than 5cm). The results confirmed our timing measurements. We assigned scores between 1 points (worst rank) and 5 points (best rank) to the votes and calculated the average scores as shown in Table 2.

CONCLUSIONS AND FUTURE WORK

We constructed two techniques enabling users to quickly navigate to different locations in different scales of a virtual scene, and to efficiently select and translate objects therein. Our experimental results show that one of these techniques, FingerGlass, significantly outperforms the current state-of-the-art techniques on touch screens for both precise selection and object translation.

FingerGlass does not require any information of the underlying scene and thus can be implemented independently on top of any existing application. In order to retain the gesture vocabulary of the underlying system, we suggest providing a modifier button in the fashion of the "Shift" or "Caps Lock" keys on computer keyboards to activate the tool temporarily or permanently.

In terms of limitations, our method requires at least three fingers to operate, and is designed for large multitouch workstations. We did not vary the screen size in our experiment. However, since three fingers occlude a significant area on small displays, it is likely that the advantage of FingerGlass decreases as the screens get smaller, compared to single-finger techniques such as Shift.

We believe that some of our findings are general enough to be applied to a wider range of applications. Therefore, we extracted a set of interaction principles for the efficient bimanual interaction with more general multiscale datasets. An example for such applications would be the modification of surfaces in 3D space. In such a system, the user could use his coarse hand to specify a small section of a surface. The view from a camera pointing along the surface's normal onto the surface would then be displayed in the magnified view. This technique would allow a user to temporarily look at scenes from a different point of view and perform operations like surface painting with his fine hand or moving small objects which are invisible from the original perspective.

The range of scales that can be explored using FingerGlass could be leveraged by allowing the user to recursively define areas of interest. By specifying a new area of interest in an existing magnified view, a new magnified view could appear, visualizing the scene at an even smaller scale.

ACKNOWLEDGEMENTS

We thank Tony DeRose, Björn Hartmann, Christine Chen and Kenrick Kin for their insightful comments and continuous support. This work was partially supported by NSF grant IIS-0812562.

REFERENCES

1. P.-A. Albinsson and S. Zhai. High precision touch screen interaction. In *Proceedings of CHI '03*, page 105, 2003.
2. C. Appert, O. Chapuis, and E. Pietriga. High-precision magnification lenses. *Proc. CHI '10*, page 273, 2010.
3. P. Baudisch, E. Cutrell, D. Robbins, M. Czerwinski, P. Tandler, B. Bederson, and A. Zierlinger. Drag-and-Pop and Drag-and-Pick. In *Proc. INTERACT 03*, 2003.
4. B. B. Bederson and J. D. Hollan. Pad++: A zooming graphical interface for exploring alternate interface physics. In *Proc. UIST '94*, pages 17–26, 1994.
5. H. Benko, A. Wilson, and P. Baudisch. Precise selection techniques for multi-touch screens. *Proceedings of CHI '06*, pages 1263–1272, 2006.
6. E. Bier, M. Stone, K. Pier, W. Buxton, and T. DeRose. Toolglass and magic lenses: the see-through interface. In *Proceedings of SIGGRAPH '93*, page 80, 1993.
7. R. Blanch, Y. Guiard, and M. Beaudouin-Lafon. Semantic pointing: improving target acquisition with control-display ratio adaptation. *Proc. CHI '04*, 2004.
8. N. Elmqvist, Y. Riche, N. Henry-Riche, and J.-D. Fekete. Mélange: Space folding for visual exploration. *IEEE transactions on visualization and computer graphics*, 16(3):468–83, 2010.
9. A. Esenther and K. Ryall. Fluid DTMouse: Better mouse support for touch-based interactions. In *Proc. AVI '06*, pages 112–115, 2006.
10. L. Findlater, A. Jansen, K. Shinohara, M. Dixon, P. Kamb, J. Rakita, and J. O. Wobbrock. Enhanced area cursors: Reducing fine pointing demands for people with motor impairments. In *Proc. UIST '10*, 2010.
11. P. M. Fitts. The Information Capacity of the Human Motor System in Controlling the Amplitude of Movement. *Journal of Experimental Psychology*, 47:381–391, 1954.
12. C. Forlines and C. Shen. DTLens: Multi-user tabletop spatial data exploration. In *Proc. UIST 2005*, pages 119–122, 2005.
13. C. Forlines, D. Wigdor, C. Shen, and R. Balakrishnan. Direct-touch vs. mouse input for tabletop displays. *Proc. CHI '07*, page 647, 2007.
14. G. W. Furnas. Generalized fisheye views. *Proc. CHI '86*, 1986.
15. G. W. Furnas and B. B. Bederson. Space-scale diagrams: understanding multiscale interfaces. *Proc. CHI '95*, 1995.
16. T. Grossman and R. Balakrishnan. The bubble cursor: enhancing target acquisition by dynamic resizing of the cursor's activation area. *Proc. CHI '05*, 2005.
17. Y. Guiard. Asymmetric Division of Labor in Human Skilled Bimanual Action: The Kinematic Chain as a Model. *Journal of Motor Behavior*, pages 486–517, 1987.
18. K. Hinckley, R. Pausch, D. Proffitt, and N. F. Kassell. Two-handed virtual manipulation. *ACM TOCHI*, 5(3):260–302, Sept. 1998.
19. K. Hornbaek, B. B. Bederson, and C. Plaisant. Navigation Patterns and Usability of Zoomable User Interfaces with and without an Overview. *ACM TOCHI*, 9(4):362–389, 2002.
20. T. Igarashi and K. Hinckley. Speed-dependent Automatic Zooming for Browsing Large Documents. In *Proc. UIST '00*, pages 139–148, 2000.
21. A. K. Karlson and B. B. Bederson. Direct Versus Indirect Input Methods for One-Handed Touchscreen Mobile Computing, 2007.
22. K. Kin, T. Miller, B. Bollensdorff, T. DeRose, B. Hartmann, and M. Agrawala. Eden: A professional multitouch tool for constructing virtual organic environments. In *Proc. CHI '11*, 2011.
23. J. D. Mackinlay, G. G. Robertson, and S. K. Card. The perspective wall: detail and context smoothly integrated. In *Proc. CHI '91*, 1991.
24. J. Mankoff, S. E. Hudson, and G. D. Abowd. Interaction techniques for ambiguity resolution in recognition-based interfaces. In *Proc. UIST '00*, pages 11–20, 2000.
25. T. Moscovich. Contact area interaction with sliding widgets. In *Proc. UIST '09*, 2009.
26. A. Olwal, S. Feiner, and S. Heyman. Rubbing and tapping for precise and rapid selection on touch-screen displays. In *Proc. CHI '08*, 2008.
27. S. Pook, E. Lecolinet, G. Vaysseix, and E. Barillot. Context and Interaction in Zoomable User Interfaces, 2000.
28. R. Potter, L. Weldon, and B. Shneiderman. Improving the accuracy of touch screens: an experimental evaluation of three strategies. *Proc. CHI '88*, 1988.
29. G. Ramos, A. Cockburn, R. Balakrishnan, and M. Beaudouin-Lafon. Pointing lenses: Facilitating stylus input through visual-and motor-space magnification. In *Proc. CHI '07*, pages 757–766, 2007.
30. G. G. Robertson and J. D. Mackinlay. The Document Lens. In *Proc. UIST '93*, 1993.
31. I. Rosenberg and K. Perlin. The UnMousePad: an interpolating multi-touch force-sensing input pad. In *Proc. SIGGRAPH '09*, 2009.
32. A. Roudaut, S. Huot, and E. Lecolinet. TapTap and MagStick: Improving one-handed target acquisition on small touch-screens. In *Proc. AVI '08*, 2008.
33. D. Schmidt, M. K. Chong, and G. Hans. IdLenses: Dynamic personal areas on shared surfaces. In *Proc. ITS '10*, 2010.
34. D. Vogel and P. Baudisch. Shift: a technique for operating pen-based interfaces using touch. In *Proc. CHI '07*, pages 657–666, 2007.
35. K. Yatani, K. Partridge, M. Bern, and M. W. Newman. Escape: a target selection technique using visually-cued gestures. *Proc. CHI '08*, 2008.

An Interactive Multi-touch Sketching Interface for Diffusion Curves

Qian Sun **Chi-Wing Fu** **Ying He**
School of Computer Engineering, Nanyang Technological University, Singapore

ABSTRACT
Diffusion curves are effective 2D vector-graphics primitives, for creating smoothly-shaded drawings with rich colors and unique styles. Conventional drawing systems for diffusion curves often require users to successively layout curve geometry and then specify colors, which is rather tedious for complex drawings. This paper proposes *a novel multi-touch sketching interface* for efficient design of 2D vector graphics with diffusion curves. In sharp contrast to previous interfaces, we develop a family of multi-touch gestures, allowing users to simultaneously sketch multiple diffusion curves and also to interactively edit and tune curve geometry and colors. Our experiments show that this not only brings novel painting experience to users but also provides a practical and effective tool for vector graphics design, useful for styles like silk painting, Disney cartoon, art poster, and photo-realistic effects. Lastly, we conduct a user study to explore the interface's intuitive and efficient drawing capability with both professional 2D artists and novice users.

Author Keywords
Multi-touch interface, Algorithms, Design

ACM Classification Keywords
H.5.2 Information Interfaces and Presentation: User interfaces; I.3.4 Graphics Utilities: Paint systems

General Terms
Design

INTRODUCTION
Diffusion curves [10] are 2D vector-graphic primitives that can effectively generate smoothly-shaded images. Basically, each diffusion curve has two pieces of information: 1) curve geometry, often defined by 2D splines; and 2) two sequences of colors, each along one side of the curve. After sketching diffusion curves on a 2D drawing canvas, we can apply the Poisson equation [2] with curve colors as boundary conditions to solve for color values over the 2D canvas. Thus, we can spread colors like heat diffusion, e.g., see Figure 1 (b&e). Lastly, since splines are used as the curve geometry, resultant drawings can have infinite resolution.

To draw with diffusion curves, users often start with a freehand-style sketch using 2D input devices like mouses and tablets. Each sketched curve is first converted into a 2D spline geometry (Bézier splines or B-splines), see Figure 1(c); then, users can specify colors along each side of the curve, see Figure 1(d). Such a procedure could be rather tedious when the drawing is complicated and requires spatially-varying colors. Moreover, users may also need to further adjust the curve geometry by adjusting the control points of the spline.

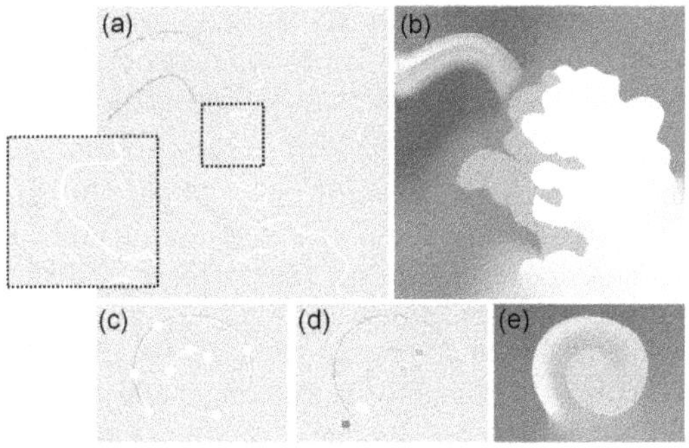

Figure 1. Diffusion curves (see (a)) enable effective generation of smoothly-shaded 2D vector-graphics (see (b)). After sketching a spline (see (c)) and specifying colors on it (see (d)), we can apply a Poisson equation solver to generate the drawing on the canvas (see (e)).

Recent boom of multi-touch technology in the market of consumer computer systems enables general users to directly use their fingers to interact with the graphical contents. Such interactions have been widely manifested in many applications on smart phones and laptops, and demonstrated to be very intuitive with general users. This paper proposes *a novel multi-touch sketching interface*, enabling interactive and practical design of 2D vector graphics with diffusion curves. We take advantages of the intuitiveness and efficiency of multi-touch to support simultaneous sketching of multiple diffusion curves and at-the-spot tuning of diffusion colors. In detail, a family of multi-touch gestures is proposed for sketching and editing diffusion curves, as well as specifying and tuning curve colors. Users can simultaneously sketch multiple diffusion curves with different colors, see Figure 2 (bottom). Finally, we developed our proposed interface into a working system and tried it with a number of users, including professional artists and novice users, demonstrating its values as a practical drawing tool.

PREVIOUS WORKS
Diffusion curves. Diffusion curves were first introduced by Orzan et al. [10] as 2D vector-graphics primitives for mod-

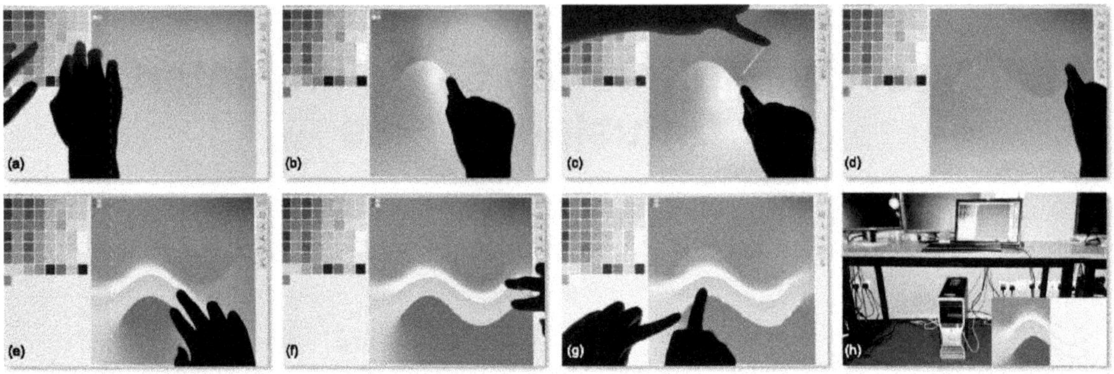

Figure 2. Our multi-touch sketching interface for diffusion curves: (a) multi-touch to select colors; (b) one-finger sketch to form a diffusion curve; (c) the second finger can help to adjust the curve geometry during the sketch; (d) complete a single curve; (e,f,g) sketch two additional curves to form a rainbow with multiple-fingers movement simultaneously; note that each curve (finger) can carry different colors during such an action; (h) our system setup: a 19" multi-touch screen and a Dell workstation; the lower-right corner shows the final image and the diffusion curve geometry.

eling images with only colors defined along region/curve boundaries; a multi-grid solver was employed to efficiently solve the Poisson equation. Later, Jeschke et al. [6] presented an alternative Laplacian solver; it can run as fast as the multi-grid solver, but is simpler to implement and feasible for arbitrary image resolutions. Moreover, they [7] also extended diffusion curves to 3D surfaces, enabling vector textures on 3D objects. Very recently, Takayama et al. [11] generalized 2D diffusion curves to 3D diffusion surfaces for modeling anisotropic solid textures.

Multi-touch interaction. Multi-touch [4, 9, 12] has been employed as an intuitive and effective interaction method in wide ranges of applications. Igarashi et al. [5] developed multi-touch interactions to intuitively manipulate 2D shapes while Bae et al. [1] presented a 3D sketching system for professional designers to create conceptual models with pen and finger gestures. Recently, Lepinski et al. [8] designed multi-touch marking menus that significantly outperform traditional marking menus while Fu et al. [3] proposed multi-touch gestures for exploring large-scale virtual space.

OUR MULTI-TOUCH SKETCHING INTERFACE

Our interface supports the following four major operations:

1) Select Colors with Multi-touch. Each diffusion curve has at least four colors, two on each side of it, to produce spatially-varying colors (by linear interpolation) along the curve geometry, see Figure 1 (a&d). In our interface, users can *multi-touch the color palette* with four fingers (see, Figure 3 (left)) to specify these boundary colors with visual feedback shown on the screen. To make it more practical, users can flexibly select or adjust one, two, three, or four colors by simultaneously touching the palette with respective number of fingers, and our system determines the color-touch match by the order of finger-screen contacts. Moreover, users can further apply multi-touch on the drawing canvas to exchange colors on diffusion curves.

2) Sketch Multiple Curves with Multi-touch. In addition, users can use multi-touch to sketch multiple diffusion curves simultaneously. Our design is motivated by the following observations on finger and hand ergonomics:

- Fingers of the same hand can naturally move together (in parallel) to sketch *curves with similar shapes* at the same time, e.g., rainbow and water wave;
- When using both hands, the non-dominant hand can easily follow the dominant hand so that associated fingers from both hands can easily draw *mirror-reflected shapes*.

To sketch multiple diffusion curves, the user can subsequently select colors for each planned curve. Associated colors for each curve are immediately shown next to the curves' endpoints as visual feedback, and users can then exercise the above ideas to *simultaneously sketch multiple curves* with one or two hands on the canvas. We found that rainbow can be easily drawn with multiple fingers of one hand while the heart shape can be easily drawn with fingers from two hands.

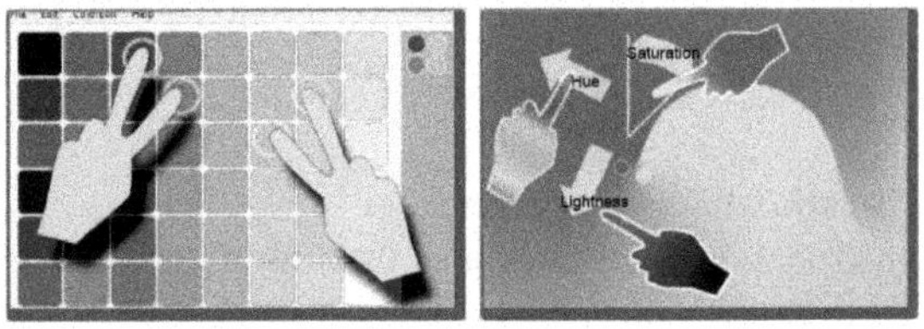

Figure 3. Multi-touch to select colors (left) and adjust colors (right).

3) Adjust Colors with Multi-touch. Users can adjust curve colors while sketching a diffusion curve; *hue, lightness and saturation* can be interactively adjusted by first multi-touching (with another finger) an empty location near the circular color tag followed by a finger drag. As shown in Figure 3 (right), dragging perpendicular and parallel to the curve's local tangent adjust the hue and lightness, respectively, at the related color tag based on the finger displacement. Performing angular change towards the opposite direction of lightness adjusts the saturation. Compared to the conventional painting interfaces which require switching to the palette panel window for color tuning, users of our interface can directly and interactively adjust colors at the spot. This strategy helps *minimize contextual switch*, thereby allowing users to concentrate on their designs on the drawing canvas.

4) Additional Features. Users can also directly edit the control points or curve segments like other works, e.g., [5]. Since diffusion curves are vector graphics which are scalable, we provide a zoom mode for users to view, edit, and sketch at appropriate scale. Supported with a real-time multi-grid solver that runs on a high-performance graphics board,

Figure 4. Paintings created by an artist with our interface; Disney cartoon, silk painting, art poster, and photo-realistic effect can be readily produced (from left to right). The artist used this system for the first time and was given 5 minutes in learning. The painting time varies from 15 to 40 minutes.

we can diffuse colors interactively while the drawing scale is changed. Users can thus sketch fine details with higher precision on important parts in their drawings. Lastly, users can also apply the at-the-spot color tuning method to adjust colors on the palette, as well as swap selected colors.

IMPLEMENTATION AND RESULTS

Hardware. Our multi-touch sketching interface was implemented and experimented on a Dell workstation T3500 with a 2.67GHz Xeon CPU, 12GB memory, a GeForce GTX295 (1792MB) graphics card, and a 3M 19" multi-touch display. See Figure 2 (lower right) for the hardware setup.

Software. To solve the Poisson equation at interactive speed, we developed a multi-grid solver on the graphics processing unit (GPU); its rough idea is to first solve for low-frequency components with a coarse domain and then iteratively refine high-frequency components with a finer domain.

Results. Figure 4 shows four example vector graphics drawings by an artist using our interface. As demonstrated in the accompanied video, our system can support interactive painting on a canvas of resolution 1920×1080; with the GPU support, it can update the visuals with multi-touch interaction at 20Hz, e.g., with the examples shown in Figure 4.

USER STUDY

We conducted a user study to explore the benefits of our multi-touch interface for general users. Our interface is compared against the conventional diffusion curves sketching interface by Orzan et al. [10]. As geometry and color are two key elements in diffusion curves painting, our goal is to measure how the interfaces help users to specify these two elements. Note that experienced artists and novice users may have very different painting styles that could lead to inaccurate measurements in the study. To counteract such discrepancy, strokes employed in our study are simple and distinctive, and after consulting with several artists and pilot-testing with some users with different levels of painting skill, two experiments with varying difficulty are designed.

Participants. Twenty-four participants were recruited in our user study, and they were divided into two equally-sized groups: G1: 7 males, 5 females, mean age 27.3; and G2: 8 males, 4 females, mean age 25.8. Among the participants, six are professional 2D and 3D artists while others are novice users. The six professional artists were split randomly and equally into the two groups.

Overall Procedure. Before going to the tasks in the experiments, we first introduced the key concepts of diffusion curves to the participants, and gave them 5 minutes to try and get familiar with the sketch-based input device. There are two stages in the user study. In the first stage (for G1), we first showed our proposed interface to the participants, and gave them 5 minutes to try the operations in the interface. Then, they were asked to complete two painting tasks (two experiments) with it. After that, we moved to the second stage and introduced the conventional interface to them. Again, we gave them another 5 minutes to try the interface. After that, they were asked to do the (same) two experiments but with the conventional interface this time. To eliminate potential discrepancy about familiarity with the interfaces, G2 did exactly the same tasks as G1 but in a reverse order when using the two interfaces. During the course of the user study, the time taken by each participant to complete a task was measured. Moreover, to help the participants (especially the novice users) complete the tasks, we showed them the expected diffusion results before starting the tasks.

Experiment #1: The first experiment is to evaluate the performance of specifying and adjusting colors on a simple diffusion curve. Participants were asked to first sketch an arbitrary stroke with four specific colors, and then increase the brightness of one color and decrease the others, see Figure 5 (left). Since a number of successive interface clicks are required to specify colors with the conventional interface, adjusting colors on an existing diffusion curve using the conventional interface with single input (mouse, tablet, or finger) is much more tedious.

In contrast, our multi-touch interface allows the participants to directly use their (four) fingers to select and adjust colors. To adjust colors, participants can simply touch one endpoint with a finger and then move another finger to a certain direction to control hue, saturation and lightness. With the multi-touch interface, participants can directly specify and adjust colors at the spot without switching frequently between the canvas and color palette. Furthermore, since the resultant drawing can be updated in real-time with the multi-touch interaction, immediate visual feedbacks are provided to the users. As shown in Figure 6, the average time to complete this experiment task with the multi-touch interface is 2.0 times shorter than that with the conventional interface.

Experiment #2: The 2nd experiment compares the multiple-curve sketching function (in multi-touch interface) with the single-stroke sketching function (in conventional interface). Sketching multiple curves with similar shapes is very common in many practical scenarios, e.g., water wave, hair strands, and rainbow. Participants were asked to sketch a rainbow

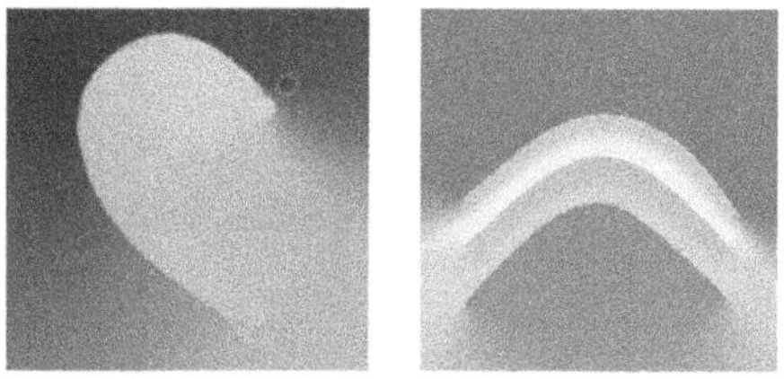

Figure 5. Tasks in Experiment 1 (left) and Experiment 2 (right).

with three strokes and six different boundary colors, see Figure 5 (right). With the conventional interface, they have to sketch the three curves one after another with just single input; thus, the curves may not result naturally with similar shapes. In contrast, the multi-touch interface allows the participants to sketch the three curves simultaneously with three fingers. This can also save roughly 69% of drawing time as compared to the conventional interface, see Figure 6.

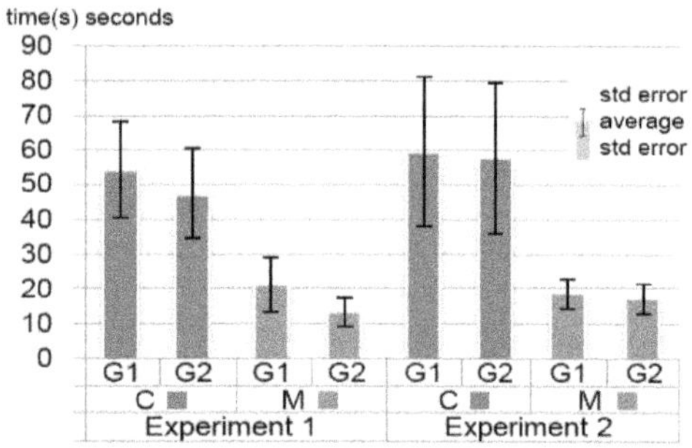

Figure 6. User study results. C: conventional; M: multi-touch.

Paired t-test. To analyze the user study data, we conducted the paired t-test with the null hypothesis *H0: the mean values of the drawing time using two interfaces are equal.* We used a significance level of 0.01, given H0 is true. As shown in Table 1, all resultant t values are larger than the critical value 2.72 with degree of freedom DOF=11 from the t-test table; hence we can reject H0 and show that our interface does perform better and help.

DOF=11	Experiment #1		Experiment #2	
Group	G1	G2	G1	G2
t value	8.9	11.03	7.12	6.74

Table 1. Resultant t-values.

Rating. After the two tasks, the participants were also asked to rate the two interfaces on their "effectiveness" and "interesting to use" on a scale of 1 to 5: 1 means "very hard to use, tedious, not satisfied at all" and 5 means "easy to use, highly effective, completely satisfied." The multi-touch interface receives average scores of 4.5 and 4.7 for "effectiveness" and "interesting to use," respectively, as compared to 3.2 and 2.9 for the conventional interface. The participants also commented that the multi-touch interface is highly intuitive for setting and tuning multiple colors, and the painting with multiple strokes in Experiment #2 is very novel; even the professional painters had never experienced this with existing 2D/3D painting systems before.

CONCLUSION

This paper presents a novel multi-touch sketching interface for efficient design of 2D vector graphics drawings with diffusion curves. In sharp contrast to the conventional interface that requires tedious working steps for constructing diffusion curves, our interface supports a family of new multi-touch gestures, enabling users to simultaneously sketch multiple curves, edit curve geometry, and interactively adjust the multi-parameter in curve colors at the spot. Using the working system we developed, we conducted a user study to show the practical value of this interface design with both professional artists and novice users. Results show that our interface not only brings new painting experience, but also provides a practical and effective tool for vector graphics design, typically useful for styles like silk painting, cartoon, art poster, and photo-realistic effects.

Acknowledgment. We thank valuable comments from anonymous reviewers; this work is supported by NRF2008IDM-IDM004-006 and A*Star SERC grant (No. 092 101 0063).

REFERENCES

1. S.-H. Bae, R. Balakrishnan, and K. Singh. ILoveSketch: as-natural-as-possible sketching system for creating 3D curve models. In *UIST '08*, pages 151–160, 2008.
2. L. Evans. *Partial Differential Equations*. Providence, 1998.
3. C.-W. Fu, W.-B. Goh, and A. Junxiang Ng. Multi-touch techniques for exploring large-scale 3D astrophysical simulations. In *CHI '10*, pages 2213–2223, 2010.
4. J. Y. Han. Low-cost multi-touch sensing through frustrated total internal reflection. In *UIST '05*, pages 115–118, 2005.
5. T. Igarashi, T. Moscovich, and J. Hughes. As-rigid-as-possible shape manipulation. In *SIGGRAPH 2005*, pages 1134–1141.
6. S. Jeschke, D. Cline, and P. Wonka. A GPU laplacian solver for diffusion curves and Poisson image editing. In *SIGGRAPH Asia 2009*. Article No. 116.
7. S. Jeschke, D. Cline, and P. Wonka. Rendering surface details with diffusion curves. In *SIGGRAPH Asia 2009*. Article No. 117.
8. G. Lepinski, T. Grossman, and G. Fitzmaurice. The design and evaluation of multitouch marking menus. In *CHI '10*, pages 2233–2242, 2010.
9. J. Matejka, T. Grossman, J. Lo, and G. Fitzmaurice. The design and evaluation of multi-finger mouse emulation techniques. In *CHI '09*, pages 1073–1082, 2009.
10. A. Orzan, A. Bousseau, H. Winnemöller, P. Barla, J. Thollot, and D. Salesin. Diffusion curves: A vector representation for smooth-shaded images. In *SIGGRAPH 2008*. Article No. 92.
11. K. Takayama, O. Sorkine, A. Nealen, and T. Igarashi. Volumetric modeling with diffusion surfaces. In *SIGGRAPH ASIA 2010*. Article No. 180.
12. D. Wigdor, J. Fletcher, and G. Morrison. Designing user interfaces for multi-touch and gesture devices. In *CHI '09*, pages 2755–2758, 2009.

Grids & Guides: Multi-Touch Layout and Alignment Tools

Mathias Frisch, Sebastian Kleinau, Ricardo Langner, Raimund Dachselt
User Interface & Software Engineering Group
Otto-von-Guericke-University Magdeburg, Germany
mfrisch@ovgu.de, {skleinau, rlangner}@st.ovgu.de, dachselt@ovgu.de

ABSTRACT
Precise alignment of graphical objects and the creation of accurate layouts are crucial activities in many applications, such as graphics design tools, presentation software or graph editors. Surface computing is very promising for these application domains but not fully explored yet. In this paper we contribute two tools which support layout tasks on interactive displays: *interactive grids* and *multi-touch alignment guides*. Both tools allow the precise positioning of graphical objects in a flexible and fluent way by multi-touch input. Direct bimanual interaction and physical metaphors are applied to arrange objects along straight lines and curves. A formative user evaluation showed promising results with regard to a productive and easy use of the tools.

Author Keywords
Layout, Alignment, Multitouch, Tabletops, Gestures

ACM Classification Keywords
H.5.2 [Information interfaces and presentation]: User Interfaces – Graphical user interfaces.

General Terms
Design, Human Factors

INTRODUCTION
Accurate positioning of graphical objects is an essential activity in many applications. In desktop publishing tools (e.g., Adobe Illustrator®) and presentation software, images or textboxes have to be aligned in a precise way to create good layouts. Graph editors are another example, in which child nodes have to be properly arranged below their parent nodes. In existing tools these tasks can be accomplished indirectly, for example by invoking functions from menus (e.g., for right alignment) or by entering values (e.g., for setting the spacing of items). Beyond that, there are techniques which allow precise positioning by direct manipulation. Users drag objects and the system provides automated assistance, for example by snapping (e.g., *snap-dragging* [1]). Objects snap to grids on the background, to the bounds of other objects or to previously created guides.

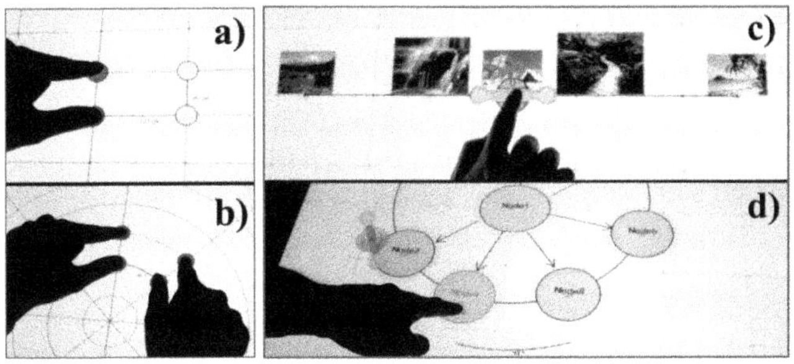

Figure 1 ***Interactive grids*****: an orthogonal grid can be adjusted by multiple fingers (a) and seamlessly changed to a radial grid (b).** ***Multi-touch alignment guides*****: objects are bound to shapes such as lines (c) or arcs (d). Alignment and spacing can be adjusted by touch input.**

However, these approaches have several drawbacks. For example, creating more complex layouts with different spacing between objects (cf. Figure 1c) or arranging objects along circular arcs (cf. Figure 1d) can be tedious.

Interactive displays supporting multi-touch interaction or even the combination of touch and pen input are very promising for graphics applications [4, 2]. Gestures allow quick mode switches and a more natural and direct way of interaction. Moreover, many tasks can be performed simultaneously by both hands. However, their potential is not fully exploited yet. Especially the creation of pleasant and precise layouts is challenging with these modalities. Therefore, tools are necessary which are tailored to multi-touch input and provide automated assistance.

In this paper we are contributing two specific tools for aligning graphical objects on multi-touch enabled displays: *interactive grids* (Figure 1 left) and *multi-touch alignment guides* (Figure 1 right). They allow path alignment tasks in a continuous flow of interaction which are difficult to achieve in existing tools. The following three interaction principles are realized by our new tools: (1) Productive use of multi-touch input and bimanual interaction. Users are able to achieve compound tasks by both sequential actions and continuous input without interrupting the workflow. (2) Flexible layouts and alignments can be created by direct manipulation of objects. Thereby, touched objects can serve as representatives of a group of objects. Manipulating them affects all other objects in the same way. (3) Finally, physical metaphors are applied. Magnetic effects and flicking and shaking gestures are used to provide natural interaction. For both tools, we conducted a formative qualitative user study which showed promising results.

RELATED WORK

Several works describe techniques for rotating and translating digital objects in a precise way applying multi-touch interaction [3, 6]. However, they focus on positioning single items and do not consider alignment tasks such as adjusting the spacing between several objects. In existing tools usually snapping mechanisms [1] are applied to align graphical objects according to alignment-objects. A widely used alignment-object is the grid. By *HyperSnapping* [5] grids are changed during dragging. We also change background grids dynamically, but apply bimanual multi-touch interaction. Furthermore, besides orthogonal grids we also consider radial grids. In order to align objects or to create symmetric shapes, several applications integrate ruler tools (e.g., [8]). Our *multi-touch alignment guides* are similar to the approaches presented by Raisamo [7]. In contrast to them, we are investigating the application of multi-touch input for aligning graphical objects, not only along straight lines, but also along other shapes.

MULTI-TOUCH ENABLED GRID

Similar to grids used in existing graphics applications our proposed *interactive grid* is located in the background of a canvas. It allows precise positioning of graphical objects by snapping [1]. In contrast to most grids which are typically adjusted by dialog boxes, the cell size of *interactive grids* can be changed directly by multi-touch input within a single fluent action. Furthermore, it is possible to switch between orthogonal and radial grids in a smooth and seamless way.

Holding a finger at a position where two grid lines intersect invokes four handles – one at each corner of the cell (Figure 1a). By moving them apart or together, the size of all cells of the grid can be adjusted. Dragging one handle changes the width and height of the cells uniformly. Dragging the edge between two adjacent handles allows the adjustment of the grid in one dimension without affecting the other one. In that way, the size of a cell can be adjusted precisely as feedback is continuously provided by displaying the distance in pixels between the handles. Furthermore, all four handles can be dragged simultaneously with up to four fingers. This allows to freely adjust the cells' width and height within a single action. These grid adjustments are typically done at the beginning of a designer's layout session, but can also be made during editing. We suggest supporting this by saving and reusing grids later on.

If one handle is fixed and one of its neighbors is deflected above a certain threshold, the orthogonal grid is changed to a radial grid (Figure 1b). Again, this can also be achieved by using four fingers simultaneously. A radial grid consists of concentric circles and diametral line segments which are evenly distributed within the disk. The center is located at the intersection point of two lines specified by the touched pairs of handles (Figure. 1b). The amount of concentric circles and the angle between two lines can be adjusted by dragging the handles or the edges between them. Thereby, feedback is given by displaying angle and distance. Graphical objects snap with their center to the grid if positioned within a certain threshold [1]. Thus, with interactive grids objects can be arranged not only along straight lines or rectangles but also along circular arcs.

However, positioning handles on touch screens in a pixel-precise way can be cumbersome. Even on commercial devices objects are often accidentally repositioned due to jitter or the intrinsic fat finger problem. For the pixel precise adjustment of the grid size, without invoking menus or entering parameters, we propose a technique called *single-step-nudging*. When users perform a short flick gesture on a handle, it moves just one pixel in the direction of the flick. Thus, the grid size can be set to a precise value after the handles were moved roughly to their target position. This is analogous to positioning tiny real world objects with slight nudges after coarse placement.

MULTI-TOUCH ALIGNMENT GUIDES

In order to address more complex tasks such as flexible object alignment and scaling, we developed *multi-touch alignment guides*. They consist of a handle (Figure 2a) combined with a geometric shape such as straight lines (Figure 1c), an arbitrary curve or a two dimensional closed shape (e.g., circles, Figure 1d). This shape is used to bind graphical objects, e.g. pictures or graph nodes, and provides constraints for positioning these items. The arrangement of bound objects can be manipulated by multi-touch input.

Manipulating Guides

Creating and deleting guides. *Multi-touch alignment guides* can be created by sketching. The type of the guide corresponds to the shape of the sketched stroke. For example, sketching a straight stroke results in a line guide which has the same length as the stroke, and sketching a circle results in a circle guide with the respective diameter. In that way, multiple guides can be created simultaneously. In order to distinguish these gestures from common sketching, we suggest starting them by holding & dragging. Holding a finger on the background and starting a drag gesture nearby with a second finger results in creating a guide. Guides can be easily deleted by dragging them off-screen or by performing a wipe gesture across them. Thereby, attached objects are not affected. In order to create line guides of infinite length we suggest dragging them from the edge of the display, as known from existing tools or holding two fingers on the canvas. Furthermore, if touch and pen input is combined [2, 4] the pen can be laid down on the display to create a guide of the same orientation and to move it in a tangible way.

Changing the size and length of a guide. A guide can be shortened by drawing a short stroke across the guide. When an infinite line guide or a circle guide is cut, handles appear at the intersection points. They can be used to adjust the length of a line guide or to create a circular arc from a circle guide. Furthermore, the diameter of a circle guide can be changed smoothly by a two-finger pinch-gesture.

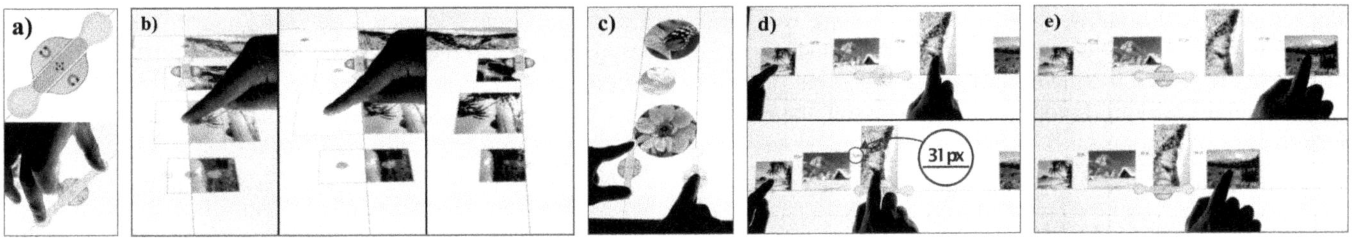

Figure 2. (a) Close-up of the handle, (b) changing the alignment by dragging an object across the guide (*all*-mode activated), (c) scaling objects by pushing two line guides together, (d) holding an object and dragging another one adjusts the spacing of objects in between, (e) *all*-mode: dragging one single object adjusts the spacing of other objects.

Repositioning the guide. A guide (and all its bound objects) can be positioned by using a handle attached to it (Figure 2a). It consists of two areas for rotation at its ends and one for translation at its center. Touching the handle with one finger constrains the interaction to translation (Figure 1c) or rotation depending on the touched area. This allows precise positioning of the guide by sequential steps of interaction as the guide snaps to the background grid. If both rotation areas are touched simultaneously by two fingers, the guide can be rotated and translated freely within a continuous flow of interaction (Figure 2a). Furthermore, the handle adapts to the current context of use. When it is touched it adjusts its size to the distance of the fingers. When it has been released, it is set back to its minimal size after a short delay. It becomes semitransparent to make it less interfering with graphical objects.

Binding and Releasing Objects

If an object is positioned near the guide within a certain threshold, it snaps to the guide automatically. Beyond that, we implemented two additional interaction techniques: *Flick & Snap* and *Collide & Snap*. Initially the guide is set to the *Flick & Snap* mode and can be positioned freely on the canvas without affecting any object. Binding a graphical object is achieved by flicking the object towards the guide. As a result, the object is animated to the guide. In that way a quick and explicit assignment of objects to several guides is possible by flicking in the respective direction. When *Collide & Snap* is activated, objects stick to the magnetic guide if they collide with it. In that way, users can move the guide across the canvas and "collect" objects (similar to [7]). In both modes an anchor point appears on the guide when the object is docked.

Switching between the two modes is achieved by pressing a button located at each side of the handle. This supports direction-independent tabletop interaction. The mode switch is possible during the movement of the guide, thus allowing a smooth way of interaction without interrupting the workflow. An object can be released by holding the object and dragging the guide away. Furthermore, it is possible to flick or to drag the object away from the guide. These three gestures are designed to be symmetric to the ones which are applied to bind objects to the guide. We consider this to be an important principle for gestural interaction.

Positioning Objects

Bound objects are manipulated directly by touch for adjusting their positions. The guide constrains the movement of the objects by its shape. A button at the handle is used to specify if a gesture affects just one object (the one which is touched) or all bound objects (*all*-mode). The *all*-mode can be considered as an intelligent way of grouping. Thereby, the touched object serves as a representative and manipulating this object affects all other bound objects in the same way. For example, all objects can be released in a single step by releasing just one object. For toggling the *all*-mode we did not introduce an additional button. Instead, the buttons for activating *Collide & Snap* change their functionality when the handle is released. This context-dependent change is possible, as moving the guide and positioning its objects cannot be done simultaneously.

Adjusting the alignment. Dragging objects across a guide results in centering objects or aligning them to the left or to the right side of the guide. While dragging, feedback is given by outlines, and when the finger is lifted, objects snap to the respective position. The *all*-mode can be activated to align all bound objects by dragging just one (Figure 2b).

Adjusting the spacing. Creating proper spacing between objects is an important and often applied task in layout applications. We support this by touching a bound object and dragging it along the guide without affecting other objects. The distance to its neighbors is displayed in pixels. If an object is dragged in *all*-mode, all other bound objects are translated as well. They are moved apart or together whereby the ratio of their spacing is maintained (Figure 2e). A similar effect is achieved by holding an object and dragging another one with a second finger. As a result, all objects in between are pushed together or moved apart (Figure 2d). Furthermore, a metaphorical "*shake*"-gesture (moving quickly back and forth) can be performed on the handle which *equally* distributes all bound objects along the guide. To avoid confusion, outlines of bound objects can be shown during shaking, whereas the actual objects remain in place before they are distributed. For pixel-precise spacing, *single-step-nudging* can be applied on bound objects, too.

Rotating and scaling. Objects can be rotated and scaled by means of a two-finger gesture. Again, in the *all*-mode all bound objects are transformed in the same way as the touched one. Additionally, we suggest combining two *line guides* to scale objects. Objects with one edge attached to a line guide are scaled by moving a second line guide to their opposite edge. Moving both guides apart or together is an elegant way of scaling all bound objects simultaneously to the same size (Figure 2c).

INITIAL USER EVALUATION

We fully implemented the *interactive grid* (orthogonal and radial) and two types of multi-touch alignment guides: a line guide (finite and infinite) and a circle guide (which can be cut and changed to arbitrary circular arcs). Both tools are integrated in a simple picture layout application and a node-link diagram editor. The former was used to conduct an initial user evaluation to investigate the tools' usability.

Apparatus and Participants. The evaluation was conducted on a multi-touch enabled SMART table (resolution: 1024x768 pixels, screen size: 57x43 cm). Ten participants took part in the study (two female, all right handed, average age: 29). Eight participants were employees of the computer science department, two of them had deeper knowledge of HCI and interaction design. The remaining two participants were professional architects and expert users of tools such as CAD programs.

Tasks and Procedure. The evaluation consisted of two parts: one for the *interactive grid,* the other for the *alignment guides*. We observed the participants during both parts and took notes about their behavior and comments. For each part the respective tool was explained to the participants. After a short training phase they were asked to solve two types of tasks: (T1) 'Align five pictures along a straight line with different spacing between the pictures' (similar to Figure1c) and (T2) 'Align five pictures on a semicircle around a sixth picture'. The target state of each task was handed to them on a printout. For T1 the size of the orthogonal grid had to be changed and the spacing of objects had to be adjusted along a line guide respectively. T2 had to be solved by the radial grid in the first part and by using a circle guide in the second part of the study. At the end, the participants were asked to fill in a usability questionnaire consisting of six items for each tool using a five-point Likert scale (1=disagree, 5=agree). The duration for both parts was about 30 minutes.

Results and Discussion. All participants successfully achieved the given tasks, and the concepts of both tools were well understood. *Single-step-nudging* and shaking the handle for equal distribution turned out to be easy and natural. The results of the questionnaire showed that the interactive grid was rated slightly better than the alignment guides: e.g., 'I quickly understood the tool' (Grid: M=4.4, SD=0.69; Guides: M=4.0, SD=0.67), 'The tool was easy to use' (M=4.1, SD=0.57; M=3.7, SD=1.01). Most participants, including both architects, agreed that it was fun to use the tools (M=4.5, SD=0.63; M=4.4, SD=0.51). They would envisage applying them in graphics programs (M=4.2, SD=0.63; M=4.2, SD=0.79).

Based on our observations we suggest the following improvements to the *interactive grid*: additional constraints for snapping the lines of the radial grid to regular angles should be added. Some participants started manipulating the grid by dragging with four fingers without invoking the handles beforehand. We suggest supporting this gesture (if not yet used for another task) as it permits interaction in the flow. Concerning the questionnaire we see the reason for the better results of the grid in its lower complexity. Beyond that, we observed that some participants had problems to reach the button for activating *collide & snap*. As a consequence, we made the button bigger. It moves back to its original size when the handle is released.

CONCLUSION AND FUTURE WORK

We presented two tools for layout and alignment tasks on interactive displays. The *interactive grid* allows adjusting the size of its cells directly and can be easily changed to a radial grid. *Multi-touch alignment guides* can be used for flexible alignment of graphical objects along different shapes. Both tools allow a continuous way of interaction as well as sequential actions by multi-touch input. They also apply physical metaphors to manipulate bound objects such as shaking or *single-step-nudging* for precise positioning. Alignment guides provide intelligent grouping of objects and change their appearance according to the context. An initial user study showed promising results for our concepts. For future work, we will create guides for shapes such as arbitrary curves. More formal user studies shall be conducted with more complex tasks, also in other domains.

REFERENCES

1. Bier, E. A. and Stone, M. C. Snap-dragging. *SIGGRAPH Comput. Graph.* 20, 4 (Aug. '86), 233-240.
2. Frisch, M., Heydekorn, J., Dachselt, R., Diagram Editing on Interactive Displays Using Multi-Touch and Pen Gestures. In *Proc. Diagrams '10*, Springer, 182-196.
3. Hancock, M. S., Carpendale, S., Vernier, F. D., Wigdor, D., and Shen, C. Rotation and Translation Mechanisms for Tabletop Interaction. In *Proc. TABLETOP 2006*. IEEE Computer Society, 79-88.
4. Hinckley, K., Yatani, K., Pahud, M., Coddington, N., Rodenhouse, J., Wilson, A., Benko, H., and Buxton, B. Manual deskterity: an exploration of simultaneous pen + touch direct input. In *Proc. CHI EA 2010*. 2793-2802.
5. Masui, T. HyperSnapping. In *Proc. HCC 2001,* IEEE Computer Society, 188-194.
6. Nacenta, M. A., Baudisch, P., Benko, H., and Wilson, A. Separability of spatial manipulations in multi-touch interfaces. In *Proc. GI 2009* ACM, 175-182.
7. Raisamo, R. An alternative way of drawing. In *Proc. CHI '99*, ACM, 175-182.
8. Zeleznik, R. C., Bragdon, A., Liu, C., and Forsberg, A. Lineogrammer: creating diagrams by drawing. In *Proc. UIST '08,* ACM, 161-170.

Fitts' Law as an Explicit Time/Error Trade-Off

Yves Guiard **Halla B. Olafsdottir** **Simon T. Perrault**
Laboratoire de traitement et de communication de l'information, CNRS, Telecom ParisTech
46 rue Barrault, 75013 Paris, France
{yves.guiard; halla; simon.perrault}@telecom-paristech.fr

ABSTRACT
The widely-held view that Fitts' law expresses a speed/accuracy trade-off is presumably correct, but it is vague. We outline a simple resource-allocation theory of Fitts' law in which movement time and error trade for each other. The theory accounts quite accurately for the data of Fitts' (1954) seminal study, as well as some fresh data of our own. In both data sets we found the time/error trade-off to obey a power law. Our data, which we could analyze more thoroughly than Fitts', are consistent with a square-root function with a single adjustable constant. We suggest that the resource-allocation framework should help combine information and energy considerations to allow a more complete account of Fitts' law.

Author Keywords
Fitts' law, resource allocation, speed/accuracy trade-off.

ACM Classification Keywords
H.5.2 User Interfaces (D.2.2, H.1.2, I.3.6)

General Terms
Experimentation, Measurement, Performance, Theory.

1. INTRODUCTION
This paper is about Fitts' law, the well-known relation that links the time it takes people to reach a target (e.g., a graphical object) with a pointer and the accuracy of their reaching action. We introduce a new formulation of Fitts' law which specifies one sense in which the law can be said to be a speed/accuracy trade-off, as traditionally assumed in HCI [12,12] as well as psychology [15,18]. A trade-off is a mutual dependency between two utilities that conflict with each other because they both draw on the same limited-resource pool: the better the performance on one front, the worse it is on the other [16,17]. Understanding how this concept applies in the context of Fitts tasks is our goal here.

A Fitts' law equation is an empirical regularity that relates mean movement time μ_T to an index of difficulty *ID* computed as a simple mathematical transform of *D/W*, the ratio of target distance *D* to target width *W*. Here are, among many others [18], four well-known formulations of the law:

$\mu_T = a * \log_2(2D/W) + b$ Fitts (1954) [2] (1)

$\mu_T = a * \log_2(D/W) + b$ Crossman (1956) [1] (2)

$\mu_T = a * \log_2(D/W + 1) + b$ MacKenzie (1992) [12] (3)

$\mu_T = a * (D/W)^b$. Meyer et al. (1990) [15] (4)

μ_T denotes average movement time (technically a mean or possibly a median, at any rate a central-trend statistic), and *a* and *b* stand for adjustable coefficients ($a>0$). Most popular within HCI is Eq. 3, known as the Shannon version of Fitts' law [11,12]. The starting point of this analysis is that Eqs. 1-4 do *not* describe a speed/accuracy trade-off.

2. THE BASIC MEASURES: TIME AND ERROR

2.1. Time Is Not Speed
First, μ_T, the dependent variable that stands on the left-hand side of Eqs. 1-4, is a time measure. In general μ_T correlates negatively with the average speed of a movement. Nevertheless it is only in casual language that one can tolerate confusion between a time measure, dimensionally [T], and a speed measure, dimensionally [LT^{-1}] [9].

2.2. Accuracy: Neither Information Nor Difficulty
Second, how the quotient of *D*/*W*, which determines the *ID* on the right-hand side of Eqs. 1-4, measures accuracy is unclear. In light of information theory [22], Fitts [2] assumed that the information conveyed by a movement is $\log_2(2D/W)$, a formula which MacKenzie [11,12] corrected to $\log_2(D/W+1)$. The information and the accuracy of movements must be linked somehow, but to our knowledge that link has not been clearly described.

Assuming that the mathematical transforms of *D/W* that feature in Eqs. 1-3 provide estimates of movement *difficulty* rather than movement information does not take us any closer to a measure of movement accuracy. In the Shannonian Fitts-MacKenzie tradition, difficulty is measured in bits and calculated, via Eqs. 1-3, from an objective property of the target layout, namely the ratio of lengths *D* and *W*. But this is just information—for lack of an operational definition of its own, it is hard to see how task difficulty might relate to accuracy.

If one wished to characterize difficulty as *subjective* effort [19], one would have the problem that none of the above *ID*s bear a monotonic relationship with this effort. There is no question that in the upper region of the *ID* spectrum (over 4 bits or so, using the Shannon *ID*), the higher the *ID*, the more difficult the task for participants. But in the lower

CHI 2011, May 7–12, 2011, Vancouver, BC, Canada.

region of the *ID* spectrum (below 2 bits or so), the *lower* the *ID*, the more difficult the task: no matter their good will, participants will systematically fail to produce large enough spreads of movement endpoints [1,4,12]. This is not too surprising. Since the kinetic-energy cost of movements varies with the square of their velocity, a Fitts task becomes difficult not only with very high but also (in a different sense of the word) with very low *ID*s. The participants' failure to comply with instructions in low-*ID* conditions just reflects their reluctance, or mere inability to produce fast enough movements because of their excessive *energetic* cost. This observation tends to be overlooked in an approach exclusively based on Shannonian information. But from the moment it is recognized that an aimed movement involves not only bits of information, but also joules of energy, it becomes clear that movement difficulty, characterized as subjective effort, can only bear a U-shaped relation with the variable known as the *ID* in Fitts' law research [7]. Information, as captured by any *ID* estimate, cannot be taken as an index of subjective difficulty.

Thus a typical Fitts' law equation expresses a relation, not between movement speed and movement accuracy, but rather between movement time and a certain dimensionless ratio whose relation with both accuracy and difficulty is unclear. We now present some distinctions which we think useful to rephrase Fitts' law as an explicit trade-off.

2.3. Relative Target Distance *D/W* vs. Relative Target Tolerance *W/D*

When Fitts [2] (p. 266) introduced his index of difficulty, he wrote $ID=-\log_2(W/2D)$, rather than $ID=\log_2(2D/W)$. These are two different mathematical writings of the same thing, and so whether the independent variable of Eqs. 1-4 is *D/W* or *W/D* might be judged an idle question. In fact that distinction is quite critical because the quotients of these two divisions designate different measures in the physical world of experimentation. The quotient of *D/W* is a measure of *relative target distance* (*RTD*)—i.e., *D* scaled to, or expressed in units of *W*. In contrast, the quotient of *W/D* is a measure of *relative target tolerance* (*RTT*)—i.e., target tolerance scaled to, or expressed in units of *D*.[1] Although it has been a tradition to formulate Fitts' law as an equation of the form $\mu_T=f(D/W)$, there is reason to prefer the inverse writing $\mu_T=f(W/D)$ [8]. First, there is a *scale of measurement* issue [26]: relative target distance or *D/W* lacks a true zero because the limiting case where $D=0$ and $W>0$, hence $D/W=0$, violates the very definition of a Fitts task—if $D=0$, no movement is required [8]. In contrast, relative target tolerance or *W/D* does enjoy a true zero: the limiting case where $W=0$ and $D>0$, hence $W/D=0$, corresponds to a zero-tolerance aiming task, which makes sense and has indeed been investigated [21]. Thus only *RTT*=*W/D*, and not *RTD*=*D/W*, runs on a *ratio* (equal-interval) scale of measurement [26]. This matters because a higher level of measurement for experimental variables means a more constraining framework for testing theoretical hypotheses [20]. For example, the *y*-intercept of an empirical regression line is interpretable only if the *x* variable has a physically-anchored zero [8].

RTT is also preferable over *RTD* for the statement of Fitts' law because any measure of accuracy, whether absolute or relative, should involve error as a component. It seems much more sensible to ground one's characterization of accuracy on a measure of tolerance (i.e., permitted error) like *RTT* than a measure of distance like *RTD*.

2.4. Task Geometry vs. Movement Performance

This section calls attention to an obvious distinction that has received little attention in the literature. On the one hand experimenters have full control over *D* and *W*, two systematic, deterministic variables that characterize the geometrical layout of targets and that serve to prescribe to participants an average amplitude and a spread of movement endpoints, respectively. On the other hand one needs to characterize the participants' actual performance. Here the elemental measures are movement duration *T* and movement amplitude *A*, from which an endpoint error can be computed as $E=A-D$. Unlike *D* and *W*, variables *T* and *A* (as well as *E*) are random variables, reflecting the natural variability of human performance. We need to distinguish *T*, *A* and *E*, to be measured at the level of individual movements, from central-trend statistics like means μ_T, μ_A, and μ_E, to be calculated over samples of movements.

We deliberately wrote Eqs. 1-4 above as $\mu_T=f(\underline{D}/W)$ rather than $\mu_T=f(\underline{A}/W)$ as has been customary since Fitts [2], because the latter notation is somewhat wobbly. If *W* unambiguously designates a property of the target layout (tolerance), it is always unclear whether the conventional symbol *A* stands for *D* (thus referring to the target layout) or μ_A (thus referring to the movement). The writing of Fitts' law becomes particularly ambiguous in this regard when *W* is replaced by *effective* width W_e to denote the tolerance that, in retrospect, would have yielded a pre-specified error percentage, given a certain spread of endpoints. Labeling this variable as "target width" suggests one is talking task geometry while W_e is a random variable of the movement.

In fact the accuracy issue can be approached in Fitts' paradigm from two markedly different, though equally legitimate, angles. In one approach, Fitts' law is all about the dependency of μ_T upon the dimensionless ratio *W/D* (or its inverse *D/W*), as suggested in the formulations we chose for Eqs. 1-4. In this approach μ_T is predicted from the task geometry, and the problem of accuracy must be phrased in terms of *D/W* or *W/D*. In the alternative approach, Fitts' law is all about the mutual dependency of two random variables, movement time and relative variable error. *RVE* seems well represented by σ_A/μ_A, a regular coefficient of variation in which σ_A and μ_A denote the standard deviation and the mean of movement amplitude [8]. Thus Fitts' law can be formulated either as $\mu_T=f(W/D)$, expressing the causal dependency of a temporal random variable upon a

[1] This study requiring a number of non-conventional distinctions and notations, the glossary placed in the final section may help.

systematically-varied geometrical variable, or alternatively as μ_T=f(σ_A/μ_A), expressing the mutual dependency of two random variables. These are what we call the *geometrical* vs. the *stochastic* version of Fitts' law.

HCI researchers, who often need to evaluate or predict pointing performance for certain target layouts, naturally adopt the former approach, assuming that movement performance is causally dependent on the target layout. It is the alternative approach, however, that paves the way for a trade-off analysis. If one wants to formulate Fitts' law as a trade-off, one needs to write the law in the form of a *mutual* dependency, with movement time depending on movement error and vice versa—it should not matter whether Fitts' law is written μ_T=f(σ_A/μ_A) or, reciprocally, σ_A/μ_A =g(μ_T).

3. A SIMPLE RESOURCE-ALLOCATION THEORY OF FITTS' LAW

Below are listed a set of basic assumptions needed for a resource-allocation theory of Fitts' law. Note that the trade-off under consideration is not between speed and accuracy, but, strictly speaking, between mean or median movement time μ_T and relative variable error *RVE*.

1. *Utility*. Movement time and relative variable error are both *negative* utilities, that is, quantities that must be minimized—the shorter the μ_T, the better the performance; the smaller the *RVE*, the better the performance.

2. *Trade-Off*. The two minimization efforts conflict with each other: the less of one negative utility, the more of the other. This is a trade-off of the min-min category.[2]

3. *Limited Resource Pool*. The trade-off results from the fact that the two concurrent minimization efforts draw from a *common pool of resources*, and this pool is *limited*. This assumption is the counterpart, within the trade-off theoretical approach, of Fitts' [2] limited-capacity channel assumption. We may designate the content of the hypothetical pool, whose nature is unknown, as the *effort*. We just need to assume, using the usual economic analogy, that some generic currency is convertible into speed and/or accuracy and that the available amount of this currency is finite, being a characteristic of every individual placed in a given situation. Devising a method for estimating that amount is our first important challenge here.

4. *Less-than-Total Resource Exploitation*. In Fitts' law experiments participants are instructed to constantly do their best —i.e., to invest 100% of their resources. Human effort, however, is subject to random fluctuations and so the amount of resource actually available to an individual at a given point in time can be less—but never more—than these 100%. The limited resource pool, in other words, must be thought of as an *upper bound*. We believe this realistic assumption, which has escaped researchers' attention until recently [25], is mandatory in any approach to Fitts' law, including the information theoretic approach.

5. *Resource allocation strategy*. Faced by resource scarcity in a Fitts task, participants can deliberately modulate the balance between their concurrent time-minimization and error-minimization efforts. Quantifying that imbalance, estimating its range of variation, and understanding its dependency upon systematically manipulated experimental conditions—different target layouts in Fitts' [2] experiment (Section 4), different verbal instructions in ours (Section 5)—constitute the second challenge of this analysis.

4. FITTS' (1954) TAPPING DATA: EVIDENCE OF A TIME/ERROR TRADE-OFF

This section aims to show that Fitts' data can indeed be reformulated explicitly as a trade-off between two conflicting utilities. Focusing on the min-min trade-off of movement time μ_T and relative variable error $RVE = \sigma_A/\mu_A$, we will introduce a simple geometrical method for characterizing quantitatively the size of the resource pool as well as the strategic imbalance.

At first sight, the suitability of Fitts' experimental protocol for a trade-off analysis of his data might seem questionable. Fitts did not ask his participants to minimize movement time and relative error concurrently—he asked them to minimize a single variable, μ_T, under a number of different constraints of relative tolerance, and so it was a systematic factor that stood for accuracy. One should bear in mind that with such a protocol, still most popular today, error actually remains a negative utility (i.e., the less of it, the better), just like movement time. It is in order to obtain from participants differing levels of *RVE* that experimenters display differing levels of *RTT*. The manipulation of target display as in [2] and instructions as in [4] may be viewed as two alternative methods with the same goal. In the former option participants are to minimize μ_T with a variety of *RVE* constraints, while in the latter they are to jointly minimize μ_T and *RVE* under a variety of speed/accuracy compromises. But both methods boil down to instructions, formulated visually and in words respectively, serving to manipulate the participants' cognitive stance in the face of the fundamental speed/accuracy dilemma.

We will consider the data Fitts [2] obtained in his famous reciprocal tapping experiment, tabulated in his Table 1 (p. 264, *light*-stylus data). The table reports movement times averaged over 16 participants, for each of 16 combination of *D* and *W*. However, Fitts did not actually record the position of movement endpoints, just tabulating percentages of target misses. Capitalizing on Fitts' report (p. 265) that undershoot and overshoot aiming errors were about equally frequent in his light-stylus experiment, we assumed μ_A=*D*. We inferred endpoint spreads from error rates using the technique described by MacKenzie [10] (Section 2.5). For each combination of *D* and *W* we computed effective width W_e (for a fixed 4% error-rate constraint, under the hypothesis of a Gaussian spread of endpoints) and then calculated $\sigma_A = W_e/4.133$.

[2] An example of a *max-max* trade-off is that between speed and accuracy, both positive utilities: the faster and the more accurate the movement, the better the performance.

Note that our analyses below separate the different levels of scale, characterized by D or μ_A, following the recommendation of Guiard [6]. We assume that the form and the size of the target display are specified by $RTT=W/D$ and D, respectively, and that the form and the size of the aimed movements are specified by RVE and μ_A, respectively.

4.1. A Power Relationship Between Movement Time and Relative Variable Error

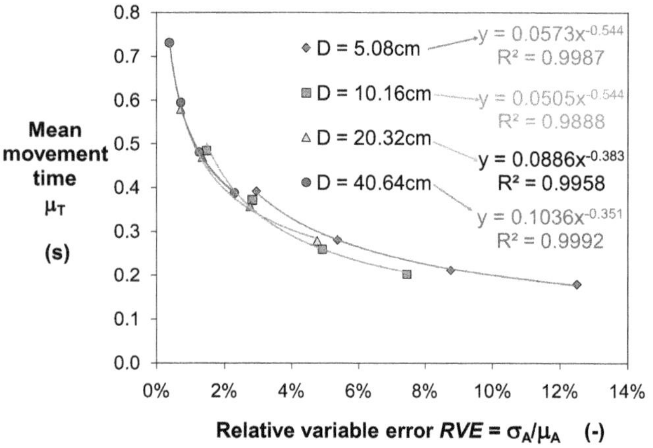

Figure 1. The trade-off of μ_T and RVE in Fitts' tapping data.

As shown in Fig. 1, Fitts' data is closely modeled, for each scale level, as a power function ($.989<r^2<.999$):

$$\mu_T = q * RVE^p \quad (5)$$

where p and q represent adjustable coefficients ($p<0$, $q>0$). Note that the logarithmic fit ($r^2=.993$ on average over the four scales) was nearly as good as the power fit ($r^2=.996$).

4.2. Amount of Resources

Eq. 5 may be rewritten as

$$\mu_T * RVE^{-p} = q \quad (6)$$

or, since we define relative variable error RVE as σ_A/μ_A, as

$$\mu_T * (\sigma_A/\mu_A)^{-p} = q. \quad (7)$$

Eq. 7 is the statement of a constant product: within each scale condition, the product of μ_T and RVE raised to the power $-p$ was conserved in Fitts' experiment despite his systematic change of the target layout and consequently of μ_T. The conservation of quantity q is illustrated in Fig. 2. For each of the four scale conditions the slope of the regression line is virtually zero—as movement time varied over a range of about 2:1, q remained remarkably stable.

In light of the trade-off theory outlined in Section 3, it is clear that the constant q specifies the average amount of resources that was available to Fitts' participants. Note that the constant q is indicative, not of an amount of resources, but of resource *scarcity*: the smaller the product of the two negative utilities, the better the performance.

The different elevations of the four flat curves of Fig. 2 show that the amount of resources available to Fitts' participants was scale dependent. The constant q reached a minimum in the D=10.16cm condition, presumably a scale optimum for Fitts' particular task conditions.

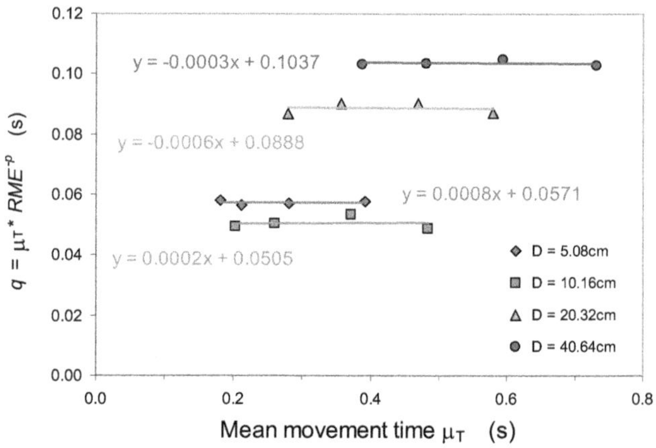

Figure 2. Conservation of the product q of Eq. 7 across the variation of μ_T, for each scale condition.

Fig. 3 plots Eq. 7 for D=40.64cm, whose best fit is μ_T=$0.1036/RVE^{0.3509}$ (r^2=.9992, see Fig. 1). Notice that the rectangle obtained by drawing straight horizontal and vertical lines to the axes from any point of the curve, whether chosen within the actual range of x values like points A, B, C, and D, or extrapolated along the curve like point E, has a constant area (if $y=q/x$, then $xy=q$). This area is no other than the coefficient q of Eq. 7, whose estimate in that particular scale condition is 0.1036s.

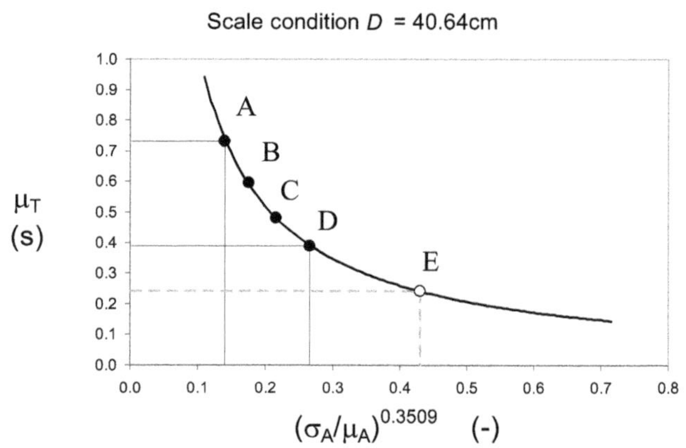

Figure 3. A plot of Eq. 7 for the D=40.64cm scale condition, where exponent p is -0.3509. ABCD are Fitts' actual four data points, E is an arbitrary extrapolation along the curve. All rectangular areas are equal.

4.3. Resource Allocation: Strategic Imbalance

If different points along the curve of Fig. 3 correspond to one and the same amount of resources, they specify different degrees of imbalance between the time- and error-minimization effort. While the product xy (the rectangular surface area in the figure) is conserved all along the curve, reflecting available resources, the ratio y/x (the rectangle's aspect ratio) changes gradually, reflecting different resource-allocation options. For any data point of the curve the actual *strategic imbalance* (*SI*) of participants can be quantitatively characterized by this aspect ratio, that is,

$$SI = \mu_T / RVE^{-p}, \quad (8)$$

or, recalling that relative variable error $RVE = \sigma_A/\mu_A$,

$$SI = \mu_T / (\sigma_A/\mu_A)^{-p}. \quad (9)$$

With this definition of the aspect ratio, which we chose to compute as y/x, the strategic imbalance SI decreases in Fig. 3 from left to right: the less cautious (and the faster) the movement, the lower the index. Thus SI correlates positively with—is an index of—the relative strength of the error-minimization component of the participant's effort.

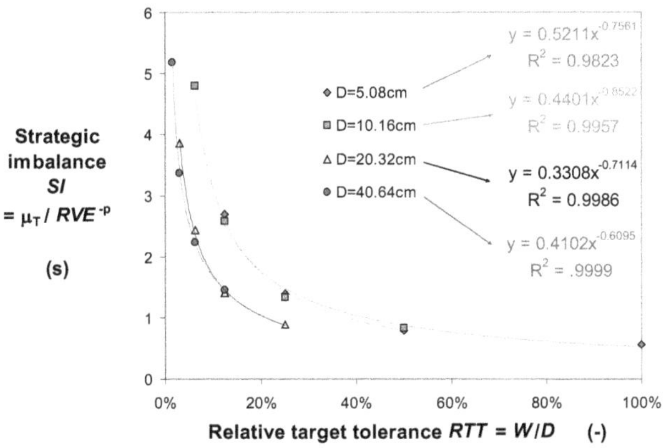

Figure 4. The *SI* as a function of *RTT* in Fitts' data.

Fig. 4 shows the dependency of the resource-allocation strategy of Fitts' participants upon *RTT*, the target-layout characteristic that Fitts used to force this strategy to vary. The dependency is highly non-linear, suggesting that the target-layout manipulation technique Fitts introduced in his 1954 study actually provided him with mediocre control over his participants' strategy. See also Fig. 5: even though Fitts raised *RTT* up to the extreme point where his two targets touched each other (i.e., W=D hence RTT=100%), *RVE* hardly exceeded 10%.

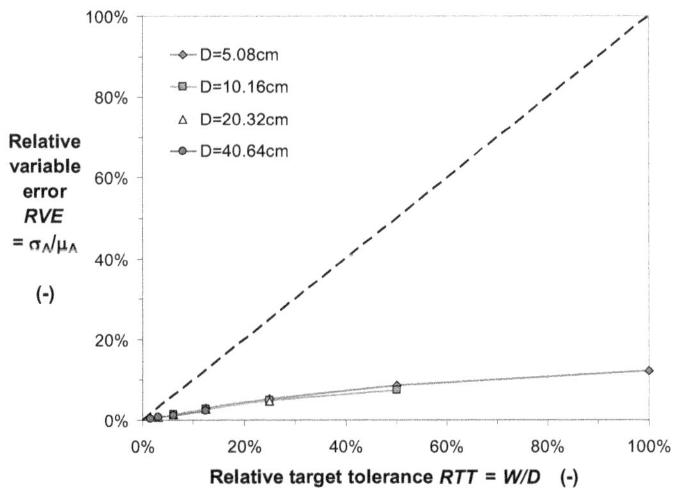

Figure 5. *RVE* as a function of *RTT*. The dashed line represents the theoretical equality *RVE*=*RTT*.

Back to Fig. 4, notice that Fitts' participants had two different strategic stances in the face of four different movement scales. For *RTT*<30%, the x ranges covered by the four curves substantially overlap, thus making it possible to compare *SI*s for geometrically-similar target layouts: Fitts' participants had about the same set of strategic imbalances in the two larger-scale conditions D=20cm and 40cm, but they apparently had another, more cautious set of strategies in the two smaller-scale conditions D=5cm and 10cm. The statistical reliability of this finding cannot be tested for lack of individual data but the pattern seems impressively consistent. One conjecture would be that because high speeds cannot be attained over small amplitudes, a scale reduction might have encouraged participants to adopt a relatively more cautious strategy.

While the pattern is quite conspicuous in the plot of Fig. 4, it is virtually undetectable in the classic plot of μ_T vs. *ID*. Also note that it could not have been deduced from our previous observation that the resource pool was maximal in Fitts' participants for 10cm movements (Fig. 2)—the aspect ratio (the quotient of μ_T/RVE^{-p}) and the surface area (the product $q=\mu_T*RVE^{-p}$) of the rectangles of Fig. 3 are two mathematically independent quantities.

4.4. Discussion

The foregoing confirms that the classic tapping data of Fitts (1954) can be satisfactorily interpreted as a trade-off between two negative utilities, time and error. Thus, not only can we view Fitts' law as the demonstration that throughput—the inverse of the law's slope, whose dimensions are bits/s—is conserved as the task *ID* is made to vary, we can just as well view the law as evidence that a certain pool of effort resources is conserved in the people across the variation of strategic imbalance. Both the information theoretic approach and the trade-off approach may help us understand Fitts' law.

5. FRESH DATA ON THE TIME/ERROR TRADE-OFF

This section reports a simple experiment which only varied task instructions so as to induce a systematic variation of the participants' strategic imbalance in the face of the concurrent time- and error-minimization efforts. Movement amplitude was invariably a comfortable 150mm.

Among our motivations for running a fresh experiment was the fact that Fitts' [2] individual data are not available. From the standpoint of resource allocation theory, one expects some quantities—notably the coefficient q of Eq. 5—to behave as within-individual constants while at the same time varying from participant to participant. Also of considerable interest is the variability of the strategic imbalance among and within individuals. Whether experimenters manipulate the target layout, as has been customary since Fitts, or speed/accuracy instructions, they face human beings with idiosyncratic strategic styles. No two participants will identically interpret instructions to move, say, as fast as possible. Nor will they show the same degree of flexibility in response to changing instructions.

Our discussion of Fitts' data above did not refer to less-than-total resource exploitation, assumption #4 of our trade-off theory, whose illustration and testing require individual data. Below we will see that this assumption is quite useful to estimate individual trade-offs.

There were two notable differences between our protocol and Fitts'. First, our aiming task was *discrete*, rather than reciprocal, our participants having to return to a fixed home position after each aimed movement. This option makes it possible to clarify the status of our temporal and spatial measures. Whereas in the reciprocal protocol μ_T is the time it takes not only to carry out a movement, but also to evaluate the error inherited from the previous movement and to prepare the next [3], in the discrete protocol μ_T measures the duration of a pure movement-execution process. Furthermore the meaning of the movement's endpoint spread σ_A is interpretable more safely in the discrete case, that variability being generated just by the execution of the movement, whereas in the reciprocal case σ_A must also reflect, to some unknown extent, the variability of the start point [3]. Finally, most pointing actions in real world HCI are discrete.

The other notable difference is that we did not visually specify tolerance *W*. We just specified *D* with two lines indicating the start point and the desired endpoint of the movement, the target being thus displayed as a single line. We manipulated the balance between the two concurrent minimization efforts by means of different sets of instructions that asked the participants to cover their whole spectrum of imbalances, from maximum speed (minimizing μ_T) to maximum accuracy (minimizing *RVE*).

5.1. Method

Participants

Sixteen volunteers participated (all right-handed, median age 27.5years, interquartile range 2.5years, four female).

Speed/Accuracy Instructions

We used five sets of instructions: 1) Max speed, 2) speed emphasis, 3) speed/accuracy balance, 4) accuracy emphasis, and 5) max accuracy. In the max-speed condition the participants were to just minimize movement time, the only requirement regarding accuracy being to refrain from committing a systematic error: no matter the dispersion of movement endpoints, participants were just to manage to terminate their movements at about the target *on average*. At the opposite extreme, the max-accuracy instructions asked participants to try to bring the cursor exactly to the target (zero pixel error), making as many corrective sub-movements and taking as much time as needed—but not more. These two extremes being defined, we simply inserted three intermediate levels of instructions, one unbiased (speed/accuracy balance) and two biased (speed emphasis, accuracy emphasis).

Apparatus and Setup

The experiment involved a 1280x1024-pixel (34.0x27.1cm) screen and a Wacom Intuos3 digitizing tablet connected to a PC running Linux Ubuntu. The screen permanently displayed two vertical lines extending from top to bottom, located 150mm apart, which marked the start point (left) and the target (right) of the movement. Both lines were 1-pixel thick and appeared in red color over a white background. Also displayed was a mobile 1-pixel thick crosshair cursor, black in color, whose motion was controlled by the stylus. The tablet being used in absolute mode with a control-display gain of 1, the hand had to move 150mm from its home position for the crosshair to reach the target.

The participant was seated at a table supporting the Wacom tablet and the screen, with a viewing distance of about 50 cm. During warm-up trials the participants were allowed to optimize the orientation of the tablet in the horizontal plane to facilitate the execution of the required left-to-right movement, the tablet being often tilted counter-clockwise. On the tablet was secured a horizontal 8-mm thick plastic ruler, along which the stylus tip was to be slid, allowing a strictly one-dimensional hand movement. The ruler offered a mechanical stop at its left end so that the start position of the stylus was standardized to the nearest screen pixel. To help initial positioning, an OK message appeared on the screen when the crosshair coincided with the start line.

We developed our own software, using Lib USB, for tablet-data acquisition, to minimize display latency relative to tablet events and to exploit the full resolution of our input device (5080dpi). The tablet coordinates were translated into pixels using floating values to maximize visual-feedback accuracy. The tablet sampling rate was approximately 100 Hz (in the range 85-125 Hz).

Procedure and Movement Measurement Algorithms

The experiment consisted of 25 blocks of 15 movements, each block being run with a given set of instructions. All five instructions were presented in one order, ascending or descending, the order being reversed from one group of five blocks to the next. The experiment lasted about 40mn per participant, including 10min of warm up.

To begin each trial the participant immobilized the screen crosshair at the start line by positioning the stylus on the tablet at the ruler stop for a few seconds. When ready, the participant moved the stylus to the target position by sliding it against the ruler, finishing up with a dwell, then lifted the stylus and, after a few seconds rest, proceeded to the next trial.

The movement start point corresponded to the place and instant where the crosshair left its home position while exhibiting positive (rightward) acceleration. Determination of the movement *endpoint* in time and space is a more subtle issue and detailed explanations about our offline algorithm were part of the instructions received by the participants. We used two different criteria, depending on the instructions condition. For the max-speed condition, where accuracy was irrelevant, our algorithm would take as the movement endpoint the *first* zeroing-out or zero-crossing of instantaneous velocity, thus ignoring any subsequent episode of velocity, whether deliberate (a corrective sub-movement) or accidental (e.g., a mechanical rebound due to arm elasticity). For the other four conditions the movement endpoint was defined as the beginning of the last dwelling period in the kinematic record, meaning that the algorithm would take into account all corrective sub-movements, if any. The criterion for a dwell was the crosshair remaining stationary for at least 100ms at least 50mm away from the home position.

5.2. Results and Discussion

Inspection of the distributions of movement times revealed some skewness, especially in the max-speed condition, hence our recourse below to median movement time (still noted μ_T) as our central-trend statistic, in place of the mean.

Systematic Error, Variable Error

On average over all participants the constant error (μ_A - 150mm) was less than 1 screen pixel in all instructions conditions but one: in the max-speed condition we found a significant 5.5mm overshoot error (t_{15}=4.50, p<.0005), a small effect (3.7%) which we will leave aside below. Rather than constant error μ_A-D, it was obviously the *variable* error σ_A (and hence RVE=σ_A/μ_A) that was massively influenced, along with μ_T, by instructions.

Effect of Instructions on Movement Time and RVE.

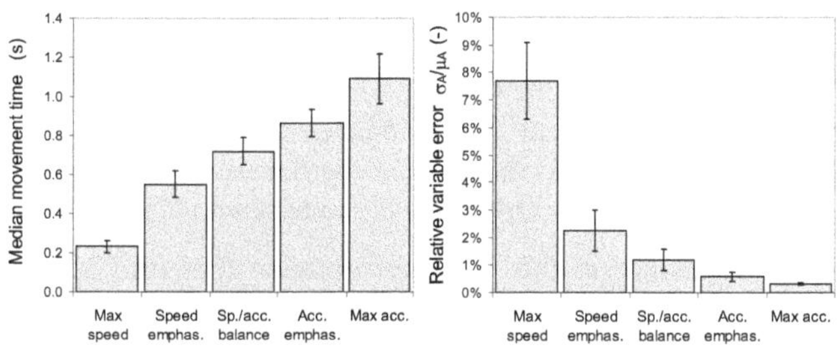

Figure 6. The effect of instructions manipulation on median μ_T and RVE, on average over our 16 participants, with 95% confidence intervals based on between-participant SDs.

With increasing emphasis on accuracy, μ_T lengthened about linearly and RVE decreased non-linearly (Fig. 6). Although the max-speed instructions imposed no constraint whatsoever on the spread of movement endpoints, RVE hardly reached 0.08 (or 8%), a finding reminiscent of Fitts' data (see Fig. 5).

Convex Front of Performance

Fig. 7 illustrates the trade-off between μ_T and RVE for one representative participant. Panel A plots all the participant's data points, one per trial block. The best fit is a power function, with quite some noise, hence a moderately impressive r^2 of .87. But let us see how assumption #4 of our resource-allocation theory—less-than-total resource exploitation—helped us exploit our data more thoroughly.

The participants were to minimize μ_T and RVE in differing proportions. Their data points may be likened with particles attracted to the West and South by two magnetic fields whose relative strengths are modulated by instructions. Viewing the scatter as a mixture of forerunning and dawdling particles, we simply assumed that the forerunners and the dawdlers were the data points under and above the curve.[3] If the resource pool is limited (Assumption #3) then forerunners must have been constrained by a hard wall—the very trade-off curve we are looking for, conceptually the borderline that separates in the graph the region of the *doable* (above the curve) from the region of the *undoable* (below). That hard wall must have prevented forerunners from spreading any further in the South-West direction. But there must be dawdlers (Assumption #4) affected by the hard-wall constraint to an attenuated extent. The data is quite consistent with this view. As shown in Fig. 7B, restricting the fit to the subset of forerunners improved the fit considerably (for this participant, from .87 to .97).

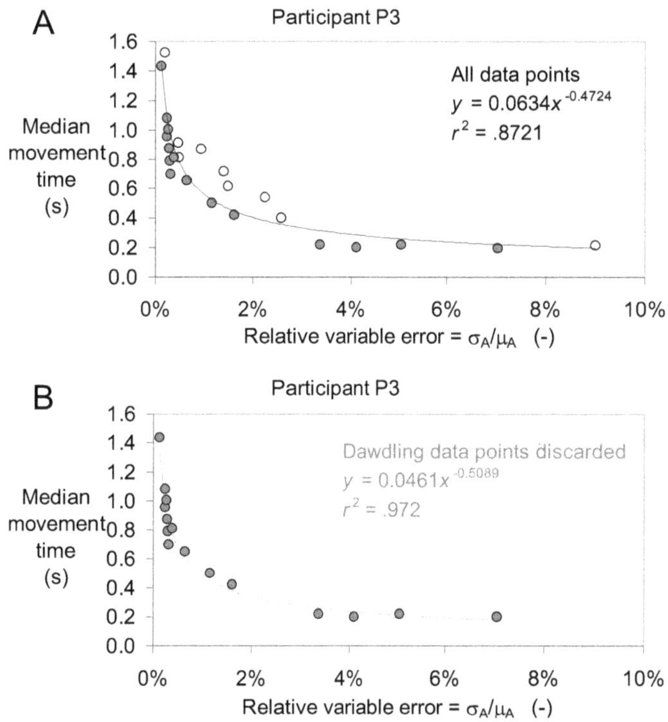

Figure 7. Convex front of performance. Panel A: a power curve is fitted to all the participant's data points; the data points under the curve (filled discs) are then selected. Panel B: a new power curve is fitted to the selected subset.

An improved fit of the power equation after elimination of dawdlers was observed in all 16 participants (Student t_{15}=8.83, p<.0001), the r^2 increasing on average from .852 to .972. We checked that, in contrast, restricting the fit to the data points resting above the first curve (i.e., selecting the dawdlers instead of the forerunners) did not improve the fit whatsoever, the r^2 changing on average over all participants from .852 to .853 (t_{15}=0.03, p=.97).

The data points that form the South-West quadrant of the convex hull of the scatter plot (shown as filled discs in Fig. 7A) are of special import: they characterize a participant's best performance. These data points must have had more than others their locations affected by resources limitations. In the rest of this report we will focus on this particular

[3] Thanks to Eric Lecolinet for suggesting this simple solution.

subset, which we call the *convex front* of performance, assumed to be the most informative about the location of the trade-off curve we are looking for.

Logarithmic, Exponential, and Power Fits

We tested the simple two-coefficient models that can accommodate the convex-down curvature evident in all our μ_T vs. *RVE* trade-off functions, the logarithmic, the exponential, and the power equation. Fitting the three candidate models to the full individual data sets (i.e., the 25 pairs of measures originating from the full set of trial blocks) resulted in the power model doing best in 10 cases (mean r^2=.853 over all participants), the exponential model doing best in four cases (mean r^2=.803) and the log model in two (mean r^2=.803). In general, the curvature was insufficient with the log and, most blatantly, the exponenttial equation. Fitting the three models again to the convex-front data, the power model was best for all but one of our 16 participants, namely Participant #11 (P11). The r^2 now ranged between .923 and .992 (on average r^2=.972, to be compared with r^2=.937 and r^2=.880 for the log and exponential model). Therefore we retained the power equation of Eq. 5 for modeling the trade-offs.[4]

A Closer Look at Individual Exponents: Evidence for a One-Coefficient Square-Root Relation

Thus, a simple power relation turned out to describe quite accurately the time/error trade-off in both Fitts' data and our own, despite our different experimental protocol. Most interestingly, the exponent p of the best-fitting power model was similar, considering the two scales conditions of Fitts' study that approximately corresponded to ours. In Fitts' data the exponent was -0.54 for D=10cm and -0.38 for D=20cm (Fig. 1); in our data, with D=15cm, the exponent was -0.47 on average. We further inquired into this issue by asking how the exponent varied with the goodness of fit and with the value taken by q, the other adjustable coefficient of Eq. 5 (see Fig. 8).

To reiterate, any individual participant produces a mixture of good and poor performance (assumption #4), but there is an infinity of ways of performing poorly and in principle only the best (convex-front) performance of that participant is informative. It should be realized that as one switches from a within- to a between-individual logic this argument works just the same. Different individuals being unequally able (or willing) to fully concentrate on a repetitive movement task, there is every reason to focus on the data of the best performers in one's quest for a consistent quantitative law. Bearing this in mind, a remarkable suggestion emerges from the data: first, the better the fit of the power model, the closer the exponent to -1/2 (Fig. 8A); second, the smaller the value of the participant's coefficient q (i.e., the better the performer, as explained in Section 4.2), the closer the exponent to -1/2 (Fig. 8B). Three individual estimates of the exponent diverged appreciably from -1/2, namely those delivered by participants P6, P8, and P11 (p=-0.60, -0.34, and -0.32, respectively), but these happened to be the sample's least credible estimates: P6 and P8 were participants for whom the power fit was distinctively worse than average (see Fig. 8A); as for P11, we can see in Fig. 8B that he ranked 15th/16 for performance, next to P8, who ranked last—a further reason to moderately trust P8's data.

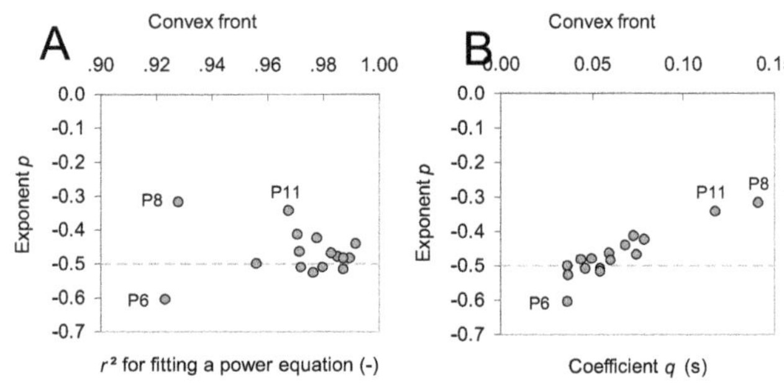

Figure 8. The exponent *p* of Eq. 5 plotted against (A) the r^2 of the power fit and (B) the value of coefficient *q*, indicative of resource-pool size. One point per individual participant.

Thus, focusing on the *best performance* (i.e., the convex front of performance) of our *best performers* (actually 13 of our 16 participants), we found that the trade-off of μ_T and *RVE* can be satisfactorily modeled in our data by a square root equation with a single adjustable constant:

$$\mu_T = q * RVE^{-1/2} \quad \text{or}$$

$$\mu_T = q / \mathrm{SQRT}(\sigma_A/\mu_A) \qquad (10)$$

where the multiplicative constant q is information about the amount of resources invested by the participant.

Constant Resource Pool and Variable Strategic Imbalance

An immediate implication of Eq. 10 is that the quantity $q = \mu_T$*SQRT(σ_A/μ_A) is conserved as the participants modulate their speed/accuracy strategy (Section 4.2). But this strategic imbalance can be quantified quite simply, as the variable ratio $SI = \mu_T$/SQRT(σ_A/μ_A) (see Section 4.3).

Fig. 9, which uses data from the same representative participant as Fig. 7, shows examples of the fit obtained with the one-coefficient model of Eq. 10 and of the within-individual conservation of q across the variation of μ_T. The orderly pattern of panel A was the rule. On average over our best 13 performers, Eq. 10 yielded r^2=.964 ($.889<r<.986$). This was significantly less than the r^2=.967 obtained with Eq. 5 (t_{12}=3.61, p=.002, one tailed), but the r^2 reduction (.003) was impressively small, given the sacrifice of one of the two free coefficients of Eq. 5.

Panel B displays a scatter plot showing no evidence of any correlation between q and μ_T. Despite a considerable 7-fold

[4] The μ_T vs. *RVE* relation involves two random variables neither of which is 'dependent' or 'independent'. In such a case the so-called standard major axis method of curve fitting is known to be preferable over traditional linear regression, which measures errors only along the vertical y axis [23]. Here both methods yielded nearly identical estimates (not surprisingly, given the very high correlations found in log-log plot between μ_T and *RVE* [23]), and so we did not depart from the ordinary least-square method.

variation, μ_T failed to exert any consistent influence on coefficient q. Indeed, considering our 13 reliable data sets, the slope of this relation (-0.0034s on average) did not significantly depart from zero (t_{12}=-1.42, p=.182, two-tailed).

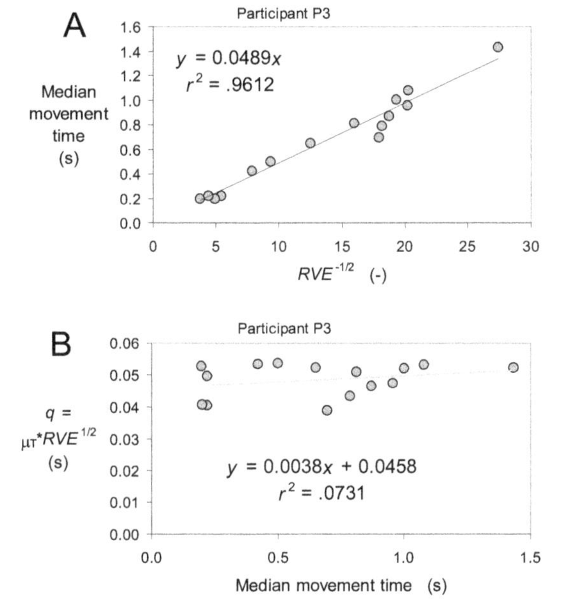

Figure 9. A representative example of (A) the fit of the one-free-coefficient model of Eq. 10 and (B) the approximate conservation of q across a seven-fold variation of μ_T.

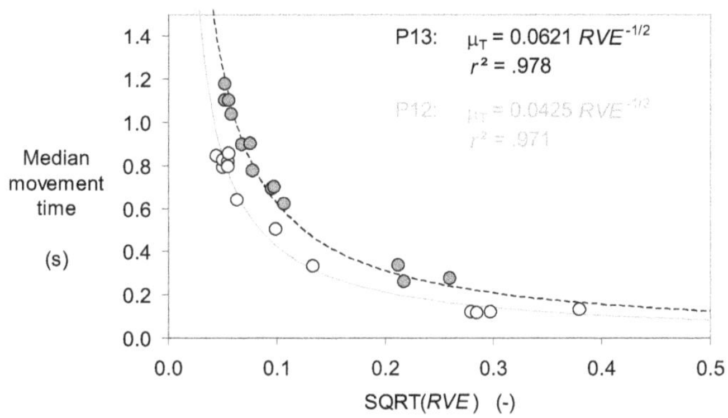

Figure 10. Comparing two individual trade-off curves.

Fig. 10 shows the trade-off curves of two individual participants whose q coefficients took distinctively different values. It is easy to see that P12 invested more resources in the task than did P13 (q=0.0425 and 0.0621, respectively). But the graph, by exhibiting different distributions of data points along their respective curves, also reveals that P12 and P13 had different *strategic preferences* for resource allocation. In response to our max-accuracy instructions P13 climbed his curve higher than P12 did his (SI_{max}=22.5 vs. 18.9), while in response to our max-speed instructions he did not explore his curve as far down as P12 did his (SI_{min}= 1.07 vs. 0.35). Thus the comparison delivers two separate pieces of evidence: beside the fact that P12 invested more resources than P13, he was more speed-biased.

IMPLICATIONS FOR HCI AND BASIC RESEARCH

In this paper we have tried to formulate with some rigor one specific sense in which Fitts' law is a speed/accuracy trade-off. The data show that indeed the law can be recast as a trade-off between two random variables, the time taken to reach a target and the relative spread of movement endpoints. Note that the trade-off we have described involves time and inaccuracy, rather than speed and accuracy. Whether Fitts' law can be recast, strictly speaking, in terms of speed and accuracy remains an open question, with some non-trivial difficulties given the multiple possible definitions of each of these two terms.

One potentially important outcome of this research is the suggestion that the mathematical description of Fitts' law can be simplified, without sacrificing much modeling precision, to a square-root equation with a single adjustable constant. For both basic-researchers and practitioners, the fewer the free coefficients of a model, the better. Based on our work currently in progress, our conjecture is that it is only for optimal scales of pointing movement that Fitts' law can be this much simplified.

The resource-allocation approach to Fitts' law helps understand that to obtain a complete understanding of target-acquisition performance we need both an intensive and a qualitative characterization. If the intensive aspect is explicitly addressed by the throughput, it seems that the information-theoretic framework has little to say about the qualitative aspect. The fact that the speed/accuracy balance is variable has been considered a worrisome complication calling for a certain correction—the substitution of effective to nominal width [1,12]—so as to end up with a single synthetic measure of performance. The correction being done, the throughput is quite insensitive to substantial variations of the speed/accuracy imbalance [4,12]. But the fact that the throughput (just like the coefficient q of our trade-off analysis) is conserved through *SI* variations does *not* mean that the latter are unimportant—a conclusion that a rapid reading of [12] might suggest. The cognitive stance controlled by speed/accuracy instructions, which strongly modulates the balance of movement times and endpoint spreads, is indeed an important factor, which does not influence throughput, but does influence another aspect of performance, the *SI*.

Reducing the data of a Fitts' law experiment to just a throughput measure, as recommended in [24], is indeed convenient for a Fitts' law practitioner but there is a cost. Suppose that, comparing two interaction techniques A and B, one finds more throughput with technique A in the presence of more errors. Assuming an appropriate adjustment for errors, the conclusion that A outperforms B may be correct but a full half of the story has been erased by the adjustment procedure. In some research contexts, especially those where safety matters critically, it may be very useful to not ignore that different interface arrangements or interaction techniques may induce different speed/accuracy imbalances in their users.

The resource allocation and the information theoretic approaches are certainly not incompatible with each other, as recognized in practice by Fitts and Radford [4], who (although they did not theorize on strategic imbalance) did manipulate speed/accuracy instructions. The right-hand side of Eq. 10 rewritten as $\log_2(\mu_T)$ less a constant = -½ $\log_2(\sigma_A/\mu_A)$ can be viewed to display bits of information. But the left-hand side of this equation, as already hinted above, is likely to call for a model involving joules of energy. Thus, one intriguing outcome of the present analysis is the suggestion that information theory should certainly participate in, but probably will not suffice to wholly account for Fitts' law.

6. ACKNOWLEGMENTS

This research has been supported by *Institut Telecom*, with a Carnot post-doctoral fellowship to HBO and a *Futur et ruptures* PhD grant to STP. We warmly thank Eric Lecolinet, Olivier Rioul, and Vincent Hayward for many stimulating discussions. Special thanks to the anonymous CHI program committee member and reviewers for an exceptionally thorough and constructive review.

7. REFERENCES

1. Crossman, E.R.F.W. (1956). The measurement of perceptual load. Unpublished PhD thesis, Univ. Birmingham, England.
2. Fitts, P.M. (1954). The information capacity of the human motor system in controlling the amplitude of movement. J. Exp. Psychol., 47, 381-391. Reprint: J. Exp. Psychol.: Gen., 1992, 121, 262-269.
3. Fitts, P.M. & Peterson, J.R. (1964). Information capacity of discrete motor responses. J. Exp. Psychol., 67, 103-112.
4. Fitts, P.M. & Radford, B.K. (1966). Information capacity of discrete motor responses under different cognitive sets. J. Exp. Psychol., 71, 475-482.
5. Guiard, Y. (2001). Disentangling relative from absolute movement amplitude in Fitts' law experiments. CHI'2001. New York: ACM Press, 315-316.
6. Guiard, Y. (2009). The problem of consistency in the design of Fitts' law experiments: Consider either target distance and width or movement form and scale. Proc. CHI'2009. New York: Sheridan Press, 1908–1918.
7. Guiard, Y. & Ferrand, T., 1998. Effets de gamme et optimum de difficulté spatiale dans une tâche de pointage de Fitts. Science et Motricité, 34, 19-25.
8. Guiard, Y. & Olafsdottir, H.B. (2010). What is a zero-difficulty movement? A scale of measurement issue in Fitts' law research. Submitted manuscript. http://hal.archives-ouvertes.fr/.
9. Hoffmann, E.R. (1996). The use of dimensional analysis in movement studies. J. Motor Behav., 28 (2), 113-123.
10. MacKenzie, I.S. (1991). Fitts' law as a performance model in human-computer interaction. PhD thesis available online: http://www.yorku.ca/mack/phd.html.
11. MacKenzie, I.S. (1989). A note on the information-theoretic basis for Fitts' law. J. Motor Behav., 21, 323-330.
12. MacKenzie, I.S. (1992). Fitts' law as a research and design tool in human-computer interaction. Human-Computer Interaction, 7, 91-139.
13. MacKenzie, I.S. & Isokoski, P. (2008). Fitts' throughput and the speed-accuracy tradeoff. Proc. CHI'2008. New York: Sheridan, 1633–1636.
14. Meehl, P.E. (1997). The problem is epistemology, not statistics. In L.L. Harlow et A. (Eds.), What if there were no significance tests? (pp. 393-425). Mahwah, NJ: Erlbaum. http://www.tc.umn.edu/~pemeehl/169ProblemIsEpistemology.pdf.
15. Meyer, D.E., Smith, J.E.K., Kornblum, S., Abrams, R.A., & Wright, C.E. (1990). Speed-accuracy trade-offs in aimed movements: Toward a theory of rapid voluntary action. In M. Jeannerod (Ed.), Attention and performance XIII (pp. 173-226). Hillsdale, NJ: Erlbaum.
16. Norman, D.A., & Bobrow, D.G. (1975). On data-limited and resource-limited processes. Cognit. Psychol., 7, 44-64.
17. Norman, D.A., & Bobrow, D.G. (1976). On the analysis of performance operating characteristics. Psychol. Rev., 83, 508-510.
18. Plamondon, R., & Alimi, A.M. (1997). Speed/accuracy trade-offs in target-directed movements. Behav. Brain Sci., 20, 279-349.
19. Rosenbaum, D.A. & Gregory, R.W. (2002). Development of a method for measuring moving-related effort: Biomechanical considerations and implications for Fitts' Law. Exp. Brain Res., 142, 365-373.
20. Roberts, S., & Pashler, H. (2000). How persuasive is a good fit? A comment on theory testing. Psychol. Rev., 107, 358-367.
21. Schmidt, R.A., Zelaznik, H.N., Hawkins, B., Frank, J.S., & Quinn, J.T. (1979). Motor-output variability: A theory for the accuracy of rapid motor acts. Psychol. Rev., 86, 415-451.
22. Shannon, C.E. (1948). A Mathematical Theory of Communic-ation. Bell System Techn. J., 27, 379-423 and 623-656.
23. Smith, R.J. (2009). Use and misuse of the reduced major axis for line-fitting. Amer. J. Phys. Anthropol., 140, 476-486.
24. Soukoreff, R. W., & MacKenzie, I.S. (2004). Towards a standard for pointing device evaluation: Perspectives on 27 years of Fitts' law research in HCI. IJHCS, 61, 751-789.
25. Soukoreff, R.W., and MacKenzie, I.S. (2009) An informatic rationale for the speed-accuracy tradeoff. Proc. SMC'2009. New York: IEEE, 2890-2896.
26. Stevens, S.S. (1946). On the theory of scales of measurement. Science, 103, No. 2684, 677-680.

8. APPENDIX: GLOSSARY OF BASIC VARIABLES

Task Geometry Measures		Physical Dimension	Unit(*)
D	Target distance	[L]	(cm)
W	Target tolerance or width	[L]	(cm)
D/W	Relative target distance (*RTD*)	[-]	
W/D	Relative target tolerance (*RTT*)	[-]	(%)
Elemental Movement Measures			
T	Movement time	[T]	(s)
A	Movement amplitude	[L]	(cm)
$E = A - D$	Endpoint error	[L]	(cm)
Movement Statistics			
μ_T	Mean or median movement time	[T]	(s)
μ_A	Mean or median movement amplitude	[L]	(cm)
$\mu_A - D$	Constant error	[L]	(cm)
σ_A	*SD* of mov. amplitude = variable error	[L]	(cm)
μ_A/σ_A	Relative movement amplitude (*RMA*)	[-]	
σ_A/μ_A	Relative variable error (*RVE*)	[-]	(%)

(*) *Note.* W being much smaller than D, it is convenient to express as a percentage relative target tolerance (*RTT=W/D*), but not its inverse relative target distance (*RTD=D/W*). Likewise, σ_A being much smaller than μ_A, it is convenient to express *RVE*, but not *RMA*, as a percentage [8].

Benchmarking Pointing Techniques with Distractors: Adding a Density Factor to Fitts' Pointing Paradigm

Renaud Blanch[1], **Michaël Ortega**[2]

[1]UJF-Grenoble 1 / UPMF-Grenoble 2 / Grenoble-INP / [2]CNRS / INRIA
Laboratoire d'Informatique de Grenoble, UMR 5217
F-38041, Grenoble, France
blanch@imag.fr, ortega@imag.fr

ABSTRACT
Fitts' pointing paradigm is widely used to conduct controlled experiments and to evaluate new interaction techniques enhancing target acquisition. Many of them change the behavior of the cursor according to various inputs, most notably the positions of potential targets. We propose to extend Fitts' paradigm in order to challenge those techniques with *distractors* (i.e., potential targets which are not the goal of the user) in a controlled manner. To reduce variability, we add a single new factor to the paradigm, the *distractor density*. We specify a distractors distribution, fully determined by this factor together with those of Fitts' task, aimed at reducing bias toward a specific technique. We also propose a preliminary extension of Fitts' law to take account of the sensitivity to the density of distractors as well as of the task difficulty. In an experiment, we compare five existing pointing techniques, and show that this extended protocol enables contrasted comparisons between them.

Author Keywords
Distractors, Fitts' law, Fitts' paradigm, pointing.

ACM Classification Keywords
H.5.2 Information Interfaces and Presentation (e.g., HCI): User Interfaces – *Evaluation/methodology, Input devices and strategies, Theory and methods.*

General Terms
Experimentation, performance, standardization, theory.

INTRODUCTION
Selecting a target by pointing is one of the most frequent tasks performed in graphical user interfaces (GUIs). This task is well modeled in the physical world by Fitts' law [12], which also holds in virtual worlds [13]. Many interaction techniques have been proposed to facilitate target acquisition in GUIs: Balakrishnan [5] offers a survey of such techniques proposed up to 2004, and new ways to enhance pointing are still regularly discovered.

Most of those enhancements rely on the system knowledge of potential target positions. This knowledge is exploited to alter the cursor behavior, either by changing its activation area (e.g., [20, 21, 28, 15]); by expanding potential targets(e.g., [30, 26]); by adapting the control-display ratio to make it "sticky" (e.g., [28, 7, 6]); or by adding "force fields" attracting the cursor (e.g., [2, 3]).

Those techniques are theoretically appealing but difficult to fully evaluate. The sole established experimental protocol shared by the HCI community is derived from Fitts' experimental paradigm. As depicted in Figure 1, it consists in the presentation of 1D pointing tasks characterized by two parameters (its amplitude (A) and its target size (W)). This experimental paradigm is adapted to conduct controlled experimental studies because it introduces only two independent variables. One limitation of such evaluations is obvious: they do not consider distractors. As reported by Ahlström *et al.* [3], in the absence of distractors, techniques such as *semantic pointing* [7] or *object pointing* [19] are tested at their optima.

The solution adopted by most researchers to evaluate the impact of distractors on their interaction technique is to conduct a less formalized experiment based on a more realistic interaction scenario. We will review some of those experiments in a later section. Let us highlight some limitations of this common practice:

- Since the design of experiments is geared towards mimicking the real world, too many independent variables are introduced and they can not be extensively explored. The analysis and the interpretation of the results are thus difficult to conduct.
- Such designs are often underspecified because they involve complex or random choices which are hard, if not impossible, to document using few words. This leads to experiments which are not reproducible.
- A corollary of the previous item is that a new experiment is often proposed for each new technique. The evaluations are then not comparable.
- The last shortcoming of such experiments is that they are designed specifically to evaluate the proposed technique and their design could be biased to favor the technique [4], either consciously or not.

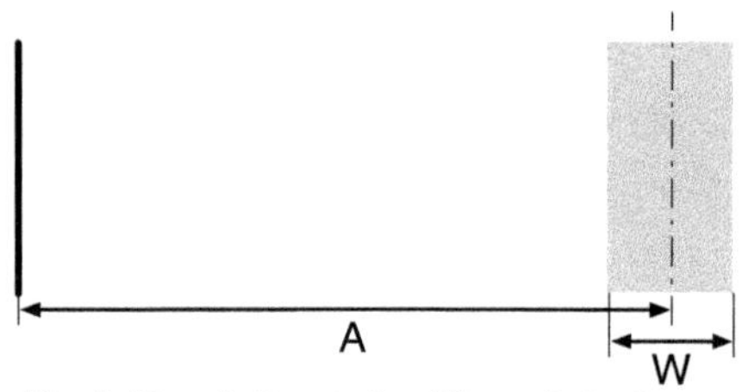

Figure 1. Fitts' 1D pointing task. The task is characterized by its amplitude (*A*) and its target width (*W*).

Our main motivation in this paper is to propose a novel experimental paradigm to address the lack of an unified way to evaluate new pointing techniques. This experimental setup could then be used as a benchmark to compare those techniques in presence of distractors. We bootstrap the process by comparing various techniques from the literature.

We first review how pointing techniques have been evaluated regarding their sensitivity to distractors. We then present the proposed experimental paradigm and how it has been designed. We also propose an extension to Fitts' law that considers the influence of distractors on performance. In the last section, this paradigm is used as a benchmark to compare different pointing techniques from the litterature.

RELATED WORK

As mentioned in the introduction, new interaction techniques enhancing target acquisition have been proposed for a while. We focus only on a set of techniques that are representative of how distractors have been handled in the past.

First, it should be noted that some consequent efforts have already been invested to unify the evaluation methodology of pointing devices or techniques and to spread those best practices into the community (e.g., the ISO standard for evaluating pointing devices [11], the recommendations of Soukoreff and MacKenzie [27] and of Zhai [29]). We do not propose "yet another framework" to evaluate pointing techniques. We propose a way to challenge techniques with distractors in a controlled manner, and this extension to the Fitts' pointing task can then be easily integrated into existing evaluation frameworks that do not currently handle the issue of distractors. The results of the experiments conducted using this paradigm can of course be evaluated using established methodologies.

Some authors have simply ignored the problem of distractors and have stuck to the established Fitts' protocol to evaluate their techniques (e.g., *semantic pointing* [7]). In this case, the technique is then evaluated in the optimal configuration: a single target known by the system. In a first experiment, the *object pointing* technique [19] is also evaluated using Fitts' paradigm. Since the cursor jumps to the closest target, it leads to a quasi-constant pointing time (i.e., the time needed to press the button). In a second experiment, the technique is evaluated in a more realistic 2D setup including distractors. Its performance is then comparable with the performance of normal pointing. Unfortunately, the 2D setup is weakly described and is impossible to reproduce.

Some authors (e.g., Keyson [22] or Worden *et al.* [28]) have addressed the issue of distractors by stressing their techniques with a worst case scenario. This illustrates that having the technique and the experimental protocol designed by the same person can introduce a bias [4], either against or in favor of the technique. While being particularly fair, this methodology has a drawback: it tests the technique for a single configuration of distractors and thus does not provide insights on its sensitivity to the amount of distractors.

Finally, other authors tested their techniques with varying distributions of distractors. The setup used to evaluate *ninja cursor* [23] is based on a "pseudo-random distribution" of distractors, presumably uniform, across the screen. They tested their technique in the presence of 1, 100 and 400 targets. Chapuis *et al.* evaluated their *DynaSpot* technique [10] with a setup proposed by Grossman and Balakrishnan for the evaluation of their *bubble cursor* technique [15]. This layout is not totally documented but its idea is to control the density of the distractors while distributing them pseudo-randomly on the path between the start of the movement toward the target and around the target itself. In those papers, the sensitivity to distractors is evaluated using this density as a factor.

We also believe that the density of distractors is the relevant factor to consider when testing the sensitivity of interaction techniques to the presence of distractors. We back up this claim in the next section.

POINTING TASK WITH DISTRACTORS

Our goal is to provide a pointing task that will challenge pointing techniques with distractors in a less biased as possible manner, and in a way that allow reproducible experiments. We want to characterize the distractors distribution by as few independent variables as possible, in order to ease the statistical analysis of the results.

In this section, we first formalize why the distractor density is the factor that should be added to the task parameterization and to the analysis of experimental results. We then present the pointing task composed of a target and several distractors, give its parametrization, and provide its design rationale.

Density as a Significant Factor

As seen in the Related Work section, researchers are aware that the presence of distractors impacts pointing techniques [23, 10, 15]. When they try to study this impact, there is a consensus among them to use the distractor density as the relevant factor to analyze how the performance is impacted by the presence of distractors.

This can be justified in an *ad hoc* manner for some techniques. For the *bubble cursor* and *object pointing*, a density of 1 (i.e., no empty space between distractors) makes the techniques identical to a normal pointing. On the other hand, a density tending towards 0 (i.e., no distractor at all) makes the target selection almost instantaneous regardless of the difficulty of the task. For *semantic pointing*, a density of 1 means that the motor scale is modified uniformly along the path toward the target and inside the target itself, and so no improvement should be observed (the index of difficulty in motor and visual space are equal). On the other hand, a density of 0 should lead to the improvements reported by Blanch *et al.* [7]. A careful analysis of other techniques should lead to similar conclusions.

A more general justification of the role that the distractor density plays can be suggested by analyzing the pointing task from an information theory point of view. The "room for improvement" in pointing tasks has been previously analyzed (e.g., by Blanch *et al.* [7]) as the mismatch between the abstract selection task —e.g., selecting 1 icon among the 32 icons on the desktop— and the actual pointing task — pointing at one of the 32×32 pixels of that icon among the 1600×1200 pixels of the screen. The former involves providing $\log_2(32) = 5$ bits to the system whereas the later consists in providing $\log_2\left(\frac{1600\times1200}{32\times32}\right) \approx 11$ bits[1]. Finding a way for not providing those $(11-5=)$ 6 extra bits is roughly the goal of all recent pointing techniques.

The *density of distractors* (ρ) gives a measure of this mismatch: $\rho = 0$ means that only the target is present —the abstract task is then a 0 bit task and the mismatch is maximal; on the other hand, $\rho = 1$ means that the space is paved with targets —the abstract and actual tasks are reunited and there is no room left for improvement using only the knowledge of the potential target positions.

The *de facto* manner authors have expressed sensitivity to distractors, the quick analysis of particular techniques, and finally the thought experiment proposed above' lead to the same conclusion: the *distractor density* is a factor that should be used to test the efficiency of pointing techniques.

Task Parameterization

A pointing task consists in a target whose size and position make the task more or less difficult. To add distractors to this task in a reproducible manner, their layout has to be specified as a function of the target geometry and of the *distractor density*. We present our proposed distribution of the distractors, explain how it is parametrized, and document the choices made while designing it.

Target Parameterization

Fitts' experimental protocol parametrizes a pointing task with 2 independent variables. The *amplitude* (A) of the task and its *width* (W) (see Figure 1 for a 1D pointing task) have long been used as factors. However, performance in *movement time* (MT) is always analyzed as function of the *index of difficulty* (ID) using Fitts' law [12]:

$$MT = a + b \times ID, \quad (1)$$

with ID expressed using Shannon formulation as advocated by MacKenzie [24]):

$$ID = \log_2\left(\frac{A}{W} + 1\right). \quad (2)$$

[1] This is not the Fitts' index of difficulty of an actual pointing task, but an upper bound of it.

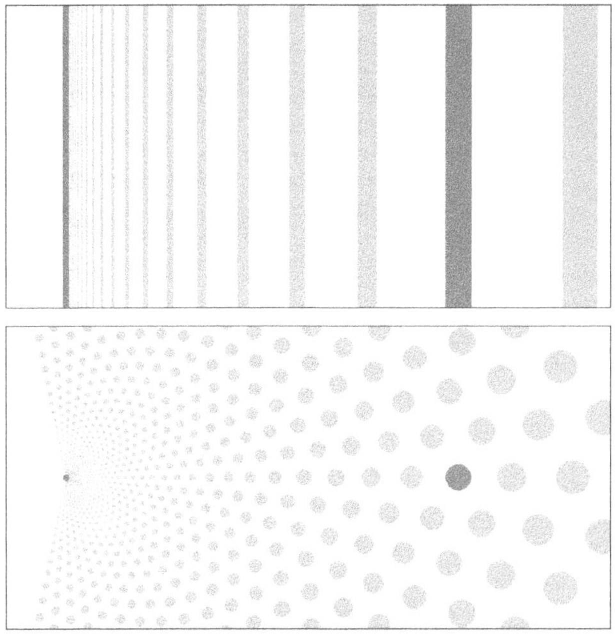

Figure 2. Self-similar tasks with distractors ($ID = 4, \rho = 0.25$). 1D (top) and 2D (bottom) tasks; distractors are grey, home is blue (left), target is red (right).

Guiard advocates for a parametrization of the task by its "form" and "scale", i.e., ID and A [17, 18]. This parametrization is formally equivalent to the use of A and W because ID, A and W are linked by Equation (2). Once ID and A are chosen, W can be computed by expressing W as a function of A and ID:

$$W = \frac{A}{2^{ID} - 1}. \quad (3)$$

As explained by Guiard, using ID and A as factors suppresses a bias widespread in the pointing experiments (namely, that high IDs are correlated with large As). We decided to use this parameterization of the target, but the distractor parameterization presented below still holds as soon as the target is specified by whichever means.

Distractors Parametrization

A question remains: given a *distractor density* (ρ), how to choose the layout of the distractors, i.e., their position and size? There are a lot of possible answers to this question. Adding as few new factors as possible is a strong requirement: the more factors are used, the more experimental trials will be needed to cover the cross product of their variation ranges. Our goal is to add the minimal number of factors that makes it possible to study the effect of distractors density. Since ρ should at least be added, we propose to stick with this minimal addition. The layout of the distractors should then be totally determined by the three factors: ID, A and ρ.

We propose a 1D layout, and since Fitts' law 2D generalization [25, 1, 16] is often used to evaluate pointing techniques in GUIs, we also provide a 2D generalization of this layout. Figure 2 illustrates those layouts with $ID = 4$ and $\rho = 0.25$

for 1D (top) and 2D (bottom) tasks. The main characteristics of the distractors are: a uniform index of difficulty equal to the target *ID* (they all have a form similar to the target modulo a scale and a rotation centered at the origin); and a uniform spatial distribution (the scaling factor between to successive distractors is constant, which makes the task self-similar). The actual 1D and 2D layout specifications are given in Appendixes.

Design Rationale

The design space of distractors layout for a given density is very large. We had to make several choices to propose the layouts presented above. We discuss here the main alternatives we faced and the rationale behind the choices we made.

"Realistic" vs. Random vs. Uniform Distribution

The first question is *should the distribution of distractors be "realistic"?*, i.e., try to mimic layouts commonly found on the desktop (e.g., as done by Ahlström *et al.* to evaluate their pointing techniques [3]). We excluded this approach because it is hard to design a "realistic" layout that can be parametrized with a single factor ρ. Choosing a single kind of layout would certainly introduce a bias toward particular techniques. Conversely, multiplying the situations to account for the diversity of reality would introduce too many variables that would make the results analysis harder.

The next question is *should some kind of randomness be introduced in the layout?*, like others have done (e.g, [15, 23]). The first problem with this approach is that real randomness leads to very disparate situations that can be properly compensated only by increasing the number of trials. For this reason, authors are often tempted to "control" the randomness (examples of such manipulation found in the literature include: ensuring that distractors do not overlap; ensuring that distractors are at a given distance from the target; ensuring a kind of uniformity of spatial distribution). The goal behind the introduction of controlled randomness is often to recreate "realistic" layouts. The produced layouts share their drawbacks (potential bias, hard to control). They are likely to be difficult to reproduce because the way randomness is introduced and controlled is hard to document.

Our final choice for a uniform distribution of the distractors is mainly backed up by the drawbacks of the alternatives but also because it is fully determinist, thus easy to reproduce. This distribution does not look "realistic" because it is very regular, but real settings often present regularities.

Equally Spaced in Space vs. in Scale

The most obvious way to distribute distractors uniformly is to use distractors having a *constant size* identical to the target and to choose a *constant step in space* to distribute them. Figure 3 presents such layouts in 1D. We have rejected this idea in favor of a *constant ID* identical to the target and a *constant step in scale*. This choices emerged while trying to solve an issue of the constant size layout. This issue is visible in Figure 3: the task at the top has a global distractor density $\rho \approx 0.31$ wile the task at the bottom has a global

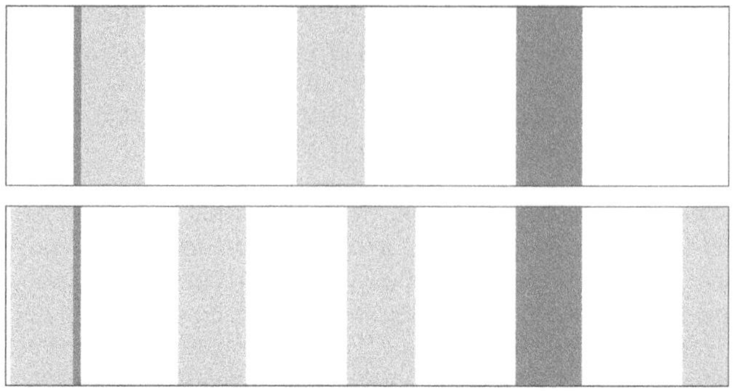

Figure 3. Evenly distributed equal-width distractors ($ID = 3$). Same local density (two distractors between the start and the target, $\rho_L \approx 0.36$) in spite of two very different global densities: $\rho \approx 0.31$ (top) and $\rho = 0.4$ (bottom).

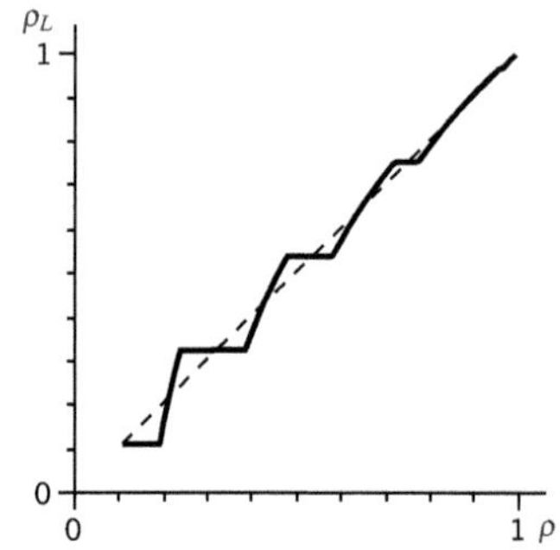

Figure 4. Local density ρ_L vs. nominal density ρ ($ID = 2.5$).

distractor density $\rho = 0.4$. However, on both paths between the start of the task and the middle of the target, exactly two distractors are present. On those paths, the proportion of space occupied by distractors is thus the same. This local density ρ_L is ≈ 0.36. The difference with the nominal ρ is $\approx +16.1\%$ for the first task and $\approx -11\%$ for the second one. Figure 4 illustrates the gap between ρ_L and ρ. The step-like shape of the curve is due to a quantization effect: different values of ρ lead to the same number of distractors on the path to the target and thus to the same ρ_L. It is likely that pointing techniques will mainly be sensitive to ρ_L rather than to ρ, and thus using ρ as a factor will probably lead to a substantial loss of statistical significance.

To confirm this hypothesis, we ran a pilot study in which a pointing technique presumably sensitive to ρ, namely *semantic pointing* [7], is tested using the constant size 1D layout. We used a single $ID = 3$, two differents $A \in \{511, 1023\}$ and 9 densities in the range $[2/15 \approx 0.13, 2/3 \approx 0.67]$ chosen at the angular points of the ρ_L vs. ρ function in order to maximize the differences between ρ_L and ρ. Two subjects performed a total of 360 trials (20 times each combination of factors). Figure 5 shows the movement time *MT* vs. the nominal density ρ on the left and vs. the local density ρ_L on the right. The similarity between the *MT* vs. ρ plot (Figure 5 left) and the ρ_L vs. ρ plot (Figure 4) is not an accident. Modeling *MT* by a linear combination of ρ and ρ_L confirms that the ρ_L parameter explains significantly the *MT* variations ($t = 3.09, p = 0.0022$) whereas ρ is rejected as a significant parameter ($t = 0{,}08$).

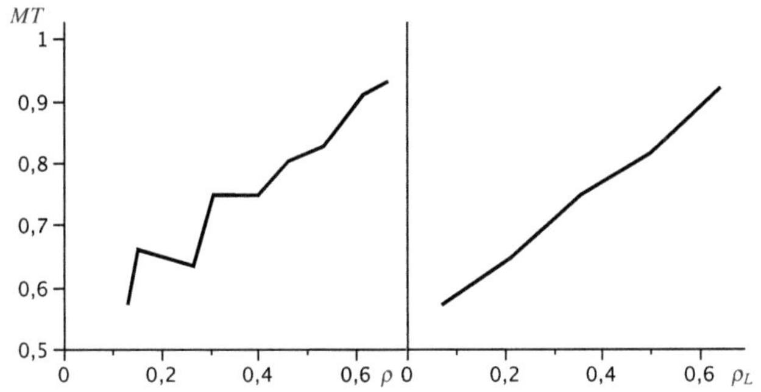

Figure 5. Semantic pointing movement time (MT in seconds) vs. nominal density ρ (left) and local density ρ_L (right) ($ID = 3$).

This pilot study shows that the naïve *constant size* approach suffers from a serious drawback: the ρ factor does not match the parameter that explains the performance. Analyzing the results would then require to transform the ρ factor into the ρ_L parameter using a non-trivial function which also depends on the *ID*. This would result in the introduction of correlated factors, which is not desirable. We have conducted this pilot study with a 1D layout, but the 2D version would probably lead to similar results since it is subject to a similar quantization at the origin.

Using the *constant ID* layout is a solution to this quantization artifact. Since it is self-similar, the distractors size tends toward zero at the origin of the task, and the local density of distractors is theoretically equal to the nominal ρ. The drawback is that it theoretically introduces an infinity of distractors. Stopping the construction when their size becomes smaller than 1 pixel (the smallest visible target on a screen) solves this issue in practice.

Other side effects of the self-similarity of the layout is that a task presents a single *ID* to the subject, and that distractor size distribution is not farther to the reality than the *constant size* layout (lots of small targets, few big targets [9]). Still, the main property of this distractor layout is the ability to accurately control the distractor density on the path of the pointing movement.

TOWARDS AN EXTENSION TO FITTS' LAW

Once a new factor is added to the parametrization of the pointing task, one can wonder how it will affect the movement time and how to account for it in Fitts' law. It obviously depends on how each specific pointing technique will take advantage of the sparseness of the task to ease the pointing but we can try some reasoning here.

As stated in the previous section, the *density of distractors* characterizes the mismatch between the abstract task —one icon among 32— and the actual pointing task —one of the pixels of the icon among the whole screen. Having a task that paves the space with distractors ($\rho = 1$) leaves no room for improvement, but if the space was only half full ($\rho = .5$), all potential targets could be made twice as big without overlapping. That would make the task easier and reduce its *ID* by roughly one bit[2]. If we reduce further the density of the task, e.g., $\rho = .25$, targets could be made four time bigger and *ID* would then decrease by 2 bits. If we define the *index of sparseness*[3] (*IS*) by:

$$IS = \log_2 \frac{1}{\rho}, \tag{4}$$

we see that it gives an approximation of the number of bits that could be gained on *ID* (e.g., $IS = 0$ for $\rho = 1$, $IS = 1$ for $\rho = .5$, $IS = 2$ for $\rho = .25$, etc.) If we hypothesize that an optimal technique could reduce *ID* by *IS* bits, the *movement time* for that optimal technique would then be:

$$MT_{opt} = a + b \times (ID - IS). \tag{5}$$

In practice however, it is more likely that different techniques will take advantage of the sparseness of the task differently. This could be measured by introducing a third parameter in Fitts' law:

$$MT = a + b \times ID - c \times IS, \tag{6}$$

where, as advocated by Zhai [29], *a* (resp. *b*) reflects the non-informational (resp. informational) aspect of input performance; and *c* quantifies the sensitivity of the technique to the presence of distractors. In this extended law, a low value for *c* means that the technique does not behave differently in the presence or in the absence of distractors (e.g., presumably the plain old mouse) and then Equation (6) falls back to the standard Fitts' law given by Equation (1). On the other hand, a value for *c* close to *b* means that the technique takes as much as possible advantage of the sparseness of the task and the law falls back to the limit case given in Equation (5).

Given the extended law formalized by Equation (6), pointing techniques could then be compared according the 2 parameters recommended by Zhai, together with a third parameter:

- *a*, the *intercept*, that measures the non-informational part of the performance;
- $1/b$, the *throughput*, that measures its sensitivity to the form of the task characterized by its *ID*; and
- c/b, the *sensitivity to distractors*, that measure its ability to make the most of the sparseness of the task, and to reduce *ID* by that proportion of *IS*.

We are aware that the extension of Fitts' law proposed in Equation (6) is only backed by reasoning and not by any actual fit of data. We acknowledge that *ID* and *IS* do probably interact, and that distractors play a role more complex than simply perturbing the pointing techniques by also modifying the perception of the task by the user. That is why we refer to Equation (6) as a *first step towards an extension to Fitts' law*, and leave further investigation in this direction for future works.

[2] The more A/W is bigger than 1 (i.e., the larger the *ID* is), the more exact is this approximation.

[3] We choose *index of sparseness* rather than *index of density* (its opposite) to avoid a possible confusion of the acronyms (*IS* vs. *ID*).

Figure 6. 2D feedbacks of *rake cursor* (left) and *Bubble cursor* (right) for the task $ID = 3$, $\rho = 0.25$.

BENCHMARKING POINTING TECHNIQUES

Having defined a pointing task from the three factors: index of difficulty (ID), task amplitude (A), and distractors density (ρ), we can use it to test the sensitivity of various techniques to those factors. Here we compare five interaction techniques: the *raw pointing* (RP) with a cursor, the *semantic pointing* (SP) technique [7], the *bubble cursor* (BC) technique [15], the *DynaSpot* (DS) technique [10], and the *rake cursor* (RC) technique [8].

This set of techniques is rather arbitrary, but our goal is to cover various strategies used to facilitate pointing: modifying the control-display ratio (SP), using a supplemental input channel (RC), or modifying the cursor activation area (BC and DS). A criterion that also motivated our selection is that those techniques are described in their respective papers with enough details to allow their precise reproduction, which is unfortunately not as common as it should be.

Pointing Technique Definition

Testing various pointing techniques made explicit the lack of definition of what is a pointing technique. We propose the following one: a pointing technique consists of handling *inputs*, providing a *picking function*, and updating a *feedback*.

Receiving relative movements from the physical pointing device and transforming it to a cursor position is the minimal *input handling*. It can involve more complex processing (e.g., for RC, mixing the mouse input and the gaze input) to maintain an internal state used by the other parts of the pointing techniques.

The *picking function* uses this internal state to compute the pixel activated when the user depresses the button of the pointing device. The picking function can be as simple as returning the cursor position (e.g., RP and SP). It can also do more complex processing such as triggering a spatial search to find the target closest to the cursor and returning the coordinates of a pixel located inside (e.g., BC).

The *feedback* usually serves the role of making the internal state of the technique and its picking function observable. It should make its behavior predictable. The minimal feedback consist of displaying a cursor arrow on the screen. It can also display the cursor activation area (BC, DS) or several arrow cursors (RC). The feedback of the BC and RC techniques is illustrated in Figure 6 for a 2D pointing task setup. Since the cursor can be outside the target that will be selected, some techniques also provide a highlight to make it observable to the user (BC, DS). In our implementation, we added this highlight to every technique because we think that its presence can affect the performance of pointing.

Implementation

The implementation we used to conduct our study is made available to the community[4] and can either serve as a reference implementation, or it can be reused as is. It includes the implementation of the techniques compared in the experiment, the implementation of the distractors layouts and the framework that drives the experiment.

Experiment

Tasks

The participants had to perform successive 2D pointing tasks. They had to move the standard cursor inside a start area (a blue disc on the middle-left of the screen), rest there for about 0.5 s. After this delay, a trial consisting of grey distractors and a red target (Figure 2 bottom) was presented and the participant had to click the target. The direction of the movement was always from the left to the right, and the participants had to come back to the start area after each trial. After each block, their error rates were displayed and they were encouraged to conform to a nominal 4% error rate by speeding up or slowing down.

Conditions and Procedure

The five *techniques* (RP, SP, BC, DS, RC) were used by each participant one after another. They always started with the *raw pointing* and the order of the four other techniques was balanced between the subjects using a latin square.

Three IDs (3, 4, 5), two As (511 and 1023 pixels), and four ISs ($\approx$ 0.74, 1.74, 2.74, 3.74) —corresponding to four ρs (0.6, 0.3, 0.15, 0.075)— were used. A randomized series of the 24 combinations was presented four times for each technique to each participant. Those four series were preceded by 12 training trials during which they were familiarized with the techniques. Each participant performed 540 pointing tasks, 480 of them being recorded.

[4] The Python/OpenGL source code is available at: http://iihm.imag.fr/blanch/projects/distractors/.

	ER	RT	MT	TT
RP	5.41	$.397 \pm .129$	$.846 \pm .193$	$1.243 \pm .268$
SP	3.28	$.376 \pm .120$	$1.021 \pm .285$	$1.397 \pm .348$
BC	3.14	$.392 \pm .135$	$.716 \pm .168$	$1.108 \pm .258$
DS	3.70	$.367 \pm .119$	$.749 \pm .177$	$1.116 \pm .243$
RC	4.89	$.470 \pm .161$	$.725 \pm .349$	$1.195 \pm .378$

Table 1. Error rate (ER in %), reaction time (RT in seconds), movement time (MT in seconds) and total time ($TT = RT + MT$ in seconds) by technique.

Subjects and Apparatus

Eight right handed unpaid adult volunteers (1 female, 7 male) served in the experiment. We used a Logitech MX 400 mouse as a pointing device, the system acceleration being discarded by reading the low level (HID) motion events. The control-display ratio was globally set to 2. For SP, it was 1 outside the distractors and 4 inside. The gaze position needed by the RC technique was acquired using a Tobii ET-17 eye tracker (17-inch 1280×800 monitor). The same monitor was used for the other techniques. The step of the RC cursor grid was fixed at 300 pixels so that the target would never be directly under a cursor at the start of a trial.

Statistical Results

The effects of the factors on the performances are explored by analyzing three dependent variables: *error rate* (ER), *reaction time* (RT) and *movement time* (MT). The *total time* (TT) of the pointing —defined as the sum of RT and MT— is also considered since for the RC technique RT is significantly different from the other ones [8]. Table 1 sums up the values[5] of those variables for the five techniques considered. The analysis of variance below use the participant as random factor and the *technique*, ID, A and IS as factors. Means are compared using Tukey's HSD tests. A total of 17 obvious outliers (among 3840 observations) caused by technical problems were removed before performing the statistics.

Error Rate

ER is 4.08% on average (very close to the 4% value users were instructed to aim for). The main significant effect on ER is contributed by ID ($F_{1,3776} = 18.74*$[6]). A second effect is found for the interaction $IS \times technique$ ($F_{4,3776} = 2.38, p = .0492$), but no other effect is present. Comparing average ERs by techniques gives no statistically significant differences. An interesting result is then that the distractor density by itself does not significantly impact the error rate.

Reaction Time

The most significant effects on RT are, from the strongest to the weakest: ID ($F_{1,3776} = 4088.25*$), IS ($F_{1,3776} = 1783.95*$), the interaction $ID \times IS$ ($F_{1,3776} = 543.65*$), and finally the technique ($F_{4,3776} = 160.61*$). Observing an effect of the technique on RT is not common in pointing experiments. Since in this case this effect is rather strong, it needs to be explained. Comparing the means of the RT by technique, confirms that *rake cursor* is significantly slower than any of the other techniques. This difference was already reported and explained for RC and RP [8], but we show here that the difference is also significant when compared to other sophisticated techniques like DS or BC. The reason is probably that with RC, the user needs to choose which cursor she will use prior to start the movement.

[5] $m \pm \sigma$ gives the mean m and standard deviation σ.

[6] $*$ denotes $p < .0001$.

Movement Time

All factors do have an effect on MT, the strongest ones being contributed by ID ($F_{1,3776} = 842.00*$) and the technique ($F_{4,3776} = 254.22*$). The interactions between the technique and each of the other factors also give significant effects. Observing so many significant effects makes them difficult to interpret. Comparing the means of the MT by technique gives two simple but interesting results: *semantic pointing* is significantly slower than any other technique, including *raw pointing*; and DS, RC and BC are not significantly different but all significantly faster than RP (and thus than SP).

Looking at the rank of each technique per participant provides an interesting result: the pattern "SP slower than RP and RP slower than BC and DS" is mostly shared (in a single case DS is slower than RP, but not significantly). On the other hand, the rank of the *rake cursor* technique exhibits a lot of variability: for two of the participants, RC is slower than RP but faster than SP, and thus ranks second worst technique; for two other participants, RC ranks third (faster than SP and RP but slower than BC and DS); while for the four remaining participants, RC ranks as the fastest technique, being even significantly faster than any other technique for three of them. This analysis shows that the performance of *rake cursor* is strongly variable among participants.

Total Time

RT being particularly high for RC, their authors also study the *total time* ($TT = RT + MT$) to allow a more fair comparison of the techniques [8]. In our case, a whole analysis of TT gives qualitative results mostly equivalent to those reported above for MT. The only difference is the rank of RC: it performs significantly better than SP and RP but it is significantly slower than BC and DS (Table 1, last column).

Analysis using Extended Fitts' Law

Table 2 summarizes the parameters obtained when fitting the MT (top) and TT (bottom) data with the extended Fitts' law (EXT) proposed in Equation (6). The first column gives the intercept (a in seconds). The second one gives the throughput *à la* Zhai ($1/b$ in bits per second) of the technique The third column gives the ratio c/b which quantifies the sensitivity to distractors, i.e., how the sparseness of the task is exploited to reduce its difficulty: $c/b = 1$ meaning that each bit of IS reduces ID by one bit; and $c/b = 0$ meaning that the density has no impact on the performance.

The remaining columns of Table 2 characterize the goodness of fit of the model using two metrics: the adjusted coefficient of determination (adj. R^2) and the Akaike information criterion (AICc). Those metrics both take into account the number of degrees of freedom of the models and thus allow comparisons with the standard Fitts' law (STD, values given in parens). For modeling TT, EXT is always better (higher

MT	a	$1/b$	c/b	adj. R^2	AICc
RP	.371	7.87	.07	.65 (.65)	-206.55 (-207.24)
SP	.513	5.49	.48	.59 (.39)	-102.87 (-69.30)
BC	.423	9.62	.46	.54 (.37)	-185.04 (-158.25)
DS	.426	10.87	.17	.34 (.33)	-152.25 (-151.92)
RC	.232	7.25	.14	.28 (.27)	-55.76 (-56.62)

TT	a	$1/b$	c/b	adj. R^2	AICc
RP	.481	4.35	.25	.68 (.61)	-112.78 (-95.68)
SP	.595	3.46	.48	.78 (.51)	-97.60 (-30.03)
BC	.489	4.57	.46	.70 (.48)	-113.02 (-66.17)
DS	.495	5.03	.33	.61 (.50)	-107.16 (-86.10)
RC	.395	4.03	.28	.57 (.49)	-56.19 (-42.78)

Table 2. Parameters of the extended Fitts' law given by Equation (6): intercept (a in seconds), througput ($1/b$ in bits per second), and sensitivity to distractors (c/b, dimensionless); adjusted coefficient of determination (adj. R^2); and the Akaike information criterion (AICc) for the movement time (top); and the total time (bottom) by technique. Numbers in parens give the corresponding values for the standard Fitts' law.

adj. R^2, lower AICc) than STD, and for MT, EXT is better or comparable to STD. It is interesting to note that EXT and STD are comparable for *RP*, *DS* and *RC*, the techniques that are the less sensitive to distractors (lowest c/b ratios).

Regarding the techniques, some observations can be made: as expected, SP is quite sensitive to *IS*, and so is BC. This is not surprising since the bubble of BC uses the empty space surrounding the target to make it effectively larger. DS is less sensitive to *IS* than BC which is also logical since the size of its activation area is bounded, and thus do not benefit of very sparse distractors distributions. On the other hand, DS has a better throughput than BC, probably because its feedback is less disturbing. So while the two techniques perform mostly the same on average, *bubble cursor* is better suited to low *ID* or low density tasks, while *DynaSpot* is better suited to high *ID* or high density tasks. Overall, *rake cursor* has the best intercept and is the enhanced technique the least sensitive to *IS*, which makes it particularly adapted to dense tasks.

CONCLUSION AND FUTURE DIRECTIONS

We have proposed an extension to Fitts' pointing paradigm that enables to quantify the sensitivity of pointing techniques to the presence of distractors. This extension adds a single factor to the two specifying a pointing task: the target density, and derives the distractors location in 1D and 2D deterministically from those three parameters. This makes possible the fair comparison of pointing techniques. We have also proposed a first step toward an extension of Fitts' law by adding a term that accounts for the sensitivity the distractors density, namely the *index of sparseness*. With those tools at hand, we have compared five pointing techniques and shown that the extended protocol and model allow more contrasted comparison of the techniques.

We believe that the use of this protocol will allow more fair comparisons of pointing techniques. To encourage its use, we release to the community a reference implementation of the distractors layout generators, a reference implementation of the interaction techniques compared in this paper, and the framework used to conduct the experiment. We hope that this repository will grow in the future, fed by the community.

In the future, we will focus our attention on the model itself. Since the interaction of *ID* and *IS* is often significant, the model may have to consider this factor also. But this interaction has to be understood first.

Regarding the protocol, two extensions are envisioned. First, the distributions of distractors presented here is not incompatible with different experimental setups, like 1D reciprocal pointing or 2D multi-directional task following the ISO 9241-9 standard. We would like to extend our experiment framework to support those task setups. Then, providing a 3D generalization of distractors layout relying also on self-similarity and distractors density should also be doable. This would allow to extend the benchmark to 3D interaction techniques, and to test the effect of distractors on the 3D generalization of Fitts' law [14].

And finally, we will add more implementation of techniques to our framework, so that it can serve as an educational resource, as well as a benchmark that allows to compare new techniques to a whole corpus of existing techniques.

ACKNOWLEDGMENTS

The authors would like to thank Olivier Chapuis, Michel Beaudouin-Lafon, Brigitte Meillon and Laurence Nigay for their insightful comments and/or their practical help on this work. Part of this work was conducted within the NOMAD project (FUI Minalogic).

APPENDIXES

1D Distractors Layout Parameterization

Having the distractors similar to the target (i.e., having the same *ID*) modulo a constant step of scale (r) means that their widths (W_i) and amplitudes (A_i) follow a geometric progression. Having the target match the distractor W_0, A_0 leads to:

$$\forall i \in \mathbb{Z}, \quad \frac{A_{i+1}}{A_i} = \frac{W_{i+1}}{W_i} = r, \tag{7}$$

$$A_i = A \times r^i, \tag{8}$$

$$W_i = W \times r^i. \tag{9}$$

To fully define the task using our parametrization (ID, A, ρ), we need to express r using those factors.

If we consider the space separating the center of to successive tasks (dotted surface in Figure 7), we can compute a local distractor density (ρ_i) in this area by dividing the length covered by the distractors by the distance separating the distractors centers:

$$\begin{aligned}\rho_i &= \frac{W_{i+1}/2 + W_i/2}{A_{i+1} - A_i} \\ &= \frac{W_i/2}{A_i} \times \frac{r+1}{r-1} \quad \text{using Equation (7)} \\ &= \frac{W/2}{A} \times \frac{r+1}{r-1} \quad \text{using Equations (8, 9).}\end{aligned} \tag{10}$$

In Equation (10), ρ_i is not anymore a function of i, which means it is the same between each successive pair of targets, i.e., that $\rho_i = \rho$ for each i. This property is a consequence of the self-similarity we have introduced in the distribution of the targets, and confirms that the global distractor density ρ is also locally respected.

Equation (10) gives:

$$\rho = \frac{r+1}{r-1} \times \rho_{min}$$
$$\iff \quad r = \frac{\rho + \rho_{min}}{\rho - \rho_{min}}, \qquad (11)$$

provided we define ρ_{min}, the lower bound for the distractor density[7], as:

$$\rho_{min} = \frac{W/2}{A} = \frac{1}{2} \times \frac{1}{2^{ID} - 1} \quad \text{using Equation (3).} \qquad (12)$$

Finally, using Equations (8, 11, 12) and (3, 9), a full parameterization of the distractors depending only on the factors (ID, A, ρ) can be derived:

$$\forall i \in \mathbb{Z}, \quad A_i = A \times \left(1 + \frac{1}{(2^{ID} - 1)\rho - 1/2}\right)^i,$$
$$W_i = \frac{A_i}{2^{ID} - 1}.$$

Those equations give an infinity of targets. In practice, constraints on a minimal size for the distractor (not less than a pixel) and a maximal distance (not more than the screen width) can be used to bound the range of i.

2D Distractor Layout Parameterization

The construction of the 2D set of distractors is a bit more complex but relies on the same principle of linking the local density to the global ρ. The global density ρ is first divided into two contributions: a tangential density ρ_t and a radial density ρ_r, such as the product of those contribution remains equal to the whole distractors density:

$$\rho_t = \sqrt{\frac{\rho}{k}},$$
$$\rho_r = \sqrt{\rho \times k} \quad \text{with } k = \frac{\pi}{4} \sin\frac{\pi}{3}. \qquad (13)$$

The constant k is chosen to create an hexagonal packing of the distractors, which is desirable because the hexagonal packing is the densest circle packing and thus allow exploring distractors density up to $\frac{\pi}{6}\sqrt{3} \approx 0.91$[8].

The tangential density ρ_t is used to link the β angle between two rays of distractors to the α half-angle under which the

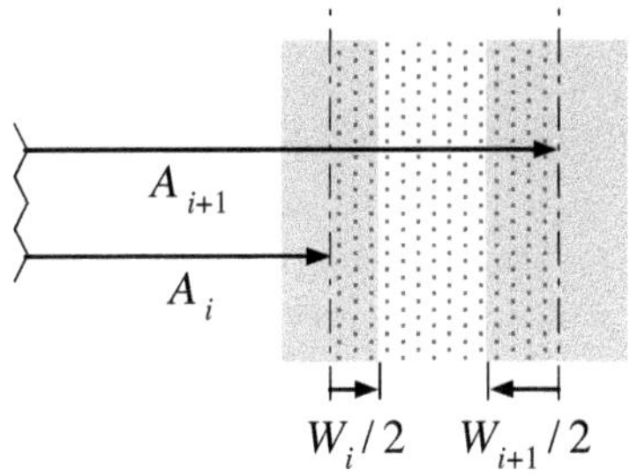

Figure 7. Computing local distractors density in 1D.

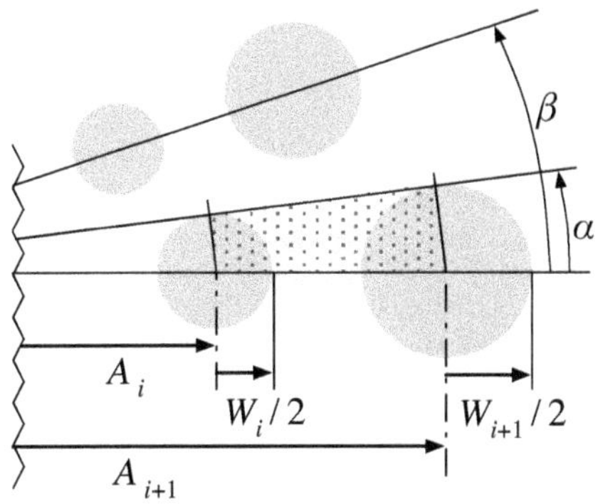

Figure 8. Computing local distractors density in 2D.

distractors are seen from the origin (see Figure 8):

$$\beta = \frac{2\alpha}{\rho_t} \quad \text{with } \alpha = \sin^{-1}\frac{W/2}{A} = \sin^{-1}\frac{1}{2} \times \frac{1}{2^{ID} - 1}. \qquad (14)$$

As for the 1D task, the scale linking the sizes of two consecutive distractors in the same ray (r) can be linked to the density by considering the dotted surface in Figure 8:

$$r = \sqrt{\frac{\pi}{\alpha - \pi/2 + \rho_r/\tan\alpha} + 1}. \qquad (15)$$

The distractors can then be defined by:

$$\forall j \in \mathbb{Z} / j \times \beta \in [-\pi/2, \pi/2], \quad \text{(each ray)}$$
$$\forall i \in \mathbb{Z}, \quad \text{(each distractor on the ray)}$$
$$A_{i,j} = \begin{cases} A \times r^i & \text{if } j \text{ is even} \\ A \times r^{i+1/2} & \text{if } j \text{ is odd} \end{cases},$$
$$W_{i,j} = \frac{A_{i,j}}{2^{ID} - 1},$$
$$\begin{pmatrix} x \\ y \end{pmatrix}_{i,j} = A_{i,j} \times \begin{pmatrix} \cos\beta j \\ \sin\beta j \end{pmatrix}. \qquad (16)$$

Equations (3, 13, 14, 15) makes it possible to express $A_{i,j}$ and $W_{i,j}$ using only the factors (ID, A, ρ) as parameters. Equation (16) gives the positions of the centers of the distractors in traditional cartesian coordinates.

[7] ρ_{min} can be seen as the task density when there is no distractor: on the path from the start towards the center of the target (A), only the half of the target present before reaching the center is not empty space ($W/2$), thus a minimal density of $\frac{W/2}{A}$.

[8] E. W. Weisstein. Circle Packing. 2008. http://mathworld.wolfram.com/CirclePacking.html

REFERENCES

1. Accot, J., and Zhai, S. Refining Fitts' law models for bivariate pointing. In *Proc. CHI'03*, ACM Press (2003), 193–200.
2. Ahlström, D. Modeling and improving selection in cascading pull-down menus using Fitts' law, the steering law and force fields. In *Proc. CHI'05*, ACM Press (2005), 61–70.
3. Ahlström, D., Hitz, M., and Leitner, G. An evaluation of sticky and force enhanced targets in multi target situations. In *Proc. NordiCHI'06* (2006), 58–67.
4. Appert, C., Beaudouin-Lafon, M., and Mackay, W. Context matters: Evaluating interaction techniques with the CIS model. In *Proc. HCI'04* (2004), 279–295.
5. Balakrishnan, R. "Beating" Fitts' law: virtual enhancements for pointing facilitation. *Int. J. Hum.-Comput. Stud. 61* (2004), 857–874.
6. Baudisch, P., Cutrell, E., Hinckley, K., and Eversole, A. Snap-and-go: helping users align objects without the modality of traditional snapping. In *Proc. CHI'05*, ACM Press (2005), 301–310.
7. Blanch, R., Guiard, Y., and Beaudouin-Lafon, M. Semantic pointing: improving target acquisition with control-display ratio adaptation. In *Proc. CHI'04*, ACM Press (2004), 519–526.
8. Blanch, R., and Ortega, M. Rake cursor: Improving pointing performance with concurrent input channels. In *Proc. CHI'09*, ACM Press (2009), 1415–1418.
9. Chapuis, O., Blanch, R., and Beaudouin-Lafon, M. Fitts' law in the wild: A field study of aimed movements. Tech. Rep. 1480, 2007. Université Paris-Sud XI.
10. Chapuis, O., Labrune, J.-B., and Pietriga, E. Dynaspot: speed-dependent area cursor. In *Proc. CHI'09*, ACM Press (2009), 1391–1400.
11. Douglas, S. A., Kirkpatrick, A. E., and MacKenzie, I. S. Testing pointing device performance and user assessment with the ISO 9241, Part 9 standard. In *Proc. CHI'99*, ACM Press (1999), 215–222.
12. Fitts, P. M. The information capacity of the human motor system in controlling the amplitude of movement. *J. of Exp. Psycho. 47* (1954), 381–391.
13. Graham, E. D., and MacKenzie, C. L. Physical versus virtual pointing. In *Proc. CHI'96*, ACM Press (1996), 292–299.
14. Grossman, T., and Balakrishnan, R. Pointing at trivariate targets in 3D environments. In *Proc. CHI'04*, ACM Press (2004), 447–454.
15. Grossman, T., and Balakrishnan, R. The bubble cursor: Enhancing target acquisition by dynamic resizing of the cursor's activation area. In *Proc. CHI'05*, ACM Press (2005), 281–290.
16. Grossman, T., and Balakrishnan, R. A probabilistic approach to modeling two-dimensional pointing. *ACM Trans. Comput.-Hum. Interact. 12*, 3 (2005), 435–459.
17. Guiard, Y. Disentangling relative from absolute amplitude in Fitts' law experiments. In *Proc. CHI'01*, ACM Press (2001), 315–316.
18. Guiard, Y. The problem of consistency in the design of Fitts' law experiments: consider either target distance and width or movement form and scale. In *Proc. CHI'09*, ACM Press (2009), 1809–1818.
19. Guiard, Y., Blanch, R., and Beaudouin-Lafon, M. Object pointing: a complement to bitmap pointing in GUIs. In *Proc. GI'04* (2004), 9–16.
20. Hoffmann, E. R. Effective target tolerance in an inverted Fitts task. *Ergonomics 38*, 4 (1995), 828–836.
21. Kabbash, P., and Buxton, W. The "Prince" technique: Fitts' law and selection using area cursors. In *Proc. CHI'95*, ACM Press (1995), 273–279.
22. Keyson, D. V. Dynamic control gain and tactile feedback in the capture of cursor movements. *Ergonomics 40*, 12 (1997), 1287–1298.
23. Kobayashi, M., and Igarashi, T. Ninja cursors: using multiple cursors to assist target acquisition on large screens. In *Proc. CHI'08*, ACM Press (2008), 949–958.
24. MacKenzie, I. S. A note on the information-theoretic basis for Fitts' law. *J. of Mot. Behav. 21* (1989), 323–330.
25. MacKenzie, I. S., and Buxton, W. Extending Fitts' law to two-dimensional tasks. In *Proc. CHI'92*, ACM Press (1992), 219–226.
26. McGuffin, M. J., and Balakrishnan, R. Fitts' law and expanding targets: Experimental studies and designs for user interfaces. *ACM Trans. Comput.-Hum. Interact. 12*, 4 (2005), 388–422.
27. Soukoreff, R. W., and MacKenzie, I. S. Towards a standard for pointing device evaluation, perspectives on 27 years of Fitts' law research in HCI. *Int. J. Hum.-Comput. Stud. 61*, 6 (2004), 751–789.
28. Worden, A., Walker, N., Bharat, K., and Hudson, S. Making computers easier for older adults to use: area cursors and sticky icons. In *Proc. CHI'97*, ACM Press (1997), 266–271.
29. Zhai, S. Characterizing computer input with Fitts' law parameters — the information and non-information aspects of pointing. *Int. J. Hum.-Comput. Stud. 61*, 6 (2004), 791–809.
30. Zhai, S., Conversy, S., Beaudouin-Lafon, M., and Guiard, Y. Human on-line response to target expansion. In *Proc. CHI'03*, ACM Press (2003), 177–184.

The Effects of Task Dimensionality, Endpoint Deviation, Throughput Calculation, and Experiment Design on Pointing Measures and Models

Jacob O. Wobbrock, Kristen Shinohara and Alex Jansen
The Information School
DUB Group
University of Washington
Seattle, WA 98195 USA
{wobbrock, kshino, ajansen7}@uw.edu

ABSTRACT
Fitts' law (1954) characterizes pointing speed-accuracy performance as *throughput*, whose invariance to target distances (A) and sizes (W) is known. However, it is unknown whether throughput and Fitts' law models in general are invariant to task dimensionality (1-D *vs.* 2-D), whether univariate (SD_x) or bivariate ($SD_{x,y}$) endpoint deviation is used, whether throughput is calculated using the mean-of-means approach or the slope-inverse approach, or whether Guiard's (2009) *Form* × *Scale* experiment design is used instead of fully crossed $A \times W$ factors. We empirically investigate the confluence of these issues, finding that Fitts' law is largely invariant across 1-D and 2-D, provided that univariate endpoint deviation (SD_x) is used in both, but that for 2-D pointing data, bivariate endpoint deviation ($SD_{x,y}$) results in better Fitts' law models. Also, the mean-of-means throughput calculation exhibits lower variance across subjects and dimensionalities than the slope-inverse calculation. In light of these and other findings, we offer recommendations for pointing evaluations, especially in 2-D. We also offer an evaluation tool called *FittsStudy* to facilitate comparisons.

Author Keywords: Fitts' law, dimensionality, endpoint deviation, effective target width, throughput, FittsStudy.

ACM Classification Keywords: H.5.2. [Information interfaces and presentation]: User interfaces—*theory and methods, evaluation/methodology.*

General Terms: Experimentation, Measurement, Theory.

INTRODUCTION
New pointing techniques regularly emerge, and often, these pointing techniques are evaluated using Fitts' law [7] to measure rapid aimed pointing performance independent of target distance (A) and size (W). Fitts' law's measure, which combines speed and accuracy, is throughput, whose invariance to the specific values of A and W is well-known. However, it is unknown whether throughput is also invariant to task dimensionality (1-D *vs.* 2-D). Although Fitts' original task used vertical ribbons and focused on 1-D horizontal pointing, the ISO 9241-9 standard [13], in recognizing the relevance of pointing to 2-D interfaces, has also prescribed a ring-of-circles target arrangement. In addition, researchers often create their own custom pointing evaluations involving 2-D targets [5], sometimes laid out in a random field [6].

Researchers have created many predictive movement time models for 2-D pointing [2,9,10,16,20]—but despite this work, the literature is almost silent on the issue of throughput calculation in 2-D. For example, it is unknown whether or not applying 1-D throughput calculations to 2-D pointing data results in equivalent throughput outcomes. It is also unknown whether univariate (SD_x) or bivariate ($SD_{x,y}$) endpoint deviation creates better models of 2-D pointing. Even the calculation of throughput itself requires further investigation, as the mean-of-means approach [26] insists on averaging indexes of difficulty and movement times, while the slope-inverse approach [30] insists on using the reciprocal of Fitts' regression slope.[1] How each calculation fares across dimensionalities and endpoint deviation schemes is unknown. Additionally, the traditional $A \times W$ experiment design has recently been exposed by Guiard [11] as introducing possible factor confounds, but the effects of the foregoing issues as they relate to his *Form* × *Scale* design are unknown. In short, there are many unanswered and interrelated questions regarding the use of Fitts' law in two-dimensional pointing studies. This paper investigates the confluence of these issues at once.

Endpoint deviation is crucial to the application of Fitts' law. Quantifying endpoint deviation is necessary for employing Crossman's correction [4] for normalizing subjects' personal speed-accuracy biases so that throughputs for a "fast but reckless" performer and a "slow and careful" performer are comparable. The ISO 9241-9 standard [13] and most prior literature [5,15,19,26,27] define the endpoint deviation, or spread of hits, as a univariate quantity computed as the standard deviation of endpoints' x-coordinates in a horizontal pointing task (SD_x). But this definition is questionable in 2-D, as it ignores any deviation in the second dimension (Δy). The comparative effects on

[1] Both approaches are mentioned, as if interchangeable, in the ISO standard [13].

throughput of using a bivariate standard deviation calculation ($SD_{x,y}$) are unknown. Given Fitts' law's origins as a 1-D model, both definitions of endpoint variability in 2-D tasks seem defensible (*cf.* [5,19]). What, then, should serve as bases for addressing these issues? In this paper, we consider invariance across dimensionalities, improved model fits, and theoretical soundness as possible answers.

This paper contributes a case for, and description of, bivariate endpoint deviation, which easily generalizes to N dimensions. It also presents results from a study of 21 subjects performing the two ISO 9241-9 pointing tasks in 1-D and 2-D layouts. Throughputs are computed using both the mean-of-means approach [26] and the slope-inverse approach [30]. The effects of univariate and bivariate endpoint deviations on throughput are examined, as are the effects of Guiard's [11] *Form* × *Scale* experiment design as an alternative to the traditional $A \times W$ experiment design.

Our key findings include that Fitts' law is largely invariant across 1-D and 2-D, provided that univariate endpoint deviation (SD_x) is used in both; but for 2-D pointing data, bivariate endpoint deviation ($SD_{x,y}$) creates better Fitts' law models than SD_x. We also find that the mean-of-means throughput calculation exhibits lower variance across subjects and dimensionalities for the same pointing data than the slope-inverse calculation. And Guiard's *Form* × *Scale* experiment design produces equivalent results with just one of three levels of A as the full $A \times W$ design, resulting in the possibility of major time savings when conducting experiments. We offer a downloadable pointing evaluation tool called *FittsStudy* that provides extensive measures and a visualization tool for exploring submovement pointing profiles.

RELATED WORK

In this section, we highlight pieces related to endpoint deviation, dimensionality, and throughput.

Endpoint Deviation

Motor psychologists (*e.g.*, [12]) have distinguished between two sources of error in rapid aimed movements: variable error (*VE*) and constant error (*CE*). Simply put, *VE* reflects the spread of hits, or endpoint deviation. By contrast, *CE* is the mean distance of endpoints from the target center. Thus, *VE* is independent of target location while *CE* is not. Crossman's correction [4] relies only on *VE*, not *CE*.

The ISO 9241-9 standard [13] and many published studies treat pointing in 2-D as having only univariate endpoint deviation (SD_x). However, Douglas *et al.* [5] provides an exception, defining 2-D endpoint deviation as a planar distance from a centroid. Unfortunately, they do not explore or discuss this choice as we do here. Murata [21] defined 2-D effective target width (W_e) directly using a bivariate joint probability distribution rather than calculating W_e using bivariate endpoint deviation ($SD_{x,y}$), which is much simpler and which has not been examined until now. Unfortunately, Murata did not compare model fits using his 2-D W_e to those using a traditional 1-D W_e, leaving the comparative utility of his technique unknown. In general, there is still no consensus as to how endpoint deviation or effective target width should be calculated in 2-D (or 3-D).

Predictive Models of 2-D Pointing

Two-dimensional Fitts' law studies have been conducted for some time (*e.g.*, [14]). Researchers have attempted to predict movement times (*MT*s) to 2-D targets for almost as long, relying on target dimensions [2,16,20] or probability distributions [9,10,24] to inform predictions. Importantly, these efforts were focused on Fitts' law's ability to predict movement times, not its related but distinct measurement of throughput. Therefore, these efforts did not deal with endpoint deviation, speed-accuracy bias correction, or throughput calculation, topics of central importance here.

Throughput Calculation

Throughput has been fundamental to Fitts' law from the beginning. Fitts himself [7] initially defined it using the mean-of-means approach. Twelve years later, as Zhai points out [30], Fitts and Radford [8] seem to switch gears, referring to the "slope constant" when discussing performance. Card *et al.* [3], who brought Fitts' law into HCI, defined throughput using the slope-inverse approach, *i.e.*, $1/b$, where b is the slope of a regression line through (*ID*, *MT*) points. MacKenzie [15] refers to both the mean-of-means and slope-inverse approaches. Twenty-five years after Card *et al.* [3], MacKenzie and Soukoreff [18] revised Card's calculations using the mean-of-means approach, finding significantly reduced throughputs. In general, Soukoreff and MacKenzie [26] have advocated for the mean-of-means approach, while Zhai [30] has advocated for the slope-inverse approach. The present study brings additional empirical evidence to this debate, especially for 2-D pointing tasks, which have thus far been mostly ignored. Although each throughput calculation results in a bits per second measure, the calculations consider different things. A reasonable approach, then, is to report both throughputs rather than adhere to one or the other.

Only using one *ID*, MacKenzie and Isokoski [19] showed that throughput remains constant across cognitive sets [8], provided that Crossman's correction [4] is used. Zhai *et al.* [31], however, has shown that Crossman's correction does not always fully correct divergent speed-accuracy biases. Nonetheless, the correction remains standard for reducing bias and equitably comparing subjects [8,15,19,26,27].

Finally, Guiard [11] has recently argued that the classic crossing of factors $A \times W$ in Fitts' law experiments introduces possible confounds, and that experiments should use *Form* × *Scale* designs instead, which amount to crossing $ID \times [A \text{ xor } W]$. Our experiment is among the first to provide results comparing both $A \times W$ and $F \times S$ designs.

ENDPOINT DEVIATION IN MULTIPLE DIMENSIONS

Humans point with different speed-accuracy biases [31] despite being issued a guideline to point as fast as achieving a 4% error rate allows [15,26]. Necessary for correcting these biases is Crossman's correction [4], which enables

Fitts' throughput, or pointing efficiency, to be properly measured. Whether using the mean-of-means throughput calculation [26] or the slope-inverse calculation [30], throughput depends on this corrected, or "effective," index of difficulty ID_e defined as

$$ID_e = \log_2\left(A_e / W_e + 1\right). \quad (1)$$

Using ID_e allows subjects making different speed-accuracy tradeoffs to be equitably compared. The faster/slower a subject points, the lower/higher his movement time but the wider/narrower his spread of hits. In Eq. 1, A_e is the average actual movement distance [26] and W_e reflects the standard deviation of endpoints as

$$W_e = 4.133 \times SD_x. \quad (2)$$

The constant term arises from the entropy of the standard normal distribution [15,27], but it is the calculation of endpoint deviation (SD_x) that interests us. As described elsewhere [13,15,19,26], SD_x is the standard deviation of endpoint coordinates along the axis of motion—by convention, the "x" indicating horizontal pointing to vertical ribbons. If we record each endpoint's x-coordinate such that negative values are undershoots and positive values are overshoots [26] (footnote 9), we would label endpoints as shown in Figure 1.

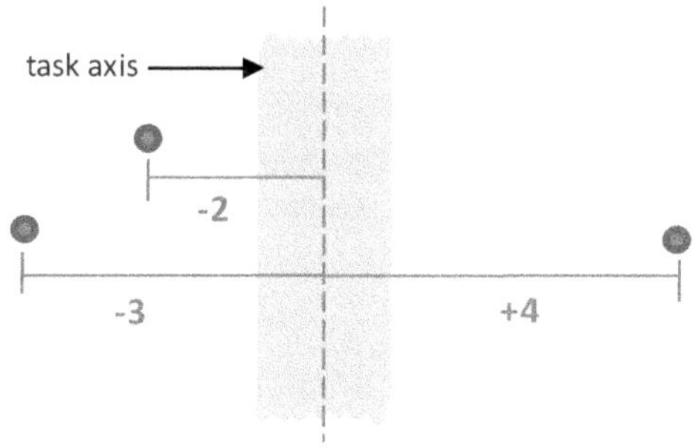

Figure 1. Vertical ribbon target with two undershoots and one overshoot.

Using the data from Figure 1 as an example, the calculation for SD_x would be:

$$SD_x = \sqrt{\frac{\sum_{i=1}^{N}(x_i - \bar{x})^2}{N-1}}, \quad (3)$$

$$= \sqrt{\frac{\left(-3+\frac{1}{3}\right)^2 + \left(-2+\frac{1}{3}\right)^2 + \left(4+\frac{1}{3}\right)^2}{2}} \approx 3.79.$$

The above calculation relies on the mean $\bar{x}$, which depends on having *signed* distances from a target center. However, in 2-D (or 3-D) pointing tasks, signed distances to target centers are untenable unless we are to discard all deviation along axes perpendicular to the task axis, turning a multidimensional task into a unidimensional one. Owing to Fitts' law's origins as a 1-D model of rapid aimed movement, it is reasonable to argue that even in 2-D pointing tasks, endpoint deviation should be regarded as univariate [19]. However, this argument forces us to ignore all deviation in one of two task dimensions, sometimes with rather absurd consequences as in Figure 2.

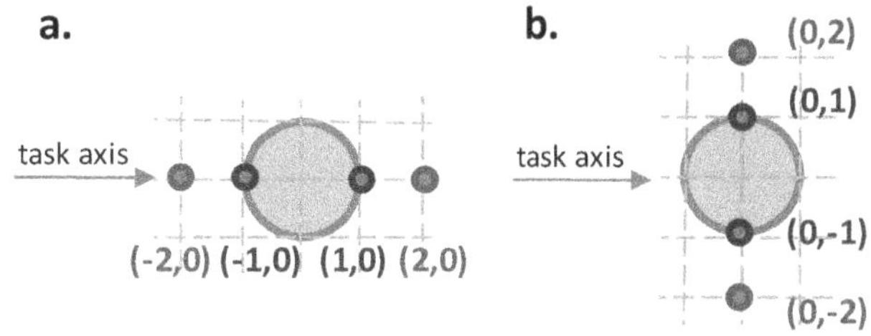

Figure 2. Given a horizontal approach, univariate endpoint deviation (SD_x) would be **(a)** rather high and **(b)** zero even though the 2-D spread of points in both cases is the same.

To date, despite years of Fitts' law research, the ramifications of the endpoint deviation calculation are unknown. Intuitively, it seems that endpoint deviation should be accounted for in all relevant task dimensions; after all, pointing to a circular target in 2-D (or spherical target in 3-D) clearly requires motor control in more than one dimension. But how, then, shall we quantify endpoint deviation in 2-D (or 3-D)? And will it produce comparable throughputs to those we observe in 1-D?

Consider Figure 3a, where using signed distances to a target's center is not feasible as it was in Figure 1. How can endpoint deviation be generalized to cover Figure 3? Clearly, *unsigned* distances from a target center do not suffice, lest the endpoint deviation of Figure 3b is considered equal to that of Figure 3a.

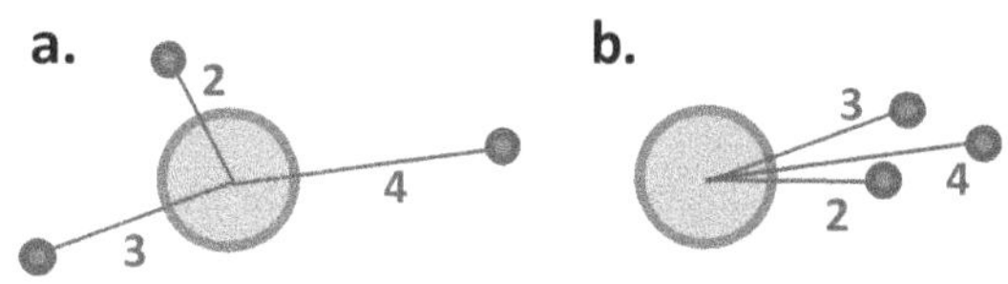

Figure 3. Endpoints at the same distances from target centers showing **(a)** a wide spread of hits, **(b)** a narrow spread of hits. The unsigned distances in (a) are the same as in (b), but clearly (a) exhibits much more endpoint deviation than (b).

Our answer lies in regarding endpoint deviation not as signed or unsigned distances from a target center, but as deviations around a center of mass. Mathematically, this notion is equally suited to 1, 2, 3, and N dimensions. As before, in Figure 4a and 4b, distances to the target center are the same, but the spread of hits differs. Now, the centroids ($\bar{x}, \bar{y}$) are also marked.

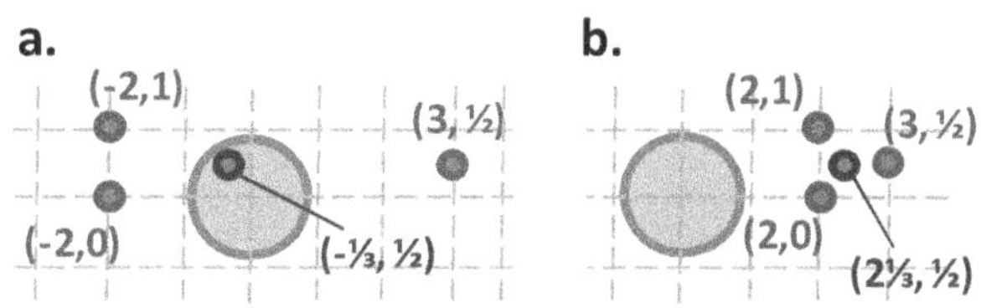

Figure 4. Three-point spreads (red) around two targets, and their centroids (blue).

The center of mass, or centroid, serves as a multidimensional mean in the *SD* calculation, now given by Eq. 4, where the deviation is the spread of hits around the centroid. In Eq. 4, we simply have substituted a 2-D distance-from-centroid formula for the 1-D distance-from-mean formula inside the parentheses of Eq. 3:

$$SD_{x,y} = \sqrt{\frac{\sum_{i=1}^{N}\left(\sqrt{(x_i-\bar{x})^2+(y_i-\bar{y})^2}\right)^2}{N-1}}. \quad (4)$$

A simplified version of Eq. 4 appears in prior work by Douglas *et al.* [5] (see Eq. 6). Applying Eq. 4 to Figures 2a and 2b yields 1.83 for both. Applying Eq. 4 to Figures 4a and 4b yields 2.93 and 0.76, respectively.

We emphasize that a spread of hits around a centroid is *not* the spread of distances from a centroid, which is a univariate deviation of 2-D distances, not a bivariate deviation of 2-D points. This incorrect definition is given for comparison as SD_{wrong} in Eq. 5.

$$SD_{wrong} = \sqrt{\frac{\sum_{i=1}^{N}(d_i-\bar{d})^2}{N-1}}, \text{ where } d_i \text{ is} \quad (5)$$

$$d_i = \sqrt{(x_i-\bar{x})^2} \text{ in 1-D, and} \quad (5a)^2$$

$$d_i = \sqrt{(x_i-\bar{x})^2+(y_i-\bar{y})^2} \text{ in 2-D.} \quad (5b)$$

If Eq. 5b were used for Figure 2a or 2b, we would get a deviation of 0.58. If it were used for Figures 4a and 4b, we would get 0.92 and 0.04, respectively. These values represent the spread of distances from the centroid, not the spread of endpoints around the centroid.

Eq. 4 is easily increased to 3-D or decreased to 1-D:

$$SD_{x,y,z} = \sqrt{\frac{\sum_{i=1}^{N}\left(\sqrt{(x_i-\bar{x})^2+(y_i-\bar{y})^2+(z_i-\bar{z})^2}\right)^2}{N-1}}, \quad (6)$$

$$SD_x = \sqrt{\frac{\sum_{i=1}^{N}\left(\sqrt{(x_i-\bar{x})^2}\right)^2}{N-1}} = \sqrt{\frac{\sum_{i=1}^{N}(x_i-\bar{x})^2}{N-1}}. \quad (7)$$

Eq. 7 shows how the deviation of 1-D coordinates around their centroid is equivalent to a standard deviation of scalars (Eq. 3). With the centroid approach, signed distances from target centers become unnecessary, and instead, 1-D coordinates can be used directly, like 2-D coordinates in Eq. 4, or 3-D coordinates in Eq. 6.

To illustrate the consistency of the centroid formulation for endpoint deviation across dimensions, consider two "equivalent" endpoint distributions in Figure 5.

In Figure 5a, univariate deviation (Eq. 7) produces 1.15. In Figure 5b, bivariate deviation (Eq. 4) also produces 1.15. (By contrast, the deviation-of-distances in Figure 5b using Eq. 5b produces 0.00 because all points are equally 1 unit from their centroid, so there is no deviation present.)

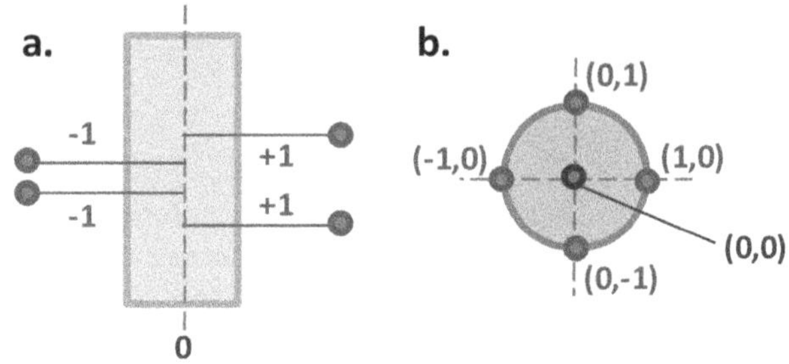

Figure 5. Two endpoint distributions for **(a)** a 1-D task, **(b)** a 2-D task. Each totals four units from their respective target center.

Thus, computing endpoint deviation as the spread of points around a center of mass unifies our calculation of deviation regardless of dimensionality. Although empirical endpoint distributions show that deviation tends to be greater along the task axis than orthogonal to it [9,21], for our purposes in quantifying *amount* of deviation, we do not care where the deviation occurs, just *that* it occurs. Endpoints 2 units up from a target center or 2 units right of a target center are each equally 2 units off the mark. Importantly, all approach angles to circular (or spherical) targets are equivalent, removing concern over target shape and approach angle in the ISO 9241-9 standard tasks [13].

Although the above formulation of endpoint deviation is consistent across dimensionalities, it remains to be seen how throughputs from 2-D tasks compare to those from 1-D tasks. Also, it is unknown whether SD_x or $SD_{x,y}$ results in better model fits for the same 2-D pointing data, how these issues interact with the two approaches to calculating throughput [26,30], or with Guiard's contention [11] that $A \times W$ factorial designs can be confounded. These questions are addressed in our experiment, described next.

METHOD

Subjects

Twenty-one subjects participated in our study. Seven were female. All were right-handed. Their average age was 29.3 years (*SD*=6.9).

Apparatus

All testing was conducted at a lab containing a 21" Samsung SyncMaster 214T flat panel monitor set to 1600×1200 resolution and a Logitech optical mouse. The computer was a Xeon CPU running Windows 7 at 3 GHz with 2 GB RAM.

We created a full-screen application called *FittsStudy* in C# to administer conditions, log data, parse files, visualize trials, and calculate results. FittsStudy was configured to administer 18 $A \times W$ conditions defined by 3 levels of A {256, 384, 512 pixels} crossed with 6 levels of W {8, 16, 32, 64, 96, 128 pixels} yielding 13 unique *ID*s ranging from 1.59 – 6.02 bits. For the 1-D task, A was measured from one vertical ribbon's center to the other, and W was the width of a ribbon. For the 2-D task, the ISO 9241-9 circular

[2] Note that Eq. 5a *will* work using signed distances from the centroid, *i.e.*, $d_i = (x_i - \bar{x})$, because in 1-D, distance is univariate. However, this calculation does not generalize to 2+ dimensions where a distance is not describable by a 1-D value.

arrangement was used [13,26], with $0.5 \cdot A$ being the radius of the target ring, and W the diameter of one circular target.

Procedure

In each of the 18 $A \times W$ conditions per session, a subject performed 23 trials, where each trial was a single attempt to click a target. In each condition, the first three trials were logged as practice and ignored, leaving 20 test trials per condition. There was no delineation between the last practice trial and the first test trial. Presentation order of the 18 $A \times W$ conditions was randomized first by A and then by W. Subjects were instructed to move as quickly as possible while maintaining an approximate 4% error rate [15]. Cumulative and condition-level error rates were displayed after each condition. Each trial only contained one click; if a target was missed, it flashed red, audibly dinged, and the next target was immediately highlighted. With each of 21 subjects completing 18 $A \times W$ conditions consisting of 20 test trials in 2 dimensionalities, 15,120 test trials were produced as part of this study.

Data Analysis

All trials were mathematically rotated to horizontal (0°) prior to analysis. Each subject's 18 $A \times W$ conditions resulted in 18 data points plotted as (ID_e, MT), where MT is average movement time and ID_e is the effective index of difficulty (Eq. 1), normalized with Crossman's correction [4] using W_e (Eq. 2), which uses endpoint deviation. For the 1-D task, SD_x was computed using Eq. 7. For the 2-D task, univariate SD_x was computed using Eq. 7 and bivariate $SD_{x,y}$ was computed using Eq. 4. Each subject's 18 (ID_e, MT) points were regressed upon to produce a Fitts' law model of the form

$$MT = a + b \cdot ID_e \quad (8)$$

and Pearson r correlation coefficient.

A subject's throughput in bits per second (bps) was calculated using both the mean-of-means approach [26], which we will designate TP_{avg}, and the slope-inverse approach [30], which we will designate TP_{inv}.

$$TP_{avg} = \frac{1}{N}\sum_{i=1}^{N}\left(\frac{ID_{e_i}}{MT_i}\right), \text{ where } N = |A| \times |W|, \quad (9)$$

$$TP_{inv} = 1/b. \quad (10)$$

Using either approach, the grand throughput for an entire experiment would be the mean throughput over all subjects.

RESULTS

Adjustment of Data

As is customary, trials flagged as spatial outliers were removed. A spatial outlier was defined from prior work [19,28] as an error whose movement was less than half the nominal distance A, or whose endpoint landed more than twice the target width W from the target center. In all, 9/7560 and 2/7560 test trials were removed from the 1-D and 2-D tasks, respectively.

Error Rates

Error rates for Fitts' law studies should be around 4% [15]. Appropriately, over all $A \times W$ conditions, the error rate for the 1-D task was 4.4% and for the 2-D task was 4.3%.

Comparison of Fitts' Law Models (*r*, *a*, *b*)

Space precludes showing Fitts' law models for all 21 subjects, but average model fits (Pearson r) and parameters (a and b) for both the 1-D vertical ribbon task and the 2-D ring-of-circles task are shown in Table 1. For the 2-D task, the exact same pointing data was analyzed using univariate (SD_x) and bivariate ($SD_{x,y}$) endpoint deviation.

The average fit of the models for the 1-D task was r=.948.[3] The average fit for the 2-D task using univariate endpoint deviation (SD_x) was r=.951. For the same 2-D data, using bivariate endpoint deviation ($SD_{x,y}$) resulted in r=.962. Paired samples t-tests show that 2-D bivariate r values were significantly higher than both the 1-D and 2-D univariate r values ($p<.05$), and that the univariate r values were not significantly different from each other.

The standard deviation of subjects' bivariate r values was lower than their univariate r values for the 2-D task (.016 *vs.* .021, respectively) given the exact same pointing data.

For model parameters, it is generally desirable to have intercepts a that are nonnegative and as close to zero as possible [26,30]. Intercepts in both 2-D models were not significantly different from those in the 1-D model, but were marginally different from each other ($t(20)$=2.04, p=.05). The 1-D, 2-D univariate, and 2-D bivariate models produced 5, 4, and 3 negative intercepts, respectively. Tests of slope parameters b showed that the 1-D and 2-D univariate slopes were not significantly different, but that both were different from the 2-D bivariate slopes ($p<.01$).

Throughput Analyses

As described above, the mean-of-means approach (TP_{avg}, Eq. 9) [26] computes the average bps over $A \times W$ conditions, and therefore accounts for the contributions of both a and b. However, averages may be affected by the range of *ID*s used, and a and b are conflated such that averages may be the same whose slopes (b) differ due to the influence of intercepts (a). By contrast, the slope-inverse approach (TP_{inv}, Eq. 10) [30] defines throughput as $1/b$. However, this approach must report a separately, and has been shown to depend upon the range of *ID*s used [26].

Univariate vs. Bivariate Throughputs (TP_{avg})

Using the mean-of-means approach, the average throughput for the 1-D task was TP_{avg}=4.85 bps (SD=0.41). The average throughput for the 2-D task with univariate endpoint deviation was TP_{avg}=4.91 bps (SD=0.43). A paired samples t-test indicates that these throughputs were not significantly different, indicating that 1-D and 2-D univariate throughputs were comparable despite changes in

[3] As Fitts himself observed [8], it is typical and appropriate for models using corrected ID_e instead of nominal ID to exhibit lower correlation coefficients (*cf.* [26,31]).

A×W design	1-D Ribbon Task, Univariate SD_x					2-D Circle Task, Univariate SD_x							2-D Circle Task, Bivariate $SD_{x,y}$						
	a	*b*	*r*	TP_{avg}	TP_{inv}	*a*	*b*	*r*	TP_{avg}	TP_{inv}	ΔTP_{avg}	ΔTP_{inv}	*a*	*b*	*r*	TP_{avg}	TP_{inv}	ΔTP_{avg}	ΔTP_{inv}
Mean	98.36	187.56	.948	4.85	5.42	74.48	192.65	.951	4.91	5.28	0.21	0.56	72.90	207.28	.962	4.49	4.90	0.36	0.72
StdDev	66.55	24.67	.027	0.41	0.71	56.01	27.09	.021	0.43	0.68	0.16	0.44	52.33	27.63	.016	0.40	0.61	0.24	0.50

Table 1. Summary results over 21 subjects for Fitts' law regression coefficients (*a* and *b*), Pearson *r* model fits, and throughput calculations (TP_{avg} and TP_{inv}) for 1-D pointing to vertical ribbons and for 2-D pointing to circles in a ring [13]. The exact same data is used for each 2-D analysis. The ΔTP_{avg} and ΔTP_{inv} columns show the absolute differences in throughputs from their respective 1-D throughputs. Because Fitts' law intercepts can be negative, means and standard deviations for those columns are of |*a*|, *i.e.*, intercepts' distance from zero.

dimensionality. The average absolute difference between subjects' 2-D univariate throughput and their 1-D throughput was ΔTP_{avg}=0.21 bps (*SD*=0.16).

The mean of 2-D bivariate throughputs was TP_{avg}=4.49 bps (*SD*=0.40), which was significantly lower than 1-D throughputs ($t(20)=-6.89$, $p<.0001$). It was also lower than the 2-D univariate throughput ($t(20)=-33.43$, $p<.0001$). The average absolute difference between subjects' 2-D bivariate throughputs and their 1-D throughputs was ΔTP_{avg}=0.36 bps (*SD*=0.24). These differences were significantly greater than the 2-D univariate differences ($t(20)=2.65$, $p<.05$).

Thus, it seems that under the mean-of-means approach to calculating throughput, for 2-D task data, univariate endpoint deviation produces throughputs closer to those obtained in the classic 1-D task. However, 2-D bivariate models fit the same data better than 2-D univariate models.

Univariate vs. Bivariate Throughputs (TP_{inv})

Using the slope-inverse approach, the average throughput for the 1-D task was TP_{inv}=5.42 bps (*SD*=0.71). The average throughput for the 2-D task with univariate endpoint deviation was TP_{inv}=5.28 bps (*SD*=0.68). These throughputs were not significantly different, indicating comparability across dimensionality as occurred for the mean-of-means approach. The average absolute difference between subjects' 2-D univariate throughput and their 1-D throughput was ΔTP_{inv}=0.56 bps (*SD*=0.44).

In comparison, the average 2-D bivariate throughput was TP_{inv}=4.90 bps (*SD*=0.61), which, like for the mean-of-means approach, was significantly lower than both 1-D throughput ($t(20)$=--3.35, $p<.01$) and 2-D univariate throughput ($t(20)=-11.11$, $p<.0001$). The average absolute difference between subjects' 2-D bivariate throughputs and their 1-D throughputs was ΔTP_{inv}=0.72 bps (*SD*=0.50). As with the mean-of-means approach, these differences were significantly greater than the 2-D univariate differences ($t(20)=2.18$, $p<.05$).

Thus, the findings from the slope-inverse approach to calculating throughput agree with those from the mean-of-means approach, but with different magnitudes.

Throughput Calculation Approaches (TP_{avg} vs. TP_{inv})

Thus far, we have compared univariate (SD_x) and bivariate ($SD_{x,y}$) endpoint deviation calculations for 2-D task data using (*i*) model fits and (*ii*) similarity to 1-D throughputs. While this was our main interest, we also reflect on the two throughput calculations, TP_{avg} and TP_{inv}. We do not advocate for one or the other here, but lend some empirical evidence to them, as prior comparisons have turned largely on principled theoretical concerns [26,30].

First, we compare the throughputs TP_{avg} and TP_{inv} from Table 1. For 1-D throughputs, at 5.42 *vs.* 4.85 bps, TP_{inv} was significantly higher among subjects than TP_{avg} ($t(20)=3.37$, $p<.01$). The same was true of 2-D univariate throughputs, at 5.28 *vs.* 4.91 bps ($t(20)=2.88$, $p<.01$), and 2-D bivariate throughputs, at 4.90 *vs.* 4.49 bps ($t(20)=3.92$, $p<.001$). Clearly, the slope-inverse calculation yields higher throughputs than the mean-of-means calculation.

Besides producing higher throughputs, TP_{inv} also had higher variance among subjects than TP_{avg}. For the 1-D task, standard deviations were 0.71 *vs.* 0.41, respectively. For the 2-D task using univariate endpoint deviation, standard deviations were 0.68 *vs.* 0.43; using bivariate endpoint deviation, standard deviations were 0.61 *vs.* 0.40.

Second, while we learned that 2-D univariate endpoint deviation produces more agreement with 1-D throughputs than 2-D bivariate endpoint deviation, we have not considered whether this result is stronger for TP_{avg} or TP_{inv}. The average absolute difference between 1-D TP_{inv} and 2-D univariate TP_{inv} was 0.56 bps, while for TP_{avg} it was 0.21 bps, a significant difference ($t(20)=3.47$, $p<.01$). For the 2-D bivariate case, ΔTP_{inv} was 0.72 bps, while ΔTP_{avg} was 0.36 bps, again a significant difference ($t(20)=2.90$, $p<.01$). Thus, in both cases, TP_{avg} agrees better between 1-D and 2-D throughputs than does TP_{inv}.

***Form × Scale* (Guiard 2009)**

Recently, Guiard [11] has argued that the typical procedure of separately manipulating *A* and *W* in Fitts' law experiments introduces potential confounds. He contends that the universally agreed upon variable of interest in Fitts' law, and the sole determiner of movement time (*MT*), is index of difficulty (*ID*), which is expressed using the equivocal ratio *A*/W. But typical experimental treatment of Fitts' law regards it as if it had three parameters—*A*, *W*, and *ID*—which introduces a confound when *A* or *W* has a disproportionate effect on *MT*. (As an example, Guiard points to Fitts' original disc-transfer experiment [7].) A remedy, Guiard argues, is to instead manipulate *Form (F)*, which is *ID*, and *Scale (S)*, which is either *A* or *W* but not both. Guiard's practical recommendation is to hold *A* constant and manipulate only *W* over the course of an experiment, thereby removing any potential confound.

In light of Guiard [11], it is conceivable that our throughput results could be affected by the traditional $A \times W$ design, and that an $F \times S$ design is worth exploring. We can retroactively

F×S design	1-D Ribbon Task, Univariate SD_x					2-D Circle Task, Univariate SD_x							2-D Circle Task, Bivariate $SD_{x,y}$						
	a	*b*	*r*	TP_{avg}	TP_{inv}	*a*	*b*	*r*	TP_{avg}	TP_{inv}	ΔTP_{avg}	ΔTP_{inv}	*a*	*b*	*r*	TP_{avg}	TP_{inv}	ΔTP_{avg}	ΔTP_{inv}
Mean	144.69	184.79	.956	4.87	5.66	84.28	198.50	.962	4.89	5.16	0.25	1.03	97.57	214.47	.969	4.49	4.78	0.43	1.22
StdDev	100.52	41.94	.053	0.41	1.19	66.10	32.86	.025	0.43	0.81	0.20	0.70	64.88	36.08	.021	0.40	0.74	0.24	0.74

Table 2. Summary results over 21 subjects for the *Form* × *Scale* design [11] using only one level of *A* (384 pixels) and all six levels of *W*. The data used for each 2-D analysis is exactly the same. Column definitions are the same as for Table 1.

apply Guiard's suggestion by retaining, for example, our middle *A* value (384 pixels) and ignoring trials for which *A* was 256 or 512 pixels. This leaves 1 *A* × 6 *W* for six (ID_e, *MT*) points per subject. Our range of nominal *ID*s becomes 2.00 – 5.61 bits. Our total test trials, excluding outliers, becomes 5039, about a third of our original amount. We re-ran our regressions and throughput analyses, this time keeping only trials for which *A*=384 pixels. Summary outcomes for our new analyses are shown in Table 2.

Comparison of Fitts' Law Models (r, a, b)

Although the average Pearson *r* model fits improved slightly in the *F*×*S* design over the *A*×*W* design, none of these improvements were statistically significant. As for the *A*×*W* design, the two univariate fits were not significantly different, and the 2-D bivariate fits were significantly higher than the 2-D univariate fits ($t(20)$=2.47, p<.05). Unlike in the *A*×*W* design, the 2-D bivariate fits were no longer better than the 1-D fits. As before, the standard deviation of model fits among subjects was low, with the 2-D bivariate model being lower than the 2-D univariate model (.021 *vs.* .025).

Although the average absolute intercept $|a|$ increased in the *F*×*S* design from the *A*×*W* design for each of the three models, these increases were not statistically significant. The standard deviation among subjects of $|a|$ increased as well, and there were more negative intercepts than previously. The 2-D univariate and bivariate intercepts were not significantly different from each other or from the 1-D intercepts.

Slope parameters *b* did not change significantly in the *F*×*S* design from the *A*×*W* design for each of the three models. As in the *A*×*W* design, in the *F*×*S* design the 1-D and 2-D univariate slopes were not significantly different from each other, but both were significantly different from the 2-D bivariate slopes (p<.01).

Univariate vs. Bivariate Throughputs (TP_{avg})

Using the mean-of-means approach to throughput calculation (Eq. 9), the *F*×*S* design produced almost identical TP_{avg} values to those from the *A*×*W* design. Within the *F*×*S* design, as in the full *A*×*W* design, 2-D univariate throughputs were not significantly different from 1-D throughputs. However, as in the *A*×*W* design, 2-D bivariate throughputs were significantly lower than 1-D throughputs ($t(20)$=-5.64, p<.0001). As before, they were also lower than 2-D univariate throughputs ($t(20)$=-23.19, p<.0001). Finally, while the absolute differences in 2-D throughputs from 1-D throughputs (ΔTP_{avg}) were not significantly different from those in the *A*×*W* design, as in the *A*×*W* design, 2-D bivariate throughputs were significantly further from 1-D throughputs than 2-D univariate throughputs ($t(20)$=2.59, p<.05). Thus, despite switching to the *F*×*S* design from the *A*×*W* design, the significance conclusions hold the same for TP_{avg}.

Univariate vs. Bivariate Throughputs (TP_{inv})

Using the slope-inverse approach to throughput calculation, the *F*×*S* design produced similar TP_{inv} values to those from the *A*×*W* design. Within the *F*×*S* design, as in the *A*×*W* design, 2-D univariate throughputs were still not significantly different from 1-D throughputs, but this time the result was only marginal ($t(20)$=-1.98, p=.06). As in the *A*×*W* design, 2-D bivariate throughputs were significantly lower than 1-D throughputs ($t(20)$=-3.59, p<.01) and 2-D univariate throughputs ($t(20)$=-9.10, p<.0001).

Until now, the findings from the *F*×*S* design mirror those from the *A*×*W* design for both TP_{avg} and TP_{inv}. However, the story changes when we examine ΔTP_{inv}. These differences grew significantly in the *F*×*S* design from the *A*×*W* design creating, on average, a discrepancy of over 1 bps per subject for both univariate ($t(20)$=3.22, p<.01) and bivariate ($t(20)$=3.47, p<.01) endpoint deviation. Thus, TP_{inv} was affected far more by the reduction of *A* to one level than was TP_{avg}. This is important in light of Zhai's [30] contention that TP_{avg} is affected more than TP_{inv} by the range of *ID*s used, and Soukoreff and MacKenzie's counter to the contrary [26]. Finally, as in the *A*×*W* design, 2-D bivariate throughputs were significantly further from 1-D throughputs than 2-D univariate throughputs ($t(20)$=2.33, p<.05). Thus, in switching to the *F*×*S* design from the *A*×*W* design, the significance conclusions are the same for TP_{inv} but the discrepancy between 2-D and 1-D throughputs grew significantly to over 1 bps.

Throughput Calculation Approaches (TP_{avg} vs. TP_{inv})

In the full *A*×*W* design, slope-inverse throughputs (TP_{inv}) were significantly higher than mean-of-means throughputs (TP_{avg}) for all three models (p<.05). However, in the *F*×*S* design, this relationship held for only 1-D throughputs ($t(20)$=2.89, p<.01). In the 2-D univariate model, although average TP_{inv} was greater than TP_{avg}, the difference was only marginal ($t(20)$=1.70, p=.10). In the 2-D bivariate model, the difference was also only marginal ($t(20)$=1.93, p=.07). The marginal results are at least due in part to the greatly increased variance among subjects' TP_{inv} values in the *F*×*S* design, which was much higher than for TP_{avg}.

In the *A*×*W* design, 2-D TP_{avg} agreed more with 1-D TP_{avg} than did 2-D TP_{inv} with 1-D TP_{inv} for both the univariate and bivariate models. In the *F*×*S* design, the same was true, with $\Delta TP_{avg} < \Delta TP_{inv}$ for univariate models ($t(20)$=5.05, p<.0001) and bivariate models ($t(20)$=4.83, p<.0001).

The resiliency of Fitts' law to changes in experimental settings is often touted as part of the law's strength. Here we have seen that in light of Guiard's [11] concern over confounding the effects on *MT* of *A*, *W*, and *ID*, switching to a $F{\times}S$ design by holding *A* constant at 384 pixels and varying only *W* has largely produced the same significance conclusions with a third of the experimental effort.

DISCUSSION

To facilitate our discussion, we first restate our key findings, each of which had statistically significant support. Findings A-F are from the full $A{\times}W$ design, while finding G specifically addresses Guiard's $F{\times}S$ design [11].

A. *Fitts' law intercepts transcend dimensionality but slopes change with endpoint deviation.* Model intercepts *a* did not change significantly from 1-D to 2-D tasks, while slopes *b* changed significantly from univariate to bivariate endpoint deviation calculations.

B. *Bivariate models fit 2-D pointing data best.* On the exact same 2-D pointing data, bivariate endpoint deviation gave better model fits, as judged by Pearson *r* coefficients, than univariate endpoint deviation.[4]

C. *2-D univariate throughputs are closest to 1-D univariate throughputs.* Using univariate endpoint deviation for 2-D pointing data gave throughputs closer to 1-D throughputs than using bivariate endpoint deviation under both the mean-of-means throughput calculation and the slope-inverse calculation.

D. *Bivariate models produce lower throughputs.* Using bivariate endpoint deviation produces lower throughputs than using univariate endpoint deviation for the same 2-D pointing data under both throughput calculation schemes. This should be no surprise, as in bivariate models, deviation is being accumulated that is ignored in univariate models. Using bivariate endpoint deviation increases W_e, decreasing ID_e for the same *MT* and thus lowering throughput.

E. *Slope-inverse throughputs are highest and exhibit most variance.* In the $A{\times}W$ design, slope-inverse throughputs were higher than mean-of-means throughputs in both dimensionalities and under both endpoint deviation schemes. They also exhibited greater variance among subjects.

F. *Mean-of-means throughputs agree most across dimensionalities.* Mean-of-means throughputs calculated from 2-D pointing data are closer to 1-D throughputs calculated the same way than are slope-inverse throughputs. This finding holds for both univariate and bivariate 2-D endpoint deviations.

G. *Guiard's [11] Form × Scale design largely upholds the above findings.* Switching to Guiard's $F{\times}S$ design instead of the traditional $A{\times}W$ design did not significantly change model fits or parameters, and findings A-D and F were categorically upheld. Finding E was upheld only for the 1-D case, although for the 2-D cases, the results were both marginal ($.05 \le p \le .10$). Additionally, the $F{\times}S$ design showed that the slope-inverse approach was more sensitive to the reduced *ID* range than the mean-of-means approach: 2-D throughputs became significantly further from 1-D throughputs, and variance among subjects increased considerably.

[4] Note that the better model fits cannot be attributed to an additional model parameter. All linear regression models are still of the form $MT = a+b{\cdot}ID_e$. Endpoint deviation is a dimensionless scalar whether it is calculated from one coordinate or two.

At this point, we are ready to ask: (*i*) how resilient is Fitts' law to changes in dimensionality?, and (*ii*) should univariate or bivariate endpoint deviation be used in 2-D studies? We take each of these questions in turn.

Fitts' Law across Dimensionalities

Is Fitts' law invariant to dimensionality? On this, our findings suggest "yes" if univariate endpoint deviation is used, and "no" if bivariate endpoint deviation is used. Put another way, as long as a 2-D task is treated with 1-D calculations, the results will be comparable to 1-D tasks. Evidence lies in the stability across dimensionalities of model intercepts and slopes (finding A) and throughputs (finding C). However, if bivariate calculations are used, then slopes (but not intercepts), model fits, and throughputs all change significantly across dimensionalities (findings A-D). However, these results do not necessarily mean that univariate deviation is most appropriate for 2-D pointing data; other considerations besides agreement with 1-D pointing studies must be weighed carefully.

Which throughput calculation seems most stable across dimensionalities? TP_{avg} produced throughputs with greater agreement across 1-D and 2-D than did TP_{inv} (finding F).

Univariate or Bivariate Endpoint Deviation in 2-D?

Above, we saw that univariate endpoint deviation calculations for 2-D pointing data cause model parameters and throughputs to better agree with 1-D pointing results. In effect, by using univariate endpoint deviation, we are treating a 2-D task as if it were a 1-D task. But does this mean univariate endpoint deviation should be used, even in 2-D pointing studies?

Agreement across dimensionalities may be an important consideration. At the same time, there are both empirical and theoretical arguments that commend a bivariate approach. Empirically, bivariate endpoint deviation produces better model fits for 2-D pointing data than univariate deviation (finding B), and as noted in footnote 4, this cannot be attributed to an increase in model parameters. Better model fits using the same data and number of parameters are no small concern, for we usually want to prize models with the best possible explanatory power. Theoretically, there is satisfaction knowing that bivariate models do not simply ignore variation in a physically relevant dimension. Although Fitts' law is a model with only one dimension for target size, this does not mean that

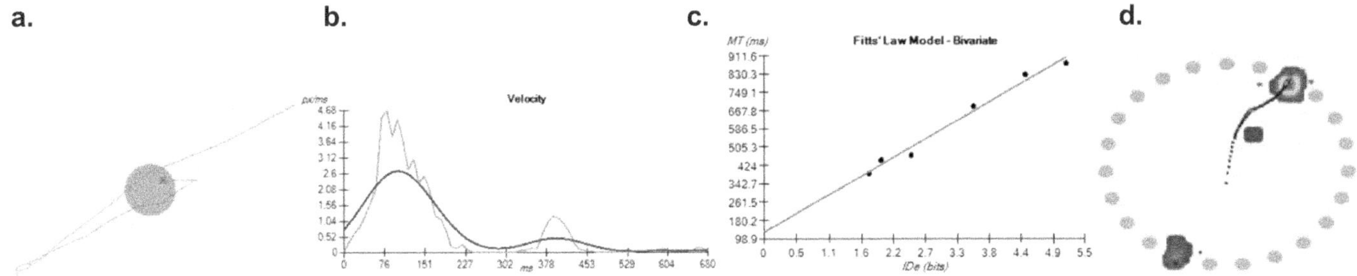

Figure 6. The *FittsStudy* tool offers **(a)** zoomable path visualizations and path analysis measures [17], **(b)** graphical submovement profiles including velocity (shown), acceleration, and jerk over time, and **(c)** Fitts' law models (shown) and pointing error models [28] using both endpoint deviation schemes and throughput calculation approaches [26,30]. **(d)** An example project by students using FittsStudy shows an eye-tracking "heat map" overlaying FittsStudy's ring-of-circles task.

targets or movements must be one-dimensional, just that size (nominal or effective) must be quantified with a dimensionless scalar reflecting *quantity* of tolerance (W) or deviation (W_e). Both SD_x and $SD_{x,y}$ achieve this.

Recommendations

In light of our findings, we recommend the following:

1. Consider using an $F{\times}S$ design by choosing one level of A and varying only W. Doing so will save considerable effort and reduce the chances of factor confounds. Alternatively, use a full $A{\times}W$ design but, afterwards, isolate a middle A value while retaining all W values and reanalyze the data as if it came from an $F{\times}S$ design. If the conclusions change, report them and investigate a disproportionate effect of A or W on MT.
2. For 2-D pointing studies, use bivariate endpoint deviation ($SD_{x,y}$), but examine results from univariate endpoint deviation (SD_x) and report them if they significantly differ.
3. If a goal is to compare results between a 1-D task and a 2-D task, compute 2-D throughputs using the mean-of-means approach (TP_{avg}) based on univariate endpoint deviation (SD_x). Doing so will cause throughputs across dimensionalities to agree best.
4. Comparisons should generally not be drawn across throughput calculation approaches, *i.e.*, comparing throughputs from the mean-of-means approach (TP_{avg}) to those from the slope-inverse approach (TP_{inv}).
5. Given the prevalence of 2-D pointing in user interfaces, we encourage the use of the ISO 9241-9 ring-of-circles task in lieu of the vertical ribbon task.

The *FittsStudy* Tool

To facilitate adoption of the foregoing recommendations, we built a downloadable software tool called *FittsStudy* (Figure 6). FittsStudy logs all pointing trials in a session in XML, from which it builds spreadsheets for statistical analysis. Although Fitts' law evaluation tools have been described in the literature [5,22,25], FittsStudy offers more features than previous tools, providing, among other things, trial browsing and zooming tools, submovement profile graphs, results from both endpoint deviation and throughput calculations, path analysis measures [17], a metronome for time-matching temporal-precision studies (*e.g.*, [23]), and models of movement times and error rates [28,29]. Future work in FittsStudy includes offering not just the vertical ribbon and ring-of-circles tasks, but also random target fields (*e.g.*, [6]), and crossing and steering tasks [1]. FittsStudy can be downloaded for free from http://depts.washington.edu/aimgroup/proj/fittsstudy/ .

FUTURE WORK

This work has made progress in clarifying the effects of task dimensionality, endpoint deviation, throughput calculation, and experiment design on Fitts' law models and measures. However, it has relied on the two suggested ISO 9241-9 task arrangements [13], both of which use regularly-shaped targets. How endpoint deviation should be calculated for irregularly-shaped targets is a topic for future work, and will almost certainly involve probabilistic accounts of endpoint distributions [9,10]. Another item for future work is examining whether the findings comparing outcomes in 1-D and 2-D transfer to 3-D pointing environments. Yet another project could investigate whether different device types other than the mouse change the pattern of results seen here.

CONCLUSION

The strength of our quantitative methods depends on deep understandings of our measures. In this paper, we have addressed Fitts' throughput and its relationship to task dimensionality, endpoint deviation, throughput calculation, and experiment design. Our findings indicate that Fitts' law is largely invariant to dimensionality (1-D *vs.* 2-D), but that this depends on using univariate endpoint deviation (SD_x), even in 2-D, which ignores deviation in the orthogonal task dimension. Bivariate endpoint deviation ($SD_{x,y}$), on the other hand, better models 2-D pointing data. We also offer support for using Guiard's [11] $F{\times}S$ experiment design to save effort and avoid possible confounds. We built FittsStudy to facilitate exploration of these issues and ease the burden of these details on researchers and evaluators.

ACKNOWLEDGEMENTS

The authors thank Ed Cutrell, I. Scott MacKenzie, T. Scott Saponas and Desney Tan. This work was supported in part by Intel Labs, Microsoft Research, and the National Science Foundation under grants IIS-0811063 and IIS-0952786.

REFERENCES

1. Accot, J. and Zhai, S. (1997). Beyond Fitts' law: Models for trajectory-based HCI tasks. *Proc. CHI '97*. New York: ACM Press, 295-302.
2. Accot, J. and Zhai, S. (2003). Refining Fitts' law models for bivariate pointing. *Proc. CHI '03*. New York: ACM Press, 193-200.
3. Card, S.K., English, W.K. and Burr, B.J. (1978). Evaluation of mouse, rate-controlled isometric joystick, step keys, and text keys for text selection on a CRT. *Ergonomics 21* (8), 601-613.
4. Crossman, E.R.F.W. (1957). The speed and accuracy of simple hand movements. In *The Nature and Acquisition of Industrial Skills*, Crossman and Seymour (eds.). Report to the Joint Committee on Individual Efficiency in Industry.
5. Douglas, S.A., Kirkpatrick, A.E. and MacKenzie, I.S. (1999). Testing pointing device performance and user assessment with the ISO 9241, Part 9 standard. *Proc. CHI '99*. New York: ACM Press, 215-222.
6. Findlater, L., Jansen, A., Shinohara, K., Dixon, M., Kamb, P., Rakita, J. and Wobbrock, J.O. (2010). Enhanced area cursors: Reducing fine-pointing demands for people with motor impairments. *Proc. UIST '10*. New York: ACM Press, 153-162.
7. Fitts, P.M. (1954). The information capacity of the human motor system in controlling the amplitude of movement. *J. Experimental Psychology 47* (6), 381-391.
8. Fitts, P.M. and Radford, B.K. (1966). Information capacity of discrete motor responses under different cognitive sets. *J. Experimental Psychology 71* (4), 475-482.
9. Grossman, T. and Balakrishnan, R. (2005). A probabilistic approach to modeling two-dimensional pointing. *ACM Transactions on Computer-Human Interaction 12* (3), 435-459.
10. Grossman, T., Kong, N. and Balakrishnan, R. (2007). Modeling pointing at targets of arbitrary shapes. *Proc. CHI '07*. New York: ACM Press, 463-472.
11. Guiard, Y. (2009). The problem of consistency in the design of Fitts' law experiments: Consider either target distance and width or movement form and scale. *Proc. CHI '09*. New York: ACM Press, 1809-1818.
12. Hancock, P.A. and Newell, K.M. (1985). The movement speed-accuracy relationship in space-time. In *Motor Behavior: Programming, Control, and Acquisition*, Heuer, Kleinbeck and Schmidt (eds.). New York: Springer-Verlag, 153-188.
13. International Organization for Standardization. (2002). Ergonomic requirements for office work with visual display terminals (VDTs)—Requirements for non-keyboard input devices. *Ref. No. ISO 9241-9:2000(E)*.
14. Jagacinski, R.J. and Monk, D.L. (1985). Fitts' law in two dimensions with hand and head movements. *J. Motor Behavior 17* (1), 77-95.
15. MacKenzie, I.S. (1992). Fitts' law as a research and design tool in human-computer interaction. *Human-Computer Interaction 7* (1), 91-139.
16. MacKenzie, I.S. and Buxton, W. (1992). Extending Fitts' law to two-dimensional tasks. *Proc. CHI '92*. New York: ACM Press, 219-226.
17. MacKenzie, I.S., Kauppinen, T. and Silfverberg, M. (2001). Accuracy measures for evaluating computer pointing devices. *Proc. CHI '01*. New York: ACM Press, 9-16.
18. MacKenzie, I.S. and Soukoreff, R.W. (2003). Card, English, and Burr (1978)—25 years later. *Extended Abstracts CHI '03*. New York: ACM Press, 760-761.
19. MacKenzie, I.S. and Isokoski, P. (2008). Fitts' throughput and the speed-accuracy tradeoff. *Proc. CHI '08*. New York: ACM Press, 1633-1636.
20. Murata, A. (1996). Empirical evaluation of performance models of pointing accuracy and speed with a PC mouse. *Int'l J. Human-Computer Interaction 8* (4), 457-469.
21. Murata, A. (1999). Extending effective target width in Fitts' law to a two-dimensional pointing task. *Int'l J. Human-Computer Interaction 11* (2), 137-152.
22. Schedlbauer, M. (2007). An extensible platform for the interactive exploration of Fitts' law and related movement time models. *Extended Abstracts CHI '07*. New York: ACM Press, 2633-2638.
23. Schmidt, R.A., Zelaznik, H., Hawkins, B., Frank, J.S. and Quinn, J.T. (1979). Motor-output variability: A theory for the accuracy of rapid motor acts. *Psychological Review 86* (5), 415-451.
24. Sheikh, I.H. and Hoffmann, E.R. (1994). Effect of target shape on movement time in a Fitts task. *Ergonomics 37* (9), 1533-1547.
25. Soukoreff, R.W. and MacKenzie, I.S. (1995). Generalized Fitts' law model builder. *Companion to CHI '95*. New York: ACM Press, 113-114.
26. Soukoreff, R.W. and MacKenzie, I.S. (2004). Towards a standard for pointing device evaluation, perspectives on 27 years of Fitts' law research in HCI. *Int'l J. Human-Computer Studies 61* (6), 751-789.
27. Welford, A.T. (1968). *Fundamentals of Skill*. London, England: Methuen.
28. Wobbrock, J.O., Cutrell, E., Harada, S. and MacKenzie, I.S. (2008). An error model for pointing based on Fitts' law. *Proc. CHI '08*. New York: ACM Press, 1613-1622.
29. Wobbrock, J.O., Jansen, A. and Shinohara, K. (2011). Modeling and predicting pointing errors in two dimensions. *Proc. CHI '11*. New York: ACM Press. To appear.
30. Zhai, S. (2004). Characterizing computer input with Fitts' law parameters–the information and non-information aspects of pointing. *Int'l J. Human-Computer Studies 61* (6), 791-809.
31. Zhai, S., Kong, J. and Ren, X. (2004). Speed-accuracy tradeoff in Fitts' law tasks—on the equivalency of actual and nominal pointing precision. *Int'l J. Human-Computer Studies 61* (6), 823-856.

The Effects of Intended Use on Target Acquisition

Regan L. Mandryk and Calvin Lough
Department of Computer Science, University of Saskatchewan
176 Thorvaldson Bldg., 110 Science Place, Saskatoon, Saskatchewan, S7N5C9
regan@cs.usask.ca, calvin.lough@usask.ca

ABSTRACT
Fitts's Law has been used extensively in HCI to describe 2D targeting; however, the controlled tasks generally used neglect aspects of real-world pointing, including how the intended use of a target affects its acquisition. We studied aiming to a target in four tasks requiring varying precision after acquisition. Our results present the first evidence that the intended use of a target affects its acquisition in terms of movement time and motion kinematics for computer aiming. Important for researchers who model 2D targeting, our results also have particular impact for HCI research that uses motion kinematics.

Author Keywords
Pointing, Fitts's Law, motion kinematics, intention

ACM Classification Keywords
H5.2. Information Interfaces and Presentation: User Interfaces - *Interaction Styles; Input devices and strategies.*

General Terms
Human Factors.

INTRODUCTION
There has been a long history of using Fitts's Law [2,6] to describe pointing on a computer display and to build models of targeting in HCI. Researchers generally use controlled tasks of a single type that represent common activities in computer use (e.g., reciprocal tapping task, docking task) to study targeting and build performance models. As results from these controlled studies begin to influence the development of interaction techniques – such as endpoint prediction-based targeting assistance – we need to consider whether there are aspects of computer aiming that laboratory experiments do not adequately represent. For example, by studying only discrete aiming tasks, we do not consider how the intended use of a target (e.g., click, dock) affects its initial acquisition.

Previous studies in human motor control have shown that intended use of a grasped disk affects the wrist kinematics of the initial reach-to-grasp movement [8]. Tasks requiring greater precision after the acquisition produced different movement times and velocity profiles. It is possible that the intended use of a target affects pointing behavior in desktop settings, as many of our models of pointing on 2D displays are derived from research on 3D aiming in the real world.

We focus on one aspect of intention – what the user will do with a target after its acquisition. We call this intention as the user plans their aiming movement to a target with its intended use in mind. We tested the effects of target use in 2D aiming with a mouse, over four tasks (targeting, double targeting, flicking, and docking), and found that the intended use of a target affects the movement time and motion kinematics of the initial target acquisition. Our results are important for researchers who model aiming on a computer, and have particular impact for HCI research that uses kinematics (e.g., endpoint prediction), or that attempts to model aiming in real-world computer use.

RELATED WORK

Models of Targeting
Woodworth [13] investigated the speed-accuracy tradeoff in aiming movements, and proposed that aiming is comprised of two phases: an initial impulse toward the target, and a deceleration phase to home-in on the target. Fitts & Peterson [2] quantified the speed-accuracy tradeoff for *discrete* aiming movements in what is now known as Fitts's Law [6]. Fitts's Law has been adapted to model computer aiming [6]. The equation quantifies the difficulty of an aiming task (the index of difficulty, ID), and demonstrates that movement time (MT) can be correlated with ID and predicted with a regression equation.

(1) $ID = log_2\left(\frac{A}{W} + 1\right)$ (2) $MT = a + b(ID)$

where A is the movement amplitude, W is the target width, and a and b are empirically-determined constants. There are various models of motor control for aiming movements, but the most successful one corresponds with Woodworth's two-phase model. The optimized initial impulse model [9] suggests that an initial ballistic movement is made towards the target, and if successful, then the task is accomplished. If not, a secondary movement is undertaken and this process repeats until the target is acquired. To optimize aiming movements under the constraints of the speed-accuracy tradeoff, movements consist of a high-velocity (ballistic) initial phase, and a series of slower, visually-guided, feedback-corrected movements (homing-in).

Motion Kinematics

MacKenzie et al. [5] examined the 3D velocity profiles of discrete aiming movements and showed that for movements of the same ID (i.e., same MT), the shape of the velocity profiles differed depending on A & W. The timing and magnitude of the peak velocity (ballistic phase) related to movement amplitude, while the proportion of time spent decelerating (homing-in phase) depended on target width. Walker reproduced the relationship between movement amplitude and peak velocity for 2D aiming with mice [12].

Kinematic measures have been used in HCI to describe differences between physical and virtual pointing [3] and to discriminate between aiming to different target shapes [11]. Velocity-based measures also have explanatory power for movement time differences. They have been used in HCI to explain the effects of sticky targets [7] and aiming across multiple displays [10]. Kinematic measures have also been used to predict the endpoint of a targeting motion [1, 4].

Motion Constraints

Marteniuk et al. [8] investigated 3D movement trajectories of the wrist for aiming under varying constraints, such as grasping a disk to either throw into a box or place in a tight-fitting well. They found that although the initial reach-to-grasp movement was the same, grasping a disk to place it into a tight-fitting well resulted in longer movement times, reflected in the lengthening of the deceleration phase. In addition, velocity just prior to grasp was higher for the throwing condition than the placing condition.

EXPERIMENT

We studied how the intended use of a target affects the motion time and kinematics of the initial targeting motion.

Experimental Setting and Protocol

Users performed a discrete aiming task [2] using a system implemented in Python on a 3.6 GHz WinXP machine, a 17-inch monitor (1280x1024 pixels), and a gaming-grade Logitech G5 optical mouse with a 2000 DPI resolution.

Task

Participants performed four different discrete aiming tasks. The initial aiming movement of each task (*subtask one*) was the same, but the tasks required different actions to be taken once the target was acquired (*subtask two*) (see Figure 1).

For the aiming subtask, participants were presented with a series of trials that first required them to select a grey start square and subsequently select a green target circle, which was presented as soon as the start square was clicked. When the cursor entered the circle, visual feedback was provided to the user by changing the colour of the circle to lighter green. Target circles were presented at three *target widths* (30, 60, and 120 pixels) and three *movement amplitudes* (150, 300, and 600 pixels), which combined to form five unique *IDs* (1.17, 1.81, 2.58, 3.46, 4.39 bits). As shown in Figure 1, the start square and target circle were always presented in a straight line along the center of the display. Descriptions of the action subtask for the four tasks follow.

Target Task: For the *target* task, users were instructed to click on a circular target when it appeared on the screen (subtask one). Once the initial target was acquired, participants returned to the start square for the next trial.

Dual Target Task: For the *dual target* task, both the primary target (green circle) and a secondary target (blue circle) were displayed. Participants were instructed to click on the primary target (subtask one) before clicking on the secondary target (subtask two). Secondary targets were presented in one of three directions (left, right, and top).

Flick Task: In the *flick* task, both the primary target and a 35-pixel green border were presented to participants at the beginning of the trial. Participants were instructed to flick the target towards the green border, which was presented in one of three directions (the left, right, or top edge). This task was intended to reflect the throwing task in [8].

Docking Task: The docking task (*dock*) required participants to first select the primary target, and then drag the target into a circular dock. The dock had a width that was 20 pixels larger than the width of the primary target, and was presented at one of three locations (left, right, and top). This task was intended to echo the fitting task in [8].

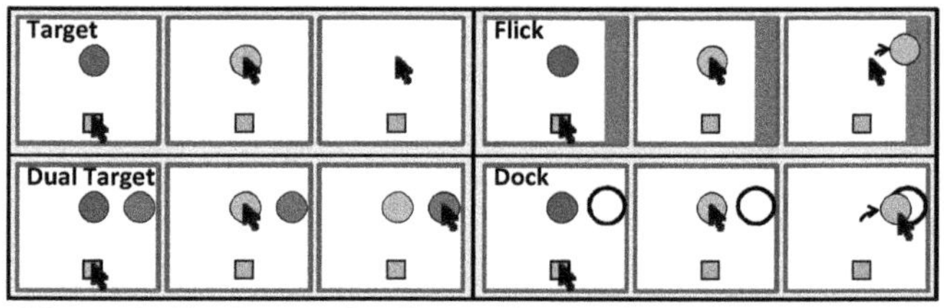

Figure 1. The four tasks. Frame 1- selecting the start square; Frame 2- the initial targeting movement (same for all tasks); Frame 3- the action to be taken with the acquired object.

The four tasks varied in the precision required in subtask two. Target and dual target were low-precision tasks; flick was medium-precision; and dock was a high-precision task.

Design

The experiment used a 4(*task*) by 3(*width*) by 3(*amplitude*) within-subjects full-factorial design. In addition, 3 targeting *directions* were presented for the *dual, flick*, and *dock* tasks. For each combination of factors, users completed 3 trial blocks (first block was training), resulting in 270 trials per participant. The order of trials within a task was random, while the order of the four tasks was fully counterbalanced.

Participants and Procedure

After filling in a consent form and demographic survey, participants were introduced to the four tasks, and were instructed to complete each trial as quickly as possible while remaining accurate. Forty-eight participants (22 female), aged 18-38 (mean 24) all used computers daily and were right-hand mouse users. The study took 20 minutes.

Data Analyses and Dependent Measures

All dependent measures focus on the initial aiming movement to the primary target (subtask one) and were determined from computer logs. Movement time (*MT*) was defined as the time from clicking on the start square until the primary target was selected. We logged errors of three types: *click errors*- when participants clicked outside of the primary target after selecting the start square; *exit errors*- when participants exited and re-entered the primary target prior to selection; *start errors*- when users moved off the start square after clicking, but before the target appeared.

Computer logs also recorded all of the mouse cursor x- and y- positions and accompanying timestamps. These were processed trial-by-trial in MATLAB and interpolated to create time-equidistant (120Hz) arrays. These arrays were differentiated to provide cursor velocity in both the x- and y- directions, then used to calculate velocity profiles, which were smoothed using a 25ms moving-average filter window. These profiles were used to calculate the motion kinematics measures including: peak velocity (pkV), time to peak velocity (tPkV), percent of time after peak velocity (%afterPkV), and click velocity (clickVel) for each trial. Click velocity was calculated as the mean velocity over the 33ms prior to selecting the primary target.

Outlier trials that took longer than three standard deviations above the mean (calculated over all trials) to complete were removed (177/12960 trials, 1.4%). We also removed trials that contained start errors (324) and click errors (360) from further analyses (684 trials, 5.3%). Due to large numbers of start errors leaving empty cells in the experiment design, three participants were removed from subsequent analyses.

After averaging over repeated trials, a one-way ANOVA tested whether *direction* in subtask two affected the initial aiming movement for flick, dock, and dual target. No difference was found (p=.851); these trials were aggregated. We conducted a RM-MANOVA on MT, PkV, tPkV, %afterPkV, ClickVel, and exit errors with ID (Equation 1) and task as factors, and with α=0.05. When the sphericity assumption was violated, the Huynh-Feldt method for adjusting the degrees of freedom was used. All pairwise comparisons used the Bonferroni correction with α=0.05.

Results

As expected, there were effects of ID on all measures (all p<.001, $.29<\eta^2<.94$). For MT, PkV, and tPkV, pairwise tests showed differences between each ID. For %afterPkV and clickVel, differences were found between each ID except for between the two smallest IDs. There were no interactions between ID and task on any of the measures except MT ($F_{9.2,403.0}$=3.6, p<.001, η^2=.08; all other p>.100). The interaction showed that there was no difference between the 2 smallest IDs for the target and dual tasks, but that all other levels of ID were different for all of the tasks.

Movement Time and Exit Errors

There was a significant effect of task on MT ($F_{2.8,120.9}$=17.5, p<0.001, η^2=.28). Pairwise comparisons showed that target and dual target were faster than flick or dock. See Figure 2.

There was no significant effect of task on exit error rates ($F_{3,132}$=.62, p=.602, η^2=.01). See Figure 2.

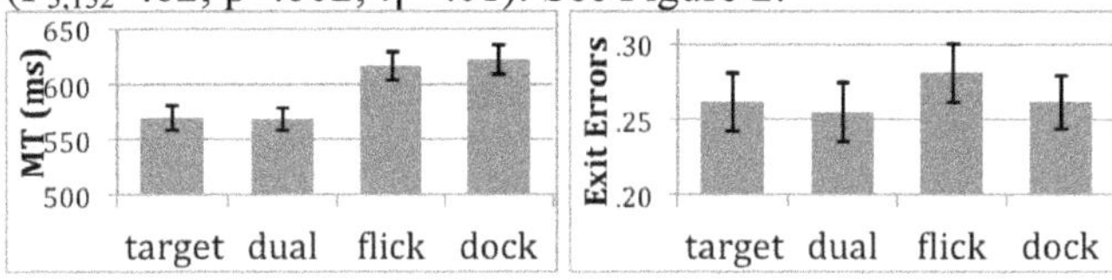

Figure 2. Means ± SE for movement time and exit errors.

Velocity-based Measures

There was a significant effect of task on PkV ($F_{3,132}$=4.7, p=.004, η^2=.10). Pairwise comparisons showed that flick had a higher PkV than target or dual target (see Figure 3).

There was a significant effect of task on clickVel ($F_{3,132}$=14.9, p<.001, η^2=.25). Pairwise comparisons showed that participants were moving faster just prior to click in target and dual target than flick or dock. See Figure 3.

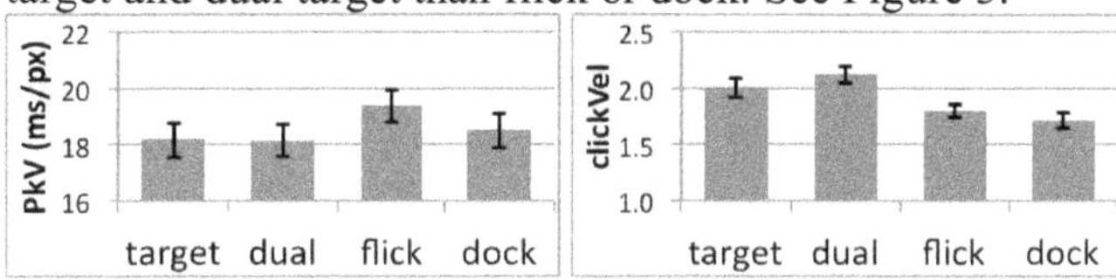

Figure 3. Means ± SE for peak velocity and click velocity.

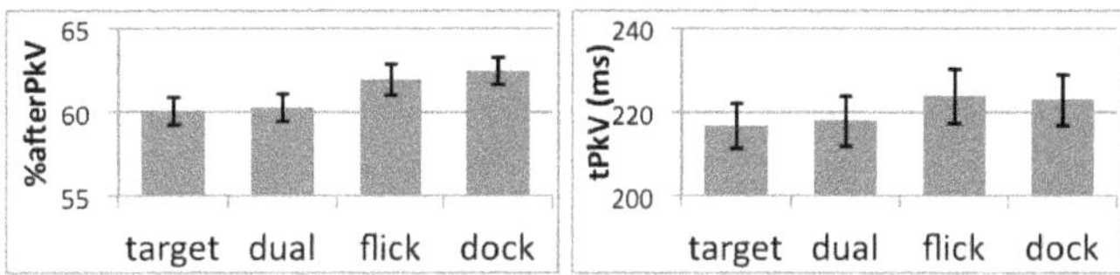

Figure 4. Means ± SE for time to peak velocity and % time after peak velocity.

There was a significant effect of task on %afterPkV ($F_{3,132}$=3.8, p=.011, η^2=.08). Pairwise comparisons showed that target and dual target had shorter deceleration phases than dock. See Figure 4. There was no significant effect of task on tPkV ($F_{2.7,117.5}$=1.0, p=.382, η^2=.02). See Figure 4.

DISCUSSION

Our results show that intended use of a target changes targeting performance with a mouse. Mirroring results for a real-world reach-to-grasp task [8], subtask one of the high-precision task (dock) had a longer movement time, longer deceleration phase, and lower velocity just prior to click, though all tasks had the same initial aiming movement. Conversely, subtask one of the lower-precision tasks (target, dual) had shorter movement times, shorter deceleration phases, and higher click velocities.

These results show that the changes in movement time can be attributed to the differences in the secondary feedback-correction phase, and not the initial ballistic phase of aiming. Mirroring [8], our results can be explained by the precision requirements; as precision of the objective increases, so does MT– the deceleration phase is lengthened and the velocity profile shape is changed through a longer proportion of movement in deceleration. We speculate that the motor planning and control for the second subtask is encapsulated within the second phase of the first subtask.

Our flick task was intended to mirror the low-precision 'throw' task in [8]; however, participants' comments made it clear that our implementation of flick required precision. We used velocity of the cursor just prior to release to give velocity to the target and did not incorporate momentum of the cursor just after release of the mouse. Users found this task to require more precision than the two targeting tasks, and our results show no differences in any of the measures between flick and dock. Future work will study alternative low-precision tasks and implementations of flick.

Relative Impact of ID and Task

Movement time is primarily determined by index of difficulty, as shown in Equation 2. The variance in MT due directly to manipulations in ID is high; η^2 for the effect of ID on MT was .94. Although the variance in MT due to task was smaller (η^2=.28), task produced significant differences. The intended use of an object has impact on the initial aiming movement to that object, although movement time will still be determined primarily by ID. Our interaction effect of ID and task on MT showed that for the two easiest targets (smallest IDs), there were no MT differences for the two low-precision tasks (target and dual target). Thus the easiest aiming movement, as defined by the combination of task and ID, did not show MT differences.

Implications for HCI

Most research in HCI that models aiming is conducted with highly-controlled tasks in an laboratory setting. Our results show that users' intended use of an object will impact the movement time and motion kinematics of the initial aiming movement to acquire the target. Researchers in HCI should acknowledge the effect of intended use on movement time and motion kinematics and be aware of how their choice of task (high or low precision) will affect their results.

Our results have particular importance for endpoint prediction. There is a recognized need for endpoint prediction to realize targeting assistance techniques that have been developed in the laboratory [4]; however, prediction techniques using motion kinematics will lose accuracy because of the variability in motion kinematics depending on intended use. Smart techniques that consider common uses of different widgets may improve accuracy.

Finally, there has been little effort to study Fitts's law in real computer use due to difficulties in data gathering and processing. For example, choosing tighter constraints on classifying targeting motions will invariably improve the model's performance. In lab studies, researchers control the task; thus, intended use has little impact on the performance of the model. To model aiming movements in real computer use, the intended or actual use of an acquired target will need to be noted and accounted for in the modeling process.

CONCLUSIONS

This research presents the first evidence that the intended use of a target affects its acquisition in terms of movement time and motion kinematics for computer aiming tasks. Our results are important for researchers who model aiming on a computer, and have particular impact for research that uses kinematics, (e.g., endpoint prediction), or that attempts to model aiming in real-world computer use.

ACKNOWLEDGEMENTS

We thank NSERC for funding and the University of Saskatchewan HCI lab and Andy Cockburn for feedback.

REFERENCES

1. Asano, T., Sharlin, E., Kitamura, Y., Takashima, K., & Kishino, F. Predictive Interaction Using the Delphian desktop. *Proc. UIST'05*, 133-141.
2. Fitts,P.M. Peterson,J.R. Information capacity of discrete motor responses. *J.Exp. Psych., 67*, 1964, 103-112.
3. Graham, E., & MacKenzie, C.L. "Physical versus virtual pointing," *Proc. CHI'96*, 292-299.
4. Lank, E., Cheng, Y., & Ruiz, J. Endpoint prediction using motion kinematics. *Proc. CHI'07*, 637–646.
5. MacKenzie, C.L., Marteniuk, R.G., Dugas, C., & Eickmeier, B. Three-dimensional movement trajectories in Fitts' task: Implications for motor control. *QJEP, 39A*, 1987, 629-647.
6. MacKenzie, I.S.. Fitts' law as a research and design tool in human-computer interaction. *JHCI, 7*, 1992, 91-139.
7. Mandryk, R.L. & Gutwin, C. Perceptibility and utility of sticky targets. *Proc. GI'08*, 65-72.
8. Marteniuk, R.G., MacKenzie, C.L., Jeannerod, M., Athenes, S., & Dugas, C. Constraints on human arm movement trajectories. *Canadian Journal of Psychology, 41(3)*, 1987, 365-378.
9. Meyer, D., Abrams, R., Kornblum, S., Wright, C., & Smith, J. Optimality in human motor performance: Ideal control of rapid aiming movements. *Psych. Review, 95,* 1988, 340-370.
10. Nacenta, M.A., Mandryk, R.L., Gutwin, C. Targeting across displayless space. *Proc. CHI '08*, 777-786.
11. Ruiz, J., Tausky, D., Bunt, A., Lank, E., & Mann, R. Analyzing the kinematics of bivariate pointing. *Proc. GI'08,* 251-258.
12. Walker, N., Meyer, D.E., & Smelter, J.B. Spatial and temporal characteristics of rapid cursor positioning movements with electromechanical mice in human-computer interaction. *Hum. Fac., 35(3)*, 1993, 431-458.
13. Woodworth,R.S. The accuracy of voluntary movements, Psych. Review Monograph, Supp., 1899, 31-114.

Modeling and Predicting Pointing Errors in Two Dimensions

Jacob O. Wobbrock, Alex Jansen, Kristen Shinohara
The Information School
DUB Group
University of Washington
Seattle, WA 98195 USA
{wobbrock, ajansen7, kshino}@uw.edu

ABSTRACT

Recently, Wobbrock *et al.* (2008) derived a predictive model of pointing accuracy to complement Fitts' law's predictive model of pointing speed. However, their model was based on one-dimensional (1-D) horizontal movement, while applications of such a model require two dimensions (2-D). In this paper, the pointing error model is investigated for 2-D pointing in a study of 21 participants performing a time-matching task on the ISO 9241-9 ring-of-circles layout. Results show that the pointing error model holds well in 2-D. If univariate endpoint deviation (SD_x) is used, regressing on N=72 observed *vs.* predicted error rate points yields R^2=.953. If bivariate endpoint deviation ($SD_{x,y}$) is used, regression yields R^2=.936. For both univariate and bivariate models, the magnitudes of observed and predicted error rates are comparable.

Author Keywords: Pointing error model, Fitts' law, metronome, movement time, error prediction, error rates.

ACM Classification Keywords: H.5.2 [Information interfaces and presentation]: User interfaces – *theory and methods*; H.1.2 [Models and principles]: User/machine systems – *human factors*.

General Terms: Experimentation, Measurement, Theory.

INTRODUCTION

Fitts' law [3,6] predicts movement time (MT) in rapid aimed pointing tasks with the following formulae:

$$MT = a + b \cdot ID, \tag{1}$$

$$ID = \log_2(A/W + 1). \tag{2}$$

ID is the task index of difficulty measured in *bits*. Task parameters are target distance A and size W, and a and b are empirical regression coefficients.

Recently, Wobbrock *et al.* [13] derived a predictive model of pointing accuracy (Eq. 3) to complement Fitts' law's predictive model of pointing speed. The independent variables in the model include target distance (A) and size (W), but now instead of predicting MT, time becomes the *actual* time taken to reach the target, MT_e. Thus, movement time becomes an *independent* variable in the accuracy model instead of the dependent result of Fitts' law. Eq. 3 uses the error function (*erf*); see footnote 1 in [13].

$$P_{error} = 1 - erf\left\{\frac{1}{A\sqrt{2}}\left[2.066 \cdot W\left(2^{\frac{MT_e - a'}{b'}} - 1\right)\right]\right\} \tag{3}$$

It is when a user's movement time may not be predictable by Fitts' law that the above pointing error model is potentially most useful. Haste, tentativeness, or extra care may cause users to point at speeds not predicted by Fitts' law. For example, in computer games, targets often appear for short durations, forcing players to rush. Another example is predicting text entry error rates on stylus keyboards for users that deliberately slow down or speed up. Yet another example is in safety-critical interfaces when trying to make controls big enough in light of space constraints to ensure a given error rate. In all instances, a pointing error model is required to make quantitative performance predictions. A current limitation, however, is that Eq. 3 was based on horizontal pointing to one-dimensional (1-D) vertical ribbon targets, but applications of a pointing error model require two dimensions (2-D).

In this paper, we investigate the accuracy of the pointing error model using the 2-D multidirectional ring-of-circles arrangement from the ISO 9241-9 standard [4,10]. As in Wobbrock *et al.*'s 1-D study [13], we use a time-matching metronome task to control MT_e as an independent variable. The metronome is paced individually for each subject by first establishing that subject's Fitts' law model.

Our findings show that the pointing error model holds well in 2-D. If univariate endpoint deviation (SD_x) is used while fitting Fitts' law, regressing on N=72 observed (y) *vs.* predicted (x) error rate points yields R^2=.953 with an equation of $y = .026 + 1.045x$. Using bivariate endpoint deviation ($SD_{x,y}$) yields R^2=.936 with an equation of $y = -.002 + 0.916x$. (Having R^2=1.00 and y=x would be a "perfect model.") Thus, both outcomes show well-fit models and comparable magnitudes of observed and predicted error rates.

REVIEW OF THE POINTING ERROR MODEL

Here, we do not re-derive the pointing error model of Eq. 3, but instead highlight aspects relevant to our inquiry. Readers are directed to prior work [13] for the derivation.

Important to the derivation of the pointing error model is the observation that endpoints in rapid aimed movements follow a normal distribution,[1] and that the entropy therein is $\log_2 \sigma\sqrt{2\pi e}$, where σ is the standard deviation of the distribution. As Welford [12] (pp. 147-148) and MacKenzie [6] explain, this results in about 96% of endpoints falling within the distribution, and about 4% falling outside. When a ~4% error rate occurs in an experiment, $\log_2 W$ accurately reflects the information in the distribution. But when subjects point with a higher error rate, their "effective" target width W_e is greater than W. When they point with an error rate less than 4%, $W_e < W$. Thus, W_e enables a *post hoc* adjustment to a 4% error rate. This is the basis for Crossman's speed-accuracy correction [1], which uses W_e instead of W in Eq. 2 and allows a "fast but careless" subject to be compared to a "slow and careful" subject. When fitting Fitts' law models to subjects, the effective index of difficulty (ID_e) in Eq. 4 replaces the nominal ID from Eq. 2, effecting Crossman's correction.

$$ID_e = \log_2(A_e/W_e + 1), \tag{4}$$

$$W_e = 4.133 \cdot SD_x \tag{5}$$

In Eq. 4, A_e reflects the mean distance of actual movements. In Eq. 5, SD_x is the univariate standard deviation of endpoint x-coordinates for an $A\times W$ condition whose data have been rotated to a reference axis (*e.g.*, 0°).

The pointing error model assumes that if a subject points at the speed with which Fitts' law predicts they should (*i.e.*, $MT_e = MT$), they will point with a ~4% error rate.[2] If they point faster than Fitts' law predicts they should (*i.e.*, $MT_e < MT$), the error rate will rise above 4%. If they point slower (*i.e.*, $MT_e > MT$), the error rate will drop below 4%.

In Eq. 3, the regression coefficients a' and b' are decorated with primes to indicate they are not from a traditional Fitts' law study but instead come from fitting Fitts' law to, ideally, a range of $MT_e \neq MT$. Put another way, a' and b' should be built upon movements spanning the speeds for which one intends to predict error rates.

Wobbrock *et al.*'s [13] investigation of the pointing error model in 1-D resulted in a model fit of R^2=.959 for N=90 observed (y) *vs.* predicted (x) points with a regression equation of $y = .007 + 0.958x$, similar to our results here.

A NOTE ON ENDPOINT DEVIATION IN 2-D

As described above, the pointing error model relies on Fitts' law regression coefficients a' and b', which arise from fitting a line to a subject's (ID_e, MT_e) points; ID_e relies on W_e, which relies on SD_x, the spread of hits. In both 1-D and 2-D, this spread of hits can be defined as a deviation of coordinates around their centroid [2,5]. A deviation of 1-D coordinates around a centroid reduces to the standard deviation formula for scalars. However, in 2-D, this reduction does not occur [14]; accordingly, we have the option of either using SD_x and ignoring deviation orthogonal to the task axis, or of using bivariate deviation $SD_{x,y}$ and capturing deviation in both dimensions. For completeness, we explore error predictions using both univariate (SD_x) and bivariate ($SD_{x,y}$) endpoint deviation as the basis for W_e and ID_e. See [14] for further discussion.

METHOD

Subjects and Apparatus

Twenty-one subjects participated in our study, of which a third were female. All subjects were right-handed. Average age was 29.3 years (SD=6.9). Subjects were run on a 21" Samsung SyncMaster 214T flat panel monitor set to 1600×1200 resolution. The computer had a Xeon CPU running Windows 7 at 3 GHz with 2 GB RAM. The input device was a Logitech optical mouse. We built a full-screen program in C♯ called *FittsStudy* [14] to facilitate the study.

Procedure

Our study consisted of two parts, both of which used the ISO 9241-9 ring-of-circles target arrangement [4,10] with 23 targets per ring. The first three of these targets were logged as practice and ignored during analysis, leaving 20 test trials per ring. A trial began immediately following the click of the previous trial and ended with a single click, regardless of whether that click hit the target. Misses were accompanied by a red flash and an audible ding.

Part 1. Subjects' individual Fitts' law models were built. FittsStudy was configured to administer 18 $A\times W$ conditions defined by 3 levels of A {256, 384, 512 pixels} and 6 levels of W {8, 16, 32, 64, 96, 128 pixels}, yielding 13 unique IDs ranging from 1.59 – 6.02 bits. Subjects' Fitts' law models were used to parameterize the metronome in part 2.

Part 2. A metronome-based time-matching study was run.[3] In this part, the same 18 $A\times W$ conditions were used, but now they were crossed with 4 levels of $MT_{\%}$ {0.6, 0.8, 1.0, 1.2}, a factor that, when multiplied by a subject's Fitts' law-predicted movement time (MT), gave the raw speed of the metronome as MT_{ms} (Eq. 6). By manipulating $MT_{\%}$ instead of raw MT_{ms}, subject-specific speed differences were accommodated.

$$MT_{ms} = MT_{\%} \times MT \tag{6}$$

The metronome was both visual and auditory, with the current circle target progressively flood-filling from the center outward and an audible "tick" playing the moment the fill completed, which was also the moment the subjects were supposed to click. After this moment, the flood fill disappeared and began to grow again.

[1] In 2-D, deviations in both x and y are normally distributed [8], but often with different extents.

[2] One can verify this by substituting $a + b \log_2(A/W + 1)$ for MT_e in Eq. 3, which gives $P_{error} = 1 - erf(2.066/\sqrt{2}) \approx .039$, about 4%.

[3] Metronomes are, of course, not part of everyday computer use, but they have been employed in motor psychology to control movement time [9]. A metronome is *not* required for the pointing error model, only the actual movement time MT_e (see Eq. 3).

In part 1, 21 subjects completed 18 $A \times W$ conditions each comprising 20 test trials for a total of 7560 trials. In part 2, the same 21 subjects completed 72 $MT_{\%} \times A \times W$ conditions each comprising 20 test trials for a total of 30,240 trials.

Analysis

When fitting Fitts' law to a subject, each $A \times W$ ring of 20 test trials resulted in one (ID_e, MT_e) point, giving 18 points for regression per subject in part 1 and 72 points in part 2. As stated above, part 1's a and b coefficients were used to set the metronome, while part 2's a' and b' coefficients were used in Eq. 3 for error rate prediction. Crossman's speed-accuracy correction [1] was used for each subject in each condition. All trials within an $A \times W$ or $MT_{\%} \times A \times W$ condition were normalized to horizontal (0°) before endpoint deviations were computed as SD_x and $SD_{x,y}$.

RESULTS

Adjustment of Data

For part 1, spatial outliers were removed. They were defined from prior work [7] as errors whose effective distances were less than half their nominal distances, or whose endpoints fell more than twice their target widths from their target centers. In all, 2 spatial outliers were removed from part 1 (0.03%). For part 2, spatial outliers were kept, but temporal outliers were removed, defined as movements whose actual durations were shorter than 75% or longer than 125% of the metronome interval. In all, 340 temporal outliers were removed from part 2 (1.12%).

Part 1, Fitts' Law Models ($A \times W$)

In part 1, the average movement time was 761 ms with an average error rate of 4.3%, close to the desired 4%. Using a mean-of-means throughput calculation [10], throughputs were 4.91 bits/s and 4.49 bits/s with univariate (SD_x) and bivariate ($SD_{x,y}$) endpoint deviation, respectively. Average Fitts' law fits were R^2=.951 and R^2=.962 for N=18 points, respectively. Thus, the a and b model values elicited for each subject in part 1 for pacing the metronome in part 2 were trustworthy.

Part 2, Pointing Error Models ($MT_{\%} \times A \times W$)

Overall Results and Fit of Fitts' Law

In part 2, the average movement time MT_e and average metronome time MT_{ms} should be close. Indeed they were, at 710 ms and 696 ms, respectively, a ratio of 1.02. The average overall error rate was 18.9%. For $MT_{\%}$=1.0, the average error rate was 6.07%, near the desired 4% rate. Throughputs were 4.83 bits/s and 4.39 bits/s using SD_x and $SD_{x,y}$, respectively. Average Fitts' law fits for N=72 points were R^2=.944 and R^2=.948, respectively. Thus, the a' and b' model values elicited for each subject and used in Eq. 3 for error rate prediction were trustworthy.

Overall Fit of the Pointing Error Model

Overall, predicted error rates were 15.6% and 20.9% using univariate (SD_x) and bivariate ($SD_{x,y}$) endpoint deviation, respectively, spanning the actual error rate of 18.9%. Figure 1 shows the N=72 points for each combination of $MT_{\%} \times A \times W$ used in the study plotted as observed (y) *vs.* predicted (x) error rates. Both SD_x and $SD_{x,y}$ result in good fits for the pointing error model with high R^2 values and regression equations near y=x. A Wilcoxon signed-rank test on absolute differences between predicted and observed error rates using each deviation scheme shows no significant difference between the SD_x and $SD_{x,y}$ models (p=.19), indicating they are comparable in fitting these data.

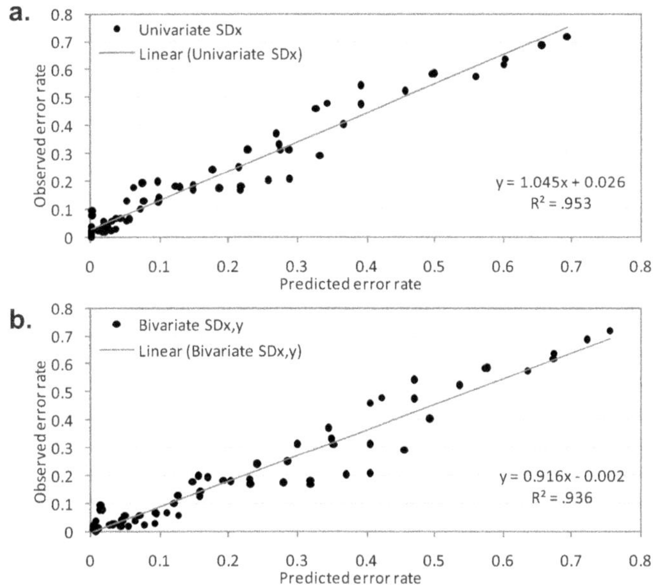

Figure 1. Error model observed (y) *vs.* predicted (x) points for our study's 72 $MT_{\%} \times A \times W$ conditions using **(a)** univariate (SD_x) and **(b)** bivariate ($SD_{x,y}$) endpoint deviation.

Effect of $MT_{\%}$ on Observed Error Rate

We found the relationship between $MT_{\%}$ and observed error rate O_{error} to be logarithmic, best fit by the equation $\ln(O_{error}) = 2.594 - 5.557 \cdot MT_{\%}$ (R^2=.807, N=72 points). Unsurprisingly, as $MT_{\%}$ increased, O_{error} significantly decreased ($\chi^2_{(3,N=72)}$=58.88, p<.0001).

Effect of ID, A and W on Observed Error Rate

In accord with Wobbrock *et al.*'s [13] 1-D study, A had no significant effect on O_{error} ($\chi^2_{(2,N=72)}$=1.31, p=.52). However, unlike Wobbrock *et al.*'s study, we found no significant effect of W on O_{error} ($\chi^2_{(5,N=72)}$=7.31, p=.20). There was also no significant effect of ID on O_{error} ($\chi^2_{(12,N=72)}$=8.15, p=.77) due to ID's combination with, and the influence of, $MT_{\%}$. Results for predicted error rates agree.

DISCUSSION

On the whole, our error model predicts well in 2-D using either univariate (SD_x) or bivariate ($SD_{x,y}$) endpoint deviation. Despite SD_x's slightly higher R^2, the two were not significantly different in their deviation from observed error rates. In general, error rate predictions using $SD_{x,y}$ were higher than those using SD_x, which makes sense given the extra movement dimension taken into account.

Despite W not causing a significant difference in observed error rates (p=.20), there was still "banding" evident. (A difference here from Wobbrock *et al.* [13] is that they used three levels of W whereas we used six.) Figure 2 shows that error rates for the smallest *W* (8 pixels) stood out from the rest. Figure 3a shows how MT_e and predicted error rates were linear in *ID*, just as Fitts' law requires. But Figure 3b shows that this linear behavior did not emerge when points were grouped by *W*. Indeed, prior work [11] has shown that error rates decrease with increases in *W even when ID is maintained*, suggesting a *W*-specific effect.

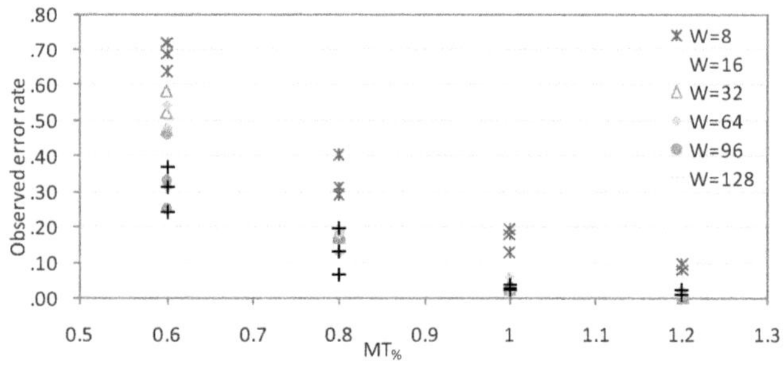

Figure 2. Error rates by $MT_{\%}$ coded by target size *W*. Levels are mixed, but some banding is clear for *W* = 8 (see Figure 7b in [13]).

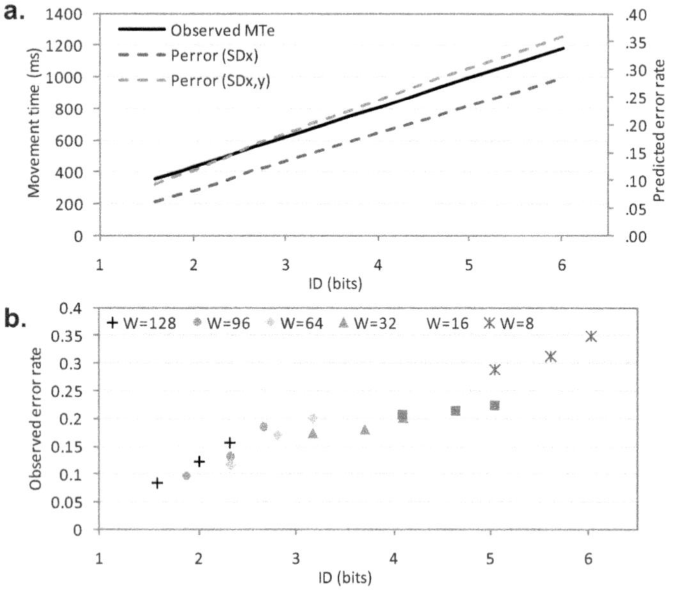

Figure 3. (a) Observed movement times are linear with index of difficulty as predicted by Fitts' law. Predicted error rates follow suit (see Figures 8a-b in [13]). **(b)** Observed error rates show some grouping by *W*, not falling on a line (see Figure 8c in [13]).

CONCLUSION AND FUTURE WORK

In this paper, we have shown that the pointing error model serves well to predict error rates from target distance (*A*) and size (*W*) and actual movement time (MT_e). Both univariate (SD_x) and bivariate ($SD_{x,y}$) endpoint deviations worked well, predicting error rates with similar differences from observed error rates. Although neither *A* nor *W* had a significant effect on observed rates, *W* seems to have a greater effect on error rates than *A*. Future work should investigate *W* further, teasing out any disproportionate effect on errors and adjusting the pointing error model accordingly. Future work should also augment the model for noncircular and irregularly-shaped targets. Performance should be predicted for a game, *e.g.*, *Whack-a-Mole*, where movement is governed by game conditions, not by Fitts' law.

ACKNOWLEDGEMENTS

The authors thank Edward Cutrell and I. Scott MacKenzie. This work was supported in part by the National Science Foundation under grants IIS-0811063 and IIS-0952786.

REFERENCES

1. Crossman, E.R.F.W. (1957). The speed and accuracy of simple hand movements. In *The Nature and Acquisition of Industrial Skills*, Crossman and Seymour (eds.). Report to the Joint Committee on Individual Efficiency in Industry.
2. Douglas, S.A., Kirkpatrick, A.E. and MacKenzie, I.S. (1999). Testing pointing device performance and user assessment with the ISO 9241, Part 9 standard. *Proc. CHI '99*. New York: ACM Press, 215-222.
3. Fitts, P.M. (1954). The information capacity of the human motor system in controlling the amplitude of movement. *J. Experimental Psychology 47* (6), 381-391.
4. International Organization for Standardization. (2002). Ergonomic requirements for office work with visual display terminals (VDTs)—Requirements for non-keyboard input devices. *Ref. No. ISO 9241-9:2000(E)*.
5. Isokoski, P. (2002). Speed-accuracy measures in a population of six mice. *Proc. APCHI '02*. Beijing, China: Science Press, 765-777.
6. MacKenzie, I.S. (1992). Fitts' law as a research and design tool in human-computer interaction. *Human-Computer Interaction 7* (1), 91-139.
7. MacKenzie, I.S. and Isokoski, P. (2008). Fitts' throughput and the speed-accuracy tradeoff. *Proc. CHI '08*. New York: ACM Press, 1633-1636.
8. Murata, A. (1999). Extending effective target width in Fitts' law to a two-dimensional pointing task. *Int'l J. Human-Computer Interaction 11* (2), 137-152.
9. Schmidt, R.A., Zelaznik, H., Hawkins, B., Frank, J.S. and Quinn, J.T. (1979). Motor-output variability: A theory for the accuracy of rapid motor acts. *Psychological Review 86* (5), 415-451.
10. Soukoreff, R.W. and MacKenzie, I.S. (2004). Towards a standard for pointing device evaluation, perspectives on 27 years of Fitts' law research in HCI. *Int'l J. Human-Computer Studies 61* (6), 751-789.
11. Wallace, S.A. and Newell, K.M. (1983). Visual control of discrete aiming movements. *Quarterly J. Experimental Psychology 35A* (2), 311-321.
12. Welford, A.T. (1968). *Fundamentals of Skill*. London, England: Methuen.
13. Wobbrock, J.O., Cutrell, E., Harada, S. and MacKenzie, I.S. (2008). An error model for pointing based on Fitts' law. *Proc. CHI '08*. New York: ACM Press, 1613-1622.
14. Wobbrock, J.O., Shinohara, K. and Jansen, A. (2011). The effects of task dimensionality, endpoint deviation, throughput calculation, and experiment design on pointing measures and models. *Proc. CHI '11*. New York: ACM Press. To appear.

Into the Wild: Challenges and Opportunities for Field Trial Methods

Barry Brown[1 2], Stuart Reeves[3] and Scott Sherwood[4]

[1] Department of Communication University of California San Diego barry@ucsd.edu

[2] Mobile Life VINN Excellence center Stockholm Sweden

[3] Horizon Digital Economy Research University of Nottingham, UK stuart@tropic.org.uk

[4] Department of Computing Science University of Glasgow UK sherwood@dcs.gla.ac.uk

ABSTRACT
Field trials of experimental systems 'in the wild' have developed into a standard method within HCI - testing new systems with groups of users in relatively unconstrained settings outside of the laboratory. In this paper we discuss methodological challenges in running user trials. Using a 'trial of trials' we examined the practices of investigators and participants - documenting 'demand characteristics', where users adjust their behaviour to fit the expectations of those running the trial, the interdependence of how trials are run and the result they produce, and how trial results can be dependent on the insights of a subset of trial participants. We develop three strategies that researchers can use to leverage these challenges to run better trials.

Author Keywords
Field trials, methods, demand characteristics, ethnography.

ACM Classification Keywords
H5.m. Information interfaces and presentation (e.g., HCI): Miscellaneous.

General Terms
Design, Experimentation, Human Factors.

INTRODUCTION
Within HCI perhaps one of the most popular methods for exploring novel technologies has been the system field trial or user study, where new systems are deployed and studied in relatively uncontrolled settings. From early on in HCI, researchers have built systems and given them to users to test in various different ways [3, 16, 28]. While early tests were usually in controlled laboratory settings, the field trial located 'in the wild' has emerged to address both diverse settings of use as well as interest in the 'unanticipated use' of systems [25]. The user trial, deployment or study has characteristics that distinguish it from other forms of deployment. While trials often involve an experimental design, there is usually a bias towards unstructured, more naturalistic experiments. Results span a mix of the qualitative and quantitative, with a open orientation towards finding out 'what happens' and drawing design principles or recommendations about users' reactions.

This paper seeks to draw lessons for how we might better conduct and present user trials in HCI. We document one trial of a photo sharing application - but not as an investigation into a system that needed to be tested but rather as a way of reflecting on user behaviour in system trials. Drawing on this trial we document three key issues that influence what happens in user trials yet are mostly absent from discussions of trial methods in HCI. *Demand characteristics* are where users in trials adjust and report on their behaviour in ways that fit with their perception of investigators' expectations. As an example, in our trial, participants discussed how they endeavoured to use our system so as to be able to be able to 'give' to those running the trial 'the results you are looking for'. *Lead participants* are where there is a reliance in reporting results from a trial on a small atypical subset of users who engage with and offer particular insight into the behaviour under investigation. In the trial discussed here one user took it on himself to organise and encourage use by others in the trial as well as offering to us insightful comments about the use of the system. Lastly *interdependence of methods and results*, describes how the way in which a particular trial is run, and the questions asked by investigators, intimately interact to narrow results and behaviour. In particular, the relationships between experimenter and participant can play as important a role in what happens in a trial as the design of the system.

We use this trial to explore how behaviours observed in trials are a product of the methods used, the orientation of investigators, interactions between participants, as well as the particular design of the system deployed. While this will come as no surprise to experienced researchers, foregrounding them allows us to explore how improve trial methodology - how we write up trials, but also how methods might better engage with the realities of trials as they are run. Our goal is to not see these issues as 'problems' with trials as such, but rather as unavoidable characteristics of trials that take place outside controlled settings, and as characteristics that can be leveraged to improve trial practice.

What are field trials?

Field trials have become a common method for studying the use of novel technologies, widely used in fields (such as HCI, Ubicomp and CSCW) where the interests of investigators goes beyond technical feasibility to exploring user understandings, practices and the eventual uses that systems might be put. What we refer to as *trials* in this paper go under a range of different names - field experiments, deployments, evaluations, field studies, technical probes - but they share a set of common features. A new system, usually developed by the researchers, is given to a set of users who are asked (often implicitly) to use the system 'naturally' outside the laboratory the system was designed in. They then use the system for anything from a few hours to a year, frequently as part of their day to day life, or with the system deployed in their home or workplace. In more experimental trials users' behaviour may be constrained with tasks set for them to carry out, while other trials eschew such controls and attempt to encourage 'natural' use. In some cases trials are run as an extension of experiments, whereas for others a more ethnographic analytic mode is adopted.

All trials involve data collected from system use, be that in the form of system logs, user interviews, observations or user reports (e.g., experience sampling). Papers focus on the technology's use, with an implicit understanding that 'the results' are produced by the users and the technology, and are not simply a function of the trial. Some go further and make claims that, based on what happens in the trial, findings can be extended to understand how similar technologies might be used if they were released commercially, or to explicitly seek to evaluate the prototype positively or negatively. There is a common interest in studying user behaviour with a prototype system so as to understand how to better design later technologies. Three diverse examples of user trials are Lee & Day's Lifelogging trial [21], Bell et al.'s Feeding Yoshi [3], or Pousman et al.'s Tableau Machine [25].

FIELD TRIALS IN THE LITERATURE

Some of the earliest technology trials come from the first half of the 1990s, as research interests migrated from testing technology in laboratory experiments to more broadly investigating interactions with technology [2]. Such was the fragile nature of first prototypes that the earliest examples are actually investigations based in research labs: Portholes at EuroPARC [11], the Active Badge system [16], and in Bell Labs various mediaspace systems [28]. Even though researchers deployed the systems within their own workplaces, their reflections offered much in terms of forming an understanding of what happened when these technologies became more widespread.

Following these pioneering studies, trials and naturalistic deployments of systems have become a core method for investigating user interactions with systems (e.g. [4, 29]). In particular, with ubiquitous computing systems, the close coupling of environment, and the concern for systems that engage with users' everyday lives, has caused the field trial to flourish as a 'standard method' (e.g. [3, 5, 27]). Indeed, the nature of ubicomp limits the power of classical laboratory studies - for example, the accuracy of location tracking can be tested in relatively controlled setting, but a study of this type tells us little about user acceptance, or how tracking might work with an individual's routine mobility. Mobility and the embedding of systems into the environment encourages deployment outside laboratories, and interest in the interweaving of technology with everyday life encourages longer trials. Of late, with the lowering of the technological hurdles for testing and deploying new applications and hardware, field trials of technology 'in the wild' lasting weeks or months have become increasingly commonplace. Within HCI the home in particular has been one important site for field studies. Situating technology within the home and exploiting the unconstrained and unanticipated use that is to be found there, researchers have sought to use them as seeding technologies and inspirations for design [26]. Taking stock of the inherent difficulties posed by such deployments, aspects of the home have also been further modified and brought back to the laboratory. The rise of 'living labs' such as MITs PlaceLab [18] enabled researchers to develop spaces in which uncertainty found in home settings could be more managed, and yet retain many aspects of field trials.

While trials have been a popular method, discussion of the field trial as a method has been relatively absent, certainly when compared to debates around other methods for examining user interactions, such as ethnography [9]. Debates around the nature of 'probes' of certain forms, particularly Hutchinson et al.'s technology probes [17] and Gaver and Rabe's cultural probes [13], are perhaps the main exceptions. Both of these approaches share a notion of a lightweight technological intervention that attempts to investigate current practice and experience to inform the design of new artefacts. Technology probes introduce new technologies that support new practices, whereas cultural probes are "a design orientated way to acquire inspirational glimpses of communities targeted for design" [6].

One radical view of user trials is that such deployments act as a kind of "breaching experiment" [9]. Crabtree argues that user trials need grapple with "the absence of practice", meaning that researchers are attempting to support through technology a set of practices which have not yet emerged, leaving us questioning what within a trial we are actually studying. Crabtree describes technology trials as "breaching experiments" - an attempt to disturb existing, taken-for-granted practices of doing things, so as to reveal how those things are done. To us this approach understates the power of trials; technology does not only disrupt but also potentially support new practices. We find in Harper et al.'s discussion of Active Badges [18] or Dourish and Adler's study of Portholes [12] more than simply the disruption of existing practice. Relatedly, Tolmie and Crabtree discuss the role of field trials in home environments [30]. Through attending to the deployment of a novel home-based technology (a video feed from a camera on a pole outside the home), they detailed how the trial participants and researchers oriented toward the technology and one another. They argue that the introduction of technology into the home disrupts 'everyday' domestic life, limiting the potential for understanding the 'everyday', something they see as the target of their studies. In contrast, Carter's et al.'s paper 'Exiting the cleanroom' [7] focuses on how we might better run trials so as to make them more 'ecologically valid' and to explore the barriers to more effective technology trials as a mode of design.

Finally, some discussions of field trials have challenged the utility of the practice itself and what it contributes to research. Davies [10] asserts that field trial-style research is costly in terms of time, but also is frequently the wrong tool for the job. If the goal is to prove that something technical is possible then usually there is no experiential concept to actually be proven - the demonstrator proves something that is already widely known, or that this point would be better demonstrated theoretically or experimentally. While Davies' points are more relevant to the specific technical goals of user trials, Kjeldskov argues that field trials provide little added user studies value, again emphasising that they are labour-intensive and that much that is found out would be better discovered in a laboratory study [20]. Whittaker et al [31] go on to argue that we should focus on constrained reference tasks and that while field trials have a role they should be used more to "modify existing task definitions for future evaluations". Rogers presents a robust response to these points demonstrating how many usability problems do not arise in the laboratory when compared to in-situ use, but also how field trials "provide a contextual backdrop against which to reflect upon the design of user experience and the mobile device sensitising us to how [our system] would (rather than should) be used in practice" [27].

EXAMINING TRIALS WITH A TRIAL

This variety of approaches towards system field trials demonstrates some of the diverse understandings of what field trials can do. While these discussions engage in productive ways with the utility of trials, or what claims can be made, our interest was in exploring what is *not* traditionally reported in trails papers - the messy details of trial practice that seldom go reported. Accordingly, we developed a trial of sorts to explore how the 'non-designed' features of a trial affected proceedings. Our goal was not to evaluate or critique trials as a method, but rather to use a trial to illustrate what we would argue are unavoidable characteristics of real world technology trials, so as to throw into relief our experiences from previous trials (e.g., [1, 3]).

Our trial had many of the trappings of a conventional study - we interviewed participants, observed them using the system and collected log data of the system's use. Just as we might use statistics to evaluate a statistical study, or ethnography to study ethnography, our goal was to use a trial to study what influences behaviour in user trials. Our interview questions, analysis and writeup focused on questions of what motivated participants to behave certain ways, and how the interactions between participants and ourselves influenced behaviour. The focus in the design and analysis was on how different interactions between participants, and between ourselves as investigators, had a role to play in participants' behaviour.

We tested an iPhone-based photo sharing system,that allowed users to distribute photos amongst a group alongside commenting on each photo. In some senses this application was fairly prosaic. The participants came from a variety of different professions and backgrounds. 20 participants were involved in our trial, split into four separate groups. As the composition of the groups, and the relationships between those involved were of particular interest for our study, we will describe these in some detail (Table 1).

Firstly, our groups varied in terms age range, and of whether they self-identified as football fans. The table also indicates the differing recruitment methods. For Groups A and D, recruitment was performed through a 'friends of friends' method (A was recruited through a family member of one of the authors, D via friends of one of the authors). Group B was recruited through University clubs, via membership of one of the authors, and Group C was recruited through press coverage, resulting in one of the members of the group contacting the authors to become a participant (and in turn recruiting his friends). Naturally, each group had a particular social configuration, which was of relevance to the way in which interaction played out during the trial. **Group A** were socially close, often exchanged SMS messages, and regularly engaged in communication together via social networking sites. For Group A we also had a 'primary contact', i.e., someone who provided an 'entry point' for us as researchers.

One of **Group B**'s pair of partners were often apart. The other three participants were friends studying at university. All group members were recruited from and acquainted with one another via a local sports club. A common interest (mountaineering) brought the researcher and participants together. Coordination and instruction was provided with all members of the group rather than via one 'primary contact'. With the exception of one member, **Group C** had attended school together and grown up alongside one

Group	A	B	C	D
Age range	24-50	Early 20s	Early 20s	Late 20s
Football fans?	N	N	Y	Y
Recruitment method	Friend-of-friend	Sports club	Press coverage	Friend-of-friend
Social configuration	Mother, daughters, niece (5f)	Two partners (2m, 2f)	Friendship group (5m)	Friendship group (3m)
	Friend of family (1f)	Friend (1f)	Cousin (1m)	Friend (1m)
Trial length	2 weeks	2 weeks	4 weeks	4 weeks

Table 1: Outline of trial groups

another for approximately ten years. The final member of this group was a cousin of one participant, and was less well-known to the larger group. This group had a primary contact who helped to distribute phones, instructions and so on. Recruited via press attention around the project, in many ways we found this produced a social distance with those participants. Lastly, and again with the exception of one member, **Group D** had grown up and attended school together. The group had know one another for approximately twenty years, except for one participant who instead knew the other members of the group via a football supporters' club.

Our data collection consisted of logged information from the trial itself (records of participants' interactions with the system), and interviews with the participants themselves at the end of the trial. During interviews, we reviewed with participants the content their group had produced. As part of this we used questions that had been developed before the trial, and questions developed over the course of the trial.

Results

Broadly, as with nearly every photo sharing system in the literature, the system was used to a *reasonable* degree, with 17 photos and 19 comments produced by each participant and roughly 1 photo or comment per day per participant. But what did the participants think about the trial itself and their own behaviour?

Demand characteristics

One key aspect of the users' descriptions of their own behaviour was what is known within the psychology literature as 'demand characteristics' [26]. Demand characteristics are where users shape or enhance their behaviour in a trial or experiment, in response to the imagined desires of the investigators. For example, users might increase their usage of a system if they assume that system usage is what the investigators are seeking, or deliberately ignore the system to reject the investigators involvement. This phenomenon is related to the well-known 'Hawthorne Effect' (while well-known, the original work that coined the term is somewhat problematic [19]).

In order to assess the importance and form of demand characteristics present in our trials, we asked participants to reflect upon how they felt the trial was run, what, if any, expectations they felt in taking part in the trial and what motivated them to engage in system use. Much of participants' motivation to use the system seemed to stem from a sense of obligation to us rather than their relationship to the system *per se*. Participants were typically eager to emphasise in interviews when they had been a 'good participant', often highlighting that they had been "us[ing] it everyday as in checking for other updates", "taking [it] to work and stuff every day", or "carrying it round all the time". Participants in the groups discussed how they attempted to assist us as experimenters, searching out ways to actually use the system: "I was just thinking what can I take photos of" or "trying to [...] think of things like on the two weeks [of the trial] ... of what to do". The desire to help us also extended to the way in which participants responded in interviews: "I was trying to make sure I had a good list [of suggestions] for you, good things for you". Participants would go as far as to account for any lack of use (as they saw it) in terms of a problem with *themselves* rather than the system ("I guess I just didn't make many comments, sorry I should I guess I should have"), whereas others suggested their less frequent use of it compared to the rest of their groups was due to *themselves* being "too boring", "[not] interesting enough". Some participants described their efforts to "show [some] willing" in spite of perhaps being "a bit of a technophobe" or even apologising for feeling "too old for it" - "[I] think oh I need to take a photograph because I was doing this the thing for you". We noted that participants treated these expectations towards 'making the system work' as obvious, normal and unremarkable ("obviously you need the data").

As part of this sense of obligation, participants also encouraged one another to use the system, and organised when they might use it together. One participant reported discussing amongst their group how they would "take [the phone] with [them] to [their] work and everyday use" so that they, as a group, "just use it when [they] could". Participants from another group described how they coordinated their use of the system such that "one of us would be at the football, and then you would text someone else to say I'm on FanPhoto tonight". Again such motivations for interacting with others, besides an interest in such interaction for its own sake, were accounted for in terms of how, as a group, they might ensure that they provided us with 'good data'. Participants also spent considerable effort interpreting the trial's purposes and the relevance of their own actions in that light. Often there would be talk of what they considered to be relevant or non-relevant activity, reflected upon the corresponding potential of activity to be 'good data' for the trial or 'irrelevant'. When interviewed, one participant, for instance, highlighted which photos and comments he considered "irrelevant" as opposed to those photos and comments that, as he put it, were "meaningful" and of being "of real consequence" (in this case, a section of a match report). Of course much of this was influenced by how we set up the trial and whether we described the system as a 'football' or general 'photo' system.

This concern for behaviour of relevance extended beyond our relationship to the participants, and also was an issue of what was relevant *between* participants themselves. In interviews participants described how they were attentive to relevance for their particular group. Thus, as one pointed out from our football fan groups, "I tried to use it more as a kind of football thing, if the football was on I'd make more of an effort", and as another mentioned, "I was more looking toward taking pictures that were relevant to an event". For Groups C and D, participants characterised importance in terms of football photos and this aspect also reinforced our presentation of the trial to participant groups. In other words, participants conducted their interaction with the system according to assumptions about the relevance of those actions to the purposes of the trial and the expectations of the experimenters. One member of Group D reported trying to keep his activity "within the guidelines" (presumably according to the way in which the system was presented at the start of the trial).

That said, participants did reflect upon their own role within the trial - for instance, in discussing "what [we] were looking for", a participant suggested he was "mostly kept in the dark" regarding the trial's details, and that he "supposed that's good really". This further highlights participants' normative attitudes towards trials, perhaps based upon previous experience of trials or common knowledge of experimental method. Participants often drew our attention towards sequences of activity that they presumed we would find useful (e.g., "this is the one I wanted to tell you about") and set aside those instances they considered less 'relevant'. As Gaver et al. points out in their own trial: "The continual engagement with the system appeared motivated as much by questions about our research agenda as by interest in what the system was saying" [15]. In one case two participants from Group C brought up in the interview a sequence in which one of them requested of the other that he update him on the progress of a game while he was attending a German language class. Similarly, in Group D, two participants both drew our attention to a sequence of photographs in which they and another participant captured a view from their positions within the stadium: "we were all at the same game but we were all in different bits of stadium … and obviously different tickets so it was quite good to like upload photos to say look this is where I am, where are you". In these instances, and throughout interviews, participants presented selections of their conduct to highlight as 'good activity'. Again, as before, these selections were driven by what participants interpreted as relevant to the purposes of the trial.

Lead participants and social relations

Alongside participants being oriented towards the trial, and each other's system use, in one group we found more formal and explicit orienting work. One participant in particular (in Group C) encouraged others in that group to engage in using the system, with the 'lead participant' (as we shall call him) making various demands on his group members. Other participants described with varying degrees how the lead participant was "out of everyone [...] very enthusiastic [...] he would kind of take a lot of photos and encourage us to take photos". In addition to encouraging others to generate content through creating content himself, he employed more direct strategies, such as asking another participant to take a photograph of his view of a stadium from his workplace (since he happened to work nearby), or emailing and text messaging others, say, to "get it out again for the game on Saturday".

This 'lead participant' also highlighted for the others why they had the system, as one participant mentioned "this is what you've got your iPhones for, this purpose". Although other participants in the group did engage in some encouraging activity, for the most part participants took their lead from this member of the group. The other groups (A, B and D) were characterised more by a sense of obligation to us as experimenters alone. As one participant reflected on the relations in his group (D), "I know the guys I wouldn't say I was really close to them but I know them and I've had some some kind of banter with them so there was there was an expectation there but to less of a degree".

More broadly, the social relations within the groups influenced the results of our various trials. As outlined earlier in our brief profile of each group, the trial groups were widely varied in terms of how they knew one another, for how long, their gender, their personal relationships with one another, how often and how much time they spent together, what their interests were and how those interests coincided with the interests of others. The relevance of social ties were formative in understanding the different patterns of interaction with and via the system. For instance, members of Group A were all equally close friends, and engaged in notably more extensive and mixed exchanges of comments than Group B. In Group B, we see far fewer exchanges due to the stratification of the group that did not occur in Group A, i.e., a less homogenous group which consisted of a couple and three close friends as opposed to a group of equally close friends. Between these two subgroups within Group B we would argue that the nature of being acquaintances influenced the reduced commenting that occurred. Group C consisted mostly of close friends who had known each other for a long time, and whose friendship was formed on the basis of common interest in football, although more recently the group had been less able to meet up for watching football together due to lifestyle changes ("back when we were younger we would have watched midweek games together sort of without fail but now we're not meeting up to watch it as much"). The system potentially offered a method by which to return to 'old times' that some participants in Group C noted as spurring their usage.

The social relations of Group C also contributed to non-participation; one member of the group did not know others so well so his participation was correspondingly less, and less 'integrated' in the social interactions (via comments) of others. In particular, he supported a different, more obscure team to the majority of the other participants, contributing to his reduced interaction via the system: "I noticed that the [other team] fans were all chatting about the game and obviously I couldn't say anything about it cause I wasn't there … so I'd say it would be good to have if it would be different if there was a fellow [team] fan".

The role of trial design and framing

Another facet of our trial was how we presented the system to the different participant groups and our role as investigators. This formed an important orienting influence in the way that participants engaged with the system, with us as experimenters and with one another. Although the instructions for actually using the system itself were delivered to each group in an identical manner (via instruction sheets), the purposes and reasons for the trial and participants' engagement with us was discussed in a way that was sensitive to the different groups. Thus, for Groups A and B, we introduced it by explaining that we had designed the system as a simple photo sharing application, and were recruiting them in order to test the quality of the software and to work out how we might iteratively improve it. For the second two groups of users (C and D) we stated that the application had been designed in order to support groups of football supporters in sharing their interests in football matches with one another, alongside a recruitment process which had been focused around football. Although the formal instructions given concerning the system were identical, in practice the differences in recruitment and in how the system was verbally framed led to key differences in use.

By and large Groups C and D directed their use around footballing events and the vast majority of their photos concerned football in some way. Group C sustained their use throughout the trial period, and their production of comments and photos was heavily oriented around ongoing football match events. As we have seen, the conduct of 'lead participants' probably contributed to this. For Group D, usage rapidly declined after the 'main events' (two football games) were over, and participation in the generation of content was more markedly slanted towards certain participants (i.e., one participant in particular contributed the majority of photos to the group, both from a trip abroad and as part of sharing his collection of football shirts). There seemed to be an important relationship between the nature of the events and participant use of the system. As one participant commented, "[The system] is better when the [football] game's better". In this way the use of the system by Groups C and D was more dependent upon events and their relative quality, which itself was directed in part by the way that we introduced the groups to the application (i.e., as an application to support football experiences). This may explain also why Group D's activity declined rapidly midway through the trial - since they as a group participated in fewer events, and their use was more event-based, the system no longer was interesting to use. In comparison, Group C sustained their use through attending many more events.

Correspondingly with the different framing we provided, Groups A and B did not engage in event-based use. Instead, photo and comment activity was woven more into workplace and home activities, which are not event-based in their nature. Interestingly, participants in both Groups C and D noted in interviews that the application could easily be "used for anything" even though participants still organised the majority of their participation around sporting events (no doubt due to the nature of their social relations being based on common interest in football). As one participant put it, whenever there was an event he deemed relevant (namely, football) he would "make more of an effort" to capture something. In spite of presenting the system in a particular way, some participants noted that they were "not sure what [we] were looking for" and since they didn't know the purposes of the trial they were not clear if they had provided us with the data they assumed we desired.

LESSONS FOR TRIAL METHODS

We make these points not as criticisms as such of the use of trials - the very inspiration for research 'in the wild' is abandoning notions of purity or simple deterministic relationships between technology and use. This discussion highlights aspects of trials that we have noted in our earlier trials, yet seldom highlighted in the published presentation. Our goal rather is that by documenting realities of how trials unfold and are influenced by these factors (demand characteristics, lead participants and trial design) we can draw lessons for how to better conduct and present trial data, how we can exploit these features so to run better trials.

Demand characteristics: investigators as participants

As outlined above one source of behaviour for trial participants is is their interpretations of what would be seen as the 'right' behaviour for those running the trial. At first blush this might seem to present a challenge to those running trials - one response would be to accentuate the distance between participants and investigators, and to attempt to adopt more neutral stance with participants. Yet this would not eliminate demand characteristics, and participants would simply resort to their own preconceptions of 'typical trial behaviour'. Demand characterises are not an example of bad methods, but are instead a fundamental part of what makes trials possible in the first place. Participation in a trial requires generosity in giving one's time and energy to taking part, particularly in trials that take place over an extended period. Even when incentives, such as payment, are given to participants this is seldom the only motivation (and if it is that can be problematic). Demand characteristics - the desire to produce something of value for those running the study - are thus fundamental to the success of trials in the first place and in many ways trials depend on demand characteristics for their feasibility.

Yet in descriptions of trials there is usually little written about how participants orientated to investigators, or how the investigators themselves saw the system being tested and the trial as it was run. What we are suggesting is the inclusion of '*investigators as participants*', seeing them as 'inside the loop', rather than controlling the trial from outside. By seeing investigators as participants in how we think through and write up trials, demand characteristics can be seen as a natural part of how trials are run. Much of what happens in a trial in this sense is an interaction between participants and investigators - one with particular obligations and requirements. On a practical level this encourages better documentation of these interactions, but also an explicit orientation to how these interactions shape users' behaviour. For example, in own trial the loaning of an expensive mobile phone for the extent of the trial acted as a considerable incentive to use the system. The 'gifting' of equipment was key in encouraging use, and thus providing usage and data for us to analyse. The arrangement of our data collection - with individuals from the groups interviewed individually also produced an individual accountability for use. As the trial developed, our own interests as investigators turned to how the relationships between participants, ourselves and how the trial was run. This in turn generated behaviour by the participants orientating to these interests. Our participants were thus very likely well-tuned to how their behaviour might be seen in terms of these relationships.

Indeed, demand characteristics can be exploited to an extent to encourage usage in trial settings. So, for example, participants could be given feedback as a trial developed on the observations that are being made, and a commentary passed on different forms of use. This would act as a way of encouraging involvement by participants in the trial, through building a reciprocal relationship. Even being explicit about what is 'expected' of participants could give participants the possibility to accept or reject those expectations explicitly. Questions about demand characteristics come into particular focus with the recent use of 'mass participation' trials, through new software distribution methods. While one might get relatively high numbers of downloads, motivating engaged use is still an open challenge here, partly due to the lack of demand characteristics amongst those who download trial software [24].

Lead participants: participants as investigators

A second methodological point concerns the role of participants themselves in trials. Frequently a subset of trial participants becomes key in how a trial is run and results are drawn. These participants - or even participant - engage with the technology and reflect on its use by themselves and others in a particularly insightful way, or alternatively work so as to encourage involvement by others who are involved in the trial. In our own trial although users gently encouraged one another to use the system, the presence of a particular highly enthusiastic 'leader' significantly drove interaction greatly in one groups. Further, the lead participant did considerable work in the interview to find interesting incidents, to offer suggestions as to what was interesting from the trial, and so on. This is not a rare event in trials in our experience, and we have frequently depended upon the insights or activities of lead users who either offer particularly astute assessments and reports of their own and others' behaviour, or go so far as to reflect upon and adjust their own practice as the trial progresses. For example, in [1] we noted how one player in particular extensively documented his own play (via video recordings), and encouraged other users to play the game more frequently.

The challenge this presents is that the use which is most interesting in terms of analysis is the use that is actually *least* typical. Yet analytically though even if only one participant uses a technology in a particularly interesting way, this atypicality is irrelevant - behaviour around technology is something that develops over time and participants are not a simple 'sample' of the greater population. Participants are being used as experts on their own activity, attempting to predict what might happen with a particular technology, to develop insight based on their use. The frequency of an observation has no relationship to insightfulness. More broadly, what we are suggesting is that *participants can be seen as investigators* themselves in the trial, with a move to acknowledging that it is through participants' own insights that the power of the trials can be focused. In some senses this echoes participatory design, yet here we are not arguing for users as designers but rather users as *analysts* of their own and others' practices.

In practical terms we see considerable potential in expanding the contribution that participants provide towards results, beyond being passive subjects. One example (drawing on the concept of lead users from technology marketing) is using blogs or the commentary of technology enthusiasts as a resource for allowing more lengthy review and discussion of technology by participants [22]. Gaver's work on cultural commentators [14] similarly explores the potential of participants as investigators for the design process. A related approach is narrative inquiry which has developed a set of methods around interviews that go into a much more lengthy examination of individuals' life histories and perspective ('working in a three dimensional narrative inquiry space' as Clandinin and Connelly [8] put it). While these methods might seem excessive, what they do is move away from the notion of participants as interchangeable 'blank slates' and engage with users as diverse active participants in the studies we run.

Trial design: diversifying methods

A final challenge identified from our trial was in how the relationships between the participants, and our framing of the system at the start of the trial, led to very different types of use between the different participants. This echoes our argument that participants are not homogeneous, and that the particular characteristics and distinctiveness of participants can lead to very different trial events. Moreover this suggests that different trials, run in different ways, can end up with very different results even if the system that is being built is exactly the same (e.g. [1]). The informal details of what goes on in the trial (the personalities of those involved, the culture it takes place in, how the system is introduced to the users) all influence trials. This suggests the value of running trials with the same systems multiple times in multiple different ways as ways of getting corpuses of diverse results. One example of this has been the diversity of experiments around location tracking technologies, systems which frequently feature very similar functionality, but via diversity in the experimental form have produced a diversity of interesting results [29].

DISCUSSION

One response to our arguments here would be that these points are already well known to those who conduct trials. Certainly, to researchers intimately involved in the production of qualitative, interpretivist research, the deep involvement of researchers in the data collection and analysis are foundational points. As Mauthner puts it, 'we are the data' [23], i.e., researchers are intimately bound to its production. Yet how this plays out in trials - as examined in our study - has a number of implications for how we might develop trial methods further.

Rejecting reproducibility

A first point is the rejection of those who advocate more standardised approaches to technology trials. There are few that are explicit in this call; one exception is Whittaker, Terveen and Nardi [31] who argue for a standardised set of trial protocols, with the use of these to support replication of experiments multiple times by different researchers. This is an aim for a comparability across experiments that is currently impossible with the diversity of approaches taken. We would suggest though that even with the best efforts of researchers, the issues that we have identified above would make such reproducibility impossible. Participants in trials are not interchangeable but are instead individuals who will relate to trials in their own way. They have a diversity of social relationships with each other and with investigators - relationships which as we have seen have a direct impact on system use. It is thus critical not to underplay both the role that we as experimenters have in the research that we do, and the natural variability of trials. It is not just that the large natural variability of humans, or variations in trial procedures, that makes the standardisation of trials impossible. It is that this goal is itself misleading - social settings involving humans and technology contain far too much variability to be reproducible in any straightforward way. While Whittaker et al.'s argument is perhaps an extreme case, the desire for comparability and standardisation in trials is not unique to them.

Moving beyond success

A second point concerns the ways in which trials suffer from the prevalent normative orientation towards 'success'. Systems and their trials in are often written in such a way as to presents the system as a success with users. This is an understandable and natural tendency - on completing a difficult technical project one wants to validate the success of at least the technical work and the ideas behind it. It is even implicit in the term 'trial', i.e., a test of suitability. This leads to the presentation of results in papers orientated in subtle ways towards highlighting users' complimentary comments on a system, or (more bluntly) only highlighting the aspects of a system that seemed to work with users in the trial. Yet clearly if one takes demand characteristics seriously, compliments about a system cannot just be quoted verbatim and taken as evidence of its straightforward success. User *compliments* are in some ways to be expected within the framework of an interview. Even usage statistics are problematic in a similar way, and although informative, should not necessarily be taken as blunt indicators of 'success'. Moreover, whatever the seeming success of a trial, how a particular technology might fare in non-trial contexts can only be broadly ascertained from what happens in that constrained setting. Recently, Gaver et al. [15] have argued that we need to acknowledge and engage with understanding failures in trials. This is something we have much sympathy for - certainly there are aspects of many of the systems which we have trialled in the past that simply did not work with users. Yet this advice could come to exacerbate the problem in that it encourages analysis in the straightforward evaluative terms of 'good or bad'. This question is not only frequently unanswerable but can limit our understandings of what is going on with technology, since each element of a system can fare differently. What happens in a trial can be indicative of the concept, that particular instantiation or even just the form factor. We would argue that we do not need to discuss failure more in HCI, but rather to break free from the premature evaluation of technologies before understanding how they interact with users and practice.

Rewriting the methods section

More boldly we would argue for innovation in how methods sections are presented in trial papers. Changing the focus of reporting trials from offering up replicable results invites a set of changes in how we describe our trials, and in particular the form that the methods section takes. Methods sections in user trials papers are, broadly speaking, written in a 'standard' way. Often this includes statistical information outlining the make up of the particular user groups. These include age, sex and some other basic contextual information such as occupation, along with some brief notion of how the users are connected. Moreover, there is a strong normative orientation in writing methods sections to presenting results as predictable, replicable and comparable. Indeed, critiquing the methods of our own papers, their orientation has been almost entirely defensive rather than documenting the actual details and tribulations that trials practically, really face. The methods sections of papers are often repetitive and anodyne, skipping much of the details of how a trial actually proceeded so as to prevent provoking reviewers.

To truly embrace the distinctiveness of trials we propose that this additional context is extended much wider and documented in greater detail. Methods sections should be more explicit about the natural contingencies and events that happen while a trial is carried out. These are not signs of a 'bad trial', but are important details that lets us understand better the differing contexts of particular trials. What is needed are methods and results sections that allow us to interpret where sources of variation come from, and the different ways in which trials are planned yet transpire in quite different ways. One example of this is [25], where a system failure resulted in an important and key research finding. Obviously, one key reason behind the formulaic nature of methods sections is the reactions of reviewers. Expanding and enriching the methods section of papers perhaps most of all will require modifications in reviewers' approaches. Frequently, there is an attempt by reviewers to find the 'fatal flaw' in a methods section and this results in methods sections written in a highly defensive manner. While this might be applicable to positivist approaches, we would argue that it is inappropriate to trials and in the longer term has had a negative impact on how methods are reported.

Lastly, we would argue for much greater innovation in methods around trials, a break away from the assumption that trials should be as 'natural' as possible. While we are not arguing that 'anything goes' in terms of methods we have some sympathy for Feyerabend who put forward an argument that, as science changes, often innovation happens as much in the methods used (and what comes to be seen as a fact) as in the actual discoveries of scientists themselves [12]. Science, as Feyerabend argued, does not rely upon a single universal notion of what is truth and how we find it; the very 'rules of the game' change as science innovates and moves into studying new phenomena. Feyerabend recommended 'methodological anarchism' as a way of increasing innovation in science - and that scientists should seek to innovate much in terms of the methods they use and in how they attempt to prove their findings.

CONCLUSION

Our goal in this paper is to focus attention on one of the key user studies methods employed in HCI. We have drawn on a 'trial of trials' - a study of a well-known, predictable technology where we focused our attention on understanding some of the complexities of how users behave in trials, rather than on the system itself. We documented the many different sources of behaviour in trials: relationships between investigators and participants, relationships between participants themselves, and the nature of trial instructions. These sources of behaviour are often neglected in trials discussions. From this we argued for three key changes in trial methods: a move away from an orientation towards the 'success' of systems; innovations to how methods sections are presented that encompass and document the reality of trials as practiced; and a broader embrace of innovation in methods, one that fully acknowledges the role that the investigator plays in user trials. In general we call for participation in an ongoing process of innovation with regard to our methods. For this to happen we would argue that there is need for a significant shift to be made by reviewers as much as practitioners.

REFERENCES

[1] Barkhuus, L., et al. Picking Pockets on the Lawn: The Development of Tactics and Strategies in a Mobile Game. In *Proceedings of UbiComp 2005, Tokyo, Japan.*, Springer Verlag (2005).

[2] Barkhuus, L. and Rode, J. From Mice to Men: 24 years of Evaluation in CHI. *Extended Proceedings of CHI 2007 (alt.chi)*(2007).

[3] Bell, M., et al. Interweaving mobile games with everyday life. In *Proceedings of CHI 2006,* ACM Press (2006), 417-426.

[4] Benford, S., et al. Experiments in inhabited TV. In *Proceedings of CHI 98,* ACM Press (1998).

[5] Benford, S., et al. The Error of our Ways: The experience of Self-Reported Position in a Location-Based Game. In *Ubicomp 2004,* Springer (2004).

[6] Boehner, K., et al. How HCI interprets the probes. In *Proceedings of CHI 2007* (2007) ACM.

[7] Carter, S., et al. Exiting the cleanroom: On ecological validity and ubiquitous computing. *Human Computer Interaction*, 23, 1 (2008), 47-99.

[8] Clandinin, D. and Connelly, F. *Narrative inquiry*. Jossey-Bass San Francisco, 2000.

[9] Crabtree, A. Taking technomethodology seriously: hybrid change in the ethnomethodology-design relationship. *Eur. J. Inf. Syst.*, 13, 3 (2004), 195-209.

[10] Davies, N. Proof-of-concept demonstrators and other evils of application-led research. *Proceedings of UbiApp Workshop, Ubicomp 2005*(2005).

[11] Dourish, P. and Adler, A. Your place or mine? Learning from long-term use of audio-video communication. *Computer Supported Cooperative Work (CSCW)*, 5, 1 (1996), 33-62.

[12] Feyerabend, P. *Against method*. Verso Books, 1993.

[13] Gaver, B., et al. Design: Cultural probes. *interactions*, 6, 1 (1999).

[14] Gaver, W. Cultural commentators: Non-native interpretations as resources for polyphonic assessment. *International journal of human-computer studies*, 65, 4 (2007), 292-305.

[15] Gaver, W., et al. Anatomy of a failure: how we knew when our design went wrong, and what we learned from it. *Proceedings of CHI 2009*(2009).

[16] Harper, R. H. R., et al. Locating systems at work. *Interacting With Computers*, 4, 3 (1992), 343-363.

[17] Hutchinson, H., et al. Technology probes: inspiring design for and with families. *CHI '03: Proceedings of the SIGCHI conference on Human factors in computing systems*(2003).

[18] Intille, S., et al. A living laboratory for the design and evaluation of ubiquitous computing technologies. In *Proceedings of CHI 2005* (2005),1941-1944 ACM New York, NY, USA.

[19] Jones, S. Was there a Hawthorne effect? *American Journal of Sociology*(1992), 451-468.

[20] Kjeldskov, J., et al. Is it worth the hassle? Exploring the added value of evaluating the usability of context-aware mobile systems in the field. In *Proceedings of MobileHCI 2004* (2004),61-73.

[21] Lee, M. L. and Dey, A. K. Lifelogging memory appliance for people with episodic memory impairment. In *Proceedings of the 10th international conference on Ubiquitous computing* (2008),44-53 ACM.

[22] Ljungblad, S. and Holmquist, L. *Transfer scenarios: grounding innovation with marginal practices*. ACM, City, 2007.

[23] Mauthner, N., et al. The data are out there, or are they? Implications for archiving and revisiting qualitative data. *Sociology*, 32, 4 (1998), 733-745.

[24] McMillan, D., et al. Further into the wild: Running worldwide trials of mobile systems. *Pervasive Computing*(2010), 210-227.

[25] Pousman, Z., et al. Living with tableau machine: a longitudinal investigation of a curious domestic intelligence. In *Proceedings of Ubicomp 2008* (2008), 370-379 ACM.

[26] Robinson, M. Design for unanticipated use. In *Proceedings of ECSCW 1993* (1993),187-202 Kluwer Academic Publishers.

[27] Rogers, Y., et al. Why It's Worth the Hassle: The Value of In-Situ Studies When Designing Ubicomp. In *Proceedings of Ubicomp 2007* (2007).

[28] Root, R. W. Design of a multi-media vehicle for social browsing. In *Proceedings of CSCW 1988* (1988) ACM Press.

[29] Smith, I. E., et al. Social Disclosure of Place: From Location Technology to Communication Practices. In *Pervasive 2005* (2005), 134-151.

[30] Tolmie, P. and Crabtree, A. Deploying research technology in the home. In *Proceedings of the 2008 ACM conference on Computer supported cooperative work* (2008),639-648 ACM.

[31] Whittaker, S., et al. Let's stop pushing the envelope and start addressing it: a reference task agenda for HCI. *Hum.-Comput. Interact.*, 15, 2 (2000), 75-106.

When a Little Knowledge Isn't a Dangerous Thing

Jacki O'Neill, David Martin
Xerox Research Centre Europe
Meylan, 38420, France
Firstname.lastname@xrce.xerox.com

Tommaso Colombino, Antonietta Grasso
Xerox Research Centre Europe
Meylan, 38420, France
Firstname.lastname@xrce.xerox.com

ABSTRACT
In this paper we compare two departments of a public administration body carrying out similar work. In one department two sections, telephony and processing, are collocated whereas in the other they are not. We demonstrate the costs of distribution, in particular how the strictly enforced division of labour and limited visibility onto the workflow of the other section causes problems when dealing with normal, natural exceptions. The setting is one of seemingly routine bureaucratic work rather than high-skilled cooperative work, thus the impact of distribution might be considered rather surprising. We argue that a key requirement for any solution is to enable practitioners on the 'shop floor' the freedom to find elegant solutions to problems.

Author Keywords
Public administration, call centres, ethnography, distributed work, collocation

ACM Classification Keywords
H5.3 Information interfaces and presentation, Group and Organization Interfaces, Organizational design

General Terms
Human factors, Design

INTRODUCTION
In this paper we describe the findings of an ethnographic study of two departments within a large European public administration body which handles benefit provision for people who are not working due to unemployment or sickness. We had the opportunity to compare how two groups, telephony and processing, in each department organized their work. The two groups were carrying out similar work in each department, except that in one they were collocated and in the other they were not. All the names of people, systems and so on, have been changed to preserve anonymity.

The overarching argument is one that is familiar, that is that, to quote Sachs [11]

"...the efficiency of work is in fact determined not so much by the logic and sequencing of task flow as by the capabilities of people for troubleshooting vexing problems in complicated situations, which inevitably arise in all workplaces."

However, this study is original as it provides the perfect opportunity to examine these issues empirically through a systematic comparison of two different departments, with similar work but with different physical ecologies. In UneDept, where telephony and processing are physically separated, hand-offs between the two sections take place almost exclusively through the technology, in keeping with the formal processes. In MediDept, by contrast, telephony and processing are collocated in the same open-plan office, enabling staff to work around the formal processes implemented in the technology to solve the everyday troubles that arise. This paper compares the operation of the two departments, focusing particularly on the implications for work organization when formal processes must be followed as opposed to the situation where local ad hoc solutions can be tried – we are particularly interested in how this relates to the handling of 'normal, natural troubles', exceptions and difficult cases.

This study is timely since advances in ICT, have led to an increasing drive towards distribution and outsourcing. In this process, elements of a business may be separated, modularized and outsourced, often with only the electronic data on systems as the means to mesh together distinct activities. Collocation is seen as unnecessary to getting the work done and may even be considered to promote inefficient interaction or idle 'chatter' [6].

RELATED WORK
The questions raised in this paper are ones at the heart of a large swathe of CHI, CSCW and organisational research; what happens when technology is used to partition and distribute or virtualise work? In the late 1980's networked distributed computer systems were heralded as a means for companies to specialize, make discrete and distribute business functions. With the rise of the outsourcing movement these arguments are still strongly in play nowadays. For example, Malone et al [7] applied Transaction Cost Theory to business computerisation, describing how parts of the business could be virtualised using ICT to make the business more efficient. They argue that since processes

can be instantiated and enabled through electronic technology, reducing the need of people to understand what other functions are doing. This work has come in for criticism at a number of levels. Kraut et al. [6] showed that the use of electronic networks does not per se lead to greater efficiency and that social communication is an enabler for the successful use of electronic networks, while curiously stating that *"Coordination through personal relationships may be less efficient, because it relies on costly and error-prone human behavior."*. In his critique Schmidt [13] examined how such an approach does not hold for cooperative work because such work is not routine and therefore requires that the actors involved communicate, negotiate and so on. In particular he described the importance of the work to coordinate the work – or articulation work. Although this has been described as invisible work we are keen, as Star [14] was, to push the point that it is not lesser work. A major feature of being able to articulate in these situations is being aware, in some way, of what is going on across the boundary. Awareness is central when we think of distribution because whereas a collocated environment provides a wealth of cues which workers use to coordinate and design their interactions [3] it becomes much harder to provide these at a distance [1,2]. Intriguingly, however, Schmidt drew a distinction between cooperative knowledge work situations and bureaucratic domains like *"public administration"* where he stated *"The Transaction Cost approach has proven to be quite useful for requirements analysis in administrative work domains."* This study allows us to examine whether this view on bureaucracy holds true.

The impact of distribution on cooperative work has been extensively studied with research comparing the work of distributed and collocated teams [8, 4]. For example, in their classic paper *Distance Matters* the Olsons pull apart the features of work which make it particularly suitable for distribution – notably that the work should be loosely coupled and it is more likely to be successful where workers have considerable common ground. Given that conflict increases when teams are distributed, Hinds [4] demonstrated how shared identity, context and spontaneous interaction can mitigate conflict. What distinguishes our work from this body of research is that rather than considering the work of cooperative teams we examine the case of bureaucratic work which, with its routine nature, would seem to be perfect for distribution and we find that similar problems arise.

METHOD AND FIELD SITES

We conducted an intensive field study (eight person weeks). The primary method was observation – shadowing the workers and listening in to the calls. The observation was supplemented by in-situ interviewing. Data was collected through field notes, photographs, audio recording and collection of artefacts. The analysis was ethnomethodological and the findings we report here were emergent i.e. even the quotes included here were delivered spontaneously within the flow of action and interaction. Thus, for example, the evident conflict between telephony and processing in UneDept was an emergent feature of the environment. The researchers did not set out to investigate conflict and did not ask questions on this.

Of the sites studied, UneDept, handled benefits for the unemployed but actively seeking work (referred to here as Unemployment Benefit (UB)); MediDept, for those unable to work because of a medical condition (Medical Benefit (MB)). Both departments deal with the processing of new claims, benefit delivery during the claim life and claim termination. We report here on the work and interrelations of two sections within each department – telephony and processing. Processing deals with the administration of claims – ensuring new claims are in order, ensuring ongoing eligibility and dealing with changes in circumstances. Telephony is a call centre for all enquiries about the ongoing claim. Operators in telephony can do some simple processing such as releasing money when there are certain types of blocks (e.g. systems glitches), changing address and bank account details. While the public administration body has customer facing offices (Work Centres) which provide general information and case workers who ensure compliance with the terms of a claim, questions about individual claims must go through telephony. Both telephony and processing use a number of computer systems in their work, some but not all of which are shared between the two groups. Core systems include:

- 'ClaimSys': a DOS-based legacy system and the main processing and payment release system. It contains all the claim details and automatically releases payment when specific conditions are completed. Citizens are paid benefit on a fortnightly basis.
- 'WorkSys': the system in the Work Centres focused on supporting and recording job search activities. It is accessible to processors and telephony.
- Email is used by all groups, with specific addresses/boxes to direct mail to particular groups.
- Telephony have two additional systems:

a) A call logging system (CLS) where they log each call they take: with call length and the citizen's government identifier (GI) - a unique mixture of numbers and letters that is the citizens key identifier.

b) A security system (SecureSys) to verify caller identity and carry out requested changes of address or bank account.

Of particular interest is the different ways in which work is physically organized. In UneDept there is a physical separation, with telephony and processing on different floors. In MediDept, telephony and processing are located in the same open plan office. Communication between Telephony and Processing in UneDept is therefore handled through formal workflows and communication channels:

1) E-mail from telephony to processing: processing must respond to the *citizen* in three days.

2) Notes on ClaimSys. The notes page on ClaimSys has a limited number of lines: ~15 lines on each of the two pages available. Once full, previous notes must be deleted so new notes can be added. Notes can be added to other systems including CLS, SecureSys and WorkSys. In WorkSys and ClaimSys the notes serve a communication function – showing key matters and progress in a claim (e.g. any mail received from the citizen is logged in the notes). In comparison CLS and SecureSys are tracking systems for telephony so each consecutive note is about a different citizen and constitutes a record of the agent's work.

3) A specific person in telephony for UneDept has the responsibility of chasing up problem cases: where three emails have been sent to processing but the citizen has not received a call back.

MediDept also uses email and notes to communicate, but because they are collocated they can talk to one another and share resources outside of the formal workflows. We will discuss the implications of this for the organisation of the work, continuity and effectiveness of service and the interrelationship between telephony and processors in the two departments. It is important to note that the department's aim in this case is distribution or virtualization, that is to be able to situate telephony anywhere in the country. In this case communication would be limited to the prescribed workflows. There are good organizational reasons for this, including: to enable processors to get on with the work of processing efficiently, without too much interruption; to enable telephony to answer the maximum number of calls (keeping caller waiting time low); and to reduce the opportunities of people giving out incorrect information and acting outside of the job role for which they have been trained. What we hope to demonstrate in this paper is that for work as inter-reliant as that of telephony and processing, when limiting communication to channels with limited interactivity, problems can arise around the smooth and effective handling of exceptional cases. We finish the paper with some design implications for addressing these issues.

FINDINGS

We saw a number of differences between the two departments which we believe are largely if not completely due to the different ecologies of the workplaces.

Collocation and work organisation

Since telephony and processing are in the same open plan office in MediDept, they have an awareness of one another's work processes and constraints, and as a consequence can develop practices to deal with the emergent and routine troubles and exceptions that characterize their workflow. The clearest illustration of this is a local arrangement for handling enquiries about medical certificates. For the first months on medical benefit a valid paper medical certificate is required. Benefits are paid fortnightly and if there is no valid certificate on the day of payment no benefit will be paid until a new one is received. The citizen gets the certificate from their healthcare professional and then either posts it to the Department or takes them to a Work Centre, to be sent internally or faxed.

During the study period, MediDept was receiving 6-800 certificates a week, and much of their ongoing work was processing them. When medical certificates are received they are input onto ClaimSys and payment can be released. When they are faxed from the Work Centre (providing both pages are received) the fax is taken as temporary proof of certificate. Medical certificates can get lost in transit (by post or fax) or given the large volumes of paper, during processing. Since healthcare professionals should not provide overlapping certificates and given that no benefit is paid if the certificate does not cover payment day, replacement is often an urgent matter. Many of the phone calls to telephony are about medical certificates:, specifically whether they have been received or why payments have not been released.

The official procedure for handling medical certificates is that when a call comes in the agent should check for it on ClaimSys. If it is not there they should handover the enquiry to processing via email. What actually happens is that the agent checks first on ClaimSys and if the medical certificate is not there but it is judged that it should be (e.g. it was faxed or it was sent by post more than five days ago) the agent will go and look for it. To facilitate this, a trolley containing the medical certificates awaiting processing has been placed in the aisle between the processors and telephony. If agents cannot find the certificate in this trolley they may check the fax machine or with whomever is inputting the medical certificates. On finding the certificate they give it to processing and reassure the caller that all is well. If the agent cannot find the certificate they may 1) advise the customer to call back 2) ask them fax across a duplicate, or 3) begin a process of further investigation. Only where the medical certificate cannot be found does the citizen need to call back – often after already faxing a duplicate. Searching for the certificates can take a few minutes and therefore runs contrary to management's wishes that agents should take the maximum number of calls.

However, let us consider what would happen if they followed the prescribed process. The processing department would have many more emails per week. The citizen would not receive such timely information and would be likely to call back more, increasing call volumes. It is likely that only after a number of calls would the citizen be asked to get a duplicate, as the steps in the process could not be joined up as they are now. Thus following the process would have a number of negative effects: 1) increased volume of emails to processors 2) increased volumes of calls to telephony 3) greater delay for customers receiving their benefit where a problem has occurred. This simple workaround enables smoother workflow and better service for the citizen. Being in the same office means that each group has awareness of the activities of the other and can use this to manage their work. In Extract 1 the citizen has received a letter asking for a new medical certificate when she has already sent one in.

Extract 1[1]

1. Caller - I got a letter saying please can you send a medical certificate by the 7th of April but it should've been received this morning - I sent one a couple of days ago
2. Operator - They do take about 4 or 5 days you know to come in Mrs C*** um
3. O - Yeah they do I'm afraid. We have had some in today and they haven't been all sorted out yet when did you send it in was it Monday or Tuesday
4. C - er what day is it today
5. *[O and C clarify it was sent on Tuesday night]*
6. O - Tuesday night so. No I mean the chances are we may not have uh you know the earliest we would get it would probably be tomorrow if that um as soon as it has been you know received you know it will be put on and a payment issued to you if you'd like to ring back say about 11 o clock tomorrow

Here, the operator uses her awareness of both what's happening today and how long the process should typically take, to deal with a citizen's call without leaving her station. She knows that today's post has come in but has not been sorted yet (turn 3), but rather than leave her station to search these she asks the caller to confirm exactly when she sent the certificate in since the caller was rather vague in her initial formulation (turn 1). Together they establish that the caller sent in the certificate on Tuesday night. The operator uses her local knowledge of normal process times and her orientation to correct procedure (i.e. that she should be answering calls) to suggest the caller ring back tomorrow – when the medical certificates are likely to have been sorted if not input into the system (turn 6). This knowledge of the best time to call in is also a product of being collocated. We can see that operators do not just flout rules willy-nilly but rather have come up with a working arrangement which serves the whole workflow and therefore the citizen best, rather than attending only to that part of the workflow within their division of labour. Another crucial feature of the work arrangement in MediDept is that they can work together to ensure that exceptions are more effectively dealt with (Extract 2).

[1] Due to recording restrictions, caller's turns were recorded only by hand and so not all callers turns were recorded.

Extract 2

1. *[Tracey from telephony comes across to processing while Becca is working on mail]:*
2. Tracy - Becca I've got Mr Signori on the phone and he wants to speak to Roy, but he's not
3. Becca - He's been paid Mr Signori
4. *[Tracey tells Becca that Roy says he can't help with the problem but that Mr Signori will speak to Becca also]*
5. Becca - Hello. Do you want to put him (he is put through), alright then, hello Mr Signori how may I help you

This example reveals how MediDept engage in ad hoc collaboration to deal with problem cases. The belief is that Mr Signori's case had been settled (turn 3). However he has called in to say his payment is missing. In UneDept the telephony operator could only send an email to processing. Here she can consult with Roy who processed the case and escalate it to the manager (Becca, turn 5). Becca's subsequent investigations reveal the payment has been sent to the wrong place so she prioritises the problem and deals with the case that day. Solving this problem in UneDept could have taken at least three days, during which time it is likely that Mr Signori would have called in a number of times, as well as delaying his benefit payment.

Distribution and work organisation

In the following extracts we look at the how having to rely extensively on formal workflows and communication channels affects the work of telephony and processing in UneDept. In Extract 3 we can see how the notes page on ClaimSys is used to manage citizen's calls. The caller, having completed a compulsory training programme, is ringing in to see what is happening with their claim. After training the citizen needs to fill in a form at the Work Centre which is then processed in the Department. The caller asserts they have filled in the form and the operator checks with a colleague about what they should do next, which is where we join the call:

Extract 3

1. *[Operator goes over to colleague]* Martin he's done the training form he did it a week late
2. Martin: so he's actually completed the form?
3. O: Yeah
4. M: is it upstairs have they received it
5. O: Um
6. M: is it in the notes
7. O: Well i-it's not, there isn't any notes
8. M: they haven't received the form then [...] *did he actually post it or give it in at*

the Work Centre

9. *O: Er um he* did it at the Work Centre

10. M: ask him to check with the Work Centre to see when they sent it to us because when they receive it upstairs in changes they always note it, isn't it? [...]But check on WorkSys hopefully there is something there. If the worst comes to the worst just send an email upstairs and ask them to look out for it [...]

11. *[O checking on WorkSys reads]: 'end of training form completed' so...*

12. M: so do an email upstairs if it was completed send an email upstairs

Given that the forms themselves are not available to them, telephony have to rely on the notes pages of ClaimSys and WorkSys, along with their knowledge of the relevant procedure, to work out what is happening. They start by discussing whether the caller has completed the post-training form. Although the caller has asserted that he has, his word alone is not enough evidence. They establish that the form has not been received 'upstairs' (i.e. in processing) as they would expect receipt to be specifically noted in the system (turns 4-8 and 10). There is however a note on WorkSys which indicates that the form has been completed (turn 13). Thus they have reconstructed that the form was completed but has not yet arrived in processing. Unlike the telephony operator dealing with medical certificates, the operator here can only rely on the presence or absence of digital traces of a document in a workflow system which may or may not be up to date. They cannot determine for sure that the document in question is or is not where it should be. The end result is that the operator has to hand off the enquiry by email (turn 12).

In another example, the caller has been asked to send in information which he claims he has already sent in – around residency entitlement. He is rather angry, but the operator only has the system notes which show that processing have asked for this information. The notes page is a limited resource, for example usually it does not contain rationales. In this case all the operator can do is assure the caller that the processors have good reason for asking for this information again and he must therefore resend it. It should be said here that the Department is not in the business of making sure citizens are happy or providing explanations for everything, but it is in the business of providing benefit to those who are eligible. In this case the system can be said to be working adequately, although it is easy to sympathise with the caller's frustration. Indeed the operator acknowledges this to the ethnographer after the call, along with a clear orientation to the division of labour:

"*I do understand his frustration with us because it's quite a lot of detailed information which he has to supply and if he's already supplied it... it's not my real position to ask why we're asking for it again...in fairness to the processors it might be that the information that they provided to us first of all just wasn't correct.*"

In many cases there may simply be no (or limited) information to give, and the caller must wait until due process is completed. Certainly there are strong notions of the timeline of a claim, e.g. for new claims, telephony would not even consider sending up an email until at least 4-6 weeks had passed.

A considerable amount of time is spent working out what is going on, what has gone wrong and what needs to be done next. In part this is because of the complexity of the benefit regulations, which change often, as benefit legislation reforms are common. The key system, ClaimSys, was designed >30 years ago to comply with completely different benefit regulations and has been adapted numerous times as the legislation changes. It is no wonder then that it does not work perfectly all the time. Problems can be located in any number of places and considerable work may be required to identify them. Solving exceptions can be time consuming and processors are constantly balancing between processing one exception vs. several straightforward claims.

It is important to understand the work involved in responding to an email. While straightforward problems are often solved rapidly more complex problems can take considerable time. Citizens may call multiple times however, telephony is often not in the best position to answer the queries. The communication systems between telephony and processing are primarily asynchronous, constrained by mode and time to be brief on content and the two sections have different views about what should constitute a note. Notes and emails work well for simple hand-offs, but are less effective in more complex cases.

To further illustrate the difference between MB and UB we can consider the following example from UB: a caller phones telephony from a Work Centre because his bank account has been closed and his benefit payment returned. He asserts that he called on Friday, but was told to wait until Monday (payment day). There are no notes to indicate this. Notes tend only to be taken when some action is performed; however without the note the operator has no evidence of this call. The payment has not yet been shown as returned on ClaimSys, so the caller needs to get a form RC2 filled out, signed by the bank and returned to the Work Centre to prove the account has been closed. This requires two appointments of ten minutes at the Work Centre. On looking at the diary system, the operator sees the first possible appointment is late afternoon (too late for the caller to get his money). Extract 4 begins with the operator telling the caller that it will not be possible to do it today (turn 1), the caller's response (turn 2) prompts the operator into further action. He gets the caller to find a floorwalker – a person whose job it is to assist with general enquiries and needs (turns 3,4). He explains the situation to the floorwalker (Mary) (turn 6).

Extract 4

1. O: Ok () Right ok well we still need to do this to get your-your one returned yeah urm I'm not going to be able to do it today
2. C - why not?
3. O: Urm unless you can get is there a floorwalker I can have a quick word with
4. O: Yeah could you grab em for us
5. *[Floorwalker comes on the phone]*
6. O: Oh hi Mary it's um James upstairs in JSA telephony. Urm this gentleman on the phone he needs to fill out a RC2 Mr B the problem is I'm having a look at the diary today and cause I need ten minutes and then about an hour gap and then ten minutes again cause he needs to go down take it down to the urm to his...

In the following omitted turns Mary agrees to do the first appointment immediately and they negotiate a provisional time (i.e. without an appointment) for the second that may allow the caller to get his money today. After the call, the operator enters detailed notes in ClaimSys, explicitly noting that no appointment has been made in the diary system, which he explains to the fieldworker:

"I put no appointment made as no space available I've put that agreed by Mary as that's what they've agreed and some people have a tendency to forget they have agreed these things so to avoid any potential problems later"

In this call the two parties from different sections work together outside of the formal process to try to ensure that the customer can get their money on the same day. They do however orientate to the formal systems and processes. Since the appointment cannot be put on the diary system it is explained in the notes. Much later in the day, when sitting with another operator, the fieldworker heard another call from the same caller. Extract 5Extract begins as the customer explains his problem (turn 1). The operator looks in ClaimSys and sees that a payment has apparently been made (turn 4), the customer asserts his desperate need for the money (turn 5), but it is not at all clear from the system details and the notes what type of payment it is.

Extract 5

1. C - I had to fill a form in because the bank has closed my account. I had to fill it in and they've taken it upstairs to xxxx. I can't get a crisis loan and I can't see why I can't get my money today
2. O: Can you just hold on
3. *[O looks in ClaimSys]*
4. O: right they have made a payment to you today. They have replaced it today er and they have replaced it for 124 pounds eighty?
5. C - can I pick it up today I'm really desperate
6. O: Er can you just hold on I just want to check payment

The operator checks payment type and sees that it looks like a counter cheque (delivered at the Work Centre at a specific time) but there is no note indicating the pick-up time. This leads to a lengthy phone interaction (> six minutes) with the processors as she tries to clarify the situation. The processors tell the operator that the cheque is in finance and she should call them. But now it is too late for finance to release the cheque as the cycle for the day is over! It is clear that although the processors completed the paperwork today they did not do so early enough for finance to release the cheque. The operator is very unhappy about this, stressing the citizen is currently on the phone. The operator returns to the caller to tell him the payment will not be made today, saying to the fieldworker just before "oh god he's going to shout". But, he has hung up. The operator is very concerned saying "That is bad news that is really, really bad" and she puts an exceptionally long note on ClaimSys (five lines) in case he calls back.

Here the formal systems of communication did not work well to expedite this matter. For the caller this involved a series of phone calls and meetings only to find out that he could not get his cheque that day. What made this procedure particularly complex is that it involved a number of parts of the organisation interacting, and clearly shows how continuity of service can break down when this interaction is purely through formal tools. Where the operator was able to speak directly about the matter to the floorwalker in the Work Centre, they were able to organise a workaround that meant that the caller had a good chance of getting their money that day. It seems that processing were unaware of the urgency of the situation and the effort that had gone into trying to arrange things. It is notable that the people in contact with the caller, who make extra efforts to sort the situation out, are not those who complete the work to resolve the situation. We are not saying that the processors do not treat people as individuals, as it is indeed often noticeable that they do. It is more that at times there is not a joined-up connection between customer contact and processing. This is a purposeful division of labour, but in the many exceptional cases it can actually result in extra work and effort.

A common complaint of telephony is that the processors do not provide adequate notes. Both groups usually only make notes when something 'significant' has happened, or some action has been undertaken. Practices also vary between individuals and it should be remembered that telephony have three places to enter notes: CLS, SecureSys and ClaimSys. For every call they log something in CLS but not always on ClaimSys, however, only the notes in ClaimSys are shared. When making a note in ClaimSys, telephony tend to describe in detail what is happening with a case. In contrast, processors only put in details of significant events or actions. For example, when a form has been sent out or received back or other matters such as "mvd to Dunstable" "mortgage housing 51.74 backdated" and so on. They certainly are unlikely to put that they have phoned the citizen but got no reply or that they started work on the case but put it to one side. This is not because the processors are being negligent, rather they have different orientations. Notes offer a restricted channel and great attention is paid to keeping notes short and concise. It is the processors who must print out the notes page for filing once filled up and decide which notes should stay and which be deleted. It is no wonder that they use the notes only for things they see as consequential or of long term interest. Cases have timelines, with key phases where the citizen is likely to contact the Department. For non-exceptional claims the citizen may call in a couple of times for simple matters. However, in exceptional cases processing can be considerably delayed meaning the citizen contacts the department frequently . In these cases it would be extremely helpful for telephony if they had a detailed understanding of what was happening. Once the delay has been resolved much of the information becomes redundant. The notes as they are currently used often do not provide the support that telephony need.

Collocation and the relationship between processors, telephony and citizens

As well as impacting the ability to organise the work around the whole workflow, whether telephony and processors are collocated or not impacts the working relationship. The staff in the two sections of MediDept are not only collocated but also cover for one another. At busy times some of the processors cover the phones, giving them direct insight into the work of telephony. Supervisors also cover the whole department at certain times (e.g. the end of the day) giving them a view onto the whole case of a citizen, rather than just a small part of it. There was much less apparent tension between the processing and telephony sections in MediDept than in UneDept.

In UneDept being limited to formal communication processes can mean the flow of work across the intra-organisational boundaries is far from smooth. To solve the problems that arise there is a liaison between telephony and processing whose job is to take action where there has been a major breakdown in the workflow. When telephony receive a call from a citizen and three emails have been sent up to processing but the caller has not had a call back then they pass the case on to the liaison by printing out the notes page and claim details page from ClaimSys and putting this into her in-tray – usually with an additional written note attached. The liaison then contacts the relevant processor to get them to handle this case as a priority – she may also call the citizen. What is particularly interesting about her work is that although this might be viewed as a case where the processors have failed in their work (since they have not responded to the citizen in a timely manner), in reality her job involves lots of persuasion to hand off these calls. She has to work to get processing to take the calls and is aware they do not always view her positively. As she says:

"and sometimes when you have to call supervisors they're not very helpful cause they feel that you are just being a nuisance contacting them even though they know it's your job. So that's not very helpful either. But I'm quite thick skinned so it doesn't really bother me but. Sometimes you get a bit fed up"

She spends time working out what is going on with the claim, partly so she can direct it to the right team but also for smoother hand-off. She parcels the cases up in particular ways to make her demands seem less burdensome (turn 3, Extract 6). Whilst she may have ten cases to pass off, she typically hands them over in batches of two or three, often with a 'difficult' case packaged with a couple of easy cases. Extract 6 gives a flavour of her work. The ClaimSys notes say "passed to rapid. John to resolve add partner. John will ring customer to advise" and an attached post-it says (about the caller) "Very aggressive. Going off his head".

Extract 6

1. Liaison: apparently it was passed to you yesterday for you to resolve um cause he hasn't had his call back and he's being very abusive to the telephony staff down here today and so they had to terminate the call so he does [softer voice] need a call back please
2. Processor: oh yeah I passed it on to somebody
3. L: cause he says nobody's called him and he's ready to burst so [gives number] do you want his GI?[gives number]. And while I'm on the line I have another one here this is a <rapid reclaim form> that was done on the 18th of March an email several emails have been sent the last one by xxx on the twenty seventh of April and his GI is [gives number] it's all in WorkSys and his surname is A***** and he would like a call back please I'll give you the mobile [gives number]
4. P: what's his complaint?
5. L: Well his is because he's done his <rapid reclaim form> since march and he hasn't he keeps phoning up emails etc someone's supposed to call him back and nothing happens
6. P: we do call them back
7. L: Mmm so why is mr F back on I don
8. P: I'll check mr F

```
9. L: Maybe it'd be helpful if the people
   that phoned back just put it in notes that
   they actually called back the customer
   then it's all there for the world to see
```

The liaison stresses the strain on her staff of dealing with these callers (turns 1 & 3). Although he takes the cases, the processor is not particularly apologetic (turns 2 & 4). When the liaison says "someone's supposed to call him back and nothing happens" (turn 5) which is a complaint that his team is not following the process he objects (turn 6). She acknowledges this it is in a rather noncommittal, but non-confrontational way (turn 7) and clearly suggests that using notes to show call backs would be helpful to telephony (turn 9). This is a request we hear her make a number of times and indeed she says to the fieldworker

```
"I mean to me it just makes sense if you
phone a customer I always put a note in
notepad. I'm now going to put a note on on
these two that I have phoned him and he says
what he's going to do but this this is what
you do you waste so much time because you
just keep going round and round and round"
```

The liaison goes on to criticise the way the processors organise their work, in particular that the supervisor should have checked that the work had been completed and the customer called. Whilst this may seem like a valid perspective from the view of telephony it does not take into account how the work is actually managed by the processors given the sheer volume of cases they have and the need to trade-off processing many easy cases vs. few hard cases. Telephony of course hear largely from the difficult cases. Since the processors are somewhat removed from the citizens this enables them to get on with the work of processing the many and meeting their targets rather than responding to incoming calls. There are many more examples we could give both from the liaison and the telephony staff but the general feeling can be summed up by the comment "there's a lack of communication big time". Another person called it 'tribal'. Tension can arise between any of the sections where work passes across the intra-organisational boundaries and it is compounded by the physical separation, just as with the work of distributed teams [4]. Such complaints and tensions were not visible in MediDept, where the staff knew one another, could see the amount of work, overhear one another and resolve workflow problems between them in ad hoc ways.

DISCUSSION

In this paper we have examined how collocation and distribution affect the working practices of two sections engaged in bureaucratic work. Previous research has focused on cooperative work and the impact of collocation/distribution on it [4,8], but there is often an assumption that more 'routine' work such as processing should be well suited to divisions of labour enacted through technology as proposed by Malone [7,13]. Indeed this is a management viewpoint subscribed to by the department, where the idea is that the data on the system backed up by notes and supplemented by unidirectional email, is enough for intra-organisational coherence. We suggest that the communication channels are *impoverished by design*; not only is it assumed that this will suffice, but it is thought that allowing more communication is inefficient. What is interesting in our findings is that as with cooperative work amongst tightly knit teams [4,8] many of the same benefits come from collocation and the same problems from distribution. Although much of the routine processing work can be adequately undertaken within this division of labour, problems arise when handling exceptional cases. It is important to understand that the exceptional cases are a problematic routine minority of cases that surface in the daily working of the Department. Often they arise due to of the complexity of the benefit regulations and they take up large amounts of time for both processors and telephony.

Pentland [10] described how the available organisational 'moves' represent (and enact) the organisation's structure and its division of labour. In UneDept the staff can, for the most part, only interact through the official workflows. Thus, the work must be completely enacted within the division of labour specified by management. There is apparent logic behind the intent of management, who fear that enabling more communication will disrupt the ability of each section to focus properly on their work. However, when we look at MediDept we see that the fears that free communication is wasteful and inefficient [cf. Kraut, 6] seem unfounded. Instead, in MediDept the workers of both sections respect the division of labour, but have an eye on how procedures enable (or restrict) the flow of work across the intra-organisational boundary. They develop ad hoc solutions only where they are needed for the good of the process as a whole, e.g. for complex cases. That is, they orientate to the sense rather than the letter of the procedures to enable the smooth running of the workflow. A bit more confidence perhaps should be had in workers to self-organise to make the workflow work. As with studies of distributed versus collocated teams, we observed a number of crucial, overlapping differences between the two departments: 1) the ability to develop informal solutions to problems, 2) the ability to understand the work of others enough to get your own work done, and 3) the working relationships between sections. We will take a closer look at these issues with a focus on notes and medical certificates, also drawing out some ideas for design.

Notes

Notes are used as the primary means of communication about a case in UneDept. Arguably they have incidentally become the key means of communication, although they are not particularly well designed for this, being restricted in amount of characters and lines. Like all communications they are recipient designed. Processors take considerable time to word their notes to try to make them understandable to others, but they tend to be designed with their fellow processors in mind and are often inadequate for telephony. There were tensions between the two sections about what notes should comprise of due to their different orientations. Telephony need to be able to reassure callers that their case is under review and so would like all actions on the case to be noted. In contrast, since they are unaware of the pressure of repeat calls to telephony, processing orientate to the limited fields in the notes page and only make notes of what they see as significant actions. It is not that they pay no attention to the work of telephony it is just that they have only a limited view of what that work consists of. Recipient design is most effective when you have a good idea about the requirements of the recipient. There are good reasons, of space and time, for limiting the amount of notes written but as they are, the notes are not a resource which would seem to be designed to fulfil the requirements of telephony.

It is possible that re-design of notes and their associated practices could improve matters somewhat. For example, more space could be provided for free text; both ephemeral and long lasting notes could be allowed to fit with the rhythms of the case (periods of intense activity and customer-interaction, followed by periods where little case work is carried out); certain conventions for abbreviations and ownership information (name, phone no.) could be promoted; and finally, people could be trained in making notes that fit with the needs of other departments.

Medical Certificates

As a contrast to the notes we can look at the medical certificates in MediDept as a shared resource that works. They reside in processing, but crucially are accessible to telephony due to collocation. The practices of 'go looking' or 'go asking' are not limited to medical certificates but this was a striking example since without the local workaround much extra work would be generated. In both departments telephony are the 'public face', whilst processors carry out back office work. The work is highly interdependent and it is important that telephony know what is happening in processing with regards to individual cases, and that situation is better in MediDept. So, what can be done to ameliorate this situation in UneDept given that management is unlikely to be persuaded by the idea of radical collocation [8]? A focus on the work at the intra-organisational boundaries could be beneficial, in particular in making visible the work of each section to the other, rather than deliberately hiding it. If we consider the case of medical certificates, taking into account current practices, it offers us an idea of how resources like case documents might be usefully shared electronically.

In the current set up, using formal channels, medical certificates can only be accessed by telephony through ClaimSys after they have been input onto the system. But, this does not take into account the actual rhythms of the case, where for the citizens there is a just-in-time process of submission and processing to ensure payment. They call in frequently around the time of submitting the certificate when often the certificate is in transit or process. For this reason the informal solution, of making them available for manual search, was developed. Telephony could confirm receipt if they had arrived or quickly flag-up missing certificates. A simple electronic solution for medical certificates would be to have a secure shared online repository between doctors and the department. This would also reduce the work required of the patient/citizen in submitting the certificates. Another solution would be to scan the medical certificates as they arrive either in the Work Centres or the sorting office, with a shared image file-store making them available to both processors and telephony. One can see how the shared image file-store could better coordinate the work of both sections around a number of different case documents for both departments.

Working Relationships

A further interesting feature of the different work arrangements is the effect on mundane office relations. In UneDept, the most ready-to-hand reasons given by staff for problems, errors or lack of response on the other side of the boundary were often negative – 'they don't do things properly'. Given the lack of insight into one another's work, and of shared context, with no means for spontaneous communication this is perhaps not surprising [4]. The contrast with the greater harmony in MediDept was apparent. This suggests that if the ecological separation of the work is to be maintained there is a need to design interfaces and processes that allow a fuller view on the on-going work activities and reasoning with possibilities for richer electronic communication when required. Greater visibility onto one another's work could offer many benefits, including reduced numbers of calls. Whilst it is certainly important that callers can get through to an operator, this is only effective if the operator can adequately resolve their problems. Otherwise they will have to call back, perhaps several times, increasing call volume and caller frustration.

CONCLUSIONS

We hope to have demonstrated within the paper that some freedom for employees to produce sensible solutions to workflow problems and the freedom to communicate and mesh together processes is vital in coordinating work in an efficient manner, particularly for non-routine and problematic cases. In many ways this echoes the argument made by Kjeld Schmidt [13] in response to more extreme versions of Transaction Cost Theory as applied to computerization in companies and sectors, maybe most well known in papers such as Malone et al. [7]. This study adds to this literature in being able to directly compare two departments doing similar types of work with two different physical ecologies. That it is in a bureaucratic setting helps us to understand this argument can apply equally well in 'routine' administration as in more typically considered cooperative work settings. Making this comparison is important for the community, as there remains a widespread perception that since computer tools enable communication, tracking and workflow, then work like this can be distributed with little cost.

In some ways this seems like a case of a problematic position in computing returning. We would argue that the reason a more extreme separation of business or administrative functions, with only electronic support, may fail is not simply a question of computer power or approach to design. Rather, views that consider human interaction necessarily wasteful and computerised workflows necessarily efficient remain problematic. We do not take an extreme opposite view but instead urge management and designers to realise that keeping the humans in the loop in a regulated manner can have a number of organisational benefits. We have shown that with open channels of communication and influence across boundaries exceptional cases are easier to deal with, and workers can share information and knowledge about each other's work that that better enables its achievement. Finally, we want to focus on knowledge and address the concern that 'a little knowledge is a dangerous thing'. In this setting management worried that if people started working across organisational boundaries they would know enough to think they could advise customers and other workers about other parts of the bureaucratic process but not enough to do so accurately [cf. 6]. It was rarely officially sanctioned. Interestingly, our research showed that workers needed to the understandings to make the processes more effective, but still oriented to the organisational boundaries and their roles within them. Thus in these situations a little knowledge is not a dangerous thing, it is vital to the functioning of the organisation.

ACKNOWLEDGMENTS

We would like to thank all the dedicated staff in The Department we met and observed during this study.

REFERENCES

1. Dourish, P & Belotti, V. (1992). Awareness and Coordination in Shared Workspaces. In proceedings of CSCW '92, pp. 107-114.
2. Erickson, T. & Kellogg, W. (2000). Social Translucence: An Approach to Designing Systems that Support Social Processes. ACM ToCHI, Vol 7, No 1, pp. 59-83.
3. Heath, C. & Luff, P. (1991). Collaborative Activity and Technology Design: Task Coordination in London Underground Control Rooms. In proceedings of ECSCW '91, Amsterdam, Netherlands, pp. 65-80.
4. Hinds, P.J. & Mortensen, M. (2005) Understanding conflict in geographically distributed teams: the moderating effects of shared identity, shared context and spontaneous communication. *Organization Science*. 16 (3). 290-307.
5. Klein, M., Dellarocas, C., and Bernstein, A. (2000) Special Issue "Adaptive Workflow Systems". Journal of CSCW. No 9 (3-4).
6. Kraut, R., Steinfield, C.Chan, A., Butler, B. & Hoag, A. (1999). Coordination and Virtualization; The Role of electronic Networks and Personal Relationships. *Organization Science*, Vol. 10, no 6, pp. 722-740.
7. Malone, T., Yates, J. & Benjamin, R. (1987). Electronic Markets and Electronic Hierarchies. *Communications of the ACM*, 30 (6) pp. 484-497.
8. Olson, J. S., Covi, L., Rocco, E., Miller, W. J., & Allie, P. (1998). A Room of Your Own: What Would it Take to Help Remote Groups Work as Well as Collocated Groups? *CHI 98* pp. 279 - 280
9. Olson, G. M., & Olson, J. S. (2000). Distance matters. Human Computer Interaction, 15, 139–178
10. Pentland, B.T. (1992) Organising moves in software support hot lines. *Administrative Science Quarterly*, 37 pp. 527-548.
11. Sachs, P. (1995). Transforming Work: Collaboration, Learning and Design. *Communications of the ACM*, Vol. 38, No 9, pp. 36-44.
12. Schmidt, K., & Bannon, L (1992): 'Taking CSCW Seriously: Supporting Articulation Work', *Journal of CSCW*, vol. 1, 1992, no. 1-2, pp. 7-40
13. Schmidt, K. (1994). The Organization of Cooperative Work: Beyond the "Leviathan" Conception of the Organization of Cooperative Work. *In Proceedings of CSCW 94*, Chapel Hill, NC, USA, pp. 101-112.
14. Star, S. L. & Strauss, A. (1999). Layers of Silence, Arenas of Voice: The Ecology of Visible and Invisible Work. Journal of CSCW, No 8, pp. 9-30

Field Trial of Tiramisu: Crowd-Sourcing Bus Arrival Times to Spur Co-Design

John Zimmerman[1], Anthony Tomasic[1], Charles Garrod[2], Daisy Yoo[1], Chaya Hiruncharoenvate[1], Rafae Aziz[3], Nikhil Ravi Thiruvengadam[4], Yun Huang[1], Aaron Steinfeld[1]

[1]Carnegie Mellon, [2]Swarthmore College, [3]University of Washington, [4]Stanford University

johnz@cs.cmu.edu

ABSTRACT

Crowd-sourcing social computing systems represent a new material for HCI designers. However, these systems are difficult to work with and to prototype, because they require a critical mass of participants to investigate social behavior. Service design is an emerging research area that focuses on how customers co-produce the services that they use, and thus it appears to be a great domain to apply this new material. To investigate this relationship, we developed Tiramisu, a transit information system where commuters share GPS traces and submit problem reports. Tiramisu processes incoming traces and generates real-time arrival time predictions for buses. We conducted a field trial with 28 participants. In this paper we report on the results and reflect on the use of field trials to evaluate crowd-sourcing prototypes and on how crowd sourcing can generate co-production between citizens and public services.

Author Keywords

Transit, service design, crowd-sourcing, field trial.

ACM Classification Keywords

H5.m. Information interfaces and presentation (e.g., HCI): Miscellaneous.

General Terms

Design, Human Factors

INTRODUCTION

The emergence of crowd-sourcing social computing systems has fundamentally changed computing. The success of services such as Wikipedia [24] (participant generated content), Travelocity [20] (participant generated reviews), Yelp [25] (participant generated location based content and reviews) and reCAPTCHA [23] (participant generated ground truth data for machine learning systems) illustrate just some of the many different forms this new technology can take and the range of problems it can address. Crowd-sourcing represents a "new material" for HCI designers to play with. However, designers lack proven design processes for creating these types of systems and lack insight into how to address issues including bootstrapping information and initiating and maintaining user participation.

Service design is an emerging discipline uniting operations research and design. Operations research has long focused on redesigning processes to improve efficiency and effectiveness; however, the transition to service design has generated a new focus on customers' experiences of a service. Interestingly, this transition mirrors the change in HCI from its traditional focus on usability to an emerging focus on user experience. Discourse in service design addresses the differences between products and services as a shift from *value-in-exchange* of goods to *value-in-use* that emerges between a customer and service provider [14]. This new perspective comes from the realization that customers have competence that service providers can use. They characterize this new perspective as *co-creation*, where value emerges through the interactions of customers and service providers [15, 16]. Crowd-sourcing social computing systems provide a rich space to investigate the intersection of HCI and service design.

Our research investigates the application of service design theory and crowd-sourcing technology to improve public services. Our intention is to help citizens who receive public services feel like co-owners. The work follows a research through design approach [27] where we design speculative systems, using methods from HCI and from service design, as a way of learning how to best design these kinds of systems. Our work began with a focus on transit commuters working as sensors in the transit network; reporting problems they experienced as a way of engaging in the "co-design" of this public service. However, fieldwork revealed that commuters had very little interest in reporting problems [26]. Instead, they wanted to know when their bus would arrive. Based on this feedback, we reframed the opportunity for service improvement of transit. We proposed that commuters could engage in co-creation of value by using the GPS enabled mobile phones they carry to generate real-time bus arrival information. Further, we speculated that if commuters engaged in frequent information exchanges with the transit service, then they would be more likely to engage in co-design activities, such as problem reporting.

CHI 2011, May 7–12, 2011, Vancouver, BC, Canada.

To further investigate the validity of our hunch and to extend our knowledge of how to effectively design crowd-sourcing systems, we developed Tiramisu ("pick me up" in Italian), a system that allows commuters to share GPS traces and report the "fullness" of a bus they are riding. The interface provides real-time, historic, and scheduled arrival times organized by stop. In addition, it allows commuters to submit reports based on their ongoing service experience. We conducted a field trial with 28 commuters who used Tiramisu for three weeks. In this paper, we provide an overview of related research, details of our prototype interaction design, results of our field trial in terms of participation in providing GPS trace information and problem reports, and reflections on how to more effectively design crowd-sourcing social computing systems.

RELATED WORK

Related work falls into three areas: crowd-sourcing, service design, and similar HCI systems.

Crowd-sourcing and participation (contribution)

Crowd-sourcing systems are difficult to prototype. They resist the tried and true HCI methods of paper prototyping and controlled lab studies, because researchers and developers cannot accurately predict if users will contribute the information needed to make a system valuable to users. In addition, researchers and developers have no tools to help them understand how many users constitute a "critical mass" needed to keep a system working. Interestingly, some early research exploring this challenge has described how researchers can use Amazon.com's Mechanical Turk as a crowd-sourcing test-bed [10].

While there has been little research on how to improve prototyping of crowd-sourcing systems, there has been a great deal of work on how to increase contribution in social computing systems. Some of the earliest work goes back to investigations of groupware. Researchers noted that many of these systems failed not for cognitive reasons (too difficult to use), but for social reasons; many workers did not enter information into these systems because they did not perceive enough individual value for their efforts [9].

A forthcoming book on the design of online communities reviews the literature on contribution and draws out approaches that system designers can take to improve contribution [11]. This work is also framed in terms of perception of value and it details three specific approaches for increasing people's contribution to a community:

- **Asking**: People are more likely to contribute if they are asked, and if they are asked specifically/individually.
- **Intrinsic Motivation**: People will contribute if they perceive an intrinsic motivation, such as their own enjoyment in doing the work. In addition, people perceive value in helping others and in helping groups of people they feel an affiliation towards.
- **Rewards**: People will contribute for different kinds of rewards including praise, increased reputation, an increase in privileges, and financial compensation.

Interestingly, there are negative consequences to haphazardly combining approaches. For example, providing rewards for work people previously performed for intrinsic reasons can reduce their perception of intrinsic value for the activity, thus negatively impacting their contribution [11].

Service Design and Co-design

In the service design community, the concept of "service" has been described as a "perspective" focused on co-creation of value between customers and service providers [6]. This idea of co-creation emerged partially out of the insight that customers can be more than consumers; they can also be a source of competence [15]. As an example, Prahalad and Ramaswamy note that in the software industry, customers commonly share their competence by becoming beta-testers [15]. Interestingly, this insight came in part because the Internet allows companies and customers to engage in dialog and also from the recognition that dialog between the customer and service provider and within communities of customers presents an opportunity for value to emerge [15].

To better understand service design, Kuusisto and Päällysaho conducted a review that revealed four types of co-production; where consumers participate in the production of the services they consume [12].

- **Consume**: Customer makes use of services and passively co-produces by creating the perception of value.
- **Co-perform**: Customer performs some of the tasks of a service.
- **Co-create**: Consumer uses resources (such as information) from a service to create their own value.
- **Co-design**: Dialog between customers and service providers around the types and form of service desired.

Service designers must take care when working on public services. Often these services function as monopolies and are not driven to improve their service offerings through competition. This is not necessarily a negative quality, as competition can diminish the importance of marginalized communities like the poor and people with disabilities, who are often the intended audience for public services. In fact, many public services exist specifically to address issues of fairness by creating a more level playing field for marginalized communities [3].

Public services have looked to technology as an approach to service improvement. Traditionally they have focused on automation and on improving the speed of service delivery. However, when public services take a more user-centered design approach, they often learn that their customers' main desires are for different services, not for automated services [2]. In detailing opportunities for public service improvement, researchers have noted seven metrics:

- **Quantity of outputs**: More services offered
- **Quality of outputs**: Speed and reliability
- **Efficiency**: More outputs for less money
- **Equity**: General sense of fairness towards citizens in terms of costs and benefits

- **Outcomes**: Increased usage of a service by the citizens or by a percentage of the citizens
- **Value**: Cost per unit of outcome
- **Consumer satisfaction**: Often a result of several of metrics above [3]

Tiramisu improves "quantity outputs" by providing real-time arrival and bus fullness information, services not currently offered.

Researchers have proposed that co-design, where customers engage in the design of the services with the provider, may be a particularly good approach for service improvement of public services. They noted three distinct beneficial outcomes: services that are more responsive to the changing needs of citizens; increased trust of the government through citizen's more positive engagement with services; and building of social capital through an increased sense of community [2].

Tiramisu attempts to operationalize the concepts of *co-production*. Specifically, we want transit commuters to *co-perform* in terms of generating bus the arrival information they desire by combining their traces with the transit service's schedule. We want commuters to engage in *co-design* through problem reporting; indicating issues that effect them enough to be worthy of the transit service's immediate attention. By conducting a field trial, we have gained insights on how to operationalize these concepts.

HCI systems in support of transit

The HCI research community has engaged in several projects at the intersections of commuting/transit and social computing. Here we discuss three working systems and detail how Tiramisu connects and provides an advance.

Researchers at the University of Washington developed a mobile system called OneBusAway that allows transit commuters to see real-time arrival information [7]. They have had great success at getting lots of participants to use this service and have noted some behavioral effects, such as an improved perception of personal safety and people choosing bus-stops farther from their currently location because the arrival time made it obvious that the bus would get them to their destination sooner. This system is similar to ours in that it focuses on the value of providing real-time bus arrival times. Tiramisu advances this work in that we have bus commuters generate the arrival time information, while their system uses GPS data logged by buses and provided by the transit service.

The Biketastic system was designed to support bike commuters [17]. Researchers conducted a proof of concept trial where participants used the system to record and share GPS traces as a way of describing a specific commute. In addition, cyclists added details of problems or challenges for a trace. This system is similar to Tiramisu in that it supports sharing GPS traces and problem reporting; however, it does not provide real-time information.

Pathfinder focused on investigating the design of systems in support of citizen science [13]. Citizen science is a philosophical approach to the practice of science where citizens in the community take on the role of research assistants, helping to collect information needed for analysis. Pathfinder intended to advance this notion by allowing citizens to participate in making sense of the data instead of limiting their role to data collection. Specifically, citizens shared information, asked questions, and proposed speculative hypotheses on commuting. Tiramisu is fundamentally different in intention from Pathfinder in that it is not designed in support of scientific sense-making by either citizens or professional scientists. Our participants share data and report problems, but they share data in terms of their own self-interest of wanting to know when a bus is coming, and they report problems with the intention of citizenship and civic engagement outside of science.

All three of these projects describe their motivation in terms of increasing sustainability through increased use of public or alternative transportation. Our work has a distinctly different intention of citizens feeling more ownership, responsibility, and control over the public services they use. Fortunately, the use of real-time arrival information has been reported to significantly increase the use of public transportation [4], and thus Tiramisu will likely have a positive impact on sustainability.

Finally, researchers have addressed the expense of commercial AVL systems by simulating a crowd-sourced AVL system for the Chicago transit service [20]. This work differs from Tiramisu in that it attempts to automatically detect when participants are riding a transit vehicle and in that it is a simulation and not a field trail.

INTERACTION DESIGN

Motivated by our fieldwork with transit commuters, discussions with a local transit agency [26], and the concepts of co-production and co-design from service design, we developed a conceptual model illustrating how information exchange between commuters and the transit service could provide a foundation from which co-design could emerge (Figure 1). We focused on crowd-sourcing the vehicle location data, literally appropriating the GPS and communication devices commuters already carry, because the transit system we were working with reported costs of approximately $70 million to install a commercial Automatic Vehicle Locator system for a mid-sized city.

In this model, transit commuters provide GPS trace data using their phones. The transit service provides planned schedule information. Based on the schedule information and the GPS traces, a computational system generates real-time arrival information.

The transit commuters we interviewed during our fieldwork shared that reporting problems and engaging in improving the transit services offerings was not their responsibility [26]. They felt that the effort to report a problem was simply too high compared to the perceived value. In working on our conceptual model, we speculated that if transit commuters accessed the arrival information and traced GPS data, then they would often have the system-in-hand. If the system displayed a screen that supports problem reports for the transit service, then, when commuters encountered a problem, having a system-in-hand would reduce the perceived effort of making a report. To capture this relationship in our conceptual model, we placed co-design above the arrival time information exchange.

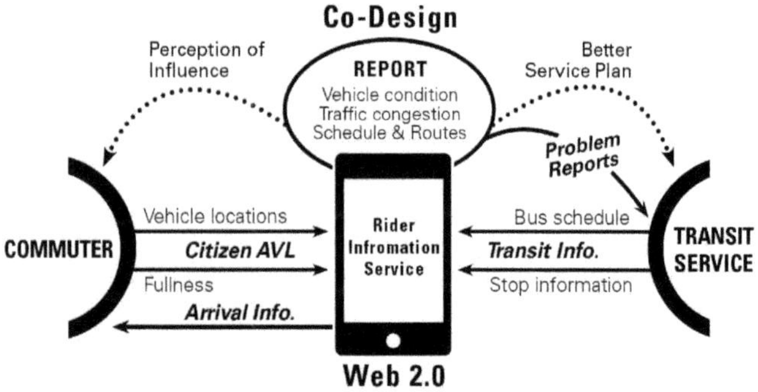

Figure 1. Conceptual model of design problem framing.

We chose to prototype and conduct the field trial using iPhones because of the critical mass of iPhone users at the time of the trail, and because the iPhone has a screen reader that supports blind and low-vision commuters. A production version of the system would need to operate on many smart phone platforms to minimize barriers to participation.

Interface Design

From the "Main Menu," users can access information on bus arrival times in three ways: nearby, search, and favorites (Figure 2A). Selecting "Nearby" transitions the interface to the "Main Map" screen, which offers a view similar to Google maps. Nearby stops appear as red pins. Selecting a pin brings up a map "annotation" with the name of the stop and the time of the next bus (Figure 2B).

Selecting the button on the annotation transitions to the "Select Route" screen, which displays a list of upcoming buses for the selected stop (Figure 2C). This screen displays real-time arrival information for a bus when there is a commuter on that bus who is sharing GPS. When this is not available, the system shows historic arrival information, assuming the system has previous trace data for this bus at this time. When neither real-time nor historic arrival information are available, the interface shows the scheduled arrival time. In designing this screen, we chose to combine real-time, historic, and schedule information as a way of addressing the bootstrapping challenge of getting crowd-sourced information into Tiramisu. Our plan is that when this app is first released, commuters will see scheduled information, and as more and more commuters use the system and trace their rides, the schedule will be replaced by real-time and historic information. We also specifically chose not to show the difference between the real-time and the scheduled arrival times. Our intention is to help commuters know when the bus is coming, and not to "shame" the transit service by revealing that their bus may be earlier or later than scheduled.

Real-time and historical data include bus fullness information, something currently not available as an estimate in the schedule provided by the transit service. Our previous fieldwork with commuters revealed their

Figure 2. Screens from Tiramisu interface.

Main Menu (A):

Main Map (B): Map with selectable stops based on location.

Select Route (C): Arrival times for selected stop.

Report (D): Select destination bus stop.

Record (E): Report fullness and share GPS trace info.

Recording (F): Update fullness and stop trace.

Report (X) Select categories.

Report (Y): Input report text and add photo.

unhappiness when they would see a bus they wanted coming towards and then have it drive past them because it was too full to allow more people to board [26]. We assumed that knowing ahead of time that a bus was full might lessen the blow of watching it drive past without stopping. Additionally, we thought commuters could use this information during rush-hour to decide if they should wait a few minutes in order to ride a bus that is less crowded. Finally, we felt fullness would benefit commuters with walkers, wheelchairs, strollers, and large bags.

Clicking on the star in the upper left corner of the "Select Route" screen (Figure 2C, underneath the C label) adds this stop to a commuter's list of favorites. Additionally, selecting favorites from the main menu (Figure 2A) transitions the interface directly to the "Select Route" screen (Figure 2C).

When commuters decide on the bus they wish to take, they select that bus from the list of arrival times, transitioning the interface to the "Destination" screen (Figure 2D). Here they select from a list of upcoming stops. Making a selection transitions the interface to the "Record" screen (Figure 2E). Once they board the bus, commuters indicate fullness and press the "Start Recording" button to share the fullness rating and the GPS trace from their phone. While tracing, Tiramisu displays the next stop (Figure 2F). At the end of the trip, commuters press a stop recording button (Figure 2F) as they exit.

Selecting "Report" from the "Main Menu" (Figure 2A), or selecting the "Report" tab at the bottom of any screen transitions the interface to the "Report" screen (Figure 2X). This allows commuters to immediately express positive or negative comments about their transit experience. Commuters categorize the report by selecting schedule, route, vehicle, driver, and bus stop. Next, they type a message and possibly provide a photo (Figure 2Y).

System Overview

Figure 3 displays a high-level functional architecture of Tiramisu. A single backend server maintains a client-server arrangement with multiple clients running on iPhones. Clients contain the user interface and a data model that records favorite stops. The server logs recorded (traced) trips, predicts arrival times, logs fullness, logs problem reports, and processes client information query requests.

To initialize the system, a GTFS [8] representation of the transit agency schedule is loaded to the database. Every thirty seconds a real-time model predicts bus arrival time and fullness for buses with trace data within the last 30 seconds. Once a day, the previous month of recorded trips are used to construct a historical model of bus arrival times and fullness. Both arrival-time prediction models first prune outliers and then regress the distance the bus must travel to a stop against the absolute time of the arrival at that stop. This model is robust against a variety of sources of error in the system, such as bad GPS information, dropped trace signals, and user error. Similarly, the real-time and historical fullness model is based on a simple average of past fullness. Models can be generated based on days of the week, weekends, and holidays. The models predict bus location and fullness approximately 20 minutes into the future.

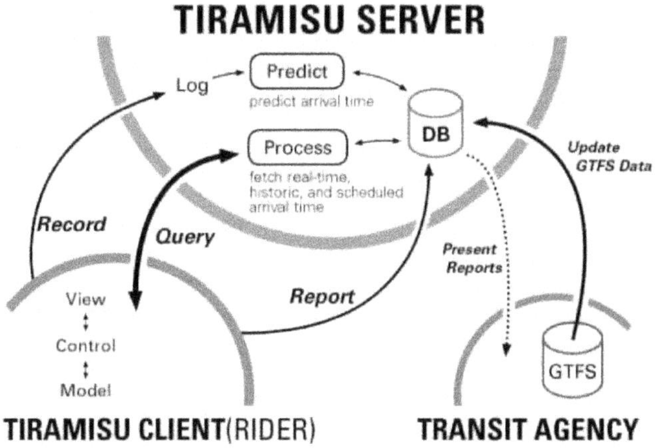

Figure 3. Functional Architecture of Tiramisu.

Client instances issue three types of requests to the server. *Trace messages* contain the client's GPS coordinates, fullness, departing-stop, destination-stop, bus route, and a trip identifier. *Reports* (containing selected options, text and an optional photo) are written directly to the database. *Informational queries* (e.g., nearest bus stops for the client) are processed against the current state of the database.

FIELD TRIAL

Typically, HCI design processes recommend an iterative process of moving from low to high fidelity prototypes. This reduces risks by addressing critical challenges before making too large of an implementation commitment. Crowd sourcing systems, however, make this iterative approach difficult. The main challenges generally have to do with acceptance of the system and participation in generating the information, and these cannot be easily investigated, with respect to a specific system, through the use of lab studies. These aspects of crowd-sourcing systems require a critical mass of participants to create the social effects of use.

In our case, we needed to know if commuters would actually share GPS traces, since this information would only help commuters downstream of their location. An individual commuter never immediately benefits from the traces they provided. Tiramisu's interaction design relies on intrinsic motivation to get commuters to share traces and report problems. In addition, during the field trial participants were paid to use the system. While creating the design, we specifically decided to not attempt to amplify people's contribution using the many approaches recommended in the literature in order to get something close to a baseline for this behavior. We also wanted to know if the co-production of the real-time arrival information would lower the barriers to co-design (problem reporting). Neither of these issues could be assessed in a lab study using paper prototypes or a roughed out technical system; therefore, we chose to conduct a field trial.

We recruited participants using electronic message systems and flyers at bus shelters. The recruiting materials indicated that participants must be regular commuters and must own an iPhone. Through selective placement of the ads, we targeted people who rode through a specific transit corridor. We wanted to reduce the number of participants needed to create a "critical mass." We recruited 28 participants: 16 fulltime students, 5 fulltime workers, and 7 part-time students who also worked fulltime.

Participants visited our lab where they took a pre-survey detailing their typical transit use and probing on their history of reporting transit issues. In addition, we loaded the Tiramisu software on their iPhone. They then left the lab and used the system for two weeks.

Near the end of two weeks of usage, we schedule an appointment for participants to return to our lab for a post survey and for payment. When they returned, we gave them the TAM 3 (Technology Acceptance Model) [5, 22]. This instrument measures perceptions of usefulness, ease of use, enjoyment in use, output quality, results from use, and behavioral intent (likelihood of use in the future). Responses use a 7-point Likert scale ranging from 1 = "extremely unlikely," to 4 = "neither," to 7 = "extremely likely." We use this instrument to get a baseline perception of the user experience and possible acceptance of Tiramisu.

While at our lab, we connected their phones; downloading the favorites they created and the impressions they experienced. The term "impression" indicates that an arrival time was displayed. For example, Figure 2C shows the "Select Route" interface screen. This screen has 5 visible impressions: 1 real-time, 1 historic, and 3 scheduled. We also conducted a semi-structured interview to find out more about their experience with Tiramisu to get arrival information, to provide traces, and to report problems. Each participant was paid $20. They were told they could continue to use Tiramisu, but that we would no longer pay.

Participants did not all start using Tiramisu on the same day. Instead, they continued to enroll over the 38 days our trial ran (Figure 4). For our analysis, we normalized the data based on an individual participant's first day, and we only included their first 21 days of use in calculating the averages. Because of the slow startup of use, participants who joined later in the trial had a higher likelihood of encountering real-time and historic data.

Throughout the trial, Tiramisu logged when and where individuals accessed bus arrival information, when and where they traced, and any problems that they reported.

During the field trial we encountered many typical challenges not usually faced in lab studies. These include a schedule change instituted by the transit agency affecting a small number of bus routes, broken and upgraded phones that required participants to return to our lab to have the software reloaded, one participant moving outside of our targeted corridor, and participants taking vacations.

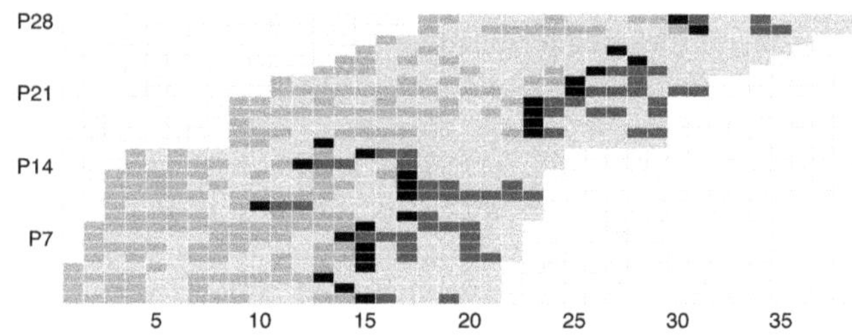

Figure 4. Ramp up of participants using the system for 21 days each over the course of the 38-day field trial. Blue indicates use of the system on a "paid" day. Black indicates the day participants were paid. Red indicates use of the system by participants after they were paid.

FINDINGS

Findings are reported in terms of **participation**, sharing GPS traces; **bootstrapping**, commuters access to real-time, historic information, and fullness information; **co-design**, contributions of problem reports; and **user experience**.

Participation

Participants provided traces (the participation rate) for approximately 56% of their sessions. A "session" happens anytime a participant accessed the arrival time information on their phone. We infer an untraced-session when participants do not start a trace within 15 minutes of a session. We calculated the participation rate by dividing sessions that contain a trace against total sessions. The participation rate is only an estimate of traces to actual "rides". We had no way to detect cases when participants boarded a bus without using Tiramisu or when they accessed the arrival time information and then chose not to ride a bus, and thus did not trace. The highest contributing participant traced 96% of their sessions and the lowest contributing participant traced 4% of their sessions.

Figure 5 shows the participation rate over time, normalized to the number of days a participant has been in the trial. Across all participants, sharing traces decreased over the course of the trial as indicated by the regression equation ($y = -0.0044x + 0.6038$) with $R^2 = 0.0551$.

Figure 5. Change in percentage of tracing over the course of the field trial in days (14-paid followed by 7-unpaid days).

There were differences in average tracing rates for different user groups. Fulltime workers traced 68% of rides; students traced 48% of rides; and participants who were both fulltime workers and part-time students traced 59% of rides.

Bootstrapping

Participants viewed 16,263 arrival impressions. These were captured when we synced their phones in our lab at the point of payment; black marks on Figure 4. Across all participants, 5.9% of the impressions they viewed showed real-time arrival times and 7.2% showed historic arrival times. Together, 13% (2,132 out of 16,263) of all impressions were created by data participants supplied and 87% came from the schedule.

In the post-survey, we asked each participant about the three types of arrival times: real-time, historic, and scheduled. Interestingly, three participants could not claim a specific preference between these three. In addition, four participants rarely if ever had the experience of having real-time or historic data available for a bus they were taking.

In general, participants really liked the real-time data, when it was available. Twenty-one participants stated that this was their favorite kind of arrival time. P28 elaborated on the difference between the printed paper schedule and the real-time: "*Although the scheduled time was* [indicating] *20-minutes later, the real time showed 2-minutes later. And the bus did come in 2-minutes*."

Two participants expressed a preference for historic data. P27: "*It was most useful when a route I was planning on taking had a historical data time with it. It was then I noticed that the historical time was closer to actual time than the published schedule*." However, 11 participants did not trust historic data. P7: "*I least trust historical data because the system is new and has not necessarily collected enough data to be useful, although this will presumably become more reliable as the amount of data increases*." One participant expressed a desire to see the scheduled data instead of historic. P18: "*I prefer scheduled time* [to historic] *because if the scheduled time is wrong, at least I can get angry at Port Authority for being inefficient*."

Twelve participants expressed distrust of scheduled data. They stated that in their experience, the buses never arrived as scheduled, and that they were always late.

In discussing the addition of fullness information, several participants expressed an appreciation for this new information. P5 described a situation where she used the system to adapt her evening commute. While using the system she saw a bus scheduled to arrive 30 minutes later than her usual bus, and the historic data showed this to typically be empty. She shared that her usual bus never had any seating. She left work a little later and the bus did in fact have many seats available.

Co-design

In the pre-survey, 3 participants answered they had previously reported problems to a transit authority within their lifetime. Over the course of our trial, 14 participants submitted 22 problem reports: 9 related to transit infrastructure, 9 related to schedule information, and 4 reporting that the Tiramisu software had crashed.

Reports on infrastructure generally addressed vehicle conditions. Examples include: *"Broken seat"* (this report included a photo of the broken seat), *"The bus died!"*, and *"The AC barely works and the inside of the bus smells like diesel fuel. It also seems to have troubles going up hills and the panel covering electronics above the driver's head is about to fall off it appears."* Interestingly, one report contained both positive and negative observations: *"The* [annunciator] *and message board are not indicating the next stop. The bus was nice and cool though."*

Several reports expressed frustration about late and missing buses. *"Late, not on time."*, *"I waited 1 hour for a 500 bus from Oakland to Highland park."*, *"No 61A, B or D has been by in the last 30 mins."* In two reports, riders attempting to explain arrival time problems: *"Traffic jam at Murray at Hazelwood in 61D."* and *"Driver eliminated upper loop in Trafford which is part of the route."*

Participants submitted 9 reports regarding errors with the arrival list. Typical comments included: *"Boarded 61D. Bus is full. It was not displayed in the arrival list." "I got on a 67E that was about 10 minutes late. It had fallen off the list of possible buses"*, *"67 not listed. Bus routes on 67 line should be updated in Tiramisu to reflect recent schedule changes."* There are four possible causes for these breakdowns. First, as mentioned in a message, a bus could deviate from the schedule enough to fall off our interface. Second, some drivers pull over to stops they have not been assigned, because commuters push the stop request button or the driver spots a waiting commuter who signals the bus. Third, there were a few errors in the schedule we received. Fourth, there was a slight schedule change during the trial and we did not incorporate this into Tiramisu.

User Experiences

In the post-use interviews, participants shared that they liked using Tiramisu. Several participants even expressed concern when we cabled their phone to our computer, fearing we would delete the software. They intended to keep using Tiramisu even without a financial reward. In fact, 26 of the 28 participants asked us to email them if a commercial version becomes available.

Results from the TAM 3 are captured in Table 1. Various analyses impression values as independent variables revealed no significant differences. These included direct analyses of impression subtypes (real-time, historic, and scheduled) as well as analyses where the independent variables described the percentage of impressions containing value-added data viewed by each participant. Since none of the comparisons generated a statistically significant result, we simply report the average rating for each category across all participants.

Participants shared how Tiramisu influenced their commuting practices. P23: "*Sometimes I don't need to look up the schedule but* [with Tiramisu] *I felt forced to look it up* ..." P31: "[Normally,] *I chat with my friends and get on whatever bus that comes. Didn't really pay attention to when exactly the bus was coming* ... [With Tiramisu,] *I often checked the* [arrival] *time*."

Table 1. Average TAM 3 ratings across all participants.

Measure	Ave	STD
Utility	5.51	1.25
Ease of use	5.56	1.55
Enjoyment	5.68	1.08
Output quality	4.82	1.60
Results of use	5.59	1.03
Behavioral Intent	5.90	1.44

In speculating on new features, two participants inquired about reporting availability for bikes on the bike rack mounted on the front of many buses. Two participants mentioned that Tiramisu would be improved if it could notify users of upcoming stops. Finally, one participant suggested that Tiramisu should automatically stop recording at the appropriate time.

Participants made many comments in terms of their phone. Several expressed concern about how much battery Tiramisu requires when sharing traces. P23: "*It sucks up your battery.*" P14 (who had an hour and a half commute): "[Tiramisu] *uses 30% of the battery from home to work*." In addition, participants expressed concern for having to explicitly stop tracing. Several noticed hours after they had exited the bus that their phone still indicated that is was "recording." Finally, several participants complained about a lack of multi-tasking on the iPhone and their desire to access other applications during their commute.

DISCUSSION

Following our analysis, we reflected on our findings. Below we highlight key insights in terms of advancing the design of Tiramisu, understanding the connection between social computing technology and service design, and prototyping social computing system via field trials. These insights are organized around the themes of participation, bootstrapping, co-design, and user experience.

Participation

During the field trial, participants traced more than half of their rides. This contribution rate seemed surprisingly high to us; however, we had no way of predicting a baseline for participation prior to the field trial. It is difficult to a claim that this is a good rate or even a "good enough" rate of participation for a crowd-sourcing social computing system to survive and flourish.

While participation seems higher than expected, it did have a slight downward trend over the course of the trial. We see three possible reasons for this. First, there was most likely a novelty effect when the app was new on the phone, and over time this effect began to diminish. Second, the earliest participants in our trial as well as participants who lived outside the main transit corridor used by other participants experienced fewer impressions of real-time and historic data, and this lack of value over time may have reduced their participation. Third, we paid participants to use Tiramisu for two week, and after the payment, they may have felt less obligated to trace their rides.

Surprisingly, students traced fewer rides than workers, and their traces were generally less valuable in terms of minutes of GPS trace, as their trips tended to be shorter; they generally lived close to school. This finding is important for others who wish to conduct field trials of these types of systems. It is important to predict which participants will receive the most value and also which participants have the most valuable information to contribute.

As mentioned, we did not choose a specific strategy to increase participation with Tiramisu. In looking at theories on contribution, we see at least three ways to proceed. We could give commuters an individual score (points) for each minute or for each stop-to-stop segment they trace. We could add this scoring and then also generate competition between groups, such as different businesses competing. Finally, we could start scoring and then charge users points (such as the number of minutes of traces they share) in order for them access the valuable real-time arrival times.

Bootstrapping

During the field trail, 28 participants created 13% of the data they experienced: impressions of real-time and historic arrival information. Once again, this seems higher than expected and again we did not have a good method of calculating how good this is or how good "good enough" is in terms of crowd-sourcing data. In particular, participation rates depend on the initial distribution of participants, which in turn affects participation rates, which in turn affects the distribution of participants, leading to a feedback-based system that is difficult to accurately model without measurements from the field.

Our design strongly benefited from the fact that we could start with a static dataset—in this case the transit schedule—which users would find to have some value in use. Tiramisu then allows users to improve this dataset by replacing instances of the static data with crowd-sourced data. This structure allowed for a slow rollout of the application. We did not need to generate an initial set of crowd-sourced data to bootstrap the system. In deciding on whether to field test a crowd-sourcing social computing system, we speculate that this model of augmenting valuable static data with more valuable crowd-sourced data decreases the risk of abandonment of the system when working with a small set of users.

Extending the transit schedule with fullness information also appeared to improve the value-in-use of Tiramisu for participants. In one case a participant was able to adjust her schedule to ride a much less crowded bus. Access to this information could potentially increase the flexibility of commuters by letting them see into situations they have not yet experienced. In the long-term, a feature like fullness might allow commuters to adjust their schedules, resulting in better load sharing across all the commuters. This information helps commuters improve their personal experience as well as others' experience with commuting.

The conflicting findings on historic arrival times surprised us. We assumed that participants would view historic as more valuable. In the next iteration of Tiramisu, we will consider the issue of trust in intelligent systems [28].

Co-design

One of the main hunches driving our design was that co-design in terms of problem reporting would increase due to participants having a phone-in-hand as they accessed the arrival time information and provided traces. The change in behavior, from 3 previous problem reports from 28 participants, to 22 problem reports from 14 of 28 participants provides some confidence that this hunch could pay off. Interestingly, the problem-reporting rate of our participants appeared to be about equal with the reported problem reporting rates of commuters with disabilities, a segment of public service users who may have higher motivation to participate in co-design due to a higher-level of dependence on this service [19].

In terms of the design, reporting problems seem like a shallow level of co-design, with a narrow focus on complaints as a measure of an issues importance. In advancing this work, it will be important to investigate if this idea of phone-in-hand would also result in increased participation of commuters in regards to more strategic planning issues, such as route and schedule changes or issues relating to taxes and budgets.

It was interesting to see participants submit reports that explained why buses were delayed; possibly in the hope the transit service could use this information to make changes. However, this action raises the possibility that commuters might be willing to share this information with each other. In reconsidering our design, we see an opportunity for commuters to add comments about an individual bus or a stop that are immediately pushed out into the system, sort of like a very localized "tweet" without the need for a special language for vehicle, stop, or route information.

In thinking about having the "system-in-hand," it is impossible for us to tell if problem-reporting contributions are linked to tracing contributions or simply to the ability to access arrival information via a mobile phone. An important advance to service design research would be a clearer investigation of the effect of commuters producing traces versus a system that simply provides this information in a mobile form. Little research has investigated how the activity of co-production changes a user's perception of the relationship they have with a service provider [1]. This analysis would get more to the heart of the co-production and co-design concepts in service design.

One concern that surfaced in our previous fieldwork from both commuters and the transit service was a lack of trust in the other commuters. Both groups felt that some commuters would maliciously produce "bad" information in terms of traces and problem reports. We did not see this effect in our field trial; however, this absence is not surprising since participants knew their behaviors were being monitored. This result offers some insight that a way to address the perceived issue of malicious behavior might be to force users of the system to give up their anonymity. This design decision is an interesting question in terms of privacy and location based technologies and in terms of governments monitoring the behavior of citizens. It may be possible to convey accountability without revealing identity [18]. This is clearly a topic for deeper investigation.

User Experience

In terms of user experience and Tiramisu, our TAM scores were quite high. Our inability to tease out more specific trends in the data suggests a ceiling effect combined with very low overall variability. Scores were uniformly high for almost all TAM indices, thereby leaving little room for differentiation on the upper end of the scale. This indicates an increased likelihood of acceptance for Tiramisu and for other systems that follow a similar design. However, this speculation is based on results of a self-selected group who volunteered for this trial. Nevertheless, these results give us confidence that the basic framing, features, and usability of the design are "good enough" to push out for a larger scale field deployment and data collection effort.

Comments from the interviews indicate that co-design of the transit service might also include co-design of Tiramisu. Participants had design ideas for new features that emerged from their use; however, our report function did not make these ideas easy to share. This desire provides further evidence of a strong connection between web 2.0 technology and opportunities for co-design.

CONCLUSIONS

Crowd-sourcing social computing systems are difficult to prototype. Iterative design techniques like testing with paper prototypes cannot investigate the critical risks of bootstrapping and contribution. In our research, we addressed this challenge by conducting a field trial of Tiramisu; a system that allows bus commuters to share GPS traces using their smart phones. Tiramisu then uses these traces to generate real-time arrival estimates of buses commuters can access on their phones. Tiramisu's design integrates theorics from service design on co-production and co-design, with the intention of getting commuters to engage more deeply with the transit service and begin to feel they can influence its service offerings.

Our field trial demonstrates that this concept works in practice. Participants were successful at tracing information and at using the real-time and historic estimates to improve their commuting experience. In addition, we noted high participation rates for explicitly sharing location traces and for reporting problems encountered with the transit service.

Acknowledgements

The Rehabilitation Engineering Research Center on Accessible Public Transportation (RERC-APT) is funded by grant number H133E080019 from the United States Department of Education through the National Institute on Disability and Rehabilitation Research. In addition, this work was partially supported by Google and by the Hillman Foundation through a grant from the Traffic21 project at Carnegie Mellon.

REFERENCES

1. Bendapudi, N. and Leone, R. P. Psychological Implications of Customer Participation in Co-Production. *Journal of Marketing*, *67*, 1 (2003), 14-28.
2. Bradwell, P. and Marr, S. *Making the Most of Collaboration an International Survey of Public Service Co-Design, DEMOS Report 23*. (2008), DEMOS, in association with PriceWaterhouseCoopers (PWC) Public Sector Research Centre, London.
3. Boyne, G. A. Sources of Public Service Improvement: A Critical Review and Research Agenda. *Journal of Public Administration Research and Theory, 13*, 3 (July 2003), 367-394.
4. Casey, C. Real-time information: Now arriving. *Metro Magazine*, http://www.metro-magazine.com/Article/Story/2003/04/Real-Time-Information-Now-Arriving.aspx (Accessed Sept 11, 2009).
5. Davis, F. D. Perceived usefulness, perceived ease of use, and user acceptance of information technology. *MIS Quarterly* (Sept. 1989), 319–339.
6. Edvardsson, B., Gustafsson, A. and Roos, I. Service Portraits in Service Research: A Critical Review. *International Journal of Service Industry Management, 16*, 1 (2005), 107-121.
7. Ferris, B., Watkins, K. and Borning, A. Onebusaway: Results from Providing Real-Time Arrival Information for Public Transit. In *Proceedings CHI*, (2010) ACM Press, 1807-1816.
8. Google GTFS: http://code.google.com/transit/spec/transit_feed_specification.html
9. Grudin, J. Why Groupware Applications Fail: Problems in Design and Evaluation. *Information Technology & People*, *4*, 3 (1989), 245-245.
10. Kittur, A., Chi, E. H. and Suh, B. Crowdsourcing User Studies with Mechanical Turk. In *Proceedings of CHI*, (2008) ACM Press, 453-456.
11. Kraut, R. E. and Resnick, R. Encouraging Contributuon to Online Communities. In Kraut, R. E., Resnick, P., Kiesler, S., Riedl, J., Konstan, J. and Chen, Y. (Eds): *Designing From Theory: Using the Social Sciences as the Basis for Building Online Communities*, (forthcoming).
12. Kuusisto, A. and Päällysaho, S. *Customer Role in Service Production and Innovation — Looking for Directions for Future Research, Report 195*, (2008) Lappeenranta University of Technology, http://akseli.tekes.fi/opencms/opencms/OhjelmaPortaali/ohjelmat/Serve/fi/Dokumenttiarkisto/Viestinta_ja_aktivointi/Julkaisut/Kuusisto_Paeaelllysaho_raportti.pdf. (Accessed: August 29, 2009).
13. Luther, K., Counts, S., Stecher, K. B., Hoff, A. and Johns, P. Pathfinder: An Online Collaboration Environment for Citizen Scientists. In *Proceedings of CHI*, (2009) ACM Press, 239-248.
14. Ng, I. C. L., Maull, R. S. and Smith, L. Embedding the New Discipline of Service Science. In *The Science of Service Systems*. H. Demirkan, J. H. Spohrer and V. Krishna (eds). Springer, 2009.
15. Prahalad, C. K. and Ramaswamy, V. Co-Opting Customer Competence. *Harvard Business Review, 78*, 1 (2000), 79-90.
16. Prahalad, C. K. and Ramaswamy, V. Co-Creating Unique Value with Customers. *Strategy & Leadership, 32*, 3 (2004), 4-9.
17. Reddy, S., Shilton, K., Denisov, G., Cenizal, C., Estrin, D. and Srivastava, M. Biketastic: Sensing and Mapping for Better Biking. In *Proceedings of CHI,* ACM Press (2010), 1817-1820.
18. Steinfeld, A. (2010). Ethics and policy implications for inclusive intelligent transportation systems. *Second International Symposium on Quality of Life Technology*.
19. Steinfeld, A., Aziz, R., Von Dehsen, L., Park, S. Y., Maisel, J., & Steinfeld, E. The value and acceptance of citizen science to promote transit accessibility. *Journal of Technology and Disability, 22*, 1-2 (2010), 73-81.
20. Thiagarajan, A., Biagioni, J., Gerlich, T., Eriksson, J. Cooperative Transit Tracking using Smart-phones. In Proceedings of SenSys, (2010) ACM Press, 85-98.
21. Travelocity: http://www.travelocity.com/
22. Venkatesh, V., and, Bala, H. Technology Acceptance Model 3 and a Research Agenda on Interventions. *Decision Sciences, 39*, 2 (May 2008), 273–315.
23. Von Ahn, L., Maurer, B., McMillen, C., Abraham, D. and Blum, M. Recaptcha: Human-Based Character Recognition Via Web Security Measures. *Science*, 321, 5895 (2008), 1465.
24. Wikipedia: http://www.wikipedia.org/
25. Yelp: http://www.yelp.com
26. Yoo, D., Zimmerman, J., Steinfeld, A., Tomasic, A, (2010): Understanding the space for co-design in riders' interactions with a transit service. In *Proceedings of CHI*, (2010) ACM Press, 1797-1806.
27. Zimmerman, J., Forlizzi, J. and Evenson, S. Research through Design as a Method for Interaction Design Research in HCI. In *Proceedings CHI*, (2007) ACM Press, 493-502.
28. Zimmerman, J. and Kurapati, K. Exposing Profiles to Build Trust in a Recommender. In *Ex. Abs. of CHI*. ACM Press (2002), 608-609.

Publics in Practice: Ubiquitous Computing at a Shelter for Homeless Mothers

Christopher A. Le Dantec[1], Robert G. Farrell[2], Jim E. Christensen[2], Mark Bailey[2], Jason B. Ellis[2], Wendy A. Kellogg[2], W. Keith Edwards[1]

[1]GVU Center
School of Interactive Computing
College of Computing, Georgia Tech
Atlanta, GA, USA
{ledantec, keith}@cc.gatech.edu

[2]IBM T. J. Watson Research Center
P.O. Box 704 Yorktown Heights,
NY 10598, USA +1 914 784-7826
{robfarr, ibmjim, mrbailey, jasone, wkellogg}
@us.ibm.com

ABSTRACT
Today, commodity technologies like mobile phones—once symbols of status and wealth—have become deeply woven into social and economic participation in Western society. Despite the pervasiveness of these technologies, there remain groups who may not have extensive access to them but who are nonetheless deeply affected by their presence in everyday life. In light of this, we designed, built, and deployed a ubiquitous computing system for one such overlooked group: the staff and residents at a shelter for homeless mothers. Our system connects mobile phones, a shared display, and a Web application to help staff and residents stay connected. We report on the adoption and use of this system over the course of a 30 week deployment, discussing the substantial impact our system had on shelter life and the broader implications for such socio-technical systems that sit at the juncture of social action and organizational coordination.

Author Keywords
Constructed Publics, Homeless, Urban Computing, Longitudinal Study, Qualitative Methods

ACM Classification Keywords
H.5.3 Group and Organization Interface: Collaborative Computing, Evaluation/methodology

General Terms
Design, Human Factors

INTRODUCTION
The presence of digital technologies in contemporary Western life is ubiquitous. Mobile phones, computers, data networks and the shared computational resources that come with them have created new opportunities for sharing [12, 29], for connecting individuals and groups in novel and meaningful ways [4, 5], and for extending participation through the democratization of information and the mobilization of civic action in a number of different civic and community based contexts [10, 26].

Despite the broad scope of human endeavor that has been positively impacted by the maturation of the field of computing, there remain, even within the riches of Western society, groups of people left out of the rapid advance of and opportunity provided by the "digital age." Being left behind is often due to a lack of economic capacity, inadequacies in education and training, and a mixture of institutional legacies that create barriers to access and participation and which serve to reinforce social marginalization. [1].

Within the United States, the urban homeless are an example of a social group that may not have extensive access to digital technologies but is nonetheless deeply affected by the pervasiveness of such technologies in everyday life. In everything from maintaining social connections to friends and family, to online registration and verification for social services, to finding and applying for employment and housing, the presence and necessity of interacting with technology has real consequences—and opportunity—for the urban homeless [21, 30, 35].

Despite the daily impact of technology on the urban homeless, few services and applications have been developed to specifically address their needs [27, 28]. Instead, typical efforts have attempted to broach the problem as one of technology access; unfortunately, such efforts are often unsuccessful because they fail to contextualize access in ways that translate into lasting technology adoption [19]. As a compounding factor, technologies deployed to the homeless need to account for the social and institutional infrastructure upon which the homeless depend [23]; purpose built systems for the homeless need to include points of interaction for the many service providers who provide care, manage resources, and act within a regulated environment [23].

The work we present here sits within this context: we have designed, built, and deployed an information system for the staff and homeless residents at an emergency night shelter. The system we designed and deployed uses elements from ubiquitous computing [34]: text and voice messaging links residents' mobile phones to a shared display in the shelter and to a collaborative desktop Web application for shelter staff. These components afford new channels of communication between the shelter staff and residents.

During the design of the system, we framed our approach as designing for two *publics*—the shelter staff as one public and the residents as the second [22]. We return to that framing here as an analytic lens to understand how the system was adopted and the role it played for the staff and residents during a 30 week deployment at the shelter. In doing so, we can begin to unpack the impact of the system on staff work practices, on identity and action of the residents, and on the social boundaries and interactions between the staff and residents. Ultimately, we found that the ubiquitous technologies we selected provided a means for the two publics to express and develop new attachments to each other as they confronted the issues affecting their lives.

BACKGROUND & SYSTEM DESIGN

We have previously detailed the fieldwork and design process used in developing our system [22, 21, 20, 23]; however, we will provide a brief overview of the system goals and key features in order to support the analysis of system use being presented here. The system—called the Community Resource Messenger (CRM)—was conceived as an intervention to let shelter staff send messages to residents about available services, reminders about appointments, and amplify their ability to help the individuals with whom they were working. The CRM was also designed to let residents make inquiries of their case manager, and to share and preserve their accumulated knowledge and experience on coping with homelessness. To address these issues, we designed and developed the CRM through a participatory process that focused on providing both staff and residents tools to support the individual and shared issues each faced.

Publics as Design Framing

To address the challenges of working with two distinct, but interwoven groups of stakeholders, we framed our design approach as one that would support and bridge two distinct but interrelated *publics*: the public of the urban homeless and the public of the staff at a specific shelter [22]. We built upon recent work within HCI [9, 8], Participatory Design [11], and Science and Technology Studies [24] that builds on John Dewey's definition of publics. For Dewey, an American pragmatist philosopher, a public is not a generic mass of people, but rather a dynamic group of stakeholders that take shape as people move to mitigate or promote particular social consequences [7]. An important part of Dewey's notion of publics is the idea that publics are both *plural* and *particular*: multiple publics exist, each constituted in response to particular shared social conditions.

Marres has further contributed to the notion of publics by arguing that the dependencies and commitments—or *attachments*—people have are critical to constituting membership in a public [24]. In particular, Marres points out that by focusing on the attachments of a public, we gain a better vantage from which to ascertain the issues around which a public forms. In particular, this foregrounding of issues enables us to move away from aligning with *a priori* groups of stakeholders, which are "usually characterized as relatively stable entities [with] established ideas, values, symbols or institutional devices" [24], and instead allows us to examine the fluid exchange of membership in a public as attachments to issues that are articulated and acted upon.

For Ehn, in considering how publics might inform participatory design, it is the articulation of issues that takes primacy as it enables a participatory design intervention to move beyond configuring materials or technology for *present* use, and instead to focus on configurations—social and material—that will facilitate *future* use [11]. This design-for-future-use—or what Ehn calls *infrastructuring* (borrowing from Star [32])—bolsters the notion of publics by arguing that participatory design can be used to *constitute* and *sustain* a public through the articulation of relationships to shared issues.

In the case of our context, the early participatory design set the groundwork for constituting and supporting the staff and residents at the shelter as two publics [22]. By so doing, we were able to foreground the *dynamic relationship* each had to a range of issues. For the shelter staff, these issues included sharing information, and coordinating care activities across different care providers—both internal staff and external agencies. For the residents, it meant understanding the social support networks and institutions upon which they depend. It also meant recognizing that while the public of the staff was stable, the public of the shelter residents was not; residents would come and go, and would not necessarily identify as part of a "homeless" public, eschewing the stigma of homelessness and more readily self-identifying as individuals overcoming adversity.

From this point of view, several specific design areas came to the fore: for the shelter staff it meant focusing on ways to help cope with resource constraints [20, 23], manage multiple relationships [16], and provide support for cooperative action as staff worked together to support several residents at a time [20, 23]; the areas of focus for the shelter residents included features to mitigate information overload [14, 21], enable continuity in maintaining social support and trusted relationships [15, 16, 21], and finally the introduction of features to address the transient and impermanent nature of membership in, and knowledge of, their public [6, 31]. We drew on these areas, derived from our understanding of previous literature as well as our own months-long fieldwork at this and other care providers, to focus our participatory design activities with the shelter staff and residents.

Participatory Design Engagement

The design process we employed engaged shelter staff and residents, both individually and together. In broad strokes, our design work was broken into three main activities. First, we held a day-long design workshop with the staff from several area service providers. This workshop was focused on identifying the goals, resources, and information flows at and between a group of service providers with whom we were working. The activities at the design workshop were largely used to understand the larger service provider ecosystem and how specific services dovetailed with each other (and where gaps were in that integration) [22, 23].

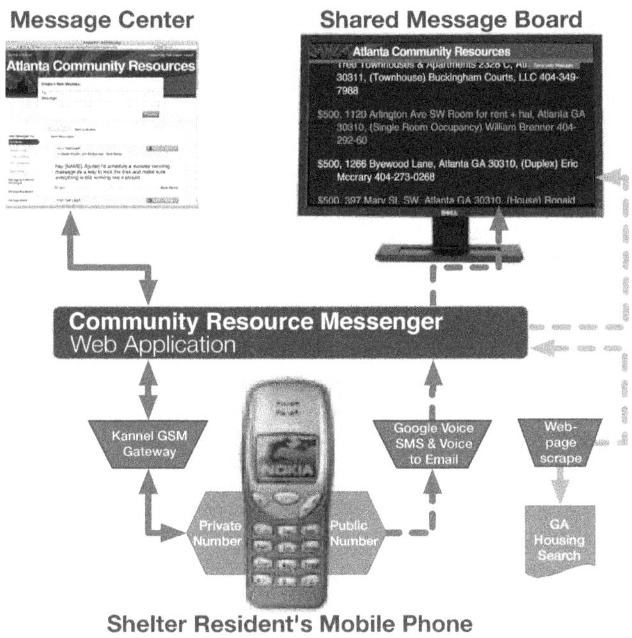

Figure 1: CRM system architecture.

The second part of our design process focused on the extended staff at the shelter where we would eventually deploy the CRM. Beginning in 2009, we met regularly with the staff. Over the ensuing months, design activities moved from initial fieldwork to understand the work practices at the shelter to defining specific CRM features. We then used progressively higher fidelity prototypes to communicate design ideas, gather feedback, and enable staff to evaluate and re-design features to better suit the way they worked.

Third and finally, we worked with the shelter residents to define the kinds of features that would support their information needs. We iterated system features and worked with the residents to engender transparency in the design process, giving them a voice in how their information would be shared with and between the staff. This was an instance of where we intentionally sought out opportunities to recognize and engage with the established power relations at the shelter: the default position of both staff and residents was that the staff knew what the residents needed and were best equipped to share that information; however, through the course of the design work and then continuing into the system deployment, residents came to a realization that their ideas were useful and helpful for each other and that they could rely on each other for information and advice [22]. To support this kind of resident-to-resident knowledge sharing—and preserve that knowledge over time—we developed features that enabled residents to act as *producers* of information rather than presuming they would only be *consumers* of information provided by the staff.

Functional Overview of the CRM

The resulting ubiquitous computing system comprised three user-facing components (see Figure 1): shelter staff accessed the system through a web interface called the Message Center, shelter residents accessed the CRM via mobile phones, and information awareness for both shelter staff and residents was provided via a shared display called the Shared Message Board. Each of these components was meant to address three different foci of activity: staff needed a central place to manage their messaging activity as well as share messages with each other to keep abreast of specific residents' needs and progress; the residents needed access to staff for help and information while away from the shelter; and staff and residents needed a way to share information with each other while co-located at the shelter.

For shelter staff, the Message Center was used to send messages directly to residents, to post information to the Shared Message Board, and to share information among the staff. Messages to residents could be addressed to multiple residents at once (similar to addressing an email to several recipients). Additionally, messages to residents could be scheduled for future and/or recurring delivery (*e.g.*, for specific future events or standing reminders about shelter meetings or other regular activities). Message sharing occurred by enabling staff to view each other's messages.

For shelter residents, access to the CRM was accomplished through basic mobile phones. In order to keep the barriers to interaction as low as possible, residents only had to send text (SMS) messages or leave voicemail at one of two phone numbers: a *private* phone number for routing messages to shelter staff and a *public* phone number for routing messages to staff and residents via the Shared Message Board. SMS messages were forwarded directly to the CRM while voicemail messages were first transcribed to text using Google Voice before being forwarded on to the system.

When co-located at the shelter, staff and residents had access to the Shared Message Board; a 24″ monitor mounted prominently near the shelter entrance, driven by a small desktop computer. The display cycled through three different information views: messages from staff originating from the Message Center, messages from residents originating from SMS and voice messages sent to the public CRM number, and external information gathered by scraping results from a housing search website.

An offsite server hosted the CRM functionality and provided telephony integration functions. All messages were stored in a MySQL database accessed through JDBC. The Message Center and Shared Message Board software components were deployed as Java web applications on Apache Tomcat along with supporting Javascript for presentation, interaction, and dynamic browser updates. Private and public SMS messages were routed using Kannel, an open source GSM gateway, and Google Voice respectively. Google Voice was also used for speech-to-text transcription of voice messages left at the public phone number.

SYSTEM DEPLOYMENT & METHODOLOGY

In February of 2010 we deployed the CRM to an emergency night shelter for single mothers and their children. The shelter allowed each family to stay for 30 days. Time beyond 30 days (up to a firm maximum of 90 days) was typically granted only under specific circumstances, such as when extra time was needed to accommodate a job transition or to allow for some flexibility for those placed on waiting lists for transitional housing programs. Additionally, the shelter was only open at night: residents had to leave by 8 AM and could only return after 4 PM, so a significant part of their day was spent away from the shelter and hence away from the staff and other sources of information.

Our deployment was built around a systematic program of semiweekly meetings with shelter staff and residents to study how the CRM was being adopted. We held two one-on-one meetings with the shelter staff each week to discuss their perspectives on the CRM. The shelter staff involved with the CRM included three women: the program director, a weekend case manager, and a night manager. The program director ran the daily case management activities and had a very hands-on, face-to-face style of working with the residents. The case manager worked with the residents during the weekends when the program director was not present. The night manager was only present in the evenings and was there primarily as an emergency contact—she had no formal case management responsibilities. We ran our meetings with the staff as open-ended interviews and discussed current system use, issues they were having with the CRM, or improvements they wanted made.

For the residents, the study experience had three main components. Starting at intake, after explaining the study and obtaining informed consent, we gathered basic demographic data about each resident, including age, education, race, and data on ownership and use of mobile phones and personal computers (including questions about specific applications, *e.g.*, SMS on the mobile phone and chat, email, and social networking sites on the PC). To ensure participating residents could use the CRM if they chose, we provided mobile phones (a Nokia E50) along with $50 worth of pre-paid credit to residents who did not have their own phone. Residents who had their own mobile phones were reimbursed for expenses incurred from interacting with the system; no other form of compensation was provided.

The second component of the study for the residents was the semiweekly meetings held with the researcher. Meetings alternated between one-on-one interviews and focus group sessions. During these interactions, we would discuss how the CRM was being used, the specific features that the residents had found useful or irrelevant, and how its use was changing from week to week. Extensive field notes were taken during these meetings, notes that were in turn used to inform subsequent interviews and focus groups.

The third and final component of the study was a one-on-one interview that occurred as each resident left the shelter. This final interview was more reflective about how they used the CRM while at the shelter, the nature of the interactions they had with shelter staff and with fellow residents via the system, and a discussion of any specific events or opportunities that arose via their use of the system.

The final source of data for this study came from observational fieldwork we engaged in during our semiweekly trips to the shelter. Each week, we took time to observe shelter life and note how staff and residents went about their routines. These observations served to inform the questions we would ask of either staff or residents, and helped us contextualize their responses.

These data—the demographic survey data, notes from one-on-one and focus group meetings with the staff and residents, the exit interview data, the field notes from our ongoing site observations, along with detailed system logs and usage reports—provided the raw materials we used to analyze CRM use and integration at the shelter. Field notes and interview data were analyzed in a rolling data analysis that allowed the lead researcher to explore specific developments among the staff and residents during the interviews and focus groups [25, 33]. System usage data was used to help provide additional context around how the system was used and to triangulate our qualitative analysis with rhythms of life at the shelter across several generations of shelter residents.

FINDINGS

The use and adoption of the CRM must be understood given the constraints of the shelter it was deployed to: the women who came to the shelter were in a period of crisis, generally in a disoriented emotional state while also experiencing difficulty in practical matters. During their initial 30 days at the shelter, they would need to find work (or better paying work), establish childcare or enroll their children in school, and they would need to secure long(er) term housing arrangements. All of these tasks were done with ample help and guidance from the shelter staff, however, direct contact time had been limited to evenings, making in-the-moment assistance nearly impossible to coordinate.

Characteristics of Shelter Residents

In total, 25 residents at the shelter participated in our study. All of the residents were female, and all but one self-identified as African American (the lone exception identifying as Hispanic). The average age of the residents was 33 years old with a maximum age of 53 and a minimum age of 20. Education level across the residents was normally distributed: four (16%) had completed some high school, 12 (48%) had high school diplomas, six (24%) completed some college, and three (12%) had a two- or four-year college degree. On average, residents stayed at the shelter for 35 days, and groups of residents would typically arrive and depart at regular intervals—what we refer to as "generations" of residents.

Mobile phone ownership was common with 19 (76%) of the residents having their own mobile phone. Of those who owned their own phone, 12 of the 19 (63%) had monthly contracts; the remaining seven (37%) used pre-paid mobile phone plans. Regardless of mobile phone ownership while at the shelter, the majority of the women used SMS messaging—22 (88%) reporting they used it regularly for staying it touch with friends and family, with self-reported message volume ranging from tens (10+) to hundreds (100+) of messages per month. Personal computer ownership was low with only five (20%) of the residents reporting owning a computer; however, all of the residents used computers at

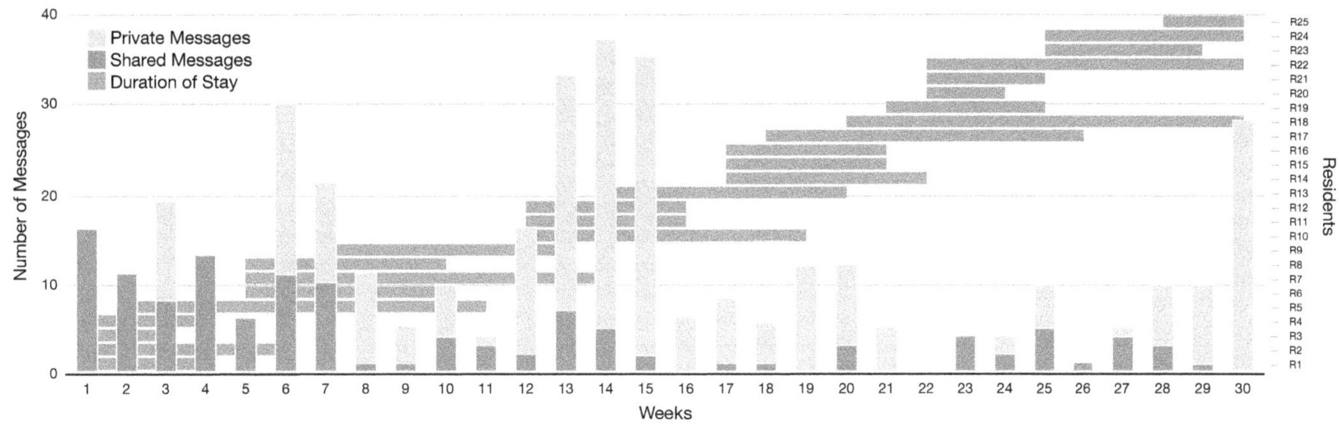

Figure 2: Weekly message volume, broken down by private/shared messages and illustrated against residents' length of stay.

least once a week through organized classes at the shelter, and the majority of the women, 18 (72%), reported using computers three or more times a week at locations like the public library, local charities, or at work. Computer use was described as including email and web at a minimum, with nearly half of the residents—12 (48%)—also reporting the use of social networking sites (*e.g.*, Facebook).

These characteristics begin to paint a picture of the technology practices of the women who came through the shelter. They were familiar with mobile phones and with using SMS—often preferring SMS as a way to keep in touch with friends and family during the day. They also understood things like Facebook and the kind of mediated interaction that takes place through online channels. These familiarities helped the residents understand the CRM and the different modes of communication it afforded, enabling us to use similes for posting messages to the Shared Message Board as like posting on a Facebook Wall.

Patterns of Use

By looking at the system usage data, we can begin to see how use of the CRM coincided with the rhythms of shelter life. Figure 2 provides detail on system use by overlaying two visualizations: the first depicts length of stay at the shelter via the horizontal bars—each bar represents a shelter resident (R1–R25 from bottom to top), the position and length of the bar indicates the week of arrival through the week of departure; the second graph is a vertically stacked bar graph (in two-tone grey) indicating the weekly total of messages sent to individuals (*i.e.*, private messages in light grey) and the weekly total of messages sent to the Shared Message Board (*i.e.*, shared messages in dark grey) by both staff and residents. By layering the data this way, we can see how the generations of residents (weeks 1–4, weeks 4–10, weeks 10–16, weeks 16–21, weeks 21–25, and weeks 25–30) coincide with message volume cycles over the 30 week deployment.

The graph in Figure 2 illustrates the processional nature of CRM use—from the messy and erratic use during initial weeks of the deployment, through to a settled pattern as staff and residents appropriated the system in support of the activities at the shelter. The irregular message volume during the first eight weeks of deployment came primarily as the staff began populating the Shared Message Board with information that had previously existed elsewhere in the shelter: phone numbers and addresses for ancillary programs, details about shelter procedure, external agencies serving specific needs, along with inspirational messages. After this initial setup work was done, the staff settled into a routine of updating the Shared Message Board as new information became available—a routine that resulted in a few messages per week.

By week 6, the staff and residents had begun to send a larger volume of private messages via the CRM—a trend that continued through week 30. The shift toward a higher volume of personal messages tracks the arrival and departure of generations of shelter residents. When a group of new residents would arrive, private message volume was low (Figure 2: weeks 4, 11, 17, 22, and 26), but would then increase and peak as individuals in that generation of residents became ready to move on (Figure 2: weeks 6, 15, 20, 25, and 30). This cycle was in part the result of residents moving from personal crisis to stability and in part the result of the case management style of the staff who would progressively give the residents more responsibility.

While this pattern generally held during our deployment, there were distinct characteristics of use within each generation of shelter residents. In particular, weeks 13–15 had a large volume of messages that did not reoccur until the very end of the deployment in week 30. To better understand what was different between the weeks of high and low message volume, we carried out a content analysis of the messages sent through the CRM. Two researchers coded each message according to one of 13 categories—topics covering specific resources like childcare, housing and employment, as well as topics like "case work" that covered coordination messages and "relationship work" that covered messages meant to establish trust and rapport. Inter-rater reliability ($\varkappa$=0.8984 with σ=0.0178) indicated a robust categorization rubric for the content exchanged via the CRM. Based on our content analysis, further details about message origin, and our qualitative experience with the lives of the women at the shelter, we are able to attribute these peaks in use to the unique way the particular residents at the shelter during weeks 13–15 and again in week 30 bonded with the staff.

Throughout the deployment, the staff accounted for 55% of the private messages (residents 45%); however, the standard deviation was quite high at ±25%; so from week to week, there was considerable variability in participation between staff and residents. During the weeks with a high-volume of messages, the split in participation between the staff and residents remained at 55%-45%, but the standard deviation dropped significantly to ±11%, indicating a much more even participation. Moreover, based on our content analysis, it was clear, throughout the deployment, that staff and residents used the CRM for coordination around specific service procedures (*e.g.*, securing long-term housing, following up on employment, or managing childcare), but during the high-use weeks in question, there were more messages that indicated a personal connection between the staff and residents (*e.g.*, "*I really enjoyed the meeting yesterday evening. Perhaps we should have more bonding and sharing experiences*", and "*Thank you, I look forward to talking to you too*"). This is important because it ties increased instrumental use of the CRM—using it to secure the services and resources necessary to move out of the shelter—with the experience of managing those resources *vis-à-vis* the relationship between staff and resident.

Overall, the cycle of use that developed with the CRM is validation that the design was appropriate, useful, and usable for the staff and residents at the shelter. Yet, it also points to two important developments with respect to how the CRM supported the two publics of shelter staff and shelter residents and how technology use can be leveraged within the broader homeless community. First, given our initial design framing of supporting two distinct publics, the CRM needed to do two things: it needed to support the articulation of common issues, some evidence of which is apparent in the content of the messages passed through the system; and it needed to support coordinated action around those articulated common issues. The staff and residents engaged in that common action when they used the CRM to share information about services and to accomplish micro-coordination to secure necessary services. It is important to point out that the action that was being taken through the CRM was new action never before possible—72% of the private messages exchanged via the CRM occurred during the day when staff had been previously unavailable to the residents—so it is not just that the CRM supported existing practices, but that it was instrumental in developing new practices.

The second point touches more generally on technology use by the homeless. As we pointed out above, the mothers at the shelter were familiar with using SMS, however, they used it almost exclusively for maintaining social relationships. This kind of social use is an important part of what digital technologies provide the homeless—a means of coping with stigma and maintaining some level of social inclusion [21, 30, 35]. However, translating non-instrumental use of technology into instrumental use has remained a challenge in no small part because the conceptual leap from viewing technology as *abstractly* useful to internalizing the *concrete* ways it can help is often difficult as the incentives remain indirect (*i.e.*, it is not always clear how mastering Word will help individuals find work) [19, 27, 28]. However, with the CRM, the incentive to interact with the system was inherently *social* as it was based on the relationship between the staff and the residents. The outcome of that social use, however, was *instrumental* in that it connected the residents to the services and help they needed to move out of the shelter and on with their lives. In short, no conceptual leap was necessary for understanding *how* the CRM could make a difference for the shelter residents.

Experiential Data

While the system usage data and content analysis help us understand what parts of the CRM were used, providing evidence of action taken via the system, the qualitative data from the semiweekly interviews and focus groups with staff and residents, along with the ethnographic observation done at the shelter, give us empirical evidence about how and to what extent system use impacted existing shelter routines. To understand this impact, we return to the notion of publics as an analytic lens for examining how the CRM affected shelter norms, how relationships between and among staff and residents were affected, and how information sharing enlisted different forms of membership in the public of shelter staff and the public of shelter resident.

Redrawing Social Boundaries

The first point we consider is the way the CRM impacted the relationship between the staff and the residents at the shelter. In particular, the adoption of the CRM for diverse communication needs initiated a redrawing of some of the boundaries between these two publics.

During weeks 10–16, conflict within the shelter began to develop around the completion of required chores. Prior to the deployment of the CRM, such conflicts were handled with face-to-face confrontations between the staff and the residents. By week 10, however, the staff had begun to rely on the ability to send messages directly to the residents in place of some of that face-to-face interaction. During a particular episode when chores—such as cleaning up after meals—were not being completed, the case worker used the CRM to send a message to several residents, writing, "*I am not sure whose turn it is but I have knocked on your door to remind you that the chore assigned to your room was not completed. Please take this opportunity to determine who needs to sweep and mop the kitchen. Thank you M—*"

This particular message marked a shift toward managing confrontation via the CRM. It also expressed a nascent tension between the case manager and program director. This tension was rooted in different notions of how to manage relationships with the residents. In particular, the program director felt that using the CRM to enforce shelter rules was not enough, and that the mothers needed to be confronted immediately when they broke those rules.

During an interview after this exchange occurred, the case manager defended her actions, asserting that sending the residents a message gave them the opportunity to correct their actions without being compelled through confrontation. In the case manager's words, "*it returned power*" to the residents, allowing them to choose how and when they would respond to the message, an example of which is provided below. This point is important on two counts. First, it highlights the tensions that arose from introducing new technologies into the shelter, and how those tensions express the dynamic way publics can reconfigure around particular issues—in this case the way shelter rules are expressed and enforced. Second, it shows how a new form of staff-resident communication was instrumental in establishing a new social boundary that reduced intrusion for the shelter residents.

The redrawing of these social boundaries was facilitated not just by the ability to message someone while they were not present, but, as the case manager noted, by the fact that "*the system [provides] a record that a message was sent.*" This record created a perceived verification that a particular message was received, displacing the need for face-to-face communication to ensure accountability by the residents. As a result, the redrawing of social boundaries within the shelter was a combination of newfound mobile and asynchronous communication capacity, along with a concomitant capability to maintain the accountabilities previously exercised through direct interaction via message persistence.

This freedom impacted the staff and residents differently. The staff could send a message to residents about a particular issue and feel they had appropriately transferred responsibility to the mother in question; the residents could choose how and when to respond to a message, thus asserting themselves without confrontation and engendering a capacity to establish boundaries according to their needs and not just according to the rules of the shelter. It is in this regard that the CRM supported the staff and residents as two distinct publics, allowing each group to respond to issues independently.

Sharing Information for Action and Identity

The next element of the CRM we consider is the Shared Message Board—a large screen mounted in the entry to the shelter (see Figure 3)—and its role in supporting the public of the shelter residents. The initial goals of the Shared Message Board were to provide a visible place for both publics—staff and residents—to share information. As the deployment unfolded, we found that the message board became more than just a place to share information, instead becoming a mechanism for surfacing common issues and establishing shared identity.

For the staff, the Shared Message Board was initially seen as a means for providing basic information to the residents consistent with the cork and whiteboards already present in the shelter. However, the impact of the Shared Message Board became apparent in a particular incident during the run-up to the Easter holiday. In the weeks before the holiday, a paper flier about a free family outing had been posted on one of the existing cork boards. While the flier was on the cork board, none of the residents asked to sign up for the event. The week before the event, however, the case

Figure 3: Shared message board and a shelter resident.

manager posted the same information on the Shared Message Board, noting in a subsequent interview that, "*as soon as it went up on the [Shared Message Board], two mothers were interested and signed up [to attend].*" She and the program director were genuinely excited about this development because it was a clear instance where information on the Shared Message Board was more actively engaged by the residents than other forms of shared information (like the existing cork boards) had ever been. One of the reasons for this was that the animated display created an expectation that new information would appear on the screen, so the residents were naturally drawn to it as a source for daily updates.

Further evidence of how the Shared Message Board impacted the residents came when the program director watched a current resident demonstrate how it worked to a new resident. The fact that senior residents were spontaneously educating new arrivals encouraged the program director that the technology was becoming an important part of the residents' routines. This in turn led the program director to request additional features for managing information on the Shared Message Board—a request that the case manager pointed out as indicative of how well the CRM had been received at the shelter, especially given the program director's initial skepticism: "*[the fact that] Ms. [program director] wants more information up is a testament to its success.*"

The Shared Message Board also supported the expression of issues among the residents and became a medium for taking action on those issues. In a message posted to the Shared Message Board during the incident when residents were not completing their chores, one resident said, "*We came to [the shelter], it was a blessing for us all and we knew the rules right away... We agreed to do them but we're not doing [them]. This is the right thing and count our blessings and ... keep it clean...*"

The prominence of the Shared Message Board in the shelter made it a focal point for the public of the shelter residents. This was seen through the way residents responded to messages posted to the Shared Message Board, it was seen in how residents took it upon themselves to induct new residents into the routines of use surrounding the Shared Message Board, and it was seen through instances of self-organization that were mediated by the Shared Message Board. In particular, posting a message reminding fellow residents of their commitments was an act of articulating and organizing action around a particular issue. But more than just managing shelter chores, we would point to this incident as one where the women at the shelter identified themselves as a cohesive group—a public—confronting common issues. It might seem mundane to organize around chores, however, for the women at the shelter, all from very different backgrounds, thrown together for a brief and tumultuous period, establishing shared identify and supporting each other was an important event. The role of the CRM in constituting this nascent and transient public came by providing a platform that helped the residents express and self-organize around these common issues.

Destabilizing a Stable Public

Finally, we turn to the ways in which the CRM impacted the work practices and responsibilities of the staff and how it altered different roles within the shelter. By adopting this system, the staff had implicitly agreed to new forms of work: they would need to update messages on the Shared Message Board and develop routines for checking messages sent to them by residents. Both of these tasks would need to be done in a timely manner and would need to be integrated into existing case management activities.

The most significant change that came with the introduction of the CRM was that the division of labor was refactored, placing most of the responsibility for updating information on the case manager. As a result, as use of the CRM became more established, it shifted the balance of power: by virtue of using the CRM to message residents and post information to the Shared Message Board, the case manager's role at the shelter was amplified. The consequence of this was that dormant ideological differences between the program director and the case manager were amplified as well.

These tensions were exposed as a result of a very specific design decision about how information would be shared among staff at the shelter. During the participatory design phase, the staff made a significant change to how the Message Center worked; instead of treating each staff login as private, the decision was made to treat the CRM like a forum where staff could see all messages [22]. The rationale was that it would help the staff better coordinate action during the handoffs from week to weekend care by enabling better contextual awareness of what was going on with each of the residents.

While this was true in use—the staff did have better awareness of ongoing communication—that awareness was limited and imperfect. The brief nature of messages sent to mobile phones (typically adhering to the 160 character limit of a single SMS message) meant that the larger conversation, one that often started during a face-to-face meeting, was difficult to ascertain. Furthermore, the forum-like qualities of the CRM became an invitation for the program director to surveil the activities of the case manager. In one specific instance, the program director reproached the case manager for contacting a former resident with what had been mistakenly interpreted as an invitation to an event for current residents. The result of this exchange was that the case manager temporarily stopped using the CRM, a fact reflected in the message volume of week 22 (see Figure 2).

More fundamental, however, was the way this interaction affected how both the case manager and the program director framed their roles within the shelter—and as such, their roles as members of the staff public. There were two factors that affected this reframing. The first was that the CRM provided the case manager an effective tool to extend her contact with the residents. By being able to message them more easily, she was able to keep in touch during the week and maintain better continuity with the mothers at the shelter. As she put it during an interview, "*I see part of my job as building rapport with the mothers*." However, by using the CRM to extend her relationship with the mothers, she initiated the second factor, which was that the case manager's heavy use of the system raised her visibility to the residents and changed some of the established power dynamics at the shelter. Prior to the CRM deployment, the program director had the most contact time with the residents and established a strict relationship with them. She enforced the rules and often made difficult decisions on how to distribute limited resources. Meanwhile, the case manager acted as a confidant and advocate for the residents, a weekend-only foil to the "tough love" provided by the program director. As the case manager began extending her relationship via the CRM, the center of influence shifted, amplifying the nurturing role of the case manager.

At its core, the issue here centers on how using the CRM redistributed power and influence along different notions of how to establish effective relationships with the residents at the shelter. While the public of the shelter staff was something we presumed as stable during the design phase [22], the CRM created an environment where the prior attachments to shared issues became altered, in this case initiating a renegotiation between the case manager and program director on how to build and maintain appropriate relationships with the residents. Yet despite these tensions, both the program director and case manager remained enthusiastic about the role CRM had in sharing information with each other and with the residents.

DISCUSSION

When we set out to design the CRM with the staff and residents of the shelter, we had an explicit goal of catalyzing and supporting two unique but interconnected publics [22]. Drawing on Dewey's notion of a public—defined as a dynamic organization of individuals formed by the desire or need to address an issue [7]—we sought to create an interactive system that would support the efforts of staff and residents in the shelter by providing a platform for exposing and articulating issues so that shared action could be taken.

A critical part of this effort to design for two publics was to design the system so that it would sustain each public over time and not just be an artifact of the specific conditions under which it was designed. Our level of success in achieving this is evidenced through the sustained system use over multiple generations of shelter residents—residents who had no part in the initial system design.

This success, however, took different forms. Whether through facilitating a redrawing of boundaries between staff and residents, or by being enlisted in the construction of shared identity, or in waking dormant tensions among the staff, use of the CRM was shaped by the social dynamics at the shelter. The role the CRM played in the shelter was expressed differently for the staff, for the residents, and for the interaction between the two, but in all cases was shaped by the social context of the shelter—the staff and residents chose to use the CRM in particular ways, and those choices had subsequent consequences on shelter life.

In particular, the destabilization and subsequent renegotiation of roles that arose among the staff is consistent with Dewey's notion of publics as mutable entities. Furthermore, it reinforces why using publics as a rubric for designing the CRM was important: publics are meant to be dynamic, and changes in the makeup and characteristics of a public should come naturally as attachments to particular issues change over time. By building for this kind of dynamism, we created a system that encoded the capability to express particular issues rather than one that encoded particular established power dynamics.

This capability to express and respond to different issues did not come from a specific desire to disrupt power dynamics at the shelter. On the contrary, it arose from a commitment on our part, as system co-designers, to provide appropriable tools to the staff and residents so that they could resolve issues as each saw fit. As use of the system developed, new strategies for confronting common issues also developed, and in the case of the staff, that use disrupted established power dynamics. The subtle point here is that the tension experienced by the staff was not one of staff versus staff or of staff versus technology, but one of evolving attachments to the issues of how to manage relationships within the shelter as facilitated by the CRM.

This kind of exploration of attachments has parallels with systems like UrbanSim or Water Wars that focus on making explicit the commitments of various stakeholders [2, 17]. However, unlike those systems, the CRM enabled immediate action to be taken on the issues expressed via the system. The staff and residents work separately or together to resolve the issues they face. The action precipitated by CRM use was specific to the homeless care community where technologies are more often deployed as procedural resources for enabling oversight and accountability [3, 18, 23]. The support provided by the CRM, however, came by way of amplifying the relationships among the staff and residents rather than by attempting to bypass those relationships with a rationalized system for managing constrained resources. We would argue that one of the reasons the residents in particular did not view the CRM as a burden was because their experience with the system was social rather than procedural: it facilitated their relationships with staff and it provided a way to further establish and share in their relationships with each other. The result of supporting the staff and residents by way of their relationships was that the CRM became a socio-technical resource for the shelter; a stable medium for sharing information that helped the staff be more effective and helped the residents feel more connected, while providing the degrees of freedom necessary to foster and sustain a number of unique relationships within the shelter.

Despite the the degrees of freedom provided by the CRM, the overarching relationship between staff was bounded by the larger context of homeless care provision. The fact that the system was situated in an emergency shelter for women displaced by homelessness meant the intrinsic need the residents had for help and guidance—the "placefullness" of the shelter [13]—ultimately shaped how the CRM was used to communicate and organize. While both staff and residents incorporated the CRM into their practices and routines the basic relationship of staff as producers and residents as consumers of information was not overtly reconfigured. In fact, the primary challenge left unaddressed by the CRM centers on how to better enlist the shelter residents as producers of information, as the source for knowledge about resources and services, rather than just as collaborative consumers. While we observed instances of production by the residents, it was not a consistent pattern of use and is something we are looking to further explore in a revised design of the CRM.

Given our experiences with the CRM, we feel there is a significant role for mobile technology in addressing the homeless, and underserved communities more generally. As we have demonstrated here through the deployment of our system, such technologies can open new lines of communication between the homeless and their care providers, leading to more efficient and frequent communications, better coordination, and improved awareness of resources and needs. The CRM is an example of a ubiquitous computing system that achieved these outcomes by empowering users to identify and respond to the social issues facing them rather than by encoding specific solutions to those issues. In addition, we also sought to further the exploration of Deweyan publics as a rubric for understanding and evaluating participatory systems. The relevance of publics for building and studying systems like the CRM is the foregrounding of issues experienced and actions taken by users without encoding particular perspectives or solutions to those issues in the technology itself; that the technology is not the solution but rather a means for users to articulate their attachments to an ever evolving set of issues.

ACKNOWLEDGEMENTS

We thank IBM Research for their generous support of this project and Nokia for providing mobile phones. We also thank the shelter staff and residents for their sustained enthusiasm during the design and deployment of the Community Resource Messenger. The first author is supported as a Microsoft Research Fellow. This research was supported by the NSF under grant IIS-0915624.

REFERENCES

1. Beegle, D.M. Overcoming the silence of generational poverty. *Talking Points*, 2003, 11–20.
2. Borning, A., Friedman, B., Davis, J. and Lin, P. Informing public deliberation: Value sensitive design of

indicators for a large-scale urban simulation. In *Proc. ECSCW 2005*, Springer-Verlag, (2005), 449–468.

3. Bovens, M. and Zourdis, S. From street-level to system-level bureaucracies: How information and communication technology is transforming administrative discretion and constitutional control. *Public Administration Review*, *62* (2), 2002, 174–184.
4. boyd, d. Feature implications of user choice: The cultural logic of "Myspace or Facebook?" *interactions*, *16* (6), 2009, 33–36.
5. Bryant, S.L., Forte, A. and Bruckman, A. Becoming wikipedian: Transformation of participation in a collaborative online encyclopedia. In *Proc. GROUP 2005*, ACM Press, (2005), 1–10.
6. Conley, D.C. Getting it together: Social and institutional obstacles to getting off the streets. *Sociological Forum*, *11* (1), 1996, 25–40.
7. Dewey, J. *The public and its problems*. Swallow Press (Henry Holt & Company), Athens, OH, 1927.
8. DiSalvo, C., Maki, J. and Martin, N. Mapmover: A case study of design-oriented research into collective expression and constructed publics. In *Proc. CHI 2007*, ACM Press, (2007), 1249–1252.
9. DiSalvo, C. Design and the construction of publics. *Design Issues*, *25* (1), 2009, 48-63.
10. DiSalvo, C., Sengers, P. and Brynjarsd'ottir, H.o. Mapping the landscape of sustainable HCI. In *Proc. CHI 2010*, ACM Press, (2010), 1975–1984.
11. Ehn, P. Participation in Design Things In *Proc. PDC 2008*, ACM Press, (2008), 92–101.
12. Grinter, R.E. and Eldridge, M. Wan2tlk?: Everyday text messaging. In *Proc. CHI 2003*, ACM Press, (2003), 441–448.
13. Harrison, S. and Dourish, P. Re-place-ing space: The roles of place and space in collaborative systems. In *Proc. CSCW 1996*, ACM Press, (1996), 67–76.
14. Hersberger, J. Are the economically poor information poor? Does the digital divide affect the homeless and access to information? *Canadian Journal of Information & Library Sciences*, *27* (3), 2002/2003, 45–63.
15. Hersberger, J. A qualitative approach to examining information transfer via social networks among homeless populations. *New Review of Information Behaviour Research*, *4* (1), 2003, 95–108.
16. Hersberger, J. The homeless and information need and services. *Reference and User Services Quarterly*, *44* (3), 2005, 199–202.
17. Hirsch, T. Water wars: Designing a civic game about water scarcity. In *Proc. DIS 2010*, ACM Press, (2010), 340–343.
18. Kling, R. Automated welfare client-tracking and service integration: The political economy of computing. *Communications of the ACM*, *21* (6), 1978, 484–493.
19. Kvasny, L. and Keil, M. The challenges of redressing the digital divide: A tale of two us cities. *Information Systems Journal*, *16* (1), 2006, 23–53.
20. Le Dantec, C.A. and Edwards, W.K. The view from the trenches: Organization, power, and technology at two nonprofit homeless outreach center. In *Proc. CSCW 2008*, ACM Press, (2008), 589–598.
21. Le Dantec, C.A. and Edwards, W.K. Designs on dignity: Perceptions of technology among the homeless. In *Proc. CHI 2008*, ACM Press, (2008), 627–636.
22. Le Dantec, C.A., Christensen, J.E., Bailey, M., Farrell, R.G., Ellis, J.B., Davis, C.M., Kellogg, W.A. and Edwards, W.K. A tale of two publics: Democratizing design at the margins. In *Proc. DIS 2010*, ACM, (2010), 11–20.
23. Le Dantec, C.A. and Edwards, W.K. Across boundaries of influence and accountability: The multiple scales of public sector information systems. In *Proc. CHI 2010*, ACM Press, (2010), 113–122.
24. Marres, N. The issues deserve more credit: Pragmatist contributions to the study of public involvement in controversy. *Social Studies of Science*, *37* (5), 2007, 759–780.
25. Miles, M.B. and Huberman, A.M. *Qualitative data analysis: An expanded sourcebook*. London, 1994.
26. Morozov, E. Iran: Downside to the "Twitter revolution". *Dissent*, *56* (4), 2009, 10–14.
27. Pinkett, R. Bridging the digital divide: Sociocultural constructionism and an asset-based approach to community technology and community building. *81st Annual Meeting of the American Educational Research Association (AERA)*, New Orleans, LA, 2000.
28. Pinkett, R. and O'Bryant, R. Building community, empowerment and self-sufficiency. *Information, Communication & Society*, *6* (2), 2003, 187–210.
29. Reingold, H. *The virtual community: Homesteading on the electronic frontier*. Addison-Wesley, 1993.
30. Roberson, J. and Nardi, B. Survival needs and social inclusion: Technology use among the homeless. In *Proc. CSCW 2010*, ACM Press, (2010), 445–448.
31. Snow, D.A. and Anderson, L. Identity work among the homeless: The verbal construction and avowal of personal identities. *The American Journal of Sociology*, *92* (6), 1987, 1336–1371.
32. Star, S.L. and Bowker, G.C. How to infrastructure. in Lievrouw, L.A. and Livingstone, S.M. eds. *The handbook of new media*, Sage, London, UK, 2002, 151–162.
33. Strauss, A. and Corbin, J. *Basics of qualitative research: Techniques and procedures for developing grounded theory*. Sage, 1998.
34. Weiser, M., Gold, R. and Brown, J.S. The origins of ubiquitous computing research at PARC in the late 1980s. *IBM Systems Journal*, *38* (4), 1999, 693–696.
35. Woelfer, J.P. and Hendry, D.G. Homeless young people's experiences with information systems: Life and work in a community technology center. In *Proc. CHI 2010*, ACM Press, (2010), 1291–1300.

Homeless Young People and Living with Personal Digital Artifacts

Jill Palzkill Woelfer and David G. Hendry
The Information School
University of Washington
Seattle, WA 98195-2840
{woelfj, dhendry}@uw.edu

ABSTRACT
This paper reports on an investigation of how homeless young people hold themselves in relation to personal digital artifacts. Twelve participants, aged 19-29, took part in semi-structured interviews. Participants answered questions about the acquisition and disposition of personal artifacts, digital and non-digital, including mobile phones, music players, and wallets. The analysis of the interview transcripts reveals that young people often part with their digital artifacts in order to meet immediate needs, including the need to create and reciprocate goodwill. This contingent holding of personal artifacts illuminates both the ordinary and extraordinary circumstances of homelessness. The paper concludes with a discussion of constraints and implications for the design of information systems for improving the welfare of homeless young people.

Author Keywords
Homeless young people, attachment, personal digital artifacts, iPods, mobile phones, access, infrastructure

ACM Classification Keywords
K.4.2 Social Issues: Miscellaneous

General Terms
Design

INTRODUCTION
Buy, sell; Beg, borrow, steal. Humans take on and part with artifacts in a seemingly endless variety of ways. In the details of particular exchanges, and holdings, much can be seen about the human capacity to survive and prosper.

In recent years HCI has become particularly interested in how people hold themselves with respect to personal digital devices. One vein of research and design has investigated how pleasurability can go hand and hand with usability and utility to improve the "user experience" [25]. Under this perspective, an overall success metric, to put it roughly, is the strength of response to such statements as "I can't live without my…." In Ghana, Africa, for example, cell phones are highly desirable, despite high ownership costs, placing mobile communication in tension with basic needs, including food [20]. Here, the key problem is perhaps to discover knowledge for how to create supremely desirable experiences and to foresee what is at stake, for persons, societies, and economies, if they are in fact realized.

In another telling example, research has shown that young people form strong attachments to music, with preferences for musical genre influencing the formation of self-identity, and other aspects of psychosocial development [1]. These findings give weight to the importance of research into the attachment for digital media and systems for creating and sharing collections [19,25].

Questions of attachment have also been framed by non-use [17]. Even in the face of prevailing social forces, some people of sufficient economic means resist adopting some technologies. In extensive field work, for example, some of the factors of non-use have been investigated at ecovillages [13]. A far-reaching finding of this work has been that deliberations concerning environmental and social sustainability related to digital technology are fraught with difficulties, evidently quite unlike making rational choices about sustainable shelter, food, and transportation. In other HCI research, it has been observed that interaction design is systemically linked with environmental sustainability, with ensoulment and attachment to digital devices – and the experiences they enable – being one central concern [5,14].

In this paper we add to this body of knowledge for human-device attachment. Specifically, we report on how the circumstances of homelessness condition young people's ability to hold digital devices and media. To anticipate what is to come, consider this participant's response to the question: *How many MP3 players have you had?*

> If you count the one that I got at the resume class, three, but technically that's not mine because I gave it to my girlfriend. So I've only owned two MP3 players. One was the little…you can buy for $8 now at the store… It took a AA or AAA battery to run. I found that and 'cause I had it for so long I decided to load it up and give it a try. And then, my 120 GB iPod, which is my pride and joy. It's MIA right

> now…Yeah, I had to pawn it. I had to get phone minutes and all sorts of wonderful fun stuff, bus fare, cigarettes, personal hygiene... Yeah, it was, like, three or four days ago…So, I'll get it back. I'm not worried about it… Every time I bring it in they say, "Wow, you have a lot of stuff on there." And that's my basis for, I've put so much money and time into it. I've so much media on it that they would never give me a decent price for it that I would never sell it, I'll just put it on a hold for a minute so I can pay a bill. [Don]

BACKGROUND

Technology and Homelessness

In the 1990s, at the time that information technology was rapidly diffusing into the U.S. middleclass, researchers asked questions about how information technology might improve the welfare of low-income families [18]. One project, for example, considered the creation of "social capital" through networked information exchanged on desktop computers at home in a low-income community [15]. Researchers, more recently, have been investigating how mobile phones can improve the quality of life of people living in relative poverty and the homeless [12,20].

Our own work has investigated the use of digital and non-digital information systems for improving the welfare of homeless young people [8,23,24]. We have observed that homeless young people eagerly adopt digital media and mobile phones [23]. Additionally, ethnographic [9] and survey [16] research, has recently reported similar results, suggesting that the adoption of digital media and devices to be widespread with sweeping implications for how homelessness is considered, mitigated, and corrected. These research findings lead to a key question: How can information systems help young people leave homelessness and not lead to further stigmatization?

Homeless Young People: Definitional Notes

Here we are not able to fully examine how the concept of "homeless youth" has been theorized in the literature or operationalized in empirical research. That said, there is a large literature on homeless youth [6,9,10,16], which shows young people generally to be present-focused, often to suffer from the effects of trauma caused by neglect or abuse early in life, and often to be distrustful of adults. At the same time, like all young people, homeless young people vigorously seek out and learn from new experiences, sometimes risky ones, and develop their identities [10].

Largely based on our collaborator's view, in this work we use the term "homeless young people" to refer to both *adolescence* (age 13 –19) and *emerging adulthood*, which has been taken to extend nearly to age 30 [21]. This lengthy, complex period of development lies beyond childhood but before young adulthood. For "homelessness," we oppose a monolithic view where the term is defined by attribute, perhaps, for example, by the absence of shelter. Rather, we support a processional view where homelessness often becomes tied to one's identity and how one perceives the world. It is related to past and ongoing circumstances, particularly concerned with how basic needs are obtained [6]. Thus, even people with shelter may consider themselves homeless if still involved with street life, if still reliant on service agencies, among other reasons.

Object Careers and Biographies

Anthropologists have observed that much can be learned about a culture by investigating the circulation of its objects [2]. Given an object: Where did it come from? How was it exchanged? How was it cared for? What are its use value and its economic value? In short, by considering objects to have "biographies" – some deemed more typical or better than others – a good deal can be learned about how a society operates and what it values. One theory that comes out of this perspective is that objects, in most if not all cultures, move through a process of "singularization" [11]. In this view, an object can first be seen as a "commodity." Then, by various personal and social processes, it can be transformed into a unique "singular" object, a digital photo album, a home, a family heirloom, a priceless work of art. Conversely, a singularized object can be commoditized, for example, remade into cash (e.g. pawning an iPod) or aged into rubbish (e.g., an obsolete computer).

Building from a different foundation [7], concerned in part with the creation and maintenance of identity, HCI has recently begun to examine how attachments become constituted with digital artifacts [13,22,25]. In general, this work seems to involve presuppositions concerning consumerism (e.g., a disposition towards purchasing things), economic means (e.g., income for discretionary spending), shelter (e.g., the "consumers" are housed in a space where objects can be stored) and familial structure (e.g., children are in touch with parents and grandparents). These are often reasonable presuppositions. However, when they do not hold, or when they are relaxed, as is the case in such communities as the Old Order Amish, ecovillages, and homeless encampments, what happens to the nature of human-object attachment, identity formation, and object biographies? We conjecture that such social configurations influence how objects are taken on, held, and parted with, with substantial implications for design.

RESEARCH SETTING

The New Tech for Youth Sessions

This work was conducted in a drop-in for homeless young people, located in urban Seattle, Washington, in a neighborhood known as the University District (U-District). Since 1993, the drop-in has offered services to homeless young people, and those transitioning out of homelessness. Recently, it has offered an 8-session, 4-week life-skills class, called *New Tech for Youth Sessions* (NTYS). In this class [8], young people develop their skills for searching and applying for jobs and work-related opportunities. As students progress through the class, they receive incentives, including a thumb drive for storing digital files and, at the last class, an 8 GB iPod and $15.00 iTunes gift card.

The iPods: Working with Tensions

Using the iPod as an incentive for completing the NTYS class raises three tensions: (1) *Might the iPod be an instrument for leaving homelessness or frivolous?* On the one hand, the iPod offers an opportunity for developing technological skills. On the other, while technology skills for iPods and iTunes might transfer to specific activities related to escaping homelessness (e.g., online searching) they are in themselves non-instrumental; (2) *Is the iPod economically justifiable or a luxury?* On the one hand, the iPod is symbolic of the mainstream, giving youth access to ordinary experiences, such as walking down the street wearing a fashionable electronic device. On the other, it can be perceived as a luxury, not fitting for people who lack basic needs; and (3) *Is the iPod commensurate with the educational effort?* On the one hand, earning the iPod may encourage feelings of accomplishment and self-worth. Certainly, an iPod is a special reward for young people who normally receive used or discarded goods. On the other, completing the 8-session NTYS class may be seen as insufficiently demanding.

Research Question

What do young people do with their iPods? If we knew, we would be better positioned to understand the tensions just described. Put broadly, therefore, the major question is twofold: How do the circumstances of poverty, on the one hand, condition the acquisition, ownership, and disposition of personal digital devices? On the other, by asking questions about personal digital devices, how they are acquired, how they are tethered to infrastructure and institutions, and so forth what can we learn about the circumstances of homelessness? We address these questions not to seek a definitive position on the iPod tensions; rather, we seek to understand what is at stake in such tensions.

METHOD

Participants

Twelve young people, four women and eight men, aged between 19 and 29 years participated in this study (*Mdn* = 21.5 years). All participants had completed an NTYS class offering, and make up a sample that covers about 17% of the population of youth that have taken a class.

To be recruited, four conditions needed to be met. The participant needed to have: (1) Been known by the staff at the drop-in and invited to join a class; (2) Successfully completed the class; (3) Remained in touch with a life-skills coordinator; and (4) Been willing to visit the U-District.

Hence, this sample is unlikely to be representative of Seattle's homeless youth. Many of Seattle's homeless young people, for example, are not in contact with the drop-in. Of those that are, some might not have been invited to participate in NTYS classes because, for example, of very limited socialization skills. Moreover, the 12 participants do not represent a random sample of NTYS graduates. Some youth, for example, having made significant progress in escaping homelessness may decline to visit the U-District.

Procedure

Participants were interviewed by the authors according to a semi-structured protocol of two phases. In the first phase, participants answered a series of closed- and open-ended questions, focused primarily on the ownership and use of mobile phones, MP3 players, wallets, and government-issued I.D.s. We chose these artifacts because they are of similar importance, commonly owned, small and usually kept on the body. In addition, we expected the rate of replacement to be higher for the two digital artifacts, since phones and MP3 players are more fragile, have value as a commodity, are subject to obsolescence, and are more easily replaced than identification. In the second phase, participants were prompted to draw a timeline and talk out the key events related to their iPods.

Depending on participants' inclinations to talk, especially about the timeline, the interviews ranged between 15–60 minutes (*Mdn* = 35.5 minutes). The interview rapport was strong, partly we think, because all participants knew at least one of the authors from the NTYS classes, where we were volunteer instructors, and because the interviews took place in a familiar location. All participants gave oral assent, with 10 participants also agreeing to audio recording. We took notes for the 2 participants who did not agree to recording. The audio recordings were transcribed, resulting in a corpus of 62,087 words (n = 10; *M* = 6,209; *SD* = 2,901). By preference, each participant received either a gift card or an iPod wall charger, each worth $5.00.

In both phases, we probed for specific information on the acquisition, maintenance, sharing, and disposition of personal artifacts. We actively avoided discussion of non-related topics, such as illegal activities and health conditions. When Irene, for example, mentioned past drug use we guided the interview towards her use of cell phones. On the other hand, illustrating the delicate balance we sought, when Greg told us that his friend lost Greg's iPod in

1. Access. Gaining access to infrastructure; Types (wireless, electricity, etc.); Skills and practical knowledge for; Folk theories; Locations; Surveillance; Constraints and limitations; Perceptions of quality
2. Circumstances of Homelessness. Living conditions; Domestic life; Sleeping places; Obtaining basic needs; Working; Play and leisure; Substance use; Conflict; Pawn shops; Institutions; Type of I.D.
3. Digital Collections. Managing digital collections; Size and types of collections; Storage and hardware; Uploading and sharing files; Maintenance; Migration; Skills and practical knowledge for
4. Friends, Family and Community. Maintaining relationships; Connections and bonds; Expressions of community; Social exchanges; Possession and ownership; Sharing resources
5. Music. Listening experiences; Locations; Devices; Perceptions and feelings about music; Names of bands and artists
6. Personal Artifacts. Types (digital devices, etc.); Experiences; Skills and practical knowledge for; Folk theories; Perceptions of quality
7. Popular Culture. References to T.V. programs, movies, video games, ring tones, etc.; Technologies; Digital media

Table 1: Topics identified after listening to the interviews.

a dumpster filled with cardboard, we *did* pose questions about how dumpsters can be used as sleeping places.

Data Analysis: Considerations and Approach

To become analytically oriented to the data, we listened to the 10 audio recordings and reviewed the notes. When a participant talked about a challenge, discussed technology use, or gave a telling account of street life we paused the recording, discussed the material, and proposed a label for the topic and a covering theme. As we progressed through the material we identified seven broad themes for organizing the topics (see Table 1).

Rather than conducting a systematic coding of the transcripts, we decided to use a narrative approach. Emphasizing the person, we chose to present each participant's stories and data as short *précis*. Thus, we sought to create "portraits," which are personal, in the young people's own voices. Addressing the research questions, we privileged material that focused on the management of digital media and the connections between devices and infrastructure (#1, #3, and #6 in Table 1). We sought, furthermore, a diversity of material. In aggregate, the 12 participant portraits cover, at least to some reasonable degree, the topics in Table 1.

FINDINGS

Musical Interests

Although not a specific topic in the interview instrument, participants talked about diverse musical interests and demonstrated a striking fluency with musical genre, artists, and bands. Therefore, working from the transcripts, we identified the names of all artists and musical genres. Intending to give both a gestalt and the particular interests of participants, Table 2 shows these data.

♂**Al**: Rhythm & Blues* ◦ Underground Hip Hop ◦ Prozac ◦ Project: Deadman[HC] ◦ Rihanna* ◦ Lea Quezada*. ♂**Bob**: Gangsta Rap ◦ Death Metal ◦ Dying Fetus[HC] ◦ Slayer ◦ Insane Clown Posse[HC] ◦ Twiztid[HC] ◦ Mickey Avalon ◦ Black Nasty ◦ Lloyd "Feel so right." ♂**Clay**: Russian/Czechoslovakian music. ♂**Don**: 300 movies, 500 CDs, 15,000 tracks. ♂**Ed**: Techno* ◦ Emo* ◦ Alternative* ◦ Machine Music* ◦ Psychopathic Records[HC] ◦ Tool ◦ Manson. ♀**Fran**: Journey ◦ Foreigner. ♂**Greg**: Ramones ◦ Charged GBH[HC] ◦ Sex Pistols ◦ Fleetwood Mac ◦ The Spits ◦ Buzzcocks ◦ Joy Division ◦ Fear ◦ Cro-Mags[HC] ◦ SamHan. ♂**Hank**: Jimmy Hendrix ◦ Pink Floyd ◦ AC/DC ◦ Alice in Chains ◦ Slayer ◦ Motorhead ◦ Sound Garden ◦ Sublime ◦ Rob Zombie ◦ Velvet Revolver. ♀**Irene**: Say Anything ◦ Patti Smith ◦ The Shins ◦ Bright Eyes ◦ The Moody Blues ◦ Led Zeppelin ◦ The Cure ◦ Pink Floyd ◦ Sinead O'Connor ◦ Blue October ◦ Bob Dylan ◦ Neil Young. ♀**Jazz**: Afroman "Colt 45" ◦ Queen "Bohemian Rhapsody," "Bicycle Race." ♀**Kay**: Black-Eyed Peas "Boom Boom Pow" ◦ 3Oh!3 "Don't Trust Me." ♂**Larry**: Harry Potter (Soundtrack).

Table 2: Music mentioned by each participant, genres underlined and songs placed in quotes. * indicates a dislike. [HC] indicates hardcore or horrorcore.

Online Access

We tabulated the data on the acquisition and disposition of digital and non-digital artifacts. Table 3 shows these data in disaggregated form, allowing, on a close reading, an examination of each participant's data as well as the distribution across all participants. Concerning online access, participants reported spending between 15 minutes and 38 hours per week online (*Mdn* = 2 hours), for email, social networking, online learning, watching videos, playing games, and similar activities.

Ownership of Personal Artifacts

All 12 participants reported that they have owned at least one mobile phone (*M* = 10; *SD* = 14.4), MP3 player (*M* = 4.4; *SD* = 3.3) and wallet (*M* = 10.2; *SD* = 9.4). In addition, at the time of the interview, all participants reported that

	Participant		Online		Mobile phone			MP3 player			Wallet			I.D.		iPod	
	Name	Age	Hrs	No.	A	No.	Age	A	No.	Age	A	No.	Age	A	Age	Fate	Age
	Al	29	¼	2	22	50	½	28	few	–	5	20	¼	3	11	Sold ♦	1 ½
	Bob	28	5	7	21	20	¼	25	11	–	7	30	24	16	¼	Lost	¼
	Clay	27	5	7	22	2	7	24	4	7	16	8	3	23	48	Traded	6
	Don	26	5	4	16	6	21	24	3	12	13	4	10	15	108	Gifted ♦	¼
	Ed	23	2	4	17	20	–	22	2	¼	5	20	36	17	¼	Sold	1
♀	Fran	22	38	15	18	1	–	21	1	12	18	1	48	16	84	Owns	12
	Greg	21	2	2	16	3	4	18	4	–	10	3	48	18	36	Lost ♦	8
	Hank	21	2	2	15	2	–	19	10	¾	13	10	24	19	24	Owns	1
♀	Irene	20	2	3	14	3	–	20	3	6	16	2	½	13	96	Gifted ♦	6
♀	Jazz	20	½	2	20	1	3	18	few	–	3	17	12	18	24	Sold ♦	1
♀	Kay	19	28	7	16	10	¼	17	3	24	12	2	–	18	12	Sold ♦	8
	Larry	19	2	5	16	2	30	15	3	17	8	5	72	17	36	Lost	¼
	Mean artifact ages (*SDs*)						8.3 (*11.2*)			8.0 (*8.1*)			25.3 (*23.4*)		40.0 (*37.0*)		3.2 (*2.3*)

Table 3: Summary of self-report responses concerning the ownership of personal digital and non-digital artifacts, showing participants' estimated age of first acquisition (A), the estimated number of artifacts owned (No.), and the length of "ownership" in months (Age). Also shown are the current ages of the 12 participants, the reported number of hours spent online (Hrs) and the frequency of access per week (No.). The symbol "–" indicates that an artifact was not owned at the time of the interview. The final column shows the fate of the iPods and the age, in months, at which point the iPod was sold, lost, gifted, or traded. The symbol ♦ refers to a fate that is related to the creation of "goodwill" (see text for details).

they had government-issued I.D. Table 3 shows the mean ages in months and the standard deviations of the artifacts, ranging from 8.0 to 40.0 months. Based on one-tailed Wilcoxon signed-rank tests, we find that I.D.s are significantly older than MP3 players ($W = 151.0$, $p = 0.029$) and mobile phones ($W = 154.0$, $p = 0.017$), and that wallets are significantly older than mobile phones ($W = 131.0$, $p = 0.045$) but not MP3 Players ($W = 125.5$, $p = 0.107$).

To estimate artifact turnover we computed ratios of the number of reported phones owned in a participant's lifetime by the number of years that he or she has owned phones. At the high end, Al reports that he has owned 50 different phones in roughly 8 years (current age: 29 years; first phone: 22), for a ratio of 50:8 (6.25/year). At the low end, Fran claims 1 phone in 5 years, for a ratio of 1:5 (0.2/year). Making these calculations for all participants, we see median rates of replacement for wallets, mobile phones, and MP3 players respectively 0.542 ($n = 12$), 0.523 ($n = 10$), and 1.0 ($n = 12$). By Wilcoxon signed-rank tests, we find a difference between wallets and MP3 players ($W=105$, $p=0.016$) but not mobile phones ($W=133$, $p=.170$).

What Happened to the iPods?

As reported in Table 3, 2 of the 12 participants continued to own their iPods, with the other iPods being sold ($n = 4$), lost ($n = 3$), gifted ($n = 2$), or traded ($n = 1$). On average, participants reported that they held on to the iPods for about 3 months after the NTYS class ($n = 10$; $M = 3.2$; $SD = 2.3$).

Portraits of Homeless Young People

We now turn to the portraits, beginning with accounts that touch upon the circumstances of homelessness in general.

Clay: The First Time I Realized that I was Homeless

Clay dresses well, speaks vividly, is upbeat, but also suffers from a serious, common illness that makes living on the street dangerous. When asked about losing a wallet, he said:

> …when I first got out here on the streets two years ago, some girl named M was the one that showed me around, and I had a couple bucks left, I was like, "Wanna go watch a movie?" So we went… [Then] we went to the Convention Center because I needed to use the restroom… I didn't think I looked too ragged, but I guess the security guard recognized her as someone that was homeless… I was like, in the restroom, and I actually had a security guard come and go like, "What are you doing in there, hurry up!"… That was the first time I felt like I was homeless.

He told of being agitated by the security guard, leaving the toilet in a hurry, without his wallet.

Clay's iPod. Clay traded for a battery-operated MP3 player, saying: "I traded that for something that I just needed to put batteries in. Because if you're around here, you can get batteries, but you can't get a laptop to recharge."

Hank: Non-Use and Utopia in Nature

Hank told us that he has limited eyesight, particularly in his left eye, due to chemotherapy in his late teens. He had owned a laptop in the past, and now uses computers at service agencies and public libraries, accessing the Internet for 1-2 hours per day. Hank was very knowledgeable about sources of free WiFi throughout the neighborhood. However, despite his domain expertise, Hank was disillusioned with technology in general and concerned about its effects on human beings:

> My opinion on computers is…it's all bad. I don't really like technology… It seems kind of redundant. We don't need it…We've got computers and all that stuff just because we got lazy… Think of how many trees it took to build one house. If we didn't build the house, we'd have so many more trees… This whole area would be covered in trees… And it would be… a much nicer and healthier place. I'd like to make my own country or something, you know?…Where we wouldn't have no big huge skyscrapers… We'd have tents, and we'd have some food around us. Yeah.

Hank's iPod. Hank had received his iPod just three weeks before his interview, and was concerned about its fragility. Although in the past he traded iPods for necessities, like a heavy jacket, he said, "I'm not going to trade this one."

Larry: Negotiating Home and Homelessness

Larry is 19, has some form of autism spectrum disorder, and loves to ride the bus. Larry talks about his father and sister at length and with great affection. He is not allowed to stay home by himself, so he relies on libraries and service agencies to provide places to go during the day. However, he told us that he had recently been banned from a library for breaking "a reasonable rule" about appropriate use of the Internet. Reflecting on this, he talked about what it feels like to be watched while using public computers:

> In respects, they aren't directly watching you. …they won't be looking directly at your screen… but off in the distance they're watching you.

Finally, just as Larry's access to home is restricted, his technology use is strongly mediated by his father, who, for example, will not allow Larry Internet access at home.

Larry's iPod. From our notes, Larry said he was attending a service agency program with other young people when his iPod disappeared. He was unsure if it had been stolen or if it had inadvertently been thrown into the trash.

Bob: Managing Digital Media

Despite his large, strong body, Bob said that he was robbed at gunpoint several weeks prior to the interview, losing his wallet and I.D. He reported that he owned an iPhone, without a working SIM card, so he thinks of it as a "fancy iPod." He also has a prepaid phone which he treats "… pretty much like a calling card where I can keep my numbers on it, throw it away when I'm done."

At several points in the interview Bob describes difficulties associated with storing music. He says "I've put a bunch of CDs on my buddy's computer just in case I get an iPod." He describes, too, an earlier time when he stored music on a laptop that he owned, but ran into difficulty synchronizing the media on the laptop with an iPod, saying:

> What happened to all my music? Like I couldn't even go into the information and read "About iPod" and says 6667 songs on here, 30 movies, like 2000 pictures.... I had to replug it and re-wipe and put it all back on again ... And it kept crashing my computer and I just broke my iPod... Somehow I finally got it to restart and sync the music up. [Then, it stopped working and] I picked up my MacBook and ripped it in half like a phone book... That was very frustrating. There went my iPod and my MacBook.

We see in this account something of the ongoing difficulty of managing media collections on fragile, unstable storage infrastructure. Even with a stable infrastructure, Bob might be unwilling to access it in public places, saying:

> I don't really like going places to use computers.... it's just uncomfortable to have nine cameras staring at you like "What are you doing with this computer?" I can't check my MySpace without just checking my MySpace. I gotta be like recorded eight different directions like some kind of, I don't know, like you're already in jail or something.

Bob's iPod. In a colorful story, Bob said: "My ex-girlfriend set me on fire and threw me down a hill, and it came out of my pocket and I never found it again. ...she threw me down the hill that we were drinking on."

Don: Collecting and Sharing Digital Media

Don, who we first met in the introduction, is in stable housing and attends community college, after many years on the street. He is a digital music collector, storing music on his computer and evidently sharing it widely with friends. He claims to have a collection of 300 movies, 500 CDs, and 15,000 tracks. Don, moreover, likes to find album covers and put them side-by-side his songs. He described using a library's computers to find album art and transferring it to an old home computer with a thumb drive.

♦*Don's iPod.* Don tells of giving the iPod to his girlfriend, but suggests a kind of joint ownership:

> Sometimes when I'm at the house and I'm bored, I might pull it out and play Klondike real fast. But for the most part it's not mine and if I had it in my possession and was using it like it was mine, I'd be more tempted to when I needed money really quick to go and throw it in the pawn shop.

Ed: Supported by Friends

Judging by the thickness of his glasses and how he talks about his sight, Ed may be legally blind. Recently released from jail, he accesses computers at friend's houses, and he also likes to read, carrying books around in his backpack:

> Like, I read anywhere from like Stephen King to *Siddhartha* or whatever. *Celestine Prophesy*, sh*t like that. Whatever's good that makes it past 100 pages.

Ed reports that he has owned over 30 CD players, and many CDs which he calls his "bibles... 'Cause I live by my music." Asked about carrying CDs, he said "it's easier just to carry an iPod." Still, about loading music onto the iPod, he said "I've never done it myself. I've just had people do it for me. 'Cause, I don't know how to." Ed volunteered that Don has been the source of music and assistance.

Ed's iPod. Ed reported that he sold his original iPod, in order to buy alcohol, indicated by a bottle he drew on his timeline and a very matter-of-fact statement. Ed did, however, have an iPod:

> My friend had, she had like a 16 gig [iPod], and then she got this one [an iPod earned by participating in a NTYS class] ...and since I'd just got out [of jail] she sold me this one so I could have my own iPod.

Ending the interview, Ed, in an expression of self-efficacy and with a twinkle in his eye toward acquainting us with "hardcore" music, took out a set of very small portable speakers from his pocket, set them up, attached his iPod to them, and shared a favorite music video, by *Twiztid*.

Al: Trading the iPod for Food, Living with Friends

Al lives in a squat. He says that "I don't really get indoors too often," so he will ask friends to check his email at the library or bring in his cell phone to be charged. When we asked how many MP3 players he's owned, he responded "I don't even know... I used to do a lot of really dumb drugs so I sold a lot of those." Now 29, he says that he got his first MP3 player when he was 28:

> I had CD players up until that point... Oh, I've had hundreds of those. Lose'em. Break'em... Once you break the lens the whole system's crap. Glorified paper weight then. 'Cause I've dropped iPods and MP3 players on the ground and they'll last a few more drops than... a CD player would.

♦*Al's iPod.* Al said he: "was staying with friends and nobody had no money. There was literally no food in the house. So I just. 'Alright [iPod] bye, bye.'" Pawning the iPod so he and his friends could eat is not likely to be inconsequential. Not only does his voice suggest sadness, later he says "I like listening to music from the time I wake until the time I go to bed. Helps keep me calm."

Fran: "I Love my iPod," LimeWire Fries Computers

Fran told us that she has a collection of 35 sunglasses. Fran once owned a mobile phone when she was 18, about 4 years ago. However, after 3 months, she cancelled the plan on the phone and gave it to a friend because "I kept buying ringtones and video games for it and stuff. And my bill was like $300 more than it should have been [per month]."

Fran currently owns a laptop computer that she uses every day. She sold her previous computer to a pawn shop after it was affected by computer viruses:

> I don't use LimeWire on my new computer. I use it on my roommate's computer, because she already had LimeWire and she's like 'Whatever. It's going to fry anyway.' But there were viruses on it [the previous computer] before the LimeWire. I was just like 'Whatever. This computer sucks. Might as well fry it some more'... It's my sister's computer and she gave it to me, ... all messed up and I thought I could fix it, but I couldn't, so I just destroyed it more.

However, when Fran took the computer to a pawn shop to sell it, "it worked for the 5 minutes that they tested it... So I just got really lucky somehow and they got screwed."

Fran's iPod. Fran still owned her iPod and had loaded, lost and then reloaded her music collection on it. Fran had blown out two pairs of earphones, "from playing the music too loud," especially in the morning when she "listen[s] to [her] music really loud…to wake [her] up." At the end of the interview, when we asked Fran if she had anything she would like to add, she simply stated, "I love my iPod."

Kay: Living with a Lockbox

Kay is enrolled in classes and was due at work after her interview. She is 19 years old, mother of an infant, and currently lives in an apartment with Fran. She keeps valuable items in a lockbox because:

> We have homeless people who come over to the house a lot and… they're my friends… but they like to take things, so I keep everything of value locked up. 'Cause, I had a piggy bank for my daughter full of like $600 in cash and change and someone emptied it.

Kay was skeptical that any of the participants would still have their iPods, saying:

> I know these kids… like when I was homeless, like I'd get iPods. Sometimes, like they wouldn't be like my iPods, but I would get iPods. And like, you know, I could have kept them, but I'd sell them, and carry around my little Discman, 'cause music is music, no matter where it's coming from. And when you're homeless, and have things of value, you'd rather have the money than the valuable thing.

♦*Kay's iPod.* Kay reported that she was happy to use another player that she had and that the iPod was just sitting in her lockbox. When one of her friends, Ed, returned from jail, she reports that she sold him the iPod so that he could listen to music, an activity that he was not able to do while incarcerated.

Greg: Music, Friends and Dumpsters

Greg loves music: "I think it kind of distracts me from the world. I put the earphones on and tune 'them' out." Greg owns his own keyboard, and has access to a piano in the transitional shelter where he is currently living. He also has a friend who had recently formed a band and is "a really good bass player."

♦ *Greg's iPod.* Greg, taken from notes, said: "I lent it out to my buddy…. He had it. He put it into the corner of a dumpster. I lent it out but he was feeling down and low. He loves music like I do. He was intoxicated. He didn't have any place to stay and it was raining." He spoke eloquently, expressing concern for his friend, and without bitterness for the lost iPod, which had over 1,000 songs.

Irene: Not Homeless Right Now

> One of my favorite things to do, because Seattle meteorologists never, I mean, they have a challenge, I'll admit it. But they're not exactly spot on all the time. So I'll go onto NOAA and I'll look at all their satellite imagery and see if I can't come up with a better, more accurate forecast than the weather man. Which usually I can.

Irene lives with her mom "in a tiny little room" and is hoping to not become homeless again. Growing up they had a computer that "was mostly just used for music and pictures, at that time, nothing else." Now, the computer is at her sister's place because her sister has room for it, and Irene says "… between me and my mom, my sister, we must have had like 2000 CDs. Like a lot."

She says that she can get power for her Zune player, which she likes better than iPods because she believes it is more compatible with Microsoft desktops, at grocery stores and gas stations. About getting power she said:

> A lot of times I lie and say it's a phone. I'm like, yeah "I need to charge my cell phone really quick." You know, and then they're more kind, like "I just need to charge my music," they're like, "Go away." [Electronics store], the library, there's lots of places especially in the U-District that you can get…free power… There's a couple places in between buildings and churches that I know of, too. So, just depends on your appearance, like if you look homeless, they're not gonna let you do it. But if you look like you're just like some random person that's like, "Oh, emergency" then they'll let you do it. It's all about how you approach them.

♦ *Irene's iPod.* Irene reports that she gave the iPod to her mother who loves it and takes it everywhere, that they learned to use iTunes together, and that the iPod is loaded with songs, saying: "She was like, 'I never thought I'd ever have something like this. I feel so cool.'"

Jazz: Using the iPod to Create Street Credibility

Jazz, a 20 year old woman, says that "All the songs I like I have memorized," and says that she does not listen to music so much. She mentioned that she has been banned from a local pawnshop. Without stable shelter, she talked about the difficulty of getting electricity, saying:

> I'm homeless! People are very stingy with their electric…. Somebody catches you charging your phone on an outlet on the outside of a building, they will yell at you until you leave.

While Jazz claimed to have had one phone in her lifetime, at the interview, she actually showed us *two* phones of the same brand and model. When we asked why she had two, she explained that one was her phone; unfortunately, it was broken but the service plan was still active. The other phone belonged to a friend; while it functioned, its service plan had expired. She then demonstrated how the SIM card could be taken out of the first phone and inserted into the second, thereby making a working phone. This act of tinkering appeared to be a source of pride.

♦ *Jazz's iPod.* In Jazz's telling, about one month after receiving the iPod, she met a person selling a dog. Taking up the opportunity, she had a friend sell her iPod at the pawnshop, and used the money to buy the dog. She, then, gave the dog to a friend.

DISCUSSION

Taking On, Holding, and Parting with Artifacts

Recall the two estimates of replacement rates of personal artifacts presented in the results: (1) The reported age of the most recently held artifact; and (2) The ratio of the reported number of artifacts of a particular kind owned by the reported number of years of owning the artifact. Given their importance, their low economical value, and their durability we expected that young people would hold onto their wallets for longer periods of time than the digital artifacts. With the small number of data points, missing data, and high variance in the data we do not find decisive evidence for this hypothesis. That said, recall that it does appear to be the case that young people in this study do hold onto their I.D.s for longer periods of time than digital artifacts (about 40 vs. 8 months), although, even so, two of the participants had replaced their I.D.s within two weeks of the interview. Part of the reason for this difference may be that I.D.s are not always held by a person; often, they are left with a case manager or reliable person for safekeeping.

Overall the data show that while participants move through mobile phones quite quickly, with median replacement rates for mobile phones and MP3 players respectively 23.0 and 11.0 months, these rates may not be too different from most people in society. For comparison, we do not know of any publicly available data on phone replacement rates, broken down by demographics. Nevertheless, a reasonable baseline might be: Owners of 2-year service plans upgrade their phones at least every 2 years and prepaid phone owners more often (Bob, recall, said of a prepaid phone "it's pretty much like a calling card"). In addition, the replacement rates for mobile phones and MP3 players appear similar to the *desired* replacement rates of college freshmen [5].

Participants often challenged our understanding for the meaning of such words as "possession" and "ownership." Recall Jazz, for example, who showed us two phones in the interview but claimed to own one phone. Whether Jazz owned one phone or two seems in doubt, perhaps hinging on technical definitions of sharing and possession. Al and Kay as well as other participants made a distinction between phones and MP3 players that were theirs and those they would "sell" or "get." Finally, recall that Don felt joint ownership for the 8 GB iPod, the one he gave to his girlfriend, expressed by his unwillingness to pawn it.

Although we did not ask about pawnshops, 8 participants mentioned them. Don's account is particularly telling for it shows how a singularized object ("my 120 GB iPod, which is my pride and joy… I've put so much money and time into it") can be turned into a commodity. In fact, Don said that he put his iPod into a pawnshop five or six times a year, sometimes paying $5 to keep the loan going. In another example, Kay said "[Once] I got stranded in Seattle. And so like I had this $300 iPod. And I was just like, well, I can just sell it and then buy it back tomorrow." While pawnshops may provide other functions (a safekeeping function), the data suggest that participants used them to convert their possessions into cash. Pawnshops, in theoretical terms, are instrumental for turning singularized objects into commodities.

Creating and Reciprocating Goodwill

In six cases (marked by the ♦), young people parted with their iPods and in the process generated some kind of goodwill. Why would Jazz buy a dog and give it to a friend? While she would not specifically tell us, a key informant suggested that it was a brilliant street move for creating credibility, for being known for giving a cool dog to a well-known person in the community. In one case, the iPod was given up to meet immediate needs of a group (Al). In other cases, they were given or sold to a close friend or family member (Don, Greg, Irene, and Kay). Goodwill appears to be quite strongly implicated in these exchanges.

Metrics of social capital, and its underlying theoretical commitments, have been used to examine the nature of homelessness and specifically to predict the risk of becoming homeless [3]. It seems likely that in some instances the iPods were used to create social capital, essential for survival on the street [10]. However, at present, we cannot offer specific evidence on if, and how, the iPods were used to create social capital. Nevertheless, if creating and reciprocating goodwill is indeed common, this process seems to contribute to the contingent nature of holding on to personal objects.

Infrastructure, Access, and Practical Knowledge

Participants revealed many challenges associated with gaining access to infrastructure. Libraries, for example, while often used to gain internet access, were also seen to be controlling and places of surveillance (Bob, Larry). Participants revealed much practical knowledge for gaining access to infrastructure in the U-District. This knowledge is both social and technical (e.g., Irene getting "emergency" power at shops and Hank knowing the locations of free wireless access). However, by being tethered to infrastructure, young people can become vulnerable. For instance, a young person may need to trespass in order to gain access to electricity, to access a social networking site, to communicate with a family member, to ask for help. But, trespassing can have severe consequences for homeless people [4]. Finally, Clay decoupled from infrastructure by trading his iPod for a battery-operated MP3 player.

The interview material is full of examples in which young people had great difficulty managing the storage of their digital media, like many families do [19]. For most youth, digital files appeared to be scattered around on older computers that were owned by family or friends. As such, access to data, and its safekeeping, was generally enabled (or not) by other people. In short, these young people in general do not have a reliable place to hold their digital materials. Impermanence of shelter and instabilities in familial and social relations appears to create a climate of unstable data storage and data migration. In turn, holding onto data so that digital artifacts can be "singularized" is difficult, without stable places for data storage and access.

Music and Listening Experiences

The participants demonstrated fluency and strong interest in music: Ed's CDs are his bibles, Greg thinks of music as a distraction, Fran listens to music to wake and Al to calm down. Infrastructure for sharing and experiencing music, clearly seen in Don's collection, is very important to this community. While musical tastes are broad (Table 2), interest in "hardcore punk" or "horrorcore hip hop" music is noteworthy for its themes of extreme violence and suicidal ideation. Preference for such dark music has been shown to correlate to substance abuse and other risk-taking behaviors [1]. Given that homeless young people are predisposed to risky behaviors [6], further study of young people's music preferences and social activities related to music – and especially the creation of social capital useful for escaping homelessness – is clearly warranted.

Reflections on Method

This work has persuaded us that the "object biographies" approach [2] does elicit a good deal of material about life circumstances, as seen in the themes and topics of Table 1 and in the portraits. We were struck by the emotive and detailed accounts that came out of straightforward questions about the taking on, holding, and parting with personal artifacts. Specifically, we underline two fundamental themes of the portraits: (1) The lives of homeless young people are very hard, directly impacting their ability to hold onto personal digital artifacts; and (2) No two young people are alike. Indeed, we chose to present the interview material as portraits to make these vital points, and not least to present young people's distinctive voices. For a second reflection, for this community of homeless young people, this work has taught us to seek out specific details concerning the creation of goodwill through the sharing of technology and media. Here, as well as in earlier work [23], the notion of "sharing" is clearly important (e.g., gifting and recall Greg's portrait). Exactly how remains for future work. Finally, it is important to note that the quantitative data that we tabulated and analyzed are self-reported. As such, these data should be treated as estimates of uncertain reliability. That said, we believe that participants were forthcoming and candid about their use of personal devices.

CONCLUSION

The principle finding of this study is that, for homeless young people in this community, being able to use digital media is largely, or perhaps always, contingent. Two additive forces appear to bring about this way of living with digital media. For one, holding onto digital artifacts, which are valuable as commodities, is always predicated on the fulfillment of other, immediate needs. In other words, to obtain food or other basic needs, it may be necessary to give up a digital artifact. But, as we have seen, immediate needs also seem to include the exchange of goodwill, which is likely crucial for survival on the street [3]. For the second force, access to necessary infrastructure is also contingent, subject to its mere availability, but also subject to the control and surveillance by people or institutions.

These forces of contingency – namely, of holding digital artifacts and of accessing infrastructure – condition the circumstances under which digital media is experienced. It is also important to note that the tethering of digital artifacts to infrastructure can make homelessness visible, perhaps amplifying these forces. In consequence, homeless young people are likely to be placed in positions where stigma and ostracism can arise by new means, specifically because of the need for infrastructure.

Yet, these two forces of contingency are surely not unique to homeless young people; it is perhaps best assumed that they apply to everyone, no matter of socioeconomic standing. Indeed, as we have discussed in prior work [23], there is an ordinariness associated with homeless young people's stories of technology. At the same time, because of the circumstance of homelessness, these stories do become extraordinary. Fundamentally, in the taking on, holding, and parting with objects we see the ever-present challenge of obtaining basic needs. In short, if the objects we have investigated in this research do in fact have "social lives" [2] then we may well consider them to be "vulnerable," just as homeless young people can be considered vulnerable.

In these social conditions – concerning shelter, familial and social relations, and discretionary income – we can discern a way of living with digital artifacts and media. Specifically, the contingent forces that we have discussed appear to present a challenge to "ensoulment" [5] and "product attachment theory" [25]. In struggling to meet immediate needs, how does one care for an object? This challenge seems most important when products are designed to support "role transition–the design of products that support the process of discovering and inventing yourself" [25, p. 395]. Yet, paradoxically, homeless young people may benefit the most from such products.

From this perspective, we propose the following constraints for designing information systems for homeless young people: (1) Technological uses are ordinary but are conditioned by the extraordinary circumstances of homelessness; (2) Digital artifacts, by their tethering to infrastructure, can subject young people to new forms of scrutiny; (3) Young people are likely to use mobile devices and media to create and reciprocate goodwill for surviving on the street; (4) Digital artifacts might be given up spontaneously or with forethought, but interest in media, especially music, is likely to persist; and (5) Young people may seek to repeatedly singularize digital devices and then later remake them as commodities.

From these constraints, one problem framing for design is to consider how media might be enabled to persist, to be ever present in this community, as access to infrastructure and devices comes and goes. Music, movies, and personal media stored and kept safe may offer a surrogate "home," albeit perhaps temporary and by no means complete. A home, nevertheless, which is real and which holds a center of gravity amongst pervasive change, personal and social complexity, and even ongoing chaos. Furthermore, and most importantly, the evident importance of goodwill suggests that the network of family and social relations be taken into account when designing artifacts aimed to help homeless young people develop personally and to escape homelessness. Perhaps devices, infrastructure, and services that enable youth to care for their media will position youth to better care for themselves. While this proposition does not in itself resolve the iPod tensions, which in part motivated this study, it does provide a direction for design.

ACKNOWLEDGMENTS

Sincere thanks to the young people for talking about their artifacts and ways of life. Special thanks to Street Youth Ministries for collaborating and to Brian Gill for statistical expertise.

REFERENCES

1. American Academy of Pediatrics, Council on Communications and Media. Policy statement – Impact of music, music lyrics, and music videos on children and youth. *Pediatrics 124*, 5 (2009), 1488-1494.
2. Appadurai, A. Introduction. In *The Social Life of Things*, A. Appadurai (Ed.). Cambridge University Press, New York, 1986, 3-63.
3. Bantchevska, D., Bartle-Haring, S., Dashora, P., Glebova, T., and Slesnick, N. Problem behaviors of homeless youth: A social capital perspective. *Journal of Human Ecology 23,* 4 (2008), 285-293.
4. Beckett, K., and Herbert, S. *Banished: The New Social Control in Urban America*. Oxford University Press, New York, 2010.
5. Blevis, E., and Stolterman, E. Ensoulment and sustainable interaction design. In *Proc. of IASDR 2007,* ACM Press (2007), 1-23.
6. Coward Bucher, C. E. Towards a needs-based typology of homeless youth. *J. Adol. Health 42* (2008), 549-554.
7. Csikszentmihalyi, M., and Rochberg-Halton, E. *The Meaning of Things: Domestic Symbols and Self.* Cambridge University Press, New York, 1981.
8. Hendry, D. G., Woelfer, J. P., Bauer, T., Fitzer, T., and Champagne, M. How to integrate digital media into a drop-in for homeless young people for deepening relationships between youth and adults. *Children and Youth. Serv. Rev.* doi: 10.1016/j.childyouth2010.11.024.
9. Karabanow, J., and Naylor, T.D. "Being hooked up": Exploring the experiences of street youth and information technologies. In *Digital Diversity*, E. D. Looker, and T. D. Naylor (Eds.). Wilfred Laurier University Press, Waterloo, ON, 2010, 161-178.
10. Kidd, S. A., and Shahar, G. Resilience in homeless youth: The key role of self-esteem. *American Journal of Orthopsychiatry 78*, 2 (2008), 163-172.
11. Kopytoff, I. The cultural biography of things: Commoditization as process. In *The Social Life of Things*, A. Appadurai (Ed.). Cambridge University Press, New York, 1986, 64-91.
12. Le Dantec, C. A., Christensen, J. E., Bailey, M., Farrell, R. G., Ellis, J. B., Danis, C. M., Kellogg, W. A., and Edwards, W. K. A tale of two publics: Democratizing design at the margins. In *Proc. DIS 2010*, ACM Press (2010), 11-20.
13. Nathan, L. *Ecovillages, Sustainability, and Information Tools*. Unpublished doctoral dissertation, University of Washington, WA, 2009.
14. Odom, W., Pierce, J., Blevis, E., and Stolterman, E. Understanding why we preserve some things and discard others in the context of interaction design. In *Proc. CHI 2009*, ACM Press (2009), 1-10.
15. Pinkett, R. D. The creating community connections project. In *Universal Usability*, J. Lazar (Ed.). John Wiley and Sons, West Sussex, England, 2007, 457-490.
16. Rice, E., Monro, W., Barman-Adhikari, A., and Young, S. D. Internet use, social networking, and HIV/AIDS risk for homeless adolescents. *J. Adol. Health 47* (2010), 610-613.
17. Satchell, C., and Dourish, P. B. Beyond the user: Use and non-use in HCI. In *Proc. OZCHI*, 2009, 9-16.
18. Schön, D. A., Sanyal, B., and Mitchell, W. J. *High Tech. for Low-Income Communities*. MIT Press, 1999.
19. Sease, R., and McDonald, D. W. Musical fingerprints: Collaboration around home media collections. In *Proc. GROUP 2009*, ACM Press (2009), 331-340.
20. Sey, A. Managing the cost of mobile communications in Ghana. In *Communication Technologies in Latin America and Africa,* Barcelona, IN3 (2010), 143-166.
21. Tanner, J. L., and Arnett, J. J. The emergence of 'emerging adulthood.' In *Handbook of Youth and Young Adulthood*, A. Furlong (Ed.). Routledge, New York, 2009, 39-45.
22. Wakkary, R., and Tanenbaum, K. A. Sustainable identity: The creativity of an everyday designer. In *Proc. CHI 2009*, ACM Press (2009), 365-374.
23. Woelfer, J. P., and Hendry D. G. Homeless young people's experiences with information systems: Life and work in a community technology center. In *Proc. CHI 2010*, ACM Press (2010), 1291-1300.
24. Woelfer, J. P., and Hendry, D. G. Stabilizing homeless young people with information and place. *JASIST 60*, 11 (2009), 2300-2312.
25. Zimmerman, J. Design for self: Making products that help people become the person they desire to be. In *Proc. CHI 2009*, ACM Press (2009), 395-404.

Improving the Safety of Homeless Young People with Mobile Phones: Values, Form and Function

Jill Palzkill Woelfer[†], Amy Iverson[†], David G. Hendry[†], Batya Friedman[†], and Brian T. Gill[‡]

[†]The Information School
University of Washington
Seattle, WA 98195-2840
{woelfj, ivera49, dhendry, batya}@uw.edu

[‡]Dept. of Mathematics
Seattle Pacific University
Seattle, WA 98119-1997
bgill@spu.edu

ABSTRACT
By their pervasiveness and by being worn on our bodies, mobile phones seem to have become intrinsic to safety. To examine this proposition, 43 participants, from four stakeholder groups (homeless young people, service providers, police officers, and community members), were asked to consider how homeless young people could use mobile phones to keep safe. Participants were asked to express their knowledge for place-based safety and to envision how mobile phones might be used to improve safety. Detailed analysis of the resulting data, which included value sketches, written value scenarios, and semi-structured discussion, led to specific design opportunities, related to values (e.g., supporting trust and desire to help others), function (e.g., documenting harms for future purposes), and form (e.g., leveraging social expectations for how mobile phones can be used to influence behavior). Together, these findings bound a design space for how mobile phones can be used to manage unsafe situations.

Author Keywords
Safety, homeless young people, mobile phones, security, Value Sensitive Design, value scenarios, value sketches

ACM Classification Keywords
K.4.2 Social Issues: Miscellaneous

General Terms
Design

INTRODUCTION
Safety is a basic human need. Not only do people wish to keep themselves and their families safe, one of the most human of acts is to come to the assistance of another in a moment of threat or accident.

Across societies and socio-economic classes, the mobile phone is fast becoming intrinsic to safety. Not only are mobile phones pervasive, they are, like eye-glasses, generally worn on human bodies or kept nearby. By being ready-to-hand, if a person encounters a potentially unsafe place or situation, or happens across an accident, the mobile phone can become an instrument for improving safety. At the same time, in some situations, the use of mobile phones may occasion moments of vulnerability and an over-reliance on its safety functions may undermine a person's overall resilience, especially if the phone malfunctions.

In situated use, moreover, the mobile phone can be seen as ambiguous, in purpose and in form. The computational and representation capacities of mobile phones are multi-faceted, suitable for pleasure, for commerce, among other purposes. In addition, the form of the mobile phone can also be transformed to suggest varying purposes. Related to safety, this ambiguity can be seen in technological adaptations. For example, in one direction, when on-board instruments detect poor driving or an accident, the car can become a mobile phone with communication functions; in the reverse, the physical form of a mobile phone can cunningly conceal a *real* gun. In a different vein, when the mobile phone is held in particular ways it can be *perceived* by others as particular things, such as a handgun.

How might mobile phones improve safety? Homeless young people, living in urban settings, present a testing case for addressing this question. One reason is that homeless youth are maturing and when they share information about their whereabouts and activities, they may benefit from the experience of caring others, like teens in stable families. For a second, homeless youth face risky situations in day-to-day life on the street. Specific technological solutions would not only be of great benefit to homeless youth, they would, in general, more fully define the design space of mobile phones and safety for all urban dwellers.

In this on-going research [24,25,26,27,28], therefore, we investigate how homeless young people manage unsafe situations. Specifically, in Seattle (the research site), we engaged homeless young people and other stakeholders and asked: How do homeless young people perceive safety in their daily lives in urban places and how do they bring mobile phones into these perceptions? What kinds of unsafe situations do they encounter? What stakeholders and institutions are implicated, and how do mobile phones interpenetrate? How do homeless youth avoid or mitigate unsafe situations, and when they do occur, how are they responded to? Finally, how do and how could the informational, communication, and form-based features of mobile phones be used to help keep young people safe?

To address these questions we engaged multiple stakeholder groups, as well as created a strong link between empirical research of current conditions and generative co-design activities that envision future possibilities. In this paper, though, we focus primarily on the empirical findings.

BACKGROUND

HCI Work Related to Homelessness and to Teen Safety

Recently the field of HCI has begun to address questions about how homeless people adopt and make use of digital and mobile technology and how specific applications can be designed to improve their welfare. One major finding of this work is that homeless people, like most people in developed and developing nations, desire digital technology in all its forms for many purposes. Moreover, homeless people are adept at overcoming economic and technological barriers to obtain access [16,26]. Additionally, through the use of digital technology in public and semi-public settings, tensions among the homeless and other urban dwellers can become prominent [18]. The need to connect personal devices to infrastructure, for example, to recharge batteries, may lead the homeless to come together into postures that are perceived as threatening by some people. We interpret these findings to suggest that the widespread diffusion of digital and mobile technologies into homeless communities is changing the nature of homelessness in ways just being discerned, with potential opportunities for equalization across social and economic classes, along with dangers of further stigmatization and entrenchment.

Another area of related work concerns a new class of mobile applications for improved safety of "homed" teenagers [4]. In short, these applications enable parents to monitor their teen's activities, providing information on what they are reading online, where they go, how they drive, who they are with, and so forth. By the availability of such intimate information, parents are called upon to balance their desire to keep their children safe with other values related to the raising of children including trust, privacy, autonomy, independence, and maturation.

Place, Homelessness, and Safety

As noted above, tensions arising from the use of mobile devices by the homeless are a contemporary example of a long-standing theme. In short, since Elizabethan times, the "homed" have often viewed the "homeless" with trepidation. Consider, for example:

> In the western world 'Home' is an ideal as well as a place – a spatially constructed ideology usually correlated with housing.... homelessness also signifies 'displacement' – an existential lack [of identity and morality] that is perhaps even more fundamental than being without shelter" [3, p. 115].

In other words, in the struggle to meet basic needs, homeless people are often forced to work against, or at least around, society's dominant norms. People without shelter become without "place." In turn, by their efforts to live, homeless people can be seen as threatening to both the physical and psychological well-being of others [6,14].

Responding to citizens' feelings of unease, city governments, including Seattle, often pass civility laws. These laws, in brief, aim to improve safety by prohibiting such public behaviors as sitting on sidewalks, sleeping in parks, and loitering in areas of drug-dealing. However, homeless people, in part, by their living circumstances and by their search for dignity often violate such prohibitions and thereby risk incarceration [22]. In fact, field work has shown that civility laws tend to be disproportionately enforced against people of lower socioeconomic standing, particularly people who are homeless [1].

The linkages between civility laws, how they are enforced, and the activities of homeless people on the real and perceived safety of city dwellers, including themselves, are complex. Here, we do not explicate them; that said, we do make two basic claims that help frame our work. First, homeless young people, in the struggle to meet basic needs, frequently encounter unsafe situations, with civility laws often being implicated. Enforcement against sleeping in public parks, for example, may lead young people to less safe sleeping situations. Second, the desire, and increasingly the need, to access digital infrastructure can also bring young people into unsafe situations. The need for electricity to recharge a phone, for example, may lead young people to trespass at secluded power outlets [24].

Value Sensitive Design

To enable a comprehensive analysis of safety and other value tensions at the research site, we drew on Value Sensitive Design [11,12,20,21], with the key theoretical constructs and methods used in this work described here:

Stakeholders. Value Sensitive Design makes a distinction between direct and indirect stakeholders. The former interact directly with the system; the latter while not interacting directly are affected by the system's use [11,12]. In the framing of this research, we assumed that homeless young people are the primary *direct* stakeholders who will adopt mobile phone technologies for keeping safe. We also assumed that other direct stakeholders might emerge as the work progressed. In addition, in prior stakeholder analysis [28] we identified three key groups of *indirect* stakeholders: service providers, police officers, and community members. Importantly, we also assumed that under certain circumstances indirect stakeholder groups might take on the role of direct stakeholders [4,8,9]. However, in keeping with our emphasis on homeless young people as the primary direct stakeholders, in the work reported here we asked all participants to consider how mobile phones might be used to keep a homeless young person safe.

Value Tensions. Prior work [5,20] has identified the importance of engaging value tensions. In our work with homeless young people we anticipated complex value tensions within an individual (e.g., a homeless young person both wanting to be self-sufficient on the street and wanting to be cared for by service providers), with an individual's relationship to a stakeholder group (e.g., at times a homeless young person might feel threatened or less safe around police and at other times the same person might call upon police for help in an unsafe situation), and among different stakeholder groups (e.g., when homeless young people's needs for physical safety, such as using a doorway of a store in order to stay dry, are in tension with community members' feelings of safety in public).

Value Sketches. For people who live in the public and must frequently move to obtain basic needs, perceptions of safety are largely situated in place and time of day. To better understand this way of life, we employed a sketching activity, called *value sketches*, which prompt participants to represent place, mobility, and safety. Sketching is a common qualitative method for uncovering knowledge for physical and conceptual structure [10,13,15,19,23]; value sketches in particular emphasize participants' values and involve a systematic analysis of the drawn elements.

Value Scenarios. While value sketches are well suited to elicit knowledge situated in place, not all types of knowledge and feelings can be most readily expressed through drawings. Stories that emphasize social and value considerations of new technologies, called value scenarios [4,21], can fill this gap. For foregrounding value implications and envisioning systemic effects, *value scenarios* were first proposed for use by designers as an extension to *use* and *problem scenarios* [2]. Here, we evolve the use of value scenarios by placing their creation in the hands of the participants to elicit ideas for how mobile phones could be used to improve the safety of homeless young people.

METHODS

Methodological Considerations

Given the complexity of homeless young people's circumstances introduced above, we took a deliberately exploratory approach. We did not want to commit to tightly focused research instruments; rather, we sought to develop instruments that would allow us to bound the design space broadly and that would lend themselves to adaptation as the work unfolded. For instance, we did not define the value "safety," instead we provided instruments which we hoped would afford the opportunity for participants to reveal their own perceptions and experiences of safety. In addition, we sought to involve a wide spectrum of stakeholders, including homeless young people, service providers, police officers, and community members. Thus, we needed to accommodate their unique characteristics by collecting data in different contexts. Finally, while the empirical work was to provide significant stand-alone data on homeless youth, mobile phones, and safety it was also undertaken with a view toward informing future co-design activities. In consequence of these considerations, the data we collected are not always completely comparable across all stakeholder groups. Accordingly, we are careful to make appropriate qualifications as needed.

The Research Setting: The U-District, Seattle, WA

This research was conducted in the University District, hereafter the *U-District*, a neighborhood located adjacent to the University of Washington. Since the 1960s, community members have developed an urban place for welcoming "wanderers" with free medical, counseling, and shelter services. Today, an alliance of nine agencies provides a continuum of care for homeless young people [25].

Researcher Stance

The research team is comprised of people with backgrounds in HCI, design, and security. We work from a design stance that seeks to both understand the situated context as well as to create meaningful change. Because of our prior volunteer work at a community technology center [26], we were able to quickly establish a trusted rapport with participants – especially important when asking questions about "safety." In varied ways our research efforts are connected with our collaborating organizations, the young people they serve, and the greater U-District. On reflection, we have also found that this work changes us, especially how we apprehend the U-District and think of the young people we have met in research and later encounter on the street. In these public encounters, we are trained to acknowledge the person but subtly, so as not to reveal our inter-personal familiarity to bystanders.

Participants, Recruitment and Data Collection Contexts

The recruitment and interviewing procedures varied somewhat by stakeholder group as follows: (1) *Homeless young people* (14 men, 5 women; ages 19–32, M=24). Service providers at one of the local agencies in the U-District recruited two same-sexed groups of homeless young people with group interviews taking place on separate days at a well known drop-in facility. (2) *Service providers* (4 women; ages 21–41, M=29; 2, 4, 36, and 72 months experience). Employees at service agencies who work with homeless young people were recruited by personal contact and interviewed as a group in their place of work. (3) *Police officers* (1 man, 1 woman; ages 38; M=38; 4 and 12.5 years experience). University police officers who have patrolled the U-District were recruited by personal contact and interviewed in their place of work. And (4) *community members* (14 men, 4 women; ages 18–84, M=52). Other people who attend school, visit, live, or work in the U-District were recruited and interviewed individually at the annual U-District Street Fair.

Special considerations for working with homeless young people. Homeless youth self-selected to be included in this research. To protect their identities they provided oral assent and participated under the auspices of a collaborating service agency. Older participants (into their early 30s) who identify with the community of homeless young people were welcomed to engage in the research activities. Following norms for remuneration at the research site, the homeless young people participants received a $25 gift card (other participants were not compensated).

Procedures

Participants in each stakeholder group completed, in this order, a value sketch, a paper and pencil survey, and a value scenario; and engaged in a semi-structured discussion concerning safety in the U-District.

Value Sketches. To gain insight into participants' perceptions of safety in the U-District for homeless youth, participants completed a value sketches activity, where they used green and red markers to indicate "safe" and "unsafe" areas respectively on a 17×20 inch map of the U-District. Of note, community members' value sketches did not address their perceptions of safe and unsafe places for homeless young people; thus, we do not report on value sketches for community members here.

Stakeholder-specific Surveys. To collect information on demographics, mobile phone use, and related topics participants completed a 3-page survey, with stakeholder-specific questions. The surveys included questions primarily on cell phone use (e.g., Homeless young people were asked "Have you ever owned a cell phone?").

Value Scenarios. To elicit ideas for how a mobile phone could help homeless young people stay safe, participants were instructed to write a value scenario, with this prompt:

> Homeless youth and young adults may face special challenges in keeping safe from harm. Please write a story about how a cell phone could help to keep a homeless youth or young adult safe. There are no right answers. The story can be as long or short as you like. It can be about a real situation or about a fictional situation.

Importantly, these instructions ask for real or fictional scenarios, with the rationale that if participants could mask some of the facts in their stories they might be more likely to reveal intimate, subversive, or otherwise risky, though plausible, ideas about the use of mobile phones.

Discussions. Finally, to provide an opportunity for open-ended conversation about safety for homeless young people, participants engaged in a discussion guided by a set of 15 questions, which were tailored to the stakeholder groups (e.g., "What kinds of things or circumstances make [*you / homeless young people*] feel [*safer / less safe*] in the U-District?" and "Imagine a situation in which [*you / a homeless youth or young adult*] might feel less safe. Can you think of a way that a cell phone could help?). For the community members, the semi-structured discussions (20–60 min.) were one-on-one and hand-written notes were taken; for all other stakeholder groups, the semi-structured discussions (60–90 min.) were audio taped and transcribed.

Coding and Reliability. Drawing on prior work [9,12], we developed coding manuals for both the value sketches and scenarios (see Tables 1 and 2). Coding manuals were developed from the homeless young people data and applied to the data for other participants. To test the inter-rater reliability for the value sketches, a second independent coder was instructed in the coding manual and re-coded all the sketches. Inter-rater reliability was assessed using Cohen's kappa, a measure of the level of agreement between two coders, with $\kappa = .788$. Inter-rater reliability for the value scenarios followed a similar procedure, with $\kappa = .815$. Two commonly referenced benchmarks for interpreting the values of Cohen's kappa are Fleiss [7], who rates any value of κ over 0.75 as excellent agreement, between 0.40 and 0.75 as intermediate to good, and below 0.40 as poor; and Landis and Koch [17], who rate a κ of 0.81 to 1.00 as "almost perfect" and between 0.61 and 0.80 as "substantial" agreement.

RESULTS

Stakeholder-Specific Surveys: Participant Backgrounds

To provide a context for understanding the data, we first establish that all stakeholder groups have some prior interaction with homeless young people and that the homeless young people we worked with had prior mobile phone experience. To begin, the service providers reported extensive ad hoc and regular weekly face-to-face interactions. Complementing their face-to-face exchanges were a variety of technologically meditated ones, including email, landline and mobile phone, MySpace or Facebook, and text messaging. The university police officers (16 years of combined experience) reported they generally interacted with homeless young people 1–10 times in a week. These face-to-face interactions included both ad hoc friendly social interactions and responding to complaints filed about or by homeless young people. In contrast, only one-third of the community member participants reported prior interactions with homeless young people, such as being asked for spare change.

In terms of prior mobile phone use, 11 of the 19 homeless young people currently own a phone (length of ownership: 2 days to 7 years; M=1.5 years) and 5 additional young people have owned a phone in the past. Additionally, more of the young women (100%) than young men (43%) currently own a phone (Fisher's exact test, $p = 0.045$).

Value Sketches

The value sketches provide a window into how participants viewed the physical space of the U-District in terms of safe and unsafe places for homeless youth. The data is anchored in place, highlighting *spots*, *paths*, and *regions*. Daytime and nighttime maps provide a means to understand the impact of daylight/daytime-activities vs. dark/nighttime-activities on perceptions of safety.

A total of 50 maps (one daytime and one nighttime map for each of the 19 homeless young people, 4 service providers, and 2 police officers) were analyzed. To analyze these maps and as shown in Table 1, our coders were instructed to begin with the identification of spots (Category I), specific locations that people can walk to; paths (Category II), along

- I. SPOT
  - A. Private
    - 1. Labeled
    - 2. Unlabeled
  - B. Public
    - 1. Bar, café, etc.
    - 2. Church, etc.
    - 3. Park
    - 4. Service agency (see Fig. 1a, 1b)
    - 5. Municipal building
    - 6. Other place
- II. PATH
  - A. Unlabeled (see Fig. 1c)
  - B. Labeled
    - 1. With safety focus
    - 2. Without safety focus
- III. REGION
  - A. Unlabeled
  - B. Labeled
    - 1. With safety focus (see Fig. 1d)
    - 2. Without safety focus
- IV. COMPOSITE
  - A. Listing
  - B. Nested
    - 1. Exceptions (see Fig. 1e)
    - 2. Elaborations

Table 1: Value sketches codes. (Uncodeable codes not shown.)

which people can walk; and regions (Category III), within which people can walk to many spots and along many paths. These features, each of which can be seen in Figure 1, were expressed through the varied use of graphic marks (e.g., spots were expressed by Xs, circles around a building, or other shapes, etc.). Overall there were a total of 146 spots, 68 paths, and 55 regions marked on the 50 maps.

Labels on the maps served multiple functions, at times acting to identify landmarks and at other times to indicate temporal, person-based, or activity-based qualifications of safety. Some participants made use of pre-existing labels on the map (e.g., University Bookstore); other participants wrote their own annotations, which were often placed in the maps' margins. Such linguistic, along with pictorial and iconographic, marks were associated by proximity, enclosure, and connectivity. For example, a green drawing of trees, labeled "Ravenna" (the name of a local park) indicates a

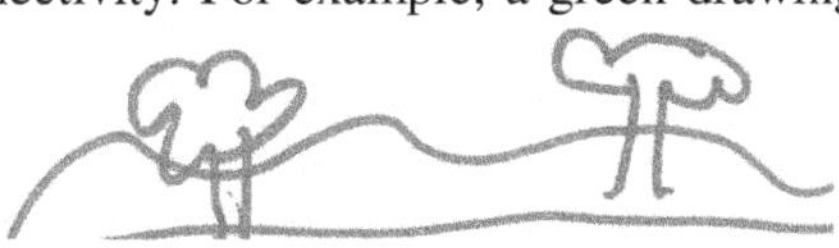

safe location whereas a red foamy beer mug, labeled "drunken danger" placed near a bar indicates an unsafe location.

Participants often employed graphic marks in combination, at times placing spots within paths, spots and paths within regions, and regions within regions. These composite visual structures (Category IV), along with linguistic marks, provide a good deal of expressive power for indicating information about place-based safety. For instance, "COP SHOP," depicted as a red rectangle, is placed on a major thoroughfare, depicted by a thick green line (see Figure 1e).

Given our emphasis on homeless young people as the direct stakeholders in this research, we now turn to two aspects of their sketches: location, the consistency with which homeless young people view specific places in their environment as safe or unsafe; and time, the overall patterns

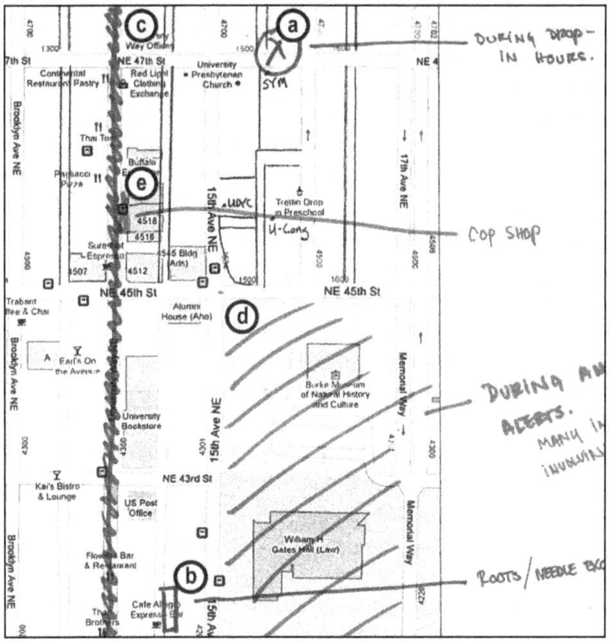

Figure 1: Value sketch (daytime), showing two spots (a and b), a path (c), a region (d), and a nested exception (e), made by a homeless young person (cropped image). Green and red represent safe and unsafe features, respectively.

with which homeless young people perceive safety in the U-District during daytime and nighttime.

In terms of location, against a background of substantial variation in the features (e.g., many features labeled on the maps were unique to a single individual), a large amount of consistency emerges in how the young people view most types of locations as either safe or unsafe. For example, the homeless young people generally consider service agencies to be safe places; service agencies were marked a total of 32 times and indicated safe in 28 cases (88%). Interestingly, while both young women and men marked service agencies as safe spots, the young women marked service agencies as safe spots on their maps more frequently than the men ($Z = -3.52$, $p = .0004$, Mann-Whitney U test). Similarly, churches were indicated safe in 10 of the 11 cases (91%) where they were marked. In terms of unsafe locations, bars were marked a total of 8 times, always indicated unsafe (100%). The youth also seemed wary of college students, with the university campus indicated unsafe on 6 of the 7 maps (86%) where it was marked and "frat row" indicated unsafe on all 4 maps (100%) where it was marked.

In terms of time of day, we expected homeless young people to view the U-District as safer during the day than during the night. Specifically, we expected young people to indicate fewer unsafe locations on their daytime than nighttime sketches. There is some suggestion that this is the case, with 29 of the 100 (29%) features marked on the daytime maps indicated unsafe as compared to 39 of the 93 (42%) nighttime features indicated as unsafe, but the difference is not statistically significant. In addition, three young people marked the entire U-District as safe during

- **I. Situation**
  - A. Reactive
    - 1. Hostile
    - 2. Accident
    - 3. Authority
    - 4. Environmental
  - B. Preventative
  - C. Secondary effect
- **II. Purpose**
  - A. Warnings
  - B. Calling for help
  - C. Maintain relationships
  - D. Documenting
  - E. Information gathering
  - F. Leveraging social expectations
  - G. Preventative
- **III. Mobile Phone Technology**
  - A. Functionality
    - 1. Traditional calling
    - 2. Customization
    - 3. Sensors
    - 4. Recording
    - 5. Technical network
    - 6. Information seeking
    - *7. Social networking*
  - B. Form
    - 1. Material
    - *2. Shape*
    - 3. Visibility
  - C. Monetary costs
- **IV. Locus of Welfare**
  - A. Self
  - B. Other

Table 2: Value scenario codes. *Italic* codes identified conceptually but not used. (Uncodeable codes not shown.)

the daytime (possibly with a few exceptions), but did not do so on their nighttime maps, perhaps indicating that the areas where they feel safe are more localized at night.

Value Scenarios

The value scenarios take off from where the value sketches end. Whereas, the value sketches provide a good deal of insight into participants' nuanced conceptions of the U-District as a place with safe and less safe physical spaces for homeless young people; the sketches tell us less about the social relationships within those spaces, subtleties tied to the situation and contexts of interactions, the nature of people's purposes, and the specific role of mobile phone technology including its functionality, form, and material costs. Participants largely freeform value scenarios brought forth all of these and other considerations.

Table 3 shows 10 illustrative scenarios, selected mainly for their coverage of the coding manual, from the 43 collected (19 homeless young people, 4 service providers, 2 police officers, and 18 community members; scenario length: 5-150 words, M=44 words). As shown in Table 2 the analysis yielded four distinct dimensions: situation, purpose, mobile phone technology, and locus of welfare. Each scenario was coded for each of the four dimensions. Complex scenarios received multiple codes within each dimension to reflect the depth and nuance of the scenario. Given our exploratory goals, we sought to uncover statistical differences in the coding of the scenarios based on stakeholder groups or gender. However, perhaps due in part to the small sample sizes, no statistically significant differences were found.

Situation refers to elements in the environment that suggest or explain why the mobile phone is used; for example, in reaction to a hostile event (Code I.A.1) or accident (I.A.2), to prevent an anticipated event from occurring (I.B), or due to secondary effects that followed from the presence of the mobile phone (I.C). *Purpose* refers to the protagonist's aims for taking action with a mobile phone; for example, to warn others of an impending event (II.A), to call for help (II.B), to document an event (II.D), or to actively leverage social expectations (II.F). *Mobile Phone Technology* refers to the technology used in the scenario; for example to the phone's functionality in making calls (III.A.1) or recoding audio or video (III.A.4), to the phone's form such as its shape (III.B.2), or the costs entailed in owning and using a mobile phone (III.C). Lastly *Locus of Welfare* refers to

H1. If you need help you can call for it. If your car runs out of gas you can call your friends to bring you some gas. And a whole bunch of other sh*t too. [Male]

H2. Some friends of mine had gone to get more beer. My phone rang, my homies called to tell me the boys were heading my way. I had enough time to put my weed away before they arrived. [Male]

H3. I would use devices in my cell phone to record law enforcement, when they choose to harass me. [Male]

H4. I don't think cell phones keep people safe because if you call the cops for seeing a crime you might get beat up later for snitching. [Male]

H5. I feel when hitching rides, with a cell phone you can be kept safe. If you're walking down the road with your thumb out and a cell phone to your ear a "weirdo" is less likely to pick you up. [Female]

H6. Once upon a time there was three little pigs, one lived in a house, one lived on the street, and the last one lived in a squat. One day a big bad wolf was looking for a squatter, the big bad wolf was out to get all the little pigs. The first little pig called the second pig, and he found the third pig through word of mouth. Thank cellphone. [Male]

H7. Usually if you have a phone people know the police are on the way. If someone is using an expensive phone, it might escalate the situation. [Male]

C1. Perhaps they might be a bit safer w/a cell phone if someone were to take advantage of them, they could call police. The question is would the police come to his/her aid? [Female]

P1. Being homeless is a challenging experience. Without a job and access to food, shelter, & other basic necessities, living on the streets is emotionally & physically draining. Having a cell phone would at least allow me to be able to call other homeless persons that I have networked with to work on attaining these difficult to get necessities. Knowing that I could call a shelter to get a bed, or 911 for an emergency would make me at least feel safer and closer to services that I need while living on the streets. Others can check on me as well to make sure that I am safe throughout the day. [Male]

S1. A man was harassing a youth in her sleeping spot. She was able to snap a picture of the man and forward it to service providers & police. With this photo the man was picked up and charge [sic]. Hopefully he will not be sexually harassing any more homeless young women. [Female]

Table 3: Value scenarios, labeled by stakeholder group: Homeless Young People (H1-H7), Community Members (C1), University Police (P1), and Service Providers (S1).

whom the protagonist directs a concern for safety, to him or herself (IV.A) or toward others (perhaps including the protagonist) (IV.B). Overall, there were a total of 50 situation, 49 purpose, 51 mobile phone technology, and 43 locus of welfare codes for the 43 scenarios.

To provide a flavor for how these dimensions and the categories within them characterize the scenarios, consider some of the exemplar scenarios presented in Table 3. For example, scenario H1 was coded as reactive/accident (I.A.2) as the protagonist faces a situation in which the mobile phone is used in direct response to "running out of gas;" calling for help (II.B), indicating the protagonist's purpose in using the mobile phone to "call your friends to bring you some gas;" traditional calling (III.A.1), to indicate the technical aspect of the mobile phone that is employed to make a "call;" and self (IV.A), to indicate that the scenario's protagonist is concerned with his own safety as in "if you [the protagonist] need help."

While allowing for rich diversity in the details and as exemplified by H1 above (see also C1, P1), one common narrative structure emerged from the data and accounted for roughly half (49%) of the scenarios. Perhaps not surprisingly and as reflected in the coding manual, this narrative structure describes reactive situations (I.A) in which the protagonist seeks help (II.B) by using a mobile phone to make a traditional phone call (III.A.1) for his or her own benefit (IV.A). Eight of the scenarios were coded with exactly this group of four codes, and an additional 13 scenarios were coded as minor variations that included at least three of these four codes. That said within this common structure, scenarios portrayed diverse situations and conveyed rich details from "staying on the street" where homeless young people are "harassed," "beat up," or "raped," to protecting "my squat" from the police, to getting "lost in the mountains," or to "running out of gas."

Other less frequently occurring patterns were also identified. For example, the codes *documenting* (for purpose) and *recording* (for functionality) were both rarely used, but tended to occur together in cases where they were used ($p = .0008$, Fisher's exact test). Scenarios H3 and S1 exemplify such a case, in one instance recording harassment from law enforcement (H3) and in the other harassment from a man on the street (S1). Only 5 scenarios were assigned the code *recording*, and 3 of the 5 were also assigned the code *documenting*; these were also the only 3 scenarios that were assigned the code *documenting*. That is, scenarios with the purpose of *documenting* always mentioned a *recording* function, showing how the coding manual represents purposes and functionality.

Working within the structured but open-ended value scenario format, participants were generative and imaginative in linking technological opportunities to problematic situations. For example, in their value scenarios homeless young people proposed "map apps to find safe places" (III.A.6), envisioned "self aware" artificial intelligence systems with "internet profiles and database access" to plan for improved safety (III.A.5), and imagined the materiality of the phone being used to "save your life by jumping in front of a bullet for you" (III.B.1).

Scenarios surfaced not only direct impacts from the mobile phone but secondary ones as well that typically resulted from the form or monetary cost of the phone. One homeless young woman wrote in H5 that when hitchhiking, visibly holding "a cell phone to your ear a 'weirdo' is less likely to pick you up." Here, the perceived benefit to safety comes from others who might cause harm "seeing" that the homeless young person could contact someone via phone; not that a particular phone call has been made.

Finally, not all uses of mobile phones were perceived as improving safety (H4, H7). For example, in H4 a homeless young man suggests that in reporting a crime to the police "you might get beat up later for snitching." In H7, another young man calls attention to the risks to safety from possessing relatively expensive technology.

DISCUSSION

On the Meaning of "Safety"

Recall that we did not define "safety;" rather we presented participants with open-ended yet structured activities to elicit their perceptions and experiences. Participants told us through sketches and stories the myriad of places, situations, and people who come together to make homeless young people more or less safe. From these materials, we have seen that safety is fundamentally situational. Homeless young people face both ordinary and extraordinary risks – running out gas (scenario H1) or getting lost in the mountains, along with chronic exposure to the possibility of harassment from police and community members (H3, S1), together with the possibility of isolated, severe violence (H4). The police are perceived to be a threat, but so too are community members, service providers, and other homeless young people. At the same time, and herein lies a major conundrum, the data also show that youth look to these same stakeholders and places, at least at times, for safety. Within this context, the coding manuals provide some specific dimensions for characterizing the uses of mobile phones for keeping safe.

On Distancing Mechanisms: Sensitivities around Safety

For many people, safety is a highly sensitive topic. Particular details about keeping safe might put a youth or his or her friends at risk, be embarrassing, or even traumatic to recall. We might expect, therefore, that some people might try to create distance between themselves and their views on safety, perhaps by obscuring some facts, using ambiguity, or stepping away from specificity. In a telling example of this sensitivity, which arose during the group discussion, one young person said: "Letting people know where I feel safe, makes me feel less safe."

Accordingly, we intentionally employed methods that provided the means for participants to control both the precision and ambiguity of the information provided. For example, in the value sketches participants could provide more or less specific information about location (e.g., labeled or unlabeled, spot vs. region). Moreover, in the value scenarios participants were not asked to differentiate between real and fictitious but plausible situations.

For both methods, indeed, it appears that some homeless young people did in fact create distance between their own experiences and what they were comfortable sharing with us. In the value sketches, three participants marked places, otherwise mundane, as safe or unsafe without indicating why (Category I.A.2). These were puzzling. Perhaps, we conjectured, the marks indicated locations of one-time altercations or places related to safety that should otherwise remain unelaborated. If so, with more focused procedures, it might be possible to elicit greater detail about these spots. However, paradoxically, by seeking to elicit greater detail, young people might be unwilling to say anything at all. We conclude, therefore, that some marks on the value sketches might be a form of "distancing," that is, conveying something important while keeping oneself out of it.

Further examples of distancing might be present in the value scenarios, where narrative forms can convey essential information but without indicating a personal connection to the events, protagonists, or conflicts. Scenario H6, a "fairy tale" about three little pigs and a big bad wolf, was such an example. Interestingly, the basic content and structure of this scenario – namely, that cell phones can be used to warn of an impending police presence – can be conveyed through different forms of writing. Scenario H2, in "realistic" style, illustrates the contrast quite well.

In a different vein, participants might create distance between themselves and their experiences by the use of language, by, for example, placing events in the passive voice or in hypothetical terms. While we have not completed a close analysis of how language might be used to "create distance" we speculate that by the use of such conditional words as "if," "would," and "could" participants might remove themselves from particular situations but convey their essential content and structure. This linguistic analysis remains for future work.

Value Tensions

For considering "relationship," instead of dichotomies or conflicting points of view, we prefer "value tensions." Value tensions capture the mutuality of relationship; they are not necessarily problematic, nor do they always cross a contentious space. Instead, tensions can keep two points of view together in balance or enable two conflicting views to coexist. This analytical orientation, in short, allows us to present and reason about relationship with nuance.

While homeless young people might help each other keep safe (H1, H2, H6, P1), by using a mobile phone to call for help, they may also be seen as "snitching" (H4), a violation of the rules of the street. The use of a phone in many situations is ambiguous – is that young person calling a "homie" or the "police?" Young people must work within this uncertainty, leading to the importance of secondary effects, leveraging social expectations, and form.

Homeless young people have complex relationships with the service providers. While young people may look to the service providers for help, they also may react negatively to particular responses and rules, as might a "homed" adolescent to his or her parent. We saw, for example, that all the young women marked service agencies as safe on their value sketches; however, in discussion they also expressed frustration with particular service providers' actions. In a similar sentiment, a young man said: "The service providers sometimes don't make me feel safe… a lot of people think they are all friendly… but it turns out they are harsh."

The relationship between homeless young people and police officers is similarly ambivalent. While the police were often seen to pose a threat (H2, H3, H6), they were also seen as potentially beneficial (H7, C1, S1). While young people's sketches do not contain a single positive statement about the police (but a fair number of negative statements), young people in discussion and in the scenarios did indicate that they would call upon the police and 911 in some emergences. At the same time, while police officers conveyed a certain dislike toward homeless young people ("It's like they own the parking lot, the donut store, the [sandwich shop],") they also appreciated the difficulty of surviving on the streets (P1).

Finally, homeless young people saw different groups of community members as safety risks. One group, called "angry Christians," was described as intolerant and violent. Concerning fraternity members a young person said: "You ever woke up to them [frat kids] rummaging through your stuff and then kicking you in the face when you said 'Get out of my stuff.'" Recall too that "frat row" and regions of the university campus were indicated to be unsafe in the value sketches. Community members used words such as "squatters," "street kids," and "Ave rats" to name the people who were perceived to make the U-District unsafe. Like the police officers, however, the scenarios showed community members to be empathetic (C1), with some scenarios envisioning communication networks specifically designed to keep homeless young people safe.

Design Opportunities

When discussing the limitations of mobile phones and when justifying new possibilities, the stakeholder groups brought forward a variety of functional criteria, operating constraints, and general desiderata for evaluating features. The general desiderata included: (1) low cost; (2) outdoor durability for repeated drops, wet, and cold; (3) flexible powering options, decoupled from infrastructure (e.g., solar recharging); (4) 24/7 reliability for emergency use; (5) independent and separate communication channels, protected from surveillance; and (6) the possibility for recovery when lost by inattention or stolen. These grounds for judging features, quite obviously, come from the circumstances of homelessness and provide a backdrop for the following opportunities for design:

Support for shifting trust relationships among homeless young people and enabling young people's desire to help others (H1, H2, H6, P1). While young people face an environment of shifting alliances, they also come to trust and rely on each other to respond to calls for help. When young people are in trouble, they could benefit from ways to reach out to trusted peers or groups, albeit the specific individuals might change quite frequently. *Technical features*: Provide capability to represent alliances, to diplomatically bring people into and out of them, to phone specific contacts, to broadcast calls for help or warnings, and to communicate without the possibility of surveillance.

Support a homeless young person's need to document abuse (H3, S1). Homeless young people described occurrences of harassment and violence, from police officers and other community members, as well as other homeless people. Documenting such events can empower young people to seek redress and, over time, may deter future harassment. *Technical features*: Provide capability to document events in real-time (e.g., audio and video recording) as they unfold, and to place such documentation into the hands of someone who or an institution that can facilitate an appropriate response.

Support a surreptitious call for help (H4, H7). Being seen or "perceived" as making contact for help or documenting a situation as it unfolds can put a homeless young person at risk, as telling of street activities to outsiders can be seen as a form of weakness or "snitching." *Technical features*: Provide capability to call and/or document a situation without being visible (e.g., eyes-free "panic" button), to represent emergency networks or trusted others, and to diplomatically bring people into and out of those networks.

Support for homeless young people as urban dwellers with specific information needs. The value sketches and scenarios capture something of the distinct perspective that homeless young people have for their physical environment (e.g., churches as places of safety, areas of parks safe at different times, etc.). *Technical features*: With location-based services, provide the capability to represent specific kinds of information that homeless people and those living in poverty might seek alongside other information about a city. Addressing this goal will foreground tensions between homeless communities and the other stakeholders [25].

Support for safe, non-stigmatized access to infrastructure. The value sketches alerted us to perceptions of safe and unsafe areas in the U-District. Recall, for example, that the university grounds, areas of student housing, and the neighborhood service center (i.e., "cop shop") were considered generally unsafe by young people. At the same time, the discussions based on the value scenarios pointed to the need for access to electricity to recharge batteries. *Technical features*: Provide access points to electricity and wireless capability at sites not considered unsafe. Moreover, enable access points to be moved to different locations so that no one location in the U-District becomes known as "that place for the homeless." One possible solution, or at least design direction, is large-sized tricycles [27] that act as mobile power and Internet connectivity sources, placed at suitable locations for all urban dwellers. Such infrastructure might mitigate the risk that homeless young people experience additional forms of stigma by the need for infrastructure.

CONCLUSIONS AND CONTRIBUTIONS

Implications for Co-Design. The coding manuals for the value sketches and the value scenarios shape a design space for further investigation of design opportunities. We intend, for example, to use the scenarios as prompts for considering specific design solutions and to use the coding manuals to situate particular solutions. In addition, we expect that value sketches, together with particular prototypes, will enable homeless young people and other co-designers to enact and envision the consequences of particular designs in action.

Contributions. In addition to the design opportunities, we: (1) Documented rich knowledge about the interaction among place, mobile phone technology, and safety for a historically underrepresented population, homeless young people; (2) Demonstrated the use of innovative open-ended yet structured methods to elicit views on a sensitive topic (personal safety) in a non-threatening and dignified manner, leaving what information to reveal and how under the control of the participant; (3) Constructed coding manuals that can be used and extended by others to analyze the relationships among place, mobile phone technology, and safety; and (4) Extended a method (i.e., value scenarios generated by participants) in Value Sensitive Design, thereby contributing to that growing literature.

Final Words. Surviving on the street requires that young people develop expertise for managing unsafe situations; mobile phones are surely implicated because of their pervasiveness and because they are worn on bodies. By investigating this setting through the systematic and synthetic analysis of place-based representations (value sketches) along with narratives of possible uses of mobile phones (value scenarios) we have been able to more fully explore the design space of mobile phones and safety. In some ways, elements of this setting are at the same time both extraordinary and ordinary [26]. Thus, much of what we have uncovered in this extraordinary setting, along with the methodological approach and methods employed, is likely to be applicable to other settings and circumstances where people look to their mobile phones for safety.

ACKNOWLEDGMENTS

Special thanks to all participants for their willingness to consider safety and mobile phones. Thanks to Sanjana Prasain for help in coding the value sketches. This research was supported in part by NSF Award CNS-0905384.

REFERENCES

1. Beckett, K., and Herbert, S. *Banished: The New Social Control in Urban America.* Oxford University Press, New York, 2010.
2. Carroll, J. M. Five reasons for scenario-based design. In *Proc. HICSS 1999*, IEEE (1999), 3051-3061.
3. Cresswell, T. *Place: A Short Introduction.* Blackwell Publishing, Oxford, 2004.
4. Czeskis, A., Dermendjieva, I., Yapit, H., Borning, A., Friedman, B., Gill, B. T., and Kohno, T. Parenting from the pocket: Value tensions and technical directions for secure and private parent-teen mobile safety. In *Proc. SOUPS 2010*, ACM Press (2010), Paper 15.
5. Denning, T., Borning, A., Friedman, B., Gill, B., Kohno, T., and Maisel, W. Patients, pacemakers, and implantable defibrillators: Human values and security for wireless implantable medical devices. In *Proc. CHI 2010*, ACM Press (2010), 917-926.
6. England, M. Stay out of drug areas: Drugs, othering and regulation of public space in Seattle, Washington. *Space and Polity 12*, 2 (2008), 197-213.
7. Fleiss, J. L., Levin, B., and Paik, M. C. *Statistical Methods for Rates and Proportions*, 3rd edition. John Wiley & Sons, New York, 2003.
8. Friedman, B., Borning, A., Davis, J. L., Gill, B. T., Kahn, Jr., P., Kriplean, T., and Lin, P. Laying the foundations for public participation and value advocacy. In *Proc. dg.o 2008*, Digital Government Society of North America (2008), 305-314.
9. Friedman, B., Höök, K., Gill, B., Eidmar, L., Sallmander Prien, C., and Severson, R. L. Personlig integritet: A comparative study of perceptions of privacy in public places in Sweden and the United States. In *Proc. NordiCHI 2008*, ACM Press (2008), 142-151.
10. Friedman, B., Hurley, D., Howe, D. C., Felten, E., and Nissenbaum, H. Users' conceptions of web security: A comparative study. *Ext. Abstracts CHI 2002*, ACM Press (2002), 746-747.
11. Friedman B., Kahn P. H., Jr., and Borning, A. Value sensitive design and information systems. In *Human-computer Interaction in Management Information Systems: Foundations*, M.E. Sharpe, Armonk, NY, 2006, 348-372.
12. Friedman, B., Kahn, P. H., Jr., Hagman, J., Severson, R. L., and Gill, B. The watcher and the watched: Social judgments about privacy in a public place. *Human-Computer Interaction 21* (2006), 235-272.
13. Gaver, W. W., Dunne, T., and Pacenti, E. Design: Cultural probes. *interactions 6*, 1 (1999), 21-29.
14. Gibson, T. A. *Securing the Spectacular City.* Lexington Books, Lanham, MA, 2004.
15. Hendry, D. G., and Efthimiadis, E. N. Conceptual models for search engines. In *Web Search: Interdisciplinary Perspectives*, A. Spink and M. Zimmer (Eds.). Springer, Berlin, 2008, 277-308.
16. Karabanow, J., and Naylor, T.D. "Being hooked up." In *Digital Diversity,* E. D. Looker, and T. D. Naylor (Eds.). Wilfred Laurier University Press, Waterloo, ON, 2010, 161-178.
17. Landis, J., and Koch, G. The measurement of observer agreement for categorical data. *Biometrics 33* (1977), 159-174.
18. Le Dantec, C. A., Christensen, J. E., Bailey, M., Farrell, R. G., Ellis, J. B., Danis, C. M., Kellogg, W. A., and Edwards, W. K. A tale of two publics. In *Proc. DIS 2010*, ACM Press (2010), 11-20.
19. Lynch, K. *The Image of the City.* The MIT Press, Cambridge, MA, 1960.
20. Miller, J. K., Friedman, B., Jancke, G., and Gill, B. Value tensions in design: The value sensitive design, development, and appropriation of a corporation's groupware system. In *Proc. GROUP 2007*, ACM Press (2007), 281-290.
21. Nathan, L. P., Klasnja, P. V., and Friedman, B. Value scenarios: A technique for envisioning systemic effects of new technologies. *Ext. Abstracts CHI 2007*, ACM Press (2007), 2585-2590.
22. Nickelsville (2010). *Declaration of a state of emergency in 2010 by and for homeless people in Seattle & King County.* http://www.nickelsvilleseattle.org/
23. Sutton, S.E., and Kemp, S. P. Integrating social science and design inquiry through interdisciplinary design charrettes. *Am. J. of Community Psychology 38* (2006), 125-139.
24. Woelfer, J. P., and Hendry, D. G. Homeless young people and living with personal digital artifacts. To appear in *Proc. CHI 2011.*
25. Woelfer, J. P., and Hendry, D. G. Designing ubiquitous information systems for a community of homeless young people. *Personal and Ubiquitous Computing*, 2010, doi: 10.1007/s00779-010-0341-5.
26. Woelfer, J. P., and Hendry, D. G. Homeless young people's experiences with information systems: Life and work in a community technology center. In *Proc. CHI 2010*, ACM Press (2010), 1291-1300.
27. Woelfer, J. P., and Hendry, D. G. Stabilizing homeless young people with information and place. *JASIST 60*, 11 (2009), 2300-2312.
28. Woelfer J. P., Yeung, M. W-M., Erdmann, C. G., and Hendry, D. G. Value considerations in an information ecology. In *Proc. AM 2008*, ASIST (2008), 248-256.

Playable Data: Characterizing the Design Space of Game-y Infographics

Nicholas Diakopoulos, Funda Kivran-Swaine, Mor Naaman
School of Communication and Information
Rutgers University
{diakop, funda, mor}@rutgers.edu

ABSTRACT
This work explores the intersection between infographics and games by examining how to embed meaningful visual analytic interactions into game mechanics that in turn impact user behavior around a data-driven graphic. In contrast to other methods of narrative visualization, games provide an alternate method for structuring a story, not bound by a linear arrangement but still providing structure via rules, goals, and mechanics of play. We designed two different versions of a game-y infographic, Salubrious Nation, and compared them to a non-game-y version in an online experiment. We assessed the relative merits of the game-y approach of presentation in terms of exploration of the visualization, insights and learning, and enjoyment of the experience. Based on our results, we discuss some of the benefits and drawbacks of our designs. More generally, we identify challenges and opportunities for further exploration of this new design space.

Author Keywords
Infographics, Visual Analytics, Games, Interaction Science

ACM Classification Keywords
H5.m. Information Interfaces and Presentation: Misc.

General Terms
Design, Experimentation, Human Factors

INTRODUCTION
In recent years there has been growing international interest in openly publishing government and other civic datasets online. The U.S. federal government's data.gov initiative has expanded since its launch in 2009 to include over 3,120 datasets ranging from national education and public health, to environmental and transportation data. Other state, local, and international bodies are rapidly moving toward transparency and civic data publishing.

In response, new outlets seeking to make sense of this growing stream of data for the public have sprung up, such as the Guardian's Datablog in the U.K. [5]. Such journalistic channels often combine interactive infographics and textual stories to explain and contextualize datasets. In this work, we consider an alternative to traditional methods of creating interactive infographics from such datasets, and explore the design space of game-like or "game-y" infographics. Such an approach would allow data from published sources to be rapidly repurposed into playable experiences that are not only engaging, but also allow for visual analysis and personal insight from the data.

We designed, built, and evaluated three different versions of an interactive data-driven infographic, Salubrious Nation, with the intent of examining the benefits and drawbacks of the game-y mode of information presentation compared to a more traditional approach. To setup the design space of game-y infographics we first draw conceptual connections between visual analytic tasks and game mechanics. We then assess the various versions of Salubrious Nation with respect to measures that are important in both information visualization and game design including how exploration of the data was affected, whether insight generation was enabled, and to what degree the experiences were engaging and enjoyable. Our study contributes insights about interaction science and the design of goal-oriented game-like visual analytic experiences, including benefits and tradeoffs of the specific designs we implemented, and of the medium in general.

RELATED WORK
Here we provide an overview of other efforts toward telling stories with data including narrative infographics, simulation, and games that incorporate raw data.

Storytelling with Information Visualization
The notion of telling a story through information graphics and visualization has been explored in various capacities in the research literature [16, 19, 21, 33] and is increasingly used in media contexts such as journalism, to build visual narratives around data. Based on a sample of 58 exemplars, Segel and Heer [33] characterized and produced a typology of different genres of narrative visualization. A pertinent design dimension of narrative visualization is the degree of ordering and interactivity - from linear and author-directed, to more free-form and user directed [16, 33].

Perhaps the most interaction-limited form of infographic storytelling is theatrical performance using graphics, which we call *histrionic visualization*. For instance, John King has used the "Magic Wall" [6], a large touch-screen display, on CNN to depict voting results during elections by walking

CHI 2011, May 7–12, 2011, Vancouver, BC, Canada.

viewers through different visuals and scenarios with the data. Another well-known example of this is Al Gore's narrated traversal of information graphics in the movie "An Inconvenient Truth". The Economist routinely produces narrated animations of some of their information graphics called videographics [4].

At the other end of the interactivity spectrum are undirected information visualizations that allow the user to freely explore the data space according to whatever is of most interest to them. A criticism of such undirected visualizations has been that they result in a *gulf of goal formation,* where users may flounder under the complexity of finding a suitable data subset to explore or choosing among available interface options [25]. In reality, most visualizations lie somewhere between the extremes of narrative storytelling and undirected exploration [33]. Landmarks or other authored waypoints provide structure, but the user is transitioned in such a way as to allow for in-between free exploration [16, 19]. In contrast, this work explores how to use game design (i.e. rules and mechanics of play) as an alternative method of structuring a narrative.

Simulation and Data-Driven Gaming

While related to interactive storytelling, games are also a cousin to simulations–procedural representations of aspects of reality [29]. Simulations (of which some are *not* games) have been used for some time to help people interactively learn and explore phenomena being modeled [11]. Models for simulations can be data-driven, however, particularly in game simulations, simplified and abstracted models tend to be preferred. Some simulated models are physical (e.g. based on known mathematical or physical relationships), while others are subjective and editorial in nature (e.g. editorial newsgames).

In contrast to games built on top of complex models or simulations, another class of games that has emerged over the past few years is more directly data-driven. Raw data, usually in the form of media such as images, videos, or text are used as inputs to the game and form objects, which the player manipulates in the course of the game. Oftentimes the goals of these games are to annotate media [17] whereas one goal of our current work is to make data-driven games analytical and insight producing experiences.

In the commercial realm, there are also games that draw on media data. For instance, Audio Surf [1] builds on the popular dynamic of music pattern games like Rock Band by allowing players to input their own music tracks. Some commercial newsgames also use data such as NewsBreaker, a twist on the classic game Breakout that incorporates RSS news headlines into the game [7]. Another game that more deeply integrates news information into the game is Scoop [9], which constructs a crossword puzzle based on real news headlines. While these designs may generally help to increase *awareness* of news information, we go beyond text or audio to incorporate the *visual analysis of raw numeric data* as central game activities.

GAME DESIGN AND INFOGRAPHICS

The concept of game-y infographics introduced here builds on fundamental elements of game design and their intersection with visual analytics and interaction science, as we describe next. We should note here that while many games do contain infographics *within* them, such as for navigation or feedback on game stats or goals, here we consider the graphic as the dominant frame and game elements as subservient to the graphic. We should also note that we are interested in the design of more *casual* games requiring a time investment of only a few minutes.

Game-y Fundamentals

Salen and Zimmerman define a *game* as "*a system in which players engage in an artificial conflict, defined by rules, that results in a quantifiable outcome*" (pg. 80 [29]). Puzzles are considered a subset of games that have a correct answer or outcome. Goals and rules are core constituents of what defines formal game systems [20]. Games also often include elements that support the conflict in the game such as scoring, competition, advancement or other reward mechanisms, and winning. The goals and structures in games serve to guide attention and motivate players' actions. Goals could include, for example, solving a puzzle, overcoming a competitor, exploring, collecting, constructing, or destructing. The design space is substantial when considering the sheer permutations of plausible systems of goals and rules that can be constructed.

In game design parlance, the salient interactivity present in a game is referred to as the *game mechanic.* According again to Salen and Zimmerman, the core game mechanic "*is the essential play activity players perform again and again in a game*" (pg. 316 [29]). For instance, in a trivia game, the core mechanic is answering questions, in a side-scroller the mechanic is to maneuver a character, and in a real-time strategy game it is to manage resources. The core mechanic can also be a compound activity composed of many actions such as simultaneous moving, aiming, and firing, as in 3D shooter games. Game mechanics can be altered by changing the existence, direction, symmetry, or semantics of relationships between objects in the game system.

Visual Analytics and Interaction Science

Visual analytics is the study of how visual interfaces amplify analytical reasoning, including both deriving insights from data, as well as producing and communicating judgments based on that analysis [34]. Research in visual analytics has examined an array of analytic activity both at the level of interactions, and representations [12, 31, 36, 38] and at the level of user intents [37]. For instance, Amar et al [12] developed a typology of low-level visual analytic tasks including *retrieve value, filter, compute derived value, find extremum, sort, range, characterize distribution, find anomalies, cluster,* and *correlate.* Applications of visual analytics are broad and span intelligence analysis [28], journalism [18], and bioinformatics [30] among others. This work extends visual analytics within the domain of journalism and data storytelling via games.

The field of *interaction science* has recently emerged as a distinct area of inquiry within visual analytics. It is defined in [27] as "*the study of methods by which humans create knowledge through the manipulation of an interface.*" The authors posit that "*the more ways a user can 'hold' their data (by changing their form or exploring them from different angles and via different transformations), the more insight will accumulate*" [27]. This developing theory suggests that the goals designed into games, reified through a game mechanic, itself composed of interactions, might provide the impetus for the exploration of a visualization parameter space. If we consider game mechanics as bundles of interactions, the concept of game-y infographics then is to creatively integrate visual analytic tasks [12] and interaction intents [37] into that bundle of interactions such that they are inexorably intertwined with accomplishing the goals of the game (See Figure 1).

This conception of game mechanics together with visual analytics gives rise to a number of questions including (1) Whether the structured and directed activity of a game motivates and engages more exploration of a visualization parameter space and of the data [22], (2) Whether visual analytic tasks embedded in game mechanics can lead to insights about the underlying data, and finally (3) Whether such a merging of analysis and gaming can be an enjoyable and fun experience. These questions are addressed in our evaluation using a combination of metrics drawn from visual analytics [15, 32] and user experience [26].

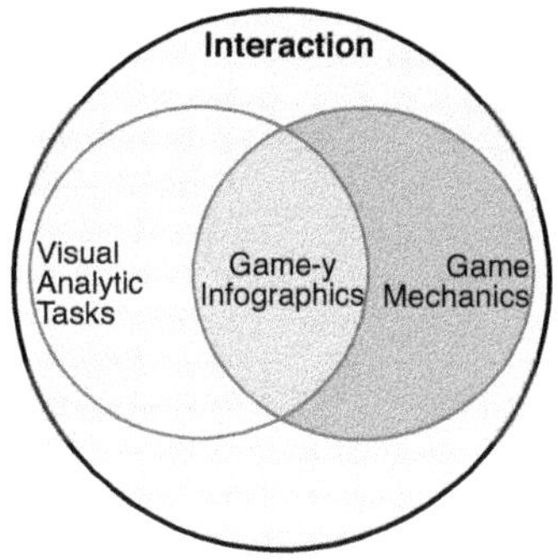

Figure 1. A conceptual diagram showing the relationship of game-y infographics, visual analytics, and game mechanics.

SALUBRIOUS NATION

To explore the space of game-y infographics and assess their benefits and limitations we designed and built three different versions of an infographic called Salubrious Nation (available online [8]). Two versions had game mechanics and the third did not. Next we discuss the data used as well as the visual, interaction, and game design of the different versions.

Dataset

As a theme for the infographics we chose national public health data as we thought this would be a compelling topic for a U.S. audience. We assembled a dataset from various online sources such as County Health Rankings [3] and the Department of Health and Human Services' Community Health Status Indicators [2]. The dataset consisted of eight health indicators geographically coded by county, including numerical values for *adult smoking rate, binge drinking rate, teen birth rate, fast food restaurants per capita, soda consumed per capita, diabetes rate, obesity rate, and heart attack death rate*. We incorporated other county-encoded demographic data acquired from the U.S. Census Bureau [10], such as population, poverty rate, life expectancy, and proportion of people over age 65.

Design

For each of our implemented versions we now describe the visual and interaction design as well as the game mechanics and visual analytic tasks supported. We primarily approached our designs via analogy by choosing mechanics popular in other casual games, such as guessing or color matching, and incorporating visual analytic tasks into these mechanics. In the design process we enumerated game interactions and their motivations (i.e. game goals) as well as how visual tasks [12] related to those interactions, taking into account visual and behavioral properties of game objects that could further enable visual analytics. We should note that these designs underwent substantive iterative revision based on feedback we obtained from play and usability testing performed using Mechanical Turk [23].

Salubrious Non-Gamey (SNG)

The non-game-y version of Salubrious Nation is shown in Figure 2a. It consists of a choropleth map as the dominant visual representation. The coloring of the map follows a spectral color sequence from yellow to red with the lighter more luminous yellow indicating "less" and the darker less luminous red indicating "more" [35]. A neutral gray is used to shade counties for which data is missing. These colors are explained in a key below the map. Above the map are instructions (instructions can also be obtained by hovering the mouse over the small question mark), a combo box for selecting the current parameter, and a slider. The slider is labeled with the minimum, maximum, and (population normalized) average for the current parameter.

As the slider is moved it displays the current value and the map is re-rendered such that the counties with a value below the slider value are shaded in yellow and yellow-orange, while the counties with a value above the slider value are shaded in orange-yellow and red. The shading transfer function is thus dynamic with the slider. Another option the user has for interacting with the map involves hovering over individual counties for details-on-demand. When the mouse is over a county the county boundary is emphasized and an overlay box pops up with the name of the county, the value of the currently selected parameter for that county, and other demographic information such as the population, poverty rate, life expectancy, and rate of people over age 65. A combo box is used to select the current parameter to visualize.

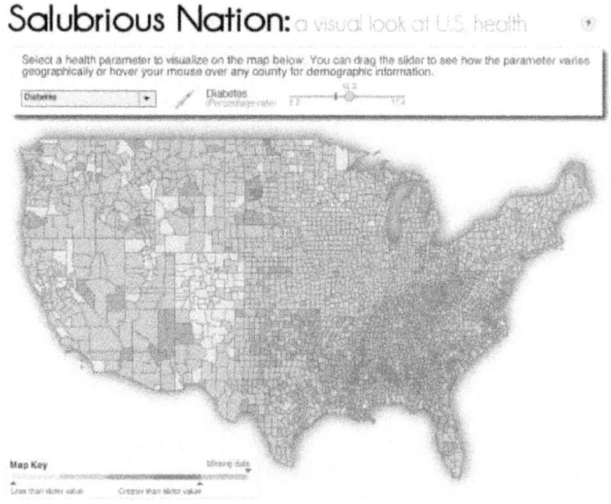

Figure 2a. Salubrious Non-Game-y - SNG

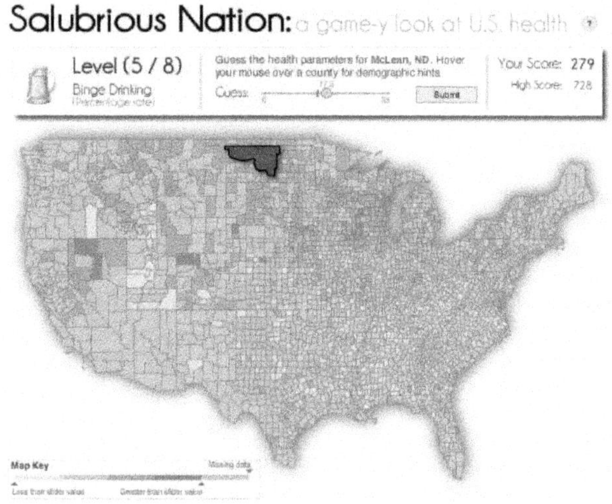

Figure 2b. Salubrious Guess - SG

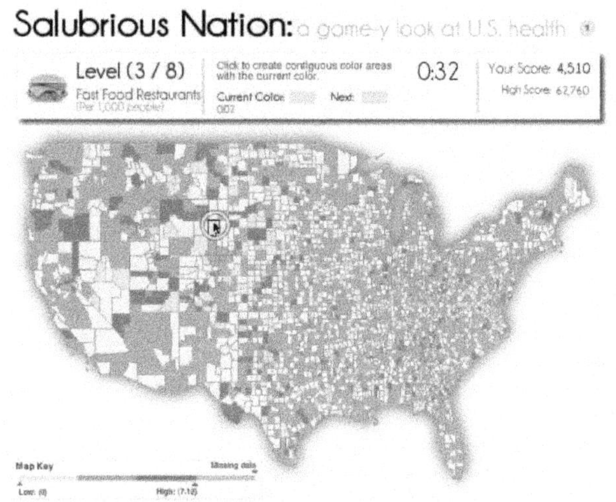

Figure 2c. Salubrious Eliminate - SE

Interaction is undirected but corresponds to analytic interaction intents and visual analytic tasks. Moving the slider enables interaction intents such as *encoding* and *connecting,* and facilitates tasks such as *characterizing* the parameter distribution geographically, seeing *anomalies* or *outliers*, and *clustering* values. The static representation of the slider also supports finding a *range* and *extremum* for the current parameter. Hovering over counties corresponds to the interaction intent of *elaboration* and supports *retrieving values* or looking for *correlations* between demographic statistics and the current parameter. Changing the parameter corresponds to a *filter* on the visible data and also supports *correlation* between parameters by flipping back and forth.

Salubrious-Guess (SG)

The first game-y design that we developed, Salubrious Guess (SG), builds on the visual representation of SNG but adds a *guessing* game mechanic that includes goals, scoring, and competition. The overall goal of the game is to accurately guess the magnitude of a given health parameter for a randomly selected target county. The player may inform their prediction using their knowledge of the health parameter in conjunction with the given demographic statistics, or using information gleaned from how the map changes color in response to manipulating the slider. The more accurate the guess, the more points the player scores. The design structures attention such that each of the eight levels consists of one health parameter and one target county. In addition to earning points, players can compete for the high score and compare their score to others' at the end of the game.

The visual representation of SG is shown in Figure 2b. and is very similar to SNG including the map, key, and slider. One exception is that the target county for each level is increased in size and highlighted in blue. An animation at the beginning of each level draws attention to the target. There is additional feedback at the top of the graphic to show the user the current level, parameter, and scores.

There is a slider similar to that of SNG that is used by the player to enter their guess for the current parameter. A submit button next to the slider enters the guess and scores it, while providing visual feedback about the correct answer. The user interacts with the graphic via the slider, which works the same way as for SNG, via hovering to obtain demographic statistics for the given county, and by hitting the submit button. The visual analytic tasks supported by SG are very similar to that of SNG except that in SG, there is *no* capability to *filter* or *correlate* between variables by flipping back and forth. Clicking the submit button supports *retrieving a value* by revealing the true value for the health parameter. After submitting a guess, the user can continue to explore the map until deciding to advance to the next level. In this interim period the hover info box also shows the exact value for the parameter.

Salubrious Eliminate (SE)

The second game-y version of Salubrious Nation that we developed explores a different part of the design space. We recognized that color matching games such as Bejewled or Snood are tremendously popular online casual games. The game mechanic entails matching groups of colors in order to eliminate game units, such as blocks or balls. We adapt this game mechanic for data in Salubrious Eliminate (SE). To do this we partition counties into low, medium, or high values based on a Z-score; each level of the parameter corresponds to a game color. Sixty percent of the counties on the map are randomly selected and colored based on their value; the other counties are left blank. The goal of the game is then to color blank areas of the map with the current color so as to create contiguous color areas. When a contiguous color area is created it is eliminated from play and the player receives points based on the size of the area cleared (i.e. the number of counties in the contiguous area). To quicken the pace time-pressure is added by having the current color switch randomly every 10 seconds and by limiting the level to 50 seconds total. As in SG each level consists of one health parameter and the player can compete for the high score and compare their score to others at the end of the game.

The visual representation of SE is somewhat different than SNG or SG (See Figure 2c). We use only three shades of color on the map and the meaning of the colors is different; it is based on the partitioning of the parameters into low, medium, and high values. The map key is labeled with the low and high values for the parameter. Additional feedback at the top of the graphic shows the current color, the upcoming next color, scores, and the amount of time left in the level. Feedback on the current color is also given by showing a colored ring around the mouse cursor. The ring blinks when the current color changes in order to draw attention to the new color.

The user interacts with SE by clicking the current color onto blank counties on the map. Creating a contiguous area scores points and eliminates those counties from play by dropping their transparency; their coloring is still apparent however so that visual trends can still be detected. In comparison to SNG or SG, SE is more limited in the range of visual analytic tasks that it supports. Clicking a county enables interaction intents including *select* and *connect* and facilitates visual analytic tasks including *characterizing the distribution*, *clustering*, and geographic *correlation*. The map key supports the tasks of identifying the *range* and *extremum* of a parameter. After the level timer expires we enable another interaction: the user can hover over the map to *retrieve values* or look for *correlations* between demographic statistics and the current parameter.

USER STUDY

We conducted a between-subjects online user study in order to compare the relative merits of the different versions of Salubrious Nation. The experiment was designed to assess the three research questions articulated earlier, namely: (1) Whether the structured and directed activity of a game motivates and engages more exploration of a visualization's parameters and data; (2) Whether visual analytic tasks embedded in a game mechanic can lead to learning, insights, or hypotheses about the data; and (3) Whether game-y infographics can be an enjoyable experience.

Procedure

The evaluation of Salubrious Nation was conducted online rather than in a lab setting in order to enhance the ecological and external validity of the study. Deploying the study in this way came at the expense of closer control of the display environment and forced us to rely on post-task recollections of insights. In order to recruit participants we published calls for participation in local university mailing lists, as well as social media sites such as Twitter. Participants were entered into a drawing to win one of two $50 gift certificates. The participants were given a URL address, and were assigned randomly to one condition of the infographic upon consenting to the study. Users were free to interact with the graphic for as long as they wanted and were asked to fill out the questionnaire when they felt they were done using the graphic.

Data Collection

We collected data by logging user interactions with the interface and from a questionnaire. We adopted several measures developed for the assessment of visual analytics tools, such as exploration and insight generation [32]. The interaction log collected data such as the time spent with the graphic and the number of entities considered via clicks, hovers, and drags. The questionnaire collected basic demographic information, Likert scale ratings of subjective impressions of the experience such as enjoyability and learning, and what we expected to be covariates such as degree of interest in public health and experience with online graphics and casual games. The questionnaire also included open-ended questions, which asked about the enjoyability of the experience and about the observations and questions users had during their experience. These open-ended responses were analyzed using affinity diagramming and iterative coding to arrive at patterns and typologies of use; insights were further categorized using a fact typology from Chen et al. [15].

Participants

One hundred forty-seven participants were recruited and assigned randomly to one of the three conditions, SNG, SG, or SE. A limitation of deploying our study online was the need to carefully vet responses and activity to exclude those that were perfunctorily participating in order to be entered into the gift certificate drawing. We excluded three participants from SNG due to no substantial log activity (i.e. they just filled out the questionnaire without using the interface), two participants from SG because they didn't complete at least half the game levels, and seven participants from SE because they didn't complete at least half the game levels. For all of the eliminated participants we verified that their questionnaire responses were largely unsubstantive. Furthermore, seven participants were excluded from the study because they did not record their user identifier on their questionnaire (which allows us to link responses to log activity). This left us with one hundred twenty seven valid participants: SNG (N=47), SG (N=41), SE (N=39). Of these participants, 64% (N=82) were female and 36% (N=45) were male. The ages of the participants ranged between 19 and 57 (M=29, SD=7.17). There were no statistically significant differences between groups on any of the demographic, interest, or experience variables measured.

RESULTS

Our analysis surfaced some key factors alluding to the benefits and drawbacks of game-y visual analytics, including aspects of the exploration of the graphic, insights and learning, and enjoyability.

Exploration of the Data and Parameter Space

Jankun-Kelly et al [22] have argued that the core activity of the visualization exploration process is manipulating different configurable variables which impact the generation of a visualization (i.e. the visualization's parameterization). Visualization exploration can be assessed by measuring metrics such as the number of entities and other parameterizations considered [32].

One measure of the amount of the data space considered is the number of unique health parameters visualized (recall there were eight parameters in total). In both game versions each parameter corresponded to a level thus in order to finish the game each parameter was considered, whereas in SNG the user was allowed to freely decide which parameters to explore. This resulted in the average number of unique parameters considered being 8.0 in SG and 7.94 in SE (one person didn't finish all eight levels) versus 5.94 in SNG. A Z-test indicates that the mean for SNG is significantly less than that for SG or SE ($p < .001$). In both game-y conditions all or almost all of the parameters were considered by every participant whereas, when left to their own inclinations, participants in the non-game-y condition only considered about 74% of the parameters on average.

Another measure of the exploration of the parameters and demographics in the graphic is how much hover activity was performed by participants (recall hovering the mouse over a county shows a detail popup with demographic statistics such as population and poverty rate). We compared the average number of hover interactions logged per user across conditions: users of SNG had the most hovers (M=532), users of SG had the next greatest amount (M=401) and users of SE had the least number (M=196). As the number of hovers was not normally distributed we applied a log transform and ran an ANOVA with post-hoc Dunnett C tests for unequal variances. Differences between SNG and SE as well as between SG and SE were significant at $p < 0.05$ indicating that participants used the hover interaction less in SE than in either SNG or SG, but there was no significant difference between SNG and SG. This is consistent with hovering being central to the mechanic in SG but non-essential to the mechanic in SE.

Besides the absolute volume of hover activity we looked at the *distribution* of hovers by plotting the aggregate density of interaction over each county for each condition. This is depicted in Figure 3 with darker counties indicating more hover interactions. The figure exposes one of the difficulties in log analysis: *intentionality*. Two salient trends apparent on the maps are artifacts of interface layout. The high density of hovers in the north-western area for SNG is a result of a drop-down combo box placed just above the map there (See Figure 2a.). The high density of hovers over Minnesota in SNG and SG is also a result of a slider (See Figure 2b) being placed above the map at that location.

However, there are other trends that are not artifacts of interface layout. For instance, in SNG there is a high density of interaction around New York and New Jersey, where the majority of the recruiting for the study was done. Perhaps unsurprisingly, people were most interested in details from the area where they reside. In SG however we see this geographic bias has disappeared–the interaction is more uniformly spread across the country. In SE the geographic bias has returned but is oriented toward larger counties. If we consider the aggregate *click* density (the primary interaction in SE) in Figure 4 then this trend towards interacting with larger counties becomes even more clear. Compared to the small counties in the eastern U.S., western counties represent faster (i.e. larger) targets to acquire, thus this interaction pattern is consistent with players optimizing the click-based game mechanic.

Between SNG and SG we can also compare the average volume of interaction with the slider to see how often that parameterization of the graphic changed. The mean per person number of slider changes for SNG was 108 and for SG it was 208. We log transformed the variable to make it normal and found a significant difference between the conditions ($F(1,80) = 10.43$ $p < .01$). The specifics of this difference become more apparent when we graph the number of slider changes logged for each tick of the slider (See Figure 5). In particular we see a much larger spike for central values of the slider indicating that participants in SG

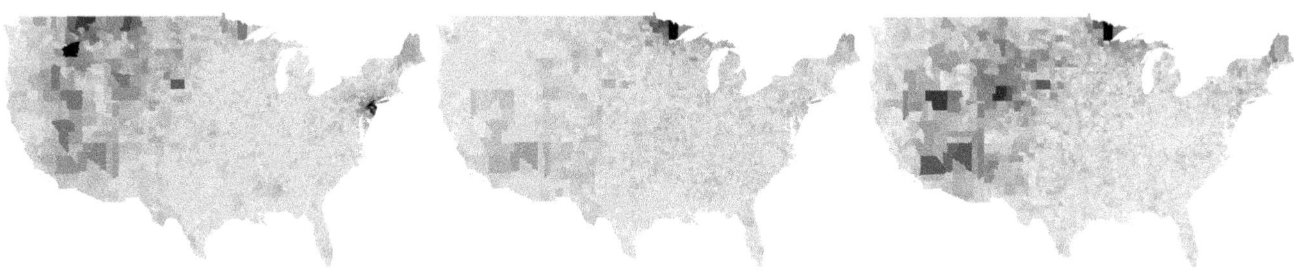

Figure 3. Normalized hover density for SNG (left), SG (middle) and SE (right).

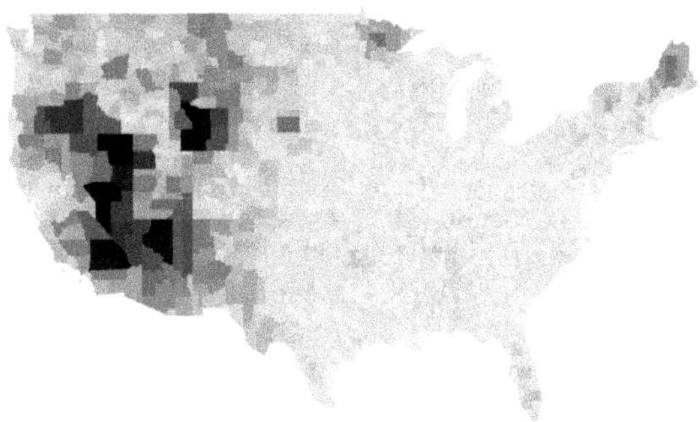

Figure 4. Normalized click map for SE

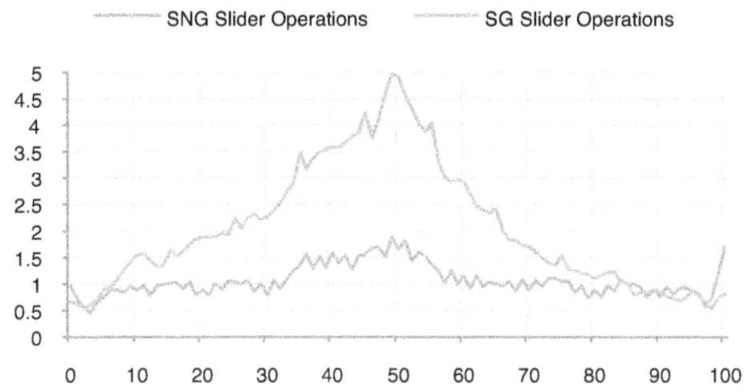

Figure 5. Average per person slider parameter exploration

moved the slider back and forth through the midpoint more often than in SNG. This interaction pattern coincides with the game mechanic: using the slider provides visual feedback with which to better inform a guess.

Insights and Learning

Having examined how the different designs of Salubrious Nation influence parameter and data exploration, we next turn to how this exploration enabled (or hindered) participants' ability to make sense of the data in terms of insights, questions, or hypotheses derived from their interaction. Here we are primarily interested in the potential of game-y infographics to engender new observations or insights and less interested in standard measures of learning such as recall, though we did also measure participants' self-reported perceptions of learning. We included two open-ended questions on the questionnaire to probe at insights, asking participants what observations, insights, or questions they had, based on their interaction with the graphic. For our analysis we adopt the definition of insight offered by Chen in [15] which corresponds to the observation of some fact (e.g. detecting an outlier) combined with an interpretation via some mental model. We manually coded the text responses using a typology of fact types [15] and present results characterizing the kinds of insights and observations reported in each condition.

SNG produced the most insights (M=1.87 per person) in comparison to the game-y versions, SG (M=0.95) and SE (M=0.54). Participants identified many different kinds of facts such as extremes, correlations and associations, geographic distributions and clusters, comparisons, and observations about the data itself such as units of measurement or missing data. Some observations were encoded as factual statements, while others were hypothetical or posed as questions, tacitly indicating some underlying observation. Responses showed that there was deductive reasoning (i.e. (dis-)confirming a tacit hypothesis) as well as ampliative abductive reasoning [14], involving the construction or promulgation of "new" hypotheses based both on the existing data as well as on some external knowledge that the participant brings to the tool. For instance, participants conjectured about the relationship of health parameters to external variables such as race, education, urbanity, and latitude with some going on to posit *causal* relationships to external variables such as literacy and education.

Users of SG generally had the same types of observations as users of SNG, albeit in lower numbers. In SG there were more questions from users about the *nature* (i.e. existence or strength) of the relationship between the given demographic statistics and the health parameters. One participant in SG wrote, "*Are the parameters displayed correlated to the health questions? Are they the best parameters to use?*". Users of SG also had more observations about associations between the demographics and the health parameters, rather than between different health parameters (SG M=0.32 per person; SNG M=0.13 per person) indicating increased attention to these relationships. In SG we begin to see people having insights not just about the data but also about the game, such as strategies for increasing points and winning: "*I tried to use the color information of the neighboring counties the most in deciding my answer values. By trying to equalize the number of counties above and below my answer, I tried to minimize my error.*"

In SE there were substantially less insights and observations about the data and more comments about how to optimize scoring in the game. For instance, one participant wrote, "*Depending on the category, regions with smaller districts tended to connect with each more than the larger regions. Hence, more points.*" Many participants, instead of reporting on observations about the data, griped about their inability to do so and complained that the game directed attention away from the data. Time pressure meant there wasn't enough time to take everything in: "*I was so focused on scoring points that I didn't notice much else about the graphic*"; "*It's hard to actually remember which areas are high or low for the stats because you concentrate hard on playing the game...*"; "*Being timed made it more of a challenge, and I ended up paying more attention to click the right colors than to being able to actually observe the map as a whole.*"

But while SE had substantially less insights about the data than SNG or SG there was an interesting relationship with interest level. We dichotomized interest level to high interest (>= 5 out of 7) and low interest (<= 4 out of 7). In SNG, high interest participants generated 64% of the insights and in SG they produce 67%. In SE the trend was reversed with 71% of insights coming from *low* interest participants. This difference is statistically significant (χ^2=9.789 $p < .01$) suggesting that although the absolute numbers were lower, SE enabled people less interested in public health to have proportionally more insights about the data.

We also measured and compared participants' self-reported learning on a seven point Likert scale ("How much do you think you learned by using the information graphic?"). We ran an ANCOVA on participants' self-reported learning with their frequency of online graphics use as a covariate ($F(2,123) = 9.885$ $p < .001$). Post-hoc Bonferroni tests showed significant differences between SNG and SE ($p < .001$) and between SG and SE ($p < .05$) but not between SNG and SG (SNG M=4.68; SG M=4.07; SE M=2.74). These results reinforce what we gleaned from our analysis of insight responses: people also *felt* they learned more in SNG or SG than in SE but the difference between SNG and SG was not statistically significant.

In both SNG and SG participants commented that they would like to see more information and knowledge explicitly communicated such as known facts for target counties, links to external information or details, explanations for differences, or contextualization and explanations for outliers and extremes. This suggests that some users approached the graphics as they would other narrative infographics and were expecting the *messaging* of *known facts* typical of that genre [33] instead of being left to their own insight generation capabilities.

Enjoyment

The last major research question we sought to address in our evaluation of Salubrious Nation was how engaging and enjoyable the experience was. On the questionnaire we asked participants to evaluate how enjoyable and fun their experience was on a Likert scale and also solicited open-ended explanations to more fully understand the ratings.

Participants in both SNG and SG often reported that their ability to have analytic insights led them to enjoy those experiences. People enjoyed seeing spatial patterns and geographic trends across regions and figuring out aspects of the data such as extremes or comparisons. In SG and SE people mentioned the game-y aspects as enjoyable as well. For instance in SG some people enjoyed the challenge and cognitive effort of the puzzle aspect. No one mentioned score as a motivator in SG, however in SE score was mentioned several times in terms of beating the high score (challenge) or just trying to score as many points as possible: "*It was fun to get a large chunk of counties and gain a lot of points at once.*" Participants in SE thought aspects of the game mechanic like clearing a big area or visually searching for areas were enjoyable.

Limitations of the interface were often the impetus for frustrations or a less enjoyable experience. In particular participants in all conditions complained of the diminutive size of the counties in the eastern U.S. as well as a lack of landmarks (e.g. cities, state boundaries) and ability to zoom and pan the map, which would help with navigation. In SE frustrations had to do with difficulty understanding the rules and goals of the game. Some participants thought it was initially unclear or not well-explained how their actions connected with the underlying data. They also complained of the time pressure and how this conflicted with their ability to focus on the data. In SG there were some complaints about the *relevance* of the targets since they were randomly generated and were likely not geographically germane to individual users. Several participants in SG also did not appreciate the guessing nature of the game. They thought it was inappropriate (and stereotyping) to be using demographics such as poverty to predict health issues; it was simply too serious an issue to be playing a game about.

Self-reported enjoyability ratings (1 to 7) showed SNG to be the most enjoyable (M=5.23), SG to be next most enjoyable (M=4.63) and SE to be least enjoyable (M=3.71). An ANOVA showed significant differences among the conditions ($F(2, 124) = 9.084$, $p < .001$) and post hoc Bonferroni tests showed significant differences between SNG and SE ($p < .001$) and between SG and SE ($p < .05$) but not between SNG and SG. Enjoyability ratings interacted with co-variates such as health interest and use of online graphics differently across conditions. In SG enjoyment ratings were positively correlated with interest in public health ($r = .508$, $p < .01$) but this correlation did not hold in the other conditions.

We compared the group main effects of public health interest to enjoyment at three levels (low=2, medium=4, high=6) and found that at low interest levels there was no significant difference in enjoyment between the conditions, but that for medium or high levels of interest there was a significant difference in enjoyment between SNG and SE ($p < .05$). We similarly compared the group main effects of use of online graphics to enjoyment at three levels (low=2, medium=4, high=6) and found that at low levels there were significant differences between SNG and SE ($p < .01$) and SG and SE ($p < .05$), but for medium levels the difference between SG and SE disappears and for high levels all differences disappear. So although SNG was overall the most enjoyable among the three, for certain subsets of participants (i.e. people minimally interested in public health and more frequent users of online graphics) the enjoyability was not significantly different.

DISCUSSION

In this paper we have begun to explore the design space and potential of game-y infographics. Our results suggest that game-y designs have benefits in terms of increased exploration of the data space. At the same time, absolute measures of insight, learning, and enjoyability were higher in SNG with important caveats such as that the proportion of insights was greater for less interested users of SE, and that content interest or use of infographics impacted the enjoyability of the designs differently. We further discuss these results and their impact on design below.

Directing Attention

Our evaluation shows that traditional infographics such as SNG generally outperformed the game-y designs across metrics of number of insights generated, self-reported learning and curiosity evoked, as well as enjoyment of the experience (though differences were often insignificantly different, especially between SNG and SG). The main contribution of our study is in showing that the primary benefit of game-y infographic designs lies with their ability to *redistribute attention*. We see substantial evidence of this when comparing metrics such as the number of unique parameters explored, counties hovered over, and slider drags. For instance, in both SG and SE levels served as structured filters on the data, essentially directing attention to each health parameter one at a time – this led users of those conditions to be exposed to more health variables than in the SNG condition.

Game goals provide mechanisms to *emphasize objects and relationships* between objects in the game. In the case of SG the relationship between the demographic statistics and the health parameters saw more questions and insights due to the predictive power of those relationships in helping the player be successful in the game. Another example is that the random nature of the target counties in SG served to more evenly distribute hover attention around the nation by pulling users away from their natural inclination to only look at locally relevant counties. In SE, the visual representation of counties led users to interact more with larger counties since they made easier targets to acquire.

Seen from this vantage point, we have shown that *game-y infographics are a mechanism to bias attention and interaction via the goals and representations embedded in the game mechanic*. For instance, data sub-sets with known lower levels of intrinsic user interest might have a bias applied to them because they are editorially deemed to be of high importance. The downsides to redistributing attention are that it requires careful authorial thought on *how* and *where* attention should be directed, and in so doing it may focus attention on objects or relationships that overlook other subtleties of the data. Finally, the very nature of game mechanics draws attention away from data and to game elements such as score or time. In particular, we found time pressure should be avoided in order to give people the requisite time to consider data as part of the game.

Another general take-away from our evaluation is that users would appreciate more explicit messaging in the graphics to teach them known facts or pieces of knowledge about the data they are interacting with. This is perhaps unsurprising since such messaging is common in information graphics and educational games [33]. This could be accomplished with more authorial effort by pre-analyzing the dataset to add context or factoids. Another less labor intensive approach would be to integrate datasets with semantic web resources such as Freebase in order to automatically link to relevant and contextual information. At the same time, designers of such experiences should consider the tradeoffs of providing information and insights explicitly versus engendering users' production of their own ampliative abductions in connection with their interactions. While the more cut and dry experience may provide more measurable "learning", an approach to engender more divergent and creative questioning may have advantages that lie outside of traditional learning. While all games are in some sense about learning [24] data-based games have the added potential to create opportunities for personal insight.

Design Challenges and Opportunities

We presented two different game designs, one based on guessing and another based on color matching. The informed guessing mechanic was largely a success whereas the timed color matching mechanic was less effective overall. Future designs might incorporate different player interaction patterns (e.g. player vs. player), game resources (e.g. lives, currency, power-ups) and goals or mechanics (e.g. collecting, building) [20].

There is substantial room for the continued exploration of the game-y infographic design space by considering different data types and different non-map-based visual representations. Some game mechanics may be more general and adaptable to different types of data whereas others may be very specific. For instance, the nature of interacting to accomplish visual tasks with temporal, hierarchical, network, text, image, or geographic data will lead to different kinds of interactions [37] and thus game mechanics for these different data types. While this is a challenge to generalizability it is also a huge opportunity to explore a range of game mechanics that may work better or worse across data types and visual representations.

Another set of design challenges arises from the definition of games as complex systems involving objects and relationships [29]. Many games are heavily *authored* experiences involving meticulous attention to designing not only object relationships and actions that can be taken in a game, but also the *particular* constellation of objects that appear at any given stage or level. Careful authorship controls for balancing difficulty and challenge as well as enriching the *semantics* via the premise and back-story of the game. In comparison, potentially *raw data*, from which a game-y infographic can be generated, may be incomplete or inconsistent, and the structure and relationships in the data may be unknown to the game designer a priori. If the data were updated, refreshed, or otherwise dynamic it could alter such relationships, disrupt the balance or challenge, and diminish the playability of the game. The design difficulty is in abstracting the data so as to impute *meaningful* objects and relationships on an uncontrolled data source. And not only must these objects and relationships be meaningful in the context of the game, they must also be meaningful for visual analysis.

A puzzle-like design, as demonstrated in SG, seems to be a promising avenue that provides a meaningful experience and also minimizes authoring costs. With the exception of the thumbnail icons used to represent each health parameter a similarly geocoded numeric dataset could easily be substituted. On the other hand, future explorations of this design space might consider a more semantically laden game aesthetic with a premise and back-story. Bonuses or other game rewards that are meaningful in the context of the data could be given for analytic tasks accomplished (e.g. a golden syringe is awarded if the county with the highest rate of diabetes is found). More semantically imbued infographic presentations have recently been shown to be more enjoyed and to improve memorability [13]. Whereas our designs were visually framed as infographics, adding more dramatic elements may make them more playful and contribute to a stronger game aesthetic.

CONCLUSIONS

In this paper we have made strides in connecting the disparate disciplines of visual analytics and game design. We have shown that although attention deficits prevail in limiting the insights and learning potential of game-y designs, such designs can redistribute players' attentional resources in interesting ways. We have shown that game-y infographics are at least as enjoyable as a non-game version under some conditions. Most importantly we have demonstrated that the goals embedded in game-y infographics can successfully motivate interactions and cause users to explore and *bias* both the exploration of parameters and the nature of insights in interesting ways. The design space for Playable Data is immense, but represents an exciting opportunity to advance interaction science by studying how different mechanics, data types, and visual representations influence exploration. Future work should further expand the spectrum of artifacts between straight infographic and casual game to better understand how that framing impacts the experience. We hope others will join us in the investigation of this space.

REFERENCES

1. http://www.audio-surf.com/
2. http://www.communityhealth.hhs.gov/
3. http://www.countyhealthrankings.org/
4. The Economist - Videographics. http://bit.ly/c3s5W2
5. http://www.guardian.co.uk/news/datablog
6. http://en.wikipedia.org/wiki/Multi-Touch_Collaboration_Wall
7. http://www.newsbreakergame.com/
8. http://www.salubriousnation.com
9. http://playscoop.com/
10. http://quickfacts.census.gov/
11. Abt, C. *Serious Games*. The Viking Press, 1970.
12. Amar, R., Eagan, J. and Stasko, J., Low-Level Components of Analytic Activity in Information Visualization. *IEEE InfoVis*, (2005).
13. Bateman, S., Mandryk, R., Gutwin, C., Genest, A., McDine, D. and Brooks, C., Useful Junk? The Effects of Visual Embellishment on Comprehension and Memorability of Charts. *Proc. CHI*, (2010).
14. Blachowicz, J. Ampliative Abduction. *International Studies in the Philosophy of Science*, *10* (2).
15. Chen, Y., Yang, J. and Ribarsky, W., Toward Effective Insight Management in Visual Analytics Systems. *PacificVis*, (2009).
16. Diakopoulos, N., Game-y Information Graphics. *CHI Extended Abstracts*, (2010).
17. Diakopoulos, N., Luther, K. and Essa, I., Audio Puzzler: Piecing Together Time-Stamped Speech Transcripts with a Puzzle Game. *ACM Multimedia*, (2008).
18. Diakopoulos, N., Naaman, M. and Kivran-Swaine, F., Diamonds in the Rough: Social Media Visual Analytics for Journalistic Inquiry. *IEEE Conference on Visual Analytics Science and Technology (VAST)*, (2010).
19. Eccles, R., Kapler, T., Harper, R. and Wright, W., Stories in GeoTime. *IEEE Visual Analytics Science and Technology (VAST)*, (2007).
20. Fullerton, T. *Game Design Workshop*. Morgan Kaufmann, 2008.
21. Gershon, N. and Page, W. What Storytelling Can Do for Information Visualization. *Communications of the ACM*, *44* (8).
22. Jankun-Kelly, T.J., Ma, K.-L. and Gertz, M. A Model and Framework for Visualization Exploration. *IEEE Trans. on Vis. and Comp. Graphics*, 13 (2)
23. Kittur, A., Chi, E.H. and Suh, B., Crowdsourcing User Studies With Mechanical Turk. *Proc. CHI*, (2008), 453-456.
24. Koster, R. *A Theory of fun for game design*. Paraglyph, 2005.
25. Lam, H. A Framework of Interaction Costs in Information Visualization. *IEEE Trans. on Vis. and Comp. Graphics*, *14* (6).
26. O'Brien, H. and Toms, E. The Development and Evaluation of a Survey to Measure User Engagement. *JASIST*, *61* (1).
27. Pike, W., Stasko, J., Chang, R. and O'Connell, T. The science of interaction. *Information Visualization*, *8* (4).
28. Pioch, N. and Everett, J., POLESTAR: Collaborative Knowledge Management and Sensemaking Tools for Intelligence Analysts. *Proc. CIKM*, (2006).
29. Salen, K. and Zimmerman, E. *Rules of Play: Game Design Fundamentals*. The MIT Press, 2003.
30. Saraiya, P., North, C. and Duca, K. An Insight-based Methodology for Evaluating Bioinformatics Visualizations. *IEEE Trans. on Vis. and Comp. Graphics*, *11* (4).
31. Schneiderman, B., The eyes have it: a task by data type taxonomy for information visualizations. *IEEE Symposium on Visual Languages*, (1996).
32. Scholtz, J., Beyond Usability: Evaluation Aspects of Visual Analytic Environments. *IEEE Symposium on Visual Analytics Science and Technology (VAST)*, (2006).
33. Segel, E. and Heer, J. Narrative Visualization: Telling Stories with Data. *IEEE Trans. on Vis. and Comp. Graphics*, *16* (6).
34. Thomas, J. and Cook, K. (eds.). *Illuminating the Path*. IEEE, 2005.
35. Ware, C. *Visual Thinking for Design*. Morgan Kaufmann, 2008.
36. Wehrend, S. and Lewis, C., A problem-oriented classification of visualization techniques. *IEEE Visualization*, (1990).
37. Yi, J.S., ah Kang, Y., Stasko, J. and Jacko, J. Toward a Deeper Understanding of the Role of Interaction in Information Visualization. *IEEE Trans. on Vis. and Comp. Graphics*, *13* (6).
38. Zhou, M. and Feiner, S., Visual Task Characterization for Automated Visual Discourse Synthesis. *Proc. CHI*, (1998).

Cardiogram: Visual Analytics for Automotive Engineers

Michael Sedlmair[1], Petra Isenberg[2], Dominikus Baur[3], Michael Mauerer[3], Christian Pigorsch[4], Andreas Butz[3]

[1]University of British Columbia, Vancouver, BC, Canada
[2]INRIA, Paris, France
[3]University of Munich, Munich, Germany
[4]BMW Group, Munich, Germany

msedl@cs.ubc.ca, petra.isenberg@inria.fr, dominikus.baur@ifi.lmu.de, michael.mauerer@cip.ifi.lmu.de, christian.pigorsch@bmw.de, butz@ifi.lmu.de

ABSTRACT
We present Cardiogram, a visual analytics system that supports automotive engineers in debugging masses of traces each consisting of millions of recorded messages from in-car communication networks. With their increasing complexity, ensuring these safety-critical networks to be error-free has become a major task and challenge for automotive engineers. To overcome shortcomings of current analysis tools, Cardiogram combines visualization techniques with a data preprocessing approach to automatically reduce complexity based on engineers' domain knowledge. In this paper, we provide the findings from an exploratory, three-year field study within a large automotive company, studying current practices of engineers, the challenges they meet and the characteristics for integrating novel visual analytics tools into their work practices. We then introduce Cardiogram, discuss how our field analysis influenced our design decisions, and present a qualitative, long-term, in-depth evaluation. Results of this study showed that our participants successfully used Cardiogram to increase the amount of analyzable information, to externalize domain knowledge, and to provide new insights into trace data. Our design approach finally led to the adoption of Cardiogram into engineers' daily practices.

Author Keywords
Visual Analytics, Visualization, Automotive

ACM Classification Keywords
H.5.0 Information Interfaces and Presentation[General]

General Terms
Design

INTRODUCTION
The field of visual analytics (VA) is continuously growing with research efforts expanding into many different domains. Visual analytics tools address the challenge of analyzing overwhelming amounts of data by combining methods from various disciplines, including information visualization (InfoVis), HCI and data analysis techniques from statistics, data mining, and others [36]. One very crucial aspect for the future of VA is to bridge the gap from research to application as the success of the field may eventually be measured by how many people will actively be using solutions in their everyday work [5]. Thus, InfoVis and VA researchers have increasingly called for more rich descriptions of novel problem domains for visual analytics and for design studies in these areas [4, 13, 14, 22] in order to gain a better understanding of everyday data analysis practices across different domains.

The research we present in this paper follows this call. We present the results of a three-year research endeavor (6 researchers / approx. 7 man-years) with the goal to develop, connect, and integrate visual analytics tools directly within an industrial work context. We worked closely with domain experts in a large automotive company to support data analysis challenges encountered during the debugging of sensor networks in modern automobiles and provided them with several solutions for their everyday work. In order to ensure that our tools would meet the requirements of the industrial work context, we engaged in a long-term problem characterization phase [13, 22], designed and tested various prototype and tool designs, and finally adopted and integrated some of them into the engineers' daily working practices. The largest of these tools, Cardiogram, is the focus of this paper.

Our work in the visual analytics domain makes three primary contributions: We first discuss our in-depth understanding from a three-year exploratory field analysis. Second, we introduce Cardiogram, a novel tool for the analysis of in-car communication traces. Cardiogram was built based on our rich understanding gathered from the field analysis and developed in close cooperation with domain experts. We discuss how we integrated the tool in the industrial work context and present the results of a qualitative, long-term, in-depth user study which showed various benefits extending current working practices of engineers. Finally, we review our experience from the domain-specific aspects of the project and discuss design decisions that led to our successful integration of visual analytics tools in a large industrial context.

While described characteristics of our application domain are meant to guide practitioners and developers in the same or similar domains, the description of our process may prove to be useful for visual analytics practitioners in many areas who wish to form closer connections to industrial partners.

CHI 2011, May 7–12, 2011, Vancouver, BC, Canada.

INDUSTRIAL BACKGROUND

Our work is situated in the domain of automotive engineering where we worked with engineers involved in the development of sensor networks in cars. An in-car sensor network consists of sensors which send information such as the vehicle's speed, actuators translating electronic information into mechanical behavior, and electronic control units (ECUs) that compute this data. Over the last years, the concentration of electronic and software components in automobiles has increased enormously resulting in highly complex in-car networks. Current networks consist of up to 100 ECUs and 300 sensors/actuators, all interconnected via several, heterogenous bus technologies (CAN, FlexRay, MOST, LIN, Ethernet) [1]. This increasing complexity has brought a variety of novel challenges such as intricate error diagnosis and recovery to automotive engineers [3, 8, 25]. ECUs of high-performance cars, for example, can deliver information at speeds of more than 1,000 readings per second over the in-car network and use this information to trigger specific actions. In the case of an airbag, for example, accelerometers send information to a microprocessor at 10ms or faster intervals and the evaluation of this data determines whether and how to inflate the airbag [1]. Transporting all relevant information typically results in more than 15,000 messages per second distributed over the network.

To verify the correctness of sensor networks, engineers log network messages via specific hardware that is installed in test cars. A one-hour log file typically consists of several GB of data with up to 50 million recorded messages. In the case an error has been occurred in a test drive, our target users' task is to inspect the log files and to identify the error source. Time and experience is needed to understand in-car communication processes and to detect sources of errors in the networks and their complex correlations. In addition, analysts cannot rely on simulations for error detection as errors are often caused by hardware or external factors. Therefore, log files are currently the only lead. These data related challenges make this work domain a prime candidate for dedicated visual analytics tools. Providing effective tools for the analysis of this data is of highest importance as the safety of the automobile and its passengers hinges on the ability of automotive engineers to understand and debug this sensor data.

RELATED WORK

We review related work of previous rich domain studies in information visualization and visual analytics and on usage of visualization in automotive engineering.

End User Integration in Visual Analytics

Recently, information visualization researchers have explicitly called for a closer integration of end-users in InfoVis/VA tool development and for the dissemination of qualitative reports on data analysis practices in real-life work contexts to ground both design and/or subsequent evaluation [4, 13, 14, 22]. Indeed, more and more InfoVis/VA projects focus on solutions for real-world, data-intensive application domains and integrate users into their development processes. Two recent examples incude a visual analytics tool for patent specialists [18] and a financial data analysis tool [35]. In our work, we used ethnographic field analysis of current practices to richly inform the design of our systems. The need to base system design on an in-depth understanding of a domain has been understood in HCI for a long time [34], and recently has also been more and more addressed by InfoVis/VA research: Tory et al. [37], for instance, conducted a qualitative analysis in the building design field, Isenberg et al. [12] studied the work of traditional collaborative data analysis, McLachlan et al. [20] worked together with system management professionals, Meyer et al. [21] with gene expression biologists, or Kincaid with oscilloscope users [17]. None of these studies so far, however, have been conducted within a large industrial setting or in our application domain.

Visualization in the Automotive Domain

Visualization in the automotive domain is most commonly used in the context of computer-aided-design, virtual reality, and scientific visualization [33]. Within scientific visualization, many techniques have focused on the analysis of physically-based (often simulated) data, such as the flow of particles for car body development [26]. Such techniques have also been integrated with information visualizations such as scatterplots and histograms for the analysis of, for example, a Diesel exhaust system [6]. While some of the scientific visualization work (e. g., [19]) shows increasing interest in integrating information visualization, considerably less work has been dedicated to the support of *electronic* engineering for car development and testing. In our own previous work, we presented several prototypes for visualizing in-car communication networks [27, 28, 30]. These systems were standalone point-solutions for specific analysis challenges and helped us to explore the design space. In this paper, we build on this work and present extended insights, a novel, fully integrated solution and its in-depth evaluation.

METHODOLOGY

We followed a general development cycle including stages of pre-design analysis, prototyping, development, and testing. Our methodology was chosen based on two main objectives: (1) Learning about the field including current practices, problems and challenges, and (2) learning about our tool and how to design and integrate it successfully in our target domain. For this purpose, we primarily focused on working closely with experts in our target domain. Both the complexity of data and analysis tasks as well as the time-constraints of the industrial work context influenced the study methods we chose and how we adopted them to these specific requirements. In spirit, our approach is similar to MILCs [32] (Multi-dimensional In-depth Long-term Case Studies) as advocated previously for information visualization for addressing the specific needs of this domain with its complex, exploratory and ill-defined tasks. Similar to the traditional MILC approach, we used a *multi-dimensional* set of study methods, and carried out *in-depth* and *long-term* investigations over a period of three years. We studied the data analysis practices of a large number of 50 expert analysts using both, their own, currently used tools and our novel tools, and did not focus on studying any tool in particular. We, thus, conducted an "ambitious" MILC as proposed for future work in [32]. Reflecting the typical structure of our target users, approx. 90% of the analysts we worked with were male and had been working in the problem domain for 2–16 years.

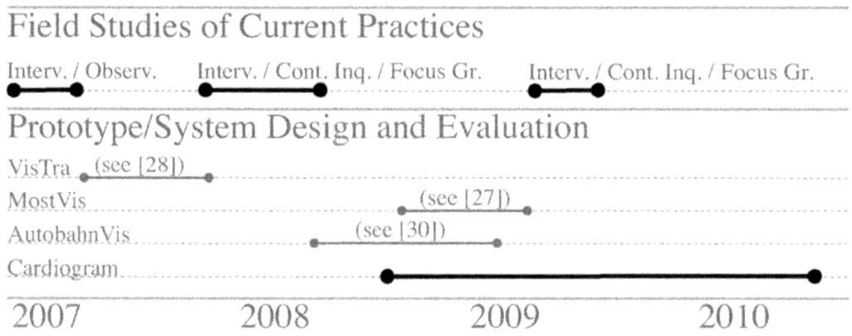

Figure 1: Overview of our development process. Black lines indicate work reported on here. Gray lines indicate phases reported on earlier.

In the following, we describe the various methods we used for studying current practices for introducing VA in our domain. We also briefly reflect on our objectives and experience using these methods for InfoVis/VA in a large company setting in order to provide other researchers with guidance for such undertakings; for a detailed description of our experience with specific evaluation requirements in large company settings we refer the reader to [29]. Our study is among one of the first in-depth endeavors of studying the complex pattern of data analysis using long-term MILCs. The time investment of three years was substantial but essential to our success later. Figure 1 provides a temporal overview of our studies as well as the different participatory tool design and evaluation phases in which we closely cooperated with our target users.

Field Studies of Current Practices

Interviews: Especially early on, we relied on semi-structured interviews to gain insights into aspects beyond what we could derive from technical documentation. Interviews provided us with a rough understanding of work practices, and showed engineers' estimations on challenges and problems as well as their ideas and approaches to overcome them. Overall, we conducted 30 1h-long interviews with both, analysts and analysis tool designers. From our notes and recordings we derived main categories of tasks and analysis challenges.

User Observation and Contextual Inquiries: In order to collect more real-life data of our experts' work practices, we started observational studies with a fly-on-the-wall technique in which we followed but did not interfere with the daily practices of the engineers. However, due to task complexity and high expertise in our domain it was not possible for a non-domain-expert to derive meaningful results through observation alone. Therefore, we chose to use contextual inquiries [11] instead which we conducted with 14 analysts (11 previously participated in interviews) in up to five 1h-long sessions per participant. Due to IPR restrictions, we solely used note-taking for data logging purposes. We used 2–3 note takers to counterbalance the lack of recording equipment. We used these results to broaden our understanding of the diversity of working practices in our domain and to verify or refute our prior findings.

Focus Groups: To evaluate, improve, and focus our findings from interviews and user observations we conducted 17 focus groups of 3–10 participants. We chose focus groups because we frequently encountered diverse and even opposed practices and statements during individual interviews. Our major goal in bringing experts together was, therefore, to form a common understanding—not just between the end users and us but also among the end users themselves. The groups consisted of varying groups of analysts, tool designers and we also invited decision makers. The latter are an important group to address in large company settings as they usually decide whether a novel solution will be integrated and funded or not. As our goal was to reach adoption of our solutions, we decided to integrate decision makers early in the process and this turned out to be essential to our success.

Participatory Design and Tool Evaluation

We augmented the methods used above with a tight collaboration with end users during the design and evaluation of our own VA tools. Both lessons learned from our previous tools but also of Cardiogram itself helped us gain additional insights into applying VA in our domain and specific challenges for VA tools and their integration into the end users' work environment. Our long-term process was, therefore, an iterative mix of current-practice field studies, tool design and tool evaluation—each of them informing another by providing us but also our end users with new insights (cf. Figure 1). For designing and evaluating our tools, including Cardiogram, we used the following methods:

Design Workshops and Personal Feedback: We designed our tools in close cooperation with end users applying a participatory design approach [16]. During several exploratory design workshops we introduced engineers to visual analytics techniques, discussed ideas, and fine-tuned possible solutions (system designs, features, etc.), and finally developed a basic concept. Next, we started developing interactive tools and provided a group of carefully chosen test engineers with frequent iterative releases and elicited feedback in personal meetings. In the case of Cardiogram, we used three different paper prototypes to evaluate early ideas, and a high-fidelity prototype before we came up with the final system presented in this paper. In doing so, we excluded alternative representation techniques and fine-tuned our approach of automatic data preprocessing (see below). A similar approach has been previously lead to success in the data analysis domain [20].

Think Aloud Protocols, Lab Studies and Field Studies: To evaluate the domain value of our tools we used both lab as well as field studies. We studied our early systems using think-aloud protocols and lab studies, investigating domain experts using our tools in artificial lab settings. While we received valuable feedback about the potentials and improvements of our tools, we did not gain insight into their usage under real-world conditions (cf. [23]). A major hindrance to gaining real-world insight on tool use was the missing close integration of our tools into current systems already in use at the company [29]. We report on how this hindrance was overcome with Cardiogram in later sections.

Informal Collaboration

Besides our formal studies, we found it invaluable for our successful integration to engage in frequent informal conversations with engineers. These conversations were, for instance, meetings at the company's cafeteria, a joint lunch, or casual discussions at the workplace. We improved our understanding of the various facets of our target domain, iteratively refined our requirements for visual analytics tools, and established successful collaborations. A drawback of informal conversations, however, is the restricted opportunity to log data for scientific rigor. In order to allow for some direct data collection we always carried notepads in case spontaneous conversations would occur. Over the three year period we collected information from roughly 80 of these spontaneous encounters, with approx. 50 different engineers.

UNDERSTANDING DATA, TASKS, AND TOOLS

In the following, we summarize the understanding we gained of our domain and its data analysis challenges by using this variety of study methods. We organize our results by task, data, current data analysis tools, and a more detailed description of practices and challenges—all of them relevant parameters for designing visual analytics tools in this domain. It is meant both as such a description to enlighten our general understanding of real-life data analysis but also as a guide to practitioners in the field. Eventually, the results of our field analysis also yielded a fundamental source for deriving the design implications we present in the 'Discussion' part.

Main Task

The main task of the automotive engineers we studied was *finding errors in in-car sensor network communication* with the goal to verify a vehicle series safety, security, and functionality. For this purpose, 1.5 years before start of production the car manufacturer produces a test vehicle fleet of about 150 test vehicles. These vehicles are driven either by specialized test drivers or by the analysis engineers themselves in order to verify the correctness of in-car networks both in ordinary as well as extreme real-world driving situations. Each test vehicle is equipped with specific hardware recording messages transported on the network. This information together with a verbal or written error report is then transferred to the analysis experts of our target group. If an error has been detected during a test drive, it is the task of the analysis engineer to locate the error source by analyzing the recorded traces (see below) and to initiate further steps to solve the problem.

Data

All communication information logged during a test drive is stored in large text files called *traces*—a temporally ordered list of all messages enriched with entries for errors that either had been automatically detected and set (e. g., pre-specified error conditions in ECU specifications) or manually annotated (e. g., pressing an "error buzzer" in the test car & manual log annotation later). Traces can get tremendously large with the duration of a test drive and the amount of logged subcomponents (state of the art: approx. 50 million messages/hour for the entire network). These traces come in different formats (depending on the recording hardware used) and are not necessarily complete (e. g., in case of failure of recording hardware). In order to handle the enormous size of traces, engineers use *journals*—as specific, pre-filtered formats to reduce trace data to a few specific message types such as error frames or fault memory entries—and manually add information such as markers, triggers or predefined events.

Current Tools

To analyze trace files, several special-purpose analysis tools were in use by our engineers. The most important ones are an in-house tool called *Carmen* as well as the commercial tool *Canalyzer* (the functionality of these tools is very similar, for a state-of-the-art function description see [38]). Both of them were considered most relevant and powerful due to their scalability and compatibility to various data formats, and the wide availability of special-purpose plugins and data interpreters. Both tools are based on the combination of different digital modules that allow an individual configuration of a tailored measuring setup. Available modules include those for data loading, interpretation, filtering, or visual representation. Typical representation modules can show dynamically interpreted lists of messages, temporal signal plots, or rudimentary overviews. To analyze traces, our experts often used one or several of these tools in combination with general-purpose tools such as text editors.

Data Analysis: Practices, Problems and Challenges

Engineers typically spent their error analysis switching between data foraging and sense-making activities [36]. Using their analysis tools they typically attempted to (a) derive a hypothesis, (b) iteratively refine the hypothesis, or (c) dismiss the hypothesis and start anew. Based on their initial hypothesis, the analysts took different approaches to finding an error. If a clear hypothesis about the error source existed, engineers commonly started to check interpreted or even raw values directly. If the hypothesis was not solid from the beginning, the error description was rather vague or if the error source was estimated to be more complex, our participants preferably started with an overview using journals and then iteratively filtered and analyzed interpreted message lists and signal plots. A main difference to regular software debugging was the inability to reproduce errors through experimentation as there is (currently) no opportunity for analysts to directly change the software of ECUs or sending additional messages to bus systems: their only means of discovering the sources were traces and journals from test runs.

Our studies showed that engineers had to track errors of varying degrees of complexity which tremendously influenced the process of finding these errors in terms of processing time, costs, and engineers involved. Simple errors outnumbered complex errors but finding and solving complex errors was often a tedious, lengthy and highly collaborative undertaking. One engineer commented *"I can track down a simple error in several minutes, but solving a complex problem can take weeks or even months"* (quote from a contextual interview, translated from German). In close cooperation with engineers we identified three main origins of complexity:

Traceability: Finding the actual source of an error proved difficult due to external circumstances such as temperature, extreme driving situations, or incorrectly specified error conditions. For example: After ending a test run, our engineers detected that all car windows would open unexpectedly. Engineers spent several weeks analyzing and trying to reproduce this error. The actual reason was a specific test case in which all four doors were simultaneously slammed shut which activated an overpressure sensor that opened the windows.

Dispersion: Many highly distributed and inter-related hard- and software systems exist in a vehicle and errors often propagate over several systems before they are automatically detected and logged. The interplay between two or more intrinsically and separately correct subsystems can lead to complex, unpredictable errors. The more dispersed errors or involved systems are, the higher the chance that they might be complex. This is also true for the above example where the actual reason was not located in the window system but in the accident security system.

Degree of trace preparation: Not every bus system or recording hardware supports journals to reduce and abstract the recorded data. Without any abstraction it can become complex and laborious to analyze message traces especially when exact error timings are not available, for example for manually recorded errors. Additionally, engineers have to be aware of the fact that measurement hardware can be the source of errors and inaccuracies in the data.

As a result of these complexities, our engineers relied on an array of different tools. Along with Carmen and Canalyzer, one engineer used another 12 tools during a 1h analysis session. He liked all his tools but was burdened by the additional work of switching between them: *"Analyzing alone is a complex task, but handling the entire overhead of using so many incoherent tools is overkill [...] each tool is a valuable part of my work but they are not well coordinated and integrated, this means a lot of additional, redundant work to me [...]"*.

CARDIOGRAM

In the following, we introduce Cardiogram, a novel tool we designed based on our current-practice field studies and on the lessons learned from our previous endeavors [27, 28, 30]. We integrated the tool into daily practices of our target users and tested it under real working conditions.

Data Analysis Requirements

The main analytics objective of Cardiogram was twofold: (a) supporting engineers in handling the masses of trace data and (b) providing new insights into temporal, logical, and behavioral aspects within the data.

1. Handling the masses of data: In our studies, we found that handling the masses of trace data is a huge practical problem. While data storage is no longer a pressing problem, analyzing all relevant data in detail is nearly impossible for engineers. In collaboration with our target users, we derived two requirements to encounter this challenge. First, *automated filtering of data* might be helpful as often only a very small subset of the data is involved in the error finding process. The reduced data can then be used as input for traditional and novel representation techniques. Second, *support for automated error detection* is required and was frequently requested by our engineers. Automatic error detection would help our target users to reduce the amount of traces to analyze but also to quickly inform initial hypotheses about errors.

2. Providing new insights: Our study also revealed that most current data representations were based on lists and simple signal-value plots. Beyond the capabilities of these tools, engineers needed to analyze timing aspects and message propagation, detect outliers and see correlation between messages and mechanical behavior. In particular, engineers needed visual support for *correlating the temporal and the logical layer* of trace messages to better understand the influence of message timing and physical behavior, and vice versa. Current techniques could not support this requirement. In addition, *novel overview* and *data abstraction techniques* are required to support better understanding of comprehensive correlations and functional dependencies in the data. Journals (see above) are a rudimentary approach for this requirement, but often

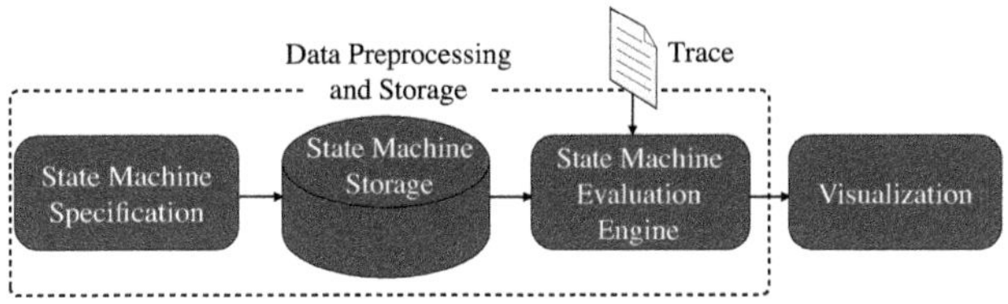

Figure 2: Workflow and components of Cardiogram.

they are not available depending on the used recording hard- and software, and—when available—are restricted to a very high level view onto traces. However, understanding comprehensive aspects on various levels of traces is essential for the detection of complex errors but as we saw, extremely difficult to retrieve directly from raw data or journals.

Design

Based on these requirements, we designed Cardiogram as two major software components: (1) A *Data Preprocessing and Storage Component* for automatic data filtering, error detection and data abstraction and (2) a *Visualization Component* for overviews of data preparation results and for gaining insight into correlations between time and logic. In terms of the sensemaking loop [36], the first component was meant to mainly aid in data foraging activities, while the visualization component was meant mainly for sense-making activities; together they allowed the engineers to switch between different activities involved in sense-making and to derive solutions to their analysis questions. Figure 2 gives an overview of the workflow in Cardiogram and shows the two basic components and its subcomponents. In the following, we describe these components in more detail:

Data Preprocessing and Storage:

This unit is responsible for the automatic preparation, abstraction and filtering of traces. To realize this, we used a model-based analysis approach utilizing state machines which was suggested for automotive system testing [2]. Our approach of using state machines for testing purposes allows for (a) reusing knowledge from software design processes, (b) specifying models for complex test cases, and (c) for automatically running these models. Our Data Preprocessing and Storage Component is made up of three subcomponents:

State Machine Specification: In order to make semantic trace interpretations automatically testable, we provide engineers with the opportunity to specify vehicle behavior in state machines. To do so, they can use a textual or a graphical editor, including an Eclipse plugin we designed, to define a set of logical vehicle states such as *"window front left open"*, transitions between states such as *"open window"*, and what events in a trace result in which transitions, e. g., *"message xy opens window"*. To test predefined conditions, each state can be additionally annotated as *error*, *warning*, or *okay*. Two main kinds of state machine designs can be specified: Verification State Machines and Context Information State Machines. Verification State Machines test a predefined situation, e. g., if a specific error condition is met or not. Context Information State Machines are more general and represent generic vehicle information such as mechanical activities (e. g., monitoring window opening) or ECU behavior. In the following, we refer to both simply as state machines.

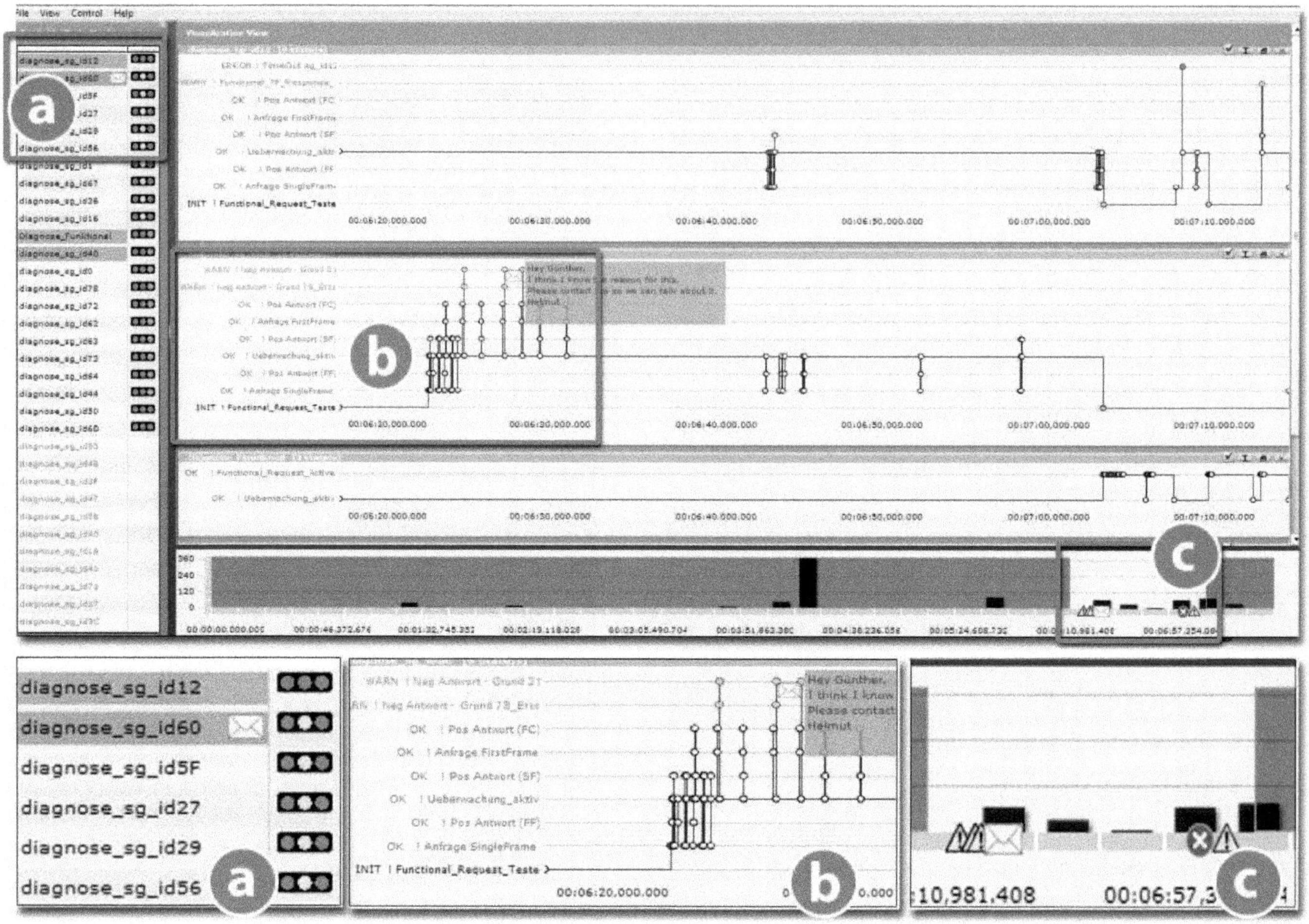

Figure 3: Screenshot of Cardiogram Visualization: (a) State Machine View showing all tested state machines ordered by relevance for bugfixing; (b) Visualization View with several detailed state/time plots showing transitions via vertical and horizontal lines and additional glyphs at target states; (c) a combined range slider/ overview bar showing the sum of all transitions within discrete time intervals.

State Machine Storage: Our target user group is located in a large company setting where thousands of employees work on highly specified tasks. To form a greater understanding based on individual expertise and to master comprehensive data analysis challenges, collaboration is indispensable. In a next step, we therefore opted for a central storage of the state machines and their descriptions in a database using a common XML format. This approach was targeted specifically at complex error analysis. By making descriptions available to all engineers they can avoid repetitive and redundant work. Previously, engineers had to spend considerable time converting data manually using different import/export formats and they specifically requested a new approach which would alleviate this burden.

State Machine Evaluation Engine: This automatic trace preprocessing unit is the heart of Cardiogram and supports the analysts by loading specific state machines, importing traces, and testing these traces with the specified state machines. Using all loaded state machines, the State Machine Evaluation Engine queries over one or more traces, identifies all occurrences of predefined transition patterns, and stores them to a temporal ordered list of transitions (similar to temporal data analysis techniques such as PatternFinder [7]). For each analyzed state machine, an additional global tag, called *aggregated state machine result*, indicates the occurrences of *error* and *warning* states which can be used for later analysis. The engine thus reduces and pre-processes the data to filtered and interpreted version of the trace(s) at hand—filtered and interpreted by the vehicle behavior the engineers had specified in state machines before. This step makes novel overview techniques possible which were particularly missing from previous tools but crucial for complex error detection.

Visualization:

The main purpose of Cardiogram's visualization (cf. Figure 3) is to support the exploration of errors, warnings, or other hints which may require further inspection because they cannot be automatically detected. In such situations, Cardiogram visualizes all state transitions of all tested state machines and helps to provide insight into incorrect vehicle states and into timing correlations between state machines, i. e., between specified vehicle behavior. Together with the three data preparation steps presented above, this visualization allows engineers to gain a novel perspective on complex dependencies of in-car networks and correlate logical with timing aspects.

Cardiogram's visualization is centered around a zoomable timeline, multiple coordinated views, and the use of consistent representation and interaction techniques. Our solution was inspired by work on previous trace visualization design studies (most importantly [10] and [24]). Similar to these solutions we chose to focus on the temporal aspect of trace data. The general setup of the visualization consists of three views, (1) the State Machine View providing an overview over all tested state machines, (2) the Visualization View allowing for investigating the timing of transitions, and (3) a Navigation/Overview Bar at the bottom.

The design of the visualization was driven by several needs uncovered during the field evaluation period:

Prioritization: The *State Machine View* (Figure 3-a) lists all state machines tested on a specific trace. It provides the contextual overview which previous tools were lacking. As requested by our target group, this list is sorted according to priority based on aggregated state machine results (first those with at least one *error* state, then the ones with at least one *warning*, etc.).

Familiarity and Fast Access: Even though our target group of engineers did not have the same academic or work background, we found that several different types of network visualizations, charts, and diagrams were in use amongst them and familiar to all. In order to support the interchange and collaboration between these engineers we decided to make use of elements from these familiar representations. We used commonly used traffic light icons next to each state machine entry in the State Machine View (Figure 3-a) to encode the aggregated state machine outcomes *error*, *warning*, *okay* using the colors red, yellow, green, and no color coding for other outcomes. By selecting a state machine from the State Machine View a similarly familiar state/time plot is shown in the Visualization View showing all transitions of this state machine according to its transition table (Figure 3-b and context). Detailed information about transitions can be retrieved by zooming in and/or hovering the mouse pointer over these dots. Note that by zooming also nearly time-equivalent transitions—appearing as vertical lines in the overview—can be resolved to their correct temporal order. Fast access to the underlying trace file is given by an integrated backlink to a traditional list presentation of the trace. Engineers were used to working with hexadecimals and regularly had to check single bytes and bits during their work. For them, raw data must always be ready at hand in order to immediately prove or discard hypotheses based on raw values. "Fast access to raw data" was one of our most requested requirements.

Time Reduction: In addition to allowing the user temporal navigation, the navigation/overview bar at the bottom of the visualization provides an overview over all transitions of selected state machines (Figure 3-c). According to a time slot size pre-defined by the user, transitions of selected state machines are subsumed and bars are added which encode the overall number of transitions in a time slot. This provides an abstracted indication about busy, calm, steady and void areas. Changes into *error* and *warning* states are indicated not only with red and yellow dots in time/state plots but also with accordingly colored, domain specific symbols (see "familiarity" above) in the overview bar. This supports fast readability of transitions and can be relevant for bugfixing.

Collaboration: Interactive annotation of the data is also supported. Each analyst can freely attach colored notes directly into a state/time plot as was done in area (b) of Figure 3. Once an annotation is set, it is displayed at the exact timestamp and state it was created at. Symbols for notes are also shown in the state machine list and in the overview bar where they indicate the position within the global timeline. These annotations can be exported together with the data and sent to a colleague for further inspection or inquiry. This supports the collaborative requirements of the large company context and helps engineers to avoid repetitive work.

Convenience Features: Based on engineers' requests during our user-centered design process, we integrated a variety of other interactive features, including: keyboard shortcuts for all features (based on familiar tools), unrestricted vertical scaling of state machine plots to provide additional overviews, minimization and closing of state machine plots, drag&drop positioning of the state machine plots and state lines to allow side-by-side comparison and new perspectives on the data, dynamic adding or subtractions of state machines to or from the overview bar, and the free configuration of nearly all system features and settings.

Integration

We spent considerable effort to closely integrate our modules with a comprehensive in-house analysis software environment, Carmen, which supports valuable back-end features such as data storage, interpretation, filtering and traditional views (e. g., message lists). During our current-practice analysis we found that many of the tools used by engineers were already integrated into this platform and therefore were powerful in terms of flexibility, compatibility, scalability, and in providing specific features for specific problems. Re-implementing all of these features for our tool would not have been possible within realistic time and budget requirements. Instead, we opted for a closely integrated solution which could be immediately used by engineers in the context of their familiar work environments and would allow them to take advantage of already supported data formats, and be combined with conventional solutions without any extra costs. Using this approach, Cardiogram has achieved wide use by our target users as unnecessary data conversions and repetitive tasks to use our tool were avoided. Integrating Cardiogram with Carmen, on the other hand, also helped us to study it under realistic conditions.

CARDIOGRAM EVALUATION

We evaluated Cardiogram in a long-term, qualitative study with expert test users rather than using quantitative measures and statistical analysis that fail to provide insights into the exploratory nature of analysis tasks [4, 23, 32]. Analysis of Cardiogram was conducted in two phases for (1) the data preprocessing and storage and (2) the visualization component. To test our novel automation and abstraction approach using state machine data preparation, we first implemented the state machine editor, database and evaluation engine (cf. Data Preprocessing and Storage components in Figure 2) and integrated it as a module in Carmen. Together with a textual representation of statistical results (number of errors/warnings occurred) and transition lists—similar to current trace practices of engineers—for detailed inspection on demand. This approach was validated in a 12-month field study with 15 domain experts—which is comparatively long by visual analytics standards. Over these 12 months, experts used the tool during their daily activities, created state machines on their own, and included the tool in their data analysis procedure. The usage length of such a single, situational session varied from several minutes up to three hours. During bi-weekly meetings with these experts we discussed their experiences with our tool and elicited feedback on their benefits and areas for improvement. As a second step, we qualitatively evaluated the Cardiogram visualization with six domain experts during a one-hour session in which they used the visualization on their own data and/or on test data sets we provided. Additionally, we received feedback from two test users who used Cardiogram for an eight week period. The results of the study uncovered several main categories of benefits for our new approach which aided in adoption and acceptance of the tool:

Results of Evaluating the Data Preprocessing Approach

Externalization of Expert Knowledge: Analysis experts created state machines to capture their expertise for verification and abstraction of complex behavior. Many of the state machines were specified to reproduce highly distributed procedures such as booting a car, starting the motor, or shutting down the vehicle. These state machines included up to 25 different states as well as clusters of sub-state machines. Each state in turn abstracted up to 15 signals in order to form combined and interpreted information about specific vehicle behavior. Externalizing this knowledge into state machines made it widely available for other engineers who benefited even without specific knowledge about this particular behavior.

Mass Analysis Instead of Sample-Tests: Our abstraction and automation techniques facilitated a broad analysis of a great number of traces. One engineer used the core components to automatically analyze 12,000 traces with 50,000 messages on average within one day. Based on the global result tags of state machines, he could isolate three important traces which he examined in more depth to verify a specific hypothesis. Previously, testing of this data relied on analyzing and debugging samples of the data, our approach however allowed the analysis of hundreds to tens of thousands of traces, and to test or verify hypotheses on a broad testing basis.

Results of Evaluating the Visualization

Correlation Between State Machines: All of our participants stated that the Cardiogram visualization was enormously helpful to understand and explore correlations between dependent state machines. For example, we saw the Cardiogram visualization being used to explore several parallel procedures involved in shutting down a car. Correct shutdowns are of high importance as errors can lead to high consumption of electricity and load on the car's battery. Shutting down a car first involves the shutdown of all relevant subsystems. One of our participants used a set of 12 state machines together with our visualization and verified the shut-down behavior of all sub-systems as well as that of the entire car. Using the visualization allowed him to compare timings, to verify correctness of temporal order, and to correlate the transitions of the state machines. This in-depth analysis was not possible previously or with the core components alone.

Trace-Related Overview of State Machine Activities: Four of our participants mentioned that the Cardiogram visualization provided a good overview over all trace-related, logical, and temporal activities. The list of all state machines showed valuable information to them on which tests had been conducted and whether they had been successful or erroneous. Freely selecting, combining, and repositioning of state machines helped them to further explore erroneous state machines and to derive correlations between them. Additionally, three participants mentioned that when zooming out, the time line provided a valuable overview over a state machine's global activities and helped to quickly detect transition peaks.

Verification and Re-Engineering of State Machines: Two of our participants used the Cardiogram visualization to verify state machines currently under construction. Loading these state machines together with a known test trace helped them to validate the correctness of transitions and to estimate possible interaction with other state machines.

Summary of Results

In summary, the analysis of the Cardiogram core components and visualization showed that the tool successfully supported the engineer's analysis requirements and addressed known challenges, most importantly it provided novel overviews and abstractions of the data, semi-automated analysis and collaborative features and, thus, allowed the engineers to avoid repetitive work. Cardiogram's abstraction and automation techniques were valuable tools for reducing and preprocessing the data and Cardiogram's visualization allowed for the analysis of comprehensive and global aspects. At the time of writing, the tool has spread within the company and is now used by more than 30 engineers on a daily and weekly basis. We recently transferred our software to the Carmen tool developers who are now extending our solutions. Extensions will include: fine-tunig of some visual encodings (e. g., larger symbols for errors and warnings in state/time plots), increasing the scalability of the visualization component (currently it can handle files with up to 100.000 transitions), and direct embedding of the tool into Carmen's core components.

DISCUSSION: RECOMMENDATIONS AND ADOPTION

While working with our domain experts and on Cardiogram we gained an in-depth understanding of the field and its visual analytics requirements. In particular, we uncovered several recommendations for developing visual analytics tools in this domain and gained insight into making them accepted and used with experts who may have had no previous experience with visual analytics tools. In the following we summarize both, the design implications that we have derived from our exploratory field analysis and from Cardiograms's design and evaluation, as well as the main aspects that we think have led to the successful adoption of Cardiogram. Some of these aspects have also been shown in other papers and domains and therefore underline their general importance (we cite some below). Others are more unique and specific for our domain. In the following we list all findings in order to provide clear and comprehensive guidance for other VA researchers in this or similar areas.

Design Implications

The following recommendations were collected for and used in the design of Cardiogram.

New Perspectives on Complex Errors: The detection of complex errors required dedicated data representations to show correlations between error sources. In particular, we uncovered a need for:

Visual overview techniques: to allow for better analysis of traces without journals and gaining insight into comprehensive aspects along traces (see also, e. g., [31]).
Perspectives beyond raw data and signal plots: No current technique supported the analysis of timings, the detection of outliers, correlations between messages, mechanical behavior, electronic data, and message propagation. Especially understanding correlations between the temporal (when has a message been sent) and the logical layer (who sent it, who received it, what software components were involved, etc.) was highly important for engineers. Not properly supported yet, all these aspects are invaluable to get a profound understanding about a trace and eventually to detect errors.
Multiple, modular, and coordinated solutions: Our group of engineers required multiple different perspectives on the data to detect complex errors (see also, e. g., [9]). Which perspectives were most relevant relied on an engineer's knowledge, preferences, as well as the underlying problem. Therefore, an unrestricted and modular combination of perspectives is instrumental. Perspectives should support coordination over time and data linking according to known techniques, but also the opportunity to work without coordination (e.g., for comparing behavior at different time stamps).
Fast access to raw data: Engineers were used to working with hexadecimals and regularly checked single bytes and bits during their work. Fast access to the familiar raw data representation to check, prove, or discard hypotheses on the sources of errors was of highest importance for them.

Handling the Masses of Data: Handling the masses of data produced in automobile testing is a huge practical challenge (see also [15]). The following approaches were successfully applied by us in Cardiogram:

Data abstraction and automated filtering: Understanding comprehensive aspects in traces is essential for complex error detection but difficult to retrieve directly from raw data. Novel data abstraction techniques were required for reproducing behavioral aspects, comprehensive correlations and functional dependencies in the data.
Support for automated error detection: Current analysis procedures rely on sample testing and a lot of recorded traces are never analyzed. Automation of this process helped engineers (a) to rapidly test a set of hypotheses, (b) to speed up the detection of common errors, and (c) to allow analyzing much more data than is achievable via manual inspection.
Avoid repetitive work and unnecessary iterations: Due to the size and complexity of recorded trace data, engineers used a large array of tools that each only supported parts of the analysis. Converting data manually is tedious and annoying and hinders the acceptance of novel solutions.

Engineer-centered Solutions: Our understanding of the work environment helped us to design solutions which closely matched the work process of our engineers.
Familiarity: Our target users had a broad background and knowledge of various data representation techniques, most importantly statistical graphics such as line plots. Supporting these well-known mental models helped to support communication with and between engineers and increasing the acceptance of new tools.
Support collaboration: Our target group was located in a large company setting with thousands of specialized employees. To form a greater understanding based on individual expertise and to master comprehensive challenges collaboration is indispensable and, therefore, should be actively supported in data analysis tools.

Adoption

Overall, the recommendations from our exploratory field analysis together with a user-centered design process helped us to design a tool that found its way into everyday routines of our analysis experts. We learned that the core ingredients to a successful deployment of our visual analytics technique in this industrial setting were (a) the approach's simplicity, (b) strong user integration throughout the entire design process, and (c) most importantly a tight integration into existing tools and workflows. Especially, with a focus on simple solutions and tight integration we deviated from our earlier visualization prototypes which tended to be feature-rich, but were never properly connected to support real-world problem solving in real environments with real data. In the following, we summarize these three main findings:

Simplicity: Our target users had demanded tools that *"simplify [my] work, not complicate it with intricate visualizations that have to be learned upfront."* Preferred were solutions with high automation and simple, easy to understand representations with an immediately apparent benefit that were explicitly tailored to their needs.

User Integration: Engineering is a complex area that requires expertise and background knowledge. As outsiders to the area we found it invaluable to counterbalance our little domain knowledge through an exploratory study of analysis practices and a user-centered design processes. This helped us to implement tailored, well-directed, and valuable solutions (see also, e. g., [20] or [21]).

Tool Integration: We also learned that in our domain tight integration of final tools with domain data and process is a crucial factor to success, adoption and an essential requirement for us to evaluate the value of our tools under real circumstances. In our case, integrating Cardiogram as a module into Carmen—a traditional and accepted tool—helped engineers to easily access the data at hand, use other common modules and draw upon multiple perspectives (see above). Especially in large companies, often a set of traditional tools already exist for a data analysis problem at hand. These tools are usually integrated into a well-defined process and re-implementing them for a research project is too expensive. However, neglecting these practices can pose additional costs for employees, for instance, due to additional data transformation efforts or tool-flipping costs. In our case, it turned out that such additional time costs were not acceptable for engineers and poorly integrated tools were disapproved of in daily work.

CONCLUSION AND FUTURE WORK

In 2006, Broy [3] wrote: "The increase of software and functionality in cars is not close to an end. In the contrary, we can expect a substantial growth in the future". This holds unchanged even four years later and is probably the strongest motivation behind the work presented. In this paper, we focused on an in-depth analysis of this application area from an VA researchers point of view. We provided results from an exploratory field study, and a novel VA tool, Cardiogram, combining data pre-processing and visualization techniques, and its evaluation in the field. We also explained and discussed our design approach and showed how it finally led to the acceptance of Cardiogram in our target domain. While our experience so far is solely based on working in our target domain, we hope that our findings can serve as reference for others who are planning to closer integrate their VA tools with real-world application domains, especially in large companies and technical environments. We encourage other researchers to report their own experience in order to broaden our general understanding about such projects and to help VA "move from research to practice" [36].

REFERENCES

1. R. Bosch GmbH. *Kraftfahrzeugtechnisches Taschenbuch.* Vieweg&Sohn Verlagsgesellschaft, 26 edition, 2007.
2. E. Bringmann and A. Krämer. Model-based Testing of Automotive Systems. In *Proc. Software Testing, Verification, and Validation*, pages 485–493. IEEE, 2008.
3. M. Broy. Challenges in automotive software engineering. In *Proc. Software Engineering (ICSE)*, pages 33–42. ACM, 2006.
4. S. Carpendale. Evaluating information visualizations. In A. Kerren, J. T. Stasko, J.-D. Fekete, and C. North, editors, *Information Visualization: Human-Centered Issues and Perspectives*, pages 19–45. Springer LNCS, 2007.
5. K. Cook. From research to reality: Visual analytics technology transition. In *VAC Views*. PNNL, Nov. 2008.
6. H. Doleisch, M. Mayer, M. Gasser, R. Wanker, and H. Hauser. Case study: Visual analysis of complex, time-dependent simulation results of a diesel exhaust system. In *Proc. EuroVis*, pages 91–96, 2004.
7. J. Fails, A. Karlson, L. Shahamat, and B. Shneiderman. A visual interface for multivariate temporal data: Finding patterns of events across multiple histories. In *Proc. VAST*, pages 167–174. IEEE, 2006.
8. H. Heinecke. Automotive system design-challenges and potential. In *Proc. Design, Automation and Test (DATE)*, pages 656–657. IEEE, 2005.
9. N. Henry and J. Fekete. Matrixexplorer: a dual-representation system to explore social networks. *IEEE Transactions on Visualization and Computer Graphics*, 12(5):677, 2006.
10. D. Holten, B. Cornelissen, and J. van Wijk. Trace Visualization Using Hierarchical Edge Bundles and Massive Sequence Views. In *Proc. of Visualizing Software for Understanding and Analysis (VISSOFT)*, pages 47–54, 2007.
11. K. Holtzblatt and S. Jones. Contextual inquiry: A participatory technique for system design. In *Participatory Design: Principles and Practices*, pages 177–210. Lawrence Erlbaum Associates, Hillsdale, NJ, USA, 1993.
12. P. Isenberg, A. Tang, and S. Carpendale. An exploratory study of visual information analysis. In *Proc. CHI*, pages 1217–1226. ACM, 2008.
13. P. Isenberg, T. Zuk, C. Collins, and S. Carpendale. Grounded evaluation of information visualizations. In *Proc. BELIV*, pages 56–63. ACM, 2008.
14. C. Johnson, R. Moorhead, T. Munzner, H. Pfister, P. Rheingans, and T. Yoo. *NIH-NSF Visualization Research Challenges Report*. IEEE Press, 2006.
15. D. Keim, E. Bak, P.and Bertini, D. Oelke, D. Spretke, and H. Ziegler. Advanced visual analytics interfaces. In *Proc. AVI*, pages 3–10. ACM, 2010.
16. F. Kensing and J. Simonsen. MUST: A method for participatory design. *Human-Computer Interaction*, 13(2):167–198, 1998.
17. R. Kincaid. Signallens: Focus+context applied to electronic time series. *IEEE Transactions on Visualization and Computer Graphics*, 16(6):900–907, 2010.
18. S. Koch, H. Bosch, M. Giereth, and T. Ertl. Iterative Integration of Visual Insights during Patent Search and Analysis. In *Proc. VAST*, pages 203–210. IEEE, 2009.
19. Z. Konyha, K. Matkovix, D. Graxanin, M. Duras, J. Juric, and H. Hauser. Interactive visual analysis of a timing chain drive using segmented curve view and other coordinated views. In *Proc. CMV*, pages 3–15. IEEE, 2007.
20. P. McLachlan, T. Munzner, E. Koutsofios, and S. North. LiveRAC: Interactive visual exploration of system management time-series data. In *Proc. CHI*, pages 1483–1492. ACM, 2008.
21. M. Meyer, T. Munzner, A. DePace, and H. Pfister. Multeesum: A tool for comparative spatial and temporal gene expression data. *IEEE Transactions on Visualization and Computer Graphics*, 16(6):908–917, 2010.
22. T. Munzner. A nested process model for visualization design and validation. *IEEE Transactions on Visualization and Computer Graphics*, 15(6):921–928, 2009.
23. C. Plaisant. The Challenge of Information Visualization Evaluation. In *Proc. AVI*, pages 109–116. ACM, 2004.
24. A. Pretorius and J. Van Wijk. Multiple views on system traces. In *Proc. PacificVis*, pages 95–102. IEEE, 2008.
25. A. Pretschner, M. Broy, I. Kruger, and T. Stauner. Software engineering for automotive systems: A roadmap. In *Future of Software Engineering*, pages 55–71. IEEE, 2007.
26. M. Schulz, F. Reck, W. Bartelheimer, and T. Ertl. Interactive visualization of fluid dynamics simulations in locally refined cartesian grids. In *Proc. VIS*, pages 413–416. IEEE, 1999.
27. M. Sedlmair, C. Bernhold, D. Herrscher, S. Boring, and A. Butz. Mostvis: An interactive visualization supporting automotive engineers in most catalog exploration. In *Proc. Information Visualisation (IV)*, pages 173–182. IEEE, 2009.
28. M. Sedlmair, W. Hintermaier, K. Stocker, T. Büring, and A. Butz. A dual-view visualization of in-car communication processes. In *Proc. Information Visualization (IV)*, pages 157–162. IEEE, 2008.
29. M. Sedlmair, P. Isenberg, D. Baur, and A. Butz. Evaluating Information Visualization in Large Companies: Challenges, Experiences and Recommendations. In *Proc. BELIV*. ACM, 2010.
30. M. Sedlmair, B. Kunze, W. Hintermaier, and A. Butz. User-centered Development of a Visual Exploration System for In-Car Communication. In *Proc. Smart Graphics*, pages 105–116. Springer, 2009.
31. B. Shneiderman. The Eyes Have It: A Task by Data Type Taxonomy for Information Visualizations. In *Proc. Visual Languages (VL)*, pages 336–343. IEEE, 1996.
32. B. Shneiderman and C. Plaisant. Strategies for evaluating information visualization tools: multi-dimensional in-depth long-term case studies. In *Proc. BELIV*. ACM, 2006.
33. J. Stevens. Visualization of Complex Automotive Data. *IEEE Computer Graphics and Applications*, 27(6):80–86, 2007.
34. L. A. Suchman. *Plans and Situated Actions*. Cambridge University Press, 1987.
35. T. Tekušová, G. Darmstadt, and T. Schreck. Visualizing Time-Dependent Data in Multivariate Hierarchic Plots-Design and Evaluation of an Economic Application. In *Proc. Information Visualization (IV)*, pages 143–150, 2008.
36. J. Thomas and K. Cook. *Illuminating the path: The research and development agenda for visual analytics*. National Visualization and Analytics Center, 2005.
37. M. Tory, S. Staub-French, B. Po, and F. Wu. Physical and Digital Artifact-Mediated Coordination in Building Design. *Proc. CSCW*, 17(4):311–351, 2008.
38. Vector Informatik GmbH. http://www.vector.com/, 03/10.

KronoMiner: Using Multi-Foci Navigation for the Visual Exploration of Time-Series Data

Jian Zhao[1] **Fanny Chevalier**[2] **Ravin Balakrishnan**[1]

[1]Department of Computer Science
University of Toronto
{jian|ravin}@dgp.toronto.edu

[2]OCAD University
Toronto
fchevalier@ocad.ca

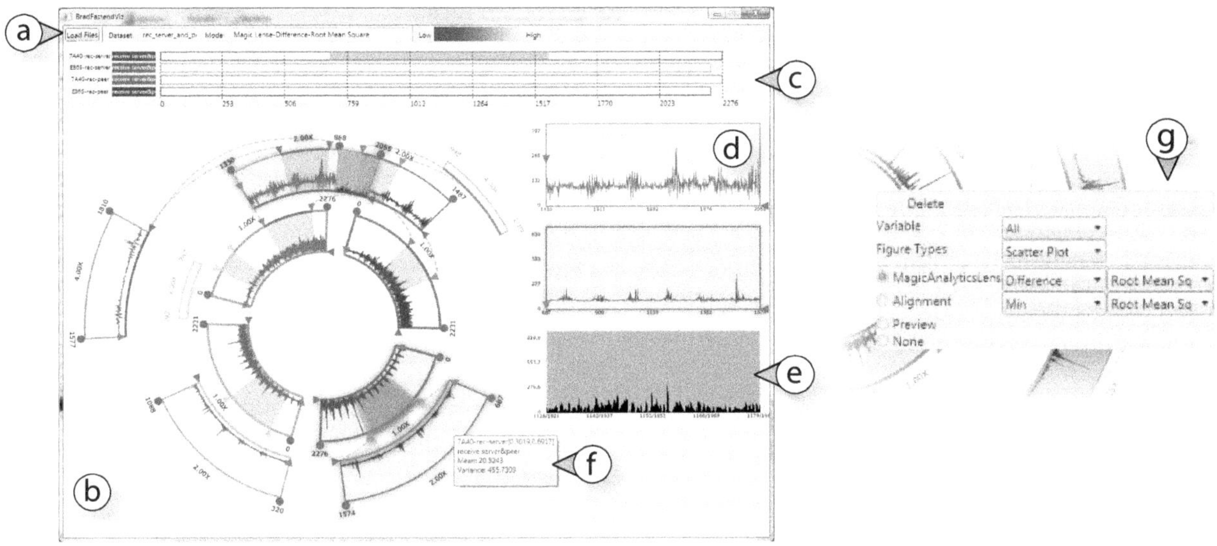

Figure 1. Exploration of four stock market datasets using KronoMiner. Left: the visualization window of KronoMiner including a (a) status bar, (b) main circular tree window (c) timeline overview, (d) four plots comparison area, displaying (e) a MagicAnalytics Lens detailed view. A tooltip (f) provides additional information on demand for each segment. Both general and context-based operations are available by invoking (g) a context menu.

ABSTRACT

The need for pattern discovery in long time-series data led researchers to develop interactive visualization tools and analytical algorithms for gaining insight into the data. Most of the literature on time-series data visualization either focus on a small number of tasks or a specific domain. We propose KronoMiner, a tool that embeds new interaction and visualization techniques as well as analytical capabilities for the visual exploration of time-series data. The interface's design has been iteratively refined based on feedback from expert users. Qualitative evaluation with an expert user not involved in the design process indicates that our prototype is promising for further research.

ACM Classification Keywords

H.5.2 User Interfaces: [Interaction Styles]

General Terms

Design, Human Factors

INTRODUCTION

The need to analyze time-series data is prevalent in various application domains ranging from business planning to intensive care medicine. Interactive visualization has proven to be an effective approach to analyze time-series, assisting doctors in diagnosis [25], helping computer network engineers optimize bandwidth usage [22], aiding finance experts market investments [5] or helping homeland security investigations [6].

Existing interactive time-series visualization tools are either domain-specific or multi-purpose. Domain-specific tools are typically designed with domain experts and are rich in specialized functionality. They are powerful for answering precise questions (e.g. what is the impact of a medical treatment? [10]) but they cannot be easily applied to other domains. They also confine users into predefined tasks and procedures, thus offering little flexibility in the exploration process and leaving little room for opportunistic discoveries. In contrast, multi-purpose tools are not restricted to a specific domain and thus target a wider audience. However, they usually only support a small number of tasks (e.g. identifying periodicity [33]) and thus require other tools to be used in conjunction for complementary but necessary exploration capabilities.

There is therefore a need for interactive time-series data visualization tools that are functional enough to support complex tasks while being flexible enough for promoting opportunistic exploration in a domain-independent manner. Not only does domain-independence make the tool accessible to a wide audience, but it also allows cross-examination of data from multiple domains and opens up new possibilities for collaboration between analysts with complementary expertise.

To address this need we propose KronoMiner, a multipurpose time-series exploration tool providing rich navigation capabilities and analytical support. KronoMiner is based on a radial display that can be drilled into details by focusing on different pieces of the data and rearranging them in a facile manner. The design of KronoMiner has been refined based on expert users' feedback at several stages of the development. Our contributions include (i) a taxonomy of design requirements gathered from experts analyzing time-series from various application domains, (ii) a review of the design space of layouts for visualizing multiple multivariate time-series, (iii) the iterative design of KronoMiner as a demonstration of the new visualization and interaction techniques in a seamless tool, and (iv) expert user feedback on our prototype.

RELATED WORK

Visual Exploration is the process of interactively browsing through different portions of a dataset to gain a better understanding of it. Not only does Visual Exploration help for hypothesis confirmation, it is also crucial for finding the unexpected and for raising new questions, especially when the users have no or only vague hypotheses about the data [31]. Although time-series data is an area of extensive study in Information Visualization research, existing interactive visualization tools for time-series data do not extensively support multipurpose Visual Exploration: they are either too specialized domain-specific tools, answering precise questions, or domain-independent but limited to a few capabilities. Relevant surveys include [24, 29].

The prevalent approach for representing temporal data is arguably timeline visualization (e.g. LifeLines [25]) in which data points are usually plotted along a uniform time axis. Other approaches use visual metaphors to represent periodic temporal data. For instance, Calendar View [32] uses a calendar display to visualize univariate time-series aggregated on a daily, weekly or monthly basis to find interesting groupings of the data. SpiraClock [7] provides continuous feedback about upcoming events by displaying them on a spiral analog clock. A similar spiral shaped time axis is used in Spiral Graph [33] to reveal cycles of a time-series. All these techniques require the data to exhibit regularity, and therefore are of a little utility for data without periodicity.

For data without apparent cycles, multi-foci interaction is required for the detailed comparison of different pieces of the data while preserving context. For example, LiveRAC [22] and Mélange [9] rely on stretch and squish navigation. They result in a single integrated view with visual distortion, even though Richter et al. [26] suggest that non-linear representation of time has negative effects on the interpretation of the data. In contrast, StackZoom [17] preserves time axis uniformity for each single sequence of a multi-resolution hierarchy dynamically built by the user. However, the multiple foci views cannot be rearranged, thereby making it difficult to compare regions of interest that are spaced out.

Time-series visualization tools also frequently integrate analytical methods to support pattern mining. For instance PatternFinder [10] assists in detecting user-defined event patterns in medical records by letting the user specify the desired sequence of events, their attributes and inter-event time spans. Although pattern mining methods help to gain insight into data, most of them require prior knowledge of the domain and of what characterizes an interesting pattern. In the context of domain-independent exploration, no specific pattern mining methods can be easily applied. Nevertheless, combining visualization with general analytical methods such as the difference plot of two variables, remains useful as an indication for tentatively identifying regions of interest. In contrast to PatternFinder, TimeSearcher2 [5] relies on such a Visual Exploration process by allowing the user to dynamically select a timebox directly on the visualization as a query by example.

When they support pattern mining, time-series interactive visualization tools usually present relevant patterns as a list sorted by matching scores to a query [10, 5], or automatically align them [25]. Since they often focus on one pattern at a time, these tools fail in providing an overview of all the relationships within and across time-series. An effective way for showing the relationships is to explicitly link the regions that match to each others using straight and curved lines. However, this can quickly lead to visual clutter because of too many link crossings. A common approach to address this problem is to bundle the links [16] and represent the data on a circular layout, as it is done in MizBee [23]. A survey of circular visualizations can be found in [8].

To summarize, despite the abundant research for visualizing time-series data, as far as we know, there is no system that extensively supports domain-independent Visual Exploration of multiple multivariate datasets. Available interactive visualization tools are either highly domain-dependent and limited to predefined tasks and procedures, or general multipurpose tools that support a very few number of tasks. With the knowledge we gained through our literature survey, we derived the design guidelines listed in the next section we used as a basis for the design of KronoMiner.

DESIGN GUIDELINES

Before enumerating the design requirements KronoMiner has been built upon, we give background on time-series data and discuss the design space of layouts for visualizing them.

Time-Series Data

Time-series are sequences of data points measured at successive times, typically at equal intervals. They consist of real numbers (e.g. temperature logs), or events (e.g. medical histories made of records of doctor visits, blood tests, etc). Time-series have the common property of being large, not only in the captured time period and number of samples, but also in the number of observed attributes [2].

The characteristics of time-series vary widely and are very dependent on the application domain. The temporal dimension itself is a special dimension that has multiple facets. Aigner et al. [2] have listed the following criteria defining the different types of time: (1) structure of time (linear vs. cyclic), (2) temporal primitive (time points vs. time intervals) and (3) time perspective (ordered time vs. branching time). In this work, we focus on non-intrinsically-periodic linear sequences of ordered time points. Nevertheless, it is possible to generalize our framework to intervals.

One of the inherent limitations of traditional time-series interactive visualization tools lies in regarding time as being an immutable and uniform dimension. Depending on the tool, Visual Exploration is usually constrained to at least one of the following: (1) *synchronism*: different attributes are usually time-aligned, making it difficult to compare delayed sequences; (2) *chronology*: time-series data is often considered as ordered data, for which successive pieces cannot be rearranged; (3) *time scale consistency*: comparing time-series simultaneously at different time scales is rarely supported. For example, squishing or stretching the time scale of server logs independently makes it possible to adjust the visualization according to response-time capacity. Some users might also look for sub-patterns or fractal behaviour [12].

Design requirements

Before designing an interactive visualization system for Visual Exploration of time-series data, we conducted an informal study with experts from different application domains to understand what features users need and how they generally carry out their exploration of time-series data. Based on their comments and the knowledge we gained through our literature survey, we derived the following design requirements.

R1: Multivariate, multiple and heterogeneous datasets. Dealing with as varied input data as possible is important for supporting multipurpose use.

(a) *multiple heterogeneous datasets:* supporting time-series from various heterogeneous sources to facilitate across-concept comparison and refrain from being domain-dependent,

(b) *multivariate data:* visualization and manipulation of both coupled and dissociated attributes,

(c) *variety of chart representations:* providing different chart representations choices.

R2: Multiple coordinated views [2]. When user actions receive immediate visual feedback, multiple views aid Visual Exploration by providing diverse perspectives of the data.

(a) *large-scale overview:* acquiring general context at any exploration state through an overview of the entire datasets help maintain a mental map of the data [28],

(b) *multi-foci, temporal hierarchies:* showing several levels of detail simultaneously in coordinated views can aid in effective browsing of the data [17],

(c) *side-by-side comparison:* side-by-side comparison is easier than comparing visually spaced-out charts or remembering previously seen views [22].

R3: Interaction. Giving users as much freedom as possible to manipulate and query the data is crucial for Visual Exploration [2].

(a) *direct manipulation:* physically manipulating graphical representations of objects has the benefit of being easy to use and learn and allows for greater system comprehension [27],

(b) *overview first, zoom & filter, details on demand:* the widely followed Shneiderman's principle [28] is recognized as effective for dealing with large datasets,

(c) *dynamic multi-foci, temporal hierarchies:* drilling down into multiple regions of interest by time brushing (i.e. manually select data on an interactive data display) eases comparison [17],

(d) *grouping, aggregating for data abstraction:* grouping several regions of interest in a single entity allows for user-defined clustering and data abstraction,

(f) *history:* maintaining the history of the exploration process is important to help users revisit important views and keep track of their exploration [14],

(e) *annotating:* annotations aid for organizing and lower memory load as they act as labels and reminders.

R4: Analytical methods. All our expert users echoed that semi-guided exploration based on statistical analysis should be considered [2].

(a) *across-concept relationships:* displaying the relationships (links, scores) resulting from the computation of classical domain-independent analytical methods provides important clues for Visual Exploration,

(b) *best match:* finding the best match between series and their matching score allows for pattern mining [5],

(c) *dynamic comparison:* displaying on-the-fly computed information (e.g. difference plot) facilitates identifying regions of interest if immediate visual update is supported while manipulating the data,

(d) *customization:* allowing for user-defined operators avoids a multipurpose tool to be too limited for specialized domain-dependent analysis.

Design Space of Layouts

Here we review different layouts that can be used to represent time-series data as a complement to Meyer and Munzner's taxonomy [23]. Figure 2 depicts the possible layouts for multivariate (a,b) and multiple (c-f) time-series datasets. Note that an exhaustive taxonomy would include spiral layouts previously described, but these ones are suited for data that exhibits a periodicity and are out of the scope of this paper.

We distinguish between multivariate data, which implies the plots to be coupled, and multiple independent datasets (that could be multivariate or not). Multivariate data can be overlaid in a single plot (Fig. 2a), but visual clutter might be overwhelming; an alternative is to stack multiple charts (Fig. 2b). Different chart types can be set for each individual plot independently without overlap, but this requires more screen real estate and might split the user's visual attention.

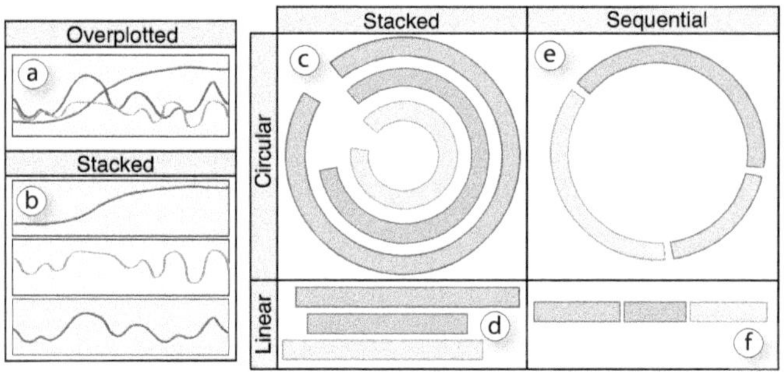

Figure 2. Design space of layouts for multiple multivariate time-series. a-b multivariate layouts, c-f multiple datasets layouts

For plotting more than one time-series dataset at a time, one can choose between a linear and a circular layout, and use stacked or sequential plots (Fig. 2). Linear layouts are more familiar to users and do not distort the data. Circular layouts are more appropriate for visualizing hierarchical structures and relationships [8]. They also succesfully apply to periodic data when spirally-shaped, but this raises issues when considering multiple series with different periodicity and time interval as the series have to be piled up in the same spiral. The sequential linear view (Fig. 2f) makes it difficult to compare time-aligned data, especially when the plots are spaced out and cannot be rearranged. The circular stacked layout (Fig. 2c) preserves time alignment, but the same data plotted on different rings is perceived differently, and may cause misinterpretation. As described next, the KronoMiner interface combines both circular (Fig. 2e) and linear (Fig. 2d) layouts.

THE KRONOMINER INTERFACE

KronoMiner is an interactive visualization tool for Visual Exploration of multiple multivariate time-series datasets. Its design relies on the aforementioned guidelines and has been iteratively refined based on experts feedback gathered at different development stages (see User Feedback section). KronoMiner aims to ease the identification and manipulation of multiple sub-pieces of interest for finer analysis, rather than providing a single global view of numerous long time-series to be analyzed as a whole. It is based on dynamic hierarchical inspection of the data at different scales and locations. The interface (Fig. 1) combines several coordinated components, taking full advantage of the individual strengths of each layout to effectively support different tasks.

Multi-Foci Hierarchy Tree

Hierarchy Tree Visualization

The main interactive exploration window (Fig. 1b) displays a circular tree structure for presenting the hierarchy of multiple foci (R2b). We have chosen a circular sequential layout for the display of the multi-foci hierarchy mainly for its compact representation of tree structures [8], but also to put selectable data within easy reach of the user [11]. Each of the tree nodes corresponds to data points within a specific range of a parent series and is displayed as a concentric arc segment on which data is plotted. The central ring contains all the available entire datasets (R1a,b). Segments belonging to different datasets can be easily distinguished by the color of their outlines. Detailed information such as timestamp bounds and time scale is displayed for each segment.

A parent-child relationship of two segments is explicitly visualized as a pair of dashed curves that link one segment to the corresponding region of interest (ROI) on its parent. Data points belonging to the ROI are duplicated in the associated segment, as a new and more detailed view of the same initial dataset. To visually reinforce the hierarchical structure, ROIs are filled in with light gray, and arcs on both of the child and parent segments are color-coded to give awareness of which portion of this data piece resides in the series. A distinguishable hue is mapped to each dataset. The dashed links as well as the lower boundary of each child segment are colored with the same hue as its parent. The luminance conveys the position in the parent series (the brighter the sooner in the parent). Moreover, when hovering over a segment, its ancestors and descendants in the hierarchy and the associated ROI in the parent are emphasized by glow effects (Fig. 1). We also indicate its location in the timeline overview (R2a, Fig. 1b), and a tooltip showing detailed information is popped-up (R3b, Fig. 1f). Duplicated data is thereby clearly pointed out by providing immediate feedback on the different coordinated views as the user interacts (R2).

Building the Hierarchy Tree

As described in this section, the whole mechanism of creating and adjusting the segments relies on the direct manipulation principle (R3a) to support a quick and effective way of drilling down into multiple locations of the datasets (R3c). To enable quick learning of the interface, all the operations for editing the hierarchy are performed on the main interactive view, by simple mouse interaction and one modifier key.

A new segment is created by directly brushing (i.e. dynamic selection in the interactive view) the ROI on any existing series in the hierarchy (R3a,c). The user is required to right click on the desired starting point — a new segment appears on the ring located one level outside from the queried data piece, and the ROI is colored with light gray. The light gray highlight delimiting the ROI and its associated segment are dynamically adjusted while the user drags the cursor, until the mouse button is released at the intended ending point, finalizing the creation. When the user needs to focus on a specific time frame, she can perform time brushing on a collection of segments belonging to a ring at once. Simultaneous creation of as many child sequences as segments present on a ring can be done in a single operation by holding the *Shift* key while brushing the time frame on one of the ring's segments.

Figure 3 depicts how the multi-foci time intervals can be adjusted by direct manipulation on the view (R3a). A OrthoZoom mechanism [3] is used to adjust ROIs in the following way: the user can look at earlier or later data points in the parent series by dragging the ROI along the ring, keeping the same time frame but at different time locations (Fig. 3a). Dragging the cursor on the radial direction towards the center (Fig. 3b) reduces the interval. Conversely, a longer interval is obtained by dragging in the opposite direction. Arrows ending the dashed curves that link a segment to its corresponding ROI are also draggable and act as sliders to adjust the ROI size (Fig. 3c). The arc segment display can also be modified: round handles placed on the extremities of each

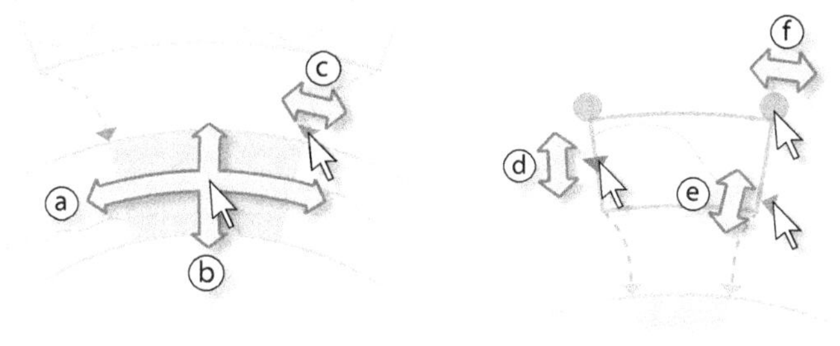

Figure 3. Left: adjusting a region of interest, (a) move and (b,c) resize. Right: adjusting a data arc segment, (d) change y-axis amplitude, (e) shif y-axis and (f) stretch or squish time

segment (Fig. 3f) allow for stretching or squishing the data representation, thus affecting the time scale used for rendering (the data always occupies all the available segment space), the ROI and the data itself remain the same. The user can also set up specific values by invoking the segment setting pop-up menu as she clicks on the segment's time scale text label on its top (Fig. 1g), both the related ROI and segment are updated in consequence. Two more controllers (Fig. 3d,e) explained later, are provided to the user for data plot visual settings.

Editing the Hierarchy Tree

Maintaining the history of the exploration process (R3f) is important to help users revisit important views and keep track of their exploration [14]. Even though we do not explicitly support navigation history, the hierarchy tree mimics exploration history since a new segment is created each time the user wants to drill down into the data and all the existing segments remain in place. When the user wants to focus on the deepest levels of the hierarchy because they correspond to the finest details, she does not require the whole hierarchy tree to be displayed in detail. In the circular representation, the deepest levels are located on the outer rings. To release space and focus visual attention, the user can shrink the inner rings (see Fig. 4) by dragging a ring towards the center of the circle view — ring interaction (Fig. 5c) is detailed later.

To avoid the view being too crowded because of the presence of too many segments, the user can also put data aside while keeping it at her disposal for later. Double clicking on a segment makes it collapse: a segment of a reduced height, not displaying any details then takes its place. Hence visual clutter is reduced, making it possible to focus on a small subset of visually detailed segments without losing the mental map of the current structure. The details can be restored anytime by a double click on a collapsed segment. Figure 1 shows examples of both collapsed and detailed segments.

Keeping the whole history of exploration is sometimes not relevant when intermediate stages are not important for the analysis. For example when a sequence of interest has been identified, the user might no longer be interested in its ancestors in the hierarchy. To get rid of unused segments, the user can enter the *Deletion mode* (discussed later) and delete either a single segment by clicking on it, or a segment and its whole sub-hierarchy while holding the *Shift* key. The deleted pieces disappear in a smooth fade out, avoiding abrupt changes in the view when deleting a whole branch.

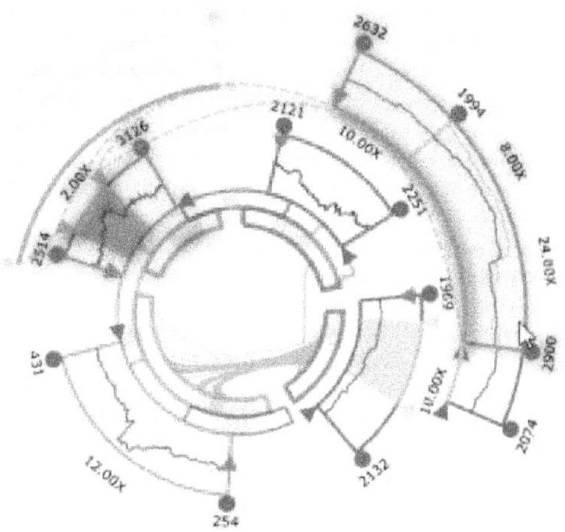

Figure 4. Example of exploration of the NYSE exchange daily open price (1970-2010) using the *Preview mode*: a phantom of the manipulated segment remains at the initial position (top left) as it is temporary overlaid on another segment for trend comparison. The inner rings have been shrunk to focus on the deepest levels of the hierarchy, and the relationships between the datasets are shown in the center.

Flexible Interaction for Visual Exploration

Adjusting the Layout for Segment Comparison

The user can freely adjust the main interactive view through classical pan (right button drag), zoom (mouse wheel) and rotate (left button drag) operations to access details. When looking at time-series data, one of the main tasks is to compare data at different locations in time. However, two segments can be spaced out in the view, even showed upside down because of the circular display. This can make the comparison more difficult than looking at side-by-side pieces (R2c). To facilitate comparison, we give the user the full freedom of rearranging the segments in the view: a segment can be rotated anywhere in its own ring. Ring jumps are also supported. Thus the segments can be freely aligned either on a stacked configuration by putting them on different rings, or overlaid to obtain overplotted data (Fig. 2a) as they are semi-transparent. We discuss later that the overlapped area can be used for analytical purposes by displaying the result of statistical functions instead of the raw data.

Looking for the unexpected is difficult and tedious and usually requires going through a lot of operations before serendipitously discovering relevant insights within the data. To avoid the user messing up her layout during the Visual Exploration, we allow for a *Preview mode* in which the current layout is maintained while the user performs a temporary analysis (e.g. dragging a segment on top of another). A phantom of the segment remains in place at its initial position, and is restored as she releases the mouse button. Figure 4 shows a temporary comparison of similar trends of open price at different time scale and location by overlaying one segment over the other in the *Preview mode*.

KronoMiner is designed to be as unconstraining as possible in terms of comparing multiple sub-pieces of several datasets. Much freedom is given to the user: segments from any loaded dataset, at any location in the dataset and rendered at any time scale can be placed anywhere in the view. Easy access

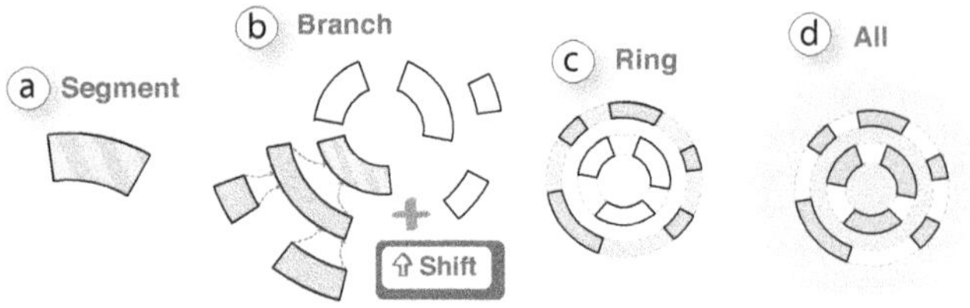

		2	Drag	Drag	Wheel
a	Select			Create and adjust a new segment	
b		Collapse Extend	Rotate Ring jump		
c				Shrink inner rings	
d			Rotate	Pan	Zoom

Figure 5. Context-based interaction. The activation area is showed in pink, and the affected elements in blue. Interaction can be performed on (a) a single segment, (b) a segment and its children branch, (c) a whole ring and (d) all rings at the same time.

to the operations through the direct manipulation techniques (R3) allows for a quick and smooth manipulation of the data with immediate visual feedback. However, giving too much freedom to the user also has its drawbacks. The hierarchy structure might not always be easy to read after reorganizing the segments. Visual cues have to be integrated to help the user maintain her mental map. To this end, we use explicit dashed links, color coding and immediate highlighting of the related branching (ancestors and children in the hierarchy) while hovering over a segment. All these techniques are designed to give as many visual cues as possible to keep awareness of the overall tree structure.

Context-based Interaction

We introduce a new context-based interaction language for the user to be able to manipulate more than one segment at a time. We exploit the current position of the cursor to determine whether the user intended to perform an action on a) a single segment, b) a segment and its whole branch, c) a single ring or d) the whole view. Figure 5 shows a summary of the different selectable groups, and the available operations for each group using the mouse buttons and the *Shift* modifier key. The pink areas correspond to all the cursor positions that determine a group, which is depicted in blue. For example, by holding the *Shift* key and dragging a segment, the user may performs a "branch" move operation (Fig. 5b) and then can rotate a segment and all its descendants in the same interaction or make them jump to different rings. Context-based interaction allows the user to adopt different strategies for Visual Exploration and optimize the interaction. For example, the rings can be used to categorize the data; each ring being dedicated to a specific group the user wants to keep related (R3d). By performing actions in the ring-mode, the user can apply the same changes to all the elements of the group in a single interaction while keeping consistency within the group.

Keeping consistency while designing direct manipulation is possible although limited: there is a finite number of ways of binding operations to the combination of mouse buttons, mouse wheel and modifier keys. Other interaction techniques such as context menu or hotbox [21] must be integrated as a complement to direct manipulation to offer more complex operations and capabilities. Following the same context-based principle just described (Fig. 5), we make available additional functionality (discussed later) on a context menu that is invoked by hitting space bar (Fig. 1e). The user can perform deletion operations and visual settings that affect a targeted set of segments, depending on the position where the menu has been invoked. The menu also contains permanent options, such as the different modes available, among which the *Preview mode* and the *Deletion mode* we introduced earlier.

The Detailed Comparison Window

Circular layouts suffer from distorting the data and might be constraining for a detailed analysis. To balance the drawbacks of the radial view, we have designed a dedicated *Detailed Comparison Window*, located on the right of the interface (Fig. 1c) where four selected segments can be displayed at a time, in a traditional linear stacked layout. To display a segment in the comparison window, the user is required to click on the desired targeted space among the four available, then click on the desired segment to be displayed. If a segment is already plotted, the new selection replaces it. The user can also right click on any of the four linear plots to clear it.

The Detailed Comparison Window was initially designed as two side-by-side plots. The current active plot was permanently showed, the second slot being reserved for the segment under the mouse cursor. One of our experts involved in the iterative design process said he *"[wanted] to be able to look at more than two plots at a time"* and that *"they should be constantly visible after [he had] selected them"*. He also reported that *"seeing them displayed on top of each others would facilitate comparison as I need them to be aligned"*. We currently support four plots, but one can easily imagine more to be visualized by making scrollable the detailed view.

To facilitate data browsing, the comparison window is enriched by interaction capabilities: the user can pan the data in the linear plot for further exploration or to control time alignment. The corresponding ROI and its associated segment are updated in the meantime. Two controllers (similar to Fig. 3d,e) are available on the duplicated linear segments, to set up y-axis amplitude and shift. We guarantee a full coordination between the two views so that the user can easily keep track of the impact of one operation on the other view. Moreover, both the arc segment and its copy are highlighted while hovering over one or the other to make it clear which data is common to the coordinated views (R2).

Dynamic Analytical Methods

When analyzing time-series data, users are commonly interested in the evolution of their data over time for detecting trends and patterns, but also anomalies. Analytical methods can help gain insight into data by automatically detecting periodicity, recurrent patterns and self-similarity [2]. However, one of the major problems is that most of these methods are heavily domain-dependent and thus cannot be applied to any type of data, and even less for comparing time-series from different application domains. Moreover, the parameters are often not self-explanatory and hence not easy to set, especially without some prior knowledge of the datasets and the characteristics of patterns of interest.

When the user has no or a vague idea of the patterns she is looking for, precise analytical computations answering specific questions are of little use. In this case, the user has to rely on Visual Exploration in order to find out the questions she does not know yet. Basic, general and domain-independent analytical computations (e.g. difference plot) are then crucial as they provide clues and suggestions of regions worth exploring deeper. Tools such as TimeSearcher2 [5] that allow for query by example pattern finding, have already demonstrated the benefit of integrating interactive visualization and analytical capabilities in a single tool. KronoMiner enriches its Visual Exploration capabilities by integrating analytical analysis support in three different ways: (1) visualization of the relationships within and between the datasets, (2) the MagicAnalytics Lens: on-the-fly computation and display of analytical methods comparing two segments, and (3) the Best Match mode: on-the-fly computation and display of the best match of two segments. We detail them in the next sections.

Showing the Relationships

Although a lot of existing interactive visualizations allow for pattern mining, to our knowledge, they all only focus on a single pattern at a time. As a consequence, they fail in providing the user with an overview of all the relationships existing within and between the datasets. In other application domains, such as Biology, it is common to represent the entire set of links representing relationships (e.g. MizBee [23] displays matching subsequences of two chromosomes). Showing all the relationships at once help the user gain a overall idea of both the closely related regions and isolated data, that are usually starting points for exploration.

In KronoMiner, we compute similar patterns using a simple brute-force similarity mining algorithm at the loading of the datasets. Any other algorithm or even predefined links can be used. Similarly to MizBee [23], the relationships within and between the different entire datasets are displayed at the center of the circular layout, connecting the data items of the main ring. The links intensity is mapped to the matching score (the darker, the higher). To make trends visually obvious we combine the edge bundling technique described in [16] with alpha blending resulting from overlapping semi-transparent links. In this way, the user has a constant access to relationships information she can use for visually mining regions of interest (R4a), thereby guiding Visual Exploration.

MagicAnalytics Lens

Detailed pairwise comparison is one of the main tasks when analyzing time-series data. It usually involves computing the correlation between the two series to compare (or subsequences of them), sometimes at a different time scale; and viewing the similarity scores of discovered patterns. Traditional statistical tools, such as Matlab, allow for a fine analysis of the data: a wide variety of predefined analytical methods are available, as well as the possibility of defining new functions. However, in such tools the user is required to specify the exact instructions (e.g. the bounds of the interval to focus on) through the use of a command line before visualizing the result. In the case that she does not know exactly what to look for, she might generate a lot of plots before finding something relevant. Not only is the process repetitive, haphazard and time-consuming, it is also distracting as the user splits her attention focusing back and forth between the command interface and the visualizations, thereby requiring she remembers what has already been explored. Moreover, these tools usually require some basic programming skills, which narrows the target audience.

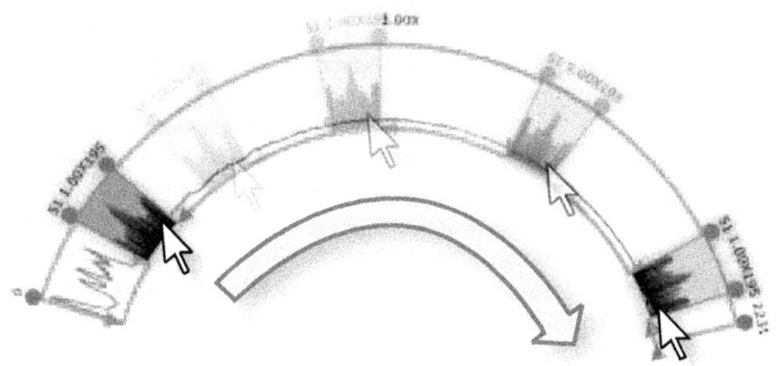

Figure 6. Example of use of the *MagicAnalytics Lens* on peer-to-peer activity logs. A segment that roughly corresponds to one day of activity is used as a lens. The lens displays the correlation plot, and the background color conveys the global root mean squares operator on a yellow-to-blue scale, in this case showing that a daily pattern is repeated as the user drags the lens along the series.

To avoid breaking the flow of the exploration process and facilitate opportunistic discovery, we introduce the *MagicAnalytics Lens*, an interactive visualization technique that computes in real time the result of a function involving two time-series, and immediately displays its result (R4c). MagicAnalytics Lens is inspired by Magic Lens [4] that affects the image inside the bounds of a shape defining the lens. In contrast to Magic Lens that uses a dedicated window as a lens applying a fixed predefined operator, MagicAnalytics Lens considers all the data pieces as a potential lens, as the displayed result depends on both the data points in the window used as a lens, and the data points under it. In Figure 6 the lens shows the cross-correlation plot between two series using the data contained in the overlapped interval. The plot is automatically updated while changing the alignment as the user moves or stretches the segment used as a lens. The background color of the lens is mapped to a computed global measure (root mean square in Fig. 6). This way, the user can very quickly assess if the current alignment compares related series. Any segment in the view can be used as a MagicAnalytics Lens, making it possible to compare data both within the original series and between the different datasets, and also data at different time scales as the user can stretch and squish the segments. A MagicAnalytics Lens can also be plotted in the synchronized Detailed Comparison Window to access the details as showed in Fig. 1c.

The MagicAnalytics Lens is made available through the contextual menu (Fig. 1g). When entering the mode, all the overlaid areas are replaced by the result of the selected functions. The current prototype integrates general functions such as the difference plot, the minimum and maximum plots, and the inner product or the root mean squares for the background, but any operator can be embedded. Ideally, the user should be able to define her own functions and then customize the tool by introducing new analysis methods on demand (R4d).

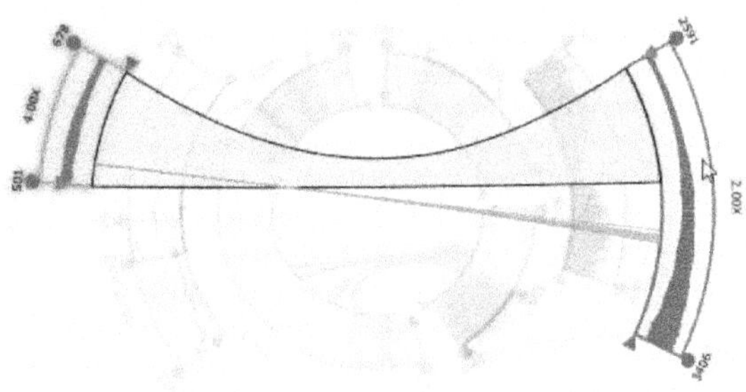

Figure 7. Example of Best Match between two segments of NYSE exchange daily open price (1970-2010) minimizing the root means square. An arch conveys the best match location, its background color is mapped to the matching scores on a yellow-to-blue scale. The pre-computed links are replicated between the two sequences. In this example, the relashionships between the segments surprisingly do not reflect the best match location and might be worth exploring further.

Finding the Best Match

There is an abundant literature about time-series statistical tools that are dedicated to pattern retrieval. Pattern discovery is an important task while analyzing time-series data as it is the preliminary step to discover new ways of defining what could characterize similarity. Allowing users to select a pattern from the data itself has been showed to be useful [5], especially in the context of Visual Exploration when the user does not have a precise idea of what she is looking for.

KronoMiner integrates a *Best Match* mode (R4b): the current selected segment defines the query pattern and hovering over a segment defines it as being the target. The best match according to a selected similarity measure is dynamically computed and displayed: an arch links the query segment to its best match within the targeted segment and the rest of the main view is faded out to avoid visual clutter (Fig. 7). The background color of the arch shape is mapped to the matching score to provide a quick indication of the similarity. We also replicate the same pre-computed relationships as showed in the center of the radial display. We thus make available the context that would otherwise be lost because of fading out. The user can access the details anytime by hovering over the arch if she needs to know the precise score value and detailed information about the two matched segments.

Similarly to the MagicAnalytics Lens, the Best Match takes into account the current time scale of the segments, thus allowing for comparing sequences at a different time scale. For example, fractal patterns within the same time series could be revealed if the user detects a high similarity between a segment and the series it comes from. The similarity function to be used is selectable through the context menu (Fig. 1g), but any other pattern mining method could be integrated.

Plot Visual Settings

For a detailed analysis, the user is able to change the plot style among the six different available (Fig. 8) in the context menu (Fig. 1g) — other types such as horizon graphs [13] or heatmaps could easily be added. Note that the amplitude and bubble plots particularly suit for radial layout as their perception is less affected by the circular deformation. We also support data display adjustments by allowing the user to alter the y-axis amplitude and shift. To do so, two draggable handles are made available on each side of a segment in both the circular main view and the comparison window (Fig. 3d,e). Dragging up and down the left handle respectively increases and decreases the amplitude. The right handle determines the position of the origin of the y axis. Dragging it up and down shifts the chart display. All the rendering settings in one of the two views are automatically reflected in the other, guarantying coordination and consistency (R2).

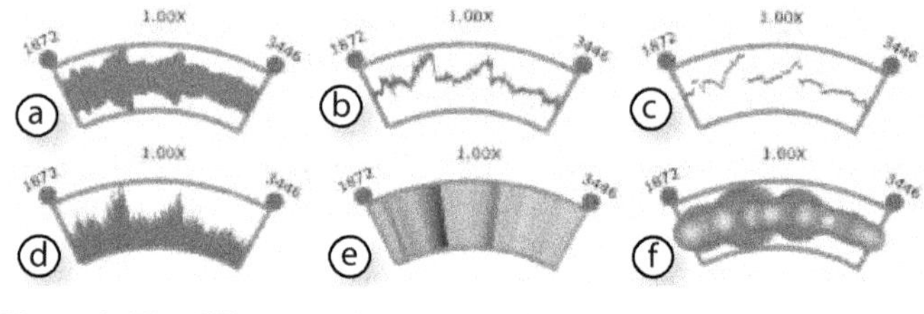

Figure 8. The different available plot styles: (a) amplitude plot, (b) line chart, (c) scatter plot, (d) histogram, (e) lines plot and (f) bubble plot.

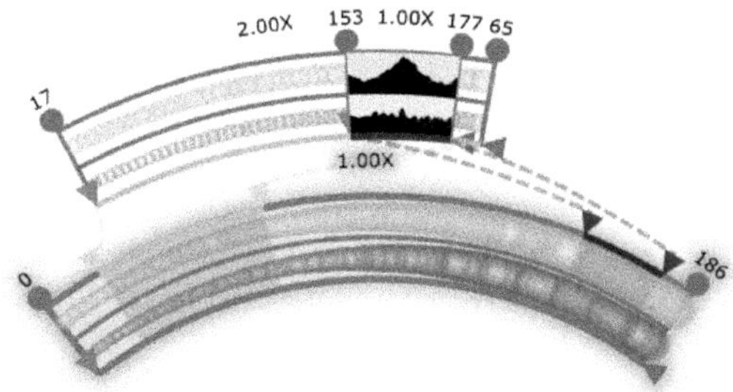

Figure 9. Example of use of the MagicAnalytics Lens on a multivariate dataset. Top plot: monthly average cost of a night's accommodation in Victoria, bottom: Consumer Price Index in Melbourne (1980-1995). The correlation plot and the background color (root means square) indicate common trends between the two segments.

One might have to deal with multiple variables while keeping them coupled. Examples include coordinates of a moving object, min/max temperatures and opening/closing price of stock market that would not make sense desynchronizing. We support multivariate datasets by piling up multiple views as showed in Figure 9. In this example, the MagicAnalytics Lens reveals a repeated pattern, but the trend is observed at a different time scale. A room price and the CPI evolve in a similar way at different times, but twice as fast the second time. Experts could make the hypothesis that there exists a correlation, and then potentially predict the phenomenom when the pattern occurs again.

Although it is possible to make rings larger to fit more than 3 variables at a time, KronoMiner does not scale to larger dimensions because of visual clutter. Design improvements (e.g. dynamic reordering and stacking) are needed to support high dimensional data. Space-efficient alternate visualizations (e.g. braided graphs [18]) would partially solve the problem but imply issues for the analytics lens design.

USER FEEDBACK

The KronoMiner interface has been iteratively refined through 4 participatory design sessions with 7 experts from different domains at different stages of the development. Each session focused respectively on Computer Network (1 expert), Medical Science (1), Weather Forecast (3) and Finances (2) and lasted 4 to 5 hours during which we introduced the tool, let the users try it and gathered feedback and requirements.

Moreover, an expert user not involved in the design process has tested the last prototype on his own data in 2 working sessions of 3 hours each. The participant is a researcher studying large scale peer-to-peer traffic data on video-on-demand websites, and usually uses Matlab. After describing the tool interface and functionalities, the user was asked to explore his data using the think-aloud protocol.

We first observed the user was clearly more comfortable with the interface during the second interview, whereas he complained *"it is difficult to remember, I have to learn"* when testing the earlier prototype. At the end of the sessions, he compared the learning process: *"It took me weeks, even months to learn how to use Matlab because I had first to learn code. I can do a lot with your tool, and I don't even have to think about it"*. We strived to make the interaction as direct as possible so as not to break the exploration flow. Context-based interaction requires training, but one cannot benefit from complex actions while always keeping straightforward interactions. We believe a novice user to be able to quickly get familiar with the different functionalities but this remains to be validated in further studies.

Our expert's dataset consisted of a month of the visiting population of two different channels, sampled from the server every 10 minutes. He first wanted to test the hypothesis that the sub-sequences of everyday's data are similar within and between channels. To do so, he brushed a ROI on one channel corresponding to what he described as *"the first day, roughly"* (he was able to identify it because of the characteristic shape of the plot). To refine his selection, he displayed the segment in the comparison window, changed the plot type to gain a better view and barely adjusted the time frame, pointing that *"it doesn't have to fit exactly, I just want a quick look"*.

The user panned the plot in the comparison window to get an overall idea of day-to-day data and possibly spot anomalies or interesting behaviour he wouldn't see in the radial representation. He adjusted the scale and the shift of the y-axis as the amplitude of the plot decreased. At some point, he mentioned *"the plot is too small now, I can't say if I see a pattern, or if it is noise. So far I've been able to barely identify a similar pattern, but now it's not possible anymore, and increasing the amplitude wouldn't help"*. He thus decided to switch to the MagicAnalytical Lens mode as a support to analyze the cross correlation. As he dragged the *"first day"* segment along the sequence, he observed a constant peak on the center of the computed plot (Fig. 6), indicating a high correlation at a zero delay. This justified part of his hypothesis and he defined the lens dragging as being *"very handy"*.

The participant roughly selected the *"last day"* data points and dragged both days segments to outer rings to gain a better view, and made them overlap, still in the MagicAnalytics Lens mode. He then dragged the first segment to sequentially compare the data from the latest day to the rest of the sequence, and validated his hypotheses as they revealed being correlated. While doing so, our user emphasized that *"In Matlab you have to generate tons of graphs. Even if you have enough space to display them, you don't have enough brain. Here, all you have to do is to simply drag [the segment]"*.

The user started to explore the data on the secondary channel. He found the daily cross correlation to be high between the two datasets, but not as strong as within the same series. After extensive navigation and digging into the data, the work space turned to be messy. Our user started to rearrange the segments: *"I need to organize"*, shrunk inner rings, and collapsed some remaining segments, as they were not of interest at this time *"I don't need this guy for now..."*. When cleaning his space, he realized he looked at many plots without noticing: *"This saves me a lot of time. Normally I have to eyeball all the data first because I don't want to go into every pieces because it is tedious"*. Further, he gathered unexpected findings as he dynamically adjusted the range of the ROI to time intervals less than a day - *"The data around midnight is similar to that around noon! It's interesting. I would have expected it is the case at other rush hours, but people should sleep at midnight. It is worthwhile to study deeper"*.

Our user was enthusiastic about analytical capabilities within a tool supporting direct manipulation. He said he wanted to explore more datasets with more variables and longer time periods using our prototype, as it would be too time-consuming with traditional tools. He mentioned that for analyzing server data, he would require to freely "*stretch the time*" as servers likely have different hardware. Hence the performance plots have to be adjusted for a fair comparison. The Best Match Mode would also be helpful as the need for mining guidance increases with the number and size of the time-series.

DISCUSSION

Look: sexy or serious?

When they do not propose a sober interface that exhibits several menus, control panels and numerous settings, tools for analysis are not taken seriously as they do not look professional. It is often that these tools are admitted to be nice-looking and pleasant to "play" with, but their appearance has a negative impact on the users' reliance. A tool that feels too easy to use might suffer from its apparent simplicity. Paradoxically, users are highly demanding for more interactivity and more user-friendly interfaces and thus create a tension between apparent profesionalism and accessibility. KronoMiner demonstrates that it remains possible to perform effective analysis while offering high interactivity in a seamless tool. There is a strong need to convince users to accept that the absence of menus and settings panels does not mean a tool is not powerful. Our user who was baffled at the beginning *"I've never seen that before"*, ended up asking us for a release of the prototype to use it for his research.

Back to the Roots

The previous observations raise the question of breaking habits. Integrating familiar interaction, and familiar representations seems to be essential for the users to feel confident and consider the tool potentially useful. Surprisingly, our expert has not been able to start any constructive exploration during our first meeting as he *"[couldn't] work without seeing somewhere some plots stacked in a linear view"*. However, he did not use the Detailed Comparison Window as much as expected during the second interview. To his own surprise, he admitted that it was reassuring to be able to get back to the traditional representation, *"I know it is there, so I feel comfortable using the tool now"*. It is difficult to make an interface feel familiar since people have different working habits, especially when targeting a wide audience. We strived to design KronoMiner to be as flexible as possible for multipurpose analysis through participatory design studies deliberately involving researchers from disparate domains, as a guarantee not to specialize to a domain and an attempt to cover common needs. By doing so, we think our tool is adapted to a wide audience. In return, it is still too general to fully support deep analysis, as our user quickly missed analytical operations he is used to apply - *"It would be great if you can add more operators to the lens"*. Allowing users to customize the tool has revealed to be crucial for functionalities extension purpose. We also believe that this would help them accept more easily new ways of interacting, as they could personalize the tool to fit with their needs.

CONCLUSION AND FUTURE WORK

This paper introduces KronoMiner, a multipurpose tool for exploring time-series datasets. KronoMiner integrates new interaction and visualization techniques in a seamless tool designed to be as unconstraining as possible so as to ease the exploration of multiple sub-pieces of interest for finer analysis. Although it does not solve all the problems, KronoMiner illustrates how multi-foci navigation enriched with general statistical tools can help users perform exploratory analysis on multiple time-series data. Feedback from experts confirmed our belief that users benefit from systems combining both improved algorithms and interactive visual interfaces to identify trends or spot anomalies. In particular, the MagicAnalytics Lens that provides an immediate visual feedback has revealed to be a promising technique.

Despite the positive early feedback, longitudinal studies still have to be run to validate our claims and better spot the limitations. We plan to provide all our experts with a release of the tool for them to try it deeper on their own data and gather their feedback. We will also encompass a mechanism for the user to be able to customize the analytical tools to study how far a general tool can support tasks the users are used to perform with their traditional specialized systems.

REFERENCES

1. W. Aigner, S. Miksch, W. Müller, H. Schumann, and C. Tominski. Visualizing time-oriented data-a systematic view. *Comput. Graph.*, 31(3):401–409, June 2007.
2. W. Aigner, S. Miksch, W. Müller, H. Schumann, and C. Tominski. Visual methods for analyzing time-oriented data. *IEEE TVCG*, 14(1):47–60, 2008.
3. C. Appert and J.-D. Fekete. Orthozoom scroller: 1d multi-scale navigation. In *Proc. CHI'06*, 21–30, 2006.
4. E. A. Bier, M. C. Stone, K. Pier, W. Buxton, and T. D. DeRose. Toolglass and magic lenses: the see-through interface. In *SIGGRAPH '93*, 73–80, 1993.
5. P. Buono, A. Aris, C. Plaisant, A. Khella, and B. Shneiderman. Interactive pattern search in time series. In *Proc. of Visualization and Data Analysis*, 175–186, 2005.
6. W. Chung, H. Chen, L. G. Chaboya, C. D. O'Toole, and H. Atabakhsh. Evaluating event visualization: a usability study of coplink spatio-temporal visualizer. *Int. J. Hum.-Comput. Stud.*, 62(1):127–157, 2005.
7. P. Dragicevic and S. Huot. Spiraclock: a continuous and non-intrusive display for upcoming events. In *Proc. CHI'02*, 604–605, 2002.
8. G. M. Draper, Y. Livnat, and R. F. Riesenfeld. A survey of radial methods for information visualization. *IEEE TVCG*, 15(5):759–776, 2009.
9. N. Elmqvist, Y. Riche, N. H. Riche, and J.-D. Fekete. Melange: Space folding for visual exploration. *IEEE TVCG*, 16(3):468–483, 2010.
10. J. Fails, A. Karlson, L. Shahamat, and B. Shneiderman. A visual interface for multivariate temporal data: Finding patterns of events across multiple histories. *Symposium On Visual Analytics Science And Technology*, 0:167–174, 2006.
11. P. Fitts and J. Peterson. Information capacity of discrete motor responses. *Jrnl of Experimental Psychology*, 67:103–112, 1964.
12. J. Gao, Y. Cao, W.-w. Tung, and J. Hu. *Multiscale Analysis of Complex Time Series: Integration of Chaos and Random Fractal Theory, and Beyond.* Wiley-Interscience, 2007.
13. J. Heer, N. Kong, and M. Agrawala. Sizing the horizon: The effects of chart size and layering on the graphical perception of time series visualizations. In *Proc. CHI'09*, 2009.
14. J. Heer, J. Mackinlay, C. Stolte, and M. Agrawala. Graphical histories for visualization: Supporting analysis, communication, and evaluation. *IEEE TVCG*, 14:1189–1196, 2008.
15. H. Hochheiser and B. Shneiderman. Dynamic query tools for time series data sets: timebox widgets for interactive exploration. *Information Visualization*, 3(1):1–18, 2004.
16. D. Holten. Hierarchical edge bundles: Visualization of adjacency relations in hierarchical data. *IEEE Transactions on Visualization and Computer Graphics*, 12:741–748, 2006.
17. W. Javed and N. Elmqvist. Stack zooming for multi-focus interaction in time-series data visualization. In *PacificVis'10*, 33–40, 2010.
18. W. Javed, B. McDonnel, and N. Elmqvist. Graphical perception of multiple time series. *IEEE TVCG*, 16(6):927–934, 2010.
19. E. J. Keogh and M. J. Pazzani. Relevance feedback retrieval of time series data. In *SIGIR'99*, 183–190, 1999.
20. R. Lopez-hernandez, D. Guilmaine, M. J. Mcguffin, and L. Barford. A layer-oriented interface for visualizing time-series data from oscilloscopes. In *PacificVis'10*, 41–48, 2010.
21. M. J. McGuffin and I. Jurisica. Interaction techniques for selecting and manipulating subgraphs in network visualizations. *IEEE TVCG*, 15(6):937–944, 2009.
22. P. McLachlan, T. Munzner, E. Koutsofios, and S. North. Liverac: interactive visual exploration of system management time-series data. In *Proc. CHI'08*, 1483–1492, 2008.
23. M. D. Meyer, T. Munzner, and H. Pfister. Mizbee: A multiscale synteny browser. *IEEE TVCG*, 15(6):897–904, 2009.
24. W. Mller and H. Schumann. Visualization methods for time-dependant data-an overview. In *Proc. of the 2003 Winter Simulation Conference*, 737–745, 2003.
25. C. Plaisant, B. Milash, A. Rose, S. Widoff, and B. Shneiderman. Lifelines: visualizing personal histories. In *Proc. CHI'96*, 221–227, 1996.
26. H. A. Richter, J. A. Brotherton, G. Abowd, and K. N. Truong. A multi-scale timeline slider for stream visualization and control. Technical report, Georgia Institute of Technology, 1999.
27. B. Shneiderman. Direct manipulation: A step beyond programming languages. *Computer*, 16:57–69, 1983.
28. B. Shneiderman. The eyes have it: A task by data type taxonomy for information visualizations. In *VL*, 336–343, 1996.
29. S. F. Silva and T. Catarci. Visualization of linear time-oriented data: A survey. *Proc. of the Int. Conf. on Web Information Systems Engineering*, 310, 2000.
30. C. Tominski, J. Abello, and H. Schumann. Axes-based visualizations with radial layouts. In *SAC'04: Proc. of the Symp. on Applied computing*, 1242–1247, 2004.
31. J. W. Tukey. *Exploratory Data Analysis*. Addison-Wesley, 1977.
32. J. J. Van Wijk. Cluster and calendar based visualization of time series data. In *Proc. INFOVIS'99*, 4–9, 1999.
33. M. Weber, M. Alexa, and W. Müller. Visualizing time-series on spirals. In *Proc. INFOVIS'01*, 7, 2001.

LifeFlow: Visualizing an Overview of Event Sequences

Krist Wongsuphasawat[1,2],
John Alexis Guerra Gómez[1,2],
Catherine Plaisant[2],
Taowei David Wang[1,2],
Ben Shneiderman[1,2]
Department of Computer Science[1] &
Human-Computer Interaction Lab[2]
University of Maryland, College Park, MD
{kristw,jguerrag,plaisant,tw7,ben}@cs.umd.edu

Meirav Taieb-Maimon[2,3]
Ben-Gurion University of the Negev[3]
Beer-Sheva, Israel
meiravta@bgu.ac.il

ABSTRACT
Event sequence analysis is an important task in many domains: medical researchers may study the patterns of transfers within the hospital for quality control; transportation experts may study accident response logs to identify best practices. In many cases they deal with thousands of records. While previous research has focused on searching and browsing, overview tasks are often overlooked. We introduce a novel interactive visual overview of event sequences called *LifeFlow*. LifeFlow is scalable, can summarize all possible sequences, and represents the temporal spacing of the events within sequences. Two case studies with healthcare and transportation domain experts are presented to illustrate the usefulness of LifeFlow. A user study with ten participants confirmed that after 15 minutes of training novice users were able to rapidly answer questions about the prevalence and temporal characteristics of sequences, find anomalies, and gain significant insight from the data.

Author Keywords
Timestamped Event Sequences, Temporal Categorical Data

ACM Classification Keywords
H.5.2 Information Interfaces and Presentation: User Interfaces—*Graphical user interfaces (GUI)*

General Terms
Design

INTRODUCTION
Event sequences are series of timestamped events. For example, Electronic Health Records (EHRs) contain doctor visits, lab results, medication orders, transfer among hospital departments etc. Highway incident logs, student records, web logs, usability study logs, are other examples.

Patient – (6:11, Arrive Hospital), (6:15, Emergency Room), (9:05, ICU), ...
Incident – (8:05, Incident Notification), (8:10, Police arrived), ...
Student – (28 Aug'07, Enter PhD program), (30 Apr'10, Proposal), ...

Event sequence analysis looks at (1) the sequence of events (e.g. Arrival→Intensive Care Unit (ICU)→Floor) and (2) time gaps between events (e.g. Emergency Room *(and after 5 hours)*→ Transfer to ICU). Medical researchers might be interested in analyzing transfer sequences in hospitals to improve the quality of care, while traffic managers are interested in analyzing incident logs to identify best practices.

Previous work on temporal data visualization can support many types of analysis, ranging from examining a single record in details to various ways of filtering and searching multiple records. They can answer questions regarding the number of records that include a specific event sequence but questions requiring an overview are not adequately supported. E.g., a question such as "What are the most common transfer patterns between services within the hospital?" requires examination of all records one by one. Being unable to see all records on the screen at once makes it difficult to spot any pattern. Squeezing a billion records into a million pixels [30] is a great challenge in information visualization. In this paper we introduce a novel interactive visual overview of event sequences called *LifeFlow*, which is scalable and can summarize not only all possible sequences but also the temporal spacing of the events within sequences. We first describe a motivating example from the medical domain, then introduce the LifeFlow visualization, review related work, describe the user interface interactive features, and finally present the results of our evaluations (two case studies and a laboratory study with ten participants). While the examples in this paper focus on the medical domain, the technique is widely applicable to other fields, such as incident management, log analysis, or the study of human activities in general. To gain a further understanding of the interactive experience, see the videos at http://www.cs.umd.edu/hcil/lifeflow.

MOTIVATING CASE STUDY
The use of information visualization to support patient care and clinical research is gaining momentum [1, 19, 9]. We have been working with physicians from the Washington Hospital Center for several years, and continuously identifying case studies that inform the design of our tools and help us

evaluate the usefulness of our approaches. This section describes a particular case study that motivated the original design of LifeFlow. It was conducted with Dr. Phuong Ho, a practicing physician in the emergency department, who was interested in analyzing sequences of patient transfers between departments for quality assurance.

Event Definitions

These terms will be used when describing the case study.
1) *ER*: Emergency Room, the section of a hospital intended to provide treatment for victims of sudden illness or trauma
2) *ICU*: Intensive Care Unit, a hospital unit in which patients requiring close monitoring and intensive care are kept
3) *IMC*: Intermediate Care, a level of medical care in a hospital that is intermediate between ICU and Floor
4) *Floor*: a hospital ward where patients receive normal care

Example question

One of Dr. Ho's particular interests was the monitoring of *bounce backs*, which occurred when a patients' level of care is decreased then increased back again urgently. E.g., a patient's condition might have improved enough to have him transferred from the ICU to Floor, but his condition worsened again and he had to be sent back to intensive care within 48 hours, suggesting he might have left the ICU too early. This pattern corresponds to a hospital quality metric that is very rarely monitored. Dr. Ho had been using an MS Excel spreadsheet to find these patients. In an interview he described the complex and time consuming effort to create the formulas and view the data. This is due in part to the fact that there are many room types and special conditions for using those rooms. We had previously worked with Dr. Ho using *LifeLines2* [35] and Similan [39] to locate patients with specific known event sequences such as the one described above. Once it had become easy to search for specific known sequences we identified other questions that could not be answered as easily; e.g.: what typically happens to patients after they leave the ER, or the ICU; what are the most common transfer patterns, what is the percentage of patients transferred from ICU to Floor and how long does it take, are there any unexpected sequences? All those new questions require a summary of all the transfer sequences and their temporal attributes. To this end, we propose *LifeFlow* to provide an overview of all transfer sequences.

LIFEFLOW DISPLAY

Figure 1 illustrates the conversion from four records of event sequences to the LifeFlow display. Raw data are displayed on a horizontal timeline with colored triangles representing events (in the same approach as LifeLines2 [35]). Each row represents one record. The transformation into LifeFlow takes two steps: aggregation and visualization.

1) *Aggregation* – All records are aggregated into a tree-based data structure called a *tree of sequences* based on the prefixes of their event sequences. For example, a record that contains event sequence Arrival → ER → ICU and a record that contains event sequence Arrival → ER → Floor, share the same prefix sequence Arrival → ER. The records are grouped event-by-event from the beginning of the event sequences to the end. In Figure 1, all records start with the

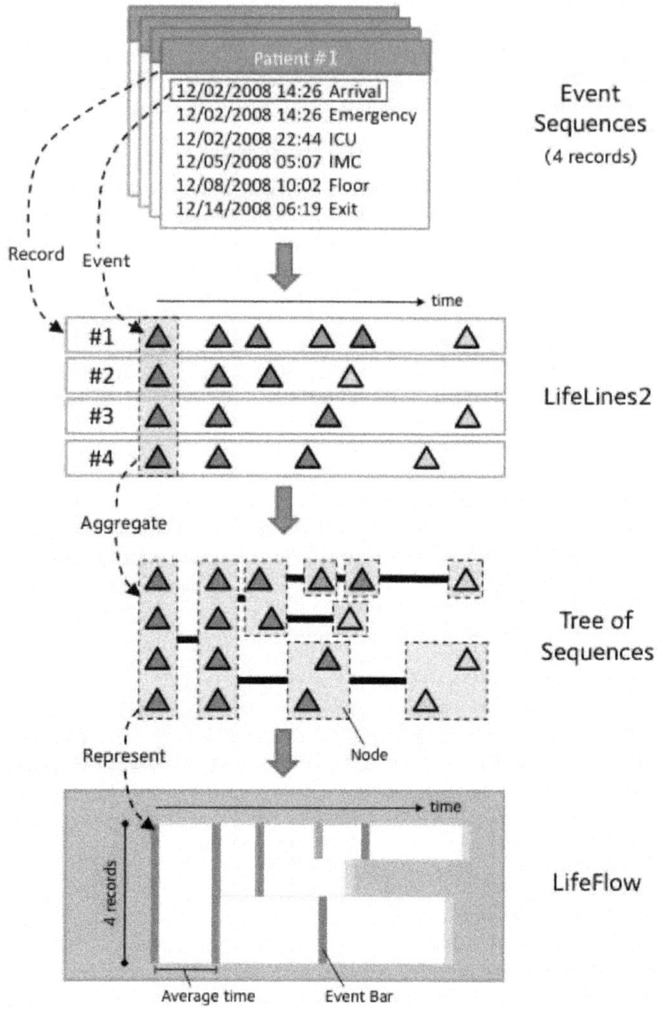

Figure 1. This diagram explains how a LifeFlow display can be constructed to summarize four records of event sequences. Raw data are represented as colored triangles on a horizontal timeline (using the traditional approach also used in LifeLines2). Each row represents one record. The records are aggregated by sequence into a data structure called a tree of sequences. The tree of sequences is then converted into LifeFlow visualization. Each tree node is represented with an event bar. The height of the bar is proportional to the number of records while its horizontal position is determined by the average time between events.

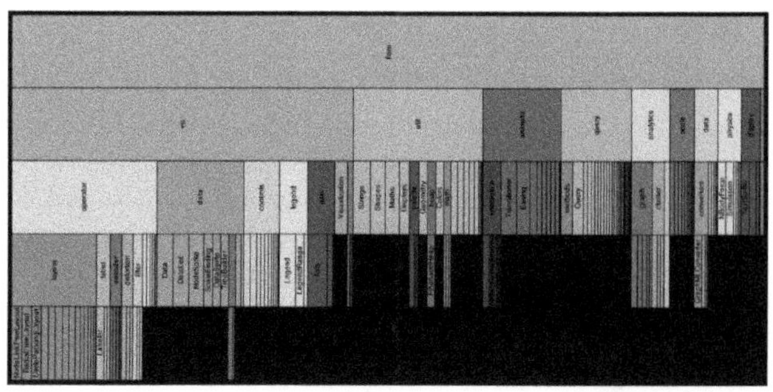

Figure 2. The Icicle Tree Visualization - the inspiration for Lifeflow - is used to display hierarchical information. The biggest rectangle on the top represents the root node. The children nodes are placed under their parent nodes. Each node's width is determined by a sum of its children's width.

blue event so they are grouped together (indicated by dashed rectangle) in to a blue tree node. Then, they all also have the pink event, so they are still grouped together into a pink node. In the next step, two of them have red events while the other two have green events so they are split into red and green nodes. Then do the same for the rest of the event sequences. In some situations, users may chose to group consecutive events of the same type together when building the tree of sequences. For example, two consecutive transfers to Floor can be treated as one transfer with the second transfer ignored. A record with sequence Arrival → ER → Floor → Floor → ICU is treated as Arrival → ER → Floor → ICU. This aggregation option can be turned on or off as needed.

2) *Visualization* – Once the tree of sequences is created, it can be visualized into the LifeFlow display. Each node of the tree is represented with a color-coded *event bar*, matching the color of the event type. The height of a bar is determined by the number of records in that node proportionally to the total number of records. E.g., the red node contains two out of four records so the height of its corresponding event bar is 50% of the total height. The horizontal gap between a bar (e.g. pink bar) and its parent (the blue bar on its left) is proportional to the mean time between the two events (blue → pink). By default, the representative time gap is the mean, but users can select other metrics, such as the median.

The LifeFlow display is scalable because it does not require additional space for a larger number of records. Users can display hundreds of records or millions of records using the same amount of screen space.

RELATED WORK

Temporal Data Visualization

Single-Record Visualization – There has been a long history of visualizing event sequences. Many systems were designed for analyzing a single record [10, 14, 18, 26, 4, 2]. The most common approach is to use a timeline-based representation. Events are placed on a horizontal timeline according to their time. One record consists of multiple rows, one for each category of events. Spiral timelines – in which angle represents time interval (time of day, days of week, months, or years)– were inspired by the cyclic nature of how we organize time and used to reveal periodic patterns in time series [8, 16, 37].

Visualization of multiple records in parallel – To support the analysis of multiple records, a common technique is to stack instances of single-record visualizations. [11, 33]. Weber *et al.*'s spiral-based visualization [37] also supports multiple records by showing each record as one ring. Those tools typically provide searching and filtering mechanisms [35, 39, 34]. In the context of our case study, users of those tools could find patients who were transferred with a specific known sequence, or find patients who were admitted to the ICU at least once, but could not find out what the common sequences are or spot anomalous sequences. Some tools allowed the users to organize records into hierarchy [7] or groups [25]. Timeline Tree [7] is a tree with timelines at the leaf nodes. Progressive Multiples [25] allow users to manually place multiple timelines in folders. However, unlike LifeFlow which provides one visual abstraction that represents multiple timelines, they do not provide any abstraction.

Visualization of combined records – To overcome the scalability issue and provide an overview, some systems provide an abstraction of multiple records [15, 3, 36]. *Continuum* [3] shows a histogram of frequency of events over time while *LifeLines2* [36] has a *temporal summary*, which is a stacked bar chart that shows the distribution of event types within each period of time. These methods can provide the distribution of events by time, which answers the questions related to the distribution, such as which type of event occurred most frequently in January 2007 or which type of event usually occurred within the first week after patients arrived at the hospital? However, the event sequences within the records are obscured and thus, it cannot answer questions related to sequences, such as where did the patient usually go directly after arrival or what is the most common transfer sequence?

Hierarchy Visualization

In LifeFlow, all records are first grouped into a hierarchical structure called a tree of sequences. Many visualizations can display hierarchical structures [32]. The most common way is to display a node-link layout in 2D [5, 38, 27], or 3D [28] or hyperbolic space [21, 24]. Space-filling techniques use implicit containment and geometry features to present a hierarchy [17, 20, 12, 6, 32]. *Icicle tree* [20, 12, 6], also called *Icicle plot*, displays hierarchical data as stacked rectangles, usually ordered from top to bottom. This visualization directly inspired our LifeFlow design (Figure 2). The root takes the entire width. Each child node is placed under its parent with the width proportional to the percentage it consumes relative to its siblings. Using these methods, the sequences of events can be represented. However, the length of time between events – which is important in many analyses – is not represented. A *phylogenetic tree* [22] is a branching diagram showing the inferred evolutionary relationships among various biological species. The edge lengths in some phylogenetic trees may be interpreted as time estimates, but each node in the tree represents only one species while each node in LifeFlow represents multiple records of event sequences. *VizTree* [23] uses a tree-based representation to detect patterns within a very long event sequences (like EKGs). For example, for a record that contains sequence of events "A,B,A,B,B,B", VizTree creates a prefix tree of all subsequences (ABA, BAB, ABB, ...), then displays the prefix tree using edge thickness to represent frequency, which can reveal frequent and rare subsequences. As with other tree-based approaches, VizTree also ignores the duration of the time gap between events. Also, VizTree focused on analyzing event sequences of length n in a single very long record rather than providing an overview of millions of records.

In summary, LifeFlow represents a new and powerful approach to aggregate event sequences, much like a compact Table of Contents is a powerful addition when there is only a search box for a full length book. LifeFlow allows users to see not only all possible sequences but also their prevalence and summarize information about the time gap between events, which is not supported by other visualizations.

LIFEFLOW INTERACTIVE FEATURES

Our working prototype of LifeFlow (Figure 3) includes the following interaction features to support exploration:

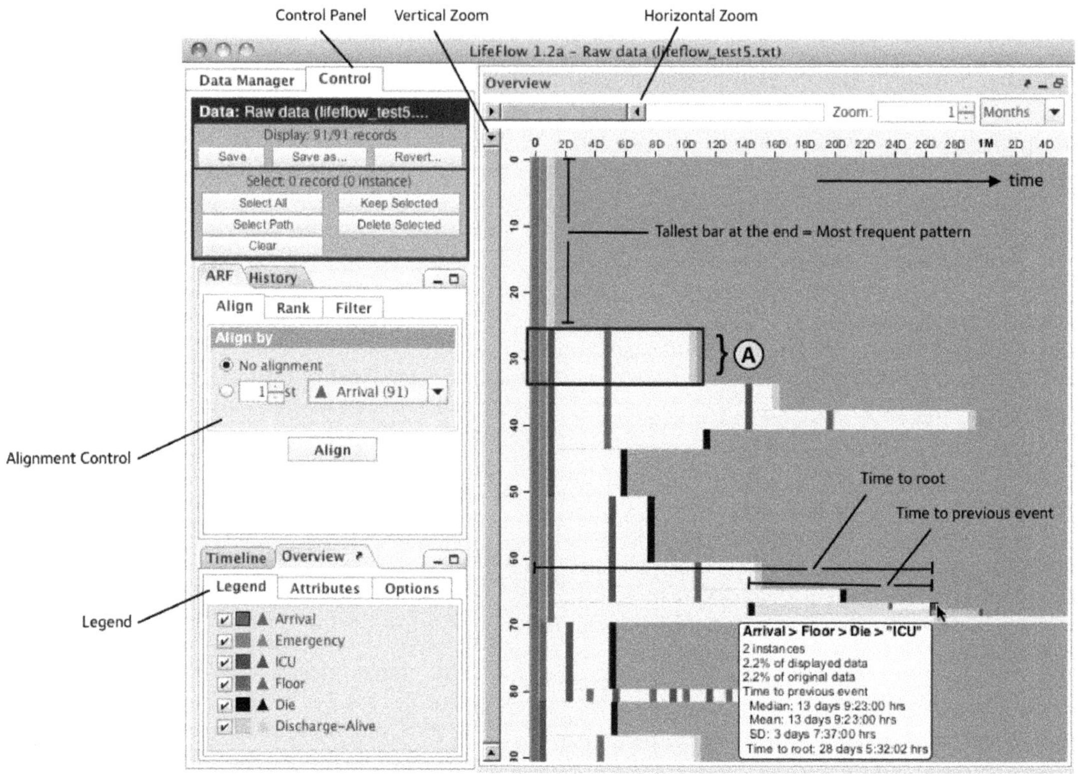

Figure 3. This screenshot of LifeFlow shows a random sample of patient transfer data based on real de-identified data (as used in the user study). The way to read sequences in LifeFlow is to read the colors (using the legend). For example the sequence (A) in the figure is Arrival (blue), Emergency (pink), ICU (red), Floor (green) and Discharge-Alive (light blue). The horizontal gap between colored bars represents the average time between events, showing that it takes approximately 4 days on average for patients to go from ICU to the floor in that (A) sequence . The height of the bars is proportional to the number of records, therefore showing the relative frequency of that sequence. The bars (e.g. Floor and Die) with same parent (Arrival → Emergency → ICU) are ordered by frequency (tallest bar on top), as you can see that Floor (green bar) is placed above Die (black bar). To find the most frequent pattern is to find the tallest bar at the end. Here it shows that the most common sequence is Arrival, Emergency then Discharge alive. Surprisingly, two patients were reported dead before transferred to ICU which indicates a data entry problem. (Please note that this is only a sample dataset and does not reflect the real performance of any hospital.)

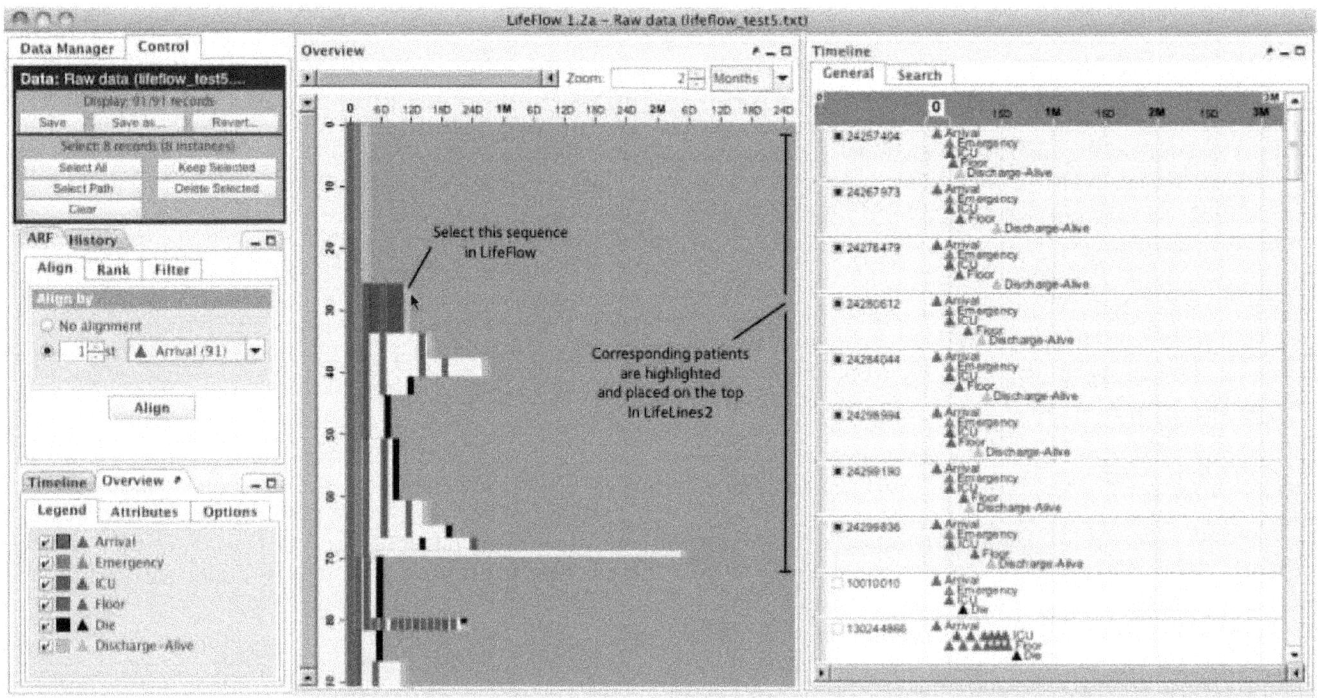

Figure 4. Here LifeFlow is used side-by-side with LifeLines2 so that individual records can be reviewed by scrolling. When a user clicks on a sequence in LifeFlow, the sequence is highlighted and all corresponding records are also highlighted and moved to the top in LifeLines2, allowing the user to examine them in more details.

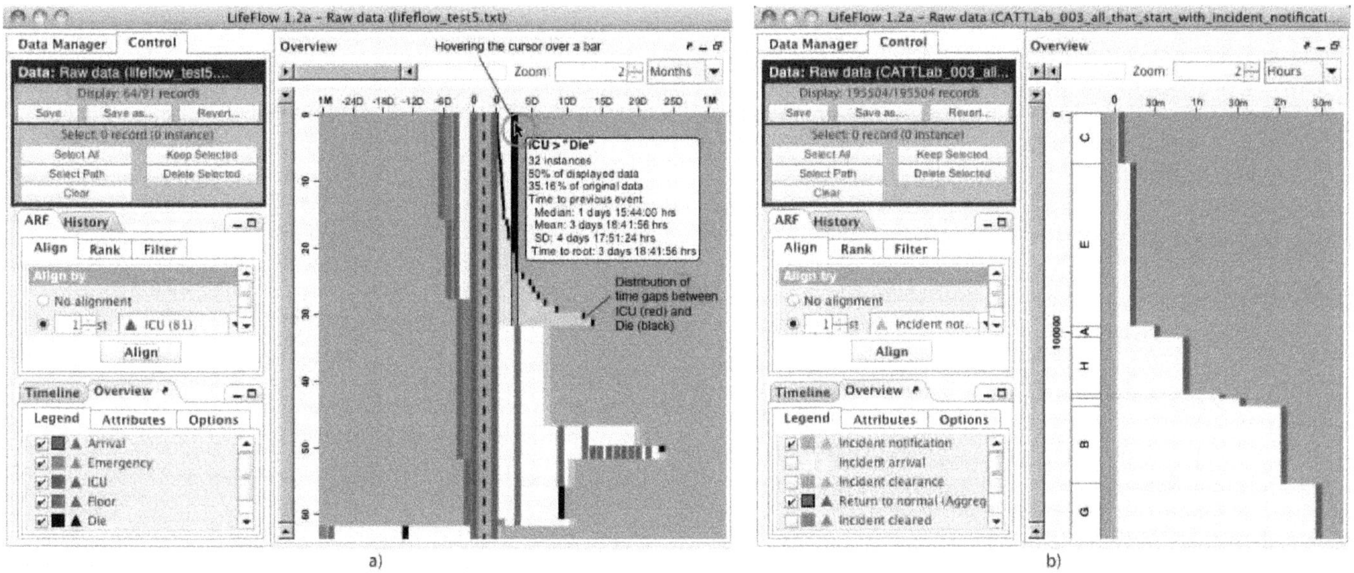

Figure 5. a) LifeFlow with alignment – The same data with Figure 3 was aligned by ICU. The user can see that the patients were most likely to die after a transfer to the ICU than any other sequence. (Please note that this is a random sample dataset and does not reflect the real performance of any hospital.) b) LifeFlow with traffic incidents data – The incidents are separated by agencies (A-G). Only "Incident Notification" and "Return to normal (aggregated)" events are shown. Other events are hidden. The agencies are sorted by a simple measure of agency performance (average time from the beginning to the end). Agency C seems to be the fastest to clear its incidents, followed by E, A, H, D, F, B and finally G.

1) *Zooming* – The horizontal zoom changes time granularity while the vertical zoom allows the users to see rare sequences in more detail.

2) *Tooltip* – When users move the mouse cursor over an event bar (Figure 3), a tooltip displays the full sequence of events, and some statistical information, such as mean time between events, standard deviation, etc.

3) *Overlay distribution of gap between events* – Hovering the cursor over a bar displays the distribution of time gaps overlaid on the Lifeflow. Figure 5a shows the distribution of length of stay in the ICU before the patients died.

4) *Sort* – Users can sort the sequences with the same parent in different ways: by the number of records that the bars represent (tallest bar on top) (Figure 3) or by the average time to previous event (shortest time on top) (Figure 5b). The default is to sort by number of records.

5) *Integration with LifeLines2* – LifeFlow can function as a standalone tool but combining with LifeLines2 facilitates exploration by allowing users to review individual records as details on demand [29]. By clicking on any event bar, users select all records that are included in that bar (Figure 4). Selected records are highlighted in the LifeLines2 view. Users can then choose to keep only the selection and remove everything else, or vice versa. In a symmetrical fashion, selecting a record in the LifeLines2 view highlights the pattern contained in that record in the LifeFlow view, allowing the users to find other records that contain the same sequence.

6) *Align* – Inspired by LifeLines2, LifeFlow allows users to choose any event type to be the *alignment* point. This supports tasks such as "what happened to the patients before and after they went to the ICU?" By default, the alignment point is not specified, so all records are aligned by the first event in the record. When users chose an alignment event, two trees of sequences are built: one tree for the sequences before the alignment (from right to left) and another tree for the sequences after the alignment (from left to right). Figure 5a shows LifeFlow with alignment. The vertical dashed line marks the aligned event. The left and right side are what happened before and after the reference point, respectively. Now one can see that in this dataset, patients most often come to ICU from Floor. After that, they often died.

7) *Including non-temporal attributes* – Records usually also contain non-temporal attributes, e.g., patient's gender. While LifeFlow does not focus on displaying those attributes, it allows users to select a non-temporal attribute and groups records by that attribute before the sequences are aggregated. LifeFlow in Figure 5b groups traffic incident records by agency before aggregating by sequence, therefore allowing simple comparison between agencies.

8) *Include/Exclude event types* – Using the legend on the left side of the screen users can check or uncheck event types to include or exclude them from the sequences. This simple functionality allows powerful transformations of the display to answer questions. E.g., in Figure 5b, the user unchecked all event types except "Incident Notification" and "Return to normal", i.e. the beginning and end of incidents. All other events that could occur during an incident are ignored and LifeFlow regenerated to show only those two event types, allowing rapid comparisons between the agencies in terms of number of incidents and average time to clear the incidents.

9) *Displaying all event bars with equal height* – When data includes a large number of sequences, it could be difficult to review the rare sequences because they are represented with very thin bars. This option displays all leaf nodes using equal height regardless of the number of records, makes it easier to review and select rare sequences.

EVALUATION

We reported two case studies in two different domains following the Multi-Dimensional In-Depth Long-Term Case Studies (MILC) [31] approach. The two studies were done in collaboration with the physicians at the Washington Hospital Center and the Center for Advanced Transportation Technology Laboratory at the University of Maryland, respectively. In addition, we conducted a user study with 10 participants.

CASE STUDY I: MEDICAL DOMAIN

As discussed in the beginning of the paper, the design of LifeFlow was motivated by the patient transfer case study. As we developed LifeFlow we continued to work with Dr. Phuong Ho to analyze more patient transfer data, and in more details. We had a 1-2 hours meeting with him approximately every two weeks for 3 months. Before the meeting he provided us with the data that he wanted to analyze, and a few initial questions. We converted the data and during the meeting sat down and looked at the data together. After discussing the questions sent in advance, he would come up with additional questions and gave feedback about the user interface, therefore closely guiding our development. We summarized the results as follows:

First impression – The first time we showed LifeFlow to Dr. Ho using patient transfer data, he was immediately enthusiastic and confident that the tool would be useful for looking at all patients who came to the hospital and in particular the emergency room (ER). He knew that many people would want to see the typical flow of the patients and the transfer time between rooms. In another meeting, we received additional feedback from the director of the Emergency Department. Finding the bounce back patients visually in the display elicited comments such as "Oh! This is very cool!" and led to a discussion of the possibilities of using this tool to analyze hospital data in the long run.

Understanding the big picture – One of the datasets we received included all 7,041 patients who came to the ER in Jan 2010. Each record contains room assignments, time that the patient was assigned to each room, and how he/she was discharged from the hospital: dead, alive, leave without being seen (LWBS) and absence without leave (AWOL). We preprocessed the data by grouping the room numbers (e.g. ER15-P, 2G06-P) into types of room (ER, ICU, IMC, Floor). In the meeting, we showed LifeFlow and Dr. Ho could review the flow of patients in the hospital. The first thing that he noticed was the most common pattern, Arrival → ER → Discharge-Alive. 4,591 (65.20%) of the patients were not admitted to the hospital (discharged directly from the ER). This is regular and consistent with what he had expected because most of the patients who visited the ER were not in severe condition and could leave immediately after they received their treatment, so we removed these 4,591 patients from the visualization to analyze other patterns. The second most common pattern, Arrival → ER → Floor → Discharge-Alive (1,016 patients, 14.43%), now became more obvious. We decided to remove it too because it was also regular. We followed the same strategy, selecting regular common sequences and removing them from the visualization to detect the uncommon cases that might be irregular. Our partner noticed that 193 patients (2.74%) left without being seen while 38 patients (0.54%) were absence without leave. These two numbers could be compared with the hospital standard for quality control. Then, our partner saw two patterns that he was interested in (Arrival → ER → Floor → IMC and Arrival → ER → Floor → ICU). These patterns correspond to another quality control metric called *step ups*, which occurs when the patients were admitted to a lower level of care (Floor), but later transferred to a higher level of care (IMC or ICU). Dr. Ho could quickly see from the visualization that the patients were transferred from Floor to ICU faster than Floor to IMC on average so he used the tooltip to see the distribution. He captured screenshots to compare with practices reported in the research literature, but also commented that the average time seemed quite good from his knowledge.

We also demonstrated the alignment and used it to analyze the transfer flow before and after the patients were admitted to the ICU. From the total 181 ICU patients, 85 (46.96%) of them were transferred from the ER and 119 (66.75%) of them were transferred to the Floor after that. However, 6 patients were transferred back from Floor to ICU (bounce backs). We saw from the distribution that one patient was transferred back in less than a day. Dr. Ho requested to see these 6 patients in more details so we clicked on the bar, which highlighted these patients in LifeLines2 view and noted down these patients' ID. In addition, he also noticed some anomalous sequences, e.g. a few patient records showed a transfer to ICU after being discharged dead, pointing to obvious error in data entry or at least reflecting the possible delays in data entry. Although we did not identify other surprising transfers (which on the other hand, reflected good quality of care), this still showed that the tool is useful for monitoring the patient transfer flow. We also received additional questions from Dr. Ho after the meeting. Some questions included clear request for alignments ("I want to see this in LifeFlow. Specifically I want to see a view that shows me where all my [ICU] patients are coming from.") indicating that he could understand what the tool is capable of and how to use it for his task.

Measuring the transfer time – Because LifeFlow can easily calculate an average time, Dr. Ho formulated many queries asking about average time, such as "Of patients who came to the ICU from the ER, what was the average time it took for transfer of the patient to the ICU? More specifically, if they went to the ICU, how long did it take from the time they had arrived at the ER to get to the ICU? Same question for IMC..." or "For all the quarters, Jan-Mar 09, Apr-Jun 09, Jul-sep 09, Oct- Dec 09 and Jan-Mar 10, I want average time from ER to 2G [which is a specific type of ICU room]."

Comparison – Another use of LifeFlow was to compare different data sets by inspecting the difference between two side-by-side LifeFlow visualizations. Dr. Ho had a hypothesis about whether IMC patients were transferred faster during the day (7am-7pm) than during the night. We opened the same dataset in two windows and filtered the records by time-of-day filtering, making the two windows contain only patients who arrived during the day and during the night, respectively. We inspected the difference between the two visualizations but no significant difference was found. In another case, we compared patients who were admitted to the IMC at least once in four quarters: Jan-Mar, Apr-Jun, Jul-Sep and Oct-Dec 2008. We opened the four datasets in four LifeFlow windows and noticed a difference in the patients who were transferred from ER to the ICU. In the first, third and fourth quarter, these patients were later transferred to IMC and Floor, with majority were transferred to the IMC. However, in the second quarter, all patients were later transferred to the IMC, suggesting further investigation whether this occurred by chance or any particular reason.

Discussion

We found that our domain expert was able to understand LifeFlow rapidly and that LifeFlow was useful to provide an overview of the entire data set, and to compare and measure the transfer times. Once the data was loaded, he could quickly see the big picture and find anomalies. Dr. Ho expressed that being able to formulate queries easily gave him more time to look at the data and formulate new hypotheses or think about other interesting questions. Although he might have been able to answer of some of the questions in SQL, it would be very difficult and error prone. He also mentioned that LifeFlow would be very useful for long-term monitoring and quality control because it provides a quick way to inspect the data from the overview. Another researcher who recently started a case study with us also gave this comment on LifeFlow: "Statistical techniques for dealing with longitudinal data generally focus on changes in continuous variables over time, and the problem of identifying patterns of sequence and temporal spacing in categorical events is not handled by standard techniques and software. This problem arises a lot in analysis of health care data, and this tool opens up a kind of study that just hasn't been possible before."

CASE STUDY II: TRANSPORTATION DOMAIN

To illustrate how LifeFlow is not in anyway limited to medical applications, we describe a second case study currently underway with the Center for Advanced Transportation Technology Lab (CATT Lab) at the University of Maryland [13]. We are using LifeFlow to examine a data set from the National Cooperative Highway Research Program (NCHRP) that includes 203,214 traffic incidents from 8 agencies. Each incident record includes a sequence of incident management events: *Incident notification* –when the agency is first notified of the incident, *Incident Arrival* –when the emergency team arrives the scene, *Lane Clearance* –when the lanes are opened, but the incident scene may be not completely cleared, *Incident cleared, Incident clearance*, and *Return to normal* –all denote the end of incidents. For ease of analysis, we aggregated all three into the new event type *Return to normal (aggregated)*. A typical sequence should start with "Incident Notification" and finish with "Return to normal (aggregated)", with the possibility of having "Incident Arrival" and "Lance Clearance" in between. In addition, the traffic incidents data includes two attributes: the agency (represented with a letter from A to H for anonymity) and the type of incident (e.g. Disabled Vehicle, Fatal Accident, etc.)

Quantifying data quality issues – After loading the dataset in LifeFlow, we immediately noticed that the Agency B contains a sequence that was more than 110 years long with 6,712 incidents. Investigating further, we found that Agency B reported the "Incident Arrival" of those incidents as January 1th 1900. Since this date is commonly used as the initial date in computer systems, this suggested that the system the Agency used to register this event might have used it as a default value. Considering these incidents as corrupted data, we removed all of them from the dataset. While it was easy to spot this problem, such anomalies can often remain undetected, and skew the results of even the simplest of analysis such as calculating the mean time to clearance. Similarly, we found and removed 48 incidents from Agency D that are about 10 months long, in which the "Incident Arrival" occurs before the "Incident Notification".

The next thing we noticed from the data was that there were many incidents that lasted exactly 24 hours, which seemed unlikely. Using the Align, Rank and Filter operators, we found that those 24-hours-long incidents have "Incident arrival" events occur in the first hour of the day (e.g. 12:30AM April 10 2009) and "Incident notification" events happened in the last hour of the same day (e.g. 11:50PM April 10 2009). This observation seemed to suggest that there were data entry problems with those incidents, indicating that the operator failed to – or was not able to – record the correct date of an event (e.g. 12:30AM Apr 11, 2009 as opposed to 12:30AM Apr 10, 2009). Similar errors were discovered for paths that are about 12 hours long, in which case the errors seem to be problems choosing between AM and PM in the date. Those anomalies were found quite easily by the computer scientist developer, who had no experience in transportation data. Finding such errors using traditional tools like SQL or manual analysis can be very difficult and time consuming, and requires experienced analysts who would suspect the existence of such errors.

Ranking the agencies' performance – In this study, we used the time from when the agencies were notified to the final clearance of the incidents as a performance measure. The time when the agency was notified can be indicated by the "Incident Notification" event. In order to compare the agencies performance, we first removed the inconsistent data (incidents that do not start with "Incident Notification"), which could be performed easily using the equal height overview feature. After the steps above, the visualization of the data can be seen in Figure 5b. Incidents are grouped by agencies. We showed only two event types ("Incident Notification" (orange) and "Return to Normal (Aggregated)" (blue)), so the horizontal length of each agency's path represents the average time from incident notification to final clearance, which reflects the performance measure for that agency. We then sorted the agencies according to the length of their paths, resulting in the fastest agency (shortest path) on the top and the slowest agency (longest path) in the bottom. From Figure 5b we could see that Agency C was the fastest agency to clear its incidents, taking about 5 minutes in average, while the slowest one was Agency G with an average of about 2 hours 27 minutes. To investigate deeper into Agency C's data, we removed the data from other agencies and looked into the different incident types reported. We found that most of the incidents that Agency C reported are "Disabled Vehicles" which had in average a time to clear of about 1 minute. Looking at the event distribution, we also found that a large number of the incidents reported "Clearance" immediately after "Incident Notification". This observation made us wonder if there is any explanation for these immediate clearances, and encouraged further analysis. In a similar fashion, we investigated Agency G, which seemed to be the slowest agency. Agency G classified their incidents in only two types "Non-ATMS Route Incident" and simply "Incident". The "Incident" incidents had an average length of about 38 minutes, which is a very good time compared to the other agencies. However, the "Non-ATMS Route Incident" incidents took in average 5 hours 14 minutes to clear. So we realized that when using the average time of all incidents from Agency G without considering the incident types, Agency G seemed to be slower than other agencies. While in fact, Agency G performed quite well for incident type "Incident".

Discussion

Although our data analysis in the case study was limited and preliminary, domain experts from the CATT Lab are conducting a more formal analysis of the data. They reviewed our work and stated that they wished LifeFlow was available earlier on when they started their own analysis. They confirmed the existence of anomalies that we had found in the data, and stated that their elimination was non-trivial when using SQL because they had to expect the errors in advance and be careful to exclude them from their analysis. However excluding all the possible erroneous sequences in a SQL query would be very difficult. In the end, they needed to review the results of SQL queries to ascertain that there were no longer any errors. Without LifeFlow, this kind of review and identification of unexpected sequences would be almost impossible. Finally, they mentioned that LifeFlow would allow them to ask more questions faster, and probably richer questions about the data. LifeFlow was also able to reveal unexpected sequences that may have been overlooked, but the tool also suggested that their prevalence is limited. We believe that using LifeFlow can assist analysts explore large datasets, such as the NCHRP traffic incident information, in ways that would be very difficult using traditional tools and might allow analysts to find richer results in less time.

USER STUDY

Our goal in this study was to investigate if LifeFlow was easy to learn, and if users could use the interface efficiently to answer representative questions. We also wanted to observe what strategies users chose and what problems they would encounter, and gather feedback and suggestions for further improvement. We used a dataset that included 91 records of hospital patient transfer (a subset of our real de-identified data, which included known anomalies to see if participants could find them). Because medical professionals have very little availability, are hard to recruit for a user study, and the data used in the study is simple enough to be understood by students, the participants we used for this study were graduate students (5 male and 5 female) from various departments of the University of Maryland. None of them was a member of the LifeFlow development team.

Procedure, Tasks and Results

Training consisted of a 12-minute video and five training questions. When the participants could answer the questions correctly, they could start the study tasks. The order of the tasks was randomly permuted across participants. The tasks were representative of the questions proposed by our domain experts during the case study, and designed to test the usability of the main interaction techniques of LifeFlow. We encouraged participants to think aloud while performing the tasks. For the first 14 tasks, observers recorded completion time and errors, if any. Because the participants needed time to understand the tasks, we gave them time to read the task description before starting the timer.

Tasks 1-9: Simple Features – The first 9 tasks required understanding the LifeFlow display and using simple interactive features such as tooltips or zooming. The tasks included questions about frequent sequences (e.g. "Where usually did the patient go after they arrived?", "What is the most common pattern?"), number of records in specified sequences (e.g. "How many patients went from arrival directly into ICU?"), time between events (e.g. "How long is the average time from ER to ICU?") and comparison between sequences (e.g. "After arriving to the ER, patients might be transferred to Floor or the ICU. Were the patients transferred from the ER to the ICU faster than from the ER to the Floor?").

Task 10-14: Advanced Features – Four tasks required using advanced features, such as alignment or using LifeFlow and LifeLines2 in combination (e.g. "Usually, where were the patients before they were admitted to the ICU for the first time?", "Retrieve the IDs of all patients with this transfer pattern." or "How many patients had the same transfer pattern as patient no.10010010?").

Results for tasks 1-14: The participants were able to perform the simple and advanced tasks quickly. They were able to use the interactions to adjust the visualization and retrieve information that was not presented in the initial view. The average $\pm$ SD completion time for the simple and advanced tasks were 14.9 ± 12.7 seconds and 15.8 ± 12.5 seconds, respectively. Please note that the participants were also narrating their actions while performing the tasks, which might have slowed them down. Only one participant made one mistake in a complex task: while retrieving the IDs of all patients who were transferred with a particularly long sequence she misread a color and could not find the correct sequence. However, she knew what she needed to do to retrieve the IDs after the sequence was found.

Task 15: Overall analysis and finding anomalies – In the last task, we asked the participants to imagine themselves as a manager who was trying to evaluate the performance of the hospital. We gave them 10 minutes to find any surprising, exceptional or impossible sequences that might indicate a problem in data entry or in hospital procedures, and explain why they thought it was a problem. We told them to report as many insights as they could in 10 minutes. We had planted three (realistic) data anomalies: 1) A few patients who died before being transferred to ICU. 2) Patients who bounce back and forth between the ICU and Floor several times. 3) Patients who stayed in the Floor for 3 months.

Results: Eight out of ten participants were able to detect all three anomalies. Two participants reported only the first two anomalies, but when we directed their attention towards the third anomaly, they explained that they had noticed it but did not think it was abnormal because some patients (e.g., cancer patients) might stay in the hospital for a long time. In addition, they also provided insight about other sequences that were possible, but undesirable from a manager's perspective, such as there were many patients who died in the Floor. They also reported surprising patterns, such as many patients were discharged alive directly from the ICU. We also observed the following common strategies: 1) Examine things that catch the eye first. 2) Scan all sequences systematically top to bottom – When they saw the normal sequence, e.g., ICU to Floor, they noted that this is good and moved on to the next sequence. 3) Align by each type of event 4) Hovering over bars with the mouse to explore distribution and detect outliers from the distribution 5) Check for more details in LifeLines2 – Although we did not display LifeLines2 at the beginning of this task, several participants opened it to use the combined view. All participants used strategies 1-3 consecutively. Three participants also followed with strategy 4. Four participants followed with strategy 5.

Debriefing: During the debrief, typical comments included: "The tool is easy to understand and easy to use.", "very easy to find common trends and uncommon sequences", "The alignment is very useful.", "In LifeFlow, it is easier to see the high level picture. With LifeLines2, you can check individuals. LifeFlow provides a great summary of the big picture." Common suggestions for improvement included increasing the bar width to make it easier to select and reorganizing the tooltip to make it more readable. Two participants also asked to analyze the data from their own research with LifeFlow.

Summary

Results suggest that users can learn to use LifeFlow in a short period of time and that LifeFlow's overview of the data allows them to understand patterns and find anomalies. There were several common strategies used when performing data analysis but not every participant used all strategies, which indicated the need for a framework to support data analysis.

CONCLUSIONS AND FUTURE WORK

Analyzing large numbers of event sequences is an important and challenging task. We introduced a new scalable visualization called LifeFlow that provides an overview of event sequences to support users' exploration, and reported on two case studies and one user study. One case study was conducted with the physicians whose questions motivated our research. The feedback from the physician was very positive. They could see clearly how this tool could be used for quality assurance in the hospital. Also, our physician partner spent less time figuring out how to specify queries and more time thinking about other interesting questions. Another case study was conducted with traffic incidents data to demonstrate the generality of the approach goes well beyond the medical domain. We were able to eliminate many errors in the data and compare different agencies' performance, thereby generating positive feedback from the domain experts. Finally, we report on a user study with ten participants which confirmed that even novice users with 15 minutes of training were able to learn to use LifeFlow and rapidly answer questions about the prevalence of interesting sequences, find anomalies, and gain significant insight from the data. We believe that LifeFlow can be applied to many other fields, where event sequences are the main focus, such as student progress analysis, usability study or web log analysis, and human activities log analysis in general. The next step of our research will focus on creating a framework to guide the data analysis, supporting comparison between datasets, integration with searching and filtering and including new interaction techniques.

ACKNOWLEDGEMENT

We would like to acknowledge the Washington Hospital Center; "Center for Integrated Transportation Systems Management, a Tier 1 Transportation Center at the University of Maryland"; and also the National Institute of Health (Grant RC1CA147489-02) for supporting this research. We also would like to thank Jen Golbeck, Tom Yeh, Sureyya Tarkan, Sigfried Gold, Nikola Ivanov, Michael VanDaniker and Michael Pack for their thoughtful comments and support.

REFERENCES

1. Aigner, W., and Miksch, S. CareVis: integrated visualization of computerized protocols and temporal patient data. *Artificial intelligence in medicine 37*, 3 (2006), 203–18.

2. Aigner, W., Miksch, S., Thurnher, B., and Biffl, S., PlanningLines: Novel Glyphs for Representing Temporal Uncertainties and Their Evaluation. *Proc. Int'l Conf. Information Visualisation* (2005), 457–463.

3. André, P., Wilson, M. L., Russell, A., Smith, D. A., Owens, A., and Schraefel, M., Continuum: designing timelines for hierarchies, relationships and scale. *Proc. ACM UIST* (2007), 101.

4. Bade, R., Schlechtweg, S., and Miksch, S., Connecting time-oriented data and information to a coherent interactive visualization. *Proc. CHI* (2004), 105–112.

5. Battista, G., Algorithms for drawing graphs: an annotated bibliography. *Computational Geometry 4*, 5 (1994), 235–282.

6. Bostock, M., and Heer, J., Protovis: a graphical toolkit for visualization. *IEEE Trans. Vis. Comput. Graphics 15*, 6 (2009), 1121–8.

7. Burch, M., Beck, F., and Diehl, S., Timeline trees: visualizing sequences of transactions in information hierarchies. *Proc. AVI* (2008), 75–82.

8. Carlis, J. V., and Konstan, J. A., Interactive visualization of serial periodic data. *Proc. ACM UIST* (1998), 29–38.

9. Chittaro, L., Visualization of patient data at different temporal granularities on mobile devices. *Proc. AVI* (2006), 484.

10. Cousins, S., and Kahn, M., The Visual Display of Temporal Information. *Artificial intelligence in medicine 3*, 6 (1991), 341–357.

11. Fails, J., Karlson, A., Shahamat, L., and Shneiderman, B., A Visual Interface for Multivariate Temporal Data: Finding Patterns of Events across Multiple Histories. *Proc. IEEE VAST* (2006), 167–174.

12. Fekete, J.-D., The InfoVis Toolkit. *Proc. IEEE Symp. Information Visualization* (2004), 167–174.

13. Guerra Gómez, J., Wongsuphasawat, K., Wang, T. D., Pack, M. and Plaisant, C., Analyzing Incident Management Event Sequences with Interactive Visualization. Transportation Research Board 90th Annual Meeting Compendium of Papers (2011).

14. Harrison, B., Owen, R., and Baecker, R., Timelines: an interactive system for the collection and visualization of temporal data. *Graphics Interface* (1994), 141.

15. Havre, S., Hetzler, E., Whitney, P., and Nowell, L., ThemeRiver: visualizing thematic changes in large document collections. *IEEE Trans. Vis. Comput. Graphics 8*, 1 (2002), 9–20.

16. Hewagamage, K., Hirakawa, M., and Ichikawa, T., Interactive visualization of spatiotemporal patterns using spirals on a geographical map. *Proc. IEEE Symp. Visual Languages* (1999), 296–303.

17. Johnson, B., and Shneiderman, B., Tree-maps: A space-filling approach to the visualization of hierarchical information structures. *Proc. IEEE Vis* (1991), 284–291.

18. Karam, G., Visualization using timelines. *Proc. ACM SIGSOFT Int'l Symp. Software testing and analysis* (1994), 125–137.

19. Klimov, D., Shahar, Y., and Taieb-Maimon, M., Intelligent visualization and exploration of time-oriented data of multiple patients. *Artificial intelligence in medicine 49*, 1 (2010), 11–31.

20. Kruskal, J., and Landwehr, J., Icicle Plots: Better Displays for Hierarchical Clustering. *The American Statistician 37*, 2 (1983), 162–168.

21. Lamping, J., The Hyperbolic Browser: A Focus+Context Technique for Visualizing Large Hierarchies. *Journal of Visual Languages & Computing 7*, 1 (1996), 33–55.

22. Letunic, I., and Bork, P., Interactive Tree Of Life (iTOL): an online tool for phylogenetic tree display and annotation. *Bioinformatics 23*, 1 (2007), 127–8.

23. Lin, J., Keogh, E., and Lonardi, S., Visualizing and discovering non-trivial patterns in large time series databases. *Information Visualization 4*, 2 (2005), 61–82.

24. Munzner, T., H3: laying out large directed graphs in 3D hyperbolic space. *Proc. VIZ '97* (1997), 2–10.

25. Phan, D., Paepcke, A., and Winograd, T., Progressive multiples for communication-minded visualization. *Proc. Graphics Interface (GI)* (2007), 225.

26. Plaisant, C., Mushlin, R., Snyder, A., Li, J., Heller, D., and Shneiderman, B., LifeLines: using visualization to enhance navigation and analysis of patient records. *Proc. AMIA Symp.* (1998), American Medical Informatics Association, 76.

27. Reingold, E., and Tilford, J., Tidier Drawings of Trees. *IEEE Trans. Softw. Eng.*, 2 (1981), 223–228.

28. Robertson, G. G., Card, S. K., and Mackinlay, J. D., Information visualization using 3D interactive animation. *Comm. of the ACM 36*, 4 (1993), 57–71.

29. Shneiderman, B., The eyes have it: a task by data type taxonomy for information visualizations. *Proc. IEEE Symp. Visual Languages* (1996), 336–343.

30. Shneiderman, B., Extreme visualization: squeezing a billion records into a million pixels. *Proc. ACM SIGMOD Conf. Management of data* (2008), 3–12.

31. Shneiderman, B., and Plaisant, C., Strategies for evaluating information visualization tools. *Proc. AVI BELIV* (2006), 1.

32. Stasko, J., and Zhang, E., Focus+context display and navigation techniques for enhancing radial, space-filling hierarchy visualizations. *Proc. IEEE Symp. Information Visualization* (2000), 57–65.

33. Vrotsou, K., Ellegard, K., and Cooper, M., Everyday Life Discoveries: Mining and Visualizing Activity Patterns in Social Science Diary Data. *Proc. Int'l Conf. Information Visualization* (2007), 130–138.

34. Vrotsou, K., Johansson, J., and Cooper, M., ActiviTree: interactive visual exploration of sequences in event-based data using graph similarity. *IEEE Trans. Vis. Comput. Graphics 15*, 6 (2009), 945–52.

35. Wang, T. D., Plaisant, C., Quinn, A. J., Stanchak, R., Murphy, S., and Shneiderman, B., Aligning temporal data by sentinel events: discovering patterns in electronic health records. *Proc. CHI* (2008), 457–466.

36. Wang, T. D., Plaisant, C., Shneiderman, B., Spring, N., Roseman, D., Marchand, G., Mukherjee, V., and Smith, M., Temporal Summaries: Supporting Temporal Categorical Searching, Aggregation and Comparison. *IEEE Trans. Vis. Comput. Graphics 15*, 6 (2009), 1049–1056.

37. Weber, M., Alexa, M., and Muller, W., Visualizing time-series on spirals. *Proc. IEEE Symp. Information Visualization* (2001), 7–13.

38. Wetherell, C., and Shannon, A., Tidy Drawings of Trees. *IEEE Trans. Softw. Eng.*, 5 (1979), 514–520.

39. Wongsuphasawat, K., and Shneiderman, B., Finding comparable temporal categorical records: A similarity measure with an interactive visualization. *Proc. IEEE VAST* (2009), 27–34.

The Photostroller

Supporting Diverse Care Home Residents in Engaging with the World

William Gaver[1], Andy Boucher[1], John Bowers[1], Mark Blythe[2], Nadine Jarvis[1], David Cameron[1], Tobie Kerridge[1], Alex Wilkie[1], Robert Phillips[1], Peter Wright[3]

[1] Interaction Research Studio
Goldsmiths, Univ. of London
initial.surname@gold.ac.uk

[2] School of Design
Northumbria University
mark.blythe@northumbria.ac.uk

[3] Department of Design
Newcastle University
p.c.wright@newcastle.ac.uk

ABSTRACT
The Photostroller is a device designed for use by residents of a care home for older people. It shows a continuous slideshow of photographs retrieved from the Flickr™ image website using a set of six predefined categories modified by a tuneable degree of 'semantic drift'. In this paper, we describe the design process that led to the Photostroller, and summarise observations made during a deployment in the care home that has lasted over two months at the time of writing. We suggest that the Photostroller balances constraint with openness, and control with drift, to provide an effective resource for the ludic engagement of a diverse group of older people with each other and the world outside their home.

Author Keywords
Older people, research through design, ludic engagement

ACM Classification Keywords
H5.m. Information interfaces and presentation (e.g., HCI): Miscellaneous.

General Terms
Design

INTRODUCTION
The Photostroller is a waist-high, portable unit whose most noticeable features are a large screen, a removable control unit (the 'tuner'), and rounded handles and wheeled legs (Figure 1). In operation, the screen shows a continuous succession of photographic images that fade from one to the next every 6 seconds in a never-ending 'slide-show'. The images are drawn from the Flickr™ website (www.flickr.com), accessed via a limited set of keywords using the dial on the tuner to select image categories, and refined by a slider on the tuner which shapes the search space (and which can also be set to hold the current image). A smaller display, set under the main screen, indicates the current search category and the title of the current image, and also gives feedback when the tuner has been adjusted.

We built the Photostroller for use by the residents of a care home in the north of England, as part a practice-based research project on technologies for older people. As with all the devices we build as an outcome of our research through design process, the Photostroller raises, and embodies positions on, a number of issues ranging from the detailed aesthetics of computational devices to ethical issues around aging. In this paper, we focus on four major themes that underlie the logic of its design. We argue that design can support older people's *ludic experiences* such as pleasure, engagement and sociability (c.f. [1, 2, 12, 14]), not just their needs for physical care. The *diversity* of 'older people', however, makes catering for these experiences a nontrivial task. We suggest that this diversity can be addressed by balancing *constraint with openness*, focusing the resources offered by a design enough to give it a clear identity, while offering requisite flexibility for those

Figure 1: The Photostroller

resources to be used and appreciated in many different ways. In addition, by balancing *control* with *drift*, systems can be simple enough that older people will interact with them [2] while still providing access to a rich body of material.

These themes and the logic that connects them became clear over the course of our research, and ultimately came to be expressed by the Photostroller itself. In the following sections, we allow the themes to emerge as we describe the process that led to our design. We start by introducing the site with which we worked, describe the observations and interventions we made there, the design process and eventual implementation of the Photostroller, and finally our observations of how the older people have been using the device. Finally, we return to these themes, and related research, in our concluding discussion.

JACOB HOUSE

Jacob House is a state funded residential care home in a city in the north of England. It caters for both permanent residents who have their own rooms and also day visitors who come two or three times a week for care and company. There were twenty-eight residents when the study began, the majority of whom are in their eighties and nineties. The oldest resident was one hundred and four years old; three of them will shortly turn one hundred. The majority of residents have high levels of dependency requiring assistance in most activities of daily living. Some of the residents also exhibit early signs of the onset of dementia.

Residents are assigned private bedrooms each having space for a small amount of furniture (e.g. an armchair, table and chairs, dresser and television). Many tend to spend their days in one of the two main sitting rooms on the ground floor. The largest (the 'main lounge') is a dining room with a shuttered counter at one end of it leading to the kitchen; dining tables and chairs are arranged around one side of the room, there are armchairs on the other side facing a large flat screen TV attached to the wall. French doors lead to an outdoor patio and garden where the older people can sit in clement weather. The second sitting room is sign-posted as the 'Quiet Room'. Armchairs are set here in an oval shape around the room, there is a large window looking out at the city walls at one end, and a fireplace along one side.

The daily routine in Jacob House is quite fixed although the residents are not obliged to follow it. Residents are served breakfast, lunch and dinner in dining rooms at fixed times; tea and coffee are served regularly throughout the day. Many residents cannot get to the dining rooms without assistance so a major part of the work of the care staff is moving them into wheelchairs using hoists. This activity punctuates the times between meals when residents have to be taken to the toilet. There is usually an afternoon activity led by a carer such as karaoke, dancing or a quiz. A hairdresser and manicurist visit once a week. Most of the residents go to bed at around eight pm although there is no compulsion to do so. Night staff check on each resident throughout the night to ensure that they have not fallen.

Observing and Intervening

Our initial view into Jacob's House took the form of regular ethnographic observations and interviews over the first months of the project. There were a number of methodological challenges in working with the older people at Jacob House. Residents found interviews demanding, quickly became tired and sometimes distressed. Moreover, although the director of the care home understood our basic intentions and welcomed us into the site, some of the staff were wary of us perhaps because of the frequency of official inspections on the one hand, and journalistic exposés in the national press of poorly-run care homes on the other.

To facilitate our engagement with Jacob House, we opened out our ethnographic stance to include various interventions and facilitated activities. These helped the residents and staff to become more familiar and comfortable with our presence as well as being of research value in themselves. The interventions served as 'tickets to talk' [15] (and importantly, on occasion, 'tickets to be silent' [3]). For instance, early in the project, we installed a Video Window, a large monitor inside the main lounge showing the view from a camera mounted on the roof of the building. This spurred a number of conversations with residents and carers. In addition, a local member of the team introduced the residents to a variety of electronic music devices, GoogleEarth and iPhone apps in a series of informal sessions that prompted a great deal of personal conversation from the older people, as well as giving some indication of their orientations to technology (for more detail, see [3]). These included a series of sessions using a data projector to display Flickr slideshows on a blank canvas hanging on the wall, using topics and search terms generated in conversations with the residents. The sessions gave rise to a rich mixture of anecdote, reminiscence and discussion, and were one of the inspirations for our eventual design.

Impressions

As the project progressed, the design team joined in several of the visits, making their own observations which supplemented, and were informed by, reports of the previous observations and interventions. In this section, we describe the overall account of Jacob's House the team developed from these various encounters, an account that served in the transition from observational study to design.

First, we were struck by how passive and sedentary the lives of the older people appeared. Most of the older people were to be found in the main lounge, sitting in one of the numerous armchairs arranged into clusters in the room, chatting, watching television or dozing off. With the institution taking care of responsibilities such as cooking, cleaning, entertainment and even movement for many of them, most of the residents appeared to submit to the rhythms and activities suggested by the carers, even though they were free not to do so. To a degree, this passivity seemed related to physical and sensory constraints. With locomotion difficult for many, as well as deteriorating eyesight, hearing, and manual dexterity, the zone of activity for many of the older people was centred closely around their person, and particularly in the areas around their laps or nearby tables.

Despite the somnolent appearance of the lounge, however, it became clear that the older people comprised an evolving and complex social community. Residents had friends and enemies, formed cliques, pursued romances and suffered jealousies. Some spent most of their time in their own rooms, preferring to avoid those who clustered in the lounges. One group of relatively active residents and day visitors started to habitually frequent the new lounge soon after its conversion from a dining room, preferring the Quiet Room to avoid the television in the main lounge.

One of the sources of the complex sociability we witnessed appeared to be the considerable diversity amongst the residents. Their differences occurred along many dimensions, including their personal histories and previous employments, current interests and orientations, preferences for sociability or solitude, attitudes towards the care home, and their immediate cognitive and physical abilities. Few topics or activities could capture the sustained attention of a majority of residents. Social alliances appeared provisional, based on overlapping preferences (say, a shared interest in birds) becoming temporarily important, but vulnerable when differences were salient. Thus some inhabitants were involved in relatively stable social groups; others were more isolated.

Thus if a complex social order underlay the residents' apparent passivity, it was nonetheless difficult to escape the impression that many of the residents were often bored and lonely. They greeted visitors with interest, if sometimes with suspicion, and occasionally complained if more attention was paid to some of them than others. They welcomed interventions that allowed them to look beyond their immediate environment – explorations of GoogleEarth or archive photography, as well as the Video Window – but seemed to value the human engagement of the researchers, artists and students as much or more than the specific activities and experiences they offered.

In addition, residents sometimes appeared deeply unhappy with their current circumstances and in dread of impending death. Early in the project we had a poignant conversation with a man who told us, tearfully, that he had travelled all over the world, from Asia to South America, but never imagined he would "end in a place like this". Several of the residents died during the course of the project, and when this happened it was traumatic for those that survived not just because they had lost a friend but also because it reminded them so forcefully of their own mortality. One resident was so terrified of death that when anyone died she would retreat to her room for two or three days.

Life at Jacob House was not as gloomy as these more distressing observations might imply, however. If the residents often appeared inactive, most also seemed cheerful. If there was occasional evidence of enmity, intolerance or envy, there were also ample signs of warmth, caring and generosity. Finally, if the older people sometimes appeared to crave more active and social engagement, this was through no fault of the staff at Jacob House, who continually demonstrated extraordinary professional dedication and personal commitment despite limited resources.

INITIAL DESIGN DIRECTIONS

Our involvement with Jacob House extended for almost two years before we started concerted work on the Photostroller. From very early on, however, we started to consider what we might design for Jacob House, exploring ideas through a variety of sketches, proposals and conversations as we learned more about the site from our observations and interventions.

For instance, an early concern was with the role of television in the care home. We were struck by the fact that the television in the main lounge was always on although it often seemed that nobody was watching it. The importance of television in care home literature is well documented [10]. It serves a number of useful social roles – it is a focal point, an excuse to gather, sometimes a ticket to talk [15]. Nonetheless, it was often ignored or irritating. This led us to experiment with systems that might have the visual intrigue of television but without the noise and narrative that can be irrelevant or distracting. We ultimately abandoned these explorations, but the Photostroller can be seen as their unintentional culmination.

Another set of concerns emerged around the notion of 'sensorimotor toys'. These built on our observation that the focus of attention and activity for many of the older people was around their laps, and also on having witnessed one of our own aging relatives repeatedly play with mechanical toys such as a Newton's Cradle. There seems to be a fascination and satisfaction in being able to engage with simple devices that exhibit the balance between predictability and chaos. Existing therapeutic tools such as the Snoezelen [5] seem to reflect this view.

Our interest in sensorimotor toys became linked with a third set of concerns, including the possibility of supporting people engaging with the end-of-life experience. It was clear from our observations that this was a paramount issue for the Jacob House residents, but despite our initial excitement about the topic we were unable to convert this to convincing design ideas.

Difficulties and an 'Experiment'

After more than a year exploring design ideas, we were still unsure whether any of them would lead to devices that a significant number of the older people would find meaningful. Our experience was that they engaged enthusiastically with activities and devices as long as these led to contact with new people but would quickly become uninterested if left to pursue them on their own. We wanted to produce a design that would not rely excessively on social scaffolding, however. Systems requiring external involvement would be difficult to sustain, given how busy the care workers at Jacob House are already. From this point of view, the system should be open to uses in which social scaffolding is a possibility, but not required.

In order to assess whether any of our lines of thinking might lead to success, we built a set of small-scale design experiments for the residents of Jacob House to try. We gathered about a dozen items for an afternoon 'show and tell' session at the care home. These included a number of purpose built devices, such as an electronically controlled laser 'spirograph', a handheld video viewer (Figure 2), and several books of thematically organised photographic prints, as well as a number of commercially available systems including the Tenori-On [13], various iPhone apps, and a set of manipulable children's toys.

Over the course of an afternoon, six of us circulated informally in the lounge, showing the things we had brought to residents, usually in small group sessions. This was an enjoyable event, and we later received very positive feedback from the care staff. Moreover, we learned a great deal about the residents in the process. However, the devices did not fare so well. Apart from their occasional suspicious reception *(Take it away! We don't want to buy it!)*, the residents greeted most of the devices with polite momentary enthusiasm *(Did you make that? How clever!)* only to discard them after a few moments. Of all the things we brought, only the video and photographs seemed to sustain interest, and at the end of the day we had to admit many of our design directions did not appear promising.

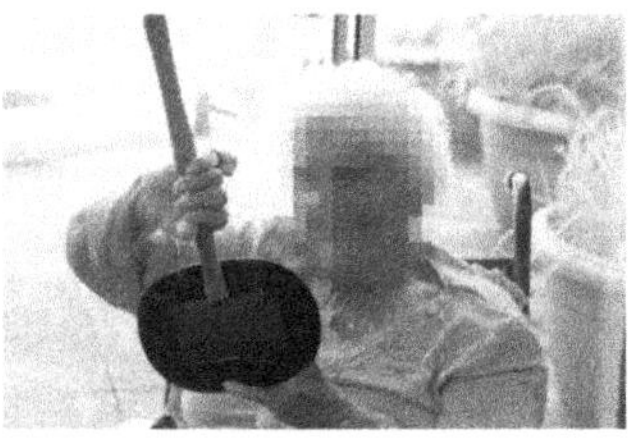

Figure 2: Using the handheld video player

After a break for reflection, the team regrouped to discuss what we had learned and how to proceed. Our interpretation of the ways the older people did and did not engage with the things we had brought them served to emphasise the older people's diversity. Insofar as they engaged with the items we brought, individuals and subgroups showed interest in different material. These observations might have encouraged us to design specialised devices around the interests of subgroups, but with the exception of the images and video even the relatively intense engagements were short-lived. Two men played who with the Tenori-On put it down after about fifteen minutes and did not engage with it again. Residents interacted with the sensorimotor toys for a few minutes, then set them aside. In general, we reached an overwhelming impression that the older people were simply not interested for long in self-contained playthings, but were keen for resources that allowed them to engage with the wider social and physical world beyond the care home. In particular, photographs – whether of historical images, or children and families, or of outer space – all sustained relatively long-lived interest, occasioning discussions ranging from anecdotes about personal or cultural history to more spiritually loaded remarks (one man started to laugh upon seeing an image of a spiral galaxy: *we're so small!*). It became clear to us that, in order to have any hope of sustained engagement from the older people, we would have to provide them resources to look beyond their immediate circumstances.

The 'show and tell' session at Jacob House was a turning point for our design work, prompting us to focus on giving the residents greater access to the world beyond the care home (cf [8]). Subsequent proposals ranged from ideas for creating electronic 'monoculars' which the older people could peer into to see video feeds from remote bird boxes, to devices that would allow the residents to specify 'sound journeys' sweeping through ambient sounds recorded in different parts of the world. Many of our ideas revolved around devices that would display slide shows drawn from Flickr. These were inspired to a great degree by the success of the sessions facilitated by our local team member. The enthusiasm these engendered was reinforced by the residents' positive reception to the photograph booklets we brought to the 'show and tell' session. Thus our speculations increasingly centred around the idea that a continuous slideshow device whose content could be steered by the residents might have lasting appeal.

THE PHOTOSTROLLER

Our initial conception of the Photostroller was that of a distributed system; a central mobile unit (the 'hub') containing the interface, processing and portable power which would wirelessly connect to various peripheral displays. We imagined that a combination of large projector displays and smaller hand-held displays would allow the device to be used in large groups such as in the lounge or dining rooms or more intimate sessions, i.e. in the residents' bedrooms. The basic idea of the interface was that the hub would contain a RFID reader whose input drives the content of photographic slideshow sourced from Flickr. Around twenty RFID tagged ornaments would visually represent the keywords they contained. These objects could be used singularly or gathered to build up more complex searches, yet the system would continue a 'chain of consciousness' browsing during periods of inactivity, slowly diverging from the original topic in a form of 'semantic drift'. This combination of control plus drift was appealing in allowing a relatively small set of initial terms to give access to a larger, and potentially serendipitous, range of images. We also imagined a keyboard interface for carers to drive the slideshow.

Refining The Design Brief

Our design development involved the co-definition of the device's physical form, interface and the basic algorithms that would control the search. We abandoned our original idea of using RFID tags embedded in ornaments, and later ideas such as mounting tokens on wire tracks like an abacus, both because these centred control too closely on the device itself and because it seemed difficult to reflect the dimension of semantic drift that was integral to the device. We began working on a different type of interaction altogether. Whereas our initial ideas centred on selecting and combining about twenty search terms, our new scheme involved directly specifying the degree of semantic drift around a smaller number of basic categories. This method reminded the team of tuning a radio, which inspired the idea of a handheld tuner in which a dial would be used to choose from a set of pre-defined themes (e.g. 'local'), and a slider would be used to choose the degree of drift in relation to that theme (e.g. 'city', 'region', 'nation' etc.).

The decision to move to a smaller handheld interface enabled the team to explore different kinds of displays. In considering likely usage scenarios we concluded that deploying multiple, unwired screens could prove complex and unreliable both socially and technically. Instead, we decided to make a mobile display unit that could be self-contained, housing both the display and its associated computation and power. The size of this display would be suitable for use by small groups and individuals; a scale of engagement that our observations suggested was prevalent in the home. This scheme provided a basic structure for developing the software and hardware for the Photostroller, as we describe in the next sections.

Software

The Photostroller software accepts input from the tuner, uses this to specify search terms, interfaces with the Flickr API to make searches and handle returns, and controls the display of results. A cache of several thousand images is maintained on the Photostroller to ensure that the slideshow runs smoothly. Much of this is relatively straightforward, so in this discussion we focus on the most challenging aspect of the design: the implementation of semantic drift.

Implementing Semantic Drift

In seeking to operationalise the notion of semantic drift, we began by exploring algorithms that could automatically generate new search terms from old ones. Our attempts in this direction were many and varied. For example, in one method, given a search term, we retrieved a pool of images and computed the most common tags Flickr users had given to those images, composing a search term from them for the next iteration. Naturally, over iterations this would diverge from the original term. However, we found that user generated tags are often idiosyncratic and search terms would quickly become opaque or get trapped into retrieving a small number of specific images again and again. We tried using databases of word associations (such as WordNet, wordnet.princeton.edu) as a source for search terms. Again, it was difficult to implement a controllable form of semantic drift as word-associations diverge rapidly (e.g. *nature – spirit – brandy*). We also experimented with the tag clusters which Flickr itself provides. However, iterating over this would often draw us back to the most common tags on Flickr (such as 'flower') or those which are most commonly used in conjunction with others (such as the brands of cameras) with the result that sequences initiated with very different search terms would nonetheless display similar sets of images after a relatively short time.

After many such attempts, we decided finally to specify search terms manually. In the final design, we use six basic categories (local, history, family, travel, space and nature) and four levels of drift, requiring twenty-four separate groups of search terms. For each group, we specify four or five searches, each involving tags specifying what we want (e.g. 'Yorkshire') and additional ones to filter undesirable results (e.g. '-pudding -terrier'). Many of the search terms contain as many as ten or twelve tags, in an attempt to negotiate the surprising, but sensible, juxtapositions of tags used by contributors to describe their images in Flickr. Nonetheless, unexpected images still appear regularly, and one of the questions we had was whether the Jacob House residents would experience these as the result of a breakdown in the system, or as interesting diversions.

Hardware

The basic hardware components of the Photostroller are a modified 17" MacBook Pro and its power transformer, as well as an XBee 1 MW module that receives control signals from an identical unit in the handheld tuner and communicates with the laptop via the USB port. Using a laptop significantly eased the implementation of the Photostroller, allowing slideshow images to be received wirelessly, locally cached and displayed according to the settings of the tuner. In addition its built-in battery allows the Photostroller to be used untethered for significant periods of time, greatly enhancing the device's portability. The disadvantage was that we had to arrange the laptop so its screen could face outwards from inside the unit's housing. To do this, we detached the hinges of the laptop and folded it backwards – a delicate operation that essentially allowed it to be 'closed' in the opposite direction than originally designed. A large green 'on' button is mounted on the side of the case and mechanically connected to the laptop power button, a similar red 'off' button in connected to a modified USB numeric keypad replicating the 'DEL' key that, when pressed, causes the Photostroller software to implement a soft shutdown. The tuner is comprised of a rotary dial and slider both connected to an Arduino Pro Mini, which is in turn connected to an XBee 1 MW module that encodes their settings as a pair of numbers to be sent to the main unit. The tuner also houses a single AA battery.

This main unit's components are mounted within a CNC-machined plywood case, which is enclosed by a powder-coated, folded sheet steel cover. The body is supported by a tubular steel frame that also forms both the legs and the curved handles. The metal cover is cut to reveal two separate areas of the laptop screen, used to clearly distinguish the image display from the smaller display that shows information about that image (including the status of the tuner, the tags used to retrieve it, its title, and, when appropriate, indications that these are being updated). The power cord emerges from the bottom of the unit, and a bracket and non-functioning socket mounted on the side allow the cord to be stowed when using battery power.

The tuner houses a rotary dial and slider, along with associated electronics and batteries, in a unit that we designed to be easy for the older people to hold and manipulate. The tuner's case was printed in three parts on an Objet Eden photopolymer 3D printer and later finished and professionally spray-painted.

Aesthetic tuning

Designing for a residential care home presents a unique situation in that there is a tension between the institutional and the domestic. Within Jacob House, efforts have been made to create a sense of domesticity both through the use of prop-like ornaments in an overtly domestic décor, and by the staff encouraging residents to personalise their rooms with belongings and photographs. Nonetheless, there is an inevitable institutional presence in the layout of the building, its furniture and fittings, and its routines.

The basic configuration of the Photostroller's housing needed to be simple, safe, robust, easy to move and straightforward to produce. To meet these requirements, we selected manufacturing processes that are commonly used for objects in such environments. However, initial design sketches tended to be too industrial in appearance, resembling medical or electronics equipment in a way we thought would discourage the residents from feeling allowed to touch or use the device. Thus a great deal of work went into refining the details of the design to make it seem less institutional and to encourage the residents to feel some ownership of it. Working with the early sketches, we began developing the form of the tubular steel frame, removing standard radii and uniform angles that reflected any mass-produced aesthetic, instead introducing more complex angles and shapes that give the Photostroller a particular stance, as if offering up the screen to the viewer, while softening the appearance. The final frame with its non-standard bends proved a huge challenge for the tube fabricators who had over 30 years of varied experience.

The handheld tuner proved to be an even greater challenge. We set ourselves the design brief that it should be able be used remotely or attached to the main body, simple to understand, easy to operate by users with limited physical ability and robust enough to withstand a fall. The main features of the tuner are a large rotary dial to select the slideshow category and a slider to control the slideshow drift. This basic two-part interaction was decided early in the process, but by prototyping these controls with cardboard models we realised we could add a third element of control by an arrangement in which the slider mechanically locks the dial when pushed to the highest position, so that the point where the two meet serves as a hold function. In the final configuration the overall shape, reminiscent of a paddle, is arranged so that the dial is embedded in a bowl-like head and the slider is mounted in the handle. Much work in refining the design of the tuner involved iterative prototyping of components on a Z-Corp powder printer in order to fulfil the ergonomic requirements of the brief, including around 40 versions of the dials and sliders, and over 20 casings.

Deciding upon a colour palette to use for the Photostroller was a particularly lengthy process, indicating how important we felt it to be. Through rendering 3D CAD models, we explored hundreds of colour treatments for the Photostroller to find an appropriate 'tone' for the device, discarding some palettes as too 'cold', others as too bright or childish. In addition we considered the effect of different colours against the LCD screen so that they would not distract from the slideshow imagery. In our final design, the main unit's case and the tuner body are both coloured 'oyster white', a creamy colour that is both subtle and warm, whilst the tubular framework is powder-coated 'mushroom' grey to contrast with the case. Inspired in part by the design of a classic *Bernina Nova 900* sewing machine, we highlighted the tuner's controls in a pure red to indicate the interactive elements.

Deployment

At the time of writing, the Photostroller has been deployed at Jacob House for more than two months. Most of the team were present at the hand-over to help with technical aspects of the deployment, to document the process photographically, and to introduce the device to residents in informal chats. By the end of the afternoon, we were hopeful of its success, as we had witnessed several residents beginning to engage with it, even introducing it to others and explaining its operation.

After the deployment, the local partner made weekly visits to Jacobs House to gather ethnographic observations and discuss the device with the residents and carers. This often involved sitting with the older people and chatting about the Photostroller as they viewed the pictures it showed. Another ethnographer on the team joined him on several occasions. What follows is an overview of their observations.

THE PHOTOSTROLLER IN JACOB HOUSE

The Photostroller has been used by a number of different people in different locations in Jacob House. A number of recognizable ways of engaging with the Photostroller have emerged depending on where it is encountered and within what kind of ongoing activity it finds a place. In this section we give a sketch of the various ways the Photostroller has been engaged with and the kinds of interactions it embeds within or brings about. Along the way, we will also discuss a number of other issues of importance with respect to our design intentions such as the effectiveness of the tuner and the drifting metaphor.

In The Quiet Room, At Large

Typically the Photostroller is to be found in what is known as 'the Quiet Room'. While the absence of a television makes the room 'quiet', the atmosphere in the Quiet Room is often lively, occasionally boisterous, and filled with conversation. It is where 'day residents' are often found. These are folk who, for example, visit Jacob House to give their carers or partners some respite, or who are making the transition into becoming full time residents. The Quiet Room is often where visiting friends or family may spend time with residents. It is a place where new relationships may be explored as it is the most likely meeting place between existing residents and potential new arrivals. In the examples we shortly discuss from the Quiet Room, participants range from 70 to 99 years old.

The Quiet Room is arranged with about eight comfortable chairs around three of the walls and with the Photostroller commonly to be found in front of the fireplace on the fourth wall. At this location it can be viewed by all those seated in the room. In this regard, it forms part of the background ambience of the room and can be surveyed from time to time if one is not involved in a more focused conversation. We have observed residents quietly watching the Photostroller in the Quiet Room, observing its procession of images between conversations. In such uses, the tuner is left in its holster and is only periodically reset, typically by John (who in many respects is the curator of the Photostroller) when he or others feel the need to view a new set of images.

In The Quiet Room, Close To

The Photostroller can also feature in conversations within the Quiet Room, sometimes being brought over closer to a small group of individuals. For example, Elaine, Nigel and Rose are clustered together with the Photostroller in front of them. Nigel is operating the tuner, which is set to show images from the 'local' category. He moves the slider down and images of London appear. He moves the slider up. "*Back to York*," he says. A picture from York's National Railway Museum appears and Rose is prompted to mention her and her family's involvement with the railways. To one of us (JB): *I used to be a member of the Museum but there were too many steps... My uncle was an engine driver from Sheffield...* As images appear from York and then Scarborough, Rose speaks of places she used to visit. This prompts Elaine and Nigel to join in and discuss a famous concert that was once staged at the York Opera House. Throughout Nigel is, from time to time, moving the slider and dial. He selects 'travel' with the slider slightly down and images related to South America appear. Elaine points to the screen and observes: *Look, a rainbow*. Elaine and Nigel then compare the importance travel has had in their lives, while Rose quietly watches the images on the Photostroller. Elaine: *Think there's places you've never been to*. Nigel: *Never wanted to go*. Elaine: *I've been to a number of places*. Nigel: *I bet you have*. Elaine: *You're a cheeky devil*. As this conversation lapses, the three of them watch the images process on the Photostroller until a picture entitled 'desert island' appears. Rose: *Oooo. That looks beautiful*. Nigel: *It does*.

This example is typical of a number of features we have observed concerning how the Photostroller is used in small group conversations. An image can prompt interaction within the group. If a topic develops of interest to, say, just two participants then others in the small group can silently watch the Photostroller in the meantime, staying part of the small group but without having to participate in the ongoing talk. As topics lapse, the Photostroller can provide means for new topics to be launched, new opportunities for reconfigured participation in the group as, for example, once Elaine and Nigel's conversation about travel lapses, Rose can initiate an exchange with Nigel where they compare their appreciation of depicted scenes.

Facilitating Engagement

While such focused small group interactions around the Photostroller can spontaneously emerge, often on the prompting of John, they can also be initiated by staff, carers, visitors or ourselves when we visit. Indeed, such parties can have a strong role in facilitating, shaping and animating (cf. [9]) the experience of the Photostroller for the residents. This is particularly notable for less able residents. For example, on one visit, one of us (MB) wheels the Photostroller into the main lounge to show it to Kate. In the next chair is Ethel, asleep. Kate is reluctant to use the tuner at first because she has just had a manicure. She also has difficulty seeing the text on the tuner as she does not have her reading glasses with her. She tells us she is 70 though in fact she is 85. MB sets the picture category to 'nature' and Kate repeatedly utters *lovely picture* as the images go by. Then she asks: *What's that?* MB: *It's a chipmunk*. Kate: *That's pretty... what's that?* MB: *They're insects*. Kate: *Ew. Creepy-crawlies*. MB moves the dial to local with the slider down towards the bottom of its throw. Kate: *That's a nice farmhouse*. MB: *The aurora borealis is in the background*. MB moves the slider up. Kate: *What's that? Is that York Minster?* MB: *Yes*. Kate: *Is that the racecourse? They've got new stands you know*.

MB is configuring Kate's experience of the Photostroller through his use of the tuner to select categories that might be of interest to her (nature, local), by responding to her questions as to what is being depicted, and by pointing out details which she might not yet have noticed (the aurora borealis). He also tries to sustain her interest by shifting the behaviour of the Photostroller, first after an image Kate finds discomforting and then after one where she seems not to respond to an unusual detail being pointed out.

During the course of this, Ethel wakes up. She is 100 years old. She has been watching the images on the Photostroller for a little while (Figure 3). *It's a new invention* she says several times. Ethel and Kate watch the images on the Photostroller for about

Figure 3: Kate and Ethel

another 15 minutes with Kate now operating the tuner as her nails have dried. Prompted by a picture of a group of soldiers, Kate describes how she was called up in the last year of World War II and served in the Observer Corps. A picture of Paris prompts Kate to tell us of a trip made there with friends when she was younger. Without her glasses, however, Kate is beginning to find the Photostroller to be tiring to view, so MB takes it over to Nancy, a resident who seldom speaks and whose words can be difficult to comprehend.

As MB steers the Photostroller through nature-images, Nancy (Figure 4) traces the pictures making a left to right gesture with her finger pointing at the screen as if scanning them. Sometimes she identifies the images and announces, e.g., *the sea!* Sometimes she reads the text below, *na nature!* Sometimes she comments. *You don't know do you? <laughter>* She points at one of the images depicting a countryside scene and starts laughing: *Trying to find it. It's like a needle in a hay, hay, haystack.* While MB (and JB) find it hard to understand all that Nancy is saying, she manifests clear and specific behaviours towards the Photostroller: pointing, scanning, laughter and utterances which seem, no matter how opaque, to be in response to the images. With the right scaffolding and attentiveness from MB, Nancy is able to engage with the Photostroller by watching the images and reacting to them.

Figure 4: Nancy's gestures

In Arthur's Room

For the staff at Jacob House, one of the most striking phenomena surrounding the Photostroller has been its adoption by Arthur. Arthur, who has learning difficulties, prefers to remain in his room rather than venture into any of the shared spaces in Jacob House. He takes his meals in his room and has a TV there though he rarely watches it, preferring to sit and gaze out of the window, which he does persistently and with great absorption during his waking hours. He rarely talks to staff who visit him, sometimes barely acknowledging their presence. From time to time, Arthur is known to shout out *Hey! Hey! Hey!* in ways that can be alarming especially for those who do not know him, but mostly he silently gazes out of the window. All day.

From time to time the Photostroller is taken by the staff into Arthur's room away from its 'usual' place in the Quiet Room. Arthur has become very attached to it, coming to regard it as "*a wedding present*" he has received. Staff will switch on the Photostroller for him, set it to a liked category such as local or nature, and place it where he can see it comfortably, typically to his left, the window being to the right of his chair.

The frames in Figure 5 give a flavour of Arthur's use of the Photostroller. In frame 1, we see Arthur looking at a picture

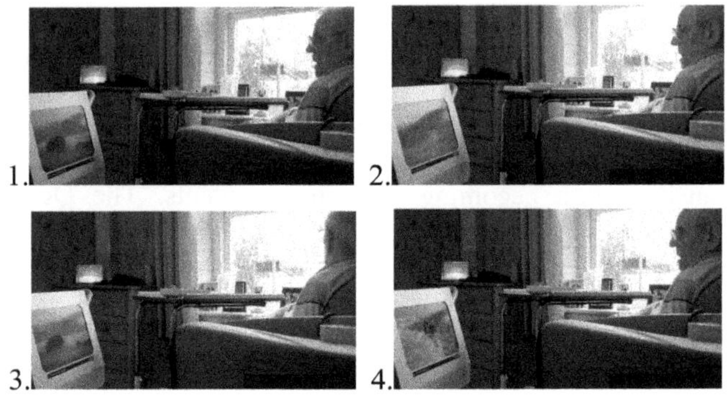

Figure 5. The Photostroller in Arthur's room

of a country scene in which a dark tree is prominent in the centre left of the image (the Photostroller is set to the category 'nature' with the slider fully down to maximize the variety of images shown). In frame 2, taken 36secs later, Arthur is looking at a dramatic image of a rocky landscape. The next image is the country scene with the dark tree again. As we see in frame 3, with this repetition, Arthur takes a look out of the window, returning to look at the next image in frame 4. Arthur's glances out of the window quite typically occur at such junctures: when an uninteresting image appears or one recurs which has just been seen. Arthur is able to shape such looks so that, if nothing interesting is found out of the window, he can return in time for the appearance of the next image.

Not only do examples like this one demonstrate Arthur's interest in the Photostroller (it is excerpted from a 28 minute video during which Arthur continually looks back and forth between the window and the Photostroller), they give a flavour of some aspects of *how* he uses it. He is able to find interest in the images without betraying his concern for the view out of the window. Indeed, the regular timing of image display and its occasional repetition gives Arthur opportunities to glance back and forth and miss very little of concern to him. The Photostroller also occasions interaction between Arthur and others who might be in the room at the time. Specific photos sometimes elicit response. At one juncture, Arthur says what sounds like *Did dub* to a photo of a parrot. As we have noted, Arthur has spoken of the Photostroller as a wedding present for him. While his speech might seem opaque or confused, staff find it remarkable that this man is speaking at all.

Steering The Photostroller

The Photostroller was designed to have autonomous 'drifting' behaviours that were nevertheless steerable using the tuner to select image category and the slider to control amount of drift. However, without facilitation from staff, visitors or ourselves, it seems that the tuner is rarely used. When the Photostroller is in the Quiet Room set back against the fireplace for all to see, the tuner customarily rests in its holster, serving more like a channel selector on an old fashioned TV than a navigation device or, say, a remote control to support idle channel hopping. Interestingly, residents often refer to the image-categories as so many 'channels'. John may be asked to 'change the channel' if the current category has exhausted its interest. It is rare for any other resident to spontaneously use the tuner though, as we have already documented, residents can do is if they are engaged in a focused activity with the Photostroller (and if their nails are dry).

While residents are sometimes bashful to pick up the tuner when invited, we have seen few instances of anyone unable to use the tuner at all once it was explained to them. 101 year old Nancy did try to make the tuner work by hovering her hand over it rather than touch either the dial or the slider, before returning to watching the images and scanning them with her finger. In many respects, as that was her principal activity with the Photostroller, there is no *need* for her to shape the flow of images. Arthur similarly finds the Photostroller to be just right for his purposes with a fixed setting (usually either nature with maximum drift or the default behaviour on switch-on: local/maximum drift).

John, who in his early 70s is one of the younger residents, shows considerable dexterity in using the tuner one-handedly, being able to curl his index finger around the dial while nudging the slider with his thumb (Figure 5). Even the most arthritic residents have had some success manipulating the tuner. The size of the slider, its 'throw', and how this is mapped, mean that one can nudge it several times to move from one extreme to another, finding different behaviours on the way, even if one's nudges are tremulous. The design of the tuner permits operation with it resting flat on a nearby table and this too helps people with severe arthritis or motor control problems.

The function of the dial is generally clear. *It changes the channel.* But we do not have clear evidence that people have grasped the drift concept, at least not as we intended. It is clear that the slider, when fully up, halts the images. Lowering the slider is more commonly conceived by contrast with this than as manifesting a controllable drift process. As John put it, lowering the slider "*gets the pictures*". This is the important matter for most uses of the Photostroller: that a satisfying variety of pictures appear and the category can be changed if new things are required. Importantly, the Photostroller does not *require* users to have an understanding of it, or use the tuner in any 'correct' fashion, or at all, to get a procession of images. Similarly, it can be used remotely or it can be reattached to the Photostroller itself. This kind of flexibility seems right for the ways the device is used.

Occasioning Stories, Appreciating Pictures

The Photostroller occasions the telling of stories, the conduct of reminiscence, and, from time to time, the display of knowledge. We have already noted memories of grand events at the Opera, Paris trips, enthusiasm for the National Railway Museum, serving in the Observer Corps. To add with a further selection from our fieldnotes, we have heard recounted Nigel's 40 year long involvement with Yorkshire football, his facility with Morse Code, Wilhelmina's uncanny effect upon animals whenever she visits a Zoo, the significance of the Grand Hotel in Scarborough (especially for Wilhelmina and her husband who have spent the week containing their wedding anniversary there every year for 49 years). All of these were elicited directly following a related photo appearing.

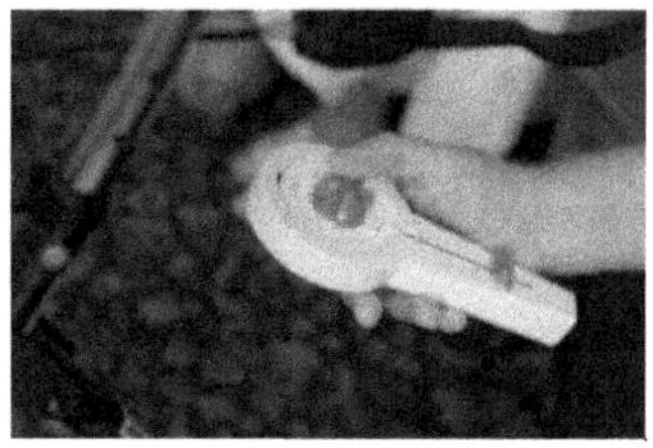

Figure 5: The Tuner

The photographs also occasion the comparison of perceptions and values, likes and dislikes. It is not always clear what a picture is *of* or why it is entitled or classified as it is. Such ambiguities and obscurities will often elicit discussion (and so are certainly not things we should have designed out). Some images are found to be beautiful. Some contain an especially lovely colour. Some images are disturbing (the wartime ones for instance) but none have been found offensive. An occasional image of an erotic content is especially well received by men and women alike as far as we have witnessed. In all these respects, the Photostroller facilitates, in a very broad but real sense, Jacob House's appreciation of photography. And it does so by flexibly embedding looking at pictures within the varied activities which are of concern to the older people we have studied: conversing, making relationships, entertaining each other, maintaining seclusion, and staying in touch.

Appreciating the Photostroller

A few residents have refused to engage with the Photostroller, apparently reflecting a reluctance to engage with any new technology. For instance, one TV room resident, on being presented with the Photostroller, said: *I don't want to see it.* For those who have explored the device, however, we have heard a range of very positive reactions. Billy, a relatively new resident, took MB on a tour of the care home and, without prompting, pointed out the Photostroller: *It's good that! Very good!* Patricia a day visitor described it as: *very nice, very interesting… because they are very good photos.* She also remarked that it was *very easy to use.* John gave a more detailed account of its appeal: *As I say it is quite interesting and it really does get you thinking and remembering things.* New views, not just remembered ones, have appeal for him: *I have seen parts of Leeds, Scarborough, I haven't seen before. It's very educational.* Staff are also enthusiastic. Sarah: *It's absolutely brilliant, the pictures are so clear.* The manager is also positive: *I love it, I really do.*

DISCUSSION

Both the Photostroller and the underlying view of aging we developed through its design contribute to the literature on support for older people. An increasing proportion of work on the elderly has suggested, often using user-centred methods [6, 14] that older people do not just need physical care, but also support for their emotional and social lives (e.g. [1, 2, 12, 14]). A variety of approaches to supporting sociability have been explored, including memory aids to help with conversation [12], online chat and game systems (e.g. [2]), and systems providing telerobotic telepresence (e.g. the Giraff, www.giraff.org, similar to Willow Garage's Texai, www.willowgarage.com). Our study is unusual in focusing on care home residents, whereas most related work focuses on supporting older people, including those with dementia, to stay at home (e.g. [4]). Most relevant to the work here are tools such as Circa, a touch screen system that provides access to a variety of media to support reminiscence [1]. However, tools such as these contrast with the Photostroller both in offering relatively complex interfaces, often implying use with caregivers, and in focusing explicitly on predefined activities.

In contrast, the combination of *control* and *drift* offered by the Photostroller seems well suited for independent use by the older people at Jacobs House and for a variety of activities. Residents (or caregivers) can use the tuner to control the category of images but, once set, images will drift by without further control, giving access to endless thematic content without requiring explicit access. As we have seen, this seems appropriate for the Jacob House residents, who often seem happy to allow their memories, musings and conversations to drift along with the imagery, but who always have the option to 'change the channel' if the content becomes unappealing. The use of drift also seems to reflect the ways that residents' conversations, as observed throughout the project, shift as new topics were prompted by previous remarks or external events.

The balance of *constraint* and *openness* the Photostroller offers also supports this flexibility. In some respects, the device can be seen as a simplified, more fit-for-purpose alternative to television. By avoiding television's narrative or commercial scripting, the system facilitates residents' ability to appropriate it into their current concerns. Its design as a specialised device to offer thematically organised photographs gives it a clear and recognisable identity, and allows a simple style of interaction appreciated by older people [2]. But it is designed to be open both in terms of its physical use – its mobility allows it to be configured for the wide variety of residents and settings within Jacob House – and in the ways the older people can engage with it. By simply presenting the photographs without a larger narrative of use, the Photostroller allows residents to orient to it as they see fit. This openness allows it not only to serve as a tool for sociability [12] or reminiscence [1], but also as a support for daydreaming, factual exchange or flights of fancy.

Most generally, and by these means, the Photostroller seems successful in providing resources for the residents' *ludic engagement* [7] both with the world outside Jacob House and with other residents within. By ludic engagement we refer to the self-motivated, non-utilitarian and fluid ways that the older people incorporate the resources offered by the Photostroller into their activities. As we have described, the Photostroller has occasioned a wide range of curiosity, anecdote, reminiscence and playful discussion that revolves both around the images it shows and the people who use it. Though it can be viewed passively, using the Photostroller often seems to involve more active engagement involving memory, interpretation, curiosity and communication. Engagement of this sort may be valuable in supporting residents' mental and social wellbeing. What seems certain is that it provides the pleasure of exploring the world's complexity and richness, a pleasure as essential to older people as it is to any of us.

ACKNOWLEDGEMENTS

This work was carried out in *The Landscapes of Cross General Engagement* project (RES-352-25-0030), which is part of the UK's Joint Councils 'New Dynamics of Ageing' Research Programme. We are deeply grateful to the residents and carers at Jacob House (not its real name) for their participation and support.

REFERENCES

1. Alm, N, Dye, R, Gowans, G, Campbell, J, Astell, A, & Ellis M (2007). A Communication Support System for Older People with Dementia. Computer 60-66.
2. Bagnall, P, Onditi, V, Rouncefield, M, Sommerville, I. (2006). Older People, Technology and Design. Gerontechnology 5(1):46-50.
3. Blythe, M, Wright, P, Bowers, J, Boucher, A, et al. (2010). Age and Experience: Ludic Engagement in a Residential Care Setting. Proc. DIS'08, 161-170.
4. Carswell, W, Mccullagh, P, Augusto, J et al. (2009). A review of the role of assistive technology for people with dementia in the hours of darkness. Technol. Health Care 17, 4, 281-304.
5. Chung, J, Lai, C, Chung, P, & French, H. (2002). Snoezelen for dementia (Cochrane Review), The Cochrane Library Update Software(3).
6. Dickenson, A & Dewsbury, G (2006). Designing computer technologies with older people. *Gerontechnology*, 5(1):1-3.
7. Gaver, W (2002). Designing for Homo Ludens. *I3 Magazine*.
8. Gaver, W, Boucher, A, Law, A, Pennington, S, Bowers, J et al. (2008). Threshold Devices: Looking out from the Home. Proc. CHI'08, 1429-1438.
9. Heath, C & vom Lehn, D Configuring Reception: (Dis)Regarding the 'Spectator' in Museums and Galleries. *Theory, Culture & Society,* 2004, 21, 43-65.
10. Kubey, R (1980). Television and Aging: Past, Present, and Future. *The Gerontologist*, 20(1), 16-35.
11. Lundell, J (2004). Obtaining feedback on advanced product concepts for elders. British HCI workshop on HCI and the Older Population.
12. Morris, M, Lundell, J, & Dishman, E. (2004). Catalyzing social interaction with ubiquitous computing. CHI'04 Late Breaking Results, 1151-1154.
13. Nishibori, Y., & Iwai, T. (2006). Tenori-On, Proc. NIME'06, 172-175.
14. Pullin, G, & Newell, A (2007). Focussing on Extra-ordinary users. Proc. HCII 2007, 253-262.

Svensson, M., & Sokoler, T. (2008). Ticket-to-Talk-Television. Proc. NordiCHI'08, 334-343.

Automics: Souvenir Generating Photoware for Theme Parks

Abigail Durrant, Duncan Rowland[1], David S. Kirk, Steve Benford, Joel Fischer, Derek McAuley

Horizon Digital Economy Research
University of Nottingham
Nottingham, UK, NG7 2TU

[1]School of Computer Science
University of Lincoln
Lincoln, UK, LN6 7TS

abigail.durrant@nottingham.ac.uk, drowland@lincoln.ac.uk, {dsk, sdb, jef, drm}@cs.nott.ac.uk,

ABSTRACT
Automics is a photo-souvenir service which utilises mobile devices to support the capture, sharing and annotation of digital images amongst groups of visitors to theme parks. The prototype service mixes individual and group photo-capture with existing in-park, on-ride photo services, to allow users to create printed photo-stories. Herein we discuss initial fieldwork in theme parks that grounded the design of Automics, our development of the service prototype, and its real-world evaluation with theme park visitors. We relate our findings on user experience of the service to a literature on mobile photoware, finding implications for the design of souvenir services.

Author Keywords
Souvenir, photoware, theme park, tourism

ACM Classification Keywords
H5.m. Information interfaces and presentation (e.g., HCI)

General Terms
Design, Human Factors.

INTRODUCTION
Digital media and photographs in particular have been of interest to the HCI community for a number of years [6]. Photography has been traditionally understood as a means for creating an impression of a moment in time and integral to practices of memory and reflection [20]. The affordances of digital media along with developments in capture and display technology [20] invite new research questions about the relationship that everyday consumers may have towards photos and photoware [1, 21] and open up interesting avenues for interaction design research.

A related area of interest within the field is in leisure practices and touristic visiting, two activities that connect to photography [2]. A recent line of inquiry considers new developments in mobile technology and their potential support for leisure and visiting. HCI researchers have considered the development and use of mobile photoware [1, 18], exploring how photo-capture and sharing enhances group experiences in mobile contexts [3, 17]. This has been seen for example in city visiting [13], rally spectating [7, 17], and, with regards mobile-*video*ware, nightclub visiting and VJing [5]. Prototype systems such as Mobiphos [13] and mGroup [17] allow the instant mobile sharing of images within a defined group. The mGroup system further enables the creation of Media Stories. These combine photo-related media and user-generated annotations in narrative threads. The authors of the two systems report ways in which they enhance the co-present social experience of visiting, with mGroup's Stories being made available afterwards as 'albums'. However, the way in which the two systems serve to support souvenir generation from visiting was not the analytical focus of the studies; and the significance that users placed on the souvenir-function was arguably under-explored.

Souvenir creation in theme parks
Our current research investigates souvenir creation in the context of visiting a theme park. Theme park settings have been little considered in the HCI literature (cf. [14, 19]), and we aim to contribute a novel set of insights in this respect whilst building on extant work on photo-related technology support for leisure and visiting. Underpinning our studies is a rationale that souvenir-making is often integral to the concept of media capture [9] and the theme park is a prominent leisure destination in which digital photography comes to the fore as a souvenir mechanism. Theme parks are also particularly intriguing to us as a 'photo-ecology', that is, a specific context in which photography is accomplished [11]. Many theme parks partner with third-party companies to provide on-ride photo (and video) capture, affording visitors access to otherwise inaccessible photo opportunities. However, given the rise in mobile photoware [1], increasing numbers of theme park visitors are to be found carrying their own media capture devices. This makes for a rich mix of digital media capture technologies in the park that is both personal and park-provided. To date, there has been no consideration in HCI or related literatures of how these diverse capture systems, *personal* and *professional*, may be meaningfully integrated in the making and delivery of souvenir products.

Theme parks are of further interest because of the social practices that they invoke. The first visit to a theme park or first 'big-ticket' ride is, for many people, a rite-of-passage event [8] and an experience that visitors want to mark for posterity with a souvenir. Theme parks are not just sites of isolated experience, they are commonly visited by groups [4]. Previous HCI studies of visiting have shown that the group dynamics of visiting shape how people wish to 'capture' and reflect on their visit [13, 17]. Further to this, recent studies on digital photography (building on a legacy of earlier research [6, 12]) elaborate complex roles played by photographers and their audiences during photo sharing and display [21]. But the negotiation of group concerns pertaining to other aspects of 'photowork' [10] (including triaging, editing and storing) remains relatively under-explored. It is evident that much photo practice is shaped by the context or 'photo-ecology' in which it occurs [11]. Indeed, the particular socio-technological features of a theme park setting present scope for extending reported understandings on a broad set of photowork concerns.

In this paper, we provide an exploration of souvenir generation in theme parks. Our research combines social scientific and technology design orientations. We begin with an ethnographically-informed account of visitor experiences relating to souvenirs. We then discuss how this study informed the design and development of a prototype 'souvenir service' (a set of integrated, supportive mechanisms) called Automics, which was based on the concept of creating and delivering photo-souvenirs combining personal and park-generated media. We then describe an 'in-the-wild' deployment and evaluation of the prototype. Our empirical work aimed to explore a new form of souvenir service but also contribute to the literatures outlined above, advancing understanding of social practices in relation to photos. As such, we illuminate the theme park as a photo-ecology and explore the intersection of digital media and group activities of capture and representation.

UNDERSTANDING CURRENT SOUVENIR PRACTICES

We began with a study of visitors' current photo practices at Alton Towers, a major UK theme park that is well known for its 'thrill rides' set among extensive gardens. Of particular relevance here is the presence of two professional 'souvenir services at the park. The Picsolve system takes photographs during a ride and offers these for sale as mounted prints at a kiosk at the ride exit. The system is optimised to take a high quality image 'that no one else can capture' and to make it available, packaged with ride branding, within minutes – it is not possible to buy the picture later on. The YourDay system captures video from major rides, mixing this with stock footage to compile a personal DVD for purchase (RFID wristbands track visitors through the rides). Neither system covers the many smaller rides and other attractions around the park.

We recruited three groups of friends or families with varied ages and intra-group social relations. *Group One* comprised friends and family gathered by Linda (47 years): her son Sam (9) and his friend Sally (10), Linda's co-facilitator at Cub Scouts Daniel (16), her work colleague Anne (40), and Anne's daughter Mel (6). Linda, Anne and Daniel had visited the park before, but it was the first time for the others. *Group Two* comprised two work colleagues Tom (36) and Lucy (25), friends Chris (21) and Mary (25), and Mary's friend Jo (28). All except Tom visited Alton Towers at least once a year. *Group Three* was an extended family, with parents Maggie and Rob (36), their children Jim (10) and Beth (7), and grandparents Alf (57) and Helen (58). Maggie described her nuclear family as annual park visitors, whereas Alf and Helen visited infrequently.

We observed these groups visiting the park on separate days during Autumn 2009. Our fieldworker travelled with them to the park, issued free day passes on arrival, and filmed them engaging in various activities throughout the day. We followed up with semi-structured interviews two weeks later, at Linda and Maggie's homes and at the workplace of Group Two, where participants were prompted to draw upon souvenirs in the course of recounting their day. We now summarise our observations.

Rites of passage

Finding the courage to take on major thrill rides was a significant feature of the day for many of our visitors and strongly reflected in their photo and souvenir practices. Sam had never been to Alton Towers before and Jim had not previously been on any of the major rides (with the exception of one), so the experiences of these younger visitors became a significant focus for their respective groups. Footage from the field captures Jim approaching Nemesis, his initial reluctance to ride, his grandparents' encouragement for him to join them on the ride, his excitement and elation on alighting, and his subsequent purchase and proud display of a souvenir medal bearing the legend 'I survived Nemesis'. Such 'rites of passage' emerged as a significant theme of the day and an overarching narrative for photo and video souvenirs. Group One labelled their YourDay DVD 'No Fear Sam' whilst Group Three labelled theirs 'Jim's First Big Rides'.

Rites of passage were important to adults too as they confronted their own fears. At interview, Linda referred to a souvenir photo of her on a Log Flume ride from a different theme park: "I went on that ride about sixteen million times to overcome a fear of going on Log Flumes, so that one was personal to me." Moreover, having to chaperone children "forced" (in Linda's own words) adults into "doing rides they wouldn't normally do".

We found examples of how the Picsolve photographs and YourDay videos supported visitors in subsequently recounting these rites of passage to others. Stock footage of rides was useful in this regard, and both Jim and Sam "loved" being able to show others the ride from a rider's perspective. However, this official documentation was not without its problems. Maggie commented on the marked difference in quality between stock footage and personal video of riders, in which it could be difficult to see faces and where people had their backs to the camera: "all you can see is the figures". The lack of control over one's own appearance in official photos and videos also proved to be controversial, as we now discuss.

Looking scared

The record of Jim's Nemesis ride, delivered by the automated souvenir systems, conflicted with the story that he wanted to promote; the photos appeared to show him looking scared. He offered alternative explanations for this, including the physical force of the ride making it hard to smile, and not knowing where the camera was located.

> **Jim:** that was only on the picture with the force of the thing - it was that powerful it wouldn't let you smile! ... On Rita, I don't know how I managed it but I knew where the camera was so I ended up smiling.
>
> **Maggie:** [Chuckles.]
>
> **Jim:** Erm, so when it does come on you just look terrified and you can hardly smile. So I don't think I really like that one.

Unfortunately for Jim, his family did not choose to buy the 'smiling' photograph from the Rita ride. Neither, however, did they purchase the Nemesis photo, due to Jim's protestations, although it was clear that they wanted to precisely because he appeared to be scared. Indeed, Maggie described her highlight of the day as being: "probably Jim coming off Nemesis, looking terrified". Jim responded immediately to Maggie's comment by saying that the photos that his father took on the day would "prove her wrong". Jim's 'terrified look' became a talking point as the day progressed and as other Picsolve cameras captured similar expressions. The 'look' became a source of entertainment, especially because the cameras captured other members looking elated. In footage of queuing for the ride Spinball Whizzer, Rob teased Jim, inviting him to "smile for the cameras, this time". The Air ride provided a further example with Jim explaining his expression on the photo (which was purchased in this case) as: "Nanny (Helen) were pushing me out of the way and I saw her hand and I was wondering 'What the heck is she doing?' ... (a)nd I thought all like getting dead worried". Therefore, the official photographic record of the day became a significant resource for the visitors to justify and even dispute their own accounts of an experience.

To buy or not to buy?

These examples also reveal how visitors struggled to decide whether or not to buy on-ride photos upon alighting, and we saw several examples of them regretting not doing so. This challenge was exacerbated by what they considered to be the relatively high cost of the printed, packaged photos as borne out at interview.

> **Maggie:** I think they're good but then you think 'I'd like that one, but we want to see what the next one's like' and then you think 'Well, maybe that one would be better'. Yeah, cause we were constantly saying we could go on later and get another photo, if we didn't like that one.
>
> **Rob:** Yeah. Whereas if you got something that saved all your photos till the end of the day - so that one's better than that one

This challenge was especially acute for families on a tight budget who wished to capture as many members as possible together, made even more complex by having to consider the inclusion of friends' children. Opinions were divided as to the merits of digital versus printed images, with people wanting access to digital copies while emphasising the long-term value of the printed versions that were displayed around their homes.

The spectator as photographer

As Jim's reference to his father suggests, visitors also took their own photos. Indeed, taking photos and recording video were significant and pleasurable aspects of the day. As it was forbidden for riders to use cameras, the task of photographing rides was taken on by spectators, or members of the party who elected not to ride but rather to wait for others riding. Taking photos could help relieve the boredom of waiting and became a central feature of the day for some. Footage from the field shows both Tom and Jo absorbed in photographing their peers on Submission and Ripsaw, two rides in which the riders remain in the view of spectators, gesturing to the riders and reviewing what had been captured. Tom, who considered himself as a hobbyist photographer, described the challenges of photographing larger coasters. He pointed to technical issues such as looking up into the light, but also not knowing when your riders would flash past after a long wait. Spectators were also involved in arranging and taking posed photos of returning riders in front of the rides, especially ones that showed them celebrating rites of passage.

'Candid Camera'

Visitors also enjoyed taking more candid images. Lucy anticipated that she could capture photos to "embarrass people with later". At interview, she talked about photos she took of her friends: "I think I probably took this one just because Jo was quite apprehensive about going on the first ride" and "this is Tom apprehensive about the first ride, cause he was really scared". 'Candid Camera' photos weren't only about being scared however.

> **Lucy**: I want to capture funny things, that's what I do. So, when I saw him [Tom] standing there yawning, I'd take a secret photo so it looked like he was really bored. Anything that was ..
>
> **Tom**: It wasn't secret - I saw you take it.
>
> **Lucy**: I'm not as stealthy as I like to think [laughs]. For me it was the fun things, the amusing moments, mundane things, fun things.

This playfulness extended after the visit with Lucy, Tom, Jo and Mary all creating Facebook albums dedicated to the visit and with various members enjoying tagging images and entering teasing comments.

Capturing the whole day

There was far more to documenting a day in the park than the rides. The spaces between the rides, the gardens and other attractions, were all deliberately themed to be part of the overall experience, and provided a backdrop for many other photos. Indeed, the park provided various sculptures and landscaped props to support this, as we saw when Group Two posed around a coffin and related Halloween props during an excursion into the Gloomy Wood. Again, visitors revealed their individual interests in this broader documentation: Jim used his camera to photograph birds and other wildlife, a personal interest, whilst the rest of his family ate lunch. Rob and Maggie commented on this.

> **Rob:** It's different, i'nt it, how kids see the day.
>
> **Maggie:** Yeah, cause you think we'd walk round and go 'Oh, it's a dog', whereas kids go 'Oh it's ***a dog***! Let's go feed the dogs!'. It's a completely different day for kids.

This dialogue demonstrates the importance of including more than just the staged, high thrill moments on rides; more prosaic experiences of the day were often deemed to be as significant within the record that was later consumed.

A PROTOTYPE PHOTO-STORY SYSTEM

Following our initial study at Alton Towers, we embarked on an iterative process to design and build a new kind of theme park souvenir service. This involved a workshop, followed by prototyping sessions and a series of site visits to test different versions of the prototype as it evolved.

Design Rationale

The study findings led us to identify an initial set of requirements for the design of photo-souvenir systems.

- **Combine professional and personal photos:** We have seen that both professional and personal systems have distinct and useful roles to play in souvenir making. Both approaches could be productively integrated.
- **Enable the playful sharing of photos.** The group-oriented nature of visiting, including taking photos, is essential to the experience. We saw how this included the playful taking and commenting of candid photos.
- **Support personal narratives**. Rather than just capturing 'in the moment' views of experience, souvenirs should embody more structured narratives, for example juxtaposing before, during and after shots to show how fears were overcome during 'rites of passage'. Moreover, it is important that individuals within the group can articulate their own, possibly divergent, accounts of the experience.
- **Involve spectators**. It is important to support spectators in being active documenters, including relieving boredom while waiting for others or even queuing.
- **Provide physical and digital forms**. Souvenirs should be appropriate for display and sharing in various physical and digital forms, from permanent objects around the home to postings on social network sites.

An approach based on photo-stories

The core idea that emerged from our design process, and that lies at the heart of our service, was to create souvenirs in the form of photo-stories – sequences of images, annotated with speech and thought bubbles and other textual captions that tell a story. Previous research has explored the potential of photo-stories, or, more broadly, 'sequential art', as a way of documenting and sharing experience. For example, the Comeks mobile phone application enabled individuals to capture, annotate and sequence photos into photo-stories and then exchange these with others as MMS messages [16], whilst [15] describes the use of photo-stories to document school lessons and, of particular relevance here, a rollercoaster ride.

The novelty of our work lies in extending these approaches to explore new forms of collective photowork to support visiting. Our prototype incorporates mobile application, features that distinguish it from previous prototypes [13, 16, 17]. This design has implications for the nature of our inquiry: it supports the creation of souvenirs by both *groups* and *individuals*, and their delivery to meet the interests of both; and it functions in conjunction with the existing professional mechanisms residing in Alton Towers. As such, our design utilises the resident systems and services to co-create highly personalised mementoes.

We were drawn to the photo-story approach because we felt it offered the potential to address our high–level design requirements. Photo-stories involve multiple images and so have the potential to *combine professional and personal photos* in a single souvenir. They can also enable *playful sharing* through capturing candid views of others, but also in captioning and annotating these. Photo-stories clearly *support narratives* – they are stories – and there is the potential to generate a unique *personal* story for each individual within a group - even when drawing on a common pool of materials. The work of capturing - but especially captioning and selecting - photos might be done during moments of 'downtime', for example when queuing for a ride or when watching and waiting for others to complete a ride. Finally, whilst photo-stories have traditionally been rendered to the *physical* printed page as comic books, there is currently a growing interest in more interactive *digital* forms, including browsing comics frame-by-frame on mobile devices [15, 16]. In short, we reasoned that our photo-story approach to design would enable us to explore how groups of individuals may collaborate to make souvenirs whilst also allowing for the integration of their content with on-ride photos generated by the park.

Automics functionality

Our design, 'Automics', is implemented with an application for Android smart-phones that enables users to capture, annotate and share photos. It also invites them to *combine* these images with Picsolve on-ride photos to produce photo-story ride souvenirs. The application was coupled with service features to deliver printed souvenirs. Automics' functionality and interface evolved over a series of three iterations of field trials. The following briefly summarises the key features of the final version.

Capture and share: A user may take a photo with the phone's inbuilt camera at anytime whereupon they are asked if they would like to save the image. Discarded images are deleted, but retained ones are immediately and anonymously distributed to other members of the users' group and also stored in a *shared pool* for the group to access via a central server in chronological order of creation (after [1]). Any images of the members captured by the Picsolve capture system are also shared and stored in the pool. Scanning and loading the Picsolve images is a manual process in the current prototype, but could be automated in a production service. Users are manually assigned to their group at the start of their visit.

Annotate and share again: The Automics application invites users to annotate any of the photos in the pool, be they user or Picsolve generated, by adding speech and thought bubbles, and captions. The smart-phone touch-screen is used to crop images to a required aspect ratio to fit a photo-story template (see below) and to enable users to place graphical elements appropriately. When completed, the annotated photo is also anonymously distributed and stored in the pool. Annotated photos can be edited many times and saved alongside the content already there, with all levels of revision being available for further editing.

Select before, on-ride and after shots: For each ride, the application asks users to select three photos that best represent their experience of 'before the ride', 'on the ride' and 'after the ride'. The 'before' and 'after' images are chosen from the group's shared pool, whilst the on-ride image is chosen from the pool of Picsolve-sourced images. Each user therefore chooses three favourite images out of all the group's captured and annotated images.

Template image created in advance using stock material

'Before' and 'after' images taken by group members

'On ride' image from official capture system

Figure 1: an Automic created by Group Three.

Construct a ride souvenir: the Automics system then automatically creates a one-page photo-story souvenir for each combination of ride and rider. The software composites the selected photos with a stock template, which includes other stock images and branding, to complete the souvenir image (Fig. 1). It should be noted that although the system prompts the user for 'before' and 'after' selections to be made, the only actual restriction actually enforced was the inclusion of an on-ride photo from Picsolve and they are free to choose any images that, to then, best represent 'before' and 'after' in the story they wish to tell. Three Automic templates were designed, one each for three selected flagship rides at the park. Towards the end of their visit, users are able to preview all the Automics they have co-created and given the option to choose one to receive as a tangible souvenir of their day. The finished Automic is printed on A4 glossy photo paper (Canon iP1900) and framed behind glass (also a manual process in the current prototype).

Notifications and prompts

The Automics system uses various notifications and prompts to try and engage users in different stages of this process. Users receive an audio-tactile notification each time a member of their group has captured or annotated a photo. We also implemented location-based prompts using to actively encourage users to engage in annotation and selection work while in the queues for rides or to take photo when near to key props around the park.

EVALUATING THE PROTOTYPE IN THE WILD

We returned to the theme park to evaluate the Automics prototype being used by groups of visitors 'in the wild', using the same ethnographic methods that we had in our initial sensitising study. Three existing social groups were recruited to use the prototype during a day-long park visit. Between them, the groups exhibited intergenerational family relations; peer relations; and differing technical proficiencies with smart-phones. All participants were frequent visitors to Alton Towers and keen to visit again. Two of the three groups responded to a snowballed advertisement, while a third was approached directly because its members had taken part in our previous study and we were interested to connect their experience of Automics to our previous findings. Group One comprised members of a nuclear family group, Gary (51) and his three children Jenny (20), Paul (19) and Daisy (14). Group Two comprised colleagues and friends: James (28), Mike (30), Martha (26) and Kate (28). Group Three comprised members of Group C (from the previous study), Jim (now 11), Beth (8) and grandparents, Alf (58) and Helen (59).

The groups were met at the park entrance on separate days and provided with complementary tickets. Before engaging with the attractions, they were taken to a room to be briefed and each person was given a smart-phone to use. The smart-phone functionality and the Automics application were explained to them, including showing an example photo-story. They were then invited to use the devices freely in the park. One researcher accompanied them for the first hour to assist with any technical queries. Another accompanied them intermittently during the day to observe. Towards the end of the day participants were invited back to discuss their experiences. Each individual was shown all of their Automics and asked to choose one to be framed and taken away as their souvenir. A final interview was then conducted at a large table with all of the media (including all iterations of annotated photos) present as paper prints. At this point each group was asked to carry out a simple triaging task in which they had to agree the best 12 images, then the best six, and finally the best one, that represented their collective day. They were also asked to lay these out in a suitable format describing why that had been chosen. The following summarises our observations.

Automatic sharing of photos

The automatic sharing of photos upon capture was a distinctive feature of Automics, and impacted considerably upon social interactions in the park, enhancing them in some instances but provoking problems in others. The capture and share function was valued for enabling people to 'do photography' together in a novel way. Gary appreciated acquiring photos from capture events that he may have missed: "I think it's really good"; "I quite like the idea of being able to share all the photos 'cause so often you've missed the shot but someone else has got it, or someone's just done something better". Gary said that this was good for allowing in-group flexibility about adopting the 'role' of Photographer: "there are times for example when you don't want to be taking photos cause you want to see the action, but if you know there's gonna be some other sucker that's gonna be taking it [laughs] you can actually concentrate on being there as opposed to taking all the photos". This worked well for non-riders who could take photos on behalf of others, such as Jim: "it was good to get other people's photos 'cause me and Grandad went on the rides so we could hardly get any photos in so Nanny took a load". All participants said that they appreciated the automatic group sharing feature. James of Group Two speculated about its potential application: "something like this would work for concerts, or a football game"; to which Martha added: "anywhere that's a group thing".

However, continual notification about the generation of content was a key problem that was echoed across groups to the point where participants became increasingly frustrated by the notifications and eventually ignored them. In Martha's words: "because one of us at any point in time was taking pictures and uploading them, it was just constant noise and vibrating". Kate added: "it would've been more useful if it wasn't ringing and vibrating every time someone uploaded a picture". Gary and Jenny of Group One said they could intuit when photos would be uploaded, not least because of being collocated and seeing each other using the application. Jenny observed that: "if I pulled it [the phone] out all of the time it would seem anti-social". She then suggested that the notifications would have greater value as part of remote communication, helping to coordinate the activities of sub-groups: "If we'd split up we could've just taken a picture of something and of course it would've just gone to everyone else and 'Oh! Okay they're by so and so ride' and just gone over there. So it's quite handy like that actually."

Captioning photos

All of our participants valued the captioning feature for enabling them to personalise content created by others. At interview, Jim, Alf and Helen discussed how a photo that Helen took of Jim alighting from Nemesis was retrieved from the shared pool and captioned by Jim:

Helen: I took the photo and then passed it from my phone to Jim's phone and then he captioned it.

Jim: Yeah!

Helen: Which is great because I didn't know that he'd done that caption and he's caught it perfectly.

Participants conveyed the social value in captioning each other's photos 'on the fly'. For Kate, captioned media resonated with contextual significance: "It was a nice way to remember what we were talking about and what made us laugh at the time". Also, the ability to caption during the day meant people could entertain each other whilst queuing by captioning whilst reading each others' captions.

Captioning was often playful, as Mike conveyed: "it was engaging, it was fun to do it... got you thinking about slapstick comments". The anonymity of contributions supported the candid: "I kinda like it when nobody notices", said Martha. This playful aspect was sometimes connected to a sense of thrill or fear. Mike referred to a photo that Martha took and he captioned and that was eventually chosen as his group's favourite: "there's a keen sense of wit when you're terrified"; "I was trying to make a joke to calm myself down". Whilst recognising how it epitomised him "being scared" in contrast to his friends, Mike observed the potential negative effect of such playful captioning: someone "more sensitive" could react badly to being made "a laughing stock".

Working to a template

Participants enjoyed co-creating souvenirs with the system, guided by prompts and an activity structure. For Helen, the panel template "focused the mind", "reminding you that at the end there was an end product". James elaborated: "It was quite nice that you'd get something at the end of the day, ... it gave us a reason to put the funny comments on".

Later in the interview, participants were invited to compare the 'Make a Panel' feature and resultant ride Automic to existing on-ride capture systems and associated products. They unanimously expressed that the detail and context afforded by the photo-story feature was appreciated and led to a bespoke souvenir. Automics was also preferred because it afforded visitors greater authorial control over how their souvenirs were fashioned: "I like that one better for the simple reason that we've got more control over it", said Helen. This included use of content authored by family or friends and, as Mike noted, "it comes from a real person rather than some machine". But this feature was not without issues: the branding of Automics and the incorporation of stock footage received mixed responses. Moreover, even though an example Automic had been shown prior to the activity, groups found it hard to conceptualise how their images would fit within a photo-story without seeing the actual templates.

Also, fitting content to a template could feel like work (running counter to the intentions of a leisure experience).

James and Martha described feeling 'forced' to create a story with a specified structure when the task didn't fit with what they were doing or how they wanted to represent their day. The triaging task at interview revealed that 'summing up' the visit did not necessarily follow a narrative structure. Some representations of the visit as-a-whole were more *thematic*. For example, for Group Two, the day was defined by 'Mike being scared'. When accounting for their triaged selections, no rite of passage or transformation was described; with the 12-print photo-story, Kate tapped sequentially on several prints saying "Mike being scared; Mike being scared; Mike being scared".

Participants described that, after using the application for a while, they composed photos with captions in mind. But the need to compose panels meant having no option but to crop photos after capture and change this composition. Jenny found this constraining: "a lot of the time I didn't want to (crop), which is quite annoying if you've just managed to get a picture of someone and they're in one place but you've got to crop". Daisy agreed: "The cropping bit was really frustrating at times". Cropping was one of many compulsory 'production tasks' that presented a barrier to photography. James said that such tasks "did really slow down the spontaneity of things"; "if you could just instantly take another photo then that might be better". Mike added: "you just want to snap and forget about it".

Automics as souvenirs of a day in the park

Although official on-ride photos were pivotal in accounts and included in the triaged collections, participants liked how Automics represented 'other aspects' of their visit, including what others were doing. At interview, all the participants showed great interest in each other's Automics, and they also saw potential in the concept of a souvenir that represented the group rather than individuals. Kate conveyed this well: "I wouldn't pay seven pounds for a picture of myself to frame and put on the wall"; "I'd rather buy a photo of the group doing something than me doing something on my own".

There was a reported benefit to the final triaging process as Helen highlighted: "actually having a look at what's going on I think that adds to the day, sitting down, choosing, having conversations – everybody joins in". Helen felt that doing this task *before the end of the visit* was part of the shared experience of being at the park. Triaging was made difficult by the large numbers of photos produced by each group – 72, 151 and 146 photos for the three groups respectively, and the need for better filters emerged. The amount of attention given to photos through captioning was understood to indicate their overall value, as Mike voiced: "I started looking for photos that had annotations on them, 'cause I thought them are the ones that are going to be best to look at, 'cause somebody has taken the time to tag it, so maybe they're the most favourite".

All participants assumed that the "raw content" would be made available to individuals alongside edited content. Having said that, the monetary cost of this content would be a determining factor in its acquisition, as Helen said: "I'd want to have all the photos but I wouldn't want to pay for them all". Helen suggested that further triaging would influence her choosing to have a digital or physical souvenir: "I would pay to say 'Well, we've got those ones, they're for the comic, but I would really like these ones too and for those I would pay to have them digitally'".

Whilst appreciating the printed souvenirs, all participants advocated distributing Automics content to social networking sites, thus embedding it in social exchanges beyond the group, beyond the park site and beyond the visit. Gary, Paul and James suggested doing this in real time, as content was being generated. But Jenny was concerned about being mis-represented through this capacity, if not by her family then by "complete strangers". Helen pointed out that sharing and captioning may be problematic in larger visiting groups with weak social ties: "in a large, possibly unconnected group such as a coach trip you have issues with people having other people having photographs of their children and doing things with them".

DISCUSSION

We now discuss the implications of our findings for photo-related souvenir generation, reflecting upon some of the issues raised and relating these back to wider HCI concerns outlined in the Introduction. Although we had structured our research around evaluating Automics in use, we were struck by the extent to which the souvenir-making activities that it supported became integral to the visitors' experiences and their social interactions in and beyond the park. To recap, our deployment aimed to explore technological support to: mobile photowork as a group concern [1, 10]; touristic and leisure visiting and its inherently social aspects [2, 4]; and the integration of professional and personal photos in the photo-ecology of the theme park.

It is important to emphasise at this point that, through designing and deploying Automics, we have additionally explored the concept of an *end-to-end souvenir service*; the design builds on our earlier insights to embrace a complex activity of souvenir production, into which cameras, photos and networked devices are embedded. Moreover, the positioning of Automics as a *service* distinguishes it from mobile photoware deployments reported elsewhere [13, 17]; its deployment has generated novel insights on souvenir generation, delivery and consumption that extend existing insights on photo-related support to visiting.

To help ground insights from our findings, we now deconstruct the souvenir generation process into a sequence of component activities: capture; annotate; triage (select); and layout and render (compose and construct a souvenir) – with 'publish' as a further optional activity. We explore how these 'workflow' elements were shaped by two fundamental tensions at play in Automics' use. These stemmed from a distribution of agency, in terms of how 'workflow' was balanced between: (i) the park system and its users (i.e. the extent to which individual users had authorial control over souvenir-generation in contrast to park control); and (ii) the in-group balancing of work (i.e. between individual visitors and their group-at-large). In the following sections, we explore how these tensions shaped visitor experience, and, by doing so, we articulate features of a theme park photo-ecology, associated socio-technical relationships, and new concerns for mobile photoware. This serves to instantiate and elaborate some of the suggested requirements raised by Ames et al [1] and extend the study of mobile tourism established by Brown and Chalmers [2].

On capture

Whereas the group creation of media content has been previously studied, a novel and valued feature of our prototype was the way in which it enabled the *role of photographer* to be shared between visitors, their friends or family, and, significantly, the photo-souvenir systems integrated into the park infrastructure. With smart-phones to hand, Automics' users were not only at liberty to capture their day as they chose, but also acquire photos of their visit captured on their behalf. Users appreciated having access to content they would not have been able to generate personally. In addition, Automics' notifications of photo opportunities were valued for promoting a more holistic representation of the day; prompts between rides shaped souvenir creation and capturing more than ride experiences.

However, the intervention of Automics in capture was not always welcome. Users voiced tensions concerning the *framing*, or *composition* of individual images. After familiarising themselves with the application, it became evident that their photos would need to be further cropped (after capture) to fit a template. They understood this active constraint as part of the workflow, and responded by framing shots with subsequent cropping in mind. But this didn't always work as intended, leading to unsatisfactory compositions. Clearly the design had not adequately fore grounded its *own* needs in terms of image standards, and in such a way that enabled users to do the fundamentals of photography, frustrating them greatly.

Aside from interaction with the service, we may consider the interplay at capture between individuals and groups of users. Evidently, there were distinct benefits to Automics facilitating capture of group activities by multiple members. 'Work' to record activities was successfully distributed within groups to ensure that, at key moments, someone was responsible for capturing events. Some felt relief to not be the sole group photographer. Beyond this, group-sharing meant that spectators to rides were afforded roles as active documenters of ride experiences, which they appreciated as did the riders they captured. This insight reflects recommendations by [1] on supporting ease of capture through 'limiting demands on attention'. Ironically though, the aforementioned interface issue over framing and cropping negatively placed demands on attention.

Users valued the automatic, real-time 'upload and share' feature (echoing [1]), with several finding this the most beneficial feature of the service. Users speculated on the potential of this feature to support sub-groupings with remote awareness and sub-group coordination, much as has been seen with users in the mGroup trials [17] and their establishment of 'common space'.

On annotation

Photo-annotation enhanced group collaboration. Bolstering findings by [1], the use of speech in *thought bubbles and captions* as a form of annotation was valued for dynamically framing and re-framing meanings of photos between people. The interface let users attach actions and intentions to individual referents and, through incremental overlays, represent multiple expressions in a way not possible with simpler annotation tools. Real-time sharing and iteration of captioned photos, enhanced by visual layering, made this photowork integral to social interaction.

Connecting to requirements above for supporting 'being at leisure', the annotation feature supported souvenir creation *as play* within the production process, and Automics became a form of entertainment in and of itself. The anonymity of photographers and editors is a distinguishing feature not present in [13, 16, 17] and turned out to be a valued aspect of the service design – and the study design – in this respect because it led to use of captioning to extend 'Candid Camera' and the subversion of others' expressions. The potential negative values of supporting Candid Camera were explored at interview, with the possibility for social embarrassment, social exclusion, or alternatively for events to be misrepresented or reinterpreted. Such speculations underlined tensions over the authorial control of images that were raised with collective annotation mechanisms more generally. These tensions gained poignancy in the context of creating lasting mementoes, suggesting that the role of captioning to support dynamic in-group dialogue could be leveraged in future souvenir designs, subject to caveats concerning misappropriation.

Tensions also emerged over the distribution of *effort* between Automics and its users. In some instances, annotating photos felt 'like work', a feeling at odds with the leisure setting. Yet perceived work needed to be balanced with desires for authorial control. The implication here is to ensure that the balance of effort in the workflow process is adequately supported so as not to overburden the user (again resonating with [1]). Automics presented one solution to this, by leveraging opportune moments for 'pushing' authoring tasks to users, e.g. in queuing 'downtime' when engaged in sociable or playful activity.

On triage

Given the orientation of Automics towards producing a material artefact, it was essential for users to select a subset of images for inclusion - to 'Make a panel'. It was clear that opportunities for this kind of triaging were somewhat dependant on the provision of a suitable technical infrastructure. Triaging large numbers of photos on a mobile device was onerous, but as a socially engaged activity, carried out at interview, it was found to be an enjoyable element of the service. This has implications for how key elements such as triaging may be delivered in a highly managed environment like a theme park. It also challenges the efficacy of giving users access to all content in the shared pool in certain situations. Algorithms could be used to determine which images are most interesting, limiting the problems encountered in a mobile deployment. This form of system-side support is advocated by [1] through automatic tagging and ascribing metadata. But again there is a tension in balancing how much the system controls the process and shapes the creative potential of users, a key insight to emerge from Automics in use.

Further to this, our participants actively appreciated the sociality of collective triaging when creating content for a shared, group souvenir of the day (at interview). This activity was a means by which they could socially consolidate their day's experience. Again, this foregrounds tensions in the group production of souvenirs and how best to integrate and represent individual and group experiences.

On layout and render

At the point at which users came to construct an Automic, the system coordinated activity. There was a rigid pre-defined template into which content could be placed. Here, the user had little control over how they used the template, the service constraining activity to make the production of a tangible souvenir more achievable. The template format suggested a narrative approach with pre-ride, on-ride (Picsolve generated), and post-ride images. Users chose to subvert this though, by inserting content which did not conform to a simple chronological narrative. Their choice of photo content sometimes reflected a much more thematic orientation to constructing a record of events. A tension emerged with how users responded to being shaped by the souvenir service; they wanted more control, but at the cost of creating a manageable service.

On publishing

A final element of the souvenir-making workflow concerns the wider publishing of Automics souvenirs. We did not prototype this element, but invited speculation on it by participants. The ability to publish to the web via social networking sites during the visit was seen as desirable. This includes both Automic souvenirs in a full but purely digital rendering, and also individual annotated images. But publishing online presented new challenges over group versus individual authorship: content could be shared widely, with various implications. The social nature of the groups we recruited, comprising family and friends, was seen as a ready means by which trust could be maintained in use of the shared media. We would argue that, in some respects, the capability of Automics to support publishing rests on the nature and scale of the group involved. This suggests the need for further inquiry on how such trust could be managed in ad hoc or temporary visitor groupings.

Posting material online would also offer some advantages to the service by serving as a means for individual elements of group records to be archived as individual representations, thus balancing the individual-group tension when it comes to producing a final souvenir.

Summary

In preceding sections we have explored the various stages of a souvenir generation process, reflecting on the tensions that arose in our Automics deployment. Two broad concerns cut through our analysis: the relative authorial control of Automics in souvenir co-creation; and group dynamics when using the service. Our reflections highlighted the importance of offering service users - in this case, theme park visitors - flexibility over the souvenir-making process. Users expressed desires to balance authorial control with the pursuit of leisure, and not to feel as if they were doing work. Equally, a core value of souvenirs was their function in representing sociality. Again this needed to be balanced with desires to preserve aspects of individual representations, and contributions to group endeavours. This specific set of requirements, relating to *the individual within the group* and the production of multiple personalised souvenirs from a shared media pool is emphasised, in contrast with previous studies that have explored interpersonal media messaging [16] or the creation of shared media albums [17].

DESIGN CONSIDERATIONS

We now consolidate these insights into considerations or sensitising issues for mobile photoware design, giving particular emphasis to souvenir-making activities.

Foreground technological constraints – Services that wish to shape user input need to make clear to users at an early stage the inherent constraints that may be imposed. This maximises the potential for users to creatively respond.

Exploit context – If souvenir services attend to context, opportune moments may be derived for 'pushing' tasks to users, thereby engaging them in 'photowork' but at the same time balancing the onerous nature of this against use of 'downtime' where other activities are less possible.

Offer souvenir defaults – Authorial control over the content and form of souvenirs should be supported, but must be balanced against a desire to not make the user feel as though they are working. If most stages of the process involve optional templates for doing photowork, this would increase authorial control whilst reducing workload, enabling the rapid generation of souvenirs.

Support rich user expression – Sequential art was successfully leveraged to enable users to express a variety of feelings and intents, and this was enhanced through supporting incremental layers of captioning.

Support group triage – The triaging task in our study demonstrated the value of group involvement in creating photo-stories *during the visit*. This suggests a need to afford space and time for collective reflection within the 'end-to-end' souvenir service structure. In the managed environment of theme parks, this suggests the potential to leverage situated displays and interactive digital surfaces.

Support individual and group representations – It is evident that souvenirs serve multiple representational functions within groups. Souvenir service designs should manage these individual and group forms of representation.

Offer extensibility – The response to web publishing as an option suggests a value in offering extensibility to service users for rendering souvenirs and distributing content to others beyond the park site and the visit. Web publishing may be a vehicle for delivering individual representations as part of an otherwise group service.

Consider privacy control – The management of content in a souvenir service that incorporates photos must explicitly consider how collective trust and anonymity is supported during the visit, and how these may devolve once souvenirs move beyond the park, including how implicit social contracts are fore grounded within the park photo-ecology and how privacy controls are made manifest.

CONCLUSIONS

Theme parks are complex socio-technical environments and rich photo-ecologies. We have explored the design and deployment of Automics, a mobile photo-souvenir service that incorporates the capture, annotation and sharing of photo-media on smart-phones. This media is combined with that generated by park systems to produce novel, personalised souvenirs. The study highlights the interplay between visitors' individual and group concerns and individual and system control of souvenir generation.

In turn, we have produced design considerations that extend the HCI literature in at least two areas: we inform the study of mobile tourism [2] with respect to souvenir generation; and we respond to mobile photoware requirements, most comprehensively articulated by [1]. We conclude that our work bolsters these requirements with empirical insights supporting the notion of integrated and flexible applications for photo-ecologies in mobile interaction. This is not least because we prototyped a *service* rather than an application. Further, by studying Automics' particular functionalities in use we reveal new challenges for mobile photoware development, relating to the creative control of content in a shared workflow, and the exploitation of context in leisure and touristic visiting.

ACKNOWLEDGEMENTS

We thank our participants and our partners Alton Towers and Picsolve. This work was funded by RCUK through the Horizon Digital Economy Research grant (EP/G065802/1).

REFERENCES

1. Ames, M., Eckles, D., Naaman, M., Spasojevic, M., and House, N. 2010. Requirements for mobile photoware. *Personal Ubiquitous Comput.* 14, 2, 95-109.
2. Brown, B. and Chalmers, M. 2003. Tourism and mobile technology. In *Proc. of ECSCW*. Kluwer, 335-354.
3. Counts, S. and Fellheimer, E. 2004. Supporting social presence through lightweight photo sharing on and off the desktop. In *Proc. of CHI* . ACM, 599-606.
4. Cross, G. S. & Walton, J. K. *The Playful Crowd: Pleasure Places in the Twentieth Century*. Columbia University Press, 2005.
5. Engström, A., Esbjörnsson, M., and Juhlin, O. 2008. Mobile collaborative live video mixing. In *Proc. of MobileHCI* . ACM, 157-166
6. Frohlich, D. M. 2004 *Audiophotography: Bringing Photos to Life with Sounds.* Springer-Verlag New York
7. Jacucci, G., Oulasvirta, A., and Salovaara, A. 2007. Active construction of experience through mobile media: a field study with implications for recording and sharing. *Personal Ubiquitous Comput.* 11, 4, 215-234
8. Jones, K. R., and Wills, J. *The Invention of the Park: From the Garden of Eden to Disney's Magic Kingdom*. Polity Press, 2005
9. Kirk, D. S., Izadi, S., Sellen, A., Taylor, S., Banks, R., and Hilliges, O. 2010. Opening up the family archive. In *Proc. of CSCW*. ACM, 261-270
10. Kirk, D., Sellen, A., Rother, C., & Wood, K. 2006. Understanding photowork. In *Proc. of CHI*. ACM, 761-770
11. Lindley, S. E., Durrant, A., Kirk, D., and Taylor, A. S. 2009. Editorial: Collocated social practices surrounding photos. *Int. J. Hum.-Comput. Stud.* 67, 12, 995-1004
12. Miller, A. D. and Edwards, W. K. 2007. Give and take: a study of consumer photo-sharing culture and practice. In *Proc. of CHI.* ACM, 347-356
13. Patel, N., Clawson, J., Voida, A., and Lyons, K. 2009. Mobiphos: A study of user engagement with a mobile collocated-synchronous photo sharing application. *Int. J. Hum.-Comput. Stud.* 67, 12, 1048-1059
14. Pausch, R., Snoddy, J., Taylor, R., Watson, S., and Haseltine, E. 1996. Disney's Aladdin: first steps toward storytelling in virtual reality, in Proc. SIGGRAPH96, ACM Press (1996), 193-203
15. Rowland, D., Porter, D., Gibson, M., Walker, K, Underwood, J. et al. 2010. Sequential Art for Science and CHI, *Extended Abstracts of CHI 2010*, ACM.
16. Salovaara, A., Appropriation of a MMS-Based Comic Creator: From System Functionalities to Resources for Action, CHI 2007, 1117-1126, San Jose, 2—7, ACM.
17. Salovaara, A., Jacucci, G., Oulasvirta, A., Saari, T., Kanerva, P., Kurvinen, E., and Tiitta, S. 2006. Collective creation and sense-making of mobile media. In *Proc. of CHI.* ACM, NY, 1211-1220
18. Sarvas, R., Oulasvirta, A., & Jacucci, G. 2005. Building social discourse around mobile photos: a systemic perspective. In *Proc. of MobileHCI*, ACM, 31-38
19. Schnädelbach H., Rennick Egglestone, S., Reeves, S., Benford, S., Walker, B., Wright, M., Performing Thrill: Designing Telemetry Systems and Spectator Interfaces for Amusement Rides, *CHI 2008*, Florence, 2008.
20. van Dijck, J. 2007. *Mediated Memories in the Digital* Age. Stanford University Press.
21. Van House, N. A. 2009. Collocated photo sharing, story-telling, and the performance of self. *Int. J. Hum.-Comput. Stud.* 67, 12, 1073-1086.

Contextual Dynamics of Group-Based Sharing Decisions

Simon Jones and Eamonn O'Neill
Department of Computer Science,
University of Bath,
Bath, BA2 7AY, UK
s.jones2@bath.ac.uk, eamonn@cs.bath.ac.uk

ABSTRACT
In this paper we investigate how decisions made while using a granular access control mechanism for sharing photographs are influenced by contextual factors and properties relating to the identities of contacts. We develop analytical models using logistic regression to understand relationships between variables that affect sharing decisions. We also investigate how predefined, static groups for privacy control cope with the challenge of sharing large amounts of content associated with numerous different contexts, and test whether they need to be adjusted to suit particular contexts.

AUTHOR KEYWORDS
Privacy, Social Media, Photo Sharing, Context-Awareness.

ACM CLASSIFICATION KEYWORDS
H5.3. Group and Organization Interfaces.

GENERAL TERMS
Human Factors, Measurement, Theory

INTRODUCTION
Disclosing personal content on social networking services can expose sensitive information about users. These services typically allow users to create connections to 'friends' such that this content can be shared amongst them and restricted from the wider public. However, these connections rarely distinguish between different types of relationship. Even within a network of 'friends', users may wish to manage the sharing of information and content with different people based on their differing relationships.

Previous work, e.g. [8, 13], has investigated the potential of automating the creation of privacy-based groups for controlling disclosure. These automated groups can reduce the burden of specifying privacy settings for each individual contact by collating contacts with which information is shared similarly. But even though group formation could be automated, the user would still have to select the appropriate groups for every piece of content that she wishes to share. There remains potential to reduce user burden even further by automatically recommending appropriate groups for sharing a particular piece of content.

Previous studies, e.g. [2, 22], have attempted to identify reasonable predictors of public vs. private settings for sharing content such as photographs, but they have generally not identified predictors that are applicable to various 'non-public' privacy settings, such as restricting access to particular subgroups within a social network. The first contribution of this paper is an investigation of the factors that affect users' decisions to share or not share content with particular contacts from their social network.

A potential barrier for group-based privacy control is that personal privacy policies are often highly dynamic and may vary depending on the current context, need and activity [18]. It may not be feasible to configure groups once in advance and have those groupings hold for all situations. Without consideration of how to share particular instances of content, preconfiguration of groups relies only on information relating to the identity of contacts, available details of their relationships and generalized notions of content sharing from previous experiences. In reality, specific properties of the content being shared may influence the salience and significance of particular group divisions, necessitating the adjustment of group memberships specifically for that context and content. Our second contribution then is an investigation into the contextual dynamics of group membership adjustment. We analyze the efficacy of both static, acontextual grouping and dynamic, contextualized grouping and identify indicators of when each is appropriate.

We conducted a longitudinal study (over 2 months) in which 22 participants used an application with granular access control for sharing photographs with their Facebook contacts. We analyzed the sharing decisions of these 22 participants for a total of 1,014 photos. From this analysis, we quantified some of the factors affecting privacy decisions and assessed whether preconfigured groups for privacy control supported these decisions.

RELATED WORK
Social networking services present many advantages for information dissemination and interpersonal communication, but the copresence of multiple social groups from different facets of a user's life can present a significant challenge for controlling privacy and online

CHI 2011, May 7–12, 2011, Vancouver, BC, Canada.

identity. Many users experience a perceived loss of control over their personal information and content when using online social networking services [12].

Default privacy settings on services such as Facebook are often configured such that content is shared uniformly with all of a user's contacts. Achieving fine-grained control is an arduous process, yet people consider such control important for presenting multiple versions of themselves [7] or for minimizing the appearance of characteristics that are contrary to an idealized version of themselves [10]. Users often resort to defensive strategies for privacy protection in the absence of easy-to-use granular controls for disclosure [14]; e.g. by not sharing content unless they are comfortable with it being seen by all of their contacts, or by adjusting their content so that it is suitable for a broader audience.

Ackerman and Mainwaring [1] emphasize that, while valued, privacy is not the users' primary task and making it an explicit task for the user can be problematic. Designing privacy management tools that do not require significant configuration effort from the user is therefore an important and worthwhile objective. Systems that automate, recommend or assist with privacy management decisions could reduce the burden placed on users while providing satisfactory levels of control. Raento and Oulasvirta [20] propose a number of design principles for supporting users with privacy management. A main principle is that privacy management tools should allow users to present themselves differently to different audiences. They suggest that this should apply even if disclosure is automated.

In order to inform the design of such tools we need to understand how people make decisions about sharing their content with social network contacts. Lederer et al. [15] found that people base sharing decisions more on the identity of the recipient than on the situation within which the information is sought. Many studies, e.g. [7, 18, 21], have shown that people want to specify groups and categories based on identities and relationships, for which they can specify appropriate disclosure settings. Jones and O'Neill [13] investigated people's rationales when grouping their contacts for the purpose of privacy control, and found six criteria, related to the identities of contacts, which were commonly considered and could inform the automated generation of privacy-based groups.

Although many contextual factors can affect privacy decisions, Lederer [15] suggests that the primary index for such decisions should be the identity of the recipient. The specific context surrounding the disclosure is secondary and has less influence on the decision. However, context cannot be ignored. Altman [3] and Palen and Dourish [19] view privacy as a dialectic and dynamic boundary regulation process, with privacy continuously negotiated and managed and boundaries refined according to context. This highlights a problem for group-based privacy controls: the context in which groups are configured may affect the configuration of group boundaries. Groups based on identity are likely to be fairly stable but not completely unaffected by context. Groups may be different when grouping in advance for 'generic privacy control' and when contemplating disclosure of particular content in the moment.

There has been little research into privacy controls that consider the combination of both salient divisions within a network of contacts, based on identity, and characteristics of relationships and network divisions that become relevant in a given context for sharing a particular piece of content. Gilbert and Karahalios [9] suggest that privacy controls based on tie strength may help to segment a user's social network into meaningful groups. But no work has so far considered the varying importance of tie strength in different contexts. Davis et al. [6] developed MMM2, a system that demonstrated how contextual information, primarily people's copresence, related to a particular piece of content could be used to offer users a list of suggested recipients with whom the user might wish to share. But they did not incorporate information about the identity of the recipients – such as strength and type of relationship – which may also influence the decision to share.

For this paper, we were interested in identifying quantifiable variables relating to both identity of contacts and contextual factors, which facilitate the understanding of an individual's decision to share or not to share a particular photograph with preconfigured sets of contacts. We were also interested in determining an additional set of variables useful for determining whether the use of preconfigured groups is appropriate in a given context and assessing the extent to which preconfigured privacy based contact groups had to be adjusted to be suitable for different contexts.

METHOD

22 participants (11 male, 11 female, mean age 27, range 19-43 years) were recruited through advertisements placed on online notice boards and notices placed around a university campus. Participants were screened through e-mail and face-to-face discussions to ensure that they used their iPhone as their primary camera, they regularly used it to take photographs (typically >20 photos per month), and they often carried it with them wherever they went, enabling photographs to be taken in different contexts.

We also ensured that all of our participants were Facebook users with established networks of contacts and that they were familiar with sharing photographs and other content using the service. Participants were offered a £50 recruitment incentive for completing the study. We did not set a target for the number of photographs they had to take. This reduced the likelihood of participants arbitrarily taking photographs to satisfy the requirements of the study and increased our confidence that they were taking photographs according to their usual reasons for doing so.

Phase 1 – Grouping Exercise

In Phase 1 participants were instructed to create their own privacy-based groups from their Facebook contacts. They could create as many or as few groups as they felt necessary for effectively controlling disclosure of their social media content, with each group containing contacts with whom they would share information/content similarly.

Jones and O'Neill [13] found that people formed privacy groups by creating and combining 'sets' of contacts based on six commonly considered criteria which represented meaningful ways of dividing their social network: Social Circles and Cliques, Tie Strength, Geographical Locations, Organizational Boundaries, Temporal Episodes, and Functional Roles. Our participants were first instructed to identify all of the distinct 'sets' of contacts resulting from dividing their network according to each of these criteria in turn. To assist them, a list of all of their Facebook contacts was provided. Each participant then sorted and aggregated her sets into discrete privacy-based groups of contacts. For example, one participant defined 3 sets of contacts based on the criterion Social Circles & Cliques: 'Family', 'Best Friends', and 'Pub Mates' (in addition to other sets based on other criteria). He then used these 3 sets to define 2 contact groups for content sharing control: Group A – 'Family and Best Friends' and Group B – 'Pub Mates'.

Jones and O'Neill [13] also found that participants typically used Tie Strength (e.g. descriptions of relationship strength) to divide sets of contacts that had been created based on the other criteria, for example splitting a single set into separate 'Strong Tie' and 'Weak Tie' sets. In Phase 1, tie strength divisions were performed last, allowing participants to subdivide any of the sets they had already created if they felt it would help them to control disclosure of content. For example, a participant based 3 contact sets on the criterion Organisational Boundaries: 'Management', 'My Office' and 'My Department'. He then split 'My Office' into 2 sets: 'Strong Ties-My Office' and 'Weak Ties-My Office'. Finally, he used these 4 sets to define 2 privacy-based groups: Group A – 'Management, My Department and Weak Ties-My Office', and Group B – 'Strong Ties-My Office'.

As participants identified the distinct sets of contacts within their network we asked them to consider including contacts that they had deleted, ignored friend requests from or refrained from adding. Users often delete friends as a way of controlling privacy. However, grouping contacts in order to make selective content sharing easier may be preferable to permanent deletion and could be considered a less "anti-social" option.

Phase 2 – Field Study

In Phase 2, the same 22 participants each had an application called 'Flickit' installed on their iPhones for 2 months. They were asked to use the Flickit application instead of the default iPhone camera application any time they wanted to take a photograph. They positioned the Flickit icon on the first screen of their iPhone, next to the default camera application so that they would be reminded to use it.

Figure 1. Providing photo meta-data and choosing sets of contacts for sharing this particular photo

Flickit is intended for managing the upload of photographs to different albums on Flickr. We used the application to replicate managing the disclosure of content with social network contacts, by mapping each of the sets that participants had created in Phase 1 to a Flickr album, using the set labels as album names.

Each time they took a photograph, users were presented with a list of their sets of contacts (Fig. 1). Participants could then decide with which sets to share the photograph. This grounded sharing decisions in a particular context, where different factors could be salient for managing group boundaries. In order to test the efficacy of preconfigured groups for managing privacy control, only the sets, rather than the groups, from Phase 1 were embedded in the interface. The privacy groups were created in Phase 1 as collated sets of contacts with which information would be shared similarly. If all of the sets that comprised a Phase 1 privacy-based group received the same sharing decision for a given photo in Phase 2, then we can infer that that group was suitably preconfigured for use in that specific context. If, however, the decision to share or not to share was not applied uniformly across different sets of contacts from within the same privacy-based group, then that group did not serve its purpose of collating contacts with whom the participant would share the same information.

Once sharing decisions had been made for all sets of contacts they were uploaded to private accounts on Flickr so that we could access them for analysis. To guard against inadvertent privacy violations, photos were not actually shared with our participants' contacts or uploaded to Facebook, but participants were instructed to treat their use of the system as if they would be, or could be in the future.

In order to reduce the risk of bias as a result of participants not uploading photos that they did not want to share with the researchers, we provided the option to upload a blank replacement image for the photograph that they had taken. In this case, we asked them to provide information about the image as if it were the photo they had taken. This method allowed us to record participants' sharing decisions without having to reveal their more sensitive photos.

CONTENT AND CONTEXT METADATA

In addition to selecting sets of contacts with whom to share photographs, participants provided related details for analysis. Flickit allowed pre-configured tags to be assigned to images, which we used to collect additional data. Our metadata collection was informed by prior research, e.g. [2, 6, 23], recording data on elements of context and content that have been shown to affect privacy decisions: Location, Event, Copresence, Content and Motivation.

We reason that these could be useful as explanatory variables for understanding sharing decisions, for use within development of recommender systems for content sharing and also for analyzing the contextual dynamics of group formation/adjustment.

Location is often indicative of significant contexts in peoples' lives. Ahern et al. [2] found that a significant portion of users have some locations in which they are more likely to take private photos, and some in which they are more likely to take public photos. We incorporated location data collection in order to investigate whether location was also useful for understanding decisions to share with particular sets of contacts, beyond the simple public vs. private distinction.

Bentley and Metcalf [4] found that events are a meaningful concept for organizing photos, and Lovett et al. [16] suggest that they may be useful for interpreting individual and group context. Events can be segmented by both location and time. We collected location and time data that had been automatically added to the photo's EXIF data by the application. To enable us to make comparisons between different types of events/locations both within and between participants, we also asked them to specify tags describing the type of event and place at which the photo was taken.

Previous work, e.g. [6], has shown that detecting people who are copresent when photographs are taken is useful for suggesting recipients. People often like to share photographs with others who have shared an experience and may have fewer privacy concerns about revealing such photos to people who were present. We therefore asked our users to give tags describing whom they were with when they took the photo.

Ahern et al. [2] found that users have content-derived patterns in making privacy decisions. We asked participants to specify tags which would help to describe the content of the image according to categories of content identified in [2]: People, Place and Object. We added an Animal category after piloting the study and finding that animals were frequently the subjects of photographs.

Some research has suggested that privacy concerns may vary according to the motivations for taking photos. For example, Miller and Edwards [17] found that for people who use photos to capture memories about which stories can later be told, privacy was the most important factor in determining whether to share photos. For others who see photography as a way to reflect on even the most mundane experiences, privacy was less of a concern. We attempted to capture people's motivations for taking photos by asking them to specify a tag from a taxonomy of motivations identified in [23]: creating and maintaining social relationships; constructing personal and group memory; self-presentation; and self-expression and functional use. Table 1 shows the tags categorized by element of context.

Category	Tags
Event/Location	*home, work, school, party, pub, nightclub, commuting*
Copresence	*alone, with friends, with family, with colleagues, with strangers*
Content	*photo of object, photo of person, photo of place, photo of animal*
Motivation	*social relationships, capture memory, self-expression, functional use*

Table 1. Tags and Content Metadata

The complete set of tags was presented to the participants for each photo that they took. They were instructed to select all applicable tags for each photo, with the option to add their own additional tags if necessary. Participants were also given a 'Description' field (Fig. 1), in which they could enter comments about their sharing decisions. If a participant tried to share a photograph and found that the sets that he had created did not provide adequate control over disclosure, he was instructed to provide a brief explanation of why this was the case, for example, if there were particular individuals whom he decided to include or exclude, or if the contacts that he wanted to share with had not been defined as a set.

Phase 3 – Post-Study Questionnaire and Interviews

Following the field study, all participants completed a questionnaire in order for us to gain further insight into how they had made sharing decisions. We followed up with individual interview sessions for the 10 participants we were able to meet face to face. The questionnaire and interviews explored the needs and practices of sharing information and examined how well the access control mechanism of the photo sharing application supported user requirements. We use some of our qualitative data to offer explanations for our quantitative findings, however a full description of our findings is beyond the scope of this paper.

ACONTEXTUAL GROUPING EXERCISE RESULTS

On average, participants used the 6 criteria to divide their contacts into 18 distinct sets (S.D.=3.85), which they then used to create a mean of 3.8 distinct privacy groups (S.D.=1.66). Fig. 2 shows a distance matrix for contacts associated with the different criteria. Distance was calculated using the frequency at which sets associated with each criterion appeared in the same privacy group, i.e. the number of times a set from criterion A was grouped with a set from criterion B. We combined these frequency measures for all groups created by all participants and calculated the average frequency to produce a complete distance matrix. Black cells (in the 75-100% region of the frequency range) indicate a strong propensity for participants to group together contacts associated with the corresponding criteria. Light and dark grey cells (in the 25-50% and 50-75% regions of the frequency range, respectively) indicate a lower frequency of contacts with the corresponding criteria being grouped together. White cells (0-25%) indicate a very low frequency of contacts grouped together with these criteria.

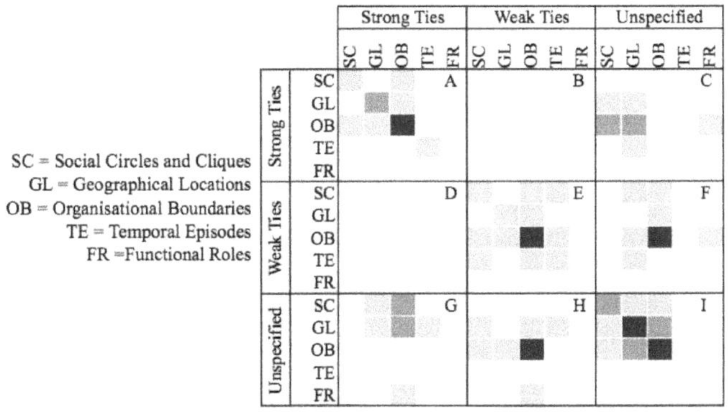

Figure 2. Distance matrix for contact sets

Figure 2 shows that there was a tendency not to mix different levels of tie strength within privacy groups. Strong ties were often grouped with other strong ties (Region A) and weak ties were often grouped with other weak ties (Region E). Contacts of different tie strengths were never combined, regardless of what other criteria they may have had in common (Regions D and B).

These results also reveal the level of granularity required in defining groups. For example, contact sets from within organizational boundaries were often merged with contact sets from within other organizational boundaries of similar tie strength to form a single group for content sharing purposes. Hence, there may be no need to separate contacts from within such contexts with fine granularity; it would suffice simply to aggregate all contacts defined by the Organizational Boundary criterion, whatever organization and therefore set they belong to, and split this 'superset' based on tie strength alone. This was also the case for Geographical Locations, albeit to a slightly lesser extent.

The same was not true for other criteria. For example, contact sets based on functional roles (relationships which are not defined by 'friendship' but some other functional reason for interacting with one another) were very rarely grouped with sets based on any other criteria, or even with contacts based on the same criterion. This indicates the need for fine granular control of these particular contacts, and highlights that different granularities are required for different relationship types within a social network.

FIELD STUDY RESULTS

In total we recorded 18,287 decisions to share or not to share a photo across all participants. We used these data to produce an analytical model for sharing decisions using logistic regression. The model provides us with a formula that computes the probability of a sharing decision as a function of the values of a number of categorical explanatory variables, in this case the metadata associated with each photograph. We were interested in identifying a set of quantifiable variables that will be useful in predictive models for selecting or recommending an appropriate audience for sharing.

Binary Logistic Regression Analysis

We conducted a hierarchical logistic regression on our dataset of sharing decisions. For our response variable we gave 'Share' responses a value of 1 and 'Do not share' a value of 0. For our binary explanatory variables we were able to use our automatically collected metadata and user selected tags relating to location, event, content, copresence, motive etc, as well as information relating to the contact's identity, such as the strength of ties and the set criteria with which the contact was associated. Incrementally adding blocks of variables to the model allowed us to examine whether the newly incorporated variables provided improved prediction ability over the preceding model; i.e. each block accounts for a certain amount of the variability observed in our 'Share Decision' measure.

Figure 3 shows the parameters for the logistic regression and our resultant analytical model of sharing decisions. B is the estimated coefficient for each variable in the model's equation. If the Wald statistic is significant ($p < 0.05$) then the parameter is useful to the model. The odds ratio; the predicted change in odds for a unit increase in the binary explanatory variable (i.e. from 0 to 1) can be calculated using Exp(B).

In the first stage of our logistic regression analysis, we examined individual differences between our 22 participants (using 21 orthogonal contrasts). We found that different participants had different propensities to share photographs, i.e. some of our participants were more inclined to share than others. We hypothesized that these differences might be associated with the participants' privacy concerns, however a test of Pearson's correlation coefficient did not reveal significant associations between coefficient/odds ratio and scores for a privacy concern questionnaire taken from [5] which participants completed at the end of Phase 1 ($r = 0.149$, n=22, $p=0.22$, n.s.).

In the second stage of our logistic regression analysis we examined the relationship between contacts' tie strength and decisions to share with them. We found that identifying both strong tie ($B=0.78$, $p<0.05$) and weak tie ($B= -1.328$, $p<0.05$) contacts offered significant influence within our model. Participants were twice as likely to share photos

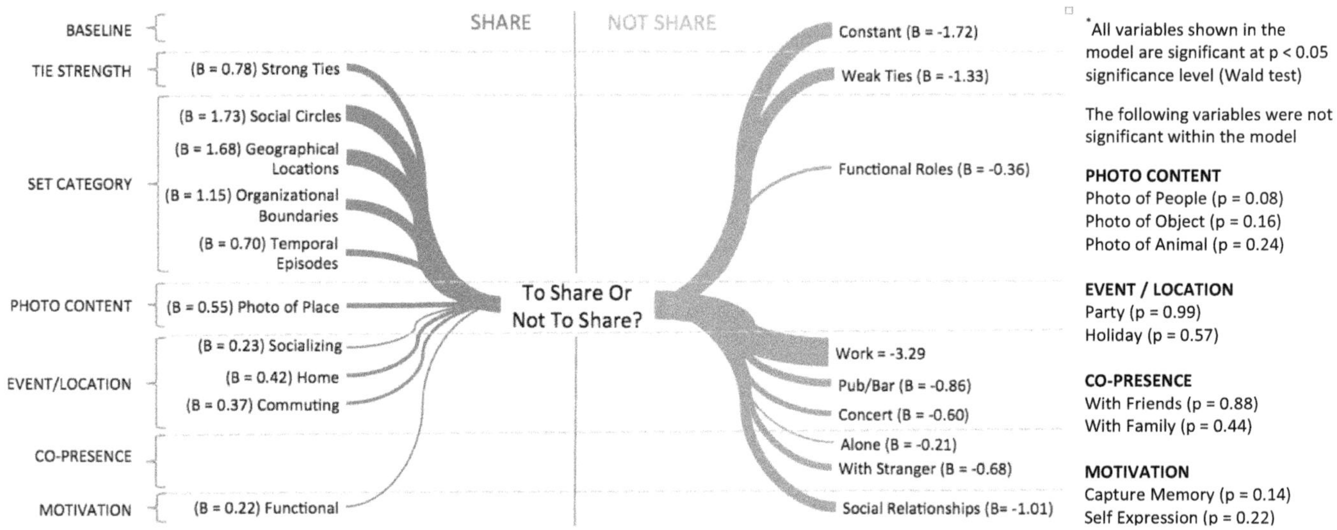

Figure 3. To Share Or Not To Share Logistic Regression Model

with contacts if they were classified as strong ties (compared to not strong ties). Weak ties were correlated with the decision not to share. Participants reported that they were often concerned about the implications of sharing personal content with people whom they did not know well, but were more comfortable sharing content with closer contacts.

In the third stage we examined whether the criteria for dividing network contacts affected sharing decisions. We found that participants were most likely to share with sets of contacts that corresponded to social circles/cliques in their network (B=1.733, $p<0.05$) and geographical locations (B=1.681, $p<0.05$), followed closely by organizational boundaries (B=1.151, $p<0.05$) and then temporal episodes (B=0.701, $p<0.05$). Only sets corresponding to functional roles (B= -0.355, $p=0.05$) decreased the odds of sharing.

In the fourth stage we examined the effects of photo content. Our model indicated that identifying whether or not a photograph contained people was not significantly useful for predicting sharing decisions (B=0.184, $p=0.08$). Results from our post-study questionnaire and interviews suggested, however, that many of our participants had considered whether there were people featured within the picture when making their sharing decisions. We discuss this subject further in the Discussion section below. Similarly, identifying that an object (B=0.131, $p=0.16$) or an animal (B=0.126, $p=0.24$) was the subject of a photograph did not offer significant predictive ability.

We found that photos of places, rather than people, objects or animals, were useful for predicting sharing decisions. This content increased the odds of sharing (B=1.731, $p<0.05$). Many of our participants commented that it was often 'easy' to make sharing decisions when the photos were of places. Generally they were more willing to share such photos due to the perception that they did not reveal personal information.

In the fifth stage we examined events and locations. Our model indicated that there was a strong decrease in the odds of sharing a photograph if it was taken at work (B= -3.292, $p<0.05$). Perhaps surprisingly, photographs taken at a bar/pub (B= -0.856, $p<0.05$), party (B= -0.004, $p<0.05$) and concert (B= -0.599, $p<0.05$) also had an overall effect of decreasing the likelihood of the photo being shared. Our participants offered a possible explanation for this observation in their interviews, commonly stating that while they took many photographs in these settings, they were the most likely to show them in embarrassing or compromising situations. Photos tagged as related to 'Holiday' did not provide statistical significance within the model (B=0.062 $p=0.57$). This suggests that participants considered other aspects of context as more important when deciding with whom to share holiday photos.

In the sixth stage we examined how the presence of others at the time of photo capture affected sharing decisions. Both being alone (B= -0.214, $p<0.05$) and the presence of strangers (B= -0.681, $p<0.05$) were negatively correlated with photographs being shared. The presence of friends (B= -0.013, $p=0.88$) and family (B=0.075, $p=0.44$) were not significant regressors within the model.

In the seventh stage of our logistic regression analysis we incorporated explanatory variables relating to the motivation for taking a photograph. Our analysis revealed that photographs taken to capture social relationships between people were less likely to be shared (B= -1.011, $p<0.05$). During our interviews it was common for participants to discuss their reluctance to share what they deemed to be photos of a more personal nature and these were often the photographs that they had taken to capture relationships with friends, family and loved ones.

Photographs that were taken to capture personal and group memories of events (B= -0.112, $p=0.14$) and those which were used as a form of self expression (B=0.109, $p=0.22$)

were not significant predictors of sharing decisions. We suggest that the motivation 'capturing personal and group memories' is too vague and encompasses such a wide range of contexts and content that it does not offer any predictive power. Many of the photos that were uploaded with the 'self expression' tag seemed to exemplify more traditional artistic and aesthetic goals of photography. We found that our participants had difficulty knowing when to assign this tag, as it was not always clear to them what constituted 'self expression'.

Our model also includes a significant constant component (B= -1.723, $p<0.05$), indicating that our participants exhibited a slight inclination not to share content unless other variables motivated them to do so.

In order to verify that the model accurately reflects sharing decisions made by our participants it was important to assess how well the model fitted our collected data.

Model Classification Measures

We assessed the fit of our classification model by examining the percentages of sharing occurrences correctly classified (Sensitivity), non-occurrences correctly classified (Specificity), sharing occurrences that were incorrect (False Positive Rate) and non-occurrences that were incorrect (False Negative Rate).

In total we included 18,287 sharing decisions (to share or not to share a particular photo with a particular set of contacts) in our analysis. 79.3% of our model's classifications were correct, indicating a reasonable fit to our data. (Sensitivity: 86.8%, Specificity: 68.7%, False Positive Rate: 21.4%, False Negative Rate: 20.3%). Our model offers a significant reduction in the number of misclassifications over the constant model, which simply shares with everyone and achieves only 50.4% accuracy.

We emphasize that we do not see our model as a ready-to-use solution for building a prediction/recommender system. Rigorous cross-validation and testing is necessary to assess how a predictive tool would work in the real world. It is still unknown precisely what level of accuracy a real recommender system would require; anything significantly better than chance might be of some use. A recommender system could engage in some confirmatory dialogue with the user or allow her to refine the recommendations, providing control while still reducing the burden of manually selecting an audience. Table 2 shows how our model classified the sharing decisions.

Observed		Predicted		
		Sharing Decision		Percentage Correct
		Not Share	Share	
Sharing Decision	Not Share	9310	1413	86.8
	Share	2364	5199	68.7
Overall Percentage				79.3

Table 2. Predicted vs. Observed Sharing Decisions

Our R^2-type statistics (Cox & Snell $R^2 = 0.467$, Nagelkerke $R^2 = 0.594$) indicate that the included explanatory variables capture a considerable amount of the data variability.

In addition to creating a single classification model for all of our participants, we used the same process to generate models for each individual participant. Our results suggest that by fitting different models to individuals based only on their own sharing decisions, the fit to our real data could be improved. Misclassifications were slightly reduced, with an average of 84.2% (S.D.=3.9%) of sharing decisions being correctly classified across the 22 individual models.

In the next section we tackle an issue that may offer the ability to identify situations in which it is not feasible to predict the outcomes of group-based privacy decisions. We examine the occurrence of situations in which sharing decisions do not align with participants' preconfigured privacy groups from Phase 1, i.e. the contexts in which these preconfigured groups needed to be significantly adjusted to provide the correct group for sharing a particular item.

GROUP ADJUSTMENT RESULTS

For each photograph we identified the contact sets, chosen via the application, with which the participant had decided to share that photo. We then calculated the extent to which the sets within each of the Phase 1 privacy-based groups received the same sharing decision. This provided us with a measure that we refer to as group cohesiveness; in other words, the degree of similarity between actual disclosure groups and preconfigured groups. Groups that have high cohesiveness are rarely adjusted, whereas groups with low cohesiveness are frequently reconfigured, perhaps according to considerations that become significant within a particular context.

For all 1,014 photos we found that, on average, 90.6% of sets within the same Phase 1 privacy group received the same disclosure settings (SD=0.09%). This suggests that the Phase 1 privacy-based groups created by participants were reasonably effective at grouping contacts with whom information would be shared similarly but that some adjustment was required. Allowing participants to specify sharing decisions at a 'Group' granularity would most often result in the correct decisions being applied to the contained sets of contacts, however, it is important that users are able to adjust groups when necessary as even a single unwanted recipient of sensitive content might nullify the benefits of the group-based approach.

We conducted a similar analysis with logistic regression, this time using group adjustment as our binary response variable. When all sets in a group were shared with uniformly, the group received a cohesiveness score of 1. If groups were adjusted, i.e. some member sets received different sharing decisions to other sets in the group, then the cohesiveness score was calculated as the largest fraction of the group to which the same setting was applied.

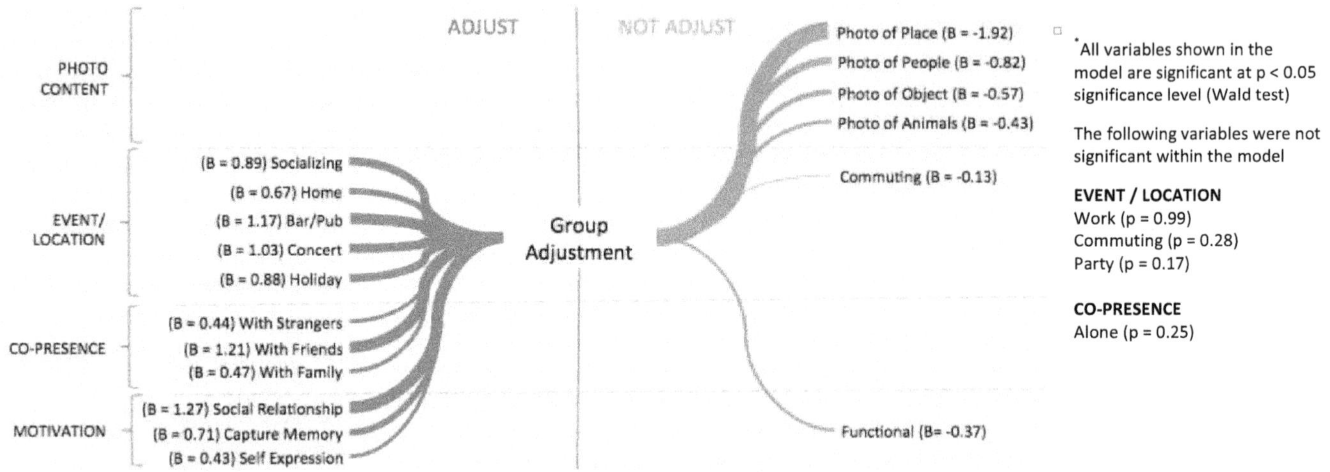

Figure 4. Group Adjustment Logistic Regression Model

We were interested to see if we could use the contextual information provided with the photographs to identify when group adjustment was most likely to take place. As this was an exploratory analysis, we set a reasonably low threshold of 0.9 for our group cohesiveness measure (i.e. 90% similarity between a Phase 1 privacy based group and the corresponding context specific sharing sets), below which we classified photos as necessitating the adjustment of preconfigured groups. It may be the case that even the slightest of adjustments become important for avoiding privacy violations. However, we were first interested to see if particular contexts required large adjustments.

Figure 4 shows the results of our logistic regression analysis and the coefficients in the model for the occurrence of group adjustment. We used the model to make statistical inferences about the contexts in which group adjustment was most marked. As with our previous model, we assessed its fit to our data, finding that the model offered a significant improvement over the naïve constant model (80.6% correct classifications). For 54.7% of sharing decisions no group adjustment took place. If groups were adjusted, on average it was by adding or removing no more than 9.4% of its sets.

A breakdown for our model is – Sensitivity: 88.0%, Specificity: 67.1%, False Positive Rate: 16.9%, False Negative Rate: 24.7%. Given the model's fit to our data, the results from the model provide reasonable predictors of group adjustment.

In the first stage of our logistic regression analysis, we examined individual differences and found that there were no significant differences in the occurrence of group adjustments between any of our participants. This implies that our participants had similar approaches to group adjustment.

In the second stage of our logistic regression analysis, we examined whether particular content was useful for predicting group adjustment. We found that all of our content related explanatory variables were useful for predicting whether groups would be adjusted ($p<0.05$). We found that photographs of people ($B= -0.822$, $p<0.05$), objects ($B= -0.565$, $p<0.05$) and animals ($B= -0.426$, $p<0.05$) had similar negative correlations with group adjustment. Photographs of places had a smaller, but still negative, effect on the odds of groups being adjusted ($B= -1.915$, $p<0.05$).

In the third stage of our logistic regression analysis, we examined events and locations. Among the remaining variables we found that neither work ($p=0.99$), 'commuting' ($B= -0.129$, $p=0.28$), nor 'party' ($B=0.339$, $p<0.17$) were significant regressors. All other variables were significant within the model and increased the odds of groups being adjusted: socializing ($B=0.885$, $p<0.05$), home ($B=0.673$, $p<0.05$), pub ($B=1.173$, $p<0.05$), concert ($B=1.033$, $p<0.05$), and holiday ($B=0.878$, $p<0.05$).

In the fourth stage of our logistic regression analysis, we examined copresence. Interestingly, we found that photos that were taken in the presence of others were correlated with privacy-based groups being significantly adjusted; this was most notable when photos were taken in the presence of friends ($B=1.206$, $p<0.05$). Being in the presence of strangers had a weaker positive correlation with groups being adjusted ($B=0.441$, $p<0.05$). Being alone was not a statistically significant predictor of group adjustment ($B= -0.163$, $p=0.25$). In the fifth stage of our logistic regression we incorporated explanatory variables relating to motivation. We found that photos for creating and maintaining social relationships were positively correlated with the adjustment of groups ($B=1.270$, $p<0.05$). The same was true for photos capturing personal and group memories ($B=0.713$, $p<0.05$) and self expression ($B=0.434$, $p<0.05$). Photos taken for functional purposes were negatively correlated with group adjustment ($B= -0.366$, $p<0.05$).

DISCUSSION

Our analysis revealed useful explanatory variables relating to the identity of contacts and the context of photo capture: namely, where and when the photo was taken, who was present at the time, what the photo was of, who was in the photo, why it was taken, the strength of the relationship to a potential recipient and the salient features of that recipient's identity with respect to divisions in the sharer's social network.

Our models offer a range of insights that may be useful to social network service designers, e.g. people are more reluctant to share photos capturing social relationships than photos taken for functional purposes; certain settings such as work, bars, concerts cause users to share less; and being a weak tie decreases the chance of being shared with in a system with granular access control.

Systems that aim to automate the process of selecting audiences for content sharing should incorporate important variables that we have identified within our models. Our findings also present design implications with respect to the configuration and adjustment of groups. Groups do not often incorporate both weak and strong ties, and fine levels of granularity are not required within groups based on organizational boundaries. Interfaces for creating groups could increase the efficiency of organizing contacts by accounting for these findings. With regard to group adjustment, our findings illustrate that systems providing group based access control should provide the ability to adjust groups after initial configuration. The frequency at which groups need to be adjusted in order to facilitate the needs of users and the contextual dynamics of sharing decisions emphasizes the importance of making this an efficient process.

Feedback from our participants in questionnaires and interviews revealed that the main criticism of the photo sharing application that they used was the effort required manually to specify granular privacy settings on a per photo basis, yet they valued the control it gave them over their privacy. Participants also found it time consuming to provide photo metadata, which was useful for our analysis. Although some of this information was automatically captured without explicit input from the participant, many features of the content and context had to be described manually by selecting appropriate tags. There are substantial bodies of work that aim to capture and describe the context of mobile devices and their users, as well as work that aims to automatically identify features of photo content. We expect that as these fields progress, our reliance on users to provide such information to predictive tools will be significantly reduced. We cannot know the extent to which machine learning will obviate the need for explicit input. Our study instead focuses on highlighting which factors matter for organizing future studies.

We found that some variables were not significantly useful for predicting sharing decisions, however a possible limitation of our approach is that these variables were not captured at an appropriate resolution. For example, we found that determining whether people are featured in a photograph was not particularly useful. But in our questionnaires and interviews, participants frequently mentioned that precisely *who* appeared in the photo was important, rather than the fact that *somebody* appeared in the photo. There are also additional variables that we were not able to control for but which participants suggested might have some influence on sharing decisions. For example, the strength of their relationship with the person in the photo mattered, as this sometimes caused them to consider not only their own privacy but also the privacy of other people in the photograph.

A possible limitation of our predictive model is that we do not consider differences between sharing decisions that are made 'in the moment', i.e. immediately after the photo has been taken, and those that are made some considerable time later. Users are sometimes uncertain about the content of, audience for, and norms regarding particular disclosures, and this uncertainty limits their ability to make the best decision at capture time [2]. Our model aims to replicate sharing decisions made by the users, with the assumption that they do not lead to privacy violations, although this may not always be true. Some of our findings suggest that users may have taken less time and/or care over privacy decisions when they were busy; e.g. photos were shared less often when users were with friends and the decisions they made correlated less with the privacy groups that they had preconfigured. Future work should look to gain further insights into the causes of these observations.

Although our study focused solely on photo sharing with social network contacts, we present our methodology as a useful outline for investigating patterns of disclosure with other types of social media content. For example, disclosure decisions for status updates may vary according to the people or subjects they reference, locations they relate to, strengths and types of relationships with potential recipients, and so on. Many of our participants told us that they would appreciate a similar method of access control for their status updates. Other privacy sensitive items of content, such as location sharing updates, e.g. using Facebook Places, create intense debate with respect to user's privacy. Assistive privacy management tools that account for the contextual dynamics of users' sharing decisions provide an opportunity to significantly reduce the burden on the user.

CONCLUSION

Our research addresses the considerable burden of exercising fine-grained control for sharing content with social network contacts. We have presented a novel approach to understanding relationships between properties of SN contacts, content, context and sharing decisions. Our work underlines the complexity of variables affecting sharing decisions but presents a manageable approach to quantifying their effects and takes a step towards better recommendation systems. We have shown that preconfigured privacy based groups which are intended to simplify and reduce the burden of controlling disclosure with individual contacts do not always provide a suitable mechanism for sharing in *all* contexts, as the groups often have to be adjusted. Furthermore, we have identified some factors that affect users' tendency to adjust these groups.

We expect that social network users will benefit from the ability to easily to share content with different people based on both their differing relationships and the specific context relating to that content. Our future work will investigate and test predictive content sharing tools and recommender systems based on our models in order to improve users' content sharing experiences.

ACKNOWLEDGMENTS

Eamonn O'Neill's research is supported by a Royal Society Industry Fellowship at Vodafone Group R&D.

REFERENCES

1. Ackerman, M. and Mainwaring, S. (2005). Privacy Issues in Human-Computer Interaction. In L. Cranor and S. Garfinkel (Eds.), Security and Usability: Designing Secure Systems that People Can Use, 381-400, Sebastopol, CA, O'Reilly.
2. Ahern, S., Eckles, D., Good, N. S., King, S., Naaman, M. and Nair, R. 2007. Over-exposed?: privacy patterns and considerations in online and mobile photo sharing. Proc. CHI '07. ACM, 357-366.
3. Altman, I. (1975). The Environment and Social Behavior: Privacy, Personal Space, Territory and Crowding. Monterey, CA: Brooks/Cole Pub. Co., Inc.
4. Bentley, F. and Metcalf, C. (2006). Flexible Views: Annotating and finding context-tagged mobile content. Ubicomp 2006 workshop on Pervasive Image Capture and Sharing.
5. Buchanan, T., Paine, C.B., Joinson, A.N. and Reips, U-D. (2007). Development of measures of online privacy concern and protection for use on the Internet, Journ. of the American Society for Information Science and Technology 58. 157–165.
6. Davis, M., Canny, J., Van House, N., Good, N., King, S., Nair, R., Burgener, C., Rinehart, B., Strickland, R., Campbell, G., Fisher, S. and Reid, N. (2005). MMM2: mobile media metadata for media sharing. Proc. MULTIMEDIA '05. ACM, 267-268.
7. DiMicco, J. M. and Millen, D. R. (2007). Identity management: multiple presentations of self in facebook. Proc. GROUP '07. ACM, 383-386.
8. Fang, L. and LeFevre, K. (2010). Privacy wizards for social networking sites. Proc. World Wide Web (WWW '10). ACM, New York, NY, USA, 351-360.
9. Gilbert, E. and Karahalios, K. (2009). Predicting tie strength with social media. CHI '09. ACM, 211-220.
10. Goffman, E. (1959). The Presentation of Self in Everyday Life. New York: Doubleday.
11. Granovetter, M. S. (1973). The Strength of Weak Ties. The American Journal of Sociology, vol. 78, no. 6, 1360–1380.
12. Hewitt, A. and Forte, A. (2006), Crossing boundaries: Identity management and student/faculty relationships on the Facebook, Proc. CSCW06. ACM.
13. Jones, S. and O'Neill, E. (2010). Feasibility of structural network clustering for group-based privacy control in social networks. SOUPS '10, vol. 485. ACM, 1-13.
14. Lampinen, A., Tamminen, S. and Oulasvirta, A. (2009). All My People Right Here, Right Now: management of group copresence on a social networking site. GROUP '09. ACM, 281-290.
15. Lederer, S. Dey, A. K. and Mankoff, J. (2002). A conceptual model and a metaphor of everyday privacy in ubiquitous computing, Intel Research, Tech. Rep. IRB-TR-02- 017.
16. Lovett, T., O'Neill, E., Pollington, D. and Irwin, J. (2009) Event-based mobile social network services, in Workshop on Context-Aware Mobile Media and Mobile Social Networks, Mobile HCI 2009.
17. Miller, A. D. and Edwards, W. K. (2007). Give and take: a study of consumer photo-sharing culture and practice. Proc. CHI '07. ACM, 347-356.
18. Olson, J., Grudin, J. and Horvitz, E. (2005). A study of preferences for sharing and privacy. CHI '05 extended abstracts. ACM, 1985–1988.
19. Palen, L. and Dourish, P. (2003). Unpacking "privacy" for a networked world. Proc. CHI '03. ACM, 129-136.
20. Raento, M. and Oulasvirta, A. (2008). Designing for privacy and self-presentation in social awareness. Personal Ubiq. Computing. 12, 7 (Oct. 2008), 527- 542.
21. Skeels, M. and Grudin, J. (2009). When social networks cross boundaries: a case study of workplace use of facebook and linkedin. Proc. GROUP '09. ACM, 95-10.
22. Tufekci, Z. (2008). Can You See Me Now? Audience and Disclosure Management in Online Social Network Sites. *Bulletin of Science and Technology Studies*. Volume 11, Number 4, June 2008 , pp. 544-564(21).
23. Van House, N., Davis, M., Ames, M., Finn, M. and Viswanathan, V. (2005). The uses of personal networked digital imaging: an empirical study of cameraphone photos and sharing. CHI '05 Extended Abstracts. ACM, 1853-1856.

Pass-Them-Around: Collaborative Use of Mobile Phones for Photo Sharing

Andrés Lucero, Jussi Holopainen, Tero Jokela
Nokia Research Center
P.O. Box 1000, FI-33721 Tampere, Finland
{andres.lucero, jussi.holopainen, tero.jokela}@nokia.com

ABSTRACT
In this paper we explore shared collocated interactions with mobile phones. We introduce a phone-based application that allows a small group of collocated people to share photos using the metaphor of passing paper photos around. The prototype encourages people to share their devices and use them interchangeably while discussing photos face-to-face. The prototype supports *ad-hoc* photo sharing in different contexts by taking into account the spatial arrangement of users around a table, measured with sensors embedded in their mobile phones. Our evaluations show that people are willing to share and connect their mobile phones to engage in collaborative interactions. Participants were able to easily share their collections of photos using our proposed interaction techniques.

Author Keywords
Collocated Interaction, Handheld Devices, Photo Sharing.

ACM Classification Keywords
H5.m. Information interfaces and presentation (e.g., HCI): Miscellaneous.

General Terms
Design, Experimentation, Human Factors.

INTRODUCTION
Mobile phones were conceived to enable communication between remote participants. While some technologies and applications have been developed to support interactions between collocated users, in general mobile devices have provided little support for local interactions. Our Social and Spatial Interactions (SSI) platform [22] extends the use of mobile devices to support shared interactions between collocated users. In this platform, the users' personal mobile devices become elements of an interaction system that is shared between all users. A key technology enabling such interactions is the ability to track the positions of mobile devices related to each other and the environment.

In the field of consumer photography, the adoption of digital imaging technologies has changed the way people see and understand photography: cheap digital cameras have become ubiquitous in our society, viewing and using photos instantly after capture has become possible, and the practically negligible cost of digital photos has lowered the barrier of photo capture [11]. Online services that support remotely sharing, distributing and commenting digital photos have emerged to challenge the traditional face-to-face sharing of paper photos. While these new sharing technologies offer many benefits over traditional methods, they lack the richness of social interaction when compared to sharing photos between collocated users [6,21].

We present the design and evaluation of the *pass-them-around* prototype, which allows a small group of collocated people to share photos. We have taken conventional sharing practices with paper photos as a starting point to see how technology could better support those practices. The evaluation of the prototype shows that people are willing to share and connect their mobile phones to engage in collaborative interactions. Participants easily shared their photo collections using our proposed interaction techniques.

The rest of this paper is structured as follows. First, we provide background information on the SSI platform and review relevant related work. Then, we describe the general design principles and interaction techniques of *pass-them-around*. Finally, we report the results of the evaluation, followed by discussion and conclusions.

BACKGROUND

Social and Spatial Interactions (SSI)
Mobile phones were originally conceived and have traditionally been utilized for personal use. The improvement in sensor and short-range communication technologies offers possibilities to explore shared use of mobile phones. In this paradigm shift, collocated users engage in collaborative activities using their devices, thus going from *personal-individual* towards *shared-multiuser* experiences and interactions. Our Social and Spatial Interactions (SSI) platform [22] extends the current individual use of these devices to support shared collocated interactions with mobile phones. The question the platform addresses is if people are willing to share their personal mobile devices and engage in collaborative interactions.

SSI Principles

The main principles of Social and Spatial Interactions are:

- *Social*: We support joint multiuser interactions by encouraging people to share their devices to reach a given goal. We have been looking into various physical and social contexts of use, e.g., office teamwork [23], sharing media content at home (this paper), and outdoor games.
- *Spatial*: We can use the relative positions of the phones with respect to each other on a flat surface to create interactions. We provide a tracking solution that is built in the phone [5], thus we do not require a dedicated infrastructure (i.e., fixed lab setting) or external equipment (e.g., infrared tower or camera) for tracking.
- *Tangible*: Tangible user interfaces (TUIs) allow people to interact with digital information by manipulating physical objects where the data is coupled with the object [17]. We explore the use of a mobile phone as a physical interface to manipulate data by performing simple actions (e.g., move, sort, group, join, spin, stack, etc.). Siftables [25] have inspired our SSI platform work.
- *Multimodal*: We use touch (i.e., touchscreen) and device gestures (i.e., gestures performed while holding a device in one's hand) as the two main user input modes. We provide multimodal feedback during the interaction, not only through visuals, but also through haptics and sound.

User-Centered Design Approach

We have been following a user-centered design (UCD) approach by involving end-users in the process of creating novel artifacts and interactions for the SSI platform. We have conducted a probes study, co-design sessions, and evaluations of prototypes. Taking these different steps has allowed us to gain a better understanding of how people might use the SSI technologies.

First, we conducted a probes study [12] with 14 mixed-nationality students where we observed people's pervasive use of (mobile) technologies. Participants reported things to us such as checking Facebook as the first thing they do in the morning (before brushing their teeth or taking a shower), or using their laptops while sharing the same table, constantly switching and transitioning between an individual and a social situation. Second, we invited five probe study participants to co-design sessions. We began each session by sharing and discussing findings from the probes with our participants to validate our results. We then presented a simple demonstrator showing the possibilities of SSI. After the demo, participants and three researchers engaged in brainstorming sessions. This work resulted in 20 possible SSI applications. Third, we took one of the 20 SSI applications and implemented it to demonstrate the potential of the SSI platform and some of its principles. The MindMap prototype [23] is a brainstorming tool that allows a workgroup to create, edit, and view virtual notes on any table. In this paper we introduce a second application from the SSI list: the *pass-them-around* prototype.

RELATED WORK

A large body of related work has influenced the design of the *pass-them-around* prototype. We have identified three main related-work areas: personal photography, collocated photo sharing, and collocated photo sharing applications.

Personal Photography

There is a rich literature on both conventional and digital personal photography and their associated practices. In the field of anthropology, Chalfen [6] studied conventional family photography and the role of photos in the home. The term Kodak Culture [6] refers to the old practice where consumers share printed photos or video footage of friends and family in a 'home mode' type of communication. Chalfen describes in detail the behavior of *storytelling* or using one's photos to tell stories *about* the pictures.

When consumers adopted digital cameras, the HCI community began a rich tradition of studying people's practices surrounding digital (and conventional) photos. Frohlich *et al.* [10] developed a set of requirements for 'Photoware' (i.e., technologies that support storing, sending and sharing photos) by studying what people do with conventional and digital photos once they have captured them. Besides the type of *storytelling* behavior reported by Chalfen, they found that people also engage in *reminiscing* talk around photos, especially when sharing photos with members who were present when the pictures were taken. Both types of behavior, *storytelling* and *reminiscing*, are what Frohlich *et al.* refer to as 'Photo-talk' [10]. Crabtree *et al.* [9] further elaborated on this work by developing requirements for distributed collaboration around digital photographs. To achieve this, they conducted a close examination of two empirical instances of conventional photo sharing. Miller and Edwards [26] looked at people from the Kodak Culture who had fully converted to digital photography to see how their practices have changed. They also studied people's digital photo sharing practices on Flickr. They found two types of practices: the Kodak Culture and 'Snapr' people. Compared to the former, 'Snaprs' are less concerned with privacy, share photos outside their existing social networks, and concentrate on *taking* pictures instead of *sharing* them.

More recently, the use of cameraphones opened a new line of research for personal photography. With their prototype, Mäkelä *et al.* [24] first studied networked digital photography enabling photo sharing that was nearly synchronous with capture. They identified that people shifted from telling stories *about* the pictures, to telling stories *with* the pictures. Koskinen *et al.* [18] looked at another type of image sharing with cameraphones via MMS. Ames *et al.* [2] conducted a 5-month study of cameraphone photography and derived a list of requirements for mobile photoware.

In their studies, several authors have found that people still rely on the printed photo as a photo-sharing object [6,9,10].

Collocated Photo Sharing

Within the larger context of personal photography, some researchers have specifically looked into collocated photo sharing practices. Lindley *et al.* [20,21] studied how people share photos at home through different means such as with loose printed photos, photo albums, cameras connected to a TV and a remote control, PCs and laptops. She proposed a set of design guidelines for photo sharing using domestic display technologies. Based on four inter-related studies on collocated photo sharing, Van House [31] identified 11 forms of face-to-face sharing: prints, photo album, self-published photographic books, slideshows (35mm slides or LCD projectors), slideshows on laptops or larger screens, framed photos (at work and at home), desktop computers, laptops, cameras, cameraphones, and online (Flickr). Each of these forms of sharing has unique advantages and limitations. She also discusses four reasons for the continuing popularity of collocated photo sharing: 1) memory, storytelling and identity, 2) relationships, 3) orality, and 4) performance. Stelmaszewska *et al.* [30] studied collocated photo sharing using cameraphones, where both capturing and sharing are done through the mobile phones. They focused their work on understanding the role of the place where sharing occurs, how and when people share photos, what determines who the photos are shared with, and what influences their sharing experience.

Collocated Photo Sharing Applications

Souvenirs [28] supports photo sharing in settings provided by the domestic environment where face-to-face can naturally occur (e.g., living room or kitchen). It links objects to photos by assigning RFID tags to physical memorabilia found in the home. Using special software, people first create a folder of photos and then place an object on an RFID reader to associate the object with the photo set. The object is later placed on the RFID reader to trigger a slideshow on a large LCD screen, or for navigation using a special physical scroll wheel. Shoebox [4] combines (physical) storage and display for digital photos. Shoebox is a box with a display at one end that can be stacked on a shelf or brought down to show photos to others. Lifting the lid and running your finger through a touch-sensitive surface on the top of the device results in navigating photos.

Other photo sharing applications use mobile phones or other portable devices to share photos. StoryTrack [3] is a portable prototype that supports local sharing of photos. People hold the device with two hands and control the viewing of images using buttons mounted on the edges of the prototype. Up to two users can view images side by side and can also share control of the presentation. The device can be passed around like a regular photo album. Additionally, audio narrations can be recorded and later played back. Ah Kun *et al.* [1] propose a network of PDAs that allows any user of a group to broadcast images on the other devices in that group. Images are transferred wirelessly using Wi-Fi. Their prototype incorporates a series of floor-control policies or software locks that determine who can control the show and when, in order to study how to best manage social interaction. Mobiphos [8] supports capturing and real-time sharing of photos among members of a collocated group using cameraphones. The application presents users with an updated stream of picture thumbnails made by the group. The display is used both as a viewfinder and a thumbnail gallery. Data is transferred between devices using Wi-Fi. Disc-O-Share [19] allows browsing and transferring photos between mobile phones (via Bluetooth) by creating three distal regions around mobile phones. Particular actions are triggered in response to entering or leaving these regions. An external camera tracks the position of the phones by reading visual markers displayed at the top of each device's screen. *Pass-them-around* differs from these applications in that it tries to emulate characteristics of sharing traditional paper photos to support a set of related practices (e.g., sequential sharing, huddling, etc.) by using the spatial arrangement of people.

DESIGN OF PASS-THEM-AROUND

Based on the findings from the SSI probes study and co-design sessions, and the relevant literature described in the previous section, we decided to design and implement the *pass-them-around* prototype that: 1) allows a small group of collocated people to share photos using the metaphor of passing printed photos around, 2) supports conventional photo sharing social practices, and 3) supports *ad-hoc* photo sharing by taking the spatial arrangement of people around a table into account.

Passing Printed Photos Metaphor (Tangibility)

The physicality of the paper photograph has important implications for photo sharing [20]. In the transition from paper to digital photographs, aspects such as the proximity of the photos to the group, access to control of the process of photo sharing, and how the group members are arranged in relation to one another have been lost. Lindley *et al.* [21] have found that people like having printed photos to hand and that being able to touch them facilitates involvement.

We use the metaphor of passing paper photos around to suggest interaction semantics. Each mobile phone device becomes a physical container of individual photos. In this way, photos regain their qualities as physical artifacts and their affordances for tangibility.

Conventional Photo Sharing Practices (Social)

The use of domestic display technologies has an impact on how people socially interact and experience collocated photo sharing [21]. It has been well documented that photo sharing is a social activity where seeing the reactions of others is an important part of showing photographs [6,21]. When viewing photos in front of a desktop computer or laptop, usually two people are seated in front of the screen (e.g., the audience) while a third person (e.g., the photographer) is *hovering* behind. As a result, it becomes difficult for the photographer to see if the audience is enjoying the photos. Passing prints around also affords the formation of group huddles or *huddling,* which amplifies the closeness inherent in conventional photo sharing.

We support conventional photo sharing practices by allowing a group of four people to discuss pictures face-to-face. Each person can use their mobile phone individually or interchangeably, to create flexible interactions within the group. We support *photo pointing* to synchronize conversation and presentation [21], and *huddling* to browse and discuss photos together in smaller groups of people.

Flexible Interaction (Spatial)

As mentioned earlier, how people are arranged with respect to one another in a photo-sharing group is very important. Moreover, there are social areas at home (e.g., kitchen, living room) and outside (e.g., bar, café) that are better suited for photo sharing. For example, photos in the center of the living room become a focal point and the open seating arrangement allows people to see one another [21].

We support *ad-hoc* photo sharing using devices enhanced with radio tracking technology [5], which allows tracking the relative positions of the devices on a flat surface. The sensors embedded in the mobile phones allow us to know where people are seated (or standing) around the table. In this way, we are able to send images between individuals and generate sequential passing of images between the devices even when people change their positions around the table. As no extra hardware is needed besides the enhanced phones, photo sharing can take place in different contexts such as over drinks at a bar or in the living room at home.

INTERACTION

The idea behind our concept is to allow a small group of collocated people to first individually browse their collections of photos and then collectively share photos as a group on any table surface. Instead of taking established digital photo sharing practices as a starting point (e.g., duplicating images, automatic slideshow mode, etc.), we took an alternative approach. Based on the rich existing literature on photoware, we tried to replicate conventional photo sharing practices (e.g., passing paper photos around, face-to-face communication, huddling, etc.) and see how technology could better support those practices.

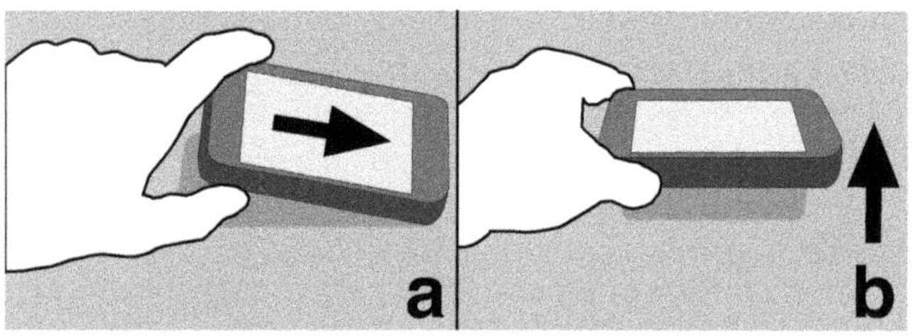

Figure 1. (a) Tilting horizontally to browse individual photo collections, and (b) tilting vertically towards the center of the table to start sharing a collection of photos.

Browsing Individual Collections

We propose a type of browsing that mimics individually flicking through a stack of paper photographs from one pile to another. After starting the application, users are presented with their individual photo collections as a pile of photos, thus the four devices display one pile each. To browse through the photos users must tilt their devices horizontally by performing a quick upward movement on either side of the device (Figure 1a) and bringing it back to a rest on the table. As a result, the photo at the top of the pile slides in the direction the device was tilted revealing the next photo in the pile. When the end of the collection is reached browsing overshoots, reverses direction and stops at the last photo. Keeping the device tilted, results in a continuous and faster browsing. Cho *et al.* [7] proposed a similar tilt user interface where the amount of browsing is proportional to the tilt angle. As an alternative, users can tap either half of the touchscreen to browse photos, which triggers a similar animation as described above for tilting.

Sharing Individual Photos *(Throwing)*

Pass-them-around supports different ways of sharing pictures. The first one is similar to passing a paper photo to another person, regardless of that person's location. This type of sharing allows for flexible one-to-one sharing of images, one at a time. To share a photo, users must first select an image by either tilting horizontally or tapping, and perform a long press on that photo. A thumbnail of the image is displayed under the user's finger, which can be moved around by dragging the finger on the touchscreen. The photo can then be thrown in any direction by flicking the thumbnail. The devices are fitted with the necessary wireless sensors to detect their current location. If no device is found in the direction the image was thrown, then the photo briefly shakes back and forth on the sender's device. However, if another device is located in the direction the photo is thrown, the photo is shown on the receiving device. The new photo fills up the screen and is displayed on top of any other existing photo. An animation shows the direction where the new photo is coming from. When the image arrives, a subtle vibration is triggered every 4 seconds to cue the receiver to flick the image back to the sender. *Throwing* takes existing multi-display reaching techniques [27], and brings them into photo sharing on mobile phones.

Sharing a Collection *(Sequential)*

The second method allows sharing photo collections as a group, closely resembling the activity of passing paper photographs around one by one, in a sequence. To start sharing a collection of photos, its owner or photographer must tilt the device vertically towards the center of the table (Figure 1b). This movement replicates the gesture for giving something out to another person. As the screen is no longer visible to the photographer when the device gesture is performed, a single intense vibration is triggered to provide feedback. When the photographer successfully shares their collection of photos with the rest of the users, the photographer's device shows the first photo of the collection, while the other devices show an empty corkboard texture. An animation showing how the three remaining devices that belong to the audience are emptied provides additional feedback to the photographer.

As previously mentioned, each mobile phone becomes a physical container of individual photos. Using horizontal tilt or tap, photos are then passed on one by one to the next person, in order. As we are able to detect the location of the devices, the photo is displayed on the next available device, even if people decide to switch positions around the table.

To investigate different social practices during photo sharing, we decided to incorporate different rules for control during browsing. For example, during *sequential* browsing the photographer decides the direction and the speed at which the photos are browsed. However, when the photographer passes their last picture around the table, then each audience member must decide when they want to pass it to the next person. In the case of passing the last photo around the table, each audience member decides the speed of browsing. These simple rules allowed us to study people's perceptions on who decides the speed of browsing.

During *sequential* photo sharing, audience members may want to inquire specific aspects of a given photo, other than the one the photographer is currently presenting. *Photo pointing* allows coordinating conversation and presentation. The audience can trigger *photo pointing* by performing a long press on a photo, which creates a copy of that photo on the remaining devices. The same user must again do a long press on the photo to stop *photo pointing* and resume *sequential* photo sharing.

Creating group huddles to closely discuss photos is a common practice in conventional photo sharing. *Pass-them-around* supports *huddling* by allowing smaller groups of people to view and discuss photos together. To connect two or more devices together, users must perform a pinch gesture on the screens of two devices (Figure 2a) [23]. Alternative ways of connecting devices include: knocking devices together to detect synchronized sounds [29], bumping devices together using accelerometer data [14], and performing pen gestures on touch-enabled devices [15].

When the devices are successfully tiled together, they display a composite larger version of the photo. By means of an animation, the current content is first removed from the devices showing the corkboard underneath, and then the new larger image slides into place. Additionally, pieces of masking tape indicate which devices have been tiled together and a distinctive scotch tape sound is played. *Sequential* photo sharing continues by considering the huddle as one physical photo container. It is also possible to tile three devices together (Figure 3). To achieve this, it is first necessary to tile two devices together for a 2x1 configuration, and then a third device can be tiled onto the existing huddle for a 3x1 configuration.

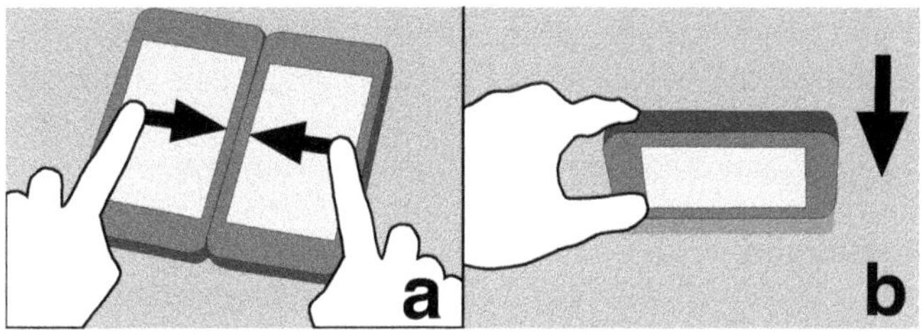

Figure 2. (a) Pinching two devices to create group huddles, and (b) tilting vertically towards oneself to stop sharing.

Figure 3. Three tiled devices during *sequential* photo share with one device acting as a controller.

Users can disconnect the devices from the shared view by simply picking them up from the table and holding them in their hands. This results in showing an overview of the corkboard. When the device is put back on the table, it resumes *sequential* sharing as an additional photo container.

To stop sharing a collection, the photographer must tilt the device vertically towards him or herself (Figure 2b). The device gesture is naturally associated to withdrawing an invitation or hiding something. A single intense vibration is triggered to signal that sharing has now stopped. The photographer can also directly obtain information on the new status of the prototype as the audience goes back to individually browsing their own collections of photos.

Sharing a Collection on a Single Display (All Tiled)

The third main method for sharing collections of photos consists of using all four devices to create a single larger tiled display. To connect four devices together, the users must first create two huddles of 2x1 devices. Then, these two huddles can be pinched together into a larger 2x2 configuration. The photographer's device is used to browse through the photos by tapping on either half of the screen.

EVALUATION

There were three main goals of the study. First, we wanted to test the ideas behind SSI and see if *pass-them-around* is a relevant prototype in the context of the SSI platform. Our second goal was to investigate the different photo-sharing strategies and social behaviors supported by the prototype. Third, we wanted to assess the proposed interaction techniques in terms of naturalness, ease of learning and use. To achieve this, we invited existing groups of friends to share their personal photos in a collocated way using the prototype. We collected qualitative data both during the photo-sharing sessions and later during semi-structured interviews. Quantitative data was collected by means of a validated questionnaire after a photo-sharing task.

Participants
The evaluation was conducted with five groups of four friends, for a total of 20 participants. We recruited groups of friends, rather than isolated individuals, so participants would feel comfortable both with one another and with the photo-sharing situation. The participants were chosen to represent a variety of user types, including parents, international students who had previously participated in the probes study and co-design sessions, and professionals. The participants varied in gender (16 male, 4 female), age (between 21 and 40), and background (14 technical, 6 non-technical). All participants owned a mobile phone, different from the one used in the study. All participants were prior digital camera and/or cameraphone owners, and five participants also had digital SLR cameras. All participants had engaged in photo sharing activities via online photo sharing sites such as Flickr or Facebook by both posting and viewing online photos.

Method
We used participants' personal photos during the evaluation so they would have a real motivation to talk about and share those photos. Each participant brought in 15 digital photos, some taken when all four friends were present (for *reminiscing* talk), and others when only the photographer was present (for *storytelling*). All the photos brought by the participants were preloaded into all four devices to avoid long transfer times while sharing photos. Each participant was provided with one device running the prototype.

Each session consisted of four parts: introduction, exploration, task, and semi-structured interview. First, we gathered participants' background information about photography and photo sharing and asked them to recall one recent occasion in which they had shared photos with families and/or friends (15 min.). Second, we briefly explained participants how to interact with the *pass-them-around* prototype. We then allowed them to freely explore the available functionality and get acquainted with the application (15 min.). Third, all four participants took turns in sharing their personal pictures with each other (30 min.). At the end of the task, we asked participants to fill-out the AttrakDiff [13] questionnaire to quantitatively measure pragmatic and hedonic aspects of the prototype. AttrakDiff measures the attractiveness of interactive products along four dimensions. Pragmatic quality (PQ) refers to the product's ability to support the achievement of behavioral goals (i.e., usability). Hedonic quality refers to the users' self: *stimulation* (HQ-S) is the product's ability to stimulate and enable personal growth (i.e., personal goals and aspirations), and *identification* (HQ-I), is the product's ability to address the need of expressing one's self through objects one owns (i.e., social aspects of product ownership). Both HQ-S and HQ-I have been found to contribute to perceived attractiveness (ATT), which describes a global value of the product based on the quality perception. Participants indicate their perception of the product by rating 28 pairs of opposite adjectives that relate to the four dimensions on a 7-point scale (-3 to 3). Finally, we had semi-structured interviews in which we asked a consistent set of open-ended questions to each group, prompting participants to walk us through some of their experiences while sharing photos using the prototype (60 min.).

Figure 4. Evaluation setup with four participants sharing photos using the devices on the round table.

The five sessions were conducted in an open meeting room area with modern and colorful furniture (Figure 4). This created the kind of cozy environment found in a bar, café, or living room. The four devices were set on a small and tall round table (60 cm. diameter x 130 cm. tall), and participants stood around the table. All sessions including the semi-structured interviews were recorded on video and transcribed. Participants were given one movie ticket each to compensate them for their time.

Affinity diagramming [16] was used to analyze the data from both the observations of use and the semi-structured interviews. Two researchers independently made notes as they watched the videos for each of the five sessions. The same two researchers collaboratively analyzed the qualitative data through several interpretation rounds. The affinity diagram supported categorization and visualization of the main themes emerging from the data. These themes form the heart of our findings section.

Implementation
We implemented *pass-them-around* on Nokia N900 mobile devices running the Maemo Linux operating system. The prototype was implemented in C++ on top of the Qt 4.6 software framework with optional OpenGL ES 2.0 rendering used for user interface graphics. Using OpenGL allowed applying fluid animations for moving, rotating and zooming the photos. In order to display events across different devices, the devices' clocks were synchronized.

As the application was running on several devices in a distributed manner, we needed to share coordination information about the application state and user actions between the devices. This was accomplished by setting up a wireless personal area network, onto which all the devices were connected. A Wi-Fi network was used on which messages sent by one device were automatically transmitted to all other devices. The devices were able to detect each other's presence with broadcast UDP packets.

The N900's internal accelerometer was used to detect when a device was picked up from the table, or when it was tilted. When the sensor showed a constant pull toward the back of the device, it was deduced that the device was on the table. When there was a constant and distinguishable pull in a given direction, it was recognized as a tilt. In all other cases, the device was considered to be in the user's hands. To simplify the device gestures, tilting vertically towards oneself was considered the same as picking up the device.

To detect people's positions around the table (e.g., to flick a photo to another device), we utilized N900 devices enhanced with radio tracking technology [5]. This particular technology tracks the angular position and distance between devices by embedding multi-antenna receivers under the devices' screen and running sensor array signal processing algorithms on each device. This allows the technology to track multiple emitters such as active RF tags or mobile phones. This radio tracking technology was conceived to track longer distances, thus the accuracy for sensing device proximity was one meter. More accurate distance measurements could for instance be used to automatically tile devices when put next to each other.

FINDINGS

In the following sections we describe the main findings from the *pass-them-around* evaluation. First, we briefly describe how participants currently share photos with family and friends. Second, we present a description of different photo-sharing practices that our findings suggest. Third, we examine people's natural social interaction during face-to-face photo sharing. Finally, we look at different aspects of spontaneous photo sharing.

Current Photo Sharing Practices

Our study confirms prior findings in photo sharing practices. Most participants reported using online services (e.g., Flickr, Picasa, Facebook) to share photos [31]. They receive feedback on the photos either through comments posted directly on the service, by chatting online, or over the phone. Other ways of sharing photos include [20,21,31]: directly showing photos from their laptop (7/20) or digital camera (4/20), connecting a digital camera, camcorder or cameraphone to a TV (4/20), using a mobile phone by either passing it around and showing photos from the display or by sending an MMS (4/20), and sending photos as email attachments (2/20). Participants said they would only order prints or print photographs to send them abroad to family members who did not have access to the technology, to frame them and hang them on the wall, and to put them in photo albums for later browsing: *"Very rarely we do this exchange of pictures on paper." [P2]*

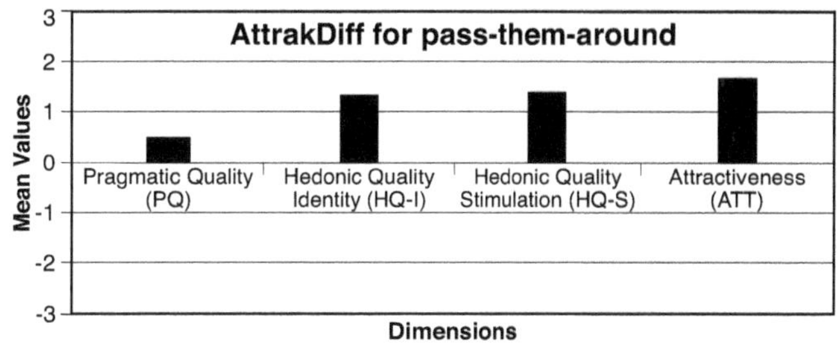

Figure 5. Mean Values along the four AttrakDiff dimensions.

Different Photo Sharing Strategies

Sequential Photo Sharing

Participants used different strategies to share photos as a group. First, participants tried *sequential* photo sharing. All participants were able to both share their collections by tilting their device vertically and browse through the photos by tilting the device horizontally, describing the gestures as *"natural."* Most participants (16/20) said that tilting horizontally for browsing was intuitive for them: *"Is tilting meant to emulate sharing printed pictures? For me tilting was nice, it was like passing a paper picture." [P18]* On the AttrakDiff questionnaire (Figure 5), the value for the attractiveness (ATT) of the prototype is located in the above-average region and thus the overall impression of the product is very attractive. The high ratings on this dimension confirm that participants thought the prototype was motivating and appealing.

About half of the participants had some trouble following the discussion of photos that were not currently displayed on their devices: *"The picture on my screen is not interesting because I am not hearing the comments about it. (...) You see the picture that was commented three pictures ago." [P12]* Participants frequently used *photo pointing* to partially solve this problem as it allowed coordinating conversation and presentation of the photos.

Photo pointing was naturally used when the photographer or the audience thought that the content was interesting. Since with *photo pointing* all participants are looking at the same photo, they tended to focus on their own devices and make comments. This was natural as in this situation there is no need to maintain the joint attention in other ways. Few participants (4/20) picked the phone up to have a closer view of the current photo. Unfortunately, in the current implementation this resulted in showing an overview of the corkboard where people can see who is connected and what is currently being displayed on their devices. This overview mode was seldom used during the evaluation: *"The overview is kind of useless." [P11]*

To our surprise, participants developed a new sharing strategy out of this need to simultaneously see the same photo that the photographer was explaining. As the photographer was unable to trigger *photo pointing,* they would pass a picture to the next participant and ask them to perform *photo pointing* instead. This allowed the photographer to remain in control of the presentation while everybody was looking at the same photo. When the photographer was done explaining a photo, they would ask the same participant to stop *photo pointing*. We call this new emerging way of photo sharing *mirrored view*.

Photo Sharing in Group Huddles

While involved in *sequential* photo sharing, participants also created *group huddles* in all sessions. All participants were able to successfully tile displays together by performing the pinch gesture. Almost all participants (19/20) thought the gesture was natural. Two participants explored new ways to pinch devices together by doing a reverse pinch (from the center towards the edges), and by trying to connect three devices with one pinch.

When a *group huddle* was created, a few photographers complained about having a different picture on their device than the one currently shown on the tiled display. The effect was more noticeable when all audience members formed a *group huddle* (3x1): *"How can I explain when I have one picture on my device and another on the (tiled) 3x1 device?" [P6]* In that case, the photographer's device is mostly used to control, so that one person is presenting and the others are watching. Regarding tiling configurations, 3x1 was used the most followed by 2x1x1 (i.e., two tiled and two individual), while two *huddles* of 2x1 devices was only used in the build up to the *all tiled* configuration.

Photo Sharing With All the Devices Tiled

Participants used the *all tiled* configuration in most sessions. Although most participants (19/20) were able to perform the sequence required to create the *all tiled* display, one participant said it required too many different steps: *"Getting (all tiled) had to be done in a specific sequence which is a bit counterintuitive." [P12]* Some participants (7/20) did not like how images were partitioned by the bezels when tiling. They proposed having the possibility to pan and zoom into the image as an alternative: *"Due to the breaking of the picture you may miss something." [P7]*

Other Ways to Share Photos

Finally, some participants (6/20) requested more flexible ways of sharing photos such as random sharing and being able to look at a specific photo while the others can continue sharing at their own pace: *"It would be nice to (...) pass a photo to two people but not to a third." [P10]*

Supporting Natural Social Interaction

In general, participants said the prototype supported natural social interaction by means of immediate verbal and non-verbal feedback. Participants used different strategies to explain the content and context of the photos to one another. The photographer usually told stories about each of the photographs and the other participants asked questions, made comments, and used gestures to point at interesting photos or parts of the photos. *Photo pointing* was often used to focus the discussion on a single photo: *"It is really nice that (here) you can pass some pictures, comment at the same time, and point out things." [P12]* Some participants expressed that the proposed type of collocated photo sharing was preferred over sharing photos online due to the lack of immediate feedback in the latter. When sharing photos online, participants use synchronous communication means such as chat or phone to get feedback: *"Explaining photos on Facebook is like giving a speech and you don't know how the audience in front of you feels." [P4]* On the two hedonic quality dimensions of AttrakDiff, i.e., identity (HQ-I) and stimulation (HQ-S), the prototype is located in the above-average region implying that people think the prototype is connective and captivating. These ratings confirm the participants' preference for sharing photos in a face-to-face situation with the help of the prototype.

As previously mentioned, we incorporated different rules for control during browsing to investigate photo sharing social practices. During *sequential* sharing, participants felt it was natural for the photographer to be in control when sharing their images by deciding the direction and speed of browsing. However, giving away the control when passing the last photo created confusion for some users (8/20). *Photo pointing* and *throwing* created similar confusion. The audience member that triggered *photo pointing* had to remember to stop it afterwards, and the recipient of a *thrown* image had to return the photo. These rules acted as social interaction inhibitors that blocked group interaction. On the AttrakDiff questionnaire (Figure 5), the prototype was only rated as average on the pragmatic quality (PQ) dimension, which means that there is room for improvement in terms of usability. These rules may have impacted the ratings on this dimension. Participants used each other's devices during the interaction regardless of its owner, apparently perceiving the prototype as one entity.

Supporting Spontaneous Photo Sharing

About half of the participants (9/20) explicitly said that the prototype allowed them to share photos spontaneously. Participants saw the potential of using the prototype in different contexts. Mobile phones and laptop computers were currently being used to show photos from their displays. While people said they carried their mobile phones with them everywhere, not all took their laptop to more informal settings such as a café or a bar: *"It is interesting as you do not carry your laptop all the time but you have the phone with you." [P7]* A few participants (5/20) said they would prefer holding the device in their hands while sharing photos rather than keeping it on a table. As an example, participants mentioned sharing while sitting on a sofa: *"It would feel more natural to hold the mobile phone in your hand than holding it on the table." [P14]*

Participants said the use of the spatial arrangement of people around a table allowed them to easily share photos. *Throwing* was an intuitive gesture to share photos, especially when sending a photo across the table to a specific person: *"I think it is a cool feature to just look at a person and just send the photo (makes a sweeping gesture)." [P14]* The different orientations of photos with respect to the viewers could potentially have been a problem, especially for the tiled configurations. However, most participants flexibly used the different tiled configurations regardless of the orientation. In some cases the photographer would see the tiled device in the right orientation, and in others it was the audience. In other cases participants would move closer to the photographer. When viewing individual photos in landscape and portrait orientations on their devices, participants would either rotate their heads, or rotate the devices, or not mind at all.

DISCUSSION

Sharing One's Own Device

The main question we were trying to answer is whether people are willing to share their devices and engage in collaborative interactions. The data collected in the *pass-them-around* evaluation shows that people were positive about sharing and connecting their devices to create a common interaction space. Participants gave similar feedback in the previous MindMap evaluation [23]. However, we are unable to fully answer this question at this point because in the evaluation participants were not using their personal devices, but the modified N900s we provided them with instead. In spite of this, there were lively discussions on using their actual devices for collaborative interactions. Some participants expressed their concerns regarding letting other people handle their phone as they may spill drinks over the phone when using it in the context of a bar or café, or unintentionally damage (i.e., scratch the backside when moving the phone on a surface), beyond the normal wear and tear that happens from daily use. However, most participants felt the benefit of engaging in *ad-hoc* collocated social interactions using the phones outweighed the potential risk of damaging the device.

Using Different Devices

Together with establishing that people are willing to share their devices, comes the fact that people have different types of mobile phones. Some participants (6/20) wondered how compatibility issues would affect collaborative interactions. The main concerns were related to different form factors, screen types and underlying technologies. First, differences in form factors between different phone models could make joint interactions such as tiling difficult, cumbersome, or even obstructive. Second, using touchless devices would require different interaction mechanisms (e.g., bumping to tile displays), which may diminish the intuitiveness of gesture-based interactions. Finally, using different touch technologies during pinching would require applying different pressure on each device: a hard touch on a resistive screen and a lighter touch on a capacitive screen. Hence, the platform would need similar device form factors and underlying technologies to be easy and intuitive to use.

Privacy Concerns

When discussing about sharing photos (or other media content) in a public environment, our participants raised their concerns on privacy. Half of the participants wanted to be able to control who they are sharing photos with and be aware of other people nearby who may be trying to join the sharing session. Having this type of control would prevent accidentally *throwing* a photo to a stranger when sharing would take place in a bar or park. The ownership of the content shared in a session was also discussed. Participants were evenly divided between those who thought the photos should only be temporarily displayed on the devices, and those who said the photos should be permanently transferred to all members of the sharing session.

Interaction Techniques

In the evaluation, participants suggested using the proposed gestures beyond the hard table surface. When seated on a couch, it is indeed more natural to share photos by taking the device in their hands. The table surface makes it easier to recognize the tilt gestures by providing a reference point. However, it is still possible to make all the gestures if people are holding their device in their hands (e.g., standing or seated next to each other), although the gestures become then harder to detect. The proposed gestures could also be used in different applications and domains. For instance, the pinch gesture could be extended to connect not only between mobile phones, but also to form a larger device ecosystem, which would include smaller jewelry-sized touch-enabled devices and larger tablet devices. The vertical tilt gesture (away from and towards oneself) could be used as a generic way to define the intention to: join and leave a session; start and stop sharing; reveal and hide something; and take or relinquish control of a situation. Finally, for our next prototype, we will be exploring the use of the *throwing* gesture in a bar context to share content between a mobile device and several public displays.

CONCLUSION

The Social and Spatial Interactions (SSI) platform explores shared collocated interactions with mobile phones. In the context of SSI, we have introduced the *pass-them-around* prototype, which allows a small group of collocated people to share photos. The prototype encourages people to share the devices and use them interchangeably while discussing photos face-to-face. We proposed different ways of sharing photos based on the metaphor of passing paper photos around. Using devices fitted with the necessary wireless sensors to detect their current location, participants were able to pass photos sequentially around the table. Additionally, the sensors allowed participants to flexibly share photos directly to another person. Evaluations with five groups of four users showed that people would be willing to share and connect their mobile phones to engage in collaborative interactions, although the idea of the SSI platform raised some concerns regarding wear and tear, compatibility and privacy. Regarding our prototype, participants were able to easily and flexibly share their collections of photos using our interaction techniques.

REFERENCES

1. Ah Kun L. M. and Marsden, G. Co-present photo sharing on mobile devices. In *Proc. MobileHCI '07*, ACM Press (2007), 277-284.
2. Ames, M., Eckles, D., Naaman, M., Spasojevic, M. and House, N. Requirements for mobile photoware. *Personal Ubiquitous Comput. 14*, 2 (2010), 95-109.
3. Balabanović, M., Chu, L. L. and Wolff, G. J. Storytelling with digital photographs. In *Proc. CHI '00*, ACM Press (2000), 564-571.
4. Banks, R. and Sellen, A. Shoebox: mixing storage and display of digital images in the home. In *Proc. TEI '09*, ACM Press (2009), 35-40.
5. Belloni, F., Kainulainen, A., Richter, A., Kalliola, K. and Koivunen, V. Multi-Emitter Tracking System for Multi-Antenna Mobile Phones. In *ICASSP 2009 Show and Tell* (2009).
6. Chalfen, R. *Snapshot Versions of Life.* Bowling Green State University Press, Bowling Green, Ohio, 1987.
7. Cho, S., Murray-Smith, R. and Kim, Y. Multi-context photo browsing on mobile devices based on tilt dynamics. In *Proc. MobileHCI '07*, ACM Press (2007), 190-197.
8. Clawson, J., Voida, A., Patel, N. and Lyons, K. Mobiphos: a collocated-synchronous mobile photo sharing application. In *Proc. MobileHCI '08*, ACM Press (2008), 187-195.
9. Crabtree, A., Rodden, T. and Mariani, J. Collaborating around collections: informing the continued development of photoware. In *Proc. CSCW '04*, ACM Press (2004), 396-405.
10. Frohlich, D., Kuchinsky, A., Pering, C., Don, A. and Ariss, S. Requirements for photoware. In *Proc. CSCW '02*, ACM Press (2002), 166-175.
11. Frohlich, D. and Fennell, J. Sound, paper and memorabilia: resources for a simpler digital photography. *Personal Ubiquitous Comput. 11*, 2 (2007), 107-116.
12. Gaver, B., Dunne, T. and Pacenti, E. Design: Cultural probes. *interactions 6*, 1 (1999), 21-29.
13. Hassenzahl, M. The interplay of beauty, goodness, and usability in interactive products. *Human-Computer Interaction 19*, 4 (2004), 319-349.
14. Hinckley, K. Synchronous gestures for multiple persons and computers. In *Proc. UIST '03*, ACM Press (2003), 149-158.
15. Hinckley, K., Ramos, G., Guimbretiere, F., Baudisch, P. and Smith, M. Stitching: pen gestures that span multiple displays. In *Proc. AVI '04*, ACM Press (2004), 23-31.
16. Holtzblatt, K., Wendell, J.B. and Wood, S. *Rapid Contextual Design.* Morgan Kaufmann, 2005.
17. Ishii, H. and Ullmer, B. Tangible bits: towards seamless interfaces between people, bits and atoms. In *Proc. CHI '97*, ACM Press (1997), 234-241.
18. Koskinen, I., Kurvinen, E. and Lehtonen, T.-K. *Mobile Image.* IT Press, 2002.
19. Kray, C., Rohs, M., Hook, J. and Kratz, S. Bridging the gap between the Kodak and the Flickr generations: A novel interaction technique for collocated photo sharing. *Int. J. Hum.-Comput. Stud. 67*, 12 (2009), 1060-1072.
20. Lindley, S. E. Designing interfaces to afford enjoyable social interactions by collocated groups. In *Proc. CHI '05*, ACM Press (2005), 1122-1123.
21. Lindley, S. and Monk, A. Designing appropriate affordances for electronic photo sharing media. In *Proc. CHI '06*, ACM Press (2006), 1031-1036.
22. Lucero, A., Keränen, J. and Jokela, T. Social and spatial interactions: shared co-located mobile phone use. In *Proc. CHI EA '10*, ACM Press (2010), 3223-3228.
23. Lucero, A., Keränen, J. and Korhonen, H. Collaborative use of mobile phones for brainstorming. In *Proc. MobileHCI '10*, ACM Press (2010), 337-340.
24. Mäkelä, A., Giller, V., Tscheligi, M. and Sefelin, R. Joking, storytelling, artsharing, expressing affection: a field trial of how children and their social network communicate with digital images in leisure time. In *Proc. CHI '00*, ACM Press (2000), 548-555.
25. Merrill, D., Kalanithi, J. and Maes, P. Siftables: towards sensor network user interfaces. In *Proc. TEI '07*, ACM Press (2007), 75-78.
26. Miller, A. D. and Edwards, W. K. Give and take: a study of consumer photo-sharing culture and practice. In *Proc. CHI '07*, ACM Press (2007), 347-356.
27. Nacenta, M., Aliakseyeu, D., Subramanian, S. and Gutwin, C. A comparison of techniques for multi-display reaching. In *Proc. CHI '05*, ACM Press (2005), 371-380.
28. Nunes, M., Greenberg, S. and Neustaedter, C. Sharing digital photographs in the home through physical mementos, souvenirs, and keepsakes. In *Proc. DIS '08*, ACM Press (2008), 250-260.
29. Rekimoto, J., Ayatsuka, Y. and Kohno, M. SyncTap: an interaction technique for mobile networking. In *Proc. MobileHCI '03*, Springer LNCS 2795 (2003), 104-115.
30. Stelmaszewska, H., Fields, B. and Blandford, A. The roles of time, place, value and relationships in collocated photo sharing with camera phones. In *Proc. British HCI '08*, BCS (2008), 141-150.
31. Van House, N. A. Collocated photo sharing, story-telling, and the performance of self. *Int. J. Hum.-Comput. Stud. 67*, 12 (2009), 1073-1086.

ClassSearch: Facilitating the Development of Web Search Skills through Social Learning

Neema Moraveji[1], Meredith Ringel Morris[2], Dan Morris[2], Mary Czerwinski[2], Nathalie Riche[2]
[1]Stanford University, Stanford, CA, USA
[2]Microsoft Research, Redmond, WA, USA
neema@moraveji.org, {merrie, dan, marycz, nath}@microsoft.com

ABSTRACT
We explore the use of social learning – improving knowledge skills by observing peer behavior – in the domain of Web search skill acquisition, focusing specifically on co-located classroom scenarios. Through a series of interviews, pilot studies, and classroom deployments, we conclude that a peripheral display of Web search activity within a classroom facilitates both social learning and teacher-led discourse. We present the ClassSearch system for shared awareness of Web search activity, which embodies principles gleaned from our iterative design process, and show results from a ClassSearch deployment in twelve middle-school classroom sessions. Finally, we highlight design suggestions and opportunities for future work while taxonomizing the space of co-located search pedagogies.

Author Keywords
Web search, education, search expertise.

ACM Classification Keywords
H.3.3. Information Systems: Search Process.

General Terms
Human factors

INTRODUCTION

Expertise in Web-based information retrieval has been studied in great detail recently [2, 32], owing largely to the increased relevance of Web search to many information needs and tasks. However, little consensus has been reached regarding how to incorporate search skills education into school curricula, and schools often have limited resources to devote specifically to Web search education.

We hypothesize that allowing expertise to spread socially among searchers will be an engaging and effective way to integrate search skills instructions into traditional classrooms. Leveraging social learning goes beyond benefits of scale: social learning theorists have long extolled the benefits of designing a sociocultural context to motivate learning. A 'community of practice' [19] provides avenues for advancing in levels of expertise, but does not exist in the domain of search. Furthermore, social learning also allows learning to occur implicitly, without courses structured around teaching search. That is, search can be learned in an authentic context [7] by building on the research process already incorporated into traditional school subjects (e.g., history, literature).

Figure 1: The ClassSearch system (shown here in a middle-school classroom deployment) provides a shared-awareness display of Web search activity within a classroom, facilitating social learning and teacher-led discourse about Web search skills. Students search using individual computers and results are shown on an instructor-controlled shared display.

In this paper, we present the design and evaluation of ClassSearch, a system to support these insights. We do so through an iterative, user-centered design process informed by feedback from 8 instructors and 8 students. We then present the results of an in situ study with 160 middle school students who used the system. The results motivate future work on systems to improve opportunities for social learning of search expertise with co-located users.

This work makes four primary contributions: (1) We introduce the use of social learning as a mechanism for Web search skill development; (2) We present results from the iterative design of a shared display for search data in classroom environments; (3) We describe the results of a deployment of ClassSearch in 12 middle school classroom sessions; (4) We discuss the design implications of our observations, and taxonomize the space of co-located search tasks and associated pedagogies.

RELATED WORK

Understanding search expertise

A variety of measures of search performance are used in information retrieval research and agreement exists that certain factors are relevant: domain expertise [2, 31], knowledge of the search engine's features [14], general literacy [17, 21], and knowledge of Web resources [31]. Condensing these disparate areas of expertise into measurable definitions of search skills, however, remains elusive. Although qualitative metrics for information literacy have been proposed [1], causes of differentiated expertise among searchers are not well-understood.

Formulating queries is particularly complex task due to its reliance upon abstraction, vocabulary, domain knowledge, and grammar. Despite this complexity, query formulation is often the focus of explicit instruction because it is so central to Web search practice [9,12].

Prior work studying the habits and behaviors of students of various ages using the Internet in directed or self-directed tasks have associated novice searchers with the inability to identify credible sources [10], issuing vague queries [4], focusing on surface features of websites [5], and limited confidence about and awareness of Web resources [8].

Supporting searchers with instruction & tools

Web search curricula have been proposed (e.g., [5, 18, 30]), though none are yet established as standards. Games [11] and inquiry-based learning [15] have been explored as methods of making search skill learning "authentic" (i.e., allowing the learner to address an actual need during instruction). Instructional guidelines have been proposed for teaching search skills [1, 9, 20, 29]. These approaches have focused on procedural learning, not social learning.

Several novel interfaces have been proposed to ease query formulation [16, 27] or visualize search result sets [26, 33]. Lin et al. [22] used visualization to give researchers deeper insight into search strategies. Navigation Flow Maps [23] enabled a categorization of search strategies among university students. PadPrints [13] used a similar visualization to facilitate within-browser reflection on search history. SearchTogether [25] and CoSearch [2] employed multi-user search visualization to facilitate collaborative search tasks. These approaches do not attempt to impart search expertise on searchers, but rather ease the process of searching itself. They are thus a complement to the present work, which explores the *transfer of expertise* among searchers.

Social learning of search expertise

The concept of imitating a skilled practitioner is perhaps the oldest and most natural form of social learning [24]. However, simply imitating the queries used or links clicked by an expert does not directly enhance a searcher's skill set; it is the mental processes underlying search that are important to imitate. This is because information needs vary from moment to moment, making the conceptual model of Web search and navigation paramount. In postulating that these processes may be socially transferred, we draw upon two theories: *legitimate peripheral participation* [19], which describes how novices in a community develop expertise, and *cognitive apprenticeship* [6], which posits that learners can imitate experts by deriving components of their thought processes, not just their behavior.

Motivation for present work

The existing literature on search expertise and social learning, coupled with existing systems for exposing Web search strategies for non-pedagogical reasons, led us to hypothesize that social learning is particularly applicable in the domain of Web search education. The subject matter in this domain varies constantly as search engines, interfaces, and corpora evolve, and limited curriculum time is presently devoted specifically to search education. These factors motivated our team to develop a system whereby search processes can be observed and discussed casually, in classrooms still focused on traditional school subjects.

INTERVIEWS WITH SEARCH INSTRUCTORS

In order to inform the development of a system to support social learning of Web search skills in classrooms, we conducted six phone interviews with teachers and librarians for one hour each. The instructors came from public schools in moderately affluent areas of the United States. This section summarizes insights drawn from these interviews.

Search curriculum

Instructors indicated that sixth grade (10-12 years old) is the earliest point at which they began teaching students about search as a skill, beginning with very focused (often single-query) tasks. As the students grow in age, they are given progressively more open-ended tasks.

One of the interviewee's schools explicitly taught search as a skill during a 7-10 day "mini-class" as part of a larger class on computer usage, but in general search skills was restricted to a single lecture or less. Of all the possible subtopics to cover in such instruction, the instructors said they focus most on query formulation and refinement, choosing a search result, and discerning credibility.

There are many different search curricula and pedagogies. One teacher remarked that teaching search is like being "an elementary school art teacher – there is no standard curriculum. The teacher decides what to do, with varying amounts of success."

The most common pedagogy was to have the instructor demonstrate search practices on a projected display at the front of the room. This might be followed by one or more discursive practices around the search task such as brainstorming possible query words as a class and listing criteria for determining a site's credibility. The students would then be "released" to do their own investigations while the instructor roams to address individual problems.

Another common teaching method was the use of side-by-side query comparisons: typically, two students working in a computer lab would execute different queries, and the results would be compared aloud.

Determining which part of a Web page is relevant to the existing query is another skill deemed important to teach. Though the use of browser shortcut keys to find keywords within a page was often mentioned to students, this functionality has low visibility and is often forgotten.

Challenges faced by instructors in class

According to interview participants, aggregate data about the class's search behavior is difficult or impossible for the instructor to glean. However, instructors told us there is a large range of search expertise in middle school classrooms. The majority of instructors we spoke with did not see themselves as experienced search experts (and students often do not always see instructors as experts), which creates an atypical dynamic in the classroom for this topic.

When an instructor approaches a student to aid in a Web search task, a form of over-the-shoulder learning [28], it is difficult and/or inefficient for the instructor to discover how the student arrived at the current navigation state (e.g., what queries they had tried, what pages they had seen). This makes search instruction very different from math, where the instructor can immediately "see the student's work" and troubleshoot individual steps. Without this affordance, feedback to students about search is often disconnected from the individual steps taken in the search process. One instructor stated: "I'd like to see what page the student is on and how they got there." Further, this over-the-shoulder approach does not scale well to typical class sizes (about 30 students), due to its inefficiency.

Teachers faced several common hurdles during search instruction. The most complex of these was communicating the algorithm for search result ranking. Furthermore, interview participants discussed students becoming preoccupied with the estimated number of results returned by a search; this is also a phenomenon we noted in our own classroom observations. This, we believe, is due to the common practice of instructors attempting to use result count as part of an easily-understood metric for search quality. This idea sometimes led to students being preoccupied with getting the "right" number of results or claiming some searches are "better" or "worse" than others based on this metric.

Another hurdle instructors faced was encouraging students to use domain-specific vocabulary, rather than colloquial terms, in their queries. Advanced operators are rarely used without a reminder from instructors.

Instructors also discussed students' perceived association between site popularity and site credibility; students often assume that large portals such as Wikipedia can be relied on for credible information. By keeping peer investigations largely invisible, this practice is reinforced. Instructors reported providing a common metric for reliability: one can judge a site in part by its domain suffix: ".edu is better than .org which is better than .com."

Logistical limitations were mentioned as well: comparing sets of search results is difficult with current tools. Results must be read aloud to the class, or students need to bring individual computers to the front of the class to attach to a projected display, disrupting class flow and prohibiting retrospective analysis of queries. In either case, it is difficult for *other* students to investigate more deeply, as only two students are participating in the exercise.

Existing tools for supporting instructors

We asked instructors about the tools they currently use during search instruction. Projectors are often used to show example searches at the front of the room. Whiteboards and chalkboards are used to enumerate query suggestions, useful sites, or related information for later reference. Teachers also mentioned monitoring software generally targeted at keeping individuals on-task and not specific to search instruction.

netTrekker [nettrekker.com] is a popular search engine to which schools purchase access; our interview participants generally worked in schools where netTrekker was the preferred search engine. The results of netTrekker are curated by a team of paid instructors, and the results can be filtered to target certain age groups. However, while instructors appreciated the high-quality information on curated sites such as netTrekker, they expressed concern that such tools do not expose students to the issues they will need to address when on the "open" Web.

THE CLASSSEARCH SYSTEM

ClassSearch architecture

Inspired by these interviews, we created ClassSearch, a system that makes aggregate (and, optionally, individual) student search data from the class visible via a large display. Instead of showing such data to the instructor alone to influence instruction, this approach makes data available to students, enabling conversations that use the data as a co-reference. ClassSearch is intended for use in a setting where the instructor has a projected display and each student has a computer workstation (such as a library, a school's computer lab, or a laptop-augmented classroom) (Figure 1).

We considered and prototyped designs that provided a separate, private display to the instructor, but discussions with instructors suggested that this would be impractical, given the degree to which instructors walk around the room during research sessions. Furthermore, instructors' lack of familiarity with multi-display systems rendered this approach prohibitively complex.

One common practice instructors described was demonstrating a search strategy on a projected display and allowing that strategy to propagate through the class. The idea that students emulate practices seen at the front of the room also informed our decision to use a shared display: in this environment, students may emulate not only instructor behavior, but peer contributions as well. This approach also follows directly from our interviewees' self-reported perceptions that they were not necessarily more skilled in search than some students.

Instructors frequently visited students at their computers, and desired a mechanism to quickly assess the search pattern that brought a student to the current browser state.

Consequently, we chose to include a component in our system that made recent query history (as opposed to complete navigation history) visible on a student's monitor, primarily to allow quick over-the-shoulder assessment by an instructor.

The ClassSearch system thus contains two components:

1) A browser add-on running on each student's computer that captures searches and Web browsing history, forwards that data to the server, and displays recent query history in a small, adjacent window.
2) A server computer, controlled by the instructor, that projects data (via the add-on) from student search behavior at the front of the room.

In this section, we describe the major features available on each system component, which were designed primarily to meet the needs identified in our preliminary interviews. For brevity, we describe only the feature set available in the final version of the software; in the following section ("Pilot Studies"), we will highlight features that were added or changed as a direct result of teacher and student pilot studies conducted around our first prototype.

Shared display

We prototyped several designs that attempted to surface complete query and navigation trails for all students, but we found that this approach did not scale well to classes at our target size (around 30 students). We experimented with abstractions that did allow this volume of data to be aggregated (such as iconic views of navigation patterns), but teachers perceived these as too high-level to support discussion around low-level search skills (though this approach will surface later in our "search strategies" view for quickly assessing individual student behavior). Through discussions with students and instructors, we identified *query terms* and *sites visited* as the most important points for discussion, leading to two of the data representations we used on our shared display.

In this section, we describe the four components available

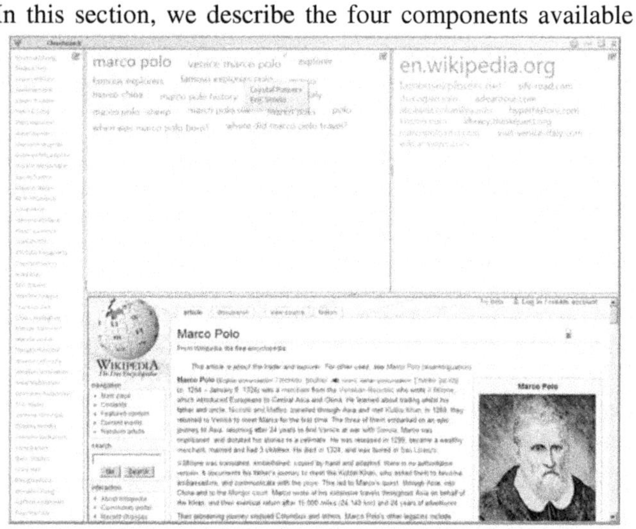

Figure 2: The shared display in its default configuration.

in various layouts in ClassSearch: *query cloud*, *site cloud*, *search strategies*, and *individual student*. When it first starts up, the ClassSearch shared display shows the query cloud and site cloud views, along with a list of students and a Web browser (Figure 2). The student list allows quick access to the search strategies view or to the individual student view (by clicking on a student's name). The Web browser supports the existing practice of instructor-led demonstration. Individual components can be maximized to occupy the entire display.

The overview window also includes a configuration dialog, which allows the instructor to save and load the state of the entire display (for resuming class sessions on subsequent days), and allows the instructor to remotely reset the browser add-on state of an individual or the entire class.

Query cloud

The *query cloud* is a view of queries that have been issued in the class (Figure 3). This view is updated in real time; it both supports discussion about query formulation and provides "hints" for students who may be having difficulty with query formulation or refinement. Our first implementation of this component used *query-level* elements, in which each query as a whole was treated as an individual term, sorted alphabetically and sized according to frequency. However, this simple approach presents two scalability issues. First of all, alphabetical sorting can quickly lead to important (common) queries disappearing below the fold; although the view is scrollable, the teacher is frequently away from the display, and the need for scrolling reduces the "at-a-glance" value of the display for students. Second, until the class has issued a large number of queries, exact query matches among students may be infrequent, limiting the value of font scaling as a means to indicate trends within the class.

We made two modifications to the query cloud to address these issues. First, we sorted the cloud by frequency (most common queries first), rather than alphabetically, to support easier observation of class trends. Second, we created an *n-gram* mode, which shows all words that appeared in queries along with any higher-order n-grams (bigrams, trigrams, etc., possibly including whole queries) if they appeared in

Figure 3: Query Cloud (n-gram view). One of the two query cloud views, in which user queries are broken up into all possible words or phrases; these are displayed in the cloud, sized according to popularity. The instructor's mouse hovers over 'volcano,' revealing the list of queries using that term.

Figure 4: Site Cloud. Pages visited by students are aggregated by site and sized by popularity. The instructor can hover over a site to see all the pages visited within that site.

two or more queries. We included both n-gram and full-query modes in the deployed version of ClassSearch.

In n-gram mode, hovering the mouse over a term shows all the queries issued that contained a particular n-gram. For the query-level view, hovering the mouse over a term optionally shows the names of all students that issued that query. Clicking a term in the query cloud shows the associated search results in an embedded browser. This functionality is intended to support discussions like "Was this a good query?" or "Let's see the search results for the three most popular queries."

Site cloud

Instructors indicated that discussion about search skills often focused on site credibility; this motivated the *site cloud* view (Figure 4), which summarizes sites visited by the class. This view supports class-wide discussion about sites and provides suggested starting points to students who may be having difficulty with a search.

The site cloud shows the sites visited by the class, sorted and sized according to frequency (for the same reason we chose to sort the query cloud according to frequency). The reason sites are aggregated, rather than showing the URLs of specific pages, is twofold. First, we anticipated instances where multiple people are visiting the same individual pages to be relatively uncommon, so collapsing within sites is more likely to show trends within a class. Second, in our observations and interviews, credibility of pages was often assessed based on heuristics concerning the site and not individual pages.

When the instructor hovers over a site, all the pages students have visited in that site are displayed in a tooltip, sorted by frequency. Clicking opens a series of browser tabs containing each student-visited page within the site. This functionality is intended to support discussions like "Did this page contain the answer we're looking for?"

Search strategies view

While the primary goal of the ClassSearch system is to promote discussion about search behavior in aggregate, instructors also expressed a desire to quickly assess individual and group progress. The shared display, however, requires careful consideration of student privacy; frequent visibility of a student's complete search history would be potentially uncomfortable and might discourage exploration. The *search strategies* view (Figure 5) attempts to

Figure 5: The *search strategies view* shows an overview of individual students' actions. Purple boxes represent queries, green boxes represent page visits. For privacy, we use pseudonyms for students throughout this paper.

balance these factors by abstracting student search patterns to allow instructors to quickly assess the progress of the class as a whole and identify students who might require assistance or students exhibiting behaviors worthy of highlighting to the rest of the class.

This view shows a graphical summary of each student's search history: purple boxes represent queries, and green boxes represent pages visited. Hovering over a purple box shows the corresponding query; hovering over a green box shows the corresponding URL. Clicking an item from the summary visualization opens the associated search results list or Web page in the browser.

Individual student view

An instructor can "drill down" on an individual student (by clicking their name in the search strategies view) to see a detailed view of that student's pages visited and queries executed during the search task (Figure 6). This view groups pages visited by query, presenting a short-term, search-centric browser history for that student, allowing quick summarization of a student's progress and search strategy. Furthermore, in cases where a student is identified as having a "good" strategy, this allows the instructor to share that student's strategy for discussion, specifically addressing our goal of transferring expertise from more-skilled to less-skilled students.

Student browser add-on

Each student's computer ran a Web browser add-on to collect search and page visit data and send that data to the teacher-controlled server computer. This component also presented a concise history of recently-executed queries on the student's monitor, attached to the bottom of the student's foreground browser window (Figure 7). This was inspired by feedback provided in preliminary interviews suggesting that over-the-shoulder assessment of students' search paths was a significant challenge for instructors as

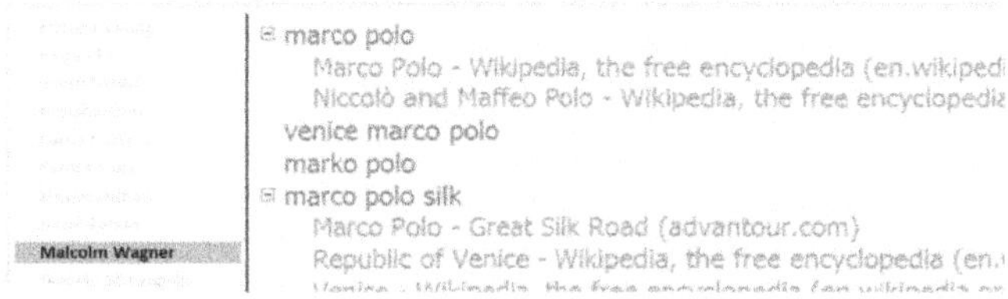

Figure 6: The *individual student view* shows the queries executed and pages visited by a specific student, summarizing the student's progress and search strategy.

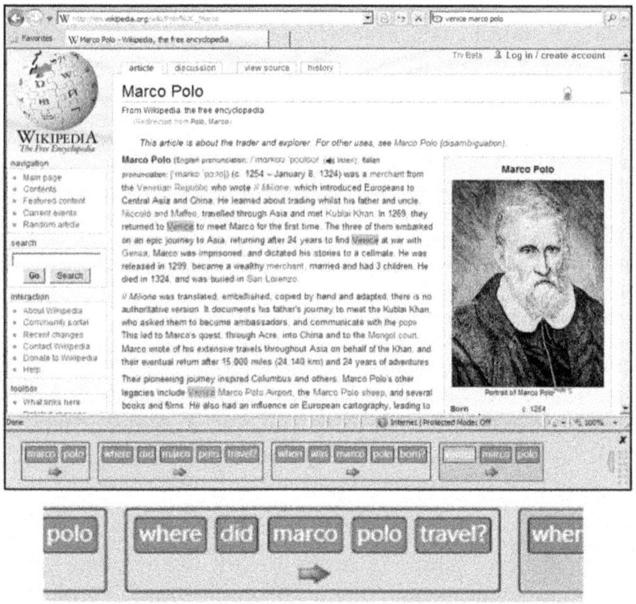

Figure 7a (top) and 7b (bottom): a) A student's browser with the add-in showing the query trail; a term has been clicked and instances of that term are highlighted in the browser. b) A close-up of the add-in showing each query, broken into terms.

they walked around the room visiting students. Queries can be concisely represented in text, and one query often summarizes an entire path of exploration, so we chose to include only queries – rather than a complete browser history – to maximize the amount of information provided to a visiting instructor while minimizing screen footprint.

Clicking any query in the history executes that query in the student's browser, and clicking any term in a query highlights occurrences of that term in the current page (Figure 7a). This functionality closely resembles a feature available in popular browser toolbars such as the Google Toolbar, and was motivated by teachers' lamenting students' inability to find relevant content within a page.

PILOT STUDIES

We conducted two pilot studies with our first iteration of ClassSearch: one with teachers and one with students in our target age range. In both cases, participants came to our lab and we created a "classroom" in a meeting room. We distributed pre- and post-surveys.

Pilot study with teachers

We brought six middle-school instructors into our lab for feedback on a small ClassSearch installation by participating in simulated classroom scenarios. Four of these instructors had also participated in our initial interviews. In the pilot study, we had each participant act as a "student," and the facilitator acted as the instructor, using search tasks adapted from [8].

Teachers remarked that being able to see which student had performed each query on the large display adds accountability. They believed this functionality would help mitigate off-task behavior, trigger interesting discussions, and group students who are doing complementary work. Instructors expressed a desire to turn off the display of student names for certain scenarios (a feature we subsequently added), but overall were not concerned with privacy in the classroom.

Instructors stressed the value of being able to delete individual terms from the display to mitigate awkward situations and to dissuade abuse. Instructors desired the ability to save and restore the state of the class's dataset because pedagogical sequences often span sessions. These features were also added after the pilot studies.

Instructors suggested that the history shown on the student's computer would discourage spending time on unrelated pages as the teacher walked around the room. Instructors also suggested that that the student history display would support discussions potentially useful for good conversations: "You can ask questions. Why'd you go here? Why'd you go there?"

Pilot study with students

Eight students entering the 6th grade came to our lab, where we set up a small ClassSearch installation. Two of the students knew each other beforehand. A researcher acted as the "instructor" and operated the shared display. The students completed four search tasks that varied in specificity, ranging from exploratory tasks to fact-finding tasks, based on tasks used by Druin et al. [8].

When asked their opinions about the query cloud, one student suggested it could help her think of a new query term, in particular by looking at the "big" (most popular) terms. In general, the students seemed focused more on the larger terms (rather than, e.g., the more unique terms or the more semantically relevant terms). One student said that her query "didn't work well" so she "looked at the query cloud and saw that 'vice president's birthday' was in a big font," so she decided to attempt that query. Another student remarked "it was easier to search when there were ideas up on the projector." When probed, the students generally acknowledged that a bigger (more popular) query does not necessarily mean a better query, and that popularity was not the only dimension upon which to evaluate queries or sites visited. Two students suggested that size of query or domain should indicate quality instead of popularity.

FIELD STUDY

ClassSearch represents a departure from existing practices of search instruction and classroom computer use. It ties individuals' usage together and creates novel feedback loops and visualizations of aggregated data that we hypothesized would impact search discourse and behavior. To investigate this hypothesis, we conducted a field study around a ClassSearch design that had been iterated to reflect the feedback from our pilot studies. Because the system presents new data in a novel format, our goals were to assess how it was appropriated and to highlight opportunities for further design iterations; a controlled, longitudinal assessment of ClassSearch's impact on learning outcomes is beyond the scope of the present work.

Participants

We conducted our field study in a public middle school (spanning grades 6-8 and ages 11-14) in an upper-middle-class suburb of Seattle. Students at the school were largely tech-savvy and regularly used computers at home. The school had a computer lab in the library that teachers used occasionally for class research projects, so computer use in class was unusual but not exceptional. Search was not given a great deal of emphasis in the school's state-defined curriculum, but was highlighted once or twice a year as part of a class library visit, typically coupled to a domain-specific research project.

For this field study, two instructors worked with us in their own classrooms. Both instructors were accustomed to the idea of using a computer with a projector at the front of the room to show students individual Web pages. Neither instructor had participated in our pilot studies.

One instructor was an eighth-grade American History teacher who used ClassSearch in four classes (approximately 50 minutes each) each day for two days in a row. Students in all four classes were conducting a research project; class time was not explicitly devoted to search instruction. The second was a sixth-grade instructor who taught search expertise in two of his classes on one day; each of these classes spanned two 50-minute sessions. Altogether, this gave us a total of six groups totaling 160 students that used the system in a total of twelve sessions.

Procedure

Prior to working with each instructor, researchers installed 30 laptop computers running the ClassSearch browser add-on in the appropriate classroom, along with an instructor (server) installation connected to a projector. We gave the instructors an opportunity to use the system the afternoon before the study began. During this session, we allowed them to test different features using a sample dataset pre-loaded into the shared display.

Students were not required to alter their normal searching practices to use either the shared display or browser add-on. They learned to use the system through real search tasks; no explicit demonstration was provided to students.

In the eighth-grade class, search expertise was not the goal of instruction, so students worked in small groups, where each group was focused on a particular research topic. For one such class, we installed a second server and projector in the classroom to explore the idea of having a shared display dedicated to a small, topic-specific group. The "main" projector was shared among the rest of the class, spanning several research groups.

FINDINGS

ClassSearch was actively used – students issued a total of 12,143 queries and visited 8,368 pages during the twelve evaluation sessions. Since our goal was to understand how teachers and students appropriated this social learning approach to search instruction, we present qualitative findings based on observations of these initial deployments. We discuss how the major features (query cloud, site cloud, and strategies view) were used, as well as unanticipated uses of the system that arose. Students used the re-finding features on their personal toolbars 411 times; however, as anticipated, the most interesting aspect of the system was the shared display, so we focus our findings there.

In general, students and teachers were enthusiastic about the technology (noting that ClassSearch was "seriously cool" and wondering "sweet, can I buy this?"). At the end of his class, one student pointed at the large display and noted "We need that *always*, so we can see what everybody is looking at and searching."

Query Cloud

Both instructors chose to keep the query cloud and site cloud open simultaneously (rather than maximizing one at the expense of the other). We had anticipated that instructors would click on items in the query cloud to display search results in order to compare and contrast the results returned by different variants of a query. In practice, though, they only clicked terms to display associated search results 11 times over the course of the observation period.

Rather than using the query cloud to explore the impact of query phrasing on results, the instructors instead valued the query cloud for the awareness it provided about synonyms, alternative phrasings, and syntax. One teacher commented that the cloud was helpful to the students because it helped them in "becoming aware of their own searching."

In particular, the query cloud enabled an awareness of aggregate behavior that was not previously possible. For instance, one teacher looked at the query cloud and noted that very few members of the class were using quotation marks when phrasing their queries. He pointed out to the class that one of the queries (*gay rights*) might be more effective if enclosed in quotations.

The query cloud also enabled the teacher to point out examples of interesting student behaviors. For example, when one student used an advanced operator in her query, the teacher called it out to the class as a point of discussion. The student explained that the operator had in fact dramatically improved her search results.

The students also paid attention to the query cloud, and it was often a topic of discussion. In particular, students were very interested in knowing who had done particular queries, and often asked about this out loud (since the list of names associated with a query was only visible if the teacher hovered his mouse over it).

Site Cloud

We anticipated that instructors would use the site cloud to select sites to visit in order to compare and contrast the quality of information found on different sites. Instructors did this occasionally, but not frequently (a total of 18 times). The teachers generally clicked on sites from *.edu* and *.org* domains in order to show the class examples of sites that they felt were credible, high-quality references.

Teachers found the site cloud valuable for spotting trends that were not previously apparent. For example, looking at which sites were large and small in the cloud, one teacher commented to his students about a trend: "people don't look at National Geographic, but it's a really good source."

The students also attended to the site cloud, as evidenced by discussions about the items it contained. In particular, the cloud prompted student discussions about the *quality* of particular sites ("the religious tolerance one is good, lots of info on it") and about the *process* of finding particular sites ("how did you search this one, Gretchen?").

Students requested an easier method to visit the sites others had found. For example, if an individual student wanted to visit a site that she noticed in the cloud, she had to type the URL into her browser – offering a shortcut to this behavior, such as the ability to "pull down" a site from the cloud, was desired. A teacher requested that students be able to indicate the quality of a site, and perhaps the site cloud font sizes could then reflect votes of quality.

Strategies View

The strategies view, which was not visible by default, was maximized 49 times, suggesting that this view was of special interest to instructors. It was generally used for short periods of time while the instructor specifically surveyed the progress of each student on the list; when the instructor walked away from the computer, he generally reset the view to display the query and site clouds. Instructors only drilled down to the individual student view 23 times.

The purple and green bars representing queries and sites in the strategies view became incorporated into the classes' vocabularies. For example, one teacher showed the strategies view and suggested that everyone in the class spend the last five minutes of the period in the "green" in order to focus on reading and taking notes on good quality sites, rather than continuing to search. Another teacher wanted to indicate that students should have completed their initial round of querying and begun reading content, and conveyed this by saying "you should probably have gotten to some green by now."

Both teachers and students desired metrics that would provide absolute indicators of search success and skill, and were eager to interpret the bars in the strategies view as such a metric. For example, referring to the strategies view, one student wondered how her search progress compared to another's, asking "am I doing well?" The bars also inspired a competitive feel among some students who assumed having longer bars was better – one even noted, "I'm going to do 1 million searches to win!" Two of the classes specifically discussed that the number of pages visited was not necessarily a meaningful metric of progress.

One teacher requested that the bars on the strategy view could indicate the duration of time a student spent on a particular page, perhaps to identify pages that might be of high quality or interesting to discuss with the entire class.

Unexpected Uses

Although ClassSearch was intended primarily as a tool to enhance search skill learning through social awareness, the teachers found additional value in the system as a means of keeping students on-task, both through their ability to monitor and address specific students' behavior and through the social pressures of behavior visibility which made students feel guilty about wandering off-task.

In the class where we introduced the second projector for the additional project groups, we were surprised to see that students not only looked at the public display for their own group (for all of the reasons mentioned earlier), but also found value in the other group's display as a glanceable summary of the other project. For example, noting the largest site "ciggyfree.com" and search term "cigarettes" gave students a quick overview of what the other group had decided to focus their inquiry on.

DISCUSSION

Our deployment of ClassSearch demonstrated that both teachers and students found pedagogical value in a public, interactive, real-time visualization of a classroom's query and browsing behavior. This simple intervention appeared to support a variety of pedagogical styles, including classes dedicated specifically to search skills instruction and classes focused on domain-specific research tasks.

Co-located search pedagogies

ClassSearch was designed for classroom scenarios in which students and instructor are co-located. However, our initial interviews, pilot studies, and field study revealed that a large spectrum of search tasks and pedagogies exists even within this space. In particular, we observed classroom tasks that varied along a continuum of individuation. We taxonomize the space of co-located search pedagogies, highlighting design recommendations to optimize ClassSearch for each scenario:

Individual topics

At the individualized end of the continuum, each student is researching a separate topic. This pedagogy was observed in eighth-grade classrooms during our field study, and is most appropriate for older students who have achieved some independence in both search and domain-specific skills. In these cases, few terms in the ClassSearch query cloud grew to large font sizes due to low overlap in usage. As a result, a student may notice query terms that may have nothing to do with his or her topic. While this presents some risk of distraction, it offers instructors a valuable opportunity for discussing overlap among related topics, and offers students lightweight awareness of other topics. Modifying ClassSearch to display structural rather than semantic commonalities among students might be a preferred alternative, for instance focusing the query cloud on trends in advanced operator use rather than keywords.

Topical sub-groups

In this type of classroom search task, the class is split into sub-groups searching for different material, but students within each group share a topic. This led to a mix of individuated and group use of ClassSearch. One practice we observed was students working together without using the display but then taking a "break" to look at the ClassSearch display for inspiration in their own tasks or to reflect on the impact that their activity had on the large display. Groups could have some sense of other groups' topics and progress. Multiple ClassSearch installations within the same room, such as the two-projector arrangement explored during our field study, can benefit this pedagogical scenario.

Shared topic

Instructors often had a theme for a class or a portion of the class that they asked students to investigate, study, or write about. An example of this was "What is your favorite Greek god and why?" In these cases, the students are all searching for different specific information but it falls under a common umbrella, and may include common queries, particular early in the task. In this class structure, students often attempted to encourage peers to visit a page they liked by pointing at their screens or at the common ClassSearch display. This frequently-observed behavior may provide a valuable opportunity for discussion of search strategies among peers. Adding the ability to "pull down" a URL from the site cloud as a jumping-off point for individual exploration, a feature requested by students in our study, would add value to this scenario.

Shared task

In settings where search skills are a primary curricular objective, an instructor may ask all the students to complete the same task, e.g., "I want everybody to type in 'birth rate Norway' into the search box." These tasks allowed the instructor to guide student attention to some extent and might be followed by a free-form query to refine the search. This type of task is most appropriate for teaching search skills explicitly, and may be appropriate for younger students with only limited search skills (this approach was observed in our field study in sixth-grade classes). When ClassSearch is used in this environment, the initial (shared) query is very large (and not very useful), but the subsequent terms are understood easily as refinements of the common original. Modifying the query cloud to use a timeline or network-layout visualization, rather than one sorted by frequency, might benefit this pedagogical approach.

Metrics of search success

By providing visualizations of aggregate information, ClassSearch provided representations of data meant to prompt reflection on the search process. While ClassSearch appears to have been successful in this respect, it was also apparent that instructors and students desired objective metrics that would indicate search skill and quality. It is not clear that such metrics exist, as defining and modeling search expertise remains an open problem [2, 31, 32].

However, both students and instructors were eager to interpret various aspects of the display as evaluative. As mentioned earlier, the length of bars in the search strategies view was sometimes interpreted as a positive indicator of students' search skill, students and teachers conflated the number of results returned with query quality, and one teacher seemed to count the number of times queries using operators such as quotations appeared in the query cloud as a metric of the class's search sophistication. Additionally, in both the pilot and field studies participants requested indicators of query and site quality in addition to popularity.

The lessons in this regard are twofold: (1) designers of search education tools should be careful to avoid interface elements that can mistakenly be interpreted as metrics, since end-users seem eager to do so, and (2) research into identifying such metrics (if they exist) would potentially be highly valued, particularly by the education community.

In addition to short-term metrics of search success, long-term metrics reflecting students' learning may also be valuable, e.g., reflecting to the teacher and/or student whether and how a student's search behavior evolves over time. Due to the short-term nature of our deployment, which prevented measuring learning outcomes, we did not endeavor to develop such metrics. Adding an additional iterative stage to our design process, such as meeting again with teachers after a moderate-length deployment of Class Search to reflect on student behaviors, might be one way to develop such metrics.

CONCLUSION

Web search skills are an increasingly necessary literacy in the digital era, but existing tools do not effectively support search instruction, nor do they enable potentially effective social pedagogies. In this paper, we proposed that using a public display to show classroom-level information regarding querying and browsing behavior can support social learning of Web search skills.

We presented the results of an iterative design process involving interviews and pilot studies with stakeholders such as teachers, librarians, and middle-school students, that revealed areas for improving upon current search skills pedagogies, and directly informed the design of ClassSearch. We described ClassSearch, and reflected on how students and teachers appropriated the system during a deployment in twelve middle-school class sessions.

We found that ClassSearch enabled new types of discussion surrounding reflection on individual students' actions and on class-level trends. In addition to identifying opportunities for further improving the system's design, our observations also enabled us to articulate a design space for classroom-based search education interventions.

Future work includes improving ClassSearch based on the feedback from our initial deployment, arranging long-term deployments to assess learning outcomes, and considering the suitability of shared displays of aggregate activity for other educational goals.

REFERENCES

1. ACRL. Objectives for Information Literacy Instruction: A Model Statement for Academic Librarians. *ACRL Standards and Guidelines*, 2001.
2. Amershi, S. and Morris, M.R. CoSearch: A System for Co-located Collaborative Web Search. *Proc CHI 2008.*
3. Bhavnani, S.K. Domain-specific search strategies for the effective retrieval of healthcare and shopping information. *CHI 2002 Extended Abstracts.*
4. Bilal, D. Children's use of the Yahooligans! Web Search Engine: I. Cognitive, Physical, and Affective Behaviors on Fact-Based Search-Tasks. *J Amer Soc for Info Sci*, 51.7 (2000), 646-5.
5. Coiro, J. Rethinking comprehension strategies to better prepare students for critically evaluating content on the Internet. *New Eng Reading Assoc J*, 39 (2003), 29-34.
6. Collins, A., Brown, J.S., Newman, S.E. Cognitive apprenticeship: Teaching the craft of reading, writing and mathematics. *Knowing Learning and Instruction*, 8.1 (1989), 453-94.
7. Dewey, J. *Democracy and Education*. New York: The Macmillan Company, 1916.
8. Druin, A., Foss, E., Hutchinson, H., Golub, E., Hatley, L. Children's roles using keyword search interfaces at home. *Proc CHI 2010.*
9. Fernández-Luna, J.M., Huete, J.F., Macfarlane, A., Efthimiadis, E.N. Teaching and learning in information retrieval. *Information Retrieval*, 12.2 (2009), 201-26.
10. Flanagin, A.J., Metzger, M.J. The perceived credibility of personal Web page information as influenced by the sex of the source. *Computers in Human Behavior*, 19.6 (2003), 683-701.
11. Halttunen, K. Sormunen, E. Learning Information Retrieval through an Educational Game. Is Gaming Sufficient for Learning? *Education for Information*, 18.4 (2000), 289-311.
12. Henry, L.A. SEARCHing for an answer: The critical role of new literacies while reading on the Internet. *The Reading Teacher*, 59 (2006), 614-27.
13. Hightower, R. R., Ring, L. T., Helfman, J. I., Bederson, B. B., Hollan, J. D. Graphical multiscale Web histories: a study of padprints. *Proc Hypertext 1998.*
14. Hölscher, C. and Strube, G. Web search behavior of Internet experts and newbies. *Computer Networks*, 33.1 (2000), 337-46.
15. Jones, G. J. An inquiry-based learning approach to teaching information retrieval. *Information Retrieval*, 12.2 (2009), 148-61.
16. Jones, S. Graphical query specification and dynamic result previews for a digital library. *Proc UIST 1998.*
17. Kodagoda, N., Wong, B. L. Effects of low & high literacy on user performance in information search and retrieval. *Brit HCI Group Ann Conf on HCI*, 2008.
18. Kuiper, E., Volman, M., Terwel, J. The Web as an Information Resource in K-12 Education: Strategies for Supporting Students in Searching and Proceedings ofessing Information. *Rev of Educ Res*, 75.3 (2005).
19. Lave, J. & Wenger, E. *Situated Learning: Legitimate Peripheral Participation*. Cambridge Univ Press, 1991.
20. Lazonder, A. Principles for designing web searching instruction. *Education and Information Technologies*, 8.2 (2003), 179-93.
21. Leu, D.J., Zawilinski, L. The New Literacies of Online Reading Comprehension. *New Eng Reading Assoc J*, 43.1 (2007), 1-7.
22. Lin, X., Liebscher, P. Marchionni, G. Graphical representations of electronic search patterns, *J Amer Soc for Info Sci*, 42.7 (1991), 469-78.
23. Lin, C., Tsai, C. Navigation Flow Map Method of Representing Students' Searching Strategies on the Web. *World Conf on Educational Multimedia, Hypermedia and Telecommunications*, 2005.
24. Meltzoff, A.N., Kuhl, P.K., Movellan,J., Sejnowski, T.J. Foundations for a New Science of Learning. *Science*, 325.5938 (2009), 284-88.
25. Morris, M.R., Horvitz, E. SearchTogether: An Interface for Collaborative Web Search. *Proc UIST 2007.*
26. Shneiderman, B., Feldman, D., Rose, A., Grau, X. F. Visualizing digital library search results with categorical and hierarchical axes. *Proc ACM Conf on Digital Libraries*, 2000,.
27. Spoerri, A. InfoCrystal: a visual tool for information retrieval & management. *Proc Intl Conf on Information and Knowledge Management*, 1993.
28. Twidale, M. B. Over the Shoulder Learning: Supporting Brief Informal Learning. *JCSCW*, 14.6 (2005), 505-547.
29. Vine, R. Real people don't do Boolean: How to teach end users to find high-quality information in the Internet. *Information Outlook*, 5.3 (2001), 16-23.
30. Walton, M., Archer, A. The Web and information literacy: scaffolding the use of web sources in a project-based curriculum. *British J Educ Tech*, 35.2 (2004), 173-86.
31. White, R., Dumais, S., Teevan, J. Characterizing the Influence of Domain Expertise on Web Search Behavior. *Proc WSDM 2009.*
32. White, R. Morris, D. Investigating the Querying and Browsing Behavior of Advanced Search Engine Users. *Proc SIGIR 2007*, 255-262.
33. Zavesky, E., Chang, S., Yang, C. Visual islands: intuitive browsing of visual search results. *Proc 2008 Intl Conf on Content-Based Image & Video Retrieval.*

Role of Available and Provided Resources in Sensemaking

Nikhil Sharma
Katz Graduate School of Business, University of Pittsburgh
268 Mervis Hall
nsharma@katz.pitt.edu
412-648-1720

ABSTRACT
Making sense of a topic often involves appropriating information and organizing themes from various existing resources. We studied how sensemakers appropriated from available online resources as well as artifacts provided by another person directly. We found that both available and provided resources affect sensemaking activities. Sensemakers added more structure in their work when online resources were easily available, but added less structure and information when they were provided relevant sensemaking artifacts from another person. We also studied how early and mature artifacts provided by another person were appropriated differently and found that mature artifacts were rated better and used more but resulted in lesser structure and information being added by the recipient. These findings have implications for the support of sensemaking activities using resources available online as well as artifacts provided by others including co-workers and friends.

Author Keywords
Sensemaking, collaboration, handoffs, representations, structure.

ACM Classification Keywords
H5.m. Information interfaces and presentation (e.g., HCI): Miscellaneous.

General Terms
Experimentation, Human Factors, Theory.

INTRODUCTION
People often engage in tasks where they confront problems that require them to find, collect, organize and understand information. This activity of creating an understanding can be referred to as 'making sense of something' or 'sensemaking'. Examples of sensemaking include topic comprehension ("what is human computer interaction"), product choice ("which HD camcorder should I buy") and diagnosis ("why is my computer not working"). Sensemaking often involves appropriating information and structure from resources like the website and artifacts created by others. The availability and quality of these resources has the potential to affect sensemaking. For example, someone engaged in a product choice task might use customer review websites and even notes and advice from a friend who recently bought a similar product. The study presented here focuses on how people incorporate available online resources and provided artifacts of varying maturity into their sensemaking. Since most sensemaking builds on existing resources, a better understanding of how people incorporate existing resources can be helpful to sensemakers and designers of sensemaking support systems.

SENSEMAKING
One testament to the importance of sensemaking is the plethora of theories, models and characteristics of sensemaking that have been developed in various fields. Among the myriad of notions of sensemaking [2,5,13] we take the model of Russell and colleagues [12] as central to our approach.

According to the Russell et al model [12], sensemaking is the process of searching for a representation and organizing information using this representation. Sensemakers need a good representation that can be used to organize information required for the task. A representation could be a schema, a framework or an organizing theme. For example, a sensemaker trying to decide which camcorder to buy could start by thinking "I have a Canon camera that I like, maybe I'll like a Canon camcorder." This representation can guide sensemakers toward information of interest. The sensemaker might search for "Canon HD camcorders" and find relevant products. Our sensemaker might rely on "customer reviews" or "recommendations" to select which camcorders out of her search are a good match. As the sensemaker finds more information, some of the information might not fit in the current representation and may build up as 'residue'. The current representation may need to be refined or 'shifted'. For instance, someone might realize that besides the brand of the camcorder (Canon) other factors like low-light performance and focusing speed also matter to her. The sensemaker might have to create a more refined representation that includes these and other aspects and then find more information about them. Once a representation has been coded sufficiently it can be used to enable action on the task at hand. The Russell et al mode, has been the basis of many sensemaking investigations [1,7,9, 10] we chose it because its crisp architecture suggests a design structure for a work environment, its cost structure principle gives a powerful dynamic for behavioral insight, and critically, it foregrounds representations in a way that can be externalized as artifacts and shared with others. The activities listed in the model can also provide the basis for coding and analyzing micro-level sensemaking activities.

Available and Provided Resources

The later stages as per the Russell et al model should involve encoding and representation modification. However, in a particularly novel situation where a representation is inaccessible, it is possible that the search for a representation may be ongoing. Thus after a fixed amount of time sensemaking activities may differ depending on how much access there is to good relevant representations. Access to 'representations' seems to be crucial in early stages of sensemaking.

Qu & Furnas [10] studied the use of online resources in sensemaking and found that besides looking for 'information' (facts and figures), people also sought out and extracted representations from web pages. They found that people used structure suggested by websites (for example navigation bars, site-maps and section headings on web pages) to create their own sensemaking representations (outlines and hierarchical folders). In this paper, hereafter this readily available online resource of representations is referred to as "available resource". For example someone trying to make sense of a camcorder may use the available resource of product page and find that a feature-list on the page can be used to create a table that can help compare various camcorders.

It is useful to point out that Qu & Furnas studied individual sensemakers in the lab setting and did not consider non-web sources of the sensemaking representations that can be just as useful. Sensemaking representations can also be appropriated from documents provided by coworkers in the work environments and by friends/family in non-work environments. For example Nelson et al [7] found sensemakers utilized annotations from friends during sensemaking. Hereafter structure provided by another person is referred to as "provided resource". For example, a friend who recently bought a camcorder can provide a sensemaker with a table she created while comparing various camcorders. Provided resources are common in handoff situations including shift changes where one worker needs to stop working and hand over existing sensemaking documents to another worker.

While available and provided resources are both useful for appropriating representations, it is useful to discriminate between them. Provided resources can be more relevant and targeted towards the task but can also be more idiosyncratic than available resources. The study presented here looks at how sensemakers extract and appropriate representations from available and provided resources.

Maturity of Provided Resources

Provided resources can vary significantly depending on many factors including how much effort and time was spent on them. This is true in many handoff scenarios. For example, in a hospital some cases might have been admitted closer to a shift change than others and may consequently have less mature 'provided' sensemaking artifacts for the recipient. Doctor notes from a case just admitted might include facts and findings that have not been connected. Early versions of artifacts can be expected to have fewer organizational themes since people's representations might still be taking shape [4]. If the provided sensemaking artifact has different elements, it is to be expected that the recipients will use the artifact differently. Artifacts that have a well-articulated representation as well as useful encoded information can be expected to be most useful to the recipient especially when other sources for good representation are scarce. In contrast, artifacts lacking organizational themes will require the recipients to develop their own representations or search for them in other places and these provided artifacts might be less useful. The study presented here also investigated the differences in appropriation of early (or less mature) and late stage (or mature) sensemaking artifacts that other people may provide.

LABORATORY STUDY

We used a sensemaking task and an in-laboratory experiment to track sensemaking progress and artifact creation in two conditions: one where representations could be easily extracted from online content and the second when a good representation was not readily available online. We then provided either early or late versions of the artifacts created by the participants to another set of participants working on the same task. We also tracked the progress of the recipients including the use of provided artifacts for those who received these provided resource.

It is also notable that representations can be internal as well as external [11]. Internal representations can take the form of mental models; external representations can include outlines, tables, notes and figures. In our work, we focus on external representations because they can be easily tracked and studied. We also focused on sensemaking behavior rather than the final outcome because it allowed the microanalysis of sensemaking activities. Even though activities relating to external artifacts creation and usage are just a small part of overall sensemaking activities, external artifacts created by people during sensemaking offered us a way to track sensemaking behavior over the period of the task.

Research Questions

The goal of the study was to answer the following questions:

1. **How do available and provided resources affect sensemaking sub-processes?** Qu & Furnas [10] examined if the availability of representations in websites affects representation construction. We intended to extend the findings to the relationship between available resources and all sub-processes of sensemaking. Additionally, we also explored how provided resources affect sensemaking sub-processes with an emphasis on representation construction.
2. **How do early and late versions of provided artifacts affect sensemaking sub-processes?** The study aimed to compare differences between the use of provided artifacts from early and late stages of sensemaking throughout the sensemaking session of the recipient. If early and late stage artifacts have different degrees of representation and information, then how are they used differently?
3. **How does provided artifact use differ based on the availability of representations online?** We also examined how and to what extent provided artifacts were used when representations were easily available online compared to when representations were not easily available online.

Sensemaking Task

The sensemaking task used in the study involved preparing to give a talk on an unfamiliar topic. This kind of "topic-comprehension" task can involve considerable sensemaking, is common in many real life situations including 'research' and has been used by others in the past to study sensemaking [10]. The participants were asked to prepare a talk using online resources on one of the two topics that have been identified for use in the study. The first topic was "tea" and the second was "drinks for the elderly". These topics were used by Qu & Furnas to study representation construction in sensemaking. Qu & Furnas chose these topics because while the topics are somewhat similar (both relate to drinks) they were different in a useful way. While there exist many well-structured websites on Tea, there were none on "drinks for elderly" topic. The lack of information on the "drinks for elderly" topic, and its ill-formed nature, called forth redefining and clarifying behavior [10]. This difference in availability of representations allows us to study it as a variable.

As the participants worked on their task they were asked to prepare an outline for the task and bookmark useful information. The outline and notes were created in Microsoft Word while bookmarks were created in the web-browser (Firefox 3.0). The participants had 50 minutes (t) to complete this task. During this time their activities and 'think aloud' [3] comments were recorded using a screen capture program (MORAE)[1]. MORAE allowed keystrokes and mouse events to be recorded along with synchronized screen images and microphone input with a resolution of 10 milliseconds. These keystrokes and mouse events were used later to detect when, where and how changes to artifacts were made during sensemaking.

Participants & equipment

The participants (n=60) were students of a large mid-western university. All participants were screened to have knowledge regarding the use of online resources but to not have knowledge regarding the task topics ("tea" or "drinks for the elderly"). The participants were between 19 and 44 years of age (median= 23 years). They came from a variety of education backgrounds ranging from chemical engineering to English literature. In order to secure participation, a subject-fee of $20 was provided. In order to motivate participants to do well in the task a bonus of $10 was promised to the top 10 percent of the subjects as judged by the quality of their outline by a subject expert. People with professional background or training in reference library work were excluded from the study. This was done because the study wanted to focus on amateurs who have search experience but are not search experts. All the participants had high English fluency.

Equipment consisted of desktop PCs with 2.66 GHz Intel Core2 Duo CPU and 3 GB RAM. The configuration included a monitor with 17-inch LCD flat screen and a keyboard and mouse. The participants used a web-browser (Firefox 3.0) to research the topic and create bookmarks and a single Microsoft Word 2008 document to create the outline and notes. MORAE screen capture ran in the background and was also used to present a post-task questionnaire that requested feedback on artifact material quality and requested biographical information.

Representation resource easily available?	**Part 1: No-artifacts provided**	**Part 2: Artifacts Provided**	
		Early Version	**Late Version**
Yes (Tea)	10	10	10
No (Elderly Drink)	10	10	10

Table 1. Conditions and Participant Counts (n = 60)

Experiment Conditions

The variables manipulated in the experiment were availability of representations, provision of artifacts and the maturity of the artifacts provided. The experiment was conducted in two parts. In the first part participants did not have access to provided artifacts but rather their artifacts were collected and were provided to the participants in the second part. Half the participants in Part 2 of the

[1] http://techsmith.com/MORAE

experiment received early stage artifacts from Part 1 participants and the other half received later stage artifact. The early stage was after 10 minutes of work (t/5) and the later stage was after 50 minutes (t).

Participants in both parts of the experiment were assigned either the topic with easily available representations ('tea') or the topic without easily available representation ('elderly drink'). So half the participants worked on the 'tea' talk task and half worked on the 'drinks for elderly' talk task. The details of participant counts can be seen in table 1.

Artifacts provided to Part 2 participants included the talk outline, notes and bookmarks from a random participant in part one of the experiment who had worked on the same task. The document containing outline and notes was made available in Microsoft Word and the accompanying bookmarks were imported into the browser.

The early and late version artifacts were used as an approximate measure of the maturity of the sensemaking and the resulting artifacts. This was based on the assumption that the longer that someone worked on it, the more mature his or her representation would be. Time was used as a variable since it was straightforward and easy to operationalize. The early time (10 minutes or t/5) was chosen after an examination of the progress of participants in Part 1 of the experiment. In Part 1, most participants (84%) had added their first set of outline elements (sections, encodings, information elements) in quick succession (with less than two minutes between them). Since we were interested in studying how early externalizations of representations affect subsequent sensemaking as compared to late externalizations, the time was picked after some externalization was accomplished. These elements were possibly based either on prior knowledge or easily found representation and information from external sources.

Individual progress did vary with some outliers who added either too little or too many sections in their outlines at the above times. In both early and late version, those artifacts with number of sections more than two standard deviations away from the respective mean were excluded (n=2) from the pool of artifacts to be handed off in the second part of the study.

Data Collection & Coding

Information gathering as well as artifact creation/use activities of the participants were tracked to enable a microanalysis of sensemaking behavior. The MORAE recordings were used to track and code for counts of various artifact related activities of the sensemakers for each minute of the session. These tracked activities were a subset of overall sensemaking activities. Other activities like creation and manipulation of internal-representations were not tracked. The sub-processes listed in the Russell et al model [12] were used to decide which activities to track and code for. To operationalize various sub-processes of sensemaking, including those delineated in the Russell et al model, the following *sensemaking activities* were coded for all the subjects:

Representation Generation

In this activity delineated by Russell et al, the sensemaker creates a representation. External representations are often composed of organizational elements (henceforth referred to as 'structure') as well as informational elements that are organized using the structure. In the current task, structure was operationalized in two ways:

- **Creating folders in bookmarks ('folder'):** The time of adding a folder in the bookmarks was captured and counts were created for the number of folders created for each minute of the session.
- **Adding sections in their outline ('section'):** The time of adding a new section or a subsection in the outline was captured and counts were created for the number of sections created for each minute of the session. Section creation was coded when text was added to create a talk organization theme rather than the addition of a fact in support of an existing section. An example was 'history of tea'.

Data Coverage

This activity involves identifying information and organizing it using the created structure [12]. There were two parts to this activity: finding/identifying relevant information (operationalized as querying below) and adding the information. If the information found cannot be encoded into an existing structure, it may just be added without being integrated (operationalized below as adding bookmarks and adding information into outline). If the information found was organized into the current structure we considered it "encoded".

- **Querying ('Q'):** Query counts were done for all queries in search engines as well as queries in websites and databases. Queries within pages were not counted. Navigational queries meant to reach a determined destination website were also not counted (e.g. Google search for 'wikipedia'). Counts were used to code the number of queries for each minute of the session.
- **Adding bookmarks ('BM-add'):** The time of bookmarking a webpage was captured and counts were created for the number of bookmarks created for each minute of the session. Here sensemakers are collecting information that is intended for encoding into the representation.
- **Adding information ('info-add'):** Counts of when people added facts to the outline or notes, putting them at the top-level of the outline without organizing them into existing sections were used to code for count totals for every minute of the section. An example of this activity was someone copying and pasting a fact into the notes (rather than in an existing outline section).

- **Encoding ('enc'):** The time of adding a piece of information or a fact to an existing section or a sub-section in the outline was captured and counts were created for each minute of the section. Encoding additions were different from section additions as the encoding additions were facts in support of a section or a sub-section. Encoding was also different from 'adding information' since encoding was an addition into an existing section rather than adding freestanding facts.

Representation Shifting

To reduce the costs of various operations in sensemaking, the sensemaker may need to "shift representations" [12]. This process was operationalized for both bookmarks and the outlines:

- **Reorganizing bookmarks ('folder-mod'):** The time of moving bookmarks to an existing folder was noted and counts were created for the modifications to structure for each minute of the session. Renaming a folder was also considered a modification event.
- **Reorganizing outline ('section-mod'):** The times of moving pieces of information or sub-sections in the outline to another section were captured and counts were created for the modifications to structure for each minute of the session. Renaming a section was also considered a modification event.

Provided Artifact Use Activities

Besides the above coding categories that were used in both parts of the experiment, some additional categories were coded for Part 2 (where artifacts were provided) of the experiment and were primarily concerned with the use of provided artifacts. We wanted to track not just when the recipients incorporated the provided artifacts into their own artifacts but also various levels of engagement with the artifact (bookmarks and outlines). The following artifact-use activities were coded:

- **Bookmark perusal ('BM-look'):** Bookmarks were imported and kept in a folder labeled 'provided bookmarks'. The *first time* when a recipient looked at the contents of the folder was noted.
- **Bookmark click ('BM-use'):** The time of clicking any one of the provided bookmarks were also noted and counts created for each minute of the session.
- **Outline perusal ('OL-look'):** The outline was provided to recipients as a word document using the outliner tool. The provided outline was collapsed and the *initial time* of expanding the provided outline for perusal was noted.
- **Outline appropriation ('OL-use'):** The time when either parts of the provided outline were incorporated into their own outline was also noted. Incorporation was done either by copying/moving parts of the provided outline to merge with their new outline or by making the provided outline the primary outline and making changes to it.

Coding was done during the sessions as well as later looking at created outlines and data captured by MORAE that included screen-capture, web-history and audio comments from the user. It should be noted that coding criteria for some categories are objective and was done from user logs. These categories included logged events and their times like: creating bookmark folders, querying, adding bookmarks, modifying bookmark folder, bookmarks, adding of outline elements (sections, encodings, information), modifying outline and using outlines. These categories were coded by the experimenter alone using browser event data. The criteria for whether an outline element was 'information', 'encoding' or a 'section' was subjective and we relied on the coder's understanding of the coding scheme. The experimenter coded these categories during the session, going to the session recording if needed. An additional coder looked at the outlines later also coded for whether an outline element was 'information', 'encoding' or 'section'. The second coder was trained using pilot data and then coded all the outlines. The inter-coder agreement for the two coders was found to be Kappa = 0.79 ($p<0.001$), 95% CI (0.77, 0.81).

Artifact Rating

Comments collected through post-experiment questionnaire were also analyzed. This information included demographic data as well as artifact ratings on a seven-point scale for the usefulness of the provided outline and the provided bookmarks as well as open-ended comments regarding these ratings.

- **Outline usefulness ('OL-rate'):** The participants rated the usefulness of the provided outline.
- **Bookmarks usefulness ('BM-rate'):** The participants rated the usefulness of the provided bookmarks.

Data Analysis

Figure 1 presents a snapshot of the collected data. For Part 1 (no artifacts provided), only *sensemaking activities* were coded. These activities included querying as well as *artifact creation activities* (BM-add, folder, folder-mod, info-add, enc, section, section-mod). *Artifact use activities* (BM look, BM-use, OL-look, OL-use) were also coded for the part 2 participants (artifacts provided) in addition to sensemaking activities.

The collected data was analyzed in two ways. First, total counts for each activity including artifact use as well as average time when a participant engaged in each activity was calculated. Means from the activity counts and times as well as artifact ratings were calculated for various conditions. Second, MANOVA [6] analysis of minute-by-minute activities was conducted.

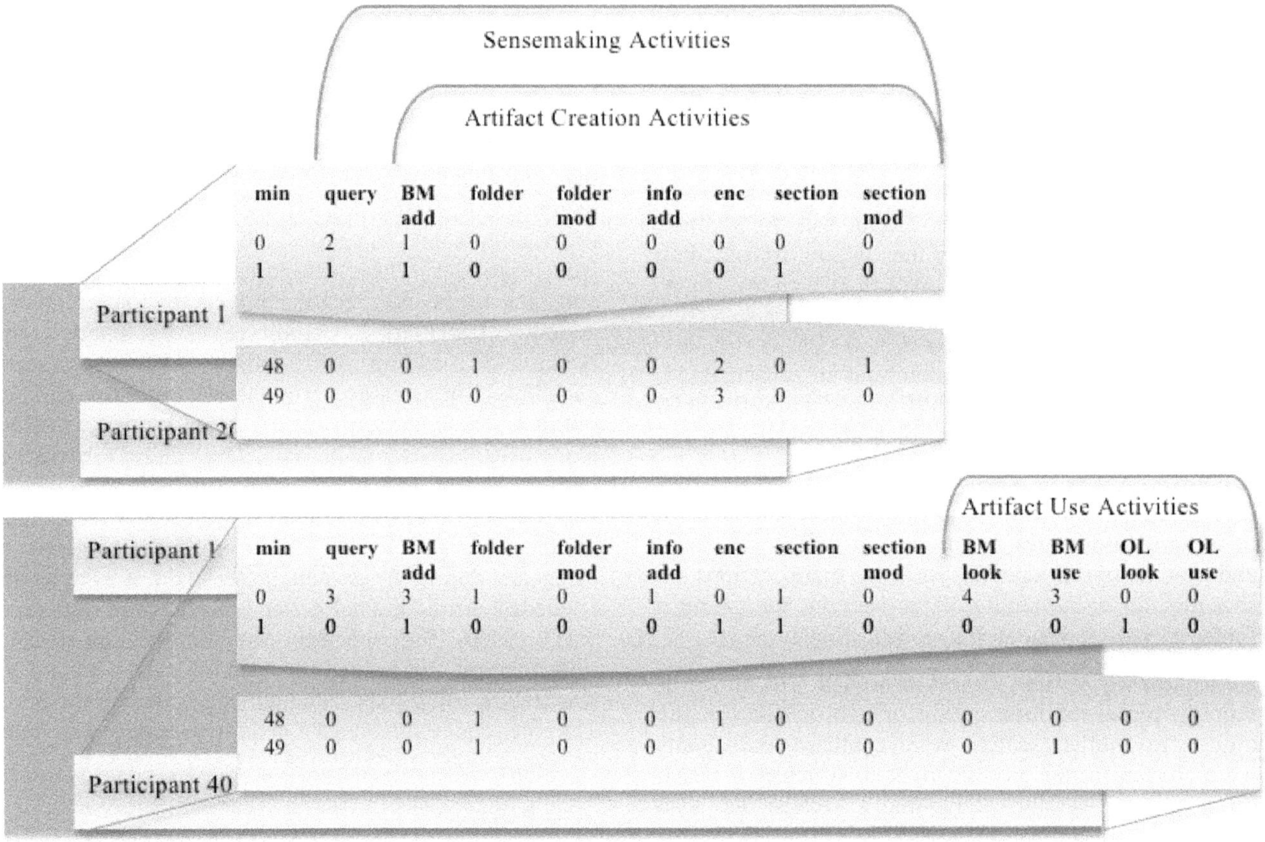

Figure 1- Snapshot of data with groups of dependent variables

Three independent variables used in the MANOVA analysis corresponded to the conditions in the study (available/no-available resource, provided/no-provided resources, early/ late provided resource). The two sets of dependent variables were: the various sensemaking activities of all the participants engaged in (query, bookmark, folder, folder-modify, information, encode, section, section-modify) and the artifact use activities which participants in Part 2 of the study engaged in (bookmark-look, bookmark-use, outline-look, outline-use). Artifact use activities and sensemaking activities were analyzed separately because Part 1 participants did not engage in artifact use activities (see Figure 1).

Hypotheses

Four groups of hypotheses relating to the three independent variables were tested using the data collected in the study. The first group is about the effects of easily available resources, the second group is about the effects of provided artifacts, the third group is about the interaction of available and provided resources and the fourth group is about the effects of maturity of provided artifacts. It should be noted that when a particular hypothesis mentions a coding category (e.g. 'artifact-use activity') all coding categories under it (e.g. BM-look, BM-use, Outline-look, Outline-read) would be applicable.

Effect of easily available resources

1. **Sensemaking activities vary based on the presence of easily available representation.** Qu & Furnas [10] found that people extracted and used structure from available web resources. We expected that sensemaking activities would differ between the two tasks because of the variation in available representations in the topics (H1.1).

Effect of provided resources

2. **Sensemaking activities vary based on the presence of provided artifacts.** As mentioned before, provided artifacts were expected to include both structure and information elements. We expected the structure elements (sections and folders) in the artifacts to help in the representation generation loop of the recipient. It was expected that overall sensemaking activities of recipients would be different from providers (H2.1). More specifically, since artifacts were expected to boost representation generation, it was expected that encoding which follows generation would occur early on average for those who had access to provided artifacts (H2.2).

Interaction of available and provided structure

3. **Provided artifact use varies in the presence of easily available structure.** Provided artifacts can be an additional source of representation besides being an information source. However, people's artifact use (BM-look, BM-use, OL-look, OL-use) was expected to differ based on how easily representations were available online (H3.1). When representations are hard to find (drinks topic), provided artifacts should serve as the predominant source of structure and information. Thus in more specific versions of H3.1: we expected provided artifacts to be used more overall (H3.2) and sooner (H3.3) during the generation loop when easily available representations are missing. We expected artifacts to be rated (Outline-usefulness, BM-usefulness) better (H3.4) by recipients when other sources of representation are not easily available (drinks task).

Effect of provided artifact maturity (early and later artifacts)

4. **Sensemaking activities and artifact use vary based on the maturity of the provided artifacts.** More representation ideas were expected to have an overall impact on sensemaking activities (H4.1), specifically later versions of artifacts would be more helpful in the generation loop and enable quicker move to encoding (H4.2).

   We also expected that early and late stage provided artifacts would be used differently (H4.3). More specifically, later versions of the provided artifacts were expected to be used more (H4.4) and sooner (H4.5) during the generation loop since they are expected to have better representation ideas. We also expected later versions of provided artifacts to be rated more useful (H4.6) by recipients because of their presumed better structure as well as informational content.

RESULTS

The collected data were analyzed to calculate mean activity counts and to calculate mean occurrence times for events. MANOVA analysis was done to analyze the effect of available resources, provided resources, interaction of available and provided resources and provided artifact maturity on various sensemaking activities. A summary of the hypotheses and their related results can be seen in Table 2.

Effect of easily available resources

Sensemaking activities vary based on the presence of easily available resources. Data from both Part 1 and Part 2 of the study were analyzed for the effect of task on activities.

1. The most general hypothesis H1.1 that sensemaking activities will differ based on available representation resources was confirmed. MANOVA analysis showed that the availability of representations (tea vs. drink tasks) significantly accounted for the variance in sensemaking activities ($p < 0.001$).

Table 2. Hypotheses & Results

Effect of:	Hypothesis		Result
Available Resources	H1.1	Variance in Sensemaking activities by topic. (MANOVA)	**p<0.001**
Provided Resources	H2.1	Variance in Sensemaking activities when artifacts provided (MANOVA)	**p<0.001**
	H2.2	Encoding earlier when resources provided	ns
Available & Provided Interaction	H3.1	Variance in artifact-use activities by task. (MANOVA)	p=0.055
	H3.2	Higher artifact use-count when resources not available	**p<0.001 (BM only)**
	H3.3	Earlier artifact use when resources not available	p= 0.076 (OL only)
	H3.4	Higher artifact rating when resources not available	ns
Provided Resource Maturity	H4.1	Variance in Sensemaking activities by provided artifact maturity (MANOVA).	**p<0.01**
	H4.2	Encoding-time earlier when late version provided	ns
	H4.3	Variance in artifact-use activities by provided artifact maturity (MANOVA).	**p<0.01**
	H4.4	Higher artifact use-count when late version provided	**p<0.05 (outlines) p<0.01 (BM)**
	H4.5	Earlier artifact use when late version provided	ns
	H4.6	Higher rating when late version provided	**p<0.05 (OL only)**

Analysis also confirmed the findings of Qu & Furnas [10] 5 years ago: that tea topic had more easily available structure that could be extracted as compared to the drinks topic. In the tea task 2.1 folders were created on average (SE=0.6), while in the drinks task, only 1 folder was created on average (SE=0.3) (differ at p< 0.05). More sections were also created in the tea task (mean=16.9, SE=1.7, p<0.01) compared to the drinks task (mean=11.5, SE=1.5).

Effect of provided resources

2. **Sensemaking activities vary based on the presence of provided artifacts.** Sensemaking activities of Part 1 and Part 2 participants were compared to evaluate the hypotheses in this group. MANOVA analysis showed that the provided artifacts accounted for the variance in sensemaking activities. The result was significant at p <0.001 and confirmed hypothesis H2.1. Surprisingly, it was found that participants who had access to provided artifacts added significantly *fewer* section, bookmarks, and information. They also had significantly fewer encodings and section modifications. There was however no significant difference in the mean encoding times of part 1 and part 2 participants, so hypothesis H2.2 was not confirmed.

Interaction of available and provided structure

3. **Provided artifact use varies in the presence of easily available resources.** Data from Part 2 of the study was used to evaluate the hypotheses in this group. MANOVA analysis showed that the topic (drinks vs. tea) accounted for the variance in artifact use activities. The result showed a strong trend (p=0.055). This shows some support for hypothesis H3.1

   We also found some positive evidence for hypothesis H3.2. People used more provided bookmarks in the drinks task (mean=6.1 bookmarks used, SE=1.2) as compared to the tea task (mean=2.8 bookmarks used (SE=1). The difference was significant at p<0.001. There was however no difference in the usage in outlines in the two different tasks, Eighty percent of participants in each task used the outline provided to them.

   Findings regarding hypothesis H3.3 were also mixed. While outlines in the drinks task were used earlier (mean usage time=6.7 minutes, SE=1.5) than in the tea task (mean usage time=11.6 minutes, SE=3.0), the results only showed a trend (p=0.076). There was no difference in the time of bookmark use. There was also no significant difference between ratings given to artifacts received by people in the tea and drinks task thus hypothesis H3.4 was also not confirmed.

Effect of provided artifact maturity (early and later artifacts)

Data from participants in part 1 of the study was used to compare the late and early versions of their artifacts to check for differences in counts of elements in the bookmarks and the outline. The comparison was done as a method-check. Early versions of provided artifacts were found to have significantly lesser structure elements. Both folder counts and section counts were significantly lower for early versions (at 10 minutes or t/5) than at finish time (t). Mean folders count at t/5 was 0 (SE=0.22) while it was 2 (SE=0.76) at 50 minutes (differ at p< 0.05). Mean section count early was 6 (SE=0.82), while it was 19 (SE=2.3) at the end (differ at p< 0.001).

4. **Sensemaking activities and artifact use vary based on the maturity of the provided artifacts.** Data from only Part 2 was analyzed to ascertain the effect of maturity on various activities. MANOVA analysis confirmed H4.1 and showed that the maturity of provided artifacts accounted for the variance in sensemaking activities. The result was significant at p<0.01. Additional analysis found that those provided with late stage/mature artifacts added lesser number of folders in their outlines and added fewer bookmarks.

   Hypothesis H4.2 regarding encoding time was not confirmed, as there was no significant difference in the mean encoding time between early and late version recipients.

   MANOVA analysis confirmed hypothesis H4.3 and showed that the provided artifact maturity accounted for the variance in artifact use. The result was significant at p<0.01. Hypothesis 4.4 regarding use count had some positive evidence. Outlines were used significantly (p<0.05) more in the late condition (19 out of 20) than in the early condition (14 out of 20). Bookmark use was also significantly higher (p<0.01) when the late artifacts were provided (mean= 6.2 bookmarks used, SE=1.4) than in the early condition (mean= 2.7 bookmarks used, SE=0.6). However this was possibly because the late condition people received more bookmarks. There was no difference in the percent of bookmarks used for the two conditions.

   There was no difference in the early and late conditions regarding the time of use of bookmarks or outlines, so there was no evidence for hypothesis H4.5.

   The results regarding ratings of early and late artifacts (hypothesis H4.6) were mixed. The outlines from the late stages were given an average rating of 6.85/10 (SE=0.54), which was significantly (p<0.05) higher than the outlines from the early stages which were rated 5/10 on average (SE=0.6). However, there was no difference in the ratings given to bookmarks in the two conditions.

DISCUSSION

The results support our hypothesis that both available web resources and provided artifacts affect sensemaking activities. The presence of easily available representations online in the tea task resulted in people adding more structure elements (folders and sections) than in the drinks task where easily available representations were lacking. This confirms earlier finding [10] that people appropriate representations from web pages (from navigational bars, page outlines and site-maps). When representations are not easily available, people need to gather information and build structure from bottom-up. Our analysis of modal activity in the early part of sensemaking (10 minutes or t/5) showed that when representations were not easily available (drinks topic), people spend time early on querying and bookmarking. In contrast, when representations were available (tea topic), the modal activities early on were adding structure (folders and sections) and encoding respectively.

The impact of provided resources was lesser sensemaking activity (information gathering, structure creation and modification). This reduced engagement in sensemaking activities could mean that either the recipients did not feel the need to do their own sensemaking or that the recipients spent a greater time trying to make sense of the provided resource rather than making sense of the actual topic.

The results also showed that available resources seem to have an effect on provided resource use. Analysis of activity counts showed that people used more of the provided outlines and bookmarks when available resources were lacking. In the words of a participant working on the drinks topic:

"It (bookmarks) gave me a basic place to start to get an idea on some of concerns around the topic"

When available resources were lacking (drink task) people also seemed to appropriate sooner from the provided outlines. In the tea task the first search query often lead people to the Wikipedia entry on 'Tea'[2]. That webpage had a sizeable article with a well-structured outline that was instantly observed by many people engaged in this task. In contrast there was no such readily available resource for the drinks task. This might have prompted an earlier reliance on the provided outline. In the words of a participant in the drinks task:

"The outline gave me an idea of where to start searching, as well as what information needed to be expanded upon and researched more thoroughly."

Results also show that the maturity of the provided resources also has an effect on the sensemaking activities of the recipient. Recipients of more mature artifacts added lesser structure and information to their own artifacts. The later versions of outlines, which had more structure content (higher number of sections and folders), were in particular used more often and rated higher by the participants as compared to the early versions.

While the findings confirmed most hypotheses there were some exceptions. The exceptions mainly seemed to relate to two aspects. First, no hypotheses relating to encoding time were confirmed. We expected that when a good representation was accessible in the form of available or provided resources, participants would start encoding sooner. However, the average encoding time did not vary based on the manipulations. One possible reason is that encoding really takes place throughout sensemaking rather than during a separate, subsequent stage. Analysis of all encodings by all participants in the study found that encoding started quite early and occurred all through the sessions. This might have resulted in there being no difference in average time of encoding between the various conditions.

A second set of unexpected results relate to the discrepancies between the two types of provided artifacts (outlines and bookmarks). For example, bookmarks were not used earlier or rated higher in the drinks task even though outlines were. One possible reason for this discrepancy is that the two kinds of artifacts served different purposes in the sensemaking activities of the recipients. While the outlines were the primary placeholder for structure and ideas, the bookmarks seemed to be a supplementary place to store more information regarding the ideas in the outline. In the words of a participant who had access to provided artifacts:

"(Bookmarks) gave me an idea where the content of outlines come from."

The bookmarks being considered supplemental and used after going through the outline might have led to their being used later in the process. Also that the bookmarks might have been considered as merely elaborating the outline rather than providing important structure might have contributed to their lower rating. This observation about the difference between bookmarks and outlines closely echo the finding of Qu & Furnas [10] about the two different artifacts.

The bookmarks were also easier to miss because they were on a sidebar in the browser. In contrast the provided outline had its own window. In the words of a recipient:

"I forgot about the existing bookmarks and therefore did not use them."

It also seemed that most participants were adept at searching for information online and felt they could get to better sources on their own. According to a recipient:

"(Bookmarks were) Not very helpful because I could easily find the information on my own once I know what to search for as provided by the given outline."

CONCLUSION & IMPLICATIONS

While other research has focused on synchronous collaboration in sensemaking [8,14] this research focused on how sensemakers asynchronously utilize resources available online as well as those provided by others like them. It has been stressed that sensemakers benefit not just from good sources of information but also from good sources of structure [9]. One common and important resource is material widely 'available' online in the form of web pages. Another useful resource is artifacts 'provided' by co-workers and friends, often as handoffs. This study

[2] http://en.wikipedia.org/wiki/Tea

focused on how these two resources affect subsequent sensemaking.

We found that both 'available' and 'provided' resources can affect the sensemaking activities during an online topic comprehension task. 'Available' resources resulted in more structure being added. In contrast 'provided' resources resulted in less structure being added by the sensemaker. This suggests that sensemakers treat available and provided resources differently and resources have different impacts on sensemaking. We also observed a reduction in sensemaking activity (structure and information addition) when people were provided with more mature resources; mature resources were used more often and were rated higher by the recipients.

Future work will attempt to clarify whether provided resources helped create a better understanding by reducing the need for representation generation and encoding and freeing up time for deeper contemplation or if the recipients were simply bogged down in the process of making sense of the provided resources. In case future investigations find that provided resources do free up more time for deeper contemplation in sensemaking, sensemakers may benefit a lot from access to 'provided' resources. Even if it is found that 'provided' resources stilt a person's understanding, the performance boost from provided resources seems encouraging for the development of systems that allow sharing of sensemaking artifacts with others.

Our study focused on only one aspect of provided resources: their maturity. Other factors like common ground between the provider and recipient can also affect how available and provided resources are utilized and will be the subject of future examination. One limitation of our study was that it involved just one kind of sensemaking scenario - topic comprehension - yet important implications can be drawn for practitioners and developers of support systems for sensemaking. For support systems and practice our results suggest that besides providing access to available resources online, supporting the sharing and reusing of sensemaking artifacts, especially from later stages can reduce sensemaking load. Provided resources may be especially useful early on when sensemakers are developing a representation. Sensemakers should be encouraged to access provided resources while starting off fresh on the task. Clear indications of the maturity of resources (for example how much time was spent on them) might be beneficial in such conditions. Sensemakers can use these indicators to choose mature material early on when they are starting on a new topic and reserve the less mature material for later information gathering and verification.

ACKNOWLEDGMENTS

George Furnas provided invaluable advice for this work. I am grateful to Michael Cohen, Karl Weick, Judy Olson & Daniel Russell for their guidance. I would also like to thank Maria Slowiaczek, Jahna Otterbacher & Libby Hemphill for their helpful comments.

REFERENCES

1. Billman, D. O.; Bier, E. A. Medical sensemaking with entity workspace. 25th Annual ACM Conference on Human Factors in Computing Systems (CHI 2007); 2007 April 28 - May 3; San Jose; CA.
2. Dervin, B. Sense-Making Theory and Practice: An overview of user interests in knowledge seeking and use. (1998) *Journal of Knowledge Management*, 2(2), 36-46.
3. Ericsson, K., & Simon, H. (May 1980). "Verbal reports as data". Psychological Review 87 (3): 215–251.
4. Furnas, G. W. "Representational Change in Sensemaking". Position Paper for Workshop on Sensemaking. CHI 2008, Florence, Italy.
5. Klein, G., Moon, B. & Hoffman, R.R. "Making Sense of Sensemaking 1: Alternative Perspectives," Intelligent Systems, vol. 21, no. 4, 2006, pp. 70–73.
6. Krzanowski, W. J. (1988) Principles of Multivariate Analysis. A User's Perspective. Oxford.
7. Nelson, L., Held C, Pirolli, P., Hong, L., Schiano D, & Chi E., With a little help from my friends: examining the impact of social annotations in sensemaking tasks, Proceedings of the 27th international conference on Human factors in computing systems, April 04-09, 2009, Boston, MA, USA
8. Paul, S. and Reddy, M. Understanding together: sensemaking in collaborative information seeking. Proceedings of the 2010 ACM conference on Computer supported cooperative work, 2010.
9. Pirolli, P. and Card, S. (2005). The sensemaking process and leverage points for analyst technology as identified through cognitive task analysis. In *Proceedings of International Conference on Intelligence Analysis*.
10. Qu Y., Furnas G.W., Sources of structure in sensemaking. CHI Extended Abstracts 2005.
11. Rogers Y., Scaife M., External Cognition (February 1997).Available: http://wwwv.cict.fr/cotcos/pjs/TheoreticalApproaches/ExtCogandRepr/ExtCogandReppaperRogers.htm
12. Russell, D. M., Stefik, M. J., Pirolli, P., Card, S. K. (1993) "Cost structure of sensemaking" Proceedings of the Conference on Human Factors in Computing Systems - INTERACT '93 and CHI '93. Amsterdam, Neth. publ by ACM, New York, NY, USA: 269-276.
13. Weick, K. E. (1995) *Sensemaking in Organizations* Thousand Oaks, CA: Sage Publications.
14. Wilson, M. L. (2010) The Exaggerated Role of Perception Within Collaborative Information Seeking. In: 2nd International Workshop on Collaborative Information Seeking, Savannah, GA, USA

Characterizing the Usability of Interactive Applications Through Query Log Analysis

Adam Fourney
afourney@cs.uwaterloo.ca

Richard Mann
mannr@uwaterloo.ca

Michael Terry
mterry@cs.uwaterloo.ca

David R. Cheriton School of Computer Science
University of Waterloo

ABSTRACT
People routinely rely on Internet search engines to support their use of interactive systems: they issue queries to learn how to accomplish tasks, troubleshoot problems, and otherwise educate themselves on products. Given this common behavior, we argue that search query logs can usefully augment traditional usability methods by revealing the primary tasks and needs of a product's user population. We term this use of search query logs *CUTS*—characterizing usability through search. In this paper, we introduce CUTS and describe an automated process for harvesting, ordering, labeling, filtering, and grouping search queries related to a given product. Importantly, this data set can be assembled in minutes, is timely, has a high degree of ecological validity, and is arguably less prone to self-selection bias than data gathered via traditional usability methods. We demonstrate the utility of this approach by applying it to a number of popular software and hardware systems.

Author Keywords
Query log analysis, Usability

ACM Classification Keywords
H.5.2 Information Interfaces and Presentation: Miscellaneous

General Terms
Human Factors

INTRODUCTION
People rely on search engines (e.g., Google[1], Yahoo![2], Bing[3], etc.) to support their use of interactive systems [5, 6]. For example, users submit search queries to locate tutorials, troubleshoot problems, or learn how to use specific features of an application. Given this behavior, search engine query logs serve as centralized repositories cataloguing the day-to-day needs of the user base of any publicly available interactive system.

In this paper, we argue that search engine query logs can be filtered and transformed into forms that usefully complement and augment data collected via traditional usability methods. We demonstrate this potential by introducing an automated process for harvesting, ordering, labeling, filtering, and grouping search queries to understand the common tasks and needs of a user base (Figure 1). We call this process *CUTS*—characterizing usability through search. Importantly, the labeled, ordered data produced by CUTS can be assembled in minutes, is timely, has a high degree of ecological validity, and is arguably much less prone to self-selection bias than traditional means of collecting data from users.

As an example of the utility of this approach, an approximation of this process can be illustrated using Google Suggest, the service that provides query completion suggestions for a given input. Given the phrase "firefox how to", Google Suggest produces a list of 10 suggested completions (Figure 2). As we will show later, these suggestions closely correspond to the 10 most popular queries matching that input.

From the list of top 10 Firefox "how to" suggestions (Figure 2), it is immediately clear that users have a number of pri-

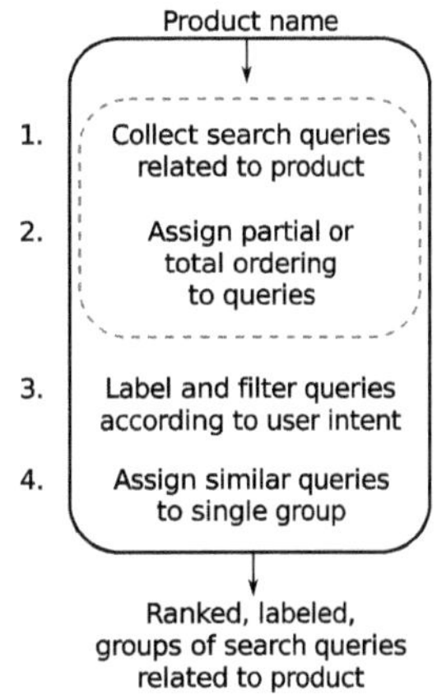

Figure 1. An overview of CUTS. Steps 1-2 are easily performed with access to raw query logs, but otherwise require approximation techniques. Step 3 utilizes our query taxonomy specialized for interactive systems.

[1] `http://www.google.com`
[2] `http://www.yahoo.com`
[3] `http://www.bing.com`

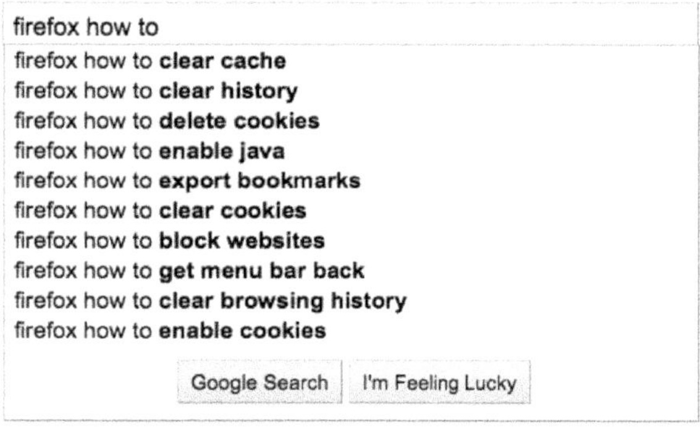

Figure 2. The top 10 suggestions provided by Google Suggest for the phrase "firefox how to".

vacy and security concerns, as evidenced by their desire to clear their cache, history, and cookies. However, the eighth item ("get menu bar back") is particularly interesting. An inspection of the Firefox user interface (version 3.6 on Windows), reveals that the top-level menu bar is easily hidden by deactivating the "Menu bar" item in Firefox's "View → Toolbars" sub-menu. However, once this action is taken, it is not easily reversed: The top-level menuing system is now hidden, removing the very means the user would employ to attempt to re-instate the menu bar. What is noteworthy about this example is that we quickly moved from data derived from query logs to a testable hypothesis regarding the usability of the software.

The contributions in this paper lie in expanding this manual process to the automated one shown in Figure 1. While seemingly straightforward, automating this process requires overcoming a number of challenges: Raw query logs are not made publicly available; there is a need to automatically determine query intent for the purposes of labeling and filtering queries (for example, to distinguish troubleshooting queries from those seeking to download the application); and differently phrased queries on the same topic should be reduced to a common canonical form. Our specific contributions, outlined below, address these challenges.

To address the problems of obtaining and ranking search queries, we demonstrate how publicly available query suggestion services (e.g., Google Suggest) and web-based tools for advertisers can be employed to create reasonable approximations of raw query logs.

We also introduce two new query classification schemes to address the need to label and filter queries. The first classification scheme is a taxonomy that extends previous search query taxonomies to include categories relevant to interactive systems. For example, this new taxonomy differentiates between queries issued to troubleshoot a problem and those seeking a tutorial. The second classification scheme considers *how* a query is phrased. We show that how a query is phrased closely corresponds to the categories of our specialized taxonomy. CUTS exploits the relationship between these two classification schemes to ascribe query intent from query phrasing.

Finally, common questions or issues are often expressed using a number of different query phrasings. To cope with this variability, we introduce a transformation that enables minor differences between queries to be ignored.

The rest of this paper is structured as follows. We first present related work, then describe our method for harvesting and ranking search queries using publicly available services. We then introduce our two classification schemes and show how they can be used to label and filter search queries. The final step of the process, grouping queries, is discussed, and a set of strategies are introduced to assist with this process. We then present a series of examples illustrating the overall utility of this approach, and conclude with a discussion of the limitations of the technique.

BACKGROUND & RELATED WORK

In recent years, researchers have demonstrated the potential for search engine query logs to model and predict real-world phenomena and events. For example, Jeremy Ginsberg *et al.* have demonstrated how query logs can be employed to help track the spread of influenza over time [10]. In this latter research, "health-seeking behaviour" is automatically detected by monitoring search terms associated with influenza (symptoms, medications, etc.). This allows the Google Flu Trends application[4] to estimate the prevalence of influenza infections on a week-to-week basis. The resultant models closely agree with data released by the Center for Disease Control (CDC), though they exhibit much less lag: Models built using query logs show a 24 hour lag in tracking flu trends, compared to the week lag of the CDC.

More generally, Richardson [24] argues that query log analysis could quickly become an indispensable tool for researchers working in such human-centric fields as anthropology, sociology, psychology, medicine, economics, and political science. He notes that query logs function as if "a survey were sent to millions of people, asking them to, every day, write down what they were interested in, thinking about, planning, and doing." Accordingly, he argues that "taken as a whole, across millions of users, ... queries constitute a measurement of the world and humanity through time" [24]. To demonstrate his point, Richardson describes a common search pattern that unfolds over the course of three to six months, starting with a user's search for "mortgage calculators". Within a week, these same users search for "realtors". About one month later, they search for legal services (e.g., "notary"), and three months later, their searches include those for home furnishing (e.g., "pottery barn"). As with Google Flu Trends, this latter example shows the potential for query logs to describe real-world phenomena.

Within the realm of interactive systems, the research literature contains many accounts of search query logs being used to improve *information interfaces*—interfaces in which finding or accessing information is a user's primary task. For example, Zhicheng Dou *et al.* demonstrate how query logs can be used to improve personalized search [8]. It is also common for website designers to use query logs to help de-

[4] `http://www.google.org/flutrends/`

termine what links should be provided in their site's top-level navigation [23]. Our work broadens these previous uses of query logs, demonstrating their utility in understanding users' needs with any publicly available interactive system.

While prior work in interactive systems has focused on using query logs to improve information interfaces, work by Brandt *et al.* has demonstrated how software developers employ search engines when creating software [6]. Through studies of developer practices, Brandt *et al.* show that software developers make extensive use of Google for a variety of programming-related tasks, such as using search to translate knowledge from one domain to another (e.g., from one programming language to another). Our work more generally considers how people employ search to support their use of interactive systems.

Importantly, all of the aforementioned research has been conducted by institutions or companies with direct access to search query logs. Access to these query logs is highly guarded, especially after the privacy problems encountered when AOL released (what they felt was) an anonymized sample of their query logs [28]. Lacking direct access to raw query logs, Bar-Yossef and Gurevich have demonstrated how statistics of these logs can be approximated using an importance sampling technique [4]. This technique estimates the popularity of certain keywords by using parameterized models (derived from the aforementioned AOL search query logs) and by sampling query completions provided by query completion suggestion services. Our work is inspired by this research, as we also use query completion suggestion services. However, we perform more exhaustive searches of the query suggestions for a specific topic (i.e., a specific interactive system), and we supplement query completion suggestions with data harvested from web-based advertising tools.

There are also a number of research endeavors which are related to CUTS, but which do not use query logs as a primary data source. In particular, many researchers have explored how logs of user interface events can be leveraged to learn about a system's usability (surveyed in [14]), or to help characterize a system's user community (e.g., [18]). In this space, David Akers *et al.* [1] have recently demonstrated that invocations of the *undo* and *erase* commands in 3D modelling software can serve as indicators of usability problems. Similarly, Amy Hurst *et al.* have shown how low-level mouse data, related to menu use, can help determine if a user is having difficulty locating an item of interest [16]. We view query log analysis as complementary to the analysis of user interface event logs, and as providing a higher-level view of the issues encountered by users. Moreover, query logs tend to more directly showcase issues regarding feature discoverability, as evidenced by the "firefox how to get the menu bar back" example noted in this paper's introduction.

Finally, online social media sites such as blogs, customer support forums, and sites hosting customer product reviews are other possible sources for understanding user needs. These sources are heavily utilized in sentiment analysis research (also known as "opinion mining") [22]. Sentiment analysis seeks to determine, from a person's writing, his or her attitude towards a particular topic. When applied to the evaluation of interactive systems, sentiment analysis can determine if a product's reviews are generally positive or negative, and can determine which aspects or features of a product typically lead to a positive or negative review. While sentiment analysis is a promising area of research, its effectiveness and scope as a tool for understanding user needs may be impacted by the effort required for users to post content to these social media outlets (compared to simply performing a web search). Conversely, query log analysis provides a view of the issues encountered by the broader user community who may not be regular contributors to the online discussion of interactive systems.

In summary, previous work demonstrates the general utility of query log analysis: it yields timely, highly ecologically valid data that can quickly lead to significant insights when studying a wide range of phenomena. However, query log analysis has not been previously applied to the problem of characterizing the overall usability of interactive systems. In the rest of this paper, we demonstrate its specific utility in the realm of interactive systems by detailing each step of the CUTS process.

QUERY HARVESTING

The core of the CUTS process lies in the analysis of search query logs. When access to raw query logs is not possible, search queries can be harvested using publicly accessible interfaces: Modern search engines provide indirect and privacy-preserving access to their logs through their query completion suggestion services [4]. In this section, we describe a process for systematically harvesting queries related to a particular interactive system using these services. We also provide evidence that the results of this method can be considered a representative sampling of the raw query logs.

Harvesting from auto-completion services

Query completion suggestion services operate as if backed by a prefix tree [4]. When viewed in this way, the characters making up a partially entered query define a path through the tree starting at the root, passing through numerous nodes. Each node contains a listing of popular queries whose prefix matches the path taken thus far. Query completion services follow the paths prescribed by partially entered queries, and return the suggestions listed at the ends of these paths.

Given the tree-like structure of these services, a standard depth-first or breadth-first tree traversal can be performed by expanding partial queries one character at a time, starting with the name of the system under investigation (Figure 3). A leaf (or external node) is reached when the completion service returns no suggestions for the given prefix.

```
firefox,
firefox a, firefox aa, firefox aaa, ...
...
firefox z, firefox za, firefox zaa, ...
```

Figure 3. Input sequence representing a depth-first traversal of Google's prefix tree rooted at "firefox".

Figure 4. The *Google Suggest* auto-completion service varies its suggestions based on the caret position.

Mining additional queries

Some search providers, such as Google, vary their query suggestions depending on the position of the caret in the search query input box (Figure 4). More specifically, Google provides a list of the top 10 completions that either begin or end with the phrases on the left or right side of the cursor. Given this behaviour, the whole tree traversal procedure can be repeated to uncover query suggestions that end with a particular suffix, providing a more complete sampling of the query logs.

By executing a systematic search of the query completion tree, many queries can be collected for a given topic. For example, on June 19th, 2010, we recorded 74,795 unique queries when performing a systematic search for queries incorporating the term "Firefox" in Google Suggest's query auto-completion database. Similar results were obtained for other systems for which we collected data (Table 1).

Application	Description	# of Query Suggestions
iPhone	A smartphone platform	476,462
Ubuntu	A Linux distribution	122,242
Photoshop	An image editor	119,791
Firefox	A web browser	74,795
Chrome	A web browser	45,499
Kindle	An eBook reader	21,621
Gimp	An image editor	14,569
Inkscape	A vector graphics editor	2,501

Table 1. Number of unique query suggestions provided by Google for various interactive systems.

Representativeness and timeliness of auto-completions

In harvesting these queries, our working assumptions are that (1) query completion services are derived from the raw query logs, (2) a given query's prevalence in these logs will have some bearing on its ranking in the list of suggestions, and (3), the suggested completions are *timely*. By "timely," we mean that query completion services assign more weight to queries performed within a recent window of time. In the following subsections, we briefly provide evidence that these assumptions are sufficiently valid for our purposes.

Representativeness of query completion suggestions

In the case of Google, some information about their query suggestion service has been published [11]. Specifically, Google's documentation notes that "All of the queries shown in (Google) Suggest have been typed previously by other Google users". Google also states:

> *Our algorithms use a wide range of information to predict the queries users are most likely to want to see. For example, Google Suggest uses data about the overall popularity of various searches to help rank the refinements it offers.* [13]

Later, when discussing the use of marketing tools to rank queries, we will provide further evidence that auto-complete suggestions have a close correspondence to the most frequently, recently performed queries.

Timeliness of query suggestions

To identify trends and new issues as they arise, it is desirable that query suggestion services emphasize recent searches over those performed in the more distant past. To study the timeliness of Google's query suggestion service, we monitored the query completion suggestions for a range of products and software applications for a period of approximately three months (June 2010 through August 2010, inclusive). Suggestions were sampled on Monday, Wednesday, and Friday on each week during this timeframe. An analysis of the collected data reveals that Google updates its auto-completion database approximately once every 14 days. These results indicate that Google is actively maintaining its query suggestion database.

Knowing the frequency with which these services are updated is advantageous, but is not sufficient for determining the extent to which current search trends are represented in query suggestions. To investigate this question, we can examine when a noteworthy event begins to appear in query suggestions. A prime candidate for exploring this question is provided by the release of the iPhone 4 on June 24th, 2010. Almost immediately, there were reports of significant signal degradation when the phone was held in a certain way [9]. The first evidence of this issue was spotted in the query suggestions on July 14th, 2010. On this date, the partial query "iphone d" resulted in Google suggesting "iphone death grip", while "iphone a" yielded "iphone antenna", and "iphone how to h" yielded "iphone how to hold". None of these queries appear in the suggestions sampled on previous dates. This corresponds to a lag of about 20 days, suggesting that the query completion services place sufficient weight on recent queries.

RANKING QUERIES

After harvesting queries, the next step is to assign an importance rank to each query. When queries are sampled from query suggestion services, detailed query frequency information is not made available (current services do not indicate how often each search is performed). We substitute this missing data in two ways. First, we complement our data set with data collected from advertising and market research tools, such as the Google AdWords Keyword Tool [12]. Second, we examine the structure of the synthesized prefix tree to obtain a *partial ordering* of the queries not covered by the market research tools. We describe each technique in turn.

Using marketing tools to assign ranks

Google provides a set of tools that can be directly applied to the problem of ranking queries. The Google AdWords Keyword Tool [12], intended to help marketers valuate keywords for advertising purposes, can be configured to report the estimated average global monthly search volume for any exact phrase. As such, it is possible to directly rank many query suggestions using this tool alone. In doing so, we again find that there is good correspondence between the harvested queries and their estimated search volume.

While many queries can be directly ranked using the Google AdWords tool, not all queries can be ranked in this way; Google AdWords provides no data for queries whose monthly search volume is below some threshold, and this threshold is reached well before the list of query suggestions has been exhausted. For example, on June 19th, 2010, we harvested 74,795 unique query suggestions for the Firefox web browser. However, Google AdWords provides search volume data for only 15,057 of those queries. In short, the search volume of about 80% of the Firefox queries falls below the threshold reported by AdWords. Accordingly, we must employ another means of ranking the remaining queries, as described next.

Generating a partial ordering

While query suggestion services do not return the frequency with which each suggested query is performed, we have argued that they operate by returning the most popular queries for a given input. We can use this behaviour to derive a *partial ordering* of the query suggestions. The key insight is this: We know that *the 10 query suggestions returned for a given prefix are more popular than all other queries later harvested that also begin with that same prefix.* An example illustrates this point.

Returning to the earlier Firefox example, the suggestion "firefox menu bar missing" appears in Google's top 10 suggestions for the prefix "firefox m". Thus, we can infer that the "firefox menu bar missing" query is more popular than the 2362 other suggestions occurring in the data set that also share the prefix of "firefox m". We say that this query has 2362 *subordinates* in order to convey this relationship.

This ranking technique provides only a partial ordering because we can only perform comparisons of a node with its ancestors and descendants in the prefix tree. We *cannot* directly compare suggestions occupying separate branches of the tree. Nevertheless, for queries whose search volume falls below the AdWords reporting threshold, a search volume-based ranking will be crudely approximated by simply sorting those queries according to their number of subordinates.

These first two steps of harvesting and ranking queries provide us with a suitable, privacy-preserving, publicly accessible replacement for raw query logs. In the remainder of the paper, our technique assumes only that one has access to a ranked list of search queries relating to the interactive system of interest.

QUERY CLASSIFICATION AND FILTERING

Given a ranked list of queries, the next step is to automatically classify queries according to the likely intent of the individual performing the search (for example, to distinguish troubleshooting queries from those seeking to download the application). Once labeled, query logs can then be filtered to select entries that are potentially related to user tasks and usability issues.

Before queries can be automatically labeled and filtered, we first need to understand the range of system-related queries that users submit to search engines. While previous work has developed a number of taxonomies for general classification of search queries (e.g., to distinguish between navigational and information-seeking queries) [7, 17, 25], we found these taxonomies too broad for our purposes. Instead, a classification scheme specialized for the domain of interactive systems is needed. Additionally, we need to understand what features of a query can be used to support automatic labeling.

In this section, we address both of these needs: We introduce a taxonomy of *query intent* specialized for interactive systems, and a second classification scheme that describes how a query is *phrased*. As we will show, in this domain, query phrasing is strongly related to query intent. Based on the aforementioned intent-phrasing relationship, we present a set of heuristics for automating the process of labeling and selecting queries of interest.

Domain-specific query intent taxonomy

Following the basic methods of grounded theory [27], we developed our query taxonomy by performing open coding on 200 randomly sampled queries regarding the GIMP software application. From this initial coding, we identified a set of common, higher-level themes, which led to our taxonomy. The resultant taxonomy includes six separate classes of interactive system queries, synthesized from the perspective of query intent:

QUERY INTENT:

- **Operation Instruction**
  Would the query be used to find instructions for performing a specific operation?
- **Troubleshooting**
  Would the query be used for troubleshooting a bug or error?
- **Reference**
  Would the query be used to find reference material? (e.g., a list of keyboard shortcuts)
- **Download**
  Would the query be used to acquire, download, or install something?
- **General Information**
  Would the query be used to find general information about the application? (e.g., product reviews or comparisons)
- **Off-topic**
  Is the query unrelated to the software / project?

Query phrasing classification scheme

In parallel with developing the former taxonomy, we also developed a classification scheme that describes how individual queries are phrased. The motivation for developing this scheme arose during our open coding sessions: In considering the range of queries, it appeared that *how* a query was phrased was very much related to the *intent* of the user. As we will show, there is indeed a relationship.

Based on the open coding of the queries, the following high-level categories of query phrasing were identified:

QUERY PHRASING:
- **Noun phrase** (e.g., gimp brushes)
- **Imperative statement** (e.g., gimp rotate text)
- **Question** (e.g., how to draw a line in gimp)
- **Statement of fact** (e.g., gimp won't start)
- **Present participle** (e.g., rotating text in gimp)
- **Other**

In the next section, we show that raters are able to achieve a high degree of inter-rater agreement when using the intent and phrasing taxonomies to label search queries. This agreement lends support to the overall utility of the taxonomies as instruments for labeling search queries.

Inter-rater reliability of the classification schemes

To establish the inter-rater reliability of these two classification schemes, two researchers applied both schemes to a set of 195 queries sampled from the GIMP and Firefox datasets. The GIMP and Firefox datasets were collected from Google Suggest on May 23rd, 2010 and June 19th, 2010 respectively. Selection of the 195 sample queries proceeded as follows: For each application, the top 50 queries (by search volume) were selected, followed by an additional 50 randomly selected queries. The resulting set of 200 samples shared 5 queries in common with the set used for the initial open coding and were thus excluded from our validation process.

In labeling this data set, we achieved an overall inter-rater reliability rate of $\kappa_{\text{intent}} = 0.76$ for query intent, and $\kappa_{\text{phrasing}} = 0.79$ for query phrasing, using the Cohen's kappa measure of rater agreement. Inter-rater reliability across the 4 sources of queries is listed in Table 2. The observed agreements are considered to be substantial [19].

Before describing how the query phrasing classification scheme can be used to identify query intent, we first show how queries are distributed across these two classification schemes. These query distributions lend additional arguments for the overall utility of this approach.

Query Source	κ_{intent}	κ_{phrasing}
Firefox, top 50	0.74 (substantial)	0.80 (substantial)
Firefox, random 50	0.86 (near perfect)	0.80 (substantial)
GIMP, top 47	0.66 (substantial)	0.72 (substantial)
GIMP, random 48	0.66 (substantial)	0.81 (near perfect)

Table 2. Inter-rater reliability for each of the four sample sets.

	Rater 1		Rater 2	
Query Intent	Freq.	%	Freq.	%
Opr. Instr.	84	43%	80	41%
Troubleshooting	15	8%	17	9%
Reference	21	11%	19	10%
Download	55	28%	62	32%
General	12	6%	12	6%
Off topic	8	4%	5	2%

Table 3. Frequencies of query intent labels for the 195 randomly selected GIMP and Firefox queries harvested from Google Suggest.

Characterizing query data

The classifications of the 195 labeled queries are summarized in Table 3. The categories we find interesting for usability analysis coincide with the first two listed in the table and the taxonomy: "Operating Instruction", and "Troubleshooting". In our sample, about half of all query suggestions fall within categories that are of interest to HCI researchers and practitioners, demonstrating the overall richness of query logs when studying interactive systems.

Relationship between query phrasing and intent

If we compare how a query is classified in each scheme, we find that how a query is phrased strongly correlates with query intent. These findings are summarized in Table 4.

Query Intent	Noun	Imperative	Question	Fact	P. Participle	Other
Opr. Inst.	0.30 (38)	0.90 (28)	0.87 (13)		1.00 (5)	
Troubleshooting	0.05 (6)			1.00 (9)		
Reference	0.14 (18)	0.03 (1)	0.13 (2)			
Download	0.42 (53)	0.07 (2)				
General:	0.09 (12)					
Off topic						1.00 (8)

Table 4. Probability of query intent given its phrasing type based on the labels assigned by rater 1. Raw frequencies are listed in parentheses. Similar values are achieved using the labels assigned by rater 2.

There are a few noteworthy observations to make in this table. As can be seen, in our sample set, if a query is phrased as an imperative statement, there is a 90% chance that the query is seeking operating instructions. A similar probability (87%) applies if the query is phrased as a question. Finally, if a query is phrased as a statement of fact, then it is almost certainly being used for troubleshooting. These relationships provide us with a set of strategies for automating the labeling of queries, which we describe next.

Heuristics for automating query labeling

In the previous section, the relationship between query phrasing and intent was established by examining labels that were *manually* assigned to queries by a pair of human raters. Automating the CUTS process requires mechanization of the query labeling step. Through further inspection of the data, we have found that certain keywords or patterns are highly indicative of each of the different phrasing types. For example, queries containing the phrase "how to" indicate questions. Once a query's phrasing has been established, we can then infer its intent using Table 4. Here we focus on queries phrased as questions, imperative statements, and statements

Labels		Pattern	Example Query
Operating Instructions	Question	**how to** ___ **in** *SystemName*	how to delete history in firefox
		SystemName **how to** ___	firefox how to clear cache
		can *SystemName* ___	can firefox block websites
		does *SystemName* ___	does firefox have private browsing
	Imperative	**use** *SystemName* ___	use firefox for windows update
		make *SystemName* ___	make firefox default browser
		SystemName **set** ___	firefox set default zoom
		create ___ **in** *SystemName*	create a new profile in firefox
		SystemName **create** ___	firefox create pdf
Troubleshooting	Fact	*SystemName* **is / isn't** ___	firefox is starting slow
		SystemName **can / can't** ___	firefox can't add bookmarks
		SystemName **will / won't** ___	firefox won't open pdf
		SystemName **does / doesn't** ___	firefox doesn't play sound
		SystemName **has / hasn't** ___	firefox has no address bar

Table 5. Filtering templates for labeling the phrasing and likely intent of queries.

of fact because these phrasing types most reliably indicate searches for instructions or troubleshooting information.

A partial list of phrasing patterns is presented in Table 5. These patterns were generated through a manual inspection of labeled data, and serve as basic heuristics for labeling different types of queries.

Many queries will not match any pattern, and will thus go unlabeled at this stage of processing. In the next section, we describe a technique for grouping related queries. When queries are grouped, labels for the individual queries are extended to the group, increasing the coverage of the labeling.

GROUPING SIMILAR QUERIES

The final step in CUTS is to reduce the variability with which queries are expressed in the data set. In query logs, common questions or issues are expressed using a number of different query phrasings. As an example, GIMP users may search "how to draw a circle in gimp", or they may simply type "gimp draw circle". Given this variability, it is desirable that similar queries be grouped, and their weights or rankings combined, in order to better estimate the prevalence of a given issue.

To group similar queries, we transform queries to a canonical form where inconsequential differences are ignored (e.g., see Table 6). This transformation applies the following rules:

- Convert inflected word forms to common word lemmas. We use the WordNet lexical database [20] to perform this transformation (e.g., "deleting cookies" becomes "delete cookie")
- Remove all instances of stop words (such as "and", "the", "to", "but", etc.)
- Remove words devoid of alphabetic letters (e.g., "3.6.10", and other non-English strings)
- Sort the query terms alphabetically.

Using this technique, it is possible to achieve a modest reduction in the size of the data set. As an example, the Firefox

"firefox lost toolbar"	
lost my toolbar firefox	firefox toolbars lost
lost firefox toolbar	firefox lost my toolbar
lost all toolbars in firefox	firefox lost all toolbars
lost toolbar in firefox	firefox lost toolbar
lost my toolbar in firefox	lost my firefox toolbar
firefox toolbar lost	

Table 6. 11 distinct queries which share the canonical representation "firefox lost toolbar".

data set of 74,795 unique queries is represented by 39,435 canonical query groups (53% of the original size). More importantly, we found that a canonical group's cardinality (number of distinct query phrasings) is directly related to the popularity of the group's overall topic or concern; compared to less popular topics, those experiencing high search volume yield logs that contain a more complete sampling of the alternative phrasings with which those queries can be expressed. Consequently, those high-volume queries tend to form groups of higher cardinality. To illustrate this point, Table 7 lists the cardinality of the canonical groups associated with the top 10 "firefox how to" queries already mentioned in the Introduction. All but the last of these queries fall within the top 99.6th percentile of group sizes, thus reinforcing the popularity of these concerns.

"Firefox how to" ...	Canonical Form	Cardinality of group
clear cache	cache clear	110
delete cookies	cookie delete	60
clear cookies	clear cookie	44
enable java	enable java	41
export bookmark	bookmark export	40
enable cookies	cookie enable	32
clear history	clear history	30
block websites	block website	29
get menu bar back	back bar get menu	16
clear browsing history	browse clear history	5

Table 7. Canonical groups associated with the top 10 "firefox how to" queries.

FINAL OUTPUT OF CUTS

The output of CUTS is a categorized and ranked list of query groups relating to the system under investigation. A sample of this output, for the Firefox application, is presented in Table 8. The final ranking of groups is determined by summing the search volumes of each group's member queries, and then sorting those groups accordingly. When search volume information is not available, a sum of subordinate counts is used instead.

Groups Containing Opr. Instr. Queries	Groups Containing Troubleshooting Queries
cache clear	not respond
clear cookie	not open pdf
cookie delete	slow
block website	crash
cookie enable	mode safe
proxy	check not spell
delete history	constant crash
...	...

Table 8. Query groups, related to Firefox, output after query harvesting, ranking, labeling, filtering and grouping.

APPLICATIONS

In this section, we apply our technique to a number of different interactive systems. Our goal here is to demonstrate the wide range of insights that can be gained using this approach. We structure this section by showing how issues related to language, desired functionality, and poor affordances can all be detected using this technique.

"Speak the user's language"

Query logs provide an excellent view of the vocabulary and terminology with which users conceive their use of interactive systems. However, this terminology does not always match that which is used by their systems. When such discrepancies arise, the associated systems can be considered to be in violation of Jakob Nielsen's "Speak the User's Language" usability heuristic [21]. We provide two examples of this problem that we identified using our technique.

Black and white, but not grayscale

The GNU Image Manipulation Program (GIMP) is an open source raster graphics editor offering similar functionality to Adobe's Photoshop application. On May 23rd, 2010, we harvested 14,559 queries relating to this software application. Analysis of the GIMP data set reveals that the terms "black" and "white" co-occur in 93 distinct queries. In each case, the queries inquire about converting color images to black and white. According to the Google AdWords tool, the query "gimp black and white" is searched an average of 590 times a month, or about once every 74 minutes.

Inspecting GIMP's interface (version 2.6) reveals that there are at least three alternative methods for converting a color image to grayscale. These methods are labeled as "grayscale", "desaturate", and "channel mixer". Such technical terms may not be familiar to a sizeable portion of GIMP's user base, as evidenced by the vocabulary used in the harvested queries. Given this finding, one could create a "black and white" command that aggregates into one command the many methods of transforming a color image into a grayscale image.

Clip, but not crop

Inkscape is an open source vector graphics editor similar to Adobe's Illustrator program. On May 22nd, 2010, we harvested 2,501 queries relating to Inkscape. Interestingly, the 8th highest volume query was "inkscape crop", with an average of 480 searches performed each month. However, being a vector graphics application, Inkscape does not have a "cropping" tool; cropping is specific to raster graphics. The equivalent operation for vector graphics is to "clip". This very popular query suggests that new Inkscape users are relying on Google to translate knowledge from one domain (i.e., raster graphics) to another domain (i.e., vector graphics). This behaviour closely resembles similar behaviour exhibited by programmers' use of Google [6]. Recognizing this issue, Inkscape could provide a "crop" command or a help entry that assists users in setting the clip for their document.

Desired functionality

In addition to identifying potential usability issues related to terminology, we found query log analysis to be an excellent source for discovering desired functionality.

Blocking unwanted calls

One popular class of queries related to Apple's iPhone product inquires about the possibility of selectively blocking unwanted calls from specific telephone numbers. While this feature is not currently supported by the device, users search for information on performing this task at least 5,800 times a month, or once every 7.5 minutes. The consensus among the user community is that the issue can be resolved by associating a silent audio clip as the ringtone of unwanted telephone numbers. That this issue is so popular suggests users would be well-served if provided with a sanctioned means of achieving this same behaviour.

Changing screen savers

Another example of identifying desired functionality emerges when analyzing the searches specific to Amazon's Kindle eBook reader. Specifically, query log analysis reveals 89 distinct phrasings of the query "how to change your kindle screensaver". The Kindle device ships with a few dozen stock images that are displayed by the device when not in use. However, these images cannot be customized by the end user. Again, the popularity of these searches suggests that such a feature would be welcomed.

Drawing shapes in GIMP

Finally, an analysis of the GIMP query data set reveals many queries related to drawing primitive shapes: Roughly 130 unique queries inquire about drawing various types of lines, 80 unique queries inquire about drawing circles, 40 queries inquire about drawing rectangles, 20 queries inquire about drawing squares, and 14 queries inquire about drawing ellipses. Moreover, the suggestions "gimp how to draw a line", and "gimp how to draw a circle" appear in the top 10 suggestions for the prefix "gimp how to", and the Google AdWords tool reports that the query "gimp draw circle" is performed an average of once an hour, each and every day. These queries are noteworthy because GIMP provides no explicit tools for drawing simple shapes. Dedicated tools for these functions would likely find great use by GIMP users.

The usability cost of poor affordances

As a final example of the types of problems that can be uncovered using query log analyses, we consider the usability cost of poor affordances and uninformative error messages.

Ubuntu's "authentication failure"

Ubuntu is currently one of the most popular GNU/Linux distributions. For reasons of security, Ubuntu disables the "root" superuser account by default, requiring users to issue the "sudo" command to gain superuser privileges. The root account has otherwise been present and used in UNIX and UNIX-like systems for decades.

While Ubuntu's policy is arguably a positive change for security, the operating system may not be adequately communicating this policy to new users: Attempts to log in as the root user (in Ubuntu version 10.04) simply result in an "authentication failure" error message. An analysis of the queries related to Ubuntu reveals nearly 130 distinct query phrasings all asking about how to access the root user account. The specific query "ubuntu login as root" is performed 720 times a month, or about once an hour. Similarly, a search for the error message "su authentication failure ubuntu" occurs about once every 7 hours. These findings suggest that users would be well served by a more helpful or detailed error message which could communicate the proper course of action when attempting to login as the root user.

DISCUSSION

In this section, we more broadly discuss issues related to using query logs to understand the needs of users of interactive systems. We begin by comparing the output of CUTS to manually curated "frequently asked questions" (i.e., FAQs). We then discuss how query log analysis can factor into existing usability practices, and enumerate various issues that may affect the rankings produced by our method.

Comparing CUTS' output to published FAQs

CUTS reveals search queries that are frequently performed by a system's users. As such, its output is directly comparable to lists of frequently asked questions (FAQs) commonly provided as documentation for many software applications. However, standard FAQs are curated by individuals, and require continual maintenance and individual judgement regarding inclusion of content. Accordingly, we expect CUTS to more accurately represent the needs of the user base over time. A comparison of our results with the GIMP FAQ lends support to this notion.

The GIMP FAQ[5] contains 25 questions/answers in the section entitled "Using GIMP." Sixteen of these issues overlap the top issues found using CUTS. The FAQ issues that don't overlap with our results tend to be quite specialized (e.g., "How do I configure X server to do global gamma correction?"). Since GIMP's user base primarily consists of casual users who perform relatively simple tasks [18], very few users will benefit from the answers to these specialized questions. In contrast, CUTS reveals a more representative set of questions related to the simple tasks users have been found to perform (e.g., "gimp how to convert to black and white").

We have also compared CUTS' results to the Firefox knowledge base (KB)[6]. Again, the CUTS data suggests many potential usability issues not directly addressed by the Firefox KB (e.g., "where do firefox downloads go"). The key point in both instances is that CUTS provides a data-driven view of user concerns that is continuously updated.

Integrating query log analysis in usability practices

Throughout the paper, we have been careful to note that query logs can be used to identify *potential* usability problems of interactive systems. While a query may *suggest* that users are experiencing difficulties with a particular aspect of the system (e.g., "gimp how to draw a circle"), further details and context are required before one can conclude the nature and severity of the issue. This additional information can be obtained using standard evaluation techniques involving users or expert evaluators. Since many methods (e.g., cognitive walkthrough) require representative tasks to be identified for evaluative purposes, CUTS can assist by supplying a ranked list of common tasks and needs.

A ranked list of common queries can also be used to assign importance to existing lists of known usability issues. The benefit of using the results of CUTS is that this ranking is derived from the search behaviour of thousands, if not millions, of users. This ranked list may also be more exhaustive than existing lists tracking usability issues. Software producers with limited resources, including volunteer-driven open source products, could thus benefit from this additional means of identifying potential usability problems.

Factors that may impact or compromise query ranking

To effectively use query analysis, it is important to understand and consider the various factors that can impact the weighting and ranking that such analysis produces. In this section, we discuss various effects that influence how often various searches are performed.

User search behaviours and query reformulation

A growing body of research (e.g., [2, 15]) examines user search behaviour. One of the practices observed is that people reformulate their queries when search results do not match their expectations or needs. As an example, a user might start with queries consisting of a few words, and then pose more detailed questions as they fail to find relevant documents in the search results [2]. As a result of this query reformulation strategy, it is conceivable that the analysis proposed in this paper artificially inflates the importance of issues for which relevant information is scarce. Reflecting on this, we note that query popularity has been observed to follow a Zipf's law distribution [26, 4]. As a result of this exponential relationship between query rank and frequency, it is unlikely that any reformulation behaviours would grossly distort the ranking of popular queries. However, the effect may be more pronounced among queries with lower search volume, suggesting a need for more work in this space.

Products with generic names

A number of products have relatively generic names (e.g., Microsoft Word, Adobe Illustrator, etc.), which can cause many irrelevant or off-topic queries to appear in query logs. A similar problem is encountered by products whose names are now synonymous with a class of operations or applications. For example, an altered digital image is often described as being "Photoshopped," regardless of which software application was used for image manipulation.

In these problematic cases, we have found our filtering techniques (e.g., "how to ___ in photoshop") are often enough to filter out the less desirable, off-topic queries.

[5] http://www.gimp.org/docs/userfaq.html
[6] http://support.mozilla.com

We also suspect that it is possible to differentiate between the uses of a word by analyzing the results that search engines return for those queries. Search engines are designed to return relevant documents, and often refine their relevance rankings by observing which pages users visit after performing searches [3]. The query-document associations recorded by search engines provide a wealth of untapped information that can further guide analysis of query logs. Use of these associations constitutes a promising area of future research.

Impact of system popularity

In the interest of preserving user privacy, query auto-completion services are unlikely to suggest queries unless those queries have been performed many times, and by many different individuals. As such, the quantity of data available for analysis by CUTS is related to the popularity of the interactive system being studied. In the extreme case, CUTS cannot be used to study systems that are not publicly available (e.g., custom software solutions, prototypes, beta software, etc.), unless one has access to internal search logs for these systems. Related to this, while CUTS is ideal for assessing usability in general, we cannot currently filter results according to particular sub-groups of users, such as novices or experts. Indeed, sub-groups in the minority are likely to be underrepresented in CUTS' output.

CONCLUSION

When faced with difficulties or questions relating to the use of interactive systems, many people routinely turn to Internet search engines as a first line of support. In this paper, we have introduced CUTS: characterizing usability through search. This process takes the name of an interactive system as input and outputs a ranked and categorized list of potential issues that users encounter with that system. These data are assembled by sampling from the query logs of top-tier Internet search engines. Importantly, the results of this process have a high degree of ecological validity, and can directly inform more formal evaluation methods by suggesting particular tasks or issues to study.

REFERENCES

1. Akers, D., Simpson, M., Jeffries, R., and Winograd, T. Undo and erase events as indicators of usability problems. In *Proc CHI '09*, ACM (New York, NY, USA, 2009), 659–668.
2. Aula, A., Khan, R. M., and Guan, Z. How does search behavior change as search becomes more difficult? In *Proc CHI '10*, ACM (New York, NY, USA, 2010), 35–44.
3. Baeza-Yates, R., and Tiberi, A. Extracting semantic relations from query logs. In *Proc KDD '07*, ACM (New York, NY, USA, 2007), 76–85.
4. Bar-Yossef, Z., and Gurevich, M. Mining search engine query logs via suggestion sampling. *Proc. VLDB Endow. 1*, 1 (2008), 54–65.
5. Barrett, R., Kandogan, E., Maglio, P. P., Haber, E. M., Takayama, L. A., and Prabaker, M. Field studies of computer system administrators: analysis of system management tools and practices. In *Proc CSCW '04*, ACM (New York, NY, USA, 2004), 388–395.
6. Brandt, J., Guo, P. J., Lewenstein, J., Dontcheva, M., and Klemmer, S. R. Two studies of opportunistic programming: interleaving web foraging, learning, and writing code. In *Proc CHI '09*, ACM (New York, NY, USA, 2009), 1589–1598.
7. Broder, A. A taxonomy of web search. *SIGIR Forum 36*, 2 (2002), 3–10.
8. Dou, Z., Song, R., and Wen, J.-R. A large-scale evaluation and analysis of personalized search strategies. In *Proc WWW '07*, ACM (New York, NY, USA, 2007), 581–590.
9. Gikas, M. Lab tests: Why Consumer Reports can't recommend the iPhone 4. *Consumer Reports* (July 2010).
10. Ginsberg, J., Mohebbi, M. H., Patel, R. S., Brammer, L., Smolinski, M. S., and Brilliant, L. Detecting influenza epidemics using search engine query data. *Nature 457* (February 2009), 1012–1014.
11. Google Corperation. Features: Google suggest. `http://www.google.com/support/websearch/bin/answer.py?hl=en\&answer=106230`, 2010.
12. Google Corperation. Google AdWords keyword tool. `https://adwords.google.com/select/KeywordToolExternal?forceLegacy=true`, 2010.
13. Google Corperation. Google suggest : FAQ. `http://labs.google.com/intl/en/suggestfaq.html`, 2010.
14. Hilbert, D. M., and Redmiles, D. F. Extracting usability information from user interface events. *ACM Computing Surveys 32*, 4 (2000), 384–421.
15. Huang, J., and Efthimiadis, E. N. Analyzing and evaluating query reformulation strategies in web search logs. In *Proc CIKM '09*, ACM (New York, NY, USA, 2009), 77–86.
16. Hurst, A., Hudson, S. E., and Mankoff, J. Dynamic detection of novice vs. skilled use without a task model. In *Proc CHI '07*, ACM (New York, NY, USA, 2007), 271–280.
17. Kellar, M., Watters, C., and Shepherd, M. A field study characterizing web-based information-seeking tasks. *J. Am. Soc. Inf. Sci. Technol. 58*, 7 (2007), 999–1018.
18. Lafreniere, B., Bunt, A., Whissell, J. S., Clarke, C. L. A., and Terry, M. Characterizing large-scale use of a direct manipulation application in the wild. In *Proc GI '10* (Toronto, Canada, 2010), 11–18.
19. Landis, J. R., and Koch, G. G. The measurement of observer agreement for categorical data. *Biometrics 33*, 1 (1977), pp. 159–174.
20. Miller, G. A. Wordnet: a lexical database for english. *Commun. ACM 38* (November 1995), 39–41.
21. Nielsen, J., and Molich, R. Heuristic evaluation of user interfaces. In *Proc CHI '90*, ACM (New York, NY, USA, 1990), 249–256.
22. Pang, B., and Lee, L. Opinion mining and sentiment analysis. *Found. Trends Inf. Retr. 2* (January 2008), 1–135.
23. Quesenbery, W., Jarrett, C., Roddis, I., Allen, S., and Stirling, V. Search Is Now Normal Behavior. What Do We Do about That. In *UPA 2008* (Baltimore, Maryland, USA, June 2008).
24. Richardson, M. Learning about the world through long-term query logs. *ACM Trans. Web 2*, 4 (2008), 1–27.
25. Rose, D. E., and Levinson, D. Understanding user goals in web search. In *Proc WWW '04*, ACM (New York, NY, USA, 2004), 13–19.
26. Saraiva, P. C., Silva de Moura, E., Ziviani, N., Meira, W., Fonseca, R., and Riberio-Neto, B. Rank-preserving two-level caching for scalable search engines. In *Proc SIGIR '01*, ACM (New York, NY, USA, 2001), 51–58.
27. Strauss, A., and Corbin, J. *Basics of Qualitative Research: Techniques and Procedures for Developing Grounded Theory*, 3rd edition ed. Sage Publications, 2008.
28. Zeller, T. AOL technology chief quits after data release. *The New York Times* (August 2006).

Determining Relevancy: How Software Developers Determine Relevant Information in Feeds

Thomas Fritz and Gail C. Murphy
University of British Columbia
{fritz,murphy}@cs.ubc.ca

ABSTRACT
Finding relevant information within the vast amount of information exchanged via feeds is difficult. Previous research into this problem has largely focused on recommending relevant information based on topicality. By not considering individual and situational factors these approaches fall short. Through a formative, interview-based study, we explored how five software developers determined relevancy of items in two kinds of project news feeds. We identified four factors that the developers used to help determine relevancy and found that placement of items in source code and team contexts can ease the determination of relevancy.

Author Keywords
News feeds, relevancy, context, interview study.

ACM Classification Keywords
H.5.3 Group and Organization Interfaces.

General Terms
Human Factors.

INTRODUCTION
Information streams—tweets, status updates from social networking services and other RSS feeds—enable users to stay aware of information that might be relevant to them. Users of such information streams face two problems. First, they must determine which streams contain information of information. Second, in many cases, not all of the information in a stream is relevant, forcing the user to separate the wheat from the chaff. Malone identified this second problem in the context of distribution lists more than twenty years ago [5].

Surprising to us, there appears to be very little formative research about the question of how to determine relevant information in a stream. Instead, the research has focused on how to recommend items within a stream, largely based on topicality; for example, the approach of Chen *et al.* [1] recommends tweets by matching terms recorded in a profile of the user and terms in the tweets. Schamber *et al.* [7] argue that a determination of relevance should go further and should involve understanding how users perceive information relative to their current situation. They suggest the use of more qualitative research methods to better understand how users determine which parts of information are relevant.

In this paper, we take this direction and present the results of a small formative study that investigated two questions: how does a user determine relevance and can the context of the situation be used to help a user to determine relevance? Our aim was to allow the formation of data-driven hypotheses that can be subjected to more detailed testing. We chose to study a team of software developers because this situation allowed us to study multiple individuals working with similar information items in a similar work environment.

Our formative study involved a team of five developers who use IBM's Rational Team Concert (RTC) environment. RTC includes a default feed reader that provides updates about several information streams, including changes to shared work items and changes to shared code. Over the period of a week, we interviewed each developer two times, presenting each with a subset of the information items in their feed reader and asked them questions related to the relevance of those items. In all, we studied 291 news items.

We found that each user had their own definition of relevance, ranging from an item being relevant because it impacted the individual's work in the present to more generic determinations that the item may help to do one's job in the future. We also found that users use the kind of information stream, the content of an item in the stream, the target of the content, their relationship with who created the item and whether or not the news had been discussed elsewhere to determine relevancy of individual items. Finally, we found that presenting news items in the context of a fragment of a developer's work appears to hold promise for easing relevancy determination. These findings lead to hypotheses that can inform future studies and that can suggest new approaches for automated support for managing information streams.

RELATED WORK
How users determine relevance of information has been considered in terms of email systems (e.g., [10]). Two of the factors for determining relevance identified in our study overlap with these findings, specifically "content" and "relation with creator". Our work independently finds these factors without presupposing that message characteristics are the only way of exploring relevancy. In addition, our work identifies that the structure of information, such as links between work items and change sets, can also play an important role in relevance determination. Another group of research showed

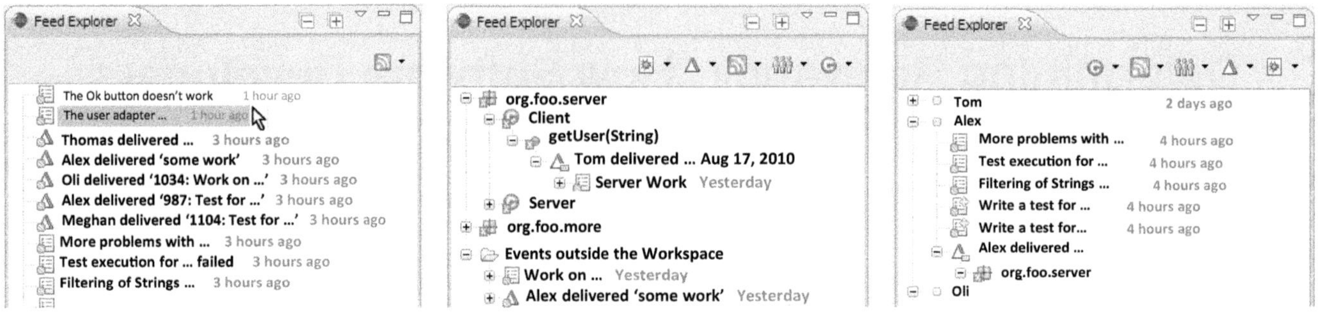

(a) Traditional List-Based Feed Reader (b) Feeds in Source Code Context (c) Feeds in Team Context

Figure 1. Presentation of Feeds.

that users frequently use sorting features to better find relevant information (e.g., [3]). Our study extends this work by investigating how context, such as the source code or the team, can help in this sorting.

A number of researchers have attempted to determine relevancy automatically using recommender-based approaches. Chen *et al.* [1] explore a variety of recommender algorithms, largely based on topic relevance, to find interesting URLs in Twitter feeds. Dabbish *et al.* [2] predict the importance of an e-mail message to a user based on predefined categories. These approaches do not try to understand how users define an item of information as relevant to their current situation.

Other research has looked at the problem of staying aware of relevant information. Palantir [6], for example, provides awareness of changes to the source code in context of a developer's workspace by decorating code in the environment as to whether or not it has been changed by someone else. In contrast, our approach focuses on a feed view of changes and considers the placement of news items in the context of a fragment of source code instead of the entire system. In addition, Palantir only indicates a change, whereas our approach presents the news item, which also provides a rational for the change, such as the work item causing the change. Treude *et al.* [9] studied how software developers use feeds in RTC for accomplishing awareness. They did not consider how developers assess the relevancy of the feeds or the items within, which is our focus in this paper.

INTERVIEW METHODOLOGY

For our study we interviewed a sample of five developers (4 male, 1 female) from a development team within a large corporation. The team was chosen based on their use of an environment that contains project feeds (IBM's RTC) and the access we were granted to their project specific changes and information. The participants had between 4 and 24 years of professional development experience (M=10 , SD=9) and at least 20 months of experience using RTC (M=23, SD=7).

We interviewed each participant twice, with four days in between the first and the second interview. In each interview, we presented the participant with a list of 30 items[1] from two default feeds that exist in RTC. One feed, *change set news*, captures changes to the code and the other feed, *work item news*, captures changes to work items, which are similar to bugs, issues or tasks. For each participant, we randomly selected the items to present from the set of all items that had occurred for the participant over the previous three days.We ensured that the presented items represented both feeds and that the participant was not the creator of the item. In each session we asked each participant to review the items and to tell us whether or not the item was relevant, how relevant the item was and why the item was relevant (or not). Participants had the option to read and explore the item and related information as much as desired. We deliberately did not define relevance for the participants to allow investigation of differing ideas of relevance between the participants.

In the first interview session, the news items were presented in a list, based on the interface of traditional feed readers (Figure 1(a)). In the second interview session, we asked the participants to review an additional 30 news items. We first showed these additional items in the context of a fragment of the related source code (Figure 1(b)). If the item was not related to the source code, it was shown in a flat list below the code. We asked the participant whether the context changed his determination of the item's relevance and whether or not the context was helpful. Next, we showed the items in terms of a team context (Figure 1(c)), in which a news item was shown underneath the team member who caused the creation of the news item. We asked the participant the same questions for the team context as for the source code context. We chose to investigate source code and team contexts because developers had earlier described this kind of information as critical to many questions they need to answer [4]. In this paper, we examine whether using this information as context can help a developer determine the relevancy of new information.

Each interview session took between 20 and 60 minutes. All interviews were recorded and the interviewer (first author of this paper) took handwritten notes. Due to the exploratory nature of our study, we parsed our data using an open coding technique to develop and identify categories of data [8].

FEEDS

A news item in the study referred to a change in a work item or a change set. In both cases, a summary of what changed was displayed, e.g. "Oli delivered 1034: Work on ...", for a change set (Figure 1(a)). Hovering over the element in the view presented the details of the change in a popup.

[1]In one case, only 21 news items were available.

During the study period, a mean of 50 (*SD*=31) items per day were available to the participant in their feed reader, created by a mean of 5 (*SD*=2) authors. Most, 46 of 50 (*SD*=32), items were about work items; the remaining 4 of 50 (*SD*=3) were about change sets.

In total, our study gathered feedback on 291 news items. Overall participants perceived 79 of the 291 (27%) news items as relevant, 24 (8%) as somewhat relevant and 188 (65%) as not relevant. Participants perceived more of the change set news items as relevant compared to work item news; participants perceived 54 of the 81 (67%) change set news items as relevant or somewhat relevant, whereas only 49 of the 210 (23%) work item news were considered relevant or somewhat relevant. Since all participants worked on the same team, many of the news items overlapped.

In the second set of interviews, we placed the items into the source code context (Figure 1(b)). Of the 150 news items considered in these interviews, 37 (25%) were related to the source code on which the team was working. All of the news items could be related to team members and could thus be shown in the context of the team member that authored the item (Figure 1(c)). More than the five developers in the study were referred to by news items so the team context involved eleven team members.

Although all participants knew of the feed reader in RTC, only one participant described using the view on a regular basis. Others just used it occasionally or very rarely. Instead, they often used other, more specialized views available within RTC to monitor changes. In particular, all participants stated that they regularly monitor changes to the source code, the information summarized in the change set news, using a view called the Pending Changes View.

USER-ORIENTED VIEW OF RELEVANCE

Each participant defined relevancy of a news item differently: a news item is relevant when it impacts the code that I am familiar with (P1), when the information is useful to me now or in the foreseeable future (P2), when it's in an area in which I am an expert of, interested in and almost are lacking expertise (P3), when it helps me to do my job at some point (P4) and if it is in an area that I see myself as a keeper or knowledgable in or critical to the project (P5).

Classification of the detailed reasons given by participants when determining relevancy suggests nine broad categories (Figure 2). Some of the categorized reasons were used mainly for identifying an item as relevant. For example, in 16 cases, participants described that the item being about a change set is why the item was relevant. Other categories are about why an item was irrelevant, such as an item being not from someone on the participant's team. Finally, some of the categorizes were used to identify items as relevant as well as irrelevant.

As described below, participants did not apply consistent criteria for determining relevancy. Although the perception of relevance is individual and situation-based, we have identified four dimensions along which participants determined

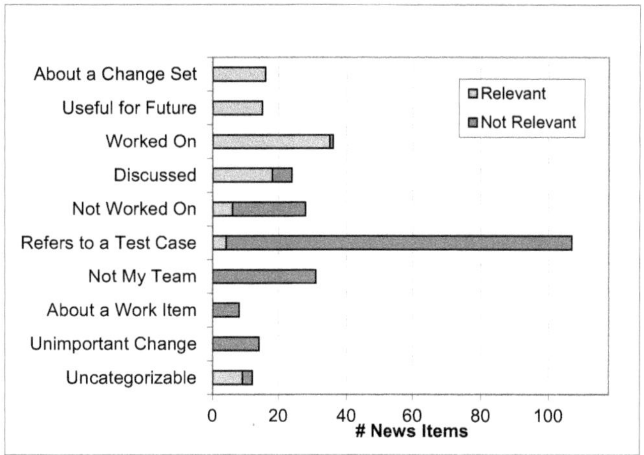

Figure 2. Categorized Reasons Developers Mentioned for Identifying a News Item as Relevant or Irrelevant.

the relevancy of an item: the content of the item, the target of the content, the relation with the creator and the previous interaction with the topic of the news item.

Content

All participants generally rated change set news as more relevant than work item news. One participant even went as far as saying that all change set news for the project are relevant but that work item news are not relevant as too many items appear and much of the information was available for the team on a physical white board (P4). This content-based approach is well-supported by today's tools that support feed subscription based on content. However, as only 67% of all change set news and 23% of work item news were considered as relevant, this statement is not well supported by the data from all participants. Furthermore, this same participant (P4) admitted that because he generally ignores work item news, he also misses questions asked of him through work items, suggesting that a content-based approach has significant drawbacks.

Other participants considered the type of the content, as opposed to the type of the feed, to determine relevance. For example, most participants stated that work item news concerning test cases were not relevant. Other factors did override these general trends. For instance, the participants described that the state of the project affects the relevancy of work item news referring to test cases. In some project states, such as when the system fails to run, work item news related to testing is more likely to be deemed relevant.

This trend of using the type of an item was also seen in other work item news deemed irrelevant, such as items on the addition of a work item to a feature (P1, P2) or on the change of a subscriber to a work item (P5).

Target of Content

The target of the content of a news item, for instance, the code to which a news item referred, was often mentioned as a reason for an item being relevant or not. One participant stated, "This is not relevant since I have not worked on that [part of the code] for a while" (P1). Another stated, "[this is relevant as] the area is related to what I worked on" (P5). As with the content, the relevance based on the target of the content is also very dependent on the situation and the individual. For instance, (P2) stated that even though an item is not in an area he worked on, it could be useful for the future and thus perceived as relevant. Tools could be built to help automate this factor of relevance determination; tracking data about which code a developer touches and changes could be used to filter information streams to only show items on which a developer does (or does not) work.

Relation with Creator

In most cases, an item created by a developer not on the direct team of the participant was perceived as less relevant (P1, P2, P4, P5). However, when the participant worked with a developer from a different team on a regular basis due to project dependencies, the item was perceived as highly relevant (P3). Some participants stated that a combination of factors may make an item relevant; for instance, if an item was created by a certain teammate and touched an area of related work it was relevant (P1). Tools could be built to support the use of combinations of factors in automating determining relevance of items.

Previous Interaction

Whether or not the news had been discussed in another setting had an impact on the perceived relevance of the corresponding news item when it appeared in the feed. Some stated that work item news were not interesting because the news had already been discussed in the planning sessions (P4). Others stated that seeing a news item related to a previously discussed issue was relevant as it confirms what is known (P3). One participant (P5) had mixed views and identified one item as relevant and another one as irrelevant based on having previously discussed these items. Providing support to automatically determine if news had been seen in another setting appears much more challenging. A better characterization of the impact of this factor would be helpful to ascertain in future studies.

CONTEXT TO REDUCE INFORMATION OVERLOAD

Although participants stated that their knowledge about the part of the code to which the news item related was used in determining relevance, only 37 of 150 (25%) were easily determined to relate to the code on which the participants worked. In 20 of the 37 (54%) cases, participants considered the source code context to be helpful. In 9 of 37 (24%) cases the participants referred to it as being somewhat helpful and in 8 (22%) cases as being not helpful. In particular, when the short form of the summary used to identify the news item was too generic, such as "delivered 2 change sets", the context provided a significant benefit to the participant in explaining the item.

When asked about source code context in general, three out of the five participants considered the placement of news items in context helpful (P1,P2,P5). One of the three stated that he "had problems with the [news items] out of context, but [for] the ones within, [he could determine relevancy] pretty quick" (P1). Another participant preferred the team context, stating that the source code context provided too much information but that the team context allows skimming over people quickly (P3). Three more participants (P1,P2,P5) conceived the team context as helpful, in particular in situations in which you do not have to work with a lot of source code, such as quality control.

CONCLUSION

A better understanding of how users determine relevance of items from feeds is needed to build better tool support to help users deal with the vast amount of information flowing to them in this form. Our study of how developers determine the relevancy of items in project-related feeds resulted in a description of four factors that impact relevancy. Only one of these factors, the type of information stream, is well-supported by today's tooling. Other factors such as the target of the content and the relationship with the creator appear plausible to develop. The fourth factor, previous interaction, requires additional study to better understand its impact in the determination of relevancy. Our study also shows that the placement of information stream items into user-oriented context, even as fragments, can be helpful in determining relevance. Further study is needed to understand how these factors generalize into other settings.

REFERENCES

1. J. Chen, R. Nairn, L. Nelson, M. Bernstein, and E. Chi. Short and tweet: experiments on recommending content from information streams. In *Proc. of CHI '10*.
2. L. A. Dabbish, R. E. Kraut, S. Fussell, and S. Kiesler. Understanding email use: predicting action on a message. In *Proc. of CHI '05*.
3. N. Ducheneaut and V. Bellotti. E-mail as habitat: an exploration of embedded personal information management. *interactions*, 2001.
4. T. Fritz and G. C. Murphy. Using information fragments to answer the questions developers ask. In *Proc. of ICSE'10*.
5. T. W. Malone, K. R. Grant, F. A. Turbak, S. A. Brobst, and M. D. Cohen. Intelligent information-sharing systems. *Commun. ACM*, 30(5), 1987.
6. A. Sarma, Z. Noroozi, and A. van der Hoek. Palantír: raising awareness among configuration management workspaces. In *Proc. of ICSE '03*.
7. L. Schamber, M. B. Eisenberg, and M. S. Nilan. A re-examination of relevance: toward a dynamic, situational definition. *Information Processing & Management*, 26, 1990.
8. A. C. Strauss and J. Corbin. *Basics of Qualitative Research: Grounded Theory Procedures and Techniques*. Sage Publications, Inc, 2nd edition, 1990.
9. C. Treude and M.-A. Storey. Awareness 2.0: staying aware of projects, developers and tasks using dashboards and feeds. In *Proc. of ICSE '10*.
10. G. D. Venolia, L. Dabbish, J. Cadiz, and A. Gupta. Supporting email workflow. Technical report, 2001.

Measuring Web Page Revisitation in Tabbed Browsing

Haimo Zhang, Shengdong Zhao
Computer Science, National University of Singapore
{z-haimo, zhaosd}@comp.nus.edu.sg
nus-hci.comp.nus.edu.sg

ABSTRACT

Browsing the web has been shown to be a highly recurrent activity. Aimed to optimize the browsing experience, extensive previous research has been carried out on users' revisitation behavior. However, the conventional definition for revisitation, which only considers page loading activities by monitoring http requests initiated by the browser, largely underestimates users' intended revisitation activities with *tabbed browsers*. Thus, we introduce a goal-oriented definition and a refined revisitation measurement based on page viewings in tabbed browsers. An empirical analysis of statistics taken from a client-side log study showed that although the overall revisitation rate remained relatively constant, tabbed browsing has introduced new behaviors warrant future investigations.

Author Keywords

Web revisitation, tabbed browsing, effective revisitation.

ACM Classification Keywords

H5.4. Information interfaces and presentation (e.g., HCI): Hypertext/Hypermedia – user issues.

General Terms

Human factors

INTRODUCTION

Browsing the web has been shown to be a highly recurrent activity [7]. Extensive research that has been conducted to understand user behavior and optimize the browsing experience focused on "web page revisitation", a term that refers to the repeated visits to previously visited web pages [3,5,6,7].

Previous studies, conducted mostly between 1994 and 2000, were mostly on non-tabbed browsers [2,5,7] and revisitation was defined as "the repeated *loading* of a web page as identified by its URL" [7].

Following this definition, the revisitation rate is calculated using the number of repeated page loading events (the difference between the total number of page loading events and the number of distinct URLs loaded, termed as the size of the URL vocabulary [7]) divided by the total number of page loading events.

While to some extent, tabbed browsing behavior can be achieved using multiple instances of non-tabbed browsers, but the pervasive usage of tabbed browsing behavior did not happen until major browsers adopted the tab feature. In 2009, Dubroy and Balakrishnan [3] conducted a study on user behaviors in Mozilla Firefox browser, highlighting the significance of tab usage in revisiting web pages. In 2010, Huang and White [4] investigated parallel browsing, specifically on how web searching tasks were performed with multiple tabs. Both papers adopted the conventional definition for revisitation and did not point out how repeated page visits in non-tabbed browsers were different from those in tabbed browsers.

Scope and Definition of Terms

From the user's perspective, the purpose of "visiting" a web page is to get information. Thus, we propose the term "effective revisitation" to describe the repetition of *obtaining information* from a web page as identified by its URL. Since the majority of web content is visual (rather than audio), we focus on revisitation of visual content in this paper.

A clear line needs to be drawn between the definition and the measurement of revisitation. Our proposed definition explains what revisitation is, rather than how it is measured. The conventional definition is somewhat misleading as it is actually a measurement of revisitations in non-tabbed browsers.

To understand why the conventional measurement for revisitation is insufficient under the tabbed browsing paradigm, several terms first need to be clarified:

• *Focused tab* or *current tab*. The current visible tab in a browser. In tabbed browsers, only the tab that is being displayed is visible. Non-tabbed browsers could be thought of as having only one tab, which is always in focus.

• *Background tabs*. They only exist in a tabbed browser. They contain opened pages, but unlike the focused tab, their content is not visible. All tabs except the focused tab are background tabs.

• *Page loading*. A page loading event is recorded whenever an http request is sent to the server.

• *Page viewing.* A page is viewable when the tab containing it is in focus. Since it is difficult to know whether the user is actually viewing a web page unless eye-tracking mechanisms are used, we assume that the user is viewing a page whenever it is displayed in the focused tab.

Limitations of the Conventional Measurement for Revisitation

In any single instances of non-tabbed browsers (since non-tabbed browsers only displays one web page, it can also be regarded as single-tabbed browsers), all web pages are loaded into the only tab, which is always in focus; so they are displayed whenever they are loaded. Therefore, the conventional measurement for revisitation is able to determine the number of page viewings through the concurrence of page loading events and page displaying events, given the assumption that page displaying equals page viewing.

In tabbed browsers, however, a page loading is not always a page displaying. The conventional measurement cannot be used to determine the number of page viewings since it would introduce two types of errors:

• *Over-count of revisitation activities.* In tabbed browsers, a background tab can be closed without being viewed. This introduces three types of over-count errors that will be counted as revisitations:

Type 1. A previously loaded-but-**not**-viewed page is loaded again and viewed;

Type 2. A previously loaded-but-**not**-viewed page is loaded again but **not** viewed; and

Type 3. A previously loaded-and-viewed page is loaded again but **not** viewed.

In all of these cases, the same page was loaded several times but viewed not more than once. They are considered revisitations in the conventional definition but should be excluded under the new definition.

• *Under-count of revisitation activities.* When users switch to a tab to display its content, which has been viewed before, no additional loading events are triggered. The conventional definition does not consider this behavior as a revisitation; our proposed definition does.

Proposed Approach for Measuring Revisitations

To accurately measure revisitation in tabbed browsing, we propose to focus on page viewings instead of page loadings. There are two types of page viewing activities in tabbed browsers:

• *Loading-based page viewing.* A web page (uniquely represented by its URL) that is loaded into the focused tab is considered viewed.

• *Tab-switching-based page viewing.* A page in a background tab is considered viewed when the tab becomes the focused tab.

The *effective revisitation rate (EffRev%)* is calculated as the number of *effective revisits* (or repeated page viewings) *(#EffRev)* divided by the total *number of page viewings (#View)*. The definitions of each term are listed below.

• *Number of page viewings (#View).* The total number of loading-based and tab-switching-based page viewings.

• *Number of effective revisits (#EffRev).* A subset of all page viewings. Effective revisits are viewings of previously viewed pages.

• *Effective revisitation rate (EffRev%).* The formula *#EffRev/#View* calculates the effective revisitation rate based on page viewings.

Note that the difference between total number of page viewings and URL vocabulary size (number of distinct URL loads) does not equal the number of effective revisits, as some URLs could have been loaded but never viewed.

The new definition and measurement prompted the following research questions:

• Using the proposed viewing-based measurement, what is the revisitation rate under the tabbed browsing paradigm? How does it differ from the results using the conventional measurement?

• How significant are the over-count and under-count errors when the conventional method is used to measure revisitations in tabbed browsers?

• Has the frequency of users' repeated page visits changed in recent years?

To answer these questions, we carried out a one-month study of 20 participants and their browsing behaviors in tabbed browsers.

A STUDY OF REVISITATION BEHAVIOR

After examining the design of Dubroy and Balakrishnan's study on tabbed browsing behavior [3], we found that both their logger and study procedure can be used for our research on revisitation. We adopted those and changed only the interview questions to target our topic.

Participants and Duration

20 participants (7 females, age range 23-26, mean 24.1) from the university community took part in the one-month study. All participants use Internet daily on Microsoft Windows Operating Systems with Mozilla Firefox as the primary browser. Participants were instructed to browse the Internet as usual. No additional demonstration or suggestion of using tabs was given prior to or during the study.

Results and Analysis

A total of 235,707 browser events were captured from the 20 participants over one-month, among which there were 89,851 page loadings and 127,344 page viewings. We do not further distinguish the type of information users try to get (whether it is advertisement, news reading, etc.). While there are different ways to define a page, we adopted the

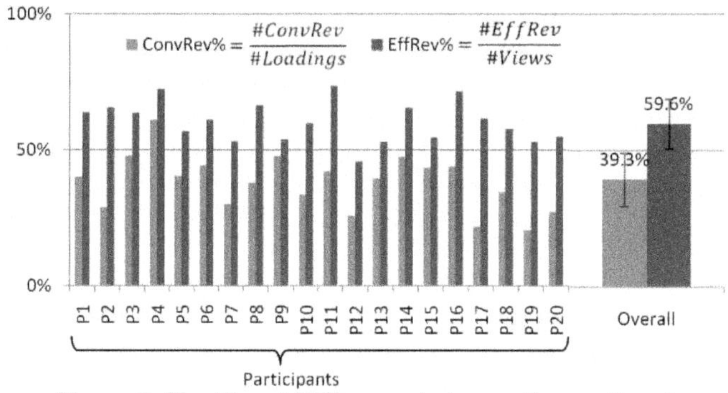

Figure 1. Significant Difference between Conventional (39.3%) and Effective (59.6%) Revisitation Rates

method of using full URL and the HTTP GET parameters to uniquely identify a web page [6].

Using the proposed viewing-based measurement, what is the revisitation rate under the tabbed browsing paradigm? How does it differ from the results using the conventional measurement?

The blue bar on the right end of figure 1 shows the overall conventional revisitation rate (39.3%, or 35,342 out of 89,851 loading events) based on page loadings, which was calculated using Tauscher and Greenberg's method [7]. The red bar besides it shows the overall effective revisitation rate (59.6%, or 75,912 out of 127,344 page viewing events) using our proposed definition and measurement. The bars on the left of the figure show revisitation rates using the two measurements for each participant.

Our calculation shows that the conventional measurement largely underestimates the amount of revisitation activities under tabbed browsing ($T_{19} = 11.25$, $p < .001$). If we break down the effective revisitation of all 75,912 events into the two types of revisitation (loading-based revisitation and tab-switching-based revisitation), the former comprises 53.0% (40,221 events) while the latter comprises 47.0% (35,691 events). This shows that tab-switching-based revisitation, which was neglected in previous studies, is about as frequent as loading-based revisitation. It reinforces the point raised by Dubroy and Balakrishnan [3] that tab switching should be considered an important means of revisitation.

How significant are the over-count and under-count errors when the conventional method is used to measure revisitations in tabbed browsers?

There are a total of 4,135 over-count error events (11.7% of all conventional revisits). Of these, 3.9% (160) are type 1, 55.2% (2,283) are type 2 and 40.9% (1,692) are type 3.

There are 38,639 under-count error events (50.9% of all effective revisits), in which revisitation activities were done with tab switching alone.

These results show that conventional measurement suffers from both over-count and under-count errors. The under-count errors are much more than over-count errors, giving rise to the overall effect that conventional measurement largely underestimates revisitations in tabbed browsing.

Has the frequency of users' repeated page visits changed in recent years?

We found four previous studies that explicitly addressed revisitation rate and present them chronologically alongside our study (table 1). The first three studies used non-tabbed browsers, while the last two studies used tabbed browsers. The study of Dubroy and Balakrishnan [3] is not included since it did not explicitly report revisitation rate.

Before the introduction of tabbed browsers, effective web revisitation activities were accurately measured as the loading of previously loaded pages. This was done in studies 1, 2 and 3, all of which have revisitation rates of above 50%.

Did the introduction of tabbed browsers change this rate? Study 4 suggested that there is a change: revisitation rate dropped to 43.7%. However, this may be misleading since the conventional measurement for revisitation was used in tabbed browsing (at least 15 out of the 25 participants in study 4 used tabbed browsers).

Our study shows that the effective revisitation rate has not dropped that dramatically (59.6% is lower than study 3's 81%, but is comparable with study 1's 61% and study 2's 58%) even with the introduction of tabbed browsers. Due to lack of tab switching data from the previous studies, we are unable to calculate effective revisitation rates for study 4.

	Catledge & Pitkow [2]	Tauscher & Greenberg [7]	McKenzie & Cockburn [5]	Obendorf & Weinreich [6,8]	Our study
Date of Study	1994	1995-1996	1999-2000	2004-2005	2010
# Participants	107	23	17	25	20
Duration	21 days	42 days	119 days	52-195 days	31 days
Revisitation Rate	61%	58%	81%	43.7%	59.6% (Effective), 39.3% (Conventional)
Browsers Used	XMosaic	XMosaic 2.6	Netscape Navigator	Partly (15/25) *Firefox 1.0*	*Firefox 3.0*
# Page Loadings	31,134	19,000	83,411	137,272	80,811 (113,243 page views)
# Distinct URLs			17,242	65,643	49,450

Table 1. Comparisons between previous studies and our study (tabbed browsers are italicized)

While our study results suggest possible reasons behind the noticeable difference between study 4 and previous studies, comparison across studies should be cautiously interpreted to consider the differences in methods and other possible limitations. The purpose of this comparison is not to judge the previous studies, but to place our study in context and to highlight any significant difference to invite further investigations.

DISCUSSION, LIMITATION AND FUTURE DIRECTIONS

While our proposed method of measuring web page revisitation shed new light into research on the topic, it is, strictly speaking, still an approximation of actual revisitation behavior. It also has issues in overcounting and undercounting page revisits.

Our definition of revisitation is "the repetition of obtaining previously seen information," but what accounts for "obtaining information" needs further clarification. Tab switching is one way of obtaining information from a web page contained in a tab. However, users may switch through tabs to find a previously opened tab or click on a tab by accident. In these cases, the tab switchings result in transient page views. Users do not actually intend to obtain information from these pages.

These tab switchings should be excluded from the calculation, and one way to do so is by excluding page views that are shorter than a certain time threshold. Table 2 tabulates number of page views, number of page revisits, and effective revisitation rates under different cut-off time thresholds.

As shown in table 2, although transient tab switchings increase the total number of page revisits, it is unlikely to significantly affect the overall revisitation rate. While applying a time threshold can help to remove some of the transient pages, determining the exact time threshold is difficult due to different scenarios and individual differences. Future research may use other methods (e.g., eye tracking) to more accurately tell whether the user is viewing the page to obtain information.

Undercounting may be caused by using multiple browser windows and revisiting non-visual contents of a page, e.g., radio stations. While these two cases happened rarely in our log study, future research in web page revisitation should take them into consideration.

Despite these limitations, we believe our method can be used as one of the important measures for future studies in web page revisitation. While it will be difficult to completely remove all issues in over and undercounting in any method of measurement, future researchers may consider reporting a percentage range, in which the actual revisitation rate resides with high probability (e.g., >95%).

Threshold (seconds)	#page revisits	#page views	EffRev rate
0	75912	127344	59.6%
1	66359	113242	58.6%
2	56653	97516	58.1%
3	46625	81322	57.3%
4	40638	71269	57.0%

Table 2. Effective revisitation rates with varying cut-off threshold in seconds

In the future, our method of measurement could be further integrated into large scale analyses of web usage [1] or existing user behaviors such as back tracking [8], to deepen our understanding of tabbed browsing and to improve user experience.

CONCLUSION

We propose a goal-oriented definition and measurement for revisitation under the tabbed browsing paradigm. Our client-side log study shows that the conventional measurement for revisitation largely underestimates revisitation activities in tabbed browsing. Although the overall revisitation rate has remained relatively steady over the years, tabbed browsing has introduced new behaviors. In the future, these need to be taken into account in studies of web page revisitation and when optimizing the browsing and revisitation experience in tabbed browsers.

ACKNOWLEDGEMENT

We thank Xiaojuan Ma and anonymous reviewers for their constructive comments and feedback. We thank members of the NUS-HCI Lab for their support. This research is supported by National University of Singapore Academic Research Fund R-252-000-375-133.

REFERENCES

1. Adar E, Teevan J, and Dumais ST. Large scale analysis of web revisitation patterns. In *Proc. CHI 2008*, ACM Press (2008), 1197-1206.
2. Catledge, L.D., Pitkow, J.E. Characterizing browsing strategies in the World-Wide Web. In *Proc. WWW 1995*, ACM Press (1995), 1065-1073.
3. Dubroy, P. and Balakrishnan, R. A study of tabbed browsing among Mozilla firefox users. In *Proc. CHI 2010*, ACM Press (2010), 673-682.
4. Huang, J. and White, R. Parallel Browsing Behavior on the Web. In *Proc. HT 2010*, ACM Press (2010).
5. McKenzie, B. and Cockburn, A. An empirical analysis of web page revisitation. *System Sciences, 2001. Proceedings of the 34th Annual Hawaii International Conference on*
6. Obendorf, H., Weinreich, H., et al. Web page revisitation revisited: implications of a long-term click-stream study of browser usage. In *Proc. CHI 2007*, ACM Press (2007), 597-606.
7. Tauscher, L. and Greenberg, S. Revisitation patterns in World Wide Web navigation. In *Proc. CHI 1997*, ACM Press (1997), 399-406.
8. Weinreich H, et al. Not quite the average: An empirical study of Web use. *ACM Trans. Web* 2008; 2(1): 1-31.

Evaluating Longitudinal Projects Combining Technology with Temporal Arts

Celine Latulipe
HCILab
University of North Carolina at Charlotte
Charlotte, NC, USA
clatulip@uncc.edu

Erin A. Carroll
HCILab
University of North Carolina at Charlotte
Charlotte, NC, USA
e.carroll@uncc.eu

Danielle Lottridge
Department of Communication
Stanford University
Stanford, CA, USA
lottridg@stanford.edu

ABSTRACT
The integration of interactive technology with temporal art such as dance is an exciting, emerging area. The design space for such collaborations is immense, with variations in sensors, visualizations, and how these interact with dancers and choreography. This paper presents the evaluation methodology and results of Dance.Draw, a longitudinal project spanning two years and three productions, which aimed to develop a deep, interdisciplinary understanding of this space. Given that this is pioneering work, there is little guidance on how to evaluate such collaborations. We describe the significant confounds in doing evaluation in this area, and we present our evolving mixed-methods approach, which includes two unique methods to address the multiple stakeholders in a holistic manner: dancer focus groups and repeated presentations. Our approach has generated insights, such as differing perspectives of audience members and the responses of dancers to technological variables. We conclude by discussing the challenges and successes of our evaluation approach.

Author Keywords
interactive dance, temporal arts, performing arts, evaluation, creativity, audience evaluation

ACM Classification Keywords
H.5.2 Information Interfaces and Presentation: User Interfaces: Evaluation/Methodology

General Terms
Human Factors

INTRODUCTION
When technologists and artists embark on large, long-term projects, the goals and outcomes span both disciplines, but it is difficult to evaluate whether the whole is greater than the sum of the parts. Part of the difficulty lies in the very different types of goals. Technologists want to innovate and measure and tend to be focused on utility. Artists are interested in expertise, pleasure, criticism and the idea that "art is set aside from ordinary life and made a dramatic focus of experience" [18]. It is possible to separately measure the outcomes using standard approaches from each discipline, but that is unlikely to measure the value of any outcomes that are interdisciplinary in nature. It is likely, given the artistic nature of choreography, that there is no single truth to be found in evaluation, but rather, insights to be gained.

This paper describes the two year process and evolution of merging technological and artistic considerations through Dance.Draw [12], which is a pioneering interactive dance project in this space. While our experience is in dance, we firmly believe that many of the evaluation methods and results presented here would generalize to other temporal arts such as theater and music. The ongoing Dance.Draw project has created three dance productions in which the motions of dancers were used as input to real-time projected visualizations. The core project challenges are three-fold: technological, methodological, and artistic. In this paper, we pay special attention to the methodological and artistic questions:

1. What are the challenges in evaluating long-term art-technology collaborations?
2. What themes emerge from the project that might be relevant to other performance-technology collaborations?
3. What methods work for evaluating this type of project?

Over the course of the project we employed a mixed-methods approach that included evaluation of over 500 audience questionnaires, audience and dancer focus groups, and experiential reflection by the production stake-holders. Our mixed-methods approach, in which we focus on evaluating success or failure from various stakeholder perspectives, stems from our user-centered design background, influenced by the specific project goals. This practice-based research contributes to the HCI field in a number of different ways. First, we demonstrate an example of long-term academic collaboration between technology and temporal arts. Second, we identify and describe the challenges and confounds in doing long-term evaluation in technology-performance projects. Third, we present evaluation results that are audience- and performer-focused, thus demonstrating a holistic methodology for studying the role of technology in something as complex and situated as dance. Fourth, we present a mixed-methods approach for evaluating the interdisciplinary success of longitudinal technology and temporal arts projects. Finally, we reflect on our evaluation to identify the successes and shortcomings, in the expectation that this will be useful for other researchers evaluating longitudinal, art-technology projects.

In this paper, we first present *Related Work*, and then describe the dance-technology *Productions* that were the subject of our longitudinal evaluations. We detail the *Evaluation Goals and Challenges* and present our *Methodology*. In *Results* we outline what we learned and how those design insights can generalize. We end with a *Discussion* of our evaluation process and results to illustrate the successes and shortcomings of the approach.

RELATED WORK

Choreographers have been integrating multimedia into their work, since the early 1960s, with Merce Cunningham leading the dance technology revolution [9]. Today there is an entire online community devoted to interactive dance [19]. Kent deSpain details a number of important dance productions that have embraced technology and explores the idea of virtual dance [8]. Technology has been integrated in many forms, shifting from productions that use digitally recorded media [17] to productions that allow dancers to control media elements [7, 13]. Mark Coniglio (founder of Troika Ranch) offered guidelines for interactive dance: performers should have room to improvise, and take advantage of interactivity; and the audience should have some understanding of the interaction. In our work, we are interested in the experiences of performers, choreographers and audience members.

In addition to dance companies, researchers are also studying interactive performances [1, 12, 14]. Lindström et al. addressed the critical issue of evaluating interactive systems for performances (using surveys), pointing out that this topic has not received enough attention [13]. While little research exists on evaluating interactive performances (this is part of the evaluation poverty described by Cockton [6]), there is literature that may be borrowed from related interactive aesthetic explorations. For example, Höök et al. consider it inappropriate to summarize the results and generalize the results beyond individuals for studies involving art [10]. This may apply to presenting responses to dance, but it is at odds with the expectations for publishing in computing. Boehner discusses the evaluation tension surrounding the conceptualization of emotional reactions into discrete categories, which may not be adequate in affective interactions [4]. She suggests instead that emotion be conceptualized as co-constructed by the participant and the evaluator.

Implicit Performance Evaluation

It is a social norm for audience members to clap at the end of a performance to express their appreciation for the effort put forth. Barkhuus and Jorgensen used applause as a method for exploring audience response by implementing a 'cheering meter' [3]. Unfortunately, clapping norms are so entrenched in the behaviors of audience members that people may clap even if they did not like the performance [15]. This makes it difficult for performers to determine what impact they are having on an audience. From an information science perspective, the information is mostly unidirectional. Performers speak of 'feeding off the energy of the audience' – while this is undoubtedly true, it is clearly a noisy signal.

Performance Surveys

One approach to effective feedback from an audience is to use surveys. Surveys can be difficult to deploy in temporal arts, as many audience members may think they are marketing-related. Lindstrom et al. deployed surveys to audience members, but it is difficult to determine the success of their survey administration, since their sample size was only 20 [13]. Stevens et al. deployed a psychometric instrument, the Audience Response Tool (ART) to record responses to a live performance [21]. A complicating factor in post-performance questionnaires is the 'peak-end' effect [11], which shows that a measure of emotional experience taken at the end of a performance or experience is strongly influenced by the peak emotion during the experience and the emotion at the tail end of the experience. This does not mean that surveys should not be used, but that their results should be analyzed with this confound in mind.

Explicit Temporal Evaluation

In the marketing and television world, numerous systems have evolved to evaluate reactions to temporal media [20], with an approach based mainly on a stimulus-response model. There is also some work in the evaluation of performances using explicit audience response reporting devices or biometric measures, such as the work of Stevens et al. who gave audience members PDAs to input their responses throughout a performance [22]. Other researchers have used biometric devices to measure participant response to temporal media and games [2, 16]. These examples point to the potential for using explicit self-report or biometric audience readings during a performance to measure reaction, which would get around the 'peak-end' effect mentioned earlier. However, there are issues to contend with in this type of evaluation, specifically the danger of the feedback device being a distraction from the performance.

The related work we have discussed shows a wide range of possible approaches to evaluation, but many are focused solely on measuring audience engagement, while our focus is more broad and encompasses evaluating the success of the project from the perspective of choreographers, dancers, technologists and audience members. In addition, few of these methods take a longitudinal approach to studying interdisciplinary work. In this paper, we address this gap.

PRODUCTIONS

To describe our experiences and the challenges of evaluating interdisciplinary work between technology and dance, we must first describe the dance productions we evaluated.

"A Mischief of *mus Musculus*" (P1 in Table 1, Figure 1) was an abstract, pure movement dance augmented with dynamic

	Production	# of dancers	Dance Genre & Choreographic Origins	Style of Visuals	Total Audience	Evaluation Methods Deployed	Dance Length	Technology Used
P1	Mus Musculus	6	Modern; Pure Movement Original Chor.	Abstract	800	Audience Surveys, Audience Focus Groups, Team Debriefings	12 min	Wireless gyro mice
P2	Whispering to Ophiuchus	7	Modern; Explicit Narrative Original Chor.	Figural & Abstract	1000	Audience Surveys, Audience & Dancer Focus Groups, Team Debriefings	22 min	logged data from acceler-ometers
P3	Bodies/ Antibodies	4	Modern with Theme Re-staged Chor.	Themed Contextual	150	Audience Surveys, Dancer Focus Groups, Informal Aud. Feedback, Team Debriefings	11 min	Wireless gyro mice & acceler-ometers

Table 1. Summary of formal Dance.Draw Productions.

Figure 1. Photo of "A Mischief of *mus Musculus*", Fall 2008.

geometrical shapes whose movement on screen was linked to the dancers' motions. The dancers carried gyroscopic wireless mice in their hands which transmitted motion signals which were used as visualization input.

Figure 2. Photo of "Whispering to Ophiuchus", Fall 2009.

"Whispering to Ophiuchus" (P2 in Table 1, Figure 2) was a narrative modern dance with a complex set of scenic properties, similar to a play. The choreography was developed in conjunction with the narrative storyline and visual production. The dancers wore wired 3D accelerometers during dance rehearsals. This logged motion data was used during performances and fed into the projected visuals, which were a mix of pre-programmed and interactive components.

Figure 3. Photo of "Bodies/Antibodies", Spring 2010.

The most recent production, "Bodies/Antibodies" (P3 in Table 1, Figure 3), was a student-choreographed modern dance piece which was re-staged, extended, and augmented with interactive visuals. The dancers wore both gyroscopic wireless mice (embedded in the torso area of the costume) and wireless 3D accelerometers (embedded in the forearm of the costume). The dancer-controlled, real-time projected visuals reflected the biological nature of the dance theme.

EVALUATION GOALS AND CHALLENGES

Evaluating a longitudinal project that crosses two very different disciplines requires sensitivity and multiple perspectives. In this section we detail the challenges in evaluating projects in which technology is embedded into an arts performance. While our experience involves dance, we believe similar challenges exist in other types of technology-augmented performance, such as music and theater.

Domain Goal Differences

Due to domain differences between computing and dance, it is challenging to decide which goals are important to each domain individually and which goals are important to further the research and practice of interactive dance. The technologists involved in the project were interested in technological advancements, developing novel interaction techniques, and understanding the impact on audience members. These were the technology 'research questions.' Participants in the project have engaged in many meta-discussions about the 'research questions' of dance. The dance specialists did not naturally think in terms of 'research questions,' but they engaged in similar processes of discovery. Choreographers often have the goal of communicating with the audience on an intellectual and/or emotional level through visual kinetics while trying to extend the boundaries of what dance looks or feels like. This is the corollary to the computer scientist's 'research questions.' For choreographers, seeing how technology can enhance dance – how the two can cooperate to form a gestalt – is also a challenging field of inquiry. They are also interested in evoking audience reactions – they want to engage the attention of the audience. If the technology is getting in the way of this goal, rather than supporting it, that would be considered a failure. The one clear, overriding goal that bridged the disciplines was the desire to understand how to balance dance and technology. It is easy to create interactive dance in which the technology overpowers the dancers or does not fit the choreography. Thus, from an aesthetic standpoint, the aim of the Dance.Draw project is to discover ways to support the creation of interactive dance in which:

- The technology is essential to the dance.
- The technology does not overpower the dancers.
- The technology and the dance are experienced as a cohesive whole.

To discover ways to support this type of interactive dance, we also need to understand how to measure these aspects of a production. Finding ways to evaluate this is a challenging part of our research, and the topic of this paper.

Dimensional Confounds

Designing in the area of interactive dance (or any other interactive temporal art) is exciting because there are so many possible dimensions to explore. However, this wide open set of possibilities also makes it difficult to ground the research and explore methodically. Consider the following possible dimensions in interactive dance design:

- The technology used for tracking dancers (computer vision, accelerometers, motion capture, floor sensors, etc.)
- The number of dancers being tracked
- The use of the captured motion (for visualizations, for sound, for lighting, for other aspects?)
- The design of the output (what type of visualizations or sound? - this is a huge design space itself)
- The development of original choreography, versus the adaptation of existing choreography
- The choreographic genre (contemporary ballet, modern, jazz, traditional dance, etc.)
- The length of the dance
- The style of music or audio accompaniment

The above list is not exhaustive, but it illustrates the immensity of the design space in creating an interactive dance piece. While many other fields also have rich design spaces, it is typically the case that one can build a variety of artifacts to test out the promising coordinates within a particular design space. Within temporal arts, the creation and staging of an interactive production is an expensive and complex undertaking, often spanning months or even years, and that production generates *one* sample pinpoint in this design space.

Contextual Confounds

Temporal arts of any kind are variable, even performances of the same production. Demographics of audience members in attendance and the timing of the performance (matinée vs. evening) may change. Also, an audience member's experience of a performance may be affected by the reaction of other audience members. The level of attendance can also impact an audience member's perception of an arts performance. Some repeat audience members become familiar with the project and bring differing levels of prior knowledge about the work to the performances.

There are some evaluation challenges that are specific to interactive dance. One issue is deciding what information to share with audience members about the technology prior to the performance, since this will have a priming effect on the audience and can impact the evaluation results. This desire to not prime the audience may be in conflict with the desire of the choreographer to help the audience have a more nuanced understanding and appreciation for the work. A follow-up issue is determining how much audience members understood of any information that is given to them in a concert program, or whether they read it at all. Related to this is the issue of vocabulary – in a newer field such as interactive dance, audiences may not be familiar with the academic vocabulary that is used to discuss and describe the work.

Many dance pieces are performed as part of a dance concert, in which an audience sees a number of different dances (typically between four and ten different pieces, often with an intermission in the middle). This setting makes it tricky when only one performance in the dance concert is to be evaluated.

Subjective Confounds

Evaluation from audience members can be further confounded by the subjective aesthetic judgments of audience members, which makes it difficult to tease out the effects of technological interventions, or to determine whether the technology was combined effectively with the choreography. It is easy to imagine designing evaluation tools (survey or focus group questions) that ask whether audience members 'liked' a specific piece. The difficulty with this type of question is the myriad factors that can influence a person's answer. An audience member may 'like' a particular performance because they know one of the dancers personally or because the music reminds them of something or because the costumes are cute. These are all valid reasons to like a performance, but they may have nothing to do with the interdisciplinary nature of the piece. In many cases, a person may like or dislike a piece, but not know why they feel that way. Similarly, a person may dislike a performance because they prefer a different dance genre, or because the person beside them said something negative about the piece. Clearly, reporting on subjective valence is tricky.

The confounds that we have outlined show that conducting evaluation of interactive dance is challenging. However, these challenges also provide an opportunity. Since there are no established approaches for doing longitudinal evaluation in a technology and temporal arts context, we have the ability to try many different techniques and explore what is most effective in helping us to address our research questions.

METHODOLOGY

Given the challenges described above, we employed an evolving mixed-methods approach to evaluation in order to understand the relative success of the productions from the multiple perspectives of performers, choreographers, technologists and audience members. We consider our approach to be unique for several reasons. First, audience members of temporal arts are typically not involved in evaluating or critiquing performances in a formal way. Second, the dancers in the research project also became research participants at the end of each dance production, by participating in focus groups. This enabled us to gain a better understanding of the full impact that this interdisciplinary project has had on them. Finally, we applied the research findings from each dance production – from team members, the audience, and the dancers – to iteratively develop our project from one dance production to the next.

Audience Feedback

Temporal arts audiences typically give feedback to performers by applauding the performance and by talking to the performers directly in post-performance gatherings. This type of feedback is noisy; there is social pressure to applaud and when speaking face-to-face with a performer, an audience member is likely to be polite and complimentary, regardless of how they felt about the performance. These types of feedback are also discrete - the entire performance is boiled down into just one or a few statements. A deeper conversation about the piece may occur between an audience member and a performer or choreographer, but this is much less frequent. Our goal is to obtain the type of deeper feedback that one might get in such conversations from a larger sample of audience members, by conducting surveys and focus groups as well as through informal feedback channels.

Surveys

We have deployed surveys in all three of the dance productions. In P1 and P2 (where the Dance.Draw productions were one of a number of dance pieces presented), our surveys were inserted inside the programs that were distributed to audience members, who were informed of the survey and told which dance the survey was about. In both cases, the Dance.Draw piece was the first performance in the program, which we believe made it easy for the audience members to complete. P3 was a single dance presentation where the surveys were handed out directly.

Audience Focus Groups and Informal Feedback

While surveys are useful for gathering feedback from large numbers of people to quantify reactions, focus groups are equally important to gather more qualitative and intricate feedback. Therefore, we hosted several formal conversations with audience members in a focus group setting. In P1 and P2, we held formal audience focus groups. These were held on campus, invitational, and were held separately from the formal dance concerts so that the only dance shown was the Dance.Draw piece. In the case of P1, the dancers performed the piece in full costume but in a performance studio, rather than on the production stage with theater lighting. In the P2 focus group a video of the dance was shown because of the intense amount of scenic elements involved in the production. In both cases, approximately half of the focus group members had seen the piece performed formally in the concert and half had not. We also gathered informal feedback from audiences after all performances, by making ourselves available in the theater lobby after each production.

Production Team Reflection

After each production, we held a debriefing session which was attended by the choreographer(s), the technologists, and any students involved in the research. The purpose of these meetings was two-fold: to find out how to improve the interdisciplinary process for future productions and also to assess the success in meeting project goals.

Dancer Focus Groups

Another unique aspect of the project evaluation is the use of performer focus groups. While the use of focus groups in HCI is not new, it is unusual to perform focus groups with the performers in an artistic piece. In P1, the dancers were part of the production team debriefing, but it was felt that they might not be honest in talking about their experiences, as the choreographer and technology members were present. Thus, starting with P2, we held separate formal Dancer Focus Groups moderated by an external expert.

Repeated Performance

During the most recent production, we employed a unique presentation format on campus. We began the presentation by having the dancers perform the piece. We then immediately asked audience members to fill out a survey, without telling them anything about the piece or the technology. There was no program to read, so the audience members were not primed in any way. Once the surveys were filled out, we gave a presentation about the project, explained the technology and project goals and answered questions. Finally, we had the dancers perform the piece a second time. We then held an audience discussion to find out how people responded to the dance the second time, knowing about the technology used and the project goals.

RESULTS

The findings from the surveys, focus groups, and reflection are clustered into four main topics: production success in terms of audience engagement; perceptions of balance between dancers and visualizations; the impact of technology awareness; and differences based on audience background. Table 2 shows demographics across all three productions.

Audience Enjoyment versus Engagement

From the beginning of this project, one of the goals was to understand the responses of audience members as a way of

Audience Background	P1	P2	P3
Dance Specialist	23.2%	21%	27.2%
Visual Arts Specialists	8%	11.8%	9.8%
Performing Arts Specialists		4.2%	4.3%
General Audience	67.4%	62.2%	57.6%
N	224	218	92
Audience Size	800	1000	97
Response Rate	28%	21.8%	94.85%

Table 2. Survey respondents' backgrounds across productions. In P1, visual arts and performing arts specialists were combined.

evaluating the interdisciplinary aspect of the work. However, it is not common practice for choreographers to have their work evaluated by general audience members. This made it challenging to select proper terminology for such surveys. This meant that as we gained experience in surveying audiences some of the terminology we used evolved. In the P1 survey, we asked audience members to rate their interest level and enjoyment of the performance, on a scale from 1 (low interest/enjoyment) to 7 (high interest/enjoyment). The mean performance interest level was 5.27 (SD=1.57) and the mean performance enjoyment was 5.19 (SD=1.69). As we progressed through the project it became clear that asking audience members how much they liked or enjoyed the performance was not useful because of the confounds we discussed earlier. Thus, while the results from the P1 survey suggest the production was well-received, we learned that it would be more valuable to look at engagement and attention. We learned that choreographers are more interested in whether a performance had an impact on the audience – whether it moved or provoked them in some (positive or negative) way. We hoped that by asking about engagement and attention, we would get away from valence issues.

In the P2 survey, we asked the audience to rate how engaging they find multimedia dances and how often P2 held their attention. Results of this survey indicate relatively high engagement (Table 3). Audience members reported that the dance production held their attention the majority of the time (M= 3.25, SD=0.71, scale: 1=No Time At All to 4=Entire Time). There was a significant correlation between the rating of multimedia dances and how much the dance production held respondents' attention (r=0.40, p<0.001).

Engagement Rating for:	P2 Mean (SD)	P3 Mean (SD)
Dance Movements	n/a	8.86 (1.24)
Visualizations	n/a	7.33 (1.88)
Performance Overall	n/a	8.93 (1.16)
Multimedia Dances	6.85 (2.36)	7.97 (1.85)

Table 3. P2 and P3 mean engagement ratings by demographic. (Scale: 1=Not Engaging to 10=Extremely Engaging).

In the most recent performance (P3), we deepened our exploration of audience engagement by asking audience members about their engagement with the dance movements, the visualizations, and the piece overall. Between P2 and P3, we found slightly higher results for P3 respondents' engagement in multimedia dance, but this was to be expected since people specifically came out to see the P3 performance. We also found that people rated the overall performance higher than multimedia dances in general and that people rated the dance movements as more engaging than the visuals (Table 3).

Balance of Technology and Dance Movements

Achieving a balance between technology and dance movements was an interdisciplinary goal in the project. In P1, respondents' average rating on the balance of dance and visualizations was 4.68 (SD=1.27) on a scale of 1 (Too much focus on dancers) to 7 (Too much focus on visualizations). While the mean indicates that we achieved an almost equal balance, we were concerned that the project goal was too obvious and that many answers centering in the middle may have been a result of the 'good participant' effect.

We continued to explore balance in P2 and P3 through the related concepts of 'distraction' and 'competition for attention.' Given that P2 included both still and moving imagery, we evaluated both of these on the P2 survey and only moving imagery on the P3 survey. We found that all ratings were near-neutral with regards to competing with dance movements (Table 4). These results appear less influenced by good participant effects because there are wide deviations in responses. A t-test found that moving images competed significantly more with dance movements than still images (t_{111}=-6.23, p<0.001). This result makes sense given that human visual perception is designed to focus on movement.

Balance Ratings:	P2 Mean (SD)	P3 Mean (SD)
Still Images	4.42 (1.24)	n/a
Moving Images	5.92 (1.88)	5.37 (2.49)

Table 4. P2 and P3 mean balance ratings for the still and moving visualizations. (Scale: 1=Did Not Compete to 10=Greatly Competed).

We also explored the issue of balance qualitatively in the P2 and P3 dancer focus groups. Note that two of the P2 dancers were also in P3, which enabled them to comment on changes over the different productions. From the dancers' perspective, there were similarities and differences between the two productions. The dancers felt that in both productions, the visuals helped to set the mood for the dance. In P2, the dancers revealed that they experienced an implicit or underlying expectation that they would be competing with the visuals for attention. In P3 the dancers felt their dancing was complemented by the visuals. One of the dancers from P3 commented, "I didn't feel like we were competing... like the technology was competing with the dancers. Whereas, it could have seemed like that before." Informal responses from audience members also explored the balance issue. One audience member in P3 commented that, "My attention was divided between the visuals and the dancers, but I liked that. It challenged me and made it more interesting. I could decide what to pay attention to at any given time."

The dancers commented on the aesthetics of the visuals: they felt that there was an improvement in the visual aesthetic from P2 to P3. In P3, the visuals were organic and had gradual rather than quick movements. They were also in neutral tones and often filled the entire screen. The dancers also commented that the P3 visuals tended to be lower on screen, behind the dancers, instead of above them as in P2. They felt that this resulted in increased visual integration.

Awareness and Impact of Technology

The technology in P1 was choreographed to be 'obvious' to the audience. The connection between the visuals and movement was underlined by the dancers' large, pronounced movements to pick up the gyroscopic mice, which caused the visualizations to appear. In the P1 survey, we asked the audience about their awareness of the technology. The program for the dance production concert explained that the dancers were controlling movement of visualizations with mice, so we asked audience members whether they read the program explanation to inform their awareness. In addition, we specifically asked if they were aware of dancers holding computer mice and if they were aware that mice controlled the movements of the projected visualizations.

Read Program?	% (N)	Awareness of mice % (N)	Awareness of visaul control % (N)
Yes	82% (184)	92.9% (171)	75.4% (138)
No	18% (40)	83.87% (33)	50% (20)

Table 5. P2 results on awareness of the technology.

A majority of the respondents reported that they read the program explanation (Table 5). Of those that read the explanation, most were aware of the mice and that the mice controlled movement of the visualizations. For those that did not read the title explanation, most were aware of the dancers holding the mice but only half were aware that the mice were controlling visualizations. Over these two groups, there were 20 respondents that did not notice the mice at all, and 76 respondents (or 34% of the total) who did not understand that the dancers were interactively controlling the visualizations. This result was unexpected since the choreography was designed to make the connection obvious.

	P2	P3
Trying to figure out tech % (N)	39.5% (47)	65.17% (63)
Enjoyed figuring out tech % (N)	74.4% (36)	87.9% (55)

Table 6. Portion of respondants in P1 and P2 trying to figure out the technology, and of those, portion who enjoyed that process.

In the focus group for P1, participants reported that they tried to figure out how the sensor technology was working. We found this behavior noteworthy, and added this question to the P2 and P3 surveys, as well as asking audience members whether or not they enjoyed that challenge (Table 6). While less than half of P2 respondents reported that they were trying to figure out how the technology worked, these respondents mostly enjoyed that challenge. P3 respondents were slightly more curious about how the technology worked and a higher percentage reported enjoying the challenge of trying to figure it out. This was not surprising because P3 was held as a feature event and likely attracted people interested in interactive dance, giving us a fully self-selected audience.

Figure Out Tech?	Competition of Still Images With Dancers	Competition of Moving Images With Dancers	Enjoyment Multimedia Dances
Trying	5.35 (3.06)	6.58 (2.6)	8.13 (1.4)
Not Trying	3.82 (2.68)	5.53 (2.83)	5.08 (2.14)
Stat. Sig.	$t_{111} = 2.81$ p = 0.01	$t_{111} = 1.99$ p = 0.05	$t_{40} = 5.23$ p < 0.001

Table 7. P2 ratings on still and moving visual competition with dancers, and how much they enjoy multimedia dances, grouped by whether the respondents were trying to figure out the technology.

There were interesting interactions with other measures, depending on whether the audience members self-identified as trying to figure out the technology. In P2, those who attempted to figure out the technology found still and moving images competed more for their attention than people not trying to figure it out (Table 7). In P3, we found that those that enjoyed figuring out the technology were more engaged in the dance movements than those who didn't ($M_F = 8.96, SD = .95$ vs. $M_{NotF} = 7.71, SD = 2.98$, $t_{55} = 2.32, p = 0.02$). These results suggest people who are very focused on technology will perceive dances differently than those who are not.

The topic of control of the devices was discussed in the dancer focus groups. Dancers reported that they expected more control from the tracking devices; in fact, they expected precise control of projected visuals (i.e. direct coupling). This result is understandable given the popularity of Wiimotes and other devices which can provide a higher level of control. However, given the complexity and varying orientation of the dancers, direct coupling was not possible in the performances. The dancers in P3 were more accepting of the loose coupling; perhaps because it was emphasized to the dancers during the production process. The gradual movement of screen visuals moderated dancers' expectations of direct coupling. Because the loose coupling was emphasized, dancers no longer felt manipulated by the visuals.

Audience Background Differences

We investigated whether there were differences in audience reactions to the performances based on the audience members' background. It is common for dance performances to attract dance specialists, art specialists, and general audience members. Therefore, in each survey, audience members classified their background training (Table 2).

In P1, we found significant differences for interest level in the dance ($F_{(2,215)} = 4.59, p = 0.01$) and enjoyment level of the dance ($F_{(2,215)} = 5.04, p = 0.01$) across the different types of audience members (Table 8). Post-hoc Tukey HSD revealed that dance specialists differed significantly from visual/performing arts specialists ($p = 0.02$) and general audience members ($p = 0.04$) for interest level in the dance. For enjoyment level, post-hoc tests only revealed a significant

Classification	Interest Level	Enjoyment
Dance Specialists	4.76 (2.01)	4.57 (2.03)
Visual/Performing Arts Specialists	5.89 (1.49)	5.61 (1.79)
General Audience	5.38 (1.35)	5.37 (1.49)

Table 8. P1 mean ratings (SD) grouped by audience background. Scale: 1 (Low) to 10 (High).

Background	Interest in Multimedia Dance	Engagement with P2
Dance	6.08 (2.80)	3.22 (0.69)
Visual Arts	6.75 (2.30)	3.17 (0.81)
Performing Arts	4.4 (3.29)	2.50 (0.58)
General Audience	7.32 (1.96)	3.23 (0.69)

Table 9. P2 respondents' mean rating (SD) of how engaging they find multimedia dances (from 1-10) and P2 engagement ratings (from 1-4).

difference between dance specialists and general audience members ($p = 0.01$). Overall, these results were not surprising, as it is expected that dance specialists would be more critical of dance performances in general.

In P2, general audience members rated their interest in multimedia dances higher than the other groups (Table 9). We observed significant differences in how often the dance held different groups' attention. Finally, there was a significant interaction between general interest in multimedia dance and attention paid to P2 ($F_{(3,107)} = 3.90, p = 0.01$). However, upon Tukey HSD pairwise testing, the only significant difference between these groups was between general audience members and performing arts specialists ($p = 0.03$). There were no significant differences based on audience background for P3. It is possible that the self-selecting nature of the P3 audience also implies an audience with more homogeneous perspectives and reactions to interactive dance.

Persistent Themes

Divided attention between projected visuals and dancers was a persistent topic across survey questions, audience focus groups, dancer focus groups and also in production debriefings. It was a design challenge to harmonize the separate elements, and the project evolved in its approach. In P1, there was a great deal of dynamic geometric activity in the projected visuals, where the movement of shapes related abstractly to dancers movements. P2 explored visuals that told a mythical story, where at times, each shape corresponded to each dancer. While the narrative was appreciated, we found more competition for attention in this piece, especially for the moving images. P3 was designed so that the visuals would be organic, with gradual movements and neutral tones to decrease competition between dancers and visuals.

We discovered that audiences have high expectations regarding the coupling of visuals and dancers. The sensing technology used thus far in the project has enabled motion detection, but not spatial positioning, thus there is no proximity coupling between a dancer and the visuals being controlled. Audience members referred to this lack of direct coupling in focus groups and in survey comments, and many did not understand the connection between visuals and dancers. From the audience perspective, trying to figure out the technology led to some unexpected behaviors: they found the visuals competed for their attention, but also reported more enjoyment. This suggests that cognitive and visual challenges may lead to increased audience engagement in dance.

From the dancer perspective, dancers were told that shapes would visually respond to their movement, which led them to exaggerate their movement in an attempt to control the shapes. In P3, loose coupling was emphasized to dancers and the gradual movement of screen visuals moderated dancer expectations of direct coupling. Thus, dancers no longer felt manipulated by visual outcomes.

Finally, we learned that disciplinary background impacted interaction with project artifacts, which became boundary objects [5]. In response to dancer requests for more communication and to see the visuals earlier in the production process, opportunities for project communication were emphasized in P2 and P3, and videos of rehearsals were placed online. In P3, dancers felt more included and empowered throughout the process, yet they also lacked awareness of the visuals. The videos were meant for the dancers and production team members to analyze the progress of the piece. However, the dancers used the videos as choreographic cleaning tools and paid little attention to the visuals. This finding is important for others in technology and temporal arts collaborations, as we found that it is necessary to clarify expectations on the use of shared artifacts.

DISCUSSION

The findings discussed in the previous section show that we have been able to learn from our evaluations and we have been making improvements in our productions and our process as a result of what we have learned. However, the saying "hindsight is 20/20" can aptly be applied as there is more that we could have done and things we could have done better. In this section, we outline the successes in our methodological approach and some things that we would do differently. We also relate our findings to the evaluation confounds identified earlier in the paper. We expect that this discussion will be relevant to other research teams that embark on long-term projects that combine temporal arts with technology.

Survey Evolution

Given that the productions change in so many ways, it is important to be willing to ask new questions in each new survey or to remove or reword questions that are not helping to answer research questions. In other words, treating the productions as controlled lab experiments in which the questions cannot change would not be useful. If we had kept the questions from the first survey throughout all three productions, we would have learned much less. As discussed earlier in the paper, there are many dimensional confounds in this type of project and there is no way treat each dance production as a controlled laboratory experiment. Instead of trying to determine the impact of any specific design dimension (such as a narrative dance versus a dance with abstract movement), we asked questions about broader, cross-cutting issues (such as balance between visualizations and dancers). We were able to address some of the contextual confounds, such as audience priming and demographic factors, by directly asking questions about them in the audience surveys.

We made a number of methodological changes to streamline inquiry into our research topics. In measuring audience engagement, we moved from evaluating enjoyment to engagement. This enabled us to effectively address the subjective confounds inherent in artistic evaluations. Above average ratings support our design choices and overall cohesion between the dance movements and visualizations. We relate this success to careful consideration of aesthetic balance between the technological and artistic aspects. Investigation into the issue of balance led to another methodological insight. Instead of directly asking for ratings on balance, we reversed the question to ask for the degree of competition. This led to what we perceive as more honest responses, as the standard deviation in responses was greater.

Audience Familiarity

Various members in the local community have seen multiple Dance.Draw performances. While some repeat audience members self-identify in audience focus groups or informal discussion by making comparisons between the shows, we have not tried to explicitly collect this information in the audience surveys. Doing so in the future will allow us to separate responses from newcomers versus returning audience members, to elucidate evolving perspectives on our work.

Repeated Performances Presentation

Our approach to presenting P3 as a feature dance presentation in which audience members were able to see the dance twice was very rewarding. This format allowed us to gather survey feedback from the audience immediately after the first performance, before any discussion about the project took place. This feedback was thus unbiased by our subsequent presentation and discussion. We then engaged with the audience, presenting the history and objectives of the project. By showing the dance a second time, the audience members were able to watch the dance and experience it with a deeper understanding. The discussion after this second showing was lively, with many people commenting about various aspects of the dance and asking more questions about the project in general. This group discussion between the project stakeholders and audience members can be considered a co-constructed experience of the dance, following the ideas of Boehner et al [4]. It is also worth noting that audience members made a point of telling us that they enjoyed seeing the dance twice, as they noticed more during the second viewing. This approach holds promise for evaluation in other domains where prototyping is not possible, and evaluation has to take place within a social context.

Performer Focus Groups

In P2, we began the practice of running performer focus groups moderated by a person not involved in creating the productions. Having an external evaluator assigned to the project from the beginning has helped us to achieve continuity and to make continual progress in refining our evaluation approaches. For the purpose of a performer focus group, we wanted honest opinions, not sycophantic responses of student dancers who were worried about their grades or being cast in future productions. Thus, having an external evaluator to moderate these focus groups has been very positive. The information collected in the focus groups helped us to understand the perspective of the performers and their thoughts on the success/failure of the production processes.

While the performer focus groups were helpful in evaluating the project, they were also useful for the dancers. The focus groups provided an important debriefing opportunity for the performers to share their thoughts about what did and did not work in the dance production process. Many of the performers have told us that they felt the focus groups were very worthwhile and some reported that they wished that there was a formal debriefing process like this after every dance they were in, because it gave them a sense of closure and an opportunity to express their thoughts. Given the low cost and ease of running the performer focus groups, it seems that this technique might be usefully deployed across temporal arts.

Technologists in the Audience

In our surveys, we tried to separate out various arts specialists from general audience members. However, we did not ask if the audience member considered themselves a 'technologist.' It would be interesting to see what percentage of the interactive dance audience labels themselves as technologists and whether they respond differently. The technologists in the project have opinions on the work, which are undoubtedly implicit in the writing of this document. However, by separating out technologist audience members, we may be able to more deeply address the domain goal differences that can make this evaluation challenging.

SUMMARY & FUTURE WORK

This papers presents findings from two years of work evaluating a pioneering interdisciplinary temporal arts and technology project. Our mixed-methods approach introduces two unique methods: performer focus groups and repeat performance presentations. Our evaluation has not generated a 'single truth,' but rather a collection of important insights, such as how the design of visuals can mediate dancers' feelings of being manipulated by technology and how production videos placed online became boundary objects through different disciplinary perspectives.

The novel methods were complemented with existing methods: audience surveys, audience focus groups and production team reflection. Over 500 survey responses were collected over the three productions, allowing us to chart how the project evolved over time. These surveys also enabled us to find significant relationships such as differing enjoyment levels based on disciplinary background. Audience members who focused on figuring out the technology found that there was more competition for their attention but also enjoyed the productions more.

Through this approach we have been able to evaluate how well we are progressing towards meeting project goals: attaining aesthetic balance between the art and technology and offering a positive and inclusive experience to dancers involved in the productions. We have learned a tremendous amount about doing this type of evaluation. In this paper we have shared our successes and failures so that others can take advantage of our lessons learned and knowledge gained.

The Dance.Draw project is ongoing and we will address our evaluation shortcomings as the project continues. We plan to add an evaluation with a panel of expert dance judges in a future production. We also plan to explore biometric evaluation techniques for audiences, performers and production team members, for both evaluation and interaction purposes.

ACKNOWLEDGMENTS

This work was funded by NSF CreativeIT (#IIS-0855882). We thank the dancers and choreographers and other collaborators who have participated in Dance.Draw. We also thank HCILab members for their feedback on this paper.

REFERENCES

1. R. Aylward and J. Paradiso. Sensemble: a wireless, compact, multi-user sensor system for interactive dance. In *Proceedings of the 2006 conference on New interfaces for musical expression*, page 139. IRCAMCentre Pompidou, 2006.

2. S. Bardzell, J. Bardzell, and T. Pace. Understanding affective interaction: Emotion, engagement, and internet videos. In *Proc. of 2009 IEEE International Conference on Affective Computing and Intelligent Interactio*, 2009.

3. L. Barkhuus and T. Jorgensen. Engaging the crowd: studies of audience-performer interaction. In *CHI'08 extended abstracts on Human factors in computing systems*, pages 2925–2930. ACM, 2008.

4. K. Boehner, P. Sengers, and S. Warner. Interfaces with the ineffable: Meeting aesthetic experience on its own terms. *ACM Transactions on Computer-Human Interaction (TOCHI)*, 15(3):1–29, 2008.

5. G. C. Bowker and S. L. Star. *Sorting things out: classification and its consequences*. MIT Press, Cambridge, MA, 1999.

6. G. Cockton. Make evaluation poverty history. In *CHI '07: alt.chi digital proceedings: http://www.viktoria.se/altchi/*, 2007.

7. M. Coniglio. The importance of being interactive. *New Visions in Performance. The Impact of New Technologies*, pages 5–12, 2004.

8. K. de Spain. Dance and technology: A pas de deux for post-humans. *Dance Research Journal*, 32(1):2–17, 2000.

9. K. Farley. Digital dance theatre: The marriage of computers, choreography and techno/human reactivity. *Body, Space and Technology*, 3(1):39–46, 2002.

10. K. Hook, P. Sengers, and G. Andersson. Sense and sensibility: evaluation and interactive art. In *Proceeding of ACM CHI 2003*, 2003.

11. D. Kahneman. *Well-being: The foundations of hedonic psychology*, pages 3–25. Russell Sage Foundation, New York, NY, USA, 1999.

12. C. Latulipe, D. Wilson, S. Huskey, M. Word, A. Carroll, E. Carroll, B. Gonzalez, V. Singh, M. Wirth, and D. Lottridge. Exploring the design space in technology-augmented dance. In *CHI EA '10: Proceedings of the 28th of the international conference extended abstracts on Human factors in computing systems*, pages 2995–3000, New York, NY, USA, 2010. ACM.

13. E. Lindström, A. Camurri, A. Friberg, G. Volpe, and M. Rinman. Affect, Attitude and Evaluation of Multisensory Performances. *Journal of New Music Research*, 34(1):69–86, 2005.

14. L. Loke and T. Robertson. Studies of dancers: Moving from experience to interaction design. *International Journal of Design*, 4(2), 2010.

15. G. Lupyan and I. Rifkin. Dynamics of applause: Modeling group phenomena through agent interaction. In *Proceedings of the 25th Annual Meeting of the Cognitive Science Society 2003*, 2003.

16. R. L. Mandryk, M. S. Atkins, and K. M. Inkpen. A continuous and objective evaluation of emotional experience with interactive play environments. In *CHI '06: Proceedings of the SIGCHI conference on Human Factors in computing systems*, pages 1027–1036, New York, NY, USA, 2006. ACM.

17. W. S. Meador, T. J. Rogers, K. O'Neal, E. Kurt, and C. Cunningham. Mixing dance realities: collaborative development of live-motion capture in a performing arts environment. *Comput. Entertain.*, 2(2):12–12, 2004.

18. S. Pinker. *The Blank Slate: The Modern Denial of Human Nature*. Viking Press, New York, NY, 2002.

19. M. B. Solano. dance-tech.net. `http://www.dance-tech.net/`.

20. D. Stayman and D. Aaker. Continuous measurement of self-report of emotional response. *Journal of Psychology and Marketing*, 10(3):199–214, 1993.

21. C. Stevens, R. Glass, E. Schubert, J. Chen, and H. Winskel. Methods for measuring audience reactions. *Proceedings of the inaugeral International Conference on Music Communication Science*, page 155, 2007.

22. C. J. Stevens, E. Schubert, R. H. Morris, M. Frear, J. Chen, S. Healey, C. Schoknecht, and S. Hansen. Cognition and the temporal arts: Investigating audience response to dance using PDAs that record continuous data during live performance. *International Journal of Human-Computer Studies*, 67(9):800 – 813, 2009.

Love, Hate, Arousal and Engagement: Exploring Audience Responses to Performing Arts

Celine Latulipe
HCILab
University of North Carolina at Charlotte
Charlotte, NC, USA
clatulip@uncc.edu

Erin A. Carroll
HCILab
University of North Carolina at Charlotte
Charlotte, NC, USA
e.carroll@uncc.edu

Danielle Lottridge
Department of Communication
Stanford University
Stanford, CA, USA
lottridg@stanford.edu

ABSTRACT
Understanding audience responses to art and performance is a challenge. New sensors are promising for measurement of implicit and explicit audience engagement. However, the meaning of biometric data, and its relationship to engagement, is unclear. We conceptually explore the audience engagement domain to uncover opportunities and challenges in the assessment and interpretation of audience engagement data. We developed a display that linked performance videos with audience biometric data and presented it to 7 performing arts experts, to explore the measurement, interpretation and application of biometric data. Experts were intrigued by the response data and reflective in interpreting it. We deepened our inquiry with an empirical study with 49 participants who watched a video of a dance performance. We related temporal galvanic skin response (GSR) data to two self-report scales, which provided insights on interpreting this measure. Our findings, which include strong correlations, support the interpretation of GSR as a valid representation of audience engagement.

Author Keywords
audience engagement, arousal, galvanic skin response

ACM Classification Keywords
H.5.2 Information Interfaces and Presentation: User Interfaces—*User-centered Design*; J.5 Computer Applications: Arts and Humanities—*Performing Arts*

General Terms
Human Factors

INTRODUCTION
In her 1991 memoir [12], choreographer Martha Graham stated, "Every dance is a kind of fever chart, a graph of the heart." Those words evoke the intricacies of artistic emotional journeys; they are also prescient, as now technology enables us to generate graphs that provide insights into experiences of dancers and audience members. The initial question that arises is how choreographers and theater directors in performance arts would use quantitative audience engagement information if it were available to them. This is a complex question because there are many facets of engagement, many possible ways to measure engagement and many possible ways to interpret and use that information once collected. The deeper cultural and moral questions are: should we collect quantitative audience engagement data? What would it mean to performing art practitioners if they could see exactly how their audiences responded?

An important and related question is "What does a biometric audience response actually mean?" It is unclear that the biometric response of an audience member collected throughout a performance actually tells us anything useful - the readings may be completely unaffected by the performance being viewed. If biometric readings really do indicate a reaction to the performance, we need to understand how those readings can be interpreted. If we can infer a reaction (its strength and/or valence) from a biometric reading, we will have a potentially powerful tool for performing arts experts.

We are motivated to explore audience feedback so that we can answer some of these questions. One way to approach the audience engagement domain is through the top-down creation, deployment, and evaluation of various combinations of software and sensors. Yet, uncertainty surrounding the appropriateness and usefulness of various sensors makes it very likely that signicant time and resources would be spent building and evaluating sensors ill-suited for the task of understanding and learning from audience engagement.

Our work is instead based on a bottom-up approach. We initially collected galvanic skin response (GSR) data from five subjects watching performance videos. We designed and implemented an application to display the audience biometric data in such a way that changes in the data are linked to the second-per-second flow of the performance. Using these recordings, we examined how seven performing arts experts interacted with audience engagement recordings of their own work or the work of their colleagues. Based on these investigations, and the interest shown in biometric audience readings by our performing arts experts, we conducted a large empirical study on the meaning of audience biometric response as measured through skin conductance. Our results show that skin conductance is a reliable indicator of emotional response to a performance, which is what our performing arts experts are most interested in.

The first part of this paper is a conceptual exploration of audience engagement - what does it mean? Should technology mediate audience engagement, and if so how should that work? We draw on literature from the performing arts, humanities, market research, psychology, psychophysiology, HCI and design. In the second part of this paper, we describe our exploratory study and the insights we gained from having performing arts experts work with sample biometric audience engagement data. In the third part of this paper, we detail an empirical study that explores the meaning of skin conductance data collected during a performance. Finally, we discuss how these different theoretical, exploratory and empirical results combine to form a clear picture of the possibilities in using biometric audience response.

AUDIENCE ENGAGEMENT

Radbourne et al. have considered measures of audience experience in performing arts and also emphasize the importance of engagement [27]. As they point out, there are many possible ways to consider audience engagement in the performing arts. Audience engagement can act as an evaluation tool to help us understand how a performance is received. We can investigate various ways to increase audience engagement by involving the audience in the production. While there is a range of audience engagement possibilities, in this work we focus on measuring audience engagement as a process tool for performing arts experts.

Temporal Art

Before continuing, it is worth noting the scope of our explorations. There are many temporal arts that could be investigated, including music, cinema, theater, dance, comedy, television, and others that are less neatly categorized. Our current work focuses primarily on dance, and secondarily on theater, and so in this discussion they will be the domains we refer to. We believe our ongoing explorations of audience engagement with dance and theater may apply to other live performances such as music, comedy and even cinema.

Television is an area where audience engagement (through various types of ratings tools) has been well-studied. In market research, continuous concurrent self-report measures have been used to indicate agreement or disagreement with a message [13] or like/dislike of a radio program [25]. We draw from market research, however there are limitations to the applicability of that work. Television is different because of the need to prevent channel switching to maintain advertising revenues. People watch television casually in their homes, and can turn it off or switch stations the moment they lose interest. This context is dramatically different than going out and paying to see a performance in a social setting.

History of Audience Interaction

The limited amount of explicit audience participation in dance has taken place within the modern dance movement. In the Judson Church Movement in the 1960s, modern dancers questioned the need for formal dance technique, thus audience involvement in a hippie sort of 'happening' often evolved [1]. In other types of audience engagement, choreographers have occasionally allowed audience members to 'yell' prompting words, either to impact the dancers' actions or as live vocal accompaniment. In theater, there is a strong history of audience interaction. One particular example is the idea of the 'spect-actor rehearsing the revolution,' where participants are invited to act out a variety of different endings [5]. Schechner describes environmental theater, in which the audience are active members of the setting [30].

There is a small amount of work in which the audience's engagement, measured through biometrics, is used as real-time input to the performance. One example is the cheering meter that measures applause during improvisational rap competitions [3]. Maynes-Aminzade et al. investigated techniques for interactively engaging a cinema audience before a show [24]. Similarly, audience preference is measured during competitive reality TV phone-in votes.

Defining Engagement

How one defines engagement is going to impact the choice of technology used to measure engagement. Intuitively, we think of engagement as related to attention and interest, and while engagement is often associated with positive valence, it is clearly possible for people to be attentive and interested with negative valence (think of disgust, terror or anger). In studying engagement we are venturing into the domain of affect and so we can look to the literature in affective computing [26, 31]. However, much of this work is aimed at presenting or generating affect, and it does not apply to measuring the engagement of audiences.

We can also look to the neurophysiology literature to better understand affect and the distinctions between valence and arousal. William James began the early accounts of how bodily reactions created emotional experience [14]. Today, neurophysiologists agree that emotions have a neurophysiological basis, precede conscious explanation and can exist outside of consciousness [19]. Zajonc describes how affective reactions are difficult to verbalize [35]. Lang describes emotions as dispositions, or states of readiness, that function to prepare and facilitate interaction with the environment [18]. When participants rated pictures, Lang found that pleasantness ratings, heart rate, and facial muscles tended to load onto one factor (valence) and interest ratings and skin conductance tended to load on another (arousal).

Emotions are often denoted by categorical labels, and they can also be conceptualized two-dimensionally, where different x,y coordinates correspond to intensities along the axes of valence (positive-negative) and arousal (sleepy-activated) [18, 29]. Theater directors and choreographers may not have in mind a specific emotional goal for their audience, but it seems unlikely that a director or choreographer would want the audience to feel bored, droopy or sleepy during a performance. Arousal is clearly important in measuring engagement. It may be interesting to measure valence during a performance, but we need to be careful about confounding two factors: how the performance makes a person feel versus how much they like the performance. Given this confound, measuring valence is considerably more complicated than measuring arousal.

Given the previous work in affect, we can state that emotional engagement is a complex phenomena that involves both valence and arousal. For the purposes of dance and theater performance, we focus on arousal, which we consider to be the most relevant component of engagement.

Current Measurement Methods

Measuring Engagement Explicitly

Audience members already give explicit feedback to performers, and performance artists talk about how they feed off the energy of their audiences. However, the bandwidth of this communication is limited and noisy. The most common measure of audience engagement and appreciation, final applause, is temporally offset from the performance itself, and prohibits that information from feeding back into the performance. More explicit methods for measuring audience engagement include post-performance surveys, focus groups and audience interviews. A complicating factor in post-performance questionnaires is the 'peak-end' effect [15], which shows that a measure of emotional experience taken immediately after an experience is strongly influenced by the peak emotion and by the emotion experienced at the tail end of the experience.

To explicitly measure engagement, audience members could use response devices similar to those that have been employed in market research, including the 'warmth monitor' [33] and the 'on-screen cursor' [4]. Mauss et al. used a slider along with physiology measures in a video-watching experiment [23]. More recently, Ranjan et al. used a slider to find differences between video conference experiences [28]. Lottridge and Chignell showed that the interface for measuring engagement matters. [20]. In a study of explicit audience reporting on dance, Stevens et al. used a system which allowed specification of a one-dimensional parameter on a handheld PDA using a stylus [34]. Their work showed that arousal is correlated with surface features of a dance more than valence.

Measuring Engagement Implicitly

There are a variety of common physiological measures that can be used to measure implicit engagement biometrically, such as GSR, heart rate, blood pressure and respiration. Combining data from a variety of measures would lead to more reliable results. All of these biometrics have some level of invasiveness - GSR requires sensors worn around the fingers, heart rate requires some type of monitor [8], etc. However, we can foresee that in the future these devices will become smaller, more sensitive and less cumbersome. Outfitting an entire audience with heart rate monitors or galvanic skin response sensors is expensive, but feasible. Given the hassle and invasiveness of such an undertaking, we need to have good reason to believe that the data obtained would be very useful. It is important to note that we consider all biometric measures to be implicit measures - although other researchers used the term 'explicit responses' in cases where they have asked participants to try to explicitly change their biometrics [17]. It is not our intent, nor would it make sense in this context, to ask users to consciously affect their biometric responses, thus we use the term 'explicit responses' to refer to conscious self-reporting.

GSR is a common biometric that measures the conductivity from sweat on the skin, which is secreted in response to autonomic nervous system arousal [7]. Lang [18] observed a linear correlation between GSR and arousal. GSR has historically been used in lie-detection, and more recently for measuring experience during video game play [21].There are also possibilities in measuring neural signals (using fMRI or fNIRs) during a performance to measure engagement, but current brain imaging technologies have serious limitations for such an undertaking. EMG measures facial muscle activation and is thus more clearly linked to affect, but also has a poor form factor for use in a theater setting.

Finally indirect, but implicit, measures of engagement are also possible. These include the use of high-resolution computer vision or thermal imaging techniques to detect facial expressions [16]. Similarly, a non-automated approach to facial action coding is possible [11]. However, the facial expressions during a performance may not be particularly illuminating, and massive parallel facial expression recognition of an audience is not currently feasible. An alternative approach may be an indirect, implicit measure of engagement through the use of seat-embedded posture detectors such as the Body Posture Measurement System (BPMS) [10]. For example, a built-in posture sensor could be coupled with an iPhone slider, or a GSR finger wrap could be paired with an engagement knob. There are a variety of combinations that could work. The benefit of these combinations is that the implicit, biometric measures could provide data even if the user forgets to explicitly indicate their engagement or is bored and just fiddles with the engagement knob. In these cases, we would expect the biometric data to help cancel out the explicit noise. Thus, the combination of such measures seems likely to lead to more reliable overall measures of engagement.

Insights and Research Questions

Assuming we have mechanisms to collect implicit or explicit audience engagement data, questions arise around parsing and making sense of the information. There are issues such as sensor noise, environmental effects, and the choice of signal processing algorithm. Ignoring all those issues and assuming that we can filter out noise, we end up with a temporal tracking of some measure that likely relates to engagement. The temporal resolution may vary, but most methods should give at least a second-by-second accounting of engagement. One of our research questions is how the performing arts experts will interpret this data.

One approach to temporal engagement data would be to treat it simply as continuous stimulus-response data. The normative assumption behind this approach is that each second, audience members are responding to the thing they just saw happen in the previous second. While a stimulus-response approach seems likely to be suitable for television [32], this approach is problematic for artistic performances. We equate it to the 'cable-news effect' - where in order to prevent people from switching channels, viewers are constantly bombarded with moving text, flashy videos and screaming commentators. We are not the first to consider this usage of biometric affect data - the idea of neuro-targeting performances for optimum engagement was proposed by Calvo-Merino et. al in a study where videos of dancers were shown to viewers inside an fMRI machine [9]. Their study used a stimulus-response approach, where they asked the viewers in the machine to rate each individual movement. As expected, participants were most engaged by the largest dance movements. To jump to the conclusion that an optimal dance contains nothing but leaps is clearly wrong. Live performances typically have a narrative structure, with a setup, a build, a climax and a denouement, or some variation on that structure. The build-up of emotion and the ups and downs that help give performances structure are clearly important, and the stimulus-response interpretation ignores this.

An alternative approach would involve semantically chunking the temporal engagement data into segments meaningful to the choreographer or theater director. The experts could be asked to define segments a priori and then be presented with pre-segmented engagement data after a performance. Alternatively, they could interactively define the segments as they investigate the data. It is possible to consider measuring both explicit (self-report) engagement levels and implicit (biometric) engagement levels to allow experts to obtain a more complete picture of audience engagement. In a study of users watching Internet videos, Bardzell et al. found it useful to triangulate affect data from various sources [2].

EXPLORATORY STUDY

Many of the technologies that could be used to measure audience engagement data are either expensive, complicated or invasive. Before anyone goes to the expense and effort of instrumenting an audience, it seems reasonable to explore how performing arts experts would construe audience engagement data. To this end, we developed an exploratory study using a small amount of audience engagement data and two different performance videos. The study is not meant to perfectly replicate live performance measurement or usage, but rather to present sample data to these experts that is reasonable and to gage their reactions to it. The study used individual arousal data collected through GSR sensors.

Methodology and Materials

Our expert user study involved showing 3 choreographers and 4 theater directors biometric response data to a dance and a theater piece, to understand how they would use information about audience engagement. Most sessions lasted approximately an hour and the expert participants were compensated with gift cards.

The participants used a custom web-based video player that added an extra layer of information, audience engagement,

Figure 1. Screen shot during session with C2. The lines topped with blue circles are segmenting lines C2 added to define semantic chunks. Between these lines the pink fill indicates the aggregate response over that segment. C2 preferred to see individualized response lines, rather than a single response line.

as measured through GSR. In other words, while the participant watched the performance, they were able to view engagement levels that corresponded to every second of the performance. Engagement levels were displayed below the video in a line graph (See Figure 1). The experts were able to interact with the data by clicking on the line graph or by sliding the seeker bar. The video player also featured a built-in ambient display in the form of a video border which changed color saturation in response to the current aggregate arousal level.

The performance that each expert watched corresponded to their respective field. Choreographers watched a dance piece entitled, *Voices*, while theater directors watched a portion of *The Crucible*. The dance was choreographed by participant C1 and the play was directed by participant T4, thus we had two participants with direct responsibility for the performances included in our study. The GSR data that was used in this study was real data collected from four members of our research lab watching videos of the dance and five members watching the play. To take into account people having different GSR baselines, we displayed the z-scores of the GSR data. Our performing arts experts were able to look at either the aggregate data or the individual engagement lines.

Procedure

Participants were introduced to the video player and the facilitator explained skin conductance using common language. The explanation was necessary because we were asking our experts to speculate on a type of data whose content was relevant, but whose form was relatively foreign to them. The participants were then invited to explore the interface and interact with the data. The session was semi-structured; the facilitator asked pre-determined questions, and followed up on topics raised by the participant.

The participants were asked to 'think aloud' as they used the video player. The sessions were recorded and we took notes that were used in a discussion at the end of each session. Interview transcripts were initially reviewed individually by the researchers to extract themes. Next we looked holistically at the data to identify patterns and relationships.

Results and Discussion

The exploratory study was not about the particular interface we designed, but was meant to explore how experts react to audience engagement data. However, we note that the experts were shown how to use the interface and seemed to have no issues using it. The participants understood that the data had been collected from people watching videos of the dance and the play, rather than live, and almost all of them thought the arousal levels would be higher if the GSR had been collected during live performances.

None of the participants seemed to notice or care about the ambient arousal level reflected in the saturation level of the video frame border. The participants were explicitly shown how to create semantic chunks along the timeline to see the aggregate arousal level for a section of a performance and two participants used this feature. C2 was enthusiastic about the ability to get average arousal for specific segments of the dance (her chunking is shown in Figure 1, stating:

> I think it's really cool – this chunking system. I like the fact that people can do this totally differently. You can get as specific or as broad as you want...

The experts investigated linkages between the data and different aspects or sections of the performances. We observed that directors interpreted high and low arousal levels and suggested various explanations. At other times, the experts made inferences on what might be causing different levels of engagement. They all noted that many factors could be influencing the arousal levels, including the music, or what people happened to be looking at, and so they were implicitly veering away from a strict stimulus-response interpretation of the data. C2 raised this attention issue, implying that she felt a stimulus-response interpretation wouldn't suffice:

> I was just watching this dancer, and I looked over at her crawling back through the thing, and I really like that. And I imagine that I might have felt aroused for a second, but for instance, I know that started a lot earlier... but that's just when I happened to notice it? So how do you think that factors into it?

C1 struggled to interpret the meaning of lower aggregate arousal during a segment of her dance when she expected higher arousal levels, and suddenly realized there might be a link to the number of dancers on stage:

> The only other thing I can think of... hmmm... we go from a duet and then suddenly you've pulled everything down and it's just one figure. Does that change how people are responding? Is there less to respond to? [] I wonder.... [], does the number of dancers on the stage have anything to do with these kind of readings?

The data doesn't necessarily provide clear direction to performing arts experts in all cases. T4 clearly understood the dangers of a stimulus-response approach to using the data and was adamantly against using it to make second-by-second adjustments to increase arousal level, stating:

> I could literally make a play where people are talking in whispers and screaming every other sentence - technically, vocally manipulate them... to keep the response constantly on an up level.

These comments demonstrate that experts evaluate a full range of possible interpretations for audience response data.

Arousal versus Valence

A theme that strongly emerged during the think aloud sessions was related to the issue of arousal versus valence. The data that our experts were shown was arousal, but they were asked if they would also be interested in valence data. Our participants were either not interested in valence at all because they considered it purely subjective, or they were only interested in getting valence if they could also get causal explanations. C2 explained:

> When you talk to people, they're only able to say what they like. It's very concentrated to what they're cognizant of...[]. I feel like there's a little less value in, 'I like this, but I didn't like this.' What I'm trying to say is, I like that you have an organic response that's subconscious, totally subconscious. I like the fact that there are these unaccountable variables that could be altering this.

All of our experts felt that valence is limited because reactions to dance and theater are subjective. T3 commented:

> ...so I'm saying that as designers and directors are trying to explore different things, it [audience engagement data] becomes very useful. It doesn't become useful for anyone in terms of 'Did they enjoy my work?' because that's so subjective and limiting.

When asked specifically if he would be interested in seeing 'like/dislike' data, T3 replied:

> I mean, I think, yeah. I think all of that stuff is good. [] But, we want to know why. [...] So yeah, like and dislike are good but only if we know why.

In interaction design, a typical goal is pleasurable experience. We can see that this stands in contrast with an artistic setting, where positive and negative emotions are equally valued; but what matters most is audience engagement. This can be a subtle aim: worthwhile experiences can be negative.

Application to Practice

All of our participants commented on how they might be able to use this type of data in their work. T2 commented:

> If this was my play I was directing right now, I would be... this section right here, is crazy. I would definitely look at that and try to figure out. What is the gender of this? Male and then we've got male... okay. And these are all females... So I would want to know what can I do to that scene to make it more interesting to males?

C3 mentioned that he would like to use our system to collect data on dance pieces that he is planning to re-stage. He also noted that he had choreographed a dance to the same piece of music as the piece shown in our study, and would like to be able to compare the audience response data from the two different dances. T4 had a related idea and talked about testing the same play with different sized audiences to see how audience size affected group dynamics and arousal.

Finally, four of our experts commented on the value of gathering audience engagement data for educational and training purposes. T2 was interested in using the data to train actors:

> But with him [referring to a point of high audience arousal while an actor is on-stage], I could be like, 'That is your moment - now what are you doing there?' Like, really working on that specific moment where the audience was a little more interested in him...

Aggregation versus Demographics

The individual line and aggregate lines supported different kinds of inquiry into the audience data. As T1 notes:

> So there is an advantage to the aggregate because it helps show a more direct correspondence between what's going on and what everyone together is experiencing. But there's also an advantage to the individual data because then you can see different responses.

C3 was intrigued by the individual data and surprised by how much difference there was between the individual responses. The data presented showed age and gender and the gender information was examined by a number of experts, but particularly T2, who examined and referred to the gender consistently. T4 was also glad to have the individual lines as he was apprehensive about catering to the average:

> I have a fear of this in some respects because to me... it's like eugenics of biology. The idea that... that you can tell... that's why I'm so glad about the individual response data. People are so diverse that as a director, as an artist... you can't deal with them as a group.

It is worth noting that it was easy to provide access to the individual lines in this exploratory study because of the small n. However, visualizing lines from an audience of 300 would be significantly more difficult. But, an aggregate measure is more statistically valid than an individual sample, as it will effectively remove much of the noise from the signals.

EMPIRICAL AUDIENCE RESPONSE STUDY

Based on the interest in audience response data shown by our performing arts experts, we wanted to take the next step in this research. The followup question, given their interest, is what does audience response data mean? To determine the feasibility and benefits of collecting this data, it is important to have a deep understanding of what the data means in a performance context. Specifically, we wanted to investigate the relationship between GSR and self-report measures of audience engagement, to understand whether the arousal measured by GSR can be accurately interpreted within the boundaries of the concept of audience engagement.

Methodology and Materials

To study the meaning of biometric audience response, we recruited 49 participants (18 male, 31 female, all students) to watch a video of an 11-minute dance performance. Ten participants were from fine arts, the rest were from other varied disciplines. Since watching a video of a dance performance is different than the experience of attending a live dance concert, we made environmental decisions to increase the participants' sense of immersion, which included projecting the dance onto a 60-inch projector screen, having the participants wear headsets to listen to the soundtrack and watch the video in a dimly lit, temperature-controlled room.

Each participant wore Thought Technology GSR fingerwraps on two fingers of their non-dominant hand, leaving their dominant hand available to rate their engagement with the performance using a physical slider. The biggest methodological challenge was determining the best way to have participants report their explicit, conscious responses to the dance performance. We wanted to give users a simple physical slider that could be used mostly eyes-free. We experimented with a number of different scales and labels to try to capture the concept of engagement with words that participants would easily relate to. During pilot studies, we found that simply labeling the slider with *No Engagement* and *High Engagement* was confusing. Participants could not detach valence from the word, and tended to only rate themselves as being engaged when they liked what they saw. Others just didn't really seem to know what we meant by engagement, and still others didn't seem to know how engaged they were. Given this, we had to investigate alternative vocabularies to help users report their engagement levels.

We finally settled on the two most promising label sets. Half of our participants were presented with a slider that had the label *Hate it!* at the bottom, the label *Love it!* at the top, and a notch in the middle to help users feel when the slider was in a neutral position (LH scale). The other half of our participants were given a slider that had the label *No Emotional Reaction* at the bottom and the label *Strong Emotional Reaction* at the top (ER scale). We anticipated that the LH scale would be more intuitive to users because it is easier to express valence than emotional reaction level. Therefore, we gave more specific instructions for the ER scale, explaining that this scale encompasses many different emotions and that strong emotional reactions could be positive or negative.

The experiment ran as a between-subjects study, with participants randomly assigned to one of the two groups. Each participant was run individually and thus we did not try to capture any of the social effects that would occur in a true performance setting. We instructed the participants that while watching the dance video, they should use their dominant hand to rate the performance using the slider, since their non-dominant hand was attached to the GSR sensor. Prior to the start of the dance performance, we captured three minutes of GSR baseline while the participants sat alone in a dimly lit room. After the baseline period, our software launched the dance performance. Participants were told:

> "Please change the location of the slider as often as necessary to reflect changes in your feelings toward the video. You should move the slider as often as your feelings change: this could be every few seconds, or if your feelings remain constant, there may be periods where the slider stays at the same location, to reflect that."

After watching the video, participants were shown a graph of their self-report ratings while the video played again. In this post-hoc interview, we asked them to explain their ratings, particularly the peaks and valleys in their data.

Data Collection and Normalization

GSR samples and slider ratings were taken every 500ms, and our study concluded with 49 participants' files consisting of 11 minutes worth of GSR data and slider ratings. After collecting the data, we applied a three-second moving average filter to both the GSR data and the self-report slider data. We smoothed the GSR data using this filter because GSR responses lag stimulus by 1-5 seconds [6]. We also smoothed the self-report responses to account for different slider reaction times between participants.

The LH slider generated readings on a scale from -50 to 50 (giving a neutral response a value of 0), while the ER scale ranged from 0 to 100. The GSR data and the LH self-report data was transformed to a scale of 0 to 100 so that correlations could be collected using the same scale. The GSR mapping transformed each participant's readings by mapping the range of minimum to maximum GSR readings to 0-100, following a process similar to Mandryk et al. [22]. This was necessary to compare the GSR results across participants (since different participants have different GSR baselines), and it was also necessary in order to perform statistical analysis between GSR readings and self-report values.

Hypotheses

Engagement is not particularly well-defined, and as mentioned previously, determining the right questions to ask of our participants in order to elicit their engagement level was difficult. We chose the emotional reaction labels because the literature suggests that the arousal level measured by GSR is most related to the intensity of emotional reactions. Thus, we anticipated a positive correlation between GSR readings and the ER slider values:

$$H_1 : R_{GSR*ER} > 0.1$$

However, our intuition led us to believe that participants would have a somewhat difficult time with the ER scale. People often have low awareness of their emotional reactions – society teaches us to keep our emotions under control in order to maintain decorum. We thought that if we asked people to react to the performance using an LH scale, that they would be much more comfortable with this. People seem to easily know whether or not they like something, even if they can't explain why. Because the LH scale has stronger reactions at both the bottom and the top of the scale, we did not anticipate a strong correlation with GSR readings. We expected the GSR ratings to fluctuate less than the LH responses:

$$H_2 : R_{GSR*LH} < 0.1$$

Our performing arts experts told us they were not interested in valance, but we thought that it might be a good surrogate for emotional reaction if we could take the absolute value of the reaction, effectively removing the valence information. Thus, we also planned to run analysis on the absolute value of the LH slider readings, which would give us larger positive numbers for stronger reactions, regardless of the valence of those reactions. We anticipated a positive correlation between GSR readings and the absolute value of the LH slider values. We also anticipated that there would be a correlation between the ER values and the absolute value of the LH values, despite these readings coming from two separate participant groups.

$$H_3 : R_{GSR*|LH|} > 0.1$$

$$H_4 : R_{ER*|LH|} > 0.1$$

Results

In our analysis, we computed the correlation between the average self-report measure of engagement and the average GSR that was collected for that measure, thus enabling comparisons within the two groups and across them. We computed correlations of the averaged responses in order to eliminate noise that is inherent in GSR sensor data. There were no significant differences in the responses between fine arts students and students from other disciplines.

We found that there was a strong, significant correlation between the ER scale and participants' GSR ($r = 0.316, p < 0.001$), allowing us to accept H1. This is a result that we expected because a strong ER should be synonymous with high arousal. On the other hand, the relationship between the LH scale and participants' GSR was weakly negative. ($r = -0.142, p < 0.001$). This allows us to accept H2.

We are also able to accept H3, in which we predicted that the absolute value of the LH scale would be strongly correlated with GSR ($r = 0.432, p < 0.001$). In fact, this correlation was stronger than the correlation between the ER scale and participants' GSR. We were very pleased with this result because it suggests that this one self-report scale, LH, can give us two dimensions of information – valence and arousal.

We anticipated in H4 that the absolute value of the LH scale would be similar to the responses from the ER scale, but the data shows a weak correlation ($r = 0.150, p < 0.001$). This weakness may be due to real differences in what participants were reporting, but may be related to the fact that the responses are from two different groups of people.

Finally, we were interested in knowing whether there would be significant correlations between the GSR readings of the two different groups. In other words, did the different self-report scales given to the two groups affect their autonomic responses? We didn't anticipate a big difference, but we did think that the stress of reporting the level of emotional reaction might cause that group's overall GSR ratings to be higher. The correlation between the GSR readings from the two groups was positive and moderate in strength ($r = 0.256, p < 0.001$). This suggests that in fact the biometric responses are not strongly impacted by the different instructions given to the two groups. There was also no statistically significant difference between the mean GSR for the ER group (51.35, SD=7.19) and the LH group (M=48.11, SD=4.24), though the mean is slightly higher for the ER group. Thus, there is no statistical evidence to support our intuition that the ER slider was more difficult to use.

Qualitative Results

In addition to correlating explicit self-report ratings to autonomic biometric readings, we had a third probe into the participant's response to the performance, which came from the post-hoc interviews in which we showed participants their self-report data while watching the video and asked them to explain their ratings. Themes emerged that elucidate the aspects of the performance that generated conscious responses.

Love/Hate Group

Participants that used the LH scale were able to list very specific aspects of the dance performance that they liked or did not like based on the dance movements and the sound score. Almost all participants agreed that they liked the faster, bigger movements, opposed to the slower movements: "These movements were just not very exciting. It was kind of slow." In addition to tempo, they also commented on specific movements: "I liked the diamond shape of the legs." "The legs in the air... they were moving, kind of like swimming. I liked that." "Right here, I think it's pretty cool what they're doing..." While there was a lot of agreement between participants on these movements, there was a certain dancer in the piece whose movements were very different than the other dancers. Some people loved her movements, while others really disliked them. For example, "I liked watching her since she was doing something completely different..." versus "I didn't like that person crawling on the ground..."

People also commented how they liked when the music became more uplifting or 'happy,' which coincided with the more 'dancy' movements that people also described liking. We also had one person who indicated that he liked a certain part of the dance because he said, "The music reminded me of some songs that I know." In this particular dance, there was a segment of the score that consisted of a voice speaking, rather than music. Few participants liked this – "I didn't really care for the guy talking." "The voice started out, and I couldn't understand it... It seemed to be just random things that I couldn't understand."

Emotional Reaction Group

People in the Emotional Reaction group did not give as many specific details about the dance performance. In general, people rated higher reactions to areas of the dance where there was more movement – "This is more what I think of as dancing – it has a beat, it's synchronous." "I was more impressed when they were up and doing stuff." Just like the LH group, people also responded to the dancer whose movements were different than the other dancers. Many people found her movements confusing and indicated a low reaction, while others responded with a high reaction to her. One person explained: "I get really happy when she's in the front dancing... and then she goes away, and I feel sad."

Participants indicated a low reaction when they were confused – "I think the reason I went down was because of the talking. It was confused why there was talking during the performance... I couldn't understand where it came into the performance." A few participants seemed to have a difficult time using the emotional reaction scale. For example, one person said, "I think that I stayed at the half way point because I didn't know what to feel." In the Emotional Reaction group, we also had one person move their slider only twice (this did not happen in the LH group) – "I didn't experience any emotions... I wasn't really bored but at the same time, I wasn't really interested." Comprehension is not well captured by the emotional reaction slider. Participants in the LH group could lower their love-hate rating if something confused them, but the mapping to the ER scale is less clear.

DISCUSSION

We opened this paper with two broad questions. First, how do performing arts experts respond to temporal biometric readings from their audience members and what would they do with that data? Second, how should biometric readings taken during a performance be interpreted? Is it reasonable to interpret them as a measure of audience engagement?

Our experts were interested and intrigued by the data in our exploratory study. The experts did not make rash judgments nor plan changes to achieve constant high arousal. Instead, they tried to understand and address unexpected or long periods of low audience arousal. They appeared to acknowledge the limitations of applying a stimulus-response interpretation to the data. T4 was specifically concerned about this:

> What worries me about the data is, I can see how producers, the people who have the money, will eradicate certain artists based upon this instantaneous feedback.

The experts were reflective in their interpretations and understood that the data was a noisy signal and that different factors could be affecting each individual's readings.

The positive response from performing arts experts and their willingness to interpret the data led us to our empirical study. We felt that before deploying a system with live audiences, we should understand the relation between galvanic skin response and audience responses to a performance. Our empirical study provides support for treating GSR as a valid measure of audience engagement - it is not simply random or unrelated to the performance. GSR readings are not only related to the performance as interpreted by arts experts, they are also strongly related to multiple conceptions of self-reported engagement by audience members. We tested two promising vocabularies to help users self-report their engagement level. The significant correlations in the GSR readings between the LH and ER groups and for the slider readings between the two groups (after the absolute value transformation of the LH readings) show that these two different framings reveal the same primitive reaction of engagement. However, the LH slider (and taking the absolute value of the ratings) gets at engagement more easily and with higher validity, given its stronger correlation with GSR.

The fact that the absolute value of participants' LH slider ratings correlated so strongly with their GSR readings is important for three reasons. First, if other researchers wish to have participants self-report on engagement, this scale was easier for participants to use, and once transformed, is a valid measure of engagement. Second, if there was interest in building audience response devices to gather both implicit biometric responses and explicit self-report responses, the LH scale would be better to use because participants have an easier time using it. Third, despite our earlier finding that performing arts experts are not interested in valence, C2 confided:

> I think having access to a graph of valence, it would be like a guilty pleasure for me to look at. [] It would be like, do people like me? Do people like my work? But I would know, as an artist, that's not interesting..."

This suggests that despite our experts' stated lack of interest in valence, there may be curiosity. Since the LH slider allows us to collect valence and a representation of engagement, it gives us more information with seemingly less cognitive effort expended by users. A system that allowed collection of both autonomic and explicit self-report data could combine the two signals to cancel noise.

CONCLUSIONS AND FUTURE WORK

We have presented a set of theoretical, exploratory and empirical results on the collection and use of temporal biometric audience response data in an effort to further understand audience engagement in the performing arts. We conclude that performing arts experts are interested in the autonomic reactions of their audience members collected throughout performances and that they are carefully reflective in interpreting such data. We showed a strong correlation between participants' explicit ratings of level of emotional reaction and their autonomic GSR responses. We also showed a strong correlation between the absolute value of love-hate ratings of a performance and participants' GSR responses. Our results support the validation of temporal GSR data as a reflection of audience engagement.

There is a difficult issue to address in this area of research: art is slow, and gsr (or other biometric measurements) are fast. It is very important to emphasize this in any work that looks to quantify and analyze responses to artwork or performance. In our exploratory study we encouraged experts to segment the data into chunks, which helped to steer them away from a second-by-second analysis of the data. In our second study, we opted to examine overall correlations across the entire data time-set to understand aggregate responses, and we did not look at second-by-second correlations related to specific events. We feel our nuanced approach is appropriate, but we admit that our work cannot capture reflective responses to art that happen after the fact.

Further, we plan to study audience biometric responses during live performances to examine patterns in live performance settings. Finally, our work represents a fundamental step in understanding biometrics as related to audience engagement. Our future work will continue to build on that understanding through several different facets to create a richer picture of audience experience and engagement.

ACKNOWLEDGEMENTS

This work was funded by an NSF CreativeIT grant (#IIS-0855882). We thank our study participants and members of the HCILab for their feedback. We would also like to acknowledge DREU students Charlotte Smail and Millicent Walsh for their assistance during the summer of 2010.

REFERENCES

1. S. Banes. Democracy's body: Judson dance theatre and its legacy. *Performing Arts Journal*, 5(2):98–107, 1981.
2. S. Bardzell, J. Bardzell, and T. Pace. Understanding affective interaction: Emotion, engagement, and internet videos. In *Proc. of 2009 IEEE International Conference on Affective Computing and Intelligent Interactio*, 2009.
3. L. Barkhuus and T. Jørgensen. Engaging the crowd: studies of audience-performer interaction. In *CHI '08: CHI '08 extended abstracts on Human factors in computing systems*, pages 2925–2930, New York, NY, USA, 2008. ACM.
4. H. Baumgartner, M. Sujan, and D. Padgett. Patterns of affective reactions to advertisements: The integration of moment-to-moment responses into overall judgments. *Journal of Marketing Research*, 34(2):219–232, 1997.
5. A. Boal. *The theatre of the oppressed*. Routledge Press, 1982.
6. W. Boucsein. *Electrodermal Activity*. Springer, 1992.
7. W. Bouscein. *Electrodermal Activity*. Plenum Press, New York, NY, USA, 1992.
8. J. F. Brosschot and J. F. Thayer. Heart rate response is longer after negative emotions than after positive emotions. *International Journal of Psychophysiology*, 50(3):181–187, 2003.

9. B. Calvo-Merino, C. Jola, D. Glaser, and P. Haggard. Towards a sensorimotor aesthetics of performing art. *Consciousness and Cognition*, 17(3):911 – 922, 2008.

10. S. D'Mello, R. W. Picard, and A. Graesser. Toward an affect-sensitive autotutor. *IEEE Intelligent Systems*, 22:53–61, 2007.

11. G. Donato, M. S. Bartlett, J. C. Hager, P. Ekman, and T. J. Sejnowski. Classifying facial actions. *IEEE Trans. Pattern Anal. Mach. Intell.*, 21(10):974–989, 1999.

12. M. Graham. *Blood Memory*. Doubleday, 1991.

13. C. Hovland, L. Lumsdaine, and F. Sheffield. *Experiments on mass communication*. Princeton University Press, Princeton, USA, 1949.

14. W. James. *The Principles of Psychology (2 vols.)*. Henry Holt (Reprinted Bristol: Thoemmes Press: 1999), New York, NY, USA, 1890.

15. D. Kahneman. *Well-being: The foundations of hedonic psychology*, pages 3–25. Russell Sage Foundation, New York, NY, USA, 1999.

16. M. M. Khan, M. Ingleby, and R. D. Ward. Automated facial expression classification and affect interpretation using infrared measurement of facial skin temperature variations. *ACM Trans. Auton. Adapt. Syst.*, 1(1):91–113, 2006.

17. K. Kuikkaniemi, T. Laitinen, M. Turpeinen, T. Saari, I. Kosunen, and N. Ravaja. The influence of implicit and explicit biofeedback in first-person shooter games. In *CHI '10: Proceedings of the 28th international conference on Human factors in computing systems*, pages 859–868, New York, NY, USA, 2010. ACM.

18. P. Lang. The emotion probe: Studies of motivation and attention. *American Psychologist*, 50(5):372–385, 1995.

19. J. LeDoux. *The Emotional Brain, the mysterious underpinnings of emotional life*. Simon & Schuster, New York, NY, USA, 1996.

20. D. Lottridge and M. Chignell. Emotrace: Tracing emotions through human-system interaction. In *HFES '09: Proceedings of the 53rd annual meeting of the Human Factors and Ergonomics Society*, pages 1541–1545. HFES, 2009.

21. R. Mandryk and M. Atkins. A fuzzy physiological approach for continuously modeling emotion during interaction with play environments. *International Journal of Human-Computer Studies*, 6(4):329–347, 2007.

22. R. L. Mandryk, M. S. Atkins, and K. M. Inkpen. A continuous and objective evaluation of emotional experience with interactive play environments. In *CHI '06: Proceedings of the SIGCHI conference on Human Factors in computing systems*, pages 1027–1036, New York, NY, USA, 2006. ACM.

23. I. Mauss, R. Levenson, L. McCarter, F. Wilhelm, and J. Gross. The tie that binds? Coherence among emotional experience, behavior, and autonomic physiology. *Emotion*, 5:175–190, 2005.

24. D. Maynes-Aminzade, R. Pausch, and S. Seitz. Techniques for interactive audience participation. In *ICMI '02: Proceedings of the 4th IEEE International Conference on Multimodal Interfaces*, page 15, Washington, DC, USA, 2002. IEEE Computer Society.

25. J. N. Peterman. The program analyzer a new technique in studying liked and disliked items in radio programs. *Journal of Applied Psychology*, 23:725–741, 1940.

26. R. W. Picard. *Affective computing*. MIT Press, Cambridge, MA, USA, 1997.

27. J. Radbourne, K. Johanson, H. Glow, and T. White. Audience experience: measuring quality in the performing arts. *International Journal of Arts Management*, 11(3):16–29, 2009.

28. A. Ranjan, J. Birnholtz, and R. Balakrishnan. Improving meeting capture by applying television production principles with audio and motion detection. In *CHI '08: Proceedings of the 26th international conference on Human factors in computing systems*, pages 227–236, New York, NY, USA, 2008. ACM.

29. J. Russel. A circumplex model of affect. *Journal of Personality and Social Psychology*, 39:1161–1178, 1980.

30. R. Schechner. *Environmental Theatre*. Applause Books, 2000.

31. N. S. Shami, J. T. Hancock, C. Peter, M. Muller, and R. Mandryk. Measuring affect in HCI: going beyond the individual. In *CHI '08 extended abstracts on Human factors in computing systems*, pages 3901–3904, New York, NY, USA, 2008. ACM.

32. S. Shapiro, D. J. MacInnis, and C. W. Park. Understanding program-induced mood effects: Decoupling arousal from valence. *Journal of Advertising*, 31(4):15–26, 2002.

33. D. Stayman and D. Aaker. Continuous measurement of self-report of emotional response. *Journal of Psychology and Marketing*, 10(3):199–214, 1993.

34. C. J. Stevens, E. Schubert, R. H. Morris, M. Frear, J. Chen, S. Healey, C. Schoknecht, and S. Hansen. Cognition and the temporal arts: Investigating audience response to dance using PDAs that record continuous data during live performance. *International Journal of Human-Computer Studies*, 67(9):800 – 813, 2009.

35. R. B. Zajonc. Feeling and thinking: Preferences need no inferences. *American Psychologist*, 35:151–175, 1980.

Designing from within: *humanaquarium*

Robyn Taylor[1], Guy Schofield[2], John Shearer[2], Jayne Wallace[2], Peter Wright[2], Pierre Boulanger[1], Patrick Olivier[2]

[1]Advanced Man-Machine Interface Laboratory
Department of Computing Science
University of Alberta
Edmonton, Canada
{rltaylor, pierreb}@ualberta.ca

[2]Culture Lab
School of Computing Science
Newcastle University, Newcastle upon Tyne, UK
{g.p.schofield, john.shearer, jayne.wallace, p.c.wright, p.l.olivier}@ncl.ac.uk

ABSTRACT
We present an experience-based approach to designing a collaborative interactive performance, *humanaquarium*. Our research explores public interaction with digital technology through the practice-based inquiry of an inter-disciplinary team of interaction designers and musicians. We present a method of designing experience from within, literally situating ourselves within the performance/use space and assuming the roles both of performers and of designers as we develop and refine the *humanaquarium* project over the course of a year's worth of public performances.

Author Keywords
Participatory performance, experience-centered design, practice-based research, interdisciplinary design, musicianship, busking, FTIR

ACM Classification Keywords
H.5.2 User Interfaces (D.2.2, H.1.2, I.3.6)

General Terms
Design

INTRODUCTION

The Baltic Centre for Contemporary Art is a large public gallery with a constantly changing programme of exhibitions. Before the opening of each new exhibition, the gallery assistants who discuss and present the work to visitors are given a brief overview of the work by a curator and are then left to live with the artworks, often spending up to eight hours a day in their company. This long-term relationship with the art leads to a gradual process of discovery over the life of the exhibition, which may last up to several months. Due to an urgent need to be able to respond to visitors' questions, assistants engage in an initial period of intensive study of the objects. Later, however, a deeper level of detail often emerges over time as conceptual and linguistic connections are untangled and made sense of. Sometimes, this occurs in solitude, but more often these leaps in understanding occur in the course of discussion, co-experiencing the works with visitors and other staff.

In this paper we present a method of research practice that leverages this long-term process of sense-making and applies it to the design cycle of the participatory performance piece, *humanaquarium* [19] (see Figure 1). Our use of performance as an investigation platform results in a design process which is literally hands-on, as the design and evaluation team also take on the roles of performers, placing themselves within the design space. This allows a co-temporal negotiation and renegotiation of the relationships between designers, participants, performers and audience. We engage in a design practice similar to that referred to by Wright and McCarthy as dialogical design [21]. Through our situatedness within the work the resultant dialogue plays out in real time.

The three researchers who comprise our production and performance team each bring to the project diverse backgrounds, with professional experience from the fields of fine art, music, computer science, interface design and curatorial practice.

Figure 1. The *humanaquarium* performance

We reflect upon a year of performing *humanaquarium* as part of an ongoing program of inquiry into engagement with digital technology in public spaces. Drawing upon the work of Benford *et al.* [1] and Sheridan *et al.* [15,16], we explore the interactive performance frame as an interplay between performers, participants and audience. Deliberately placing ourselves as performers within this frame over an extended period of time, we experience directly and immediately the results of our design interventions and their impact on the performance experience.

humanaquarium was intended to use existing creative practice to investigate specific design concerns regarding participant engagement with publically situated interactive technology. *humanaquarium* was structured from the outset to facilitate ongoing evaluation and revision over an extended period, allowing us to gradually re-imagine content and interaction strategies in response to a deepening understanding of the design space gained through performing the work in public.

The project has two interconnected elements: a physical interface comprising the hardware and software components of the performance space itself (hereafter referred to as 'the box'), and a performance practice designed to best exploit the affordances of the interface. We use the term '*humanaquarium*' to describe what is conventionally considered to be the performance – everything which occurs in the course of deploying the work in a public setting. The *humanaquarium* performance centers around interaction with a 1.5 metre cube, inside of which sit two live musicians (authors Taylor and Schofield). The structure is faced with a transparent acrylic frustrated total internal reflection (FTIR) screen [11]. The system translates the position of touches into audio visual effects that alter the musicians' performance as they play. In this way, participants can 'jam' with the performers in order to collaboratively control the audio-visual content of each *humanaquarium* performance.

Performing from within the interface allows us a unique vantage point from which to explore participant experience with the *humanaquarium* project. We propose that this method of research provides a valuable complement to more traditional forms of experimental investigation, leveraging perspectives from the inside as well as the outside of the design space, and allowing design insights to emerge through the performance experiences we share with the audiences

We begin this paper with a discussion of situated, long-term research practice, and introduce the *humanaquarium* project. We present the methodology that we used to design *humanaquarium*, beginning with an investigation of a previous piece of participatory art that we used to define the design space and identify emergent concerns about participant engagement. We describe our initial concept for *humanaquarium* and how it was iteratively refined using practice-based research. We describe the insights into public behavior we gained from incorporating performance practice into our research process, and explore how designing the *humanaquarium* art piece from within yielded insight into overarching tendencies and trends including intuitive shifts in design focus occurring almost unconsciously at the time.

RESEARCH IN THE WILD

Goffman's use of theatrical analogy to describe human behaviour in social settings proposes that all social interaction bears similarity to dramatic performance – individuals choose to manipulate their *presentation of self* [10] in order to be esteemed by their peers. We suggest that exploring how people conduct themselves within a literally theatrical, improvisational context can afford us insight into how people experience technology in conspicuous public settings. *humanaquarium* was conceived as an application of performance practice to the exploration of public behaviour, intended to be developed and presented outside the laboratory. To date, *humanaquarium* has been performed in over forty performances at eight different venues. It has been sited in lobbies and exhibition halls, marine labs and museums, affording us extended immersion in the practice of developing an interface 'in the wild'.

Our research practice stems from our awareness that investigating human experience in the laboratory is necessarily exclusive of many of the contextual factors found in real world environments. Our approach builds upon an existing body of human-computer interaction research which prioritizes depth of insight by using long term studies of small participant groups in authentic settings. Approaches such as Gaver *et al.*'s long-term installations of unique technologies into people's homes [9], or Wallace's crafting of bespoke jewellery pieces for individual subjects [20] are situated outside the laboratory, allowing a genuine interrogation of the cultural context under investigation. The duration of these projects allows for rich insight to be evolved over time as the process of sense-making [14] allows elements of the investigation to be appropriated by the subjects. Intentionally developing and refining an investigation while situated within an authentic environment allows research interventions and inquiries to evolve in response to emergent ideas observed in practice [6]. We suggest that our investigatory approach bears similarity to Boehner *et al.*'s situated study of the *Affector* interface [3], allowing appropriation of the project to develop over time. While *humanaquarium*'s audience is necessarily new with each presentation of the work, the performance and design team remain constant, allowing our understanding of the experience to be enriched by its unfolding trajectory.

Creative practice has previously been used as an interrogative tool. For example, Gaver uses cultural commentators – professionals from the fields of cinema and documentary – to provide a polyphonic account of the design process "in which a multiplicity of perspectives encourages a multi-layered assessment" [7, p.292]. Hook *et al.* also use documentary specifically to provoke discussion and elicit design response from participants [12]. These processes, however, still position the creative practitioner as an outside observer or commentator, and follow a classical design trajectory in which the designer and user take turns proposing and responding to artefacts in a strict temporal sequence. In *humanaquarium* we collapse this staggered proposition-response cycle to a real-time dialogue where the designer/performer and user propose solutions to each other, literally face to face. Taking active roles as performers during the investigatory process sites us inside the artefact that facilitates the dialogue. We leverage our own engagement in the process as a means of obtaining insight perceptible from within the experience itself.

Using performance as our investigatory tool allows us to draw upon art theoretical accounts providing perspective on the relationship between the viewer and the object. When planning a 2D image, a sculptural work or a performance, artists often take great care in considering the structure of the experience they are preparing for the viewer [2]. Krauss [13] describes tableau sculptures as existing in theatrical terms, with the viewer's movement around the work placing it in dramatic time. Suchman describes experiencing a creative work as determined not only by the content of the work, but by the relationship between the artefact and the viewer within a specific situation and context [17]. McCarthy and Wright's framework for describing experience [14] has previously been applied to the understanding of aesthetic content [22], examining not only the created artefact, but also its sociocultural context. We adopt their framework as part of our pragmatic approach using performance practice in the design process.

HUMANAQUARIUM: INTERFACE AND PERFORMANCE

The interface used in the *humanaquarium* performance is a large and virtually featureless aluminium and plywood box, painted a neutral grey. The front wall of the box is a transparent pane of acrylic allowing viewers to peer inside. Inside the box sit a soprano (Taylor) and mandolin/synth player (Schofield), whose musical performance is augmented by visuals projected onto the rear wall of the box. The *humanaquarium* is situated in an area where it can be encountered by passersby, with the third member of the team (Shearer) facilitating their interaction.

FTIR [11] is used to monitor participants' touches via infrared LEDs in the edges of the acrylic window and a camera mounted in the ceiling of the box. Max/MSP/Jitter translates this data into MIDI messages which are then sent to Ableton Live to control audio processing and synthesis, in some instances controlling the orchestration of the piece by cross-fading between different instruments, and in others adjusting audio properties of the instruments and voice. Jitter is used to combine visualizations derived from the singer's vocal performance with visual effects (created from multiple video layers) controlled by the position of participant touches. A video layer consisting of a distinct animated element which directly mirrors the position of touches is used to reinforce the legibility of the connection between the interaction and the performance. Further detail explaining the implementation of *humanaquarium* can be found in a previous publication [19]. Videos are available online at http://www.humanaquarium.org

humanaquarium performances range from ten to thirty minutes, the length being largely determined by the siting of the interface and presence of passersby. During each performance, members of the audience may at any time take an active part in the performance by moving their hands across the window (see Figure 2) as the musicians play. The performance trajectory varies according to the interactions of passersby, with the musicians controlling the instruments available to participants and, in effect, 'jamming' with them. Performances end either when participants lose interest and move away or, more frequently, when the musicians decide that the piece has reached a natural end because the emergent structure of the performance suggests a finale.

Figure 2. Participants interact with *humanaquarium*

INITIALLY DEFINING THE DESIGN SPACE

The *humanaquarium* project is the second in our series of performances designed to explore audience engagement with creative experiences. We began the design process for *humanaquarium* by examining our experiences with a previous work created by members of our design team, a stage-based participatory performance, *dream.Medusa* [18].

In *dream.Medusa*, four selected audience members joined a live singer (Taylor) on the stage. Taylor's singing controlled a responsive visualization which could be influenced and adapted by the four participants who used hand-held devices to control features of the visualizations and collaborate with Taylor to create the visual component of the piece. The participants were not instructed in how to operate the deliberately ambiguous interface (a featureless metallic tube containing accelerometers which transmitted participant gestures to the visualization engine) but were encouraged to improvise and explore the gestural space during the development of the performance. The participants were located centre-stage with Taylor, so they were visible to the audience who could watch how their gestures influenced the performance and could see the resulting visualizations projected on the backdrop of the stage.

dream.Medusa had originally been commissioned by the Nuit Blanche festival in Toronto, and was subsequently performed in a variety of international festival contexts over the course of a year. During that year, we were able to observe and interact with numerous participants in a variety of cultural contexts as they experienced the work. Often we were able to engage participants in discussion after the conclusion of the performances. Participants were consistently enthusiastic to discuss what they deemed to be a novel and stimulating experience (taking part in an improvisational multimedia performance in a public setting). They were often surprisingly forthcoming and frank in their feedback, describing how the risk-taking aspect of performing an improvisational and unknown piece of work in a public setting made them acutely aware of their relationship to the audience. Participants reported a heightened sense of vulnerability, knowing they were being watched and possibly judged by their peers, but also described feeling creatively empowered knowing that they were contributing to the execution of the performance that was being experienced by the group.

Our experiences with *dream.Medusa* highlighted a number of factors influencing participant engagement in interactive performance scenarios. Identifying these factors provided the starting point for the design of *humanaquarium*:

• Stage fright: the stage-based nature of the traditional performance medium increased participants' concerns about being observed, making mistakes and appearing foolish in front of the audience

• Collaboration: participants wanted an understanding of how they were permitted to interact with one another, what the boundaries of shared interaction were, and how they could create shared effects

• Legibility: participants wanted to know how their actions affected the performance development, and to understand the domain space of what actions they could take.

Although the process of designing, performing and then evaluating *dream.Medusa* had produced interesting feedback about user engagement, we realized that this did not fully leverage the dialogical potential offered by the designer taking the role of performer during the performance. *dream.Medusa* was in most respects composed traditionally, with a fixed temporal structure. Although it allowed improvisation and participation it was presented from the outset as a finished piece and was performed with minimal variation between repetitions. When designing *humanaquarium*, we decided to leave the structure of the performance open, allowing the possibility of ongoing refinement. The presence of the designers allowed immediate adaptation of the work in response to the shared performance experience.

Four threads of experience

We saw a need to adopt a theoretical framework with which to focus our understanding of the performance experience and the interplay of the various roles involved. We used McCarthy and Wright's pragmatic approach to structure an investigation of participant experience in *dream.Medusa* [18]. Using their practice of addressing technology within its sociocultural context, we examined participatory performance in terms of its *threads of experience* [14].

McCarthy and Wright frame experience in terms of its *sensual, emotional, spatio-temporal,* and *compositional* elements. Rather than partitioning experience in a reductionist manner, they suggest using each of these elements to filter the examination of experiential phenomena. Being mindful of the interplay and overlap between each of these threads can provide new insight into complex scenarios in which addressing the social and cultural context is fundamental to understanding what is taking place.

When one considers multimedia art, the **sensual** characteristics of the media content figure prominently in the discussion. The artist's crafted audio-visual content provides sensory stimulation both to the audience and to the participants, shaping their instinctive and visceral response to the work. Additional sensory information is provided from the environment (the sounds of other activities in the background, the scent of the space in which the performance takes place, etc.) also influencing the way in which the experience is perceived by those involved.

The experience of the participatory performance is **emotionally** shaped by the ongoing casting of each individual's role – at different times during the performance, each individual may consider him/herself to be fulfilling the role of 'performer', 'participant' or 'observer'[16]. Each of those roles carries with it social context and expectation, while framing the individual's emotions as well as the emotions they ascribe to the other people sharing the performance frame.

Spatio-temporal factors describe the influence of the setting and context in which the performance is enacted. Venues and events have perceived cultural contexts that imbue weight and meaning to the actions taking place within. It is therefore important to consider how the understood prestige of the performance setting, the degree of public exposure, and the perceived openness and accessibility of the environment influences the experience of each participant. Also relevant to a discussion of spatio-temporal issues are the concepts of ephemerality and non-repeatability. Collaborative performance is strongly affected by the unpredictable contributions of the individuals gathered together at a specific point in time.

The **compositional** narrative experienced by those taking part in a participatory performance consists not only of the artistic or aesthetic 'story arc' of the performance itself, but also of the processes of discovering the art piece, choosing to pay attention to it, possibly choosing to interact, and formulating an impression of the ongoing experience. This narrative arc experienced by participants, audience and performers as well as the creative and development teams is integral to the sense-making process of understanding the experience.

Addressing the participants' observations and our own insights within the context of McCarthy and Wright's four threads of experience, we conducted a simple theoretical thematic analysis of participant interviews and observations we had made about the *dream.Medusa* experience. We codified observations in terms of how they related to the various threads of experience. Temporarily narrowing our focus to sequentially explore each thread in turn helped us to unpick the insights contained within the body of complexly interrelated sociotechnical observations. It enabled us to scrutinize elements participants had found enjoyable about the performance experience, and also recognize the source of issues participants had raised regarding barriers to their enjoyment and engagement with the performance interface.

THE *HUMANAQUARIUM* DESIGN

The next stage in our process required to use what we had learned from *dream.Medusa* to inspire initial design decisions for *humanaquarium* which could later be refined as we experienced and re-evaluated the piece in public settings. We began the creative process by considering each thread of experience in isolation. We considered how manipulating each thread in turn could allow us to address our previously identfied concerns of stage fright, collaboration and legibility in interactive performance. This strategy generated the key ideas used to inform the design of *humanaquarium*.

One of *dream.Medusa*'s major creative goals was to immerse audience and participants in the performance, hoping that they would feel enchanted and engaged with the collaborative experience. Many of the decisions we made when considering the sensual and compositional aspects of the performance were done in the hopes of promoting engagement and immersion. The performance was characterized by an ethereal soundtrack with sweeping strings and a pulsing bass rhythm. Visually, *dream.Medusa* was equally hypnotic, with vividly-coloured images of jellyfish slowly drifting across the screen. Participants described how the audio-visual content focused their senses and helped them immerse themselves in the performance, losing track of time as they focused on the sensual aspects of the experience. We were encouraged by these reports, as a diminished awareness of the passage of time is a signifier of immersion or flow, as reported by Csikszentmihalyi [5], indicating to us that our crafting of the performance's sensual and compositional elements had been successful in promoting participant engagement. We decided to include similarly styled audio-visual content in *humanaquarium*.

Participants had reported that although they did not always understand the functionality of the ambiguous gestural interface of *dream.Medusa*, they felt increasingly engaged with the work simply because they believed that their actions impacted its execution. We decided that the ludic ambiguity [8] and playfulness of the interface was an interesting avenue of exploration, and that we could use *humanaquarium* to investigate further how legibility of interaction affected participant engagement and satisfaction.

Negative issues that were brought up in discussion with participants often focused on issues triggered by aspects of the emotional and spatio-temporal elements of the participatory performance experience. People reported fears of appearing foolish in public, of overstepping personal boundaries in terms of personal space on the stage, or of failing to operate the technology properly during the performance and upsetting the artist responsible for the conception of the work. This feedback suggested to us that the stage-based nature along with the pressure and formality of the *dream.Medusa* performance was increasing participants' feelings of stage fright. The visibility and conspicuousness of participants' interactions exacerbated their occasional frustration with the ambiguity of the interface due to their natural social desire to appear competent in public. We were eager to investigate how participants would interact with a participatory creative environment if the stressors triggered by the theatrical context of *dream.Medusa* were reduced.

We decided that exploring a less intimidating manner of performance would be beneficial. Drawing upon the improvisational tradition of busking (a casual, street-based form of performance) we designed *humanaquarium* to be experienced in a less formal context, hoping that novice, untrained participants would find this platform more comfortable and accessible. Eliminating the need for participants to take part in a traditionally staged performance also reduced the level of commitment required. Interacting with two street performers residing in a glass fronted box is an inherently transient act. When participants no longer wished to interact they could move away from the interface, leaving the performance frame.

The very site of interaction (the transparent FTIR surface of the box) was also a response to the emotional and interpersonal issues raised during the *dream.Medusa* experiences. Participants had reported feeling uneasy being in close proximity to Taylor as she sang. Most audiences would naturally have no experience of the sheer volume and dynamic energy projected by a classical singer who is engaging in the physically demanding act of producing supported sound. Participants described it as fascinating yet somewhat uncomfortable, as they wanted to observe but felt that they weren't sure if it was appropriate to stare. The transparent front of the aquarium provided a physical and metaphorical boundary between participant and performer, increasing the socially appropriate space between them, while maintaining the performer's ability to make eye contact and indicate approval and encouragement of the participatory actions.

INVESTIGATION AND REFINEMENT METHODOLOGY

Once the *humanaquarium* was built, the third phase of our design process involved launching the performance into the public sphere, continually refining the design based on our ongoing understanding of the performance experience.

Earlier we discussed the process of gradual sense-making experienced by art gallery assistants over the course of an exhibition and how this led us to a novel investigative methodology in which we situated ourselves within the design. Living with *humanaquarium* over a period of time allowed us to make sense of it in new ways as it became integrated into our existing creative practices. We suggest that investigating public interaction with technology through the medium of performance demands a long-term approach, as changes in context across performance repetitions affected not only the participants who encountered *humanaquarium,* but also our own engagement and perception of the interactive experience. By deciding to place ourselves within the work as performers as well as designers, we gained the advantage not only of a co-temporal and co-spatial proximity to both the users and the artefact – in this case the *humanaquarium* performance – but also of offering it up to the filter of our own creative practice over an extended period of time.

Performance Practice

A crucial factor in designing for *humanaquarium* was planning for live shows. By conceiving of *humanaquarium* as a 'show' – a performance in the theatrical sense with a beginning, an end and a musical trajectory between the two – we committed to a form of practice where the creators of the piece would necessarily be occupied and immersed in the work during performances. During a performance of *humanaquarium*, Taylor and Schofield (within the box) had to consciously engage the audience, play and sing around each other, monitor the changing state of the interface for faults in the computer vision system or audio/visual processing software and react to both the participants' physical actions outside the box and the consequent effect on their own musical output. Shearer (outside the box) watched for faults and performed the duty of sound engineer by listening and watching the musicians intently and gesturing for changes in volume etc. As well as these tasks, in some cases Shearer acted as a 'ringer' by demonstrating the interaction potential to particularly shy audiences.

In addition to performing these tasks it was crucial to the development of the research trajectory for us to consciously observe and reflect upon the unfolding performance. Performances were videotaped, and immediately after each show, all three members of the team individually took written notes, anecdotally recording their impressions of the performance. Critical incidents such as unusual audience actions were recorded.

It became rapidly apparent that the design of *humanaquarium* enabled the research team to observe the experience from perspectives that were both literally and figuratively diverse. The performers inside the box had a very different visual perspective on the performance than did the external observers. They could see the faces of the participants through the acrylic window and were able to recount experiences and communications that were shared between themselves and the participants as they watched one another through the glass. The performers were also uniquely positioned to observe smaller, more subtle communications and interactions between participants who had a perception of relative privacy when standing in front of the box with their backs to the observing audience.

In addition to the observations afforded to them due to their physical vantage point inside the installation, the performers' roles as creative practitioners immersed in the execution of the piece allowed them to reflect upon the experience from a perspective of enriched investment. Their observations of the experience were fundamentally filtered by the instinctive audience evaluation and self-monitoring practiced by seasoned performers when engaged in their craft. Taylor and Schofield documented their self-evaluation of their own musical performances and described their tacit perception of how well the show had been received from their perspective as the performers of the work. The team was, however, aware that these observations would inevitably be influenced and coloured by their inherently self-conscious nature.

Shearer, observing from the outside of the performance space, was able to provide a different accounting of the work. Observing from an external vantage point, he could see a much larger area of the room. He could observe how audience members approached *humanaquarium* and how they behaved before, during, and after interacting with the performance. Shearer could also evaluate the aesthetics of the performance from a removed, arguably more objective standpoint, as he was monitoring the action remotely rather than as an immersed participant.

During the course of the year we had occasion to augment our usual documentation practice with more formalized investigatory studies, where the reports of the core team members were augmented by the annotations of a newly introduced observer previously unfamiliar with the performance, and where participants were interviewed for feedback after the performance event had concluded.

After each performance, we reviewed our notes and videos, discussed what was successful about the performance, and addressed what we felt could be changed in order to improve subsequent presentations. We then filed the notes and videotapes so that we could revisit them at a later date in order to explore how our design decisions and perceptions evolved over time.

Iterative Revision Process

A fundamental component of the *humanaquarium* design process was our awareness of how growing familiar with our own performance platform over a period of time increased our ability to use the art piece as an opportunity for exploration. In contrast to *dream.Medusa* where the performance content was fixed and remained relatively constant over the year in which it was performed, we specifically designed *humanaquarium* to be easily adaptable and changeable. We theorized that over the course of numerous performances (at the time of writing we have performed *humanaquarium* over forty times) we would want to adjust the audio-visual content and the interaction strategies in order to respond to participant feedback and our own experiences and perceptions of *humanaquarium*'s strengths and weaknesses.

We deliberately made technical decisions which would allow us to rapidly reconfigure *humanaquarium*'s creative content and interaction mappings. By defining the relationships between participant touches and system reactions in the visual programming environment of Max/MSP, we were able to make changes to the way participants' actions affected system output without recompiling code – enabling us to make minor revisions on-site during the intervals between performances.

We very consciously decided to present *humanaquarium* in a form which was simultaneously finished and unfinished. In our earliest performances, we were acutely aware that our performance was essentially being tested `in-the-wild', and we accepted that we were going to be unable to truly predict how our audience would choose to interact with the performance. From an artistic standpoint, this presented the performers with an opportunity that was at once both exhilarating and anxiety-provoking – they were aware that they would have to experience the resulting performance in a public context (for better or for worse!) and use their artistry and professional skill to react to participant behaviour truly on-the-fly.

We deliberately scheduled an initial run of small-scale performances scheduled two weeks apart, in order to maximize the opportunity to review, revise, and remount different versions of the performance. The rapid turnaround time between iterations allowed us to immerse and focus ourselves in a very immediate and intense process of creative design development. Many of these revisions centered upon improving system legibility by adjusting the mapping between participant touch and audio-visual response.

As the design stabilized and we began presenting the piece in more prestigious contexts (international festivals and exhibitions) we were able to take more time between revisions, permitting more labor-intensive changes such as the addition of an entirely new selection of new audio-visual content and motifs.

After-the-fact reflection

At the end of the year, our core production team scheduled a dedicated review session in order to discuss the project in terms of the progressions and insights we felt had been achieved over the course of the year.

Initially we assembled a recollected narrative of the project's trajectory constructed out of the notes associated with each performance. We discussed the key issues which had emerged during each performance repetition, and identified how these issues had inspired us to modify or adapt *humanaquarium*'s design in response. With this retrospective created, we then reviewed the video documentation, exploring from this more temporally removed perspective how our intended modifications had actually impacted subsequent iterations of the performance.

This after-the-fact exercise afforded us the opportunity to make a holistic assessment of how *humanaquarium*'s evolving design trajectory addressed the issues and challenges originally targeted in the project brief. We also found that a retrospective look at the year's progression raised some previously undiscovered discussion points about the emerging tensions evident in this experience-centered design approach. Reviewing the entirety of the video documentation made it evident to us that our motivations were simultaneously being influenced by concerns regarding aesthetics and usability, and that these concerns occasionally were in conflict, as we discuss later in this paper.

IMPACT OF OUR DESIGN DECISIONS

By conducting ongoing evaluation and monitoring over the course of the year as well as retrospectively assessing the progression of *humanaquarium*'s design, we were able to examine how we had addressed the design concerns we had originally intended to explore.

Stage Fright

The setup of *humanaquarium* was intended, as much as possible to overcome the intimidating nature of traditional stage performances. As previously discussed, the spatio-temporal and emotional aspects of the performance were calculated to minimize stage fright and facilitate fearless engagement with the work. Seating the musicians at ground level, physically separating the performers from the participants, and enclosing the performance environment within a small space were all expected to reduce the sense of invasion of personal space and ease the emotional aspects of transition [15] between the roles of passive audience member and active participant in the performance. By placing the performance space in non-theatrical venues, we hoped to dispel the sense that *humanaquarium* was a traditional theatrical experience which required the audience to arrange themselves in a particular way as passive observers of the performance. We hoped that this would minimize the anxiety inherent in audience members consciously identifying themselves as part of a formal performance, with all of the concomitant social factors associated with such a high stress situation. Certain factors were retained in order to facilitate the audience's understanding of the situation – the window could still be read as a proscenium, encouraging viewing from the front, and the musicians were costumed and played conventional instruments. However, casting the scenario as a busking performance meant that participants were free to join or leave at any point, reducing the level of commitment required to take part.

The chief source of discomfort for participants, unsurprisingly, still seemed to be the presence of other audience members. While many audience members came forward to explore and interact with the box, some were still reluctant to relinquish the anonymity of the crowd and would form a horseshoe (see Figure 3), observing the action from several metres away.

Figure 3. Observers, participants

Collaboration

When designing *humanaquarium* we were interested in developing a set of affordances that would facilitate collaboration between performers/designers and audience/participants. The FTIR technology which formed the basis of *humanaquarium*'s interactive screen allows for multiple touches to be tracked and used in the performance. In designing compositions for *humanaquarium*, we attempted to build in responses which took into account multiple participants interacting with the entire area of the screen. In one particular paradigm, we divided the screen horizontally into three areas, allowing separate control of three separate instruments. In practice, however, we very quickly found that in nearly every case, adult participants were very reluctant to use the central portion of the screen.

In every performance, audience members approached the glass and seemed able to cope with their extreme proximity to the performers, suggesting that the ameliorating effect of the transparent barrier had been successful in reducing social anxiety in that regard. However, we noticed that many audience members chose to hover at the edges of the frame rather than placing themselves directly in front of the screen, enabling themselves to stay out of the performers' field of vision. Nearly everyone was extremely careful about blocking the view from audience members behind them. Participants would usually restrict themselves to one side of the screen, and stake out an area of the glass with which to play. The exception to this otherwise consistent phenomenon was small children (see Figure 2), who rarely seemed to have any anxieties about either their extreme closeness to the performers or the effect of their presence on other audience members, often standing directly in the middle of the screen.

As previously discussed, the audience was provided with few cues as to how to interact with *humanaquarium*. The screen was apparently an ordinary piece of acrylic and bore little resemblance to any kind of traditional musical instrument or electronic interface. In order to explore whether audience members would be able to determine its functionality from each other's efforts or whether approaching the glass would be a natural response to the performance we avoided using explicit graphical instructions of any kind. We occasionally met with a certain amount of trepidation concerning the interface: on several occasions audience members caused an abrupt effect on the audio when they touched the screen, and instantly gestured an apology for their perceived 'mistake'.

Due to the types of events at which *humanaquarium* has been shown, most audiences were aware that the performance involved some kind of interaction on their part. However, we occasionally encountered situations where audience members would initially install themselves in front of the box and wait to be entertained. We decided to intervene with gestures from inside the box if necessary to begin the collaboration and surmised that one of the musicians placing an outstretched hand on the glass would elicit a mirrored gesture from participants. This was borne out consistently. Participants were in general very willing to interact directly with the performers, making eye contact and watching their actions closely. We noticed a willingness to take cues in the form of gestures which helped us clarify some of the interactions in otherwise complex parts of performances.

Legibility

In *humanaquarium*, legibility was from the beginning an important factor. As we found in *dream.Medusa* that participants wanted to know how their actions affected the performance development, and to understand the domain space of what actions they could take, we consciously strove to make *humanaquarium* as legible as possible in terms of the connection between the actions of the performers, the participants and the system itself, without resorting to actual graphical instructions.

After the initial hurdle of beginning to engage participants, we quickly found that there was some variation in how well different audiences were reading the interaction. By scheduling multiple performances of *humanaquarium* at each venue, we were able to experiment with strategies to engage audience members at different levels, structuring the same shows slightly differently across repetitions. One particular approach which we adopted from very early on was a gradual increase in musical complexity - using 'tutorial' passages in the composition so that solo instruments or voices could be clearly heard and the control paradigm discovered. As discussed, if necessary, we would intervene with gestures, if for instance, participants were attempting actions that the system did not support well, such as very rapid or light touches.

We came to realize that certain controls were easy to discern, for example, the vertical axis of the screen mapped easily to balance between high and low synth lines. Other, more subtle controls were sometimes missed, such as variations in the tempo of arpeggiators or vocal panning effects. We realized quite quickly, to our surprise, that although legibility was important to some participants, it was quite possible to engage many audiences with the most basic forms of participation. Some audience members were apparently content to experiment with the first controls they discovered. Children in particular, would often watch the performers enthralled, while keeping one hand motionless on the glass for the duration of the performance. They appeared aware that their participation was required but otherwise had no desire to collaborate actively with the performers, choosing simply to register their presence and participation in the experience. For participants, knowing that their actions were in some way necessary to the outcome of the performance seemed to increase their investment in the experience, whether or not they chose to experiment with the full range of controls.

REFLECTIONS ON A YEAR OF PRACTICE

We began this discussion considering the experiences of gallery staff living with artworks over extended periods of time. Their unpicking of the artworks through conversations with each other and visitors would over time form a polyphonic account of the work, incorporating perspectives that had evolved from the shared experience. The voice that was always missing from this conversation was that of the creator him/herself. The gallery staff effectively took on the role of interpreter, conveying their own understanding of the artist's intentions at one remove, necessarily filtering the work through their own experience of it.

Approaches such as Gaver's [7] cultural commentators or Hook *et al*'s [12] use of documentary as an investigatory tool similarly use an outsider's account of a design and then communicate it back to the designer. Due to their external vantage point they offer an intriguing set of perspectives from outside the design space. In the design of *humanaquarium* we deliberately decided to attempt the inverse of this approach, seeking a more central perspective by designing from within, engaging in a direct dialogue with the user. Situating ourselves within the design and taking the role of performer during the *humanaquarium* performance we were able to add the voice of the designer directly to a phase of the design process from which it would normally be absent. While this manner of investigation is necessarily self-reflective in nature, placing ourselves inside the design provided us with a combination of first-hand experience and simultaneous dialogical exchange with users, leading us to a number of insights that may have been overlooked in a traditional design process.

Crucially, while Gaver's and Hook's approaches involve the creation of what could be termed secondary artefacts to explore the design space (e.g. documentaries and cultural commentaries), our practice-based investigation allowed our design process to focus entirely on the artefact under consideration: the *humanaquarium* performance. This approach was advantageous in that it allowed super-rapid prototyping of new design revisions and periods of simultaneous design proposition and response. A particular challenge of this approach, however, was that we had to adapt the complexity of our design interventions to account for the real-world time frame of the performance schedule.

Living with the piece for a year and integrating it fully with our creative practice led to a gradual reframing of the design space. Simultaneous with the evolution of *humanaquarium*'s design, we experienced a deepening understanding of our instincts as performers. In reviewing a year of performing and developing for *humanaquarium*, we realized certain factors were being constantly re-negotiated, sometimes unconsciously shifting the priority focus during the design process.

Each musician came to the project with nearly 20 years of experience in traditional stage performance and playing with other performers, either in jazz/improvisational contexts or in the performance of rehearsed pieces. However, the unique setup of *humanaquarium* necessitated careful consideration of our roles as performers. We had begun preparing performances for *humanaquarium* with the initial hypothesis that allowing users the creative agency to structure and control the sensual components of the experience would increase user engagement. As time progressed, however, and we gained in confidence as performers, we began to introduce more complex structures, musical motifs and visual narratives and began to interact more with each other musically. A tension emerged between our instincts and desires as musicians to make more complex and (to us) more satisfying musical pieces, and the necessity to retain a simplicity and transparency in our compositions which would allow passing viewers to instantly collaborate with us. Upon reviewing footage of early performances, we realized that in creating more intricate, polished shows, we had inadvertently sacrificed some of the unpredictability of the medium: something which we had always thought important. The combination of being able to look back on a large number of design iterations coupled with a deeply personal experience of each performance allowed us to identify and learn from embedded trends such as these.

In *humanaquarium*, we drew upon experience gained from working both in the arts and in HCI. When asked whether we had considered particular elements of the design 'as artists' or 'as HCI designers' we realized that in most cases the answer was both – the concerns of the one inextricably intertwined with the other. This meant that when tensions arose between the goals of one discipline or the other there was no linguistic barrier to overcome. Moreover, as we experienced each performance first hand, we were able to learn not only from participants' accounts of the experience but multiple readings of our own, informed by the differing perspectives of our dual practice.

ACKNOWLEDGMENTS
This work has been part-funded by the Research Councils UK Digital Economy Research Hub SiDE: Social Inclusion through the Digital Economy.

REFERENCES

1. Benford, S., Crabtree, A., Reeves, S., Sheridan, J., Dix, A., Flintham, M. and Drozd, A. The Frame of the Game: Blurring the Boundary between Fiction and Reality in Mobile Experiences. In Proceedings of the SIGCHI conference on Human Factors in computing systems, pages 427–436. ACM New York, NY, USA, 2006.
2. Bishop, C. Installation Art a Critical History. London: Tate, 2005.
3. Boehner, K., Sengers, P.,Warner, S. Interfaces with the ineffable: Meeting aesthetic experience on its own terms, ACM Transactions on Computer-Human Interaction (TOCHI), v.15 n.3, p.1-29. 2008.
4. Braun, V. and Clarke, V. Using Thematic analysis in Psychology. Qualitative Research in Psychology, 3, 2, 77-101. 2006.
5. Csikszentmihalyi, M. Flow: the psychology of optimal experience. New York: Harper & Row, 1990.
6. Design-Based Research Collective. Design-based research: An emerging paradigm for educational inquiry. *Educational Researcher, 32*(1), 5-8. 2003.
7. Gaver, W. Cultural commentators: Non-native interpretations as resources for polyphonic assessment, International Journal of Human-Computer Studies, v.65 n.4, p.292-305, April, 2007
8. Gaver, W. The video window: my life with a ludic system. Personal and Ubiquitous Computing, 10(2):60–65, 2006.
9. Gaver, W., Boucher, A., Law, A., Pennington, S., Bowers, J., Beaver, J., Humble, J., Kerridge, T., Villar, N. and Wilkie, A. Threshold devices: looking out from the home. 2008.
10. Goffman, E. Presentation of Self in Everyday Life. Doubleday Anchor Books, New York. 1959.
11. Han, J.Y. Low-cost multi-touch sensing through frustrated total internal reflection. In Proc. of UIST'05. pp. 115-118.
12. Hook, J., Green, D. and Olivier, P. A short film about VJs: Using documentary film to engage performers in design. Extended Abstracts of the ACM Conference on Human Factors in Computing Systems (CHI'09), 2009.
13. Krauss, R. Passages in Modern Sculpture. Cambridge Mass: The MIT Press, 1977.
14. McCarthy, J. and Wright, P. Technology as experience. The MIT Press, 2004.
15. Sheridan, J.G., Bryan-Kinns, N. and Bayliss, A. Encouraging witting participation and performance in digital live art, Proc. of the 21st British CHI Group Annual Conference on HCI. United Kingdom, 2007.
16. Sheridan, J., Dix, A., Lock, S. and Bayliss, A. Understanding Interaction in Ubiquitous Guerrilla Performances in Playful Arenas. In Proceedings of HCI, pages 3–18. Springer, 2004.
17. Suchman, L.A. Human-Machine Reconfigurations: Plans and Situated Actions, Cambridge University Press, New York, NY, 2006
18. Taylor, R., Boulanger, P., Olivier, P., Wallace, J. Exploring participatory performance to inform the design of collaborative public interfaces. CHI Extended Abstracts 2009: 3721-372
19. Taylor, R., Schofield, G., Shearer, J., Wallace, J., Boulanger, P., Olivier, P. *humanaquarium*: A Participatory Performance System. In Proceedings. of the 2010 Conference on New Interfaces for Musical Expression, pp. 440-443, 2010.
20. Wallace, J. Emotionally charged: a Practice-Centred Enquiry of Digital Jewellery and Personal Emotional Significance. PhD thesis, Sheffield Hallam University, 2007.
21. Wright, P. and McCarthy, J. Experience-Centered Design: Designers, Users, and Communities in Dialogue. Morgan Claypool, 2010.
22. Wright, P., Wallace, J. and McCarthy, J. Aesthetics and experience-centered design. ACM Transactions on Computer-Human Interaction. 15(3). 2008

CHI 2011 Author Index

CHI 2011 Author Index

CHI 2011 Author Index

CHI 2011 Author Index

CHI 2011 Author Index

CHI 2011 Author Index

CHI 2011 Author Index

CHI 2011 Author Index

CHI 2011 Author Index

CHI 2011 Author Index

CHI 2011 Author Index

CHI 2011 Author Index

CHI 2011 Author Index

CHI 2011 Author Index

CHI 2011 Author Index

CHI 2011 Author Index

CHI 2011 Author Index

www.ingramcontent.com/pod-product-compliance
Ingram Content Group UK Ltd.
Pitfield, Milton Keynes, MK11 3LW, UK
UKHW051454290926
15471UKWH00008B/1198

9 781450 313629